P9-DMO-759

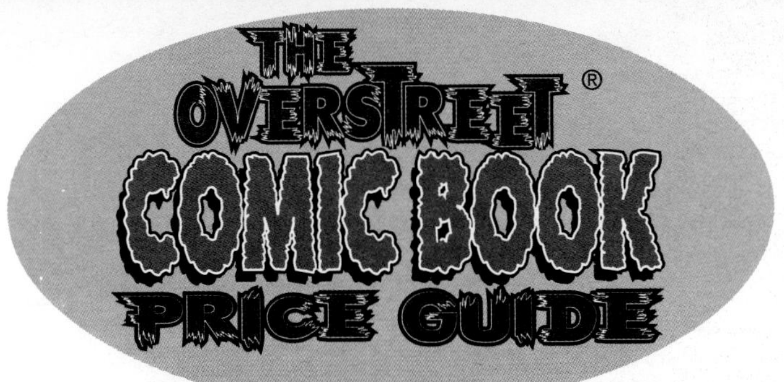

30th Edition

COMICS FROM 1842-PRESENT INCLUDED
FULLY ILLUSTRATED CATALOGUE & EVALUATION GUIDE

by ROBERT M. OVERSTREET

GEMSTONE PUBLISHING

J. C. Vaughn • **Executive Editor**
Arnold T. Blumberg • **Editor**
Mark Huesman • **Pricing Coordinator**
Brenda Busick • **Creative Director**
Kimberly Grover • **Administrative Assistant**

SPECIAL CONTRIBUTORS TO THIS EDITION

Robert L. Beerbohm • Arnold T. Blumberg • Landon Chesney
M. Thomas Inge • Matt Nelson • Richard D. Olson, Ph.D. • J. C. Vaughn

SENIOR ADVISORS FOR OVER 25 YEARS

Dave Alexander • Landon Chesney • Bruce Hamilton • Michelle Nolan
Terry Stroud • Harry B. Thomas •Doug Sulipa • Raymond S. True

SENIOR ADVISORS FOR OVER 20 YEARS

Gary M. Carter • Bill Cole • Gene Seger • Steve Geppi • Stan Gold
M. Thomas Inge • Phil Levine • Richard Olson • Ron Pussell
David R. Smith • John K. Snyder

SPECIAL ADVISORS TO THIS EDITION

Dave Anderson • David J. Anderson, D.D.S. • Robert L. Beerbohm • Jon Berk • Steve Borock
John Chruscinski • Gary Colabuono • Larry Curcio • Gary Dolgoff • Joe Dungan • Conrad Eschenberg
Richard Evans • Stephen Fishler • Philip J. Gaudino • Steve Gentner • Michael Goldman • Jamie Graham
Daniel Greenhalgh • Eric Groves • Gary Guzzo • John Grasse • Mark Haspel • John Hone • John Hauser
George Huang • Bill Hughes • Rob Hughes • Ed Jaster • Joseph Koch • Joe Mannarino • Rick Manzella
Harry Matetsky • Jon McClure • Matt Nelson • Hugh O'Kennon • Michael Naiman • Josh Nathanson
James Payette • Todd Reznik • "Doc" Robinson • Robert Rogovin • Rory Root • Robert Roter • Chuck Rozanski
Matt Schiffman • Dave Smith • Laura Sperber • Tony Starks • Joel Thingvall • Joe Vereneault • Frank Verzyl
John Verzyl • Rose Verzyl • Jerry Weist • Mark Wilson • Harley Yee • Vincent Zurzolo, Jr.

HarperResource
An Imprint of HarperCollins*Publishers*

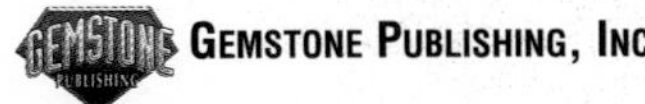
GEMSTONE PUBLISHING, INC.

Serious Comic Book Collectors, Also Look For
THE OVERSTREET COMIC BOOK GRADING GUIDE
By Robert M. Overstreet and Gary M. Carter

Important Notice. All of the information, including valuations, in this book has been compiled from the most reliable sources, and every effort has been made to eliminate errors and questionable data. Nevertheless, the possibility of error always exists in a work of such immense scope. The publisher will not be held responsible for losses which may occur in the purchase, sale, or other transaction of items because of information contained herein. Readers who feel they have discovered errors are invited to *write* and inform us so that the errors may be corrected in subsequent editions.

Cover Illustrations by: Three Ghoulunatics with Drusilla painting by Al Feldstein; science fiction cover by Al Williamson, colored by Marie Severin; used with permission.

THE OVERSTREET COMIC BOOK PRICE GUIDE (30th Edition) is an original publication of Gemstone Publishing, Inc. and HarperCollins. This edition has never before appeared in book form.

HARPERCOLLINS Publishers, Inc.
10 East 53rd Street
New York, New York 10022

HarperCollins books may be purchased for educational, business, or sales promotional use. For information, please write to: Special Markets Department, HarperCollins Publishers, Inc., 10 East 53rd Street, New York, New York 10022.

Overstreet is a registered trademark of Gemstone Publishing, Inc.
Published by arrangement with Gemstone Publishing.
ISBN: 006-095-7344

First HarperCollins Printing: March 2000

10 9 8 7 6 5 4 3 2 1

TABLE OF CONTENTS

ACKNOWLEDGEMENTS

Mark Arnold (Harvey data); Larry Bigman (Frazetta-Williamson data); Glenn Bray (Kurtzman data); Gary Carter (DC data); J. B. Clifford Jr. (EC data); Gary Coddington (Superman data); Wilt Conine (Fawcett data); Dr. S. M. Davidson (Cupples & Leon data); Al Dellinges (Kubert data); David Gerstein (Walt Disney Comics data); Kevin Hancer (Tarzan data); Charles Heffelfinger and Jim Ivey (March of Comics listing); R. C. Holland and Ron Pussell (Seduction and Parade of Pleasure data); Grant Irwin (Quality data); Richard Kravitz (Kelly data); Phil Levine (giveaway data); Dan Malan & Charles Heffelfinger (Classic Comics data); Fred Nardelli (Frazetta data); Michelle Nolan (love comics); Mike Nolan (MLJ, Timely, Nedor data); George Olshevsky (Timely data); Scott Pell ('50s data); Greg Robertson (National data); Don Rosa (Late 1940s to 1950s data); Matt Schiffman (Bronze Age data); Frank Scigliano (Little Lulu data); Gene Seger (Buck Rogers data); Rick Sloane (Archie data); David R. Smith, Archivist, Walt Disney Productions (Disney data); Tony Starks (Silver and Bronze Age data); Don and Maggie Thompson (Four Color listing); Mike Tiefenbacher & Jerry Sinkovec (Atlas and National data); Raymond True & Philip J. Gaudino (Classic Comics data); Jim Vadeboncoeur Jr. (Williamson and Atlas data); Kim Weston (Disney and Barks data); Cat Yronwode (Spirit data); Andrew Zerbe and Gary Behymer (M. E. data).

I will always be indebted to my good friend Landon Chesney for his help in putting together the feature article as well as allowing me to publish one of his "Frank Fearnot" strips. Chesney is considered by many to be one of early fandom's top writers and illustrators and resides in Cleveland, Tennessee.

In celebration of the EC "New Trend"'s 50th anniversary, we are fortunate to have covers by two EC greats, Al Feldstein and Al Williamson. Feldstein's Ghoulunatics cover painting is one of his best yet! The science fiction cover by Williamson, beautifully colored by Marie Severin, is inspired as well. Thanks to all for creating such great covers and especially to Wendy Bucci Gaines for her kind permission to use her famous characters!

Thanks Matt Nelson for rewriting the restored comics section. This has been needed for a long time.

I want to personally thank each advisor that attended the May 1999 meeting in Baltimore. We discussed many topics important to the future health of our market. We salute the good people at CGC who came down to discuss certified grading with us. This provided a forum to field questions from dozens of Overstreet advisors. Credit is due my two grading advisors, Steve Borock and Mark Haspel of Comics Guaranty Corp., for reviewing the new grading changes in this edition.

Tribute is also given to Chuck Rozanski for his voluminous contribution of pricing data for this edition which included internet sales.

My gratitude is given to Chris Pedrin, known for his extensive published research on DC war comics, for checking the accuracy of and providing needed data for this and previous editions of the guide. Thanks, Chris, from me and all of fandom for your excellent contribution to this area of research.

Thanks to Stephen Fishler and Marc Patten for "How to Sell Your Comic Collection;" to Dr. Richard Olson for grading and Yellow Kid information; to Tom Inge for his "Chronology of the American Comic Book"; to Arnold T. Blumberg for his introduction to the Promotional Comics section; to Robert Beerbohm and Richard Olson for their introductions to the Platinum Age and Golden Age sections; to Bill Blackbeard of the San Francisco Academy of Comic Art for his Platinum Age cover photos; to Bill Spicer and Zetta DeVoe (Western Publishing Co.) for their contribution of data; and especially to Bill for his kind permission to reprint portions of his and Jerry Bails' America's Four Color Pastime.

Thanks again Doug Sulipa, Jon McClure and Tony Starks for continuing to provide detailed Bronze Age data! Harry Thomas, Stephen Fishler, Jim Payette, Rob Rogovin, Joe Vereneault, John Verzyl, Frank Verzyl, Josh Nathanson, Vincent Zurzolo Jr., Ed Jaster, Ron Pussell, Dave Alexander, Mark Wilson and Terry Stroud supplied detailed pricing data, market reviews or other material in this edition.

Acknowledgement is also due to the following people who generously contributed much needed data/photographs for this edition: Jim Alberico, Henrik Andreasen, Stephen Baer, Stephen Barrington, Robert Beerbohm, Jonathan Bennett, Peter Bilelis, David T. Breth, Mike Browning, Howard Leroy Davis, Phil Davis, Paul Ellner, Brandon Finkler, David R. George, Mike Hayes, Tim Holl, David Kell, Joseph Latino, James Ludwig, Jordan Lund, William Mahan, Greg Z. Manos, Robert Mathis, Howard E. Michaels Jr., John Mlachnik, Stan Molson, Buddy Paige, Dennis Petilli, Matt Poslusny, Robert Quesinberry, Benn Ray, Craig Smith, Tom Sodano, Jim Stangas, West Stephan, Jeff Walker, Murray R. Ward, Doug Wheeler, John Witek, and Eddie Wolowski.

Finally, special credit is due our talented production staff for their assistance with this edition; to Arnold T. Blumberg (Editor), Brenda Busick (Art Director), and Mark Huesman (Pricing Coordinator), as well as to our Executive Editor, J. C. Vaughn, for their valuable contributions to this edition. Thanks to my wife, Caroline, for her encouragement and support on such a tremendous project, and to all who placed ads in this edition.

No. 27
MAY, 1939
Detective
COMICS
10¢

No. 1
SPRING ISSUE
BATMAN

ACTION
COMICS
10¢

WHIZ
COMICS
10¢
GANGWAY FOR CAPTAIN MARVEL!

10¢
MARVEL
COMICS
ACTION MYSTERY ADVENTURE

DIAMOND
INTERNATIONAL GALLERIES
WANTED

COME VISIT OUR NEW YORK CITY SHOWROOM! (OPEN WEEKDAYS, BY APPT ONLY.)
FOUR COLOR COMICS
BUY
WHY YOU SHOULD CALL US BEFORE YOU SELL YOUR COLLECTION OF COMICS, ARTWORK OR MEMORABILIA:
SELL
We make it easy! No waiting for payment, No song and dance about grading. We'll come to you: Anywhere, Anytime! FOUR COLOR COMICS takes the risk out of selling. Treat yourself to an honest, straight-forward experience—Sell your collection to us and walk away with more money in your pocket and a smile on your face.
And if you're looking to buy comics, original artwork or memorabilia, give us a call first! We probably already have that elusive issue or object you've been searching for—and at a price you'll like!
CALL ROBERT ROGOVIN!
(212) 675-6990
THE JOKER © 1939, 1998 DC COMICS, ALL RIGHTS RESERVED

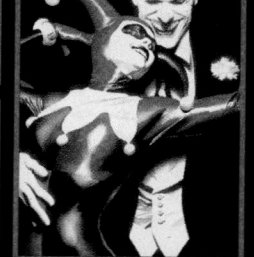

HISTORY with a twist

Exhuming the "New Trend" On its 50th Anniversary

by ARNOLD T. BLUMBERG

*Welcome to **THE OVERSTREET COMIC BOOK PRICE GUIDE**. With this edition we celebrate 30 years of bringing you the most exhaustively researched and accurate information on the hobby of comic book collecting. We also share this anniversary year with another venerable comic book icon now celebrating 50 years since its original debut — the EC Comics "New Trend" titles, some of the most impressive and influential comic book creations ever published. Join us now as we take a look back at what made the EC era such a pivotal moment in comic book history, and enjoy some personal recollections by EC and 30th edition **OVERSTREET** cover artists Al Feldstein and Al Williamson, as well as a unique walk down memory lane by the **GUIDE**'s own creator, Robert M. Overstreet. So what are you waiting for, kiddees? An invitation written in blood? Hahahahaha!*

DAWN OF THE UNDEAD

Over fifty years after O. Henry (born William Sidney Porter) popularized the concept of the ironic twist ending with stories like "The Gift of the Magi" and "The Ransom of Red Chief," and a few years before TV writer Rod Serling would cement the literary gimmick in the pop culture consciousness through an eerie anthology series called *The Twilight Zone*, a comic book company originally known as Educational Comics decided to try something a bit different. Guided by publisher Bill Gaines, the son of the company's original owner, what emerged not only changed the face of comic books and entertainment but inspired actions that would forever affect the relationship between the government, so-called arbiters of morality and comic book publishers, as well as our own perception of the very notion of creative and artistic freedom.

In April 1950, the first of EC Comics' "New Trend" titles appeared: **Crypt of Terror** and **The Vault of Horror**. Soon after, other series such as **Weird Science**, **Weird Fantasy**, and more stuffed comic racks everywhere, and kids were introduced to a new era in comic book storytelling. Containing admittedly edgy, occasionally grotesque images of brutality and violence, the EC titles were a showcase for a stable of talent that used the horror and sci-fi genres to tell tales that had never been seen before in that form. Stories of adventures beyond the stars and on strange, alien worlds, and frightening fables of nightmarish creatures that rose from the grave to exact revenge on the living — all of these and more filled the pages of EC's "New Trend," seen by many as perhaps the greatest single achievement of the comic book medium at that time.

What distinguished EC Comics from their contemporaries and balanced the obvious and arguably excessive use of gore and violence* was an astonishing evolution of the comic book form to tell stories that had never been attempted by any other publisher. Much more than simple tales of terror, EC's "New Trend" blended the device of the ironic or surprise twist ending with surprisingly literate narratives and a heightened social awareness that enabled EC to comment on many of the most taboo subjects of the day while couching their commentary in the form of disposable comic book entertainment.

The EC comics of this period are supreme examples of comic literature, and the topics they tackled were far more challenging than anything Superman was battling over at DC.

*Note: It should be stressed that the graphic content of the "New Trend" was a noticeable mid-stream shift in tone away from the more classic horror of the earlier EC comics. While it proved to be a successful business decision meant to bolster the line's popularity and play to the desires of the larger audience, it did offend some fans who felt the gore was not only out of place but made it difficult to bring EC comics home to sensitive parents! This would prove to be the seeds of EC's downfall, as we will read later.

DEADLY SERIOUS

While other comic books appropriated the clichés of the pulp fiction and Saturday matinee serial genres, EC quietly borrowed from the traditions of science fiction and fantasy literature...often a bit too over-zealously, as many of their classic tales are none-too-subtly altered versions of published SF and horror stories from the likes of Edgar Allan Poe and Ray Bradbury. In Bradbury's case, he was such a fan of the EC titles that he allowed them to continue adapting his works, further blurring the line between EC Comics and "legitimate" sci-fi literature. This liberal but admirable

use of literary source material resulted in some of the most finely crafted and socially aware stories of the Golden Age.

While many of these stories functioned on a pure entertainment level, there were always other shades of meaning to be found, and no doubt at least some readers were able to appreciate the thought that creators like Harvey Kurtzman, Al Williamson, Al Feldstein, Bill Elder, Bernard Krigstein, Jack Davis, and others put into their work. EC Comics spoke of the human condition, and even their most visceral horror tales often had a kernel of commentary about the nature of human cruelty, justice and a strong streak of morality either upheld or subverted. In their science fiction titles, however, the social consciousness of EC Comics was at its most expressive, dealing with verboten topics like racism and ethnic hatred, religion, and even the very forces soon to threaten EC itself — rampant and blind censorship of artistic and literary ideas.

These were controversial and heady subjects to be sure, particularly for young readers, but EC forged ahead with stories that never shied away from the harder issues. "He Walked Among Us," for example, is a famous story that dared to question the nature of organized religion and suggest that a Christ-like figure named Kraft, in actuality an astronaut from another world, could be mistaken for a deity due to his advanced technology and killed by those fearful of such change. Is the origin of Christianity too a misinterpretation of historical fact? EC dared to pose the question.

Other tales like "In Gratitude," a simple but emotionally powerful portrait of a soldier returning home, took on the charged topic of racial inequality. The soldier brings home the body of a dead friend who saved his life, but when his parents and the entire town refuse to allow him to be buried where he wishes, he berates everyone at a rally celebrating his return. His friend cannot share in this celebration because of his selfless sacrifice, he tells them, and now he's denied his proper resting place...only because he is black. EC employs their now familiar twist ending to deliver a very potent punch, and another boundary is shattered by the pioneering publisher.

"The Reformers" is an oft-quoted and reprinted tale from the EC library, mainly because it has the added irony of dealing with the very censorship soon to engulf EC itself. A team of zealots arrives on a serene world to preach the need for reform. Unfortunately, this world has no need for reform. People are free to pursue whatever entertainment they like, express whatever thoughts they wish, and there is no crime or excessive indulgence. It is in short a paradise where the freedom of action and ideas is allowed to flourish. The reformers are not needed, so they plot to create the evil this society has purged in order to make themselves useful and allow them to preach their doctrine. That's when they receive a message from home base. The satanic figure on their screen tells them they must leave and not attempt to preach reform there. "That place just can't be tormented," their leader informs them. "That's...Heaven!" Placing religious and moral reformers in the service of the Devil himself, "The Reformers" champions the cause of free speech and the need to allow people to choose their own opinions and forms of expression.

Although the "New Trend" is perhaps best known for its sci-fi and horror titles, those weren't the only genres being explored by EC at the time. **Crime SuspenStories**, **Two-Fisted Tales**, and **Frontline Combat** were portraying the worlds of crime and war with the same level of literary and artistic accomplishment, just as pre-Trend EC series devoted to western and romance stories had set new standards for comics. The "New Trend" was the full flowering of the medium at the height of the Golden Age and a major success for EC; it was perhaps inevitable, then, that this company would face its own ironic twist ending.

DEAD END

By now, most comic book aficionados know this part of the story by heart, but given the principles with which it deals, it certainly bears repeating. At the height of America's obsession with eradicating the "Communist threat" — an umbrella title given to all forms of excessive governmental investigation into the lives of its citizenry, culminating in the horrific "witch-hunts" led by Senator Joseph McCarthy that resulted in the blacklisting of countless Hollywood actors, actresses, directors, and writers — Senator Estes Kefauver was looking for his own crusade, and found it in the allegations of Mafia involvement in the magazine distribution industry. Unfortunately for EC, this soon led to a subcommittee charged with investigating the comic book industry as well, which opened a door for the architect of EC's downfall, Dr. Frederic Wertham.

Wertham was a psychiatrist whose pet peeve was comic books. In numerous articles, as well as an infamous volume titled **Seduction of the Innocent** (1954), Wertham put forth the rather thinly supported theory that, based on his own limited sampling of children and comic book readers, comics were directly responsible for all manner of juvenile delinquency, crime, and sexual perversion in American society. Through various women's magazines in particular, titles clearly aimed at mothers who would be most receptive to his alarmist material, Wertham argued that comics were nothing less than an evil influence on the minds of our youth and should be dealt with.

Kefauver's investigation of the magazine distribution industry coincided with Wertham's crusade when the committee charged with delving into the comics scene adopted Wertham's theories and works as the basis for further investigation of the medium. **Seduction of the Innocent** purported to provide examples of the deranged, offensive tales children were reading in comics and offered incendiary commentary that turned the spotlight on an entire storytelling form. When it came time for the industry and the medium to defend itself, the entire enterprise virtually fell on the shoulders on one man — a single publisher who was called to testify before the Senate subcommittee and basically defend the very existence of comics before the eyes of the country and the world. Naturally, due to the content of his comics, the man chosen as the scapegoat was Bill Gaines.

Gaines' shaky testimony is legendary in comic book circles, but although the performance was less than exemplary, it did succeed in holding things at bay long enough for the rest of the industry to react. While EC Comics took the full brunt of the blast from the Senate investigation, the rest of the comic book world pondered the future. Never before or since in history has an entire entertainment medium been put on trial solely on the basis of certain specific content choices, and the results were similarly historic. The other comic book publishers, fearing what may happen next, decided to create a voluntary

organization that would serve as an industry-wide censorship board, evaluating and regulating the content of all comics that carried its seal of approval. Dubbed the Comics Code Authority, this system would significantly curtail the portrayal of violence, criminal and sexual activity, and numerous other "objectionable" pursuits, in all comic books published under their banner.

EC suffered a massive blow as a result of the investigation, and was forced to discontinue its entire line of "New Trend" titles (the only survivor was **Mad**, which was subsequently altered from comic to magazine format, becoming a major pop culture success story of its own before finally being acquired by DC and Time-Warner). In an attempt to survive and retain its readership, EC scrambled to find new ways to operate in the post-Wertham era, but found the path a difficult one. Hampered by the extremely stringent requirements of the Code, EC desperately tried to find new avenues for storytelling, resulting in a series of comics known as the "New Direction" titles. Featuring such thrilling topics as the "adventures" of doctors and psychiatrists in titles like **MD** and **Psychoanalysis** (perhaps a none too subtle dig at the source of EC's grief), the "New Direction" line was not nearly as successful as the "New Trend," and although these comics featured the same artists and writers, they were never as good as their predecessors either.

BUT WHEN HIS BODY WAS SENT BACK HERE, IT WASN'T GOOD ENOUGH TO BE BURIED IN FAIR-LAWN CEMETERY. IT WASN'T GOOD ENOUGH BECAUSE ITS SKIN WASN'T THE RIGHT COLOR...

DEAD AGAIN

Half a century later, despite the attempt to stamp out the "influence" of the "New Trend" titles from EC, they remain some of the most fondly remembered and respected comics of the period. Although the "New Trend" played a role in the comic medium's first (and so far, only) major brush with censorship and almost total catastrophe, leading to the demise of the 'offending' titles, a massive reorganization of EC's output and the establishment of a regulatory body that today is viewed as something of a dinosaur, there is no denying that the line's importance in comic book history goes far beyond its political and economic significance. The "New Trend" titles represent some of the finest examples of comic book storytelling in the medium up to that point, and serve as shining examples of a cohesive team of creators pushing the boundaries of the form in design as well as content.

Today, the EC Comics style has become a part of our collective pop culture memory, influencing whole new generations of storytellers in comics and other media as well. Writers like Stephen King (*Carrie*, *Salem's Lot*) and filmmakers like George Romero (*Night of the Living Dead*, *Martin*) have paid homage to the EC horror clichés with their loving tribute, the cult anthology film *Creepshow*, while the EC stories themselves were given new life through a hit HBO series that borrowed its title (and its rotting host) from the vaults of EC itself. Titled *Tales From the Crypt*, the series ran for six seasons and adapted countless original EC tales with the Crypt-Keeper (voiced by John Kassir) providing his unique, pun-filled commentary on the macabre proceedings. The show was helmed by big-name Hollywood producers like Joel Silver and Robert Zemeckis...more of those poor kids permanently damaged by EC Comics, no doubt.

The comic book medium itself survived, of course, and although the "New Trend" came to a premature end, its lessons were not soon forgotten, either politically or creatively. Thanks to longtime publisher fans like Russ Cochran, these seminal issues are still available for old and new comic book fans to enjoy. They are a timeless record of the artform's full flowering in the 1950s, and despite their occasionally edgy and even grotesque subject matter, they demonstrate how the medium can excite, entertain, and yes, even educate through the simple combination of words and pictures on the page. EC taught us all about what comics might be capable of, for good or bad, and enlightened us about our world and the dangers of judging others on the basis of race or color.

Well, what do you know, it turns out they *were* Educational Comics after all. How's *that* for a twist ending?

TELL US YOUR STORY!

We're interested in hearing from past and present EC collectors as we revamp the EC portion of our website, **www.gemstonepub.com**.

Did you get them off the newsstand when they first came out, or are you a newcomer to EC fandom? Do you collect for value or for the stories? What grabs you about them? Do you like the art? The stories? Both? Are they just great comics or are they your favorites? Let us know!

e-mail **eccollector@gemstonepub.com**

Or write to
EC Collector
The Overstreet Comic Book Price Guide
Gemstone Publishing, Inc.
1966 Greenspring Drive, Suite LL-3
Timonium, MD 21093

EC, MAD and BEYOND

Al Feldstein

by J.C. Vaughn

One of the first things Al Feldstein admits is that he didn't know fans would still be eagerly collecting EC comics 44 years after they stopped making them.

"If I did, I'd probably be a lot richer," he laughs, "because at the time I had at my disposal boxes of mint copies of everything we were doing. I would take two copies, one for bound volumes of my work that I kept as a record and one to bring home to my kids. I never kept back issues, which of course in later years proved to be idiotic because they became so valuable. Who knew back then that they would become collectors' items?"

He noted that in recent years record prices have been brought at auction for Bill Gaines' file copies.

"The interesting thing about Bill Gaines' collection," he says, "was it was never saved because he thought they would be valuable. Twelve copies of each issue were wrapped and put away first in his desk and eventually stored in a vault strictly for the Post Office's second class postal requirements. He wanted a record that he had complied with the postal requirements for text pieces and minimal advertising."

Of course it's not only the comics that have done well at auction.

"I noticed that one of my science fiction covers recently sold for something like $8,000 or $10,000, some ridiculous amount. I think I got paid $35 or $40 for it," he laughs. "Who knew?"

Feldstein says he continues to see a lot of enthusiasm for the EC recreation art that he's painted, and his originals are also doing very well. Far from the swirl and hubbub of New York, he lives and maintains a studio in Montana, with a mile and quarter of the Yellowstone River rolling through his property. There, numerous subjects from animals to people to vast landscapes are captured in his many works since he retired from **MAD**.

MEETING BILL GAINES

Feldstein first met Bill Gaines when Gaines was taking over the business following the death of his father. The two immediately hit it off and drafted a contract to create a teen comic entitled **Going Steady With Peggy**.

The three-issue contract Feldstein signed even gave him a chunk of the speculative profits of the comic. The teen market was starting to fade, however, and Gaines may have rethought his contractual generosity, so **Going Steady With Peggy** never happened. He agreed to tear up the contract and work on other titles together.

TREND SETTERS

"I would ask Bill, 'Why are we following trends?' Simon and Kirby would start a trend. Everyone would follow," he says. "The innovators always last. When the teenage market started to soften, **Archie** still lasted even though everything else was getting hurt. Same with the romance market. The Simon and Kirby books lasted longer than the imitators," he says.

"Bill and I used to go to Roller Derby together a lot. We chatted about the things we loved when we were kids. I remembered listening to Arch Obler's *Witch's Tale*, *Lights Out*, and *The Inner Sanctum*. I said 'Why don't we do real Gothic horror in comics?' I admit that there were dabblings in that genre—there was **Adventures into the Unknown**, for one—but it wasn't what I had in mind. That's how I got the Crypt-Keeper and Vault-Keeper started. Bill was a little cautious. He wanted to try them out. So he introduced them in **Crime Patrol** and **War Against Crime** (with *The Crypt of Terror* in **Crime Patrol** and *The Vault of Horror* in **War Against Crime**). That's how we got started in the horror business," he says.

THE EC FAMILY

Feldstein says the EC staff and freelancers quickly became more than just creative people doing business together.

"It was a family of mutual admiration and chiding and suggestions," he says. "It was a creative atmosphere. It was really a lot fun to be working for us. [As a result of his experiences as a freelance writer and artist] there were many things that I instituted with Bill. Every artist would get paid the day he brought his artwork in and a new job would be waiting for him. He would not have to take his portfolio around and go looking for another job to feed his family. We kept our artists

occupied. If there were any changes, we had a board so they could do them right there. Later on with **MAD** and the New Direction titles at EC, the writers got paid the day their script was accepted. That was something I personally pushed. Comics for some reason or other had very little respect for writers. They would get paid $5 to $7 per page for writing and the artists were getting $25 to $30 for artwork. I felt this was ridiculous. If it wasn't for the written word, a good story, there wouldn't be any artwork worth a damn. You can have Frank Frazetta doing a fantastic page of artwork, but it's not going to entertain people on a story level without a good story. This was especially true with **MAD** where we needed innovation, creativity and new ideas every day. I eventually got the writers on a par with the artists."

Feldstein was also excited by his own development as a writer. An important change was marked when he began working with Ray Bradbury's short stories.

"When I started to adapt Bradbury's stories to comics, I was so impressed with his writing that I started to emulate it in my own captions and dialogue for our original stories. I got a little wordy, but he was very effective. I really think I did him justice with the adaptations, and the artists certainly contributed to that.

He was very pleased with the results. I have collections of his works that he autographed for me with very sweet comments that I treasure. I never met him. We never talked directly. Some day I really should get in touch with him just to reminisce," he says.

An important part of the EC family's ambiance was that it wasn't all business. Some of the fun of it was just that: fun.

"We had a rather gullible stockroom boy named Anthony," he says. "He was an interesting neighborhood kid who came in to help out with the mailings, the Fan-Addict Club and subscriptions. He was a nice kid. One day Bill, Johnny Craig and I had this idea that we were going to ride Anthony on this twin brother of Bill's called 'Rex.' We said he was a nasty character and that if he came into the office Anthony should steer clear of him."

Rex was identical to Bill except for an ear-to-ear scar that crossed at the mouth.

"We would put a rubber cement scar on Bill and then 'Rex' would come storming into the office when Bill Gaines was out. He would mess up the place, snarl at everybody and steal things. He drove Anthony crazy. It was something that went on for a long time. He never quite figured that Rex only showed up when Bill was away," Feldstein says.

"One day, back when there were wire recorders, we recorded Rex's voice snarling at Anthony about something. We called from one of the other offices, Bill answered the phone and gave it to Anthony, saying 'It's Rex.' This snarling voice got on and yelled at him while he was there with Bill in the office. This convinced the kid that there were two different people because Bill was sitting there looking at him," he said.

"We had a great time."

PROBLEMS FOR EC

From the start, though, distribution wasn't good. Though Feldstein says there were 300,000 or more copies of each issue, they were hamstrung.

"We were with a second class distributor, Leader News. They were very weak," he says. And weak turned worse when the Senate hearings on the influence of comics on adolescents came about. Leader News had also been publishing EC knock-offs and went into bankruptcy.

"Bill was really caught," he says. "He owed people money. That was really it for us as a publisher other than **MAD**, which Bill was able to get into a better distributor, American News

Company."

The successful titles of EC's "New Trend" line that included **Tales from the Crypt**, **Vault of Horror** and others were killed with the advent of the Comics Code. Gaines tried to keep them going with the "New Direction" Code-approved titles, but they were faced with the same distribution problems. Because of that, Feldstein says, they didn't ever really had a chance to establish an audience.

Next came the Picto-Fiction titles, with their illustrated stories in a magazine format, but none of the titles were successful. From the entire EC line, only **MAD** survived. Though forgotten by many fans, this line did leave at least one memorable legacy.

"If you're really an astute fan, and you're looking for through some of the Picto-Fiction where I wrote more than one story, you'll see I used the pseudonym Alfred E. Newman. This is prior to me taking over **MAD**. When I decided to use this grinning idiot as the **MAD** mascot, even though Harvey had played with the face, I gave him my pseudonym," Feldstein says.

HUMOR IN A JUGULAR VEIN

"**MAD** was a special kind of magazine,'" he says. "It was a satire and social commentary magazine, and I directed it that way when I took over. [It] reinforced the beliefs that young people had but weren't seeing in print elsewhere. We were putting it into print."

"Back when I first took over, I was determined to give the creators credit. I started working on the first masthead, but I didn't want to change it every issue, so I wrote 'The Usual Gang of Idiots.' It's still there," he laughs.

After a long tenure, though, he felt it was time to call it quits. "At the end of my contract in May of 1984, I decided to retire. I felt that **MAD** was not long for this world unless something was done, and I could not budge Bill on the changes I thought were important," he says.

"There had been a slide. We had reached a peak of about 2.8 million copies per issue. When I left, it was down to 1.75 million," he continues. "It really grieves me to see it today under 300,000, which is where I picked it up from Harvey when I first took over in 1956."

The time at EC and **MAD** gave him the opportunity to work with an amazing array of creators. Of them, who did he really like working with? "Everybody on the staff. I didn't work with any people I didn't like or didn't feel were professional," he says.

He does have a problem, though, with the lack of credit he has received.

"I've lived with this Kurtzman cult even though

I took over the magazine in 1956 and turned it into a rather American icon of social criticism, I was never able to undo cult attachment of Harvey. There were articles written about us in the '70s about our effect on the 'Make Love Not War' population, the burning of bras, the tearing up of draft cards and so on. They never once credited me and said it was done by Harvey Kurtzman. Harvey stopped doing **MAD** in 1956 and this stuff was taking place in the '60s and '70s. It was a problem for me from an ego point of view," he says.

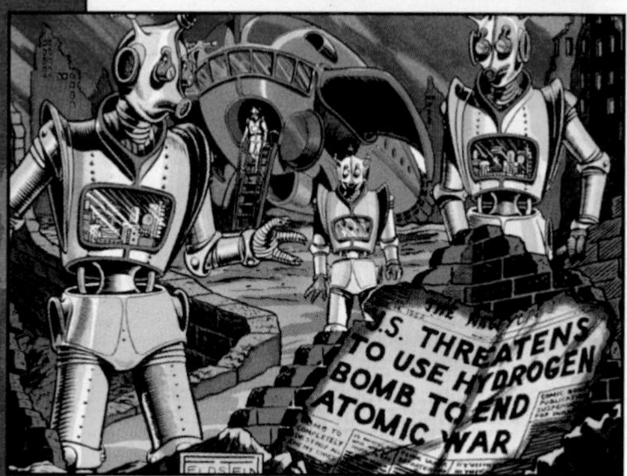

"Now that I go to conventions and I'm trying to straighten out the history, I go around saying that Bill Gaines and I had a cash and credit arrangement. He paid me cash and he took the credit," he laughs.

BEYOND EC & MAD

Asked to pinpoint a few favorite pieces of work, he says he doesn't really have favorites among his stories.

"At this point, 47 to 50 years later, I don't remember which were my favorites. I know that as I did each story I enjoyed it. I thought it was a good job. Some were a little formulaic and on some we took the easy way out, but some were very clever and well constructed. Some I was very proud of in terms of the ones we called our 'preachies,' which were pleas for tolerance, racial equality and justice. We were doing things that weren't done in comics in those days," he says.

As for the enthusiasts, original Fan-Addicts and newcomers alike, what would Feldstein tell them of the enduring legacy of EC comics?

"I'd tell them they're crazy for spending the kind of money they're spending on collecting them," he laughs, "but only because I'm jealous."

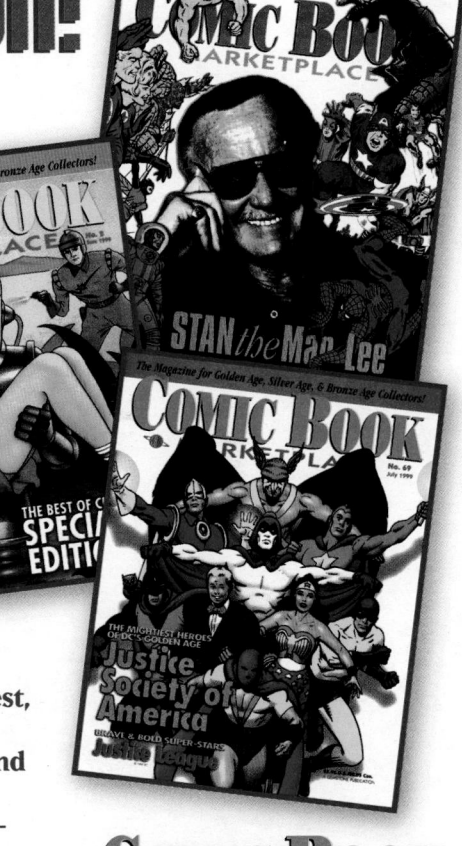

See Next Page for Ordering Information →

IT STARTED WITH FLASH GORDON-FLIGHTS TO EC & BEYOND with AL WILLIAMSON

By J.C. Vaughn

*It started with **Flash Gordon**, the 1940s action-filled, meticulously illustrated adventure comic strip by Alex Raymond. **The Spirit**, Will Eisner's smoky creation, Hal Foster's exquisitely rendered **Prince Valiant** and other strips followed close behind.*

In Spanish, of course.

Fans and historians know Al Williamson for his highly evocative art over the last fifty years. Many, though, don't know the full scope or variety of his efforts.

*He has worked on everything from pencilling and inking stories in EC's **Weird Science-Fantasy** in the '50s to inking John Romita, Jr. on **Daredevil** for Marvel in the '90s, stopping along the way for a highly respected run on the daily and Sunday **Star Wars** strip with the late writer Archie Goodwin.*

During his career, he has worked with the proverbial Who's Who of comic book talent. The list of names includes John Prentice (the artist who took over ***Rip Kirby*** *in 1956 following the death of its creator, Alex Raymond), Roy G. Krenkel, Angelo Torres, Wally Wood, Joe Orlando and the rest of the EC gang.*

When publisher Bill Gaines and writer/editor Al Feldstein brought that group together, they must have known in some sense the amazing level of talent they had assembled. There is equally no way they could have known what a permanent impression they would make on the industry or the art form.

Williamson, along with artists such as Wally Wood, Harvey Kurtzman, and others carved out a distinctive – and as it turns out, lasting – niche in American comics with the quality of their work on the EC line.

Although it has been 50 years since the "New Trend" began and almost 45 since it ended, today's top creators routinely cite the horror, crime and science fiction comics that comprised the "New Trend" as being among the most influential comics in the history of the medium.

While more experienced fans might know Williamson for his EC work, younger enthusiasts might know him exclusively for his inking abilities. Then as now, he maintained a distinctive style that is neither entirely old school nor entirely new, containing elements both classical and innovative.

Many comic book artists know acclaim from fans or from fellow professionals. Williamson is one of those rare artists who unquestionably has both.

SOUTH AMERICA

For a young Al Williamson growing up in Colombia, the world of comics held incredible fascination. His wonderment was encouraged by his mother, who regularly bought comics for him (she would read them, too). Her favorite, he says, was **The Spirit**, printed in Mexico, and he quickly developed a liking for it as well.

It wasn't his favorite, though. That honor was reserved for Alex Raymond's legendary run on **Flash Gordon**.

Even **Flash Gordon** wasn't his favorite from the beginning, though.

"The first artist to inspire me was an Argentine artist called Carlos Clemen, then Bill Everett, creator of Amazing Man and Sub-Mariner," he says.

Thoroughly revved up by the Buster Crabbe serial, *Flash Gordon Conquers the Universe*, and the realization that Hollywood was making movies from comics, he was hooked.

"I was immediately taken with it and really just overwhelmed by it," he once told an interviewer. "It took over my life at the age of ten."[1]

With the excitement of the serial and the subsequent introduction to Hal Foster's work on **Prince Valiant**, Williamson's career was set in motion.

"I started drawing in school every chance I got," he says.

NORTH AMERICA

When his parents split up and his mother decided to return to North America, Williamson wasn't all that concerned with the differences he would experience or the situations that might confront him. He had *other* priorities.

This was where comics were done," he said. "This is where Alex Raymond lives."

In 1943 Williamson and his mother settled in San Francisco where he promptly began to devour his daily helping of Raymond's **Flash Gordon**. Then the unthinkable happened. Well, unthinkable to a 12-year-old fan at any rate.

Raymond joined the war effort and his duties on the strip were taken over by Austin Briggs. No reflection on Briggs, but he just wasn't Raymond, whose departure was not sufficiently explained. Not that any justification would have sufficed for the young Williamson.

"The next year my mother and I moved to New York. I went to the office of King Features Syndicate, owners of the strip, and demanded an explanation," he says. He was 13 years old.

"A lady there was very nice and she offered me proofs of Briggs' strips, but I turned them down. I suppose it wasn't very polite, but I didn't want them," he says with a laugh.

EC-A WORLD OF ITS OWN

Becoming an artist is different for each individual. Williamson described himself as "pretty much self-taught," although he counts the high standards of influences such as Roy Krenkel and Frank Frazetta as benchmarks.

"I was working with Frank on **John Wayne Comics**, and this particular scene called for John Wayne and a sidekick to be going along when a rabbit darts out in front of them. Frank said, 'I've never drawn a rabbit.' He closed his eyes for a moment, then drew a great looking rabbit," he says.

He had made his first successful foray into comic book art in **Famous Funnies**. "I did a couple of spot illustrations," he says. That title, ironically, had been the first American comic book he had ever seen.

In the process of breaking in, he became friends with a few of the artists working for publisher William M. Gaines at EC Comics.

"Wally Wood and Joe Orlando kept on telling me to come up and meet Bill," he says. "I finally met him at a party at Wally's. I was 20 or so. He was always very nice, but he demanded respect. You knew you couldn't mess around with a deadline."

Williamson says Gaines was quick to give him a chance, but that chance came with the caveat "If you're late, you don't work for me again."

"If the deadline was in two weeks, I made it in two weeks, but Bill always made a production of it, like he didn't think I was going to make or he'd been sweating over it all day," he laughs.

Not that Williamson didn't cut it close.

"I was a goof off," he said. "I would have a bunch of my friends come over the night before an assignment was due and we'd knock it out. It wasn't the most professional situation, but it was a great time."

The camaraderie of those late night sessions was one of the perks of working for EC. Even though Williamson was the youngest (he was 20 when he started), he got along well with the other creators.

"They were all sweethearts," he says. "They were all good artists in that group, and they were good people, too."

THE END OF EC

When Senate hearings – inspired by Dr. Frederic Wortham's claims about the influence of comic books on youngsters – came about, so did the Comics Code. The Code put an end to the axes in heads, hangings, electrocutions and other graphic depictions on the covers of the "New Trend" titles, although they had never really been a big factor on the science fiction titles with which Williamson was more associated.

On the heels of the demise of the "New Trend," Gaines launched the "New Direction" titles; Williamson's artwork was featured prominently in **Valor**. It, though, like all the "New Direction" titles was short-lived.

"I don't think any of us thought about how long it would last," he says of his time at EC. "It was sad when it was over, but Bill had **MAD** and I was already working for Stan Lee doing westerns over at Marvel [then Atlas], so it wasn't as if I lost my livelihood."

AFTER EC

After the end of EC's comic book line, Williamson worked for several other publishers. He also ended up working with John Prentice on the newspaper strip **Rip Kirby**.

"Johnny was wonderful to work with. He was very patient, but he was the best schooling I could have had on meeting a deadline. He always made it clear how important that was," he says.

Rip Kirby, of course, was not the end of Williamson's newspaper work. In addition to a run on **Secret Agent X-9** he teamed up with his old friend Archie Goodwin for a long, respected run on the **Star**

Wars strip. He remembers the collaboration fondly and identifies him as his favorite writer to work with.

"When King Features called me to do this strip, I immediately thought of Archie to write it," he says. "We had lunch. Archie said to me, 'I'll write if you draw it,' and I said, 'I'll draw it if you write it,' and that's how we got together for that."

Goodwin, who launched Marvel's creator-owned Epic line, had also worked for Warren, but was best known as a writer-editor for DC Comics.

"Archie was very good," he says. "He wrote a story you could draw. He wrote with the artist in mind."

Another great DC Comics editor Julie Schwartz switched the track of Williamson's career by offering him an inking assignment. Here he could still inject elements of style and detail, but he could work without the time consuming undertaking of designing and laying out each page. In other words, he could work faster.

As a result, a whole generation of comic book fans grew up knowing Williamson more as an inker than as a pencil artist. Whether it was over Curt Swan's pencils on a Superman comic or John Romita, Jr. on **Darvedevil: Man Without Fear**, his inks tend to bring their own elements to a story without suborning the style of the penciler.

In 1995 he illustrated a 2-issue **Flash Gordon** series for Marvel with his good friend Mark Schultz, creator of **Xenozoic Tales**.

"It was hard work, but fun," he says.

PLACE IN HISTORY

Al Williamson continues to ply his craft in the comics industry, accepting both inking and full illustration assignments. He works from 9 to 5 each day at his Pennsylvania home, taking an hour for lunch.

If he pauses to reflect on the place in history earned by the EC creators, he does not do so indulgently. Instead of a prideful comment about the importance of what they achieved or how he has never yet missed a deadline, one is more likely to get a comment about what a good group of guys his fellow artists were.

While he originally kept copies of all the ECs (over time he gave them to friends), he eventually kept only the science fiction and the war titles. He still enjoys what he does, and if he laments certain directions the industry has gone in, he doesn't dwell on them.

"Sometimes it seems just a little bit hard to believe that I've been in this business for 50 years," he laughs.

1 **Comic Book Marketplace #51**, September 1997, Gemstone Publishing, Inc., p. 21.

THE MON CALAMARI HAVE WAGED THEIR OWN BATTLE AGAINST THE EMPIRE FOR SOME TIME, LUKE... NOW THEY'VE JOINED THE REBEL ALLIANCE!
TO EVACUATE OUR YAVIN HEADQUARTERS, WE NEED A DIVERSION FOR THE IMPERIALS... I'M MEETING WITH THE MON CALAMARI LEADER, ADMIRAL ACKBAR, TO SEE IF THEY CAN SUPPLY IT!
BETTER STRAP IN BACK THERE, PRINCESS! WE'RE APPROACHING OUR RENDEZVOUS COORDINATES... TIME TO DROP FROM HYPERSPACE!
11-23

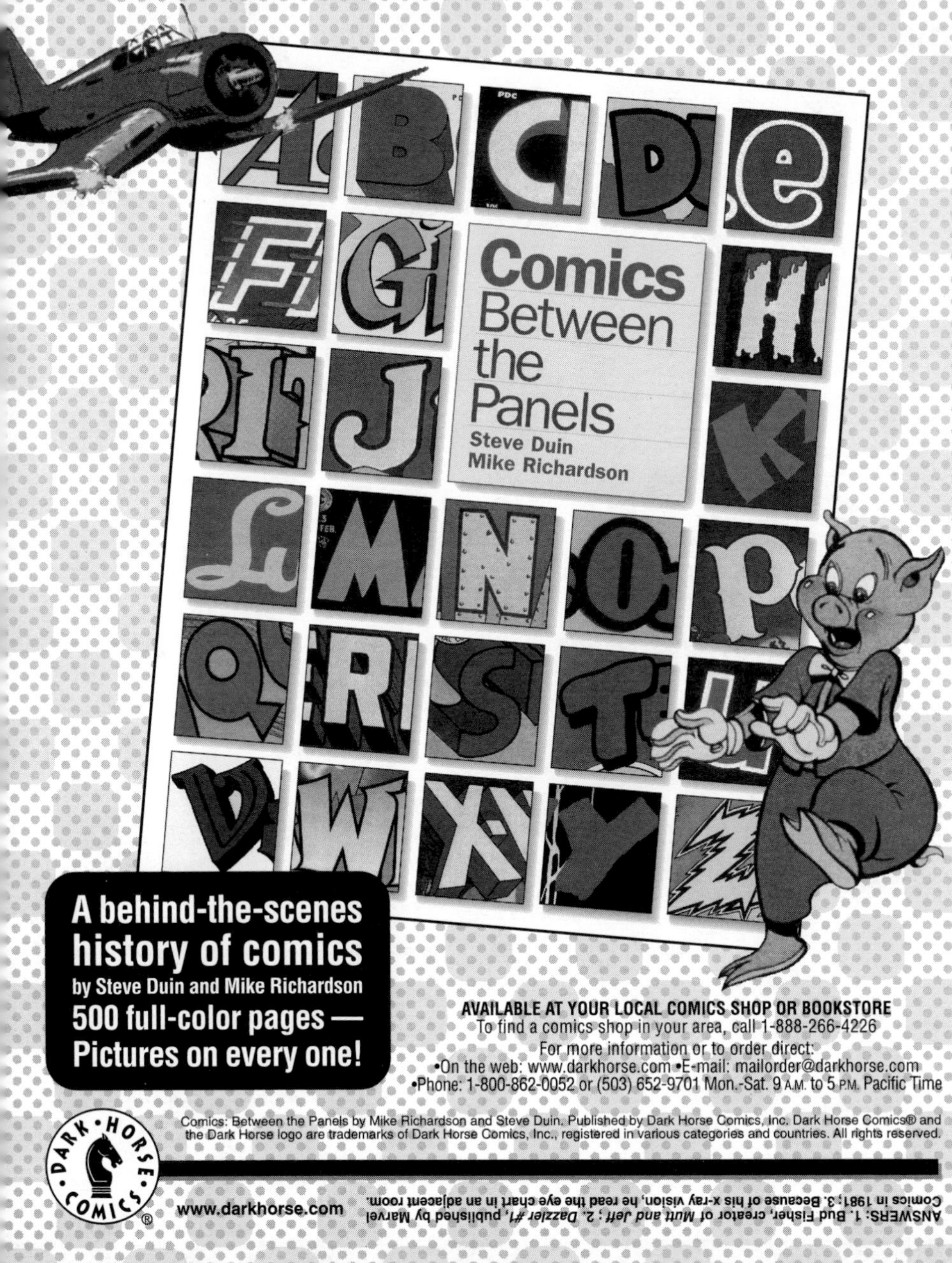

The 1940s *Daredevil.* © LEV

Breakfast entertainment! © DC

Welcome to a unique event in the history of The Overstreet Comic Book Price Guide. In 30 years, Bob Overstreet has never written a feature article for this book, but now, for the first time, he celebrates (and illustrates!) his 30th anniversary as the definitive source of accurate comic book information with an affectionate look back at his childhood and the comics that made him the fan he remains today. Presented here is the history of Bob Overstreet that led into the Comic Book Price Guide. Bob talks about his early days as a comic book fan, and the weird and wonderful world of EC Comics. So join us, kiddies, for a real dead-time story! Hahahahaha!

After receiving my copy of Bill Schelly's **Fandom 's**

Finest Comics #3 recently, I started thinking about those early days back in 1952 when I first met Landon Chesney and became an EC fan. It's all coming back to me now—the correspondence, the price lists, the artwork, all the memories. My god! It was 1952 and Chesney and I were both only 13 years old! Maybe it's fate, but for some reason I did save all my correspondence and price lists from those early years and recently re-read the dozens of letters. Interestingly, fans were a lot more sophisticated than you may realize. The same condition grades were already in use in the early 1950s, back when there was really no accepted standard.

Before getting into my involvement with ECs, let's go back a few years to when comic books were just comic books. We bought them to read and enjoy, spending most of our time doing the things that kids did to have fun—flip gun wars, roller skating, riding slow-moving trains coming into the train yard, pole vaulting, fishing, riding bicycles, roller-skating and girl watching. It was sometime after the war, and my older brother, Jerry, and I lived perfectly normal happy lives being uprooted all the time, moving from place to place, from school to school, never really settling down anywhere. We had a dresser drawer full of comic books consisting of the usual dog-eared funny animal and superhero fare. As Dad read the morning paper, I was reading **Fox and the Crow** while eating my breakfast, which was usually a bowl of Kix. Yes, I did order that Atomic Bomb ring back in 1947 that was advertised on the Kix box!

© LEV

PLAYING DAREDEVIL

In 1949 we moved to Tuskaloosa, Alabama when I was eleven years old and in the 6th grade. One day we decided to play **Daredevil**—you know, the old red and blue one. My brother Jerry and I climbed up a telephone pole and hand-walked the power line clear across the highway to the other side! When we got halfway across, we were too scared to turn back. We played at a lumber yard close by where there were huge stacks of lumber, some 10 to 15 feet high. The stacks were different distances apart and we would run and jump across, increasing the distance as we thought we could make it just like Daredevil would have done. We practiced running and jumping and pole vaulting to build up our physical prowess.

The House of Glass

THE COMIC BOOK HOUSE

In an open field behind where we lived there was this small house with large glass windows all around. When Jerry and I looked through the glass we saw stacks and stacks of comic books just sitting there. We didn't understand why the comic books were there, but I remember standing there, staring in at all these wonderful comic books and wishing that someday, I would have stacks of my own. Recently I discussed this with my older brother, and he remembered that the comics only had 3/4th covers, which meant that they were returns waiting for destruction or underground sale.

ICE CREAM FOR A SONG

One day there was this talent contest held at the local movie theater. It was advertised on the radio, and they promised a full quart of ice cream to everyone that participated. I couldn't let this one slip by! I've never had a full quart of ice cream before! So I worried about what to do at the talent show. My dad suggested that I sing a song, and he offered to teach me one that would be a sure hit.

"BESIDE A WESTERN WATER TANK,ONE COLD NOVEMBER DAY – INSIDE AN EMPTY BOXCAR, A DYING HOBO LAY. – GULP!"
YANK!
Original artwork by Bob Overstreet

The title of the song was "Dying Hobo!" and it was an old railroad song from the 1930s. Ever heard of it?

When I showed up at the theater the piano player asked me what my song was, and then said "that's okay, I can play anything. Just tell me what it is when you go on." Finally my turn came, and there I was standing center stage. The announcer asked me what I was going to sing, and I told him "Dying Hobo!" Well, they had never heard of it and I began to sing the lyrics while the piano tried to catch up. It was a disaster! Very soon, there was this guy on the side of the stage with a big wooden hook and looking very mean. My brother Jerry was sitting in the front row booing and getting the whole audience to do the same. He started throwing tomatoes and the guy with the hook finally got me. How embarrassing! What a kid will do for a quart of ice cream.

We left Tuskaloosa and moved back to Cleveland, Tennessee in 1950, where my older brother and I were both in the same classroom—he was in the eighth grade and I was in the seventh—with the same teacher. We lived in the country and had to ride the bus to this small school on the edge of town. The next year we moved closer to town and I was sent to Arnold School for the eighth grade. It was here that I met Landon Chesney.

BIRTH OF AN EC FAN

Chesney invited me over to his house one day to look at his EC collection, which was a stack of comics carefully stored in a small cardboard box. These comic books were special. As Chesney put it, "ECs were the best written and best drawn comic

Clockwise: *Weird Fantasy #11*. A long bicycle ride to acquire this baby! *Haunt of Fear #11*. My first back issue! *Crime SuspenStories #11*. My first Crime off the stands! *Vault of Horror #15 (#4)*, found in an old box of comics! All © WMG.

books ever produced! Yesiree, they never insulted your intelligence and the stories were all great, each with a twist ending. It's fascinating to see how these artists laid out their stories with the special lighting effects and the unusual angles." He would say, "see how Craig handles the folds in cloth, the brush strokes are perfectly executed." He would turn to a Feldstein story and say "look here, the stories by this artist are heavy in atmosphere." After further doses of the likes of "Ghastly" Ingels, Wally Wood and Harvey Kurtzman, I was hooked! A new EC fan was born!

THE COLLECTION BEGINS

Until then, it never occurred to me that a comic book was something you collect. The idea of putting runs together was fascinating and I was ready to get started. The very next issues on the stands began my collection. But where would one find all the issues that came before? It seemed impossible, especially to a 13-year-old who had no money.

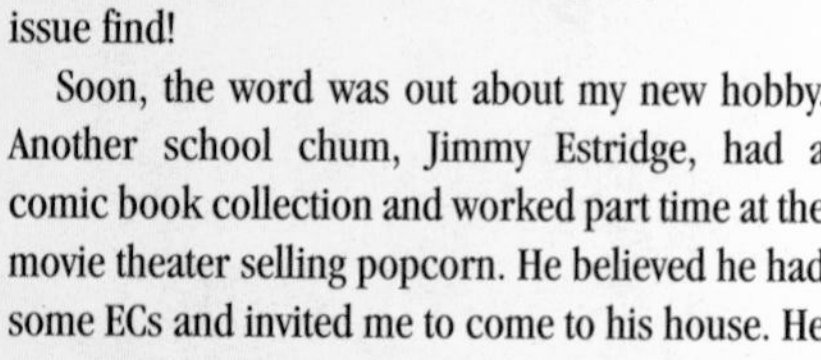

One day at school there was a magic show, and I was working selling snacks and drinks to the other students. There was this kid sitting there on the stands reading **Haunt of Fear** #11. Gadzooks, a back issue! I asked him if he would sell it. He said that he would, but had to finish reading it first, so I waited. This was exciting, my first back issue find!

Soon, the word was out about my new hobby. Another school chum, Jimmy Estridge, had a comic book collection and worked part time at the movie theater selling popcorn. He believed he had some ECs and invited me to come to his house. He lived on the south side of town—a long bicycle ride—but I scored again, getting **Weird Fantasy** #11, my second back issue find!

A new acquaintance (Bill Smalling) that lived a couple miles out of town on George- town Road invited me over for the weekend. His father ran the movie projector at the Princess Theater downtown. Bill had a box of comic books, and here I acquired a dog-eared copy of **Vault of Horror** #15 with a chunk out of the cover. This book was a whopping two years old! It felt like I had discovered an ancient Egyptian tomb-piece! The current **Vault** on the stands was #24, which meant that I still had to find #1-14 and #15-23 to catch up. It was years later before I knew #12 was actually the first issue.

My first **Crime SuspenStories** off the stands was #11, and the first **Haunt** was #12. Since my only transportation was via bicycle, it was very difficult to go too far out of my neighborhood to buy ECs off the stands. There was a small local grocery store on Harle Avenue that had a comic book rack. Chesney and I had the owner, Mrs. Gladys Pierce, special order two each of all the ECs. She would hold these for us to pick up on the way home from school.

At 13 years of age, Chesney and I were both interested in cartoon art and were especially impressed with the EC style, which became our criterion for excellence. L.C. was already an accomplished artist at that time, having done hundreds of "Frank Fearnot" (his character) cartoon strips. He once said that he had enough of these to run as a daily in a newspaper for two years. His flare for cartoon art was inspired, and it came easy for him.

He could pencil up a scene quickly which bursted with excitement!*

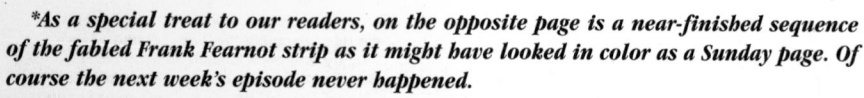

As a special treat to our readers, on the opposite page is a near-finished sequence of the fabled Frank Fearnot strip as it might have looked in color as a Sunday page. Of course the next week's episode never happened.

FRANK FEARNOT

CHESNEY–

AND THE ZOO CAPER!!

by Landon Chesney

Fandom remembers Chesney for his more serious EC style narratives such as "Life Battery," but at a very early age, before there was a fandom, he entertained himself by penciling dozens of these Fearnot strips. The stories were set up in four panel sequences with the storyline often continuing as in this example. This is pure Chesney! A rare insight into the humorous vein of one of fandom's greatest artists and story-tellers!

Will Frank solve the riddle of the gator? Tune in next week for the conclusion!

THE HAUNTED HOUSE

We lived in the small town of Cleveland, Tennessee, and there was an old, vacant two-story house downtown that had a reputation for being haunted. Strange lights and ghostly images were seen moving about inside late at night. As the story goes, this house belonged to a doctor who died in the upstairs bedroom. They could not settle the estate, so the house stayed completely furnished and locked up for years, just as it was the night of his death. White sheets were placed over all the furniture, giving a spooky aura to the place at night!

One of our favorite Kurtzman stories was "House of Horror" which appeared in **Haunt Of Fear** #15(#1). Remembering this EC story which was about a haunted house, Chesney and I got a few of our friends and went to this house to "act out" this famous EC story. It was close to midnight, and it was going to be a test of courage. One by one, we all were given a single match with instructions to enter the house in the dark and find our way into the living room. Then we had to creep up the spiral staircase to the second floor, down a dark, narrow hallway loaded with test tubes, flasks and surgical instruments, and finally to the bedroom where the doctor died. We then had to strike the match in the window for those outside to see, to prove we "made it." Of course, Chesney went first (he had more courage than the rest of us put together), and I went second. While inching my way through the dark house, feeling my way along, I was so scared that if I heard a pin drop, I would have been out of there! Finally, I made it to the bedroom and struck the match. That night we all learned about fear and how it felt having your hair stand on end. This was one of many trips that we took into the unknown.

With hair beginning to rise, we entered the forbidden zone!

THE CEMETERY

Soon we were ready to create our own horror stories, but inspiration was needed. What was it really like being in a graveyard at the stroke of midnight—the witching hour? How did it feel seeing a full werewolf moon coming up over gravestones or casting eerie shadows around a cemetery loaded with creepy mausoleums? To find out, we went to Cemetery Hill, Cleveland's oldest and largest graveyard. This was scary and inspiring, but there were only a few mausoleums and they weren't that impressive. We wondered where could we find the ultimate graveyard? The closest large city was Atlanta—a two hour drive. So, on the first free weekend, we were off.

Not knowing where any of the cemeteries were, we stopped at a filling station and got directions to Atlanta's largest and best cemetery. Here was some of the most ornate grave decor you could imagine. We hit pay dirt! We found a nice spacious mausoleum with a decorated iron spiked fence. We sat on top of a large tombstone with pad and pencil in hand sketching out this beautiful scene. This would be just the thing for an opening sequence in one of our horror stories. As we were sketching away, we heard muffled voices coming from behind. The voices came louder and louder. Finally we turned around and there was a large group of people collecting around the very gravestone where we were sitting! We burned leather and didn't stop until we reached our car and made it out of there and back to Cleveland.

Houdini was known for his levitation tricks. He always said that there was an explaination for all of his illusions, although some have never been explained to this very day.

HOUDINI AND THE OCCULT

Chesney also had an interest in magic and was a fan of Houdini. Houdini was an enigma. Not only was he the best escape artist ever, but he prided himself on performing the ultimate illusions, such as levitation and other tricks that could not be easily explained. His interest in the occult was such that he never attended a seance that he couldn't expose. His famous reward of $10,000 to any occultist that could fool him was legendary. He promised his wife that after his death, if there was any way to do it, he would contact her, but he never did. The complexities of Houdini challenged Chesney's mind and we spent many nights talking about it. We were both intrigued and aspired to be like Houdini.

Chesney concocted a straight jacket which he would have a friend put on him. He would suddenly disappear behind a screen and, voila!, come out in seconds completely free (just like Houdini). He also designed a small stock, like the ones from the middle ages, made of two-by-fours that were hinged, opening at the top, with two holes cut out for locking in your hands. He would have a friend put this on him, lock the padlock and hold the key. He would disappear behind a screen and within seconds appear with his hands out, completely free! He would then hand the still locked stock to his astonished friend. Yes, it was fun being an escape artist like Houdini.

WATCH ME DISAPPEAR!!
Original artwork by Bob Overstreet

The secret hideaway!

A rare 1950s shot of Chesney in his cloak and hat.

THE TRUNK ESCAPE

In 1952, Chesney had a black top hat and cloak (like Dracula's) which he wore to play a villain. He found this old bell-top trunk which we decided to set up with a false bottom. We dug this deep ditch at his house, reliving some of the great EC horror stories where someone was digging a grave. Our hole was about eight feet long and five feet deep when we finished. We put a piece of plywood over the top of the ditch, which had a trap door at one end. At the other end, we cut a hole and nailed down this hollow log that was just big enough for us to stand inside it from below and peer out of the knotholes. We then took the trunk with the false bottom and set it on top of the plywood. The rest of the area around the trunk was camouflaged with dirt and grass so that it looked like there was just an old trunk sitting on the ground. I would hide below the trunk and Chesney, wearing his cloak and hat, would lure one of the neighborhood kids to follow him. When he had someone watching, he would open the trunk, get in, and go through the false bottom and disappear.

The kid would open the trunk to find Chesney had completely vanished while I would be looking at the whole scene through the knothole in the stump.

The Devil Comes A'Knockin'!

THE DEVIL APPEARS

We both lived in small houses which were probably built back in the 1930s or '40s. His bedroom entrance was off the back porch. Since I was staying over one night, we got this bright idea about summoning up the Devil. If we could get the Devil to actually appear, this would be proof of his existence! To make this work, we thought, all religious literature had to be removed from the room. Having done this, we began swearing at the Devil, demanding that he appear, daring him over and over again! We would have had a heart attack if he did show up! In Chesney's small bedroom he had a bed-light that cast eerie shadows on the wall. We were startled by one of these shadows that at first appeared to have horns. As the night wore on, our demands for proof dwindled.

We were finally willing to accept three knocks on the door as proof of his existence. We went to bed and were startled to hear three loud knocks on the bedroom door! The knocks were so loud that they woke Chesney's father, who immediately came out to investigate. The porch lights went on and he came barging into our bedroom only to find two scared-stiff teenagers! He asked us who was knocking? We were too scared to tell him the truth. Was it the Devil that really knocked on our door that night? Perhaps, but we never tried that again to find out!

VOICES IN THE NIGHT

Occasionally, Chesney would hear faint music and voices coming from somewhere in his bedroom at night. This was really eerie until we figured out it was probably his bed springs picking up signals from a radio tower a couple miles away. Spending the night with Chesney was often a hair-raising experience. You were always entertained but had to be prepared for anything!

MAIL-ORDER ECs

When I began buying ECs off the stands in 1952, my allowance was around ten cents a week, just enough to buy four ECs a month. In a couple years, I had a paper route and began making a little money. This enabled me to buy some back issues through the mail. Chesney and I became close friends competing with each other for back-issue ECs. In 1954, Chesney kept coming up with these great, never before seen, early issues. Eventually he gave me his source, a guy named Billy Hoover. EC fans may remember this name because Billy always stamped his name and address in the centerfold of all the comics he sold. Soon Billy was sending me his latest list of ECs for sale. He had a large collection of mostly ECs, westerns and

Whispering bedsprings!

Disneys, and had been buying and selling comic books since 1950. His lists were typed on whatever paper he could find—tissue paper, paper sacks, colored paper—whatever he could cram into his typewriter. Like Chesney and I, Billy enjoyed drawing and coloring comics too. We would draw something and send it to him for coloring, and he would mail us books to read and return. How many collectors today can 'borrow' a book through the mail?

SUMMER CAMP

At the age of 15, I was offered a summer job as counselor at a boy's camp on Guntersville Lake, Alabama. The very first day there, a sharp kid got me into a game of blackjack and took away my whole summer's spending money. I had to live just on the three meals served each day. I was also in charge of a house of kids. When they learned about my collection, they made fun of it so much that when I returned home, the comic books had to go.

I'd been interested in Indian arrowheads and crystals for years (another story), and one day a friend showed me a beautiful quartz crystal and offered to trade a box full of them for my EC collection. Still remembering the ridicule received at camp, I made the trade. Of couse, the very next day, my senses returned, but it was too late! This kid traded my ECs to Gene Eberly, a close friend of Chesney's. Chesney ended up with my collection by trading Gene a fairly new BB gun for the comics. What a deal! He then called and offered them back to me at two for a quarter, keeping the ones he needed. So for a long, long time, I had to feed my old pal quarters to get my collection back. This was the first of many lessons to come in my collecting career. At least I was able to get them back!

EXPLORING OUR UNIVERSE

We were at that impressionable age where everything was questionable. We developed an intense interest in the mysteries of the universe as well as the subjects delved into by EC comics, such as ghosts, haunted houses, vampires, werewolves, ghouls, graveyards, mausoleums, mental telepathy, moving objects, seances, ouija boards, levitation, spiritual photography, UFOs, and many other paranormal and pseudo-scientific concepts.

We both shared a group of friends, most of whom were adults, that were involved in various scientific fields. One of them was Chester Patterson, a machinist who helped me design and make parts for my telescope. He engineered a nice rack-and-pinion focusing mechanism which worked beautifully. Chet built himself a small one-room laboratory next to his house. Here he conducted experiments in micro-biology, growing cultures in petri dishes and experimenting with antibiotics. He had a wonderful microscope which he used in various experiments. Chesney and I would meet with Chet on a weekly basis to discuss all aspects of epistemology (the essence of knowledge) which breaks down into science and philosophy. Besides all branches of science, we discussed the essence of matter and space/time concepts such as relativity. Chet introduced us to subjects and levels of thought that would not have been possible on our own.

Chester became a good friend and encouraged me in astronomy. We also went on geological hunts into North Carolina looking for gemstones. He taught me how to identify the crystal cleavage of corumdum and soon I was finding some real rubies and sapphires, not to mention the basic metamorphic and crystalline rock samples.

Chesney and I had another older friend, Jack West, who had a telescope, knew photography and was well read in history, philosophy and the sciences. As kids, we were impressed because Jack submitted a sunspot count every day to Mount Polamar, the famous observatory that housed the largest telescope in the world!. He would project the sun's image onto a piece of white cardboard where you could easily see and count all the storms on the sun's disk. Jack shared our interests and even collected a few comic books. I still remember the copy of **Strange Adventures** #1 he had, the one with the **Destination: Moon** cover.

Jack taught me astronomy and photography. He had an extensive library, encouraging me to read and start my own library. Chesney and I would spend many hours visiting with Jack each week. We experimented photographing model rockets with special lighting effects, shooting lightning at night and taking pictures through his telescope. We even shot lighting effects on our faces, to be utilized later in comic book stories. Jack was also very good at firing a pistol and throwing a hatchet and knife. He taught us how to safely do all these things. We would have contests among ourselves. We sure did have fun in those days.

Strange Adventures #1, © DC

Another elder friend of mine, actually a friend of my father, was J. L. Van Wagoner, with whom Chesney did not get along. He invited us over to his house for discussions. Van was from the old school, which required patience to learn from him. His stories were long and drawn-out, but when the end came, it was always thought-provoking and worth the wait. Chesney didn't have the patience required and soon dropped out of the discussions. Chesney kept saying "get to the point, Van, get to the point!" Van's specialties were philosophy, fossils and history. His wife baked the best rum cakes you would ever put into your mouth.

BUYING THEM OFF THE STANDS

All through high school, my EC collection came together by systematically buying each EC right off the stands. Every week, it was like Christmas! It's hard to explain today how important and exciting it was the day the ECs came out. Of all the events in my life up to that time, this was the most anticipated. The night before this blessed event, I couldn't eat or sleep. That day at school would always be the longest day of the year, and finally, there it was—the rack of comic books containing that week's treat, all for just a dime a piece!

Chesney and I were there in the early period and stayed with EC to the very end. We witnessed all the changes as they occurred. Since the first two years of "New Trend"s were so difficult to obtain back then, we could only imagine what the covers and stories were like, not having seen them. I remember having dreams of finding a collection of old ECs and looking at the covers for the first time, wild covers that only the imagination of a 14 year old could create. Of course, as the years passed, we were able to finally see all the real EC covers, and we were never disappointed.

THE BIRTH OF EC

Years later, we came to understand more about the history of EC, the weird numbering of the early issues, and all the forces at work that propelled Bill Gaines into doing what he did. After World War II, with the surrender of Germany and Japan, the superhero characters had lost the main reason for their existance – to fight the axis powers!

There were no villains left to fight, except the common criminals that were always there. Consequently, fan support for the superhero went into a decline. Men and women in the armed services all read comic books and they, for the most part, went home which created a huge decline in sales. After the war, the comic industry began experimenting with other types of comic books. Crime, love, teenage, westerns, funny animal, and a host of other genres began to appear. At this time EC.was mimmicking the other publishers with titles such as **Crime Patrol**, **Moon Girl**, **Modern Love, Gunfighter, Animal Fables** and others.

Then, in 1950, out of nowhere, this small, obscure comic publisher, EC, launched their brilliant NEW TREND In Comic Magazines! The publisher, Bill Gaines, introduced two bombshells at the same time! The very first series ever, composed of three different titles, based on gothic horror: **Crypt of Terror, Haunt of Fear** and **Vault of Horror**, and a science fiction series base on two titles: **Weird Fantasy** and **Weird Science!** These books were not the normal comic fare. All the stories were beautifully plotted, with twist endings, and crisp, exciting illustrations, the quality of which had never been seen before. From the beginning, these comic books were written for teenage to college age readers.

Other publishers followed EC's lead and began their horror and science fiction titles. Late in the year, EC put out **Crime SuspenStories** now giving them a trilogy of powerfull genres that continued to get the attention of the entire comics market! In 1951, EC got into the Korean war with their explosive titles **Frontline Combat** and **Two-Fisted Tales**! War comics like no other war comics you have ever read. These two titles started the whole genre of war comics to follow which are still coming out today. Interestingly, it was not World War II that started the genre, it was the Korean War!

We were thrilled to see the appearance of **Shock SuspenStories #1**, but noticed a slight drop in quality in the whole lineup from that point on. As fans we felt that the addiition of another title gave the staff less time to work on the rest of the line resulting in jobs being rushed to meet the deadline. Recently Chesney remarked "The drop in quality is most noticeable in the difference between **Crime SuspenStories** #9 and #10. Even the paper seems less substantial and the printing occasionally looked smudgey. Craig dropped his thick-line approach and went for a thinner, more illustration-like look. I thought his brushier approach suited the horror and crime genres better. And I dont think he ever did a more imagina-

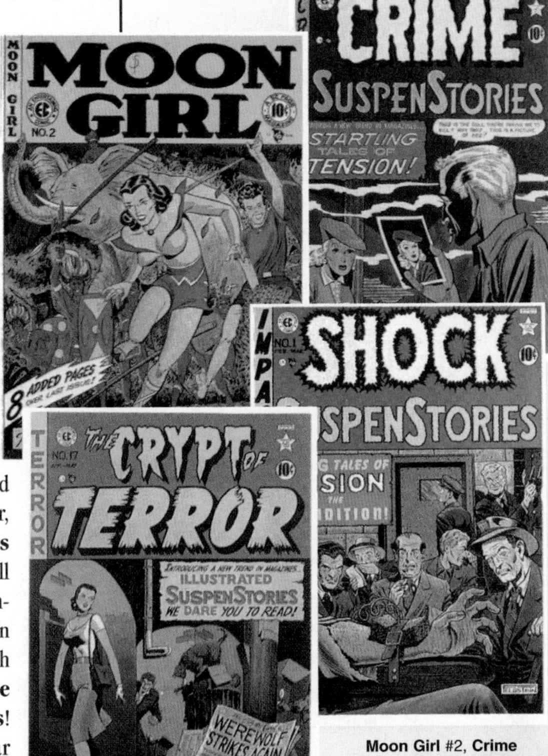

Moon Girl #2, **Crime SuspenStories #1, Crypt of Terror** #17, **Shock SuspenStories** #1,all © WMG tive cover than that attic scene on #9. Anyway, the debut of **Shock** proved, to my mind at least, the (sob) last gasp of the New Trend."

THE DEATH OF EC

Over the next two years, we saw the house style begin to change with the addition of new artists and writers. The horror stories were evolving into more graphic, stomach turning, blood and gore scenes. This is in contrast to the early years where these scenes were left up to each reader to visualize on his own. There is more impact on the reader seeing an expression of horror on the face of a person looking at a horrible scene than actually showing the scene itself. With the way horror comics were going, we knew it wouldn't last. As a true fan, I continued to buy every issue even though my parents were beginning to object. They actually did throw away a few of the more grotesque issues. The 1990s popular HBO series, **Tales From The Crypt**, adapted EC stories and took blood and gore to levels unimaginable back in the 1950s.

In 1955 Chesney decided to join the Air Force and see the world while I stayed in Cleveland, graduating from high school in 1956. Over the next several years Chesney and I kept in touch. He was in the service and I was struggling trying to make ends meet and finding a career.

EC was gone! We knew it back in 1954, and the "New Direction" titles of 1955 just didn't fill that void. EC was over, my collection was stored away, and I never thought it would ever connect with my life again.

THE FLYING SAUCER SIGHTING

The rage of the 1950s was this new American pastime of sky watching for UFOs. Since the name "Flying Saucer" was coined back in 1947 by Kenneth Arnold, thousands of sightings have occured worldwide, and continue to this very day. In 1954 Bill Gaines and Al Feldstein were quick to respond to the public interest in this developing field. Feldstein (recent communication) got in touch with Donald Keyhoe, who headed up the Air Force's "Project Bluebook" to get some of the best UFO stories they had. These were adapted and published in a special issue of **Weird Science Fantasy** (#26), where EC challenged the Air Force.

As EC fans, we were thrilled with this development. During the 1950s many nights were spent out with my telescope looking up to the stars. If anything unusual was flying around, I would see it.

Then in the Fall of 1956 when Chesney was home on leave, I took him to an astronomy class meeting one night at the observatory in Chattanooga, TN. It was dusk. Chesney and I were looking to the West. Suddenly, there it was! An orange colored disc with a dome on top. It was coming straight at us and wobbling, like it was riding on a cushion of air. It quickly disappeared into the lights of the city. To see a real flying saucer was considered the "ultimate experience" for a 1950s EC fan.

OUR FIRST COMIC BOOK STORY

After a few years Chesney came home from the Air Force. This was in the late 1950s. It didn't take long until we were both getting the itch to finally get that EC story done. You know, the one we had always wanted to do, but just didn''t.

Since we both loved Kurtzman''s 1950 classic "House of Horror," and in memory of the old haunted house that iniated us into the occult, we decided to do a takeoff on this theme. After work, we got together at night and began the task of creating the "masterpiece." The title of our yarn became "A Study In Horror." Inspired by the classic EC house style initiated by Feldstein, Craig and Kurtzman, we began creating the layouts using shadows, odd camera angles and sound effects. We drew ourselves as the main characters in the storyline. Bill Spicer, one of our early EC correspondents was launching a new fanzine, **Fantasy Illustrated**, and needed fresh fan material. Chesney drew the cover to the first issue and our story soon appeared in issue #3.

A rare early Polaroid shot of Overstreet inking page two of "Study." Taken in the late 1950s.

We had now reignited the old EC fever and began anew our quest of getting more involved with dealers and fans across the country. This gave each of us the opportunity of finally finishing our EC collections. Both of us were still missing issues. In 1961, Harry Thomas, a local fan who we met through the Southern Fandom Group reintroduced us to 1940s costumed hero comics.

Little did I know that a decade away my life would take such a dramatic turn with the appearance of the very first issue of The **Overstreet Comic Book Price Guide**!

Title page to "House Of Horror" which appeared in Haunt Of Fear #15(#1). This is the story that inspired our "A Study In Horror," along with another story we heard from our mutual friend, Jack West. Jack told us that he saw an ad in a North Carolina newspaper offering a reward to anyone that would stay in this mansion, reputed to be haunted. It was too far away for us to make the trip, but we did the next best thing. We put it into a comic book story. By the way, "A Study In Horror" was our first full fledged comic book story. as a team. As the EC story goes, some upper classmen took some freshmen to a haunted house for initiation into their fraternity. Each one was given a lantern and told to wave it at them from the 1st and 2nd floor windows, then go up to the attic and wait.

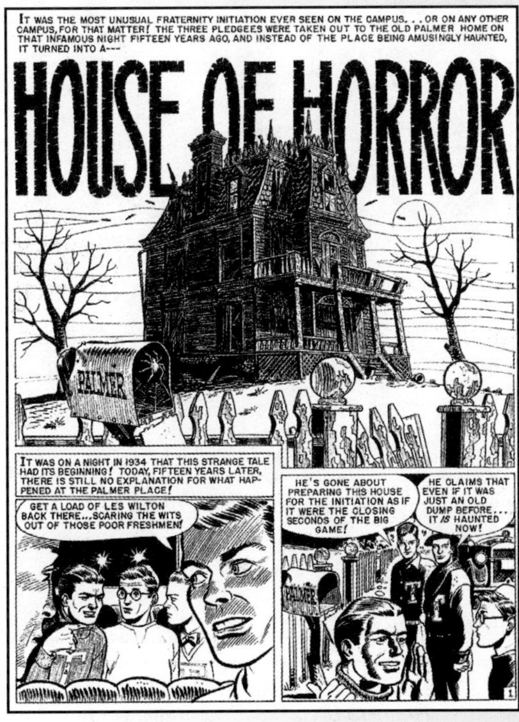

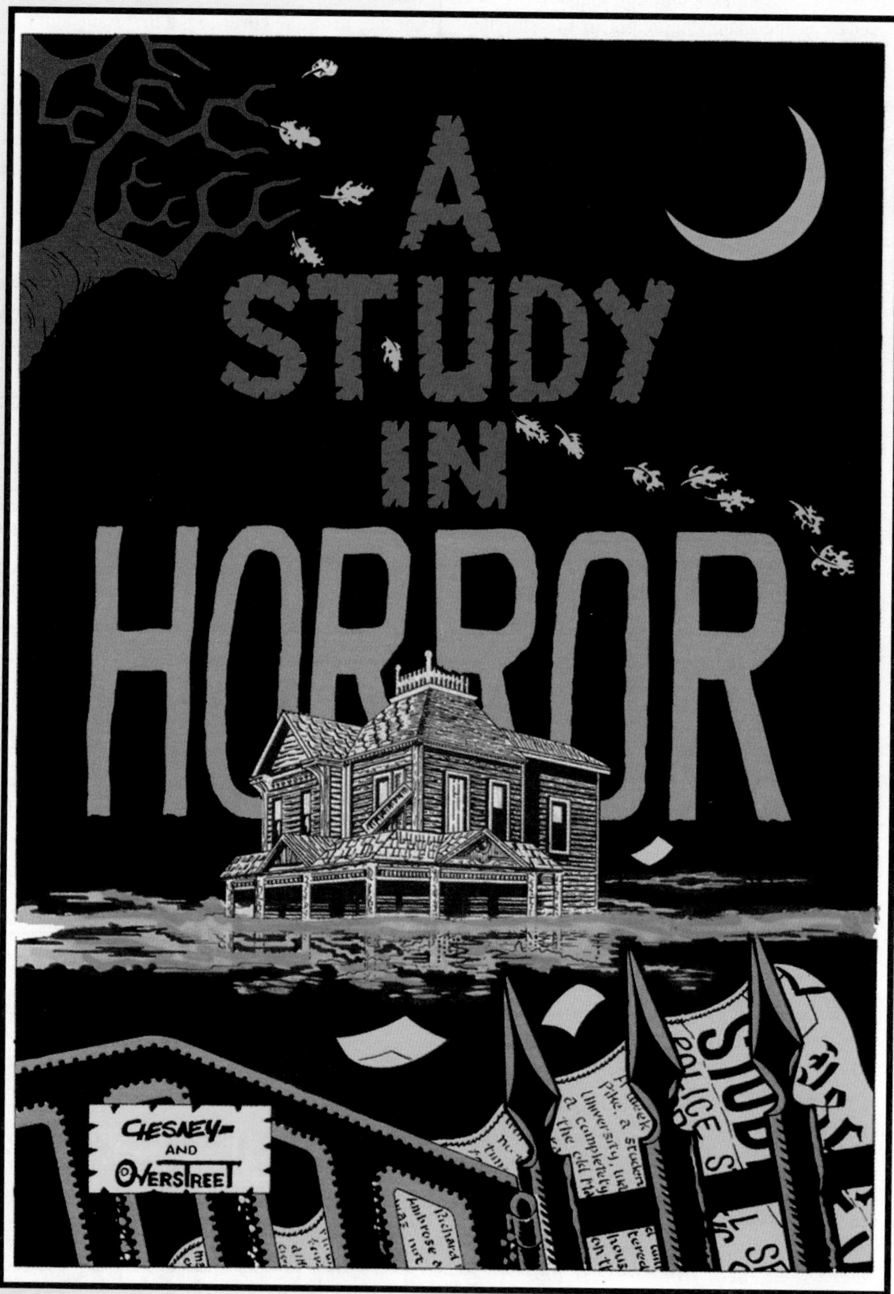

A Study In Horror was inspired by EC's "House of Horror," which appeared in Haunt of *Fear #15* (#1), 1950. Naturally, we found our own real, live haunted house to act out the scenes in this story!

The following story was originally written and drawn back in the 1950s by Chesney and Overstreet and was published in the early 1960s by Bill Spicer in a black and white format. Now as a special treat to our readers, here it is–**IN FULL COLOR FOR THE FIRST TIME!** The storyline was recently rewritten by today's Chesney and Overstreet for two reasons. One was to make the dialog fit better into today's world and the other to create an interesting "twist" on the original theme where the story repeats itself. So, let the story begin.....

ON THE MOONLIT CAMPUS OF A LARGE MIDWESTERN UNIVERSITY, A JOURNALISM MAJOR NAMED SIDNEY PIKE IS INTERRUPTED IN HIS WORK...
HEY SID! GUESS WHAT I FOUND IN A BACK ISSUE OF THE COLLEGE NEWSPAPER!
WHAT IS IT, STEVE?
OKAY... THIS GOES BACK SOME 30 YEARS! "TWO STUDENTS FROM STATE U. DECIDED TO SPEND THE NIGHT IN A HAUNTED HOUSE... ON A DARE! THE NEXT MORNING ONE WAS FOUND INSANE AND THE OTHER HAD VANISHED!"
SAY! LETS SEE THAT!
WELL, I'LL BE DARNED! I ALWAYS THOUGHT THAT STORY WAS A GAG! SOME KIND OF URBAN MYTH OR WHATEVER...
YEAH! A FOLK TALE WITH NO BASIS IN FACT!
YOU KNOW SOMETHING, STEVE? THIS IS REALLY INTRIGUING! LIKE, WHAT REALLY HAPPENED TO THE GUY WHO VANISHED?! I MEAN... C'MON... PEOPLE DON'T JUST VANISH!!
...AND WHAT ABOUT THE GUY WHO WENT BONKERS? DID HE RECOVER?? OR IS HE STILL LOCKED AWAY SOMEWHERE?
ITS HIGH TIME I TESTED MY SKILLS AS AN INVESTIGATIVE REPORTER!! I THINK I'LL FOLLOW UP ON THIS! WHY DON'T YOU COME ALONG?!
W-WHAT?! ME SPEND THE NIGHT IN A HAUNTED HOUSE?!
YEAH!! WHY NOT!
...ASSUMING THE PLACE IS STILL STANDING, THAT'S A GREAT IDEA! SO FAR WE'VE GOT MORE QUESTIONS THAN ANSWERS, BUT I'VE GOT AN IDEA FOR A SHORTCUT! I'M GONNA CONTACT THE ALUMNI OFFICE AND SEE IF THEY HAVE A CURRENT ADDRESS ON ALDOUS MANOR!
WHO'S ALDOUS MANOR?!
TECH
HE OWNS THE PROPERTY!

AS STORM CLOUDS LOOM ON THE HORIZON, SID AND STEVE CONTINUE ON THEIR UNUSUAL JOURNEY TO THE SMALL VILLAGE WHERE ALDOUS MANOR LIVES.
YOU'VE COME TO THE RIGHT PLACE, BOYS!
THANKS FOR SEEING US ON SUCH SHORT NOTICE! THIS SHOULD PROVE INTERESTING FOR MY THESIS ON THE PARANORMAL!!
A.M. MANOR

MAKE YOURSELVES COMFORTABLE, BOYS, AND I'LL SKETCH A LITTLE BACKGROUND ON THE HOUSE FOR YOU!!
WHAT WE'VE HEARD SO FAR IS FACINATING, MISTER MANOR!

FASCINATING—YES—AND PERHAPS A LITTLE MORE THAN THAT— YOU SEE THE HOUSE IS TIED IN DIRECTLY WITH MY FAMILY AND, SINCE THE HOUSE WAS FIRST BUILT OVER 70 YEARS AGO NO LESS THAN 5 MEMBERS OF THE MANORS CLAN HAVE MET... SINGULARLY STRANGE FATES THERE!

HOW-HOW WAS THAT, SIR?

TWO WERE FOUND HANGED IN AN UPPER CHAMBER OF THE HOUSE CALLED THE GREEN ROOM — THE OTHER THREE DISAPPEARED — VANISHED WITHOUT A TRACE— PERHAPS I SHOULD EXPLAIN THAT THEY HAD ALL SLEPT IN THE GREEN ROOM THE NIGHT OF THEIR DISAPPEARANCE—THE NEXT MORNING THERE WAS NO EVIDENCE OF ANYONE EVEN HAVING PASSED THE NIGHT THERE — IT WAS AS IF—AS IF THEY HAD NEVER EVEN --- EXISTED---
BUT SURELY, MR. MANOR—THERE IS SOME EXPLANATION!

NONE—SAVE AN OLD LEGEND THAT HAS BEEN HANDED DOWN THROUGH THE FAMILY— BUT EVEN IT IS SO PREPOSTEROUS THAT ONLY THE MOST SUPERSTITIOUS COULD GIVE IT CREDENCE—

PLEASE GO ON MR. MANOR

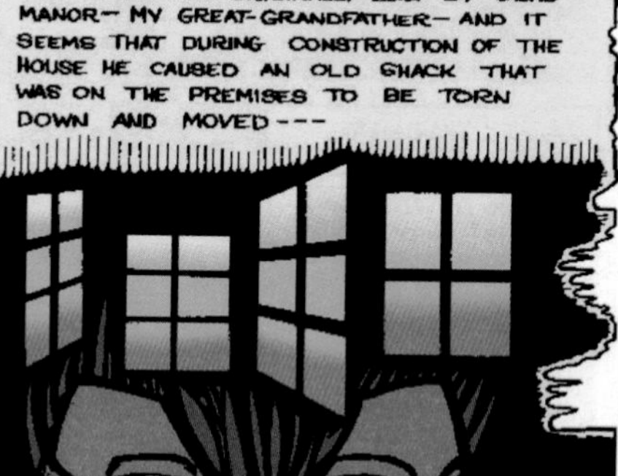
THE HOUSE WAS ORIGINALLY BUILT BY SILAS MANOR— MY GREAT-GRANDFATHER— AND IT SEEMS THAT DURING CONSTRUCTION OF THE HOUSE HE CAUSED AN OLD SHACK THAT WAS ON THE PREMISES TO BE TORN DOWN AND MOVED---

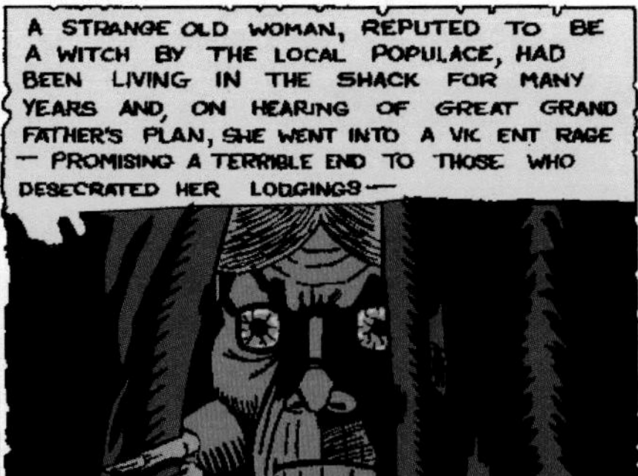
A STRANGE OLD WOMAN, REPUTED TO BE A WITCH BY THE LOCAL POPULACE, HAD BEEN LIVING IN THE SHACK FOR MANY YEARS AND, ON HEARING OF GREAT GRAND FATHER'S PLAN, SHE WENT INTO A VIC ENT RAGE — PROMISING A TERRIBLE END TO THOSE WHO DESECRATED HER LODGINGS—

SOME SAY THAT ON HER DEATH BED SHE SCREAMED WORDS OF A LONG DEAD LANGUAGE TO THE HEAVENS — PLACING A CURSE ON THE MANOR HOUSE AND ALL WHO SHOULD LIVE WITH IN ITS WALLS...
GREAT-GRAND FATHER WAS FOUND HANGED THE NEXT MORNING—

... AND SO, GENTLEMEN, THAT IS THE STORY OF THE MANOR'S CURSE!

WELL— ITS NOT TOO DIFFERENT FROM MOST OF THE OLD LEGENDS I'VE RESEARCHED ON — IN FACT, I'D SAY IT WAS TYPICAL, EH STEVE?
YEAH—TYPICAL!
THEN, YOU'LL UNDER TAKE TO STAY IN THE HOUSE OVERNIGHT!

RIGHT YOU ARE, SIR, IN FACT WE'LL BEGIN AT ONCE!
EXCELLENT— I'LL HAVE MY CAR BROUGHT ROUND AND SHOW YOU THE WAY—

LATER— ON AN OLD DESERTED BACK ROAD ...
WHAT'S THAT STRANGE NOISE MR. MANOR? HEH HEH... KINDA REMINDS ME OF THE MUSIC TRACK FROM PSYCHO!
THOSE ARE CRICKETS, SIDNEY! YOU BOYS NEED TO GET OUT OF THE CITY AND INTO THE COUNTRY MORE!
WOW, STEVE! THERE'S THE HOUSE DEAD-AHEAD ...AND YOU KNOW WHAT? IT BEARS AN UN-CANNY RESEMB-LANCE TO...
YEAH... I KNOW, SID! I KNOW! KEEP AT IT AND YOU'RE GOING TO TALK ME OUT OF GOING ALONG ON THIS EXPEDITION!
SKEE!SKEE!SKEE!SKEE!SKEE!S

AS THE CAR ROLLS TO A STOP, THE SOUND OF INSECTS IN THE SURROUNDING FOLIAGE GIVES WAY TO SILENCE...
WELL, SID... STEVE... IT'S NOT TO LATE TO CHANGE YOUR MINDS!
WE'LL BE FINE, MR MANOR! JUST DON'T FORGET TO PICK US UP IN THE MORNING!!
THE BOYS WATCH IN SILENCE AS THE TAILLIGHTS OF THE CAR DISAPPEAR IN THE GATHERING DUSK....AND THEN...
WHAT DO YOU THINK, SID? IS THE OLD BOY HAVING US ON?
PROBABLY! BUT... EVERYTHING'S GRIST FOR THE MILL! WHAT 'HAUNTED HOUSE' STORY WOULD BE COMPLETE WITHOUT AN "ANCESTRAL CURSE" LURKING IN THE BACKGROUND?
AND DID YOU HEAR WHAT HE SAID ABOUT THE LANTERN? ITS THE SAME ONE HIS CLASSMATES USED 30 YEARS AGO!
OH, THAT'S JUST TERRIFIC! I CAN'T TELL YOU HOW THRILLED I AM TO HEAR THAT... YIKE! WHAT'S THAT?
RUMBLE!
ATMOSPHERE! I LOVE IT! YOU KNOW...I'VE BEEN GIVING SOME THOUGHT TO WHAT HAPPENED THAT NIGHT...AND I DON'T REALLY THINK IT HAD ANYTHING TO DO WITH THE HOUSE... OR ANYTHING SUPERNATURAL!
YOU DON'T KNOW WHAT A LOAD OFF THAT IS! BY ALL MEANS... LET'S HEAR IT!!
OKAY—SUPPOSE THE GUY WHO WENT INSANE WAS ON THE BRINK ANY WAY...MAYBE HE'D HAVE FLIPPED OUT IF HE'D STAYED IN THE DORM THAT NIGHT...
...OR WENT BOWLING OR SOMETHING! OKAY, SHERLOCK, HOW ABOUT THE GUY WHO VANISHED?!
EVEN EASIER! MAYBE HE WAS UNDER SOME KIND OF PRESSURE! YOU KNOW... HOME... FAMILY... SCHOOL... A LOVE AFFAIR GONE SOUR... AND HE JUST DECIDED TO VAMOOSE!
YEAH, I KNOW THE FEELING!!! LIKE... NOW! FOR INSTANCE!
RUMBLE BOOM!

C'MON, WILL YA? THIS IS FUN! ADMIT IT! HEY! CHECK IT OUT... THIS HAS GOT TO BE THE GREEN ROOM!
WHOAA! YOU MEAN THE ROOM WHERE THEY HANGED THEMSELVES?!

SAY... IS IT JUST ME... OR HAS IT GOTTEN COLDER ALLUVA SUDDEN? CRIMINY! IT FEELS LIKE A COLD-STORAGE UNIT IN HERE!
AND NOT A STICK OF FURNITURE IN THE PLACE... WHY DO YOU SUPPOSE THAT IS??

YOU'RE RIGHT! THERE WAS FURNITURE IN ALL THE OTHER ROOMS BUT...
STEVE?

WHAT TH... HOW'D HE DO THAT?! HE SNUCK OUT ON ME WITHOUT MAKING A SOUND!

STEVE!
STEVE!
STEVE STEVE
STEVE

OKAY! I GET IT! MY PAL, THE WISE GUY PUT ONE OVER ON ME! AND NOW I'M SUPPOSED TO PANIC OR SOMETHING... WELL, TWO CAN PLAY THAT GAME!!

CRIPES! WHAT IS GOING ON HERE?! IT... IT SOUNDS LIKE PEOPLE ARE MOVING FURNITURE AROUND BUT... THERE'S NO FURNI-TURE UP THERE!!
THUMP THUMP TH

OMIGOSH--WHAT IF STEVE BAILED OUT ON ME?! HE COULD BE HALFWAY BACK TO MR. MANOR'S PLACE BY NOW! WAIT! I'M FALLING INTO HIS TRAP! GOTTA STAY CALM!

YOW

NO! I DROPPED THE LANTERN!

SMASH!

TERRIFIC! THIS IS ALL WE NEED! HOW ARE WE GONNA NAVIGATE OUR WAY OUTTA THIS MASO-LEUM? BLACKER THAN PITCH! WAIT... GOT MATCHES HERE SOMEWHERE...
SCRATCH

AH!

THE GREEN ROOM! THAT'S WHERE THE RASCAL IS HIDING! PRETTY SLICK! BUT HE FORGOT ONE THING

LOCKED!! HOW COULD IT BE LOCKED?! STEVE, OPEN UP! THE PLACE IS SWARMING WITH RATS! WE GOTTA GET OUTTA HERE!! C'MON WILL YA! THIS IS NO TIME FOR . . .
BOOM!

I KNOW YOU'RE IN THERE, OKAY?! THE DOOR WAS WIDE OPEN WHEN I LEFT! I'M CERTAIN OF IT! ENOUGH ALREADY WITH THE MIND GAMES! I'M NOT GETTING MATERIAL HERE I CAN USE IN MY STORY! HELLO?! HELLO!!

OKAY, THAT'S IT! I'M OUTTA HERE. YA HEAR ME? I'M LEAVIN' WITHOUT YOU! THE LANTERN'S BROKEN AND I'VE GOT ONE LOUSY MATCH TO GET BACK DOWN THE STAIRS... DAMN!!
SCRATCH
SCRATCH

SQUEA-EEAK
WHAT WAS THAT?

THE DOOR— ITS OPEN NOW!

C'MON, STEVE— FUN TIMES OVER NOW, HUH? — YOU MANAGED TO SCARE THE OLD GHOST HUNTER — NOW C'MON

STEVE!

Iscariot News
STUDENT VANISHES
POLICE STILL SEARCHING FOR MISSING STUDENT
A week has passed since Sidney
Pike, a student at State
University, was found with
a completely shattered mind
in the old Manors house,
the search still continues
for Steve Stiles although
no trace of him has been
found. Pikes condition is
better and officials are
MIND SHATTERED

WILL

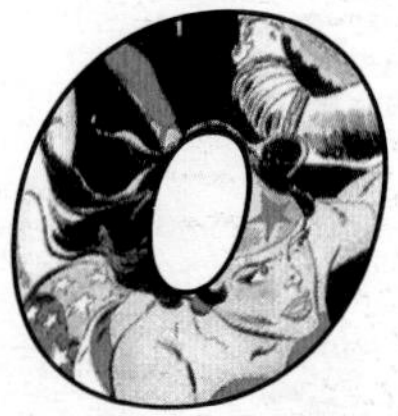

BE AN EXPLOSIVE YEAR?

by Robert M. Overstreet

As we stand on the threshold of a new era, there's no better time to take stock of the comic book market and examine what an amazing transformation is taking place right before our eyes. Although it's too early to tell what effect some of the changes noted below will have on the future of the market as we move into the 21st century, it seems certain that the hobby as we have known it will soon alter significantly. We hope to remain at the forefront of that change and observe its effects as we move beyond our 30th edition.

Before we take a closer look at the many currents running through the market this past year, we should briefly discuss some of the more significant developments that will certainly affect the future of the hobby in general terms. 1999 was undeniably a year of innovation in all areas, and some of those innovations are only now beginning to take hold in a market that has remained much the same for years.

INTERNET SALES: If there's one word that's on the lips of every Overstreet advisor, dealer, collector, or casual comic book fan, it's eBay...or its philosophical equivalent, anyway. Almost becoming synonymous with the internet itself (which has a far more sweeping effect on the hobby, as we will soon see), this auction site and its many imitators has stepped in and provided a whole new avenue for buying and selling comics that never existed before. Many dealers reported good sales in the developing internet market. Although grading may not be accurate here, tons of lower grade comic books in the less than $100 category were selling to new collectors entering the field for the first time. Prices realized varied from above to well below guide list. At this early stage the internet market is challenging and chaotic, and next year should see even more sales as this market continues to reach more and more people. Dealers complained that due to the internet, collections are now much harder to buy since the collector can now sell direct through web sites such as eBay and cut out the middle man.

Now that dealers have a chance to advertise virtually for free on the internet via their own websites and auctions (although organized auction sites do incur fees for items auctioned), barriers are being broken across the board. Collectors who could never collect Golden Age or other previously high-priced or unobtainable material have found an avenue for locating reasonably priced comics. eBay and other auctions have breathed life into the back issue market and give a good indication of what truly sells, but the progress comes at a price. Will freedom of the internet adversely affect the brick and mortar stores, or kill conventional buying and selling altogether? While it seems unlikely, there's no doubt that electronic collecting is here to stay, and perhaps it's not all isolated. Reports indicate that some convention and mail order activity is up thanks to the internet, which has introduced heretofore casual collectors into the hobby and encouraged them to seek bargains elsewhere as well. Older collectors may also be led back into classic routes of collecting thanks to a new burst of energy provided by the internet.

One note of warning: while eBay and other auction sales are encouraging and seem to be revitalizing the hobby, they bring with them a number of important cautions. "Caveat Emptor" is the watchword of the day as buyers and sellers often do business with little real knowledge of the market or the true value of the items auctioned. Many of the new collectors brought into the hobby via the internet are relatively uninformed and are often willing to pay 5-10 times guide for comics in their area of interest (particularly in pop culture categories like television and film). There are also some rather uncouth trading practices in use today, such as "sniping," in which a buyer sneaks onto an auction in the last seconds and puts in a final bid, and numerous instances of fraud being perpetrated on buyers who do not exercise caution. With auction sites proliferating and more new collectors coming to comics every day who have no interest or concern about proper grading or value, how will this affect the hobby and the ways in which we track and reflect pricing data? These will be the challenges we will face in the next century of collecting.

PROFESSIONAL GRADING: 1999 also saw the introduction of a new service in the industry, a process by which collectors can certify their comics and establish an easily agreed upon grade through the auspices of CGC. Also providing the means to preserve the certified comics through a specially-designed sealable holder, CGC has now changed the way we think about high-end collecting. Response to the certification of comics seemed positive, although it was very late in the year before CGC had everything in place to launch the project at full steam. They intended to have examples on display at the November New York show, but last-minute technical problems prevented this from happening. It was reported to us that several dealers have been selectively buying up high grade Golden and Silver Age books for certification. Since the grading company will be checking the books for whiteness of paper, restoration and other defects as well as certifying its authenticity and grade, investors from other collectible fields will now be able to buy into the comic market with confidence. Look out! This could become a very volatile part of the market in coming years, as the certification process almost guarantees an influx of non-comic collector investors, at least initially. We will be watching this trend very closely in the coming months to see what effect certification has on the comic book market, but it's a distinct probability that certified books will soon bring new record prices for high-grade key issues.

THEME COLLECTING/THE "CHARLTON" PHENOMENON: If the internet has done anything to the comic book market, it's shifted interest from more traditional collecting strategies to those focusing on specific pop culture or genre "themes." As new, uninformed collectors enter the market with their own likes and dislikes, the hobby has found itself faced with a number of new trends, including bargain hunting and rabid collecting of previously undistinguished or undervalued companies and titles. As we will see later, Charlton appears to lead the way in this category as demand skyrockets for all titles by this company, and for many other traditionally non-collected comics as well. Copies can sell for as much as 10 to 20 times guide! They aren't the only ones benefiting from this new fixation on theme collecting, as humor, teen, sports, and other genres quickly rise in interest. Risqué content such as bikini panels, tiny character cameos, parodies of TV, comic, film, rock group appearances, art by stalwarts like Kirby, Byrne, Wrightson, Perez, and Adams, superheroine titles -- all these and more are categories sought after by a new breed of collector. Some are even collecting purely based on cover theme, such as UFO/flying saucers, mermaids, time machines, space/SF/rockets, cross-dressing, bondage, politically incorrect, crossovers, black people (esp. pre-1970), last issues, #100s, cheerleaders, chess, Satan, dinosaurs, dragons, errors, monsters, Halloween, paper dolls, motorcycles, Mounties, nudity, out of character, religion, robots, slavery/slaves, spanking panels, superhero, swipes, Titanic, various wars (Civil, WWII, etc.) and much, much more. Look for this trend to continue and even grow in force as more and more internet-based collectors enter the market looking for bargains and their favorite topics.

CHANGES IN THIS GUIDE: Many of the more recent titles have been consolidated into standard price groupings of issues with a minimum price of $2.00 for NM listed. Golden Age spreads have been reduced again to bring the guide into balance with the market. Some new discoveries are included as well as more classic covers in this edition. The Bronze Age listings have again been expanded to show the more important issues that are selling at higher prices. You will notice a new format and type style in many sections designed to give the book a better appearance throughout and usher in a new era for the guide as we celebrate our 30th anniversary.

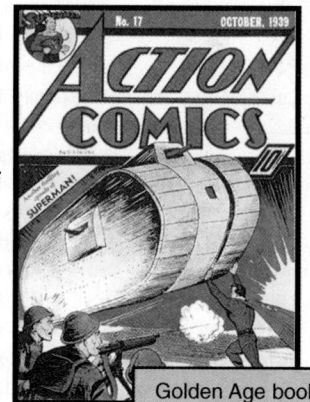

© DC

Golden Age books such as this **Action Comics** #17 are in high demand.

CONVENTIONS: There was a noticeable decrease in back-issue dealers at the San Diego show in 1999. We were told that tables have become expensive and that their internet and mailing list sales have picked up, replacing the need to go to a convention (see above). All dealers reported a strong market in 1999 and anticipate the same next year. All of the following information was gleaned from reports provided to us by dealers and collectors over the course of the year. Without further ado, let's see what happened in the comic book market in 1999!

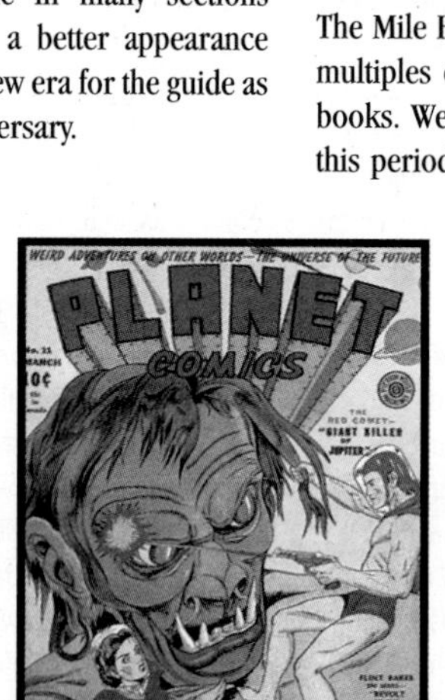

© FH

The Mile High **Planet** run brought multiples of guide list! **Planet** #11 shown.

MARKET REPORT BY AGE

GOLDEN AGE: This era remains a cornerstone of the hobby, and demand is now far outstripping supply. The back issue market is alive and well. Reports received throughout 1999 indicate that Golden Age books were in high demand, selling in all grades. With high grade copies vanishing, demand for copies in less than FN has increased. These books typically sell over guide. High demand titles include classics like Batman, Superman, Flash, Green Lantern, and very elusive high grade copies of Action Comics. Other titles also showing substantial interest include Planet Comics, Green Llama, Airboy and Airfighter, Frankenstein, Wings, Contact, Captain America, Wonder Woman, and Quality and MLJ titles.

Horror comics were selling at above guide levels, continuing their upward climb from previous years. High demand for the key bizarre covers was noticed where record sales occurred at multiples of guide list. The Mile High Planet run again changed hands at multiples of guide list along with other pedigree books. We see no let-up in demand for books of this period! Perhaps the only drawback here is a recurring one; many of these books are still too pricey for the average collector, and as a result the trend continues toward great deals on eye-catching books. Other collectors have shifted to collecting covers as opposed to traditional runs, with interest high on Schomburg, Kamen, L. B. Cole, or Baker covers (especially bondage covers). Demand is high for WWII superhero covers as well.

While superhero titles remain strong in this era, Timely, horror, and Good Girl comics are also quick sellers, routinely fetching above guide prices in high grade. Even books with primitive restoration sell, but move slower and for less money than their unretouched counterparts. More specific examination of trends in Golden Age sales can be found in our key sales lists and in the genre and company breakdowns featured later in this article.

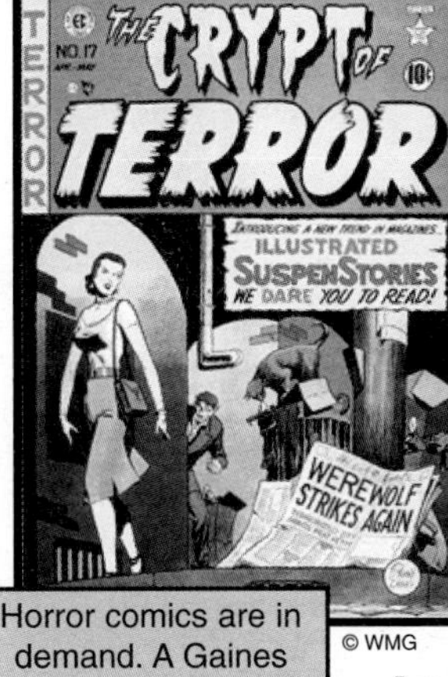

Horror comics are in demand. A Gaines **Crypt of Terror** #17 sold for $6600!

ATOM AGE: This era appears to be selling well, although some areas are cooling off. Without a doubt, the hottest genre of the Atom Age is horror, with strong demand evident for horror and sci-fi titles from Avon and Atlas. Demand for horror titles has resulted in over guide sales for high and low grade copies. Strong sales have also been reported on EC horror, Frontline Combat, and Two-Fisted Tales (EC Gaines file copies are selling for record prices). DC superhero titles are the runaway best sellers of the genre, with Batman and Superman performing best in all grades. Many collectors are acquiring F to FN copies for under $300!

TV and movie tie-in titles like I Love Lucy and The Three Stooges, DC mystery/sci-fi (Mystery in Space, Strange Adventure, House of Mystery and House of Secrets), and romance titles are all experiencing high demand. Fox is the leader in romance, with all titles beginning with "My" selling well. 1950s Archies are selling well, and demand is high for the Carl Barks Duck One-Shots and early WD Comics & Stories, which are elusive in high grade copies. Other successful genres include Giants, which sell well in low and high grade due to scarcity of high grade copies, Good Girl comics like Phantom Lady, and specific artist appearances. Key figures in this area include L. B. Cole, Wolverton, Ditko, Baker, Kirby, Kubert, and Frazetta.

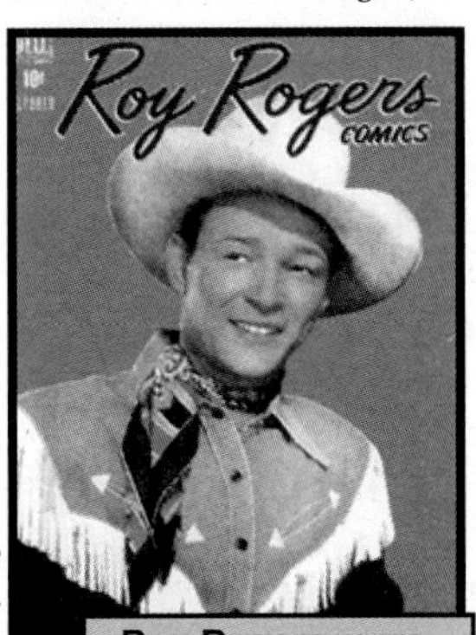

Roy Rogers represents one of the popular western series.

Westerns are selling at an average rate, with personality photo covers performing the best (Gene Autry, Roy Rogers and the Lone Ranger are leaders). However, the king of slow sellers has to be 1950s Dell funny animals(Uncle Scrooge, Donald Duck, Walt Disney's Comics and Stories, Looney Tunes). Notable exceptions include Uncle Scrooge FC #386 (#1) and various Little Lulus, all of which are hard to find in decent grades. Marginal sales are also reported in other humor, funny animal and teen titles.

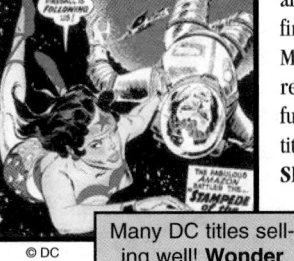

Many DC titles selling well! **Wonder Woman** #99 shown.

SILVER AGE: According to many, this era represents the area of collecting most impacted by the advent of internet commerce. Rabid interest in low grade copies via auction sites has energized this market, but resulted in moderate sales from other sources like conventions and mail order operations. Many books in lesser grades are being heavily discounted through the internet, while high grade copies are in demand and fetching above guide prices with some record sales reported on key issues. The internet influx may deplete the inventory of Silver Age books as all the new collectors seek out their favorites, but the energy this is bringing to the market may serve to revitalize this area for next year.

Another trend seems to be a loss of interest

from completists, particularly in Marvel titles, mainly due to the constant restarting of titles that has eroded consumer faith in the stability of traditional collecting of runs. With no commitment from the publisher as far as preserving the history and continuity of their series, there is a corresponding loss of energy on the part of collectors as well. DC, on the other hand, with their continuously numbered titles well into the high hundreds, now have an asset no one else can claim, inspiring collectors interested in runs to turn to that company instead. Since most activity in this era is focused on the "Big Two," Marvel and DC, here are some specific observations on the performance of each company this past year:

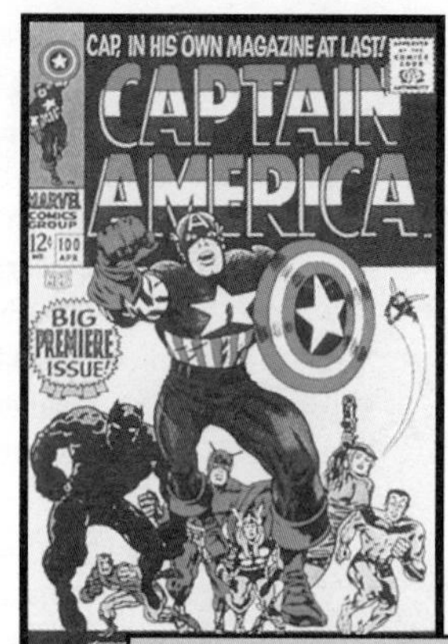

© MAR

Strictly graded late '60s Marvels are in demand, such as this **Captain America** #100.

DC: With a new demand reported from outside the US and Canada, DC is experiencing strong sales in many areas, particularly with obscure titles, 100 pagers, annuals and specials. High grade copies of DC sell well and above guide, while many collectors are seeking Silver Age DC in GD to FN+. Thanks to a good supply and intense internet competition, above guide sales on insignificant material are rarely seen. Prices are expected to remain steady in this area. Hot titles selling well (if graded accurately) include some of the usual suspects: Action Comics, Adventure Comics, Batman (HOT), Brave and the Bold (more are seeking keys in high grade), Detective 80 page Giants (HOT HOT HOT), Flash, Jimmy Olsen and Lois Lane, Mystery in Space (Adam Strange-HOT), Showcase, Sugar and Spice (frequently requested and hard to find), Superman, and Wonder Woman (highly undervalued and HOT). DC War comics are in high demand, with middle to high grade extremely scarce. Most sought after titles include Our Army at War, GI Combat, Star Spangled War Stories, and Our Fighting Forces, all selling at 100% of guide for MT copies. Other titles like Flash, Green Lantern and Justice League of America move decently, while Aquaman, Blackhawk, House of Mystery (the Martian Manhunter issues) and House of Secrets (Dial H for Hero) are slow sellers.

MARVEL: Despite the impact of Marvel's historical disdain, back issues are still selling well, and in some cases, collectors are not willing to pay guide. A basic rule of thumb is that 1965-1970 Marvels are performing well if strictly graded. Key titles are as expected: Amazing Spider-Man, Avengers (particularly #57-100), Captain America, Captain Marvel, Daredevil #1-#30, FF #1-#30 (HOT), Journey Into Mystery, and Silver Surfer #1 & #2. Anthology titles like Strange Tales, Tales of Suspense and Tales to Astonish are showing more interest and are becoming harder to find. Thor sells at and above guide in lower grades, while X-Men demand has dropped. Steranko, Barry Smith, and Neal Adams issues are the exceptions, going for 50% above guide in GD to FN. These are becoming scarce due to low print runs.

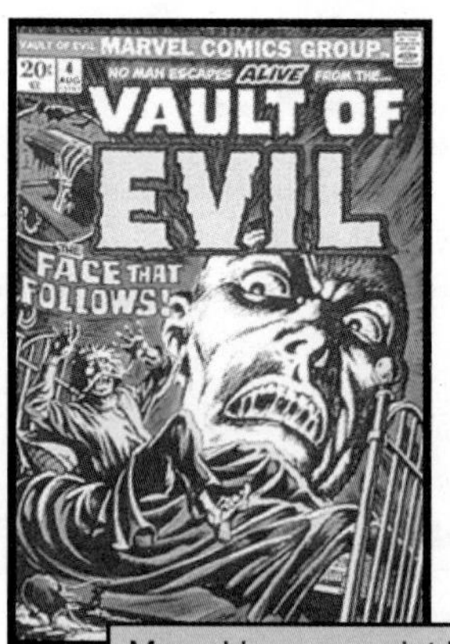

© MAR

Marvel horror reprint books are in demand, such as **Vault of Evil** #4 shown.

BRONZE AGE: In an era that is finally moving far enough away in time to generate substantial collector interest (aided by internet sales), reports indicate that low grade copies are selling well across the board due to scarcity. Marvel horror reprints areexcellent sellers, followed closely by Wonder Woman. Comic magazines are also selling well, with Eerie publications selling fast and above guide. Skywald sells very fast, and Vampirella remains the best-selling Warren title, although all pre-1980 Warrens are selling well. Many collectors are buying over-sized treasuries, digests, and Famous First DC comics, all of which are selling well and usually at guide. '70s comics must be in nice shape, adhering to the trend in collectors demanding good condition, well graded copies, but even low grades will sell as long as the price is right.

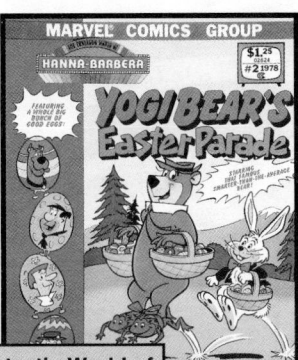

The **Funtastic World of Hanna-Barbera** #2 is among the hot books.

© MAR

This is the most requested era for many dealers, with teen, love, reprint, magazine and western comics quickly becoming elusive due to low guide prices. Demand for strict NM copies is growing, and there is definitely a much smaller supply than expected. Low priced NM copies are now bringing 150-300% of guide!

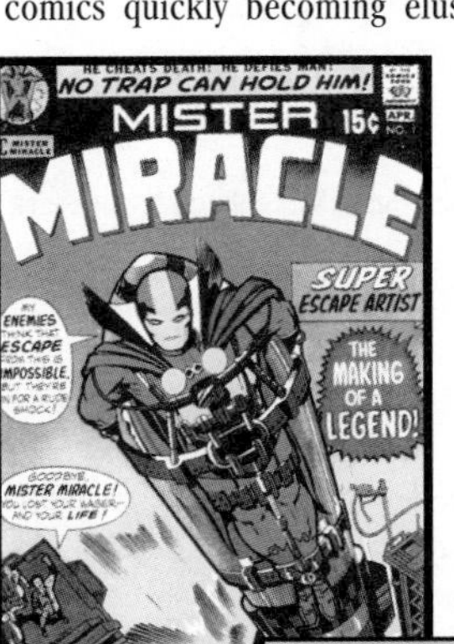

© DC

Kirby books like **Mister Miracle** #1 move very well.

All 15 and 20 cent books are in hot demand and undervalued. Best sellers in this era include: My Love, Our Love Story, Marvel Treasury, digests, all magazines, all reprints, all horror, western, giants, Spidey, British editions, all TV, cartoon, Hanna Barbera, Kirby, anything NM, Millie, Patsy, Chili, Crazy, all minor keys, Epic, Planet of the Apes, Foom, Groo #100 up, all humor, Marvel Age, giveaways, memorabilia, Fireside books, paperbacks, war and even Star titles! Some specific observations tied to activity in sales of the "Big Two" publishers follow:

DC: Freedom Fighters is hot, and the black cover on #1 makes NM copies hard to find. The Freedom Fighters intro in J.L.A. #107, #108 are also hot. Offbeat titles are making a splash, with requested series like Kamandi, Demon (#1 undervalued), and Plastic Man leading the pack. Kirby titles and art are naturally drawing attention, and titles like Forever People, New Gods, and earlier Mr. Miracles (#1-9) move very well. In the mainline superhero series, Superman and Batman family titles are seeing movement, with Batgirl covers on Batman selling best. Also selling well are Action Comics, Adventure Comics, Brave and the Bold, Detective Comics, Flash, Lois Lane, Jimmy Olsen, Wonder Woman, Weird War Tales, Weird Western Tales, and other DC war comics. Much harder to find and in high demand are the DC horror titles like Ghost, Unexpected, Witching Hour, Secrets of Sinister House, Sinister House of Secret Love, and House of Mystery. These are solid sellers but growing scarce. 52 and 100 pagers are also sought after and hard to find in NM. Some of these sell better than Silver Age!

MARVEL: Hulk #181, Giant Size X-Men #1 and X-Men #94 are the "Big Three" for many dealers, and sell fast in NM for well over guide. These huge key books also sell well in lower grades. X-Men #94-142 is a solid selling run, while other hot Marvel 15-25 cent books include: Amazing Adventures, Amazing Spider-Man (HOT), Avengers, Captain America, Daredevil, Defenders, Fantastic Four, Hulk, Marvel Spotlight, Thor, Tomb of Dracula (#2-5 are hot), and Werewolf by Night. Giant Size books are picking up steam, scarce and extremely rare in high grade, with Thor, Iron Man, Captain America most sought after and selling at 1.5 times guide in F/VF. Marvel 30/35 cent

© MAR

Hulk #181 sells fast for many dealers.

variants had their biggest increase this year, although most dealers think the market is limited for these books, and Marvel's B&W books are selling well, particularly Planet of the Apes and Deadly Hands of Kung Fu. These sell over guide in VF or better. Even Savage Sword of Conan is finding new life, while reprint series are decent sellers. Kirby titles are on the rise, including Eternals, Devil Dinosaur, 2001: A Space Odyssey. Interestingly, the worst sales have been reported in titles like Ms. Marvel, Howard the Duck, Machine Man (1st), Omega the Unknown, Logan's Run and Micronauts.

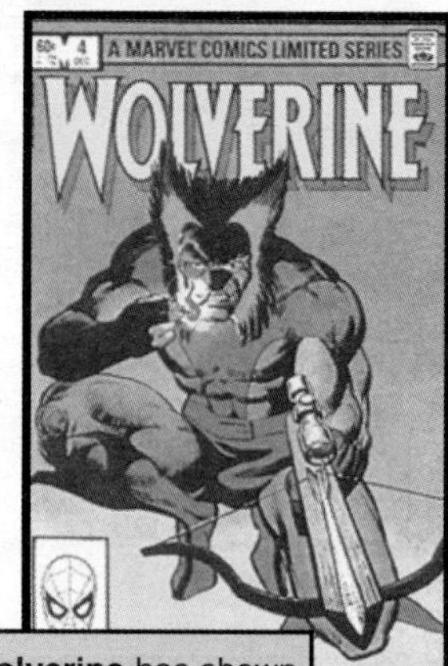

Wolverine has shown a surge in demand. #4, 1982 shown.

© MAR

MODERN AGE: Continuing the shift in emphasis to the later eras in comics, the Modern Age has shown some interesting activity in the last year. The key word is manga, manga, manga! Thanks to the electrifying effect of titles like Pokemon and Dragon Ball Z, manga and manga style comics are on a definite upswing, even positively influencing other all-ages sales like Archie. Here are some specific observations:

DC: The new Batgirl (in Shadow of the Bat #83, $25) is fueling interest in the Batman books. The animated Batgirl also sells well (Batman Adventures #12 NM $5), while Batman titles themselves are moderate. DC 80-page Giants and the Flash are doing well, as are issues of JLA and Nightwing #1-20. Wonder Woman demand has increased, and recent back issues sell well. Two of 1998's hottest titles, Battlechasers and Danger Girl, have seen a large drop in interest thanks to serious delays throughout 1999. Vertigo titles have stopped generating much interest, with the exception of Invisibles (selling at 2 times guide), Preacher, Transmetropolitan, and the Trenchcoat Brigade mini-series.

Danger Girl #1. This title is losing its steam!

© Atomico

MARVEL: Stalwarts like Amazing Spider-Man and Captain America are experiencing moderate sales, while Wolverine has had a surge in demand. Marvel graphic novels, especially Marvel Masterworks, are selling well as collectors seek reasonably priced reprints of classic stories. Current Marvels selling well include Thunderbolts, which are selling a bit above guide, the Marvel Knights line, especially The Inhumans, and Spider-Girl (a near-future character who is the only surviving member of a mostly failed subset of titles). This character's first appearance in What If? #105 is hard to find, fetching $25-30 in some instances.

MOVIE/TV TIE-INS: Star Wars back issues are sluggish, with the exception of Marvel's Star Wars #107, and Dark Horse's Crimson Empire, Mara Jade, and Shadows of the Empire, all tie-ins that came out pre-Phantom Menace with low print runs. TV tie-ins like Simpsons and Buffy the Vampire Slayer are doing well, while Xena and X-Files titles are way down due to a lack of new issues. A basic rule of thumb in this area is that all licensed books tend to show high demand at the outset, tapering off by the 9th or 10th issues.

MISCELLANEOUS: Viz Comics has successful manga titles like Pokemon, Dragon Ball Z and Sailor Moon (first issues of the last two titles have been reported as selling for $25 each). The only consistent back issue sellers for Image are Spawn and Witchblade. Late '70s and early '80s long-running titles are in short supply, and when found in high grade sell easily, while discounted copies from that era also perform well. Early independents like PC, Eclipse and Continuity are good sellers. "Bad girl" books seem to be losing steam, although Vampirella is up a little and perhaps performing even better than when new. As with the Marvel

Masterworks and DC Archives, other collections and trade paperbacks are the answer to readers looking for expensive hard to find issues in affordable packaging.

MARKET REPORT BY GENRE

While there are certainly many more genre categories in comic book collecting, here are some highlights from 1999 and a survey of the trends observed in the past year:

ARTIST ISSUES: Kirby comics, as might be expected, lead the way, with 1948-1960 Kirby selling 20% over guide in lower grades and 30-40% in higher grades. Frazetta covers and art sell 20-50% over guide. Alex Toth art comics go for 20-50% above guide (non-DC only). Other notable trends in special artist issues, as well as specific examples of those already noted, are discussed in other sections of this report.

COMIC DIGESTS: Fast becoming one of the strongest sellers, this category suffers from short supply and high demand. DC digests are red hot, especially Best of DC #41 and up. These digests had small print runs and are therefore very hard to find. Undocumented and unpublished stories appear in some digest comics, featuring notable material from Canceled Comics Cavalcade. Best of DC #10 is hot, as it contains an all-new original Penguin origin story. Other popular digests include: Golden Comic Digests, Hanna Barbera titles (which bring 200-300% guide!), Fiction Illustrated #3, Shocking Tales #1, Archie Superhero #1 and #2, all Mystery Comic digests, all GK story digests, Adventure, Jonah Hex, Betty and Veronica, Madhouse, Pat the Brat. Newer Harvey digests of the early '90s had thin covers and were heavily wrinkled due to overgluing. Now that collectors are seeking them out, it's doubtful any exist in NM. Also scarce are pre-1980 digests in FN or better. Keep an eye on this area of collecting.

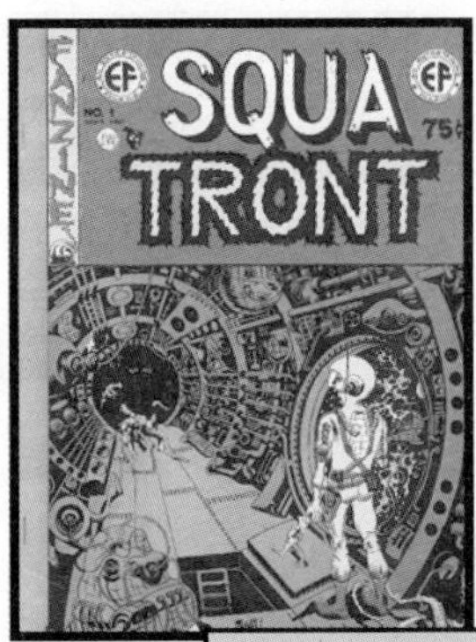

© Jerry Weist

Fanzines have been revitalized. **Squa Tront** #1 shown.

FANZINES: As yet another byproduct of the internet influx, eBay has revitalized once unimportant or overlooked peripheral collectibles and merchandise. Another growing market is the collection of fanzines, many of which exist in untold quantities with undocumented character appearances and work by many major artists and writers. These 'zines, often relegated to clearance bins in the past and now existing mostly in low grade and in permanent collections, are now commanding multiples of cover price. Even '80s issues are sought after, as are fanzines with art and stories by Steve Ditko, Wally Wood, Joe Orlando, and Jack Kirby. Popular titles include: Foom, Amazing World of DC, Charlton Bullseye, Comics Interview, Comics Journal, Spa Fon, Squa-Tront, Witzend, Comic Feature, RBCC, and other obscure titles.

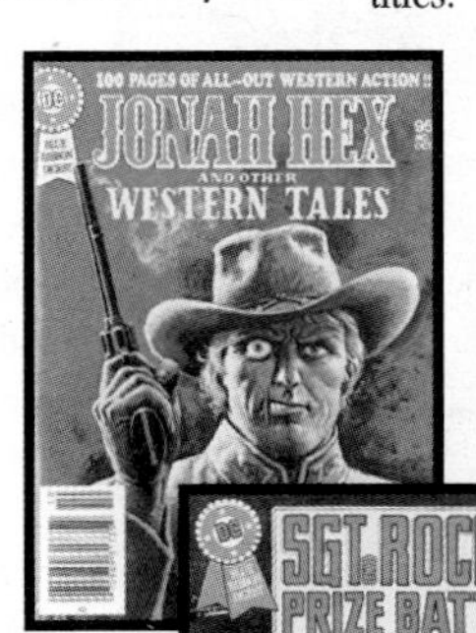

© DC

Comic Digests are in demand. **Jonah Hex** #1 & **Best of DC** #18 shown.

FOREIGN AND CANADIAN COMICS: A strong market niche, these feature reprints of popular characters. Charlie Chaplin, Laurel and Hardy, and the Phantom are among the stars featured, and many foreign editions contain cheap reprints of great SA and GA titles. The UK has produced hundreds of hardcover comic and illustrated text story "Annuals," many based on popular US TV, cartoon, and comic book characters of the '50s through the '90s. Many annuals feature original non-US material. UK titles with no US counterparts include: She-Ra, Dangerman, Go-Bots, Dukes of Hazzard, Charlie's Angels, CHiPs, Mork and Mindy, Starsky and Hutch, Knight Rider, and more. This category shows fast growth.

Collectors are also seeking

Canadian editions of the May to August 1968 Gold Key variants with 15 cent cover prices. These books are going up in demand and 1940s-'50s editions exist at a ratio of about 1 to every 10 domestic copies. Original material B&W Canadian editions are very rare, with no more than 5 copies extant on most. VG copies bring $35-100 for average non-key issues. Marvel and DC newsstand copies are in demand as well, with 1 to 2 copies for every 100 on market. These often bring double guide in VG or less, and they exist on all comics with newsstand distribution in their respective time periods (Marvel 10/82-8/86; DC 10/82-9/88).

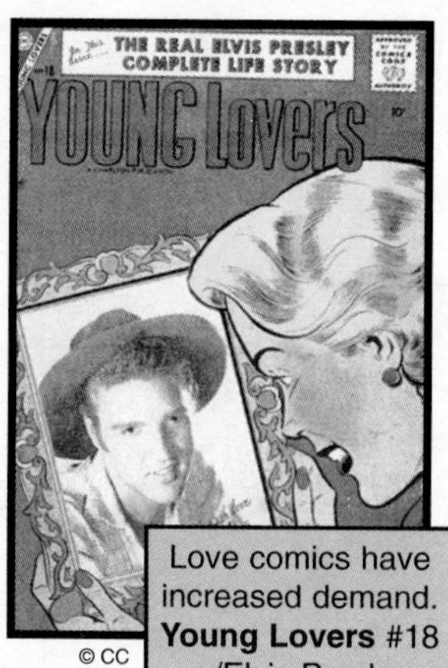

© CC

Love comics have increased demand. **Young Lovers** #18 w/Elvis Presley photo cover is a hot item!

GOOD GIRL ART: The more obscure the art, the more collectors want it, and this is a unique genre in that it overlaps many others (notations about significant sales or other "Good Girl" data is distributed throughout this report in the appropriate categories). Collectors are fighting for existing copies of this genre.

HUMOR & PARODY MAGAZINES: Except for MAD, humor books are hard to keep in stock, with keys bringing in 200% of guide or more. Cracked and Sick (very scarce) are often undervalued and overlooked by the market. As with most internet-driven collector trends, guide value is irrelevant to buyers here, and they are willingly pay multiples of guide based on pop culture interests.

© WP

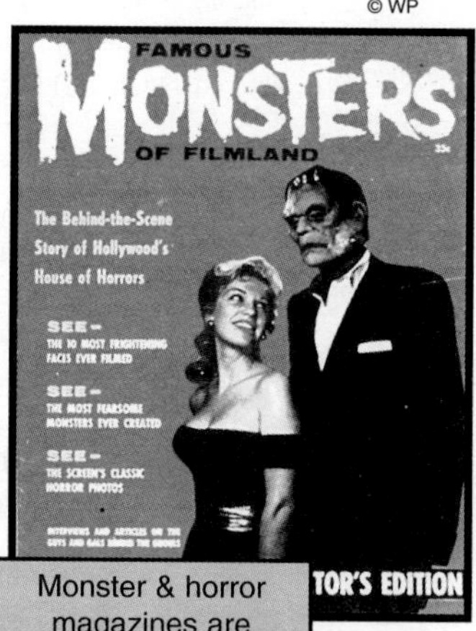

Monster & horror magazines are increasing in demand. **Famous Monsters** #1 shown.

MAGAZINES: Famous Monsters and obscure Dell and horror magazines from the late '60s and early '70s are increasing in demand, as are copies of Weird Worlds, Witches, Tales From the Tomb, and Weird Tales (Eerie Publications), titles similar to pre-Code horror from the '50s. These magazines usually sell on eBay for $10 to $15 a piece. Monsters lead the pack with Warren titles like Eerie and Creepy in demand. Vampirella is selling well again after some overexposure. Later Warren issues are scarce. Tales of the Zombie is hot, and Deadly Hands of Kung Fu and Savage Sword of Conan are also showing increased demand.

MOVIE/TV/PERSONALITY TIE-INS: A very strong and fast growing category thanks to the internet influx, bargains abound here and even '80s titles are strong, bringing over low guide prices. Although there are many subcategories of such tie-ins (some of which are covered throughout this market report), TV cartoons have a big following, and new collectors are eagerly snapping up examples everywhere they can find them.

RELIGION: This is a hot market, with Spire titles and Treasure Chest moving well. Many issues are now hard to find and some may not exist! Marvel and Frontier titles, Crusader, Cosmics, and DC treasury Bible are solid sellers. Other obscure titles that sell immediately upon discovery are: Hansi, Tom Landry, Johnny Cash, and all Spire Archies. Most collectors in this category are merely looking for decent reading copies and pay over guide prices for them.

ROMANCE: Collectors in this genre are now more selective. Giant sized issues are good sellers, while bikini covers sell very well. Women's Lib covers are sparking interest, as are hippie issues and other examples of bad taste. Collectors entering the market and looking for unresearched exciting finds are gravitating to the unusual stories and good artwork. Sought after titles include Young Love, Young Lovers and Summer Love.

WAR: DC is without a doubt leading in this genre,

and Atlas is close behind. There are still plenty of bargains to be found here. Our Army at War is sought after, with issues #82-198 in any condition selling above guide. GI Combat is on the increase (#67, 87, 114), as well as Grandenetti and gray tone covers and pre-Code Atlas war comics.

WESTERNS: DC titles are increasing, while Atlas is hot depending on the featured artist. Hopalong Cassidy leads Fawcett, which otherwise has moderate sales, and Dell titles are slow apart from movie and TV tie-ins.

© CC

Charltons are elusive and HOT! **Hot Rods & Racing Cars** #1 shown.

MISCELLANEOUS: Teen comics from the '60s, like Harvey's Bunny or Charlton's Go-Go, with artwork or photos of rock stars, sell at guide when they can be found. Other Charltons in demand are Frank Merriwell at Yale, Hercules and Hot Rods & Racing Cars. Monkeyshines, Calling All Kids, Men of Battle and all King comics are selling, especially cartoons and reading library issues, while ACG horror and superhero titles are steady, with humor and love titles picking up steam,. Other oddball titles that bring 150%-200% of guide include: Fatman, Capt. Marvel (MF Enterprises), Henry Brewster, True Comics & Adventure Stories. All Skywald, both magazine and giant comics, are in short supply and in high demand. Tower special artist issues and Tippy Teen titles are on the move as well. Fast Willie Jackson is in demand for $10 each and up. Solid sales have been reported in pre-Code horror from all publishers except EC, which may be slower due to reprints. High grade material is harder to find and sought after. Although a peripheral category of comic collectible, the venerable pulps have experienced some increased demand. Nice copies of low number classic strip reprints like Sparkler and Popular are experiencing limited demand. Copies of Crackajack and Fritzi Ritz sell steadily.

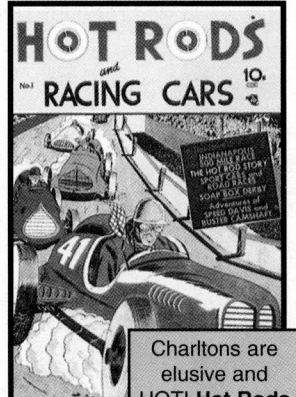

© AP

Giants are hot: **Archie's Giant Series Magazine** #2 shown.

MARKET REPORT BY COMPANY

As with the genre section, some of our market data focused on many of the major publishers in the hobby both past and present. Here are some examples of 1999 activity in those categories:

ARCHIE COMICS: This company shows steady growth with unknown parodies surfacing. Giants, especially squarebound, are red hot. Sabrina (with its TV connection) and Josie are top sellers (Josie #45-#50 and Sabrina #1-#10 bring over 200% of guide!), and that trend includes any appearances and cameos as well. While teen superheroes are heating up, Betty & Veronica lead the pack in the mainline titles. High demand also reported for Little Archie, '70s digests, Cheryl Blossom, and all Red Circle titles. '80s Mighty Crusaders, Mighty Comics and Shadow are going up, and the Spire issues are hot. '80s Katy Keene issues bring top dollar from paper doll collectors, while Sonic the Hedgehog (based on the Sega Genesis and other video games) is blazing hot, fetching from $5-$20 each!! Christmas and Archie #1 treasuries are rare in any condition, and NM

Black Knight is an Atlas book on top of many want lists. #2 shown.

© MAR

copies could go for 400% of guide!

ATLAS: One cannot overstate the demand for pre-superhero Atlas and Marvel. Collectors are buying crime, horror, war, western and even love titles vigorously. In demand are Black Knight, Rawhide Kid (Kirby) and Yellow Claw.

ATLAS/SEABOARD: Everyone is scrambling to get a full set of this company's output, now slowly being recognized as fertile and overlooked collecting ground. #3 and #4 issues are elusive. Devilina, Thrilling Adventure, and Weird Tales of the Macabre #2s are low print items, scarce and in big demand. Movie Monsters had four issues: #1 is uncommon, #2 and #3 are scarce, and #4 is rare. Also rare and hot at 200% guide is Gothic Romances #1, while Vicki #1 and #2 are sought after with #3 and #4 scarce. Demand in this area is about ten times the supply!

Fawcett had some of the best Golden Age covers. **Captain Marvel Adventures** #13 shown.

© FAW

CHARLTON: This is perhaps the fastest growing market and full of surprises; forget high grade copies on most of these titles! Dealers couldn't give them away a few years ago, and now completists are having a tough time on love titles as everything is selling in all grades. All 1983 and newer titles had low runs and are tough to find, with Emergency, Ronald McDonald and Haunted Love blazing hot and fetching multiples of guide! Additional hot titles: all Hanna Barbera, '60s war, Bionic Woman, Charlton Bullseye, David Cassidy, all Byrne issues, all love, Partridge Family, Scooby Doo, all superhero, Phantom, Six Million Dollar Man, Space 1999, all magazines, soap opera love and romance, all TV, Bugaloos, Ditko and artist issues, GoGo, Hanna Barbera Parade, Hong Kong Phooey, Ponytail, Speed Buggy, Wheelie and the Chopper Bunch. Solid sellers were hot genres like horror, war, western, hot rod, and cartoon titles. Horror first issues are high in demand and going for above guide, while some collectors are actively seeking issues by Ditko, Aparo, Newton and other key artists. Keep an eye on this one!

DC: Everything pre-1985 is selling. Hot titles include: Wonder Woman, anything with the JLA or JSA, Shazam, Super Friends, all war, Supergirl, all Giants, all treasuries, all digests, all western, all horror/mystery, all humor, all romance, artist books, most minor keys and crossovers, undervalued 15 and 20 cent cover price issues, Amazing World of DC, memorabilia, all paperbacks, all Kirby, Whitman variants, Gothic Love! Silver Age humor, love, and war titles, plus short run series like Batlash, Hot Wheels, Capt. Action, Creeper and Wonder Woman were frequently requested. All grades are selling in this area.

DELL: Now standing as the underachievers in today's market after a period of dumping across the board, Dell showed slightly increased demand for low number Four Colors, Looney Tunes, Little Lulu, Bugs Bunny, and Pogo. There is also interest in low number Walt Disney's Comics and Stories, which are tough to find in high grade. File copies lulled collectors looking for high grade copies into a false sense of security, and in the 1962 transition year to Gold Key they remain unavailable and on many want lists. Hanna Barbera and TV titles are the most requested, with war, horror, and TV in high demand. Looney Tunes picked up, as did other popular titles: Air War, Beverly Hillbillies, Bewitched, Combat, Dracula, Frankenstein, Ghost Stories, Hogan's Heroes, Jungle War, Kona, Laurel & Hardy, Lone Ranger, Melvin Monster, Monkees, Ponytail, Outer Limits, Quick Draw McGraw, Tarzan, Thirteen, Turok, and Werewolf.

FAWCETT: A steady and reliable seller, Fawcett slowed slightly, and offers some Golden Age bargains. Mainstream non-superhero titles like Nyoka, Hoppy the Marvel Bunny and Six-Gun Heroes were popular, but sales were led by titles like Captain Marvel Adventures, Spy Smasher and Captain Midnight.

FICTION HOUSE: Also a steady seller, collectors were seeking copies of Planet, Fight, Rangers,

Jungle, Jumbo, and Wings, as well as obscure titles like Cowgirl Romances and Indians. Collectors prefer higher grade copies but look for low numbers in lesser grades too. Demand from Good Girl art collectors led to good sales in this area.

GOLD KEY: Now featuring lower prices than Dell, these books sell twice as fast. 1962 and early '63 issues had low print runs and are an underestimated good investment. Hanna Barbera leads the pack, while other hot titles include: Addams Family, Amazing Chan, Banana Splits, Battle of the Planets, Dr. Solar #1-15, Occult Files of Dr. Spector, Fat Albert, HB Fun-In, Happy Days, HR Pufnstuf, King Kong treasury, Krofft Supershow, Lancelot Link, Land of the Giants, Lidsville, Looney Tunes, Lost in Space #1-20, Magnus #1-10, Mighty Samson, Phantom, Scooby Doo, Smokey Bear, Super TV Heroes, Tarzan, Top Cat, Turok, Twilight Zone, UFO, Wacky Races, Wacky Witch, Wally, and Yosemite Sam. As usual, movie and TV titles are selling well, and Disney titles are in short supply with demand on the upswing. Uncle Scrooge and Donald Duck lead the way there, while others like Little Lulu, Dr. Solar and Magnus are also still in demand. Phantom is selling despite a very short supply, and Tarzan is also doing well with a similar shortage. Horror titles are the slowest selling in this category.

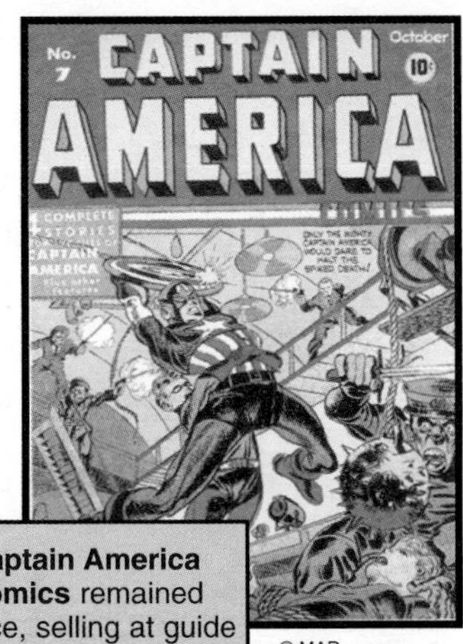

Captain America Comics remained scarce, selling at guide levels. #7 shown.

© MAR

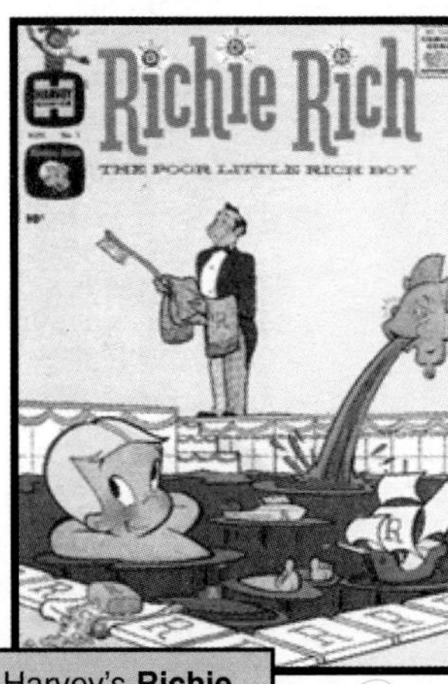

Harvey's **Richie Rich** #1 in high demand!

© HARV

HARVEY: Key books in the first 20 issues of most series are in high demand, with collector desire increasing on low numbers of Casper, Little Dot, Sad Sack, Richie Rich, Little Lotta, Hot Stuff, Spooky, and Little Audrey. There is a distinct demand for early titles like Speed and Green Hornet, as well as '60s titles like the teen Bunny. While superheroes move slowly, everything is selling from new to old, and in all grades. Giants and digests are hot. Other titles in demand include Harvey Pop, Rock Happening, Blondie, Felix, Wendy, Spirit, Spyman, and Unearthly Spectacular.

QUALITY: There is currently demand for low numbers of Crack, Hit, Military, Police and Smash, with copies in short supply. Jack Cole and Lou Fine art is driving demand. Interest in Blackhawk, Plastic Man and Modern is moderate.

TIMELY: This area is definitely still strong although demand is strongest in lower grades. Collectors are still seeking copies in high and middle grades, however. Captain America remains the leading title, with others like All Winners, Marvel Mystery, Miss Fury, Sub-Mariner, Human Torch, and related titles also sought after. High grade copies sell over guide while lesser grades fetch 100-200% of guide.

WALT DISNEY: 8/80-12/80 Whitmans are a big problem for collectors, with Donald Duck #222, Scrooge #179, and Mickey #208 all scarcer even than Golden Age issues! Endless reprints seem to hold down value, and non-reprinted issues are better sellers. The most requested titles include WD Comics Digest (GK), WD Paint Book, most Whitmans, Beagle Boys, Classic Cartoon movie titles, Annette titles, Zorro, Jungle Book treasury, Gladstone Digests, all Don Rosa issues, Moby Duck, Phantom Blot, Scarecrow, Showcase, Super Goof, and Winnie the Pooh.

WARREN: Most Warren series are not that scarce and are in high demand. Early numbers of Creepy and Eerie are in relatively low supply, and special artist issues are in high demand. As usual,

Vampirella is still hot and never stops selling well, although the title is emerging from a bit of a slump after some overexposure due to the modern era Harris titles. Notable areas of interest in this category include Blazing Combat #1 and anthology, Comix International #1, Creepy #146, Vampirella #91-113, Vampirella Annual #1, Vampirella Special #1, Help, After Hours, Spacemen, Wildest Westerns, Famous Monsters #81-120, Odd World of Richard Corben, all paperbacks and Goblin.

Copies of **Phantom Lady** like this #23 still bring a premium.

© FOX

WHITMAN: This is fast becoming a strong market, with pre-1980 variants of Gold Key editions now bringing full guide to multiples of guide on lower priced issues. Completists are hunting them down but having a hard time finding them. Theme collectors are seeking these issues too. The Pre-Pack only 8-12/80 issues are nearly non-existent and bring 200-500% of guide even in VG! An Uncle Scrooge #179 (file copy) sold for an astonishing $1250 late in the year. The 1982 no date code issues are also elusive, bringing 100-200% of guide. The 101 known DC Whitman variants, 3/78-8/80 are scarce in better than VG with most VF copies an easy sale at $10 each. With a ratio of about 1-4 extant copies for every 100 direct copies on the market, this is a potentially fertile area for more activity.

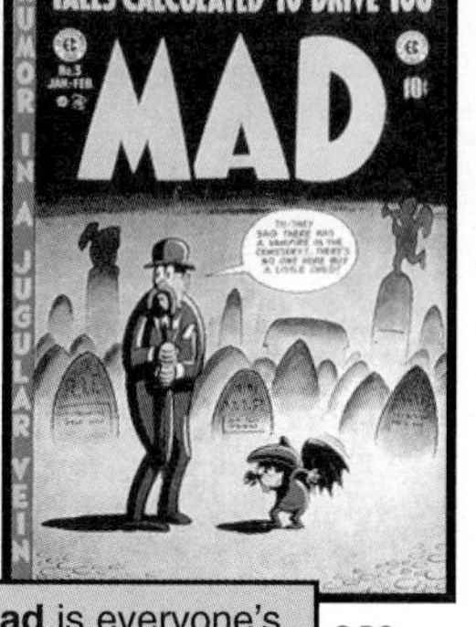

Mad is everyone's favorite! #3 shown.

© DC

MISCELLANEOUS: Demand has reached a plateau for Centaur titles, while EC is enjoying increased demand for horror and sci-fi. MAD is very popular and sought after by all ages; it's often the most avidly collected title by the largest age range in some areas. Fox comics sell well, with superheroes selling at 100-200% of guide in lesser grades and 185-375% in high grade. Continued strong demand for early Lou Fine covers is apparent, and Fox titles like Phantom Lady, Dagar, Rulah, and Zoot are as hot as ever. Gleason titles showing some movement are Silver Streak, Daredevil, and early issues of Boy, while MLJ is still strong, with undiminished demand for superhero titles. Copies are scarce. With an almost non-existent supply, demand is high for Tower titles, led by Wally Wood books and the teen Archie knock-offs.

CONCLUSION

So where does the comic book market stand at this dramatic time in history? Whether you believe the new millennium is approaching or has already begun, there's no doubt that the comic book hobby has already passed a crucial turning point, but the ramifications of that event have yet to be measured. With the influence of the internet, the hobby has experienced a stunning shift in emphasis away from traditional collecting to innovative new ways of celebrating the medium and our mutual love of comics. Whether we will look back on 1999 as the beginning of the end or the start of a bright new era in the hobby remains to be seen, but chances are comics will remain an exciting and viable collectible for years to come, perhaps even ushering in another millennium before all is said and done. Stay tuned...

Special Thanks to the many Overstreet advisors who contributed individual market reports, trend analyses, sales data, and more for the composition of this market report, including David T. Alexander, Dave Anderson, Lauren Becker, Samuel D. Catalino, Gary Colabuono, DJ's Comics, Gary Dolgoff, Bob Ficarra, Eric J. Groves, Ed Jaster, Phil Mateer, Joshua Nathanson, Matt Nelson, Terry O'Neill, Redbeard's Book Den, David H. Sincere, Tony Starks, Doug Sulipa, Michael Tierney, and Tropic Comics.

KEY COMICS SOLD IN 1999

The following lists of sales were reported to Gemstone during the year and represent only a small portion of the total amount of important books that have sold.

GOLDEN-ATOM AGE SALES

Action Comics #18 VG (restored) $315
Action Comics #27 VG $235
Action Comics #57 VG/F $170
Adventure Comics #40 VF $50,000
Adventure Comics #46 VG $600
Adventure Comics #48 VF- $16,000
Adventure Comics #56 F/VF $900
Adventure Comics #58 Restored VF/NM $900
Adventure Comics #74 Restored VG/FN $1000
Adventure Comics #87 VG/F $225
Adventure Comics #88 F+ $400
Adventure Comics #93 G/VG $160
Adventure Comics #94 VG/F $230
Adventure Comics #237 VF/NM $225
Adventure Comics #246 VF/NM $225
All American #27 VG- $350
All American #27 VG- $400
All American #30 FN+ $460
All American #47 FN $315
All Flash #1 VF/NM $16,000
All Flash #2 G/VG $300
All Flash #4 G/VG $150
All Flash #5 G/VG $150
All Flash #7 VG $175
All Flash #19 VG/F $225
All Flash #30 VF $375
All Flash Mile High run of about 20 issues at 5 time guide (trade)
All Star Comics #1 Restored FN $1000
All Winners #12 apparent NM (restored) $350
Baffling Mysteries #20 VF/NM $255
Batman #1 G/VG $5500
Batman #1 VG- $6250, appears FN but extensive restoration and recreation back cover $4400
Batman #2 VG $2000
Batman #11 F+ $300
Batman #11 F/VF $220
Batman #19 VG $207
Big All American Comics G- $750
Captain America Comics #1 VG+ $10,000
Captain America Comics #3 Restored VG+ $1200
Captain America Comics #5 (missing two wraps) $200
Captain America Comics #9 VG/VG+ $850
Captain America Comics #11 VF (restored) $600
Captain America Comics #12 VF $1200
Captain America Comics #15 VG+ $640
Captain America Comics #16 VF+ (Olshevsky copy, small tr. seal) $2500
Captain America Comics #32 G+ (glue) $150
Captain America Comics #33 VG- $400
Captain America Comics #36 F $150
Captain America Comics #41 G/VG (no centerfold) $60
Captain America Comics #47 Restored VG+ $200
Captain America Comics #50 VG (centerfold out) $100
Captain America Comics #52 FN- $375
Captain America Comics #53 FN- $375
Captain America Comics #74 (Canadian edition) 1/2" spine split otherwise VF/NM $2075
Captain Marvel #8 F/VF $320
Captain Marvel #13 VG- $100
Captain Marvel #23 VF+ $425
Captain Marvel #26 F/VF $200
Captain Marvel #29 VF+ $300
Captain Marvel #51 VF/NM $135
Captain Marvel #52 NM+ $250
Captain Marvel Jr. #11 VG $100
Captain Midnight #10 F/VF $280
Claire Voyant #4 FN $240
Comic Cavalcade #11 VF $385
Comic Cavalcade #20 VG+ $200
Daring Mystery Comics #4 VF/NM (Nova Scotia pedigree) $2000
Dell Giant Christmas Parade #1 F/VF $230
Dell Giant Vacation Parade #1 F/VF $335
Detective Comics #3 apparent VF/NM (restored) $6000
Detective Comics #19 FN- (restored) $1075
Detective Comics #27 FN $80,000
Detective Comics #28 apparent VF/NM (professional restoration) $4600
Detective Comics #29 NM (Allentown) $70,000 (trade)
Detective Comics #38 Restored FN $2500
Detective Comics #62 FN+ $450
Exciting #58 VF/NM $600
Famous Funnies #214 VF/NM $1300
Fantastic Comics #8 VF- $615
Flash Comics #10 G/VG $250
Flash Comics #24 VG/F $425
Flash Comics #85 F- $215
Flash Comics (Wheaties Giveaway) G $300
Four Color (Volcano Valley) #147 VF/NM $1000 (Salida Copy)
Four Color Comics #108 F/VF $550
Four Color Comics #159 F/VF $320
Four Color Comics #178 G $75
Four Color Comics #238 F/VF $225
Green Lantern #8 VG/F $400
Marvel Family #2 FN+ $255
Marvel Family #3 FN+ $200
Marvel Family #4 VG/VG- $51
Marvel Family #5 FN $65
Marvel Family #7 FN- $64
Marvel Mystery #4 GD $1000
Marvel Mystery #47 Restored G/VG $150
Marvel Mystery #48 VG $225
Marvel Mystery #51 Restored G $100
More Fun #52,53 (Larson) double NM guide
More Fun #60 Restored FN $400
More Fun #62 VG- $500
More Fun #67 VF- (cleaned cover, top staple reinforced) $2400
More Fun #68 GD+ $200
More Fun #70 G $285
More Fun #73 VF $10,500
New Fun #1 G/VG $17,000
Reform School Girls VG+ $800
San Francisco copies of Sensation Comics #49 NM, #53 NM+ and Star Spangled #28 NM/MT $3400 for the lot
Sensation #1 (Mile High) $80,000 (trade)
Sensation #2-33 + 20 other Mile High issues at 5 times guide (cash and trade)
Sensation Comics #7 VG/F $230

Sensation Comics #9 VG $185
Sensation Comics #10 VG/F $230
Sensation Comics #22 VG $125
Sensation Comics #29 VG/F $160
Sensation Comics #32 VG/F $115
Sensation Comics #33 VG $100
Sensation Comics #35 VG/F $100
Sensation Comics #43 VG+ $100
Sensation Comics #53 VG/F $70
Sensation Comics #72 FN $110
Sensation Comics #75 F/VF $125
Sensation Comics #102 VG- $80
Slave Girl #1 VF/NM (Bethlehem copy) $1050
Space Detective #3 F/VF (Bethlehem copy) $230
Star Spangled #16 NM/M (Mile High copy) $4070
Sub-Mariner Comics #8 VF/NM $2000
Sub-Mariner Comics #19 Restored F- $350
Sub-Mariner Comics #39 VG $150
Superman #1 apparent F/VF (restored, new back cover) $5000 (to a dealer who then sold it for $7500)
Superman #18 VG- $200
Superman #21 VG- $150
Superman #25 VF/VF+ $750
Suspense Comics #6 VG- $350
Suspense Comics #9 G $250
Suspense Comics #10 G $250
Suspense Comics #11 VG- $200 (piece out)
Suspense Comics #12 Restored VF/NM $500
Tales of Horror #1 FN- $105
Thing #15 F/VF $325
Thrilling #70 VF/NM $450
Underworld Crime #7 VG- $200
USA Comics #14 VG/F $285
Weird Fantasy #23 VF+ $157.50
Whiz #1 Restored VG/FN $5000
Witches Tales #25 VG $175
Wonder Woman #4 VG+ $325
Wonder Woman #6 VG/F $270
Wonder Woman #8 VG $140
Wonder Woman #10 VG/F $275
Wonder Woman #13 FN- $235
Wonder Woman #18 FN $245
Wonder Woman #27 VG $150
Wonder Woman #30 VG/F $170
Wonder Woman #39 VG $95
Wonder Woman #40 VG+ $110
World's Finest #9 VG $295
World's Finest #11 F/VF $550
World's Finest #12 F/VF $550
Young Allies #1 NM- $9000
Young Men #24 G/VG $800

SILVER-BRONZE AGE SALES

Action Comics #252 FN- (color touch and glue on spine) $200
Amazing Fantasy #15 VG++ $2000
Amazing Spider-Man #1 VG/F $1800, G/VG $775
Amazing Spider-Man #3 NM- $2400, VF/NM $1750, VG+ $275, NM- (restored) $475
Amazing Spider-Man #4 NM- $1850, NM- $1650
Amazing Spider-Man #8 NM (arrival date) $1050
Amazing Spider-Man #16 VF+ $280
Amazing Spider-Man #25 VF/NM $250
Amazing Spider-Man #26 VF/NM $225
Amazing Spider-Man #27 VF/NM $240
Amazing Spider-Man #28 NM (Winnepeg) $725
Amazing Spider-Man #35 NM/NM+ $230, VF+ $95
Amazing Spider-Man #50 NM- $370
Amazing Spider-Man Annual #1 FN+ $200
Avengers #1 VF/VF+ $1600, FN $515, FN+ $700
Avengers #2 NM $900
Avengers #13 NM $235
Brave and the Bold #28 VG- $600
Brave and the Bold #34 VF/NM $1800
Daredevil #1 VF $920
Fantastic Four #1 F- $350
Fantastic Four #1 VG/F $1750, VG (trimmed, tear seal) $1500
Fantastic Four #2 G+ $250
Fantastic Four #9 VF- $300
Fantastic Four #11 VG/F $130
Fantastic Four #22 NM $185
Fantastic Four #48 NM- $800, NM $1000, NM/MT $1365
Fantastic Four #58 NM/NM- $75
Fantastic Four #60 NM $80
Hawkman #1 NM (glossy, white pages) $875, VF+ $490
Hulk #1 VG/F $1200
Hulk #2 G $108
Hulk #102 NM+ $250
Hulk #181 FN- $125
Journey into Mystery #62 FN+ $90
Journey Into Mystery #83 G $275
Journey Into Mystery #86 VF/NM $385
Journey Into Mystery #117 NM- $105
Justice League #13 NM $250
Showcase #6 F/VF $2350
Showcase #8 VG $950
Showcase #22 VG $525
Showcase #31 FN $77
Showcase #32 VG $51
Silver Surfer #1 VF+ $265
Strange Tales #1 VG+ $800
Strange Tales #3 VG+ $195
Strange Tales #74 FN+ $70
Strange Tales #97 F/VF $225
Tales of Suspense #1 VG+ $00
Tales of Suspense #2 VG $100
Tales of Suspense #10 FN/VF $178
Tales of Suspense #32 VG $65
Tales of Suspense #39 NM+ (Pacific Coast Collection) $11,200
Tales of Suspense #39 VG $425, VG $475
Tales of Suspense #39 VG $500
Tales of Suspense #59 VF+ $240
Tales to Astonish #10 VG- $75
Tales to Astonish #18 VG $65
Tales to Astonish #27 F/VF $875, VG $450, VF+ $2000
Tales to Astonish #35 FN $225
Tales to Astonish #57 VF+ $100
X-Men #1 (rusty staples otherwise VF) $1800, VG/F $780, G $325
X-Men #1 NM++(Pacific Coast Collection) $22,400
X-Men #2 NM++(Pacific Coast Collection) $5,426
X-Men #3 NM++(Pacific Coast Collection) $2,072
X-Men #5 VF/NM $420
X-Men #8 VF+ $175
X-Men #10 VF/NM $225
X-Men #19 NM/MT $240, VF+ $100
X-Men #26 NM/MT $190
X-Men #29 VF/NM $90
X-Men #35 NM $165
X-Men Lot (#1 VG, #2 VG/F, #3 VG+) $940 (25% off)

Bronze Age Sales:

Amazing Spider-Man #121 NM+ $145, NM/NM+ $135
Conan #1 VF/NM $175, F/VF $90
Conan #5 NM $60
Hulk #181 NM $500, NM+ $595, MT $800
Giant-Size X-Men #1 NM/MT $575, FN $80

The following tables denote the rate of appreciation of the top Golden Age, Platinum Age, Silver Age and Bronze Age books, as well as selected genres over the past year. The retail value for a Near Mint copy of each book (or VF where a Near Mint copy is not known to exist) in 2000 is compared to its value in 1999. The rate of return for 2000 over 1999 is given. The place in rank is given for each comic by year, with its corresponding value in highest known grade. These tables can be very useful in forecasting trends in the market place. For instance, the investor might want to know which book is yielding the best dividend from one year to the next, or one might just be interested in seeing how the popularity of books changes from year to year. For instance, *Motion Picture Funnies Weekly* #1 was in 43rd place in 1999 and has increased to 32rd place in 2000. Premium books are also included in these tables and are denoted with an asterisk(*).

The following tables are meant as a guide to the investor. However, it should be pointed out that trends may change at anytime and that some books can meet market resistance with a slowdown in price increases, while others can develop into real comers from a presently dormant state. In the long run, if the investor sticks to the books that are appreciating steadily each year, he shouldn't go very far wrong.

TOP GOLDEN AGE BOOKS

2000 OVER 1999 GUIDE VALUES

ISSUE NO.	2000 RANK	2000 NM PRICE	1999 RANK	1999 NM PRICE	$ INCR.	% INCR.
Action Comics #1	1	$200,000	1	$185,000	$15,000	8%
Detective Comics #27	2	$175,000	2	$165,000	$10,000	6%
Superman #1	3	$140,000	3	$130,000	$10,000	8%
Marvel Comics #1	4	$125,000	4	$115,000	$10,000	9%
All-American Comics #16	5	$70,000	5	$65,000	$5,000	8%
Batman #1	6	$65,000	6	$63,000	$2,000	3%
Whiz Comics #2 (#1)	7	$64,000	7	$63,000	$1,000	2%
Flash Comics #1	8	$60,000	8	$57,000	$3,000	5%
Captain America Comics #1	9	$58,000	9	$56,000	$2,000	4%
Detective Comics #1	10	VF $50,000	10	VF $50,000	$0	0%
More Fun Comics #52	11	$50,000	11	$48,000	$2,000	4%
New Fun Comics #1	12	VF $39,000	12	VF $38,000	$1,000	3%
Detective Comics #33	13	$36,000	13	$35,000	$1,000	3%
Adventure Comics #40	14	$34,000	14	$33,000	$1,000	3%
All Star Comics #3	15	$31,500	16	$31,000	$500	2%
Detective Comics #38	16	$31,000	17	$30,000	$1,000	3%
More Fun Comics #53	17	$30,000	15	$32,000	-$2,000	-6%
Captain Marvel Adventures #1	18	$28,500	18	$28,000	$500	2%
Green Lantern #1	19	$28,000	19	$27,000	$1,000	4%
Detective Comics #29	20	$26,000	21	$25,000	$1,000	4%
Detective Comics #31	21	$26,000	22	$25,000	$1,000	4%
All Star Comics #8	22	$25,500	20	$25,000	$500	2%
New York World's Fair 1939	23	$24,000	23	$24,000	$0	0%
Famous Funnies-Series 1 #1	24	$22,500	24	$22,000	$500	2%
Human Torch #2 (#1)	25	$22,000	25	$21,000	$1,000	5%
Sensation Comics #1	26	$22,000	26	$21,000	$1,000	5%
Action Comics #2	27	$21,000	27	$20,000	$1,000	5%
Sub-Mariner Comics #1	28	$21,000	30	$20,000	$1,000	5%
Adventure Comics #48	29	$20,000	28	$20,000	$0	0%
* Century Of Comics nn	30	VF $20,000	34	VF $17,000	$3,000	18%
Marvel Mystery Comics #2	31	$20,000	29	$20,000	$0	0%
* Motion Picture Funnies Weekly #1	32	$20,000	43	$15,000	$5,000	33%
New Fun Comics #6	33	VF $19,000	31	VF $18,500	$500	3%
Marvel Mystery Comics #9	34	$18,500	32	$18,000	$500	3%
Wonder Woman #1	35	$18,000	33	$17,500	$500	3%
Daring Mystery Comics #1	36	$17,000	35	$16,500	$500	3%
Jumbo Comics #1	37	VF $17,000	36	VF $16,500	$500	3%
New Comics #1	38	VF $17,000	38	VF $16,000	$1,000	6%
New Fun Comics #2	39	VF $17,000	37	VF $16,500	$500	3%
Walt Disney's Comics & Stories #1	40	$16,500	39	$16,000	$500	3%

ISSUE NO.	2000 RANK	2000 NM PRICE	1999 RANK	1999 NM PRICE	$ INCR.	% INCR.
Famous Funnies #1	41	$16,000	40	$15,500	$500	3%
Detective Comics #28	42	$15,500	41	$15,000	$500	3%
Marvel Mystery Comics #5	43	$15,500	42	$15,000	$500	3%
All Winners Comics #1	44	$15,000	44	$14,500	$500	3%
Amazing Man Comics #5	45	$14,750	45	$14,500	$250	2%
Action Comics #3	46	$14,500	47	$14,000	$500	4%
World's Best Comics #1	47	$14,500	48	$14,000	$500	4%
Action Comics #7	48	$14,300	50	$13,000	$1,300	10%
Detective Comics #2	49	VF $14,300	46	VF $14,300	$0	0%
Wonder Comics #1	50	$14,000	49	$13,500	$500	4%
All Flash #1	51	$13,000	54	$12,500	$500	4%
New York World's Fair 1940	52	$13,000	51	$13,000	$0	0%
Silver Streak #6	53	$13,000	61	$12,000	$1,000	8%
Wow Comics #1	54	$13,000	55	$12,500	$500	4%
All-American Comics #17	55	$12,500	52	$12,500	$0	0%
All-American Comics #19	56	$12,500	53	$12,500	$0	0%
Archie Comics #1	57	$12,500	62	$11,500	$1,000	9%
Big Book of Fun Comics #1	58	VF $12,500	57	VF $12,000	$500	4%
Double Action #2	59	$12,500	58	$12,000	$500	4%
Mystic Comics #1	60	$12,500	59	$12,000	$500	4%
New Book of Comics #1	61	VF $12,500	60	VF $12,000	$500	4%
All Star Comics #1	62	$12,000	56	$12,000	$0	0%
Batman #2	63	$11,500	65	$11,200	$300	3%
* Funnies on Parade nn	64	$11,500	68	$11,000	$500	5%
More Fun Comics #14	65	VF $11,500	63	VF $11,500	$0	0%
More Fun Comics #55	66	$11,500	64	$11,500	$0	0%
Four Color Ser. 1 (Donald Duck) #4	67	$11,000	71	$10,500	$500	5%
Mickey Mouse Magazine #1	68	$11,000	69	$11,000	$0	0%
More Fun Comics #73	69	$11,000	72	$10,500	$500	5%
Pep Comics #22	70	$11,000	78	$10,000	$1,000	10%
Silver Streak #1	71	$11,000	73	$10,500	$500	5%
Suspense Comics #3	72	$11,000	80	$10,000	$1,000	10%
Daredevil Comics #1	73	$10,500	84	$9,500	$1,000	11%
Looney Tunes and Merrie Melodies #1	74	$10,500	77	$10,000	$500	5%
Detective Comics #3	75	VF $10,200	74	VF $10,200	$0	0%
Action Comics #10	76	$10,000	82	$9,500	$500	5%
Adventure Comics #61	77	$10,000	66	$11,000	-$1,000	-9%
Adventure Comics #72	78	$10,000	75	$10,000	0	0%
Adventure Comics #73	79	$10,000	67	$11,000	-$1,000	-9%
Captain America Comics #2	80	$10,000	76	$10,000	$0	0%
Four Color Ser. 1 (Mickey Mouse) #16	81	VF $10,000	88	VF $9,000	$1,000	11%
Red Raven Comics #1	82	$10,000	79	$10,000	$0	0%
Superman #2	83	$10,000	81	$9,700	$300	3%
USA Comics #1	84	$10,000	85	$9,500	$500	5%
Young Allies Comics #1	85	$10,000	86	$9,500	$500	5%
Comics Magazine #1	86	VF $9,600	83	VF $9,500	$100	1%
Big All-American #1	87	$9,500	70	$10,800	-$1,300	-12%
Mystery Men Comics #1	88	$9,500	87	$9,400	$100	1%
Planet Comics #1	89	$9,500	89	$9,000	$500	6%
Marvel Mystery Comics #3	90	$9,000	90	$8,600	$400	5%
Green Giant Comics #1	91	$8,800	91	$8,500	$300	4%
Famous Funnies Carnival of Comics nn	92	$8,500		$8,000	$500	6%
More Fun Comics #54	93	$8,400	92	$8,400	0	0%
Action Comics #4	94	$8,300	94	$8,000	$300	4%
Action Comics #5	95	$8,300	95	$8,000	$300	4%
Action Comics #6	96	$8,300	96	$8,000	$300	4%
Captain America Comics #3	97	$8,200	93	$8,200	$0	0%
New Fun Comics #3	98	VF $8,200		VF $8,000	$200	3%
New Fun Comics #4	99	VF $8,200		VF $8,000	$200	3%
New Fun Comics #5	100	VF $8,200		VF $8,000	$200	3%

TOP 10 PLATINUM AGE BOOKS

2000 OVER 1999 GUIDE VALUES

TITLE/ISSUE#	2000 RANK	2000 VF PRICE	1999 RANK	1999 VF PRICE	$ INCR.	% INCR.
Mickey Mouse Book (2nd printing)-variant	1	FN $12,000	1	FN $12,000	$0	0%
Mickey Mouse Book (1st printing)	2	$11,000	2	$11,000	$0	0%
Mickey Mouse Book (2nd printing)	3	$10,000	3	$10,000	$0	0%
Yellow Kid in McFadden Flats	4	FN $8,500	4	FN $8,000	$500	6%
Buster Brown and His Resolutions 1903	5	FN $4,000	5	FN $3,200	$800	25%
* Buster Brown's Blue Ribbon #1 1904	6	$3,600	9	$3,600	$0	0%
Dreams of the Rarebit Fiend	7	FN $3,000	6	FN $2,680	$320	11%
Little Sammy Sneeze	8	FN $3,000	7	FN $2,660	$340	12%
Pore Li'l Mose	9	FN $3,000	8	FN $2,000	$1,000	50%
Little Nemo 1906	10	FN $2,800	10	FN $2,335	$465	20%

TOP 10 SILVER AGE BOOKS

2000 OVER 1999 GUIDE VALUES

TITLE/ISSUE#	2000 RANK	2000 NM PRICE	1999 RANK	1999 NM PRICE	$ INCR.	% INCR.
Amazing Fantasy #15	1	$25,000	1	$27,000	-$2,000	-7%
Showcase #4	2	$25,000	2	$25,000	$0	0%
Fantastic Four #1	3	$19,000	3	$19,000	$0	0%
Amazing Spider-Man #1	4	$18,000	4	$18,000	$0	0%
Incredible Hulk #1	5	$12,000	5	$12,000	$0	0%
Showcase #8	6	$12,000	6	$12,000	$0	0%
Showcase #9	7	$6,700	7	$6,500	$200	3%
X-Men #1	8	$6,200	8	$6,000	$200	3%
Detective Comics #225	9	$5,600	9	$5,600	$0	0%
Flash #105(#1)	10	$5,600	10	$5,500	$100	2%

TOP 10 BRONZE AGE BOOKS

2000 OVER 1999 GUIDE VALUES

TITLE/ISSUE#	2000 RANK	2000 NM PRICE	1999 RANK	1999 NM PRICE	$ INCR.	% INCR.
Star Wars #1 (35¢ cover price)	1	$530	1	$510	$20	4%
Giant-Size X-Men #1	2	$490	2	$480	$10	2%
House of Secrets #92	3	$490	3	$470	$20	4%
Incredible Hulk #181	4	$480	4	$465	$15	3%
X-Men #94	5	$460	5	$440	$20	5%
DC 100 Page Super Spectacular #5	6	$420	6	$400	$20	5%
X-Men #98 (30¢ cover price)	7	$280	7	$280	$0	0%
X-Men #99 (30¢ cover price)	8	$280	8	$280	$0	0%
Vampirella #113	9	$270	T9	$250	$20	8%
Vampirella Annual #1	10	$260	T9	$250	$10	4%

TOP 10 CRIME BOOKS

2000 OVER 1999 GUIDE VALUES

TITLE/ISSUE#	2000 RANK	2000 NM PRICE	1999 RANK	1999 NM PRICE	$ INCR.	% INCR.
Crime Does Not Pay #22	1	$1,700	1	$1,650	$50	3%
True Crime Comics #2	2	$1,050	2	$1,020	$30	3%
Crime Does Not Pay #23	3	$975	3	$950	$25	3%
Crimes By Women #1	4	$960	4	$920	$40	4%
Crime Does Not Pay #24	5	$775	5	$750	$25	3%
True Crime Comics #3	6	$775	6	$750	$25	3%
The Killers #1	7	$750	7	$720	$30	4%
True Crime Comics #4	8	$700	8	$680	$20	3%
The Killers #2	9	$650	9	$630	$20	3%
True Crime Comics Vol. 2 #1	10	$625	10	$600	$25	4%

TOP 10 HORROR BOOKS

2000 OVER 1999 GUIDE VALUES

TITLE/ISSUE#	2000 RANK	2000 NM PRICE	1999 RANK	1999 NM PRICE	$ INCR.	% INCR.
Vault of Horror #12	1	$4,000	1	$3,800	$200	5%
Tales of Terror Annual #1	2	VF $3,200	2	VF $3,200	$0	0%
Journey into Mystery #1	3	$2,800	3	$2,650	$150	6%
Eerie #1	4	$2,600	5	$2,400	$200	8%
Strange Tales #1	5	$2,600	4	$2,500	$100	4%
Crypt of Terror #17	6	$2,350	6	$2,200	$150	7%
Haunt of Fear #15	7	$2,350	7	$2,200	$150	7%
Crime Patrol #15	8	$2,000	8	$1,900	$100	5%
House of Mystery #1	9	$1,700	9	$1,650	$50	3%
Tales to Astonish #1	10	$1,500	10	$1,500	$0	0%

TOP 10 ROMANCE BOOKS

2000 OVER 1999 GUIDE VALUES

TITLE/ISSUE#	2000 RANK	2000 NM PRICE	1999 RANK	1999 NM PRICE	$ INCR.	% INCR.
Giant Comics Edition #12	1	$825	1	$750	$75	10%
Intimate Confessions #1	2	$560	2	$540	$20	4%
Giant Comics Edition #9	3	$480	3	$460	$20	4%
Giant Comics Edition #15	4	$450	5	$430	$20	5%
Romance Trail #1	5	$450	4	$440	$10	2%
Young Lovers #18	6	$440	6	$420	$20	5%
DC 100 Page Super Spectacular #5	7	$420	7	$400	$20	5%
Giant Comics Edition #13	8	$420	8	$395	$25	6%
Secret Hearts #1	9	$410	9	$390	$20	5%
Personal Love #32	10	$385		$360	$25	7%

TOP 10 SCI-FI BOOKS

2000 OVER 1999 GUIDE VALUES

TITLE/ISSUE#	2000 RANK	2000 NM PRICE	1999 RANK	1999 NM PRICE	$ INCR.	% INCR.
Mystery In Space #1	1	$2,600	1	$2,600	$0	0%
Strange Adventures #1	2	$2,600	2	$2,500	$100	4%
Showcase (Adam Strange) #17	3	$2,100	3	$2,100	$0	0%
Showcase (Space Ranger) #15	4	$1,750	4	$1,700	$50	3%
Journey Into Unknown Worlds #36	5	$1,700	6	$1,600	$100	6%
Fawcett Movie (Man From Planet X) #15	6	$1,650	5	$1,650	$0	0%
Strange Adventures #9	7	$1,600	7	$1,500	$100	7%
Weird Fantasy #13 (#1)	8	$1,600	8	$1,500	$100	7%
Weird Science #12 (#1)	9	$1,600	9	$1,500	$100	7%
Weird Science-Fantasy Annual 1952	10	$1,500	10	$1,500	$0	0%

TOP 10 WESTERN BOOKS

2000 OVER 1999 GUIDE VALUES

TITLE/ISSUE#	2000 RANK	2000 NM PRICE	1999 RANK	1999 NM PRICE	$ INCR.	% INCR.
Gene Autry Comics #1	1	$7,200	1	$7,000	$200	3%
*Lone Ranger Ice Cream 1939	2	VF $5,500	3	VF $4,200	1,300	31%
*Lone Ranger Ice Cream 1939 2nd	3	VF $5,500				(new listing)
Hopalong Cassidy #1	4	$4,800	2	$4,600	$200	4%
*Red Ryder Victory Patrol '42	5	$4,000				(new listing)
*Red Ryder Victory Patrol '43	6	$3,750	4	$3,600	$150	4%
*Red Ryder Victory Patrol '44	7	$3,550	5	$3,400	$150	4%
*Tom Mix Ralston #1	8	$3,000	6	$2,700	$300	11%
Red Ryder Comics #1	9	$2,600	7	$2,500	$100	4%
Roy Rogers Four Color #38	10	$2,200	8	$2,000	$200	10%

METROPOLIS
COLLECTIBLES
873 Broadway, Suite 201 New York, NY 10011
Tel: (212) 260-4147 Fax: (212) 260-4304
Toll Free: 1-800-229-6387
email: buying@metropoliscomics.com Web: www.metropoliscomics.com

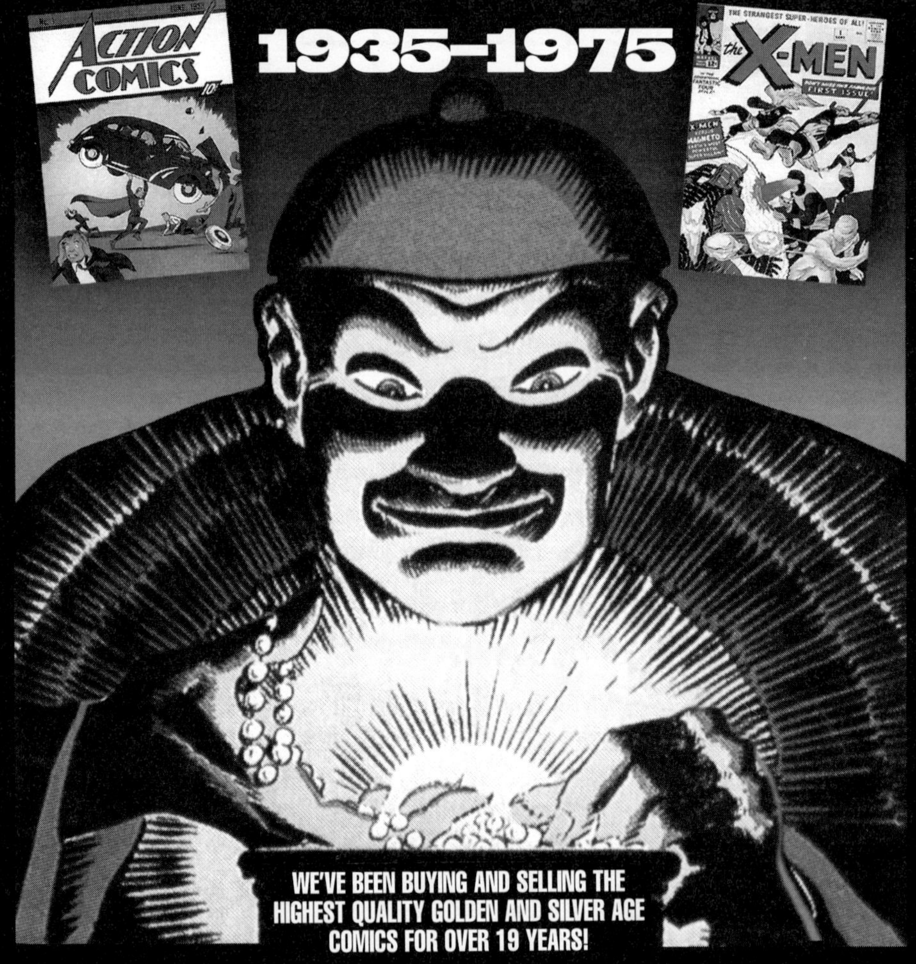
1935–1975
ACTION COMICS
THE STRANGEST SUPER-HEROES OF ALL!
the X-MEN
FIRST ISSUE!
X-MEN
MAGNETO
WE'VE BEEN BUYING AND SELLING THE HIGHEST QUALITY GOLDEN AND SILVER AGE COMICS FOR OVER 19 YEARS!

AMAZING
FANTASY
SPIDER MAN
© MARVEL COMICS

FOUR COLOR
COMICS
BUYING PRE-1955 POSTERS
I buy, sell, and collect movie posters and theater displays. I can and will pay you the highest price for your poster or collection of posters. Call me before you sell.
Of particular interest:
EARLY DISNEY
UNIVERSAL HORROR
1950'S SCIENCE-FICTION
1930'S POSTERS
115 West 27th St.
New York, NY 10001
Tel: (212) 675-6990
Fax: (212) 675-6145
Keybooks@aol.com
www.fourColorComics.com
D.W. GRIFFITH'S MIGHTY SPECTACLE
THE BIRTH OF A NATION
FOUNDED ON THOMAS DIXON'S THE CLANSMAN
THE DAY THE EARTH STOOD STILL
MICHAEL RENNIE · PATRICIA NEAL · HUGH MARLOWE
FRANKENSTEIN meets THE WOLF MAN
ILONA MASSEY
BELA
Charlie
UNITED ARTISTS PICTURE
KONG
FAY WRAY · ROBT. ARMSTRONG
BRUCE CABOT
EDGAR WALLACE
JOEL McCREA
CYNTHIA

FOUR COLOR
COMICS
BUYING PRE-1980 LINE-ART
I buy, sell, and collect original comic art. I can and will pay you the highest price for your art. Call me before you sell.
Of particular interest:
GOLDENAGE ART
DC SILVERAGE ART
MARVEL SILVERAGE ART
EC COVER ART
FRAZETTA, KIRBY, DITKO, BARKS
115 West 27th St.
New York, NY 10001
Tel: (212) 675-6990
Fax: (212) 675-6145
Keybooks@aol.com
www.fourColorComics.com
THE AMAZING SPIDER-MAN
"SPIDER-MAN NO MORE!"
THOR BATTLES THE INCREDIBLE HULK!
RAREBIT FIEND
GYRO GEARLOOSE
I BROUGHT THE ROC TO LIFE!
TALES CALCULATED TO DRIVE YOU MAD
NICK FURY, AGENT OF S.H.I.E.L.D.!
"TO FREE A BRAIN SLAVE"

DID YOU TURN INTO A
MONSTER
THE LAST TIME YOU RECEIVED
A MAIL ORDER?
If this looks familiar, treat yourself to honest grading and fair pricing by buying your Silver and Golden Age comics from us!
At FOUR COLOR COMICS, we specialize in treating the customer right and we unconditionally guarantee every book we sell!
Fantastic Four
10¢
FOUR COLOR
COMICS
NY SHOWROOM (By Appointment Only): 115 West 27th St, New York, NY 10001 (212) 675-6990 Fax:(212) 675-6145
IF YOU'VE GOT BOOKS TO SELL, CALL IMMEDIATELY: (212) 675-6990
DESIGN: ARNIE SAWYER All artwork: © DC COMICS, © MARVEL ENTERTAINMENT GROUP, INC

ORIGINAL ART WANTED

If you have any of the ORIGINAL BLACK AND WHITE ARTWORK to these COVERS/interiors (even if they are not for sale), please contact me so I can leave you with an offer (and I can stop looking for it). Cash Paid or will trade other art or comics (Gold, Silver, Modern).

PLEASE SAVE THIS LIST, it's good forever.

******PLEASE NOTE: I am NOT looking for the comic books themselves!!!******

ALL ART LISTED IS FOR ORIGINAL B&W COVER ART UNLESS OTHERWISE NOTED!

Interior art indicated in italics.

Avengers #161

Hulk #207

X-Men #121

Adventure #452

Justice League #148

Showcase #94

NEAL ADAMS
Action #466
DC 1978 Calendar Cover - Disasters

ROSS ANDRU
Superman #334, 338, 341, 349

JIM APARO
Adventure #452 (Aquaman)
Aquaman #62, 63
Batman #294
Brave & Bold #130, 136, 139
Manbat #2
Showcase #94, 95, 96 (Doom Patrol)

RICH BUCKLER
Action #478, 483
All-Star Comics #69
Astonishing Tales #26, 27 (Deathlok)
DC Super Stars #10 (Strange Sports)
Freedom Fighters #9, 10, 14
Iron Man Annual #3
Justice League #148, 158
Kamandi #47, 50, 52, 56, 60
Secret Society Super Villians Spectacular (DC Special Series #6)
Superman #327
Super Team Family #8 (Challengers)
New Gods #14, 15
Teen Titans (old) #50-53
X-Men #97

BOB BUDIANSKY
Ghost Rider #40, 43
Marvel 2-in-1 #49
X-Men #120

JOHN BUSCEMA
Fantastic Four #202
Thor #262

SAL BUSCEMA
Hulk #207 (interior pages)
What If? #17 (old)

JOHN BYRNE
****Avengers #181 (interiors), 186-190
****(No one will pay more for Byrne Avengers covers /interiors)
Capt. America #248
Champions #11 (Pages 1-3)
Fantastic Four (ANY covers #211-267!)

Iron Man #109
Marvel Team-Up (ANY covers!)
Marvel 2-in-1 (ANY covers), *any interiors #53-58*
Secret Origins Annual #1 (Doom Patrol)
Spec. Spider-Man #17
Super Villain Team-Up #14
X-Men #108-142 (ANY covers & *interiors*)

ERNIE CHAN(CHUA)
Batman #282
Champions #17
DC Super Stars #8 (Of Space), #9 (Man Behind the Gun)
Flash #243
Invaders #29
Justice League #132
Kamandi #45, 48, 49
Secret Society Super Villains #1-5
Teen Titans (old) #44

DAVE COCKRUM
Avengers #169, 175
Battlestar Galactica #1, 2
Hulk #207
Human Fly #3
Iron Man #110
Star Wars #17
Super Villain Team-Up #12
****X-Men Giant Size #1, #94-126, 145-147
(**ANY covers/pages**)

GENE COLAN
Dr. Strange #27
Tomb of Dracula #64
What If? #17 (old) (Ghost Rider/Capt. Marvel/Spiderwoman)

DICK DILLIN
DC Presents #13, 14
DC Super Stars #10 (Strange Sports) (interior pages)
Justice League #144, 147, 148 (*also interiors #144, 147*), 168, 171, 173

STEVE DITKO
Shade #3, 7

KEITH GIFFEN
Defenders #44
(ANY interior pages)

DICK GIORDANO
Batman #300
Superboy & Legion #253

MIKE GOLDEN
Mirconauts #3-17

MIKE GRELL
Green Lantern #92, 100
Superboy & Legion #228, 230, 231

BOB HALL
Champions #16 (*Interiors*)
Human Fly #17
ANY Squadron Supreme Covers
Super Villain Team-Up #14 (ANY Interior Pages)

RICK HOBERG
Star Wars #2

CARMINE INFANTINO
Star Wars #14,15,19,22

GIL KANE
Avengers #130, 141
Captain America #216
Champions #11, 16
Jungle Action (Black Panther) #14
Marvel Team-Up #23
Star Wars #8

MIKE KALUTA
Batman Family #17

JACK KIRBY
Capt. America #202 (cover + page 14)
Defenders #44
Invaders #14, 15
Kamandi (ANY covers)
Weird Wonder Tales #18

ALAN KUPPERBERG
Invaders #37, 38
Marvel's Greatest Comics #81

BOB LAYTON
Iron Man #121, 127, 135, 139 (others considered)
Marvel Premiere #47 (Ant Man)
Squadron Supreme (ANY covers)
What If? #32 (old)

GARCIA LOPEZ
Action #481, 482, 484
DC Special Series #5 (Superman Spect.), #11 (Flash Spectacular)
Untold Legend of Batman #2

AL MILGROM
Al Star Comics #70

Amazing Spider-Man #194
Defenders #74
Firestorm (old) #2, 3
Flash #268
Invaders #41
Secret Society Super Villains #10
Shogun Warriors (ANY covers)
Skull the Slayer #1

FRANK MILLER
Daredevil #158-181 (Covers & Splashes)
Dark Knight (ANY pgs)
X-Men Annual #3

MIKE NASSER
Kobra #6, 7
Spectacular Spider-Man #37

DON NEWTON
Avengers Annual #9
New Gods #12 (Splash page)

GEORGE PEREZ
******AVENGERS** #160-168, 170-174, 181, 183-185, 191, 192, 194-201, Avengers Ann. #8 (especially #161, 181), *interiors wanted* #161, 162, 167,
Korvac TPB Cover,
****(No one will pay/trade more for Perez Avengers covers!)
Batman Outsiders #5
Fantastic Four (ANY cover)
Infinity Gauntlet (ANY cover)
Justice League #184, 195, 196, 197, 207, 209, 219, 220 (**any** other covers considered)
Marvel Fanfare #10-12
Marvel Premiere #45-46 (Manwolf)
Marvel 2-in-1 #42 50,51,57,58,61-63
(**ANY** *interiors #53-58*)
New Teen Titans #1-50, Annual #3
New Titans (Baxter) #1-5
War of the Gods #1
X-Men #112, Annual #3 (interior pages)
Also looking for "oddball" titles Perez did from 1975-1987

KEITH POLLARD
Iron Man #108, 111, 112 Marvel 2-in-1 #55

FRANK ROBBINS
Human Fly #10

MARSHALL ROGERS
Mr. Miracle (DC House Ad Page–1977), #19-25

JOHN ROMITA, JR.
Avengers #176
Defenders #62
Iron Man #114-117

ALEX ROSS
Marvels #0-4 (ANY splashes/pages)
Kingdom Come (various pages)

PAUL RYAN
Squadron Supreme (ANY covers)

KURT SCHAFFENBERGER
Action #474

ALEX SCHOMBURG
Invaders Ann. #1 (Also Human Torch pages)

JIM STARLIN
Justice League #185

JOE STATON
All Star Comics #71-73
"DC Explosion" (DC House Ad page –1978)
New Gods #19
Showcase #97, 99 (Power Girl) (Splash #94)
Superboy & Legion #249

CHIC STONE
Marvel 2-in-1 #48

HERB TRIMPE
Godzilla #3
Marvel Spotlight #12 (Son of Satan)

DAVE WENZEL
Avengers #177 (interiors)

ALAN WEISS
Human Fly #7
Shazam! (1977) #34

WALLY WOOD
All-Star Comics #64

RON WILSON
Marvel Premiere #55
Marvel 2-in-1 #37
Captain America #230

ARTISTS UNKNOWN
Super Villain Team-Up #15 (Doom-Red Skull)

Godzilla #3

Avengers #160

Superboy/Legion #228

Iron Man #110

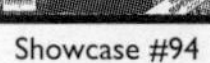

Freedom Fighters #10

Avengers #183

Please Contact: JONATHAN MANKUTA
75 McArthur Lane, Smithtown, NY 11787
Phone –1-631-864-2281 (Leave message if no answer)
e-mail JONMANKUTA@AOL.COM • SEE MY OTHER ADS ON PAGES 134 & 135

This is what I ask myself every time I hear of a significant collection being sold for less money than I would pay, and I wasn't contacted. You have nothing to lose and everything to gain by contacting me. I have purchased many of the major collections over the years. We are serious about buying your comics and paying you the most for them.

If you have comics or related items for sale, please call or send a list for my quote. Remember, no collection is too large or small, even if it's $200,000 or more.

These are some of the high prices I will pay for comics. Percentages stated will be paid for any grade unless otherwise noted, and are based on the Overstreet Guide.

—JAMES F. PAYETTE

Action #2–20	85%	Detective #28–100	60%
Action #21–200	65%	Detective #27 (Mint)	125%
Action #1 (Mint)	125%	Green Lantern #1 (Mint)	150%
Adventure #247	75%	Jackie Gleason #1–12	70%
All American #16 (Mint)	150%	Keen Detective Funnies	70%
All Star #8	70%	Ken Maynard	70%
Amazing Man	70%	More Fun #7–51	75%
Amazing Mystery Funnies	70%	New Adventure #12–31	80%
The Arrow	70%	New Comics #1–11	70%
Batman #2–100	60%	New Fun #1–6	70%
Batman #1 (Mint)	150%	Sunset Carson	70%
Bob Steele	70%	Superman #1 (Mint)	150%
Detective #1–26	85%	Whip Wilson	70%

We are also paying 70% of Guide for the following:

All Winners
Andy Devine
Captain America (1st)
Congo Bill
Detective Eye
Detective Picture Stories
Funny Pages
Funny Picture Stories
Hangman
Jumbo 1–10
Mystery Men
Marvel Mystery
Tim McCoy
Wonder Comics (Fox 1 & 2)

BUYING & SELLING GOLDEN AND SILVER AGE COMICS SINCE 1975

I JUST DON'T GET IT!
We are paying 65% of Guide for the following:
Adventure 32–100
All American
All Flash
All New
All Select
All Top 8–18
Blonde Phantom
Blue Beetle 47–57
Brenda Starr 1–12
Catman
Crash
Daring Mystery
Fantastic
Flash (1st)
Hit 1–20
Human Torch
John Wayne
JO-JO 7–29
Kid Komics
Miss Fury
More Fun 52–107
Mysterious Adventure
Mystic (1st)
National 1–23
New Book of Comics
Pep 1–40
Phantom Lady
Phantom Stranger
Rangers 1-20
Rulah
Science (Fox)
Sensation
Silver Streak 1–17
Smash
Speed 1–20
Strange Tales 1–100
Sub-Mariner (1st)
U.S.A.
Weird Comics
Zoot 7–16
We are paying 55% of Guide for the following:
Adventure 101–200
Adv. of Bob Hope 1–50
Adv. of Jerry Lewis 1–50
Adv. of Ozzie & Harriet
Airboy
Air Fighters
All Star
Amazing Spiderman 1–10
America's Greatest
Blackhawk 9–110
Brave & the Bold 1–20
Bulletman
Captain Marvel
Captain Marvel Jr.
Captain Midnight
Challengers 1–10
Comic Cavalcade 1–29
Daredevil 1st 1–20
Dollman
Fantastic Four 1–10
Fight 1–30
Frontier Fighters
Green Hornet 1–20
Green Lantern (1st)
House of Mystery 1–50
House of Secrets 1–25
Ibis
Journey Into Mystery 1–80
Jumbo 11–50
Jungle 1–50
Lash Larue 1–46
Leading 1–14
Legend of D. Boone
Marvel Family
Mary Marvel
Master
Military
Modern
Movie Comics (D.C.)
My Greatest Adv. 1–50
Mystery in Space 1–50
Nickel
Planet
Police 1–20
Saint
Shadow (1st)
Showcase 1–20
Shield Wizard
Spy Smasher
Star Spangled
Superman 1–125
Superman's Pal 1–30
Strange Adventure 1–120
Superboy 1–50
Tomahawk 1–30
Top-Notch
W.D. Comics & Stories 1–40
Whiz
World's Finest 1–110
Young Allies
Zip 1–39
We are also paying 50–100% of Guide for many other titles. Comics must be properly graded and complete. Please send your listing of comics for sale or a list of comics you wish to purchase. We are dealing in Marvels, D.C.'s, Western, Funny Material and much more! Please send one dollar for our current retail listing of comics in stock. We will travel for large collections or, if you're passing through the area, call for an appointment.
JAMES F. PAYETTE
Rare Books & Comics
P.O Box 750 • Bethlehem, NH 03574
Phone 603-869-2097 • Fax 603-869-3475
COMICS GUARANTY, LLC Charter Member Dealer
CREDENTIALS
Special Advisor to Overstreet Guide 1985–1998
Member AACBC 1990–1998
Member AACBC Authenticating, Certification, and Grading committee for Sotheby's 1991–1998
CBG Customer Service Award Winner for many years
Experience as Dealer/Collector since 1975
PLEASE SEE MY OTHER ADS FOR FURTHER REFERENCE

PACIFIC COMIC EXCHANGE, INC.

SELLERS: Please contact The Exchange if you would like to *consign* these or other books at full market value or sell your collection directly at competitive prices.

CGSA	M	NM/M	++ + NM --	VFN/NM	++ + VFN --	FN/VFN	+ FN --	VG/FN	+ VG	G/VG	G	Fr/G	Fr	Pr
	100 - 91	90	88,85,80,75	70	68,65,63,60,55	50	45,40,35	30	25,20	15	10	8	6	3
OVERSTREET -	10.0	9.8	9.7,9.6,9.4,9.2	9.0	8.8,8.5,8.3,8.0,7.5	7.0	6.5,6.0,5.5	5.0	4.5,4.0	3.0	2.0	1.5	1.0	.5

© DC

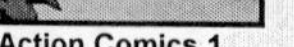
Action Comics 1

© DC

Detective Comics 27

© MEG

Marvel Comics 1

	G 10	VG 20	FN 40	VFN 60	NM 80	NM/M 90
Action Comics 1	$30,000	$50,000	$100,000	$150,000	$300,000	$600,000
Detective Comics 27	$25,000	$45,000	$85,000	$125,000	$250,000	$450,000
Marvel Comics 1	$12,000	$20,000	$40,000	$60,000	$120,000	$300,000

Wanted Immediately in VFN 60 - NM/M 90

	VFN 60	NM 80	NM/M 90		VFN 60	NM 80	NM/M 90
Action Comics 1	$150,000	$300,000	$600,000	Green Lantern 1 (SA)	$1,250	$4,000	$7,500
Adventure Comics 40	$25,000	$50,000	$120,000	Green Lantern 1 (GA)	$12,500	$30,000	$75,000
Adventure Comics 210	$1,500	$3,500	$7,500	Incredible Hulk 1	$5,000	$12,000	$30,000
Adventure Comics 247	$2,250	$6,000	$12,000	Jimmy Olsen 1	$3,000	$9,000	$15,000
All Star Comics 3	$16,000	$35,000	$120,000	Journey Into Mystery 83	$1,800	$5,000	$12,000
All Star Comics 8	$13,000	$30,000	$100,000	Justice League 1	$1,500	$5,000	$10,000
All-American Comics 16	$40,000	$80,000	$175,000	Lois Lane 1	$2,000	$4,500	$9,000
Amazing Fantasy 15	$10,000	$27,000	$50,000	Marvel Comics 1	$60,000	$120,000	$300,000
Amazing Spider-Man 1	$6,000	$18,000	$35,000	More Fun Comics 52	$30,000	$75,000	$150,000
Batman 1	$33,000	$80,000	$180,000	More Fun Comics 55	$6,500	$13,500	$30,000
Batman 100	$1,350	$2,500	$5,000	Sensation Comics 1	$10,000	$24,000	$65,000
Captain America 1	$30,000	$70,000	$150,000	Showcase 4	$12,000	$30,000	$60,000
Detective Comics 1	$50,000	$100,000	$225,000	Showcase 22	$1,800	$5,500	$11,000
Detective Comics 27	$125,000	$250,000	$485,000	Sub-Mariner Comics 1	$10,000	$20,000	$60,000
Detective Comics 33	$20,000	$45,000	$100,000	Superman 1	$75,000	$150,000	$400,000
Detective Comics 38	$18,000	$35,000	$100,000	Superman 100	$1,200	$3,000	$6,000
Fantastic Four 1	$7,500	$25,000	$50,000	Suspense Comics 3	$8,000	$25,000	$50,000
Flash Comics 1	$30,000	$75,000	$165,000	Wonder Woman 1	$9,000	$25,000	$50,000
Flash Comics 104	$3,500	$8,000	$20,000	X-Men 1	$2,500	$9,000	$20000

See complete catalog at www.pcei.com

Corporate Office:
337 S. Robertson Blvd. Ste 203, Beverly Hills, CA 90211
Tel: (310) 544-4936, Fax: (310) 544-4900

Shipping Address:
P.O. Box 2629 Palos Verdes Pen., CA 90274
E-Mail: sales@pcei.com, www.pcei.com

VISA MasterCard

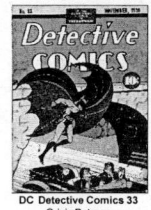

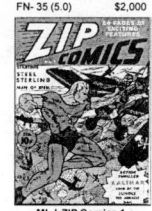

Sold.

That is all you will be able to say when you are dealing with Harley Yee. My prices paid out are among the highest. You are always able to receive cash immediately. There is no collection that is too small because I will travel anywhere to view your collection.

I have over 14 years experience and I'm also a senior advisor to the *Overstreet Price Guide.* You will always receive prompt, professional service. I specialize in the Golden and Silver Age.

HARLEY
YEE

P.O. Box 51758
Livonia, MI 48151-5758
voice: 800.731.1029 or 734.421.7921
fax: 734.421.7928

Call or write for a free catalog.

ORIGINAL ART WANTED

If you have any of the ORIGINAL BLACK AND WHITE ARTWORK to these COVERS/interiors (even if they are not for sale), please contact me so I can leave you with an offer (and I can stop looking for it). Cash Paid or will trade other art or comics (Gold, Silver, Modern).

PLEASE SAVE THIS LIST, it's good forever.

******PLEASE NOTE: I am NOT looking for the comic books themselves!!!******

ALL ART LISTED IS FOR ORIGINAL B&W COVER ART UNLESS OTHERWISE NOTED!

Interior art indicated in italics.

Avengers #189

X-Men #111

Justice League #207

All-Star #70

SSSV #8

Marvel 2-in-1 #55

NEAL ADAMS
Action #466
DC 1978 Calendar Cover - Disasters

ROSS ANDRU
Superman #334, 338, 341, 349

JIM APARO
Adventure #452 (Aquaman)
Aquaman #62, 63
Batman #294
Brave & Bold #130, 136, 139
Manbat #2
Showcase #94, 95, 96 (Doom Patrol)

RICH BUCKLER
Action #478, 483
All-Star Comics #69
Astonishing Tales #26, 27 (Deathlok)
DC Super Stars #10 (Strange Sports)
Freedom Fighters #9, 10, 14
Iron Man Annual #3
Justice League #148, 158
Kamandi #47, 50, 52, 56, 60
Secret Society Super Villians Spectacular (DC Special Series #6)
Superman #327
Super Team Family #8 (Challengers)
New Gods #14, 15
Teen Titans (old) #50-53
X-Men #97

BOB BUDIANSKY
Ghost Rider #40, 43
Marvel 2-in-1 #49
X-Men #120

JOHN BUSCEMA
Fantastic Four #202
Thor #262

SAL BUSCEMA
Hulk #207 (interior pages)
What If? #17 (old)

JOHN BYRNE
****Avengers #181 (interiors),186-190
****(No one will pay more for Byrne Avengers covers /interiors)
Capt. America #248
Champions #11 (Pages 1-3)
Fantastic Four (ANY covers #211-267!)
Iron Man #109
Marvel Team-Up (ANY covers!)
Marvel 2-in-1 (ANY covers), *any interiors #53-58*
Secret Origins Annual #1 (Doom Patrol)
Spec. Spider-Man #17
Super Villain Team-Up #14
X-Men #108-142 (ANY covers & *interiors*)

ERNIE CHAN(CHUA)
Batman #282
Champions #17
DC Super Stars #8 (Of Space), #9 (Man Behind the Gun)
Flash #243
Invaders #29
Justice League #132
Kamandi #45, 48, 49
Secret Society Super Villains #1-5
Teen Titans (old) #44

DAVE COCKRUM
Avengers #169, 175
Battlestar Galactica #1, 2
Hulk #207
Human Fly #3
Iron Man #110
Star Wars #17
Super Villain Team-Up #12
****X-Men Giant Size #1, #94-126, 145-147 (**ANY covers/pages**)

GENE COLAN
Dr. Strange #27
Tomb of Dracula #64
What If? #17 (old) (Ghost Rider/Capt. Marvel/Spiderwoman)

DICK DILLIN
DC Presents #13, 14
DC Super Stars #10 (Strange Sports) (interior pages)
Justice League #144, 147, 148 (*also interiors #144, 147*), 168, 171, 173

STEVE DITKO
Shade #3, 7

KEITH GIFFEN
Defenders #44 (ANY interior pages)

DICK GIORDANO
Batman #300
Superboy & Legion #253

MIKE GOLDEN
Mirconauts #3-17

MIKE GRELL
Green Lantern #92, 100
Superboy & Legion #228, 230, 231

BOB HALL
Champions #16 (*Interiors*)
Human Fly #17
ANY Squadron Supreme Covers
Super Villain Team-Up #14 (ANY Interior Pages)

RICK HOBERG
Star Wars #2

CARMINE INFANTINO
Star Wars #14,15,19,22

GIL KANE
Avengers #130, 141
Captain America #216
Champions #11, 16
Jungle Action (Black Panther) #14
Marvel Team-Up #23
Star Wars #8

MIKE KALUTA
Batman Family #17

JACK KIRBY
Capt. America #202 (cover + page 14)
Defenders #44
Invaders #14, 15
Kamandi (ANY covers)
Weird Wonder Tales #18

ALAN KUPPERBERG
Invaders #37, 38
Marvel's Greatest Comics #81

BOB LAYTON
Iron Man #121, 127, 135, 139 (others considered)
Marvel Premiere #47 (Ant Man)
Squadron Supreme (ANY covers)
What If? #32 (old)

GARCIA LOPEZ
Action #481, 482, 484
DC Special Series #5 (Superman Spect.), #11 (Flash Spectacular)
Untold Legend of Batman #2

AL MILGROM
Al Star Comics #70
Amazing Spider-Man #194
Defenders #74
Firestorm (old) #2, 3
Flash #268
Invaders #41
Secret Society Super Villains #10
Shogun Warriors (ANY covers)
Skull the Slayer #1

FRANK MILLER
Daredevil #158-181 (Covers & Splashes)
Dark Knight (ANY pgs)
X-Men Annual #3

MIKE NASSER
Kobra #6, 7
Spectacular Spider-Man #37

DON NEWTON
Avengers Annual #9
New Gods #12 (Splash page)

GEORGE PEREZ
******AVENGERS** #160-168, 170-174, 181, 183-185, 191, 192, 194-201, Avengers Ann. #8 (especially #161, 181), *interiors wanted* #161, 162, 167,
Korvac TPB Cover,
****(No one will pay/trade more for Perez Avengers covers!)
Batman Outsiders #5
Fantastic Four (ANY cover)
Infinity Gauntlet (ANY cover)
Justice League #184, 195, 196, 197, 207, 209, 219, 220 (**any** other covers considered)
Marvel Fanfare #10-12
Marvel Premiere #45-46 (Manwolf)
Marvel 2-in-1 #42 50,51,57,58,61-63 (**ANY** *interiors #53-58*)
New Teen Titans #1-50, Annual #3
New Titans (Baxter) #1-5
War of the Gods #1
X-Men #112, Annual #3 (interior pages)
Also looking for "oddball" titles Perez did from 1975-1987

KEITH POLLARD
Iron Man #108, 111, 112 Marvel 2-in-1 #55

FRANK ROBBINS
Human Fly #10

MARSHALL ROGERS
Mr. Miracle (DC House Ad Page–1977), #19-25

JOHN ROMITA, JR.
Avengers #176
Defenders #62
Iron Man #114-117

ALEX ROSS
Marvels #0-4 (ANY splashes/pages)
Kingdom Come (various pages)

PAUL RYAN
Squadron Supreme (ANY covers)

KURT SCHAFFENBERGER
Action #474

ALEX SCHOMBURG
Invaders Ann. #1 (Also Human Torch pages)

JIM STARLIN
Justice League #185

JOE STATON
All Star Comics #71-73
"DC Explosion" (DC House Ad page –1978)
New Gods #19
Showcase #97, 99 (Power Girl) (Splash #94)
Superboy & Legion #249

CHIC STONE
Marvel 2-in-1 #48

HERB TRIMPE
Godzilla #3
Marvel Spotlight #12 (Son of Satan)

DAVE WENZEL
Avengers #177 (interiors)

ALAN WEISS
Human Fly #7
Shazam! (1977) #34

WALLY WOOD
All-Star Comics #64

RON WILSON
Marvel Premiere #55
Marvel 2-in-1 #37
Captain America #230

ARTISTS UNKNOWN
Super Villain Team-Up #15 (Doom-Red Skull)

Jungle Action #14

Green Lantern #92

Captain America #202

Brave & Bold #136

Human Fly #10

Flash #243

Please Contact: JONATHAN MANKUTA
75 McArthur Lane, Smithtown, NY 11787
Phone –1-631-864-2281 (Leave message if no answer)
e-mail JONMANKUTA@AOL.COM

SILVER AGE
12¢
BUYING
COMICS
107
APR.
ALL COMICS, ALL GRADES
•WILL TRAVEL TO YOU!
•WILL PAY MORE!
•WILL PAY CASH!
©MARVEL COMICS
SELLING
the LARGEST SELECTION of SILVER AGE in N.Y.C. WITHOUT APPOINTMENT
•COMPETITIVE PRICING!
•STRICT GRADING!
•MAIL ORDER ANYWHERE
•WANT LIST SERVICE
•FREE CATALOGUE
•OPEN 7 DAYS

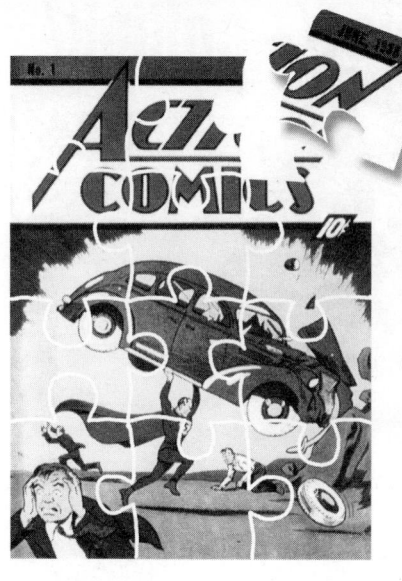

the GOBLIN'S DEN
37 Pinesmoke Cr.
ssissauga, Ontario, Canada
/ 3L4
#(905)848-0559 Fax#(416)622-0574
ail:GOBLINS@ionsys.com
ALWAYS
Buying & Selling
Pre-1977
Comics
We also buy: Action Figures, Model Kits &
emorabilia
Highest Prices Paid for quality pre-code Horror,
ime & Good Girl
DAN ORGILL '98.
(AFTER ROMITA)

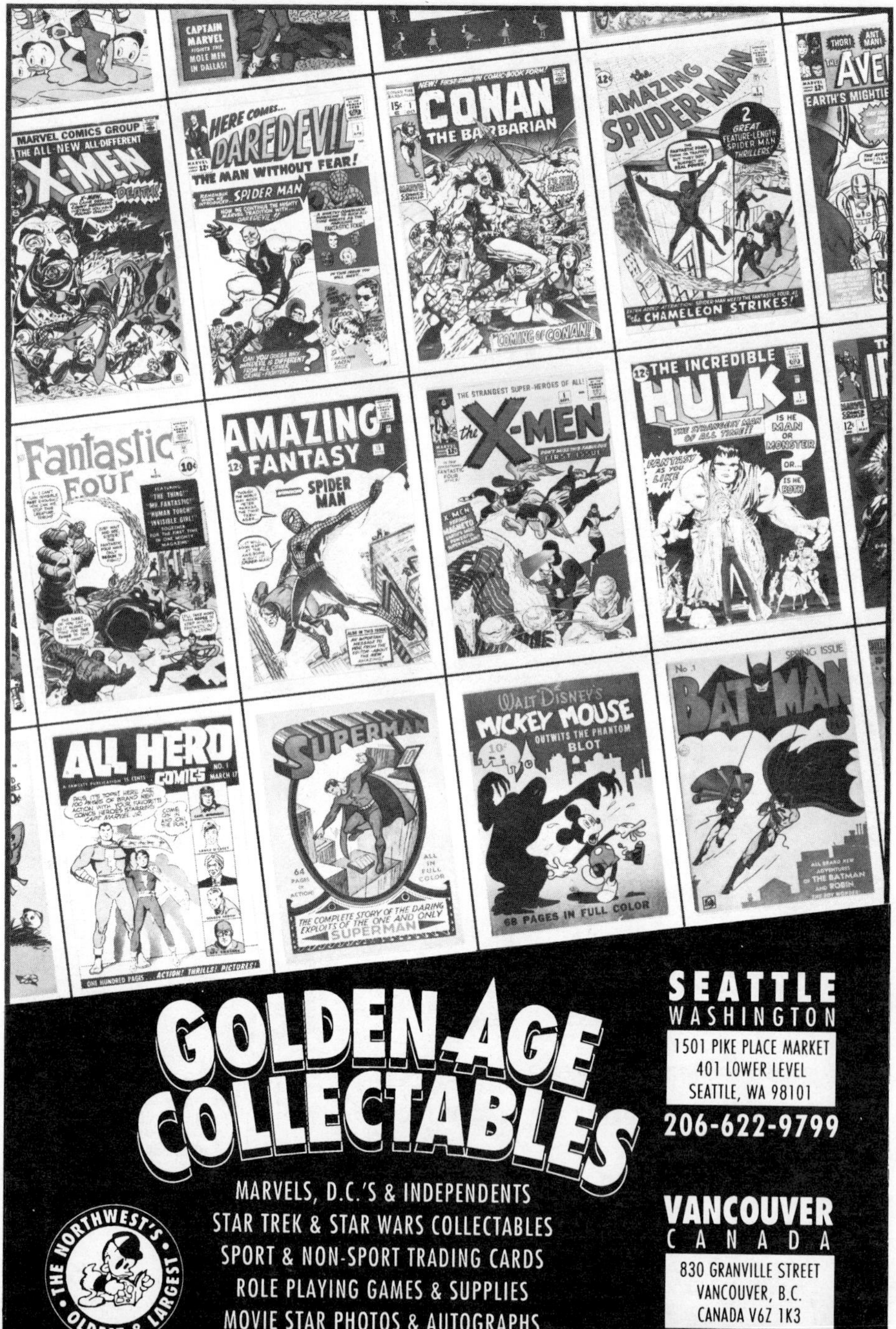

jaster collectibles

BUYING:

Aggressively buying comics, pulps and original art, all genres

Honest appraisals

Top prices paid

Complete collections are our specialty

Will travel to view larger collections

30 years of collecting and dealer experience

Our goal is a mutually beneficial transaction

Largest buyer in Chicago and the Midwest

Phone 888 913 8944 www.nearmint.com

Comics 10¢
APRIL
PHANTOM LADY
MAY, 1939
10¢
AMERICA
SUB-MARIN
HITLER'S BERCHTESG
THE Shado
DEATH'S BRIGHT FINGER

Some Things
Just Arent
Right...
... and we're not helping.
PARIS

MOTOR CITY COMICS
Gold & Silver Age
NOW OPEN
Come Visit Our Warehouse
by appointment only
WE ALSO DEAL IN PULPS
& ORIGINAL ART
Batman, Spectre, Green Lantern © DC Comics

JOHN VERZYL AND DAUGHTER ROSE, "HARD AT WORK."

John Verzyl started collecting comic books in 1965, and within ten years he had amassed thousands of Golden and Silver Age comic books. In 1979, with his wife Nanette, he opened "COMIC HEAVEN," a retail store devoted entirely to the buying and selling of comic books.

Over the years, John Verzyl has come to be recognized as an authority in the field of comic books. He has served as a special advisor to the "Overstreet Comic Book Price Guide" for the last ten years. Thousands of his "mint" comics were photographed for Ernst Gerber's newly-released "Photo-Journal Guide To Comic Books." His tables and displays at the annual San Diego Comic Convention and the Chicago Comic Convention draw customers from all over the country.

The first COMIC HEAVEN AUCTION was held in 1987, and today his Auction Catalogs are mailed out to more than ten thousand interested collectors and dealers.

Comic Heaven
John and Nanette Verzyl
P.O. Box 900
Big Sandy, TX 75755
1-903-636-5555

Congratulations! We at Gemstone welcome you to the hobby of comic books. This book is the most comprehensive reference work available on comics. It is also respected and used by dealers and collectors everywhere. The Overstreet price is the accepted price around the world, and we have not earned this privilege easily. Through hard work, diligence and constant contact with the market for decades, Overstreet has become the most trusted name in comics.

HOW TO USE THIS BOOK

This volume is an accurate, detailed alphabetical list of comic books and their retail values. Comic books are listed by title, regardless of company. Prices listed are shown in Good, Fine and Near Mint condition with many key books priced in an additional Very Fine grade. Comic books that fall in between the grades listed can be priced simply with the following procedure: Very Good is half way between Good and Fine; Very Fine is half way between Fine and Near Mint (unless a VF price is already shown). The older true Mint books usually bring a premium over the Near Mint price. Books in Fair bring 50 to 70% of the Good price. Some books only show a Very Fine price as the highest grade. The author has not been able to determine if these particular books exist in better than Very Fine condition, thus the omission of a Near Mint price. Most comic books are listed in groups, i.e., 11-20, 21-30, 31-50, etc.

The prices listed opposite these groupings represent the value of each issue in that group. More detailed information is given for individual comic books. If you are looking for a particular character, consult the first appearance indexes which will help you locate the correct title and issue. This book also contains hundreds of ads covering all aspects of this hobby. Whether you are buying or selling, the advertising sections can be of tremendous benefit to you.

NEW COMIC BOOKS

This book lists all new comic books at cover price, regardless of their performance in the secondary market. In many cases, new comics are not worth their cover price in the secondary market, and collectors may pay pennies on the dollar for copies of these issues. Nevertheless, since these comics have yet to establish themselves as collectors' items, they are listed at full cover price. It should also be noted that regarding polybagged comics, it is the official policy of **The Overstreet Comic Book Price Guide** to grade comics regardless of whether they are still sealed in their polybag or not. If opened, the polybag and its contents should be preserved separately so that all components of the original package remain together.

COMIC BOOK VALUES

All values listed in this book are in U.S. currency and are retail prices based on (but not limited to) reports from our extensive network of experienced advisors which include convention sales, mail order, auctions, unpublished personal sales and stores. Overstreet, with several decades of market experience, has developed a unique and comprehensive system for gathering, documenting, averaging and pricing data on comic books. The end result is a true fair market value for your use. We have earned the reputation for our cautious, conservative approach to pricing comic books. You, the collector, can be assured that the prices listed in this volume are the most accurate and useful in print.

IMPORTANT NOTE: This book is not a dealer's price list, although some dealers may base their prices on the values listed. The true value of any comic book is what you are willing to pay. Prices listed herein are an indication of what collectors (not dealers) would probably pay. For one reason or another, these collectors might want certain books badly, or else need specific issues to complete their runs and so are willing to pay more.

DEALERS' POSITION: Dealers are not in a position to pay the full prices listed, but work on a percentage depending largely on the amount of investment required and the quality of material offered. Usually they will pay from 20 to 70% of the list price depending on how long it will take them to sell the collection after making the investment; the higher the demand and better the condition, the more the percentage. Most dealers are faced with expenses such as advertising, travel, telephone and mailing, rent, employee salaries, plus convention costs. These costs must all be factored in before the books are sold. The high demand books usually sell right away but there are many other titles that are difficult to sell due to low demand. Sometimes a dealer will have costs tied up in this types of books for several years before finally moving them. Remember, his position is that of handling, demand, and overhead. Most dealers are victims of these economics.

HOW COMICS ARE LISTED

Comic books are listed alphabetically by title. The true title of a comic book can usually be found listed with the publisher's information, or indicia, often found at the bottom of the first page. Titles that appear on the front cover can vary from the official title listed inside.

Comic book titles, sequence of issues, dates of first and last issues, publishing companies, origin and special issues are listed when known. Prominent and collectible artists are also pointed out (usually in footnotes). Page counts will always include covers. Most comic books began with a #1, but occasionally many titles began with an odd number. There is a reason for this. Publishers had to register new titles with the post office for 2nd class permits. The registration fee was expensive. To avoid this expense, many publishers would continue the numbering of new titles from old defunct titles. For instance, **Weird Science** #12 (1st issue) was continued from the defunct **Saddle Romances** #11 (the last issue). In doing this, the publishers hoped to avoid having to register new titles. However, the post office would soon discover the new title and force the publisher to pay the registration fee as well as to list the correct number. For instance, the previous title mentioned began with #12 (1st issue). Then #13 through #15 were published. The next issue became #5 after the Post Office correction. Now the sequence of published issues (see the listings) is #12-15, 5-on. This created a problem in early fandom for the collector because the numbers 12-15 in this title were duplicated.

WHAT COMICS ARE LISTED

The Guide lists primarily American comic books due to space limitations. The earliest comic books date back to 1897 and are included in their own section under <u>The Platinum Age</u>. These books basically reprinted newspaper strips and were published in varying sizes, usually with cardboard covers, but sometimes as hardbacks. The format of **Funnies On Parade**, published in 1933 (saddle-stitched), soon became the standard for the modern comic book, although squarebound versions were also published. Most of these formats that appeared on newsstands will be included.

NEW COMIC LISTINGS

The 1980s and '90s have experienced an explosion of publishers with hundreds of new titles appearing in black & white and color. Many of these comics are listed in this book, but not all due to space limitation. We will attempt to list complete information only on those titles that show some collector interest. The selection of titles to include is constantly being monitored by our board of advisors. Please do not contact us to list your new comic books. Listings are determined by the marketplace. However, we are interested in receiving review copies of all new comic books published.

GRADING

For complete, detailed information on grading and restoration, consult the **Overstreet Comic Book Grading Guide**. Copies are available through all normal distribution channels or can be ordered direct from the publisher by sending $12 plus $2 postage and handling. You can also call Gemstone toll free at 1-888-375-9800.

The Overstreet Comic Book Grading Card, known as the **ONE** and **OWL Card** is also available. This card has two functions. The **ONE Card** (**O**verstreet's **N**umerical **E**quivalent) is used to convert grading condition terms to the new numerical grading system. The **OWL Card** (**O**verstreet's **W**hiteness **L**evel) is used for grading the whiteness of paper. The color scale on the **OWL Card** is simply placed over the interior comic book paper. The paper color is matched with the color on the card to get the **OWL** number. The **ONE/OWL Card** may be ordered direct from the publisher by sending $1.30 per card.

HOW TO GRADE

Before a comic book's true value can be assessed, its condition or state of preservation must be determined. In all comic books, the better the condition the more desirable and valuable the book. Comic books in **MINT** condition will bring several times the price of the same book in **POOR** condition. Therefore it is very important to be able to properly grade your books. Comics should be graded from the inside out, so the following comic book areas should be examined before assigning a final grade.

Check inside pages, inside spine and covers and outside spine and covers for any tears, markings, brittleness, tape, soiling, chunks out or other defects that would affect the grade. After all the above steps have been taken, then the reader can begin to consider an overall grade for his or her book. The grading of a comic book is done by simply looking at the book and describing its condition, which may range from absolutely perfect newsstand condition **MINT** to extremely worn, dirty, and torn **POOR**.

Numerous variables influence the evaluation of a comic book's condition and all must be considered in the final evaluation. Although the grade of a comic book is based upon an accumulation of defects, some defects may be more extreme for a particular grade as long as other acceptable listed defects are almost non-existent. As grading is the most subjective aspect of determining a comic's value, it is very important that the grader be careful not to allow wishful thinking to influence what the eyes see. It is also very important to realize that older comics in **MINT** condition are extremely scarce and are rarely advertised for sale; most of the higher grade comics advertised range from **VERY FINE** to **NEAR MINT**.

GRADING DEFINITIONS

Note: This edition uses both the traditional grade abbreviations and the **ONE** number throughout the listings. The **O**verstreet **N**umerical **E**quivalent (**ONE**) spread range is given with each grade.

MINT (MT) (ONE 9.9-10.0): Near perfect in every way. Only the most subtle bindery or printing defects are allowed. Cover is flat with no surface wear. Cover inks are bright with high reflectivity and minimal fading. Corners are cut square and sharp. Staples are generally centered, clean with no rust. Cover is generally well centered and firmly secured to interior pages. Paper is supple and fresh. Spine is tight and flat.

NEAR MINT/MINT (NM/MT) (ONE 9.8): A comic book that has enough positive qualities to make it better than a NM+, but has enough detracting qualities to keep it from being a MT 9.9. In most cases the comic book has a better appearance than a NM+.

NEAR MINT (NM) (ONE 9.2-9.7): Nearly perfect with only minor imperfections allowed. This grade should have no corner or impact creases, stress marks should be almost invisible, and bindery tears must be less than 1/16 inch. A couple of very tiny color flecks, or a combination of the above that keeps the book from being perfect, where the overall eye appeal is less than Mint drops the book into this grade. Only the most subtle binding and/or printing defects allowed. Cover is flat with no surface wear. Cover inks are bright with high reflectivity and minimum of fading. Corners are cut square and sharp with ever so slight blunting permitted. Staples are generally centered, clean with no rust. Cover is well centered and firmly secured to interior pages. Paper is supple and like new. Spine is tight and flat.

VERY FINE/NEAR MINT (VF/NM) (ONE 9.0): A comic book that has enough positive qualities to make it better than a VF+, but has enough detracting qualities to keep it from being a NM-. In most cases the comic book has a better appearance than a VF+.

VERY FINE (VF) (ONE 7.5-8.5): An excellent copy with outstanding eye appeal. Sharp, bright and clean with supple pages. Cover is relatively flat with almost no surface wear. Cover inks are generally bright with moderate to high reflectivity. Staples may show some discoloration. Spine may have a couple of almost insignificant transverse stress lines and is almost completely flat. A barely unnoticeable 1/4 inch crease is acceptable, if color is not broken. Pages and covers can be yellowish/tannish (at the least, but not brown and will usually be off-white to white).

FINE/VERY FINE (FN/VF) (ONE 7.0): A comic book that has enough positive qualities to make it better than a FN+, but has enough detracting qualities to keep it from being a VF-. In most cases the comic book has a better appearance than a FN+.

FINE (FN) (ONE 5.5-6.5): An above-average copy that shows minor wear but is still relatively flat and clean with no significant creasing or other serious defects. Eye appeal is somewhat reduced because of slight surface wear and possibly a small defect such as a few slight cross stress marks on spine or a very slight spine split (1/4"). A Fine condition comic book appears to have been read a few times and has been handled with moderate care. Compared to a VF, cover inks are beginning to show a significant reduction in reflectivity but it is still a highly collectible and desirable book.Pages and interior covers may be tan, but pages must still be fairly supple with no signs of brittleness.

VERY GOOD/FINE (VG/FN) (ONE 5.0): A comic book that has enough positive qualities to make it better than a VG+, but has enough detracting qualities to keep it from being a FN-. In most cases the comic book has a better appearance than a VG+.

VERY GOOD (VG) (ONE 3.5-4.5): The average used comic book. A comic in this grade shows some wear, can have a reading or center crease or a moderately rolled spine, but has not accumulated enough total defects to reduce eye appeal to the point that it is not a desirable copy. Some discoloration, fading and even minor soiling is allowed. As much as a 1/4" triangle can be missing out of the corner or edge. A missing square piece (1/8" by 1/8") is also acceptable. Store stamps, name stamps, arrival dates, initials, etc. have no effect on this grade. Cover and interior pages can have some minor tears and folds and the centerfold may be detached at one staple. The cover may also be loose, but not completely detached. Common bindery and printing defects do not affect grade. Pages and inside covers may be brown but not brittle. Tape should never be used for comic book repair; however many VG condition comics have minor tape repair.

GOOD/VERY GOOD (GD/VG) (ONE 3.0): A comic book that has enough positive qualities to keep it better than a GD+, but has enough detracting qualities to keep it from being a VG-. In most cases the comic book has a better appearance than a GD+.

GOOD (GD) (ONE 1.8-2.5): A copy in this grade has all pages and covers, although there may be small pieces missing inside; the largest piece allowed from front or back cover is a 1/2" triangle or a square 1/4" by 1/4". Books in this grade are commonly creased, scuffed, abraded, soiled and may have as much as a 2" spine split, but are still completely readable. Often paper quality is low but not brittle. Cover reflectivity is low and in some cases completely absent. This grade can have a moderate accumulation of defects but still maintains its basic structural integrity.

FAIR/GOOD (FR/GD) (ONE 1.5): A comic book that has enough positive qualities to keep it better than a FR+, but has enough detracting qualities to keep it from being a GD-. In most cases the comic book has a better appearance than a FR+.

NEW TEN POINT GRADING SYSTEM

10.0	Mint
9.9	Mint
9.8	Near Mint/Mint
9.6	Near Mint +
9.4	Near Mint
9.2	Near Mint -
9.0	Very Fine/Near Mint
8.5	Very Fine +
8.0	Very Fine
7.5	Very Fine -
7.0	Fine/Very Fine
6.5	Fine +
6.0	Fine
5.5	Fine -
5.0	Very Good/Fine
4.5	Very Good +
4.0	Very Good
3.5	Very Good -
3.0	Good/Very Good
2.5	Good +
2.0	Good
1.8	Good -
1.5	Fair/Good
1.0	Fair
0.5	Poor

FAIR (FR) (ONE 1.0): A copy in this grade is usually soiled, ragged and possibly unattactive. Creases, tears and/or folds are prevalent. Spine may be split up to 2/3rds its entire length. Staples may be gone. Up to 1/10th of the front cover may be missing. These books are readable although soiling, staining, tears, markings or chunks missing may moderately interfere with reading the complete story. Some collectors consider this the lowest collectible grade because comic books in lesser condition are usually defaced and/or brittle. Very often paper quality is low and may have slight brittleness around the edges but not in the central portions of the pages. Comic books in this grade may have a clipped coupon so long as it is noted along side of the nomenclature; ie: "Fair (1.0) Coupon Clipped." Valued at 50-70% of good.

POOR (PR) (ONE 0.5): Most comic books in this grade have been sufficiently degraded to the point that copies may have extremely severe stains, missing staples, brittleness, mildew or moderate to heavy cover abrasion to the point that some cover inks are indistinct/absent. Comic books in this grade can have small chunks missing and pieces out of pages. They may have been defaced with paints, varnishes, glues, oil, indelible markers or dyes. Covers may be split the entire length of the book, but both halves must be present and basically still there with some chunks missing. A page(s) may be missing as long as it is noted along side of the nomenclature; ie: " POOR (0.5) 2nd Page Missing." Value depends on extent of defects but would average about 1/3 of GOOD.

DUST JACKETS

Many of the early strip reprint comics were printed in hardback with dust jackets. Books with dust jackets are worth more. The value can increase from 20 to 50 percent depending on the rarity of book. Usually, the earlier the book, the greater the percentage. Unless noted, prices listed are without dust jackets. The condition of the dust jacket should be graded independently of the book itself.

RESTORED COMICS

When restoration of comics first began, it was a collection of crude, damaging attempts to preserve or fix comics exhibiting defects like tears or missing pieces. At first using tape, glue and color pens, restoration soon evolved, utilizing more advanced techniques like chemical baths and deacidification. Today, professional restorers work in a quickly maturing field using methods that have stood the test of time. There is still a stigma attached to restoration, however, often due to a lack of knowledge about how restored comics relate to the market.

Many restored comics are unnecessarily put through the process, begging the question, 'when should I restore my comics?' If a comic is in VG or better, do not restore it. Restoration is meant to preserve deteriorating comics, taking an ugly pile of loose pages and restoring them to an attractive form that can be handled and enjoyed. In the case of comics in VG or higher grades, the book is already an attractive item and restoration would be excessive.

The value of the comic should also be high enough to justify restoration. With prices of $30-$75 an hour to restore a comic, only very valuable books should be candidates. It's recommended to avoid restoring Silver Age comics, apart from key issues, due to their relative availability. Restored Silver Age comics also do not rise in value as much as a restored Golden Age comic.

Bindery chips, a common defect in Golden Age comics, are considered printing defects and are relatively acceptable in the market. Restoration on such a defect by itself would usually be considered excessive. Books with brown or brittle pages are usually not good candidates either. Even though the comic will look better, its page quality will still rate a lower grade. Bleaching and other treatments can be used, but are expensive, frowned upon and not very effective. Only the most expensive books should ever be considered for page treatment. Similarly, books missing covers and interior pages are poor candidates for restoration. A comic must be relatively complete to be successfully restored.

Preventative restoration, widely used and accepted by collectors, consists of "non-additive" restoration on a book with one or two major defects. A prime example would be a $2,000 book in Fine that has a 2" piece of tape on the cover. Removal of the tape improves the value and appearance of the book. The process is cheap and quick, and nothing is "added" to the comic, such as Japan paper or color touch (see the glossary for definitions). Although it's always imperative to disclose any and all restoration work on a book, some collectors don't even view these simple repairs as restoration. Other defects fixable by "preventative" techniques are water stains, warping, dirt or writing, rusty staples, and spine rolls. These minor fixes work best with books above VG, the one exception to the rule noted earlier.

Once restored, a comic's value depends upon several factors:

The amount of restoration: In general, the more restoration has been performed, the less the comic is worth compared to its apparent grade value. A lightly restored book will be valued higher than a book with heavy restoration in the same apparent grade.

The "before" and "restored" grades: As a rule of thumb, consider these formulae:

Golden Age key issues:
(guide value of comic before restoration)
+(guide value of comic's apparent grade)/2.5

Golden Age common issues:
(guide value of comic before restoration)
+(guide value of comic's apparent grade)/2.0

Silver Age issues:
(guide value of comic before restoration)
+(guide value of comic's apparent grade)/3.0

These formulae serve only as a benchmark. Each book is unique and may vary in pricing.

The market demand: This is highly subjective, but the higher the demand, the likelier your restored book will fetch its apparent grade price. Consequently, if the comic is slow on the market, a restored copy may be less than the value derived from the above formulae.

The market value: The market fluctuates widely on restored copies of expensive books. A small variance in perception of what a restored copy is worth can mean a difference of thousands of dollars on high end comics (see formulae above). Values tend to be more stable on common books.

Age of the comic: The younger a comic, the less likely the book will increase in value significantly from restoration. This applies mainly to Silver Age comics, as noted earlier.

Armed with this knowledge and a good understanding of the market, you should be able to make an informed decision about restoration. When in doubt, contact a reputable dealer or collector who is familiar with restored comics in the marketplace.

SCARCITY OF COMICS

1897-1933 Comics: Most of these books are bound with thick cardboard covers and are very rare to non-existent in VF or better condition. Due to their extreme age, paper browning is very common. Brittleness could be a problem.

1933-1940 Comics: There are many issues from this period that are very scarce in any condition, especially from the early to mid-1930s. Surviving copies of any particular issue range from a handful to several hundred. Near Mint to Mint copies are virtually non-existent with known examples of any particular issue limited to five or fewer copies. Most surviving copies are in FN-VF or less condition. Brittleness or browning of paper is fairly common and could be a problem.

1941-1952 Comics: Surviving comic books would number from less than 100 to several thousand copies of each issue. Near Mint to Mint copies are a little more common but are still relatively scarce with only a dozen or so copies in this grade existing of any particular issue. Exceptions would be recent warehouse finds of most Dell comics (6-100 copies, but usually 30 or less), and Harvey comics (1950s-1970s) surfacing. Due to low paper quality of the late 1940s and 1950s, many comics from this period are rare in Near Mint to Mint condition. Most remaining copies are VF or less. Browning of paper could be a problem.

1953-1959 Comics: As comic book sales continued to drop during the 1950s, production values were lowered resulting in cheaply printed comics. For this reason, high grade copies are extremely rare. Many Atlas and Marvel comics have chipping along the trimmed edges (Marvel chipping) which reduces even more the number of surviving high grade copies.

1960-1979 Comics: Early '60s comics are rare in Near Mint to Mint condition. Most copies of early '60s Marvels and DCs grade no higher than VF. Many early keys in NM or MT exist in numbers less than 10-20 of each. Mid-'60s to late-'70s books in high grade are more common due to the hoarding of comics that began in the mid-'60s.

1980-Present: Comics of today are common in high grade. VF to NM is the standard rather than the exception.

When you consider how few Golden and Silver Age books exist compared to the current market, you will begin to appreciate the true rarity of these early books. In many cases less than 5-10 copies exist of a particular issue in Near Mint to Mint condition, while most of the 1930s books do not exist in this grade at all.

COLLECTING COMICS

New comic books are available in many different kinds of stores. Grocery stores, drug stores, Wal-Mart, K-Mart, book stores, comic book stores and card and comics specialty shops are a few examples. Local flea markets and, of course, comic book conventions in your area are excellent sources for new and old comic books.

Most collectors begin by buying new issues in Mint condition directly off the newsstand or from their local comic store. (Subscription copies are available from several mail-order services, and often the publishers themselves.) Each week new comics appear on the stands that are destined to become true collectors' items. The trick is to locate a store that carries a complete line of comics. In several localities this may be difficult. Most collectors frequent several magazine stands in order not to miss something they want. Even then, it pays to keep in close contact with collectors in other areas. Sooner or later, nearly every collector has to rely upon a friend in Fandom or a dealer to obtain for him an item that is unavailable locally (see ads in this book).

Before you buy any comic to add to your collection, you should carefully inspect its condition. Unlike stamps and coins, defective comics are generally not highly prized. The cover should be properly cut and printed. Remember that every blemish or sign of wear depreciates the beauty and value of your comics.

The serious collector usually buys extra copies of popular titles. He may trade these multiples for items unavailable locally (for example, foreign comics), or he may store the multiples for resale at some future date. Such speculation is, of course, a gamble. Selecting the right investment books is tricky business that requires special knowledge. With experience, the beginner will improve his buying skills. Remember, if you play the new comics market, be prepared to buy and sell fast as values rise and fall rapidly.

Today's comic books offer a wide variety of subjects, art styles and writers to satisfy even the most discriminating fan. Whether it's the latest new hot title or company, or one of many popular titles that have been around for a long time, the comic book fan has a broad range from which to pick. Print runs of many popular titles have dropped over the past few years, creating the possibility of a true rarity occurring when demand outstrips supply. Less "gimmicky" covers are seen these days, but occasionally an eye-catching specialty cover will appear, such as the Superman new costume issue (#123) that glows-in-the-dark. Some cover variants continue to appear as well. "Bad Girl" and horror titles have been popular along with the standard superhero fare. The collector should always stay informed about the new trends developing in this fast-moving market. Since the market fluctuates greatly, and there is a vast array of comics to choose from, it's recommended first and foremost that you collect what you enjoy reading; that way, despite any value changes, you will always maintain a sense of personal satisfaction with your collection.

POLYBAGGED COMICS: It is the official policy of this Guide to grade comics regardless of whether they are still sealed in their polybag or not. Sealed comics in bags are not always in MINT condition and could even be damaged. The value should not suffer as long as the bag (opened) and all of its original manufactured contents are preserved and kept together.

COLLECTING ON A BUDGET: Collectors check out their local newsstand or comic specialty store for the latest arrivals. Hundreds of brand new comic books are displayed each week for the collector, much more than anyone can afford to purchase. Today's reader must be careful and budget his money wisely in choosing what to buy.

COLLECTING ARTISTS: Many collectors enjoy favorite artists and follow their work from issue to issue, title to title, company to company. In recent years, some artists have achieved "star" status.

Autograph signings occur at all major comic conventions as well as special promotions with local stores. Fans line up by the hundreds at such events to meet these superstars. Some of the current top artists of new comics are: Todd McFarlane, Alex Ross, Jim Lee, Michael Turner, Marc Silvestri, Rob Liefeld, Chris Bachalo, J. Scott Campbell, Humberto Ramos, and Adam and Andy Kubert. Original artwork from these artists have been bringing record prices at auctions and from dealers' lists.

COLLECTING BY COMPANIES: Some collectors become loyal to a particular company and only collect its titles. It's another way to specialize and collect in a market that expands faster than your pocket book.

COLLECTING #1 ISSUES: For decades, comic enthusiasts have always collected first (#1) issues. This is yet another way to control spending and build an interesting collection for the future. #1 issues have everything going for them--some introduce new characters, while others are underprinted, creating a rarity factor. #1 issues cross many subjects as well as companies, and make for an intriguing collection.

BACK ISSUES

A back issue is any comic currently not available on the stands. Collectors of current titles often want to find the earlier issues in order to complete the run. Thus a back issue collector is born. Comic books have been published and collected for over 100 years. However, the earliest known comic book dealers didn't appear until the late 1930s. But today, there are hundreds of dealers that sell old comic books (See ads in this book).

LOCATING BACK ISSUES: The first place to begin, of course, is with your collector friends who may have unwanted back issues or duplicates for sale. Look in the yellow pages, or call the Comic Shop Locator Service at 1-888-COMIC-BOOK, to see if you have a comic book store available. If you do, they would know of other collectors in your area. Advertising in local papers could get good results. Go to regional markets and look for comic book dealers. There are many trade publications in the hobby that would put you in touch with out-of-town dealers. This Annual Guide has ads buying and selling old comic books. Some dealers publish regular price lists of old comic books for sale. Get on their mailing list.

Putting a quality collection of old comics together takes a lot of time, effort and money. Many old comics are not easy to find. Persistence and luck play a big part in acquiring needed issues. Most quality collections are put together over a long period of time by placing mail orders with dealers and other collectors.

Comics of early vintage are extremely expensive if they are purchased through a regular dealer or collector. Unless you have unlimited funds to invest in your hobby, you will find it necessary to restrict your collecting in certain ways. However you define your collection, you should be careful to set your goals well within affordable limits.

PRESERVATION & STORAGE

Comic books are fragile and easy to damage. Most dealers and collectors hesitate to let anyone personally handle their rare comics. It is common courtesy to ask permission before handling another person's comic book. Most dealers would prefer to remove the comic from its bag and show it to the customer themselves. In this way, if the book is damaged, it would be the dealer's responsibility–not the customer's. Remember, the slightest crease or chip could render an otherwise Mint book to Near Mint or even Very Fine.

Consult the **Overstreet Comic Book Grading Guide** and learn the proper way to hold a comic book. The following steps are provided to aid the novice in the proper handling of comic books: 1. Remove the comic from its protective sleeve or bag very carefully. 2. Gently lay the comic (unopened) in the palm of your hand so that it will stay relatively flat and secure. 3. You can now leaf through the book by carefully rolling or flipping the pages with the thumb and forefinger of your other hand. Caution: Be sure the book always remains relatively flat or slightly rolled. Avoid creating stress points on the covers with your fingers and be particularly cautious in bending covers back too far on Mint books. 4. After examining the book, carefully insert it back into the bag or protective sleeve. Watch corners and edges for folds or tears as you replace the book. Always keep tape completely away while inserting a comic in a bag.

Comic books should also be protected from the elements as well as the dangers of light, heat, and humidity. This can easily be achieved with proper storage. Improper storage methods will be detrimental to the "health" of your collection, and may even quicken its deterioration.

Store comic books away from direct light sources, especially florescent which contains high levels of ultraviolet (UV) radiation. UV lights are like sunlight, and will quickly fade the cover inks. Tungsten filament lighting is safer than florescent but should still be used at brief intervals. Remember, exposure to light accumulates damage, so store your collection in a cool, dark place away from windows.

Temperatures must also be carefully regulated. Fungus and mold thrives in higher temperatures, so the lower the temperature, the longer the life of your collection.

Atmospheric pollution is another problem associated with long term storage of paper. Sulfuric dioxide which can occur from automobile exhaust will cause paper to turn yellow over a period of time. For this reason, it is best not to store your valuable comics close to a garage. Some of the best preserved comic books known were protected from exposure to the air such as the Gaines EC collection. These books were carefully wrapped in paper at time of publication, and completely sealed from the air. Each package was then sealed in a box and stored in a closet in New York. After over 40 years of storage when the packages were opened, you could instantly catch the odor of fresh newsprint; the paper was snow white and supple, and the cover inks were as brilliant as the day they were printed. This illustrates how important it is to protect your comics from the atmosphere.

Like UV, high relative humidity (rh) can also be damaging to paper. Maintaining a low and stable relative humidity, around 50%, is crucial; varying humidity will only damage your collection.

Care must be taken when choosing materials for storing your comics. Many common items such as plastic bags, boards, and boxes may not be as safe as they seem. Some contain chemicals that will actually help to destroy your collection rather than save it. Always purchase materials designed for long-term storage, such as Mylar type "D" sleeves and acid-free boards and boxes. Polypropylene and polyethylene bags, while safe for temporary storage, should be changed every three to five years.

Comics are best stored vertically in boxes. For shelving, make sure that comics do not come into direct contact with the shelving surface. Use acid-free boards as a buffer between shelves comics. Also, never store comics directly on the floor; elevate them 6-10 inches to allow for flooding. Similarly, never store your collection directly against a wall, particularly an outside wall. Condensation and poor air circulation will encourage mold and fungus growth.

When handling your high grade comics, wash your hands first, eliminating harmful oils from the skin before coming into contact with the books. Lay the comic on a flat surface and slowly turn the pages. This will minimize the stress to the staples and spine. With these guidelines, your collection should enjoy a long life and maintain a reasonable condition and value.

BUYING & SELLING

Whether you're a new collector just starting to acquire comics or a long-time collector now interested in selling a collection, by purchasing this Guide, you have begun the long process necessary to successfully buy and sell comics.

SELLING YOUR COMICS

If you are planning to sell a collection, you must first decide what category listed below best describes your collection. As a rule of thumb, the lower categories will need less detail provided in your inventory list. A collection of key late '30s DCs will require you to list exact titles, numbers, and grades, as well as possible restoration information. If, however, you have 20,000 miscellaneous '80s and '90s comics for sale, a rough list of the number of books and publishers should be enough. The categories are:

1. PLATINUM AGE (1897-1932): The supply is very scarce. More people are becoming interested in these early books due to comics passing their

100th birthday. Moderate interest among average dealers, but high interest with dealers that specialize in this material. A detailed list will be necessary paying attention to brittleness, damage and pages missing. Dealers will pay up to a high percentage of Guide list for key titles.

2. GOLDEN AGE, All Grades (1933 - pre-1956): The most desirable. A detailed inventory will be necessary. Key higher grade books are easier to sell, but lower grades in most titles show the best selling potential, due to the fact that many collectors cannot afford a $20,000 VF book but may be able to afford a GD for only $2,000. Highest demand is for the superhero titles such as **Batman**, **Superman**, **Human Torch**, etc. The percentage of Guide that dealers will pay for your collection will vary depending on condition and contents. A collection of low demand titles will not bring the same percentage as a collection of prime titles.

3. High Grade SILVER AGE (1956-mid 1960s): A detailed inventory will be necessary. There are always investors looking for VF or better books from this period. Dealers will usually pay a high percentage of Guide list for these high grade books. Silver Age below VF will fall into category #4.

4. Low Grade SILVER AGE: Spanning books lower than VF from the late '50s to 1970, this category exhibits the average grade of most collections. Consequently, the supply of this material is much more common than category #2. This means that you could be competing with many other similar collections being offered at the same time. You will have to shop this type of collection to get the best price, and be prepared to sell at a significant discount if you find a willing buyer with good references.

5. MODERN AGE (post-1970): Certain titles from the early 1970s in high grade are showing increasing demand. However, many books from the 1980s to the 1990s are in low demand with the supply for the most part always being of high grade books. These collections are typified by long runs of certain titles and/or publishers. A detailed inventory will not be necessary. Contact local comic stores or buyers first to gauge their level of interest. Dealing with buyers outside your area should be avoided if possible.

IMPORTANT: Many of the 1980s and 1990s books are listed at cover price. This indicates that these books have not established a collector's value. When selling books of this type, the true market value could be 20-50% of cover price or less.

6. BULK (post-1980 in quantities greater than 5,000): These collections usually contain multiple copies of the same issues. It is advisable to price on a per-book basis (2¢ and 20¢ each). Do NOT attempt an inventory list, and only contact buyers who advertise buying in bulk quantity.

You should never deal with a buyer without fully checking their references. For additional verification, consult The Better Business Bureau; the local BBB may be able to help you in establishing a buyer's credibility, as well as assisting in resolving any disputes. **The Overstreet Comic Book Price Guide** and **Comic Book Marketplace** are also recognized authorities. Advertised dealers will likely have a more established reputation.

Potential buyers will be most concerned with the retail value of your entire collection, which may be more or less than Guide depending what you have and their current demand. Some rare early books in VF or NM may bring a price over Guide list while other titles in lower grade may sell for a price under Guide list. Most vintage books, however, will sell for around the Guide price. However, 1980s or 1990s books that list at cover price may only be worth a percentage of that price. You must then decide on what percentage you would be willing to accept for your collection, taking into account how the collection breaks down into fast, moderate and slow moving books. To expect someone to pay full retail is unrealistic. You will have to be flexible in order to close a deal.

Many buyers may want to purchase only certain key or high grade books from your collection, almost always favoring the buyer. While you may be paid a high percentage of retail, you will find that "cherry-picked" collections are much more difficult to sell. Furthermore, the percentage of retail that you will receive for a "cherry-picked" collection will be much lower than if the collection had been left intact. Remember, key issues and/or high grade issues make or break a collection. Selling on consignment, another popular option in today's market, could become a breeding ground for cherry-pickers, so again, always check a dealer's references thoroughly.

Some collectors may choose to sell their comic books on a piecemeal basis, requiring much greater care and detail in preparing an inventory list and grading comics for sale. You will be able to realize a higher percentage of retail by selling your collection this way, but the key books will certainly sell first, leaving a significant portion of the collection unsold. You will need to keep repricing and discounting your books to encourage buyers.

You can advertise your collection in trade publications or through mass mailings. If you sell books through the mail, you must also establish a reasonable return policy, as some books will unquestionably be returned. Check the local post office and/or UPS regarding the various rates and services available for shipping your books. Marketing your books at conventions is another option. As a dealer, you will also incur overhead expenses such as postage, mailing and display supplies, advertising costs, etc.

In all cases, be willing to establish trust with a prospective buyer. By following the procedures outlined here, you will be able to sell your collection successfully, for a fair price, with both parties walking away satisfied. After all, collecting comic books is supposed to be fun; it only becomes a chore if you let it.

WHERE TO BUY AND SELL

Throughout this book you will find the advertisements of many reputable dealers who sell back-issue comics magazines. If you are an inexperienced collector, be sure to compare prices before you buy. When a dealer is selected (ask for references), send him a small order (under $100) first to check out his grading accuracy, promptness in delivery, guarantees of condition advertised, and whether he will accept returns when dissatisfied. Never send cash through the mail. Send money orders or checks for your personal protection. Beware of bargains, as the items advertised sometimes do not exist but are only a fraud to get your money.

The Price Guide is indebted to everyone who placed ads in this volume. Your mentioning this book when dealing with the advertisers would be greatly appreciated.

COMIC CONVENTIONS

The first comic book conventions, or cons, were originally conceived as the comic book counterpart to science fiction fandom conventions. There were many attempts to form successful national cons, but they were all stillborn. It is interesting that after only three relatively organized years of existence, the first comic con was held. Of course, its magnitude was nowhere near as large as most established cons held today.

What is a comic con? Dealers, collectors, fans, publishers, distributors, manufacturers, whatever they call themselves can be found trading, selling, and buying the adventures of their favorite characters for hours on end. Additionally most cons have guests of honor, usually professionals in the field of comic art, either writers, artists, or editors. The committees put together panels for the con attendees in which the assembled pros talk about certain areas of comics, most of the time fielding questions from the assembled audience. At cons one can usually find displays of various and sundry things, usually toys, thousands of comic books, original art, and more. There can be the showing of movies or videos. Of course there is always the chance to get together with friends at cons and just talk about comics. One also has a good opportunity to make new friends who have similar interests and with whom one can correspond after the convention is over.

It is difficult to describe accurately what goes on at a con. The best way to find out is to go to one and see for yourself. The largest cons are WonderCon (April), Pittsburgh (April), San Diego (July), Chicago (July), and Atlanta (July). For accurate dates and addresses, consult ads in this edition as well as some of the adzines. Please remember when writing for convention information to include a self addressed, stamped envelope for reply.

It's possible to discern two distinct and largely unrelated movements in the history of Comics Fandom. The first began around 1953 as a response to the the trend-setting EC lines of comics. The first true comics fanzines of this movement were short-lived. Bob Stewart's **EC FAN BULLETIN** was a hectographed newsletter that ran two issues about six months apart; Jimmy Taurasi's **FANTASY COMICS**, a newsletter devoted to all science-fiction comics of the period, was a monthly that ran for about six months. These were followed by other newsletters such as Mike May's **EC FAN JOURNAL**, and George Jennings' **EC WORLD PRESS**. EC fanzines of a wider and more critical scope appeared somewhat later. Two of the finest were **POTRZEBIE**, from a number of fans, and Ron Parker's **HOOHAH**. Gauging from the response that **POTRZEBIE** received from an EC letter column plug, Ted White estimated the average age of EC fans at 9 to 13, while many were actually in their mid-teens. This was discouraging to many fanzine editors hoping to reach an older audience. Consequently, many gave up their efforts on behalf of Comics Fandom, especially with the demise of the EC groups, and turned to SF (science fiction) fandom with its longer tradition and older membership. While the flourish of fan activity in response to the EC comics was certainly noteworthy, it never developed into a full-fledged, independent, and self-sustaining movement.

The second movement began in 1960, largely as a response to (and later stimulus for) the reappearance of the costumed hero and the Second Heroic Age of Comics. Most historians date the Second Heroic Age from **Flash** #105, February 1959. The letter departments of Julius Schwartz (editor at National Periodicals), and later those of Stan Lee (Marvel Group) and Bill Harris (Gold Key) were influential in bringing comics readers into Fandom. Sparks were lit among SF fans first, when experienced fan writers, who were part of an established tradition, produced the first in a series of articles on '40s comics–ALL IN COLOR FOR A DIME. The series was introduced in **XERO** #1 (September 1960), a general SF fanzine edited and published by Dick Lupoff.

Meanwhile, outside SF fandom, Jerry Bails and Roy Thomas, two comics fans of long-standing, conceived the first true comics fanzine in response to the Second Heroic Age, **ALTER EGO**, appearing in March 1961. The first issues were widely circulated, and profoundly influenced the comics fan movement, attracting many fans in their twenties and thirties, unlike the earlier EC fan following. Many of these older fans had been collectors for years but were largely unknown to each other. Joined by scores of new, younger fans, this group formed the nucleus of a self-sustaining and still growing movement. Although it has borrowed a few appropriate SF terms, Comics Fandom of the '60s was an independent movement without the advantages and disadvantages of a longer tradition. What Comics Fandom did derive from SF fans was largely thanks to fanzines produced by so-called double fans, the most notable being **COMIC ART**, edited and published by Don and Maggie Thompson.

The **ROCKET'S BLAST COMIC COLLECTOR** by G.B. Love was the first sucessful adzine in the early 1960s and was instrumental in the development of the comics market. G.B. remembers beginning his fanzine **THE ROCKET'S BLAST** in late 1961. Only six copies of the first 4 page issue were printed. Soon after Mr. Love had a letter published in **MYSTERY IN SPACE**, telling all about his new fanzine. His circulation began to grow. Buddy Saunders, a well known comic book store owner, designed the first **ROCKET'S BLAST** logo and was an artist on the publication for many years thereafter. With issue #29 he took over **THE COMICOLLECTOR** fanzine from Biljo White and combined it with **ROCKET'S BLAST** to form the **RBCC**. He remembers that the **RBCC** hit its highest circulation of 2,500 around 1971. Many people who wrote, drew or otherwise contributed to the **RBCC** went on to become well known writers, artists, dealers and store-owners in the comics field.

FOREIGN EDITION COMICS

One interesting and relatively inexpensive source of early vintage comics is the foreign market. Many American newspaper and magazine strips are reprinted abroad (in English and in other languages) months and even years after they appear in the States. By arranging trades with foreign collectors, one can obtain substantial runs of American comic book reprints and newspaper strips dating back years. These reprints are often in black and white, and sometimes the reproduction is poor. Once interest in foreign-published comics has been piqued, a collector might become interested in original strips from these countries.

NEWSPAPER STRIPS

Collecting newspaper comic strips is somewhat different than collecting comic books, although it can be equally satisfying. Most strip collectors begin by clipping strips from their local paper, but soon branch out to out-of-town papers. Naturally this can become more expensive and more frustrating, as it is easy to miss out-of-town editions. Consequently, most strip collectors work out trade agreements with collectors in other cities. This usually means saving local strips for trade only.

Back issues of some newspaper comic strips are also occasionally available from dealers. Prices vary greatly depending on age, condition, and demand.

ORIGINAL ART

Some enthusiasts collect original comic book and strip art. These mostly black and white, inked drawings are usually done on illustration paper at about 30 percent larger than the original printed panels. Because original art is a one-of-a-kind article, it is highly prized and can be difficult to obtain.

Interest in original comic art has increased tremendously in the past few years because more current art is available now that companies return originals to the artists, who then either sell the work themselves at cons, or through agents and dealers. The best way to find the piece you want is to scour cons and get on as many art dealers' mailing lists as possible. Although the masters' works from the Golden and Silver Ages bring fine art prices, most current work is available at moderate prices, with something for everyone at various costs, from Kirby to McFarlane, Ditko to Bachalo.

TOYS AND MORE

In the past ten years or so, interest in collecting comic-related merchandise has soared. Comic book and toy shows are often dominated by toys and related products.

Action figures and limited edition statues based on comic characters are currently the most popular. Highly successful toy action figure lines based on Batman, Spawn, Spider-Man, and many others cram toy store shelves. Statues and figurines, either painted or in kit form, are very popular higher-end collectibles. Statues of characters like Witchblade, Sandman, Shi, and many more draw collector attention through print, web, and convention advertising.

Numerous other tie-in products based on comic characters are released every year and seem to represent a large percentage of the collectible market today. Books like **Hake's Price Guide to Character Toys**, and periodicals like **Collecting Figures** and **Toyfare** track the collectibility of these items.

COVER BAR CODES

Today's comic books are cover-coded for the direct sales (comic shop, newsstand, and foreign markets). They are all first printings, with the special coding being the only difference. The comics sold to the comic shops have to be coded differently, as they are sold on a no-return basis while newsstand comics are not. The Price Guide has not detected any price difference between these versions. Currently, the difference is easily detected by looking at the front cover bar code (a box located at the lower left). The bar code used to be filled in for newsstand sales and left blank or contain a character for comic shop sales. Now, as you can see here, direct sale editions are clearly marked, both versions containing the bar code.

Newsstand

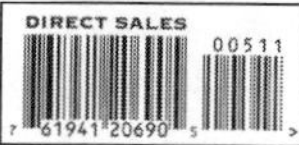

Direct Sales (DC)

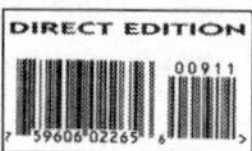

Direct Edition (Marvel)

MARVEL REPRINTS

In recent years Marvel has reprinted some of their comics. There has been confusion in identifying the reprints from the originals, but in 99% of the cases, the reprints have listed "reprint," or "2nd printing," etc. in the indicia, along with a later copyright date in some cases. Some Marvel 2nd printings have a gold logo. The only known exceptions are a few of the movie books such as **Star Wars**, the **Marvel Treasury Editions**, and tie-ins such as **G.I. Joe**. These books were reprinted and not identified as reprints. The **Star Wars** reprints have a large diamond with no date and a blank UPC symbol on the cover. Others had cover variations such as a date missing or different colors. Beginning in mid-1990, all Marvel 2nd printings have a gold logo.

Gold Key and other comics were also sold with a Whitman label. Even though collectors may prefer one label over the other, the Price Guide does not differentiate in the price. Beginning in 1980, all comics produced by Western carried the Whitman label.

PUBLISHERS' CODES

The following abbreviations are used with cover reproductions throughout the book for copyright purposes:

AC-(Americomics)
ACE-Ace Periodicals
ACG-American Comics Group
AJAX-Ajax-Farrell
AP-Archie Publications
ATLAS-Atlas Comics (see below)
AVON-Avon Periodicals
BP-Better Publications
C & L-Cupples & Leon
CC-Charlton Comics
CEN-Centaur Publications
CCG-Columbia Comics Group
CG-Catechetical Guild
CHES-Harry 'A' Chesler
CLDS-Classic Det. Stories
CM-Comics Magazine
DC-DC Comics, Inc.
DEF-Defiant Comics
DELL-Dell Publishing Co.
DH-Dark Horse
DMP-David McKay Publishing
DS-D. S. Publishing Co.
EAS-Eastern Color Printing Co.
EC-E. C. Comics
ECL-Eclipse Comics
ENWIL-Enwil Associates
EP-Elliott Publications
ERB-Edgar Rice Burroughs
FAW-Fawcett Publications
FC-First Comics
FF-Famous Funnies
FH-Fiction House Magazines
FOX-Fox Features Syndicate
GIL-Gilberton
GK-Gold Key
GP-Great Publications
HARV-Harvey Publications
H-B-Hanna-Barbera
HILL-Hillman Periodicals
HOKE-Holyoke Publishing Co.
IM-Image Comics
KING-King Features Syndicate
LEV-Lev Gleason Publications
MAL-Malibu Comics
MAR-Marvel Characters, Inc.
ME-Magazine Enterprises
MLJ-MLJ Magazines
MS-Mirage Studios
NOVP-Novelty Press
PG-Premier Group
PINE-Pines
PMI-Parents' Magazine Institute
PRIZE-Prize Publications
QUA-Quality Comics Group
REAL-Realistic Comics
RH-Rural Home
S & S-Street and Smith Publishers
SKY-Skywald Publications
STAR-Star Publications
STD-Standard Comics
STJ-St. John Publishing Co.
SUPR-Superior Comics
TC-Tower Comics
TM-Trojan Magazines
TOBY-Toby Press
TOPS-Tops Comics
UFS-United Features Syndicate
VAL-Valiant
VITL-Vital Publications
WDC-The Walt Disney Company
WEST-Western Publishing Co.
WHIT-Whitman Publishing Co.
WHW-William H. Wise
WMG-William M. Gaines (E. C.)
WP-Warren Publishing Co.
YM-Youthful Magazines
Z-D-Ziff-Davis Publishing Co.

TIMELY/MARVEL/ATLAS

"A Marvel Magazine" and "Marvel Group" were the designations used between December 1946 and May 1947 for the Timely/Marvel/Atlas group of comics during that period, although these taglines were not used on all of the titles/issues during that time. The Timely Comics symbol was used between July 1942 and September 1942, although again not on all titles/issues during the period. The round "Marvel Comic" symbol was used between February 1949 and June 1950. An early Comics Code symbol (star and bar) was used between April 1952 and February 1955. The Atlas globe symbol was used between December 1951 and September 1957. The M over C symbol (signifying the beginning of Marvel Comics as we know it today) was introduced in July 1961 and remained until the price increased to 12 cents in February 1962. We present here the publishers' codes for the Timely/Marvel/Atlas group of comics:

ACI-Animirth Comics, Inc.
AMI-Atlas Magazines, Inc.
ANC-Atlas News Co., Inc.
BPC-Bard Publishing Corp.
BFP-Broadcast Features Pubs.
CBS-Crime Bureau Stories
CLDS-Classic Detective Stories
CCC-Comic Combine Corp.
CDS-Current Detective Stories
CFI-Crime Files, Inc.
CmPI-Comedy Publications, Inc.
CmPS-Complete Photo Story
CnPC-Cornell Publishing Corp.
CPC-Chipiden Publishing Corp.
CPI-Crime Publications, Inc.
CPS-Canam Publishing Sales Corp.
CSI-Classics Syndicate, Inc.
DCI-Daring Comics, Inc.
EPC-Euclid Publishing Co.
EPI-Emgee Publications, Inc.
FCI-Fantasy Comics, Inc.
FPI-Foto Parade, Inc.
GPI-Gem Publishing, Inc.
HPC-Hercules Publishing Corp.
IPS-Interstate Publishing Corp.
JPI-Jaygee Publications, Inc.
LBI-Lion Books, Inc.
LCC-Leading Comic Corp.
LMC-Leading Magazine Corp.
MALE-Male Publishing Corp.
MAP-Miss America Publishing Corp.
MCI-Marvel Comics, Inc.
MgPC-Margood Publishing Corp.
MjMC-Marjean Magazine Corp.
MMC-Mutual Magazine Corp.
MPC-Medalion Publishing Corp.
MPI-Manvis Publications, Inc.
NPI-Newsstand Publications, Inc.
NPP-Non-Pareil Publishing Corp.
OCI-Official Comics, Inc.
OMC-Official Magazine Corp.
OPI-Olympia Publications, Inc.
PPI-Postal Publications, Inc.
PrPI-Prime Publications, Inc.
RCM-Red Circle Magazines, Inc.
SAI-Sports Actions, Inc.
SePI-Select Publications, Inc.
SnPC-Snap Publishing Co.
SPC-Select Publishing Co.
SPI-Sphere Publications, Inc.
TCI-Timely Comics, Inc.
TP-Timely Publications
20 CC-20th Century Comics Corp.
USA-U.S.A. Publications, Inc.
VPI-Vista Publications, Inc.
WFP-Western Fiction Publishing
WPI-Warwick Publications, Inc.
YAI-Young Allies, Inc.
ZPC-Zenith Publishing Co., Inc.

COMIC BOOK ARTISTS

Many of the more popular artists in the business are specially noted in the listings. When more than one artist worked on a story, their names are separated by a (/). The first name did the pencil drawings and the second the inks. When two or more artists work on a story, only the most prominent will be noted in some cases. We wish all good artists could be listed, but due to space limitation, only the most popular can. The following list of artists are considered to be either the most collected in the comic field or are historically significant. Artists designated below with an (*) indicate that only their most noted work will be listed. The rest will eventually have all their work shown as the information becomes available. This list could change from year to year as new artists come into prominence:

Adams, Arthur
Adams, Neal
Aparo, Jim
Bachalo, Chris
Bagley, Mark
Baker, Matt
Barks, Carl
Beck, C. C.
*Brunner, Frank
*Buscema, John
Byrne, John
Campbell, J. Scott
Capullo, Greg
*Check, Sid
Colan, Gene
Cole, Jack
Cole, L. B.
Craig, Johnny
Crandall, Reed
Darrow, Geof
Davis, Jack
Disbrow, Jayson
*Ditko, Steve
Eisner, Will
*Elder, Bill
Evans, George
Everett, Bill
Feldstein, Al
Fine, Lou
Foster, Harold
Fox, Matt
Frazetta, Frank
Gibbons, Dave
*Giffen, Keith
Golden, Michael
Gottfredson, Floyd
*Guardineer, Fred
Gustavson, Paul
*Heath, Russ
Howard, Wayne
*Infantino, Carmine
Ingels, Graham
Jones, Jeff
Kamen, Jack
Kane, Bob
*Kane, Gil
Kelly, Walt
Kieth, Sam
Kinstler, E. R.
Kirby, Jack
Krenkel, Roy
Krigstein, Bernie
Kubert, Adam
Kubert, Andy
*Kubert, Joe
Kurtzman, Harvey
Lapham, Dave
Larsen, Erik
Lee, Jae
Lee, Jim
Liefeld, Rob
Madureira, Joe
Manning, Russ
McFarlane, Todd
McWilliams, Al
Meskin, Mort
Mignola, Mike
Miller, Frank
Moreira, Ruben
*Morisi, Pete
*Newton, Don
Nostrand, Howard
Orlando, Joe
Pakula, Mac
*Palais, Rudy
*Perez, George
Portacio, Whilce
Powell, Bob
Quesada, Joe
Raboy, Mac
Ramos, Humberto
Raymond, Alex
Ravielli, Louis
*Redondo, Nestor
Rogers, Marshall
Ross, Alex
Schomburg, Alex
Sears, Bart
Siegel & Shuster
Silvestri, Marc
Simon & Kirby (S&K)
*Simonson, Walt
Smith, Paul
Stanley, John
*Starlin, Jim
Steranko, Jim
Stevens, Dave
Texeira, Mark
Thibert, Art
Torres, Angelo
Toth, Alex
Turner, Michael
Tuska, George
Ward, Bill
Williamson, Al
Windsor-Smith, Barry
Woggon, Bill
Wolverton, Basil
Wood, Wallace
Wrightson, Bernie
Zeck, Mike

ARTISTS' FIRST WORK

Adams, Neal - (1 pg.) **Archie's Jokebook Mag.** #41, 9/59; (1st on Batman, cvr only) **Detective Comics** #370, 12/67; (1st Warren art) **Creepy** #14
Aparo, Jim - **Go-Go** #1, 6/66
Balent, Jim - **Sgt. Rock** #393, 10/84
Barks, Carl - (art only) **Donald Duck Four Color** #9, 8/42; (scripts only) **Large Feature Comic** #7, ca. Spring 1942
Broderick, Pat - (cover & art) **Planet of Vampires** #1, 2/75
Brunner, Frank - (fan club sketch) **Creepy** #10, 1965
Buckler, Rich - **Flash Gordon** #10, 11/67
Burnley, Jack - (cover & art) **NY World's Fair** nn, '40
Buscema, John - (1st at Marvel) **Strange Tales** #150, 11/66
Byrne, John - **Nightmare** #20, 8/74; (1st at DC) **Untold Legend of the Batman** #1, 7/80; (1st at Marvel) **Giant-Size Dracula** #5, 6/75
Capullo, Greg - (1st on X-Force) **X-Force Annual** #1, '92
Colan, Gene - **Wings Comics** #53, 1/45
Cole, Jack - (1 pg.) **Star Comics** #11, 4/38
Crandall, Reed - **Hit Comics** #10, 4/41
Davis, Jack - (cartoon) **Tip Top Comics** #32, 12/38
Ditko, Steve - (1st publ.) **Black Magic** V4#3, 11-12/53 (1st drawn story), **Fantastic Fears** #5, 1-2/54
Everett, Bill - **Amazing Mystery Funnies** V1#2, 9/38
Fine, Lou - (1st cvr) **Wonder Comics** #2, 6/39; **Jumbo Comics** #4, 12/38
Frazetta, Frank - **Tally-Ho Comics** nn, 12/44
Garney, Ron - **G. I. Joe, A Real American Hero** #110, 3/91
Giffen, Keith - (1 pg.) **Deadly Hands of Kung-Fu** #17, 11/75; (1st story) **Deadly Hands of Kung-Fu** #22, 4?/76; (tied w/Deadly Hands) **Amazing Adventures** #35, 3/76
Golden, Michael - **Marvel Classics Comics** #28, '77
Grell, Mike - **Adventure Comics** #435, 9-10/74
Hamner, Cully - **Green Lantern: Mosaic** #1, 6/92
Hughes, Adam - **Blood of Dracula** #1, 11/87
Ingels, Graham art at E.C. - **Saddle Justice** #4, Sum '48
Jurgens, Dan - **Warlord** #53, 1/82
Kaluta, Michael - **Teen Confessions** #59, 12/69
Kelly, Walt - **New Comics** #1, 12/35
Keown, Dale - **Samurai** #13, 1987; **Nth Man the Ultimate Ninja** #8, 1/90; (1st at Marvel); (1st on Hulk) **Incredible Hulk** #367, 3/90
Kieth, Sam - **Primer** #5, 11?/83
Kirby, Jack - **Jumbo Comics** #1, 9/38;
Kubert, Adam/Andy/Joe art - **Sgt. Rock** #422, 7/88
Kurtzman, Harvey - **Tip Top Comics** #36, 4/39; (1st at E.C.) **Lucky Fights It Through** nn, 1949
Larsen, Erik - **Megaton** #1, 11/83
Lee, Jae - **Marvel Comics Presents** #85, '91
Lee, Jim - (1st at Marvel) **Alpha Flight** #51, 10/87; (1st on X-Men) **X-Men** #248?, ?/89; (art on Punisher) **Punisher War Journal** #1, 11/88
Liefeld, Rob - (1st at DC) **Warlord** #131, 9/88; (1st at Marvel) **X-Factor** #40, 4?/89; (1st full story) **Megaton** #8, 8/87; (inside front cover only) **Megaton** #5, 6/86
Lim, Ron - (art on Silver Surfer) **Silver Surfer Ann.** #1, '88
Matsuda, Jeff - **Brigade** #0, 9/93
Mayer, Sheldon - **New Comics** #1, 12/35
McFarlane, Todd - **Coyote** #11, ?/85; (1st full story) **All Star Squadron** #47, 7/85; (1st on Hulk) **Incredible Hulk** #330, 4/87
Medina, Angel - (pin-up only) **Megaton** #3, 2/86
Mignola, Mike - **Marvel Fanfare** #15, 5/83
Miller, Frank - (1st on Batman) **DC Special Series** #21, Spr '80; (1st on Daredevil) **Spectacular Spider-Man** #27, 2/79
Newton, Don - **Many Ghosts of Dr. Graves** #45, 5/74
Perez, George - (1st at DC) **Flash** #289, 9/80; (2 pgs.) **Astonishing Tales** #25, 8/74
Portacio, Whilce - (1st on X-Men) **X-Men** #201, 1/86
Pulido, Brian - **Evil Ernie** #1, 12/91
Quesada, Joe - (1st on X-Factor) **X-Factor Ann.** #7, '92
Raboy, Mac - (1st cover for Fawcett) **Master Comics** #21, 12/41
Ramos, Humberto - (1st U.S. work) **Hardwire** #15, 6/94
Romita, John - **Strange Tales** #4, 12/51; (1st at Marvel) **Daredevil** #12, 1/66
Romita, John Jr. - (1st complete story) **Iron Man** #115, 10/78
Ross, Alex - **The Terminator: The Burning Earth** V2#1, 3/90
Shuster, Joe - (cover) **New Adv. Comics** #16, 6/37
Siegel & Shuster - **New Fun Comics** #6, 10/35
Simon & Kirby - **Blue Bolt** #2, 7/40
Simonson, Walter - **Magnus, Robot Fighter** #10, 5/65
Smith, Paul - (1 pg. pin-up) **King Conan** #7, 9/81; (1st full story) **Marvel Fanfare** #1, 3/82
Steranko, Jim - **Spyman** #1, Sep '66; (1st at Marvel) **Strange Tales** #151, 12/66
Swan, Curt - **Dick Cole** #1, 12-1/48-49
Talbot, Bryan - (1st U.S. work) **Hellblazer Annual** #1, Summer '89
Thomas, Roy - (scripts) **Son of Vulcan** #50, 1/66
Torres, Angelo - **Crime Mysteries** #13, 5/54
Turner, Mike - **Cyberforce Origins-Stryker**, 2/95
Weeks, Lee - **Tales of Terror** #5, 11/85
Weiss, Alan - (illo) **Blue Beetle** #5, 3-4/65
Williamson, Al - (1st at E.C.) **Tales From the Crypt** #31, 9/52; (text illos) **Famous Funnies** #169, 8/48
Windsor-Smith, Barry - **X-Men** #53, 2/69
Wood, Wally - (1st at E.C.) **Saddle Romances** #10, 1-2/50
Wrightson, Bernie - **House of Mystery** #179, 4/68; (1st at Marvel) **Chamber of Darkness** #7, 10/70; (1st cover) **Web of Horror** #3, 4/70; (fan club sketch) **Creepy** #9
Zeck, Mike - (illos) **Barney and Betty Rubble** #11, 2/75

The American Comic Book: 1842-2000

THE MARKETING OF A MEDIUM

by Arnold T. Blumberg

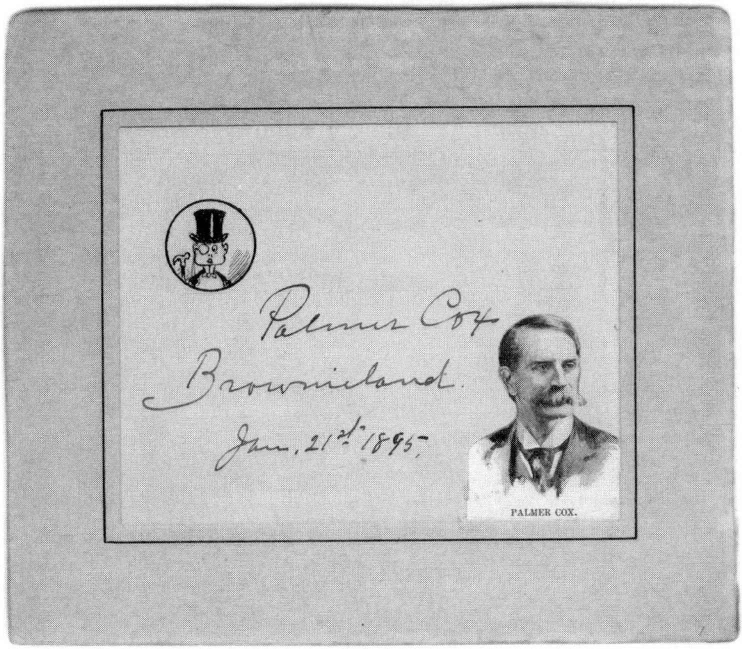

A very rare piece indeed, this represents one of the few existing examples of Palmer Cox's signature, as Cox always printed his name on his art. The character depicted in the upper left, "The Dude," represents a typical New Yorker and was Cox's favorite.

For the first time in the history of ***The Overstreet Comic Book Price Guide****, we are listing premium and giveaway comics (now collectively referred to as "promotional comics" in this edition) in their own section. Besides attempting to present the information on such comics in a clearer, more organized way than in the past (traditionally these comics have been listed throughout the guide and at the end of related titles), we hope that by setting promotional comics apart, we can draw attention to this fertile but as yet poorly represented area of comic book history.*

One of the best examples of the Brownies' proliferation into all kinds of merchandise. This rare Luden's Cough Drop ad (1890s) is the earliest known character die-cut sign.

Everyone wants something for free. It's in our nature to look for the quick fix, the good deal, the complimentary gift. We long to hit the lottery and quit our job, to win the trip around the world, or find that pot of gold at the end of the proverbial rainbow. Collectors in particular are certainly built to appreciate the notion of the "free gift," since it not only means a new item to collect and enjoy, but no risk or obligation in order to acquire it.

Ah, but there's the rub, because things are not always what they seem, and "free gifts" usually come with a price. As the saying goes, "there's no such thing as a free lunch," so if it seems too good to be true, it probably is. This is the case even in the world of comics, where premiums and giveaways have a familiar agenda hidden behind the bright colors and fanciful stories. But where did it all begin?

EXTRA EXTRA

As we learn more about the early history of the comic book industry through continual investigation and the publishing of articles like those regularly featured in this book, we gain a much greater understanding of the financial and creative forces at work in shaping the medium, but perhaps one of the most intriguing and least recognized factors that influenced the dawn of comics is the concept of the premium or giveaway. (Note: Some of the historical information referenced in this article is derived from material also presented in Robert L. Beerbohm's introductory article to the Platinum Age and Modern Age sections.)

The birth of the comic book as we know it today is intimately connected with the development of the comic strip in American newspapers and their use as an advertising and marketing tool for staple products such as bread, milk, and cereal. From the very beginning, comic characters have played several roles in pop culture, entertaining the youth of the country while also (sometimes none too subtly) acting as hucksters for whatever corporation foots the bill. From important staples to frivolous material produced simply to make a buck, these products have utilized the comics medium to sell, sell, sell. And what better way to hook a prospective customer than to give them "something for nothing?"

Although comic characters were already being aggressively merchandised all around the world by the mid-1890s--as with, for example, Palmer Cox's **The Brownies**--the real starting point for the success of comics as a giveaway marketing mechanism can be traced to the introduction of **The Yellow Kid**, Richard Outcault's now legendary newspaper strip.

Newspaper publishers had already recognized that comic strips could boost circulation as well as please sponsors and advertisers by drawing more eyes to the page, so Sunday "supplements" were introduced to entice fans. Outcault's creation cemented the theory with proof of comic characters' marketing and merchandising power.

Soon after, Outcault (who had most likely been inspired by Cox's merchandising success with **The Brownies** in the first place) caught lightning in a bottle once more with **Buster Brown**, who has the distinction of being America's first nationally licensed comic strip character. Soon, comic strips proliferated throughout the nation's newspapers, offering companies the chance to license recognizable personas as their own personal pitchmen (or women or animals...). Comic character merchandise wasn't far behind, resulting in a boom of future collectibles now catalogued in volumes like **Hake's Price Guide to Character Toys**.

Comic books themselves were at the heart of this movement, and giveaway and premium collections of comic strips not only appealed to children and adults alike, but provided the impetus for the birth of the modern comic book format itself. It could be said that without the concept of the giveaway comic or the marketing push behind it, there would be no comic book industry as we have it today.

Thanks to men like Harry I. Wildenberg of Eastern Printing and companies like Gulf Oil (who liked Wildenberg's idea of an advertising-driven comics tabloid and produced **Gulf Comic Weekly**), the modern comic came into being around 1932-33.

What most people agree was the first modern format comic, **Funnies on Parade**, was released as a result of this growing merchandising movement, and sparked by the success of Wildenberg's and Gulf Oil's grand experiment. Through the auspices of Proctor & Gamble, **Funnies on Parade** was printed and given away in the Spring of 1933.

Perhaps one of the earliest examples of the business world acknowledging and investigating the influence of the comic book on modern pop culture and American enterprise. FORTUNE Magazine, April 1933.

A medium was born, and a marketing tool had completed its first step in the long road to maturity.

The impact of this new approach to advertising was not lost on the business world. Contrary to modern belief, comic books were hardly discounted by the adults of the time, at least not those who had the marketing savvy to recognize an opportunity--or a threat--when they saw one.

READ ALL ABOUT IT

In the April 1933 issue of **Fortune** magazine, an article titled "The Funny Papers" trumpeted the arrival of comics as a force to be reckoned with in the world of advertising and business, and what's more, a force to fear as well. At first providing a brief survey of the newspaper comic strip business (which for many of the magazine's readers must have seemed a foreign topic for serious discussion), the article goes on to examine the incredible financial draw of comics and their characters:

"Between 70 and 75 per cent {sic} of the readers of any newspaper follow its comic sections regularly...Even the advertiser has succumbed to the comic, and in 1932 spent well over $1,000,000 for comic-paper space."

"Comic Weekly is the comic section of seventeen Hearst Sunday papers...Advertisers who market their wares through balloon-speaking manikins {sic} may enjoy the proximity of Jiggs, Maggie, Barney Google, and other funny Hearst headliners."

Although the article continues to cast the notion of relying on comic strip material to sell product in a negative light, actually suggesting that advertisers who utilize comics are violating unspoken rules of "advertising decorum" and bringing themselves "down to the level" of comics (and since when have advertisers been stalwart preservers of good taste and high moral standards), there is no doubt that they are viewing comics in a new light. The comic characters have arrived by 1933...and they're ready to help sell your merchandise too.

THE MARCH OF WAR AND BEYOND

Through the relentless currents of time, comic strips, books, and the characters that starred in them became more and more an intrinsic part of American culture. During the turmoil of the Great Depression and World War

II, comic characters in print and celluloid form entertained while informing and selling at the same time, and premium and giveaway comics came well and truly into their own, pushing everything from loaves of bread to war bonds.

In the 1950s and '60s, there was a shift in focus as the power of giveaway and premium comics was applied to more altruistic endeavors than simply selling something. Comic book format pamphlets, fully illustrated and often inventively written, taught children about banking, money, the dangers of poison and other household products, and even chronicled moments in American history. The comic book as giveaway was now not only a marketing gimmick--it was a tool for educating as well.

The 1970s and '80s saw another boom in premium and giveaway comics. Every product imaginable seemed to have a licensing deal with a comic book character, usually one of the prominent flag bearers of the Big Two, Marvel or DC. Spider-Man fought bravely against the Beetle for the benefit of All Detergent; Captain America allied himself with the Campbell Kids; and Superman helped a class of computer students beat a disaster-conjuring foe at his own game with the help of Radio Shack Tandy computers.

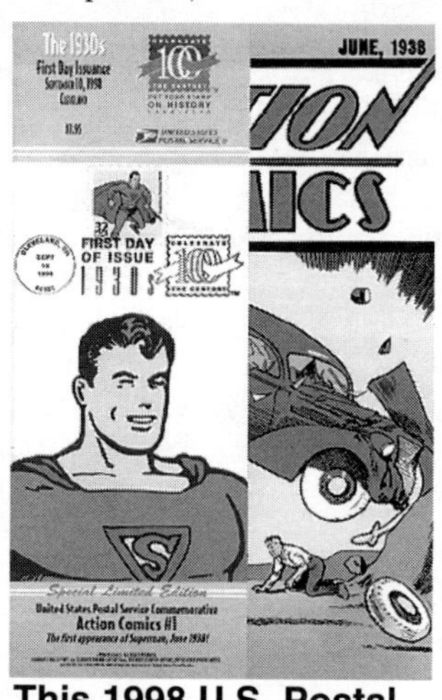

This 1998 U.S. Postal Service premium is one of the most recent examples of the continuing popularity of promotional comics.

Newspapers rediscovered the power of comics, not just with enlarged strip supplements but with actual comic books. Spider-Man, the Hulk, and others turned up as giveaway comic extras in various American newspapers (including Chicago and Dallas publications), while a whole series of public information comics like those produced decades earlier used superheroes to caution children about the dangers of smoking, drugs, and child abuse.

Comics also turned up in a plethora of other toy products as the 1980s introduced kids to the joy of electronic games and action figures. Supplementary comics provided "free" with action figure and video game packages told the backstory about the product, adding depth to the play experience while providing an extra incentive to buy. Comics became an intrinsic part of the Atari line of video cartridges, for example, eventually spawning its own full-blown newsstand series as well.

Today, premium comics continue to thrive and are still utilized as a valuable marketing and promotional tool. "Free" comics are still packaged with action figures and video games, and offered as mail-away premiums from a variety of product manufacturers. The comic industry itself has expanded its use of giveaway comics to self-promote as well, with "ashcan" and other giveaway editions turning up at conventions and comic shops to advertise upcoming series and special events. Many of these function as old-fashioned premiums, with a coupon or other response required from the reader to receive the comic.

As for the supplements and giveaways printed all those years ago, they have spawned a collectible fervor all their own, thanks to their atypical distribution and frequent rarity. For that and the desire to delve deeper into comics history, we hope that by focusing more directly on this genre, we can enhance our understanding of this vital component in the development and history of the modern comic book.

Whether you're a collector or not, we're all motivated by that desire to get something for nothing. For as long as consumers are enticed by the notion of the "free gift," promotional comics will remain a vital marketing component in many business models, but they will also continue to fight the stigma that has long been associated with the industry as a whole. "Respectable" sources like **Fortune** may have taken notice of the power of comic-related advertising 67 years ago, but after all this time comics still fight an uphill battle to establish some measure of dignity for the medium. Perhaps the higher visibility of promotional comics will eventually prove to be a deciding factor in that intellectual war.

See ya in the funny papers.

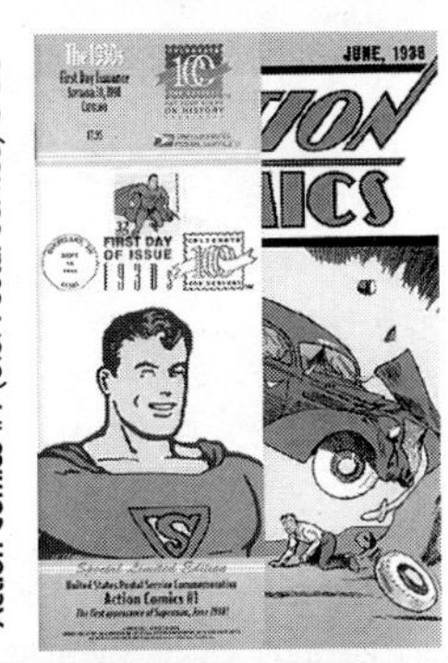

Action Comics #1 (U.S. Postal Service) © DC

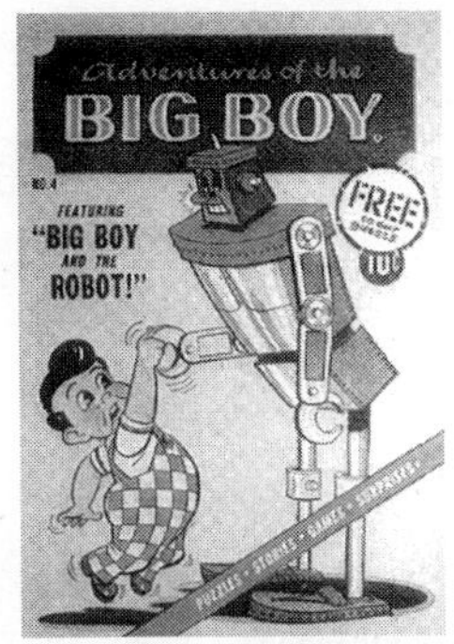

Adventures of the Big Boy #4 © Timely

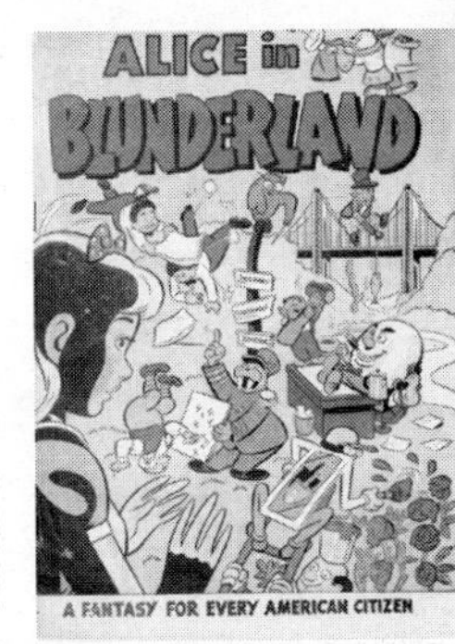

Alice in Blunderland © Industrial Services

GD2.0 FN6.0 NM9.4

ACTION COMICS
DC Comics: 1947 - 1998 (Giveaway)
1 (1976, 1983) paper cover w/10¢ price, 16pgs. in color; reprints complete Superman story from #1 ('38) 2.25 6.75 18.00
1 (1976) Safeguard Giveaway; paper cover w/"free", 16pgs. in color; reprints complete Superman story from #1 ('38) 2.50 7.50 20.00
1 (1987 Nestle Quik; 1988, 50¢) 1.00 3.00 7.50
1 (1998 U.S. Postal Service, $7.95) Reprints entire issue; extra outer half-cover contains First Day Issuance of 32¢ Superman stamp with Sept. 10, 1998 Cleveland, OH postmark 7.95
Theater (1947, 32 pgs., 6-1/2 x 8-1/4", nn)-Vigilante story based on Columbia Vigilante serial; no Superman-c or story 66.00 198.00 525.00

ADVENTURE COMICS
IGA: No date (early 1940s) (Paper-c, 32 pgs.)
Two diff. issues; Super-Mystery-r from 1941 24.00 72.00 190.00

ADVENTURE IN DISNEYLAND
Walt Disney Productions (Dist. by Richfield Oil): May, 1955 (Giveaway, soft-c., 16 pgs)
nn 9.50 28.00 75.00

ADVENTURES OF G. I. JOE
1969 (3-1/4x7") (20 & 16 pgs.)
First Series: 1-Danger of the Depths. 2-Perilous Rescue. 3-Secret Mission to Spy Island. 4-Mysterious Explosion. 5-Fantastic Free Fall. 6-Eight Ropes of Danger. 7-Mouth of Doom. 8-Hidden Missile Discovery. 9-Space Walk Mystery. 10-Fight for Survival. 11-The Shark's Surprise.
Second Series: 2-Flying Space Adventure. 4-White Tiger Hunt. 7-Capture of the Pygmy Gorilla. 12-Secret of the Mummy's Tomb.
Third Series: Reprinted surviving titles of First Series. Fourth Series: 13-Adventure Team Headquarters. 14-Search For the Stolen Idol.
each.... 1.25 3.75 10.00

ADVENTURES OF MARGARET O'BRIEN, THE
Bambury Fashions (Clothes): 1947 (20 pgs. in color, slick-c, regular size) (Premium)
In "The Big City" movie adaptation (scarce) 20.00 60.00 140.00

ADVENTURES OF STUBBY, SANTA'S SMALLEST REINDEER, THE
W. T. Grant Co.: nd (early 1940s) (Giveaway, 12 pgs.)
nn 4.25 13.00 28.00

ADVENTURES OF THE BIG BOY
Timely Comics/Webs Adv. Corp./Illus. Features: 1956 - No. 466, 1996? (Giveaway) (East & West editions of early issues)
1-Everett-a 150.00 425.00 850.00
2-Everett-a 50.00 125.00 275.00
3-5 25.00 75.00 125.00
6-10: 6-Sci/fic issue 10.00 50.00 100.00
11-20 5.00 15.00 50.00
21-30 3.00 10.00 28.00
31-50 2.00 6.00 16.00
51-100 1.00 2.80 7.00
101-150 2.40 6.00
151-240 5.00
241-265,267-269,271-300: 3.00
266-Superman x-over 2.50 7.50 20.00
270-TV's Buck Rogers-c/s 2.50 7.50 20.00
301-400 2.50
401-466 2.00
1-50 ('76-'84,Paragon Prod.) (...Shoney's Big Boy) .50
Summer, 1959 issue, large size 11.00 33.00 75.00
NOTE: No. 467 was completed but never published.

ADVENTURES WITH SANTA CLAUS
Promotional Publ. Co. (Murphy's Store): No date (early 50's) (9-3/4x 6-3/4", 24 pgs., giveaway, paper-c)
nn-Contains 8 pgs. ads 4.25 13.00 28.00
16 pg. version 4.25 13.00 28.00

AIR POWER (CBS TV & the U.S. Air Force Presents)
Prudential Insurance Co.: 1956 (5-1/4x7-1/4", 32 pgs., giveaway, soft-c)
nn-Toth-a? Based on 'You Are There' TV program by Walter Cronkite 11.00 33.00 75.00

ALICE IN BLUNDERLAND
Industrial Services: 1952 (Paper cover, 16 pgs. in color)
nn-Facts about big government waste and inefficiency 14.00 43.00 100.00

ALICE IN WONDERLAND
Western Printing Company/Whitman Publ. Co.: 1965; 1982
Meets Santa Claus(1950s), nd, 16 pgs. 4.15 12.50 25.00
Rexall Giveaway(1965, 16 pgs., 5x7-1/4) Western Printing (TV, Hanna-Barbera) 2.50 7.50 24.00
Wonder Bakery Giveaway(16 pgs, color, nn, nd) (Continental Baking Company, 1969) 2.50 7.50 25.00
1-(Whitman; 1982)-r/4-Color #331 1.60 4.00

ALICE IN WONDERLAND MEETS SANTA
No publisher: nd (6-5/8x9-11/16", 16 pgs., giveaway, paper-c)
nn 11.00 33.00 75.00

ALL NEW COMICS
Harvey Comics: Oct, 1993 (Giveaway, no cover price, 16 pgs.)(Hanna-Barbera)
1-Flintstones, Scooby Doo, Jetsons, Yogi Bear & Wacky Races previews for upcoming Harvey's new Hanna-Barbera line-up 2.00
NOTE: Material previewed in Harvey giveaway was eventually published by Archie.

AMAZING SPIDER-MAN, THE
Marvel Comics Group
Aim Toothpaste Giveaway (36 pgs., reg. size)-1 pg. origin recap; Green Goblin-c/story 1.25 3.75 10.00
Aim Toothpaste Giveaway (16 pgs., reg. size)-Dr. Octopus app. 1.25 3.75 10.00
All Detergent Giveaway (1979, 36 pgs.), nn-Origin-r 2.00 6.00 15.00
GiveawayY-Acme & Dingo Children's Boots (1980)-Spider-Woman app. 2.00 6.00 15.00
Amazing Spider-Man nn (1990, 6-1/8x9", 28 pgs.)-Shan-Lon giveaway; r/ Amazing Spider-Man #303 w/McFarlane-c/a 1.00 4.00 8.00
...& Power Pack (1984, nn)(Nat'l Committee for Prevention of Child Abuse (two versions, mail offer & store giveaway)-Mooney-a; Byrne-c
Mail offer 1.00 3.00 10.00
Store giveaway 3.00
...& The Hulk (Special Edition)(6/8/80; 20 pgs.)-Supplement to Chicago Tribune (giveaway) 2.00 6.00 15.00
...& The Incredible Hulk (1981, 1982; 36 pgs.)-Sanger Harris or May D&F supplement to Dallas Times, Dallas Herald, Denver Post, Kansas City Star, Tulsa World; Foley's supplement to Houston Chronicle (1982, 16 pgs.)-"Great Rodeo Robbery"; The Jones Store-giveaway (1983, 16 pgs.) 2.25 6.75 18.00
...and the New Mutants Featuring Skids nn (National Committee for Prevention of Child Abuse/K-Mart giveaway)-Williams-c(i) 5.00
...Captain America, The Incredible Hulk, & Spider-Woman (1981) (7-11 Stores giveaway; 36 pgs.) 1.10 3.30 9.00
...: Danger in Dallas (1983) (Supplement to Dallas Times Herald) giveaway 1.10 3.30 9.00
...: Danger in Denver (1983) (Supplement to Denver Post) giveaway for May D&F stores 1.10 3.30 9.00
..., Fire-Star, And Ice-Man at the Dallas Ballet Nutcracker (1983; supplement to Dallas Times Herald)-Mooney-p 1.40 4.15 11.00
Giveaway-Esquire Magazine (2/69)-Miniature-Still attached 9.00 27.00 100.00
Giveaway-Eye Magazine (2/69)-Miniature-Still attached 8.50 25.50 85.00

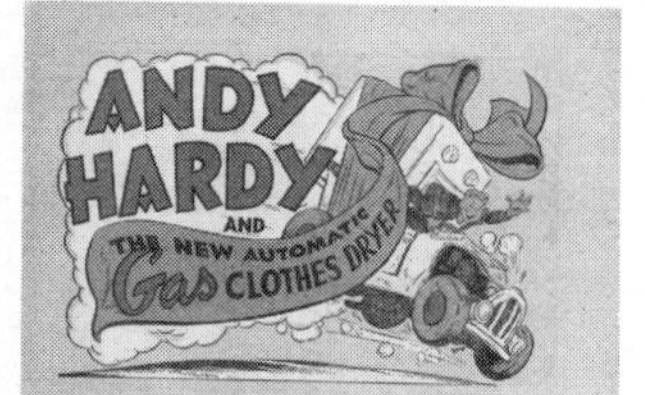

Andy Hardy Comics © WEST

Batman and Other DC Classics #1 © DC

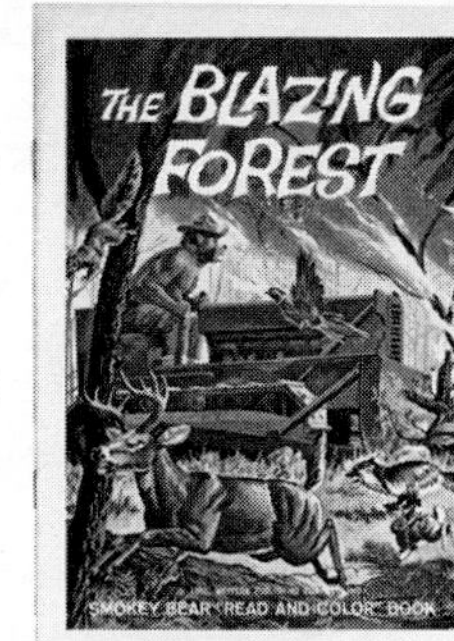

The Blazing Forest nn © WEST

	GD2.0	FN6.0	NM9.4
..., Storm & Powerman (1982; 20 pgs.)(American Cancer Society) giveaway		2.40	6.00
...Vs. The Hulk (Special Edition; 1979, 20 pgs.)(Supplement to Columbus Dispatch)-Giveaway	1.50	4.50	12.00
...Vs. The Prodigy (Giveaway, 16 pgs. in color (1976, 5x6-1/2")-Sex education; (1 million printed; 35-50¢)	2.50	7.50	20.00

AMERICA MENACED!
Vital Publications: 1950 (Paper-c)

nn-Anti-communism estimated value... 200.00

AMERICAN COMICS
Theatre Giveaways (Liberty Theatre, Grand Rapids, Mich. known): 1940's

Many possible combinations. "Golden Age" superhero comics with new cover added and given away at theaters. Following known: Superman #59, Capt. Marvel #20, Capt. Marvel Jr. #5, Action #33, Classics Comics #8, Whiz #39. Value would vary with book and should be 70-80 percent of the original.

ANDY HARDY COMICS
Western Printing Co.:

	GD2.0	FN6.0	NM9.4
...& the New Automatic Gas Clothes Dryer (1952, 5x7-1/4", 16 pgs.) Bendix Giveaway (soft-c)	7.50	22.50	45.00

APACHE HUNTER
Creative Pictorials: 1954 (18 pgs. in color) (promo copy) (saddle stitched)

	GD2.0	FN6.0	NM9.4
nn-Severin, Heath stories	17.00	51.00	120.00

ARCHIE AND HIS GANG (Zeta Beta Tau Presents...)
Archie Publications: Dec. 1950 (St. Louis National Convention giveaway)

	GD2.0	FN6.0	NM9.4
nn-Contains new cover stapled over Archie Comics #47 (11-12/50) on inside; produced for Zeta Beta Tau	15.00	45.00	105.00

ARCHIE COMICS
Archie Publications

	GD2.0	FN6.0	NM9.4
...And His Friends Help Raise Literacy Awareness In Mississippi nn (3/94)-Giveaway			4.00
...And the History of Electronics nn (5/90, 36 pgs.)-Radio Shack giveaway; Howard Bender-c/a			5.00
Mini-Comics (1970-Fairmont Potato Chips Giveaway-Miniature)(8 issues-nn's., 8 pgs. each)	2.50	7.50	20.00
Official Boy Scout Outfitter (1946, 9-1/2x6-1/2, 16 pgs.)-B. R. Baker Co. (Scarce)	47.00	141.00	375.00
Shoe Store giveaway (1948, Feb?)	17.00	51.00	120.00

ARCHIE SHOE-STORE GIVEAWAY
Archie Publications: 1944-49 (12-15 pgs. of games, puzzles, stories like Superman-Tim books, No nos. - came out monthly)

	GD2.0	FN6.0	NM9.4
(1944-47)-issues	13.00	33.00	90.00
2/48-Peggy Lee photo-c	10.00	30.00	70.00
3/48-Marylee Robb photo-c	10.00	30.00	65.00
4/48-Gloria De Haven photo-c	10.00	30.00	70.00
5/48,6/48,7/48	10.00	30.00	65.00
8/48-Story on Shirley Temple	11.00	33.00	75.00
10/48-Archie as Wolf on cover	12.00	36.00	85.00
5/49-Kathleen Hughes photo-c	8.35	25.00	50.00
7/49	8.35	25.00	50.00
8/49-Archie photo-c from radio show	14.00	43.00	100.00
10/49-Gloria Mann photo-c from radio show	10.00	30.00	70.00
11/49,12/49	8.00	24.00	48.00

ARCHIE'S JOKE BOOK MAGAZINE (See Joke Book ...)
Archie Publications

	GD2.0	FN6.0	NM9.4
Drug Store Giveaway (No. 39 w/new-c)	4.00	12.00	24.00

ARCHIE'S TEN ISSUE COLLECTOR'S SET (Title inside of cover only)
Archie Publications: June, 1997 - No. 10, June, 1997 ($1.50, 20 pgs.)

1-10: 1,7-Archie. 2,8-Betty & Veronica. 3,9-Veronica. 4-Betty. 5-World of Archie. 6-Jughead. 10-Archie and Friends 2.00

ASTRO COMICS
American Airlines (Harvey): 1968 - 1979 (Giveaway)

Reprints of Harvey comics. 1968-Hot Stuff. 1969-Casper, Spooky, Hot Stuff, Stumbo the Giant, Little Audrey, Little Lotta, & Richie Rich reprints.

	GD2.0	FN6.0	NM9.4
1970-r/Richie Rich #97 (all scarce)	2.25	6.75	18.00
1973-r/Richie Rich #122. 1975-Wendy. 1975-Richie Rich & Casper. 1977-r/Richie Rich & Casper #20. 1978-r/Richie Rich & Casper #25. 1979-r/Richie Rich & Casper #30 (scarce)	2.25	6.75	18.00

ATARI FORCE
DC Comics: 1982 - No. 5, 1983

	GD2.0	FN6.0	NM9.4
1-3 (1982, 5X7", 52 pgs.)-Given away with Atari games			4.00
4,5 (1982-1983, 52 pgs.)-Given away with Atari games (scarcer)	1.00	2.80	7.00

AURORA COMIC SCENES INSTRUCTION BOOKLET
Aurora Plastics Co.: 1974 (6-1/4x9-3/4," 8 pgs., slick paper)
(Included with superhero model kits)

	GD2.0	FN6.0	NM9.4
181-140-Tarzan; Neal Adams-a	5.00	10.00	25.00
182-140-Spider-Man.	7.00	20.00	35.00
183-140-Tonto(Gil Kane art). 184-140-Hulk. 185-140-Superman. 186-140-Superboy. 187-140-Batman. 188-140-The Lone Ranger(1974-by Gil Kane). 192-140-Captain America(1975). 193-140-Robin	3.00	8.00	22.00

BACK TO THE FUTURE
Harvey Comics

Special nn (1991, 20 pgs.)-Brunner-c; given away at Universal Studios in Florida 2.00

BALTIMORE COLTS
American Visuals Corp.: 1950 (Giveaway)

	GD2.0	FN6.0	NM9.4
nn-Eisner-c	47.00	141.00	375.00

BAMBI (Disney)
K. K. Publications (Giveaways)/Whitman Publ. Co.: 1941, 1942, 1984

	GD2.0	FN6.0	NM9.4
1941-Horlick's Malted Milk & various toy stores; text & pictures; most copies mailed out with store stickers on-c	50.00	125.00	250.00
1942-Same as 4-Color #12, but no price (Same as '41 issue?) (Scarce)	75.00	200.00	400.00
1-(Whitman, 1984; 60¢)-r/4-Color #186		2.40	6.00

BATMAN
DC Comics: 1966-1989

Batman and Other DC Classics 1 (1989, giveaway)-DC Comics/Diamond Comic Distributors; Batman origin-r/Batman #47, Camelot 3000-r by Bolland, Justice League-r('87), New Teen Titans-r by Perez. 1.00

Kellogg's Poptarts comics (1966, Set of 6, 16 pgs.); All were folded and placed in

Poptarts boxes. Infantino art on Catwoman and Joker issues.

"The Man in the Iron Mask", "The Penguin's Fowl Play", "The Joker's Happy Victims", "The Catwoman's Catnapping Caper", "The Mad Hatter's Hat Crimes", "The Case of the Batman II"

	GD2.0	FN6.0	NM9.4
each....	3.00	9.00	30.00
Pizza Hut giveaway (12/77)-exact-r of #122,123; Joker-c/story		2.40	6.00
Prell Shampoo giveaway (1966, 16 pgs.)- "The Joker's Practical Jokes" (6-7/8x3-3/8")	3.20	9.60	32.00

BATMAN RECORD COMIC
National Periodical Publications: 1966 (one-shot)

	GD2.0	FN6.0	NM9.4
1-With record (still sealed)	12.50	38.00	125.00
Comic only	7.00	21.00	70.00

BEETLE BAILEY
Charlton Comics: 1969-1970 (Giveaways)

	GD2.0	FN6.0	NM9.4
Bold Detergent ('69)-same as regular issue (#67)	1.00	3.00	8.00
Cerebral Palsy Assn. V2#71('69) - V2#73(#1,1/70)	1.00	3.00	8.00
Red Cross (1969, 5x7", 16 pgs., paper-c)	1.00	3.00	8.00

BIG JIM'S P.A.C.K.
Mattel, Inc. (Marvel Comics): No date (1975) (16 pgs.)

	GD2.0	FN6.0	NM9.4
nn-Giveaway with Big Jim doll; Buscema/Sinnott-c/a	2.00	6.00	20.00

BLACK GOLD

Bozo the Clown © DELL

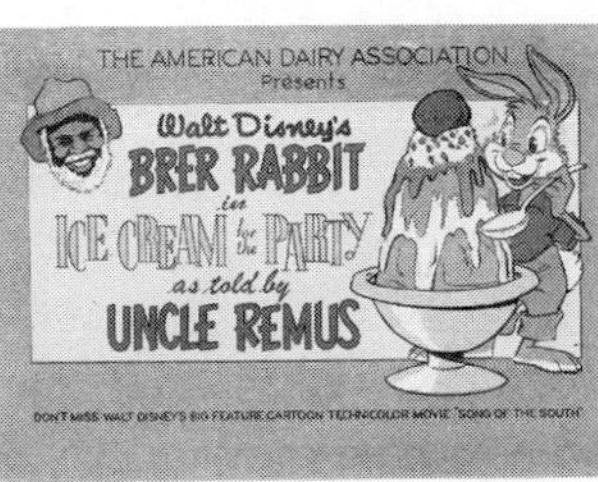

Brer Rabbit in "Ice Cream For The Party" © WDC

GD2.0 FN6.0 NM9.4

Esso Service Station (Giveaway): 1945? (8 pgs. in color)
nn-Reprints from True Comics 6.00 18.00 35.00

BLAZING FOREST, THE (See Forest Fire and Smokey The Bear)
Western Printing: 1962 (20 pgs., 5x7", slick-c)
nn-Smokey The Bear fire prevention 1.00 3.00 10.00

BLESSED PIUS X
Catechetical Guild (Giveaway): No date (Text/comics, 32 pgs., paper-c)
nn 4.00 10.00 20.00

BLONDIE COMICS
Harvey Publications: 1950-1964
1950 Giveaway 5.35 16.00 32.00
1962,1964 Giveaway 1.75 5.25 14.00
N. Y. State Dept. of Mental Hygiene Giveaway-(1950) Regular size; 16 pgs.; no # 2.50 7.50 20.00
N. Y. State Dept. of Mental Hygiene Giveaway-(1956) Regular size; 16 pgs.; no # 2.00 6.00 16.00
N. Y. State Dept. of Mental Hygiene Giveaway-(1961) Regular size; 16 pgs.; no # 1.75 5.25 14.00

BLOOD IS THE HARVEST
Catechetical Guild: 1950 (32 pgs., paper-c)
(Scarce)-Anti-communism (13 known copies) 106.00 320.00 850.00
Black & white version (5 known copies), saddle stitched 40.00 120.00 290.00
Untrimmed version (only one known copy); estimated value-$600
NOTE: *In 1979 nine copies of the color version surfaced from the old Guild's files plus the five black & white copies.*

BLUE BIRD CHILDREN'S MAGAZINE, THE
Graphic Information Service: V1#2, 1957 - No. 10 1958 (16 pgs., soft-c, regular size)
V1#2-10: Pat, Pete & Blue Bird app. 4.00

BLUE BIRD COMICS
Various Shoe Stores/Charlton Comics: Late 1940's - 1964 (Giveaway)
nn(1947-50)(36 pgs.)-Several issues; Human Torch, Sub-Mariner app. in some 20.00 60.00 125.00
1959-Li'l Genius, Timmy the Timid Ghost, Wild Bill Hickok (All #1) 2.00 6.00 20.00
1959-(6 titles; all #2) Black Fury #1,4,5, Freddy #4, Li'l Genius, Timmy the Timid Ghost #4, Masked Raider #4, Wild Bill Hickok (Charlton) 2.00 6.00 20.00
1959-(#5) Masked Raider #21 2.00 6.00 20.00
1960-(6 titles)(All #4) Black Fury #8,9, Masked Raider, Freddy #8,9, Timmy the Timid Ghost #9, Li'l Genius #7,9 (Charlt.) 2.00 6.00 15.00
1961,1962-(All #10's) Atomic Mouse #12,13,16, Black Fury #11,12, Freddy, Li'l Genius, Masked Raider, Six Gun Heroes, Texas Rangers in Action, Timmy the Ghost, Wild Bill Hickok, Wyatt Earp #3,11-13,16-18 (Charlton) 2.00 6.00 15.00
1963-Texas Rangers #17 (Charlton) 1.00 2.80 7.00
1964-Mysteries of Unexplored Worlds #18, Teenage Hotrodders #18, War Heroes #18 (Charlton) 1.10 3.30 9.00
1965-War Heroes #18 5.00
NOTE: *More than one issue of each character could have been published each year. Numbering is sporadic.*

BOB & BETTY & SANTA'S WISHING WHISTLE
Sears Roebuck & Co.: 1941 (Christmas giveaway, 12 pgs.)
nn 11.00 33.00 75.00

BOBBY BENSON'S B-BAR-B RIDERS (Radio)
Magazine Enterprises/AC Comics
...in the Tunnel of Gold-(1936, 5-1/4x8"; 100 pgs.) Radio giveaway by Hecker-H.O. Company(H.O. Oats); contains 22 color pgs. of comics, rest in novel form 10.00 30.00 60.00
...And The Lost Herd-same as above 10.00 30.00 60.00

BOBBY SHELBY COMICS

GD2.0 FN6.0 NM9.4

Shelby Cycle Co./Harvey Publications: 1949
nn 4.00 10.00 20.00

BOYS' RANCH
Harvey Publications: 1951
Shoe Store Giveaway #5,6 (Identical to regular issues except Simon & Kirby centerfold replaced with ad) 25.00 75.00 150.00

BOZO THE CLOWN (TV)
Dell Publishing Co.: 1961
Giveaway-1961, 16 pgs., 3-1/2x7-1/4", Apsco Products 4.00 12.00 40.00

BRER RABBIT IN "ICE CREAM FOR THE PARTY"
American Dairy Association: 1955 (5x7-1/4", 16 pgs., soft-c) (Walt Disney) (Premium)
nn-(Scarce) 50.00 150.00 325.00

BUCK ROGERS (In the 25th Century)
Kelloggs Corn Flakes Giveaway: 1933 (6x8", 36 pgs)
370A-By Phil Nowlan & Dick Calkins; 1st Buck Rogers radio premium & 1st app. in comics (tells origin) (Reissued in 1995) 100.00 350.00 500.00
with envelope 175.00 450.00 600.00

BUGS BUNNY (Puffed Rice Giveaway)
Quaker Cereals: 1949 (32 pgs. each, 3-1/8x6-7/8")
A1-Traps the Counterfeiters, A2-Aboard Mystery Submarine, A3- Rocket to the Moon, A4-Lion Tamer, A5-Rescues the Beautiful Princess, B1-Buried Treasure, B2-Outwits the Smugglers, B3-Joins the Marines, B4-Meets the Dwarf Ghost, B5-Finds Aladdin's Lamp, C1-Lost in the Frozen North, C2-Secret Agent, C3-Captured by Cannibals, C4-Fights the Man from Mars, C5-And the Haunted Cave
each.... 8.35 25.00 50.00

BUGS BUNNY (3-D)
Cheerios Giveaway: 1953 (Pocket size) (15 titles)
each.... 10.00 30.00 60.00

BULLETMAN
Fawcett Publications
Well Known Comics (1942)-Paper-c, glued binding; printed in red (Bestmaid/Samuel Lowe giveaway) 20.00 65.00 125.00

BULLS-EYE (Cody of The Pony Express No. 8 on)
Charlton: 1955
Great Scott Shoe Store giveaway-Reprints #2 with new cover 20.00 75.00 150.00

BUSTER BROWN
Various Publishers: 1904 - 1912 (3x5" to 5x7"; sizes vary)(Advertising premium booklets)

GD2.0 FN6.0 VF8.0

The Brown Shoe Company, St. Louis, USA
Set of five books (5x7", 16 pgs., color)
Brown's Blue Ribbon Book of Jokes and Jingles Book 1 (nn, 1904)-By R. F. Outcault; Buster Brown & Tige, Little Tommy Tucker, Jack & Jill, Little Boy Blue, Dainty Jane; The Yellow Kid app. on back-c (1st comic book premium) 514.00 2056.00 3600.00
Buster Brown's Blue Ribbon Book of Jokes and Jingles Book 2 (1905)-Original color art by Outcault 229.00 916.00 1600.00
Buster's Book of Jokes & Jingles Book 3 (1909)-r/Blue Ribbon post cards not signed by R.F. Outcault 229.00 916.00 1600.00
Buster's Book of Instructive Jokes and Jingles Book 4 (1910)-Original color art not signed by R.F. Outcault 229.00 916.00 1600.00
...Book of Travels nn (1912, 3x5")-Original color art not signed by Outcault 100.00 400.00 700.00
NOTE: *Estimated 5 to 6 known copies exist of books #1-4.*

The Buster Brown Bread Company
"Buster Brown" Bread Book of Rhymes, The nn (1904, 4x6", 12 pgs.)-Original color art not signed by R.F. Outcault 136.00 544.00 950.00

The Buster Brown Stocking Company

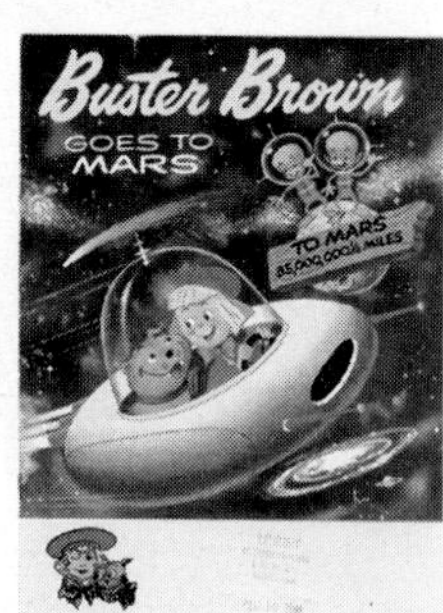

Buster Brown Comics -Goes to Mars © Brown Shoe Co.

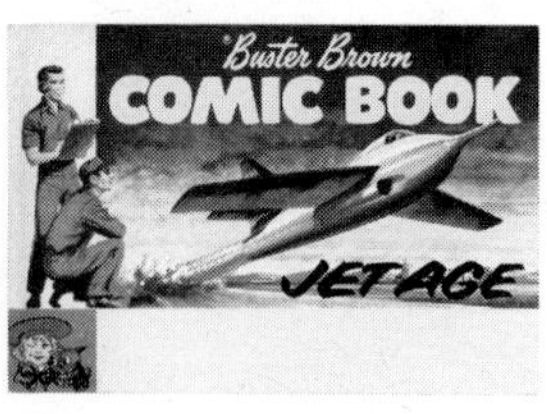

Buster Brown Comics -In the Jet Age © Brown Shoe Co.

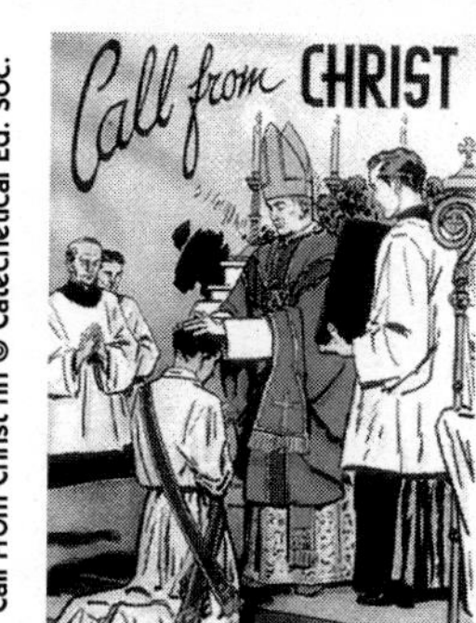

Call From Christ nn © Catechetical Ed. Soc.

	GD2.0	FN6.0	NM9.4
Buster Brown Drawing Book, The nn (nd, 5x6", 20 pgs.)-B&W reproductions of 1903 R.F. Outcault art to trace	100.00	300.00	500.00
Collins Baking Company			
Buster Brown Drawing Book nn (1904, 3x5", 12 pgs.)-Original B&W art to trace not signed by R.F. Outcault	100.00	300.00	500.00
C. H. Morton, St. Albans, VT			
Merry Antics of Buster Brown, Buddy Tucker & Tige nn (nd, 3-1/2x5-1/2", 16 pgs.)-Original B&W art by R.F. Outcault	68.00	272.00	475.00
Frederick A. Stokes Co.			
...Abroad (1904, 8x10-1/4, 86 pgs., B&W, hard-c)-R. F. Outcault-a (Rare)	143.00	572.00	1000.00
...Abroad (1904, B&W, 67 pgs.)-R. F. Outcault-a	143.00	572.00	1000.00
...My Resolutions (1906, 10x8", B&W, 68 pgs.)-R.F. Outcault-a (Rare)	200.00	800.00	1350.00
Ivan Frank & Company			
Buster Brown nn (1904, 3x5", 12 pgs.)-B&W repros of R. F. Outcault Sunday pages (First premium to actually reproduce Sunday comic pages – may be first premium comic book?)	100.00	350.00	750.00
Pond's Extract			
Buster Brown's Experiences With Pond's Extract nn (1904, 4-1/2x6-3/4", 28 pgs.)-Original color art by R.F. Outcault (may be the first premium comic book with original art)	150.00	750.00	1200.00
Ringen Stove Company			
Quick Meal Steel Ranges nn (nd, 3x5", 16 pgs.)-Original B&W art not signed by R.F. Outcault	61.00	244.00	425.00
Saalfield Company Muslin Books			
(1)...Goes Fishing (1907, 6-7/8x6-1/8", 24 pgs., color)-r/1905 Sunday comics page by Outcault(Rare)	60.00	150.00	250.00
(2)...Plays Indian (1907, 6-7/8x6-1/8", 24 pgs., color)-r/1905 Sunday comics page by Outcault(Rare)	50.00	140.00	200.00
(3)...Plays Cowboy (1907, 6-3/4x6", 10 pgs., color)-r/1905 Sunday comics page by Outcault(Rare)	50.00	140.00	200.00
(4)...And The Donkey (1907, 6-7/8x6-1/8", 24 pgs., color)-r/1905 Sunday comics page by Outcault (Rare)	50.00	140.00	200.00
No Publisher Listed			
The Drawing Book nn (1906, 3-9/16x5", 8 pgs.)-Original B&W art to trace not signed by R.F. Outcault	75.00	300.00	475.00

BUSTER BROWN COMICS (Radio)(Also see My Dog Tige in Promotional sec.)
Brown Shoe Co: 1945 - No. 43, 1959 (No. 5: paper-c)

	GD2.0	FN6.0	NM9.4
nn, nd (#1,scarce)-Featuring Smilin' Ed McConnell & the Buster Brown gang "Midnight" the cat, "Squeaky" the mouse & "Froggy" the Gremlin; covers mention diff. shoe stores. Contains adventure stories	62.00	187.00	500.00
2	19.00	58.00	135.00
3,5-10	10.00	30.00	70.00
4 (Rare)-Low print run due to paper shortage	16.00	47.00	110.00
11-20	7.50	22.50	45.00
21-24,26-28	5.35	16.00	32.00
25,33-37,40,41-Crandall-a in all	10.00	30.00	65.00
29-32-"Interplanetary Police Vs. the Space Siren" by Crandall (pencils only #29)	10.00	30.00	65.00
38,39,42,43	5.35	16.00	32.00

BUSTER BROWN COMICS (Radio)
Brown Shoe Co: 1950s

	GD2.0	FN6.0	NM9.4
...Goes to Mars (2/58-Western Printing), slick-c, 20 pgs., reg. size	11.00	33.00	75.00
...In "Buster Makes the Team!" (1959-Custom Comics)	7.50	22.50	45.00
...In The Jet Age ('50s), slick-c, 20 pgs., 5x7-1/4"	10.00	30.00	70.00
...Of the Safety Patrol ('60-Custom Comics)	4.25	13.00	28.00
...Out of This World ('59-Custom Comics)	7.35	22.00	44.00
...Safety Coloring Book ('58, 16 pgs.)-Slick paper	6.70	20.00	40.00

CALL FROM CHRIST
Catechetical Educational Society: 1952 (Giveaway, 36 pgs.)

	GD2.0	FN6.0	NM9.4
nn	3.00	7.50	15.00

CANCELLED COMIC CAVALCADE
DC Comics, Inc.: Summer, 1978 - No. 2, Fall, 1978 (8-1/2x11", B&W)
(Xeroxed pgs. on one side only w/blue cover and taped spine)

1-(412 pgs.) Contains xeroxed copies of art for: Black Lightning #12, cover to #13; Claw #13, 14; The Deserter #1; Doorway to Nightmare #6; Firestorm #6; The Green Team #2,3.
2-(532 pgs.) Contains xeroxed copies of art for: Kamandi #60 (including Omac), #61; Prez #5; Shade #9 (including The Odd Man); Showcase #105 (Deadman), 106 (The Creeper); The Vixen #1; and covers to Army at War #2, Battle Classics #3, Demand Classics #1 & 2, Dynamic Classics #3, Mr. Miracle #26, Ragman #6, Weird Mystery #25 & 26, & Western Classics #1 & 2. (Rare) (One set sold in 1989 for $1,200.00)

NOTE: *In June, 1978, DC cancelled several of their titles. For copyright purposes, the unpublished original art for these titles was xeroxed, bound in the above books, published and distributed. Only 35 copies were made.*

CAP'N CRUNCH COMICS (See Quaker Oats)
Quaker Oats Co.: 1963; 1965 (16 pgs.; miniature giveaways; 2-1/2x6-1/2")

	GD2.0	FN6.0	NM9.4
(1963 titles)- "The Picture Pirates", "The Fountain of Youth", "I'm Dreaming of a Wide Isthmus". (1965 titles)- "Bewitched, Betwitched, & Betweaked", "Seadog Meets the Witch Doctor", "A Witch in Time"	8.00	20.00	50.00

CAPTAIN ACTION (Toy)
National Periodical Publications

	GD2.0	FN6.0	NM9.4
...& Action Boy('67)-Ideal Toy Co. giveaway (1st app. Captain Action)	20.00	60.00	125.00

CAPTAIN AMERICA
Marvel Comics Group

	GD2.0	FN6.0	NM9.4
...& The Campbell Kids (1980, 36pg. giveaway, Campbell's Soup/U.S. Dept. of Energy)	1.00	3.00	8.00
...Goes To War Against Drugs(1990, no #, giveaway)-Distributed to direct sales shops; 2nd printing exists			4.00
...Meets The Asthma Monster (1987, no #, giveaway, Your Physician and Glaxo, Inc.)		2.40	6.00
...Vs. Asthma Monster (1990, no #, giveaway, Your Physician & Allen & Hanbury's)			4.00

CAPTAIN AMERICA COMICS
Timely/Marvel Comics: 1954

	GD2.0	FN6.0	NM9.4
Shoestore Giveaway #77	56.00	170.00	450.00

CAPTAIN ATOM
Nationwide Publishers

	GD2.0	FN6.0	NM9.4
...- Secret of the Columbian Jungle (16 pgs. in color, paper-c, 3-3/4x5-1/8")-Fireside Marshmallow giveaway	4.15	12.50	25.00

CAPTAIN FORTUNE PRESENTS
Vital Publications: 1955 - 1959 (Giveaway, 3-1/4x6-7/8", 16 pgs.)

	GD2.0	FN6.0	NM9.4
"Davy Crockett in Episodes of the Creek War", "Davy Crockett at the Alamo", "In Sherwood Forest Tells Strange Tales of Robin Hood" ('57), "Meets Bolivar the Liberator" ('59), "Tells How Buffalo Bill Fights the Dog Soldiers" ('57), "Young Davy Crockett"	2.00	5.00	10.00

CAPTAIN GALLANT (...of the Foreign Legion) (TV)
Charlton Comics

	GD2.0	FN6.0	NM9.4
Heinz Foods Premium (#1?)(1955; regular size)-U.S. Pictorial; contains Buster Crabbe photos; Don Heck-a		2.40	6.00

CAPTAIN MARVEL ADVENTURES
Fawcett Publications

	GD2.0	FN6.0	NM9.4
Bond Bread Giveaways-(24 pgs.; pocket size-7-1/4x3-1/2"; paper cover): "...& the Stolen City" ('48), "The Boy Who Never Heard of Capt. Marvel", "Meets the Weatherman" -(1950)(reprint) each....	35.00	100.00	200.00

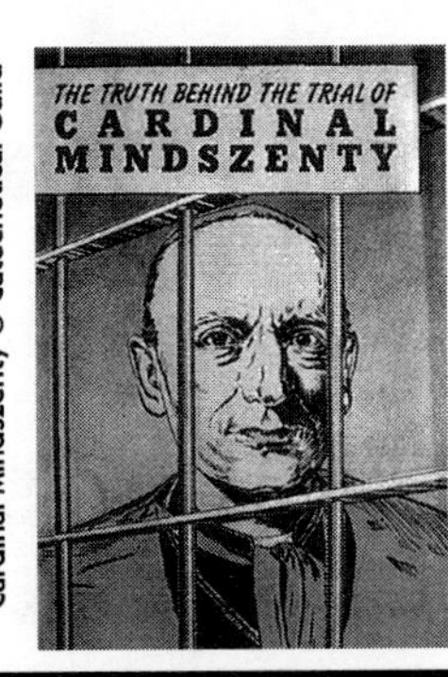

Cardinal Mindszenty © Catechetical Guild

Cheerios Premiums © WDC

Cheerios Premiums © WDC

GD2.0 FN6.0 NM9.4

...Well Known Comics (1944; 12 pgs.; 8-1/2x10-1/2")-printed in red & in blue; soft-c; glued binding)-Bestmaid/Samuel Lowe Co. giveaway 20.00 75.00 150.00

CAPTAIN MARVEL ADVENTURES
Fawcett Publications (Wheaties Giveaway): 1945 (6x8", full color, paper-c)

nn- "Captain Marvel & the Threads of Life" plus 2 other stories (32 pgs.) 75.00 250.00 500.00

NOTE: *All copies were taped at each corner to a box of Wheaties and are never found in Fine or Mint condition. Prices listed for each grade include tape.*

CAPTAIN MARVEL AND THE LTS. OF SAFETY
Ebasco Services/Fawcett Publications: 1950 - 1951 (3 issues - no No.'s)

	GD2.0	FN6.0	VF8.0
nn (#1) "Danger Flies a Kite" ('50, scarce),	200.00	600.00	1200.00
nn (#2)"Danger Takes to Climbing" ('50),	175.00	500.00	1000.00
nn (#3)"Danger Smashes Street Lights" ('51)	175.00	500.00	1000.00

CAPTAIN MARVEL, JR.
Fawcett Publications: (1944; 12 pgs.; 8-1/2x10-1/2")

GD2.0 FN6.0 NM9.4

...Well Known Comics (Printed in blue; paper-c, glued binding)-Bestmaid/Samuel Lowe Co. giveaway 11.00 32.00 80.00

CARDINAL MINDSZENTY (The Truth Behind the Trial of...)
Catechetical Guild Education Society: 1949 (24 pgs., paper cover)

nn-Anti-communism 6.70 20.00 40.00
Press Proof-(Very Rare)-(Full color, 7-1/2x11-3/4", untrimmed)
Only two known copies 150.00
Preview Copy (B&W, stapled), 18 pgs.; contains first 13 pgs. of Cardinal Mindszenty and was sent out as an advance promotion.
Only one known copy 150.00 - 200.00

NOTE: *Regular edition also printed in French. There was also a movie released in 1949 called "Guilty of Treason" which is a fact-based account of the trial and imprisonment of Cardinal Mindszenty by the Communist regime in Hungary.*

CARNIVAL OF COMICS
Fleet-Air Shoes: 1954 (Giveaway)

nn-Contains a comic bound with new cover; several combinations possible; Charlton's Eh! known 3.00 7.50 15.00

CARVEL COMICS (Amazing Advs. of Capt. Carvel)
Carvel Corp. (Ice Cream): 1975 - No. 5, 1976 (25¢; #3-5: 35¢) (#4,5: 3-1/4x5")

1-3 3.00
4,5(1976)-Baseball theme 1.00 2.80 7.00

CASE OF THE WASTED WATER, THE
Rheem Water Heating: 1972? (Giveaway)

nn-Neal Adams-a 3.20 9.50 35.00

CASPER SPECIAL
Target Stores (Harvey): nd (Dec, 1990) (Giveaway with $1.00 cover)

Three issues-Given away with Casper video 4.00

CASPER, THE FRIENDLY GHOST (Paramount Picture Star...)(2nd Series)
Harvey Publications

American Dental Association (Giveaways):
...'s Dental Health Activity Book-1977 2.00 7.00
...Presents Space Age Dentistry-1972 .90 2.70 9.00
..., His Den, & Their Dentist Fight the Tooth Demons-1974 .90 2.70 9.00

CENTURY OF COMICS
Eastern Color Printing Co.: 1933 (100 pgs.) (Probably the 3rd comic book)

Bought by Wheatena, Milk-O-Malt, John Wanamaker, Kinney Shoe Stores, & others to be used as premiums and radio giveaways. No publisher listed.

	GD2.0	FN6.0	VF8.2
nn-Mutt & Jeff, Joe Palooka, etc. reprints	3500.00	11,000.00	20,000.00

CHEERIOS PREMIUMS (Disney)
Walt Disney Productions: 1947 (16 titles, pocket size, 32 pgs.)

	GD2.0	FN6.0	NM9.4
Set "W"			
W1-Donald Duck & the Pirates	10.00	30.00	60.00
W2-Bucky Bug & the Cannibal King	4.00	12.00	24.00
W3-Pluto Joins the F.B.I.	4.00	12.00	24.00
W4-Mickey Mouse & the Haunted House	5.35	16.00	32.00
Set "X"			
X1-Donald Duck, Counter Spy	10.00	30.00	60.00
X2-Goofy Lost in the Desert	4.00	11.00	22.00
X3-Br'er Rabbit Outwits Br'er Fox	4.00	11.00	22.00
X4-Mickey Mouse at the Rodeo	5.35	16.00	32.00
Set "Y"			
Y1-Donald Duck's Atom Bomb by Carl Barks. Disney has banned reprinting this book	90.00	270.00	725.00
Y2-Br'er Rabbit's Secret	4.00	11.00	22.00
Y3-Dumbo & the Circus Mystery	5.00	15.00	30.00
Y4-Mickey Mouse Meets the Wizard	5.35	16.00	32.00
Set "Z"			
Z1-Donald Duck Pilots a Jet Plane (not by Barks)	10.00	30.00	60.00
Z2-Pluto Turns Sleuth Hound	4.00	11.00	22.00
Z3-The Seven Dwarfs & the Enchanted Mtn.	5.35	16.00	32.00
Z4-Mickey Mouse's Secret Room	5.35	16.00	32.00

CHEERIOS 3-D GIVEAWAYS (Disney)
Walt Disney Productions: 1954 (24 titles, pocket size) (Glasses were cut-outs on boxes)

Glasses only... 5.70 17.00 40.00
(Set 1) 1-Donald Duck & Uncle Scrooge, the Firefighters
2-Mickey Mouse & Goofy, Pirate Plunder
3-Donald Duck's Nephews, the Fabulous Inventors
4-Mickey Mouse, Secret of the Ming Vase
5-Donald Duck with Huey, Dewey, & Louie; ...the Seafarers (title on 2nd page)
6-Mickey Mouse, Moaning Mountain
7-Donald Duck, Apache Gold
8-Mickey Mouse, Flight to Nowhere (per book) 7.85 23.50 55.00
(Set 2) 1-Donald Duck, Treasure of Timbuktu
2-Mickey Mouse & Pluto, Operation China
3-Donald Duck in the Magic Cows
4-Mickey Mouse & Goofy, Kid Kokonut
5-Donald Duck, Mystery Ship
6-Mickey Mouse, Phantom Sheriff
7-Donald Duck, Circus Adventures
8-Mickey Mouse, Arctic Explorers (per book) 7.85 23.50 55.00
(Set 3) 1-Donald Duck & Witch Hazel
2-Mickey Mouse in Darkest Africa
3-Donald Duck & Uncle Scrooge, Timber Trouble
4-Mickey Mouse, Rajah's Rescue
5-Donald Duck in Robot Reporter
6-Mickey Mouse, Slumbering Sleuth
7-Donald Duck in the Foreign Legion
8-Mickey Mouse, Airwalking Wonder (per book).... 7.85 23.50 55.00

CHESTY AND COPTIE (Disney)
Los Angeles Community Chest: 1946 (Giveaway, 4pgs.)

nn-(One known copy) by Floyd Gottfredson 91.00 274.00 775.00

CHESTY AND HIS HELPERS (Disney)
Los Angeles War Chest: 1943 (Giveaway, 12 pgs., 5-1/2x7-1/4")

nn-Chesty & Coptie 62.00 185.00 525.00

CHRISTMAS ADVENTURE, THE
S. Rose (H. L. Green Giveaway): 1963 (16 pgs.)

nn 1.10 3.30 9.00

CHRISTMAS AT THE ROTUNDA (Titled Ford Rotunda Christmas Book 1957 on) (Regular size)
Ford Motor Co. (Western Printing): 1954 - 1961 (Given away every Christmas at one location)

Christmas is Coming

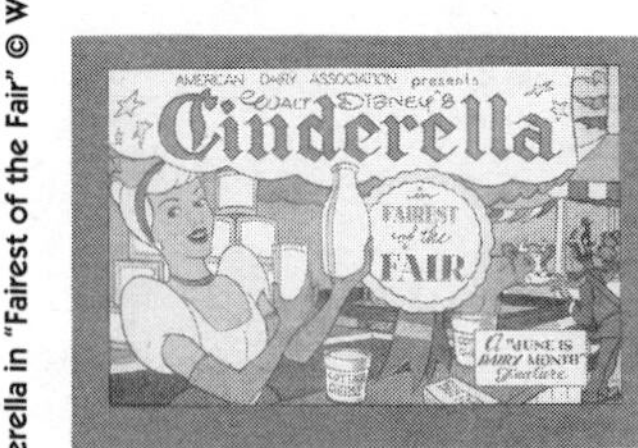

Cinderella in "Fairest of the Fair" © WDC

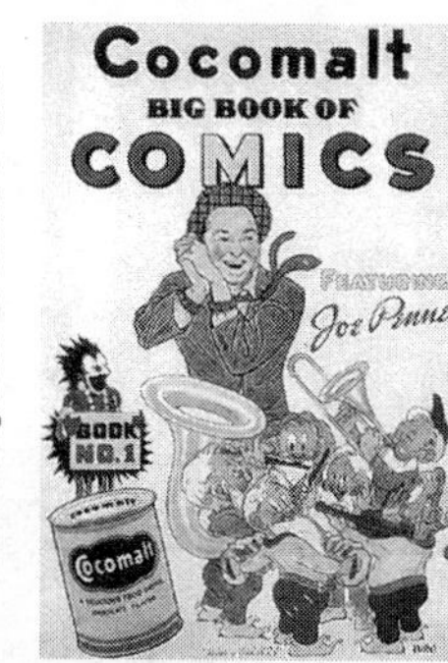

Cocomalt Big Book of Comics © CHES

	GD2.0	FN6.0	NM9.4
1954-56 issues (nn's)	5.00	15.00	30.00
1957-61 issues (nn's)	4.00	12.00	24.00

CHRISTMAS CAROL, A
Sears Roebuck & Co.: No date (1942-43) (Giveaway, 32 pgs., 8-1/4x10-3/4", paper cover)

nn-Comics & coloring book 18.00 54.00 125.00

CHRISTMAS CAROL, A
Sears Roebuck & Co.: 1940s ? (Christmas giveaway, 20 pgs.)

nn-Comic book & animated coloring book 16.00 47.00 110.00

CHRISTMAS CAROLS
Hot Shoppes Giveaway: 1959? (16 pgs.)

nn 3.60 9.00 18.00

CHRISTMAS COLORING FUN
H. Burnside: 1964 (20 pgs., slick-c, B&W)

nn 1.50 4.50 12.00

CHRISTMAS DREAM, A
Promotional Publishing Co.: 1950 (Kinney Shoe Store Giveaway, 16 pgs.)

nn 4.00 11.00 22.00

CHRISTMAS DREAM, A
J. J. Newberry Co.: 1952? (Giveaway, paper cover, 16 pgs.)

nn 4.00 10.00 20.00

CHRISTMAS DREAM, A
Promotional Publ. Co.: 1952 (Giveaway, 16 pgs., paper cover)

nn 4.00 10.00 20.00

CHRISTMAS FUN AROUND THE WORLD
No publisher: No date (early 50's) (16 pgs., paper cover)

nn 4.00 11.00 22.00

CHRISTMAS IS COMING!
No publisher: No date (early 50's?) (Store giveaway, 16 pgs.)

nn 4.00 10.00 18.00

CHRISTMAS JOURNEY THROUGH SPACE
Promotional Publishing Co.: 1960

nn-Reprints 1954 issue Jolly Christmas Book with new slick cover
2.50 7.50 25.00

CHRISTMAS ON THE MOON
W. T. Grant Co.: 1958 (Giveaway, 20 pgs., slick cover)

nn 8.35 25.00 50.00

CHRISTMAS PLAY BOOK
Gould-Stoner Co.: 1946 (Giveaway, 16 pgs., paper cover)

nn 8.35 25.00 50.00

CHRISTMAS ROUNDUP
Promotional Publishing Co.: 1960

nn-Marv Levy-c/a 1.25 3.75 10.00

CHRISTMAS STORY CUT-OUT BOOK, THE
Catechetical Guild: No. 393, 1951 (15¢, 36 pgs.)

393-Half text & half comics 5.35 16.00 32.00

CHRISTMAS USA (Through 300 Years) (Also see Uncle Sam's...)
Promotional Publ. Co.: 1956 (Giveaway)

nn-Marv Levy-c/a 2.00 5.00 10.00

CHRISTMAS WITH SNOW WHITE AND THE SEVEN DWARFS
Kobackers Giftstore of Buffalo, N.Y.: 1953 (16 pgs., paper-c)

nn 5.85 17.50 35.00

CHRISTOPHERS, THE
Catechetical Guild: 1951 (Giveaway, 36 pgs.) (Some copies have 15¢ sticker)

nn-Stalin as Satan in Hell 25.00 75.00 175.00

GD2.0 FN6.0 NM9.4

CINDERELLA IN "FAIREST OF THE FAIR"
American Dairy Association (Premium): 1955 (5x7-1/4", 16 pgs., soft-c) (Walt Disney)

nn 10.00 30.00 70.00

CINEMA COMICS HERALD
Paramount Pictures/Universal/RKO/20th Century Fox/Republic:
1941 - 1943 (4-pg. movie "trailers", paper-c, 7-1/2x10-1/2")(Giveaway)

	GD2.0	FN6.0	NM9.4
"Mr. Bug Goes to Town" (1941)	10.00	30.00	60.00
"Bedtime Story"	5.85	17.50	35.00
"Lady For A Night", John Wayne, Joan Blondell ('42)	12.00	36.00	85.00
"Reap The Wild Wind" (1942)	8.70	26.00	52.00
"Thunder Birds" (1942)	8.00	24.00	48.00
"They All Kissed the Bride"	8.00	24.00	48.00
"Arabian Nights" (nd)	8.00	24.00	48.00
"Bombardie" (1943)	8.00	24.00	48.00
"Crash Dive" (1943)-Tyrone Power	8.00	24.00	48.00

NOTE: *The 1941-42 issues contain line art with color photos. 1943 issues are line art.*

CLASSICS GIVEAWAYS (Classic Comics reprints)

12/41–Walter Theatre Enterprises (Huntington, WV) giveaway containing #2 (orig.) w/new generic-c (only 1 known copy) 113.00 339.00 900.00

1942–Double Comics containing CC#1 (orig.) (diff. cover) (not actually a giveaway) (very rare) (also see Double Comics) (only one known copy)
218.00 654.00 1850.00

12/42–Saks 34th St. Giveaway containing CC#7 (orig.) (diff. cover) (very rare; only 6 known copies) 714.00 2142.00 5000.00

2/43–American Comics containing CC#8 (orig.) (Liberty Theatre giveaway) (different cover) (only one known copy) (see American Comics)
163.00 490.00 1300.00

12/44–Robin Hood Flour Co. Giveaway - #7-CC(R) (diff. cover) (rare) (edition probably 5 [22]) 300.00 900.00 2400.00

NOTE: How are above editions determined without CC covers? 1942 is dated 1942, and CC#1-first reprint did not come out until 5/43. 12/42 and 2/43 are determined by blue note at bottom of first text page only in original edition. 12/44 is estimated from page width each reprint edition had progressively slightly smaller page width.

1951–Shelter Thru the Ages (C.I. Educational Series) (actually Giveaway by the Ruberoid Co.) (16 pgs.) (contains original artwork by H. C. Kiefer) (there are 5 diff. back cover ad variations: "Ranch" house ad, "Igloo" ad, "Doll House" ad, "Tree House" ad & blank)(scarce) 88.00 264.00 700.00

1952–George Daynor Biography Giveaway (CC logo) (partly comic book/pictures/newspaper articles) (story of man who built Palace Depression out of junkyard swamp in NJ) (64 pgs.)(very rare; only 3 known copies, one missing-bc) 857.00 2571.00 6300.00

1953–Westinghouse/Dreams of a Man (C.I. Educational Series) (Westinghouse bio./Westinghouse Co. giveaway) (contains original artwork by H. C. Kiefer) (16 pgs.) (also French/Spanish/Italian versions)
(scarce) 84.00 252.00 675.00

NOTE: Reproductions of 1951, 1952, and 1953 exist with color photocopy covers and black & white photocopy interior ("W.C.N. Reprint") 2.00 5.00 10.00

1951-53–Coward Shoe Giveaways (all editions very rare); 2 variations of back-c ad exist:
With back-c photo ad: 5 (87), 12 (89), 22 (85), 32 (85),49 (85), 69 (87), 72 (no HRN), 80 (0), 91 (0), 92 (0), 96 (0), 98 (0), 100 (0), 101 (0), 103-105 (all Os) 42.00 126.00 340.00
With back-c cartoon ad: 106-109 (all 0s), 110 (111), 112 (0)
47.00 141.00 400.00

1956–Ben Franklin 5-10 Store Giveaway (#65-PC with back cover ad) (scarce) 39.00 117.00 290.00

1956–Ben Franklin Insurance Co. Giveaway (#65-PC with diff. back cover ad) (very rare) 71.00 213.00 600.00

11/56–Sealtest Co. Edition - #4 (135) (identical to regular edition except for Sealtest logo printed, not stamped, on front cover) (only two copies known to exist) 43.00 129.00 350.00

1958–Get-Well Giveaway containing #15-CI (new cartoon-type cover) (Pressman Pharmacy) (only one copy known to exist)
39.00 117.00 300.00

1967-68–Twin Circle Giveaway Editions - all HRN 166, with back cover ad

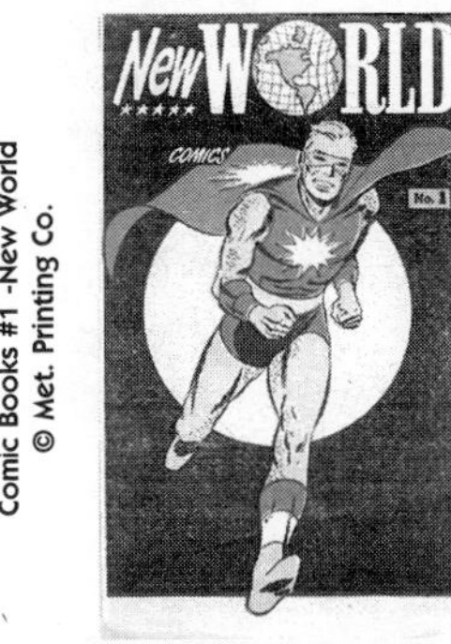

Comic Books #1 -New World © Met. Printing Co.

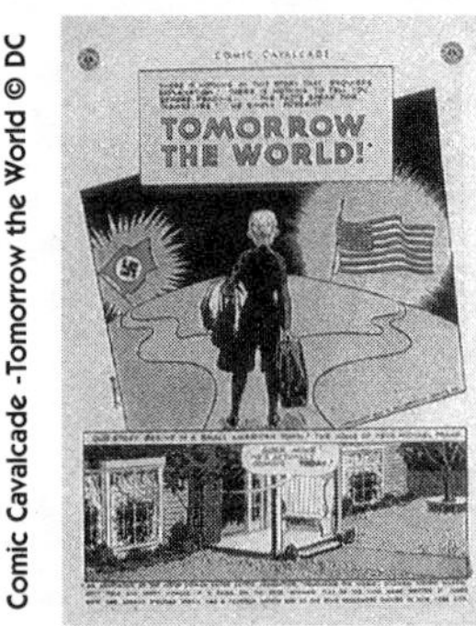

Comic Cavalcade -Tomorrow the World © DC

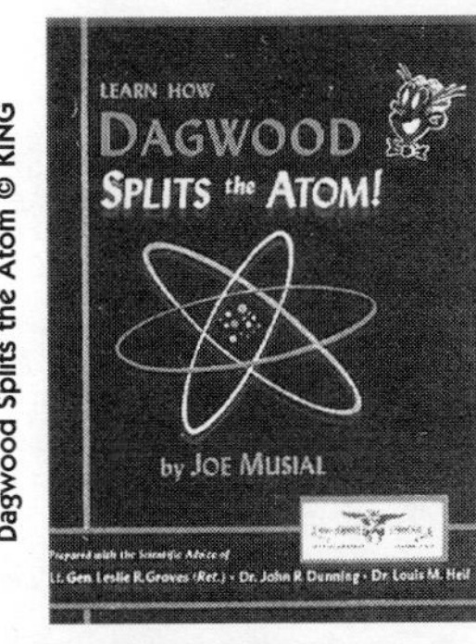

Dagwood Splits the Atom © KING

	GD2.0	FN6.0	NM9.4
for National Catholic Press.			
2(R68), 4(R67), 10(R68), 13(R68)	3.00	9.00	30.00
48(R67), 128(R68), 535(576-R68)	3.50	10.50	35.00
16(R68), 68(R67)	5.00	15.00	50.00
12/69–Christmas Giveaway ("A Christmas Adventure") (reprints Picture Parade #4-1953, new cover) (4 ad variations)			
Stacy's Dept. Store	2.50	7.50	25.00
Anne & Hope Store	5.50	16.50	55.00
Gibson's Dept. Store (rare)	5.50	16.50	55.00
"Merry Christmas" & blank ad space	2.50	7.50	25.00

CLIFF MERRITT SETS THE RECORD STRAIGHT
Brotherhood of Railroad Trainsmen: Giveaway (2 different issues)

...and the Very Candid Candidate by Al Williamson 3.00
...Sets the Record Straight by Al Williamson (2 different-c: one by Williamson, the other by McWilliams) 3.00

CLYDE BEATTY COMICS (Also see Crackajack Funnies)
Commodore Productions & Artists, Inc.

...African Jungle Book('56)-Richfield Oil Co. 16 pg. giveaway, soft-c 11.00 33.00 75.00

C-M-O COMICS
Chicago Mail Order Co.(Centaur): 1942 - No. 2, 1942 (68 pgs., full color)

1-Invisible Terror, Super Ann, & Plymo the Rubber Man app. (all Centaur costume heroes) 81.00 245.00 650.00
2-Invisible Terror, Super Ann app. 53.00 159.00 425.00

COCOMALT BIG BOOK OF COMICS
Harry 'A' Chesler (Cocomalt Premium): 1938 (Reg. size, full color, 52 pgs.)

1-(Scarce)-Biro-c/a; Little Nemo by Winsor McCay Jr., Dan Hastings; Jack Cole, Guardineer, Gustavson, Bob Wood-a 225.00 675.00 1800.00

COMIC BOOK (Also see Comics From Weatherbird)
American Juniors Shoe: 1954 (Giveaway)

Contains a comic rebound with new cover. Several combinations possible. Contents determines price.

COMIC BOOK MAGAZINE
Chicago Tribune & other newspapers: 1940 - 1943 (Similar to Spirit Sections) (7-3/4x10-3/4"; full color; 16-24 pgs. ea.)

1940 issues	8.35	25.00	50.00
1941, 1942 issues	5.85	17.50	35.00
1943 issues	5.35	16.00	32.00

NOTE: *Published weekly. Texas Slim, Kit Carson, Spooky, Josie, Nuts & Jolts, Lew Loyal, Brenda Starr, Daniel Boone, Captain Storm, Rocky, Smokey Stover, Tiny Tim, Little Joe, Fu Manchu appear among others. Early issues had photo stories with pictures from the movies; later issues had comic art.*

COMIC BOOKS (Series 1)
Metropolitan Printing Co. (Giveaway): 1950 (16 pgs.; 5-1/4x8-1/2"; full color; bound at top; paper cover)

1-Boots and Saddles; intro The Masked Marshal	5.00	15.00	30.00
1-The Green Jet; Green Lama by Raboy	29.00	86.00	200.00
1-My Pal Dizzy (Teen-age)	2.80	7.00	14.00
1-New World; origin Atomaster (costumed hero)	9.00	27.00	55.00
1-Talullah (Teen-age)	2.80	7.00	14.00

COMIC CAVALCADE
All-American/National Periodical Publications

Giveaway (1944, 8 pgs., paper-c, in color)-One Hundred Years of Co-operation-r/Comic Cavalcade #9 75.00 225.00 600.00
Giveaway (1945, 16 pgs., paper-c, in color)-Movie "Tomorrow The World" (Nazi theme); r/Comic Cavalcade #10 100.00 300.00 800.00
Giveaway (c. 1944-45; 8 pgs, paper-c, in color)-The Twain Shall Meet-r/Comic Cavalcade #8 75.00 225.00 600.00

COMIC SELECTIONS (Shoe store giveaway)
Parents' Magazine Press: 1944-46 (Reprints from Calling All Girls, True Comics, True Aviation, & Real Heroes)

1 4.15 12.50 25.00

	GD2.0	FN6.0	NM9.4
2-5	3.60	9.00	18.00

COMICS FROM WEATHER BIRD (Also see Comic Book, Edward's Shoes, Free Comics to You & Weather Bird)
Weather Bird Shoes: 1954 - 1957 (Giveaway)
Contains a comic bound with new cover. Many combinations possible. Contents would determine price. Some issues do not contain complete comics, but only parts of comics.Value equals 40 to 60 percent of contents.

COMICS READING LIBRARIES (Educational Series)
King Features (Charlton Publ.): 1973, 1977, 1979 (36 pgs. in color) (Giveaways)

R-01-Tiger, Quincy		2.00	6.00
R-02-Beetle Bailey, Blondie & Popeye	.90	2.70	9.00
R-03-Blondie, Beetle Bailey		2.00	6.00
R-04-Tim Tyler's Luck, Felix the Cat	1.60	4.80	16.00
R-05-Quincy, Henry		2.00	6.00
R-06-The Phantom, Mandrake	1.60	4.80	16.00
1977 reprint(R-04)	.90	2.70	9.00
R-07-Popeye, Little King	1.10	3.30	11.00
R-08-Prince Valiant(Foster), Flash Gordon	2.00	6.00	20.00
1977 reprint	1.30	3.90	13.00
R-09-Hagar the Horrible, Boner's Ark	.90	2.70	9.00
R-10-Redeye, Tiger		2.00	6.00
R-11-Blondie, Hi & Lois		2.00	6.00
R-12-Popeye-Swee'pea, Brutus	1.10	3.30	11.00
R-13-Beetle Bailey, Little King		2.00	6.00
R-14-Quincy-Hamlet		2.00	6.00
R-15-The Phantom, The Genius	1.10	3.30	11.00
R-16-Flash Gordon, Mandrake	2.00	6.00	20.00
1977 reprint	1.10	3.30	11.00
Other 1977 editions....			5.00
1979 editions(68pgs.)			5.00

NOTE: *Above giveaways available with purchase of $45.00 in merchandise. Used as a reading skills aid for small children.*

COMMANDMENTS OF GOD
Catechetical Guild: 1954, 1958

300-Same contents in both editions; diff-c 2.80 7.00 14.00

COMPLIMENTARY COMICS
Sales Promotion Publ.: No date (1950's) (Giveaway)

1-Strongman by Powell, 3 stories 6.70 20.00 40.00

CRACKAJACK FUNNIES (Giveaway)
Malto-Meal: 1937 (Full size, soft-c, full color, 32 pgs.)(Before No. 1?)

nn-Features Dan Dunn, G-Man, Speed Bolton, Buck Jones, The Nebbs, Clyde Beatty, Freckles, Major Hoople, Wash Tubbs 100.00 300.00 800.00

CROSLEY'S HOUSE OF FUN (Also see Tee and Vee Crosley...)
Crosley Div. AVCO Mfg. Corp.: 1950 (Giveaway, paper cover, 32 pgs.)

nn-Strips revolve around Crosley appliances 4.25 13.00 26.00

DAGWOOD SPLITS THE ATOM (Also see Topix V8#4)
King Features Syndicate: 1949 (Science comic with King Features characters) (Giveaway)

nn-Half comic, half text; Popeye, Olive Oyl, Henry, Mandrake, Little King, Katzenjammer Kids app. 7.50 22.50 45.00

DAISY LOW OF THE GIRL SCOUTS
Girl Scouts of America: 1954, 1965 (16 pgs., paper-c)

1954-Story of Juliette Gordon Low	4.00	10.00	20.00
1965	1.00	3.00	8.00

DAN CURTIS GIVEAWAYS
Western Publishing Co.:1974 (3x6", 24 pgs., reprints)

1-Dark Shadows	1.00	3.00	8.00
2,6-Star Trek	1.25	3.75	10.00

3-5,7-9: 3-The Twilight Zone. 4-Ripley's Believe It or Not! 5-Turok, Son of Stone (partial-r/Turok #78) 7-The Occult Files of Dr. Spektor. 8-Dagar the

Davy Crockett © WDC

Dick Tracy Sheds Light on the Mole © WEST

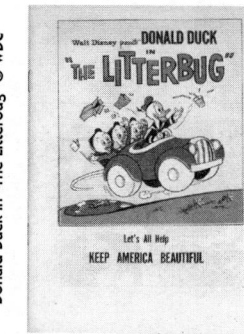

Donald Duck in "The Litterbug" © WDC

GD2.0 FN6.0 NM9.4

Invincible. 9-Grimm's Ghost Stories 5.00

DANNY KAYE'S BAND FUN BOOK
H & A Selmer: 1959 (Giveaway)

nn 5.85 17.50 35.00

DAREDEVIL
Marvel Comics Group: 1993

...Vs. Vapora 1 (Engineering Show Giveaway, 16 pg.)–Intro Vapora 3.00

DAVY CROCKETT (TV)
Dell Publishing Co./Gold Key

...Christmas Book (no date, 16 pgs., paper-c)-Sears giveaway 5.85 17.50 35.00
...Safety Trails (1955, 16pgs, 3-1/4x7")-Cities Service giveaway 7.50 22.50 45.00

DAVY CROCKETT
Charlton Comics

Hunting With... nn ('55, 16 pgs.)-Ben Franklin Store giveaway (Publ.-S. Rose) 5.00 15.00 30.00

DAVY CROCKETT
Walt Disney Prod.: (1955, 16 pgs., 5x7-1/4", slick, photo-c)
...In the Raid at Piney Creek-American Motors giveaway 7.50 22.50 45.00

DC SPOTLIGHT
DC Comics : 1985 (50th anniversary special) (giveaway)

1-Includes profiles on Batman:The Dark Knight & Watchmen 3.00

DENNIS THE MENACE
Hallden (Fawcett)

...& Dirt ('59,'68)-Soil Conservation giveaway; r-# 36; Wiseman-c/a 2.40 6.00
...Away We Go('70)-Caladayl giveaway 2.40 6.00
...Coping with Family Stress-giveaway 4.00
...Takes a Poke at Poison('61)-Food & Drug Admin. giveaway; Wiseman-c/a 2.40 6.00
...Takes a Poke at Poison-Revised 1/66, 11/70, 1972, 1974, 1977, 1981 4.00

DETECTIVE COMICS (Also see other Batman titles)
National Periodical Publications/DC Comics

27 (1984)-Oreo Cookies giveaway (32 pgs., paper-c) r-/Det. 27, 38 & Batman No. 1 (1st Joker) 5.00 15.00 30.00

DICK TRACY GIVEAWAYS
1939 - 1958; 1990

Buster Brown Shoes Giveaway (1940s?, 36 pgs. in color); 1938-39-r by Gould 36.00 107.00 250.00
Gillmore Giveaway (See Superbook)
...Hatful of Fun (No date, 1950-52, 32pgs.; 8-1/2x10")-Dick Tracy hat promotion; Dick Tracy games, magic tricks. Miller Bros. premium 18.00 54.00 125.00
Motorola Giveaway (1953)-Reprints Harvey Comics Library #2; "The Case of the Sparkle Plenty TV Mystery" 5.00 15.00 30.00
Original Dick Tracy by Chester Gould, The (Aug, 1990, 16 pgs., 5-1/2x8-1/2")-Gladstone Publ.; Bread Giveaway 2.50 7.50 25.00
Popped Wheat Giveaway (1947, 16 pgs. in color)-1940-r; Sig Feuchtwanger Publ.; Gould-a 2.40 6.00 12.00
...Presents the Family Fun Book; Tip Top Bread Giveaway, no date or number (1940, Fawcett Publ., 16 pgs. in color)-Spy Smasher, Ibis, Lance O'Casey app. 56.00 170.00 450.00
Same as above but without app. of heroes & Dick Tracy on cover only 14.00 43.00 100.00
Service Station Giveaway (1958, 16 pgs. in color)(regular size, slick cover)-Harvey Info. Press 3.60 9.00 18.00
Shoe Store Giveaway (Weatherbird)(1939, 16 pgs.)-Gould-a 13.50 41.00 95.00

DICK TRACY SHEDS LIGHT ON THE MOLE
Western Printing Co.: 1949 (16 pgs.) (Ray-O-Vac Flashlights giveaway)

nn-Not by Gould 6.70 20.00 40.00

DICK WINGATE OF THE U.S. NAVY
Superior Publ./Toby Press: 1951; 1953 (no month)

nn-U.S. Navy giveaway 4.00 10.00 20.00
1(1953, Toby)-Reprints nn issue? (same-c) 4.00 10.00 20.00

DIG 'EM
Kellogg's Sugar Smacks Giveaway: 1973 (2-3/8x6", 16 pgs.)

nn-4 different issues 5.00

DOC CARTER VD COMICS
Health Publications Institute, Raleigh, N. C. (Giveaway): 1949 (16 pgs. in color) (Paper-c)

nn 19.00 58.00 135.00

DONALD AND MICKEY MERRY CHRISTMAS (Formerly Famous Gang Book Of Comics)
K. K. Publ./Firestone Tire & Rubber Co.: 1943 - 1949 (Giveaway, 20 pgs.)
Put out each Christmas; 1943 issue titled "Firestone Presents Comics" (Disney)

1943-Donald Duck-r/WDC&S #32 by Carl Barks 68.00 205.00 750.00
1944-Donald Duck-r/WDC&S #35 by Barks 64.00 191.00 700.00
1945- "Donald Duck's Best Christmas", 8 pgs. Carl Barks; intro. & 1st app. Grandma Duck in comic books 91.00 273.00 1000.00
1946-Donald Duck in "Santa's Stormy Visit", 8 pgs. Carl Barks 65.00 198.00 725.00
1947-Donald Duck in "Three Good Little Ducks", 8 pgs. Carl Barks 65.00 198.00 725.00
1948-Donald Duck in "Toyland", 8 pgs. Carl Barks 65.00 198.00 725.00
1949-Donald Duck in "New Toys", 8 pgs. Barks 59.00 177.00 650.00

DONALD DUCK
K. K. Publications: 1944 (Christmas giveaway, paper-c, 16 pgs.)(2 versions)
nn-Kelly cover reprint 75.00 225.00 750.00

DONALD DUCK AND THE RED FEATHER
Red Feather Giveaway: 1948 (8-1/2x11", 4 pgs., B&W)

nn 15.00 45.00 150.00

DONALD DUCK IN "THE LITTERBUG"
Keep America Beautiful: 1963 (5x7-1/4", 16 pgs., soft-c) (Disney giveaway)

nn 3.20 9.60 32.00

DONALD DUCK "PLOTTING PICNICKERS" (See Frito-Lay Giveaway)

DONALD DUCK'S SURPRISE PARTY
Walt Disney Productions: 1948 (16 pgs.) (Giveaway for Icy Frost Twins Ice Cream Bars)

nn-(Rare)-Kelly-c/a 314.00 943.00 2200.00

DOT AND DASH AND THE LUCKY JINGLE PIGGIE
Sears Roebuck Co.: 1942 (Christmas giveaway, 12 pgs.)

nn-Contains a war stamp album and a punch out Jingle Piggie bank 10.00 30.00 60.00

DOUBLE TALK (Also see Two-Faces)
Feature Publications: No date (1962?) (32 pgs., full color, slick-c)
Christian Anti-Communism Crusade (Giveaway)

nn-Sickle with blood-c 8.00 24.00 80.00

DUMBO (Walt Disney's..., The Flying Elephant)
Weatherbird Shoes/Ernest Kern Co.(Detroit)/ Wieboldt's (Chicago): 1941 (K.K. Publ. Giveaway)

nn-16 pgs., 9x10" (Rare) 47.00 140.00 375.00
nn-52 pgs., 5-1/2x8-1/2", slick cover in color; B&W interior; half text, half reprints 4-Color No. 17 (Dept. store) 29.00 86.00 200.00

DUMBO WEEKLY
Walt Disney Prod.: 1942 (Premium supplied by Diamond D-X Gas Stations)

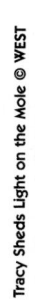

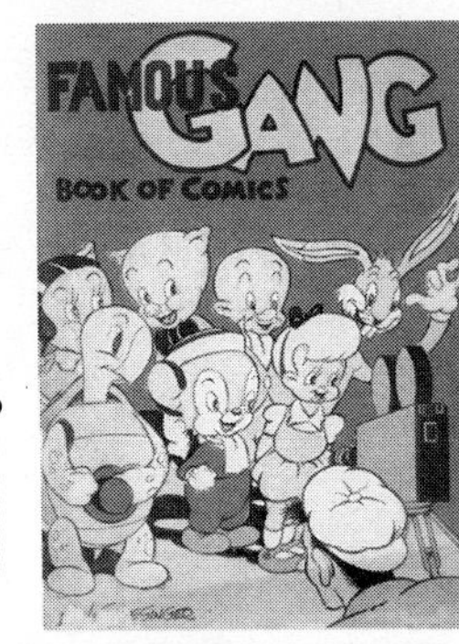

Famous Gang Book of Comics © WDC

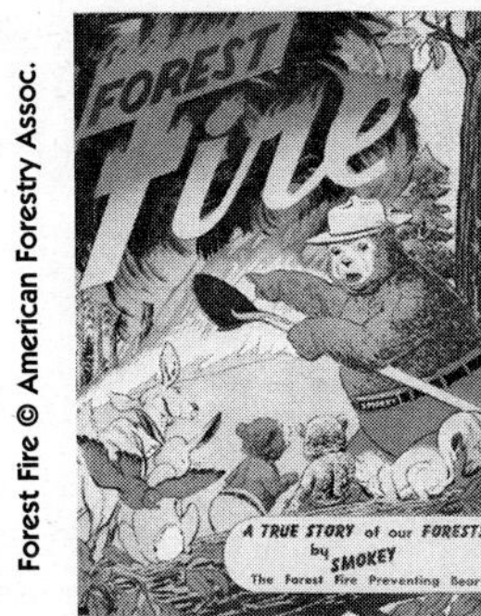

Forest Fire © American Forestry Assoc.

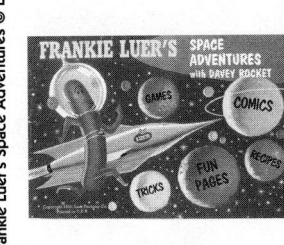

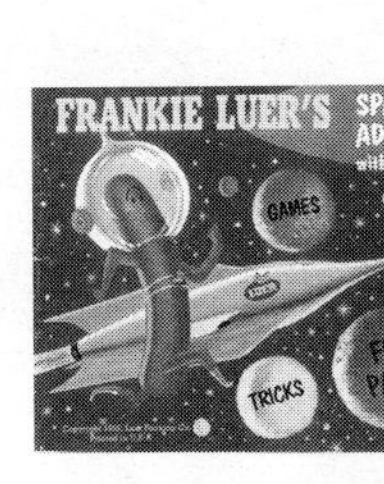

Frankie Luer's Space Adventures © Luer

GD2.0 FN6.0 NM9.4

1 75.00 225.00 600.00
2-16 18.00 54.00 150.00
Binder only 375.00
NOTE: *A cover and binder came separate at gas stations. Came with membership card.*

EAT RIGHT TO WORK AND WIN
Swift & Company: 1942 (16 pgs.) (Giveaway)

Blondie, Henry, Flash Gordon by Alex Raymond, Toots & Casper, Thimble Theatre(Popeye), Tillie the Toiler, The Phantom, The Little King, & Bringing up Father - original strips just for this book -(in daily strip form which shows what foods we should eat and why) 50.00 150.00 300.00

EDWARD'S SHOES GIVEAWAY
Edward's Shoe Store: 1954 (Has clown on cover)

Contains comic with new cover. Many combinations possible. Contents determines price, 50-60 percent of original. (Similar to Comics From Weatherbird & Free Comics to You)

ELSIE THE COW
D. S. Publishing Co.
Borden's cheese comic picture bk ("40, giveaway) 18.00 54.00 125.00
Borden Milk Giveaway-(16 pgs., nn) (3 ishs, 1957) 13.50 41.00 95.00
Elsie's Fun Book(1950; Borden Milk) 13.50 41.00 95.00
Everyday Birthday Fun With... (1957; 20 pgs.)(100th Anniversary); Kubert-a 13.50 41.00 95.00

ESCAPE FROM FEAR
Planned Parenthood of America: 1956, 1962, 1969 (Giveaway, 8 pgs. full color) (On birth control)
1956 edition 8.75 26.25 65.00
1962 edition 4.50 13.50 45.00
1969 edition 2.50 7.50 22.00

EVEL KNIEVEL
Marvel Comics Group (Ideal Toy Corp.): 1974 (Giveaway, 20 pgs.)
nn-Contains photo on inside back-c 2.50 7.50 22.00

FAMOUS COMICS (Also see Favorite Comics)
Zain-Eppy/United Features Syndicate: No date; Mid 1930's (24 pgs., paper-c)
nn-Reprinted from 1933 & 1934 newspaper strips in color; Joe Palooka, Hairbreadth Harry, Napoleon, The Nebbs, etc. (Many different versions known) 50.00 250.00 375.00

FAMOUS FAIRY TALES
K. K. Publ. Co.: 1942; 1943 (32 pgs.); 1944 (16 pgs.) (Giveaway, soft-c)
1942-Kelly-a 40.00 120.00 325.00
1943-r-/Fairy Tale Parade No. 2,3; Kelly-a 34.00 101.00 235.00
1944-Kelly-a 30.00 90.00 210.00

FAMOUS FUNNIES -A CARNIVAL OF COMICS
Eastern Color: 1933 **GD2.0 FN6.0 VF8.0 NM9.4**
(Probably the second comic book), 36 pgs., no date given, no publisher, no number; contains strip reprints of The Bungle Family, Dixie Dugan, Hairbreadth Harry, Joe Palooka, Keeping Up With the Jones, Mutt & Jeff, Reg'lar Fellers, S'Matter Pop, Strange As It Seems, and others. This book was sold by M. C. Gaines to Wheatena, Milk-O-Malt, John Wanamaker, Kinney Shoe Stores, & others to be given away as premiums and radio giveaways (1933).
895.00 2685.00 5370.00 8500.00

FAMOUS GANG BOOK OF COMICS (Becomes Donald & Mickey Merry Christmas 1943 on)
Firestone Tire & Rubber Co.: Dec, 1942 (Christmas giveaway, 32 pgs., paper-c)
GD2.0 FN6.0 NM9.4
nn-(Rare)-Porky Pig, Bugs Bunny, Mary Jane & Sniffles, Elmer Fudd; r/Looney Tunes 60.00 180.00 600.00

FATHER OF CHARITY
Catechetical Guild Giveaway: No date (32 pgs.; paper cover)
nn 2.40 6.00 12.00

FAVORITE COMICS (Also see Famous Comics)
Grocery Store Giveaway (Diff. Corp.) (detergent): 1934 (36 pgs.)
Book 1-The Nebbs, Strange As It Seems, Napoleon, Joe Palooka, Dixie Dugan, S'Matter Pop, Hairbreadth Harry, etc. reprints 75.00 225.00 600.00
Book 2,3 50.00 150.00 400.00

GD2.0 FN6.0 NM9.4

FAWCETT MINIATURES (See Mighty Midget)
Fawcett Publications: 1946 (3-3/4x5", 12-24 pgs.) (Wheaties giveaways)
Captain Marvel "And the Horn of Plenty"; Bulletman story 15.00 45.00 105.00
Captain Marvel "& the Raiders From Space"; Golden Arrow story 15.00 45.00 105.00
Captain Marvel Jr. "The Case of the Poison Press!" Bulletman story 15.00 45.00 105.00
Delecta of the Planets; C. C. Beck art; B&W inside; 12 pgs.; 3 printing variations (coloring) exist 24.00 73.00 170.00

FIGHT FOR FREEDOM
National Assoc. of Mfgrs./General Comics: 1949, 1951 (Giveaway, 16 pgs.)
nn-Dan Barry-c/a; used in **POP**, pg. 102 5.70 17.00 35.00

FIRE AND BLAST
National Fire Protection Assoc.: 1952 (Giveaway, 16 pgs., paper-c)
nn-Mart Baily A-Bomb-c; about fire prevention 16.00 47.00 110.00

FLASH COMICS
National Periodical Publications: 1946 (6-1/2x8-1/4", 32 pgs.) (Wheaties Giveaway)
nn-Johnny Thunder, Ghost Patrol, The Flash & Kubert Hawkman app.; Irwin Hasen-c/a 300.00 1100.00
NOTE: *All known copies were taped to Wheaties boxes and are never found in mint condition. Copies with light tape residue bring the listed prices in all grades*

FLASH GORDON
Dell Publishing Co.
Macy's Giveaway(1943)-(Rare)-20 pgs.; not by Raymond 59.00 176.00 470.00

FLASH GORDON
Harvey Comics: 1951 (16 pgs. in color, regular size, paper-c) (Gordon Bread giveaway)
1,2: 1-r/strips 10/24/37 - 2/6/38. 2-r/strips 7/14/40 - 10/6/40; Reprints by Raymond each.... 1.50 4.50 10.00
NOTE: *Most copies have brittle edges.*

FOREST FIRE (Also see The Blazing Forest and Smokey The Bear)
American Forestry Assn.(Commerical Comics): 1949 (dated-1950) (16 pgs., paper-c)
nn-Intro/1st app. Smokey The Forest Fire Preventing Bear; created by Rudy Wendelein; Wendelein/Sparling-a; 'Carter Oil Co.' on back-c of original 17.00 51.00 120.00

FOREST RANGER HANDBOOK
Wrather Corp.: 1967 (5x7", 20 pgs., slick-c)
nn-WIth Corey Stuart & Lassie photo-c 2.25 6.75 18.00

FORGOTTEN STORY BEHIND NORTH BEACH, THE
Catechetical Guild: No date (8 pgs., paper-c)
nn 2.80 7.00 14.00

48 FAMOUS AMERICANS
J. C. Penney Co. (Cpr. Edwin H. Stroh): 1947 (Giveaway) (Half-size in color)
nn-Simon & Kirby-a 11.50 34.00 80.00

FRANKIE LUER'S SPACE ADVENTURES
Luer Packing Co.: 1955 (5x7", 36 pgs., slick-c)
nn- With Davey Rocket 3.00 7.50 15.00

FREDDY
Charlton Comics
Schiff's Shoes Presents... #1 (1959)-Giveaway 1.00 3.00 8.00

FREE COMICS TO YOU FROM... (name of shoe store) (Has clown on cover & another with a rabbit) (Like comics from Weather Bird & Edward's Shoes)
Shoe Store Giveaway: Circa 1956, 1960-61

Contains a comic bound with new cover - several combinations possible; some Harvey titles known. Contents determine price.

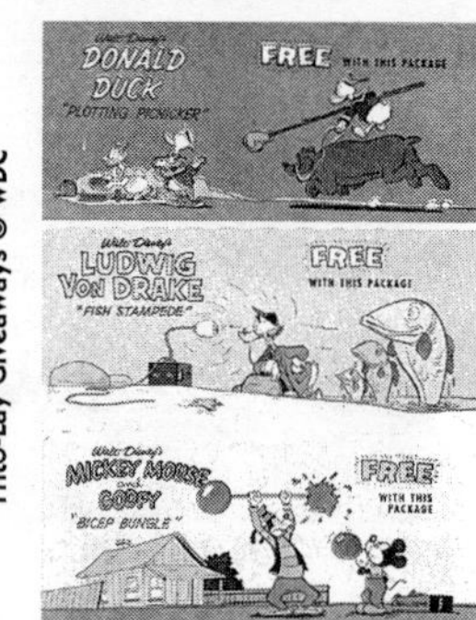

Frito-Lay Giveaways © WDC

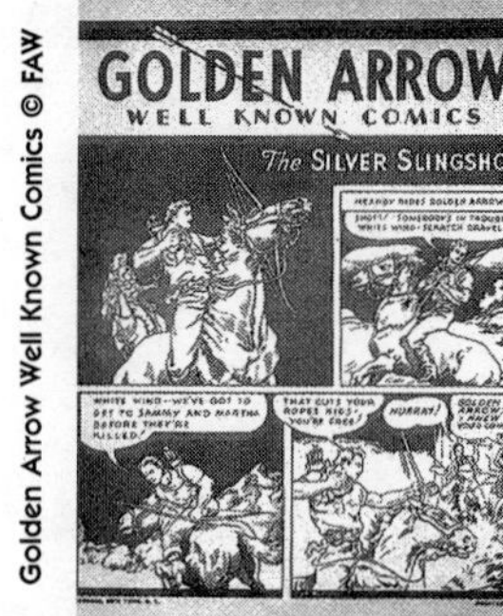

Golden Arrow Well Known Comics © FAW

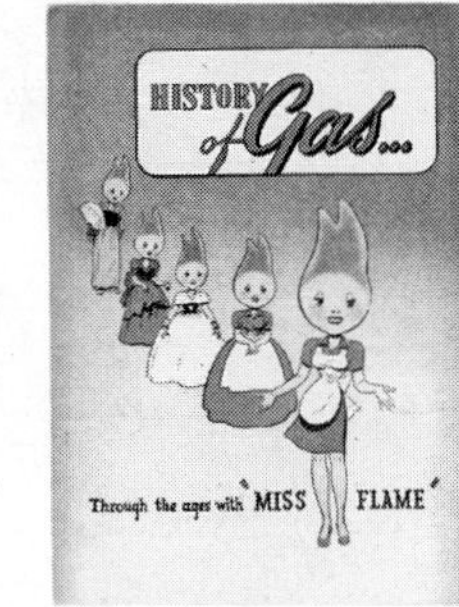

History of Gas © American Gas Assoc.

GD2.0 FN6.0 NM9.4

FREEDOM TRAIN
Street & Smith Publications: 1948 (Giveaway)

nn-Powell-c w/mailer 20.00 75.00 150.00

FRIENDLY GHOST, CASPER, THE (Becomes Casper... #254 on)
Harvey Publications

American Dental Assoc. giveaway-Small size (1967, 16 pgs.) 2.50 7.50 20.00

FRITO-LAY GIVEAWAY
Frito-Lay: 1962 (3-1/4x7", soft-c, 16 pgs.) (Disney)

nn-Donald Duck "Plotting Picnickers" 5.00 15.00 50.00
nn-Ludwig Von Drake "Fish Stampede" 3.20 9.60 32.00
nn- Mickey Mouse & Goofy "Bicep Bungle" 3.80 11.40 38.00

FRONTIER DAYS
Robin Hood Shoe Store (Brown Shoe): 1956 (Giveaway)

1 3.20 8.00 16.00

FUNNIES ON PARADE (Premium)(See Toy World Funnies)
Eastern Color Printing Co.: 1933 (Probably the 1st comic book) (36 pgs., slick cover) No date or publisher listed

GD2.0 FN6.0 VF8.0 NM9.4

nn-Contains Sunday page reprints of Mutt & Jeff, Joe Palooka, Hairbreadth Harry, Reg'lar Fellers, Skippy, & others (10,000 print run). This book was printed for Proctor & Gamble to be given away & came out before Famous Funnies or Century of Comics. 1045.00 3136.00 6270.00 11,500.00

FUNNY PICTURE STORIES (Comic Pages V3#4 on)
Comics Magazine Co./Centaur Publications GD2.0 FN6.0 NM9.4

Laundry giveaway (16-20 pgs., 1930s)-slick-c 30.00 100.00 200.00

FUNNY STUFF
National Periodical Publications (Wheaties Giveaway): 1946 (6-1/2x8-1/4")

nn-(Scarce)-Dodo & the Frog, Three Mouseketeers, etc.; came taped to Wheaties box; never found in better than fine 150.00 400.00 –

GABBY HAYES WESTERN (Movie star)
Fawcett Publications

Quaker Oats Giveaway nn's(#1-5, 1951, 2-1/2x7") (Kagran Corp.)-...In Tracks of Guilt, ...In the Fence Post Mystery, ...In the Accidental Sherlock, ... In the Frame-Up, ...In the Double Cross Brand known 11.00 33.00 75.00

GARY GIBSON COMICS (Donut club membership)
National Dunking Association: 1950 (Included in donut box with pin and card)

1-Western soft-c, 16 pgs.; folded into the box 2.50 7.50 20.00

GENE AUTRY COMICS
Dell Publishing Co.

...Adventure Comics And Play-Fun Book ('47)-32 pgs., 8x6-1/2"; games, comics, magic (Pillsbury premium) 35.00 150.00 300.00
Quaker Oats Giveaway(1950)-2-1/2x6-3/4"; 5 different versions; "Death Card Gang", "Phantoms of the Cave", "Riddle of Laughing Mtn.", "Secret of Lost Valley", "Bond of the Broken Arrow" (came in wrapper)
each... 14.00 43.00 100.00
3-D Giveaway(1953)-Pocket-size; 5 different 14.00 43.00 100.00

GENE AUTRY TIM (Formerly Tim) (Becomes Tim in Space)
Tim Stores: 1950 (Half-size) (B&W Giveaway)

nn-Several issues (All Scarce) 13.00 39.00 90.00

G. I. COMICS (Also see Jeep & Overseas Comics)
Giveaways: 1945 - No. 73?, 1946 (Distributed to U. S. Armed Forces)

1-73-Contains Prince Valiant by Foster, Blondie, Smilin' Jack, Mickey Finn, Terry & the Pirates, Donald Duck, Alley Oop, Moon Mullins & Capt. Easy strip reprints (at least 73 issues known to exist) 8.35 25.00 50.00

GOLDEN ARROW
Fawcett Publications

...Well Known Comics (1944; 12 pgs.; 8-1/2x10-1/2"; paper-c; glued binding)-Bestmaid/Samuel Lowe giveaway; printed in green 9.15 27.00 55.00

GOLDILOCKS & THE THREE BEARS
K. K. Publications: 1943 (Giveaway)

nn 10.00 30.00 70.00

GREAT PEOPLE OF GENESIS, THE
David C. Cook Publ. Co.: No date (Religious giveaway, 64 pgs.)

nn-Reprint/Sunday Pix Weekly 2.80 7.00 14.00

GREAT SACRAMENT, THE
Catechetical Guild: 1953 (Giveaway, 36 pgs.)

nn 2.80 7.00 14.00

GULF FUNNY WEEKLY (Gulf Comic Weekly No. 1-4)(See Standard Oil Comics)
Gulf Oil Company (Giveaway): 1933 - No. 422, 5/23/41 (in full color; 4 pgs.; tabloid size to 2/3/39; 2/10/39 on, regular comic book size)(early issues undated)

1 75.00 300.00 600.00
2-5 30.00 100.00 200.00
6-30 18.00 54.00 125.00
31-100 13.00 39.00 90.00
101-196 8.35 25.00 50.00
197-Wings Winfair begins(1/29/37); by Fred Meagher beginning in 1938 27.00 81.00 190.00
198-300 (Last tabloid size) 14.00 43.00 100.00
301-350 (Regular size) 8.35 25.00 50.00
351-422 5.85 17.50 35.00

GULLIVER'S TRAVELS
Macy's Department Store: 1939, small size

nn-Christmas giveaway 14.00 42.00 85.00

GUN THAT WON THE WEST, THE
Winchester-Western Division & Olin Mathieson Chemical Corp.: 1956 (Giveaway, 24 pgs.)

nn-Painted-c 5.00 15.00 30.00

HAPPINESS AND HEALING FOR YOU (Also see Oral Roberts'...)
Commercial Comics: 1955 (36 pgs., slick cover) (Oral Roberts Giveaway)

nn 9.15 27.00 55.00
NOTE: *The success of this book prompted Oral Roberts to go into the publishing business himself to produce his own material.*

HAWTHORN-MELODY FARMS DAIRY COMICS
Everybody's Publishing Co.: No date (1950's) (Giveaway)

nn-Cheerie Chick, Tuffy Turtle, Robin Koo Koo, Donald & Longhorn Legends 1.60 4.00 8.00

HENRY ALDRICH COMICS (TV)
Dell Publishing Co.

Giveaway (16 pgs., soft-c, 1951)-Capehart radio 2.00 6.00 22.00

HERE IS SANTA CLAUS
Goldsmith Publishing Co. (Kann's in Washington, D.C.): 1930s (16 pgs., 8 in color) (stiff paper covers)

nn 9.30 28.00 65.00

HERE'S HOW AMERICA'S CARTOONISTS HELP TO SELL U.S. SAVINGS BONDS
Harvey Comics: 1950? (16 pgs., giveaway, paper cover)

Contains: Joe Palooka, Donald Duck, Archie, Kerry Drake, Red Ryder, Blondie & Steve Canyon 17.00 51.00 120.00

HISTORY OF GAS
American Gas Assoc.: Mar, 1947 (Giveaway, 16 pgs.)

nn-Miss Flame narrates 5.00 15.00 30.00

HONEYBEE BIRDWHISTLE AND HER PET PEPI (Introducing...)
Newspaper Enterprise Assoc.: 1969 (Giveaway, 24 pgs., B&W, slick cover)

nn-Contains Freckles newspaper strips with a short biography of Henry

How Stalin Hopes We Will Destroy America © Joe Lowe Co.

If the Devil Could Talk © Catechetical Guild

Jo-Joy © W.T. Grant Dept. Stores

GD2.0 FN6.0 NM9.4

Fornhals (artist) & Fred Fox (writer) of the strip 4.00 12.00 40.00

HOPALONG CASSIDY
Fawcett Publications

Grape Nuts Flakes giveaway (1950,9x6") 15.00 45.00 105.00
...& the Mad Barber (1951 Bond Bread giveaway)-7x5"; used in **SOTI**, pgs. 308,309 25.00 75.00 175.00
...Meets the Brend Brothers Bandits (1951 Bond Bread giveaway, color, paper-c, 16pgs. 3-1/2x7")-Fawcett Publ. 12.00 36.00 85.00
...Strange Legacy (1951 Bond Bread giveaway) 12.00 36.00 85.00
White Tower Giveaway (1946, 16pgs., paper-c) 12.00 36.00 85.00

HOPPY THE MARVEL BUNNY (WELL KNOWN COMICS)
Fawcett Publications: 1944 (8-1/2x10-1/2", paper-c)
Bestmaid/Samuel Lowe (printed in red or blue) 10.00 30.00 60.00

HOT STUFF, THE LITTLE DEVIL
Harvey Publications (Illustrated Humor):1963
Shoestore Giveaway 1.20 3.60 12.00

HOW STALIN HOPES WE WILL DESTROY AMERICA
Joe Lowe Co. (Pictorial Media): 1951 (Giveaway, 16 pgs.)
nn 50.00 150.00 400.00

HURRICANE KIDS, THE (Also See Magic Morro, The Owl, Popular Comics #45)
R.S. Callender: 1941 (Giveaway, 7-1/2x5-1/4", soft-c)
nn-Will Ely-a. 10.00 30.00 60.00

IF THE DEVIL WOULD TALK
Roman Catholic Catechetical Guild/Impact Publ.: 1950; 1958 (32 pgs.; paper cover; in full color)
nn-(Scarce)-About secularism (20-30 copies known to exist); very low distribution 81.00 245.00 650.00
1958 Edition-(Impact Publ.); art & script changed to meet church criticism of earlier edition; 80 plus copies known to exist 25.00 75.00 175.00
Black & White version of nn edition; small size; only 4 known copies exist 29.00 86.00 200.00

NOTE: *The original edition of this book was printed and killed by the Guild's board of directors. It is believed that a very limited number of copies were distributed. The 1958 version was a complete bomb with very limited, if any, circulation. In 1979, 11 original, 4 1958 reprints, and 4 B&W's surfaced from the Guild's old files in St. Paul, Minnesota.*

IN LOVE WITH JESUS
Catechetical Educational Society: 1952 (Giveaway, 36 pgs.)
nn 4.00 10.00 22.00

INTERSTATE THEATRES' FUN CLUB COMICS
Interstate Theatres: Mid 1940's (10¢ on cover) (B&W cover) (Premium)
Cover features MLJ characters looking at a copy of Top-Notch Comics, but contains an early Detective Comic on inside; many combinations possible 8.35 25.00 50.00

IRON HORSE GOES TO WAR, THE
Association of American Railroads: 1960 (Giveaway, 16 pgs.)
nn-Civil War & railroads 4.00 12.00 25.00

IS THIS TOMORROW?
Catechetical Guild: 1947 (One Shot) (3 editions) (52 pgs.)
1-Theme of communists taking over the USA; (no price on cover) Used in **POP**, pg. 102 14.00 43.00 100.00
1-(10¢ on cover) 21.00 64.00 150.00
1-Has blank circle with no price on cover 23.00 69.00 160.00
Black & White advance copy titled "Confidential" (52 pgs.)-Contains script and art edited out of the color edition, including one page of extreme violence showing mob nailing a Cardinal to a door; (only two known copies) 50.00 200.00 400.00

NOTE: *The original color version first sold for 10 cents. Since sales were good, it was later printed as a giveaway. Approximately four million in total were printed. The two black and white copies listed plus two other versions as well as a full color untrimmed version surfaced in 1979 from the Guild's old files in St. Paul, Minnesota.*

IT'S FUN TO STAY ALIVE
National Automobile Dealers Association: 1948 (Giveaway, 16 pgs., heavy stock paper)
Featuring: Bugs Bunny, The Berrys, Dixie Dugan, Elmer, Henry, Tim Tyler, Bruce Gentry, Abbie & Slats, Joe Jinks, The Toodles, & Cokey; all art copyright 1946-48 drawn especially for this book.

JACK & JILL VISIT TOYTOWN WITH ELMER THE ELF
Butler Brothers (Toytown Stores): 1949 (Giveaway, 16 pgs., paper cover)
nn 4.00 10.00 20.00

JACK ARMSTRONG (Radio)(See True Comics)
Parents' Institute: 1949
12-Premium version(distr. in Chicago only); Free printed on upper right-c; no price (Rare) 21.00 64.00 150.00

JACKPOT OF FUN COMIC BOOK
DCA Food Ind.: 1957, giveaway
nn-Features Howdy Doody 10.00 30.00 60.00

JEEP COMICS
R. B. Leffingwell & Co.: 1945 - 1946
1-46(Giveaways)-Strip reprints in all; Tarzan, Flash Gordon, Blondie, The Nebbs, Little Iodine, Red Ryder, Don Winslow, The Phantom, Johnny Hazard, Katzenjammer Kids; distr. to U.S. Armed Forces from 1945-1946 5.00 15.00 30.00

JINGLE BELLS CHRISTMAS BOOK
Montgomery Ward (Giveaway): 1971 (20 pgs., B&W inside, slick-c)
nn 2.00

JOAN OF ARC
Catechetical Guild (Topix) (Giveaway): No date (28 pgs.)
nn 10.00 30.00 65.00
NOTE: *Unpublished version exists which came from the Guild's files.*

JOE PALOOKA (2nd Series
Harvey Publications
...Body Building Instruction Book (1958 B&M Sports Toy giveaway, 16pgs., 5-1/4x7")-Origin 10.00 30.00 60.00
...Fights His Way Back (1945 Giveaway, 24 pgs.) Family Comics 17.00 51.00 120.00
...in Hi There! (1949 Red Cross giveaway, 12 pgs., 4-3/4x6") 9.15 27.00 55.00
...in It's All in the Family (1945 Red Cross giveaway, 16 pgs., regular size) 10.00 30.00 70.00

JOE THE GENIE OF STEEL
U.S. Steel Corp., Pittsburgh, PA: 1950 (16 pgs.)
nn 4.00 10.00 20.00

JOHNNY JINGLE'S LUCKY DAY
American Dairy Assoc.: 1956 (16 pgs.; 7-1/4x5-1/8") (Giveaway) (Disney)
nn 4.00 12.00 24.00

JO-JOY (The Adventures of...)
W. T. Grant Dept. Stores: 1945 - 1953 (Christmas gift comic, 16 pgs., 7-1/16x10-1/4")
1945-53 issues 4.25 13.00 26.00

JOLLY CHRISTMAS BOOK (See Christmas Journey Through Space)
Promotional Publ. Co.: 1951; 1954; 1955 (36 pgs.; 24 pgs.)
1951-(Woolworth giveaway)-slightly oversized; no slick cover; Marv Levy-c/a 6.70 20.00 40.00
1954-(Hot Shoppes giveaway)-regular size-reprints 1951 issue; slick cover added; 24 pgs.; no ads 6.70 20.00 40.00
1955-(J. M. McDonald Co. giveaway)-reg. size 5.00 15.00 30.00

JUMPING JACKS PRESENTS THE WHIZ KIDS
Jumping Jacks Stores giveaway: 1978 (In 3-D) with glasses (4 pgs.)
nn 1.00

JUNGLE BOOK FUN BOOK, THE (Disney)

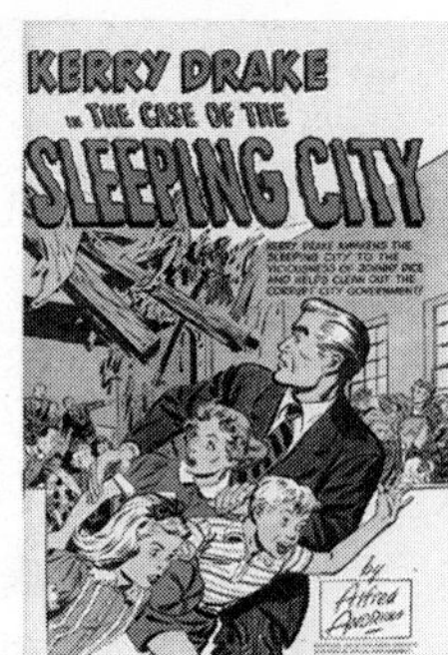

Kerry Drake Detective Cases © Publ. Synd.

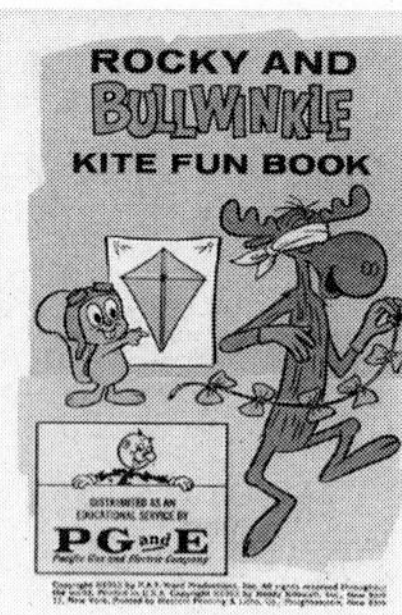

Kite Fun Book 1963 © Jay Ward

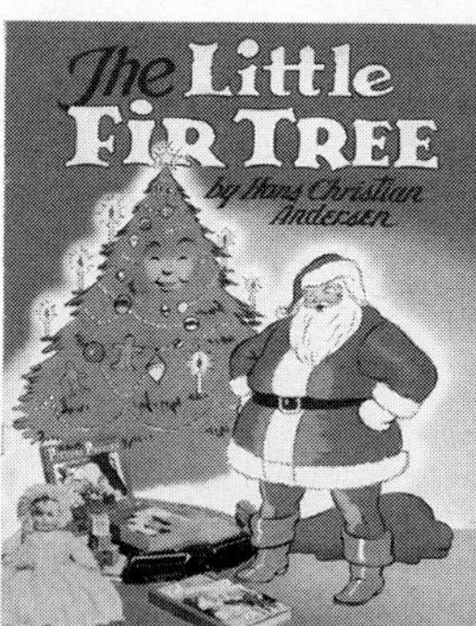

Little Fir Tree © W.T. Grant

Baskin Robbins: 1978
nn-Ice Cream giveaway 1.50 4.50 12.00

KASCO KOMICS
Kasko Grainfeed (Giveaway): 1945; No. 2, 1949 (Regular size, paper-c)
1(1945)-Similar to Katy Keene; Bill Woggon-a; 28 pgs.; 6-7/8x9-7/8" 17.00 51.00 120.00
2(1949)-Woggon-c/a 13.00 39.00 90.00

KATY AND KEN VISIT SANTA WITH MISTER WISH
S. S. Kresge Co. : 1948 (Giveaway, 16 pgs., paper-c)
nn 4.25 13.00 26.00

KERRY DRAKE DETECTIVE CASES
Publisher's Syndicate
...in the Case of the Sleeping City-(1951)-16 pg. giveaway for armed forces; paper cover 4.25 13.00 26.00

KEY COMICS
Key Clothing Co./Peterson Clothing: 1951 - 1956 (32 pgs.) (Giveaway)
Contains a comic from different publishers bound with new cover. Cover changed each year. Many combinations possible. Distributed in Nebraska, Iowa, & Kansas. Contents would determine price, 40-60 percent of original.

KIRBY'S SHOES COMICS
Kirby's Shoes: 1959 (8 pgs., soft-c)
nn-Features Kirby the Golden Bear 1.00 3.00 8.00

KITE FUN BOOK
Pacific, Gas & Electric/Sou. California Edison/Florida Power & Light/ Missouri Public Service Co.: 1953 - 1981 (16pgs, 5x7-1/4", soft-c)
1953-Pinocchio Learns About Kites (Disney) 47.00 141.00 375.00
1954-Donald Duck Tells About Kites-Fla. Power, S.C.E. & version with label issues-Barks pencils-8 pgs.; inks-7 pgs. (Rare) 400.00 1200.00 2800.00
1954-Donald Duck Tells About Kites-P.G.&E. issue -7th page redrawn changing middle 3 panels to show P.G.&E. in story line; (All Barks; last page Barks pencils only) Scarce 247.00 741.00 2100.00
1955-Brer Rabbit in "A Kite Tail" (Disney) 34.00 103.00 240.00
1956-Woody Woodpecker (Lantz) 14.00 43.00 100.00
1957-?
1958-Tom And Jerry (M.G.M.) 10.00 30.00 60.00
1960-Porky Pig (Warner Bros.) 4.50 13.50 45.00
1960-Bugs Bunny (Warner Bros.) 4.50 13.50 45.00
1961-Huckleberry Hound (Hanna-Barbera) 5.50 16.50 55.00
1962-Yogi Bear (Hanna-Barbera) 3.50 10.50 35.00
1963-Rocky and Bullwinkle (TV)(Jay Ward) 10.00 30.00 100.00
1963-Top Cat (TV)(Hanna-Barbera) 4.50 13.50 45.00
1964-Magilla Gorilla (TV)(Hanna-Barbera) 4.00 12.00 40.00
1965-Jinks, Pixie and Dixie (TV)(Hanna-Barbera) 2.80 8.00 28.00
1965-Tweety and Sylvester (Warner); S.C.E. version with Reddy Kilowatt app. 1.50 4.50 12.00
1966-Secret Squirrel (Hanna-Barbera); S.C.E. version with Reddy Kilowatt app. 6.50 19.50 65.00
1967-Beep! Beep! The Road Runner (TV)(Warner) 2.50 7.50 20.00
1968-Bugs Bunny (Warner Bros.) 2.50 7.50 22.00
1969-Dastardly and Muttley (TV)(Hanna-Barbera) 4.00 12.00 40.00
1970-Rocky and Bullwinkle (TV)(Jay Ward) 7.00 21.00 70.00
1971-Beep! Beep! The Road Runner (TV)(Warner) 2.25 6.75 18.00
1972-The Pink Panther (TV) 1.50 4.50 12.00
1973-Lassie (TV) 2.80 8.40 28.00
1974-Underdog (TV) 2.25 6.75 18.00
1975-Ben Franklin 1.00 2.80 7.00
1976-The Brady Bunch (TV) 2.50 7.50 20.00
1977-Ben Franklin 1.00 2.80 7.00
1977-Popeye 1.75 5.25 14.00
1978-Happy Days (TV) 1.75 5.25 14.00
1979-Eight is Enough (TV) 1.75 5.25 14.00
1980-The Waltons (TV, released in 1981) 1.75 5.25 14.00

KNOW YOUR MASS
Catechetical Guild: No. 303, 1958 (35¢, 100 Pg. Giant) (Square binding)
303-In color 4.00 10.00 20.00

K. O. PUNCH, THE (Also see Lucky Fights It Through)
E. C. Comics: 1948 (Educational giveaway)
nn-Feldstein-splash; Kamen-a 94.00 282.00 750.00

KOREA MY HOME (Also see Yalta to Korea)
Johnstone and Cushing: nd (1950s)
nn-Anti-communist; Korean War 24.00 73.00 170.00

KRIM-KO KOMICS
Krim-ko Chocolate Drink: 5/18/35 - No. 6, 6/22/35; 1936 - 1939 (weekly)
1-(16 pgs., soft-c, Dairy giveaways)-Tom, Mary & Sparky Advs. by Russell Keaton, Jim Hawkins by Dick Moores, Mystery Island! by Rick Yager begin 14.00 43.00 100.00
2-6 (6/22/35) 10.00 30.00 70.00
Lola, Secret Agent; 184 issues, 4 pg. giveaways - all original stories each.... 7.00 21.00 42.00

LABOR IS A PARTNER
Catechetical Guild Educational Society: 1949 (32 pgs., paper-c)
nn-Anti-communism 19.00 58.00 135.00
Confidential Preview-(8-1/2x11", B&W, saddle stitched)-only one known copy; text varies from color version, advertises next book on secularism (If the Devil Would Talk) 21.00 64.00 150.00

LADY AND THE TRAMP IN "BUTTER LATE THAN NEVER"
American Dairy Assoc. (Premium): 1955 (16 pgs., 5x7-1/4", soft-c) (Disney)
nn 11.00 33.00 75.00

LASSIE (TV)
Dell Publ. Co
The Adventures of... nn-(Red Heart Dog Food giveaway, 1949)-16 pgs, soft-c; 1st app. Lassie in comics 30.00 125.00 250.00

LIFE OF THE BLESSED VIRGIN
Catechetical Guild (Giveaway): 1950 (68pgs.) (square binding)
nn-Contains "The Woman of the Promise" & "Mother of Us All" rebound 4.25 13.00 28.00

LI'L ABNER (Al Capp's) (Also see Natural Disasters!)
Harvey Publ./Toby Press
...& the Creatures from Drop-Outer Space-nn (Job Corps giveaway; 36 pgs., in color)(entire book by Frank Frazetta) 29.00 88.00 205.00
...Joins the Navy (1950) (Toby Press Premium) 15.00 50.00 85.00
...by Al Capp Giveaway (Circa 1955, nd) 15.00 50.00 85.00

LITTLE ALONZO
Macy's Dept. Store: 1938 (B&W, 5-1/2x8-1/2")(Christmas giveaway)
nn-By Ferdinand the Bull's Munro Leaf 8.35 25.00 50.00

LITTLE DOT
Harvey Publications
Shoe store giveaway 2 3.80 11.40 38.00

LITTLE FIR TREE, THE
W. T. Grant Co. : nd (1942) (8-1/2x11") (12 pgs. with cover, color & B&W, heavy paper) (Christmas giveaway)
nn-Story by Hans Christian Anderson; 8 pg. Kelly-r/Santa Claus Funnies (not signed); X-Mas-c
(One copy in Mint sold for $1750.00 in 1986 & another copy in VF sold for $1000.00 in 1991)

LITTLE KLINKER
Little Klinker Ventures: Nov, 1960 (20 pgs.) (slick cover) (Montgomery Ward Giveaway)
nn 1.50 4.50 12.00

LITTLE MISS SUNBEAM COMICS
Magazine Enterprises/Quality Bakers of America

Lone Ranger Cheerios © Lone Ranger Ent.

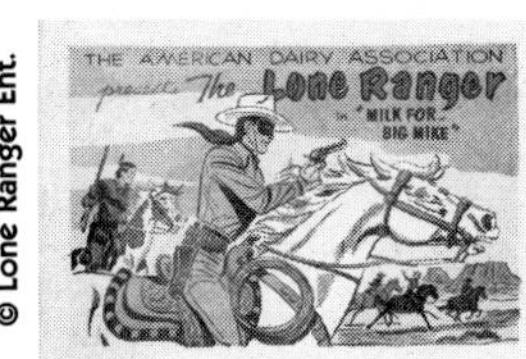

Lone Ranger in "Milk For Big Mike" © Lone Ranger Ent.

March of Comics #4 © WDC

GD2.0 FN6.0 NM9.4

Bread Giveaway 1-4(Quality Bakers, 1949-50)-14 pgs. each 5.00 15.00 30.00
Bread Giveaway (1957,61; 16pgs, reg. size) 4.75 13.00 28.00

LITTLE ORPHAN ANNIE
David McKay Publ./Dell Publishing Co.

Junior Commandos Giveaway (same-c as 4-Color #18, K.K. Publ.)(Big Shoe Store); same back cover as '47 Popped Wheat giveaway; 16 pgs; flag-c; r/strips 9/7/42-10/10/42 30.00 125.00 250.00
Popped Wheat Giveaway ('47)-16 pgs. full color; reprints strips from 5/3/40 to 6/20/40 2.00 5.00 10.00
Quaker Sparkies Giveaway (1940) 21.00 64.00 150.00
Quaker Sparkies Giveaway (1941, full color, 20 pgs.); "LOA and the Rescue"; r/strips 4/13/39-6/21/39 & 7/6/39-7/17/39. "LOA and the Kidnappers"; r/strips 11/28/38-1/28/39 19.00 58.00 135.00
Quaker Sparkies Giveaway (1942, full color, 20 pgs.); "LOA and Mr. Gudge"; r/strips 2/13/38-3/21/38 & 4/18/37-5/30/37. "LOA and the Great Am" 17.00 51.00 120.00

LITTLE TREE THAT WASN'T WANTED, THE
W. T. Grant Co. (Giveaway): 1960, (Color, 28 pgs.)

nn-Christmas giveaway 1.50 4.50 12.00

LONE RANGER, THE
Dell Publishing Co.

Cheerios Giveaways (1954, 16 pgs., 2-1/2x7", soft-c) #1- "The Lone Ranger, His Mask & How He Met Tonto". #2- "The Lone Ranger & the Story of Silver" each.... 20.00 60.00 120.00
Doll Giveaways (Gabriel Ind.)(1973, 3-1/4x5")- "The Story of The Lone Ranger" & "The Carson City Bank Robbery" 1.50 4.50 12.00
How the Lone Ranger Captured Silver Book(1936)-Silvercup Bread giveaway 100.00 300.00 500.00
...In Milk for Big Mike (1955, Dairy Association giveaway), soft-c; 5x7-1/4", 16 pgs. 20.00 60.00 125.00
Legend of The Lone Ranger (1969, 16 pgs., giveaway)-Origin The Lone Ranger 3.00 9.00 30.00
Merita Bread giveaway (1954, 16 pgs., 5x7-1/4")- "How to Be a Lone Ranger Health & Safety Scout" 25.00 75.00 150.00

LONE RANGER COMICS, THE
Lone Ranger, Inc. : Book 1, 1939(inside) (shows 1938 on-c) (52 pgs. in color; regular size) (Ice cream mail order) **GD2.0 FN6.0 VF8.0**

Book 1-(Scarce)-The first western comic devoted to a single character; not by Vallely 850.00 3000.00 5000.00
2nd version w/large full color promo poster pasted over centerfold & a smaller poster pasted over back cover; includes new additional premiums not originally offered (Rare) 900.00 3200.00 5500.00

LUCKY FIGHTS IT THROUGH (Also see The K. O. Punch)
Educational Comics: 1949 (Giveaway, 16 pgs. in color, paper-c) **GD2.0 FN6.0 NM9.4**

nn-(Very Rare)-1st Kurtzman work for E. C.; V.D. prevention 125.00 375.00 1000.00
nn-Reprint in color (1977) 2.00
NOTE: *Subtitled "The Story of That Ignorant, Ignorant Cowboy". Prepared for Communications Materials Center, Columbia University.*

LUDWIG VON DRAKE (See Frito-Lay Giveaway)

MACO TOYS COMIC
Maco Toys/Charlton Comics: 1959 (Giveaway, 36 pgs.)

1-All military stories featuring Maco Toys 1.25 3.75 10.00

MAGIC MORRO (Also see Super Comics #21, The Owl, & The Hurricane Kids)
K. K. Publications: 1941 (7-1/2x5-1/4, giveaway, soft-c)

nn-Ken Ernst-a. 12.00 36.00 85.00

MAGIC OF CHRISTMAS AT NEWBERRYS, THE
E. S. London: 1967 (Giveaway) (B&W, slick-c, 20 pgs.)

nn 2.40 6.00

GD2.0 FN6.0 NM9.4

MAJOR INAPAK THE SPACE ACE
Magazine Enterprises (Inapac Foods): 1951 (20 pgs.) (Giveaway)

1-Bob Powell-c/a 2.00
NOTE: *Many warehouse copies surfaced in 1973.*

MAMMY YOKUM & THE GREAT DOGPATCH MYSTERY
Toby Press: 1951 (Giveaway)

nn-Li'l Abner 18.00 54.00 125.00
nn-Reprint (1956) 4.25 13.00 28.00

MAN OF PEACE, POPE PIUS XII
Catechetical Guild: 1950 (See Pope Pius XII... & To V2#8)

nn-All Powell-a 4.25 13.00 28.00

MARCH OF COMICS (Boys' and Girls'...#3-353)
K. K. Publications/Western Publishing Co.: 1946 - No. 488, April, 1982 (#1-4 are not numbered) (K.K. Giveaway) (Founded by Sig Feuchtwanger)

Early issues were full size, 32 pages, and were printed with and without an extra cover of slick stock, just for the advertiser. The binding was stapled if the slick cover was added; otherwise, the pages were glued together at the spine. Most 1948 - 1951 issues were full size,24 pages, pulp covers. Starting in 1952 they were half-size and 32 pages with slick covers.1959 and later issues had only 16 pages plus covers. 1952 -1959 issues read oblong; 1960 and later issues read upright. All have new stories except where noted.

nn (#1, 1946)-Goldilocks; Kelly back-c (16 pgs., stapled) 36.00 107.00 250.00
nn (#2, 1946)-How Santa Got His Red Suit; Kelly-a (11 pgs., r/4-Color #61 from 1944) (16pgs., stapled) 36.00 107.00 250.00
nn (#3, 1947)-Our Gang (Walt Kelly) 46.00 137.00 340.00
nn (#4)-Donald Duck by Carl Barks, "Maharajah Donald", 28 pgs.; Kelly-c? (Disney) 857.00 2571.00 7000.00
5-Andy Panda (Walter Lantz) 21.50 64.00 150.00
6-Popular Fairy Tales; Kelly-c; Noonan-a(2) 25.00 75.00 175.00
7-Oswald the Rabbit 24.00 71.00 165.00
8-Mickey Mouse, 32 pgs. (Disney) 71.00 215.00 500.00
9(nn)-The Story of the Gloomy Bunny 11.00 33.00 75.00
10-Out of Santa's Bag 10.00 30.00 70.00
11-Fun With Santa Claus 8.35 25.00 55.00
12-Santa's Toys 8.35 25.00 55.00
13-Santa's Surprise 8.35 25.00 55.00
14-Santa's Candy Kitchen 8.35 25.00 55.00
15-Hip-It-Ty Hop & the Big Bass Viol 8.35 25.00 50.00
16-Woody Woodpecker (1947)(Walter Lantz) 16.00 47.00 110.00
17-Roy Rogers (1948) 29.00 86.00 200.00
18-Popular Fairy Tales 13.00 39.00 90.00
19-Uncle Wiggily 11.00 33.00 75.00
20-Donald Duck by Carl Barks, "Darkest Africa", 22 pgs.; Kelly-c (Disney) 500.00 1500.00 4000.00
21-Tom and Jerry 13.00 39.00 90.00
22-Andy Panda (Lantz) 11.50 34.00 80.00
23-Raggedy Ann & Andy; Kerr-a 17.00 49.00 115.00
24-Felix the Cat, 1932 daily strip reprints by Otto Messmer 27.00 81.00 190.00
25-Gene Autry 27.00 81.00 190.00
26-Our Gang; Walt Kelly 26.00 79.00 185.00
27-Mickey Mouse; r/in M. M. #240 (Disney) 50.00 150.00 350.00
28-Gene Autry 26.00 79.00 185.00
29-Easter Bonnet Shop 5.85 17.50 40.00
30-Here Comes Santa 5.35 16.00 32.00
31-Santa's Busy Corner 5.35 16.00 32.00
32-No book produced
33-A Christmas Carol (12/48) 5.35 16.00 32.00
34-Woody Woodpecker 11.50 34.00 80.00
35-Roy Rogers (1948) 29.00 86.00 200.00
36-Felix the Cat(1949); by Messmer; '34 strip-r 24.00 71.00 165.00
37-Popeye 18.00 54.00 125.00
38-Oswald the Rabbit 10.00 30.00 58.00
39-Gene Autry 26.00 79.00 185.00
40-Andy and Woody 10.00 30.00 58.00

March of Comics #72 © KING

March of Comics #75 © WB

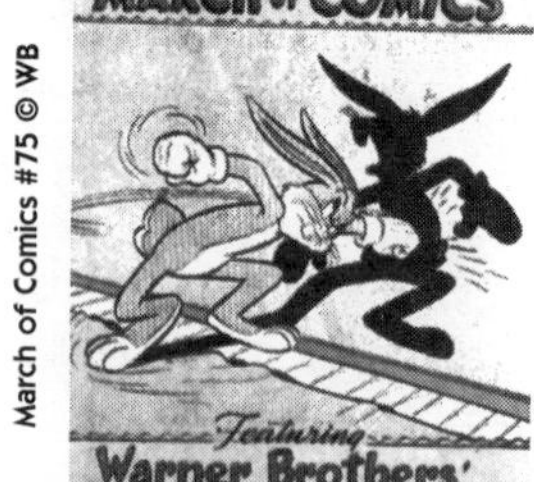

March of Comics #125 © ERB

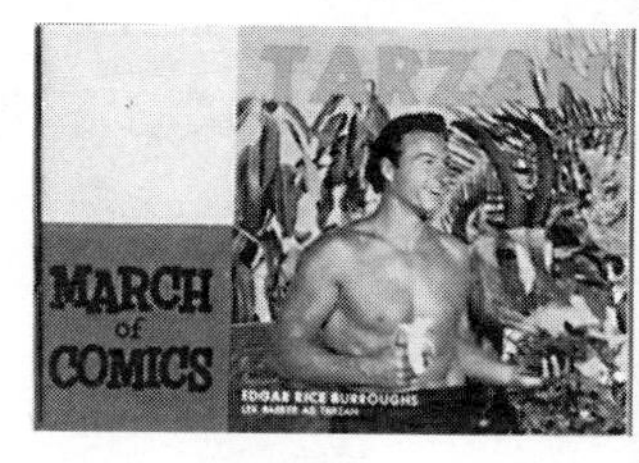

	GD2.0	FN6.0	NM9.4
41-Donald Duck by Carl Barks, "Race to the South Seas", 22 pgs.; Kelly-c	500.00	1500.00	3500.00
42-Porky Pig	10.00	30.00	65.00
43-Henry	8.00	24.00	48.00
44-Bugs Bunny	11.00	33.00	75.00
45-Mickey Mouse (Disney)	39.00	116.00	270.00
46-Tom and Jerry	11.00	33.00	75.00
47-Roy Rogers	25.00	75.00	175.00
48-Greetings from Santa	4.25	13.00	26.00
49-Santa Is Here	4.25	13.00	26.00
50-Santa Claus' Workshop (1949)	4.25	13.00	26.00
51-Felix the Cat (1950) by Messmer	19.00	58.00	135.00
52-Popeye	15.00	45.00	105.00
53-Oswald the Rabbit	10.00	30.00	58.00
54-Gene Autry	23.00	69.00	160.00
55-Andy and Woody	8.70	26.00	52.00
56-Donald Duck; not by Barks; Barks art on back-c (Disney)	36.00	109.00	255.00
57-Porky Pig	8.70	26.00	60.00
58-Henry	6.35	19.00	38.00
59-Bugs Bunny	10.00	30.00	65.00
60-Mickey Mouse (Disney)	35.00	105.00	245.00
61-Tom and Jerry	8.70	26.00	52.00
62-Roy Rogers	24.00	71.00	165.00
63-Welcome Santa (1/2-size, oblong)	4.25	13.00	26.00
64(nn)-Santa's Helpers (1/2-size, oblong)	4.25	13.00	26.00
65(nn)-Jingle Bells (1950) (1/2-size, oblong)	4.25	13.00	26.00
66-Popeye (1951)	13.00	39.00	90.00
67-Oswald the Rabbit	8.50	25.50	52.00
68-Roy Rogers	21.50	64.00	150.00
69-Donald Duck; Barks-a on back-c (Disney)	31.00	94.00	220.00
70-Tom and Jerry	8.00	24.00	48.00
71-Porky Pig	8.50	25.50	52.00
72-Krazy Kat	10.00	30.00	65.00
73-Roy Rogers	19.00	56.00	130.00
74-Mickey Mouse (1951)(Disney)	29.00	86.00	200.00
75-Bugs Bunny	8.70	26.00	52.00
76-Andy and Woody	8.00	24.00	48.00
77-Roy Rogers	18.00	54.00	125.00
78-Gene Autry (1951); last regular size issue	17.00	51.00	120.00
79-Andy Panda (1952, 5x7" size)	4.25	13.00	28.00
80-Popeye	11.50	34.00	80.00
81-Oswald the Rabbit	5.00	15.00	30.00
82-Tarzan; Lex Barker photo-c	19.00	58.00	135.00
83-Bugs Bunny	6.70	20.00	40.00
84-Henry	4.00	12.00	24.00
85-Woody Woodpecker	4.00	12.00	24.00
86-Roy Rogers	13.50	41.00	95.00
87-Krazy Kat	8.70	26.00	52.00
88-Tom and Jerry	5.70	17.00	34.00
89-Porky Pig	4.00	12.00	24.00
90-Gene Autry	13.00	39.00	90.00
91-Roy Rogers & Santa	13.00	39.00	90.00
92-Christmas with Santa	4.00	10.00	20.00
93-Woody Woodpecker (1953)	4.00	12.00	24.00
94-Indian Chief	10.00	30.00	70.00
95-Oswald the Rabbit	4.00	12.00	24.00
96-Popeye	10.00	30.00	68.00
97-Bugs Bunny	5.70	17.00	34.00
98-Tarzan; Lex Barker photo-c	21.00	62.00	145.00
99-Porky Pig	4.00	12.00	24.00
100-Roy Rogers	10.70	32.00	75.00
101-Henry	4.00	11.00	22.00
102-Tom Corbett (TV)('53, early app).; painted-c	17.00	49.00	115.00
103-Tom and Jerry	4.00	12.00	24.00
104-Gene Autry	11.00	33.00	75.00
105-Roy Rogers	11.00	33.00	75.00
106-Santa's Helpers	4.00	11.00	22.00
107-Santa's Christmas Book - not published			
108-Fun with Santa (1953)	4.00	11.00	22.00
109-Woody Woodpecker (1954)	4.00	11.00	22.00
110-Indian Chief	5.70	17.00	34.00
111-Oswald the Rabbit	4.00	11.00	22.00
112-Henry	4.00	10.00	20.00
113-Porky Pig	4.00	11.00	22.00
114-Tarzan; Russ Manning-a	21.00	62.00	145.00
115-Bugs Bunny	4.25	13.00	28.00
116-Roy Rogers	11.00	33.00	75.00
117-Popeye	10.00	30.00	68.00
118-Flash Gordon; painted-c	13.50	41.00	95.00
119-Tom and Jerry	4.00	11.00	22.00
120-Gene Autry	11.00	33.00	75.00
121-Roy Rogers	11.00	33.00	75.00
122-Santa's Surprise (1954)	3.60	9.00	18.00
123-Santa's Christmas Book	3.60	9.00	18.00
124-Woody Woodpecker (1955)	4.00	10.00	20.00
125-Tarzan; Lex Barker photo-c	19.00	58.00	135.00
126-Oswald the Rabbit	4.00	10.00	20.00
127-Indian Chief	5.70	17.00	35.00
128-Tom and Jerry	4.00	10.00	20.00
129-Henry	3.40	8.50	17.00
130-Porky Pig	4.00	10.00	20.00
131-Roy Rogers	11.00	33.00	75.00
132-Bugs Bunny	4.00	12.00	24.00
133-Flash Gordon; painted-c	12.00	36.00	85.00
134-Popeye	8.00	24.00	48.00
135-Gene Autry	10.00	30.00	68.00
136-Roy Rogers	10.00	30.00	68.00
137-Gifts from Santa	2.80	7.00	14.00
138-Fun at Christmas (1955)	2.80	7.00	14.00
139-Woody Woodpecker (1956)	4.00	10.00	20.00
140-Indian Chief	5.70	17.00	35.00
141-Oswald the Rabbit	4.00	10.00	20.00
142-Flash Gordon	12.00	36.00	85.00
143-Porky Pig	4.00	10.00	20.00
144-Tarzan; Russ Manning-a; painted-c	18.00	54.00	125.00
145-Tom and Jerry	4.00	10.00	20.00
146-Roy Rogers; photo-c	11.00	33.00	75.00
147-Henry	3.00	7.50	15.00
148-Popeye	8.00	24.00	48.00
149-Bugs Bunny	4.00	11.00	22.00
150-Gene Autry	10.00	30.00	68.00
151-Roy Rogers	10.00	30.00	68.00
152-The Night Before Christmas	2.80	7.00	14.00
153-Merry Christmas (1956)	2.80	7.00	14.00
154-Tom and Jerry (1957)	4.00	10.00	20.00
155-Tarzan; photo-c	18.00	54.00	125.00
156-Oswald the Rabbit	4.00	10.00	20.00
157-Popeye	6.70	20.00	40.00
158-Woody Woodpecker	4.00	10.00	20.00
159-Indian Chief	5.70	17.00	35.00
160-Bugs Bunny	4.00	11.00	22.00
161-Roy Rogers	10.00	30.00	58.00
162-Henry	3.00	7.50	15.00
163-Rin Tin Tin (TV)	7.50	22.50	50.00
164-Porky Pig	4.00	10.00	20.00
165-The Lone Ranger	10.00	30.00	65.00
166-Santa and His Reindeer	2.80	7.00	14.00
167-Roy Rogers and Santa	10.00	30.00	58.00
168-Santa Claus' Workshop (1957)	2.80	7.00	14.00
169-Popeye (1958)	6.70	20.00	40.00
170-Indian Chief	5.70	17.00	35.00
171-Oswald the Rabbit	3.60	9.00	18.00
172-Tarzan	13.50	41.00	95.00

March of Comics #205 © Terry Toons

March of Comics #233 © Jay Ward

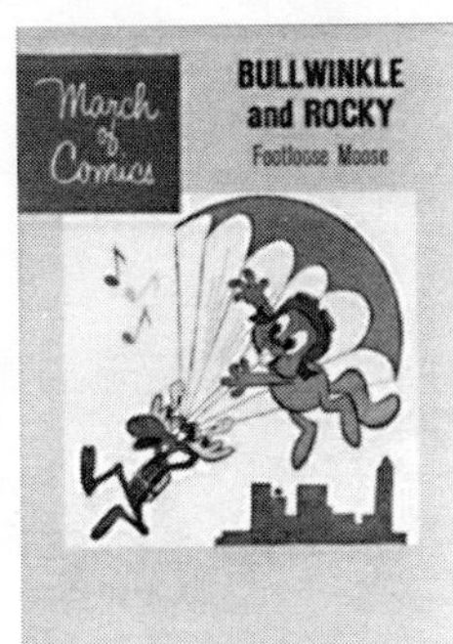

March of Comics #290 © WEST

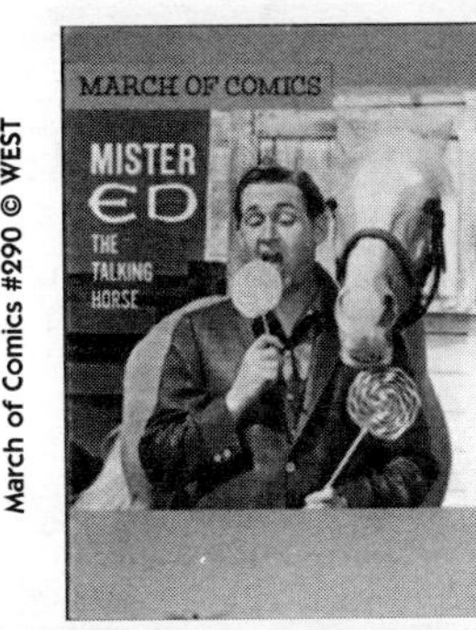

	GD2.0	FN6.0	NM9.4
173-Tom and Jerry	3.60	9.00	18.00
174-The Lone Ranger	10.00	30.00	65.00
175-Porky Pig	3.60	9.00	18.00
176-Roy Rogers	9.15	27.00	55.00
177-Woody Woodpecker	3.60	9.00	18.00
178-Henry	3.00	7.50	15.00
179-Bugs Bunny	3.60	9.00	18.00
180-Rin Tin Tin (TV)	6.50	19.50	45.00
181-Happy Holiday	2.00	5.00	10.00
182-Happi Tim	3.20	8.00	16.00
183-Welcome Santa (1958)	2.40	6.00	12.00
184-Woody Woodpecker (1959)	3.20	8.00	16.00
185-Tarzan; photo-c	13.00	39.00	90.00
186-Oswald the Rabbit	3.20	8.00	16.00
187-Indian Chief	5.35	16.00	32.00
188-Bugs Bunny	3.20	8.00	16.00
189-Henry	2.80	7.00	14.00
190-Tom and Jerry	3.20	8.00	16.00
191-Roy Rogers	8.35	25.00	50.00
192-Porky Pig	3.20	8.00	16.00
193-The Lone Ranger	10.00	30.00	60.00
194-Popeye	5.85	17.50	35.00
195-Rin Tin Tin (TV)	6.00	18.00	40.00
196-Sears Special - not published			
197-Santa Is Coming	2.40	6.00	12.00
198-Santa's Helpers (1959)	2.40	6.00	12.00
199-Huckleberry Hound (TV)(1960, early app.)	7.15	21.50	50.00
200-Fury (TV)	5.35	16.00	32.00
201-Bugs Bunny	3.20	8.00	16.00
202-Space Explorer	9.15	27.50	55.00
203-Woody Woodpecker	2.80	7.00	14.00
204-Tarzan	10.00	30.00	70.00
205-Mighty Mouse	6.35	19.00	38.00
206-Roy Rogers; photo-c	8.35	25.00	50.00
207-Tom and Jerry	2.80	7.00	14.00
208-The Lone Ranger; Clayton Moore photo-c	12.00	36.00	85.00
209-Porky Pig	2.80	7.00	14.00
210-Lassie (TV)	6.35	19.00	38.00
211-Sears Special - not published			
212-Christmas Eve	2.40	6.00	12.00
213-Here Comes Santa (1960)	2.40	6.00	12.00
214-Huckleberry Hound (TV)(1961)	6.00	18.00	40.00
215-Hi Yo Silver	6.00	18.00	40.00
216-Rocky & His Friends (TV)(1961); predates Rocky and His Fiendish Friends #1 (see Four Color #1128)	10.00	30.00	70.00
217-Lassie (TV)	5.70	17.00	35.00
218-Porky Pig	2.80	7.00	14.00
219-Journey to the Sun	5.35	16.00	32.00
220-Bugs Bunny	3.20	8.00	16.00
221-Roy and Dale; photo-c	7.50	22.50	45.00
222-Woody Woodpecker	2.80	7.00	14.00
223-Tarzan	10.00	30.00	70.00
224-Tom and Jerry	2.80	7.00	14.00
225-The Lone Ranger	7.50	22.50	45.00
226-Christmas Treasury (1961)	2.40	6.00	12.00
227-Letters to Santa (1961)	2.40	6.00	12.00
228-Sears Special - not published?			
229-The Flintstones (TV)(1962); early app.; predates 1st Flintstones Gold Key issue (#7)	10.00	30.00	70.00
230-Lassie (TV)	5.00	15.00	30.00
231-Bugs Bunny	3.20	8.00	16.00
232-The Three Stooges	10.00	30.00	65.00
233-Bullwinkle (TV) (1962, very early app.)	11.00	32.00	75.00
234-Smokey the Bear	4.00	10.00	20.00
235-Huckleberry Hound (TV)	6.00	18.00	40.00
236-Roy and Dale	5.85	17.50	35.00
237-Mighty Mouse	4.70	14.00	28.00

	GD2.0	FN6.0	NM9.4
238-The Lone Ranger	7.50	22.50	45.00
239-Woody Woodpecker	2.80	7.00	14.00
240-Tarzan	9.15	27.50	60.00
241-Santa Claus Around the World	2.00	5.00	10.00
242-Santa's Toyland (1962)	2.00	5.00	10.00
243-The Flintstones (TV)(1963)	9.15	27.50	55.00
244-Mister Ed (TV); early app.; photo-c	5.85	17.50	35.00
245-Bugs Bunny	3.20	8.00	16.00
246-Popeye	4.35	13.00	26.00
247-Mighty Mouse	4.70	14.00	28.00
248-The Three Stooges	10.00	30.00	65.00
249-Woody Woodpecker	2.80	7.00	14.00
250-Roy and Dale	5.85	17.50	35.00
251-Little Lulu & Witch Hazel	14.00	43.00	100.00
252-Tarzan; painted-c	9.15	27.50	55.00
253-Yogi Bear (TV)	7.15	21.50	50.00
254-Lassie (TV)	5.35	16.00	32.00
255-Santa's Christmas List	2.40	6.00	12.00
256-Christmas Party (1963)	2.40	6.00	12.00
257-Mighty Mouse	4.70	14.00	28.00
258-The Sword in the Stone (Disney)	9.15	27.50	55.00
259-Bugs Bunny	3.20	8.00	16.00
260-Mister Ed (TV)	4.70	14.00	28.00
261-Woody Woodpecker	2.80	7.00	14.00
262-Tarzan	8.35	25.00	50.00
263-Donald Duck; not by Barks (Disney)	10.00	30.00	65.00
264-Popeye	4.35	13.00	26.00
265-Yogi Bear (TV)	5.70	17.00	35.00
266-Lassie (TV)	4.15	12.50	25.00
267-Little Lulu; Irving Tripp-a	11.50	34.00	80.00
268-The Three Stooges	10.00	30.00	60.00
269-A Jolly Christmas	2.00	5.00	10.00
270-Santa's Little Helpers	2.00	5.00	10.00
271-The Flintstones (TV)(1965)	9.15	27.50	60.00
272-Tarzan	8.35	25.00	50.00
273-Bugs Bunny	3.20	8.00	16.00
274-Popeye	4.35	13.00	26.00
275-Little Lulu; Irving Tripp-a	10.00	30.00	65.00
276-The Jetsons (TV)	16.00	47.00	110.00
277-Daffy Duck	3.20	8.00	16.00
278-Lassie (TV)	4.15	12.50	25.00
279-Yogi Bear (TV)	5.70	17.00	35.00
280-The Three Stooges; photo-c	10.00	30.00	60.00
281-Tom and Jerry	2.40	6.00	12.00
282-Mister Ed (TV)	4.70	14.00	28.00
283-Santa's Visit	2.40	6.00	12.00
284-Christmas Parade (1965)	2.40	6.00	12.00
285-Astro Boy (TV); 2nd app. Astro Boy	41.00	122.00	300.00
286-Tarzan	7.50	22.50	45.00
287-Bugs Bunny	3.20	8.00	16.00
288-Daffy Duck	2.80	7.00	14.00
289-The Flintstones (TV)	8.50	26.00	60.00
290-Mister Ed (TV); photo-c	4.00	12.00	24.00
291-Yogi Bear (TV)	5.00	15.00	30.00
292-The Three Stooges; photo-c	10.00	30.00	60.00
293-Little Lulu; Irving Tripp-a	9.15	27.50	55.00
294-Popeye	4.35	13.00	26.00
295-Tom and Jerry	2.40	6.00	12.00
296-Lassie (TV); photo-c	4.00	11.00	22.00
297-Christmas Bells	2.40	6.00	12.00
298-Santa's Sleigh (1966)	2.40	6.00	12.00
299-The Flintstones (TV)(1967)	8.50	26.00	60.00
300-Tarzan	7.50	22.50	45.00
301-Bugs Bunny	2.80	7.00	14.00
302-Laurel and Hardy (TV); photo-c	5.00	15.00	30.00
303-Daffy Duck	2.00	5.00	10.00
304-The Three Stooges; photo-c	9.15	27.50	55.00

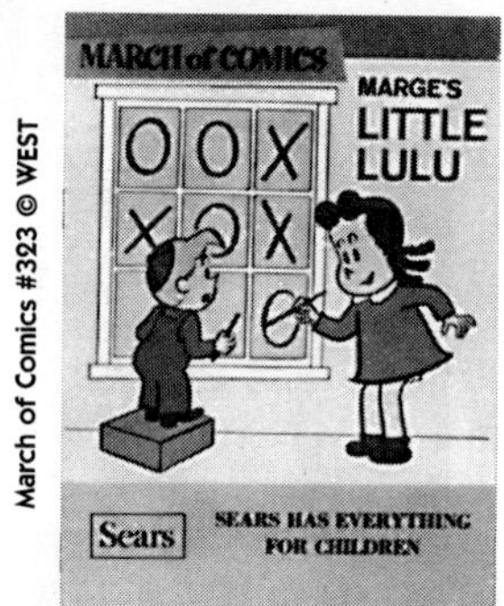

March of Comics #323 © WEST

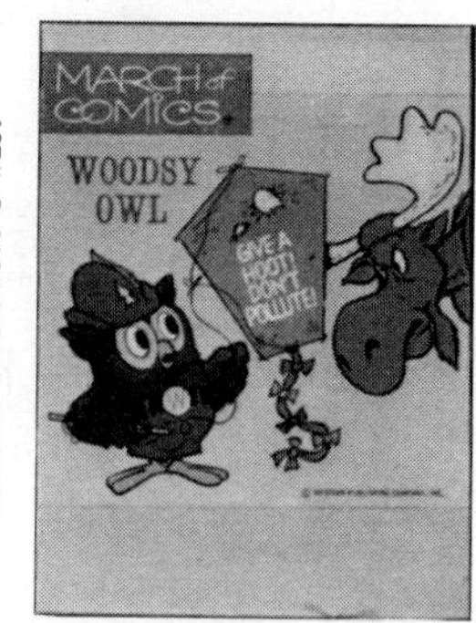

March of Comics #395 © WEST

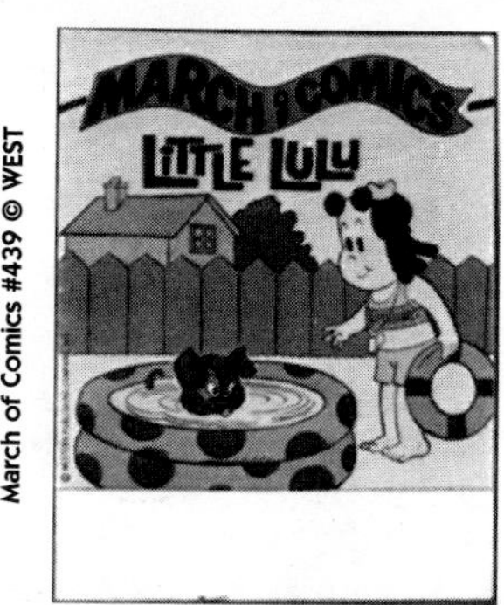

March of Comics #439 © WEST

	GD2.0	FN6.0	NM9.4
305-Tom and Jerry	2.00	5.00	10.00
306-Daniel Boone (TV); Fess Parker photo-c	5.85	17.50	40.00
307-Little Lulu; Irving Tripp-a	7.50	22.50	45.00
308-Lassie (TV); photo-c	4.00	11.00	22.00
309-Yogi Bear (TV)	4.25	13.00	28.00
310-The Lone Ranger; Clayton Moore photo-c	12.00	36.00	85.00
311-Santa's Show	2.40	6.00	12.00
312-Christmas Album (1967)	2.40	6.00	12.00
313-Daffy Duck (1968)	2.00	5.00	10.00
314-Laurel and Hardy (TV)	4.70	14.00	28.00
315-Bugs Bunny	2.80	7.00	14.00
316-The Three Stooges	7.50	22.50	45.00
317-The Flintstones (TV)	7.15	21.50	50.00
318-Tarzan	6.70	20.00	40.00
319-Yogi Bear (TV)	4.25	13.00	28.00
320-Space Family Robinson (TV); Spiegle-a	14.00	43.00	100.00
321-Tom and Jerry	2.00	5.00	10.00
322-The Lone Ranger	6.70	20.00	40.00
323-Little Lulu; not by Stanley	4.35	13.00	26.00
324-Lassie (TV); photo-c	4.00	11.00	22.00
325-Fun with Santa	2.40	6.00	12.00
326-Christmas Story (1968)	2.40	6.00	12.00
327-The Flintstones (TV)(1969)	7.15	21.50	50.00
328-Space Family Robinson (TV); Spiegle-a	14.00	43.00	100.00
329-Bugs Bunny	2.80	7.00	14.00
330-The Jetsons (TV)	11.50	34.00	80.00
331-Daffy Duck	2.00	5.00	10.00
332-Tarzan	5.35	16.00	32.00
333-Tom and Jerry	2.00	5.00	10.00
334-Lassie (TV)	4.00	10.00	20.00
335-Little Lulu	4.35	13.00	26.00
336-The Three Stooges	7.50	22.50	45.00
337-Yogi Bear (TV)	4.25	13.00	28.00
338-The Lone Ranger	6.70	20.00	40.00
339-(Was not published)			
340-Here Comes Santa (1969)	2.40	6.00	12.00
341-The Flintstones (TV)	7.15	21.50	50.00
342-Tarzan	5.35	16.00	32.00
343-Bugs Bunny	2.40	6.00	12.00
344-Yogi Bear (TV)	4.15	12.50	25.00
345-Tom and Jerry	2.00	5.00	10.00
346-Lassie (TV)	4.00	10.00	20.00
347-Daffy Duck	2.00	5.00	10.00
348-The Jetsons (TV)	10.00	30.00	70.00
349-Little Lulu; not by Stanley	4.00	11.00	22.00
350-The Lone Ranger	5.00	15.00	30.00
351-Beep-Beep, the Road Runner (TV)	2.80	7.00	14.00
352-Space Family Robinson (TV); Spiegle-a	14.00	43.00	100.00
353-Beep-Beep, the Road Runner (1971) (TV)	2.80	7.00	14.00
354-Tarzan (1971)	4.70	14.00	28.00
355-Little Lulu; not by Stanley	4.00	11.00	22.00
356-Scooby Doo, Where Are You? (TV)	7.15	21.50	50.00
357-Daffy Duck & Porky Pig	2.00	5.00	10.00
358-Lassie (TV)	4.00	10.00	20.00
359-Baby Snoots	2.80	7.00	14.00
360-H. R. Pufnstuf (TV); photo-c	7.15	21.50	50.00
361-Tom and Jerry	2.00	5.00	10.00
362-Smokey the Bear (TV)	2.00	5.00	10.00
363-Bugs Bunny & Yosemite Sam	2.40	6.00	12.00
364-The Banana Splits (TV); photo-c	5.70	17.00	40.00
365-Tom and Jerry (1972)	2.00	5.00	10.00
366-Tarzan	4.35	13.00	26.00
367-Bugs Bunny & Porky Pig	2.40	6.00	12.00
368-Scooby Doo (TV)(4/72)	5.70	17.00	40.00
369-Little Lulu; not by Stanley	3.60	9.00	18.00
370-Lassie (TV); photo-c	4.00	10.00	20.00
371-Baby Snoots	2.40	6.00	12.00

	GD2.0	FN6.0	NM9.4
372-Smokey the Bear (TV)	2.00	5.00	10.00
373-The Three Stooges	6.70	20.00	40.00
374-Wacky Witch	2.00	5.00	10.00
375-Beep-Beep & Daffy Duck (TV)	2.00	5.00	10.00
376-The Pink Panther (1972) (TV)	2.80	7.00	14.00
377-Baby Snoots (1973)	2.40	6.00	12.00
378-Turok, Son of Stone; new-a	16.00	47.00	110.00
379-Heckle & Jeckle New Terrytoons (TV)	2.00	5.00	10.00
380-Bugs Bunny & Yosemite Sam	2.00	5.00	10.00
381-Lassie (TV)	3.20	8.00	16.00
382-Scooby Doo, Where Are You? (TV)	5.00	15.00	30.00
383-Smokey the Bear (TV)	1.60	4.00	8.00
384-Pink Panther (TV)	2.00	5.00	10.00
385-Little Lulu	3.00	7.50	15.00
386-Wacky Witch	1.60	4.00	8.00
387-Beep-Beep & Daffy Duck (TV)	1.60	4.00	8.00
388-Tom and Jerry (1973)	1.60	4.00	8.00
389-Little Lulu; not by Stanley	3.00	7.50	15.00
390-Pink Panther (TV)	1.60	4.00	8.00
391-Scooby Doo (TV)	4.15	12.50	25.00
392-Bugs Bunny & Yosemite Sam	1.20	3.00	6.00
393-New Terrytoons (Heckle & Jeckle) (TV)	1.20	3.00	6.00
394-Lassie (TV)	2.40	6.00	12.00
395-Woodsy Owl	1.20	3.00	6.00
396-Baby Snoots	1.60	4.00	8.00
397-Beep-Beep & Daffy Duck (TV)	1.20	3.00	6.00
398-Wacky Witch	1.20	3.00	6.00
399-Turok, Son of Stone; new-a	13.00	39.00	90.00
400-Tom and Jerry	1.20	3.00	6.00
401-Baby Snoots (1975) (r/#371)	1.60	4.00	8.00
402-Daffy Duck (r/#313)	1.00	2.50	5.00
403-Bugs Bunny (r/#343)	1.20	3.00	6.00
404-Space Family Robinson (TV)(r/#328)	10.00	30.00	70.00
405-Cracky	1.00	2.50	5.00
406-Little Lulu (r/#355)	2.40	6.00	12.00
407-Smokey the Bear (TV)(r/#362)	1.20	3.00	6.00
408-Turok, Son of Stone; c-r/Turok #20 w/changes; new-a	9.30	28.00	65.00
409-Pink Panther (TV)	1.00	2.50	5.00
410-Wacky Witch	.80	2.00	4.00
411-Lassie (TV)(r/#324)	2.40	6.00	12.00
412-New Terrytoons (1975) (TV)	.80	2.00	4.00
413-Daffy Duck (1976)(r/#331)	.80	2.00	4.00
414-Space Family Robinson (r/#328)	9.30	28.00	65.00
415-Bugs Bunny (r/#329)	.80	2.00	4.00
416-Beep-Beep, the Road Runner (r/#353)(TV)	.80	2.00	4.00
417-Little Lulu (r/#323)	2.40	6.00	12.00
418-Pink Panther (r/#384) (TV)	.80	2.00	4.00
419-Baby Snoots (r/#377)	1.00	2.50	5.00
420-Woody Woodpecker	.80	2.00	4.00
421-Tweety & Sylvester	.80	2.00	4.00
422-Wacky Witch (r/#386)	.80	2.00	4.00
423-Little Monsters	1.00	2.50	5.00
424-Cracky (12/76)	.80	2.00	4.00
425-Daffy Duck	.80	2.00	4.00
426-Underdog (TV)	5.00	15.00	30.00
427-Little Lulu (r/#335)	1.60	4.00	8.00
428-Bugs Bunny	.60	1.50	3.00
429-The Pink Panther (TV)	.60	1.50	3.00
430-Beep-Beep, the Road Runner (TV)	.60	1.50	3.00
431-Baby Snoots	.80	2.00	4.00
432-Lassie (TV)	1.20	3.00	6.00
433-437: 433-Tweety & Sylvester. 434-Wacky Witch. 435-New Terrytoons (TV). 436-Wacky Advs. of Cracky. 437-Daffy Duck	.60	1.50	3.00
438-Underdog (TV)	4.15	12.50	25.00
439-Little Lulu (r/#349)	1.60	4.00	8.00
440-442,444-446: 440-Bugs Bunny. 441-The Pink Panther (TV). 442-Beep-			

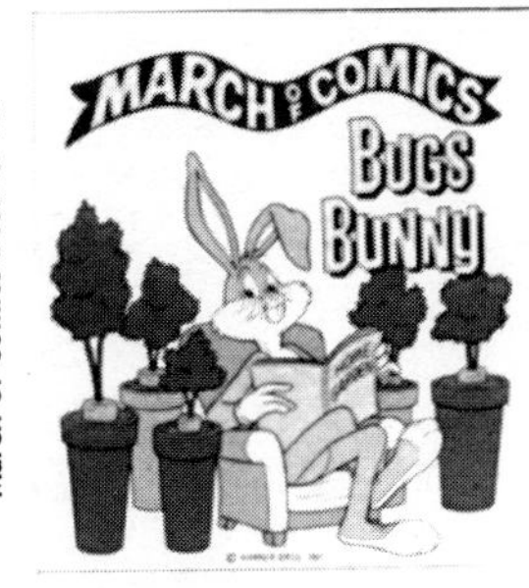

March of Comics #452 © WB

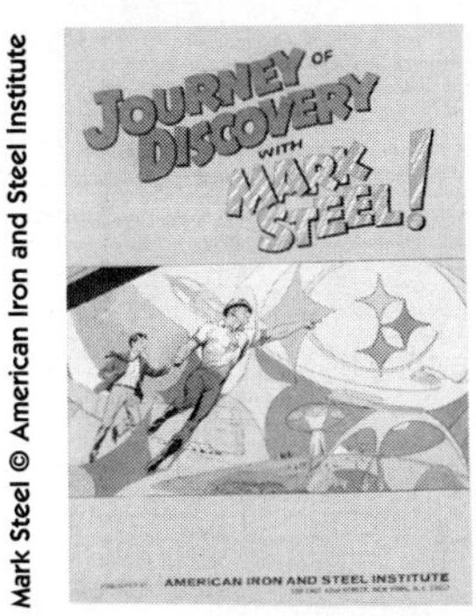

Mark Steel © American Iron and Steel Institute

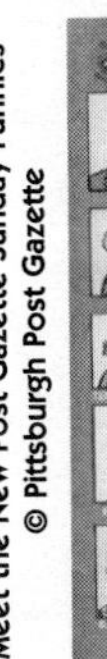
Meet the New Post Gazette Sunday Funnies © Pittsburgh Post Gazette

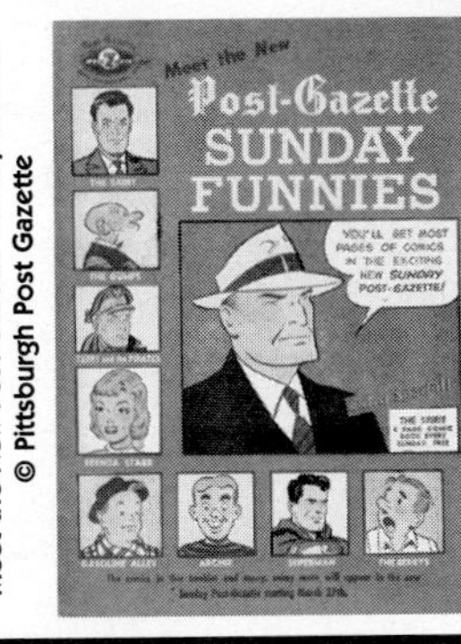

GD2.0 FN6.0 NM9.4

Beep, the Road Runner (TV). 444-Tom and Jerry. 445-Tweety and Sylvester. 446-Wacky Witch .60 1.50 3.00
443-Baby Snoots .80 2.00 4.00
447-Mighty Mouse 1.20 3.00 6.00
448-455,457,458: 448-Cracky. 449-Pink Panther (TV). 450-Baby Snoots 451-Tom and Jerry. 452-Bugs Bunny. 453-Popeye. 454-Woody Woodpecker. 455-Beep-Beep, the Road Runner (TV). 457-Tweety & Sylvester. 458-Wacky Witch .60 1.50 3.00
456-Little Lulu (r/#369) 1.20 3.00 6.00
459-Mighty Mouse 1.20 3.00 6.00
460-466: 460-Daffy Duck. 461-The Pink Panther (TV). 462-Baby Snoots. 463-Tom and Jerry. 464-Bugs Bunny. 465-Popeye. 466-Woody Woodpecker .60 1.50 3.00
467-Underdog (TV) 4.00 10.00 20.00
468-Little Lulu (r/#385) .80 2.00 4.00
469-Tweety & Sylvester .60 1.50 3.00
470-Wacky Witch .60 1.50 3.00
471-Mighty Mouse .80 2.50 5.00
472-474,476-478: 472-Heckle & Jeckle(12/80). 473-Pink Panther(1/81)(TV). 474-Baby Snoots. 476-Bugs Bunny. 477-Popeye. 478-Woody Woodpecker .60 1.50 3.00
475-Little Lulu (r/#323) .80 2.00 4.00
479-Underdog (TV) 3.00 7.50 15.00
480-482: 480-Tom and Jerry. 481-Tweety and Sylvester. 482-Wacky Witch .60 1.50 3.00
483-Mighty Mouse .80 2.00 5.00
484-487: 484-Heckle & Jeckle. 485-Baby Snoots. 486-The Pink Panther (TV). 487-Bugs Bunny .60 1.50 3.00
488-Little Lulu (4/82) (r/#335) .80 2.00 4.00

MARGARET O'BRIEN (See The Adventures of...)

MARK STEEL
American Iron & Steel Institute: 1967, 1968, 1972 (Giveaway) (24 pgs.)
1967,1968- "Journey of Discovery with..."; Neal Adams art 2.50 7.50 20.00
1972- "...Fights Pollution"; N. Adams-a 1.25 3.75 10.00

MARVEL COLLECTOR'S EDITION: X-MEN
Marvel Comics: 1993 (3-3/4x6-1/2")
1-4-Pizza Hut giveaways 3.00

MARVEL COMICS PRESENTS
Marvel Comics: 1988 (4 1/4 x 6 1/4, 20 pgs.)
...Mini Comic Giveaway (4 different issues)
nn-Alf 1.00 3.00 8.00
nn-Flintstone Kids 1.00 3.00 8.00
nn-Spider-Man-reprints Amazing Spider-Man #1 1.00 2.80 7.00
nn-X-Men-reprints X-Men #53; B. Smith-a 1.00 2.80 7.00

MARVEL MINI-BOOKS
Marvel Comics Group: 1966 (50 pgs., B&W; 5/8x7/8") (6 different issues) (Smallest comics ever published) (Marvel Mania Giveaways)
Captain America, Millie the Model, Spider-Man, Sgt. Fury, Hulk, Thor 6.00 18.00 65.00
NOTE: *Each came in six different color covers, usually one color: Pink, yellow, green, etc.*

MARY'S GREATEST APOSTLE (St. Louis Grignion de Montfort)
Catechetical Guild (Topix) (Giveaway): No date (16 pgs.; paper cover)
nn 2.80 7.00 14.00

MASKED PILOT, THE (See Popular Comics #43)
R.S. Callender: 1939 (7-1/2x5-1/4", 16 pgs., premium, non-slick-c)
nn-Bob Jenney-a 10.00 30.00 70.00

McCRORY'S CHRISTMAS BOOK
Western Printing Co: 1955 (36 pgs., slick-c) (McCrory Stores Corp. giveaway)
nn-Painted-c 3.60 9.00 18.00

McCRORY'S TOYLAND BRINGS YOU SANTA'S PRIVATE EYES
Promotional Publ. Co.: 1956 (16 pgs.) (Giveaway)
nn-Has 9 pg. story plus 7 pgs. toy ads 2.80 7.00 14.00

McCRORY'S WONDERFUL CHRISTMAS
Promotional Publ. Co.: 1954 (20 pgs., slick-c) (Giveaway)
nn 3.60 9.00 18.00

MEET HIYA A FRIEND OF SANTA CLAUS
Julian J. Proskauer/Sundial Shoe Stores, etc.: 1949 (18 pgs.?, paper-c)-(Giveaway)
nn 5.85 17.50 35.00

MEET THE NEW POST GAZETTE SUNDAY FUNNIES
Pittsburgh Post Gazette: 3/12/49 (7-1/4x10-1/4", 16 pgs., paper-c)
Commercial Comics (insert in newspaper)
Dick Tracy by Gould, Gasoline Alley, Terry & the Pirates, Brenda Starr, Buck Rogers by Yager, The Gumps, Peter Rabbit by Fago, Superman, Funnyman by Siegel & Shuster, The Saint, Archie, & others done especially for this book. A fine copy sold at auction in 1985 for $276.00.
Estimated value.... $300 – $800

MEN OF COURAGE
Catechetical Guild: 1949
Bound Topix comics-V7#2,4,6,8,10,16,18,20 4.00 10.00 20.00

MEN WHO MOVE THE NATION
Publisher unknown: (Giveaway) (B&W)
nn-Neal Adams-a 4.25 13.00 26.00

MERRY CHRISTMAS, A
K. K. Publications (Child Life Shoes): 1948 (Giveaway)
nn 5.00 15.00 30.00

MERRY CHRISTMAS
K. K. Publications (Blue Bird Shoes Giveaway): 1956 (7-1/4x5-1/4")
nn 4.00 10.00 20.00

MERRY CHRISTMAS FROM MICKEY MOUSE
K. K. Publications: 1939 (16 pgs.) (Color & B&W) (Shoe store giveaway)
nn-Donald Duck & Pluto app.; text with art (Rare); c-reprint/Mickey Mouse Mag. V3#3 (12/37)(Rare) 300.00 1200.00 2400.00

MERRY CHRISTMAS FROM SEARS TOYLAND (See Santa's Christmas Comic)
Sears Roebuck Giveaway: 1939 (16 pgs.) (Color)
nn-Dick Tracy, Little Orphan Annie, The Gumps, Terry & the Pirates 100.00 500.00 1000.00

MICKEY MOUSE (Also see Frito-Lay Giveaway)
Dell Publ. Co
...& Goofy Explore Business(1978) 4.00
...& Goofy Explore Energy(1976-1978, 36 pgs.); Exxon giveaway in color; regular size 4.00
...& Goofy Explore Energy Conservation(1976-1978)-Exxon 4.00
...& Goofy Explore The Universe of Energy(1985, 20 pgs.); Exxon giveaway in color; regular size 3.00
The Perils of Mickey nn (1993, 5-1/4x7-1/4", 16 pgs.)-Nabisco giveaway w/ games, Nabisco coupons & 6 pgs. of stories; Phantom Blot app. 2.00

MICKEY MOUSE MAGAZINE
Walt Disney Productions: V1#1, Jan, 1933 - V1#9, Sept, 1933 (5-1/4x7-1/4")
No. 1-3 published by Kamen-Blair (Kay Kamen, Inc.)
GD2.0 FN6.0 VF8.0
(Scarce)-Distributed by dairies and leading stores through their local theatres. First few issues had 5¢ listed on cover, later ones had no price.
V1#1 500.00 2000.00 4000.00
2-9 200.00 500.00 1000.00

MICKEY MOUSE MAGAZINE
Walt Disney Productions: V1#1, 11/33 - V2#12, 10/35 (Mills giveaways issued by different dairies)
GD2.0 FN6.0 NM9.4
V1#1 225.00 750.00 1500.00
2-12: 2-X-Mas issue 75.00 250.00 500.00
V2#1-12: 2-X-Mas issue. 4-St. Valentine-c 50.00 175.00 350.00
V4#1 (Giveaway) 50.00 175.00 350.00

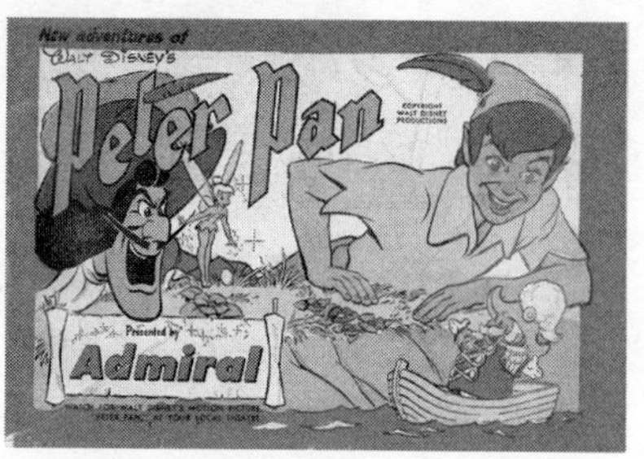

New Adventures of Peter Pan © WDC

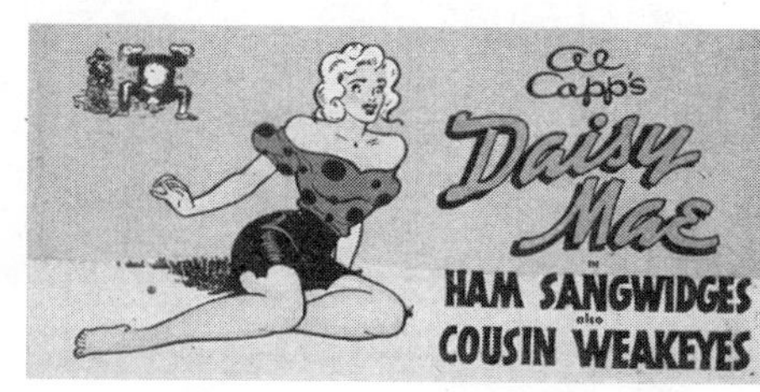

Oxydol-Dreft #2 © Oxydol-Dreft

GD2.0 FN6.0 NM9.4

MIGHTY ATOM, THE
Whitman
Giveaway(1959, '63, Whitman)-Evans-a 2.00 6.00 15.00
Giveaway ('64r, '65r, '66r, '67r, '68r, '73r, '76r)-Evans-r? 2.40 6.00

MINUTE MAN
Sovereign Service Station giveaway: No date (16 pgs., B&W, paper-c blue & red)
nn-American history 2.00 5.00 10.00

MINUTE MAN ANSWERS THE CALL, THE
By M. C. Gaine: 1942 (4 pgs.) (Giveaway inserted in Jr. JSA Membership Kit)
nn-Sheldon Moldoff-a 21.00 64.00 150.00

MIRACLE ON BROADWAY
Broadway Comics: Dec, 1995 (Giveaway)
1-Ernie Colon-c/a; Jim Shooter &Co. story; 1st known digitally printed comic book; 1st app. Spire & Knights on Broadway (1150 print run) 20.00
NOTE: *Miracle on Broadway was a limited edition comic given to 1100 VIPs in the entertainment industry for the 1995 Holiday Season.*

MISS SUNBEAM (See Little Miss Sunbeam Comics)

MR. BUG GOES TO TOWN (See Cinema Comics Herald)
K.K. Publications: 1941 (Giveaway, 52 pgs.)
nn-Cartoon movie (scarce) 75.00 300.00 600.00

MOTHER OF US ALL
Catechetical Guild Giveaway: 1950? (32 pgs.)
nn 2.00 5.00 10.00

MOTION PICTURE FUNNIES WEEKLY (Amazing Man #5 on?)
First Funnies, Inc.: 1939 (Giveaway)(B&W, 36 pgs.)
No month given; last panel in Sub-Mariner story dated 4/39
(Also see Colossus, Green Giant & Invaders No. 20)
1-Origin & 1st printed app. Sub-Mariner by Bill Everett (8 pgs.); Fred Schwab-c; reprinted in Marvel Mystery #1 with color added over the craft tint which was used to shade the black & white version; Spy Ring, American Ace (reprinted in Marvel Mystery #3) app. (Rare)-only eight (8) known copies,one near mint with white pages, the rest with brown pages. 4000.00 10,000.00 20,000.00
Covers only to #2-4 (set) 500.00
NOTE: The only eight known copies (with a ninth suspected) were discovered in 1974 in the estate of the deceased publisher. Covers only to issues No. 2-4 were also found which evidently were printed in advance along with #1. #1 was to be distributed only through motion picture movie houses. However, it is believed that only advanced copies were sent out and the motion picture houses not going for the idea. Possible distribution at local theaters in Boston suspected. The last panel of Sub-Mariner contains a rectangular box with "Continued Next Week" printed in it. When reprinted in Marvel Mystery, the box was left in with lettering omitted.

MY DOG TIGE (Buster Brown's Dog)
Buster Brown Shoes: 1957 (Giveaway)
nn 5.00 20.00 30.00

MY GREATEST THRILLS IN BASEBALL
Mission of California: Date? (16 pg. Giveaway)
nn-By Mickey Mantle 75.00 200.00 500.00

NATURAL DISASTERS!
Graphic Information Service/ Civil Defense: 1956 (16 pgs., soft-c)
nn-Al Capp Li'l Abner-c; Li'l Abner cameo (1 panel); narrated by Mr. Civil Defense 10.00 50.00 75.00

NAVY: HISTORY & TRADITION
Stokes Walesby Co./Dept. of Navy: 1958 - 1961 (nn) (Giveaway)
1772-1778, 1778-1782, 1782-1817, 1817-1865, 1865-1936, 1940-1945:
1772-1778-16 pg. in color 4.25 13.00 28.00
1861: Naval Actions of the Civil War: 1865-36 pg. in color; flag-c 4.25 13.00 28.00

NEW ADVENTURE OF WALT DISNEY'S SNOW WHITE AND THE SEVEN DWARFS, A (See Snow White Bendix Giveaway)

NEW ADVENTURES OF PETER PAN (Disney)
Western Publishing Co.: 1953 (5x7-1/4", 36 pgs.) (Admiral giveaway)
nn 13.00 40.00 90.00

NEW TEEN TITANS, THE
DC Comics: Nov. 1983
nn(11/83-Keebler Co. Giveaway)-In cooperation with "The President's Drug Awareness Campaign"; came in Presidential envelope w/letter from White House (Nancy Reagan) 1.00
nn-(re-issue of above on Mando paper for direct sales market); American Soft Drink Ind. version; I.B.M. Corp. version 1.00

OLD GLORY COMICS
Chesapeake & Ohio Railway: 1944 (Giveaway)
nn-Capt. Fearless reprint 5.85 17.50 35.00

ON THE AIR
NBC Network Comic: 1947 (Giveaway, paper-c)
nn-(Rare) 30.00 100.00 175.00

OUT OF THE PAST A CLUE TO THE FUTURE
E. C. Comics (Public Affairs Comm.): 1946? (16 pgs.) (paper cover)
nn-Based on public affairs pamphlet "What Foreign Trade Means to You" 24.00 71.00 165.00

OUTSTANDING AMERICAN WAR HEROES
The Parents' Institute: 1944 (16 pgs., paper-c)
nn-Reprints from True Comics 4.00 12.00 24.00

OVERSEAS COMICS (Also see G.I. Comics & Jeep Comics)
Giveaway (Distributed to U.S. Armed Forces): 1944 - No. 105?, 1946 (7-1/4x10-1/4"; 16 pgs. in color)
23-105-Bringing Up Father (by McManus), Popeye, Joe Palooka, Dick Tracy, Superman, Gasoline Alley, Buz Sawyer, Li'l Abner, Blondie, Terry & the Pirates, Out Our Way 5.85 17.50 35.00

OWL, THE (See Crackajack Funnies #25 & Popular Comics #72)(Also see The Hurricane Kids & Magic Morro
Western Pub. Co./R.S. Callender: 1940 (Giveaway)(7-1/2x5-1/4")(Soft-c, color)
nn-Frank Thomas-a 21.00 64.00 150.00

OXYDOL-DREFT
Oxydol-Dreft:1950 (Set of 6 pocket-size giveaways; distributed through the mail as a set) (Scarce)
1-3: 1-Li'l Abner. 2-Daisy Mae. 3-Shmoo 13.00 40.00 90.00
4-John Wayne; Williamson/Frazetta-c from John Wayne #3 17.00 51.00 120.00
5-Archie 14.00 43.00 100.00
6-Terrytoons Mighty Mouse 13.00 40.00 90.00
NOTE: *Set is worth more with original envelope.*

PADRE OF THE POOR
Catechetical Guild: nd (Giveaway) (16 pgs., paper-c)
nn 3.00 7.50 15.00

PAUL TERRY'S HOW TO DRAW FUNNY CARTOONS
Terrytoons, Inc. (Giveaway): 1940's (14 pgs.) (Black & White)
nn-Heckle & Jeckle, Mighty Mouse, etc. 12.00 36.00 85.00

PETER PAN (See New Adventures of Peter Pan)

PETER PENNY AND HIS MAGIC DOLLAR
American Bankers Association, N. Y. (Giveaway): 1947 (16 pgs.; paper-c; regular size)
nn-(Scarce)-Used in **SOTI**, pg. 310, 311 17.00 51.00 120.00
Diff. version (7-1/4x11")-redrawn, 16 pgs., paper-c 10.00 30.00 65.00

PETER WHEAT (The Adventures of...)
Bakers Associates Giveaway: 1948 - 1956? (16 pgs. in color) (paper covers)
nn(No.1)-States on last page, end of 1st Adventure of...; Kelly-a 30.00 120.00 240.00
nn(4 issues)-Kelly-a 19.00 75.00 150.00
6-10-All Kelly-a 15.00 45.00 105.00
11-20-All Kelly-a 13.00 40.00 90.00

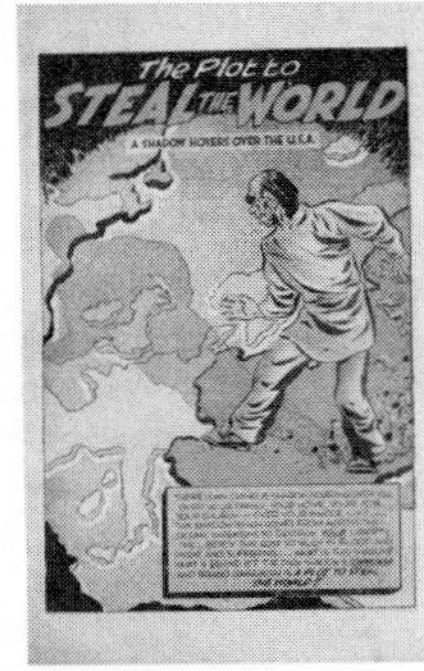

Plot to Steal the World © Work & Unity Group

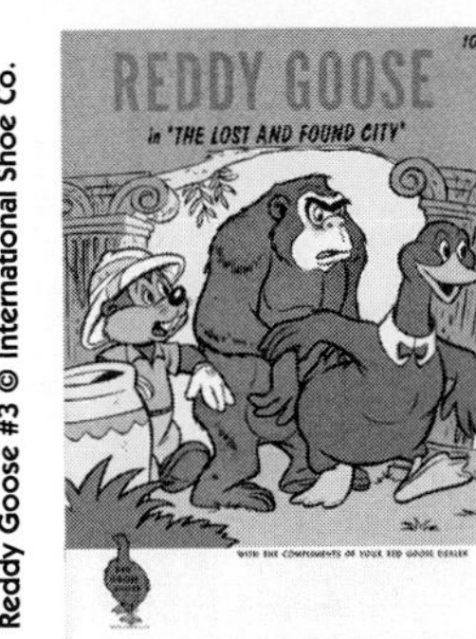

Reddy Goose #3 © International Shoe Co.

Reddy Kilowatt #2 © E.C.

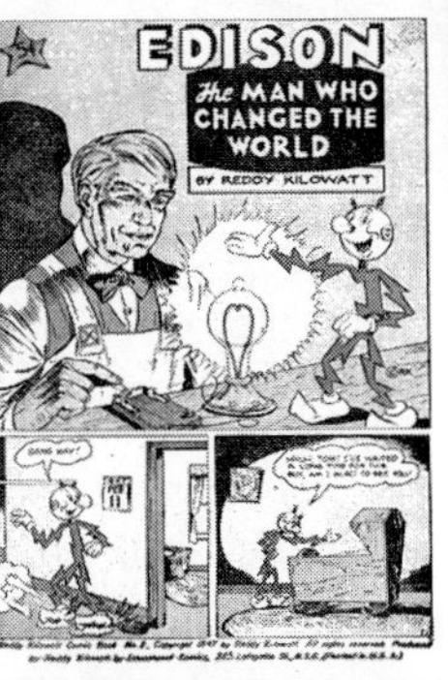

GD2.0 FN6.0 NM9.4

21-35-All Kelly-a 11.00 33.00 75.00
36-66 8.35 25.00 50.00
...Artist's Workbook ('54, digest size) 8.35 25.00 50.00
...Four-In-One Fun Pack (Vol. 2, '54), oblong, comics w/puzzles 10.00 30.00 60.00
...Fun Book ('52, 32 pgs., paper-c, B&W & color, 8-1/2x10-3/4")-Contains cut-outs, puzzles, games, magic & pages to color 12.00 36.00 85.00
NOTE: *Al Hubbard art #36 on; written by Del Connell.*

PETER WHEAT NEWS
Bakers Associates: 1948 - No. 30, 1950 (4 pgs. in color)
Vol. 1-All have 2 pgs. Peter Wheat by Kelly 25.00 100.00 200.00
2-10 18.00 54.00 125.00
11-20 11.00 33.00 75.00
21-30 8.35 25.00 50.00
NOTE: *Early issues have no date & **Kelly** art.*

PINOCCHIO
Cocomalt/Montgomery Ward Co.: 1940 (10 pgs.; giveaway, linen-like paper)
nn-Cocomalt edition 24.00 71.00 165.00
nn-store edition 19.00 58.00 135.00

PIUS XII MAN OF PEACE
Catechetical Guild: No date (12 pgs.; 5-1/2x8-1/2") (B&W)
nn-Catechetical Guild Giveaway 4.00 12.00 24.00

PLOT TO STEAL THE WORLD, THE
Work & Unity Group: 1948, 16pgs., paper-c
nn-Anti commumism 19.00 56.00 140.00

POCAHONTAS
Pocahontas Fuel Company (Coal): 1941 - No. 2, 1942
nn(#1), 2-Feat. life story of Indian princess Pocahontas & facts about Pocahontas coal, Pocahontas, VA. 16.00 48.00 120.00

POLL PARROT
Poll Parrot Shoe Store/International Shoe
K. K. Publications (Giveaway): 1950 - No. 4, 1951; No. 2, 1959 - No. 16, 1962
1 ('50)-Howdy Doody; small size 25.00 75.00 150.00
2-4('51)-Howdy Doody 15.00 62.00 125.00
2('59)-16('62): 2-The Secret of Crumbley Castle. 5-Bandit Busters. 7-The Make-Believe Mummy. 8-Mixed Up Mission('60). 10-The Frightful Flight. 11-Showdown at Sunup. 12-Maniac at Mubu Island. 13-...and the Runaway Genie. 14-Bully for You. 15-Trapped In Tall Timber. 16-...& the Rajah's Ruby('62) 2.25 6.75 18.00

POPEYE
Whitman
Bold Detergent giveaway (Same as regular issue #94) 5.00
Quaker Cereal premium (1989, 16pp, small size,4 diff.)(Popeye & the Time Machine,--On Safari, --& Big Foot, --vs. Bluto) 1.85 5.50 15.00

POPEYE
Charlton (King Features) (Giveaway): 1972 - 1974 (36 pgs. in color)
E-1 to E-15 (Educational comics) 1.00 2.80 7.00
nn-Popeye Gettin' Better Grades-4 pgs. used as intro. to above giveaways (in color) 1.00 2.80 7.00

POPSICLE PETE FUN BOOK (See All-American Comics #6)
Joe Lowe Corp.: 1947, 1948
nn-36 pgs. in color; Sammy 'n' Claras, The King Who Couldn't Sleep & Popsicle Pete stories, games, cut-outs 11.00 33.00 75.00
Adventure Book ('48)-Has Classics ad with checklist to HRN #343 (Great Expectations #43) 10.00 30.00 65.00

PORKY'S BOOK OF TRICKS
K. K. Publications (Giveaway): 1942 (8-1/2x5-1/2", 48 pgs.)
nn-7 pg. comic story, text stories, plus games & puzzles 50.00 225.00 450.00

GD2.0 FN6.0 NM9.4

POST GAZETTE (See Meet the New...)

POWER RECORD COMICS
Marvel Comics/Power Records: 1974 - 1978 ($1.49, 7x10" comics, 20 pgs. with 45 R.P.M. record)
PR10-Spider-Man-r/from #124,125; Man-Wolf app. PR11-Hulk-r. PR12-Captain America-r/#168. PR13-Fantastic Four-r/#126. PR14-Frankenstein-Ploog-r/#1. PR15-Tomb of Dracula-Colan-r/#2. PR16-Man-Thing-Ploog-r/#5. PR17-Werewolf By Night-Ploog-r/Marvel Spotlight #2. PR18-Planet of the Apes-r. PR19-Escape From the Planet of the Apes-r. PR20-Beneath the Planet of the Apes-r. PR21-Battle for the Planet of the Apes-r. PR24-Spider-Man II-New-a begins. PR25-Star Trek "Passage to Moauv". PR26-Star Trek "Crier in Emptiness." PR27-Batman "Stacked Cards"; N. Adams-a(p). PR28-Superman "Alien Creatures". PR29-Space: 1999 "Breakaway". PR30-Batman; N. Adams-r/Det.(7 pgs.). PR31-Conan-N. Adams-a; reprinted in Conan #116. PR32-Space: 1999 "Return to the Beginning". PR33-Superman-G.A. origin, Buckler-a(p). PR34-Superman. PR35-Wonder Woman-Buckler-a(p). PR36-Holo-Man. PR37-Robin Hood. PR39-Huckleberry Finn. PR40-Davy Crockett. PR41-Robinson Crusoe. PR42-20,000 Leagues Under the Sea. PR46-Star Trek "The Robot Masters". PR47-Little Women
With record; each... 2.50 7.50 20.00

PURE OIL COMICS (Also see Salerno Carnival of Comics, 24 Pages of Comics, & Vicks Comics)
Pure Oil Giveaway: Late 1930's (24 pgs., regular size, paper-c)
nn-Contains 1-2 pg. strips; i.e., Hairbreadth Harry, Skyroads, Buck Rogers by Calkins & Yager, Olly of the Movies, Napoleon, S'Matter Pop, etc.
Also a 16 pg. 1938 giveaway w/Buck Rogers 50.00 140.00 285.00

QUAKER OATS (Also see Cap'n Crunch)
Quaker Oats Co.: 1965 (Giveaway) (2-1/2x5-1/2") (16 pgs.)
"Plenty of Glutton", starring Quake & Quisp; 2.50 7.50 20.00
"Lava Come-Back", "Kite Tale" 4.00

REAL FUN OF DRIVING!!, THE
Chrysler Corp.: 1965, 1967 (Regular size)
nn-Schaffenberger-a (12 pgs.) 3.00

REAL HIT
Fox Features Publications: 1944 (Savings Bond premium)
1-Blue Beetle-r 19.00 56.00 130.00
NOTE: *Two versions exist, with and without covers. The coverless version has the title, No. 1 and price printed at top of splash page.*

RED BALL COMIC BOOK
Parents' Magazine Institute: 1947 (Red Ball Shoes giveaway)
nn-Reprints from True Comics 3.00 7.50 15.00

REDDY GOOSE
International Shoe Co. (Western Printing): No #, 1958?; No. 2, Jan, 1959 - No. 16, July, 1962 (Giveaway)
nn (#1) 5.00 15.00 50.00
2-16 3.00 9.00 30.00

REDDY KILOWATT (5¢) (Also see Story of Edison)
Educational Comics (E. C.): 1946 - No. 2, 1947; 1956 - 1960 (no month) (16 pgs., paper-c)
nn-Reddy Made Magic (1946, 5¢) 12.00 36.00 85.00
nn-Reddy Made Magic (1958) 8.35 25.00 50.00
2-Edison, the Man Who Changed the World (3/4" smaller than #1) (1947, 5¢) 12.00 36.00 85.00
...Comic Book 2 (1954)- "Light's Diamond Jubilee" 9.00 27.00 55.00
...Comic Book 2 (1958, 16 pgs.)- "Wizard of Light" 8.35 25.00 50.00
...Comic Book 3 (1956, 8 pgs.)- "The Space Kite"; Orlando story; regular size 8.35 25.00 50.00
...Comic Book 3 (1960, 8 pgs.)- "The Space Kite"; Orlando story; regular size 4.60 13.80 46.00
NOTE: *Several copies surfaced in 1979.*

REDDY MADE MAGIC
Educational Comics (E. C.): 1956, 1958 (16 pgs., paper-c)
1-Reddy Kilowatt-r (splash panel changed) 11.00 33.00 75.00
1 (1958 edition) 6.70 20.00 40.00

RED ICEBERG, THE
Impact Publ. (Catechetical Guild): 1960 (10¢, 16 pgs., Communist propaganda)

Red Ryder Victory Patrol 1942 © DELL

Roy Rogers Comics © DELL

Salute to the Boy Scouts
© Association of American Railroads

GD2.0 FN6.0 NM9.4

nn-(Rare)- 'We The People' back-c 30.00 90.00 300.00
2nd version- 'Impact Press' back-c 31.00 93.00 310.00
3rd version-"Explains comic" back-c 31.00 93.00 310.00

NOTE: *This book was the Guild's last anti-communist propaganda book and had very limited circulation. 3 - 4 copies surfaced in 1979 from the defunct publisher's files. Other copies do turn up.*

RED RYDER COMICS
Dell Publ. Co.

Buster Brown Shoes Giveaway (1941, color, soft-c, 32 pgs.) 27.00 81.00 190.00
Red Ryder Super Book of Comics (1944, paper-c, 32 pgs.; blank back-c) Magic Morro app. 29.00 86.00 200.00
Red Ryder Victory Patrol-nn(1942, 32 pgs.)(Langendorf bread; includes cut-out membership card and certificate, order blank and "Slide-Up" decoder, and a Super Book of Comics in color (same content as Super Book #4 w/diff. cover (Pan-Am)) (Rare) 444.00 1333.00 4000.00
Red Ryder Victory Patrol-nn(1943, 32 pgs.)(Langendorf bread; includes cut-out "Rodeomatic" radio decoder, order coupon for "Magic V-Badge", cut-out membership card and certificate and a full color Super Book of comics comic book) (Rare) 416.00 1250.00 3750.00
Red Ryder Victory Patrol-nn(1944, 32 pgs.)-r-/#43,44; comic has a paper-c & is stapled inside a triple cardboard fold-out-c; contains membership card, decoder, map of R.R. home range, etc. Herky app. (Langendorf Bread give-away; sub-titled 'Super Book of Comics')(Rare) 394.00 1183.00 3550.00
Wells Lamont Corp. giveaway (1950)-16 pgs. in color; regular size; paper-c; 1941-r 25.00 75.00 175.00

RIPLEY'S BELIEVE IT OR NOT!
Harvey Publications

J. C. Penney giveaway (1948) 8.35 25.00 50.00

ROBIN HOOD (New Adventures of...)
Walt Disney Productions: 1952 (Flour giveaways, 5x7-1/4", 36 pgs.)

"New Adventures of Robin Hood", "Ghosts of Waylea Castle", & "The Miller's Ransom" each.... 4.25 13.00 26.00

ROBIN HOOD'S FRONTIER DAYS (...Western Tales, Adventures of... #1)
Shoe Store Giveaway (Robin Hood Stores): 1956 (20 pgs., slick-c)(7 issues?)

nn 4.25 13.00 28.00
nn-Issues with Crandall-a 7.70 23.00 48.00

ROCKETS AND RANGE RIDERS
Richfield Oil Corp.: May, 1957 (Giveaway, 16 pgs., soft-c)

nn-Toth-a 17.00 51.00 120.00

ROUND THE WORLD GIFT
National War Fund (Giveaway): No date (mid 1940's) (4 pgs.)

nn 12.00 36.00 85.00

ROY ROGERS COMICS
Dell Publishing Co.

...& the Man From Dodge City (Dodge giveaway, 16 pgs., 1954)-Frontier, Inc. (5x7-1/4") 14.00 43.00 100.00
Official Roy Rogers Riders Club Comics (1952; 16 pgs., reg. size, paper-c) 40.00 150.00 300.00

RUDOLPH, THE RED-NOSED REINDEER
Montgomery Ward: 1939 (2,400,000 copies printed); Dec, 1951 (Giveaway)

Paper cover-1st app. in print; written by Robert May; ill. by Denver Gillen 13.00 39.00 90.00
Hardcover version 17.00 51.00 120.00
1951 Edition (Has 1939 date)-36 pgs., slick-c printed in red & brown; pulp interior printed in four mixed-ink colors: red, green, blue & brown 8.35 25.00 50.00
1951 Edition with red-spiral promotional booklet printed on high quality stock, 8-1/2"x11", in red & brown, 25 pages composed of 4 fold outs, single sheets and the Rudolph comic book inserted (rare) 50.00 150.00 400.00

SAD CASE OF WAITING ROOM WILLIE, THE
American Visuals Corp. (For Baltimore Medical Society): (nd, 1950?) (14 pgs. in color; paper covers; regular size)

nn-By Will Eisner (Rare) 48.00 144.00 385.00

SAD SACK COMICS
Harvey Publications: 1957-1962

Armed Forces Complimentary copies, HD #1-40 (1957-1962) 1.00 2.80 7.00

SALERNO CARNIVAL OF COMICS (Also see Pure Oil Comics, 24 Pages of Comics, & Vicks Comics)
Salerno Cookie Co.: Late 1930s (Giveaway, 16 pgs, paper-c)

nn-Color reprints of Calkins' Buck Rogers & Skyroads, plus other strips from Famous Funnies 50.00 150.00 400.00

SALUTE TO THE BOY SCOUTS
Association of American Railroads: 1960 (16 pgs.)

nn-History of scouting and the railroad 2.25 6.75 18.00

SANTA AND POLLYANNA PLAY THE GLAD GAME
Sales Promotion: Aug, 1960 (16 pgs.) (Disney giveaway)

nn 1.75 5.25 14.00

SANTA & THE BUCCANEERS
Promotional Publ. Co.: 1959 (Giveaway)

nn-Reprints 1952 Santa & the Pirates 1.25 3.75 10.00

SANTA & THE CHRISTMAS CHICKADEE
Murphy's: 1974 (Giveaway, 20 pgs.)

nn 2.40 6.00

SANTA & THE PIRATES
Promotional Publ. Co.: 1952 (Giveaway)

nn-Marv Levy-c/a 2.80 7.00 14.00

SANTA CLAUS FUNNIES (Also see The Little Fir Tree)
W. T. Grant Co./Whitman Publishing: nd; 1940 (Giveaway, 8x10"; 12 pgs., color & B&W, heavy paper)

nn-(2 versions- no date and 1940) 13.00 39.00 90.00

SANTA ON THE JOLLY ROGER
Promotional Publ. Co. (Giveaway): 1965

nn-Marv Levy-c/a 2.40 6.00

SANTA! SANTA!
R. Jackson: 1974 (20 pgs.) (Montgomery Ward giveaway)

nn 4.00

SANTA'S CHRISTMAS COMIC VARIETY SHOW (See Merry Christmas From Sears Toyland)
Sears Roebuck & Co.: 1943 (24 pgs.)

Contains puzzles & new comics of Dick Tracy, Little Orphan Annie, Moon Mullins, Terry & the Pirates, etc. 75.00 300.00 600.00

SANTA'S CHRISTMAS TIME STORIES
Premium Sales, Inc.: nd (Late 1940s) (16 pgs., paper-c) (Giveaway)

nn 5.35 16.00 32.00

SANTA'S CIRCUS
Promotional Publ. Co.: 1964 (Giveaway, half-size)

nn-Marv Levy-c/a 1.00 3.00 8.00

SANTA'S FUN BOOK
Promotional Publ. Co.: 1951, 1952 (Regular size, 16 pgs., paper-c) (Murphy's giveaway)

nn 3.20 8.00 16.00

SANTA'S GIFT BOOK
No Publisher: No date (16 pgs.)

nn-Puzzles, games only 2.80 7.00 14.00

SANTA'S NEW STORY BOOK
Wallace Hamilton Campbell: 1949 (16 pgs., paper-c) (Giveaway)

Sergeant Preston of the Yukon © Quaker Cereals

Snow White and the Seven Dwarfs in "Milky Way" © WDC

GD2.0 FN6.0 NM9.4

nn 5.00 15.00 30.00

SANTA'S REAL STORY BOOK
Wallace Hamilton Campbell/W. W. Orris: 1948, 1952 (Giveaway, 16 pgs.)
nn 4.25 13.00 28.00

SANTA'S RIDE
W. T. Grant Co.: 1959 (Giveaway)
nn 2.00 6.00 16.00

SANTA'S RODEO
Promotional Publ. Co.: 1964 (Giveaway, half-size)
nn-Marv Levy-a 1.00 2.80 7.00

SANTA'S SECRET CAVE
W.T. Grant Co.: 1960 (Giveaway, half-size)
nn 1.75 5.25 14.00

SANTA'S SECRETS
Sam B. Anson Christmas giveaway: 1951, 1952? (16 pgs., paper-c)
nn-Has games, stories & pictures to color 3.60 9.00 18.00

SANTA'S STORIES
K. K. Publications (Klines Dept. Store): 1953 (Regular size, paper-c)
nn-Kelly-a 17.00 51.00 120.00
nn-Another version (1953, glossy-c, half-size, 7-1/4x5-1/4")-Kelly-a 11.50 34.00 80.00

SANTA'S SURPRISE
K. K. Publications: 1947 (Giveaway, 36 pgs., slick-c)
nn 6.00 18.00 36.00

SANTA'S TOYTOWN FUN BOOK
Promotional Publ. Co.: 1953 (Giveaway)
nn-Marv Levy-c 2.40 6.00 12.00

SERGEANT PRESTON OF THE YUKON
Quaker Cereals: 1956 (4 comic booklets) (Soft-c, 16 pgs., 7x2-1/2" & 5x2-1/2") Giveaways
"How He Found Yukon King", "The Case That Made Him A Sergeant", "How Yukon King Saved Him From The Wolves", "How He Became A Mountie" each... 10.00 50.00 75.00

SHERIFF OF COCHISE, THE (TV)
Mobil: 1957 (16 pgs.) Giveaway
nn-Schaffenberger-a 3.00 7.50 15.00

SKATING SKILLS
Custom Comics, Inc./Chicago Roller Skates: 1957 (36 & 12 pgs.; 5x7", two versions) (10¢)
nn-Resembles old ACG cover plus interior art 3.20 8.00 16.00

SKIPPY'S OWN BOOK OF COMICS (See Popular Comics)
No publisher listed: 1934 (Giveaway, 52 pgs., strip reprints)
nn-(Scarce)-By Percy Crosby 450.00 1350.00 4500.00
Published by Max C. Gaines for Phillip's Dental Magnesia to be advertised on the Skippy Radio Show and given away with the purchase of a tube of Phillip's Tooth Paste. This is the first four-color comic book of reprints about one character.

SKY KING "RUNAWAY TRAIN" (TV)
National Biscuit Co.: 1964 (Regular size, 16 pgs.)
nn 20.00 50.00 75.00

SLAM BANG COMICS
Post Cereal Giveaway: No. 9, No date
9-Dynamic Man, Echo, Mr. E, Yankee Boy app. 8.35 25.00 50.00

SMILIN' JACK
Dell Publishing Co.
Popped Wheat Giveaway (1947)-1938 strip reprints; 16 pgs. in full color 5.00
Shoe Store Giveaway-1938 strip reprints; 16 pgs. 4.25 13.00 28.00
Sparked Wheat Giveaway (1942)-16 pgs. in full color 4.25 13.00 28.00

SMOKEY STOVER
Dell Publishing Co.
General Motors giveaway (1953) 5.00 15.00 35.00
National Fire Protection giveaway(1953 & 1954)-16 pgs., paper-c 5.00 15.00 35.00

SMOKEY THE BEAR (See Forest Fire for 1st app.)
Dell Publ. Co.: 1959
True Story of..., The -U.S. Forest Service giveaway-Publ. by Western Printing Co.; reprints 1st 16 pgs. of Four Color #932 3.20 8.00 16.00
1964,1969 reprints 3.20 8.00 16.00

SNOW FOR CHRISTMAS
W. T. Grant Co.: 1957 (16 pgs.) (Giveaway)
nn 3.60 9.00 18.00

SNOW WHITE AND THE SEVEN DWARFS
Bendix Washing Machines: 1952 (32 pgs., 5x7-1/4", soft-c) (Disney)
nn 11.00 33.00 75.00

SNOW WHITE AND THE SEVEN DWARFS
Promotional Publ. Co.: 1957 (Small size)
nn 4.00 10.50 21.00

SNOW WHITE AND THE SEVEN DWARFS
Western Printing Co.: 1958 (16 pgs, 5x7-1/4", soft-c) (Disney premium)
nn- "Mystery of the Missing Magic" 6.70 20.00 40.00

SNOW WHITE AND THE 7 DWARFS IN "MILKY WAY"
American Dairy Assoc.: 1955 (16 pgs., soft-c, 5x7-1/4") (Disney premium)
nn 11.00 33.00 75.00

SPACE GHOST COAST TO COAST
Cartoon Network: Apr, 1994 (giveaway to Turner Broadcasting employees)
1-8 pgs.; origin of Space Ghost 4.00

SPACE PATROL (TV)
Ziff-Davis Publishing Co. (Approved Comics)
...'s Special Mission (8 pgs., B&W, Giveaway) 75.00 260.00 525.00

SPECIAL DELIVERY
Post Hall Synd.: 1951 (32 pgs.; B&W) (Giveaway)
nn-Origin of Pogo, Swamp, etc.; 2 pg. biog. on Walt Kelly (One copy sold in 1980 for $150.00)

SPECIAL EDITION (U. S. Navy Giveaways)
National Periodical Publications: 1944 - 1945 (Regular comic format with wording simplified, 52 pgs.)
1-Action (1944)-Reprints Action #80 59.00 177.00 500.00
2-Action (1944)-Reprints Action #81 59.00 177.00 500.00
3-Superman (1944)-Reprints Superman #33 59.00 177.00 500.00
4-Detective (1944)-Reprints Detective #97 62.00 185.00 525.00
5-Superman (1945)-Reprints Superman #34 59.00 177.00 500.00
6-Action (1945)-Reprints Action #84 59.00 177.00 500.00
NOTE: ***Wayne Boring** c-1, 2, 6. **Dick Sprang** c-4.*

SPIRIT, THE (Weekly Comic Book)
Will Eisner: 6/2/40 - 10/5/52 (16 pgs.; 8 pgs.) (no cover) (in color)
(Distributed through various newspapers and other sources)
NOTE: **Eisner** script, pencils/inks for the most part from 6/2/40-4/26/42; a few stories assisted by Jack Cole, Fine, Powell and Kotsky.
6/2/40(#1)-Origin/1st app. The Spirit; reprinted in Police #11; Lady Luck (Brenda Banks)(1st app.) by Chuck Mazoujian & Mr. Mystic (1st. app.) by S. R. (Bob) Powell begin 65.00 195.00 550.00
6/9/40(#2) 31.00 92.00 225.00
6/16/40(#3)-Black Queen app. in Spirit 18.00 54.00 135.00
6/23/40(#4)-Mr. Mystic receives magical necklace 15.00 45.00 110.00
6/30/40(#5) 15.00 45.00 110.00
7/7/40(#6)-1st app.: Spirit carplane; Black Queen app. in Spirit

The Spirit 6/16/40 © Will Eisner

The Spirit 8/4/40 © Will Eisner

The Spirit 3/12/50 © Will Eisner

	GD2.0	FN6.0	NM9.4
	15.00	45.00	110.00
7/14/40(#7)-8/4/40(#10): 7/21/40-Spirit becomes fugitive wanted for murder	12.00	36.00	90.00
8/11/40-9/22/40	11.00	33.00	80.00
9/29/40-Ellen drops engagement with Homer Creep	10.00	30.00	70.00
10/6/40-11/3/40	10.00	30.00	70.00
11/10/40-The Black Queen app.	10.00	30.00	70.00
11/17/40, 11/24/40	10.00	30.00	70.00
12/1/40-Ellen spanking by Spirit on cover & inside; Eisner-1st 3 pgs., J. Cole rest	14.00	43.00	110.00
12/8/40-3/9/41	8.35	25.00	55.00
3/16/41-Intro. & 1st app. Silk Satin	13.00	39.00	95.00
3/23/41-6/1/41: 5/11/41-Last Lady Luck by Mazoujian; 5/18/41-Lady Luck by Nick Viscardi begins, ends 2/22/42	8.35	25.00	55.00
6/8/41-2nd app. Satin; Spirit learns Satin is also a British agent	10.00	30.00	75.00
6/15/41-1st app. Twilight	10.00	30.00	65.00
6/22/41-Hitler app. in Spirit	8.35	25.00	55.00
6/29/41-1/25/42,2/8/42	6.00	18.00	45.00
2/1/42-1st app. Duchess	10.00	30.00	65.00
2/15/42-4/26/42-Lady Luck by Klaus Nordling begins 3/1/42	6.70	20.00	50.00
5/3/42-8/16/42-Eisner/Fine/Quality staff assists on Spirit	4.30	13.00	32.00
8/23/42-Satin cover splash; Spirit by Eisner/Fine although signed by Fine	10.00	30.00	70.00
8/30/42,9/27/42-10/11/42,10/25/42-11/8/42-Eisner/Fine/Quality staff assists on Spirit	4.30	13.00	32.00
9/6/42-9/20/42,10/18/42-Fine/Belfi art on Spirit; scripts by Manly Wade Wellman	3.00	9.00	22.00
11/15/42-12/6/42,12/20/42,12/27/42,1/17/43-4/18/43,5/9/43-8/8/43-Wellman/ Woolfolk scripts, Fine pencils, Quality staff inks	3.00	9.00	22.00
12/13/42,1/3/43,1/10/43,4/25/43,5/2/43-Eisner scripts/layouts; Fine pencils, Quality staff inks	3.75	11.25	28.00
8/15/43-Eisner script/layout; pencils/inks by Quality staff; Jack Cole-a	2.40	7.20	18.00
8/22/43-12/12/43-Wellman/Woolfolk scripts, Fine pencils, Quality staff inks; Mr. Mystic by Guardineer-10/10/43-10/24/43	2.40	7.20	18.00
12/19/43-8/13/44-Wellman/Woolfolk/Jack Cole scripts; Cole, Fine & Robin King-a; Last Mr. Mystic-5/14/44	2.20	6.50	16.00
8/20/44-12/16/45-Wellman/Woolfolk scripts; Fine art with unknown staff assists	2.20	6.50	16.00

NOTE: *Scripts/layouts by Eisner, or Eisner/Nordling, Eisner/Mercer or Spranger/Eisner; inks by Eisner or Eisner/Spranger in issues 12/23/45-2/2/47.*

	GD2.0	FN6.0	NM9.4
12/23/45-1/6/46: 12/23/45-Christmas-c	4.00	12.00	30.00
1/13/46-Origin Spirit retold	6.40	19.00	48.00
1/20/46-1st postwar Satin app.	5.30	16.00	40.00
1/27/46-3/10/46: 3/3/46-Last Lady Luck by Nordling	4.00	12.00	30.00
3/17/46-Intro. & 1st app. Nylon	5.30	16.00	40.00
3/24/46,3/31/46,4/14/46	4.00	12.00	30.00
4/7/46-2nd app. Nylon	4.70	14.00	35.00
4/21/46-Intro. & 1st app. Mr. Carrion & His Pet Buzzard Julia	6.40	19.00	48.00
4/28/46-5/12/46,5/26/46-6/30/46: Lady Luck by Fred Schwab in issues 5/5/46-11/3/46	4.00	12.00	30.00
5/19/46-2nd app. Mr. Carrion	4.70	14.00	35.00
7/7/46-Intro. & 1st app. Dulcet Tone & Skinny	5.60	17.00	42.00
7/14/46-9/29/46	4.00	12.00	30.00
10/6/46-Intro. & 1st app. P'Gell	6.40	19.00	48.00
10/13/46-11/3/46,11/16/46-11/24/46	4.00	12.00	30.00
11/10/46-2nd app. P'Gell	5.00	15.00	38.00
12/1/46-3rd app. P'Gell	4.70	14.00	35.00
12/8/46-2/2/47	3.50	10.50	26.00

NOTE: *Scripts, pencils/inks by Eisner except where noted in issues 2/9/47-12/19/48.*

	GD2.0	FN6.0	NM9.4
2/9/47-7/6/47: 6/8/47-Eisner self satire	3.50	10.50	26.00
7/13/47- "Hansel & Gretel" fairy tales	5.30	16.00	40.00
7/20/47-Li'L Abner, Daddy Warbucks, Dick Tracy, Fearless Fosdick parody; A-Bomb blast-c	5.60	17.00	42.00
7/27/47-9/14/47	3.50	10.50	26.00
9/21/47-Pearl Harbor flashback	4.30	13.00	32.00
9/28/47-1st mention of Flying Saucers in comics-3 months after 1st sighting in Idaho on 6/25/47	9.30	28.00	70.00
10/5/47- "Cinderella" fairy tales	5.30	16.00	40.00
10/12/47-11/30/47	3.50	10.50	26.00
12/7/47-Intro. & 1st app. Powder Pouf	6.40	19.00	48.00
12/14/47-12/28/47	3.50	10.50	26.00
1/4/48-2nd app. Powder Pouf	4.70	14.00	35.00
1/11/48-1st app. Sparrow Fallon; Powder Pouf app.	4.70	14.00	35.00
1/18/48-He-Man ad cover; satire issue	4.70	14.00	35.00
1/25/48-Intro. & 1st app. Castanet	5.60	17.00	42.00
2/1/48-2nd app. Castanet	4.00	12.00	30.00
2/8/48-3/7/48	3.50	10.50	26.00
3/14/48-Only app. Kretchma	4.00	12.00	30.00
3/21/48,3/28/48,4/11/48-4/25/48	3.50	10.50	26.00
4/4/48-Only app. Wild Rice	4.00	12.00	30.00
5/2/48-2nd app. Sparrow	3.50	10.50	26.00
5/9/48-6/27/48,7/11/48,7/18/48: 6/13/48-TV issue	3.50	10.50	26.00
7/4/48-Spirit by Andre Le Blanc	2.70	8.00	20.00
7/25/48-Ambrose Bierce's "The Thing" adaptation classic by Eisner/ Grandenetti	9.30	28.00	70.00
8/1/48-8/15/48,8/29/48-9/12/48	3.50	10.50	26.00
8/22/48-Poe's "Fall of the House of Usher" classic by Eisner/Grandenetti	9.30	28.00	70.00
9/19/48-Only app. Lorelei	5.00	15.00	38.00
9/26/48-10/31/48	3.50	10.50	26.00
11/7/48-Only app. Plaster of Paris	5.00	15.00	38.00
11/14/48-12/19/48	3.50	10.50	26.00

NOTE: *Scripts by Eisner or Feiffer or Eisner/Feiffer or Nordling. Art by Eisner with backgrounds by Eisner, Grandenetti, Le Blanc, Stallman, Nordling, Dixon and/or others in issues 12/26/48-4/1/51 except where noted.*

	GD2.0	FN6.0	NM9.4
12/26/48-Reprints some covers of 1948 with flashbacks	3.50	10.50	26.00
1/2/49-1/16/49	3.50	10.50	26.00
1/23/49,1/30/49-1st & 2nd app. Thorne	5.00	15.00	38.00
2/6/49-8/14/49	3.50	10.50	26.00
8/21/49,8/28/49-1st & 2nd app. Monica Veto	5.00	15.00	38.00
9/4/49,9/11/49	3.50	10.50	26.00
9/18/49-Love comic cover; has gag love comic ads on inside	5.00	15.00	38.00
9/25/49-Only app. Ice	4.30	13.00	32.00
10/2/49,10/9/49-Autumn News appears & dies in 10/9 issue	4.30	13.00	32.00
10/16/49-11/27/49,12/18/49,12/25/49	3.50	10.50	26.00
12/4/49,12/11/49-1st & 2nd app. Flaxen	4.00	12.00	30.00
1/1/50-Flashbacks to all of the Spirit girls-Thorne, Ellen, Satin, & Monica	6.70	20.00	50.00
1/8/50-Intro. & 1st app. Sand Saref	9.30	28.00	70.00
1/15/50-2nd app. Saref	6.70	20.00	50.00
1/22/50-2/5/50	3.50	10.50	26.00
2/12/50-Roller Derby issue	4.70	14.00	35.00
2/19/50-Half Dead Mr. Lox - Classic horror	4.70	14.00	35.00
2/26/50-4/23/50,5/14/50,5/28/50,7/23/50-9/3/50	3.50	10.50	26.00
4/30/50-Script/art by Le Blanc with Eisner framing	1.85	5.60	14.00
5/7/50,6/4/50-7/16/50-Abe Kanegson-a	1.85	5.60	14.00
5/21/50-Script by Feiffer/Eisner, art by Blaisdell, Eisner framing	1.85	5.60	14.00
9/10/50-P'Gell returns	5.00	15.00	38.00
9/17/50-1/7/51	3.50	10.50	26.00
1/14/51-Life Magazine cover; brief biography of Comm. Dolan, Sand Saref, Silk Satin, P'Gell, Sammy & Willum, Darling O'Shea, & Mr. Carrion & His Pet Buzzard Julia, with pin-ups by Eisner	5.00	15.00	38.00
1/21/51,2/4/51-4/1/51	3.50	10.50	26.00
1/28/51- "The Meanest Man in the World" classic by Eisner			

Story of Harry S. Truman © DNC

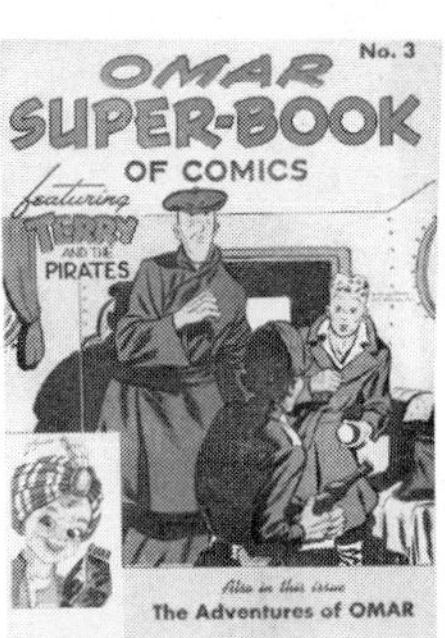

Super Book of Comics #3 © WEST

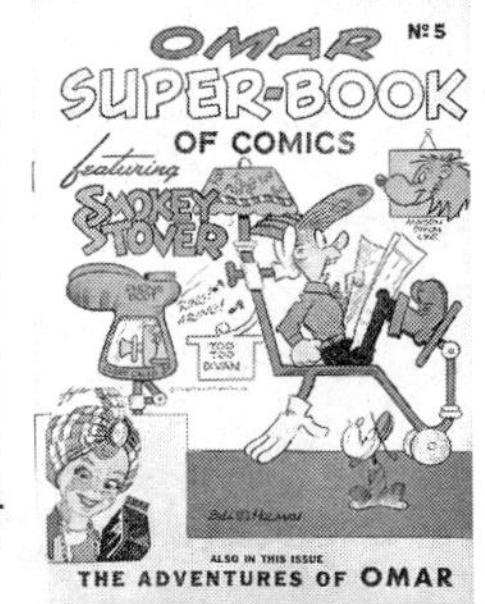

Super Book of Comics #5 © WEST

GD2.0 FN6.0 NM9.4

	GD2.0	FN6.0	NM9.4
	5.00	15.00	38.00
4/8/51-7/29/51,8/12/51-Last Eisner issue	3.50	10.50	26.00
8/5/51,8/19/51-7/20/52-Not Eisner	1.85	5.60	14.00
7/27/52-(Rare)-Denny Colt in Outer Space by Wally Wood; 7 pg. S/F story of E.C. vintage	32.00	95.00	235.00
8/3/52-(Rare)- "Mission...The Moon" by Wood	32.00	95.00	235.00
8/10/52-(Rare)- "A DP On The Moon" by Wood	32.00	95.00	235.00
8/17/52-(Rare)- "Heart" by Wood/Eisner	27.00	81.00	200.00
8/24/52-(Rare)- "Rescue" by Wood	32.00	95.00	235.00
8/31/52-(Rare)- "The Last Man" by Wood	32.00	95.00	235.00
9/7/52-(Rare)- "The Man in The Moon" by Wood	32.00	95.00	235.00
9/14/52-(Rare)-Eisner/Wenzel-a	8.75	27.00	70.00
9/21/52-(Rare)- "Denny Colt, Alias The Spirit/Space Report" by Eisner/Wenzel	11.50	34.00	85.00
9/28/52-(Rare)- "Return From The Moon" by Wood	32.00	95.00	235.00
10/5/52-(Rare)- "The Last Story" by Eisner	11.50	34.00	85.00

Large Tabloid pages from 1946 on (Eisner) - Price 200 percent over listed prices.
NOTE: *Spirit sections came out in both large and small format. Some newspapers went to the 8-pg. format months before others. Some printed the pages so they cannot be folded into a small comic book section; these are worth less. (Also see Three Comics & Spiritman).*

SPY SMASHER
Fawcett Publications

	GD2.0	FN6.0	NM9.4
Well Known Comics (1944, 12 pgs., 8-1/2x10-1/2"), paper-c, glued binding, printed in green; Bestmaid/Samuel Lowe giveaway	15.00	45.00	105.00

STANDARD OIL COMICS (Also see Gulf Funny Weekly)
Standard Oil Co.: 1933 (Giveaway, tabloid size, 4 pgs. in color)

	GD2.0	FN6.0	NM9.4
1-Series has original art	50.00	150.00	400.00
2-5	20.00	60.00	150.00
6-14: 14-Fred Opper strip, 1 pg.	11.00	33.00	75.00

STAR TEAM
Marvel Comics Group: 1977 (6-1/2x5", 20 pgs.) (Ideal Toy Giveaway)

	GD2.0	FN6.0	NM9.4
nn	1.00	3.00	8.00

STEVE CANYON COMICS
Harvey Publications

	GD2.0	FN6.0	NM9.4
Dept. Store giveaway #3(6/48, 36pp)	10.00	30.00	70.00
...'s Secret Mission (1951, 16 pgs., Armed Forces giveaway); Caniff-a	10.00	30.00	65.00
Strictly for the Smart Birds (1951, 16 pgs.)-Information Comics Div. (Harvey) Premium	9.35	28.00	56.00

STORIES OF CHRISTMAS
K. K. Publications: 1942 (Giveaway, 32 pgs., paper cover)

	GD2.0	FN6.0	NM9.4
nn-Adaptation of "A Christmas Carol"; Kelly story "The Fir Tree"; Infinity-c	37.00	111.00	260.00

STORY HOUR SERIES (Disney)
Whitman Publ. Co.: 1948, 1949; 1951-1953 (36 pgs., paper-c) (4-3/4x6-1/2")
Given away with subscription to Walt Disney's Comics & Stories

	GD2.0	FN6.0	NM9.4
nn(1948)-Mickey Mouse and the Boy Thursday	12.00	36.00	85.00
nn(1948)-Mickey Mouse the Miracle Master	12.00	36.00	85.00
nn(1948)-Minnie Mouse and Antique Chair	12.00	36.00	85.00
nn(1949)-The Three Orphan Kittens(B&W & color)	7.50	22.50	45.00
nn(1949)-Danny-The Little Black Lamb	7.50	22.50	45.00
800(1948)-Donald Duck in "Bringing Up the Boys"	18.00	54.00	125.00
1953 edition	11.00	33.00	75.00
801(1948)-Mickey Mouse's Summer Vacation	10.00	30.00	65.00
1951, 1952 editions	4.25	13.00	28.00
802(1948)-Bugs Bunny's Adventures	8.35	25.00	50.00
803(1948)-Bongo	5.70	17.00	35.00
804(1948)-Mickey and the Beanstalk	8.35	25.00	50.00
805-15(1949)-Andy Panda and His Friends	6.70	20.00	40.00
806-15(1949)-Tom and Jerry	7.50	22.50	45.00
808-15(1949)-Johnny Appleseed	5.70	17.00	35.00
1948, 1949 Hard Cover Edition of each....	$3.00 - $5.00 more.		

STORY OF EDISON, THE
Educational Comics: 1956 (16 pgs.) (Reddy Killowatt)

	GD2.0	FN6.0	NM9.4
nn-Reprint of Reddy Kilowatt #2(1947)	8.35	25.00	50.00

STORY OF HARRY S. TRUMAN, THE
Democratic National Committee: 1948 (Giveaway, regular size, soft-c, 16 pg.)

	GD2.0	FN6.0	NM9.4
nn-Gives biography on career of Truman; used in **SOTI**, pg. 311	14.00	43.00	100.00

STRANGE AS IT SEEMS
McNaught Syndicate: 1936 (B&W, 5x7", 24 pgs.)

	GD2.0	FN6.0	NM9.4
nn-Ex-Lax giveaway	4.00	10.00	20.00

SUGAR BEAR
Post Cereal Giveaway: No date, circa 1975? (2-1/2x4-1/2", 16 pgs.)

	GD2.0	FN6.0	NM9.4
"The Almost Take Over of the Post Office", "The Race Across the Atlantic", "The Zoo Goes Wild" each...			5.00

SUPER BOOK OF COMICS
Western Publishing Co.: nd (1942-1943?) (Soft-c, 32 pgs.) (Pan-Am/Gilmore Oil/Kelloggs premiums)

	GD2.0	FN6.0	NM9.4
nn-Dick Tracy (Gilmore)-Magic Morro app.	44.00	132.00	350.00
1-Dick Tracy & The Smuggling Ring; Stratosphere Jim app. (Rare) (Pan-Am)	44.00	132.00	350.00
1-Smilin' Jack, Magic Morro (Pan-Am)	13.00	39.00	125.00
2-Smilin' Jack, Stratosphere Jim (Pan-Am)	13.00	39.00	125.00
2-Smitty, Magic Morro (Pan-Am)	13.00	39.00	125.00
3-Captain Midnight, Magic Morro (Pan-Am)	36.00	107.00	250.00
3-Moon Mullins?	13.00	39.00	125.00
4-Red Ryder, Magic Morro (Pan-Am). Same content as Red Ryder Victory Patrol comic w/diff. cover	21.00	64.00	150.00
4-Smitty, Stratosphere Jim (Pan-Am)	13.00	39.00	125.00
5-Don Winslow, Magic Morro (Gilmore)	21.00	64.00	150.00
5-Don Winslow, Stratosphere Jim (Pan-Am)	21.00	64.00	150.00
5-Terry & the Pirates	25.00	75.00	175.00
6-Don Winslow, Stratosphere Jim (Pan-Am)-McWilliams-a	21.00	64.00	150.00
6-King of the Royal Mounted, Magic Morro (Pan-Am)	21.00	64.00	150.00
7-Dick Tracy, Magic Morro (Pan-Am)	29.00	86.00	200.00
7-Little Orphan Annie	14.00	43.00	100.00
8-Dick Tracy, Stratosphere Jim (Pan-Am)	25.00	75.00	175.00
8-Dan Dunn, Magic Morro (Pan-Am)	14.00	43.00	100.00
9-Terry & the Pirates, Magic Morro (Pan-Am)	25.00	75.00	175.00
10-Red Ryder, Magic Morro (Pan-Am)	21.00	64.00	150.00

SUPER-BOOK OF COMICS
Western Publishing Co.: (Omar Bread & Hancock Oil Co. giveaways)
1944 - No. 30, 1947 (Omar); 1947 - 1948 (Hancock) (16 pgs.)

Note: The Hancock issues are all exact reprints of the earlier Omar issues. The issue numbers were removed in some of the reprints.

	GD2.0	FN6.0	NM9.4
1-Dick Tracy (Omar, 1944)	24.00	73.00	170.00
1-Dick Tracy (Hancock, 1947)	18.00	54.00	125.00
2-Bugs Bunny (Omar, 1944)	8.35	25.00	50.00
2-Bugs Bunny (Hancock, 1947)	6.70	20.00	40.00
3-Terry & the Pirates (Omar, 1944)	13.00	39.00	90.00
3-Terry & the Pirates (Hancock, 1947)	11.50	34.00	80.00
4-Andy Panda (Omar, 1944)	8.35	25.00	50.00
4-Andy Panda (Hancock, 1947)	6.70	20.00	40.00
5-Smokey Stover (Omar, 1945)	6.70	20.00	40.00
5-Smokey Stover (Hancock, 1947)	5.00	15.00	30.00
6-Porky Pig (Omar, 1945)	8.35	25.00	50.00
6-Porky Pig (Hancock, 1947)	6.70	20.00	40.00
7-Smilin' Jack (Omar, 1945)	8.35	25.00	50.00
7-Smilin' Jack (Hancock, 1947)	6.70	20.00	40.00
8-Oswald the Rabbit (Omar, 1945)	6.70	20.00	40.00
8-Oswald the Rabbit (Hancock, 1947)	5.00	15.00	30.00
9-Alley Oop (Omar, 1945)	14.00	43.00	100.00

Super Book of Comics #9 © WEST

Superman (mini) © DC

Superman's Christmas Adventure © DC

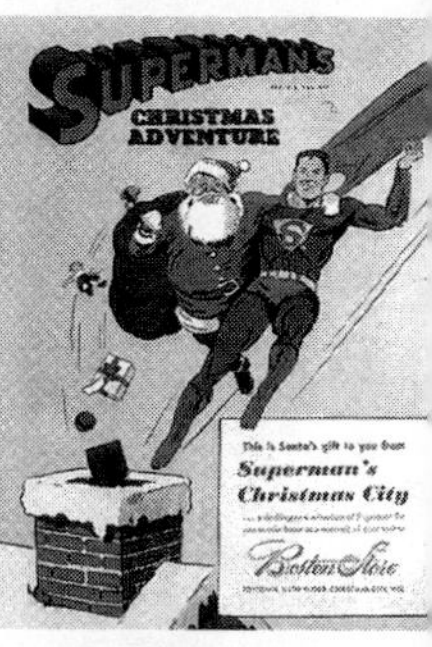

	GD2.0	FN6.0	NM9.4
9-Alley Oop (Hancock, 1947)	13.00	39.00	90.00
10-Elmer Fudd (Omar, 1945)	6.70	20.00	40.00
10-Elmer Fudd (Hancock, 1947)	5.00	15.00	30.00
11-Little Orphan Annie (Omar, 1945)	9.15	27.00	55.00
11-Little Orphan Annie (Hancock, 1947)	7.50	22.50	45.00
12-Woody Woodpecker (Omar, 1945)	6.70	20.00	40.00
12-Woody Woodpecker (Hancock, 1947)	5.00	15.00	30.00
13-Dick Tracy (Omar, 1945)	14.00	43.00	100.00
13-Dick Tracy (Hancock, 1947)	13.00	39.00	90.00
14-Bugs Bunny (Omar, 1945)	6.70	20.00	40.00
14-Bugs Bunny (Hancock, 1947)	5.00	15.00	30.00
15-Andy Panda (Omar, 1945)	5.85	17.50	35.00
15-Andy Panda (Hancock, 1947)	5.00	15.00	30.00
16-Terry & the Pirates (Omar, 1945)	13.00	39.00	90.00
16-Terry & the Pirates (Hancock, 1947)	10.00	30.00	70.00
17-Smokey Stover (Omar, 1946)	6.70	20.00	40.00
17-Smokey Stover (Hancock, 1948?)	5.00	15.00	30.00
18-Porky Pig (Omar, 1946)	5.85	17.50	35.00
18-Porky Pig (Hancock, 1948?)	5.00	15.00	30.00
19-Smilin' Jack (Omar, 1946)	6.70	20.00	40.00
nn-Smilin' Jack (Hancock, 1948)	5.00	15.00	30.00
20-Oswald the Rabbit (Omar, 1946)	5.85	17.50	35.00
nn-Oswald the Rabbit (Hancock, 1948)	5.00	15.00	30.00
21-Gasoline Alley (Omar, 1946)	9.15	27.00	55.00
nn-Gasoline Alley (Hancock, 1948)	7.50	22.50	45.00
22-Elmer Fudd (Omar, 1946)	5.85	17.50	35.00
nn-Elmer Fudd (Hancock, 1948)	5.00	15.00	30.00
23-Little Orphan Annie (Omar, 1946)	8.35	25.00	50.00
nn-Little Orphan Annie (Hancock, 1948)	6.70	20.00	40.00
24-Woody Woodpecker (Omar, 1946)	5.85	17.50	35.00
nn-Woody Woodpecker (Hancock, 1948)	5.00	15.00	30.00
25-Dick Tracy (Omar, 1946)	13.00	39.00	90.00
nn-Dick Tracy (Hancock, 1948)	10.00	30.00	70.00
26-Bugs Bunny (Omar, 1946))	5.85	17.50	35.00
nn-Bugs Bunny (Hancock, 1948)	5.00	15.00	30.00
27-Andy Panda (Omar, 1946)	5.85	17.50	35.00
27-Andy Panda (Hancock, 1948)	5.00	15.00	30.00
28-Terry & the Pirates (Omar, 1946)	13.00	39.00	90.00
28-Terry & the Pirates (Hancock, 1948)	10.00	30.00	70.00
29-Smokey Stover (Omar, 1947)	5.85	17.50	35.00
29-Smokey Stover (Hancock, 1948)	5.00	15.00	30.00
30-Porky Pig (Omar, 1947)	5.85	17.50	35.00
30-Porky Pig (Hancock, 1948)	5.00	15.00	30.00
nn-Bugs Bunny (Hancock, 1948)-Does not match any Omar book	5.00	15.00	30.00

SUPER CIRCUS (TV)
Cross Publishing Co.

	GD2.0	FN6.0	NM9.4
1-(1951, Weather Bird Shoes giveaway)	6.70	20.00	40.00

SUPERGEAR COMICS
Jacobs Corp.: 1976 (Giveaway, 4 pgs. in color, slick paper)

	GD2.0	FN6.0	NM9.4
nn-(Rare)-Superman, Lois Lane; Steve Lombard app. (500 copies printed, over half destroyed?)	1.50	4.50	12.00

SUPERGIRL
DC Comics: 1984, 1986 (Giveaway, Baxter paper)

	GD2.0	FN6.0	NM9.4
nn-(American Honda/U.S. Dept. Transportation) Torres-c/a			1.25

SUPER HEROES PUZZLES AND GAMES
General Mills Giveaway (Marvel Comics Group): 1979 (32 pgs., regular size)

	GD2.0	FN6.0	NM9.4
nn-Four 2-pg. origin stories of Spider-Man, Captain America, The Hulk, & Spider-Woman	2.00	6.00	15.00

SUPERMAN
National Periodical Publ./DC Comics

	GD2.0	FN6.0	NM9.4
72-Giveaway(9-10/51)-(Rare)-Price blackened out; came with banner wrapped around book; without banner	69.00	206.00	556.00
72-Giveaway with banner	97.00	290.00	775.00
Kelloggs Giveaway-(2/3 normal size, 1954)-r-two stories/Superman #55	34.00	103.00	240.00
...Meets the Quik Bunny (1987, Nestles Quik premium, 36 pgs.)			3.00
Pizza Hut Premiums (12/77)-Exact reprints of 1950s comics except for paid ads (set of 6 exist?); Vol. 1-r#97 (#113-r also known)			4.00
Radio Shack Giveaway-36 pgs. (7/80) "The Computers That Saved Metropolis", Starlin/Giordano-a; advertising insert in Action #509, New Advs. of Superboy #7, Legion of Super-Heroes #265, & House of Mystery #282. (All comics were 68 pgs.) Cover of inserts printed on newsprint. Giveaway contains 4 extra pgs. of Radio Shack advertising that inserts do not			3.00
Radio Shack Giveaway-(7/81) "Victory by Computer"			2.00
Radio Shack Giveaway-(7/82) "Computer Masters of Metropolis"			2.00

SUPERMAN AND THE GREAT CLEVELAND FIRE
National Periodical Publ.: 1948 (Giveaway, 4 pgs., no cover) (Hospital Fund)

	GD2.0	FN6.0	NM9.4
nn-In full color	75.00	250.00	500.00

SUPERMAN (Miniature)
National Periodical Publ.: 1942; 1955 - 1956 (3 issues, no #'s, 32 pgs.)
The pages are numbered in the 1st issue: 1-32; 2nd: 1A-32A, and 3rd: 1B-32B

	GD2.0	FN6.0	NM9.4
No date-Py-Co-Pay Tooth Powder giveaway (8 pgs.; circa 1942)	84.00	253.00	675.00
1-The Superman Time Capsule (Kellogg's Sugar Smacks)(1955)	56.00	169.00	450.00
1A-Duel in Space (1955)	50.00	150.00	400.00
1B-The Super Show of Metropolis (also #1-32, no B)(1955)	50.00	150.00	400.00

NOTE: *Numbering variations exist. Each title could have any combination-#1, 1A, or 1B.*

SUPERMAN RECORD COMIC
National Periodical Publications: 1966 (Golden Records)

	GD2.0	FN6.0	NM9.4
(With record)-Record reads origin of Superman from comic; came with iron-on patch, decoder, membership card & button; comic-r/Superman #125,146	19.00	58.00	135.00
Comic only	12.00	36.00	85.00

SUPERMAN'S BUDDY (Costume Comic)
National Periodical Publications: 1954 (4 pgs., slick paper-c; one-shot) (Came in box w/costume)

	GD2.0	FN6.0	NM9.4
1-w/box & costume	125.00	375.00	1000.00
Comic only	59.00	176.00	470.00
1-(1958 edition)-Printed in 2 colors	17.00	49.00	115.00

SUPERMAN'S CHRISTMAS ADVENTURE
National Periodical Publications: 1940, 1944 (Giveaway, 16 pgs.)
Distributed by Nehi drinks, Bailey Store, Ivey-Keith Co., Kennedy's Boys Shop, Macy's Store, Boston Store

	GD2.0	FN6.0	NM9.4
1(1940)-Burnley-a; F. Ray-c/r from Superman #6 (Scarce)-Superman saves Santa Claus. Santa makes real Superman Toys offered in 1940. 1st merchandising story	550.00	2200.00	4400.00
nn(1944) w/Santa Claus & X-mas tree-c	112.00	450.00	1000.00
nn(1944) w/Candy cane & Superman-c	100.00	400.00	900.00

SUPERMAN-TIM (Becomes Tim)
Superman-Tim Stores/National Periodical Publ.: Aug, 1942 - May, 1950 (Half size) (B&W Giveaway w/2 color covers) (Publ. monthly 2/43 on)

	GD2.0	FN6.0	NM9.4
8/42 (#1)-All have Superman illos.	125.00	500.00	1000.00
1/43 (#2)	41.00	124.00	330.00
2/43 (#3)	41.00	124.00	330.00
3/43 (#4)	41.00	124.00	330.00
4/43, 5/43, 6/43, 7/43, 8/43	39.00	118.00	275.00
9/43, 10/43, 11/43, 12/43	34.00	103.00	240.00
1/44-12/44	26.00	79.00	185.00
1/45-5/45, 8-12/45, 1/46-8/46	24.00	71.00	165.00
6/45-Classic Superman-c	26.00	77.00	180.00
7/45-Classic Superman flag-c	26.00	77.00	180.00
9/46-1st stamp album issue	75.00	250.00	500.00
10/46-1st Superman story	34.00	103.00	240.00
11/46, 12/46, 1/47-8/47 issues-Superman story in each; 2/47-Infinity-c.			

Swamp Fox © WDC

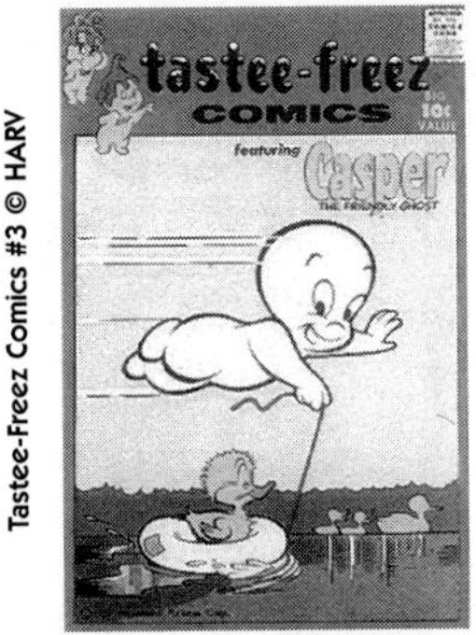
Tastee-Freez Comics #3 © HARV

Tilly and Ted - Tinkertotland © W.T. Grant Co.

	GD2.0	FN6.0	NM9.4
All 36 pgs.	34.00	103.00	240.00
9/47-Stamp album issue & Superman story	44.00	132.00	350.00
10/47, 11/47, 12/47-Superman stories (24 pgs.)	34.00	103.00	240.00
1/48-7/48,10/48, 11/48, 2/49, 4/49-11/49	27.00	81.00	190.00
8/48-Contains full page ad for Superman-Tim watch giveaway	26.00	79.00	185.00
9/48-Stamp album issue	36.00	107.00	250.00
1/49-Full page Superman bank cut-out	26.00	79.00	185.00
3/49-Full page Superman boxing game cut-out	26.00	79.00	185.00
12/49-3/50, 5/50-Superman stories	30.00	90.00	210.00
4/50-Superman story, baseball stories; photo-c without Superman	27.00	81.00	190.00

NOTE: *All issues have Superman illustrations throughout. The page count varies depending on whether a Superman-Tim comic story is inserted. If it is, the page count is either 36 or 24 pages. Otherwise all issues are 16 pages. Each issue has a special place for inserting a full color Superman stamp. The stamp album issues had spaces for the stamps given away the past year. The books were mailed as a subscription premium. The stamps were given away free (or when you made a purchase) only when you physically came into the store.*

SWAMP FOX, THE
Walt Disney Productions: 1960 (14 pgs, small size) (Canada Dry Premiums)

Titles: (A)-Tory Masquerade, (B)-Turnabout Tactics, (C)-Rindau Rampage; each came in paper sleeve, books 1,2 & 3; Set with sleeves	6.00	18.00	60.00
Comic only	1.85	5.50	15.00

SYNDICATE FEATURES (Sci/fi)
Harry A. Chesler Syndicate: V1#3, 11/15/37 (Tabloid size, 3 colors, 4 pgs.) (Editors premium)(Came folded)

V1#3-Dan Hastings daily strips-Guardineer-a	500.00	1500.00	2500.00

TASTEE-FREEZ COMICS
Harvey Comics: 1957 (10¢, 36 pgs.)(6 different issues given away)

1,3: 1-Little Dot. 3-Casper	3.80	11.40	38.00
2,4,5: 2-Rags Rabbit. 4-Sad Sack. 5-Mazie	2.40	7.20	24.00
6-Dick Tracy	3.50	10.50	35.00

TAYLOR'S CHRISTMAS TABLOID
Dept. Store Giveaway: Mid 1930s, Cleveland, Ohio (Tabloid size; in color)

nn-(Very Rare)-Among the earliest pro work of Siegel & Shuster; one full color page called "The Battle in the Stratosphere", with a pre-Superman look; Shuster art thoughout. (Only 1 known copy)
Estimated value... 3000.00

TEE AND VEE CROSLEY IN TELEVISION LAND COMICS
(Also see Crosley's House of Fun)
Crosley Division, Avco Mfg. Corp. : 1951 (52 pgs.; 8x11"; paper cover; in color) (Giveaway)

Many stories, puzzles, cut-outs, games, etc.	5.00	15.00	30.00

TENNESSEE JED (Radio)
Fox Syndicate? (Wm. C. Popper & Co.): nd (1945) (16 pgs.; paper cover; regular size; giveaway)

nn	30.00	100.00	200.00

TENNIS (...For Speed, Stamina, Strength, Skill)
Tennis Educational Foundation: 1956 (16 pgs.; soft cover; 10¢)

Book 1-Endorsed by Gene Tunney, Ralph Kiner, etc. showing how tennis has helped them	5.00	15.00	30.00

TERRY AND THE PIRATES
Dell Publishing Co.: 1939 - 1953 (By Milton Caniff)

Buster Brown Shoes giveaway(1938)-32 pgs.; in color	29.00	86.00	200.00
Canada Dry Premiums-Books #1-3(1953, 36 pgs.; 2x5")-Harvey; #1-Hot Shot Charlie Flies Again; 2-In Forced Landing; 3-Dragon Lady in Distress)	17.00	51.00	120.00
Gambles Giveaway (1938, 16 pgs.)	10.00	30.00	60.00
Gillmore Giveaway (1938, 24 pgs.)	10.00	30.00	65.00
Popped Wheat Giveaway(1938)-Strip reprints in full color; Caniff-a			5.00
Shoe Store giveaway (Weatherbird)(1938, 16 pgs., soft-c)(2-diff.)	10.00	30.00	60.00
Sparked Wheat Giveaway(1942, 16 pgs.)-In color	10.00	30.00	60.00

TERRY AND THE PIRATES
Libby's Radio Premium: 1941 (16 pgs.; reg. size)(shipped folded in the mail)

	GD2.0	FN6.0	VF8.0
"Adventure of the Ruby of Genghis Khan" - Each pg. is a puzzle that must be completed to read the story	300.00	1000.00	1800.00

THAT THE WORLD MAY BELIEVE
Catechetical Guild Giveaway: No date (16 pgs.) (Graymoor Friars distr.)

	GD2.0	FN6.0	NM9.4
nn	1.60	4.00	8.00

350 YEARS OF AMERICAN DAIRY FOODS
American Dairy Assoc.: 1957 (5x7", 16 pgs.)

nn-History of milk	3.00	7.50	15.00

THUMPER (Disney)
Grosset & Dunlap: 1942 (50 cents, 32pgs., hardcover book, 7"x8-1/2" w/dust jacket)

nn-Given away (along with a copy of Bambi) for a $2.00, 2-year subscription to WDC&S in 1942. (Xmas offer). Book only	16.00	47.00	110.00
Dust jacket only	9.15	27.00	55.00

TILLY AND TED-TINKERTOTLAND
W. T. Grant Co.: 1945 (Giveaway, 20 pgs.)

nn-Christmas comic	6.35	19.00	38.00

TIM (Formerly Superman-Tim; becomes Gene Autry-Tim)
Tim Stores: June, 1950 - Oct, 1950 (B&W, half-size)

4 issues; 6/50, 9/50, 10/50 known	8.35	25.00	50.00

TIM AND SALLY'S ADVENTURES AT MARINELAND
Marineland Restaurant & Bar, Marineland, CA: 1957 (5x7", 16 pgs., soft-c)

nn-copyright Oceanarium, Inc.	1.60	4.00	8.00

TIM IN SPACE (Formerly Gene Autry Tim; becomes Tim Tomorrow)
Tim Stores: 1950 (1/2 size giveaway) (B&W)

nn	5.35	16.00	32.00

TIM TOMORROW (Formerly Tim In Space)
Tim Stores: 8/51, 9/51, 10/51, Christmas, 1951 (5x7-3/4")

nn-Prof. Fumble & Captain Kit Comet in all	5.35	16.00	32.00

TOM MIX (...Commandos Comics #10-12)
Ralston-Purina Co.: Sept, 1940 - No. 12, Nov, 1942 (36 pgs.); 1983 (one-shot)
Given away for two Ralston box-tops; 1983 came in cereal box

1-Origin (life) Tom Mix; Fred Meagher-a	300.00	1500.00	3000.00
2	106.00	319.00	850.00
3-9	66.00	197.00	525.00
10-12: 10-Origin Tom Mix Commando Unit; Speed O'Dare begins; Japanese sub-c. 12-Sci/fi-c	53.00	160.00	425.00
1983- "Taking of Grizzly Grebb", Toth-a; 16 pg. miniature	1.85	5.50	15.00

TOM SAWYER COMICS
Giveaway: 1951? (Paper cover)

nn-Contains a coverless Hopalong Cassidy from 1951; other combinations known	4.00	10.00	20.00

TOPPS COMICS PRESENTS
Topps Comics: No. 0, 1993 (Giveaway, B&W, 36 pgs.)

0-Dracula vs. Zorro, Teenagents, Silver Star, & Bill the Galactic Hero 2.00

TOWN THAT FORGOT SANTA, THE
W. T. Grant Co.: 1961 (Giveaway, 24 pgs.)

nn	2.00	6.00	16.00

TOY WORLD FUNNIES (See Funnies On Parade)
Eastern Color Printing Co.: 1933 (36 pgs., slick cover, Golden Eagle and Wanamaker giveaway)

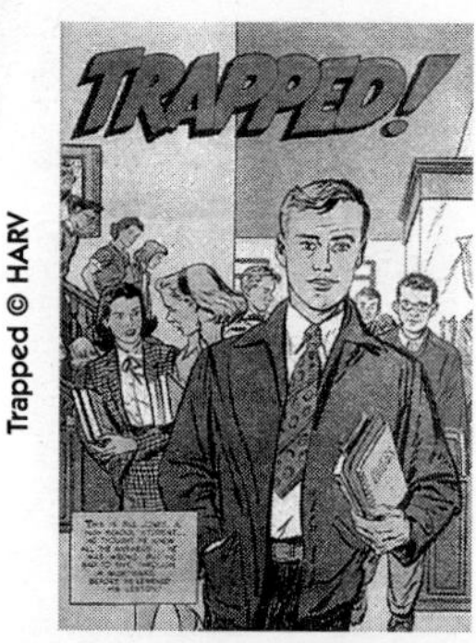

Trapped © HARV

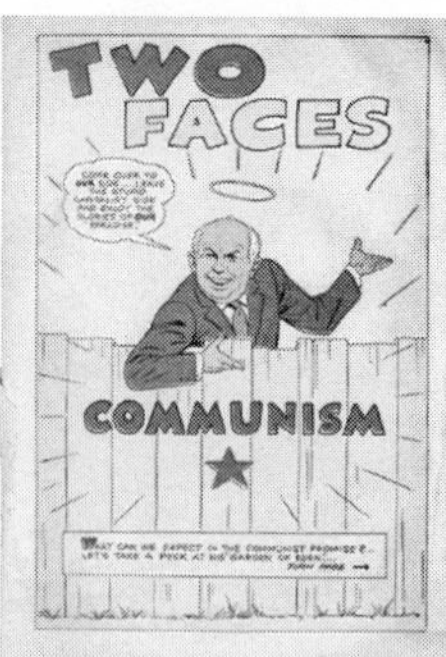

Two Faces of Communism © CACC

Unkept Promise © Legion of Truth

nn-Contains contents from Funnies On Parade/Century Of Comics. A rare varia tion of Funnies On Parade; same format, similar contents, same cover except for large Santa placed in certer (value will be based on sale)

TRAPPED
Harvey Publications (Columbia Univ. Press): 1951 (Giveaway, soft-c, 16 pgs)

nn-Drug education comic (30,000 printed?) distributed to schools.; mentioned in **SOTI**, pgs. 256,350 1.60 4.00 8.00

NOTE: *Many copies surfaced in 1979 causing a setback in price; beware of trimmed edges, because many copies have a brittle edge.*

TRIP TO OUTER SPACE WITH SANTA
Sales Promotions, Inc/Peoria Dry Goods: 1950s (paper-c)

nn-Comics, games & puzzles 4.00 10.00 20.00

TRIP WITH SANTA ON CHRISTMAS EVE, A
Rockford Dry Goods Co.: No date (Early 1950s) (Giveaway, 16 pgs., paper-c)

nn 4.00 10.00 20.00

TRUTH BEHIND THE TRIAL OF CARDINAL MINDSZENTY, THE (See Cardinal Mindszenty)

24 PAGES OF COMICS (No title) (Also see Pure Oil Comics, Salerno Carnival of Comics, & Vicks Comics)
Giveaway by various outlets including Sears: Late 1930s

nn-Contains strip reprints-Buck Rogers, Napoleon, Sky Roads, War on Crime 50.00 125.00 275.00

TWO FACES OF COMMUNISM (Also see Double Talk)
Christian Anti-Communism Crusade, Houston, Texas: 1961 (Giveaway, paper-c, 36 pgs.)

nn 12.00 36.00 90.00

2001, A SPACE ODYSSEY (Movie)
Marvel Comics Group

Howard Johnson giveaway (1968, 8pp); 6 pg. movie adaptation, 2 pg. games, puzzles; McWilliams-a 3.00

UNCLE SAM'S CHRISTMAS STORY
Promotional Publ. Co.: 1958 (Giveaway)

nn-Reprints 1956 Christmas USA 1.50 4.50 12.00

UNKEPT PROMISE
Legion of Truth: 1949 (Giveaway, 24 pgs.)

nn-Anti-alcohol 9.15 27.00 55.00

UNTOUCHABLES, THE (TV)
Leaf Brands, Inc.

Topps Bubblegum premiums produced by Leaf Brands, Inc.-2-1/2x4-1/2", 8 pgs. (3 diff. issues) "The Organization, Jamaica Ginger, The Otto Frick Story (drug), 3000 Suspects, The Antidote, Mexican Stakeout, Little Egypt, Purple Gang, Bugs Moran Story, & Lily Dallas Story" 2.50 7.50 20.00

VICKS COMICS (See Pure Oil Comics, Salerno Carnival of Comics & 24 Pages of Comics)
Eastern Color Printing Co. (Vicks Chemical Co.): nd (circa 1938) (Giveaway, 68 pgs. in color)

nn-Famous Funnies-r (before #40); contains 5 pgs. Buck Rogers (4 pgs. from F.F. #15, & 1 pg. from #16) Joe Palooka, Napoleon, etc. app. 69.00 206.00 550.00

nn-16 loose, untrimmed page giveaway; paper-c; r/Famous Funnies #14; Buck Rogers, Joe Palooka app. 26.00 79.00 185.00

WALT DISNEY'S COMICS & STORIES
K.K. Publications: 1942-1963 known (7-1/3"x10-1/4", 4 pgs. in color, slick paper) (folded horizontally once or twice as mailers) (Xmas subscription offer)

1942 mailer-r/Kelly cover to WDC&S 25; 2-year subscription + two Grosset & Dunlap hardcover books (32-pages each), of Bambi and of Thumper, offered for $2.00; came in an illustrated C&S envelope with an enclosed postage paid envelope (Rare) Mailer only 18.00 55.00 185.00
with envelopes 25.00 75.00 250.00

1947,1948 mailer 12.00 37.00 125.00

1949 mailer-A rare Barks item: Same WDC&S cover as 1942 mailer, but with art changed so that nephew is handing teacher Donald a comic book rather than an apple, as originally drawn by Kelly. The tiny, 7/8"x1-1/4" cover shown was a rejected cover by Barks that was intended for C&S 110, but was redrawn by Kelly for C&S 111. The original art has been lost and this is its only app. (Rare) 35.00 105.00 350.00

1950 mailer-P.1 r/Kelly cover to Dell Xmas Parade 1 (without title); p.2 r/Kelly cover to C&S 101 (w/o title), but with the art altered to show Donald reading C&S 122 (by Kelly); hardcover book, "Donald Duck in Bringing Up the Boys" given with a $1.00 one-year subscription; P.4 r/full Kelly Xmas cover to C&S 99 (Rare) 12.00 37.00 125.00

1953 mailer-P.1 r/cover Dell Xmas Parade 4 (w/o title); insides offer "Donald Duck Full Speed Ahead," a 28-page, color, 5-5/8"x6-5/8" book, not of the Story Hour series; P.4 r/full Barks C&S 148 cover (Rare) 8.00 25.00 85.00

1963 mailer-Pgs. 1,2 & 4 r/GK Xmas art; P.3 r/a 1963 C&S cover (Scarce) 5.00 15.00 50.00

NOTE: *It is assumed a different mailer was printed each Xmas for at least twenty years. A 1952 mailer is known.*

GD2.0 FN6.0 NM9.4

WALT DISNEY'S COMICS & STORIES
Walt Disney Productions: 1943 (36 pgs.) (Dept. store Xmas giveaway)

nn-X-Mas-c with Donald & the Boys; Donald Duck by Jack Hannah; Thumper by Ken Hultgren 42.00 127.00 425.00

WATCH OUT FOR BIG TALK
Giveaway: 1950

nn-Dan Barry-a; about crooked politicians 4.25 13.00 26.00

WEATHER-BIRD (See Comics From..., Dick Tracy, Free Comics to You... Super Circus & Terry and the Pirates)
International Shoe Co./Western Printing Co.: 1958 - No. 16, July, 1962 (Shoe store giveaway)

1 3.00 9.00 30.00
2-16 1.85 5.50 15.00

NOTE: *The numbers are located in the lower bottom panel, pg. 1. All feature a character called Weather-Bird.*

WEATHER BIRD COMICS (See Comics From Weather Bird)
Weather Bird Shoes: 1957 (Giveaway)

nn-Contains a comic bound with new cover. Several combinations possible; contents determines price (40 - 60 percent of contents).

WHAT DO YOU KNOW ABOUT THIS COMICS SEAL OF APPROVAL?
No publisher listed (DC Comics Giveaway): nd (1955) (4 pgs., slick paper-c)

nn-(Rare) 56.00 169.00 450.00

WHAT'S BEHIND THESE HEADLINES
William C. Popper Co.: 1948 (16 pgs.)

nn-Comic insert "The Plot to Steal the World" 5.35 16.00 32.00

WHEATIES (Premiums)
Walt Disney Productions: 1950 & 1951 (32 titles, pocket-size, 32 pgs.)

(Set A-1 to A-8, 1950)

A-1-Mickey Mouse & the Disappearing Island, A-5-Mickey Mouse, Roving Reporter each... 5.00 15.00 30.00

A-2-Grandma Duck, Homespun Detective, A-6-Li'l Bad Wolf, Forest Ranger, A-7-Goofy, Tightrope Acrobat, A-8-Pluto & the Bogus Money each... 4.15 12.50 25.00

A-3-Donald Duck & the Haunted Jewels, A-4-Donald Duck & the Giant Ape each... 8.35 25.00 50.00

(Set B-1 to B-8, 1950)

B-1-Mickey Mouse & the Pharoah's Curse, B-4-Mickey Mouse & the Mystery Sea Monster each... 5.00 15.00 30.00

B-2-Pluto, Canine Cowpoke, B-5-Li'l Bad Wolf in the Hollow Tree Hideout, B-7-Goofy & the Gangsters each... 4.15 12.50 25.00

B-3-Donald Duck & the Buccaneers, B-6-Donald Duck,Trail Blazer, B-8 Donald Duck, Klondike Kid each... 8.35 25.00 50.00

(Set C-1 to C-8, 1951)

Vicks Comics © EAS

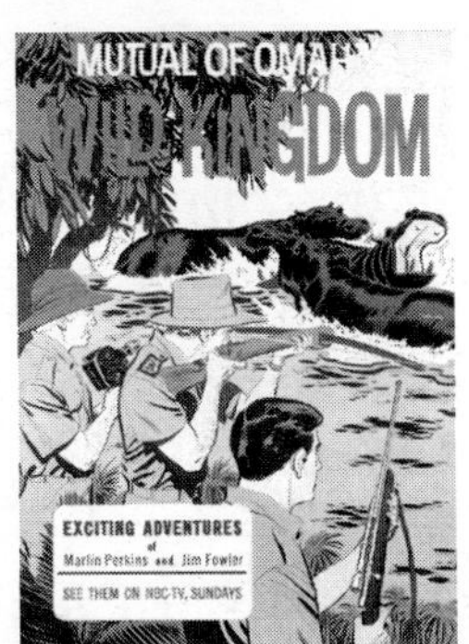

Wild Kingdom © WEST

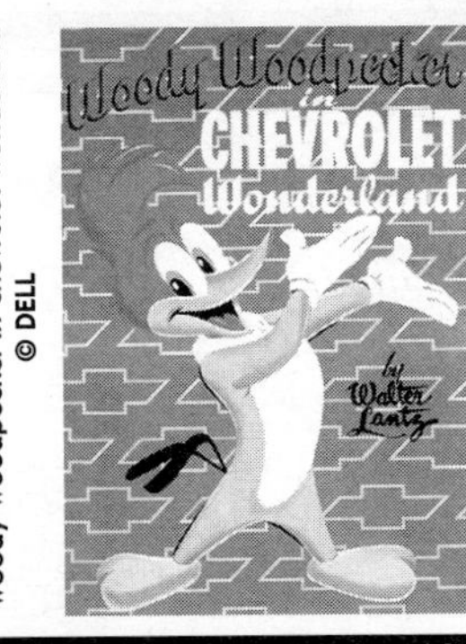

Woody Woodpecker in Chevrolet Wonderland © DELL

GD2.0 FN6.0 NM9.4

C-1-Donald Duck & the Inca Idol, C-5-Donald Duck in the Lost Lakes, C-8-Donald Duck Deep-Sea Diver each... 8.35 25.00 50.00
C-2-Mickey Mouse & the Magic Mountain, C-6-Mickey Mouse & the Stagecoach Bandits each... 5.00 15.00 30.00
C-3-Li'l Bad Wolf, Fire Fighter, C-4-Gus & Jaq Save the Ship, C-7-Goofy, Big Game Hunter each... 4.15 12.50 25.00

(Set D-1 to D-8, 1951)

D-1-Donald Duck in Indian Country, D-5-Donald Duck, Mighty Mystic each... 8.35 25.00 50.00
D-2-Mickey Mouse and the Abandoned Mine, D-6-Mickey Mouse & the Medicine Man each... 5.00 15.00 30.00
D-3-Pluto & the Mysterious Package, D-4-Bre'r Rabbit's Sunken Treasure, D-7-Li'l Bad Wolf and the Secret of the Woods, D-8-Minnie Mouse, Girl Explorer each... 4.15 12.50 25.00

NOTE: *Some copies lack the Wheaties ad.*

WHIZ COMICS (Formerly Flash Comics & Thrill Comics #1)
Fawcett Publications

Wheaties Giveaway(1946, Miniature, 6-1/2x8-1/4", 32 pgs.); all copies were taped at each corner to a box of Wheaties and are never found in very fine or mint condition; "Capt. Marvel & the Water Thieves", plus Golden Arrow, Ibis, Crime Smasher stories 100.00 400.00 –

WILD KINGDOM (TV)
Western Printing Co.: 1965 (Giveaway, regular size, slick-c, 16 pgs.)

nn-Mutual of Omaha's... 1.75 5.25 14.00

WISCO/KLARER COMIC BOOK (Miniature)
Marvel Comics/Vital Publ./Fawcett Publ.: 1948 - 1964 (3-1/2x6-3/4", 24 pgs.)

Given away by Wisco "99" Service Stations, Carnation Malted Milk, Klarer Health Wieners, Fleers Dubble Bubble Gum, Rodeo All-Meat Wieners, Perfect Potato Chips, & others; see ad in Tom Mix #21

Blackstone & the Gold Medal Mystery (1948) 7.50 22.50 45.00
Blackstone "Solves the Sealed Vault Mystery" (1950) 7.50 22.50 45.00
Blaze Carson in "The Sheriff Shoots It Out" (1950) 7.50 22.50 45.00
Captain Marvel & Billy's Big Game (r/Capt. Marvel Adv. #76) 31.00 92.00 215.00

(Prices vary widely on this book)

China Boy in "A Trip to the Zoo" #10 (1948) 4.25 13.00 26.00
Indoors-Outdoors Game Book 2.00 5.00 10.00
Jim Solar Space Sheriff in "Battle for Mars", "Between Two Worlds", "Conquers Outer Space", "The Creatures on the Comet", "Defeats the Moon Missile Men", "Encounter Creatures on Comet", "Meet the Jupiter Jumpers", "Meets the Man From Mars", "On Traffic Duty", "Outlaws of the Spaceways", "Pirates of the Planet X", "Protects Space Lanes", "Raiders From the Sun", "Ring Around Saturn", "Robots of Rhea", "The Sky Ruby", "Spacetts of the Sky", "Spidermen of Venus", "Trouble on Mercury" 6.35 19.00 38.00
Johnny Starboard & the Underseas Pirates (1948) 4.00 10.00 20.00
Kid Colt in "He Lived by His Guns" (1950) 8.35 25.00 50.00
Little Aspirin as "Crook Catcher" #2 (1950) 2.40 6.00 12.00
Little Aspirin in "Naughty But Nice" #6 (1950) 2.40 6.00 12.00
Return of the Black Phantom (not M.E. character)(Roy Dare)(1948) 5.00 15.00 30.00
Secrets of Magic 2.80 7.00 14.00
Slim Morgan "Brings Justice to Mesa City" #3 2.80 7.00 14.00
Super Rabbit(1950)-Cuts Red Tape, Stops Crime Wave! 10.00 30.00 65.00
Tex Farnum, Frontiersman (1948) 3.60 9.00 18.00
Tex Taylor in "Draw or Die, Cowpoke!" (1950) 5.35 16.00 32.00
Tex Taylor in "An Exciting Adventure at the Gold Mine" (1950) 5.00 15.00 30.00
Wacky Quacky in "All-Aboard" 1.60 4.00 8.00
When School Is Out 1.60 4.00 8.00
Willie in a "Comic-Comic Book Fall" #1 2.00 5.00 10.00
Wonder Duck "An Adventure at the Rodeo of the Fearless Quacker!" (1950) 9.15 27.50 55.00
Rare uncut version of three; includes Capt. Marvel, Tex Farnum, Black Phantom Estimated value... $325.00
Rare uncut version of three; includes China Boy, Blackstone, Johnny Starboard & the Underseas Pirates Estimated value... $95.00

WOMAN OF THE PROMISE, THE
Catechetical Guild: 1950 (General Distr.) (Paper cover, 32 pgs.)

nn 4.00 10.00 20.00

WONDERFUL WORLD OF DUCKS (See Golden Picture Story Book)
Colgate Palmolive Co.: 1975

1-Mostly-r 4.00

WONDER WOMAN
DC Comics: 1977

Pizza Hut Giveaways (12/77)-Reprints #60,62 2.00

WONDER WORKER OF PERU
Catechetical Guild: No date (5x7", 16 pgs., B&W, giveaway)

nn 4.00 10.00 20.00

WOODY WOODPECKER
Dell Publishing Co.

Clover Stamp-Newspaper Boy Contest('56)-9 pg. story-(Giveaway) 5.00 15.00 30.00
In Chevrolet Wonderland(1954-Giveaway)(Western Publ.)-20 pgs., full story line; Chilly Willy app. 21.00 64.00 150.00
...Meets Scotty MacTape(1953-Scotch Tape giveaway)-16 pgs., full size 21.00 64.00 150.00

WOOLWORTH'S CHRISTMAS STORY BOOK
Promotional Publ. Co.(Western Printing Co.): 1952 - 1954 (16 pgs., paper-c) (See Jolly Christmas Book)

nn 5.00 15.00 30.00

NOTE: *1952 issue-Marv Levy c/a.*

WOOLWORTH'S HAPPY TIME CHRISTMAS BOOK
F. W. Woolworth Co.(Whitman Publ. Co.): 1952 (Christmas giveaway, 36 pgs.)

nn 5.00 15.00 30.00

WORLD'S FINEST COMICS
National Periodical Publ./DC Comics

Giveaway (c. 1944-45, 8 pgs., in color, paper-c)-Johnny Everyman-r/World's Finest 20.00 80.00 175.00
Giveaway (c. 1949, 8 pgs., in color, paper-c)- "Make Way For Youth" r/World's Finest; based on film of same name 18.00 70.00 150.00

WORLD'S GREATEST SUPER HEROES
DC Comics (Nutra Comics) (Child Vitamins, Inc.): 1977 (Giveaway, 3-3/4x3-3/4", 24 pgs.)

nn-Batman & Robin app.; health tips 1.00 3.00 8.00

XMAS FUNNIES
Kinney Shoes: No date (Giveaway, paper cover, 36 pgs.?)

Contains 1933 color strip-r; Mutt & Jeff, etc. 50.00 200.00 300.00

YALTA TO KOREA (Also see Korea My Home)
M. Phillip Corp. (Republican National Committee): 1952 (Giveaway, paper-c)

nn-(8 pgs.)-Anti-communist propaganda book 20.00 60.00 140.00

YOGI BEAR (TV)
Dell Publishing Co.

Giveaway ('84, '86)-City of Los Angeles, "Creative First Aid" & "Earthquake Preparedness for Children" 4.00

YOUR TRIP TO NEWSPAPERLAND
Philadelphia Evening Bulletin (Printed by Harvey Press): June, 1955 (14x11-1/2", 12 pgs.)

nn-Joe Palooka takes kids on newspaper tour 4.25 13.00 26.00

The American Comic Book: 1842-1932

IN THE BEGINNING: NEW DISCOVERIES BEYOND THE PLATINUM AGE

by Robert L. Beerbohm & Richard D. Olson, PhD
©2000

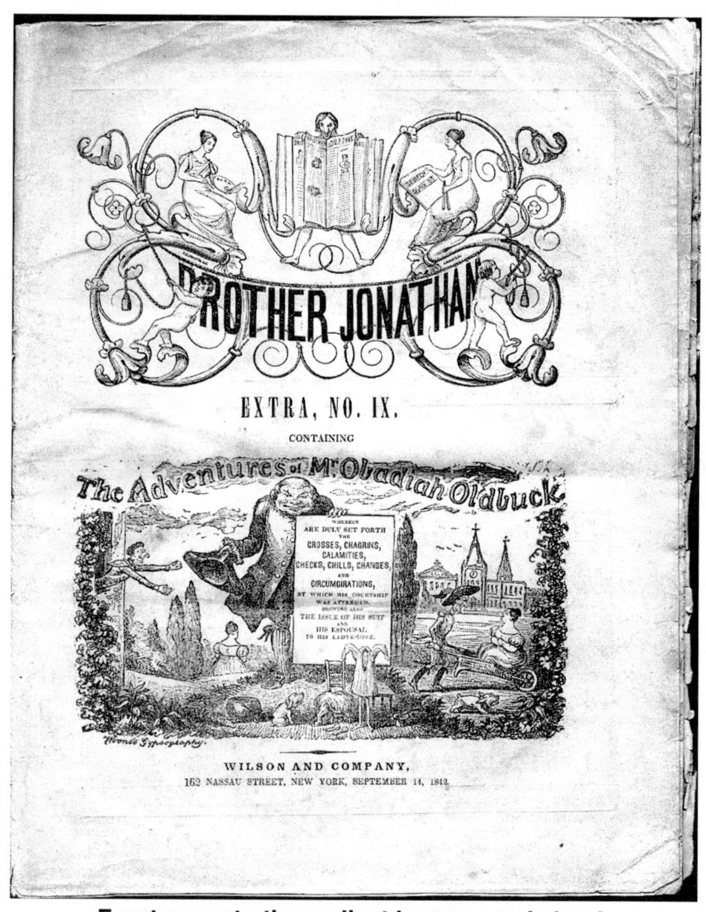

Front cover to the earliest known comic book published in America, The Adventures of Obadiah Oldbuck, Sept. 1842, Wilson & Co. NY.

Adventures of Obadiah Oldbuck, 1842. Page 8 of a 40 page graphic novel by Rudolph Topffer...the history books have to be rewritten.

The story of the success of the comic strip as we know it today is tied closely to the companies who sponsored them and paid licenses to the copyright holder for the purpose of advertising products. What mainly keeps the Platinum Age from being collected as much as later era comics is simply a general lack of awareness as well as the extreme rarity of many of these volumes, especially in any type of high grade. Many Platinum Age books are much rarer than so-called Golden Age comic books, yet despite this rarity, **Mutt & Jeff**, **Bringing Up Father**, **The Katzenjammer Kids**, and many more were as popular, if not more so, than **Superman** and **Batman** when they were introduced. **Superman** #1 sold out three printings totaling 900,000 copies, yet on any given day in the same year (1939), as just one example, over 100 million people were reading the adventures of Chic Young's **Blondie** in the funny pages. Recent research has come up with some more amazing rediscoveries. There is much that can be learned and applied to today's comics market by a simple historical examination of the medium's evolution.

The first known cartoon printed on paper in the **New World** was in a Puritan children's book first published in 1646. Titled simply "The Burning of Mr. John Rogers," it showed in flaming graphic detail what happens to those who stray from the flock and have to be burned at the stake. Wertham would have had a field day with this one! The first cartoon published in a newspaper in America is generally credited to Benjamin Franklin's "God Helps Those Who Help Themselves," in his periodical **Plain Truth** (1747). Other panel cartoons soon followed all over America, many utilizing word balloons. In 1753 his famous "Join Or Die" snake parts was published.

According to **The New York Times** (Sept. 3, 1904), the first American comic book was issued as a supplement to Brother Jonathan (New York, Sept. 14, 1842). It was a reprint of Rudolphe Töpffer's **The Adventures of Obadiah Oldbuck**, and it was 40 pages in length, side-stitched, printed on both sides of the paper with six to twelve panels per page, and measuring 8 1/2" x 11". One copy missing its outer wrap turned up in Oakland, California in late 1998, confirming its existence. You can take a look at the earliest known American comic book at www.reuben.org/evry/obadiah.html. Another whole complete copy turned up four months later in the Northeast, which is the copy pictured here for the first time in well over a century. This serves to push back the concept of what we think a comic book might be by well over 50 years. We thank Doug Wheeler for kindly sharing it with us. It bears further close scrutiny by the international comics scholar community.

Töpffer, who was Swiss, created at least eight widely published comic books which might also be called "graphic novels." Jerry Robinson, in his authoritative 1974 history book **The Comics**, wrote that "Töpffer is considered by some histori-

The first known cartoon in North America, "The Burning of Mr. John Rogers," 1646.

ans the inventor of the picture story, as he called it, and consequently the father of today's comics." Many other comics historians of equal stature have written just as eloquently about the man who invented the modern comic strip in 1827. By 1841, Töpffer's picture stories had been translated into over half a dozen languages including rare British editions; the American **Obadiah Oldbuck** is a reprint of this reprint. One more British reprint was printed in America by 1846 by Wilson & Company, titled **Wonderful Adventures of Batchelor Butterfly**. In 1849 Wilson reprinted **Obadiah** with a new title, **Mishaps and Adventures of Obadiah Oldbuck**, this time strip-shaped, with certain panels deleted and some of the text altered to smooth over these deletions. Töpffer's comic books remained in print beginning in the 1850s through another publisher named Dick & Fitzgerald in the USA until at least 1877. Over 100 years later, even though he is widely acknowledged in Europe as the father of the comic book graphic novel, Töpffer remains relatively obscure on this side of the Atlantic.

As the third millennium dawns next year, we keep rediscovering many other comic books printed, distributed and widely read in America throughout the 1800s which are little known today due to their extreme rarity. During the last decade, serious collectors have begun looking into the dim past and are steadily expanding their awareness of these earlier comic books. As knowledge grows in this area, we hope to report more about what we tentatively dub "Victorian Age" comic books.

The first graphic advertising utilizing fold-out comic strips appeared several years after the Civil War, initially sponsored by cereal and tobacco companies. At first these ads contained young kids, then animals of all kinds. With the immigrant influx of the 1870s and '80s, fairies soon dominated the scene. Palmer Cox's **The Brownies** were the first North American comics-type characters to be internationally merchandised. For over a quarter of a century, Cox deftly combined the popular advertising motifs of animals and fairies into a wonderful, whimsical world of society at its best and worst. Cox's (1840-1924) first work in **St. Nicholas**, a magazine for children, was in the March 1879 issue, titled "The Wasp and the Bee." He began his famous creation with his trademark verse and art with a creation entitled **The Brownies' Ride** in the February 1883 issue.

The Brownies' first book was issued by 1887, titled **The Brownies: Their Book**; many more followed. Cox also added a run of his hugely popular characters in **Ladies Home Journal** from October 1891 through February 1895, as well as a special on December 1910. With the 1892-93 World's Fair, the merchandising exploded with a host of products, including pianos, paper dolls and other figurines, chairs, stoves, puzzles, cough drops, coffee, soap, boots, candy, and many more. Brownies material was being produced in Europe as well as the United States.

Cox ran The Brownies as a newspaper strip in the **San Francisco Examiner** during 1898 and in the **New York World** in 1900. It was syndicated from 1903 through 1907. He seems to have retired from regularly drawing The Brownies with the January 1914 issue of **St. Nicholas** when he was 74. A wealthy man, he lived to the ripe old age of 84. Shortly before he died, he did a special commemorative Brownies for the October 1924 **St. Nicholas** issue, titled "The Wasp - a Rhyme."

By the mid-1890s, while keeping careful track of quickly rising circulations of magazines with graphic humor such as **Harper's**, **Puck**, **St. Nicholas**, **Judge**, **Life** and **Truth**, New York based newspaper publishers began to recognize that illustrated humor would sell extra papers.

Thus was born the Sunday "comic supplement." Most of the regular favorites were under contract with these magazines; however, there was an artist working for **Truth** who wasn't. Roy L McCardell, then a staffer at **Puck**, informed Morrill Goddard, Sunday editor of **The New York World**, that he knew someone who could fit what was needed at the then largest newspaper in America.

Richard F. Outcault (1863-1928) first introduced his street children strip in the June 2, 1894 issue of **Truth**, somewhat inspired by Michael Angelo Woolf's slum kids single panel cartoons in Life which had begun in the mid 1880s. It's also possible that Outcault's **Hogan's Alley** cast, including the Yellow Kid, was inspired by Charles W. Saalburg's **The Ting Ling Kids** which began in the **Chicago Inter-Ocean** by May 1894. By 1895 Saalburg was Art Director in charge of coloring for the new color printing press at the **New York World**. Edward Harrigan's play "O'Reilly and the Four Hundred," which had a song beginning with the words "Down in Hogan's Alley..." likely provided direct inspiration.

By the November 18, 1894 issue of the **World**, Outcault was working for Goddard and Saalburg. Outcault produced a successful Sunday newspaper sequential comic strip in color with "The Origin of a New Species" on the back page in the World's first colored Sunday supplement. Long time pro Walt McDougall, a famous cartoonist reputed to have turned the 1884 Presidential race with a single cartoon that ran in the **World**, handled the cartoon art on the front page. Earlier, **The World** began running full page color single panels on May 21, 1893. McDougall did various other page panels during 1893, but it was January 28, 1894 when the first sequence of comic pictures in a newspaper appeared in panels in the same format as our comic strips today. It was a full page cut up into nine panels, and the sequence was drawn entirely in pantomime, with no words. This historic page was drawn by Mark Fenderson.

The second page to appear in panels was an eight panel strip from February 4, 1894, also lacking words except for the title. This page was a collaboration between Walt McDougall and Mark Fenderson titled "The Unfortunate Fate of a Well-Intentioned Dog." From then on, many full page color strips by McDougall and Fenderson appeared; they were the first cartoonists to draw for the Sunday newspaper comic section. It was Outcault, however, who soon became the most famous cartoonist featured. After first appearing in black and white in Pulitzer's **The New York World** on February 17, 1895 and again on March 10, 1895, **The Yellow Kid** was introduced to the public in color on May 5, 1895.

THE BROWNIES' RIDE.

BY PALMER COX.

PALMER COX

ONE night a cunning brownie band
Was roaming through a farmer's land,
And while the rogues went prying round,
The farmer's mare at rest they found;

And peeping through the stable-door,
They saw the harness that she wore:
The whip was hanging on the wall,
Old Mag was grinding in the stall;

The Brownies by Palmer Cox, 1883, were the earliest known recurring comic characters merchandised in North America.

Some have erroneously reported in scholarly journals that perhaps it was Frank Ladendorf's "Uncle Reuben," first introduced May 26, 1895, which became the first regularly recurring comics character in newspapers. This is wrong, as even Outcault's "Yellow Kid" began in Pulitzer's paper a good three months before **Uncle Reuben**. Until firm evidence to the contrary comes to light, that honor will forever be enshrined with Jimmy Swinnerton's **Little Bears** cartoon characters, found all over inside Hearst's **San Francisco Examiner** as early as 1892. Though never actually a comic strip, they nonetheless were the earliest presently known recurring comics characters in American newspapers. There never was a strip titled **Little Bears and Tigers**, as the Tigers portion was strictly for New York consumption when Hearst ordered Swinnerton to move to the Big Apple to compete better in the brewing comic strip wars.

The Yellow Kid is widely recognized today as the first newspaper comic strip to demonstrate without a doubt that the general public was ready for full color comics. **The Yellow Kid** was the first in the USA to show that (1) comics could increase newspaper sales, and that (2) comic characters could be merchandised. **The Yellow Kid** was the headlining spark of what soon became dubbed by Hearst as "eight pages of polychromatic effulgence that makes the rainbow look like a lead pipe."

Ongoing research suggests that Palmer Cox's fabulous success with **The Brownies** was a direct inspiration for Richard Outcault's future merchandising work. The ultimate proof lies in the fourth Yellow Kid cartoon, which appeared in the February 9, 1895 issue of **Truth**. It was reprinted in the **New York World** eight days later on February 17, 1895, becoming the first Yellow Kid cartoon in the newspapers. The caption read "FOURTH WARD BROWNIES. MICKEY, THE ARTIST (adding a finishing touch) Dere, Chimmy! If Palmer Cox wuz t' see yer, he'd git yer copyrighted in a minute." The Yellow Kid was widely licensed in the greater New York area for all kinds of products, including gum and cigarette cards, toys, pin backs, cookies, post cards, tobacco products, and appliances. There was also a short-lived humor magazine from Street & Smith named **The Yellow Kid**, featuring exquisite Outcault covers, plus a 196-page comic book from Dillingham & Co. known as **The Yellow Kid in McFadden's Flats**, dated to early 1897. In addition, there were several Yellow Kid plays produced, spawning other collectibles like show posters, programs and illustrated sheet music. (For those interested in more information regarding the Yellow Kid, it is available on the Internet at www.neponset.com/yellowkid.)

Mickey Dugan burned brightly for a few years as Outcault secured a copyright on the character with the United States Government by Sept. 1896. By the time he completed the necessary paper work, however, hundreds of business people nationwide had pirated the image of The Yellow Kid and plastered it all over every product imaginable; mothers were even dressing their newborns to look like Dugan. (Outcault, however, kept regularly utilizing images of **The Yellow Kid** in his comics style advertising work confirmed as late as 1915.) Outcault soon found himself in a maelstrom not of his choosing, which probably pushed him to eventually drop the character. Outcault's creation went back and forth between newspaper giants Pulitzer and Hearst until Bennett's New York Herald mercifully snatched the cartoonist away in 1900 to do what amounted to a few relatively short-run strips. Later, he did one particular strip for a year - a satire of rural black America titled **Pore Li'l Mose**, and then his newer creation, **Buster Brown**, debuted May 4, 1902. Mose had a very rare comic book collection published in 1902 by Cupples & Leon, now highly sought after by today's savvy collectors. Outcault continued drawing him in the background of occasional **Buster Brown** strips for many years to come.

"Fourth Ward Brownies," artwork by Richard F. Outcault, Feb. 17, 1895. First appearance in Pulitzer's NY World. Note the Yellow Kid, second from left.

William Randolph Hearst loved the comic strip medium ever since he was a lit-

Earliest known display ad for comic books found in The Three Fun Makers, 1908, with 27 titles then in print. Note cover price says 60 cents per copy.

tle boy growing up on **Max & Moritz** by Wilhelm Busch in American collected book editions translated from the original German (these collections were first published in book form in 1870, serving as the influence for **The Katzenjammer Kids**). One of the ways Hearst responded to losing Outcault in 1900 was by purchasing the highly successful 23 year old humor magazine **Puck** from its founder, Joseph Keppler. With **Puck** and its exclusive cartoonist contracts, he got, among others, the very popular F. M. Howarth and Frederick Burr Opper's undivided attention. Opper had first burst upon the comics scene in America back in 1880. Within a year Hearst had transformed this **National Lampoon** of its day into the colored Sunday comics section, **Puck-The Comic Weekly**. At first featuring Rudolph Dirk's **The Katzenjammer Kids** (1897), **Happy Hooligan** and other fine strips by the wildly popular Opper and a few others including Rudolph's brother Gus Dirks, the Hearst comic section steadily added more strips; for decades to come, there wasn't anything else that could compete with **Puck**. Hearst hired the best of the best and transformed **Puck** into the most popular comics section anywhere.

Outcault, meanwhile, followed in Palmer Cox's footprints a decade later by using the nexus of a World's Fair as a jumping off venue. **Buster Brown** was an instant sensation when he debuted as the new merchandising mascot of the Brown Shoe Company at the 1904 St. Louis World's Fair in a special Buster Brown Shoes pavilion. The character has the honor of being the first nationally licensed comic strip character in America. Many hundreds of different **Buster Brown** premiums have been issued. Comic books by Frederick A. Stokes Company featuring **Buster Brown & His Dog Tige** began as early as 1903 with **Buster Brown and His Resolutions**, simultaneously published in several different languages throughout the world.

After a few years, Buster and Outcault returned to Hearst in late 1905, joining what soon became the flagship of the comics world. Buster's popularity quickly spread all over the United States and then the world as he single-handedly spawned the first great comics licensing dynasty. For years, there were little people traveling from town to town performing as **Buster Brown** and selling shoes while accompanied by small dogs named Tige. Many other highly competitive licensed strips would soon follow. We suggest checking out **Hake's Price Guide to Character Toys** for

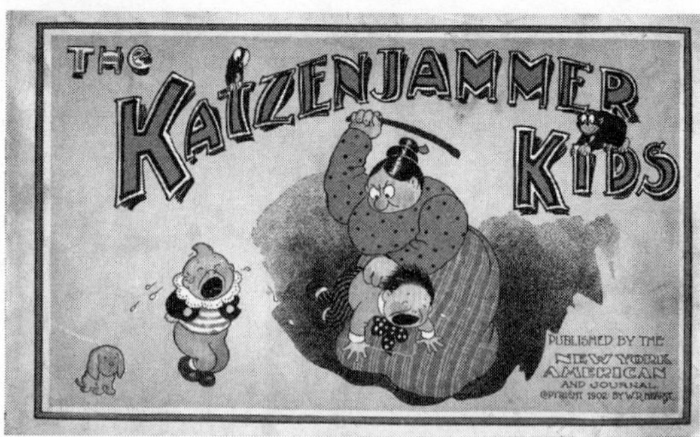

Top, The Katzenjammer Kids by Rudolph Dirks, WR Hearst (86 pages), 1902. Bottom, Happy Hooligan and His Brother... by F. Opper, also Hearst (86 pages), 1902.

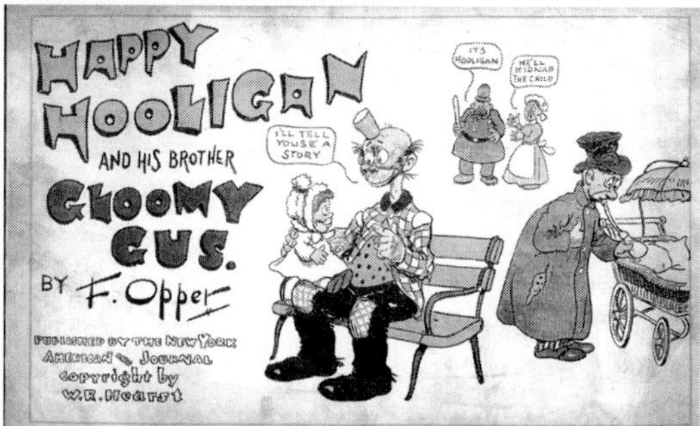

information on several hundred **Buster Brown** competitors, as well as several pages of the more fascinating **Buster Brown** material.

Soon there were many comic strip syndicates not only offering hundreds of various comic strips but also offering to license the characters for any company interested in paying the fee. The history of the comic strips with wide popularity since **The Yellow Kid** has been intertwined with give-away premiums and character-based, store-bought merchandise of all kinds. Since its infancy as a profitable art form unto itself with **The Yellow Kid**, the comic strip world has profited from selling all sorts of "stuff" to the public featuring their favorite character or strip as its motif. American business gladly responded to the desire for comic character memorabilia with thousands of fun items to enjoy and collect. Most of the early comics were not aimed specifically at kids, though children understandably enjoyed them as well.

The comic book has generally been associated with almost all of the licensed merchandise in this century. In the Platinum Age section beginning right after this essay, you will find a great many comic books in varied formats and sizes published before the advent of the first successful monthly newsstand comic book, **Famous Funnies**. What drove each of these evolutionary format changes was the need by their producers to make money. Following are some "new" highlights recently rediscovered. Space precludes mentioning others.

In 1892, Charles Scribner's Sons published A. B. Frost's **Bull Calf and Other Tales**, measuring 8 1/2 x 6 3/4. It contains sequential comic strip art on quite a few pages as well as single panel cartoons. By 1898, Charles Scribner's Sons also issued E.W. Kemble's **The Billy Goat and Other Comicalities** as a 112 page hardcover measuring 8 1/2 x 6 3/4, which also has sequential comic strip pages.

Another very significant format was F. M. Howarth's **Funny Folks**, published in 1899 by E. P. Dutton and drawn from color as well as black and white pages of **Puck**. This rather large hardcover volume measured 16 1/2 wide by 12 tall. It contains numerous sequential comic strip pages as well as single gag illustrations. Howarth's art was a joy to behold and deserves wider recognition.

By October 1900, Hearst had already caused F. Opper's **Folks In Funnyville** to be collected by publisher R. H. Russell, NY in a 12 x 9 hard cover format from his **New York Journal American Humorist** section. At the end of 1900, Carl Shultze's **Vaudevilles and Other Things** had its first edition published by Isaac H. Blanchard Co., NY. It measures 10 1/2 wide x 13 tall with 22 pages including covers. Each interior page is a 2 to 7 panel comic strip with lots of color.

There was also a recently unearthed 2nd printing of **Vaudevilles**, dating sometime after 1901, with the inscription "From the Originator of the 'Foxy Grandpa' Series" at the bottom of its front cover. This note is lacking on the earlier first edition, and it also switches format size to 11 tall and 13 inches wide.

E. W. Kemble's **The Blackberries** had a color collection by 1901, also published by R. H. Russell, NY, as well as a few other comic-related volumes by Kemble still to be unearthed and properly identified. If you have information you wish to share, please send it to the authors of this essay for future updates.

Confirmed this year for the first time is the exact format of Hearst's 1902 **The Katzenjammer Kids** and **Happy Hooligan And His Brother Gloomy Gus**. They both measure 15 5/16 wide x 10 inches tall and contain 88 pages including covers. Confirmed this year also is the fact that there are two separate editions with different covers for the pictured 1902 first edition and a 1903 Frederick Stokes edition of **Katzenjammer Kids** with differing contents. They appear to be two different books entirely, and what confuses many collectors is that they have identical indicia title pages, as does an entirely different **KK** from 1905.

Settling on a popular size of 17" wide by 11" tall, comic books were soon available that featured Charles "Bunny" Shultze's **Foxy Grandpa**, Rudolph Dirk's **The Katzenjammer Kids**, Winsor McCay's **Little Sammy Sneeze**, **Rarebit Fiend** and **Little Nemo**, and Fred Opper's **Happy Hooligan** and **Maud**, in addition to dozens of **Buster Brown** comic books. For well over a decade, these large-size, full-color volumes were the norm, retailing for 50 cents. These collections offered Sunday comics at full-size with only one side printed on a page. **The Outbursts of Everett True** by A. D. Condo and J. W. Raper was first published by Saalfield in 1907 in a 88 page hardcover collection. It may qualify as the first daily comic strip collection as it predates the newly dethroned first **Mutt & Jeff** collection by 3 years. Condo & Raper's creation began a regular run several times a week in daily newspapers in 1905 and lasted until 1927, when Condo got too sick to continue. This same **Everett True** collection was later truncated a bit by Saalfield in 1921 to 56 strips in just 32 pages measuring the 10x10 Cupples & Leon size. By 1908 Stokes had a large backlist of full color comic books for sale at 60 cents each. Some of these titles date back to 1903 and were reprinted over and over as demanded warranted. Note the number of titles in the adjacent advertisement pulled from the back of **The Three Fun Makers**.

With the ever-increasing popularity of Bud Fisher's new daily strip sensation, **Mutt & Jeff**, a new format was created for reprinting daily strips in black and white, a hardcover book about 15" wide by 5" tall, published by Ball starting in 1910, for five volumes. In 1912 Ball also branched out to at least the just unearthed **Doings of the Van Loons** by Fred. I. Leipziger. This rare comic book is the same exact format as the Ball **Mutt & Jeff** books and is listed for the first time this year.

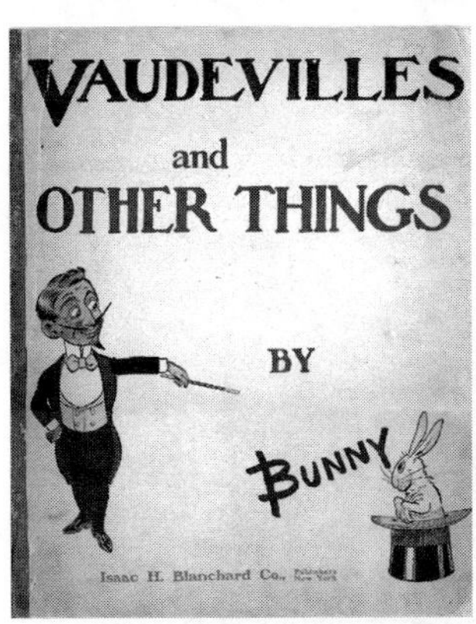

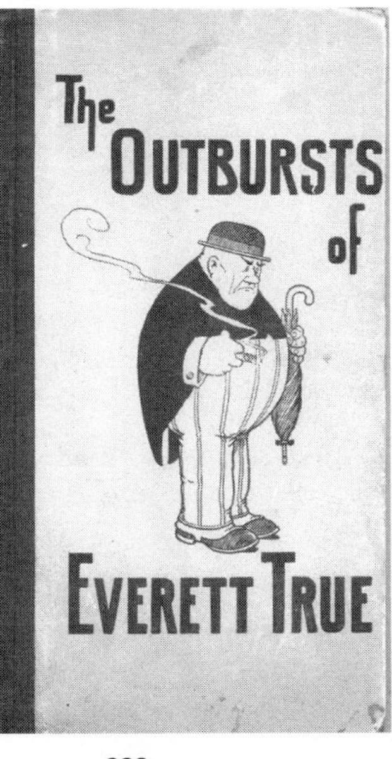

Above, Vaudevilles and Other Things by Carl "Bunny" Schultze, 1900. Right, The Outbursts of Everett True, 1907. Very scarce first edition.

The next significant evolutionary change occurred in 1919, when Cupples & Leon began issuing their black and white daily strip reprint books in a new aforementioned format, about 10" wide by 10" tall, with four panels reprinted per page in a two by two matrix. These books were 52 pages for 25 cents, and the first editions featured **Bringing Up Father** and **Mutt &**

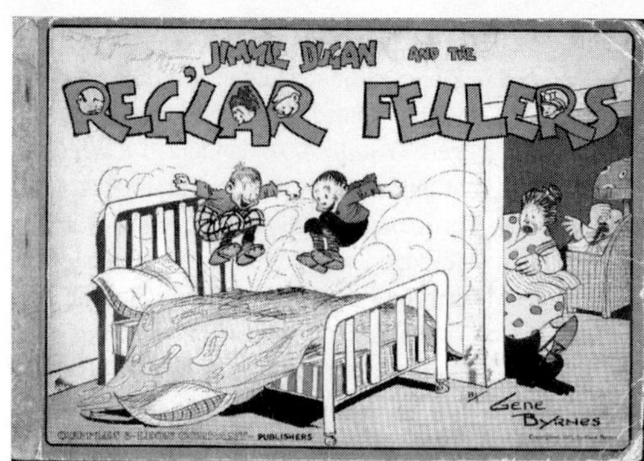

Reg'lar Fellers by Gene Byrne, 1921, one of the last two oblong large size comic books.

Jeff. By 1921 the last of the oblong (11x15 approx. size) color comic books were issued, with Cupples & Leon's **Jimmie Dugan** And **The Reg'lar Fellers** by Gene Byrne and EmBee's **The Trouble Of Bringing Up Father** by self publisher George McManus. Of special historical interest, Embee issued the first 10 cent monthly comic book, **Comic Monthly**, with a first issue dated January 1922. A dozen 8 1/2" by 9" issues were published, each featuring solo adventures of popular King Features strips. The monthly 10 cent comic book concept had finally arrived, though it would be more than a decade before it became successful.

In 1926, Cupples & Leon added a new 7" wide by 9" tall format with **Little Orphan Annie**, **Smitty**, and others. These books were issued in both soft cover and hardcover editions with dust jackets, and became extremely popular at 60 cents per copy. Dell began publishing all original material in **The Funnies** in late 1929 in a larger tabloid format. At least three dozen issues were published before Delacorte threw in the towel. Even the extremely popular **Big Little Book**, introduced in 1932, can be viewed as a smaller version of the existing formats. The competition amongst publishers now included Dell, McKay, Sonnet. Saalfield and Whitman. The 1930s saw a definite shift in merchandising comic strip material from adults to children. This was the decade when Kellogg's placed **Buck Rogers** on the map, and when Ovaltine issued tons of **Little Orphan Annie** material. Merchandising pioneers Sam Gold and Kay Kamen spearheaded this transformation.

Upwards of a thousand of these **Funnies On Parade** precursors, in all formats, were published through 1935 and were very popular. Toward the end of this era, beautiful collections of **Popeye**, **Mickey Mouse**, **Dick Tracy**, and many others were published which today command ever higher prices on the open market as they are rediscovered by the advanced collector.

Each year, this Platinum Age section grows as advanced collectors continue to report in with new finds. We encourage readers to help with this section of the book, as each new data entry is very important. For further information on this earlier fascinating era of American comic books, check out Robert L. Beerbohm's "The American Comic Book 1897-1932," originally printed in the 27th edition of **The Overstreet Comic Book Price Guide** and on Gemstone's web site at www.gemstonepub.com. Robert may be contacted at beerbohm @teknetwork.com. Also for interested collectors: A Platinum Age discussion group is now available at www.onelist.com/subscribe/Platinum AgeComics.

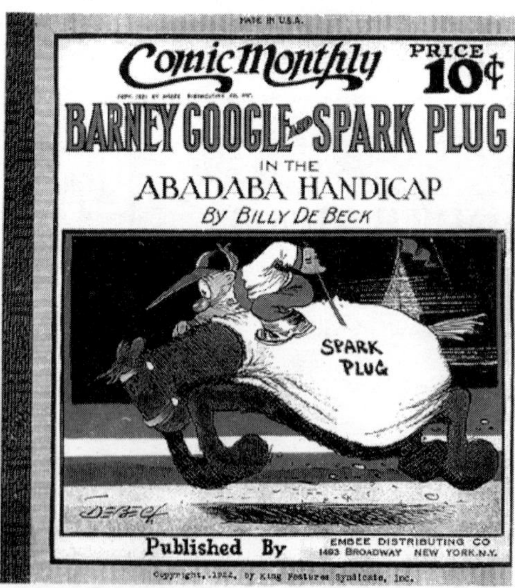

Comic Monthly #11, Nov. 1922, EmBee Publishing Co., is the first monthly newsstand comic book series.

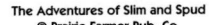

The Adventures of Slim and Spud
© Prairie Farmer Pub. Co.

All the Funny Folks
© World Press Today, Inc.

Bringing Up Father #1
© C&L

GD2.0 FN6.0 VF8.0

ADVENTURES OF HAWKSHAW (See Hawkshaw The Detective)
The Saalfield Publishing Co.: 1917 (9-3/4x13-1/2", 48 pgs., Color & two-tone)
nn-By Gus Mager (only 24 pgs. of strips, reverse of each pg. is blank) 43.00 172.00 300.00
nn-1927 Reprints 1917 issue 37.00 148.00 260.00

ADVENTURES OF MICKEY MOUSE, THE
David McKay Co., Inc.: Book I, 1931 - Book II, 1932 (5-1/2"x8-1/2", 32 pgs.)
Book I-First Disney book, by strict definition (1st printing-50,000 copies)(see Mickey Mouse Book by Bibo & Lang). Illustrated text refers to Clarabelle Cow as "Carolyn" and Horace Horsecollar as "Henry". The name "Donald Duck" appears with a non-costumed generic duck on back cover & inside, not in the context of the character that later debuted in the Wise Little Hen.
Hardback w/characters on back-c 71.00 284.00 500.00
Softcover w/characters on back-c 36.00 144.00 250.00
Version without characters on back-c 43.00 172.00 300.00
Book II-Less common than Book I. Character development brought into conformity with the Mickey Mouse cartoon shorts and syndicated strips. Captain Church Mouse, Tanglefoot, Peg-Leg Pete and Pluto appear with Mickey & Minnie 43.00 172.00 300.00

ADVENTURES OF SLIM AND SPUD, THE
Prairie Farmer Publ. Co.: 1924 (3-3/4x 9-3/4", 104 pgs., B&W strip reprints)
nn 41.00 164.00 290.00

ADVENTURES OF WILLIE GREEN, THE
Frank M. Acton Co.: 1915 (50¢, 8-1/2X16", B&W, soft-c)
Book 1-By Harris Brown; strip-r 46.00 184.00 325.00

AIN'T IT A GRAND & GLORIOUS FEELING? (Also see Mr. & Mrs.)
Whitman Publishing Co.: 1922 (9x9-3/4", 52 pgs., stiff cardboard-c)
nn-1921 daily strip-r; B&W, color-c; Briggs-a 43.00 172.00 300.00
nn-(9x9-1/2", 28pgs., stiff cardboard-c)-Sunday strip-r in color (inside front-c says "More of the Married Life of Mr. & Mrs".) 32.00 128.00 225.00

ALL THE FUNNY FOLKS
World Press Today, Inc.: 1926 (11-1/2x8-1/2", 112 pgs., color, hard-c)
nn-Barney Google, Spark Plug, Jiggs & Maggie, Tillie The Toiler, Happy Hooligan, Hans & Fritz, Toots & Casper, etc. 90.00 360.00 635.00

ALONG THE FIRING LINE WITH ROGER BEAN
Chas. B. Jackson: 1916 (6x17", 66 pgs., B&W, hard-c)
3-By Chic Jackson (1915 daily strips) 51.00 204.00 360.00

ALPHONSE & GASTON & LEON
Hearst's New York American & Journal: 1902,1903 (15-1/4x10", Sunday strip reprints in color)
nn-(1902)By Fred Opper 300.00 1200.00 -
nn-(1903)-reprint 240.00 960.00 -

ANGELIC ANGELINA
Cupples & Leon Company: 1909 (11-1/2x17", 30 pgs., 2 colors)
nn-By Munson Paddock 54.00 214.00 375.00

BANANA OIL
MS Publ. Co.: 1924 (52 pgs., B&W)
nn-Milt Gross-a; not reprints 57.00 228.00 400.00

BARNEY GOOGLE AND SPARK PLUG (See Comic Monthly & Giant Comic Album)
Cupples & Leon Co.: 1923 - No. 6, 1928 (52 pgs., B&W, daily strip-r)
1 (nn)-By Billy DeBeck 55.00 220.00 385.00
2-6 43.00 172.00 300.00
NOTE: *Started in 1918 as newspaper strip; Spark Plug began 1922, 1923.*

BILLY GOAT AND OTHER COMICALITIES, THE
Frederick A. Stokes: 1898 (8-1/2 x 6-3/.4")(116 pgs., Hardcover)
nn 100.00 400.00 -

BILLY THE BOY ARTIST'S BOOK OF FUNNY PICTURES
C.M.Clark Publishing Co.: 1910 (9X12", cardboard-c, Boston Globe)
nn-strip-r; strip app. 1898-1956 in Globe 68.00 272.00 475.00

BLACKBERRIES, THE
R. H. Russell: 1901 (9"x12", color, hard-c)
nn-By E. W. Kemble 238.00 950.00 -

BOBBY THATCHER & TREASURE CAVE
Altemus Co.: 1932 (7x9", 86 pgs., B&W, hard-c)
nn-Reprints; Storm-a 24.00 96.00 170.00

BOBBY THATCHER'S ROMANCE
The Bell Syndicate/Henry Altemus Co.: 1931 (7x8-3/4")
nn-By Storm 24.00 96.00 170.00

BRINGING UP FATHER
Star Co. (King Features): 1917 (16-1/2x5-1/2", 100 pgs., B&W, cardboard-c)
nn-(Rare)-Daily strip reprints by George McManus (no price on-c) 129.00 516.00 900.00

BRINGING UP FATHER
Cupples & Leon Co.: 1919 - No. 26, 1934 (10x10", 52 pgs., B&W, stiff cardboard-c) (No. 22 is 9-1/4x9-1/2")
1-Daily strip-r by George McManus in all 86.00 344.00 600.00
2-10 43.00 172.00 300.00
11-26 (Scarcer) 50.00 200.00 350.00
The Big Book 1(1926)-Thick book (hardcover); 10-1/4x10-1/4", 142 pgs. 121.00 484.00 850.00
The Big Book 2(1929) 96.00 384.00 675.00
NOTE: *The Big Books contain 3 regular issues rebound and probably w/dust jackets.*

BUDDY TUCKER (see Buster Brown Nuggets)

BUDDY TUCKER & HIS FRIENDS (Also see Buster Brown)
Cupples & Leon Co.: 1906 (11x17", color)
nn-1905 Sunday strip-r by R. F. Outcault 225.00 900.00 -

BUFFALO BILL'S PICTURE STORIES
Street & Smith Publications: 1909 (Soft cardboard cover)
nn 54.00 214.00 375.00

BUGHOUSE FABLES
Embee Distributing Co. (King Features): 1921 (10¢, 4x4-1/2", 48 pgs.)
1-Barney Google 39.00 156.00 275.00

BUG MOVIES
Dell Publishing Co.: 1931 (52 pgs., B&W)
nn-Not reprints; Stookie Allen-a 32.00 128.00 225.00

BULL CALF AND OTHER TALES
Charles Scribner's Sons: 1892 (116 pgs., 7"Tx9"w)(hard cover)
nn 100.00 400.00 -

BUSTER BROWN (Also see Brown's Blue Ribbon Book of Jokes and Jingles & Buddy Tucker & His Friends)
(Also see Buster Brown listings in the Promotional Comics section)
Frederick A. Stokes Co.: 1903 - 1916 (Daily strip-r in color)
(1)...& His Resolutions (1903, 11-1/4x16", 66 pgs.) by R. F. Outcault (Rare)-1st nationally distributed comic. Distr. through Sears & Roebuck(Rare) 1000.00 4000.00 -
(2)...His Dog Tige & Their Troubles (1904, 11-1/4x16-1/4", 66 pgs.)(Rare) 350.00 1400.00 -
(3)...Pranks (1905, 11-1/4x16-3/8", 66 pgs.)(Rare)

Buster Brown's Amusing Capers
© C&L

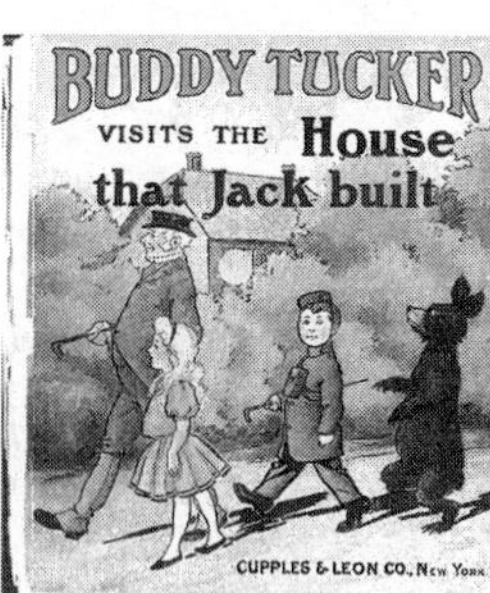

Buster Brown Nuggets #10
© C&L

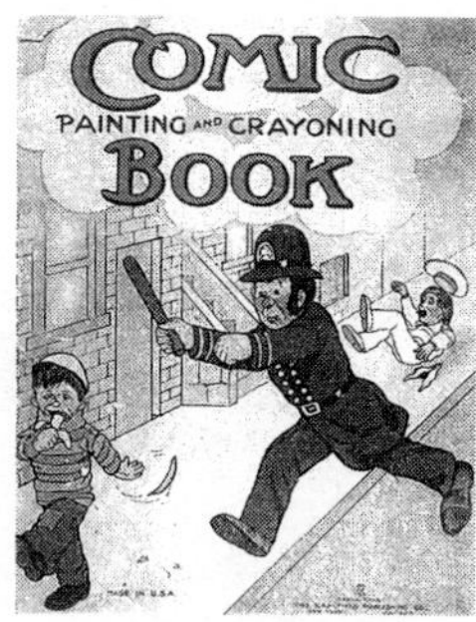

Comic Painting and Crayoning Book
© Saalfield Publ.

	GD2.0	FN6.0	VF8.0
	300.00	1200.00	-
(4)...Antics (1906, 11x16-3/8", 66 pgs.)(Rare)	300.00	1200.00	-
(5)...And Company (1906, 11x16-1/2", 66 pgs.)(Scarce)	225.00	900.00	-
(6)...Mary Jane & Tige (1906, 11-1/4x16, 66 pgs.)(Scarce)	225.00	900.00	-
(7) Collection of Buster Brown Comics (1908)(Scarce)	175.00	700.00	-
(8)...Up to Date (1910, 10-1/8x15-3/4", 66 pgs.)(Rare)	171.00	684.00	1200.00
(9)... Fun And Nonsense (1911, 10-1/8x15-3/4", 62 pgs.)	150.00	600.00	1050.00
(10)...The Fun Maker (1912, 10-1/8x15-3/4", 66 pgs.)(Rare)-Yellow Kid (4 pgs.)	150.00	600.00	1050.00
(11)...At Home (1913, 10-1/8x15-3/4", 56 pgs.)	135.00	540.00	950.00
(12)...The Little Rogue (1916, 10-1/8x15-3/4", 62 pgs.) (Rare)	135.00	540.00	950.00
(13)...And Tige Here Again	125.00	500.00	875.00
(14)...The Real Buster Brown	125.00	500.00	875.00

NOTE: *Rarely found in fine or mint condition.*

BUSTER BROWN
Cupples & Leon Co./N. Y. Herald Co.: 1906 - 1917 (11x17", color, strip-r) (By R. F. Outcault)

	GD2.0	FN6.0	VF8.0
(1A)...His Dog Tige & Their Jolly Times (1906, 11x16, 46 pgs.)	229.00	916.00	1600.00
(1B)...His Dog Tige And Their Jolly Times (1906, 11-3/8x16-5/8", 68 pgs.)	128.00	512.00	900.00
(2)...Latest Frolics (1906, 11-3/8x16-5/8", 66 pgs.)	128.00	512.00	900.00
(3)...Amusing Capers (1908, 58 pgs.)	100.00	400.00	700.00
(4)...The Busy Body (1909, 11-3/8x16-5/8", 62 pgs.)	100.00	400.00	700.00
(5)...On His Travels (1910, 11x16", 46 pgs.)	93.00	372.00	650.00
(6)...Happy Days (1911, 11-3/8x16-5/8", 58 pgs.)	93.00	372.00	650.00
(7)...In Foreign Lands (1912)	93.00	372.00	650.00
(8)...And His Pets (1913, 11x16", 46 pgs.)	93.00	372.00	650.00
(9)...Funny Tricks (1914, 11-3/8x16-5/8", 58 pgs.)	93.00	372.00	650.00
(10)...And the Cat (1917)	93.00	372.00	650.00

NOTE: *Rarely found in fine or mint condition.*

BUSTER BROWN (Also see listings in the Promotional Comics section)

BUSTER BROWN NUGGETS
Cupples & Leon Co./N.Y.Herald Co.: 1907 (1905, 7-1/2x6-1/2", 36 pgs., color, strip-r, hard-c)(By R. F. Outcault)

	GD2.0	FN6.0	VF8.0
(1) Buster Brown Goes Fishing	33.00	134.00	235.00
(2) Buster Brown Goes Swimming	33.00	134.00	235.00
(3) Buster Brown Plays Indian	33.00	134.00	235.00
(4) Buster Brown Goes Shooting	33.00	134.00	235.00
(5) Buster Brown Plays Cowboy	33.00	134.00	235.00
(6) Buster Brown On Uncle Jack's Farm	33.00	134.00	235.00
(7) Buster Brown Tige And The Bull	33.00	134.00	235.00
(8) Buster Brown And Uncle Buster	33.00	134.00	235.00
(9) Buddy Tucker Meets Alice in Wonderland	33.00	134.00	235.00
(10) Buddy Tucker Visits The House That Jack Built	33.00	134.00	235.00

BUSTER BROWN'S AUTOBIOGRAPHY
Frederick A. Stokes Co.: 1907 (B&W, 10x8", 71 pgs.) (16 color plates & 36 B&W illos)

	GD2.0	FN6.0	VF8.0
nn	57.00	228.00	400.00

BUTTONS & FATTY IN THE FUNNIES
Whitman Publishing Co.: nd (1927)(10-1/4"x15-1/2", 28pg., color)

	GD2.0	FN6.0	VF8.0
W936-Signed "M.E.B.", probably Merrill Blosser; strips in color copyright The Brooklyn Daily Eagle; thought to be one of the first two western Publ. Co. books (very rare)	61.00	244.00	425.00

CHARLIE CHAPLIN
Essanay/M. A. Donohue & Co.: 1917 (9x16", B&W, large size soft-c)

	GD2.0	FN6.0	VF8.0
Series 1, #315-Comic Capers (9-3/4x15-3/4")-18pgs. by Segar; Series 1, #316-In the Movies	200.00	800.00	1400.00
Series 1, #317-Up in the Air, #318-In the Army	200.00	800.00	1400.00
Funny Stunts-(12-1/2x16-3/8", color)	164.00	656.00	1150.00

NOTE: *All contain **Segar** -a; pre-Thimble Theatre.*

CHASING THE BLUES
Doubleday Page: 1912 (7-1/2x10", 52 pgs., B&W, hard-c)

	GD2.0	FN6.0	VF8.0
nn-by Rube Goldberg	121.00	484.00	850.00

CLANCY THE COP
Dell Publishing Co.: 1930 - No. 2, 1931 (10x10", 52 pgs., B&W, cardboard-c) (not-r)

	GD2.0	FN6.0	VF8.0
1,2-Vep-a	40.00	162.00	285.00

CLIFFORD MCBRIDE'S IMMORTAL NAPOLEON & UNCLE ELBY
The Castle Press: 1932 (12x17"; soft-c cartoon book)

	GD2.0	FN6.0	VF8.0
nn-Intro. by Don Herod	36.00	144.00	250.00

COMIC MONTHLY
Embee Dist. Co.: Jan, 1922 - No. 12, Dec, 1922 (10¢, 8-1/2"x9", 28 pgs., 2-color covers) (1st monthly newsstand comic publication) (Reprints 1921 B&W dailies)

	GD2.0	FN6.0	VF8.0
1-Polly & Her Pals	193.00	772.00	1350.00
2-Mike & Ike by Rube Goldberg	114.00	456.00	800.00
3-S'Matter, Pop?	71.00	284.00	500.00
4-Barney Google	114.00	456.00	800.00
5-Tillie the Toiler	71.00	284.00	500.00
6-12: 6-Indoor Sports. 7-Little Jimmy. 8-Toots and Casper. 9,10-Foolish Questions. 11-Barney Google & Spark Plug in the Abadaba Handicap. 12-Polly & Her Pals	71.00	284.00	500.00

COMIC PAINTING AND CRAYONING BOOK
Saalfield Publ. Co.: 1917 (10x13-1/2", 32 pgs.) (No price on-c)

	GD2.0	FN6.0	VF8.0
nn-Tidy Teddy by F. M. Follett, Clarence the Cop, Mr. & Mrs. Butt-In; regular comic stories to read or color	43.00	172.00	300.00

DAFFYDILS
Cupples & Leon Co.: 1911 (6x8", 52 pgs., B&W, hard-c)

	GD2.0	FN6.0	VF8.0
nn-By Tad	43.00	172.00	300.00

DEADWOOD GULCH
Dell Publishing Co.: 1931 (52 pgs., B&W)

	GD2.0	FN6.0	VF8.0
nn-By Charles "Boody" Rogers	25.00	100.00	175.00

DICK TRACY & DICK TRACY JR. CAUGHT THE RACKETEERS, HOW
Cupples & Leon Co.: 1933 (7x8-1/2", 88pgs., hard-c) (See Treasure Box of Famous Comics)

	GD2.0	FN6.0	VF8.0
2-(Numbered on pg. 84)-Continuation of Stooge Viller book (daily strip reprints from 8/3/33 thru 11/8/33)(Rarer than #1)	79.00	316.00	550.00
With dust jacket...	118.00	472.00	825.00

DICK TRACY & DICK TRACY JR. AND HOW THEY CAPTURED "STOOGE" VILLER
Cupples & Leon Co.: 1933 (7x8-1/2", 100 pgs., hard-c, one-shot)
Reprints 1932 & 1933 Dick Tracy daily strips

	GD2.0	FN6.0	VF8.0
nn(No.1)-1st app. of "Stooge" Viller	79.00	316.00	550.00
with dust jacket...	118.00	472.00	825.00

DOINGS OF THE DOO DADS, THE
Detroit News (Universal Feat. & Specialty Co.): 1922 (50¢, 7-3/4x7-3/4", 34 pgs, B&W, red & white-c, square binding)

	GD2.0	FN6.0	VF8.0
nn-Reprints 1921 newspaper strip "Text & Pictures" given away as prize in the Detroit News Doo Dads contest; by Arch Dale	40.00	162.00	285.00

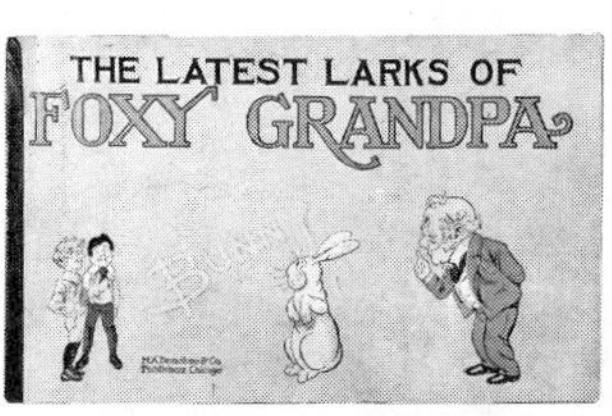

Foxy Grampa: The Latest Larks of...
© Frederick A. Stokes

The Funnies #1
© DELL

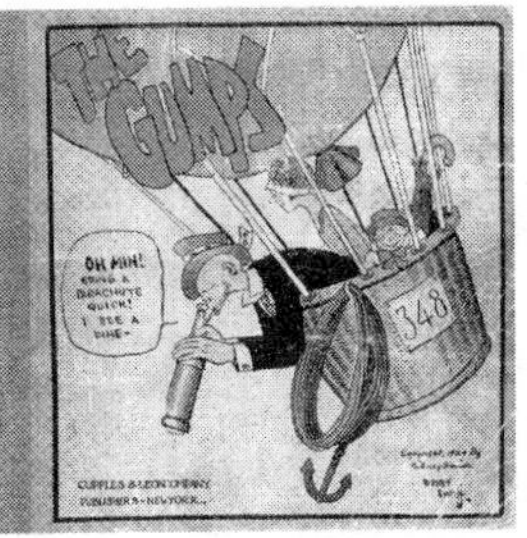

The Gumps nn (1924)
© C&L

GD2.0 FN6.0 VF8.0

DOINGS OF THE VAN-LOONS
Ball Publications: 1912 (5-3/4X15-1/2"", 68pg., B&W, hard-c)

	GD2.0	FN6.0	VF8.0
nn-By Fred I. Leipziger	71.00	214.00	500.00

DOLLY DIMPLES & BOBBY BOONCE'
Cupples & Leon Co.: 1933 (7x8-3/4")

nn-Grace Drayton-a	24.00	96.00	165.00

DREAMS OF THE RAREBIT FIEND
Doffield & Co.?: 1905

nn-By Winsor McCay (Very Rare) (Three copies known to exist) Estimated value....	750.00	3000.00	-

FELIX
Henry Altemus Company: 1931 (6-1/2"x8-1/4", 52 pgs., color, hard-c w/dust jacket)

1-3-Sunday strip reprints of Felix the Cat by Otto Messmer. Book No. 2 r/1931 Sunday panels mostly two to a page in a continuity format oddly arranged so each tier of panels reads across two pages, then drops to the next tier. (Books 1 & 3 have not been documented.)(Rare)

Each	104.00	416.00	725.00
With dust jacket	150.00	600.00	1050.00

FELIX THE CAT BOOK
McLoughlin Bros.: 1927 (8"x15-3/4", 52 pgs, half in color-half in B&W)

nn-Reprints 23 Sunday strips by Otto Messmer from 1926 & 1927, every other one in color, two pages per strip. (Rare)	200.00	800.00	1400.00
260-Reissued (1931), reformatted to 9-1/2"x10-1/4" (same color plates, but one strip per every three pages), retitled ("Book" dropped from title) and abridged (only eight strips repeated from first issue, 28 pgs.).(Rare)	79.00	316.00	550.00

FOLKS IN FUNNYVILLE
R.H. Russell: 1900 (12"Tx9"w)(cardboard-c)

nn-Reprinted from Hearst's NY Journal American Humorist supplements	225.00	900.00	-

FOOLISH QUESTIONS (Boxed card set)
Wallie Dorr Co., N.Y.: 1919 (5-1/4x3-3/4")(box & card backs are red)

nn-Boxed set w/52 B&W comics on cards; each a single panel gag complete set w/box	64.00	193.00	450.00

FOXY GRANDPA (Also see The Funnies, 1st series)
N. Y. Herald/Frederick A. Stokes Co./M. A. Donahue & Co./Bunny Publ. (L. R. Hammersly Co.): 1901 - 1916 (Strip-r in color, hard-c)

1901-9x15" in color-N. Y. Herald	225.00	900.00	-
1902- "Latest Larks of...", 32 pgs., 9-1/2x15-1/2"	138.00	550.00	-
1902- "The Many Advs. of...", 9x12", 148 pgs., Hammersly Co.	145.00	580.00	-
1903- "Latest Advs.", 9x15", 24 pgs., Hammersly Co.	138.00	550.00	-
1903- "...'s New Advs.", 10x15", 32 pgs., Stokes	138.00	550.00	-
1904- "Up to Date", 10x15", 28 pgs., Stokes	125.00	500.00	800.00
1905- "& Flip Flaps", 9-1/2x15-1/2", 52 pgs.	125.00	500.00	800.00
1905- "The Latest Advs. of", 9x15", 28, 52, & 66 pgs, M.A. Donohue Co.; re-issue of 1902 issue	85.00	340.00	600.00
1905- "Latest Larks of", 9-1/2x15-1/2", 52 pgs., Donahue; re-issue of 1902 issue	85.00	340.00	600.00
1905- "Latest Larks of", 9-1/2x15-1/2", 24 pg. edition, Donahue; re-issue of 1902 issue	85.00	340.00	600.00
1905- "Merry Pranks of", 9-1/2x15-1/2", 52 pgs., Donahue	85.00	340.00	600.00
1906- "Frolics", 10x15", 30 pgs., Stokes	85.00	340.00	600.00
1907?-"...& the Boys, 10x15", color, Stokes, 60ç	85.00	340.00	600.00
1908?-"...Surprises", 10x15, color, Stokes, 60ç	85.00	340.00	600.00
1908?- "Triumphs", 10x15"	85.00	340.00	600.00
1908?- "...& Little Brother", 10x15"	85.00	340.00	600.00
1911- "Latest Tricks", r-1910,1911 Sundays-Stokes Co.	85.00	340.00	600.00
1914-(9-1/2x15-1/2", 24 pgs.)-6 color cartoons/page, Bunny Publ.	71.00	284.00	500.00
1916- "Merry Book", 10x15", Stokes	71.00	284.00	500.00

FOXY GRANDPA SPARKLETS SERIES
M. A. Donahue & Co.: 1908 (6-1/2x7-3/4"; 24 pgs., color)

"... Rides the Goat", "...& His Boys", "...Playing Ball", "...Fun on the Farm", "...Fancy Shooting", "...Show the Boys Up Sports",... "Plays Santa Claus" each....	85.00	340.00	600.00
900- "Playing Ball"; Bunny illos; 8 pgs., linen like pgs., no date	62.00	248.00	435.00

FUNNIES, THE (Also see Comic Cuts)
Dell Publishing Co.: 1929 - No. 36, 10/18/30 (10¢; 5¢ No. 22 on) (16 pgs.)
Full tabloid size in color; not reprints; published every Saturday

1-My Big Brudder, Johnathan, Jazzbo & Jim, Foxy Grandpa, Sniffy, Jimmy Jams & other strips begin; first four-color comic newsstand publication; also contains magic, puzzles & stories	171.00	684.00	1200.00
2-21 (1930, 30¢)	50.00	200.00	350.00
22(nn-7/12/30-5¢)	36.00	144.00	250.00
23(nn-7/19/30-5¢), 24(nn-7/26/30-5¢), 25(nn-8/2/30), 26(nn-8/9/30), 27(nn-8/16/30), 28(nn-8/23/30), 29(nn-8/30/30), 30(nn-9/6/30), 31(nn-9/13/30), 32(nn-9/20/30), 33(nn-9/27/30), 34(nn-10/4/30), 35(nn-10/11/30), 36(nn, no date-10/18/30) each....	36.00	144.00	250.00

FUNNY FOLK
E. P. Dutton: 1899 (12"x16-1/2", half in color-half in B&W, hard-c) (Reprints cartoons from Puck)

nn	325.00	1300.00	-

GASOLINE ALLEY (Also see Popular Comics & Super Comics)
Reilly & Lee Publishers: 1929 (7x8-3/4", B&W daily strip-r, hard-c)

nn-By King (96 pgs.)	46.00	184.00	320.00

GUMPS, THE
Landfield-Kupfer/Cupples & Leon No. 2: No. 1, 1918 - No. 6, 1921; 1924 - No. 8, 1931 (10x10", 52 pgs., B&W)

Book No. 1(1918)(Rare)-cardboard-c, 5-1/4x13-1/3", 64 pgs., daily strip-r by Sidney Smith	150.00	600.00	1050.00
Book No.2(1918)-(Rare); 5-1/4x13-1/3"; paper cover; 36 pgs. daily strip reprints by Sidney Smith	104.00	416.00	725.00
Book No. 3-6 (Rare)	57.00	228.00	400.00
nn(1924)-By Sidney Smith	61.00	244.00	425.00
2,3	39.00	156.00	270.00
4-7	33.00	132.00	230.00
8-(10x14"); 36 pgs.; B&W; National Arts Co.	33.00	132.00	230.00

GUMPS, ANDY AND MIN, THE
Landfield-Kupfer Printing Co., Chicago/Morrison Hotel: nd (1920s) (Giveaway, 5-1/2"x14", 20 pgs., B&W, soft-c)

nn-Strip-r by Sidney Smith; art & logo embossed on cover w/hotel restaurant menu on back-c or a hotel promo ad; 4 diff. issues known	43.00	172.00	300.00

HANS UND FRITZ
The Saalfield Publishing Co.: 1929 (10x13-1/2", 28 pgs., B&W)

193-(Rare)-By R. Dirks; contains 1916 Sunday strip reprints of Katzenjammer Kids & Hawkshaw the Detective	104.00	416.00	725.00

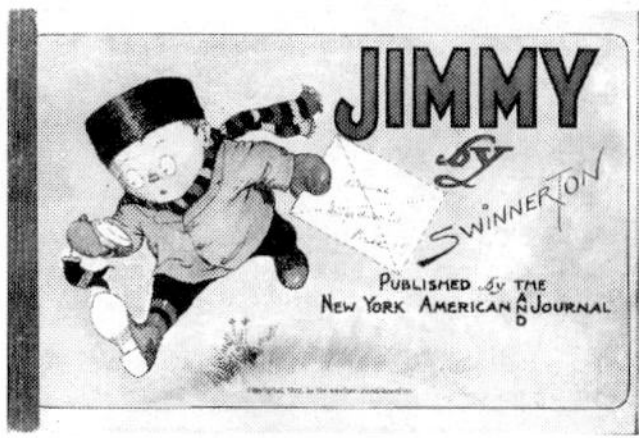

Jimmy
© NY American & Journal

Little Nemo 1906
© Doffield & Co.

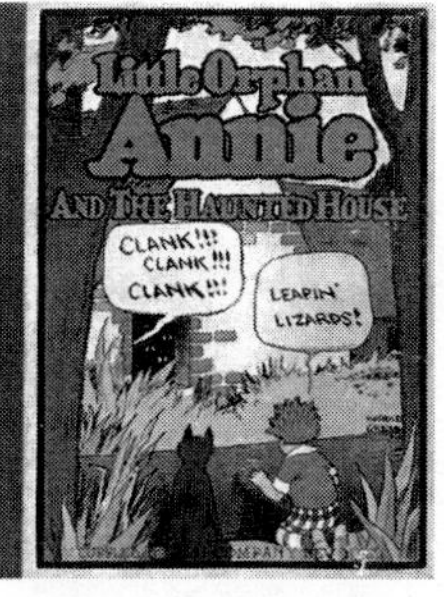

Little Orphan Annie #3 - The Haunted House
© C&L

	GD2.0	FN6.0	VF8.0
...The Funny Larks Of (1927) reprints 1916 strips; Halloween-c	82.00	328.00	575.00
...The Funny Larks Of 2(1929)	79.00	316.00	550.00

HAPPY HOOLIGAN (See Alphonse...)
Hearst's New York American & Journal: 1902,1903

Book 1-(1902)-"And His Brother Gloomy Gus", By Fred Opper; has 1901-02-r; (yellow & black)(86 pgs.)(10x15-1/4")	175.00	700.00	-
50 Pg. Edition(1903)-10x15" 18 pgs. in color	157.00	628.00	-

HAPPY HOOLIGAN (See The Travels of...)
Frederick A. Stokes Co.: 1908 (10x15", cardboard-c)

1908-"Handy--", 32 pgs, color	93.00	372.00	-
1908?-"--Home Again", 68 pgs., 60ç in color; by F. Opper; full color-c	112.00	450.00	-

HAPPY HOOLIGAN (Story of...)
McLoughlin Bros.: No. 281, 1932 (9-1/2x12", 16 pgs., soft-c)

281-Three-color text, pictures on heavy paper	64.00	193.00	450.00

HAROLD TEEN (Adventures of...)
Cupples & Leon Co.: 1929-31 (52 pgs., cardboard-c)

nn-B&W daily strip reprints by Carl Ed	41.00	164.00	290.00

HAWKSHAW THE DETECTIVE (See Advs. of..., Hans Und Fritz & Okay)
The Saalfield Publishing Co.: 1917 (10-1/2x13-1/2", 24 pgs., B&W Sunday strip-r)

nn-By Gus Mager	41.00	164.00	290.00

HENRY
David McKay Co.: 1935 (25¢, soft-c)

Book 1-By Carl Anderson	50.00	200.00	350.00

HOME, SWEET HOME
M.S. Publishing Co.: 1925 (10-1/4x10")

nn-By Tuthill	33.00	134.00	235.00

HOW THEY DRAW PROHIBITION
Association Against Prohibition: 1930 (10x9-1/2", 100 pgs.)

nnSingle panel and multi-panel comics (rare)	71.00	285.00	500.00

IT HAPPENS IN THE BEST FAMILIES
Powers Photo Engraving Co.: 1920 (52 pgs.)(9-1/2x10-3/4")

nn-By Briggs; B&W Sunday strips-r	28.00	112.00	195.00
Special Railroad Edition (30¢)-r/strips from 1914-1920	24.00	96.00	170.00

JIMMIE DUGAN AND THE REG'LAR FELLERS
Cupples & Leon: 1921, 46 pgs. (11"x16")

nn-By Gene Byrne; Ties with "The Troubles With Bringing up Father" by EmBee (#21) as last of this size	71.00	284.00	500.00

JIMMY (James Swinnerton)
N. Y. American & Journal: 1905 (10x15", 40 pgs., color)

nn	125.00	500.00	-

JIMMY AND HIS SCRAPES
Frederick A. Stokes: 1908?, (10x15", 60ç, cardboard-c)

nn-In color	57.00	228.00	400.00

JIMMY, STORY OF
McLoughlin Bros.:1932 (9'1/2"X12", 16 pgs., soft cover)

nn	64.00	193.00	450.00

JOE PALOOKA
Cupples & Leon Co.: 1933 (52 pgs., B&W daily strip-r)

nn-(Scarce)-by Fisher	114.00	456.00	800.00

JUST KIDS
McLoughlin Bros.: No. 283, 1932 (9-1/2x12", 16 pgs., paper-c)

	GD2.0	FN6.0	VF8.0
283-Three-color text, pictures on heavy paper	21.00	84.00	145.00

KATZENJAMMER KIDS, THE (Also see Hans Und Fritz)
New York American & Journal: 1902,1903 (10x15-1/4", 86 pgs., color)
(By Rudolph Dirks; strip 1st appeared in 1898) © W.R. Hearst

1902 (Rare)(red & black); has 1901-02 strips	350.00	1400.00	-
1903 (Rare)-reprint	275.00	1100.00	-
1905?-The Cruise of the, 10x15", 60ç, in color	175.00	700.00	-
1905-A Series of Comic Pictures, 10x15", 40 pgs. in color	175.00	700.00	-
1905-Tricks of...(10x15)	175.00	700.00	-
1906-Stokes-10x16", 32 pgs. in color	150.00	600.00	-
1910-The Komical...(10x15)	79.00	316.00	600.00
1921-Embee Dist. Co., 10x16", 20 pgs. in color	64.00	256.00	450.00

KEEPING UP WITH THE JONESES
Cupples & Leon Co.: 1920 - No. 2, 1921 (9-1/4x9-1/4", 52 pgs., B&W daily strip-r)

1,2-By Pop Momand	37.00	148.00	260.00

LADY BOUNTIFUL
Saalfield Publ. Co./Press Publ. Co.: 1917 (10-1/4x13-1/2", 24 pgs., B&W, cardboard-c)

nn-By Gene Carr; 2 panels per page	37.00	148.00	260.00

LIFE'S LITTLE JOKES
M.S. Publ. Co.: No date (1924) (52 pgs., B&W)

nn-By Rube Goldberg	61.00	244.00	425.00

LILY OF THE ALLEY IN THE FUNNIES
Whitman Publishing Co.(one of their first two books)**:** No date (1927) (10-1/4x15-1/2"; 28 pgs., color)

W936 - By T. Burke (Rare)	57.00	228.00	400.00

LITTLE ANNIE ROONEY
David McKay Co.: 1935 (25¢, soft-c)

Book 1	43.00	172.00	300.00

LITTLE JOHNNY & THE TEDDY BEARS
Reilly & Britton Co.: 1907 (10x14", 32 pgs.; green, red, black interior color)

nn-By J. R. Bray-a/Robert D. Towne-s	57.00	228.00	400.00

LITTLE NEMO (...in Slumberland)
Doffield & Co.(1906)/Cupples & Leon Co.(1909): 1906, 1909 (Sunday strip-r in color, cardboard covers)

1906-11x16-1/2" by Winsor McCay; 30 pgs. (Rare)	700.00	2800.00	-
1909-10x14" by Winsor McCay (Rare)	600.00	2400.00	-

LITTLE ORPHAN ANNIE (See Treasure Box of Famous Comics)
Cupples & Leon Co.: 1926 - 1934 (7x8-3/4", 100 pgs., B&W daily strip-r, hard-c)

1(1926)-Little Orphan Annie	50.00	200.00	350.00
1(1926)-softback (see Treasure Box...)			
2('27)-In the Circus	36.00	144.00	250.00
2('28)-softback (36 pgs.)	30.00	120.00	210.00
3('28)-The Haunted House	36.00	144.00	250.00
3('28)-softback (36 pgs.)	30.00	120.00	210.00
4('29)-Bucking the World	36.00	144.00	250.00
5('30)-Never Say Die	30.00	120.00	210.00
6('31)-Shipwrecked	30.00	120.00	210.00
7('32)-A Willing Helper	24.00	96.00	170.00
8('33)-In Cosmic City	24.00	96.00	170.00
9('34)-Uncle Dan (Rare)	43.00	172.00	300.00

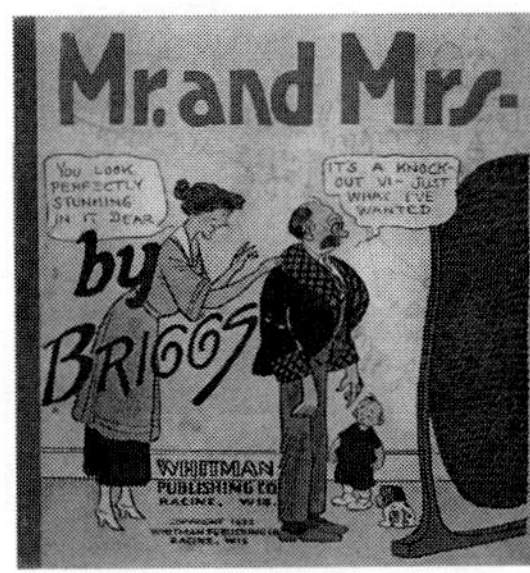

Mr. & Mrs.
© WHIT

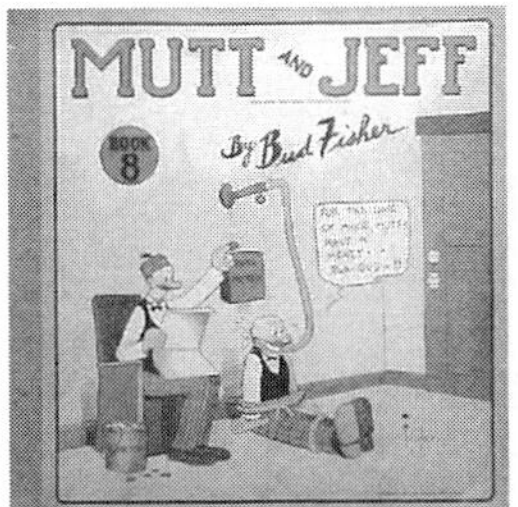

Mutt & Jeff #8
© Ball Publ.

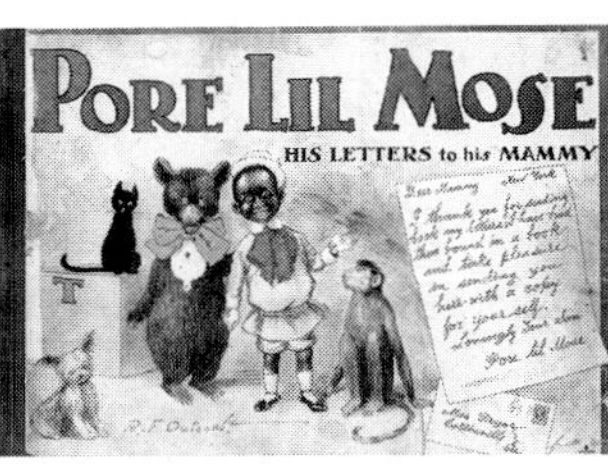

Pore Li'l Mose
© WHIT

GD2.0 FN6.0 VF8.0 GD2.0 FN6.0 VF8.0

NOTE: *Each book reprints dailies from the previous year.*

LITTLE SAMMY SNEEZE
New York Herald Co.: 1905 (11x16-1/2", 28 pgs., color)

nn-By Winsor McCay (Rare) 750.00 3000.00 -
NOTE: *Rarely found in fine to mint condition.*

LITTLE SKEEZIX BOOKS (Also see Skeezix)
Reilly & Lee Co.: No date (1927-28?) Boxed set of three Skeezix books)

nn-Box with 3 issues of Skeezix (possibly remaindered). Skeezix & Pal, Skeezix at the Circus, Skeezix & Uncle Walt known. Set... 80.00 320.00 550.00

MAUD
Frederick A. Stokes Co.: 1906 - 1908? (10x15-1/2", cardboard-c)

1906, By Fred Opper (Scarce), 32pgs. color 200.00 800.00 -
1908?--The Matchless, 10x15" in color 150.00 600.00
1908?--The Mirthful Mule, 10x15" in color 150.00 600.00

MICKEY MOUSE BOOK
Bibo & Lang: 1930-1931 (9"x12", stapled-c, 20 pgs., 4 printings)

nn-First Disney licensed publication (a magazine, not a book–see first book, Adventures of Mickey Mouse). Contains story of how Mickey met Walt and got his name; games, cartoons & song "Mickey Mouse (You Cute Little Feller)," written by Irving Bibo; Minnie, Clarabelle Cow, Horace Horsecollar & caricature of Walt shaking hands with Mickey. The changes made with the 2nd printing have been verified by billing affidavits in the Walt Disney Archives and include:Two Win Smith Mickey strips from 4/15/30 and 4/17/30 added to page 8 & back-c; "Printed in U.S.A." added to front cover; Bobette Bibo's age of 11 years added to title page; faulty type on the word "tail" corrected top of page 3; the word "start" added to bottom of page 7, removing the words "start 1 2 3 4" from the top of page 7; music and lyrics were rewritten on pages 12-14. A green ink border was added beginning with 2nd printing and some covers have inking variations. Art by Albert Barbelle, drawn in an Ub Iwerks style. Total circulation : 97,938 copies varying from 21,000 to 26,000 per printing.

1st printing. Contains the song lyrics **censored** in later printings, "When little Minnie's pursued by a big bad villain we feel so bad then we're glad when you up and kill him." Attached to the Nov. 15, 1930 issue of the Official Bulletin of the Mickey Mouse Club notes: "Attached to this Bulletin is a new Mickey Mouse Book that has just been published." This is thought to be the reason why a slightly disproportionate larger number of copies of the first printing still exist 1200.00 5400.00 11,000.00
2nd printing with a theater/advertising. Christmas greeting added to inside front cover (1 copy known with Dec. 27, 1930 date) ---- 12,000.00 ----
2nd-4th printings 1100.00 5000.00 10,000.00
NOTE: Theater/advertising copies do not qualify as separate printings. Most copies are missing pages 9 & 10 which had a puzzle to be cut out. *Puzzle (pages 9 and 10) cut out or missing, subtract 60% to 75%.*

MICKEY MOUSE COMIC
David McKay Co.: 1931 - No. 4, 1934 (10"x9-3/4", 52 pgs., cardboard-c)
(Later reprints exist)

1(1931)-Reprints Floyd Gottfredson daily strips in black & white from 1930 & 1931, including the famous two week sequence in which Mickey tries to commit suicide 214.00 856.00 1500.00
2(1932)-1st app. of Pluto reprinted from 7/8/31 daily. All pgs. from 1931 164.00 656.00 1150.00
3(1933)-Reprints 1932 & 1933 Sunday pages in color, one strip per page, including the "Lair of Wolf Barker" continuity pencilled by Gottfredson and inked by Al Taliaferro & Ted Thwaites. First app. Mickey's nephews, Morty & Ferdie, one identified by name of Mortimer Fieldmouse, not to be confused with Uncle Mortimer Mouse who is introduced in the Wolf Barker story 214.00 856.00 1500.00
4(1934)-1931 dailies, include the only known reprint of the infamous strip of 2/4/31 where the villainous Kat Nipp snips off the end of Mickey's tail with a pair of scissors 121.00 484.00 850.00

MILITARY WILLY
J. I. Austen Co.: 1907 (7x9-1/2", 14 pgs., every other page in color, stapled)

nn-By F. R. Morgan 54.00 216.00 375.00

MISCHIEVOUS MONKS OF CROCODILE ISLE, THE
J. I. Austen Co., Chicago: 1908 (8-1/2x11-1/2", 12 pgs., 4 pgs. in color)

nn-By F. R. Morgan; reads longwise 78.00 312.00 550.00

MR. & MRS. (Also see Ain't It A Grand and Glorious Feeling?)
Whitman Publishing Co.: 1922 (9x9-1/2", 52 & 28 pgs., cardboard-c)

nn-By Briggs (B&W, 52 pgs.) 36.00 144.00 250.00
nn-28 pgs.-(9x9-1/2")-Sunday strips-r in color 39.00 156.00 275.00

MONKEY SHINES OF MARSELEEN
Cupples & Leon Co.: 1909 (11-1/2x17", 28 pgs. in two colors)

nn-By Norman E. Jennett 54.00 216.00 375.00

MOON MULLINS
Cupples & Leon Co.: 1927 - 1933 (52 pgs., B&W daily strip-r)

Series 1('27)-By Willard 57.00 228.00 400.00
Series 2('28), Series 3('29), Series 4('30) 39.00 156.00 275.00
Series 5('31), 6('32), 7('33) 36.00 144.00 250.00
Big Book 1('30)-B&W 50.00 200.00 350.00

MUTT & JEFF (...Cartoon, The)
Ball Publications: 1910 - No. 5, 1916 (5-3/4x15-1/2", B&W, hard-c)

1(1910)(68 pgs., 50¢) 186.00 744.00 1300.00
2,3: 2(1911, 68 pgs.)-Opium den panels; Jeff smokes opium (pipe dreams). 3(1912, 68 pgs.) 96.00 384.00 675.00
4(1915)(68 pgs., 50¢)(Rare) 96.00 384.00 675.00
5(1916)(68 pgs.)(Rare)-Photos of Fisher, 1st pg. 171.00 684.00 1200.00
NOTE: *Mutt & Jeff first appeared in newspapers in 1908. Cover variations exist showing Mutt & Jeff reading various newspapers; i.e., The Oregon Journal, The American, and The Detroit News. Reprinting of each issue began soon after publication. No. 5 may not have been reprinted. Values listed include the reprints.*

MUTT & JEFF
Cupples & Leon Co.: No. 6, 1919 - No. 22, 1933? (9-1/2x9-1/2", 52 pgs., B&W dailies, stiff-c)

6-22-By Bud Fisher 57.00 228.00 400.00
NOTE: *Later issues are somewhat rarer.*
nn(1920)-(Advs. of...) 16x11"; 20 pgs.; reprints 1919 Sunday strips 93.00 372.00 650.00
Big Book nn(1926, 144 pgs., hardcovers) 114.00 456.00 800.00
w/dust jacket 193.00 772.00 1350.00
Big Book 1(1928)-Thick book (hardcovers) 114.00 456.00 800.00
w/dust jacket (rare) 183.00 732.00 1275.00
Big Book 2(1929)-Thick book (hardcovers) 114.00 456.00 800.00
w/dust jacket (rare) 183.00 732.00 1275.00
NOTE: *The Big Books contain three previous issues rebound.*

MUTT & JEFF
Embee Publ. Co.: 1921 (9x15")

nn-Sunday strips in color (Rare) 143.00 572.00 1000.00

NEBBS, THE
Cupples & Leon Co.: 1928 (52 pgs., B&W daily strip-r)

nn-By Sol Hess; Carlson-a 40.00 160.00 280.00

NEWLYWEDS
Saalfield Publ. Co.: 1907; 1917 (cardboard-c)

...& Their Baby' by McManus; Saalfield, (1907, 13x10", 52 pgs.); daily strips in full color 150.00 600.00 -

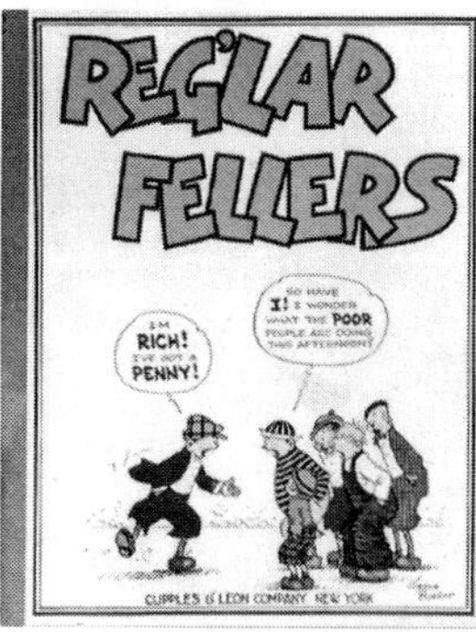

Reg'lar Fellers #1
© C&L

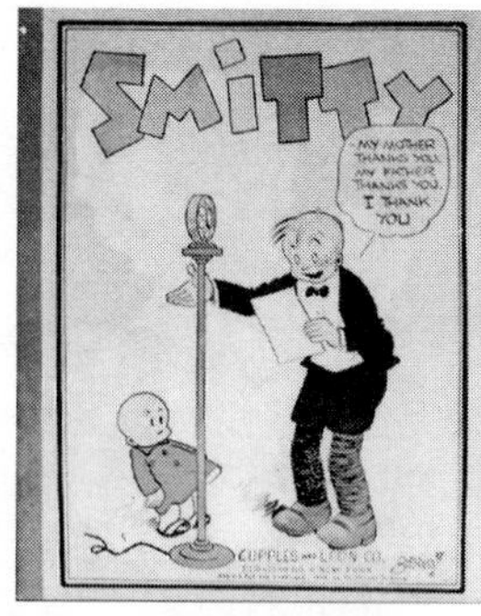

Smitty (Treasure Book of Famous Comics)
© C&L

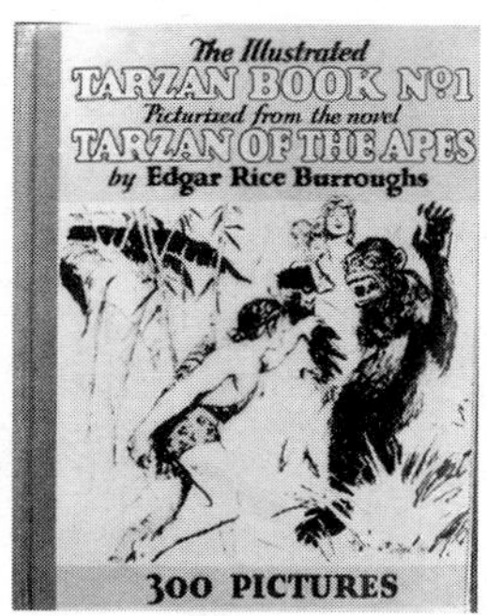

Tarzan Book
© Grosset & Dunlap

GD2.0 FN6.0 VF8.0 GD2.0 FN6.0 VF8.0

...& Their Baby's Comic Pictures, The, by McManus, Saalfield, (1917, 14x10", 22 pgs, oblong, cardboard-c); reprints 'Newlyweds' (Baby Snookums strips) mainly from 1916; blue cover; says for painting & crayoning, but some pages in color. (Scarce) 70.00 280.00 490.00

NIPPY'S POP
The Saalfield Publishing Co.: 1917 (10-1/2x13-1/2", B&W, Sunday strip-r)
nn-32 pgs. 37.00 148.00 260.00

OH, MAN (A Bully Collection of Those Inimitable Humor Cartoons)
P.F. Volland & Co.: 1919 (8-1/2x13")
nn-By Briggs 37.00 148.00 260.00

OH SKIN-NAY!
P.F. Volland & Co.: 1913 (8-1/2x13")
nn-The Days Of Real Sport by Briggs 37.00 148.00 260.00

ON AND OFF MOUNT ARARAT (also see Tigers)
Heart's New York American & Journal: 1902, 86pgs. 10x15-1/4"
nn-Noah's ark satire by Jimmy Swinnerton 125.00 500.00 -

ON THE LINKS
Associated Feature Service: Dec, 1926 (9x10", 48 pgs.)
nn-Daily strip-r 22.00 88.00 155.00

OUTBURSTS OF EVERETT TRUE, THE
Saalfield Publ. Co.(Werner Co.): 1907 (92 pgs.)(5-1/4"w x 9-7/16" tall);1921 (32 pgs., B&W)(10x10")
1907 (2-4 panel strips-r)-By A.D. Condo & J.W. Raper71.00 284.00 500.00
1921-Full color-c; reprints 56 of 88 cartoons from1907 ed. 34.00 136.00 240.00

PECKS BAD BOY
Thompson of Chicago (by Walt McDougal): 1906 - 1908 (11-1/4x15-3/4", strip-r)
...& Cousin Cynthia(1907)-In color 71.00 284.00 500.00
...& His Chums (1908)-Hardcover; in full color; 16 pgs. 71.00 284.00 500.00
Advs. of...And His Country Cousins (1906)-In color, 18 pgs., oblong 71.00 284.00 500.00
Advs. of...in Pictures (1908)-In color; Stanton & Van V. Liet Co. 71.00 284.00 500.00

PERCY & FERDIE
Cupples & Leon Co.: 1921 (10x10", 52 pgs., B&W dailies, cardboard-c)
nn-By H. A. MacGill (Rare) 61.00 244.00 425.00

PETER RABBIT
John H. Eggers Co. The House of Little Books Publishers: 1922 - 1923 (9-1/4x6-1/4", paper-c)
B1-B4-(Rare)-(Set of 4 books which came in a cardboard box)-Each book reprints half of a Sunday page per page and contains 8 B&W and 2 color pages; by Harrison Cady
each.... 43.00 172.00 300.00
Box only 57.00 228.00 400.00

PINK LAFFIN
Whitman Publishing Co.: 1922 (9x12")(Strip-r)
...the Lighter Side of Life, ...He Tells 'Em, ...and His Family, ...Knockouts; Ray Gleason-a (All rare)
each... 26.00 104.00 185.00

PORE LI'L MOSE
New York Herald Publ. by Grand Union Tea
Cupples & Leon Co.: 1902 (10-1/2x15", 30 pgs., color)
nn-By R. F. Outcault; 1 pg. strips about early Negroes (Very rare) 1000.00 3000.00 -

REG'LAR FELLERS (See All-American Comics, Jimmie Dugan & The..., Popular Comics & Treasure Box of Famous Comics)
Cupples & Leon Co./MS Publishng Co.: 1921 - 1929
1(1921)-52 pgs. B&W dailies (Cupples & Leon, 10x10") 40.00 160.00 285.00
1925, 48 pgs. B&W dailies (MS Publ.) 36.00 144.00 250.00
Hardcover (1929, 96 pgs.)-B&W reprints 49.00 196.00 340.00

ROGER BEAN, R. G. (Regular Guy)
The Indiana News Co.: 1915 - No. 5, 1917 (4-3/4x16", 34 pgs., B&W, cardboard-c) (No. 1 & 4 bound on side, No. 3 bound at top)
1-By Chic Jackson (48 pgs.)(Scarce) 46.00 184.00 320.00
2-5 (Scarce) 31.00 124.00 220.00
Baby Grand Edition #3 (10x10") 31.00 124.00 220.00

SAM AND HIS LAUGH
Frederick A. Stokes: 1908? (10x15", cardboard-c)
nn-In color 57.00 228.00 400.00

SCHOOL DAYS
Harper & Bros.: 1919 (9x8", 104 pgs.)
nn-By Clare Victor Dwiggins 36.00 142.00 250.00

SILK HAT HARRY'S DIVORCE SUIT
M. A. Donoghue & Co.: 1912 (5-3/4x15-1/2", B&W)
Newspaper-r by Tad (Thomas Dorgan) 26.00 104.00 180.00

SKEEZIX (Also see Gasoline Alley & Little Skeezix Books)
Reilly & Lee Co.: 1925 - 1928 (Strip-r, soft covers) (pictures & text)
...and Uncle Walt (1924)-Origin 26.00 104.00 180.00
...and Pal (1925) 21.00 84.00 150.00
...at the Circus (1926) 21.00 84.00 150.00
...& Uncle Walt (1927) 21.00 84.00 150.00
...Out West (1928) 21.00 84.00 150.00
Hardback Editions... 34.00 136.00 235.00

SKIPPY
No publisher listed: Circa 1920s (10x8", 16 pgs., color/B&W cartoons)
nn-By Percy Crosby 81.00 322.00 565.00

S'MATTER POP?
Saalfield Publ. Co.: 1917 (10x14", 44 pgs., B&W, cardboard-c)
nn-By Charlie Payne; in full color; pages printed on one side 41.00 164.00 290.00

SMITTY (See Treasure Box of Famous Comics)
Cupples & Leon Co.: 1928 - 1933 (9-1/2x9-1/2", 52 pgs., B&W strip-r, cardboard-c)
1928-(96 pgs. 7x8-3/4") 41.00 164.00 290.00
1929-At the Ball Game, 1930-The Flying Office Boy, 1931-The Jockey, 1932-In the North Woods each... 31.00 124.00 220.00
1933-At Military School 31.00 124.00 220.00
Hardback Editions-(7x8-1/4", 100 pgs.)(Rare)-With dust jacket
each... 40.00 160.00 280.00

STRANGE AS IT SEEMS
Blue-Star Publishing Co.: 1932 (64 pgs., B&W, square binding)
1-Newspaper-r 32.00 128.00 225.00
NOTE: *Published with and without No. 1 and price on cover.*
Ex-Lax giveaway(1936, B&W, 24 pgs., 5x7")-McNaught Synd. 13.00 52.00 90.00

Tillie the Toiler #5
© C&L

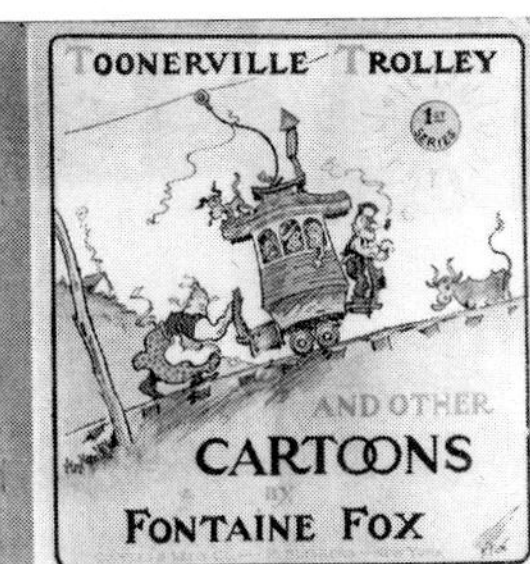

Toonerville Trolley #1
© C&L

Yellow Kid in McFadden's Flats
© G.W. Dillingham Co.

GD2.0 FN6.0 VF8.0

TAILSPIN TOMMY STORY & PICTURE BOOK
McLoughlin Bros.: No. 266, 1931? (nd) (10-1/2x10", color strip-r)
266-By Forrest 34.00 136.00 240.00

TAILSPIN TOMMY (Also see Famous Feature Stories & The Funnies)
Cupples & Leon Co.: 1932 (100 pgs., hard-c)
nn-(Rare)-B&W strip reprints from 1930 by Hal Forrest & Glenn Claffin 43.00 172.00 300.00

TARZAN BOOK (The Illustrated...)
Grosset & Dunlap: 1929 (7x9", 80 pgs.)
1(Rare)-Contains 1st B&W Tarzan newspaper comics from 1929. Cloth reinforced spine & dust jacket (50¢); Foster-c
with dust jacket... 82.00 328.00 575.00
without dust jacket... 33.00 132.00 230.00
2nd Printing(1934, 25¢, 76 pgs.)-4 Foster pgs. dropped; paper spine, circle in lower right cover with 25¢ price. The 25¢ is barely visible on some copies 31.00 124.00 220.00
1967-House of Greystoke reprint-7x10", using the complete 300 illustrations/ text from the 1929 edition minus the original indicia, foreword, etc. Initial version bound in gold paper & sold for $5.00. Officially titled **Burroughs Biblophile #2**. A very few additional copies were bound in heavier blue paper.
Gold binding... 2.25 6.75 18.00
Blue binding... 2.50 7.50 24.00

TARZAN OF THE APES TO COLOR
Saalfield Publishing Co.: No. 988, 1933 (10-3/4x15-1/4", 24 pgs) (Coloring book)
988-(Very Rare)-Contains 1929 daily reprints with some new art by Hal Foster. Two panels blown up large on each page with one at the top of opposing pages on every other double-page spread. Believed to be the only time these panels appeared in color. Most color panels are reproduced a second time in b&w to be colored 257.00 1028.00 1800.00

THIMBLE THEATRE STARRING POPEYE
Sonnet Publishing Co.: 1931 - No. 2, 1932 (25¢, B&W, 52 pgs.)(Rare)
1-Daily strip serial-r in both by Segar 157.00 628.00 1100.00
2 136.00 544.00 950.00
NOTE: *The very first Popeye reprint book. Popeye first entered Thimble Theatre in 1929.*

THREE FUNMAKERS, THE
Stokes and Company: 1908 (10x15", 64 pgs., color) (1904-06 Sunday strip-r)
nn-Maude, Katzenjammer Kids, Happy Hooligan 275.00 1100.00 -

"TIGE" HIS STORY
Frederick A. Stokes Co.: 1905 (10x8", 63 pgs., B&W) (63 illos.)
nn 125.00 500.00 -

TIGERS (Also see On and Off Mount Ararat)
Hearst's New York American & Journal: 1902, 86pgs. 10x15-1/4"
nn-Funny animal strip-r by Jimmy Swinnerton 125.00 500.00 -

TILLIE THE TOILER
Cupples & Leon Co.: 1925 - No. 8, 1933 (52 pgs., B&W, daily strip-r)
nn (#1) 46.00 184.00 325.00
2-8 34.00 136.00 240.00
NOTE: *First strip appearance was January, 1921.*

TOM SAWYER & HUCK FINN
Stoll & Edwards Co.: 1925 (10-3/4x10", 52 pgs, stiff covers)(Sunday strips in color)
nn-By Dwiggins; 1923, 1924-r 35.00 140.00 245.00

GD2.0 FN6.0 VF8.0

TOONERVILLE TROLLEY
Cupples & Leon Co.: 1921 (52 pgs., B&W, daily strip-r)
1-By Fontaine Fox 54.00 216.00 375.00

TRAVELS OF HAPPY HOOLIGAN, THE
Frederick A. Stokes Co.: 1906 (10-1/4x15-3/4", 32 pgs., cardboard covers)
nn-Contains reprints from 1905 100.00 400.00 -

TREASURE BOX OF FAMOUS COMICS
Cupples & Leon Co.: Mid 1930's (6-7/8x8-1/2", 36 pgs, soft covers) (Boxed set of 5 books)
Little Orphan Annie (1926) 21.00 84.00 150.00
Reg'lar Fellers (1928) 19.00 76.00 130.00
Smitty (1928) 19.00 76.00 130.00
Harold Teen (1931) 19.00 76.00 130.00
How Dick Tracy & Dick Tracy Jr. Caught The Racketeers (1933) 26.00 104.00 185.00
Softcover set of five books in box 160.00 640.00 1125.00
Box only 57.00 228.00 400.00
NOTE: *Dates shown are copyright dates; all books actually came out in 1934 or later. The softcovers are abbreviated versions of the hardcover editions listed under each character.*

TRIALS OF LULU AND LEANDER, THE
William A. Stokes Co.: 1906 (10x16", 32 pgs. in color)
nn-By F. M. Howarth 125.00 500.00 -

TROUBLE OF BRINGING UP FATHER, THE
Embee Publ. Co.: 1921 (9x15", Sunday-r in color)
nn-(Rare) 75.00 300.00 525.00

VAUDEVILLES AND OTHER THINGS
Isaac H. Blandiard Co.: 1900 (10-1/2x13", 22 pgs., color), 1901 (11X13")
nn-By Bunny (Scarce) 200.00 800.00 -
nn-2nd print. "By the creator of Foxy Grandpa" on-c 150.00 600.00 -

WILLIE WESTINGHOUSE EDISON SMITH THE BOY INVENTOR
William A. Stokes Co.: 1906 (10x16", 36 pgs. in color)
nn-By Frank Crane (Scarce) 175.00 700.00 -

WINNIE WINKLE
Cupples & Leon Co.: 1930 - No. 4, 1933 (52 pgs., B&W daily strip-r)
1 39.00 156.00 275.00
2-4 26.00 104.00 185.00

YELLOW KID, THE (Magazine)(becomes The Yellow Kid Book #10 on)
Howard Ainslee & Co., N.Y.: Mar. 20, 1897 - #9, July 17, 1897 (5¢, B&W w/color covers, 52p., stapled)
1-R.F. Outcault Yellow kid on-c only #1-6. The same Yellow Kid color ad app. on back-c #1-6 (advertising the New York Sunday Journal) 650.00 2600.00 -
2 (4/3/97) 350.00 1400.00 -
3-6 (#6, 6/5/97) 243.00 975.00 -
7-9 (Yellow Kid not on-c) 106.00 425.00 -
NOTE: Richard Outcault's Yellow Kid from the Hearst New York American represents the very first successful comic strip in America. Eventually the first prototype comic books appeared reprinting these early strips. This magazine is listed here due to historical importance but is not a comic book.

YELLOW KID IN MCFADDEN'S FLATS, THE
G. W. Dillingham Company, New York: 1897 (50¢, 5 1/2x7 1/2", 196 pgs., B&W, squarebound)
nn-The first "comic" book; E. W. Townsend narrative w/R. F. Outcault Sunday comic page art-r & some original drawings 4750.00 8500.00 -

The American Comic Book: 1933-PRESENT

THE GOLDEN AGE AND BEYOND: ORIGINS OF THE MODERN COMIC BOOK

by Robert L. Beerbohm & Richard D. Olson, PhD

Standard Oil Comics Weekly #14, 1933. Newly discovered comics tabloid, same size as Gulf Funny Weekly. But where are the earlier issues that supposedly exist?

The formats that comic publishing pioneer Cupples & Leon popularized in 1919, although similar in appearance to comics of the Golden Age, are quite different in appearance from today's comics. Even so, the books and those formats were consistently successful until 1929, when they had to compete against The Great Depression; the Depression eventually won. One major reason for a format change was that at a cost of 25¢ per book for the 10" x 10" cardboard style and 60¢ for the 7" x 8 1/2" dustjacketed hardcovers, the price became increasingly prohibitive for most consumers already stifled by the crushed economy. As a result, all Cupples & Leon style books published between 1929-1935 are much rarer than their earlier counterparts because most Americans had little money to spend after paying for necessities like food and shelter.

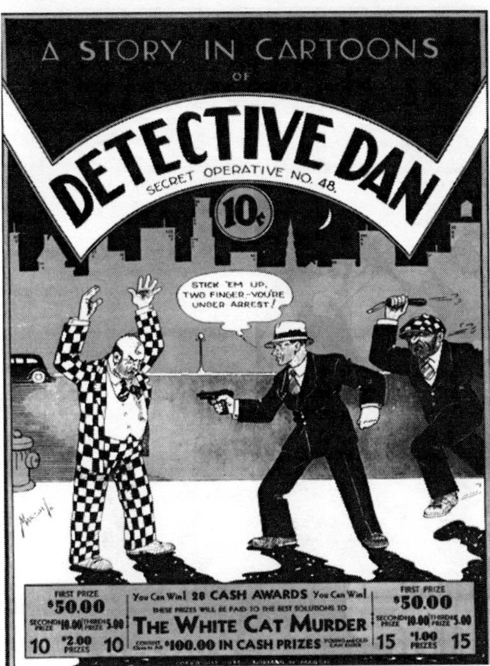

Detective Dan, early 1933, Humor Publishing Co. The first original newsstand comic book and direct inspiration for Siegel and Shuster to convert Superman into a comic book.

By the early 1930s, the era of the Prestige Format black & white reprint comic book was over. In 1932-33 a lot of format variations arose, collecting such newspaper strips as **Bobby Thatcher**, **Bringing Up Father**, **Buck Rogers**, **Dick Tracy**, **Happy Hooligan**, **Joe Palooka**, **Just Kids**, **The Little King**, **Little Orphan Annie**, **Men of Daring**, **Mickey Mouse**, **Moon Mullins**, **Mutt & Jeff**, **Smitty**, **Tailspin Tommy**, **Tarzan**, **Thimble Theater starring Popeye**, **Tillie the Toiler**, **Winnie Winkle**, and the **Highlights of History** series. With the 1933 newsstand appearance of Humor's **Detective Dan**, **Adventures of Detective Ace King**, **Bob Scully**, **Two Fisted Hick Detective**, and others, these little understood original material comic books were the direct inspiration for Jerry Siegel and Joe Shuster to transform their fanzine character **The Superman** from **Science Fiction** #3 (January 1933) into a comic strip that would stand as a watershed mark in American pop culture. The stage was set for a new frontier.

Prior to Humor's very rare output, there was Embee's **Comic Monthly**'s dozen issues in 1922, and several dozen of Dell's **The Funnies** tabloid in 1929-30. All except **Comic Monthly** contained only original material and still failed. With another format change, however, including four colors, double page counts and a hefty price reduction (starting for free as promotional premiums due to the nationwide numbing effects of worldwide deflation), the birthing pangs of the modern American comic book occurred in late 1932. Created out of desperation, to keep the printing presses rolling, the modern American comic book was born when a 45-year-old sales manager for Eastern Color Printing Company of New York reinvented the format.

Harry I. Wildenberg's job was to come up with ideas that would sell color printing for Eastern, a company which also printed the comic sections for a score of newspapers, including the **Boston Globe**, the **Brooklyn Times**, the **Providence Journal**, and the **Newark Ledger**. Down-time meant less take-home pay, so Wildenberg was always racking his brains for something to fit the color presses. He was fascinated by the miles of funny sheets which rolled off Eastern's presses

Famous Funnies #1, July 1934, was the first successful newsstand comic book, and it ran until 1955.

each week, and he constantly sought new ways to exploit their commercial possibilities. If the funny papers were this popular, he reasoned, they should prove a good advertising medium. He decided to suggest a comics tabloid to one of his clients.

That client, Gulf Oil Company, liked the idea, and hired a few artists to create an original comic called **Gulf Comic Weekly**. The comic was dated April 1933 and was 10 1/2" x 15". It was the first comic to be advertised nationally on the radio beginning April 30th. Its first artists were Stan Schendel doing **The Uncovered Wagon**, Victor doing **Curly and the Kids**, and Svess on a strip named **Smileage**. All were full page, full color comic strips. Wildenberg promptly had Eastern print this four page comic, making it probably the first tabloid newsprint comic published for American distribution outside of a newspaper in the 20th Century. Wildenberg and Gulf were astonished when the tabloids were grabbed up as fast as Gulf service stations could offer them. Distribution shot up to 3,000,000 copies a week after Gulf changed the name to **Gulf Funny Weekly**. The series remained a tabloid until early 1939 and ran for 422 issues until May 23, 1941.

Recent research has also turned up "new" unrediscovered comics material from other oil companies from this same time span of 1933-34. Perhaps spurred by the runaway success of **Gulf Funny Weekly**, these other oil companies found they had to compete with licensed comic strip material of their own in order to remain profitable. The authors of this essay are actively soliciting help in uncovering more information regarding the following:

There are at least 14 issues (and possibly many more) of a four page tabloid-size full color comics giveaway titled **Standard Oil Comics**, dating from 1933. The issues seen so far contain Fred Opper's **Si and Mirandi**, an older couple who interact with perennial favorites, **Happy Hooligan** and **Maud the Mule**. Other strips include **Pesty And His Pop** and **Smiling Slim** by Sid Hicks. Considering the concept of **Gulf Funny Weekly** has been well known for decades while **Standard Oil Comics** remains virtually unknown, our guess is **Gulf Comic Weekly** began first and ran many years longer than Rockefeller's version.

Beginning with the March-April 1934 issue of **Shell Globe** (V4 #2), characters from Bud Fisher (**Mutt & Jeff**) and Fontaine Fox (**Toonerville Folks**) were licensed to sell gas & oil for this company. 52,000 eight foot standees were made for Fisher's **Mutt and Jeff** and Fox's **Powerful Katrinka and the Skipper** for placement around 13,000 Shell gas stations. Augmenting them was an army of 250,000 miniature figures of the same characters. In addition, more than 1,000,000 play masks were given away to children along with more than 285,000 window stickers. If that wasn't enough, hundreds of thousands of 3x5 foot posters featuring these characterswere released in conjunction with twenty-four sheet outdoor billboards. Radio announcements of this promotion began running April 7th, 1934. It is presently unknown if Shell had a comics tabloid created to give away to customers.

The idea for creating an actual comic book, however, did not occur to Wildenberg until later in 1933, when he was idly folding a newspaper in halves then in quarters. As he looked at the twice-folded paper, it occurred to him that it was a convenient book size (actually it was late stage "Dime Novel" size, which companies like Street & Smith were pumping out). The format had its heyday from the 1880s through the 1910s, having been invented by the firm of Beadle and Adam in 1860 in more of a digest format. According to a 1942 article by Max Gaines, another contributing factor in the development of the format was an inspection of a promotional folder published by the Ledger Syndicate, in which four-color Sunday comic pages were printed in 7" x 9".

According to a 1949 interview with Wildenberg, he thought "why not a comic book? It would have 32 or 64 pages and make a fine item for concerns which distribute premiums." Wildenberg obtained publishing rights to certain Associated, Bell, Fisher, McNaught and Public Ledger Syndicate comics, had an artist make up a few dummies by hand, and then had his sales staff walk them around to his biggest advertisers. Wildenberg received a telegram from Proctor & Gamble for an order of a million copies for a 32-page color comic magazine called **Funnies on Parade**. The entire print run was given away in just a few weeks in the Spring of 1933.

Also working for Eastern Color at this same time were quite a few future legends of the comics business, such as Max Gaines, Lev Gleason and a fellow named Harold Moore (all sales staff directly underneath the supervision of Wildenberg), Sol Harrison as a color separator, and George Dougherty Sr. as a printer. All of them worked on the **Funnies on Parade** project. Morris Margolis was brought in from Charlton

Publications in Derby, Connecticut to solve binding problems centered on getting the pages in proper numerical sequence on that last fold to "modern" comic book size. All were infected with the comics bug for mostof the rest of their lives.

The success of **Funnies on Parade** quickly led to Eastern publishing additional giveaway books in the same format by late 1933, including the 32 page **Famous Funnies A Carnival of Comics**, the 100 page **A Century of Comics** and **Skippy's Own Book of Comics**; the latter became the first "new" format comic book about a single character. These thicker issues had press runs of up to 500,000 per title. The idea that anyone would pay for them seemed fantastic to Wildenberg, so Max Gaines stickered ten cents on several dozen of the latest premium, **Famous Funnies A Carnival of Comics**, as a test, and talked a couple newsstands into participating in this experiment. The copies sold out over the weekend and newsies asked for more.

Eastern sales staffers then approached Woolworth's. The late Oscar Fitz-Alan Douglas, sales brains of Woolworth, showed some interest, but after several months of deliberation decided the book would not give enough value for ten cents. Kress, Kresge, McCrory, and several other dime stores turned them down even more abruptly. Wildenberg next went to George Hecht, editor of **Parents Magazine**, and tried to persuade him to run a comic supplement or publish a "higher level" comic magazine. Hecht also frowned on the idea.

In Wildenberg's 1949 interview, he

Not to be outdone, Shell Oil began a huge comics promotion in March 1934 to compete with Gulf and Standard Oil.

noted that "even the comic syndicates couldn't see it. 'Who's going to read old comics?' they asked." With the failures of **Comic Monthly** and **The Funnies** still fresh in some minds, no one could see why children would pay ten cents for a comic magazine when they could get all they want for free in a Sunday newspaper. But Wildenberg had become convinced that children as well as grown-ups were not getting all the comics they wanted in the Sunday papers; otherwise, the **Gulf Comic Weekly** and the premium comics would not have met with such success. Wildenberg said, "I decided that if boys and girls were willing to work for premium coupons to obtain comic books, they might be willing to pay ten cents on the newsstands." This conviction was also strengthened by Max Gaines' ten cent sticker experiment.

George Janosik, the president of Eastern Color, then called on George Delacorte to form a 50-50 joint venture to publish and market a comic book "magazine" for retail sales, but American News turned them down cold. The magazine monopoly also remembered Delacorte's abortive **The Funnies** from just a few years before. After much discussion on how to proceed, Delacorte finally agreed to publish it and a partnership was formed. They printed 40,000 copies for distribution to a few chain stores. Known today as **Famous Funnies Series One**, half of its pages came from reprints of the reprints in **Funnies on Parade** and **Famous Funnies A Carnival of Comics**.

With 68 full-color pages at only ten cents a piece, it sold out in thirty days with not a single returned copy. Delacorte refused to print a second edition. "Advertisers won't use it," he complained. "They say it's not dignified enough." The profit, however, was approximately $2,000. This particular edition is the rarest of all these early Eastern comic book experiments.

In early 1934, while riding the train, another Eastern Color employee named Harold A. Moore read an account from a prominent New York newspaper that indicated they owed much of their circulation success to their comics section. Mr. Moore went back to Harry Gold, President of American News, with the article in hand. He succeeded in acquiring a print order for 250,000 copies for a proposed monthly comics magazine. In May 1934, **Famous Funnies** #1 (with a July cover date) hit the newsstands with Steven O. Douglass as its only editor (even though Harold Moore was listed as such in #1) until it ceased publication some twenty years later. It was a 64-page version of the 32-page giveaways, and more importantly, it still sold for a dime! The first issue lost $4,150.60. Ninety percent of the copies sold out and a second issue dated September debuted in July. From then on, the comic book was published monthly. **Famous Funnies** also began carrying original material, apparently as early as the second issue. With #3, **Buck Rogers** took center stage and stayed there for the next twenty years, with covers by Frank Frazetta -- some of his best comics work ever.

Delacorte got cold feet and sold back his interest to Eastern, even though the seventh issue cleared a profit of $2,664.25. Wildenberg emphasized that Eastern could make a manufacturer's

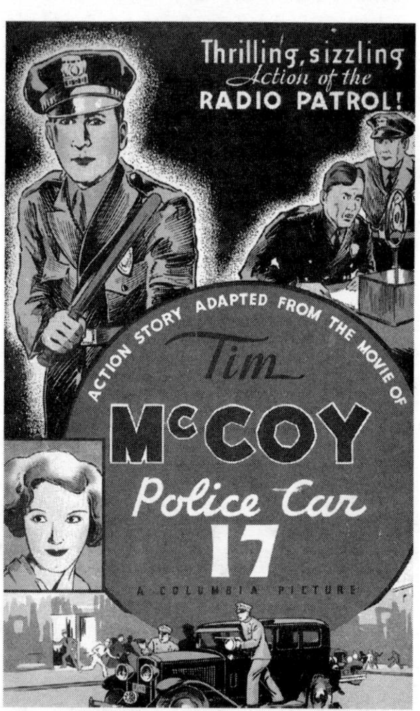

Tim McCoy Police Car 17, Whitman's first comic (1934), and also the first movie adaptation comic book. This has been a sleeper for too long.

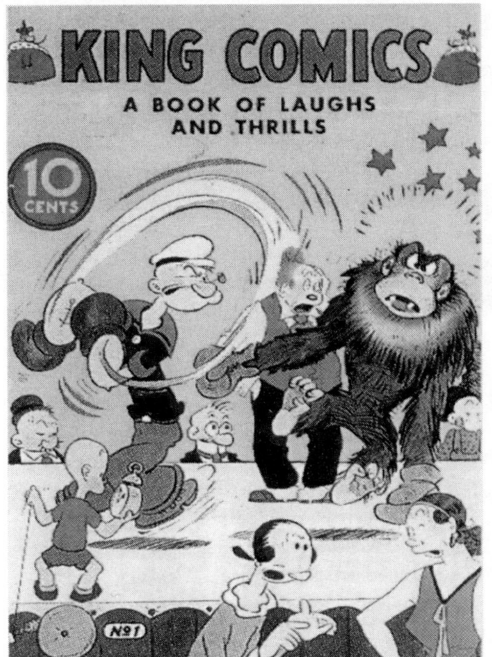

King Comics #1, April 1936, marking King Features Syndicate's entry into the new 64 page color comic market and featuring the first appearances of Flash Gordon, Popeye, and Mandrake the Magician.

profit by printing its own books as well as the publishing profits once it was distributed. Every issue showed greater sales than the preceding one, until within a year, close to a million 64-page books were being sold monthly at ten cents apiece; Eastern received the lion's share of the receipts, and soon found it was netting $30,000 per issue. The comic syndicates received $640 ($10 a page) for publishing rights. Original material could be obtained from budding professionals for just $5 a page. According to Will Eisner in R. C. Harvey's **The Art of the Comic Book**, the prices then paid for original material had a long range effect of keeping creator wages low for years.

Initially, Eastern's experiment was eyed with skepticism by the publishing world, but within a year or so after **Famous Funnies** was nonchalantly placed on sale alongside slicker magazines like **Atlantic Monthly** or **Harper's**, at least five other competitors entered the field. In late 1934, pulp writer turned publisher Major Wheeler-Nicholson introduced **New Fun** #1 at almost tabloid-size containing all original material. Around this same time, Whitman brought out the first original material movie adaptation, **Tim McCoy Police Car 17**, in the tabloid New Fun format with stiff card covers. A few years before, they had introduced the new comics formats known as the **Big Little Book** and the **Big Big Book**. The **BLB** and **BBB** formats would go toe-to-toe with Eastern's creation throughout the 1930s, but Eastern would win out.

The very last 10" x 10" comic books pioneered by Cupples & Leon were published in mid-1935 by the David McKay Company. In late 1935, Max Gaines (with his youthful assistant Sheldon Mayer) reached an agreement with George Delacorte (who was re-entering the comic book business a third time) and McClure Syndicate (a growing newspaper comic strip enterprise) to reprint newspaper comic strips in **Popular Comics**. Also by late 1935, Lev Gleason, another pioneer who participated in **Funnies on Parade**, had become the first editor of United Feature's own **Tip Top Comics**. In 1939 he would begin publishing his own titles, creating the crime comic book as a separate popular genre by 1942 with **Crime Does Not Pay**.

Industry giant King Features introduced **King Comics** #1 (April 1936) through publisher David McKay, with Ruth Plumly Thompson as editor. McKay had already been issuing various format comic books with King Feature characters for a few years, including **Mickey Mouse**, **Henry**, **Popeye** and **Secret Agent X-9**, wherein Dashiell Hammett received cover billing and Alex Raymond was listed simply as "illustrator." McKay readily adapted to this format. Soon most young comic book illustrators were copying Raymond's style.

The following month, William Cook and John Mahon, former disgruntled employees of Wheeler-Nicholson, brought out **The Comics Magazine** #1 (May 1936). This was followed by

In the early 1950s, Carl Barks increased the circulation of WDCS to over 4 million per issue, and in 1952 his creation, Uncle Scrooge, got his own comic book, selling over a million an issue while the superhero slumbered.

Henle Publishing issuing **Wow**, which contained the earliest comics work of Will Eisner, Bob Kane, Dick Briefer and others. By the end of 1936, Cook and Mahon pioneered the first single theme comic books: **Funny Picture Stories** (adventure), **Detective Picture Stories** (crime), and **Western Picture Stories** (the Western). The company would eventually be known historically as Centaur Comics, and serve as the subject of endless debate among fan historians regarding their earliest origins.

Almost forty years after the first newspaper strip comic book compilations were issued at the dawn of international popularity for American comic strips, the race was on to get out of the starting block. In late 1937 Major Wheeler-Nicholson stumbled when he couldn't pay his printing bill to Harry Donenfeld. In a recent intervew, Harry's son, Irwin, said "in 1932 my father and Paul Sampliner started Independent News with Jack Liebowitz as the accountant. The company was begun with Paul Sampliner's mother's money. If it hadn't been for her investments into building the distribution as well as purchasing color printing presses, there might never have been a DC Comics."

Soon after the Major lost control of his company, **Action Comics** #1 was published with a cover date of June 1938, and the Golden Age of superhero comics had begun. Early in 1938 at McClure Syndicate, Max Gaines and Shelly Mayer showed editor Vin Sullivan a many times rejected sample strip. Sullivan then talked Harry Donenfeld, Paul Sampliner and Jack Liebowitz into publishing Jerry Siegel and Joe Shuster's creation, **The Last Son of Krypton**. This was followed in 1939 by a lucrative partnership for Gaines with the Detective Comics people in the All-American Comics Group.

While there's a great deal of controversy surrounding such labeling, the Golden Age is often viewed these days as beginning with **Action Comics** #1 and continuing through the end of World War II. There was a time not that long ago that the newspaper reprint comic book was collected with more fervor than the heroic comics of the '40s. **Feature Book** #26, **Four Color** #10 and **Single Series** #20 were the holy grails of collecting.

The Atom Age began in early 1946, revamping the industry once again as circulations soon hit their all-time highs with over a billion issues sold a year. By the early 1950s one in three periodicals sold in the USA was a comic book. This continued until the advent of the self-censoring, industry-stifling Comics Code, created in response to a public outcry spearheaded by Dr. Frederic Wertham's tirade against the American comics industry, published in book form as **Seduction of the Innocent**.

It took a year or two to recover from that moralistic assault, with many historians concluding that the Silver Age of Superheroes began with the publication of **Showcase** #4 in 1956, continuing through those turbulent times until Jack Kirby left Marvel for DC in 1969. Others point to the 1952 releases of Kurtzman's **MAD** #1 and Bark's **Uncle Scrooge Four Color** #386 (#1) as true Silver, since those titles soon broke the "million sold per issue" mark when the rest of the comic book industry was reeling from the effects of the public uproar fueled by Wertham.

The Bronze Age has been generally stated to begin when the Code approved newsstand comic book industry raised its standard cover price from 12 to 15 cents. As circulations plummeted after the **Batman** TV craze wore off by 1968 and the superhero glut withered on the stands, out in San Francisco cartoonist Robert Crumb's creator-owned **Zap Comics** #1 appeared, printed by Charles Plymell. Soon thereafter, Jay Lynch and Skip Williamson brought out **Bijou Funnies**, Gilbert Shelton self-published **Feds N Heads** and Crumb let S. Clay Wilson, Victor Moscoso and Rick Griffin into **Zap**.

As originally published by the Print Mint beginning with #2, **Zap Comics** almost single-handedly spawned an industry with tremendous growth in alternative comix running through the 1970s. During this decade the San Francisco Bay Area was an intense hotbed of comix being issued without a comics code "seal of approval" from companies such as Rip Off Press, Last Gasp, San Francisco Comic Book Company, Cpmpany & Sons, Weirdom Publications, Star*Reach, and Comics & Comix. Kitchen Sink prospered for many years in Wisconsin and many small press comix publishers scattered across the USA and Canada issued single titles.

With the advent of the Direct Market by 1979, the last 20 years have generally been called The Modern Age, although there are hints of a new age emerging since the mid-1990s. In each of the above Ages, however, the secret for consumers and collectors has remained the same: buy what you enjoy. We did, and we're still collectors today!

(portions excerpted from **Comic Book Store Wars**. Those portions ©1999 Robert Beerbohm. E-mail: beerbohm@teknetwork.com)

Zap Comics #1, Feb. 1968, paved the way for the introduction of the Direct Market and has sold over a million copies, continuously in print for over 30 years. Last Gasp's first comic was Slow Death #1 (1970), below left, with a cover by Greg Irons. Bijou Funnies #8 (1973) by Kitchen Sink sports a cover by Harvey Kurtzman!

Abbott and Costello #4 © STJ

Ace Comics #50 © DMP

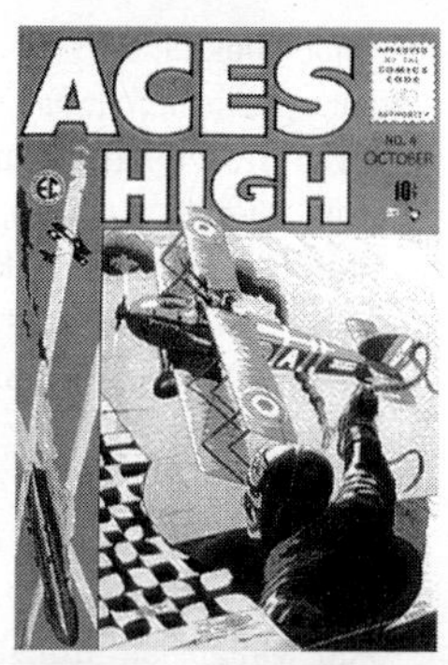

Aces High #4 © WMG

GD2.0 FN6.0 NM9.4

The correct title listing for each comic book can be determined by consulting the indicia (publication data) on the beginning interior pages of the comic. The official title is determined by those words of the title in capital letters only, and not by what is on the cover.

Titles are listed in this book as if they were one word, ignoring spaces, hyphens, and apostrophes, to make finding titles easier. Comic books listed should be assumed to be in color unless noted "B&W".

Comic publishers are invited to send us sample copies for possible inclusion in future guides.

Near Mint is the highest value listed in this price guide. True mint books from the 1970s through the present do exist, so the Near Mint value listed should be interpreted as a Mint value for those books.

A-1 (See A-One)

AARON STRIPS
Image Comics: Apr, 1997 - No. 4, Oct, 1997;
Amazing Aaron Prod.: No. 5, Jan, 1999 - Present ($2.95, B&W)
1-6-Reprints Adventures of Aaron newspaper strips 3.00

ABBIE AN' SLATS (...With Becky No. 1-4) (See Comics On Parade, Fight for Love, Giant Comics Edition 2, Giant Comics Editions #1, Sparkler Comics, Tip Topper, Treasury of Comics, & United Comics)
United Features Syndicate: 1940; March, 1948 - No. 4, Aug, 1948 (Reprints)

	GD2.0	FN6.0	NM9.4
Single Series 25 ('40)	37.00	111.00	260.00
Single Series 28	31.00	92.00	215.00
1 (1948)	16.00	47.00	110.00
2-4: 3-r/Sparkler #68-72	9.15	27.50	55.00

ABBOTT AND COSTELLO (...Comics)(See Giant Comics Editions #1 & Treasury of Comics)
St. John Publishing Co.: Feb, 1948 - No. 40, Sept, 1956 (Mort Drucker-a in most issues)

	GD2.0	FN6.0	NM9.4
1	50.00	150.00	400.00
2	27.00	81.00	190.00
3-9 (#8, 8/49; #9, 2/50)	17.00	51.00	120.00
10-Son of Sinbad story by Kubert (new)	21.00	62.00	145.00
11,13-20 (#11, 10/50; #13, 8/51; #15, 12/52)	12.00	36.00	85.00
12-Movie issue	13.50	41.00	95.00
21-30: 28-r/#8. 30-Painted-c	10.00	30.00	65.00
31-40: 33,38-Reprints	7.50	22.50	45.00
3-D #1 (11/53, 25¢)-Infinity-c	35.00	105.00	245.00

ABBOTT AND COSTELLO (TV)
Charlton Comics: Feb, 1968 - No. 22, Aug, 1971 (Hanna-Barbera)

	GD2.0	FN6.0	NM9.4
1	6.00	18.00	60.00
2	3.20	9.60	32.00
3-10	2.80	8.40	28.00
11-22	2.50	7.50	20.00

ABC (See America's Best TV Comics)

ABE SAPIEN: DRUMS OF THE DEAD
Dark Horse Comics: Mar, 1998 ($2.95, one-shot)
1-McDonald-s/Thompson-a. Hellboy back-up; Mignola-s/a/c 3.00

A. BIZARRO
DC Comics: Jul, 1999 - No. 4, Oct, 1999 (2.50, limited series)
1-4-Gerber-s/Bright-a 2.50

ABOMINATIONS (See Hulk)
Marvel Comics: Dec, 1996 - No. 3, Feb, 1997 (1.50, limited series)
1-3-Future Hulk storyline 2.00

GD2.0 FN6.0 NM9.4

ABRAHAM LINCOLN LIFE STORY (See Dell Giants)

ABRAHAM STONE
Marvel Comics (Epic): July, 1995 - No. 2, Aug, 1995 ($6.95, limited series)
1,2-Joe Kubert-s/a 1.00 2.80 7.00

ABSENT-MINDED PROFESSOR, THE
Dell Publishing Co.: Apr, 1961 (Disney)
Four Color #1199-Movie, photo-c 6.40 19.00 70.00

ABSOLUTE VERTIGO
DC Comics (Vertigo): Winter, 1995 (99¢, mature)
nn-1st app. Preacher. Previews upcoming titles including Jonah Hex: Riders of the Worm, The Invisibles (King Mob), The Eaters, Ghostdancing & Preacher 1.00 3.00 8.00

ABYSS, THE (Movie)
Dark Horse Comics: June, 1989 - No. 2, July, 1989 ($2.25, limited series)
1,2-Adaptation of film; Kaluta & Moebius-a 2.25

ACCLAIM ADVENTURE ZONE
Acclaim Books: 1997 ($4.50, digest size)
1-Short stories of Turok, Troublemakers, Ninjak and others 4.50

ACE COMICS
David McKay Publications: Apr, 1937 - No. 151, Oct-Nov, 1949 (All contain some newspaper strip reprints)

	GD2.0	FN6.0	NM9.4
1-Jungle Jim by Alex Raymond, Blondie, Ripley's Believe It Or Not, Krazy Kat begin (1st app. of each)	300.00	900.00	2700.00
2	94.00	282.00	750.00
3-5	60.00	180.00	485.00
6-10	45.00	135.00	360.00
11-The Phantom begins (1st app., 2/38) (in brown costume)	71.00	213.00	570.00
12-20	40.00	120.00	280.00
21-25,27-30	34.00	102.00	240.00
26-Origin & 1st app. Prince Valiant (5/39); begins series?	90.00	270.00	725.00
31-40: 37-Krazy Kat ends	24.00	72.00	170.00
41-60	18.00	54.00	125.00
61-64,66-76-(7/43; last 68 pgs.)	16.00	48.00	110.00
65-(8/42)-Flag-c	17.00	51.00	115.00
77-84 (3/44; all 60 pgs.)	13.00	39.00	90.00
85-99 (52 pgs.)	11.00	33.00	75.00
100 (7/45; last 52 pgs.)	12.00	36.00	85.00
101-134: 128-(11/47)-Brick Bradford begins. 134-Last Prince Valiant (all 36 pgs.)	9.15	27.50	55.00
135-151: 135-(6/48)-Lone Ranger begins	8.35	25.00	50.00

ACE KELLY (See Tops Comics & Tops In Humor)

ACE KING (See Adventures of Detective...)

ACES
Acme Press (Eclipse): Apr, 1988 - No. 5, Dec, 1988 ($2.95, B&W, magazine)
1-5 3.00

ACES HIGH
E.C. Comics: Mar-Apr, 1955 - No. 5, Nov-Dec, 1955

	GD2.0	FN6.0	NM9.4
1-Not approved by code	15.50	46.50	155.00
2	9.50	28.00	95.00
3-5	8.00	24.00	80.00

NOTE: *All have stories by* ***Davis, Evans, Krigstein,*** *and* ***Wood. Evans*** *c-1-5.*

ACES HIGH
Gemstone Publishing: Apr, 1999 - No. 5, Aug, 1999 ($2.50)
1-5-Reprints E.C. issues 2.50
Annual 1 ($13.50) r/#1-5 13.50

ACTION ADVENTURE (War) (Formerly Real Adventure)
Gillmor Magazines: V1#2, June, 1955 - No. 4, Oct, 1955
V1#2-4 4.00 12.00 24.00

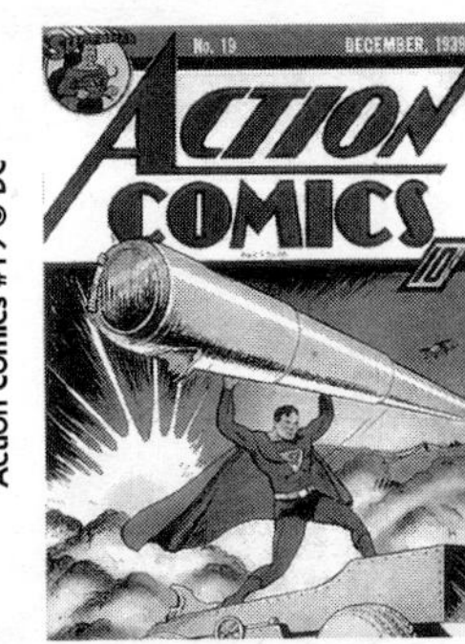

Action Comics #19 © DC

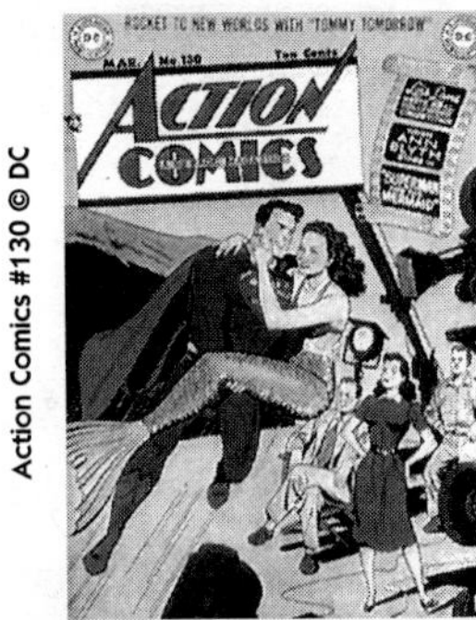

Action Comics #130 © DC

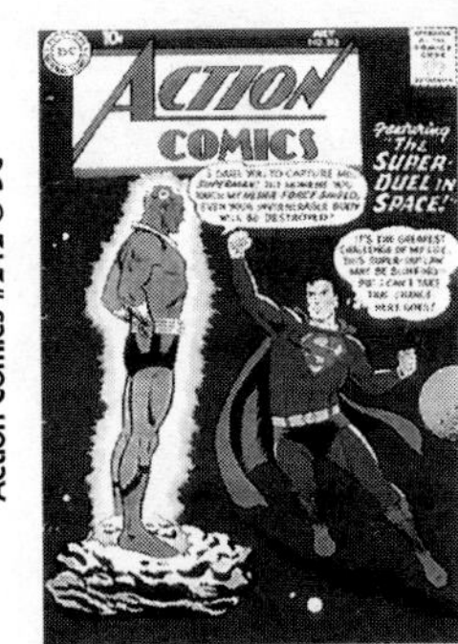

Action Comics #242 © DC

GD2.0 FN6.0 NM9.4 GD2.0 FN6.0 NM9.4

ACTION COMICS (...Weekly #601-642) (Also see The Comics Magazine #1, More Fun #14-17 & Special Edition) (Also see Promotional Comics section)
National Periodical Publ./Detective Comics/DC Comics: 6/38 - No. 583, 9/86; No. 584, 1/87 - Present

GD2.0 FN6.0 VF8.0 NM9.4

1-Origin & 1st app. Superman by Siegel & Shuster, Marco Polo, Tex Thompson, Pep Morgan, Chuck Dawson & Scoop Scanlon; 1st app. Zatara & Lois Lane; Superman story missing 4 pgs. which were included when reprinted in Superman #1; Clark Kent works for Daily Star; story continued in #2 30,000.00 70,000.00 110,000.00 200,000.00

1-Reprint, Oversize 13-1/2x10". **WARNING:** This comic is an exact reprint of the original except for its size. DC published it in 1974 with a second cover titling it as a Famous First Edition. There have been many reported cases of the outer cover being removed and the interior sold as the original edition. The reprint with the new outer cover removed is practically worthless. See Famous First Edition for value.

GD2.0 FN6.0 NM9.4

1(1993)-Came w/Reign of Superman packs 1.50
2-O'Mealia non-Superman covers thru #6 2300.00 6900.00 21,000.00
3 (Scarce)-Superman apps. in costume in only one panel 1600.00 4800.00 14,500.00
4-6: 6-1st Jimmy Olsen (called office boy) 900.00 2700.00 8300.00
7-2nd Superman cover 1600.00 4800.00 14,300.00
8,9 700.00 2100.00 6000.00
10-3rd Superman cover by Siegel & Shuster 1100.00 3200.00 10,000.00
11,14: 14-Clip Carson begins, ends #41; Zatara-c 337.00 1010.00 3200.00
12-Has 1 pg. Batman ad for Det. #27 (5/39); Zatara sci-fi cover 347.00 1040.00 3300.00
13-Shuster Superman-c; last Scoop Scanlon 579.00 1737.00 5500.00
15-Guardineer Superman-c; Detective Comics ad 484.00 1452.00 4600.00
16 276.00 828.00 2350.00
17-Superman cover; last Marco Polo 379.00 1137.00 3600.00
18-Origin 3 Aces; 1st X-Ray Vision? 276.00 828.00 2350.00
19-Superman covers begin; has full pg. ad for New York World's Fair 1939 337.00 1010.00 3200.00
20-The 'S' left off Superman's chest; Clark Kent works at 'Daily Star' 331.00 993.00 3150.00
21-Has 2 ads for More Fun #52 (1st Spectre) 250.00 750.00 2000.00
22,24,25: 24-Kent at Daily Planet. 25-Last app. Gargantua T. Potts, Tex Thompson's sidekick 237.00 711.00 1900.00
23-1st app. Luthor (w/red hair) & Black Pirate; Black Pirate by Moldoff; 1st mention of The Daily Planet (4/40)-Has 1 panel ad for Spectre in More Fun 579.00 1737.00 5500.00
26-28,30 200.00 600.00 1600.00
29-1st Lois Lane-c (10/40) 237.00 711.00 1900.00
31,32: 32-Intro/1st app. Krypto Ray Gun in Superman story by Burnley 125.00 375.00 1000.00
33-Origin Mr. America; Superman by Burnley; has half page ad for All Star Comics #3 156.00 468.00 1250.00
34-36,38,39: 36-Robot cover 122.00 366.00 975.00
37,40: 37-Origin Congo Bill. 40-(9/41)-Intro/1st app. Star Spangled Kid & Stripesy; Jerry Siegel photo 131.00 393.00 1050.00
41 112.00 336.00 900.00
42-1st app./origin Vigilante; Bob Daley becomes Fat Man; origin Mr. America's magic flying carpet; The Queen Bee & Luthor app; Black Pirate ends; not in #41 162.00 486.00 1300.00
43-46,48-50: 44-Fat Man's i.d. revealed to Mr. America. 45-1st app. Stuff (Vigilante's oriental sidekick) 112.00 336.00 900.00
47-1st Luthor cover in comics (4/42) 162.00 486.00 1300.00
51-1st app. The Prankster 112.00 336.00 900.00
52-Fat Man & Mr. America become the Ameri-commandos; origin Vigilante retold; classic Superman and back-ups-c 116.00 348.00 925.00
53-60: 56-Last Fat Man. 57-2nd Lois Lane-c in Action (3rd anywhere, 2/43). 59-Kubert Vigilante begins?, ends #70. 60-First app. Lois Lane as Super-woman 74.00 222.00 590.00
61-Historic Atomic Radiation-c (6/43) 72.00 213.00 580.00
62,63,65-70: 63-Last 3 Aces 68.00 204.00 545.00
64-Intro Toyman 78.00 234.00 625.00
71-79: 74-Last Mr. America 62.00 186.00 500.00
80-2nd app. & 1st Mr. Mxyztplk-c (1/45) 90.00 270.00 720.00
81-90: 83-Intro Hocus & Pocus 61.00 183.00 490.00
91-99: 93-X-Mas-c. 99-1st small logo (8/46) 59.00 177.00 470.00
100 122.00 366.00 975.00
101-Nuclear explosion-c (10/46) 122.00 366.00 975.00
102-120: 102-Mxyztplk-c. 105,117-X-Mas-c 57.00 171.00 460.00
121-126,128-140: 135,136,138-Zatara by Kubert 52.00 156.00 415.00
127-Vigilante by Kubert; Tommy Tomorrow begins (12/48, see Real Fact #6) 61.00 183.00 485.00
141-157,159-161: 151-Luthor/Mr. Mxyztplk/Prankster team-up. 156-Lois Lane as Super Woman. 160- Last 52 pgs. 49.00 147.00 390.00
158-Origin Superman retold 112.00 336.00 900.00
162-180: 168,176-Used in **POP**, pg. 90. 173-Robot-c 42.00 126.00 335.00
181-201: 191-Intro. Janu in Congo Bill. 198-Last Vigilante. 201-Last pre-code issue 40.00 120.00 315.00
202-220: 212-(1/56)-Includes 1956 Superman calendar that is part of story. 40.00 88.00 295.00
221-240: 221-1st S.A. issue. 224-1st Golden Gorilla story. 228-(5/57)-Kongorilla in Congo Bill story (Congorilla try-out) 33.00 99.00 230.00
241,243-251: 241-Batman x-over. 248-Origin/1st app. Congorilla; Congo Bill renamed Congorilla. 251-Last Tommy Tomorrow 26.00 79.00 185.00
242-Origin & 1st app. Brainiac (7/58); 1st mention of Shrunken City of Kandor 108.00 325.00 1400.00
252-Origin & 1st app. Supergirl (5/59); intro new Metallo 125.00 348.00 1400.00
253-2nd app. Supergirl 43.00 129.00 385.00
254-1st meeting of Bizarro & Superman-c/story 30.00 90.00 260.00
255-1st Bizarro Lois Lane-c/story & both Bizarros leave Earth to make Bizarro World 22.00 66.00 190.00
256-260: 259-Red Kryptonite used 15.00 45.00 120.00
261-1st X-Kryptonite which gave Streaky his powers; last Congorilla in Action; origin & 1st app. Streaky The Super Cat 18.00 54.00 125.00
262,264-266,268-270 13.00 39.00 110.00
263-Origin Bizarro World 16.50 50.00 140.00
267(8/60)-3rd Legion app; 1st app. Chameleon Boy, Colossal Boy, & Invisible Kid, 1st app. of Supergirl as Superwoman. 41.00 123.00 375.00
271-275,277-282: 274-Lois Lane as Superwoman; 282-Last 10¢ issue 9.50 28.50 80.00
276(5/61)-6th Legion app; 1st app. Brainiac 5, Phantom Girl, Triplicate Girl, Bouncing Boy, Sun Boy, & Shrinking Violet; Supergirl joins Legion 20.00 60.00 170.00
283(12/61)-Legion of Super-Villains app. 1st 12¢ 9.50 28.50 95.00
284(1/62)-Mon-el app. 9.50 28.50 95.00
285(2/62)-12th Legion app; Brainiac 5 cameo; Supergirl's existence revealed to world; JFK & Jackie cameos 9.50 28.50 95.00
286-292,294-300: 286(3/62)-Legion of Super Villains app. 287(4/62)-15th Legion app.(cameo). 288-Mon-el app.; r-origin Supergirl. 289(6/62)-16th Legion app. (Adult); Lightning Man & Saturn Woman's marriage 1st revealed. 290(7/62)-17th Legion app. (cameo); Phantom Girl app. 1st Supergirl emergency squad 291,292,294-299: 291-1st meeting Supergirl & Mr. Mxyzptlk. 292-2nd app. Superhorse (see Adv. #293). 297-Mon-el app. 298-Legion cameo. 300-(5/63) 6.50 19.50 65.00
293-Origin Comet (Superhorse) 9.50 28.50 95.00
301-308,310-320: 304-Origin & 1st app. Black Flame (9/63). 306-Brainiac 5, Mon-el app. 307-Saturn Girl app.313-Batman app. 314-retells origin Supergirl; J.L.A. x-over. 317-Death of Nor-Kan of Kandor. 319-Shrinking Violet app. 3.20 9.60 32.00
309-(2/64)-Legion app.; Batman & Robin-c & cameo; JFK app. (he died 11/22/63; on stands same time as death) 3.80 11.40 38.00
321-333,335-340: 336-Origin Akvar (Flamebird). 340-Origin, 1st app. of the Parasite 2.60 7.80 26.00
334-Giant G-20; origin Supergirl, Streaky, Superhorse & Legion (all-r) 6.00 18.00 60.00
341-346,348-359: 341-Batman app. in Supergirl back-up story. 342-UFO story. 344-Batman x-over. 345-Allen Funt/Candid Camera story. 350-Batman, Green Arrow & Green Lantern app. in Supergirl back-up story. 358-Superboy meets

Action Comics #484 © DC

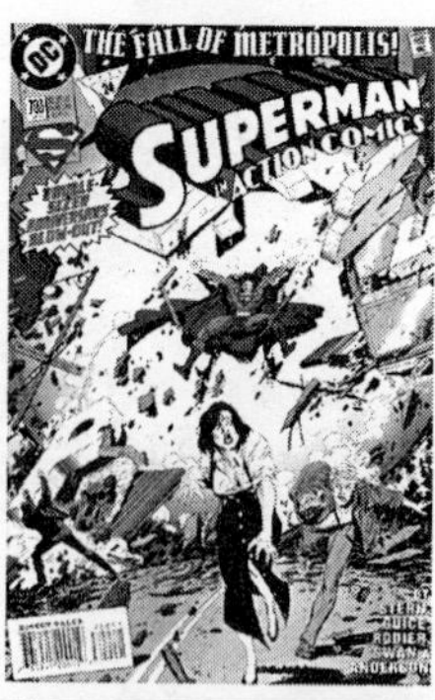
Action Comics #700 © DC

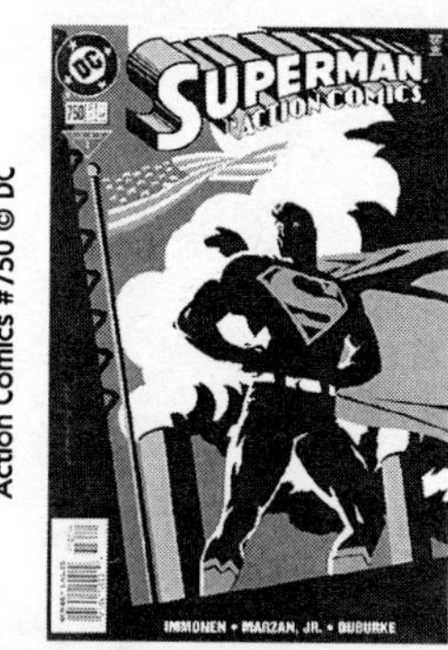
Action Comics #750 © DC

GD2.0 FN6.0 NM9.4

Supergirl 2.50 7.50 20.00

347,360-Giant Supergirl G-33,G-45; 347-Origin Comet-r plus Bizarro story. 360-Legion-r; r/origin Supergirl 4.20 12.60 42.00

361-372,374-378: 361-2nd app. Parasite. 363-366-Leper/Death story. 365-JLA & Legion app. 366-JLA app. 370-New facts about Superman's origin. 376-Last Supergirl in Action. 377-Legion begins (thru #392). 378-Last 12¢ issue 2.00 6.00 16.00

373-Giant Supergirl G-57; Legion-r 3.60 10.80 36.00

379-399,401: 388-Sgt. Rock app. 392-Batman-c/app.; last Legion in Action; Saturn Girl gets new costume. 393-401-All Superman issues. 1.50 4.50 12.00

400 2.50 7.50 20.00

402-Last 15¢ issue; Superman vs. Supergirl duel 2.25 6.75 18.00

403-413: All 52 pg. issues. 411-Origin Eclipso-(r). 413-Metamorpho begins, ends #418 2.25 6.75 18.00

414-424: 419-Intro. Human Target. 421-Intro Capt. Strong; Green Arrow begins. 422,423-Origin Human Target 1.10 3.30 9.00

425-Neal Adams-a(p); The Atom begins 2.00 6.00 16.00

426-431,433-436,438,439 2.40 6.00

432-1st S.A. Toyman app (2/74). 1.40 4.15 11.00

437,443-(100 pg. Giants) 2.50 7.50 22.00

440-1st Grell-a on Green Arrow 1.40 4.15 11.00

441,442,444-448: 441-Grell-a on Green Arrow continues 2.40 6.00

449-(68 pgs.) 1.00 3.00 8.00

450-483,485-499: 454-Last Atom. 456-Grell Jaws-c. 458-Last Green Arrow. 466-Batman, Flash app. 485-Adams-c. 487,488-(44 pgs.). 487-Origin & 1st app. Microwave Man; origin Atom retold 4.50

482,487-492,495,496,498,504,505,507,508-Whitman variants (no cover price) 1.10 3.30 9.00

484-Earth II Superman & Lois Lane wed; 40th anniversary issue(6/78) 2.40 6.00

500-($1.00, 68 pgs.)-Infinity-c; Superman life story; shows Legion statues in museum 2.40 6.00

501-551,554-582: 511-514-Airwave II solo stories. 513-The Atom begins. 517-Aquaman begins; ends #541. 521-1st app. The Vixen. 532,536-New Teen Titans cameo. 535,536-Omega Men app. 544-(Mando paper, 68 pgs.)-Origins new Luthor & Brainiac; Omega Men cameo. 544-Shuster-a (pin-up); article by Siegel. 546-J.L.A., New Teen Titans app. 551-Starfire becomes Red-Star 2.50

552,553-Animal Man-c & app. (2/84 & 3/84) 4.50

583-Alan Moore scripts; last Earth 1 Superman story (cont'd from Superman #423) 2.40 6.00

584-599: 584-Byrne-a begins; New Teen Titans app. 586-Legends x-over. 596-Millennium x-over; Spectre app. 598-1st app. Checkmate 3.00

600-($2.50, 84 pgs., 5/88) 2.40 6.00

601-642-Weekly issues ($1.50, 52 pgs.): 601-Re-intro The Secret Six. 611-614-: Catwoman stories (new costume in #611). 613-618-Nightwing stories 2.25

643-Superman & monthly issues begin again; Perez-c/a/scripts begin; swipes cover to Superman #1 3.00

644-649,651-661,663-666,668-673,675-682: 645-1st app. Maxima. 654-Part 3 of Batman storyline. 655-Free extra 8 pgs. 660-Death of Lex Luthor. 661-Begin $1.00-c. 675-Deathstroke cameo. 679-Last $1.00 issue 2.50

650-($1.50, 52 pgs.)-Lobo cameo (last panel) 3.00

662-Clark Kent reveals i.d. to Lois Lane; story continued in Superman #53 4.00

667-($1.75, 52 pgs.) 2.50

674-Supergirl logo & c/story (reintro) 5.00

683-Doomsday cameo 2.50

683,685-2nd & 3rd printings 2.00

684-Doomsday battle issue 3.00

685,686-Funeral for a Friend issues; Supergirl app. 2.50

687-($1.95)-Collector's Ed.w/die-cut-c 2.50

687-($1.50)-Newsstand Edition with mini-poster 2.00

688-694,696-699,701-703-($1.50): 688-Guy Gardner-c/story. 697-Bizarro-c/story. 703-(9/94)-Zero Hour 2.00

695-($2.50)-Collector's Edition w/embossed foil-c 2.50

700-($2.95, 68 pgs.)-Fall of Metropolis Pt 1; Pete Ross marries Lana Lang; Curt Swan & Murphy Anderson inks 3.00

GD2.0 FN6.0 NM9.4

700-Platinum 10.00

700-Gold 15.00

0(10/94), 704(11/94)-710-719,721-731: 710-Begin $1.95-c. 714-Joker app. 719-Batman-c/app. 721-Mr. Mxyzptlk app. 723-Brainiac as Superman; Dave Johnson-c.727-Final Night x-over. 2.00

720-Lois breaks off engagement w/Clark 3.00

720-2nd print. 2.00

732-749,751-758: 732-New powers. 733-New costume, Ray app. 738-Immonen-s/a(p) begins. 741-Legion app. 744-Millennium Giants x-over. 745-747-70's-style Superman vs. Prankster. 753-JLA-c/app. 757-Hawkman-c 2.00

750-($2.95) 3.00

#1,000,000 (11/98) Gene Ha-c; 853rd Century x-over 2.00

Annual 1-6('87-'94, $2.95)-1-Art Adams-c/a(p); Batman app. 2-Perez-c/a(i) 3-Armageddon 2001. 4-Eclipso vs. Shazam. 5-Bloodlines; 1st app. Loose Cannon. 6-Elseworlds story 3.00

Annual 7,9 ('95, '97, $3.95)-7-Year One story. 9-Pulp Heroes sty 4.00

Annual 8 (1996, $2.95)-Legends of the Dead Earth story 3.00

NOTE: ***Supergirl's*** *origin in 262, 280, 285, 291, 305, 309.* **N. Adams** *c-356, 358, 359, 361-364, 366, 367, 370-374, 377-379i, 398-400, 402, 404,405, 419p, 466, 468, 469, 473i, 485.* **Aparo** *a-642.* **Austin** *c/a-682i.* **Baily** *a-24, 25.* **Boring** *a-164, 194, 211, 223, 233, 241, 250, 261, 266-268, 346, 348, 352, 356, 357.* **Burnley** *a-28-33; c-48?, 53-55, 58, 59?, 60-63, 65, 66p, 67p, 70p, 71p, 79p, 82p, 84-86p, 90-92p, 93p?, 94p, 107p, 108p.* **Byrne** *a-584-598p, 599i, 600p; c-584-591, 596-600.* **Ditko** *a-642.* **Giffen** *a-560, 563, 565, 577, 579; c-539, 560, 563, 565, 577, 579.* **Grell** *a-440-442, 444-446, 450-452, 456-458; c-456.* **Guardineer** *a-24, 25; c-8, 11, 12, 14-16, 18. 25.* **Guice** *a(p)-676-681, 683-698, 700; c-683, 685, 686, 687(direct), 688-693i, 694-696, 697i, 698-700.* **Infantino** *a-642.* **Kaluta** *c-613.* **Bob Kane's** *Clip Carson-14-41.* **Gil Kane** *a-443r, 493r, 539-541, 544-546, 551-554, 601-605, 642; c-535p, 540, 541, 544p, 545-549, 551-554, 580, 627.* **Kirby** *c-638.* **Meskin** *a-42-121(most).* **Mignola** *a-600, Annual 2; c-c-614.* **Moldoff** *a-23-25, 443r.* **Mooney** *a-667p.* **Mortimer** *c-153, 154, 159-172, 174, 178-181, 184, 186-189, 191-193, 196, 200, 206.* **Orlando** *a-617p; c-621.* **Perez** *a-600i, 643-652p, Annual 2p; c-529p, 602, 643-651, Annual 2p.* **Quesada** *c-Annual 4p.* **Fred Ray** *c-34, 36-46, 50-52.* **Siegel & Shuster** *a-1-27.* **Paul Smith** *c-608.* **Starlin** *a-509; c-631.* **Leonard Starr** *a-597i(part),* **Staton** *a-525p, 526p, 531p, 535p, 536p.* **Swan/Moldoff** *c-281, 286, 287, 293, 298, 334.* **Thibert** *c-676, 677p, 678-681, 684.* **Toth** *a-406, 407, 413, 431; c-616.* **Tuska** *a-486p, 550.* **Williamson** *a-568i.* **Zeck** *c-Annual 5*

ACTION FORCE (Also see G.I. Joe European Missions)
Marvel Comics Ltd. (British): Mar, 1987 - No. 40?, 1988 ($1.00, weekly, magazine)

1,3: British G.I. Joe series. 3-w/poster insert 3.50

2,4-40 2.00

ACTION GIRL
Slave Labor Graphics: Oct, 1994 - Present ($2.50/$2.75, B&W)

1-17: 4-Begin $2.75-c 2.75

1-6 ($2.75, 2nd printings): All read 2nd Print in indicia. 1-(2/96). 2-(10/95). 3-(2/96). 4-(7/96). 5-(2/97). 6-(9/97) 2.75

1-4 ($2.75, 3rd printings): All read 3rd Print in indicia. 2.75

ACTION PLANET COMICS
Action Planet: 1996 - No. 3, Sept, 1997 ($3.95, B&W, 44 pgs.)

1-3: 1-Intro Monster Man by Mike Manley & other stories 4.00

Giant Size Action Planet Halloween Special (1998, $5.95, oversized) 2.40 6.00

ACTUAL CONFESSIONS (Formerly Love Adventures)
Atlas Comics (MPI): No. 13, Oct, 1952 - No. 14, Dec, 1952

13,14 5.35 16.00 32.00

ACTUAL ROMANCES (Becomes True Secrets #3 on?)
Marvel Comics (IPS): Oct, 1949 - No. 2, Jan, 1950 (52 pgs.)

1 10.00 30.00 65.00

2-Photo-c 6.70 20.00 40.00

ADAM AND EVE
Spire Christian Comics (Fleming H. Revell Co.): 1975,1978 (35¢/49¢)

nn-By Al Hartley 5.00

ADAM STRANGE (Also see Green Lantern #132, Mystery In Space #53 & Showcase #17)
DC Comics: 1990 - No. 3, 1990 ($3.95, 52 pgs, limited series, squarebound)

Book One - Three: Andy & Adam Kubert-c/a 4.00

ADAM-12 (TV)

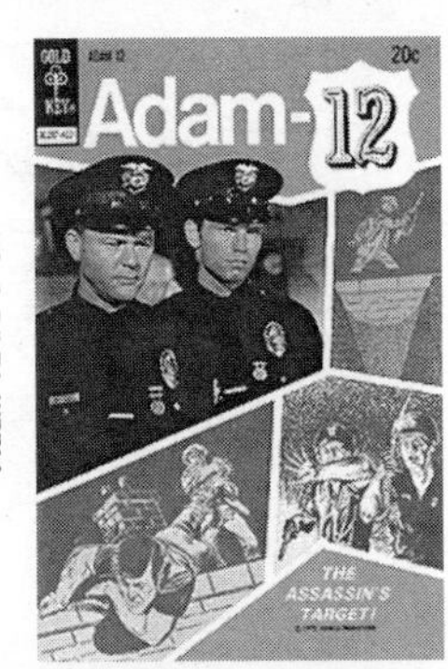

Adam-12 #2 © GK

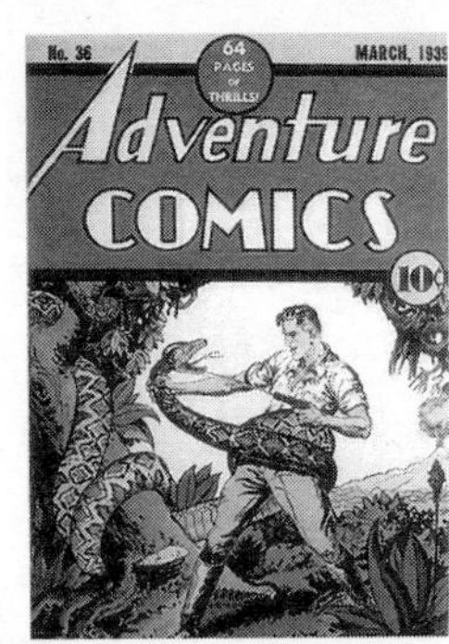

Adventure Comics #36 © DC

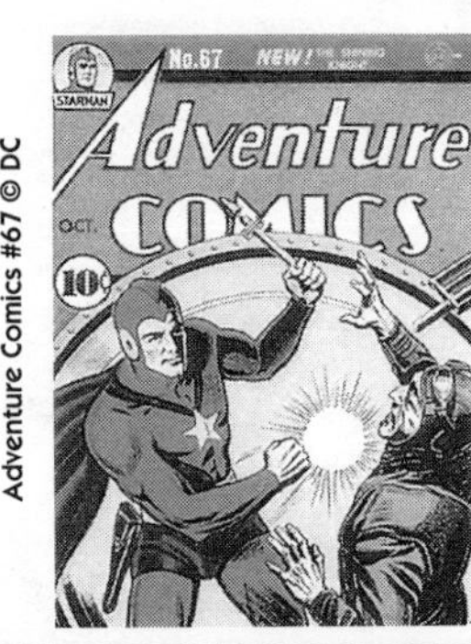

Adventure Comics #67 © DC

GD2.0 FN6.0 NM9.4

Gold Key: Dec, 1973 - No. 10, Feb, 1976 (Photo-c)
1 5.50 16.50 60.00
2-10 2.50 7.50 22.00

ADDAM OMEGA
Antarctic Press: Feb, 1997 - No. 4, Aug, 1997 ($2.95, B&W)
1-4 3.00

ADDAMS FAMILY (TV cartoon)
Gold Key: Oct, 1974 - No. 3, Apr, 1975 (Hanna-Barbera)
1 8.25 25.00 90.00
2,3 5.00 15.00 55.00

ADLAI STEVENSON
Dell Publishing Co.: Dec, 1966
12-007-612-Life story; photo-c 2.25 7.00 25.00

ADOLESCENT RADIOACTIVE BLACK BELT HAMSTERS (See Clint)
Comic Castle/Eclipse Comics: 1986 - No. 9, Jan, 1988 ($1.50, B&W)
1-9: 1st & 2nd printings exist 2.00
1-Limited Edition 3.00
1-In 3-D (7/86) 2.00
2-4 ($2.50) 2.50
Massacre The Japanese Invasion #1 (8/89, $2.00) 2.00

ADRENALYNN (See The Tenth)
Image Comics: Aug, 1999 - Present ($2.50)
1,2-Tony Daniel-s/Marty Egeland-a; origin of Adrenalynn 2.50

ADULT TALES OF TERROR ILLUSTRATED (See Terror Illustrated)

ADVANCED DUNGEONS & DRAGONS (Also see TSR Worlds)
DC Comics: Dec, 1988 - No. 36, Dec, 1991 (Newsstand #1 is Holiday, 1988-89) ($1.25/$1.50/$1.75)
1-Based on TSR role playing game 3.50
2-36: 25-$1.75-c begins 2.00
Annual 1 (1990, $3.95, 68 pgs.) 4.00

ADVENTURE BOUND
Dell Publishing Co.: Aug, 1949
Four Color 239 4.25 13.00 48.00

ADVENTURE COMICS (Formerly New Adventure)(...Presents Dial H For Hero #479-490)
National Periodical Publications/DC Comics: No. 32, 11/38 - No. 490, 2/82; No. 491, 9/82 - No. 503, 9/83
32-Anchors Aweigh (ends #52), Barry O'Neil (ends #60, not in #33), Captain Desmo (ends #47), Dale Daring (ends #47), Federal Men (ends #70), The Golden Dragon (ends #36), Rusty & His Pals (ends #52) by Bob Kane, Todd Hunter (ends #38) and Tom Brent (ends #39) begin
466.00 1400.00 3200.00
33-38: 37-Cover used on Double Action #2 216.00 650.00 1500.00
39(6/39):-Jack Wood begins, ends #42; 1st mention of Marijuana in comics
216.00 650.00 1500.00
GD2.0 FN6.0 VF8.0 NM9.4
40-(Rare, 7/39, on stands 6/10/39)-The Sandman begins by Bert Christman (who died in WWII); believed to be 1st conceived story (see N.Y. World's Fair for 1st published app.); Socko Strong begins, ends #54
3500.00 10,500.00 21,000.00 34,000.00
GD2.0 FN6.0 NM9.4
41-O'Mealia-c 466.00 1400.00 4200.00
42,44-Sandman-c by Flessel. 44-Opium story 600.00 1800.00 5400.00
43,45 288.00 864.00 2400.00
46,47-Sandman covers by Flessel. 47-Steve Conrad Adventurer begins, ends #76 411.00 1230.00 3700.00
GD2.0 FN6.0 VF8.0 NM9.4
48-Intro & 1st app. The Hourman by Bernard Baily; Baily-c (Hourman c-48,50,52-59) 1750.00 5250.00 10,500.00 20,000.00
GD2.0 FN6.0 NM9.4
49,50: 50-Cotton Carver by Jack Lehti begins, ends #64
225.00 675.00 1800.00
51,60-Sandman-c: 51-Sandman-c by Flessel. 288.00 864.00 2400.00
52-59: 53-1st app. Jimmy "Minuteman" Martin & the Minutemen of America in Hourman; ends #78. 58-Paul Kirk Manhunter begins (1st app.), ends #72
200.00 600.00 1600.00
GD2.0 FN6.0 VF8.0 NM9.4
61-1st app. Starman by Jack Burnley (4/41); Starman c-61-72; Starman by Burnley in #61-80 909.00 2730.00 5460.00 10,000.00
GD2.0 FN6.0 NM9.4
62-65,67,68,70: 67-Origin & 1st app. The Mist; classic Burnley-c 70-Last Federal Men 169.00 507.00 1350.00
66-Origin/1st app. Shining Knight (9/41) 206.00 618.00 1650.00
69-1st app. Sandy the Golden Boy (Sandman's sidekick) by Paul Norris (in a Bob Kane style); Sandman dons new costume 181.00 543.00 1450.00
71-Jimmy Martin becomes costumed aide to the Hourman; 1st app.Hourman's Miracle Ray machine 156.00 468.00 1250.00
GD2.0 FN6.0 VF8.0 NM9.4
72-1st Simon & Kirby Sandman (3/42, 1st DC work)
818.00 2454.00 4910.00 10,000.00
73-Origin Manhunter by Simon & Kirby; begin new series; Manhunter-c
909.00 2730.00 5460.00 10,000.00
GD2.0 FN6.0 NM9.4
74-78,80: 74-Thorndyke replaces Jimmy, Hourman's assistant; new Sandman-c begin by S&K. 75-Thor app. by Kirby; 1st Kirby Thor (see Tales of the Unexpected #16). 77-Origin Genius Jones; Mist story. 80-Last S&K Manhunter & Burnley Starman 175.00 525.00 1400.00
79-Classic Manhunter-c 194.00 582.00 1550.00
81-90: 83-Last Hourman. 84-Mike Gibbs begins, ends #102
112.00 336.00 900.00
91-Last Simon & Kirby Sandman 94.00 282.00 750.00
92-99,101,102: 92-Last Manhunter. 101-Shining Knight origin retold. 102-Last Starman, Sandman, & Genius Jones; most-S&K-c (Genius Jones cont'd in More Fun #108) 91.00 273.00 725.00
100-S&K-c 119.00 357.00 950.00
103-Aquaman, Green Arrow, Johnny Quick & Superboy all move over from More Fun Comics #107; 8th app. Superboy; Superboy-c begin; 1st small logo (4/46) 275.00 825.00 2200.00
104 94.00 282.00 750.00
105-110 67.00 201.00 540.00
111-120: 113-X-Mas-c 61.00 183.00 490.00
121-126,128-130: 128-1st meeting Superboy & Lois Lane
55.00 165.00 440.00
127-Brief origin Shining Knight retold 57.00 171.00 460.00
131-141,143-149: 132-Shining Knight 1st return to King Arthur time; origin aide Sir Butch 45.00 135.00 360.00
142-Origin Shining Knight & Johnny Quick retold 51.00 153.00 410.00
150,151,153,155,157,159,161,163-All have 6 pg. Shining Knight stories by Frank Frazetta. 159-Origin Johnny Quick 55.00 165.00 440.00
152,154,156,158,160,162,164-169: 166-Last Shining Knight. 168-Last 52 pg. issue 41.00 123.00 320.00
170-180 40.00 120.00 295.00
181-199: 189-B&W and color illo in **POP** 40.00 120.00 285.00
200 (5/54) 47.00 141.00 425.00
201-208: 207-Last Johnny Quick (not in 205) 33.00 100.00 280.00
209-Last pre-code issue; origin Speedy 35.00 105.00 295.00
GD2.0 FN6.0 VF8.0 NM9.4
210-1st app. Krypto (Superdog)-c/story (3/55)
230.00 690.00 1500.00 3000.00
GD2.0 FN6.0 NM9.4
211-213,215-220: 220-Krypto app. 31.00 92.00 260.00
214-2nd app. Krypto 44.00 132.00 400.00
221-246: 229-1st S.A. issue. 237-1st Intergalactic Vigilante Squadron (6/57)
25.00 75.00 215.00
GD2.0 FN6.0 VF8.0 NM9.4
247(4/58)-1st Legion of Super Heroes app.; 1st app. Cosmic Boy, Lightning Boy (later Lightning Lad in #267), & Saturn Girl (origin)
307.00 920.00 2150.00 4400.00

Adventure Comics #248 © DC

Adventure Comics #293 © DC

Adventure Comics 80 Page Giant #1 © DC

GD2.0 FN6.0 NM9.4 — **GD2.0 FN6.0 NM9.4**

GD2.0 FN6.0 NM9.4

248-252,254,255-Green Arrow in all: 255-Intro. Red Kryptonite in Superboy (used in #252 but with no effect) 19.00 58.00 165.00

253-1st meeting of Superboy & Robin; Green Arrow by Kirby in #250-255 (also see World's Finest #96-99) 26.00 78.00 220.00

256-Origin Green Arrow by Kirby 56.00 168.00 560.00

257-259: 258-Green Arrow x-over in Superboy 16.00 48.00 135.00

260-1st Silver-Age origin Aquaman (5/59) 61.00 183.00 610.00

261-265,268,270: 262-Origin Speedy in Green Arrow. 270-Congorilla begins, ends #281,283 13.00 39.00 110.00

266-(11/59)-Origin & 1st app. Aquagirl (tryout, not same as later character) 14.00 42.00 120.00

267(12/59)-2nd Legion of Super Heroes; Lightning Boy now called Lightning Lad; new costumes for Legion 77.00 231.00 770.00

269-Intro. Aqualad (2/60); last Green Arrow (not in #206) 25.00 74.00 210.00

271-Origin Luthor retold 27.00 81.00 230.00

272-274,277-280: 279-Intro White Kryptonite in Superboy. 280-1st meeting Superboy-Lori Lemaris 12.00 35.00 100.00

275-Origin Superman-Batman team retold (see World's Finest #94) 22.00 65.00 185.00

276-(9/60) Re-intro Metallo (3rd app?); story similar to Superboy #49 13.00 39.00 110.00

281,284,287-289: 281-Last Congorilla. 284-Last Aquaman in Adv. 287,288-Intro Dev-Em, the Knave from Krypton. 287-1st Bizarro Perry White & J. Olsen. 288-Bizarro-c. 289-Legion cameo (statues) 10.50 32.00 90.00

282(3/61)-5th Legion app; intro/origin Star Boy 19.00 56.00 160.00

283-Intro. The Phantom Zone 19.00 56.00 160.00

285-1st Tales of the Bizarro World-c/story (ends #299) in Adv. (see Action #255) 16.50 50.00 140.00

286-1st Bizarro Mxyzptlk; Bizarro-c 14.00 42.00 120.00

290(11/61)-9th Legion app; origin Sunboy in Legion (last 10¢ issue) 19.00 56.00 160.00

291,292,295-298: 291-1st 12¢ ish, (12/61). 292-1st Bizarro Lana Lang & Lucy Lane. 295-Bizarro-c; 1st Bizarro Titano 7.50 22.50 75.00

293(2/62)-13th Legion app; Mon-el & Legion Super Pets (1st app./origin) app. (1st Superhorse). 1st Bizarro Luthor & Kandor 12.00 36.00 120.00

294-1st Bizarro Marilyn Monroe, Pres. Kennedy. 10.00 30.00 100.00

299-1st Gold Kryptonite (8/62) 8.00 24.00 80.00

300-Tales of the Legion of Super-Heroes series begins (9/62); Mon-el leaves Phantom Zone (temporarily), joins Legion 32.00 96.00 360.00

301-Origin Bouncing Boy 12.50 37.50 125.00

302-305: 303-1st app. Matter-Eater Lad. 304-Death of Lightning Lad in Legion 8.50 25.50 85.00

306-310: 306-Intro. Legion of Substitute Heroes. 307-1st app. Element Lad in Legion. 308-1st app. Lightning Lass in Legion 7.50 22.50 75.00

311-320: 312-Lightning Lad back in Legion. 315-Last new Superboy story; Colossal Boy app. 316-Origins & powers of Legion given. 317-Intro. Dream Girl in Legion; Lightning Lass becomes Light Lass; Hall of Fame series begins. 320-Dev-Em 2nd app. 6.00 18.00 60.00

321-Intro Time Trapper 5.00 15.00 50.00

322-330: 327-Intro/1st app. Lone Wolf in Legion. 329-Intro The Bizarro Legionnaires 4.20 12.60 42.00

331-340: 337-Chlorophyll Kid & Night Girl app. 340-Intro Computo in Legion 3.50 10.50 35.00

341-Triplicate Girl becomes Duo Damsel 2.50 7.50 25.00

342-345,347,350,351: 345-Last Hall of Fame; returns in 356,371. 351-1st app. White Witch 2.50 7.50 20.00

346-1st app. Karate Kid, Princess Projectra, Ferro Lad, & Nemesis Kid. 2.80 8.40 28.00

348,349: 348-Origin Sunboy; intro Dr. Regulus in Legion. 349-Intro Universo & Rond Vidar 2.50 7.50 20.00

352,354-360: 355-Insect Queen joins Legion (4/67) 2.00 6.00 16.00

353-Death of Ferro Lad in Legion 2.50 7.50 24.00

361-364,366,368-370: 369-Intro Mordru in Legion 1.85 5.50 15.00

365,367: 365-Intro Shadow Lass; lists origins & powers of L.S.H. 367-New Legion headquarters. 2.25 6.75 18.00

371,372: 371-Intro. Chemical King. 372-Timber Wolf & Chemical King join. 2.25 6.75 18.00

373,374,376-380: 372-Intro. Tornado Twins (Flash descendants). 374-Article on comics fandom. 380-Last Legion in Adventure; last 12¢-c 1.85 5.50 15.00

375-Intro Quantum Queen & The Wanderers 2.25 6.75 18.00

381-Supergirl begins; 1st full length Supergirl story & her 1st solo book (6/69) 6.50 19.50 65.00

382-389,391-396,398 2.00 6.00 16.00

390-Giant Supergirl G-69 3.20 9.60 32.00

397-1st app. new Supergirl 2.50 7.50 20.00

399-Unpubbed G.A. Black Canary story 2.50 7.50 20.00

400-New costume for Supergirl (12/70) 2.50 7.50 25.00

401,402: 402-Last 15¢-c 1.50 4.50 12.00

403-68 pg. Giant G-81; Legion-r/#304,305,308,312 3.00 9.00 30.00

404-408-(20¢-c) 1.25 3.75 10.00

409,410,411-(52 pgs.) 1.75 5.25 14.00

412-(52 pgs.) Reprints origin & 1st app. of Animal Man from Strange Adventures #180 2.25 6.75 18.00

413-415,417-420-(52 pgs.): 413-Hawkman by Kubert r/B&B #44; G.A. Robot-man-r/Det. #178; Zatanna by Morrow. 414-r-2nd Animal Man/Str. Advs. #184. 415-Animal Man-r/Str. Adv.#190 (origin recap). . 417-Morrow Vigilante; Frazetta Shining Knight-r/Adv. #161; origin The Enchantress; no Zatanna. 418-Prev. unpub. Dr. Mid-Nite story from 1948; no Zatanna. 420-Animal Man-r/Str. Adv. #195 2.00 6.00 16.00

416-Also listed as DC 100 Pg. Super Spectacular #10; Golden Age-r; r/1st app. Black Canary from Flash #86; no Zatanna (see DC 100 Pg. Super Spectacular #10 for price)

421-424,427: Last Supergirl in Adventure. 427-Last Vigilante 1.10 3.30 9.00

425-New look, content change to adventure; Kaluta-c; Toth-a, origin Capt. Fear 2.25 6.75 18.00

426-1st Adventurers Club. 1.40 4.15 11.00

428-Origin/1st app. Black Orchid (c/story, 6-7/73) 3.50 10.50 35.00

429,430-Black Orchid-c/stories 2.25 6.75 18.00

431-Spectre by Aparo begins, ends #440. 3.80 11.40 38.00

432-439-Spectre app. 433-437-Cover title is Weird Adv. Comics. 436-Last 20¢ issue. 2.25 6.75 18.00

440-New Spectre origin. 2.50 7.50 24.00

441,442,444,448-458: 441-452-Aquaman app. 450-Weather Wizard app. in Aquaman story. 449-451-Martian Manhunter app. 453-458-Superboy app. 453-Intro. Mighty Girl. 457,458-Eclipso app. 4.00

443,445-447: 443-Fisherman app. 445-447-The Creeper app. 446-Flag-c 1.00 3.00 7.00

459,460 (68 pgs.): 459-New Gods/Darkseid storyline concludes from New Gods #19 (#459 is dated 9-10/78) without missing a month. 459-Flash (ends #466), Deadman (ends #466), Wonder Woman (ends #464), Green Lantern (ends #460). 460-Aquaman (ends #478) 1.75 5.25 14.00

461,462 ($1.00, 68 pgs.): 461-Justice Society begins; ends 466. 461,462-Death Earth II Batman 1.75 5.25 14.00

463-466 ($1.00 size, 68 pgs.) 1.10 3.30 9.00

467-Starman by Ditko & Plastic Man begins; 1st app. Prince Gavyn (Starman). 1.25 3.75 10.00

468-490: 470-Origin Starman. 479-Dial 'H' For Hero begins, ends #490. 478-Last Starman & Plastic Man. 480-490: Dial 'H' For Hero 3.50

491-503: 491-100pg. Digest size begins; r/Legion of Super Heroes/Adv. #247, 267; Spectre, Aquaman, Superboy, S&K Sandman, Black Canary-r & new Shazam by Newton begin. 492,495,496,499-S&K Sandman-r/Adventure in all. 493-Challengers of the Unknown begins by Tuska w/brief origin. 493-495, 497-499-G.A. Captain Marvel-r. 494-499-Spectre-r/Spectre 1-3, 5-7. 496-Capt. Marvel Jr. new-s, Cockrum-a. 498-Mary Marvel new-s; Plastic Man-r begin; origin Bouncing Boy-r/ #301. 500-Legion-r (Digest size, 148 pgs.). 501-503: G.A.-r 1.75 5.25 14.00

... 80 Page Giant (10/98, $4.95) Wonder Woman, Shazam, Superboy, Supergirl Green Arrow, Legion, Bizarro World stories 5.00

NOTE: *Bizarro covers-285, 286, 288, 294, 295, 329. Vigilante app.-420, 426, 427.* **N. Adams** *a(r)-495i-498i; c-365-369, 371-373, 375-379, 381-383.* **Aparo** *a-431-433, 434i, 435, 436, 437i, 438i,*

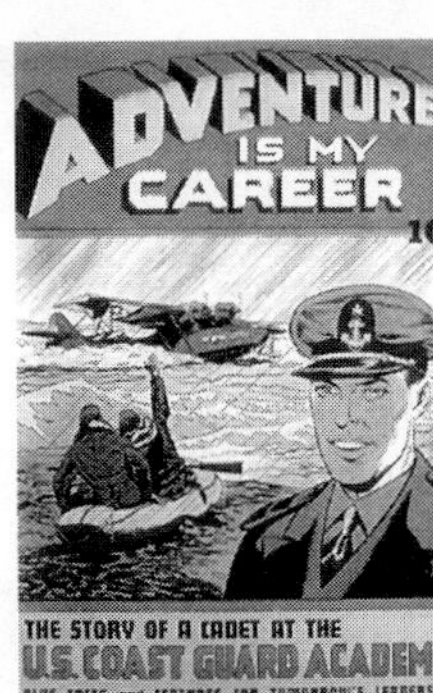

Adventure is My Career © Conde Nast

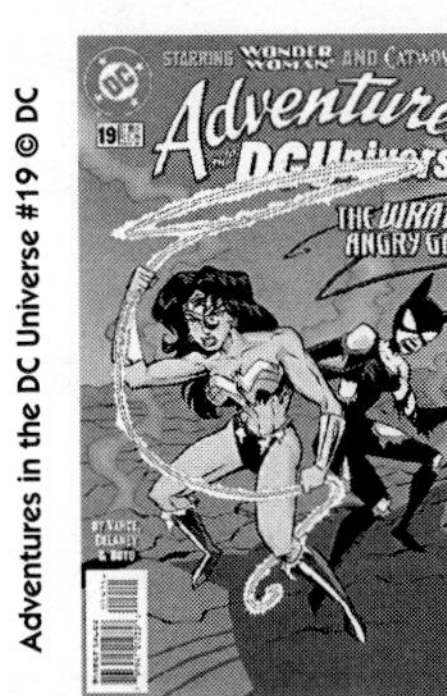

Adventures in the DC Universe #19 © DC

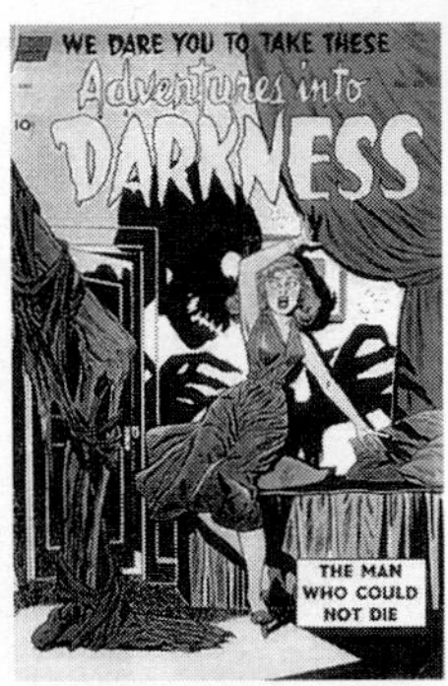

Adventures into Darkness #10 © STD

GD2.0 FN6.0 NM9.4

439-452, 503r; c-431-452. ***Austin*** *a-449i 451i.* ***Bernard Baily*** *c-48, 50, 52-59.* ***Bolland*** *c-475.* ***Burnley*** *c-61-72, 116-120p.* ***Chaykin*** *a-438.* ***Ditko*** *a-467-478p; c-467p.* ***Creig Flessel*** *c-32, 33, 40, 42, 44, 46, 47, 51, 60.* ***Giffen*** *c-491p-494p, 500p.* ***Grell*** *a-435-437, 440.* ***Guardineer*** *c-34, 35, 45.* ***Infantino*** *a-416r.* ***Kaluta*** *c-425.* ***Bob Kane*** *a-38.* ***G. Kane*** *a-414r, 425; c-496-499, 537.* ***Kirby*** *a-250-256.* ***Kubert*** *a-413.* ***Meskin*** *a-81,127.* ***Moldoff*** *a-494i; c-49.* ***Morrow*** *a-413-415, 417, 422, 502r, 503r.* ***Netzer/Nasser*** *a-449-451.* ***Newton*** *a-459-461, 464-466, 491p, 492p.* ***Paul Norris*** *a-69.* ***Orlando*** *a-457p, 458p.* ***Perez*** *c-484-486, 490p.* ***Simon/Kirby*** *a-503r; c-73-97, 100-102.* ***Starlin*** *c-471.* ***Staton*** *a-445-447i, 456-458p, 459, 460, 461p-465p, 466,467p-478p, 502p(r); c-458, 461(back).* ***Toth*** *a-418, 419, 425, 431, 495p-497p.* ***Tuska*** *a-494p.*

ADVENTURE COMICS (Also see All Star Comics 1999 crossover titles)
DC Comics: May, 1999 ($1.99, one-shot)

1-Golden Age Starman and the Atom; Snejbjerg-a 2.00

ADVENTURE INTO MYSTERY
Atlas Comics (BFP No. 1/OPI No. 2-8): May, 1956 - No. 8, July, 1957

1-Powell s/f-a; Forte-a; Everett-c 30.00 90.00 270.00
2-Flying Saucer story 17.00 51.00 150.00
3,6-Everett-c 14.00 42.00 125.00
4-7: 4-Williamson-a, 4 pgs; Powell-a. 5-Everett-c/a, Orlando-a. 7-Torres-a; Everett-c 15.00 45.00 135.00
8-Moriera, Sale, Torres, Woodbridge-a, Severin-c 14.00 42.00 125.00

ADVENTURE IS MY CAREER
U.S. Coast Guard Academy/Street & Smith: 1945 (44 pgs.)

nn-Simon, Milt Gross-a 18.00 54.00 125.00

ADVENTURERS, THE
Aircel Comics/Adventure Publ.: Aug, 1986 - No. 10, 1987? ($1.50, B&W)
V2#1, 1987 - V2#9, 1988; V3#1, Oct, 1989 - V3#6, 1990

1-Peter Hsu-a 3.00
1-Cover variant, limited ed. 5.00
1-2nd print (1986); 1st app. Elf Warrior 2.00
2,3, 0 (#4, 12/86)-Origin, 5-10, Book II, reg. & Limited Ed. #1 2.00
Book II, #2,3,0,4-7 2.00
Book III, #1 (10/89, $2.25)-Reg. & limited-c, Book III, #2-6 2.25

ADVENTURES (No. 2 Spectacular... on cover)
St. John Publishing Co.: Nov, 1949 - No. 2, Feb, 1950 (No. 1 ...in Romance on cover) (Slightly larger size)

1(Scarce); Bolle, Starr-a(2) 25.00 75.00 175.00
2(Scarce)-Slave Girl; China Bombshell app.; Bolle, L. Starr-a 40.00 120.00 285.00

ADVENTURES FOR BOYS
Bailey Enterprises: Dec, 1954

nn-Comics, text, & photos 5.35 16.00 32.00

ADVENTURES IN PARADISE (TV)
Dell Publishing Co.: Feb-Apr, 1962

Four Color#1301 3.60 11.00 40.00

ADVENTURES IN ROMANCE (See Adventures)

ADVENTURES IN SCIENCE (See Classics Illustrated Special Issue)

ADVENTURES IN THE DC UNIVERSE
DC Comics: Apr, 1997 - No. 19, Oct, 1998 ($1.75/$1.95/$1.99)

1-Animated style in all: JLA-c/app 4.00
2-11,13-17,19: 2-Flash app. 3-Wonder Woman. 4-Green Lantern. 6-Aquaman. 7-Shazam Family. 8-Blue Beetle & Booster Gold. 9-Flash. 10-Legion. 11-Green Lantern & Wonder Woman. 13-Impulse & Martian Manhunter. 14-Superboy/Flash race 3.00
12,18-JLA-c/app 3.50
Annual 1(1997, $3.95)-Dr. Fate, Impulse, Rose & Thorn, Superboy, Mister Miracle app. 4.00

ADVENTURES IN 3-D
Harvey Publications: Nov, 1953 - No. 2, Jan, 1954 (25¢)

1-Nostrand, Powell-a, 2-Powell-a 17.00 51.00 120.00

ADVENTURES INTO DARKNESS (See Seduction of the Innocent 3-D)
Better-Standard Publications/Visual Editions: No. 5, Aug, 1952- No. 14, 1954

5-Katz-c/a; Toth-a(p) 32.00 96.00 225.00
6-Tuska, Katz-a 19.00 57.00 130.00
7-9: 7-Katz-c/a. 8,9-Toth-a(p) 20.00 60.00 140.00
10-12: 10,11-Jack Katz-a. 12-Toth?; lingerie panel 17.00 51.00 120.00
13-Toth-a(p); Cannibalism story cited by T. E. Murphy articles 20.00 60.00 140.00
14 13.50 41.00 95.00

NOTE: ***Fawcette*** *a-13.* ***Moriera*** *a-5.* ***Sekowsky*** *a-10, 11, 13(2).*

ADVENTURES INTO TERROR (Formerly Joker Comics)
Marvel/Atlas Comics (CDS): No. 43, Nov, 1950 - No. 31, May, 1954

43(#1) 60.00 180.00 480.00
44(#2, 2/51)-Sol Brodsky-c 40.00 120.00 320.00
3(4/51), 4 25.00 75.00 175.00
5-Wolverton-c panel/Mystic #6; Rico-c panel also; Atom Bomb story 30.00 90.00 210.00
6,8: 8-Wolverton text illo r-/Marvel Tales #104 24.00 72.00 165.00
7-Wolverton-a "Where Monsters Dwell", 6 pgs.; Tuska-c; Maneely-c panels 52.00 156.00 420.00
9,10,12-Krigstein-a. 9-Decapitation panels 21.00 63.00 150.00
11,13-20 18.00 54.00 125.00
21-24,26-31 16.00 48.00 110.00
25-Matt Fox-a 21.00 63.00 150.00

NOTE: ***Ayers*** *a-21.* ***Colan*** *a-3, 5, 14, 21, 24, 25, 28, 29; c-27.* ***Colletta*** *a-30.* ***Everett*** *c-13, 21, 25.* ***Fass*** *a-28, 29.* ***Forte*** *a-28.* ***Heath*** *a-43, 44, 4-6, 22, 24, 26; c-43, 9, 11.* ***Lazarus*** *a-7.* ***Maneely*** *a-7(3 pg.), 10, 11, 21., 22 c-15, 29.* ***Don Rico*** *a-4, 5(3 pg.).* ***Sekowsky*** *a-43, 3, 4.* ***Sinnott*** *a-8, 9, 11, 28.* ***Tuska*** *a-14; c-7.*

ADVENTURES INTO THE UNKNOWN
American Comics Group: Fall, 1948 - No. 174, Aug, 1967 (No. 1-33: 52 pgs.)

(1st continuous series Supernatural comic; see Eerie #1)

1-Guardineer-a; adapt. of 'Castle of Otranto' by Horace Walpole 181.00 543.00 1450.00
2,3: 3-Feldstein-a (9 pgs) 70.00 210.00 560.00
4,5: 5-'Spirit Of Frankenstein' series begins, ends #12 (except #11) 37.00 111.00 260.00
6-10 30.00 90.00 210.00
11-16,18-20: 13-Starr-a 24.00 72.00 170.00
17-Story similar to movie 'The Thing' 29.00 87.00 200.00
21-26,28-30 19.00 57.00 135.00
27-Williamson/Krenkel-a (8 pgs.) 25.00 75.00 175.00
31-50: 38-Atom bomb panels 16.00 48.00 110.00
51-(1/54)-(3-D effect-c/story)-Only white cover 34.00 102.00 235.00
52-58: (3-D effect-c/stories with black covers). 52-E.C. swipe/Haunt Of Fear #14 31.00 93.00 220.00
59-3-D effect story only; new logo 25.00 75.00 175.00
60-Woodesque-a by Landau 11.00 33.00 75.00
61-Last pre-code issue (1-2/55) 11.00 33.00 75.00
62-70 5.50 16.50 55.00
71-90 4.00 12.00 40.00
91,96(#95 on inside),107,116-All have Williamson-a 5.50 16.50 55.00
92-95,97-99,101-106,108-115,117-127: 109-113,118-Whitney painted-c 3.50 10.50 35.00
100 4.00 12.00 40.00
128-Williamson/Krenkel/Torres-a(r)/Forbidden Worlds #63; last 10¢ issue 3.50 10.50 35.00
129-152-3,157: 153,157-Magic Agent app. 3.00 9.00 30.00
154-Nemesis series begins (origin), ends #170 3.50 10.50 35.00
155,156,158-167,170-174 2.80 8.40 28.00
168-Ditko-a(p) 3.50 10.50 35.00
169-Nemesis battles Hitler 3.00 9.00 30.00

NOTE: *"Spirit of Frankenstein" series in 5, 6, 8-10, 12, 16.* ***Buscema*** *a-100, 106, 108-110, 158r, 165r.* ***Cameron*** *a-34.* ***Craig*** *a-152, 160.* ***Goode*** *a-45, 47, 60.* ***Landau*** *a-51, 59-63.* ***Lazarus*** *a-34, 48, 51, 52, 56, 58, 79, 87; c-31-56, 58.* ***Reinman*** *a-102, 111, 112, 115-118, 124, 130, 137, 141, 145, 164.* ***Whitney*** *c-12-30, 57, 59-on (most.)* ***Torres/Williamson*** *a-116.*

ADVENTURES INTO WEIRD WORLDS
Marvel/Atlas Comics (ACI): Jan, 1952 - No. 30, June, 1954

1-Atom bomb panels 50.00 150.00 400.00

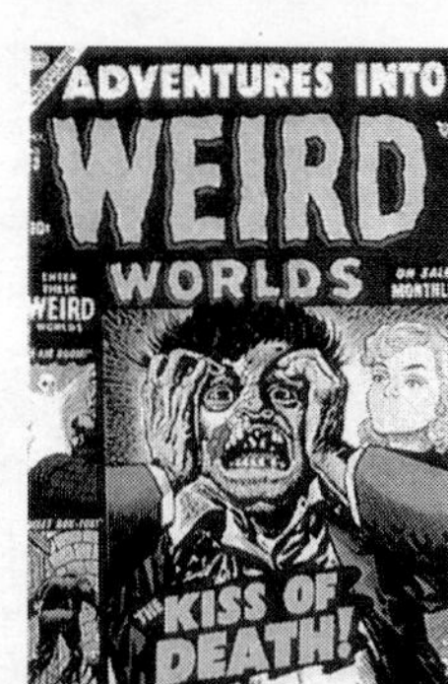

Adventures into Weird Worlds #23 © MAR

Adventures of Barry Ween, Boy Genius #1 © Judd Winick

Adventures of Bob Hope #19 © DC

	GD2.0	FN6.0	NM9.4
2-Sci/fic stories (2); one by Maneely	35.00	105.00	245.00
3-10: 7-Tongue ripped out. 10-Krigstein, Everett-a	24.00	72.00	165.00
11-21: 21-Hitler in Hell story	19.00	57.00	135.00
22-26: 24-Man holds hypo & splits in two	17.00	51.00	115.00
27-Matt Fox end of world story-a; severed head-c	34.00	102.00	240.00
28-Atom bomb story; decapitation panels	19.00	57.00	135.00
29,30	13.50	41.00	95.00

NOTE: ***Ayers** a-8, 26. **Everett** a-4, 5; c-6, 8, 10-13, 18, 19, 22, 24, 25; a-4, 25. **Fass** a-7. **Forte** a-21, 24. **Al Hartley** a-2. **Heath** a-1, 4, 17, 22; c-7, 9, 20. **Maneely** a-2, 3, 11, 20, 22, 23, 25; c-1, 3, 22, 25-27, 29. **Reinman** a-24, 28. **Rico** a-13. **Robinson** a-13. **Sinnott** a-25, 30. **Tuska** a-1, 2, 12, 15. **Whitney** a-7. **Wildey** a-28. Bondage c-22.*

ADVENTURES IN WONDERLAND
Lev Gleason Publications: April, 1955 - No. 5, Feb, 1956 (Jr. Readers Guild)

	GD2.0	FN6.0	NM9.4
1-Maurer-a	10.00	30.00	60.00
2-4	5.85	17.50	35.00
5-Christmas issue	6.70	20.00	40.00

ADVENTURES OF AARON
Image Comics: Mar, 1997 - No. 3, Sept, 1997 (2.95, B&W)

1,2,100(#3),3(#4) — 3.00

ADVENTURES OF ALAN LADD, THE
National Periodical Publ.: Oct-Nov, 1949 - No. 9, Feb-Mar, 1951 (All 52 pgs.)

	GD2.0	FN6.0	NM9.4
1-Photo-c	90.00	270.00	725.00
2-Photo-c	49.00	147.00	390.00
3-6: Last photo-c	40.00	120.00	285.00
7-9	32.00	96.00	225.00

NOTE: ***Dan Barry** a-1. **Moreira** a-3-7.*

ADVENTURES OF ALICE (Also see Alice in Wonderland & ...at Monkey Island)
Civil Service Publ./Pentagon Publishing Co.: 1945

	GD2.0	FN6.0	NM9.4
1	10.00	30.00	70.00
2-Through the Magic Looking Glass	10.00	30.00	60.00

ADVENTURES OF BARON MUNCHAUSEN, THE
Now Comics: July, 1989 - No. 4, Oct, 1989 ($1.75, limited series)

1-4: Movie adaptation — 2.00

ADVENTURES OF BARRY WEEN, BOY GENIUS, THE
Image Comics: Mar, 1999 - No. 3, May, 1999 ($2.95, B&W, limited series)

1-3-Judd Winick-s/a — 3.00
TPB (Oni Press, 11/99, $8.95) — 8.95

ADVENTURES OF BAYOU BILLY, THE
Archie Comics: Sept, 1989 - No. 5, June, 1990 ($1.00)

1-5: Esposito-c/a(i). 5-Kelley Jones-c — 2.50

ADVENTURES OF BOB HOPE, THE (Also see True Comics #59)
National Per. Publ.: Feb-Mar, 1950 - No. 109, Feb-Mar, 1968 (#1-10: 52pgs.)

	GD2.0	FN6.0	NM9.4
1-Photo-c	156.00	468.00	1250.00
2-Photo-c	74.00	222.00	590.00
3,4-Photo-c	44.00	132.00	350.00
5-10	40.00	120.00	290.00
11-20	23.00	69.00	160.00
21-31 (2-3/55; last precode)	15.00	45.00	105.00
32-40	8.50	25.50	85.00
41-50	7.00	21.00	70.00
51-70	5.00	15.00	50.00
71-93	3.00	9.00	30.00
94-Aquaman cameo	3.50	10.50	35.00
95-1st app. Super-Hip & 1st monster issue (11/65)	4.50	13.50	45.00
96-105: Super-Hip and monster stories in all. 103-Batman, Robin, Ringo Starr cameos	3.00	9.00	30.00
106-109-All monster-c/stories by N. Adams-c/a	4.50	13.50	45.00

NOTE: *Buzzy in #34. Kitty Karr of Hollywood in #15, 17-20, 23, 28. Liz in #26, 109. Miss Beverly Hills of Hollywood in #7, 8, 10, 13, 14. Miss Melody Lane of Broadway in #15. Rusty in #23, 25. Tommy in #24. No 2nd feature in #2-4, 6, 8, 11, 12, 28-108.*

ADVENTURES OF CAPTAIN AMERICA
Marvel Comics: Sept, 1991 - No. 4, Jan, 1992 ($4.95, 52 pgs., squarebound, limited series)

1-4: 1-Embossed-c; Fabian Nicieza scripts; Kevin Maguire-c/a(p) begins, ends #3. 2-4-Austin-c/a(i) — 5.00

ADVENTURES OF CYCLOPS AND PHOENIX (Also See Askani'son & The Further Adventures of Cyclops And Phoenix)
Marvel Comics: May, 1994 - No. 4, Aug, 1994 ($2.95, limited series)

1-4-Characters from X-Men — 4.00
Trade paperback ($14.95)-reprints #1-4 — 15.00

ADVENTURES OF DEAN MARTIN AND JERRY LEWIS, THE
(The Adventures of Jerry Lewis #41 on) (See Movie Love #12)
National Periodical Publications: July-Aug, 1952 - No. 40, Oct, 1957

	GD2.0	FN6.0	NM9.4
1	87.00	261.00	700.00
2-3 pg origin on how they became a team	44.00	132.00	350.00
3-10: 3- I Love Lucy text featurette	23.00	69.00	160.00
11-19: Last precode (2/55)	14.00	42.00	100.00
20-30	11.50	34.00	80.00
31-40	10.00	30.00	60.00

ADVENTURES OF DETECTIVE ACE KING, THE (Also see Bob Scully-- & Detective Dan)
Humor Publ. Corp.: No date (1933) (36 pgs., 9-1/2x12") (10¢, B&W, one-shot) (paper-c)

	GD2.0	FN6.0	VF8.0
Book 1-Along with Detective Dan, the first comic w/original art & the first of a single theme.; Not reprints; Ace King by Martin Nadle (The American Sherlock Holmes). A Dick Tracy look-alike	267.00	800.00	1600.00

ADVENTURES OF EVIL AND MALICE, THE
Image Comics: June, 1999 - No. 4 ($3.50, limited series)

	GD2.0	FN6.0	NM9.4
1-Jimmie Robinson-s/a			4.00
2			3.50

ADVENTURES OF FELIX THE CAT, THE
Harvey Comics: May, 1992 ($1.25)

1-Messmer-r — 2.00

ADVENTURES OF FORD FAIRLANE, THE
DC Comics: May, 1990 - No. 4, Aug, 1990 ($1.50, limited series, mature)

1-4: Andrew Dice Clay movie tie-in; Don Heck inks — 2.00

ADVENTURES OF HOMER COBB, THE
Say/Bart Prod. : Sept, 1947 (Oversized)
(Published in the U.S., but printed in Canada)

	GD2.0	FN6.0	NM9.4
1-(Scarce)-Feldstein-c/a	28.00	84.00	195.00

ADVENTURES OF HOMER GHOST (See Homer The Happy Ghost)
Atlas Comics: June, 1957 - No. 2, Aug, 1957

	GD2.0	FN6.0	NM9.4
V1#1,2	6.70	20.00	40.00

ADVENTURES OF JERRY LEWIS, THE (Adventures of Dean Martin & Jerry Lewis No. 1-40)(See Super DC Giant)
National Periodical Publ.: No. 41, Nov, 1957 - No. 124, May-June, 1971

	GD2.0	FN6.0	NM9.4
41	6.00	18.00	60.00
42-60	5.00	15.00	50.00
61-67,69-73,75-80	3.80	11.40	38.00
68,74-Photo-c (movie)	4.50	13.50	45.00
81,82,85-87,90,91,93,94,96,98,99: 93-Beatles parody as babies	2.60	7.80	26.00
83,84,88: 83-1st Monsters-c/s. 84-Jerry as a Super-hero-c/s. 88-1st Witch, Miss Kraft	3.00	9.00	30.00
89-Bob Hope app.; Wizard of Oz & Alfred E. Neuman in MAD parody	2.60	7.80	26.00
92-Superman cameo	3.60	10.80	36.00
95-1st Uncle Hal Wack-A-Buy Camp-c/s	3.00	9.00	30.00
97-Batman/Robin/Joker-c/story; Riddler & Penguin app; Dick Sprang-c.	5.50	16.50	55.00
100	3.20	9.60	32.00
101,103,104-Neal Adams-c/a	4.50	13.50	45.00

Adventures of Mighty Mouse #7 © STJ

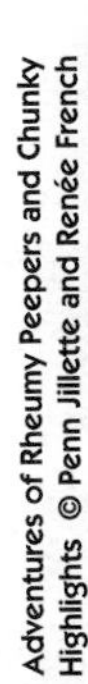
Adventures of Rheumy Peepers and Chunky Highlights © Penn Jillette and Renée French

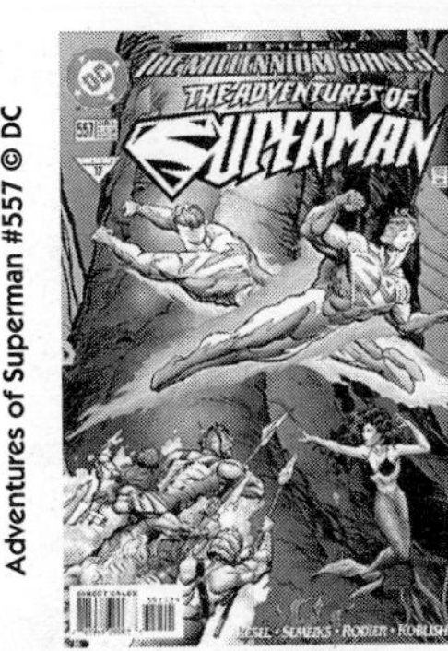

Adventures of Superman #557 © DC

GD2.0 FN6.0 NM9.4

102-Beatles app.; Neal Adams c/a 6.00 18.00 60.00
105-Superman x-over 3.80 11.40 38.00
106-111,113-116 2.50 7.50 20.00
112,117: 112-Flash x-over. 117-W. Woman x-over 3.60 10.80 36.00
118-124 2.00 6.00 16.00
NOTE: *Monster-c/s-90,93,96,98,101. Wack-A-Buy Camp-c/s-96,99,102,107,108.*

ADVENTURES OF JO-JOY, THE (See Jo-Joy)

ADVENTURES OF LASSIE, THE (See Lassie)

ADVENTURES OF LUTHER ARKWRIGHT, THE
Valkyrie Press/Dark Horse Comics: Oct, 1987 - No. 9, Jan, 1989 ($2.00, B&W)
V2, #1, Mar, 1990 - V2#9, 1990 ($1.95, B&W)

1-9: 1-Alan Moore intro., V2#1-9 (Dark Horse): r-1st series; new-c 4.00
TPB (1997, $14.95) r/#1-9 w/Michael Moorcock intro. 15.00

ADVENTURES OF MIGHTY MOUSE (Mighty Mouse Adventures No. 1)
St. John Publishing Co.: No. 2, Jan, 1952 - No. 18, May, 1955

2 24.00 73.00 170.00
3-5 12.00 36.00 85.00
6-18 10.00 30.00 60.00

ADVENTURES OF MIGHTY MOUSE (2nd Series)
(Two No. 144's; formerly Paul Terry's Comics; No. 129-137 have nn's)
(Becomes Mighty Mouse No. 161 on)
St. John/Pines/Dell/Gold Key: No. 126, Aug, 1955 - No. 160, Oct, 1963

126(8/55), 127(10/55), 128(11/55)-St. John 7.15 21.50 50.00
nn(129, 4/56)-144(8/59)-Pines 4.20 12.60 42.00
144(10-12/59)-155(7-9/62) Dell 3.25 10.00 35.00
156(10/62)-160(10/63) Gold Key 3.65 11.00 40.00
NOTE: *Early issues titled "Paul Terry's Adventures of ...."*

ADVENTURES OF MIGHTY MOUSE (Formerly Mighty Mouse)
Gold Key: No. 166, Mar, 1979 - No. 172, Jan, 1980

166-172 4.00

ADVS. OF MR. FROG & MISS MOUSE (See Dell Junior Treasury No. 4)

ADVENTURES OF OZZIE & HARRIET, THE (See Ozzie & Harriet)

ADVENTURES OF PATORUZU
Green Publishing Co.: Aug, 1946 - Winter, 1946

nn's-Contains Animal Crackers reprints 4.15 12.50 25.00

ADVENTURES OF PINKY LEE, THE (TV)
Atlas Comics: July, 1955 - No. 5, Dec, 1955

1 26.00 78.00 185.00
2-5 16.00 48.00 110.00

ADVENTURES OF PIPSQUEAK, THE (Formerly Pat the Brat)
Archie Publications (Radio Comics): No. 34, Sept, 1959 - No. 39, July, 1960

34 3.20 9.60 32.00
35-39 2.50 7.50 22.00

ADVENTURES OF QUAKE & QUISP, THE (See Quaker Oats "Plenty of Glutton")

ADVENTURES OF REX THE WONDER DOG, THE (Rex...No. 1)
National Periodical Publications: Jan-Feb, 1952 - No. 45, May-June, 1959; No. 46, Nov-Dec, 1959

1-(Scarce)-Toth-c/a 103.00 309.00 875.00
2-(Scarce)-Toth-c/a 51.00 153.00 435.00
3-(Scarce)-Toth-a 39.00 117.00 335.00
4,5 31.00 93.00 250.00
6-10 23.00 69.00 185.00
11-Atom bomb-c/story 26.00 78.00 210.00
12-19: 19-Last precode (1-2/55) 14.00 42.00 110.00
20-46 10.00 30.00 80.00
NOTE: ***Infantino, Gil Kane** art in 5-19 (most)*

ADVENTURES OF RHEUMY PEEPERS AND CHUNKY HIGHLIGHTS, THE
Oni Press: Feb, 1999 ($2.95, B&W, one-shot)

nn-Penn Jillette-s/Renée French-a 3.00

GD2.0 FN6.0 NM9.4

ADVENTURES OF ROBIN HOOD, THE (Formerly Robin Hood)
Magazine Enterprises (Sussex Publ. Co.): No. 7, 9/57 - No. 8, 11/57
(Based on Richard Greene TV Show)

7,8-Richard Greene photo-c. 7-Powell-a 15.00 45.00 105.00

ADVENTURES OF ROBIN HOOD, THE
Gold Key: Mar, 1974 - No. 7, Jan, 1975 (Disney cartoon) (36 pgs.)

1(90291-403)-Part-r of $1.50 editions 1.50 4.50 12.00
2-7: 1-7 are part-r 1.00 3.00 7.00

ADVENTURES OF SNAKE PLISSKEN
Marvel Comics: Jan, 1997 ($2.50, one-shot)

1-Based on Escape From L.A. movie; Brereton-c 2.50

ADVENTURES OF SPIDER-MAN, THE (TV cartoon)
Marvel Comics: Apr, 1996 - No. 12, Mar, 1997 (99¢)

1-12: Based on animated television show. 2.00

ADVENTURES OF SUPERBOY, THE (See Superboy, 2nd Series)

ADVENTURES OF SUPERMAN (Formerly Superman)
DC Comics: No. 424, Jan, 1987 - No. 499, Feb, 1993;
No. 500, Early June, 1993 - Present

424 3.00
425-462: 426-Legends x-over. 432-1st app. Jose Delgado who becomes Gangbuster in #434. 436-Byrne scripts begin. 436,437-Millennium x-over. 438-New Brainiac app. 440-Batman app. 449-Invasion 2.50
463-Superman/Flash race; cover swipe/Superman #199 5.00
464-Lobo-c & app. (pre-dates Lobo #1) 3.00
465-495: 467-Part 2 of Batman story. 473-Hal Jordan, Guy Gardner x-over. 477-Legion app. 491-Last $1.00-c. 480-($1.75, 52 pgs.). 495-Forever People-c/story; Darkseid app. 2.50
496,197: 496-Doomsday cameo. 497-Doomsday battle issue 3.00
496,497-2nd printings 2.00
498,499-Funeral for a Friend; Supergirl app. 2.50
498-2nd & 3rd printings 2.00
500-($2.95, 68 pgs.)-Collector's edition w/card 3.50
500-($2.50, 68 pgs.)-Regular edition w/different-c 2.50
500-Platinum edition 2.25 6.80 25.00
501-($1.95)-Collector's edition with die-cut-c 2.00
501-($1.50)-Regular edition w/mini-poster & diff.-c 2.00
502-516: 502-Supergirl-c/story. 508-Challengers of the Unknown app. 510-Bizarro-c/story. 516-(9/94)-Zero Hour 2.50
505-($2.50)-Holo-grafx foil-c edition 2.50
0,517-523: 0-(10/94). 517-(11/94) 2.00
524-549,551-571: 524-Begin $1.95-c. 527-Return of Alpha Centurion (Zero Hour) 533-Impulse c/app. 535-Luthor-c/app. 536-Brainiac app. 537-Parasite app. 540-Final Night x-over. 541 Superboy-c/app.;Lois and Clark honeymoon. 545-New powers. 546-New costume. 551-Cyborg app. 555-Red & Blue Supermen battle. 557-Millennium Giants x-over, 558-560: Superman Silver Age-style story; Krypto app. 561-Begin $1.99-c. 565-JLA app. 2.00
550-($3.50)-Double sized 3.50
#1,000,000 (11/98) Gene Ha-c; 853rd Century x-over 3.00
Annual 1 (1987, $1.25, 52 pgs.)-Starlin-c & scripts 4.00
Annual 2,3 (1990, 1991, $2.00, 68 pgs.): 2-Byrne-c/a(i); Legion '90 (Lobo) app. 3-Armageddon 2001 x-over 3.00
Annual 4-6 ('92-'94, $2.50, 68 pgs.): 4-Guy Gardner/Lobo-c/story; Eclipso storyline; Quesada-c(p). 5-Bloodlines storyline. 6-Elseworlds sty. 3.00
Annual 7,9('95, '97, $3.95)-7-Year One story. 9-Pulp Heroes sty 4.00
Annual 8 (1996, $2.95)-Legends of the Dead Earth story 3.00
NOTE: ***Erik Larsen** a-431.*

ADVENTURES OF THE DOVER BOYS
Archie Comics (Close-up): September, 1950 - No. 2, 1950 (No month given)

1,2 8.35 25.00 50.00

ADVENTURES OF THE FLY (The Fly #1-6; Fly Man No. 32-39; See The Double Life of Private Strong, The Fly, Laugh Comics & Mighty Crusaders)
Archie Publications/Radio Comics: Aug, 1959 - No. 30, Oct, 1964; No. 31, May, 1965

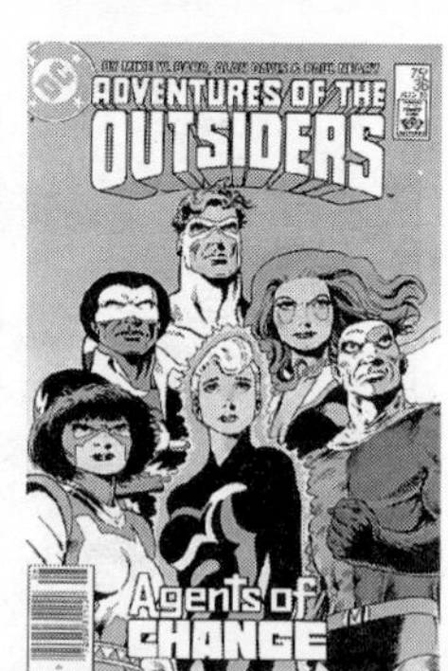

Adventures of the Outsiders #36 © DC

Adventures on the Planet of the Apes #10 © MAR

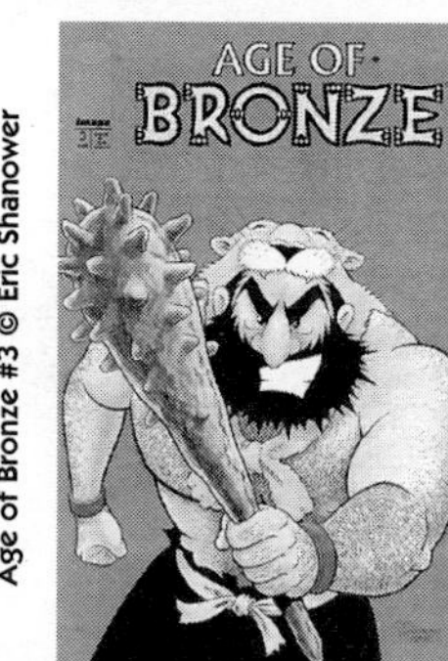

Age of Bronze #3 © Eric Shanower

1-Shield app.; origin The Fly; S&K-c/a 45.00 135.00 540.00
2-Williamson, S&K-a 28.00 84.00 280.00
3-Origin retold; Davis, Powell-a 22.00 66.00 220.00
4-Neal Adams-a(p)(1 panel); S&K-c; Powell-a; 2 pg. Shield story 12.00 36.00 120.00
5-10: 7-1st S.A. app. Black Hood (7/60). 8-1st S.A. app. Shield (9/60). 9-Shield app. 9-1st app. Cat Girl. 10-Black Hood app. 8.00 24.00 80.00
11-13,15-20: 13-1st app. Fly Girl w/o costume. 16-Last 10¢ issue. 20-Origin Fly Girl retold 5.00 15.00 50.00
14-Origin & 1st app. Fly Girl in costume 6.50 19.50 65.00
21-30: 23-Jaguar cameo. 27-29-Black Hood 1 pg. strips. 30-Comet x-over (1st S.A. app.) in Fly Girl 3.20 9.60 32.00
31-Black Hood, Shield, Comet app. 3.50 10.50 35.00
NOTE: ***Simon** c-2-4. **Tuska** a-1. Cover title to #31 is Flyman; Advs. of the Fly inside.*

ADVENTURES OF THE JAGUAR, THE (See Blue Ribbon Comics, Laugh Comics & Mighty Crusaders)
Archie Publications (Radio Comics): Sept, 1961 - No. 15, Nov, 1963
1-Origin Jaguar (1st app?) by J. Rosenberger 17.00 51.00 170.00
2,3: 3-Last 10¢ issue 8.50 25.50 85.00
4-6-Catgirl app. (#4's-c is same as splash pg.) 6.50 19.50 65.00
7-10 5.00 15.00 50.00
11-15: 13,14-Catgirl, Black Hood app. in both 4.00 12.00 40.00

ADVENTURES OF THE MASK (TV cartoon)
Dark Horse Comics: Jan, 1996 - No. 12, Dec, 1996 ($2.50)
1-12: Based on animated series 2.50

ADVENTURES OF THE NEW MEN (Formerly Newmen #1-21)
Maximum Press: No. 22, Nov, 1996; No. 23, March, 1997 ($2.50)
22,23-Sprouse-c/a 2.50

ADVENTURES OF THE OUTSIDERS, THE (Formerly Batman & The Outsiders; also see The Outsiders)
DC Comics: No. 33, May, 1986 - No. 46, June, 1987
33-46: 39-45-r/Outsiders #1-7 by Aparo 2.00

ADVENTURES OF THE SUPER MARIO BROTHERS (See Super Mario Bros.)
Valiant: 1990 - No. 9, Oct, 1991 ($1.50)
V2#1 3.50
2-9 2.50

ADVENTURES OF THE THING, THE (Also see The Thing)
Marvel Comics: Apr, 1992 - No. 4, July, 1992, ($1.25, limited series)
1-4: 1-r/Marvel Two-In-One #50 by Byrne; Kieth-c. 2-4-r/Marvel Two-In-One #80,51 & 77; 2-Ghost Rider-c/story. 3-Miller-r 2.00

ADVENTURES OF THE X-MEN, THE (TV cartoon)
Marvel Comics: Apr, 1996 - No. 12, Mar, 1997 (99¢)
1-12: Based on television show. 2.00

ADVENTURES OF TINKER BELL (See Tinker Bell, 4-Color No. 896 & 982)

ADVENTURES OF TOM SAWYER (See Dell Junior Treasury No. 10)

ADVENTURES OF YOUNG DR. MASTERS, THE
Archie Comics (Radio Comics): Aug, 1964 - No. 2, Nov, 1964
1 2.25 6.75 18.00
2 1.50 4.50 12.00

ADVENTURES ON OTHER WORLDS (See Showcase #17 & 18)

ADVENTURES ON THE PLANET OF THE APES
Marvel Comics Group: Oct, 1975 - No. 11, Dec, 1976
1-Planet of the Apes-r in color; Starlin-c 1.50 4.50 12.00
2-5, 6-11 1.00 2.80 7.00
5-7-(30¢-c variants, limited distribution) 2.80 8.40 28.00
NOTE: ***Alcala** a-6-11r. **Buckler** c-2p. **Nasser** c-7. **Starlin** c-6. **Tuska** a-1-5r.*

AFRICA
Magazine Enterprises: 1955
1(A-1#137)-Cave Girl, Thun'da; Powell-c/a(4) 22.00 66.00 155.00

GD2.0 FN6.0 NM9.4

AFRICAN LION (Disney movie)
Dell Publishing Co.: Nov, 1955
Four Color #665 4.50 13.50 50.00

AFTER DARK
Sterling Comics: No. 6, May, 1955 - No. 8, Sept, 1955
6-8-Sekowsky-a in all 8.35 25.00 50.00

AGAINST BLACKSHARD 3-D (Also see SoulQuest)
Sirius Comics: August, 1986 ($2.25)
1 2.25

AGENT LIBERTY SPECIAL (See Superman, 2nd Series)
DC Comics: 1992 ($2.00, 52 pgs, one-shot)
1-1st solo adventure; Guice-c/a(i) 2.00

AGENT THREE-ZERO
Galaxinovels, Inc.: Sept, 1993 ($3.95, 52 pgs.)
1-Polybagged with card & mini-poster; Platt-c/a(1st work) 4.00

AGENT THREE–ZERO: THE BLUE SULTANS QUEST/ BLUE SULTAN–GALAXI FACT FILES
Galaxi Novels: 1994 ($2.95, color w/text-no comics, limited series)
1-($2.95)-Flip book w/Blue Sultan 3.00
1-($3.95)-Polybagged w/trading card; flip book w/Blue Sultan 4.00
1-($5.95)-Platinum embossed edition; flip book w/ Blue Sultan 6.00

AGENTS OF LAW (Also see Comic's Greatest World)
Dark Horse Comics: Mar, 1995 - No.6, Sept, 1995 ($2.50)
1-6: 5-Predator app. 6-Predator app.; death of Law 2.50

AGE OF APOCALYPSE: THE CHOSEN
Marvel Comics: Apr, 1995 ($2.50, one-shot)
1-Wraparound-c 2.50

AGE OF BRONZE
Image Comics: Nov, 1998 - Present ($2.95, B&W, limited series)
1-5-Eric Shanower-c/s/a 3.00
...Special (6/99, $2.95) Story of Agamemnon and Menelaus 3.00

AGE OF HEROES, THE
Halloween Comics/Image Comics #3 on: 1996 - Present ($2.95, B&W)
1-5: James Hudnall scripts; John Ridgway-c/a 3.00
...Special ($4.95) r/#1,2 5.00
...Special 2 ($6.95) r/#3,4 7.00
...Wex 1 ('98, $2.95) Hudnall-s/Angel Fernandez-a 3.00

AGE OF INNOCENCE: THE REBIRTH OF IRON MAN
Marvel Comics: Feb, 1996 ($2.50, one-shot)
1-New origin of Tony Stark 3.00

AGE OF REPTILES
Dark Horse Comics: Nov, 1993 - No. 4, Feb, 1994 ($2.50, limited series)
1-4: Delgado-c/a/scripts in all 2.50

AGE OF REPTILES: THE HUNT
Dark Horse Comics: May, 1996 - No. 5, Sept, 1996 ($2.95, limited series)
1-5: Delgado-c/a/scripts in all; wraparound-c 3.00

AGGIE MACK
Four Star Comics Corp./Superior Comics Ltd.: Jan, 1948 - No. 8, Aug, 1949
1-Feldstein-a, "Johnny Prep" 30.00 90.00 210.00
2,3-Kamen-c 16.00 47.00 110.00
4-Feldstein "Johnny Prep"; Kamen-c 21.00 62.00 145.00
5-8-Kamen-c/a 17.00 49.00 115.00

AGGIE MACK
Dell Publishing Co.: Apr - Jun, 1962
Four Color #1335 2.75 8.00 30.00

AIR ACE (Formerly Bill Barnes No. 1-12)

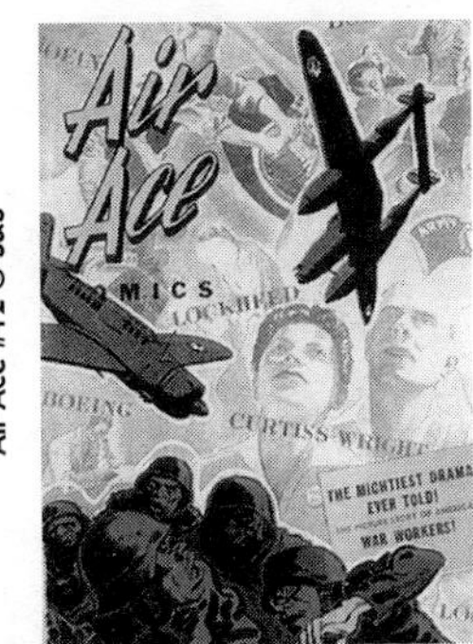

Air Ace #12 © S&S

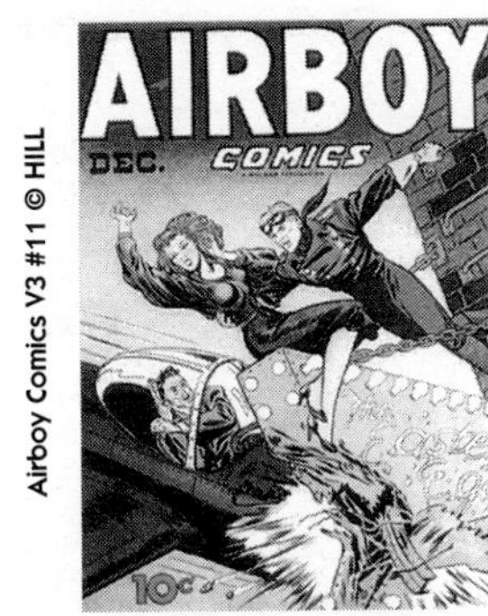

Airboy Comics V3 #11 © HILL

Alan Moore's Awesome Universe Handbook © Awesome Ent.

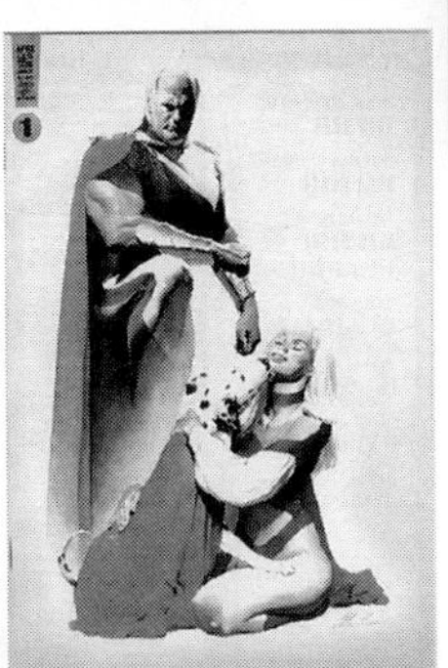

Street & Smith Publications: V2#1, Jan, 1944 - V3#8(No. 20), Feb-Mar, 1947

	GD2.0	FN6.0	NM9.4
V2#1	27.00	81.00	190.00
V2#2-Classic-c	16.00	47.00	110.00
V2#3-12: 7-Powell-a	12.00	36.00	85.00
V3#1-6	10.00	30.00	65.00
V3#7-Powell bondage-c/a; all atomic issue	20.00	60.00	140.00
V3#8 (V5#8 on-c)-Powell-c/a	11.00	33.00	75.00

AIRBOY (Also see Airmaidens, Skywolf, Target: Airboy & Valkyrie)
Eclipse Comics: July, 1986 - No. 50, Oct, 1989 (#1-8, 50¢, 20 pgs., bi-weekly; #9-on, 36pgs.; #34-on monthly)

	GD2.0	FN6.0	NM9.4
1-49: 2-1st Marisa; Skywolf gets new costume. 3-The Heap begins. 5-Valkyrie returns; Dave Stevens-c. 9-Begin $1.25-c; Skywolf begins. 11-Origin of G.A. Airboy & his plane Birdie. 28-Mr. Monster vs. The Heap. 33-Begin $1.75-c. 38-40-The Heap by Infantino. 41-r/1st app. Valkyrie from Air Fighters. 42-Begin $1.95-c. 46,47-part-r/Air Fighters. 48-Black Angel-r/A.F			2.00
50 ($4.95, 52 pgs.)-Kubert-c			5.00

NOTE: ***Evans*** c-21. ***Gulacy*** c-7, 20. ***Spiegle*** a-34, 35, 37. ***Ken Steacy*** painted c-17, 33.

AIRBOY COMICS (Air Fighters Comics No. 1-22)
Hillman Periodicals: V2#11, Dec, 1945 - V10#4, May, 1953 (No V3#3)

	GD2.0	FN6.0	NM9.4
V2#11	66.00	198.00	525.00
12-Valkyrie app.	43.00	129.00	340.00
V3#1,2(no #3)	37.00	111.00	260.00
4-The Heap app. in Skywolf	33.00	100.00	230.00
5-8,10,11: 6-Valkyrie app.	27.00	81.00	190.00
9-Origin The Heap	33.00	100.00	230.00
12-Skywolf & Airboy x-over; Valkyrie app.	37.00	111.00	260.00
V4#1-Iron Lady app.	31.00	93.00	220.00
2,3,12: 2-Rackman begins	22.00	66.00	155.00
4-Simon & Kirby-c	25.00	75.00	175.00
5-11-All S&K-a	24.00	72.00	165.00
V5#1-4,6-11: 4-Infantino Heap. 10-Origin The Heap	16.00	48.00	110.00
5-Skull-c.	18.00	54.00	125.00
12-Krigstein-a(p)	19.00	57.00	130.00
V6#1-3,5-12: 6,8-Origin The Heap	16.00	48.00	110.00
4-Origin retold	20.00	60.00	140.00
V7#1-12: 7,8,10-Origin The Heap	16.00	48.00	110.00
V8#1-3,5-12	14.00	42.00	100.00
4-Krigstein-a	15.00	45.00	105.00
V9#1-4,6-12: 2-Valkyrie app. 7-One pg. Frazetta ad	11.50	34.00	80.00
5(#100)	13.00	39.00	90.00
V10#1-4	11.00	33.00	75.00

NOTE: ***Barry*** *a-V2#3, 7.* ***Bolle*** *a-V4#12.* ***McWilliams*** *a-V3#7, 9.* ***Powell*** *a-V7#2, 3, V8#1, 6.* ***Starr*** *a-V5#1, 12.* ***Dick Wood*** *a-V4#12. Bondage-c V5#8.*

AIRBOY MEETS THE PROWLER
Eclipse Comics: Aug, 1987 ($1.95, one-shot)

	GD2.0	FN6.0	NM9.4
1-John Snyder, III-c/a			2.00

AIRBOY-MR. MONSTER SPECIAL
Eclipse Comics: Aug, 1987 ($1.75, one-shot)

	GD2.0	FN6.0	NM9.4
1			2.00

AIRBOY VERSUS THE AIR MAIDENS
Eclipse Comics: July, 1988 ($1.95)

	GD2.0	FN6.0	NM9.4
1			2.00

AIR FIGHTERS CLASSICS
Eclipse Comics: Nov, 1987 - No. 6, May, 1989 ($3.95, 68 pgs., B&W)

	GD2.0	FN6.0	NM9.4
1-6: Reprints G.A. Air Fighters #2-7. 1-Origin Airboy			4.00

AIR FIGHTERS COMICS (Airboy Comics #23 (V2#11) on)
Hillman Periodicals: Nov, 1941; No. 2, Nov, 1942 - V2#10, Fall, 1945

	GD2.0	FN6.0	NM9.4
V1#1-(Produced by Funnies, Inc.); Black Commander only app.	200.00	600.00	1600.00
2(11/42)-(Produced by Quality artists & Biro for Hillman); Origin & 1st app. Airboy & Iron Ace; Black Angel (1st app.), Flying Dutchman & Skywolf (1st app.) begin; Fuje-a; Biro-c/a	289.00	867.00	2600.00
3-Origin/1st app. The Heap; origin Skywolf; 2nd Airboy app./c	150.00	450.00	1200.00
4	105.00	315.00	840.00
5,6	80.00	240.00	640.00
7-12	67.00	200.00	540.00
V2#1,3-9: 5-Flag-c; Fuje-a. 7-Valkyrie app.	60.00	180.00	480.00
2-Skywolf by Giunta; Flying Dutchman by Fuje; 1st meeting Valkyrie & Airboy (she worked for the Nazis in beginning); 1st app. Valkyrie (11/43)	94.00	282.00	750.00
10-Origin The Heap & Skywolf	67.00	200.00	540.00

NOTE: ***Fuje*** *a-V1#2, 5, 7, V2#2, 3, 5, 7-9.* ***Giunta*** *a-V2#2, 3, 7, 9.*

AIRFIGHTERS MEET SGT. STRIKE SPECIAL, THE
Eclipse Comics: Jan, 1988 ($1.95, one-shot, stiff-c)

	GD2.0	FN6.0	NM9.4
1-Airboy, Valkyrie, Skywolf app.			2.00

AIR FORCES (See American Air Forces)

AIRMAIDENS SPECIAL
Eclipse Comics: August, 1987 ($1.75, one-shot, Baxter paper)

	GD2.0	FN6.0	NM9.4
1-Marisa becomes La Lupina (origin)			2.00

AIR RAIDERS
Marvel Comics (Star Comics)/Marvel #3 on: Nov, 1987- No. 5, Mar, 1988 ($1.00)

	GD2.0	FN6.0	NM9.4
1-5			2.00

AIRTIGHT GARAGE, THE
Marvel Comics (Epic Comics): July, 1993 - No. 4, Oct, 1993 ($2.50, limited series)

	GD2.0	FN6.0	NM9.4
1-4: Moebius-c/a/scripts			2.50

AIR WAR STORIES
Dell Publishing Co.: Sept-Nov, 1964 - No. 8, Aug, 1966

	GD2.0	FN6.0	NM9.4
1-Painted-c; Glanzman-c/a begins	2.80	8.40	28.00
2-8: 2-Painted-c (all painted?)	2.25	6.75	18.00

AKIKO
Sirius: Mar, 1996 - Present ($2.50, B&W)

	GD2.0	FN6.0	NM9.4
1-Crilley-c/a/scripts in all			5.00
2			4.00
3-10			3.00
11-24 ($2.50), 25-($2.95, 32 pgs.)-w/Asala back-up pages			3.00
26-34			2.50
TPB Volume 1 ('97, $14.95) r/#1-7			15.00
TPB Volume 2,3 ('98, '99, $11.95) 2-r/#8-13. 3- r/#14-18			12.00

AKIKO ON THE PLANET SMOO
Sirius: Dec, 1995 ($3.95, B&W)

	GD2.0	FN6.0	NM9.4
V1#1-($3.95)-Crilley-c/a/scripts; gatefold-c	1.00	2.80	7.00
Ashcan ('95, mail offer)			2.00
Hardcover V1#1 (12/95, $19.95, B&W, 40 pgs.)			20.00

AKIRA
Marvel Comics (Epic Comics): Sept, 1988 - No. 38, Dec, 1995 ($3.50/$3.95/$6.95, deluxe, 68 pgs.)

	GD2.0	FN6.0	NM9.4
1	2.50	7.50	20.00
1,2-2nd printings (1989, $3.95)			4.00
2-5	1.10	3.30	9.00
6-16	1.00	3.00	7.00
17-33: 17-$3.95-c begins		2.40	6.00
34-38: 34-(1994)-$6.95-c begins. 35-37: 35-(1995). 37-Texieira back-up, Gibbons, Williams pin-ups. 38-Moebius, Allred, Pratt, Toth, Romita, Van Fleet, O'Neill, Madureira pin-ups.	1.00	3.00	8.00

ALADDIN & HIS WONDERFUL LAMP (See Dell Jr Treasury #2)

ALAN LADD (See The Adventures of...)

ALAN MOORE'S AWESOME UNIVERSE HANDBOOK
Awesome Entertainment: Apr, 1999 - Present ($2.95, B&W)

	GD2.0	FN6.0	NM9.4
1-Alan Moore-text/ Alex Ross-sketch pages and 2 covers			3.00

ALAN MOORE'S SONGBOOK
Caliber Comics: 1998 ($5.95, B&W)

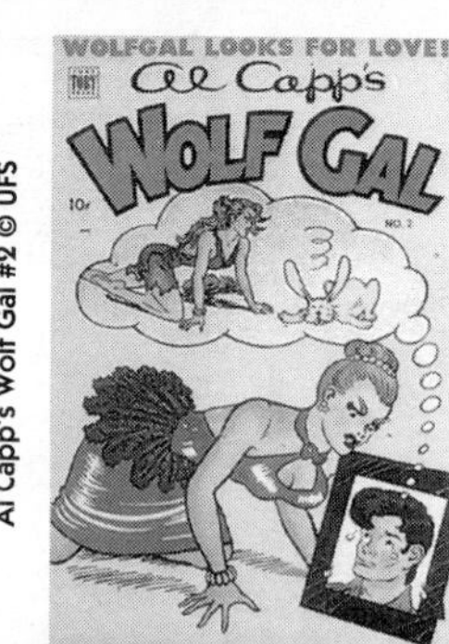

Al Capp's Wolf Gal #2 © UFS

Alarming Tales #5 © HARV

Alien Legion #2 © MAR

1-Alan Moore song lyrics w/illust. by various 6.00

ALARMING ADVENTURES
Harvey Publications: Oct, 1962 - No. 3, Feb, 1963

1-Crandall/Williamson-a 7.00 21.00 70.00
2-Williamson/Crandall-a 4.50 13.50 45.00
3 4.00 12.00 40.00

NOTE: ***Bailey** a-1, 3. **Crandall** a-1p, 2i. **Powell** a-2(2). **Severin** c-1-3. **Torres** a-2? **Tuska** a-1. **Williamson** a-1i, 2p.*

ALARMING TALES
Harvey Publications (Western Tales): Sept, 1957 - No. 6, Nov, 1958

1-Kirby-c/a(4); Kamandi prototype story by Kirby 21.00 64.00 150.00
2-Kirby-a(4) 17.00 51.00 120.00
3,4-Kirby-a. 4-Powell, Wildey-a 11.50 34.00 80.00
5-Kirby/Williamson-a; Wildey-a; Severin-c 13.00 39.00 90.00
6-Williamson-a?; Severin-c 11.00 33.00 75.00

ALBEDO
Thoughts And Images: Apr, 1985 - No. 14, Spring, 1989 (B&W)

0-Yellow cover; 50 copies 3.50 10.50 35.00
0-White cover, 450 copies 2.25 6.75 18.00
0-Blue, 1st printing, 500 copies 2.25 6.75 18.00
0-Blue, 2nd printing, 1000 copies 1.25 3.75 10.00
0-3rd & 4th printing 4.00
1-Dark red; 1st app. Usagi Yojimbo 1.25 3.75 10.00
1-Bright red 2.40 6.00
2 4.00
3-14, Vol. 2; 1-10 2.50

ALBEDO ANTHROPOMORPHICS
Antarctic Press: Spring, 1994

V3#1-Steve Gallacci-c/a 2.00

ALBERTO (See The Crusaders)

ALBERT THE ALLIGATOR & POGO POSSUM (See Pogo Possum)

ALBUM OF CRIME (See Fox Giants)

ALBUM OF LOVE (See Fox Giants)

AL CAPP'S DOGPATCH (Also see Mammy Yokum)
Toby Press: No. 71, June, 1949 - No. 4, Dec, 1949

71(#1)-Reprints from Tip Top #112-114 24.00 71.00 165.00
2-4: 4-Reprints from Li'l Abner #73 16.00 47.00 110.00

AL CAPP'S SHMOO (Also see Oxydol-Dreft & Washable Jones & Shmoo)
Toby Press: July, 1949 - No. 5, Apr, 1950 (None by Al Capp)

1 39.00 116.00 270.00
2-5: 3-Sci-fi trip to moon. 4-X-Mas-c; origin/1st app. Super-Shmoo
26.00 79.00 185.00

AL CAPP'S WOLF GAL
Toby Press: 1951 - No. 2, 1952

1,2-Edited-r from Li'l Abner #63,64 34.00 101.00 235.00

ALEXANDER THE GREAT (Movie)
Dell Publishing Co.: No. 688, May, 1956

Four Color 688-Buscema-a; photo-c 6.00 19.00 68.00

ALF (TV) (See Star Comics Digest)
Marvel Comics: Mar, 1988 - No. 50, Feb, 1992 ($1.00)

1-(Giant) Photo-c 4.00
2-49: 22-X-Men parody 2.50
50-($1.75, 52 pgs.)-Final issue; photo-c 3.00
Annual 1-3: 2-Sienkiewicz-c 3.00
...Comics Digest 1 (1988)-Reprints Alf #1,2 1.00 3.00 8.00
Holiday Special 1,2 ('88, Wint. '89, 68 pgs.) 3.00
Spring Special 1 (Spr/89, $1.75, 68 pgs.) 3.00

ALFRED HARVEY'S BLACK CAT
Lorne-Harvey Productions: 1995 ($3.50, B&W/color)

1-Origin by Mark Evanier & Murphy Anderson; contains history of Alfred Harvey & Harvey Publications; 5 pg. B&W Sad Sack story; Hildebrandts-c 4.00

ALGIE
Timor Publ. Co.: Dec, 1953 - No. 3, 1954

1-Teenage 4.15 12.50 25.00
1-Misprint exists w/Secret Mysteries #19 inside 5.00 15.00 30.00
2,3 3.60 9.00 18.00
Accepted Reprint #2(nd) 2.50 4.50 12.00
Super Reprint #15 1.25 3.75 10.00

ALIAS:
Now Comics: July, 1990 - No. 5, Nov, 1990 ($1.75)

1-5: 1-Sienkiewicz-c 2.00

ALICE (New Adventures in Wonderland)
Ziff-Davis Publ. Co.: No. 10, 7-8/51 - No. 2, 11-12/51

10-Painted-c; Berg-a 21.00 62.00 145.00
11-Dave Berg-a 11.50 34.00 80.00
2-Dave Berg-a 10.00 30.00 70.00

ALICE AT MONKEY ISLAND (See The Adventures of Alice)
Pentagon Publ. Co. (Civil Service): No. 3, 1946

3 8.00 24.00 48.00

ALICE IN WONDERLAND (Disney; see Advs. of Alice, Dell Jr. Treasury #1, The Dreamery, Movie Comics,Walt Disney Showcase #22, and World's Greatest Stories)
Dell Publishing Co.: No. 24, 1940; No. 331, 1951; No. 341, July, 1951

Single Series 24 (#1)(1940) 40.00 120.00 320.00
Four Color 331, 341-"Unbirthday Party w/... 14.00 41.00 150.00

ALIEN ENCOUNTERS (Replaces Alien Worlds)
Eclipse Comics: June, 1985 - No. 14, Aug, 1987 ($1.75, Baxter paper, mature)

1-14: Nudity, strong language in all. 9-Snyder-a 3.00

ALIEN LEGION (See Epic & Marvel Graphic Novel #25)
Marvel Comics (Epic Comics): 4/84 - No. 20, 9/87

nn-With bound-in trading card 4.00
2-20: 2-$1.50-c 3.00

ALIEN LEGION (2nd Series): **Marvel Comics (Epic Comics):** 8/1987 (indicia) (10/87 on-c) - No. 18, 8/90 V2#1-18 2.00

ALIEN LEGION: (Series of titles; all Marvel/Epic Comics)
--BINARY DEEP, 1993 ($3.50, one-shot, 52 pgs.), nn-With bound-in trading card 3.50
--JUGGER GRIMROD, 8/92 ($5.95, one-shot, 52 pgs.) Book 1 2.40 6.00
--ONE PLANET AT A TIME, 5/93 - Book 3, 7/93 ($4.95, squarebound, 52 pgs.)
Book 1-3: Hoang Nguyen-a 5.00
--ON THE EDGE (The... #2 & 3), 11/90 - No. 3, 1/91 ($4.50, 52 pgs.)
1-3 4.50
--TENANTS OF HELL, '91 - No. 2, '1 ($4.50, squarebound, 52 pgs.)
Book 1,2-Stroman-c/a(p) 4.50

ALIEN NATION (Movie)
DC Comics: Dec, 1988 ($2.50; 68 pgs.)

1-Adaptation of film; painted-c 2.50

ALIEN RESURRECTION (Movie)
Dark Horse Comics: Oct, 1997 - No. 2, Nov, 1997 ($2.50; limited series)

1,2-Adaptation of film; Dave McKean-c 2.50

ALIENS, THE (Captain Johner and...)(Also see Magnus Robot Fighter...)
Gold Key: Sept-Dec, 1967; No. 2, May, 1982

1-Reprints from Magnus #1,3,4,6-10; Russ Manning-a in all
2.50 7.50 22.00
2-Same contents as #1 5.50

ALIENS (Movie) (See Alien: The Illustrated..., Dark Horse Comics & Dark Horse Presents #24)

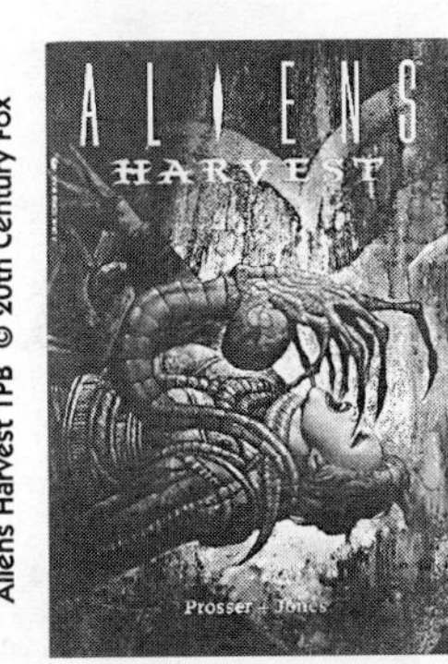

Aliens Harvest TPB © 20th Century Fox

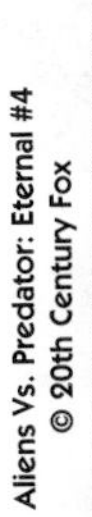
Aliens Vs. Predator: Eternal #4 © 20th Century Fox

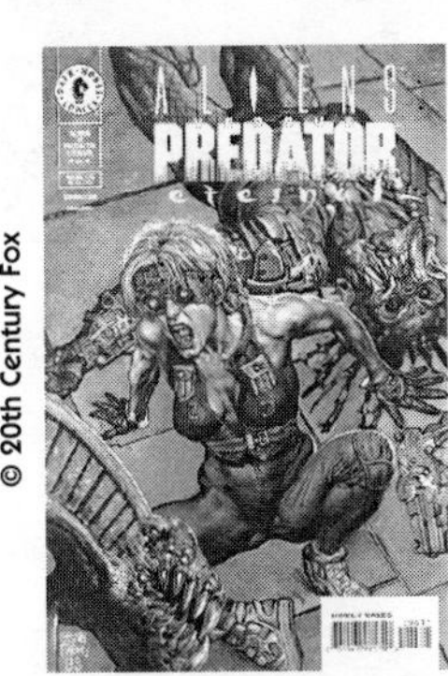

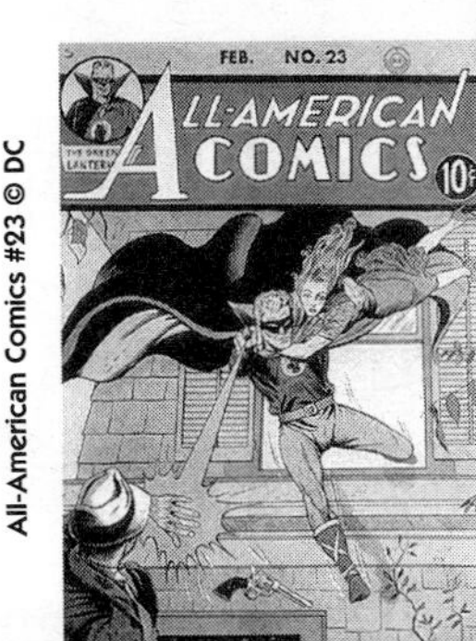

All-American Comics #23 © DC

GD2.0 FN6.0 NM9.4

Dark Horse Comics: May, 1988 - No. 6, July, 1989 ($1.95, B&W, limited series)
1-Based on movie sequel;1st app. Aliens in comics 1.75 5.25 14.00
1-2nd - 6th printings; 4th w/new inside front-c 2.00
2 1.00 2.80 7.00
2-2nd & 3rd printing, 3-6-2nd printings 2.00
3 5.00
4-6 3.50
Mini Comic #1 (2/89, 4x6")-Was included with Aliens Portfolio 4.00
Collection 1 ($10.95,)-r/#1-6 plus Dark Horse Presents #24 plus new-a 12.00
Collection 1-2nd printing (1991, $11.95)-On higher quality paper than 1st print; Dorman painted-c 12.00
Hardcover ('90, $24.95, B&W)-r/1-6, DHP #24 25.00
Platinum Edition - (See Dark Horse Presents: Aliens Platinum Edition) -

ALIENS
Dark Horse Comics: V2#1, Aug, 1989 - No. 4, 1990 ($2.25, limited series)
V2#1-Painted art by Denis Beauvais 4.50
1-2nd printing (1990), 2-4 2.25

ALIENS: (Series of titles, all Dark Horse)
--ALCHEMY, 10/97 - No. 3, 11/97 ($2.95),1-3-Corben-c/a, Arcudi-s 3.00
--APOCALYPSE - THE DESTROYING ANGELS, 1/99 - No. 4, 4/99 ($2.95)
1-4-Doug Wheatly-a/Schultz-s 3.00
--BERSERKERS, 1/95 - No. 4, 4/95 ($2.50) 1-4 2.50
--COLONIAL MARINES, 1/93 - No. 10, 7/94 ($2.50) 1-10 2.50
--EARTH ANGEL. 8/94 ($2.95) 1-Byrne-a/story; wraparound-c 3.00
--EARTH WAR, 6/90 - No. 4, 10/90 ($2.50) 1-All have Sam Kieth-a & Bolton painted-c 4.50
1-2nd printing, 3,4 2.50
2 3.50
--GENOCIDE, 11/91 - No. 4, 2/92 ($2.50) 1-4-Arthur Suydam painted-c. 4-Wraparound-c, poster 2.50
--GLASS CORRIDOR, 6/98 ($2.95) 1-David Lloyd-s/a 3.00
--HARVEST (See Aliens: Hive)
--HAVOC, 6/97 - No. 2, 7/97 ($2.95) 1,2: Schultz-s, Kent Williams-c, 40 artists including Art Adams, Kelley Jones, Duncan Fegredo, Kevin Nowlan 3.00
--HIVE, 2/92 - No. 4,5/92 ($2.50) 1-4: Kelley Jones-c/a in all 3.00
...Harvest TPB ('98, $16.95) r/series; Bolton-c 17.00
--KIDNAPPED, 12/97 - No. 3, 2/98 ($2.50) 1-3 2.50
--LABYRINTH, 9/93 - No. 4, 1/94 ($2.50)1-4: 1-Painted-c 2.50
--LOVESICK, 12/96 ($2.95) 1 3.00
--MONDO HEAT, 2/96 ($2.50) nn-Sequel to Mondo Pest 2.50
--MONDO PEST, 4/95 ($2.95, 44 pgs.)nn-r/Dark Horse Comics #22-24 3.00
--MUSIC OF THE SPEARS, 1/94 - No. 4, 4/94 ($2.50) 1-4 2.50
--PIG, 3/97 ($2.95)1 3.00
--PREDATOR: THE DEADLIEST OF SPECIES, 7/93 - No. 12,8/95 ($2.50)
1-Bolton painted-c; Guice-a(p) 4.50
1-Embossed foil platinum edition 10.00
2-12: Bolton painted-c. 2,3-Guice-a(p) 3.00
--PURGE, 8/97 ($2.95) nn-Hester-a 3.00
--ROGUE, 4/993 - No. 4, 7/93 ($2.50)1-4: Painted-c 2.50
--SACRIFICE, 5/93 ($4.95, 52 pgs.) nn-P. Milligan scripts; painted-c/a 5.00
--SALVATION, 11/93 ($4.95, 52 pgs.)nn-Mignola-c/a(p); Gibbons script 5.00
--SPECIAL, 6/97 ($2.50) 1 2.50
--STALKER, 6/98 ($2.50)1-David Wenzel-s/a 2.50
--STRONGHOLD, 5/94 - No. 4, 9/94 ($2.50) 1-4 2.50
--SURVIVAL, 2/98 - No. 3, 4/98 ($2.95)1-3-Tony Harris-c 3.00

ALIENS VS. PREDATOR (See Dark Horse Presents #36)
Dark Horse Comics: June, 1990 - No. 4, Dec, 1990 ($2.50, limited series)
1-Painted-c 1.00 3.00 7.00
1-2nd printing 3.00
0-(7/90, $1.95, B&W)-r/Dark Horse Pres. #34-36 1.10 3.30 9.00
2,3 5.00
4-Dave Dorman painted-c 4.00
Annual (7/99, $4.95) Jae Lee-c 5.00
--VS. PREDATOR: BOOTY, 1/96 ($2.50) nn-painted-c 2.50
--VS. PREDATOR: DUEL, 3/95 - No. 2, 4/95 ($2.50) 1,2 2.50
--VS. PREDATOR: ETERNAL, 6/98 - No. 4, 9/98 ($2.50)1-4: Edginton-s/Maleev-a; Fabry-c 2.50
--VS. PREDATOR: WAR, No. 0, 5/95 - No. 4, 8/95 ($2.50) 0-4: Corben painted-c 2.50
--WRAITH, 7/98 ($2.95)1-Jay Stephens-s 3.00

ALIEN TERROR (See 3-D Alien Terror)

ALIEN: THE ILLUSTRATED STORY (Also see Aliens)
Heavy Metal Books: 1980 ($3.95, soft-c, 8x11")
nn-Movie adaptation; Simonson-a 1.85 5.50 15.00

ALIEN 3 (Movie)
Dark Horse Comics: June, 1992 - No. 3, July, 1992 ($2.50, limited series)
1-3: Adapts 3rd movie; Suydam painted-c 2.50

ALIEN WORLDS (Also see Eclipse Graphic Album #22)
Pacific Comics/Eclipse: Dec, 1982 - No. 9, Jan, 1985
1,2,4: 2,4-Dave Stevens-c/a 5.00
3,5-9: 2.50
3-D No. 1-Art Adams 1st published art 5.00

ALISTER THE SLAYER
Midnight Press: Oct, 1995 ($2.50)
1-Boris-c 2.50

ALL-AMERICAN COMICS (...Western #103-126, ...Men of War #127 on; also see The Big All-American Comic Book)
All-American/National Periodical Publ.: April, 1939 - No. 102, Oct, 1948
1-Hop Harrigan (1st app.), Scribbly by Mayer (1st DC app.), Toonerville Folks, Ben Webster, Spot Savage, Mutt & Jeff, Red White & Blue (1st app.), Adv. in the Unknown, Tippie, Reg'lar Fellers, Skippy, Bobby Thatcher, Mystery Men of Mars, Daiseybelle, Wiley of West Point begin 832.00 2500.00 5800.00
2-Ripley's Believe It or Not begins, ends #24 232.00 700.00 1600.00
3-5: 5-The American Way begins, ends #10 168.00 505.00 1180.00
6,7: 6-Last Spot Savage; Popsicle Pete begins, ends #26, 28. 7-Last Bobby Thatcher 140.00 425.00 975.00
8-The Ultra Man begins & 1st-c app. 210.00 625.00 1400.00
9,10: 10-X-Mas-c 130.00 400.00 900.00
11-15: 11-Ultra Man-c. 12-Last Toonerville Folks. 15-Last Tippie & Reg'lar Fellars; Ultra Man-c 125.00 375.00 850.00

GD2.0 FN6.0 VF8.0 NM9.4

16-(Rare)-Origin/1st app. Green Lantern by Sheldon Moldoff (c/a)(7/40) & begin series; appears in costume on-c & only one panel inside; created by Martin Nodell. Inspired in 1940 by a switchman's green lantern that would give trains the go ahead to proceed.
7000.00 21,000.00 42,000.00 70,000.00

GD2.0 FN6.0 NM9.4

17-2nd Green Lantern 1090.00 3270.00 12,500.00
18-N.Y. World's Fair-c/story 800.00 2400.00 8,000.00

GD2.0 FN6.0 VF8.0 NM9.4

19-Origin/1st app. The Atom (10/40); last Ultra Man
1090.00 3270.00 6540.00 12,500.00

GD2.0 FN6.0 NM9.4

20-Atom dons costume; Ma Hunkle becomes Red Tornado (1st app.)(1st DC costumed heroine, before Wonder Woman, 11/40); Rescue on Mars begins, ends #25; 1 pg. origin Green Lantern 400.00 1200.00 3600.00
21-23: 21-Last Wiley of West Point & Skippy. 23-Last Daiseybelle; 3 Idiots begin, end #82 250.00 750.00 2000.00
24-Sisty & Dinky become the Cyclone Kids; Ben Webster ends; origin Dr. Mid-

All-American Comics #102 © DC

All-American Men of War #3 © DC

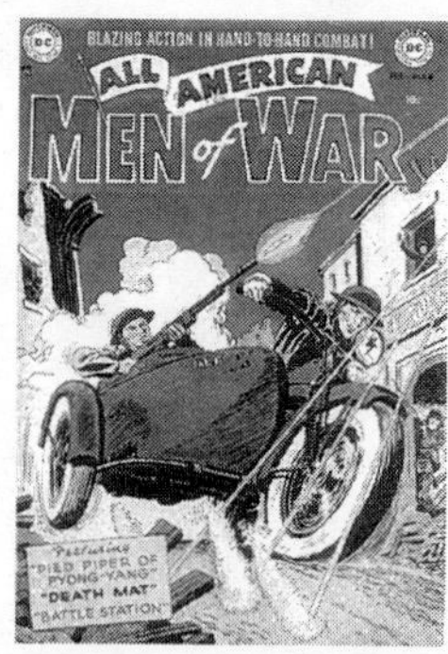

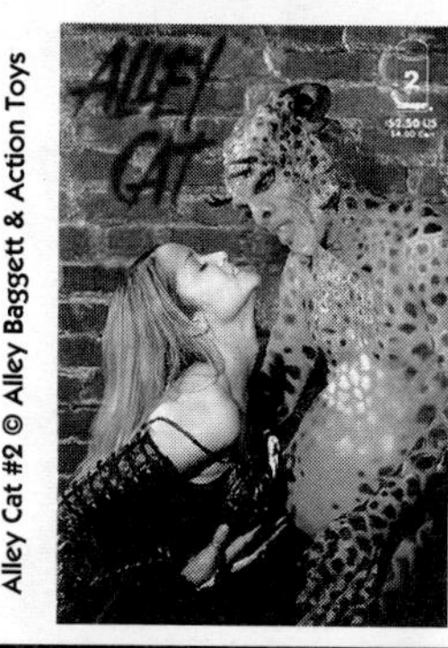

Alley Cat #2 © Alley Baggett & Action Toys

GD2.0 FN6.0 NM9.4

Nite & Sargon, The Sorcerer in text with app. 294.00 882.00 2600.00

GD2.0 FN6.0 VF8.0 NM9.4

25-Origin & 1st story app. Dr. Mid-Nite by Stan Asch; Hop Harrigan becomes Guardian Angel; last Adventure in the Unknown 800.00 2400.00 4800.00 8000.00

GD2.0 FN6.0 NM9.4

26-Origin/1st story app. Sargon, the Sorcerer 333.00 1000.00 3000.00
27: #27-32 are misnumbered in indicia with correct No. appearing on-c. Intro. Doiby Dickles, Green Lantern's sidekick 355.00 1065.00 3200.00
28-Hop Harrigan gives up costumed i.d. 156.00 468.00 1250.00
29,30 156.00 468.00 1250.00
31-40: 35-Doiby learns Green Lantern's i.d. 116.00 348.00 925.00
41-50: 50-Sargon ends 97.00 291.00 780.00
51-60: 59-Scribbly & the Red Tornado ends 84.00 252.00 670.00
61-Origin/1st app. Solomon Grundy (11/44) 422.00 1266.00 3800.00
62-70: 70-Kubert Sargon; intro Sargon's helper, Maximillian O'Leary 78.00 234.00 625.00
71-88: 71-Last Red White & Blue. 72-Black Pirate begins (not in #74-82); last Atom. 73-Winky, Blinky & Noddy begins, ends #82. 79,83-Mutt & Jeff-c. 67.00 201.00 540.00
89-Origin & 1st app. Harlequin 97.00 291.00 780.00
90-99: 90-Origin/1st app. Icicle. 99-Last Hop Harrigan 87.00 261.00 700.00
100-1st app. Johnny Thunder by Alex Toth (8/48); western theme begins (Scarce) 181.00 543.00 1450.00
101-Last Mutt & Jeff (Scarce) 122.00 366.00 980.00
102-Last Green Lantern, Black Pirate & Dr. Mid-Nite (Scarce) 244.00 732.00 1950.00

NOTE: *No Atom in 47, 62-69.* **Kinstler** *Black Pirate-89.* **Stan Aschmeier** *a (Dr. Mid-Nite) 25-84; c-7.* **Mayer** *c-1, 2(part), 6, 10.* **Moldoff** *c-16-23.* **Nodell** *c-31.* **Paul Reinman** *a (Green Lantern)-53-55p, 56-84, 87; (Black Pirate)-83-88, 90; c-52, 55-76, 78, 80, 81, 87.* **Toth** *a-88, 92, 96, 98-102; c(p)-92, 96-102. Scribbly by* **Mayer** *in #1-59. Ultra Man by* **Mayer** *in #8-19.*

ALL-AMERICAN COMICS (Also see All Star Comics 1999 crossover titles)
DC Comics: May, 1999 ($1.99, one-shot)

1-Golden Age Green Lantern and Johnny Thunder; Barreto-a 2.00

ALL-AMERICAN MEN OF WAR (Previously All-American Western)
National Periodical Publ.: No. 127, Aug-Sept, 1952 - No. 117, Sept-Oct, 1966

127 (#1, 1952) 72.00 216.00 865.00
128 (1952) 47.00 141.00 560.00
2(12-1/'52-53)-5 41.00 123.00 455.00
6-Devil Dog story; Ghost Squadron story 31.00 93.00 310.00
7-10: 8-Sgt. Storm Cloud-s 31.00 93.00 310.00
11-18: 17-1st Frogman-s in this title. 18-Last precode (2/55) 29.00 87.00 290.00
19-27: 21-Easy Co. prototype 20.00 60.00 200.00
28 (12/55)-1st Sgt. Rock prototype; Kubert-a 25.00 75.00 250.00
29,30,32-Wood-a 21.00 63.00 210.00
31,33-38,40: 34-Gunner prototype-s. 35-Greytone-c. 36-Little Sure Shot prototype-s. 38-1st S.A. issue 16.50 50.00 165.00
39 (11/56)-2nd Sgt. Rock prototype; 1st Easy Co.? 22.00 66.00 220.00
41-50: 42-46-Tankbusters-c/s. 42-Pre-Sgt. Rock Easy Co. c/s. 48-Easy Co.-c/s w/Nick app.; Kubert-a 13.50 41.00 135.00
51-56,58-62,65,66: 61-Gunner-c/s 10.00 30.00 100.00
57(5/58),63,64 -Pre-Sgt. Rock Easy Co. c/s 13.00 39.00 130.00
67-1st Gunner & Sarge by Andru & Esposito 28.00 84.00 280.00
68,69: 68-2nd app. Gunner & Sarge. 69-1st Tank Killer-c/s 13.00 39.00 130.00
70 10.00 30.00 100.00
71-80: 71,72,76-Tank Killer-c/s. 74-Minute Commandos-c/s 7.00 21.00 70.00
81,84-88: 88-Last 10¢ issue 6.50 19.50 65.00
82-Johnny Cloud begins(1st app.), ends #117 11.50 34.00 115.00
83-2nd Johnny Cloud 7.00 21.00 70.00
89-100: 89-Battle Aces of 3 Wars begins, ends #98 4.20 12.60 42.00
101-111,113-117: 111,114,115-Johnny Cloud. 117-Johnny Cloud-c & 3-part story 3.20 9.60 32.00

GD2.0 FN6.0 NM9.4

112-Balloon Buster series begins, ends #114,116 3.50 10.50 35.00

NOTE: *Frogman stories in 17, 38, 44, 45, 50, 51, 53, 55-58, 63, 65, 66, 72, 76, 77.* **Colan** *a-112.* **Drucker** *a-47, 58, 61, 63, 65, 69, 71, 74, 77.* **Grandenetti** *c(p)-127, 128, 2-17(most).* **Heath** *a-14, 27, 32, 38, 41, 45, 47, 50, 51, 55-58, 62, 64, 71, 75, 76, 78, 95, 111-117; c-85, 91, 94-96, 100, 101, 110-112, others?* **Infantino** *a-8.* **Kirby** *a-29.* **Krigstein** *a-128('52), 2, 3, 5.* **Kubert** *a-22, 24, 28, 29, 33, 34, 36, 38, 39, 41-43, 47-50, 52, 53, 55, 56, 59, 60, 63-65, 69, 71-73, 76, 102, 103, 105, 106, 108, 114; c-41, 44, 52, 54, 55, 58, 64, 69, 76, 77, 79, 102-106, 108, 113-117, others? Tank Killer in 69, 71, 76 by* **Kubert. P. Reinman** *c-55, 57, 61, 62, 71, 72, 74-76, 80.* **J. Severin** *a-58.*

ALL-AMERICAN SPORTS
Charlton Comics: Oct, 1967

1 2.50 7.50 20.00

ALL-AMERICAN WESTERN (Formerly All-American Comics; Becomes All-American Men of War)
National Periodical Publications: No. 103, Nov, 1948 - No. 126, June-July, 1952 (103-121: 52 pgs.)

103-Johnny Thunder & his horse Black Lightning continues by Toth, ends #126; Foley of The Fighting 5th, Minstrel Maverick, & Overland Coach begin; Captain Tootsie by Beck; mentioned in Love and Death 47.00 141.00 375.00
104-Kubert-a 37.00 111.00 260.00
105,107-Kubert-a 31.00 93.00 215.00
106,108-110,112: 112-Kurtzman's "Pot-Shot Pete" (1 pg.) 23.00 69.00 160.00
111,114-116-Kubert-a 25.00 75.00 175.00
113-Intro. Swift Deer, J. Thunder's new sidekick (4-5/50); classic Toth-c; Kubert-a 27.00 81.00 190.00
117-126: 121-Kubert-a; bondage-c 19.00 57.00 130.00

NOTE: **G. Kane** *c(p)-119, 120, 123.* **Kubert** *a-103-105, 107, 111, 112(1 pg.), 113-116, 121.* **Toth** *a 103-126; c(p)-103-116, 121, 122, 124-126. Some copies of #125 have #12 on-c.*

ALL COMICS
Chicago Nite Life News: 1945

1 12.00 36.00 85.00

ALLEGRA
Image Comics (WildStorm): Aug, 1996 - No. 4, Dec, 1996 ($2.50)

1-4 2.50

ALLEY CAT (Alley Baggett)
Image Comics: July, 1999 - Present ($2.50)

Preview Edition -Diamond Dateline supplement 8.00
Prelude 5.00
Prelude w/variant-c 8.00
1-Photo-c 2.50
1-Painted-c by Dorian 3.50
1-Another Universe Edition, 1-Wizard World Edition 7.00
2,3 2.50
Lingerie Edition (10/99, $4.95) Photos, pin-ups, cover gallery 5.00
...Vs. Lady Pendragon ('99, $3.00) Stinsman-c 3.00

ALLEY OOP (See The Comics, The Funnies, Red Ryder and Super Book #9)
Dell Publishing Co.: No. 3, 1942

Four Color 3 (#1) 47.00 141.00 525.00

ALLEY OOP
Argo Publ.: Nov, 1955 - No. 3, Mar, 1956 (Newspaper reprints)

1 16.00 47.00 110.00
2,3 11.00 33.00 75.00

ALLEY OOP
Dell Publishing Co.: 12-2/62-63 - No. 2, 9-11/63

1,2 4.50 13.50 50.00

ALLEY OOP
Standard Comics: No. 10, 1947 - No. 18, Oct, 1949

10 23.00 69.00 160.00
11-18: 17,18-Schomburg-c 17.00 51.00 120.00

ALLEY OOP ADVENTURES

All-Famous Police Cases #10 © STAR

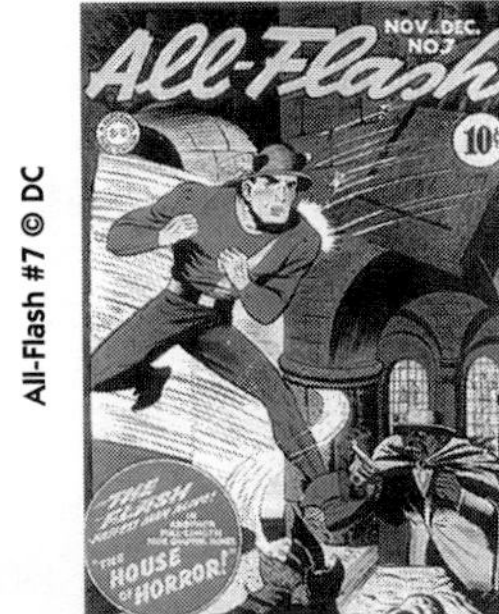

All-Flash #7 © DC

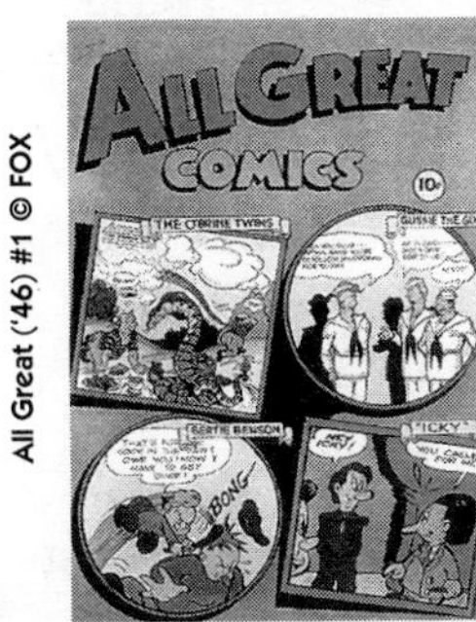

All Great ('46) #1 © FOX

GD2.0 FN6.0 NM9.4

GD2.0 FN6.0 NM9.4

Antarctic Press: Aug, 1998 - Present ($2.95)
1-3-Jack Bender-s/a 3.00

ALL-FAMOUS CRIME (Formerly Law Against Crime #1-3; becomes All-Famous Police Cases #6 on)
Star Publications: No. 4, 2/50 - No. 5, 5/50; No. 8, 5/51 - No. 10, 11/51
4 (#1-1st series)-Formerly Law-Crime 24.00 73.00 170.00
5 (#2) 16.00 47.00 110.00
8 (#3-2nd series) 15.00 45.00 105.00
9 (#4)-Used in **SOTI**, illo- "The wish to hurt or kill couples in lovers' lanes is a not uncommon perversion;" L.B. Cole-c/a(r)/Law-Crime #3 30.00 90.00 210.00
10 (#5)-Becomes All-Famous Police Cases #6 13.50 41.00 95.00
NOTE: *All have **L.B. Cole** covers.*

ALL FAMOUS CRIME STORIES (See Fox Giants)

ALL-FAMOUS POLICE CASES (Formerly All Famous Crime #10 [#5])
Star Publications: No. 6, Feb, 1952 - No. 16, Sept, 1954
6 15.00 45.00 105.00
7,8: 7-Baker story; . 8-Marijuana story 13.50 41.00 95.00
9-16 12.00 36.00 85.00
NOTE: ***L. B. Cole** c-all; a-15, 1pg. **Hollingsworth** a-15.*

ALL-FLASH (...Quarterly No. 1-5)
National Per. Publ./All-American: Summer, 1941 - No. 32, Dec-Jan, 1947-48
GD2.0 FN6.0 VF8.0 NM9.4
1-Origin The Flash retold by E. E. Hibbard; Hibbard c-1-10,12-14,16,31p. 1182.00 3546.00 7092.00 13,000.00
GD2.0 FN6.0 NM9.4
2-Origin recap 312.00 936.00 2500.00
3,4 162.00 486.00 1300.00
5-Winky, Blinky & Noddy begins (1st app.), ends #32 119.00 357.00 950.00
6-10 97.00 291.00 780.00
11-13: 12-Origin/1st The Thinker. 13-The King app. 85.00 255.00 680.00
14-Green Lantern cameo 97.00 291.00 780.00
15-20: 18-Mutt & Jeff begins, ends #22 71.00 213.00 570.00
21-31 56.00 168.00 450.00
32-Origin/1st app. The Fiddler; 1st Star Sapphire 97.00 291.00 780.00
NOTE: *Book length stories in 2-13, 16. Bondage c-31, 32. **Martin Nodell** c-15, 17-28.*

ALL FOR LOVE (Young Love V3#5-on)
Prize Publications: Apr-May, 1957 - V3#4, Dec-Jan, 1959-60
V1#1 6.00 18.00 60.00
2-6: 5-Orlando-c 3.50 10.50 35.00
V2#1-5(1/59), 5(3/59) 2.50 7.50 24.00
V3#1(5/59), 1(7/59)-4: 2-Powell-a 1.85 5.50 15.00

ALL FUNNY COMICS
Tilsam Publ./National Periodical Publications (Detective): Winter, 1943-44 - No. 23, May-June, 1948
1-Genius Jones (1st app.), Buzzy (1st app., ends #4), Dover & Clover (see More Fun #93) begin; Bailey-a 47.00 141.00 375.00
2 23.00 69.00 160.00
3-10 13.50 41.00 95.00
11-13,15,18,19-Genius Jones app. 13.00 39.00 90.00
14,17,20-23 10.00 30.00 60.00
16-DC Super Heroes app. 31.00 93.00 220.00

ALL GOOD
St. John Publishing Co.: Oct, 1949 (50¢, 260 pgs.)
nn-(8 St. John comics bound together) 60.00 180.00 480.00
NOTE: *Also see Li'l Audrey Yearbook & Treasury of Comics.*

ALL GOOD COMICS (See Fox Giants)
Fox Features Syndicate: No.1, Spring, 1946 (36 pgs.)
1-Joy Family, Dick Transom, Rick Evans, One Round Hogan 23.00 69.00 160.00

ALL GREAT (See Fox Giants)
Fox Feature Syndicate: 1946 (36 pgs.)
1-Crazy House, Bertie Benson Boy Detective, Gussie the Gob 23.00 69.00 160.00

ALL GREAT
William H. Wise & Co.: nd (1945?) (132 pgs.)
nn-Capt. Jack Terry, Joan Mason, Girl Reporter, Baron Doomsday; Torture scenes 39.00 117.00 270.00

ALL GREAT COMICS (Formerly Phantom Lady #13? Dagar, Desert Hawk No. 14 on)
Fox Features Syndicate: No. 14, Oct, 1947 - No. 13, Dec, 1947 (Newspaper strip reprints)
14(#12)-Brenda Starr & Texas Slim-r (Scarce) 53.00 159.00 425.00
13-Origin Dagar, Desert Hawk; Brenda Starr (all-r); Kamen-c; Dagar covers begin 50.00 150.00 400.00

ALL-GREAT CONFESSIONS (See Fox Giants)

ALL GREAT CRIME STORIES (See Fox Giants)

ALL GREAT JUNGLE ADVENTURES (See Fox Giants)

ALL HALLOW'S EVE
Innovation Publishing: 1991 ($4.95, 52 pgs.)
1-Painted-c/a 5.00

ALL HERO COMICS
Fawcett Publications: Mar, 1943 (100 pgs., cardboard-c)
1-Capt. Marvel Jr., Capt. Midnight, Golden Arrow, Ibis the Invincible, Spy Smasher, Lance O'Casey; 1st Banshee O'Brien; Raboy-c 150.00 450.00 1200.00

ALL HUMOR COMICS
Quality Comics Group: Spring, 1946 - No. 17, December, 1949
1 18.00 54.00 125.00
2-Atomic Tot story; Gustavson-a 10.00 30.00 65.00
3-9: 3-Intro Kelly Poole who is cover feature #3 on. 5-1st app. Hickory? 8-Gustavson-a 5.85 16.00 35.00
10-17 4.25 12.00 26.00

ALLIANCE, THE
Image Comics (Shadowline Ink): Aug, 1995 - No. 3, Nov, 1995 ($2.50)
1-3: 2-(9/95) 2.50

ALL LOVE (...Romances No. 26)(Formerly Ernie Comics)
Ace Periodicals (Current Books): No. 26, May, 1949 - No. 32, May, 1950
26 (No. 1)-Ernie, Lily Belle app. 8.35 25.00 50.00
27-L. B. Cole-a 11.50 34.00 80.00
28-32 5.00 15.00 30.00

ALL-NEGRO COMICS
All-Negro Comics: June, 1947 (15¢)
1 (Rare) 300.00 900.00 2700.00
NOTE: *Seldom found in fine or mint condition; many copies have brown pages.*

ALL-NEW COLLECTORS' EDITION (Formerly Limited ...)
DC Comics, Inc.: Jan, 1978 - Vol. 8, No. C-62, 1979 (No. 54-58: 76 pgs.)
C-53-Rudolph the Red-Nosed Reindeer 3.50 10.50 35.00
C-54-Superman Vs. Wonder Woman 2.50 7.50 25.00
C-55-Superboy & the Legion of Super-Heroes; Wedding of Lightning Lad & Saturn Girl; Grell-c/a 2.80 8.40 28.00
C-56-Superman Vs. Muhammad Ali: story & wraparound N. Adams-c/a 3.50 10.50 35.00
C-58-Superman Vs. Shazam 2.50 7.50 22.00
C-60-Rudolph's Summer Fun(8/78) 3.00 9.00 30.00
C-61-(See Famous First Edition-Superman #1)
C-62-Superman the Movie (68 pgs.; 1979)-Photo-c from movie plus photos inside (also see DC Special Series #25) 1.75 5.25 14.00
NOTE: ***Buckler** a-C-58; c-C-58*

ALL-NEW COMICS (...Short Story Comics No. 1-3)
Family Comics (Harvey Publications): Jan, 1943 - No. 14, Nov, 1946; No. 15, Mar-Apr, 1947 (10 x 13-1/2")

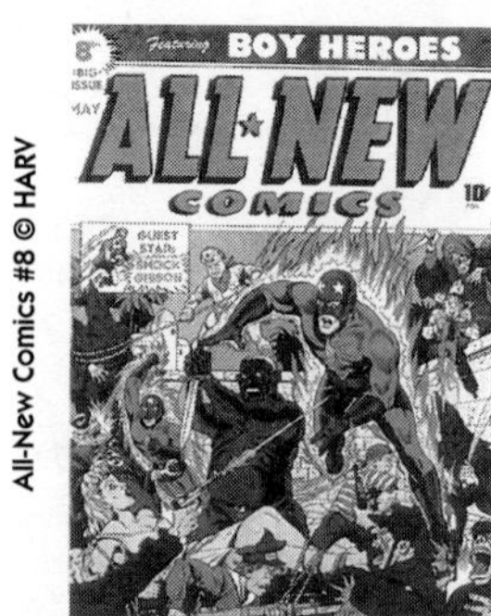

All-New Comics #8 © HARV

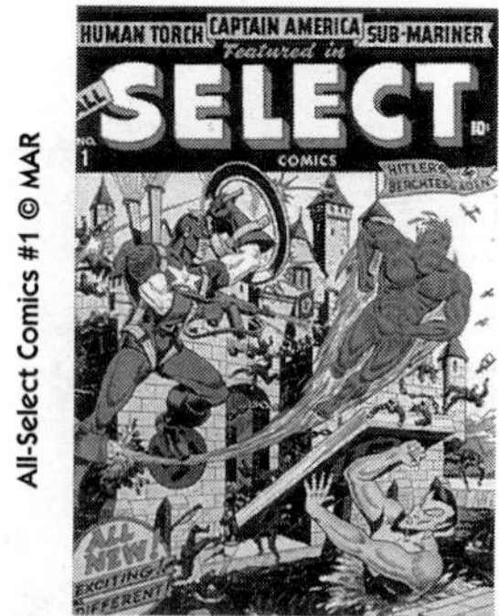

All-Select Comics #1 © MAR

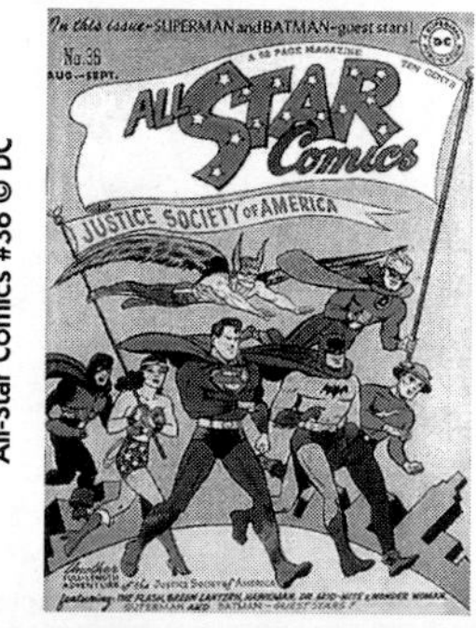

All-Star Comics #36 © DC

GD2.0 FN6.0 NM9.4

1-Steve Case, Crime Rover, Johnny Rebel, Kayo Kane, The Echo, Night Hawk, Ray O'Light, Detective Shane begin (all 1st app.?); Red Blazer on cover only; Sultan-a 275.00 825.00 2200.00
2-Origin Scarlet Phantom by Kubert 97.00 291.00 780.00
3 72.00 216.00 580.00
4 57.00 171.00 460.00
5-9: 5-Schomburg-c thru #11. 6-The Boy Heroes & Red Blazer (text story) begin, end #12; Black Cat app.; intro. Sparky in Red Blazer. 7-Kubert, Powell-a; Black Cat & Zebra app. 8,9: 8-Shock Gibson app.; Kubert, Powell-a; Schomburg-c. 9-Black Cat app.; Kubert-a 62.00 186.00 500.00
10-13: 10-The Zebra app. (from Green Hornet Comics); Kubert-a(3). 11-Girl Commandos, Man In Black app. 12-Kubert-a. 13-Stuntman by Simon & Kirby; Green Hornet, Joe Palooka, Flying Fool app.; Green Hornet-c 56.00 168.00 450.00
14-The Green Hornet & The Man in Black Called Fate by Powell, Joe Palooka app.; J. Palooka-c by Ham Fisher 52.00 156.00 420.00
15-(Rare)-Small size (5-1/2x8-1/2"; B&W; 32 pgs.). Distributed to mail subscribers only. Black Cat and Joe Palooka app. Estimated value....$250-350

NOTE: *Also see Boy Explorers No. 2, Flash Gordon No. 5, and Stuntman No. 3.* ***Powell*** *a-11.* ***Schomburg*** *c-5-11. Captain Red Blazer & Spark on c-5-11 (w/Boy Heroes #12).*

ALL-OUT WAR
DC Comics: Sept-Oct, 1979 - No. 6, Aug, 1980 ($1.00, 68 pgs.)

1-The Viking Commando(origin), Force Three(origin), & Black Eagle Squadron begin 5.00
2-6 3.00

NOTE: ***Ayers*** *a(p)-1-6.* ***Elias*** *r-2.* ***Evans*** *a-1-6.* ***Kubert*** *c-16.*

ALL PICTURE ADVENTURE MAGAZINE
St. John Publishing Co.: Oct, 1952 - No. 2, Nov, 1952 (100 pg. Giants, 25¢, squarebound)

1-War comics 25.00 75.00 175.00
2-Horror-crime comics 39.00 117.00 270.00

NOTE: *Above books contain three St. John comics rebound; variations possible.* ***Baker*** *art known in both.*

ALL PICTURE ALL TRUE LOVE STORY
St. John Publishing Co.: Oct., 1952 - No. 2, Nov., 1952 (100 pgs., 25¢)

1-Canteen Kate by Matt Baker 44.00 132.00 350.00
2--Baker c/a 29.00 87.00 200.00

ALL-PICTURE COMEDY CARNIVAL
St. John Publishing Co.: October, 1952 (100 pgs., 25¢)(Contains 4 rebound comics)

1-Contents can vary; Baker-a 40.00 120.00 320.00

ALL REAL CONFESSION MAGAZINE (See Fox Giants)

ALL ROMANCES (Mr. Risk No. 7 on)
A. A. Wyn (Ace Periodicals): Aug, 1949 - No. 6, June, 1950

1 9.15 27.00 55.00
2 4.15 12.50 25.00
3-6 4.00 10.00 20.00

ALL-SELECT COMICS (Blonde Phantom No. 12 on)
Timely Comics (Daring Comics): Fall, 1943 - No. 11, Fall, 1946

1-Capt. America (by Rico #1), Human Torch, Sub-Mariner begin; Black Widow story (4 pgs.); Classic Schomburg-c 800.00 2400.00 8000.00
2-Red Skull app. 312.00 936.00 2500.00
3-The Whizzer begins 194.00 582.00 1550.00
4,5-Last Sub-Mariner 131.00 393.00 1050.00
6-9: 6-The Destroyer app. 8-No Whizzer 109.00 327.00 875.00
10-The Destroyer & Sub-Mariner app.; last Capt. America & Human Torch issue 109.00 327.00 875.00
11-1st app. Blonde Phantom; Miss America app.; all Blonde Phantom-c by Shores 225.00 675.00 1800.00

NOTE: ***Schomburg*** *c-1-10.* ***Sekowsky*** *a-7. #7 & 8 show 1944 in indicia, but should be 1945.*

ALL SPORTS COMICS (Formerly Real Sports Comics; becomes All Time Sports Comics No. 4 on)
Hillman Periodicals: No. 2, Dec-Jan, 1948-49; No. 3, Feb-Mar, 1949

GD2.0 FN6.0 NM9.4

2-Krigstein-a(p), Powell, Starr-a 34.00 102.00 240.00
3-Mort Lawrence-a 23.00 69.00 160.00

ALL STAR COMICS (All Star Western No. 58 on)
National Periodical Publ./All-American/DC Comics: Sum, '40 - No. 57, Feb-Mar, '51; No. 58, Jan-Feb, '76 -No. 74, Sept-Oct, '78

GD2.0 FN6.0 VF8.0 NM9.4

1-The Flash (#1 by E.E. Hibbard), Hawkman(by Shelly), Hourman(by Bernard Baily), The Sandman(by Creig Flessel), The Spectre(by Baily), Biff Bronson, Red White & Blue(ends #2) begin; Ultra Man's only app. (#1-3 are quarterly; #4 begins bi-monthly issues) 1100.00 3300.00 6600.00 12,000.00

GD2.0 FN6.0 NM9.4

2-Green Lantern (by Martin Nodell), Johnny Thunder begin; Green Lantern figure swipe from the cover of All-American Comics #16; Flash figure swipe from the cover of Flash Comics #8; Moldoff/Bailey-c (cut & paste-c.) 500.00 1500.00 4500.00

GD2.0 FN6.0 VF8.0 NM9.4

3-Origin & 1st app. The Justice Society of America (Win/40); Dr. Fate & The Atom begin, Red Tornado cameo 2865.00 8600.00 17,200.00 31,500.00
3-Reprint, Oversize 13-1/2x10". **WARNING:** This comic is an exact reprint of the original except for its size. DC published it in 1974 with a second cover titling it as a Famous First Edition. There have been many reported cases of the outer cover being removed and the interior sold as the original edition. The reprint with the new outer cover removed is practically worthless. See Famous First Edition for value.

GD2.0 FN6.0 NM9.4

4-1st adventure for J.S.A. 500.00 1500.00 4500.00
5-1st app. Shiera Sanders as Hawkgirl (1st costumed super-heroine, 6-7/41) 430.00 1290.00 3900.00
6-Johnny Thunder joins JSA 300.00 900.00 2400.00
7-Batman, Superman, Flash cameo; last Hourman; Doiby Dickles app. 311.00 933.00 2800.00

GD2.0 FN6.0 VF8.0 NM9.4

8-Origin & 1st app. Wonder Woman (12-1/41-42)(added as 9 pgs. making book 76 pgs.; origin cont'd in Sensation #1; see W.W. #1 for more detailed origin); Dr. Fate dons new helmet; Hop Harrigan text stories & Starman begin; Shiera app.; Hop Harrigan JSA guest; Starman & Dr. Mid-Nite become members 2318.00 6950.00 13,900.00 25,500.00

GD2.0 FN6.0 NM9.4

9,10: 9-JSA's girlfriends cameo; Shiera app.; J. Edgar Hoover of FBI made associate member of JSA. 10-Flash, Green Lantern cameo; Sandman new costume 281.00 843.00 2250.00
11-Wonder Woman begins; Spectre cameo; Shiera app. 287.00 861.00 2300.00
12-Wonder Woman becomes JSA Secretary 262.00 786.00 2100.00
13,15: Sandman w/Sandy in #14 & 15. 15-Origin & 1st app. Brain Wave; Shiera app. 237.00 711.00 1900.00
14-(12/42) Junior JSA Club begins; w/membership offer & premiums 244.00 731.00 1950.00
16-20: 19-Sandman w/Sandy. 20-Dr. Fate & Sandman cameo 175.00 525.00 1400.00
21-23: 21-Spectre & Atom cameo; Dr. Fate by Kubert; Dr. Fate, Sandman end. 22-Last Hop Harrigan; Flag-c. 23-Origin/1st app. Psycho Pirate; last Spectre & Starman 156.00 468.00 1250.00
24-Flash & Green Lantern cameo; Mr. Terrific only app.; Wildcat, JSA guest; Kubert Hawkman begins; Hitler-c 156.00 468.00 1250.00
25-27: 25-Flash & Green Lantern start again. 26-Robot-c. 27-Wildcat, JSA guest (#24-26: only All-American imprint) 131.00 393.00 1050.00
28-32 119.00 357.00 950.00
33-Solomon Grundy & Doiby Dickles app; classic Solomon Grundy cover. Last Solomon Grundy G.A. app. 300.00 900.00 2500.00
34,35-Johnny Thunder cameo in both 112.00 336.00 900.00
36-Batman & Superman JSA guests 275.00 825.00 2200.00
37-Johnny Thunder cameo; origin & 1st app. Injustice Society; last Kubert Hawkman 150.00 450.00 1200.00
38-Black Canary begins; JSA Death issue 175.00 525.00 1400.00
39,40: 39-Last Johnny Thunder 106.00 318.00 850.00
41-Black Canary joins JSA; Injustice Society app. (2nd app.?) 106.00 318.00 850.00
42-Atom & the Hawkman don new costumes 106.00 318.00 850.00

All-Star Squadron #41 © DC

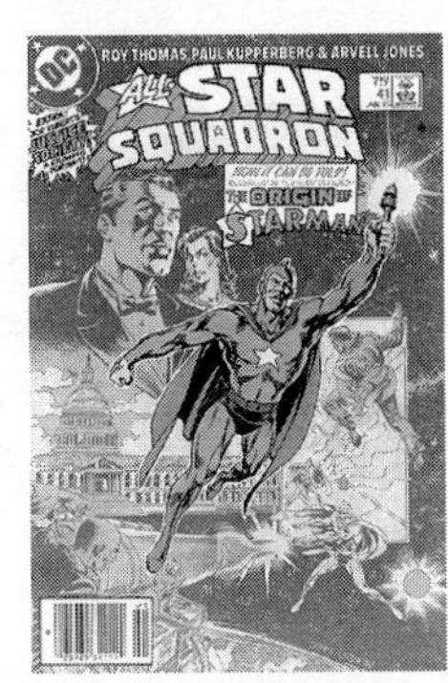

All Star Western #93 © DC

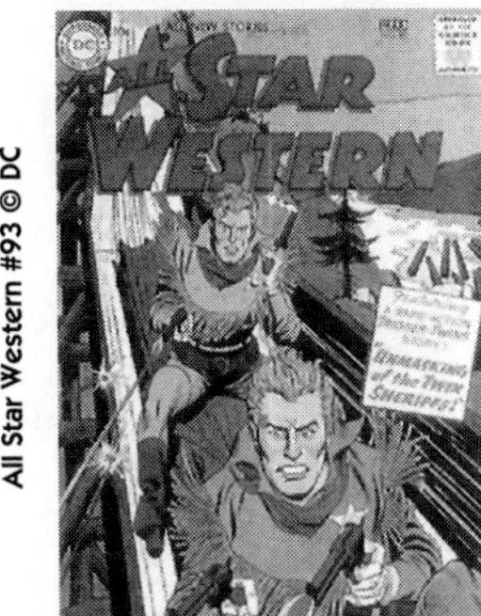

All Top Comics #9 © FOX

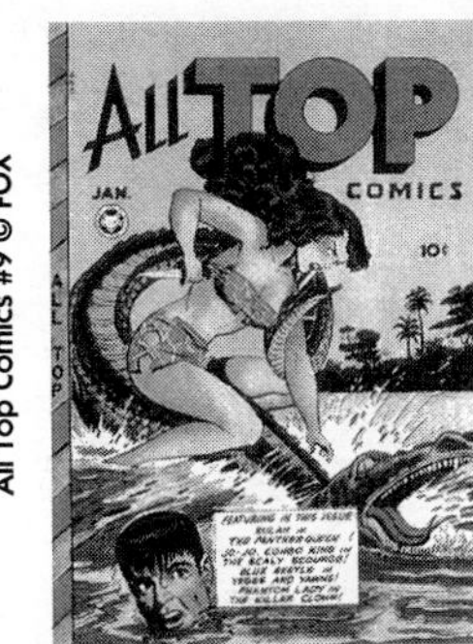

43-49,51-56: 43-New logo; Robot-c. 55-Sci/Fi story. 56-Robot-c 106.00 318.00 850.00
50-Frazetta art, 3 pgs. 119.00 357.00 950.00
57-Kubert-a, 6 pgs. (Scarce); last app. G.A. Green Lantern, Flash & Dr.Mid-Nite 156.00 468.00 1200.00
V12 #58-(1976) JSA (Flash, Hawkman, Dr. Mid-Nite, Wildcat, Dr. Fate, Green Lantern, Star Spangled Kid, & Robin) app.; intro Power Girl. 1.85 5.50 15.00
V12 #59-68,70-74(1976-78) 1.00 3.00 8.00
V12 #69-1st Earth-2 Huntress (Helena Wayne) 1.85 5.50 15.00

NOTE: *No Atom-27, 36; no Dr. Fate-13; no Flash-8, 9, 11-23; no Green Lantern-8, 9,11-23; Hawkman in 1-57 (only one to app. in all 57 issues); no Johnny Thunder-5, 36; no Wonder Woman-9, 10, 23. Book length stories in 4-9, 11-14, 18-22, 25, 26, 29, 30, 32-36, 42, 43. Johnny Peril in #42-46, 48, 49, 51, 52,54-57.* **Baily** *a-1-10, 12, 13, 14i, 15-20.* **Burnley** *Starman-8-13; c-12, 13.* **Grell** *c-58.* **E.E. Hibbard** *c-3, 4, 6-10.* **Infantino** *c-40.* **Kubert** *Hawkman-24-30, 33-37.* **Lampert/Baily/Flessel** *c-1, 2.* **Moldoff** *Hawkman-3-23; c-11.* **Mart Nodell** *c-25i, 26i, 27-32.* **Purcell** *c-5.* **Simon & Kirby** *Sandman 14-17, 19.* **Staton** *a-66-74p. c-74p.* **Toth** *a-37(2), 38(2), 40, 41; c-38, 41.* **Wood** *a-58i-63i, 64, 65; c-63i, 64, 65. Issues 1-7, 9-16 are 68 pgs.; #8 is 76 pgs.; #17-19 are 60 pgs.; #20-57 are 52 pgs.*

ALL STAR COMICS (Also see crossover 1999 editions of Adventure, All-American, National, Sensation, Smash, Star Spangled and Thrilling Comics)
DC Comics: May, 1999 - No. 2, May, 1999 ($2.95, bookends for JSA x-over)

1,2-Justice Society in World War 2; Robinson-s/Johnson-c 3.00
...80-Page Giant (9/99, $4.95) Phantom Lady app. 5.00

ALL STAR INDEX, THE
Independent Comics Group (Eclipse): Feb, 1987 ($2.00, Baxter paper)

1 3.00

ALL-STAR SQUADRON (See Justice League of America #193)
DC Comics: Sept, 1981 - No. 67, Mar, 1987

1-Original Atom, Hawkman, Dr. Mid-Nite, Robotman (origin), Plastic Man, Johnny Quick, Liberty Belle, Shining Knight begin 4.00
2-46,48,49: 4, 7-Spectre app. 5-Danette Reilly becomes new Firebrand. 8-Re-intro Steel, the Indestructable Man. 12-Origin G.A. Hawkman retold. 23-Origin/1st app. The Amazing Man. 24-Batman app. 25-1st app. Infinity, Inc. (9/83), 26-Origin Infinity, Inc. (2nd app.); Robin app. 27-Dr. Fate vs. The Spectre. 30-35-Spectre app. 33-Origin Freedom Fighters of Earth-X. 36,37-Superman vs. Capt. Marvel; Ordway-c. 41-Origin Starman 3.00
47-Origin Dr. Fate; McFarlane-a (1st full story)/part-c (7/85) 5.00
50-Double size; Crisis x-over 4.00
51-67: 51-56-Crisis x-over. 61-Origin Liberty Belle. 62-Origin The Shining Knight. 63-Origin Robotman. 65-Origin Johnny Quick. 66-Origin Tarantula 3.00
Annual 1-3: 1(11/82)-Retells origin of G.A. Atom, Guardian & Wildcat; Jerry Ordway's 1st pencils for DC.(1st work was inking Carmine Infantino in House of Mystery #94) 2(11/83)-Infinity, Inc. app. 3(9/84) 3.00

NOTE: **Buckler** *a-1-5; c-1, 3-5, 51.* **Kubert** *c-2, 7-18. JLA app. in 14, 15. JSA app. in 4, 14, 15, 19, 27, 28.*

ALL-STAR STORY OF THE DODGERS, THE
Stadium Communications: Apr, 1979 ($1.00)

1 .90 2.70 8.00

ALL STAR WESTERN (Formerly All Star Comics No. 1-57)
National Periodical Publ.: No. 58, Apr-May, 1951 - No. 119, June-July, 1961

58-Trigger Twins (ends #116), Strong Bow, The Roving Ranger & Don Caballero begin 43.00 129.00 340.00
59,60: Last 52 pgs. 23.00 69.00 160.00
61-66: 61-64-Toth-a 19.00 57.00 135.00
67-Johnny Thunder begins; Gil Kane-a 23.00 69.00 160.00
68-81: Last precode (2-3/55) 10.00 30.00 70.00
82-98: 97-1st S.A. issue 10.00 30.00 65.00
99-Frazetta-r/Jimmy Wakely #4 10.00 30.00 70.00
100 10.00 30.00 70.00
101-107,109-116,118,119 8.00 24.00 48.00
108-Origin J. Thunder; J. Thunder logo begins 19.00 57.00 135.00
117-Origin Super Chie 11.50 34.00 80.00

NOTE: **Gil Kane** *c(p)-58, 59, 61, 63, 64, 68, 69, 70-95(most), 97-199(most).* **Infantino** *art in most issues. Madame .44 app.-#117-119.*

ALL-STAR WESTERN (Weird Western Tales No. 12 on)
National Periodical Publications: Aug-Sept, 1970 - No. 11, Apr-May, 1972

1-Pow-Wow Smith-r; Infantino-a 3.00 9.00 30.00
2-6: 2-Outlaw begins; El Diablo by Morrow begins; has cameos by Williamson, Torres, Kane, Giordano & Phil Seuling. 3-Origin El Diablo. 5-Last Outlaw issue. 6-Billy the Kid begins, ends #8 1.75 5.25 14.00
7-9-(52 pgs.) 9-Frazetta-a, 3pgs.(r) 2.25 6.75 18.00
10-(52 pgs.) Jonah Hex begins (1st app., 2-3/72) 20.00 60.00 200.00
11-(52 pgs.) 2nd app. Jonah Hex 10.00 30.00 100.00

NOTE: **Neal Adams** *c-2-5;* **Aparo** *a-5.* **G. Kane a***-3, 4, 6, 8.* **Kubert** *a-4r, 7-9r.* **Morrow** *a-2-4, 10, 11. No. 7-11 have 52 pgs..*

ALL SURPRISE (Becomes Jeanie #13 on) (Funny animal)
Timely/Marvel (CPC): Fall, 1943 - No. 12, Winter, 1946-47

1-Super Rabbit, Gandy & Sourpuss begin 29.00 86.00 200.00
2 13.00 39.00 90.00
3-10,12 10.00 30.00 70.00
11-Kurtzman "Pigtales" art 11.50 34.00 80.00

ALL TEEN (Formerly All Winners; All Winners & Teen Comics No. 21 on)
Marvel Comics (WFP): No. 20, January, 1947

20-Georgie, Mitzi, Patsy Walker, Willie app.; Syd Shores-c 10.00 30.00 60.00

ALL-TIME SPORTS COMICS (Formerly All Sports Comics)
Hillman Per.: V2No. 4, Apr-May, 1949 - V2No. 7, Oct-Nov, 1949 (All 52 pgs.)

V2#4 21.00 64.00 150.00
5-7: 5-(V1#5 inside)-Powell-a; Ty Cobb sty. 7-Krigstein-p; Walter Johnson & Knute Rockne sty 16.00 47.00 110.00

ALL TOP
William H. Wise Co.: 1944 (132 pgs.)

Capt. V, Merciless the Sorceress, Red Robbins, One Round Hogan, Mike the M.P., Snooky, Pussy Katnip app. 28.00 84.00 195.00

ALL TOP COMICS (My Experience No. 19 on)
Fox Features Synd./Green Publ./Norlen Mag.: 1945; No. 2, Sum, 1946 - No. 18, Mar, 1949; 1957 - 1959

1-Cosmo Cat & Flash Rabbit begin (1st app.) 21.00 64.00 150.00
2 (#1-7 are funny animal) 10.00 30.00 70.00
3-7 8.35 25.00 50.00
8-Blue Beetle, Phantom Lady, & Rulah, Jungle Goddess begin (11/47); Kamen-c 212.00 636.00 1700.00
9-Kamen-c 109.00 327.00 875.00
10-Kamen bondage-c 119.00 357.00 950.00
11-13,15-17: 11-Rulah-c. 15-No Blue Beetle 95.00 285.00 760.00
14-No Blue Beetle; used in **SOTI**, illo- "Corpses of colored people strung up by their wrists" 119.00 357.00 950.00
18-Dagar, Jo-Jo app; no Phantom Lady or Blue Beetle 61.00 183.00 490.00
6(1957-Green Publ.)-Patoruzu the Indian; Cosmo Cat on cover only. 6(1958-Literary Ent.)-Muggy Doo; Cosmo Cat on cover only. 6(1959-Norlen)-Atomic Mouse; Cosmo Cat on cover only. 6(1959)-Little Eva. 6(Cornell)-Supermouse on-c 4.00 10.00 20.00

NOTE: *Jo-Jo by* **Kamen***-12,18.*

ALL TRUE ALL PICTURE POLICE CASES
St. John Publishing Co.: Oct, 1952 - No. 2, Nov, 1952 (100 pgs.)

1-Three rebound St. John crime comics 40.00 120.00 290.00
2-Three comics rebound 29.00 86.00 200.00

NOTE: *Contents may vary.*

ALL-TRUE CRIME (...Cases No. 26-35; formerly Official True Crime Cases)
Marvel/Atlas Comics: No. 26, Feb, 1948 - No. 52, Sept, 1952 (OFI #26,27/CFI #28,29/LCC #30-46/LMC #47-52)

26(#1)-Syd Shores-c 29.00 86.00 200.00
27(4/48)-Electric chair-c 20.00 60.00 140.00
28-41,43-48,50-52: 35-37-Photo-c 10.00 30.00 60.00
42,49-Krigstein-a. 49-Used in **POP**, Pg 79 10.00 30.00 70.00

NOTE: **Robinson** *a-47, 50.* **Shores** *c-26.* **Tuska** *a-48(3).*

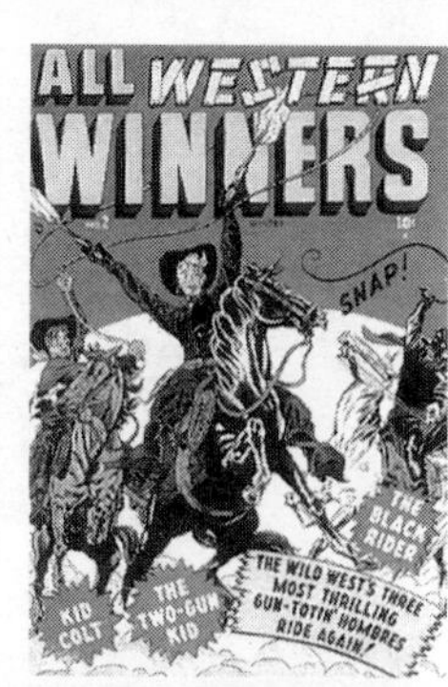

All Western Winners #2 © MAR

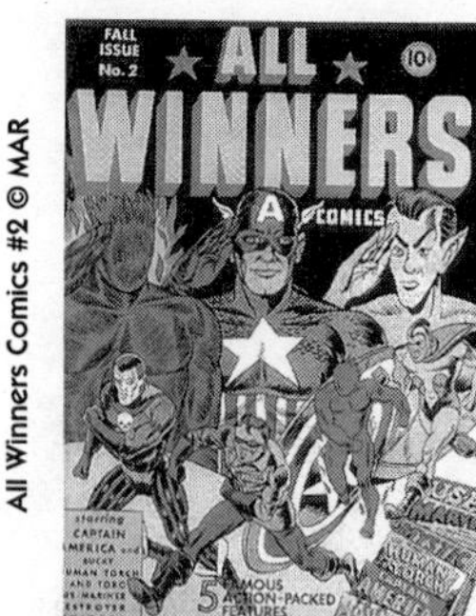

All Winners Comics #2 © MAR

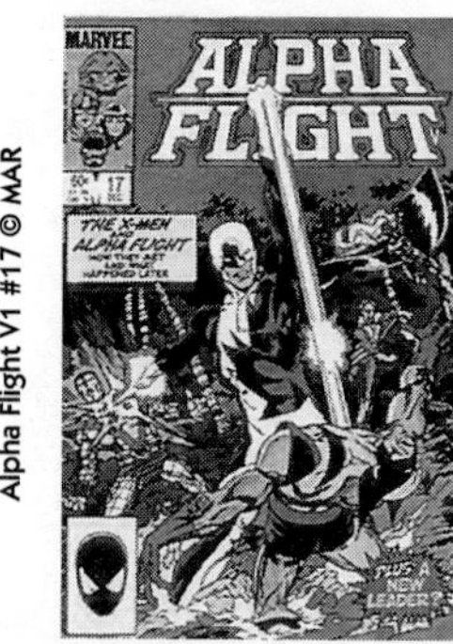

Alpha Flight V1 #17 © MAR

ALL-TRUE DETECTIVE CASES (Kit Carson No. 5 on)
Avon Periodicals: Feb-Mar, 1954 - No. 4, Aug-Sept, 1954

	GD2.0	FN6.0	NM9.4
1	24.00	73.00	170.00
2-Wood-a	19.00	58.00	135.00
3-Kinstler-c	10.00	30.00	70.00
4-r/Gangsters And Gun Molls #2; Kamen-a	17.00	51.00	120.00
nn(100 pgs.)-7 pg. Kubert-a, Kinstler back-c	37.00	111.00	260.00

ALL TRUE ROMANCE (...Illustrated No. 3)
Artful Publ. #1-3/Harwell(Comic Media) #4-20?/Ajax-Farrell(Excellent Publ.) No. 22 on/Four Star Comic Corp.: 3/51 - No. 20, 12/54; No. 22, 3/55 - No. 30?, 7/57; No. 3(#31), 9/57;No. 4(#32), 11/57; No. 33, 2/58 - No. 34, 3/58

	GD2.0	FN6.0	NM9.4
1 (3/51)	14.00	43.00	100.00
2 (10/51; 11/51 on-c)	7.50	22.50	45.00
3(12/51) - #5(5/52)	6.35	19.00	38.00
6-Wood-a, 9 pgs. (exceptional)	15.00	45.00	105.00
7-10	5.00	15.00	30.00
11-13,16-19 (9/54)	4.00	12.00	24.00
14-Marijuana story	4.25	13.00	28.00
20,22: Last precode issue (Ajax, 3/55)	4.00	10.00	20.00
23-27,29,30	3.20	8.00	16.00
28 (9/56)-L. B. Cole, Disbrow-a	9.15	27.00	55.00
3,4,33,34 (Farrell, '57- '58)	2.80	7.00	14.00

ALL WESTERN WINNERS (Formerly All Winners; becomes Western Winners with No. 5; see Two-Gun Kid No. 5)
Marvel Comics(CDS): No. 2, Winter, 1948-49 - No. 4, April, 1949

	GD2.0	FN6.0	NM9.4
2-Black Rider (origin & 1st app.) & his horse Satan, Kid Colt & his horse Steel, & Two-Gun Kid & his horse Cyclone begin; Shores c-2-4	77.00	231.00	620.00
3-Anti-Wertham editorial	40.00	120.00	290.00
4-Black Rider i.d. revealed; Heath, Shores-a	40.00	120.00	290.00

ALL WINNERS COMICS (All Teen #20) (Also see Timely Presents: ...)
USA No. 1-7/WFP No. 10-19/YAI No. 21: Summer, 1941 - No. 19, Fall, 1946; No. 21, Winter, 1946-47; (No #20) (No. 21 continued from Young Allies No. 20)

	GD2.0	FN6.0	VF8.0	NM9.4
1-The Angel & Black Marvel only app.; Capt. America by Simon & Kirby, Human Torch & Sub-Mariner begin (#1 was advertised as All Aces); 1st app. All-Winners Squad in text story by Stan Lee	1364.00	4090.00	8180.00	15,000.00

	GD2.0	FN6.0	NM9.4
2-The Destroyer & The Whizzer begin; Simon & Kirby Captain America	422.00	1266.00	3800.00
3	275.00	825.00	2200.00
4-Classic War-c by Al Avison	277.00	862.00	2500.00
5	181.00	543.00	1450.00
6-The Black Avenger only app.; no Whizzer story; Hitler, Hirohito & Mussolini-c	206.00	618.00	1650.00
7-10	156.00	468.00	1250.00
11,13-18: 11-1st Atlas globe on-c (Winter, 1943-44; also see Human Torch #14). 14-16-No Human Torch	120.00	360.00	960.00
12-Red Skull story; last Destroyer; no Whizzer story	144.00	432.00	1150.00
19-(Scarce)-1st story app. & origin All Winners Squad (Capt. America & Bucky, Human Torch & Toro, Sub-Mariner, Whizzer, & Miss America; r-in Fantasy Masterpieces #10	355.00	1065.00	3200.00
21-(Scarce)-All Winners Squad; bondage-c	311.00	933.00	2800.00

NOTE: ***Everett*** *Sub-Mariner-1, 3, 4;* ***Burgos*** *Torch-1, 3, 4.* ***Schomburg*** *c-1, 7-18.* ***Shores*** *c-19p, 21.*

(2nd Series - August, 1948, Marvel Comics (CDS))
(Becomes All Western Winners with No. 2)

	GD2.0	FN6.0	NM9.4
1-The Blonde Phantom, Capt. America, Human Torch, & Sub-Mariner app.	271.00	813.00	1900.00

ALL YOUR COMICS (See Fox Giants)
Fox Feature Syndicate (R. W. Voight): Spring, 1946 (36 pgs.)

	GD2.0	FN6.0	NM9.4
1-Red Robbins, Merciless the Sorceress app.	17.00	51.00	120.00

ALMANAC OF CRIME (See Fox Giants)

AL OF FBI (See Little Al of the FBI)

ALPHA AND OMEGA
Spire Christian Comics (Fleming H. Revell): 1978 (49¢)

	GD2.0	FN6.0	NM9.4
nn			5.00

ALPHA CENTURION (See Superman, 2nd Series & Zero Hour)
DC Comics: 1996 ($2.95, one-shot)

	GD2.0	FN6.0	NM9.4
1			3.00

ALPHA FLIGHT (See X-Men #120,121 & X-Men/Alpha Flight)
Marvel Comics: Aug, 1983 - No. 130, Mar, 1994 (#52-on are direct sales only)

	GD2.0	FN6.0	NM9.4
1-Byrne-a begins (52pgs.)-Wolverine & Nightcrawler cameo			3.00
2-12,14-16,18-32,35-50: 2-Vindicator becomes Guardian; origin Marrina & Alpha Flight. 3-Concludes origin Alpha Flight. 6-Origin Shaman. 7-Origin Snowbird. 10,11-Origin Sasquatch. 12-(52 pgs.)-Death of Guardian. 16-Wolverine cameo. 20-New headquarters. 25-Return of Guardian. 28-Last Byrne issue. 39-47,49-Portacio-a(i). 50-Double size; Portacio-a(i)			2.50
13,17,33,34: 13-Wolverine app. 17-X-Men x-over (70% r-/X-Men #109); Wolverine cameo. 33-X-Men (Wolverine) app. 34-Origin Wolverine			3.00
51-Jim Lee's 1st work at Marvel (10/87); Wolverine cameo; 1st Jim Lee Wolverine; Portacio-a(i)			5.00
52,53-Wolverine app.; Lee-a on Wolverine; Portacio-a(i); 53-Lee/Portacio-a			2.50
54-105: 54,63,64-No Jim Lee-a. 54-Portacio-a(i). 55-62-Jim Lee-a(p). 71-Intro The Sorcerer (villain). 74-Wolverine, Spider-Man & The Avengers app. 89-Original Guardian returns. 75-Double size ($1.95, 52 pgs.). 87-90-Wolverine 4 part story w/Jim Lee-c. 91-Dr. Doom app. 94-F.F. x-over. 99-Galactus, Avengers app. 100-($2.00, 52 pgs.)-Avengers & Galactus app.102-Intro Weapon Omega. 104-Last $1.50-c			2.00
106-Northstar revelation issue			2.50
106-2nd printing (direct sale only)			2.00
107-119,121-129: 107-X-Factor x-over. 110-112-Infinity War x-overs. 110, 111-Wolverine app. (brief). 111-Thanos cameo			2.00
120-($2.25)-Polybagged w/Paranormal Registration Act poster			2.25
130-($2.25, 52 pgs.)			2.50
Annual 1,2 (9/86, 12/87))			2.00
Special V2#1(6/92, $2.50, 52 pgs.)-Wolverine-c/story			2.50

NOTE: ***Austin*** *c-1i, 2i, 53i.* ***Byrne*** *c-81, 82.* ***Guice*** *c-85, 91-99.* ***Jim Lee*** *a(p)-51, 53, 55-62, 64; c-53, 87-90.* ***Mignola*** *a-29-31p.* ***Whilce Portacio*** *a(i)-39-47, 49-54.*

ALPHA FLIGHT (2nd Series)
Marvel Comics: Aug, 1997 - No. 20, Mar, 1999 ($2.99/$1.99)

	GD2.0	FN6.0	NM9.4
1-($2.99)-Wraparound cover		2.40	6.00
2,3: 2-Variant-c			4.00
4-11,13-20: 8,9-Wolverine-c/app.			3.00
12-($2.99) Death of Sasquatch; wraparound-c			4.00
.../Inhumans '98 Annual ($3.50) Raney-a			3.50

ALPHA FLIGHT: IN THE BEGINNING
Marvel Comics: July, 1997 ($1.95, one-shot)

	GD2.0	FN6.0	NM9.4
(-1)-Flashback w/Wolverine			2.00

ALPHA FLIGHT SPECIAL
Marvel Comics: July, 1991 - No. 4, Oct, 1991 ($1.50, limited series)

	GD2.0	FN6.0	NM9.4
1-4: 1-3-r-A. Flight #97-99 w/covers. 4-r-A.Flight #100			2.00

ALPHA KORPS
Diversity Comics: Sept, 1996 ($2.50)

	GD2.0	FN6.0	NM9.4
1-Origin/1st app. Alpha Korps			2.50

ALPHA WAVE
Darkline Comics: Mar, 1987 ($1.75, 36 pgs.)

	GD2.0	FN6.0	NM9.4
1			2.00

ALTERED IMAGE
Image Comics: Apr, 1998 - No. 3, Sept, 1998 ($2.50, limited series)

	GD2.0	FN6.0	NM9.4
1-3-Spawn, Witchblade, Savage Dragon; Valentino-s/a			3.00

ALTER EGO

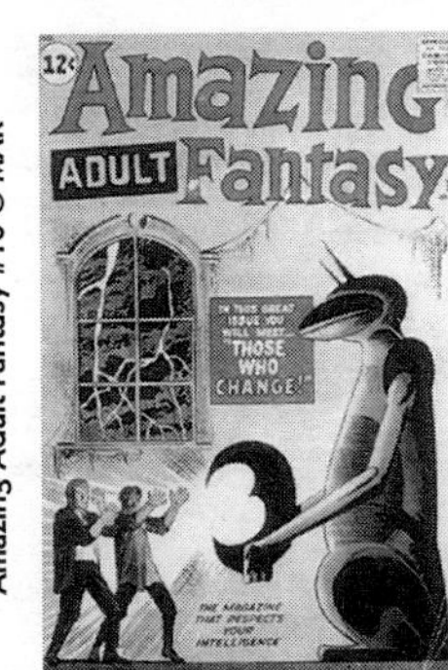

Amazing Adult Fantasy #10 © MAR

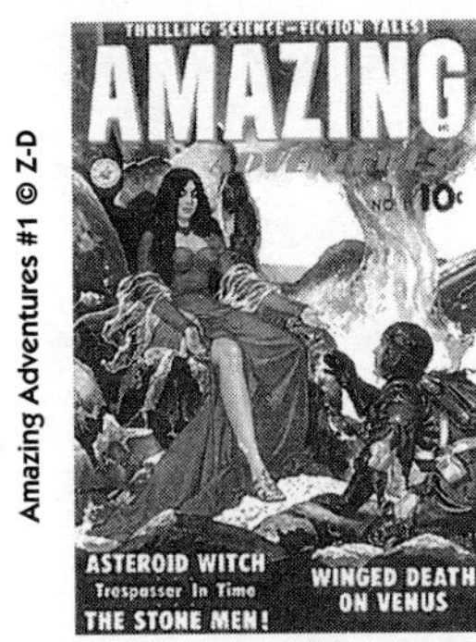

Amazing Adventures #1 © Z-D

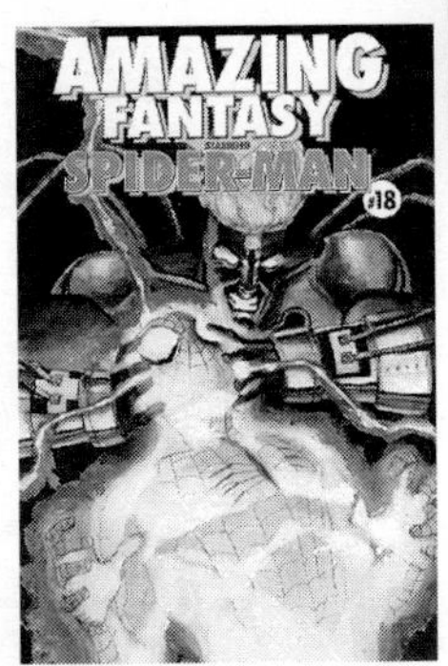

Amazing Fantasy #18 © MAR

GD2.0 FN6.0 NM9.4

First Comics: May, 1986 - No. 4, Nov, 1986 (Mini-series)
1-4 2.00

ALVIN (TV) (See Four Color Comics No. 1042)
Dell Publishing Co.: Oct-Dec, 1962 - No. 28, Oct, 1973
12-021-212 (#1) 8.00 25.00 90.00
2 4.50 13.50 50.00
3-10 3.60 11.00 40.00
11-28 2.75 8.00 30.00
Alvin For President (10/64) 2.90 8.70 32.00
...& His Pals in Merry Christmas with Clyde Crashcup & Leonardo 1
(02-120-402)-(12-2/64) 7.00 21.00 70.00
Reprinted in 1966 (12-023-604 4.50 13.50 50.00

ALVIN & THE CHIPMUNKS
Harvey Comics: July, 1992 - No. 5, May, 1994
1-5 2.00

AMALGAM AGE OF COMICS, THE: THE DC COMICS COLLECTION
DC Comics: 1996 ($12.95, trade paperback)
nn-r/Amazon, Assassins, Doctor Strangefate, JLX, Legends of the Dark Claw, & Super Soldier 13.00

AMANDA AND GUNN
Image Comics: Apr, 1997 - No. 4, Oct, 1997 ($2.95, B&W, limited series)
1-4 3.00

AMAZING ADULT FANTASY (Formerly Amazing Adventures #1-6; becomes Amazing Fantasy #15)
Marvel Comics Group (AMI): No. 7, Dec, 1961 - No. 14, July, 1962
7-Ditko-c/a begins, ends #14 48.00 144.00 575.00
8-Last 10¢ issue 40.00 120.00 450.00
9-13: 12-1st app. Mailbag. 13-Anti-communist sty 38.00 114.00 420.00
14-Prototype issue (Professor X) 40.00 120.00 465.00

AMAZING ADVENTURE FUNNIES (Fantoman No. 2 on)
Centaur Publications: June, 1940 - No. 2, Sept. 1940
1-The Fantom of the Fair by Gustavson (r/Amaz. Mystery Funnies V2#7,V2#8), The Arrow, Skyrocket Steele From the Year X by Everett (r/AMF #2); Burgos-a 175.00 525.00 1400.00
2-Reprints; Published after Fantoman #2 112.00 336.00 900.00
NOTE: ***Burgos*** *a-1(2).* ***Everett*** *a-1(3).* ***Gustavson*** *a-1(5), 2(3).* ***Pinajian*** *a-2.*

AMAZING ADVENTURES (Also see Boy Cowboy & Science Comics)
Ziff-Davis Publ. Co.: 1950; No. 1, Nov, 1950 - No. 6, Fall, 1952 (Painted covers)
1950 (no month given) (8-1/2x11) (8 pgs.) Has the front & back cover plus Schomburg story used in Amazing Advs. #1 (Sent to subscribers of Z-D s/f magazines & ordered through mail for 10¢. Used to test market)
Estimated value... 300.00
1-Wood, Schomburg, Anderson, Whitney-a 67.00 200.00 540.00
2-5: 2-Schomburg-a. 2,4,5-Anderson-a. 3,5-Starr-a 34.00 102.00 240.00
6-Krigstein-a 36.00 108.00 250.00

AMAZING ADVENTURES (Becomes Amazing Adult Fantasy #7 on)
Atlas Comics (AMI)/Marvel Comics No. 3 on: June, 1961 - No. 6, Nov, 1961
1-Origin Dr. Droom (1st Marvel-Age Superhero) by Kirby; Kirby/Ditko-a (5 pgs.) Ditko & Kirby-a in all; Kirby monster c-1-6 104.00 312.00 1250.00
2 44.00 132.00 525.00
3-6: 6-Last Dr. Droom 40.00 120.00 450.00

AMAZING ADVENTURES
Marvel Comics Group: Aug, 1970 - No. 39, Nov, 1976
1-Inhumans by Kirby(p) & Black Widow (1st app. in Tales of Suspense #52) double feature begins 4.00 12.00 40.00
2-4: 2-F.F. brief app. 4-Last Inhumans by Kirby 2.00 6.00 16.00
5-8: Adams-a(p); 8-Last Black Widow; last 15¢-c 2.50 7.50 25.00
9,10: Magneto app. 10-Last Inhumans (origin-r by Kirby)
1.75 5.25 14.00
11-New Beast begins(1st app. in mutated form; origin in flashback); X-Men cameo in flashback (#11-17 are X-Men tie-ins) 7.50 22.50 75.00

GD2.0 FN6.0 NM9.4

12-17: 13-Brotherhood of Evil Mutants x-over from X-Men. 15-X-Men app.
17-Last Beast (origin); X-Men app. 2.50 7.50 20.00
18-War of the Worlds begins (5/73); 1st app. Killraven; Neal Adams-a(p)
2.00 6.00 16.00
19-35,38,39: 35-Giffen's first published story (art), along with Deadly Hands of Kung-Fu #22 (3/76) 2.40 6.00
36,37-(Regular 25¢ edition)(7-8/76) 2.40 6.00
36,37-(30¢-c variants, limited distribution) 2.50 7.50 20.00
NOTE: ***N. Adams*** *c-6-8.* ***Buscema*** *a-1p, 2p.* ***Colan*** *a-3-5p, 26p.* ***Ditko*** *a-24r.* ***Everett*** *a(i)3-5, 7-9.* ***Giffen*** *a-35i, 38p.* ***G. Kane*** *c-11, 25p, 29p.* ***Ploog*** *a-12i.* ***Russell*** *a-27-32, 34-37, 39; c-28, 30-32, 33i, 34, 35, 37, 39i.* ***Starliing*** *a-17.* ***Starlin*** *c-15p, 16, 17, 27.* ***Sutton*** *a-11-15p.*

AMAZING ADVENTURES
Marvel Comics Group: Dec, 1979 - No. 14, Jan, 1981
V2#1-Reprints story/X-Men #1 & 38 (origins) 4.00
2-14: 2-6-Early X-Men-r. 7,8-Origin Iceman 3.00
NOTE: ***Byrne*** *c-6p, 9p.* ***Kirby*** *a-1-14r; c-7, 9.* ***Steranko*** *a-12r.* ***Tuska*** *a-7-9.*

AMAZING ADVENTURES
Marvel Comics: July, 1988 ($4.95, squarebound, one-shot, 80 pgs.)
1-Anthology; Austin, Golden-a 5.00

AMAZING ADVENTURES OF CAPTAIN CARVEL AND HIS CARVEL CRUSADERS, THE (See Carvel Comics)

AMAZING CHAN & THE CHAN CLAN, THE (TV)
Gold Key: May, 1973 - No. 4, Feb, 1974 (Hanna-Barbera)
1-Warren Tufts-a in all 2.50 7.50 20.00
2-4 1.75 5.25 14.00

AMAZING COMICS (Complete Comics No. 2)
Timely Comics (EPC): Fall, 1944
1-The Destroyer, The Whizzer, The Young Allies (by Sekowsky), Sergeant Dix; Schomburg-c 175.00 525.00 1400.00

AMAZING DETECTIVE CASES (Formerly Suspense No. 2?)
Marvel/Atlas Comics (CCC): No. 3, Nov, 1950 - No. 14, Sept, 1952
3 24.00 72.00 170.00
4-6 13.50 41.00 95.00
7-10 12.00 36.00 85.00
11,12,14: 11-(3/52)-Change to horror 20.00 60.00 140.00
12-Krigstein-a 20.00 60.00 140.00
13-(Scarce)-Everett-a; electrocution-c/story 26.00 78.00 180.00
NOTE: ***Colan*** *a-9.* ***Maneely*** *c-13.* ***Sekowsky*** *a-12.* ***Sinnott*** *a-13.* ***Tuska*** *a-10.*

AMAZING FANTASY (Formerly Amazing Adult Fantasy #7-14)
Atlas Magazines/Marvel: #15, Aug, 1962 (Sept, 1962 shown in indicia); #16, Dec, 1995 - #18, Feb, 1996
GD2.0 FN6.0 VF8.0 NM9.4
15-Origin/1st app. of Spider-Man by Ditko (11 pgs.); 1st app. Aunt May & Uncle Ben; Kirby/Ditko-c 1000.00 3000.00 10,000.00 25,000.00
GD2.0 FN6.0 NM9.4
16-18 ('95-'96, $3.95): Kurt Busiek scripts; painted-c/a 4.00

AMAZING GHOST STORIES (Formerly Nightmare)
St. John Publishing Co.: No. 14, Oct, 1954 - No. 16, Feb, 1955
14-Pit & the Pendulum story by Kinstler; Baker-c 29.00 86.00 200.00
15-r/Weird Thrillers #5; Baker-c, Powell-a 20.00 60.00 140.00
16-Kubert reprints of Weird Thrillers #4; Baker-c; Roussos, Tuska-a; Kinstler-a (1 pg.) 21.00 62.00 145.00

AMAZING HIGH ADVENTURE
Marvel Comics: 8/84; No. 2, 10/85; No. 3, 10/86 - No. 5, 1987 ($2.00)
1-5: 3,4-Baxter paper 2.00
NOTE: ***Bissette*** *a-4.* ***Bolton*** *c/a-4.* ***Severin*** *a-1, 3.* ***Paul Smith*** *a-2.* ***Williamson*** *a-2i.*

AMAZING-MAN COMICS (Formerly Motion Picture Funnies Weekly?) (Also see Stars And Stripes Comics)
Centaur Publications: No. 5, Sept, 1939 - No. 26, Jan, 1942
GD2.0 FN6.0 VF8.0 NM9.4
5(#1)(Rare)-Origin/1st app. A-Man the Amazing Man by Bill Everett; The Cat-Man by Tarpe Mills (also #8), Mighty Man by Filchock, Minimidget &

Amazing-Man Comics #9 © CEN

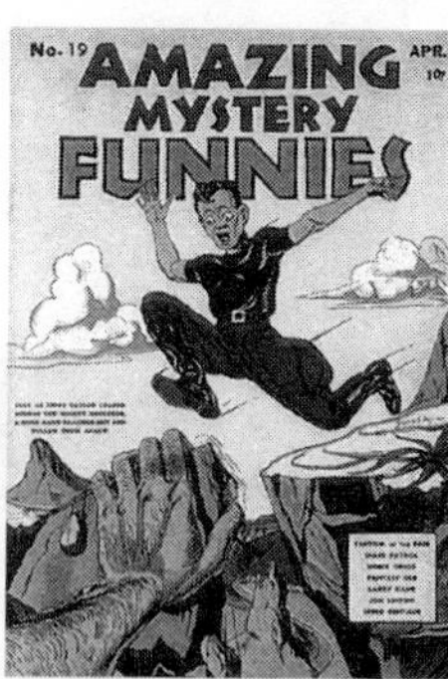

Amazing Mystery Funnies #19 © CEN

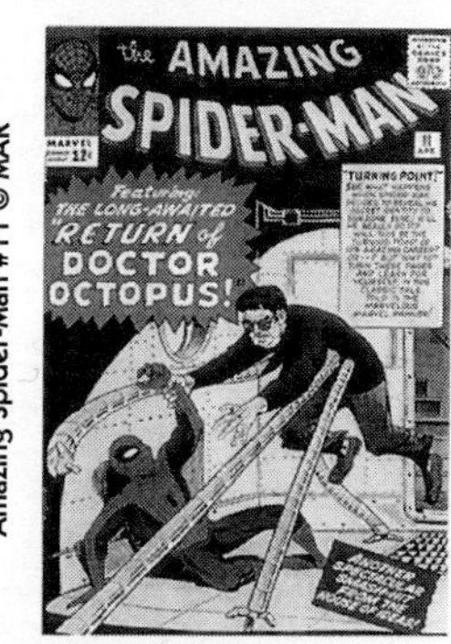

Amazing Spider-Man #11 © MAR

sidekick Ritty, & The Iron Skull by Burgos begins
1340.00 4020.00 80400.00 14,750.00

GD2.0 FN6.0 NM9.4

6-Origin The Amazing Man retold; The Shark begins; Ivy Menace by Tarpe Mills app. 294.00 882.00 2650.00
7-Magician From Mars begins; ends #11 200.00 600.00 1600.00
8-Cat-Man dresses as woman 137.00 411.00 1100.00
9-Magician From Mars battles the 'Elemental Monster,' swiped into The Spectre in More Fun #54 & 55. Ties w/Marvel Mystery #4 for 1st Nazi War-c on a comic (2/40) 137.00 411.00 1150.00
10,11: 11-Zardi, the Eternal Man begins; ends #16; Amazing Man dons costume; last Everett issue 120.00 360.00 960.00
12,13 105.00 315.00 840.00
14-Reef Kinkaid, Rocke Wayburn (ends #20), & Dr. Hypno (ends #21) begin; no Zardi or Chuck Hardy 87.00 261.00 700.00
15,17-20: 15-Zardi returns; no Rocke Wayburn. 17-Dr. Hypno returns; no Zardi 74.00 222.00 590.00
16-Mighty Man's powers of super strength & ability to shrink & grow explained; Rocke Wayburn returns; no Dr. Hypno; Al Avison (a character) begins, ends #18 (a tribute to the famed artist) 79.00 237.00 630.00
21-Origin Dash Dartwell (drug-use story); origin & only app. T.N.T.
74.00 222.00 590.00
22-Dash Dartwell, the Human Meteor & The Voice app; last Iron Skull & The Shark; Silver Streak app. (classic-c) 77.00 231.00 615.00
23-Two Amazing Man stories; intro/origin Tommy the Amazing Kid; The Marksman only app. 72.00 216.00 575.00
24-King of Darkness, Nightshade, & Blue Lady begin; end #26; 1st app. Super-Ann 72.00 216.00 550.00
25,26 (Scarce): Meteor Martin by Wolverton in both; 26-Electric Ray app.
109.00 327.00 875.00

NOTE: ***Everett** a-5-11; c-5-11. **Gilman** a-14-20. **Giunta/Mirando** a-7-10. **Sam Glanzman** a-14-16, 18-21, 23. **Louis Glanzman** a-6, 9-11, 14-21; c-13-19, 21. **Robert Golden** a-9. **Gustavson** a-6; c-22, 23. **Lubbers** a-14-21. **Simon** a-10. **Frank Thomas** a-6, 9-11, 14, 15, 17-21.*

AMAZING MYSTERIES (Formerly Sub-Mariner Comics No. 31)
Marvel Comics (CCC): No. 32, May, 1949 - No. 35, Jan, 1950 (1st Marvel Horror Comic)

32-The Witness app. 75.00 225.00 600.00
33-Horror format 32.00 96.00 225.00
34,35: Changes to Crime. 34,35-Photo-c 18.00 54.00 125.00

AMAZING MYSTERY FUNNIES
Centaur Publications: Aug, 1938 - No. 24, Sept, 1940 (All 52 pgs.)

V1#1-Everett-c(1st); Dick Kent Adv. story; Skyrocket Steele in the Year X on cover only 300.00 900.00 2700.00
2-Everett 1st-a (Skyrocket Steele) 175.00 525.00 1400.00
3 87.00 261.00 700.00
3(#4, 12/38)-nn on cover, #3 on inside; bondage-c
78.00 234.00 625.00
V2#1-4,6: 2-Drug use story. 3-Air-Sub DX begins by Burgos. 4-Dan Hastings, Hastings, Sand Hog begins (ends #5). 6-Last Skyrocket Steele
72.00 216.00 575.00
5-Classic Everett-c 92.00 276.00 740.00
7 (Scarce)-Intro. The Fantom of the Fair & begins; Everett, Gustavson, Burgos-a 300.00 900.00 2700.00
8-Origin & 1st app. Speed Centaur 122.00 366.00 975.00
9-11: 11-Self portrait and biog. of Everett; Jon Linton begins; early Robot cover (11/39) 72.00 216.00 575.00
12 (Scarce)-1st Space Patrol; Wolverton-a (12/39); new costume Phantom of the Fair 187.00 561.00 1500.00
V3#1(#17, 1/40)-Intro. Bullet; Tippy Taylor serial begins, ends #24 (continued in The Arrow #2) 72.00 216.00 575.00
18,20: 18-Fantom of the Fair by Gustavson 69.00 207.00 550.00
19,21-24: Space Patrol by Wolverton in all 87.00 261.00 750.00

NOTE: ***Burgos** a-V2#3-9. **Eisner** a-V1#2, 3(2). **Everett** a-V1#2-4, V2#1, 3-6; c-V1#1-4,V2#3, 5, 18. **Filchock** a-V2#9. **Flessel** a-V2#6. **Guardineer** a-V1#4, V2#4-6; **Gustavson** a-V2#4, 5, 9-12, V3#1, 18, 19; c-V2#7, 9, 12, V3#1, 21, 22; **McWilliams** a-V2#9, 10. **TarpeMills** a-V2#2, 4-6, 9-12, V3#1. **Leo Morey**(Pulp artist) c-V2#10; text illo-V2#11. **FrankThomas** a-6-V2#11. **Webster** a-V2#4.*

AMAZING SAINTS
Logos International: 1974 (39¢)

nn-True story of Phil Saint 5.00

AMAZING SCARLET SPIDER
Marvel Comics: Nov, 1995 - No. 2, Dec, 1995 ($1.95, limited series)

1,2: Replaces "Amazing Spider-Man" for two issues 2.00

AMAZING SPIDER-MAN, THE (See All Detergent Comics, Amazing Fantasy, America's Best TV Comics, Aurora, Deadly Foes of Spider-Man, Fireside Book Series, Giant-Size Spider-Man, Giant Size Super-Heroes Featuring..., Marvel Collectors Item Classics, Marvel Fanfare, Marvel Graphic Novel, Marvel Spec. Ed., Marvel Tales, Marvel Team-Up, Marvel Treasury Ed., Nothing Can Stop the Juggernaut, Official Marvel Index To..., Peter Parker..., Power Record Comics, Spectacular..., Spider-Man, Spider-Man Digest, Spider-Man Saga, Spider-Man 2099, Spider-Man Vs. Wolverine, Spidey Super Stories, Strange Tales Annual #2, Superman Vs. ..., Try-Out Winner Book, Web of Spider- Man & Within Our Reach)

AMAZING SPIDER-MAN, THE
Marvel Comics Group: March, 1963 - No. 441, Nov, 1998

GD2.0 FN6.0 VF8.0 NM9.4

1-Retells origin by Steve Ditko; 1st Fantastic Four x-over (ties w/F.F. #12 as first Marvel x-over); intro. John Jameson & The Chameleon; Spider-Man's 2nd app.; Kirby/Ditko-c; Ditko-c/a #1-38
700.00 2100.00 7000.00 18,000.00

GD2.0 FN6.0 NM9.4

1-Reprint from the Golden Record Comic set 7.50 22.50 75.00
with record (1966) 15.00 45.00 150.00
2-1st app. the Vulture & the Terrible Tinkerer 214.00 642.00 3000.00
3-1st full-length story; Human Torch cameo; intro. & 1st app. Doc Octopus; Spider-Man pin-up by Ditko 161.00 483.00 2100.00
4-Origin & 1st app. The Sandman (see Strange Tales #115 for 2nd app.); Intro. Betty Brant & Liz Allen 142.00 426.00 1700.00
5-Dr. Doom app. 121.00 363.00 1450.00
6-1st app. Lizard 104.00 312.00 1250.00
7,8,10: 7-Vs. The Vulture; 1st monthly issue. 8-Fantastic Four app. in back-up story by Kirby/Ditko. 10-1st app. Big Man & The Enforcers
67.00 200.00 800.00
9-Origin & 1st app. Electro (2/64) 75.00 225.00 900.00
11,12: 11-1st app. Bennett Brant. 12-Doc Octopus unmasks Spider-Man-c/story
41.00 123.00 475.00
13-1st app. Mysterio 55.00 165.00 665.00

GD2.0 FN6.0 VF8.0 NM9.4

14-(7/64)-1st app. The Green Goblin (c/story)(Norman Osborn); Hulk x-over
133.00 400.00 800.00 1600.00

GD2.0 FN6.0 NM9.4

15-1st app. Kraven the Hunter; 1st mention of Mary Jane Watson (not shown) 49.00 147.00 585.00
16-Spider-Man battles Daredevil (1st x-over 9/64); still in old yellow costume
35.00 105.00 385.00
17-2nd app. Green Goblin (c/story); Human Torch x-over (also in #18 & #21)
49.00 147.00 585.00
18-1st app. Ned Leeds who later becomes Hobgoblin; Fantastic Four back-up story; 3rd app. Sandman 35.00 105.00 380.00
19-Sandman app. 31.00 93.00 310.00
20-Origin & 1st app. The Scorpion 35.00 105.00 385.00
21-2nd app. The Beetle (see Strange Tales #123) 25.00 75.00 255.00
22-1st app. Princess Python 23.00 69.00 230.00
23-3rd app. The Green Goblin-c/story; Norman Osborn app.
31.00 93.00 350.00
24 21.00 62.00 205.00
25-(6/65)-1st app. Mary Jane Watson (cameo; face not shown); 1st app. Spencer Smythe; Norman Osborn app. 25.00 75.00 250.00
26-4th app. The Green Goblin-c/story; 1st app. Crime Master; dies in #27
28.00 84.00 280.00
27-5th app. The Green Goblin-c/story; Norman Osborn app.
26.00 78.00 260.00
28-Origin & 1st app. Molten Man (9/65, scarcer in high grade)
33.00 100.00 370.00
29,30 16.00 48.00 160.00

Amazing Spider-Man #39 © MAR

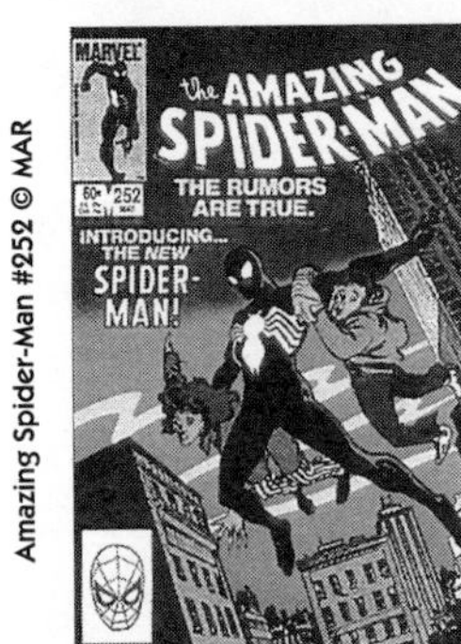

Amazing Spider-Man #252 © MAR

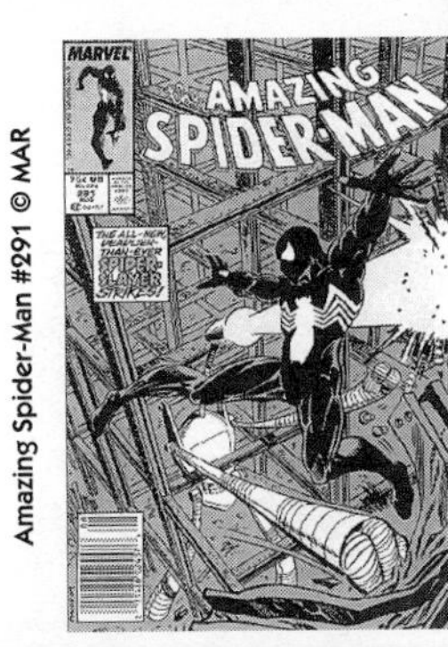

Amazing Spider-Man #291 © MAR

GD2.0 FN6.0 NM9.4

31-38: 31-1st app. Harry Osborn who later becomes 2nd Green Goblin, Gwen Stacy & Prof. Warren. 34-4th app. Kraven the Hunter. 36-1st app. Looter. 37-Intro. Norman Osborn. 38-(7/66)-2nd app. Mary Jane Watson (cameo; face not shown); last Ditko issue 16.00 48.00 160.00
39-The Green Goblin-c/story; Green Goblin's i.d. revealed as Norman Osborn; Romita-a begins (8/66; see Daredevil #16 for 1st Romita-a on Spider-Man) 21.50 65.00 215.00
40-1st told origin The Green Goblin-c/story 31.00 93.00 315.00
41-1st app. Rhino 16.50 50.00 165.00
42-(11/66)-3rd app. Mary Jane Watson (cameo in last 2 panels); 1st time face is shown 13.50 41.00 135.00
43-49: 44,45-2nd & 3rd app. The Lizard. 46-Intro. Shocker. 47-M. J. Watson & Peter Parker 1st date. 47-Green Goblin cameo; Harry & Norman Osborn app. 47,49-5th & 6th app. Kraven the Hunter 9.50 28.50 95.00
50-1st app. Kingpin (7/67) 36.00 108.00 400.00
51-2nd app. Kingpin 15.50 47.00 155.00
52-60: 52-1st app. Joe Robertson & 3rd app. Kingpin. 56-1st app. Capt. George Stacy. 57,58-Ka-Zar app. 59-1st app. Brainwasher (alias Kingpin); 1st-c app. M. J. Watson 7.00 21.00 70.00
61-74: 67-1st app. Randy Robertson. 69-Kingpin-c. 69,70-Kingpin app. 73-1st app. Silvermane. 74-Last 12¢ issue 5.00 15.00 50.00
75-89,91-93,95,99: 78,79-1st app. The Prowler. 83-1st app. Schemer & Vanessa (Kingpin's wife). 84,85-Kingpin-c/story. 86-Re-intro & origin Black Widow in new costume. 93-1st app. Arthur Stacy 4.00 12.00 40.00
90-Death of Capt. Stacey 5.50 16.50 55.00
94-Origin retold 7.00 21.00 70.00
96-98-Green Goblin app. (97,98-Green Goblin-c); drug books not approved by CCA 8.50 25.50 85.00
100-Anniversary issue (9/71); Green Goblin cameo (2 pgs.) 17.50 52.00 175.00
101-1st app. Morbius the Living Vampire; Wizard cameo; last 15¢ issue (10/71) 12.50 38.00 125.00
101-Silver ink 2nd printing (9/92, $1.75) 2.00
102-Origin & 2nd app. Morbius (25¢, 52 pgs.) 8.50 25.50 85.00
103-118: 104,111-Kraven the Hunter-c/stories. 108-1st app. Sha-Shan. 109-Dr. Strange-c/story (6/72). 110-1st app. Gibbon. 113-1st app. Hammerhead. 116-118-reprints story from Spectacular Spider-Man Mag. in color with some changes 3.00 9.00 30.00
119,120-Spider-Man vs. Hulk (4 & 5/73) 4.50 13.50 45.00
121-Death of Gwen Stacy (6/73) (killed by Green Goblin) (reprinted in Marvel Tales #98 & 192) 11.00 33.00 125.00
122-Death of The Green Goblin-c/story (7/73) (reprinted in Marvel Tales #99 & 192) 13.00 39.00 140.00
123,125-128: 123-Cage app. 125-Man-Wolf origin. 127-1st mention of Harry Osborn becoming Green Goblin 2.50 7.50 25.00
124-1st app. Man-Wolf (9/73) 3.60 11.00 36.00
129-1st app. Jackal & The Punisher (2/74) 14.50 44.00 160.00
130-133,138-141,152-154,160: 131-Last 20¢ issue. 139-1st app. Grizzly. 140-1st app. Glory Grant. 1.50 4.50 12.00
134-(7/74); 1st app. Tarantula; Harry Osborn discovers Spider-Man's ID; Punisher cameo 3.00 9.00 30.00
135-2nd full Punisher app. (8/74) 4.50 13.50 45.00
136-Reappearance of The Green Goblin (Harry Osborn; Norman Osborn's son) 4.00 12.00 40.00
137-Green Goblin-c/story (2nd Harry Osborn) 3.50 10.50 35.00
142,143-Gwen Stacy clone cameos: 143-1st app. Cyclone 2.50 7.50 22.00
144-147: 144-Full app. of Gwen Stacy clone. 145,146-Gwen Stacy clone story line continues. 147-Spider-Man learns Gwen Stacy is clone 2.00 6.00 16.00
148-Jackal revealed 2.50 7.50 24.00
149-Spider-Man clone story begins, clone dies (?); origin of Jackal 3.50 11.00 35.00
150-Spider-Man decides he is not the clone 1.85 5.50 15.00
151-Spider-Man disposes of clone body 1.50 4.50 12.00
155-159-(Regular 25¢ editions). 159- Last 25¢ issue(8/76) 1.50 4.50 12.00
155-159-(30¢-c variants, limited distribution) 3.60 11.00 36.00
161-Nightcrawler app. from X-Men; Punisher cameo; Wolverine & Colossus app. 1.50 4.50 12.00
162-Punisher, Nightcrawler app.; 1st Jigsaw 1.50 4.50 12.00
163-168,181-190: 167-1st app. Will O' The Wisp. 181-Origin retold; gives life history of Spidey; Punisher cameo in flashback (1 panel). 182-(7/78)-Peter 's first proposal to Mary Jane, but she refuses 1.00 3.00 8.00
169-173-(Regular 30¢ edition). 169-Clone story recapped. 171-Nova app. 1.00 3.00 8.00
169-173-(35¢-c variants, limited dist.)(6-10/77) 3.20 9.60 32.00
174,175-Punisher app. 1.50 4.50 12.00
176-180-Green Goblin app 1.85 5.50 15.00
191-193,195-199,203-208,210-219: 193-Peter & Mary Jane break up. 196-Faked death of Aunt May. 203-2nd app. Dazzler. 209-1st app. Calypso (Kraven's girlfriend). 210-1st app. Madame Web. 212-1st app. Hydro Man; origin Sandman 1.00 2.80 7.00
194-1st app. Black Cat 1.75 5.25 14.00
200-Giant origin issue (1/80) 2.25 6.75 18.00
201,202-Punisher app. 1.25 3.75 10.00
209-Origin & 1st app. Calypso (10/80) 1.00 2.80 7.00
220-237: 225-(2/82)-Foolkiller-c/story. 226,227-Black Cat returns. 236-Tarantula dies. 234-Free 16 pg. insert "Marvel Guide to Collecting Comics". 235-Origin Will-'O-The-Wisp 2.40 6.00
238-(3/83)-1st app. Hobgoblin (Ned Leeds); came with skin "Tattooz" decal. **Note:** The same decal appears in the more common Fantastic Four #252 which is being removed & placed in this issue as incentive to increase value (Value listed is with or without tattooz) 5.00 15.00 50.00
239-2nd app. Hobgoblin & 1st battle w/Spidey 3.00 9.00 30.00
240-243,246-248: 241-Origin The Vulture. 243-Reintro Mary Jane Watson after 4 year absence 5.00
244-3rd app. Hobgoblin (cameo) 1.00 3.00 8.00
245-(10/83)-4th app. Hobgoblin (cameo); Lefty Donovan gains powers of Hobgoblin & battles Spider-Man 1.50 4.50 12.00
249-251: 3 part Hobgoblin/Spider-Man battle. 249-Retells origin & death of 1st Green Goblin. 251-Last old costume 1.25 3.75 10.00
252-Spider-Man dons new black costume (5/84); ties with Marvel Team-Up #141 & Spectacular Spider-Man #90 for 1st new costume (See Marvel S-H Secret Wars #8) 2.50 7.50 25.00
253-1st app. The Rose 2.40 6.00
254-258: 256-1st app. Puma. 257-Hobgoblin cameo; 2nd app. Puma; M. J. Watson reveals she knows Spidey's i.d. 258-Hobgoblin app. (minor) 5.00
259-Full Hobgoblin app.; Spidey back to old costume; origin Mary Jane Watson 1.00 3.00 8.00
260-Hobgoblin app. 2.40 6.00
261-Hobgoblin-c/story; painted-c by Vess 1.00 2.80 7.00
262-Spider-Man unmasked; photo-c 5.00
263,264,266-274,277-280,282,283: 274-Zarathos (The Spirit of Vengeance) app. 277-Vess back-up art. 279-Jack O'Lantern-c/story. 282-X-Factor x-over 3.50
265-1st app. Silver Sable (6/85) 2.40 6.00
265-Silver ink 2nd printing ($1.25) 2.00
275-($1.25, 52 pgs.)-Hobgoblin-c/story; origin-r by Ditko 1.25 3.75 10.00
276-Hobgoblin app. 2.40 6.00
281-Hobgoblin battles Jack O'Lantern 1.00 2.60 6.50
284,285: 284-Punisher cameo; Gang War story begins; Hobgoblin-c/story. 285-Punisher app.; minor Hobgoblin app. 1.00 2.80 7.00
286-288: 286-Hobgoblin-c & app. (minor). 287-Hobgoblin app. (minor). 288-Full Hobgoblin app.; last Gang War 2.40 6.00
289-(6/87, $1.25, 52 pgs.)-Hobgoblin's i.d. revealed as Ned Leeds; death of Ned Leeds; Macendale (Jack O'Lantern) becomes new Hobgoblin (1st app.) 2.25 6.75 18.00
290-292,295-297: 290-Peter proposes to Mary Jane. 292-She accepts; leads into Amazing Spider-Man Annual #21 4.00
293,294-Part 2 & 5 of Kraven story from Web of Spider-Man. 294-Death of Kraven 2.40 6.00

Amazing Spider-Man #355 © MAR

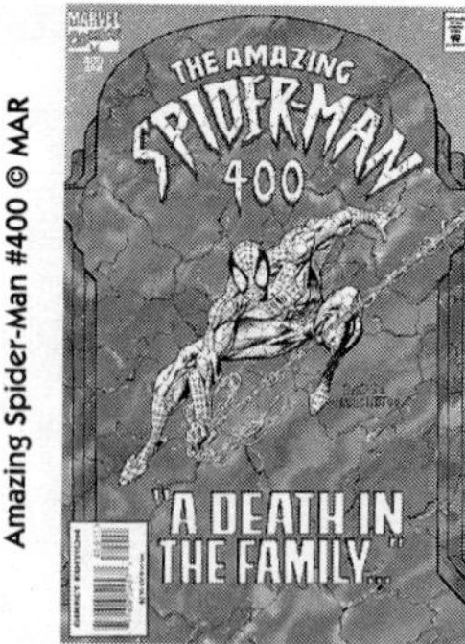

Amazing Spider-Man #400 © MAR

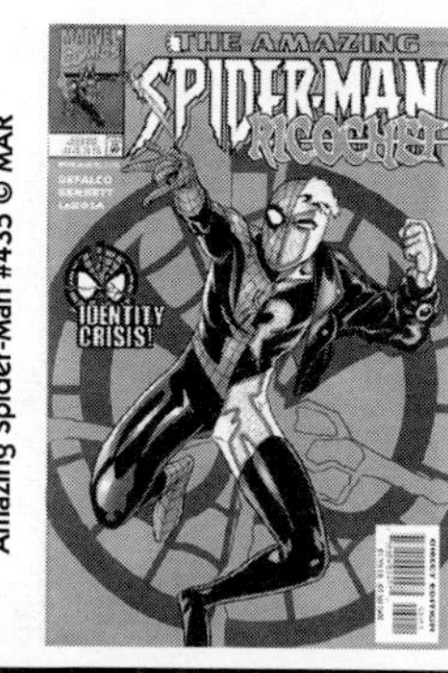

Amazing Spider-Man #435 © MAR

GD2.0 FN6.0 NM9.4

298-Todd McFarlane-c/a begins (3/88); 1st app. Eddie Brock who becomes Venom; (cameo on last pg.) 2.50 7.50 25.00
299-1st app. Venom with costume (cameo) 1.85 5.50 15.00
300 ($1.50, 52 pgs.; 25th Anniversary)-1st full Venom app.; last black costume (5/88) 5.50 16.50 55.00
301-305: 301 ($1.00 issues begin). 304-1st bi-weekly issue 1.00 3.00 8.00
306-311,313,314: 306-Swipes-c from Action #1. 315-317-Venom app. 2.40 6.00
312-Hobgoblin battles Green Goblin 1.25 3.75 10.00
315-317-Venom app. 1.25 3.75 10.00
318-323,325: 319-Bi-weekly begins again 5.00
324-Sabretooth app.; McFarlane cover only 2.40 6.00
326,327,329: 327-Cosmic Spidey continues from Spectacular Spider-Man (no McFarlane-c/a) 3.00
328-Hulk x-over; last McFarlane issue 1.00 2.80 7.00
330,331-Punisher app. 331-Minor Venom app. 3.00
332,333-Venom-c/story 2.40 6.00
334-336,338-343: 341-Tarantula app. 3.00
337-Hobgoblin app. 3.50
344-1st app. Cletus Kasady (Carnage) 1.00 3.00 8.00
345-1st full app. Cletus Kasady; Venom cameo on last pg. 1.10 3.30 9.00
346,347-Venom app. 5.00
348,349,351-359: 348-Avengers x-over. 351,352-Nova of New Warriors app. 353-Darkhawk app.; brief Punisher app. 354-Punisher cameo & Nova, Night Thrasher (New Warriors), Darkhawk & Moon Knight app. 357,358-Punisher, Darkhawk, Moon Knight, Night Thrasher, Nova x-over. 358-3 part gatefold-c; last $1.00-c. 360-Carnage cameo 2.50
350-($1.50, 52pgs.)-Origin retold; Spidey vs. Dr. Doom; pin-ups; Uncle Ben app. 3.00
360-Carnage cameo 3.00
361-Intro Carnage (the Spawn of Venom); begin 3 part story; recap of how Spidey's alien costume became Venom 1.00 3.00 8.00
361-($1.25)-2nd printing; silver-c 2.50
362,363-Carnage & Venom-c/story 5.00
362-2nd printing 2.00
364,366-374,376-387: 364-The Shocker app. (old villain). 366-Peter's parents-c/story. 369-Harry Osborn back-up (Gr. Goblin II). 373-Venom back-up. 374-Venom-c/story. 376-Cardiac app. 378-Maximum Carnage part 3. 381,382-Hulk app. 383-The Jury app. 384-Venom/carnage app. 387-New costume Vulture 2.00
365-($3.95, 84 pgs.)-30th anniversary issue w/silver hologram on-c; Spidey/Venom/Carnage pull-out poster; contains 5 pg. preview of Spider-Man 2099 (1st app.); Spidey's origin retold; Lizard app.; reintro Peter's parents in Stan Lee 3 pg. text w/illo (story continues thru #370). 4.00
365-Second printing; gold hologram on-c 2.00
375-($3.95, 68 pgs.)-Holo-grafx foil-c; vs. Venom story; ties into Venom: Lethal Protector #1; Pat Olliffe-a. 4.00
388-($2.25, 68 pgs.)-Newsstand edition; Venom back-up & Cardiac & chance back-up 2.25
388-($2.95, 68 pgs.)-Collector's edition w/foil-c 3.00
389-396,398,399,401-420: 389-$1.50-c begins; bound-in trading card sheet; Green Goblin app. 394-Power & Responsibility Pt. 2. 396-Daredevil-c & app. 403-Carnage app. 406-1st New Doc Octopus. 407-Human Torch, Silver Sable, Sandman app. 409-Kaine, Rhino app. 410-Carnage app. 414-The Rose app. 415-Onslaught story; Spidey vs. Sentinels. 416-Epilogue to Onslaught; Garney-a(p); Williamson-a(i) 2.00
390-($2.95)-Collector's edition polybagged w/16 pg. insert of new animated Spidey TV show plus animation cel 3.00
394-($2.95, 48 pgs.)-Deluxe edition; flip book w/Birth of a Spider-Man Pt. 2; silver foil both-c 3.00
397-($2.25)-Flip book w/Ultimate Spider-Man 2.25
400-($2.95)-Death of Aunt May 3.00
400-($3.95)-Death of Aunt May; embossed double-c 5.00
400-Collector's Edition; white-c 1.00 3.00 8.00
408-($2.95) Polybagged version with TV theme song cassette 8.00

GD2.0 FN6.0 NM9.4

421-424, -1 (7/97)($1.95-c) 2.00
425-($2.99)-48 pgs., wraparound-c 3.00
426,428-433: 426-Begin $1.99-c. 432-Spiderhunt pt. 2 2.00
427-($2.25) Return of Dr. Octopus; double gatefold-c 2.25
434-440: 434-Double cover with "Amazing Ricochet #1". 438-Daredevil app. 439-Avengers-c/app. 440-Byrne-s 2.00
441-Final issue; Byrne-s 3.00
Annual 1 (1964, 72 pgs.)-Origin Spider-Man; 1st app. Sinister Six (Dr. Octopus, Electro, Kraven the Hunter, Mysterio, Sandman, Vulture) (41 pg. story); plus gallery of Spidey foes 56.00 168.00 675.00
Annual 2 (1965, 25¢, 72 pgs.)-Reprints from #1,2,5 plus new Doctor Strange story 25.00 75.00 250.00
Special 3 (11/66, 25¢, 72 pgs.)-Avengers & Hulk x-over; Doctor Octopus-r from #11,12; Romita-a 9.00 27.00 90.00
Special 4 (11/67, 25¢, 68 pgs.)-Spidey battles Human Torch (new 41 pg. story) 8.50 25.50 85.00
Special 5 (11/68, 25¢, 68 pgs.)-New 40 pg. Red Skull story; 1st app. Peter Parker's parents; last annual with new-a 8.00 24 00 80.00
Special 6 (11/69, 25¢, 68 pgs.)-Reprints 41 pg. Sinister Six story from annual #1 plus 2 Kirby/Ditko stories (r) 3.50 10.50 35.00
Special 7 (12/70, 25¢, 68 pgs.)-All-r(#1,2) 3.50 10.50 35.00
Special 8 (12/71)-All-r 3.50 10.50 35.00
King Size 9 ('73)-Reprints Spectacular Spider-Man (mag.) #2; 40 pg. Green Goblin-c/story (re-edited from 58 pgs.) 3.50 10.50 35.00
Annual 10 (1976)-Origin Human Fly (vs. Spidey); new-a begins 1.85 5.50 15.00
Annual 11-13 ('77-'79)-12 -Spider-Man vs. Hulk-r/#119,120. 3-Byrne/Austin-a (new) 1.25 3.75 10.00
Annual 14 (1980)-Miller-c/a(p), 40pgs. 1.50 4.50 12.00
Annual 15 (1981)-Miller-c/a(p); Punisher app. 1.50 4.50 12.00
Annual 16-20: 16 (1982)-Origin/1st app. new Capt. Marvel (female heroine). 17 (1983). 18 (1984). 19 (1985). 20 (1986)-Origin Iron Man of 2020 2.40 6.00
Annual 21 (1987)-Special wedding issue; newsstand & direct sale versions exist & are worth same 1.25 3.75 10.00
Annual 22 (1988, $1.75, 68 pgs.)-1st app. Speedball; Evolutionary War x-over; Daredevil app. 2.40 6.00
Annual 23 (1989, $2.00, 68 pgs.)-Atlantis Attacks; origin Spider-Man retold; She-Hulk app.; Byrne-c; Liefeld-a(p), 23 pgs. 4.00
Annual 24 (1990, $2.00, 68 pgs.)-Ant-Man app. 3.00
Annual 25 (1991, $2.00, 68 pgs.)-3 pg. origin recap; Iron Man app.; 1st Venom solo story; Ditko-a (6 pgs.) 5.00
Annual 26 (1992, $2.25, 68 pgs.)-New Warriors-c/story; Venom solo story cont'd in Spectacular Spider-Man Annual #12 4.00
Annual 27,28 ('93, '94, $2.95, 68 pgs.)-27-Bagged w/card; 1st app. Annex. 28-Carnage-c/story; Rhino & Cloak and Dagger back-ups 3.00
'96 Special-($2.95, 64 pgs.)-"Blast From The Past" 4.00
'97 Special-($2.99)-Wraparound-c,Sundown app. 4.00
Super Special 1 (4/95, $3.95)-Flip Book 4.00
...: Skating on Thin Ice 1(1990, $1.25, Canadian)-McFarlane-c; anti-drug issue 1.10 3.30 9.00
...: Skating on Thin Ice 1 (2/93, $1.50, American) 3.00
...: Double Trouble 2 (1990, $1.25, Canadian) 2.40 6.00
...: Double Trouble 2 (2/93, $1.50, American) 2.00
...: Hit and Run 3 (1990, $1.25, Canadian)-Ghost Rider-c/story 1.10 3.30 9.00
...: Hit and Run 3 (2/93. $1.50, American) 2.00
... : Carnage (6/93, $6.95)-r/ASM #344,345,359-363 1.00 2.80 7.00
...: Chaos in Calgary 4 (Canadian; part of 5 part series) 1.75 5.25 14.00
...: Chaos in Calgary 4 (2/93, $1.50, American) 2.00
...: Deadball 5 (1993, $1.60, Canadian)-Green Goblin-c/story; features Montreal Expos 2.25 6.75 18.00

Note: Prices listed above are for English Canadian editions. French editions are worth double.

...: Soul of the Hunter nn (8/92, $5.95, 52 pgs.)-Zeck-c/a(p) 2.40 6.00
Parallel Lives (1990, $8.95, 68pgs.)-Graphic novel 1.10 3.30 9.00

Amazing Spider-Man V2 #5 © MAR

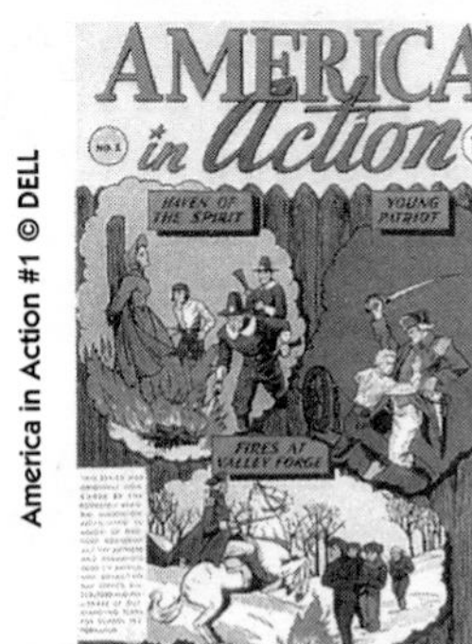

America in Action #1 © DELL

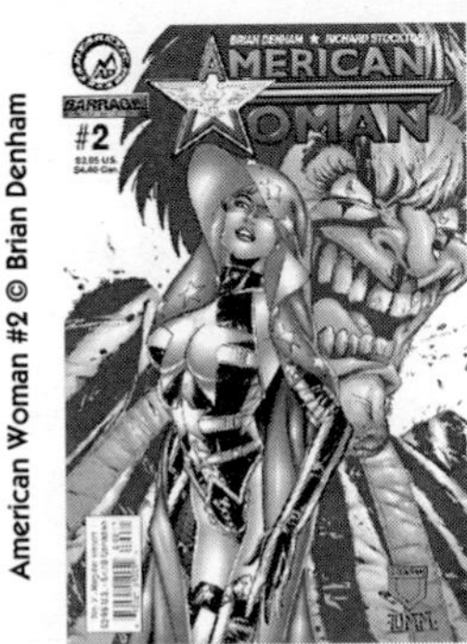

American Woman #2 © Brian Denham

GD2.0 FN6.0 NM9.4

NOTE: ***Austin*** *a(i)-248, 335, 337, Annual 13; c(i)-188, 241, 242, 248, 331, 334, 343, Annual 25.* ***J. Buscema*** *a(p)-72, 73, 76-81, 84, 85.* ***Byrne*** *a-189p, 190p, 206p, Annual 3r, 6r, 7r, 13p; c-189p, 268, 296, Annual 12.* ***Ditko*** *a-1-38, Annual 1, Special 3(r), 2, 24(2); c-1i, 2-38.* ***Guice*** *c/a-Annual 18i.* ***Gil Kane*** *a(p)-89-105, 120-124, 150, Annual 10, 12i, 24p; c-90p, 96, 98, 99, 101-105p, 129p, 131p, 132p, 137-140p, 143p, 148p, 149p, 151p, 153p, 160p, 161p, Annual 10p, 24.* ***Kirby*** *a-8.* ***Erik Larsen*** *a-324, 327, 329-350; c-327, 329-350, 354i, Annual 25.* ***McFarlane*** *a-298p, 299p, 300-303, 304-323p, 325p, 328; c-298-325, 328.* ***Miller*** *c-218, 219.* ***Mooney*** *a-65i, 67-82i, 84-88i, 173i, 178i, 189i, 190i, 192i, 193i, 196-202i, 207i, 211-219i, 221i, 222i, 226i, 227i, 229-233i, Annual 11i, 17i.* ***Nasser*** *c-228p.* ***Nebres*** *a-Annual 24i.* ***Russell*** *c-357i.* ***Simonson*** *c-222, 337i.* ***Starlin*** *a-113i, 114i, 187p.* ***Williamson*** *a-365i.*

AMAZING SPIDER-MAN (Volume 2)
Marvel Comics: Jan, 1998 - Present ($2.99/$1.99)

1-($2.99)-Byrne-a 4.00
1-($6.95) Dynamic Forces variant-c by the Romitas 1.00 3.00 10.00
2-($1.99) Two covers -by John Byrne and Andy Kubert 3.00
3-10: 4-Fantastic Four app. 5-Spider-Woman-c 2.00
1999 Annual (6/99, $3.50) Buscema-a 3.50

AMAZING WILLIE MAYS, THE
Famous Funnies Publ.: No date (Sept, 1954)

nn 70.00 280.00 560.00

AMAZING WORLD OF SUPERMAN (See Superman)

AMAZING X-MEN
Marvel Comics: Mar, 1995 - No.4, July, 1995 ($1.95, limited series)

1-Age of Apocalypse 3.00
2-4 2.00

AMAZON
Comico: Mar, 1989 - No. 3, May, 1989 ($1.95, limited series)

1-3: Ecological theme 2.00

AMAZON (Also see Marvel Versus DC #3 & DC Versus Marvel #4)
DC Comics (Amalgam): Apr, 1996 ($1.95, one-shot)

1-John Byrne-c/a/scripts 2.00

AMAZON ATTACK 3-D
The 3-D Zone: Sept, 1990 ($3.95, 28 pgs.)

1-Chaykin-a 4.00

AMAZON WOMAN (1st Series)
FantaCo: Summer, 1994 - No. 2, Fall, 1994 ($2.95, B&W, limited series, mature)

1,2: Tom Simonton-c/a/scripts 3.00

AMAZON WOMAN (2nd Series)
FantaCo: Feb, 1996 - No. 4, May, 1996 ($2.95, B&W, limited series, mature)

1-4: Tom Simonton-a/scripts 3.00

AMAZON WOMAN: INVADERS OF TERROR
FantaCo: 1996 ($5.95, B&W, one-shot, mature)

nn-Tom Simonton-a/scripts 2.40 6.00

AMBUSH (See Zane Grey, Four Color 314)

AMBUSH BUG (Also see Son of...)
DC Comics: June, 1985 - No. 4, Sept, 1985 (75¢, limited series)

1-4: Giffen-c/a in all 2.00
Nothing Special 1 (9/92, $2.50, 68pg.)-Giffen-c/a 2.50
Stocking Stuffer (2/86, $1.25)-Giffen-c/a 2.00

AMERICA AT WAR - THE BEST OF DC WAR COMICS (See Fireside Book Series)

AMERICA IN ACTION
Dell(Imp. Publ. Co.)/Mayflower House Publ.: 1942; Winter, 1945 (36 pgs.)

1942-Dell-(68 pgs.) 16.00 47.00 110.00
1-(1945)-Has 3 adaptations from American history; Kiefer, Schrotter & Webb-a 11.00 33.00 75.00

AMERICAN, THE
Dark Horse Comics: July, 1987 - No. 8, 1989 ($1.50/$1.75, B&W)

1-8: ($1.50) 2.00
Collection ($5.95, B&W)-Reprints 2.40 6.00

GD2.0 FN6.0 NM9.4

Special 1 (1990, $2.25, B&W) 2.25

AMERICAN AIR FORCES, THE (See A-1 Comics)
William H. Wise(Flying Cadet Publ. Co./Hasan(No.1)/Life's Romances/ Magazine Ent. No. 5 on): Sept-Oct, 1944-No. 4, 1945; No. 5, 1951-No. 12, 1954

1-Article by Zack Mosley, creator of Smilin' Jack 13.00 39.00 90.00
2-4 8.70 26.00 52.00

NOTE: *All part comic, part magazine. Art by* **Whitney, Chas. Quinlan, H. C. Kiefer,** *and* ***Tony Dipreta.***

5(A-1 45)(Formerly Jet Powers), 6(A-1 54), 7(A-1 58), 8(A-1 65), 9(A-1 67), 10(A-1 74), 11(A-1 79), 12(A-1 91) 5.70 17.00 34.00

NOTE: ***Powell*** *c/a-5-12.*

AMERICAN FLAGG! (See First Comics Graphic Novel 3,9,12,21 & Howard Chaykin's..)
First Comics: Oct, 1983 - No. 50, Mar, 1988

1-Chaykin-c/a begins 2.00
2-50: 21-27-Alan Moore scripts. 31-Origin Bob Violence 2.00
Special 1 (11/86)-Introduces Chaykin's Time^2 2.00

AMERICAN FREAK: A TALE OF THE UN-MEN
DC Comics (Vertigo): Feb, 1994 - No. 5, Jun, 1994 ($1.95, mini-series, mature)

1-5 2.00

AMERICAN GRAPHICS
Henry Stewart: No. 1, 1954; No. 2, 1957 (25¢)

1-The Maid of the Mist, The Last of the Eries (Indian Legends of Niagara) (sold at Niagara Falls) 10.00 30.00 60.00
2-Victory at Niagara & Laura Secord (Heroine of the War of 1812) 6.35 19.00 38.00

AMERICAN INDIAN, THE (See Picture Progress)

AMERICAN LIBRARY
David McKay Publ.: 1943 - No. 6, 1944 (15¢, 68 pgs., B&W, text & pictures)

nn (#1)-Thirty Seconds Over Tokyo (movie) 34.00 103.00 240.00
nn (#2)-Guadalcanal Diary; painted-c (only 10¢) 26.00 77.00 180.00
3-6: 3-Look to the Mountain. 4-Case of the Crooked Candle (Perry Mason). 5-Duel in the Sun. 6-Wingate's Raiders 11.50 34.00 80.00

AMERICAN: LOST IN AMERICA, THE
Dark Horse Comics: July, 1992 - No. 4, Oct, 1992 ($2.50, limited series)

1-4: 1-Dorman painted-c. 2-Joe Phillips painted-c. 3-Mignola-c. 4-Jim Lee-c. 2.50

AMERICAN SPLENDOR: (Series of titles)
Dark Horse Comics: Aug, 1996 - Sept, 1999 ($2.95, B&W, all one-shots)

--**COMIC-CON COMICS** (8/96) 1-H. Pekar script. --**MUSIC COMICS** (11/97) nn-H. Pekar-s/Sacco-a; r/Village Voice jazz strips. --**ODDS AND ENDS** (12/97) 1-Pekar-s. --**ON THE JOB** (5/97) 1-Pekar-s. --**A STEP OUT OF THE NEST** (8/94) 1-Pekar-s. --**TERMINAL** (9/99) 1-Pekar-s. --**TRANSATLANTIC** (7/98) 1-"American Splendour" on cover; Pekar-s 3.00

AMERICAN SPLENDOR: WINDFALL
Dark Horse Comics: Sept, 1995 - No. 2, Oct,1995 ($3.95, B&W, limited series)

1,2-Pekar script 4.00

AMERICAN TAIL: FIEVEL GOES WEST, AN
Marvel Comics: Early Jan, 1992 - No. 3, Early Feb, 1992 ($1.00, limited series)

1-3-Adapts Universal animated movie; Wildman-a 2.00

AMERICAN WOMAN
Antarctic Press (Barrage Studios): Jun, 1998 - No. 2 ($2.95)

1,2: 1-Denham-s/a. 2-Stockton-s 3.00

AMERICA'S BEST COMICS
Nedor/Better/Standard Publications: Feb, 1942; No. 2, Sept, 1942 - No. 31, July, 1949 (New logo with #9)

1-The Woman in Red, Black Terror, Captain Future, Doc Strange, The Liberator, & Don Davis, Secret Ace begin 225.00 675.00 1800.00
2-Origin The American Eagle; The Woman in Red ends 87.00 261.00 700.00

America's Greatest Comics #7 © FAW

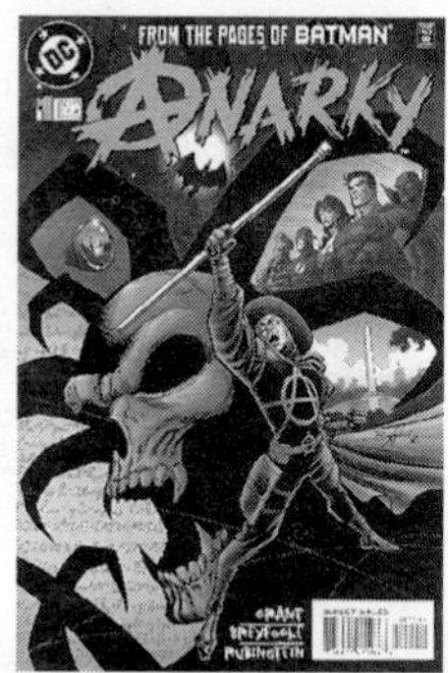

Anarky (2nd series) #1 © DC

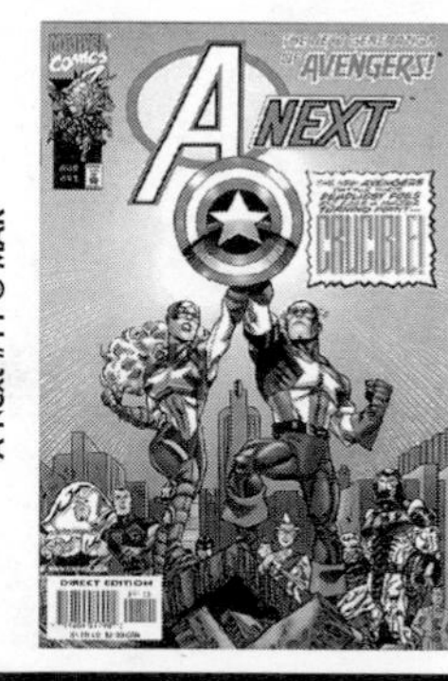

A-Next #11 © MAR

3-Pyroman begins (11/42, 1st app.; also see Startling Comics #18, 12/42) 66.00 200.00 525.00
4-6: 5-Last Capt. Future (not in #4); Lone Eagle app. 6-American Crusader app. 50.00 150.00 400.00
7-Hitler, Mussolini & Hirohito-c 69.00 208.00 550.00
8-Last Liberator 45.00 135.00 360.00
9-The Fighting Yank begins; The Ghost app. 55.00 165.00 440.00
10,12-21: 10-Flag-c. 14-American Eagle ends. 21-Infinity-c. 42.00 126.00 340.00
11-Hirohito & Tojo-c. (10/44) 45.00 135.00 360.00
22-Capt. Future app. 40.00 120.00 300.00
23-Miss Masque begins; last Doc Strange 47.00 141.00 375.00
24-Miss Masque bondage-c 45.00 135.00 360.00
25-Last Fighting Yank; Sea Eagle app. 40.00 120.00 280.00
26-31: 26-The Phantom Detective & The Silver Knight app.; Frazetta text illo & some panels in Miss Masque. 27,28-Commando Cubs. 27-Doc Strange. 28-Tuska Black Terror. 29-Last Pyroman 40.00 120.00 280.00
NOTE: *American Eagle not in 3, 8, 9, 13. Fighting Yank not in 10, 12. Liberator not in 2, 6, 7. Pyroman not in 9, 11, 14-16, 23, 25-27.* ***Schomburg (Xela)*** *c-5, 7-31. Bondage c-18, 24.*

AMERICA'S BEST TV COMICS (TV)
American Broadcasting Co. (Prod. by Marvel Comics): 1967 (25¢, 68 pgs.)
1-Spider-Man, Fantastic Four (by Kirby/Ayers), Casper, King Kong, George of the Jungle, Journey to the Center of the Earth stories (promotes new TV cartoon show) 13.50 40.00 95.00

AMERICA'S BIGGEST COMICS BOOK
William H. Wise: 1944 (196 pgs., one-shot)
1-The Grim Reaper, The Silver Knight, Zudo, the Jungle Boy, Commando Cubs, Thunderhoof app. 40.00 120.00 300.00

AMERICA'S FUNNIEST COMICS
William H. Wise: 1944 - No. 2, 1944 (15¢, 80 pgs.)
nn(#1), 2 27.00 81.00 190.00

AMERICA'S GREATEST COMICS
Fawcett Publications: May?, 1941 - No. 8, Summer, 1943 (15¢, 100 pgs., soft cardboard-c)
1-Bulletman, Spy Smasher, Capt. Marvel, Minute Man & Mr. Scarlet begin; Classic Mac Raboy-c. 1st time that Fawcett's major super-heroes appear together as a group on a cover. Fawcett's 1st squarebound comic. 275.00 825.00 2200.00
2 137.00 411.00 1100.00
3 97.00 291.00 775.00
4,5: 4-Commando Yank begins; Golden Arrow, Ibis the Invincible & Spy Smasher cameo in Captain Marvel 73.00 219.00 585.00
6,7: 7-Balbo the Boy Magician app.; Captain Marvel, Bulletman cameo in Mr. Scarlet 67.00 200.00 535.00
8-Capt. Marvel Jr. & Golden Arrow app.; Spy Smasher x-over in Capt. Midnight; no Minute Man or Commando Yank 67.00 200.00 535.00

AMERICA'S SWEETHEART SUNNY (See Sunny, ...)

AMERICA VS. THE JUSTICE SOCIETY
DC Comics: Jan, 1985 - No. 4, Apr, 1985 ($1.00, limited series)
1-Double size; Alcala-a(i) in all 4.00
2-4: 3,4-Spectre cameo 3.00

AMERICOMICS
Americomics: April, 1983 - No. 6, Mar, 1984 ($2.00, Baxter paper/slick paper)
1-Intro/origin The Shade; Intro. The Slayer, Captain Freedom and The Liberty Corps; Perez-c 3.00
1,2-2nd printings ($2.00) 2.00
2-6: 2-Messenger app. & 1st app. Tara on Jungle Island. 3-New & old Blue Beetle battle. 4-Origin Dragonfly & Shade. 5-Origin Commando D. 6-Origin the Scarlet Scorpion 2.00
Special 1 (8/83, $2.00)-Sentinels of Justice (Blue Beetle, Captain Atom, Nightshade & The Question) 3.00

AMETHYST
DC Comics: Jan, 1985 - No. 16, Aug, 1986 (75¢)
1-16: 8-Fire Jade's i.d. revealed, Special 1 (10/86, $1.25) 2.00
1-4 (11/87 - 2/88)(Limited series) 2.00

AMETHYST, PRINCESS OF GEMWORLD (See Legion of Super-Heroes #298)
DC Comics: May, 1983 - No. 12, Apr, 1984 (Maxi-series)
1-(60¢) 2.00
1,2-(35¢): tested in Austin & Kansas City 2.50 7.50 20.00
2-12: Perez-c(p) #6-11, Annual 1(9/84) 2.00
NOTE: ***Perez*** *c-4i, 5-11p.*

AMY RACECAR COLOR SPECIAL (See Stray Bullets)
El Capitán Books: July, 1997 ($2.95, one-shot)
1-David Laphan-a/scripts 3.00

ANARCHO DICTATOR OF DEATH (See Comics Novel)

ANARKY (See Batman titles)
DC Comics: May, 1997 - No. 4, Aug, 1997 ($2.50, limited series)
1 3.50
2-4 2.50

ANARKY (See Batman titles)
DC Comics: May, 1999 - Present ($2.50)
1-6: 1-JLA app.; Grant-s/Breyfogle-a. 3-Green Lantern app. 2.50

ANCHORS ANDREWS (The Saltwater Daffy)
St. John Publishing Co.: Jan, 1953 - No. 4, July, 1953
(Anchors the Saltwater... No. 4)
1-Canteen Kate by Matt Baker (9 pgs.) 19.00 56.00 130.00
2-4 5.85 17.50 35.00

ANDY & WOODY (See March of Comics No. 40, 55, 76)

ANDY BURNETT (TV, Disney)
Dell Publishing Co.: Dec, 1957
Four Color 865-Photo-c 9.00 27.00 100.00

ANDY COMICS (Formerly Scream Comics; becomes Ernie Comics)
Current Publications (Ace Magazines): No. 20, June, 1948-No. 21, Aug, 1948
20,21: Archie-type comic 5.85 17.50 35.00

ANDY DEVINE WESTERN
Fawcett Publications: Dec, 1950 - No. 2, 1951
1 53.00 160.00 425.00
2 40.00 120.00 310.00

ANDY GRIFFITH SHOW, THE (TV)(1st show aired 10/3/60)
Dell Publishing Co.: #1252, Jan-Mar, 1962 - #1341, Apr-Jun, 1962
Four Color 1252(#1), 1341-Photo-c 32.00 95.00 350.00

ANDY HARDY COMICS (See Movie Comics #3 by Fiction House)
Dell Publishing Co.: April, 1952 - No. 6, Sept-Nov, 1954
Four Color 389(#1) 2.70 8.00 30.00
Four Color 447,480,515,5,6 2.25 6.80 25.00

ANDY PANDA (Also see Crackajack Funnies #39, The Funnies, New Funnies & Walter Lantz...)
Dell Publishing Co.: 1943 - No. 56, Nov-Jan, 1961-62 (Walter Lantz)
Four Color 25(#1, 1943) 48.00 143.00 525.00
Four Color 54(1944) 30.00 89.00 325.00
Four Color 85(1945) 15.50 46.00 170.00
Four Color 130(1946),154,198 9.50 29.00 105.00
Four Color 216,240,258,280,297 6.25 18.50 68.00
Four Color 326,345,358 3.80 11.50 40.00
Four Color 383,409 2.90 8.70 32.00
16(11-1/52-53) - 30 1.60 4.80 16.00
31-56 1.00 3.00 10.00
(See March of Comics #5, 22, 79, & Super Book #4, 15, 27.)

A-NEXT (See Avengers)
Marvel Comics: Oct, 1998 - No. 12, Sept, 1999 ($1.99)
1-Next generation of Avengers; Frenz-a 2.50
2-12: 2-Two covers. 3-Defenders app. 2.00

Angela TPB © Todd McFarlane Prod.

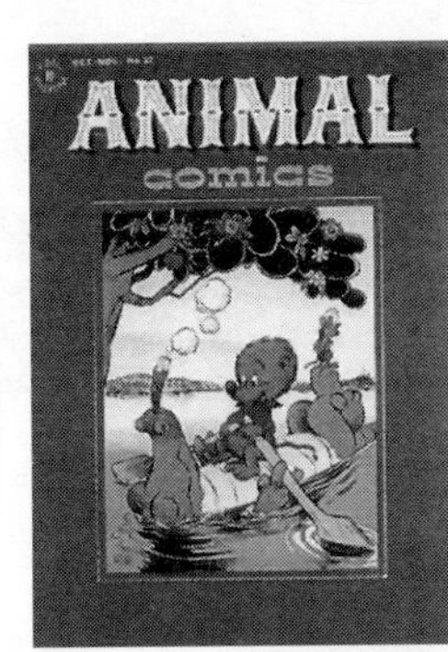

Animal Comics #17 © DELL

Animaniacs #51 © Warner Bros.

	GD2.0	FN6.0	NM9.4

ANGEL
Dell Publishing Co.: Aug, 1954 - No. 16, Nov-Jan, 1958-59

	GD2.0	FN6.0	NM9.4
Four Color 576(#1, 8/54)	2.25	6.75	25.00
2(5-7/55) - 16	1.50	4.50	12.00

ANGELA
Image Comics (Todd McFarlane Productions): Dec, 1994 - No. 3, Feb, 1995 ($2.95, limited series)

	GD2.0	FN6.0	NM9.4
1-Gaiman scripts & Capullo-c/a in all; Spawn app.	2.50	7.50	20.00
2	1.85	5.50	15.00
3	1.85	5.50	15.00
Special Edition (1995)-Pirate Spawn-c	3.00	9.00	30.00
Special Edition (1995)-Angela-c	3.00	9.00	30.00
Trade paperback ($9.95, 1995) reprints #1-3 & Special Ed. w/additional pin-ups.			10.00

ANGELA/GLORY: RAGE OF ANGELS (See Glory/Angela: Rage of Angels)
Image Comics (Todd McFarlane Productions): Mar, 1996 ($2.50, one-shot)

	GD2.0	FN6.0	NM9.4
1-Liefeld-c/Cruz-a(p); Darkchylde preview flip book			4.00
1-Variant-c			4.00

ANGEL AND THE APE (Meet Angel No. 7) (See Limited Collector's Edition C-34 & Showcase No. 77)
National Periodical Publications: Nov-Dec, 1968 - No. 6, Sept-Oct, 1969

	GD2.0	FN6.0	NM9.4
1-(11-12/68)-Not Wood-a	3.50	10.50	35.00
2-6-Wood inks in all	2.50	7.50	22.00

ANGEL AND THE APE (2nd Series)
DC Comics: Mar, 1991 - No. 4, June, 1991 ($1.00, limited series)

	GD2.0	FN6.0	NM9.4
1-4			2.00

ANGEL FIRE
Crusade Comics: June, 1997 - No. 3, Oct, 1997 ($2.95, limited series)

	GD2.0	FN6.0	NM9.4
1-3: 1-(3 variant covers). 3-B&W			3.00

ANGEL LOVE
DC Comics: Aug, 1986 - No. 8, Mar, 1987 (75¢, limited series)

	GD2.0	FN6.0	NM9.4
1-8, Special 1 (1987, $1.25, 52 pgs.)			2.00

ANGEL OF LIGHT, THE (See The Crusaders)

ANIMA
DC Comics: Mar, 1994 - No. 15, July, 1995 ($1.75/$1.95/$2.25)

	GD2.0	FN6.0	NM9.4
1-7,0,8-15: 7-(9/94)-Begin $1.95-c; Zero Hour x-over			2.50

ANIMAL ADVENTURES
Timor Publications/Accepted Publ. (reprints): Dec, 1953 - No. 3, May?, 1954

	GD2.0	FN6.0	NM9.4
1-Funny animal	5.35	16.00	32.00
2,3: 2-Featuring Soopermutt (2/54)	4.00	10.00	20.00
1-3 (reprints, nd)	2.00	5.00	10.00

ANIMAL ANTICS (Movie Town... No. 24 on)
National Periodical Publ: Mar-Apr, 1946 - No. 23, Nov-Dec, 1949 (All 52 pgs.?)

	GD2.0	FN6.0	NM9.4
1-Raccoon Kids begins by Otto Feur; some-c by Grossman; Seaman Sy Wheeler by Kelly in some issues	44.00	132.00	350.00
2	25.00	75.00	175.00
3-10: 10-Post-c/a	15.00	45.00	105.00
11-23: 14,15,18,19-Post-a	10.00	30.00	70.00

ANIMAL COMICS
Dell Publishing Co.: Dec-Jan, 1941-42 - No. 30, Dec-Jan, 1947-48

	GD2.0	FN6.0	NM9.4
1-1st Pogo app. by Walt Kelly (Dan Noonan art in most issues)	90.00	270.00	900.00
2-Uncle Wiggily begins	45.00	135.00	450.00
3,5	32.00	96.00	320.00
4,6,7-No Pogo	19.00	57.00	190.00
8-10	23.00	69.00	230.00
11-15	14.00	42.00	140.00
16-20	9.50	28.50	95.00
21-30: 24-30- "Jigger" by John Stanley	7.00	21.00	70.00

NOTE: ***Dan Noonan*** *a-18-30.* ***Gollub*** *art in most later issues; c-29, 30.* ***Kelly*** *c-7-26.*

ANIMAL CRACKERS (Also see Adventures of Patoruzu)
Green Publ. Co./Norlen/Fox Feat.(Hero Books): 1946; No. 31, July, 1950; No. 9, 1959

	GD2.0	FN6.0	NM9.4
1-Super Cat begins (1st app.)	16.00	47.00	110.00
2	9.15	27.00	55.00
3-10 (Exist?)	4.15	12.50	25.00
31(Fox)-Formerly My Love Secret	5.85	17.50	35.00
9(1959-Norlen)-Infinity-c	3.60	9.00	18.00
nn, nd ('50s), no publ.; infinity-c	3.60	9.00	18.00

ANIMAL FABLES
E. C. Comics (Fables Publ. Co.): July-Aug, 1946 - No. 7, Nov-Dec, 1947

	GD2.0	FN6.0	NM9.4
1-Freddy Firefly (clone of Human Torch), Korky Kangaroo, Petey Pig, Danny Demon begin	40.00	120.00	280.00
2-Aesop Fables begin	25.00	75.00	175.00
3-6	20.00	60.00	140.00
7-Origin Moon Girl	56.00	169.00	450.00

ANIMAL FAIR (Fawcett's...)
Fawcett Publications: Mar, 1946 - No. 11, Feb, 1947

	GD2.0	FN6.0	NM9.4
1	24.00	73.00	170.00
2	11.50	34.00	80.00
3-6	9.15	27.00	55.00
7-11	6.70	20.00	40.00

ANIMAL FUN
Premier Magazines: 1953 (25¢, came w/glasses)

	GD2.0	FN6.0	NM9.4
1-(3-D)-Ziggy Pig, Silly Seal, Billy & Buggy Bear	34.00	103.00	240.00

ANIMAL MAN (See Action Comics #552, 553, DC Comics Presents #77, 78, Secret Origins #39, Strange Adventures #180 & Wonder Woman #267, 268)
DC Comics (Vertigo imprint #57 on): Sept, 1988 - No. 89, Nov, 1995 ($1.25/$1.50/$1.75/$1.95/$2.25, mature)

	GD2.0	FN6.0	NM9.4
1-Grant Morrison scripts begin, ends #26			5.00
2-Superman cameo			3.00
3-49,51-55,57-89: 6-Invasion tie-in. 9-Manhunter-c/story. 24-Arkham Asylum story; Bizarro Superman app. 25-Inferior Five app. 26-Morrison apps. in story; part photo-c (of Morrison?). 68-Photo-c			2.25
50-($2.95, 52 pgs.)-Last issue w/Veitch scripts			3.00
56-($3.50, 68 pgs.)			3.50
Annual 1 (1993, $3.95, 68 pgs.)-Bolland-c; Children's Crusade Pt. 3			4.00

NOTE: ***Bolland*** *c-1-63. 71-**Sutton**-a(i)*

ANIMAL MYSTIC (See Dark One...)
Cry For Dawn/Sirius: 1993 - No. 4, 1995 ($2.95?/$3.50, B&W)

	GD2.0	FN6.0	NM9.4
1	2.50	7.50	25.00
1-Alternate	5.00	15.00	50.00
1-2nd printing		2.40	6.00
2	2.50	7.50	20.00
2,3-2nd prints (Sirius)			4.00
3,4: 4-Color poster insert, Linsner-s	1.25	3.75	10.00
TPB ($14.95) r/			15.00

ANIMAL MYSTIC WATER WARS
Sirius: 1996 - Present ($2.95, limited series)

	GD2.0	FN6.0	NM9.4
1-6-Dark One-c/a/scripts			5.00

ANIMAL WORLD, THE (Movie)
Dell Publishing Co.: No. 713, Aug, 1956

	GD2.0	FN6.0	NM9.4
Four Color 713	2.75	8.00	30.00

ANIMANIACS (TV)
DC Comics: May, 1995 - Present ($1.50/$1.75/$1.95/$1.99)

	GD2.0	FN6.0	NM9.4
1-54: 13-Manga issue. 19-X-Files parody; Miran Kim-c; Adlard-a (4 pgs.). 26-E.C. parody-c. 34-Xena parody. 43-Pinky and the Brain take over			3.00
A Christmas Special (12/94, $1.50, "1" on-c)			2.50

ANIMATED COMICS
E. C. Comics: No date given (Summer, 1947?)

	GD2.0	FN6.0	NM9.4
1 (Rare)	67.00	202.00	540.00

Annex #2 © MAR

A-1Comics #35 © ME

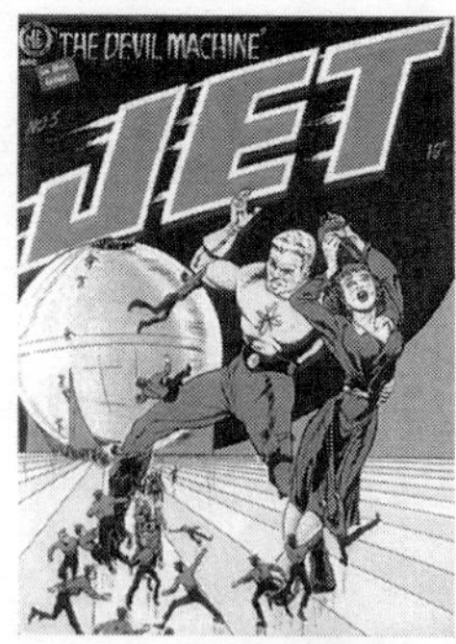

A-1Comics #77 © ME

GD2.0 FN6.0 NM9.4 | GD2.0 FN6.0 NM9.4

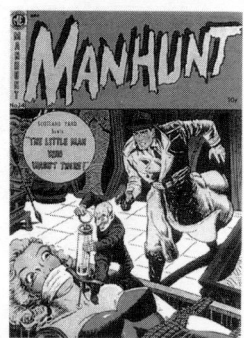

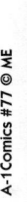

ANIMATED FUNNY COMIC TUNES (See Funny Tunes)

ANIMATED MOVIE-TUNES (Movie Tunes No. 3)
Margood Publishing Corp. (Timely): Fall, 1945 - No. 2, Sum, 1946

1,2-Super Rabbit, Ziggy Pig & Silly Seal 20.00 60.00 140.00

ANIMAX
Marvel Comics (Star Comics): Dec, 1986 - No. 4, June, 1987

1-4: Based on toys 2.00

ANNE RICE'S THE MUMMY OR RAMSES THE DAMNED
Millennium Publications: Oct, 1990 - No. 12, 1991 ($2.50, limited series)

1-12: Adapts novel; Mooney-p in all 2.50

ANNETTE (Disney, TV)
Dell Publishing Co.: No. 905, May, 1958; No. 1100, May, 1960
(Mickey Mouse Club)

Four Color 905-Annette Funicello photo-c 26.00 78.00 285.00
Four Color 1100-...'s Life Story (Movie); A. Funicello photo-c
21.00 63.00 230.00

ANNEX
Marvel Comics: Aug, 1994 - No. 4, Nov, 1994 ($1.75)

1-4: 1-Spider-Man app. 2.00

ANNIE
Marvel Comics Group: Oct, 1982 - No. 2, Nov, 1982 (60¢)

1,2-Movie adaptation 2.00
Treasury Edition ($2.00, tabloid size) 1.85 5.50 15.00

ANNIE OAKLEY (See Tessie The Typist #19, Two-Gun Kid & Wild Western)
Marvel/Atlas Comics(MPI No. 1-4/CDS No. 5 on): Spring, 1948 - No. 4, 11/48; No. 5, 6/55 - No. 11, 6/56

1 (1st Series, 1948)-Hedy Devine app. 40.00 120.00 320.00
2 (7/48, 52 pgs.)-Kurtzman-a, "Hey Look", 1 pg; Intro. Lana; Hedy Devine app; Captain Tootsie by Beck 26.00 77.00 180.00
3,4 21.00 64.00 150.00
5 (2nd Series, 1955)-Reinman-a ; Maneely-c 15.00 45.00 105.00
6-9: 6,8-Woodbridge-a. 9-Williamson-a (4 pgs.) 11.50 34.00 80.00
10,11: 11-Severin-c 10.00 30.00 70.00

ANNIE OAKLEY AND TAGG (TV)
Dell Publishing Co./Gold Key: 1953 - No. 18, Jan-Mar, 1959; July, 1965
(Gail Davis photo-c #3 on)

Four Color 438 (#1) 14.00 41.00 150.00
Four Color 481,575 (#2,3) 8.00 23.00 85.00
4(7-9/55)-10 6.40 19.00 70.00
11-18(1-3/59) 5.50 16.50 60.00
1(7/65-Gold Key)-Photo-c (c-r/#6) 4.50 13.50 50.00
NOTE: *Manning a-13. Photo back c-4, 9, 11.*

ANOTHER WORLD (See Strange Stories From...)

ANTARCTIC PRESS JAM 1996
Antarctic Press: Dec, 1996 ($2.95, one-shot)

1 3.00

ANTHRO (See Showcase #74)
National Periodical Publications: July-Aug, 1968 - No. 6, July-Aug, 1969

1-(7-8/68)-Howie Post-a in all 4.20 12.60 42.00
2-6: 6-Wood-c/a (inks) 2.50 7.50 25.00

ANTONY AND CLEOPATRA (See Ideal, a Classical Comic)

ANYTHING GOES
Fantagraphics Books: Oct, 1986 - No. 6, 1987 ($2.00, #1-5 color & B&W/#6 B&W, limited series)

1-6: 1-Flaming Carrot app. (1st in color?); G. Kane-c. 2-6: 2-Miller-c(p); Alan Moore scripts; Kirby-a; early Sam Kieth-a (2 pgs.). 3-Capt. Jack, Cerebus app.; Cerebus-c by N. Adams. 4-Perez-c. 5-3rd color Teenage Mutant Ninja Turtles app. 3.00

A-1
Marvel Comics (Epic Comics): 1992 - No. 4, 1993 ($5.95, limited ser., mature)

1-4: 3-Bisley-c 2.00 6.00

A-1 COMICS (A-1 appears on covers No. 1-17 only)(See individual title listings.) (1st two issues not numbered.)
Life's Romances Publ.-No. 1/Compix/Magazine Ent.: 1944 - No. 139, Sept-Oct, 1955 (No #2)

(See Individual Alphabetical listings for prices)

nn-Kerry Drake, Johnny Devildog, Rocky, Streamer Kelly (slightly large size)	1-Dotty Dripple (1 pg.), Mr. Ex, Bush Berry, Rocky, Lew Loyal (20 pgs.)
9-Texas Slim (all)	2-8,10-Texas Slim & Dirty Dalton, The Corsair, Teddy Rich, Dotty Dripple, Inca Dinca, Tommy Tinker, Little Mexico & Tugboat Tim, The Masquerader & others. 7-Corsair-c/s. 8-Intro. Rodeo Ryan
11-Teena; Ogden Whitney-c	
12,15-Teena	
13-Guns of Fact & Fiction (1948). Used in **SOTI**, pg. 19; Ingels & Johnny Craig-a	14-Tim Holt Western Adventures #1 (1948)
16-Vacation Comics; The Pixies, Tom Tom, Flying Fredd, & Koko & Kola	17-Tim Holt #2; photo-c; last issue to carry A-1 on cover (9-10/48)
18,20-Jimmy Durante; photo covers	
19-Tim Holt #3; photo-c	21-Joan of Arc (1949)-Movie adapta tion; Ingrid Bergman photo-covers & interior photos; Whitney-a
22-Dick Powell (1949)-Photo-c	
23-Cowboys and Indians #6; Doc Holiday-c/story	24-Trail Colt #1-Frazetta-r in-Manhunt #13; Ingels-c; L. B. Cole-a
25-Fibber McGee & Molly (1949) (Radio)	
26-Trail Colt #2-Ingels-c	27-Ghost Rider #1(1950)-Origin
28-Christmas-(Koko & Kola #6) ("50)	29-Ghost Rider #2-Frazetta-c (1950)
30-Jet Powers #1-Powell-a	31-Ghost Rider #3-Frazetta-c & origin ('51)
32-Jet Powers #2	
33-Muggsy Mouse #1('51)	34-Ghost Rider #4-Frazetta-c (1951)
35-Jet Powers #3-Williamson/Evans-a	36-Muggsy Mouse #2; Racist-c
37-Ghost Rider #5-Frazetta-c (1951)	38-Jet Powers #4-Williamson/Wood-a
39-Muggsy Mouse #3	40-Dogface Dooley #1('51)
41-Cowboys 'N' Indians #7 (1951)	42-Best of the West #1-Powell-a
43-Dogface Dooley #2	44-Ghost Rider #6
45-American Air Forces #5-Powell-c/a	46-Best of the West #2
47-Thun'da, King of the Congo #1-Frazetta-c/a('52)	48-Cowboys 'N' Indians #8
	49-Dogface Dooley #3
50-Danger Is Their Business #11 ('52)-Powell-a	51-Ghost Rider #7 ('52)
	52-Best of the West #3
53-Dogface Dooley #4	54-American Air Forces #6(8/52)-Powell-a
55-U.S. Marines #5-Powell-a	
56-Thun'da #2-Powell-c/a	57-Ghost Rider #8
58-American Air Forces #7-Powell-a	59-Best of the West #4
60-The U.S. Marines #6-Powell-a	61-Space Ace #5(1953)-Guardineer-a
62-Starr Flagg, Undercover Girl #5 (#1) reprinted from A-1 #24	63-Manhunt #13-Frazetta
	64-Dogface Dooley #5
65-American Air Forces #8-Powell-a	66-Best of the West #5
67-American Air Forces #9-Powell-a	68-U.S. Marines #7-Powell-a
69-Ghost Rider #9(10/52)	70-Best of the West #6
71-Ghost Rider #10(12/52)-Vs. Frankenstein	72-U.S. Marines #8-Powell-a(3)
	73-Thun'da #3-Powell-c/a
74-American Air Forces #10-Powell-a	75-Ghost Rider #11(3/52)
76-Best of the West #7	77-Manhunt #14
78-Thun'da #4-Powell-c/a	79-American Air Forces #11-Powell-a
80-Ghost Rider #12(6/52)-One-eyed Devil-c	81-Best of the West #8
	82-Cave Girl #11(1953)-Powell-c/a; origin (#1)
83-Thun'da #5-Powell-c/a	
84-Ghost Rider #13(7-8/53)	85-Best of the West #9
86-Thun'da #6-Powell-c/a	87-Best of the West #10(9-10/53)
88-Bobby Benson's B-Bar-B Riders #20	89-Home Run #3-Powell-a; Stan Musial photo-c
90-Red Hawk #11(1953)-Powell-c/a	
91-American Air Forces #12-Powell-a	92-Dream Book of Romance #5-Photo-c; Guardineer-a
93-Great Western #8('54)-Origin The Ghost Rider; Powell-a	94-White Indian #11-Frazetta-a(r); Powell-c
95-Muggsy Mouse #4	
96-Cave Girl #12, with Thun'da;	97-Best of the West #11

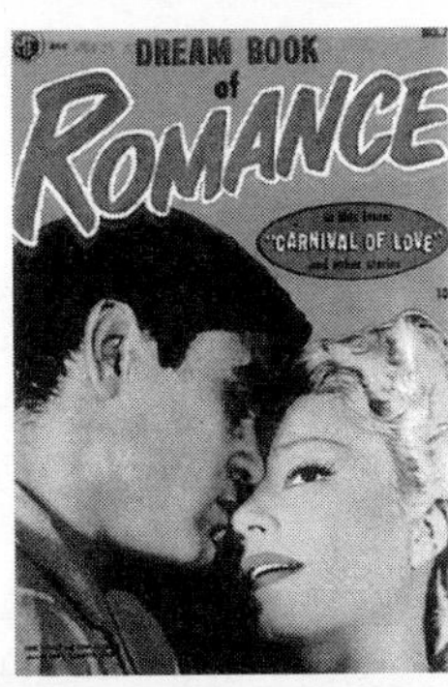

A-1Comics #109 © ME

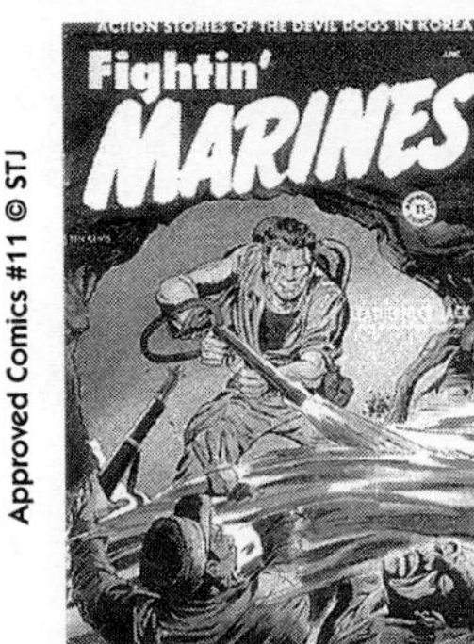

Approved Comics #11 © STJ

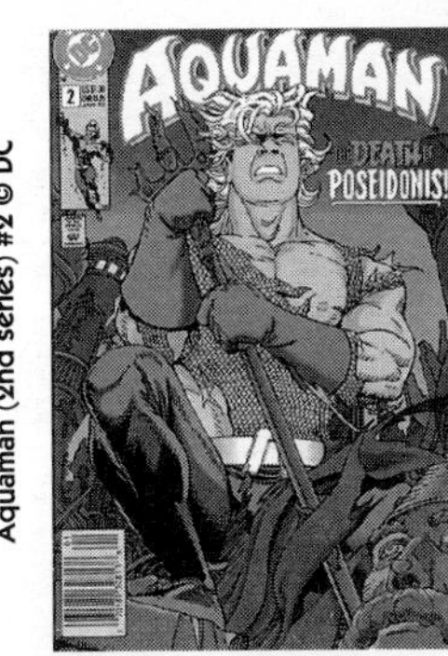

Aquaman (2nd series) #2 © DC

GD2.0 FN6.0 NM9.4

Powell-c/a
99-Muggsy Mouse #5
101-White Indian #12-Frazetta-a(r)
101-Dream Book of Romance #6 (4-6/54); Marlon Brando photo-c; Powell, Bolle, Guardineer-a
105-Great Western #9-Ghost Rider app.; Powell-a, 6 pgs.; Bolle-c
107-Hot Dog #1
108-Red Fox #15 (1954)-L.B. Cole c/a; Powell-a
110-Dream Book of Romance #8 (10/54)-Movie photo-c
112-Ghost Rider #14 ('54)
114-Dream Book of Love #2-Guardineer, Bolle-a; Piper Laurie, Victor Mature photo-c
118-Undercover Girl #7-Powell-c
120-Badmen of the West #2
121-Mysteries of Scotland Yard #1; reprinted from Manhunt (5 stories)
124-Dream Book of Romance #8 (10-11/54)
126-I'm a Cop #2-Powell-a
128-I'm a Cop #3-Powell-a
130-Strongman #1-Powell-a (2-3/55)
132-Strongman #2
134-Strongman #3
136-Hot Dog #4
138-The Avenger #4-Powell-c/a
98-Undercover Girl #6-Powell-c
100-Badmen of the West #1-Meskin-a(?)
103-Best of the West #12-Powell-a
104-White Indian #13-Frazetta-a(r) ('54)
106-Dream Book of Love #1 (6-7/54) -Powell, Bolle-a; Montgomery Clift, Donna Reed photo-c
109-Dream Book of Romance #7 (7-8/54). Powell-a; movie photo-c
111-I'm a Cop #1 ('54); drug mention story; Powell-a
113-Great Western #10; Powell-a
115-Hot Dog #3
116-Cave Girl #13-Powell-c/a
117-White Indian #14
119-Straight Arrow's Fury #1 (origin); Fred Meagher-c/a
122-Black Phantom #1 (11/54)
123-Dream Book of Love #3 (10-11/54)-Movie photo-c
125-Cave Girl #14-Powell-c/a
127-Great Western #11('54)-Powell-a
129-The Avenger #1('55)-Powell-c
131-The Avenger #2('55)-Powell-c/a
133-The Avenger #3-Powell-c/a
135-White Indian #15
137-Africa #1-Powell-c/a(4)
139-Strongman #4-Powell-a

NOTE: ***Bolle** a-110. Photo-c-17-22, 89, 92, 101, 106, 109, 110, 114, 123, 124.*

APACHE
Fiction House Magazines: 1951

	GD2.0	FN6.0	NM9.4
1	20.00	60.00	140.00
I.W. Reprint No. 1-r/#1 above	2.50	7.50	22.00

APACHE KID (Formerly Reno Browne; Western Gunfighters #20 on) (Also see Two-Gun Western & Wild Western)
Marvel/Atlas Comics(MPC No. 53-10/CPS No. 11 on): No. 53, 12/50 - No. 10, 1/52; No. 11, 12/54 - No. 19, 4/56

	GD2.0	FN6.0	NM9.4
53(#1)-Apache Kid & his horse Nightwind (origin), Red Hawkins by Syd Shores begins	33.00	99.00	230.00
2(2/51)	16.00	47.00	110.00
3-5	11.00	33.00	75.00
6-10 (1951-52): 7-Russ Heath-a	10.00	30.00	60.00
11-19 (1954-56)	7.50	22.50	45.00

NOTE: ***Heath** a-7. c-11, 13. **Maneely** a-53; c-53(#1), 12, 14-16. **Powell** a-14. **Severin** c-17.*

APACHE MASSACRE (See Chief Victorio's...)

APACHE TRAIL
Steinway/America's Best: Sept, 1957 - No. 4, June, 1958

	GD2.0	FN6.0	NM9.4
1	10.00	30.00	70.00
2-4: 2-Tuska-a	6.70	20.00	40.00

APE (Magazine)
Dell Publishing Co.: 1961 (52 pgs., B&W)

	GD2.0	FN6.0	NM9.4
1-Comics and humor	2.80	8.40	28.00

APOLLO SMILE
Eagle Wing Press: July, 1998 - Present ($2.95)

	GD2.0	FN6.0	NM9.4
1,2-Manga			3.00

APPARITION
Caliber Comics: 1995 ($3.95, 52 pgs., B&W)

	GD2.0	FN6.0	NM9.4
1 ($3.95)			4.00
V2#1-6 ($2.95)			3.00
Visitations			4.00

APPLESEED
Eclipse Comics: Sept, 1988 - Book 4, Vol. 4, Aug, 1991 ($2.50/$2.75/$3.50, 52/68 pgs, B&W)

	GD2.0	FN6.0	NM9.4
Book One, Vol. 1-5: 5-(1/89), Book Two, Vol. 1(2/89) -5(7/89): Art Adams-c, Book Three, Vol. 1(8/89) -4 ($2.75), Book Three, Vol. 5 ($3.50), Book Four, Vol. 1 (1/91) - 4 (8/91) ($3.50, 68 pgs.)			4.00

APPLESEED DATABOOK
Dark Horse Comics: Apr, 1994 - No. 2, May, 1994 ($3.50, B&W, limited series)

	GD2.0	FN6.0	NM9.4
1,2: 1-Flip book format			3.50

APPROVED COMICS
St. John Publishing Co. (Most have no c-price): March, 1954 - No. 12, Aug, 1954 (All painted-c)

	GD2.0	FN6.0	NM9.4
1-The Hawk #5-r	10.00	30.00	65.00
2-Invisible Boy (3/54)-Origin; Saunders-c	16.00	47.00	110.00
3-Wild Boy of the Congo #11-r (4/54)	10.00	30.00	65.00
4,5: 4-Kid Cowboy-r. 5-Fly Boy-r	10.00	30.00	65.00
6-Daring Adv.-r (5/54); Krigstein-a(2); Baker-c	11.50	34.00	80.00
7-The Hawk #6-r	10.00	30.00	65.00
8-Crime on the Run (6/54); Powell-a; Saunders-c	10.00	30.00	65.00
9-Western Bandit Trails #3-r, with new-c; Baker-c/a	11.50	34.00	80.00
11-Fightin' Marines #3-r (8/54); Canteen Kate app; Baker-c/a	12.00	36.00	85.00
12-North West Mounties #4-r(8/54); new Baker-c	12.00	36.00	85.00

AQUAMAN (See Adventure #260, Brave & the Bold, DC Comics Presents #5, DC Special #28, DC Special Series #1, DC Super Stars #7, Detective, JLA, Justice League of America, More Fun #73, Showcase #30-33, Super DC Giant, Super Friends, and World's Finest Comics)

AQUAMAN (1st Series)
National Periodical Publications/DC Comics: Jan-Feb, 1962 - #56, Mar-Apr, 1971; #57, Aug-Sept,1977 - #63, Aug-Sept, 1978

	GD2.0	FN6.0	NM9.4
1-(1-2/62)-Intro. Quisp	54.00	162.00	650.00
2	27.00	81.00	270.00
3-5	15.00	45.00	150.00
6-10	9.00	27.00	95.00
11-20: 11-1st app. Mera. 18-Aquaman weds Mera; JLA cameo	8.00	24.00	80.00
21-32: 23-Birth of Aquababy. 26-Huntress app.(3-4/66). 29-1st app. Ocean Master, Aquaman's step-brother. 30-Batman & Superman-c & cameo	4.50	13.50	45.00
33-1st app. Aqua-Girl (see Adventure #266)	5.00	15.00	50.00
34-40: 40-Jim Aparo's 1st DC work (8/68)	3.00	9.00	30.00
41-46,47,49: 45-Last 12¢-c	2.50	7.50	20.00
48-Origin reprinted	2.50	7.50	22.00
50-52-Deadman by Neal Adams	4.80	14.40	48.00
53-56('71): 56-1st app. Crusader; last 15¢-c	1.00	3.00	8.00
57('77)-63: 58-Origin retold		2.40	6.00

NOTE: ***Aparo** a-40-45, 46p, 47-59; c-58-63. **Nick Cardy** c-1-39. **Newton** a-60-63.*

AQUAMAN (1st limited series)
DC Comics: Feb, 1986 - No. 4, May, 1986 (75¢, limited series)

	GD2.0	FN6.0	NM9.4
1-New costume; 1st app. Nuada of Thierna Na Oge.			5.00
2-4: 3-Retelling of Aquaman & Ocean Master's origins.			3.50
Special 1 (1988, $1.50, 52 pgs.)			3.50

NOTE: ***Craig Hamilton** c/a-1-4p. **Russell** c-2-4i.*

AQUAMAN (2nd limited series)
DC Comics: June, 1989 - No. 5, Oct, 1989 ($1.00, limited series)

	GD2.0	FN6.0	NM9.4
1-5: Giffen plots/breakdowns; Swan-a(p).			2.50
Special 1 (Legend of..., $2.00, 1989, 52 pgs.)-Giffen plots/breakdowns; Swan-a(p).			2.50

AQUAMAN (2nd Series)
DC Comics: Dec, 1991 - No. 13, Dec, 1992 ($1.00/$1.25)

	GD2.0	FN6.0	NM9.4
1-5			2.00
6-13: 6-Begin $1.25-c. 9-Sea Devils app.			2.00

AQUAMAN (3rd Series)(Also see Atlantis Chronicles)
DC Comics: Aug, 1994 - Present ($1.50/$1.75/$1.95/$1.99)

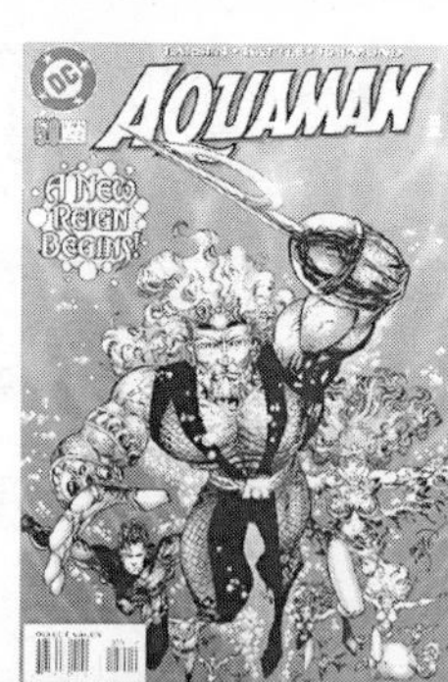

Aquaman (3rd series) #50 © DC

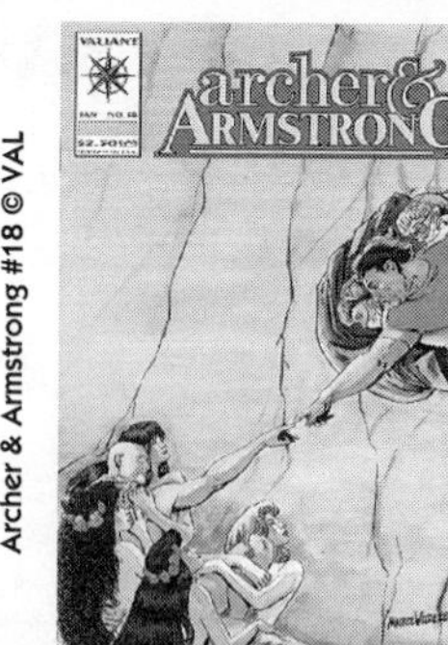

Archer & Armstrong #18 © VAL

Archie Americana Series, Best of the Sixties TPB © AP

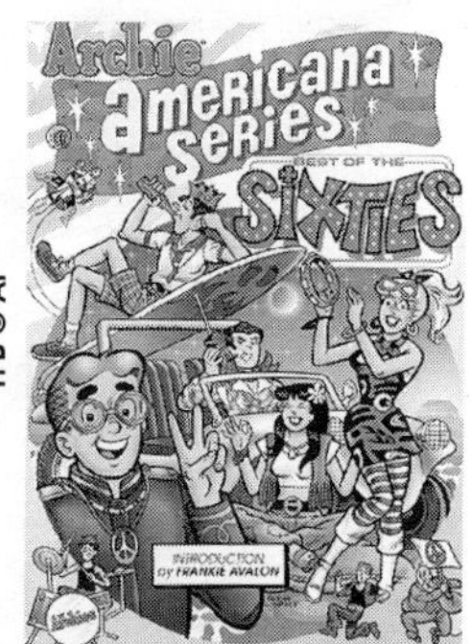

GD2.0 FN6.0 NM9.4

1-(8/94)-Peter David scripts begin; reintro Dolphin 1.00 2.80 7.00
2-(9/94)-Aquaman loses hand 1.00 3.00 8.00
0-(10/94)-Aquaman replaces lost hand w/hook. 1.00 2.80 7.00
3-8: 3-(11/94)-Superboy-c/app. 4-Lobo app. 6-Deep Six app. 4.00
9-42,44-53: 9-Begin $1.75-c. 10-Green Lantern app. 11-Reintro Mera. 15-Reintro Kordax. 16-vs. JLA. 18-Reintro Ocean Master & Atlan (Aquaman's father). 19-Reintro Garth (Aqualad). 23-1st app. Deep Blue (Neptune Perkins & Tsunami's daughter). 23,24-Neptune Perkins, Nuada, Tsunami, Arion, Power Girl, & The Sea Devils app. 26-Final Night. 28-Martian Manhunter-c/app. 29-Black Manta-c/app. 32-Swamp Thing-c/app. 37-Genesis x-over 41-Maxima-c/app. 44-G.A. Flash & Sentinel app. 50-Larsen-s begins. 53-Superman app. 2.00
43-Millennium Giants x-over; Superman-c/app. 3.00
#1,000,000 (11/98) 853rd Century x-over 3.00
Annual 1 (1995, $3.50)-Year One story 3.50
Annual 2 (1996, $2.95)-Legends of the Dead Earth story 3.00
Annual 3 (1997, $3.95)-Pulp Heroes story 4.00
Annual 4,5 ('98, '99, $2.95)-4-Ghosts; Wrightson-c. 5-JLApe 3.00
...Secret Files 1 (12/98, $4.95) Origin-s and pin-ups 5.00
NOTE: ***Art Adams**-c, Annual 5. **Mignola** c-6. **Simonson** c-15.*

AQUAMAN: TIME & TIDE (3rd limited series) (Also see Atlantis Chronicles)
DC Comics: Dec, 1993 - No. 4, Mar, 1994 ($1.50, limited series)

1-4: Peter David scripts; origin retold. 3.00
Trade paperback ($9.95) 10.00

AQUANAUTS (TV)
Dell Publishing Co.: May - July, 1961

Four Color 1197-Photo-c 6.25 18.50 70.00

ARABIAN NIGHTS (See Cinema Comics Herald)

ARACHNOPHOBIA (Movie)
Hollywood Comics (Disney Comics): 1990 ($5.95, 68 pg. graphic novel)

nn-Adaptation of film; Spiegle-a 6.00
Comic edition ($2.95, 68 pgs.) 3.00

ARAKNIS
Mushroom Comics: 1995 - No. 4, 1996 ($2.50, limited series)

1-4: 3-w/pin-ups 2.50

ARAKNIS
Mushroom Comics: No. 0, Apr, 1996 - No. 2, 1996 ($2.95/$2.50)

0-(4/96, $2.95) 3.00
0-Special Edition 5.00
1,2: 1-Ongoing series (5/96) 2.50
1-Special Edition; polybagged w/certificate 10.00

ARAKNIS: RETRIBUTION
Morningstar Productions: May, 1997 ($2.50, unfinished limited series)

1-Ortiz Brothers-s/a 2.50

ARAK/SON OF THUNDER (See Warlord #48)
DC Comics: Sept, 1981 - No. 50, Nov, 1985

1-50: 1-Origin; 1st app. Angelica, Princess of White Cathay. 3-Intro Valda, The Iron Maiden. 12-Origin Valda. 20-Origin Angelica. 24,50-(52 pgs.) 2.00
Annual 1(10/84) 2.00

ARCANA (Also see Books of Magic limited & ongoing series and Mister E)
DC Comics (Vertigo): 1994 ($3.95, 68 pgs., annual)

1-Bolton painted-c; Children's Crusade/Tim Hunter story 4.00

ARCANUM
Image Comics (Top Cow Productions): Apr, 1997 - No. 8, Feb, 1998 ($2.50)

1/2 Gold Edition 15.00
1-Brandon Peterson-s/a(p), 1-Variant-c, 4-American Ent. Ed. 4.00
2-8 3.00
3-Variant-c 2.40 6.00

ARCHANGEL (See Uncanny X-Men, X-Factor & X-Men)
Marvel Comics: Feb, 1996 ($2.50, B&W, one-shot)

1-Milligan story 2.50

ARCHER & ARMSTRONG
Valiant: July (June inside), 1992 - No. 26, Oct, 1994 ($2.50)

0-(7/92)-B. Smith-c/a; Reese-i assists 3.00
0-(Gold Logo) 6.00
1-7,9-26: 1-(8/92)-Origin & 1st app. Archer; Miller-c; B. Smith/Layton-a. 2-2nd app Turok(c/story); Smith/Layton-a; Simonson-c. 3,4-Smith-c&a(p) & scripts. 10-2nd app. Ivar. 10,11-B. Smith-c. 21,22-Shadowman app. 22-w/bound-in trading card. 25-Eternal Warrior app. 26-Flip book w/Eternal Warrior #26 2.50
8-($4.50, 52 pgs.)-Combined with Eternal Warrior #8; B. Smith-c/a & scripts; 1st app. Ivar the Time Walker 4.50

ARCHIE (See Archie Comics) (Also see Christmas & Archie, Everything's..., Explorers of the Unknown, Jackpot, Little..., Oxydol-Dreft, Pep, Riverdale High, Teenage Mutant Ninja Turtles Adventures & To Riverdale and Back Again)

ARCHIE AMERICANA SERIES, BEST OF THE FORTIES
Archie Publications: 1991 ($10.95, trade paperback)

V1-r/early strips from 1940's; intro. by Steven King. 1.40 4.15 11.00

ARCHIE AMERICANA SERIES, BEST OF THE FIFTIES
Archie Publications: 1991 ($8.95, trade paperback)

V2-r/strips from 1950's; 1.50 4.50 12.00
2nd printing (1998, $9.95) 10.00

ARCHIE AMERICANA SERIES, BEST OF THE SIXTIES
Archie Publications: 1995 ($9.95, trade paperback)

V3-r/strips from 1960's; intro. by Frankie Avalon. 10.00

ARCHIE AMERICANA SERIES, BEST OF THE SEVENTIES
Archie Publications: 1997 ($9.95, trade paperback)

V4-r/strips from 1970's 10.00

ARCHIE AND BIG ETHEL
Spire Christian Comics (Fleming H. Revell Co.): 1982 (69¢)

nn-(Low print run) 5.00

ARCHIE & FRIENDS
Archie Comics: Dec, 1992 - Present ($1.25/$1.50/$1.75/$1.79, bi-monthly)

1 4.00
2,4,10-14,17,18,20-Sabrina app. 20-Archie's Band-c 3.00
3,5-9,16 2.50
15-Babewatch-s with Sabrina app. 5.00
19-Josie and the Pussycats app.; E.T. parody-c/s 4.00
21-40 2.00

ARCHIE AND ME (See Archie Giant Series Mag. #578, 591, 603, 616, 626)
Archie Publications: Oct, 1964 - No. 161, Feb, 1987

1 15.00 45.00 150.00
2 7.50 22.50 75.00
3-5 4.00 12.00 40.00
6-10 2.50 7.50 22.00
11-20 1.85 5.50 15.00
21(6/68)-26,28-30: 21-UFO story. 26-X-Mas-c 1.50 4.50 12.00
27-Groovyman & Knowman superhero-s; UFO-sty 2.25 6.75 18.00
31-42: 37-Japan Expo '70-c/s 1.00 3.00 8.00
43-63-(All Giants): 43-(8/71) Mummy-s. 44-Mermaid-s. 49-Josie & the Pussycats c/app. 62-Elvis cameo-c. 63-(2/74) 1.50 4.50 12.00
64-66,68-99-(Regular size): 85-Bicentennial-s. 98-Collectors Comics 2.40 6.00
67-Sabrina app.(8/74) 1.00 3.00 8.00
100-(4/78) 1.00 3.00 8.00
101-120: 107-UFO-s 4.00
121(8/80)-159: 134-Riverdale 2001 3.00
160,161: 160-Origin Mr. Weatherbee. 161-Last issue 4.00

ARCHIE AND MR. WEATHERBEE
Spire Christian Comics (Fleming H. Revell Co.): 1980 (59¢)

nn 5.00

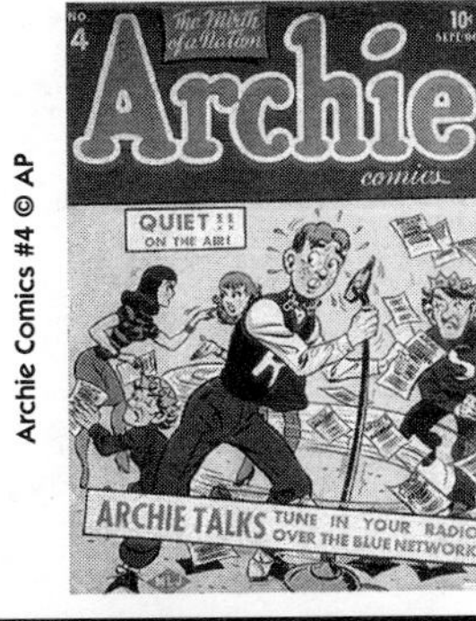

Archie Comics #4 © AP

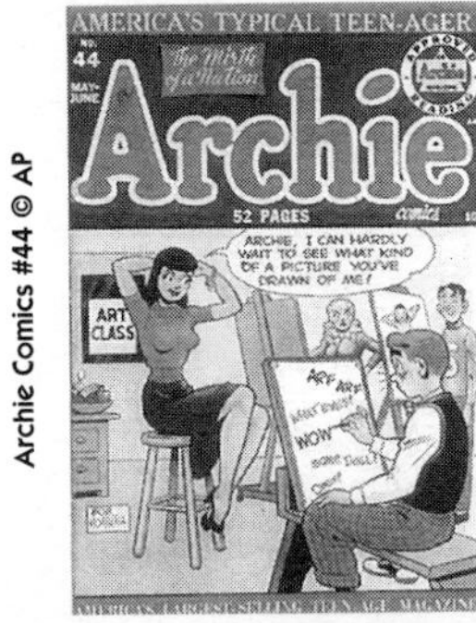

Archie Comics #44 © AP

Archie Comics #422 © AP

GD2.0 FN6.0 NM9.4

ARCHIE...ARCHIE ANDREWS, WHERE ARE YOU? (...Comics Digest #9, 10; ...Comics Digest Mag. No. 11 on)
Archie Publications: Feb, 1977 - Present (Digest size, 160-128 pgs., quarterly)

1 2.50 7.50 20.00
2,3,5,7-9-N. Adams-a; 8-r-/origin The Fly by S&K. 9-Steel Sterling-r 1.50 4.50 12.00
4,6,10 ($1.00/$1.50): 17-Katy Keene story 1.10 3.30 9.00
11-20 1.00 2.80 7.00
21-50,100 5.00
51-70 4.00
71-117: 113-Begin $1.95-c 3.00

ARCHIE AS PUREHEART THE POWERFUL (Also see Archie Giant Series #142, Jughead as Captain Hero, Life With Archie & Little Archie)
Archie Publications (Radio Comics): Sept, 1966 - No. 6, Nov, 1967

1-Super hero parody 7.50 22.50 75.00
2 5.00 15.00 50.00
3-6 3.50 10.50 35.00

NOTE: *Evilheart cameos in all. Title: Archie As Pureheart the Powerful #1-3; ...As Capt. Pureheart-#4-6.*

ARCHIE AT RIVERDALE HIGH (See Archie Giant Series Magazine #573, 586, 604 & Riverdale High)
Archie Publications: Aug, 1972 - No. 113, Feb, 1987

1 5.00 15.00 50.00
2 2.50 7.70 25.00
3-5 2.25 6.75 18.00
6-10 1.50 4.50 12.00
11-30 1.00 3.00 8.00
31(12/75)-46,48-50(12/77): 47-Betty mud wrestling-s 2.40 6.00
47-Archie in drag-s 1.00 3.00 8.00
51-80,100 (12/84) 5.00
81(8/81)-88, 91,93-95,97,98: 96-Anti-smoking issue 4.00
89,90-Early Cheryl Blossom app. 90-Archies Band app. 4.00
92,96,99-Cheryl Blossom app. 4.00
101,102,104-109,111,112: 102-Ghost-c 3.00
103-Archie dates Cheryl Blossom-s 1.00 3.00 8.00
110,113: 110-Godzilla-s. 113-Last issue 4.00

ARCHIE COMICS (Archie #114 on; 1st Teen-age comic; Radio show aired 6/2/45 by NBC)
MLJ Magazines No. 1-19/Archie Publ.No. 20 on: Winter, 1942-43 - No. 19, 3-4/46; No. 20, 5-6/46 - Present

GD2.0 FN6.0 VF8.0 NM9.4
1 (Scarce)-Jughead, Veronica app.; 1st app. Mrs. Andrews 1136.00 3408.00 6816.00 12,500.00

GD2.0 FN6.0 NM9.4
2 278.00 834.00 2500.00
3 (60 pgs.)(scarce) 231.00 693.00 1850.00
4,5: 4-Article about Archie radio series 120.00 360.00 960.00
6,8-10: 6-X-Mas-c. 87.00 261.00 700.00
7-1st definitive love triangle story 90.00 270.00 725.00
11-20: 15,17,18-Dotty & Ditto by Woggon. 16-Woggon-a 56.00 168.00 450.00
21-30: 23-Betty & Veronica by Woggon. 25-Woggon-a. 30-Coach Piffle app., a Coach Kleets prototype. 34-Pre-Dilton try-out (named Dilbert) 40.00 120.00 290.00
31-40 23.00 69.00 160.00
41-50 16.00 48.00 110.00
51-60: (1954) 51-Katy Keene app. 7.50 22.50 75.00
61-70 (1954): 65-70, Katy Keene app. 6.00 18.00 60.00
71-80: 72-74-Katy Keene app. 4.80 14.40 48.00
81-99: 94-1st Coach Kleets 3.80 11.40 38.00
100 5.00 15.00 50.00
101-122,124-130 (1962) 2.50 7.50 24.00
123-UFO-c/s; Vampire-s 2.60 7.80 26.00
131-157,159,160 1.85 5.50 15.00
158-Archie in drag story 1.85 5.50 18.00
161(2/66)-182,184,186-195,197-199: 168-Superhero gag-c. 176,178-Twiggy-c 1.25 3.75 10.00
183-1st Caveman Archie gang story 1.75 5.25 14.00
185-1st "The Archies" Band story 1.75 5.25 14.00
196 (12/69)-1st Cricket O'Dell 2.50 7.50 20.00
200 (6/70) 1.50 4.50 12.00
201-230(11/73): 213-Sabrina/Josie-c cameos. 229-Lost Child issue 1.00 2.80 7.00
231-260(3/77): 253-Tarzan parody 2.40 6.00
261-282, 284-299 5.00
283(8/79)-Cover/story plugs "International Children's Appeal" which was a fraudulent charity, according to TV's 20/20 news program broadcast July 20, 1979 2.40 6.00
300(1/81)-Anniversary issue 2.40 6.00
301-321,323-325,327-335,337-350: 323-Cheryl Blossom pin-up 3.00
322-E.T. story 4.00
326-Early Cheryl Blossom story 1.25 3.75 10.00
336-Michael Jackson/Boy George parody 4.00
351-399: 356-Calgary Olympics Special. 393-Infinity-c; 1st comic book printed on recycled paper 2.50
400 (6/92)-Shows 1st meeting of Little Archie and Veronica 5.00
401-428 2.00
429-Love Showdown part 1 4.00
430-492: 467- "A Storm Over Uniforms" x-over parts 3,4 2.00
Annual 1 ('50)-116 pgs. (Scarce) 162.00 486.00 1300.00
Annual 2 ('51) 81.00 243.00 650.00
Annual 3 ('52) 50.00 150.00 400.00
Annual 4,5 (1953-54) 37.00 111.00 260.00
Annual 6-10 (1955-59): 8-(100 pgs.). 10-(84 pgs.) Elvis record on-c 14.00 42.00 140.00
Annual 11-15 (1960-65): 12,13-(84 pgs.) 14,15-(68 pgs.) 6.00 18.00 60.00
Annual 16-20 (1966-70)(all 68 pgs.): 20-Archie's band-c 2.50 7.50 25.00
Annual 21-26 (1971-75): 21,22 (68 pgs.). 22,23-Archie's band-s. 23-Archie's band/Josie/Sabrina-c. 23-26-(52 pgs.). 25-Cavemen-s 1.50 4.50 12.00
Annual Digest 27 ('75) 2.50 7.50 24.00
...28-30 2.00 6.00 16.00
...31-34 1.50 4.50 12.00
...35-40 (...Magazine #35 on) 1.10 3.30 9.00
...41-65 ('94) 4.00
...66-69 2.00
...All-Star Specials(Winter '75, $1.25)-6 remaindered Archie comics rebound in each; titles: "The World of Giant Comics", "Giant Grab Bag of Comics", "Triple Giant Comics" & "Giant Spec. Comics 2.50 7.50 25.00
Special Edition-Christmas With Archie 1(1/75)-Treasury (rare) 4.00 12.00 40.00

NOTE: *Archies Band-s-185, 188-192, 197, 198, 201, 204, 205, 208, 209, 215, 329, 330; Band-c-191, 330. Cavemen Archie Gang-s-183, 192, 197, 208, 210, 220, 223, 282, 333, 335, 338, 340.* ***Al Fagly*** *c-17-35.* ***Bob Montana*** *c-38, 41-50, 58, Annual 1-4.* ***Bill Woggon*** *c-53, 54.*

ARCHIE COMICS DIGEST (...Magazine No. 37-95)
Archie Publications: Aug, 1973 - Present (Small size, 160-128 pgs.)

1 6.80 20.50 75.00
2 4.00 12.00 40.00
3-5 3.00 9.00 30.00
6-10 2.25 6.75 18.00
11-33: 32,33-The Fly-r by S&K 1.25 3.75 10.00
34-60 1.00 3.00 8.00
61-80,100 2.40 6.00
81-99 5.00
101-140: 36-Katy Keene story 4.00
141-165 3.00
166-169 2.00

NOTE: ***Neal Adams*** *a-1, 2, 4, 5, 19-21, 24, 25, 27, 29, 31, 33. X-mas c-88, 94, 100, 106.*

ARCHIE COMICS PRESENTS: THE LOVE SHOWDOWN COLLECTION
Archie Publications: 1994 ($4.95, squarebound)

Archie Giant Series Magazine #136 © AP

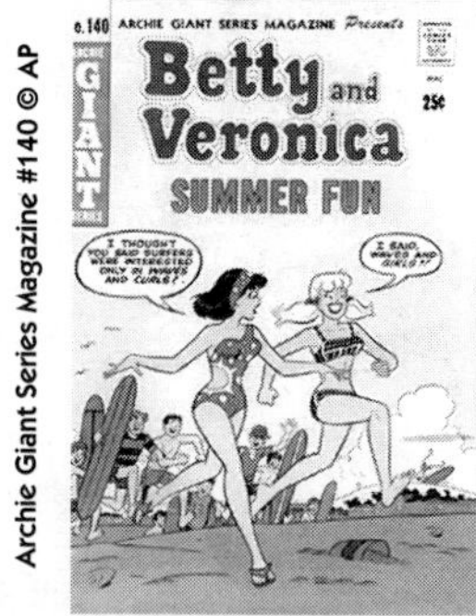

Archie Giant Series Magazine #140 © AP

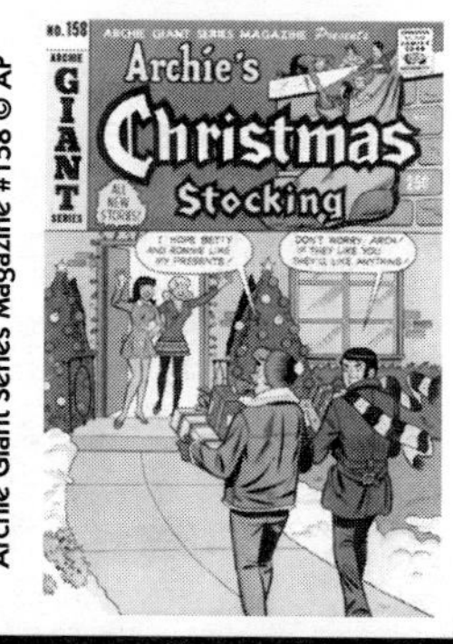

Archie Giant Series Magazine #158 © AP

nn-r/Archie #429, Betty #19, Betty & Veronica #82, & Veronica #39 6.00

ARCHIE GETS A JOB
Spire Christian Comics (Fleming H. Revell Co.): 1977
nn 6.00

ARCHIE GIANT SERIES MAGAZINE
Archie Publications: 1954 - No. 632, July, 1992 (No #36-135, no #252-451) (#1 not code approved) (#1-233 are Giants; #12-184 are 68 pgs.,#185-194,197-233 are 52 pgs.; #195,196 are 84 pgs.; #234-up are 36 pgs.)

1-Archie's Christmas Stocking 112.00 336.00 900.00
2-Archie's Christmas Stocking('55) 68.00 204.00 550.00
3-6-Archie's Christmas Stocking('56- '59) 47.00 141.00 375.00
7-10: 7-Katy Keene Holiday Fun(9/60); Bill Woggon-c. 8-Betty & Veronica Summer Fun(10/60); baseball story w/Babe Ruth & Lou Gehrig. 9-The World of Jughead (12/60). 10-Archie's Christmas Stocking(1/61) 31.00 94.00 250.00
11,13,16,18: 11-Betty & Veronica Spectacular (6/61). 13-Betty & Veronica Summer Fun (10/61). 16-Betty & Veronica Spectacular (6/62). 18-Betty & Veronica Summer Fun (10/62) 23.00 69.00 180.00
12,14,15,17,19,20: 12-Katy Keene Holiday Fun (9/61). 14-The World of Jughead (12/61); Vampire-s. 15-Archie's Christmas Stocking (1/62). 17-Archie's Jokes (9/62); Katy Keene app. 19-The World of Jughead (12/62). 20-Archie's Christmas Stocking (1/63) 12.00 36.00 120.00
21,23,26,28: 21-Betty & Veronica Spectacular (6/63). 23-Betty & Veronica Summer Fun (10/63). 26-Betty & Veronica Spectacular (6/64). 28-Betty & Veronica Summer Fun (9/64) 9.00 27.00 90.00
22,24,25,27,29,30: 22-Archie's Jokes (9/63). 24-The World of Jughead (12/63). 25-Archie's Christmas Stocking (1/64). 27-Archie's Jokes (8/64). 29-Around the World with Archie (10/64); Doris Day-s. 30-The World of Jughead (12/64) 7.00 21.00 70.00
31-35,136-141: 31-Archie's Christmas Stocking (1/65). 32-Betty & Veronica Spectacular (6/65). 33-Archie's Jokes (8/65). 34-Betty & Veronica Summer Fun (9/65). 35-Around the World with Archie (10/65). 136-The World of Jughead (12/65). 137-Archie's Christmas Stocking (1/66). 138-Betty & Veronica Spectacular (6/66). 139-Archie's Jokes (6/66). 140-Betty & Veronica Summer Fun (8/66). 141-Around the World with Archie (9/66) 5.50 16.50 55.00
36-135-Do not exist
142-Archie's Super-Hero Special (10/66)-Origin Capt. Pureheart, Capt. Hero, and Evilheart 6.00 18.00 60.00
143-The World of Jughead(12/66); Capt. Hero-c/s; Man From R.I.V.E.R.D.A.L.E., Pureheart, Superteen app. 3.50 10.50 35.00
144-160: 144-Archie's Christmas Stocking (1/67). 145-Betty & Veronica Spectacular (6/67). 146-Archie's Jokes (6/67). 147-Betty & Veronica Summer Fun (8/67) 148-World of Archie (9/67). 149-World of Jughead (10/67). 150-Archie's Christmas Stocking (1/68). 151-World of Archie (2/68). 152-World of Jughead (2/68). 153-Betty & Veronica Spectacular (6/68). 154-Archie Jokes (6/68). 155-Betty & VeronicaSummer Fun (8/68). 156-World of Archie (10/68). 157-World of Jughead (12/68). 158-Archie's Christmas Stocking (1/69). 159-Betty & Veronica Christmas Spectacular (1/69). 160-World of Archie (2/69); Frankenstein-s each... 2.50 7.50 25.00
161-World of Jughead (2/69); Super-Jughead-s; 11 pg.early Cricket O'Dell-s 2.50 7.50 25.00
162-183: 162-Betty & Veronica Spectacular (6/69). 163-Archie's Jokes(8/69). 164-Betty & Veronica Summer Fun (9/69). 165-World of Archie (9/69). 166-World of Jughead (9/69). 167-Archie's Christmas Stocking (1/70). 168-Betty & Veronica Christmas Spect. (1/70). 169-Archie's Christmas Love-In (1/70). 170-Jughead's Eat-Out Comic Book Mag. (12/69). 171-World of Archie (2/70). 172-World of Jughead (2/70). 173-Betty & Veronica Spectacular (6/70). 174-Archie's Jokes (8/70). 175-Betty & Veronica Summer Fun (9/70). 176-Li'l Jinx Giant Laugh-Out (8/70). 177-World of Archie (9/70). 178-World of Jughead (9/70). 179-Archie's Christmas Stocking(1/71). 180-Betty & Veronica Christmas Spect. (1/71). 181-Archie's Christmas Love-In (1/71). 182-World of Archie (2/71). 183-World of Jughead (2/71)-Last squarebound
each... 2.25 6.75 18.00
184-189,193,194,197-199 (52 pgs.): 184-Betty & Veronica Spectacular (6/71). 185-Li'l Jinx Giant Laugh-Out (6/71). 186-Archie's Jokes (8/71). 187-Betty & Veronica Summer Fun (9/71). 188-World of Archie (9/71). 189-World of Jughead (9/71). 193-World of Archie (3/72).194-World of Jughead (4/72). 197-Betty & Veronica Spectacular (6/72). 198-Archie's Jokes (8/72). 199-Betty & Veronica Summer Fun (9/72)
each... 2.00 6.00 16.00
190-192: 190-Archie's Christmas Stocking (12/71); Sabrina on-c. 191-Betty & Veronica Christmas Spect.(2/72); Sabrina app.. 192-Archie's Christmas Love-In (1/72); Archie Band-c/s 2.50 7.50 20.00
195-(84 pgs.)-Li'l Jinx Christmas Bag (1/72). 2.50 7.50 25.00
196-(84 pgs.)-Sabrina's Christmas Magic (1/72) 4.00 12.00 40.00
200-(52 pgs.)-World of Archie (10/72) 2.50 7.50 22.00
201-206,208-219,221-230,232,233 (All 52 pgs.): 201-Betty & Veronica Spectacular (10/72). 202-World of Jughead (11/72). 203-Archie's Christmas Stocking (12/72). 204-Betty & Veronica Christmas Spectacular (2/73). 205-Archie's Christmas Love-In (1/73). 206-Li'l Jinx Christmas Bag (12/72). 208-World of Archie (3/73). 209-World of Jughead (4/73). 210-Betty & Veronica Spectacular (6/73). 211-Archie's Jokes (8/73). 212-Betty & Veronica Summer Fun (9/73). 213-World of Archie (10/73). 214-Betty & Veronica Spectacular (10/73). 215-World of Jughead (11/73). 216-Archie's Christmas Stocking (12/73). 217-Betty & Veronica Christmas Spectacular (2/74). 218-Archie's Christmas Love-In (1/74). 219-Li'l Jinx Christmas Bag (12/73). 221-Betty & Veronica Spectacular (Advertised as World of Archie) (6/74). 222-Archie's Jokes (advertised as World of Jughead) (8/74). 223-Li'l Jinx (8/74). 224-Betty & Veronica Summer Fun (9/74). 225-World of Archie (9/74). 226-Betty & Veronica Spectacular (10/74). 227-World of Jughead (10/74). 228-Archie's Christmas Stocking (12/74). 229-Betty & Veronica Christmas Spectacular (12/74). 230-Archie's Christmas Love-In (1/75). 232-World of Archie (3/75). 233-World of Jughead (4/75)
each... 1.10 3.30 9.00
207,220,231,243: Sabrina's Christmas Magic. 207-(12/72). 220-(12/73). 231-(1/75). 243-(1/76)
each... 1.85 5.50 15.00
234-242,244-251 (36 pgs.): 234-Betty & Veronica Spectacular (6/75). 235-Archie's Jokes (8/75). 236-Betty & Veronica Summer Fun (9/75). 237-World of Archie (9/75) 238-Betty & Veronica Spectacular (10/75). 239-World of Jughead (10/75). 240-Archie's Christmas Stocking (12/75). 241-Betty & Veronica Christmas Spectacular (12/75). 242-Archie's Christmas Love-In (1/76). 244-World of Archie (3/76). 245-World of Jughead (4/76). 246-Betty & Veronica Spectacular (6/76). 247-Archie's Jokes (8/76). 248-Betty & Veronica Summer Fun (9/76). 249-World of Archie (9/76). 250-Betty & Veronica Spectacular (10/76). 251-World of Jughead
each.... 1.00 3.00 8.00
252-451-Do not exist
452-454,456-466,468-478, 480-490,492-499: 452-Archie's Christmas Stocking (12/76). 453-Betty & Veronica Christmas Spectacular (12/76). 454-Archie's Christmas Love-In (1/77). 456-World of Archie (3/77). 457-World of Jughead (4/77). 458-Betty & Veronica Spectacular (6/77). 459-Archie's Jokes (8/77)-Shows 8/76 in error. 460-Betty & Veronica Summer Fun (9/77). 461-World of Archie (9/77). 462-Betty & Veronica Spectacular (10/77). 463-World of Jughead (10/77). 464-Archie's Christmas Stocking (12/77). 465-Betty & Veronica Christmas Spectacular (12/77). 466-Archie's Christmas Love-In (1/78). 468-World of Archie (2/78). 469-World of Jughead (2/78). 470-Betty & Veronica Spectacular(6/78). 471-Archie's Jokes (8/78). 472-Betty & Veronica Summer Fun (9/78). 473-World of Archie (9/78). 474-Betty & Veronica Spectacular (10/78). 475-World of Jughead (10/78). 476-Archie's Christmas Stocking (12/78). 477-Betty & Veronica Christmas Spectacular (12/78). 478-Archie's Christmas Love-In (1/79). 480-The World of Archie (3/79). 481-World of Jughead (4/79). 482-Betty & Veronica Spectacular (6/79). 483-Archie's Jokes (8/79). 484-Betty & Veronica Summer Fun(9/79). 485-The World of Archie (9/79). 486-Betty & Veronica Spectacular(10/79). 487-The World of Jughead (10/79). 488-Archie's Christmas Stocking (12/79). 489-Betty & Veronica Christmas Spectacular (1/80). 490-Archie's Christmas Love-in (1/80). 492-The World of Archie (2/80). 493-The World of Jughead (4/80). 494-Betty & Veronica Spectacular (6/80). 495-Archie's Jokes (8/80). 496-Betty & Veronica Summer Fun (9/80). 497-The World of Archie (9/80). 498-Betty & Veronica Spectacular (10/80). 499-The World of Jughead (10/80).
each... 2.40 6.00

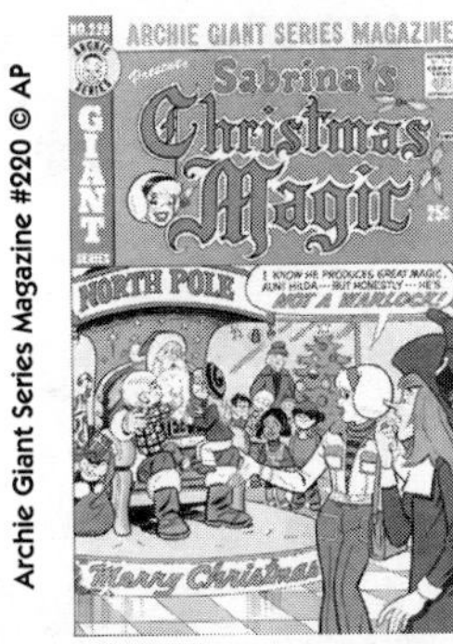
Archie Giant Series Magazine #220 © AP

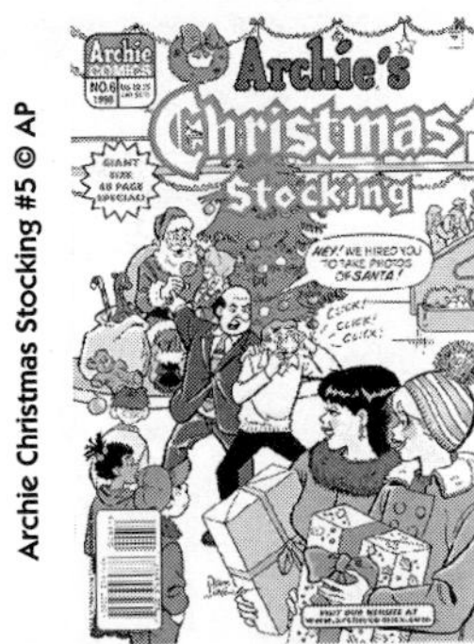
Archie Christmas Stocking #5 © AP

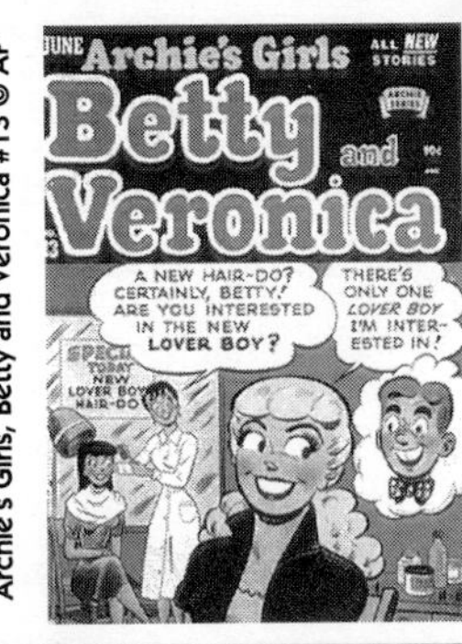
Archie's Girls, Betty and Veronica #13 © AP

GD2.0 FN6.0 NM9.4

455,467,479,491,503-Sabrina's Christmas Magic: 455-(1/77). 467-(1/78). 479-(1/79) Dracula/Werewolf-s. 491-(1/80), 503(1/81) 1.50 4.50 12.00
500-Archie's Christmas Stocking (12/80) 1.10 3.30 9.00
501-514,516-527,529-532,534-539,541-543,545-550: 501-Betty & Veronica Christmas Spectacular (12/80). 502-Archie's Christmas Love-in (1/81). 504-The World of Archie (3/81). 505-The World of Jughead (4/81). 506-Betty & Veronica Spectacular (6/81). 507-Archie's Jokes (8/81). 508-Betty & Veronica Summer Fun (9/81). 509-The World of Archie (9/81). 510-Betty & Vernonica Spectacular (9/81). 511-The World of Jughead (10/81). 512-Archie's Christmas Stocking (12/81). 513-Betty & Veronica Christmas Spectacular (12/81). 514-Archie's Christmas Love-in (1/82). 516-The World of Archie (3/82). 517-The World of Jughead (4/82). 518-Betty & Veronica Spectacular (6/82). 519-Archie's Jokes (8/82). 520-Betty & Veronica Summer Fun (9/82). 521-The World of Archie (9/82). 522-Betty & Veronica Spectacular (10/82). 523-The World of Jughead (10/82).524-Archie's Christmas Stocking (1/83). 525-Betty and Veronica Christmas Spectacular (1/83). 526-Betty and Veronica Spectacular (5/83). 527-Little Archie (8/83). 529-Betty and Veronica Summer Fun (8/83). 530-Betty and Veronica Spectacular (9/83). 531-The World of Jughead (9/83). 532-The World of Archie (10/83). 534-Little Archie (1/84). 535-Archie's Christmas Stocking (1/84). 536-Betty and Veronica Christmas Spectacular (1/84). 537-Betty and Veronica Spectacular (6/84). 538-Little Archie (8/84). 539-Betty and Veronica Summer Fun (8/84). 541-Betty and Veronica Spectacular (9/84). 542-The World of Jughead (9/84). 543-The World of Archie (10/84). 545-Little Archie (12/84). 546-Archie's Christmas Stocking (12/84). 547-Betty and Veronica Christmas Spectacular (12/84). 548-?. 549-Little Archie. 550-Betty and Veronica Summer Fun each... 1.00 3.00 8.00
515,528,533,540,544: 515-Sabrina's Christmas Magic (1/82). 528-Josie and the Pussycats (8/83). 533-Sabrina; Space Pirates by Frank Bolling (10/83). 540-Josie and the Pussycats (8/84). 544-Sabrina the Teen-Age Witch (10/84). each... 1.25 3.75 10.00
551,562,571,584,597-Josie and the Pussycats 1.00 2.80 7.00
552-561,563-570,572-583,585-596,598-600: 552-Betty & Veronica Spectacular. 553-The World of Jughead. 554-The World of Archie. 555-Betty's Diary. 556-Little Archie (1/86). 557-Archie's Christmas Stocking (1/86). 558-Betty & Veronica Christmas Spectacular (1/86). 559-Betty & Veronica Spectacular. 560-Little Archie. 561-Betty & Veronica Summer Fun. 563-Betty & Veronica Spectacular. 564-World of Jughead. 565-World of Archie. 566-Little Archie. 567-Archie's Christmas Stocking. 568-Betty & Veronica Christmas Spectacular. 569-Betty & Veronica Spring Spectacular. 570-Little Archie. 571-Dracula-c/s. 572-Betty & Veronica Summer Fun. 573-Archie At Riverdale High. 574-World of Archie. 575-Betty & Veronica Spectacular. 576-Pep. 577-World of Jughead. 578-Archie And Me. 579-Archie's Christmas Stocking. 580-Betty and Veronica Christmas Spectacular. 581-Little Archie Christmas Special. 582-Betty & Veronica Spring Spectacular. 583-Little Archie. 585-Betty & Veronica Summer Fun. 586-Archie At Riverdale High. 587-The World of Archie (10/88); 1st app. Explorers of the Unknown. 588-Betty & Veronica Spectacular. 589-Pep (10/88). 590-The World of Jughead. 591-Archie & Me. 592-Archie's Christmas Stocking. 593-Betty & Veronica Christmas Spectacular. 594-Little Archie. 595-Betty & Veronica Spring Spectacular. 596-Little Archie. 598-Betty & Veronica Summer Fun. 599-The World of Archie (10/89); 2nd app. Explorers of the Unknown. 600-Betty and Veronica Spectacular each.... 4.00
601,602,604-609,611-629: 601-Pep. 602-The World of Jughead. 604-Archie at Riverdale High. 605-Archie's Christmas Stocking. 606-Betty and Veronica Christmas Spectacular. 607-Little Archie. 608-Betty and Veronica Spectacular. 609-Little Archie. 611-Betty and Veronica Summer Fun. 612-The World of Archie. 613-Betty and Veronica Spectacular. 614-Pep (10/90). 615-Veronica's Summer Special. 616-Archie and Me. 617-Archie's Christmas Stocking. 618-Betty & Veronica Christmas Spectacular. 619-Little Archie. 620-Betty and Veronica Spectacular. 621-Betty and Veronica Summer Fun. 622-Josie & the Pussycats; not published. 623-Betty and Veronica Spectacular. 624-Pep Comics. 625-Veronica's Summer Special. 626-Archie and Me. 627-World of Archie. 628-Archie's Pals 'n' Gals Holiday Special. 629-Betty & Veronica Christmas Spectacular. each.... 2.50
603-Archie and Me; Titanic app. 4.00
610-Josie and the Pussycats 4.00
630-632: 630-Archie's Christmas Stocking. 631-Archie's Pals 'n' Gals. 632-Betty & Veronica Spectacular 2.25

NOTE: *Archies Band-c-173,180,192; s-189,192. Archie Cavemen-165,225,232,244,249. Little Sabrina-527,534,538,545,556,566. UFO-s-178,487,594.*

ARCHIE MEETS THE PUNISHER (Same contents as The Punisher Meets Archie)
Marvel Comics & Archie Comics Publ.: Aug, 1994 ($2.95, 52 pgs., one-shot)
1-Batton Lash story, J. Buscema-a on Punisher, S. Goldberg-a on Archie 4.00

ARCHIE'S ACTIVITY COMICS DIGEST MAGAZINE
Archie Enterprises: 1985 - No. 4? (Annual, 128 pgs., digest size)

1	1.00	2.80	7.00
2-4			5.00

ARCHIE'S CAR
Spire Christian Comics (Fleming H. Revell co.): 1979 (49¢)
nn 5.00

ARCHIE'S CHRISTMAS LOVE-IN (See Archie Giant Series Mag. No. 169, 181,192, 205, 218, 230, 242, 454, 466, 478, 490, 502, 514)

ARCHIE'S CHRISTMAS STOCKING (See Archie Giant Series Mag. No. 1-6,10, 15, 20, 25, 31, 137, 144, 150, 158, 167, 179, 190, 203, 216, 228, 240, 452, 464, 476, 488, 500, 512, 524, 535, 546, 557, 567, 579, 592, 605, 617, 630)

ARCHIE'S CHRISTMAS STOCKING
Archie Comics: 1993 -Present ($2.00, 52 pgs.)(Bound-in calendar poster in all)
1-5: 1-Dan DeCarlo-c/a 3.00
6,7: 6-(1998, $2.25). 7-(1999, $2.29) 2.29

ARCHIE'S CLEAN SLATE
Spire Christian Comics (Fleming H. Revell Co.): 1973 (35/49¢)
1 (Some issues have nn) 2.40 6.00

ARCHIE'S DATE BOOK
Spire Christian comics (Fleming H. Revell Co.): 1981
nn 5.00

ARCHIE'S DOUBLE DIGEST QUARTERLY MAGAZINE
Archie Comics: 1981 - Present ($1.95/$2.75/$2.95, 256 pgs.) (A.D.D. Magazine No. 10 on)

1	2.25	6.75	18.00
2-10; 6-Katy Keene story.	1.25	3.75	10.00
11-30: 29-Pureheart story	1.00	3.00	8.00
31-50			5.00
51-70,100			4.00
71-99,101-113			3.00

ARCHIE'S FAMILY ALBUM
Spire Christian Comics (Fleming H. Revell Co.): 1978 (39¢, 36 pgs.)
nn 5.00

ARCHIE'S FESTIVAL
Spire Christian Comics (Fleming H. Revell Co.): 1980 (49¢)
nn 5.00

ARCHIE'S GIRLS, BETTY AND VERONICA (Becomes Betty & Veronica)(Also see Veronica)
Archie Publications (Close-Up): 1950 - No. 347, Apr, 1987

1	150.00	450.00	1200.00
2	72.00	216.00	575.00
3-5	45.00	135.00	350.00
6-10: 6-Dan DeCarlo's 1st Archie work; Betty's 1st ponytail. 10-Katy Keene app. (2 pgs.)	40.00	120.00	280.00
11-20: 11,13,14,17-19-Katy Keene app. 17-Last pre-code issue (3/55). 20-Debbie's Diary (2 pgs.)	28.00	84.00	195.00
21-30: 27,30-Katy Keene app. 29-Tarzan	20.00	60.00	140.00
31-43,45-50: 41-Marilyn Monroe and BrigitteBardot mentioned. 45-Fabian 1 pg. photo & bio. 46-Bobby Darin 1 pg. photo & bio	12.00	36.00	85.00

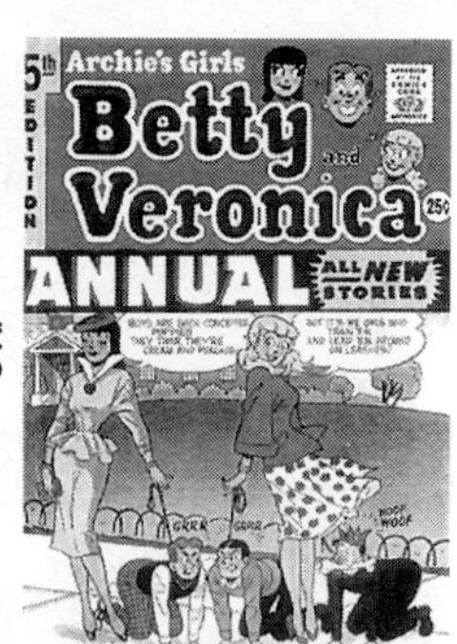

Archie's Girls, Betty and Veronica Annual #5 © AP

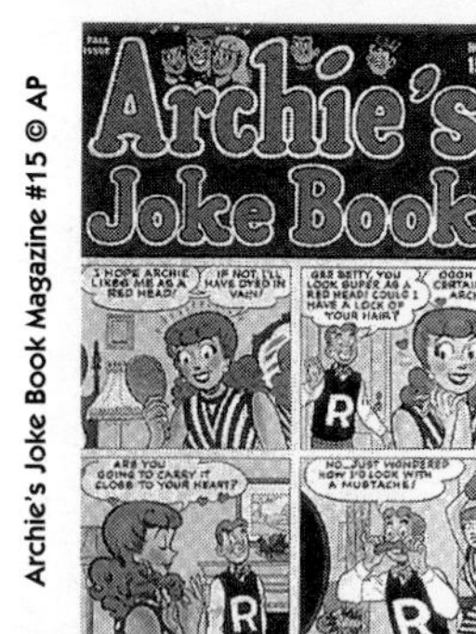

Archie's Joke Book Magazine #15 © AP

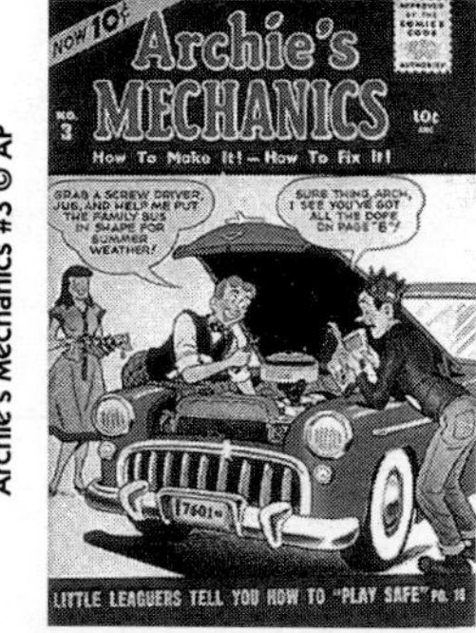

Archie's Mechanics #3 © AP

	GD2.0	FN6.0	NM9.4
44-Elvis Presley 1 pg. photo & bio	13.50	41.00	95.00
51-55,57-74: 73-Sci-fi-c	6.50	19.50	65.00
56-Elvis and Bobby Darin records parody	7.00	21.00	70.00
75-Betty & Veronica sell souls to Devil	12.00	36.00	120.00
76-99: 82-Bobby Rydell 1 pg. illustrated bio; Elvis mentioned on-c. 84-Connie Francis 1 pg. illustrated bio	3.50	10.50	35.00
100	4.50	13.50	45.00
101-117,120 (12/65): 113-Monsters-s	2.50	7.50	22.00
118-(10/65) 1st app./origin Superteen (also see Betty & Me #3)	4.00	12.00	40.00
119-2nd app./last Superteen story	2.60	7.80	26.00
121,122,124-126,128-140 (8/67): 135,140-Mod-c. 136-Slave Girl-s	2.00	6.00	16.00
123-"Jingo"-Ringo parody-c	1.85	5.50	15.00
127-Beatles Fan Club-s	2.50	7.50	24.00
141-156,158-180 (12/70): 164-Archies Band	1.50	4.50	12.00
157-Archies Band	2.25	6.75	18.00
181-193,195-199	1.10	3.30	9.00
194-Sabrina-c/s	1.75	5.25	14.00
200-(8/72)	1.50	4.50	12.00
201-205,207,209,211-215,217-240	1.00	3.00	8.00
206,208,216-Sabrina c/app. 206-Josie-c. 210-Sabrina app.	1.50	4.50	12.00
241 (1/76)-270 (6/78)		2.40	6.00
271-299: 281-UFO-s			5.00
300 (12/80)-Anniversary issue		2.40	6.00
301-309,311-319			3.50
310-John Travolta parody story			5.00
320 (10/82)-1st Cheryl Blossom	1.85	5.50	15.00
321,322-Cheryl Blossom app.	1.50	4.50	12.00
323,326,327,330,331,333-347: 333-Monsters-s			3.00
324,325-Crickett O'Dell app.			5.00
328-Cheryl Blossom app.	1.00	3.00	8.00
329,332: 329-Betty dressed as Madonna. 332-Superhero costume party			4.00
Annual 1 (1953)	84.00	252.00	675.00
Annual 2(1954)	40.00	120.00	315.00
Annual 3-5 (1955-1957)	33.00	99.00	230.00
Annual 6-8 (1958-1960)	21.00	64.00	150.00

ARCHIE'S HOLIDAY FUN DIGEST
Archie Comics: 1997 - Present ($1.75/$1.95/$1.99, annual)

	GD2.0	FN6.0	NM9.4
1-4-Christmas stories			2.00

ARCHIE'S JOKEBOOK COMICS DIGEST ANNUAL (See Jokebook...)

ARCHIE'S JOKE BOOK MAGAZINE (See Joke Book ...)
Archie Publ: 1953 - No. 3, Sum, 1954; No. 15, Fall, 1954 - No. 288, 11/82 (subtitled...Laugh-In #127-140; ...Laugh-Out #141-194)

	GD2.0	FN6.0	NM9.4
1953-One Shot (#1)	84.00	252.00	650.00
2	44.00	132.00	350.00
3 (no #4-14)	37.00	111.00	260.00
15-20: 15-Formerly Archie's Rival Reggie #14; last pre-code issue (Fall/54). 15-17-Katy Keene app.	21.00	64.00	150.00
21-30	13.00	39.00	90.00
31-40,42,43: 42-Bio of Ed "Kookie" Byrnes. 43-story about guitarist Duane Eddy	10.00	30.00	60.00
41-1st professional comic work by Neal Adams (9/59), 1 pg.	21.00	64.00	150.00
44-47-N. Adams-a in all, 1-3 pgs.	11.50	34.00	80.00
48-Four pgs. N. Adams-a	12.00	36.00	85.00
49-56,58-60 (1962)	2.60	7.80	26.00
57-Elvis mentioned; Marilyn Monroe cameo	3.00	9.00	30.00
61-80 (8/64): 66-(12¢ cover)	2.00	6.00	16.00
66-(15¢ cover variant)	2.50	7.50	25.00
81-89,91,92,94-99	1.50	4.50	12.00
90,93: 90-Beatles gag. 93-Beatles cameo	2.25	6.75	18.00
100 (5/66)	2.00	6.00	16.00
101,103-117,119-123,127,129,131-140 (9/69): 105-Superhero gag-c. 108-110-Archies Archers Band-s. 116-Beatles/Monkees/Bob Dylan cameos (posters)	1.25	3.75	10.00
102 (7/66) Archie Band prototype-c; Elvis parody panel, Rolling Stones mention	2.00	6.00	16.00
118,124,125,126,128,130: 118-ArchieBand-c; Veronica & Groovers band-s. 124-Archies Band-c/app. 125-Beatles cameo (poster). 126,130-Monkees cameo. 128-Veronica/Archies Band app.	2.00	6.00	16.00
141-173,175-181,183-199	1.00	3.00	8.00
174-Sabrina-c. 182-Sabrina cameo	1.25	3.75	10.00
200 (9/74)	1.25	3.75	10.00
201-230 (3/77)			5.00
231-239,241-288			4.00
240-Elvis record-c			5.00

NOTE: *Archies Band-c-118,124,147,172; 1 pg.-s-127,128,138,140,143,147,167; 2 pg.-s-124,131, 155. Sabrina app.-247,248,252-259,261,262,264,266-270,274,277,284-286.*

ARCHIE'S JOKES (See Archie Giant Series Mag. No. 17, 22, 27, 33, 139, 146, 154, 163, 174, 186, 198, 211, 222, 235, 247, 459, 471, 483, 495, 519)

ARCHIE'S LOVE SCENE
Spire Christian Comics (Fleming H. Revell Co.): 1973 (35¢/49¢/no price)

	GD2.0	FN6.0	NM9.4
1-(35¢ Edition)	1.00	3.00	8.00
1-(49¢ Edition/no price) (Some copies have nn)		2.40	6.00

ARCHIE'S MADHOUSE (Madhouse Ma-ad No. 67 on)
Archie Publications: Sept, 1959 - No. 66, Feb, 1969

	GD2.0	FN6.0	NM9.4
1-Archie begins	22.00	66.00	220.00
2	11.00	33.00	110.00
3-5	7.50	22.50	75.00
6-10	5.00	15.00	50.00
11-17 (Last w/regular characters)	3.80	11.40	38.00
18-21,29: 18-New format begins	2.50	7.50	25.00
22-1st app. Sabrina, the Teen-age Witch (10/62)	18.00	54.00	180.00
23,24-Sabrina app.	4.50	13.50	45.00
25,26,28-Sabrina app. 25-1st app. Captain Sprocket (4/63)	4.00	12.00	40.00
27-Sabrina-c; no story	3.50	10.50	35.00
30,34,38-40: No Sabrina. 34-Bordered-c begin.	2.00	6.00	16.00
31,32-Sabrina app.?	2.00	6.00	16.00
33,37-Sabrina app.	3.20	9.60	32.00
35-Beatles cameo. No Sabrina	3.20	9.60	22.00
36-1st Salem the Cat w/Sabrina story	4.00	12.00	40.00
41-48,51-57,60-62,64-66; No Sabrina 43-Mighty Crusaders cameo. 44-Swipes Mad #4 (Super-Duperman) in "Bird Monsters From Outer Space"	1.50	4.50	12.00
49,50,58,59,63-Sabrina stories	2.50	7.50	22.00
Annual 1 (1962-63) no Sabrina	6.50	19.50	65.00
Annual 2 (1964) no Sabrina	4.00	12.00	40.00
Annual 3 (1965)-Origin Sabrina the Teen-Age Witch	6.50	19.50	65.00
Annual 4,5('66-68)(Becomes Madhouse Ma-ad Annual #7 on); no Sabrina	2.25	6.75	18.00
Annual 6 (1969)-Sabrina the Teen-Age Witch-sty	3.50	10.50	35.00

NOTE: *Cover title to #61-65 is "Madhouse" and to #66 is "Madhouse Ma-ad Jokes".*

ARCHIE'S MECHANICS
Archie Publications: Sept, 1954 - No. 3, 1955

	GD2.0	FN6.0	NM9.4
1-(15¢; 52 pgs.)	75.00	225.00	600.00
2-(10¢)-Last pre-code issue	46.00	138.00	365.00
3-(10¢)	40.00	120.00	300.00

ARCHIE'S ONE WAY
Spire Christian Comics (Fleming H. Revell Co.): 1972 (35¢/39¢/49¢, 36 pgs.)

	GD2.0	FN6.0	NM9.4
nn-(35¢ Edition)	1.00	3.00	8.00
nn-(39¢, 49¢, no price editions)		2.40	6.00

ARCHIE'S PAL, JUGHEAD (Jughead No. 127 on)
Archie Publications: 1949 - No. 126, Nov, 1965

	GD2.0	FN6.0	NM9.4
1 (1949)-1st app. Moose (see Pep #33)	125.00	375.00	1000.00
2 (1950)	59.00	177.00	475.00
3-5	40.00	120.00	290.00

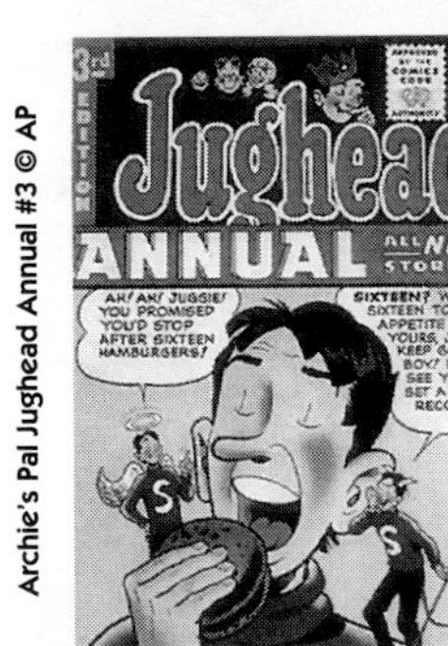

Archie's Pal Jughead Annual #3 © AP

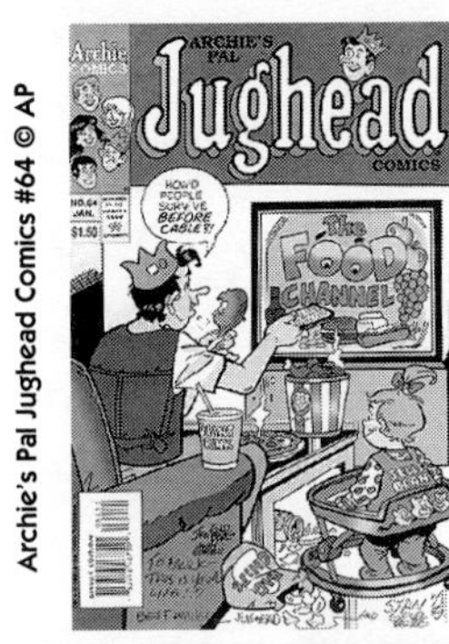

Archie's Pal Jughead Comics #64 © AP

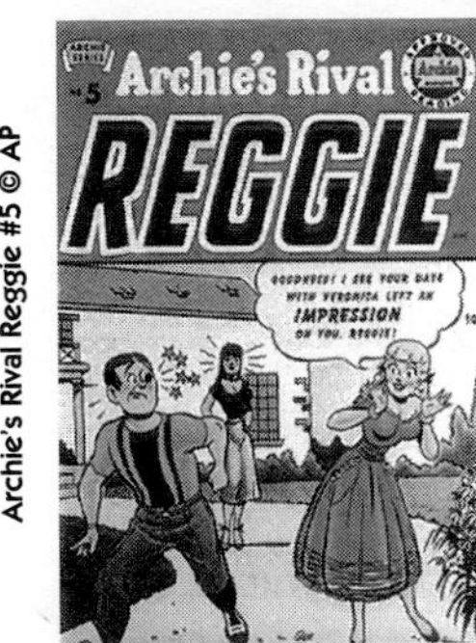

Archie's Rival Reggie #5 © AP

	GD2.0	FN6.0	NM9.4
6-10: 7-Suzie app.	28.00	84.00	195.00
11-20	17.00	51.00	120.00
21-30: 23-25,28-30-Katy Keene app. 23-Early Dilton-s. 28-Debbie's Diary app.	11.50	34.00	80.00
31-50: 49-Archies Rock 'N' Rollers band-c	5.00	15.00	50.00
51-70: 67-Betty seducing Jughead-c. 68-Early Archie Gang Cavemen-s	3.00	9.00	30.00
71-76,81-84,87,89-99: 72-Jughead dates Betty & Veronica	2.25	6.75	18.00
77,78,80,85,86,88-Horror/Sci-Fi-c	2.50	7.50	20.00
79-Creature From the Black Lagoon-c	3.00	9.00	30.00
100	2.50	7.50	20.00
101-Return of Big Ethyl	2.50	7.50	20.00
102-126	1.75	5.25	14.00
Annual 1 (1953, 25¢)	52.00	156.00	420.00
Annual 2 (1954, 25¢)-Last pre-code issue	37.00	111.00	260.00
Annual 3-5 (1955-57, 25¢)	26.00	78.00	180.00
Annual 6-8 (1958-60, 25¢)	16.00	48.00	110.00

ARCHIE'S PAL JUGHEAD COMICS (Formerly Jughead #1-45)
Archie Comic Publ.: No. 46, June, 1993 - Present ($1.25/$1.50/$1.75/$1.79)

	GD2.0	FN6.0	NM9.4
46-124: 100-"A Storm Over Uniforms" x-over part 1,2			2.00

ARCHIE'S PALS 'N' GALS (Also see Archie Giant Series Magazine #628)
Archie Publ: 1952-53 - No. 6, 1957-58; No. 7, 1958 - No. 224, Sept, 1991 (...All News Stories on-c #49-59)

	GD2.0	FN6.0	NM9.4
1-(116 pgs., 25¢)	70.00	210.00	560.00
2(Annual)('54, 25¢)	40.00	120.00	290.00
3-5(Annual, '55-57, 25¢): 3-Last pre-code issue	29.00	87.00	200.00
6-10('58-'60)	17.00	51.00	115.00
11-18,20 (84 pgs.): 12-Harry Belafonte 2 pg. photos & bio 17-B&V paper dolls	10.00	30.00	60.00
19-Marilyn Monroe app.	11.00	33.00	75.00
21,22,24-28,30 (68 pgs.)	4.00	12.00	40.00
23-(Wint./62) 6 pg. Josie-s with Pepper and Melody (1st app.?); Betty in towel pin-up	6.00	18.00	60.00
29-Beatles satire (68 pgs.)	6.00	18.00	60.00
31(Wint. 64/65)-39 -(68 pgs.)	3.50	10.50	35.00
40-Early Superteen-s; with Pureheart	5.00	15.00	50.00
41(8/67)-43,45-50(2/69) (68 pgs.)	2.50	7.50	25.00
44-Archies Band-s; WEB cameo	3.00	9.00	30.00
51(4/69),52,55-64(6/71): 62-Last squarebound	2.25	6.75	18.00
53-Archies Band-c/s	2.50	7.50	25.00
54-Satan meets Veronica-s	2.50	7.50	25.00
65(8/70),67-70,73-81,83(6/74) (52 pgs.)	1.75	5.25	14.00
66,82-Sabrina-c	2.50	7.50	20.00
71,72-Two part drug story (8/72,9/72)	2.25	6.75	18.00
75-Archies Band-s	2.50	7.50	20.00
84-99	1.00	3.00	8.00
100 (12/75)	1.25	3.75	10.00
101-130(3/79): 125,126-Riverdale 2001-s		2.40	6.00
131-160,162-170 (7/84)			4.50
161 (11/82) 2nd app./1st solo Cheryl Blossom-s and pin-up; 1st Jason Blossom	2.50	7.50	20.00
171-173,175,177-197,199: 197-G. Colan-a			3.00
174,176,198: 174-New Archies Band-s. 176-Cyndi Lauper-c. 198-Archie gang on strike at Archie Ent. offices			5.00
200(9/88)-Illiteracy-s			5.00
201,203-224: Later issues $1.00 cover			2.00
202-Explains end of Archie's jalopy; Dezerland-c/s; James Dean cameo			4.00

NOTE: *Archies Band-c-45,47,49,53,56; s-44,53,75,174. UFO-s-50,63,209,220.*

ARCHIE'S PALS 'N' GALS DOUBLE DIGEST MAGAZINE
Archie Comic Publications: Nov, 1992 - Present ($2.50/$2.75/$2.95/$2.99)

	GD2.0	FN6.0	NM9.4
1-3: 1-Capt. Hero story; Pureheart app. 2-Superduck story; Little Jinx in all		2.40	6.00
4-29: 4-Begin $2.75-c.			4.00
30-45: 40-Begin $2.99-c			3.00

ARCHIE'S PARABLES
Spire Christian Comics (Fleming H. Revell Co.): 1973,1975 (39/49¢, 36 pgs.)

	GD2.0	FN6.0	NM9.4
nn-By Al Hartley; 39¢ Edition	1.00	3.00	8.00
49¢, no price editions		2.40	6.00

ARCHIE'S R/C RACERS (Radio controlled cars)
Archie Comics: Sept, 1989 - No. 10, Mar, 1991 (95¢/$1)

	GD2.0	FN6.0	NM9.4
1,2,5-7,10: 5-Elvis parody. 7-Supervillain-c/s. 10-UFO-c/s			4.00
3,4,8,9			3.00

ARCHIE'S RIVAL REGGIE (Reggie & Archie's Joke Book #15 on)
Archie Publications: 1950 - No. 14, Aug, 1954

	GD2.0	FN6.0	NM9.4
1-Reggie 1st app. in Jackpot Comics #5	72.00	216.00	575.00
2	40.00	120.00	285.00
3-5	28.00	84.00	195.00
6-10	20.00	60.00	140.00
11-14: Katy Keene in No. 10-14, 1-2 pgs.	14.00	38.00	100.00

ARCHIE'S RIVERDALE HIGH (See Riverdale High)

ARCHIE'S ROLLER COASTER
Spire Christian Comics (Fleming H. Revell Co.): 1981 (69¢)

	GD2.0	FN6.0	NM9.4
nn		2.40	6.00

ARCHIE'S SOMETHING ELSE
Spire Christian Comics (Fleming H. Revell Co.): 1975 (39/49¢, 36 pgs.)

	GD2.0	FN6.0	NM9.4
nn -Hell's Angels Biker on motorcycle-c		2.40	6.00
Barbour Christian Comics Edtion (1986, no price listed)	1.00	3.00	8.00

ARCHIE'S SONSHINE
Spire Christian Comics (Fleming H. Revell Co.): 1973, 1974 (39/49¢, 36 pgs.)

	GD2.0	FN6.0	NM9.4
39¢ Edition	1.00	3.00	8.00
49¢, no price editions		2.40	6.00

ARCHIE'S SPORTS SCENE
Spire Christian Comics (Fleming H. Revell Co.): 1983 (no cover price)

	GD2.0	FN6.0	NM9.4
nn			5.00

ARCHIE'S SPRING BREAK
Archie Comics: 1996 - Present ($2.00, 48 pgs., annual)

	GD2.0	FN6.0	NM9.4
1-4: 1,2-Dan DeCarlo-c			2.25

ARCHIE'S STORY & GAME COMICS DIGEST MAGAZINE
Archie Enterprises: Nov, 1986 - Present ($1.25/$1.35/$1.50/$1.95, 128 pgs., digest-size)

	GD2.0	FN6.0	NM9.4
1: Many copies pre-marked in run	1.50	4.50	12.00
2-10	1.00	3.00	8.00
11-20		2.40	6.00
21-38			3.00
39-42-($1.95)			2.00

ARCHIE'S SUPER HERO SPECIAL (See Archie Giant Series Mag. No. 142)

ARCHIE'S SUPER HERO SPECIAL (...Comics Digest Mag. 2)
Archie Publications (Red Circle): Jan, 1979 - No. 2, Aug, 1979(95¢, 148 pgs.)

	GD2.0	FN6.0	NM9.4
1-Simon & Kirby r-/Double Life of Pvt. Strong #1,2; Black Hood, The Fly, Jaguar, The Web app.	1.50	4.50	12.00
2-Contains contents to the never published Black Hood #1; origin Black Hood; N. Adams, Wood, McWilliams, Morrow, S&K-a(r); N. Adams-c. The Shield, The Fly, Jaguar, Hangman, Steel Sterling, The Web, The Fox-r	1.25	3.75	10.00

ARCHIE'S SUPER TEENS
Archie Comic Publications, Inc.: 1994 - No. 4, 1996 ($2.00, 52 pgs.)

	GD2.0	FN6.0	NM9.4
1-4: 1-Staton/Esposito-c/a; pull-out poster. 2-Fred Hembeck script; Bret Blevins/Terry Austin-a			2.00

ARCHIE'S TV LAUGH-OUT ("...Starring Sabrina" on-c #1-50)
Archie Publications: Dec, 1969 - No. 106, Apr, 1986 (#1-7: 68 pgs.)

	GD2.0	FN6.0	NM9.4
1-Sabrina begins, thru #106	8.00	24.00	80.00
2 (68 pgs.)	4.00	12.00	40.00
3-6 (68 pgs.)	2.50	7.50	24.00

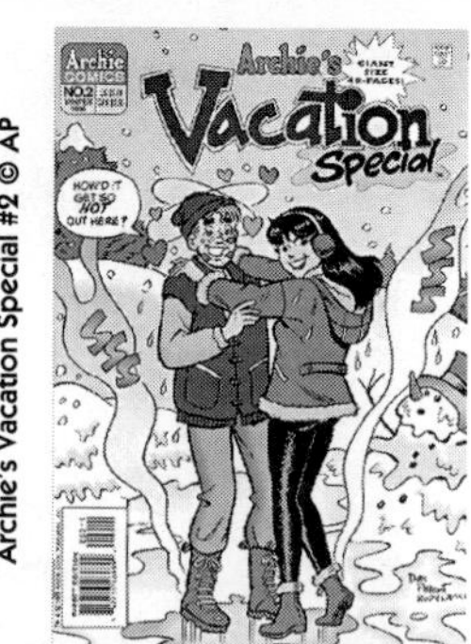

Archie's Vacation Special #2 © AP

Aria #2 © Haberlin & Holguin

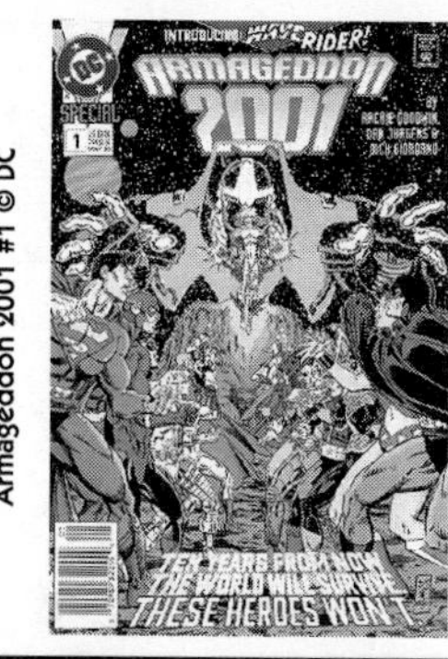

Armageddon 2001 #1 © DC

GD2.0 FN6.0 NM9.4

7-Josie begins, thru #105; Archie's & Josie's Bands cover logos begin 5.00 15.00 50.00
8-23 (52 pgs.): 10-1st Josie on-c. 12-1st Josie and Pussycats on-c. 14-Beatles cameo on poster 2.50 7.50 22.00
24-40: 37,39,40-Bicenntennial-c 1.50 4.50 12.00
41,47,56: 41-Alexandra rejoins J&P band. 47-Fonz cameo; voodoo-s. 56-Fonz parody; B&V with Farrah hair-c 1.75 5.25 14.00
42-46,48-55,57-60 1.10 3.30 9.00
61-68,70-80: 63-UFO-s. 79-Mummy-s 2.40 6.00
69-Sherlock Holmes parody 5.00
81-90,94,95,97-99: 84 Voodoo-s 4.00
91-Early Cheryl Blossom-s; Sabrina/Archies Band-c 1.50 4.50 12.00
92-A-Team parody 2.40 6.00
93-(2/84) Archie in drag-s; Hill Street Blues-s; Groucho Marx parody; cameo parody app. of Batman, Spider-Man, Wonder Woman and others 1.00 3.00 8.00
96-MASH parody-s; Jughead in drag; Archies Band-c 2.40 6.00
100-(4/85) Michael Jackson parody-c/s; J&P band and Archie band on-c 1.25 3.75 10.00
101-104-Lower print run. 104-Miami Vice parody-c 2.40 6.00
105-Wrestling/Hulk Hogan parody-c; J&P band-s 1.00 2.80 7.00
106-Last issue; low print run (scarce) 1.00 2.80 7.00

NOTE: ***Dan DeCarlo-a*** *78-up(most),* ***c-89-up(most). Archies Band-s*** *2,7,9-11,15,20,25,37,64,65,67,68,70,73,76,78,79,83,84,86,90,96,100,101;* ***Archies Band-c*** *2,17,20,91,94,96,99-103.* ***Josie-s*** *12,21,26,35,52,78,80,90.* ***Josie-c*** *10,91,94.* ***Josie and the Pussycats (as a band in costume)-s*** *7,9,10,37,38,41,42,66,84,99-101,105.* ***Josie w/Pussycats member Valerie &/or Melody-s*** *17,20,22,25,27-29,31,33,36,39,40,43-51,53-65,67-77,79,81-83,85-89,92-94,102-104.* ***Josie w/Pussycats band-c*** *12,14,17,18,22,24.* ***Sabrina-s*** *1-9,11-86,88-106.* ***Sabrina-c*** *1-18,21,23,27,49,91,94.*

ARCHIE'S VACATION SPECIAL
Archie Publications: Winter, 1994? - Present ($2.00/$2.25/$2.29, annually)
1-7 2.25

ARCHIE'S WEIRD MYSTERIES (TV)
Archie Comics: Feb, 2000 - Present ($1.79)
1 2.00

ARCHIE'S WORLD
Spire Christian Comics (Fleming H. Revell Co.): 1973, 1976 (39/49¢)
39¢ Edition 1.00 3.00 8.00
49¢, no price editions 2.40 6.00

ARCHIE 3000
Archie Comics: May, 1989 - No. 16, July, 1991 (75¢/95¢/$1.00)
1,16: 16-Aliens-c/s 3.00
2-15: 6-Begin $1.00-c; X-Mas-c 2.00

ARCOMICS PREMIERE
Arcomics: July, 1993 ($2.95)
1-1st lenticular-c on a comic (flicker-c) 3.00

AREA 88
Eclipse Comics/VIZ Comics #37 on: May 26, 1987 - No. 42, 1989 ($1.50/$1.75, B&W)
1-42: 1,2-2nd printings exist 2.00

AREALA: ANGEL OF WAR (See Warrior Nun titles)
Antarctic Press: Sept, 1998 - No. 4, June, 1999 ($2.95/$2.99, color/B&W)
1-4: 3,4-B&W. 4-($2.99-c) 3.00

ARENA
Alchemy Studios: Jan, 1990 ($1.50, 7x10-1/8", 20 pgs.)
1-Science fiction 2.00
1-Signed & numbered ed. (500 copies) 3.00

ARGUS (See Flash, 2nd Series) (Also see Showcase '95 #1,2)
DC Comics: Apr, 1995 - No. 6, Oct, 1995 ($1.50, limited series)
1-6: 4-Begin $1.75-c 2.00

ARIA
Image Comics (Avalon Studios): Jan, 1999 - Present ($2.50)
Preview (11/98, $2.95) 5.00
1-Anacleto-c/a 4.00
1-Variant-c by Michael Turner 1.00 2.80 7.00
1-($10.00) Alternate-c by Turner 1.25 3.75 10.00
1,2-(Blanc & Noir) Black and white printing of pencil art 3.00
1-(Blanc & Noir) DF Edition 7.00
2-4: 2,4-Anacleto-c/a. 3-Martinez-a 2.50

ARIANE AND BLUEBEARD (See Night Music #8)

ARIEL & SEBASTIAN (See Cartoon Tales & The Little Mermaid)

ARION, LORD OF ATLANTIS (Also see Warlord #55)
DC Comics: Nov, 1982 - No. 35, Sept, 1985
1-35: 1-Story cont'd from Warlord #62, Special #1 (11/85) 2.00

ARION THE IMMORTAL (Also see Showcase '95 #7)
DC Comics: July, 1992 - No. 6, Dec, 1992 ($1.50, limited series)
1-6: 4-Gustovich-a(i) 2.00

ARISTOCATS (See Movie Comics & Walt Disney Showcase No. 16)

ARISTOKITTENS, THE (...Meet Jiminy Cricket No. 1)(Disney)
Gold Key: Oct, 1971 - No. 9, Oct, 1975
1 2.50 7.50 22.00
2-5,7-9 1.60 4.85 13.00
6-(52 pgs.) 2.00 6.00 16.00

ARIZONA KID, THE (Also see The Comics & Wild Western)
Marvel/Atlas Comics(CSI): Mar, 1951 - No. 6, Jan, 1952
1 21.00 64.00 150.00
2-4: 2-Heath-a(3) 11.00 33.00 75.00
5,6 10.00 30.00 65.00

NOTE: ***Heath*** *a-1-3; c-1-3.* ***Maneely*** *c-4-6.* ***Morisi*** *a-4-6.* ***Sinnott*** *a-6.*

ARK, THE (See The Crusaders)

ARKAGA
Image Comics: Sept, 1997 ($2.95, one-shot)
1-Jorgensen-s/a 3.00

ARMAGEDDON: ALIEN AGENDA
DC Comics: Nov, 1991 - No. 4, Feb, 1992 ($1.00, limited series)
1-4 2.00

ARMAGEDDON FACTOR, THE
AC Comics: 1987 - No. 2, 1987; No. 3, 1990 ($1.95)
1,2: Sentinels of Justice, Dragonfly, Femforce 2.00
3-($3.95, color)-Almost all AC characters app. 4.00

ARMAGEDDON: INFERNO
DC Comics: Apr, 1992 - No. 4, July, 1992 ($1.00, limited series)
1-4: Many DC heroes app. 3-A. Adams/Austin-a 2.50

ARMAGEDDON 2001
DC Comics: May, 1991 - No. 2, Oct, 1991 ($2.00, squarebound, 68 pgs.)
1-Features many DC heroes; intro Waverider 3.00
1-2nd & 3rd printings; 3rd has silver ink-c 2.00
2 2.50

ARMATURE
Olyoptics: Nov, 1996 - No. 2, ($2.95, limited series)
1,2-Steve Oliff-c/s/a; Maxx app. 3.00

ARMED & DANGEROUS
Acclaim Comics (Armada): Apr, 1996 - No.4, July, 1996 ($2.95, B&W)
1-4-Bob Hall-c/a & scripts 3.00
Special 1 (8/96, $2.95, B&W)-Hall-c/a & scripts. 3.00

ARMED & DANGEROUS HELL'S SLAUGHTERHOUSE
Acclaim Comics (Armada): Oct, 1996 - No. 4, Jan, 1997 ($2.95, B&W)
1-4: Hall-c/a/scripts. 3.00

ARMOR (AND THE SILVER STREAK)

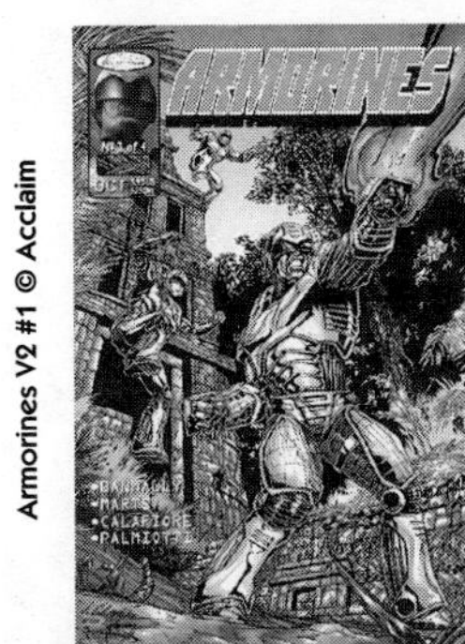

Armorines V2 #1 © Acclaim

Artbabe V2 #3 © Fantagraphics

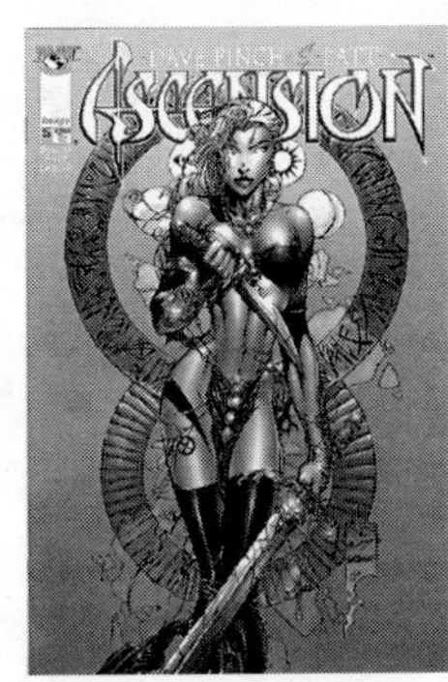

Ascension #5 © Banning & Finch

GD2.0 FN6.0 NM9.4

Continuity Comics: Sept, 1985 - No.13, Apr, 1992 ($2.00)

1-13: 1-Intro/origin Armor & the Silver Streak; Neal Adams-c/a. 7-Origin Armor; Nebres-i 2.00

ARMOR (DEATHWATCH 2000)
Continuity Comics: Apr, 1993 - No.6, Nov, 1993 ($2.50)

1-6: 1-3-Deathwatch 2000 x-over 2.50

ARMORED TROOPER VOTOMS (Manga)
CPM Comics: July, 1996 ($2.95)

1 3.00

ARMORINES (See X-O Manowar #25)
Valiant: June, 1994 - No. 12, June, 1995 ($2.25)

1-12: 7-Wraparound-c. 12-Byrne-c/swipe (X-Men, 1st Series #138) 2.25

ARMORINES (Volume 2)
Acclaim Comics: Oct, 1999 - No. 4 ($3.95, limited series)

1-Calafiore & P. Palmiotti-a 3.95

ARMY AND NAVY COMICS (Supersnipe No. 6 on)
Street & Smith Publications: May, 1941 - No. 5, July, 1942

	GD2.0	FN6.0	NM9.4
1-Cap Fury & Nick Carter	47.00	141.00	375.00
2-Cap Fury & Nick Carter	29.00	86.00	200.00
3,4: 4-Jack Farr-c/a	20.00	60.00	140.00
5-Supersnipe app.; see Shadow V2#3 for 1st app.; Story of Douglas MacArthur; George Marcoux-c/a	47.00	141.00	375.00

ARMY ATTACK
Charlton Comics: July, 1964 - No. 4, Feb, 1965; V2#38, July, 1965 - No. 47, Feb, 1967

	GD2.0	FN6.0	NM9.4
V1#1	3.00	9.00	30.00
2-4(2/65)	2.25	6.75	18.00
V2#38(7/65)-47 (formerly U.S. Air Force #1-37)	1.85	5.50	15.00

NOTE: ***Glanzman** a-1-3. **Montes/Bache** a-44.*

ARMY AT WAR (Also see Our Army at War & Cancelled Comic Cavalcade)
DC Comics: Oct-Nov, 1978

1-Kubert-c; all new story and art 5.00

ARMY OF DARKNESS (Movie)
Dark Horse Comics: Nov, 1992 - No. 2, Dec, 1992; No. 3, Oct, 1993 ($2.50, limited series)

1-3-Bolton painted-c/a 2.50

ARMY SURPLUS KOMIKZ FEATURING CUTEY BUNNY
Army Surplus Komikz/Eclipse Comics: 1982 - No. 5, 1985 ($1.50, B&W)

1-Cutey Bunny begins 5.00
2-5: 5-(Eclipse)-JLA/X-Men/Batman parody 3.00

ARMY WAR HEROES (Also see Iron Corporal)
Charlton Comics: Dec, 1963 - No. 38, June, 1970

	GD2.0	FN6.0	NM9.4
1	3.20	9.60	32.00
2-10	2.50	7.50	22.00
11-21,23-30: 24-Intro. Archer & Corp. Jack series	2.00	6.50	16.00
22-Origin/1st app. Iron Corporal series by Glanzman	2.50	7.50	20.00
31-38	1.25	3.75	10.00
Modern Comics Reprint 36 ('78)			4.00

NOTE: ***Montes/Bache** a-1, 16, 17, 21, 23-25, 27-30.*

AROUND THE BLOCK WITH DUNC & LOO (See Dunc and Loo)

AROUND THE WORLD IN 80 DAYS (Movie) (See A Golden Picture Classic)
Dell Publishing Co.: Feb, 1957

	GD2.0	FN6.0	NM9.4
Four Color 784-Photo-c	5.75	17.00	63.00

AROUND THE WORLD UNDER THE SEA (See Movie Classics)

AROUND THE WORLD WITH ARCHIE (See Archie Giant Series Mag. #29, 35, 141)

AROUND THE WORLD WITH HUCKLEBERRY & HIS FRIENDS (See Dell Giant No. 44)

ARRGH! (Satire)

GD2.0 FN6.0 NM9.4

Marvel Comics Group: Dec, 1974 - No. 5, Sept, 1975 (25¢)

	GD2.0	FN6.0	NM9.4
1	2.00	6.00	16.00
2-5	1.25	3.75	10.00

NOTE ***Alcala** a-2; c-3. **Everett** a-1r, 2r. **Maneely** a-4r. **Sekowsky** a-1p. **Sutton** a-1, 2.*

ARROW (See Protectors)
Malibu Comics: Oct, 1992 ($1.95, one-shot)

1-Moder-a(p) 2.00

ARROW, THE (See Funny Pages)
Centaur Publications: Oct, 1940 - No. 2, Nov, 1940; No. 3, Oct, 1941

	GD2.0	FN6.0	NM9.4
1-The Arrow begins(r/Funny Pages)	288.00	862.00	2300.00
2,3: 2-Tippy Taylor serial continues from Amazing Mystery Funnies #24. 3-Origin Dash Dartwell, the Human Meteor; origin The Rainbow-r; bondage-c	119.00	356.00	950.00

NOTE: ***Gustavson** a-1, 2; c-3.*

ARROWHEAD (See Black Rider and Wild Western)
Atlas Comics (CPS): April, 1954 - No. 4, Nov, 1954

	GD2.0	FN6.0	NM9.4
1-Arrowhead & his horse Eagle begin	15.00	45.00	105.00
2-4: 4-Forte-a	10.00	30.00	65.00

NOTE: ***Heath** c-3. **Jack Katz** a-3. **Maneely** c-2. **Pakula** a-2. **Sinnott** a-1-4; c-1.*

ARSENAL (Teen Titans' Speedy)
DC Comics: Oct, 1998 - No. 4, Jan, 1999 ($2.50, limited series)

1-4: Grayson-s. 1-Black Canary app. 2-Green Arrow app. 2.50

ARSENAL SPECIAL (See New Titans, Showcase '94 #7 & Showcase '95 #8)
DC Comics: 1996 ($2.95, one-shot)

1 3.00

ARTBABE
Fantagraphics Books: May, 1996 - Apr, 1999 ($2.50/$2.95/$3.50, B&W)

V1 #5, V2 #1-3 3.00
#4-($3.50) 3.50

ARTEMIS: REQUIEM (Also see Wonder Woman, 2nd Series #90)
DC Comics: June, 1996 - No. 6, Nov, 1996 ($1.75, limited series)

1-6: Messner-Loebs scripts & Ed Benes-c/a in all. 1,2-Wonder Woman app. 3.00

ARTESIA
Sirius Entertainment: Jan, 1999 - No. 6, June, 1999 ($2.95)

1-6-Mark Smylie-s/a 3.00

ART OF ZEN INTERGALACTIC NINJA, THE
Entity Comics: 1994 - No. 2, 1994 ($2.95)

1,2 3.00

ARZACH (See Moebius...)
Dark Horse Comics: 1996 ($6.95, one-shot)

	GD2.0	FN6.0	NM9.4
nn-Moebius-c/a/scripts	1.00	2.80	7.00

ASCENSION
Image Comics (Top Cow Productions): Oct, 1997 - Present ($2.50)

	GD2.0	FN6.0	NM9.4
Preview	1.00	2.80	7.00
Preview Gold Edition			10.00
Preview San Diego Edition	1.85	5.50	15.00
0			5.00
1/2	1.00	3.00	8.00
1-David Finch-s/a(p)/Batt-s/a(i)			5.00
1-Variant-c w/Image logo at lower right	1.00	3.00	8.00
2-6			4.00
7-20			3.00
Fan Club Edition	1.25	3.75	10.00

...COLLECTED EDITION
1998 - Present ($4.95, squarebound)

	GD2.0	FN6.0	NM9.4
1,2: 1-r/#1,2. 2-r/#3,4		2.40	6.00

ASH
Event Comics: Nov, 1994 - No. 6, Dec, 1995; No. 0, May, 1996 ($2.50/$3.00)

Ash: Fire and Crossfire #1 © Quesada & Palmiotti

Astonishing #34 © ATLAS

Astonishing Tales #2 © MAR

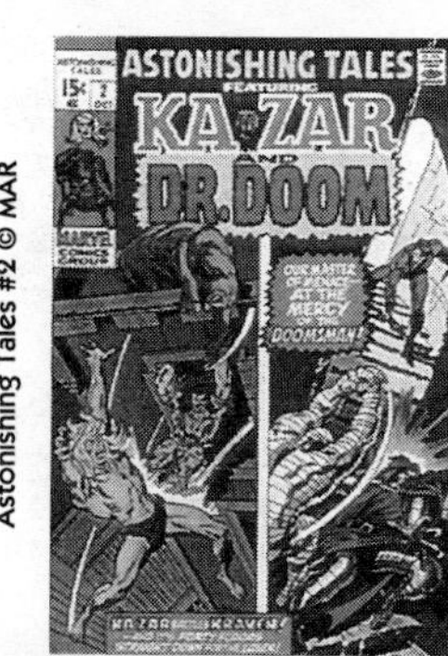

GD2.0 FN6.0 NM9.4

0-Present & Future (Both 5/96, $3.00, foil logo-c)-w/pin-ups 3.00
0-Blue Foil logo-c (Present and Future) (1000 each) 5.00
0-Silver Prism logo-c (Present and Future) (500 each) 12.00
0-Red Prism logo-c (Present and Future) (250 each) 20.00
0-Gold Hologram logo-c (Present and Future) (1000 each) 10.00
1-Quesada-p/story; Palmiotti-i/story: Barry Windsor-Smith pin-up 1.85 5.50 15.00
2-Mignola Hellboy pin-up 1.00 3.30 9.00
3,4: 3-Big Guy pin-up by Geoff Darrow. 4-Jim Lee pin-up 6.00
4-Fahrenheit Gold 9.00
4-6-Fahrenheit Red (5,6-1000) 10.00
4-6-Fahrenheit White 15.00
5, 6-Double-c w/Hildebrandt Bros.-a, Quesada & Palmiotti. 6-Texiera-c 4.00
5,6-Fahrenheit Gold (2000) 5.00
6-Fahrenheit White (500)-Texiera-c 15.00
Volume 1 (1996, $14.95, TPB)-r/#1-5, intro by James Robinson 15.00

ASH: CINDER & SMOKE
Event Comics: May, 1997 - No. 6, Oct, 1997 ($2.95, limited series)
1-6:Ramos-a/Waid, Augustyn-s in all
2-6-variant covers by Ramos and Quesada 3.00

ASH: FILES
Event Comics: Mar, 1997 ($2.95, one-shot)
1-Comics w/text 3.00

ASH: FIRE AND CROSSFIRE
Event Comics: Jan, 1999 - No. 5 ($2.95, limited series)
1,2-Robinson-s/Quesada & Palmiotti-c/a 3.00

ASH: FIRE WITHIN, THE
Event Comics: Sept, 1996 - No. 2, Jan, 1997 ($2.95, unfinished limited series)
1,2:Quesada & Palmiotti-c/s/a 3.00

ASH/ 22 BRIDES
Event Comics: Dec, 1996 - No. 2, Apr, 1997 ($2.95, limited series)
1,2:Nicieza-s/Ramos-c/a 3.00

ASKANI'SON (See Adventures of Cyclops & Phoenix limited series)
Marvel Comics: Jan, 1996 - No. 4, May, 1996 ($2.95, limited series)
1-4: Story cont'd from Advs. of Cyclops & Phoenix; Lobdell/Loeb story; Gene Ha-c/a(p) 3.00
TPB (1997, $12.99) r/#1-4; Gene Ha painted-c 13.00

ASSASSINETTE
Pocket Change Comics: 1994 - No.7, 1995? ($2.50, B&W)
1-7: 1-Silver foil-c 2.50

ASSASSINETTE HARDCORE
Pocket Change Comics: 1995 - No.2, 1995 ($2.50, B&W, limited series)
1,2 2.50

ASSASSINS
DC Comics (Amalgam): Apr, 1996 ($1.95)
1 2.00

ASSASSINS, INC.
Silverline Comics: 1987 - No. 2, 1987 ($1.95)
1,2 2.00

ASTER
Entity Comics: Oct, 1994 - No. 4, 1995 ($2.95)
0-4: 1,3,4-Foil Logo. 2-Foil-c. 3-Variant-c exists. 3.00

ASTER: THE LAST CELESTIAL KNIGHT
Entity Comics: 1995 - No. 3, 1996 ($2.50)
1-3 2.50

ASTONISHING (Formerly Marvel Boy No. 1, 2)
Marvel/Atlas Comics(20CC): No. 3, Apr, 1951 - No. 63, Aug, 1957
3-Marvel Boy continues; 3-5-Marvel Boy-c 87.00 261.00 700.00
4-6-Last Marvel Boy; 4-Stan Lee app. 60.00 180.00 480.00

GD2.0 FN6.0 NM9.4

7-10: 7-Maneely s/f story. 10-Sinnott s/f story 28.00 84.00 195.00
11,12,15,17,20 24.00 72.00 170.00
13,14,16,18,19-Krigstein-a. 18-Jack The Ripper sty 26.00 78.00 180.00
21,22,24 22.00 66.00 155.00
23-E.C. swipe "The Hole In The Wall" from Vault Of Horror #16 22.00 66.00 155.00
25,29: 25-Crandall-a. 29-Decapitation-c 20.00 60.00 140.00
26-28 18.00 54.00 125.00
30-Tentacled eyeball story 23.00 69.00 160.00
31-37-Last pre-code issue 17.00 51.00 115.00
38-43,46,48-52,56,58,59,61 12.00 36.00 85.00
44,45,47,53-55,57,60: 44-Crandall swipe/Weird Fantasy #22. 45,47-Krigstein-a. 53-Ditko-a. 54-Torres-a, 55-Crandall, Torres-a. 57-Williamson/Krenkel-a (4 pgs.). 60-Williamson/Mayo-a (4 pgs.) 13.50 41.00 95.00
62,63: 62-Torres, Powell-a. 63-Woodbridge-a 13.00 39.00 90.00

NOTE: ***Ayers*** *a-16.* ***Berg*** *a-36, 53, 56.* ***Cameron*** *a-50.* ***Gene Colan*** *a-12, 20, 29, 56.* ***Ditko*** *a-53.* ***Drucker*** *a-41, 62.* ***Everett*** *a-3-6(3), 6, 10, 12, 37, 47, 48, 58; c-3-5, 13,15, 16, 18, 29, 47, 49, 51, 53-55, 57, 59-63.* ***Fass*** *a-11, 34.* ***Forte*** *a-53, 58, 60.* ***Fuje*** *a-11.* ***Heath*** *a-8, 29; c-8, 9, 19, 22, 25, 26.* ***Kirby*** *a-56.* ***Lawrence*** *a-28, 37, 38, 42.* ***Maneely*** *a-7(2); c-7, 31, 33, 34, 56.* ***Moldoff*** *a-33.* ***Morisi*** *a-10, 60.* ***Morrow*** *a-52, 61.* ***Orlando*** *a-47, 58, 61.* ***Pakula*** *a-10.* ***Powell*** *a-43, 44, 48.* ***Ravielli*** *a-28.* ***Reinman*** *a-32, 34, 38.* ***Robinson*** *a-20.* ***J. Romita*** *a-7, 18, 24, 43, 57,61.* ***Roussos*** *a-55.* ***Sale*** *a-28, 38, 59; c-32.* ***Sekowsky*** *a-13.* ***Severin*** *c-46.* ***Shores*** *a-16, 60.* ***Sinnott*** *a-11, 30.* ***Whitney*** *a-13.* ***Ed Win*** *a-20. Canadian reprints exist.*

ASTONISHING TALES (See Ka-Zar)
Marvel Comics Group: Aug, 1970 - No. 36, July, 1976 (#1-7: 15¢; #8: 25¢)
1-Ka-Zar (by Kirby(p) #1,2; by B. Smith #3-6) & Dr. Doom (by Wood #1-4; by Tuska #5,6; by Colan #7,8) double feature begins; Kraven the Hunter-c/story; Nixon cameo 3.60 10.80 36.00
2-Kraven the Hunter-c/story; Kirby, Wood-a 2.25 6.75 18.00
3-6: B. Smith-p; Wood-a-#3,4. 5,6-Red Skull 2-part story 2.50 7.50 25.00
7-Last 15¢ issue 1.75 5.25 14.00
8-(25¢, 52 pgs.)-Last Dr. Doom 2.50 7.50 20.00
9-Lorna-r/Lorna #14 1.50 4.50 12.00
10-B. Smith/Sal Buscema-a. 1.50 4.50 12.00
11-Origin Ka-Zar & Zabu 1.75 5.25 14.00
12-2nd app.Man-Thing; by Neal Adams (see Savage Tales #1 for 1st app.) 2.50 7.50 20.00
13-3rd app.Man-Thing 2.00 6.00 16.00
14-20: 14-Jann of the Jungle-r (1950s). 19-Starlin-a(p). 20-Last Ka-Zar 2.40 6.00
21-(12/73)-It! the Living Colossus begins, ends #24 (see Supernatural Thrillers #1) 2.00 6.00 16.00
22-24: 23,24-Fin Fang Foom app. 1.50 4.50 12.00
25-1st app. Deathlok the Demolisher; full length stories begin, end #36; Perez's 1st work, 2 pgs. (8/74) 2.50 7.50 24.00
26-28,30 1.00 2.80 7.00
29-r/origin/1st app. Guardians of the Galaxy from Marvel Super-Heroes #18 plus-c w/4 pgs. omitted; no Deathlok story 1.00 2.80 7.00
31-34: 31-Watcher-r/Silver Surfer #3 2.40 6.00
35,36-(Regular 25¢ edition)(5,7/76) 2.40 6.00
35,36-(30¢-c, low distribution) 2.50 7.50 20.00

NOTE: ***Buckler*** *a-13i, 16p, 25, 26p, 27p, 28, 29p-36p; c-13, 25p, 26-30, 32-35p, 36.* ***John Buscema*** *a-9, 12p-14p, 16p; c-4-6p, 12p.* ***Colan*** *a-7p, 8p.* ***Ditko*** *a-21r.* ***Everett*** *a-6i.* ***G. Kane*** *a-11p, 15p; c-9, 10p, 11p, 14, 15p, 21p.* ***McWilliams*** *a-30i.* ***Starlin*** *a-19p; c-16p.* ***Sutton & Trimpe*** *a-8.* ***Tuska*** *a-5p, 6p, 8p.* ***Wood*** *a-1-4.* ***Wrightson*** *c-31i.*

ASTONISHING X-MEN
Marvel Comics: Mar, 1995 - No.4, July, 1995 ($1.95, limited series)
1-Age of Apocalypse 4.00
2-4 3.00

ASTONISHING X-MEN
Marvel Comics: Sept, 1999 - No.3, Nov, 1999 ($2.50, limited series)
1-New team, Cable & X-Man app.; Peterson-a 2.50

ASTRO BOY (TV) (See March of Comics #285 & The Original...)
Gold Key: August, 1965 (12¢)

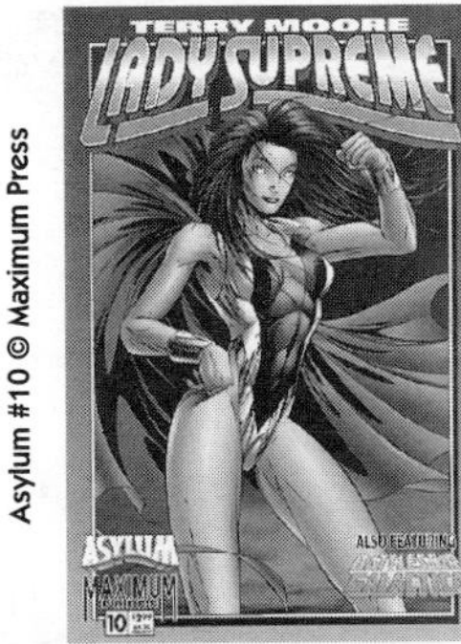

Asylum #10 © Maximum Press

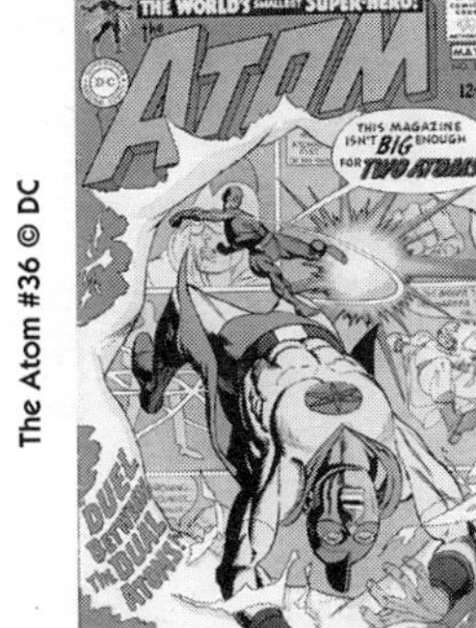

The Atom #36 © DC

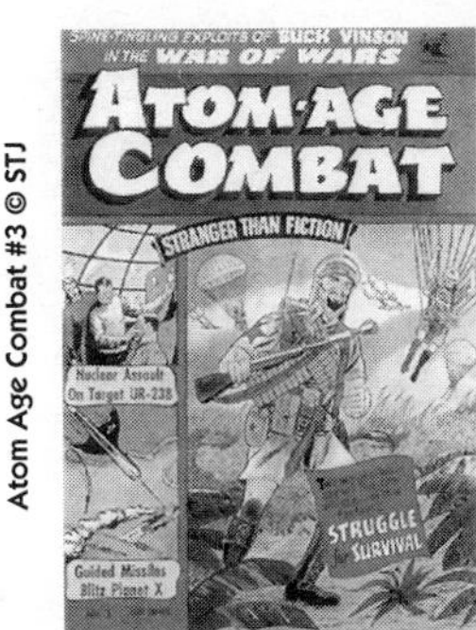

Atom Age Combat #3 © STJ

GD2.0 FN6.0 NM9.4

1(10151-508)-Scarce;1st app. Astro Boy in comics 42.00 125.00 460.00

ASTRO CITY (See Kurt Busiek's Astro City)

ASYLUM
Millennium Publications: 1993 ($2.50)

1-3: 1-Bolton-c/a; Russell 2-pg. illos 2.50

ASYLUM
Maximum Press: Dec, 1995 - No. 11, Jan, 1997 ($2.95/$2.99, anthology) (#1-6 are flip books)

1-10: 1-Warchild by Art Adams, Beanworld, Avengelyne, Battlestar Galactica. 2-Intro Mike Deodato's Deathkiss; Cybrid story begins, ends #5. 4-1st app.Christian; painted Battlestar Galactica story begins. 5-Intro Black Seed (formerly Black Flag) by Dan Fraga; B&W Christian story. 6-Intro Bionix (Six Million Dollar Man & the Bionic Woman). 7-Begin $2.99-c; Don Simpson's Megaton Man; Black Seed pinup. 8-B&W-a. 9- Foot Soldiers & Kid Supreme. 10-Lady Supreme by Terry Moore-c/app. 4.00

ATARI FORCE (Also see Promotional comics section)
DC Comics: Jan, 1984 - No. 20, Aug, 1985 (Mando paper)

1-20: 1-(1/84)-Intro Tempest, Packrat, Babe, Morphea, & Dart 2.00
Special 1 (4/86) 2.00
NOTE: ***Byrne*** *c-Special 1i.* ***Giffen*** *a-12p, 13i.* ***Rogers*** *a-18p, Special 1p.*

A-TEAM, THE (TV)
Marvel Comics Group: Mar, 1984 - No. 3, May, 1984

1-3 2.00
1,2-(Whitman bagged set) w/75¢-c 2.40 6.00
3-(Whitman, no bag) w/75¢-c 2.40 6.00

ATLANTIS CHRONICLES, THE (Also see Aquaman, 3rd Series & Aquaman: Time & Tide)
DC Comics: Mar, 1990 - No. 7, Sept, 1990 ($2.95, limited series, 52 pgs.)

1-7: 1-Peter David scripts. 7-True origin of Aquaman; nudity panels 3.25

ATLANTIS, THE LOST CONTINENT
Dell Publishing Co.: May, 1961

Four Color #1188-Movie, photo-c 9.00 27.00 100.00

ATLAS (See 1st Issue Special)

ATLAS
Dark Horse Comics: Feb, 1994 - No. 4, 1994 ($2.50, limited series)

1-4 2.50

ATOM, THE (See Action #425, All-American #19, Brave & the Bold, D.C. Special Series #1, Detective, Flash Comics #80, Power Of The Atom, Showcase #34 -36 , Super Friends, Sword of The Atom, Teen Titans & World's Finest)

ATOM, THE (...& the Hawkman No. 39 on)
National Periodical Publ.: June-July, 1962 - No. 38, Aug-Sept, 1968

1-(6-7/62)-Intro Plant-Master; 1st app. Maya 63.00 188.00 750.00
2 30.00 90.00 300.00
3-1st Time Pool story; 1st app. Chronos (origin) 19.00 57.00 190.00
4,5: 4-Snapper Carr x-over 15.00 45.00 150.00
6,8-10: 8-Justice League, Dr. Light app. 10.00 30.00 100.00
7-Hawkman x-over (6-7/63; 1st Atom & Hawkman team-up); 1st app. Hawkman since Brave & the Bold tryouts 26.00 78.00 260.00
11-15: 13-Chronos-c/story 7.00 21.00 70.00
16-20: 19-Zatanna x-over 5.00 15.00 50.00
21-28,30: 28-Chronos-c/story 4.00 12.00 40.00
29-1st solo Golden Age Atom x-over in S.A. 14.00 42.00 140.00
31-35,37,38: 31-Hawkman x-over. 37-Intro. Major Mynah; Hawkman cameo 4.00 12.00 40.00
36-G.A. Atom x-over 5.00 15.00 50.00
NOTE: ***Anderson*** *a-1-11i, 13i; c-inks-1-25, 31-35, 37.* ***Sid Greene*** *a-8i-37i.* ***Gil Kane*** *a-1p-37p; c-1p-28p, 29, 33p, 34.* ***George Roussos*** *38i* ***Mike Sekowsky*** *38p Time Pool stories also in 6, 9,12, 17, 21, 27, 35.*

ATOM ,THE (See Tangent Comics/ The Atom)

ATOM AGE (See Classics Illustrated Special Issue)

ATOM-AGE COMBAT
St. John Publishing Co.: June, 1952 - No. 5, Apr, 1953; Feb, 1958

1-Buck Vinson in all 41.00 123.00 325.00
2-Flying saucer story 26.00 79.00 185.00
3,5: 3-Mayo-a (6 pgs.). 5-Flying saucer-c/story 21.00 64.00 150.00
4 (Scarce) 26.00 77.00 180.00
1(2/58-St. John) 17.00 51.00 120.00

ATOM-AGE COMBAT
Fago Magazines: Nov, 1958 - No. 3, Mar, 1959

1-All have Dick Ayers-c/a 25.00 75.00 175.00
2,3: 2-A-Bomb explosion-c 19.00 56.00 130.00

ATOMAN
Spark Publications: Feb, 1946 - No. 2, April, 1946

1-Origin & 1st app. Atoman; Robinson/Meskin-a; Kidcrusaders, Wild Bill Hickok, Marvin the Great app. 56.00 168.00 450.00
2-Robinson/Meskin-a; Robinson c-1,2 40.00 120.00 325.00

ATOM & HAWKMAN, THE (Formerly The Atom)
National Periodical Publ: No. 39, Oct-Nov, 1968 - No. 45, Oct-Nov, 1969

39-43: 40-41-Kubert/Anderson-a. 43-(7/69)-Last 12¢ issue; 1st app. Gentleman Ghost 3.50 10.50 35.00
44,45: 44-(9/69)-1st 15¢-c; origin Gentleman Ghost 3.50 10.50 35.00
NOTE: ***M. Anderson*** *a-39, 40i, 41i, 43, 44.* ***Sid Greene*** *a-40i-45i.* ***Kubert*** *a-40p, 41p; c-39-45.*

ATOM ANT (TV) (See Golden Comics Digest #2) (Hanna-Barbera)
Gold Key: January, 1966 (12¢)

1(10170-601)-1st app. Atom Ant, Precious Pup, and Hillbilly Bears 28.00 85.00 320.00

ATOM ANT & SECRET SQUIRREL
Archie Publications: Nov, 1995 - No. 12 ($1.50, bi-monthly)

1-12-Hanna-Barbera characters 2.00

ATOMIC AGE
Marvel Comics (Epic Comics): Nov, 1990 - No. 4, Feb, 1991 ($4.50, limited series, squarebound, 52 pgs.)

1-4: Williamson-a(i) 4.50

ATOMIC ATTACK (True War Stories; formerly Attack, first series)
Youthful Magazines: No. 5, Jan, 1953 - No. 8, Oct, 1953 (1st story is sci/fi in all issues)

5-Atomic bomb-c; science fiction stories in all 37.00 111.00 260.00
6-8 23.00 69.00 160.00

ATOMIC BOMB
Jay Burtis Publications: 1945 (36 pgs.)

1-Airmale & Stampy 50.00 150.00 400.00

ATOMIC BUNNY (Formerly Atomic Rabbit)
Charlton Comics: No. 12, Aug, 1958 - No. 19, Dec, 1959

12 11.00 33.00 75.00
13-19 6.70 20.00 40.00

ATOMIC COMICS
Daniels Publications (Canadian): Jan, 1946 (Reprints, one-shot)

1-Rocketman, Yankee Boy, Master Key app. 34.00 103.00 240.00

ATOMIC COMICS
Green Publishing Co.: Jan, 1946 - No. 4, July-Aug, 1946 (#1-4 were printed w/o cover gloss)

1-Radio Squad by Siegel & Shuster; Barry O'Neal app.; Fang Gow cover-r/ Detective Comics (Classic-c) 131.00 393.00 1050.00
2-Inspector Dayton; Kid Kane by Matt Baker; Lucky Wings, Congo King, Prop Powers (only app.) begin 60.00 180.00 480.00
3,4: 3-Zero Ghost Detective app.; Baker-a(2) each; 4-Baker-c 40.00 120.00 320.00

ATOMIC KNIGHTS (See Strange Adventures #117)

ATOMIC MOUSE (TV, Movies) (See Blue Bird, Funny Animals, Giant Comics Edition & Wotalife Comics)

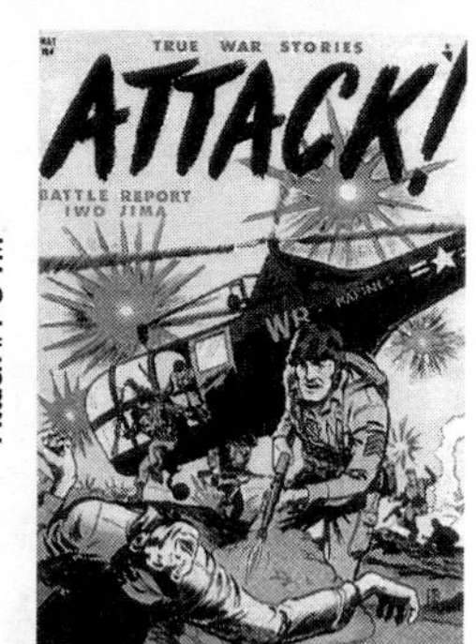

Attack #1 © YM

Authentic Police Cases #10 © STJ

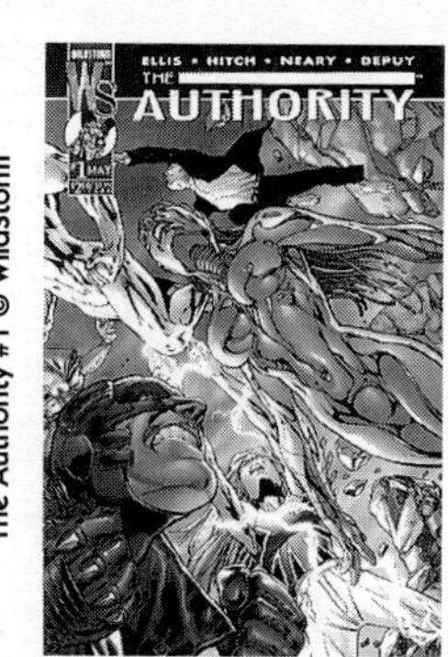

The Authority #1 © WildStorm

GD2.0 FN6.0 NM9.4

Capitol Stories/Charlton Comics: 3/53 - No. 54, 6/63; No. 1, 12/84; V2#10, 9/85 - No. 13, ?/86

1-Origin & 1st app.; Al Fago-c/a in all? 31.00 94.00 220.00
2 11.50 34.00 80.00
3-10: 5-Timmy The Timid Ghost app.; see Zoo Funnies 10.00 30.00 65.00
11-13,16-25 5.35 16.00 32.00
14,15-Hoppy The Marvel Bunny app. 7.50 22.50 45.00
26-(68 pgs.) 10.00 30.00 70.00
27-40: 36,37-Atom The Cat app. 4.25 13.00 28.00
41-54 3.00 7.50 15.00
1 (1984)-Low print run 4.00
V2#10 (10/85) -13-Fago-r. #12(1/86)-Low print run 3.00

ATOMIC RABBIT (Atomic Bunny #12 on; see Giant Comics #3 & Wotalife)
Charlton Comics: Aug, 1955 - No. 11, Mar, 1958

1-Origin & 1st app.; Al Fago-c/a in all? 27.00 81.00 190.00
2 11.00 33.00 75.00
3-10 7.50 22.50 45.00
11-(68 pgs.) 11.00 33.00 75.00

ATOMIC SPY CASES
Avon Periodicals: Mar-Apr, 1950 (Painted-c)

1-No Wood-a; A-bomb blast panels; Fass-a 30.00 90.00 210.00

ATOMIC THUNDERBOLT, THE
Regor Company: Feb, 1946 (one-shot)

1-Intro. Atomic Thunderbolt & Mr. Murdo 56.00 168.00 450.00

ATOMIC WAR!
Ace Periodicals (Junior Books): Nov, 1952 - No. 4, Apr, 1953

1-Atomic bomb-c 85.00 255.00 680.00
2,3: 3-Atomic bomb-c 55.00 165.00 440.00
4-Used in **POP**, pg. 96 & illo. 55.00 165.00 440.00

ATOMIK ANGELS
Crusade Comics: May, 1996 - No. 4, Nov. 1996 ($2.50)

1-4: 1-Freefall from Gen 13 app 3.00
1-Variant-c 4.00
Intrep-Edition (2/96, B&W, giveaway at launch party)-Previews Atomik Angels #1; includes Billy Tucci interview. 4.00

ATOM SPECIAL (See Atom & Justice League of America)
DC Comics: 1993/1995 ($2.50/$2.95)(68pgs.)

1,2: 1-Dillon-c/a. 2-McDonnell-a/Bolland-c/Peyer-s 3.00

ATOM THE CAT (Formerly Tom Cat; see Giant Comics #3)
Charlton Comics: No. 9, Oct, 1957 - No. 17, Aug, 1959

9 9.15 27.00 55.00
10,13-17 5.00 15.00 30.00
11,12: 11(64 pgs)-Atomic Mouse app. 12(100 pgs.) 10.00 30.00 70.00

ATTACK
Youthful Mag./Trojan No. 5 on: May, 1952 - No. 4, Nov, 1952; No. 5, Jan, 1953 - No. 5, Sept, 1953

1-(1st series)-Extreme violence 27.00 81.00 190.00
2,3-Both Harrison-c/a; bondage, whipping 13.00 39.00 90.00
4-Krenkel-a (7 pgs.); Harrison-a (becomes Atomic Attack #5 on) 13.50 41.00 95.00
5-(#1, Trojan, 2nd series) 11.00 33.00 75.00
6-8 (#2-4), 5 8.35 25.00 50.00

ATTACK
Charlton Comics: No. 54, 1958 - No. 60, Nov, 1959

54 (25¢, 100 pgs.) 10.00 30.00 65.00
55-60 4.00 11.00 22.00

ATTACK!
Charlton Comics: 1962 - No. 15, 3/75; No. 16, 8/79 - No. 48, 10/84

nn(#1)-('62) Special Edition 3.20 9.60 32.00
2('63), 3(Fall, '64) 2.50 7.50 22.00
V4#3(10/66), 4(10/67)-(Formerly Special War Series #2; becomes Attack At Sea V4#5) 2.00 6.00 16.00
1(9/71) 2.00 6.00 16.00
2-5: 4-American Eagle app. 1.50 4.50 12.00
6-15(3/75): 1.10 3.30 9.00
16(8/79) - 40 3.00
41-47 Low print run 4.00
48(10/84)-Wood-r; S&K-c 5.00
Modern Comics 13('78)-r 3.00
NOTE: ***Sutton*** *a-9,10,13.*

ATTACK!
Spire Christian Comics (Fleming H. Revell Co.): 1975 (39¢/49¢, 36 pgs.)

nn 5.00

ATTACK AT SEA (Formerly Attack!, 1967)
Charlton Comics: V4#5, Oct, 1968

V4#5 2.00 6.00 16.00

ATTACK ON PLANET MARS (See Strange Worlds #18)
Avon Periodicals: 1951

nn-Infantino, Fawcette, Kubert & Wood-a; adaptation of Tarrano the Conqueror by Ray Cummings 70.00 210.00 560.00

ATTITUDE LAD
Slave Labor Graphics: Apr, 1994 - No. 3, Nov, 1994 ($2.95, B&W)

1-3 3.00

AUDREY & MELVIN (Formerly Little...)(See Little Audrey & Melvin)
Harvey Publications: No. 62, Sept, 1974

62 1.00 3.00 8.00

AUGIE DOGGIE (TV) (See Hanna-Barbera Band Wagon, Quick-Draw McGraw, Spotlight #2, Top Cat & Whitman Comic Books)
Gold Key: October, 1963 (12¢)

1-Hanna-Barbera character 17.00 50.00 185.00

AUTHENTIC POLICE CASES
St. John Publishing Co.: 2/48 - No. 6, 11/48; No. 7, 5/50 - No. 38, 3/55

1-Hale the Magician by Tuska begins 39.00 116.00 270.00
2-Lady Satan, Johnny Rebel app. 24.00 73.00 170.00
3-Veiled Avenger app.; blood drainage story plus 2 Lucky Coyne stories; used in **SOTI**, illo. from Red Seal #16 41.00 124.00 330.00
4,5: 4-Masked Black Jack app. 5-Late 1930s Jack Cole-a(r); transvestism story 24.00 73.00 170.00
6-Matt Baker-c; used in **SOTI**, illo- "An invitation to learning", r-in Fugitives From Justice #3; Jack Cole-a; also used by the N.Y. Legis. Comm. 44.00 132.00 350.00
7,8,10-14: 7-Jack Cole-a; Matt Baker-a begins #8, ends #?; Vic Flint in #10-14. 10-12-Baker-a(2 each) 20.00 60.00 140.00
9-No Vic Flint 16.00 47.00 110.00
15-Drug-c/story; Vic Flint app.; Baker-c 20.00 60.00 140.00
16,18,20,21,23: Baker-a(i) 12.00 36.00 85.00
17,19,22-Baker-c 13.50 41.00 95.00
24-28 (All 100 pgs.): 26-Transvestism 23.00 69.00 160.00
29-32 7.50 22.50 45.00
33-38: 33-Transvestism; Baker-c. 34-Baker-c; r/#95. 35-Baker-c/a(2); r/#10 36-r/#11; Vic Flint strip-r; Baker-c/a(2) unsigned. 37-Baker-c; r/#17. 38-Baker-c/a; r/#18 11.00 33.00 75.00
NOTE: ***Matt Baker*** *c-6-16, 17, 19, 22, 27, 29, 31-38; a-13, 16. Bondage c-1, 3.*

AUTHORITY, THE
DC Comics (WildStorm): May, 1999 - Present ($2.50)

1-5: 1-Wraparound-c; Warren Ellis-s/Bryan Hitch and Paul Neary-a 3.00

AUTOMATON
Image Comics (Flypaper Press): Sept, 1998 - No. 3, 1998 ($2.95, lim. series)

1-3-R.A. Jones-s/Peter Vale-a 3.00

AUTUMN

Avengelyne V2 #7 © Rob Liefeld

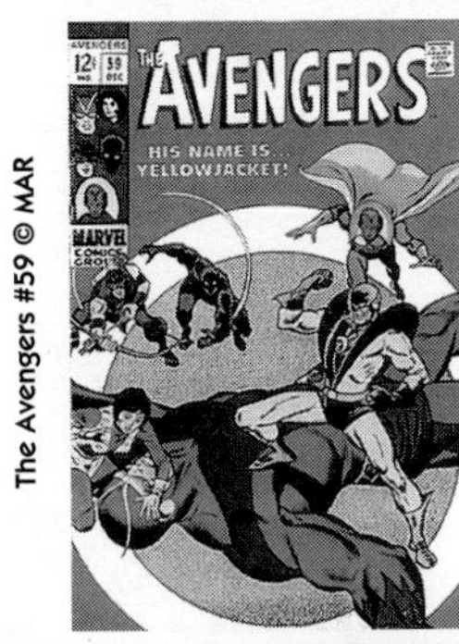

The Avengers #59 © MAR

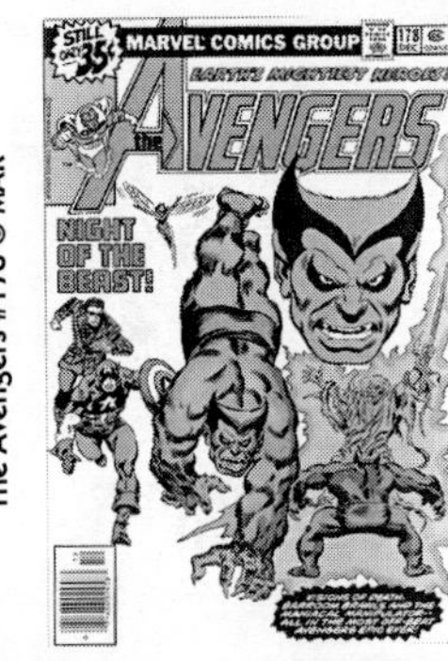

The Avengers #178 © MAR

GD2.0 FN6.0 NM9.4

Caliber Comics: 1995 - No. 3, 1995 ($2.95, B&W)
1-3 3.00

AUTUMN ADVENTURES (Walt Disney's...)
Disney Comics: Autumn, 1990; No. 2, Autumn, 1991 ($2.95, 68 pgs.)
1-Donald Duck-r(2) by Barks, Pluto-r, & new-a 3.50
2-D. Duck-r by Barks; new Super Goof story 3.50

AVATAR
DC Comics: Feb, 1991 - No. 3, Apr, 1991 ($5.95, limited series, 100 pgs.)
1-3: Based on TSR's Forgotten Realms 2.40 6.00

AVENGEBLADE
Maximum Press: July, 1996 - No. 2, Aug, 1996 ($2.99, limited series)
1,2: Bad Girls parody 3.00

AVENGELYNE
Maximum Press: May, 1995 - No. 3, July, 1995 ($2.50/$3.50, limited series)
1/2 1.85 5.50 15.00
1/2 Platinum 20.00
1-Newstand ($2.50)-Photo-c; poster insert 1.00 3.00 8.00
1-Direct Market ($3.50)-Chromium-c; poster 1.10 3.30 9.00
1-Glossy edition 3.00 9.00 30.00
1-Gold 15.00
2-3: 2-Polybagged w/card 4.00
3-Variant-c; Deodato pin-up 2.40 6.00
...Swimsuit (8/95, $2.95)-Pin-ups/photos. 3-Variant-c exist (2 photo, 1 Liefeld-a) 5.00
...Swimsuit (1/96, $3.50, 2nd printing)-photo-c 5.00
Trade paperback (12/95, $9.95) 10.00

AVENGELYNE
Maximum Press: V2#1, Apr, 1996 - No. 14, Apr, 1997 ($2.95/$2.50)
V2#1-Four covers exist (2 photo-c). 5.00
V2#2-Three covers exist (1 photo-c); flip book w/Darkchylde 2.25 6.75 18.00
V2#0, 3-14: 0-(10/96).3-Flip book w/Priest preview. 4-Cybrid app; w/Darkchylde/Avengelyne poster. 5-Flip book w/Blindside. 6-Divinity-c/app. 4.00
...Bible (10/96, $3.50) 3.50

AVENGELYNE (Volume 3)
Awesome Comics: Mar, 1999 - Present ($2.50)
1-Fraga & Liefeld-a 2.50

AVENGELYNE: ARMAGEDDON
Maximum Press: Dec, 1996 - No. 3, Feb, 1997 ($2.99, limited series)
1-3-Scott Clark-a(p) 4.00

AVENGELYNE: DEADLY SINS
Maximum Press: Feb, 1996 - No. 2, Mar, 1996 ($2.95, limited series)
1,2: 1-Two-c exist (1 photo, 1 Liefeld-a). 2-Liefeld-c; Pop Mhan-a(p). 3.00

AVENGELYNE/GLORY
Maximum Press: Sept, 1995 ($3.95, one-shot)
1-Chromium-c 5.00
1-Variant-c 2.40 6.00

AVENGELYNE/GLORY: GODYSSEY, THE (See Glory/...)
Maximum Press: Sept, 1996 ($2.99, one-shot)
1-Two covers (1 photo) 3.00

AVENGELYNE/GLORY SWIMSUIT SPECIAL
Maximum Press: June, 1996 ($2.95)
1-Pin-ups & photos of Avengelyne and Glory; photo-c (variant illos-c. also exists) 4.00

AVENGELYNE/POWER
Maximum Press: Nov, 1995 - No.3, Jan, 1996 ($2.95, limited series)
1-3: 1,2-Liefeld-c. 3-Three variant-c. exist (1 photo-c) 3.00
1-Variant-c 3.50

GD2.0 FN6.0 NM9.4

AVENGELYNE • PROPHET
Maximum Press: May, 1996; No. 2, Feb. 1997 ($2.95, unfinished lim. series)
1,2-Liefeld-c/a(p) 3.00

AVENGELYNE/ WARRIOR NUN AREALA (See Warrior Nun/...)
Maximum Press: Nov, 1996 ($2.99, one-shot)
1 4.00

AVENGER, THE (See A-1 Comics)
Magazine Enterprises: Feb-Mar, 1955 - No. 4, Aug-Sept, 1955
1(A-1 #129)-Origin 39.00 116.00 270.00
2(A-1 #131), 3(A-1 #133) Robot-c, 4(A-1 #138) 25.00 75.00 175.00
IW Reprint #9('64)-Reprints #1 (new cover) 2.50 7.50 24.00
NOTE: *Powell a-2-4; c-1-4.*

AVENGERS, THE (TV)(Also see Steed and Mrs. Peel)
Gold Key: Nov, 1968 ("John Steed & Emma Peel" cover title) (15¢)
1-Photo-c 22.00 66.00 240.00

AVENGERS, THE (See Essential..., Giant-Size..., Kree/Skrull War Starring..., Marvel Graphic Novel #27, Marvel Super Action, Marvel Super Heroes('66), Marvel Treasury Ed., Marvel Triple Action, Solo Avengers, Tales Of Suspense #49, West Coast Avengers & X-Men Vs....)

AVENGERS, THE (The Mighty Avengers on cover only #63-69)
Marvel Comics Group: Sept, 1963 - No. 402, Sept, 1996
GD2.0 FN6.0 VF8.0 NM9.4
1-Origin & 1st app. The Avengers (Thor, Iron Man, Hulk, Ant-Man, Wasp); Loki app. 171.00 514.00 1111.00 2400.00
GD2.0 FN6.0 NM9.4
2-Hulk leaves Avengers 52.00 156.00 620.00
3-1st Sub-Mariner x-over (outside the F.F.); Hulk & Sub-Mariner team-up & battle Avengers; Spider-Man cameo (1/64) 35.00 105.00 385.00
4-Revival of Captain America who joins the Avengers; 1st Silver Age app. of Captain America & Bucky (3/64) 125.00 375.00 1500.00
4-Reprint from the Golden Record Comic set 7.50 22.50 75.00
With Record (1966) 11.00 33.00 110.00
5-Hulk app. 22.50 68.00 225.00
6-8: 6-Intro/1st app. original Zemo & his Masters of Evil. 8-Intro Kang 18.00 54.00 180.00
9-Intro Wonder Man who dies in same story 18.50 55.00 185.00
10-Intro/1st app. Immortus; early Hercules app. (11/64) 15.50 47.00 155.00
11-Spider-Man-c & x-over (12/64) 18.50 55.00 185.00
12-15: 15-Death of original Zemo 11.50 34.00 115.00
16-New Avengers line-up (Hawkeye, Quicksilver, Scarlet Witch join; Thor, Iron Man, Giant-Man, Wasp leave) 12.50 38.00 125.00
17-19: 19-Intro/1st app. Swordsman; origin Hawkeye (8/65) 8.50 25.50 85.00
20-22: Wood inks 5.50 16.50 55.00
23-30: 23-Romita Sr. inks (1st Silver Age Marvel work). 25-Dr. Doom-c/story. 28-Giant-Man becomes Goliath (5/66) 4.00 12.00 40.00
31-40 2.80 8.40 28.00
41-47,49-52,54-56: 43,44-1st app. Red Guardian. 46-Ant-Man returns (re-intro, 11/67) 47-Magneto-c/story. 52-Black Panther joins; 1st app. The Grim Reaper. 54-1st app. new Masters of Evil. 56-Zemo app; story explains how Capt. America became imprisoned in ice during WWII, only to be rescued in Avengers #4 2.50 7.50 24.00
48-Origin/1st app. new Black Knight (1/68) 2.50 7.50 25.00
53-X-Men app. 3.50 10.50 35.00
57-1st app. S.A. Vision (10/68) 7.00 21.00 70.00
58-Origin The Vision 4.80 14.40 48.00
59-65: 59-Intro. Yellowjacket. 60-Wasp & Yellowjacket wed. 63-Goliath becomes Yellowjacket; Hawkeye becomes the new Goliath. 65-Last 12¢ issue 2.50 7.50 22.00
66,67-B. Smith-a 2.60 7.80 26.00
68-70: 70-Nighthawk on cover 1.85 5.50 15.00
71-1st app. The Invaders (12/69); 1st app. Nighthawk; Black Knight joins 3.20 9.60 32.00
72-79,81,82,84-86,88-91: 82-Daredevil app. 88-Written by Harlan Ellison

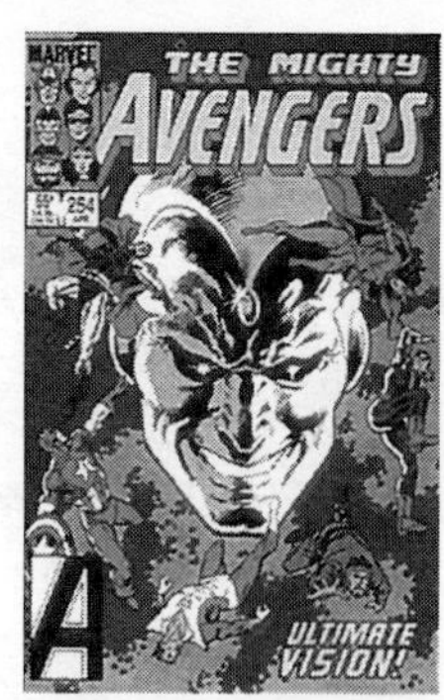

The Avengers #254 © MAR

AVENGERS
THOR! IRON MAN! THE HULK! ANT-MAN! and the WASP!
MARVEL AGE OF COMICS!

The Avengers #1 1/2 © MAR

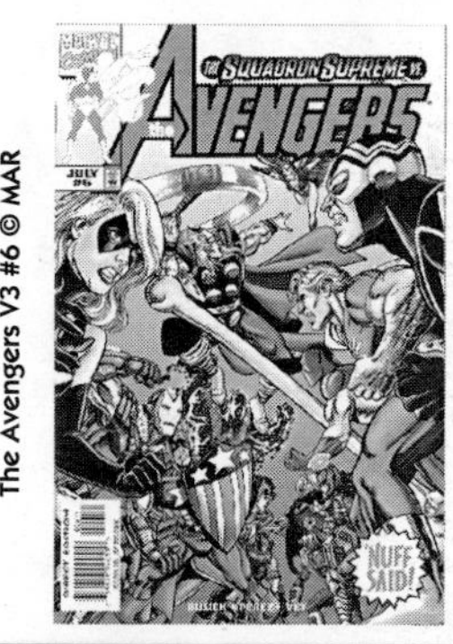

The Avengers V3 #6 © MAR

GD2.0 FN6.0 NM9.4

1.75 5.25 14.00
80-Intro. Red Wolf (9/70) 2.50 7.50 22.00
83-Intro. The Liberators (Wasp, Valkyrie, Scarlet Witch, Medusa & the Black Widow) 2.50 7.50 24.00
87-Origin The Black Panther 2.80 8.40 28.00
92-Last 15¢ issue; Neal Adams-c 2.25 6.75 18.00
93-(52 pgs.)-Neal Adams-c/a 5.00 15.00 55.00
94-96-Neal Adams-c/a 3.50 10.50 35.00
97-G.A. Capt. America, Sub-Mariner, Human Torch, Patriot, Vision, Blazing Skull, Fin, Angel, & new Capt. Marvel x-over 2.25 6.75 18.00
98,99: 98-Goliath becomes Hawkeye; Smith c/a(i). 99-Smith-c, Smith/Sutton-a 2.50 7.50 22.00
100-(6/72)-Smith-c/a; featuring everyone who was an Avenger 6.25 18.50 70.00
101-106,108,109: 101-Harlan Ellison scripts 1.50 4.50 12.00
107-Starlin-a(p) 1.85 5.50 15.00
110,111-X-Men app. 2.50 7.50 22.00
112-1st app. Mantis 2.00 6.00 16.00
113-115,119-124,126-130: 123-Origin Mantis 1.25 3.75 10.00
116-118-Defenders/Silver Surfer app. 2.00 6.00 16.00
125-Thanos-c & brief app. 2.00 6.00 16.00
131-133,136-140: 136-Ploog-r/Amazing Advs. #12 1.00 3.00 8.00
134,135-True origin Vision 1.25 3.75 10.00
141-143,145,152-163 2.40 6.00
144-Origin & 1st app. Hellcat 1.10 3.30 9.00
146-149-(Reg.25¢ editions)(4-7/76) 2.40 6.00
146-149-(30¢-c variants, limited distribution) 1.60 4.80 16.00
150-Kirby-a(r); new line-up: Capt. America, Scarlet Witch, Iron Man, Wasp, Yellowjacket, Vision & The Beast 1.00 3.00 8.00
150-(30¢-c variant, limited distribution) 1.80 5.40 18.00
151-Wonder Man returns w/new costume 1.00 3.00 8.00
160-164-(35¢-c variants, limited dist.)(6-10/77) 2.50 7.50 24.00
164-166: Byrne-a 1.00 2.80 7.00
167-180: 168-Guardians of the Galaxy app. 174-Thanos cameo. 176-Starhawk app. 3.50
181-191-Byrne-a: 181-New line-up: Capt. America, Scarlet Witch, Iron Man, Wasp, Vision, Beast & The Falcon. 183-Ms. Marvel joins. 185-Origin Quicksilver & Scarlet Witch 5.00
192-199,201-213,215-262: 195-1st Taskmaster. 211-New line-up: Capt. America, Iron Man, Tigra, Thor, Wasp & Yellowjacket. 213-Yellowjacket leaves. 215,216-Silver Surfer app. 216-Tigra leaves. 217-Yellowjacket & Wasp return. 221-Hawkeye & She-Hulk join. 227-Capt. Marvel (female) joins; origins of Ant-Man, Wasp, Giant-Man, Goliath, Yellowjacket, & Avengers. 230-Yellowjacket quits. 231-Iron Man leaves. 232-Starfox (Eros) joins. 234-Origin Quicksilver, Scarlet Witch. 236-New logo. 238-Origin Blackout. 239-Avengers app. on David Letterman show. 240-Spider-Woman revived. 250-($1.00, 52 pgs.) 2.50
200-(10/80, 52 pgs.)-Ms. Marvel leaves. 3.50
214-Ghost Rider-c/story 5.00
263-1st app. X-Factor (1/86)(story continues in Fantastic Four #286) 5.00
264-299: 272-Alpha Flight app. 291-$1.00 issues begin. 297-Black Knight, She-Hulk & Thor resign. 298-Inferno tie-in 2.50
300 (2/89, $1.75, 68 pgs.)-Thor joins; Simonson-a 2.50
301-325,327,329-343: 302-Re-intro Quasar. 305-Byrne scripts begin. 314-318-Spider-Man x-over. 320-324-Alpha Flight app. (320-cameo). 327-2nd app. Rage. 341,342-New Warriors app. 343-Last $1.00-c 2.00
326-1st app. Rage (11/90) 3.00
328,344-349,351-359,361,362,364,365,367: 328-Origin Rage. 365-Contains coupon for Hunt for Magneto contest 2.00
350-($2.50, 68 pgs.)-Double gatefold-c showing-c to #1; r/#53 w/cover in flip book format; vs. The Starjammers 2.50
360-($2.95, 52 pgs.)-Embossed all-foil-c; 30th ann. 3.50
363-($2.95, 52 pgs.)-All silver foil-c 3.00
366-($3.95, 68 pgs.)-Embossed all gold foil-c 4.00
368,370-374,376-399: 368-Bloodties part 1; Avengers/X-Men x-over. 374-bound-in trading card sheet. 380-Deodato-a. 390,391-"The Crossing." 395-Death of "old" Tony Stark; wraparound-c. 2.00
369-($2.95)-Foil embossed-c; Bloodties part 5 3.00
375-($2.00, 52 pgs.)-Regular ed.; Thunderstrike returns; leads into Malibu Comics' Black September. 2.00
375-($2.50, 52 pgs.)-Collector's ed. w/bound-in poster; leads into Malibu Comics' Black September. 2.50
400-402: Waid-s; 402-Deodato breakdowns; cont'd in X-Men #56 & Onslaught: Marvel Universe. 4.00
Special 1 (9/67, 25¢, 68 pgs.)-New-a; original & new Avengers team-up 6.50 19.50 65.00
Special 2 (9/68, 25¢, 68 pgs.)-New-a; original vs. new Avengers 3.50 10.50 35.00
Special 3 (9/69, 25¢, 68 pgs.)-r/Avengers #4 plus 3 Capt. America stories by Kirby (art); origin Red Skull 2.50 7.50 24.00
Special 4 (1/71, 25¢, 68 pgs.)-Kirby-r/Avengers #5,6 1.85 5.50 15.00
Special 5 (1/72)-Spider-Man x-over 1.85 5.50 15.00
Annual 6 (11/76) 1.00 3.00 8.00
Annual 7 (11/77)-Starlin-c/a; Warlock dies; Thanos app. 2.25 6.75 18.00
Annual 8 (1978)-Dr. Strange, Ms. Marvel app. 2.40 6.00
Annual 9 (1979)-Newton-a(p) 5.00
Annual 10 (1981)-Golden-p; X-Men cameo; 1st app. Rogue & Madelyne Pryor 2.50 7.50 20.00
Annual 11-18: 11(1982)-Vs. The Defenders. 12('83), 13('84), 14('85),15('86), 16('87), 17 ('88)-Evolutionary War x-over, 18('89)-Atlantis Attacks 3.50
Annual 19-23 (90-'94, 68 pgs.). 22-Bagged/card 3.00
Marvel Double Feature...Avengers/Giant-Man #379 ($2.50, 52 pgs.)-Same as Avengers #379 w/Giant-Man flip book 2.50
The Yesterday Quest ($6.95)-r/#181,182,185-187 1.00 2.80 7.00
Under Siege ('98, $16.95, TPB) r/#270,271,273-277 17.00
...: Visionaries ('99, $16.95)-r/early George Perez art 17.00

NOTE: ***Austin*** *c(i)-157, 167, 168, 170-177, 181, 183-188, 198-201, Annual 8.* ***John Buscema*** *a-41-44p, 46p, 47p, 49, 50, 51-62p, 74-77, 79-85, 87-91, 97, 105p, 121p, 124p,125p, 152, 153p, 255-279p, 281-302p; c-41-66, 68-71, 73-91, 97-99, 178, 256-259p, 261-279p, 281-302p.* ***Byrne*** *a-164-166p, 181-191p, 233p, Annual 13i, 14p; c-186-190p, 233p, 260, 305p; scripts-305-312.* ***Colan*** *a(p)-63-65, 111, 206-208, 210, 211; c(p)-65, 206-208, 210, 211.* ***Ditko*** *a-Annual 13.* ***Guice*** *a-Annual 12p.* ***Don Heck*** *a-9-15, 17-40, 157.* ***Kane*** *c-37p, 159p.* ***Kane/Everett*** *c-97.* ***Kirby*** *a-1-8p, Special 3r, 4r(p); c-1-30, 148, 151-158; layouts-14-16.* ***Ron Lim*** *c(p)-335-341.* ***Miller*** *c-193p.* ***Mooney*** *a-86i, 179p, 180p.* ***Nebres*** *a-178i; c-179i.* ***Newton*** *a-204p, Annual 9p.* ***Perez*** *a(p)-141, 143, 144, 148, 150, 154, 155, 160, 161, 162, 167,168, 170, 171, 194-196, 198-202, Annual 6, 8; c(p)-160-162, 164-166, 170-174, 181,183-185, 191, 192, 194-201, 379-382, Annual 8.* ***Starlin*** *c-121, 135.* ***Staton*** *a-127-134i.* ***Tuska*** *a-47i,48i, 51i, 53i, 54i, 106p, 107p, 135p, 137-140p, 163p. Guardians of the Galaxy app. in #167, 168, 170, 173, 175, 181.*

AVENGERS, THE (Volume Two)
Marvel Comics: V2#1, Nov, 1996 - No. 13, Nov, 1997 ($2.95/$1.95/$1.99)
(Produced by Extreme Studios)

1-($2.95)-Heroes Reborn begins; intro new team (Captain America, Swordsman, Scarlet Witch, Vision, Thor, Hellcat & Hawkeye); 1st app. Avengers Island; Loki & Enchantress app.; Rob Liefeld-p & plot; Chap Yaep-p; Jim Valentino scripts; variant-c exists 4.00
1-($1.95)-Variant-c 5.00
2-12: 2,3-Jeph Loeb scripts begin, Kang app. 4-Hulk-c/app. 5-Thor/Hulk battle; 2 covers. 10,11,13-"World War 3"-pt. 2, x-over w/Image characters. 12-($2.99) "Heroes Reunited"-pt. 2 4.00

AVENGERS, THE (Volume Three)
Marvel Comics: Feb, 1998 - Present ($2.99/$1.99)

1-($2.99, 48 pgs.) Busiek-s/Perez-a/wraparound-c; Avengers reassemble after Heroes Return 5.00
1-Variant Heroes Return cover 1.00 2.80 7.00
1-Rough Cut-Features original script and pencil pages 3.00
2-($1.99)Perez-c, 2-Lago painted-c 3.00
3,4: 3-Wonder Man-c/app. 4-Final roster chosen; Perez poster 2.50
5-11: 5,6-Squadron Supreme-c/app. 8-Triathlon-c/app. 2.00
12-($2.99) Thunderbolts app. 3.00
13-21: 13-New Warriors app. 16-18-Ordway-s/a. 19-Ultron returns 2.00
#11/2 (12/99, $2.50) Timm-c/a/Stern-s; 1963-style issue 2.50
.../ Squadron Supreme '98 Annual ($2.99) 3.00
1999 Annual (7/99, $3.50) Manco-a 3.50

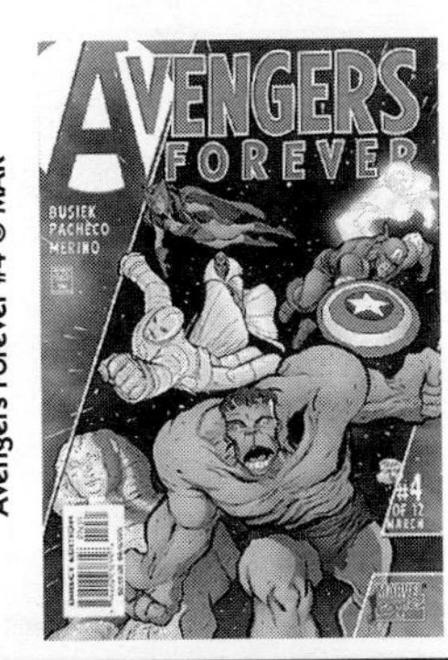

Avengers Forever #4 © MAR

Aviation Cadets nn © S&S

Azrael #60 © DC

GD2.0 FN6.0 NM9.4

Ultron Unleashed TPB (8/99, $3.50) reprints early app. 3.50
Wizard #0-Ultron Unlimited prelude 1.00

AVENGERS COLLECTOR'S EDITION, THE
Marvel Comics: 1993 (Ordered through mail w/candy wrapper, 20 pgs.)
1-Contains 4 bound-in trading cards 3.00

AVENGERS FOREVER
Marvel Comics: Dec, 1998 - No. 12, Feb, 2000 ($2.99)
1-Busiek-s/Pacheco-a in all 4.00
2-12: 4-Four covers. 6-Two covers 3.00

AVENGERS LOG, THE
Marvel Comics: Feb, 1994 ($1.95)
1-Gives history of all members; Perez-c 2.00

AVENGERS SPOTLIGHT (Formerly Solo Avengers #1-20)
Marvel Comics: No. 21, Aug, 1989 - No. 40, Jan, 1991 (75¢/$1.00)
21-40: 21-Byrne-c/a. 26-Acts of Vengeance story. 31-34-U.S. Agent series. 36-Heck-i. 37-Mortimer-i. 40-The Black Knight app. 2.00

AVENGERS STRIKEFILE
Marvel Comics: Jan, 1994 ($1.75, one-shot)
1 2.00

AVENGERS: THE CROSSING
Marvel Comics: July, 1995 ($4.95, one-shot)
1-Deodato-c/a; 1st app. Thor's new costume 5.00

AVENGERS: THE LEGEND
Marvel Comics: Oct, 1996 ($3.95, one-shot)
1-Tribute issue 4.00

AVENGERS: THE TERMINATRIX OBJECTIVE
Marvel Comics: Sept, 1993 - No. 4, Dec, 1993 ($1.25, limited series)
1 ($2.50)-Holo-grafx foil-c 2.50
2-4-Old vs. current Avengers 2.00

AVENGERS: TIMESLIDE
Marvel Comics: Feb, 1996 ($4.95, one-shot)
1-Foil-c 5.00

AVENGERS/ULTRAFORCE (See Ultraforce/Avengers)
Marvel Comics: Oct, 1995 ($3.95, one-shot)
1-Wraparound foil-c by Perez 4.00

AVENGERS UNPLUGGED
Marvel Comics: Oct, 1995 - No. 6, Aug, 1996 (99¢, bi-monthly)
1-6 2.00

AVENGERS WEST COAST (Formerly West Coast Avengers)
Marvel Comics: No. 48, Sept, 1989 - No. 102, Jan, 1994 ($1.00/$1.25)
48,49: 48-Byrne-c/a & scripts continue thru #57 2.00
50-Re-intro original Human Torch 3.00
51-99: 54-Cover swipe/F.F. #1. 70-Spider-Woman app. 75 (52 pgs.)-Fantastic Four x-over78-Last $1.00-c. 79-Dr. Strange x-over. 84-Origin Spider-Woman retold; Spider-Man app. (also in #85,86). 87,88-Wolverine-c/story. 93-95-Darkhawk app. 2.00
100-($3.95, 68 pgs.)-Embossed all red foil-c 4.00
101,102: 101-X-Men x-over 3.00
Annual 5-8 ('90- '93, 68 pgs.)-5,6-West Coast Avengers in indicia. 7-Darkhawk app. 8-Polybagged w/card 3.00

AVIATION ADVENTURES AND MODEL BUILDING
Parents' Magazine Institute: No. 16, Dec, 1946 - No. 17, Feb, 1947 (True Aviation Advs. ...No. 15)
16,17-Half comics and half pictures 6.70 20.00 40.00

AVIATION CADETS
Street & Smith Publications: 1943
nn 16.00 47.00 110.00

GD2.0 FN6.0 NM9.4

A-V IN 3-D
Aardvark-Vanaheim: Dec, 1984 ($2.00, 28 pgs. w/glasses)
1-Cerebus, Flaming Carrot, Normalman & Ms. Tree 3.00

AWAKENING, THE
Image Comics: Oct, 1997 - No. 4, Apr, 1998 ($2.95, B&W, limited series)
1-4-Stephen Blue-s/c/a 3.00

AWESOME ADVENTURES
Awesome Entertainment: Aug, 1999 ($2.50)
1-Alan Moore-s/ Steve Skroce-a; Youngblood story 2.50

AWESOME HOLIDAY SPECIAL
Awesome Entertainment: Dec, 1997 ($2.50, one-shot)
1-Flip book w/covers of Fighting American & Coven. Holiday stories also featuring Kaboom and Shaft by regular creators. 3.00
1-Gold Edition 5.00

AWFUL OSCAR (Formerly & becomes Oscar Comics with No. 13)
Marvel Comics: No. 11, June, 1949 - No. 12, Aug, 1949
11,12 8.35 25.00 50.00

AWKWARD UNIVERSE
Slave Labor Graphics: 12/95 ($9.95, graphic novel)
nn 10.00

AXA
Eclipse Comics: Apr, 1987 - No. 2, Aug, 1987 ($1.75)
1,2 2.00

AXEL PRESSBUTTON (Pressbutton No. 5; see Laser Eraser &...)
Eclipse Comics: Nov, 1984 - No. 6, July, 1985 ($1.50/$1.75, Baxter paper)
1-6: Reprints Warrior (British mag.). 1-Bolland-c; origin Laser Eraser & Pressbutton 2.50

AXIS ALPHA
Axis Comics: Feb, 1994 ($2.50, one-shot)
V1-Previews Axis titles including, Tribe, Dethgrip, B.E.A.S.T.I.E.S. & more; Pitt app. in Tribe story. 3.00

AZRAEL (...Agent of the Bat #47 on)(Also see Batman: Sword of Azrael)
DC Comics: Feb, 1995 - Present ($1.95/$2.25)
1-Dennis O'Neil scripts begin 2.40 6.00
2,3 5.00
4-46,48-60: 5,6-Ras Al Ghul app. 13-Nightwing-c/app. 15-Contagion Pt. 5 (Pt. 4 on-c). 16-Contagion Pt. 10. 22-Batman-c/app. 23, 27-Batman app. 27,28-Joker app. 35-Hitman app. 36-39-Batman, Bane app. 50-New costume. 53-Joker-c/app. 56,57,60-New Batgirl app. 3.00
47-($3.95) Flip book with Batman: Shadow of the Bat #80 5.00
#1,000,000 (11/98) Giarrano-a 2.25
Annual 1 (1995, $3.95)-Year One story 4.00
Annual 2 (1996, $2.95)-Legends of the Dead Earth story 3.00
Annual 3 (1997, $3.95)-Pulp Heroes story; Orbik-c 4.00
Plus (12/96, $2.95)-Question-c/app. 3.00

AZRAEL/ ASH
DC Comics: 1997 ($4.95, one-shot)
1-O'Neil-s/Quesada, Palmiotti-a 5.00

AZTEC ACE
Eclipse Comics: Mar, 1984 - No. 15, Sept, 1985 ($2.25/$1.50/$1.75, Baxter paper)
1-$2.25-c (52 pgs.) 2.50
2-15: 2-Begin 36 pgs. 2.00
NOTE: ***N. Redondo** a-1i-8i, 10i. c-6-8i.*

AZTEK: THE ULTIMATE MAN
DC Comics: Aug, 1996 - No. 10, May 1997 ($1.75)
1-1st app. Aztek & Synth; Grant Morrison & Mark Millar scripts in all 4.00
2-9: 2-Green Lantern app. 3-1st app. Death-Doll. 4-Intro The Lizard King. 5-Origin. 6-Joker app.; Batman cameo. 7-Batman app. 8-Luthor app. 9-vs. Parasite-c/app. 3.00

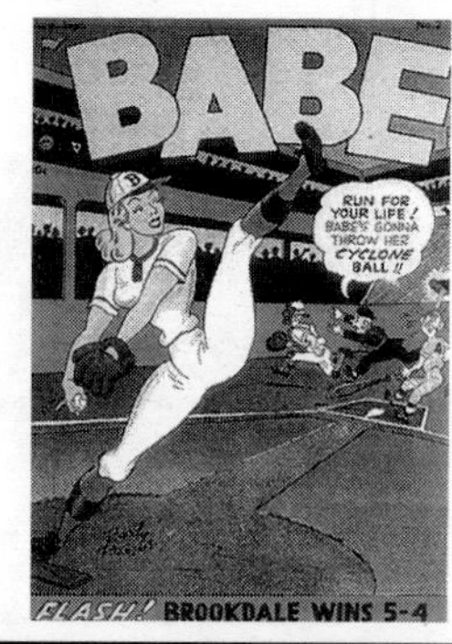

Babe #2 © PRIZE

Baby Huey #4 © HARV

Babylon 5 #11 © Warner Bros.

	GD2.0	FN6.0	NM9.4
10-JLA-c/app.	1.25	3.75	10.00

NOTE: ***Breyfogle** c-5p. **N. Steven Harris** a-1-5p. **Porter** c-1p. **Wieringo** c-2p.*

BABE (...Darling of the Hills, later issues)(See Big Shot and Sparky Watts)
Prize/Headline/Feature: June-July, 1948 - No. 11, Apr-May, 1950

	GD2.0	FN6.0	NM9.4
1-Boody Rogers-a	20.00	60.00	140.00
2-Boody Rogers-a	12.00	36.00	85.00
3-11-All by Boody Rogers	11.00	33.00	75.00

BABE
Dark Horse Comics (Legend): July, 1994 - No. 4, Jan, 1994 ($2.50, lim. series)

	GD2.0	FN6.0	NM9.4
1-4: John Byrne-c/a/scripts; ProtoTykes back-up story			2.50

BABE RUTH SPORTS COMICS (Becomes Rags Rabbit #11 on?)
Harvey Publications: April, 1949 - No. 11, Feb, 1951

	GD2.0	FN6.0	NM9.4
1-Powell-a	39.00	116.00	270.00
2-Powell-a	26.00	79.00	185.00
3-11: Powell-a in most	21.00	64.00	150.00

NOTE: *Baseball c-2-4, 9. Basketball c-1, 6. Football c-5. Yogi Berra c/story-8. Joe DiMaggio c/story-3. Bob Feller c/story-4. Stan Musial c-9.*

BABES IN TOYLAND (Disney, Movie) (See Golden Pix Story Book ST-3)
Dell Publishing Co.: No. 1282, Feb-Apr, 1962

	GD2.0	FN6.0	NM9.4
Four Color 1282-Annette Funicello photo-c	11.00	34.00	125.00

BABES OF BROADWAY
Broadway Comics: May, 1996 ($2.95, one-shot)

	GD2.0	FN6.0	NM9.4
1-Pin-ups of Broadway Comics' female characters; Alan Davis, Michael Kaluta, J. G. Jones, Alan Weiss, Guy Davis & others-a; Giordano-c.			3.00

BABE 2
Dark Horse Comics (Legend): Mar, 1995 - No. 2, May, 1995 ($2.50, lim. series)

	GD2.0	FN6.0	NM9.4
1,2: John Byrne-c/a/scripts			2.50

BABY HUEY
Harvey Comics: No. 100, Oct, 1990 - No. 101, Nov, 1990; No. 1, Oct, 1991 - No. 9, June, 1994 ($1.00/$1.25/$1.50, quarterly)

	GD2.0	FN6.0	NM9.4
100,101,1,2 ($1.00): 1-Cover says "Big Baby Huey"			4.00
3-9 ($1.25-$1.50)			2.50

BABY HUEY AND PAPA (See Paramount Animated...)
Harvey Publications: May, 1962 - No. 33, Jan, 1968 (Also see Casper The Friendly Ghost)

	GD2.0	FN6.0	NM9.4
1	16.00	48.00	160.00
2	7.50	22.50	75.00
3-5	5.00	15.00	50.00
6-10	2.60	7.80	26.00
11-20	2.25	6.75	18.00
21-33	1.85	5.50	15.00

BABY HUEY DIGEST
Harvey Publications: June, 1992 (Digest-size, one-shot)

	GD2.0	FN6.0	NM9.4
1-Reprints			5.00

BABY HUEY DUCKLAND
Harvey Publications: Nov, 1962 - No. 15, Nov, 1966 (25¢ Giants, 68 pgs.)

	GD2.0	FN6.0	NM9.4
1	12.00	36.00	120.00
2-5	5.00	15.00	50.00
6-15	2.60	7.80	26.00

BABY HUEY, THE BABY GIANT (Also see Big Baby Huey, Casper, Harvey Hits #22, Harvey Comics Hits #60, & Paramount Animated Comics)
Harvey Publ: 9/56 - #97, 10/71; #98, 10/72; #99, 10/80; #100, 10/90 - #102?

	GD2.0	FN6.0	NM9.4
1-Infinity-c	38.00	114.00	380.00
2	18.50	55.00	185.00
3-Baby Huey takes anti-pep pills	12.00	36.00	120.00
4,5	9.00	27.00	90.00
6-10	5.00	15.00	50.00
11-20	3.60	10.80	36.00
21-40	2.50	7.50	25.00
41-60	2.25	6.75	18.00
61-79 (12/67)	1.85	5.50	15.00
80(12/68) - 95-All 68 pg. Giants	2.50	7.50	20.00
96,97-Both 52 pg. Giants	1.85	5.50	15.00
98-99: Regular size		2.40	6.00
100-102 ($1.00)			3.00

BABYLON 5 (TV)
DC Comics: Jan, 1995 - No. 11, Dec, 1995 ($1.95/$2.50)

	GD2.0	FN6.0	NM9.4
1	2.25	6.75	18.00
2-5	1.75	5.25	14.00
6-11: 7-Begin $2.50-c	1.50	4.50	12.00
... The Price of Peace (1998, $9.95, TPB) r/#1-4,11			10.00

BABYLON 5: IN VALEN'S NAME
DC Comics: Mar, 1998 - No. 3, May, 1998 ($2.50, limited series)

	GD2.0	FN6.0	NM9.4
1-3			4.00

BABY SNOOTS (Also see March of Comics #359, 371, 396, 401, 419, 431,443, 450, 462, 474, 485)
Gold Key: Aug, 1970 - No. 22, Nov, 1975

	GD2.0	FN6.0	NM9.4
1	2.50	7.50	20.00
2-11	1.25	3.75	10.00
12-22: 22-Titled Snoots, the Forgetful Elefink		2.40	6.00

BACCHUS (Also see Eddie Campbell's ...)
Harrier Comics (New Wave): 1988 - No. 2, Aug, 1988 ($1.95, B&W)

	GD2.0	FN6.0	NM9.4
1,2: Eddie Campbell-c/a/scripts.			2.00

BACHELOR FATHER (TV)
Dell Publishing Co.: No. 1332, 4-6/62 - No. 2, 1962

	GD2.0	FN6.0	NM9.4
Four Color 1332 (#1), 2-Written by Stanley	7.25	22.00	80.00

BACHELOR'S DIARY
Avon Periodicals: 1949 (15¢)

	GD2.0	FN6.0	NM9.4
1(Scarce)-King Features panel cartoons & text-r; pin-up, girl wrestling photos; similar to Sideshow	40.00	120.00	280.00

BACK DOWN THE LINE
Eclipse Books: 1991 (Mature adults, 8-1/2 x 11", 52 pgs.)

	GD2.0	FN6.0	NM9.4
nn (Soft-c, $8.95)-Bolton-c/a			9.00
nn (Limited Hard-c, $29.95)			30.00

BACKLASH (Also see The Kindred)
Image Comics (WildStorm Prod.): Nov,1994 - No. 32, May, 1997 ($1.95/$2.50)

	GD2.0	FN6.0	NM9.4
1-Double-c; variant-double-c			3.00
2-7,9-32: 5-Intro Mindscape; 2 pinups. 19-Fire From Heaven Pt 2. 20-Fire From Heaven Pt 10. 31-WildC.A.T.S app.			2.50
8-($1.95, newsstand)-Wildstorm Rising Pt. 8			2.50
8-($2.50, direct market)-Wildstorm Rising Pt. 8			2.50
25-($3.95)-Double-size			4.00
...& Taboo's African Holiday (9/99, $5.95) Booth-s/a(p)			6.00

BACKLASH/SPIDER-MAN
Image Comics (WildStorm Productions): Aug, 1996 - No. 2, Sept, 1996 ($2.50, limited series)

	GD2.0	FN6.0	NM9.4
1,2: Pike (villain from WildC.A.T.S) & Venom app.			2.50

BACK TO THE FUTURE (Movie, TV cartoon)
Harvey Comics: Nov, 1991 - No. 4, June, 1992 ($1.25)

	GD2.0	FN6.0	NM9.4
1-4: 1,2-Gil Kane-c; based on animated cartoon			2.00

BACK TO THE FUTURE: FORWARD TO THE FUTURE
Harvey Comics: Oct, 1992 - No. 3, Feb, 1993 ($1.50, limited series)

	GD2.0	FN6.0	NM9.4
1-3			2.00

BAD BOY
Oni Press: Dec, 1997 ($4.95, one-shot)

	GD2.0	FN6.0	NM9.4
1-Frank Miller-s/Simon Bisley-a/painted-c			5.00

BAD COMPANY
Quality Comics/Fleetway Quality #15 on: Aug, 1988 - No. 19?, 1990 ($1.50/$1.75, high quality paper)

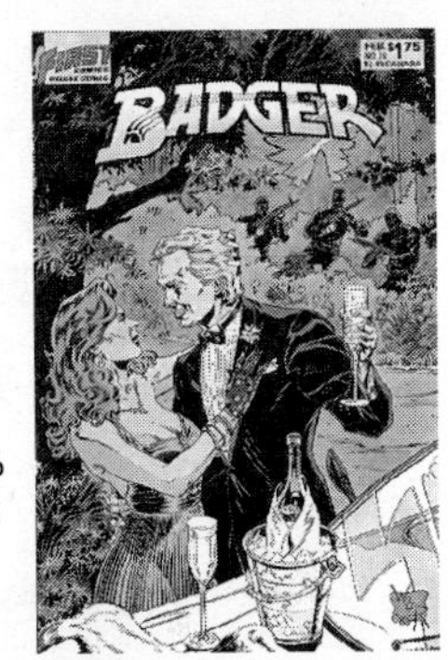

Badger #20 © First Pub. Inc.

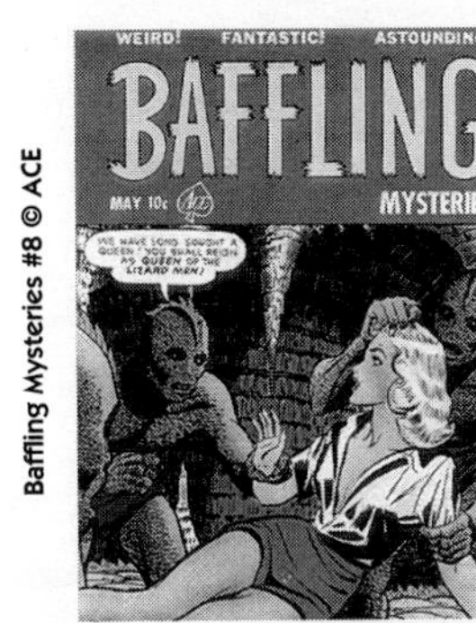

Baffling Mysteries #8 © ACE

Ball and Chain #1 © Stray Thoughts Inc.

GD2.0 FN6.0 NM9.4

1-19: 5,6-Guice-c 2.00

BAD EGGS, THE
Acclaim Comics (Armada): June, 1995 - No. 8, Jan, 1997 ($2.95)
1-8: Layton scripts; Perlin-a. 5-8-"That Dirty Yellow Mustard." 5-William Shatner app. 3.00

BADGE OF JUSTICE
Charlton Comics: No. 22, 1/55 - No. 23, 3/55; 4/55 - No. 4, 10/55
22(1/55) 10.00 30.00 65.00
23(3/55), 1 6.70 20.00 40.00
2-4 5.00 15.00 30.00

BADGER, THE
Capital Comics(#1-4)/First Comics: Dec, 1983 - No. 70, Apr, 1991; V2#1, Spring, 1991
1 3.00
2-70: 52-54-Tim Vigil-c/a 2.00
50-($3.95, 52 pgs.) 4.00
V2#1 (Spring, 1991, $4.95) 5.00

BADGER, THE
Image Comics: V3#78, May, 1997 - Present ($2.95, B&W)
78-Cover lists #1, Baron-s 3.00
79/#2, 80/#3, 81(indicia lists #80)/#4,82-88/#5-11 3.00

BADGER GOES BERSERK
First Comics: Sept, 1989 - No. 4, Dec, 1989 ($1.95, lim. series, Baxter paper)
1-4: 2-Paul Chadwick-c/a(2pgs.) 2.50

BADGER: SHATTERED MIRROR
Dark Horse Comics: July, 1994 - No. Oct, 1994 ($2.50, limited series)
1-4 2.50

BADGER: ZEN POP FUNNY-ANIMAL VERSION
Dark Horse Comics: July, 1994 - No. 2, Aug, 1994 ($2.50, limited series)
1,2 2.50

BADLANDS
Vortex Comics: May, 1990 ($3.00, glossy stock, mature)
1-Chaykin-c 3.00

BADLANDS
Dark Horse Comics: July, 1991 - No. 6, Dec, 1991 ($2.25, B&W, limited series)
1-6: 1-John F. Kennedy-c; reprints Vortex Comics issue 2.25

BADMEN OF THE WEST
Avon Periodicals: 1951 (Giant) (132 pgs., painted-c)
1-Contains rebound copies of Jesse James, King of the Bad Men of Deadwood, Badmen of Tombstone; other combinations possible. Issues with Kubert-a... 36.00 107.00 250.00

BADMEN OF THE WEST! (See A-1 Comics)
Magazine Enterprises: 1953 - No. 3, 1954
1(A-1 100)-Meskin-a? 23.00 69.00 160.00
2(A-1 120), 3: 2-Larsen-a 14.00 43.00 100.00

BADMEN OF TOMBSTONE
Avon Periodicals: 1950
nn 13.50 41.00 95.00

BADROCK (Also see Youngblood)
Image Comics (Extreme Studios): Mar, 1995 - No. 2, Jan, 1996 ($1.75/$2.50)
1-Variant-c (3) 3.00
2-Liefeld-c/a & story; Savage Dragon app, flipbook w/Grifter/Badrock #2; variant-c exist 2.50
Annual 1(1995,$2.95)-Arthur Adams-c 3.00
Annual 1 Commemorative ($9.95)-3,000 printed 10.00
.../Wolverine (6/96, $4.95, squarebound)-Sauron app; pin-ups; variant-c exists 5.00
.../Wolverine (6/96)-Special Comicon Edition 5.00

GD2.0 FN6.0 NM9.4

BADROCK AND COMPANY (Also see Youngblood)
Image Comics (Extreme Studios): Sept, 1994 - No.6, Feb, 1995 ($2.50)
1-6 : 6-Indicia reads "October 1994"; story cont'd in Shadowhawk #17 2.50

BAFFLING MYSTERIES (Formerly Indian Braves No. 1-4; Heroes of the Wild Frontier No. 26-on)
Periodical House (Ace Magazines): No. 5, Nov, 1951 - No. 26, Oct, 1955
5 31.00 94.00 220.00
6-24: 8-Woodish-a by Cameron. 10-E.C. Crypt Keeper swipe on-c. 24-Last pre-code issue 19.00 56.00 130.00
25-Reprints; surrealistic-c 16.00 47.00 110.00
26-Reprints 13.00 39.00 90.00
NOTE: *Cameron a-8, 10, 16-18, 20-22. Colan a-5, 11, 25r/5. Sekowsky a-5, 6, 22. Bondage c-20, 23. Reprints in 18(1), 19(1), 24(3).*

BALBO (See Master Comics #33 & Mighty Midget Comics)

BALDER THE BRAVE
Marvel Comics Group: Nov, 1985 - No. 4, 1986 (Limited series)
1-4: Simonson-c/a; character from Thor 2.00

BALLAD OF HALO JONES, THE
Quality Comics: Sept, 1987 - No. 12, Aug, 1988 ($1.25/$1.50)
1-12: Alan Moore scripts in all 2.00

BALL AND CHAIN
DC Comics (Homage): Nov, 1999 - No. 4 ($2.50, limited series)
1-Lobdell-s/Garza-a 2.50

BALLISTIC (Also See Cyberforce)
Image Comics (Top Cow Productions): Sept, 1995 - No. 3, Dec, 1995 ($2.50, limited series)
1-3: Wetworks app, Turner-c/a 3.00

BALLISTIC ACTION
Image Comics (Top Cow Productions): May, 1996 ($2.95, one-shot)
1-Pin-ups of Top Cow characters participating in outdoor sports 3.00

BALLISTIC IMAGERY
Image Comics (Top Cow Productions): Jan, 1996 ($2.50, anthology, one-shot)
1-Cyberforce app. 2.50

BALLISTIC/ WOLVERINE
Image Comics (Top Cow Productions): Feb, 1997 ($2.95, one-shot)
1-Devil's Reign pt. 4; Witchblade cameo (1 page) 3.00

BALOO & LITTLE BRITCHES (Disney)
Gold Key: Apr, 1968
1-From the Jungle Book 2.80 8.40 28.00

BAMBI (Disney) (See Movie Classics, Movie Comics, and Walt Disney Showcase No. 31)
Dell Publishing Co.: No. 12, 1942; No. 30, 1943; No. 186, Apr, 1948
Four Color 12-Walt Disney's... 52.00 157.00 575.00
Four Color 30-Bambi's Children (1943) 52.00 157.00 575.00
Four Color 186-Walt Disney's...; reprinted as Movie Classic Bambi #3 (1956) 16.00 47.00 175.00

BAMBI (Disney)
Grosset & Dunlap: 1942 (50¢, 7"x8-1/2", 32pg, hard-c w/dust jacket)
nn-Given away w/a copy of Thumper for a $2.00, 2-yr. subscription to WDC&S in 1942 (Xmas offer). Book only 19.00 56.00 130.00
w/dust jacket 30.00 90.00 210.00

BAMM BAMM & PEBBLES FLINTSTONE (TV)
Gold Key: Oct, 1964 (Hanna-Barbera)
1 8.25 25.50 85.00

BANANA SPLITS, THE (TV) (See Golden Comics Digest & March of Comics No. 364)
Gold Key: June, 1969 - No. 8, Oct, 1971 (Hanna-Barbera)

Barbie Fashion #14 © Mattel, Inc.

The Barker #7 © QUA

Barnyard Comics #13 © Nedor

	GD2.0	FN6.0	NM9.4
1-Photo-c on all	10.00	30.00	100.00
2-8	6.00	18.00	60.00

BAND WAGON (See Hanna-Barbera Band Wagon)

BANDY MAN, THE
Caliber: 1996 - No. 3, ($2.95, B&W, limited series)

	GD2.0	FN6.0	NM9.4
1-3-Stephan Petrucha scripts; 1-Jill Thompson-a; Miran Kim-c			3.00

BANG-UP COMICS
Progressive Publishers: Dec, 1941 - No. 3, June, 1942

	GD2.0	FN6.0	NM9.4
1-Cosmo Mann & Lady Fairplay begin; Buzz Balmer by Rick Yager in all (origin #1)	91.00	273.00	725.00
2,3	47.00	141.00	380.00

BANNER COMICS (Becomes Captain Courageous No. 6)
Ace Magazines: No. 3, Sept, 1941 - No. 5, Jan, 1942

	GD2.0	FN6.0	NM9.4
3-Captain Courageous (1st app.) & Lone Warrior & Sidekick Dicky begin; Jim Mooney-c	100.00	300.00	800.00
4,5: 4-Flag-c	61.00	183.00	490.00

BARABBAS
Slave Labor Graphics: Aug, 1986 - No. 2, Nov, 1986 ($1.50, B&W, lim. series)

	GD2.0	FN6.0	NM9.4
1,2			2.00

BARBARIANS, THE
Atlas Comics/Seaboard Periodicals: June, 1975

	GD2.0	FN6.0	NM9.4
1-Origin, only app. Andrax; Iron Jaw app.			4.00

BARBIE
Marvel Comics: Jan, 1991 - No. 66, Apr, 1996 ($1.00/$1.25/$1.50)

	GD2.0	FN6.0	NM9.4
1-Polybagged w/Barbie Pink Card; Romita-c	1.10	3.30	9.00
2-49,51-66			5.00
50-(Giant)		2.40	6.00

BARBIE & KEN
Dell Publishing Co.: May-July, 1962 - No. 5, Nov-Jan, 1963-64

	GD2.0	FN6.0	NM9.4
01-053-207(#1)-Based on Mattel toy dolls	35.00	106.00	390.00
2-4	25.00	76.00	280.00
5 (Rare)	31.00	93.00	340.00

BARBIE FASHION
Marvel Comics: Jan, 1991 - No. 63, Jan, 1996 ($1.00/$1.25/$1.50)

	GD2.0	FN6.0	NM9.4
1-Polybagged w/doorknob hanger	1.10	3.30	9.00
2-49,51-63: 4-Contains preview to Sweet XVI. 14-Begin $1.25-c			5.00
50-(Giant)		2.40	6.00

BARBI TWINS, THE
Topps Comics: 1995 ($2.50/$5.00)

	GD2.0	FN6.0	NM9.4
1-Razor app.			2.50
Swimsuit Art Calendar ($5.00)-art by Linsner, Bradstreet, Hughes; Julie Bell-c			5.00

BARB WIRE (See Comics' Greatest World)
Dark Horse Comics: Apr, 1994 - No. 9, Feb, 1995 ($2.00/$2.50)

	GD2.0	FN6.0	NM9.4
1-9: 1-Foil logo			2.50
Trade paperback (1996, $8.95)-r/#2,3,5,6 w/Pamela Anderson bio			9.00

BARB WIRE: ACE OF SPADES
Dark Horse Comics: May, 1996 - No. 4, Sept, 1996 ($2.95, limited series)

	GD2.0	FN6.0	NM9.4
1-4: Chris Warner-c/a(p)/scripts; Tim Bradstreet-c/a(i) in all			3.00

BARB WIRE COMICS MAGAZINE SPECIAL
Dark Horse Comics: May, 1996 ($3.50, B&W, magazine, one-shot)

	GD2.0	FN6.0	NM9.4
nn-Adaptation of film; photo-c; poster insert.			3.50

BARB WIRE MOVIE SPECIAL
Dark Horse Comics: May, 1996 ($3.95, one-shot)

	GD2.0	FN6.0	NM9.4
nn-Adaptation of film; photo-c; 1st app. new look			4.00

BARKER, THE (Also see National Comics #42)
Quality Comics Group/Comic Magazine: Autumn, 1946 - No. 15, Dec, 1949

	GD2.0	FN6.0	NM9.4
1	19.00	56.00	130.00
2	10.00	30.00	65.00
3-10	7.50	22.50	45.00
11-14	5.00	15.00	30.00
15-Jack Cole-a(p)	5.85	17.50	35.00

NOTE: ***Jack Cole*** *art in some issues.*

BARNABY
Civil Service Publications Inc.: 1945 (25¢,102 pgs., digest size)

	GD2.0	FN6.0	NM9.4
V1#1-r/Crocket Johnson strips from 1942	3.00	7.50	15.00

BARNEY AND BETTY RUBBLE (TV) (Flintstones' Neighbors)
Charlton Comics: Jan, 1973 - No. 23, Dec, 1976 (Hanna-Barbera)

	GD2.0	FN6.0	NM9.4
1	3.00	9.00	30.00
2-11: 11(2/75)-1st Mike Zeck-a (illos)	1.85	5.50	15.00
12-23	1.25	3.75	10.00

BARNEY BAXTER (Also see Magic Comics)
David McKay/Dell Publishing Co./Argo: 1938 - No. 2, 1956

	GD2.0	FN6.0	NM9.4
Feature Books 15(McKay-1938)	27.00	82.00	300.00
Four Color 20(1942)	26.00	78.00	285.00
4,5	11.00	33.00	120.00
1,2 (1956-Argo)	8.35	25.00	50.00

BARNEY BEAR ...
Spire Christian Comics (Fleming H. Revell Co.): 1977-1981

	GD2.0	FN6.0	NM9.4
...Home Plate nn-(1979, 49¢), ...Lost and Found nn-(1979, 49¢), Out of The Woods nn-(1980, 49¢), Sunday School Picnic nn-(1981, 69¢, The Swamp Gang!-(1977, 39¢)			5.00

BARNEY GOOGLE & SNUFFY SMITH
Dell Publishing Co./Gold Key: 1942 - 1943; April, 1964

	GD2.0	FN6.0	NM9.4
Four Color 19(1942)	38.00	113.00	415.00
Four Color 40(1944)	22.00	66.00	240.00
Large Feature Comic 11(1943)	24.00	71.00	260.00
1(10113-404)-Gold Key (4/64)	3.50	10.50	35.00

BARNEY GOOGLE & SNUFFY SMITH
Toby Press: June, 1951 - No. 4, Feb, 1952 (Reprints)

	GD2.0	FN6.0	NM9.4
1	11.50	34.00	80.00
2,3	7.50	22.50	45.00
4-Kurtzman-a "Pot Shot Pete", 5 pgs.; reprints John Wayne #5	11.50	34.00	80.00

BARNEY GOOGLE AND SNUFFY SMITH
Charlton Comics: Mar, 1970 - No. 6, Jan, 1971

	GD2.0	FN6.0	NM9.4
1	2.50	7.50	20.00
2-6	1.60	4.85	13.00

BARNYARD COMICS (Dizzy Duck No. 32 on)
Nedor/Polo Mag./Standard(Animated Cartoons): June, 1944 - No. 31, Sept, 1950; No. 10, 1957

	GD2.0	FN6.0	NM9.4
1 (nn, 52 pgs.)-Funny animal	19.00	56.00	130.00
2 (52 pgs.)	10.00	30.00	65.00
3-5	6.70	20.00	40.00
6-12,16	5.35	16.00	32.00
13-15,17,21,23,26,27,29-All contain Frazetta text illos	7.50	22.50	45.00
18-20,22,24,25-All contain Frazetta-a & text illos	10.00	30.00	70.00
28,30,31	4.00	10.00	20.00
10 (1957)(Exist?)	2.00	5.00	10.00

BARRY M. GOLDWATER
Dell Publishing Co.: Mar, 1965 (Complete life story)

	GD2.0	FN6.0	NM9.4
12-055-503-Photo-c	3.00	9.00	30.00

BARRY WINDSOR-SMITH: STORYTELLER
Dark Horse Comics: Oct, 1996 - No. 9, July, 1997 ($4.95, oversize)

	GD2.0	FN6.0	NM9.4
1-9: 1-Intro Young Gods, Paradox Man & the Freebooters; Barry Smith-c/a/scripts			5.00

Baseball Comics #1 © Will Eisner

Basil #2 © STJ

Batman #6 © DC

GD2.0 FN6.0 NM9.4

Preview 4.00

BAR SINISTER (Also see Shaman's Tears)
Acclaim Comics (Windjammer): Jun, 1995 - No. 4, Sept, 1995 ($2.50, lim. series)

1-4: Mike Grell-c/a/scripts 2.50

BARTMAN (Also see Simpson's Comics & Radioactive Man)
Bongo Comics: 1993 - No. 6, 1994 ($1.95/$2.25)

1-($2.95)-Foil-c; bound-in jumbo Bartman poster 4.00
2-6: 3-w/trading card 2.50

BASEBALL COMICS
Will Eisner Productions: Spring, 1949 (Reprinted later as a Spirit section)

1-Will Eisner-c/a 68.00 202.00 540.00

BASEBALL COMICS
Kitchen Sink Press: 1991 ($3.95, coated stock)

1-r/1949 ish. by Eisner; contains trading cards 5.00

BASEBALL HEROES
Fawcett Publications: 1952 (one-shot)

nn (Scarce)-Babe Ruth photo-c; baseball's Hall of Fame biographies 75.00 225.00 600.00

BASEBALL'S GREATEST HEROES
Magnum Comics: Dec, 1991 - No. 2, May, 1992 ($1.75)

1-Mickey Mantle #1; photo-c; Sinnott-a(p) 3.00
2-Brooks Robinson #1; photo-c; Sinnott-a(i) 2.00

BASEBALL THRILLS
Ziff-Davis Publ. Co.: No. 10, Sum, 1951 - No. 3, Sum, 1952
(Saunders painted-c No.1,2)

10(#1)-Bob Feller, Musial, Newcombe & Boudreau stories 40.00 120.00 300.00
2-Powell-a(2)(Late Sum, '51); Feller, Berra & Mathewson stories 29.00 86.00 200.00
3-Kinstler-c/a; Joe DiMaggio story 29.00 86.00 200.00

BASEBALL THRILLS 3-D
The 3-D Zone: May, 1990 ($2.95, w/glasses)

1-New L.B. Cole-c; life stories of Ty Cobb & Ted Williams 5.00

BASICALLY STRANGE (Magazine)
John C. Comics (Archie Comics Group): Dec, 1982 ($1.95, B&W)

1-(21,000 printed; all but 1,000 destroyed; pgs. out of sequence) 1.75 5.25 14.00
1-Wood, Toth-a; Corben-c; reprints & new art 1.25 3.75 10.00

BASIC HISTORY OF AMERICA ILLUSTRATED
Pendulum Press: 1976 (B&W) (Soft-c $1.50; Hard-c $4.50)

07-1999-America Becomes a World Power 1890-1920. 07-2251-The Industrial Era 1865-1915. 07-226x-Before the Civil War 1830-1860. 07-2278-Americans Move Westward 1800-1850. 07-2286-The Civil War 1850-1876; Redondo-a. 07-2294-The Fight for Freedom 1750-1783. 07-2308-The New World 1500-1750. 07-2316-Problems of the New Nation 1800-1830. 07-2324-Roaring Twenties and the Great Depression 1920-1940. 07-2332-The United States Emerges 1783-1800. 07-2340-America Today 1945-1976. 07-2359-World War II 1940-1945

BASIL (...the Royal Cat)
St. John Publishing Co.: Jan, 1953 - No. 4, Sept, 1953

1-Funny animal 5.00 15.00 30.00
2-4 3.20 8.00 16.00
I.W. Reprint 1 1.00 3.00 8.00

BASIL WOLVERTON'S FANTASTIC FABLES
Dark Horse Comics: Oct, 1993 - No. 2, Dec, 1993 ($2.50, B&W, limited series)

1,2-Wolverton-c/a(r) 4.00

BASIL WOLVERTON'S GATEWAY TO HORROR
Dark Horse Comics: June, 1988 ($1.75, B&W, one-shot)

1-Wolverton-r 4.00

BASIL WOLVERTON'S PLANET OF TERROR
Dark Horse Comics: Oct, 1987 ($1.75, B&W, one-shot)

1-Wolverton-r; Alan Moore-c 4.00

BATGIRL ADVENTURES (See Batman Adventures, The)
DC Comics: Feb, 1998 ($2.95, one-shot) (Based on animated series)

1-Harley Quinn and Poison Ivy app.; Timm-c 4.00

BATGIRL SPECIAL
DC Comics: 1988 ($1.50, one-shot, 52 pgs)

1-Kitson-a/Mignola-c 1.00 2.80 7.00

BAT LASH (See DC Special Series #16, Showcase #76, Weird Western Tales)
National Periodical Publications: Oct-Nov, 1968 - No. 7, Oct-Nov, 1969
(All 12¢ issues)

1-(10-11/68)-2nd app. Bat Lash 2.80 8.40 28.00
2-7 2.00 6.00 16.00

BATMAN (See Anarky, Aurora, The Best of DC #2, Blind Justice, The Brave & the Bold, Cosmic Odyssey, DC 100-Page Super Spec. #14,20, DC Special, DC Special Series, Detective, Dynamic Classics, 80-Page Giants, Gotham By Gaslight, Gotham Nights, Greatest Batman Stories Ever Told, Greatest Joker Stories Ever Told, Heroes Against Hunger, JLA,The Joker, Justice League of America, Justice League Int., Legends of the Dark Knight, Limited Coll. Ed., Man-Bat, Nightwing, Power Record Comics, Real Fact #5, Robin, Saga of Ra's Al Ghul, Shadow of the..., Star Spangled, Super Friends, 3-D Batman, Untold Legend of..., Wanted... & World's Finest Comics)

BATMAN
National Per. Publ./Detective Comics/DC Comics: Spring, 1940 - Present
(#1-5 were quarterly)

GD2.0 FN6.0 VF8.0 NM9.4

1-Origin The Batman reprinted (2 pgs.) from Det. #33 w/splash from #34 by Bob Kane; see Detective #33 for 1st origin; 1st app. Joker (2 stories intended for 2 separate issues of Det. Comics which would have been 1st & 2nd app.); splash pg. to 2nd Joker story is similar to cover of Det. #40 (story intended for #40); 1st app. The Cat (Catwoman)(1st villainess in comics); has Batman story (w/Hugo Strange) without Robin originally planned for Det. #38; mentions location (Manhattan) where Batman lives (see Det. #31). This book was created entirely from the inventory of Det. Comics; 1st Batman/Robin pin-up on back-c; has text piece & photo of Bob Kane 5,416.00 16,250.00 35,200.00 65,000.00

1-Reprint, oversize 13-1/2x10". **WARNING:** This comic is an exact duplicate reprint of the original except for its size. DC published it in 1974 with a second cover titling it as a Famous First Edition. There have been many reported cases of the outer cover being removed and the interior sold as the original edition. The reprint with the new outer cover removed is practically worthless. See Famous First Edition for value.

GD2.0 FN6.0 NM9.4

2-2nd app. The Joker; 2nd app. Catwoman (out of costume) in Joker story; 1st time called Catwoman
NOTE: A 15¢-c for Canadian distr. exists.
1100.00 3300.00 11,500.00
3-3rd app Catwoman (1st in costume & 1st costumed villainess); 1st Puppet Master app.; classic Kane & Moldoff-c 740.00 2220.00 7400.00
4-3rd app. The Joker (see Det. #45 for 4th); 1st mention of Gotham City in a Batman comic (on newspaper)(Win/40) 600.00 1800.00 6000.00
5-1st app. the Batmobile with its bat-head front 430.00 1290.00 4300.00
6,7: 7-Bullseye-c 400.00 1200.00 3600.00
8-Infinity-c. 333.00 1000.00 3000.00
9-10:9-1st Batman x-mas story; Burnley-c. 10-Catwoman story (gets new costume) 311.00 933.00 2800.00
11-Classic Joker-c by Ray/Robinson (3rd Joker-c, 6-7/42); Joker & Penguin app. 600.00 1800.00 5400.00
12,15: 15-New costume Catwoman 275.00 825.00 2200.00
13-Jerry Siegel (Superman's co-creator) appears in a Batman story. 288.00 864.00 2450.00
14-2nd Penguin-c; Penguin app. (12-1/42-43) 288.00 864.00 2450.00
16-Intro/origin Alfred (4-5/43); cover is a reverse of #9 cover by Burnley; 1st small logo 463.00 1390.00 4400.00
17,19,20: 17-Penguin app. 19-Joker app. 20-1st Batmobile-c (12-1/43-44) 188.00 564.00 1500.00
18-Hitler, Hirohito, Mussolini-c. 237.00 711.00 1900.00
21,22,24,26,28-30: 21-1st skinny Alfred in Batman (2-3/44). 21,30-Penguin app. 22-1st Alfred solo-c/story (Alfred solo stories in 22-32,36); Catwoman &

Batman #49 © DC

Batman #139 © DC

Batman #227 © DC

	GD2.0	FN6.0	NM9.4
The Cavalier app. 28-Joker story	137.00	411.00	1100.00
23-Joker-c/story	200.00	600.00	1600.00
25-Only Joker/Penguin team-up; 1st team-up between two major villains	206.00	618.00	1650.00
27-Burnley Christmas-c; Penguin app.	181.00	543.00	1450.00
31,32,34-36,39: 32-Origin Robin retold. 35-Catwoman story (in new costume w/o cat head mask). 36-Penguin app.	103.00	309.00	825.00
33-Christmas-c	116.00	348.00	925.00
37,40,44-Joker-c/stories	137.00	411.00	1100.00
38-Penguin-c/story	116.00	348.00	925.00
41,45,46: 41-1st Sci-fi cover/story in Batman; Penguin app.(6-7/47). 45-Christmas-c/story; Catwoman story; Vicki Vale app. (1st app?)	78.00	234.00	625.00
42,43: 42-2nd Catwoman-c (1st in Batman)(8-9/47); Catwoman story also. 43-Penguin-c/story	100.00	300.00	800.00
47-1st detailed origin The Batman (6-7/48); 1st Bat-signal-c this title (see Detective #108); Batman tracks down his parent's killer and reveals i.d. to him	300.00	900.00	2700.00
48-1000 Secrets of the Batcave; r-in #203; Penguin story	103.00	309.00	825.00
49-Joker-c/story; 1st app. Mad Hatter; Vicki Vale app.	162.00	486.00	1300.00
50-Two-Face impostor app.	87.00	261.00	700.00
51,54,56,57,59: 57-Centerfold is a 1950 calendar. 59-1st app. Deadshot; Batman in the future-c/story	75.00	225.00	600.00
52,55-Joker-c/stories	97.00	291.00	775.00
53,58,60,61: 58-Penguin-c. 61-Origin Batman Plane II	84.00	252.00	675.00
62-Origin Catwoman; Catwoman-c	112.00	336.00	900.00
63,80-Joker stories. 63-Flying saucer story(2-3/51)	69.00	207.00	550.00
64,67,70-72,74-77,79: 70-Robot-c. 72-Last 52 pg. issue. 74-Used in **POP**, Pg. 90. 79-Vicki Vale in "The Bride of Batman"	59.00	177.00	475.00
65,69,84-Catwoman-c/stories. 84-Two-Face app.	67.00	200.00	540.00
66,73-Joker-c/stories. 66-Pre-2nd Batman & Robin team try-out. 73-Vicki Vale story	79.00	237.00	635.00
68,81-Two-Face-c/stories	62.00	186.00	500.00
78-(8-9/53)-Roh Kar, The Man Hunter from Mars story-the 1st lawman of Mars to come to Earth (green skinned)	75.00	225.00	600.00
82,83,85-89: 86-Intro Batmarine (Batman's submarine). 89-Last pre-code issue	56.00	168.00	450.00
90,91,93-99: 97-2nd app. Bat-Hound-c/story; Joker app. 99-(4/56)-Last G.A. Penguin app.	47.00	141.00	375.00
92-1st app. Bat-Hound-c/story	62.00	186.00	500.00
100-(6/56)	243.00	729.00	1950.00
101-(8/56)-Clark Kent x-over who protects Batman's i.d. (3rd story)	50.00	150.00	400.00
102-104,106-109: 103-1st S.A. issue; 3rd Bat-Hound-c/story	39.00	117.00	350.00
105-1st Batwoman in Batman (2nd anywhere)	50.00	150.00	450.00
110-Joker story	40.00	120.00	360.00
111-120: 112-1st app. Signalman (super villain). 113-1st app. Fatman; Batman meets his counterpart on Planet X w/a chest plate similar to S.A. Batman's design (yellow oval w/black design inside).	33.00	100.00	300.00
121- Origin/1st app. of Mr. Zero (Mr. Freeze).	40.00	120.00	360.00
122,124-126,128,130: 124-2nd app. Signal Man. 126-Batwoman-c/story. 128-Batwoman cameo. 130-Lex Luthor app.	22.00	66.00	200.00
123,127: 123-Joker story; Bat-Hound app. 127-(10/59)-Batman vs. Thor the Thunder God-c/story; Joker story; Superman cameo	25.00	75.00	225.00
129-Origin Robin retold; bondage-c; Batwoman-c/story (reprinted in Batman Family #8)	27.00	81.00	240.00
131-135,137-139,141-143: 131-Intro 2nd Batman & Robin series (see #66; also in #135,145,154,159,163). 133-1st Bat-Mite in Batman (3rd app. anywhere). 134-Origin The Dummy (not Vigilante's villain). 139-Intro 1st original Bat-Girl; only app. Signalman as the Blue Bowman. 141-2nd app. original Bat-Girl. 143-(10/61)-Last 10¢ issue	17.00	51.00	155.00
136-Joker-c/story	20.00	60.00	180.00
140,144-Joker stories. 140-Batwoman-c/story; Superman cameo. 144-(12/61)-1st 12¢ issue	16.00	48.00	160.00
145,148-Joker-c/stories	17.00	51.00	170.00
146,147,149,150	11.50	34.00	115.00
151-154,156-158,160-162,164-168,170: 152-Joker story. 156-Ant-Man/Robin team-up(6/63). 164-New Batmobile(6/64) new look & Mystery Analysts series begins	9.00	27.00	90.00
155-1st S.A. app. The Penguin (5/63)	30.00	81.00	300.00
159,163-Joker-c/stories. 159-Bat-Girl app.	11.00	33.00	110.00
169-2nd SA Penguin app.	12.00	36.00	120.00
171-1st Riddler app.(5/65) since Dec. 1948	36.00	108.00	390.00
172-175,177,178,180,184	5.50	16.50	55.00
176-(80-Pg. Giant G-17); Joker-c/story; Penguin app. in strip-r; Catwoman reprint	7.50	22.50	75.00
179-2nd app. Silver Age Riddler	12.00	36.00	120.00
181-Batman & Robin poster insert; intro. Poison Ivy	14.00	42.00	140.00
182,187-(80 Pg. Giants G-24, G-30); Joker-c/stories	6.50	19.50	65.00
183-2nd app. Poison Ivy	9.00	27.00	90.00
185-(80 Pg. Giant G-27)	6.50	19.50	65.00
186-Joker-c/story	6.00	18.00	60.00
188,191,192,194-196,199	3.20	9.60	32.00
189-1st S.A. app. Scarecrow; retells origin of G.A. Scarecrow from World's Finest #3(1st app.)	7.00	21.00	70.00
190-Penguin app.	3.50	10.50	35.00
193-(80-Pg. Giant G-37)	5.50	16.50	55.00
197-4th S.A. Catwoman app. cont'd from Det. #369; 1st new Batgirl app. in Batman (5th anywhere)	5.50	16.50	55.00
198-(80-Pg. Giant G-43); Joker-c/story-r/World's Finest #61; Catwoman-r/ Det. #211; Penguin-r; origin-r/#47	6.50	19.50	65.00
200-(3/68)-Joker cameo; retells origin of Batman & Robin; 1st Neal Adams work this title (cover only)	12.00	36.00	120.00
201-Joker story	3.50	10.50	35.00
202,204-207,209,210	2.50	7.50	24.00
203-(80 Pg. Giant G-49); r/#48, 61, & Det. 185; Batcave Blueprints	4.50	13.50	45.00
208-(80 Pg. Giant G-55); New origin Batman by Gil Kane plus 3 G.A. Batman reprints w/Catwoman, Vicki Vale & Batwoman	4.50	13.50	45.00
211,212,: 212-Last 12¢ issue	2.50	7.50	24.00
213-(80-Pg. Giant G-61); 30th anniversary issue (7-8/69); origin Alfred (r/Batman #16), Joker(r/Det. #168), Clayface; new origin Robin with new facts	5.90	17.70	65.00
214-217: 214-Alfred given a new last name- "Pennyworth" (see Detective #96)	2.50	7.50	22.00
218-(80-Pg. Giant G-67)	4.50	13.50	45.00
219-Neal Adams-a	4.00	12.00	40.00
220,221,224-227,229-231	2.50	7.50	20.00
222-Beatles take-off; art lesson by Joe Kubert	3.50	10.50	35.00
223,228,233-(80-Pg. Giants G-73,G-79,G-85)	3.80	11.40	38.00
232-N. Adams-a. Intro/1st app. Ras Al Ghul; origin Batman & Robin retold; last 15¢ issue	8.00	23.00	85.00
234-(9/71)-1st modern app. of Harvey Dent/Two-Face; (see World's Finest #173 for Batman as Two-Face; only S.A. mention of character); N. Adams-a; 52 pg. issues begin, end #242	10.00	30.00	110.00
235,236,239-242: 239-XMas-c. 241-Reprint/#5	2.50	7.50	22.00
237-N. Adams-a. G.A. Batman-r/Det. #37; 1st app. The Reaper; Wrightson/Ellison plots	5.00	15.00	50.00
238-Also listed as DC 100 Page Super Spectacular #8; Batman, Legion, Aquaman-r; G.A. Atom, Sargon (r/Sensation #57), Plastic Man (r/Police #14) stories; Doom Patrol origin-r; N. Adams wraparound-c (see DC 100 Pg. Super Spectacular #8 for price)			
243-245-Neal Adams-a	3.50	10.50	35.00
246-250,252,253: 246-Scarecrow app. 253-Shadow-c & app.	2.50	7.50	20.00
251-(9/73)-N. Adams-c/a; Joker-c/story	5.00	15.00	55.00
254,256-259,261-All 100 pg. editions; part-r: 254-(2/74)-Man-Bat-c & app. 256-Catwoman app. 257-Joker & Penguin app. 258-The Cavalier-r. 259-Shadow-c/app.	2.50	7.50	24.00

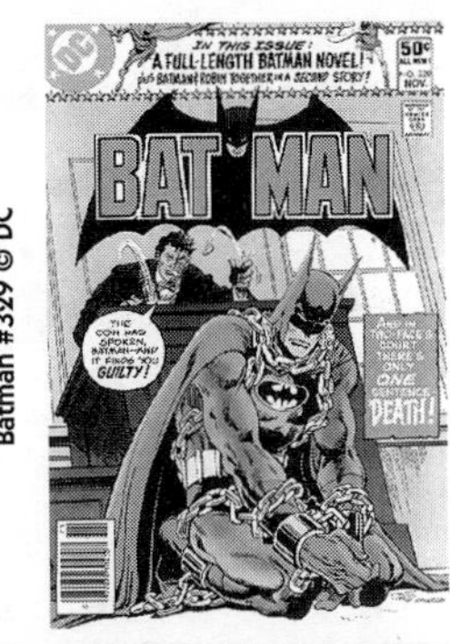

Batman #329 © DC

Batman #463 © DC

Batman #563 © DC

GD2.0 FN6.0 NM9.4

255-(100 pgs.)-N. Adams-c/a; tells of Bruce Wayne's father who wore bat costume & fought crime (r/Det. #235); r/story Batman #22 4.00 12.00 40.00
260-Joker-c/story (100 pgs.) 4.00 12.00 40.00
262 (68pgs.) 2.50 7.50 22.00
263,264,266-285,287-290,292,293,295-299: 266-Catwoman back to old costume 1.50 4.50 12.00
265-Wrightson-a(i) 1.60 4.85 13.00
286,291,294: 294-Joker-c/stories 1.85 5.50 15.00
300-Double-size 2.25 6.75 18.00
301-(7/78)-320,322-331,333-352: 304-(44 pgs.). 306-3rd app. Black Spider. 308-Mr. Freeze app. 310-1st modern app. The Gentleman Ghost in Batman; Kubert-c. 311-Batgirl-c/story; Batgirl reteams w/Batman. 312,314,346-Two-Face-c/stories. 313-2nd app. Calendar Man. 316-Robin returns. 318-Intro Firebug. 319-2nd modern age app. The Gentleman Ghost; Kubert-c. 322-324-Catwoman (Selina Kyle) app. 322,323-Cat-Man cameos (1st in Batman, 1 panel each). 323-1st meeting Catwoman & Cat-Man. 324-1st full app. Cat-Man this title. 344-Poison Ivy app. 345-1st app. new Dr. Death. 345,346,351-7 pg. Catwoman back-ups 1.10 3.30 9.00
321,353,359-Joker-c/stories. 1.25 3.75 10.00
332-Catwoman's 1st solo. 1.25 3.75 10.00
354-356,358,360-365,369,370: 361-1st app Harvey Bullock 2.40 6.00
357-1st app. Jason Todd (3/83); see Det. #524; 1st app. Croc (cameo) 1.25 3.75 10.00
366-Jason Todd 1st in Robin costume; Joker-c/story 1.25 3.75 10.00
367-Jason in red & green costume (not as Robin) 2.40 6.00
368-1st new Robin in costume (Jason Todd) 1.00 2.80 7.00
371-399,401-403: 371-Cat-Man-c/story; brief origin Cat-Man (cont'd in Det. #538). 386,387-Intro Black Mask (villain). 380-391-Catwoman app. 398-Catwoman & Two-Face app. 401-2nd app. Magpie (see Man of Steel #3 for 1st). 403-Joker cameo 4.00

NOTE: *Most issues between 397 & 432 were reprinted in 1989 and sold in multi-packs. Some are not identified as reprints but have newer ads copyrighted after cover dates. 2nd and 3rd printings exist.*

400 ($1.50, 68pgs.)-Dark Knight special; intro by Stephen King; Art Adams/Austin-a 2.25 6.75 18.00
404-Miller scripts begin (end 407); Year 1; 1st modern app. Catwoman (2/87) 1.10 3.30 9.00
405-407: 407-Year 1 ends (See Det. Comics for Year 2) 2.40 6.00
408-410: New Origin Jason Todd (Robin) 5.00
411-416,421-425: 411-Two-face app. 412-Origin/1st app. Mime. 414-Starlin scripts begin, end #429. 416-Nightwing-c/story. 423-McFarlane-c 4.00
417-420: "Ten Nights of the Beast" storyline 5.00
426-($1.50, 52 pgs.)- "A Death In The Family" storyline begins, ends #429 1.25 3.75 10.00
427- "A Death In The Family" part 2. 1.10 3.30 9.00
428-Death of Robin (Jason Todd) 1.00 2.80 7.00
429-Joker-c/story; Superman app. 5.00
430-432 3.00
433-435-Many Deaths of the Batman story by John Byrne-c/scripts 3.00
436-Year 3 begins (ends #439); origin original Robin retold by Nightwing (Dick Grayson); 1st app. Timothy Drake (8/89) 3.00
436-441: 436-2nd printing. 437-Origin Robin cont. 440,441: "A Lonely Place of Dying" Parts 1 & 3 2.50
442-1st app. Timothy Drake in Robin costume 3.00
443-456,458,459,462-464: 445-447-Batman goes to Russia. 448,449-The Penguin Affair Pts 1 & 3. 450-Origin Joker. 450,451-Joker-c/stories. 452-454-Dark Knight Dark City storyline; Riddler app. 455-Alan Grant scripts begin, ends #466, 470. 464-Last solo Batman story; free 16 pg. preview of Impact Comics line 2.50
457-Timothy Drake officially becomes Robin & dons new costume 3.00
457-Direct sale edition (has #000 in indicia) 3.00
460,461,465-487: 460,461-Two part Catwoman story. 465-Robin returns to action with Batman. 470-War of the Gods x-over. 475,476-Return of Scarface-c/story. 476-Last $1.00-c.477,478-Photo-c 2.50
488-Cont'd from Batman: Sword of Azrael #4; Azrael-c & app. 1.00 2.80 7.00
489-Bane-c/story; 1st app. Azrael in Bat-costume 4.00
490-Riddler-c/story; Azrael & Bane app. 5.00
491,492: 491-Knightfall lead-in; Joker-c/story; Azrael & Bane app.; Kelley Jones-c begin. 492-Knightfall part 1; Bane app. 4.00
492-Platinum edition (promo copy) 10.00
493-496: 493-Knightfall Pt. 3. 494-Knightfall Pt. 5; Joker-c & app. 495-Knightfall Pt. 7; brief Bane & Joker apps. 496-Knightfall Pt. 9, Joker-c/story; Bane cameo. 3.00
497-(Late 7/93)-Knightfall Pt. 11; Bane breaks Batman's back; B&W outer-c; Aparo-a(p); Giordano-a(i) 4.00
497-499: 497-2nd printing. 497-Newsstand edition w/o outer cover. 498-Knightfall part 15; Bane & Catwoman-c & app. (see Showcase 93 #7 & 8) 499-Knightfall Pt. 17; Bane app. 2.50
500-($2.50, 68 pgs.)-Knightfall Pt. 19; Azrael in new Bat-costume; Bane-c/story 2.50
500-($3.95, 68 pgs.)-Collector's Edition w/die-cut double-c w/foil by Joe Quesada & 2 bound-in post cards 4.50
501-508,510,511: 501-Begin $1.50-c. 501-508-Knightquest. 503,504-Catwoman app. 507-Ballistic app.; Jim Balent-a(p). 510-KnightsEnd Pt. 7. 511-(9/94)-Zero Hour; Batgirl-c/story 2.00
509-($2.50, 52 pgs.)-KnightsEnd Pt. 1 2.50
0,512-514,516-518: 0-(10/94)-Origin retold. 512-(11/94)-Dick Grayson assumes Batman role 2.50
515-Special Ed.($2.50)-Kelley Jones-a begins; all black embossed-c; Troika Pt. 1 3.00
515-Regular Edition 2.50
519-534,536-549: 519-Begin $1.95-c. 521-Return of Alfred, 522-Swamp Thing app. 525-Mr. Freeze app. 527,528-Two Face app. 529-Contagion Pt. 6. 530-532-Deadman app. 533-Legacy prelude. 534-Legacy Pt. 5. 536-Final Night x-over; Man-Bat-c/app. 540,541-Spectre-c-app. 544-546-Joker & The Demon. 548,549-Penguin-c/app. 2.50
530-532 ($2.50)-Enhanced edition; glow-in-the-dark-c. 3.00
535-(10/96, $2.95)-1st app. The Ogre 3.00
535-(10/96, $3.95)-1st app. The Ogre; variant, cardboard, foldout-c 4.00
550-($3.50)-Collector's Ed., includes 4 collector cards; intro. Chase, return of Clayface; Kelley Jones-c 3.50
550-($2.95)-Standard Ed.; Williams & Gray-c 2.95
551,552,554-562: 551,552-Ragman c/app. 554-Cataclysm pt. 12. 2.00
553-Cataclysm pt.3 4.00
563-No Man's Land; Joker-c by Campbell; Bob Gale-s 2.40 6.00
564-569: 569-New Batgirl-c/app. 3.00
570-572: 572-Joker and Harley app. 2.00
#1,000,000 (11/98) 853rd Century x-over 2.00
Annual 1 (8-10/61)-Swan-c 54.00 162.00 650.00
Annual 2 28.00 85.00 285.00
Annual 3 (Summer, '62)-Joker-c/story 29.00 88.00 295.00
Annual 4,5 13.00 39.00 130.00
Annual 6,7 (7/64, 25¢, 80 pgs.) 10.00 30.00 100.00
Annual V5#8 (1982)-Painted-c 1.00 2.80 7.00
Annual 9,10,12: 9(7/85). 10(1986). 12(1988, $1.50) 5.00
Annual 11 (1987, $1.25)-Penguin-c/story; Alan Moore scripts 6.00
Annual 13 (1989, $1.75, 68 pgs.)-Gives history of Bruce Wayne, Dick Grayson, Jason Todd, Alfred, Comm. Gordon, Barbara Gordon (Batgirl) & Vicki Vale; Morrow-i 4.00
Annual 14-17 ('90-'93, 68 pgs.)-14-Origin Two-Face. 15-Armageddon 2001 x-over; Joker app. 15 (2nd printing). 16-Joker-c/s; Kieth-c. 17 (1993, $2.50, 68 pgs.)-Azrael in Bat-costume; intro Ballistic 4.00
Annual 18 (1994, $2.95) 3.00
Annual 19 (1995, $3.95)-Year One story; retells Scarecrow's origin 4.00
Annual 20 (1996, $2.95)-Legends of the Dead Earth story; Giarrano-a 3.00
Annual 21 (1997, $3.95)-Pulp Heroes story 4.00
Annual 22,23 ('98, '99, $2.95)-22-Ghosts; Wrightson-c. 23-JLApe; Art Adams-c 3.00
Special 1 (4/84)-Mike W. Barr story; Golden-c/a 5.00

NOTE: ***Art Adams** a-400p. **Neal Adams** c-200, 203, 210, 217, 219-222, 224-227, 229, 230, 232, 234, 236-241, 243-246, 251, 255, Annual 14. **Aparo** a-414-420, 426-435, 440-448, 450, 451,*

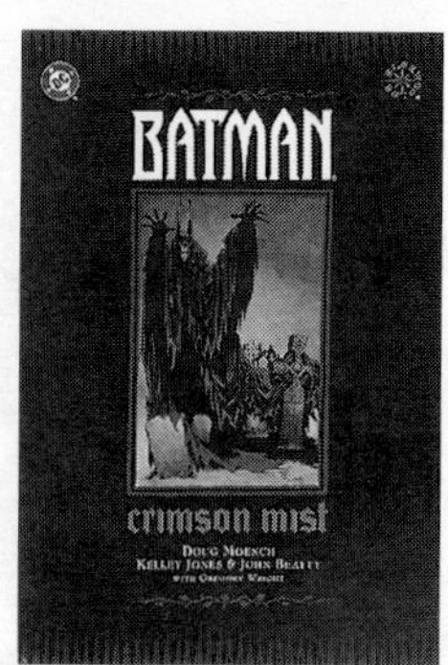

Batman: Crimson Mist HC © DC

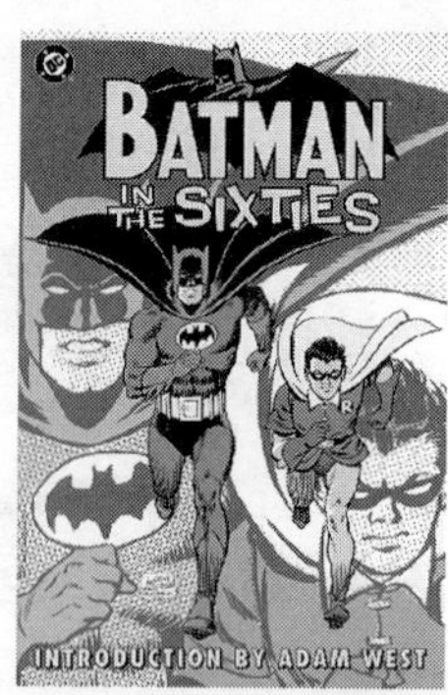

Batman in the Sixties TPB © DC

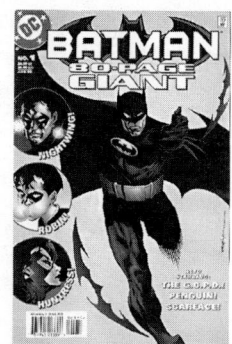

Batman 80-Page Giant #1 © DC

GD2.0 FN6.0 NM9.4

480-483, 486-491, 494-500; c-414-416, 481, 482, 463i, 486, 487i. ***Bolland*** *a-400; c-445-447.* ***Burnley*** *a-10, 12-18, 20, 22, 25, 27; c-9, 15, 16, 27, 28p, 40p, 42p.* ***Byrne*** *c-401, 433-435, 533-535, Annual 11.* ***Travis Charest*** *c-488-490p.* ***Colan*** *a-340p, 343-345p, 348-351p, 373p, 383p; c-343p, 345p, 350p.* ***J. Cole*** *a-238r.* ***Cowan*** *a-Annual 10p.* ***Golden*** *a-295p, 303p, 484, 485.* ***Alan Grant*** *scripts-455-466, 470, 474-476, 479, 480, Annual 16(part).* ***Grell*** *a-287, 288p, 289p, 290; c-287-290.* ***Infantino/Anderson*** *c-167, 173, 175, 181, 186, 191, 192, 194, 195, 198, 199.* ***Kelley Jones*** *a-513-519, 521-525, 527; c-491-499, 500(newsstand), 501-510, 513.* ***Kaluta*** *c-242, 248, 253, Annual 12.* ***G. Kane/Anderson*** *c-178-180.* ***Bob Kane*** *a-1, 2, 5; c-1-5, 7, 17.* ***G. Kane*** *a-(r)-254, 255, 259, 261, 353i.* ***Kubert*** *a-238r, 400; c-310, 319p, 327, 328, 344.* ***McFarlane*** *c-423.* ***Mignola*** *c-426-429, 452-454, Annual 18.* ***Moldoff*** *c-101-140.* ***Moldoff/Giella*** *a-164-175, 177-181, 183, 184, 186.* ***Moldoff/Greene*** *a-169, 172-174, 177-179, 181, 184.* ***Mooney*** *a-255r.* ***Morrow*** *a-Annual 13i.* ***Newton*** *a-305, 306, 328p, 331p, 332p, 337p, 338p, 346p, 352-357p, 360-372p, 374-378p; c-374p, 378p.* ***Nino*** *a-Annual 9.* ***Irv Novick*** *c-201, 202.* ***Perez*** *a-400; c-436-442.* ***Fred Ray*** *c-8, 10; w/****Robinson****-11.* ***Robinson/Roussos*** *a-12-17, 20, 22, 24, 25, 27, 28, 31, 33, 37.* ***Robinson*** *a-12, 14, 18, 22-32,34, 36, 37, 255r, 260r, 261r; c-6, 8, 10, 12-15, 18, 21, 24, 26, 30, 37, 39.* ***Simonson*** *a-300p, 312p, 321p; c-300p, 312p, 366, 413i.* ***P. Smith*** *a-Annual 9.* ***Dick Sprang*** *c-19, 20, 22, 23, 25, 29, 31-36, 38, 51, 55, 66, 73, 76.* ***Starlin*** *c/a-402.* ***Staton*** *a-334.* ***Sutton*** *a-400.* ***Wrightson*** *a-265i, 400; c-320r. Bat-Hound app. in 92, 97, 103, 123, 125, 133, 156, 158. Bat-Mite app. in 133, 136, 144, 146, 158, 161. Batwoman app. in 105, 116, 122, 125, 128, 129, 131, 133, 139, 140, 141, 144, 145, 150, 151, 153, 154, 157, 159, 162, 163.* ***Zeck*** *c-417-420. Catwoman back-ups in 332, 345, 346, 348-351. Joker app. in 1, 2, 4, 5, 7-9, 11-13, 19, 20, 23, 25, 28, 32 & many more. Robin solo back-up stories in 337-339, 341-343.*

BATMAN (Books and trade paperbacks)
...: A LONELY PLACE OF DYING (1990, $3.95, 132 pgs.)-r/Batman #440-442 & New Titans #60,61; Perez-c 4.00
...: ANARKY TPB (1999, $12.95) r/early appearances 13.00
...AND DRACULA: RED RAIN nn (1991, $24.95)-Hard-c.; Elseworlds storyline 30.00
...AND DRACULA: Red Rain nn (1992, $9.95)-SC 10.00
ARKHAM ASYLUM Hard-c (1989, $24.95) 30.00
ARKHAM ASYLUM Soft-c ($14.95) 15.00
BIRTH OF THE DEMON Hard-c (1992, $24.95)-Origin of Ras al Ghul 25.00
BIRTH OF THE DEMON Soft-c (1993, $12.95) 13.00
BLIND JUSTICE nn (1992, $7.50)-r/Det. #598-600 7.50
BLOODSTORM (1994, $24.95,HC) Kelley Jones-c/a 28.00
BRIDE OF THE DEMON Hard-c (1990, $19.95) 20.00
BRIDE OF THE DEMON Soft-c ($12.95) 13.00
...: CASTLE OF THE BAT ($5.95)-Elseworlds story 6.00
...: CATACLYSM ('99, $17.95)-r/ story arc 18.00
...: COLLECTED LEGENDS OF THE DARK KNIGHT nn (1994, $12.95)-r/Legends of the Dark Knight #32-34,38,42,43 13.00
...: CRIMSON MIST (1999, $24.95,HC)-Elseworlds story Doug Moench-s/Kelley Jones-c/a 25.00
...: DARK JOKER-THE WILD (1993, $24.95,HC)-Elseworlds story Doug Moench-s/Kelley Jones-c/a 25.00
...: DARK JOKER-THE WILD (1993, $9.95,SC) 10.00
...DARK KNIGHT DYNASTY nn (1997, $24.95)-Hard-c.; 3 Elseworlds stories; Barr-s/ S. Hampton painted-a, Gary Frank, McDaniel-a(p) 25.00
...DEADMAN: DEATH AND GLORY nn (1996, $24.95)-Hard-c.; Robinson-s/ Estes-c/a 25.00
...DEADMAN: DEATH AND GLORY ($12.95)-SC 13.00
DEATH IN THE FAMILY (1988, $3.95, trade paperback)-r/Batman #426-429 by Aparo 5.00
DEATH IN THE FAMILY: (2nd - 5th printings) 4.00
DIGITAL JUSTICE nn (1990, $24.95, Hard-c.)-Computer generated art 25.00
... FACES (1995, $9.95, TPB) 10.00
FOUR OF A KIND TPB (1998, $14.95)-r/1995 Year One Annuals featuring Poison Ivy, Riddler, Scarecrow, & Man-Bat 15.00
...GOTHIC (1992, $12.95, TPB)-r/Legends of the Dark Knight #6-10 13.00
...: HAUNTED KNIGHT-(1997,12.95) r/ Halloween sp.. 13.00
... IN THE SIXTIES TPB ($19.95) Intro. by Adam West 20.00
... LEGACY-(1996,17.95) reprints Legacy 18.00
...: THE MANY DEATHS OF THE BATMAN (1992, $3.95, 84 pgs.)-r/Batman #433-435 w/new Byrne-c 4.00
...: THE MOVIES (1997, $19.95)-r/movie adaptions of Batman, Batman Returns, Batman Forever, Batman and Robin 20.00
...: PREY (1992, $12.95)-Gulacy/Austin-a 13.00
...: PRODIGAL (1997, $14.95)-Gulacy/Austin-a 15.00

GD2.0 FN6.0 NM9.4

SHAMAN (1993, $12.95)-r/Legends/D.K. #1-5 13.00
...: SON OF THE DEMON Hard-c (9/87, $14.95) 30.00
...: SON OF THE DEMON limited signed & numbered Hard-c (1,700) 45.00
...: SON OF THE DEMON Soft-c w/new-c ($8.95) 10.00
...: SON OF THE DEMON Soft-c (1989, $9.95, 2nd printing - 4th printing) 10.00
...: TALES OF THE DEMON (1991, $17.95, 212 pgs.)-Intro by Sam Hamm; reprints by N. Adams(3) & Golden; contains Saga of Ra's Al Ghul #1 18.00
...: TEN NIGHTS OF THE BEAST (1994, $5.95)-r/Batman #417-420 6.00
...:THE LAST ANGEL (1994, $12.95, TPB) 13.00
...: THRILLKILLER (1998, $12.95, TPB)-r/series & Thrillkiller '62 13.00
...: VENOM (1993, $9.95, TPB)-r/Legends of the Dark Knight #16-20; embossed-c 10.00
YEAR ONE Hard-c (1988, $12.95) 18.00
YEAR ONE (1988, $9.95, TPB)-r/Batman #404-407 by Miller; intro by Miller 10.00
YEAR ONE (TPB, 2nd & 3rd printings) 10.00
YEAR TWO (1990, $9.95, TPB)-r/Det. 575-578 by McFarlane; wraparound-c 10.00

BATMAN (one-shots)
... ABDUCTION, THE (1998, $5.95) 6.00
... & ROBIN (1997, $5.95)-Movie adaption 6.00
...: ARKHAM ASYLUM - TALES OF MADNESS (5/98, $2.95) Cataclysm x-over pt. 16; Grant-s/Taylor-a 3.00
... : BANE (1997, $4.95)-Dixon-s/Burchett-a; Stelfreeze-c; cover interlocks w/Batman:(Batgirl, Mr. Freeze, Poison Ivy) 5.00
... : BATGIRL (1997, $4.95)-Puckett-s/Haley,Kesel-a; Stelfreeze-c; cover interlocks w/Batman:(Bane, Mr. Freeze, Poison Ivy) 5.00
... : BATGIRL (6/98, $1.95)-Girlfrenzy; Balent-a 2.00
... : BLACKGATE (1/97, $3.95) Dixon-s 4.00
... : BLACKGATE - ISLE OF MEN (4/98, $2.95) Cataclysm x-over pt. 8; Moench-s/Aparo-a 3.00
... BOOK OF SHADOWS, THE (1999, $5.95) 6.00
BROTHERHOOD OF THE BAT (1995, $5.95)-Elseworlds-s 6.00
... BULLOCK'S LAW (8/99, $4.95) Dixon-s 5.00
.../CAPTAIN AMERICA (1996, $5.95, DC/Marvel) Elseworlds story; Byrne-c/s/a 6.00
... : CATWOMAN DEFIANT nn (1992, $4.95, prestige format)-Milligan scripts; cover interlocks w/Batman: Penguin Triumphant; special foil logo. 5.00
... : DARK ALLEGIANCES (1996, $5.95)-Elseworlds story, Chaykin-c/a. 6.00
... : DARK KNIGHT GALLERY (1995, $3.50)-Pin-ups by Pratt, Balent, & others. 3.50
...:DEATH OF INNOCENTS (12/96, $3.95)-O'Neil-s/ Staton-a(p) 4.00
.../DEMON (1996, $4.95)-Alan Grant scripts 5.00
... 80-PAGE GIANT (8/98, $4.95) Stelfreeze-c 5.00
... FOREVER (1995, $5.95, direct market) 6.00
... FOREVER (1995, $3.95, newsstand) 4.00
FULL CIRCLE nn (1991, $5.95, stiff-c, 68 pgs.)-Sequel to Batman: Year Two 6.00
...GALLERY, The 1 (1992, $2.95)-Pin-ups by Miller, N. Adams & others 3.00
...GOTHAM BY GASLIGHT (1989, $3.95) 4.00
.../GREEN ARROW: THE POISON TOMORROW nn (1992, $5.95, square-bound, 68 pgs.)-Netzer-c/a 6.00
HOLY TERROR nn (1991, $4.95, 52 pgs.)-Elseworlds story 5.00
.../HOUDINI: THE DEVIL'S WORKSHOP (1993, $5.95) 6.00
... :HUNTRESS/SPOILER - BLUNT TRAUMA (5/98, $2.95) Cataclysm pt. 13 Dixon-s/Barreto & Sienkiewicz-a 3.00
...: IN DARKEST KNIGHT nn (1994, $4.95, 52 pgs.)-Elseworlds story; Batman w/Green Lantern's ring. 5.00
...:JOKER'S APPRENTICE (5/99, $3.95) Von Eeden-a 4.00
...:JUDGE DREDD: JUDGEMENT ON GOTHAM nn (1991, $5.95, 68 pgs.) Grant/Wagner scripts; Simon Bisley-c/a 6.00
...:JUDGE DREDD: JUDGEMENT ON GOTHAM nn (2nd printing) 6.00

Batman: Nosferatu © DC

Batman and Superman: World's Finest #1 © DC

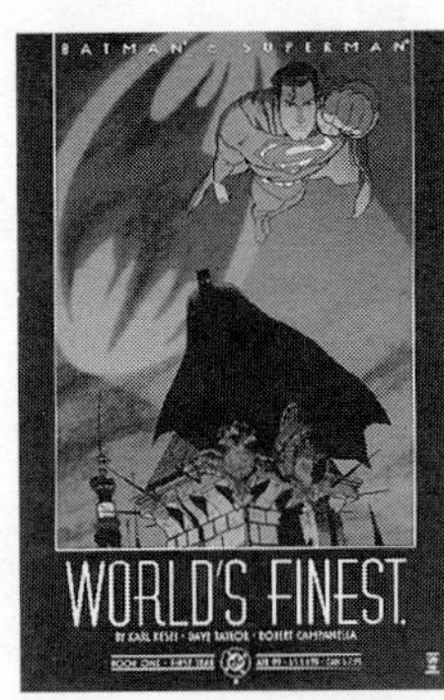

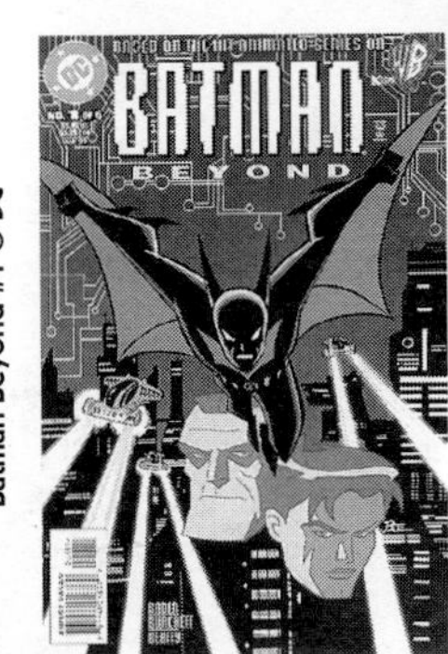

Batman Beyond #1 © DC

GD2.0 FN6.0 NM9.4

...:JUDGE DREDD: THE ULTIMATE RIDDLE (1995, $4.95) 5.00
...:JUDGE DREDD: VENDETTA IN GOTHAM (1993, $5.95) 6.00
...: KNIGHTGALLERY (1995, $3.50)-Elseworlds sketchbook. 3.50
...: MASK OF THE PHANTASM (1994, $2.95)-Movie adapt. 3.00
...: MASK OF THE PHANTASM (1994, $4.95)-Movie adapt. 5.00
...: MASQUE (1997, $6.95)-Elseworlds; Grell-c/s/a 7.00
...: MASTER OF THE FUTURE nn (1991, $5.95, 68 pgs.)-Elseworlds storyline; sequel to Gotham By Gaslight; embossed-c 6.00
...: MITEFALL (1995, $4.95)-Alan Grant script, Kevin O'Neill-a 5.00
... : MR. FREEZE (1997, $4.95)-Dini-s/Buckingham-a; Stelfreeze-c; cover interlocks w/Batman:(Bane, Batgirl, Poison Ivy) 5.00
...: NOSFERATU (1999, $5.95) McKeever-a 6.00
...: PENGUIN TRIUMPHANT nn (1992, $4.95)-Staton-a(p); special foil logo 5.00
...•PHANTOM STRANGER nn (1997, $4.95) nn-Grant-s/Ransom-a 5.00
... : PLUS (2/97, $2.95) Arsenal-c/app. 3.00
... : POISON IVY (1997, $4.95)-J.F. Moore-s/Apthorp-a; Stelfreeze-c; cover interlocks w/Batman:(Bane, Batgirl, Mr. Freeze) 5.00
.../PUNISHER: LAKE OF FIRE (1994, $4.95, DC/Marvel) 5.00
... :REIGN OF TERROR ('99, $4.95) Elseworlds 5.00
...RETURNS MOVIE SPECIAL (1992, $3.95) 4.00
...RETURNS MOVIE PRESTIGE (1992, $5.95, squarebound)-Dorman painted-c 6.00
...:RIDDLER-THE RIDDLE FACTORY (1995, $4.95)-Wagner script 5.00
...: SCARECROW 3-D (12/98, $3.95) w/glasses 4.00
...: SCAR OF THE BAT nn (1996, $4.95)-Elseworlds story; Max Allan Collins script; Barreto-a. 5.00
... :SCOTTISH CONNECTION (1998, $5.95) Quitely-a 6.00
... :SEDUCTION OF THE GUN nn (1992, $2.50, 68 pgs.) 2.50
.../SPAWN: WAR DEVIL nn (1994, $4.95, 52 pgs.) 5.00
.../SPIDER-MAN (1997, $4.95) Dematteis-s/Nolan & Kesel-a 5.00
... : THE ABDUCTION ('98, $5.95) 6.00
... :THE BLUE, THE GREY, & THE BAT nn (1992, $5.95, 68 pgs.)-Weiss/Lopez-a 6.00
... :THE KILLING JOKE (1988, deluxe 52 pgs., mature readers)-Bolland-c/a; Alan Moore scripts. 12.00
...: THE KILLING JOKE (2nd thru 8th printings) 3.50
...: THE OFFICIAL COMIC ADAPTATION OF THE WARNER BROS. MOTION PICTURE (1989, $2.50, regular format, 68 pgs.)-Ordway-c. 3.00
...: THE OFFICIAL COMIC ADAPTATION OF THE WARNER BROS. MOTION PICTURE (1989, $4.95, prestige format, 68 pgs.)-same interiors but different-c than regular format. 5.00
...: TWO-FACE-CRIME AND PUNISHMENT-(1995, $4.95)-Scott McDaniel-a 5.00
... : TWO FACES (11/98, $4.95) Elseworlds 5.00
...: VENGEANCE OF BANE SPECIAL 1 (1992, $2.50, 68 pgs.)-Origin & 1st app. Bane (see Batman #491) 1.00 3.00 10.00
...: VENGEANCE OF BANE SPECIAL 1 (2nd printing) 2.50
....:VENGEANCE OF BANE II nn (1995, $3.95)-sequel 4.00
...Vs. THE INCREDIBLE HULK (1995, $3.95)-r/DC Special Series #27 4.00
...: VILLAINS SECRET FILES (10/98, $4.95) Origin-s 5.00

BATMAN ADVENTURES, THE (Based on animated series)
DC Comics: Oct, 1992 - No. 36, Oct, 1995 ($1.25/$1.50)

1-Penguin-c/story 3.00
1 ($1.95, Silver Edition)-2nd printing 2.00
2-6,8-19: 2,12-Catwoman-c/story. 3-Joker-c/story. 5-Scarecrow-c/story. 10-Riddler-c/story. 11-Man-Bat-c/story. 12-Batgirl & Catwoman-c/story. 16-Joker-c/story; begin $1.50-c. 18-Batgirl-c/story. 19-Scarecrow-c/story. 2.50
7-Special edition polybagged with Man-Bat trading card 4.00
20-24,26-32: 26-Batgirl app. 2.00
25-($2.50, 52 pgs.)-Superman app. 2.50
33-36: 33-Begin $1.75-c 2.00
Annual 1,2 ('94, '95): 2-Demon-c/story; Ra's al Ghul app. 3.50
Holiday Special 1 (1995, $2.95) 3.50

GD2.0 FN6.0 NM9.4

The Collected Adventures Vol. 1,2 ('93, '95, $5.95) 6.00
TPB ('98, $7.95) r/#1-6; painted wraparound-c 8.00

BATMAN ADVENTURES, THE: MAD LOVE
DC Comics: Feb, 1994 ($3.95/$4.95)

1-Origin of Harley Quinn; Dini-s/Timm-c/a 1.50 4.50 12.00
1-($4.95, Prestige format) new Timm painted-c 2.40 6.00

BATMAN ADVENTURES, THE: THE LOST YEARS (TV)
DC Comics: Jan, 1998 - No. 5, May, 1998 ($1.95) (Based on animated series)

1-5-Leads into Fall '97's new animated episodes. 4-Tim Drake becomes Robin. 5-Dick becomes Nightwing 3.00

BATMAN/ALIENS
DC Comics/Dark Horse: Mar, 1997 - No. 2, Apr, 1997 ($4.95, lim. series)

1,2: Wrightson-c/a. 5.00
TPB-(1997, $14.95) w/prequel from DHP #101,102 15.00

BATMAN AND ROBIN ADVENTURES (TV)
DC Comics: Nov, 1995 - No. 25, Dec, 1997 ($1.75) (Based on animated series)

1-Dini-s. 5.00
2-24: 2-4-Dini script. 4-Penguin-c/story. 5-Joker-c/story; Poison Ivy, Harley Quinn-c/app. 9-Batgirl & Talia-c/story. 10-Ra's Al Ghul-c/story 11-Man-Bat app. 12-Bane-c/app. 13-Scarecrow-c/app. 15 Deadman-c/app. 16-Catwoman-c/app. 18-Joker-c/app. 24-Poison Ivy app. 3.00
25-($2.95, 48 pgs.) 3.00
Annual 1,2 (11/96, 11/97): 1-Phantasm-c/app. 2-Zatara and Zatanna-c/app. 4.00
...: Sub-Zero(1998, $3.95) Adaption of animated video 4.00

BATMAN AND SUPERMAN ADVENTURES: WORLD'S FINEST
DC Comics: 1997 ($6.95, square-bound, one-shot) (Based on animated series)

1-Adaption of animated crossover episode; Dini-s/Timm-c. 7.00

BATMAN AND SUPERMAN: WORLD'S FINEST
DC Comics: Apr, 1999 - No. 10 ($4.95/$1.99, limited series)

1-($4.95, squarebound) Taylor-a 5.00
2-6-($1.99) 5-Batgirl app. 2.00

BATMAN AND THE OUTSIDERS (The Adventures of the Outsiders#33 on) (Also see Brave & The Bold #200 & The Outsiders) (Replaces The Brave and the Bold)
DC Comics: Aug, 1983 - No. 32, Apr, 1986 (Mando paper #5 on)

1-Batman, Halo, Geo-Force, Katana, Metamorpho & Black Lightning begin. 3.00
2-32: 5-New Teen Titans x-over. 9-Halo begins. 11,12-Origin Katana. 18-More facts about Metamorpho's origin. 28-31-Lookers origin. 32-Team disbands 2.00
Annual 1,2 (9/84, 9/85): 2-Metamorpho & Sapphire Stagg wed 2.50

NOTE: ***Aparo*** *a-1-9, 11-13p, 16-20; c-1-4, 5i, 6-21, Annual 1, 2.* ***B. Kane*** *a-3r.* ***Layton*** *a-19i, 20i.* ***Lopez*** *a-3p. Miller c-Annual 1.* ***Perez*** *c-5p.* ***B. Willingham*** *a-14p.*

BATMAN: BANE OF THE DEMON
DC Comics: Mar, 1998 - No. 4, June, 1998 ($1.95, limited series)

1-4-Dixon-s/Nolan-a; prelude to Legacy x-over 2.00

BATMAN BEYOND (Based on animated series)(Mini-series)
DC Comics: Mar, 1999 - No. 6, Aug, 1999 ($1.99)

1-6: 1,2-Adaption of pilot episode, Timm-c 2.00

BATMAN BEYOND (Based on animated series)(Continuing series)
DC Comics: Nov, 1999 - Present ($1.99)

1-Rousseau-a; Batman vs. Batman 2.00

BATMAN: BLACK & WHITE
DC Comics: June, 1996 - No. 4, Sept, 1996 ($2.95, B&W, limited series)

1-Stories by McKeever, Timm, Kubert, Chaykin, Goodwin; Jim Lee-c; Allred inside front-c; Moebius inside back-c 4.00
2-4: 2-Stories by Simonson, Corben, Bisley & Gaiman; Miller-c. 3-Stories by M. Wagner, Janson, Sienkiewicz, O'Neil & Kristiansen; B. Smith-c; Russell inside front-c; Silvestri inside back-c. 4-Stories by Bolland, Goodwin & Gianni,

Batman: Dark Victory #1 © DC

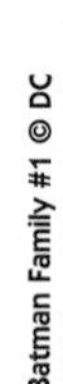

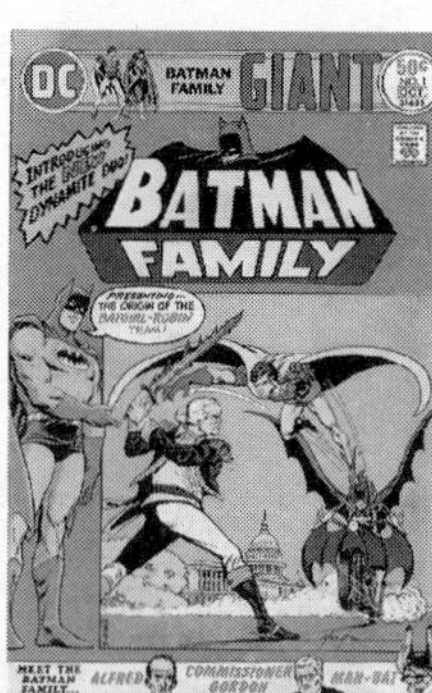

Batman Family #1 © DC

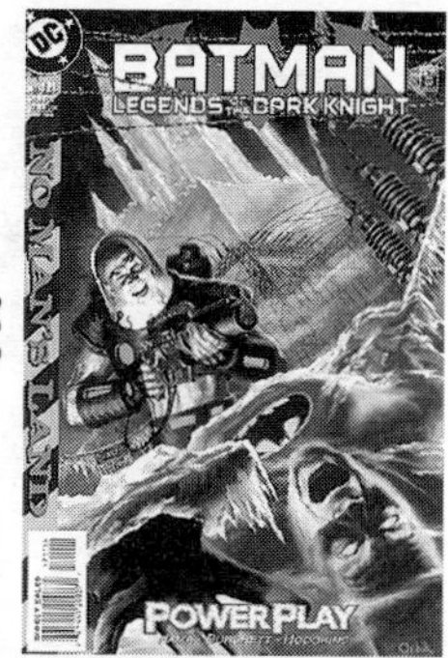

Batman: Legends of the Dark Knight #121 © DC

GD2.0 FN6.0 NM9.4

Strnad & Nowlan, O'Neil & Stelfreeze; Toth-c; pin-ups by Neal Adams & Alex Ross 3.00
Hardcover ('97, $39.95) r/series w/new art & cover plate 40.00

BATMAN: BOOK OF THE DEAD
DC Comics: Jun, 1999 - No. 2, July, 1999 ($4.95, limited series, prestige format)
1,2-Elseworlds; Kitson-a 5.00

BATMAN: CATWOMAN DEFIANT (See Batman one-shots)

BATMAN CHRONICLES, THE
DC Comics: Summer, 1995 - Present ($2.95, quarterly)
1-3,5-18: 1-Dixon/Grant/Moench script. 3-Bolland-c. 5-Oracle Year One story, Richard Dragon app.,Chaykin-c. 6-Kaluta-c; Ra's Al Ghul story. 7-Superman-c /app.11-Paul Pope-s/a. 12-Cataclysm pt. 10. 18-No Man's Land 3.50
4-Hitman story by Ennis, Contagion tie-in; Balent-c 1.10 3.30 9.00
...Gallery (3/97, $3.50) Pin-ups 3.50
...Gauntlet, The (1997, $4.95, one-shot) 5.00

BATMAN: DARK KNIGHT OF THE ROUND TABLE
DC Comics: 1999 - No. 2, 1999 ($4.95, limited series, prestige format)
1,2-Elseworlds; Giordano-a 5.00

BATMAN: DARK VICTORY
DC Comics: 1999 - No. 12, 2000 ($4.95/$1.95, limited series)
Wizard #0 Preview 1.00
1-($4.95) Loeb-s/Sale-c/a 5.00

BATMAN FAMILY, THE
National Periodical Pub./DC Comics: Sept-Oct, 1975 - No. 20, Oct-Nov, 1978 (#1-4, 17-on: 68 pgs.) (Combined with Detective Comics with No. 481)
1-Origin/2nd app. Batgirl-Robin team-up (The Dynamite Duo); reprints plus one new story begins; N. Adams-a(r); r/1st app. Man-Bat from Det. #400 2.00 6.00 16.00
2-5: 2-r/Det. #369. 3-Batgirl & Robin learn each's i.d.; r/Batwoman app. from Batman #105. 4-r/1st Fatman app. from Batman #113. 5-r/1st Bat-Hound app. from Batman #92 1.25 3.75 10.00
6,9-Joker's daughter on cover (1st app?) 1.75 5.25 14.00
7,8,14-16: 8-r/Batwoman app.14-Batwoman app. 15-3rd app. Killer Moth. 16-Bat-Girl cameo (last app. in costume until New Teen Titans #47) 1.00 3.00 8.00
10-1st revival Batwoman; Cavalier app.; Killer Moth app. 1.85 5.50 15.00
11-20: 11-13-Rogers-a(p): 11-New stories begin; Man-Bat begins. 13-Batwoman cameo. 17-($1.00 size)-Batman, Huntress begin; Batwoman & Catwoman 1st meet. 18-20: Huntress by Staton in all. 20-Origin Ragman retold 1.50 4.50 12.00
NOTE: ***Aparo** a-17; c-11-16. **Austin** a-12i. **Chaykin** a-14p. **Michael Golden** a-15-17,18-20p. **Grell** a-1; c-1. **Gil Kane** a-2r. **Kaluta** c-17, 19. **Newton** a-13. **Robinson** a-1r, 3i(r), 9r. **Russell** a-18i, 19i. **Starlin** a-17; c-18, 20.*

BATMAN: GCPD
DC Comics: Aug, 1996 - No. 4, Nov, 1996 ($2.25, limited series)
1-4: Features Jim Gordon; Aparo/Sienkiewicz-a 2.25

BATMAN: GORDON OF GOTHAM
DC Comics: June, 1998 - No. 4, Sept, 1998 ($1.95, limited series)
1-4: Gordon's early days in Chicago 2.25

BATMAN: GORDON'S LAW
DC Comics: Dec, 1996 - No. 3, Feb, 1997 ($1.95, limited series)
1-3: Dixon-s/Janson-c/a 2.00

BATMAN: GOTHAM ADVENTURES (TV)
DC Comics: June, 1998 - Present ($2.95/$1.95)
1-($2.95) Based on Kids WB Batman animated series 3.00
2-3-($1.95): 2-Two-Face-c/app. 2.50
4-17: 4-Begin $1.99-c. 5-Deadman-c. 13-MAD #1 cover swipe 2.50

BATMAN: GOTHAM NIGHTS II (First series listed under Gotham Nights)
DC Comics: Mar, 1995 - No. 4, June, 1995 ($1.95, limited series)

GD2.0 FN6.0 NM9.4

1-4 2.00

BATMAN/GRENDEL (1st limited series)
DC Comics: 1993 - No. 2, 1993 ($4.95, limited series, squarebound; 52 pgs.)
1,2: Batman vs. Hunter Rose. 1-Devil's Riddle; Matt Wagner-c/a/scripts. 2-Devil's Masque; Matt Wagner-c/a/scripts 2.40 6.00

BATMAN/GRENDEL (2nd limited series)
DC Comics: June, 1996 - No. 2, July, 1996 ($4.95, limited series, squarebound)
1,2: Batman vs. Grendel Prime. 1-Devil's Bones; Matt Wagner-c/a/s 5.00

BATMAN: HARLEY QUINN
DC Comics: 1999 ($5.95, prestige format)
1-Intro. of Harley Quinn into regular DC continuity; Dini-s/Alex Ross-c 8.00
1-(2nd printing) 6.00

BATMAN/ HELLBOY/STARMAN
DC Comics/Dark Horse: Jan, 1999 - No. 2, Feb, 1999 ($2.50, limited series)
1,2: Robinson-s/Mignola-a. 2-Harris-c 2.50

BATMAN/ JUDGE DREDD "DIE LAUGHING"
DC Comics: 1998 - No. 2, 1999 ($4.95, limited series, squarebound)
1,2: 1-Fabry-c/a. 2-Jim Murray-c/a 5.00

BATMAN: KNIGHTGALLERY (See Batman one-shots)

BATMAN: LEGENDS OF THE DARK KNIGHT (Legends of the Dark...#1-36)
DC Comics: Nov, 1989 - Present ($1.50/$1.75/$1.95/$1.99)
1- "Shaman" begins, ends #5; outer cover has four different color variations, all worth same 5.00
2-10- "Gothic" by Grant Morrison (scripts) 3.00
11-15: 11-15-Gulacy/Austin-a. 13-Catwoman app. 3.00
16-Intro drug Bane uses; begin Venom story 1.00 2.80 7.00
17-20 5.00
21-49,51-63: 38-Bat-Mite-c/story. 46-49-Catwoman app. w/Heath-c/a. 51-Ragman app.; Joe Kubert-c. 59,60,61-Knightquest x-over. 62,63-KnightsEnd Pt. 4 & 10 3.00
50-($3.95, 68 pgs.)-Bolland embossed gold foil-c; Joker-c/story; pin-ups by Chaykin, Simonson, Williamson, Kaluta, Russell, others 5.00
64,0,65-99: 64-(9/94)-Begin $1.95-c. 0-(10/94)-Quesada/Palmiotti-c; various artists on story. 71-73-James Robinson-s, J. Watkiss-c/a. 74,75-Ted McKeever-c/a/s. 76-78-Scott Hampton-c/a/s. 81-Card insert. 83,84-Ellis-s. 85-Robinson-s. 91-93-Ennis-s. 94-Michael T. Gilbert-s/a. 3.00
100-($3.95) Alex Ross painted-c; gallery by various 5.00
101-115: 101-Ezquerra-a. 102-104-Robinson-s 2.50
116-No Man's Land stories begin; Huntress-c 4.00
117-125: 120-ID of new Batgirl revealed. 122-Harris-c 3.00
126-128 2.00
Annual 1-7 ('91-'97, $3.50-$3.95, 68 pgs.): 1-Joker app. 2-Netzer-c/a. 3-New Batman (Azrael) app. 4-Elseworlds story. 5-Year One; Man-Bat app. 6-Legend of the Dead Earth story. 7-Pulp Heroes story 4.00
Halloween Special 1 (12/93, $6.95, 84 pgs.)-Embossed & foil stamped-c 1.00 3.00 8.00
Batman Madness-...Halloween Special (1994, $4.95) 5.00
Batman Ghosts-...Halloween Special (1995, $4.95) 5.00
NOTE: ***Aparo** a-Annual 1. **Chaykin** scripts-24-26. **Giffen** a-Annual 1. **Golden** a-Annual 1. **Alan Grant** scripts-38, 52, 53. **Gil Kane** c/a-24-26. **Mignola** a-54; c-54, 62. **Morrow** a-Annual 3i. **Quesada** a-Annual 1. **James Robinson** scripts- 71-73. **Russell** c/a-42, 43. **Sears** a-21, 23; c-21, 23. **Zeck** a-69, 70; c-69, 70.*

BATMAN-LEGENDS OF THE DARK KNIGHT: JAZZ
DC Comics: Apr, 1995 - No. 3, June, 1995 ($2.50, limited series)
1-3 2.50

BATMAN: MANBAT
DC Comics: Oct, 1995 - No. 3, Dec, 1995 ($4.95, limited series)
1-3-Elseworlds-Delano-script; Bolton-a. 5.00
TPB-(1997, $14.95) r/#1-3 15.00

BATMAN: MITEFALL (See Batman one-shots)

BATMAN MINIATURE (See Batman Kellogg's)

Batman: No Man's Land #0 © DC

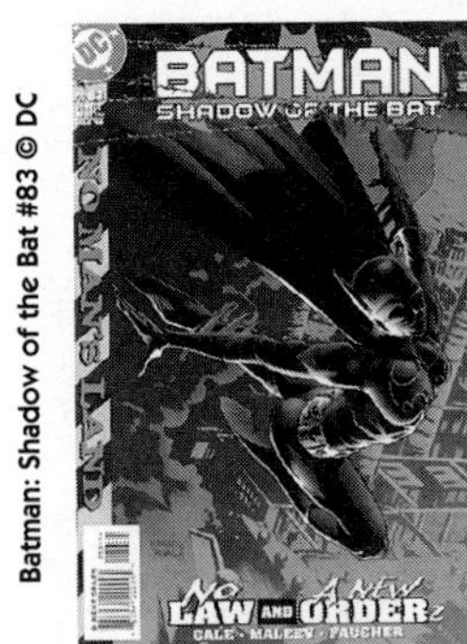

Batman: Shadow of the Bat #83 © DC

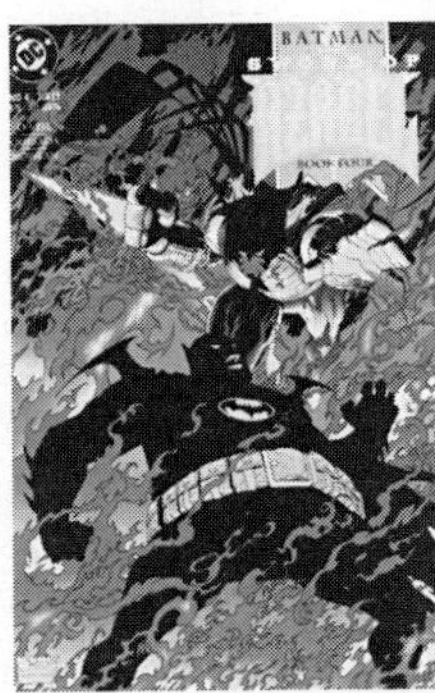

Batman: Sword of Azrael #4 © DC

GD2.0 FN6.0 NM9.4

BATMAN: NO MAN'S LAND (Also see 1999 Batman titles)
DC Comics: (one shots)

nn (3/99, $2.95) Alex Ross-c; Bob Gale-s; begins year-long story arc 3.00
Collector's Ed. (3/99, $3.95) Ross lenticular-c 5.00
#0 (: Ground Zero on cover) (12/99, $4.95) Orbik-c 5.00
...: Gallery (7/99, $3.95) Jim Lee-c 4.00
...: Secret Files (12/99, $4.95) Maleev-c 5.00
TPB ('99, $12.95) r/early No Man's Land stories; new Batgirl early app.
No Law and a New Order TPB(1999, $5.95) Ross-c 6.00

BATMAN: PENGUIN TRIUMPHANT (See Batman one-shots)

BATMAN/PREDATOR III: BLOOD TIES
DC Comics/Dark Horse Comics: Nov, 1997 - No. 4, Feb, 1998 ($1.95, lim. series)

1-4: Dixon-s/Damaggio-c/a 2.00
TPB-(1998, $7.95) r/#1-4 8.00

BATMAN RETURNS MOVIE SPECIAL (See Batman one-shots)

BATMAN: RIDDLER-THE RIDDLE FACTORY (See Batman one-shots)

BATMAN: RUN, RIDDLER, RUN
DC Comics: 1992 - Book 3, 1992 ($4.95, limited series)

Book 1-3: Mark Badger-a & plot 5.00

BATMAN: SECRET FILES
DC Comics: Oct, 1997 ($4.95)

1-New origin-s and profiles 5.00

BATMAN: SHADOW OF THE BAT
DC Comics: June, 1992 - No. 94, Feb, 2000 ($1.50/$1.75/$1.95/$1.99)

1-The Last Arkham-c/story begins; Alan Grant scripts in all 4.00
1-($2.50)-Deluxe edition polybagged w/poster, pop-up & book mark 5.00
2-7: 4-The Last Arkham ends. 7-Last $1.50-c 3.00
8-28: 14,15-Staton-a(p). 16-18-Knightfall tie-ins. 19-28-Knightquest tie-ins w/Azrael as Batman. 19,20-Painted-c. 25-Silver ink-c; anniversary issue 2.50
29-($2.95, 52 pgs.)-KnightsEnd Pt. 2 3.00
30,31,0,32-72: 30-KnightsEnd Pt. 8. 31-(9.94)-Begin $1.95-c; Zero Hour. 0-(10/94). 32-(11/94). 33-Robin-c. 35-Troika-Pt.2. 43,44-Cat-Man & Catwoman-c. 48-Contagion Pt. 1; card insert. 49-Contagion Pt.7. 56,57,58-Poison Ivy-c/app. 62-Two-Face app. 69,70-Fate app. 2.50
35-($2.95)-Variant embossed-c 3.00
73,74,76-78: Cataclysm x-over pts. 1,9. 76-78-Orbik-c 2.00
75-($2.95) Mr. Freeze & Clayface app.; Orbik-c 3.00
79,81,82: 79-Begin $1.99-c; Orbik-c 2.00
80-($3.95) Flip book with Azrael #47 5.00
83-No Man's Land; intro. new Batgirl (Huntress) 12.00
84,85-No Man's Land 4.00
86-94: 87-Deodato-a. 90-Harris-c. 92-Superman app. 3.00
#1,000,000 (11/98) 853rd Century x-over; Orbik-c 2.00
Annual 1-5 ('93-'97 $2.95-$3.95, 68 pgs.): 3-Year One story; Poison Ivy app. 4-Legends of the Dead Earth story; Starman cameo. 5-Pulp Heroes story; Poison Ivy app. 4.00

BATMAN-SPAWN: WAR DEVIL (See Batman one-shots)

BATMAN SPECTACULAR (See DC Special Series No. 15)

BATMAN: SWORD OF AZRAEL (Also see Azrael & Batman #488,489)
DC Comics: Oct, 1992 - No. 4, Jan, 1993 ($1.75, limited series)

1-Wraparound gatefold-c; Quesada-c/a(p) in all; 1st app. Azrael 1.00 3.00 8.00
2-4: 4-Cont'd in Batman #488 5.00
Silver Edition 1-4 (1993, $1.95)-Reprints #1-4 2.00
Trade Paperback (1993, $9.95)-Reprints #1-4 10.00
Trade Paperback Gold Edition 15.00

BATMAN: THE CULT
DC Comics: 1988 - No. 4, Nov, 1988 ($3.50, deluxe limited series)

1-Wrightson-a/painted-c in all 5.00
2-4 4.00
Trade Paperback ('91, $14.95)-New Wrightson-c 15.00

BATMAN: THE DARK KNIGHT RETURNS
DC Comics: Mar, 1986 - No. 4, 1986 ($2.95, squarebound, limited series)

1-Miller story & c/a(p); set in the future 3.00 9.00 30.00
1,2-2nd & 3rd printings, 3-2nd printing 2.40 6.00
2-Carrie Kelly becomes 1st female Robin 1.85 5.50 15.00
3-Death of Joker; Superman app. 1.10 3.30 9.00
4-Death of Alfred; Superman app. 1.00 2.80 7.00
Hard-c, signed & numbered edition ($40.00)(4000 copies) 250.00
Hard-c, trade edition 40.00
Soft-c, trade edition (1st printing only) 1.85 5.50 15.00
Soft-c, trade edition (2nd thru 8th printings) 1.10 3.30 9.00
10th Anniv. Slipcase set ('96, $100.00): Signed & numbered hard-c edition (10,000 copies), sketchbook, copy of script for #1, 2 colorprints 100.00
10th Anniv. Hard-c ('96, $45.00) 45.00
10th Anniv. Soft-c ('97, $14.95) 15.00
NOTE: *The #2 second printings can be identified by matching the grey background colors on the inside front cover and facing page. The inside front cover of the second printing has a dark grey background which does not match the lighter grey of the facing page. On the true 1st printings, the backgrounds are both light grey. All other issues are clearly marked.*

BATMAN: THE KILLING JOKE (See Batman one-shots)

BATMAN: THE LONG HALLOWEEN
DC Comics: Oct, 1996 - No. 13, Oct, 1997 ($2.95/$4.95, limited series)

1-($4.95)-Loeb-s/Sale-c/a in all 1.00 3.00 8.00
2-5($2.95): 2-Solomon Grundy-c/app. 3-Joker-c/app., Catwoman, Poison Ivy app. 2.00 6.00
6-10: 6-Poison Ivy-c. 7-Riddler-c/app. 5.00
11,12 4.00
13-($4.95, 48 pgs.)-Killer revelations 5.00
HC-($29.95) r/series 30.00
SC-($19.95) 20.00

BATMAN: THE OFFICIAL COMIC ADAPTATION OF THE WARNER BROS. MOTION PICTURE (See Batman one-shots)

BATMAN: THE ULTIMATE EVIL
DC Comics: 1995 ($5.95, limited series, prestige format)

1,2-Barrett, Jr. adaptation of Vachss novel. 6.00

BATMAN 3-D (Also see 3-D Batman)
DC Comics: 1990 ($9.95, w/glasses, 8-1/8x10-3/4")

nn-Byrne-a/scripts; Riddler, Joker, Penguin & Two-Face app. plus r/1953 3-D Batman; pin-ups by many artists 1.50 4.50 12.00

BATMAN: TOYMAN
DC Comics: Nov, 1998 - No. 4, Feb, 1999 ($2.25, limited series)

1-4-Hama-s 2.25

BATMAN: TWO-FACE-CRIME AND PUNISHMENT (See Batman one-shots)

BATMAN: TWO-FACE STRIKES TWICE
DC Comics: 1993 - No. 2, 1993 ($4.95, 52 pgs.)

1,2-Flip book format w/Staton-a (G.A. side) 5.00

BATMAN VERSUS PREDATOR
DC Comics/Dark Horse Comics: 1991 - No. 3, 1992 ($4.95/$1.95, limited series) (1st DC/Dark Horse x-over)

1 (Prestige format, $4.95)-1 & 3 contain 8 Batman/Predator trading cards; Andy & Adam Kubert-a; Suydam painted-c 6.00
1-3 (Regular format, $1.95)-No trading cards 4.00
2,3-(Prestige)-2-Extra pin-ups inside; Suydam-c 5.00
TPB (1993, $5.95, 132 pgs.)-r/#1-3 w/new introductions & forward plus new wraparound-c by Gibbons 6.00

BATMAN VERSUS PREDATOR II: BLOODMATCH
DC Comics: Late 1994 - No. 4, 1995 ($2.50, limited series)

1-4-Huntress app.; Moench scripts; Gulacy-a 2.50
TPB (1995, $6.95)-r/#1-4 7.00

Battle #4 © MAR

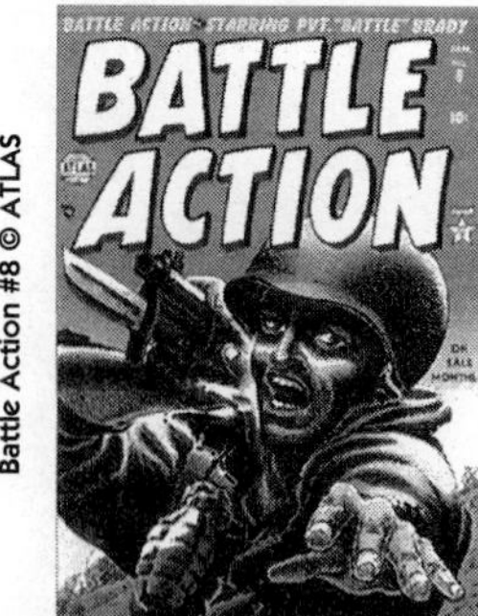

Battle Action #8 © ATLAS

Battle Chasers #4 © Joe Madureira

BATMAN VS. THE INCREDIBLE HULK (See DC Special Series No. 27)

BATMAN/ WILDCAT
DC Comics: Apr, 1997 - No.3, June, 1997 ($2.25, mini-series)

	GD2.0	FN6.0	NM9.4
1-3: Dixon/Smith-s: 1-Killer Croc app.			2.25

BAT MASTERSON (TV) (Also see Tim Holt #28)
Dell Publishing Co.: Aug-Oct, 1959; Feb-Apr, 1960 - No. 9, Nov-Jan, 1961-62

	GD2.0	FN6.0	NM9.4
Four Color 1013 (#1) (8-10/59)	11.00	34.00	125.00
2-9: Gene Barry photo-c on all. 2-Two different back-c exist	5.50	16.50	60.00

BATS (See Tales Calculated to Drive You Bats)

BATS, CATS & CADILLACS
Now Comics: Oct, 1990 - No. 2, Nov, 1990 ($1.75)

	GD2.0	FN6.0	NM9.4
1,2: 1-Gustovich-a(i); Snyder-c			2.00

BAT-THING
DC Comics (Amalgam): June, 1997 ($1.95, one-shot)

	GD2.0	FN6.0	NM9.4
1-Hama-s/Damaggio & Sienkiewicz-a			2.00

BATTLE
Marvel/Atlas Comics(FPI #1-62/ Male #63 on): Mar, 1951 - No. 70, Jun, 1960

	GD2.0	FN6.0	NM9.4
1	29.00	86.00	200.00
2	13.00	39.00	90.00
3-10: 4-1st Buck Pvt. O'Toole. 10-Pakula-a	10.00	30.00	65.00
11-20: 11-Check-a	8.35	25.00	50.00
21,23-Krigstein-a	10.00	30.00	60.00
22,24-36: 32-Tuska-a. 36-Everett-a	6.35	19.00	38.00
37-Kubert-a (Last precode, 2/55)	7.00	21.00	42.00
38-40,42-48	5.35	16.00	32.00
41,49: 41-Kubert/Moskowitz-a. 49-Davis-a	7.00	21.00	42.00
50-54,56-58	5.00	15.00	30.00
55-Williamson-a (5 pgs.)	7.50	22.50	45.00
59-Torres-a	5.85	17.50	35.00
60-62: 60,62-Combat Kelly app. 61-Combat Casey app.	5.00	15.00	30.00
63-Ditko-a	10.00	30.00	60.00
64-66-Kirby-a. 66-Davis-a; has story of Fidel Castro in pre-Communism days (an admiring profile)	10.00	30.00	70.00
67,68: 67-Williamson/Crandall-a (4 pgs.); Kirby, Davis-a. 68-Kirby/Williamson-a (4 pgs.); Kirby/Ditko-a	11.00	33.00	75.00
69,70: 69-Kirby-a. 70-Kirby/Ditko-a	10.00	30.00	65.00

NOTE: ***Andru*** *a-37.* ***Berg*** *a-38, 14, 60-62.* ***Colan*** *a-33, 55.* ***Everett*** *a-36, 50, 70; c-56, 57.* ***Heath*** *a-6, 9, 13, 31, 69; c-6, 9, 12, 26, 35, 37.* ***Kirby*** *c-64-69.* ***Maneely*** *a-4, 6, 31, 61; c-4, 33, 59, 61.* ***Orlando*** *a-47.* ***Powell*** *a-53, 55.* ***Reinman*** *a-8, 9, 26, 32.* ***Robinson*** *a-9, 39.* ***Romita*** *a-26.* ***Severin*** *a-28, 32-34, 66-69; c-36, 55.* ***Sinnott*** *a-33, 37.* ***Woodbridge*** *a-52, 55.*

BATTLE ACTION
Atlas Comics (NPI): Feb, 1952 - No. 12, 5/53; No. 13, 11/54 - No. 30, 8/57

	GD2.0	FN6.0	NM9.4
1-Pakula-a	23.00	69.00	160.00
2	11.50	34.00	80.00
3,4,6,7,9,10: 6-Robinson-c/a. 7-Partial nudity	7.00	21.00	42.00
5-Used in **POP**, pg. 93,94	7.50	22.50	45.00
8-Krigstein-a	8.35	25.00	50.00
11-15 (Last precode, 2/55)	7.00	21.00	42.00
16-29: 27,30-Torres-a	6.35	19.00	38.00

NOTE: *Battle Brady app. 5-7, 10-12.* ***Berg*** *a-3.* ***Check*** *a-11.* ***Everett*** *a-7; c-13, 25.* ***Heath*** *a-3, 8, 18; c-3,15, 18, 21.* ***Maneely*** *a-1; c-5.* ***Reinman*** *a-1.* ***Robinson*** *a-6, 7; c-6.* ***Shores*** *a-7(2).* ***Sinnott*** *a-3.* ***Woodbridge*** *a-28, 30.*

BATTLE ATTACK
Stanmor Publications: Oct, 1952 - No. 8, Dec, 1955

	GD2.0	FN6.0	NM9.4
1	10.00	30.00	65.00
2	5.85	17.50	35.00
3-8: 3-Hollingsworth-a	4.15	12.50	25.00

BATTLE BEASTS
Blackthorne Publishing: Feb, 1988 - No. 4, 1988 ($1.50/$1.75, B&W/color)

	GD2.0	FN6.0	NM9.4
1-4: 1-3- (B&W)-Based on Hasbro toys. 4-Color			2.00

BATTLE BRADY (Formerly Men in Action No. 1-9; see 3-D Action)
Atlas Comics (IPC): No. 10, Jan, 1953 - No. 14, June, 1953

	GD2.0	FN6.0	NM9.4
10: 10-12-Syd Shores-c	13.00	39.00	90.00
11-Used in **POP**, pg. 95 plus B&W & color illos	9.15	27.00	55.00
12-14	7.50	22.50	45.00

BATTLE CHASERS
Image Comics (Cliffhanger): Apr, 1998 - No. 4, Dec, 1998;
DC Comics (Cliffhanger): No. 5, May, 1999 - Present ($2.50)

	GD2.0	FN6.0	NM9.4
Prelude (2/98)	1.25	3.75	10.00
Prelude Gold Ed.			10.00
1-Madureira & Sharrieff-s/Madureira-a(p)/Charest-c	4.00	10.00	20.00
1-American Ent. Ed. w/"racy" cover	4.00	10.00	20.00
1-Gold Edition			18.00
1-Chromium cover			100.00
1-2nd printing		2.40	6.00
2	1.00	3.00	8.00
2-Dynamic Forces BattleChrome cover	4.00	10.00	20.00
3-Red Monika cover by Madureira			5.00
4-6: 4-Four covers. 6-Back-up by Warren-s/a			4.00
...Collected Edition 1,2 (11/98, 5/99, $5.95) 1-r/#1,2. 2-r/#3,4			6.00

BATTLE CLASSICS (See Cancelled Comic Cavalcade)
DC Comics: Sept-Oct, 1978 (44 pgs.)

	GD2.0	FN6.0	NM9.4
1-Kubert-r; new Kubert-c			5.00

BATTLE CRY
Stanmor Publications: 1952 (May) - No. 20, Sept, 1955

	GD2.0	FN6.0	NM9.4
1	11.50	34.00	80.00
2	6.70	20.00	40.00
3,5-10: 8-Pvt. Ike begins, ends #13,17	4.15	12.50	25.00
4-Classic E.C. swipe	6.35	19.00	38.00
11-20	4.00	11.00	22.00

NOTE: ***Hollingsworth*** *a-9; c-20.*

BATTLEFIELD (War Adventures on the...)
Atlas Comics (ACI): April, 1952 - No. 11, May, 1953

	GD2.0	FN6.0	NM9.4
1-Pakula, Reinman-a	19.00	58.00	135.00
2-5: 2-Heath, Maneely, Pakula, Reinman-a	10.00	30.00	65.00
6-11	6.70	20.00	40.00

NOTE: ***Colan*** *a-11.* ***Everett*** *a-8.* ***Heath*** *a-1, 2, 5p; c-2, 8, 9, 11.* ***Ravielli*** *a-11.*

BATTLEFIELD ACTION (Formerly Foreign Intrigues)
Charlton Comics: No. 16, Nov, 1957 - No. 62, 2-3/66; No. 63, 7/80 - No. 89, 11/84

	GD2.0	FN6.0	NM9.4
V2#16	5.35	16.00	32.00
17,20-30	3.60	9.00	18.00
18,19-Check-a (2 stories in #18)	2.50	7.50	20.00
31-62(1966)	1.85	5.50	15.00
63-80(1983-84)			4.00
81-83,85-89 (Low print run)			5.00
84-Kirby reprints; 3 stories	1.00	2.80	7.00

NOTE: ***Montes/Bache*** *a-43, 55, 62.* ***Glanzman*** *a-87r.*

BATTLE FIRE
Aragon Magazine/Stanmor Publications: Apr, 1955 - No. 7, 1955

	GD2.0	FN6.0	NM9.4
1	8.35	25.00	50.00
2	4.15	12.50	25.00
3-7	3.20	8.00	16.00

BATTLE FOR A THREE DIMENSIONAL WORLD
3D Cosmic Publications: May, 1983 (20 pgs., slick paper w/stiff-c, $3.00)

	GD2.0	FN6.0	NM9.4
nn-Kirby c/a in 3-D; shows history of 3-D		2.40	6.00

BATTLEFORCE
Blackthorne Publishing: Nov, 1987 - No. 2, 1988 ($1.75, color/B&W)

	GD2.0	FN6.0	NM9.4
1,2: Based on game. 1-In color. 2-B&W			2.00

BATTLE FOR INDEPENDENTS, THE (Also See Cyblade/Shi & Shi/Cyblade: The Battle For Independents)

Battlefront #3 © MAR

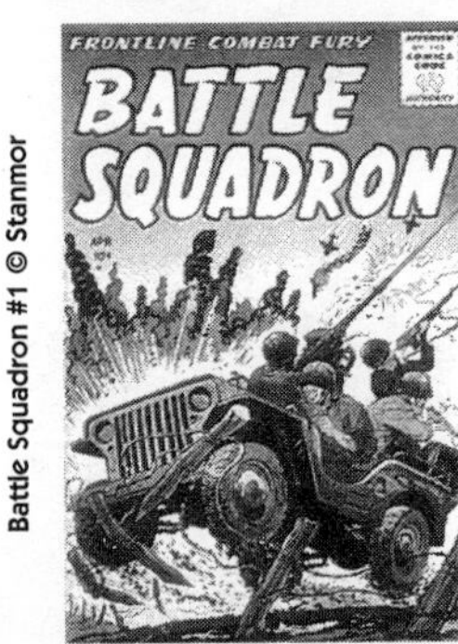

Battle Squadron #1 © Stanmor

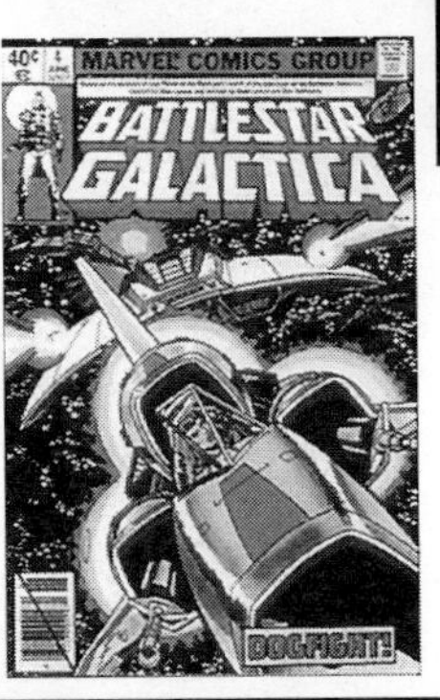

Battlestar Galactica #4 © MAR

GD2.0 FN6.0 NM9.4

Image Comics (Top Cow Productions)/Crusade Comics: 1995 ($29.95)
nn-boxed set of all editions of Shi/Cyblade & Cyblade/Shi plus new variant. 4.00 12.00 40.00

BATTLE FOR THE PLANET OF THE APES (See Power Record Comics)

BATTLEFRONT
Atlas Comics (PPI): June, 1952 - No. 48, Aug, 1957

	GD2.0	FN6.0	NM9.4
1-Heath-c	26.00	77.00	180.00
2-Robinson-a(4)	12.00	36.00	85.00
3-5-Robinson-a(4) in each	10.00	30.00	70.00
6-10: Combat Kelly in No. 6-10	10.00	30.00	60.00
11-22,24-28: 14,16-Battle Brady app. 22-Teddy Roosevelt & His Rough Riders story. 28-Last pre-code (2/55)	6.70	20.00	40.00
23,43-Check-a	7.50	22.50	45.00
29-39,41,44-47	5.35	16.00	32.00
40,42-Williamson-a	8.35	25.00	50.00
48-Crandall-a	6.70	20.00	40.00

NOTE: Ayers *a-19, 32.* **Berg** *a-44.* **Colan** *a-21, 22, 32, 33, 40.* **Drucker** *a-28, 29.* **Everett** *a-44.* **Heath** *c-23, 26, 27, 29, 32.* **Maneely** *a-22, 23; c-2, 13, 22, 35.* **Morisi** *a-42.* **Morrow** *a-41.* **Orlando** *a-47.* **Powell** *a-19, 21, 25, 29, 32, 40, 47.* **Robinson** *a-1-4, 5(4); c-4, 5.* **Robert Sale** *a-19.* **Severin** *a-32; c-40.* **Woodbridge** *a-45, 46.*

BATTLEFRONT
Standard Comics: No. 5, June, 1952

	GD2.0	FN6.0	NM9.4
5-Toth-a	13.50	41.00	95.00

BATTLE GROUND
Atlas Comics (OMC): Sept, 1954 - No. 20, Aug, 1957

	GD2.0	FN6.0	NM9.4
1	19.00	58.00	135.00
2-Jack Katz-a	10.00	30.00	65.00
3,4-Last precode (3/55)	7.50	22.50	45.00
5-8,10	6.70	20.00	40.00
9,11,13,18: 9-Krigstein-a. 11,13,18-Williamson-a in each	9.15	27.00	55.00
12,15-17,19,20	6.35	19.00	38.00
14-Kirby-a	10.00	30.00	60.00

NOTE: **Ayers** *a-13.* **Colan** *a-11, 13.* **Drucker** *a-7, 12, 13, 20.* **Heath** *c-2, 5, 13.* **Maneely** *a-19; c-1, 19.* **Orlando** *a-17.* **Pakula** *a-11.* **Severin** *a-5, 12, 19. c-20.* **Tuska** *a-11.*

BATTLE HEROES
Stanley Publications: Sept, 1966 - No. 2, Nov, 1966 (25¢)

	GD2.0	FN6.0	NM9.4
1,2	1.85	5.50	15.00

BATTLE OF THE BULGE (See Movie Classics)

BATTLE OF THE PLANETS (TV)
Gold Key/Whitman No. 6 on: 6/79 - No. 10, 12/80
(Based on syndicated cartoon by Sandy Frank)

	GD2.0	FN6.0	NM9.4
1: Mortimer a-1-4,7-10	1.10	3.30	9.00
2-6,10		2.40	6.00
7,8(11/80),9 (3-pack only?)	1.50	4.50	12.00

BATTLE REPORT
Ajax/Farrell Publications: Aug, 1952 - No. 6, June, 1953

	GD2.0	FN6.0	NM9.4
1	8.35	25.00	50.00
2-6	5.00	15.00	30.00

BATTLE SQUADRON
Stanmor Publications: April, 1955 - No. 5, Dec, 1955

	GD2.0	FN6.0	NM9.4
1	6.70	20.00	40.00
2-5: 3-Iwo Jima & flag-c	4.00	12.00	24.00

BATTLESTAR GALACTICA (TV) (Also see Marvel Comics Super Special #8)
Marvel Comics Group: Mar, 1979 - No. 23, Jan, 1981

	NM9.4
1: 1-5 adapt TV episodes	5.00
2-23: 1-3-Partial-r	4.00

NOTE: **Austin** *c-9i, 10i.* **Golden** *c-18.* **Simonson** *a(p)-4, 5, 11-13, 15-20, 22, 23; c(p)-4, 5,11-17, 19, 20, 22, 23.*

BATTLESTAR GALACTICA (TV) (Also see Asylum)
Maximum Press: July, 1995 - No.4, Nov, 1995 ($2.50, limited series)

	NM9.4
1-4: Continuation of TV series	4.00
Trade paperback (12/95, $12.95)-reprints series	13.00

BATTLESTAR GALACTICA: APOLLO'S JOURNEY (TV)
Maximum Press: Apr, 1996 - No. 3, June, 1996 ($2.95, limited series)
1-3: Richard Hatch scripts 4.00

BATTLESTAR GALACTICA: JOURNEY'S END (TV)
Maximum Press: Aug, 1996 - No. 4, Nov, 1996 ($2.99, limited series)
1-4-Continuation of the T.V. series 4.00

BATTLESTAR GALACTICA: SPECIAL EDITION (TV)
Maximum Press: Jan, 1997 ($2.99, one-shot)
1-Fully painted; Scalf-c/s/a; r/Asylum 3.00

BATTLESTAR GALACTICA: STARBUCK (TV)
Maximum Press: Dec, 1995 - No. 3, Mar, 1996 ($2.50, limited series)
1-3 3.00

BATTLESTAR GALACTICA: THE COMPENDIUM (TV)
Maximum Press: Feb, 1997 ($2.99, one-shot)
1 3.00

BATTLESTAR GALACTICA: THE ENEMY WITHIN (TV)
Maximum Press: Nov, 1995 - No. 3, Feb, 1996 ($2.50, limited series)
1-3: 3-Indicia reads Feb, 1995 in error. 2.50

BATTLESTAR GALACTICA (TV)
Realm Press: Dec, 1997 - No. 5, July, 1998 ($2.99)

	NM9.4
1-5-Chris Scalf-s/painted-a/c	3.00
...Search For Sanctuary (9/98) Scalf & Kuhoric-s	3.00

BATTLESTAR GALACTICA: SEASON III
Realm Press: June/July, 1999 - Present ($2.99)

	NM9.4
1-3: 1-Kuhoric-s/Scalf & Scott-a; Scalf-c. 2-Covers oby Scalf and Stinsman. 3-Two covers	3.00
1-Variant-c by Jae Lee	3.00
1999 Tour Book (5/99, $2.99)	3.00
1999 Tour Book Convention Edition (6.99)	7.00

BATTLESTONE (Also see Brigade & Youngblood)
Image Comics (Extreme): Nov, 1994 - No. 2, Dec, 1994 ($2.50, limited series)
1,2-Liefeld plots 2.50

BATTLE STORIES (See XMas Comics)
Fawcett Publications: Jan, 1952 - No. 11, Sept, 1953

	GD2.0	FN6.0	NM9.4
1-Evans-a	13.00	39.00	90.00
2	7.50	22.50	45.00
3-11	5.85	17.50	35.00

BATTLE STORIES
Super Comics: 1963 - 1964
Reprints #10-12,15-18: 10-r/U.S Tank Commandos #? 11-r/? 11, 12,17-r/Monty Hall #?; 13-Kintsler-a (1pg).15-r/American Air Forces #7 by Powell; Bolle-r. 18-U.S. Fighting Air Force #? 1.10 3.30 9.00

BATTLETECH (See Blackthorne 3-D Series #41 for 3-D issue)
Blackthorne Publishing: Oct, 1987 - No. 6, 1988 ($1.75/$2.00)

	NM9.4
1-6: Based on game. 1-Color. 2-Begin B&W	2.00
Annual 1 ($4.50, B&W)	4.50

BATTLETECH
Malibu Comics: Feb, 1995 ($2.95)
0 3.00

BATTLETECH FALLOUT
Malibu Comics: Dec, 1994 - No. 4, Mar, 1995 ($2.95)

	FN6.0	NM9.4
1-4-Two edi. exist #1; normal logo		3.00
1-Gold version w/foil logo stamped "Gold Limited Edition		8.00
1-Full-c holographic limited edition	2.40	6.00

BATTLETIDE (Death's Head II & Killpower...)

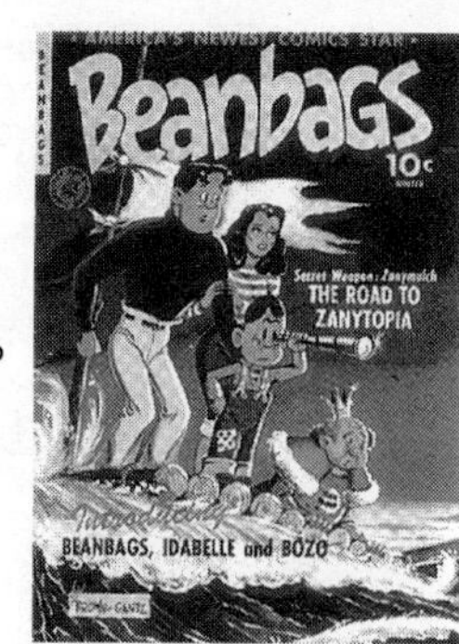

Beanbags #1 © Z-D

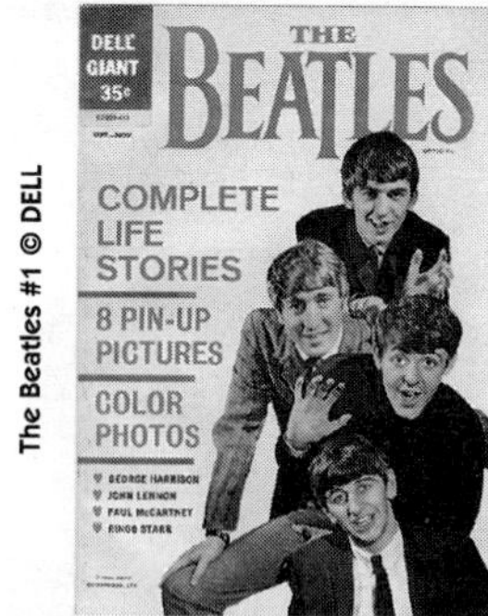

The Beatles #1 © DELL

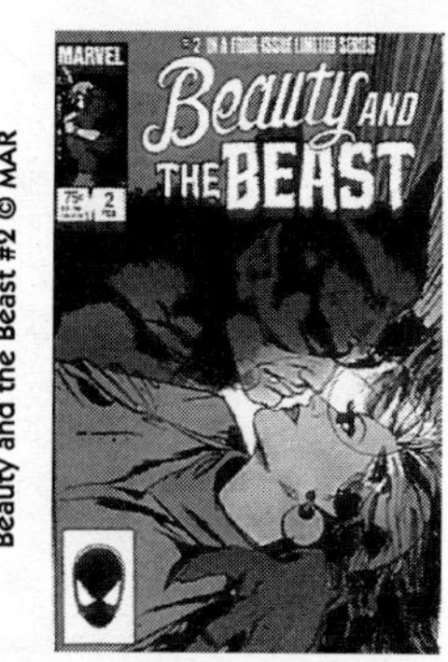

Beauty and the Beast #2 © MAR

GD2.0 FN6.0 NM9.4

Marvel Comics UK, Ltd.: Dec, 1992 - No. 4, Mar, 1993 ($1.75, mini-series)
1-4: Wolverine, Psylocke, Dark Angel app. 2.00

BATTLETIDE II (Death's Head II & Killpower...)
Marvel Comics UK, Ltd.: Aug, 1993 - No. 4, Nov, 1993 ($1.75, mini-series)
1-($2.95)-Foil embossed logo 3.00
2-4: 2-Hulk-c/story 2.00

BATTLEZONES: DREAM TEAM 2 (See Dream Team)
Malibu Comics (Ultraverse): Mar, 1996 ($3.95)
1-pin-ups between Marvel & Malibu characters by Mike Wieringo, Phil Jimenez, Mike McKone, Cully Hamner, Gary Frank & others 4.00

BAYWATCH COMIC STORIES (TV) (Magazine)
Acclaim Comics (Armada): May, 1996 - No. 4, 1997 ($4.95) (Photo-c on all)
1-4: Photo comics based on TV show 5.00

BEACH BLANKET BINGO (See Movie Classics)

BEAGLE BOYS, THE (Walt Disney)(See The Phantom Blot)
Gold Key: 11/64; No. 2, 11/65; No. 3, 8/66 - No. 47, 2/79 (See WDC&S #134)

	GD2.0	FN6.0	NM9.4
1	3.20	9.60	32.00
2-5	2.00	6.00	16.00
6-10	1.50	4.50	12.00
11-20: 11,14,19-r	1.10	3.30	9.00
21-30: 27-r		2.40	6.00
31-47			4.00

BEAGLE BOYS VERSUS UNCLE SCROOGE
Gold Key: Mar, 1979 - No. 12, Feb, 1980

	GD2.0	FN6.0	NM9.4
1	1.25	3.75	10.00
2-12: 9-r			5.00

BEANBAGS
Ziff-Davis Publ. Co. (Approved Comics): Winter, 1951 - No. 2, Spring, 1952

	GD2.0	FN6.0	NM9.4
1,2	10.00	30.00	65.00

BEANIE THE MEANIE
Fago Publications: 1958 - No. 3, May, 1959

	GD2.0	FN6.0	NM9.4
1-3	4.00	12.00	24.00

BEANY AND CECIL (TV) (Bob Clampett's...)
Dell Publishing Co.: Jan, 1952 - 1955; July-Sept, 1962 - No. 5, July-Sept, 1963

	GD2.0	FN6.0	NM9.4
Four Color 368	25.00	75.00	275.00
Four Color 414,448,477,530,570,635(1/55)	16.00	47.00	170.00
01-057-209 (#1)	15.00	45.00	165.00
2-5	10.00	30.00	110.00

BEAR COUNTRY (Disney)
Dell Publishing Co.: No. 758, Dec, 1956

	GD2.0	FN6.0	NM9.4
Four Color 758-Movie	4.50	13.50	50.00

BEAST (See X-Men)
Marvel Comics: May, 1997 - No. 3, 1997 ($2.50, mini-series)
1-3-Giffen-s/Nocon-a 3.00

B.E.A.S.T.I.E.S. (Also see Axis Alpha)
Axis Comics: Apr, 1994 ($1.95)
1-Javier Saltares-c/a/scripts 2.00

BEATLES, THE (See Girls' Romances #109, Go-Go, Heart Throbs #101, Herbie #5, Howard the Duck Mag. #4, Laugh #166, Marvel Comics Super Special #4, My LittleMargie #54, Not Brand Echh, Strange Tales #130, Summer Love, Superman's Pal Jimmy Olsen #79, Teen Confessions #37, Tippy's Friends & Tippy Teen)

BEATLES, THE (Life Story)
Dell Publishing Co.: Sept-Nov, 1964 (35¢)
1-(Scarce)-Stories with color photo pin-ups; Paul S. Newman-s 41.00 123.00 500.00

BEATLES EXPERIENCE, THE
Revolutionary Comics: Mar, 1991 - No. 8, 1991 ($2.50, B&W, limited series)
1-8: 1-Gold logo 3.00

GD2.0 FN6.0 NM9.4

BEATLES YELLOW SUBMARINE (See Movie Comics under Yellow...)

BEAUTIFUL PEOPLE
Slave Labor Graphics: Apr, 1994 ($4.95, 8-1/2x11", one-shot)
nn 5.00

BEAUTIFUL STORIES FOR UGLY CHILDREN
DC Comics (Piranha Press): 1989 - No. 30, 1991 ($2.00/$2.50, B&W, mature)
V1-12-30: 12-$2.50-c begins 2.50
A Cotton Candy Autopsy ($12.95, B&W)-Reprints 1st two volumes 13.00

BEAUTY AND THE BEAST, THE
Marvel Comics Group: Jan, 1985 - No. 4, Apr, 1985 (limited series)
1-4: Dazzler & the Beast from X-Men; Sienkiewicz-c on all 2.00

BEAUTY AND THE BEAST (Graphic novel)(Also see Cartoon Tales & Disney's New Adventures of...)
Disney Comics: 1992
nn-($4.95, prestige edition)-Adapts animated film 5.00
nn-($2.50, newsstand edition) 2.50

BEAUTY AND THE BEAST
Disney Comics: Sept., 1992 - No. 2, 1992 ($1.50, limited series)
1,2 2.00

BEAUTY AND THE BEAST: PORTRAIT OF LOVE (TV)
First Comics: May, 1989 - No. 2, Mar, 1990 ($5.95, 60 pgs., squarebound)
1,2: 1-Based on TV show, Wendy Pini-a/scripts. 2-...: Night of Beauty; by Wendy Pini 2.40 6.00

BEAVER VALLEY (Movie)(Disney)
Dell Publishing Co.: No. 625, Apr, 1955

	GD2.0	FN6.0	NM9.4
Four Color 625	5.50	16.50	60.00

BEAVIS AND BUTTHEAD (MTV's...)(TV cartoon)
Marvel Comics: Mar, 1994 - No. 28, June, 1996 ($1.95)
1-Silver ink-c. 1, 2-Punisher & Devil Dinosaur app. 3.00
1-2nd printing 2.00
2,3: 2-Wolverine app. 3-Man-Thing, Spider-Man, Venom, Carnage, Mary Jane & Stan Lee cameos; John Romita, Sr. art (2 pgs.) 2.00
4-28: 5-War Machine, Thor, Loki, Hulk, Captain America & Rhino cameos. 6-Psylocke, Polaris, Daredevil & Bullseye app. 7-Ghost Rider & Sub-Mariner app. 8-Quasar & Eon app.9-Prowler & Nightwatch app. 11-Black Widow app. 12-Thunderstrike & Bloodaxe app. 13-Night Thrasher app. 14-Spider-Man 2099 app. 15-Warlock app. 16-X-Factor app. 25-Juggernaut app. 2.00

BECK & CAUL INVESTIGATIONS
Gauntlet Comics (Caliber): Jan, 1994 - No. 5, 1995? ($2.95, B&W)
1-5 3.00
Special 1 ($4.95) 5.00

BEDKNOBS AND BROOMSTICKS (See Walt Disney Showcase No. 6 & 50)

BEDLAM!
Eclipse Comics: Sept, 1985 - No. 2, Sept, 1985 (B&W-r in color)
1,2: Bissette-a 2.00

BEDTIME STORY (See Cinema Comics Herald)

BEELZELVIS
Slave Labor Graphics: Feb, 1994 ($2.95, B&W, one-shot)
1 3.00

BEEP BEEP, THE ROAD RUNNER (TV)(See Daffy & Kite Fun Book)
Dell Publishing Co./Gold Key No. 1-88/Whitman No. 89 on: July, 1958 - No. 14, Aug-Oct, 1962; Oct, 1966 - No. 105, 1983

	GD2.0	FN6.0	NM9.4
Four Color 918 (#1, 7/58)	8.50	26.00	95.00
Four Color 1008,1046 (11-1/59-60)	4.40	13.00	48.00
4(2-4/60)-14(Dell)	3.25	10.00	36.00
1(10/66, Gold Key)	4.20	12.60	42.00
2-5	3.00	9.00	30.00
6-14	2.50	7.50	20.00
15-18,20-40	1.85	5.50	15.00

Ben Casey #5 © Bing Crosby Prod.

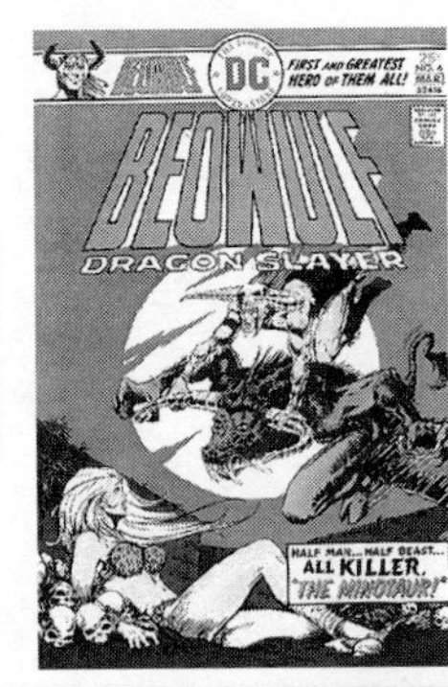

Beowulf #6 © DC

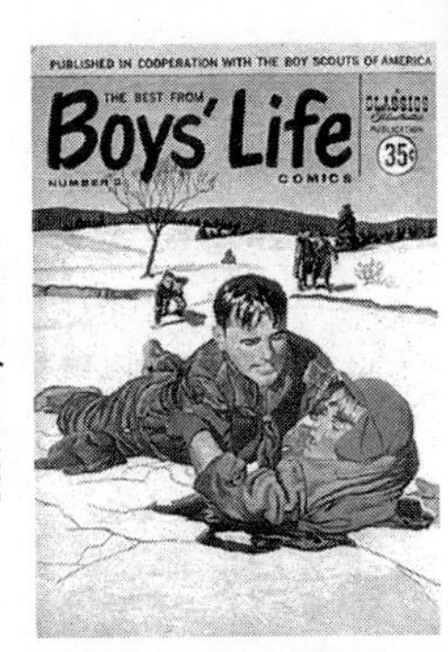

Best of Boy's Life #2 © GIL

	GD2.0	FN6.0	NM9.4
19-With pull-out poster	2.80	8.40	28.00
41-50	1.25	3.75	10.00
51-70	1.00	2.80	7.00
71-88			4.00
89,90,94-101		2.40	6.00
91(8/80), 92(9/80), 93 (3-pack?)	1.25	3.75	10.00
102-105 (All #90189 on-c; nd or date code; pre-pack?)	1.00	3.00	8.00

NOTE: *See March of Comics #351, 353, 375, 387, 397, 416, 430, 442, 455. #5, 8-10, 35, 53, 59-62, 68-r; 96-102, 104 are 1/3-r.*

BEETLE BAILEY (See Comics Reading Library, Giant Comic Album & Sarge Snorkel)
Dell Publishing Co./Gold Key #39-53/King #54-66/Charlton #67-119/ Gold Key #120-131/Whitman #132: #459, 5/53 - #38, 5-7/62; #39, 11/62 - #53, 5/66; #54, 8/66 - #65, 12/67;#67, 2/69 - #119, 11/76; #120, 4/78 - #132, 4/80

	GD2.0	FN6.0	NM9.4
Four Color 469 (#1)-By Mort Walker	9.00	27.00	100.00
Four Color 521,552,622	4.50	13.50	50.00
5(2-4/56)-10(5-7/57)	3.60	11.00	40.00
11-20(4-5/59)	2.75	8.00	30.00
21-38(5-7/62)	2.50	7.50	20.00
39-53(5/66)	2.00	6.00	16.00
54-65 (No. 66 publ. overseas only?)	1.75	5.25	14.00
67-69: 69-Last 12¢ issue	1.50	4.50	12.00
70-99	1.25	3.75	10.00
100	1.65	4.85	13.00
101-119	1.00	2.80	7.00
120-132			4.00

BEETLE BAILEY
Harvey Comics: V2#1, Sept, 1992 - V2#9, Aug, 1994 ($1.25/$1.50)

	GD2.0	FN6.0	NM9.4
V2#1-4			3.00
5-9-($1.50)			2.00
Big Book 1(11/92),2(5/93)(Both $1.95, 52 pgs.)			3.00
Giant Size V2#1(10/92),2(3/93)(Both $2.25,68 pgs.)			3.00

BEETLEJUICE (TV)
Harvey Comics: Oct, 1991 ($1.25)

	GD2.0	FN6.0	NM9.4
1			2.00

BEETLEJUICE CRIMEBUSTERS ON THE HAUNT
Harvey Comics: Sept, 1992 - No. 3, Jan, 1993 ($1.50, limited series)

	GD2.0	FN6.0	NM9.4
1-3			2.00

BEE 29, THE BOMBARDIER
Neal Publications: Feb, 1945

	GD2.0	FN6.0	NM9.4
1-(Funny animal)	23.00	69.00	160.00

BEHIND PRISON BARS
Realistic Comics (Avon): 1952

	GD2.0	FN6.0	NM9.4
1-Kinstler-c	29.00	86.00	200.00

BEHOLD THE HANDMAID
George Pflaum: 1954 (Religious) (25¢ with a 20¢ sticker price)

	GD2.0	FN6.0	NM9.4
nn	4.00	10.00	20.00

BELIEVE IT OR NOT (See Ripley's...)

BEN AND ME (Disney)
Dell Publishing Co.: No. 539, Mar, 1954

	GD2.0	FN6.0	NM9.4
Four Color 539	3.00	9.00	32.00

BEN BOWIE AND HIS MOUNTAIN MEN
Dell Publishing Co.: 1952 - No. 17, Nov-Jan, 1958-59

	GD2.0	FN6.0	NM9.4
Four Color 443 (#1)	5.50	16.50	60.00
Four Color 513,557,599,626,657	2.75	8.00	30.00
7(5-7/56)-11: 11-Intro/origin Yellow Hair	2.75	8.00	30.00
12-17	2.25	6.75	24.00

BEN CASEY (TV)
Dell Publishing Co.: June-July, 1962 - No. 10, June-Aug, 1965 (Photo-c)

	GD2.0	FN6.0	NM9.4
12-063-207 (#1)	4.50	13.50	50.00
2(10/62),3,5-10	3.20	9.60	35.00
4-Marijuana & heroin use story	3.65	11.00	40.00

BEN CASEY FILM STORY (TV)
Gold Key: Nov, 1962 (25¢) (Photo-c)

	GD2.0	FN6.0	NM9.4
30009-211-All photos	7.00	21.00	75.00

BENEATH THE PLANET OF THE APES (See Movie Comics & Power Record Comics)

BEN FRANKLIN (See Kite Fun Book)

BEN HUR
Dell Publishing Co.: No. 1052, Nov, 1959

	GD2.0	FN6.0	NM9.4
Four Color 1052-Movie, Manning-a	9.00	27.00	100.00

BEN ISRAEL
Logos International: 1974 (39¢)

	GD2.0	FN6.0	NM9.4
nn			6.00

BEOWULF (Also see First Comics Graphic Novel #1)
National Periodical Publications: Apr-May, 1975 - No. 6, Feb-Mar, 1976

	GD2.0	FN6.0	NM9.4
1			5.00
2-6: 4-Dracula-c/s. 5-Flying saucer-c/story			4.00

BERLIN
Black Eye Productions: Apr, 1996 - Present ($2.50/$2.95, B&W)

	GD2.0	FN6.0	NM9.4
1-4: Jason Lutes-c/a/scripts.			2.50
5,6-($2.95)			3.00

BERNI WRIGHTSON, MASTER OF THE MACABRE
Pacific Comics/Eclipse Comics No. 5: July, 1983 - No. 5, Nov, 1984 ($1.50, Baxter paper)

	GD2.0	FN6.0	NM9.4
1-5: Wrightson-c/a(r). 4-Jeff Jones-r (11 pgs.)			4.00

BERRYS, THE (Also see Funny World)
Argo Publ.: May, 1956

	GD2.0	FN6.0	NM9.4
1-Reprints daily & Sunday strips & daily Animal Antics by Ed Nofziger	5.00	15.00	30.00

BERZERKERS (See Youngblood V1#2)
Image Comics (Extreme Studios): Aug, 1995 - No. 3, Oct, 1995 ($2.50, limited series)

	GD2.0	FN6.0	NM9.4
1-3: Beau Smith scripts, Fraga-a			2.50

BEST COMICS
Better Publications: Nov, 1939 - No. 4, Feb, 1940(Large size, reads sideways)

	GD2.0	FN6.0	NM9.4
1-(Scarce)-Red Mask begins(1st app.) & c/s-all. Contains 6 pg. Boston Celtics photo story	75.00	225.00	600.00
2-4: 4-Cannibalism story	47.00	141.00	375.00

BEST FROM BOY'S LIFE, THE
Gilberton Company: Oct, 1957 - No. 5, Oct, 1958 (35¢)

	GD2.0	FN6.0	NM9.4
1-Space Conquerors & Kam of the Ancient Ones begin, end #5; Bob Cousy photo/story	10.00	30.00	70.00
2,3,5	6.35	19.00	38.00
4-L.B. Cole-a	7.50	22.50	45.00

BEST LOVE (Formerly Sub-Mariner Comics No. 32)
Marvel Comics (MPI): No. 33, Aug, 1949 - No. 36, April, 1950 (Photo-c 33-36)

	GD2.0	FN6.0	NM9.4
33-Kubert-a	11.00	33.00	75.00
34	6.35	19.00	38.00
35,36-Everett-a	8.00	24.00	48.00

BEST OF BUGS BUNNY, THE
Gold Key: Oct, 1966 - No. 2, Oct, 1968

	GD2.0	FN6.0	NM9.4
1,2-Giants	4.50	13.50	45.00

BEST OF DC, THE (Blue Ribbon Digest) (See Limited Coll. Ed. C-52)
DC Comics: Sept-Oct, 1979 - No. 71, Apr, 1986 (100-148 pgs; mostly reprints)

	GD2.0	FN6.0	NM9.4
1,2,5-9: 1-Superman, w/"Death of Superman"-r. 2-Batman 40th Ann. Special. 5-Best of 1979. 6,8-Superman. 7-Superboy. 9-Batman, Creeper app.		2.40	6.00
3-Superfriends	1.25	3.70	10.00

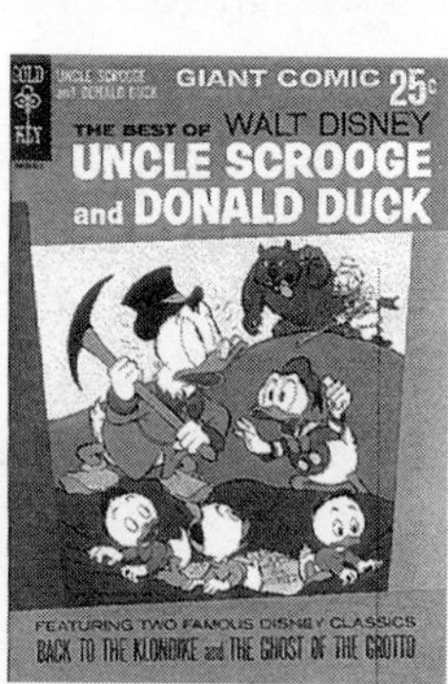

Best of Uncle Scrooge and Donald Duck #1 © WDC

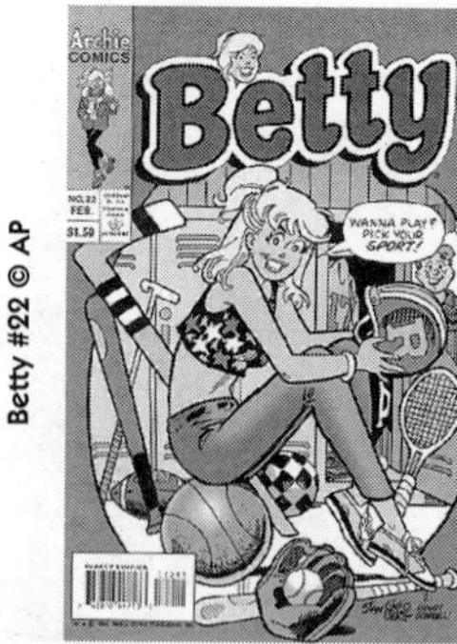

Betty #22 © AP

Betty and Me #16 © AP

GD2.0 FN6.0 NM9.4

4-Rudolph the Red Nosed Reindeer 1.25 3.70 10.00
10-Secret Origins of Super Villains; 1st ever Penguin origin-s 1.85 5.50 15.00
11-20: 11-The Year's Best Stories. 12-Superman Time and Space Stories. 13-Best of DC Comics Presents. 14-Origins of Batman Villains. 15-Superboy 16-Superman Anniv. 17-Supergirl. 18-Teen Titans new-s., Adams, Kane-a; Perez-c. 19-Superman. 20-World's Finest 2.40 6.00
21-Justice Society 1.00 3.00 8.00
22-27: 22-Christmas; unpublished Sandman story w/Kirby-a. 23-(148 pgs.)-Best of 1981. 24 Legion, new story and 16 pgs. new costumes. 25-Superman. 26-Brave & Bold. 27-Superman vs. Luthor 1.00 3.00 8.00
28,29: 28-Binky, Sugar & Spike app. 29-Sugar & Spike, 3 new stories; new Stanley & his Monster story 1.25 3.75 10.00
30-36,38,40: 30-Detective Comics. 31-JLA. 32-Superman. 33-Secret origins of Legion Heroes and Villains. 34-Metal Men; has #497 on-c from Adv. Comics. 35-The Year's Best Comics Stories(148 pgs.). 36-Superman vs. Kryptonite. 38-Superman. 40-World of Krypton 1.00 3.00 8.00
37,39: 37-"Funny Stuff", Mayer-a. 39-Binky 1.25 3.75 10.00
41,43,45,47,49,53,55,58,60,63,65,68,70: 41-Sugar & Spike new stories with Mayer-a. 43,49,55-Funny Stuff. 45,53,70-Binky. 47,58,65,68-Sugar & Spike. 60-Plop!; Wood-c(r) & Aragonés-r (5/85). 63-Plop!; Wrightson-a(r) 1.85 5.50 15.00
42,44,46,48,50-52,54,56,57,59,61,62,64,66,67,69,71: 42,56-Superman vs. Aliens. 44,57,67-Superboy & LSH. 46-Jimmy Olsen. 48-Superman Team-ups 50-Year's best Superman. 51-Batman Family. 52 Best of 1984. 54,56,59-Superman. 61-(148 pgs.)Year's best. 62-Best of Batman 1985. 69-Year's best Team stories. 71-Year's best 1.25 3.75 10.00

NOTE: ***N. Adams*** *a-2r, 14r, 18r, 26, 51.* ***Aparo*** *a-9, 14, 26, 30; c-9, 14, 26.* ***Austin*** *a-51i.* ***Buckler*** *a-40p; c-16, 22.* ***Giffen*** *a-50, 52; c-33p.* ***Grell*** *a-33p.* ***Grossman*** *a-37.* ***Heath*** *a-26.* ***Infantino*** *a-10r, 18.* ***Kaluta*** *a-40.* ***G. Kane*** *a-10r, 18r; c-40, 44.* ***Kubert*** *a-10r, 21, 26.* ***Layton*** *a-21.* ***S. Mayer*** *c-29, 37, 41, 43, 47; a-28, 29, 37, 41, 43, 47, 58, 65, 68.* ***Moldoff*** *c-64p.* ***Morrow*** *a-40; c-40.* ***W. Mortimer*** *a-39p.* ***Newton*** *a-5, 51.* ***Perez*** *a-24, 50p; c-18, 21, 23.* ***Rogers*** *a-14, 51p.* ***Simonson*** *a-11r.* ***Spiegle*** *a-52.* ***Starlin*** *a-51.* ***Staton*** *a-5, 21.* ***Tuska*** *a-24.* ***Wolverton*** *a-60.* ***Wood*** *a-60, 63; c-60, 63.* ***Wrightson*** *a-60. New art in #14, 18, 24.*

BEST OF DENNIS THE MENACE, THE
Hallden/Fawcett Publications: Summer, 1959 - No. 5, Spring, 1961 (100 pgs.)

1-All reprints; Wiseman-a 6.50 19.50 65.00
2-5 4.50 13.50 45.00

BEST OF DONALD DUCK, THE
Gold Key: Nov, 1965 (12¢, 36 pgs.)(Lists 2nd printing in indicia)

1-Reprints Four Color #223 by Barks 6.40 19.00 70.00

BEST OF DONALD DUCK & UNCLE SCROOGE, THE
Gold Key: Nov, 1964 - No. 2, Sept, 1967 (25¢ Giants)

1(30022-411)('64)-Reprints 4-Color #189 & 408 by Carl Barks; cover of F.C. #189 redrawn by Barks 6.40 19.00 70.00
2(30022-709)('67)-Reprints 4-Color #256 & "Seven Cities of Cibola" & U.S. #8 by Barks 6.40 19.00 70.00

BEST OF HORROR AND SCIENCE FICTION COMICS
Bruce Webster: 1987 ($2.00)

1-Wolverton, Frazetta, Powell, Ditko-r 4.00

BEST OF MARMADUKE, THE
Charlton Comics: 1960

1-Brad Anderson's strip reprints 2.60 7.80 26.00

BEST OF MS. TREE, THE
Pyramid Comics: 1987 - No. 4, 1988 ($2.00, B&W, limited series)

1-4 2.00

BEST OF THE BRAVE AND THE BOLD, THE (See Super DC Giant)
DC Comics: Oct, 1988 - No. 6, Jan, 1989 ($2.50, limited series)

1-6: Neal Adams-r, Kubert-r & Heath-r in all 4.00

BEST OF THE WEST (See A-1 Comics)
Magazine Enterprises: 1951 - No. 12, April-June, 1954

1(A-1 42)-Ghost Rider, Durango Kid, Straight Arrow, Bobby Benson begin 40.00 120.00 320.00

GD2.0 FN6.0 NM9.4

2(A-1 46) 21.00 64.00 150.00
3(A-1 52), 4(A-1 59), 5(A-1 66) 18.00 54.00 125.00
6(A-1 70), 7(A-1 76), 8(A-1 81), 9(A-1 85), 10(A-1 87), 11(A-1 97), 12(A-1 103) 13.00 39.00 90.00

NOTE: ***Bolle*** *a-9.* ***Borth*** *a-12.* ***Guardineer*** *a-5, 12.* ***Powell*** *a-1, 12.*

BEST OF UNCLE SCROOGE & DONALD DUCK, THE
Gold Key: Nov, 1966 (25¢)

1(30030-611)-Reprints part 4-Color #159 & 456 & Uncle Scrooge #6,7 by Carl Barks 6.40 19.00 70.00

BEST OF WALT DISNEY COMICS, THE
Western Publishing Co.: 1974 ($1.50, 52 pgs.) (Walt Disney)
(8-1/2x11" cardboard covers; 32,000 printed of each)

96170-Reprints 1st two stories less 1 pg. each from 4-Color #62 2.50 7.60 28.00
96171-Reprints Mickey Mouse and the Bat Bandit of Inferno Gulch from 1934 (strips) by Gottfredson 2.50 7.60 28.00
96172-r/Uncle Scrooge #386 & two other stories 2.50 7.60 28.00
96173-Reprints "Ghost of the Grotto" (from 4-Color #159) & "Christmas on Bear Mountain" (from 4-Color #178) 2.50 7.60 28.00

BEST ROMANCE
Standard Comics (Visual Editions): No. 5, Feb-Mar, 1952 - No. 7, Aug, 1952

5-Toth-a; photo-c 11.50 34.00 80.00
6,7-Photo-c 5.00 15.00 30.00

BEST SELLER COMICS (See Tailspin Tommy)

BEST WESTERN (Formerly Terry Toons? or Miss America Magazine
Marvel Comics (IPC): V7#24(#57)?; Western Outlaws & Sheriffs No. 60 on)
No. 58, June, 1949 - No. 59, Aug, 1949

58,59-Black Rider, Kid Colt, Two-Gun Kid app.; both have Syd Shores-c 20.00 60.00 140.00

BETTIE PAGE COMICS
Dark Horse Comics: Mar, 1996 ($3.95)

1-Dave Stevens-c; Blevins & Heath-a; Jaime Hernandez pin-up 4.50

BETTIE PAGE COMICS: SPICY ADVENTURE
Dark Horse Comics: Jan, 1997 ($2.95, one-shot, mature)

nn-Silke-c/s/a 3.50

BETTY (See Pep Comics #22 for 1st app.)
Archie Comics: Sept, 1992 - Present ($1.25/$1.50/$1.75/$1.79)

1 4.00
2-18,20-24: 20-1st Super Sleuther-s 2.50
19-Love Showdown part 2 4.00
25-Pin-up page of Betty as Marilyn Monroe, Madonna, Lady Di 4.00
26-82: 57- "A Storm Over Uniforms" x-over part 5,6 2.00

BETTY AND HER STEADY (Going Steady with Betty No. 1)
Avon Periodicals: No. 2, Mar-Apr, 1950

2 9.15 27.00 55.00

BETTY AND ME
Archie Publications: Aug, 1965 - No. 200, Aug, 1992

1 9.00 27.00 90.00
2,3: 3-Origin Superteen 4.50 13.50 45.00
4,5,7,8: Superteen in new costume #4-7; dons new helmet in #5, ends #8. 3.00 9.00 30.00
6,10: Girl from R.I.V.E.R.D.A.L.E. 2.50 7.50 22.00
9,11-15,17-20(4/69): 9-UFO-s 1.80 5.40 18.00
16-Classic cover; w/risqué cover dialogue .90 2.70 20.00
21,24-35: 33-Paper doll page 1.10 3.30 9.00
22-Archies Band-s 1.50 4.50 12.00
23-I Dream of Jeannie parody 2.00 6.00 16.00
36(8/71),37,41-55 (52 pgs.) : 42-Betty as vamp-s 1.75 5.25 14.00
38-Sabrina app. 2.50 7.50 20.00
39-Josie and Sabrina cover cameos 2.00 6.00 16.00
40-Archie & Betty share a cabin 2.00 6.00 16.00

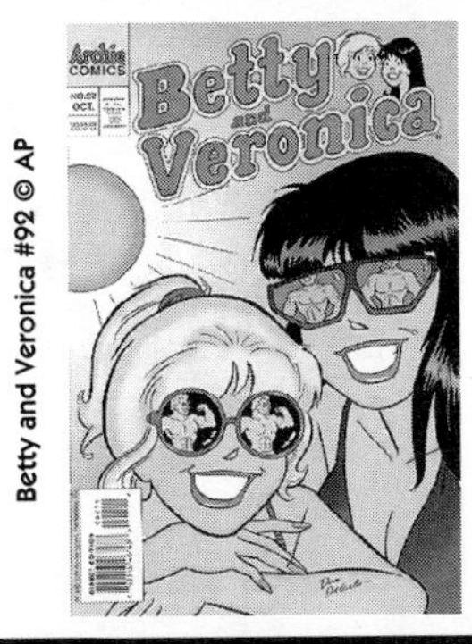

Betty and Veronica #92 © AP

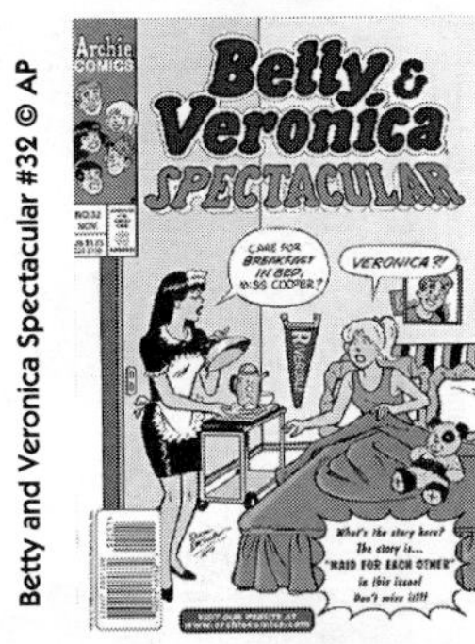

Betty and Veronica Spectacular #32 © AP

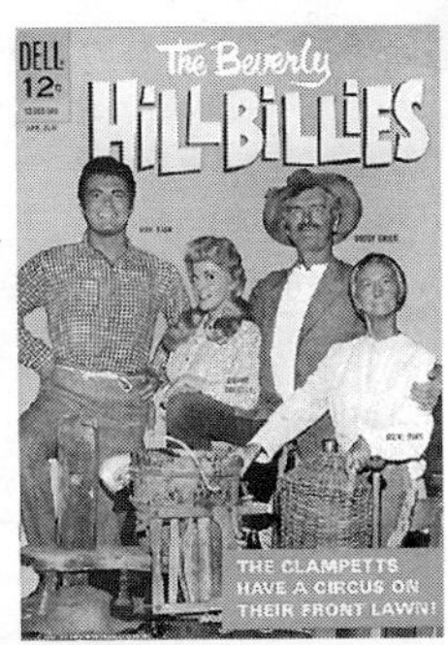

Beverly Hillbillies #9 © Filmway

56(4/71)-80(12/76): 79 Betty Cooper mysteries thru #86. 79-81-Drago the Vampire-s 1.00 2.80 7.00
81-99: 83-Harem-c. 84-Jekyll & Hyde-c/s 5.00
100(3/79) 1.00 2.80 7.00
101,118: 101-Elvis mentioned. 118-Tarzan mentioned 4.00
102-117,119-130(9/82): 103,104-Space-s. 124-DeCarlo-c begins 3.50
131-138,140,142-147,149-154,156-158: 135,136-Jason Blossom app. 136-Cheryl Blossom cameo. 137-Space-s. 138-Tarzan parody 2.50
139,141,148: 139-Katy Keene collecting-s; Archie in drag-s. 141-Tarzan parody-s. 148-Cyndi Lauper parody-s 4.00
155,159,160(8/87): 155-Archie in drag-s. 159-Superhero gag-c. 160-Wheel of Fortune parody 3.00
161-169,171-199 2.00
170-New Archie Superhero-s 3.00
200 4.00

BETTY AND VERONICA (Also see Archie's Girls...)
Archie Enterprises: June, 1987 - Present (75¢ /$1.25/$1.50/$1.75/$1.79)

1,82-Love Showdown part 3 4.00
2-10 3.00
11-81,83-144 2.00
Summer Fun 1 (1994, $2.00, 52 pgs. plus poster) 2.00

BETTY & VERONICA ANNUAL DIGEST (...Digest Magazine #1-4, 44 on; ...Comics Digest Mag. #5-43)
Archie Publications: Nov, 1980 - Present ($1.00/$1.50/$1.75/$1.95/$1.99, digest size)

1 2.25 6.75 18.00
2-10: 2(11/81-Katy Keene story), 3(8/82) 1.25 3.75 10.00
11-30 1.00 2.80 7.00
31-50 5.00
51-70 3.00
71-109 2.00

BETTY & VERONICA ANNUAL DIGEST MAGAZINE
Archie Comics: Sept, 1989 - Present ($1.50/$1.75/$1.79, 128 pgs.)

1 5.00
2-10: 9-Neon ink logo 4.00
11-17: 16-Begin $1.79-c 3.00

BETTY & VERONICA CHRISTMAS SPECTACULAR (See Archie Giant Series Magazine #159, 168, 180, 191, 204, 217, 229, 241, 453, 465, 477, 489, 501, 513, 525, 536, 547, 558, 568, 580, 593, 606, 618)

BETTY & VERONICA DOUBLE DIGEST MAGAZINE
Archie Enterprises: 1987 - Present ($2.25/$2.75/$1.50/$2.79/$2.95/$2.99, digest size, 256 pgs.)(...Digest #12 on)

1 1.10 3.30 9.00
2-10 5.00
11-25: 5,17-Xmas-c. 16-Capt. Hero story 3.50
26-85 3.00

BETTY & VERONICA SPECTACULAR (See Archie Giant Series Mag. #11, 16, 21, 26, 32, 138, 145, 153, 162, 173, 184, 197, 201, 210, 214, 221, 226, 234, 238, 246, 250, 458, 462, 470, 482, 486, 494, 498, 506, 510, 518, 522, 526, 530, 537, 552, 559, 563, 569, 575, 582, 588, 600, 608, 613, 620, 623, and Betty & Veronica)

BETTY AND VERONICA SPECTACULAR
Archie Comics: Oct, 1992 - Present ($1.25/$1.50/$1.75)

1 3.00
2-39: 1-Dan DeCarlo-c/a 2.00

BETTY & VERONICA SPRING SPECTACULAR (See Archie Giant Series Magazine #569, 582, 595)

BETTY & VERONICA SUMMER FUN (See Archie Giant Series Mag. #8, 13, 18, 23, 28, 34, 140, 147, 155, 164, 175, 187, 199, 212, 224, 236, 248, 460, 484, 496, 508, 520, 529, 539, 550, 561, 572, 585, 598, 611, 621)
Archie Comics: 1994 - Present ($2.00/$2.29)

1-5 2.00
6-($2.29) 2.29

BETTY BOOP'S BIG BREAK
First Publishing: 1990 ($5.95, 52 pgs.)

nn-By Joshua Quagmire; 60th anniversary ish. 6.00

BETTY PAGE 3-D COMICS
The 3-D Zone: 1991 ($3.95, "7-1/2x10-1/4," 28 pgs., no glasses)

1-Photo inside covers; back-c nudity 5.00

BETTY'S DIARY (See Archie Giant Series Magazine No. 555)
Archie Enterprises: April, 1986 - No. 40, Apr, 1991 (#1:65¢; 75¢/95¢)

1 4.00
2-10 3.00
11-40 2.00

BETTY'S DIGEST
Archie Enterprises: Nov, 1996 - Present ($1.75/$1.79)

1,2 2.00

BEVERLY HILLBILLIES (TV)
Dell Publishing Co.: 4-6/63 - No. 18, 8/67; No. 19, 10/69; No. 20, 10/70; No. 21, Oct, 1971

1-Photo-c 15.00 45.00 165.00
2-Photo-c 8.00 24.00 90.00
3-9: All have photo covers 5.50 16.50 60.00
10: No photo cover 3.80 11.50 40.00
11-21: All have photo covers. 18-Last 12¢ issue. 19-21-Reprint #1-3 (covers and insides) 4.50 13.50 50.00

NOTE: *#1-9, 11-21 are photo covers.*

BEWARE (Formerly Fantastic; Chilling Tales No. 13 on)
Youthful Magazines: No. 10, June, 1952 - No. 12, Oct, 1952

10-E.A. Poe's Pit & the Pendulum adaptation by Wildey; Harrison/Bache-a; atom bomb and shrunken head-c 43.00 128.00 340.00
11-Harrison-a; Ambrose Bierce adapt. 31.00 94.00 220.00
12-Used in **SOTI**, pg. 388; Harrison-a 31.00 94.00 220.00

BEWARE
Trojan Magazines/Merit Publ. No. ?: No. 13, 1/53 - No. 16, 7/53; No. 5, 9/53 - No. 15, 5/55

13(#1)-Harrison-a 45.00 135.00 360.00
14(#2, 3/53)-Krenkel/Harrison-c; dismemberment, severed head panels 31.00 94.00 220.00
15,16(#3, 5/53; #4, 7/53)-Harrison-a 24.00 73.00 170.00
5,9,12,13 24.00 73.00 170.00
6-Ill. in **SOTI**- "Children are first shocked and then desensitized by all this brutality." Corpse on cover swipe/V.O.H. #26; girl on cover swipe/Advs. Into Darkness #10 47.00 141.00 375.00
7,8-Check-a 24.00 73.00 170.00
10-Frazetta/Check-c; Disbrow, Check-a 55.00 165.00 440.00
11-Disbrow-a; heart torn out, blood drainage 28.00 84.00 195.00
14,15: 14-Myron Fass-c. 15-Harrison-a 21.00 64.00 150.00

NOTE: ***Fass** a-5, 6, 8; c-6, 11, 14. **Forte** a-8. **Hollingsworth** a-15(#3), 16(#4), 9; c-16(#4), 8, 9. **Kiefer** a-16(#4), 5, 6, 10.*

BEWARE (Becomes Tomb of Darkness No. 9 on)
Marvel Comics Group: Mar, 1973 - No. 8, May, 1974 (All reprints)

1-Everett-c; Kirby & Sinnott-r ('54) 2.00 6.00 16.00
2-8: 2-Forte, Colan-r. 6-Tuska-a. 7-Torres-r/Mystical Tales #7 1.40 4.15 11.00

NOTE: ***Infantino** a-4r. **Gil Kane** c-4. **Wildey** a-7r.*

BEWARE TERROR TALES
Fawcett Publications: May, 1952 - No. 8, July, 1953

1-E.C. art swipe/Haunt of Fear #5 & Vault of Horror #26 40.00 120.00 320.00
2 27.00 81.00 190.00
3-7 21.00 64.00 150.00
8-Tothish-a; people being cooked-c 24.00 73.00 170.00

NOTE: ***Andru** a-2. **Bernard Bailey** a-1; c-1-5. **Powell** a-1, 2, 8. **Sekowsky** a-2.*

BEWARE THE CREEPER (See Adventure, Best of the Brave & the Bold, Brave & the Bold, 1st Issue Special, Flash #318-323, Showcase #73, World's

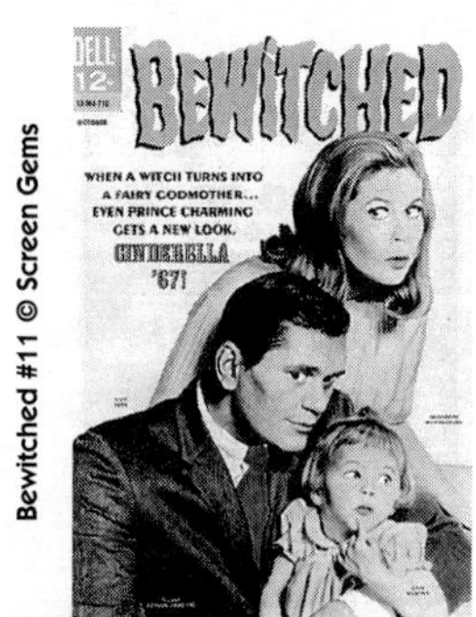

Bewitched #11 © Screen Gems

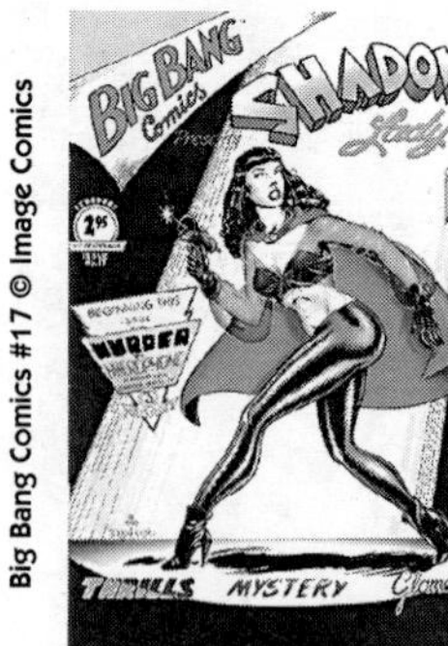

Big Bang Comics #17 © Image Comics

Big Chief Wahoo #5 © EAS

GD2.0 FN6.0 NM9.4

Finest #249)
National Periodical Publications: May-June, 1968 - No. 6, Mar-Apr, 1969 (All 12¢ issues)

1-(5-6/68)-Classic Ditko-c; Ditko-a in all 6.50 19.50 65.00
2-6: 2-5-Ditko-c. 6-Gil Kane-c 4.20 12.60 42.00

BEWITCHED (TV)
Dell Publishing Co.: 4-6/65 - No. 11, 10/67; No. 12, 10/68 - No. 13, 1/69; No. 14, 10/69

1-Photo-c 14.00 41.00 150.00
2-No photo-c 7.00 21.00 75.00
3-13-All have photo-c. 12-Reprints #1 5.00 15.00 55.00
14-No photo-c; reprints #2 3.20 9.50 35.00

BEYOND, THE
Ace Magazines: Nov, 1950 - No. 30, Jan, 1955

1-Bakerish-a(p) 40.00 120.00 280.00
2-Bakerish-a(p) 24.00 71.00 165.00
3-10: 10-Woodish-a by Cameron 15.00 45.00 105.00
11-20: 18-Used in **POP**, pgs. 81,82 12.00 36.00 85.00
21-26,28-30 11.50 34.00 80.00
27-Used in **SOTI**, pg. 111 12.00 36.00 85.00
NOTE: ***Cameron** a-10, 11p, 12p, 15, 16, 21-27, 30; c-20. **Colan** a-6, 13, 17. **Sekowsky** a-2, 3, 5, 7, 11, 14, 27r. No. 1 was to appear as Challenge of the Unknown No. 7.*

BEYOND THE GRAVE
Charlton Comics: July, 1975 - No. 6, June, 1976; No. 7, Jan, 1983 - No. 17, Oct, 1984

1-Ditko-a (6 pgs.); Sutton painted-c 1.85 5.50 15.00
2-6: 2-5-Ditko-a; Ditko c-2,3,6 1.25 3.75 10.00
7-17: ('83-'84) Reprints. 13-Aparo-c(r). 15-Sutton-c (low print run)2.40 6.00
Modern Comics Reprint 2('78) 3.00
NOTE: ***Howard** a-4. **Kim** a-1. **Larson** a-4, 6.*

BIBLE TALES FOR YOUNG FOLK (...Young People No. 3-5)
Atlas Comics (OMC): Aug, 1953 - No. 5, Mar, 1954

1 24.00 73.00 170.00
2-Everett, Krigstein-a 17.00 51.00 120.00
3-5: 4-Robinson-c 13.00 39.00 90.00

BIG (Movie)
Hit Comics (Dark Horse Comics): Mar, 1989 ($2.00)

1-Adaptaiton of film; Paul Chadwick-c 2.00

BIG ALL-AMERICAN COMIC BOOK, THE (See All-American Comics)
All-American/National Per. Publ.: 1944 (132 pgs., one-shot) (Early DC Annual)

GD2.0 FN6.0 VF8.0 NM9.4
1-Wonder Woman, Green Lantern, Flash, The Atom, Wildcat, Scribbly, The Whip, Ghost Patrol, Hawkman by Kubert (1st on Hawkman), Hop Harrigan, Johnny Thunder, Little Boy Blue, Mr. Terrific, Mutt & Jeff app.; Sargon on cover only; cover by Kubert/Hibbard/Mayer/others 800.00 2400.00 5950.00 9,500.00

BIG BABY HUEY (Also see Baby Huey)
Harvey Comics: Oct, 1991 - No. 4, Mar, 1992 ($1.00, quarterly)

GD2.0 FN6.0 NM9.4
1-4 2.50

BIG BANG COMICS (Becomes Big Bang #4)
Caliber Press: Spring, 1994 - No. 4, Feb, 1995 ($1.95, limited series)

0-4: 0-Alex Ross-c. 2.00
Your Big Book of Big Bang Comics TPB ('98, $11.00) r/#0-2 11.00

BIG BANG COMICS (Volume 2)
Image Comics (Highbrow Entertainment): V2#1, May, 1996 - Present ($1.95/$2.50/$2.95)

1-23: 1-Mighty Man app.2-4-S.A. Shadowhawk app.5-Begin $2.95-c. 6-Curt Swan/Murphy Anderson-c. 7-Begin B&W. 12-Savage Dragon-c/app. 15-Bissette-c. 16,17,21-Shadow Lady 3.00
24,25-($3.95): 24-History of Big Bang Comics Vol. 1 4.00

GD2.0 FN6.0 NM9.4

BIG BLACK KISS
Vortex Comics: Sep, 1989 - No, 3, Nov, 1989 ($3.75, B&W, lim. series, mature)

1-3-Chaykin-s/a 4.00

BIG BLOWN BABY (Also see Dark Horse Presents)
Dark Horse Comics: Aug, 1996 - No. 4, Nov, 1996 ($2.95, lim. series, mature)

1-4: Bill Wray-c/a/scripts 3.00

BIG BOOK OF ..., THE
DC Comics (Paradox Press): 1994 - Present (B&W)($12.95 - $14.95)
nn-...**BAD**,1998 ($14.95),...**CONSPIRACIES**, 1995 ($12.95), ...**DEATH**,1994 ($12.95), ...**FREAKS**, 1996 ($14.95), ...**GRIMM**, 1999 ($14.95), ...**HOAXES**, 1996 ($14.95), ...**LITTLE CRIMINALS**,1996 ($14.95), ...**LOSERS**,1997 ($14.95), **MARTYRS**, 1997 ($14.95), ...**SCANDAL**,1997 ($14.95), ...**THE WEIRD WILD WEST**,1998 ($14.95), ...**THUGS**, 1997 ($14.95), ...**UNEXPLAINED**, 1997 ($14.95), ...**URBAN LEGENDS**, 1994 ($12.95), ...**VICE**, 1999 ($14.95), ...**WEIRDOS**, 1995 ($12.95) 12.95 - 14.95 ea.

BIG BOOK OF FUN COMICS (See New Book of Comics)
National Periodical Publications: Spring, 1936 (Large size, 52 pgs.)
(1st comic book annual & DC annual) **GD2.0 FN6.0 VF8.0**
1 (Very rare)-r/New Fun #1-5 2083.00 6250.00 12,500.00

BIG BOOK ROMANCES
Fawcett Publications: Feb, 1950 (no date given) (148 pgs.)
GD2.0 FN6.0 NM9.4
1-Contains remaindered Fawcett romance comics - several combinations possible 36.00 107.00 250.00

BIG BOY (See Adventures of the Big Boy)

BIG BRUISERS
Image Comics (WildStorm Productions): July, 1996 ($3.50, one-shot)

1-Features Maul from WildC.A.T.S, Impact from Cyberforce & Badrock from Youngblood; wraparound-c 3.50

BIG CHIEF WAHOO
Eastern Color Printing/George Dougherty (distr. by Fawcett): July, 1942 - No. 7, Wint., 1943/44?(no year given)(Quarterly)

1-Newspaper-r (on sale 6/15/42) 40.00 120.00 315.00
2-Steve Roper app. 22.00 66.00 155.00
3-5: 4-Chief is holding a Katy Keene comic 17.00 49.00 115.00
6-7 11.50 34.00 80.00
NOTE: *Kerry Drake in some issues.*

BIG CIRCUS, THE (Movie)
Dell Publishing Co.: No. 1036, Sept-Nov, 1959

Four Color 1036-Photo-c 5.50 16.50 60.00

BIG COUNTRY, THE (Movie)
Dell Publishing Co.: No. 946, Oct, 1958

Four Color 946-Photo-c 6.40 19.00 70.00

BIG DADDY ROTH (Magazine)
Millar Publications: Oct-Nov, 1964 - No. 4, Apr-May, 1965 (35¢)

1-Toth-a 14.00 42.00 140.00
2-4-Toth-a 10.50 32.00 105.00

BIG GUY AND RUSTY THE BOY ROBOT, THE (Also See Madman Comics #6,7 & Martha Washington Stranded In Space)
Dark Horse (Legend): July, 1995 - No. 2, Aug, 1995 ($4.95, oversize, lim. series)

1,2-Frank Miller scripts & Geoff Darrow-c/a 1.10 3.30 9.00
Trade paperback (10/96, $14.95)-r/1,2 w/cover gallery 15.00

BIG HERO ADVENTURES (See Jigsaw)

BIG JON & SPARKIE (Radio)(Formerly Sparkie, Radio Pixie)
Ziff-Davis Publ. Co.: No. 4, Sept-Oct, 1952 (Painted-c)

4-Based on children's radio program 18.00 54.00 125.00

BIG LAND, THE (Movie)
Dell Publishing Co.: No. 812, July, 1957

Big Shot Comics #46 © CCG

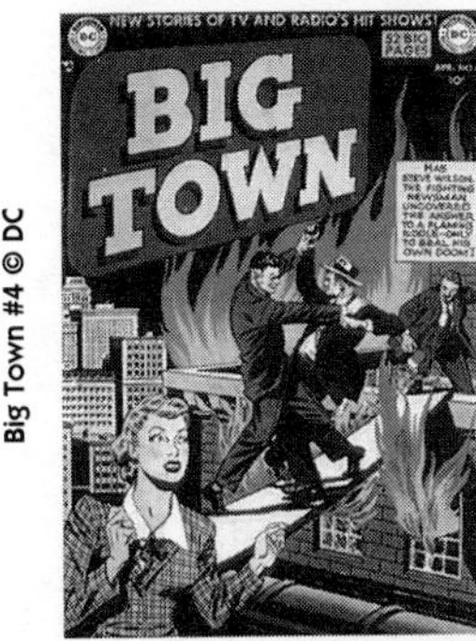

Big Town #4 © DC

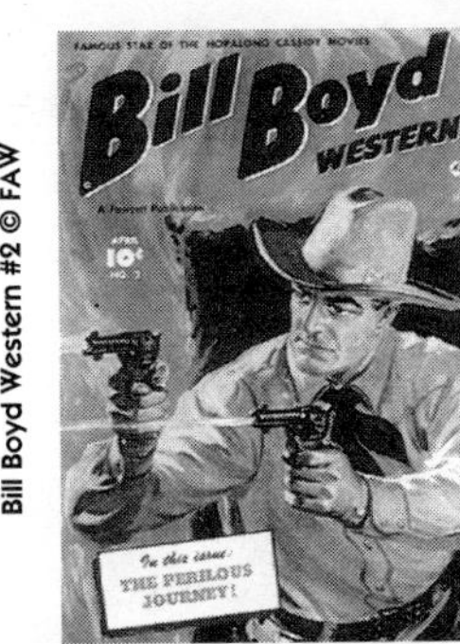

Bill Boyd Western #2 © FAW

GD2.0 FN6.0 NM9.4

Four Color 812-Alan Ladd photo-c 9.00 27.00 100.00

BIG RED (See Movie Comics)

BIG SHOT COMICS
Columbia Comics Group: May, 1940 - No. 104, Aug, 1949

1-Intro. Skyman; The Face (1st app.; Tony Trent), The Cloak (Spy Master), Marvelo, Monarch of Magicians, Joe Palooka, Charlie Chan, Tom Kerry, Dixie Dugan, Rocky Ryan begin; Charlie Chan moves over from Feature Comics #31 (4/40). 200.00 600.00 1600.00
2 75.00 225.00 600.00
3-The Cloak called Spy Chief; Skyman-c 71.00 213.00 500.00
4,5 50.00 150.00 400.00
6-10: 8-Christmas-c 40.00 120.00 320.00
11-14: 14-Origin & 1st app. Sparky Watts (6/41) 40.00 120.00 290.00
15-Origin The Cloak 40.00 120.00 320.00
16-20 31.00 94.00 220.00
21-23,26,27,29,30: 29-Intro. Capt. Yank; Bo (a dog) newspaper strip-r by Frank Beck begin, ends #104. 30-X-Mas-c 26.00 77.00 180.00
24,25: 24-Tojo-c. 25-Hitler-c 27.00 81.00 190.00
28-Hitler, Tojo & Mussolini-c 37.00 111.00 260.00
31,33-40 19.00 58.00 135.00
32-Vic Jordan newspaper strip reprints begin, ends #52; Hitler, Tojo & Mussolini-c 25.00 75.00 175.00
41-50: 42-No Skyman. 43-Hitler-c. 46-Hitler, Tojo-c. 50-Origin The Face retold 16.00 47.00 110.00
51-56,58-60 13.00 39.00 90.00
57-Hitler, Tojo Halloween mask-c 16.00 47.00 110.00
61-70: 63 on-Tony Trent, the Face 10.00 30.00 70.00
71-80: 73-The Face cameo. 74-(2/47)-Mickey Finn begins. 74,80-The Face app. in Tony Trent. 78-Last Charlie Chan strip-r 10.00 30.00 65.00
81-90: 85-Tony Trent marries Babs Walsh. 86-Valentines-c 9.15 27.00 55.00
91-99,101-104: 69-94-Skyman in Outer Space. 96-Xmas-c 7.50 22.50 45.00
100 10.00 30.00 60.00

NOTE: ***Mart Bailey*** *art on "The Face" No. 1-104.* ***Guardineer*** *a-5. Sparky Watts by* ***Boody Rogers****-No. 14-42, 77-104, (by others No. 43-76). Others than Tony Trent wear "The Face" mask in No. 46-63, 93. Skyman by* ***Ogden Whitney****-No. 1, 2, 4, 12-37, 49, 70-101. Skyman covers-No. 1, 3, 7-12, 14, 16, 20, 27, 89, 95, 100.*

BIG TEX
Toby Press: June, 1953

1-Contains (3) John Wayne stories-r with name changed to Big Tex 10.00 30.00 60.00

BIG-3
Fox Features Syndicate: Fall, 1940 - No. 7, Jan, 1942

1-Blue Beetle, The Flame, & Samson begin 200.00 600.00 1600.00
2 85.00 255.00 680.00
3-5 60.00 180.00 480.00
6,7: 6-Last Samson. 7-V-Man app. 50.00 150.00 400.00

BIG TOP COMICS, THE (TV's Great Circus Show)
Toby Press: 1951 - No. 2, 1951 (No month)

1,2 8.35 25.00 50.00

BIG TOWN (Radio/TV) (Also see Movie Comics, 1946)
National Periodical Publ: Jan, 1951 - No. 50, Mar-Apr, 1958 (No. 1-9: 52pgs.)

1-Dan Barry-a begins 60.00 180.00 480.00
2 34.00 103.00 240.00
3-10 19.00 56.00 130.00
11-20 13.00 39.00 90.00
21-31: Last pre-code (1-2/55) 10.00 30.00 70.00
32-50 8.35 25.00 50.00

BIG VALLEY, THE (TV)
Dell Publishing Co.: June, 1966 - No. 5, Oct, 1967; No. 6, Oct, 1969

1: Photo-c #1-5 3.80 11.50 42.00
2-6: 6-Reprints #1 2.20 6.50 24.00

GD2.0 FN6.0 NM9.4

BIKER MICE FROM MARS (TV)
Marvel Comics: Nov, 1993 - No. 3, Jan, 1994 ($1.50, limited series)

1-3: 1-Intro Vinnie, Modo & Throttle. 2-Origin 2.00

BILL & TED'S BOGUS JOURNEY
Marvel Comics: Sept, 1991 ($2.95, squarebound, 84 pgs.)

1-Adapts movie sequel 3.00

"BILL AND TED'S EXCELLENT ADVENTURE" MOVIE ADAPTATION
DC Comics: 1989 (No cover price)

nn-Torres-a. 2.00

BILL & TED'S EXCELLENT COMIC BOOK (Movie)
Marvel Comics: Dec, 1991 - No. 12, 1992 ($1.00/$1.25)

1-12: 3-Begin $1.25-c 2.00

BILL BARNES COMICS (...America's Air Ace Comics No. 2 on)
(Becomes Air Ace V2#1 on; also see Shadow Comics)
Street & Smith Publications: Oct, 1940(No. month given) - No. 12, Oct, 1943

1-23 pgs.-comics; Rocket Rooney begins 75.00 225.00 600.00
2-Barnes as The Phantom Flyer app.; Tuska-a 40.00 120.00 320.00
3-5 34.00 103.00 240.00
6-12 29.00 86.00 200.00

BILL BATTLE, THE ONE MAN ARMY (Also see Master Comics No. 133)
Fawcett Publications: Oct, 1952 - No. 4, Apr, 1953 (All photo-c)

1 11.00 33.00 75.00
2 7.00 21.00 42.00
3,4 5.85 17.50 35.00

BILL BLACK'S FUN COMICS
Paragon #1-3/Americomics #4: Dec, 1982 - No. 4, Mar, 1983 ($1.75, Baxter paper)(1st AC comic)

1-Intro. Capt. Paragon, Phantom Lady & Commando D (#1-3 are B&W fanzines; 8-1/2x11") 2.00
2-4: 4-($2.00, color)-Origin Nightfall (formerly Phantom Lady); Nightveil app. 3-Kirby-c. 4-Kirby-a 2.00

BILL BOYD WESTERN (Movie star; see Hopalong Cassidy & Western Hero)
Fawcett Publ: Feb, 1950 - No. 23, June, 1952 (1-3,7,11,14-on: 36 pgs.)

1-Bill Boyd & his horse Midnite begin; photo front/back-c 49.00 146.00 390.00
2-Painted-c 28.00 84.00 195.00
3-Photo-c begin, end #23; last photo back-c 21.00 64.00 150.00
4-6(52 pgs.) 17.00 51.00 120.00
7,11(36 pgs.) 13.50 41.00 95.00
8-10,12,13(52 pgs.) 14.00 43.00 100.00
14-22 13.00 39.00 90.00
23-Last issue 14.00 43.00 100.00

BILL BUMLIN (See Treasury of Comics No. 3)

BILL ELLIOTT (See Wild Bill Elliott)

BILLI 99
Dark Horse Comics: Sept, 1991 - No. 4, 1991 ($3.50, B&W, lim. series, 52 pgs.)

1-4: Tim Sale-c/a 3.50

BILL STERN'S SPORTS BOOK
Ziff-Davis Publ. Co.(Approved Comics): Spring-Sum, 1951 - V2#2, Win, 1952

V1#10-(1951) 19.00 58.00 135.00
2-(Sum/52; reg. size) 14.00 43.00 100.00
V2#2-(1952, 96 pgs.)-Krigstein, Kinstler-a 19.00 58.00 135.00

BILL THE BULL: ONE SHOT, ONE BOURBON, ONE BEER
Boneyard Press: Dec, 1994 ($2.95, B&W, mature)

1 3.00

BILL THE CLOWN
Slave Labor Graphics: Feb, 1992 ($2.50, one-shot)

1,1-(2nd printing, 4/93, $2.95) 3.00
Comedy Isn't Pretty 1 (11/92, $2.50) 3.00

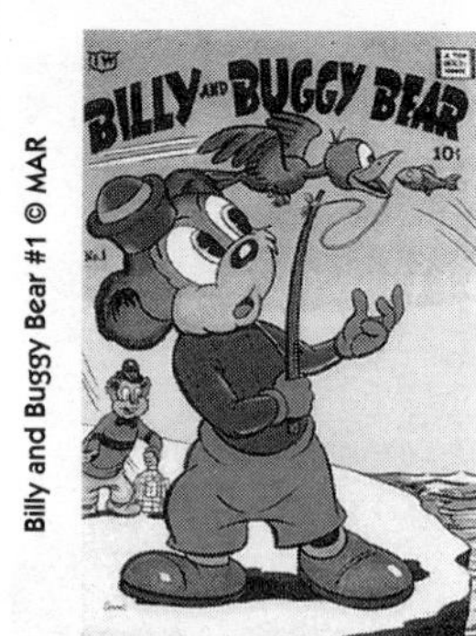

Billy and Buggy Bear #1 © MAR

Billy the Kid #5 © TOBY

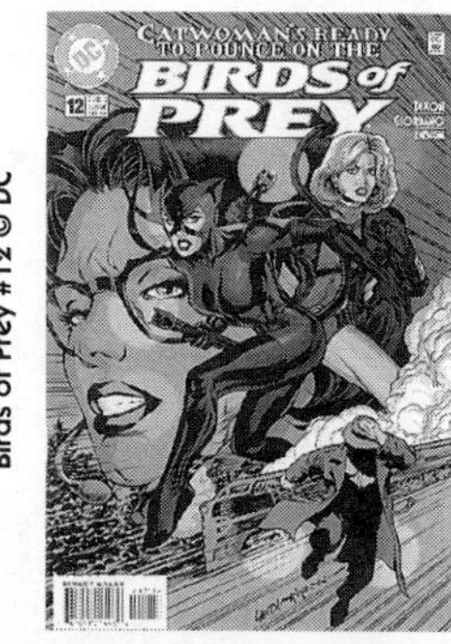

Birds of Prey #12 © DC

GD2.0 FN6.0 NM9.4

Death & Clown White 1 (9/93, $2.95) 3.00

BILLY AND BUGGY BEAR (See Animal Fun)
I.W. Enterprises/Super: 1958; 1964

I.W. Reprint #1, #7('58)-All Surprise Comics #?(Same issue-r for both) 1.10 3.30 9.00
Super Reprint #10(1964) 1.10 3.30 9.00

BILLY BUCKSKIN WESTERN (2-Gun Western No. 4)
Atlas Comics (IMC No. 1/MgPC No. 2,3): Nov, 1955 - No. 3, Mar, 1956

1-Mort Drucker-a; Maneely-c/a 13.50 41.00 95.00
2-Mort Drucker-a 10.00 30.00 70.00
3-Williamson, Drucker-a 11.00 33.00 75.00

BILLY BUNNY (Black Cobra No. 6 on)
Excellent Publications: Feb-Mar, 1954 - No. 5, Oct-Nov, 1954

1 6.70 20.00 40.00
2 4.00 11.00 22.00
3-5 3.60 9.00 18.00

BILLY BUNNY'S CHRISTMAS FROLICS
Farrell Publications: 1952 (25¢ Giant, 100 pgs.)

1 18.00 54.00 125.00

BILLY COLE
Cult Press: May, 1994 - No. 4, Aug, 1994 ($2.75, B&W, limited series)

1-4 2.75

BILLY MAKE BELIEVE
United Features Syndicate: No. 14, 1939

Single Series 14 29.00 86.00 200.00

BILLY NGUYEN, PRIVATE EYE
Caliber Press: V2#1, 1990 ($2.50)

V2#1 2.50

BILLY THE KID (Formerly The Masked Raider; also see Doc Savage Comics & Return of the Outlaw)
No. 9, Nov, 1957 - No. 121, Dec, 1976; No. 122, Sept, 1977 - No. 123,
Charlton Publ. Co.: Oct, 1977; No. 124, Feb, 1978 - No. 153, Mar, 1983

9 10.00 30.00 60.00
10,12,14,17-19: 12-2 pg Check-sty 5.85 17.50 35.00
11-(68 pgs.)-Origin & 1st app. The Ghost Train 8.35 25.00 50.00
13-Williamson/Torres-a 7.00 21.00 42.00
15-Origin; 2 pgs. Williamson-a 7.00 21.00 42.00
16-Williamson-a, 2 pgs. 6.70 20.00 40.00
20-26-Severin-a(3-4 each) 7.00 21.00 42.00
27-30: 30-Masked Rider app. 2.50 7.50 24.00
31-40 2.25 6.75 18.00
41-60 1.85 5.50 15.00
61-65 1.25 3.75 10.00
66-Bounty Hunter series begins. 1.60 4.85 13.00
67-80: Bounty Hunter series; not in #79,82,84-86 1.25 3.75 10.00
81-90: 87-Last Bounty Hunter 1.00 2.80 7.00
91-123: 110-Dr. Young of Boothill app. 111-Origin The Ghost Train. 117-Gunsmith & Co., The Cheyenne Kid app. 2.40 6.00
124(2/78)-153 4.00
Modern Comics 109 (1977 reprint) 3.00

NOTE: ***Boyette*** *a-91-110.* ***Kim*** *a-73.* ***Morsi*** *a-12,14.* ***Sattler*** *a-118-123.* ***Severin*** *a(r)-121-129, 134; c-23, 25.* ***Sutton*** *a-111.*

BILLY THE KID ADVENTURE MAGAZINE
Toby Press: Oct, 1950 - No. 30, 1955

1-Williamson/Frazetta-a (2 pgs) r/from John Wayne Adventure Comics #2; photo-c 30.00 90.00 210.00
2-Photo-c 10.00 30.00 60.00
3-Williamson/Frazetta "The Claws of Death", 4 pgs. plus Williamson art 33.00 99.00 230.00
4,5,7,8,10: 4,7-Photo-c 6.70 20.00 40.00
6-Frazetta assist on "Nightmare"; photo-c 13.50 41.00 95.00
9-Kurtzman Pot-Shot Pete; photo-c 11.00 33.00 75.00
11,12,15-20: 11-Photo-c 6.35 19.00 38.00
13-Kurtzman-r/John Wayne #12 (Genius) 7.00 21.00 42.00
14-Williamson/Frazetta; r-of #1 (2 pgs.) 10.00 30.00 65.00
21,23-30 5.00 15.00 30.00
22-Williamson/Frazetta-r(1pg.)/#1; photo-c 6.35 19.00 38.00

BILLY THE KID AND OSCAR (Also see Fawcett's Funny Animals)
Fawcett Publications: Winter, 1945 - No. 3, Summer, 1946 (Funny animal)

1 13.50 41.00 95.00
2,3 10.00 30.00 65.00

BILLY WEST (Bill West No. 9,10)
Standard Comics (Visual Editions): 1949-No. 9, Feb, 1951; No. 10, Feb, 1952

1 11.00 33.00 75.00
2 6.35 19.00 38.00
3-6,9,10 4.25 13.00 28.00
7,8-Schomburg-c 5.70 17.00 34.00

NOTE: ***Celardo*** *a-1-6, 9; c-1-3.* ***Moreira*** *a-3.* ***Roussos*** *a-2.*

BING CROSBY (See Feature Films)

BINGO (...Comics) (H. C. Blackerby)
Howard Publ.: 1945 (Reprints National material)

1-L. B. Cole opium-c 30.00 90.00 210.00

BINGO, THE MONKEY DOODLE BOY
St. John Publishing Co.: Aug, 1951; Oct, 1953

1(8/51)-By Eric Peters 5.35 16.00 32.00
1(10/53) 4.00 12.00 24.00

BINKY (Formerly Leave It to...)
National Periodical Publ./DC Comics: No. 72, 4-5/70 - No. 81, 10-11/71; No. 82, Summer/77

72-76 2.00 6.00 16.00
77-79: (68pgs.). 77-Bobby Sherman 1pg. story w/photo. 78-1 pg. sty on Barry Williams of Brady Bunch. 79-Osmonds 1pg. story 3.00 9.00 30.00
80,81 (52pgs.)-Sweat Pain story 2.50 7.50 22.00
82 (1977, one-shot) 1.50 4.50 12.00

BINKY'S BUDDIES
National Periodical Publications: Jan-Feb, 1969 - No. 12, Nov-Dec, 1970

1 3.50 10.50 35.00
2-12 2.00 6.00 16.00

BIONEERS
Mirage Publishing: Aug, 1994 ($2.75)

1-w/bound-in trading card 2.75

BIONIC WOMAN, THE (TV)
Charlton Publications: Oct, 1977 - No. 5, June, 1978

1 1.00 3.00 8.00
2-5 5.00

BIRDS OF PREY (Also see Black Canary/Oracle: Birds of Prey)
DC Comics: Jan,1999 - Present ($1.99)

1-Dixon-s/Land-c/a 4.00
2-12: 6-Nightwing-c/app. 2.50
TPB (1999, $17.95) r/ previous series and one-shots 18.00

BIRDS OF PREY: BATGIRL
DC Comics: Feb,1998 ($2.95, one-shot)

1-Dixon-s/Frank-c 4.00

BIRDS OF PREY: MANHUNT
DC Comics: Sept, 1996 - No. 4, Dec, 1996 ($1.95, limited series)

1-4: Features Black Canary, Oracle, Huntress, & Catwoman; Chuck Dixon scripts; Gary Frank-c on all. 1-Catwoman cameo only 5.00

NOTE: ***Gary Frank*** *c-1-4.* ***Matt Haley*** *a-1-4p.* ***Wade Von Grawbadger*** *a-1i.*

BIRDS OF PREY: REVOLUTION
DC Comics: 1997 ($2.95, one-shot)

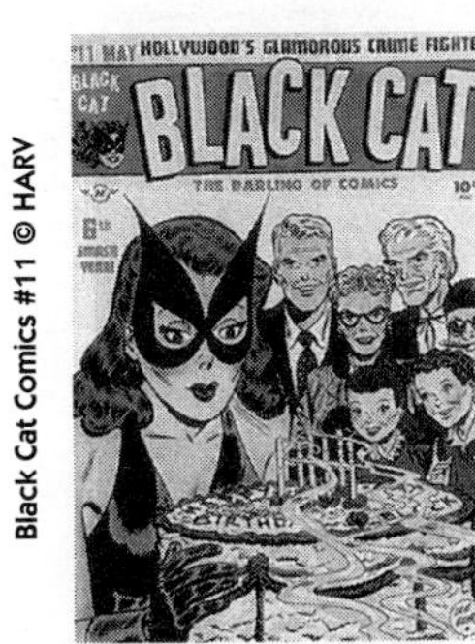
Bishop The Last X-Man #1 © MAR

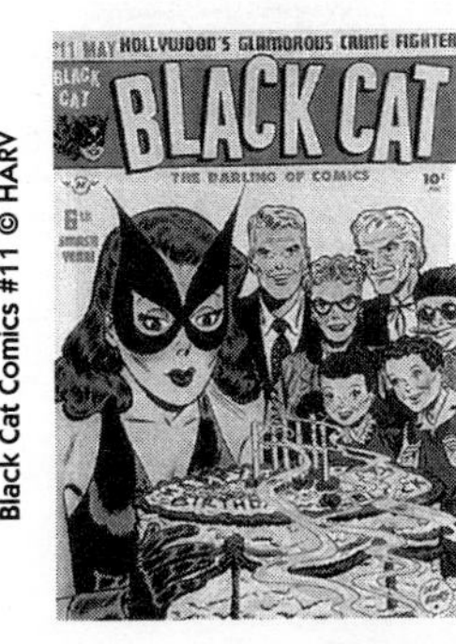

Black Cat Comics #11 © HARV

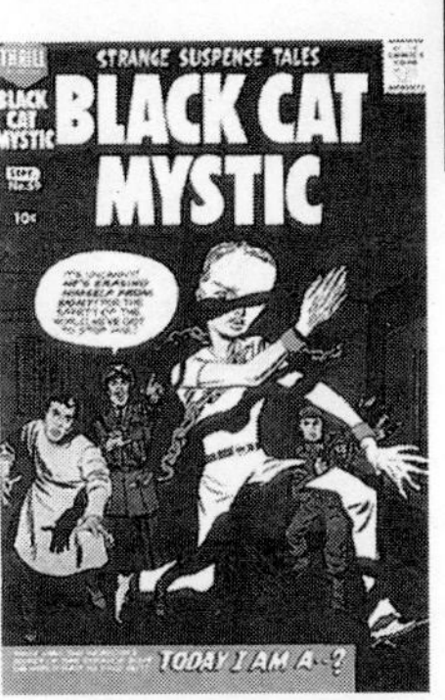

Black Cat Mystic #59 © HARV

GD2.0 FN6.0 NM9.4

GD2.0 FN6.0 NM9.4

1-Frank-c/Dixon-s 3.50

BIRDS OF PREY: THE RAVENS
DC Comics: June,1998 ($1.95, one-shot)

1-Dixon-s; Girlfrenzy issue 3.00

BIRDS OF PREY: WOLVES
DC Comics: Oct, 1997 ($2.95, one-shot)

1-Dixon-s/Giordano & Faucher-a 3.50

BIRTH CAUL, THE
Eddie Campbell Comics: 1999 ($5.95, B&W, one-shot)

1-Alan Moore-s/Eddie Campbell-a 6.00

BIRTH OF THE DEFIANT UNIVERSE, THE
Defiant Comics: May, 1993

nn-contains promotional artwork & text; limited print run of 1000 copies. 1.25 3.75 10.00

BISHOP (See Uncanny X-Men & X-Men)
Marvel Comics: Dec, 1994 - No.4, Mar, 1995 ($2.95, limited series)

1-4: Foil-c 3.00

BISHOP THE LAST X-MAN
Marvel Comics: Oct, 1999 - Present ($2.99)

1-Jeanty-a 3.00

BISHOP: XAVIER SECURITY ENFORCER
Marvel Comics: Jan, 1998 - No.3, Mar, 1998 ($2.50, limited series)

1-3: Ostrander-s 3.00

BIZARRE ADVENTURES (Formerly Marvel Preview)
Marvel Comics Group: No. 25, 3/81 - No. 34, 2/83 (#25-33: Magazine-$1.50)

25,26: 25-Lethal Ladies. 26-King Kull; Bolton-c/a 1.00 2.80 7.00
27,28: 27-Phoenix, Iceman & Nightcrawler app. 28-The Unlikely Heroes; Elektra by Miller; Neal Adams-a 1.10 3.30 9.00
29,30,32,33: 29-Stephen King's Lawnmower Man. 30-Tomorrow; 1st app. Silhouette. 32-Gods; Thor-c/s. 33-Horror; Dracula app.; photo-c 2.40 6.00
31-After The Violence Stops; new Hangman story; Miller-a 1.00 3.00 8.00
34 ($2.00, Baxter paper, comic size)-Son of Santa; Christmas special; Howard the Duck by Paul Smith 5.00

NOTE: ***Alcala*** *a-27i.* ***Austin*** *a-25i, 28i.* ***Bolton*** *a-26, 32.* ***J. Buscema*** *a-27p, 29, 30p; c-26.* ***Byrne*** *a-31 (2 pg.).* ***Golden*** *a-25p, 28p.* ***Perez*** *a-27p.* ***Rogers*** *a-25p.* ***Simonson*** *a-29; c-29.* ***Paul Smith*** *a-34.*

BLACK AND WHITE (See Large Feature Comic, Series I)

BLACK & WHITE (Also see Codename: Black & White)
Image Comics (Extreme): Oct,1994 - No. 3, Jan,1995 ($1.95, limited series)

1-3: Thibert-c/story 2.00

BLACK & WHITE MAGIC
Innovation Publishing: 1991 ($2.95, 98 pgs., B&W w/30 pgs. color, square-bound)

1-Contains rebound comics w/covers removed; contents may vary 3.00

BLACKBALL COMICS
Blackball Comics: Mar, 1994 ($3.00)

1-Trencher-c/story by Giffen; John Pain by O'Neill 3.00

BLACKBEARD'S GHOST (See Movie Comics)

BLACK BEAUTY (See Son of Black Beauty)
Dell Publishing Co.: No. 440, Dec, 1952

Four Color 440 2.75 8.00 30.00

BLACK CANARY (See All Star Comics #38, Flash Comics #86, Justice League of America #75 & World's Finest #244)
DC Comics: Nov, 1991 - No. 4, Feb, 1992 ($1.75, limited series)

1-4 2.00

BLACK CANARY
DC Comics: Jan, 1993 - No. 12, Dec, 1993 ($1.75)

1-12: 8-The Ray-c/story. 9,10-Huntress-c/story 2.00

BLACK CANARY/ORACLE: BIRDS OF PREY (Also see Showcase '96 #3)
DC Comics: 1996 ($3.95, one-shot)

1-Chuck Dixon scripts & Gary Frank-c/a. 1.00 2.80 7.00

BLACK CAT COMICS (...Western #16-19; ...Mystery #30 on)
(See All-New #7,9, The Original Black Cat, Pocket & Speed Comics)
Harvey Publications (Home Comics): June-July, 1946 - No. 29, June, 1951

1-Kubert-a; Joe Simon c-1-3 62.00 187.00 500.00
2-Kubert-a 36.00 107.00 250.00
3,4: 4-The Red Demons begin (The Demon #4 & 5) 29.00 86.00 200.00
5,6,7: 5,6-The Scarlet Arrow app. in ea. by Powell; S&K-a in both. 6-Origin Red Demon. 7-Vagabond Prince by S&K plus 1 more story 36.00 107.00 250.00
8-S&K-a; Kerry Drake begins, ends #13 31.00 94.00 220.00
9-Origin Stuntman (r/Stuntman #1) 37.00 111.00 260.00
10-20: 14,15,17-Mary Worth app. plus Invisible Scarlet O'Neil-#15,20,24 24.00 71.00 165.00
21-26 19.00 58.00 135.00
27,28: 27-Used in **SOTI**, pg. 193; X-Mas-c; 2 pg. John Wayne story. 28-Intro. Kit, Black Cat's new sidekick 21.00 62.00 145.00
29-Black Cat bondage-c; Black Cat stories 20.00 60.00 140.00

BLACK CAT MYSTERY (Formerly Black Cat; ...Western Mystery #54; ...Western #55,56;...Mystery #57; ...Mystic #58-62; Black Cat #63-65)
Harvey Publications: No. 30, Aug, 1951 - No. 65, Apr, 1963

30-Black Cat on cover only 25.00 75.00 175.00
31,32,34,37,38,40 19.00 58.00 135.00
33-Used in **POP**, pg. 89; electrocution-c 21.00 62.00 145.00
35-Atomic disaster cover/story 22.00 66.00 155.00
36,39-Used in **SOTI**: #36-Pgs. 270,271; #39-Pgs. 386-388 24.00 71.00 165.00
41-43 19.00 58.00 135.00
44-Eyes, ears, tongue cut out; Nostrand-a 20.00 60.00 140.00
45-Classic "Colorama" by Powell; Nostrand-a 34.00 103.00 240.00
46-49,51-Nostrand-a in all 20.00 60.00 140.00
50-Check-a; classic Warren Kremer?-c showing a man's face burning away 44.00 132.00 350.00
52,53 (r/#34 & 35) 12.00 36.00 85.00
54-Two Black Cat stories (2/55, last pre-code) 16.00 47.00 110.00
55,56-Black Cat app. 12.00 36.00 85.00
57(7/56)-Kirby-c 11.00 33.00 75.00
58-60-Kirby-a(4). 58,59-Kirby-c. 60,61-Simon-c 16.00 47.00 110.00
61-Nostrand-a; "Colorama" r/#45 16.00 47.00 110.00
62 (3/58)-E.C. story swipe 10.00 30.00 70.00
63-65: Giants(10/62,1/63, 4/63); Reprints; Black Cat app. 63-origin Black Kitten. 65-1 pg. Powell-a 13.50 41.00 95.00

NOTE: ***Kremer*** *a-37, 39, 43; c-36, 37, 47.* ***Meskin*** *a-51.* ***Palais*** *a-30, 31(2), 32(2), 33-35, 37-40.* ***Powell*** *a-32-35, 36(2), 40, 41, 43-53, 57.* ***Simon*** *c-63-65.* ***Sparling*** *a-44. Bondage c-32, 34, 43.*

BLACK COBRA (Bride's Diary No. 4 on) (See Captain Flight #8)
Ajax/Farrell Publications(Excellent Publ.): No. 1, 10-11/54; No. 6(No. 2), 12-1/54-55; No. 3, 2-3/55

1-Re-intro Black Cobra & The Cobra Kid (costumed heroes) 29.00 86.00 200.00
6(#2)-Formerly Billy Bunny 17.00 51.00 120.00
3-(Pre-code)-Torpedoman app. 16.00 47.00 110.00

BLACK CONDOR (Also see Crack Comics, Freedom Fighters & Showcase '94 #10,11)
DC Comics: June, 1992 - No. 12, May, 1993 ($1.25)

1-12: 1-10,12-Heath-c. 9,10-The Ray app. 12-Batman-c/scripts 2.00

BLACK CROSS SPECIAL (See Dark Horse Presents)
Dark Horse Comics: Jan, 1988 ($1.75, B&W, one-shot)(Reprints & new-a)

1-1st & 2nd print; 2nd has 2pgs new-a 2.00

Black Diamond Western #16 © LEV

Black Goliath #1 © MAR

Blackhawk #41 © QUA

GD2.0 FN6.0 NM9.4

BLACK CROSS: DIRTY WORK (See Dark Horse Presents)
Dark Horse Comics: Apr, 1997 ($2.95, one-shot)

1-Chris Warner-c/s/a 3.00

BLACK DIAMOND
Americomics: May, 1983 - No. 5, 1984 (no month)($2.00-$1.75, Baxter paper)

1-3-Movie adapt.; 1-Colt back-up begins 2.50
4,5 2.00

NOTE: Bill Black a-1i; c-1. Gulacy c-2-5. Sybil Danning photo back-c-1.

BLACK DIAMOND WESTERN (Formerly Desperado No. 1-8)
Lev Gleason Publ: No. 9, Mar, 1949 - No. 60, Feb, 1956 (No. 9-28: 52 pgs.)

9-Black Diamond & his horse Reliapon begin; origin & 1st app. Black Diamond 19.00 56.00 130.00
10 10.00 30.00 60.00
11-15 7.50 22.50 45.00
16-28(11/49-11/51)-Wolverton's Bing Bang Buster 10.00 30.00 60.00
29-40: 31-One pg. Frazetta anti-drug ad 5.00 15.00 30.00
41-50,53-59 4.15 12.50 25.00
51-3-D effect-c/story 12.00 36.00 85.00
52-3-D effect story 11.50 34.00 80.00
60-Last issue 5.35 16.00 32.00

NOTE: Biro c-9-35?. Fass a-58, c-54-56, 58. Guardineer a-9, 15, 18. Kida a-9. Maurer a-10. Ed Moore a-16. Morisi a-55. Tuska a-10, 48.

BLACK DRAGON, THE
Marvel Comics (Epic Comics): 5/85 - No. 6, 10/85 (Baxter paper, mature)

1-6: 1-Chris Claremont story & John Bolton-c/a in all. 2.50

BLACK DRAGON, THE
Dark Horse Comics: Apr, 1996 ($17.95, B&W, trade paperback)

nn-Reprints Epic Comics limited series; intro by Anne McCaffrey 18.00

BLACK FLAG (See Asylum #5)
Maximum Press: Jan, 1995 - No.4, 1995; No. 0, July, 1995 ($2.50, B&W) (No. 0 in color)

Preview Edition (6/94, $1.95, B&W)-Fraga/McFarlane-c. 2.00
0-4: 0-(7/95)-Liefeld/Fraga-c. 1-(1/95). 3.00
1-Variant cover 5.00
2,4-Variant covers 3.00

NOTE: Fraga a-0-4, Preview Edition; c-1-4. Liefeld/Fraga c-0. McFarlane/Fraga c-Preview Edition.

BLACK FURY (Becomes Wild West No. 58) (See Blue Bird)
Charlton Comics Group: May, 1955 - No. 57, Mar-Apr, 1966 (Horse stories)

1 6.35 19.00 38.00
2 3.60 9.00 18.00
3-10 2.80 7.00 14.00
11-15,19,20 2.00 5.00 10.00
16-18-Ditko-a 6.35 19.00 38.00
21-30 1.00 2.80 7.00
31-57 5.00

BLACK GOLIATH
Marvel Comics Group: Feb, 1976 - No. 5, Nov, 1976

1-Tuska-a(p) thru #3 2.40 6.00
2-5: 2-4-(Regular 25¢ editions). 4-Kirby-c 4.00
2-4-(30¢-c variants, limited distribution)(4,6,8/76) 2.00 6.00 16.00

BLACKHAWK (Formerly Uncle Sam #1-8; see Military & Modern Comics)
Comic Magazines(Quality)No. 9-107(12/56); National Periodical PublicationsNo. 108(1/57)-250; DC Comics No. 251 on: No. 9, Winter, 1944 - No. 243, 10-11/68; No. 244, 1-2/76 - No. 250, 1-2/77; No. 251, 10/82 - No. 273, 11/84

9 (1944) 300.00 900.00 2700.00
10 (1946) 106.00 318.00 850.00
11-15: 14-Ward-a; 13,14-Fear app. 70.00 210.00 560.00
16-20: 20-Ward Blackhawk 56.00 168.00 450.00
21-30 (1950) 44.00 132.00 350.00
31-40: 31-Chop Chop by Jack Cole 36.00 107.00 250.00
41-49,51-60: 42-Robot-c 29.00 86.00 200.00
50-1st Killer Shark; origin in text 31.00 94.00 220.00
61,62: 61-Used in **POP**, pg. 91. 62-Used in **POP**, pg. 92 & color illo 25.00 75.00 175.00
63-70,72-80: 65-H-Bomb explosion panel. 66-B&W & color illos **POP**. 70-Return of Killer Shark; atomic explosion panel. 75-Intro. Blackie the Hawk 23.00 69.00 160.00
71-Origin retold; flying saucer-c; A-Bomb panels 26.00 79.00 185.00
81-86: Last precode (3/55) 21.00 64.00 150.00
87-92,94-99,101-107: 91-Robot-c. 105-1st S.A. 17.00 51.00 120.00
93-Origin in text 18.00 54.00 125.00
100 21.00 64.00 150.00
108-1st DC issue (1/57); re-intro. Blackie, the Hawk, their mascot; not in #115 40.00 120.00 450.00
109-117: 117-(10/57)-Mr. Freeze app. 15.00 45.00 150.00
118-(11/57)-Frazetta-r/Jimmy Wakely #4 (3 pgs.) 16.00 48.00 160.00
119-130 (11/58): 120-Robot-c 10.00 30.00 100.00
131-140 (2/59): 133-Intro. Lady Blackhawk 7.50 22.50 75.00
141-150,152-163,165,166: 141-Catman returns-c/s. 143-Kurtzman-r/Jimmy Wakely #4. 150-(7/60)-King Condor returns. 166-Last 10¢ issue 5.50 16.50 55.00
151-Lady Blackhawk receives & loses super powers 6.00 18.00 60.00
164-Origin retold 6.50 19.50 65.00
167-180 3.00 9.00 30.00
181-190 2.50 7.50 22.00
191-196,199,201,202,204-210: 196-Combat Diary series begins. 2.25 6.75 18.00
197-New look for Blackhawks 2.50 7.50 22.00
198,200: 198-Origin retold 2.50 7.50 22.00
203-Origin Chop Chop (12/64) 2.50 7.50 22.00
211-227,229-243(1968): 230-Blackhawks become superheroes; JLA cameo 242-Return to old costumes 1.75 5.25 14.00
228-Batman, Green Lantern, Superman, The Flash cameos. 2.00 6.00 16.00
244 ('76) -250: 250-Chuck dies 4.00
251-273: 251-Origin retold; Black Knights return. 252-Intro Domino. 253-Part origin Hendrickson. 258-Blackhawk's Island destroyed. 259-Part origin Chop-Chop. 265-273 (75¢ cover price) 2.00

NOTE: Chaykin a-260; c-257-260, 262. Crandall a-10, 11, 13, 16?, 18-20, 22-26, 30-33, 35p, 36(2), 37, 38?, 39-44, 46-50, 52-58, 60, 63, 64, 66, 67; c-14-20, 22-63(most except #28-33, 36, 37, 39). Evans a-244, 245,246i, 248-250i. G. Kane c-263, 264. Kubert c-244, 245. Newton a-266p. Severin a-257.Spiegle a-261-267, 269-273; c-265-272. Toth a-260p. Ward a-16-27(Chop Chop, 8pgs. ea.); pencilled stories-No. 17-63(approx.). Wildey a-268. Chop Chop solo stories in #10-95?

BLACKHAWK
DC Comics: Mar, 1988 - No. 3, May, 1988 ($2.95, limited series, mature)

1-3: Chaykin painted-c/a/scripts 3.00

BLACKHAWK (Also see Action Comics #601)
DC Comics: Mar, 1989 - No. 16, Aug, 1990 ($1.50, mature)

1-6,8-16: 16-Crandall-c swipe 2.00
7-($2.50, 52 pgs.)-Story-r/Military #1 2.50
Annual 1 (1989, $2.95, 68 pgs.)-Recaps origin of Blackhawk, Lady Blackhawk, and others 3.00
Special 1 (1992, $3.50, 68 pgs.)-Mature readers 3.50

BLACKHAWK INDIAN TOMAHAWK WAR, THE
Avon Periodicals: 1951 (Also see Fighting Indians of the Wild West)

nn-Kinstler-c; Kit West story 18.00 54.00 125.00

BLACK HEART ASSASSIN
Iguana Comics: Jan, 1994 ($2.95)

1 3.00

BLACK HOLE (See Walt Disney Showcase #54) (Disney, movie)
Whitman Publishing Co.: Mar, 1980 - No. 4, Sept, 1980

11295(#1) (1979, Golden, $1.50-c, 52 pgs., graphic novel; 8 1/2x11") Photo-c; Spiegle-a. 1.50 4.50 16.00
1-4: 1,2-Movie adaptation. 2-4-Spiegle-a. 3-McWilliams-a; photo-c.

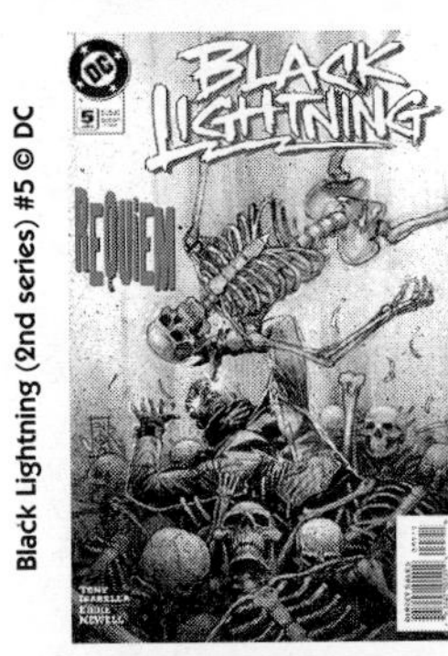

Black Lightning (2nd series) #5 © DC

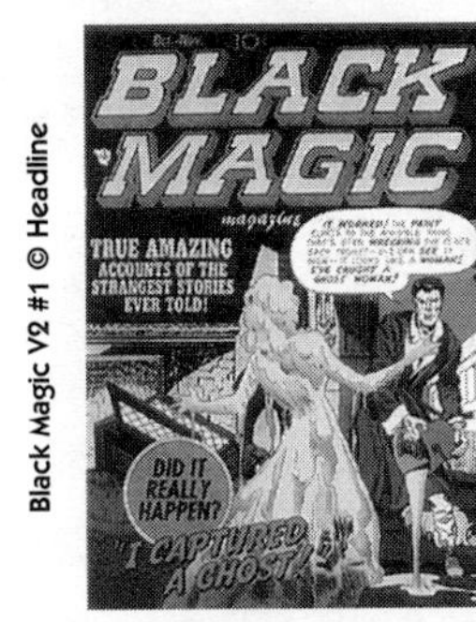

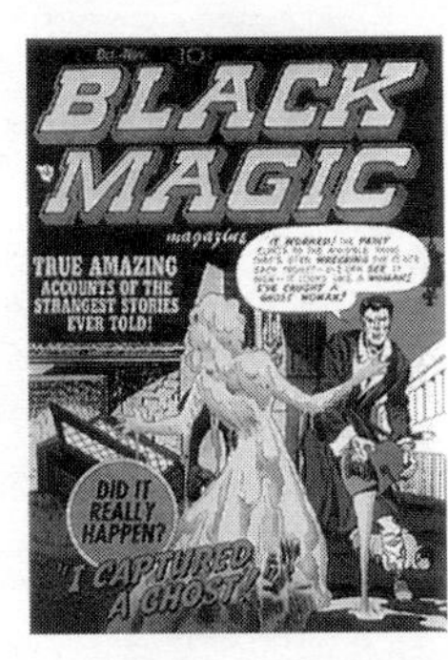

Black Magic V2 #1 © Headline

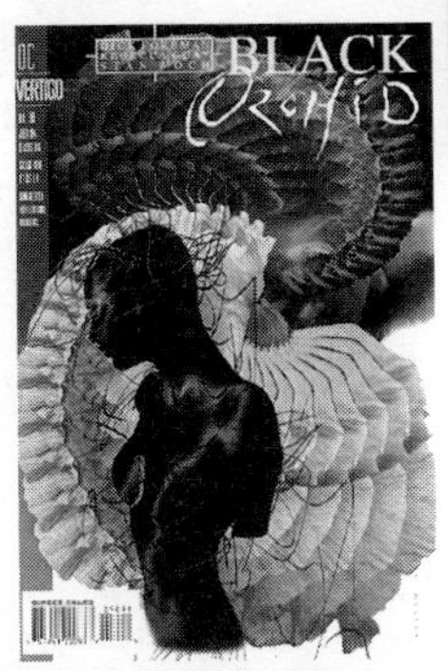

Black Orchid #10 © DC

	GD2.0	FN6.0	NM9.4
3,4-New stories		2.40	6.00

BLACK HOOD, THE (See Blue Ribbon, Flyman & Mighty Comics)
Red Circle Comics (Archie): June, 1983 - No. 3, Oct, 1983 (Mandell paper)

	GD2.0	FN6.0	NM9.4
1-Morrow, McWilliams, Wildey-a; Toth-c			3.00
2,3: MLJ's The Fox by Toth-c/a. 3-Morrow-a			2.00

(Also see Archie's Super-Hero Special Digest #2)

BLACK HOOD
DC Comics (Impact Comics): Dec, 1991 - No. 12, Dec, 1992 ($1.00)

	GD2.0	FN6.0	NM9.4
1-12: 11-Intro The Fox. 12-Origin Black Hood			2.00
Annual 1 (1992, $2.50, 68 pgs.)-w/Trading card			2.50

BLACK HOOD COMICS (Formerly Hangman #2-8; Laugh Comics #20 on; also see Black Swan, Jackpot, Roly Poly & Top-Notch #9)
MLJ Magazines: No. 9, Wint., 1943-44 - No. 19, Sum., 1946 (on radio in 1943)

	GD2.0	FN6.0	NM9.4
9-The Hangman & The Boy Buddies cont'd	100.00	300.00	800.00
10-Hangman & Dusty, the Boy Detective app.	57.00	171.00	455.00
11-Dusty app.; no Hangman	43.00	128.00	340.00
12-18: 14-Kinstler blood-c. 17-Hal Foster swipe from Prince Valiant; 1st issue with "An Archie Magazine" on-c	40.00	120.00	300.00
19-I.D. exposed; last issue	50.00	150.00	400.00

NOTE: *Hangman by **Fuje** in 9, 10. **Kinstler** a-15, c-14-16.*

BLACK JACK (Rocky Lane's...; formerly Jim Bowie)
Charlton Comics: No. 20, Nov, 1957 - No. 30, Nov, 1959

	GD2.0	FN6.0	NM9.4
20	8.35	25.00	50.00
21,27,29,30	5.00	15.00	30.00
22-(68 pgs.)	7.50	22.50	45.00
23-Williamson/Torres-a	7.00	21.00	42.00
24-26,28-Ditko-a	9.15	27.00	55.00

BLACK KNIGHT, THE
Toby Press: May, 1953; 1963

	GD2.0	FN6.0	NM9.4
1-Bondage-c	23.00	69.00	160.00
Super Reprint No. 11 (1963)-Reprints 1953 issue	2.50	7.50	20.00

BLACK KNIGHT, THE (Also see The Avengers #48, Marvel Super Heroes & Tales To Astonish #52)
Atlas Comics (MgPC): May, 1955 - No. 5, April, 1956

	GD2.0	FN6.0	NM9.4
1-Origin Crusader; Maneely-c/a	82.00	246.00	625.00
2-Maneely-c/a(4)	58.00	174.00	460.00
3-5: 4-Maneely-c/a. 5-Maneely-c, Shores-a	45.00	135.00	360.00

BLACK KNIGHT (Also see Avengers & Ultraforce)
Marvel Comics: June, 1990 - No. 4, Sept, 1990 ($1.50, limited series)

	GD2.0	FN6.0	NM9.4
1-4: 1-Original Black Knight returns			2.00

NOTE: ***Buckler** c-1-4p*

BLACK KNIGHT: EXODUS
Marvel Comics: Dec, 1996 ($2.50, one-shot)

	GD2.0	FN6.0	NM9.4
1-Raab-s; Apocalypse-c/app.			2.50

BLACK LAMB, THE
DC Comics (Helix): Nov, 1996 - No, 6, Apr, 1997 ($2.50, limited series)

	GD2.0	FN6.0	NM9.4
1-6: Tim Truman-c/a/scripts			2.50

BLACK LIGHTNING (See The Brave & The Bold, Cancelled Comic Cavalcade, DC Comics Presents #16, Detective #490 and World's Finest #257)
National Periodical Publ./DC Comics: Apr, 1977 - No. 11, Sept-Oct, 1978

	GD2.0	FN6.0	NM9.4
1,11: 1-Origin Black Lightning. 11-The Ray new solo story			5.00
2,3,6-10:			3.50
4,5-Superman-c/s. 4-Intro Cyclotronic Man			4.00

NOTE: ***Buckler** c-1-3p, 6-11p. #11 is 44 pgs.*

BLACK LIGHTNING (2nd Series)
DC Comics: Feb, 1995 - No. 13, Feb, 1996 ($1.95/$2.25)

	GD2.0	FN6.0	NM9.4
1-5-Tony Isabella scripts begin, ends #8			3.00
6-13: 6-Begin $2.25-c. 13-Batman-c/app.			3.00

BLACK MAGIC (...Magazine) (Becomes Cool Cat V8#6 on)
Crestwood Publ. V1#1-4,V6#1-V7#5/Headline V1#5-V5#3,V7#6-V8#5: 10-11/50 - V4#1, 6-7/53: V4#2, 9-10/53 - V5#3, 11-12/54; V6#1, 9-10/57 - V7#2, 11-12/58: V7#3, 7-8/60 - V8#5, 11-12/61
(V1#1-5, 52pgs.; V1#6-V3#3, 44pgs.)

	GD2.0	FN6.0	NM9.4
V1#1-S&K-a, 10 pgs.; Meskin-a(2)	80.00	240.00	800.00
2-S&K-a, 17 pgs.; Meskin-a	40.00	120.00	360.00
3-6(8-9/51)-S&K, Roussos, Meskin-a	36.00	107.00	325.00
V2#1(10-11/51),4,5,7(#13),9(#15),12(#18)-S&K-a	26.00	77.00	210.00
2,3,6,8,10,11(#17)	18.00	52.00	140.00
V3#1(#19, 12/52) - 6(#24, 5/53)-S&K-a	20.00	60.00	160.00
V4#1(#25, 6-7/53), 2(#26, 9-10/53)-S&K-a(3-4)	22.00	64.00	170.00
3(#27, 11-12/53)-S&K-a; Ditko-a (2nd published-a); also see Captain 3-D, Daring Love #1, Strange Fantasy #9, & Fantastic Fears #5 (Fant. Fears was 1st drawn, but not 1st publ.)	40.00	120.00	350.00
4(#28)-Eyes ripped out/story-S&K, Ditko-a	30.00	90.00	240.00
5(#29, 3-4/54)-S&K, Ditko-a	23.00	68.00	180.00
6(#30, 5-6/54)-S&K, Powell?-a	18.00	52.00	140.00
V5#1(#31, 7-8/54 - 3(#33, 11-12/54)-S&K-a	14.00	43.00	115.00
V6#1(#34, 9-10/57), 2(#35, 11-12/57)	8.50	26.00	60.00
3(1-2/58) - 6(7-8/58)	8.50	26.00	60.00
V7#1(9-10/58) - 3(7-8/60)	7.00	21.00	50.00
4(9-10/60), 5(11-12/60)-Torres-a	8.50	26.00	60.00
6(1-2/61)-Powell-a(2)	7.00	21.00	50.00
V8#1(3-4/61)-Powell-c/a	7.00	21.00	50.00
2(5-6/61)-E.C. story swipe/W.F. #22; Ditko, Powell-a	8.50	26.00	60.00
3(7-8/61)-E.C. story swipe/W.F. #22; Powell-a(2)	8.50	26.00	60.00
4(9-10/61)-Powell-a(5)	7.00	21.00	50.00
5-E.C. story swipe/W.S.F. #28; Powell-a(3)	8.50	26.00	60.00

NOTE: ***Bernard Baily** a-V4#6?, V5#3(2). **Grandenetti** a-V2#3, 11. **Kirby** c-V1#1-6, V2#1-12, V3#1-6, V4#1, 2, 4-6, V5#1-3. **McWilliams** a-V3#2i. **Meskin** a-V1#1(2), 2, 3, 4(2), 5(2), 6, V2/1, 2, 3(2), 4(3), 5, 6(2), 7-9, 11, 12i, V3#1(2), 5, 6, V5#1(2), 2. **Orlando** a-V6#1, 4, V7#2; c-V6/1-6. **Powell** a-V5#1?. **Roussos** a-V1#3-5, 6(2), V2#3(2), 4, 5(2), 6, 8, 9, 10(2), 11, 12p, V3#1(2), 2i, 5, V5#2. **Simon** a-V2#12, V3#2, V7#5? c-V4#3?, V7#3?, 4, 5?, 6?, V8#1-5. **Simon & Kirby** a-V1#1, 2(2), 3-6, V2#1, 4, 5, 7, 9, 12, V3#1-6, V4#1(3), 2(4), 3(2), 4(2), 5, 6, V5#1-3; c-V2#1. **Leonard Starr** a-V1#1. **Tuska** a-V6#3, 4. **Woodbridge** a-V7#4.*

BLACK MAGIC
National Periodical Publications: Oct-Nov, 1973 - No. 9, Apr-May, 1975

	GD2.0	FN6.0	NM9.4
1-S&K reprints	2.50	7.50	22.00
2-8-S&K reprints	1.50	4.50	12.00
9-S&K reprints	1.85	5.50	15.00

BLACK MAGIC
Eclipse International: Apr, 1990 - No. 4, Oct, 1990 ($2.75, B&W, mini-series)

	GD2.0	FN6.0	NM9.4
1-($3.50, 68pgs.)-Japanese manga			3.50
2-4 ($2.75, 52 pgs.)			3.00

BLACKMAIL TERROR (See Harvey Comics Library)

BLACK MASK
DC Comics: 1993 - No. 3, 1994 ($4.95, limited series, 52 pgs.)

	GD2.0	FN6.0	NM9.4
1-3			5.00

BLACK OPS
Image Comics (WildStorm): Jan, 1996 - No. 5, May, 1996 ($2.50, lim. series)

	GD2.0	FN6.0	NM9.4
1-5			2.50

BLACK ORCHID (See Adventure Comics #428 & Phantom Stranger)
DC Comics: Holiday, 1988-89 - No. 3, 1989 ($3.50, lim. series, prestige format)

	GD2.0	FN6.0	NM9.4
Book 1,3: Gaiman scripts & McKean painted-a in all		2.40	6.00
Book 2-Arkham Asylum story; Batman app.	1.00	2.80	7.00

BLACK ORCHID
DC Comics: Sept, 1993 - No. 22, June, 1995 ($1.95/$2.25)

	GD2.0	FN6.0	NM9.4
1-22: Dave McKean-c all issues			2.25
1-Platinum Edition			12.00
Annual 1 (1993, $3.95, 68 pgs.)-Children's Crusade			4.00

BLACKOUTS (See Broadway Hollywood...)

BLACK PANTHER, THE (Also see Avengers #52, Fantastic Four #52, Jungle Action & Marvel Premiere #51-53)

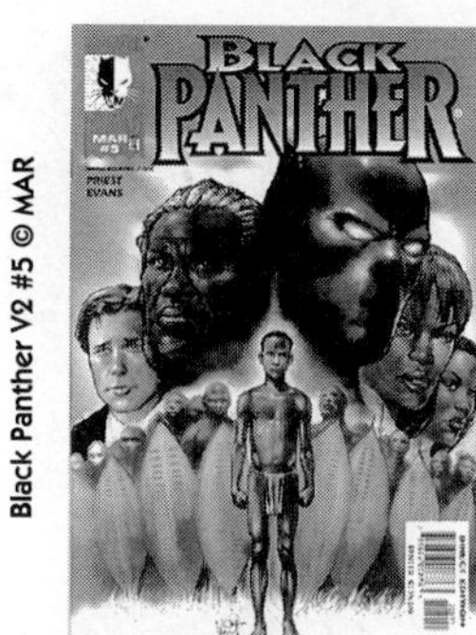

Black Panther V2 #5 © MAR

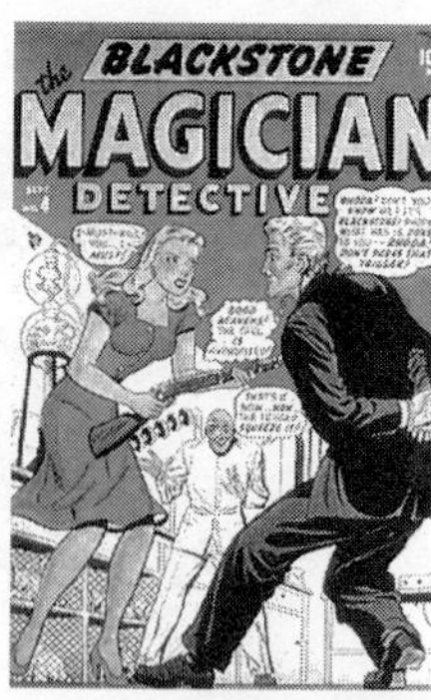

Blackstone, The Magician #4 © MAR

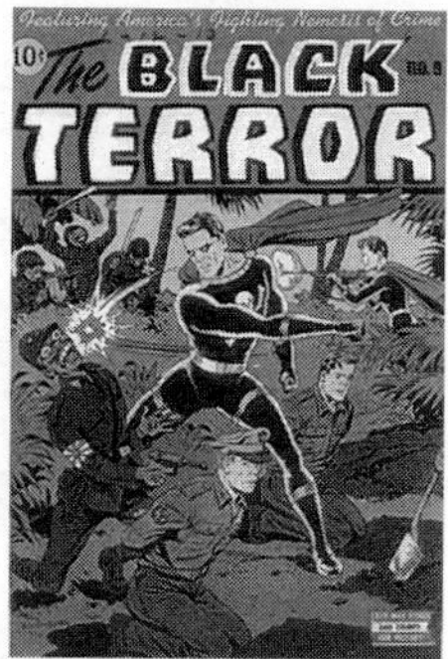

Black Terror #9 © Pub. Ent. Ltd.

GD2.0 FN6.0 NM9.4

Marvel Comics Group: Jan, 1977 - No. 15, May, 1979

1 1.75 5.25 14.00
2-13: 4,5-(Regular 30¢ editions) 1.00 2.80 7.00
4,5-(35¢-c variants, limited dist.)(7,9/77) 2.50 7.50 24.00
14,15-Avengers x-over 1.10 3.30 9.00
NOTE: ***J. Buscema*** *c-15p.* ***Kirby*** *c/a & scripts-1-12.* ***Layton*** *c-13i.*

BLACK PANTHER
Marvel Comics Group: July, 1988 - No. 4, Oct, 1988 ($1.25)

1-4 2.00

BLACK PANTHER (Marvel Knights)
Marvel Comics: Nov, 1998 - Present ($2.50)

1-Texeira-a/c; Priest-s 5.00
1-($6.95) DF edition w/Quesada& Palmiotti-c 7.00
2-4: 2-Two covers by Texeira and Timm. 3-Fantastic Four app. 3.00
5-10: 5-Evans-a. 6-8-Jusko-a. 8-Avengers-c/app. 2.50

BLACK PANTHER: PANTHER'S PREY
Marvel Comics: 1991 - No. 4, 1991 ($4.95, squarebound, lim. series, 52 pgs.)

1-4 5.00

BLACK PEARL, THE
Dark Horse Comics: Sept, 1996 - No. 5, Jan, 1997 ($2.95, limited series)

1-5: Mark Hamill scripts 3.00

BLACK PHANTOM (See Tim Holt #25, 38)
Magazine Enterprises: Nov, 1954 (one-shot) (Female outlaw)

1 (A-1 #122)-The Ghost Rider story plus 3 Black Phantom stories; Headlight-c/a 38.00 114.00 265.00

BLACK PHANTOM
AC Comics: 1989 - No. 3, 1990 ($2.50, B&W; #2 color)(Reprints & new-a)

1-3: 1-Ayers-r, Bolle-r/B.P. #1-3-Redmask-r 2.75

BLACK PHANTOM, RETURN OF THE (See Wisco)

BLACK RIDER (Western Winners #1-7; Western Tales of Black Rider #28-31; Gunsmoke Western #32 on)(See All Western Winners, Best Western, Kid Colt, Outlaw Kid, Rex Hart, Two-Gun Kid, Two-Gun Western, Western Gunfighters, Western Winners, & Wild Western)
Marvel/Atlas Comics(CDS No. 8-17/CPS No. 19 on): No. 8, 3/50 - No. 18, 1/52; No. 19, 11/53 - No. 27, 3/55

8 (#1)-Black Rider & his horse Satan begin; 36 pgs; Stan Lee photo-c as Black Rider) 40.00 120.00 325.00
9-52 pgs. begin, end #14 22.00 66.00 155.00
10-Origin Black Rider 26.00 79.00 185.00
11-14: 14-Last 52pgs. 16.00 47.00 110.00
15-19: 19-Two-Gun Kid app. 13.50 41.00 95.00
20-Classic-c; Two-Gun Kid app. 15.00 45.00 105.00
21-27: 21-23-Two-Gun Kid app. 24,25-Arrowhead app. 26-Kid Colt app. 27-Last issue; last precode. Kid Colt app. The Spider (a villain) burns to death 12.00 36.00 85.00
NOTE: ***Ayers*** *c-22.* ***Jack Keller*** *a-15, 26, 27.* ***Maneely*** *a-14; c-16, 17, 25, 27.* ***Syd Shores*** *a-19, 21, 22, 23(3), 24(3), 25-27; c-19, 21, 23.* ***Sinnott*** *a-24, 25.* ***Tuska*** *a-12, 19-21.*

BLACK RIDER RIDES AGAIN!, THE
Atlas Comics (CPS): Sept, 1957

1-Kirby-a(3); Powell-a; Severin-c 24.00 73.00 170.00

BLACK SEPTEMBER (Also see Avengers/Ultraforce, Ultraforce (1st series) #10 & Ultraforce/Avengers)
Malibu Comics (Ultraverse): 1995 ($1.50, one-shot)

Infinity-Intro to the newUltraverse; variant-c exists. 2.00

BLACKSTONE (See Super Magician Comics & Wisco Giveaways)

BLACKSTONE, MASTER MAGICIAN COMICS
Vital Publ./Street & Smith Publ.: Mar-Apr, 1946 - No. 3, July-Aug, 1946

1 27.00 81.00 190.00
2,3 19.00 56.00 130.00

GD2.0 FN6.0 NM9.4

BLACKSTONE, THE MAGICIAN (...Detective on cover only #3 & 4)
Marvel Comics (CnPC): No. 2, May, 1948 - No. 4, Sept, 1948 (No #1) (Cont'd from E.C. #1?)

2-The Blonde Phantom begins, ends #4 56.00 169.00 450.00
3,4: 3-Blonde Phantom by Sekowsky 40.00 120.00 300.00

BLACKSTONE, THE MAGICIAN DETECTIVE FIGHTS CRIME
E. C. Comics: Fall, 1947

1-1st app. Happy Houlihans 46.00 137.00 365.00

BLACK SWAN COMICS
MLJ Magazines (Pershing Square Publ. Co.): 1945

1-The Black Hood reprints from Black Hood No. 14; Bill Woggon-a; Suzie app. 22.00 66.00 155.00

BLACK TARANTULA (See Feature Presentations No. 5)

BLACK TERROR (See America's Best Comics & Exciting Comics)
Better Publications/Standard: Winter, 1942-43 - No. 27, June, 1949

1-Black Terror, Crime Crusader begin 275.00 825.00 2200.00
2 100.00 300.00 800.00
3 70.00 210.00 560.00
4,5 59.00 177.00 470.00
6-10: 7-The Ghost app. 52.00 156.00 415.00
11-20: 20-The Scarab app. 41.00 124.00 330.00
21-Miss Masque app. 46.00 138.00 365.00
22-Part Frazetta-a on one Black Terror story 41.00 124.00 330.00
23,25-27 40.00 120.00 310.00
24-Frazetta-a (1/4 pg.) 40.00 120.00 320.00
NOTE: ***Schomburg (Xela)*** *c-2-27; bondage c-2, 17, 24.* ***Meskin*** *a-27.* ***Moreira*** *a-27.* ***Robinson/Meskin*** *a-23, 24(3), 25, 26.* ***Roussos/Mayo*** *a-24.* ***Tuska*** *a-26, 27.*

BLACK TERROR, THE (Also see Total Eclipse)
Eclipse Comics: Oct, 1989 - No. 3, June, 1990 ($4.95, 52 pgs., squarebound, limited series)

1-3: Beau Smith & Chuck Dixon scripts; Dan Brereton painted-c/a 5.00

BLACKTHORNE 3-D SERIES
Blackthorne Publishing Co.: May, 1985 - No. 80, 1989 ($2.25/$2.50)

1-Sheena in 3-D #1. D. Stevens-c/retouched-a 4.00
2-10: 2-MerlinRealm in 3-D #1. 3-3-D Heroes #1. Goldyn in 3-D #1. 5-Bizarre 3-D Zone #1. 6-Salimba in 3-D #1. 7-Twisted Tales in 3-D #1. 8-Dick Tracy in 3-D #1. 9-Salimba in 3-D #2. 10-Gumby in 3-D #1 4.00
11-19: 11-Betty Boop in 3-D #1. 12-Hamster Vice in 3-D #1. 13-Little Nemo in 3-D #1. 14-Gumby in 3-D #2. 15-Hamster Vice #6 in 3-D. 16-Laffin' Gas #6 in 3-D. 17-Gumby in 3-D #3. 18-Bullwinkle and Rocky in 3-D #1. 19-The Flintstones in 3-D #1. 4.00
20,26,35,39,52,62-G.I. Joe in 3-D. 62-G.I. Joe Annual 5.00
21-24,27-28: 21-Gumby in 3-D #4. 22-The Flintstones in 3-D #2. 23-Laurel & Hardy in 3-D #1. 24-Bozothe Clown in 3-D #1. 27-Bravestarr in 3-D #1. 28- Gumby in 3-D #5. 4.00
25,29,37-The Transformers in 3-D 5.00
30-Star Wars in 3-D #1 1.50 4.50 12.00
31-34,36,38,40: 31-The California Raisins in 3-D #1. 32-Richie Rich & Casper in 3-D #1. 33-Gumby in 3-D #6. 34-Laurel & Hardy in 3-D #2. 36-The Flintstones in 3-D #3. 38-Gumby in 3-D #7. 40-Bravestarr in 3-D #2 4.00
41-46,49,50: 41-Battletech in 3-D #1. 42-The Flintstones in 3-D #4. 43-Underdog in 3-D #1 44-The California Raisins in 3-D #2. 45-Red Heat in 3-D #1 (movie adapt.). 46-The California Raisins in 3-D #3. 49-Rambo in 3-D #1. 49-Sad Sack in 3-D #1. 50-Bullwinkle For President in 3-D #1 4.00
47,48-Star Wars in 3-D #2,3 1.00 3.00 8.00
51,53-60: 51-Kull in 3-D #1. 53-Red Sonja in 3-D #1. 54-Bozo in 3-D #2. 55-Waxwork in 3-D #1 (movie adapt.). 56. 57-Casper in 3-D #1. 58-Baby Huey in 3-D #1. 59-Little Dot in 3-D #1. 60-Solomon Kane in 3-D #1 4.00
61,63-80: 61-Werewolf in 3-D #1. 63-The California Raisins in 3-D #4. 64-To Die For in 3-D #1. 65-Capt. Holo in 3-D #1. 66-Playful Little Audrey in 3-D #1. 67-Kull in 3-D #2. 68. 69-The California Raisins in 3-D #5. 70-Wendy in 3-D #1. 71. 72-Sports Hall of Shame #1. 73. 74-The Noid in 3-D #1. 75-Moonwalker in 3-D #1 (Michael Jackson movie adapt.). 76-79. 80-The

Black Widow #1 © MAR

Blade Runner #1 © MAR

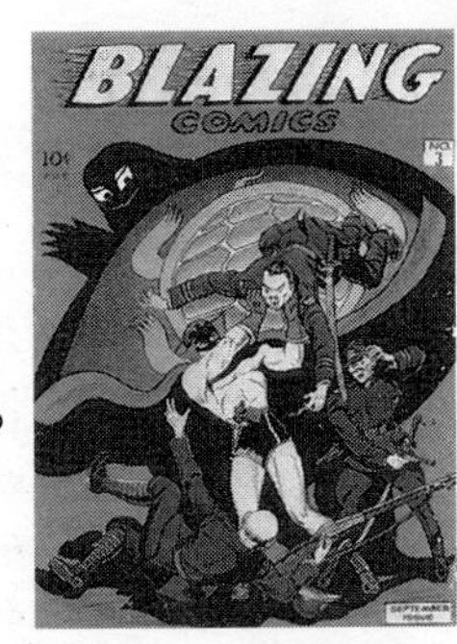

Blazing Comics #3 © Enwil

GD2.0 FN6.0 NM9.4

Noid in 3-D #2 4.00

BLACK WIDOW (Marvel Knights)
Marvel Comics: May, 1999 - No. 3, Aug, 1999 ($2.99, limited series)
1-(June on-c) Devin Grayson-s/J.G. Jones-c/a; Daredevil app. 4.00
1-Variant-c by Jones 4.00
2,3 3.00
...Web of Intrigue (6/99, $3.50) r/origin & early appearances 3.50

BLACKWULF
Marvel Comics: June, 1994 - No. 10, Mar, 1995 ($1.50)
1-($2.50)-Embossed-c; Angel Medina-a 2.50
2-10 2.00

BLADE (The Vampire Hunter)
Marvel Comics: Mar, 1998 ($3.50, one-shot)
1-Colan-a(p)/Christopher Golden-s 3.50

BLADE (The Vampire Hunter)
Marvel Comics: Nov, 1998 - No. 3, Jan, 1999 ($3.50/$2.99)
1-($3.50) Contains Movie insider pages; McKean-a 3.50
2,3-($2.99): 2-Two covers 3.00
...Sins of the Father (10/98, $5.99) Sears-a 6.00

BLADE OF THE IMMORTAL (Manga)
Dark Horse Comics: June, 1996 - Present ($2.95/$3.95, B&W)
1-10: 2-#1 on cover in error 4.00
11,19,20,34-($3.95, 48 pgs.): 34-Food one-shot 4.00
12-18,21-33,35-37: 12-Begin Dreamsong. 21-Begin On Silent Wings. 29-Begin Dark Shadow. 35-Begin Heart of Darkness 4.00

BLADE RUNNER (Movie)
Marvel Comics Group: Oct, 1982 - No. 2, Nov, 1982
1,2-r/Marvel Super Special #22; 1-Williamson-c/a. 2-Williamson-a 2.00

BLADESMEN UNDERSEA
Blue Comet Press: 1994 ($3.50, B&W)
1-Polybagged w/trading card 3.50

BLADE: THE VAMPIRE-HUNTER
Marvel Comics: July, 1994 - No. 10, Apr, 1995 ($1.95)
1-($2.95)-Foil-c 4.00
2-10 3.00

BLAIR WITCH PROJECT, THE (Movie companion, not adaption)
Oni Press: July, 1999 ($2.95, B&W, one-shot)
1-(1st printing) History of the Blair Witch, art by Edwards, Mireault, and Davis; Van Meter-s; only the stick figure is red on the cover 15.00
1-(2nd printing) Stick figure and title lettering are red on cover 5.00
1-(3rd printing) Stick figure, title, and creator credits are red on cover 3.00
DF Glow in the Dark variant-c ($10.00) 10.00

BLAST (Satire Magazine)
G & D Publications: Feb, 1971 - No. 2, May, 1971
1-Wrightson & Kaluta-a/Everette-c 5.50 16.50 55.00
2-Kaluta-c/a 3.80 11.40 38.00

BLAST CORPS
Dark Horse Comics: Oct, 1998 ($2.50, one-shot, based on Nintendo game)
1-Reprints from Nintendo Power magazine; Mahn-a 2.50

BLASTERS SPECIAL
DC Comics: 1989 ($2.00, one-shot)
1-Peter David scripts; Invasion spin-off 2.00

BLAST-OFF (Three Rocketeers)
Harvey Publications (Fun Day Funnies): Oct, 1965 (12¢)
1-Kirby/Williamson-a(2); Williamson/Crandall-a; Williamson/Torres/Krenkel-a; Kirby/Simon-c 4.20 12.60 42.00

BLAZE
Marvel Comics: Aug, 1994 - No. 12, July, 1995 ($1.95)
1-($2.95)-Foil embossed-c 3.00
2-12: 2-Man-Thing-c/story 2.00

BLAZE CARSON (Rex Hart #6 on)(See Kid Colt, Tex Taylor, Wild Western, Wisco)
Marvel Comics (USA): Sept, 1948 - No. 5, June, 1949
1: 1,2-Shores-c 26.00 77.00 180.00
2,4,5: 4-Two-Gun Kid app. 5-Tex Taylor app. 19.00 56.00 130.00
3-Used by N.Y. State Legis. Comm. (injury to eye splash); Tex Morgan app. 20.00 60.00 140.00

BLAZE: LEGACY OF BLOOD (See Ghost Rider & Ghost Rider/Blaze)
Marvel Comics (Midnight Sons imprint): Dec, 1993 - No. 4, Mar, 1994 ($1.75, limited series)
1-4 2.00

BLAZE THE WONDER COLLIE (Formerly Molly Manton's Romances #1?)
Marvel Comics(SePI): No. 2, Oct, 1949 - No. 3, Feb, 1950 (Both have photo-c)
2(#1), 3-(Scarce) 22.00 66.00 155.00

BLAZING BATTLE TALES
Seaboard Periodicals (Atlas): July, 1975
1-Intro. Sgt. Hawk & the Sky Demon; Severin, McWilliams, Sparling-a; Thorne-c 5.00

BLAZING COMBAT (Magazine)
Warren Publishing Co.: Oct, 1965 - No. 4, July, 1966 (35¢, B&W)
1-Frazetta painted-c on all 15.00 45.00 150.00
2 4.00 12.00 40.00
3,4: 4-Frazetta half pg. ad 3.00 9.00 30.00
...Anthology (reprints from No. 1-4) 4.20 12.60 42.00
NOTE: *Above has art by* ***Colan, Crandall, Evans, Morrow, Orlando, Severin, Torres, Toth, Williamson,*** *and* ***Wood.***

BLAZING COMBAT: WORLD WAR I AND WORLD WAR II
Apple Press: Mar, 1994 ($3.75, B&W)
1,2: 1-r/Colan, Toth, Goodwin, Severin, Wood-a. 2-r/Crandall, Evans, Severin, Torres, Williamson-a 3.75

BLAZING COMICS
Enwil Associates/Rural Home: 6/44 - #3, 9/44; #4, 2/45; #5, 3/45; #5(V2#2), 3/55 - #6(V2#3), 1955?
1-The Green Turtle, Red Hawk, Black Buccaneer begin; origin Jun-Gal 47.00 141.00 375.00
2-5: 3-Briefer-a. 5-(V2#2 inside) 33.00 99.00 230.00
5(3/55, V2#2-inside)-Black Buccaneer-c, 6(V2#3-inside, 1955)-Indian/Japanese-c 13.00 39.00 90.00
NOTE: *No. 5 & 6 contain remaindered comics rebound and the contents can vary. Cloak & Daggar, Will Rogers, Superman 64, Star Spangled 130, Kaanga known. Value would be half of contents.*

BLAZING SIXGUNS
Avon Periodicals: Dec, 1952
1-Kinstler-c/a; Larsen/Alascia-a(2), Tuska?-a; Jesse James, Kit Carson, Wild Bill Hickok app. 14.00 43.00 100.00

BLAZING SIXGUNS
I.W./Super Comics: 1964
I.W. Reprint #1,8,9: 1-r/Wild Bill Hickok #26, Western True Crime #? & Blazing Sixguns #1 by Avon; Kinstler-c. 8-r/Blazing Western #?; Kinstler-c. 9-r/Blazing Western #1; Ditko-r; Kintsler-c reprinted from Dalton Boys #1. 1.50 4.50 12.00
Super Reprint #10,11,15,16: 10,11-r/The Rider #2,1. 15-r/Silver Kid Western #?. 16-r/Buffalo Bill #?; Wildey-r; Severin-c. 17(1964)-r/Western True Crime #? 1.50 4.50 12.00
12-Reprints Bullseye #3; S&K-a 3.00 9.00 30.00
18-r/Straight Arrow #? by Powell; Severin-c 1.60 4.85 13.00

BLAZING SIX-GUNS (Also see Sundance Kid)
Skywald Comics: Feb, 1971 - No. 2, Apr, 1971 (52 pgs.)
1-The Red Mask, Sundance Kid begin, Avon's Geronimo reprint by Kinstler;

Blazing West #3 © ACG

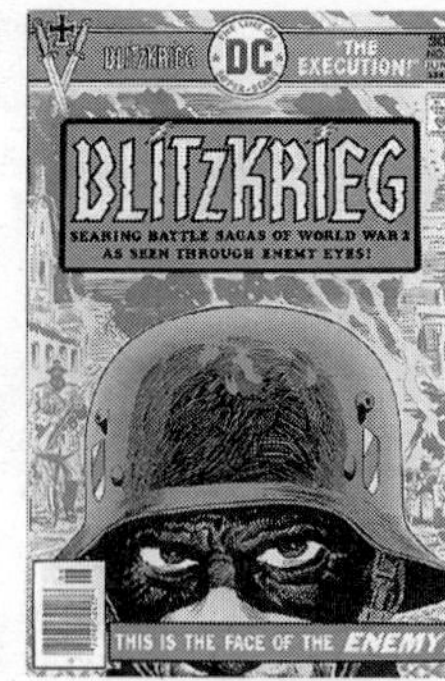

Blitzkrieg #3 © DC

Blood: A Tale #2 © JM DeMatteis & Kent Williams

	GD2.0	FN6.0	NM9.4
Wyatt Earp app.	1.50	4.50	12.00
2-Wild Bill Hickok, Jesse James, Kit Carson-r plus M.E. Red Mask-r	1.10	3.30	9.00

BLAZING WEST (Also see The Hooded Horseman)
American Comics Group (B&I Publ./Michel Publ.): Fall, 1948 - No. 22, Mar-Apr, 1952

	GD2.0	FN6.0	NM9.4
1-Origin & 1st app. Injun Jones, Tenderfoot & Buffalo Belle; Texas Tim & Ranger begins, ends #13	19.00	58.00	135.00
2,3	10.00	30.00	65.00
4-Origin & 1st app. Little Lobo; Starr-a	8.35	25.00	50.00
5-10: 5-Starr-a	7.00	21.00	42.00
11-13	5.35	16.00	32.00
14-Origin & 1st app. The Hooded Horseman	10.00	30.00	70.00
15-22: 15,16,18,19-Starr-a	7.50	22.50	45.00

BLAZING WESTERN
Timor Publications: Jan, 1954 - No. 5, Sept, 1954

	GD2.0	FN6.0	NM9.4
1-Ditko-a (1st Western-a?); text story by Bruce Hamilton	14.00	43.00	100.00
2-4	6.35	19.00	38.00
5-Disbrow-a	6.70	20.00	40.00

BLEAT
Slave Labor Graphics: Aug, 1995 ($2.95)

	GD2.0	FN6.0	NM9.4
1			3.00

BLIND JUSTICE (Also see Batman: Blind Justice)
DC Comics/Diamond Comic Distributors: 1989 (Giveaway, squarebound)

	GD2.0	FN6.0	NM9.4
nn-Contains Detective #598-600 by Batman movie writer Sam Hamm, w/covers; published same time as originals?			2.00

BLINDSIDE
Image Comics (Extreme Studios): Aug, 1996 ($2.50)

	GD2.0	FN6.0	NM9.4
1-Variant-c exists			2.50

BLIP
Marvel Comics Group: 2/1983 - 1983 (Video game mag. in comic format)

	GD2.0	FN6.0	NM9.4
1-1st app. Donkey Kong & Mario Bros. in comics, 6pgs. comics; photo-c		2.40	6.00
2-Spider-Man photo-c; 6pgs. Spider-Man comics w/Green Goblin	1.00	2.80	7.00
3,4,6			3.50
5-E.T., Indiana Jones; Rocky-c			4.00
7-6pgs. Hulk comics; Pac-Man & Donkey Kong Jr. Hints			5.00

BLISS ALLEY
Image Comics: July, 1997 - No. 2($2.95, B&W)

	GD2.0	FN6.0	NM9.4
1,2-Messner-Loebs-s/a			3.00

BLITZKRIEG
National Periodical Publications: Jan-Feb, 1976 - No. 5, Sept-Oct, 1976

	GD2.0	FN6.0	NM9.4
1-Kubert-c on all	3.00	9.00	30.00
2-5	2.25	6.75	18.00

BLONDE PHANTOM (Formerly All-Select #1-11; Lovers #23 on)(Also see Blackstone, Marvel Mystery, Millie The Model #2, Sub-Mariner Comics #25 & Sun Girl)
Marvel Comics (MPC): No. 12, Winter, 1946-47 - No. 22, Mar, 1949

	GD2.0	FN6.0	NM9.4
12-Miss America begins, ends #14	137.00	412.00	1100.00
13-Sub-Mariner begins (not in #16)	84.00	253.00	675.00
14,15: 15-Kurtzman's "Hey Look"	78.00	234.00	625.00
16-Captain America with Bucky story by Rico(p), 6 pgs.; Kurtzman's "Hey Look" (1 pg.)	106.00	318.00	850.00
17-22: 22-Anti Wertham editorial	70.00	212.00	565.00

NOTE: ***Shores** c-12-18.*

BLONDIE (See Ace Comics, Comics Reading Libraries, Dagwood, Daisy & Her Pups, Eat Right to Work..., King & Magic Comics)
David McKay Publications: 1942 - 1946

	GD2.0	FN6.0	NM9.4
Feature Books 12 (Rare)	64.00	192.00	640.00
Feature Books 27-29,31,34(1940)	19.00	56.00	130.00
Feature Books 36,38,40,42,43,45,47	17.00	51.00	120.00
...1944 (Hard-c, 1938, B&W, 128 pgs.)-1944 daily strip-r	13.50	41.00	95.00

BLONDIE & DAGWOOD FAMILY
Harvey Publ. (King Features Synd.): Oct, 1963 - No. 4, Dec, 1965 (68 pgs.)

	GD2.0	FN6.0	NM9.4
1	2.40	7.20	24.00
2-4	1.40	4.20	14.00

BLONDIE COMICS (...Monthly No. 16-141)
David McKay #1-15/Harvey #16-163/King #164-175/Charlton #177 on: Spring, 1947 - No. 163, Nov, 1965; No. 164, Aug, 1966 - No. 175, Dec, 1967; No. 177, Feb, 1969 - No. 222, Nov, 1976

	GD2.0	FN6.0	NM9.4
1	24.00	73.00	170.00
2	11.50	34.00	80.00
3-5	10.00	30.00	60.00
6-10	7.50	22.50	45.00
11-15	5.35	16.00	32.00
16-(3/50; 1st Harvey issue)	6.70	20.00	40.00
17-20: 20-(3/51)-Becomes Daisy & Her Pups #21 & Chamber of Chills #21	3.00	9.00	30.00
21-30	2.50	7.50	22.00
31-50	2.25	6.75	18.00
51-80	2.00	6.00	16.00
81-99	1.75	5.25	14.00
100	2.25	6.75	18.00
101-124,126-130	1.50	4.50	12.00
125 (80 pgs.)	2.50	7.50	25.00
131-136,138,139	1.10	3.30	9.00
137,140-(80 pgs.)	2.50	7.50	22.00
141-147,149-154,156,160,164-167	1.50	4.50	12.00
148,155,157-159,161-163 are 68 pgs.	2.50	7.50	20.00
168-175	1.00	3.00	8.00
177-199 (no #176)	1.00	2.80	7.00
200	1.25	3.75	10.00
201-222: 211,212-1st & 2nd app. Super Dagwood		2.40	6.00
Blondie, Dagwood & Daisy 1(100 pgs., 1953)	18.00	54.00	125.00

BLOOD
Marvel Comics (Epic Comics): Feb, 1988 - No. 4, Apr, 1988 ($3.25, mature)

	GD2.0	FN6.0	NM9.4
1-4: DeMatteis scripts & Kent Williams-c/a			3.50

BLOOD AND GLORY (Punisher & Captain America)
Marvel Comics: Oct, 1992 - No. 3, Dec, 1992 ($5.95, limited series)

	GD2.0	FN6.0	NM9.4
1-3: 1-Embossed wraparound-c			6.00

BLOOD & ROSES: FUTURE PAST TENSE (Bob Hickey's...)
Sky Comics: Dec, 1993 ($2.25)

	GD2.0	FN6.0	NM9.4
1-Silver ink logo			2.25

BLOOD & ROSES: SEARCH FOR THE TIME-STONE (Bob Hickey's...)
Sky Comics: Apr, 1994 ($2.50)

	GD2.0	FN6.0	NM9.4
1			2.50

BLOOD AND SHADOWS
DC Comics (Vertigo): 1996 - Book 4, 1996 ($5.95, squarebound, mature)

	GD2.0	FN6.0	NM9.4
Books 1-4: Joe R. Lansdale scripts; Mark A. Nelson-c/a.			6.00

BLOOD: A TALE
DC Comics (Vertigo): Nov, 1996 - No. 4, Feb, 1997 ($2.95, limited series)

	GD2.0	FN6.0	NM9.4
1-4: Reprints Epic series w/new-c; DeMatteis scripts; Kent Williams-c/a			3.00

BLOODBATH
DC Comics: Early Dec, 1993 - No. 2, Late Dec, 1993 ($3.50, 68 pgs.)

	GD2.0	FN6.0	NM9.4
1-Neon ink-c; Superman app.; new Batman-c /app.			3.50
2-Hitman 2nd app.	1.00	2.80	7.00

BLOODFIRE
Lightning Comics: June, 1993 - No. 12, May, 1994 ($2.95)

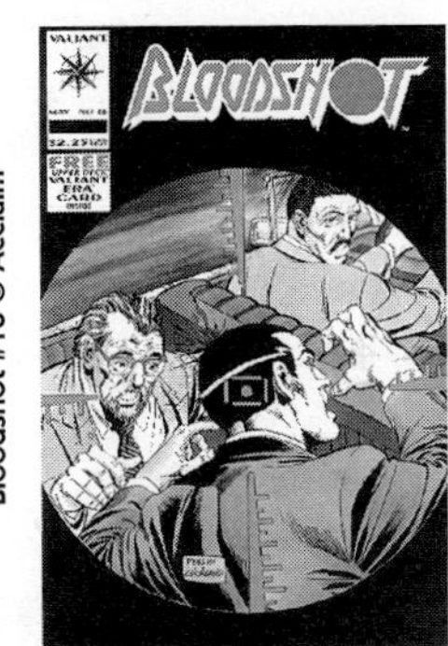

Bloodshot #16 © Acclaim

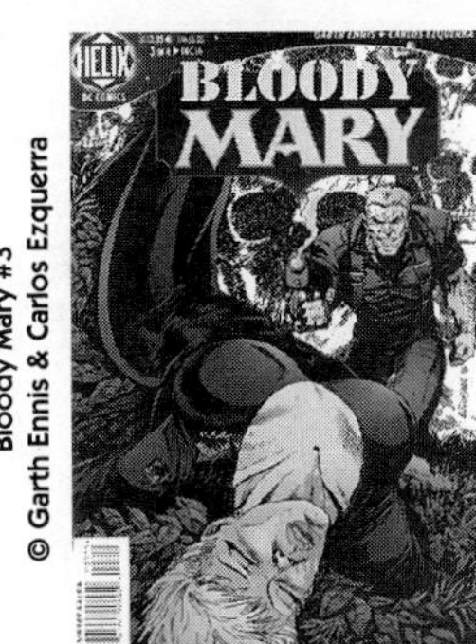

Bloody Mary #3 © Garth Ennis & Carlos Ezquerra

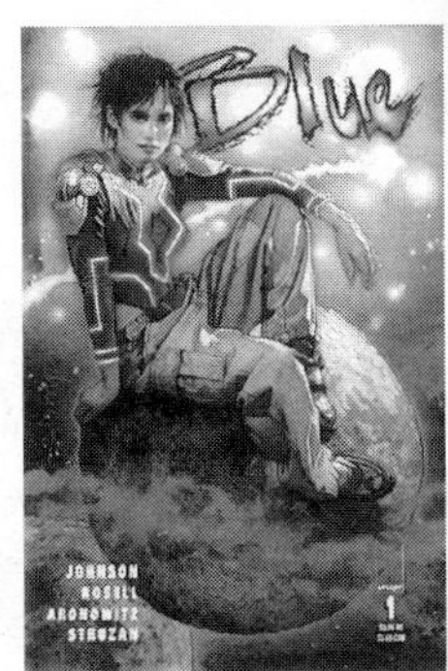

Blue #1 © Greg Aronowitz and Drew Struzan

GD2.0 FN6.0 NM9.4

1-($3.50)-Foil-c; 1st app. Bloodfire 3.50
2-12: 2-Origin; contracts HIV virus via transfusion. 5-Polybagged w/card & collectors warning on bag. 12-(5/94) 3.00
0-(Indicia reads June 1994, May on-c, $3.50) 3.50
.../Hellina 1 (7/95, $3.00) 3.00
.../Hellina 1 (7/95, $9.95)-Nude edition; Deodato-c 10.00
.../Hellina (8/95, $9.95)-Commemorative edition 10.00

BLOODLINES: A TALE FROM THE HEART OF AFRICA (See Tales From the Heart of Africa)
Marvel Comics (Epic Comics): 1992 ($5.95, 52 pgs.)
1-Story cont'd from Tales From... 6.00

BLOOD OF DRACULA
Apple Comics: Nov, 1987 - No. 20?, 1990 ($1.75/$1.95, B&W)($2.25 #14,16 on)
11-14,16-20: 110-Chadwick-c. 4,16-19-Lost Frankenstein pgs. by Wrightson 3.00
15-Contains stereo flexidisc ($3.75) 3.75

BLOOD OF THE INNOCENT (See Warp Graphics Annual)
WaRP Graphics: 1/7/86 - No. 4, 1/28/86 (Weekly mini-series, mature)
1-4 2.00

BLOODPACK
DC Comics: Mar, 1995 - No. 4, June,1995 ($1.50, limited series)
1-4 2.00

BLOODPOOL
Image Comics (Extreme): Aug, 1995 - No. 4, Nov, 1995 ($2.50, limited series)
1-4: Jo Duffy scripts in all 2.50
Special (3/96, $2.50)-Jo Duffy scripts 2.50
Trade Paperback (1996, $12.95)-r/#1-4 13.00

BLOOD REIGN SAGA
London Night Studios: 1996 ($3.00, B&W, mature)
1-"Encore Edition" 3.00

BLOODSCENT
Comico: Oct, 1988 ($2.00, one-shot, Baxter paper)
1-Colan-p 2.00

BLOODSEED
Marvel Comics (Frontier Comics): Oct, 1993 - No. 2, Nov, 1993 ($1.95)
1,2: Sharp/Cam Smith-a 2.00

BLOODSHOT (See Eternal Warrior #4 & Rai #0)
Valiant/Acclaim Comics (Valiant): Nov, 1992 - No. 51, Aug, 1996 ($2.25/$2.50)
1-($3.50)-Chromium embossed-c by B. Smith w/poster 4.00
2-5,8-14: 3-$2.25-c begins; cont'd in Hard Corps #5. 4-Eternal Warrior-c/story. 5-Rai & Eternal Warrior app. 14-(3/94)-Reese-c(i) 2.50
6,7-1st app. Ninjak (out of costume). 7-In costume 3.00
0-(3/94, $3.50)-Wraparound chromium-c by Quesada(p); origin 3.50
0-Gold variant 6.00
15(4/94)-51: 16-w/bound-in trading card. 51-Bloodshot dies? 2.50
Yearbook 1 (1994, $3.95) 4.00
Special 1 (3/94, $5.95)-Zeck-c/a(p) 6.00

BLOODSHOT (Volume Two)
Acclaim Comics (Valiant): July, 1997 - No. 16, Oct, 1998 ($2.50)
1-16: 1-Two covers. 5-Copycat-c. X-O Manowar-c/app 3.00

BLOODSTRIKE (See Supreme V2#3)
Image Comics (Extreme Studios): 1993 - No. 22, May, 1995; No. 25, May, 1994 ($1.95/$2.50)
1-22, 25: Liefeld layouts in early issues. 1-Blood Brothers prelude. 2-1st app. Lethal. 5-1st app. Noble. 9-Black and White part 6 by Art Thibert; Liefeld pin-up. 9,10-Have coupon #3 & 7 for Extreme Prejudice #0. 10-(4/94). 11-(7/94). 16:Platt-c; Prophet app. 17-19-polybagged w/card . 25-(5/94)-Liefeld/Fraga-c 3.00

NOTE: ***Giffen** story/layouts-4-6.* ***Jae Lee** c-7, 8.* ***Rob Liefeld** layouts-1-3.* ***Art Thibert** c-6i.*

BLOODSTRIKE ASSASSIN
Image Comics (Extreme Studios): June, 1995 - No. 3, Aug, 1995; No. 0, Oct, 1995 ($2.50, limited series)
0-3: 3-(8/95)-Quesada-c. 0-(10/95)-Battlestone app. 3.00

BLOOD SWORD, THE
Jademan Comics: Aug, 1988 - No. 53, Dec, 1992 ($1.50/$1.95, 68 pgs.)
1-53: Kung Fu stories 2.50

BLOOD SWORD DYNASTY
Jademan Comics: 1989 -No. 41, Jan, 1993 ($1.25, 36 pgs.)
1-41: Ties into Blood Sword 2.50

BLOOD SYNDICATE
DC Comics (Milestone): Apr, 1993 - No. 35, Feb, 1996 ($1.50/-$3.50)
1-($2.95)-Collector's Edition; polybagged with poster, trading card, & acid-free backing board (direct sale only) 3.50
1-9,11-24,26,27,29,33-34: 8-Intro Kwai. 15-Byrne-c. 16-Worlds Collide Pt. 6; Superman-c/app.17-Worlds Collide Pt. 13. 29-(99¢); Long Hot Summer x-over 2.00
10,28,30-32: 10-Simonson-c. 30-Long Hot Summer x-over 2.50
25-($2.95, 52 pgs.) 3.00
35-Kwai disappears; last issue 3.50

BLOODWULF
Image Comics (Extreme): Feb, 1995 - No. 4, May, 1995 ($2.50, limited series)
1-4: 1-Liefeld-c w/4 diferent captions & alternate-c. 2.50
Summer Special (8/95, $2.50)-Jeff Johnson-c/a; Supreme app; story takes place between Legend of Supreme #3 & Supreme #23. 2.50

BLOODY MARY
DC Comics (Helix): Oct, 1996 - No. 4, Jan, 1997 ($2.25, limited series)
1-4: Garth Ennis scripts; Ezquerra-c/a in all 3.50

BLOODY MARY: LADY LIBERTY
DC Comics (Helix): Sept, 1997 - No. 4, Dec, 1997 ($2.50, limited series)
1-4: Garth Ennis scripts; Ezquerra-c/a in all 3.00

BLUE
Image Comics (Action Toys): Aug, 1999 - Present ($2.50)
1-Aronowitz-s/Struzan-c 2.50

BLUEBEARD
Slave Labor Graphics: Nov, 1993 - No. 3, Mar, 1994 ($2.95, B&W, lim. series)
1-3: James Robinson scripts. 2-(12/93) 3.00
Trade paperback (6/94, $9.95) 10.00
Trade paperback (2nd printing, 7/96, $12.95)-New-c 13.00

BLUE BEETLE, THE (Also see All Top, Big-3, Mystery Men & Weekly Comic Magazine)
Fox Publ. No. 1-11, 31-60; Holyoke No. 12-30: Winter, 1939-40 - No. 57, 7/48; No. 58, 4/50 - No. 60, 8/50

	GD2.0	FN6.0	NM9.4
1-Reprints from Mystery Men #1-5; Blue Beetle origin; Yarko the Great-r/from Wonder/Wonderworld 2-5 all by Eisner; Master Magician app.; (Blue Beetle in 4 different costumes)	400.00	1200.00	3600.00
2-K-51-r by Powell/Wonderworld 8,9	144.00	432.00	1150.00
3-Simon-c	100.00	300.00	800.00
4-Marijuana drug mention story	67.00	200.00	540.00
5-Zanzibar The Magician by Tuska	61.00	183.00	490.00
6-Dynamite Thor begins (1st); origin Blue Beetle	58.00	174.00	465.00
7,8-Dynamo app. in both. 8-Last Thor	54.00	162.00	435.00
9-12: 9,10-The Blackbird & The Gorilla app. in both. 10-Bondage/hypo-c 11(2/42)-The Gladiator app. 12(6/42)-The Black Fury app.	48.00	144.00	385.00
13-V-Man begins (1st app.), ends #18; Kubert-a	58.00	174.00	465.00
14,15-Kubert-a in both. 14-Intro. side-kick (c/text only), Sparky (called Spunky #17-19)	50.00	150.00	400.00
16-18: 17-Brodsky-c	40.00	120.00	310.00
19-Kubert-a	40.00	120.00	320.00
20-Origin/1st app. Tiger Squadron; Arabian Nights begin	44.00	132.00	350.00

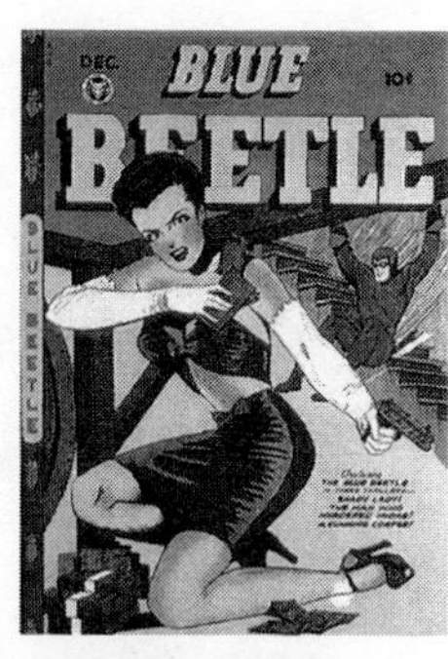

The Blue Beetle #51 © FOX

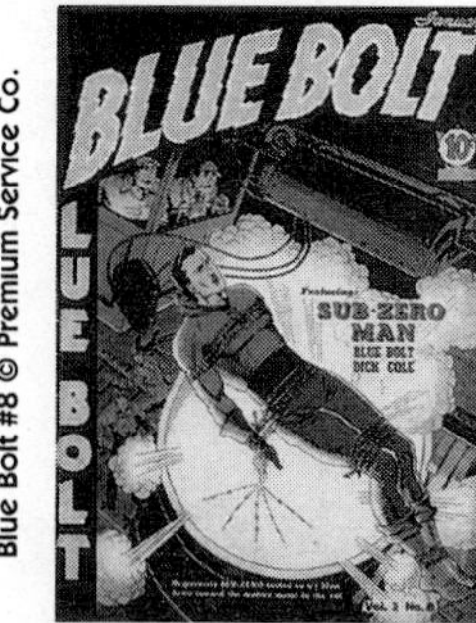

Blue Bolt #8 © Premium Service Co.

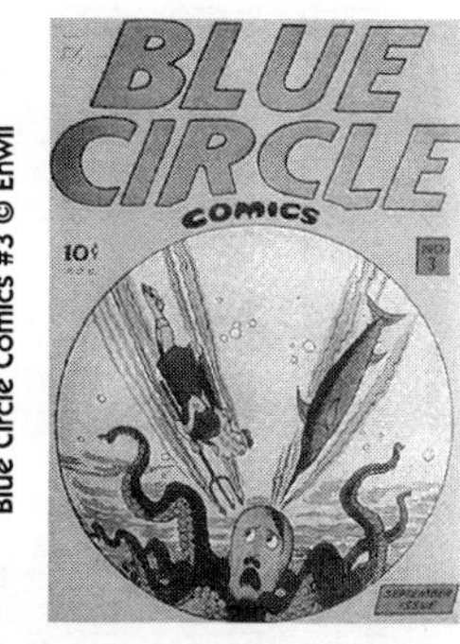

Blue Circle Comics #3 © Enwil

GD2.0 FN6.0 NM9.4

21-26: 24-Intro. & only app. The Halo. 26-General Patton story & photo
33.00 100.00 230.00
27-Tamaa, Jungle Prince app. 30.00 90.00 210.00
28-30(2/44) 27.00 81.00 190.00
31(6/44), 33,34,36-40: 34-38-"The Threat from Saturn" serial.
25.00 75.00 175.00
32-Hitler-c 36.00 108.00 250.00
35-Extreme violence 30.00 90.00 210.00
41-45 23.00 69.00 160.00
46-The Puppeteer app. 26.00 78.00 180.00
47-Kamen & Baker-a begin 109.00 327.00 875.00
48-50 87.00 261.00 700.00
51,53 74.00 222.00 590.00
52-Kamen bondage-c; true crime stories begin 111.00 332.00 885.00
54-Used in **SOTI**. Illo, "Children call these 'headlights' comics"
119.00 357.00 950.00
55-57: 56-Used in **SOTI**, pg. 145. 57(7/48)-Last Kamen issue; becomes Western Killers? 72.00 216.00 580.00
58(4/50)-60-No Kamen-a 16.00 47.00 110.00

NOTE: ***Kamen*** *a-47-51, 53, 55-57; c-47, 49-52.* ***Powell*** *a-4(2). Bondage-c 9-12, 46, 52.*

BLUE BEETLE (Formerly The Thing; becomes Mr. Muscles No. 22 on) (See Charlton Bullseye & Space Adventures)
Charlton Comics: No. 18, Feb, 1955 - No. 21, Aug, 1955

18,19-(Pre-1944-r). 18-Last pre-code issue. 19-Bouncer, Rocket Kelly-r
19.00 58.00 135.00
20-Joan Mason by Kamen 24.00 73.00 170.00
21-New material 17.00 51.00 120.00

BLUE BEETLE (Unusual Tales #1-49; Ghostly Tales #55 on)(See Captain Atom #83 & Charlton Bullseye)
Charlton Comics: V2#1, June, 1964 - V2#5, Mar-Apr, 1965; V3#50, July, 1965 - V3#54, Feb-Mar, 1966; #1, June, 1967 - #5, Nov, 1968

V2#1-Origin/1st S.A. app. Dan Garrett-Blue Beetle 6.50 19.50 65.00
2-5: 5-Weiss illo; 1st published-a? 4.50 13.50 45.00
V3#50-54-Formerly Unusual Tales 4.50 13.50 45.00
1(1967)-Question series begins by Ditko 9.00 27.00 90.00
2-Origin Ted Kord-Blue Beetle (see Capt. Atom #83 for 1st Ted Kord Blue Beetle); Dan Garrett x-over 4.00 12.00 40.00
3-5 (All Ditko-c/a in #1-5) 3.20 9.60 32.00
1,3(Modern Comics-1977)-Reprints 4.00

NOTE: *#6 only appeared in the fanzine 'The Charlton Portfolio.'*

BLUE BEETLE (Also see Americomics, Crisis On Infinite Earths, Justice League & Showcase '94 #2-4)
DC Comics: June, 1986 - No. 24, May, 1988

1-Origin retold; intro. Firefist 3.00
2-24: 2-Origin Firefist. 5-7-The Question app. 11-14-New Teen Titans x-over. 20-Justice League app. 20,21-Millennium tie-ins 2.00

BLUEBERRY (See Lt. Blueberry & Marshal Blueberry)
Marvel Comics (Epic Comics): 1989 - No. 5, 1990 ($12.95/$14.95, graphic novel)

1,3,4,5-($12.95)-Moebius-a in all 13.00
2-($14.95) 15.00

BLUE BOLT
Funnies, Inc. No. 1/Novelty Press/Premium Group of Comics: June, 1940 - No. 101 (V10#2), Sept-Oct, 1949

V1#1-Origin Blue Bolt by Joe Simon, Sub-Zero Man, White Rider & Super Horse, Dick Cole, Wonder Boy & Sgt. Spook (1st app. of each)
278.00 833.00 2500.00
2-Simon & Kirby's 1st art & 1st super-hero (Blue Bolt)
150.00 450.00 1200.00
3-1 pg. Space Hawk by Wolverton; 2nd S&K-a on Blue Bolt (same cover date as Red Raven #1); 1st time S&K names app. in a comic; Simon-c
125.00 375.00 1000.00
4,5-S&K-a in each; 5-Everett-a begins on Sub-Zero
112.00 338.00 900.00
6,8-10-S&K-a 100.00 300.00 800.00

GD2.0 FN6.0 NM9.4

7-S&K-c/a 112.00 336.00 900.00
11,12: 11-Robot-c 106.00 318.00 850.00
V2#1-Origin Dick Cole & The Twister; Twister x-over in Dick Cole, Sub-Zero, & Blue Bolt; origin Simba Karno who battles Dick Cole thru V2#5 & becomes main supporting character V2#6 on; battle-c 34.00 103.00 240.00
2-Origin The Twister retold in text 27.00 81.00 190.00
3-5: 5-Intro. Freezum 24.00 73.00 170.00
6-Origin Sgt. Spook retold 20.00 60.00 140.00
7-12: 7-Lois Blake becomes Blue Bolt's costume aide; last Twister. 12-Text-sty by Mickey Spillaine 17.00 51.00 120.00
V3#1-3 13.50 41.00 95.00
4-12: 4-Blue Bolt abandons costume 10.00 30.00 70.00
V4#1-Hitler, Tojo, Mussolini-c 18.00 54.00 125.00
V4#2-12: 3-Shows V4#3 on-c, V4#4 inside (9-10/43). 5-Infinity-c. 8-Last Sub-Zero 10.00 30.00 60.00
V5#1-8, V6#1-3,5-10, V7#1-12 9.15 27.00 55.00
V6#4-Racist cover 10.00 30.00 65.00
V8#1-6,8-12, V9#1-5,7,8, V10#1(#100),V10#2(#101)-Last Dick Cole, Blue Bolt
8.35 25.00 50.00
V8#7,V9#6,9-L. B. Cole-c 17.00 51.00 120.00

NOTE: ***Everett*** *c-V1#4, 11, V2#1, 2.* ***Gustavson*** *a-V1#1-12, V2#1-7.* ***Kiefer*** *c-V3#1.* ***Rico*** *a-V6#10, V7#4. Blue Bolt not in V9#8.*

BLUE BOLT (Becomes Ghostly Weird Stories #120 on; continuation of Novelty Blue Bolt) (...Weird Tales of Terror #111,...Weird Tales #112-119)
Star Publications: No. 102, Nov-Dec, 1949 - No. 119, May-June, 1953

102-The Chameleon, & Target app. 31.00 92.00 215.00
103,104-The Chameleon app. 104-Last Target 29.00 86.00 200.00
105-Origin Blue Bolt (from #1) retold by Simon; Chameleon & Target app.; opium den story 45.00 135.00 360.00
106-Blue Bolt by S&K begins; Spacehawk reprints from Target by Wolverton begin, ends #110; Sub-Zero begins; ends #109 43.00 128.00 340.00
107-110: 108-Last S&K Blue Bolt reprint. 109-Wolverton-c(r)/inside Spacehawk splash. 110-Target app. 40.00 120.00 325.00
111,112: 111-Red Rocket & The Mask-r; last Blue Bolt; 1pg. L. B. Cole-a 112-Last Torpedo Man app. 40.00 120.00 295.00
113-Wolverton's Spacehawk-r/Target V3#7 40.00 120.00 315.00
114,116: 116-Jungle Jo-r 40.00 120.00 295.00
115-Sgt. Spook app. 40.00 120.00 315.00
117-Jo-Jo & Blue Bolt-r 40.00 120.00 300.00
118-"White Spirit" by Wood 40.00 120.00 315.00
119-Disbrow/Cole-c; Jungle Jo-r 40.00 120.00 300.00
Accepted Reprint #103(1957?, nd) 10.00 30.00 65.00

NOTE: ***L. B. Cole*** *c-102-108, 110 on.* ***Disbrow*** *a-112(2), 113(3), 114(2), 115(2), 116-118.* ***Hollingsworth*** *a-117.* ***Palais*** *a-112r. Sci/Fi c-105-110. Horror c-111.*

BLUE BULLETEER, THE (Also see Femforce Special)
AC Comics: 1989 ($2.25, B&W, one-shot)

1-Origin by Bill Black; Bill Ward-a 3.00

BLUE BULLETEER (Also see Femforce Special)
AC Comics: 1996 ($5.95, B&W, one-shot)

1-Photo-c 2.40 6.00

BLUE CIRCLE COMICS (Also see Roly Poly Comic Book)
Enwil Associates/Rural Home: June, 1944 - No. 5, Mar, 1945; No. 6, 1950s

1-The Blue Circle begins (1st app.); origin & 1st app. Steel Fist
26.00 79.00 185.00
2 18.00 54.00 125.00
3-Hitler parody-c 20.00 60.00 140.00
4-6: 5-Last Steel Fist. 6-(1950s)-Colossal Features-r
10.00 30.00 70.00

BLUE DEVIL (See Fury of Firestorm #24, Underworld Unleashed, Starman #38)
DC Comics: June, 1984 - No. 31, Dec, 1986 (75¢/$1.25)

1 3.00
2-31: 4-Origin Nebiros. 7-Gil Kane-a. 8-Giffen-a. 17,18-Crisis x-over 2.00
Annual 1 (11/85)-Team-ups w/Black Orchid, Creeper, Demon, Madame Xanadu, Man-Bat & Phantom Stranger 2.00

Blue Ribbon Comics #4 © MLJ

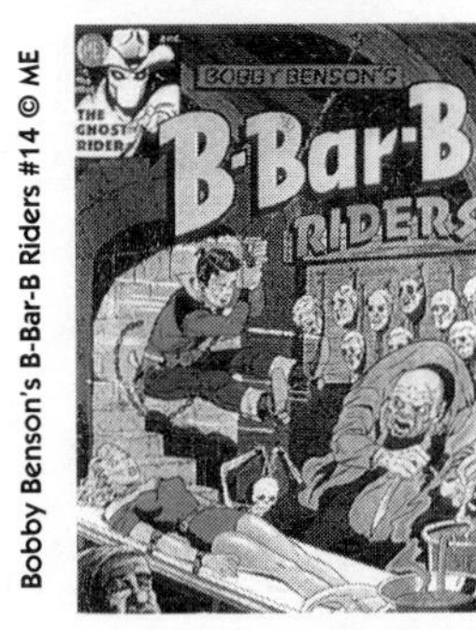

Bobby Benson's B-Bar-B Riders #14 © ME

Bob Steele Western #3 © FAW

GD2.0 FN6.0 NM9.4

BLUE PHANTOM, THE
Dell Publishing Co.: June-Aug, 1962

1(01-066-208)-by Fred Fredericks 2.80 8.40 28.00

BLUE RIBBON COMICS (...Mystery Comics No. 9-18)
MLJ Magazines: Nov, 1939 - No. 22, Mar, 1942 (1st MLJ series)

1-Dan Hastings, Richy the Amazing Boy, Rang-A-Tang the Wonder Dog begin (1st app. of each); Little Nemo app. (not by W. McCay); Jack Cole-a(3) 300.00 900.00 2600.00
2-Bob Phantom, Silver Fox (both in #3), Rang-A-Tang Club & Cpl. Collins begin (1st app. of each); Jack Cole-a 121.00 363.00 965.00
3-J. Cole-a 83.00 249.00 665.00
4-Doc Strong, The Green Falcon, & Hercules begin (1st app. each); origin & 1st app. The Fox & Ty-Gor, Son of the Tiger 87.00 261.00 700.00
5-8: 8-Last Hercules; 6,7-Biro, Meskin-a. 7-Fox app. on-c 62.00 186.00 500.00
9-(Scarce)-Origin & 1st app. Mr. Justice (2/41) 262.00 786.00 2100.00
10-13: 12-Last Doc Strong. 13-Inferno, the Flame Breather begins, ends #19; Devil-c 96.00 288.00 765.00
14,15,17,18: 15-Last Green Falcon 83.00 249.00 665.00
16-Origin & 1st app. Captain Flag (9/41) 159.00 477.00 1275.00
19-22: 20-Last Ty-Gor. 22-Origin Mr. Justice retold 83.00 249.00 665.00

NOTE: ***Biro*** *c-3-5; a-2 (Cpl. Collins & Scoop Cody).* ***S. Cooper*** *c-9-17. 20-22 contain "Tales From the Witch's Cauldron" (same strip as "Stories of the Black Witch" in Zip Comics). Mr. Justice c-9-18. Captain Flag c-16(w/Mr. Justice), 19-22.*

BLUE RIBBON COMICS (Becomes Teen-Age Diary Secrets #4)(See Heckle & Jeckle)
Blue Ribbon (St. John): Feb, 1949 - No. 6, Aug, 1949

1,3-Heckle & Jeckle 9.15 27.00 55.00
2(4/49)-Diary Secrets; Baker-c 19.00 56.00 130.00
4(6/49)-Teen-Age Diary Secrets; Baker c/a(2) 19.00 58.00 135.00
5(8/49)-Teen-Age Diary Secrets; Oversize; photo-c; Baker-a(2)- Continues as Teen-Age Diary Secrets 25.00 75.00 175.00
6-Dinky Duck(8/49) 4.00 12.00 24.00

BLUE-RIBBON COMICS
Red Circle Prod./Archie Ent. No. 5 on: Nov, 1983 - No. 14, Dec, 1984

1-S&K-r/Advs. of the Fly #1,2; Williamson/Torres-r/Fly #2; Ditko-c 4.00
2-14: 3-Origin Steel Sterling. 5-S&K Shield-r. 6,7-The Fox app. 8-Toth centerspread. 8,11-Black Hood. 12-Thunder Agents. 13-Thunder Bunny. 14-Web & Jaguar 3.00

NOTE: ***N. Adams*** *a(r)-8.* ***Buckler*** *a-4i.* ***Nino*** *a-2i.* ***McWilliams*** *a-8.* ***Morrow*** *a-8.*

BLUE STREAK (See Holyoke One-Shot No. 8)

BLYTHE (Marge's)
Dell Publishing Co.: No. 1072, Jan-Mar, 1960

Four Color 1072 4.50 13.50 50.00

B-MAN (See Double-Dare Adventures)

BO (Tom Cat #4 on) (Also see Big Shot #29 & Dixie Dugan)
Charlton Comics Group: June, 1955 - No. 3, Oct, 1955 (A dog)

1-3: Newspaper reprints by Frank Beck 7.00 21.00 42.00

BOATNIKS, THE (See Walt Disney Showcase No. 1)

BOB BURDEN'S ORIGINAL MYSTERYMEN PRESENTS
Dark Horse Comics: 1999 - Present ($2.95)

1-3-Bob Burden-s/Sadowski-a(p) 3.00

BOBBY BENSON'S B-BAR-B RIDERS (Radio) (See Best of The West, The Lemonade Kid & Model Fun)
Magazine Enterprises/AC Comics: May-June, 1950 - No. 20, May-June, 1953

1-The Lemonade Kid begins; Powell-a (Scarce) 43.00 128.00 340.00
2 17.00 49.00 115.00
3-5: 4,5-Lemonade Kid-c (#4-Spider-c) 13.00 39.00 90.00
6-8,10 11.50 34.00 80.00
9,11,13-Frazetta-c; Ghost Rider in #13-15 by Ayers-a. 13-Ghost Rider-c 33.00 99.00 230.00
12,17-20: 20-(A-1 #88) 11.00 33.00 75.00
14-Decapitation/Bondage-c & story; classic horror-c 21.00 64.00 150.00
15-Ghost Rider-c 16.00 47.00 110.00
16-Photo-c 13.00 39.00 90.00
1 (1990, $2.75, B&W)-Reprints; photo-c & inside covers 2.75

NOTE: ***Ayers*** *a-13-15, 20.* ***Powell*** *a-1-12(4 ea.), 13(3), 14-16(Red Hawk only); c-1-8,1 0, 12. Lemonade Kid in most 1-13.*

BOBBY COMICS
Universal Phoenix Features: May, 1946

1-By S. M. Iger 7.50 22.50 45.00

BOBBY SHERMAN (TV)
Charlton Comics: Feb, 1972 - No. 7, Oct, 1972

1-Based on TV show "Getting Together" 3.50 10.50 35.00
2-7: 4-Photo-c 2.50 7.50 24.00

BOB COLT (Movie star)(See XMas Comics)
Fawcett Publications: Nov, 1950 - No. 10, May, 1952

1-Bob Colt, his horse Buckskin & sidekick Pablo begin; photo front/back-c begin 43.00 129.00 345.00
2 30.00 90.00 210.00
3-5 24.00 71.00 165.00
6-Flying Saucer story 20.00 60.00 140.00
7-10: 9-Last photo back-c 19.00 56.00 130.00

BOB HOPE (See Adventures of... & Calling All Boys #12)

BOB MARLEY, TALE OF THE TUFF GONG (Music star)
Marvel Comics: Aug, 1994 - No, 3, Nov, 1994 ($5.95, limited series)

1-3 2.40 6.00

BOB POWELL'S TIMELESS TALES
Eclipse Comics: March, 1989 ($2.00, B&W)

1-Powell-r/Black Cat #5 (Scarlet Arrow), 9 & Race for the Moon #1 2.00

BOB SCULLY, THE TWO-FISTED HICK DETECTIVE (Also see Advs. of Detective Ace King and Detective Dan)
Humor Publ. Co.: No date (1933) (36 pgs., 9-1/2x11", B&W, paper-c; 10¢-c)

nn-By Howard Dell; not reprints 81.00 244.00 650.00

BOB SON OF BATTLE
Dell Publishing Co.: No. 729, Nov, 1956

Four Color 729 2.75 8.00 30.00

BOB STEELE WESTERN (Movie star)
Fawcett Publications/AC Comics: Dec, 1950 - No. 10, June, 1952; 1990

1-Bob Steele & his horse Bullet begin; photo front/back-c begin 56.00 167.00 445.00
2 32.00 96.00 225.00
3-5: 4-Last photo back-c 24.00 73.00 170.00
6-10: 10-Last photo-c 19.00 56.00 130.00
1 (1990, $2.75, B&W)-Bob Steele & Rocky Lane reprints; photo-c & inside covers 2.75

BOB SWIFT (Boy Sportsman)
Fawcett Publications: May, 1951 - No. 5, Jan, 1952

1 9.15 27.00 55.00
2-5: Saunders painted-c #1-5 5.00 15.00 30.00

BOB, THE GALACTIC BUM
DC Comics: Feb, 1995 - No. 4, June, 1995 ($1.95, limited series)

1-4: 1-Lobo app. 2.50

BODY BAGS
Dark Horse Comics (Blanc Noir): Sept, 1996 - No. 4, Jan, 1997 ($2.95, mini-series, mature)(1st Blanc Noir series)

1-Jason Pearson-c/a/scripts in all. 1-Intro Clownface & Panda. 1.00 3.00 8.00
2 1.25 3.75 10.00
3,4 2.40 6.00

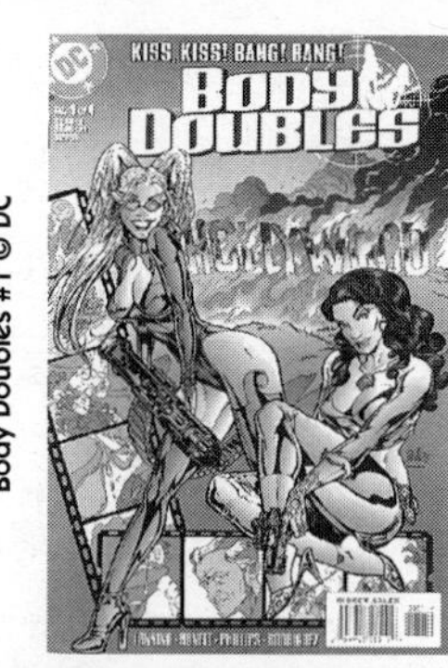

Body Doubles #1 © DC

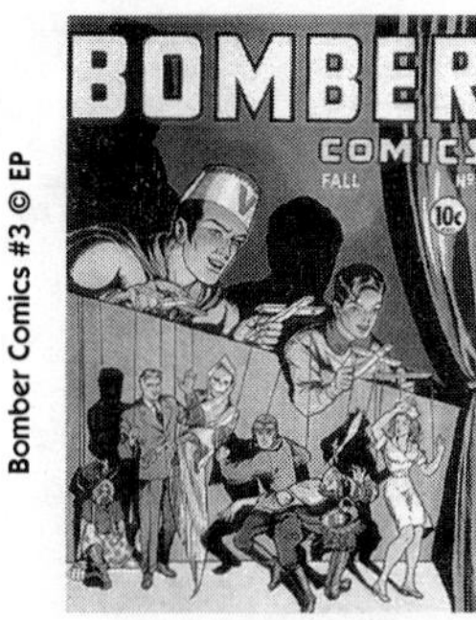

Bomber Comics #3 © EP

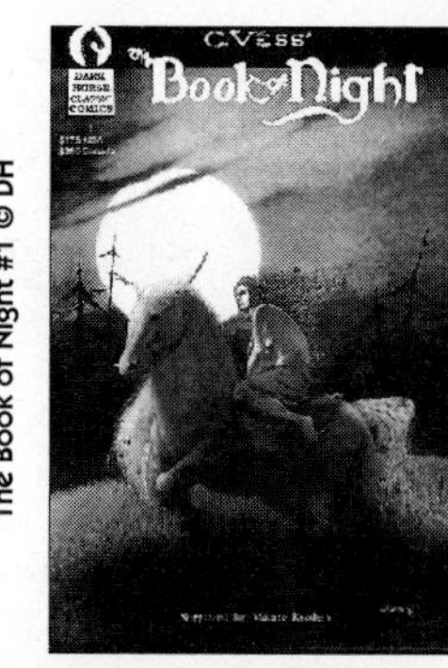

The Book of Night #1 © DH

GD2.0 FN6.0 NM9.4

BODYCOUNT (Also see Casey Jones & Raphael)
Image Comics (Highbrow Entertainment): Mar, 1996 - No. 4, July, 1996 ($2.50, limited series)

1-4: Kevin Eastman-a(p)/scripts; Simon Bisley-c/a(i); Turtles app. 2.50

BODY DOUBLES (See Resurrection Man)
DC Comics: Oct, 1999 - No. 4 ($2.50, limited series)

1,2-Lanning & Abnett-s. 2-Black Canary app. 2.50
...(Villains) (2/98, $1.95, one-shot) 1-Pearson-c; Deadshot app. 2.00

BOFFO LAFFS
Paragraphics: 1986 - No. 5 ($2.50/$1.95)

1-($2.50) First comic cover with hologram 2.50
2-5 2.00

BOHOS
Image Comics (Flypaper Press): June, 1998 - Present ($2.95)

1-3-Whorf-s/Penaranda-a 3.00

BOLD ADVENTURES
Pacific Comics: Oct, 1983 - No. 3, June, 1984 ($1.50)

1-Time Force, Anaconda, & The Weirdling begin 2.00
2,3: 2-Soldiers of Fortune begins. 3-Spitfire 2.00
NOTE: ***Kaluta** c-3. **Nebres** a-1-3. **Nino** a-2, 3. **Severin** a-3.*

BOLD STORIES (Also see Candid Tales & It Rhymes With Lust)
Kirby Publishing Co.: Mar, 1950 - July, 1950 (Digest size, 144 pgs.)

March issue (Very Rare) - Contains "The Ogre of Paris" by Wood 120.00 360.00 960.00
May issue (Very Rare) - Contains "The Cobra's Kiss" by Graham Ingels (21 pgs.) 103.00 309.00 825.00
July issue (Very Rare) - Contains "The Ogre of Paris" by Wood 90.00 272.00 725.00

BOLT AND STAR FORCE SIX
Americomics: 1984 ($1.75)

1-Origin Bolt & Star Force Six 2.00
Special 1 (1984, $2.00, 52pgs., B&W) 2.00

BOMBARDIER (See Bee 29, the Bombardier & Cinema Comics Herald)

BOMBAST
Topps Comics: 1993 ($2.95, one-shot) (Created by Jack Kirby)

1-Polybagged w/Kirbychrome trading card; Savage Dragon app.; Kirby-c; has coupon for Amberchrome Secret City Saga #0 3.00

BOMBA THE JUNGLE BOY (TV)
National Periodical Publ.: Sept-Oct, 1967 - No. 7, Sept-Oct, 1968 (12¢)

1-Intro. Bomba; Infantino/Anderson-c 2.50 7.50 22.00
2-7 2.00 6.00 16.00

BOMBER COMICS
Elliot Publ. Co./Melverne Herald/Farrell/Sunrise Times: Mar, 1944 - No. 4, Winter, 1944-45

1-Wonder Boy, & Kismet, Man of Fate begin 62.00 187.00 500.00
2-Hitler-c 40.00 120.00 300.00
3: 2-4-Have Classics Comics ad to HRN 20 39.00 116.00 270.00
4-Hitler, Tojo & Mussolini-c; Sensation Comics #13-c/swipe; has Classics Comics ad to HRN 20. 50.00 150.00 400.00

BONANZA (TV)
Dell/Gold Key: June-Aug, 1960 - No. 37, Aug, 1970 (All Photo-c)

Four Color 1110 (6-8/60) 34.00 102.00 375.00
Four Color 1221,1283, & #01070-207, 01070-210 16.00 49.00 180.00
1(12/62-Gold Key) 17.00 52.00 190.00
2 8.75 26.50 95.00
3-10 7.00 20.00 75.00
11-20 5.50 16.50 60.00
21-37: 29-Reprints 4.50 13.50 50.00

BONE

GD2.0 FN6.0 NM9.4

Cartoon Books/Image Comics #21 on: July, 1991 - Present ($2.95, B&W)

1-Jeff Smith-c/a in all 7.00 21.00 75.00
1-2nd printing 1.50 4.50 12.00
1-3rd thru 5th printings 4.00
2-1st printing 4.00 12.25 45.00
2-2nd & 3rd printings 5.00
3-1st printing 3.50 10.50 35.00
3-2nd thru 4th printings 4.00
4,5 1.85 5.50 15.00
6-10 1.00 3.00 8.00
11-36: 21-1st Image issue 4.00
13 1/2 1.50 4.50 12.00
13 1/2 (Gold) 1.85 5.50 15.00
1-26-($2.95): 1-Image reprints begin w/new-c. 2-Allred pin-up. 3.00
Holiday Special (1993, giveaway) 3.00
Sourcebook-San Diego Edition 3.00
Complete Bone Adventures Vol 1,2 ('93, '94, $12.95, r/#1-6 & #7-12) 13.00
Volume 1-($19.95, hard-c)-"Out From Boneville" 20.00
Volume 1-($12.95, soft-c) 13.00
Volume 2,5-($22.95, hard-c)-"The Great Cow Race" & "Rock Jdaw" 23.00
Volume 2,5($14.95, soft-c) 15.00
Volume 3,4-($24.95, hard-c)-"Eyes of the Storm" & "The Dragonslayer" 25.00
Volume 3,4-($16.95, soft-c) 17.00
Volume 6-($15.95, soft-c)-"Old Man's Cave" 16.00
NOTE: *Printings not listed sell for cover price.*

BONGO (See Story Hour Series)

BONGO & LUMPJAW (Disney, see Walt Disney Showcase #3)
Dell Publishing Co.: No. 706, June, 1956; No. 886, Mar, 1958

Four Color 706 (#1) 4.50 13.50 50.00
Four Color 886 3.80 11.50 40.00

BON VOYAGE (See Movie Classics)

BOOF
Image Comics (Todd McFarlane Prod.): July, 1994 - No. 6, Dec, 1994 ($1.95)

1-6 2.00

BOOF AND THE BRUISE CREW
Image Comics (Todd McFarlane Prod.): July, 1994 - No. 6, Dec, 1994 ($1.95)

1-6 2.00

BOOK AND RECORD SET (See Power Record Comics)

BOOK OF ALL COMICS
William H. Wise: 1945 (196 pgs.)(Inside f/c has Green Publ. blacked out)

nn-Green Mask, Puppeteer & The Bouncer 39.00 116.00 270.00

BOOK OF ANTS, THE
Artisan Entertainment: 1998 ($2.95, B&W)

1-Based on the movie Pi; Aronofsky-s 3.00

BOOK OF BALLADS AND SAGAS, THE
Green Man Press: Oct, 1995 - Present ($2.95/$3.50/$3.25, B&W)

1-4: 1-Vess-c/a; Gaiman story. 3.50

BOOK OF COMICS, THE
William H. Wise: No date (1944) (25¢, 132 pgs.)

nn-Captain V app. 39.00 116.00 270.00

BOOK OF FATE, THE (See Fate)
DC Comics: Feb, 1997 - No. 12, Jan, 1998 ($2.25/$2.50)

1-12: 4-Two-Face-c/app. 6-Convergence. 11-Sentinel app. 3.00

BOOK OF LOVE (See Fox Giants)

BOOK OF NIGHT, THE
Dark Horse Comics: July, 1987 - No. 3, 1987 ($1.75, B&W)

1-3: Reprints from Epic Illustrated; Vess-a 2.25
TPB-r/#1-3 15.00
Hardcover-Black-c with red crest 100.00

Books of Magic #52 © DC

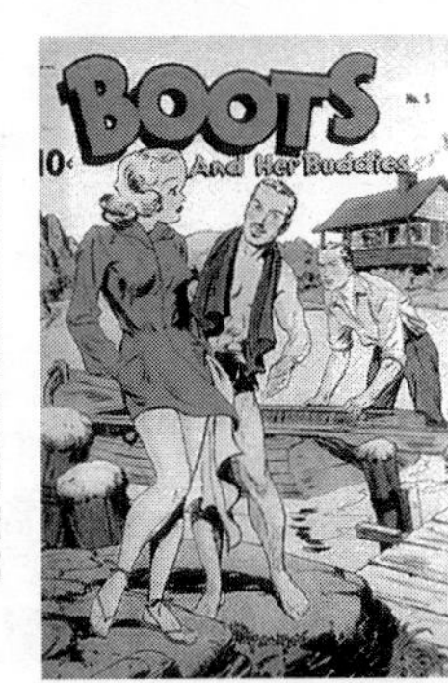

Boots and Her Buddies #5 © STD

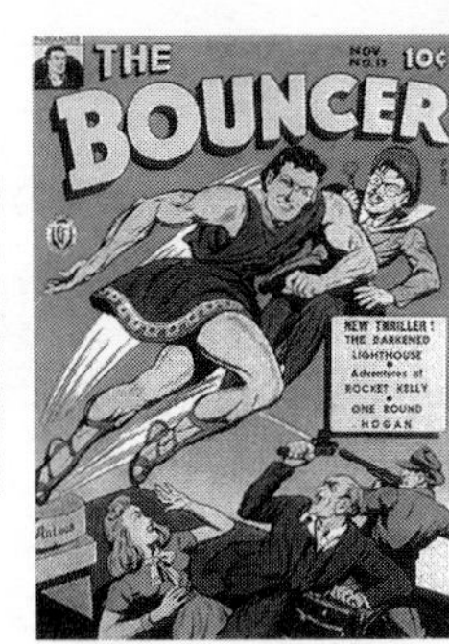

The Bouncer #13 © FOX

GD2.0 FN6.0 NM9.4

Hardcover w/slipcase (1991) signed and numbered 50.00

BOOK OF THE DEAD
Marvel Comics: Dec, 1993 - No. 4, Mar, 1994 ($1.75, limited series, 52 pgs.)

1-4: 1-Ploog Frankenstein & Morrow Man-Thing-r begin; Wrightson-r/Chamber of Darkness #7. 2-Morrow new painted-c; Chaykin/Morrow Man-Thing; Krigstein-r/Uncanny Tales #54; r/Fear #10. 3-r/Astonishing Tales #10 & Starlin Man-Thing. 3,4-Painted-c 3.00

BOOKS OF FAERIE, THE
DC Comics (Vertigo): Mar, 1997 - No. 3, May,1997 ($2.50, limited series)

1-3-Gross-a 2.50
TPB (1998, $14.95) r/#1-3 & Arcana Annual #1 15.00

BOOKS OF FAERIE, THE :AUBERON'S TALE
DC Comics (Vertigo): Aug, 1998 - No. 3, Oct,1998 ($2.50, limited series)

1-3-Gross-a 3.00

BOOKS OF FAERIE, THE :MOLLY'S STORY
DC Comics (Vertigo): Sept, 1999 - No. 4, Dec,1999 ($2.50, limited series)

1,2-Ney Rieber-s/Mejia-a 3.00

BOOKS OF MAGIC
DC Comics: 1990 - No. 4, 1991 ($3.95, 52 pgs., limited series, mature)

1-Bolton painted-c/a; Phantom Stranger app.; Gaiman scripts in all
1.10 3.30 9.00
2,3: 2-John Constantine, Dr. Fate, Spectre, Deadman app. 3-Dr. Occult app.; minor Sandman app. 2.40 6.00
4-Early Death-c/app. (early 1991) 1.00 2.80 7.00
Trade paperback-($19.95)-Reprints limited series 20.00

BOOKS OF MAGIC
DC Comics (Vertigo): May, 1994 - Present ($1.95/$2.50, mature)

1-Charles Vess-c 1.50 4.50 12.00
1-Platinum 2.50 7.50 20.00
2,3 1.00 2.80 7.00
4-Death app. 1.00 2.80 7.00
5-14; Charles Vess-c 4.00
15-50: 15-$2.50-c begins. 22-Kaluta-c. 25-Death-c/app; Bachalo-c 3.00
51-65: 51-Peter Gross-s/a begins. 55-Medley-a 2.50
Annual 1,2 (2/97, 2/98, $3.95) 4.00
Bindings (1995, $12.95, TPB)-r/#1-4 13.00
Girl in the Box (1999, $14.95, TPB)-r/#26-32 15.00
Reckonings (1997, $12.95, TPB)-r/#14-20 13.00
Summonings (1996, $17.50, TPB)-r/#5-13, Vertigo Rave #1 17.50
Transformations (1998, $12.95, TPB)-r/#21-25 13.00

BOONDOGGLE
Knight Press: Mar, 1995 - No. 4 ($2.95, B&W)

1-4: Stegelin-c/a/scripts 3.00

BOONDOGGLE
Caliber Press: Jan, 1997 - Present ($2.95, B&W)

1,2: Stegelin-c/a/scripts 3.00

BOOSTER GOLD (See Justice League #4)
DC Comics: Feb, 1986 - No. 25, Feb, 1988 (75¢)

1 3.00
2-25: 4-Rose & Thorn app. 6-Origin. 6,7,23-Superman app. 8,9-LSH app. 22-JLI app. 24,25-Millennium tie-ins 2.00
NOTE: ***Austin** c-22i. **Byrne** c-23i.*

BOOTS AND HER BUDDIES
Standard Comics/Visual Editions/Argo (NEA Service):
No. 5, 9/48 - No. 9, 9/49; 12/55 - No. 3, 1956

5-Strip-r 15.00 45.00 105.00
6,8 10.00 30.00 70.00
7-(Scarce)-Spanking panels(3) 11.50 34.00 80.00
9-(Scarce)-Frazetta-a (2 pgs.) 25.00 75.00 175.00
1-3(Argo-1955-56)-Reprints 5.00 15.00 30.00

GD2.0 FN6.0 NM9.4

BOOTS & SADDLES (TV)
Dell Publ. Co.: No. 919, July, 1958; No. 1029, Sept, 1959; No. 1116, Aug, 1960

Four Color 919 (#1)-Photo-c 7.00 22.00 80.00
Four Color 1029, 1116-Photo-c 4.50 13.50 50.00

BORDERLINE
Friction Press: June, 1992 ($2.25, B&W)

0-Ashcan edition; 1st app. of Cliff Broadway 2.00
1-Painted-c 3.00
1-Special Edition (bagged w/ photo, S&N) 4.00

BORDER PATROL
P. L. Publishing Co.: May-June, 1951 - No. 3, Sept-Oct, 1951

1 11.00 33.00 75.00
2,3 8.35 25.00 50.00

BORDER WORLDS (Also see Megaton Man)
Kitchen Sink Press: 7/86 - No. 7, 1987; V2#1, 1990 - No. 4, 1990 ($1.95-$2.00, B&W, mature)

1-7, V2#1-4: Donald Simpson-c/a/scripts 3.00

BORIS KARLOFF TALES OF MYSTERY (TV) (...Thriller No. 1,2)
Gold Key: No. 3, April, 1963 - No. 97, Feb, 1980

3-5-(Two #5's, 10/63,11/63): 5-(10/63)-11 pgs. Toth-a.
3.00 9.00 30.00
6-8,10: 10-Orlando-a 2.50 7.50 24.00
9-Wood-a 2.80 8.40 28.00
11-Williamson-a, 8 pgs.; Orlando-a, 5 pgs. 2.80 8.40 28.00
12-Torres, McWilliams-a; Orlando-a(2) 2.50 7.50 22.00
13,14,16-20 2.25 6.75 18.00
15-Crandall 2.50 7.50 20.00
21-Jeff Jones-a(3 pgs.) "The Screaming Skull" 2.50 7.50 20.00
22-Last 12¢ issue 1.75 5.25 14.00
23-30: 23-Reprint; photo-c 1.75 5.25 12.00
31-50: 36-Weiss-a 1.10 3.30 9.00
51-74: 74-Origin & 1st app. Taurus 1.00 2.80 7.00
75-79,87-97: 90-r/Torres, McWilliams-a/#12; Morrow-c 5.00
80-86-(52 pgs.) 1.00 3.00 8.00
Story Digest 1(7/70-Gold Key)-All text/illos.; 148pp. 3.00 9.00 30.00
(See Mystery Comics Digest No. 2, 5, 8, 11, 14, 17, 20, 23, 26)
NOTE: ***Bolle** a-51-54, 56, 58, 59. **McWilliams** a-12, 14, 18, 19, 72, 80, 81, 93. **Orlando** a-11-15, 21. Reprints: 78, 81-86, 88, 90, 92, 95, 97.*

BORIS KARLOFF THRILLER (TV) (Becomes Boris Karloff Tales...)
Gold Key: Oct, 1962 - No. 2, Jan, 1963 (80 pgs.)

1-Photo-c 5.90 18.00 65.00
2 4.00 12.00 45.00

BORIS THE BEAR
Dark Horse Comics/Nicotat Comics #13 on: Aug, 1986 - No. 34, 1990 ($1.50/$1.75/$1.95, B&W)

1, Annual 1 (1988, $2.50) 3.00
1 (2nd printing),2,3,4A,4B,5-12, 14-34: 8-(44 pgs.) 2.00
13-1st Nicotat Comics issue 3.00

BORIS THE BEAR INSTANT COLOR CLASSICS
Dark Horse Comics: July, 1987 - No. 3, 1987 ($1.75/$1.95)

1-3 2.00

BORN AGAIN
Spire Christian Comics (Fleming H. Revell Co.): 1978 (39¢)

nn-Watergate, Nixon, etc. 5.00

BOUNCER, THE (Formerly Green Mask #9)
Fox Features Syndicate: 1944 - No. 14, Jan, 1945

nn(1944, #10?) 26.00 77.00 180.00
11(#1)(9/44)-Origin; Rocket Kelly, One Round Hogan app.
21.00 64.00 150.00
12-14: 14-Reprints no # issue 17.00 51.00 120.00

BOUNTY GUNS (See Luke Short's..., Four Color 739)

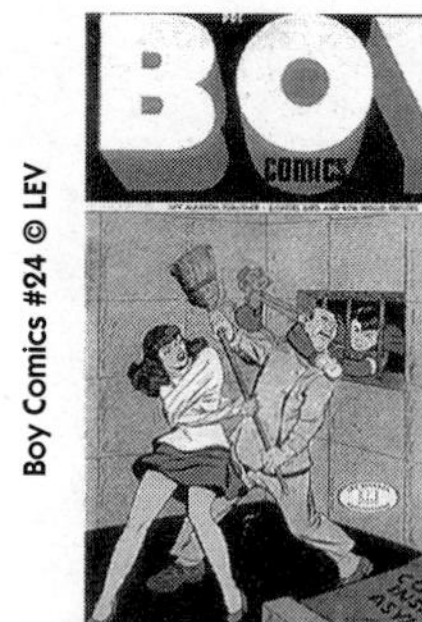

Boy Comics #24 © LEV

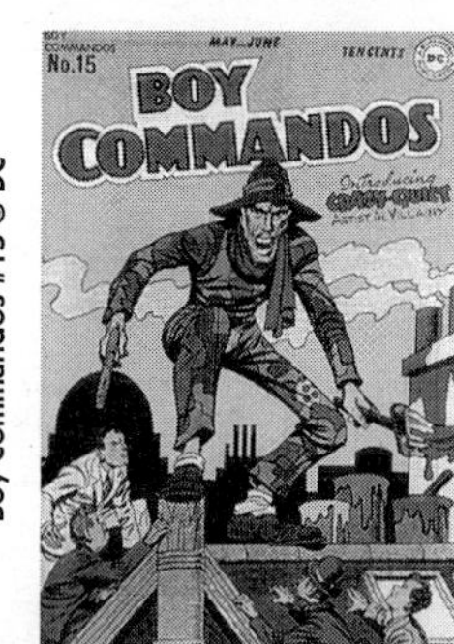

Boy Commandos #15 © DC

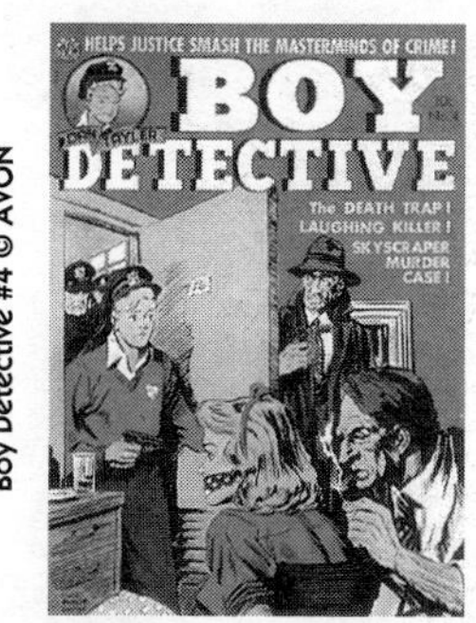

Boy Detective #4 © AVON

BOX OFFICE POISON
Antarctic Press: 1996 - Present ($2.95, B&W)

	GD2.0	FN6.0	NM9.4
1-Alex Robinson-s/a in all			4.00
2-13, ...Kolor Karnival 1 (5/99, $2.99)			3.00
...Super Special 0 (5/97, $4.95)			5.00
Sherman's March: Collected BOP Vol. 1 (9/98, $14.95) r/#0-4			15.00

BOY AND HIS 'BOT, A
Now Comics: Jan, 1987 ($1.95)

	GD2.0	FN6.0	NM9.4
1-A Holiday Special			2.00

BOY AND THE PIRATES, THE (Movie)
Dell Publishing Co.: No. 1117, Aug, 1960

	GD2.0	FN6.0	NM9.4
Four Color 1117-Photo-c	5.50	16.50	60.00

BOY COMICS (Captain Battle No. 1 & 2; Boy Illustories No. 43-108) (Stories by Charles Biro)(Also see Squeeks)
Lev Gleason Publ. (Comic House): No. 3, Apr, 1942 - No. 119, Mar, 1956

	GD2.0	FN6.0	NM9.4
3(No.1)-Origin Crimebuster, Bombshell & Young Robin Hood; Yankee Longago, Case 1001-1008, Swoop Storm, & Boy Movies begin; 1st app. Iron Jaw; Crimebuster's pet monkey Squeeks begins	288.00	862.00	2400.00
4-Hitler, Tojo, Mussolini-c	119.00	357.00	950.00
5	87.00	261.00	700.00
6-Origin Iron Jaw; origin & death of Iron Jaw's son; Little Dynamite begins, ends #39; 1st Iron Jaw-c	250.00	750.00	2000.00
7-Flag & Hitler, Tojo, Mussolini-c	81.00	243.00	650.00
8-Death of Iron Jaw; Iron Jaw-c	87.00	261.00	700.00
9-Iron Jaw-c	78.00	234.00	625.00
10-Return of Iron Jaw; classic Biro-c; Iron Jaw-c	119.00	357.00	950.00
11-Classic Iron Jaw-c	75.00	225.00	600.00
12,13	55.00	165.00	440.00
14-Iron Jaw-c	58.00	174.00	465.00
15-Death of Iron Jaw	70.00	210.00	560.00
16,18-20	37.00	111.00	260.00
17-Flag-c	40.00	120.00	280.00
21-29,31,32-(All 68 pgs.). 28-Yankee Longago ends. 32-Swoop Storm & Young Robin Hood end	24.00	73.00	170.00
30-(68 pgs.)-Origin Crimebuster retold	36.00	107.00	250.00
33-40: 34-Crimebuster story(2); suicide-c/story	18.00	54.00	125.00
41-50	16.00	47.00	110.00
51-59: 57-Dilly Duncan begins, ends #71	14.00	43.00	100.00
60-Iron Jaw returns	16.00	47.00	110.00
61-Origin Crimebuster & Iron Jaw retold	18.00	54.00	125.00
62-Death of Iron Jaw explained	17.00	51.00	120.00
63-73: 63-McWilliams-a. 73-Frazetta 1-pg. ad	12.00	36.00	85.00
74-88: 80-1st app. Rocky X of the Rocketeers; becomes "Rocky X" #101; Iron Jaw, Sniffer & the Deadly Dozen in 80-118	10.00	30.00	65.00
89-92-The Claw serial app. in all	10.00	30.00	70.00
93-Claw cameo; Rocky X by Sid Check	10.00	30.00	65.00
94-97,99	10.00	30.00	60.00
98,100: 98-Rocky X by Sid Check	10.00	30.00	65.00
101-107,109,111,119: 111-Crimebuster becomes Chuck Chandler. 119-Last Crimebuster	8.35	25.00	50.00
108,110,112-118-Kubert-a	10.00	30.00	60.00

(See Giant Boy Book of Comics)
NOTE: *Boy Movies in 3-5,40,41. Iron Jaw app.-3, 4, 6, 8, 10, 11, 13-15; returns-60-62, 68, 69, 72-79, 81-118.* ***Biro*** *c-all.* ***Briefer*** *a-5, 13, 14, 16-20 among others.* ***Fuje*** *a-55, 18 pgs.* ***Palais*** *a-14, 16, 17, 19, 20 among others.*

BOY COMMANDOS (See Detective #64 & World's Finest Comics #8)
National Periodical Publications: Winter, 1942-43 - No. 36, Nov-Dec, 1949

	GD2.0	FN6.0	NM9.4
1-Origin Liberty Belle; The Sandman & The Newsboy Legion x-over in Boy Commandos; S&K-a, 48 pgs.; S&K cameo? (classic-c)	470.00	1410.00	4700.00
2-Last Liberty Belle; Hitler-c; S&K-a, 46 pgs.	150.00	450.00	1200.00
3-S&K-a, 45 pgs.	100.00	300.00	800.00
4-6: 6-S&K-a	69.00	206.00	550.00
7-10	47.00	141.00	375.00
11-Infinity-c	36.00	107.00	250.00
12-14,16,18-19-More S&K	27.00	81.00	190.00
15-1st app. Crazy Quilt, their arch nemesis	29.00	86.00	200.00
17,20-Sci/fi-c/stories	30.00	90.00	210.00
21,22,25: 22-Judy Canova x-over	21.00	62.00	145.00
23-S&K-c/a(all)	25.00	75.00	175.00
24-1st costumed superhero satire-c (11-12/47).	24.00	73.00	170.00
26-Flying Saucer story (3-4/48)-4th of this theme; see The Spirit 9/28/47(1st), Shadow Comics V7#10 (2nd, 1/48) & Captain Midnight #60 (3rd, 2/48)	23.00	69.00	160.00
27,28,30: 30-Cleveland Indians story	20.00	60.00	140.00
29-S&K story (1)	22.00	66.00	155.00
31-35: 32-Dale Evans app. on-c & in story. 34-Intro. Wolf, their mascot	19.00	58.00	135.00
36-Intro The Atomobile c/sci-fi story (Scarce)	31.00	94.00	220.00

NOTE: *Most issues signed by* ***Simon & Kirby*** *are not by them.* ***S&K*** *c-1-9, 13, 14, 17, 21, 23, 24, 30-32.* ***Feller*** *c-30.*

BOY COMMANDOS
National Per. Publ.: Sept-Oct, 1973 - No. 2, Nov-Dec, 1973 (G.A. S&K reprints)

	GD2.0	FN6.0	NM9.4
1,2: 1-Reprints story from Boy Commandos #1 plus-c & Detective #66 by S&K. 2-Infantino/Orlando-c	1.10	3.30	9.00

BOY COWBOY (Also see Amazing Adventures & Science Comics)
Ziff-Davis Publ. Co.: 1950 (8 pgs. in color)

	GD2.0	FN6.0	NM9.4
nn-Sent to subscribers of Ziff-Davis mags. & ordered through mail for 10¢; used to test market for Kid Cowboy Estimated value			150.00

BOY DETECTIVE
Avon Periodicals: May-June, 1951 - No. 4, May, 1952

	GD2.0	FN6.0	NM9.4
1	18.00	54.00	125.00
2,3: 3-Kinstler-c	11.00	33.00	75.00
4-Kinstler-c	13.50	41.00	95.00

BOY EXPLORERS COMICS (Terry and The Pirates No. 3 on)
Family Comics (Harvey Publ.): May-June, 1946 - No. 2, Sept-Oct, 1946

	GD2.0	FN6.0	NM9.4
1-Intro The Explorers, Duke of Broadway, Calamity Jane & Danny Dixon... Cadet; S&K-c/a, 24 pgs.	57.00	172.00	460.00
2-(Scarce)-Small size (5-1/2x8-1/2"; B&W; 32 pgs.) Distributed to mail subscribers only; S&K-a Estimated value			$250.00-$400.00

(Also see All New No. 15, Flash Gordon No. 5, and Stuntman No. 3)

BOY ILLUSTORIES (See Boy Comics)

BOY LOVES GIRL (Boy Meets Girl No. 1-24)
Lev Gleason Publications: No. 25, July, 1952 - No. 57, June, 1956

	GD2.0	FN6.0	NM9.4
25(#1)	6.35	19.00	38.00
26,27,29-33: 30-33-Serial, 'Loves of My Life	4.00	11.00	22.00
34-42: 39-Lingerie panels	3.60	9.00	18.00
28-Drug propaganda story	4.15	12.50	25.00
43-Toth-a	5.85	17.50	35.00
44-50: 50-Last pre-code (2/55)	3.00	7.50	15.00
51-57: 57-Ann Brewster-a	2.20	5.50	11.00

BOY MEETS GIRL (Boy Loves Girl No. 25 on)
Lev Gleason Publications: Feb, 1950 - No. 24, June, 1952 (No. 1-17: 52 pgs.)

	GD2.0	FN6.0	NM9.4
1-Guardineer-a	8.35	25.00	50.00
2	4.25	13.00	28.00
3-10	4.00	12.00	24.00
11-24	4.00	10.00	20.00

NOTE: ***Briefer*** *a-24.* ***Fuje*** *c-3,7. Painted-c 1-17. Photo-c 19-21, 23.*

BOYS' AND GIRLS' MARCH OF COMICS (See March of Comics)

BOYS' RANCH (Also see Western Tales & Witches' Western Tales)
Harvey Publ.: Oct, 1950 - No. 6, Aug, 1951 (No.1-3, 52 pgs.; No. 4-6, 36 pgs.)

	GD2.0	FN6.0	NM9.4
1-S&K-c/a(3)	59.00	177.00	475.00
2-S&K-c/a(3)	41.00	123.00	325.00
3-S&K-c/a(2); Meskin-a	40.00	120.00	290.00
4-S&K-c/a, 5 pgs.	36.00	107.00	250.00
5,6-S&K-c, splashes & centerspread only; Meskin-a			

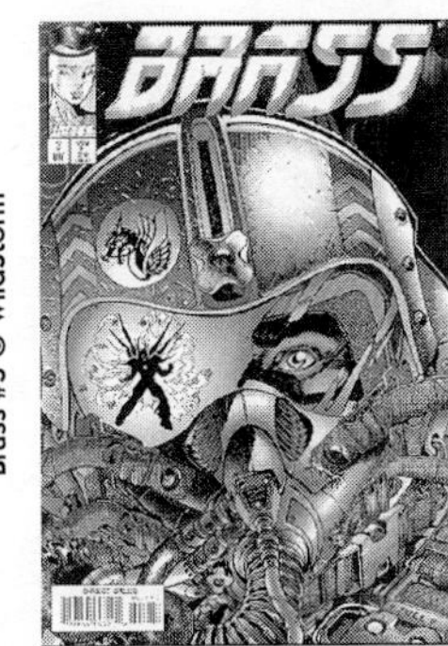

Brass #3 © WildStorm

The Brave and the Bold #12 © DC

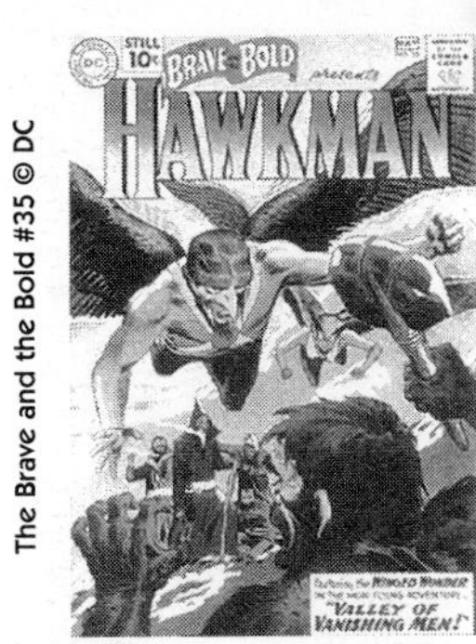

The Brave and the Bold #35 © DC

GD2.0 FN6.0 NM9.4

20.00 60.00 140.00

BOZO (Larry Harmon's Bozo, the World's Most Famous Clown)
Innovation Publishing: 1992 ($6.95, 68 pgs.)

1-Reprints Four Color #285(#1) 1.00 2.80 7.00

BOZO THE CLOWN (TV) (Bozo No. 7 on)
Dell Publishing Co.: July, 1950 - No. 4, Oct-Dec, 1963

Four Color 285(#1) 17.00 52.00 190.00
2(7-9/51)-7(10-12/52) 10.00 30.00 110.00
Four Color 464,508,551,594(10/54) 8.00 25.00 90.00
1(nn, 5-7/62) 5.50 16.50 60.00
2 - 4(1963) 4.50 13.50 50.00

BOZZ CHRONICLES, THE
Marvel Comics (Epic Comics): Dec, 1985 - No. 6, 1986 (Lim. series, mature)

1-6-Logan/Wolverine look alike in 19th century 2.00

BRADLEYS, THE (Also see Hate)
Fantagraphics Books: Apr, 1999 - No. 6 ($2.95, B&W, limited series)

1-4-Reprints Peter Bagge's-s/a 3.00

BRADY BUNCH, THE (TV)(See Kite Fun Book and Binky #78)
Dell Publishing Co.: Feb, 1970 - No. 2, May, 1970

1 8.65 26.00 95.00
2 6.35 19.00 70.00

BRAIN, THE
Sussex Publ. Co./Magazine Enterprises: Sept, 1956 - No. 7, 1958

1-Dan DeCarlo-a in all including reprints 8.35 25.00 50.00
2,3 4.25 13.00 28.00
4-7 4.00 10.00 20.00
I.W. Reprints #1-4,8-10('63),14: 2-Reprints Sussex #2 with new cover added 1.25 3.75 10.00
Super Reprint #17,18(nd) 1.25 3.75 10.00

BRAINBANX
DC Comics (Helix): Mar, 1997 - No. 6, Aug, 1997 ($2.50, limited series)

1-6: Elaine Lee-s/Temujin-a 2.50

BRAIN BOY
Dell Publishing Co.: Apr-June, 1962 - No. 6, Sept-Nov, 1963 (Painted c-#1-6)

Four Color 1330(#1)-Gil Kane-a; origin 12.00 37.00 135.00
2(7-9/62),3-6: 4-Origin retold 7.00 20.00 75.00

BRAM STOKER'S BURIAL OF THE RATS (Movie)
Roger Corman's Cosmic Comics: Apr, 1995 - No.3, June, 1995 ($2.50)

1-3: Adaptation of film; Jerry Prosser scripts 2.50

BRAM STOKER'S DRACULA (Movie)(Also see Dracula: Vlad the Impaler)
Topps Comics: Oct, 1992 - No. 4, Jan, 1993 ($2.95, limited series, polybagged)

1-(1st & 2nd printing)-Adaptation of film begins; Mignola-c/a in all; 4 trading cards & poster;photo scenes of movie 3.00
1-Crimson foil edition (limited to 500) 10.00
2-Bound-in poster & cards 3.00
2-4: 2-Bound-in poster & cards. 4 trading cards in both. 3-Contains coupon to win 1 of 500 crimson foil-cedition of #1. 4-Contains coupon to win 1 of 500 uncut sheets of all 16 trading cards 3.00

BRAND ECHH (See Not Brand Echh)

BRAND NEW YORK: WHAT JUSTICE
Comic Box Inc.: July, 1997 ($3.95, B&W&Red)

1-Zoltan-s/a, Peter Avanti-s 4.00

BRAND OF EMPIRE (See Luke Short's...Four Color 771)

BRASS
Image Comics (WildStorm Productions): Aug, 1996 - No. 3, May, 1997 ($2.50, limited series)

1-($4.50) Folio Ed.; oversized 4.50
1-3: Wiesenfeld-s/Bennett-a. 3-Grunge & Roxy(Gen 13) cameo 2.50

GD2.0 FN6.0 NM9.4

BRATPACK/MAXIMORTAL SUPER SPECIAL
King Hell Press: 1996 ($2.95, B&W, limited series)

1,2: Veitch-s/a 3.00

BRATS BIZARRE
Marvel Comics (Epic/Heavy Hitters): 1994 - No. 4, 1994 ($2.50, limited series)

1-4: All w/bound-in trading cards 2.50

BRAVADOS, THE (See Wild Western Action)
Skywald Publ. Corp.: Aug, 1971 (52 pgs., one-shot)

1-Red Mask, The Durango Kid, Billy Nevada-r; Bolle-a; 3-D effect story 1.25 3.75 10.00

BRAVE AND THE BOLD, THE (See Best Of... & Super DC Giant) (Replaced by Batman & The Outsiders)
National Periodical Publ./DC Comics: Aug-Sept, 1955 - No. 200, July, 1983

1-Viking Prince by Kubert, Silent Knight, Golden Gladiator begin; part Kubert-c 214.00 642.00 2800.00
2 100.00 300.00 1200.00
3,4 53.00 159.00 635.00
5-Robin Hood begins (4-5/56, 1st DC app.), ends #15; see Robin Hood Tales #7 57.00 171.00 685.00
6-10: 6-Robin Hood by Kubert; last Golden Gladiator app.; Silent Knight; no Viking Prince. 8-1st S.A. issue 40.00 120.00 460.00
11-22,24: 12,14-Robin Hood-c. 18,21-23-Grey tone-c. 22-Last Silent Knight. 24-Last Viking Prince by Kubert (2nd solo book) 31.00 93.00 350.00
23-Viking Prince origin by Kubert; 1st B&B single theme issue & 1st Viking Prince solo book 40.00 120.00 460.00
25-1st app. Suicide Squad (8-9/59) 34.00 102.00 375.00
26,27-Suicide Squad 30.00 90.00 300.00

GD2.0 FN6.0 VF8.0 NM9.4

28-(2-3/60)-Justice League intro./1st app.; origin/1st app. Snapper Carr 300.00 900.00 2250.00 5100.00
29-Justice League (4-5/60)-2nd app. battle the Weapons Master; robot-c 150.00 450.00 1050.00 2250.00
30-Justice League (6-7/60)-3rd app.; vs. Amazo 128.00 384.00 832.00 1800.00

GD2.0 FN6.0 NM9.4

31-1st app. Cave Carson (8-9/60); scarce in high grade; 1st try-out series 31.00 93.00 325.00
32,33-Cave Carson 21.50 64.00 215.00

GD2.0 FN6.0 VF8.0 NM9.4

34-Origin/1st app. Silver-Age Hawkman, Hawkgirl & Byth by Kubert (2-3/61); 1st S.A. Hawkman tryout series; all predate Hawkman #1 133.00 400.00 865.00 1850.00

GD2.0 FN6.0 NM9.4

35-Hawkman by Kubert (4-5/61)-2nd app. 40.00 120.00 485.00
36-Hawkman by Kubert; origin & 1st app. Shadow Thief (6-7/61)-3rd app. 37.00 111.00 410.00
37-Suicide Squad (2nd tryout series) 22.50 68.00 225.00
38,39-Suicide Squad. 38-Last 10¢ issue 19.50 58.00 195.00
40,41-Cave Carson Inside Earth (2nd try-out series). 40-Kubert-a. 41-Meskin-a 14.00 42.00 140.00
42-Hawkman by Kubert (2nd tryout series) 28.00 84.00 285.00
43-Hawkman by Kubert; more detailed origin 33.00 100.00 330.00
44-Hawkman by Kubert; grey-tone-c 24.00 72.00 240.00
45-49-Strange Sports Stories by Infantino 6.50 19.50 65.00
50-The Green Arrow & Manhunter From Mars (10-11/63); 1st Manhunter x-over outside of Detective (pre-dates House of Mystery #143); team-ups begin 16.50 50.00 165.00
51-Aquaman & Hawkman (12-1/63-64); pre-dates Hawkman #1 22.00 66.00 220.00
52-(2-3/64)-3 Battle Stars; Sgt. Rock, Haunted Tank, Johnny Cloud, & Mlle. Marie team-up for 1st time by Kubert (c/a) 15.00 45.00 150.00
53-Atom & The Flash by Toth 6.50 19.50 65.00
54-Kid Flash, Robin & Aqualad; 1st app./origin Teen Titans (6-7/64) 26.00 78.00 260.00
55-Metal Men & The Atom 5.00 15.00 50.00

The Brave and the Bold #61 © DC

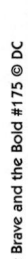

The Brave and the Bold #72 © DC

The Brave and the Bold #175 © DC

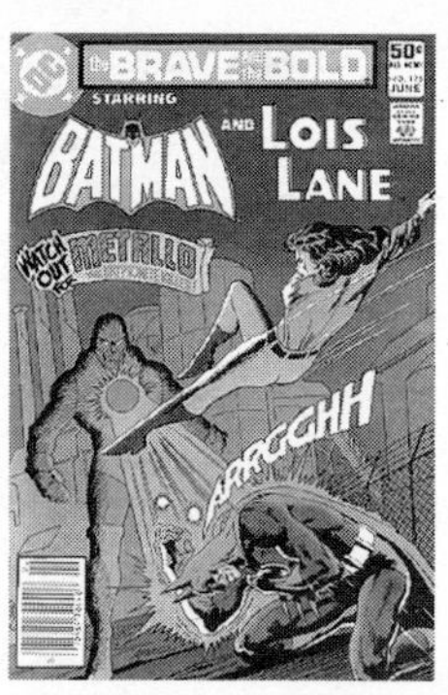

GD2.0 FN6.0 NM9.4

56-The Flash & Manhunter From Mars 5.00 15.00 50.00
57-Origin & 1st app. Metamorpho (12-1/64-65) 14.50 44.00 145.00
58-2nd app. Metamorpho by Fradon 7.50 22.50 75.00
59-Batman & Green Lantern; 1st Batman team-up in Brave and the Bold 9.50 28.50 95.00
60-Teen Titans (2nd app.)-1st app. new Wonder Girl (Donna Troy), who joins Titans (6-7/65) 9.00 27.00 90.00
61-Origin Starman & Black Canary by Anderson 11.50 34.00 115.00
62-Origin Starman & Black Canary cont'd. 62-1st S.A. app. Wildcat (10-11/65); 1st S.A. app. of G.A. Huntress 9.50 28.50 95.00
63-Supergirl & Wonder Woman 5.00 15.00 50.00
64-Batman Versus Eclipso (see H.O.S. #61) 6.00 18.00 60.00
65-Flash & Doom Patrol (4-5/66) 2.80 8.40 28.00
66-Metamorpho & Metal Men (6-7/66) 2.80 8.40 28.00
67-Batman & The Flash by Infantino; Batman team-ups begin, end #200 (8-9/66) 4.50 13.50 45.00
68-Batman/Metamorpho/Joker/Riddler/Penguin-c/story; Batman as Bat-Hulk (Hulk parody) 6.50 19.50 65.00
69-Batman & Green Lantern 3.20 9.60 32.00
70-Batman & Hawkman; Craig-a(p) 3.20 9.60 32.00
71-Batman & Green Arrow 3.20 9.60 32.00
72-Spectre & Flash (6-7/67); 4th app. The Spectre; predates Spectre #1 3.80 11.40 38.00
73-Aquaman & The Atom 3.00 9.00 30.00
74-Batman & Metal Men 3.00 9.00 30.00
75-Batman & The Spectre (12-1/67-68); 6th app. Spectre; came out between Spectre #1 & #2 3.40 10.20 34.00
76-Batman & Plastic Man (2-3/68); came out between Plastic Man #8 & #9 3.00 9.00 30.00
77-Batman & The Atom 3.00 9.00 30.00
78-Batman, Wonder Woman & Batgirl 3.00 9.00 30.00
79-Batman & Deadman by Neal Adams (8-9/68); early Deadman app. 5.50 16.50 55.00
80-Batman & Creeper (10-11/68); N. Adams-a; early app. The Creeper; came out between Creeper #3 & #4 4.20 12.60 42.00
81-Batman & Flash; N. Adams-a 4.20 12.60 42.00
82-Batman & Aquaman; N. Adams-a; origin Ocean Master retold (2-3/69) 4.20 12.60 42.00
83-Batman & Teen Titans; N. Adams-a (4-5/69) 4.20 12.60 42.00
84-Batman (G.A., 1st S.A. app.) & Sgt. Rock; N. Adams-a; last 12¢ issue (6-7/69) 4.20 12.60 42.00
85-Batman & Green Arrow; 1st new costume for Green Arrow by Neal Adams (8-9/69) 4.50 13.50 45.00
86-Batman & Deadman (10-11/69); N. Adams-a; story concludes from Strange Adventures #216 (1-2/69) 4.20 12.60 42.00
87-Batman & Wonder Woman 2.50 7.50 26.00
88-Batman & Wildcat 2.50 7.50 26.00
89-Batman & Phantom Stranger (4-5/70); early Phantom Stranger app. (came out between Phantom Stranger #6 & 7 2.50 7.50 24.00
90-Batman & Adam Strange 2.50 7.50 24.00
91-Batman & Black Canary (8-9/70) 2.50 7.50 24.00
92-Batman; intro the Bat Squad 2.50 7.50 24.00
93-Batman-House of Mystery; N. Adams-a 3.50 10.50 35.00
94-Batman-Teen Titans 2.50 7.50 20.00
95-Batman & Plastic Man 2.50 7.50 20.00
96-Batman & Sgt. Rock; last 15¢ issue 2.50 7.50 20.00
97-Batman & Wildcat; 52 pg. issues begin, end #102; reprints origin & 1st app. Deadman from Strange Advs. #205 2.50 7.50 22.00
98-Batman & Phantom Stranger; 1st Jim Aparo Batman-a? 2.50 7.50 22.00
99-Batman & Flash 2.50 7.50 22.00
100-(2-3/72, 25¢, 52 pgs.)-Batman-Gr. Lantern-Gr. Arrow-Black Canary-Robin; Deadman-r by Adams/Str. Advs. #210 4.20 12.60 42.00
101-Batman & Metamorpho; Kubert Viking Prince 2.00 6.00 16.00
102-Batman-Teen Titans; N. Adams-a(p) 2.50 7.50 20.00
103-107,109,110: Batman team-ups: 103-Metal Men. 104-Deadman. 105-Wonder Woman. 106-Green Arrow. 107-Black Canary. 109-Demon.
110-Wildcat 1.10 3.30 9.00
108-Sgt. Rock 1.75 5.25 14.00
111-Batman/Joker-c/story 1.75 5.25 14.00
112-117: All 100 pgs.; Batman team-ups: 112-Mr. Miracle. 113-Metal Men; reprints origin/1st Hawkman from Brave and the Bold #34; r/origin Multi-Man/ Challengers #14. 114-Aquaman. 115-Atom; r/origin Viking Prince from #23; r/Dr. Fate/Hourman/Solomon Grundy/Green Lantern from Showcase #55. 116-Spectre. 117-Sgt. Rock; last 100 pg. issue 2.50 7.50 20.00
118-Batman/Wildcat/Joker-c/story 1.75 5.25 14.00
119,121-123,125-128,132-140: Batman team-ups: 119-Man-Bat. 121-Metal Men. 122-Swamp Thing. 123-Plastic Man/Metamorpho. 125-Flash. 126-Aquaman. 127-Wildcat. 128-Mr. Miracle. 132-Kung-Fu Fighter. 133-Deadman. 134-Green Lantern. 135-Metal Men. 136-Metal Men/Green Arrow. 137-Demon. 138-Mr. Miracle. 139-Hawkman. 140-Wonder Woman 1.00 2.80 7.00
120-Kamandi(68 pgs.) 1.25 3.75 10.00
124-Sgt. Rock` 1.25 3.75 10.00
129,130-Batman/Green Arrow/Atom parts 1 & 2; Joker & Two Face-c/stories 1.50 4.50 12.00
131-Batman & Wonder Woman vs. Catwoman-c/sty 1.10 3.30 9.00
141-Batman/Black Canary vs. Joker-c/story 1.50 4.50 12.00
142-160: Batman team-ups: 142-Aquaman. 143-Creeper; origin Human Target (44 pgs.). 144-Green Arrow; origin Human Target part 2 (44 pgs.). 145-Phantom Stranger. 146-G.A. Batman/Unknown Soldier. 147-Supergirl. 148-Plastic Man; X-Mas-c. 149-Teen Titans. 150-Anniversary issue; Superman. 151-Flash. 152-Atom. 153-Red Tornado. 154-Metamorpho. 155-Green Lantern. 156-Dr. Fate. 157-Batman vs. Kamandi (ties into Kamandi #59). 158-Wonder Woman. 159-Ra's Al Ghul. 160-Supergirl. 2.40 6.00
161-181,183-190,192-195,198,199: Batman team-ups: 161-Adam Strange. 162-G.A. Batman/Sgt. Rock. 163-Black Lightning. 164-Hawkman. 165-Man-Bat. 166-Black Canary; Nemesis (intro) back-up story begins, ends #192; Penguin-c/story. 167-G.A. Batman/Blackhawk; origin Nemesis. 168-Green Arrow. 169-Zatanna. 170-Nemesis. 171-Scalphunter.172-Firestorm. 173-Guardians of the Universe. 174-Green Lantern. 175-Lois Lane 176-Swamp Thing. 177-Elongated Man. 178-Creeper. 179-Legion. 180-Spectre. 181-Hawk & Dove. 183-Riddler. 184-Huntress. 185-Green Arrow. 186-Hawkman. 187-Metal Men. 188,189-Rose & the Thorn. 190-Adam Strange. 192-Superboy vs. Mr. I.Q. 193-Nemesis. 194-Flash. 195-I...Vampire 198-Karate Kid. 199-Batman vs. The Spectre 4.00
182-G.A. Robin; G.A. Starman app.; 1st modern app. G.A. Batwoman 5.00
191-Batman/Joker-c/story; Nemesis app. 1.00 3.00 8.00
196-Ragman; origin Ragman retold. 2.40 6.00
197-Catwoman; Earth II Batman & Catwoman marry; 2nd modern app. of G.A. Batwoman 1.00 3.00 8.00
200-Double-sized (64 pgs.); printed on Mando paper; Earth One & Earth Two Batman app. in separate stories; intro/1st app. Batman & The Outsiders 1.10 3.30 9.00

NOTE: ***Neal Adams*** *a-79-86, 93, 100r, 102; c-75, 76, 79-86, 88-90, 93, 95, 99, 100r.* ***M. Anderson*** *a-115r; c-72i, 96i.* ***Andru/Esposito*** *c-25-27.* ***Aparo*** *a-98, 100-102, 104-125, 126i, 127-136, 138-145, 147, 148i, 149-152, 154, 155, 157-162, 168-170, 173-178, 180-182, 184, 186 189i, 191i-193i, 195, 196, 200; c-105-109, 111-136, 137i, 138-175, 177, 180-184, 186-200.* ***Austin*** *a-166i.* ***Bernard Baily*** *c-32, 33, 58.* ***Buckler*** *a-185, 186p; c-137, 178p, 185p, 186p.* ***Giordano*** *a-143, 144.* ***Infantino*** *a-67p, 72p, 97r, 98r, 115r, 172p, 183p, 190p, 194p; c-45-49, 67p, 69p, 70p, 72p, 96p, 98r.* ***Kaluta*** *c-176.* ***Kane*** *a-115r; c-59, 64.* ***Kubert*** *&/or* ***Heath*** *a-1-24; reprints-101, 113, 115, 117.* ***Kubert*** *a-99r; c-22-24, 34-36, 40, 42-44, 52.* ***Mooney*** *a-114r.* ***Mortimer*** *a-64, 69.* ***Newton*** *a-153p, 156p, 165p.* ***Irv Novick*** *c-1(part), 2-21.* ***Fred Ray*** *a-78r.* ***Roussos*** *a-50, 76i, 114r.* ***Staton*** *148p. 52 pgs.-97, 100; 68 pgs.-120; 100 pgs.-112-117.*

BRAVE AND THE BOLD, THE
DC Comics: Dec, 1991 - No. 6, June, 1992 ($1.75, limited series)

1-6: Green Arrow, The Butcher, The Question in all; Grell scripts in all 2.00
NOTE: ***Grell*** *c-3, 4-6.*

BRAVE AND THE BOLD SPECIAL, THE (See DC Special Series No. 8)

BRAVE EAGLE (TV)
Dell Publishing Co.: No. 705, June, 1956 - No. 929, July, 1958

Four Color 705 (#1)-Photo-c 5.50 16.50 60.00
Four Color 770, 816, 879 (2/58), 929-All photo-c 2.75 8.00 30.00

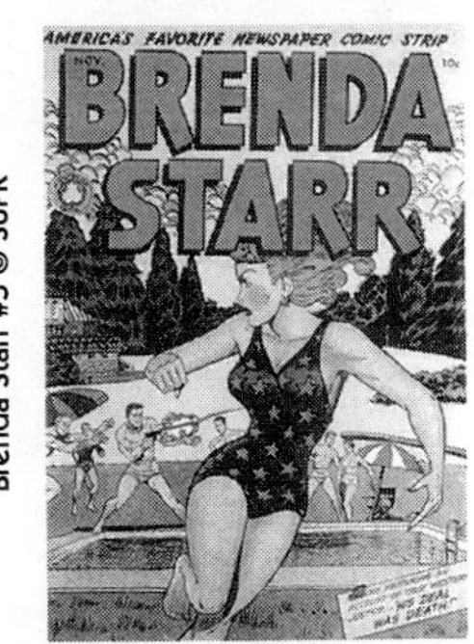

Brenda Starr #5 © SUPR

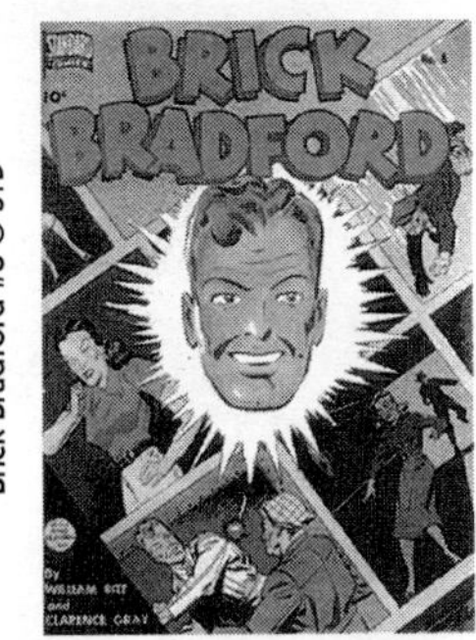

Brick Bradford #8 © STD

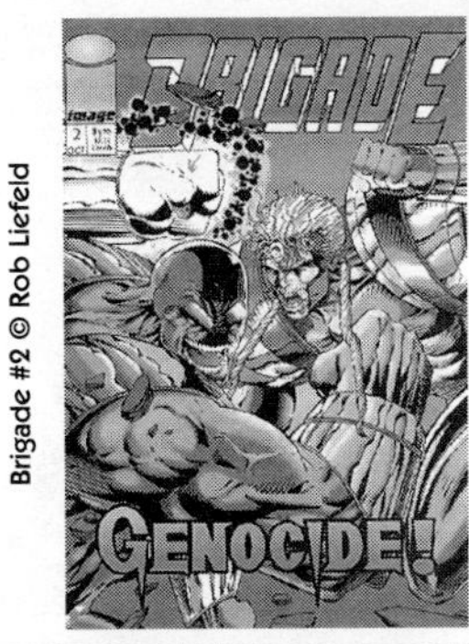

Brigade #2 © Rob Liefeld

GD2.0 FN6.0 NM9.4

BRAVE ONE, THE (Movie)
Dell Publishing Co.: No. 773, Mar, 1957

	GD2.0	FN6.0	NM9.4
Four Color 773-Photo-c	4.50	13.50	50.00

BRAVURA
Malibu Comics (Bravura): 1995 (mail-in offer)

0-wraparound holographic-c; short stories and promo pin-ups of Chaykin's Power &Glory, Gil Kane's & Steven Grant's Edge, Starlin's Breed, & Simonson's Star Slammers.			5.00
1 1/2			7.00

BREAKNECK BLVD.
MotioN Comics/Slave Labor Graphics Vol. 2: No. 0, Feb, 1994 - No. 2, Nov, 1994; Vol. 2#1, Jul, 1995 - #6, Dec., 1996 ($2.50/$2.95, B&W)

0-2, V2#1-6: 0-Perez/Giordano-c			3.00

BREAK-THRU (Also see Exiles V1#4)
Malibu Comics (Ultraverse): Dec, 1993 - No. 2, Jan, 1994 ($2.50, 44 pgs.)

1,2-Perez-c/a(p); has x-overs in Ultraverse titles			2.50

BREATHTAKER
DC Comics: 1990 - No. 4, 1990 ($4.95, 52 pgs., prestige format, mature)

Book 1-4: Mark Wheatley-painted-c/a & scripts; Marc Hempel-a			5.00
TPB (1994, $14.95) r/#1-4; intro by Neil Gaiman			15.00

'BREED
Malibu Comics (Bravura): Jan, 1994 - No. 6, 1994 ($2.50, limited series)

1-6: 1-(48 pgs.)-Origin & 1st app. of 'Breed by Starlin; contains Bravura stamps; spot varnish-c. 2-5-contains Bravura stamps. 6-Death of Rachel			3.00
...:Book of Genesis (1994, $12.95)-reprints #1-6			13.00

'BREED II
Malibu Comics (Bravura): Nov, 1994 - No. 6, Apr, 1995 ($2.95, limited series)

1-6: Starlin-c/a/scripts in all. 1-Gold edition			3.00

BREEZE LAWSON, SKY SHERIFF (See Sky Sheriff)

BRENDA LEE STORY, THE
Dell Publishing Co.: Sept, 1962

01-078-209	8.00	23.00	85.00

BRENDA STARR (Also see All Great)
Four Star Comics Corp./Superior Comics Ltd.: No. 13, 9/47; No. 14, 3/48; V2#3, 6/48 - V2#12, 12/49

V1#13-By Dale Messick	75.00	225.00	600.00
14-Kamen bondage-c	78.00	234.00	625.00
V2#3-Baker-a?	64.00	192.00	510.00
4-Used in **SOTI**, pg. 21; Kamen bondage-c	75.00	225.00	600.00
5-10	61.00	183.00	490.00
11,12 (Scarce)	62.00	186.00	500.00

NOTE: *Newspaper reprints plus original material through #6. All original #7 on.*

BRENDA STARR (...Reporter)(Young Lovers No. 16 on?)
Charlton Comics: No. 13, June, 1955 - No. 15, Oct, 1955

13-15-Newspaper-r	36.00	107.00	250.00

BRENDA STARR REPORTER
Dell Publishing Co.: Oct, 1963

1	14.00	44.00	160.00

BRER RABBIT (See Kite Fun Book, Walt Disney Showcase #28 and Wheaties)
Dell Publishing Co.: No. 129, 1946; No. 208, Jan, 1949; No. 693, 1956 (Disney)

Four Color 129 (#1)-Adapted from Disney movie "Song of the South"	27.00	82.00	300.00
Four Color 208 (1/49)	11.00	32.00	120.00
Four Color 693-Part-r 129	8.00	25.00	90.00

BRIAN BOLLAND'S BLACK BOOK
Eclipse Comics: July, 1985 (one-shot)

1-British B&W-r in color			2.00

BRICK BRADFORD (Also see Ace Comics & King Comics)
King Features Syndicate/Standard: No. 5, July, 1948 - No. 8, July, 1949 (Ritt & Grey reprints)

5	18.00	54.00	125.00
6-Robot-c (by Schomburg?).	26.00	77.00	180.00
7-Schomburg-c. 8-Says #7 inside, #8 on-c	13.50	41.00	95.00

BRIDE'S DIARY (Formerly Black Cobra No. 3)
Ajax/Farrell Publ.: No. 4, May, 1955 - No. 10, Aug, 1956

4 (#1)	6.35	19.00	38.00
5-8	4.00	12.00	24.00
9,10-Disbrow-a	5.85	17.50	35.00

BRIDES IN LOVE (Hollywood Romances & Summer Love No. 46 on)
Charlton Comics: Aug, 1956 - No. 45, Feb, 1965

1	9.15	27.00	55.00
2	5.00	15.00	30.00
3-6,8-10	2.50	7.50	24.00
7-(68 pgs.)	3.20	9.60	32.00
11-20	1.85	5.50	15.00
21-45	1.10	3.30	9.00

BRIDES ROMANCES
Quality Comics Group: Nov, 1953 - No. 23, Dec, 1956

1	11.00	33.00	75.00
2	5.85	17.50	35.00
3-10: Last precode (3/55)	4.25	13.00	28.00
11-17,19-22: 15-Baker-a(p)?; Colan-a	4.00	10.00	20.00
18-Baker-a	5.35	16.00	32.00
23-Baker-c/a	8.00	24.00	48.00

BRIDE'S SECRETS
Ajax/Farrell(Excellent Publ.)/Four-Star: Apr-May, 1954 - No. 19, May, 1958

1	10.00	30.00	65.00
2	5.35	16.00	32.00
3-6: Last precode (3/55)	4.00	12.00	24.00
7-11,13-19: 18-Hollingsworth-a	4.00	11.00	22.00
12-Disbrow-a	4.25	13.00	26.00

BRIDE-TO-BE ROMANCES (See True...)

BRIGADE
Image Comics (Extreme Studios): Aug, 1992 - No. 4, 1993 ($1.95, lim. series)

1-Liefeld part plots/scripts in all, Liefeld-c(p); contains 2 Brigade trading cards; 1st app. Genocide			3.00
1-Gold foil stamped logo edition			8.00
2-Contains coupon for Image Comics #0 & 2 trading cards			3.00
2-With coupon missing			2.00
3-Contains 2 bound-in trading cards; 1st Birds of Prey			2.50
4-Flip book format featuring Youngblood #5			2.50

BRIGADE
Image Comics (Extreme): V2#1, May, 1993 - V2#22, July, 1995 ($1.95/$2.50)

V2#1-22: 1-Gatefold-c; Liefeld co-plots; Blood Brothers part 1; Bloodstrike app.; 1st app. Boone & Hacker. 2-(6/93, V2#1 on inside)-Foil merricote-c (news stand ed. w/out foil-c exists). 3-1st app. Roman; Perez-c(i); Liefeld scripts. 6-1st app. Coral & Worlok. 6-8-Thibert-c(i). 8-Liefeld scripts; Black and White part 5 by Art Thibert. 8,9-Coupons #2 & 6 for Extreme Prejudice #0 bound-in. 11-(8/94, $2.50) WildC.A.T.S app. 16-Polybagged w/ trading card. 19-Glory app. 20 (Regular-c.)-Troll, Supreme, Shadowhawk, Glory,Vanguard, & Roman form new team. 22-"Supreme Apocalypse" Pt. 4; Marv Wolfman scripts; polybagged w/ trading card			2.50
0-(9/93)-Liefeld scripts; 1st app. Warcry; Youngblood & Wildcats app.; Thibert-c(i)			2.50
20-(Variant-c. by Quesada & Palmiotti)-Troll, Supreme, Shadowhawk, Glory, Vanguard, & Roman form new team.			2.50
Sourcebook 1 (8/94, $2.95)			3.00

BRIGAND, THE (See Fawcett Movie Comics No. 18)

BRINGING UP FATHER
Dell Publishing Co.: No. 9, 1942 - No. 37, 1944

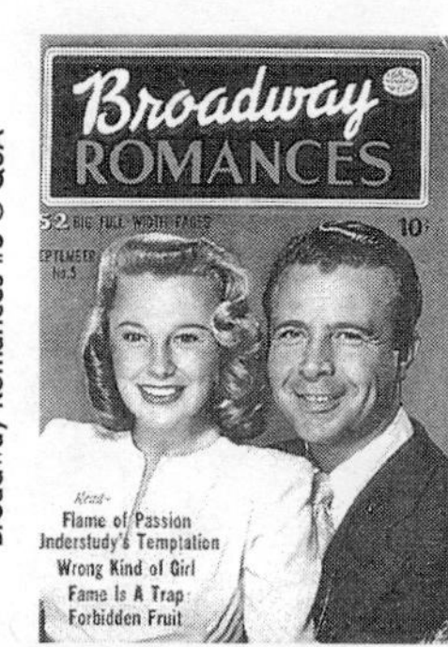

Broadway Romances #5 © QUA

Brother Power, The Geek #1 © DC

Buccaneers #21 © QUA

	GD2.0	FN6.0	NM9.4
Large Feature Comic 9	19.00	57.00	210.00
Four Color 37	19.00	57.00	210.00

BRING BACK THE BAD GUYS
Marvel Comics: 1998($24.95, TPB)

1-Reprints stories of Marvel villains' secrets 25.00

BRING ON THE BAD GUYS (See Fireside Book Series)

BRINKE OF DESTRUCTION
High-Top and Brinke Stevens: Dec, 1995 - Jan, 1997($2.95)

1-3: 1-Boris-c. 2-Julie Bell-c. 3-Garris-c 3.00
Holiday Special ($6.99)-Comic w/audio tape .85 2.60 7.00

BRINKE OF DISASTER
Revenge Entertainment Group: 1996 ($2.25, B&W, one-shot)

nn-Photo-c 2.25

BRINKE OF ETERNITY
Chaos! Comics: Apr, 1994 ($2.75, one-shot)

1 3.00
1-Signed Edition 4.00

BROADWAY HOLLYWOOD BLACKOUTS
Stanhall: Mar-Apr, 1954 - No. 3, July-Aug, 1954

1	10.00	30.00	70.00
2,3	7.50	22.50	45.00

BROADWAY ROMANCES
Quality Comics Group: January, 1950 - No. 5, Sept, 1950

1-Ward-c/a (9 pgs.); Gustavson-a	33.00	99.00	230.00
2-Ward-a (9 pgs.); photo-c	24.00	73.00	170.00
3-5: All-Photo-c	11.00	33.00	75.00

BROKEN ARROW (TV)
Dell Publishing Co.: No. 855, Oct, 1957 - No. 947, Nov, 1958

Four Color 855 (#1)-Photo-c	5.00	15.00	54.00
Four Color 947-Photo-c	4.00	12.00	45.00

BROKEN CROSS, THE (See The Crusaders)

BRONCHO BILL (See Comics On Parade, Sparkler & Tip Top Comics)
United Features Syndicate/Standard(Visual Editions) No. 5-on: 1939 - 1940; No. 5, 1?/48 - No. 16, 8?/50

Single Series 2 ('39)	47.00	142.00	380.00
Single Series 19 ('40)(#2 on cvr)	40.00	120.00	325.00
5	12.00	36.00	85.00
6(4/48)-10(4/49)	7.50	22.50	45.00
11(6/49)-16	5.85	17.50	35.00

NOTE: ***Schomburg** c-6, 7, 9-13, 16.*

BROOKLYN DREAMS
DC Comics (Paradox Press): 1994, ($4.95, B&W, limited series, mature)

1-4 5.00

BROOKS ROBINSON (See Baseball's Greatest Heroes #2)

BROTHER BILLY THE PAIN FROM PLAINS
Marvel Comics Group: 1979 (68pgs.)

1-B&W comics, satire, Jimmy Carter-c & x-over w/Brother Billy peanut jokes. Joey Adams-a (scarce) 2.25 6.75 18.00

BROTHER POWER, THE GEEK (See Saga of Swamp Thing Annual & Vertigo Visions)
National Periodical Publications: Sept-Oct, 1968 - No. 2, Nov-Dec, 1968

1-Origin; Simon-c(i?)	4.00	12.00	40.00
2	2.50	7.50	20.00

BROTHERS, HANG IN THERE, THE
Spire Christian Comics (Fleming H. Revell Co.): 1979 (49¢)

nn 5.00

BROTHERS OF THE SPEAR (Also see Tarzan)
Gold Key/Whitman No. 18: June, 1972 - No. 17, Feb, 1976; No. 18, May, 1982

	GD2.0	FN6.0	NM9.4
1	2.80	8.40	28.00
2-Painted-c begin, end #17	1.75	5.25	14.00
3-10	1.10	3.30	9.00
11-18: 12-Line drawn-c. 13-17-Spiegle-a. 18-r/#2; Leopard Girl-r			5.00

BROTHERS, THE CULT ESCAPE, THE
Spire Christian Comics (Fleming H. Revell Co.): 1980 (49¢)

nn 4.00

BROWNIES (See New Funnies)
Dell Publishing Co.: No. 192, July, 1948 - No. 605, Dec, 1954

Four Color 192(#1)-Kelly-a	11.50	34.00	125.00
Four Color 244(9/49), 293 (9/50)-Last Kelly c/a	10.00	30.00	110.00
Four Color 337(7-8/51), 365(12-1/51-52), 398(5/52)	3.00	10.00	36.00
Four Color 436(11/52), 482(7/53), 522(12/53), 605	3.00	9.00	32.00

BRUCE GENTRY
Better/Standard/Four Star Publ./Superior No. 3: Jan, 1948 - No. 8, Jul, 1949

1-Ray Bailey strip reprints begin, end #3; E. C. emblem appears as a monogram on stationery in story; negligee panels	43.00	129.00	345.00
2,3	35.00	105.00	245.00
4-8	24.00	73.00	170.00

NOTE: ***Kamenish** a-2-7; c-1-8.*

BRUCE LEE (Also see Deadly Hands of Kung Fu)
Malibu Comics: July, 1994 - No. 6, Dec, 1994 ($2.95, 36 pgs.)

1-6: 1-(44 pgs.)-Mortal Kombat prev., 1st app. in comics. 2,6-(36 pgs.) 4.00

BRUCE JONES' OUTER EDGE
Innovation: 1993 ($2.50, B&W, one-shot)

1-Bruce Jones-c/a/script 2.50

BRUCE WAYNE: AGENT OF S.H.I.E.L.D. (Also see Marvel Versus DC #3 & DC Versus Marvel #4)
Marvel Comics (Amalgam): Apr, 1996 ($1.95, one-shot)

1-Chuck Dixon scripts & Cary Nord-c/a. 2.00

BRUISER
Anthem Publications: Feb, 1994 ($2.45)

1 2.45

BRUTE, THE
Seaboard Publ. (Atlas): Feb, 1975 - No. 3, July, 1975

1,3: 1-Origin & 1st app; Sekowsky-a(p). 3-Brunner/Starlin/Weiss-a(p) 5.00
2-Sekowsky-a(p) 4.00

BRUTE & BABE
Ominous Press: July, 1994 - No. 2, Aug, 1994

1-($3.95, 8 tablets plus-c)-"...It Begins..."; tablet format 4.00
2-($2.50, 36 pgs.)-"Mael's Rage", 2-(40 pgs.)-Stiff additional variant-c 2.50

BRUTE FORCE
Marvel Comics: Aug, 1990 - No. 4, Nov, 1990 ($1.00, limited series)

1-4: Animal super-heroes 2.00

BUBBLEGUM CRISIS: GRAND MAL
Dark Horse Comics: Mar, 1994 - No. 4, June, 1994 ($2.50, limited series)

1-4-Japanese manga 2.50

BUCCANEER
I. W. Enterprises: No date (1963)

I.W. Reprint #1(r-/Quality #20), #8(r-/#23): Crandall-a in each 2.50 7.50 22.00

BUCCANEERS (Formerly Kid Eternity)
Quality Comics: No. 19, Jan, 1950 - No. 27, May, 1951 (No. 24-27: 52 pgs.)

19-Captain Daring, Black Roger, Eric Falcon & Spanish Main begin; Crandall-a	47.00	141.00	375.00
20,23-Crandall-a	34.00	103.00	240.00
21-Crandall-c/a	40.00	120.00	300.00
22-Bondage-c	28.00	84.00	195.00

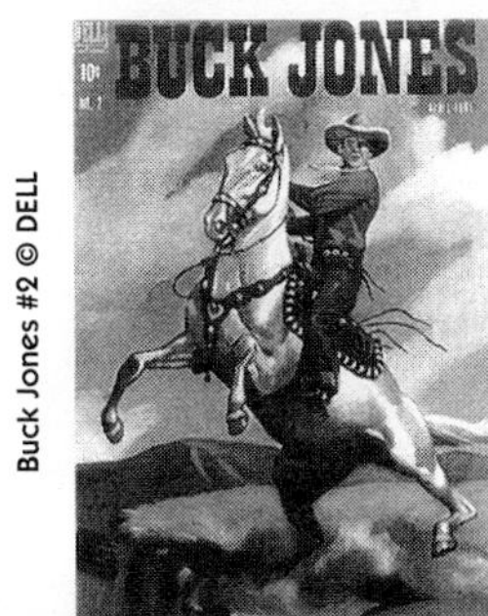

Buck Jones #2 © DELL

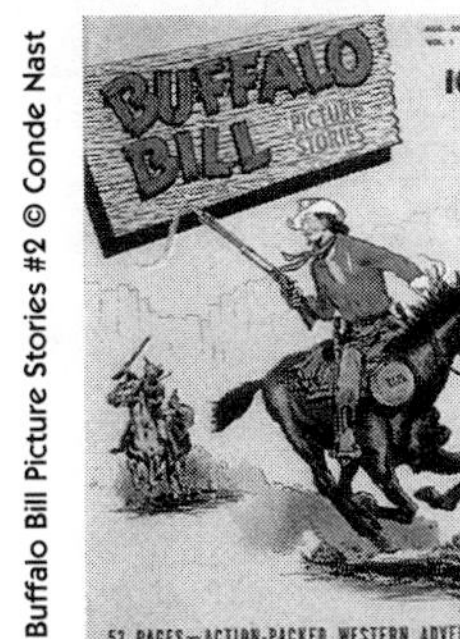

Buffalo Bill Picture Stories #2 © Conde Nast

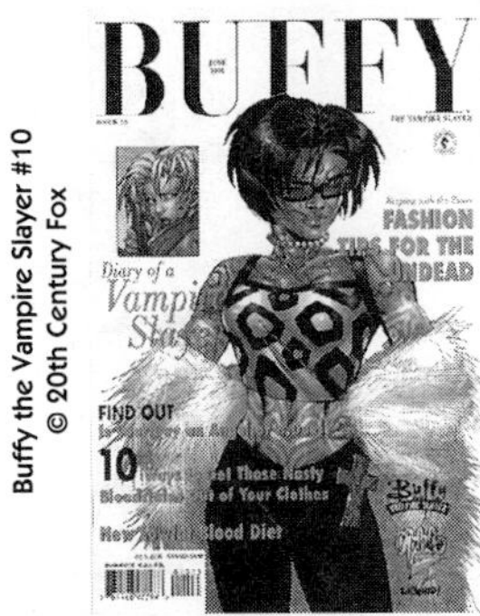

Buffy the Vampire Slayer #10 © 20th Century Fox

GD2.0 FN6.0 NM9.4

24-26: 24-Adam Peril, U.S.N. begins. 25-Origin & 1st app. Corsair Queen. 26-last Spanish Main 24.00 71.00 165.00
27-Crandall-c/a 36.00 107.00 250.00
Super Reprint #12 (1964)-Crandall-r/#21 2.50 7.50 25.00

BUCCANEERS, THE (TV)
Dell Publishing Co.: No. 800, 1957

Four Color 800-Photo-c 6.40 19.00 70.00

BUCKAROO BANZAI (Movie)
Marvel Comics Group: Dec, 1984 - No. 2, Feb, 1985

1,2-Movie adaptation; r/Marvel Super Special #33 2.00

BUCK DUCK
Atlas Comics (ANC): June, 1953 - No. 4, Dec, 1953

1-Funny animal stories in all 13.00 39.00 90.00
2-4: 2-Ed Win-a(5) 6.70 20.00 40.00

BUCK JONES (Also see Crackajack Funnies, Famous Feature Stories, Master Comics #7 & Wow Comics #1, 1936)
Dell Publishing Co.: No. 299, Oct, 1950 - No. 850, Oct, 1957 (All Painted-c)

Four Color 299(#1)-Buck Jones & his horse Silver-B begin; painted back-c begins, ends #5 11.00 34.00 125.00
2(4-6/51) 6.00 18.00 65.00
3-8(10-12/52) 5.00 15.00 55.00
Four Color 460,500,546,589 4.50 13.50 50.00
Four Color 652,733,850 2.75 8.00 30.00

BUCK ROGERS (Also see Famous Funnies, Pure Oil Comics, Salerno Carnival of Comics, 24 Pages of Comics, & Vicks Comics)
Famous Funnies: Winter, 1940-41 - No. 6, Sept, 1943

1-Sunday strip reprints by Rick Yager; begins with strip #190; Calkins-c 300.00 900.00 2700.00
2 (7/41)-Calkins-c 125.00 375.00 1000.00
3 (12/41), 4 (7/42) 106.00 318.00 850.00
5,6: 5-Story continues with Famous Funnies No. 80; Buck Rogers, Sky Roads. 6-Reprints of 1939 dailies; contains B.R. story "Crater of Doom" (2 pgs.) by Calkins not-r from Famous Funnies 94.00 282.00 750.00

BUCK ROGERS
Toby Press: No. 100, Jan, 1951 - No. 9, May-June, 1951

100(#7)-All strip-r begin 27.00 81.00 190.00
101(#8), 9-All Anderson-a(1947-49-r/dailies) 21.00 64.00 150.00

BUCK ROGERS (...in the 25th Century No. 5 on) (TV)
Gold Key/Whitman No. 7 on: Oct, 1964; No. 2, July, 1979 - No. 16, May, 1982 (No #10)

1(10128-410, 12¢)-1st S.A. app. Buck Rogers & 1st new B. R. in comics since 1933 giveaway; painted-c; back-c pin-up 5.00 15.00 55.00
2(7/79)-6: 3,4,6-Movie adaptation; painted-c 5.00
7,11 (Whitman) 2.40 6.00
8-10 (prepack)(scarce) 1.25 3.75 10.00
12-16 4.00
Giant Movie Edition 11296(64pp, Whitman, $1.50), reprints GK #2-4 minus cover; tabloid size; photo-c (See Marvel Treasury) 2.25 6.75 18.00
Giant Movie Edition 02489(Western/Marvel, $1.50), reprints GK #2-4 minus cover 2.00 6.00 16.00

NOTE: ***Bolle** a-2p,3p, Movie Ed.(p). **McWilliams** a-2i,3i, 5-11, Movie Ed.(i). Painted c-1-9,11-13.*

BUCK ROGERS (Comics Module)
TSR, Inc.: 1990 - No. 10, 1991 ($2.95, 44 pgs.)

1-10 (1990): 1-Begin origin in 3 parts. 2-Indicia says #1. 2,3-Black Barney back-up story. 4-All Black Barney issue; B. B.-c. 5-Indicia says #6; Black Barney-c & lead story; Buck Rogers back-up story. 10-Flip book (72pgs.) 3.00

BUCKSKIN (TV)
Dell Publishing Co.: No. 1011, July, 1959 - No. 1107, June-Aug, 1960

Four Color 1011 (#1)-Photo-c 6.40 19.00 70.00
Four Color 1107-Photo-c 5.50 16.50 60.00

BUCKY O'HARE (Funny Animal)
Continuity Comics: 1988 ($5.95, graphic novel)

1-Michael Golden-c/a(r); r/serial-Echo of Futurepast #1-6. 2.40 6.00
Deluxe Hardcover ($40, 52pg, 8x11") 40.00

BUCKY O'HARE
Continuity Comics: Jan, 1991 - No. 5, 1991 ($2.00)

1-6: 1-Michael Golden-c/a 2.50

BUDDIES IN THE U.S. ARMY
Avon Periodicals: Nov, 1952 - No. 2, 1953

1-Lawrence-c 11.50 34.00 80.00
2-Mort Lawrence-c/a 8.35 25.00 50.00

BUFFALO BEE (TV)
Dell Publishing Co.: No. 957, Nov, 1958 - No. 1061, Dec-Feb, 1959-60

Four Color 957 (#1) 9.00 27.00 100.00
Four Color 1002 (8-10/59), 1061 6.00 18.00 65.00

BUFFALO BILL (See Frontier Fighters, Super Western Comics &Western Action Thrillers)
Youthful Magazines: No. 2, Oct, 1950 - No. 9, Dec, 1951

2-Annie Oakley story 11.50 34.00 80.00
3-9: 2-4-Walter Johnson-c/a. 9-Wildey-a 8.00 24.00 48.00

BUFFALO BILL CODY (See Cody of the Pony Express)

BUFFALO BILL, JR. (TV) (See Western Roundup)
Dell/Gold Key: Jan, 1956 - No. 13, Aug-Oct, 1959; 1965 (All photo-c)

Four Color 673 (#1) 5.75 17.00 63.00
Four Color 742,766,798,828,856(11/57) 4.00 12.00 45.00
7(2-4/58)-13 3.00 10.00 36.00
1(6/65, Gold Key)-Photo-c(r/F.C. #798); photo-b/c 3.00 10.00 36.00

BUFFALO BILL PICTURE STORIES
Street & Smith Publications: June-July, 1949 - No. 2, Aug-Sept, 1949

1,2-Wildey, Powell-a in each 12.00 36.00 85.00

BUFFY THE VAMPIRE SLAYER (Based on the TV series)
Dark Horse Comics: 1998 - Present ($2.95)

1-Bennett-a/Watson-s; Art Adams-c 5.00
1-Variant photo-c 5.00
1-Gold foil logo Art Adams-c 15.00
1-Gold foil logo photo-c 20.00
2-11-Regular and photo-c. 4-7-Gomez-a. 5,8-Green-c 4.00
Wizard #1/2 12.00

BUFFY THE VAMPIRE SLAYER: ANGEL
Dark Horse Comics: May, 1999 - No. 3, July, 1999 ($2.95, limited series)

1-3-Gomez-a; Matsuda-c & photo-c for each 3.00

BUFFY THE VAMPIRE SLAYER: SPIKE AND DRU
Dark Horse Comics: Apr, 1999; No. 2, Oct, 1999 ($2.95)

1,2-Photo-c 3.00

BUFFY THE VAMPIRE SLAYER: THE ORIGIN (Adapts movie screenplay)
Dark Horse Comics: Jan, 1999 - No. 3, Mar, 1999 ($2.95, limited series)

1-3-Brereton-s/Bennett-a; reg & photo-c for each 3.00

BUG
Marvel Comics: Mar, 1997 ($2.99, one-shot)

1-Micronauts character 3.00

BUGALOOS (TV)
Charlton Comics: Sept, 1971 - No. 4, Feb, 1972

1 2.80 8.40 28.00
2-4 2.25 6.75 18.00

NOTE: *No. 3(1/72) went on sale late in 1972 (after No. 4) with the 1/73 issues.*

BUGBOY
Image Comics: June, 1998 ($3.95, B&W, one-shot)

1-Mark Lewis-s/a 4.00

Bugs Bunny (1st mini-series) #2 © Warner Bros.

Bulletman #7 © FAW

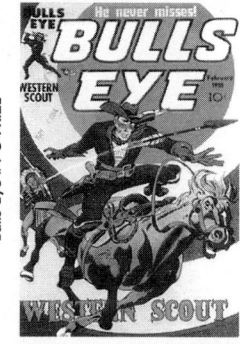

Bulls-Eye #4 © PRIZE

BUGHOUSE (Satire)
Ajax/Farrell (Excellent Publ.): Mar-Apr, 1954 - No. 4, Sept-Oct, 1954

	GD2.0	FN6.0	NM9.4
V1#1	18.00	54.00	125.00
2-4	11.00	33.00	75.00

BUGS BUNNY (See The Best of..., Camp Comics, Comic Album #2, 6, 10, 14, Dell Giant #28, 32, 46, Dynabrite, Golden Comics Digest #1, 3, 5, 6, 8, 10, 14, 15, 17, 21, 26, 30, 34, 39, 42, 47, Kite Fun Book, Large Feature Comic #8, Looney Tunes and Merry Melodies, March of Comics #44, 59, 75, 83, 97, 115, 132, 149, 160, 179, 188, 201, 220, 231, 245, 259, 273, 287, 301, 315, 329, 343, 363, 367, 380, 392, 403, 415, 428, 440, 452, 464, 476, 487, Porky Pig, Puffed Wheat, Story Hour Series #802, Super Book #14, 26 and Whitman Comic Books)

BUGS BUNNY (See Dell Giants for annuals)
Dell Publishing Co./Gold Key No. 86-218/Whitman No. 219 on: 1942 - No. 245, 1983

	GD2.0	FN6.0	NM9.4
Large Feature Comic 8(1942)-(Rarely found in fine-mint condition)	109.00	327.00	1200.00
Four Color 33 ('43)	109.00	327.00	1200.00
Four Color 51	35.00	105.00	385.00
Four Color 88	20.00	60.00	220.00
Four Color 123('46),142,164	15.00	45.00	165.00
Four Color 187,200,217,233	10.00	30.00	110.00
Four Color 250-Used in **SOTI**, pg. 309	11.00	33.00	120.00
Four Color 266,274,281,289,298('50)	8.00	25.00	90.00
Four Color 307,317(#1),327(#2),338,347,355,366,376,393	7.00	20.00	75.00
Four Color 407,420,432(10/52)	5.50	16.50	60.00
Four Color 498(9/53),585(9/54), 647(9/55)	4.50	13.50	50.00
Four Color 724(9/56),838(9/57),1064(12/59)	3.60	11.00	40.00
28(12-1/52-53)-30	3.50	10.50	38.00
31-50	3.00	9.00	30.00
51-85(7-9/62)	2.50	7.50	20.00
86(10/62)-88-Bugs Bunny's Showtime-(25¢, 80pgs.)	5.00	15.00	55.00
89-99	2.00	6.00	16.00
100	2.25	6.75	18.00
101-118: 118-Last 12¢ issue	1.50	4.50	12.00
119-140	1.10	3.30	9.00
141-170	1.00	2.80	7.00
171-218			4.00
219,220,225-237: 229-Swipe of Barks story/WDC&S #223			4.50
221(9/80),222(11/80)-Pre-pack?	1.50	4.50	12.00
223 (1/81),224 (3/81)-Low distr.	1.00	3.00	8.00
238-245 (#90070 on-c, nd, nd code; pre-pack?	1.25	3.75	10.00

NOTE: *Reprints-100, 102, 104, 123, 143, 144, 147, 167, 173, 175-177, 179-185, 187, 190.*

	GD2.0	FN6.0	NM9.4
...Comic-Go-Round 11196-(224 pgs.)($1.95)(Golden Press, 1979)	2.50	7.50	20.00
...Winter Fun 1(12/67-Gold Key)-Giant	3.20	9.60	32.00

BUGS BUNNY
DC Comics: June, 1990 - No. 3, Aug, 1990 ($1.00, limited series)

1-3: Daffy Duck, Elmer Fudd, others app. 2.00

BUGS BUNNY (...Monthly on-c)
DC Comics: 1993 - No. 3, 1994? ($1.95)

1-3-Bugs, Porky Pig, Daffy, Road Runner 3.00

BUGS BUNNY & PORKY PIG
Gold Key: Sept, 1965 (Paper-c, giant, 100 pgs.)

	GD2.0	FN6.0	NM9.4
1(30025-509)	7.00	20.00	80.00

BUGS BUNNY'S ALBUM (See Bugs Bunny, Four Color No. 498,585,647,724)

BUGS BUNNY LIFE STORY ALBUM (See Bugs Bunny, Four Color No. 838)

BUGS BUNNY MERRY CHRISTMAS (See Bugs Bunny, Four Color No. 1064)

BULLET CROW, FOWL OF FORTUNE
Eclipse Comics: Mar, 1987 - No. 2, Apr, 1987 ($2.00, B&W, limited series)

1,2-The Comic Reader-r & new-a 2.00

BULLETMAN (See Fawcett Miniatures, Master Comics, Mighty Midget Comics, Nickel Comics & XMas Comics)
Fawcett Publications: Sum, 1941 - #12, 2/12/43; #14, Spr, 1946 - #16, Fall, 1946 (No #13)

	GD2.0	FN6.0	NM9.4
1-Silver metallic-c	311.00	933.00	2800.00
2-Raboy-c	144.00	432.00	1150.00
3,5-Raboy-c each	104.00	312.00	835.00
4	91.00	273.00	730.00
6-10: 7-Ghost Stories told by night watchman of cemetery begins; Eisnerish-a; hidden message "Chic Stone is a jerk"	75.00	225.00	600.00
11,12,14-16 (nn 13): 12-Robot-c	56.00	168.00	450.00

NOTE: ***Mac Raboy*** *c-1-3, 5, 6, 10. "Bulletman the Flying Detective" on cover #8 on.*

BULLETPROOF MONK
Image Comics (Flypaper Press): 1998 - No. 3, 1999 ($2.95, limited series)

1-3-Oeming-a 3.00

BULLETS AND BRACELETS (Also see Marvel Versus DC #3 & DC Versus Marvel #4)
Marvel Comics (Amalgam): Apr, 1996 ($1.95)

1-John Ostrander script & Gary Frank-c/a 2.00

BULLS-EYE (Cody of The Pony Express No. 8 on)
Mainline No. 1-5/Charlton No. 6,7: 7-8/54-No. 5, 3-4/55; No. 6, 6/55; No. 7, 8/55

	GD2.0	FN6.0	NM9.4
1-S&K-c, 2 pgs.-a	50.00	150.00	400.00
2-S&K-c/a	43.00	128.00	340.00
3-5-S&K-c/a(2 each). 4-Last pre-code issue (1-2/55). 5-Censored issue with tomahawks removed in battle scene	37.00	111.00	260.00
6-S&K-c/a	30.00	90.00	210.00
7-S&K-c/a(3)	37.00	111.00	260.00

BULLS-EYE COMICS (Formerly Komik Pages #10; becomes Kayo #12)
Harry 'A' Chesler: No. 11, 1944

	GD2.0	FN6.0	NM9.4
11-Origin K-9, Green Knight's sidekick, Lance; The Green Knight, Lady Satan, Yankee Doodle Jones app.	40.00	120.00	290.00

BULLWHIP GRIFFIN (See Movie Comics)

BULLWINKLE (...and Rocky No. 20 on; See March of Comics #233 and Rocky & Bullwinkle)(TV) (Jay Ward)
Dell/Gold Key: 3-5/62 - #11, 4/74; #12, 6/76 - #19, 3/78; #20, 4/79 - #25, 2/80

	GD2.0	FN6.0	NM9.4
Four Color 1270 (3-5/62)	18.00	55.00	200.00
01-090-209 (Dell, 7-9/62)	14.00	44.00	160.00
1(11/62, Gold Key)	13.00	39.00	145.00
2(2/63)	7.50	22.50	85.00
3(4/72)-11(4/74-Gold Key)	4.00	12.00	45.00
12-14: 12(6/76)-Reprints. 13(9/76), 14-New stories	2.25	6.75	18.00
15-25	1.25	3.75	10.00
Mother Moose Nursery Pomes 01-530-207 (5-7/62, Dell)	18.00	55.00	200.00

NOTE: *Reprints: 6, 7, 20-24.*

BULLWINKLE (...& Rocky No. 2 on)(TV)
Charlton Comics: July, 1970 - No. 7, July, 1971

	GD2.0	FN6.0	NM9.4
1	5.00	15.00	50.00
2-7	3.50	10.50	35.00

BULLWINKLE AND ROCKY
Star Comics/Marvel Comics No. 3 on: Nov, 1987 - No. 9, Mar, 1989

1-9: 3,5,8-Dudley Do-Right app. 4-Reagan-c 3.00

BUMMER
Fantagraphics Books: June, 1995 ($3.50, B&W, mature)

1 3.50

BUNNY (Also see Rock Happening)
Harvey Publications: Dec, 1966 - No. 20, Dec, 1971; No. 21, Nov, 1976

	GD2.0	FN6.0	NM9.4
1-68 pg. Giants begin	5.50	16.50	55.00
2-10	3.20	9.60	32.00
11-18: 18-Last 68 pg. Giant	2.60	7.80	26.00
19-21-52 pg. Giants: 21-Fruitman app.	2.50	7.50	22.00

BURKE'S LAW (TV)
Dell Publ.: 1-3/64; No. 2, 5-7/64; No. 3, 3-5/65 (All have Gene Barry photo-c)

Buster Crabbe #3 © FF

Buzzy #6 © DC

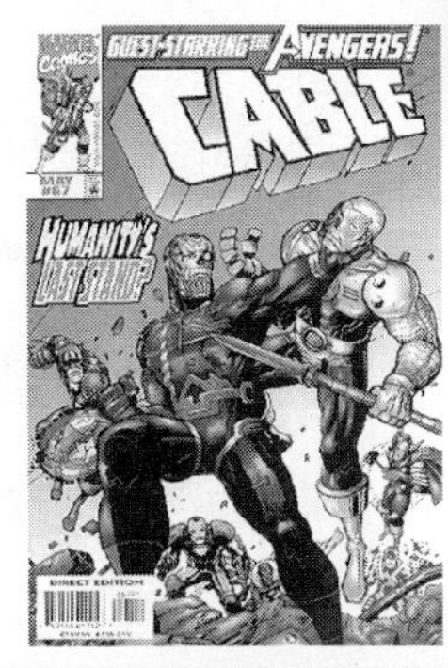

Cable #67 © MAR

GD2.0 FN6.0 NM9.4

1-Photo-c 4.00 12.00 45.00
2,3-Photo-c 3.00 9.00 35.00

BURNING ROMANCES (See Fox Giants)

BUSTER BEAR
Quality Comics Group (Arnold Publ.): Dec, 1953 - No. 10, June, 1955

1-Funny animal 9.15 27.50 55.00
2 4.25 13.00 28.00
3-10 4.00 11.00 22.00
I.W. Reprint #9,10 (Super on inside) 2.00 5.00 10.00

BUSTER BROWN COMICS (See Promotional Comics section)

BUSTER BUNNY
Standard Comics(Animated Cartoons)/Pines: Nov, 1949 - No. 16, Oct, 1953

1-Frazetta 1 pg. text illo. 9.15 27.00 55.00
2 4.25 13.00 28.00
3-16: 15-Racist-c 4.00 10.00 20.00

BUSTER CRABBE (TV)
Famous Funnies Publ.: Nov, 1951 - No. 12, 1953

1-1st app.(?) Frazetta anti-drug ad; text story about Buster Crabbe & Billy the Kid 34.00 103.00 240.00
2-Williamson/Evans-c; text story about Wild Bill Hickok & Pecos Bill 36.00 107.00 250.00
3-Williamson/Evans-c/a 40.00 120.00 280.00
4-Frazetta-c/a, 1pg.; bondage-c 45.00 135.00 360.00
5-Frazetta-c; Williamson/Krenkel/Orlando-a, 11pgs. (per Mr. Williamson) 109.00 327.00 875.00
6,8 17.00 51.00 120.00
7-Frazetta one pg. ad 19.00 56.00 130.00
9-One pg. Frazetta Boy Scouts ad (1st?) 16.00 47.00 110.00
10-12 10.00 30.00 70.00
NOTE: Eastern Color sold 3 dozen each NM file copies of #s 9-12 a few years ago.

BUSTER CRABBE (The Amazing Adventures of...)(Movie star)
Lev Gleason Publications: Dec, 1953 - No. 4, June, 1954

1,4: 1-Photo-c. 4-Flash Gordon-c 21.00 62.00 145.00
2,3-Toth-a 19.00 58.00 135.00

BUTCH CASSIDY
Skywald Comics: June, 1971 - No. 3, Oct, 1971 (52 pgs.)

1-Red Mask reprint, retitled Maverick; Bolle-a; Sutton-a 1.50 4.50 12.00
2,3: 2-Whip Wilson-r. 3-Dead Canyon Days reprint/Crack Western No. 63; Sundance Kid app.; Crandall-a 1.10 3.30 9.00

BUTCH CASSIDY (...& the Wild Bunch)
Avon Periodicals: 1951

1-Kinstler-c/a 17.00 51.00 120.00
NOTE: ***Reinman** story; Issue number on inside spine.*

BUTCH CASSIDY (See Fun-In No. 11 & Western Adventure Comics)

BUTCHER, THE (Also see Brave and the Bold, 2nd Series))
DC Comics: May, 1990 - No. 5, Sept, 1990 ($1.50, mature)

1-5: 1-No indicia inside 2.00

BUZ SAWYER (Sweeney No. 4 on)
Standard Comics: June, 1948 - No. 3, 1949

1-Roy Crane-a 21.00 64.00 150.00
2-Intro his pal Sweeney 12.00 36.00 85.00
3 10.00 30.00 70.00

BUZ SAWYER'S PAL, ROSCOE SWEENEY (See Sweeney)

BUZZ BUZZ COMICS MAGAZINE
Horse Press: May, 1996 ($4.95, B&W, over-sized magazine)

1-Paul Pope-c/a/scripts; Moebius-a 5.00

BUZZY (See All Funny Comics)
National Periodical Publications/Detective Comics: Winter, 1944-45 - No. 75, 1-2/57; No. 76, 10/57; No. 77, 10/58

GD2.0 FN6.0 NM9.4

1 (52 pgs. begin); "America's favorite teenster" 27.00 81.00 190.00
2 (Spr, 1945) 13.00 39.00 90.00
3-5 10.00 30.00 60.00
6-10 6.35 19.00 38.00
11-20 5.35 16.00 32.00
21-30 4.00 12.00 24.00
31,35-38 4.00 10.00 20.00
32-34,39-Last 52 pgs. Scribbly story by Mayer in each (these four stories were done for Scribbly #14 which was delayed for a year) 4.00 12.00 24.00
40-77: 62-Last precode (2/55) 3.60 9.00 18.00

BUZZY THE CROW (See Harvey Comics Hits #60 & 62, Harvey Hits #18 & Paramount Animated Comics #1)

BY BIZARRE HANDS
Dark Horse Comics: Apr, 1994 - No. 3, June, 1994 ($2.50, B&W, mature)

1-3: Lansdale stories 2.50

CABBOT: BLOODHUNTER (Also see Bloodstrike & Bloodstrike: Assassin)
Maximum Press: Jan, 1997 ($2.50, one-shot)

1-Rick Veitch-a/script; Platt-c; Thor, Chapel & Prophet cameos 2.50

CABLE (See Ghost Rider &..., & New Mutants #87)
Marvel Comics: May, 1993 - Present ($3.50/$1.95/$1.50)

1-($3.50, 52 pgs.)-Gold foil & embossed-c; Thibert a-1-4p; c-1-3 3.50
2-15: 3-Extra 16 pg. X-Men/Avengers ann. preview. 4-Liefeld-a assist; last Thibert-a(p). 6-8-Reveals that Baby Nathan is Cable; gives background on Stryfe. 9-Omega Red-c/story. 11-Bound-in trading card sheet 2.50
16-Newsstand edition 2.50
16-Enhanced edition 8.00
17-20-($1.95)-Deluxe edition, 20-w/bound in '95 Fleer Ultra cards 3.00
17-20-($1.50)-Standard edition 2.50
21-24, 26-44, -1(7/97): 21-Begin $1.95-c; return from Age of Apocalyse. 24-Grizzly dies. 28-vs. Sugarman; Mr. Sinister app. 30-X-Man-c/app.; Exodus app. 31-vs. X-Man. 32-Post app. 33-Post-c/app; Mandarin app (flashback); includes "Onslaught Update". 34-Onslaught x-over; Hulk-c/app.; Apocalypse app (cont'd in Hulk #444). 35-Onslaught x-over; Apocalypse vs. Cable. 36-w/card insert. 38-Weapon X-c/app; Psycho Man & Micronauts app. 40-Scott Clark-a(p). 41-Bishop-c/app. 2.50
25 ($3.95)-Foil gatefold-c 4.00
45-49,51-72: 45-Operation Zero Tolerance. 51-1st Casey-s. 54-Black Panther. 55-Domino-c/app. 62-Nick Fury-c/app.63-Stryfe-c/app. 67,68-Avengers-c/app. 71-Liefeld-a 2.50
50-($2.99) Double sized w/wraparound-c 3.00
.../Machine Man '98 Annual ($2.99) Wraparound-c 3.00
.../X-Force '96 Annual ($2.95) Wraparound-c 3.00
...'99 Annual ($3.50) vs. Sinister; computer photo-c 3.50
...Second Genesis 1 (9/99, $3.99) r/New Mutants #99, 100 and X-Force #1; Liefeld-c 4.00

CABLE - BLOOD AND METAL (Also see New Mutants #87 & X-Force #8)
Marvel Comics: Oct, 1992 - No. 2, Nov, 1992 ($2.50, limited series, 52 pgs.)

1-Fabian Nicieza scripts; John Romita, Jr.-c/a in both; Cable vs. Stryfe; 2nd app. of The Wild Pack (becomes The Six Pack); wraparound-c. 3.50
2-Prelude to X-Cutioner's Song 2.50

CADET GRAY OF WEST POINT (See Dell Giants)

CADILLACS & DINOSAURS (TV)
Marvel Comics (Epic Comics): Nov, 1990 - No. 6, Apr, 1991 ($2.50, limited series, coated paper)

1-6: r/Xenozoic Tales in color w/new-c 2.50
...In 3-D #1 (7/92, $3.95, Kitchen Sink)-With glasses 5.00

CADILLACS AND DINOSAURS (TV)
Topps Comics: V2#1, Feb, 1994 - V2#9, 1995 ($2.50, limited series)

V2#1-($2.95)-Collector's edition w/Stout-c & bound-in poster; Buckler-a; foil stamped logo; Giordano-a in all 2.40 6.00

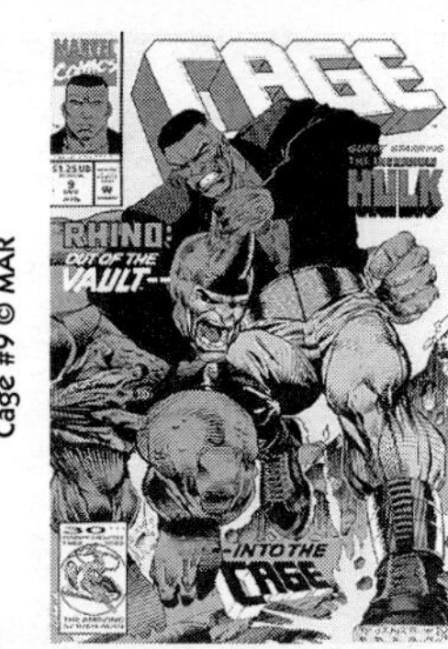

Cage #9 © MAR

Calling All Boys #8 © PMI

Camelot 3000 #9 © DC

V2#1-9: 1-Newsstand edition w/Giordano-c. 2,3-Collector's editions w/Stout-c & posters. 2,3-Newsstand ed. w/Giordano-c; w/o posters. 4-6-Collectors & Newsstand editions; Kieth-c. 7-9-Linsner-c 3.00

CAFFEINE
Slave Labor Graphics: Jan, 1996 - Present ($2.95, B&W)

1-9 3.00

CAGE (Also see Hero for Hire, Power Man & Punisher)
Marvel Comics: Apr, 1992 - No. 20, Nov, 1993 ($1.25)

1-20: 3-Punisher-c & minor app. 9-Rhino-c/story; Hulk cameo. 10-Rhino & Hulk-c/story. 12-(52 pgs.)-Iron Fist app. 2.00

CAGED HEAT 3000 (Movie)
Roger Corman's Cosmic Comics: Nov, 1995 - No. 3, Jan, 1996 ($2.50)

1-3: Adaptation of film 2.50

CAGES
Tundra Publ.: 1991 - No. 10, May, 1996 ($3.50/$3.95/$4.95, limited series)

1-Dave McKean-c/a in all 1.50 4.50 12.00
2-Misprint exists 1.00 3.00 8.00
3-9: 5-$3.95-c begins 4.00
10-($4.95) 5.00

CAIN'S HUNDRED (TV)
Dell Publishing Co.: May-July, 1962 - No. 2, Sept-Nov, 1962

nn(01-094-207) 2.50 7.50 20.00
2 1.75 5.25 14.00

CAIN/VAMPIRELLA FLIP BOOK
Harris Comics: Oct, 1994 ($6.95, one-shot, squarebound)

nn-contains Cain #3 & #4; flip book is r/Vampirella story from 1993 Creepy Fearbook. 1.00 3.00 7.50

CALIBER PRESENTS
Caliber Press: Jan, 1989 - No. 24, 1991 ($1.95/$2.50, B&W, 52 pgs.)

1-Anthology; 1st app. The Crow; Tim Vigil-c/a 5.50 16.50 60.00
2-Deadworld story; Tim Vigil-a 1.00 3.00 8.00
3-24: 15-24 ($3.50, 68 pgs.) 3.50

CALIBER PRESENTS: CINDERELLA ON FIRE
Caliber Press: 1994 ($2.95, B&W, mature)

1 3.00

CALIBER SPOTLIGHT
Caliber Press: May, 1995 ($2.95, B&W)

1-Kabuki app 3.50

CALIBRATIONS
Caliber: 1996 - No. 5 (99¢, anthology)

1-5: 1-Jill Thompson-c/a. 1,2-Atmospherics by Warren Ellis 2.50

CALIFORNIA GIRLS
Eclipse Comics: June, 1987 - No. 8, May, 1988 ($2.00, 40 pgs, B&W)

1-8: All contain color paper dolls 2.00

CALLING ALL BOYS (Tex Granger No. 18 on)
Parents' Magazine Institute: Jan, 1946 - No. 17, May, 1948 (Photo c-1-5,7,8)

1 11.00 33.00 75.00
2-Contains Roy Rogers article 5.85 17.50 35.00
3-7,9,11,14-17: 6-Painted-c. 11-Rin Tin Tin photo on-c; Tex Granger begins. 14-J. Edgar Hoover photo on-c. 15-Tex Granger-c begin 4.00 12.00 24.00
8-Milton Caniff story 6.70 20.00 40.00
10-Gary Cooper photo on-c 6.35 19.00 38.00
12-Bob Hope photo on-c 10.00 30.00 60.00
13-Bing Crosby photo on-c 8.35 25.00 50.00

CALLING ALL GIRLS
Parents' Magazine Institute: Sept, 1941 - No. 89, Sept, 1949 (Part magazine, part comic)

1 13.00 39.00 90.00
2-Photo-c 7.50 22.50 45.00
3-Shirley Temple photo-c 9.15 27.00 55.00
4-10: 4,5,7,9-Photo-c. 9-Flag-c 5.00 15.00 30.00
11-Tina Thayer photo-c; Mickey Rooney photo-b/c; B&W photo inside of Gary Cooper as Lou Gehrig in "Pride of Yankees" 5.00 15.00 30.00
12-20 4.00 12.00 24.00
21-39,41-43(10-11/45)-Last issue with comics 3.60 9.00 18.00
40-Liz Taylor photo-c 10.00 30.00 65.00
44-51(7/46)-Last comic book size issue 3.20 8.00 16.00
52-89 2.80 7.00 14.00

NOTE: ***Jack Sparling*** *art in many issues; becomes a girls' magazine "Senior Prom" with #90.*

CALLING ALL KIDS (Also see True Comics)
Parents' Magazine Institute: Dec-Jan, 1945-46 - No. 26, Aug, 1949

1-Funny animal 10.00 30.00 70.00
2 5.35 16.00 32.00
3-10 3.20 8.00 16.00
11-26 2.80 7.00 14.00

CALVIN (See Li'l Kids)

CALVIN & THE COLONEL (TV)
Dell Publishing Co.: No. 1354, Apr-June, 1962 - No. 2, July-Sept, 1962

Four Color 1354(#1) 7.00 22.00 80.00
2 4.50 13.50 50.00

CAMBION
Slave Labor Graphics: Dec, 1995 - No. 2, Feb, 1996 ($2.95, B&W)

1,2 3.00

CAMELOT 3000
DC Comics: Dec, 1982 - No. 11, July, 1984; No. 12, Apr, 1985 (Direct sales, maxi series, Mando paper)

1-12: 1-Mike Barr scripts & Brian Bolland-c/a begin. 5-Intro Knights of New Camelot 2.50
TPB (1988, $12.95) r/#1-12 15.00

NOTE: ***Austin*** *a-7i-12i.* ***Bolland*** *a-1-12p; c-1-12.*

CAMERA COMICS
U.S. Camera Publishing Corp./ME: July, 1944 - No. 9, Summer, 1946

nn (7/44) 24.00 71.00 165.00
nn (9/44) 19.00 58.00 135.00
1(10/44)-The Grey Comet 19.00 58.00 135.00
2 13.00 39.00 90.00
3-Nazi WW II-c; photos 11.50 34.00 80.00
4-9: All half photos 11.00 33.00 75.00

CAMP CANDY (TV)
Marvel Comics: May, 1990 - No. 6, Oct, 1990 ($1.00, limited series)

1-6: Post-c/a(p); featuring John Candy 2.00

CAMP COMICS
Dell Publishing Co.: Feb, 1942 - No. 3, April, 1942 (All have photo-c)

1- "Seaman Sy Wheeler" by Kelly, 7 pgs.; Bugs Bunny app.; Mark Twain adaptation 53.00 159.00 425.00
2-Kelly-a, 12 pgs.; Bugs Bunny app. 47.00 141.00 375.00
3-(Scarce)-Dave Berg & Walt Kelly-a 53.00 159.00 425.00

CAMP RUNAMUCK (TV)
Dell Publishing Co.: Apr, 1966

1-Photo-c 2.50 7.50 28.00

CAMPUS LOVES
Quality Comics Group (Comic Magazines): Dec, 1949 - No. 5, Aug, 1950

1-Ward-c/a (9 pgs.) 30.00 90.00 210.00
2-Ward-c/a 23.00 69.00 160.00
3-5: 5-Spanking panels (2) 11.50 34.00 80.00

NOTE: ***Gustavson*** *a-1-5. Photo c-3-5.*

CAMPUS ROMANCE (...Romances on cover)
Avon Periodicals/Realistic: Sept-Oct, 1949 - No. 3, Feb-Mar, 1950

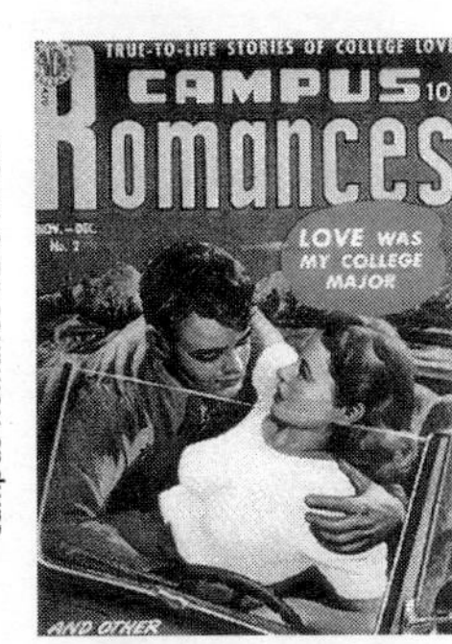

Campus Romance #2 © AVON

Canteen Kate #2 © STJ

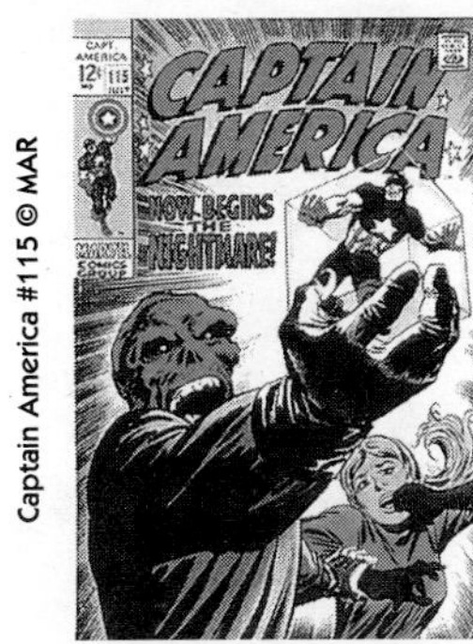

Captain America #115 © MAR

GD2.0 FN6.0 NM9.4

1-Walter Johnson-a; c-/Avon paperback #348 21.00 64.00 150.00
2-Grandenetti-a; c-/Avon paperback #151; spanking panel
16.00 47.00 110.00
3-c-/Avon paperback #201 16.00 47.00 110.00
Realistic reprint 6.70 20.00 40.00

CANADA DRY PREMIUMS (See Swamp Fox, The & Terry & The Pirates)

CANDID TALES (Also see Bold Stories & It Rhymes With Lust)
Kirby Publ. Co.: April, 1950; June, 1950 (Digest size) (144 pgs.) (Full color)

nn-(Scarce) Contains Wood female pirate story, 15 pgs., and 14 pgs. in June issue; Powell-a 88.00 264.00 700.00
NOTE: *Another version exists with Dr. Kilmore by Wood; no female pirate story.*

CANDY
William H. Wise & Co.: Fall, 1944 - No. 3, Spring, 1945

1-Two Scoop Scuttle stories by Wolverton 38.00 114.00 265.00
2,3-Scoop Scuttle by Wolverton, 2-4 pgs. 28.00 84.00 195.00

CANDY (Teen-age)(Also see Police Comics #37)
Quality Comics Group (Comic Magazines): Autumn, 1947 - No. 64, Jul, 1956

1-Gustavson-a 21.00 64.00 150.00
2-Gustavson-a 11.00 33.00 75.00
3-10 7.50 22.50 45.00
11-30 5.00 15.00 30.00
31-63 4.25 13.00 28.00
64-Ward-c(p)? 4.25 13.00 28.00
Super Reprint No. 2,10,12,16,17,18('63- '64):17-Candy #12
1.50 4.50 12.00
NOTE: ***Jack Cole*** *1-2 pg. art in many issues.*

CANNON (See Heroes, Inc. Presents Cannon)

CANNONBALL COMICS
Rural Home Publishing Co.: Feb, 1945 - No. 2, Mar, 1945

1-The Crash Kid, Thunderbrand, The Captive Prince & Crime Crusader begin; skull-c 75.00 225.00 600.00
2-Devil-c 60.00 180.00 480.00

CANTEEN KATE (See All Picture All True Love Story & Fightin' Marines)
St. John Publishing Co.: June, 1952 - No. 3, Nov, 1952

1-Matt Baker-c/a 48.00 144.00 385.00
2-Matt Baker-c/a 40.00 120.00 315.00
3-(Rare)-Used in **POP**, pg. 75; Baker-c/a 47.00 141.00 375.00

CAP'N QUICK & A FOOZLE (Also see Eclipse Mag. & Monthly)
Eclipse Comics: July, 1984 - No. 3, Nov, 1985 ($1.50, color, Baxter paper)

1-3-Rogers-c/a 2.00

CAPTAIN ACTION (Toy)
National Periodical Publications: Oct-Nov, 1968 - No. 5, June-July, 1969 (Based on Ideal toy)

1-Origin; Wood-a; Superman-c app. 9.50 28.50 95.00
2,3,5-Kane/Wood-a 6.00 18.00 60.00
4 4.50 13.50 45.00

CAPTAIN AERO COMICS (Samson No. 1-6; also see Veri Best Sure Fire &Veri Best Sure Shot Comics)
Holyoke Publishing Co.: V1#7(#1), Dec, 1941 - V2#4(#10), Jan, 1943; V3#9(#11), Sept, 1943 -V4#3(#17), Oct, 1944; #21, Dec, 1944 - #26, Aug, 1946 (No #18-20)

V1#7(#1)-Flag-Man & Solar, Master of Magic, Captain Aero, Cap Stone, Adventurer begin 150.00 450.00 1200.00
8-10: 8(#2)-Pals of Freedom app. 9(#3)-Alias X begins; Pals of Freedom app. 10(#4)-Origin The Gargoyle; Kubert-a 74.00 222.00 590.00
11,12(#5,6)-Kubert-a; Miss Victory in #6 61.00 183.00 490.00
V2#1,2(#7,8): 8-Origin The Red Cross; Miss Victory app.; Brodsky-c(i)
40.00 120.00 290.00
3(#9)-Miss Victory app. 34.00 101.00 235.00
4(#10)-Miss Victory app. 26.00 79.00 185.00
V3#9 - V3#13(#11-15): 11,15-Miss Victory app. 21.00 64.00 150.00

GD2.0 FN6.0 NM9.4

V4#2(#16) 20.00 60.00 140.00
V4#3(#17), 21-24-L. B. Cole covers. 22-Intro/origin Mighty Mite.
25 36.00 107.00 250.00
26--L. B. Cole S/F-c; Palais-a(2) (scarce) 75.00 225.00 600.00
NOTE: ***L.B. Cole*** *c-17.* ***Hollingsworth*** *a-23.* ***Infantino*** *a-23, 26.* ***Schomburg*** *c-15, 16.*

CAPTAIN AMERICA (See Adventures of..., All-Select, All Winners, Aurora, Avengers #4, Blood and Glory, Captain Britain 16-20, Giant-Size..., The Invaders, Marvel Double Feature, Marvel Fanfare, Marvel Mystery, Marvel Super-Action, Marvel Super Heroes V2#3, Marvel Team-Up, Marvel Treasury Special, Power Record Comics, USA Comics, Young Allies & Young Men)

CAPTAIN AMERICA (Formerly Tales of Suspense #1-99) (Captain America and the Falcon #134-223 & Steve Rogers: Captain America #444-454 appears on cover only)
Marvel Comics Group: No. 100, Apr, 1968 - No. 454, Aug, 1996

100-Flashback on Cap's revival with Avengers & Sub-Mariner; story continued from Tales of Suspense #99; Kirby-c/a begins 20.00 60.00 300.00
101-The Sleeper-c/story; Red Skull app. 5.00 15.00 50.00
102-108: 102-Sleeper-c/s. 103,104-Red Skull-c/sty 3.00 9.00 30.00
109-Origin Capt. America retold 5.00 15.00 50.00
110,111,113-Classic Steranko-c/a: 110-Rick becomes Cap's partner; Hulk x-over; 1st app. Viper. 111-Death of Steve Rogers. 113-Cap's funeral
5.00 15.00 50.00
112-Origin retold; last Kirby-c/a 3.00 9.00 30.00
114,115: 115-Last 12¢ issue 2.50 7.50 20.00
116,118-120 2.25 6.75 18.00
117-1st app. The Falcon (9/69) 4.50 13.50 45.00
121-136,139,140: 121-Retells origin. 133-The Falcon becomes Cap's partner; origin Modok. 140-Origin Grey Gargoyle retold 1.25 3.75 10.00
137,138-Spider-Man x-over 1.50 4.50 12.00
141,142: 142-Last 15¢ issue 1.00 2.80 7.00
143-(52 pgs). 1.25 3.75 10.00
144-153,156-171,176-179: 144-New costume Falcon. 153-1st app. (cameo) Jack Monroe. 155-158-Cap's strength increased. 160-1st app. Solarr. 164-1st app. Nightshade. 176-End of Capt. America 2.40 6.00
154-1st full app. Jack Monroe (Nomad)(10/72) 1.10 3.30 9.00
155-Origin; redrawn w/Falcon added; origin J. Monroe
1.10 3.30 9.00
172-175: X-Men x-over 1.25 3.75 10.00
180-Intro/origin of Nomad (Steve Rogers) 1.00 2.80 7.00
181-Intro/origin new Cap. 2.40 6.00
182,184-192,194,195: 186-True origin The Falcon 4.00
183-Death of new Cap; Nomad becomes Cap 2.40 6.00
193-Kirby-a returns 1.00 3.00 8.00
196-199-(Regular 25¢ edition)(4-7/76) 4.00
196-199-(30¢-c variants, limited distribution) 2.00 6.00 16.00
200-(Regular 25¢ edition)(8/76) 2.40 6.00
200-(30¢-c variant, limited distribution) 2.50 7.50 24.00
201-214-Kirby-c/a 5.00
215-240,242-246: 215-Retells Cap's origin. 216-r/story from Strange Tales #114. 217-1st app. Marvel Man (later Quasar). 229-Marvel Man app. 230-Battles Hulk-c/story cont'd in Hulk #232. 233-Death of Sharon Carter. 234,235-Daredevil x-over; 235(7/79)-Miller-a(p). 244,245-Miller-c. 3.00
210-214-(35¢-c variants, limited dist.)(6-10/77) 1.50 4.50 12.00
241-Punisher app.; Miller-c. 1.00 3.00 8.00
241-2nd print 2.00
247-255-Byrne-a. 255-Origin; Miller-c. 4.00
256-281,284,285,289-322,324-326,328-331: 264-Old X-Men cameo in flash-back. 265,266-Nick Fury & Spider-Man app. 267-1st app. Everyman. 269-1st Team America. 279-(3/83)-Contains Tattooz skin decals. 281-1950s Bucky returns. 284-Patriot (Jack Mace) app. 285-Death of Patriot. 298-Origin Red Skull. 328-Origin & 1st app. D-Man 2.00
282-Bucky becomes new Nomad (Jack Monroe) 4.00
282-Silver ink 2nd print ($1.75) w/original date (6/83) 2.00
283,327,333-340: 283-2nd app. Nomad. 327-Capt. Amer. battles Super Patriot. 333-Intro & origin new Captain (Super Patriot). 339-Fall of the Mutants tie-in 3.00
286-288-Deathlok app. 2.50
323-1st app. new Super Patriot (see Nick Fury) 4.00

Captain America V3 #2 © MAR

Captain America V3 #14 © MAR

Captain America Comics #57 © MAR

GD2.0 FN6.0 NM9.4

332-Old Cap resigns 5.00
341-343,345-349 2.00
344-($1.50, 52 pgs.)-Ronald Reagan cameo 2.50
350-($1.75, 68 pgs.)-Return of Steve Rogers (original Cap) to original costume 3.00
351-382,384-396: 351-Nick Fury app. 354-1st app. U.S. Agent (6/89, see Avengers West Coast)373-Bullseye app. 375-Daredevil app. 386-U.S. Agent app. 387-389-Red Skull back-up stories. 396-Last $1.00-c. 396,397-1st app. all new Jack O'Lantern 2.00
383-($2.00, 68 pgs.)-50th anniversary issue; Red Skull story; Jim Lee-c(i) 3.00
397-399,401-424,425: 402-Begin 6 part Man-Wolf story w/Wolverine in #403-407. 405-410-New Jack O'Lantern app. in back-up story. 406-Cable & Shatterstar cameo. 407-Capwolf vs. Cable-c/story. 408-Infinity War x-over; Falcon solo back-up. 423-Vs. Namor-c/story 2.00
400-($2.25, 84 pgs.)-Flip book format w/double gatefold-c; r/Avengers #4 plus-c; contains cover pin-ups. 2.50
425-($2.95, 52 pgs.)-Embossed Foil-c ed.n; Fighting Chance Pt. 1 3.00
425-($1.75, 52 pgs.)-Regular edition 2.00
426-443,446,447,449-453: 427-Begin $1.50-c; bound-in trading card sheet. 449-Thor app. 450-"Man Without A Country" storyline begins, ends #453; Bill Clinton app; variant-c exists. 451-1st app.Cap's new costume. 452-Machinesmith app. 453-Cap gets old costume back; Bill Clinton app. 2.00
444-Mark Waid scripts & Ron Garney-c/a(p) begins, ends #454; Avengers app. 5.00
445,454: 445-Sharon Carter & Red Skull return. 3.00
448-($2.95, double-sized issue)-Waid script & Garney-c/a; Red Skull dies? 3.50
Special 1(1/71)-Origin retold 2.60 7.80 26.00
Special 2(1/72)-Colan-r/Not Brand Echh; all-r 1.75 5.25 14.00
Annual 3,4('76,'77, 52 pgs.)-Kirby-c/a(new); 4-Magneto-c/story (34 pgs.) 1.10 3.30 9.00
Annual 5-7: (52 pgs.)('81-'83) 4.00
Annual 8(9/86)-Wolverine-c/story 1.50 4.50 12.00
Annual 9-13('90-'94, 68 pgs.)-9-Nomad back-up. 10-Origin retold (2 pgs.). 11-Falcon solo story. 12-Bagged w/card. 13-Red Skull-c/story 3.00
...ASHCAN EDITION ('95, 75¢) 2.00
...: DEATHLOK LIVES! nn(10/93, $4.95)-r/#286-288 5.00
...DRUG WAR 1-(1994, $2.00, 52 pgs.)-New Warriors app. 2.00
...MAN WITHOUT A COUNTRY (1998, $12.99, TPB)-r/#450-453 13.00
...MEDUSA EFFECT 1 (1994, $2.95, 68 pgs.)-Origin Baron Zemo 3.00
...OPERATION REBIRTH (1996, $9.95)-r/#445-448 10.00
...STREETS OF POISON ($15.95)-r/#372-378 16.00
...: THE MOVIE SPECIAL nn (5/92, $3.50, 52 pgs.)-Adapts movie; printed on coated stock; The Red Skull app. 3.50

NOTE: ***Austin*** *c-225i, 239i, 246i.* ***Buscema*** *a-115p, 217p; c-136p, 217, 297.* ***Byrne*** *c-223(part), 238, 239, 247p-254p, 290, 291, 313p; a-247-254p, 255, 313p, 350.* ***Colan*** *a(p)-116-137, 256, Annual 5; c(p)-116-123, 126, 129.* ***Everett*** *a-136i, 137i; c-126i.* ***Garney*** *a(p)-444-454.* ***Gil Kane*** *a-145p; c-147p, 149p, 150p, 170p, 172-174, 180, 181p, 183-190p, 215, 216, 220, 221.* ***Kirby*** *a(p)-100-109, 112, 193-214, 216, Special 1, 2(layouts), Annual 3, 4; c-100-109, 112, 126p, 193-214.* ***Ron Lim*** *a(p)-366, 368-378, 380-386; c-366p, 368-378p, 379, 380-393p.* ***Miller*** *c-241p, 244p, 245p, 255p, Annual 5.* ***Mooney*** *a-149i.* ***Morrow*** *a-144.* ***Perez*** *c-243p, 246p.* ***Robbins*** *c(p)-183-187, 189-192, 225.* ***Roussos*** *a-140i, 168i.* ***Starlin/Sinnott*** *c-162.* ***Sutton*** *a-244i.* ***Tuska*** *a-112i, 215p, Special 2.* ***Waid*** *scripts-444-454.* ***Williamson*** *a-313i.* ***Wood*** *a-127i.* ***Zeck*** *a-263-289; c-300.*

CAPTAIN AMERICA (Volume Two)
Marvel Comics: V2#1, Nov, 1996 - No. 13, Nov, 1997($2.95/$1.95/$1.99)
(Produced by Extreme Studios)

1-($2.95)-Heroes Reborn begins; Rob Liefeld-c/a; Jeph Loeb scripts; reintro Nick Fury 5.00
1-($2.95)-(Variant-c)-Liefeld-c/a 5.00
1-(7/96, $2.95)-(Exclusive Comicon Ed.)-Liefeld-c/a 1.00 2.80 7.00
2-1113: 5-Two-c. 6-Cable-c/app. 13--"World War 3"-pt. 4, x-over w/Image 2.50
12-($2.99) "Heroes Reunited"-pt. 4 3.50

CAPTAIN AMERICA (Vol. Three) (Also see Capt. America: Sentinel of Liberty)
Marvel Comics: Jan, 1998 - Present ($2.99/$1.99)

1-($2.99) Mark Waid-s/Ron Garney-a 4.00
1-Variant cover 2.40 6.00
2-($1.99): 2-Two covers 3.00
3-11: 3-Returns to old shield. 4-Hawkeye app. 5-Thor-c/app. 7-Andy Kubert-c/a begin. 9-New shield 2.50
12-($2.99) Battles Nightmare; Red Skull back-up story 3.50
13-17,19-Red Skull returns 2.00
18-($2.99) Cap vs. Korvac in the Future 3.00
20-22: 20,21-Sgt. Fury back-up story painted by Evans 2.00
.../Citizen V '98 Annual ($3.50) Busiek & Kesel-s 3.50
1999 Annual ($3.50) Flag Smasher app. 3.50

CAPTAIN AMERICA COMICS
Timely/Marvel Comics (TCI 1-20/CmPS 21-68/MjMC 69-75/Atlas Comics (PrPI 76-78): Mar, 1941 - No. 75, Jan, 1950; No. 76, 5/54 - No. 78, 9/54
(No. 74 & 75 titled Capt. America's Weird Tales)

	GD2.0	FN6.0	VF8.2	NM9.4
1-Origin & 1st app. Captain America & Bucky by S&K; Hurricane, Tuk the Caveboy begin by S&K; 1st app. Red Skull; Hitler-c (by Simon?); intro of the "Capt. America Sentinels of Liberty Club" (advertised on inside front-c.); indicia reads Vol. 2, Number 1	4,833.00	14,500.00	31,415.00	58,000.00

	GD2.0	FN6.0	NM9.4
2-S&K Hurricane; Tuk by Avison (Kirby splash); classic Hitler-c	950.00	2850.00	10,000.00
3-Classic Red Skull-c & app; Stan Lee's 1st text (1st work for Marvel)	863.00	2589.00	8200.00
4-1st full pg. panel in comics	575.00	1725.00	4900.00
5	485.00	1455.00	4600.00
6-Origin Father Time; Tuk the Caveboy ends	442.00	1326.00	4100.00
7-Red Skull app.; classic-c	485.00	1455.00	4600.00
8-10-Last S&K issue, (S&K centerfold #6-10)	375.00	1125.00	3300.00
11-Last Hurricane, Headline Hunter; Al Avison Captain America begins, ends #20; Avison-c(p)	325.00	975.00	2900.00
12-The Imp begins, ends #16; last Father Time	305.00	915.00	2700.00
13-Origin The Secret Stamp; classic-c	325.00	975.00	2900.00
14,15	305.00	915.00	2700.00
16-Red Skull unmasks Cap; Red Skull-c	366.00	1100.00	3200.00
17-The Fighting Fool only app.	275.00	825.00	2200.00
18-classic-c	275.00	825.00	2200.00
19-Human Torch begins #19	218.00	654.00	1750.00
20-Sub-Mariner app.; no H. Torch	218.00	654.00	1750.00
21-25: 25-Cap drinks liquid opium	206.00	618.00	1650.00
26-30: 27-Last Secret Stamp; last 68 pg. issue. 28-60 pg. issues begin.	194.00	582.00	1550.00
31-35,38-40: 34-Centerfold poster of Cap	169.00	507.00	1350.00
36-Classic Hitler-c	262.00	786.00	2100.00
37-Red Skull app.	212.00	636.00	1700.00
41-45,47: 41-Last Jap War-c. 47-Last German War-c	150.00	450.00	1200.00
46-German Holocaust-c; classic	175.00	525.00	1400.00
48-58,60	120.00	360.00	960.00
59-Origin retold	288.00	864.00	2400.00
61-Red Skull-c/story	231.00	693.00	1850.00
62,64,65: 65-Kurtzman's "Hey Look"	156.00	468.00	1250.00
63-Intro/origin Asbestos Lady	162.00	486.00	1300.00
66-Bucky is shot; Golden Girl teams up with Captain America & learns his i.d; origin Golden Girl	169.00	507.00	1350.00
67-73: 67-Captain America/Golden Girl team-up; Mxyztplk swipe; last Toro in Human Torch. 68,70-Sub-Mariner/Namora, and Captain America/Golden Girl team-up in each. 69-Human Torch/Sun Girl team-up. 70-Science fiction-c/story. 71-Anti Wertham editorial; The Witness, Bucky app.	162.00	486.00	1300.00
74-(Scarce)(1949)-Titled "Captain America's Weird Tales"; Red Skull-c & app.; classic-c	422.00	1266.00	3800.00
75(2/50)-Titled "C.A.'s Weird Tales"; no C.A. app.; horror cover/stories	162.00	486.00	1300.00
76-78(1954): Human Torch/Toro stories; all have communist-c/stories	97.00	291.00	775.00

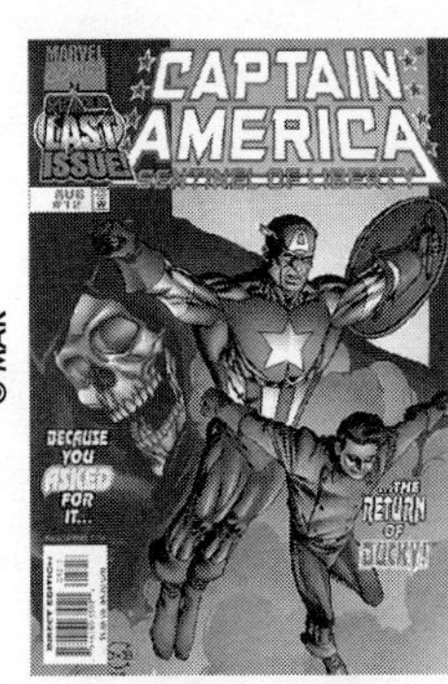

Captain America: Sentinel of Liberty #12 © MAR

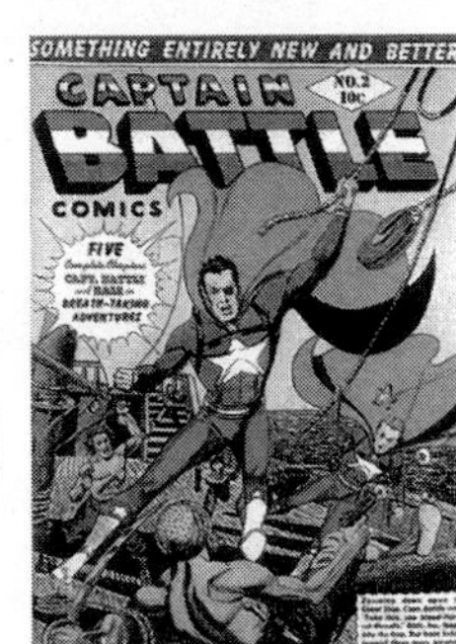

Captain Battle #2 © LEV

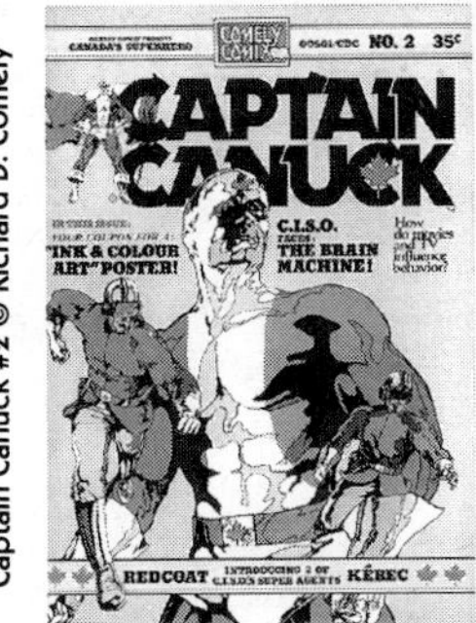

Captain Canuck #2 © Richard D. Comely

GD2.0 FN6.0 NM9.4

132-Pg. Issue (B&W-1942)(Canadian)-Has blank inside-c and back-c; contains Marvel Mystery #33 & Capt. America #18 w/cover from Capt. America #22; same contents as Marvel Mystery annual 2000.00 6000.00 12000.00

NOTE: *Crandall a-2i, 3i, 9i, 10i. **Kirby** c-8p. **Rico** c-69-71. **Romita** c-77, 78. **Schomburg** c-3, 4, 26-29, 31, 33, 37-39, 41, 42, 45-54, 58. **Sekowsky** c-55, 56. **Shores** c-1, 2, 5-7, 11i, 20-25, 30, 32, 34, 35, 40, 57, 59-67. **S&K** c-1, 2, 5-7, 9, 10. Bondage c-3, 7, 15, 16, 34, 38.*

CAPTAIN AMERICA/NICK FURY: BLOOD TRUCE
Marvel Comics: Feb, 1995 ($5.95, one-shot, squarebound)

nn-Chaykin story 2.40 6.00

CAPTAIN AMERICA, SENTINEL OF LIBERTY (See Fireside Book Series)

CAPTAIN AMERICA: SENTINEL OF LIBERTY
Marvel Comics: Sept, 1998 - No. 12, Aug, 1999 ($1.99)

1-Waid-s/Garney-a 3.00
1-Rough Cut ($2.99) Features original script and pencil pages 3.00
2-5: 2-Two-c; Invaders WW2 story 2.00
6-($2.99) Iron Man-c/app. 3.00
7-11: 8-Falcon-c/app. 9-Falcon poses as Cap 2.00
12-($2.99) Final issue; Bucky-c/app. 3.00

CAPTAIN AMERICA SPECIAL EDITION
Marvel Comics Group: Feb, 1984 - No. 2, Mar, 1984 ($2.00, Baxter paper)

1-Steranko-c/a(r) in both; r/ Captain America #110,111 3.50
2-Reprints the scarce Our Love Story #5, and C.A. #113 5.00

CAPTAIN AMERICA: THE LEGEND
Marvel Comics: Sept, 1996 ($3.95, one-shot)

1-Tribute issue; wraparound-c 4.00

CAPTAIN AND THE KIDS, THE (See Famous Comics Cartoon Books)

CAPTAIN AND THE KIDS, THE (See Comics on Parade, Katzenjammer Kids, Okay Comics & Sparkler Comics)
United Features Syndicate/Dell Publ. Co.: 1938 -12/39; Sum, 1947 - No. 32, 1955; Four Color No. 881, Feb, 1958

Single Series 1(1938) 87.00 262.00 700.00
Single Series 1(Reprint)(12/39- "Reprint" on-c) 47.00 141.00 375.00
1(Summer, 1947-UFS)-Katzenjammer Kids 13.50 41.00 95.00
2 7.15 21.50 50.00
3-10 6.70 20.00 40.00
11-20 4.25 13.00 28.00
21-32(1955) 4.00 12.00 24.00
50th Anniversary issue-(1948)-Contains a 2 pg. history of the strip, including an account of the famous Supreme Court decision allowing both Pulitzer & Hearst to run the same strip under different names 10.00 30.00 60.00
Special Summer issue, Fall issue (1948) 6.35 19.00 38.00
Four Color 881 (Dell) 2.75 8.00 30.00

CAPTAIN ATOM
Nationwide Publishers: 1950 - No. 7, 1951 (5¢, 5x7-1/4", 52 pgs.)

1-Science fiction 37.00 111.00 260.00
2-7 20.00 60.00 140.00

CAPTAIN ATOM (Formerly Strange Sus. Stories #77)(Also see Space Adv.)
Charlton Comics: V2#78, Dec, 1965 - V2#89, Dec, 1967

V2#78-Origin retold; Bache-a (3 pgs.) 7.50 22.50 75.00
79-82: 79-1st app. Dr. Spectro; 3 pg. Ditko cut & paste /Space Adventures #24. 82-Intro. Nightshade (9/66) 4.50 13.50 45.00
83-86: Ted Kord Blue Beetle in all. 83-(11/66)-1st app. Ted Kord. 84-1st app. new Captain Atom 4.00 12.00 40.00
87-89: Nightshade by Aparo in all 4.00 12.00 40.00
83-85(Modern Comics-1977)-reprints 4.00

NOTE: ***Aparo** a-87-89. **Ditko** c/a(p) 78-89. #90 only published in fanzine 'The Charlton Bullseye' #1, 2.*

CAPTAIN ATOM (Also see Americomics & Crisis On Infinite Earths)
DC Comics: Mar, 1987 - No. 57, Sept, 1991 (Direct sales only #35 on)

1-(44 pgs.)-Origin/1st app. with new costume 3.00
2-49: 5-Firestorm x-over. 6-Intro. new Dr. Spectro. 11-Millennium tie-in 14-Nightshade app. 16-Justice League app. 17-$1.00-c begins; Swamp Thing app. 20-Blue Beetle x-over. 24,25-Invasion tie-in 2.00
51057: 50-($2.00, 52 pgs.). 57-War of the Gods x-over 2.50
Annual 1,2 ('88, '89)-1-Intro Major Force 2.50

GD2.0 FN6.0 NM9.4

CAPTAIN BATTLE (Boy Comics #3 on) (See Silver Streak Comics)
New Friday Publ./Comic House: Summer, 1941 - No. 2, Fall, 1941

1-Origin Blackout by Rico; Captain Battle begins (1st appeared in Silver Streak #10, 5/41) 116.00 347.00 925.00
2 78.00 234.00 625.00

CAPTAIN BATTLE (2nd Series)
Magazine Press/Picture Scoop No. 5: No. 3, Wint, 1942-43 - No. 5, Sum, 1943 (#3: 52pgs., nd)(#5: 68pgs.)

3-Origin Silver Streak-r/SS#3; origin Lance Hale-r/Silver Streak; Simon-a(r) 66.00 197.00 525.00
4,5: 5-Origin Blackout retold 46.00 139.00 370.00

CAPTAIN BATTLE, JR.
Comic House (Lev Gleason): Fall, 1943 - No. 2, Winter, 1943-44

1-The Claw vs. The Ghost 97.00 291.00 775.00
2-Wolverton's Scoop Scuttle; Don Rico-c/a; The Green Claw story is reprinted from Silver Streak #6 78.00 234.00 625.00

CAPTAIN BEN DIX
Bendix Aviation Corporation: 1943 (Small size)

nn 6.70 20.00 40.00

CAPTAIN BRITAIN (Also see Marvel Team-Up No. 65, 66)
Marvel Comics International: Oct. 13, 1976 - No. 39, July 6, 1977 (Weekly)

1-Origin; with Capt. Britain's face mask inside 1.50 4.50 12.00
2-Origin, part II; Capt. Britain's Boomerang inside 1.00 2.80 7.00
3-11: 3,8-Vs. Bank Robbers. 4-7-Vs. Hurricane. 9-11: Vs. Dr. Synne 4.00
12-27: (scarce)-12,13-Vs. Dr. Synne. 14,15-Vs. Mastermind. 16-20-With Capt. America; 17 misprinted & color section reprinted in #18. 21-23,25,26-With Capt. America. 24-With C.B.'s Jet Plane inside. 27-Origin retold 1.50 4.50 12.00
28-32,36-39: 28-32-Vs. Lord Hawk. 36-Star Sceptre. 37-39-Vs. Highwayman & Munipulator 3.00
33-35-More on origin 3.50
Annual (1978, Hardback, 64 pgs.)-Reprints #1-7 with pin-ups of Marvel characters 1.10 3.30 9.00
Summer Special (1980, 52 pgs.)-Reprints 3.00

NOTE: *No. 1, 2, & 24 are rarer in mint due to inserts. Distributed in Great Britain only. Nick Fury-r by **Steranko** in 1-20, 24-31, 35-37. Fantastic Four-r by **J. Buscema** in all. New **Buscema**-a in 24-30. Story from No. 39 continues in Super Spider-Man (British weekly) No. 231-247. Following cancellation of his series, new Captain Britain stories appeared in "Super Spider-Man" (British weekly) No. 231-247. Captain Britain stories which appear in Super-Spider-Man No 248-253 are reprints of Marvel Team-Up No. 65&66. Capt. Britain strips also appeared in Hulk Comic (weekly) 1, 3-30, 42-55, 57-60, in Marvel Superheroes (monthly) 377-388, in Daredevils (monthly) 1-11, Mighty World of Marvel (monthly) 7-16 & Captain Britain (monthly) 1-14. Issues 1-23 have B&W & color, paper-c, & are 32 pgs. Issues 24 on are all B&W w/glossy-c & are 36 pgs.*

CAPTAIN CANUCK
Comely Comix (Canada) (All distr. in U. S.): 7/75 - No. 4, 7/77; No. 4, 7-8/79 - No. 14, 3-4/81

1-1st app. Bluefox 4.50
2,3(5-7/76)-2-1st app. Dr. Walker, Redcoat & Kebec. 3-1st app. Heather 3.50
4(1st printing-2/77)-10x14-1/2"; (5.00); B&W; 300 copies serially numbered and signed with one certificate of authenticity 8.00 23.00 85.00
4(2nd printing-7/77)-11x17", B&W; only 15 copies printed; signed by creator Richard Comely, serially #'d and two certificates of authenticity inserted; orange cardboard covers (Very Rare) 11.00 33.00 120.00
4-14: 4(7-8/79)-1st app. Tom Evans & Mr. Gold; origin The Catman. 5-Origin Capt. Canuck's powers; 1st app. Earth Patrol & Chaos Corps. 8-Jonn 'The Final Chapter'. 9-1st World Beyond. 11-1st 'Chariots of Fire' story 2.50
Special Collectors Pack (polybagged) 1.00 3.00 8.00
Summer Special 1(7-9/80, 95¢, 64 pgs.) 2.00

NOTE: *30,000 copies of No. 2 were destroyed in Winnipeg.*

Captain Fearless Comics #1 © HOKE

Captain Flight Comics #10 © Four Star

Captain Jet #4 © Farrell

GD2.0 FN6.0 NM9.4

CAPTAIN CARROT AND HIS AMAZING ZOO CREW (Also see New Teen Titans & Oz-Wonderland War)
DC Comics: Mar, 1982 - No. 20, Nov, 1983

1-20: 1-Superman app. 3-Re-intro Dodo & The Frog. 9-Re-intro Three Mouseketeers, the Terrific Whatzit. 10,11- Pig Iron reverts back to Peter Porkchops. 20-The Changeling app. 2.00

CAPTAIN CARVEL AND HIS CARVEL CRUSADERS (See Carvel Comics)

CAPTAIN CONFEDERACY
Marvel Comics (Epic Comics): Nov, 1991 - No. 4, Feb, 1992 ($1.95)

1-4: All new stories 2.00

CAPTAIN COURAGEOUS COMICS (Banner #3-5; see Four Favorites #5)
Periodical House (Ace Magazines): No. 6, March, 1942

6-Origin & 1st app. The Sword; Lone Warrior, Capt. Courageous app.; Capt. moves to Four Favorites #5 in May 75.00 225.00 600.00

CAPT'N CRUNCH COMICS (See Cap'n...)

CAPTAIN DAVY JONES
Dell Publishing Co.: No. 598, Nov, 1954

Four Color 598 3.60 11.00 40.00

CAPTAIN EASY (See The Funnies & Red Ryder #3-32)
Hawley/Dell Publ./Standard(Visual Editions)/Argo: 1939 - No. 17, Sept, 1949; April, 1956

nn-Hawley(1939)-Contains reprints from The Funnies & 1938 Sunday strips by Roy Crane 85.00 255.00 680.00
Four Color 24 (1943) 41.00 123.00 450.00
Four Color 111(6/46) 14.00 41.00 150.00
10(Standard-10/47) 11.00 33.00 75.00
11-17: All contain 1930s & '40s strip-r 9.15 27.00 55.00
Argo 1(4/56)-Reprints 6.70 20.00 40.00
NOTE: *Schomburg c-13, 16.*

CAPTAIN EASY & WASH TUBBS (See Famous Comics Cartoon Books)

CAPTAIN ELECTRON
Brick Computer Science Institute: Aug, 1986 ($2.25)

1-Disbrow-a 2.25

CAPTAIN EO 3-D (Disney)
Eclipse Comics: July, 1987 (Eclipse 3-D Special #18, $3.50, Baxter)

1-Adapts 3-D movie 3.50
1-2-D limited edition 5.00
1-Large size (11x17", 8/87)-Sold only at Disney Theme parks ($6.95) 1.50 4.50 12.00

CAPTAIN FEARLESS COMICS (Also see Holyoke One-Shot #6, Old Glory Comics & Silver Streak #1)
Helnit Publishing Co. (Holyoke Publ. Co.): Aug, 1941 - No. 2, Sept, 1941

1-Origin Mr. Miracle, Alias X, Captain Fearless, Citizen Smith Son of the Unknown Soldier; Miss Victory (1st app.) begins (1st patriotic heroine? before Wonder Woman) 81.00 244.00 650.00
2-Grit Grady, Captain Stone app. 50.00 150.00 400.00

CAPTAIN FLAG (See Blue Ribbon Comics #16)

CAPTAIN FLASH
Sterling Comics: Nov, 1954 - No. 4, July, 1955

1-Origin; Sekowsky-a; Tomboy (female super hero) begins; only pre-code issue; atomic rocket-c 40.00 120.00 280.00
2-4: 4-Flying saucer invasion-c 21.00 64.00 150.00

CAPTAIN FLEET (Action Packed Tales of the Sea)
Ziff-Davis Publishing Co.: Fall, 1952

1-Painted-c 14.00 43.00 100.00

CAPTAIN FLIGHT COMICS
Four Star Publications: Mar, 1944 - No. 10, Dec, 1945; No. 11, Feb-Mar, 1947

nn 40.00 120.00 300.00
2-4: 4-Rock Raymond begins, ends #7 23.00 69.00 160.00
5-Bondage, classic torture-c; Red Rocket begins; the Grenade app. (scarce) 75.00 225.00 600.00
6 21.00 64.00 150.00
7-10: 7-L. B. Cole covers begin, end #11. 8-Yankee Girl begins; intro. Black Cobra & Cobra Kid & begins. 9-Torpedoman app.; last Yankee Girl; Kinstler-a. 10-Deep Sea Dawson, Zoom of the Jungle, Rock Raymond, Red Rocket, & Black Cobra app; bondage-c 40.00 120.00 325.00
11-Torpedoman, Blue Flame (Human Torch clone) app.; last Black Cobra, Red Rocket; classic L. B. Cole robot-c (scarce) 75.00 225.00 600.00

CAPTAIN GALLANT (...of the Foreign Legion) (TV) (Texas Rangers in Action No. 5 on?)
Charlton Comics: 1955; No. 2, Jan, 1956 - No. 4, Sept, 1956

Non-Heinz version (#1)-Buster Crabbe photo on-c; full page Buster Crabbe photo inside front-c 10.00 30.00 60.00
2-4: Buster Crabbe in all 8.35 25.00 50.00

CAPTAIN GLORY
Topps Comics: Apr, 1993 ($2.95) (Created by Jack Kirby)

1-Polybagged w/Kirbychrome trading card; Ditko-a & Kirby-c; has coupon for Amberchrome Secret City Saga #0 3.00

CAPTAIN HERO (See Jughead as...)

CAPTAIN HERO COMICS DIGEST MAGAZINE
Archie Publications: Sept, 1981

1-Reprints of Jughead as Super-Guy 1.00 3.00 8.00

CAPTAIN HOBBY COMICS
Export Publication Ent. Ltd. (Dist. in U.S. by Kable News Co.): Feb, 1948 (Canadian)

1 6.35 19.00 38.00

CAPT. HOLO IN 3-D (See Blackthorne 3-D Series #65)

CAPTAIN HOOK & PETER PAN (Movie)(Disney)
Dell Publishing Co.: No. 446, Jan, 1953

Four Color 446 8.00 25.00 90.00

CAPTAIN JET (Fantastic Fears No. 7 on)
Four Star Publ./Farrell/Comic Media: May, 1952 - No. 5, Jan, 1953

1-Bakerish-a 19.00 56.00 130.00
2 11.00 33.00 75.00
3-5,6(?) 10.00 30.00 60.00

CAPTAIN JOHNER & THE ALIENS
Valiant: May, 1995 - No. 2, May, 1995 ($2.95, shipped in same month)

1,2: Reprints Magnus Robot Fighter 4000 A.D. back-up stories; new Paul Smith-c 3.00

CAPTAIN JUSTICE (TV)
Marvel Comics: Mar, 1988 - No. 2, Apr, 1988 (limited series)

1,2-Based on True Colors television series. 2.00

CAPTAIN KANGAROO (TV)
Dell Publishing Co.: No. 721, Aug, 1956 - No. 872, Jan, 1958

Four Color 721 (#1)-Photo-c 13.00 40.00 145.00
Four Color 780, 872-Photo-c 11.00 34.00 125.00

CAPTAIN KIDD (Formerly Dagar; My Secret Story #26 on)(Also see Comic Comics & Fantastic Comics)
Fox Feature Syndicate: No. 24, June, 1949 - No. 25, Aug, 1949

24,25: 24-Features Blackbeard the Pirate 13.50 41.00 95.00

CAPTAIN MARVEL (See All Hero, All-New Collectors' Ed., America's Greatest, Fawcett Miniature, Gift, Legends, Limited Collectors' Ed., Marvel Family, Master No. 21, Mighty Midget Comics, Shazam, Special Edition Comics, Whiz, Wisco, World's Finest #253 and XMas Comics)

CAPTAIN MARVEL (Becomes ...Presents the Terrible 5 No. 5)
M. F. Enterprises: April, 1966 - No. 4, Nov, 1966 (25¢ Giants)

nn-(#1 on pg. 5)-Origin; created by Carl Burgos 2.50 7.50 25.00
2-4: 3-(#3 on pg. 4)-Fights the Bat 2.00 6.00 16.00

CAPTAIN MARVEL (Marvel's Space-Born Super-Hero! Captain Marvel #1-6;

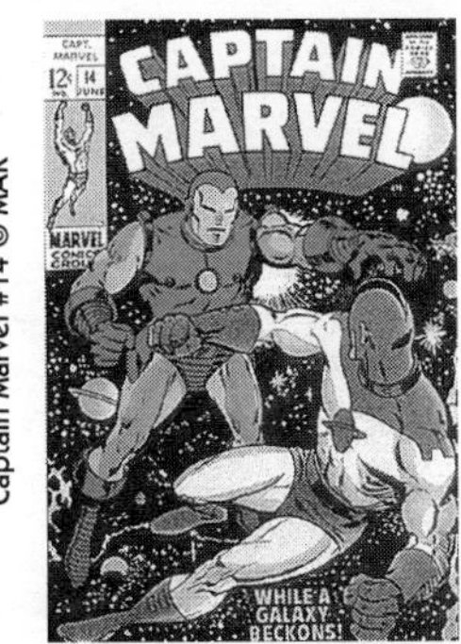

Captain Marvel #14 © MAR

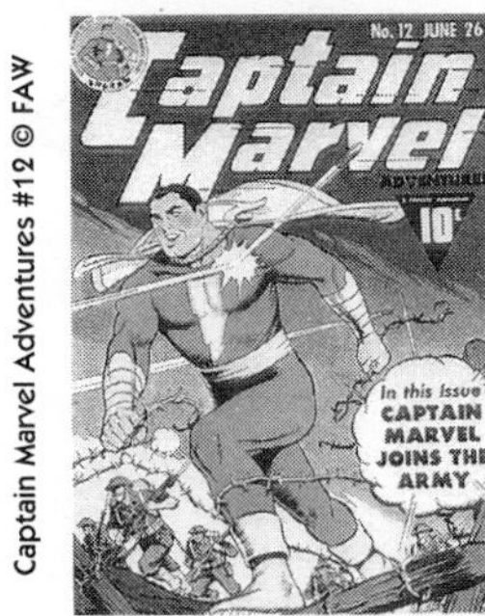

Captain Marvel Adventures #12 © FAW

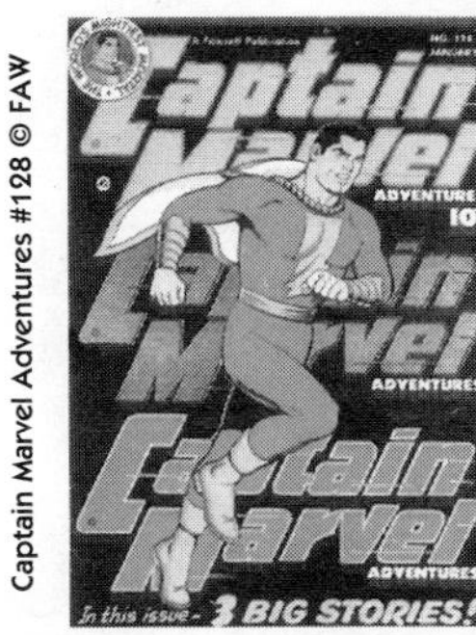

Captain Marvel Adventures #128 © FAW

GD2.0 FN6.0 NM9.4

see Giant-Size..., Life Of..., Marvel Graphic Novel #1, Marvel Spotlight V2#1 & Marvel Super-Heroes #12)
Marvel Comics Group: May, 1968 - No. 19, Dec, 1969; No. 20, June, 1970 - No. 21, Aug, 1970; No. 22, Sept, 1972 - No. 62, May, 1979

1 6.00 18.00 60.00
2-Super Skrull-c/story 2.50 7.50 20.00
3-5: 4-Captain Marvel battles Sub-Mariner 1.50 4.50 12.00
6-11: 11-Capt. Marvel given great power by Zo the Ruler; Smith/Trimpe-c; Death of Una 1.10 3.30 9.00
12-21: 14-Capt. Marvel vs. Iron Man; last 12¢ issue. 16,17-New costume. 21-Capt. Marvel battles Hulk; last 15¢ issue 1.00 2.80 7.00
22-24 2.40 6.00
25,26: 25-Starlin-c/a begins; Starlin's 1st Thanos saga begins (3/73), ends #34; Thanos cameo (5 panels). 26-Minor Thanos app. (see Iron Man #55); 1st Thanos-c 1.75 5.25 14.00
27,28-1st & 2nd full app. Thanos. 28-Thanos-c/s 1.25 3.75 10.00
29,30-Thanos cameos. 29-C.M. gains more powers 1.00 3.00 8.00
31,32: Thanos app. 31-Last 20¢ issue. 32-Thanos-c 1.25 3.75 10.00
33-Thanos-c & app.; Capt. Marvel battles Thanos; 1st origin Thanos 1.75 5.25 12.00
34-1st app. Nitro; C.M. contracts cancer which eventually kills him; last Starlin-c/a 1.00 3.00 8.00
35-43,46-50,53-56,58-62: 36-R-origin/1st app. Capt. Marvel from Marvel Super-Heroes #12. 39-Origin Watcher. 41,43-Wrightson part inks; #43-c(i). 49-Starlin & Weiss-p assists. 58-Thanos cameo 2.50
44,45-(Regular 25¢ editions)(5,7/76) 2.50
44,45-(30¢-c variants, limited distribution) 2.40 6.00
51,52-(Regular 30¢ editions)(7,9/77) 2.50
51,52-(35¢-c variants, limited distribution) 2.40 6.00
57-Thanos appears in flashback 2.40 6.00

*NOTE: **Alcala** a-35. **Austin** a-46i, 49-53i; c-52i. **Buscema** a-18p-21p. **Colan** a(p)-1-4; c(p)-1-4, 8, 9. **Heck** a-5-10p, 16p. **Gil Kane** a-17-21p; c-17-24p, 37p, 53. **Starlin** a-36. **McWilliams** a-40i. #25-34 were reprinted in The Life of Captain Marvel.*

CAPTAIN MARVEL
Marvel Comics: Nov, 1989 ($1.50, one-shot, 52 pgs.)

1-Super-hero from Avengers; new powers 2.00

CAPTAIN MARVEL
Marvel Comics: Feb, 1994 ($1.75, 52 pgs.)

1-(Indicia reads Vol 2 #2)-Minor Captain America app. 2.00

CAPTAIN MARVEL
Marvel Comics: Dec, 1995 - No. 6, May, 1996 ($2.95/$1.95)

1 ($2.95)-Advs. of Mar-Vell's son begins; Fabian Nicieza scripts; foil-c 3.00
2-6: 2-Begin $1.95-c 2.00

CAPTAIN MARVEL ADVENTURES (See Special Edition Comics for pre #1)
Fawcett Publications: 1941 (March) - No. 150, Nov, 1953
(#1 on stands 1/16/41)

GD2.0 FN6.0 VF8.2 NM9.4

nn(#1)-Captain Marvel & Sivana by Jack Kirby. The cover was printed on unstable paper stock and is rarely found in Fine or Mint condition; blank back inside-c 2375.00 7125.00 14,250.00 28,500.00

GD2.0 FN6.0 NM9.4

2-(Advertised as #3, which was counting Special Edition Comics as the real #1); Tuska-a 389.00 1167.00 3500.00
3-Metallic silver-c 262.00 786.00 2100.00
4-Three Lt. Marvels app. 181.00 543.00 1450.00
5 137.00 411.00 1100.00
6-10: 9-1st Otto Binder scripts on Capt. Marvel 106.00 318.00 850.00
11-15: 12-Capt. Marvel joins the Army. 13-Two pg. Capt. Marvel pin-up. 15-Comic cards on back-c begin, end #26 84.00 252.00 675.00
16,17: 17-Painted-c 79.00 237.00 630.00
18-Origin & 1st app. Mary Marvel & Marvel Family (12/11/42); painted-c; Mary Marvel by Marcus Swayze 194.00 582.00 1550.00
19-Mary Marvel x-over; Christmas-c 66.00 200.00 530.00
20,21-Attached to the cover, each has a miniature comic just like the Mighty Midget Comics #11, except that each has a full color promo ad on the back cover. Most copies were circulated without the miniature comic. These issues with miniatures attached are very rare, and should not be mistaken for copies with the similar Mighty Midget glued in its place. The Mighty Midgets had blank back covers except for a small victory stamp seal. Only the Capt. Marvel and Captain Marvel Jr. No. 11 miniatures have been positively documented as having been affixed to these covers. Each miniature was only partially glued by its back cover to the Captain Marvel comic making it easy to see if it's the genuine miniature rather than a Mighty Midget.
with comic attached.... 330.00 990.00 3300.00
20-Without miniature 62.00 186.00 500.00
21-Without miniature; Hitler-c 78.00 234.00 625.00
22-Mr. Mind serial begins; 1st app. Mr. Mind 87.00 261.00 700.00
23-25 59.00 177.00 475.00
26-30: 26-Flag-c. 29-1st Mr. Mind-c & 1st app. (his voice was heard over the radio before now)(11/43) 50.00 150.00 400.00
31-35: 35-Origin Radar (5/44, see Master #50) 46.00 138.00 365.00
36-40: 37-Mary Marvel x-over 40.00 120.00 310.00
41-46: 42-Christmas-c. 43-Capt. Marvel 1st meets Uncle Marvel (1st app.); Mary Batson cameo. 46-Mr. Mind serial ends 35.00 105.00 245.00
47-50 32.00 96.00 225.00
51-53,55-60: 51-63-Bi-weekly issues. 52-Origin & 1st app. Sivana Jr.; Capt. Marvel Jr. x-over 27.00 81.00 190.00
54-Special oversize 68 pg. issue 28.00 84.00 195.00
61-The Cult of the Curse serial begins 32.00 96.00 225.00
62-65-Serial cont.; Mary Marvel x-over in #65 27.00 81.00 190.00
66-Serial ends; Atomic War-c 31.00 93.00 215.00
67-77,79: 69-Billy Batson's Christmas; Uncle Marvel, Mary Marvel, Capt. Marvel Jr. x-over. 71-Three Lt. Marvels app. 79-Origin Mr. Tawny 24.00 72.00 170.00
78-Origin Mr. Atom 28.00 84.00 195.00
80-Origin Capt. Marvel retold 53.00 159.00 425.00
81-84,86-90: 81,90-Mr. Atom app. 82-Infinity-c. 86-Mr. Tawny app. 23.00 69.00 160.00
85-Freedom Train issue 29.00 87.00 200.00
91-99: 96-Mr. Tawny app. 22.00 66.00 155.00
100-Origin retold; silver metallic-c 40.00 120.00 325.00
101-115,117-120 21.00 63.00 150.00
116-Flying Saucer issue (1/51) 24.00 72.00 170.00
121-Origin retold 30.00 90.00 210.00
122-137,139-149: 141-Pre-code horror story "The Hideous Head-Hunter". 142-used in **POP**, pgs. 92,96 21.00 63.00 145.00
138-Flying Saucer issue (11/52) 25.00 75.00 175.00
150-(Low distribution) 39.00 117.00 270.00

*NOTE: **Swayze** a-12, 14, 15, 18, 19, 40; c-12, 15, 19.*

CAPTAIN MARVEL AND THE GOOD HUMOR MAN (Movie)
Fawcett Publications: 1950

nn-Partial photo-c w/Jack Carson & the Captain Marvel Club Boys 46.00 137.00 365.00

CAPTAIN MARVEL COMIC STORY PAINT BOOK (See Comic Story...)

CAPTAIN MARVEL, JR. (See Fawcett Miniatures, Marvel Family, Master Comics, Mighty Midget Comics, Shazam & Whiz Comics)

CAPTAIN MARVEL, JR.
Fawcett Publications: Nov, 1942 - No. 119, June, 1953 (No #34)

1-Origin Capt. Marvel Jr. retold (Whiz #25); Capt. Nazi app. Classic Raboy-c 450.00 1350.00 4500.00
2-Vs. Capt. Nazi; origin Capt. Nippon 188.00 564.00 1500.00
3 100.00 300.00 800.00
4-Classic Raboy-c 109.00 327.00 875.00
5-Vs. Capt. Nazi 94.00 282.00 750.00
6-8: 8-Vs. Capt. Nazi 72.00 216.00 575.00
9,10: 9-Classic flag-c. 10-Hitler-c 75.00 225.00 600.00
11,12,15-Capt. Nazi app. 60.00 180.00 480.00
13-Hitler-c 56.00 168.00 450.00
14,16-20: 14-X-Mas-c. 16-Capt. Marvel & Sivana x-over. 19-Capt. Nazi & Capt. Nippon app. 53.00 159.00 425.00
21-30: 25-Flag-c 40.00 120.00 320.00

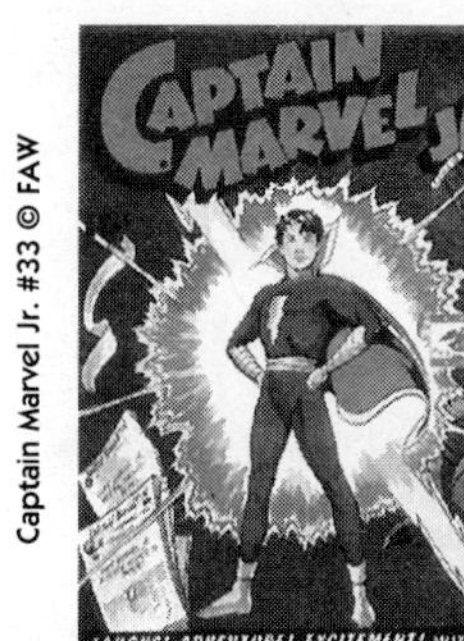

Captain Marvel Jr. #33 © FAW

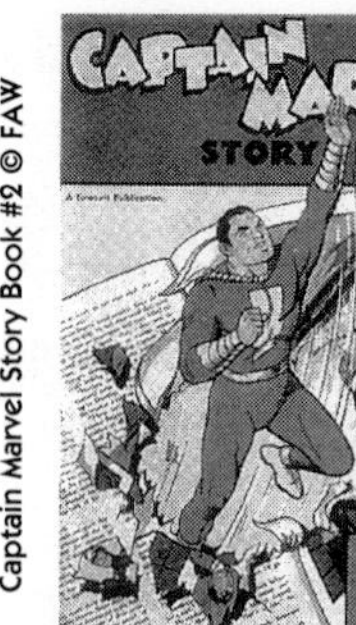

Captain Marvel Story Book #2 © FAW

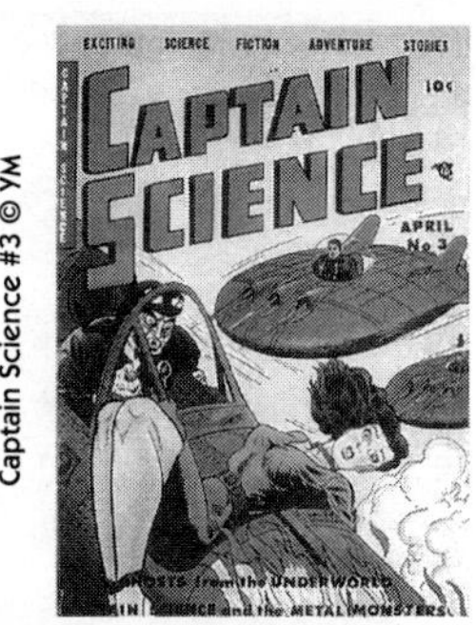

Captain Science #3 © YM

GD2.0 FN6.0 NM9.4

31-33,36-40: 37-Infinity-c 30.00 90.00 210.00
35-#34 on inside; cover shows origin of Sivana Jr. which is not on inside. Evidently the cover to #35 was printed out of sequence and bound with contents to #34 30.00 90.00 210.00
41-70: 42-Robot-c. 53-Atomic Bomb-c/story 22.00 66.00 155.00
71-99,101-104: 104-Used in **POP**, pg. 89 16.00 47.00 110.00
100 19.00 58.00 135.00
105-114,116-118: 116-Vampira, Queen of Terror app. 119-Electric chair-c 14.00 43.00 100.00
115-Injury to eye-c; Eyeball story w/injury-to-eye panels 26.00 77.00 180.00
119-Electric chair-c (scarce) 32.00 96.00 225.00
NOTE: ***Mac Raboy** c-1-28, 30-32, 57, 59 among others.*

CAPTAIN MARVEL PRESENTS THE TERRIBLE FIVE
M. F. Enterprises: Aug, 1966; V2#5, Sept, 1967 (No #2-4) (25¢)
1 2.50 7.50 22.00
V2#5-(Formerly Captain Marvel) 1.75 5.25 14.00

CAPTAIN MARVEL'S FUN BOOK
Samuel Lowe Co.: 1944 (1/2" thick) (cardboard covers)(25¢)
nn-Puzzles, games, magic, etc.; infinity-c 34.00 103.00 240.00

CAPTAIN MARVEL SPECIAL EDITION (See Special Edition)

CAPTAIN MARVEL STORY BOOK
Fawcett Publications: Summer, 1946 - No. 4, Summer?, 1948
1-Half text 54.00 163.00 435.00
2-4 40.00 120.00 290.00

CAPTAIN MARVEL THRILL BOOK (Large-Size)
Fawcett Publications: 1941 (B&W w/color-c)
GD2.0 FN6.0 VF8.2
1-Reprints from Whiz #8,10, & Special Edition #1 (Rare) 260.00 780.00 2600.00
NOTE: *Rarely found in Fine or Mint condition.*

CAPTAIN MIDNIGHT (TV, radio, films) (See The Funnies, Popular Comics & Super Book of Comics)(Becomes Sweethearts No. 68 on)
Fawcett Publications: Sept, 1942 - No. 67, Fall, 1948 (#1-14: 68 pgs.)
GD2.0 FN6.0 NM9.4
1-Origin Captain Midnight, star of radio and movies; Captain Marvel cameo on cover 288.00 862.00 2300.00
2-Smashes the Jap Juggarnaut 131.00 393.00 1050.00
3-5: Grapples the Gremlins 95.00 285.00 760.00
6-10: 9-Raboy-c. 10-Raboy Flag-c 69.00 207.00 550.00
11-20: 11,17,18-Raboy-c. 16 (1/44) 50.00 150.00 400.00
21-30: 22-War savings stamp-c. 24-Jap flag sunburst-c. 40.00 120.00 300.00
31-40 30.00 90.00 210.00
41-59,61-67: 50-Sci/fi theme begins? 24.00 71.00 165.00
60-Flying Saucer issue (2/48)-3rd of this theme; see The Spirit 9/28/47(1st), Shadow Comics V7#10 (2nd, 1/48) & Boy Commandos #26 (4th, 3-4/48) 31.00 94.00 220.00

CAPTAIN NICE (TV)
Gold Key: Nov, 1967 (one-shot)
1(10211-711)-Photo-c 6.00 18.00 65.00

CAPTAIN N: THE GAME MASTER (TV)
Valiant Comics: 1990 - No. 6? ($1.95, thick stock, coated-c)
1-6: 4-6-Layton-c 2.00

CAPTAIN PARAGON (See Bill Black's Fun Comics)
Americomics: Dec, 1983 - No. 4, 1985
1-4: 1-Intro/1st app. Ms. Victory 2.00

CAPTAIN PARAGON AND THE SENTINELS OF JUSTICE
AC Comics: April, 1985 - No. 6, 1986 ($1.75)
1-6: 1-Capt. Paragon, Commando D., Nightveil, Scarlet Scorpion, Stardust & Atoman begin 2.00

GD2.0 FN6.0 NM9.4

CAPTAIN PLANET AND THE PLANETEERS (TV cartoon)
Marvel Comics: Oct, 1991 - No. 12, Oct, 1992 ($1.00/$1.25)
1-N. Adams painted-c 3.00
2-12: 3-Romita-c 2.00

CAPTAIN POWER AND THE SOLDIERS OF THE FUTURE (TV)
Continuity Comics: Aug, 1988 - No. 2, 1988 ($2.00)
1,2: 1-Neal Adams-c/layouts/inks; variant-c exists. 3.00

CAPTAIN PUREHEART (See Archie as...)

CAPTAIN ROCKET
P. L. Publ. (Canada): Nov, 1951
1 40.00 120.00 300.00

CAPT. SAVAGE AND HIS LEATHERNECK RAIDERS (...And His Battlefield Raiders #9 on)
Marvel Comics Group (Animated Timely Features): Jan, 1968 - No. 19, Mar, 1970 (See Sgt. Fury No. 10)
1-Sgt. Fury & Howlers cameo 2.50 7.50 22.00
2,7,11: 2-Origin Hydra. 1-5,7-Ayers/Shores-a. 7-Pre-"Thing" Ben Grimm story. 11-Sgt. Fury app. 1.75 5.25 14.00
3-6,8-10,12-14: 14-Last 12¢ issue 1.50 4.50 12.00
15-19 1.25 3.75 10.00

CAPTAIN SCIENCE (Fantastic No. 8 on)
Youthful Magazines: Nov, 1950 - No. 7, Dec, 1951
1-Wood-a; origin; 2 pg. text w/ photos of George Pal's "Destination Moon." 78.00 234.00 625.00
2 40.00 120.00 310.00
3,6,7; 3,6-Bondage c-swipes/Wings #94,91 40.00 120.00 280.00
4,5-Wood/Orlando-c/a(2) each 75.00 225.00 600.00
NOTE: ***Fass** a-4. Bondage c-3, 6, 7.*

CAPTAIN SILVER'S LOG OF SEA HOUND (See Sea Hound)

CAPTAIN SINBAD (Movie Adaptation) (See Fantastic Voyages of... & Movie Comics)

CAPTAIN STERNN: RUNNING OUT OF TIME
Kitchen Sink Press: Sept, 1993 - No. 5, 1994 ($4.95, limited series, coated stock, 52 pgs.)
1-5: Berni Wrightson-c/a/scripts 5.00
1-Gold ink variant 10.00

CAPTAIN STEVE SAVAGE (...& His Jet Fighters, No. 2-13)
Avon Periodicals: 1950 - No. 8, 1/53; No. 5, 9-10/54 - No. 13, 5-6/56
nn(1st series)-Wood art, 22 pgs. (titled "...Over Korea") 37.00 111.00 260.00
1(4/51)-Reprints nn issue (Canadian) 15.00 45.00 105.00
2-Kamen-a 10.00 30.00 65.00
3-11 (#6, 9-10/54, last precode) 6.70 20.00 40.00
12-Wood-a (6 pgs.) 11.00 33.00 75.00
13-Check, Lawrence-a 7.50 22.50 45.00
NOTE: ***Kinstler** c-2-5, 7-9, 11. **Lawrence** a-8. **Ravielli** a-5, 9.*
5(9-10/54-2nd series)(Formerly Sensational Police Cases) 6.70 20.00 40.00
6-Reprints nn issue; Wood-a 10.00 30.00 65.00
7-13: 9,10-Kinstler-c. 10-r/cover #2 (1st series). 13-r/cover #8 (1st series) 4.25 13.00 26.00

CAPTAIN STONE (See Holyoke One-Shot No. 10)

CAPT. STORM (Also see G. I. Combat #138)
National Periodical Publications: May-June, 1964 - No. 18, Mar-Apr, 1967 (Grey tone c-8)
1-Origin 3.80 11.40 38.00
2-18: 3,6,13-Kubert-a. 4-Colan-a. 12-Kubert-c 2.80 8.40 28.00

CAPTAIN 3-D (Super hero)
Harvey Publications: December, 1953 (25¢, came with 2 pairs of glasses)
1-Kirby/Ditko-a (Ditko's 3rd published work tied with Strange Fantasy #9, see also Daring Love #1 & Black Magic V4 #3); shows cover in 3-D on inside;

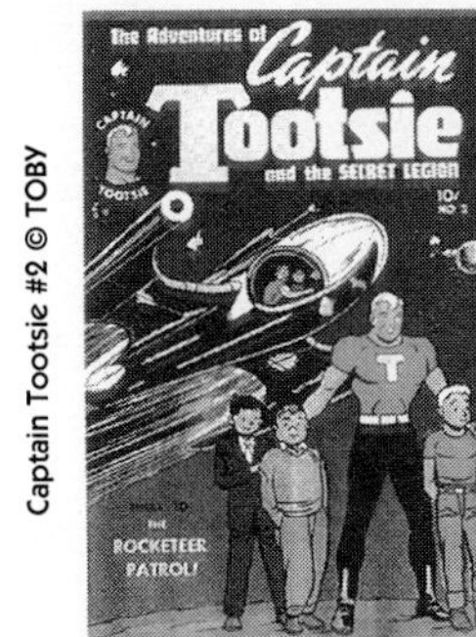

Captain Tootsie #2 © TOBY

Captain Video #6 © FAW

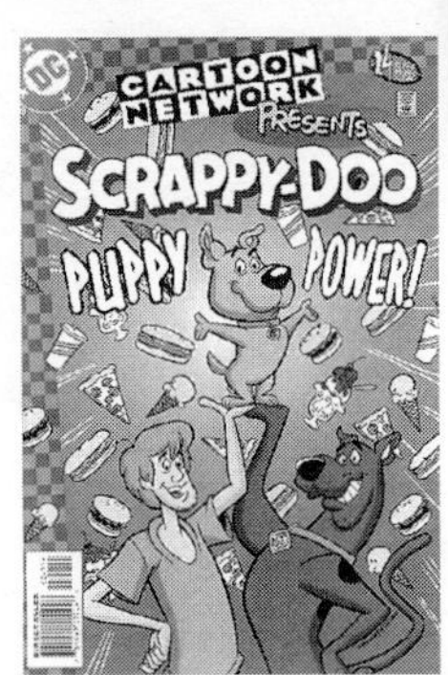

Cartoon Network Presents #24 © H-B

GD2.0 FN6.0 NM9.4

Kirby/Meskin-c (Half price without glasses) 10.00 30.00 70.00

CAPTAIN THUNDER AND BLUE BOLT
Hero Comics: Sept, 1987 - No. 10, 1988 ($1.95)
1-10: 1-Origin Blue Bolt. 3-Origin Capt. Thunder. 6-1st app. Wicket. 8-Champions x-over 2.00

CAPTAIN TOOTSIE & THE SECRET LEGION (Advs. of…)(Also see Monte Hale #30,39 & Real Western Hero)
Toby Press: Oct, 1950 - No. 2, Dec, 1950
1-Not Beck-a; both have sci/fi covers 29.00 86.00 200.00
2-The Rocketeer Patrol app.; not Beck-a 18.00 54.00 125.00

CAPTAIN TRIUMPH (See Crack Comics #27)

CAPTAIN VENTURE & THE LAND BENEATH THE SEA (See Space Family Robinson)
Gold Key: Oct, 1968 - No. 2, Oct, 1969
1-r/Space Family Robinson serial; Spiegle-a 4.00 12.00 40.00
2-Spiegle-a 3.50 10.50 35.00

CAPTAIN VICTORY AND THE GALACTIC RANGERS
Pacific Comics: Nov, 1981 - No. 13, Jan, 1984 ($1.00, direct sales, 36-48 pgs.) (Created by Jack Kirby)
1-13: 1-1st app. Mr. Mind. 3-N. Adams-a 2.00
Special 1-(10/83)-Kirby c/a(p) 2.00
NOTE: ***Conrad*** *a-10, 11.* ***Ditko*** *a-6.* ***Kirby*** *a-1-3p; c-1-13.*

CAPTAIN VIDEO (TV) (See XMas Comics)
Fawcett Publications: Feb, 1951 - No. 6, Dec, 1951 (No. 1,5,6-36pgs.; 2-4, 52pgs.) (All photo-c)
1-George Evans-a(2) 106.00 319.00 850.00
2-Used in **SOTI**, pg. 382 69.00 207.00 550.00
3-6-All Evans-a except #5 mostly Evans 58.00 174.00 465.00
NOTE: *Minor* ***Williamson*** *assists on most issues. Photo c-1, 5, 6; painted c-2-4.*

CAPTAIN WILLIE SCHULTZ (Also see Fightin' Army)
Charlton Comics: No. 76, Oct, 1985 - No. 77, Jan, 1986
76,77-Low print run 2.00

CAPTAIN WIZARD COMICS (See Meteor, Red Band & Three Ring Comics)
Rural Home: 1946
1-Capt. Wizard dons new costume; Impossible Man, Race Wilkins app. 29.00 86.00 200.00

CARE BEARS (TV, Movie)(See Star Comics Magazine)
Star Comics/Marvel Comics No. 15 on: Nov, 1985 - No. 20, Jan, 1989
1-20: Post-a begins. 11-$1.00-c begins. 13-Madballs app. 2.00

CAREER GIRL ROMANCES (Formerly Three Nurses)
Charlton Comics: June, 1964 - No. 78, Dec, 1973
V4#24-31 1.50 4.50 12.00
32-Elvis Presley, Herman's Hermits, Johnny Rivers line drawn-c 9.00 27.00 90.00
33-50 1.25 3.75 10.00
51-78 1.00 2.80 7.00

CAR 54, WHERE ARE YOU? (TV)
Dell Publishing Co.: Mar-May, 1962 - No. 7, Sept-Nov, 1963; 1964 - 1965 (All photo-c)
Four Color 1257(#1, 3-5/62) 6.40 19.00 70.00
2(6-8/62)-7 3.60 10.80 40.00
2,3(10-12/64), 4(1-3/65)-Reprints #2,3,&4 of 1st series 2.25 6.75 25.00

CARL BARKS LIBRARY OF WALT DISNEY'S GYRO GEARLOOSE COMICS AND FILLERS IN COLOR, THE
Gladstone: 1993 ($7.95, 8-1/2x11", limited series, 52 pgs.)
1-6: Carl Barks reprints 1.00 3.00 10.00

CARL BARKS LIBRARY OF WALT DISNEY'S COMICS AND STORIES IN COLOR, THE
Gladstone: Jan, 1992 - No. 51, Mar, 1996 ($8.95, 8-1/2x11", 60 pgs.)
1,2,6,8-51: 1-Barks Donald Duck-r/WDC&S #31-35; 2-r/#36,38-41; 6-r/#57-61; 8-r/#67-71; 9-r/#72-76; 10-r/#77-81; 11-r/#82-86; 12-r/#87-91; 13-r/#92-96; 14-r/#97-101; 15-r/#102-106; 16-r/#107-111; 17-r/#112,114,117,124,125; 18-r/#126-130; 19-r/#131,132(2),133,134; 20-r/#135-139; 21-r/#140-144; 22-r/#145-149; 23-r/#150-154; 24-r/#155-159; 25-r/#160-164; 26-r/#165-169; 27-r/#170-174;28-r/#175-179; 29-r/#180-184; 30-r/#185-189; 31-r/#190-194; 32-r/#195-199;33-r/#200-204; 34-r/#205-209; 35-r/#210-214; 36-r/#215-219; 37-r/#220-224; 38-r/#225-229; 39-r/#230-234; 40-r/#235-239; 41-r/#240-244; 42r/#245-249; 43-r/#250-254; 44-50; All contain one Heroes & Villains trading card each 1.00 3.00 10.00
3,4,7: 3-r/#42-46. 4-r/#47-51. 7-r/#62-66. 1.50 4.50 15.00
5-r/#52-56 2.00 6.00 20.00

CARL BARKS LIBRARY OF WALT DISNEY'S DONALD DUCK ADVENTURES IN COLOR, THE
Gladstone: 1994 - Present ($7.95/$9.95, 44-68 pgs., 8-1/2"x11") (all contain one Donald Duck trading card each)
1-16-Carl Barks-r: 1-r/FC #9; 2-r/FC #29; 3-r/FC #62; 4-r/FC #108; 5-r/FC #147 & #79(Mickey Mouse); 6-r/MOC #4, Cheerios "Atom Bomb," D.D. Tells About Kites; 7-r/FC #159. 8-r/FC #178 & 189. 9-r/FC #199 & 203; 10-r/FC 223 & 238; 11-r/Christmas Parade #1 & 2; 12-r/FC #296; 13-r/FC #263; 14-r/MOC #20 & 41; 15-r/FC 275 & 282; 16-r/FC #291&300; 17-r/FC #308 & 318; 18-r/Vac. Parade #1 & Summer Fun #2; 19-r/FC #328 & 367 1.20 3.60 12.00

CARL BARKS LIBRARY OF WALT DISNEY'S DONALD DUCK CHRISTMAS STORIES IN COLOR, THE
Gladstone: 1992 ($7.95, 44pgs., one-shot)
nn-Reprints Firestone giveaways 1945-1949 1.50 4.50 15.00

CARL BARKS LIBRARY OF WALT DISNEY'S UNCLE SCROOGE COMICS ONE PAGERS IN COLOR, THE
Gladstone: 1992 - No. 2, 1993 ($8.95, limited series, 60 pgs., 8-1/2x11")
1-Carl Barks one pg. reprints 2.50 7.50 25.00
2-Carl Barks one pg. reprints 1.50 4.50 15.00

CARNAGE: IT'S A WONDERFUL LIFE
Marvel Comics: Oct, 1996 ($1.95, one-shot)
1-David Quinn scripts 3.00

CARNAGE: MIND BOMB
Marvel Comics: Feb, 1996 ($2.95, one-shot)
1-Warren Ellis script; Kyle Hotz-a 3.00

CARNATION MALTED MILK GIVEAWAYS (See Wisco)

CARNEYS, THE
Archie Comics: Summer, 1994 ($2.00, 52 pgs)
1-Bound-in pull-out poster 2.50

CARNIVAL COMICS (Formerly Kayo #12; becomes Red Seal Comics #14)
Harry 'A' Chesler/Pershing Square Publ. Co.: 1945
nn (#13)-Guardineer-a 16.00 47.00 110.00

CAROLINE KENNEDY
Charlton Comics: 1961 (one-shot)
nn-Interior photo covers of Kennedy family 8.50 25.50 85.00

CAROUSEL COMICS
F. E. Howard, Toronto: V1#8, April, 1948
V1#8 5.75 17.00 34.00

CARTOON KIDS
Atlas Comics (CPS): 1957 (no month)
1-Maneely-c/a; Dexter The Demon, Willie The Wise-Guy, Little Zelda app. 10.00 30.00 65.00

CARTOON NETWORK PRESENTS
DC Comics: Aug, 1997 - No. 24, Aug, 1999 ($1.75-$1.99, anthology)
1-24: 1-Dexter's Lab. 2-Space Ghost. 12-Bizarro World 2.00

Cartoon Network Starring... #1 © DC

Carvers #2 © Flypaper Press

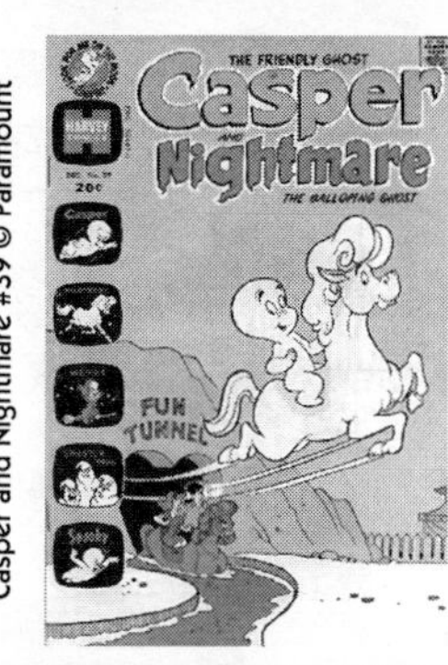

Casper and Nightmare #39 © Paramount

	GD2.0	FN6.0	NM9.4
1-Platinum Edition			2.00

CARTOON NETWORK STARRING... (Anthology)
DC Comics: Sept, 1999 - Present ($1.99)

1-Powerpuff Girls			2.00

CARTOON TALES (Disney's...)
W.D. Publications (Disney): nd, nn (1992) ($2.95, 6-5/8x9-1/2", 52 pgs.)

nn-Ariel & Sebastian - Serpent Teen; Beauty and the Beast ; A Tale of of Enchantment; Darkwing Duck - Just Us Justice Ducks; 101 Dalmations - Canine Classics; Tale Spin - Surprise in the Skies; Uncle Scrooge - Blast to the Past 4.00

CARVERS
Image Comics (Flypaper Press): 1998 - No. 3, 1999 ($2.95)

1-3-Pander Bros.-a/Fleming-s			3.00

CAR WARRIORS
Marvel Comics (Epic): June, 1991 - No. 4, Sept, 1991 ($2.25, lim. series)

1-4: 1-Says April in indicia			2.25

CASE OF THE SHOPLIFTER'S SHOE (See Perry Mason, Feature Book No.50)

CASE OF THE WINKING BUDDHA, THE
St. John Publ. Co.: 1950 (132 pgs.; 25¢; B&W; 5-1/2x7-5-1/2x8")

nn-Charles Raab-a; reprinted in Authentic Police Cases No. 25	26.00	79.00	185.00

CASEY-CRIME PHOTOGRAPHER (Two-Gun Western No. 5 on)(Radio)
Marvel Comics (BFP): Aug, 1949 - No. 4, Feb, 1950

1-Photo-c; 52 pgs.	21.00	64.00	150.00
2-4: Photo-c	14.00	43.00	100.00

CASEY JONES (TV)
Dell Publishing Co.: No. 915, July, 1958

Four Color 915-Alan Hale photo-c	4.50	13.50	50.00

CASEY JONES & RAPHAEL (See Bodycount)
Mirage Studios: Oct, 1994 ($2.75, unfinished limited series)

1-Bisley-c; Eastman story & pencils			2.75

CASEY JONES: NORTH BY DOWNEAST
Mirage Studios: June, 1994? - No. 2, July, 1994 ($2.75, limited series)

1,2-Rick Veitch script & pencils; Kevin Eastman story & inks			2.75

CASPER ADVENTURE DIGEST
Harvey Comics: V2#1, Oct, 1992 - V2#8, Apr, 1994 ($1.75/$1.95, digest-size)

V2#1: Casper, Richie Rich, Spooky, Wendy			4.00
2-8			3.00

CASPER AND...
Harvey Comics: Nov, 1987 - No. 12, June, 1990 (.75/$1.00, all reprints)

1-Ghostly Trio			4.00
2-12: 2-Spooky; begin $1.00-c. 3-Wendy. 4-Nightmare. 5-Ghostly Trio. 6-Spooky. 7-Wendy. 8-Hot Stuff. 9-Baby Huey. 10-Wendy.11-Ghostly Trio. 12-Spooky			3.00

CASPER AND FRIENDS
Harvey Comics: Oct, 1991 - No. 5, July, 1992 ($1.00/$1.25)

1-Nightmare, Ghostly Trio, Wendy, Spooky			4.00
2-5			3.00

CASPER AND FRIENDS MAGAZINE: Mar, 1997 - No. 3, July, 1997 ($3.99)

1-3			4.00

CASPER AND NIGHTMARE (See Harvey Hits# 37, 45, 52, 56, 59, 62, 65, 68,71, 75)

CASPER AND NIGHTMARE (Nightmare & Casper No. 1-5)
Harvey Publications: No. 6, 11/64 - No. 44, 10/73; No. 45, 6/74 - No. 46, 8/74 (25¢)

6: 68 pg. Giants begin, ends #32	3.80	11.40	38.00
7-10	2.60	7.80	26.00
11-20	1.80	5.40	18.00

	GD2.0	FN6.0	NM9.4
21-37: 33-37-(52 pg. Giants)	1.40	4.20	14.00
38-46	1.00	3.00	8.00

NOTE: *Many issues contain reprints.*

CASPER AND SPOOKY (See Harvey Hits No. 20)
Harvey Publications: Oct, 1972 - No. 7, Oct, 1973

1	2.20	6.60	22.00
2-7	1.20	3.60	12.00

CASPER AND THE GHOSTLY TRIO
Harvey Pub.: Nov, 1972 - No. 7, Nov, 1973; No. 8, Aug, 1990 - No. 10, Dec, 1990

1	2.20	6.60	22.00
2-7	1.20	3.60	12.00
8-10			4.00

CASPER AND WENDY
Harvey Publications: Sept, 1972 - No. 8, Nov, 1973

1: 52 pg. Giant	2.20	6.60	22.00
2-8	1.20	3.60	12.00

CASPER BIG BOOK
Harvey Comics: V2#1, Aug, 1992 - No. 3, May, 1993 ($1.95, 52 pgs.)

V2#1-Spooky app.			4.00
2,3			3.00

CASPER CAT (See Dopey Duck)
I. W. Enterprises/Super: 1958; 1963

1,7:1-Wacky Duck #?.7-Reprint, Super No. 14('63)	1.10	3.30	9.00

CASPER DIGEST (...Magazine #?; ...Halloween Digest #8, 10)
Harvey Publications: Oct, 1986 - No. 18, Jan, 1991 ($1.25/$1.75, digest-size)

1	1.00	3.00	8.00
2-18: 11-Valentine-c. 18-Halloween-c			5.00

CASPER DIGEST (...Magazine #? on)
Harvey Comics: V2#1, Sept, 1991 - V2#14, Nov, 1994 ($1.75/$1.95, digest-size)

V2#1			4.00
2-14			3.00

CASPER DIGEST STORIES
Harvey Publications: Feb, 1980 - No. 4, Nov, 1980 (95¢, 132 pgs., digest size)

1	1.20	3.60	12.00
2-4	1.00	2.80	7.00

CASPER DIGEST WINNERS
Harvey Publications: Apr, 1980 - No. 3, Sept, 1980 (95¢, 132 pgs., digest size)

1	1.20	3.60	12.00
2,3	1.00	2.80	7.00

CASPER ENCHANTED TALES DIGEST
Harvey Comics: May, 1992 - No. 10, Oct, 1994 ($1.75, digest-size, 98 pgs.)

1-Casper, Spooky, Wendy stories			4.00
2-10			3.00

CASPER GHOSTLAND
Harvey Comics: May, 1992 ($1.25)

1			3.00

CASPER GIANT SIZE
Harvey Comics: Oct, 1992 - No. 4, Nov, 1993 ($2.25, 68 pgs.)

V2#1-4-Casper, Wendy, Spooky stories			4.00

CASPER HALLOWEEN TRICK OR TREAT
Harvey Publications: Jan, 1976 (52 pgs.)

1	2.00	6.00	20.00

CASPER IN SPACE (Formerly Casper Spaceship)
Harvey Publications: No. 6, June, 1973 - No. 8, Oct, 1973

6-8	1.00	3.00	10.00

CASPER'S GHOSTLAND
Harvey Publications: Winter, 1958-59 - No. 97, 12/77; No. 98, 12/79 (25¢)

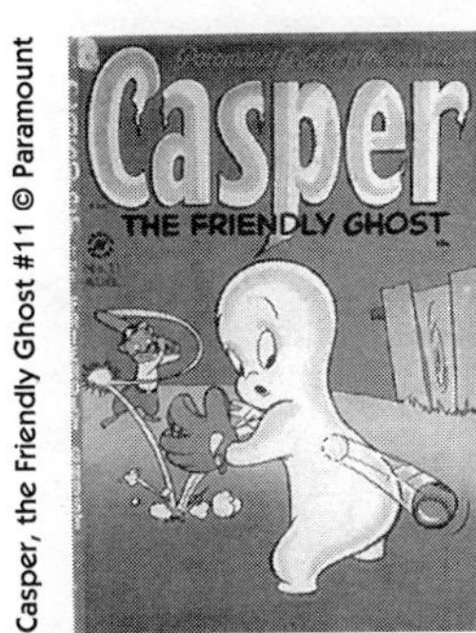

Casper, the Friendly Ghost #11 © Paramount

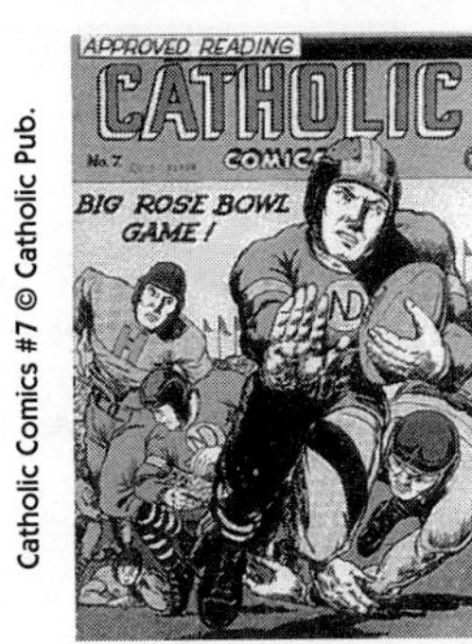

Catholic Comics #7 © Catholic Pub.

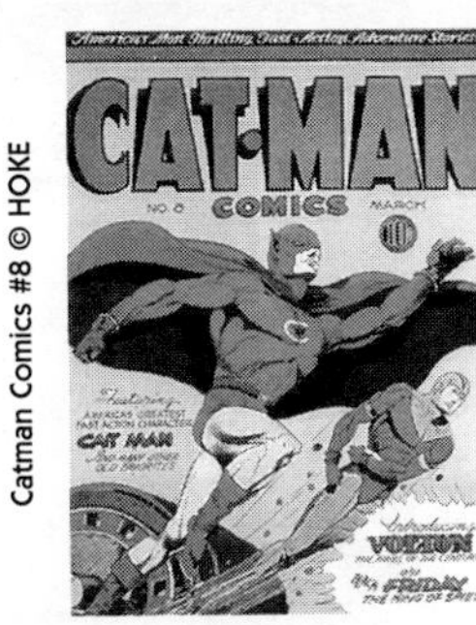

Catman Comics #8 © HOKE

	GD2.0	FN6.0	NM9.4
1-84 pgs. begin, ends #10	16.00	48.00	160.00
2	8.50	25.50	85.00
3-10	6.00	18.00	60.00
11-20: 11-68 pgs. begin, ends #61. 13-X-Mas-c	4.50	13.50	45.00
21-40	3.40	10.20	34.00
41-61	1.80	5.40	18.00
62-77: 62-52 pgs. begin	1.00	3.00	10.00
78-98: 94-X-Mas-c		2.40	6.00

NOTE: *Most issues contain reprints w/new stories.*

CASPER SPACESHIP (Casper in Space No. 6 on)
Harvey Publications: Aug, 1972 - No. 5, April, 1973

	GD2.0	FN6.0	NM9.4
1: 52 pg. Giant	2.20	6.60	22.00
2-5	1.20	3.60	12.00

CASPER STRANGE GHOST STORIES
Harvey Publications: October, 1974 - No. 14, Jan, 1977 (All 52 pgs.)

	GD2.0	FN6.0	NM9.4
1	1.80	5.40	18.00
2-14	1.20	3.60	12.00

CASPER, THE FRIENDLY GHOST (See America's Best TV Comics, Famous TV Funday Funnies, The Friendly Ghost..., Nightmare &..., Richie Rich and..., Tastee-Freez, Treasury of Comics, Wendy the Good Little Witch & Wendy Witch World)

CASPER, THE FRIENDLY GHOST (Becomes Harvey Comics Hits No. 61 (No. 6), and then continued with Harvey issue No. 7)(1st Series)
St. John Publishing Co.: Sept, 1949 - No. 5, Aug, 1951

	GD2.0	FN6.0	NM9.4
1(1949)-Origin & 1st app. Baby Huey & Herman the Mouse (1st time the name Casper app. in any media, even films)	156.00	468.00	1250.00
2,3 (2/50 & 8/50)	67.00	200.00	540.00
4,5 (3/51 & 8/51)	52.00	156.00	415.00

CASPER, THE FRIENDLY GHOST (Paramount Picture Star...)(2nd Series)
Harvey Publications (Family Comics): No. 7, Dec, 1952 - No. 70, July, 1958
Note: No. 6 is Harvey Comics Hits No. 61 (10/52)

	GD2.0	FN6.0	NM9.4
7-Baby Huey begins, ends #9	31.00	93.00	310.00
8,9	17.50	52.00	175.00
10-Spooky begins (1st app., 6/53), ends #70?	19.00	57.00	190.00
11-18: Alfred Harvey app. in story	10.50	32.00	105.00
19-1st app. Nightmare (4/54)	14.00	42.00	140.00
20-Wendy the Witch begins (1st app., 5/54)	17.50	52.00	175.00
21-30: 24-Infinity-c	8.00	24.00	80.00
31-40	5.50	16.50	55.00
41-50	4.50	13.50	45.00
51-70 (Continues as Friendly Ghost... 8/58)	4.00	12.00	40.00

CASPER THE FRIENDLY GHOST (Formerly The Friendly Ghost...)(3rd Series)
Harvey Comics: No. 254, July, 1990 - No. 260, Jan, 1991 ($1.00)

	GD2.0	FN6.0	NM9.4
254-260			2.50

CASPER THE FRIENDLY GHOST (4th Series)
Harvey Comics: Mar, 1991 - No. 28, Nov, 1994 ($1.00/$1.25/$1.50)

	GD2.0	FN6.0	NM9.4
1-Casper becomes Mighty Ghost; Spooky & Wendy app.			4.00
2-10: 7,8-Post-a			3.00
11-28-($1.50)			2.00

CASPER T.V. SHOWTIME
Harvey Comics: Jan, 1980 - No. 5, Oct, 1980

	GD2.0	FN6.0	NM9.4
1	1.00	3.00	8.00
2-5			5.00

CASSETTE BOOKS (Classics Illustrated)
Cassette Book Co./I.P.S. Publ.: 1984 (48 pgs, b&w comic with cassette tape)

NOTE: *This series was illegal. The artwork was illegally obtained, and the Classics Illustrated copyright owner, Twin Circle Publ. sued to get an injunction to prevent the continued sale of this series. Many C.I. collectors obtained copies before the 1987 injunction, but now they are already scarce. Here again the market is just developing, but sealed mint copies of com ic and tape should be worth at least $25.*

1001 (CI#1-A2)New-PC 1002(CI#3-A2)CI-PC 1003(CI#13-A2)CI-PC
1004(CI#25)CI-LDC 1005(CI#10-A2)New-PC 1006(CI#64)CI-LDC

CASTILIAN (See Movie Classics)

CASTLE WAITING
Olio: 1997 - No. 7, 1999 ($2.95, B&W)

	GD2.0	FN6.0	NM9.4
1-7: Linda Medley-s/a			3.00
Hiatus Issue (1999) Crilley-c; short stories and previews			3.00

CASUAL HEROES
Image Comics (Motown Machineworks): Apr, 1996 ($2.25, unfinished lim. series

	GD2.0	FN6.0	NM9.4
1-Steve Rude-c			2.25

CAT, T.H.E. (TV) (See T.H.E. Cat)

CAT, THE (See Movie Classics)

CAT, THE (Female hero)
Marvel Comics Group: Nov, 1972 - No. 4, June, 1973

	GD2.0	FN6.0	NM9.4
1-Origin & 1st app. The Cat (who later becomes Tigra); Mooney-a(i); Wood-c(i)/a(i)	2.50	7.50	20.00
2,3: 2-Marie Severin/Mooney-a. 3-Everett inks	1.50	4.50	12.00
4-Starlin/Weiss-a(p)	1.75	5.25	14.00

CATALYST: AGENTS OF CHANGE (Also see Comics' Greatest World)
Dark Horse Comics: Feb, 1994 - No.7, Nov, 1994 ($2.00, limited series)

	GD2.0	FN6.0	NM9.4
1-7: 1-Foil stamped logo			2.00

CAT & MOUSE
EF Graphics (Silverline): Dec, 1988 ($1.75, color w/part B&W)

	GD2.0	FN6.0	NM9.4
1-1st printing (12/88, 32 pgs.), 1-2nd printing (5/89, 36 pgs.)			2.00

CAT FROM OUTER SPACE (See Walt Disney Showcase #46)

CATHOLIC COMICS (See Heroes All Catholic...)
Catholic Publications: June, 1946 - V3#10, July, 1949

	GD2.0	FN6.0	NM9.4
1	29.00	86.00	200.00
2	15.00	45.00	105.00
3-13(7/47)	13.00	39.00	90.00
V2#1-10	10.00	30.00	60.00
V3#1-10: Reprints 10-part Treasure Island serial from Target V2#2-11 (see Key Comics #5)	10.00	30.00	65.00

CATHOLIC PICTORIAL
Catholic Guild: 1947

	GD2.0	FN6.0	NM9.4
1-Toth-a(2) (Rare)	39.00	116.00	270.00

CATMAN COMICS (Formerly Crash Comics No. 1-5)
Holyoke Publishing Co./Continental Magazines V2#12, 7/44 on:
5/41 - No. 17, 1/43; No. 18, 7/43 - No. 22, 12/43; No. 23, 3/44 - No. 26, 11/44; No. 27, 4/45 - No. 30, 12/45; No. 31, 6/46 - No. 32, 8/46

	GD2.0	FN6.0	NM9.4
1(V1#6)-Origin The Deacon & Sidekick Mickey, Dr. Diamond & Rag-Man; The Black Widow app.; The Catman by Chas. Quinlan & Blaze Baylor begin	311.00	933.00	2900.00
2(V1#7)	112.00	336.00	900.00
3(V1#8)-The Pied Piper begins; classic Hitler, Stalin & Mussolini-c	94.00	282.00	750.00
4(V1#9)	85.00	255.00	680.00
5(V2#10)-Origin Kitten; The Hood begins (c-redated), 6,7(V2#11,12)	69.00	207.00	550.00
8(V2#13,3/42)-Origin Little Leaders; Volton by Kubert begins (his 1st comic book work)	85.00	255.00	680.00
9,10(V2#14,15): 10-Origin Blackout retold; Phantom Falcon begins	56.00	168.00	450.00
11 (V3#1)-Kubert-a	56.00	168.00	450.00
12 (V3#2), 14, 15, 17, 18(V3#8, 7/43)	50.00	150.00	400.00
13-(scarce)	69.00	207.00	550.00
16,19,20: 16 (V3#5)-Hitler, Tojo, Mussolini, Stalin-c. 19 (V2#6)-Hitler, Tojo, Mussolini-c. 20 (V2#7): Classic Hitler-c	66.00	198.00	525.00
21- 23 (V2#10, 3/44)	44.00	132.00	350.00
nn(V3#13, 5/44)-Rico-a; Schomburg bondage-c	40.00	120.00	325.00
nn(V2#12, 7/44, nn(V3#1, 9/44)-Origin The Golden Archer; Leatherface app.	40.00	120.00	310.00
nn(V3#2, 11/44)-L. B. Cole-c	72.00	216.00	575.00
27-Origin Kitten retold; L. B. Cole Flag-c	78.00	234.00	625.00

Catseye #1 © Hyperwerks

Catwoman #57 © DC

Cavewoman: Rain #2 © Budd Root

	GD2.0	FN6.0	NM9.4
28-Catman learns Kitten's I.D.; Dr. Macabre, Deacon app.; L. B. Cole c/a	81.00	243.00	650.00
29-32-L. B. Cole-c; bondage-#30	72.00	216.00	575.00

NOTE: ***Fuje** a-11, 29(3), 30. **Palais** a-11, 29(2), 30(2), 32; c-25(7/44). **Rico** a-11(2).*

CATSEYE
Hyperwerks Comics: Dec, 1998 - No. 4, June, 1999 ($2.95)

1-4-Altstaetter-s/a 3.00

CAT TALES (3-D)
Eternity Comics: Apr, 1989 ($2.95)

1-Felix the Cat-r in 3-D 4.00

CATWOMAN (Also see Action Comics Weekly #611, Batman #404-407, Detective Comics, & Superman's Girlfriend Lois Lane #70, 71)
DC Comics: Feb, 1989 - No. 4, May, 1989 ($1.50, limited series, mature)

1	1.25	3.75	10.00
2-4: 3-Batman cameo. 4-Batman app.	1.10	3.30	9.00
Her Sister's Keeper (1991, $9.95, trade paperback)-r/#1-4			10.00

CATWOMAN (Also see Showcase '93, Showcase '95 #4, & Batman #404-407)
DC Comics: Aug, 1993 - Present ($1.50-$1.99)

1-($1.95)-Embossed-c; Bane app.; Balent c-1-10; a-1-10p 4.00
2,3,0,2-20: 3-Bane flashback cameo. 4-Brief Bane app. 6,7-Knightquest tie-ins; Batman (Azrael) app. 8-1st app. Zephyr. 12-KnightsEnd pt. 6. 13-new Knights End Aftermath.14-(9/94)-Zero Hour. 0-(10/94)-Origin retold 3.00
21-24, 26-30, 33-49: 21-$1.95-c begins. 28,29-Penguin cameo app. 36-Legacy pt. 2. 38-40-Year Two; Batman, Joker, Penguin & Two-Face app. 46-Two-Face app. 2.00
25,31,32: 25-($2.95)-Robin app. 31-Contagion pt. 4 (Reads pt. 5 on-c). 32-Contagion pt. 9. 3.00
50-($2.95, 48 pgs.)-New armored costume 3.00
50-($2.95, 48 pgs.)-Collector's Ed.w/metallic ink-c 3.00
51-75: 51-Huntress-c/app. 54-Grayson-s begins. 56-Cataclysm pt.6. 57-Poison Ivy-c/app.63-65-Joker-c/app.72-No Man's Land; Ostrander-s begins 2.50
#1,000,000 (11/98) 853rd Century x-over 2.00
Annual 1 (1994, $2.95, 68 pgs.)-Elseworlds story; Batman app.; no Balent-a 3.00
Annual 2,4 ('95, '97, $3.95)-2-Year One story. 4-Pulp Heroes 4.00
Annual 3 (1996, $2.95)-Legends of the Dead Earth story 3.00
...Plus 1 (11/97, $2.95) Screamqueen (Scare Tactics) app. 3.00
TPB ($9.95) r/#15-19, Balent-c 10.00

CATWOMAN/ GUARDIAN OF GOTHAM
DC Comics: 1999 - No. 2, 1999 ($5.95, limited series)

1-Elseworlds; Moench-s/Balent-a 6.00

CATWOMAN/VAMPIRELLA: THE FURIES
DC Comics/Harris Publ.: Feb, 1997 ($4.95, squarebound, one-shot, 46 pgs.) (1st DC/Harris x-over)

nn-Reintro Pantha; Chuck Dixon scripts; Jim Balent-c/a 5.00

CATWOMAN/WILDCAT
DC Comics: Aug, 1998 - No. 4, Nov, 1998 ($2.50, limited series)

1-Chuck Dixon & Beau Smith-s; Stelfreeze-c 3.00

CAUGHT
Atlas Comics (VPI): Aug, 1956 - No. 5, Apr, 1957

1	20.00	60.00	140.00
2-4: 3-Maneely, Pakula, Torres-a. 4-Maneely-a	10.00	30.00	70.00
5-Crandall, Krigstein-a	11.50	34.00	80.00

NOTE: ***Drucker** a-2. **Heck** a-4. **Severin** c-1, 2, 4, 5. **Shores** a-4.*

CAVALIER COMICS
A. W. Nugent Publ. Co.: 1945; 1952 (Early DC reprints)

2(1945)-Speed Saunders, Fang Gow	20.00	60.00	140.00
2(1952)	10.00	30.00	70.00

CAVE GIRL (Also see Africa)
Magazine Enterprises: No. 11, 1953 - No. 14, 1954

11(A-1 82)-Origin; all Cave Girl stories	41.00	124.00	330.00
12(A-1 96), 13(A-1 116), 14(A-1 125)-Thunda by Powell in each	32.00	96.00	225.00

NOTE: ***Powell** c/a in all.*

CAVE GIRL
AC Comics: 1988 ($2.95, 44 pgs.) (16 pgs. of color, rest B&W)

1-Powell-r/Cave Girl #11; Nyoka photo back-c from movie; Powell/Bill Black-c; Special Limited Edition on-c 3.00

CAVE KIDS (TV) (See Comic Album #16)
Gold Key: Feb, 1963 - No. 16, Mar, 1967 (Hanna-Barbera)

1	6.00	18.00	65.00
2-5	3.20	9.60	32.00
6-16: 7,12-Pebbles & Bamm Bamm app. 16-1st Space Kidettes	2.50	7.50	22.00

CAVEWOMAN
Basement Comics: Jan, 1994 - No. 6, 1995 ($2.95)

1	3.50	10.50	35.00
2	2.50	7.50	20.00
3-6	1.50	4.50	12.00

CAVEWOMAN MEETS EXPLORERS
Basement Comics: 1997 ($2.95, B&W, one-shot)

1 3.00

CAVEWOMAN: MISSING LINK
Basement Comics: 1997 - No. 4, 1998 ($2.95, B&W, limited series)

1-4 3.00

CAVEWOMAN: RAIN
Caliber: 1996 - No. 8, 1998 ($2.95, limited series)

1-8, 8-Alternate cover 4.00
8-Green foil cover 5.00

CELESTINE (See Violator Vs. Badrock #1)
Image Comics (Extreme): May, 1996 - No. 2, June, 1996 ($2.50, limited series)

1,2: Warren Ellis scripts 2.50

CENTURION OF ANCIENT ROME, THE
Zondervan Publishing House: 1958 (no month listed) (B&W, 36 pgs.)

(Rare) All by Jay Disbrow	32.00	96.00	225.00

CENTURIONS (TV)
DC Comics: June, 1987 - No. 4, Sept, 1987 (75¢, limited series)

1-4 2.00

CENTURY: DISTANT SONS
Marvel Comics: Feb, 1996 ($2.95, one-shot)

1-Wraparound-c 3.00

CENTURY OF COMICS (See Promotional Comics section)

CEREBUS BI-WEEKLY
Aardvark-Vanaheim: Dec. 2, 1988 - No. 26, Nov. 11, 1989 ($1.25, B&W)

Reprints Cerebus The Aardvark#1-26

1-16, 18, 19, 21-26:			2.50
17-Hepcats app.	1.85	5.50	15.00
20-Milk & Cheese app.	2.50	7.50	20.00

CEREBUS: CHURCH & STATE
Aardvark-Vanaheim: Feb, 1991 - No. 30, Apr, 1992 ($2.00, B&W, bi-weekly)

1-30: r/Cerebus #51-80 2.50

CEREBUS: HIGH SOCIETY
Aardvark-Vanaheim: Feb, 1990 - No. 25, 1991 ($1.70, B&W)

1-25: r/Cerebus #26-50 2.50

CEREBUS JAM
Aardvark-Vanaheim: Apr, 1985

1-Eisner, Austin, Dave Sim-a (Cerebus vs. Spirit) 5.00

CEREBUS THE AARDVARK (See A-V in 3-D, Nucleus, Power Comics)

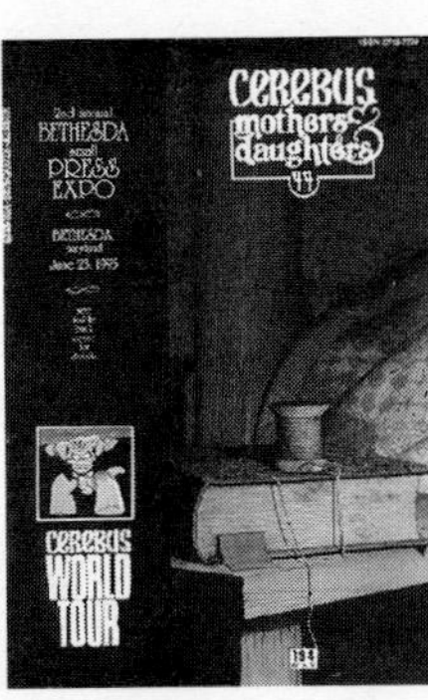

Cerebus #194 © Dave Sim and Gerhard

Challengers of the Unknown (1st) #4 © DC

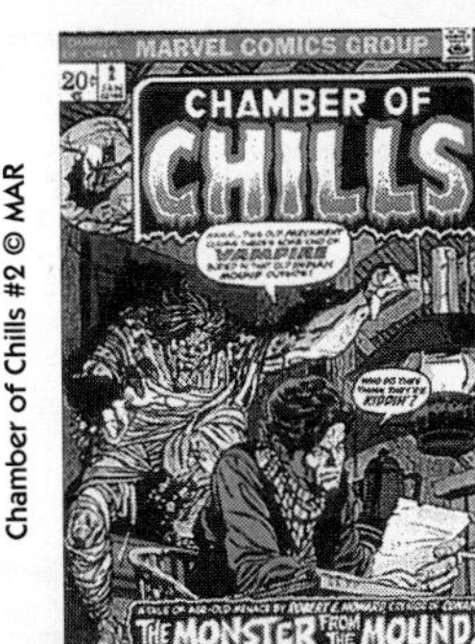

Chamber of Chills #2 © MAR

GD2.0 FN6.0 NM9.4

Aardvark-Vanaheim: Dec, 1977 - Present ($1.70/$2.00/$2.25, B&W)

0 — 3.00
0-Gold — 20.00
1-1st app. Cerebus; 2000 print run; most copies poorly printed — 21.00 63.00 230.00

Note: *There is a counterfeit version known to exist. It can be distinguished from the original in the following ways: inside cover is glossy instead of flat, black background on the front cover is blotted or spotty. Reports show that a counterfeit #2 also exists.*

2-Dave Sim art in all — 6.35 19.00 70.00
3-Origin Red Sophia — 5.50 16.50 60.00
4-Origin Elrod the Albino — 4.00 12.00 40.00
5,6 — 3.50 10.50 35.00
7-10 — 2.50 7.50 22.00
11,12: 11-Origin The Cockroach — 2.25 6.75 18.00
13-15: 14-Origin Lord Julius — 1.10 3.30 9.00
16-20, 23-30: 23-Preview of Wandering Star by Teri S. Wood. 26-High Society begins,ends #50 — 2.40 6.00
21-B. Smith letter in letter column — 2.50 7.50 25.00
22-Low distribution; no cover price — 1.50 4.50 12.00
31-Origin Moonroach — 1.00 2.80 7.00
32-40, 53-Intro. Wolveroach (cameo) — 5.00
41-50,52: 52-Church & State begins, ends #111; Cutey Bunny app. — 4.00
51,54: 51-Cutey Bunny app. 54-1st full Wolveroach story — 2.40 6.00
55,56-Wolveroach app.; Normalman back-ups by Valentino — 4.50
57-245: 61,62: Flaming Carrot app. 65-Gerhard begins. 104-Flaming Carrot app. 112/113-Double issue. 114-Jaka's Story begins, ends #136. 139-Melmoth begins, ends #150. 175-($2.25, 44 pgs). 151-Mothers & Daughters begins, ends #200. 201-Guys storyline begins; Eddie Campbell's Bacchus app. 220-231-Rick's Story. 232-Going Home begins — 2.50
151-153-2nd printings — 2.25
Free Cerebus (Giveaway, 1991-92?, 36 pgs.)-All-r — 2.00

CHAIN GANG WAR
DC Comics: July, 1993 - No. 12, June, 1994 ($1.75)

1-($2.50)-Embossed silver foil-c, Dave Johnson-c/a — 2.50
2-4,6-12: 3-Deathstroke app. 4-Brief Deathstroke app. 6-New Batman (Azrael) cameo. 11-New Batman-c/story. 12-New Batman app. — 2.00
5-($2.50)-Foil-c; Deathstroke app; new Batman cameo (1 panel) — 2.50

CHAINS OF CHAOS
Harris Comics: Nov, 1994 - No. 3, Jan, 1995 ($2.95, limited series)

1-3-Re-Intro of The Rook w/ Vampirella — 3.00

CHALLENGE OF THE UNKNOWN (Formerly Love Experiences)
Ace Magazines: No. 6, Sept, 1950 (See Web Of Mystery No. 19)

6- "Villa of the Vampire" used in N.Y. Joint Legislative Comm. Publ; Sekowsky-a — 27.00 81.00 190.00

CHALLENGER, THE
Interfaith Publications/T.C. Comics: 1945 - No. 4, Oct-Dec, 1946

nn; nd; 32 pgs.; Origin the Challenger Club; Anti-Fascist with funny animal filler — 37.00 111.00 260.00
2-4: Kubert-a; 4-Fuje-a — 29.00 86.00 200.00

CHALLENGERS OF THE FANTASTIC
Marvel Comics (Amalgam): June 1997 ($1.95, one-shot)

1-Karl Kesel-s/Tom Grummett-a — 2.00

CHALLENGERS OF THE UNKNOWN (See Showcase #6, 7, 11, 12, Super DC Giant, and Super Team Family)
National Per. Publ./DC Comics: 4-5/58 - No. 77, 12-1/70-71; No. 78, 2/73 - No. 80, 6-7/73; No. 81, 6-7/77 - No. 87, 6-7/78

1-(4-5/58)-Kirby/Stein-a(2); Kirby-c — 162.00 485.00 2100.00
2-Kirby/Stein-a(2) — 64.00 193.00 770.00
3-Kirby/Stein-a(2) — 55.00 165.00 660.00
4-8-Kirby/Wood-a plus cover to #8 — 44.00 133.00 530.00
9,10 — 26.00 78.00 260.00
11-15: 11-Grey tone-c. 14-Origin/1st app. Multi-Man (villain) — 17.50 53.00 175.00
16-22: 18-Intro. Cosmo, the Challengers Spacepet. 22-Last 10¢ issue — 12.00 36.00 120.00
23-30 — 6.00 18.00 60.00
31-Retells origin of the Challengers — 6.50 19.50 65.00
32-40 — 3.00 9.00 30.00
41-60: 43-New look begins. 48-Doom Patrol app. 49-Intro. Challenger Corps. 51-Sea Devils app. 55-Death of Red Ryan. 60-Red Ryan returns — 2.25 6.75 18.00
61-68: 64,65-Kirby origin-r, parts 1 & 2. 66-New logo. 68-Last 12¢ issue. — 1.10 3.30 9.00
69-73,75-80: 69-1st app. Corinna. 77-Last 15¢ issue — 5.00
74-Deadman by Tuska/Adams; 1 pg. Wrightson-a — 1.85 5.50 15.00
81,83-87: 81-(6-7/77). 83-87-Swamp Thing app. — 2.40 6.00
82-Swamp Thing begins, c/s — 1.10 3.30 9.00

NOTE: ***N. Adams** c-67, 68, 70, 72, 74i, 81i. **Buckler** c-83-86p. **Giffen** a-83-87p. **Kirby** a-75-80r; c-75, 77, 78. **Kubert** c-64, 66, 69, 76, 79. **Nasser** c/a-81p, 82p. **Tuska** a-73. **Wood** r-76.*

CHALLENGERS OF THE UNKNOWN
DC Comics: Mar, 1991 - No. 8, Oct, 1991 ($1.75, limited series)

1-Jeph Loeb scripts & Tim Sale-a in all (1st work together); Bolland-c — 2.50
2-8: 2-Superman app. 3-Dr. Fate app. 6-G. Kane-c(p). 7-Steranko-c/swipe by Art Adams — 2.50

NOTE: ***Art Adams** c-7. **Hempel** c-5. **Gil Kane** c-6p. **Sale** a-1-8; c-3, 8. **Wagner** c-4.*

CHALLENGERS OF THE UNKNOWN
DC Comics: Feb, 1997 - No. 18, July, 1998 ($2.25)

1-18: 1-Intro new team; Leon-c/a(p) begins. 4-Origin of new team. 11,12-Batman app. 15-Millennium Giants x-over; Superman-c/app. — 2.50

CHALLENGE TO THE WORLD
Catechetical Guild: 1951 (10¢, 36 pgs.)

nn — 4.00 10.00 20.00

CHAMBER OF CHILLS (Formerly Blondie Comics #20; ...of Clues No. 27 on)
Harvey Publications/Witches Tales: No. 21, June, 1951 - No. 26, Dec, 1954

21 (#1) — 40.00 120.00 290.00
22,24 (#2,4) — 26.00 77.00 180.00
23 (#3)-Excessive violence; eyes torn out — 29.00 86.00 200.00
5(2/52)-Decapitation, acid in face scene — 29.00 86.00 200.00
6-Woman melted alive — 27.00 81.00 190.00
7-Used in **SOTI**, pg. 389; decapitation/severed head panels — 26.00 77.00 180.00
8-10: 8-Decapitation panels — 21.00 64.00 150.00
11,12,14 — 16.00 47.00 110.00
13,15-24-Nostrand-a in all. 13,21-Decapitation panels. 18-Atom bomb panels. 20-Nostrand-c — 23.00 69.00 160.00
25,26 — 13.00 39.00 90.00

NOTE: *About half the issues contain bondage, torture, sadism, perversion, gore, cannabalism, eyes ripped out, acid in face, etc. **Elias** c-4-11, 14-19, 21-26. **Kremer** a-12, 17. **Palais** a-21(1), 23. **Nostrand/Powell** a-13, 15, 16. **Powell** a-21, 23, 24('51), 5-8, 11, 13, 18-21, 23-25. Bondage-c-21, 24('51), 7. 25-r/#5; 26-r/#9.*

CHAMBER OF CHILLS
Marvel Comics Group: Nov, 1972 - No. 25, Nov, 1976

1-Harlan Ellison adaptation — 2.25 6.75 18.00
2-5: 2-1st app. John Jakes (Brak the Barbarian) — 1.40 4.15 11.00
6-25: 22,23-(Regular 25¢ editions) — 1.10 3.30 9.00
22,23-(30¢-c variants, limited distribution)(5,7/76) — 2.80 8.40 28.00

NOTE: ***Adkins** a-1i, 2i. **Brunner** a-2-4; c-4. **Chaykin** a-4. **Ditko** r-14, 16, 19, 23, 24. **Everett** a-3i, 11r,21r. **Heath** a-1r. **Gil Kane** c-2p. **Kirby** r-11, 18, 19, 22. **Powell** a-13r. **Russell** a-1p, 2p. **Williamson/Mayo** a-13r. **Robert E. Howard** horror story adaptation-2, 3.*

CHAMBER OF CLUES (Formerly Chamber of Chills)
Harvey Publications: No. 27, Feb, 1955 - No. 28, April, 1955

27-Kerry Drake-r/#19; Powell-a; last pre-code — 10.00 30.00 70.00
28-Kerry Drake — 7.50 22.50 45.00

CHAMBER OF DARKNESS (Monsters on the Prowl #9 on)
Marvel Comics Group: Oct, 1969 - No. 8, Dec, 1970

1-Buscema-a(p) — 4.50 13.50 45.00
2,3: 2-Neal Adams scripts. 3-Smith, Buscema-a — 2.50 7.50 24.00

The Champions #13 © MAR

Chapel #2 © Rob Liefeld

Charlie Chan #9 © CC

4-A Conanesque tryout by Smith (4/70); reprinted in Conan #16; Marie Severin/Everett-c 4.00 12.00 40.00
5,8: 5-H.P. Lovecraft adaptation. 8-Wrightson-c 2.25 6.75 18.00
6 1.75 5.25 14.00
7-Wrightson-c/a, 7pgs. (his 1st work at Marvel); Wrightson draws himself in 1st & last panels; Kirby/Ditko-r; last 15¢-c 2.25 6.75 18.00
1-(1/72; 25¢ Special) 2.50 7.50 22.00
NOTE: ***Adkins/Everett*** *a-8.* ***Buscema*** *a-Special 1r.* ***Craig*** *a-5.* ***Ditko*** *a-6-8r.* ***Heck*** *a-1, 2, 8, Special 1r.* ***Kirby*** *a(p)-4, 5, 7r.* ***Kirby/Everett*** *c-5.* ***Severin/Everett*** *c-6.* ***Shores*** *a-2, 3i, Special 1r.* ***Sutton*** *a-1, 2i, 4, 7, Special 1r.* ***Wrightson*** *c-7, 8.*

CHAMP COMICS (Formerly Champion No. 1-10)
Worth Publ. Co./Champ Publ./Family Comics(Harvey Publ.): No. 11, Oct, 1940 - No. 29, March, 1944

11-Human Meteor cont'd. from Champion 84.00 252.00 675.00
12-17,20: 14,15-Crandall-c. 20-The Green Ghost app. 62.00 186.00 500.00
18,19-Simon-c. 19-The Wasp app. 78.00 234.00 625.00
21-29: 22-The White Mask app. 23-Flag-c. 24-Hitler, Tojo & Mussolini-c 50.00 150.00 400.00

CHAMPION (See Gene Autry's...)

CHAMPION COMICS (Formerly Speed Comics #1?; Champ Comics No. 11 on)
Worth Publ. Co.(Harvey Publications): No. 2, Dec, 1939 - No. 10, Aug, 1940 (no No.1)

2-The Champ, The Blazing Scarab, Neptina, Liberty Lads, Jungleman, Bill Handy, Swingtime Sweetie begin 150.00 450.00 1200.00
3-7: 7-The Human Meteor begins? 72.00 216.00 575.00
8-10: 8-Simon-c. 9-1st S&K-c (1st collaboration together). 10-Bondage-c by Kirby 131.00 394.00 1050.00

CHAMPIONS, THE
Marvel Comics Group: Oct, 1975 - No. 17, Jan, 1978

1-Origin & 1st app. The Champions (The Angel, Black Widow, Ghost Rider, Hercules, Iceman); Venus x-over 1.75 5.25 14.00
2-4,8-14,16,17: 2,3-Venus x-over. 11-14,17-Byrne-a 1.10 3.30 9.00
5-7-(Regular 25¢ edition)(4-8/76) 6-Kirby-c 1.10 3.30 9.00
5-7-(30¢-c variants, limited distribution) 2.80 8.40 28.00
15-(Regular 30¢ edition)(9/77)-Byrne-a 1.10 3.30 9.00
15-(35¢-c variant, limited distribution) 2.80 8.40 28.00
NOTE: ***Buckler/Adkins*** *c-3.* ***Byrne*** *a-11-15, 17.* ***Kane/Adkins*** *c-1.* ***Kane/Layton*** *c-11.* ***Tuska*** *a-3p, 4p, 6p, 7p. Ghost Rider c-1-4, 7, 8, 10, 14, 16, 17 (4, 10, 14 are more prominent).*

CHAMPIONS (Game)
Eclipse Comics: June, 1986 - No. 6, Feb, 1987 (limited series)

1-6: 1-Intro Flare; based on game. 5-Origin Flare 2.00

CHAMPIONS (Also see The League of Champions)
Hero Comics: Sept, 1987 - No. 12, 1989 ($1.95)

1-12: 1-Intro The Marksman & The Rose. 14-Origin Malice 2.00
Annual 1(1988, $2.75, 52pgs.)-Origin of Giant 2.75

CHAMPION SPORTS
National Periodical Publications: Oct-Nov, 1973 - No. 3, Feb-Mar, 1974

1 2.50 7.50 20.00
2,3 1.50 4.50 12.00

CHANNEL ZERO
Image Comics: Feb, 1998 - No. 5 ($2.95, B&W, limited series)

1-5, ...Dupe (1/99) -Brian Wood-s/a 3.00

CHAOS (See The Crusaders)

CHAOS! BIBLE
Chaos! Comics: Nov, 1995 ($3.30, one-shot)

1-Profiles of characters & creators 3.50

CHAOS EFFECT, THE
Valiant: 1994

Alpha (Giveaway w/trading card checklist) 2.00
Alpha-Gold variant, Omega-Gold variant 5.00
Omega (11/94, $2.25); Epilogue Pt. 1, 2 (12/94, 1/95; $2.95) 3.00

CHAOS! GALLERY
Chaos! Comics: Aug, 1997 ($2.95, one-shot)

1-Pin-ups of characters 3.00

CHAOS! QUARTERLY
Chaos! Comics: Oct, 1995 -No. 3, May, 1996 ($4.95, quarterly)

1-3: 1-anthology; Lady Death-c by Julie Bell. 2-Boris "Lady Demon"-c 5.00
1-Premium Edition (7,500) 25.00

CHAPEL (Also see Youngblood & Youngblood Strikefile #1-3)
Image Comics (Extreme Studios): No. 1 Feb, 1995 - No. 2, Mar, 1995 ($2.50, limited series)

1,2 2.50

CHAPEL (Also see Youngblood & Youngblood Strikefile #1-3)
Image Comics (Extreme Studios): V2 #1, Aug, 1995 - No. 7, Apr, 1996 ($2.50)

V2#1-7: 4-Babewatch x-over. 5-vs. Spawn. 7-Shadowhawk-c/app; Shadowhunt x-over 2.50
#1-Quesada & Palmiotti variant-c 2.50

CHAPEL (Also see Youngblood & Youngblood Strikefile #1-3)
Awesome Entertainment: Sept, 1997 ($2.99, one-shot)

1 (Reg. & alternate covers) 3.00

CHARLEMAGNE (Also see War Dancer)
Defiant Comics: Mar, 1994 - No. 5, July, 1994 ($2.50)

1/2 (Hero Illustrated giveaway)-Adam Pollina-c/a.
1-(3/94, $3.50, 52 pgs.)-Adam Pollina-c/a. 3.50
2,3,5: Adam Pollina-c/a. 2-War Dancer app. 5-Pre-Schism issue. 2.50
4-($3.25, 52 pgs.) 3.25

CHARLIE CHAN (See Big Shot Comics, Columbia Comics, Feature Comics & The New Advs. of...)

CHARLIE CHAN (The Adventures of...) (Zaza The Mystic No. 10 on) (TV)
Crestwood(Prize) No. 1-5; Charlton No. 6(6/55) on: 6-7/48 - No. 5, 2-3/49; No.6, 6/55 - No. 9, 3/56

1-S&K-c, 2 pgs.; Infantino-a 72.00 216.00 575.00
2-5-S&K-c: 3-S&K-c/a 47.00 141.00 375.00
6 (6/55-Charlton)-S&K-c 34.00 103.00 240.00
7-9 17.00 51.00 120.00

CHARLIE CHAN
Dell Publishing Co.: Oct-Dec, 1965 - No. 2, Mar, 1966

1-Springer-a 3.65 11.00 40.00
2 2.25 6.75 25.00

CHARLIE McCARTHY (See Edgar Bergen Presents...)
Dell Publishing Co.: No. 171, Nov, 1947 - No. 571, July, 1954 (See True Comics #14)

Four Color 171 24.00 71.00 260.00
Four Color 196-Part photo-c; photo back-c 16.50 49.00 180.00
1(3-5/49)-Part photo-c; photo back-c 14.00 44.00 160.00
2-9(7/52; #5,6-52 pgs.) 6.40 19.00 70.00
Four Color 445,478,527,571 4.50 13.50 50.00

CHARLTON BULLSEYE
CPL/Gang Publications: 1975 - No. 5, 1976 ($1.50, B&W, bi-monthly, magazine format)

1: 1 & 2 are last Capt. Atom by Ditko/Byrne intended for the never published Capt. Atom #90; Nightshade app.; Jeff Jones-a 3.00 9.00 30.00
2-Part 2 Capt. Atom story by Ditko/Byrne 2.50 7.50 20.00
3-Wrong Country by Sanho Kim 1.85 5.50 15.00
4-Doomsday + 1 by John Byrne 1.85 5.50 15.00
5-Doomsday + 1 by Byrne, The Question by Toth; Neal Adams back-c; Toth-c 2.60 7.80 26.00

CHARLTON BULLSEYE
Charlton Publications: June, 1981 - No. 10, Dec, 1982; Nov, 1986

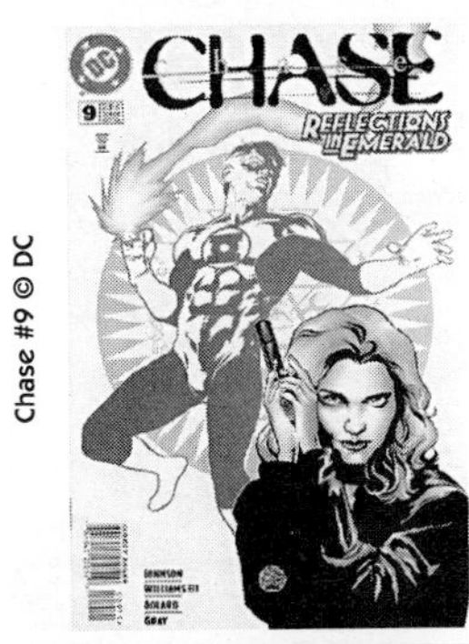

Chase #9 © DC

Cheryl Blossom #21 © AP

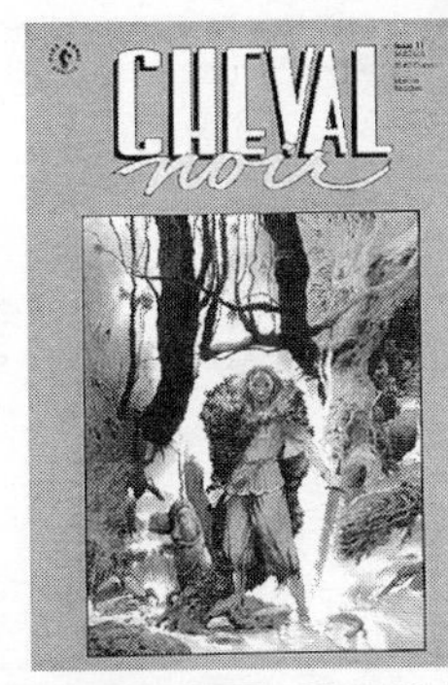

Cheval Noir #11 © DH

GD2.0 FN6.0 NM9.4

1-Blue Beetle, The Question app.; 1st app. Rocket Rabbit 4.00
2-10: 2-1st app. Neil The Horse; Rocket Rabbit app. 4-Vanguards. 6-Origin & 1st app. Thunderbunny 3.00
Special 1,2: 1(11/86) (Half in B&W). 2-Atomic Mouse app. (1987) 4.00

CHARLTON CLASSICS
Charlton Comics: Apr, 1980 - No. 9, Aug, 1981
1 5.00
2-9 3.00

CHARLTON CLASSICS LIBRARY (1776)
Charlton Comics: V10 No.1, Mar, 1973 (one-shot)
1776 (title) - Adaptation of the film musical "1776"; given away at movie theatres 1.50 4.50 12.00

CHARLTON PREMIERE (Formerly Marine War Heroes)
Charlton Comics: V1#19, July, 1967; V2#1, Sept, 1967 - No. 4, May, 1968
V1#19, V2#1,2,4: V1#19-Marine War Heroes. V2#1-Trio; intro. Shape, Tyro Team & Spookman. 2-Children of Doom. 4-Unlikely Tales; Aparo, Ditko-a 2.25 6.75 18.00
V2#3-Sinistro Boy Fiend; Blue Beetle & Peacemaker x-over 2.50 7.50 20.00

CHARLTON SPORT LIBRARY - PROFESSIONAL FOOTBALL
Charlton Comics: Winter, 1969-70 (Jan. on cover) (68 pgs.)
1 2.60 7.80 26.00

CHASE (See Batman #550 for 1st app.)
DC Comics: Feb, 1998 - No. 9, Oct, 1998; #1,000,000 Nov, 1998 ($2.50)
1-9: Williams III & Gray-a. 1-Includes 4 Chase cards. 4-Teen Titans app. 7,8-Batman app. 9-GL Hal Jordan-c/app. 2.50
#1,000,000 (11/98) Final issue; 853rd Century x-over 2.50

CHASSIS
Millenium Publications: 1996 - No. 2 ($2.95)
1,2: 1-Adam Hughes-c 3.00

CHASTITY: LUST FOR LIFE
Chaos! Comics: May, 1999 - No. 3, July, 1999 ($2.95, limited series)
1-3-Nutman-s/Benes-c/a 3.00

CHASTITY: ROCKED
Chaos! Comics: Nov, 1998 - No. 4, Feb, 1999 ($2.95, limited series)
1-4-Nutman-s/Justiniano-c/a 3.00

CHASTITY: THEATER OF PAIN
Chaos! Comics: Feb, 1997 - No. 3, June, 1997 ($2.95, limited series)
1-3-Pulido-s/Justiniano-c/a 3.00
TPB (1997, $9.95) r/#1-3 10.00

CHECKMATE (TV)
Gold Key: Oct, 1962 - No. 2, Dec, 1962
1-Photo-c on both 4.50 13.50 50.00
2 4.00 12.00 45.00

CHECKMATE! (See Action Comics #598)
DC Comics: Apr, 1988 - No. 33, Jan, 1991 ($1.25)
1-33: 13: New format begins 2.00
NOTE: ***Gil Kane*** *c-2, 4, 7, 8, 10, 11, 15-19.*

CHERYL BLOSSOM (See Archie's Girls, Betty and Veronica #320 for 1st app.)
Archie Publications: Sept, 1995 - No. 3, Nov, 1995 ($1.50, limited series)
1-3, Special 1-4 ('95, '96, $2.00) 2.50

CHERYL BLOSSOM (Cheryl's Summer Job)
Archie Publications: July, 1996 - No. 3, Sept, 1996 ($1.50, limited series)
1-3 2.00

CHERYL BLOSSOM (...Goes Hollywood)
Archie Publications: Dec, 1996 - No. 3, Feb, 1997 ($1.50, limited series)
1-3 2.00

CHERYL BLOSSOM
Archie Publications: Apr, 1997 - Present ($1.50/$1.75/$1.79)
1-26: 1-7-Dan DeCarlo-c/a 2.00

CHESTY SANCHEZ
Antarctic Press: Nov, 1995 - No. 2, Mar, 1996 ($2.95, B&W)
1,2 3.00
...Super Special (2/99, $5.99) 6.00

CHEVAL NOIR
Dark Horse Comics: 1989 - No. 48, Nov, 1993 ($3.50, B&W, 68 pgs.)
1-8,10 ($3.50): 6-Moebius poster insert 3.50
9,11,13,15,17,20,22 ($4.50, 84 pgs.) 4.50
12,18,19,21,23,25,26 ($3.95): 12-Geary-a; Mignola-c. 26-Moebius-a begins 4.00
14 ($4.95, 76 pgs.)(7 pgs. color) 5.00
16,24 ($3.75): 16-19-Contain trading cards 3.75
27-48 ($2.95): 33-Snyder III-c 3.00
NOTE: ***Bolland*** *a-2, 6, 7, 13, 14.* ***Bolton*** *a-2, 4, 45; c-4, 20.* ***Chadwick*** *c-13.* ***Dorman*** *painted c-16.* ***Geary*** *a-13, 14.* ***Kelley Jones*** *c-27.* ***Kaluta*** *a-6; c-6, 18.* ***Moebius*** *c-5, 9, 26.* ***Dave Stevens*** *c-1, 7.* ***Sutton*** *painted c-36.*

CHEYENNE (TV)
Dell Publishing Co.: No. 734, Oct, 1956 - No. 25, Dec-Jan, 1961-62
Four Color 734(#1)-Clint Walker photo-c 16.00 47.00 170.00
Four Color 772,803: Clint Walker photo-c 7.00 20.00 75.00
4(8-10/57) - 25: 4-9,13-25-Clint Walker photo-c. 10-12-Ty Hardin photo-c 4.50 13.50 50.00

CHEYENNE AUTUMN (See Movie Classics)

CHEYENNE KID (Formerly Wild Frontier No. 1-7)
Charlton Comics: No. 8, July, 1957 - No. 99, Nov, 1973
8 (#1) 5.85 17.50 35.00
9,15-19 4.00 11.00 22.00
10-Williamson/Torres-a(3); Ditko-c 9.15 27.00 55.00
11-(68 pgs.)-Cheyenne Kid meets Geronimo 10.00 30.00 70.00
12-Williamson/Torres-a(2) 10.00 30.00 70.00
13-Williamson/Torres-a (5 pgs.) 6.35 19.00 38.00
14-Williamson-a (5 pgs.?) 6.35 19.00 38.00
20-22,24,25-Severin c/a(3) each 2.50 7.50 24.00
23,27-29 1.50 4.50 12.00
26,30-Severin-a 2.25 6.75 18.00
31-59 1.50 4.50 12.00
60-80: 66-Wander by Aparo begins, ends #87 1.00 3.00 8.00
81-99: . Apache Red begins #88, origin in #89 2.40 6.00
Modern Comics Reprint 87,89(1978) 3.00

CHIAROSCURO (THE PRIVATE LIVES OF LEONARDO DA VINCI)
DC Comics (Vertigo): July, 1995 - No. 10, Apr, 1996 ($2.50/$2.95, limited series, mature)
1-9 2.50
10-($2.95) 3.00

CHICAGO MAIL ORDER (See C-M-O Comics)

CHI-CHIAN
Sirius Entertainment: 1997 - No. 6, 1998 ($2.95, limited series)
1-6-Voltaire-s/a 3.00

CHIEF, THE (Indian Chief No. 3 on)
Dell Publishing Co.: No. 290, Aug, 1950 - No. 2, Apr-June, 1951
Four Color 290(#1), 2 4.50 13.50 50.00

CHIEF CRAZY HORSE (See Wild Bill Hickok #21)
Avon Periodicals: 1950 (Also see Fighting Indians of the Wild West!)
nn-Fawcette-c 20.00 60.00 140.00

CHIEF VICTORIO'S APACHE MASSACRE (See Fight Indians of/Wild West!)
Avon Periodicals: 1951
nn-Williamson/Frazetta-a (7 pgs.); Larsen-a; Kinstler-c

Children of the Voyager #3 © MAR

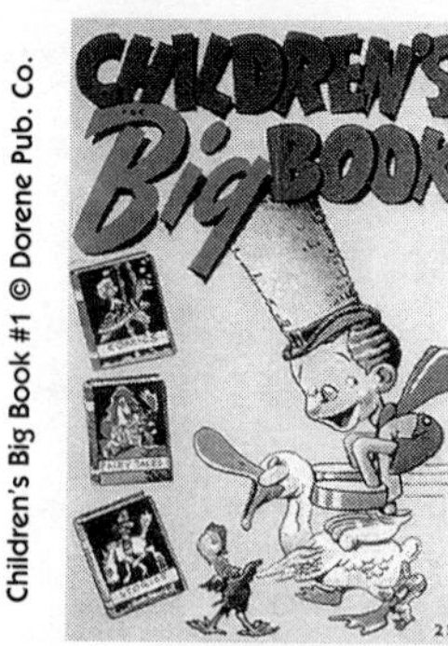

Children's Big Book #1 © Dorene Pub. Co.

C.H.I.X. #1 © Studiosaurus

	GD2.0	FN6.0	NM9.4
	40.00	120.00	320.00

CHILDHOOD'S END
Image Comics: Oct, 1997 ($2.95, B&W)

	GD2.0	FN6.0	NM9.4
1-Bourne-s/Calafiore-a			3.00

CHILDREN OF FIRE
Fantagor Press: Nov, 1987 - No. 3, 1988 ($2.00, limited series)

	GD2.0	FN6.0	NM9.4
1-3: by Richard Corben			2.00

CHILDREN OF THE VOYAGER (See Marvel Frontier Comics Unlimited)
Marvel Frontier Comics: Sept, 1993 - No. 4, Dec, 1993 ($1.95, limited series)

	GD2.0	FN6.0	NM9.4
1-($2.95)-Embossed glow-in-the-dark-c			3.00
2-4			2.00

CHILDREN'S BIG BOOK
Dorene Publ. Co.: 1945 (25¢, stiff-c, 68 pgs.)

	GD2.0	FN6.0	NM9.4
nn-Comics & fairy tales; David Icove-a	10.00	30.00	70.00

CHILDREN'S CRUSADE, THE
DC Comics (Vertigo): Dec, 1993 - No. 2, Jan, 1994 ($3.95, limited series)

	GD2.0	FN6.0	NM9.4
1,2-Neil Gaiman scripts & Chris Bachalo-a; framing issues for Children's Crusade x-over			4.00

CHILD'S PLAY: THE SERIES (Movie)
Innovation Publishing: May, 1991 - #3, 1991 ($2.50, 28pgs.)

	GD2.0	FN6.0	NM9.4
1-3			2.50

CHILD'S PLAY 2 THE OFFICIAL MOVIE ADAPTATION (Movie)
Innovation Publishing: 1990 - No. 3, 1990 ($2.50, bi-weekly limited series)

	GD2.0	FN6.0	NM9.4
1-3: Adapts movie sequel			2.50

CHILI (Millie's Rival)
Marvel Comics Group: 5/69 - No. 17, 9/70; No. 18, 8/72 - No. 26, 12/73

	GD2.0	FN6.0	NM9.4
1	5.00	15.00	50.00
2-5	2.50	7.50	24.00
6-17	2.00	6.00	16.00
18-26	1.25	3.75	10.00
Special 1(12/71)	3.00	9.00	30.00

CHILLER
Marvel Comics (Epic): Nov, 1993 - No. 2, Dec, 1993 ($7.95, lim. series)

	GD2.0	FN6.0	NM9.4
1,2-(68 pgs.)	1.00	3.00	8.00

CHILLING ADVENTURES IN SORCERY (...as Told by Sabrina #1, 2) (Red Circle Sorcery No. 6 on)
Archie Publications (Red Circle Productions): 9/72 - No. 2, 10/72; No. 3, 10/73 - No. 5, 2/74

	GD2.0	FN6.0	NM9.4
1-Sabrina cameo	3.00	9.00	30.00
2-Sabrina cameo	1.50	4.50	15.00
3-5: Morrow-c/a, all	1.10	3.30	9.00

CHILLING TALES (Formerly Beware)
Youthful Magazines: No. 13, Dec, 1952 - No. 17, Oct, 1953

	GD2.0	FN6.0	NM9.4
13(No.1)-Harrison-a; Matt Fox-c/a	47.00	142.00	380.00
14-Harrison-a	34.00	103.00	240.00
15-Has #14 on-c; Matt Fox-c; Harrison-a	40.00	120.00	290.00
16-Poe adapt.-'Metzengerstein'; Rudyard Kipling adapt.- 'Mark of the Beast,' by Kiefer; bondage-c	29.00	86.00	200.00
17-Matt Fox-c; Sir Walter Scott & Poe adapt.	37.00	111.00	260.00

CHILLING TALES OF HORROR (Magazine)
Stanley Publications: V1#1, 6/69 - V1#7, 12/70; V2#2, 2/71 - V2#5, 10/71 (50¢, B&W, 52 pgs.)

	GD2.0	FN6.0	NM9.4
V1#1	4.50	13.50	45.00
2-7: 7-Cameron-a	3.00	9.00	30.00
V2#2,3,5: 2-Spirit of Frankenstein-r/Adventures into the Unknown #16	2.60	7.80	26.00
V2#4-r/9 pg. Feldstein-a from Adventures into the Unknown #3	3.00	9.00	30.00

NOTE: *Two issues of V2#2 exist, Feb, 1971 and April, 1971.*

CHILLY WILLY
Dell Publ. Co.: No. 740, Oct, 1956 - No. 1281, Apr-June, 1962 (Walter Lantz)

	GD2.0	FN6.0	NM9.4
Four Color 740 (#1)	3.60	11.00	40.00
Four Color 852 (2/58),967 (2/59),1017 (9/59), 1074 (2-4/60),1122 (8/60), 1177 (4-6/61), 1212 (7-9/61), 1281	2.75	8.00	30.00

CHINA BOY (See Wisco)

CHIP 'N' DALE (Walt Disney)(See Walt Disney's C&S #204)
Dell Publishing Co./Gold Key/Whitman No. 65 on: Nov, 1953 - No. 30, June-Aug, 1962; Sept, 1967 - No. 83, 1982

	GD2.0	FN6.0	NM9.4
Four Color 517(#1)	7.00	22.00	80.00
Four Color 581,636	4.50	13.50	50.00
4(12/55-2/56)-10	3.80	11.40	42.00
11-30	2.90	8.70	32.00
1(Gold Key, 1967)-Reprints	2.00	6.00	22.00
2-10	1.00	3.00	10.00
11-20		2.40	6.00
21-64,70-77			3.00
65,66 (Whitman)			4.00
67-69 (3-pack? 1980)	1.00	3.00	8.00
78-83 (All #90214; 3-pack?, nd, dn code	1.00	2.80	7.00

NOTE: *All Gold Key/Whitman issues have reprints except No. 32-35, 38-41, 45-47. No. 23-28, 30-42, 45-47, 49 have new covers.*

CHIP 'N DALE RESCUE RANGERS
Disney Comics: June, 1990 - No. 19, Dec, 1991 ($1.50)

	GD2.0	FN6.0	NM9.4
1-19: New stories; 1,2-Origin			2.00

CHITTY CHITTY BANG BANG (See Movie Comics)

C.H.I.X.
Image Comics (Studiosaurus): Jan, 1998 ($2.50)

	GD2.0	FN6.0	NM9.4
1-Dodson, Haley, Lopresti, Randall, and Warren-s/c/a			3.00
1-($5.00) "X-Ray Variant" cover			5.00
C.H.I.X. That Time Forgot 1 (8/98, $2.95)			3.00

CHOICE COMICS
Great Publications: Dec, 1941 - No. 3, Feb, 1942

	GD2.0	FN6.0	NM9.4
1-Origin Secret Circle; Atlas the Mighty app.; Zomba, Jungle Fight, Kangaroo Man, & Fire Eater begin	150.00	450.00	1200.00
2	79.00	237.00	635.00
3-Double feature; Features movie "The Lost City" (classic cover); continued from Great Comics #3	112.00	337.00	900.00

CHOO CHOO CHARLIE
Gold Key: Dec, 1969

	GD2.0	FN6.0	NM9.4
1-John Stanley-a (scarce)	9.00	26.00	95.00

CHRISTIAN (See Asylum)
Maximum Press: Jan, 1996 ($2.99, one-shot)

	GD2.0	FN6.0	NM9.4
1-Pop Mhan-a			3.00

CHRISTIAN HEROES OF TODAY
David C. Cook: 1964 (36 pgs.)

	GD2.0	FN6.0	NM9.4
nn	1.25	3.75	10.00

CHRISTMAS (Also see A-1 Comics)
Magazine Enterprises: No. 28, 1950

	GD2.0	FN6.0	NM9.4
A-1 28	5.00	15.00	30.00

CHRISTMAS ADVENTURE, A (See Classics Comics Giveaways, 12/69)

CHRISTMAS ALBUM (See March of Comics No. 312)

CHRISTMAS ANNUAL
Golden Special: 1975 ($1.95, 100 pgs., stiff-c)

	GD2.0	FN6.0	NM9.4
nn-Reprints Mother Goose stories with Walt Kelly-a	3.00	9.00	30.00

CHRISTMAS & ARCHIE
Archie Comics: Jan, 1975 ($1.00, 68 pgs., 10-1/4x13-1/4")

	GD2.0	FN6.0	NM9.4
1	3.50	10.50	38.00

CHRISTMAS BELLS (See March of Comics No. 297)

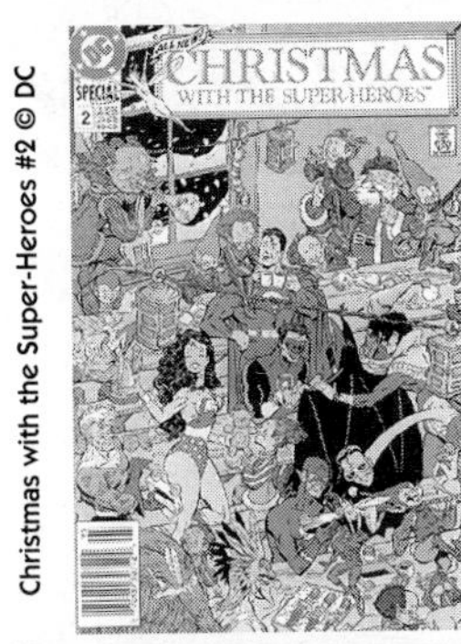

Christmas with the Super-Heroes #2 © DC

Chronos #7 © DC

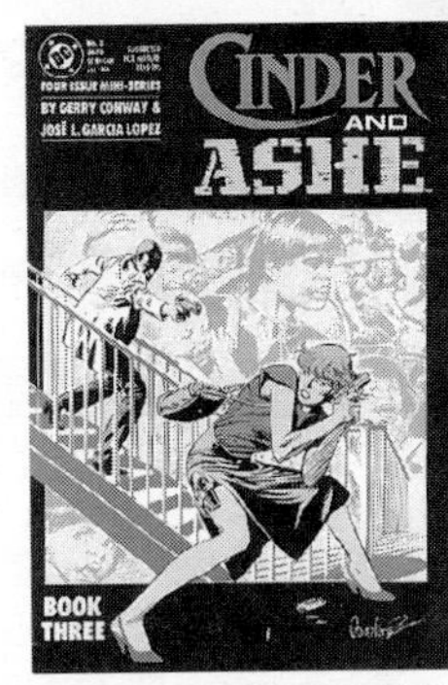

Cinder and Ashe #3 © DC

CHRISTMAS CARNIVAL
Ziff-Davis Publ. Co./St. John Publ. Co. No. 2: 1952 (25¢, one-shot, 100 pgs.)

	GD2.0	FN6.0	NM9.4
nn	29.00	86.00	200.00
2-Reprints Ziff-Davis issue plus-c	16.00	47.00	110.00

CHRISTMAS CAROL, A (See March of Comics No. 33)

CHRISTMAS EVE, A (See March of Comics No. 212)

CHRISTMAS IN DISNEYLAND (See Dell Giants)

CHRISTMAS PARADE (See Dell Giant No. 26, Dell Giants, March of Comics No. 284, Walt Disney Christmas Parade & Walt Disney's...)

CHRISTMAS PARADE (Walt Disney's)
Gold Key: Jan, 1963 (no month listed) - No. 9, Jan, 1972 (#1,5: 80 pgs.; #2-4,7-9: 36 pgs.)

	GD2.0	FN6.0	NM9.4
1 (30018-301)-Giant	7.70	22.00	85.00
2-6: 2-r/F.C. #367 by Barks. 3-r/F.C. #178 by Barks. 4-r/F.C. #203 by Barks. 5-r/Christ. Parade #1 (Dell) by Barks; giant. 6-r/Christmas Parade #2 (Dell) by Barks (64 pgs.); giant	5.50	16.50	60.00
7-Pull-out poster (half price w/o poster)	3.65	11.00	40.00
8-r/F.C. #367 by Barks; pull-out poster	5.50	16.50	60.00
9	2.75	8.00	30.00

CHRISTMAS PARTY (See March of Comics No. 256)

CHRISTMAS STORIES (See Little People No. 959, 1062)

CHRISTMAS STORY (See March of Comics No. 326)

CHRISTMAS STORY BOOK (See Woolworth's Christmas Story Book)

CHRISTMAS TREASURY, A (See Dell Giants & March of Comics No. 227)

CHRISTMAS WITH ARCHIE
Spire Christian Comics (Fleming H. Revell Co.): 1973, 1974 (49¢, 52 pgs.)

	GD2.0	FN6.0	NM9.4
nn			6.00

CHRISTMAS WITH MOTHER GOOSE
Dell Publishing Co.: No. 90, Nov, 1945 - No. 253, Nov, 1949

	GD2.0	FN6.0	NM9.4
Four Color 90 (#1)-Kelly-a	17.00	52.00	190.00
Four Color 126 ('46), 172 (11/47)-By Walt Kelly	13.00	39.00	145.00
Four Color 201 (10/48), 253-By Walt Kelly	11.25	34.00	125.00

CHRISTMAS WITH SANTA (See March of Comics No. 92)

CHRISTMAS WITH THE SUPER-HEROES (See Limited Collectors' Edition)
DC Comics: 1988; No. 2, 1989 ($2.95)

	GD2.0	FN6.0	NM9.4
1,2: 1-(100 pgs.)-All reprints; N. Adams-r, Byrne-c; Batman, Superman, JLA, LSH Christmas stories; r-Miller's 1st Batman/DC Special Series #21. 2-(68 pgs.)-Superman by Chadwick; Batman, Wonder Woman, Deadman, Gr. Lantern, Flash app.; Morrow-a; Enemy Ace by Byrne; all new-a			3.50

CHROMA-TICK, THE (...Special Edition, #1,2) (Also see The Tick)
New England Comics Press: Feb, 1992 - No. 8, Nov, 1993 ($3.95/$3.50, 44 pgs.)

	GD2.0	FN6.0	NM9.4
1,2-Includes serially numbered trading card set			4.00
3-8 ($3.50, 36 pgs.): 6-Bound-in card			3.50

CHROME
Hot Comics: 1986 - No. 3, 1986 ($1.50, limited series)

	GD2.0	FN6.0	NM9.4
1-3			2.00

CHROMIUM MAN, THE
Triumphant Comics: Aug, 1993 - No.10, May, 1994 ($2.50)

	GD2.0	FN6.0	NM9.4
1-1st app. Mr. Death; all serially numbered			2.50
2-10: 2-1st app. Prince Vandal. 3-1st app. Candi, Breaker & Coil. 4,5-Triumphant Unleashed x-over. 8,9-(3/94). 10-(5/94)			2.50
0-(4/94)-Four color-c, 0-All pink-c & all blue-c; no cover price			2.50

CHROMIUM MAN: VIOLENT PAST, THE
Triumphant Comics: Jan, 1994 - No. 2, Jan, 1994 ($2.50, limited series)

	GD2.0	FN6.0	NM9.4
1,2-Serially numbered to 22,000 each			2.50

CHRONICLES OF CORUM, THE (Also see Corum...)
First Comics: Jan, 1987 - No. 12, Nov, 1988 ($1.75/$1.95, deluxe series)

	GD2.0	FN6.0	NM9.4
1-12: Adapts Michael Moorcock's novel			2.00

CHRONOS
DC Comics: Mar, 1998 - No. 11, Feb. 1999 ($2.50)

	GD2.0	FN6.0	NM9.4
1-11-J.F. Moore-s/Guinan-a			2.50
#1,000,000 (11/98) 853rd Century x-over			2.50

CHRONOWAR (Manga)
Dark Horse Comics: Aug, 1996 - No. 9, Apr, 1997 ($2.95, limited series)

	GD2.0	FN6.0	NM9.4
1-9			3.00

CHUCKLE, THE GIGGLY BOOK OF COMIC ANIMALS
R. B. Leffingwell Co.: 1945 (132 pgs., one-shot)

	GD2.0	FN6.0	NM9.4
1-Funny animal	20.00	60.00	140.00

CHUCK NORRIS (TV)
Marvel Comics (Star Comics): Jan, 1987 - No. 4, July, 1987

	GD2.0	FN6.0	NM9.4
1-3: Ditko-a			3.00
4-No Ditko-a (low print run)			5.00

CHUCK WAGON (See Sheriff Bob Dixon's...)

CICERO'S CAT
Dell Publishing Co.: July-Aug, 1959 - No. 2, Sept-Oct, 1959

	GD2.0	FN6.0	NM9.4
1,2-Cat from Mutt & Jeff	3.00	9.00	35.00

CIMARRON STRIP (TV)
Dell Publishing Co.: Jan, 1968

	GD2.0	FN6.0	NM9.4
1-Stuart Whitman photo-c	3.20	9.50	35.00

CINDER AND ASHE
DC Comics: May, 1988 - No. 4, Aug, 1988 ($1.75, limited series)

	GD2.0	FN6.0	NM9.4
1-4: Mature readers			2.00

CINDERELLA (Disney) (See Movie Comics)
Dell Publishing Co.: No. 272, Apr, 1950 - No. 786, Apr, 1957

	GD2.0	FN6.0	NM9.4
Four Color 272	9.00	27.00	100.00
Four Color 786-Partial-r 272	5.50	16.50	60.00

CINDERELLA
Whitman Publishing Co.: Apr, 1982

	GD2.0	FN6.0	NM9.4
nn-Reprints 4-Color #272			4.00

CINDERELLA LOVE
Ziff-Davis/St. John Publ. Co. No. 12 on: No. 10, 1950; No. 11, 4-5/51; No. 12, 9/51; No. 4, 10-11/51 - No. 11, Fall, 1952; No. 12, 10/53 - No. 15, 8/54; No. 25, 12/54 - No. 29, 10/55 (No #16-24)

	GD2.0	FN6.0	NM9.4
10(#1)(1st Series, 1950)-Painted-c	13.00	39.00	90.00
11(#2, 4-5/51)-Crandall-a; Saunders painted-c	10.00	30.00	60.00
12(#3, 9/51)-Photo-c	7.00	21.00	42.00
4-8: 4,6,7-Photo-c	5.85	17.50	35.00
9-Kinstler-a; photo-c	7.50	22.50	45.00
10,11(Fall/'52), 14: 10,11-Photo-c. 14-Baker-a	7.00	21.00	42.00
12(St. John-10/53)-#13:13-Painted-c.	5.35	16.00	32.00
15(8/54)-Matt Baker-c	8.35	25.00	50.00
25(2nd Series)(Formerly Romantic Marriage)	5.35	16.00	32.00
26-Baker-c; last precode (2/55)	8.35	25.00	50.00
27,29: Both Matt Baker-c	8.35	25.00	50.00
28	4.00	12.00	24.00

CINDY COMICS (...Smith No. 39, 40; Crime Can't Win No. 41 on)(Formerly Krazy Komics) (See Junior Miss & Teen Comics)
Timely Comics: No. 27, Fall, 1947 - No. 40, July, 1950

	GD2.0	FN6.0	NM9.4
27-Kurtzman-a, 3 pgs: Margie, Oscar begin	19.00	58.00	135.00
28-31-Kurtzman-a	11.50	34.00	80.00
32-40: 33-Georgie story; anti-Wertham editorial	8.35	25.00	50.00

NOTE: *Kurtzman's "Hey Look"-#27(3), 29(2), 30(2), 31; "Giggles 'n' Grins"-28.*

CIRCUS (...the Comic Riot)
Globe Syndicate: June, 1938 - No. 3, Aug, 1938

1-(Scarce)-Spacehawks (2 pgs.), & Disk Eyes by Wolverton (2 pgs.), Pewee Throttle by Cole (2nd comic book work; see Star Comics V1#11), Beau Gus,

Cisco Kid Comics #1 © B. Bailey

Claire Voyant #4 © STD

Clandestine #10 © MAR

GD2.0 FN6.0 NM9.4

Ken Craig & The Lords of Crillon, Jack Hinton by Eisner, Van Bragger by Kane 785.00 2355.00 5500.00
2,3-(Scarce)-Eisner, Cole, Wolverton, Bob Kane-a in each 393.00 1180.00 2750.00

CIRCUS BOY (TV) (See Movie Classics)
Dell Publishing Co.: No. 759, Dec, 1956 - No. 813, July, 1957

Four Color 759 (#1)-The Monkees' Mickey Dolenz photo-c 10.50 31.50 115.00
Four Color 785 (4/57),813-Mickey Dolenz photo-c 10.00 30.00 110.00

CIRCUS COMICS
Farm Women's Pub. Co./D. S. Publ.: 1945 - No. 2, Jun, 1945; Wint., 1948-49

1-Funny animal 11.50 34.00 80.00
2 8.35 25.00 50.00
1(1948)-D.S. Publ.; 2 pgs. Frazetta 24.00 73.00 170.00

CIRCUS OF FUN COMICS
A. W. Nugent Publ. Co.: 1945 - No. 3, Dec, 1947 (A book of games & puzzles)

1 13.00 39.00 90.00
2,3 8.35 25.00 50.00

CISCO KID, THE (TV)
Dell Publishing Co.: July, 1950 - No. 41, Oct-Dec, 1958

Four Color 292(#1)-Cisco Kid, his horse Diablo, & sidekick Pancho & his horse Loco begin; painted-c begin 22.00 66.00 240.00
2(1/51)-5 9.50 28.50 105.00
6-10 7.00 22.00 80.00
11-20 6.40 19.00 70.00
21-36-Last painted-c 4.50 13.50 50.00
37-41: All photo-c 9.00 27.00 100.00
NOTE: ***Buscema** a-40.* ***Ernest Nordli** painted c-5-16, 20, 35.*

CISCO KID COMICS
Bernard Bailey/Swappers Quarterly: Winter, 1944 (one-shot)

1-Illustrated Stories of the Operas: Faust; Funnyman by Giunta; Cisco Kid (1st app.) & Superbaby begin; Giunta-c 40.00 120.00 310.00

CITIZEN SMITH (See Holyoke One-Shot No. 9)

CITY OF THE LIVING DEAD (See Fantastic Tales No. 1)
Avon Periodicals: 1952

nn-Hollingsworth-c/a 40.00 120.00 310.00

CITY SURGEON (Blake Harper...)
Gold Key: August, 1963

1(10075-308)-Painted-c 3.20 9.60 32.00

CIVIL WAR MUSKET, THE (Kadets of America Handbook)
Custom Comics, Inc.: 1960 (25¢, half-size, 36 pgs.)

nn 2.50 7.50 22.00

CLAIRE VOYANT (Also see Keen Teens)
Leader Publ./Standard/Pentagon Publ.: 1946 - No. 4, 1947 (Sparling strip reprints)

nn 56.00 168.00 450.00
2,4: 2-Kamen-c. 4-Kamen bondage-c 44.00 132.00 355.00
3-Kamen bridal-c; contents mentioned in Love and Death, a book by Gershom Legman(1949) referenced by Dr. Wertham in **SOTI** 53.00 159.00 425.00

CLANDESTINE (Also see Marvel Comics Presents & X-Men: ClanDestine)
Marvel Comics: Oct, 1994 - No.12, Sept, 1995 ($2.95/$2.50)

1-($2.95)-Alan Davis-c/a(p)/scripts & Mark Farmer-c/a(i) begin, ends #8; Modok app.; Silver Surfer cameo; gold foil-c 3.00
2-12: 2-Wraparound-c. 2,3-Silver Surfer app. 5-Origin of ClanDestine. 6-Capt. America, Hulk, Spider-Man, Thing & Thor-c; Spider-Man cameo. 7-Spider-Man-c/app; Punisher cameo. 8-Invaders & Dr. Strange app. 9-12-Modok app. 10-Captain Britain-c/app. 11-Sub-Mariner app 2.50
Preview (10/94, $1.50) 2.00

CLASH

GD2.0 FN6.0 NM9.4

DC Comics: 1991 - No. 3, 1991 ($4.95, limited series, 52 pgs.)

Book One - Three: Adam Kubert-c/a 5.00

CLASSIC COMICS/ILLUSTRATED - INTRODUCTION
by Dan Malan

Further revisions have been made to help in understanding the **Classics** section. **Classics** reprint editions prior to 1963 had either incorrect dates or no dates listed. Those reprint editions should be identified only by the highest number on the reorder list (HRN). Past price guides listed what were calculated to be approximately correct dates, but many people found it confusing for the price guide to list a date not listed in the comic itself.

We have also attempted to clear up confusion about edition variations, such as color, printer, etc. Such variations will be identified by letters. Editions will now be determined by three categories. Original edition variations will be Edition 1A, 1B, etc. All reprint editions prior to 1963 will be identified by HRN only. All reprint editions from 9/63 on will be identified by the correct date listed in the comic.

We have also included new information on four recent reprintings of **Classics** not previously listed. From 1968-1976 Twin Circle, the Catholic newspaper, serialized over 100 **Classics** titles. That list can be found under non-series items at the end of this section. In 1972 twelve **Classics** were reissued as **Now Age Books Illustrated**. They are listed under **Pendulum Illustrated Classics**. In 1982, 20 **Classics** were reissued, adapted for teaching English as a second language. They are listed under **Regents Illustrated Classics**. Then in 1984, six **Classics** were reissued with cassette tapes. See the listing under **Cassette Books**.

UNDERSTANDING CLASSICS ILLUSTRATED
by Dan Malan

Since **Classics Illustrated** is the most complicated comic book series, with all its reprint editions and variations, with changes in covers and artwork, with a variety of means of identifying editions, and with the most extensive worldwide distribution of any comic-book series; therefore this introductory section is provided to assist you in gaining expertise about this series.

THE HISTORY OF CLASSICS

The **Classics** series was the brain child of Albert L. Kanter, who saw in the new comic-book medium a means of introducing children to the great classics of literature. In October of 1941 his Gilberton Co. began the **Classic Comics** series with **The Three Musketeers**, with 64 pages of storyline. In those early years, the struggling series saw irregular schedules and numerous printers, not to mention variable art quality and liberal story adaptations. With No.13 the page total was reduced to 56 (except for No. 33, originally scheduled to be No. 9), and with No. 15 the coming-next ad on the outside back cover moved inside. In 1945 the Jerry Iger Shop began producing all new CC titles, beginning with No. 23. In 1947 the search for a classier logo resulted in **Classics Illustrated**, beginning with No. 35, **Last Days of Pompeii**. With No. 45 the page total dropped again to 48, which was to become the standard.

Two new developments in 1951 had a profound effect upon the success of the series. One was the introduction of painted covers, instead of the old line drawn covers, beginning with No. 81, **The Odyssey**. The second was the switch to the major national distributor Curtis. They raised the cover price from 10 to 15 cents, making it the highest priced comic-book, but it did not slow the growth of the series, because they were marketed as books, not comics. Because of this higher quality image, **Classics** flourished during the fifties while other comic series were reeling from outside attacks. They diversified with their new **Juniors**, **Specials**, and **World Around Us** series.

Classics artwork can be divided into three distinct periods. The pre-Iger era (1941-44) was mentioned above for its variable art quality. The Iger era (1945-53) was a major improvement in art quality and adaptations. It came to be dominated by artists Henry Kiefer and Alex Blum, together accounting for some 50 titles. Their styles gave the first real personality to the series. The EC era (1954-62) resulted from the demise of the EC horror series, when many of their artists made the major switch to classical art.

But several factors brought the production of new CI titles to a complete halt in 1962. Gilberton lost its 2nd class mailing permit. External factors like television, cheap paperback books, and Cliff Notes were all eating away at their market. Production halted with No.167, **Faust**, even though many more titles were

Classic Comics #1 © GIL

Classic Comics #2 © GIL

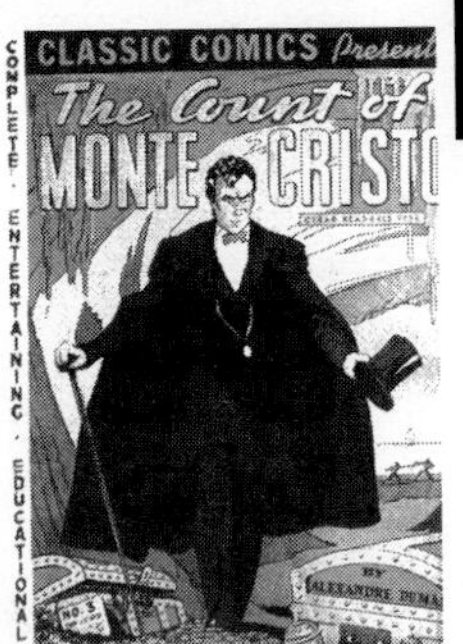

Classic Comics #3 © GIL

already in the works. Many of those found their way into foreign series, and are very desirable to collectors. In 1967, **Classics Illustrated** was sold to Patrick Frawley and his Catholic publication, Twin Circle. They issued two new titles in 1969 as part of an attempted revival, but succumbed to major distribution problems in 1971. In 1988, the trio: First Publishing, Berkley Press, and Classics Media Group acquired the use rights for the old CI series art, logo, and name from the Frawley Group. So far they have used only the name in the new series, but do have plans to reprint the old CI.

One of the unique aspects of the **Classics Illustrated** (CI) series was the proliferation of reprint variations. Some titles had as many as 25 editions. Reprinting began in 1943. Some **Classic Comics** (CC) reprints (r) had the logo format revised to a banner logo, and added a motto under the banner. In 1947 CC titles changed to the CI logo, but kept their line drawn covers (LDC). In 1948, Nos. 13, 18, 29 and 41 received second covers (LDC2), replacing covers considered too violent, and reprints of Nos. 13-44 had pages reduced to 48, except for No. 26, which had 48 pages to begin with.

Starting in the mid-1950s, 70 of the 80 LDC titles were reissued with new painted covers (PC). Thirty of them also received new interior artwork (A2). The new artwork was generally higher quality with larger art panels and more faithful but abbreviated storylines. Later on, there were 29 second painted covers (PC2), mostly by Twin Circle. Altogether there were 199 interior art variations (169 (O)s and 30 A2 editions) and 272 different covers (169 (O)s, four LDC2s, 70 new PCs of LDC (O)s, and 29 PC2s). It is mildly astounding to realize that there are nearly 1400 different editions in the U.S. CI series.

FOREIGN CLASSICS ILLUSTRATED

If U.S. Classics variations are mildly astounding, the veritable plethora of foreign CI variations will boggle your imagination. While we still anticipate additional discoveries, we presently know about series in 25 languages and 27 countries. There were 250 new CI titles in foreign series, and nearly 400 new foreign covers of U.S. titles. The 1400 U.S. CI editions pale in comparison to the 4000 plus foreign editions. The very nature of CI lent itself to flourishing as an international series. Worldwide, they published over one billion copies! The first foreign CI series consisted of six Canadian Classic Comic reprints in 1946.

The following chart shows when CI series first began in each country:
1946: Canada. 1947: Australia. 1948: Brazil/The Netherlands. 1950: Italy. 1951: Greece/Japan/Hong Kong(?)/England/Argentina/Mexico. 1952: West Germany. 1954: Norway. 1955: New Zealand/South Africa. 1956: Denmark/Sweden/Iceland. 1957: Finland/France. 1962: Singapore(?). 1964: India (8 languages). 1971: Ireland (Gaelic). 1973: Belgium(?) /Philippines(?) & Malaysia(?).

Significant among the early series were Brazil and Greece. In 1950, Brazil was the first country to begin doing its own new titles. They issued nearly 80 new CI titles by Brazilian authors. In Greece in 1951 they actually had debates in parliament about the effects of Classics Illustrated on Greek culture, leading to the inclusion of 88 new Greek History & Mythology titles in the CI series.

But by far the most important foreign CI development was the joint European series which began in 1956 in 10 countries simultaneously. By 1960, CI had the largest European distribution of any American publication, not just comics! So when all the problems came up with U.S. distribution, they literally moved the CI operation to Europe in 1962, and continued producing new titles in all four CI series. Many of them were adapted and drawn in the U.S., the most famous of which was the British CI #158A. Dr. No, drawn by Norman Nodel. Unfortunately, the British CI series ended in late 1963, which limited the European CI titles available in English to 15. Altogether there were 82 new CI art titles in the joint European series, which ran until 1976.

IDENTIFYING CLASSICS EDITIONS

HRN: This is the highest number on the reorder list. It should be listed in ( ) after the title number. It is crucial to understanding various CI editions.

ORIGINALS (O): This is the all-important First Edition. To determine (O)s,there is one primary rule and two secondary rules (with exceptions):

Rule No. 1: All (O)s and only (O)s have coming-next ads for the next number. **Exceptions**: No. 14(15) (reprint) has an ad on the last inside text page only. No. 14(0) also has a full-page outside back cover ad (also rule 2). Nos.55(75) and 57(75) have coming-next ads. (Rules 2 and 3 apply here). Nos. 168(0) and 169(0) do not have coming-next ads. No.168 was never reprinted; No. 169(0) has HRN (166). No. 169(169) is the only reprint.

Rule No. 2: On nos.1-80, all (O)s and only (O)s list 10c on the front cover. **Exceptions**: Reprint variations of Nos. 37(62), 39(71), and 46(62) list 10c on the front cover. (Rules 1 and 3 apply here.)

Rule No. 3: All (O)s have HRN close to that title No. **Exceptions**: Some reprints also have HRNs close to that title number: a few CC(r)s, 58(62), 60(62), 149(149), 152(149) 153(149), and title nos. in the 160's. (Rules 1 and 2 apply here.)

DATES: Many reprint editions list either an incorrect date or no date. Since Gilberton apparently kept track of CI editions by HRN, they often left the (O) date on reprints. Often, someone with a CI collection for sale will swear that all their copies are originals. That is why we are so detailed in pointing out how to identify original editions. Except for original editions, which should have a coming-next ad, etc., all CI dates prior to 1963 are incorrect! So you want to go by HRN only if it is (165) or below, and go by listed date if it is 1963 or later. There are a few (167) editions with incorrect dates. They could be listed either as (167) or (62/3), which is meant to indicate that they were issued sometime between late 1962 and early 1963.

COVERS: A change from CC to LDC indicates a logo change, not a cover change; while a change from LDC to LDC2, LDC to PC, or from PC to PC2 does indicate a new cover. New PCs can be identified by HRN, and PC2s can be identified by HRN and date. Several covers had color changes, particularly from purple to blue.

Notes: If you see 15 cents in Canada on a front cover, it does not necessarily indicate a Canadian edition. Editions with an HRN between 44 and 75, with 15 cents on the cover are Canadian. Check the publisher's address. An HRN listing two numbers with a / between them indicates that there are two different reorder lists in the front and back covers. Official Twin Circle editions have a full-page back cover ad for their TC magazine, with no CI reorder list. Any CI with just a Twin Circle sticker on the front is not an official TC edition.

TIPS ON LISTING CLASSICS FOR SALE

It may be easy to just list Edition 17, but Classics collectors keep track of CI editions in terms of HRN and/or date, (O) or (r), CC or LDC, PC or PC2, A1 or A2, soft or stiff cover, etc. Try to help them out. For originals, just list (0), unless there are variations such as color (Nos. 10 and 61), printer (Nos. 18-22), HRN (Nos. 95, 108, 160), etc. For reprints, just list HRN if it's (165) or below. Above that, list HRN and date. Also, please list type of logo/cover/art for the convenience of buyers. They will appreciate it.

CLASSIC COMICS (Also see Best from Boys Life, Cassette Books, Famous Stories, Fast Fiction, Golden Picture Classics, King Classics, Marvel Classics Comics, Pendulum Illustrated Classics, Picture Parade, Picture Progress, Regents Ill. Classics, Spitfire, Stories by Famous Authors, Superior Stories, and World Around Us.)

CLASSIC COMICS (Classics Illustrated No. 35 on)
Elliot Publishing #1-3 (1941-1942)/Gilberton Publications #4-167 (1942-1967) /Twin Circle Pub. (Frawley) #168-169 (1968-1971):
10/41 - No. 34, 2/47; No. 35, 3/47 - No. 169, Spring 1969
(Reprint Editions of almost all titles 5/43 - Spring 1971)
(Painted Covers (0)s No. 81 on, and (r)s of most Nos. 1-80)

Abbreviations:
A–Art; C or c–Cover; CC–Classic Comics; CI–Classics Ill.;
Ed–Edition; LDC–Line Drawn Cover; PC–Painted Cover; r–Reprint

1. The Three Musketeers

Ed	HRN	Date	Details	A	C	GD2.0	FN6.0	NM9.4
1	–	10/41	Date listed-1941; Elliot Pub; 68 pgs.	1	1	430.00	1290.00	4400.00
2	10	–	10¢ price removed on all (r)s; Elliot Pub; CC-r	1	1	33.00	100.00	250.00
3	15	–	Long Isl. Ind. Ed.; CC-r	1	1	24.00	72.00	180.00
4	18/20		Sunrise Times Ed.; CC-r	1	1	16.00	48.00	120.00
5	21	–	Richmond Courier	1	1	15.00	44.00	110.00

Classic Comics #4 © GIL

Classic Comics #5 © GIL

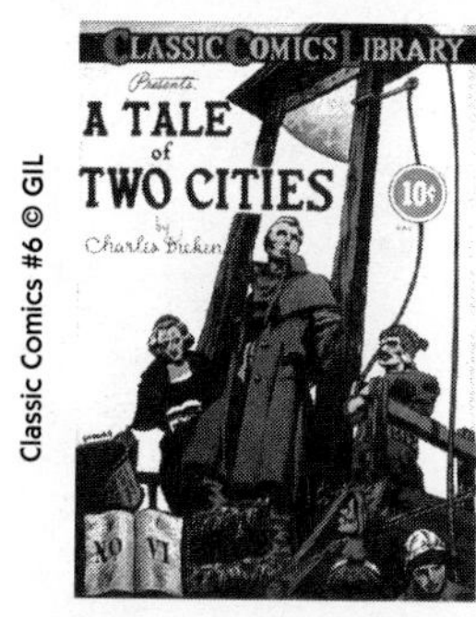

Classic Comics #6 © GIL

Ed	HRN	Date	Details	A	C	GD2.0	FN6.0	NM9.4
			Ed.; CC-r					
6	28	1946	CC-r	1	1	13.00	39.00	90.00
7	36	–	LDC-r	1	1	6.40	19.00	45.00
8	60	–	LDC-r	1	1	5.00	15.00	30.00
9	64	–	LDC-r	1	1	4.00	11.00	22.00
10	78	–	C-price 15¢;LDC-r	1	1	4.00	10.00	20.00
11	93	–	LDC-r	1	1	4.00	10.00	20.00
12	114	–	Last LDC-r	1	1	3.20	8.00	16.00
13	134	–	New-c; old-a; 64 pg. PC-r	1	2	3.60	9.00	18.00
14	143	–	Old-a; PC-r; 64 pg.	1	2	2.80	7.00	14.00
15	150	–	New-a; PC-r; Evans/Crandall-a	2	2	3.20	8.00	16.00
16	149	–	PC-r	2	2	2.00	5.00	8.00
17	167	–	PC-r	2	2	2.00	5.00	8.00
18	167	4/64	PC-r	2	2	2.00	5.00	8.00
19	167	1/65	PC-r	2	2	2.00	5.00	8.00
20	167	3/66	PC-r	2	2	2.00	5.00	8.00
21	166	11/67	PC-r	2	2	2.00	5.00	8.00
22	166	Spr/69	C-price 25¢ ; stiff-c; PC-r	2	2	2.00	5.00	8.00
23	169	Spr/71	PC-r; stiff-c	2	2	2.00	5.00	8.00

2. Ivanhoe

Ed	HRN	Date	Details	A	C	GD2.0	FN6.0	NM9.4
1	(O)	12/41?	Date listed-1941; Elliot Pub; 68 pgs.	1	1	212.00	635.00	1800.00
2	10	–	Price & 'Presents' removed; Elliot Pub; CC-r	1	1	29.00	88.00	220.00
3	15	–	Long Isl. Ind. ed.; CC-r	1	1	19.00	56.00	140.00
4	18/20		Sunrise Times ed.; CC-r	1	1	16.00	48.00	120.00
5	21	–	Richmond Courier ed.; CC-r	1	1	15.00	44.00	110.00
6	28	1946	Last 'Comics'-r	1	1	12.00	36.00	90.00
7	36	–	1st LDC-r	1	1	7.00	21.00	50.00
8	60	–	LDC-r	1	1	5.00	15.00	30.00
9	64	–	LDC-r	1	1	4.00	12.00	24.00
10	78	–	C-price 15¢; LDC-r	1	1	4.00	10.00	20.00
11	89	–	LDC-r	1	1	3.60	9.00	18.00
12	106	–	LDC-r	1	1	3.00	7.50	15.00
13	121	–	Last LDC-r	1	1	3.00	7.50	15.00
14	136	–	New-c&a; PC-r	2	2	4.00	10.00	20.00
15	142	–	PC-r	2	2	2.00	5.00	9.00
16	153	–	PC-r	2	2	2.00	5.00	9.00
17	149	–	PC-r	2	2	2.00	5.00	9.00
18	167	–	PC-r	2	2	2.00	5.00	8.00
19	167	5/64	PC-r	2	2	2.00	5.00	8.00
20	167	1/65	PC-r	2	2	2.00	5.00	8.00
21	167	3/66	PC-r	2	2	2.00	5.00	8.00
22A	166	9/67	PC-r	2	2	2.00	5.00	8.00
22B	166	–	Center ad for Children's Digest & Young Miss; rare; PC-r	2	2	10.00	30.00	75.00
23	166	R/68	C-Price 25¢; PC-r	2	2	2.00	5.00	8.00
24	169	Win/69	Stiff-c	2	2	2.00	5.00	8.00
25	169	Win/71	PC-r; stiff-c	2	2	2.00	5.00	8.00

3. The Count of Monte Cristo

Ed	HRN	Date	Details	A	C	GD2.0	FN6.0	NM9.4
1	(O)	3/42	Elliot Pub; 68 pgs.	1	1	135.00	406.00	1150.00
2	10	–	Conray Prods; CC-r	1	1	25.00	76.00	190.00
3	15	–	Long Isl. Ind. ed.; CC-r	1	1	20.00	60.00	150.00
4	18/20		Sunrise Times ed.; CC-r	1	1	17.00	52.00	130.00
5	20	–	Sunrise Times ed.; CC-r	1	1	15.00	46.00	115.00
6	21	–	Richmond Courier ed.; CC-r	1	1	15.00	44.00	110.00
7	28	1946	CC-r; new Banner logo	1	1	11.00	34.00	85.00
8	36	–	1st LDC-r	1	1	7.00	21.00	50.00
9	60	–	LDC-r	1	1	5.00	15.00	30.00
10	62	–	LDC-r	1	1	5.70	17.00	34.00
11	71	–	LDC-r	1	1	4.00	11.00	22.00
12	87	–	C-price 15¢; LDC-r	1	1	4.00	10.00	20.00
13	113	–	LDC-r	1	1	3.00	7.50	15.00
14	135	–	New-c&a; PC-r; Cameron-a	2	2	3.60	9.00	18.00
15	143	–	PC-r	2	2	2.00	5.00	9.00
16	153	–	PC-r	2	2	2.00	5.00	9.00
17	161	–	PC-r	2	2	2.00	5.00	9.00
18	167	–	PC-r	2	2	2.00	5.00	8.00
19	167	7/64	PC-r	2	2	2.00	5.00	8.00
20	167	7/65	PC-r	2	2	2.00	5.00	8.00
21	167	7/66	PC-r	2	2	2.00	5.00	8.00
22	166	R/68	C-price 25¢; PC-r	2	2	2.00	5.00	8.00
23	169	–	Win/69 Stiff-c; PC-r	2	2	2.00	5.00	8.00

4. The Last of the Mohicans

Ed	HRN	Date	Details	A	C	GD2.0	FN6.0	NM9.4
1	(O)	8/42	Date listed-1942; Gilberton #4(0) on; 68 pgs.	1	1	112.00	335.00	950.00
2	12	–	Elliot Pub; CC-r	1	1	25.00	76.00	190.00
3	15	–	Long Isl. Ind. ed.; CC-r	1	1	20.00	60.00	150.00
4	20	–	Long Isl. Ind. ed.; CC-r; banner logo	1	1	17.00	50.00	125.00
5	21	–	Queens Home News ed.; CC-r	1	1	15.00	46.00	115.00
6	28	1946	Last CC-r; new	1	1	12.00	36.00	90.00
7	36	–	1st LDC-r	1	1	7.00	21.00	50.00
8	60	–	LDC-r	1	1	5.00	15.00	30.00
9	64	–	LDC-r	1	1	4.00	11.00	22.00
10	78	–	C-price 15¢; LDC-r	1	1	4.00	10.00	20.00
11	89	–	LDC-r	1	1	3.60	9.00	18.00
12	117	–	Last LDC-r	1	1	3.00	7.50	15.00
13	135	–	New-c; PC-r	1	2	3.60	9.00	18.00
14	141	–	PC-r	1	2	2.20	5.50	11.00
15	150	–	New-a; PC-r; Severin, L.B. Cole-a	2	2	4.00	10.00	20.00
16	161	–	PC-r	2	2	2.00	5.00	8.00
17	167	–	PC-r	2	2	2.00	5.00	8.00
18	167	6/64	PC-r	2	2	2.00	5.00	8.00
19	167	8/65	PC-r	2	2	2.00	5.00	8.00
20	167	8/66	PC-r	2	2	2.00	5.00	8.00
21	166	R/67	C-price 25¢; PC-r	2	2	2.00	5.00	8.00
22	169	Spr/69	Stiff-c; PC-r	2	2	2.00	5.00	8.00

5. Moby Dick

Ed	HRN	Date	Details	A	C	GD2.0	FN6.0	NM9.4
1A	(O)	9/42	Date listed-1942; Gilberton; 68 pgs.	1	1	141.00	424.00	1200.00
1B			inside-c, rare free promo			212.00	635.00	1800.00
2	10	–	Conray Prods; Pg. 64 changed from 105 title list to letter from Editor; CC-r	1	1	27.00	80.00	200.00
3	15	–	Long Isl. Ind. ed.;	1	1	23.00	68.00	170.00

Classic Comics #7 © GIL

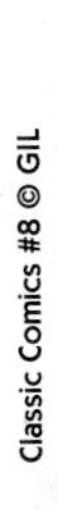
Classic Comics #8 © GIL

Classic Comics #9 © GIL

Ed	HRN	Date	Details	A	C	GD2.0	FN6.0	NM9.4
			Pg. 64 changed from Letter to the Editor to Ill. poem-Concord Hymn; CC-r					
4	18/20	–	Sunrise Times ed.; CC-r	1	1	17.00	52.00	130.00
5	20	–	Sunrise Times ed.; CC-r	1	1	17.00	50.00	125.00
6	21	–	Sunrise Times ed.; CC-r	1	1	15.00	46.00	115.00
7	28	1946	CC-r; new banner logo	1	1	13.00	40.00	100.00
8	36	–	1st LDC-r	1	1	7.00	21.00	50.00
9	60	–	LDC-r	1	1	5.00	15.00	30.00
10	62	–	LDC-r	1	1	5.70	17.00	34.00
11	71	–	LDC-r	1	1	4.00	12.00	24.00
12	87	–	C-price 15¢; LDC-r	1	1	4.00	11.00	22.00
13	118	–	LDC-r	1	1	3.60	9.00	18.00
14	131	–	New c&a; PC-r	2	2	4.00	10.00	20.00
15	138	–	PC-r	2	2	2.00	5.00	9.00
16	148	–	PC-r	2	2	2.00	5.00	9.00
17	158	–	PC-r	2	2	2.00	5.00	9.00
18	167	–	PC-r	2	2	2.00	5.00	8.00
19	167	6/64	PC-r	2	2	2.00	5.00	8.00
20	167	7/65	PC-r	2	2	2.00	5.00	8.00
21	167	3/66	PC-r	2	2	2.00	5.00	8.00
22	166	9/67	PC-r	2	2	2.00	5.00	8.00
23	166	Win/69	New-c & c-price 25¢; Stiff-c; PC-r	2	3	3.00	7.50	15.00
24	169	Win/71	PC-r	2	3	2.80	7.00	14.00

6. A Tale of Two Cities

Ed	HRN	Date	Details	A	C	GD2.0	FN6.0	NM9.4
1	(O)	10/42	Date listed-1942; 68 pgs. Zeckerberg c/a	1	1	112.00	335.00	950.00
2	14	–	Elliot Pub; CC-r	1	1	24.00	72.00	180.00
3	18	–	Long Isl. Ind. ed.; CC-r	1	1	19.00	56.00	140.00
4	20	–	Sunrise Times ed.; CC-r	1	1	17.00	50.00	125.00
5	28	1946	Last CC-r; new banner logo	1	1	12.00	36.00	90.00
6	51	–	1st LDC-r	1	1	6.40	19.00	45.00
7	64	–	LDC-r	1	1	4.30	13.00	26.00
8	78	–	C-price 15¢; LDC-r	1	1	4.00	11.00	22.00
9	89	–	LDC-r	1	1	3.00	7.50	15.00
10	117	–	LDC-r	1	1	3.00	7.50	15.00
11	132	–	New-c&a; PC-r; Joe Orlando-a	2	2	4.00	10.00	20.00
12	140	–	PC-r	2	2	1.50	4.00	8.00
13	147	–	PC-r	2	2	1.50	4.00	8.00
14	152	–	PC-r; very rare	2	2	17.00	52.00	130.00
15	153	–	PC-r	2	2	2.00	5.00	9.00
16	149	–	PC-r	2	2	2.00	5.00	9.00
17	167	–	PC-r	2	2	2.00	5.00	8.00
18	167	6/64	PC-r	2	2	2.00	5.00	8.00
19	167	8/65	PC-r	2	2	2.00	5.00	8.00
20	166	5/67	PC-r	2	2	2.00	5.00	8.00
21	166	Fall/68	New-c & 25¢; PC-r	2	3	3.60	9.00	18.00
22	169	Sum/70	Stiff-c; PC-r	2	3	2.80	7.00	14.00

7. Robin Hood

Ed	HRN	Date	Details	A	C	GD2.0	FN6.0	NM9.4
1	(O)	12/42	Date listed-1942; first Gift Box ad-bc; 68 pgs.	1	1	82.00	247.00	700.00
2	12	–	Elliot Pub; CC-r	1	1	23.00	70.00	175.00
3	18	–	Long Isl. Ind. ed.; CC-r	1	1	17.00	52.00	130.00
4	20	–	Nassau Bulletin ed.; CC-r	1	1	16.00	48.00	120.00
5	22	–	Queens Cty. Times ed.; CC-r	1	1	15.00	44.00	110.00
6	28	–	CC-r	1	1	13.00	40.00	95.00
7	51	–	LDC-r	1	1	6.40	19.00	45.00
8	64	–	LDC-r	1	1	4.25	13.00	28.00
9	78	–	LDC-r	1	1	4.00	10.00	20.00
10	97	–	LDC-r	1	1	3.60	9.00	18.00
11	106	–	LDC-r	1	1	3.00	7.50	15.00
12	121	–	LDC-r	1	1	3.00	7.50	15.00
13	129	–	New-c; PC-r	1	2	4.00	10.00	20.00
14	136	–	New-a; PC-r	2	2	4.00	10.00	20.00
15	143	–	PC-r	2	2	2.00	5.00	9.00
16	153	–	PC-r	2	2	2.00	5.00	9.00
17	164	–	PC-r	2	2	2.00	5.00	8.00
18	167	–	PC-r	2	2	2.00	5.00	8.00
19	167	6/64	PC-r	2	2	2.00	5.00	8.00
20	167	5/65	PC-r	2	2	2.00	5.00	8.00
21	167	7/66	PC-r	2	2	2.00	5.00	8.00
22	166	12/67	PC-r	2	2	2.00	5.00	8.00
23	169	Sum/69	Stiff-c; c-price 25¢; PC-r	2	2	2.00	5.00	8.00

8. Arabian Nights

Ed	HRN	Date	Details	A	C	GD2.0	FN6.0	NM9.4
1	(O)	2/43	Original; 68 pgs. Lilian Chestney-c/a	1	1	141.00	424.00	1200.00
2	17	–	Long Isl. ed.; pg. 64 changed from Gift Box ad to Letter from British Medical Worker; CC-r	1	1	52.00	155.00	440.00
3	20	–	Nassau Bulletin; Pg. 64 changed from letter to article-Three Men Named Smith; CC-r	1	1	43.00	129.00	350.00
4A	28	1946	CC-r; new banner logo, slick-c	1	1	31.00	92.00	230.00
4B	28	1946	Same, but w/stiff-c	1	1	31.00	92.00	230.00
5	51	–	LDC-r	1	1	21.00	64.00	160.00
6	64	–	LDC-r	1	1	17.00	52.00	130.00
7	78	–	LDC-r	1	1	16.00	48.00	120.00
8	164	–	New-c&a; PC-r	2	2	15.00	44.00	110.00

9. Les Miserables

Ed	HRN	Date	Details	A	C	GD2.0	FN6.0	NM9.4
1A	(O)	3/43	Original; slick paper cover; 68 pgs.	1	1	82.00	247.00	700.00
1B	(O)	3/43	Original; rough, pulp type-c; 68 pgs.	1	1	103.00	309.00	875.00
2	14	–	Elliot Pub; CC-r	1	1	25.00	76.00	190.00
3	18	3/44	Nassau Bul. Pg. 64 changed from Gift Box ad to Bill of Rights article; CC-r	1	1	21.00	62.00	155.00
4	20	–	Richmond Courier ed.; CC-r	1	1	17.00	50.00	125.00
5	28	1946	Gilberton; pgs. 60-64 rearranged/ illos added; CC-r	1	1	13.00	38.00	95.00
6	51	–	LDC-r	1	1	7.00	21.00	50.00
7	71	–	LDC-r	1	1	5.65	17.00	34.00
8	87	–	C-price 15¢; LDC-r	1	1	5.00	15.00	30.00
9	161	–	New-c&a; PC-r	2	2	5.00	15.00	30.00

Classic Comics #10 © GIL

Classic Comics #11 © GIL

Classic Comics #13 © GIL

Ed	HRN	Date	Details	A	C	GD2.0	FN6.0	NM9.4
10	167	9/63	PC-r	2	2	2.80	7.00	14.00
11	167	12/65	PC-r	2	2	2.80	7.00	14.00
12	166	R/1968	New-c & price 25¢; PC-r	2	3	4.00	10.00	20.00

10. Robinson Crusoe (Used in **SOTI**, pg. 142)

Ed	HRN	Date	Details	A	C	GD2.0	FN6.0	NM9.4
1A	(O)	4/43	Original; Violet-c; 68 pgs; Zuckerberg c/a	1	1	71.00	212.00	600.00
1B	(O)	4/43	Original; blue-grey-c, 68 pgs.	1	1	79.00	238.00	675.00
2A	14	–	Elliot Pub; violet-c; 68 pgs; CC-r	1	1	27.00	80.00	200.00
2B	14	–	Elliot Pub; blue-grey-c; CC-r	1	1	24.00	72.00	180.00
3	18	–	Nassau Bul. Pg. 64 changed from Gift Box ad to Bill of Rights article; CC-r	1	1	17.00	52.00	130.00
4	20	–	Queens Home News ed.; CC-r	1	1	15.00	46.00	115.00
5	28	1946	Gilberton; pg. 64 changes from Bill of Rights to WWII article-One Leg Shot Away; last CC-r	1	1	12.00	36.00	90.00
6	51	–	LDC-r	1	1	6.40	19.00	45.00
7	64	–	LDC-r	1	1	5.00	15.00	30.00
8	78	–	C-price 15¢; LDC-r	1	1	4.00	11.00	22.00
9	97	–	LDC-r	1	1	4.00	10.00	20.00
10	114	–	LDC-r	1	1	3.00	7.50	15.00
11	130	–	New-c; PC-r	1	2	3.30	10.00	20.00
12	140	–	New-a; PC-r	2	2	3.30	10.00	20.00
13	153	–	PC-r	2	2	1.60	4.00	8.00
14	164	–	PC-r	2	2	1.50	3.50	7.00
15	167	–	PC-r	2	2	1.50	3.50	7.00
16	167	7/64	PC-r	2	2	2.00	5.50	11.00
17	167	5/65	PC-r	2	2	2.00	5.50	11.00
18	167	6/66	PC-r	2	2	2.00	5.00	8.00
19	166	Fall/68	C-price 25¢; PC-r	2	2	2.00	5.00	8.00
20	166	R/68	(No Twin Circle ad)	2	2	2.00	5.00	9.00
21	169	Sm/70	Stiff-c; PC-r	2	2	2.00	5.00	9.00

11. Don Quixote

Ed	HRN	Date	Details	A	C	GD2.0	FN6.0	NM9.4
1	10	5/43	First (O) with HRN list; 68 pgs.	1	1	77.00	229.00	650.00
2	18	–	Nassau Bulletin ed.; CC-r	1	1	23.00	68.00	170.00
3	21	–	Queens Home News ed.; CC-r	1	1	17.00	52.00	130.00
4	28	–	CC-r	1	1	13.00	38.00	95.00
5	110	–	New-PC; PC-r	1	2	4.70	14.00	28.00
6	156	–	Pgs. reduced 68 to 52; PC-r	1	2	3.00	7.50	15.00
7	165	–	PC-r	1	2	2.00	5.00	10.00
8	167	1/64	PC-r	1	2	2.00	5.00	10.00
9	167	11/65	PC-r	1	2	2.00	5.00	10.00
10	166	R/1968	New-c & price 25¢; PC-r	1	3	4.00	11.00	22.00

12. Rip Van Winkle and the Headless Horseman

Ed	HRN	Date	Details	A	C	GD2.0	FN6.0	NM9.4
1	11	6/43	Original; 68 pgs.	1	1	77.00	229.00	650.00
2	15	–	Long Isl. Ind. ed.; CC-r	1	1	22.00	66.00	165.00
3	20	–	Long Isl. Ind. ed.;	1	1	17.00	52.00	130.00
4	22	–	Queens Cty. Times ed.; CC-r	1	1	15.00	44.00	110.00
5	28	–	CC-r	1	1	12.00	36.00	90.00
6	60	–	1st LDC-r	1	1	6.00	18.00	40.00
7	62	–	LDC-r	1	1	4.25	13.00	26.00
8	71	–	LDC-r	1	1	4.00	10.00	20.00
9	89	–	C-price 15¢; LDC-r	1	1	3.30	9.00	18.00
10	118	–	LDC-r	1	1	3.00	7.50	15.00
11	132	–	New-c; PC-r	1	2	4.00	10.00	20.00
12	150	–	New-a; PC-r	2	2	4.00	10.00	20.00
13	158	–	PC-r	2	2	2.00	5.00	9.00
14	167	–	PC-r	2	2	2.00	5.00	9.00
15	167	12/63	PC-r	2	2	2.00	5.00	8.00
16	167	4/65	PC-r	2	2	2.00	5.00	8.00
17	167	4/66	PC-r	2	2	2.00	5.00	8.00
18	166	R/1968	New-c&price 25¢; PC-r; stiff-c	2	3	2.80	7.00	14.00
19	169	Sm/70	PC-r; stiff-c	2	3	2.20	5.50	11.00

13. Dr. Jekyll and Mr. Hyde (Used in **SOTI**, pg. 143)(1st horror comic?)

Ed	HRN	Date	Details	A	C	GD2.0	FN6.0	NM9.4
1	12	8/43	Original 60 pgs.	1	1	111.00	335.00	950.00
2	15	–	Long Isl. Ind. ed.; CC-r	1	1	32.00	96.00	240.00
3	20	–	Long Isl. Ind. ed.; CC-r	1	1	22.00	66.00	165.00
4	28	–	No c-price; CC-r	1	1	17.00	50.00	125.00
5	60	–	New-c; Pgs. reduced from 60 to 52; H.C. Kiefer-c; LDC-r	1	2	6.00	18.00	40.00
6	62	–	LDC-r	1	2	5.00	15.00	30.00
7	71	–	LDC-r	1	2	4.00	12.00	24.00
8	87	–	Date returns (erroneous); LDC-r	1	2	4.00	11.00	22.00
9	112	–	New-c&a; PC-r; Cameron-a	2	3	4.25	13.00	28.00
10	153	–	PC-r	2	3	2.00	5.00	9.00
11	161	–	PC-r	2	3	2.00	5.00	9.00
12	167	–	PC-r	2	3	2.00	5.00	8.00
13	167	8/64	PC-r	2	3	2.00	5.00	8.00
14	167	11/65	PC-r	2	3	2.00	5.00	8.00
15	166	R/68	C-price 25¢; PC-r	2	3	2.00	5.00	8.00
16	169	Wn/69	PC-r; stiff-c	2	3	2.00	5.00	8.00

14. Westward Ho!

Ed	HRN	Date	Details	A	C	GD2.0	FN6.0	NM9.4
1	13	9/43	Original; last outside bc coming-next ad; 60 pgs.	1	1	182.00	547.00	1550.00
2	15	–	Long Isl. Ind. ed.; CC-r	1	1	55.00	166.00	470.00
3	21	–	Queens Home News; Pg. 56 changed from coming-next ad to Three Men Named Smith; CC-r	1	1	42.00	126.00	335.00
4	28	1946	Gilberton; Pg. 56 changed again to WWII article-Speaking for America; last CC-r	1	1	35.00	104.00	260.00
5	53	–	Pgs. reduced from 60 to 52; LDC-r	1	1	32.00	96.00	240.00

15. Uncle Tom's Cabin (Used in **SOTI**, pgs. 102, 103)

Ed	HRN	Date	Details	A	C	GD2.0	FN6.0	NM9.4
1	14	11/43	Original; Outside-bc ad: 2 Gift Boxes; 60 pgs.; color var. on-c; green trunk,root on left & brown trunk,	1	1	65.00	194.00	550.00

Classic Comics #15 © GIL

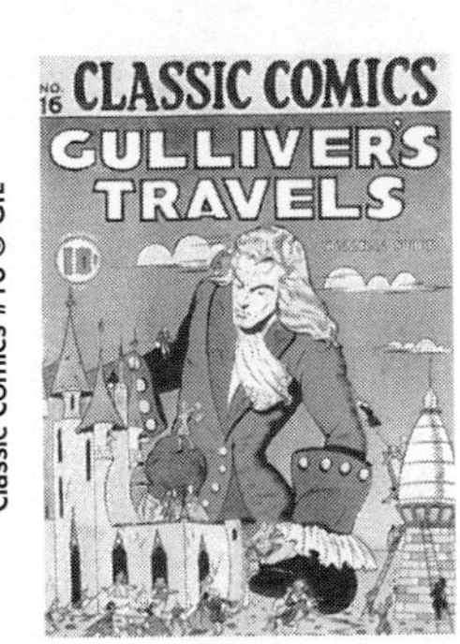

Classic Comics #16 © GIL

Classic Comics #17 © GIL

Ed	HRN	Date	Details	A	C	GD2.0	FN6.0	NM9.4
			root on left					
2	15	–	Long Isl. Ind. listed- bottom inside-fc; also Gilberton listed bottom-pg. 1; CC-r; green root vs. brown root var. occurs again	1	1	24.00	72.00	180.00
3	21	–	Nassau Bulletin ed.; CC-r	1	1	19.00	56.00	140.00
4	28	–	No c-price; CC-r	1	1	13.00	38.00	95.00
5	53	–	Pgs. reduced 60 to 52; LDC-r	1	1	6.40	19.00	45.00
6	71	–	LDC-r	1	1	5.00	15.00	30.00
7	89	–	C-price 15¢; LDC-r	1	1	4.25	13.00	28.00
8	117	–	New-c/lettering changes; PC-r	1	2	4.00	10.00	20.00
9	128	–	'Picture Progress' promo; PC-r	1	2	2.00	6.00	12.00
10	137	–	PC-r	1	2	2.00	5.00	9.00
11	146	–	PC-r	1	2	2.00	5.00	9.00
12	154	–	PC-r	1	2	2.00	5.00	9.00
13	161	–	PC-r	1	2	2.00	5.00	8.00
14	167	–	PC-r	1	2	2.00	5.00	8.00
15	167	6/64	PC-r	1	2	2.00	5.00	8.00
16	167	5/65	PC-r	1	2	2.00	5.00	8.00
17	166	5/67	PC-r	1	2	2.00	5.00	8.00
18	166	Wn/69	New-stiff-c; PC-r	1	3	2.80	8.40	14.00
19	169	Sm/70	PC-r; stiff-c	1	3	2.40	7.20	12.00

16. Gullivers Travels

Ed	HRN	Date	Details	A	C	GD2.0	FN6.0	NM9.4
1	15	12/43	Original-Lilian Chestney c/a; 60 pgs.	1	1	66.00	198.00	560.00
2	18/20	–	Price deleted; Queens Home News ed; CC-r	1	1	21.00	64.00	160.00
3	22	–	Queens Cty. Times ed.; CC-r	1	1	17.00	50.00	125.00
4	28	–	CC-r	1	1	12.00	36.00	90.00
5	60	–	Pgs. reduced to 48; LDC-r	1	1	5.80	17.00	35.00
6	62	–	LDC-r	1	1	4.25	13.00	26.00
7	78	–	C-price 15¢; LDC-r	1	1	4.00	11.00	22.00
8	89	–	LDC-r	1	1	3.00	9.00	18.00
9	155	–	New-c; PC-r	1	2	4.00	10.00	20.00
10	165	–	PC-r	1	2	2.00	5.00	8.00
11	167	5/64	PC-r	1	2	2.00	5.00	8.00
12	167	11/65	PC-r	1	2	2.00	5.00	8.00
13	166	R/1968	C-price 25¢; PC-r	1	2	2.00	5.00	8.00
14	169	Wn/69	PC-r; stiff-c	1	2	2.00	5.00	8.00

17. The Deerslayer

Ed	HRN	Date	Details	A	C	GD2.0	FN6.0	NM9.4
1	16	1/44	Original; Outside-bc ad: 3 Gift Boxes; 60 pgs.	1	1	57.00	171.00	485.00
2A	18	–	Queens Cty Times (inside-fc); CC-r	1	1	22.00	66.00	165.00
2B	18	–	Gilberton (bottom-pg. 1); CC-r; Scarce	1	1	32.00	96.00	240.00
3	22	–	Queens Cty. Times ed.; CC-r	1	1	17.00	52.00	130.00
4	28	–	CC-r	1	1	13.00	38.00	95.00
5	60	–	Pgs.reduced to 52; LDC-r	1	1	6.00	18.00	40.00
6	64	–	LDC-r	1	1	4.00	12.00	24.00
7	85	–	C-price 15¢; LDC-r	1	1	3.60	9.00	18.00
8	118	–	LDC-r	1	1	3.00	7.50	15.00
9	132	–	LDC-r	1	1	3.00	7.50	15.00
10	167	11/66	Last LDC-r	1	1	2.80	7.00	14.00
11	166	R/1968	New-c & price 25¢; PC-r	1	2	4.00	10.00	20.00
12	169	Spr/71	Stiff-c; letters from parents & educators; PC-r	1	2	2.80	7.00	14.00

18. The Hunchback of Notre Dame

Ed	HRN	Date	Details	A	C	GD2.0	FN6.0	NM9.4
1A	17	3/44	Orig.; Gilberton ed; 60 pgs.	1	1	76.00	229.00	650.00
1B	17	3/44	Orig.; Island Pub. Ed.; 60 pgs.	1	1	68.00	203.00	575.00
2	18/20	–	Queens Home News ed.; CC-r	1	1	24.00	72.00	180.00
3	22	–	Queens Cty. Times ed.; CC-r	1	1	18.00	54.00	135.00
4	28	–	CC-r	1	1	15.00	46.00	115.00
5	60	–	New-c; 8pgs. deleted; Kiefer-c; LDC-r	1	2	6.00	18.00	38.00
6	62	–	LDC-r	1	2	4.00	12.00	24.00
7	78	–	C-price 15¢; LDC-r	1	2	4.00	11.00	22.00
8A	89	–	H.C.Kiefer on bottom right-fc; LDC-r	1	2	4.00	10.00	20.00
8B	89	–	Name omitted; LDC-r	1	2	4.25	13.00	28.00
9	118	–	LDC-r	1	2	3.60	9.00	18.00
10	140	–	New-c; PC-r	1	3	4.25	13.00	28.00
11	146	–	PC-r	1	3	4.00	10.00	20.00
12	158	–	New-c&a; PC-r; Evans/Crandall-a	2	4	4.00	11.00	22.00
13	165	–	PC-r	2	4	2.00	5.00	9.00
14	167	9/63	PC-r	2	4	2.00	5.00	9.00
15	167	10/64	PC-r	2	4	2.00	5.00	9.00
16	167	4/66	PC-r	2	4	2.00	5.00	8.00
17	166	R/1968	New price 25¢; PC-r	2	4	2.00	5.00	8.00
18	169	Sp/70	Stiff-c; PC-r	2	4	2.00	5.00	8.00

19. Huckleberry Finn

Ed	HRN	Date	Details	A	C	GD2.0	FN6.0	NM9.4
1A	18	4/44	Orig.; Gilberton ed.; 60 pgs.	1	1	47.00	142.00	400.00
1B	18	4/44	Orig.; Island Pub.; 60 pgs.	1	1	51.00	154.00	435.00
2	18	–	Nassau Bulletin ed.; fc-price 15¢-Canada; no coming-next ad; CC-r	1	1	23.00	68.00	170.00
3	22	–	Queens City Times ed.; CC-r	1	1	17.00	52.00	130.00
4	28	–	CC-r	1	1	12.00	36.00	90.00
5	60	–	Pgs. reduced to 48; LDC-r	1	1	5.85	17.00	35.00
6	62	–	LDC-r	1	1	4.25	13.00	26.00
7	78	–	LDC-r	1	1	4.00	10.00	20.00
8	89	–	LDC-r	1	1	3.60	9.00	18.00
9	117	–	LDC-r	1	1	3.00	7.50	15.00
10	131	–	New-c&a; PC-r	2	2	3.60	9.00	18.00
11	140	–	PC-r	2	2	2.00	5.00	9.00
12	150	–	PC-r	2	2	2.00	5.00	9.00
13	158	–	PC-r	2	2	2.00	5.00	9.00
14	165	–	PC-r (scarce)	2	2	3.60	9.00	18.00
15	167	–	PC-r	2	2	2.00	5.00	8.00
16	167	6/64	PC-r	2	2	2.00	5.00	8.00
17	167	6/65	PC-r	2	2	2.00	5.00	8.00
18	167	10/65	PC-r	2	2	2.00	5.00	8.00

Classic Comics #21 © GIL

Classic Comics #23 © GIL

Classic Comics #24 © GIL

Ed	HRN	Date	Details	A	C	GD2.0	FN6.0	NM9.4
19	166	9/67	PC-r	2	2	2.00	5.00	8.00
20	166	Win/69	C-price 25¢; PC-r; stiff-c	2	2	2.00	5.00	8.00
21	169	Sm/70	PC-r; stiff-c	2	2	2.00	5.00	8.00

20. The Corsican Brothers

Ed	HRN	Date	Details	A	C	GD2.0	FN6.0	NM9.4
1A	20	6/44	Orig.; Gilberton ed.; bc-ad: 4 Gift Boxes; 60 pgs.	1	1	41.00	124.00	330.00
1B	20	6/44	Orig.; Courier ed.; 60 pgs.	1	1	39.00	117.00	300.00
1C	20	6/44	Orig.; Long Island Ind. ed.; 60 pgs.	1	1	39.00	117.00	300.00
2	22	–	Queens Cty. Times ed.; white logo banner; CC-r	1	1	19.00	56.00	140.00
3	28	–	CC-r	1	1	17.00	52.00	130.00
4	60	–	CI logo; no price; 48 pgs.; LDC-r	1	1	15.00	46.00	115.00
5A	62	–	LDC-r; Classics Ill. logo at top of pgs.	1	1	13.00	38.00	95.00
5B	62	–	w/o logo at top of pg. (scarcer)	1	1	14.00	42.00	105.00
6	78	–	C-price 15¢; LDC-r	1	1	12.00	36.00	90.00
7	97	–	LDC-r	1	1	11.00	32.00	80.00

21. 3 Famous Mysteries ("The Sign of the 4", "The Murders in the Rue Morgue", "The Flayed Hand")

Ed	HRN	Date	Details	A	C	GD2.0	FN6.0	NM9.4
1A	21	7/44	Orig.; Gilberton ed.; 60 pgs.	1	1	87.00	261.00	740.00
1B	21	7/44	Orig. Island Pub. Co.; 60 pgs.	1	1	89.00	268.00	760.00
1C	21	7/44	Original; Courier Ed.; 60 pgs.	1	1	76.00	229.00	650.00
2	22	–	Nassau Bulletin ed.; CC-r	1	1	35.00	104.00	260.00
3	30	–	CC-r	1	1	27.00	82.00	205.00
4	62	–	LDC-r; 8 pgs. deleted; LDC-r	1	1	21.00	64.00	160.00
5	70	–	LDC-r	1	1	19.00	58.00	145.00
6	85	–	C-price 15¢; LDC-r	1	1	17.00	50.00	125.00
7	114	–	New-c; PC-r	1	2	17.00	50.00	125.00

22. The Pathfinder

Ed	HRN	Date	Details	A	C	GD2.0	FN6.0	NM9.4
1A	22	10/44	Orig.; No printer listed; ownership statement inside fc lists Gilberton & date; 60 pgs.	1	1	42.00	127.00	340.00
1B	22	10/44	Orig.; Island Pub. ed.; 60 pgs.	1	1	39.00	116.00	290.00
1C	22	10/44	Orig.; Queens Cty Times ed. 60 pgs.	1	1	39.00	116.00	290.00
2	30	–	C-price removed; CC-r	1	1	13.00	38.00	95.00
3	60	–	Pgs. reduced to 52; LDC-r	1	1	5.00	15.00	30.00
4	70	–	LDC-r	1	1	4.00	12.00	24.00
5	85	–	C-price 15¢; LDC-r	1	1	4.00	10.00	20.00
6	118	–	LDC-r	1	1	3.60	9.00	18.00
7	132	–	LDC-r	1	1	3.00	7.50	15.00
8	146	–	LDC-r	1	1	3.00	7.50	15.00
9	167	11/63	New-c; PC-r	1	2	4.25	13.00	28.00
10	167	12/65	PC-r	1	2	3.00	7.50	15.00
11	166	8/67	PC-r	1	2	3.00	7.50	15.00

23. Oliver Twist (1st Classic produced by the Iger Shop)

Ed	HRN	Date	Details	A	C	GD2.0	FN6.0	NM9.4
1	23	7/45	Original; 60 pgs.	1	1	40.00	120.00	315.00
2A	30	–	Printers Union logo on bottom left-fc same as 23(Orig.) (very rare); CC-r	1	1	29.00	88.00	220.00
2B	30	–	Union logo omitted; CC-r	1	1	12.00	36.00	90.00
3	60	–	Pgs. reduced to 48; LDC-r	1	1	5.30	16.00	32.00
4	62	–	LDC-r	1	1	4.25	13.00	26.00
5	71	–	LDC-r	1	1	4.00	11.00	22.00
6	85	–	C-price 15¢; LDC-r	1	1	4.00	10.00	20.00
7	94	–	LDC-r	1	1	3.00	7.50	15.00
8	118	–	LDC-r	1	1	3.00	7.50	15.00
9	136	–	New-PC, old-a; PC-r	1	2	3.60	9.00	18.00
10	150	–	Old-a; PC-r	1	2	2.80	7.00	14.00
11	164	–	Old-a; PC-r	1	2	3.20	8.00	16.00
12	164	–	New-a; PC-r; Evans/Crandall-a	2	2	4.25	14.00	28.00
13	167	–	PC-r	2	2	3.00	7.50	15.00
14	167	8/64	PC-r	2	2	2.00	5.00	8.00
15	167	12/65	PC-r	2	2	2.00	5.00	8.00
16	166	R/1968	New 25¢; PC-r	2	2	2.00	5.00	8.00
17	169	Win/69	Stiff-c; PC-r	2	2	2.00	5.00	8.00

24. A Connecticut Yankee in King Arthur's Court

Ed	HRN	Date	Details	A	C	GD2.0	FN6.0	NM9.4
1	9/45	–	Original	1	1	37.00	110.00	275.00
2	30	–	No price circle; CC-r	1	1	11.00	34.00	85.00
3	60	–	8 pgs. deleted; LDC-r	1	1	5.00	15.00	30.00
4	62	–	LDC-r	1	1	4.25	13.00	26.00
5	71	–	LDC-r	1	1	4.00	11.00	24.00
6	87	–	C-price 15¢; LDC-r	1	1	4.00	10.00	20.00
7	121	–	LDC-r	1	1	3.60	9.00	18.00
8	140	–	New-c&a; PC-r	2	2	4.00	10.00	20.00
9	153	–	PC-r	2	2	2.00	5.00	9.00
10	164	–	PC-r	2	2	2.00	5.00	8.00
11	167	–	PC-r	2	2	2.00	5.00	8.00
12	167	7/64	PC-r	2	2	2.00	5.00	8.00
13	167	6/66	PC-r	2	2	2.00	5.00	8.00
14	166	R/1968	C-price 25¢; PC-r	2	2	2.00	5.00	8.00
15	169	Spr/71	PC-r; stiff-c	2	2	2.00	5.00	8.00

25. Two Years Before the Mast

Ed	HRN	Date	Details	A	C	GD2.0	FN6.0	NM9.4
1	10/45	–	Original; Webb/Heames-a&c	1	1	37.00	110.00	275.00
2	30	–	Price circle blank; CC-r	1	1	11.00	34.00	85.00
3	60	–	8 pgs. deleted; LDC-r	1	1	5.00	15.00	30.00
4	62	–	LDC-r	1	1	4.25	13.00	26.00
5	71	–	LDC-r	1	1	4.00	10.00	20.00
6	85	–	C-price 15¢; LDC-r	1	1	3.60	9.00	18.00
7	114	–	LDC-r	1	1	3.00	7.50	15.00
8	156	–	3 pgs. replaced by fillers; new-c; PC-r	1	2	4.00	10.00	20.00
9	167	12/63	PC-r	1	2	2.00	5.00	8.00
10	167	12/65	PC-r	1	2	2.00	5.00	8.00
11	166	9/67	PC-r	1	2	2.00	5.00	8.00
12	169	Win/69	C-price 25¢; stiff-c PC-r	1	2	2.00	5.00	8.00

26. Frankenstein (2nd horror comic?)

Ed	HRN	Date	Details	A	C

Classic Comics #26 © GIL

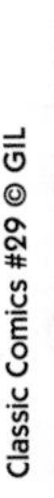

Classic Comics #29 © GIL

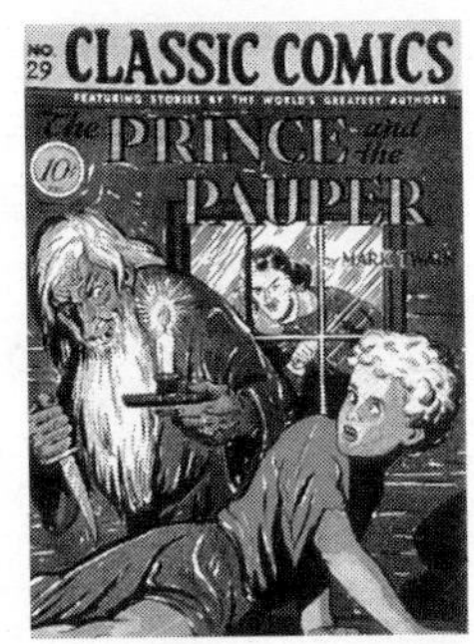

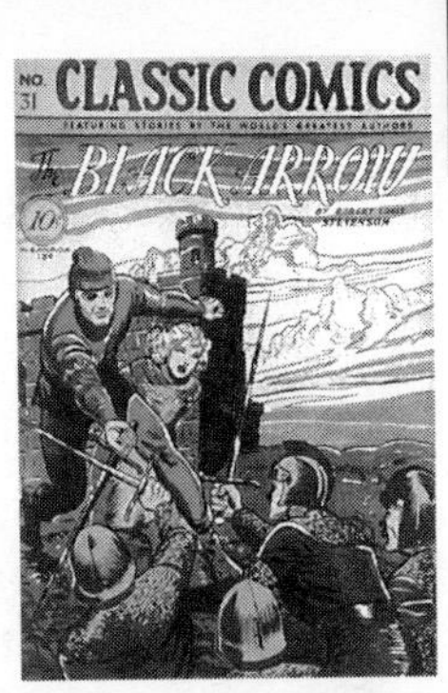

Classic Comics #31 © GIL

Ed	HRN	Date	Details	A	C	GD2.0	FN6.0	NM9.4
1	26	12/45	Orig.; Webb/Brewster a&c; 52 pgs.	1	1	88.00	265.00	750.00
2A	30	–	Price circle blank; no indicia; CC-r	1	1	27.00	80.00	200.00
2B	30	–	With indicia; scarce; CC-r	1	1	31.00	94.00	235.00
3	60	–	LDC-r	1	1	13.00	40.00	100.00
4	62	–	LDC-r	1	1	12.00	36.00	90.00
5	71	–	LDC-r	1	1	5.85	17.00	35.00
6A	82	–	C-price 15¢; soft-c LDC-r	1	1	5.00	15.00	30.00
6B	82	–	Stiff-c; LDC-r	1	1	6.30	19.00	38.00
7	117	–	LDC-r	1	1	3.60	9.00	18.00
8	146	–	New Saunders-c; PC-r	1	2	4.00	11.00	22.00
9	152	–	Scarce; PC-r	1	2	6.00	18.00	40.00
10	153	–	PC-r	1	2	2.00	5.00	9.00
11	160	–	PC-r	1	2	2.00	5.00	9.00
12	165	–	PC-r	1	2	2.00	5.00	8.00
13	167	–	PC-r	1	2	2.00	5.00	8.00
14	167	6/64	PC-r	1	2	2.00	5.00	8.00
15	167	6/65	PC-r	1	2	2.00	5.00	8.00
16	167	10/65	PC-r	1	2	2.00	5.00	8.00
17	166	9/67	PC-r	1	2	2.00	5.00	8.00
18	169	Fall/69	C-price 25¢; stiff-c PC-r	1	2	2.00	5.00	8.00
19	169	Spr/71	PC-r; stiff-c	1	2	2.00	5.00	8.00

27. The Adventures of Marco Polo

Ed	HRN	Date	Details	A	C	GD2.0	FN6.0	NM9.4
1	4/46	–	Original	1	1	39.00	117.00	300.00
2	30	–	Last 'Comics' reprint; CC-r	1	1	12.00	36.00	90.00
3	70	–	8 pgs. deleted; no c-price; LDC-r	1	1	4.25	13.00	28.00
4	87	–	C-price 15¢; LDC-r	1	1	4.00	10.00	20.00
5	117	–	LDC-r	1	1	2.80	7.00	14.00
6	154	–	New-c; PC-r	1	2	3.60	9.00	18.00
7	165	–	PC-r	1	2	2.00	5.00	8.00
8	167	4/64	PC-r	1	2	2.00	5.00	8.00
9	167	6/66	PC-r	1	2	2.00	5.00	8.00
10	169	Spr/69	New price 25¢; stiff-c; PC-r	1	2	2.00	5.00	8.00

28. Michael Strogoff

Ed	HRN	Date	Details	A	C	GD2.0	FN6.0	NM9.4
1	6/46	–	Original	1	1	39.00	117.00	310.00
2	51	–	8 pgs. cut; LDC-r	1	1	12.00	36.00	90.00
3	115	–	New-c; PC-r	1	2	4.25	13.00	26.00
4	155	–	PC-r	1	2	2.80	7.00	14.00
5	167	11/63	PC-r	1	2	2.20	5.50	11.00
6	167	7/66	PC-r	1	2	2.20	5.50	11.00
7	169	Sm/69	C-price 25¢; stiff-c PC-r	1	3	2.80	7.00	14.00

29. The Prince and the Pauper

Ed	HRN	Date	Details	A	C	GD2.0	FN6.0	NM9.4
1	7/46	–	Orig.; "Horror"-c	1	1	53.00	159.00	450.00
2	60	–	8 pgs. cut; new-c by Kiefer; LDC-r	1	2	5.80	17.00	35.00
3	62	–	LDC-r	1	2	4.25	13.00	28.00
4	71	–	LDC-r	1	2	4.00	10.00	20.00
5	93	–	LDC-r	1	2	3.60	9.00	18.00
6	114	–	LDC-r	1	2	3.00	7.50	15.00
7	128	–	New-c; PC-r	1	3	3.60	9.00	18.00
8	138	–	PC-r	1	3	2.00	5.00	9.00
9	150	–	PC-r	1	3	2.00	5.00	9.00
10	164	–	PC-r	1	3	2.00	5.00	8.00
11	167	–	PC-r	1	3	2.00	5.00	8.00
12	167	7/64	PC-r	1	3	2.00	5.00	8.00
13	167	11/65	PC-r	1	3	2.00	5.00	8.00
14	166	R/68	C-price 25¢; PC-r	1	3	2.00	5.00	8.00
15	169	Sm/70	PC-r; stiff-c	1	3	2.00	5.00	8.00

30. The Moonstone

Ed	HRN	Date	Details	A	C	GD2.0	FN6.0	NM9.4
1	9/46	–	Original; Rico-c/a	1	1	39.00	117.00	300.00
2	60	–	LDC-r; 8pgs. cut	1	1	6.00	18.00	40.00
3	70	–	LDC-r	1	1	5.80	17.00	35.00
4	155	–	New L.B. Cole-c; PC-r	1	2	6.30	19.00	38.00
5	165	–	PC-r; L.B. Cole-c	1	2	4.00	10.00	20.00
6	167	1/64	PC-r; L.B. Cole-c	1	2	2.00	5.00	10.00
7	167	9/65	PC-r; L.B. Cole-c	1	2	2.00	5.00	9.00
8	166	R/1968	C-price 25¢; PC-r	1	2	2.00	5.00	8.00

31. The Black Arrow

Ed	HRN	Date	Details	A	C	GD2.0	FN6.0	NM9.4
1	10/46	–	Original	1	1	29.00	88.00	220.00
2	51	–	Cl logo; LDC-r 8pgs. deleted	1	1	5.30	16.00	32.00
3	64	–	LDC-r	1	1	4.00	10.00	20.00
4	87	–	C-price 15¢; LDC-r	1	1	3.60	9.00	18.00
5	108	–	LDC-r	1	1	3.00	7.50	15.00
6	125	–	LDC-r	1	1	2.80	7.00	14.00
7	131	–	New-c; PC-r	1	2	3.60	9.00	18.00
8	140	–	PC-r	1	2	2.00	5.00	9.00
9	148	–	PC-r	1	2	2.00	5.00	9.00
10	161	–	PC-r	1	2	2.00	5.00	8.00
11	167	–	PC-r	1	2	2.00	5.00	8.00
12	167	7/64	PC-r	1	2	2.00	5.00	8.00
13	167	11/65	PC-r	1	2	2.00	5.00	8.00
14	166	R/1968	C-price 25¢; PC-r	1	2	2.00	5.00	8.00

32. Lorna Doone

Ed	HRN	Date	Details	A	C	GD2.0	FN6.0	NM9.4
1	12/46	–	Original; Matt Baker c&a	1	1	37.00	110.00	275.00
2	53/64	–	8 pgs. deleted; LDC-r	1	1	7.50	22.00	45.00
3	85	–	C-price 15¢; LDC-r; Baker c&a	1	1	5.80	17.00	35.00
4	118	–	LDC-r	1	1	4.00	10.00	20.00
5	138	–	New-c; old-c becomes new title pg.; PC-r	1	2	4.00	10.00	20.00
6	150	–	PC-r	1	2	2.00	5.00	8.00
7	165	–	PC-r	1	2	2.00	5.00	8.00
8	167	1/64	PC-r	1	2	2.00	5.00	10.00
9	167	11/65	PC-r	1	2	2.00	5.00	10.00
10	166	R/1968	New-c; PC-r	1	3	4.00	10.00	20.00

33. The Adventures of Sherlock Holmes

Ed	HRN	Date	Details	A	C	GD2.0	FN6.0	NM9.4
1	33	1/47	Original; Kiefer-c; contains Study in Scarlet & Hound of the Baskervilles; 68 pgs.	1	1	112.00	335.00	950.00
2	53	–	"A Study in Scarlet" (17 pgs.) deleted; LDC-r	1	1	42.00	127.00	340.00
3	71	–	LDC-r	1	1	33.00	100.00	250.00
4A	89	–	C-price 15¢; LDC-r	1	1	27.00	80.00	200.00
4B	89	–	Kiefer's name omitted from-c	1	1	28.00	84.00	210.00

34. Mysterious Island (Last "Classic Comic")

Ed	HRN	Date	Details	A	C

Classics Illustrated #37 © GIL

Classics Illustrated #39 © GIL

Classics Illustrated #42 © GIL

						GD2.0	FN6.0	NM9.4
1	2/47	–	Original; Webb/Heames-c/a	1	1	39.00	117.00	300.00
2	60	–	8 pgs. deleted; LDC-r	1	1	5.80	17.00	35.00
3	62	–	LDC-r	1	1	4.25	13.00	26.00
4	71	–	LDC-r	1	1	5.80	17.00	35.00
5	78	–	C-price 15¢ in circle; LDC-r	1	1	4.00	11.00	22.00
6	92	–	LDC-r	1	1	4.00	10.00	20.00
7	117	–	LDC-r	1	1	3.00	7.50	15.00
8	140	–	New-c; PC-r	1	2	3.60	9.00	18.00
9	156	–	PC-r	1	2	2.00	5.00	9.00
10	167	10/63	PC-r	1	2	2.00	5.00	8.00
11	167	5/64	PC-r	1	2	2.00	5.00	8.00
12	167	6/66	PC-r	1	2	2.00	5.00	8.00
13	166	R/1968	C-price 25¢; PC-r	1	2	2.00	5.00	8.00

35. Last Days of Pompeii (First "Classics Illustrated")

Ed	HRN	Date	Details	A	C	GD2.0	FN6.0	NM9.4
1	–	3/47	Original; LDC; Kiefer-c/a	1	1	39.00	117.00	300.00
2	161	–	New c&a; 15¢; PC-r; Kirby/Ayers-a	2	2	5.00	15.00	30.00
3	167	1/64	PC-r	2	2	3.20	8.00	16.00
4	167	7/66	PC-r	2	2	3.20	8.00	16.00
5	169	Spr/70	New price 25¢; stiff-c; PC-r	2	2	3.20	8.00	16.00

36. Typee

Ed	HRN	Date	Details	A	C	GD2.0	FN6.0	NM9.4
1	4/47	–	Original	1	1	21.00	62.00	155.00
2	64	–	No c-price; 8 pg. ed.; LDC-r	1	1	6.30	19.00	38.00
3	155	–	New-c; PC-r	1	2	3.60	9.00	18.00
4	167	9/63	PC-r	1	2	2.00	5.00	10.00
5	167	7/65	PC-r	1	2	2.00	5.00	10.00
6	169	Sm/69	C-price 25¢; stiff-c PC-r	1	2	2.00	5.00	10.00

37. The Pioneers

Ed	HRN	Date	Details	A	C	GD2.0	FN6.0	NM9.4
1	37	5/47	Original; Palais-c/a	1	1	15.00	44.00	110.00
2A	62	–	8 pgs. cut; LDC-r; price circle blank	1	1	4.25	13.00	26.00
2B	62	–	10¢; LDC-r;	1	1	23.00	70.00	175.00
3	70	–	LDC-r	1	1	3.60	9.00	18.00
4	92	–	15¢; LDC-r	1	1	3.00	7.50	15.00
5	118	–	LDC-r	1	1	2.80	7.00	14.00
6	131	–	LDC-r	1	1	2.80	7.00	14.00
7	132	–	LDC-r	1	1	2.80	7.00	14.00
8	153	–	LDC-r	1	1	2.80	7.00	14.00
9	167	5/64	LDC-r	1	1	2.00	5.00	10.00
10	167	6/66	LDC-r	1	1	2.00	5.00	10.00
11	166	R/1968	New-c; 25¢; PC-r	1	2	4.00	10.00	20.00

38. Adventures of Cellini

Ed	HRN	Date	Details	A	C	GD2.0	FN6.0	NM9.4
1	6/47	–	Original; Froehlich c/a	1	1	27.00	80.00	200.00
2	164	–	New-c&a; PC-r	2	2	3.60	9.00	18.00
3	167	12/63	PC-r	2	2	2.00	5.00	10.00
4	167	7/66	PC-r	2	2	2.00	5.00	10.00
5	169	Spr/70	Stiff-c; new price 25¢; PC-r	2	2	2.40	6.00	12.00

39. Jane Eyre

Ed	HRN	Date	Details	A	C	GD2.0	FN6.0	NM9.4
1	7/47	–	Original	1	1	26.00	78.00	195.00
2	60	–	No c-price; 8 pgs. cut; LDC-r	1	1	5.30	16.00	32.00
3	62	–	LDC-r	1	1	4.25	13.00	28.00
4	71	–	LDC-r; c-price 10¢	1	1	4.00	12.00	24.00
5	92	–	C-price 15¢; LDC-r	1	1	4.00	10.00	20.00
6	118	–	LDC-r	1	1	3.60	9.00	18.00
7	142	–	New-c; old-a; PC-r	1	2	4.00	11.00	22.00
8	154	–	Old-a; PC-r	1	2	3.60	9.00	18.00
9	165	–	New-a; PC-r	2	2	4.00	11.00	22.00
10	167	12/63	PC-r	2	2	3.60	9.00	18.00
11	167	4/65	PC-r	2	2	3.20	8.00	16.00
12	167	8/66	PC-r	2	2	3.20	8.00	16.00
13	166	R/1968	New-c; PC-r	2	3	7.50	22.50	45.00

40. Mysteries ("The Pit and the Pendulum", "The Advs. of Hans Pfall" & "The Fall of the House of Usher")

Ed	HRN	Date	Details	A	C	GD2.0	FN6.0	NM9.4
1	8/47	–	Original; Kiefer-c/a, Froehlich, Griffiths-a	1	1	57.00	169.00	480.00
2	62	–	LDC-r; 8pgs. cut	1	1	23.00	70.00	175.00
3	75	–	LDC-r	1	1	20.00	60.00	150.00
4	92	–	C-price 15¢; LDC-r	1	1	16.00	48.00	120.00

41. Twenty Years After

Ed	HRN	Date	Details	A	C	GD2.0	FN6.0	NM9.4
1	9/47	–	Original; 'horror'-c	1	1	39.00	117.00	300.00
2	62	–	New-c; no c-price 8 pgs. cut; LDC-r; Kiefer-c	1	2	5.80	17.00	35.00
3	78	–	C-price 15¢; LDC-r	1	2	4.15	12.50	25.00
4	156	–	New-c; PC-r	1	3	3.60	9.00	18.00
5	167	12/63	PC-r	1	3	1.60	4.00	8.00
6	167	11/66	PC-r	1	3	1.60	4.00	8.00
7	169	Spr/70	New price 25¢; stiff-c; PC-r	1	3	1.60	4.00	8.00

42. Swiss Family Robinson

Ed	HRN	Date	Details	A	C	GD2.0	FN6.0	NM9.4
1	42	10/47	Orig.; Kiefer-c&a;	1	1	19.00	58.00	145.00
2A	62	–	8 pgs. cut; outside bc: Gift Box ad; LDC-r	1	1	5.30	16.00	32.00
2B	62	–	8 pgs. cut; outside-bc: Reorder list; scarce; LDC-r	1	1	8.50	26.00	60.00
3	75	–	LDC-r	1	1	4.00	11.00	22.00
4	93	–	LDC-r	1	1	4.00	10.00	20.00
5	117	–	LDC-r	1	1	3.60	9.00	18.00
6	131	–	New-c; old-a; PC-r	1	2	3.60	9.00	18.00
7	137	–	Old-a; PC-r	1	2	2.35	7.00	14.00
8	141	–	Old-a; PC-r	1	2	2.35	7.00	14.00
9	152	–	New-a; PC-r	2	2	3.60	9.00	18.00
10	158	–	PC-r	2	2	1.60	4.00	8.00
11	165	–	PC-r	2	2	2.80	7.00	14.00
12	167	12/63	PC-r	2	2	2.00	5.00	10.00
13	167	4/65	PC-r	2	2	1.50	3.50	7.00
14	167	5/66	PC-r	2	2	1.50	3.50	7.00
15	166	11/67	PC-r	2	2	1.50	3.50	7.00
16	169	Spr/69	PC-r; stiff-c	2	2	1.50	3.50	7.00

43. Great Expectations (Used in **SOTI**, pg. 311)

Ed	HRN	Date	Details	A	C	GD2.0	FN6.0	NM9.4
1	11/47	–	Original; Kiefer-a/c	1	1	81.00	244.00	690.00
2	62	–	No c-price; 8 pgs. cut; LDC-r	1	1	47.00	141.00	400.00

44. Mysteries of Paris (Used in **SOTI**, pg. 323)

Ed	HRN	Date	Details	A	C	GD2.0	FN6.0	NM9.4
1A	44	12/47	Original; 56 pgs.; Kiefer-c/a	1	1	62.00	185.00	525.00
1B	44	12/47	Orig.; printed on	1	1	68.00	203.00	575.00

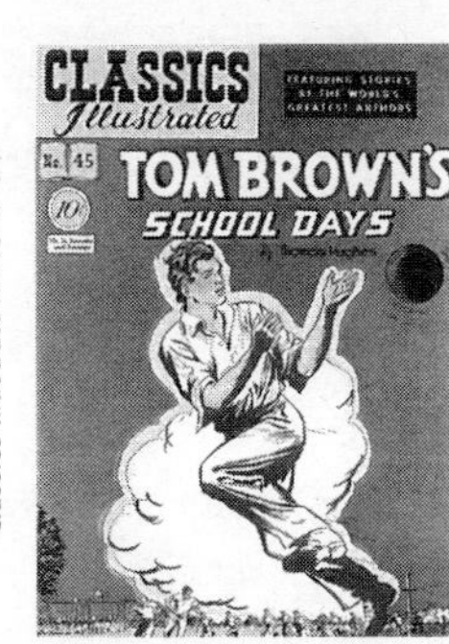

Classics Illustrated #45 © GIL

Classics Illustrated #47 © GIL

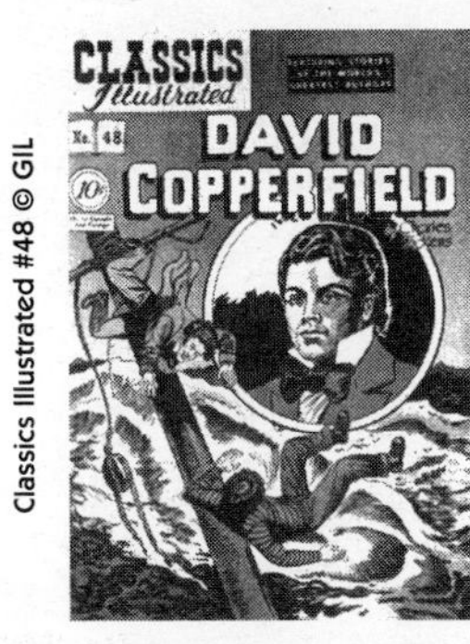

Classics Illustrated #48 © GIL

Ed	HRN	Date	Details	A	C	GD2.0	FN6.0	NM9.4
			white/heavier paper; (rare)					
2A	62	–	8 pgs. cut; outside-bc: Gift Box ad; LDC-r	1	1	27.00	80.00	200.00
2B	62	–	8 pgs. cut; outside-bc: reorder list; LDC-r	1	1	27.00	80.00	200.00
3	78	–	C-price 15¢; LDC-r	1	1	23.00	68.00	170.00

5. Tom Brown's School Days

Ed	HRN	Date	Details	A	C	GD2.0	FN6.0	NM9.4
1	44	1/48	Original; 1st 48pg. issue	1	1	13.00	38.00	95.00
2	64	–	No c-price; LDC-r	1	1	5.80	17.00	35.00
3	161	–	New-c&a; PC-r	2	2	3.00	7.50	15.00
4	167	2/64	PC-r	2	2	2.00	5.00	10.00
5	167	8/66	PC-r	2	2	2.00	5.00	10.00
6	166	R/1968	C-price 25¢; PC-r	2	2	2.00	5.00	10.00

6. Kidnapped

Ed	HRN	Date	Details	A	C	GD2.0	FN6.0	NM9.4
1	47	4/48	Original; Webb-c/a	1	1	12.00	36.00	90.00
2A	62	–	Price circle blank; LDC-r	1	1	4.25	13.00	28.00
2B	62	–	C-price 10¢; rare; LDC-r	1	1	27.00	82.00	205.00
3	78	–	C-price 15¢; LDC-r	1	1	4.00	11.00	22.00
4	87	–	LDC-r	1	1	3.60	9.00	18.00
5	118	–	LDC-r	1	1	3.00	7.50	15.00
6	131	–	New-c; PC-r	1	2	3.60	9.00	18.00
7	140	–	PC-r	1	2	2.00	5.00	9.00
8	150	–	PC-r	1	2	2.00	5.00	9.00
9	164	–	Reduced pg.width; PC-r	1	2	2.00	5.00	8.00
10	167	–	PC-r	1	2	2.00	5.00	8.00
11	167	3/64	PC-r	1	2	2.00	5.00	8.00
12	167	6/65	PC-r	1	2	2.00	5.00	8.00
13	167	12/65	PC-r	1	2	2.00	5.00	8.00
14	166	9/67	PC-r	1	2	2.00	5.00	8.00
15	166	Win/69	New price 25¢; PC-r; stiff-c	1	2	2.00	5.00	8.00
16	169	Sm/70	PC-r; stiff-c	1	2	2.00	5.00	8.00

7. Twenty Thousand Leagues Under the Sea

Ed	HRN	Date	Details	A	C	GD2.0	FN6.0	NM9.4
1	47	5/48	Orig.; Kiefer-a&c;	1	1	12.00	36.00	90.00
2	64	–	No c-price; LDC-r	1	1	4.25	13.00	28.00
3	78	–	C-price 15¢; LDC-r	1	1	4.00	10.00	20.00
4	94	–	LDC-r	1	1	3.60	9.00	18.00
5	118	–	LDC-r	1	1	3.00	7.50	15.00
6	128	–	New-c; PC-r	1	2	3.60	9.00	18.00
7	133	–	PC-r	1	2	2.40	6.00	12.00
8	140	–	PC-r	1	2	1.60	4.00	9.00
9	148	–	PC-r	1	2	1.60	4.00	9.00
10	156	–	PC-r	1	2	1.60	4.00	9.00
11	165	–	PC-r	1	2	1.60	4.00	9.00
12	167	–	PC-r	1	2	1.60	4.00	9.00
13	167	3/64	PC-r	1	2	1.60	4.00	9.00
14	167	8/65	PC-r	1	2	1.60	4.00	9.00
15	167	10/66	PC-r	1	2	1.60	4.00	9.00
16	166	R/1968	C-price 25¢; new-c PC-r	1	3	2.40	6.00	12.00
17	169	Spr/70	Stiff-c; PC-r	1	3	2.80	7.00	14.00

8. David Copperfield

Ed	HRN	Date	Details	A	C	GD2.0	FN6.0	NM9.4
1	47	6/48	Original; Kiefer-c/a	1	1	13.00	38.00	95.00
2	64	–	Price circle replaced by motif of boy reading; LDC-r	1	1	4.25	13.00	28.00
3	87	–	C-price 15¢; LDC-r	1	1	3.60	9.00	18.00
4	121	–	New-c; PC-r	1	2	3.00	7.50	15.00
5	130	–	PC-r	1	2	2.00	5.00	9.00
6	140	–	PC-r	1	2	2.00	5.00	9.00
7	148	–	PC-r	1	2	2.00	5.00	9.00
8	156	–	PC-r	1	2	2.00	5.00	9.00
9	167	–	PC-r	1	2	2.00	5.00	8.00
10	167	4/64	PC-r	1	2	2.00	5.00	8.00
11	167	6/65	PC-r	1	2	2.00	5.00	8.00
12	166	5/67	PC-r	1	2	2.00	5.00	8.00
13	166	R/67	PC-r; C-price 25¢	1	2	2.40	7.20	12.00
14	166	Spr/69	C-price 25¢; stiff-c PC-r	1	2	2.00	5.00	8.00
15	169	Win/69	Stiff-c; PC-r	1	2	2.00	5.00	8.00

49. Alice in Wonderland

Ed	HRN	Date	Details	A	C	GD2.0	FN6.0	NM9.4
1	47	7/48	Original; 1st Blum a & c	1	1	17.00	50.00	125.00
2	64	–	No c-price; LDC-r	1	1	6.30	19.00	38.00
3A	85	–	C-price 15¢; soft-c LDC-r	1	1	5.00	15.00	30.00
3B	85	–	Stiff-c; LDC-r	1	1	5.80	17.00	35.00
4	155	–	New PC, similar to orig.; PC-r	1	2	5.00	15.00	30.00
5	165	–	PC-r	1	2	4.00	11.00	22.00
6	167	3/64	PC-r	1	2	3.60	9.00	18.00
7	167	6/66	PC-r	1	2	3.60	9.00	18.00
8A	166	Fall/68	New-c; soft-c; 25¢ c-price; PC-r	1	3	5.00	15.00	30.00
8B	166	Fall/68	New-c; stiff-c; 25¢ c-price; PC-r	1	3	9.00	27.00	55.00

50. Adventures of Tom Sawyer (Used in **SOTI**, pg. 37)

Ed	HRN	Date	Details	A	C	GD2.0	FN6.0	NM9.4
1A	51	8/48	Orig.; Aldo Rubano a&c	1	1	13.00	38.00	95.00
1B	51	9/48	Orig.; Rubano c&a	1	1	13.00	38.00	95.00
1C	51	9/48	Orig.; outside-bc: blue & yellow only; rare	1	1	19.00	58.00	145.00
2	64	–	No c-price; LDC-r	1	1	4.00	12.00	24.00
3	78	–	C-price 15¢; LDC-r	1	1	3.60	9.00	18.00
4	94	–	LDC-r	1	1	3.00	7.50	15.00
5	117	–	LDC-r	1	1	2.80	7.00	14.00
6	132	–	LDC-r	1	1	2.80	7.00	14.00
7	140	–	New-c; PC-r	1	2	3.60	9.00	18.00
8	150	–	PC-r	1	2	2.00	5.00	10.00
9	164	–	New-a; PC-r	2	2	3.60	9.00	18.00
10	167	–	PC-r	2	2	2.00	5.00	10.00
11	167	1/65	PC-r	2	2	2.00	5.00	8.00
12	167	5/66	PC-r	2	2	2.00	5.00	8.00
13	166	12/67	PC-r	2	2	2.00	5.00	8.00
14	169	Fall/69	C-price 25¢; stiff-c; PC-r	2	2	2.00	5.00	8.00
15	169	Win/71	PC-r	2	2	2.00	5.00	8.00

51. The Spy

Ed	HRN	Date	Details	A	C	GD2.0	FN6.0	NM9.4
1A	51	9/48	Original; inside-bc illo: Christmas Carol	1	1	11.00	34.00	85.00
1B	51	9/48	Original; inside-bc illo: Man in Iron Mask	1	1	11.00	34.00	85.00
1C	51	8/48	Original; outside-bc: full color	1	1	11.00	34.00	85.00
1D	51	8/48	Original; outside-bc: blue & yellow only;	1	1	15.00	46.00	115.00

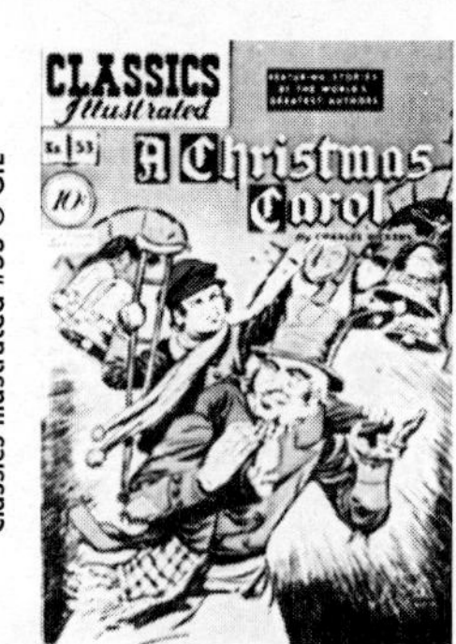

Classics Illustrated #53 © GIL

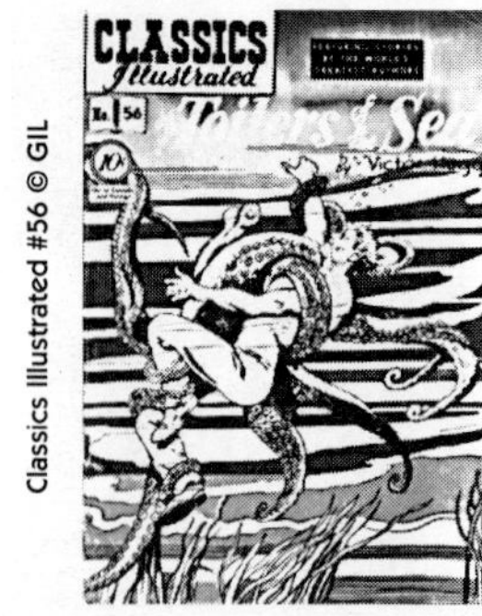

Classics Illustrated #56 © GIL

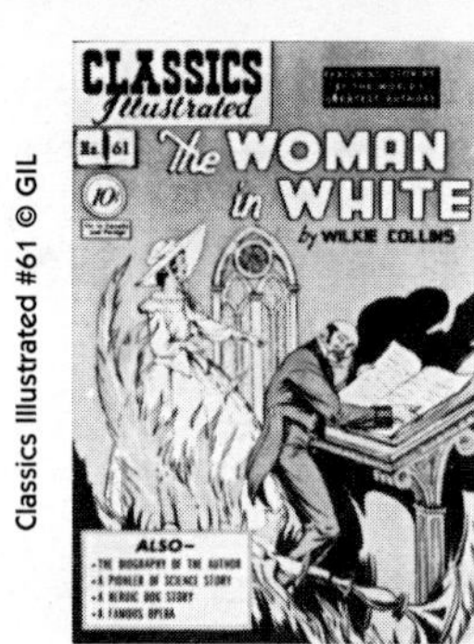

Classics Illustrated #61 © GIL

Ed	HRN	Date	Details	A	C	GD2.0	FN6.0	NM9.4
			scarce					
2	89	–	C-price 15¢; LDC-r	1	1	4.00	11.00	22.00
3	121	–	LDC-r	1	1	3.60	9.00	18.00
4	139	–	New-c; PC-r	1	2	3.60	9.00	18.00
5	156	–	PC-r	1	2	2.00	5.00	9.00
6	167	11/63	PC-r	1	2	2.00	5.00	8.00
7	167	7/66	PC-r	1	2	2.00	5.00	8.00
8A	166	Win/69	C-price 25¢; soft-c; scarce; PC-r	1	2	4.00	10.00	20.00
8B	166	Win/69	C-price 25¢; stiff-c; PC-r	1	2	2.00	5.00	8.00

52. The House of the Seven Gables

Ed	HRN	Date	Details	A	C	GD2.0	FN6.0	NM9.4
1	53	10/48	Orig.; Griffiths a&c	1	1	11.00	34.00	85.00
2	89	–	C-price 15¢; LDC-r	1	1	4.00	11.00	22.00
3	121	–	LDC-r	1	1	3.60	9.00	18.00
4	142	–	New-c&a; PC-r; Woodbridge-a	2	2	4.00	10.00	20.00
5	156	–	PC-r	2	2	2.00	5.00	9.00
6	165	–	PC-r	2	2	2.00	5.00	8.00
7	167	5/64	PC-r	2	2	2.00	5.00	10.00
8	167	3/66	PC-r	2	2	2.00	5.00	8.00
9	166	R/1968	C-price 25¢; PC-r	2	2	2.00	5.00	8.00
10	169	Spr/70	Stiff-c; PC-r	2	2	2.00	5.00	8.00

53. A Christmas Carol

Ed	HRN	Date	Details	A	C	GD2.0	FN6.0	NM9.4
1	53	11/48	Original & only ed; Kiefer-c/a	1	1	15.00	46.00	115.00

54. Man in the Iron Mask

Ed	HRN	Date	Details	A	C	GD2.0	FN6.0	NM9.4
1	55	12/48	Original; Froehlich-a, Kiefer-c	1	1	11.00	32.00	80.00
2	93	–	C-price 15¢; LDC-r	1	1	4.25	13.00	26.00
3A	111	–	(O) logo lettering; scarce; LDC-r	1	1	5.85	17.00	35.00
3B	111	–	New logo as PC; LDC-r	1	1	4.00	12.00	24.00
4	142	–	New-c&a; PC-r	2	2	4.00	10.00	20.00
5	154	–	PC-r	2	2	2.00	5.00	9.00
6	165	–	PC-r	2	2	2.00	5.00	8.00
7	167	5/64	PC-r	2	2	2.00	5.00	8.00
8	167	4/66	PC-r	2	2	2.00	5.00	8.00
9A	166	Win/69	C-price 25¢; soft-c PC-r	2	2	4.00	10.00	20.00
9B	166	Win/69	Stiff-c	2	2	2.00	5.00	8.00

55. Silas Marner (Used in **SOTI**, pgs. 311, 312)

Ed	HRN	Date	Details	A	C	GD2.0	FN6.0	NM9.4
1	55	1/49	Original-Kiefer-c	1	1	11.00	34.00	85.00
2	75	–	Price circle blank; 'Coming Next' ad; LDC-r	1	1	4.25	13.00	28.00
3	97	–	LDC-r	1	1	3.60	9.00	18.00
4	121	–	New-c; PC-r	1	2	3.60	9.00	18.00
5	130	–	PC-r	1	2	2.00	5.00	9.00
6	140	–	PC-r	1	2	2.00	5.00	9.00
7	154	–	PC-r	1	2	2.00	5.00	9.00
8	165	–	PC-r	1	2	2.00	5.00	8.00
9	167	2/64	PC-r	1	2	2.00	5.00	8.00
10	167	6/65	PC-r	1	2	2.00	5.00	8.00
11	166	5/67	PC-r	1	2	2.00	5.00	8.00
12A	166	Win/69	C-price 25¢; soft-c PC-r	1	2	4.00	10.00	20.00
12B	166	Win/69	C-price 25¢; stiff-c PC-r	1	2	2.00	5.00	8.00

56. The Toilers of the Sea

Ed	HRN	Date	Details	A	C	GD2.0	FN6.0	NM9.4
1	55	2/49	Original; A.M. Froehlich-c/a	1	1	20.00	60.00	150.00
2	165	–	New-c&a; PC-r; Angelo Torres-a	2	2	5.80	17.00	35.00
3	167	3/64	PC-r	2	2	4.00	10.00	20.00
4	167	10/66	PC-r	2	2	4.00	10.00	20.00

57. The Song of Hiawatha

Ed	HRN	Date	Details	A	C	GD2.0	FN6.0	NM9.4
1	55	3/49	Original; Alex Blum-c/a	1	1	11.00	34.00	85.00
2	75	–	No c-price w/15¢ sticker; 'Coming Next' ad; LDC-r	1	1	4.25	13.00	28.00
3	94	–	C-price 15¢; LDC-r	1	1	4.00	11.00	22.00
4	118	–	LDC-r	1	1	3.60	9.00	18.00
5	134	–	New-c; PC-r	1	2	3.60	9.00	18.00
6	139	–	PC-r	1	2	2.00	5.00	9.00
7	154	–	PC-r	1	2	2.00	5.00	9.00
8	167	–	Has orig.date; PC-r	1	2	2.00	5.00	8.00
9	167	9/64	PC-r	1	2	2.00	5.00	8.00
10	167	10/65	PC-r	1	2	2.00	5.00	8.00
11	166	F/1968	C-price 25¢; PC-r	1	2	2.00	5.00	8.00

58. The Prairie

Ed	HRN	Date	Details	A	C	GD2.0	FN6.0	NM9.4
1	60	4/49	Original; Palais c/a	1	1	11.00	34.00	85.00
2A	62	–	No c-price; no coming-next ad; LDC-r	1	1	6.40	19.00	45.00
2B	62		10¢ (rare)	1	1	15.00	46.00	115.00
3	78	–	C-price 15¢ in dbl. circle; LDC-r	1	1	4.00	11.00	22.00
4	114	–	LDC-r	1	1	3.60	9.00	18.00
5	131	–	LDC-r	1	1	3.00	7.50	15.00
6	132	–	LDC-r	1	1	3.00	7.50	15.00
7	146	–	New-c; PC-r	1	2	3.60	9.00	18.00
8	155	–	PC-r	1	2	2.00	5.00	9.00
9	167	5/64	PC-r	1	2	2.00	5.00	8.00
10	167	4/66	PC-r	1	2	2.00	5.00	8.00
11	169	Sm/69	New price 25¢; stiff-c; PC-r	1	2	2.00	5.00	8.00

59. Wuthering Heights

Ed	HRN	Date	Details	A	C	GD2.0	FN6.0	NM9.4
1	60	5/49	Original; Kiefer-c/a	1	1	13.00	38.00	95.00
2	85	–	C-price 15¢; LDC-r	1	1	5.30	16.00	32.00
3	156	–	New-c; PC-r	1	2	4.00	10.00	20.00
4	167	1/64	PC-r	1	2	2.00	5.00	10.00
5	167	10/66	PC-r	1	2	2.00	5.00	10.00
6	169	Sm/69	C-price 25¢; stiff-c; PC-r	1	2	2.00	5.00	10.00

60. Black Beauty

Ed	HRN	Date	Details	A	C	GD2.0	FN6.0	NM9.4
1	62	6/49	Original; Froehlich-c/a	1	1	11.00	34.00	85.00
2	62	–	No c-price; no coming-next ad; LDC-r (rare)	1	1	14.00	42.00	105.00
3	85	–	C-price 15¢; LDC-r	1	1	4.25	13.00	26.00
4	158	–	New L.B. Cole-c/a; PC-r	2	2	5.00	15.00	30.00
5	167	2/64	PC-r	2	2	2.80	7.00	14.00
6	167	3/66	PC-r	2	2	2.80	7.00	14.00
7	166	R/1968	New-c&price, 25¢; PC-r	2	3	6.80	20.00	48.00

61. The Woman in White

Classics Illustrated #64 © GIL

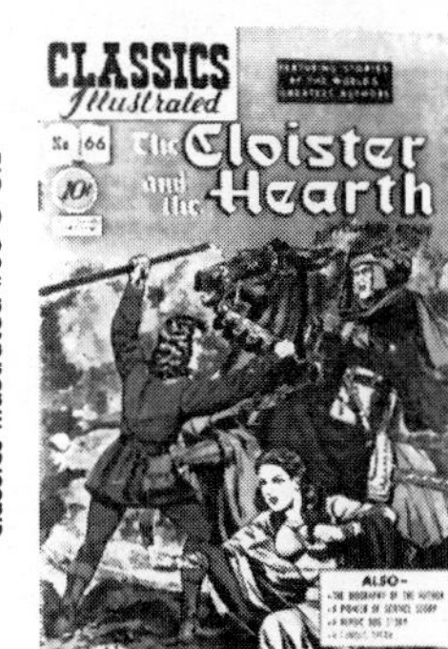

Classics Illustrated #66 © GIL

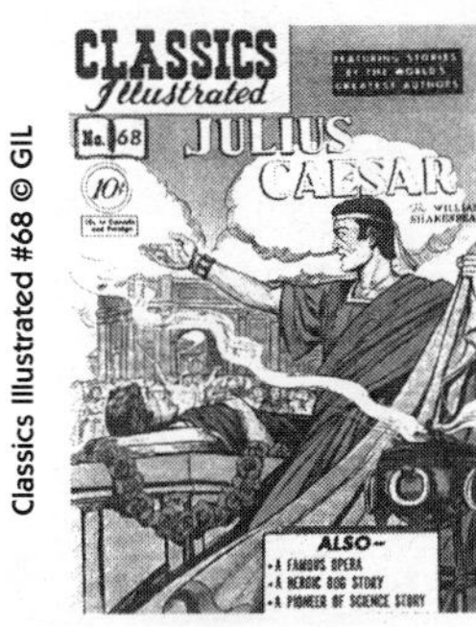

Classics Illustrated #68 © GIL

Ed	HRN	Date	Details	A	C	GD2.0	FN6.0	NM9.4
1A	62	7/49	Original; Blum-c/a fc-purple; bc: top illos light blue	1	1	13.00	38.00	95.00
1B	62	7/49	Original; Blum-c/a fc-pink; bc: top illos light violet	1	1	13.00	38.00	95.00
2	156	–	New-c; PC-r	1	2	4.00	12.00	24.00
3	167	1/64	PC-r	1	2	3.00	7.50	15.00
4	166	R/1968	C-price 25¢; PC-r	1	2	3.00	7.50	15.00

62. Western Stories ("The Luck of Roaring Camp" and "The Outcasts of Poker Flat")

Ed	HRN	Date	Details	A	C	GD2.0	FN6.0	NM9.4
1	62	8/49	Original; Kiefer-c/a	1	1	11.00	32.00	80.00
2	89	–	C-price 15¢; LDC-r	1	1	4.25	13.00	26.00
3	121	–	LDC-r	1	1	4.00	10.00	20.00
4	137	–	New-c; PC-r	1	2	3.60	9.00	18.00
5	152	–	PC-r	1	2	2.00	5.00	8.00
6	167	10/63	PC-r	1	2	2.00	5.00	8.00
7	167	6/64	PC-r	1	2	2.00	5.00	8.00
8	167	11/66	PC-r	1	2	2.00	5.00	8.00
9	166	R/1968	New-c&price 25¢; PC-r	1	3	3.60	9.00	18.00

63. The Man Without a Country

Ed	HRN	Date	Details	A	C	GD2.0	FN6.0	NM9.4
1	62	9/49	Original; Kiefer-c/a	1	1	11.00	34.00	85.00
2	78	–	C-price 15¢ in double circle; LDC-r	1	1	4.25	13.00	26.00
3	156	–	New-c, old-a; PC-r	1	2	4.00	11.00	22.00
4	165	–	New-a & text pgs.; PC-r; A. Torres-a	2	2	4.00	10.00	20.00
5	167	3/64	PC-r	2	2	2.00	5.00	8.00
6	167	8/66	PC-r	2	2	2.00	5.00	8.00
7	169	Sm/69	New price 25¢; stiff-c; PC-r	2	2	2.00	5.00	8.00

64. Treasure Island

Ed	HRN	Date	Details	A	C	GD2.0	FN6.0	NM9.4
1	62	10/49	Original; Blum-c/a	1	1	12.00	36.00	85.00
2A	82	–	C-price 15¢; soft-c LDC-r	1	1	4.00	12.00	24.00
2B	82	–	Stiff-c; LDC-r	1	1	4.35	13.00	26.00
3	117	–	LDC-r	1	1	4.00	10.00	20.00
4	131	–	New-c; PC-r	1	2	3.60	9.00	18.00
5	138	–	PC-r	1	2	2.00	5.00	9.00
6	146	–	PC-r	1	2	2.00	5.00	9.00
7	158	–	PC-r	1	2	2.00	5.00	9.00
8	165	–	PC-r	1	2	2.00	5.00	8.00
9	167	–	PC-r	1	2	2.00	5.00	8.00
10	167	6/64	PC-r	1	2	2.00	5.00	8.00
11	167	12/65	PC-r	1	2	2.00	5.00	8.00
12A	166	10/67	PC-r	1	2	2.00	5.00	8.00
12B	166	10/67	w/Grit ad stapled in book	1	2	11.00	34.00	85.00
13	169	Spr/69	New price 25¢; stiff-c; PC-r	1	2	2.00	5.00	9.00
14	–	1989	Long John Silver's Seafood Shoppes; $1.95, First/Berkley Publ.; Blum-r	1	2		.80	2.00

65. Benjamin Franklin

Ed	HRN	Date	Details	A	C	GD2.0	FN6.0	NM9.4
1	64	11/49	Original; Kiefer-c; Iger Shop-a	1	1	11.00	34.00	85.00
2	131	–	New-c; PC-r	1	2	4.00	10.00	20.00
3	154	–	PC-r	1	2	2.00	5.00	10.00
4	167	2/64	PC-r	1	2	2.00	5.00	9.00
5	167	4/66	PC-r	1	2	2.00	5.00	9.00
6	169	Fall/69	New price 25¢; stiff-c; PC-r	1	2	2.00	5.00	9.00

66. The Cloister and the Hearth

Ed	HRN	Date	Details	A	C	GD2.0	FN6.0	NM9.4
1	67	12/49	Original & only ed; Kiefer-a & c	1	1	23.00	70.00	175.00

67. The Scottish Chiefs

Ed	HRN	Date	Details	A	C	GD2.0	FN6.0	NM9.4
1	67	1/50	Original; Blum-a&c	1	1	10.00	30.00	75.00
2	85	–	C-price 15¢; LDC-r	1	1	4.25	13.00	26.00
3	118	–	LDC-r	1	1	4.00	10.00	20.00
4	136	–	New-c; PC-r	1	2	4.00	10.00	20.00
5	154	–	PC-r	1	2	2.00	5.00	10.00
6	167	11/63	PC-r	1	2	2.40	6.00	12.00
7	167	8/65	PC-r	1	2	2.00	5.00	10.00

68. Julius Caesar (Used in **SOTI**, pgs. 36, 37)

Ed	HRN	Date	Details	A	C	GD2.0	FN6.0	NM9.4
1	70	2/50	Original; Kiefer-c/a	1	1	9.30	28.00	70.00
2	85	–	C-price 15¢; LDC-r	1	1	4.00	12.00	24.00
3	108	–	LDC-r	1	1	3.60	10.00	20.00
4	156	–	New L.B. Cole-c; PC-r	1	2	4.00	11.00	22.00
5	165	–	New-a by Evans, Crandall; PC-r	2	2	4.00	11.00	22.00
6	167	2/64	PC-r	2	2	2.00	5.00	8.00
7	167	10/65	Tarzan books inside cover; PC-r	2	2	2.00	5.00	8.00
8	166	R/1967	PC-r	2	2	2.00	5.00	8.00
9	169	Win/69	PC-r; stiff-c	2	2	2.00	5.00	8.00

69. Around the World in 80 Days

Ed	HRN	Date	Details	A	C	GD2.0	FN6.0	NM9.4
1	70	3/50	Original; Kiefer-c/a	1	1	9.30	28.00	70.00
2	87	–	C-price 15¢; LDC-r	1	1	4.00	12.00	24.00
3	125	–	LDC-r	1	1	4.00	10.00	20.00
4	136	–	New-c; PC-r	1	2	4.00	10.00	20.00
5	146	–	PC-r	1	2	2.00	5.00	9.00
6	152	–	PC-r	1	2	2.00	5.00	9.00
7	164	–	PC-r	1	2	2.00	5.00	8.00
8	167	–	PC-r	1	2	2.00	5.00	8.00
9	167	7/64	PC-r	1	2	2.00	5.00	8.00
10	167	11/65	PC-r	1	2	2.00	5.00	8.00
11	166	7/67	PC-r	1	2	2.00	5.00	8.00
12	169	Spr/69	C-price 25¢; stiff-c; PC-r	1	2	2.00	5.00	8.00

70. The Pilot

Ed	HRN	Date	Details	A	C	GD2.0	FN6.0	NM9.4
1	71	4/50	Original; Blum-c/a	1	1	9.00	26.00	65.00
2	92	–	C-price 15¢; LDC-r	1	1	4.25	13.00	26.00
3	125	–	LDC-r	1	1	4.00	10.00	20.00
4	156	–	New-c; PC-r	1	2	4.00	11.00	22.00
5	167	2/64	PC-r	1	2	2.80	7.00	14.00
6	167	5/66	PC-r	1	2	2.20	5.50	11.00

71. The Man Who Laughs

Ed	HRN	Date	Details	A	C	GD2.0	FN6.0	NM9.4
1	71	5/50	Original; Blum-c/a	1	1	15.00	46.00	115.00
2	165	–	New-c&a; PC-r	2	2	9.00	26.00	65.00
3	167	4/64	PC-r	2	2	8.00	24.00	55.00

72. The Oregon Trail

Ed	HRN	Date	Details	A	C	GD2.0	FN6.0	NM9.4
1	73	6/50	Original; Kiefer-c/a	1	1	9.00	26.00	65.00
2	89	–	C-price 15¢; LDC-r	1	1	4.25	13.00	26.00
3	121	–	LDC-r	1	1	4.00	10.00	20.00
4	131	–	New-c; PC-r	1	2	4.00	10.00	20.00

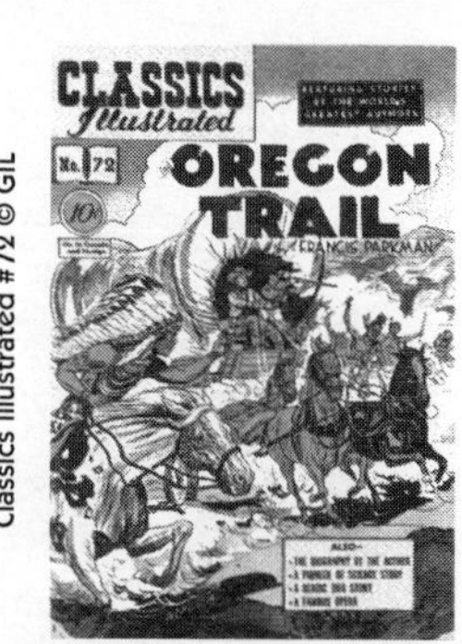

Classics Illustrated #72 © GIL

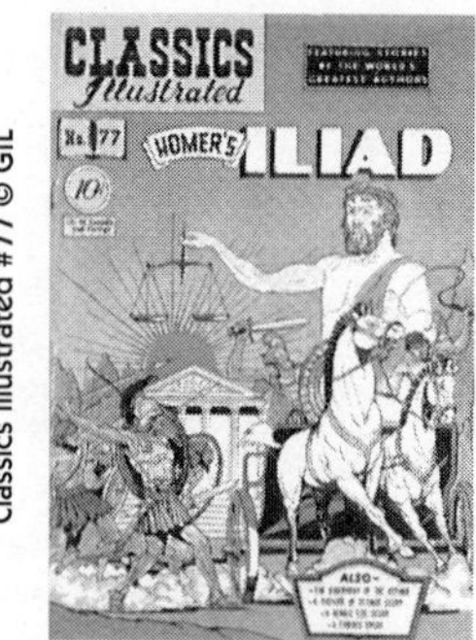

Classics Illustrated #77 © GIL

Classics Illustrated #78 © GIL

Ed	HRN	Date	Details	A	C	GD2.0	FN6.0	NM9.4
5	140	–	PC-r	1	2	2.00	5.00	9.00
6	150	–	PC-r	1	2	2.00	5.00	9.00
7	164	–	PC-r	1	2	2.00	5.00	8.00
8	167	–	PC-r	1	2	2.00	5.00	8.00
9	167	8/64	PC-r	1	2	2.00	5.00	8.00
10	167	10/65	PC-r	1	2	2.00	5.00	8.00
11	166	R/1968	C-price 25¢; PC-r	1	2	2.00	5.00	8.00

73. The Black Tulip

Ed	HRN	Date	Details	A	C	GD2.0	FN6.0	NM9.4
1	75	7/50	1st & only ed.; Alex Blum-c/a	1	1	30.00	90.00	225.00

74. Mr. Midshipman Easy

Ed	HRN	Date	Details	A	C	GD2.0	FN6.0	NM9.4
1	75	8/50	1st & only edition	1	1	30.00	90.00	225.00

75. The Lady of the Lake

Ed	HRN	Date	Details	A	C	GD2.0	FN6.0	NM9.4
1	75	9/50	Original; Kiefer-c/a	1	1	9.00	26.00	65.00
2	85	–	C-price 15¢; LDC-r	1	1	4.25	13.00	28.00
3	118	–	LDC-r	1	1	4.00	11.00	22.00
4	139	–	New-c; PC-r	1	2	4.00	10.00	20.00
5	154	–	PC-r	1	2	2.00	5.00	9.00
6	165	–	PC-r	1	2	2.00	5.00	8.00
7	167	4/64	PC-r	1	2	2.00	5.00	8.00
8	167	5/66	PC-r	1	2	2.00	5.00	8.00
9	169	Spr/69	New price 25¢; stiff-c; PC-r	1	2	2.00	5.00	8.00

76. The Prisoner of Zenda

Ed	HRN	Date	Details	A	C	GD2.0	FN6.0	NM9.4
1	75	10/50	Original; Kiefer-c/a	1	1	8.50	26.00	60.00
2	85	–	C-price 15¢; LDC-r	1	1	4.25	13.00	26.00
3	111	–	LDC-r	1	1	4.00	10.00	20.00
4	128	–	New-c; PC-r	1	2	4.00	10.00	20.00
5	152	–	PC-r	1	2	2.00	5.00	9.00
6	165	–	PC-r	1	2	2.00	5.00	8.00
7	167	4/64	PC-r	1	2	2.00	5.00	8.00
8	167	9/66	PC-r	1	2	2.00	5.00	8.00
9	169	Fall/69	New price 25¢; stiff-c; PC-r	1	2	2.00	5.00	8.00

77. The Iliad

Ed	HRN	Date	Details	A	C	GD2.0	FN6.0	NM9.4
1	78	11/50	Original; Blum-c/a	1	1	8.50	26.00	60.00
2	87	–	C-price 15¢; LDC-r	1	1	4.25	13.00	28.00
3	121	–	LDC-r	1	1	4.00	10.00	20.00
4	139	–	New-c; PC-r	1	2	3.60	9.00	18.00
5	150	–	PC-r	1	2	2.00	5.00	9.00
6	165	–	PC-r	1	2	2.00	5.00	8.00
7	167	10/63	PC-r	1	2	2.00	5.00	8.00
8	167	7/64	PC-r	1	2	2.00	5.00	8.00
9	167	5/66	PC-r	1	2	2.00	5.00	8.00
10	166	R/1968	C-price 25¢; PC-r	1	2	2.00	5.00	8.00

78. Joan of Arc

Ed	HRN	Date	Details	A	C	GD2.0	FN6.0	NM9.4
1	78	12/50	Original; Kiefer-c/a	1	1	8.50	26.00	60.00
2	87	–	C-price 15¢; LDC-r	1	1	4.25	13.00	26.00
3	113	–	LDC-r	1	1	4.00	10.00	20.00
4	128	–	New-c; PC-r	1	2	4.00	10.00	20.00
5	140	–	PC-r	1	2	2.00	5.00	9.00
6	150	–	PC-r	1	2	2.00	5.00	9.00
7	159	–	PC-r	1	2	2.00	5.00	9.00
8	167	–	PC-r	1	2	2.00	5.00	8.00
9	167	12/63	PC-r	1	2	2.00	5.00	8.00
10	167	6/65	PC-r	1	2	2.00	5.00	8.00
11	166	6/67	PC-r	1	2	2.00	5.00	8.00
12	166	Win/69	New-c&price, 25¢; PC-r; stiff-c	1	3	4.00	11.00	22.00

79. Cyrano de Bergerac

Ed	HRN	Date	Details	A	C	GD2.0	FN6.0	NM9.4
1	78	1/51	Orig.; movie promo inside front-c; Blum-c/a	1	1	8.50	26.00	60.00
2	85	–	C-price 15¢; LDC-r	1	1	4.25	13.00	26.00
3	118	–	LDC-r	1	1	4.00	10.00	20.00
4	133	–	New-c; PC-r	1	2	4.00	10.00	20.00
5	156	–	PC-r	1	2	2.80	7.00	14.00
6	167	8/64	PC-r	1	2	2.80	7.00	14.00

80. White Fang (Last line drawn cover)

Ed	HRN	Date	Details	A	C	GD2.0	FN6.0	NM9.4
1	79	2/51	Orig.; Blum-c/a	1	1	8.50	26.00	60.00
2	87	–	C-price 15¢; LDC-r	1	1	4.25	13.00	28.00
3	125	–	LDC-r	1	1	4.00	10.00	20.00
4	132	–	New-c; PC-r	1	2	3.60	9.00	18.00
5	140	–	PC-r	1	2	2.00	5.00	9.00
6	153	–	PC-r	1	2	2.00	5.00	9.00
7	167	–	PC-r	1	2	2.00	5.00	8.00
8	167	9/64	PC-r	1	2	2.00	5.00	8.00
9	167	7/65	PC-r	1	2	2.00	5.00	8.00
10	166	6/67	PC-r	1	2	2.00	5.00	8.00
11	169	Fall/69	New price 25¢; PC-r; stiff-c	1	2	2.00	5.00	8.00

81. The Odyssey (1st painted cover)

Ed	HRN	Date	Details	A	C	GD2.0	FN6.0	NM9.4
1	82	3/51	First 15¢ Original; Blum-c	1	1	8.00	24.00	55.00
2	167	8/64	PC-r	1	1	2.80	7.00	14.00
3	167	10/66	PC-r	1	1	2.80	7.00	14.00
4	169	Spr/69	New, stiff-c; PC-r	1	2	4.00	10.00	20.00

82. The Master of Ballantrae

Ed	HRN	Date	Details	A	C	GD2.0	FN6.0	NM9.4
1	82	4/51	Original; Blum-c	1	1	6.30	19.00	38.00
2	167	8/64	PC-r	1	1	3.60	9.00	18.00
3	166	Fall/68	New, stiff-c; PC-r	1	2	4.00	10.00	20.00

83. The Jungle Book

Ed	HRN	Date	Details	A	C	GD2.0	FN6.0	NM9.4
1	85	5/51	Original; Blum-c Bossert/Blum-a	1	1	6.30	19.00	38.00
2	110	–	PC-r	1	1	2.00	6.00	12.00
3	125	–	PC-r	1	1	2.00	5.00	9.00
4	134	–	PC-r	1	1	2.00	5.00	9.00
5	142	–	PC-r	1	1	2.00	5.00	9.00
6	150	–	PC-r	1	1	2.00	5.00	9.00
7	159	–	PC-r	1	1	2.00	5.00	9.00
8	167	–	PC-r	1	1	2.00	5.00	8.00
9	167	3/65	PC-r	1	1	2.00	5.00	8.00
10	167	11/65	PC-r	1	1	2.00	5.00	8.00
11	167	5/66	PC-r	1	1	2.00	5.00	8.00
12	166	R/1968	New c&a; stiff-c; PC-r	2	2	4.00	10.00	20.00

84. The Gold Bug and Other Stories ("The Gold Bug", "The Tell-Tale Heart", "The Cask of Amontillado")

Ed	HRN	Date	Details	A	C	GD2.0	FN6.0	NM9.4
1	85	6/51	Original; Blum-c/a; Palais, Laverly-a	1	1	10.00	30.00	75.00
2	167	7/64	PC-r	1	1	9.30	28.00	65.00

85. The Sea Wolf

Ed	HRN	Date	Details	A	C	GD2.0	FN6.0	NM9.4
1	85	7/51	Original; Blum-c/a	1	1	4.25	13.00	28.00
2	121	–	PC-r	1	1	2.00	5.00	9.00
3	132	–	PC-r	1	1	2.00	5.00	9.00
4	141	–	PC-r	1	1	2.00	5.00	9.00
5	161	–	PC-r	1	1	2.00	5.00	8.00

Classics Illustrated #87 © GIL

Classics Illustrated #89 © GIL

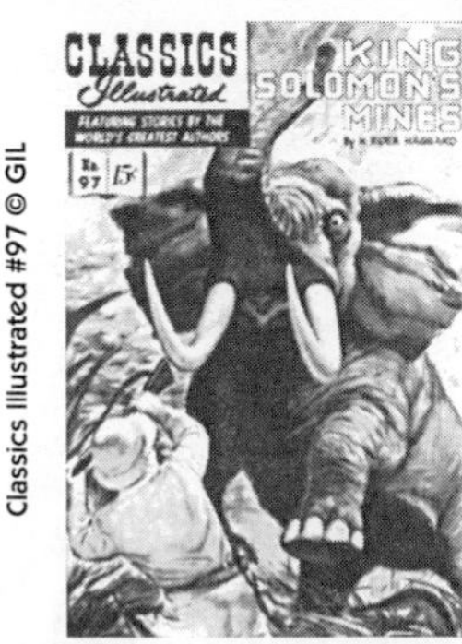

Classics Illustrated #97 © GIL

Ed	HRN	Date	Details	A	C	GD2.0	FN6.0	NM9.4
6	167	2/64	PC-r	1	1	2.00	5.00	8.00
7	167	11/65	PC-r	1	1	2.00	5.00	8.00
8	169	Fall/69	New price 25¢; stiff-c; PC-r	1	1	2.00	5.00	8.00

86. Under Two Flags

Ed	HRN	Date	Details	A	C	GD2.0	FN6.0	NM9.4
1	87	8/51	Original; first delBourgo-a	1	1	4.25	13.00	26.00
2	117	–	PC-r	1	1	2.00	6.00	12.00
3	139	–	PC-r	1	1	2.00	5.00	10.00
4	158	–	PC-r	1	1	2.00	5.00	10.00
5	167	2/64	PC-r	1	1	2.00	5.00	8.00
6	167	8/66	PC-r	1	1	2.00	5.00	8.00
7	169	Sm/69	New price 25¢; stiff-c; PC-r	1	1	2.00	5.00	8.00

87. A Midsummer Nights Dream

Ed	HRN	Date	Details	A	C	GD2.0	FN6.0	NM9.4
1	87	9/51	Original; Blum c/a	1	1	4.25	13.00	28.00
2	161	–	PC-r	1	1	2.00	5.00	9.00
3	167	4/64	PC-r	1	1	2.00	5.00	8.00
4	167	5/66	PC-r	1	1	2.00	5.00	8.00
5	169	Sm/69	New price 25¢; stiff-c; PC-r	1	1	2.00	5.00	8.00

88. Men of Iron

Ed	HRN	Date	Details	A	C	GD2.0	FN6.0	NM9.4
1	89	10/51	Original	1	1	4.25	13.00	28.00
2	154	–	PC-r	1	1	2.00	5.00	10.00
3	167	1/64	PC-r	1	1	2.00	5.00	8.00
4	166	R/1968	C-price 25¢; PC-r	1	1	2.00	5.00	8.00

89. Crime and Punishment (Cover illo. in **POP**)

Ed	HRN	Date	Details	A	C	GD2.0	FN6.0	NM9.4
1	89	11/51	Original; Palais-a	1	1	5.00	15.00	30.00
2	152	–	PC-r	1	1	2.00	5.00	10.00
3	167	4/64	PC-r	1	1	2.00	5.00	8.00
4	167	5/66	PC-r	1	1	2.00	5.00	8.00
5	169	Fall/69	New price 25¢ stiff-c; PC-r	1	1	2.00	5.00	8.00

90. Green Mansions

Ed	HRN	Date	Details	A	C	GD2.0	FN6.0	NM9.4
1	89	12/51	Original; Blum-c/a	1	1	4.25	13.00	28.00
2	148	–	New L.B. Cole-c; PC-r	1	2	3.00	7.50	15.00
3	165	–	PC-r	1	2	2.00	5.00	8.00
4	167	4/64	PC-r	1	2	2.00	5.00	8.00
5	167	9/66	PC-r	1	2	2.00	5.00	8.00
6	169	Sm/69	New price 25¢; stiff-c; PC-r	1	2	2.00	5.00	8.00

91. The Call of the Wild

Ed	HRN	Date	Details	A	C	GD2.0	FN6.0	NM9.4
1	92	1/52	Orig.; delBourgo-a	1	1	4.25	13.00	28.00
2	112	–	PC-r	1	1	2.00	5.00	10.00
3	125	–	'Picture Progress' on back-c; PC-r	1	1	2.00	5.00	10.00
4	134	–	PC-r	1	1	2.00	5.00	10.00
5	143	–	PC-r	1	1	2.00	5.00	10.00
6	165	–	PC-r	1	1	2.00	5.00	10.00
7	167	–	PC-r	1	1	2.00	5.00	8.00
8	167	4/65	PC-r	1	1	2.00	5.00	8.00
9	167	3/66	PC-r	1	1	2.00	5.00	8.00
10	166	11/67	PC-r	1	1	2.00	5.00	8.00
11	169	Spr/70	New price 25¢; stiff-c; PC-r	1	1	2.00	5.00	8.00

92. The Courtship of Miles Standish

Ed	HRN	Date	Details	A	C	GD2.0	FN6.0	NM9.4
1	92	2/52	Original; Blum-c/a	1	1	4.25	13.00	26.00
2	165	–	PC-r	1	1	2.00	5.00	9.00
3	167	3/64	PC-r	1	1	2.00	5.00	9.00
4	166	5/67	PC-r	1	1	2.00	5.00	9.00
5	169	Win/69	New price 25¢ stiff-c; PC-r	1	1	2.00	5.00	9.00

93. Pudd'nhead Wilson

Ed	HRN	Date	Details	A	C	GD2.0	FN6.0	NM9.4
1	94	3/52	Orig.; Kiefer-c/a;	1	1	4.25	13.00	28.00
2	165	–	New-c; PC-r	1	2	2.40	6.00	12.00
3	167	3/64	PC-r	1	2	2.00	5.00	10.00
4	166	R/1968	New price 25¢; soft-c; PC-r	1	2	2.00	5.00	10.00

94. David Balfour

Ed	HRN	Date	Details	A	C	GD2.0	FN6.0	NM9.4
1	94	4/52	Original; Palais-a	1	1	4.25	13.00	28.00
2	167	5/64	PC-r	1	1	2.80	7.00	14.00
3	166	R/1968	C-price 25¢; PC-r	1	1	2.80	7.00	14.00

95. All Quiet on the Western Front

Ed	HRN	Date	Details	A	C	GD2.0	FN6.0	NM9.4
1A	96	5/52	Orig.; del Bourgo-a	1	1	9.30	28.00	70.00
1B	99	5/52	Orig.; del Bourgo-a	1	1	7.50	22.50	52.00
2	167	10/64	PC-r	1	1	4.00	10.00	20.00
3	167	11/66	PC-r	1	1	4.00	10.00	20.00

96. Daniel Boone

Ed	HRN	Date	Details	A	C	GD2.0	FN6.0	NM9.4
1	97	6/52	Original; Blum-a	1	1	4.00	12.00	24.00
2	117	–	PC-r	1	1	2.00	5.00	9.00
3	128	–	PC-r	1	1	2.00	5.00	9.00
4	132	–	PC-r	1	1	2.00	5.00	9.00
5	134	–	"Story of Jesus" on back-c; PC-r	1	1	2.00	5.00	9.00
6	158	–	PC-r	1	1	2.00	5.00	9.00
7	167	1/64	PC-r	1	1	2.00	5.00	8.00
8	167	5/65	PC-r	1	1	2.00	5.00	8.00
9	167	11/66	PC-r	1	1	2.00	5.00	8.00
10	166	Win/69	New-c; price 25¢; PC-r; stiff-c	1	2	2.80	7.00	14.00

97. King Solomon's Mines

Ed	HRN	Date	Details	A	C	GD2.0	FN6.0	NM9.4
1	96	7/52	Orig.; Kiefer-a	1	1	4.00	12.00	24.00
2	118	–	PC-r	1	1	2.00	5.00	10.00
3	131	–	PC-r	1	1	2.00	5.00	10.00
4	141	–	PC-r	1	1	2.00	5.00	10.00
5	158	–	PC-r	1	1	2.00	5.00	10.00
6	167	2/64	PC-r	1	1	2.00	5.00	8.00
7	167	9/65	PC-r	1	1	2.00	5.00	8.00
8	169	Sm/69	New price 25¢; stiff-c; PC-r	1	1	2.00	5.00	8.00

98. The Red Badge of Courage

Ed	HRN	Date	Details	A	C	GD2.0	FN6.0	NM9.4
1	98	8/52	Original	1	1	4.25	13.00	26.00
2	118	–	PC-r	1	1	2.00	5.00	10.00
3	132	–	PC-r	1	1	2.00	5.00	10.00
4	142	–	PC-r	1	1	2.00	5.00	10.00
5	152	–	PC-r	1	1	2.00	5.00	10.00
6	161	–	PC-r	1	1	2.00	5.00	10.00
7	167	–	Has orig.date; PC-r	1	1	2.00	5.00	10.00
8	167	9/64	PC-r	1	1	2.00	5.00	10.00
9	167	10/65	PC-r	1	1	2.00	5.00	10.00
10	166	R/1968	New-c&price 25¢; PC-r; stiff-c	1	2	3.60	9.00	18.00

99. Hamlet (Used in **POP**, pg. 102)

Ed	HRN	Date	Details	A	C	GD2.0	FN6.0	NM9.4
1	98	9/52	Original; Blum-a	1	1	4.25	13.00	28.00
2	121	–	PC-r	1	1	2.00	5.00	10.00

Classics Illustrated #100 © GIL

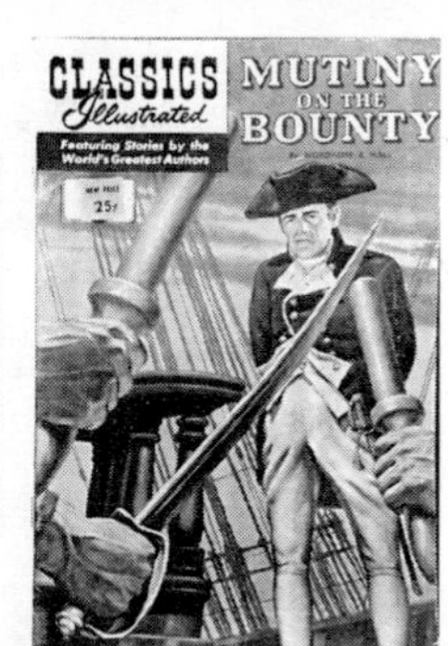

Classics Illustrated #102 © GIL

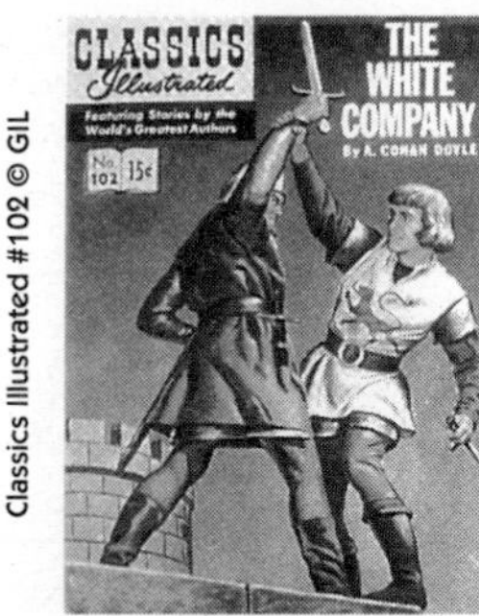

Classics Illustrated #108 © GIL

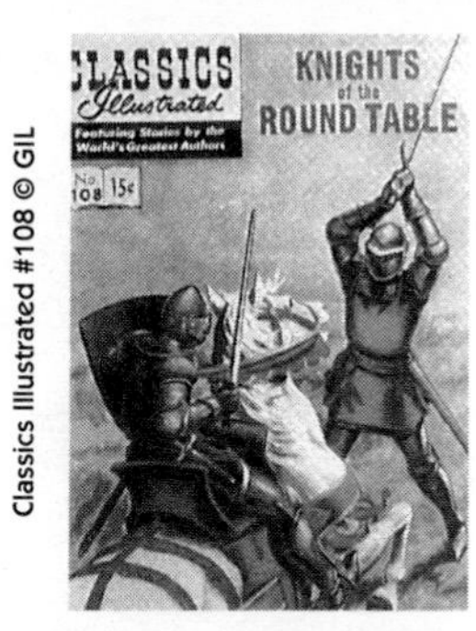

Ed	HRN	Date	Details	A	C	GD2.0	FN6.0	NM9.4
3	141	–	PC-r	1	1	2.00	5.00	10.00
4	158	–	PC-r	1	1	2.00	5.00	10.00
5	167	–	Has orig.date; PC-r	1	1	2.00	5.00	8.00
6	167	7/65	PC-r	1	1	2.00	5.00	8.00
7	166	4/67	PC-r	1	1	2.00	5.00	8.00
8	169	Spr/69	New-c&price 25¢; PC-r; stiff-c	1	2	3.60	9.00	18.00

100. Mutiny on the Bounty

Ed	HRN	Date	Details	A	C	GD2.0	FN6.0	NM9.4
1	100	10/52	Original	1	1	4.00	12.00	24.00
2	117	–	PC-r	1	1	2.00	5.00	10.00
3	132	–	PC-r	1	1	2.00	5.00	10.00
4	142	–	PC-r	1	1	2.00	5.00	10.00
5	155	–	PC-r	1	1	2.00	5.00	10.00
6	167	–	Has orig. date;PC-r	1	1	2.00	5.00	8.00
7	167	5/64	PC-r	1	1	2.00	5.00	8.00
8	167	3/66	PC-r	1	1	2.00	5.00	8.00
9	169	Spr/70	PC-r; stiff-c	1	1	2.00	5.00	8.00

101. William Tell

Ed	HRN	Date	Details	A	C	GD2.0	FN6.0	NM9.4
1	101	11/52	Original; Kiefer-c delBourgo-a	1	1	4.00	12.00	24.00
2	118	–	PC-r	1	1	2.00	5.00	10.00
3	141	–	PC-r	1	1	2.00	5.00	10.00
4	158	–	PC-r	1	1	2.00	5.00	10.00
5	167	–	Has orig.date; PC-r	1	1	2.00	5.00	8.00
6	167	11/64	PC-r	1	1	2.00	5.00	8.00
7	166	4/67	PC-r	1	1	2.00	5.00	8.00
8	169	Win/69	New price 25¢; stiff-c; PC-r	1	1	2.00	5.00	8.00

102. The White Company

Ed	HRN	Date	Details	A	C	GD2.0	FN6.0	NM9.4
1	101	12/52	Original; Blum-a	1	1	7.50	22.50	52.00
2	165	–	PC-r	1	1	4.00	10.00	22.00
3	167	4/64	PC-r	1	1	4.00	10.00	22.00

103. Men Against the Sea

Ed	HRN	Date	Details	A	C	GD2.0	FN6.0	NM9.4
1	104	1/53	Original; Kiefer-c; Palais-a	1	1	4.25	13.00	28.00
2	114	–	PC-r	1	1	3.20	8.00	16.00
3	131	–	New-c; PC-r	1	2	4.00	10.00	20.00
4	158	–	PC-r	1	2	2.80	7.00	14.00
5	149	–	White reorder list; came after HRN-158; PC-r	1	2	4.00	12.00	24.00
6	167	3/64	PC-r	1	2	2.00	5.00	10.00

104. Bring 'Em Back Alive

Ed	HRN	Date	Details	A	C	GD2.0	FN6.0	NM9.4
1	105	2/53	Original; Kiefer-c/a	1	1	4.00	12.00	24.00
2	118	–	PC-r	1	1	2.00	5.00	9.00
3	133	–	PC-r	1	1	2.00	5.00	9.00
4	150	–	PC-r	1	1	2.00	5.00	9.00
5	158	–	PC-r	1	1	2.00	5.00	9.00
6	167	10/63	PC-r	1	1	2.00	5.00	8.00
7	167	9/65	PC-r	1	1	2.00	5.00	8.00
8	169	Win/69	New price 25¢; stiff-c; PC-r	1	1	2.00	5.00	8.00

105. From the Earth to the Moon

Ed	HRN	Date	Details	A	C	GD2.0	FN6.0	NM9.4
1	106	3/53	Original; Blum-a	1	1	4.00	12.00	24.00
2	118	–	PC-r	1	1	2.00	5.00	9.00
3	132	–	PC-r	1	1	2.00	5.00	9.00
4	141	–	PC-r	1	1	2.00	5.00	9.00
5	146	–	PC-r	1	1	2.00	5.00	9.00
6	156	–	PC-r	1	1	2.00	5.00	9.00
7	167	–	Has orig. date; PC-r	1	1	2.00	5.00	8.00
8	167	5/64	PC-r	1	1	2.00	5.00	8.00
9	167	5/65	PC-r	1	1	2.00	5.00	8.00
10A	166	10/67	PC-r	1	1	2.00	5.00	8.00
10B	166	10/67	w/Grit ad stapled in book	1	1	10.00	30.00	75.00
11	169	Sm/69	New price 25¢; stiff-c; PC-r	1	1	2.00	5.00	8.00
12	169	Spr/71	PC-r	1	1	2.00	5.00	8.00

106. Buffalo Bill

Ed	HRN	Date	Details	A	C	GD2.0	FN6.0	NM9.4
1	107	4/53	Orig.; delBourgo-a	1	1	4.00	11.00	22.00
2	118	–	PC-r	1	1	2.00	5.00	9.00
3	132	–	PC-r	1	1	2.00	5.00	9.00
4	142	–	PC-r	1	1	2.00	5.00	9.00
5	161	–	PC-r	1	1	2.00	5.00	8.00
6	167	3/64	PC-r	1	1	2.00	5.00	8.00
7	166	7/67	PC-r	1	1	2.00	5.00	8.00
8	169	Fall/69	PC-r; stiff-c	1	1	2.00	5.00	8.00

107. King of the Khyber Rifles

Ed	HRN	Date	Details	A	C	GD2.0	FN6.0	NM9.4
1	108	5/53	Original	1	1	4.00	12.00	24.00
2	118	–	PC-r	1	1	2.00	5.00	9.00
3	146	–	PC-r	1	1	2.00	5.00	9.00
4	158	–	PC-r	1	1	2.00	5.00	9.00
5	167	–	Has orig.date; PC-r	1	1	2.00	5.00	8.00
6	167	–	PC-r	1	1	2.00	5.00	8.00
7	167	10/66	PC-r	1	1	2.00	5.00	8.00

108. Knights of the Round Table

Ed	HRN	Date	Details	A	C	GD2.0	FN6.0	NM9.4
1A	108	6/53	Original; Blum-a	1	1	4.25	13.00	28.00
1B	109	6/53	Original; scarce	1	1	5.70	17.00	36.00
2	117	–	PC-r	1	1	2.00	5.00	9.00
3	165	–	PC-r	1	1	2.00	5.00	8.00
4	167	4/64	PC-r	1	1	2.00	5.00	8.00
5	166	4/67	PC-r	1	1	2.00	5.00	8.00
6	169	Sm/69	New price 25¢; stiff-c; PC-r	1	1	2.00	5.00	8.00

109. Pitcairn's Island

Ed	HRN	Date	Details	A	C	GD2.0	FN6.0	NM9.4
1	110	7/53	Original; Palais-a	1	1	4.25	13.00	28.00
2	165	–	PC-r	1	1	2.00	5.00	10.00
3	167	3/64	PC-r	1	1	2.00	5.00	10.00
4	166	6/67	PC-r	1	1	2.00	5.00	10.00

110. A Study in Scarlet

Ed	HRN	Date	Details	A	C	GD2.0	FN6.0	NM9.4
1	111	8/53	Original	1	1	10.00	30.00	75.00
2	165	–	PC-r	1	1	8.50	26.00	60.00

111. The Talisman

Ed	HRN	Date	Details	A	C	GD2.0	FN6.0	NM9.4
1	112	9/53	Original; last H.C. Kiefer-a	1	1	4.00	12.00	28.00
2	165	–	PC-r	1	1	2.00	5.00	9.00
3	167	5/64	PC-r	1	1	2.00	5.00	9.00
4	166	Fall/68	C-price 25¢; PC-r	1	1	2.00	5.00	9.00

112. Adventures of Kit Carson

Ed	HRN	Date	Details	A	C	GD2.0	FN6.0	NM9.4
1	113	10/53	Original; Palais-a	1	1	4.25	13.00	26.00
2	129	–	PC-r	1	1	2.00	5.00	9.00
3	141	–	PC-r	1	1	2.00	5.00	9.00
4	152	–	PC-r	1	1	2.00	5.00	9.00
5	161	–	PC-r	1	1	2.00	5.00	8.00
6	167	–	PC-r	1	1	2.00	5.00	8.00

Classics Illustrated #118 © GIL

Classics Illustrated #123 © GIL

Classics Illustrated #124 © GIL

Ed	HRN	Date	Details	A	C	GD2.0	FN6.0	NM9.4
7	167	2/65	PC-r	1	1	2.00	5.00	8.00
8	167	5/66	PC-r	1	1	2.00	5.00	8.00
9	166	Win/69	New-c&price 25¢; PC-r; stiff-c	1	2	2.80	7.00	14.00

113. The Forty-Five Guardsmen

Ed	HRN	Date	Details	A	C	GD2.0	FN6.0	NM9.4
1	114	11/53	Orig.; delBourgo-a	1	1	6.50	19.50	45.00
2	166	7/67	PC-r	1	1	2.50	7.50	25.00

114. The Red Rover

Ed	HRN	Date	Details	A	C	GD2.0	FN6.0	NM9.4
1	115	12/53	Original	1	1	6.50	19.50	45.00
2	166	7/67	PC-r	1	1	2.50	7.50	25.00

115. How I Found Livingstone

Ed	HRN	Date	Details	A	C	GD2.0	FN6.0	NM9.4
1	116	1/54	Original	1	1	8.30	25.00	58.00
2	167	1/67	PC-r	1	1	3.60	10.80	36.00

116. The Bottle Imp

Ed	HRN	Date	Details	A	C	GD2.0	FN6.0	NM9.4
1	117	2/54	Orig.; Cameron-a	1	1	8.30	25.00	58.00
2	167	1/67	PC-r	1	1	3.60	10.80	36.00

117. Captains Courageous

Ed	HRN	Date	Details	A	C	GD2.0	FN6.0	NM9.4
1	118	3/54	Orig.; Costanza-a	1	1	6.85	21.50	48.00
2	167	2/67	PC-r	1	1	2.25	6.75	18.00
3	169	Fall/69	New price 25¢; stiff-c; PC-r	1	1	2.25	6.75	18.00

118. Rob Roy

Ed	HRN	Date	Details	A	C	GD2.0	FN6.0	NM9.4
1	119	4/54	Original; Rudy & Walter Palais-a	1	1	8.30	25.00	58.00
2	167	2/67	PC-r	1	1	3.60	10.80	36.00

119. Soldiers of Fortune

Ed	HRN	Date	Details	A	C	GD2.0	FN6.0	NM9.4
1	120	5/54	Schaffenberger-a	1	1	6.00	18.00	42.00
2	166	3/67	PC-r	1	1	2.25	6.75	18.00
3	169	Spr/70	New price 25¢; stiff-c; PC-r	1	1	2.25	6.75	18.00

120. The Hurricane

Ed	HRN	Date	Details	A	C	GD2.0	FN6.0	NM9.4
1	121	6/54	Orig.; Cameron-a	1	1	6.00	18.00	42.00
2	166	3/67	PC-r	1	1	2.60	7.80	26.00

121. Wild Bill Hickok

Ed	HRN	Date	Details	A	C	GD2.0	FN6.0	NM9.4
1	122	7/54	Original	1	1	4.00	10.00	20.00
2	132	–	PC-r	1	1	2.00	5.00	9.00
3	141	–	PC-r	1	1	2.00	5.00	9.00
4	154	–	PC-r	1	1	2.00	5.00	9.00
5	167	–	PC-r	1	1	2.00	5.00	8.00
6	167	8/64	PC-r	1	1	2.00	5.00	8.00
7	166	4/67	PC-r	1	1	2.00	5.00	8.00
8	169	Win/69	PC-r; stiff-c	1	1	2.00	5.00	8.00

122. The Mutineers

Ed	HRN	Date	Details	A	C	GD2.0	FN6.0	NM9.4
1	123	9/54	Original	1	1	4.00	12.00	28.00
2	136	–	PC-r	1	1	2.00	5.00	9.00
3	146	–	PC-r	1	1	2.00	5.00	9.00
4	158	–	PC-r	1	1	2.00	5.00	9.00
5	167	11/63	PC-r	1	1	2.00	5.00	8.00
6	167	3/65	PC-r	1	1	2.00	5.00	8.00
7	166	8/67	PC-r	1	1	2.00	5.00	8.00

123. Fang and Claw

Ed	HRN	Date	Details	A	C	GD2.0	FN6.0	NM9.4
1	124	11/54	Original	1	1	4.00	12.00	28.00
2	133	–	PC-r	1	1	2.00	5.00	9.00
3	143	–	PC-r	1	1	2.00	5.00	9.00
4	154	–	PC-r	1	1	2.00	5.00	9.00
5	167	–	Has orig.date; PC-r	1	1	2.00	5.00	8.00
6	167	9/65	PC-r	1	1	2.00	5.00	8.00

124. The War of the Worlds

Ed	HRN	Date	Details	A	C	GD2.0	FN6.0	NM9.4
1	125	1/55	Original; Cameron-c/a	1	1	6.30	19.00	38.00
2	131	–	PC-r	1	1	2.00	5.00	10.00
3	141	–	PC-r	1	1	2.00	5.00	10.00
4	148	–	PC-r	1	1	2.00	5.00	10.00
5	156	–	PC-r	1	1	2.00	5.00	10.00
6	165	–	PC-r	1	1	2.00	5.00	12.00
7	167	–	PC-r	1	1	2.00	5.00	9.00
8	167	11/64	PC-r	1	1	2.00	5.00	10.00
9	167	11/65	PC-r	1	1	2.00	5.00	9.00
10	166	R/1968	C-price 25¢; PC-r	1	1	2.00	5.00	9.00
11	169	Sm/70	PC-r; stiff-c	1	1	2.00	5.00	9.00

125. The Ox Bow Incident

Ed	HRN	Date	Details	A	C	GD2.0	FN6.0	NM9.4
1	3/55	–	Original; Picture Progress replaces reorder list	1	1	4.00	10.00	20.00
2	143	–	PC-r	1	1	2.00	5.00	9.00
3	152	–	PC-r	1	1	2.00	5.00	9.00
4	149	–	PC-r	1	1	2.00	5.00	9.00
5	167	–	PC-r	1	1	2.00	5.00	8.00
6	167	11/64	PC-r	1	1	2.00	5.00	8.00
7	166	4/67	PC-r	1	1	2.00	5.00	8.00
8	169	Win/69	New price 25¢; stiff-c; PC-r	1	1	2.00	5.00	8.00

126. The Downfall

Ed	HRN	Date	Details	A	C	GD2.0	FN6.0	NM9.4
1	5/55	–	Orig.; 'Picture Progress' replaces reorder list; Cameron-c/a	1	1	4.00	12.00	28.00
2	167	8/64	PC-r	1	1	2.40	6.00	12.00
3	166	R/1968	C-price 25¢; PC-r	1	1	2.40	6.00	12.00

127. The King of the Mountains

Ed	HRN	Date	Details	A	C	GD2.0	FN6.0	NM9.4
1	128	7/55	Original	1	1	4.00	12.00	28.00
2	167	6/64	PC-r	1	1	2.00	5.00	10.00
3	166	F/1968	C-price 25¢; PC-r	1	1	2.00	5.00	10.00

128. Macbeth (Used in **POP**, pg. 102)

Ed	HRN	Date	Details	A	C	GD2.0	FN6.0	NM9.4
1	128	9/55	Orig.; last Blum-a	1	1	4.00	12.00	28.00
2	143	–	PC-r	1	1	2.00	5.00	9.00
3	158	–	PC-r	1	1	2.00	5.00	9.00
4	167	–	PC-r	1	1	2.00	5.00	8.00
5	167	6/64	PC-r	1	1	2.00	5.00	8.00
6	166	4/67	PC-r	1	1	2.00	5.00	8.00
7	166	R/1968	C-Price 25¢; PC-r	1	1	2.00	5.00	8.00
8	169	Spr/70	Stiff-c; PC-r	1	1	2.00	5.00	8.00

129. Davy Crockett

Ed	HRN	Date	Details	AC		GD2.0	FN6.0	NM9.4
1	129	11/55	Orig.; Cameron-a	1	1	10.00	30.00	75.00
2	167	9/66	PC-r	1	1	8.50	26.00	60.00

130. Caesar's Conquests

Ed	HRN	Date	Details	A	C	GD2.0	FN6.0	NM9.4
1	130	1/56	Original; Orlando-a	1	1	5.35	16.00	32.00
2	142	–	PC-r	1	1	2.00	5.00	9.00
3	152	–	PC-r	1	1	2.00	5.00	9.00
4	149	–	PC-r	1	1	2.00	5.00	9.00

Classics Illustrated #131 © GIL

Classics Illustrated #138 © GIL

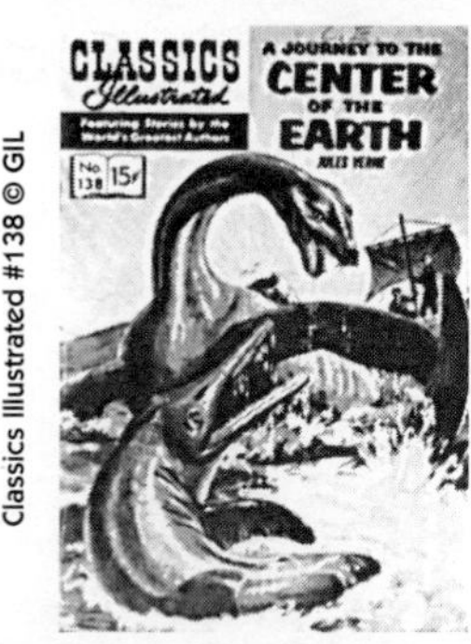

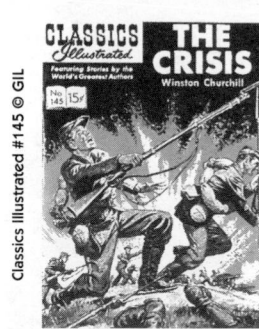

Classics Illustrated #145 © GIL

Ed	HRN	Date	Details	A	C	GD2.0	FN6.0	NM9.4
5	167	–	PC-r	1	1	2.00	5.00	8.00
6	167	10/64	PC-r	1	1	2.00	5.00	8.00
7	167	4/66	PC-r	1	1	2.00	5.00	8.00

131. The Covered Wagon

Ed	HRN	Date	Details	A	C	GD2.0	FN6.0	NM9.4
1	131	3/56	Original	1	1	4.00	10.00	20.00
2	143	–	PC-r	1	1	2.00	5.00	9.00
3	152	–	PC-r	1	1	2.00	5.00	9.00
4	158	–	PC-r	1	1	2.00	5.00	9.00
5	167	–	PC-r	1	1	2.00	5.00	8.00
6	167	11/64	PC-r	1	1	2.00	5.00	8.00
7	167	4/66	PC-r	1	1	2.00	5.00	8.00
8	169	Win/69	New price 25¢; stiff-c; PC-r	1	1	2.00	5.00	8.00

132. The Dark Frigate

Ed	HRN	Date	Details	A	C	GD2.0	FN6.0	NM9.4
1	132	5/56	Original	1	1	4.00	12.00	28.00
2	150	–	PC-r	1	1	2.00	5.00	10.00
3	167	1/64	PC-r	1	1	2.00	5.00	9.00
4	166	5/67	PC-r	1	1	2.00	5.00	9.00

133. The Time Machine

Ed	HRN	Date	Details	A	C	GD2.0	FN6.0	NM9.4
1	132	7/56	Orig.; Cameron-a	1	1	5.35	16.00	32.00
2	142	–	PC-r	1	1	2.00	5.00	10.00
3	152	–	PC-r	1	1	2.00	5.00	10.00
4	158	–	PC-r	1	1	2.00	5.00	10.00
5	167	–	PC-r	1	1	2.00	5.00	9.00
6	167	6/64	PC-r	1	1	2.20	5.50	11.00
7	167	3/66	PC-r	1	1	2.00	5.00	9.00
8	166	12/67	PC-r	1	1	2.00	5.00	9.00
9	169	Win/71	New price 25¢; stiff-c; PC-r	1	1	2.00	5.00	8.00

134. Romeo and Juliet

Ed	HRN	Date	Details	A	C	GD2.0	FN6.0	NM9.4
1	134	9/56	Original; Evans-a	1	1	4.00	12.00	28.00
2	161	–	PC-r	1	1	2.00	5.00	9.00
3	167	9/63	PC-r	1	1	2.00	5.00	8.00
4	167	5/65	PC-r	1	1	2.00	5.00	8.00
5	166	6/67	PC-r	1	1	2.00	5.00	8.00
6	166	Win/69	New c&price 25¢; stiff-c; PC-r	1	2	4.00	10.00	20.00

135. Waterloo

Ed	HRN	Date	Details	A	C	GD2.0	FN6.0	NM9.4
1	135	11/56	Orig.; G. Ingels-a	1	1	4.00	12.00	28.00
2	153	–	PC-r	1	1	2.00	5.00	9.00
3	167	–	PC-r	1	1	2.00	5.00	8.00
4	167	9/64	PC-r	1	1	2.00	5.00	8.00
5	166	R/1968	C-price 25¢; PC-r	1	1	2.00	5.00	8.00

136. Lord Jim

Ed	HRN	Date	Details	A	C	GD2.0	FN6.0	NM9.4
1	136	1/57	Original; Evans-a	1	1	4.00	12.00	28.00
2	165	–	PC-r	1	1	2.00	5.00	8.00
3	167	3/64	PC-r	1	1	2.00	5.00	8.00
4	167	9/66	PC-r	1	1	2.00	5.00	8.00
5	169	Sm/69	New price 25 ¢; stiff-c; PC-r	1	1	2.00	5.00	8.00

137. The Little Savage

Ed	HRN	Date	Details	A	C	GD2.0	FN6.0	NM9.4
1	136	3/57	Original; Evans-a	1	1	4.00	12.00	28.00
2	148	–	PC-r	1	1	2.00	5.00	9.00
3	156	–	PC-r	1	1	2.00	5.00	9.00
4	167	–	PC-r	1	1	2.00	5.00	8.00
5	167	10/64	PC-r	1	1	2.00	5.00	8.00
6	166	8/67	PC-r	1	1	2.00	5.00	8.00
7	169	Spr/70	New price 25¢; stiff-c; PC-r	1	1	2.00	5.00	8.00

138. A Journey to the Center of the Earth

Ed	HRN	Date	Details	A	C	GD2.0	FN6.0	NM9.4
1	136	5/57	Original	1	1	6.00	18.00	40.00
2	146	–	PC-r	1	1	2.00	5.00	10.00
3	156	–	PC-r	1	1	2.00	5.00	10.00
4	158	–	PC-r	1	1	2.00	5.00	10.00
5	167	–	PC-r	1	1	2.00	5.00	8.00
6	167	6/64	PC-r	1	1	2.40	6.00	12.00
7	167	4/66	PC-r	1	1	2.40	6.00	12.00
8	166	R/68	C-price 25¢; PC-r	1	1	2.00	5.00	8.00

139. In the Reign of Terror

Ed	HRN	Date	Details	A	C	GD2.0	FN6.0	NM9.4
1	139	7/57	Original; Evans-a	1	1	4.00	10.00	20.00
2	154	–	PC-r	1	1	2.00	5.00	10.00
3	167	–	Has orig.date; PC-r	1	1	2.00	5.00	8.00
4	167	7/64	PC-r	1	1	2.00	5.00	8.00
5	166	R/1968	C-price 25¢; PC-r	1	1	2.00	5.00	8.00

140. On Jungle Trails

Ed	HRN	Date	Details	A	C	GD2.0	FN6.0	NM9.4
1	140	9/57	Original	1	1	4.00	10.00	20.00
2	150	–	PC-r	1	1	2.00	5.00	9.00
3	160	–	PC-r	1	1	2.00	5.00	9.00
4	167	9/63	PC-r	1	1	2.00	5.00	8.00
5	167	9/65	PC-r	1	1	2.00	5.00	8.00

141. Castle Dangerous

Ed	HRN	Date	Details	A	C	GD2.0	FN6.0	NM9.4
1	141	11/57	Original	1	1	5.70	17.00	35.00
2	152	–	PC-r	1	1	2.00	5.00	9.00
3	167	–	PC-r	1	1	2.00	5.00	9.00
4	166	7/67	PC-r	1	1	2.00	5.00	9.00

142. Abraham Lincoln

Ed	HRN	Date	Details	A	C	GD2.0	FN6.0	NM9.4
1	142	1/58	Original	1	1	5.35	16.00	32.00
2	154	–	PC-r	1	1	2.00	5.00	9.00
3	158	–	PC-r	1	1	2.00	5.00	9.00
4	167	10/63	PC-r	1	1	2.00	5.00	8.00
5	167	7/65	PC-r	1	1	2.00	5.00	8.00
6	166	11/67	PC-r	1	1	2.00	5.00	8.00
7	169	Fall/69	New price 25¢; stiff-c; PC-r	1	1	2.00	5.00	8.00

143. Kim

Ed	HRN	Date	Details	A	C	GD2.0	FN6.0	NM9.4
1	143	3/58	Original; Orlando-a	1	1	4.15	12.50	25.00
2	165	–	PC-r	1	1	2.00	5.00	8.00
3	167	11/63	PC-r	1	1	2.00	5.00	8.00
4	167	8/65	PC-r	1	1	2.00	5.00	8.00
5	169	Win/69	New price 25¢; stiff-c; PC-r	1	1	2.00	5.00	8.00

144. The First Men in the Moon

Ed	HRN	Date	Details	A	C	GD2.0	FN6.0	NM9.4
1	143	5/58	Original; Wood-bridge/Williamson/Torres-a	1	1	5.00	15.00	30.00
2	152	–	(Rare)-PC-r	1	1	6.40	19.00	45.00
3	153	–	PC-r	1	1	2.00	5.00	9.00
4	161	–	PC-r	1	1	2.00	5.00	8.00
5	167	–	PC-r	1	1	2.00	5.00	8.00
6	167	12/65	PC-r	1	1	2.00	5.00	8.00
7	166	Fall/68	New-c&price 25¢; PC-r; stiff-c	1	2	3.25	8.00	16.00
8	169	Win/69	Stiff-c; PC-r	1	2	2.40	6.00	12.00

145. The Crisis

Ed	HRN	Date	Details	A	C

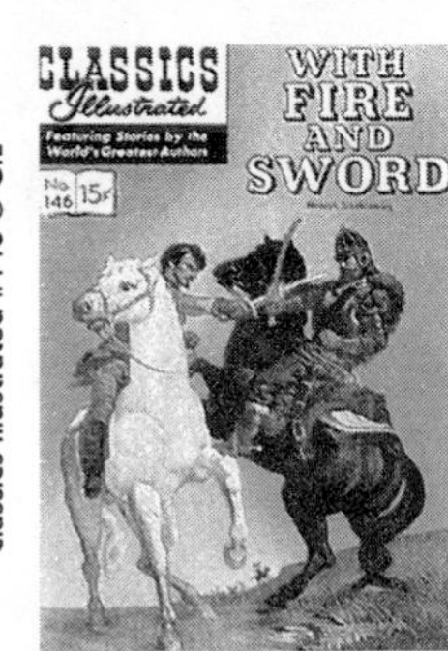
Classics Illustrated #146 © GIL

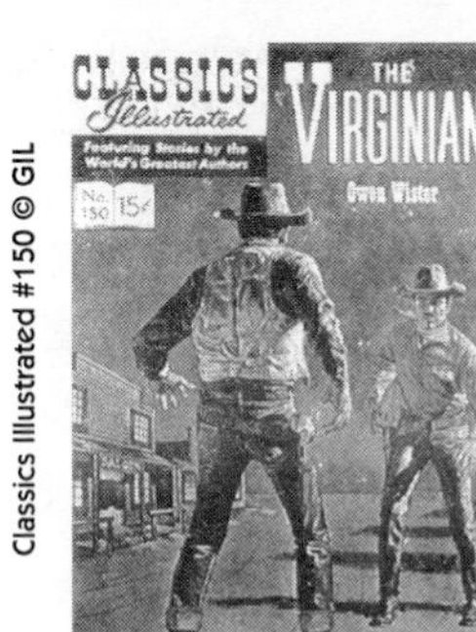
Classics Illustrated #150 © GIL

Classics Illustrated #152 © GIL

Ed	HRN	Date	Details	A	C	GD2.0	FN6.0	NM9.4
1	143	7/58	Original; Evans-a	1	1	4.00	12.00	28.00
2	156	–	PC-r	1	1	2.00	5.00	9.00
3	167	10/63	PC-r	1	1	2.00	5.00	8.00
4	167	3/65	PC-r	1	1	2.00	5.00	8.00
5	166	R/68	C-price 25¢; PC-r	1	1	2.00	5.00	8.00

146. With Fire and Sword

Ed	HRN	Date	Details	A	C	GD2.0	FN6.0	NM9.4
1	143	9/58	Original; Woodbridge-a	1	1	5.35	16.00	32.00
2	156	–	PC-r	1	1	2.00	6.00	12.00
3	167	11/63	PC-r	1	1	2.00	5.00	10.00
4	167	3/65	PC-r	1	1	2.00	5.00	10.00

147. Ben-Hur

Ed	HRN	Date	Details	A	C	GD2.0	FN6.0	NM9.4
1	147	11/58	Original; Orlando-a	1	1	4.15	12.50	25.00
2	152	–	Scarce; PC-r	1	1	5.00	15.00	30.00
3	153	–	PC-r	1	1	2.00	5.00	9.00
4	158	–	PC-r	1	1	2.00	5.00	9.00
5	167	–	Orig.date; but PC-r	1	1	2.00	5.00	8.00
6	167	2/65	PC-r	1	1	2.00	5.00	8.00
7	167	9/66	PC-r	1	1	2.00	5.00	8.00
8A	166	Fall/68	New-c&price 25¢; PC-r; soft-c	1	2	4.00	10.00	20.00
8B	166	Fall/68	New-c&price 25¢; PC-r; stiff-c; scarce	1	2	5.35	16.00	32.00

148. The Buccaneer

Ed	HRN	Date	Details	A	C	GD2.0	FN6.0	NM9.4
1	148	1/59	Orig.; Evans/Jenny-a; Saunders-c	1	1	4.15	12.50	25.00
2	568	–	Juniors list only PC-r	1	1	2.00	5.00	10.00
3	167	–	PC-r	1	1	2.00	5.00	8.00
4	167	9/65	PC-r	1	1	2.00	5.00	8.00
5	169	Sm/69	New price 25¢; PC-r; stiff-c	1	1	2.00	5.00	8.00

149. Off on a Comet

Ed	HRN	Date	Details	A	C	GD2.0	FN6.0	NM9.4
1	149	3/59	Orig.;G.McCann-a; blue reorder list	1	1	4.00	12.00	28.00
2	155	–	PC-r	1	1	2.00	5.00	9.00
3	149	–	PC-r; white reorder list; no coming-next ad	1	1	2.00	5.00	9.00
4	167	12/63	PC-r	1	1	2.00	5.00	8.00
5	167	2/65	PC-r	1	1	2.00	5.00	8.00
6	167	10/66	PC-r	1	1	2.00	5.00	8.00
7	166	Fall/68	New-c & price 25¢; PC-r	1	2	3.60	9.00	18.00

150. The Virginian

Ed	HRN	Date	Details	A	C	GD2.0	FN6.0	NM9.4
1	150	5/59	Original	1	1	5.70	17.00	36.00
2	164	–	PC-r	1	1	3.00	7.50	15.00
3	167	10/63	PC-r	1	1	4.00	10.00	20.00
4	167	12/65	PC-r	1	1	3.00	7.50	15.00

151. Won By the Sword

Ed	HRN	Date	Details	A	C	GD2.0	FN6.0	NM9.4
1	150	7/59	Original	1	1	5.35	16.00	32.00
2	164	–	PC-r	1	1	2.40	6.00	12.00
3	167	10/63	PC-r	1	1	2.40	6.00	12.00
4	166	7/67	PC-r	1	1	2.40	6.00	12.00

152. Wild Animals I Have Known

Ed	HRN	Date	Details	A	C	GD2.0	FN6.0	NM9.4
1	152	9/59	Orig.; L.B. Cole c/a	1	1	6.00	18.00	40.00
2A	149	–	PC-r; white reorder list; no coming-next ad; IBC: Jr. list #572	1	1	2.00	5.00	9.00
2B	149	–	PC-r; inside-bc: Jr. list to #555	1	1	2.00	5.00	10.00
2C	149	–	PC-r; inside-bc: has World Around Us ad; scarce	1	1	4.00	10.00	20.00
3	167	9/63	PC-r	1	1	2.00	5.00	8.00
4	167	8/65	PC-r	1	1	2.00	5.00	8.00
5	169	Fall/69	New price 25¢; stiff-c; PC-r	1	1	2.00	5.00	8.00

153. The Invisible Man

Ed	HRN	Date	Details	A	C	GD2.0	FN6.0	NM9.4
1	153	11/59	Original	1	1	6.00	18.00	40.00
2A	149	–	PC-r; white reorder list; no coming-next ad; inside-bc: Jr. list to #572	1	1	2.00	5.00	10.00
2B	149	–	PC-r; inside-bc: Jr. list to #555	1	1	2.20	5.50	11.00
3	167	–	PC-r	1	1	2.00	5.00	8.00
4	167	2/65	PC-r	1	1	2.00	5.00	8.00
5	167	9/66	PC-r	1	1	2.00	5.00	8.00
6	166	Win/69	New price 25¢; PC-r; stiff-c	1	1	2.00	5.00	8.00
7	169	Spr/71	Stiff-c; letters spelling 'Invisible Man' are 'solid' not 'invisible;' PC-r	1	1	2.00	5.00	8.00

154. The Conspiracy of Pontiac

Ed	HRN	Date	Details	A	C	GD2.0	FN6.0	NM9.4
1	154	1/60	Original	1	1	3.80	11.40	38.00
2	167	11/63	PC-r	1	1	2.80	7.00	14.00
3	167	7/64	PC-r	1	1	2.80	7.00	14.00
4	166	12/67	PC-r	1	1	2.80	7.00	14.00

155. The Lion of the North

Ed	HRN	Date	Details	A	C	GD2.0	FN6.0	NM9.4
1	154	3/60	Original	1	1	5.35	16.00	32.00
2	167	1/64	PC-r	1	1	2.40	6.00	12.00
3	166	R/1967	C-price 25¢; PC-r	1	1	2.00	5.00	10.00

156. The Conquest of Mexico

Ed	HRN	Date	Details	A	C	GD2.0	FN6.0	NM9.4
1	156	5/60	Orig.; Bruno Premiani-c/a	1	1	5.35	16.00	32.00
2	167	1/64	PC-r	1	1	2.00	5.00	10.00
3	166	8/67	PC-r	1	1	2.00	5.00	10.00
4	169	Spr/70	New price 25¢; stiff-c; PC-r	1	1	2.00	5.00	8.00

157. Lives of the Hunted

Ed	HRN	Date	Details	A	C	GD2.0	FN6.0	NM9.4
1	156	7/60	Orig.; L.B. Cole-c	1	1	4.00	12.00	38.00
2	167	2/64	PC-r	1	1	2.80	7.00	14.00
3	166	10/67	PC-r	1	1	2.80	7.00	14.00

158. The Conspirators

Ed	HRN	Date	Details	A	C	GD2.0	FN6.0	NM9.4
1	156	9/60	Original	1	1	6.00	18.00	36.00
2	167	7/64	PC-r	1	1	2.80	7.00	14.00
3	166	10/67	PC-r	1	1	2.80	7.00	14.00

159. The Octopus

Ed	HRN	Date	Details	A	C	GD2.0	FN6.0	NM9.4
1	159	11/60	Orig.; Gray Morrow-a; L.B. Cole-c	1	1	6.00	18.00	38.00
2	167	2/64	PC-r	1	1	2.40	6.00	12.00
3	166	R/1967	C-price 25¢; PC-r	1	1	2.40	6.00	12.00

Classics Illustrated #164 © GIL

Classics Illustrated #165 © GIL

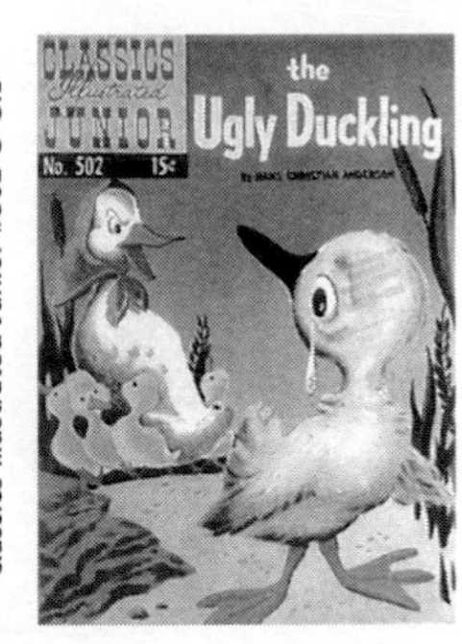

Classics Illustrated Junior #502 © GIL

160. The Food of the Gods

Ed	HRN	Date	Details	A	C	GD2.0	FN6.0	NM9.4
1A	159	1/61	Original	1	1	6.00	18.00	38.00
1B	160	1/61	Original; same, except for HRN	1	1	5.80	17.00	35.00
2	167	1/64	PC-r	1	1	2.40	6.00	12.00
3	166	6/67	PC-r	1	1	2.40	6.00	12.00

161. Cleopatra

Ed	HRN	Date	Details	A	C	GD2.0	FN6.0	NM9.4
1	161	3/61	Original	1	1	6.00	18.00	38.00
2	167	1/64	PC-r	1	1	3.20	8.00	16.00
3	166	8/67	PC-r	1	1	3.20	8.00	16.00

162. Robur the Conqueror

Ed	HRN	Date	Details	A	C	GD2.0	FN6.0	NM9.4
1	162	5/61	Original	1	1	6.00	18.00	38.00
2	167	7/64	PC-r	1	1	2.80	7.00	14.00
3	166	8/67	PC-r	1	1	2.80	7.00	14.00

163. Master of the World

Ed	HRN	Date	Details	A	C	GD2.0	FN6.0	NM9.4
1	163	7/61	Original; Gray Morrow-a	1	1	6.00	18.00	36.00
2	167	1/65	PC-r	1	1	2.80	7.00	14.00
3	166	R/1968	C-price 25¢; PC-r	1	1	2.80	7.00	14.00

164. The Cossack Chief

Ed	HRN	Date	Details	A	C	GD2.0	FN6.0	NM9.4
1	164	(1961)	Orig.; nd(10/61?)	1	1	6.00	18.00	36.00
2	167	4/65	PC-r	1	1	2.80	7.00	14.00
3	166	Fall/68	C-price 25¢; PC-r	1	1	2.80	7.00	14.00

165. The Queen's Necklace

Ed	HRN	Date	Details	A	C	GD2.0	FN6.0	NM9.4
1	164	1/62	Original; Morrow-a	1	1	6.00	18.00	36.00
2	167	4/65	PC-r	1	1	2.80	7.00	14.00
3	166	Fall/68	C-price 25¢; PC-r	1	1	2.80	7.00	14.00

166. Tigers and Traitors

Ed	HRN	Date	Details	A	C	GD2.0	FN6.0	NM9.4
1	165	5/62	Original	1	1	9.00	28.00	65.00
2	167	2/64	PC-r	1	1	4.00	11.00	22.00
3	167	11/66	PC-r	1	1	4.00	11.00	22.00

167. Faust

Ed	HRN	Date	Details	A	C	GD2.0	FN6.0	NM9.4
1	165	8/62	Original	1	1	14.00	41.00	95.00
2	167	2/64	PC-r	1	1	6.00	18.00	40.00
3	166	6/67	PC-r	1	1	6.00	18.00	40.00

168. In Freedom's Cause

Ed	HRN	Date	Details	A	C	GD2.0	FN6.0	NM9.4
1	169	Win/69	Original; Evans/ Crandall-a; stiff-c; 25¢; no coming-next ad;	1	1	16.00	48.00	120.00

169. Negro Americans The Early Years

Ed	HRN	Date	Details	A	C	GD2.0	FN6.0	NM9.4
1	166	Spr/69	Orig. & last issue; 25¢; Stiff-c; no coming-next ad; other sources indicate publication date of 5/69	1	1	12.00	36.00	90.00
2	169	Spr/69	Stiff-c	1	1	6.40	19.00	45.00

NOTE: *Many other titles were prepared or planned but were only issued in British/European series.*

CLASSIC PUNISHER (Also see Punisher)
Marvel Comics: Dec, 1989 ($4.95, B&W, deluxe format, 68 pgs.)

1-Reprints Marvel Super Action #1 & Marvel Preview #2 plus new story 5.00

CLASSICS ILLUSTRATED
First Publishing/Berkley Publishing: Feb, 1990 - No. 27, July, 1991 ($3.75/$3.95, 52 pgs.)

1-27: 1-Gahan Wilson-c/a. 4-Sienkiewicz painted-c/a. 6-Russell scripts/layouts. 7-Spiegle-a. 9-Ploog-c/a. 16-Staton-a. 18-Gahan Wilson-c/a; 20-Geary-a. 26-Aesop's Fables (6/91). 26,27-Direct sale only 4.00

CLASSICS ILLUSTRATED
Acclaim Books/Twin Circle PublishingCo.: Feb, 1997 - Present ($4.99, digest-size) (Each book contains study notes)

A Christmas Carol-(12/97), A Connecticut Yankee in King Arthur's Court-(5/97), All Quiet on the Western Front-(1/98), A Midsummer's Night Dream-(4/97) Around the World in 80 Days-(1/98), A Tale of Two Cities-(2/97)Joe Orlando-r, Captains Courageous-(11/97), Crime and Punishment-(3/97), Dr. Jekyll and Mr. Hyde-(10/97), Don Quixote-(12/97), Frankenstein-(10/97), Great Expectations-(4/97), Hamlet-(3/97), Huckleberry Finn-(3/97), Jane Eyre-(2/97), Kidnapped-(1/98), Les Miserables-(5/97), Lord Jim-(9/97), Macbeth-(5/97), Moby Dick-(4/97), Oliver Twist-(5/97), Robinson Crusoe-(9/97), Romeo & Juliet-(2/97), Silas Marner-(11/97), The Call of the Wild-(9/97), The Count of Monte Cristo-(1/98), The House of the Seven Gables-(9/97), The Iliad-(12/97), The Invisible Man-(10/97), The Last of the Mohicans-(12/97), The Master of Ballantrae-(11/97), The Odyssey-(3/97), The Prince and the Pauper-(4/97), The Red Badge Of Courage-(9/97), Tom Sawyer-(2/97) Wuthering Heights-(11/97) 5.00

NOTE: *Stories reprinted from the original Gilberton Classic Comics and Classics Illustrated.*

CLASSICS ILLUSTRATED GIANTS
Gilberton Publications: Oct, 1949 (One-Shots - "OS")

These Giant Editions, all with new Kiefer front and back covers, were advertised from 10/49 to 2/52. They were 50¢ on the newsstand and 60¢ by mail. They are actually four Classics in one volume. All the stories are reprints of the Classics Illustrated Series. NOTE: There were also British hardback Adventure & Indian Giants in 1952, with the same covers but different contents: Adventure - 2, 7, 10; Indian - 17, 22, 37, 58. They are also rare.

	GD2.0	FN6.0	NM9.4
"An Illustrated Library of Great Adventure Stories" - reprints of No. 6,7,8,10 (Rare); Kiefer-c	129.00	387.00	1100.00
"An Illustrated Library of Exciting Mystery Stories" - reprints of No. 30,21,40, 13 (Rare)	141.00	423.00	1200.00
"An Illustrated Library of Great Indian Stories" - reprints of No. 4,17,22,37 (Rare)	129.00	387.00	1100.00

INTRODUCTION TO CLASSICS ILLUSTRATED JUNIOR

Collectors of Juniors can be put into one of two categories: those who want any copy of each title, and those who want all the originals. Those seeking every original and reprint edition are a limited group, primarily because Juniors have no changes in art or covers to spark interest, and because reprints are so low in value it is difficult to get dealers to look for specific reprint editions.

In recent years it has become apparent that most serious Classics collectors seek Junior originals. Those seeking reprints seek them for low cost. This has made the previous note about the comparative market value of reprints inadequate. Three particular reprint editions are worth even more. For the 535-Twin Circle edition, see Giveaways. There are also reprint editions of 501 and 503 which have a full-page bc ad for the very rare Junior record. Those may sell as high as $10-$15 in mint. Original editions of 557 and 558 also have that ad.

There are no reprint editions of 577. The only edition, from 1969, is a 25 cent stiff-cover edition with no ad for the next issue. All other original editions have coming-next ad. But 577, like C.I. #168, was prepared in 1962 but not issued. Copies of 577 can be found in 1963 British/European series, which then continued with dozens of additional new Junior titles.

PRICES LISTED BELOW ARE FOR ORIGINAL EDITIONS, WHICH HAVE AN AD FOR THE NEXT ISSUE.

NOTE: *Non HRN 576 copies- many are written on or colored . Reprints with 576 HRN are worth about 1/3 original prices. All other HRN #'s are 1/2 original price*

CLASSICS ILLUSTRATED JUNIOR
Famous Authors Ltd. (Gilberton Publications): Oct, 1953 - Spring, 1971

	GD2.0	FN6.0	NM9.4
501-Snow White & the Seven Dwarfs; Alex Blum-a	10.00	30.00	70.00
502-The Ugly Duckling	7.50	22.50	45.00
503-Cinderella	4.25	13.00	28.00

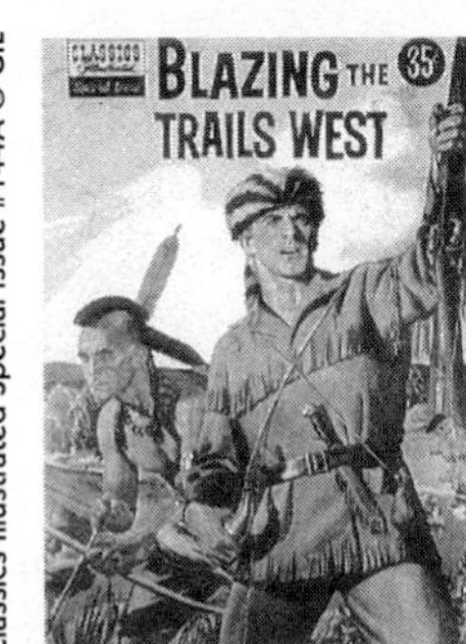

Classics Illustrated Special Issue #144A © GIL

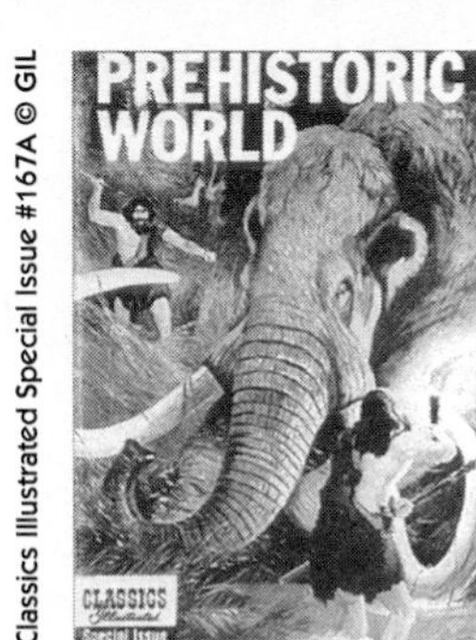

Classics Illustrated Special Issue #167A © GIL

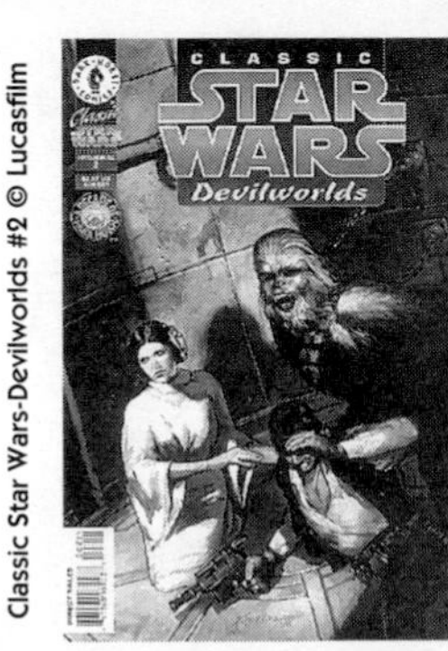

Classic Star Wars-Devilworlds #2 © Lucasfilm

GD2.0 FN6.0 NM9.4

504-512: 504-The Pied Piper. 505-The Sleeping Beauty. 506-The Three Little Pigs. 507-Jack & the Beanstalk. 508-Goldilocks & the Three Bears. 509-Beauty and the Beast. 510-Little Red Riding Hood. 511-Puss-N Boots. 512-Rumpelstiltskin 4.00 10.00 20.00
513-Pinocchio 4.25 13.00 28.00
514-The Steadfast Tin Soldier 7.00 21.00 42.00
515-Johnny Appleseed 4.00 10.00 20.00
516-Aladdin and His Lamp 4.25 13.00 26.00
517-519: 517-The Emperor's New Clothes. 518-The Golden Goose. 519-Paul Bunyan 4.00 10.00 20.00
520-Thumbelina 4.25 13.00 28.00
521-King of the Golden River 4.00 10.00 20.00
522,523,530: 522-The Nightingale. 523-The Gallant Tailor. 530-The Golden Bird 3.60 9.00 18.00
524-The Wild Swans 4.25 13.00 26.00
525,526: 525-The Little Mermaid. 526-The Frog Prince 4.25 13.00 26.00
527-The Golden-Haired Giant 4.00 10.00 20.00
528-The Penny Prince 4.00 10.00 20.00
529-The Magic Servants 4.00 10.00 20.00
531-Rapunzel 4.00 10.00 20.00
532-534: 532-The Dancing Princesses. 533-The Magic Fountain. 534-The Golden Touch 3.20 8.00 16.00
535-The Wizard of Oz 5.85 17.50 35.00
536-The Chimney Sweep 4.00 10.00 20.00
537-The Three Fairies 4.00 12.00 24.00
538-Silly Hans 3.20 8.00 16.00
539-The Enchanted Fish 4.25 13.00 28.00
540-The Tinder-Box 4.25 13.00 28.00
541-Snow White & Rose Red 3.60 9.00 18.00
542-The Donkey's Tale 3.60 9.00 18.00
543-The House in the Woods 4.00 10.00 20.00
544-The Golden Fleece 5.00 15.00 30.00
545-The Glass Mountain 3.60 9.00 18.00
546-The Elves & the Shoemaker 3.60 9.00 18.00
547-The Wishing Table 4.00 10.00 20.00
548-551: 548-The Magic Pitcher. 549-Simple Kate. 550-The Singing Donkey. 551-The Queen Bee 3.20 8.00 16.00
552-The Three Little Dwarfs 4.00 10.00 20.00
553,556: 553-King Thrushbeard. 556-The Elf Mound 3.20 8.00 16.00
554-The Enchanted Deer 4.25 13.00 26.00
555-The Three Golden Apples 3.60 9.00 18.00
557-Silly Willy 4.00 12.00 24.00
558-The Magic Dish; L.B. Cole-c; soft and stiff-c exist on original 5.35 16.00 32.00
559-The Japanese Lantern; 1 pg. Ingels-a; L.B. Cole-c 5.35 16.00 32.00
560-The Doll Princess; L.B. Cole-c 5.35 16.00 32.00
561-Hans Humdrum; L.B. Cole-c 3.60 9.00 18.00
562-The Enchanted Pony; L.B. Cole-c 5.35 16.00 32.00
563,565-567,570: 563-The Wishing Well; L.B. Cole-c. 565-The Silly Princess; L.B. Cole-c. 566-Clumsy Hans; L.B. Cole-c. 567-The Bearskin Soldier; L.B. Cole-c. 570-The Pearl Princess 3.20 8.00 16.00
564-The Salt Mountain; L.B.Cole-c. 568-The Happy Hedgehog; L.B. Cole-c. 4.00 10.00 20.00
569,573: 569-The Three Giants.573-The Crystal Ball 3.60 9.00 18.00
571,572: 571-How Fire Came to the Indians. 572-The Drummer Boy 4.25 13.00 28.00
574-Brightboots 3.60 9.00 18.00
575-The Fearless Prince 4.00 12.00 24.00
576-The Princess Who Saw Everything 5.00 15.00 30.00
577-The Runaway Dumpling 6.00 18.00 36.00

NOTE: *Prices are for original editions. Last reprint - Spring, 1971.* ***Costanza*** *&* ***Schaffenberger*** *art in many issues.*

CLASSICS ILLUSTRATED SPECIAL ISSUE
Gilberton Co.: (Came out semi-annually) Dec, 1955 - Jul, 1962 (35¢, 100 pgs.)

129-The Story of Jesus (titled ...Special Edition) "Jesus on Mountain" cover 7.85 23.50 55.00
"Three Camels" cover (12/58) 10.00 30.00 75.00
"Mountain" cover (no date)-Has checklist on inside b/c to HRN #161 & different testimonial on back-c 7.00 21.00 42.00
"Mountain" cover (1968 re-issue; has white 50¢ circle) 6.70 20.00 40.00
132A-The Story of America (6/56); Cameron-a 7.50 22.50 45.00
135A-The Ten Commandments(12/56) 6.70 20.00 40.00
138A-Adventures in Science(6/57); HRN to 137 5.85 17.50 35.00
138A-(6/57)-2nd version w/HRN to 149 4.25 13.00 28.00
138A-(12/61)-3rd version w/HRN to 149 5.85 17.50 35.00
141A-The Rough Rider (Teddy Roosevelt)(12/57); Evans-a 6.70 20.00 40.00
144A-Blazing the Trails West(6/58)- 73 pgs. of Crandall/Evans plus Severin-a 6.35 19.00 38.00
147A-Crossing the Rockies(12/58)-Crandall/Evans-a 6.70 20.00 40.00
150A-Royal Canadian Police(6/59)-Ingels, Sid Check-a 6.70 20.00 40.00
153A-Men, Guns & Cattle(12/59)-Evans-a (26 pgs.); Kinstler-a 6.70 20.00 40.00
156A-The Atomic Age(6/60)-Crandall/Evans, Torres-a 6.70 20.00 40.00
159A-Rockets, Jets and Missiles(12/60)-Evans, Morrow-a 6.70 20.00 40.00
162A-War Between the States(6/61)-Kirby & Crandall/Evans-a; Ingels-a 12.00 36.00 90.00
165A-To the Stars(12/61)-Torres, Crandall/Evans, Kirby-a 6.70 20.00 40.00
166A-World War II('62)-Torres, Crandall/Evans, Kirby-a 9.30 28.00 65.00
167A-Prehistoric World(7/62)-Torres & Crandall/Evans-a; two versions exist (HRN to 165 & HRN to 167) 9.30 28.00 65.00
nn Special Issue-The United Nations (1964; 50¢; scarce); this is actually part of the European Special Series, which cont'd on after the U.S. series stopped issuing new titles in 1962. This English edition was prepared specifically for sale at the U.N. It was printed in Norway 28.00 83.00 220.00

NOTE: *There was another U.S. Special Issue prepared in 1962 with artwork by* ***Torres*** *entitled World War I. Unfortunately, it was never issued in any English-language edition. It was issued in 1964 in West Germany, The Netherlands, and some Scandanavian countries, with another edition in 1974 with a new cover.*

CLASSICS LIBRARY (See King Classics)

CLASSIC STAR WARS (Also see Star Wars)
Dark Horse Comics: Aug, 1992 - No. 20, June, 1994 ($2.50)

1-Begin Star Wars strip-r by Williamson; Williamson redrew portions of the panels to fit comic book format 2.40 6.00
2-10: 8-Polybagged w/Star Wars Galaxy trading card. 8-M. Schultz-c 4.00
11-19: 13-Yeates-c. 17-M. Schultz-c. 19-Evans-c 3.00
20-($3.50, 52 pgs.)-Polybagged w/trading card 3.50
Escape To Hoth TPB ($16.95) r/#15-20 1.70 5.10 17.00
The Rebel Storm TPB - r/#8-14 1.70 5.10 17.00
Trade paperback ($29.95, slip-cased)-Reprints all movie adaptations 30.00

NOTE: *Williamson c-1-5,7,9,10,14,15,20.*

CLASSIC STAR WARS: (Title series). **Dark Horse Comics**

--A NEW HOPE, 6/94 - No. 2, 7/94 ($3.95)
1,2: 1-r/Star Wars #1-3, 7-9 publ; 2-r/Star Wars #4-6, 10-12 publ. by Marvel Comics 4.00

--DEVILWORLDS, 8/96 - No.2, 9/96 ($2.50s)1,2: r/Alan Moore-s 2.50

--HAN SOLO AT STARS' END, 3/97 - No.3, 5/97 ($2.95s)
1-3: r/strips by Alfredo Alcala 3.00

--RETURN OF THE JEDI, 10/94 - No.2, 11/94 ($3.50)
1,2: 1-r/1983-84 Marvel series; polybagged with w/trading card 3.50

--THE EARLY ADVENTURES, 8/94 - No. 9, 4/95 ($2.50)1-9 2.50

--THE EMPIRE STRIKES BACK, 8/94 - No. 2, 9/94 ($3.95)
1-r/Star Wars #39-44 published by Marvel Comics 4.00

CLASSIC X-MEN (Becomes X-Men Classic #46 on)

Clerks Holiday Special #1 © View Askew

Climax! #1 © Gilmore

Cloak & Dagger (2nd series) #4 © MAR

Marvel Comics Group: Sept, 1986 - No. 45, Mar, 1990

1-Begins-r of New X-Men 3.00
2-10: 10-Sabretooth app. 2.50
11-43: 11-1st origin of Magneto in back-up story. 17-Wolverine-c. 27-r/X-Men #121. 26-r/X-Men #120; Wolverine-c/app. 35-r/X-Men #129. 39-New Jim Lee back-up story (2nd-a on X-Men). 43-Byrne-c/a(r); $1.75, double-size 2.00

NOTE: ***Art Adams*** *c(p)-1-10, 12-16, 18-23.* ***Austin*** *c-10,15-21,24-28i.* ***Bolton*** *back up stories in 1-28,30-35.* ***Williamson*** *c-12-14i.*

CLAW (See Capt. Battle, Jr. Daredevil Comics & Silver Streak Comics)

CLAW THE UNCONQUERED (See Cancelled Comic Cavalcade)
National Periodical Publications/DC Comics: 5-6/75 - No. 9, 9-10/76; No. 10, 4-5/78 - No. 12, 8-9/78

1-1st app. Claw 5.00
2-12: 3-Nudity panel. 9-Origin 4.00

NOTE: ***Giffen*** *a-8-12p.* ***Kubert*** *c-10-12.* ***Layton*** *a-9i, 12i.*

CLAY CODY, GUNSLINGER
Pines Comics: Fall, 1957

1-Painted-c 5.00 15.00 30.00

CLEAN FUN, STARRING "SHOOGAFOOTS JONES"
Specialty Book Co.: 1944 (10¢, B&W, oversized covers, 24 pgs.)

nn-Humorous situations involving Negroes in the Deep South
White cover issue... 9.15 27.00 55.00
Dark grey cover issue... 10.00 30.00 65.00

CLEMENTINA THE FLYING PIG (See Dell Jr. Treasury)

CLEOPATRA (See Ideal, a Classical Comic No. 1)

CLERKS: THE COMIC BOOK (Also see Oni Double Feature #1)
Oni Press: Feb, 1998 ($2.95, B&W, one-shot)

1-Kevin Smith-s 1.50 4.50 12.00
1-Second printing 4.00
...Holiday Special (12/98, $2.95) Smith-s 3.00

CLIFFHANGER (See Battle Chasers, Crimson, and Danger Girl)
WildStorm Prod./Wizard Press: 1997 (Wizard supplement)

0-Sketchbook preview of Cliffhanger titles 1.25 3.75 10.00

CLIMAX! (Mystery)
Gillmor Magazines: July, 1955 - No. 2, Sept, 1955

1,2 12.00 36.00 85.00

CLINT (Also see Adolescent Radioactive Black Belt Hamsters)
Eclipse Comics: Sept, 1986 - No. 2, Jan, 1987 ($1.50, B&W)

1,2 2.00

CLINT & MAC (TV, Disney)
Dell Publishing Co.: No. 889, Mar, 1958

Four Color 889-Alex Toth-a, photo-c 12.00 35.00 135.00

CLIVE BARKER'S BOOK OF THE DAMNED: A HELLRAISER COMPANION
Marvel Comics (Epic): Oct, 1991 - No. 3, Nov, 1992 ($4.95, semi-annual)

Volume 1-3-(52 pgs.): 1-Simon Bisley-c. 2-(4/92). 3-(11/92)-McKean-a (1 pg.) 5.00

CLIVE BARKER'S HELLRAISER (Also see Epic, Hellraiser Nightbreed –Jihad, Revelations, Son of Celluloid, Tapping the Vein & Weaveworld)
Marvel Comics (Epic Comics): 1989 - No. 20, 1993 ($4.50-6.95, mature readers, quarterly, 68 pgs.)

Book 1-4,10-16,18,19: Based on Hellraiser & Hellbound movies; Bolton-c/a; Spiegle & Wrightson-a (graphic album). 10-Foil-c. 12-Sam Kieth-a 5.00
Book 5-9 ($5.95): 7-Bolton-a. 8-Morrow-a 6.00
Book 17-Alex Ross-a, 34 pgs. 1.25 3.75 10.00
Book 20-By Gaiman/McKean 7.00
...Dark Holiday Special ('92, $4.95)-Conrad-a 5.00
...Spring Slaughter 1 ('94, $6.95, 52 pgs.)-Painted-c 7.00
...Summer Special 1 ('92, $5.95, 68 pgs.) 6.00

GD2.0 FN6.0 NM9.4

CLIVE BARKER'S NIGHTBREED (Also see Epic)
Marvel Comics (Epic Comics): Apr, 1990 - No. 25, Mar, 1993 ($1.95/$2.25/$2.50, mature readers)

1-25: 1-4-Adapt horror movie. 5-New storie; Guice-a(p) 2.50

CLIVE BARKER'S THE HARROWERS
Marvel Comics (Epic Comics): Dec, 1993 - No. 6, May, 1994 ($2.50)

1-($2.95)-Glow-in-the-dark-c; Colan-c/a in all 3.00
2-6 2.50

NOTE: ***Colan*** *a(p)-1-6; c-1-3, 4p, 5p.* ***Williamson*** *a(i)-2, 4, 5(part).*

CLOAK AND DAGGER
Ziff-Davis Publishing Co.: Fall, 1952

1-Saunders painted-c 24.00 73.00 170.00

CLOAK AND DAGGER (Also see Marvel Fanfare)
Marvel Comics Group: Oct, 1983 - No. 4, Jan, 1984 (Mini-series) (See Spectacular Spider-Man #64)

1-4-Austin-c/a(i) in all. 4-Origin 2.00

CLOAK AND DAGGER (2nd Series)(Also see Marvel Graphic Novel #34 & Strange Tales)
Marvel Comics Group: July, 1985 - No. 11, Jan, 1987

1-11: 9-Art Adams-p 2.00
...And Power Pack (1990, $7.95, 68 pgs.) 8.00

NOTE: ***Mignola*** *c-7, 8.*

CLOAK AND DAGGER (3rd Series listed as Mutant Misadventures Of...)

CLOBBERIN' TIME
Marvel Comics: Sept, 1995 ($1.95) (Based on card game)

nn-Overpower game guide; Ben Grimm story 2.00

CLONEZONE SPECIAL
Dark Horse Comics/First Comics: 1989 ($2.00, B&W)

1-Back-up series from Badger & Nexus 2.00

CLOSE ENCOUNTERS (See Marvel Comics Super Special & Marvel Special Edition)

CLOSE SHAVES OF PAULINE PERIL, THE (TV?)
Gold Key: June, 1970 - No. 4, March, 1971

1 2.50 7.50 22.00
2-4 2.00 6.00 16.00

CLOWN COMICS (No. 1 titled Clown Comic Book)
Clown Comics/Home Comics/Harvey Publ.: 1945 - No. 3, Win, 1946

nn (#1) 10.00 30.00 70.00
2,3 7.00 21.00 42.00

CLOWNS, THE (I Pagliacci)
Dark Horse Comics: 1998 ($2.95, B&W, one-shot)

1-Adaption of the opera; P. Craig Russell-script 3.00

CLUBHOUSE RASCALS (#1 titled ...Presents?) (Also see Three Rascals)
Sussex Publ. Co. (Magazine Enterprises): June, 1956 - No. 2, Oct, 1956

1,2: The Brain app. 5.35 16.00 32.00

CLUB "16"
Famous Funnies: June, 1948 - No. 4, Dec, 1948

1-Teen-age humor 11.00 33.00 75.00
2-4 6.70 20.00 40.00

CLUE COMICS (Real Clue Crime V2#4 on)
Hillman Periodicals: Jan, 1943 - No. 15(V2#3), May, 1947

1-Origin The Boy King, Nightmare, Micro-Face, Twilight, & Zippo
103.00 309.00 825.00
2 49.00 147.00 390.00
3-5 37.00 111.00 260.00
6,8,9: 8-Palais-c/a(2) 28.00 84.00 195.00
7-Classic torture-c 40.00 120.00 310.00
10-Origin/1st app. The Gun Master & begin series; content changes to crime
28.00 84.00 195.00

Clue Comics #7 © HILL

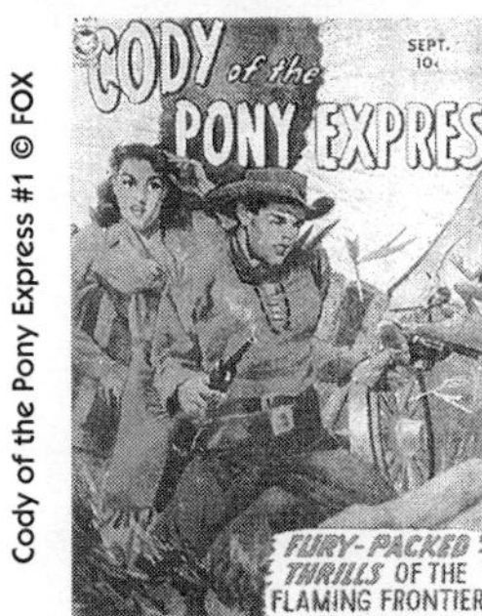

Cody of the Pony Express #1 © FOX

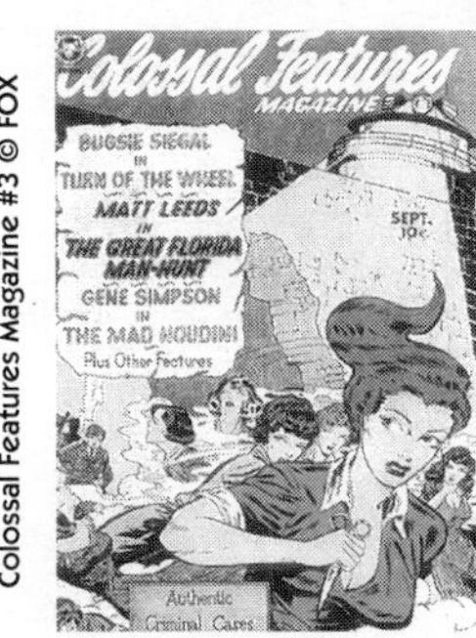

Colossal Features Magazine #3 © FOX

GD2.0 FN6.0 NM9.4

11 19.00 58.00 135.00
12-Origin Rackman; McWilliams-a, Guardineer-a(2) 25.00 75.00 175.00
V2#1-Nightmare new origin; Iron Lady app.; Simon & Kirby-a 45.00 135.00 340.00
V2#2-S&K-a(2)-Bondage/torture-c; man attacks & kills people with electric iron. Infantino-a 45.00 135.00 360.00
V2#3-S&K-a(3) 45.00 135.00 360.00

CLUELESS SPRING SPECIAL (TV)
Marvel Comics: May, 1997 ($3.99, magazine sized, one-shot)
1-Photo-c from TV show 4.00

CLUTCHING HAND, THE
American Comics Group: July-Aug, 1954
1 34.00 103.00 240.00

CLYDE BEATTY COMICS (Also see Crackajack Funnies)
Commodore Productions & Artists, Inc.: October, 1953 (84 pgs.)
1-Photo front/back-c; movie scenes and comics 26.00 79.00 185.00

CLYDE CRASHCUP (TV)
Dell Publishing Co.: Aug-Oct, 1963 - No. 5, Sept-Nov, 1964
1-All written by John Stanley 12.00 36.00 130.00
2-5 11.00 33.00 120.00

COBALT BLUE (Also see Power Comics)
Innovation Publishing: Sept, 1989 - No. 2, Oct, 1989 ($1.95, 28 pgs.)
1,2-Gustovich-c/a/scripts 2.00
The Graphic Novel ($6.95, color, 52 pgs.)-r/1,2 7.00

CODE BLUE
Image Comics (Jet-Black): Apr, 1998 ($2.95, B&W)
1-Jimmie Robinson-s/a 3.00

CODE NAME: ASSASSIN (See 1st Issue Special)

CODENAME: DANGER
Lodestone Publishing: Aug, 1985 - No. 4, May, 1986 ($1.50)
1-4 2.00

CODENAME DOUBLE IMPACT
High Impact Entertainment: 1997 ($2.95, B&W)
1,2 3.00

CODENAME: FIREARM (Also see Firearm)
Malibu Comics (Ultraverse): June, 1995 - No. 5, Sept, 1995 ($2.95, bimonthly limited series)
0-5: 0-2-Alec Swan back-up story by James Robinson 3.00
NOTE: ***Perez*** *c-0.*

CODENAME: GENETIX
Marvel Comics UK: Jan, 1993 - No. 4, May, 1993 ($1.75, limited series)
1-4: Wolverine in all 2.00

CODENAME SPITFIRE (Formerly Spitfire And The Troubleshooters)
Marvel Comics Group: No. 10, July, 1987 - No. 13, Oct, 1987
10-13: 10-Rogers-c/a 2.00

CODENAME: STRYKE FORCE (Also See Cyberforce V1#4 & Cyberforce/Stryke Force: Opposing Forces ($1.95-$2.25)
Image Comics (Top Cow Productions): Jan, 1994 - No. 14, Sept, 1995
0,1-14: 1-12-Silvestri stories, Peterson-a. 4-Stormwatch app. 14-Story continues in Cyberforce/Stryke Force: Opposing Forces; Turner-a 2.25
1-Gold, 1-Blue 4.00

CODE NAME: TOMAHAWK
Fantasy General Comics: Sept, 1986 ($1.75, high quality paper)
1-Sci/fi 2.00

CODE OF HONOR
Marvel Comics: Feb, 1997 - No. 4, May, 1997 ($5.95, limited series)
1-4-Fully painted by various; Dixon-s 6.00

GD2.0 FN6.0 NM9.4

CODY OF THE PONY EXPRESS (See Colossal Features Magazine)
Fox Features Syndicate: Sept, 1950 - No. 3, Jan, 1951 (See Women Outlaws)
1-3 (Actually #3-5). 1-Painted-c 12.00 36.00 85.00

CODY OF THE PONY EXPRESS (Buffalo Bill...) (Outlaws of the West #11 on; Formerly Bullseye)
Charlton Comics: No. 8, Oct, 1955; No. 9, Jan, 1956; No. 10, June, 1956
8-Bullseye on splash pg; not S&K-a 6.70 20.00 40.00
9,10: Buffalo Bill app. in all 4.25 13.00 28.00

CODY STARBUCK (1st app. in Star Reach #1)
Star Reach Productions: July, 1978 (2nd printing exists)
nn-Howard Chaykin-c/a 6.00
NOTE: *Both printings say First Printing. True first printing is on lower-grade paper, somewhat off-register, and snow in snow sequence has green tint.*

CO-ED ROMANCES
P. L. Publishing Co.: November, 1951
1 6.35 19.00 38.00

COFFEE WORLD
World Comics: Oct, 1995 ($1.50, B&W, anthology)
1-Shannon Wheeler's Too Much Coffee Man story 2.00

COLLECTORS DRACULA, THE
Millennium Publications: 1994 - No. 2, 1994 ($3.95, color/B&W, 52 pgs., limited series)
1,2-Bolton-a (7 pgs.) 4.00

COLLECTORS ITEM CLASSICS (See Marvel Collectors Item Classics)

COLONIA
Colonia Press: 1998 ($2.95, B&W)
1-3-Jeff Nicholson-s/a 3.00

COLORS IN BLACK
Dark Horse Comics: Mar, 1995 - No. 4, June, 1995 ($2.95, limited series)
1-4 3.00

COLOSSAL FEATURES MAGAZINE (Formerly I Loved) (See Cody of the Pony Express)
Fox Features Syndicate: No. 33, 5/50 - No. 34, 7/50; No. 3, 9/50 (Based on Columbia serial)
33,34: Cody of the Pony Express begins. 33-Painted-c. 34-Photo-c 13.00 39.00 90.00
3-Authentic criminal cases 12.00 36.00 85.00

COLOSSAL SHOW, THE (TV)
Gold Key: Oct, 1969
1 4.20 12.60 42.00

COLOSSUS (See X-Men)
Marvel Comics: Oct, 1997 ($2.99, 48 pgs., one-shot)
1-Raab-s/Hitch & Nealy-a, wraparound-c 3.00

COLOSSUS COMICS (See Green Giant & Motion Picture Funnies Weekly)
Sun Publications (Funnies, Inc.?): March, 1940
1-(Scarce)-Tulpa of Tsang(hero); Colossus app. 355.00 1067.00 3200.00
NOTE: *Cover by artist that drew Colossus in Green Giant Comics.*

COLOUR OF MAGIC, THE (Terry Pratchett's...)
Innovation Publishing: 1991 - No. 4, 1991 ($2.50, limited series)
1-4: Adapts 1st novel of the Discworld series 3.00

COLT .45 (TV)
Dell Publishing Co.: No. 924, 8/58 - No. 1058, 11-1/59-60; No. 4, 2-4/60 - No. 9, 5-7/61
Four Color 924(#1)-Wayde Preston photo-c on all 9.00 27.00 100.00
Four Color 1004,1058, #4,5,7-9: 1004-Photo-b/c 7.00 20.00 75.00
6-Toth-a 8.00 23.00 85.00

COLUMBIA COMICS
William H. Wise Co.: 1943

Combat #1 © MAR

Combat Kelly #1 © MAR

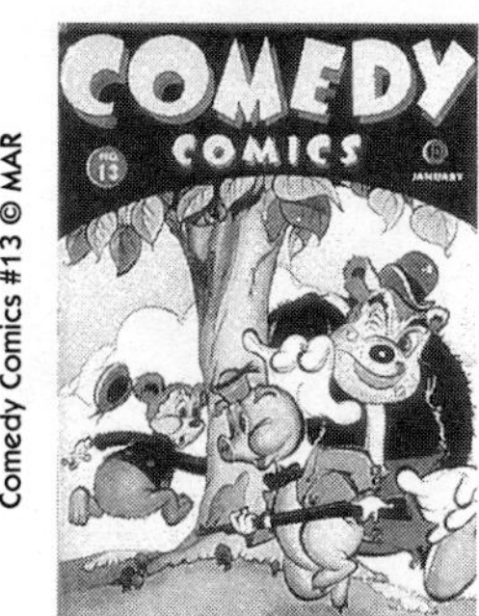

Comedy Comics #13 © MAR

	GD2.0	FN6.0	NM9.4
1-Joe Palooka, Charlie Chan, Capt. Yank, Sparky Watts, Dixie Dugan app.	27.00	81.00	190.00

COLUMBUS
Dark Horse Comics: Sept, 1992 ($2.50, B&W, one-shot)

1-Yeates painted-c			2.50

COMANCHE (See Four Color No. 1350)

COMANCHEROS, THE
Dell Publishing Co.: No. 1300, Mar-May, 1962

Four Color 1300-Movie, John Wayne photo-c	14.00	44.00	160.00

COMBAT
Atlas Comics (ANC): June, 1952 - No. 11, April, 1953

1	21.00	64.00	150.00
2-Heath-c/a	11.00	32.00	75.00
3,5-9,11: 9-Robert Q. Sale-a	8.35	25.00	50.00
4-Krigstein-a	9.15	27.00	55.00
10-B&W and color illos. in **POP**	8.35	25.00	50.00

NOTE: *Combat Casey in 7-11.* ***Heath*** *c-1, 2, 9.* ***Maneely*** *a-1; c-3.* ***Pakula*** *a-1.* ***Reinman*** *a-1.*

COMBAT
Dell Publishing Co.: Oct-Nov, 1961 - No. 40, Oct, 1973 (No #9)

1	3.80	12.60	42.00
2,3,5:	2.40	7.80	26.00
4-John F. Kennedy c/story (P.T. 109)	2.90	8.70	32.00
6,7,8(4-6/63), 8(7-9/63)	2.00	6.00	22.00
10-26: 26-Last 12¢ issue	1.60	4.80	16.00
27-40(reprints #1-14). 30-r/#4	1.30	4.00	12.00

NOTE: ***Glanzman*** *c/a-1-27, 28-40r.*

COMBAT CASEY (Formerly War Combat)
Atlas Comics (SAI): No. 6, Jan, 1953 - No. 34, July, 1957

6 (Indicia shows 1/52 in error)	13.00	39.00	90.00
7-Spanking panel	8.35	25.00	50.00
8-Used in **POP**, pg. 94	7.00	21.00	42.00
9	6.35	19.00	38.00
10,13-19-Violent art by R. Q. Sale; Battle Brady x-over #10	10.00	30.00	70.00
11,12,20-Last Precode (2/55)	6.35	19.00	38.00
21-34	5.35	16.00	32.00

NOTE: ***Everett*** *a-6.* ***Heath*** *c-10, 17, 19, 30.* ***Maneely*** *c-6, 8.* ***Powell*** *a-29(5), 30(5), 34.* ***Severin*** *c-26, 33.*

COMBAT KELLY
Atlas Comics (SPI): Nov, 1951 - No. 44, Aug, 1957

1-1st app. Combat Kelly; Heath-a	26.00	77.00	180.00
2	12.00	36.00	85.00
3-10	10.00	30.00	60.00
11-Used in **POP**, pgs. 94,95 plus color illo.	8.35	25.00	50.00
12-Color illo. in **POP**	8.35	25.00	50.00
13-16	6.35	19.00	38.00
17-Violent art by R. Q. Sale; Combat Casey app.	10.00	30.00	70.00
18-20,22-44: 18-Battle Brady app. 28-Last precode (1/55). 38-Green Berets story (8/56)	6.35	19.00	38.00
21-Transvestism-c	6.70	20.00	40.00

NOTE: ***Berg*** *a-8, 12-14, 16, 17, 19-23, 25, 26, 28, 31-36, 42-44; c-2.* ***Colan*** *a-42.* ***Heath*** *a-4; c-31.* ***Lawrence*** *a-23.* ***Maneely*** *a-4(2), 6, 7(3), 8; c-4, 5, 7, 8, 10, 25.* ***R.Q. Sale*** *a-17, 25.* ***Severin*** *c-41, 42.* ***Whitney*** *a-5.*

COMBAT KELLY (...and the Deadly Dozen)
Marvel Comics Group: June, 1972 - No. 9, Oct, 1973

1-Intro & origin new Combat Kelly; Ayers/Mooney-a; Severin-c (20¢)	1.85	5.50	15.00
2,5-8	1.10	3.30	9.00
3,4: 3-Origin. 4-Sgt. Fury-c/s	1.50	4.50	12.00
9-Death of the Deadly Dozen	1.75	5.25	14.00

COMBINED OPERATIONS (See The Story of the Commandos)

COMEBACK (See Zane Grey 4-Color 357)

GD2.0 FN6.0 NM9.4

COMEDY CARNIVAL
St. John Publishing Co.: no date (1950's) (100 pgs.)

nn-Contains rebound St. John comics	34.00	103.00	240.00

COMEDY COMICS (1st Series) (Daring Mystery #1-8) (Becomes Margie Comics #35 on)
Timely Comics (TCI 9,10): No. 9, April, 1942 - No. 34, Fall, 1946

9-(Scarce)-The Fin by Everett, Capt. Dash, Citizen V, & The Silver Scorn app.; Wolverton-a; 1st app. Comedy Kid; satire on Hitler & Stalin; The Fin, Citizen V & Silver Scorn cont. from Daring Mystery	247.00	741.00	2100.00
10-(Scarce)-Origin The Fourth Musketeer, Victory Boys; Monstro, the Mighty app.	176.00	529.00	1500.00
11-Vagabond, Stuporman app.	47.00	141.00	375.00
12,13	13.50	41.00	95.00
14-Origin/1st app. Super Rabbit (3/43) plus-c	47.00	141.00	375.00
15-20	12.00	36.00	85.00
21-32	10.00	30.00	65.00
33-Kurtzman-a (5 pgs.)	11.50	34.00	80.00
34-Intro Margie; Wolverton-a (5 pgs.)	18.00	54.00	125.00

COMEDY COMICS (2nd Series)
Marvel Comics (ACI): May, 1948 - No. 10, Jan, 1950

1-Hedy, Tessie, Millie begin; Kurtzman's "Hey Look" (he draws himself)	33.00	99.00	230.00
2	12.00	36.00	85.00
3,4-Kurtzman's "Hey Look" (?&3)	13.50	41.00	95.00
5-10	7.50	22.50	45.00

COMET, THE (See The Mighty Crusaders & Pep Comics #1)
Red Circle Comics (Archie): Oct, 1983 - No. 2, Dec, 1983

1,2: 1-Re-intro & origin The Comet; The American Shield begins. 2-Origin continues. Nino & Infantino art in both			2.00

COMET, THE
DC Comics (Impact Comics): July, 1991 - No. 18, Dec, 1992 ($1.00/$1.25)

1			2.50
2-18: 4-Black Hood app. 6-Re-intro Hangman. 8-Web x-over. 10-Contains Crusaders trading card. 4-Origin. Netzer(Nasser) c(p)-11,14-17			2.00
Annual 1 (1992, $2.50, 68 pgs.)-Contains Impact trading card; Shield back-up story			2.50

COMET MAN, THE (Movie)
Marvel Comics Group: Feb, 1987 - No. 6, July, 1987 (limited series)

1-6: 3-Hulk app. 4-She Hulk shower scene c/s. Fantastic 4 app. 5-Fantastic 4 app.			2.00

NOTE: ***Kelley Jones*** *a-1-6p.*

COMIC ALBUM (Also see Disney Comic Album)
Dell Publishing Co.: Mar-May, 1958 - No. 18, June-Aug, 1962

1-Donald Duck	7.00	22.00	80.00
2-Bugs Bunny	3.60	11.00	40.00
3-Donald Duck	5.50	16.50	60.00
4-6,8-10: 4-Tom & Jerry. 5-Woody Woodpecker. 6,10-Bugs Bunny. 8-Tom & Jerry. 9-Woody Woodpecker	2.75	8.00	30.00
7,11,15: Popeye. 11-(9-11/60)	3.60	11.00	40.00
12-14: 12-Tom & Jerry. 13-Woody Woodpecker. 14-Bugs Bunny	2.75	8.00	30.00
16-Flintstones (12-2/61-62)-3rd app. Early Cave Kids app.	6.40	19.00	70.00
17-Space Mouse (3rd app.)	3.60	11.00	40.00
18-Three Stooges; photo-c	6.40	19.00	70.00

COMIC BOOK
Marvel Comics-#1/Dark Horse Comics-#2: 1995 ($5.95, oversize)

1-Spumco characters by John K.	1.00	2.80	7.00
2-(Dark Horse)		2.40	6.00

COMIC CAPERS
Red Circle Mag./Marvel Comics: Fall, 1944 - No. 6, Summer, 1946

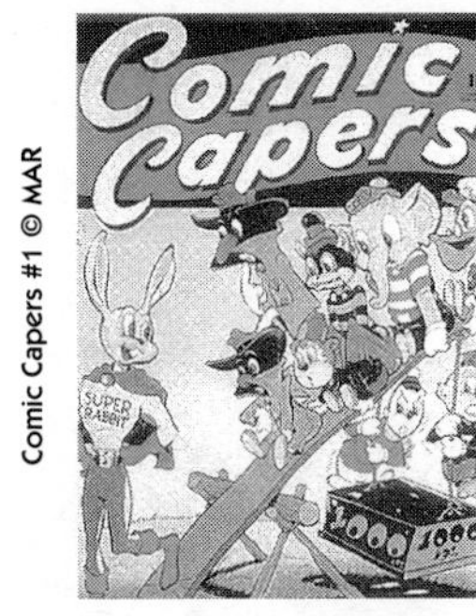

Comic Capers #1 © MAR

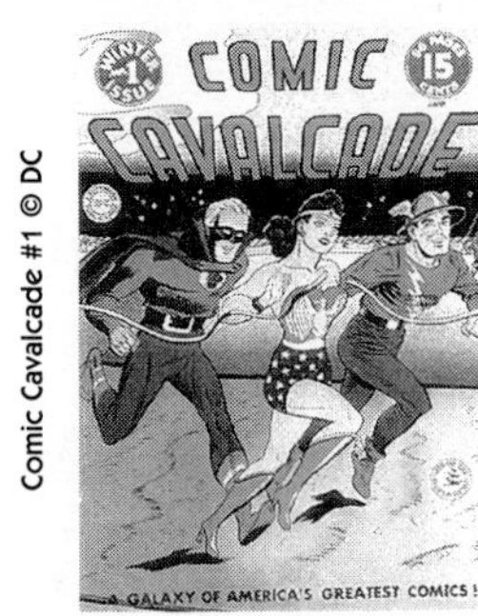

Comic Cavalcade #1 © DC

The Comics #6 © DELL

GD2.0 FN6.0 NM9.4

1-Super Rabbit, The Creeper, Silly Seal, Ziggy Pig, Sharpy Fox begin 24.00 73.00 170.00
2 12.00 36.00 85.00
3-6 10.00 30.00 70.00

COMIC CAVALCADE
All-American/National Periodical Publications: Winter, 1942-43 - No. 63, June-July, 1954 (Contents change with No. 30, Dec-Jan, 1948-49 on)

GD2.0 FN6.0 VF8.0 NM9.4

1-The Flash, Green Lantern, Wonder Woman, Wildcat, The Black Pirate by Moldoff (also #2), Ghost Patrol, and Red White & Blue begin; Scribbly app.; Minute Movie 800.00 2400.00 4800.00 8000.00

GD2.0 FN6.0 NM9.4

2-Mutt & Jeff begin; last Ghost Patrol & Black Pirate; Minute Movies 225.00 675.00 1800.00
3-Hop Harrigan & Sargon, the Sorcerer begin; The King app. 162.00 486.00 1300.00
4,5: 4-The Gay Ghost, The King, Scribbly, & Red Tornado app. 5-Christmas-c. 5-Prints ad for Jr. JSA membership kit that includes "The Minute Man Answers The Call" 137.00 411.00 1100.00
6-10: 7-Red Tornado & Black Pirate app.; last Scribbly. 9-Fat & Slat app.; X-Mas-c 105.00 315.00 840.00
11,12,14,16-20: 12-Last Red White & Blue. 19-Christmas-c 87.00 261.00 700.00
13-Solomon Grundy app.; X-Mas-c 144.00 432.00 1150.00
15-Johnny Peril begins (1st app.,6-7/46), ends #29 (See Danger Trail & Sensation Mystery) 97.00 291.00 775.00
21-23: 23-Harry Lampert-c (Toth swipes) 84.00 252.00 675.00
24-Solomon Grundy x-over in Green Lantern 103.00 309.00 825.00
25-28: 25-Black Canary app.; X-Mas-c. 26-28-Johnny Peril app. 28-Last Mutt & Jeff 72.00 216.00 575.00
29-(10-11/48)-Last Flash, Wonder Woman, Green Lantern & Johnny Peril; Wonder Woman invents "Thinking Machine"; 2nd computer in comics (after Flash Comics #52); Leave It to Binky story (early app.) 84.00 252.00 675.00
30-(12-1/48-49)-The Fox & the Crow, Dodo & the Frog & Nutsy Squirrel begin 40.00 120.00 320.00
31-35 23.00 69.00 160.00
36-49 16.00 47.00 110.00
50-62(Scarce) 20.00 60.00 140.00
63(Rare) 33.00 99.00 230.00

NOTE: ***Grossman*** *a-30-63.* ***E.E. Hibbard*** *c-(Flash only)-1-4, 7-14, 16-19, 21.* ***Sheldon Mayer*** *a(2-3)-40-63.* ***Moulson*** *c(G.L.)-7, 15.* ***Nodell*** *c(G.L.)-9.* ***H.G. Peter*** *c(W. Woman only)-1, 3-21, 24.* ***Post*** *a-31, 36.* ***Purcell*** *c(G.L.)-2-5, 10.* ***Reinman*** *a(Green Lantern)-4-6, 8, 9, 13, 15-21; c(Gr. Lantern)-6, 8, 19.* ***Toth*** *a(Green Lantern)-26-28; c-27. Atom app.-22, 23.*

COMIC COMICS
Fawcett Publications: Apr, 1946 - No. 10, Feb, 1947

1-Captain Kidd; Nutty Comics #1 in indicia 12.00 36.00 85.00
2-10-Wolverton-a, 4 pgs. each. 5-Captain Kidd app. Mystic Moot by Wolverton in #2-10? 13.50 41.00 95.00

COMIC CUTS (Also see The Funnies)
H. L. Baker Co., Inc.: 5/19/34 - 7/28/34 (5¢, 24 pgs.) (Tabloid size in full color) (Not reprints; published weekly; created for newsstand sale)

V1#1 - V1#7(6/30/34), V1#8(7/14/34), V1#9(7/28/34)-Idle Jack strips 10.00 30.00 60.00

COMIC LAND
Fact and Fiction Publ.: March, 1946

1-Sandusky & the Senator, Sam Stupor, Sleuth, Marvin the Great, Sir Passer, Phineas Gruff app.; Irv Tirman & Perry Williams art 13.00 39.00 90.00

COMICO CHRISTMAS SPECIAL
Comico: Dec, 1988 ($2.50, 44pgs.)

1-Rude/Williamson-a; Dave Stevens-c 3.00

COMICO COLLECTION
Comico: 1987 ($9.95, slipcased collection)

nn-Contains exclusive Grendel: Devil's Vagary, 9 random Comico comics, a poster and newsletter in black slipcase w/silver ink 25.00

COMICO PRIMER (See Primer)

COMIC PAGES (Formerly Funny Picture Stories)
Centaur Publications: V3#4, July, 1939 - V3#6, Dec, 1939

V3#4-Bob Wood-a 69.00 207.00 550.00
5,6: 6-Schwab-c 52.00 156.00 420.00

COMICS (See All Good)

COMICS, THE
Dell Publ. Co.: Mar, 1937 - No. 11, Nov, 1938 (Newspaper strip-r; bi-monthly)

1-1st app. Tom Mix in comics; Wash Tubbs, Tom Beatty, Myra North, Arizona Kid, Erik Noble & International Spy w/Doctor Doom begin 175.00 525.00 1400.00
2 81.00 243.00 650.00
3-11: 3-Alley Oop begins 66.00 200.00 525.00

COMICS AND STORIES (See Walt Disney's Comics and Stories)

COMICS & STORIES (Also see Wolf & Red)
Dark Horse Comics: Apr, 1996 - No. 3, June, 1996 ($2.95, limited series) (Created by Tex Avery)

1-3: Wolf & Red app; reads Comics and Stories on-c. 1-Terry Moore-a. 2-Reed Waller-a. 3.00

COMICS CALENDAR, THE (The 1946...)
True Comics Press (ordered through the mail): 1946 (25¢, 116 pgs.) (Stapled at top)

nn-(Rare) Has a "strip" story for every day of the year in color 40.00 120.00 300.00

COMICS DIGEST (Pocket size)
Parents' Magazine Institute: Winter, 1942-43 (B&W, 100 pgs)

1-Reprints from True Comics (non-fiction World War II stories) 9.15 27.00 55.00

COMICS EXPRESS
Eclipse Comics: Nov, 1989 - No. 2, Jan, 1990 ($2.95, B&W, 68pgs.)

1,2: Collection of strip-r; 2(12/89-c, 1/90 inside) 3.00

COMICS FOR KIDS
London Publ. Co./Timely: 1945 (no month); No. 2, Sum, 1945 (Funny animal)

1,2-Puffy Pig, Sharpy Fox 13.00 39.00 90.00

COMICS' GREATEST WORLD
Dark Horse Comics: Jun, 1993 - V4#4, Sept, 1993 ($1.00, weekly, lim. series)

Arcadia (Wk 1): V1#1,2,4: 1-X: Frank Miller-c. 2-Pit Bulls. 4-Monster. 2.00
1-B&W Press Proof Edition (1500 copies) 1.25 3.75 10.00
1-Silver-c; distr. retailer bonus w/print & cards 1.00 3.00 8.00
3-Ghost, Dorman-c; Hughes-a 4.00
Retailer's Prem. Emb. Silver Foil Logo-r/V1#1-4 1.25 3.75 10.00
Golden City (Wk 2: V2#1-4: 1-Rebel; Ordway-c. 2-Mecha; Dave Johnson-c. 3-Titan; Walt Simonson-c. 4-Catalyst; Perez-c. 2.00
1-Gold-c; distr. retailer bonus w/print & cards. 2.40 6.00
Retailer's Prem. Embos. Gold Foil Logo-r/V2#1-4 1.00 3.00 8.00
Steel Harbor (Week 3): V3#1-Barb Wire; Dorman-c; Gulacy-a(p) 4.00
2-4: 2-The Machine. 3-Wolfgang. 4-Motorhead 2.00
1-Silver-c; distr. retailer bonus w/print & cards 1.00 3.00 8.00
Retailer's Prem. Emb. Red Foil Logo-r/V3#1-4. 1.25 3.75 10.00
Vortex (Week 4): V4#1-4: 1-Division 13; Dorman-c. 2-Hero Zero; Art Adams-c. 3-King Tiger; Chadwick-a(p); Darrow-c. 4-Vortex; Miller-c. 2.00
1-Gold-c; distr. retailer bonus w/print & cards. 2.40 6.00
Retailer's Prem. Emb. Blue Foil Logo-r/V4#1-4. 1.00 3.00 8.00

COMICS' GREATEST WORLD: OUT OF THE VORTEX (See Out of The Vortex)

COMICS HITS (See Harvey Comics Hits)

COMICS MAGAZINE, THE (...Funny Pages #3)(Funny Pages #6 on)
Comics Magazine Co. (1st Comics Mag./Centaur Publ.): May, 1936 - No. 5, Sept, 1936 (Paper covers)

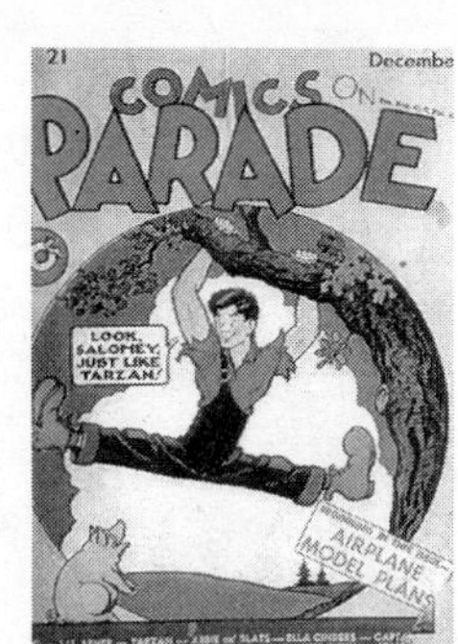

Comics on Parade #21 © UFS

Commander Battle and the Atomic Sub #3 © ACG

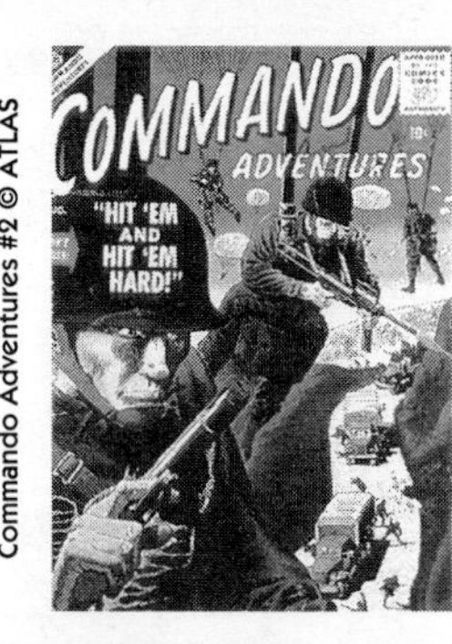

Commando Adventures #2 © ATLAS

GD2.0 FN6.0 VF8.0
1-1st app. Dr. Mystic (a.k.a. Dr. Occult) by Siegel & Shuster (the 1st app. of a Superman prototype in comics). Dr. Mystic is not in costume but later appears in costume as a more pronounced prototype in More Fun #14-17. (1st episode of "The Koth and the Seven"; continues in More Fun #14; originally scheduled for publication at DC). 1 pg. Kelly-a; Sheldon Mayer-a 1200.00 3600.00 9600.00
GD2.0 FN6.0 NM9.4
2-Federal Agent (a.k.a. Federal Men) by Siegel & Shuster; 1 pg. Kelly-a 237.00 711.00 1900.00
3-5 193.00 579.00 1500.00

COMICS NOVEL (Anarcho, Dictator of Death)
Fawcett Publications: 1947
1-All Radar; 51 pg anti-fascism story 29.00 88.00 205.00

COMICS ON PARADE (No. 30 on are a continuation of Single Series)
United Features Syndicate: Apr, 1938 - No. 104, Feb, 1955
1-Tarzan by Foster; Captain & the Kids, Little Mary Mixup, Abbie & Slats, Ella Cinders, Broncho Bill, Li'l Abner begin 300.00 900.00 3000.00
2 (Tarzan & others app. on-c of #1-3,17) 118.00 354.00 1000.00
3 94.00 282.00 800.00
4,5 71.00 213.00 600.00
6-10 47.00 141.00 400.00
11-16,18-20 41.00 123.00 325.00
17-Tarzan-c 45.00 135.00 385.00
21-29: 22-Son of Tarzan begins. 22,24,28-Tailspin Tommy-c. 29-Last Tarzan issue 33.00 100.00 250.00
30-Li'l Abner 21.00 64.00 160.00
31-The Captain & the Kids 15.00 44.00 110.00
32-Nancy & Fritzi Ritz 12.00 36.00 90.00
33,36,39,42-Li'l Abner 17.00 52.00 130.00
34,37,40-The Captain & the Kids (10/41,6/42,3/43) 15.00 44.00 110.00
35,38-Nancy & Fritzi Ritz. 38-Infinity-c 12.00 36.00 90.00
41-Nancy & Fritzi Ritz 9.30 28.00 70.00
43-The Captain & the Kids 15.00 44.00 110.00
44)3/44),47,50: Nancy & Fritzi Ritz 9.30 28.00 70.00
45-Li'l Abner 15.00 44.00 110.00
46,49-The Captain & the Kids 12.00 36.00 90.00
48-Li'l Abner (3/45) 15.00 44.00 110.00
51,54-Li'l Abner 12.00 36.00 90.00
52-The Captain & the Kids (3/46) 8.50 26.00 60.00
53,55,57-Nancy & Fritzi Ritz 8.50 26.00 60.00
56-The Captain & the Kids (r/Sparkler) 8.50 26.00 60.00
58-Li'l Abner; continues as Li'l Abner #61? 12.00 36.00 90.00
59-The Captain & the Kids 6.85 21.00 48.00
60-70-Nancy & Fritzi Ritz 6.85 21.00 48.00
5.70 17.00 35.00
71-99,101-104-Nancy & Sluggo. 71-76-Nancy only 5.70 17.00 35.00
100-Nancy & Sluggo 6.50 19.50 45.00
Special Issue, 7/46; Summer, 1948 - The Captain & the Kids app. 5.70 17.00 35.00
NOTE: Bound Volume (Very Rare) includes No. 1-12; bound by publisher in pictorial comic boards & distributed at the 1939 World's Fair and through mail order from ads in comic books (also see Tip Top) 235.00 706.00 2000.00
NOTE: *Li'l Abner reprinted from Tip Top.*

COMICS REVUE
St. John Publ. Co. (United Features Synd.): June, 1947 - No. 5, Jan, 1948
1-Ella Cinders & Blackie 10.00 30.00 65.00
2,4: 2-Hap Hopper (7/47). 4-Ella Cinders (9/47) 7.50 22.50 45.00
3,5: 3-Iron Vic (8/47). 5-Gordo No. 1 (1/48) 6.70 20.00 40.00

COMIC STORY PAINT BOOK
Samuel Lowe Co.: 1943 (Large size, 68 pgs.)
1055-Captain Marvel & a Captain Marvel Jr. story to read & color; 3 panels in color per pg. (reprints) 62.00 186.00 625.00

COMIX BOOK
Marvel Comics Group/Krupp Comics Works No. 4,5: 1974 - No. 5, 1976
($1.00, B&W, magazine)
1-Underground comic artists; 2 pgs. Wolverton-a 2.50 7.50 24.00
2,3: 2-Wolverton-a (1 pg.) 2.25 6.75 18.00
4(2/76), 4(5/76), 5 (Low distribution) 2.50 7.50 20.00
NOTE: *Print run No. 1-3: 200-250M; No. 4&5: 10M each.*

COMIX INTERNATIONAL
Warren Magazines: Jul, 1974 - No. 5, Spring, 1977 (Full color, stiff-c, mail only)
1-Low distribution; all Corben story remainders from Warren 7.00 21.00 75.00
2,4: 2-Wood, Wrightson-r. 4-printing w/Corben sty 2.50 7.50 25.00
3-5: 4-(printing without Corben story). 4-Crandall-a. 5-Spirit story 2.50 7.50 20.00
NOTE: *No. 4 had two printings with extra **Corben** story in one. No. 3 may also have a variation. No. 3 has two Jeff Jones reprints from Vampirella.*

COMMANDER BATTLE AND THE ATOMIC SUB
Amer. Comics Group (Titan Publ. Co.): Jul-Aug, 1954 - No. 7, Aug-Sep, 1955
1 (3-D effect)-Moldoff flying saucer-c 45.00 135.00 360.00
2,4-7: 2-Moldoff-c. 4-(1-2/55)-Last pre-code; Landau-a. 5-3-D effect story (2 pgs.). 6,7-Landau-a. 7-Flying saucer-c 30.00 90.00 210.00
3-H-Bomb-c; Atomic Sub becomes Atomic Spaceship 31.00 94.00 220.00

COMMANDO ADVENTURES
Atlas Comics (MMC): June, 1957 - No. 2, Aug, 1957
1,2-Severin-c. 2-Drucker-a? 9.15 27.00 55.00

COMMANDO YANK (See The Mighty Midget Comics & Wow Comics)

COMPLETE BOOK OF COMICS AND FUNNIES
William H. Wise & Co.: 1944 (25¢, one-shot, 196 pgs.)
1-Origin Brad Spencer, Wonderman; The Magnet, The Silver Knight by Kinstler, & Zudo the Jungle Boy app. 40.00 120.00 290.00

COMPLETE BOOK OF TRUE CRIME COMICS
William H. Wise & Co.: No date (Mid 1940's) (25¢, 132 pgs.)
nn-Contains Crime Does Not Pay rebound (includes #22) 100.00 300.00 800.00

COMPLETE COMICS (Formerly Amazing Comics No. 1)
Timely Comics (EPC): No. 2, Winter, 1944-45
2-The Destroyer, The Whizzer, The Young Allies & Sergeant Dix; Schomburg-c 144.00 431.00 1150.00

COMPLETE GUIDE TO THE DEADLY ARTS OF KUNG FU AND KARATE
Marvel Comics: 1974 (68 pgs., B&W magazine)
V1#1-Bruce Lee-c and 5 pg. story (scarce) 3.00 9.00 30.00

COMPLETE LOVE MAGAZINE (Formerly a pulp with same title)
Ace Periodicals (Periodical House): V26#2, May-June, 1951 - V32#4(#191), Sept, 1956
V26#2-Painted-c (52 pgs.) 5.85 17.50 35.00
V26#3-6(2/52), V27#1(4/52)-6(1/53) 4.15 12.50 25.00
V28#1(3/53), V28#2(5/53), V29#3(7/53)-6(12/53) 4.00 10.00 20.00
V30#1(2/54), V30#1(#176, 4/54),2,4-6(#181, 1/55) 4.00 10.00 20.00
V30#3(#178)-Rock Hudson photo-c 4.25 13.00 26.00
V31#1(#182, 3/55)-Last precode 4.00 10.00 20.00
V31#2(5/55)-6(#187, 1/56) 3.00 7.50 15.00
V32#1(#188, 3/56)-4(#191, 9/56) 3.00 7.50 15.00
NOTE: *(34 total issues). Photo-c V27#5-on. Painted-c V26#3.*

COMPLETE MYSTERY (True Complete Mystery No. 5 on)
Marvel Comics (PrPI): Aug, 1948 - No. 4, Feb, 1949 (Full length stories)
1-Seven Dead Men 43.00 128.00 340.00
2-4: 2-Jigsaw of Doom! 3-Fear in the Night; Burgos-c/a (28 pgs.). 4-A Squealer Dies Fast 40.00 120.00 300.00

COMPLETE ROMANCE
Avon Periodicals: 1949
1-(Scarce)-Reprinted as Women to Love 39.00 116.00 270.00

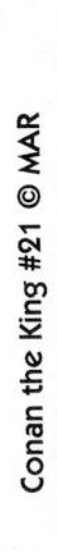
Conan the Barbarian #11 © MAR

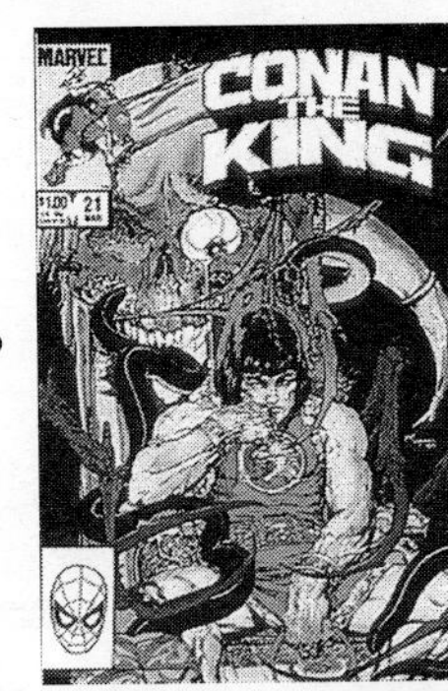

Conan the King #21 © MAR

Concrete - Fragile Creature #2 © DH

CONAN (See Chamber of Darkness #4, Giant-Size..., Handbook of..., King Conan, Marvel Graphic Novel #19, 28, Marvel Treasury Ed., Power Record Comics, Robert E. Howard's.., Savage Sword of Conan, and Savage Tales)

CONAN: (Title Series): Marvel Comics

CONAN, 8/95 - No. 11, 6/96 ($2.95), 1-11: 4-Malibu Comic's Rune app. 3.00

...CLASSIC, 6/94 - No. 11, 4/95 ($1.50), 1-11: 1-r/Conan #1 by B. Smith, r/covers w/changes. 2-11-r/Conan #2-11 by Smith. 2-Bound w/cover to Conan The Adventurer #2 by mistake 2.00

...DEATH COVERED IN GOLD, 9/99 - No. 3, 11/99 ($2.99), 1-3-Roy Thomas-s/John Buscema-a 3.00

...RETURN OF STYRM, 9/98 - No. 3, 11/98 ($2.99), 1-3-Parente & Soresina-a; painted-c 3.00

...RIVER OF BLOOD, 6/98 - No. 3, 8/98 ($2.50), 1-3 2.50

...SCARLET SWORD, 12/98 - No. 3, 2/99 ($2.99), 1-3-Thomas-s/Raffaele-a 3.00

CONAN SAGA, THE
Marvel Comics: June, 1987 - No. 97, Apr, 1995 ($2.00/$2.25, B&W, magazine)

1-Barry Smith-r 1-9,11; new Barry Smith-c 1-9 2.00
2-27: 13,15-Boris-c. 17-Adams-r. 18,25-Chaykin-r. 22-r/Giant-Size Conan 1,2 2.00
28-97 ($2.25): 31-Red Sonja-r by N. Adams/SSOC #1; 1 pg. Jeff Jones-r. 32-Newspaper strip-r begin by Buscema. 33-Smith/Conrad-a. 39-r/Kull #1('71) by Andru/Wood. 44-Swipes-c/Savage Tales #1. 57-Brunner-r/SSOC #30. 66-r/Conan Annual #2 by Buscema. 79-r/Conan #43-45 w/Red Sonja. 85-Based on Conan #57-63 2.25

NOTE: ***J. Buscema** r-32-on; c-86. **Chaykin** r-34. **Chiodo** painted c-63, 65, 66, 82. **G. Colan** a-47p. **Jusko** painted c-64, 83. **Kaluta** c-84. **Nino** a-37. **Ploog** a-50. **N. Redondo** painted c-48, 50, 51, 53, 57, 62. **Simonson** r-50-54, 56. **B. Smith** r-51. **Starlin** c-34. **Williamson** r-50i.*

CONAN THE ADVENTURER
Marvel Comics: June, 1994 - No. 14, July, 1995 ($1.50)

1-($2.50)-Embossed foil-c; Kayaran-a 2.50
2-14 2.00
2-Contents are Conan Classics #2 by mistake 2.00

CONAN THE BARBARIAN
Marvel Comics: Oct, 1970 - No. 275, Dec, 1993

	GD2.0	FN6.0	NM9.4
1-Origin/1st app. Conan (in comics) by Barry Smith; 1st app. Kull (cameo); #1-9 are 15¢ issues	17.00	52.00	190.00
2	6.50	19.00	70.00
3-(Low distribution in some areas)	11.00	33.00	120.00
4,5	5.00	15.00	50.00
6-9: 8-Hidden panel message, pg. 14. 9-Last 15¢-c	3.20	9.60	32.00
10,11 (25¢ giants): 10-Black Knight-r; Kull story by Severin	4.20	12.60	42.00
12,13: 12-Wrightson-c(i)	2.50	7.50	20.00
14,15-Elric app.	3.20	9.60	32.00
16,19,20: 16-Conan-r/Savage Tales #1	2.25	6.75	18.00
17,18-No Barry Smith-a	1.10	3.30	9.00
21,22: 22-Has reprint from #1	1.85	5.50	15.00
23-1st app. Red Sonja (2/73)	2.50	7.50	24.00
24-1st full Red Sonja story; last Smith-a	2.50	7.00	20.00
25-John Buscema-c/a begins			6.00
26-30			5.00
31-36,38-57,59,60: 44,45-N. Adams-i(Crusty Bunkers). 45-Adams-c. 48-Origin retold. 59-Origin Belit			4.00
37-Neal Adams-c/a; last 20¢ issue; contains pull-out subscription form	1.10	3.30	9.00
58-2nd Belit app. (see Giant-Size Conan #1)			5.00
61-65-(Regular 25¢ editions)(4-8/76)			3.00
61-65-(30¢-c variants, limited distribution)	1.50	4.50	12.00
66-99: 68-Red Sonja story cont'd from Marvel Feature #7. 84-Intro. Zula. 85-Origin Zula. 87-r/Savage Sword of Conan #3 in color			3.00
100-(52 pg. Giant)-Death of Belit			4.00
101-274: 116-r/Power Record Comic PR31. 115-Double size. 200-(52 pgs.). 250-(60 pgs.). 232-Young Conan storyline begins; Conan is born. 244-Return of Zula. 262-Adapted from R.E. Howard story			2.00
275-($2.50, 68 pgs.)-Final issue; painted-c			3.00
King Size 1(1973, 35¢)-Smith-r/#2,4; Smith-c	1.50	4.50	12.00
Annual 2(1976, 50¢)-New full length story			4.00
Annual 3-12: 3('78)-Chaykin/N. Adams-r/SSOC #2. 4('78)-New full length story. 5(1979)-New full length Buscema story & part-c, 6(1981)-Kane-c/a. 7('82)-Based on novel "Conan of the Isles" (new-a). 8(1984), 9(1984), 10(1986). 11(1986). 12(1987)			2.00
Special Edition 1 (Red Nails)			3.50

NOTE: ***Arthur Adams** c-248, 249. **Neal Adams** a-116r(i); c-49i. **Austin** a-125, 126; c-125i, 126i. **Brunner** c-17i. c-40. **Buscema** a-25-36p, 38, 39, 41-56p, 58-63p, 65-67p, 68, 70-78p, 84-86p, 88-91p, 93-126p, 136p, 140, 141-144p, 146-158p, 159, 161, 162, 163p, 165-185p, 187-190p, Annual 2(3pgs.). 3-5p, 7p; c(p)-26, 36, 44, 46, 52, 56, 58, 59, 64, 65, 72, 78-80, 83-91, 93-103, 105-126, 136-151, 155-159, 161, 162, 168, 169, 171, 172, 174, 175, 178-185, 188, 189, Annual 4, 5, 7. **Chaykin** a-79-83. **Golden** c-152. **Kaluta** c-167. **Gil Kane** a-12p, 17p, 18p, 127-130, 131-134p; c-12p, 17p, 18p, 23, 25, 27-32, 34, 35, 38, 39, 41-43, 45-51, 53-55, 57, 60-63, 65-71, 73p, 76p, 127-134. **Jim Lee** c-242. **McFarlane** c-241p. **Ploog** a-57. **Russell** a-21; c-251i. **Simonson** c-135. **B. Smith** a-1-11p, 12, 13-15p, 16, 19-21, 23, 24; c-1-11, 13-16, 19-24p. **Starlin** a-64. **Wood** a-47r. Issue Nos. 3-5, 7-9, 11, 16-18, 21, 23, 25, 27-30, 35, 37, 38, 42, 45, 52, 57, 58, 65, 69-71, 73, 79-83, 99, 100, 104, 114, Annual 2 have original Robert E. Howard stories adapted. Issues #32-34 adapted from Norvell Page's novel **Flame Winds**.*

CONAN THE BARBARIAN (Volume 2)
Marvel Comics: July, 1997 - No. 3, Oct, 1997 ($2.50, limited series)

1-3-Castellini-a 2.50

CONAN THE BARBARIAN MOVIE SPECIAL (Movie)
Marvel Comics Group: Oct, 1982 - No. 2, Nov, 1982

1,2-Movie adaptation; Buscema-a 2.00

CONAN THE BARBARIAN: THE USURPER
Marvel Comics: Dec, 1997 - No. 3, Feb, 1998 ($2.50, limited series)

1-3-Dixon-s 2.50

CONAN THE DESTROYER (Movie)
Marvel Comics Group: Jan, 1985 - No. 2, Mar, 1985

1,2-r/Marvel Super Special 2.00

CONAN THE KING (Formerly King Conan)
Marvel Comics Group: No. 20, Jan, 1984 - No. 55, Nov, 1989

20-55: 48-55 ($1.50) 2.00

NOTE: ***Kaluta** c-20-23, 24i, 26, 27, 30, 50, 52. **Williamson** a-37i; c-37i, 38i.*

CONAN: THE LORD OF THE SPIDERS
Marvel Comics: Mar, 1998 - No. 3, May, 1998 ($2.50, limited series)

1-3-Roy Thomas-s/Raffaele-a 2.50

CONAN THE SAVAGE
Marvel Comics: Aug, 1995 - No. 10, May, 1996 ($2.95, B&W, Magazine)

1-10: 1-Bisley-c. 4-vs. Malibu Comic's Rune. 5,10-Brereton-c 3.00

CONAN VS. RUNE (Also See Conan #4)
Marvel Comics: Nov, 1995 ($2.95, one-shot)

1-Barry Smith-c/a/scripts 3.00

CONCRETE (Also see Dark Horse Presents & Within Our Reach)
Dark Horse Comics: March, 1987 - No. 10, Nov, 1988 ($1.50, B&W)

	GD2.0	FN6.0	NM9.4
1-Paul Chadwick-c/a in all	1.25	3.75	10.00
1-2nd print			3.00
2		2.40	6.00
3-Origin			5.00
4-10			4.00
A New Life 1 (1989, $2.95, B&W)-r/#3,4 plus new-a (11 pgs.)			3.00
Celebrates Earth Day 1990 ($3.50, 52 pgs.)		2.40	6.00
Color Special 1 (2/89, $2.95, 44 pgs.)-r/1st two Concrete apps. from Dark Horse Presents #1,2 plus new-a		2.40	6.00
Land And Sea 1 (2/89, $2.95, B&W)-r/#1,2		2.40	6.00
Odd Jobs 1 (7/90, $3.50)-r/5,6 plus new-a			3.50

CONCRETE: (Title series), Dark Horse Comics

--ECLECTICA, 4/93 - No. 2, 5/93 ($2.95) 1,2 3.00

--FRAGILE CREATURE, 6/91 - No. 4, 2/92 ($2.50) 1-4 2.50

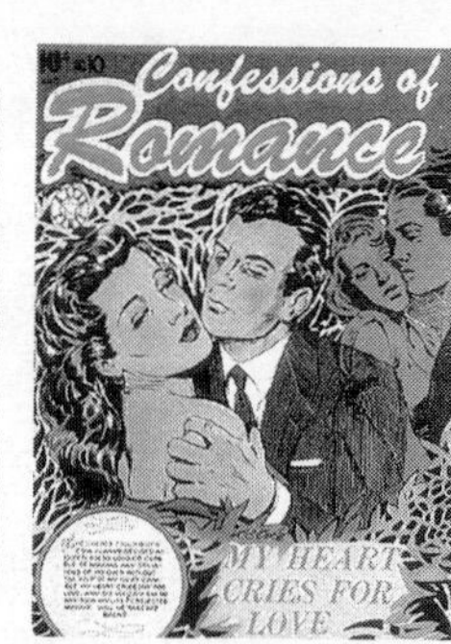

Confessions of Romance #10 © STAR

Congo Bill (1st series) #1 © DC

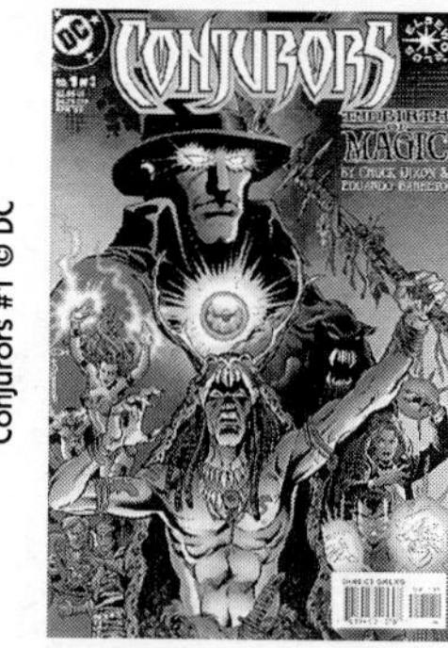

Conjurors #1 © DC

GD2.0 FN6.0 NM9.4

--**KILLER SMILE,** (Legend), 7/94 - No. 4, 10/94 ($2.9) 1-4 3.00

--**STRANGE ARMOR,** 12/97 - No. 5, 5/98 ($2.95, color) 1-5-Chadwick-s/c/a; retells origin 3.00

--**THINK LIKE A MOUNTAIN,** (Legend), 3/96 - No. 6, 8/96 ($2.95)
1-6: Chadwick-a/scripts & Darrow-c in all 3.00

CONDORMAN (Walt Disney)
Whitman Publishing: Oct, 1981 - No. 3, Jan, 1982
1-3: 1,2-Movie adaptation; photo-c 4.00

CONEHEADS
Marvel Comics: June, 1994 - No. 4, 1994 ($1.75, limited series)
1-4 2.00

CONFESSIONS ILLUSTRATED (Magazine)
E. C. Comics: Jan-Feb, 1956 - No. 2, Spring, 1956

	GD2.0	FN6.0	NM9.4
1-Craig, Kamen, Wood, Orlando-a	16.00	47.00	110.00
2-Craig, Crandall, Kamen, Orlando-a	13.50	41.00	95.00

CONFESSIONS OF LOVE
Artful Publ.: Apr, 1950 - No. 2, July, 1950 (25¢, 7-1/4x5-1/4", 132 pgs.)

	GD2.0	FN6.0	NM9.4
1-Bakerish-a	26.00	79.00	185.00
2-Art & text; Bakerish-a	15.00	45.00	105.00

CONFESSIONS OF LOVE (Formerly Startling Terror Tales #10; becomes Confessions of Romance No. 7 on)
Star Publications: No. 11, 7/52 - No. 14, 1/53; No. 4, 3/53- No. 6, 8/53

	GD2.0	FN6.0	NM9.4
11-13: 12,13-Disbrow-a	13.50	41.00	95.00
14,5,6	10.00	30.00	70.00
4-Disbrow-a	11.50	34.00	80.00

NOTE: *All have* ***L. B. Cole*** *covers.*

CONFESSIONS OF ROMANCE (Formerly Confessions of Love)
Star Publications: No. 7, Nov, 1953 - No. 11, Nov, 1954

	GD2.0	FN6.0	NM9.4
7	13.50	41.00	95.00
8	10.00	30.00	70.00
9-Wood-a	13.00	39.00	90.00
10,11-Disbrow-a	11.50	34.00	80.00

NOTE: *All have* ***L. B. Cole*** *covers.*

CONFESSIONS OF THE LOVELORN (Formerly Lovelorn)
American Comics Group (Regis Publ./Best Synd. Features): No. 52, Aug, 1954 - No. 114, June-July, 1960

	GD2.0	FN6.0	NM9.4
52 (3-D effect)	28.00	84.00	195.00
53,55	8.35	25.00	50.00
54 (3-D effect)	28.00	84.00	195.00
56-Anti-communist propaganda story, 10 pgs; last pre-code (2/55)	10.00	30.00	65.00
57-90,100	4.25	13.00	28.00
91-Williamson-a	8.35	25.00	50.00
92-99,101-114	4.00	11.00	22.00

NOTE: ***Whitney*** *a-most issues; c-52, 53. Painted c-106, 107.*

CONFIDENTIAL DIARY (Formerly High School Confidential Diary; Three Nurses #18 on)
Charlton Comics: No. 12, May, 1962 - No. 17, Mar, 1963

	GD2.0	FN6.0	NM9.4
12-17	2.00	6.00	16.00

CONGO BILL (See Action Comics & More Fun Comics #56)
National Periodical Publication: Aug-Sept, 1954 - No. 7, Aug-Sept, 1955

	GD2.0	FN6.0	VF8.0
1 (Scarce)	91.00	273.00	725.00
2,7 (Scarce)	71.00	213.00	565.00
3-6 (Scarce). 4-Last pre-code issue	60.00	180.00	480.00

NOTE: *(Rarely found in fine to mint condition.)* ***Nick Cardy*** *c-1-7.*

CONGO BILL
DC Comics (Vertigo): Oct, 1999 - No. 4, Jan, 2000 ($2.95, limited series)

	GD2.0	FN6.0	NM9.4
1,2-Corben-c			3.00

CONGORILLA (Also see Actions Comics #224)
DC Comics: Nov, 1992 - No. 4, Feb, 1993 ($1.75, limited series)
1-4: 1,2-Brian Bolland-c 2.00

CONJURORS
DC Comics: Apr, 1999 - No. 3, Jun, 1999 ($2.95, limited series)
1-3-Elseworlds; Phantom Stranger app.; Barreto-c/a 3.00

CONNECTICUT YANKEE, A (See King Classics)

CONQUEROR, THE
Dell Publishing Co.: No., 690, Mar, 1956

	GD2.0	FN6.0	NM9.4
Four Color 690-Movie, John Wayne photo-c	14.00	44.00	160.00

CONQUEROR COMICS
Albrecht Publishing Co.: Winter, 1945

	GD2.0	FN6.0	NM9.4
nn	19.00	56.00	130.00

CONQUEROR OF THE BARREN EARTH (See The Warlord #63)
DC Comics: Feb, 1985 - No. 4, May, 1985 (Limited series)
1-4: Back-up series from Warlord 2.00

CONQUEST
Store Comics: 1953 (6¢)

	GD2.0	FN6.0	NM9.4
1-Richard the Lion Hearted, Beowulf, Swamp Fox	5.00	15.00	30.00

CONQUEST
Famous Funnies: Spring, 1955

	GD2.0	FN6.0	NM9.4
1-Crandall-a, 1 pg.; contains contents of 1953 ish.	4.00	11.00	22.00

CONSPIRACY
Marvel Comics: Feb, 1998 - No. 2, Mar, 1998 ($2.99, limited series)
1,2-Painted art by Korday/Abnett-s 3.00

CONSTRUCT
Caliber (New Worlds): 1996 - No. 6, 1997 ($2.95, B&W, limited series)
1-6: Paul Jenkins scripts 3.00

CONTACT COMICS
Aviation Press: July, 1944 - No. 12, May, 1946

	GD2.0	FN6.0	NM9.4
nn-Black Venus, Flamingo, Golden Eagle, Tommy Tomahawk begin	47.00	141.00	380.00
2-5: 3-Last Flamingo. 3,4-Black Venus by L. B. Cole. 5-The Phantom Flyer app.	40.00	120.00	290.00
6,11-Kurtzman's Black Venus; 11-Last Golden Eagle, last Tommy Tomahawk; Feldstein-a	40.00	120.00	320.00
7-10	36.00	107.00	250.00
12-Sky Rangers, Air Kids, Ace Diamond app.; L.B. Cole sci-fi cover	62.00	186.00	500.00

NOTE: ***L. B. Cole*** *a-3, 9; c-1-12.* ***Giunta*** *a-3.* ***Hollingsworth*** *a-5, 7, 10.* ***Palais*** *a-11, 12.*

CONTEMPORARY MOTIVATORS
Pendelum Press: 1977 - 1978 ($1.45, 5-3/8x8", 31 pgs., B&W)

	GD2.0	FN6.0	NM9.4
14-3002 The Caine Mutiny; 14-3010 Banner in the Sky; 14-3029 God Is My Co-Pilot; 14-3037 Guadalcanal Diary; 14-3045 Hiroshima; 14-3053 Hot Rod; 14-3061 Just Dial a Number; 14-3088 The Diary of Anne Frank; 14-3096 Lost Horizon		2.40	6.00
14-307x Star Wars			10.00

NOTE: *Also see Pendulum Illustrated Classics. Above may have been distributed the same.*

CONTEST OF CHAMPIONS (See Marvel Super-Hero...)

CONTEST OF CHAMPIONS II
Marvel Comics: Sept, 1999 - No. 5 ($2.50, limited series)
1,2-Claremont-s/Jimenez-a 2.50

CONTRACTORS
Eclipse Comics: June, 1987 ($2.00, B&W, one-shot)
1-Funny animal 2.00

CONVOCATIONS: A MAGIC THE GATHERING GALLERY
Acclaim Comics (Armada): Jan, 1996 ($2.50, one-shot)
1-pin-ups by various artists including Kaluta, Vess, and Dringenberg 2.50

Coo Coo Comics #42 © STD

Cosmic Ray #1 © Stephen Blue

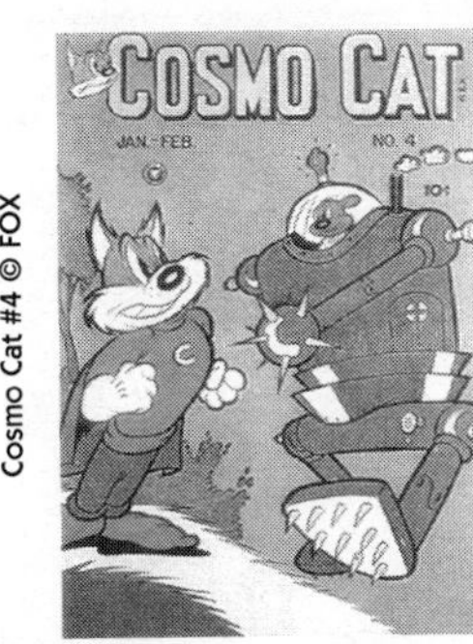

Cosmo Cat #4 © FOX

GD2.0 FN6.0 NM9.4

COO COO COMICS (...the Bird Brain No. 57 on)
Nedor Publ. Co./Standard (Animated Cartoons): Oct, 1942 - No. 62, Apr, 1952

	GD2.0	FN6.0	NM9.4
1-Origin/1st app. Super Mouse & begin series (cloned from Superman); the first funny animal super hero series (see Looney Tunes #5 for 1st funny animal super hero)	29.00	86.00	200.00
2	13.00	39.00	90.00
3-10: 10-(3/44)	8.00	24.00	48.00
11-33: 33-1 pg. Ingels-a	5.85	17.50	35.00
34-40,43-46,48-Text illos by Frazetta in all. 36-Super Mouse covers begin	10.00	30.00	65.00
41-Frazetta-a (6-pg. story & 3 text illos)	17.00	51.00	120.00
42,47-Frazetta-a & text illos.	12.00	36.00	85.00
49-(1/50)-3-D effect story; Frazetta text illo	10.00	30.00	70.00
50,51-3-D effect-c only. 50-Frazetta text illo	10.00	30.00	65.00
52-62: 56-Last Supermouse?	4.25	13.00	28.00

"COOKIE" (Also see Topsy-Turvy)
Michel Publ./American Comics Group(Regis Publ.): Apr, 1946 - No. 55, Aug-Sept, 1955

	GD2.0	FN6.0	NM9.4
1-Teen-age humor	20.00	60.00	140.00
2	10.00	30.00	70.00
3-10	7.50	22.50	45.00
11-20	5.85	17.50	35.00
21-23,26,28-30	4.25	13.00	26.00
24,25,27-Starlett O'Hara stories	5.00	15.00	30.00
31-34,37-50,52-55	4.00	12.00	24.00
35,36-Starlett O'Hara stories	4.25	13.00	28.00
51-(10-11/54) 8pg. TrueVision 3-D effect story	8.35	25.00	50.00

COOL CAT (Formerly Black Magic)
Prize Publications: V8#6, Mar-Apr, 1962 - V9#2, July-Aug, 1962

	GD2.0	FN6.0	NM9.4
V8#6, nn(V9#1, 5-6/62), V9#2	2.50	7.50	24.00

COOL WORLD (Movie)
DC Comics: Apr, 1992 - No. 4, Sept, 1992 ($1.75, limited series)

1-4: Prequel to animated/live action movie by Ralph Bakshi. 1-Bakshi-c. Bill Wray inks in all 2.00
Movie Adaptation nn ('92, $3.50, 68pg.)-Bakshi-c 3.50

COPPER CANYON (See Fawcett Movie Comics)

COPS (TV)
DC Comics: Aug, 1988 - No. 15, Aug, 1989 ($1.00)

1 ($1.50, 52 pgs.)-Based on Hasbro Toys 2.50
2-15: 14-Orlando-c(p) 2.00

COPS: THE JOB
Marvel Comics: June, 1992 - No. 4, Sept, 1992 ($1.25, limited series)

1-4: All have Jusko scripts & Golden-c 2.00

CORBEN SPECIAL, A
Pacific Comics: May, 1984 (one-shot)

1-Corben-c/a; E.A. Poe adaptation 4.00

CORKY & WHITE SHADOW (Disney, TV)
Dell Publishing Co.: No. 707, May, 1956 (Mickey Mouse Club)

	GD2.0	FN6.0	NM9.4
Four Color 707-Photo-c	6.40	19.00	70.00

CORLISS ARCHER (See Meet Corliss Archer)

CORMAC MAC ART (Robert E. Howard's...)
Dark Horse Comics: 1990 - No. 4, 1990 ($1.95, B&W, mini-series)

1-4: All have Bolton painted-c; Howard adapts. 2.00

CORNY'S FETISH
Dark Horse Comics: Apr, 1998 ($4.95, B&W, one-shot)

1-Renée French-s/a; Bolland-c 5.00

CORPORAL RUSTY DUGAN (See Holyoke One-Shot #2)

CORPSES OF DR. SACOTTI, THE (See Ideal a Classical Comic)

CORSAIR, THE (See A-1 Comics No. 5, 7, 10)

CORTEZ AND THE FALL OF THE AZTECS
Tome Press: 1993 ($2.95, B&W, limited series)

1,2 3.00

CORUM: THE BULL AND THE SPEAR (See Chronicles Of Corum)
First Comics: Jan, 1989 - No. 4, July, 1989 ($1.95)

1-4: Adapts Michael Moorcock's novel 2.00

COSMIC BOOK, THE
Ace Comics: Dec, 1986 - No. 1, 1987 ($1.95)

1,2: 1-(44pgs.)-Wood, Toth-a. 2-(B&W) 2.00

COSMIC BOY (Also see The Legion of Super-Heroes)
DC Comics: Dec, 1986 - No. 4, Mar, 1987 (limited series)

1-4: Legends tie-ins all issues 2.00

COSMIC ODYSSEY
DC Comics: 1988 - No. 4, 1988 ($3.50, limited series, squarebound)

1-4: Reintro. New Gods into DC continuity; Superman, Batman, Green Lantern (John Stewart) app; Starlin scripts, Mignola-c/a in all. 2-Darkseid merges Demon & Jason Blood (separated in Demon limited series #4); John Stewart responsible for the death of a star system. 4.00
Trade paperback-r/#1-4. 20.00

COSMIC POWERS
Marvel Comics: Mar, 1994 - No. 6, Aug, 1994 ($2.50, limited series)

1-6: 1-Ron Lim-c/a(p). 1,2-Thanos app. 2-Terrax. 3-Ganymede & Jack of Hearts app. 2.50

COSMIC POWERS UNLIMITED
Marvel Comics: May, 1995 - No. 5, May, 1996 ($3.95, quarterly)

1-5 4.00

COSMIC RAY
Image Comics: June, 1999 - Present ($2.95, B&W)

1,2-Steven Blue-s/a 3.00

COSMO CAT (Becomes Sunny #11 on; also see All Top & Wotalife Comics)
Fox Publications/Green Publ. Co./Norlen Mag.: July-Aug, 1946 - No. 10, Oct, 1947; 1957; 1959

	GD2.0	FN6.0	NM9.4
1	27.00	81.00	190.00
2	13.50	41.00	95.00
3-Origin (11-12/46)	18.00	54.00	125.00
4-10: 4-Robot-c	9.15	27.00	55.00
2-4(1957-Green Publ. Co.)	4.25	13.00	28.00
2-4(1959-Norlen Mag.)	4.00	11.00	22.00
I.W. Reprint #1	1.75	5.25	14.00

COSMO THE MERRY MARTIAN
Archie Publications (Radio Comics): Sept, 1958 - No. 6, Oct, 1959

	GD2.0	FN6.0	NM9.4
1-Bob White-a in all	13.50	41.00	95.00
2-6	10.00	30.00	65.00

COTTON WOODS
Dell Publishing Co.: No. 837, Sept, 1957

	GD2.0	FN6.0	NM9.4
Four Color 837	2.75	8.00	30.00

COUGAR, THE (Cougar No. 2)
Seaboard Periodicals (Atlas): April, 1975 - No. 2, July, 1975

1,2: 1-Adkins-a(p). 2-Origin; Buckler-c(p) 4.00

COUNTDOWN (See Movie Classics)

COUNT DUCKULA (TV)
Marvel Comics: Nov, 1988 - No. 15, Jan, 1991 ($1.00)

1-7,9-15: Dangermouse back-ups. 3.00
8-Geraldo Rivera photo-c/& app.; Sienkiewicz-a(i) 4.00

COUNT OF MONTE CRISTO, THE
Dell Publishing Co.: No. 794, May, 1957

	GD2.0	FN6.0	NM9.4
Four Color 794-Movie, Buscema-a	8.00	25.00	90.00

Coven #6 © Awesome

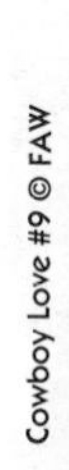
Cowboy Love #9 © FAW

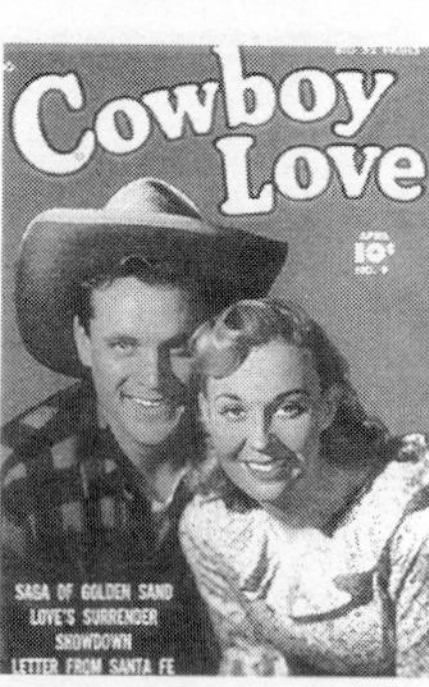

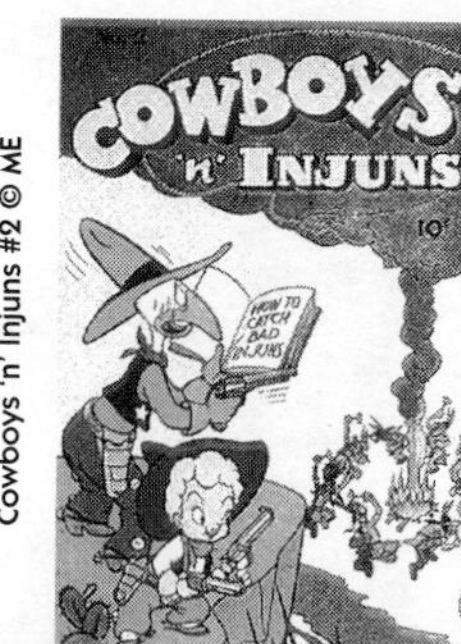

Cowboys 'n' Injuns #2 © ME

COURAGE COMICS
J. Edward Slavin: 1945

	GD2.0	FN6.0	NM9.4
1,2,77	7.85	23.50	55.00

COURTSHIP OF EDDIE'S FATHER (TV)
Dell Publishing Co.: Jan, 1970 - No. 2, May, 1970

	GD2.0	FN6.0	NM9.4
1-Bill Bixby photo-c on both	3.45	10.35	38.00
2	2.90	8.70	32.00

COVEN
Awesome Entertainment: Aug, 1997 - No. 5, Mar, 1998 ($2.50)

	GD2.0	FN6.0	NM9.4
Preview	1.00	3.00	8.00
1-Loeb-s/Churchill-a; Churchill-c	1.00	3.00	8.00
1-Liefeld variant-c	1.00	2.80	7.00
1-Pollina variant-c	1.00	3.00	8.00
1-American Entertainment Ed.	1.00	3.00	8.00
1-American Entertainment Gold Ed.			10.00
1-Fan Appreciation Ed.(3/98); new Churchill-c			3.00
1-Fan Appreciation Gold Ed.			10.00
1+ :Includes B&W art from Kaboom	1.25	3.75	10.00
1+ :Gold Ed.			7.50
1+ :Red Foil cover			12.00
2-Regular-c w/leaping Fantom		2.40	6.00
2-Variant-c w/circle of candles	1.00	3.00	8.00
2-American Entertainment Gold Ed.			8.00
2-Dynamic Forces Gold Ed.			10.00
3-6-Contains flip book preview of ReGex			3.00
3-White variant-c	1.00	2.80	7.00
3,4: 3-Halloween wraparound-c. 4-Purple variant-c			3.00
4-Dynamic Forces Ed.			5.00
4,5-Dynamic Forces Gold Ed.	1.00	3.00	8.00
5-Dynamic Forces Ed.			4.00
...Black & White (9/98) Short stories			3.00
...Fantom Special (2/98) w/sketch pages			5.00
...Fantom Special Gold Ed.			10.00

COVEN
Awesome Entertainment: Jan, 1999 - Present ($2.50)

	GD2.0	FN6.0	NM9.4
1-3: 1-Loeb-s/Churchill-a; 6 covers by various. 2-Supreme-c/app. 3-Flip book w/Kaboom preview			2.50
... Dark Origins (7/99, 2.50) w/Lionheart gallery			2.50

COVERED WAGONS, HO (Disney, TV)
Dell Publishing Co.: No. 814, June, 1957 (Donald Duck)

	GD2.0	FN6.0	NM9.4
Four Color 814-Mickey Mouse app.	4.50	13.50	50.00

COWBOY ACTION (Formerly Western Thrillers No. 1-4; Becomes Quick-Trigger Western No. 12 on)
Atlas Comics (ACI): No. 5, March, 1955 - No. 11, March, 1956

	GD2.0	FN6.0	NM9.4
5	12.00	36.00	85.00
6-10: 6-8-Heath-c	10.00	30.00	60.00
11-Williamson-a (4 pgs.); Baker-a	10.00	30.00	70.00

NOTE: ***Ayers** a-8. **Drucker** a-6. **Maneely** c/a-5, 6. **Severin** c-10. **Shores** a-7.*

COWBOY COMICS (Star Ranger #12, Stories #14)(Star Ranger Funnies #15)
Centaur Publishing Co.: No. 13, July, 1938 - No. 14, Aug, 1938

	GD2.0	FN6.0	NM9.4
13-(Rare)-Ace and Deuce, Lyin Lou, Air Patrol, Aces High, Lee Trent, Trouble Hunters begin	119.00	356.00	950.00
14-Filchock-c	84.00	253.00	675.00

NOTE: ***Guardineer** a-13, 14. **Gustavson** a-13, 14.*

COWBOY IN AFRICA (TV)
Gold Key: Mar, 1968

	GD2.0	FN6.0	NM9.4
1(10219-803)-Chuck Connors photo-c	4.00	12.00	40.00

COWBOY LOVE (Becomes Range Busters?)
Fawcett Publications/Charlton Comics No. 28 on: 7/49 - V2#10, 6/50; No. 11, 1951; No. 28, 2/55 - No. 31, 8/55

	GD2.0	FN6.0	NM9.4
V1#1-Rocky Lane photo back-c	19.00	56.00	130.00
2	6.70	20.00	40.00
V1#3,4,6 (12/49)	5.85	17.50	35.00
5-Bill Boyd photo back-c (11/49)	7.50	22.50	45.00
V2#7-Williamson/Evans-a	10.00	30.00	60.00
V2#8-11	4.25	13.00	28.00
V1#28 (Charlton)-Last precode (2/55) (Formerly Romantic Story?)	4.25	13.00	28.00
V1#29-31 (Charlton; becomes Sweetheart Diary #32 on)	4.15	12.50	25.00

NOTE: ***Powell** a-10. **Marcus Swayze** a-2, 3. Photo c-1-11. No. 1-3, 5-7, 9, 10 are 52 pgs.*

COWBOY ROMANCES (Young Men No. 4 on)
Marvel Comics (IPC): Oct, 1949 - No. 3, Mar, 1950 (All photo-c & 52 pgs.)

	GD2.0	FN6.0	NM9.4
1-Photo-c	23.00	69.00	160.00
2-William Holden, Mona Freeman "Streets of Laredo" photo-c	14.00	43.00	100.00
3-Photo-c	12.00	36.00	85.00

COWBOYS 'N' INJUNS (...and Indians No. 6 on)
Com No. 1-5/Magazine Enterprises No. 6 on: 1946 - No. 5, 1947; No. 6, 1949 - No. 8, 1952

	GD2.0	FN6.0	NM9.4
1	11.00	33.00	75.00
2-5-All funny animal western	8.35	25.00	50.00
6(A-1 23)-Half violent, half funny; Ayers-a	10.00	30.00	65.00
7(A-1 41, 1950), 8(A-1 48)-All funny	7.50	22.50	45.00
I.W. Reprint No. 1,7 (Reprinted in Canada by Superior, No. 7)	1.75	5.25	14.00
Super Reprint #10 (1963)	1.75	5.25	14.00

COWBOY WESTERN COMICS (TV)(Formerly Jack In The Box; Becomes Space Western No. 40-45 & Wild Bill Hickok & Jingles No. 68 on; title:Cowboy Western Heroes No. 47 & 48; Cowboy Western No. 49 on)
Charlton (Capitol Stories): No. 17, 7/48 - No. 39, 8/52; No. 46, 10/53; No. 47, 12/53; No. 48, Spr, '54;
No. 49, 5-6/54 - No. 67, 3/58 (nn 40-45)

	GD2.0	FN6.0	NM9.4
17-Jesse James, Annie Oakley, Wild Bill Hickok begin; Texas Rangers app.	18.00	54.00	125.00
18,19-Orlando-c/a. 18-Paul Bunyan begins. 19-Wyatt Earp story	11.00	33.00	75.00
20-25: 21-Buffalo Bill story. 22-Texas Rangers-c/story. 24-Joel McCrea photo-c & adaptation from movie "Three Faces West". 25-James Craig photo-c & adaptation from movie "Northwest Stampede"	10.00	30.00	65.00
26-George Montgomery photo-c and adaptation from movie "Indian Scout"; 1 pg. bio on Will Rogers	11.50	34.00	80.00
27-Sunset Carson photo-c & adapts movie "Sunset Carson Rides Again" plus 1 other Sunset Carson story	57.00	171.00	460.00
28-Sunset Carson line drawn-c; adapts movies "Battling Marshal" & "Fighting Mustangs" starring Sunset Carson	33.00	99.00	230.00
29-Sunset Carson line drawn-c; adapts movies "Rio Grande" with Sunset Carson & "Winchester '73" w/James Stewart plus 5 pg. life history of Sunset Carson featuring Tom Mix	33.00	99.00	230.00
30-Sunset Carson photo-c; adapts movie "Deadline" starring Sunset Carson plus 1 other Sunset Carson story	57.00	171.00	460.00
31-34,38,39,47-50 (no #40-45): 50-Golden Arrow, Rocky Lane & Blackjack (r?) stories	8.35	25.00	50.00
35,36-Sunset Carson-c/stories (2 in each). 35-Inside front-c photo of Sunset Carson plus photo on-c	33.00	99.00	230.00
37-Sunset Carson stories (2)	21.00	62.00	145.00
46-(Formerly Space Western)-Space western story	20.00	60.00	140.00
51-57,59-66: 51-Golden Arrow(r?) & Monte Hale-r renamed Rusty Hall. 53,54-Tom Mix-r. 55-Monte Hale story(r?). 66-Young Eagle story. 67-Wild Bill Hickok and Jingles-c/story	5.85	17.50	35.00
58-(1/56, 15¢, 68 pgs.)-Wild Bill Hickok, Annie Oakley & Jesse James stories; Forgione-a	8.35	25.00	50.00
67-(15¢, 68 pgs.)-Williamson/Torres-a, 5 pgs.	10.00	30.00	65.00

NOTE: *Many issues trimmed 1" shorter. **Maneely** a-67(5). Inside front/back photo c-29.*

COWGIRL ROMANCES (Young Men No. 4 on)
Marvel Comics (CCC): No. 28, Jan, 1950 (52 pgs.)

	GD2.0	FN6.0	NM9.4
28(#1)-Photo-c	20.00	60.00	140.00

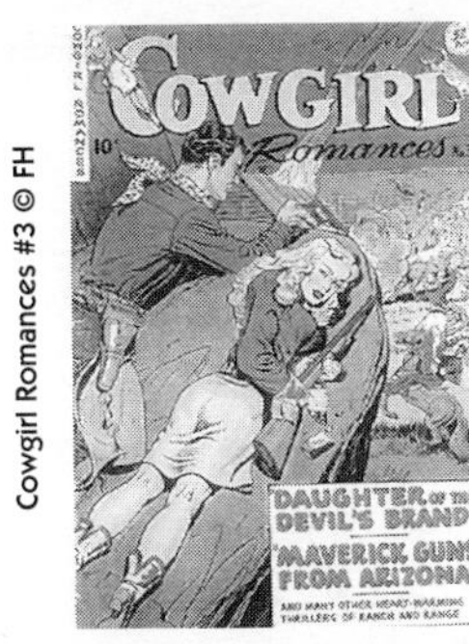
Cowgirl Romances #3 © FH

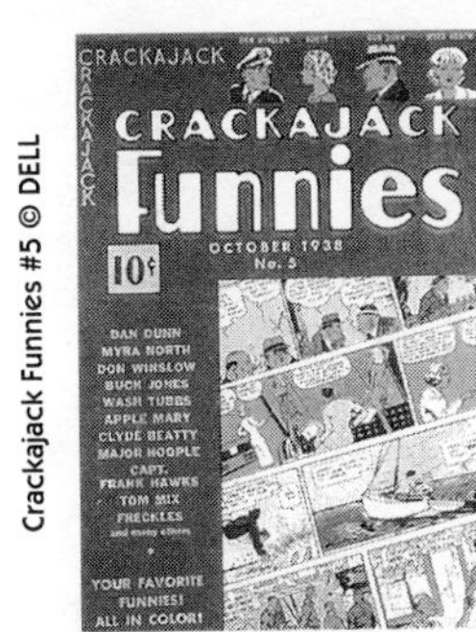
Crackajack Funnies #5 © DELL

Crack Comics #18 © QUA

COWGIRL ROMANCES
Fiction House Magazines: 1950 - No. 12, Winter, 1952-53 (No. 1-3: 52 pgs.)

1-Kamen-a 33.00 99.00 230.00
2 17.00 49.00 115.00
3-5: 5-12-Whitman-c (most) 15.00 45.00 105.00
6-9,11,12 13.50 41.00 95.00
10-Frazetta?/Williamson?-a; Kamen?/Baker-a; r/Mitzi story from Movie Comics #4 w/all new dialogue 31.00 94.00 220.00

COW PUNCHER (...Comics)
Avon Periodicals: Jan, 1947; No. 2, Sept, 1947 - No. 7, 1949

1-Clint Cortland, Texas Ranger, Kit West, Pioneer Queen begin; Kubert-a; Alabam stories begin 40.00 120.00 300.00
2-Kubert, Kamen/Feldstein-a; Kamen-c 34.00 103.00 240.00
3-5,7: 3-Kiefer story 24.00 73.00 170.00
6-Opium drug mention story; bondage, headlight-c; Reinman-a 31.00 92.00 215.00

COWPUNCHER
Realistic Publications: 1953 (nn) (Reprints Avon's No. 2)

nn-Kubert-a 10.00 30.00 70.00

COWSILLS, THE (See Harvey Pop Comics)

COYOTE
Marvel Comics (Epic Comics): June, 1983 - No. 16, Mar, 1986

1-10,15: 7-10-Ditko-a 2.00
11-1st McFarlane-a. 2.40 6.00
12-14,16: 12-14-McFarlane-a. 14-Badger x-over. 16-Reagan c/app. 4.00

CRACKAJACK FUNNIES (Also see The Owl)
Dell Publishing Co.: June, 1938 - No. 43, Jan, 1942

1-Dan Dunn, Freckles, Myra North, Wash Tubbs, Apple Mary, The Nebbs, Don Winslow, Tom Mix, Buck Jones, Major Hoople, Clyde Beatty, Boots begin 237.00 711.00 1900.00
2 97.00 291.00 775.00
3 69.00 207.00 550.00
4 52.00 156.00 420.00
5-Nude woman on cover 55.00 165.00 440.00
6-8,10: 8-Speed Bolton begins (1st app.) 41.00 123.00 325.00
9-(3/39)-Red Ryder strip-r begin by Harman; 1st app. in comics & 1st cover app. 122.00 366.00 975.00
11-14 40.00 120.00 310.00
15-Tarzan text feature begins by Burroughs (9/39); not in #26,35 43.00 129.00 340.00
16-24: 18-Stratosphere Jim begins (1st app., 12/39). 23-Ellery Queen begins plus-c (1st comic book app., 5/40) 33.00 99.00 230.00
25-The Owl begins (1st app., 7/40); in new costume #26 by Frank Thomas (also see Popular Comics #72) 75.00 225.00 600.00
26-30: 28-Part Owl-c 50.00 150.00 400.00
31-Owl covers begin, end #42 52.00 156.00 420.00
32-Origin Owl Girl 56.00 168.00 450.00
33-38: 36-Last Tarzan issue. 37-Cyclone & Midge begin (1st app.) 44.00 132.00 350.00
39-Andy Panda begins (intro/1st app., 9/41) 53.00 159.00 425.00
40-42: 42-Last Owl-c. 40.00 120.00 300.00
43-Terry & the Pirates-r 36.00 108.00 250.00
NOTE: *McWilliams art in most issues.*

CRACK COMICS (Crack Western No. 63 on)
Quality Comics Group: May, 1940 - No. 62, Sept, 1949

1-Origin & 1st app. The Black Condor by Lou Fine, Madame Fatal, Red Torpedo, Rock Bradden & The Space Legion; The Clock, Alias the Spider (by Gustavson), Wizard Wells, & Ned Brant begin; Powell-a; Note: Madame Fatal is a man dressed as a woman 440.00 1320.00 4400.00
2 225.00 675.00 1800.00
3 150.00 450.00 1200.00
4 131.00 363.00 1050.00
5-10: 5-Molly The Model begins. 10-Tor, the Magic Master begins 100.00 300.00 800.00
11-20: 13-1 pg. J. Cole-a. 15-1st app. Spitfire 87.00 261.00 700.00
21-24: 23-Pen Miller begins; continued from National Comics #22. 24-Last Fine Black Condor 67.00 200.00 540.00
25,26: 26-Flag-c 55.00 165.00 440.00
27-(1/43)-Intro & origin Captain Triumph by Alfred Andriola (Kerry Drake artist) & begin series 100.00 300.00 800.00
28-30 44.00 132.00 350.00
31-39: 31-Last Black Condor 28.00 84.00 195.00
40-46 20.00 60.00 140.00
47-57,59,60-Capt. Triumph by Crandall 21.00 64.00 150.00
58,61,62-Last Captain Triumph 13.50 41.00 95.00
NOTE: *Black Condor by* ***Fine:*** *No. 1, 2, 4-6, 8, 10-24; by* ***Sultan:*** *No. 3, 7; by* ***Fugitani:*** *No. 9.* ***Cole*** *a-34.* ***Crandall*** *a-61(unsigned); c-48, 49, 51-61.* ***Guardineer*** *a-17.* ***Gustavson*** *a-1, 13, 17.* ***McWilliams*** *a-15-27. Black Condor c-2, 4, 6, 8, 10, 12, 14, 16, 18, 20-26. Capt. Triumph c-27-62. The Clock c-1, 3, 5, 7, 9, 11, 13, 15, 17, 19.*

CRACKED (Magazine) (Satire) (Also see The 3-D Zone #19)
Major Magazines(#1-212)/Globe Communications(#213 on): Feb-Mar, 1958 - Present

1-One pg. Williamson-a; Gunsmoke-s 12.50 38.00 125.00
2-1st Shut-Ups & Bonus Cut-Outs; Frankenstein-s 6.00 18.00 60.00
3-5 4.50 13.50 45.00
6-10: 7-Reprints 1st 6 covers on-c. 8-Frankenstein-c. 10-Wolverton-a 3.50 10.50 35.00
11-12, 13(nn,3/60), 2.80 8.40 28.00
14-17, 18(nn,2/61), 19,20: 14-Kirby-a 2.60 7.80 26.00
21-27(11/62), 27(No.28, 2/63; mis-#d), 29(5/63) 2.50 7.50 24.00
30-40(11/64): 37-Beatles and Superman cameos 2.50 7.50 22.00
41-45,47-56,59,60: 47,49,52-Munsters. 51-Beatles inside-c 59-Laurel and Hardy photos 2.50 7.50 20.00
46,57,58: 46,58-Man From U.N.C.L.E. 46-Beatles. 57-Rolling Stones 2.50 7.50 20.00
61-80: 62-Beatles cameo. 69-Batman, Superman app. 70-(8/68) Elvis cameo. 71-Garrison's Gorillas; W.C. Fields photos 1.75 5.25 14.00
81-99: 99-Alfred E. Neuman on-c 1.75 5.25 14.00
100 2.50 7.50 20.00
101-119: 104-Godfather-c/s. 108-Archie Bunker-s. 112,119-Kung Fu (TV) 113-Tarzan-s. 115-MASH. 117-Cannon. 118-The Sting-c/s 1.25 3.75 10.00
120(12/74) Six Million Dollar Man-c/s; Ward-a 1.75 5.25 14.00
121,122,124-126,128-133,136-140: 121-American Graffiti. 122-Korak-c/s. 124,131-Godfather-c/s. 128-Capone-c. 129,131-Jaws. 132-Baretta-c/s. 133-Space 1999. 136-Laverne and Shirley/Fonz-c. 137-Travolta/Kotter-c/s. 138-Travolta/Laverne and Shirley/Fonz-c. 139-Barney Miller-c/s. 140-King Kong-c/s; Fonz-s 1.25 3.75 10.00
123-Planet of the Apes-c/s; Six Million Dollar Man 1.75 5.25 14.00
127,134,135: 127-Star Trek-c/s; Ward-a. 134-Fonz-c/s; Starsky and Hutch. 135-Bionic Woman-c/s; Ward-a 1.50 4.50 12.00
141,151-Charlie's Angels-c/s. 151-Frankenstein 1.50 4.50 12.00
142,143,150,152-155,157: 142-MASH-c/s. 143-Rocky-c/s; King Kong-s. 150-(5/78) Close Encounters-c/s. 152-Close Enc./Star Wars-c/s. 153-Close Enc./Fonz-c/s. 154-Jaws II-c/s; Star Wars-s. 155-Star Wars/Fonz-c 1.25 3.75 10.00
144,149,156,158-160: 144-Fonz/Happy Days-c. 149-Star Wars/Six Mil.$ Man-c/s. 156-Grease/Travolta-c. 158-Mork & Mindy. 159-Battlestar Galactica-c/s; MASH-s. 160-Superman-c/s 1.40 4.15 11.00
145,147-Both have insert postcards: 145-Fonz/Rocky/L&S-c/s. 147-Star Wars-s; Farrah photo page (missing postcards-1/2 price) 2.25 6.75 18.00
1146,148: 46-Star Wars-c/s with stickers insert (missing stickers-1/2 price). 148-Star Wars-c/s with inside-c color poster 2.50 7.50 20.00
161,170-Ward-a: 161-Mork & Mindy-c/s. 170-Dukes of Hazzard-c/s 1.00 3.00 8.00
162,165-168,171,172,175-178,180-Ward-a: 162-Sherlock Holmes-s. 165-Dracula-c/s. 167-Mork-c/s. 168,175-MASH-c/s. 168-Mork-s. 172-Dukes of Hazzard/CHiPs-c/s. 176-Barney Miller-c/s 1.00 2.80 7.00
163,179:163-Postcard insert; Mork & Mindy-c/s. 179-Insult cards insert; Popeye, Dukes of Hazzard-c/s 2.00 6.00 16.00

Cracked #233 © Globe Communications Corp.

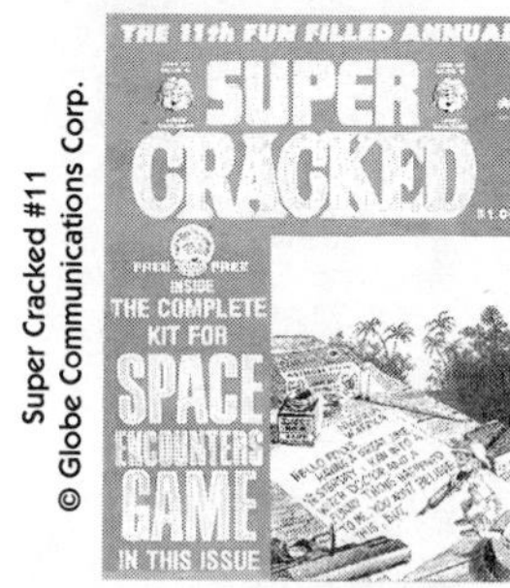

Super Cracked #11 © Globe Communications Corp.

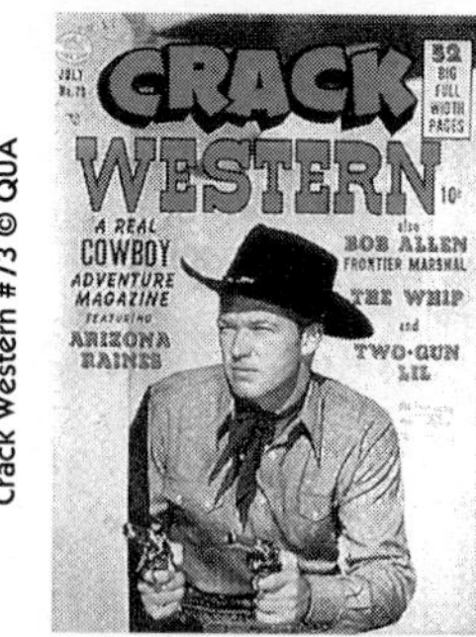

Crack Western #73 © QUA

GD2.0 FN6.0 NM9.4

164,169,173,174: 164-Alien movie-c/s; Mork & Mindy-s. 169-Star Trek. 173,174-Star Wars-Empire Strikes Back. 173-SW poster 1.25 3.75 10.00

181,182,185-191,193,194,196-198-most Ward-a: 182-MASH-c/s. 185-Dukes of Hazzard-c/s; Jefferson-s. 187-Love Boat. 188-Fall Guy-s. 189-Fonz/Happy Days-c. 190,194-MASH-c/s. 191-Magnum P.I./Rocky-c; Magnum-s. 193-Knight Rider-s. 196-Dukes of Hazzard/Knight Rider-c/s. 198-Jaws III-c/s; Fall Guy-s 2.40 6.00

183,184,192,195,199,200-Ward-a in all: 183-Superman-c/s. 184-Star Trek-c/s. 192-E.T.-c/s; Rocky-s. 195-E.T.-c/s. 199-Jabba-c; Star Wars-s. 200-(12/83) 1.00 2.80 7.00

201,203,210-A-Team-c/s 5.00

202,204-206,211-224,226,227,230-233: 202-Knight Rider-s. 204-Magnum P.I.; A-Team-s. 206-Michael Jackson/Mr. T-c/s. 212-Prince-s; Cosby-s. 213-Monsters issue-c/s. 215-Hulk Hogan/Mr. T-c/s. 216-Miami Vice-s; James Bond-s. 217-Rambo-s; Cosby-s; A-Team-s. 218-Rocky-c/s. 219-Arnold/Commando-c/s; Rocky-s; Godzilla. 220-Rocky-c/s. 221-Stephen King app. 223-Miami Vice-s. 224-Cosby-s. 226-29th Anniv.; Tarzan-s; Aliens-s; Family Ties-s. 227-Cosby, Family Ties, Miami Vice-s. 230-Monkees-c/s; Elvis on-c; Gumby-s. 232-Alf, Cheers, StarTrek-s. 233-Superman/James Bond-c/s; Robocop, Predator-s 4.00

207-209,225,234: 207-Michael Jackson-c/s. 208-Indiana Jones-c/s. 209-Michael Jackson/Gremlins-c/s; Star Trek III-s. 225-Schwarzenegger/Stallone/G.I. Joe-c/s. 234-Don Martin-a begins; Batman/Robocop/Clint Eastwood-c/s 2.40 6.00

228,229: 228-Star Trek-c/s; Alf, Pee Wee Herman-s. 229-Monsters issue-c/s; centerfold with many superheroes 2.40 6.00

235,239,243,249: 235-1st Martin-c; Star Trek:TNG-s; Alf-s. 239-Beetlejuice-c/s; Mike Tyson-s. 243-X-Men and other heroes app. 249-Batman/Indiana Jones/Ghostbusters-c/s 2.40 6.00

236,244,245,248: 236-Madonna/Stallone-c/s; Twilight Zone-s. 244-Elvis-c/s; Martin-c. 245-Roger Rabbit-c/s. 248-Batman issue 2.40 6.00

237,238,240-242,246,247,250: 237-Robocop-s. 238-Rambo-c/s; Star Trek-s. 242-Dirty Harry-s, Ward-a. 246-Alf-s; Star Trek-s., Ward-a. 247-Star Trek-s. 250-Batman/Ghostbusters-s 4.00

251-253,255,256,259,261-265,275-278,281,284,286-297,299: 252-Star Trek-s. 253-Back to the Future-c/s. 255-TMNT-c/s. 256-TMNT-c/s; Batman, Bart Simpson on-c. 259-Die Hard II, Robocop-s. 261-TMNT, Twin Peaks-s. 262-Rocky-c/s; Rocky Horror-s. 265-TMNT-s. 276-Aliens III, Batman-s. 277-Clinton-c. 284-Bart Simpson-c; 90210-s. 297-Van Damme-s/photo-c. 299-Dumb & Dumber-c/s 4.00

254,257,266,267,272,280,282,285,298,300: 254-Back to the Future, Punisher-s; Wolverton-a, Batman-s, Ward-a. 257-Batman, Simpsons-s; Spider-Man and other heroes app. 266-Terminator-c/s. 267-Toons-c/s. 272-Star Trek VI-s. 280-Swimsuit issue. 282-Cheers-c/s. 285-Jurassic Park-c/s. 298-Swimsuit issue; Martin-c. 300-(8/95) Brady Bunch-c/s 5.00

258,260,274,279,283: 258-Simpsons-c/s; Back to the Future-s. 260-Spider-Man-c/s; Simpsons-s. 274-Batman-c/s. 279-Madonna-c/s. 283-Jurassic Park-c/s; Wolverine app. inside back-c 5.00

301-305,307-341 2.50

306-Toy Story-c/s 4.00

Biggest... (Winter, 1977) 1.75 5.25 14.00

Biggest, Greatest... nn('65) 3.20 9.60 32.00

Biggest, Greatest... 2('66) - #5('69) 2.50 7.50 20.00

Biggest, Greatest... 6('70) - #12('76) 2.00 6.00 16.00

...Blockbuster 1,2 ('88) 2.40 6.00

...Digest 1(Fall, '86, 148 pgs.) - #5 2.40 6.00

...Collectors' Edition 4 ('73; formerly ...Special) 1.50 4.50 12.00

5-10 1.50 4.50 12.00

11-30: 23-Ward-a 1.10 3.30 9.00

31-50 1.00 2.80 7.00

51-70 5.00

71-84: 83-Elvis, Batman parodies 4.00

...Party Pack 1,2('88) 4.00

...Shut-Ups (2/72-'72; Cracked Spec. #3) 1 2.50 7.50 20.00

2 1.50 4.50 12.00

...Special 3('73; formerly Cracked Shut-Ups; ...Collectors' Edition#4 on) 1.00 3.00 8.00

GD2.0 FN6.0 NM9.4

Extra Special... 1('76) 1.50 4.50 12.00

Extra Special... 2('76) 1.00 3.00 8.00

Giant... nn('65) 4.00 12.00 40.00

Giant... 2('66)-5('69) 2.80 8.40 28.00

Giant...6('70)-12('76) 2.50 7.50 22.00

Giant...nn(9/77)-24 1.85 5.50 15.00

Giant...25-35 1.50 4.50 12.00

Giant...36-48('87) 1.00 3.00 8.00

King Sized... 1('67) 3.80 11.40 38.00

King Sized... 2('68)-5('71) 2.60 7.80 26.00

King Sized... 6('72)-11('77) 2.50 7.50 22.00

King Sized... 12-17 1.50 4.50 12.00

King Sized... 18-22 (Sum/'86) 1.00 3.00 8.00

Super... 1('68) 3.00 9.00 30.00

Super... 2('69)-5 2.60 7.80 26.00

Super... 6-10 2.50 7.50 20.00

Super... 11-16 2.00 6.00 16.00

Super... 17-24('88) 1.50 4.50 12.00

Super... 1('87, 100 pgs.)-Severin & Elder-a 1.00 3.00 8.00

NOTE: ***Burgos*** *a-1-10.* ***Colan*** *a-257.* ***Davis*** *a-5, 11-17, 24, 40, 80; c-12-14, 16.* ***Elder*** *a-5, 6, 10-13; c-10.* ***Everett*** *a-1-10, 23-25, 61; c-1.* ***Heath*** *a-1-3, 6, 13, 14, 17, 110; c-6.* ***Jaffee*** *a-5, 6.* ***Don Martin*** *c-235, 244, 247, 259, 261, 264.* ***Morrow*** *a-8-10.* ***Reinman*** *a-1-4.* ***Severin*** *c/a-in most all issues.* ***Shores*** *a-3-7.* ***Torres*** *a-7-10.* ***Ward*** *a-22-24, 27, 35, 40, 120-193, 195, 197-205, 242, 244, 246, 247, 250, 252-257.* ***Williamson*** *a-1 (1 pg.).* ***Wolverton*** *a-10 (2 pgs.), Giant nn('65).* ***Wood*** *a-27, 35, 40. Alfred E. Neuman c-177, 200, 202. Batman c-234, 248, 249, 256, 274. Captain America c-256. Christmas c-234, 243. Spider-Man c-260. Star Trek c-127, 169, 207, 228. Star Wars c-145, 146, 148, 149, 152, 155, 173, 174, 199. Superman c-183, 233. #144, 146 have free full-color pre-glued stickers. #145, 147, 155, 163 have free full-color postcards. #123, 137, 154, 157 have free iron-ons.*

CRACKED MONSTER PARTY
Globe Communications: July, 1988 - No. 26, 1990?

1 1.50 4.50 12.00

2-10 1.00 3.00 8.00

11-26 5.00

CRACKED'S FOR MONSTERS ONLY
Major Magazines: Sept, 1969 - No. 9, Sept, 1969

1 3.00 9.00 30.00

2-9 2.00 6.00 16.00

CRACKED SPACED OUT
Globe Communications: Fall, 1993 - No. 4, 1994?

1-4 3.00

CRACK WESTERN (Formerly Crack Comics; Jonesy No. 85 on)
Quality Comics Group: No. 63, Nov, 1949 - No. 84, May, 1953
(36 pgs., 63-68,74-on)

63(#1)-Ward-c; Two-Gun Lil (origin & 1st app.)(ends #84), Arizona Ames, his horse Thunder (with sidekick Spurs & his horse Calico), Frontier Marshal (ends #70), & Dead Canyon Days (ends #69) begin; Crandall-a 21.00 64.00 150.00

64,65: 64-Ward-c. Crandall-a in both. 16.00 47.00 110.00

66,68-Photo-c. 66-Arizona Ames becomes A. Raines (ends #84) 13.50 41.00 95.00

67-Randolph Scott photo-c; Crandall-a 16.00 47.00 110.00

69(52pgs.)-Crandall-a 13.50 41.00 95.00

70(52pgs.)-The Whip (origin & 1st app.) & his horse Diablo begin (ends #84); Crandall-a 13.50 41.00 95.00

71(52pgs.)-Frontier Marshal becomes Bob Allen F. Marshal (ends #84); Crandall-c/a 16.00 47.00 110.00

72(52pgs.)-Tim Holt photo-c 13.00 39.00 90.00

73(52pgs.)-Photo-c 10.00 30.00 60.00

74-76,78,79,81,83-Crandall-c. 83-Crandall-a(p) 11.50 34.00 80.00

77,80,82 8.35 25.00 50.00

84-Crandall-c/a 13.00 39.00 90.00

NOTE: ***Crandall*** *c-71p, 74-81, 83p(w/****Cuidera****-i).*

CRASH COMICS (Catman Comics No. 6 on)
Tem Publishing Co.: May, 1940 - No. 5, Nov, 1940

Crash Ryan #1 © MAR

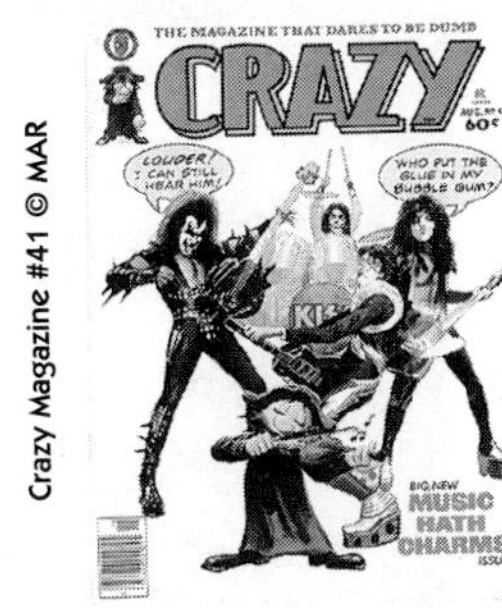
Crazy Magazine #41 © MAR

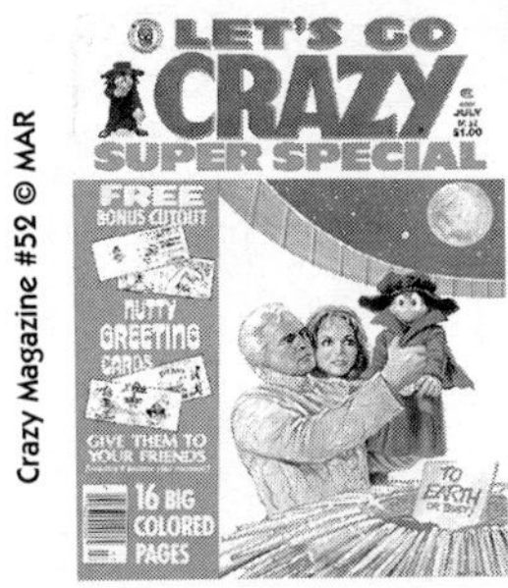
Crazy Magazine #52 © MAR

GD2.0 FN6.0 NM9.4

	GD2.0	FN6.0	NM9.4
1-The Blue Streak, Strongman (origin), The Perfect Human, Shangra begin (1st app. of each); Kirby-a	288.00	862.00	2400.00
2-Simon & Kirby-a	144.00	432.00	1150.00
3,5-Simon & Kirby-a	125.00	375.00	1000.00
4-Origin & 1st app. The Catman; S&K-a	288.00	862.00	2400.00

NOTE: *Solar Legion by **Kirby** No. 1-5 (5 pgs. each). Strongman c-1-4. Catman c-5.*

CRASH DIVE (See Cinema Comics Herald)

CRASH METRO AND THE STAR SQUAD
Oni Press: May, 1999 ($2.95, B&W, one-shot)

1-Allred-s/Ontiveros-a 3.00

CRASH RYAN (Also see Dark Horse Presents #44)
Marvel Comics (Epic): Oct, 1984 - No. 4, Jan, 1985 (Baxter paper, lim. series)

1-4 2.00

CRAZY (Also see This Magazine is Crazy)
Atlas Comics (CSI): Dec, 1953 - No. 7, July, 1954

1-Everett-c/a	25.00	75.00	175.00
2	18.00	54.00	125.00
3-7: 4-I Love Lucy satire. 5-Satire on censorship	15.00	45.00	105.00

NOTE: ***Ayers** a-5. **Berg** a-1, 2. **Burgos** c-5, 6. **Drucker** a-6. **Everett** a-1-4. **Al Hartley** a-4. **Heath** a-3, 7; c-7. **Maneely** a-1-7, c-3, 4. **Post** a-3-6. Funny monster c-1-4.*

CRAZY (Satire)
Marvel Comics Group: Feb, 1973 - No. 3, June, 1973

1-Not Brand Echh-r; Beatles cameo (r)	2.25	6.75	18.00
2,3-Not Brand Echh-r; Kirby-a	1.50	4.50	12.00

CRAZY MAGAZINE (Satire)
Oct, 1973 - No. 94, Apr, 1983 (40-90¢, B&W magazine)
Marvel Comics: (#1, 44 pgs; #2-90, reg. issues, 52 pgs; #92-95, 68 pgs)'

1-Wolverton(1 pg.), Bode-a; 3 pg. photo story of Neal Adams & Dick Giordano; Harlan Ellison story; TV Kung Fu sty. 2.80 8.40 28.00

2-"Live & Let Die" c/s; 8pgs; Adams/Buscema-a; McCloud w5 pgs. Adams-a; Kurtzman's "Hey Look" 2 pg.-r 2.50 7.50 20.00

3-5: 3-"High Plains Drifter" w/Clint Eastwood c/s; Waltons app; Drucker, Reese-a. 4-Shaft-c/s; Ploog-a; Nixon 3 pg. app; Freas-a. 5-Michael Crichton's "Westworld" c/s; Nixon app. 1.85 5.50 15.00

6,7,18: 6-Exorcist c/s; Nixon app. 7-TV's Kung Fu c/s; Nixon app.; Ploog & Freas-a. 18-Six Million Dollar Man/Bionic Woman c/s; Welcome Back Kotter story 1.50 4.50 12.00

8-10: 8-Serpico c/s; Casper parody; TV's Police Story. 9-Joker cameo; Chinatown story; Eisner s/a begins; Has 1st 8 covers on-c. 10-Playboy Bunny-c; M. Severin-a; Lee Marrs-a begins; "Deathwish" story 1.25 3.75 10.00

11-17,19: 11-Towering Inferno. 12-Rhoda. 13-"Tommy" the Who Rock Opera. 14-Mandingo. 15-Jaws story. 16-Santa/Xmas-c; "Good Times" TV story; Jaws. 17-Bi-Centennial ish; Baretta; Woody Allen. 19-King Kong c/s; Reagan, J. Carter, Howard the Duck cameos, "Laverne & Shirley" 1.00 3.00 8.00

20,24,27: 20-Bi-Centennial-c; Space 1999 sty; Superheroes song sheet, 4pgs. 24-Charlies Angels. 27-Charlies Angels/Travolta/Fonz-c; Bionic Woman sty 1.50 4.50 12.00

21-23,25,26,28-30: 21-Starskey & Hutch. 22-Mount Rushmore/J. Carter-c; TV's Barney Miller; Superheroes spoof. 23-Santa/Xmas-c; "Happy Days" sty; "Omen" sty. 25-J. Carter-c/s; Grandenetti-a begins; TV's Alice; Logan's Run. 26-TV Stars-c; Mary Hartman, King Kong. 28-Donny & Marie Osmond-c/s; Marathon Man. 29-Travolta/Kotter-c; "One Day at a Time", Gong Show. 30-1977, 84 pgs. w/bonus; Jaws, Baretta, King Kong, Happy Days 1.00 3.00 8.00

31,33-35,38,40: 31-"Rocky"-c/s; TV game shows. 33-Peter Benchley's "Deep". 34-J. Carter-c; TV's "Fish". 35-Xmas-c with Fonz/Six Million Dollar Man/ Wonder Woman/Darth Vader/Travolta, TV's "Mash" & "Family Matters". 38-Close Encounters of the Third Kind-c/s. 40-"Three's Company-c/s 2.40 6.00

32-Star Wars/Darth Vader-c/s; "Black Sunday" 1.85 5.50 15.00

36,42,47,49: 36-Farrah Fawcett/Six Million Dollar Man-c; TV's Nancy Drew & Hardy Boys; 1st app. Howard The Duck in Crazy, 2 pgs. 42-84 pgs. w/bonus; TV Hulk/Spider-Man-c; Mash, Gong Show, One Day at a Time, Disco, Alice. 47-Battlestar Galactica xmas-c; movie "Foul Play". 49-1979, 84 pgs. w/bonus; Mork & Mindy-c; Jaws, Saturday Night Fever, Three's Company 1.00 3.00 8.00

37-1978, 84 pgs. w/bonus. Darth Vader-c; Barney Miller, Laverne & Shirley, Good Times, Rocky, Donny & Marie Osmond, Bionic Woman 1.50 4.50 12.00

39,44: 39-Saturday Night Fever-c/s. 44-"Grease"-c w/Travolta/O. Newton-John 1.25 3.75 10.00

41-Kiss-c & 1pg. photos; Disaster movies, TV's "Family", Annie Hall 2.80 8.40 28.00

43,45,46,48,51: 43-Jaws-c; Saturday Night Fever; Stallone's "Fist".43-E.C. swipe from Mad #131 45-Travolta/O. Newton-John/J. Carter-c; Eight is Enough. 46-TV Hulk-c/s; Punk Rock. 48-"Wiz"-c, Battlestar Galactica-s. 51-Grease/Mork & Mindy/D&M Osmond-c, Mork & Mindy-sty. "Boys from Brazil" 2.40 6.00

50,58: 50-Superman movie-c/sty, Playboy Mag., TV Hulk, Fonz; Howard the Duck, 1 pg. 58-1980, 84 pgs. w/32 pg. color comic bonus insert-Full reprint of Crazy Comic #1, Battlestar Galactica, Charlie's Angels, Starsky & Hutch 1.50 4.50 12.00

52,59,60,64: 52-1979, 84 pgs. w/bonus. Marlon Brando-c; TV Hulk, Grease. Kiss, 1 pg. photos. 59-Santa Ptd-c by Larkin; "Alien", "Moonraker", Rocky-2, Howard the Duck, 1 pg. 60-Star Trek w/Muppets-c; Star Trek sty; 1st app/origin Teen Hulk; Severin-a. 64-84 pgs. w/bonus Monopoly game satire. "Empire Strikes Back", 8 pgs,.One Day at a Time. 1.50 4.50 12.00

53,54,65,67-70: 53-"Animal House"-c/sty; TV's "Vegas", Howard the Duck, 1 pg. 54-Love at First Bite-c/sty, Fantasy Island sty, Howard the Duck 1 pg. 65-(Has #66 on-c, Aug/'80). "Black Hole" w/Janson-a; Kirby,Wood/Severin-a(r), 5 pgs. Howard the Duck, 3 pgs.; Broderick-a; Buck Rogers, Mr. Rogers. 67-84 pgs. w/bonus; TV's Kung Fu, Excorcist; Ploog-a(r). 68-American Gigalo, Dukes of Hazzard, Teen Hulk; Howard the Duck, 3 pgs. Broderick-a; Monster sty/5 pg. Ditko-a(r). 69-Obnoxio the Clown-c/sty; Stephen King's "Shining", Teen Hulk, Richie Rich, Howard the Duck, 3pgs; Broderick-a. 70-84 pgs. Towering Inferno, Daytime TV; Trina Robbins-a 2.40 6.00

55-57,61,63: 55-84 pgs. w/bonus; Love Boat, Mork & Mindy, Fonz, TV Hulk. 56-Mork/Rocky/J. Carter-c; China Syndrome. 57-TV Hulk with Miss Piggy-c, Dracula, Taxi, Muppets. 61-1980, 84 pgs. Adams-a(r), McCloud, Pro wrestling, Casper, TV's Police Story. 63-Apocalypse Now-Coppola's cult movie; 3rd app. Teen Hulk, Howard the Duck, 3 pgs. 1.00 3.00 8.00

62-Kiss Ptd-c & 2 pg. app; Quincy, 2nd app. Teen Hulk 2.50 7.50 25.00

66-Sept/'80, Empire Strikes Back-c/sty; Teen Hulk by Severin, Howard the Duck, 3pgs. by Broderick 1.25 3.75 10.00

71,72,75-77,79: 71-Blues Brothers parody, Teen Hulk, Superheroes parody, WKRP in Cincinnati, Howard the Duck, 3pgs. by Broderick. 72-Jackie Gleason/Smokey & the Bandit II-c/sty, Shogun, Teen Hulk. Howard the Duck, 3pgs. by Broderick. 75-Flash Gordon movie c/sty; Teen Hulk, Cat in the Hat, Howard the Duck 3pgs. by Broderick. 76-84 pgs. w/bonus; Monster-sty w/ Crandall-a(r), Monster-stys(2) w/Kirby-a(r), 5pgs. ea; Mash, TV Hulk, Chinatown. 77-Popeye movie/R. Williams-c/sty; Teen Hulk, Love Boat, Howard the Duck 3 pgs. 79-84 pgs. w/bonus color stickers; has new material; "9 to 5" w/Dolly Parton, Teen Hulk, Magnum P.I., Monster-sty w/5pgs, Ditko-a(r), "Rat" w/Sutton-a(r), Everett-a, 4 pgs.(r) 2.40 6.00

73,74,78,80: 73-84 pgs. w/bonus Hulk/Spiderman Finger Puppets-c & bonus; "Live & Let Die, Jaws, Fantasy Island. 74-Dallas/"Who Shot JR"-c/sty; Elephant Man, Howard the Duck 3pgs. by Broderick. 78-Clint Eastwood-c/sty; Teen Hulk, Superheroes parody, Lou Grant. 80-Star Wars, 2 pg. app; "Howling", TV's "Greatest American Hero" 1.00 3.00 8.00

81,84,86,87,89: 81-.Superman Movie II-c/sty; Wolverine cameo, Mash, Teen Hulk. 84-American Werewolf in London, Johnny Carson app; Teen Hulk. 86-Time Bandits-c/sty; Private Benjamin. 87-Rubix Cube-c; Hill Street Blues, "Ragtime", Origin Obnoxio the Clown; Teen Hulk. 89-Burt Reynolds "Sharkeys Machine", Teen Hulk 2.40 6.00

82-X-Men-c w/new Byrne-a, 84 pgs. w/new material; Fantasy Island, Teen Hulk, "For Your Eyes Only", Spiderman/Human Torch-r by Kirby/Ditko; Sutton-a(r); Rogers-a; Hunchback of Notre Dame, 5 pgs. 1.85 5.50 15.00

83-Raiders of the Lost Ark-c/sty; Hart to Hart; Reese-a; Teen Hulk

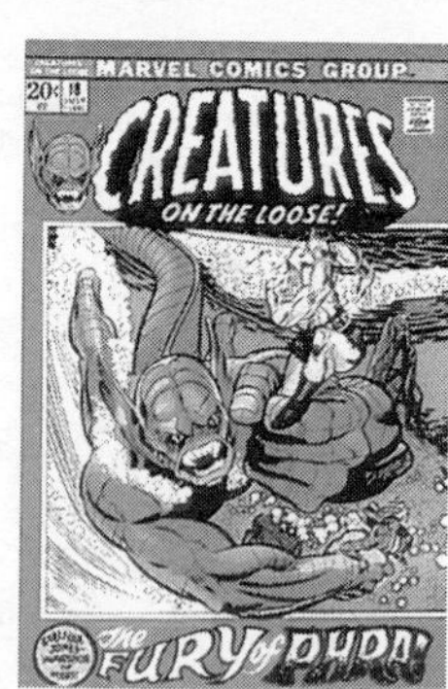

Creatures on the Loose #18 © MAR

The Creeper #5 © DC

Creepy #6 © Warren

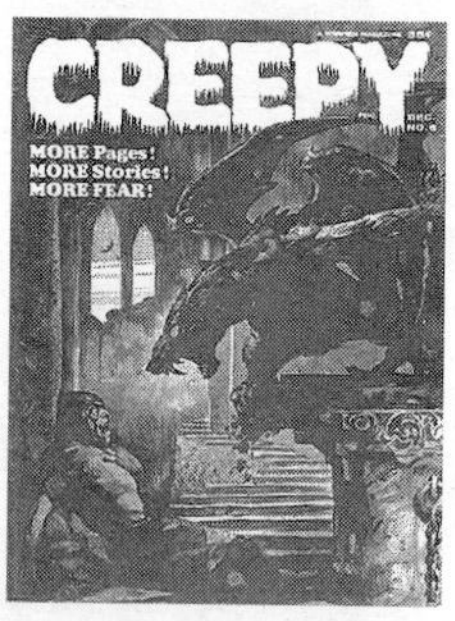

GD2.0 FN6.0 NM9.4

1.25 3.75 10.00

85,88: 85-84 pgs; Escape from New York, Teen Hulk; Kirby-a(r), 5 pgs, Posiedon Adventure, Flintstones, Sesame Street. 88-84 pgs. w/bonus Dr. Strange Game; some new material; Jeffersons, X-Men/Wolverine, 10 pgs.; Byrne-a; Apocalypse Now, Teen Hulk 1.00 3.00 8.00

90-94: 90-Conan-c/sty; M. Severin-a; Teen Hulk. 91-84 pgs, some new materi al; Bladerunner-c/sty, "Deathwish-II, Teen Hulk, Black Knight, 10 pgs.-'50s-r w/Maneely-a. 92-Wrath of Khan Star Trek-c/sty; Joanie & Chachi, Teen Hulk. 93-"E.T."-c/sty, Teen Hulk, Archie Bunkers Place, Dr. Doom Game. 94-Poltergeist, Smurfs, Teen Hulk, Casper, Avengers parody-8pgs. Adams-a. 1.50 4.50 12.00

Crazy Summer Special #1 (Sum, '75, 100 pgs.)-Nixon, TV Kung Fu, Babe Ruth, Joe Namath, Waltons, McCloud, Chariots of the Gods 1.75 5.25 14.00

NOTE: **N. Adams** *a-2, 61r, 94p.* **Austin** *a-82i.* **Buscema** *a-2, 82.* **Byrne** *c-82p.* **Nick Cardy** *c-7, 8, 10, 12-16, Super Special 1.* **Crandall** *a-76r.* **Ditko** *a-68r, 79r, 82r.* **Drucker** *a-3.* **Eisner** *a-9-16.* **Kelly Freas** *c-1-6, 9, 11; a-7.* **Kirby/Wood** *a-66r.* **Ploog** *a-1, 4, 7, 67r, 73r.* **Rogers** *a-82.* **Sparling** *a-92.* **Wood** *a-65r. Howard the Duck in 36, 50, 51, 53, 54, 59, 63, 65, 66, 68, 69, 71, 72, 74, 75, 77. Hulk in 46, c-42, 46, 57, 73. Star Wars in 32, 66; c-37.*

CRAZYMAN
Continuity Comics: Apr, 1992 - No. 3, 1992 ($2.50, high quality paper)

1-($3.95, 52 pgs.)-Embossed-c; N. Adams part-i 4.00
2,3 ($2.50): 2-N. Adams/Bolland-c 2.50

CRAZYMAN
Continuity Comics: V2#1, 5/93 - No. 4, 1/94 ($2.50, high quality paper)

V2#1-4: 1-Entire book is die-cut. 2-(12/93)-Adams-c(p) & part scripts. 3-(12/93). 4-Indicia says #3, Jan. 1993 2.50

CRAZY, MAN, CRAZY (Magazine) (Becomes This Magazine is...?) (Formerly From Here to Insanity)
Humor Magazines (Charlton): V2#1, Dec, 1955 - V2#2, June, 1956

V2#1,V2#2-Satire; Wolverton-a, 3 pgs. 12.00 36.00 85.00

CREATURE, THE (See Movie Classics)

CREATURE
Antarctic Press: Oct, 1997 - Present ($2.95, B&W)

1,2-Don Walker-s/a 3.00

CREATURES OF THE ID
Caliber Press: 1990 ($2.95, B&W)

1-Frank Einstein (Madman) app.; Allred-a 3.80 11.50 40.00

CREATURES ON THE LOOSE (Formerly Tower of Shadows No. 1-9)(See Kull)
Marvel Comics: No. 10, March, 1971 - No. 37, Sept, 1975 (New-a & reprints)

10-(15¢)-1st full app. King Kull; see Kull the Conqueror; Wrightson-a 3.60 10.80 36.00
11-15: 15-Last 15¢ issue 1.75 5.25 14.00
16-Origin Warrior of Mars (begins, ends #21) 1.40 4.15 11.00
17-20 1.00 2.80 7.00
21-Steranko-c 1.10 3.30 9.00
22-Steranko-c; Thongor stories begin 1.40 4.15 11.00
23-29-Thongor-c/stories 5.00
30-Manwolf begins 1.50 4.50 12.00
31-33 1.10 3.30 9.00
34-37 1.00 2.80 7.00

NOTE: **Crandall** *a-13.* **Ditko** *r-15, 17, 18, 20, 22, 24, 27, 28.* **Everett** *a-16i(new).* **Matt Fox** *r-21i.* **Howard** *a-26i.* **Gil Kane** *a-16p, 17p, 19i; c-16, 17, 19, 20, 25, 29, 33p, 35p, 36p.* **Kirby** *a-10-15r, 16(2)r, 17r, 19r.* **Morrow** *a-20, 21.* **Perez** *a-33-37; c-34p.* **Shores a-11. innott** *r-21.* **Sutton** *c-10.* **Tuska** *a-31p, 32p.*

CREECH, THE
Image Comics: Oct, 1997 - No. 3, Dec, 1997 ($1.95/$2.50, limited series)

1-3: 1-Capullo-s/c/a(p) 2.50
TPB (1999, $9.95) r/#1-3, McFarlane intro. 10.00

CREED
Hall of Heroes Comics: Dec, 1994 - No. 2, Jan, 1995 ($2.50, B&W)

1 1.85 5.50 15.00
2 1.50 4.50 12.00

GD2.0 FN6.0 NM9.4

CREED
Lightning Comics: June, 1995 - Present ($2.75/$3.00, B&W/color)

1-($2.75) 4.00
1-($3.00, color) 4.50
1-($9.95)-Commemorative Edition 10.00
1-TwinVariant Edition (1250? print run) 10.00
1-Special Edition; polybagged w/certificate 4.00
1 Gold Collectors Edition; polybagged w/certificate 3.00
2,3-($3.00, color)-Butt Naked Edition & regular-c 3.00
3-($9.95)-Commemorative Edition; polybagged w/certificate & card 10.00

CREED: CRANIAL DISORDER
Lightning Comics: Oct, 1996 ($3.00, one-shot)

1-3-Two covers 3.00
1-($5.95)-Platinum Edition 6.00
2,3-($9.95)Ltd.l Edition 10.00

CREED/TEENAGE MUTANT NINJA TURTLES
Lightning Comics: May, 1996 ($3.00, one-shot)

1-Kaniuga-a(p)/scripts; Laird-c; variant-c exists 3.00
1-($9.95)-Platinum Edition 10.00
1-Special Edition; polybagged w/certificate 5.00

CREED: USE YOUR DELUSION
Avatar Press: Jan, 1998 - No. 2, Feb, 1998 ($3.00, B&W)

1,2-Kaniuga-s/c/a 3.00
1,2-($4.95) Foil cover 5.00

CREEPER, THE (See Beware... , Showcase #73 & 1st Issue Special #7)
DC Comics: Dec, 1997 - No. 11; #1,000,000 Nov, 1998 ($2.50)

1-11-Kaminski-s/Martinbrough-a(p). 7,8-Joker-c/app. 3.00
#1,000,000 (11/98) 853rd Century x-over 2.50

CREEPSVILLE
Laughing Reindeer Press: V2#1, Winter, 1995 ($4.95)

V2#1-Comics w/text 5.00

CREEPY (See Warren Presents)
Warren Publishing Co./Harris Publ. #146: 1964 - No. 145, Feb, 1983; No. 146, 1985 (B&W, magazine)

1-Frazetta-a (his last story in comics?); Jack Davis-c; 1st Warren all comics magazine 8.65 26.00 95.00
2: 2-Frazetta-c & 1 pg. strip 4.35 13.00 48.00
3-13: 3-7,9-11-Frazetta-c. 7-Frazetta 1 pg. strip. 9-Creepy fan club sketch by Wrightson (1st published-a); has 1/2 pg. anti-smoking strip by Frazetta. 10-Brunner fan club sketch (1st published work) 2.50 7.50 25.00
14-Neal Adams 1st Warren work 2.80 8.40 28.00
15-31,33-37,39-47,49: 15-17,27-Frazetta-c 2.50 7.50 22.00
32-Frazetta-c; Harlan Ellison sty 3.80 11.40 38.00
38 (scarce) 3.20 9.60 32.00
48,55,65-(1973, 1974, 1975 Annuals) #55 & 65 contain an 8 pg. slick comic insert. 2.50 7.50 24.00
50-Vampirella-c 2.80 8.40 28.00
51,54,56-64: All contain an 8 pg. slick comic insert in middle 2.50 7.50 20.00
52,53,66-112,114-140: 93-Sports issue. 96-Aliens issue. 102-All monster issue. 121-All Severin-r issue. 125-All N. Adams-r issue. 137-All Williamson-r issue. 139-All Toth-r issue 1.10 3.30 9.00
113-All Wrightson-r issue 1.40 4.15 11.00
141-145 (low dist.) 144-Giant, $2.25; Frazetta-c 1.85 5.50 15.00
146 ($2.95)-1st from Harris; resurrection issue 5.00 15.00 55.00
Year Book '68-'70: '70-Neal Adams, Ditko-a(r) 3.20 9.60 32.00
Annual 1971,1972 3.20 9.60 32.00
1993 Fearbook ($3.95)-Harris Publ. Vampirella app. 3.20 9.60 32.00

NOTE: *All issues contain many good artists works:* **Neal Adams, Brunner, Corben, Craig (Taycee), Crandall, Ditko, Evans, Frazetta, Heath, Jeff Jones, Krenkel, McWilliams, Morrow, Nino, Orlando, Ploog, Severin, Torres, Toth, Williamson, Wood, & Wrightson**; *covers by* **Crandall, Davis, Frazetta, Morrow, San Julian, Todd/Bode**; *Otto Binder's "Adam Link" stories in No. 2, 4, 6, 8, 9, 12, 13, 15 with* **Orlando** *art.* **Frazetta** *c-2-7, 9-11, 15-17, 27, 32, 83r, 89r, 91r.* **E.A. Poe** *adaptations in 66, 69, 70.*

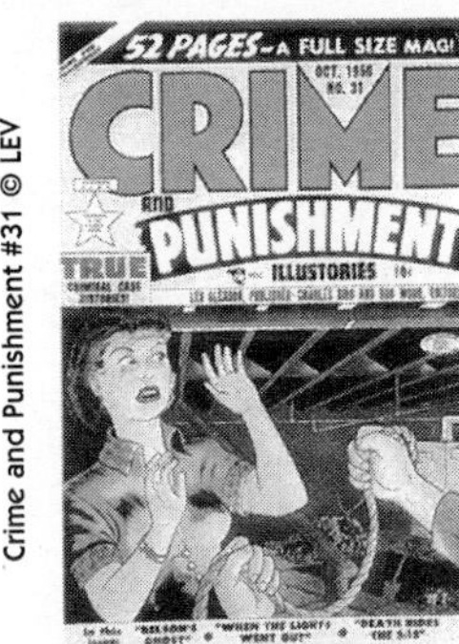

Crime and Punishment #31 © LEV

Crime Clinic #11 (#2) © Z-D

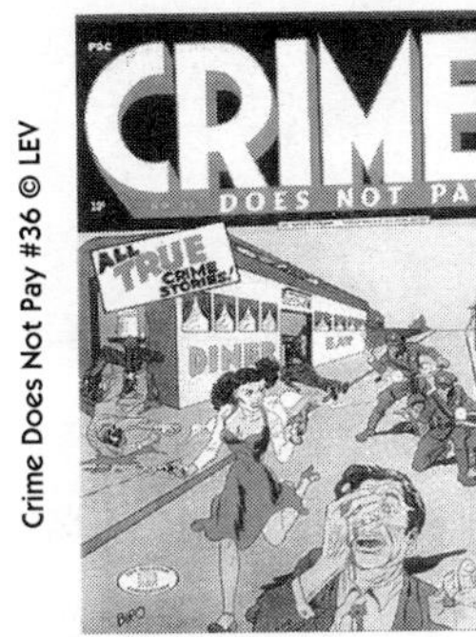

Crime Does Not Pay #36 © LEV

CREEPY THINGS
Charlton Comics: July, 1975 - No. 6, June, 1976

	GD2.0	FN6.0	NM9.4
1	1.50	4.50	12.00
2-6: Ditko-a in 3,5. Sutton c-3,4	1.00	2.80	7.00
Modern Comics Reprint 2-6(1977)			4.00

NOTE: *Larson a-2,6. Sutton a-1,2,4,6. Zeck a-2.*

CREMATOR
Chaos! Comics: Dec, 1998 - No. 5, May, 1999 ($2.95, limited series)

	GD2.0	FN6.0	NM9.4
1-5-Leonardo Jimenez-s/a			3.00

CRIME AND JUSTICE (Rookie Cop? No. 27 on)
Capitol Stories/Charlton Comics: March, 1951 - No. 26, Sept, 1955

	GD2.0	FN6.0	NM9.4
1	30.00	90.00	210.00
2	10.00	30.00	65.00
3-8,10-13: 6-Negligee panels	9.15	27.00	55.00
9-Classic story "Comics Vs. Crime"	21.00	64.00	150.00
14-Color illos in **POP**; gory story of man who beheads women	16.00	47.00	110.00
15-17,19-26; 15-Negligee panels	5.85	17.50	35.00
18-Ditko-a	23.00	69.00	160.00

NOTE: *Alascia c-20. Ayers a-17. Shuster a-19-21; c-19. Bondage c-11, 12.*

CRIME AND PUNISHMENT (Title inspired by 1935 film)
Lev Gleason Publications: April, 1948 - No. 74, Aug, 1955

	GD2.0	FN6.0	NM9.4
1-Mr. Crime app. on-c	30.00	90.00	210.00
2	16.00	47.00	110.00
3-Used in **SOTI**, pg. 112; injury-to-eye panel; Fuje-a	19.00	56.00	130.00
4,5	11.50	34.00	80.00
6-10	10.00	30.00	65.00
11-20	9.15	27.00	55.00
21-30	7.00	21.00	42.00
31-38,40-44,46: 46-One pg. Frazetta-a	5.85	17.50	35.00
39-Drug mention story "The 5 Dopes"	10.00	30.00	60.00
45- "Hophead Killer" drug story	10.00	30.00	60.00
47-57,60-65,70-74:	5.85	17.50	35.00
58-Used in **POP**, pg. 79	6.35	19.00	38.00
59-Used in **SOTI**, illo "What comic-book America stands for"	26.00	77.00	180.00
66-Toth-c/a(4); 3-D effect issue (3/54); 1st "Deep Dimension" process	35.00	105.00	245.00
67- "Monkey on His Back" heroin story; 3-D effect issue	30.00	90.00	210.00
68-3-D effect issue; Toth-c (7/54)	26.00	77.00	180.00
69- "The Hot Rod Gang" dope crazy kids	10.00	30.00	65.00

NOTE: *Biro c-most. Everett a-31. Fuje a-3, 4, 12, 13, 17, 18, 20, 26, 27. Guardineer a-2-4, 10, 14, 17, 18, 20, 26-28, 32, 38-44. Kinstler c-69. McWilliams a-41, 48, 49. Tuska a-28, 30, 51, 64, 70.*

CRIME AND PUNISHMENT: MARSHALL LAW TAKES MANHATTAN
Marvel Comics (Epic Comics): 1989 ($4.95, 52 pgs., direct sales only, mature)

	GD2.0	FN6.0	NM9.4
nn-Graphic album featuring Marshall Law			5.00

CRIME CAN'T WIN (Formerly Cindy Smith)
Marvel/Atlas Comics (TCI 41/CCC 42,43,4-12): No. 41, 9/50 - No. 43, 2/51; No. 4, 4/51 - No. 12, 9/53

	GD2.0	FN6.0	NM9.4
41(#1)	24.00	73.00	170.00
42(#2)	13.50	41.00	95.00
43(#3)-Horror story	16.00	47.00	110.00
4(4/51),5-12: 10-Possible use in **SOTI**, pg. 161	10.00	30.00	70.00

NOTE: *Robinson a-9-11. Tuska a-43.*

CRIME CASES COMICS (Formerly Willie Comics)
Marvel/Atlas Comics(CnPC No.24-8/MJMC No.9-12): No. 24, 8/50 - No. 27, 3/51; No. 5, 5/51 - No. 12, 7/52

	GD2.0	FN6.0	NM9.4
24 (#1, 52 pgs.)-True police cases	15.00	45.00	105.00
25-27(#2-4): 27-Morisi-a	10.00	30.00	70.00
5-12: 11-Robinson-a. 12-Tuska-a	10.00	30.00	60.00

CRIME CLINIC
Ziff-Davis Publishing Co.: No. 10, July-Aug, 1951 - No. 5, Summer, 1952

	GD2.0	FN6.0	NM9.4
10(#1)-Painted-c; origin Dr. Tom Rogers	25.00	75.00	175.00
11(#2),4,5: 4,5-Painted-c	17.00	51.00	120.00
3-Used in **SOTI**, pg. 18	18.00	54.00	125.00

NOTE: *All have painted covers by Saunders. Starr a-10.*

CRIME CLINIC
Slave Labor Graphics: May, 1995 - No. 2, Oct, 1995 ($2.95, B&W, limited series)

	GD2.0	FN6.0	NM9.4
1,2			3.00

CRIME DETECTIVE COMICS
Hillman Periodicals: Mar-Apr, 1948 - V3#8, May-June, 1953

	GD2.0	FN6.0	NM9.4
V1#1-The Invisible 6, costumed villains app; Fuje-c/a, 15 pgs.	25.00	75.00	175.00
2,5: 5-Krigstein-a	10.00	30.00	70.00
3,4,6,7,10-12: 6-McWilliams-a	10.00	30.00	60.00
8-Kirbyish-a by McCann	10.00	30.00	60.00
9-Used in **SOTI**, pg. 16 & "Caricature of the author in a position comic book publishers wish he were in permanently" illo.	33.00	99.00	230.00
V2#1,4,7-Krigstein-a: 1-Tuska-a	10.00	30.00	65.00
2,3,5,6,8-12 (1-2/52)	6.35	19.00	38.00
V3#1-Drug use-c	6.70	20.00	40.00
2-8	5.35	16.00	32.00

NOTE: *Briefer a-11, V3#1. Kinstlerish-a by McCann-V2#7, V3#2. Powell a-10, 11. Starr a-10.*

CRIME DETECTOR
Timor Publications: Jan, 1954 - No. 5, Sept, 1954

	GD2.0	FN6.0	NM9.4
1	17.00	51.00	120.00
2	10.00	30.00	60.00
3,4	9.15	27.00	55.00
5-Disbrow-a (classic)	18.00	54.00	125.00

CRIME DOES NOT PAY (Formerly Silver Streak Comics No. 1-21)
Comic House/Lev Gleason/Golfing (Title inspired by film):
No. 22, June, 1942 - No. 147, July, 1955 (1st crime comic)

	GD2.0	FN6.0	NM9.4
22(23 on cover, 22 on indicia)-Origin The War Eagle & only app.; Chip Gardner begins; #22 was rebound in Complete Book of True Crime (Scarce)	212.00	636.00	1700.00
23 (Scarce)	122.00	366.00	975.00
24-Intro. & 1st app. Mr. Crime (Scarce)	97.00	291.00	775.00
25-30: 27-Classic Bird-c. 30-Wood and Biro app.	55.00	165.00	440.00
31-40	36.00	107.00	250.00
41-Origin & 1st app. Officer Common Sense	26.00	77.00	180.00
42-Electrocution-c	31.00	94.00	220.00
43-46,48-50: 44,45,50 are 68 pg. issues	17.00	51.00	120.00
47-Electric chair-c	30.00	90.00	210.00
51-70: 63,64-Possible use in **SOTI**, pg. 306. 63-Contains Biro & Gleason's self censorship code of 12 listed restrictions (5/48)	15.00	45.00	105.00
71-99: 87-Chip Gardner begins, ends #100	11.50	34.00	80.00
100	12.00	36.00	85.00
101-104,107-110: 102-Chip Gardner app	10.00	30.00	60.00
105-Used in **POP**, pg. 84	10.00	30.00	70.00
106,114-Frazetta-a, 1 pg.	10.00	30.00	60.00
111-Used in **POP**, pgs. 80 & 81; injury-to-eye sty illo	10.00	30.00	60.00
112,113,115-130	7.00	21.00	42.00
131-140	5.35	16.00	32.00
141,142-Last pre-code issue; Kubert-a(1)	9.15	27.00	55.00
143-Kubert-a in one story	9.15	27.00	55.00
144-146	5.35	16.00	32.00
147-Last issue (scarce); Kubert-a	11.50	34.00	80.00
1(Golfing-1945)	5.85	17.50	35.00
The Best of...(1944, 128 pgs.)-Series contains 4 rebound issues	75.00	225.00	600.00
...1945 issue	56.00	168.00	450.00
...1946-48 issues	41.00	124.00	330.00
...1949-50 issues	40.00	120.00	285.00

Crime Files #6 © STD

Crime Must Lose #7 © MAR

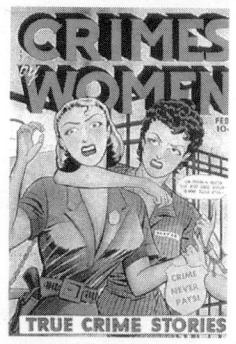

Crimes By Women #11 © FOX

...1951-53 issues 32.00 96.00 225.00

NOTE: *Many issues contain violent covers and stories. Who Dunnit by* ***Guardineer****-39-42, 44-105, 108-110; Chip Gardner by* ***Bob Fujitani (Fuje)****-88-103.* ***Alderman*** *a-29, 41-44, 49.* ***Dan Barry*** *a-75.* ***Biro*** *c-1-76, 122, 142.* ***Briefer*** *a-29(2), 30, 31, 33, 37, 39.* ***G. Colan*** *a-105.* ***Fuje*** *c-88, 89, 91-94, 96, 98, 99, 102, 103.* ***Guardineer*** *a-57, 71.* ***Kubert*** *c-143.* ***Landau*** *a-118.* ***Maurer*** *a-29, 39, 41, 42.* ***McWilliams*** *a-91, 93, 95, 100-103.* ***Palais*** *a-30, 33, 37, 39, 41-43, 44(2), 46, 49.* ***Powell*** *a-146, 147.* ***Tuska*** *a-48, 50(2), 51, 52, 56, 57(2), 60-64, 66, 67, 71. Painted c-87-102. Bondage c-43, 62, 98.*

CRIME EXPOSED
Marvel Comics (PPI)/Marvel Atlas Comics (PrPI): June, 1948; Dec, 1950 - No. 14, June, 1952

1(6/48) 29.00 86.00 200.00
1(12/50) 18.00 54.00 125.00
2 12.00 36.00 85.00
3-9,11,14 10.00 30.00 65.00
10-Used in **POP**, pg. 81 10.00 30.00 70.00
12-Krigstein & Robinson-a 10.00 30.00 70.00
13-Used in **POP**, pg. 81; Krigstein-a 11.00 33.00 75.00

NOTE: ***Maneely*** *c-8.* ***Robinson*** *a-11, 12.* ***Tuska*** *a-3, 4.*

CRIMEFIGHTERS
Marvel Comics (CmPS 1-3/CCC 4-10): Apr, 1948 - No. 10, Nov, 1949

1-Some copies are undated & could be reprints 23.00 69.00 160.00
2,3: 3-Morphine addict story 12.00 36.00 85.00
4-10: 6-Anti-Wertham editorial. 9,10-Photo-c 10.00 30.00 70.00

CRIME FIGHTERS (...Always Win)
Atlas Comics (CnPC): No. 11, Sept, 1954 - No. 13, Jan, 1955

11-13: 11-Maneely-a,13-Pakula, Reinman, Severin-a
10.00 30.00 70.00

CRIME-FIGHTING DETECTIVE (Shock Detective Cases No. 20 on; formerly Criminals on the Run)
Star Publications: No. 11, Apr-May, 1950 - No. 19, June, 1952
(Based on true crime cases)

11-L. B. Cole-c/a (2 pgs.); L. B. Cole-c on all 17.00 51.00 120.00
12,13,15-19: 17-Young King Cole & Dr. Doom app. 13.00 39.00 90.00
14-L. B. Cole-c/a, r/Law-Crime #2 15.00 45.00 105.00

CRIME FILES
Standard Comics: No. 5, Sept, 1952 - No. 6, Nov, 1952

5-1pg. Alex Toth-a; used in **SOTI**, pg. 4 (text) 23.00 69.00 160.00
6-Sekowsky-a 11.50 34.00 80.00

CRIME ILLUSTRATED (Magazine)
E. C. Comics: Nov-Dec, 1955 - No. 2, Spring, 1956 (25¢, Adult Suspense Stories on-c)

1-Ingels & Crandall-a 13.50 41.00 95.00
2-Ingels & Crandall-a 11.50 34.00 80.00

NOTE: ***Craig*** *a-2.* ***Crandall*** *a-1, 2; c-2.* ***Evans*** *a-1.* ***Davis*** *a-2.* ***Ingels*** *a-1, 2.* ***Krigstein/Crandall*** *a-1.* ***Orlando*** *a-1, 2; c-1.*

CRIME INCORPORATED (Formerly Crimes Incorporated)
Fox Features Syndicate: No. 2, Aug, 1950; No. 3, Aug, 1951

2 25.00 75.00 175.00
3(1951)-Hollingsworth-a 19.00 56.00 130.00

CRIME MACHINE (Magazine)
Skywald Publications: Feb, 1971 - No. 2, May, 1971 (B&W)

1-Kubert-a(2)(r)(Avon) 4.50 13.50 50.00
2-Torres, Wildey-a; violent-c/a 3.20 9.60 32.00

CRIME MUST LOSE! (Formerly Sports Action?)
Sports Action (Atlas Comics): No. 4, Oct, 1950 - No. 12, April, 1952

4-Ann Brewster-a in all; c-used in N.Y. Legis. Comm. documents
17.00 51.00 120.00
5-12: 9-Robinson-a. 11-Used in **POP**, pg. 89 11.50 34.00 80.00

CRIME MUST PAY THE PENALTY (Formerly Four Favorites; Penalty #47, 48)
Ace Magazines (Current Books): No. 33, Feb, 1948; No. 2, Jun, 1948 - No. 48, Jan, 1956

33(#1, 2/48)-Becomes Four Teeners #34? 30.00 90.00 210.00
2(6/48)-Extreme violence; Palais-a? 19.00 58.00 135.00
3,4,8: 3- "Frisco Mary" story used in Senate Investigation report, pg. 7. 4,8-Transvestism stories 13.50 41.00 95.00
5-7,9,10 10.00 30.00 60.00
11-20-Drug story "Dealers in White Death" 9.15 27.00 55.00
21-32,34-40,42-48 6.35 19.00 38.00
33(7/53)- "Dell Fabry-Junk King" drug story; mentioned in Love and Death
10.00 30.00 60.00
41-reprints "Dealers in White Death" 6.70 20.00 40.00

NOTE: ***Cameron*** *a-29-31, 34, 35, 39-41.* ***Colan*** *a-20, 31.* ***Kremer*** *a-3, 37r.* ***Larsen*** *a-32.* ***Palais*** *a-5?,37.*

CRIME MUST STOP
Hillman Periodicals: October, 1952 (52 pgs.)

V1#1(Scarce)-Similar to Monster Crime; Mort Lawrence, Krigstein-a
61.00 182.00 485.00

CRIME MYSTERIES (Secret Mysteries #16 on; combined with Crime Smashers #7 on)
Ribage Publ. Corp. (Trojan Magazines): May, 1952 - No. 15, Sept, 1954

1-Transvestism story; crime & terror stories begin 48.00 144.00 385.00
2-Marijuana story (7/52) 36.00 109.00 255.00
3-One pg. Frazetta-a 31.00 92.00 215.00
4-Cover shows girl in bondage having her blood drained; 1 pg. Frazetta-a
48.00 144.00 385.00
5-10 25.00 75.00 175.00
11,12,14 24.00 71.00 165.00
13-(5/54)-Angelo Torres 1st comic work (inks over Check's pencils); Check-a
31.00 92.00 215.00
15-Acid in face-c 36.00 109.00 255.00

NOTE: ***Fass*** *a-13; c-4, 10.* ***Hollingsworth*** *a-10-13, 15; c-2, 12, 13, 15.* ***Kiefer*** *a-4.* ***Woodbridge*** *a-13? Bondage-c-1, 8, 12.*

CRIME ON THE RUN (See Approved Comics #8)

CRIME ON THE WATERFRONT (Formerly Famous Gangsters)
Realistic Publications: No. 4, May, 1952 (Painted cover)

4 28.00 84.00 195.00

CRIME PATROL (Formerly International #1-5; International Crime Patrol #6; becomes Crypt of Terror #17 on)
E. C. Comics: No. 7, Summer, 1948 - No. 16, Feb-Mar, 1950

7-Intro. Captain Crime 54.00 162.00 460.00
8-14: 12-Ingels-a 46.00 138.00 395.00
15-Intro. of Crypt Keeper (inspired by Witches Tales radio show) & Crypt of Terror (see Tales From the Crypt #33 for origin); used by N.Y. Legis. Comm.; last pg. Feldstein-a 222.00 666.00 2000.00
16-2nd Crypt Keeper app.; Roussos-a 144.00 432.00 1300.00

NOTE: ***Craig*** *c/a in most issues.* ***Feldstein*** *a-9-16.* ***Kiefer*** *a-8, 10, 11.* ***Moldoff*** *a-7.*

CRIME PHOTOGRAPHER (See Casey...)

CRIME REPORTER
St. John Publ. Co.: Aug, 1948 - No. 3, Dec, 1948 (Indicia shows Oct.)

1-Drug club story 44.00 132.00 355.00
2-Used in **SOTI**: illo- "Children told me what the man was going to do with the red-hot poker;" r/Dynamic #17 with editing; Baker-c; Tuska-a
67.00 200.00 535.00
3-Baker-c; Tuska-a 37.00 111.00 260.00

CRIMES BY WOMEN
Fox Features Syndicate: June, 1948 - No. 15, Aug, 1951; 1954
(True crime cases)

1-True story of Bonnie Parker 120.00 360.00 960.00
2,3: 3-Used in **SOTI**, pg. 234 64.00 192.00 510.00
4,5,7-9,11-15: 8-Used in **POP**.14-Spanking panel r/from All Famous Crime Stories (1949) (Fox Giant) 55.00 165.00 440.00
6-Classic girl fight-c; acid-in-face panel 61.00 183.00 485.00
10-Used in **SOTI**, pg. 72; girl fight-c 57.00 171.00 460.00
54(M.S. Publ.-'54)-Reprint; (formerly My Love Secret)

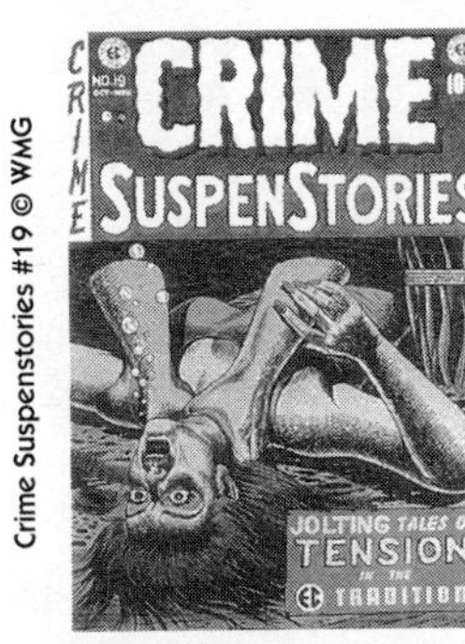

Crime Suspenstories #19 © WMG

Crimson #3 © Humberto Ramos

Crisis on Infinite Earths #4 © DC

26.00 77.00 180.00

CRIMES INCORPORATED (Formerly My Past)
Fox Features Syndicate: No. 12, June, 1950 (Crime Incorporated No. 2 on)

12 13.50 41.00 95.00

CRIMES INCORPORATED (See Fox Giants)

CRIME SMASHER (See Whiz #76)
Fawcett Publications: Summer, 1948 (one-shot)

1-Formerly Spy Smasher 40.00 120.00 310.00

CRIME SMASHERS (Becomes Secret Mysteries No. 16 on)
Ribage Publishing Corp.(Trojan Magazines): Oct, 1950 - No. 15, Mar, 1953

1-Used in **SOTI**, pg. 19,20, & illo "A girl raped and murdered;" Sally the Sleuth begins 74.00 223.00 595.00
2-Kubert-c 40.00 120.00 295.00
3,4 32.00 96.00 225.00
5-Wood-a 39.00 118.00 275.00
6,8-11: 8-Lingerie panel 24.00 71.00 165.00
7-Female heroin junkie story 25.00 75.00 175.00
12-Injury to eye panel; 1 pg. Frazetta-a 26.00 77.00 180.00
13-Used in **POP**, pgs. 79,80; 1 pg. Frazetta-a 26.00 77.00 180.00
14,15 21.00 64.00 150.00

NOTE: ***Hollingsworth** a-14. **Kiefer** a-15. Bondage c-7, 9.*

CRIME SUSPENSTORIES (Formerly Vault of Horror No. 12-14)
E. C. Comics: No. 15, Oct-Nov, 1950 - No. 27, Feb-Mar, 1955

15-Identical to #1 in content; #1 printed on outside front cover. #15 (formerly "The Vault of Horror") printed and blackened out on inside front cover with Vol. 1, No. 1 printed over it. Evidently, several of No. 15 were printed before a decision was made not to drop the Vault of Horror and Haunt of Fear series. The print run was stopped on No. 15 and continued on No. 1. All of No. 15 were changed as described above. 117.00 352.00 1175.00
1 90.00 270.00 900.00
2 49.00 148.00 470.00
3-5: 3-Poe adaptation. 3-Old Witch stories begin 34.00 101.00 320.00
6-10 28.00 83.00 250.00
11,12,14,15: 15-The Old Witch guest stars 21.00 63.00 190.00
13,16-Williamson-a 24.00 72.00 215.00
17-Williamson/Frazetta-a (6 pgs.) 26.00 78.00 235.00
18,19: 19-Used in **SOTI**, pg. 235 18.00 53.00 160.00
20-Cover used in **SOTI**, illo "Cover of a children's comic book" 23.00 70.00 210.00
21,24-27: 24- "Food For Thought" similar to "Cave In" in Amazing Detective Cases #13 (1952) 11.50 35.00 105.00
22,23-Used in Senate investigation on juvenile delinquency. 22-Ax decapitation-c 18.00 53.00 160.00

NOTE: ***Craig** a-1-21; c-1-18, 20-22. **Crandall** a-18-26. **Davis** a-4, 5, 7, 9-12, 20. **Elder** a-17,18. **Evans** a-15, 19, 21, 23, 25, 27; c-23, 24. **Feldstein** c-19. **Ingels** a-1-12, 14, 15, 27. **Kamen** a-2, 4-18, 20-27; c-25-27. **Krigstein** a-22, 24, 25, 27. **Kurtzman** a-1, 3. **Orlando** a-16, 22, 24, 26. **Wood** a-1, 3. Issues No. 11-15 have E. C. "quickie" stories. No. 25 contains the famous "Are You a Red Dupe?" editorial. Ray Bradbury adaptations-15, 17.*

CRIME SUSPENSTORIES
Russ Cochran/Gemstone Publ.: Nov, 1992 - Present ($1.50/$2.00/$2.50)

1-24:Reprints Crime SuspenStories series 2.50

CRIMINALS ON THE RUN (Formerly Young King Cole)
(Crime Fighting Detective No. 11 on)
Premium Group (Novelty Press): V4#1, Aug-Sep, 1948-#10, Dec-Jan, 1949-50

V4#1-Young King Cole continues 28.00 84.00 195.00
2-6: 6-Dr. Doom app. 24.00 71.00 165.00
7-Classic "Fish in the Face" c by L. B. Cole 46.00 138.00 370.00
V5#1,2 (#8,9),10: 9,10-L. B. Cole-c 21.00 62.00 145.00

NOTE: *Most issues have **L. B. Cole covers. McWilliams** a-V4#6, 7, V5#2; c-V4#5.*

CRIMSON (Also see Cliffhanger #0)
Image Comics (Cliffhanger Productions): May, 1998 - No. 7, Dec, 1998;
DC Comics (Cliffhanger Prod.): No. 8, Mar, 1999 - Present ($2.50)

1-Humberto Ramos-a/Augustyn-s 5.00
1-Variant-c by Warren 8.00
1-Chromium-c 20.00
2-Ramos-c with street crowd, 2-Variant-c by Art Adams 3.00
2-Dynamic Forces CrimsonChrome cover 15.00
3-7: 3-Ramos Moon background-c. 7-3-covers by Ramos, Madureira, & Campbell 3.00
8-12: 8-First DC issue 2.50
DF Premiere Ed. 1998 ($6.95) covers by Ramos and Jae Lee 7.00
Loyalty and Loss TPB ('99, $12.95) r/#1-6 13.00

CRIMSON AVENGER, THE (See Detective Comics #20 for 1st app.)(Also see Leading Comics #1 & World's Best/Finest Comics)
DC Comics: June, 1988 - No. 4, Sept, 1988 ($1.00, limited series)

1-4 2.00

CRIMSON NUN
Antarctic Press: May, 1997 - No. 4, Nov, 1997 ($2.95, limited series)

1-4 3.00

CRIMSON PLAGUE
Event Comics: June, 1997 ($2.95)

1-George Perez-a 3.00

CRISIS ON INFINITE EARTHS (Also see Official... Index and Legends of the DC Universe)
DC Comics: Apr, 1985 - No. 12, Mar, 1986 (maxi-series)

1-1st DC app. Blue Beetle & Detective Karp from Charlton; Perez-c on all 1.10 3.30 9.00
2-6: 6-Intro Charlton's Capt. Atom, Nightshade, Question, Judomaster, Peacemaker & Thunderbolt into DC Universe 1.00 3.00 8.00
7-Double size; death of Supergirl 1.10 3.30 9.00
8-Death of the Flash (Barry Allen) 1.50 4.50 12.00
9-11: 9-Intro. Charlton's Ghost into DC Universe. 10-Intro. Charlton's Banshee, Dr. Spectro, Image, Punch & Jewellee into DC Universe; Starman (Prince Gavyn) dies. 1.00 3.00 8.00
12-(52 pgs.)-Deaths of Dove, Kole, Lori Lemaris, Sunburst, G.A. Robin & Huntress; Kid Flash becomes new Flash; 3rd & final DC app. of the 3 Lt. Marvels; Green Fury gets new look (becomes Green Flame in Infinity, Inc. #32) 1.00 3.00 8.00
Slipcased Hardcover (1998, $99.95) Wraparound dust-jacket cover by Pérez and Alex Ross; sketch pages by Pérez; intro by Wolfman 110.00

CRITICAL MASS (See A Shadowline Saga: Critical Mass)

CRITTERS (Also see Usagi Yojimbo Summer Special)
Fantagraphics Books: 1986 - No. 50, 1990 ($1.70/$2.00, B&W)

1-Cutey Bunny, Usagi Yojimbo app. 5.00
2-22,24-49: 3,6,7,10,11,14,38-Usagi Yojimbo app. 11-Christmas Special (68 pgs.); Usagi Yojimbo. 22-Watchmen parody; two diff. covers exist 2.00
23-With Alan Moore Flexi-disc ($3.95) 5.00
50 ($4.95, 84 pgs.)-Neil the Horse, Capt. Jack, Sam & Max & Usagi Yojimbo app.; Quagmire, Shaw-a 5.00
Special 1 (1/88, $2.00) 2.00

CROSS
Dark Horse Comics: No. 0, Oct, 1995 - No. 6, Apr, 1995 ($2.95, limited series, mature)

0-6: Darrow-c & Vachss scripts in all 3.00

CROSS AND THE SWITCHBLADE, THE
Spire Christian Comics (Fleming H. Revell Co.): 1972 (35-49¢)

1-Some issues have nn 5.00

CROSSFIRE
Spire Christian Comics (Fleming H. Revell Co.): 1973 (39/49¢)

nn 5.00

CROSSFIRE (Also see DNAgents)
Eclipse Comics: 5/84 - No. 17, 3/86; No. 18, 1/87 - No. 26, 2/88 ($1.50, Baxter paper)(#18-26 (B&W)

1-11,14-26: 1-DNAgents x-over; Spiegle-c/a begins 2.00
12,13-Death of Marilyn Monroe. 12-Dave Stevens-c 3.00

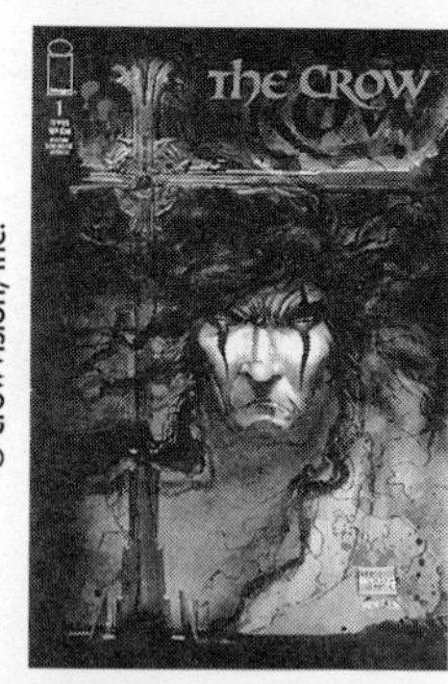

The Crow (Image Comics) #1 © CrowVision, Inc.

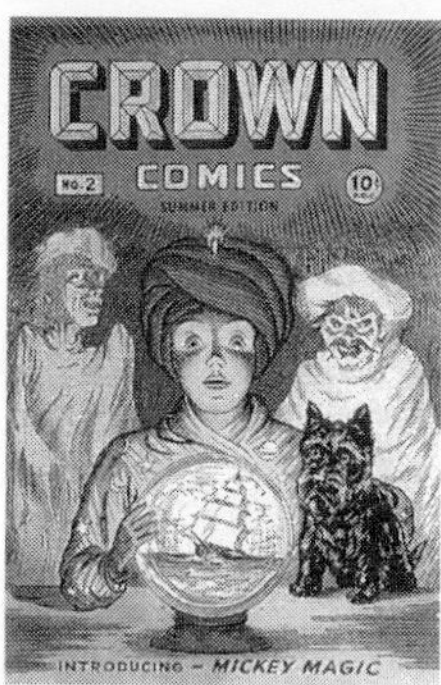

Crown Comics #2 © Golfing

Cryin' Lion #2 © WHW

GD2.0 FN6.0 NM9.4

GD2.0 FN6.0 NM9.4

CROSSFIRE AND RAINBOW (Also see DNAgents)
Eclipse Comics: June, 1986 - No. 4, Sept, 1986 ($1.25, deluxe format)

1-3: Spiegle-a. 4-Dave Stevens-c 2.00

CROSSING THE ROCKIES (See Classics Illustrated Special Issue)

CROSSROADS
First Comics: July, 1988 - No. 5, Nov, 1988 ($3.25, lim. series, deluxe format)

1-5 3.25

CROW, THE (Also see Caliber Presents)
Caliber Press: Feb, 1989 - No. 4, 1989 ($1.95, B&W, limited series)

1-James O'Barr-c/a/scripts 5.50 16.50 60.00
1-3-2nd printing 1.00 3.00 8.00
2-4 3.00 9.00 30.00
2-3rd printing 2.40 6.00

CROW, THE
Tundra Publishing, Ltd.: Jan, 1992 - No. 3, 1992 ($4.95, B&W, 68 pgs.)

1-3: 1-r/#1,2 of Caliber series. 2-r/#3 of Caliber series w/new material. 3-All new material 1.00 3.00 8.00

CROW, THE
Kitchen Sink Press: 1/96 - No. 3, 3/96 ($2.95, B&W)

1-3: James O'Barr-c/scripts 3.00
#0-A Cycle of Shattered Lives (12/98, $3.50) new story by O'Barr 3.50

CROW, THE
Image Comics (Todd McFarlane Prod.): Feb, 1999 - Present ($2.50)

1-7: 1-Two covers by McFarlane and Kent Williams; Muth-s 2.50

CROW, THE: CITY OF ANGELS (Movie)
Kitchen Sink Press: July, 1996 - No. 3, Sept, 1996 ($2.95, limited series)

1-3: Adaptation of film; two-c (photo & illos.). 1-Vincent Perez interview 3.00

CROW, THE: FLESH AND BLOOD
Kitchen Sink Press: May, 1996 - No. 3, July, 1996 ($2.95, limited series)

1-3: O'Barr-c 3.00

CROW, THE: RAZOR - KILL THE PAIN
London Night Studios: Apr, 1998 - No.3, July, 1998 ($2.95, B&W, lim. series)

1-3-Hartsoe-s/O'Barr-painted-c 3.00
0(10/98) Dorien painted-c, Finale (2/99) 3.00
The Lost Chapter (2/99, $4.95), Tour Book-(12/97) pin-ups; 4 diff.-c 5.00

CROW, THE: WAKING NIGHTMARES
Kitchen Sink Press: Jan, 1997 - No.4, 1998 ($2.95, B&W, limited series)

1-4-Miran Kim-c 3.00

CROW, THE: WILD JUSTICE
Kitchen Sink Press: Oct, 1996 ($2.95, B&W, unfinished limited series)

1-Prosser-s/Adlard-a 3.00

CROWN COMICS
Golfing/McCombs Publ.: Wint, 1944-45; No. 2, Sum, 1945 - No. 19, July, 1949

1- "The Oblong Box" E.A. Poe adaptation 34.00 103.00 240.00
2,3-Baker-a; 3-Voodah by Baker 23.00 69.00 160.00
4-6-Baker-c/a; Voodah app. #4,5 24.00 73.00 170.00
7-Feldstein, Baker, Kamen-a; Baker-c 23.00 69.00 160.00
8-Baker-a; Voodah app. 21.00 62.00 145.00
9-11,13-19: Voodah in #10-19. 13-New logo 12.00 36.00 85.00
12-Master Marvin by Feldstein, Starr-a; Voodah-c 13.00 39.00 90.00
NOTE: ***Bolle** a-11, 13-16, 18, 19; c-11p, 15. **Powell** a-19. **Starr** a-11-13; c-11i.*

CRUCIBLE
DC Comics (Impact): Feb, 1993 - No. 6, July, 1993 ($1.25, limited series)

1-6:1-(99¢)-Neon ink-c. 1,2-Quesada-c(p). 1-4-Quesada layouts 2.00

CRUEL AND UNUSUAL
DC Comics (Vertigo): June, 1999 - No. 4, Sept, 1999 ($2.95, limited series)

1-4-Delano & Peyer-s/McCrea-c/a 3.00

CRUSADER FROM MARS (See Tops in Adventure)
Ziff-Davis Publ. Co.: Jan-Mar, 1952 - No. 2, Fall, 1952 (Painted-c)

1-Cover is dated Spring 69.00 206.00 550.00
2-Bondage-c 53.00 159.00 425.00

CRUSADER RABBIT (TV)
Dell Publishing Co.: No. 735, Oct, 1956 - No. 805, May, 1957

Four Color 735 (#1) 31.00 93.00 340.00
Four Color 805 24.00 70.00 260.00

CRUSADERS, THE (Religious)
Chick Publications: 1974 - Vol. 16, 1985 (39/69¢, 36 pgs.)

Vol.1-Operation Bucharest ('74). Vol.2-The Broken Cross ('74). Vol.3-Scarface ('74). Vol.4-Exorcists ('75). Vol.5-Chaos ('75) 5.00
Vol.6-Primal Man? ('76)-(Disputes evolution theory). Vol.7-The Ark-(claims proof of existence, destroyed by Bolsheviks). Vol.8-The Gift-(Life story of Christ). Vol.9-Angel of Light-(Story of the Devil). Vol.10-Spellbound?-(Tells how rock music is Satanical & produced by witches). 11-Sabotage?. 12-Alberto. 13-Double Cross. 14-The Godfathers. (No. 6-14 low in distribution; loaded in religious propaganda.). 15-The Force. 16-The Four Horsemen 5.00

CRUSADERS (Southern Knights No. 2 on)
Guild Publications: 1982 (B&W, magazine size)

1-1st app. Southern Knights 5.00

CRUSADERS, THE (Also see Black Hood, The Jaguar, The Comet, The Fly, Legend of the Shield, The Mighty... & The Web)
DC Comics (Impact): May, 1992 - No. 8, Dec, 1992 ($1.00/$1.25)

1-8-Contains 3 Impact trading cards 2.00

CRUSH, THE
Image Comics (Motown Machineworks): Jan, 1996 - No. 5, July, 1996 ($2.25, limited series)

1-5: Baron scripts 3.00

CRY FOR DAWN
Cry For Dawn Pub.: 1989 - No. 9 ($2.25, B&W, mature)

1 9.00 27.00 100.00
1-2nd printing 3.00 9.00 30.00
1-3rd printing 2.50 7.50 20.00
2 4.50 13.50 45.00
2-2nd printing 1.10 3.30 9.00
3 3.00 9.00 30.00
4-6 2.25 6.75 18.00
5-2nd printing 5.00
7-9 1.75 5.25 14.00
4-9-Signed & numbered editions 2.50 7.50 25.00
...Calendar (1993) 35.00

CRYIN' LION COMICS
William H. Wise Co.: Fall, 1944 - No. 3, Spring, 1945

1-Funny animal 13.50 41.00 95.00
2-Hitler app. 11.00 33.00 75.00
3 10.00 30.00 60.00

CRYPT
Image Comics (Extreme): Aug, 1995 - No.2, Oct. 1995 ($2.50, limited series)

1,2-Prophet app. 2.50

CRYPTIC WRITINGS OF MEGADETH
Chaos! Comics: Sept, 1997 - Present ($2.95, quarterly)

1-4-Stories based on song lyrics by Dave Mustaine 3.00

CRYPT OF DAWN (see Dawn)
Sirius: 1996 ($2.95, B&W, limited series)

1-Linsner-c/s; anthology. 5.00
2, 3 (2/98) 4.00
4,5: 4- (6/98), 5-(11/98) 3.00
Ltd. Edition 20.00

CRYPT OF SHADOWS

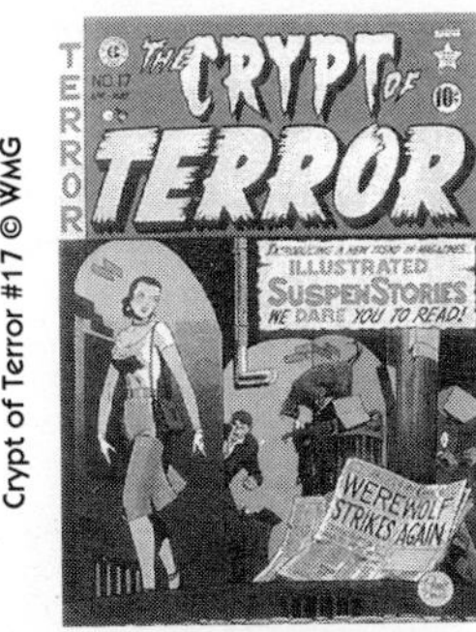

Crypt of Terror #17 © WMG

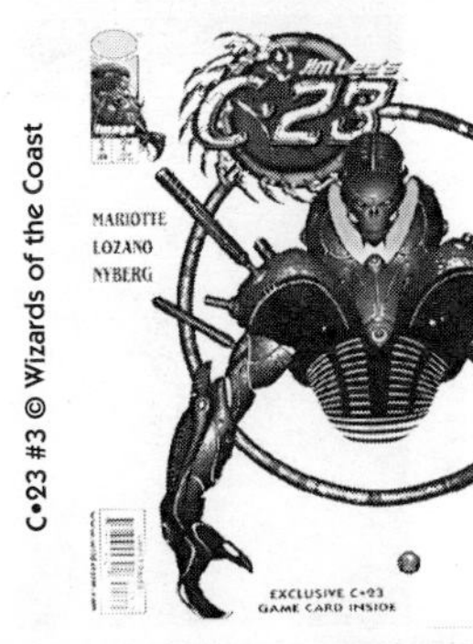

C•23 #3 © Wizards of the Coast

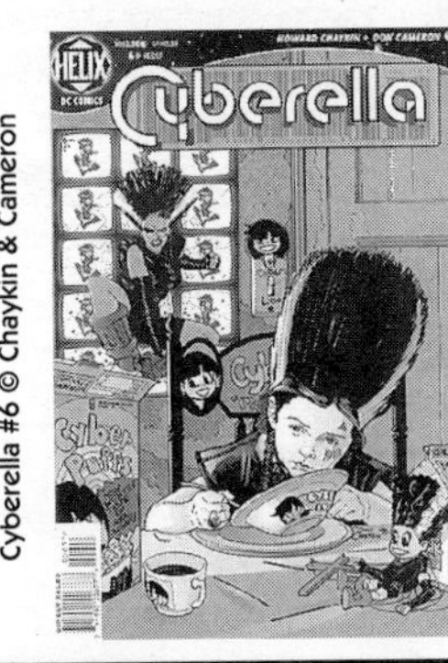

Cyberella #6 © Chaykin & Cameron

GD2.0 FN6.0 NM9.4

Marvel Comics Group: Jan, 1973 - No. 21, Nov, 1975 (#1-9 are 20¢)

1-Wolverton-r/Advs. Into Terror #7 2.00 6.00 16.00
2-10: 2-Starlin/Everett-c 1.50 4.50 12.00
11-21: 18,20-Kirby-a 1.00 3.00 8.00

NOTE: ***Briefer** a-2r. **Ditko** a-13r, 18-20r. **Everett** a-6, 14r; c-2i. **Heath** a-1r. **Gil Kane** c-1, 6. **Mort Lawrence** a-1r, 8r. **Maneely** a-2r. **Moldoff** a-8. **Powell** a-12r, 14r. **Tuska** a-2r.*

CRYPT OF TERROR (Formerly Crime Patrol; Tales From the Crypt No. 20 on)
E. C. Comics: No. 17, Apr-May, 1950 - No. 19, Aug-Sept, 1950

17-1st New Trend to hit stands 235.00 705.00 2350.00
18,19 134.00 403.00 1275.00

NOTE: ***Craig** c/a-17-19. **Feldstein** a-17-19. **Ingels** a-19. **Kurtzman** a-18. **Wood** a-18. Canadian reprints known; see Table of Contents.*

C•23 (Jim Lee's...) (Based on Wizards of the Coast card game)
Image Comics: Apr, 1998 - No. 8, Nov, 1998 ($2.50)

1-8: 1,2-Choi & Mariotte-s/ Charest-c. 2-Variant-c by Jim Lee. 4-Ryan Benjamin-c. 5,8-Corben var-c. 6-Flip book with Planetary preview; Corben-c 3.00

CUD
Fantagraphics Books: 8/92 - No. 8, 12/94 ($2.25-$2.75, B&W, mature)

1-8: Terry LaBan scripts & art in all. 6-1st Eno & Plum 3.00

CUD COMICS
Dark Horse Comics: Jan, 1995 - Present ($2.95, B&W)

1-8: Terry LaBan-c/a/scripts. 5-Nudity; marijuana story 3.00
Eno and Plum TPB (1997, $12.95) r/#1-4, DHP #93-95 13.00

CUPID
Marvel Comics (U.S.A.): Dec, 1949 - No. 2, Mar, 1950

1-Photo-c 13.00 39.00 90.00
2-Betty Page ('50s pin-up queen) photo-c; Powell-a (see My Love #4) 28.00 84.00 195.00

CURIO
Harry 'A' Chesler: 1930's(?) (Tabloid size, 16-20 pgs.)

nn 19.00 58.00 135.00

CURLY KAYOE COMICS (Boxing)
United Features Syndicate/Dell Publ. Co.: 1946 - No. 8, 1950; Jan, 1958

1 (1946)-Strip-r (Fritzi Ritz); biography of Sam Leff, Kayoe's artist 16.00 47.00 110.00
2 9.15 27.00 55.00
3-8 6.70 20.00 40.00
United Presents...(Fall, 1948) 5.00 15.00 30.00
Four Color 871 (Dell, 1/58) 1.80 5.50 20.00

CURSE OF DRACULA, THE
Dark Horse Comics: July, 1998 - No. 3, Sept, 1998 ($2.95, limited series)

1-3-Wolfman-s/Colan-a 3.00

CURSE OF DREADWOLF
Lightning Comics: Sept, 1994 ($2.75, B&W)

1 2.75

CURSE OF RUNE (Becomes Rune, 2nd Series)
Malibu Comics (Ultraverse): May, 1995 - No. 4, Aug, 1995 ($2.50, lim. series)

1-4: 1-Two covers form one image 2.50

CURSE OF THE SPAWN
Image Comics (Todd McFarlane Prod.): Sept, 1996 - No. 29, Mar, 1999 ($1.95)

1-Dwayne Turner-a(p) 1.00 2.80 7.00
1-B&W Edition 2.25 6.75 18.00
2-3 5.00
4-10 3.00
11-13: 12-Movie photo-c of Melinda Clarke (Priest) 2.50
14-26 2.00

CURSE OF THE WEIRD
Marvel Comics: Dec, 1993 - No. 4, Mar, 1994 ($1.25, limited series)
(Pre-code horror-r)

GD2.0 FN6.0 NM9.4

1-4: 1,3,4-Wolverton-r(1-Eye of Doom; 3-Where Monsters Dwell; 4-The End of the World). 2-Orlando-r. 4-Zombie-r by Everett; painted-c 2.50

NOTE: ***Briefer** r-2. **Jack Davis** a-4r. **Ditko** a-1r, 2r, 4r; c-1r. **Everett** r-1. **Heath** r-1-3. **Kubert** r-3. **Wolverton** a-1r, 3r, 4r.*

CUSTER'S LAST FIGHT
Avon Periodicals: 1950

nn-Partial reprint of Cowpuncher #1 17.00 49.00 115.00

CUTEY BUNNY (See Army Surplus Komikz Featuring...)

CUTIE PIE
Junior Reader's Guild (Lev Gleason): May, 1955 - No. 3, Dec, 1955; No. 4, Feb, 1956; No. 5, Aug, 1956

1 5.85 17.50 35.00
2-5: 4-Misdated 2/55 4.00 10.00 20.00

CUTTING EDGE
Marvel Comics: Dec, 1995 ($2.95)

1-Hulk-c/story; Messner-Loebs scripts 3.00

CYBERCITY
CPM Comics: Sept, 1995- Present ($2.95, bi-monthly)

Part One #1,2; Part Two #1,2; Part Three #1,2 3.00

CYBERELLA
DC Comics (Helix): Sept, 1996 - No. 12, Aug, 1997 ($2.25/$2.50)
(1st Helix series)

1-12: 1-5-Chaykin & Cameron-a. 1,2-Chaykin-c. 3-5-Cameron-c 2.50

CYBERFORCE
Image Comics (Top Cow Productions): Oct, 1992 - No. 4, 1993; No. 0, Sept, 1993 ($1.95, limited series)

1-Silvestri-c/a in all; coupon for Image Comics #0; 1st Top Cow Productions title. 1.00 3.00 8.00
1-With coupon missing 2.00
2-4,0: 2-(3/93). 3-Pitt-c/story. 4-Codename: Stryke Force back-up (1st app.); foil-c. 0-(9/93)-Walt Simonson-c/a/scripts 3.00

CYBERFORCE
Image Comics (Top Cow Productions)/Top Cow Comics No. 28 on:
V2#1, Nov, 1993 - No. 35, Sept. 1997 ($1.95)

V2#1-24: 1-7-Marc Silvestri/Keith Williams-c/a. 8-McFarlane-c/a. 10-Painted variant-c exists. 18-Variant-c exists. 23-Velocity-c. 2.50
1-3: 1-Gold Logo-c. 2-Silver embossed-c. 3-Gold embossed-c 10.00
1-(99¢, 3/96, 2nd printing) 2.00
25-($3.95)-Wraparound, foil-c 4.00
26-35: 28-(11/96)-1st Top Cow Comics iss. Quesada & Palmiotti's Gabriel app. 27-Quesada & Palmiotti's Ash app. 2.50
Annual 1,2 (3/95, 8/96, $2.50, $2.95) 3.00

NOTE: *Annuals read Volume One in the indica.*

CYBERFORCE ORIGINS
Image Comics (Top Cow Productions): Jan, 1995 - No. 3, Nov, 1995 ($2.50)

1-Cyblade (1/95) 5.00
1-Cyblade (3/96, 99¢, 2nd printing) 2.00
1A-Exclusive Ed.; Tucci-c 4.00
2,3: 2-Stryker (2/95)-1st Mike Turner-a. 3-Impact 2.50

CYBERFORCE/STRYKEFORCE: OPPOSING FORCES (See Codename: Stryke Force #15)
Image Comics (Top Cow Productions): Sept, 1995 - No.2, Oct, 1995 ($2.50, limited series)

1,2: 2-Stryker disbands Strykeforce. 2.50

CYBERFORCE UNIVERSE SOURCEBOOK
Image Comics (Top Cow Productions): Aug, 1994/Feb, 1995 ($2.50)

1,2-Silvestri-c 2.50

CYBERFROG
Hall of Heroes: June, 1994 - No. 2, Dec, 1994 ($2.50, B&W, limited series)

1,2 2.50

Cyclone Comics #5 © Bilbara

Cy-Gor #1 © Todd McFarlane Prod.

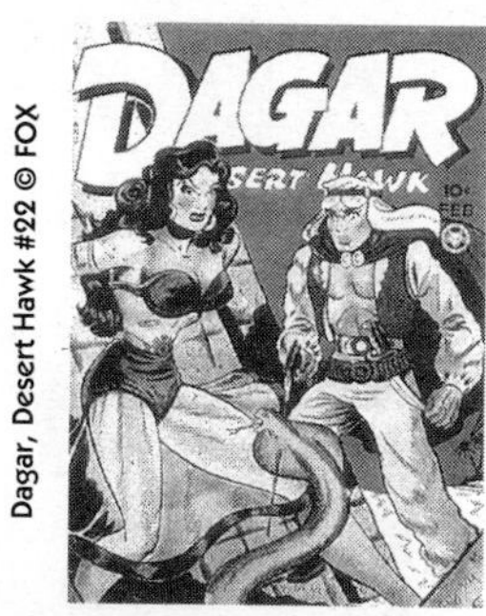

Dagar, Desert Hawk #22 © FOX

CYBERFROG
Harris Comics: Feb, 1996 - No. 3, Apr, 1996 ($2.95)
0-3: Van Sciver-c/a/scripts. 2-Variant-c exists 5.00

CYBERFROG: (Title series), **Harris Comics**
--RESERVOIR FROG, 9/96 - No. 2, 10/96 ($2.95) 1,2: Van Sciver-c/a/scripts; wraparound-c 3.00
--RD ANNIVERSARY SPECIAL, 1/97 - #2, ($2.50, B&W) 1,2 2.50
--VS. CREED, 7/97 ($2.95, B&W)1 3.00

CYBERNARY (See Deathblow #1)
Image Comics (WildStorm Productions): Nov, 1995 - No.5, Mar, 1996 ($2.50)
1-5 2.50

CYBERPUNK
Innovation Publishing: Sept, 1989 - No. 2, Oct, 1989 ($1.95, 28 pgs.) Book 2, #1, May, 1990 - No. 2, 1990 ($2.25, 28 pgs.)
1,2, Book 2 #1,2:1,2-Ken Steacy painted-covers (Adults) 2.25

CYBERPUNK: THE SERAPHIM FILES
Innovation Publishing: Nov, 1990 - No. 2, Dec, 1990 ($2.50, 28 pgs., mature)
1,2: 1-Painted-c; story cont'd from Seraphim 2.50

CYBERPUNX
Image Comics (Extreme Studios): Mar, 1996 ($2.50)
1 3.00

CYBERRAD
Continuity Comics: 1991 - No. 7, 1992 ($2.00)(Direct sale & newsstand-c variations)
V2#1, 1993 ($2.50)
1-7: 5-Glow-in-the-dark-c by N. Adams (direct sale only). 6-Contains 4 pg. fold-out poster; N. Adams layouts 2.00
V2#1-($2.95, direct sale ed.)-Die-cut-c w/B&W hologram on-c; Neal Adams sketches 3.00
V2#1-($2.50, newsstand ed.)-Without sketches 2.50

CYBERRAD DEATHWATCH 2000 (Becomes CyberRad w/#2, 7/93)
Continuity Comics: Apr, 1993 - No. 2, 1993 ($2.50)
1,2: 1-Bagged w/2 cards; Adams-c & layouts & plots. 2-Bagged w/card; Adams scripts 2.50

CYBER 7
Eclipse Comics: Mar, 1989 - #7, Sept, 1989; V2#1, Oct, 1989 - #10, 1990 ($2.00, B&W)
1-7, Book 2 #1-10: Stories translated from Japanese 2.00

CYBLADE/ GHOST RIDER
Marvel Comics /Top Cow Productions: Jan 1997 ($2.95, one-shot)
1-Devil's Reign pt. 2 4.00

CYBLADE/SHI (Also see Battle For The Independents & Shi/Cyblade: The Battle For The Independents)
Image Comics (Top Cow Productions): 1995 ($2.95, one-shot)

	GD2.0	FN6.0	NM9.4
San Diego Preview	2.50	7.50	20.00
1-($2.95)-1st app. Witchblade	2.500	4.50	12.00
1-($2.95)-variant-c; Tucci-a	1.00	3.00	8.00

CYBRID
Maximum Press: July, 1995; No. 0, Jan, 1997 ($2.95/$3.50)
1-(7/95) 3.00
0-(1/97)-Liefeld-a/script; story cont'd in Avengelyne #4 3.50

CYCLONE COMICS (Also see Whirlwind Comics)
Bilbara Publishing Co.: June, 1940 - No. 5, Nov, 1940

	GD2.0	FN6.0	NM9.4
1-Origin Tornado Tom; Volton (the human generator), Tornado Tom, Kingdom of the Moon, Mister Q begin (1st app. of each)	141.00	422.00	1125.00
2,3	70.00	210.00	560.00
4,5	56.00	167.00	445.00

CYCLOPS: RETRIBUTION
Marvel Comics: 1994 ($5.95, trade paperback)

	GD2.0	FN6.0	NM9.4
nn-r/Marvel Comics Presents #17-24		2.40	6.00

CY-GOR (See Spawn #38 for 1st app.)
Image Comics (Todd McFarlane Prod.): July, 1999 - Present ($2.50)
1-Veitch-s 2.50

CYNTHIA DOYLE, NURSE IN LOVE (Formerly Sweetheart Diary)
Charlton Publications: No. 66, Oct, 1962 - No. 74, Feb, 1964

	GD2.0	FN6.0	NM9.4
66-74	1.75	5.25	14.00

DAEMONSTORM
Caliber Comics: 1997 ($3.95, one-shot)
1-McFarlane-c 4.00

DAEMONSTORM: STORMWALKER
Caliber Comics: 1997 ($3.95, B&W, one-shot)
nn 4.00

DAFFY (Daffy Duck No. 18 on)(See Looney Tunes)
Dell Publishing Co./Gold Key No. 31-127/Whitman No. 128 on: #457, 3/53 - #30, 7-9/62; #31, 10-12/62 - #145, 1983 (No #132,133)

	GD2.0	FN6.0	NM9.4
Four Color 457(#1)-Elmer Fudd x-overs begin	8.00	25.00	90.00
Four Color 536,615('55)	4.00	12.00	45.00
4(1-3/56)-11('57)	2.70	8.10	30.00
12-19(1958-59)	1.80	5.40	20.00
20-40(1960-64)	1.75	5.25	14.00
41-60(1964-68)	1.50	4.50	12.00
61-90(1969-74)-Road Runner in most	1.00	3.00	6.00
91-110		2.40	6.00
111-127			4.00
128,134-141			5.00
129(8/80), 130,131 (pre-pack?)	1.25	3.75	10.00
142-145(#90029 on-c; nd, nd code, pre-pack?)	1.00	2.80	7.00
Mini-Comic 1 (1976; 3-1/4x6-1/2")			5.00

NOTE: *Reprint issues-No.41-46, 48, 50, 53-55, 58, 59, 65, 67, 69, 73, 81, 96, 103-108; 136-142, 144, 145(1/3-2/3-r). (See March of Comics No. 277, 288, 303, 313, 331, 347, 357,375, 387, 397, 402, 413, 425, 437, 460).*

DAFFY TUNES COMICS
Four-Star Publications: June, 1947; No. 12, Aug, 1947

	GD2.0	FN6.0	NM9.4
nn	7.50	22.50	45.00
12-Al Fago-c/a; funny animal	6.35	19.00	38.00

DAGAR, DESERT HAWK (Captain Kidd No. 24 on; formerly All Great)
Fox Features Syndicate: No. 14, Feb, 1948 - No. 23, Apr, 1949 (No #17,18)

	GD2.0	FN6.0	NM9.4
14-Tangi & Safari Cary begin; Good bondage-c/a	75.00	225.00	600.00
15,16-E. Good-a; 15-Bondage-c	46.00	138.00	365.00
19,20,22: 19-Used in **SOTI**, pg. 180 (Tangi)	40.00	120.00	305.00
21,23: 21- "Bombs & Bums Away" panel in "Flood of Death" story used in **SOTI.** 23-Bondage-c	43.00	129.00	345.00

NOTE: *Tangi by **Kamen**-14-16, 19, 20; c-20, 21.*

DAGAR THE INVINCIBLE (Tales of Sword & Sorcery...) (Also see Dan Curtis Giveaways & Gold Key Spotlight)
Gold Key: Oct, 1972 - No. 18, Dec, 1976; No. 19, Apr, 1982

	GD2.0	FN6.0	NM9.4
1-Origin; intro. Villains Olstellon & Scor	2.50	7.50	20.00
2-5: 3-Intro. Graylin, Dagar's woman; Jarn x-over	1.00	3.00	8.00
6-1st Dark Gods story		2.40	6.00
7-10: 9-Intro. Torgus. 10-1st Three Witches story		2.40	6.00
11-18: 13-Durak & Torgus x-over; story continues in Dr. Spektor #15. 14-Dagar's origin retold. 18-Origin retold			5.00
19-Origin-r/#18			4.00

NOTE: *Durak app. in 7, 12, 13. Tragg app. in 5, 11.*

DAGWOOD (Chic Young's) (Also see Blondie Comics)
Harvey Publications: Sept, 1950 - No. 140, Nov, 1965

	GD2.0	FN6.0	NM9.4
1	12.50	37.00	125.00
2	6.50	19.50	65.00
3-10	5.00	15.00	50.00
11-20	4.00	12.00	40.00

Daisy and Her Pups #8 © KFS

Dale Evans Comics #7 © DC

Danger #6 © Comic Media

	GD2.0	FN6.0	NM9.4
21-30	3.50	10.50	35.00
31-50	3.00	9.00	30.00
51-70	2.20	6.60	22.00
71-100	1.60	4.80	16.00
101-128,130,135	1.20	3.60	12.00
129,131-134,136-140-All are 68-pg. issues	2.00	6.00	20.00

NOTE: *Popeye and other one page strips appeared in early issues.*

DAI KAMIKAZE!
Now Comics: June, 1987 - No. 12, Aug, 1988 ($1.75)

1-12: 1-1st app. Speed Racer; 2nd print exists — 2.00

DAILY BUGLE (See Spider-Man)
Marvel Comics: Dec, 1996 - No. 3, Feb, 1997 ($2.50, B&W, limited series)

1-3-Paul Grist-s — 2.50

DAISY AND DONALD (See Walt Disney Showcase No. 8)
Gold Key/Whitman No. 42 on: May, 1973 - No. 59, 1984 (no No. 48)

	GD2.0	FN6.0	NM9.4
1-Barks-r/WDC&S #280,308	2.50	7.50	22.00
2-5: 4-Barks-r/WDC&S #224	1.50	4.50	12.00
6-10	1.00	3.00	8.00
11-20		2.40	6.00
21-41: 32-r/WDC&S #308			5.00
42-44 (Whitman)		2.40	6.00
45 (8/80),46-(pre-pack?)	2.25	6.75	18.00
47-(12/80)-Only distr. in Whitman 3-pack	3.60	10.80	36.00
48(3/81)-50(8/81): 50-r/#3	1.10	3.30	9.00
51-54: 51-Barks-r/4-Color #1150. 52-r/#2	1.00	2.80	7.00
55-59-(all #90284 on-c, nd, nd code, pre-pack?)	1.40	4.15	11.00

DAISY & HER PUPS (Blondie's Dogs)(Formerly Blondie Comics #20)
Harvey Publications: No. 21, 7/51 - No. 27, 7/52; No. 8, 9/52 - No. 18, 5/54

	GD2.0	FN6.0	NM9.4
21 (#1)-Blondie's dog Daisy and her 5 pups led by Elmer begin. Rags Rabbit app	4.00	12.00	40.00
22-27 (#2-7): 26,27 have No. 6 & 7 on cover but No. 26 & 27 on inside. 23,25-The Little King app. 24-Bringing Up Father by McManus app. 25-27-Rags Rabbit app.	2.50	7.50	25.00
8-18: 8,9-Rags Rabbit app. 8,17-The Little King app. 11-The Flop Family Swan begins. 22-Cookie app. 11-Felix The Cat app. by 17,18-Popeye app.	1.80	5.40	18.00

DAISY COMICS
Eastern Color Printing Co.: Dec, 1936 (5-1/4x7-1/2")

	GD2.0	FN6.0	NM9.4
nn-Joe Palooka, Buck Rogers (2 pgs. from Famous Funnies No. 18), Napoleon Flying to Fame, Butty & Fally	34.00	103.00	240.00

DAISY DUCK & UNCLE SCROOGE PICNIC TIME (See Dell Giant #33)

DAISY DUCK & UNCLE SCROOGE SHOW BOAT (See Dell Giant #55)

DAISY DUCK'S DIARY (See Dynabrite Comics, & Walt Disney's C&S #298)
Dell Publishing Co.: No. 600, Nov, 1954 - No. 1247, Dec-Fef, 1961-62 (Disney)

	GD2.0	FN6.0	NM9.4
Four Color 600 (#1)	6.00	18.00	65.00
Four Color 659, 743 (11/56)	5.00	15.00	55.00
Four Color 858 (11/57), 948 (11/58), 1247 (12-2/61-62)	4.00	12.00	45.00
Four Color 1055 (11-1/59-60), 1150 (12-1/60-61)-By Carl Barks)	9.00	27.00	100.00

DAISY HANDBOOK
Daisy Manufacturing Co.: 1946; No. 2, 1948 (10¢, pocket-size, 132 pgs.)

	GD2.0	FN6.0	NM9.4
1-Buck Rogers, Red Ryder; Wolverton-a(2 pgs.)	40.00	120.00	280.00
2-Captain Marvel & Ibis the Invincible, Red Ryder, Boy Commandos & Robotman; Wolverton-a (2 pgs.); contains 8 pg. color catalog	40.00	120.00	280.00

DAISY MAE (See Oxydol-Dreft)

DAISY'S RED RYDER GUN BOOK
Daisy Manufacturing Co.: 1955 (25¢, pocket-size, 132 pgs.)

	GD2.0	FN6.0	NM9.4
nn-Boy Commandos, Red Ryder; 1pg. Wolverton-a	26.00	77.00	180.00

DAKKON BLACKBLADE ON THE WORLD OF MAGIC: THE GATHERING
Acclaim Comics (Armada): June, 1996 ($5.95, one-shot)

	GD2.0	FN6.0	NM9.4
1-Jerry Prosser scripts; Rags Morales-c/a.		2.40	6.00

DAKOTA LIL (See Fawcett Movie Comics)

DAKOTA NORTH
Marvel Comics Group: June, 1986 - No. 5, Feb, 1987

1-5 — 2.00

DAKTARI (Ivan Tors) (TV)
Dell Publishing Co.: July, 1967 - No. 3, Oct, 1968; No. 4, Sept, 1969 (All have photo-c)

	GD2.0	FN6.0	NM9.4
1	2.80	8.40	28.00
2-4	2.50	7.50	20.00

DALE EVANS COMICS (Also see Queen of the West...)
National Periodical Publications: Sept-Oct, 1948 - No. 24, July-Aug, 1952 (No. 1-19: 52 pgs.)

	GD2.0	FN6.0	NM9.4
1-Dale Evans & her horse Buttermilk begin; Sierra Smith begins by Alex Toth	96.00	287.00	765.00
2-Alex Toth-a	46.00	139.00	370.00
3-11-Alex Toth-a	31.00	92.00	215.00
12-20: 12-Target-c	14.00	43.00	100.00
21-24	16.00	47.00	110.00

NOTE: *Photo-c-1, 2, 4-14.*

DALGODA
Fantagraphics Books: Aug, 1984 - No. 8, Feb, 1986 (High quality paper)

1- Fujitake-c/a in all — 2.50
2-7: 2,3-Debut Grimwood's Daughter. 8-Alan Moore story — 2.00

DALTON BOYS, THE
Avon Periodicals: 1951

	GD2.0	FN6.0	NM9.4
1-(Number on spine)-Kinstler-c	16.00	47.00	110.00

DAMAGE
DC Comics: Apr, 1994 - No. 20, Jan, 1996 ($1.75/$1.95)

1-20: 6-(9/94)-Zero Hour. 0-(10/94). 7-(11/94). 14-Ray app. — 2.50

DAMAGE CONTROL (See Marvel Comics Presents #19)
Marvel Comics: 5/89 - No. 4, 8/89; V2#1, 12/89 - No. 4, 2/90 ($1.00) V3#1, 6/91 - No. 4, 9/91 ($1.25, all are limited series)

V1#1-4,V2#1-4,V3#1-4: V1#4-Wolverine app. V2#2,4-Punisher app. 1-Spider-Man app. 2-New Warriors app. 3,4-Silver Surfer app. 4-Infinity Gauntlet parody — 2.00

DAMNED
Image Comics (Homage Comics): June, 1997 - No. 4, Sept, 1997 ($2.50, limited series)

1-4-Steven Grant-s/Mike Zeck-c/a in all — 2.50

DANCES WITH DEMONS (See Marvel Frontier Comics Unlimited)
Marvel Frontier Comics: Sept, 1993 - No. 4, Dec, 1993 ($1.95, limited series)

1-($2.95)-Foil embossed-c — 3.00
2-4 — 2.00

DANDEE
Four Star Publications: 1947

	GD2.0	FN6.0	NM9.4
nn	6.35	19.00	38.00

DAN DUNN (See Crackajack Funnies, Detective Dan, Famous Feature Stories & Red Ryder)

DANDY COMICS (Also see Happy Jack Howard)
E. C. Comics: Spring, 1947 - No. 7, Spring, 1948

	GD2.0	FN6.0	NM9.4
1-Funny animal; Vince Fago-a in all; Dandy in all	34.00	103.00	240.00
2	25.00	75.00	175.00
3-7: 3-Intro Handy Andy who is c-feature #3 on	19.00	56.00	130.00

DANGER
Comic Media/Allen Hardy Assoc.: Jan, 1953 - No. 11, Aug, 1954

	GD2.0	FN6.0	NM9.4
1-Heck-c/a	17.00	51.00	120.00

Danger Girl #4 © J. Scott Campbell

Dan'l Boone #1 © ME

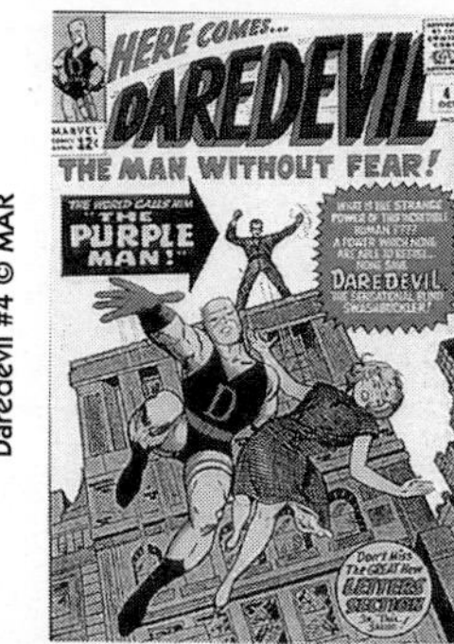

Daredevil #4 © MAR

GD2.0 FN6.0 NM9.4

2,3,5,7,9-11: 10.00 30.00 65.00
6- "Narcotics" story; begin spy theme 10.00 30.00 70.00
4-Marijuana cover/story 11.50 34.00 80.00
8-Bondage/torture/headlights panels 13.00 39.00 90.00
NOTE: *Morisi a-2, 5, 6(3), 10; c-2. Contains some reprints from Danger & Dynamite.*

DANGER (Jim Bowie No. 15 on) (Formerly Comic Media title)
Charlton Comics Group: No. 12, June, 1955 - No. 14, Oct, 1955
12(#1) 9.15 27.00 55.00
13,14: 14-r/#12 6.70 20.00 40.00

DANGER
Super Comics: 1964
Super Reprint #10-12 (Black Dwarf; #10-r/Great Comics #1 by Novack. #11-r/Johnny Danger #1. #12-r/Red Seal #14), #15-r/Spy Cases #26. #16-Unpublished Chesler material (Yankee Girl), #17-r/Scoop #8 (Capt. Courage & Enchanted Dagger), #18(nd)-r/Guns Against Gangsters #5 (Gun-Master, Annie Oakley, The Chameleon; L.B. Cole-r)
1.75 5.25 14.00

DANGER AND ADVENTURE (Formerly This Magazine Is Haunted; Robin Hood and His Merry Men No. 28 on)
Charlton Comics: No. 22, Feb, 1955 - No. 27, Feb, 1956
22-Ibis the Invincible-c/story; Nyoka app.; last pre-code issue
10.00 30.00 65.00
23-Lance O'Casey-c/story; Nyoka app.; Ditko-a thru #27
11.50 34.00 80.00
24-27: 24-Mike Danger& Johnny Adventure begin 8.35 25.00 50.00

DANGER GIRL (Also see Cliffhanger #0)
Image Comics (Cliffhanger Productions): Mar, 1998 - No. 4, Dec, 1998;
DC Comics (Cliffhanger Prod.): No. 5, Mar, 1999 - Present ($2.95/$2.50)
Preview-Bagged in DV8 #14 Voyager Pack 4.00
Preview Gold Edition 8.00
1-($2.95) Hartnell & Campbell-s/Campbell/Garner-a 1.00 3.00 8.00
1-($4.95) Chromium cover 45.00
1-American Entertainment Ed. 8.00
1-American Entertainment Gold Ed., 1-Tourbook edition 10.00
1-"Danger-sized" ed.; over-sized format 3.00 9.00 30.00
2-($2.50) 4.00
2-Smoking Gun variant cover, 2-Platinum Ed., 2-Dynamic Forces Omnichrome variant-c 1.85 5.50 15.00
2-Gold foil cover 12.00
2-Ruby red foil cover 50.00
3,4-3-c by Campbell, Charest and Adam Hughes. 4-Big knife variant-c 3.00
3,5: 3-Gold foil cover. 5-DF Bikini variant-c 10.00
4-6 2.50
San Diego Preview (8/98, B&W) flip book w/Wildcats preview 5.00
... :The Dangerous Collection n(8/98; r-#1), 2-(11/98, $5.95) r/#2,3 6.00
... :The Dangerous Collection nn, 2-($10.00) Gold foil logo 10.00

DANGER IS OUR BUSINESS!
Toby Press: 1953(Dec.) - No. 10, June, 1955
1-Captain Comet by Williamson/Frazetta-a, 6 pgs. (science fiction)
43.00 128.00 340.00
2 11.50 34.00 80.00
3-10 10.00 30.00 70.00
I.W. Reprint #9('64)-Williamson/Frazetta-r/#1; Kinstler-c
11.00 33.00 75.00

DANGER IS THEIR BUSINESS (Also see A-1 Comic)
Magazine Enterprises: No. 50, 1952
A-1 50-Powell-a 13.00 39.00 90.00

DANGER MAN (TV)
Dell Publishing Co.: No. 1231, Sept-Nov, 1961
Four Color 1231-Patrick McGoohan photo-c 10.00 30.00 110.00

DANGER TRAIL (Also see Showcase #50, 51)
National Periodical Publ.: July-Aug, 1950 - No. 5, Mar-Apr, 1951 (52 pgs.)
1-King Faraday begins, ends #4; Toth-a in all 112.00 336.00 900.00

GD2.0 FN6.0 NM9.4

2 80.00 240.00 640.00
3-(Rare) one of the rarest early '50s DCs 112.00 336.00 900.00
4,5: 5-Johnny Peril-c/story (moves to Sensation Comics #107); new logo (also see Comic Cavalcade #15-29) 67.00 200.00 540.00

DANGER TRAIL
DC Comics: Apr, 1993 - No. 4, July, 1993 ($1.50, limited series)
1-4: Gulacy-c on all 2.00

DANGER UNLIMITED (See San Diego Comic Con Comics #2 & Torch of Liberty Special)
Dark Horse (Legend): Feb, 1994 - No. 4, May, 1994 ($2.00, limited series)
1-4: Byrne-c/a/scripts in all; origin stories of both original team (Doc Danger, Thermal, Miss Mirage, & Hunk) & future team (Thermal, Belebet, & Caucus). 1-Intro Torch of Liberty & Golgotha (cameo) in back-up story. 4-Hellboy & Torch of Liberty cameo in lead story 2.00
Trade paperback (1995, $14.95)-r/#1-4; includes last pg. originally cut from #4 15.00

DAN HASTINGS (See Syndicate Features)

DANIEL BOONE (See The Exploits of..., Fighting... Frontier Scout...,The Legends of... & March of Comics No. 306)
Dell Publishing Co.: No. 1163, Mar-May, 1961
Four Color 1163-Marsh-a 4.50 13.50 50.00

DANIEL BOONE (TV) (See March of Comics No. 306)
Gold Key: Jan, 1965 - No. 15, Apr, 1969 (All have Fess Parker photo-c)
1 8.00 24.00 90.00
2 4.00 12.00 45.00
3-5 3.50 10.50 35.00
6-15 2.50 7.50 22.00

DAN'L BOONE
Sussex Publ. Co.: Sept, 1955 - No. 8, Sept, 1957
1 14.00 43.00 100.00
2 9.15 27.00 55.00
3-8 6.70 20.00 40.00

DANNY BLAZE (...Firefighter) (Nature Boy No. 3 on)
Charlton Comics: Aug, 1955 - No. 2, Oct, 1955
1 10.00 30.00 65.00
2 8.35 25.00 50.00

DANNY DINGLE (See Sparkler Comics)
United Features Syndicate: No. 17, 1940
Single Series 17 24.00 73.00 170.00

DANNY THOMAS SHOW, THE (TV)
Dell Publishing Co.: No. 1180, Apr-June, 1961 - No. 1249, Dec-Feb, 1961-62
Four Color 1180-Toth-a, photo-c 15.00 44.00 160.00
Four Color 1249-Manning-a, photo-c 15.00 44.00 160.00

DARBY O'GILL & THE LITTLE PEOPLE (Movie)(See Movie Comics)
Dell Publishing Co.: 1959 (Disney)
Four Color 1024-Toth-a; photo-c. 9.00 27.00 100.00

DAREDEVIL (...& the Black Widow #92-107 on-c only; see Giant-Size...,Marvel Advs., Marvel Graphic Novel #24, Marvel Super Heroes, '66 & Spider-Man &...)
Marvel Comics Group: Apr, 1964 - No. 380, Oct, 1998
GD2.0 FN6.0 VF8.0 NM9.4
1-Origin/1st app. Daredevil; reprinted in Marvel Super Heroes #1 (1966); death of Battling Murdock; intro Foggy Nelson & Karen Page; Everett-c/a
135.00 405.00 875.00 1900.00
GD2.0 FN6.0 NM9.4
2-Fantastic Four cameo; 2nd app. Electro (Spidey villain); Thing guest star
40.00 120.00 475.00
3-Origin & 1st app. The Owl (villain) 31.00 93.00 310.00
4-The Purple Man app. 27.00 82.00 275.00
5-Minor costume change; Wood-a begins 19.00 57.00 190.00
6,8-10: 8-Origin/1st app. Stilt-Man 13.00 39.00 130.00

Daredevil #100 © MAR

Daredevil #376 © MAR

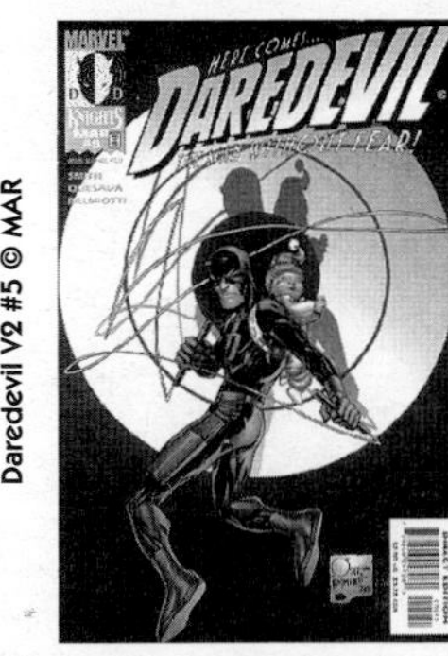

Daredevil V2 #5 © MAR

GD2.0 FN6.0 NM9.4

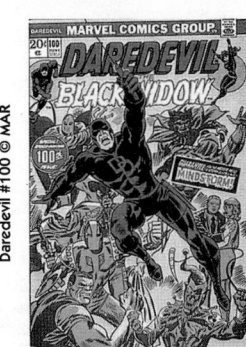

7-Daredevil battles Sub-Mariner & dons new red costume (4/65) 25.00 75.00 250.00
1-15: 12-1st app. Plunderer; Ka-Zar app. 13-Facts about Ka-Zar's origin; Kirby-a 6.00 18.00 60.00
6,17-Spider-Man x-over. 16-1st Romita-a on Spider-Man (5/66) 9.00 27.00 90.00
8-20: 18-Origin & 1st app. Gladiator 4.50 13.50 45.00
1-26,28-30: 24-Ka-Zar app. 3.00 9.00 30.00
7-Spider-Man x-over 3.20 9.40 32.00
1-40: 38-Fantastic Four x-over; cont'd in F.F. #73. 39-1st Exterminator (later becomes Death-Stalker) 2.50 7.50 22.00
1,42,44-49: 41-Death Mike Murdock. 42-1st app. Jester. 45-Statue of Liberty photo-c 2.00 6.00 16.00
3,50-53: 43-Daredevil battles Captain America; origin partially retold. 50-52-B. Smith-a. 53-Origin retold; last 12¢ issue 2.50 7.50 20.00
4-56,58-60: 54-Spider-Man cameo. 56-1st app. Death's Head (9/69); story cont'd in #57 (not same as new Death's Head) 1.75 5.25 14.00
7-Reveals i.d. to Karen Page; Death's Head app. 1.85 5.50 15.00
1-76,78-80: 79-Stan Lee cameo. 80-Last 15¢ issue 1.50 4.50 12.00
7-Spider-Man x-over 1.85 5.50 15.00
1-Oversize issue; Black Widow begins (11/71). 2.50 7.50 20.00
2-99: 83-B. Smith layouts/Weiss-p. 87-Electro-c/story 1.50 4.50 12.00
00-Origin retold 2.50 7.50 20.00
01-104,106-120: 107-Starlin-c; Thanos cameo. 113-1st app. Deathstalker (cameo). 114-1st full app. Deathstalker 1.00 3.00 8.00
05-Origin Moondragon by Starlin (12/73); Thanos cameo in flashback (early app.) 1.50 4.50 12.00
21-130,137: 124-1st app. Copperhead; Black Widow leaves. 126-1st new Torpedo 5.00
31-Origin/1st app. new Bullseye (see Nick Fury #15) 2.25 6.75 18.00
32-136-(Regular 25¢ editions). 132-Bullseye app. 2.40 6.00
32-136-(30¢-c variants, limited distribution)(4-8/76) 1.75 5.25 14.00
38-Ghost Rider-c/story; Death's Head is reincarnated; Byrne-a .85 2.60 7.00
39-147,149-157: 142-Nova cameo. 146-Bullseye app. 150-1st app. Paladin. 151-Reveals i.d. to Heather Glenn. 155-Black Widow returns. 156-The 1960s Daredevil app. 4.00
48-(Regular 30¢ edition)(9/77) 4.00
48-(35¢-c, limited distribution) 1.25 3.75 10.00
58-Frank Miller art begins (5/79); origin/death of Deathstalker (see Captain America #235 & Spectacular Spider-Man #27 3.50 10.50 35.00
59 2.50 7.50 20.00
60,161,163,164,169: 163-Hulk cameo. 164-Origin retold. 169-Electra app. 1.50 4.50 12.00
62-Ditko-a; no Miller-a 5.00
65-167,170 1.10 3.30 9.00
68-Origin/1st app. Elektra 4.00 12.00 40.00
71-175: 174,175-Elektra app. 2.40 6.00
76-180-Elektra app. 178-Cage app. 179-Anti-smoking issue mentioned in the Congressional Record 5.00
31-(52 pgs.)-Death of Elektra; Punisher cameo out of costume 1.25 3.75 10.00
32-184-Punisher app. by Miller (drug issues) 4.00
35-191: 187-New Black Widow. 189-Death of Stick. 190-($1.00, 52 pgs.)-Elektra returns, part origin. 191-Last Miller Daredevil 3.00
92-195,197-226,228-237,239,240,242-247: 197,200-Bullseye app. 208-Harlan Ellison scripts borrowed from Avengers TV episode "House that Jack Built". 219-Miller-c/script. 226-Frank Miller plots begin. 228-233-Last Miller scripts 2.00
96-Wolverine app. 1.00 2.80 7.50
27-Miller scripts begin 3.00
38,248,249: 238-Mutant Massacre; Sabretooth app. 248,249-Wolverine app. 4.00
41,250,251,253,258:: 241-Todd McFarlane-a(p) 250-1st app. Bullet. 258-Intro The Bengal (a villain) 2.00

GD2.0 FN6.0 NM9.4

252,255,256,258,260: 252-(52 pgs.); Fall of the Mutants. 255,256-2nd & 3rd app. Typhoid Mary. 259,260-Typhoid Mary app. 260-(52 pgs.) 3.00
254-Origin & 1st app. Typhoid Mary (5/88) 1.00 2.80 7.50
257-Punisher app. (x-over w/Punisher #10) 5.00
261-318: 270-1st app. Black Heart. 272-Intro Shotgun (villain). 282-Silver Surfer app. (cameo in #281). 283-Capt. America app. 297-Typhoid Mary app.; Kingpin storyline begins. 293-Punisher app. 292-D. G. Chichester scripts begin. 295-Ghost Rider app. 300-($2.00, 52 pgs.)-Kingpin story ends. 303-Re-intro the Owl. 304-Garney-c/a. 305,306-Spider-Man-c. 309-Punisher-c.; Terror app. 310-Calypso-c. 2.00
319-Prologue to Fall From Grace; Elektra returns 4.00
319-2nd printing w/black-c 2.00
320-Fall From Grace Pt 1 4.00
321-Fall From Grace regular ed.; Pt 2; new costume; Venom app. 2.00
321-($2.00)-Wraparound Glow-in-the-dark-c ed. 4.00
322-Fall From Grace Pt 3; Eddie Brock app. 3.00
323,324-Fall From Grace Pt. 4 & 5: 323-Vs. Venom-c/story. 324-Morbius-c/story 2.00
325-($2.50, 52 pgs.)-Fall From Grace ends; contains bound-in poster 2.50
326-349,351-353: 326-New logo. 328-Bound-in trading card sheet. 330-Gambit app. 348-1st Cary Nord art in DD (1/96);"Dec" on-c. 353-Karl Kesel scripts; Nord-c/a begins; Mr. Hyde-c/app. 2.00
350-($2.95)-Double-sized 3.00
350-($3.50)-Double-sized; gold ink-c 3.50
354-374,376-379: Kesel scripts, Nord-c/a in all. 354-$1.50-c begins. 355-Larry Hama layouts; Pyro app. 358-Mysterio-c/app. 359-Absorbing Man cameo. 360-Absorbing Man-c/app. 361-Black Widow-c/app. 363-Gene Colan-a(p) begins. 368-Omega Red-c/app. 372-Ghost Rider-c/app.376-379-"Flying Blind", DD goes undercover for S.H.I.E.L.D 2.00
375-($2.99) Wraparound-c; Mr. Fear-c/app. 3.00
380-($2.99) Final issue; flashback story 4.00
Special 1(9/67, 25¢, 68 pgs.)-New art/story 3.50 10.50 35.00
Special 2,3: 2(2/71, 25¢, 52 pgs.)-Entire book has Powell/Wood-r; Wood-c. 3(1/72)-Reprints 1.25 3.75 10.00
Annual 4(10/76) 2.00 6.00
Annual 4(#5)-10: ('89-94 68 pgs.)-5-Atlantis Attacks. 6-Sutton-a. 7-Guice-a (7 pgs.). 8-Deathlok-c/story. 9-Polybagged w/card. 10 3.00
.../DEADPOOL- (Annual '97, $2.99)-Wraparound-c 3.00
...:FALL FROM GRACE TPB ($19.95)-r #319-325 20.00
.../PUNISHER TPB (1988, $4.95)-r/D.D. #182-184 (all printings) 5.00

NOTE: ***Art Adams** c-238p, 239. **Austin** a-191i; c-151i, 200i. **John Buscema** a-136, 137p, 234p, 235p; c-86p, 136i, 137p, 142, 219. **Byrne** c-200p, 201, 203, 223. **Capullo** a-286p. **Colan** a(p)-20-49, 53-82, 84-98, 100, 110, 112, 124, 153, 154, 156, 157, Spec. 1p; c(p)-20-42, 44-49, 53-60, 71, 92, 98, 138, 153, 154, 156, 157, Annual 1. **Craig** a-50i, 52i. **Ditko** a-162, 234p, 235p, 264p; c-162. **Everett** c/a-1; inks-21, 83. **Garney** c/a-304. **Gil Kane** a-141p, 146-148p, 151p; c(p)-85, 90, 91, 93, 94, 115, 116, 119, 120, 125-128, 133, 139, 147, 152. **Kirby** c-2-4, 5p, 12p, 13p, 43, 136p. **Layton** c-202. **Miller** scripts-168-182, 183(part), 184-191, 219, 227-233; a-158-161p, 163-184p, 191p; c-158-161p, 163-184p, 185-189, 190p, 191. **Orlando** a-2-4p. **Powell** a-9p, 11p, Special 1r, 2r. **Simonson** c-199, 236p. **B. Smith** a-236p; c-51p, 52p, 217. **Starlin** a-105p. **Steranko** c-44i. **Tuska** a-39i, 145p. **Williamson** a(i)-237, 239, 240, 243, 248-257, 259-282, 283(part), 284, 285, 287, 288(part), 289(part), 293-300; c(i)-237, 243, 244, 248-257, 259-263, 265-278, 280-289, Annual 8. **Wood** a-5-8, 9i, 10, 11i, Spec. 2i; c-5i, 6-11, 164i.*

DAREDEVIL (Volume 2) (Marvel Knights)
Marvel Comics: Nov, 1998 - Present ($2.50)

1-Kevin Smith-s/Quesada & Palmiotti-a 4.00
1-($6.95) DF Edition w/Quesada & Palmiotti var.-c 7.00
1-($6.00) DF Sketch Ed. w/B&W-c 6.00
2-Two covers by Campbell and Quesada/Palmiotti 5.00
3-8: 4,5-Bullseye app. 8-Spider-Man-c/app. 2.50
TPB ($9.95) r/#1-3 10.00
Visionaries TPB ($19.95) r/#1-8; Ben Affleck intro. 20.00

DAREDEVIL/ BATMAN (Also see Batman/Daredevil)
Marvel Comics/ DC Comics: 1997 ($5.99, one-shot)

nn-McDaniel-c/a 2.40 6.00

DAREDEVIL/ SHI (See Shi/ Daredevil)
Marvel Comics/ Crusade Comics: Feb,1997 ($2.95, limited series)

1 3.00

Daredevil Comics #2 © LEV

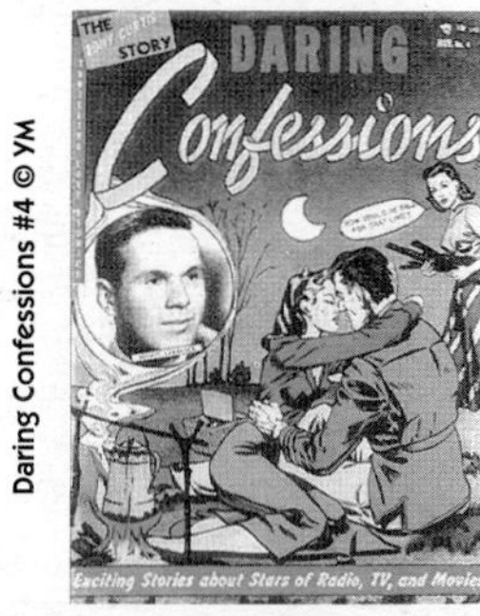

Daring Confessions #4 © YM

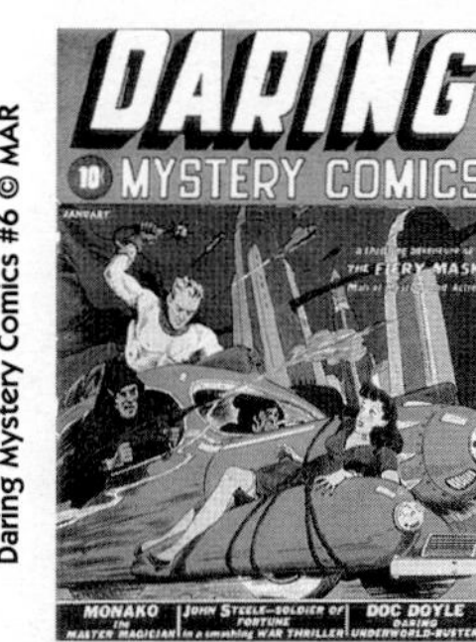

Daring Mystery Comics #6 © MAR

DAREDEVIL THE MAN WITHOUT FEAR
Marvel Comics: Oct, 1993 - No. 5, Feb, 1994 ($2.95, limited series) (foil embossed covers)

1-5: Miller scripts; Romita, Jr./Williamson-c/a 4.00
Hardcover 100.00
Trade paperback 20.00

DAREDEVIL COMICS (See Silver Streak Comics)
Lev Gleason Publications (Funnies, Inc. No. 1): July, 1941 - No. 134, Sept, 1956 (Charles Biro stories)

GD2.0 FN6.0 VF8.0 NM9.4
1-No. 1 titled "Daredevil Battles Hitler"; The Silver Streak, Lance Hale, Cloud Curtis, Dickey Dean, Pirate Prince team up w/Daredevil and battle Hitler; Daredevil battles the Claw; Origin of Hitler feature story. Hitler photo app. on-c 950.00 2850.00 5700.00 10,500.00

GD2.0 FN6.0 NM9.4
2-London, Pat Patriot (by Reed Crandall), Nightro, Real American No. 1 (by Briefer #2-11), Dickie Dean, Pirate Prince, & Times Square begin; intro. & only app. The Pioneer, Champion of America 289.00 867.00 2600.00
3-Origin of 13 181.00 543.00 1450.00
4 156.00 468.00 1250.00
5-Intro. Sniffer & Jinx; Ghost vs. Claw begins by Bob Wood, ends #20 122.00 366.00 975.00
6-(#7 in indicia) 103.00 309.00 825.00
7-10: 8-Nightro ends 87.00 261.00 700.00
11-London, Pat Patriot end; classic bondage/torture-c 100.00 300.00 800.00
12-Origin of The Claw; Scoop Scuttle by Wolverton begins (2-4 pgs.), ends #22, not in #21 137.00 411.00 1100.00
13-Intro. of Little Wise Guys (10/42) 116.00 348.00 925.00
14 62.00 186.00 500.00
15-Death of Meatball 91.00 273.00 725.00
16,17 57.00 171.00 460.00
18-New origin of Daredevil (not same as Silver Streak #6) 122.00 366.00 975.00
19,20 49.00 147.00 390.00
21-Reprints cover of Silver Streak #6 (on inside) plus intro. of The Claw from Silver Streak #1 84.00 252.00 675.00
22-30: 27-Bondage/torture-c 40.00 120.00 290.00
31-Death of The Claw 78.00 234.00 625.00
32-37,39,41: 35-Two Daredevil stories begin, end #68 (35-41 are 64 pgs.) 29.00 86.00 200.00
38-Origin Daredevil retold from #18 40.00 120.00 325.00
42-50: 42-Intro. Kilroy in Daredevil; 1 panel Steranko-a 23.00 69.00 160.00
51-69-Last Daredevil issue (12/50) 16.00 47.00 110.00
70-Little Wise Guys take over book; McWilliams-a; Hot Rock Flanagan begins, ends #80 13.00 39.00 90.00
71-79,81: 79-Daredevil returns 10.00 30.00 70.00
80-Daredevil x-over 11.00 33.00 75.00
82,90,100: 82,90-One pg. Frazetta ad in both 10.00 30.00 70.00
83-89,91-99,101-134 10.00 30.00 60.00
NOTE: ***Biro*** *c/a-all?* ***Bolle*** *a-125.* ***Maurer*** *a-75.* ***McWilliams*** *a-73, 75, 79, 80.*

DARING ADVENTURES (Also see Approved Comics)
St. John Publishing Co.: Nov, 1953 (25¢, 3-D, came w/glasses)

1 (3-D)-Reprints lead story from Son of Sinbad #1 by Kubert 35.00 105.00 245.00

DARING ADVENTURES
I.W. Enterprises/Super Comics: 1963 - 1964

I. W. Reprint #8-r/Fight Comics #53; Matt Baker-a 4.50 13.50 45.00
I.W. Reprint #9-r/Blue Bolt #115; Disbrow-a(3) 5.00 15.00 50.00
Super Reprint #10,11('63)-r/Dynamic #24,16; 11-Marijuana story; Yankee Boy app.; Mac Raboy-a 2.80 8.40 28.00
Super Reprint #12('64)-Phantom Lady from Fox (r/#14 only? w/splash pg. omitted); Matt Baker-a 12.00 36.00 120.00
Super Reprint #15('64)-r/Hooded Menace #1 7.00 21.00 70.00
Super Reprint #16('64)-r/Dynamic #12 2.50 7.50 22.0
Super Reprint #17('64)-r/Green Lama #3 by Raboy 3.80 11.40 38.0
Super Reprint #18-Origin Atlas from unpublished Atlas Comics #1 3.00 9.00 30.0

DARING COMICS (Formerly Daring Mystery) (Jeanie Comics No. 13 on)
Timely Comics (HPC): No. 9, Fall, 1944 - No. 12, Fall, 1945

9-Human Torch, Toro & Sub-Mariner begin 111.00 333.00 885.0
10-12: 10-The Angel only app. 11,12-The Destroyer app. 94.00 282.00 750.0
NOTE: ***Schomburg*** *c-9-11.* ***Sekowsky*** *c-12? Human Torch, Toro & Sub-Mariner c-9-12.*

DARING CONFESSIONS (Formerly Youthful Hearts)
Youthful Magazines: No. 4, 11/52 - No. 7, 5/53; No. 8, 10/53

4-Doug Wildey-a; Tony Curtis story 12.00 36.00 85.0
5-8: 5-Ray Anthony photo on-c. 6,8-Wildey-a 10.00 30.00 65.0

DARING ESCAPES
Image Comics: Sept, 1998 - No. 4, Mar, 1999 ($2.95/$2.50, mini-series)

1-Houdini; following app. in Spawn #19,20 3.0
2-4-($2.50) 2.5

DARING LOVE (Radiant Love No. 2 on)
Gilmor Magazines: Sept-Oct, 1953

1–Steve Ditko's 1st published work (1st drawn was Fantastic Fears #5)(Also See Black Magic #27)(scarce) 40.00 120.00 280.0

DARING LOVE (Formerly Youthful Romances)
Ribage/Pix: No. 15, 12/52; No. 16, 2/53-c, 4/53-Indicia; No. 17-4/53-c & indicia

15 10.00 30.00 65.0
16,17: 17-Photo-c 9.15 27.00 55.0
NOTE: ***Colletta*** *a-15.* ***Wildey*** *a-17.*

DARING LOVE STORIES (See Fox Giants)

DARING MYSTERY COMICS (Comedy Comics No. 9 on; title changed to Daring Comics with No. 9)
Timely Comics (TPI 1-6/TCI 7,8): 1/40 - No. 5, 6/40; No. 6, 9/40; No. 7, 4/41 - No. 8, 1/42

GD2.0 FN6.0 VF8.0 NM9.4
1-Origin The Fiery Mask (1st app.) by Joe Simon; Monako, Prince of Magic (1st app.), John Steele, Soldier of Fortune (1st app.), Doc Doyle (1st app.) begin; Flash Foster & Barney Mullen, Sea Rover only app; bondage-c 1416.00 4248.00 8500.00 17,000.0

GD2.0 FN6.0 NM9.
2-(Rare)-Origin The Phantom Bullet (1st & only app.); The Laughing Mask & Mr. E only app.; Trojak the Tiger Man begins, ends #6; Zephyr Jones & K-4 & His Sky Devils app., also #4 620.00 1860.00 6200.0
3-The Phantom Reporter, Dale of FBI, Breeze Barton, Captain Strong & Marvex the Super-Robot only app.; The Purple Mask begins 370.00 1110.00 3700.0
4,5: 4-Last Purple Mask; Whirlwind Carter begins; Dan Gorman, G-Man app. 5-The Falcon begins (1st app.); The Fiery Mask, Little Hercules app. by Sagendorf in the Segar style; bondage-c 288.00 864.00 2400.0
6-Origin & only app. Marvel Boy by S&K; Flying Flame, Dynaman, & Stuporman only app.; The Fiery Mask by S&K; S&K-c 355.00 1065.00 3200.0
7-Origin The Blue Diamond, Captain Daring by S&K, The Fin by Everett, The Challenger, The Silver Scorn & The Thunderer by Burgos; Mr. Millions app 288.00 864.00 2600.0
8-Origin Citizen V; Last Fin, Silver Scorn, Capt. Daring by Borth, Blue Diamond & The Thunderer; Kirby & part solo Simon-c; Rudy the Robot only app.; Citizen V, Fin & Silver Scorn continue in Comedy #9 250.00 750.00 2000.0
NOTE: ***Schomburg*** *c-1-4, 7.* ***Simon*** *a-2, 3, 5. Cover features: 1-Fiery Mask; 2-Phantom Bullet; Purple Mask; 4-G-Man; 5-The Falcon; 6-Marvel Boy; 7, 8-Multiple characters.*

DARING NEW ADVENTURES OF SUPERGIRL, THE
DC Comics: Nov, 1982 - No. 13, Nov, 1983 (Supergirl No. 14 on)

1-Origin retold; Lois Lane back-ups in #2-12 4.0
2-13: 8,9-Doom Patrol app. 13-New costume; flag-c 2.5
NOTE: ***Buckler*** *c-1p, 2p.* ***Giffen*** *c-3p, 4p.* ***Gil Kane*** *c-6, ,8, 9, 11-13.*

Dark Angel #6 © MAR

Darkchylde The Legacy #1 © Randy Queen

Darkhawk #43 © MAR

ARK, THE
ontinum Comics: Nov, 1990 - No. 4, Feb, 1993; V2#1, May, 1993 - V2#7, pr?, 1994 ($1.95)
1-4: 1-Bright-p; Panosian, Hanna-i; Stroman-c. 2-(1/92)-Stroman-c/a(p). 4-Perez-c & part-i 3.00
2#1,V2#2-6: V2#1-Red foil Bart Sears-c. V2#1-Red non-foil variant-c. V2#1-2nd printing w/blue foil Bart Sears-c. V2#2-Stroman/Bryant-a. 3-Perez-c(i). 3-6-Foil-c. 4-Perez-c & part-i;bound-in trading cards. 5,6-(2,3/94)-Perez-c(i). 7-(B&W)-Perez-c(i) 2.00
onvention Book 1 ,2(Fall/94, 10/94)-Perez-c 2.00

ARK ANGEL (Formerly Hell's Angel)
arvel Comics UK, Ltd.: No. 6, Dec, 1992 - No. 16, Dec, 1993 ($1.75)
6-8,13-16: 6-Excalibur-c/story. 8-Psylocke app. 2.00
9-12-Wolverine/X-Men app. 3.00

ARKCHYLDE
aximum Press #1-3/ Image Comics #4 on: June, 1996 - No. 5, Sept, 1997 2.95/ $2.50)

	GD	FN	NM
1-Randy Queen-c/a/scripts; "Roses" cover		2.40	6.00
1-American Entertainment Edition-wraparound-c		2.40	6.00
1-"Fashion magazine-style" variant-c	1.00	2.80	7.00
1-Special Comicon Edition (contents of #1) Winged devil variant-c			5.00
1-($2.50)-Remastered Ed.-wraparound-c			4.00
2(Reg-c),2-Spiderweb and Moon variant-c	1.00	2.80	7.00
3(Reg-c),3-"Kalvin Clein" variant-c by Drew			4.00
4(Reg-c), 4-Variant-c		2.40	6.00
5			4.00
5-B&W Edition, 5-Dynamic Forces Gold Ed.	1.00	3.00	8.00
0-(3/98, $2.50)			2.50
0-American Entertainment Ed.			4.00
0-Dynamic Forces Ed.			5.00
0-Dynamic Forces Gold Ed.	1.00	2.80	7.00
/2-WIzard offer			4.00
/2 Variant-c		2.40	6.00
/2 Gold Ed.	1.00	3.00	9.00

. The Descent TPB ('98, $19.95) r/#1-5; bagged with Darkchylde The Legacy Preview Special 1998; listed price is for TPB only 20.00

ARKCHYLDE SKETCH BOOK
nage Comics (Dynamic Forces): 1998
1-Regular-c 8.00
1-DarkChrome cover 16.00

ARKCHYLDE SUMMER SWIMSUIT SPECTACULAR
C Comics (WildStorm): Aug, 1999 ($3.95, one-shot)
1-Pin-up art by various 4.00

ARKCHYLDE SWIMSUIT ILLUSTRATED
nage Comics: 1998 ($2.50, one-shot)
1-Pin-up art by various 2.50
1-(6.95) Variant cover 7.00
1-American Entertainment Ed. 3.00
1-Dynamic Forces Ed. 4.00
1-Dynamic Forces Gold Ed. 6.00
1-Chromium cover 15.00

ARKCHYLDE THE DIARY
nage Comics: June, 1997 ($2.50, one-shot)
1-Queen-c/s/ art by various 2.50
1-Variant-c 5.00
1-Holochrome variant-c 8.00

ARKCHYLDE THE LEGACY
nage Comics/DC (WildStorm) #3 on: Aug, 1998 - Present ($2.50)
1-3: 1-Queen-c. 2-Two covers by Queen and Art Adams 2.50

ARK CLAW ADVENTURES
C Comics (Amalgam): June, 1997 ($1.95, one-shot)
1-Templeton-c/s/a & Burchett-a 2.00

DARK CRYSTAL, THE (Movie)
Marvel Comics Group: April, 1983 - No. 2, May, 1983
1,2-Adaptation of film 2.00

DARK DOMINION
Defiant: Oct, 1993 - No. 10, July, 1994 ($2.50)
1-10-Len Wein scripts begin. 4-Free extra 16 pgs. 7-9-J.G. Jones-c/a. 10-Pre-Schism issue; Shooter/Wein script; John Ridgway-a 2.50

DARKER IMAGE (Also see Deathblow, The Maxx, & Bloodwulf)
Image Comics: Mar, 1993 ($1.95, one-shot)
1-The Maxx by Sam Kieth begins; Bloodwulf by Rob Liefeld & Deathblow by Jim Lee begin (both 1st app.); polybagged w/1 of 3 cards by Kieth, Lee or Liefeld 2.50
1-B&W interior pgs. w/silver foil logo 6.00

DARKEWOOD
Aircel Publishing: 1987 - No. 5, 1988 ($2.00, 28pgs, limited series)
1-5 2.00

DARK FANTASIES
Dark Fantasy: 1994 - No. 8, 1995 ($2.95)

	GD	FN	NM
1-Test print Run (3,000)-Linsner-c	1.00	3.00	8.00
1-Linsner-c			5.00
2-9: 2-4 (Deluxe), 2-4 (Regular), 5-8 (Deluxe; $3.95)			4.00
5-8 (Regular; $3.50)			3.50

DARK GUARD
Marvel Comics UK: Oct, 1993 - No. 4, Jan, 1994 ($1.75)
1-($2.95)-Foil stamped-c 3.00
2-4 2.00

DARKHAWK
Marvel Comics: Mar, 1991 - No. 50, Apr, 1995 ($1.00/$1.25/$1.50)
1-Origin/1st app. Darkhawk; Hobgoblin cameo 3.00
2-24,26-48: 2-Spider-Man & Hobgoblin app. 3-Spider-Man & Hobgoblin app. 6-Capt. America & Daredevil x-over. 9-Punisher app. 11,12-Tombstone app. 13,14-Venom-c/story. 19-Spider-Man & Brotherhood of Evil Mutants-c/story. 20-Spider-Man app. 22-Ghost Rider-c/story. 23-Origin begins, ends #25. 27-New Warriors-c/story. 35-Begin 3 part Venom story. 39-Bound-in trading card sheet 2.00
25,50: (52 pgs.)-Red holo-grafx foil-c w/double gatefold poster; origin of Darkhawk armor revealed. 3.00
Annual 1-3 ('92-'94,68 pgs.)-1-Vs. Iron Man. 2 -Polybagged w/card 3.00

DARKHOLD: PAGES FROM THE BOOK OF SINS (See Midnight Sons Unltd)
Marvel Comics (Midnight Sons imprint #15 on): Oct, 1992 - No. 16, Jan, 1994
1-($2.75, 52 pgs.)-Polybagged w/poster by Andy & Adam Kubert; part 4 of Rise of the Midnight Sons storyline 2.75
2-10,12-16: 3-Reintro Modred the Mystic (see Marvel Chillers #1). 4-Sabertooth-c/sty. 5-Punisher & Ghost Rider app. 15-Spot varnish-c. 15,16-Siege of Darkness part 4&12 2.00
11-($2.25)-Outer-c is a Darkhold envelope made of black parchment w/gold ink 2.25

DARK HORSE CLASSICS (Title series), **Dark Horse Comics**
1992 ($3.95, B&W, 52 pgs. nn's: The Last of the Mohicans. 20,000 Leagues Under the Sea 4.00

DARK HORSE CLASSICS, 5/96 ($2.95) 1-r/Predator: Jungle Tales 3.00

--ALIENS VERSUS PREDATOR, 2/97 - No. 6, 7/97 ($2.95,) 1-6: r/Aliens Versus Predator 3.00

--GODZILLA: KING OF THE MONSTERS, 4/98 ($2.95) 1-6: 1-r/Godzilla: Color Special; Art Adams-a 3.00

--STAR WARS: DARK EMPIRE, 3/97 - No. 6, 8/97 ($2.95) 1-6: r/Star Wars: Dark Empire 3.00

--TERROR OF GODZILLA, 8/98 - No. 6, 1/99 ($2.95) 1-6-r/manga Godzilla in color; Art Adams-c 3.00

Dark Horse Presents Annual 1997 © DH

Darkminds #1 © Dreamwave Prod.

Dark Mysteries #6 © Merit Pub.

DARK HORSE COMICS
Dark Horse Comics: Aug, 1992 - No. 25, Sept, 1994 ($2.50)

1-Dorman double gategold painted-c; Predator, Robocop, Timecop (3-part) & Renegade stories begin 3.00
2-6,11-25: 2-Mignola-c. 3-Begin 3-part Aliens story; Aliens-c. 4-Predator-c. 6-Begin 4 part Robocop story. 12-Begin 2-part Aliens & 3-part Predator stories. 13-Thing From Another World begins w/Nino-a(i). 15-Begin 2-part Aliens: Cargo story. 16-Begin 3-part Predator story. 17-Begin 3-part Star Wars: Droids story & 3-part Aliens: Alien story; Droids-c. 19-Begin 2-part X story; X cover 2.50
7-Begin Star Wars: Tales of the Jedi 3-part story 1.00 2.80 7.00
8-1st app. X and begins; begin 4-part James Bond 2.40 6.00
9,10: 9-Star Wars ends. 10-X ends; Begin 3-part Predator & Godzilla stories 4.00

NOTE: ***Art Adams** c-11.*

DARK HORSE DOWN UNDER
Dark Horse Comics: June, 1994 - No. 3, Oct, 1994 ($2.50, B&W, limited series)

1-3 2.50

DARK HORSE MONSTERS
Dark Horse Comics: Feb, 1997 ($2.95, one-shot)

1-reprints 3.00

DARK HORSE PRESENTS
Dark Horse Comics: July, 1986 - Present ($1.50-$2.95, B&W)

1-1st app. Concrete by Paul Chadwick 1.25 3.75 10.00
1-2nd printing (1988, $1.50) 2.25
1-Silver ink 3rd printing (1992, $2.25)-Says 2nd printing inside 2.25
2-9: 2-6,9-Concrete app. 4.00
10-1st app. The Mask; Concrete app. 1.25 3.75 10.00
11-19,21-23: 11-19,21-Mask stories. 12,14,16,18,22-Concrete app. 15(2/88). 17-All Roachmill issue 3.00
20-(68 pgs.)-Concrete, Flaming Carrot, Mask 1.25 3.75 10.00
24-Origin Aliens-c/story (11/88); Mr. Monster app. 1.80 5.40 18.00
25-31,33,37-41,44,45,47-50: 28-(52 pgs.)-Concrete app.; Mr. Monster story (homage to Graham Ingels). 33-(44 pgs.). 38-Concrete. 40-(52 pgs.)-1st Argosy story. 44-Crash Ryan. 48-50-Contain 2 trading cards. 50-S/F story by Perez 3.00
32,34,35: 32-(68 pgs.)-Annual; Concrete, American. 34-Aliens-c/story. 35-Predator-c/story 4.00
36-1st Aliens Vs. Predator story; painted-c, 36-Variant line drawn-c 5.00
42,43,46,51-57: 42,43-Aliens-c/stories. 46-Prequel to new Predator II mini-series 51-53-Sin City by Frank Miller, parts 2-4; 51,53-Miller-c (see D.H.P. Fifth Anniv. Special for pt. 1). 54-The Next Men begins(1st app.) by Byrne (9/91); Miller-a. 55-2nd app. The Next Men; parts 5 & 6 of Sin City by Miller; Homocide by Morrow in both. 54-Morrow-c; 55-Miller-c. 56-(68 pg. annual)-part prologue to Aliens: Genocide; part 7 of Sin City by Miller; Next Men by Byrne. 57-(52 pgs.)-Part 8 of Sin City by Miller; Next Men by Byrne; Byrne & Miller-c; Alien Fire story; swipes cover to Daredevil #1 3.00
58-66,68-79,81-84-($2.25): 58,59-Part 9,10 Sin City by Miller; Alien Fire stories. 60,61-Part 11,12 Sin City by Miller. 62-Last Sin City (entire book by Miller, c/a;52 pgs.). 64-Dr. Giggles begins (1st app.), ends #66; Boris the Bear story. 66-New Concrete-c/story by Chadwick. 71-Begin 3 part Dominque story by Jim Balent; Balent-c. 72-(3/93)-Begin 3-part Eudaemon (1st app.) story by Nelson. 3.00
67-($3.95, 68 pgs.)-Begin 3-part prelude to Predator: Race War mini-series; Oscar Wilde adapt. by Russell 4.00
80-Art Adams-c/a (Monkeyman & O'Brien) 4.00
85-87,92-99,101-108: 85-Begin $2.50-c. 92, 93, 95-Too Much Coffee Man. 101-Aliens c/a by Wrightson, story by Paul Pope. 103-Kirby gatefold-c. 106-Big Blown Baby by Bill Wray. 107-Mignola-c/a 3.00
88-91-Hellboy by Mignola. 4.00
100-1-Intro Lance Blastoff by Miller; Milk & Cheese by Evan Dorkin 4.00
100-2-100-5: 100-2-Hellboy-c by Wrightson; Hellboy story by Mignola; includes Roberta Gregory & Paul Pope stories. 100-3-Darrow-c, Concrete by Chadwick; Pekar story. 100-4-Gibbons-c: Miller story, Geary story/a. 100-5-Allred-c, Adams, Dorkin, Pope 3.00
109-125: 109-Begin $2.95-c; Paul Pope-c. 110-Ed Brubaker-a/scripts. 114-Flip books begin; Lance Blastoff by Miller; Star Slammers by Simonson. 115-Miller-c. 117-Aliens-c/app. 118-Evan Dorkin-c/a. 119-Monkeyman & O'Brien. 124-Predator. 125-Nocturnals 3.00
126-($3.95, 48 pgs.)-Flip book: Nocturnals, Starship Troopers 4.00
127-134,136-140: 127-Nocturnals. 129-The Hammer. 132-134-Warren-a 3.00
135-($3.50) The Mark 3.50
141-All Buffy the Vampire Slayer issue 4.00
142-145: 142-Mignola-c. 143-Tarzan 3.00
Annual 1997 ($4.95, 64 pgs.)-Flip book; Body Bags, Aliens. Pearson-c; stories by Allred & Stephens, Pope, Smith & Morrow 1.00 3.00 8.00
Annual 1998 ($4.95, 64 pgs.) 1st Buffy the Vampire Slayer comic app.; Hellboy story and cover by Mignola 1.00 2.80 7.00
...Aliens Platinum Edition (1992)-r/DHP #24,43,43,56 & Special 11.00
...Fifth Anniversary Special nn (4/91, $9.95)-Part 1 of Sin City by Frank Miller (c/a); Aliens, Aliens vs. Predator, Concrete, Roachmill, Give Me Liberty & The American stories 10.00
The One Trick Rip-off (1997, $12.95, TPB)-r/stories from #101-112 13.00

NOTE: ***Geary** a-59, 60. **Miller** a-Special, 51-53, 55-62; c-59-62, 100-1; c-51, 53, 55, 59-62, 100-1. **Moebius** a-63; c-63, 70. **Vess** a-78; c-75, 78.*

DARK KNIGHT (See Batman: The Dark Knight Returns & Legends of the...)

DARKLON THE MYSTIC (Also see Eerie Magazine #79,80)
Pacific Comics: Oct, 1983 (one-shot)

1-Starlin-c/a(r) 2.00

DARKMAN (Movie)
Marvel Comics: Sept, 1990; Oct, 1990 - No. 3, Dec, 1990 ($1.50)

1 (9/90, $2.25, B&W mag., 68 pgs.)-Adaptation of film 3.00
1-3: Reprints B&W magazine 2.00

DARKMAN
Marvel Comics: V2#1, Apr, 1993 -No. 6, Sept, 1993 ($2.95, limited series)

V2#1 ($3.95, 52 pgs.) 4.00
2-6 3.00

DARK MANSION OF FORBIDDEN LOVE, THE (Becomes Forbidden Tales of Dark Mansion No. 5 on)
National Periodical Publ.: Sept-Oct, 1971 - No. 4, Mar-Apr, 1972 (52 pgs.)

1 11.00 33.00 120.00
2-4: 2-Adams-c. 3-Jeff Jones-c 3.80 11.50 40.00

DARKMINDS
Image Comics (Dreamwave Prod.): July, 1998 - No. 8, Apr, 1999 ($2.50)

1-Manga; Pat Lee-s/a; 2 covers 1.25 3.75 10.00
1-2nd printing 2.50
2 .0-(1/99, $5.00) Story and sketch pages 5.00
3-8, 1/2 (5/99, $2.50) Story and sketch pages 2.50
... Collected 1,2 (1/99,3/99; $7.95) 1-r/#1-3. 2-r/#4-6 8.00

DARK MYSTERIES (Thrilling Tales of Horror & Suspense)
"Master" - "Merit" Publications: June-July, 1951 - No. 25?, 1955

1-Wood-c/a (8 pgs.) 92.00 276.00 735.00
2-Wood/Harrison-c/a (8 pgs.) 62.00 186.00 500.00
3-9: 7-Dismemberment, hypo blood drainage stys 36.00 107.00 250.00
10-Cannibalism story; witch burning-c 38.00 114.00 265.00
11-13,15-18: 11-Severed head panels. 13-Dismemberment-c/story. 17-The Old Gravedigger host 26.00 79.00 185.00
14-Several E.C. Craig swipes 27.00 81.00 190.00
19-Injury-to-eye panel; E.C. swipe; torture-c 35.00 105.00 245.00
20-Female bondage, blood drainage story 32.00 96.00 225.00
21,22: 21-Devil-c. 22-Last pre-code issue, misdated 3/54 instead of 3/55 19.00 58.00 135.00
23-25 (#25-Exist?) 16.00 47.00 110.00

NOTE: ***Cameron** a-1, 2. **Myron Fass** c/a-21. **Harrison** a-3, 7; c-3. **Hollingsworth** a-7-17, 20, 21, 23. **Wildey** a-5. Woodish art by **Fleishman**-9; c-10, 14-17. Bondage c-10, 18, 19.*

DARK NEMESIS (VILLAINS) (See Teen Titans)
DC Comics: Feb, 1998 ($1.95, one-shot)

The Darkness #13 © Top Cow Prod.

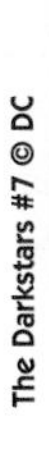

The Darkstars #7 © DC

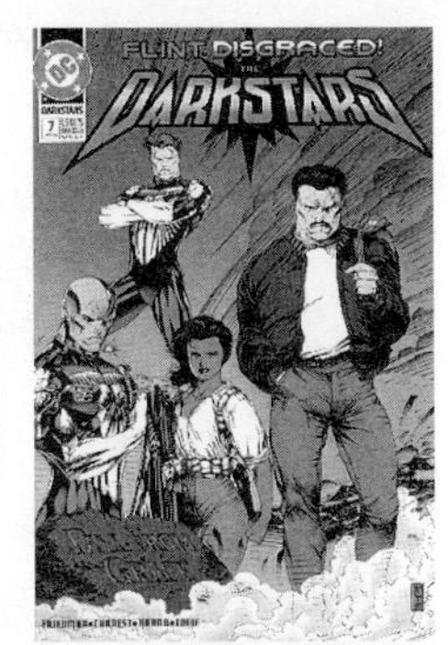

Darling Romance #1 © AP

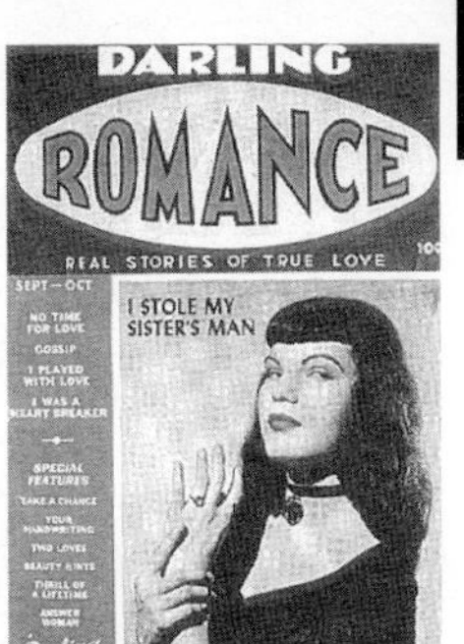

GD2.0 FN6.0 NM9.4

1-Jurgens-s/Pearson-c 2.00

DARKNESS, THE (See Witchblade #10)
Image Comics (Top Cow Productions): Dec, 1996 - Present ($2.50)

Special Preview Edition-(7/96, B&W)-Ennis script; Silvestri-a(p) 2.25 6.75 18.00
0 2.50 7.50 20.00
0-Gold Edition 22.00
1/2 2.00 6.00 16.00
1/2-Christmas-c 3.00 9.00 30.00
1-Ennis-s/Silvestri-a, 1-Black variant-c 1.85 5.50 15.00
1-Platinum variant-c 30.00
1,2: 1-Fan Club Ed. 1.25 3.75 10.00
3-5 2.40 6.00
6-10: 9,10-Witchblade "Family Ties" x-over pt. 2,3 5.00
7-Variant-c w/concubine 1.50 4.50 12.00
8-American Entertainment 1.85 5.50 15.00
8-American Entertainment Gold Ed. 20.00
9-American Entertainment Gold Ed. 10.00
10-American Entertainment Gold Ed. 15.00
11-Regular Ed.; Ennis-s/Silverstri & D-Tron-c 4.00
11-Nine (non-chromium) variant-c (Benitez, Cabrera, the Hildebrandts, Finch, Keown, Peterson, Portacio, Tan, Turner 6.00
11-Chromium-c by Silvestri & Batt 40.00
12-19: 13-Begin Benitez-a(p) 3.00
20-24 2.50
25-($3.99) Two covers (Benitez, Silvestri) 4.00
Holiday Pin-up-American Entertainment 1.00 3.00 8.00
Holiday Pin-up Gold Ed.-American Entertainment 14.00
Infinity #1 (8/99, $3.50) Lobdell-s 3.50
Prelude-American Entertainment 1.00 2.80 7.00
Prelude Gold Ed.-American Entertainment 14.00
Wizard ACE Ed.- Reprints #1 2.25 6.75 18.00
...Collected Editions #1-4 ($4.95, trade paperback) 1-r/#1,2. 2-r/#3,4. 3- r/#5,6. 4- r/#7,8 5.00
...Collected Editions #5 ($5.95, trade paperback) r/#11,12 6.00
Deluxe Collected Editions #1 (12/98, $14.95, TPB) r/#1-6 & Preview 15.00

DARKNESS/ BATMAN
Image Comics (Top Cow Productions): Aug, 1999 ($5.95, one-shot)

1-Silvestri, Finch, Lansing-a(p) 6.00

DARK ONE'S THIRD EYE
Sirius Entertainment: 1996; Dec, 1998 ($4.95, B&W)

nn-Dark One-a; squarebound; pinups, Vol. 2-(12/98) 5.00

DARK OZ
Arrow Comics: 1997 - No. 5 ($2.75, B&W, limited series)

1-Bill Bryan-a 2.75

DARKSEID (VILLAINS) (See Jack Kirby's New Gods and New Gods)
DC Comics: Feb, 1998 ($1.95, one-shot)

1-Byrne-s/Pearson-c 2.00

DARKSEID VS. GALACTUS: THE HUNGER
DC Comics: 1995 ($4.95, one-shot) (1st DC/Marvel x-over by John Byrne)

nn-John Byrne-c/a/script 5.00

DARK SHADOWS
Steinway Comic Publ. (Ajax)(America's Best): Oct, 1957 - No. 3, May, 1958

1 15.00 45.00 105.00
2,3 11.50 34.00 80.00

DARK SHADOWS (TV) (See Dan Curtis Giveaways)
Gold Key: Mar, 1969 - No. 35, Feb, 1976 (Photo-c: 1-7)

1(30039-903)-With pull-out poster (25¢) 30.00 90.00 260.00
1-With poster missing 9.00 27.00 100.00
2 7.00 22.00 80.00
3-With pull-out poster 15.00 45.00 120.00
3-With poster missing 5.50 16.50 60.00
4-7: 7-Last photo-c 6.40 19.00 70.00
8-10 5.00 15.00 55.00
11-20 4.00 12.00 45.00
21-35: 30-Last painted-c 3.00 9.00 35.00
Story Digest 1 (6/70, 148pp.)-Photo-c 8.00 25.00 90.00

DARK SHADOWS (TV) (See Nightmare on Elm Street)
Innovation Publishing: June, 1992 - No. 4, Spring, 1993 ($2.50, limited series, coated stock)

1-Based on 1991 NBC TV mini-series; painted-c 4.00
2-4 3.00

DARK SHADOWS: BOOK TWO
Innovation Publishing: 1993 - No. 4, July, 1993 ($2.50, limited series)

1-4-Painted-c. 4-Maggie Thompson scripts 3.00

DARK SHADOWS: BOOK THREE
Innovation Publishing: Nov, 1993 ($2.50)

1-(Whole #9) 3.00

DARKSIDE
Maximum Press: Oct, 1996 ($2.99, one-shot)

1-Avengelyne-c/app. 3.00

DARKSTARS, THE
DC Comics: Oct, 1992 - No. 38, Jan, 1996 ($1.75/$1.95)

1-1st app. The Darkstars 3.00
2-24,0,25-38: 5-Hawkman & Hawkwoman app. 18-20-Flash app.. 24-(9/94)-Zero Hour. 0-(10/94). 25-(11/94). 30-Green Lantern app. 31-...vs. Darkseid. 32-Green Lantern app. 2.50

NOTE: ***Travis Charest*** *a(p)-4-7; c(p)-2-5; c-6-11.* ***Stroman*** *a-1-3; c-1.*

DARK TOWN
Mad Monkey Press: 1995 ($3.95, magazine-size, quarterly)

1-Kaja Blackley scripts; Vanessa Chong-a 4.00

DARKWING DUCK (TV cartoon) (Also see Cartoon Tales)
Disney Comics: Nov, 1991 - No. 4, Feb, 1992 ($1.50, limited series)

1-4: Adapts hour-long premiere TV episode 2.00

DARLING LOVE
Close Up/Archie Publ. (A Darling Magazine): Oct-Nov, 1949 - No. 11, 1952 (no month) (52 pgs.)(All photo-c?)

1-Photo-c 16.00 47.00 110.00
2-Photo-c 10.00 30.00 65.00
3-8,10,11: 3-6-photo-c 8.35 25.00 50.00
9-Krigstein-a 10.00 30.00 60.00

DARLING ROMANCE
Close Up (MLJ Publications): Sept-Oct, 1949 - No. 7, 1951 (All photo-c)

1-(52 pgs.)-Photo-c 21.00 64.00 150.00
2 10.00 30.00 65.00
3-7 9.15 27.00 55.00

DARQUE PASSAGES (See Master Darque)
Acclaim (Valiant): April, 1998 ($2.50)

1-Christina Z.-s/Manco-c/a 2.50

DART (Also see Freak Force & Savage Dragon)
Image Comics (Highbrow Entertainment): Feb, 1996 - No. 3, May, 1996 ($2.50, limited series)

1-3 3.00

DASTARDLY & MUTTLEY (See Fun-In No. 1-4, 6 and Kite Fun Book)

DATE WITH DANGER
Standard Comics: No. 5, Dec, 1952 - No. 6, Feb, 1953

5,6-Secret agent stories: 6-Atom bomb story 8.35 25.00 50.00

DATE WITH DEBBI (Also see Debbi's Dates)
National Periodical Publ.: Jan-Feb, 1969 - No. 17, Sept-Oct, 1971; No. 18, Oct-Nov, 1972

A Date With Judy #7 © DC

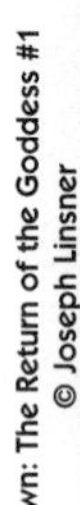
Dawn: The Return of the Goddess #1 © Joseph Linsner

The Dazzler #32 © MAR

	GD2.0	FN6.0	NM9.4
1-Teenage	4.00	12.00	40.00
2-5,17-(52 pgs) James Taylor sty.	2.25	6.75	18.00
6-12,18-Last issue	2.00	6.00	16.00
13-16-(68 pgs.): 14-1 pg. story on Jack Wild. 15-Marlo Thomas/"That Girl" sty	2.50	7.50	20.00

DATE WITH JUDY, A (Radio/TV, and 1948 movie)
National Periodical Publications: Oct-Nov, 1947 - No. 79, Oct-Nov, 1960 (No. 1-25: 52 pgs.)

	GD2.0	FN6.0	NM9.4
1-Teenage	27.00	81.00	190.00
2	13.00	39.00	90.00
3-10	10.00	30.00	70.00
11-20	6.70	20.00	40.00
21-40	5.35	16.00	32.00
41-45: 45-Last pre-code (2-3/55)	4.25	13.00	28.00
46-79: 79-Drucker-c/a	4.00	11.00	22.00

DATE WITH MILLIE, A (Life With Millie No. 8 on)(Teenage)
Atlas/Marvel Comics (MPC): Oct, 1956 - No. 7, Aug, 1957; Oct, 1959 - No. 7, Oct, 1960

	GD2.0	FN6.0	NM9.4
1(10/56)-(1st Series)-Dan DeCarlo-a in #1-7	24.00	73.00	170.00
2	12.00	36.00	85.00
3-7	10.00	30.00	60.00
1(10/59)-(2nd Series)	13.00	39.00	90.00
2-7	10.00	30.00	60.00

DATE WITH PATSY, A (Also see Patsy Walker)
Atlas Comics: Sept, 1957 (One-shot)

	GD2.0	FN6.0	NM9.4
1-Starring Patsy Walker	10.00	30.00	70.00

DAVID AND GOLIATH (Movie)
Dell Publishing Co.: No. 1205, July, 1961

	GD2.0	FN6.0	NM9.4
Four Color 1205-Photo-c	5.50	16.50	60.00

DAVID CASSIDY (TV)(See Partridge Family, Swing With Scooter #33 & Time For Love #30)
Charlton Comics: Feb, 1972 - No. 14, Sept, 1973

	GD2.0	FN6.0	NM9.4
1-Most have photo covers	4.00	12.00	40.00
2-5	2.50	7.50	22.00
6-14	2.60	7.80	26.00

DAVID LADD'S LIFE STORY (See Movie Classics)

DAVY CROCKETT (See Dell Giants, Fightin..., Frontier Fighters, It's Game Time, Power Record Comics, Western Tales & Wild Frontier)

DAVY CROCKETT (Frontier Fighter...)
Avon Periodicals: 1951

	GD2.0	FN6.0	NM9.4
nn-Tuska?, Reinman-a; Fawcette-c	17.00	51.00	120.00

DAVY CROCKETT (...King of the Wild Frontier No. 1,2)(TV)
Dell Publishing Co./Gold Key: 5/55 - No. 671, 12/55; No. 1, 12/63; No. 2, 11/69 (Walt Disney)

	GD2.0	FN6.0	NM9.4
Four Color 631(#1)-Fess Parker photo-c	16.75	50.00	185.00
Four Color 639-Photo-c	13.25	40.00	145.00
Four Color 664,671(Marsh-a)-Photo-c	12.00	37.00	135.00
1(12/63-Gold Key)-Fess Parker photo-c; reprints	12.00	37.00	135.00
2(11/69)-Fess Parker photo-c; reprints	3.60	11.00	40.00

DAVY CROCKETT (...Frontier Fighter #1,2; Kid Montana #9 on)
Charlton Comics: Aug, 1955 - No. 8, Jan, 1957

	GD2.0	FN6.0	NM9.4
1	9.15	27.00	55.00
2	5.85	17.50	35.00
3-8	4.25	13.00	26.00

DAWN
Sirius Entertainment: June, 1995 - No. 6, 1996 ($2.95)

	GD2.0	FN6.0	NM9.4
1/2-w/certificate		2.40	6.00
1/2-Variant-c	1.85	5.50	15.00
1-Linsner-c/a	1.00	2.80	7.00
1-Black Light Edition	1.25	3.75	10.00
1-White Trash Edition	1.85	5.50	15.00
1-Look Sharp Edition	3.00	9.00	30.00
2-4: Linsner-c/a			4.00
2-Variant-c, 3-Limited Edition	1.85	5.50	15.00
4-6-Vibrato-c			3.00
4, 5-Limited Edition	1.25	3.75	10.00
6-Limited Edition	1.50	4.50	12.00
Lucifer's Halo TPB (11/97, $19.95) r/Drama, Dawn #1-6 plus 12 pages of new artwork			20.00

DAWN: THE RETURN OF THE GODDESS
Sirius Entertainment: Apr, 1999 - No. 4 ($2.95, limited series)

	GD2.0	FN6.0	NM9.4
1-Linsner-s/a			3.00

DAYDREAMERS (See Generation X)
Marvel Comics: Aug, 1997 - No. 3, Oct, 1997 ($2.50, limited series)

	GD2.0	FN6.0	NM9.4
1-3-Franklin Richards, Howard the Duck, Man-Thing app.			2.50

DAYS OF THE MOB (See In the Days of the Mob)

DAZEY'S DIARY
Dell Publishing Co.: June-Aug, 1962

	GD2.0	FN6.0	NM9.4
01-174-208: Bill Woggon-c/a	3.20	9.50	35.00

DAZZLER, THE (Also see Marvel Graphic Novel & X-Men #130)
Marvel Comics Group: Mar, 1981 - No. 42, Mar, 1986

	GD2.0	FN6.0	NM9.4
1,22,24,27,28,38: 1-X-Men app. 22 (12/82)-vs. Rogue Battle-c/sty. 24-Full app. Rogue w/Powerman (Iron Fist). 27-Rogue app. 28-Full app. Rogue; ystique app. 38-Wolverine-c/app.; X-Men app.			3.00
2-21,23,25,26,29-37,39-42: 2-X-men app. 10,11-Galactus app. 21-Double size; photo-c. 23-Rogue/Mystique 1 pg. app. 26-Jusko-c. 33-Michael Jackson thriller swipe-c/sty. 40-Secret Wars II. 42-Beast-c/sty			2.00

NOTE: *No. 1 distributed only through comic shops.* ***Alcala*** *a-1i, 2i.* ***Chadwick*** *a-38-42p; c(p)-39 41, 42.* ***Guice*** *a-38i, 42i; c-38, 40.*

DC CHALLENGE
DC Comics: Nov, 1985 - No. 12, Oct, 1986 ($1.25, maxi-series)

	GD2.0	FN6.0	NM9.4
1-12: 1-Colan-a. 2,8-Batman-c/app. 4-Gil Kane-c/a			2.00

NOTE: *Batman app. in 1-4, 6-12. Joker app. in 7.* ***nfantino*** *a-3.* ***Ordway*** *c-12.* ***Swan/Austin*** *c 10.*

DC COMICS PRESENTS
DC Comics: July-Aug, 1978 - No. 97, Sept, 1986 (Superman team-ups in all)

	GD2.0	FN6.0	NM9.4
1-4th & final Superman/Flash race	.85	2.60	7.00
2-10: 2-Part 2 of Superman/Flash race. 4-Metal Men. 6-Green Lantern. 8-Swamp Thing. 9-Wonder Woman			4.00
11-25,27-40,42-46,48-50,52-71,73-76,79-83: 13,43,80-Legion of Super-Heroes. 19-Batgirl. 31,58-Robin. 35-Man-Bat. 42-Sandman. 52-Doom Patrol. 82-Adam Strange. 83-Batman & Outsiders.			3.00
26-(10/80)-Green Lantern; intro Cyborg, Starfire, Raven (1st app. New Teen Titans in 16 pg. preview); Starlin-c/a; Sargon the Sorcerer back-up	1.75	5.25	14.00
41,72,77,78,97: 41-Superman/Joker-c/story. 72-Joker/Phantom Stranger-c/story.77,78-Animal Man app. (77-c also). 97-Phantom Zone			4.00
47-He-Man-c/s (1st app. in comics)		2.40	6.00
51,84,85: 51-Preview insert (16 pgs.) of He-Man (2nd app.). 84-Challengers of the Unknown; Kirby-c/s. 85-Swamp Thing; Alan Moore scripts			5.00
86-96: 86-88-Crisis x-over. 88-Creeper			3.00
Annual 1,4: 1(9/82)-G.A. Superman. 4(10/85)-Superwoman			3.00
Annual 2,3: 2(7/83)-Intro/origin Superwoman. 3(9/84)-Shazam.			3.00

NOTE: ***Adkins*** *a-2, 54; c-2.* ***Buckler*** *a-33, 34; c-30, 33, 34.* ***Giffen*** *a-39; c-59.* ***Gil Kane*** *a-28, 35 Annual 3; c-48p, 56, 58, 60, 62, 64, 68, Annual 2, 3.* ***Kirby*** *c/a-84.* ***Kubert*** *c/a-66.* ***Morrow*** *c/a-65* ***Newton*** *c/a-54p.* ***Orlando*** *c-53i.* ***Perez*** *a-26p, 61p; c-38, 61, 94.* ***Starlin*** *a-26-29p, 36p, 37p; c 26-29, 36, 37, 93.* ***Toth*** *a-84.* ***Williamson*** *i-79, 85, 87.*

DC GRAPHIC NOVEL (Also see DC Science Fiction...)
DC Comics: Nov, 1983 - No. 7, 1986 ($5.95, 68 pgs.)

	GD2.0	FN6.0	NM9.4
1-3,5,7: 1-Star Raiders. 2-Warlords; not from regular Warlord series. 3-The Medusa Chain; Ernie Colon story/a. 5-Me and Joe Priest; Chaykin-c. 7-Space Clusters; Nino-c/a.	1.40	4.15	11.00
4-The Hunger Dogs by Kirby; Darkseid kills Himon from Mister Miracle &			

DC One Million #4 © DC

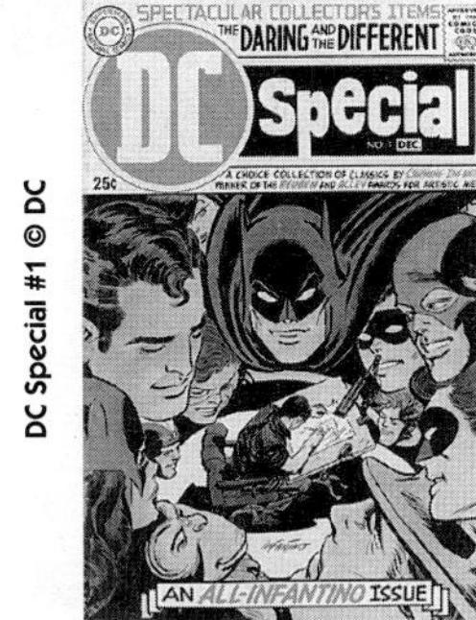

DC Special #1 © DC

DC Special #29 © DC

destroys New Genesis 2.50 7.50 25.00
6-Metalzoic; Sienkiewicz-c ($6.95) 1.25 3.75 10.00

DC/MARVEL: ALL ACCESS (Also see DC Versus Marvel & Marvel Versus DC)
DC Comics: 1996 - No. 4, 1997 ($2.95, limited series)

1-4: 1-Superman & Spider-Man app. 2-Robin & Jubilee app. 3-Dr. Strange & Batman-c/app., X-Men , JLA app. 4-X-Men vs. JLA-c/app. rebirth of Amalgam 3.00

DC/MARVEL: CROSSOVER CLASSICS II
DC Comics: 1998 ($14.95, TPB)

1-Reprints Batman/Punisher: Lake of Fire, Punisher/Batman: Deadly Knights, Silver Surfer/Superman, Batman & Capt. America 15.00

DC 100 PAGE SUPER SPECTACULAR
(Title is 100 Page... No. 14 on)(Square bound) (Reprints, 50¢)
National Periodical Publications: No. 4, Summer, 1971 - No. 13, 6/72; No. 14, 2/73 - No. 22, 11/73 (No #1-3)

4-Weird Mystery Tales; Johnny Peril & Phantom Stranger; cover & splashes by Wrightson; origin Jungle Boy of Jupiter 11.30 34.00 125.00
5-Love Stories; Wood inks (7 pgs.)(scarcer) 35.00 105.00 420.00
6- "World's Greatest Super-Heroes"; JLA, JSA, Spectre, Johnny Quick, Vigilante & Hawkman; contains unpublished Wildcat story; N. Adams wrap-around-c; r/JLA #21,22 10.50 32.00 115.00
7-(Also listed as Superman #245) Air Wave, Kid Eternity, Hawkman-r; Atom-r/Atom #3 3.20 9.50 35.00
8-(Also listed as Batman #238) Batman, Legion, Aquaman-r; G.A. Atom, Sargon (r/Sensation #57), Plastic Man (r/Police #14) stories; Doom Patrol origin-r; N. Adams wraparound-c 6.75 20.00 75.00
9-(Also listed as Our Army at War #242) Kubert-c 6.00 18.00 65.00
10-(Also listed as Adventure Comics #416) Golden Age-reprints; r/1st app. Black Canary from Flash #86; no Zatanna 4.50 13.50 50.00
11-(Also listed as Flash #214) origin Metal Men-r/Showcase #37; never before pubbed G.A. Flash story. 4.00 12.00 45.00
12-14: 12-(Also listed as Superboy #185) Legion-c/story; Teen Titans, Kid Eternity (r/Hit #46), Star Spangled Kid-r(S.S. #55). 13-(Also listed as Superman #252) Ray(r/Smash #17), Black Condor, (r/Crack #18), Hawkman(r/Flash #24); Starman-r/Adv. #67; Dr. Fate & Spectre-r/More Fun #57; N. Adams-c. 14-Batman-r/Detective #31,32,156; Atom-r/Showcase #34 3.20 9.50 35.00
15-22: 15-r/2nd Boy Commandos/Det. #64. 17-JSA-r/All Star #37 (10-11/47, 38 pgs.), Sandman-r/Adv. #65 (8/41), JLA #23 (11/63) & JLA #43 (3/66). 20-Batman-r/Det. #66,68, Spectre; origin Two-Face. 21-Superboy; r/Brave & the Bold #54. 22-r/All-Flash #13. 1.80 5.40 20.00

NOTE: ***Anderson*** *r-11, 14, 18i, 22.* ***B. Baily*** *r-18, 20.* ***Burnley*** *r-18, 20.* ***Crandall*** *r-14p, 20.* ***Drucker*** *r-4.* ***Grandenetti*** *a-22(2)r.* ***Heath*** *a-22r.* ***Infantino*** *r-17, 20, 22.* ***G. Kane*** *r-18.* ***Kirby*** *r-15.* ***Kubert*** *r-6, 7, 16, 17; c-16, 19.* ***Manning*** *a-19r.* ***Meskin*** *r-4, 22.* ***Mooney*** *r-15, 21.* ***Toth*** *r-17, 20.*

DC ONE MILLION (Also see crossover #1,000,000 issues)
DC Comics: Nov, 1998 - No. 4, Nov, 1998 ($2.95/$1.99, weekly lim. series)

1-($2.95) JLA travels to the 853rd century; Morrison-s 3.00
2-4-($1.99) 2.00
... Eighty-Page Giant (8/99, $4.95) 5.00
TPB ('99, $14.95) r/#1-4 and several x-over stories 15.00

DC SCIENCE FICTION GRAPHIC NOVEL
DC Comics: 1985 - No. 7, 1987 ($5.95)

SF1-SF7: SF1-Hell on Earth by Robert Bloch; Giffen-p. SF2-Nightwings by Robert Silverberg; G. Colan-p. SF3-Frost & Fire by Bradbury. SF4-Merchants of Venus. SF5-Demon With A Glass Hand by Ellison; M. Rogers-a. SF6-The Magic Goes Away by Niven. SF7-Sandkings by George R.R. Martin 1.10 3.30 9.00

DC SILVER AGE CLASSICS
DC Comics: 1992 ($1.00, all reprints)

...Action Comics #252-r/1st Supergirl. Adventure Comics #247-r/1st Legion of S.H. The Brave and the Bold #28-r/1st JLA. Detective Comics #225-r/1st Martian Manhunter. Detective Comics #327-r/1st new look Batman. Green Lantern #76-r/Green Lantern/Gr. Arrow. House of Secrets #92-r/1st Swamp Thing. Showcase #4-r/1st S.A. Flash. Showcase #22-r/1st S.A. Green Lantern 2.00
...Sugar and Spike #99; 2 unpublished stories 4.00

DC SPECIAL (Also see Super DC Giant)
National Per. Publ.: 10-12/68 - No. 15, 11-12/71; No. 16, Spr/75 - No. 29, 8-9/77

1-All Infantino issue; Flash, Batman, Adam Strange-r; begin 68 pg. issues, end #21 3.80 11.40 38.00
2-Teen humor; Binky, Buzzy, Harvey app. 5.90 18.00 65.00
3-All-Girl issue; unpubl. GA Wonder Woman story 4.00 12.00 40.00
4-15: 4-Horror (1st Abel cameo). 5-All Kubert issue; Viking Prince, Sgt. Rock-r. 6-Western. 7,9,13-Strangest Sports. 11-Monsters. 12-Viking Prince; Kubert-c/a (r/B&B almost entirely). 15-G.A. Plastic Man origin-r/Police #1; origin Woozy by Cole; 14,15-(52 pgs.) 2.50 7.50 24.00
16-27: 16-Super Heroes Battle Super Gorillas; r/Capt. Storm #1, 1st Johnny Cloud/All-Amer. Men of War #82. 17-Early S.A. Green Lantern-r. 22-Origin Robin Hood. 26-Enemy Ace on-c only. 27-Captain Comet story 1.25 3.75 10.00
28,29: 28-Earth Shattering Disaster Stories; Legion of Super-Heroes story. 29-New "The Untold Origin of the Justice Society"; Staton-a 1.75 5.25 14.00

NOTE: ***N. Adams*** *c-3, 4, 6, 11, 29.* ***Grell*** *a-20; c-17, 20.* ***Heath*** *a-12r.* ***G. Kane*** *a-6p, 13r, 17r, 19-21r.* ***Kirby*** *a-4,11.* ***Kubert*** *a-6r, 12r, 22.* ***Meskin*** *a-10.* ***Moreira*** *a-10.* ***Staton*** *a-29p.* ***Toth*** *a-13, 20r. #1-15: 25¢; 16-27: 50¢; 28, 29: 60¢. #1-13, 16-21: 68 pgs.; 14, 15: 52 pgs.; 25-27: oversized.*

DC SPECIAL BLUE RIBBON DIGEST
DC Comics: Mar-Apr, 1980 - No. 24, Aug, 1982

1,2,4,5: 1-Legion reprints. 2-Flash. 4-Green Lantern. 5-Secret Origins; new Zatara and Zatanna 1.00 3.00 8.00
3-Justice Society 1.50 4.50 12.00
6-10: 6-Ghosts. 7-Sgt. Rock's Prize Battle Tales. 8-Legion. 9-Secret Origins. 10-Warlord-"The Deimos Saga"-Grell-s/c/a 1.00 3.00 8.00
11-19: 11-Justice League. 12-Haunted Tank; reprints 1st app. 13-Strange Sports Stories. 14-UFO Invaders; Adam Strange app. 15-Secret Origins of Super Villains; JLA app. 16-Green Lantern/Green Arrow-r; all Adams-a. 17-Ghosts. 18-Sgt. Rock;Kubert front & back-c. 19-Doom Patrol; new Perez-c 1.50 4.50 10.00
20-Dark Mansion of Forbidden Love (scarce) 3.00 9.00 30.00
21-24: 21-Our Army at War. 22-Secret Origins. 23-Green Arrow, w/new 7 pg. story. 24-House of Mystery; new Kubert wraparound-c 1.50 4.50 12.00

NOTE: ***N. Adams*** *a-16(6)r, 17r, 23r; c-16.* ***Aparo*** *a-6r, 24r; c-23.* ***Grell*** *a-8, 10; c-10.* ***Heath*** *a-14.* ***Infantino*** *a-15r.* ***Kaluta*** *a-17r.* ***Gil Kane*** *a-15r, 22r.* ***Kirby*** *a-5, 9, 23r.* ***Kubert*** *a-3, 18r, 21r; c-7, 12, 14, 17, 18, 21, 24.* ***Morrow*** *a-24r.* ***Orlando*** *a-17r, 22r; c-1, 20.* ***Toth*** *a-21r, 24r.* ***Wood*** *a-3, 17r, 24r.* ***Wrightson*** *a-16r, 17r, 24r.*

DC SPECIAL SERIES
National Periodical Publications/DC Comics: 9/77 - No. 16, Fall, 1978; No. 17, 8/79 - No. 27, Fall, 1981 (No. 18, 19, 23, 24 - digest size, 100 pgs.; No. 25-27 - Treasury sized)

1-"5-Star Super-Hero Spectacular 1977"; Batman, Atom, Flash, Green Lantern, Aquaman, in solo stories, Kobra app.; N. Adams-c 1.50 4.50 12.00
2(#1)-"The Original Swamp Thing Saga 1977"-r/Swamp Thing #1&2 by Wrightson; new Wrightson wraparound-c. 1.00 2.80 7.00
3,4,6-8: 3-Sgt Rock. 4-Unexpected. 6-Secret Society of Super Villains, Jones-a. 7-Ghosts Special. 8-Brave and Bold w/ new Batman, Deadman & Sgt Rock team-up 1.10 3.30 9.00
5-"Superman Spectacular 1977"-(84 pg, $1.00)-Superman vs. Brainiac & Lex Luthor, new 63 pg. story 1.50 4.50 12.00
9-Wonder Woman; Ditko-a (11 pgs.) 1.50 4.50 12.00
10-"Secret Origins of Superheroes Special 1978"-(52. pgs)-Dr. Fate, Lightray & Black Canary-c/new origin stories; Staton, Newton-a 1.10 3.30 9.00
11-"Flash Spectacular 1978"-(84 pgs.) Flash, Kid Flash, GA Flash & Johnny Quick vs. Grodd; Wood-i on Kid Flash chapter 1.25 3.75 10.00
12-"Secrets of Haunted House Special Spring 1978" 1.10 3.30 9.00
13-"Sgt. Rock Special Spring 1978", 50 pg new story 1.10 3.30 9.00
14,17,20-"Original Swamp Thing Saga", Wrightson-a: 14-Sum '78, r/#3,4. 17-Sum '79 r/#5-7. 20-Jan/Feb '80, r/#8-10 1.10 3.30 9.00
15-"Batman Spectacular Summer 1978", Ra's Al Ghul-app.; Golden-a.

DC Super-Stars #16 © DC

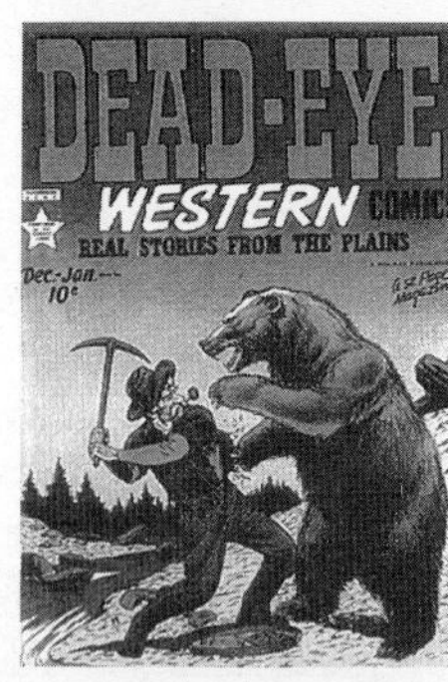

Dead-Eye Western Comics #7 © HILL

Dead Corpse #4 © Hinz & Pugh

GD2.0 FN6.0 NM9.4

Rogers-a/front & back-c 1.40 4.15 11.00
16-"Jonah Hex Spectacular Fall 1978"; death of Jonah Hex, Heath-a; Bat Lash and Scalphunter stories 3.20 9.60 32.00
18,19-Digest size: 18-"Sgt. Rock's Prize Battle Tales Fall 1979". 19-"Secret Origins of Super-Heroes Fall 1979"; origins Wonder Woman (new-a),r/Robin, Batman-Superman team, Aquaman, Hawkman and others 1.40 4.15 11.00
21-"Super-Star Holiday Special Spring 1980", Frank Miller-a in "Batman--Wanted Dead or Alive" (1st Batman story); Jonah Hex, Sgt. Rock, Superboy &LSH and House of Mystery/Witching Hour-c/stories 2.25 6.75 18.00
22-"G.I. Combat Sept. 1980", Kubert-c. Haunted Tank-s 1.10 3.30 9.00
23,24-Digest size: 23-World's Finest-r. 24-Flash 1.50 4.50 12.00
V5#25-($2.95)-"Superman II, the Adventure Continues Summer 1981"; photos from movie & photo-c (see All-New Coll. Ed. C-62) 1.50 4.50 12.00
26-($2.50)-"Superman and His Incredible Fortress of Solitude Summer 1981" 1.50 4.50 12.00
27-($2.50)-"Batman vs. The Incredible Hulk Fall 1981" 2.50 7.50 20.00

NOTE: ***Aparo** c-8. **Heath** a-12i, 16. **Infantino** a-19r. **Kirby** a-23, 19r. **Kubert** c-13, 19r. **Nasser/Netzer** a-1, 10i, 15. **Newton** a-10. **Nino** a-4, 7. **Starlin** c-12. **Staton** a-1. **Tuska** a-19r. #25 & 26. were advertised as All-New Collectors' Edition C-63, C-64. #26 was originally planned as All-New Collectors' Ed. C-30?; has C-630 & A.N.C.E. on cover.*

DC SUPER-STARS
National Periodical Publications/DC Comics: March, 1976 - No. 18, Winter, 1978 (No.3-18: 52 pgs.)

1-(68 pgs.)-Re-intro Teen Titans (predates T. T. #44 (11/76); tryout iss.) plus r/Teen Titans; W.W. as girl was original Wonder Girl 1.75 5.25 14.00
2-7,9,11,12,16: 2,4,6,8-Adam Strange; 2-(68 pgs.)-r/1st Adam Strange/Hawkman team-up from Mystery in Space #90 plus Atomic Knights origin-r. 3-Legion issue. 4-r/Tales/Unexpected #45 1.10 3.30 9.00
8-r/1st Space Ranger from Showcase #15, Adam Strange-r/Mystery in Space #89 & Star Rovers-r/M.I.S. #80 1.50 4.50 12.00
10-Strange Sports Stories; Batman/Joker-c/story 1.25 3.75 10.00
13-Sergio Aragonés Special 1.75 5.25 14.00
14,15,18: 15-Sgt. Rock 1.25 3.75 10.00
17-Secret Origins of Super-Heroes (origin of The Huntress); origin Green Arrow by Grell; Legion app.; Earth II Batman & Catwoman marry (1st revealed; also see B&B #197 & Superman Family #211) 1.75 5.25 14.00

NOTE: ***M. Anderson** r-2, 4, 6. **Aparo** c-7, 14, 18. **Austin** a-11i. **Buckler** a-14p; c-10. **Grell** a-17. **G. Kane** a-1r, 10r. **Kubert** c-15. **Layton** c/a-16i, 17i. **Mooney** a-4r, 6r. **Morrow** c/a-11r. **Nasser** a-11. **Newton** c/a-16p. **Staton** a-17; c-17. No. 10, 12-18 contain all new material; the rest are reprints. #1 contains new and reprint material.*

DCU HEROES SECRET FILES
DC Comics : Feb, 1999 ($4.95, one-shot)

1-Origin-s and pin-ups; new Star Spangled Kid app. 5.00

DC UNIVERSE HOLIDAY BASH
DC Comics: 1997- 1999 ($3.95)

I,II-(X-mas '96,'97) Christmas stories by various 4.00
III (1999, for Christmas '98, $4.95) 5.00

DC UNIVERSE: TRINITY
DC Comics: Aug, 1993 - No. 2, Sept, 1993 ($2.95, 52 pgs, limited series)

1,2-Foil-c; Green Lantern, Darkstars, Legion app. 3.50

DCU VILLAINS SECRET FILES
DC Comics: Apr, 1999 ($4.95, one-shot)

1-Origin-s and profile pages 5.00

DC VERSUS MARVEL (See Marvel Versus DC) (Also see Amazon, Assassins, Bruce Wayne: Agent of S.H.I. E. L.D., Bullets & Bracelets, Doctor Strangefate, JLX, Legend of the Dark Claw, Magneto & The Magnetic Men, Speed Demon, Spider-Boy, Super Soldier, X-Patrol)
DC Comics: No. 1, 1996, No. 4, 1996 ($3.95, limited series)

1,4: 1-Marz script, Jurgens-a(p); 1st app. of Access. 4.00
.../Marvel Versus DC ($12.95, trade paperback) r/1-4 13.00

D-DAY (Also see Special War Series)

GD2.0 FN6.0 NM9.4

Charlton Comics (no No. 3): Sum/63; No. 2, Fall/64; No. 4, 9/66; No. 5, 10/67; No. 6, 11/68

1,2: 1(1963)-Montes/Bache-c. 2(Fall,'64)-Wood-a(4) 2.80 8.40 28.00
4-6('66-'68)-Montes/Bache-a #5 2.00 6.00 16.00

DEAD AIR
Slave Labor Graphics: July, 1989 ($5.95, graphic novel)

nn-Mike Allred's 1st published work 6.00

DEAD CORPSe
DC Comics (Helix): Sept, 1998 - No. 4, Dec, 1998 ($2.50, limited series)

1-4-Pugh-a/Hinz-s 2.50

DEAD END CRIME STORIES
Kirby Publishing Co.: April, 1949 (52 pgs.)

nn-(Scarce)-Powell, Roussos-a; painted-c 48.00 144.00 385.00

DEAD-EYE WESTERN COMICS
Hillman Periodicals: Nov-Dec, 1948 - V3#1, Apr-May, 1953

V1#1-(52 pgs.)-Krigstein, Roussos-a 17.00 51.00 120.00
V1#2,3-(52 pgs.) 10.00 30.00 60.00
V1#4-12-(52 pgs.) 5.85 17.50 35.00
V2#1,2,5-8,10-12: 1-7-(52 pgs.) 4.25 13.00 28.00
3,4-Krigstein-a 6.70 20.00 40.00
9-One pg. Frazetta ad 4.25 13.00 28.00
V3#1 4.15 12.50 25.00

NOTE: ***Briefer** a-V1#8. Kinstleresque stories by **McCann**-12, V2#1, 2, V3#1. **McWilliams** a-V1#5. **Ed Moore** a-V1#4.*

DEADFACE: DOING THE ISLANDS WITH BACCHUS
Dark Horse Comics: July, 1991 - No. 3, Sept, 1991 ($2.95, B&W, lim. series)

1-3: By Eddie Campbell 3.00

DEADFACE: EARTH, WATER, AIR, AND FIRE
Dark Horse Comics: July, 1992 - No. 4, Oct, 1992 ($2.50, B&W, limited series; British-r)

1-4: By Eddie Campbell 2.50

DEAD IN THE WEST
Dark Horse Comics: Oct, 1993 - No. 2, Mar, 1994 ($3.95, B&W, 52 pgs.)

1,2-Timothy Truman-c 4.00

DEAD KING (See Evil Ernie)
Chaos! Comics: May, 1998 - No. 4, Aug, 1998, ($2.95, limited series)

1-4-Fisher-s 3.00

DEADLIEST HEROES OF KUNG FU (Magazine)
Marvel Comics Group: Summer, 1975 (B&W)(76 pgs.)

1 -Bruce Lee vs. Carradine painted-c; TV Kung Fu, 4pgs. photos/article; Enter the Dragon, 24 pgs. photos/article w/ Bruce Lee; Bruce Lee photo pinup 2.25 6.75 18.00

DEADLINE USA
Dark Horse Comics: Apr, 1992 - No. 8, Nov, 1992 ($3.95, B&W, 52 pgs.)

1-8: Johnny Nemo w/Milligan scripts in all 4.00

DEADLY DUO, THE
Image Comics (Highbrow Entertainment): Nov, 1994 - No. 3, Jan, 1995 ($2.50, limited series)

1-3: 1-Ist app. of Kill Cat 2.50

DEADLY DUO, THE
Image Comics (Highbrow Entertainment): June, 1995 - No. 4, Oct, 1995 ($2.50, limited series)

1-4: 1-Spawn app. 2-Savage Dragon app. 3-Gen 13 app. 2.50

DEADLY FOES OF SPIDER-MAN (See Lethal Foes of...)
Marvel Comics: May, 1991 - No. 4, Aug, 1991 ($1.00, limited series)

1-4: 1-Punisher, Kingpin, Rhino app. 2.00

DEADLY HANDS OF KUNG FU, THE (See Master of Kung Fu)

Deadly Hands of Kung-Fu #4 © MAR

Dead of Night #1 © MAR

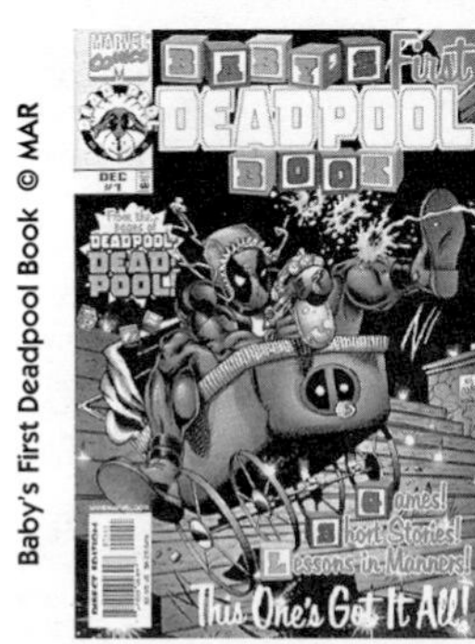

Baby's First Deadpool Book © MAR

GD2.0 FN6.0 NM9.4

Marvel Comics Group: April, 1974 - No. 33, Feb, 1977 (75¢) (B&W, magazine)

1(V1#4 listed in error)-Origin Sons of the Tiger; Shang-Chi, Master of Kung Fu begins (ties w/Master of Kung Fu #17 as 3rd app. Shang-Chi); Bruce Lee painted-c by Neal Adams; 2pg. memorial photo pinup w/8 pgs. photos/articles; TV Kung Fu, 9 pgs. photos/articles; 15 pgs. Starlin-a. 2.60 7.80 26.00

2-Adams painted-c; 1st time origin of Shang-Chi, 34 pgs. by Starlin. TV Kung Fu, 6 pgs. ph/a w/2 pg. pinup. Bruce Lee, 11 pgs. ph/a 2.50 7.50 22.00

3,4,7,10: 3-Adams painted-c; Gulacy-a. Enter the Dragon, photos/articles, 8 pgs. 4-TV Kung Fu painted-c by Neal Adams; TV Kung Fu 7 pg. article/art; Fu Manchu; Enter the Dragon, 10 pg. photos/article w/Bruce Lee. 7-Bruce Lee painted-c & 9 pgs. photos/articles-Return of Dragon plus 1 pg. photo pinup. 10-(3/75)-Iron Fist painted-c & 34 pg. sty-Early app. 2.50 6.50 16.00

5,6: 5-1st app. Manchurian, 6 pgs. Gulacy-a. TV Kung Fu, 4 pg. article; re books w/Barry Smith-a. Capt. America-sty, 10 pgs. Kirby-a(r). 6-Bruce Lee photos/article, 6 pgs.; 15 pgs. early Perez-a 1.75 5.25 14.00

8,9,11: 9-Iron Fist, 2 pg. Preview pinup; Nebres-a. 11-Billy Jack painted-c by Adams; 17 pgs. photos/article 1.40 4.15 11.00

12,13: 12-James Bond painted-c by Adams; 14 pg. photos/article. 13-16 pgs. early Perez-a; Piers Anthony, 7 pgs. photos/article 1.10 3.30 9.00

14-Classic Bruce Lee painted-c by Adams. Lee pinup by Chaykin. Lee 16 pg. photos/article w/2 pgs. Green Hornet TV 3.40 10.20 34.00

15,19: 15-Sum, '75 Giant Annual #1. 20pgs. Starlin-a. Bruce Lee photo pinup & 3 pg photos/article re book; Man-Thing app. Iron Fist-c/sty; Gulacy-a 18pgs. 19-Iron Fist painted-c & series begins; 1st White Tiger 1.50 4.50 12.00

16,18,20: 16-1st app. Corpse Rider, a Samurai w/Sanho Kim-a. 20-Chuck Norris painted-c & 16 pgs. interview w/photos/article; Bruce Lee vs. C. Norris pinup by Ken Barr. Origin The White Tiger, Perez-a 1.25 3.75 10.00

17-Bruce Lee painted-c by Adams; interview w/R. Clouse, director Enter Dragon 7 pgs. w/B. Lee app. 1st Giffen-a (1pg. 11/75) 2.50 7.50 22.00

21-Bruce Lee 1pg. photos/article 1.00 3.00 8.00

22,30-32: 22-1st app. Jack of Hearts (cameo). 1st Giffen sty-a (along w/Amazing Adv. #35, 3/76). 30-Swordquest-c/sty & conclusion; Jack of Hearts app. 31-Jack of Hearts app; Staton-a. 32-1st Daughters of the Dragon -c/sty, 21 pgs. M. Rogers-a/Claremont-sty; Iron Fist pinup 1.40 4.15 11.00

23-26,29: 23-1st full app. Jack of Hearts. 24-Iron Fist-c & centerfold pinup. early Zeck-a; Shang Chi pinup; 6 pgs. Piers Anthony text sty w/Perez/Austin-a; Jack of Hearts app. early Giffen-a. 25-1st app. Shimuru, "Samurai", 20 pgs. Mantlo-sty/Broderick-a; "Swordquest"-c & begins 17 pg. sty by Sanho Kim; 11 pg. photos/article; partly Bruce Lee. 26-Bruce Lee painted-c & pinup; 16 pgs. interviews w/Kwon & Clouse; talk about B. Lee re-filming of B. Lee legend. 29-Ironfist vs. Shang Chi battle-c/sty; Jack of Hearts app. 1.75 5.25 14.00

27 1.10 3.30 9.00

28-All Bruce Lee Special Issue; (1st time in comics). Bruce Lee painted-c by Ken Barr & pinup. 36 pgs. comics chronicaling Bruce Lee's life; 15 pgs. B. Lee photos/article (Rare in high grade) 4.20 12.60 42.00

33-Shang Chi-c/sty; Classic Daughters of the Dragon, 21 pgs. M. Rogers-a/Claremont-sty with Nudity; Bob Wall interview, photos/article, 14 pgs. 1.75 5.25 14.00

...Special Album Edition 1(Summer, '74)-Iron Fist-c/story (early app., 3rd?); 10 pgs. Adams-i; Shang Chi/Fu Manchu, 10 pgs.; Sons of Tiger, 11 pgs.; TV Kung Fu, 6 pgs. photos/article 2.25 6.75 18.00

NOTE: ***Bruce Lee:*** *1-7, 14, 15, 17, 25, 26, 28.* ***Kung Fu (TV):*** *1, 2, 4.* ***Jack of Hearts:*** *22, 23, 29-33.* ***Shang Chi Master of Kung Fu:*** *1-9, 11-18, 29, 31, 33.* ***Sons of Tiger:*** *1, 3, 4, 6-14, 16-19.* ***Swordquest:*** *25-27, 29-33.* ***White Tiger:*** *19-24, 26, 27, 29-33.* ***N. Adams*** *a-1i(part), 27i; c-1, 2-4, 11, 12, 14, 17.* ***Giffen*** *a-22p, 24p.* ***G. Kane*** *a-23p.* ***Kirby*** *a-5r.* ***Nasser*** *a-27p, 28.* ***Perez*** *a(p)-6-14, 16, 17, 19, 21.* ***Rogers*** *a-26, 32, 33.* ***Starlin*** *a-1, 2r, 15r.* ***Staton*** *a-28p, 31, 32.*

DEADMAN (See The Brave and the Bold & Phantom Stranger #39)
DC Comics: May, 1985 - No. 7, Nov, 1985 ($1.75, Baxter paper)

1-7: 1-Deadman-r by Infantino, N. Adams in all. 5-Batman-c/story-r/Str. Advs. 7-Batman-r 3.00

GD2.0 FN6.0 NM9.4

DEADMAN
DC Comics: Mar, 1986 - No. 4, June, 1986 (75¢, limited series)

1-4: Lopez-c/a. 4-Byrne-c(p) 2.00

DEADMAN: EXORCISM
DC Comics: 1992 - No. 2, 1992 ($4.95, limited series, 52 pgs.)

1,2: Kelley Jones-c/a in both 5.00

DEADMAN: LOVE AFTER DEATH
DC Comics: 1989 - No. 2, 1990 ($3.95, 52 pgs., limited series, mature)

Book One, Two: Kelley Jones-c/a in both. 1-contains nudity 4.00

DEAD OF NIGHT
Marvel Comics Group: Dec, 1973 - No. 11, Aug, 1975

1-Horror reprints 1.75 5.25 14.00
2-10: 10-Kirby-a 1.10 3.30 9.00
11-Intro Scarecrow; Kane/Wrightson-c 2.00 6.00 16.00

NOTE: ***Ditko*** *r-7, 10.* ***Everett*** *c-2.* ***Sinnott*** *r-1.*

DEAD OR ALIVE - A CYBERPUNK WESTERN
Image Comics (Shok Studio): Apr, 1998 - No. 4, July, 1998 ($2.50, lim. series)

1-4 3.00

DEADPOOL (See New Mutants #98)
Marvel Comics: Aug, 1994 - No. 4, Nov, 1994 ($2.50, limited series)

1: Mark Waid's 1st Marvel work; Ian Churchill-c/a 4.00
2--4 3.00

DEADPOOL
Marvel Comics: Jan, 1997 - Present ($2.95/$1.95/$1.99)

1-($2.95)-Wraparound-c 4.00
2-Begin-$1.95-c. 3.00
3-10,12-22,24: 4-Hulk-c/app. 12-Variant-c. 14-Begin McDaniel-a. 22-Cable app. 2.00
11-($3.99)-Deadpool replaces Spider-Man from Amazing Spider-Man #47; Kraven, Gwen Stacy app. 5.00
23,25-($2.99); 23-Dead Reckoning pt. 1; wraparound-c 3.00
26-32: 27-Wolverine-c/app. 2.00
.../Death '98 Annual ($2.99) Kelly-s, ... Team-Up (12/98, $2.99) Widdle Wade-c/app., Baby's First Deadpool Book (12/98, $2.99), Encyclopædia Deadpoolica (12/98, $2.99) Synopses 3.00
Mission Improbable TPB (9/98, $14.95) r/#1-5 15.00
#0 ('98, bagged with Wizard #87) 2.00

DEADPOOL: THE CIRCLE CHASE (See New Mutants #98)
Marvel Comics: Aug, 1993 - No. 4, Nov, 1993 ($2.00, limited series)

1-($2.50)-Embossed-c 4.00
2-4 3.00

DEADSHOT (See Batman #59, Detective Comics #474, & Showcase '93 #8)
DC Comics: Nov, 1988 - No. 4, Feb, 1989 ($1.00, limited series)

1-4 2.00

DEADSIDE (See Shadowman)
Acclaim Comics: Feb, 1999 - No. 4, ($2.50, limited series)

1-3-Jenkins-s/Haselden-Wood-a 2.50

DEAD WHO WALK, THE (See Strange Mysteries, Super Reprint #15, 16)
Realistic Comics: 1952 (one-shot)

nn 47.00 141.00 375.00

DEADWORLD (Also see The Realm)
Arrow Comics/Caliber Comics: Dec, 1986 - No. 26 ($1.50/$1.95/#15-28: $2.50, B&W, mature)

1-26: 5-26-Graphic covers, 5-26: Tame covers 2.50
...Archives 1-3 (1992, $2.50) 2.50

DEAN MARTIN & JERRY LEWIS (See Adventures of...)

DEAR BEATRICE FAIRFAX
Best/Standard Comics (King Features): No. 5, Nov, 1950 - No. 9, Sept, 1951 (Vern Greene art)

Dear Beatrice Fairfax #6 © STD

Deathblow #13 © Aegis Ent.

Deathlok (3rd series) #1 © MAR

GD2.0 FN6.0 NM9.4

5-All have Schomburg air brush-c 9.15 27.00 55.00
6-9 5.85 17.50 35.00

DEAR HEART (Formerly Lonely Heart)
Ajax: No. 15, July, 1956 - No. 16, Sept, 1956

15,16 5.35 16.00 32.00

DEAR LONELY HEART (...Illustrated No. 1-6)
Artful Publications: Mar, 1951; No. 2, Oct, 1951 - No. 8, Oct, 1952

1 16.00 47.00 110.00
2 7.50 22.50 45.00
3-Matt Baker Jungle Girl story 17.00 51.00 120.00
4-8 6.70 20.00 40.00

DEAR LONELY HEARTS (Lonely Heart #9 on)
Harwell Publ./Mystery Publ. Co. (Comic Media): Aug, 1953 -No. 8, Oct, 1954

1 10.00 30.00 65.00
2-8 6.35 19.00 38.00

DEARLY BELOVED
Ziff-Davis Publishing Co.: Fall, 1952

1-Photo-c 15.00 45.00 105.00

DEAR NANCY PARKER
Gold Key: June, 1963 - No. 2, Sept, 1963

1-Painted-c on both 2.60 7.80 26.00
2 2.50 7.50 20.00

DEATHBLOW (Also see Darker Image)
Image Comics (WildStorm Productions): May (Apr. inside), 1993 - No. 29, Aug, 1996 ($1.75/$1.95/$2.50)

0-(8/96, $2.95, 32 pgs.)-r/Darker Image w/new story & art; Jim Lee & Trevor Scott-a; new Jim Lee-c 3.00
1-($2.50)-Red foil stamped logo on black varnish-c; Jim Lee-c/a; flip-book side has Cybernary -c/story (#2 also) 2.50
1-($1.95)-Newsstand version w/o foil-c & varnish 2.00
2-29:: 2-(8/93)-Lee-a; with bound-in poster. 2-($1.75)-Newsstand ver sion w/o poster. 4-Jim Lee-c. 5-9: Jim Lee-c in all. 13-W/pinup poster by Tim Sale & Jim Lee. 16 ($1.95, Newsstand)-Wildstorm Rising Pt. 6. 16. ($2.50, Direct Market)-Wildstorm Rising Pt. 617-Variant "Chicago Comicon" edition exists. 20,21-Gen 13 app. 23-Backlash-c/app. 24,25-Grifter-c/app; Gen 13 & Dane from Wetworks app. 28-Deathblow dies. 29-Memorial issue 2.50
5-Alternate Portacio-c (Forms larger picture when combined with alternate-c for Gen 13 #5, Kindred #3, Stormwatch #10, Team 7 #1, Union #0, Wetworks #2 & WildC.A.T.S # 11) 2.40 6.00

DEATHBLOW BYBLOWS
DC Comics (WildStorm): Nov, 1999 - No. 3 ($2.95, limited series)

1-Alan Moore-s/Jim Baikie-a 2.95

DEATHBLOW/WOLVERINE
Image Comics (WildStorm Productions)/ Marvel Comics: Sept, 1996 - No. 2, Feb, 1997 ($2.50, limited series)

1,2: Wiesenfeld-s/Bennett-a 2.50
TPB (1997, $8.95) r/#1,2 9.00

DEATHDEALER
Verotik: July, 1995 - No. 4, July, 1997 ($5.95)

1-Frazetta-c; Bisley-a 1.00 3.00 8.00
1-2nd print, 2-4-($6.95)-Frazetta-c; embossed logo 1.00 2.80 7.00

DEATHLOK (Also see Astonishing Tales #25)
Marvel Comics: July, 1990 - No. 4, Oct, 1990 ($3.95, limited series, 52 pgs.)

1-4: 1,2-Guice-a(p). 3,4-Denys Cowan-a, c-4 4.00

DEATHLOK
Marvel Comics: July, 1991 - No. 34, Apr, 1994 ($1.75)

1-Silver ink cover; Denys Cowan-c/a(p) begins 2.50
2-18,20-24,26-34: 2-Forge (X-Men) app. 3-Vs. Dr. Doom. 5-X-Men & F.F. x-over. 6,7-Punisher x-over. 9,10-Ghost Rider-c/story. 16-Infinity War x-over. 17-Jae Lee-c. 22-Black Panther app. 27-Siege app. 2.00

GD2.0 FN6.0 NM9.4

19-($2.25)-Foil-c 2.25
25-($2.95, 52 pgs.)-Holo-grafx foil-c 3.00
Annual 1 (1992, $2.25, 68 pgs.)-Guice-p; Quesada-c(p) 3.00
Annual 2 (1993, $2.95, 68 pgs.)-Bagged w/card; intro Tracer 3.00
NOTE: *Denys Cowan a(p)-9-13, 15, Annual 1; c-9-12, 13p, 14.* ***Guice/Cowan*** *c-8.*

DEATHLOK
Marvel Comics: Sept, 1999 - Present ($1.99)

1,2: 1-Casey-s/Manco-a. 2-Two covers 2.00

DEATHLOK SPECIAL
Marvel Comics: May, 1991 - No. 4, June, 1991 ($2.00, bi-weekly lim. series)

1-4: r/1-4(1990) w/new Guice-c #1,2; Cowan c-3,4 2.00
1-2nd printing w/white-c 2.00

DEATHMARK
Lightning Comics: Dec, 1994 ($2.95, B&W)

1 3.00

DEATHMATE
Valiant (Prologue/Yellow/Blue)/Image Comics (Black/Red/Epilogue): Sept, 1993 - Epilogue (#6), Feb, 1994 ($2.95/$4.95, limited series)

Preview-(7/93, 8 pgs.) 2.00
Prologue (#1)–Silver foil; Jim Lee/Layton-c; B. Smith/Lee-a; Liefeld-a(p) 3.00
Prologue–Special gold foil ed. of silver ed. 4.00
Black (#2)-(9/93, $4.95, 52 pgs.)-Silvestri/Jim Lee-c; pencils by Peterson/Silvestri/Capullo/Jim Lee/Portacio; 1st story app. Gen 13 telling their rebellion against the Troika (see WildC.A.T.S. Trilogy) 7.00
Black-Special gold foil edition 1.00 3.00 8.00
Yellow (#3)-(10/93, $4.95, 52 pgs)-Yellow foil-c; Indicia says Prologue Sept 1993 by mistake; 3rd app. Ninjak; Thibert-c(i) 5.00
Yellow-Special gold foil edition 6.00
Blue (#4)-(10/93, $4.95, 52 pgs.)-Thibert blue foil-c(i); Reese-a(i) 5.00
Blue-Special gold foil edition 6.00
Red (#5), Epilogue (#6)-(2/94, $2.95)-Silver foil Quesada/Silvestri-c; Silvestri-a(p) 3.00

DEATH METAL
Marvel Comics UK: Jan, 1994 - No. 4, Apr, 1994 ($1.95, limited series)

1-4: 1-Silver ink-c. Alpha Flight app. 2.00

DEATH METAL VS. GENETIX
Marvel Comics UK: Dec, 1993 - No. 2, Jan, 1994 (Limited series)

1-($2.95)-Polybagged w/2 trading cards 3.00
2-($2.50)-Polybagged w/2 trading cards 2.50

DEATH OF CAPTAIN MARVEL (See Marvel Graphic Novel #1)

DEATH OF MR. MONSTER, THE (See Mr. Monster #8)

DEATH OF SUPERMAN (See Superman, 2nd Series)

DEATH RACE 2020
Roger Corman's Cosmic Comics: Apr, 1995 - No. 8, Nov, 1995 ($2.50)

1-8: Sequel to the Movie 2.50

DEATH RATTLE (Formerly an Underground)
Kitchen Sink Press: V2#1, 10/85 - No. 18, 1988, 1994 ($1.95, Baxter paper, mature)

V2#1-7,9-18: 1-Corben-c. 2-Unpubbed Spirit story by Eisner. 5-Robot Woman-r by Wolverton. 6-B&W issues begin. 10-Savage World-r by by Williamson/ Torres/ Krenkel/Frazetta from Witzend #1. 16-Wolverton Spacehawk-r 2.00
8-(12/86)-1st app. Mark Schultz's Xenozoic Tales/Cadillacs & Dinosaurs 3.00
8-(1994)-r plus interview w/Mark Schultz 2.00

DEATH'S HEAD (See Daredevil #56, Dragon's Claws #5 & Incomplete...)
Marvel Comics: Dec, 1988 - No. 10, Sept, 1989 ($1.75)

1-Dragon's Claws spin-off 4.00
2-Fantastic Four app.; Dragon's Claws x-over 3.00
3-10: 8-Dr. Who app. 9-F. F. x-over; Simonson-c(p) 3.00
...Gold 1 (1/94, $3.95, 68 pgs.)-Gold foil-c 5.00

Death's Head II #9 © MAR

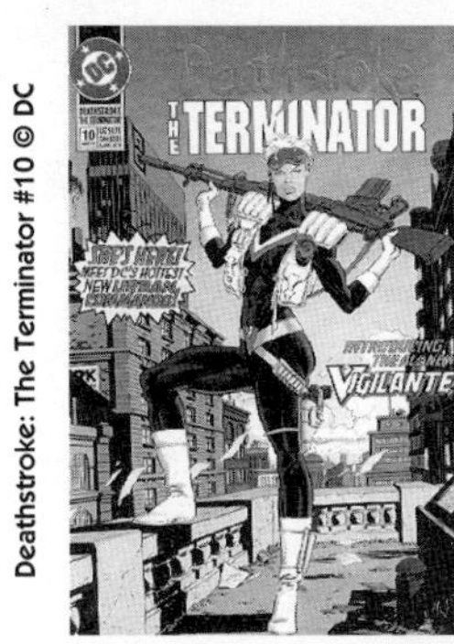

Deathstroke: The Terminator #10 © DC

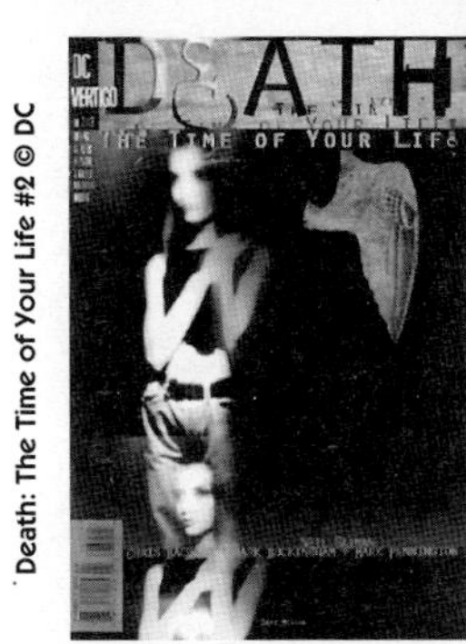

Death: The Time of Your Life #2 © DC

GD2.0 FN6.0 NM9.4

DEATH'S HEAD II (Also see Battletide)
Marvel Comics UK, Ltd.: Mar, 1992 - No. 4, June (May inside), 1992 ($1.75, color, limited series)

1-4: 2-Fantastic Four app. 4-Punisher, Spider-Man , Daredevil, Dr. Strange, Capt. America & Wolverine in the year 2020 — 2.50
1,2-Silver ink 2nd printiings — 2.50

DEATH'S HEAD II (Also see Battletide)
Marvel Comics UK, Ltd.: Dec, 1992 - No. 16, Mar, 1994 ($1.75/$1.95)

V2#1-13,15,16: 1-Gatefold-c. 1-4-X-Men app.15-Capt. America & Wolverine app. — 2.00
14-($2.95)-Foil flip-c w/Death's Head II Gold #0 — 3.00

DEATH'S HEAD II & THE ORIGIN OF DIE CUT
Marvel Comics UK, Ltd.: Aug, 1993 - No. 2, Sept, 1993 (limited series)

1-($2.95)-Embossed-c — 3.00
2 ($1.75) — 2.00

DEATHSTROKE: THE TERMINATOR (Deathstroke: The Hunted #0-47; Deathstroke #48-60) (Also see Marvel & DC Present, New Teen Titans #2, New Titans, Showcase '93 #7,9 & Tales of the Teen Titans #42-44)
DC Comics: Aug, 1991 - No. 60, June, 1996 ($1.75-$2.25)

1-New Titans spin-off; Mike Zeck c-1-28 — 4.00
1-Gold ink 2nd printing ($1.75) — 2.00
2 — 3.00
3-40,0(10/94),41(11/94)-49,51-60: 6,8-Batman cameo. 7,9-Batman-c/story. 9-1st new Vigilante (female) in cameo. 10-1st full app. new Vigilante; Perez-i. 13-Vs. Justice League; TeamTitans cameo on last pg. 14-Total Chaos, part 1; TeamTitans-c/story cont'd in New Titans #90. 15-Total Chaos, part 4. 40-(9/94). 0-(10/94)-Begin Deathstroke, The Hunted, ends #47. — 2.50
50 ($3.50) — 3.50
Annual 1-4 ('92-'95, 68 pgs.): 1-Nightwing & Vigilante app.; minor Eclipso app. 2-Bloodlines Deathstorm; 1st app. Gunfire. 3-Elseworlds story. 4-Year One story — 4.00

NOTE: ***Golden*** *a-12.* ***Perez*** *a-11i.* ***Zeck*** *c-Annual 1, 2.*

DEATH: THE HIGH COST OF LIVING (See Sandman #8) (Also see the Books of Magic limited & ongoing series)
DC Comics (Vertigo): Mar, 1993 - No. 3, May, 1993 ($1.95, limited series)

1-Bachalo/Buckingham-a; Dave McKean-c; Neil Gaiman scripts in all — 2.40 — 6.00
1-Platinum edition — 25.00
2 — 5.00
3-Pgs. 19 & 20 had wrong placement — 3.00
3-Corrected version w/pgs. 19 & 20 facing each other; has no-c & ads for Sebastion O & The Geek added — 4.00
Death Talks About Life-giveaway about AIDS prevention — 4.00
Hardcover (1994, $19.95)-r/#1-3 & Death Talks About Life; intro. by Tori Amos. — 20.00
Trade paperback (6/94, $12.95, Titan Books)-r/#1-3 & Death Talks About Life; prism-c — 13.00

DEATH: THE TIME OF YOUR LIFE (See Sandman #8)
DC Comics (Vertigo): Apr, 1996 - No. 3, July, 1996 ($2.95, limited series)

1-3: Neil Gaiman story & Bachalo/Buckingham-a; Dave McKean-c. 2-(5/96). — 3.00
Hardcover (1997, $19.95)-r/#1-3 w/3 new pages & gallery art by various artists — 20.00
Trade paperback (1997, $12.95)-r/#1-3 & Visions of Death gallery; Intro. by Claire Danes — 13.00

DEATH 3
Marvel Comics UK: Sept, 1993 - No. 4, Dec, 1993 ($1.75, limited series)

1-($2.95)-Embossed-c — 3.00
2-4 — 2.00

DEATH VALLEY (Cowboys and Indians)
Comic Media: Oct, 1953 - No. 6, Aug, 1954

GD2.0 FN6.0 NM9.4

	GD2.0	FN6.0	NM9.4
1-Billy the Kid; Morisi-a; Andru/Esposito-c/a	10.00	30.00	60.00
2-Don Heck-c	5.85	17.50	35.00
3-6: 3,5-Morisi-a. 5-Discount-a	5.00	15.00	30.00

DEATH VALLEY (Becomes Frontier Scout, Daniel Boone No.10-13)
Charlton Comics: No. 7, 6/55 - No. 9, 10/55 (Cont'd from Comic Media series)

	GD2.0	FN6.0	NM9.4
7-9: 8-Wolverton-a (half pg.)	5.00	15.00	30.00

DEATHWISH
DC Comics (Milestone Media): Dec, 1994 - No. 4, Mar, 1995 (2.50, lim. series)

1-4 — 2.50

DEATH WRECK
Marvel Comics UK: Jan, 1994 - No. 4, Apr, 1994 ($1.95, limited series)

1-4: 1-Metallic ink logo; Death's Head II app. — 2.00

DEBBIE DEAN, CAREER GIRL
Civil Service Publ.: April, 1945 - No. 2, July, 1945

	GD2.0	FN6.0	NM9.4
1,2-Newspaper reprints by Bert Whitman	12.00	36.00	85.00

DEBBI'S DATES (Also see Date With Debbi)
National Periodical Publications: Apr-May, 1969 - No. 11, Dec-Jan, 1970-71

	GD2.0	FN6.0	NM9.4
1	3.80	11.40	38.00
2,3,5,7-11	2.00	6.00	16.00
4-Neal Adams text illo	2.80	8.40	28.00
6-Superman cameo	4.00	12.00	40.00

DECADE OF DARK HORSE, A
Dark Horse Comics: Jul, 1996 - No. 4, Oct, 1996 ($2.95, B&W/color, lim. series)

1-4: 1-Sin City-c/story by Miller; Grendel by Wagner; Predator. 2-Star Wars wraparound-c. 3-Aliens-c/story; Nexus, Mask stories — 3.00

DECAPITATOR (Randy Bowen's...)
Dark Horse Comics: Jun, 1998 - No. 4, ($2.95)

1-4-Bowen-s/art by various. 1-Mahnke-c. 3-Jones-c — 4.00

DECEPTION, THE
Image Comics (Flypaper Press): 1999 - No. 3, 1999 ($2.95, B&W, mini-series)

1-3-Horley painted-c — 3.00

DEEP, THE (Movie)
Marvel Comics Group: Nov, 1977

1-Infantino-c/a — 3.00

DEEP DARK FANTASIES
Dark Fantasy Productions: Oct, 1995 ($4.50/$4.95, B&W)

1-($4.50)-Clive Barker-c, anthology — 4.50
1-($4.95)-Red foil logo-c — 5.00

DEFCON 4
Image Comics (WildStorm Productions): Feb, 1996 - No. 4, Sept, 1996 ($2.50, limited series)

	GD2.0	FN6.0	NM9.4
1/2	1.10	3.30	9.00
1/2 Gold-(1000 printed)			14.00
1-Main Cover by Mat Broome & Edwin Rosell			3.00
1-Hordes of Cymulants variant-c by Michael Golden			5.00
1-Backs to the Wall variant-c by Humberto Ramos & Alex Garner			5.00
1-Defcon 4-Way variant-c by Jim Lee	1.00	2.80	7.00
2-4			2.50

DEFENDERS, THE (TV)
Dell Publishing Co.: Sept-Nov, 1962 - No. 2, Feb-Apr, 1963

	GD2.0	FN6.0	NM9.4
12-176-211(#1)	3.20	9.50	35.00
12-176-304(#2)	2.50	7.50	28.00

DEFENDERS, THE (Also see Giant-Size..., Marvel Feature, Marvel Treasury Edition, Secret Defenders & Sub-Mariner #34, 35; The New...#140-on)
Marvel Comics Group: Aug, 1972 - No. 152, Feb, 1986

	GD2.0	FN6.0	NM9.4
1-The Hulk, Doctor Strange, Sub-Mariner begin	5.50	16.50	60.00
2-Silver Surfer x-over	3.00	9.00	30.00
3-5: 3-Silver Surfer x-over. 4-Valkyrie joins	2.50	7.50	20.00

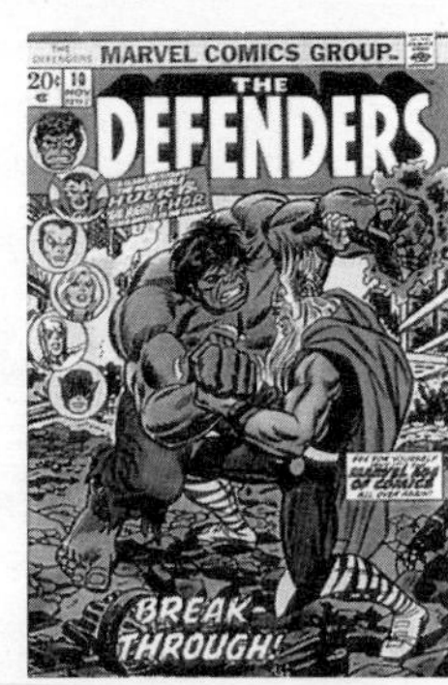

The Defenders #10 © MAR

Deity Preview © Hyperwerks

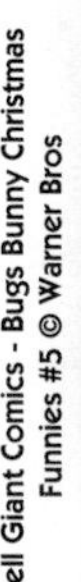
Dell Giant Comics - Bugs Bunny Christmas Funnies #5 © Warner Bros

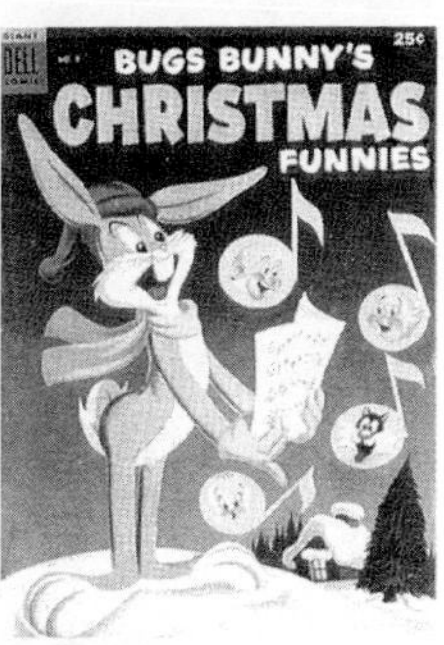

6,7: 6-Silver Surfer x-over 1.85 5.50 15.00
8,9,11: 8-11-Defenders vs. the Avengers (Crossover with Avengers #115-118)
8,11-Silver Surfer x-over 2.50 7.50 20.00
10-Hulk vs. Thor battle 2.50 7.50 25.00
12-14: 12-Last 20¢ issue 1.00 3.00 8.00
15,16-Magneto & Brotherhood of Evil Mutants app. from X-Men
1.25 3.75 10.00
17-20: 17-Power Man x-over (11/74) 2.40 6.00
21-25: 24,25-Son of Satan app. 5.00
26-29-Guardians of the Galaxy app. (#26 is 8/75; pre-dates Marvel Presents #3): 28-1st full app. Starhawk (cameo #27). 29-Starhawk joins Guardians
2.40 6.00
30-33,39-50: 31,32-Origin Nighthawk. 44-Hellcat joins. 45-Dr. Strange leaves. 47-49-Early Moon Knight app. (5/77) 4.00
34-38-(Regular 25¢ editions): 35-Intro New Red Guardian 4.00
34-38-(30¢-c variants, limited distribution)(4-8/76) 1.85 5.50 15.00
51-60: 53-1st app. Lunatik (cameo, Lobo lookalike). 55-Origin Red Guardian; Lunatik cameo. 56-1st full Lunatik story 3.00
61-75: 61-Lunatik & Spider-Man app. 70-73-Lunatik (origin #71). 73-75-Foolkiller II app. (Greg Salinger). 74-Nighthawk resigns 2.50
76-95,97-99,101-124,126-149,151: 77-Origin Omega. 78-Original Defenders return thru #101. 94-1st Gargoyle. 101-Silver Surfer-c & app. 104-The Beast joins. 105-Son of Satan joins. 106-Death of Nighthawk. 120,121-Son of Satan-c/stories. 122-Final app. Son of Satan (2 pgs.). 129-New Mutants cameo (3/84, early x-over) 2.00
96-Ghost Rider app. 4.00
100-(52 pgs.)-Hellcat (Patsy Walker) revealed as Satan's daughter 5.00
125,150: 125-(52 pgs.)-Intro new Defenders. 150-(52 pgs.)-Origin Cloud 4.00
152-(52 pgs.)-Ties in with X-Factor & Secret Wars II 2.50
Annual 1 (1976, 52 pgs.)-New book-length story 1.25 3.75 10.00

NOTE: ***Art Adams*** *c-142p.* ***Austin*** *a-53i; c-65i, 119i, 145i.* ***Frank Bolle*** *a-7i, 10i, 11i.* ***Buckler*** *c(p)-34, 38, 76, 77, 79-86, 90, 91.* ***J. Buscema*** *c-66.* ***Giffen*** *a-42-49p, 50, 51-54p.* ***Golden*** *a-53p, 54p; c-94, 96.* ***Guice*** *c-129.* ***G. Kane*** *c(p)-13, 16, 18, 19, 21-26, 31-33, 35-37, 40, 41, 52, 55.* ***Kirby*** *c-42-45.* ***Mooney*** *a-3i, 31-34i, 62i, 63i, 85i.* ***Nasser*** *c-88p.* ***Perez*** *c(p)-51, 53, 54.* ***Rogers*** *c-98.* ***Starlin*** *c-110.* ***Tuska*** *a-57p. Silver Surfer in No. 2, 3, 6, 8-11, 92, 98-101, 107, 112-115, 122-125.*

DEFENDERS OF DYNATRON CITY
Marvel Comics: Feb, 1992 - No. 6, July, 1992 ($1.25, limited series)
1-6-Lucasarts characters. 2-Origin 2.00

DEFENDERS OF THE EARTH (TV)
Marvel Comics (Star Comics): Jan, 1987 - No. 4, July, 1987
1-4: The Phantom, Mandrake The Magician, Flash Gordon begin. 3-Origin Phantom. 4-Origin Mandrake 3.00

DEFINITIVE DIRECTORY OF THE DC UNIVERSE, THE (See Who's Who...)

DEITY (Also see Kosmic Kat)
Hyperwerks Comics: Sept, 1997 - No. 6, Apr, 1998, ($2.95, limited series)
1-6, 0(5/98) 4.00
1-Variant-c 5.00
2-6,0-Variant covers 3.00
0-NDC Edition 4.00
0-NDC Silver Ed. 8.00
0-NDC Gold Ed. 12.00

DEITY (Volume 2)
Hyperwerks Comics: Sept, 1998 - No. 5 ($2.95)
Preview (6/98) Flip book with Lady Pendragon preview 3.00
1-5: 1-Flip book w/Catseye preview 3.00

DEITY:REVELATIONS (Volume 3)
Hyperwerks Comics: July, 1999 - Present ($2.95)
1-Alstaetter and Napton-s/a 3.00

DELECTA OF THE PLANETS (See Don Fortune & Fawcett Miniatures)

DELLA VISION (...The Television Queen) (Patty Powers #4 on)
Atlas Comics: April, 1955 - No. 3, Aug, 1955
1-Al Hartley-c 14.00 43.00 100.00

GD2.0 FN6.0 NM9.4

2,3 10.00 30.00 70.00

DELL GIANT COMICS

Dell Publishing began to release square bound comics in 1949 with a 132-page issue called Christmas Parade #1. The covers were of a heavier stock to accommodate the increased number of pages. The books proved profitable at 25 cents, but the average number of pages was quickly reduced to 100. Ten years later they were converted to a numbering system similar to the Four Color Comics, for greater ease in distribution and the page counts cut back to mostly 84 pages. The label "Dell Giant" began to appear on the covers in 1954. Because of the size of the books and the heavier, less pliant cover stock, they are rarely found in high grade condition, and with the exception of a small quantity of copies released from Western Publishing's warehouse–are almost never found in near mint.

	GD2.0	FN6.0	VF8.0	NM9.4
Abraham Lincoln Life Story 1(3/58)	5.00	15.00	30.00	90.00
Bugs Bunny Christmas Funnies 1(11/50, 116pp)	13.50	40.50	91.00	240.00
...Christmas Funnies 2(11/51, 116pp)	9.00	27.00	54.00	160.00
...Christmas Funnies 3-5(11/52-11/54,)-Becomes Christmas Party #6	8.00	24.00	48.00	145.00
...Christmas Funnies 7-9(12/56-12/58)	7.00	21.00	42.00	130.00
...Christmas Party 6(11/55)-Formerly Bugs Bunny Christmas Funnies	6.00	18.00	36.00	105.00
...County Fair 1(9/57)	9.00	27.00	54.00	160.00
...Halloween Parade 1(10/53)	8.50	25.50	51.00	150.00
...Halloween Parade 2(10/54)-Trick 'N' Treat Halloween Fun #3 on	7.00	21.00	42.00	130.00
...Trick 'N' Treat Halloween Fun 3,4(10/55-10/56)-Formerly Halloween Parade #2	8.00	24.00	48.00	140.00
...Vacation Funnies 1(7/51, 112pp)	13.50	40.50	81.00	240.00
...Vacation Funnies 2('52)	10.50	31.50	63.00	190.00
...Vacation Funnies 3-5('53-'55)	8.00	24.00	48.00	145.00
...Vacation Funnies 6-9('54-6/59)	7.00	21.00	42.00	130.00
Cadet Gray of West Point 1(4/58)-Williamson-a, 10pgs.; Buscema-a; photo-c	5.00	15.00	30.00	90.00
Christmas In Disneyland 1(12/57)-Barks-a, 18 pgs.	21.00	63.00	126.00	380.00
Christmas Parade 1(11/49)(132 pgs.)(1st Dell Giant)-Donald Duck (25pgs. by Barks, r-in G.K. Christmas Parade #5); Mickey Mouse & other film oriented stories; Cinderella (prior to movie), 7 Dwarfs, Bambi & Thumper, So Dear To My Heart, Flying Mouse, Dumbo, Cookieland & others	47.00	141.00	282.00	850.00
Christmas Parade 2('50)-Donald Duck (132 pgs.)(25 pgs. by Barks, r-in G.K. Christmas Parade #6). Mickey, Pluto, Chip & Dale, etc. Contents shift to a holiday expansion of W.D. C&S type format	36.00	108.00	216.00	650.00
Christmas Parade 3-7('51-'55, #3-116pgs; #4-7, 100 pgs.)	10.00	30.00	60.00	180.00
Christmas Parade 8(12/56)-Barks-a, 8 pgs.	18.00	54.00	108.00	320.00
Christmas Parade 9(12/58)-Barks-a, 20 pgs.	21.00	63.00	126.00	380.00
Christmas Treasury, A 1(11/54)	6.50	19.50	40.00	115.00
Davy Crockett, King Of The Wild Frontier 1(9/55)-Fess Parker photo-c; Marsh-a	14.50	43.50	87.00	260.00
Disneyland Birthday Party 1(10/58)-Barks-a, 16 pgs. r-by Gladstone	21.00	63.00	126.00	380.00
Donald and Mickey In Disneyland 1(5/58)	9.00	27.00	54.00	160.00
Donald Duck Beach Party 1(7/54)-Has an Uncle Scrooge story (not by Barks) that prefigures the later rivalry with Flintheart Glomgold and tells of Scrooge's wild rivalry with another millionaire	11.00	33.00	66.00	200.00
...Beach Party 2(1955)-Lady & Tramp	8.50	25.50	50.00	150.00
...Beach Party 3-5(1956-58)	8.50	25.50	50.00	150.00
...Beach Party 6(8/59, 84pp)-Stapled	5.50	16.50	33.00	100.00
Donald Duck Fun Book 1,2(1953 & 10/54)-Games, puzzles, comics & cut-outs (very rare in unused condition)(most copies commonly have defaced interior pgs.)	30.50	91.50	183.00	550.00

Dell Giant Comics - Pogo Parade © Walt Kelly

Dell Giant Comics - Peter Pan Treasure Chest © WDC

Dell Giant Comics - Summer Fun #2 © WDC

GD2.0 FN6.0 NM9.4

Donald Duck In Disneyland 1(9/55)-1st Disneyland Dell Giant
11.00 33.00 66.00 200.00
Golden West Rodeo Treasury 1(10/57) 7.00 21.00 42.00 125.00
Huey, Dewey and Louie Back To School 1(9/58)
7.00 21.00 42.00 120.00
Lady and The Tramp 1(6/55) 14.00 42.00 84.00 250.00
Life Stories of American Presidents 1(11/57)-Buscema-a
4.00 12.00 24.00 75.00
Lone Ranger Golden West 3(8/55)-Formerly Lone Ranger Western Treasury
14.50 43.50 87.00 260.00
Lone Ranger Movie Story nn(3/56)-Origin Lone Ranger in text; Clayton Moore photo-c 27.00 81.00 162.00 490.00
...Western Treasury 1(9/53)-Origin Lone Ranger, Silver, & Tonto; painted cover
16.00 48.00 96.00 290.00
...Western Treasury 2(8/54)-Becomes Lone Ranger Golden West #3
10.50 31.50 63.00 185.00
Marge's Little Lulu & Alvin Story Telling Time 1(3/59)-r/#2,5,3,11,30,10,21,17,8, 14,16; Stanley-a 11.00 33.00 66.00 195.00
...& Her Friends 4(3/56)-Tripp-a 9.00 27.00 54.00 165.00
...& Her Special Friends 3(3/55)-Tripp-a 11.00 33.00 66.00 200.00
...& Tubby At Summer Camp 5,2: 5(10/57)-Tripp-a. 2(10/58)-Tripp-a
9.00 27.00 54.00 165.00
...& Tubby Halloween Fun 6,2: 6(10/57)-Tripp-a. 2(10/58)-Tripp-a
9.00 27.00 54.00 165.00
...& Tubby In Alaska 1(7/59)-Tripp-a 9.00 27.00 54.00 165.00
...On Vacation 1(7/54)-r/4C-110,14,4C-146,5,4C-97,4,4C-158,3,1;Stanley-a
20.00 60.00 120.00 360.00
...& Tubby Annual 1(3/53)-r/4C-165,4C-74,4C-146,4C-97,4C-158, 4C-139, 4C-131; Stanley-a (1st Lulu Dell Gnt) 24.50 73.50 147.00 435.00
...& Tubby Annual 2('54)-r/4C-139,6,4C-115,4C-74,5,4C-97,3,4C-146,18; Stanley-a 21.50 64.50 130.00 390.00
Marge's Tubby & His Clubhouse Pals 1(10/56)-1st app. Gran'pa Feeb;1st app. Janie; written by Stanley; Tripp-a 10.50 31.50 63.00 190.00
Mickey Mouse Almanac 1(12/57)-Barks-a, 8pgs.
21.50 64.50 130.00 390.00
...Birthday Party 1(9/53)-r/entire 48pgs. of Gottfredson's "Mickey Mouse in Love Trouble" from WDC&S 36-39. Quality equal to original. Also reprints one story each from 4-Color 27, 29, & 181 plus 6 panels of highlights in the career of Mickey Mouse 26.00 78.00 156.00 470.00
...Club Parade 1(12/55)-r/4-Color 16 with some death trap scenes redrawn by Paul Murry & recolored with night turned into day; quality less than original
20.00 60.00 120.00 360.00
...In Fantasy Land 1(5/57) 10.00 30.00 60.00 180.00
...In Frontier Land 1(5/56)-Mickey Mouse Club issue
10.00 30.00 60.00 180.00
...Summer Fun 1(8/58)-Mobile cut-outs on back-c; becomes Summer Fun with #2 10.00 30.00 60.00 180.00
Moses & The Ten Commandments 1(8/57)-Not based on movie; Dell's adaptation; Sekowsky-a 4.00 12.00 24.00 70.00
Nancy & Sluggo Travel Time 1(9/58) 5.50 16.50 33.00 95.00
Peter Pan Treasure Chest 1(1/53, 212pp)-Disney; contains 54-page movie adaptation & other P. Pan stories; plus Donald & Mickey stories w/P. Pan; a 32-page retelling of "D. Duck Finds Pirate Gold" with yellow beak, called "Capt. Hook & the Buried Treasure" 83.50 250.00 500.00 1500.00
Picnic Party 6,7(7/55-6/56)(Formerly Vacation Parade)-Uncle Scrooge, Mickey & Donald 8.50 25.50 50.00 150.00
Picnic Party 8(7/57)-Barks-a, 6pgs 18.00 54.00 108.00 320.00
Pogo Parade 1(9/53)-Kelly-a(r-/Pogo from Animal Comics in this order: #11,13,21,14,27,16,23,9,18,15,17) 23.50 70.50 141.00 425.00
Raggedy Ann & Andy 1(2/55) 12.00 36.00 72.00 220.00
Santa Claus Funnies 1(11/52)-Dan Noonan -A Christmas Carol adaptation
6.50 19.50 39.00 115.00
Silly Symphonies 1(9/52)-Redrawing of Gotfredson's Mickey Mouse strip of "The Brave Little Tailor;" 2 Good Housekeeping pages (from 1943); Lady and the Two Siamese Cats, three years before "Lady & the Tramp;" a retelling of Donald Duck's first app. in "The Wise Little Hen" & other stories based on 1930's Silly Symphony cartoons 23.50 70.50 141.00 425.00

GD2.0 FN6.0 NM9.4

Silly Symphonies 2(9/53)-M. Mouse in "The Sorcerer's Apprentice", 2 Good Housekeeping pages (from 1944); The Pelican & the Snipe, Elmer Elephant, Peculiar Penguins, Little Hiawatha, & others
21.00 63.00 126.00 380.00
Silly Symphonies 3(2/54)-r/Mickey & The Beanstalk (4-Color #157, 39pgs.), Little Minnehaha, Pablo, The Flying Gauchito, Pluto, & Bongo, & 2 Good Housekeeping pages (1944) 18.00 54.00 108.00 320.00
Silly Symphonies 4(8/54)-r/Dumbo (4-Color 234), Morris The Midget Moose, The Country Cousin, Bongo, & Clara Cluck
18.00 54.00 108.00 320.00
Silly Symphonies 5-8: 5(2/55)-r/Cinderella (4-Color 272), Bucky Bug, Pluto, Little Hiawatha, The 7 Dwarfs & Dumbo, Pinocchio. 6(8/55)-r/Pinocchio (WDC&S 63), The 7 Dwarfs & Thumper (WDC&S 45), M. Mouse "Adventures With Robin Hood" (40 pgs.), Johnny Appleseed, Pluto & Peter Pan, & Bucky Bug; Cut-out on back-c. 7(2/57)-r/Reluctant Dragon, Ugly Duckling, M. Mouse & Peter Pan, Jiminy Cricket, Peter & The Wolf, Brer Rabbit, Bucky Bug; Cut-out on back-c. 8(2/58)-r/Thumper Meets The 7 Dwarfs (4-Color #19), Jiminy Cricket, Niok, Brer Rabbit; Cut-out on back-c
15.00 45.00 90.00 270.00
Silly Symphonies 9(2/59)-r/Paul Bunyan, Humphrey Bear, Jiminy Cricket, The Social Lion, Goliath II; cut-out on back-c
14.00 42.00 84.00 250.00
Sleeping Beauty 1(4/59) 23.50 70.50 141.00 425.00
Summer Fun 2(8/59, 84pp, stapled binding)(Formerly Mickey Mouse...)-Barks-a(2), 24 pgs. 21.00 63.00 126.00 380.00
Tarzan's Jungle Annual 1(8/52)-Lex Barker photo on-c of #1,2
11.00 33.00 66.00 200.00
...Annual 2(8/53) 8.50 25.50 50.00 150.00
...Annual 3-7('54-9/58)(two No. 5s)-Manning-a-No. 3,5-7; Marsh-a in No. 1-7 plus painted-c 1-7 7.00 21.00 42.00 125.00
Tom And Jerry Back To School 1(9/56) 10.50 31.50 63.00 190.00
...Picnic Time 1(7/58) 8.00 24.00 48.00 145.00
...Summer Fun 1(7/54)-Droopy written by Barks
13.00 39.00 78.00 230.00
...Summer Fun 2-4(7/55-7/57) 5.50 16.50 32.00 95.00
...Toy Fair 1(6/58) 8.00 24.00 48.00 145.00
...Winter Carnival 1(12/52)-Droopy written by Barks
18.00 54.00 108.00 320.00
...Winter Carnival 2(12/53)-Droopy written by Barks
15.00 45.00 90.00 265.00
...Winter Fun 3(12/54) 5.50 16.50 31.00 95.00
...Winter Fun 4-7(12/55-11/58) 4.50 13.50 27.00 80.00
Treasury of Dogs, A 1(10/56) 4.50 13.50 28.00 85.00
Treasury of Horses, A (9/55) 4.50 13.50 28.00 85.00
Uncle Scrooge Goes To Disneyland 1(8/57p)-Barks-a, 20pgs.r-by Gladstone
21.00 63.00 126.00 380.00
Vacation In Disneyland 1(8/58) 9.00 27.00 54.00 160.00
Vacation Parade 1(7/50, 132pp)-Donald Duck & Mickey Mouse; Barks-a, 55 pgs. 66.50 200.00 400.00 1200.00
Vacation Parade 2(7/51,116pp) 22.00 66.00 133.00 400.00
Vacation Parade 3-5(7/52-7/54)-Becomes Picnic Party No. 6 on. #4-Robin Hood Advs. 10.50 31.50 63.00 190.00
Western Roundup 1(6/52)-Photo-c; Gene Autry, Roy Rogers, Johnny Mack Brown, Rex Allen, & Bill Elliott begin; photo back-c begin, end No. 14,16,18
19.50 58.50 117.00 350.00
Western Roundup 2(2/53)-Photo-c 10.50 31.00 62.00 190.00
Western Roundup 3-5(7-9/53 - 1-3/54)-Photo-c
8.50 25.50 50.00 150.00
Western Roundup 6-10(4-6/54 - 4-6/55)-Photo-c
8.00 24.00 48.00 140.00
Western Roundup 11-17,25-Photo-c; 11-13,16,17-Manning-a. 11-Flying A's Range Rider, Dale Evans begin 7.00 21.00 42.00 130.00
Western Roundup 18-Toth-a; last photo-c; Gene Autry ends
7.50 22.50 45.00 135.00
Western Roundup 19-24-Manning-a. 19-Buffalo Bill Jr. begins (7-9/57; early app.). 19,20,22-Toth-a. 21-Rex Allen, Johnny Mack Brown end. 22-Jace Pearson's Texas Rangers, Rin Tin Tin, Tales of Wells Fargo (2nd app., 4-6/58) &

Dell Giant Comics #23 © DELL

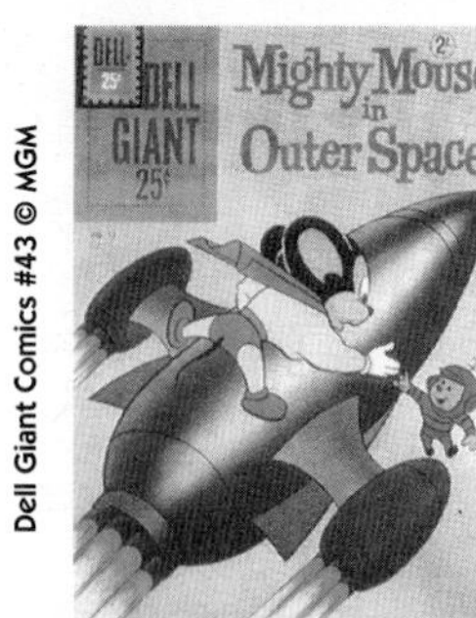

Dell Giant Comics #43 © MGM

The Demon (2nd series) #18 © DC

GD2.0 FN6.0 NM9.4

Wagon Train (2nd app.) begin 6.50 19.00 38.00 115.00
Woody Woodpecker Back To School 1(10/52)
8.00 24.00 48.00 140.00
...Back To School 2-4,6('53-10/57)-County Fair No. 5
5.50 16.50 32.00 95.00
...County Fair 5(9/56)-Formerly Back To School
5.50 16.50 32.00 95.00
...County Fair 2(11/58) 4.50 13.50 27.00 80.00

DELL GIANTS (Consecutive numbering)
Dell Publishing Co.: No. 21, Sept, 1959 - No. 55, Sept, 1961 (Most 84 pgs., 25¢)

21-(#1)-M.G.M.'s Tom & Jerry Picnic Time (84pp, stapled binding)-Painted-c
9.00 27.00 54.00 160.00
22-Huey, Dewey & Louie Back to School (Disney; 10/59, 84pp, square binding begins) 6.50 19.50 40.00 120.00
23-Marge's Little Lulu & Tubby Halloween Fun (10/59)-Tripp-a
9.00 27.00 54.00 160.00
24-Woody Woodpecker's Family Fun (11/59)(Walter Lantz)
6.50 19.50 39.00 115.00
25-Tarzan's Jungle World(11/59)-Marsh-a; painted-c
8.50 25.50 50.00 150.00
26-Christmas Parade(Disney; 12/59)-Barks-a, 16pgs.; Barks draws himself on wanted poster pg. 13 18.00 54.00 108.00 320.00
27-Man in Space r-/4-Color 716,866, & 954 (100 pgs., 35¢)(Disney)(TV)
8.00 24.00 48.00 145.00
28-Bugs Bunny's Winter Fun (2/60) 8.00 24.00 48.00 145.00
29-Marge's Little Lulu & Tubby in Hawaii (4/60)-Tripp-a
8.50 25.50 50.00 150.00
30-Disneyland USA(Disney; 6/60) 7.00 21.00 42.00 130.00
31-Huckleberry Hound Summer Fun (7/60)(TV)(HannaBarbera)-Yogi Bear & Pixie & Dixie app. 10.50 31.50 63.00 190.00
32-Bugs Bunny Beach Party 4.50 13.50 27.00 85.00
33-Daisy Duck & Uncle Scrooge Picnic Time (Disney; 9/60)
7.00 21.00 42.00 130.00
34-Nancy & Sluggo Summer Camp (8/60)
5.50 16.50 33.00 100.00
35-Huey, Dewey & Louie Back to School (Disney; 10/60)-1st app. Daisy Duck's Nieces, April, May & June 8.50 25.50 50.00 150.00
36-Marge's Little Lulu & Witch Hazel Halloween Fun (10/60)-Tripp-a
8.50 25.50 50.00 150.00
37-Tarzan, King of the Jungle (11/60)-Marsh-a; painted-c
8.00 24.00 48.00 140.00
38-Uncle Donald & His Nephews Family Fun (Disney; 11/60)-Cover painting based on a pencil sketch by Barks 10.50 31.50 63.00 190.00
39-Walt Disney's Merry Christmas (Disney; 12/60)-Cover painting based on a pencil sketch by Barks 10.50 31.50 63.00 190.00
40-Woody Woodpecker Christmas Parade (12/60)(Walter Lantz)
4.50 13.50 27.00 85.00
41-Yogi Bear's Winter Sports (12/60)(TV)(Hanna-Barbera)-Huckleberry Hound, Pixie & Dixie, Augie Doggie app. 10.50 31.50 63.00 190.00
42-Marge's Little Lulu & Tubby in Australia (4/61)
9.00 27.00 54.00 160.00
43-Mighty Mouse in Outer Space (5/61) 17.00 51.00 102.00 305.00
44-Around the World with Huckleberry and His Friends (7/61)(TV)(Hanna-Barbera)-Yogi Bear, Pixie & Dixie, Quick Draw McGraw, Augie Doggie app.; 1st app. Yakky Doodle 10.50 31.50 63.00 190.00
45-Nancy & Sluggo Summer Camp (8/61)
4.50 13.50 27.00 85.00
46-Bugs Bunny Beach Party (8/61) 4.50 13.50 27.00 85.00
47-Mickey & Donald in Vacationland (Disney; 8/61)
6.50 19.50 40.00 120.00
48-The Flintstones (No. 1)(Bedrock Bedlam)(7/61)(TV)(Hanna-Barbera) 1st app. in comics 16.00 48.00 95.00 285.00
49-Huey, Dewey & Louie Back to School (Disney; 9/61)
6.50 19.50 40.00 120.00
50-Marge's Little Lulu & Witch Hazel Trick 'N' Treat (10/61)
8.50 25.50 50.00 150.00
51-Tarzan, King of the Jungle by Jesse Marsh (11/61)-Painted-c
6.00 18.00 35.00 105.00
52-Uncle Donald & His Nephews Dude Ranch (Disney; 11/61)
5.50 16.50 33.00 100.00
53-Donald Duck Merry Christmas (Disney; 12/61)
5.50 16.50 33.00 100.00
54-Woody Woodpecker's Christmas Party (12/61)-Issued after No. 55
5.50 16.50 33.00 100.00
55-Daisy Duck & Uncle Scrooge Showboat (Disney; 9/61)
6.50 19.50 40.00 120.00
NOTE: All issues printed with & without ad on back cover.

DELL JUNIOR TREASURY
Dell Publishing Co.: June, 1955 - No. 10, Oct, 1957 (15¢) (All painted-c)

	GD2.0	FN6.0	NM9.4
1-Alice in Wonderland; r/4-Color #331 (52 pgs.)	9.50	28.50	105.00
2-Aladdin & the Wonderful Lamp	6.35	19.00	70.00
3-Gulliver's Travels (1/56)	5.50	16.50	60.00
4-Adventures of Mr. Frog & Miss Mouse	6.00	18.00	65.00
5-The Wizard of Oz (7/56)	6.35	19.00	70.00
6-10: 6-Heidi (10/56). 7-Santa and the Angel. 8-Raggedy Ann and the Camel with the Wrinkled Knees. 9-Clementina the Flying Pig. 10-Adventures of Tom Sawyer	5.50	16.50	60.00

DEMOLITION MAN
DC Comics: Nov, 1993 - No. 4, Feb, 1994 ($1.75, color, limited series)

1-4-Movie adaptation 2.00

DEMON, THE (See Detective Comics No. 482-485)
National Periodical Publications: Aug-Sept, 1972 - V3#16, Jan, 1974

1-Origin; Kirby-c/a in all 2.50 7.50 20.00
2-5 1.25 3.75 10.00
6-16 2.40 6.00

DEMON, THE (1st limited series)(Also see Cosmic Odyssey #2)
DC Comics: Nov, 1986 - No. 4, Feb, 1987 (75¢, limited series)
(#2 has #4 of 4 on-c)

1-4: Matt Wagner-a(p) & scripts in all. 4-Demon & Jason Blood become separate entities. 2.50

DEMON, THE (2nd Series)
DC Comics: July, 1990 - No. 57, May, 1995 ($1.50/$1.75/$1.95)

1-Grant scripts begin, ends #39: 1-4-Painted-c 4.00
2-42,46,47: 3,8-Batman app. (cameo #4). 12-Bisley painted-c. 12-15,21-Lobo app. (1 pg. cameo #11). 19-($2.50, 44 pgs.)-Lobo poster stapled inside. 23-Robin app. 28-Superman-c/story; begin $1.75-c. 29-Superman app. 31, 33-39-Lobo app. 40-Garth Ennis scripts begin. 2.50
43-45-Hitman app. 2.40 6.00
46-48 Return of The Haunted Tank-c/s. 48-Begin $1.95-c. 4.00
49,51,0-(10/94),55-57: 51-(9/94) 2.50
50 ($2.95, 52 pgs.) 3.00
52-54-Hitman-s 4.00
Annual 1 (1992, $3.00, 68 pgs.)-Eclipso-c/story 3.00
Annual 2 (1993, $3.50, 68 pgs.)-1st app. of Hitman 1.85 5.50 15.00
NOTE: *Alan Grant scripts in #1-16, 20, 21, 23-25, 30-39, Annual 1.* ***Wagner*** *a/scripts-22.*

DEMON DREAMS
Pacific Comics: Feb, 1984 - No. 2, May, 1984

1,2-Mostly r-/Heavy Metal 2.00

DEMONGATE
Sirius Entertainment: May, 1996 - Present ($2.50, B&W)

1-10-Bao Lin Hum/Steve Blevins-s/a 2.50

DEMON GUN
Crusade Ent.: June, 1996 - No. 3, Jan, 1997 ($2.95, B&W, limited series)

1-3: Gary Cohn scripts in all. 2-(10/96) 3.00

DEMON-HUNTER
Seaboard Periodicals (Atlas): Sept, 1975

Dennis the Menace #2 © FAW

Dennis the Menace #98 © FAW

Dennis the Menace and His Friends #21 © FAW

	GD2.0	FN6.0	NM9.4
1-Origin; Buckler-c/a			4.00

DEMON KNIGHT: A GRIMJACK GRAPHIC NOVEL
First Publishing: 1990 ($8.95, 52 pgs.)

nn-Flint Henry-a			9.00

DENNIS THE MENACE (TV with 1959 issues) (Becomes ...Fun Fest Series; See The Best of... & The Very Best of...)(...Fun Fest on-c only to #156-166)
Standard Comics/Pines No.15-31/Hallden (Fawcett) No.32 on: 8/53 - #14, 1/56; #15, 3/56 - #31, 11/58; #32, 1/59 - #166, 11/79

1-1st app. Dennis, Mr. & Mrs. Wilson, Ruff & Dennis' mom & dad; Wiseman-a, written by Fred Toole-most issues	51.00	154.00	410.00
2	26.00	79.00	185.00
3-10: 8-Last pre-code issue	15.00	45.00	105.00
11-20	11.50	34.00	80.00
21-30: 22-1st app. Margaret w/blonde hair	9.15	27.00	55.00
31-1st app. Joey	6.70	20.00	40.00
32-40(1/60): 37-A-Bomb blast panel. 39-1st app. Gina (11/59)	5.35	16.00	32.00
41-60(7/62)	2.50	7.50	20.00
61-80(9/65),100(1/69)	1.75	5.25	14.00
81-99	1.50	4.50	12.00
101-117: 102-Last 12¢ issue	1.00	3.00	8.00
118(1/72)-131 (All 52 pages)	1.10	3.30	9.00
132(1/74)-166		2.40	6.00

NOTE: ***Wiseman** c/a-1-46, 53, 68, 69.*

DENNIS THE MENACE (Giants) (No. 1 titled Giant Vacation Special; becomes Dennis the Menace Bonus Magazine No. 76 on)
(#1-8,18,23,25,30,38: 100 pgs.; rest to #41: 84 pgs.; #42-75: 68 pgs.)
Standard/Pines/Hallden(Fawcett): Summer, 1955 - No. 75, Dec, 1969

nn-Giant Vacation Special(Summ/55-Standard)	19.00	56.00	130.00
nn-Christmas issue (Winter '55)	16.00	47.00	110.00
2-Giant Vacation Special (Summer '56-Pines)	14.00	43.00	100.00
3-Giant Christmas issue (Winter '56-Pines)	13.00	39.00	90.00
4-Giant Vacation Special (Summer '57-Pines)	12.00	36.00	85.00
5-Giant Christmas issue (Winter '57-Pines)	12.00	36.00	85.00
6-In Hawaii (Giant Vacation Special)(Summer '58-Pines)	11.50	34.00	80.00
6-In Hawaii (Summer '59-Hallden)-2nd printing; says 3rd large printing on-c 6-In Hawaii (Summer '60)-3rd printing; says 4th large printing on-c 6-In Hawaii (Summer '62)-4th printing; says 5th large printing on-c each....	8.35	25.00	50.00
6-Giant Christmas issue (Winter '58)	11.00	33.00	75.00
7-In Hollywood (Winter '59-Hallden)	5.00	15.00	50.00
7-In Hollywood (Summer '61)-2nd printing	3.50	10.50	35.00
8-In Mexico (Winter '60, 100 pgs.-Hallden/Fawcett)	5.00	15.00	50.00
8-In Mexico (Summer '62, 2nd printing)	3.50	10.50	35.00
9-Goes to Camp (Summer '61, 84 pgs.)-1st CCA approved issue	5.00	15.00	50.00
9-Goes to Camp (Summer '62)-2nd printing	3.50	10.50	35.00
10-12: 10-X-Mas issue (Winter '61), 11-Giant Christmas issue (Winter '62), 12-Triple Feature (Winter '62)	5.50	16.50	55.00
13-17: 13-Best of Dennis the Menace (Spring '63)-Reprints, 14-And His Dog Ruff (Summer '63), 15-In Washington, D.C. (Summer '63), 16-Goes to Camp (Summer '63)-Reprints No. 9, 17-& His Pal Joey (Winter '63)	3.00	9.00	30.00
18-In Hawaii (Reprints No. 6)	2.50	7.50	25.00
19-Giant Christmas issue (Winter '63)	3.50	10.50	35.00
20-Spring Special (Spring '64)	3.50	10.50	35.00
21-40 (Summer '66): 30-r/#6	2.50	7.50	20.00
41-60 (Fall '68)	1.75	5.25	14.00
61-75 (12/69): 68-Partial-r/#6	1.50	4.50	12.00

NOTE: ***Wiseman** c/a-1-8, 12, 14, 15, 17, 20, 22, 27, 28, 31, 35, 36, 41, 49.*

DENNIS THE MENACE
Marvel Comics Group: Nov, 1981 - No. 13, Nov, 1982

1-New-a		2.40	6.00
2-13: 2-New art. 3-Part-r. 4,5-r. 5-X-Mas-c & issue, 7-Spider Kid-c/sty			4.00

NOTE: ***Hank Ketcham** c-most; a-3, 12. **Wiseman** a-4, 5.*

DENNIS THE MENACE AND HIS DOG RUFF
Hallden/Fawcett: Summer, 1961

1-Wiseman-c/a	6.50	19.50	45.00

DENNIS THE MENACE AND HIS FRIENDS
Fawcett Publ.: 1969; No. 5, Jan, 1970 - No. 46, April, 1980 (All reprints)

Dennis the Menace & Joey No. 2 (7/69)	2.00	6.00	16.00
Dennis the Menace & Ruff No. 2 (9/69)	2.00	6.00	16.00
Dennis the Menace & Mr. Wilson No. 1 (10/69)	2.50	7.50	22.00
Dennis & Margaret No. 1 (Winter '69)	2.50	7.50	22.00
5-20: 5-Dennis the Menace & Margaret. 6-...& Joey. 7-...& Ruff. 8-...& Mr. Wilson	1.10	3.30	9.00
21-37	1.00	2.80	7.00
38-46 (Digest size, 148 pgs., 4/78, 95¢)	1.10	3.30	9.00

NOTE: *Titles rotate every four issues, beginning with No. 5.*

DENNIS THE MENACE AND HIS PAL JOEY
Fawcett Publ.: Summer, 1961 (10¢) (See Dennis the Menace Giants No. 45)

1-Wiseman-c/a	6.50	19.50	45.00

DENNIS THE MENACE AND THE BIBLE KIDS
Word Books: 1977 (36 pgs.)

1-10: 1-Jesus. 2-Joseph. 3-David. 4-The Bible Girls. 5-Moses. 6-More About Jesus. 7-The Lord's Prayer. 8-Stories Jesus told. 9-Paul, God's Traveller. 10-In the Beginning		2.40	6.00

NOTE: ***Ketcham** c/a in all.*

DENNIS THE MENACE BIG BONUS SERIES
Fawcett Publications: No. 10, Feb, 1980 - No. 11, Apr, 1980

10,11			5.00

DENNIS THE MENACE BONUS MAGAZINE (Formerly Dennis the Menace Giants Nos. 1-75)(...Big Bonus Series on-c for #174-194)
Fawcett Publications: No. 76, 1/70 - No. 95, 7/71; No. 95, 7/71; No. 97, '71; No. 194, 10/79; (No. 76-124: 68 pgs.; No. 125-163: 52 pgs.; No. 164 on: 36 pgs.)

76-90(3/71)	1.10	3.30	9.00
91-95, 97-110(10/72): Two #95's with same date(7/71) A-Summer Games, and B-That's Our Boy. No #96	1.00	3.00	8.00
111-150		2.40	6.00
151-194: 166-Indicia printed backwards			5.00

DENNIS THE MENACE COMICS DIGEST
Marvel Comics Group: April, 1982 - No. 3, Aug, 1982 ($1.25, digest-size)

1-3-Reprints	1.00	3.00	8.00
1-Mistakenly printed with DC emblem on cover	1.50	4.50	12.00

NOTE: ***Ketcham** c-all. **Wiseman** a-all. A few thousand #1's were published with a DC emblem on cover.*

DENNIS THE MENACE FUN BOOK
Fawcett Publications/Standard Comics: 1960 (100 pgs.)

1-Part Wiseman-a	6.00	18.00	60.00

DENNIS THE MENACE FUN FEST SERIES (Formerly Dennis the Menace #166)
Hallden (Fawcett): No. 16, Jan, 1980 - No. 17, Mar, 1980 (40¢)

16,17-By Hank Ketcham			3.00

DENNIS THE MENACE POCKET FULL OF FUN!
Fawcett Publications (Hallden): Spring, 1969 - No. 50, March, 1980 (196 pgs.) (Digest size)(Scarce in VF or better)

1-Reprints in all issues	4.00	12.00	40.00
2-10	2.50	7.50	25.00
11-20	2.00	6.00	16.00
21-28	1.25	3.75	10.00
29-50: 35,40,46-Sunday strip-r	1.00	2.80	7.00

NOTE: *No. 1-28 are 196 pgs.; No. 29-36: 164 pgs.; No. 37: 148 pgs.; No. 38 on: 132 pgs. No. 8, 11, 15, 21, 25, 29 all contain strip reprints.*

DENNIS THE MENACE TELEVISION SPECIAL

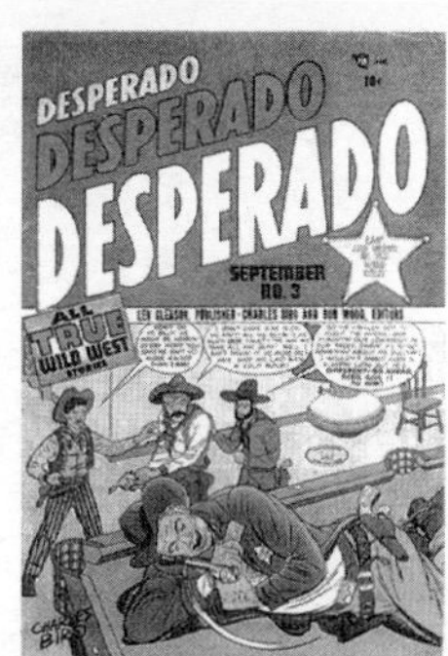

Desperado #3 © LEV

Desperados #5 © Aegis Ent.

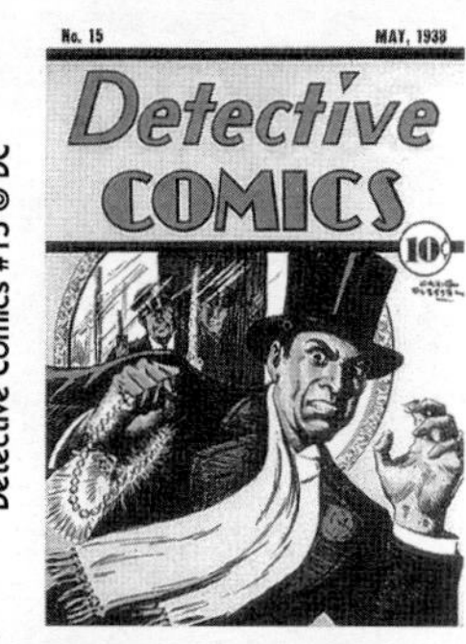

Detective Comics #15 © DC

Fawcett Publ. (Hallden Div.): Summer, 1961 - No. 2, Spring, 1962 (Giant)

1 5.50 16.50 55.00
2 3.00 9.00 30.00

DENNIS THE MENACE TRIPLE FEATURE
Fawcett Publications: Winter, 1961 (Giant)

1-Wiseman-c/a 5.50 16.50 55.00

DEPUTY, THE (TV)
Dell Publishing Co.: No. 1077, Feb-Apr, 1960 - No. 1225, Oct-Dec, 1961 (all-Henry Fonda photo-c)

Four Color 1077 (#1)-Buscema-a 12.00 35.00 130.00
Four Color 1130 (9-11/60)-Buscema-a,1225 9.00 27.00 100.00

DEPUTY DAWG (TV) (Also see New Terrytoons)
Dell Publishing Co./Gold Key: Oct-Dec, 1961 - No. 1299, 1962; No. 1, Aug, 1965

Four Color 1238,1299 10.00 30.00 110.00
1(10164-508)(8/65)-Gold Key 10.00 30.00 120.00

DEPUTY DAWG PRESENTS DINKY DUCK AND HASHIMOTO-SAN (TV)
Gold Key: August, 1965

1(10159-508) 9.50 286.00 105.00

DESERT GOLD (See Zane Grey 4-Color 467)

DESIGN FOR SURVIVAL (Gen. Thomas S. Power's...)
American Security Council Press: 1968 (36 pgs. in color) (25¢)

nn-Propaganda against the Threat of Communism-Aircraft cover; H-Bomb panel 2.50 7.50 20.00
Twin Circle Edition-Cover shows panels from inside 1.50 4.50 12.00

DESPERADO (Becomes Black Diamond Western No. 9 on)
Lev Gleason Publications: June, 1948 - No. 8, Feb, 1949 (All 52 pgs.)

1-Biro-c on all; contains inside photo-c of Charles Biro, Lev Gleason & Bob Wood 13.00 39.00 90.00
2 7.50 22.50 45.00
3-Story with over 20 killings 8.00 24.00 48.00
4-8 5.85 17.50 35.00

NOTE: ***Barry** a-2. **Fuje** a-4, 8. **Guardineer** a-5-7. **Kida** a-3-7. **Ed Moore** a-4, 6.*

DESPERADOES
Image Comics (Homage): Sept, 1997 - No. 5, June, 1998 ($2.50/$2.95)

1-Mariotte-s/Cassaday-c/a 3.00
2-5-($2.95) 3.00
...: A Moment's Sunlight TPB ('98, $16.95) r/#1-5 17.00

DESPERATE TIMES (See Savage Dragon)
Image Comics: Jun, 1998 - No. 4, Dec, 1998 ($2.95, B&W)

1-4-Chris Eliopoulos-s/a 3.00

DESTINATION MOON (See Fawcett Movie Comics, Space Adventures #20, 23, & Strange Adventures #1)

DESTINY: A CHRONICLE OF DEATHS FORETOLD (See Sandman)
DC Comics (Vertigo): 1997 - No.3, 1998 ($5.95, limited series)

1-3-Kwitney-s in all: 1-Williams & Zulli-a, Williams painted-c. 2-Williams & Scott Hampton-painted-c/a. 3-Williams & Guay-a 2.40 6.00

DESTROY!!
Eclipse Comics: 1986 ($4.95, B&W, magazine-size, one-shot)

1 5.00
3-D Special 1-r-/#1 ($2.50) 4.00

DESTROYER, THE
Marvel Comics: Nov, 1989 - No. 9, Jun, 1990 ($2.25, B&W, magazine, 52 pgs.)

1-Based on Remo Williams movie, paperbacks 2.25
2-9: 2-Williamson part inks. 4-Ditko-a 2.25

DESTROYER, THE
Marvel Comics: V2#1, March, 1991 ($1.95, 52 pgs.)
V3#1, Dec, 1991 - No. 4, Mar, 1992 ($1.95, mini-series)

V2#1,V3#1-4: Based on Remo Williams paperbacks. V3#1-4-Simonson-c. 3-Morrow-a 2.00

DESTROYER, THE (Also see Solar, Man of the Atom)
Valiant: Apr, 1995 ($2.95, color, one-shot)

0-Indicia indicates #1 3.00

DESTROYER DUCK
Eclipse Comics: Feb, 1982 - No. 7, May, 1984 (#2-7: Baxter paper) ($1.50)

1-Origin Destroyer Duck; 1st app. Groo; Kirby-c/a(p) 2.40 6.00
2-5: 2-Starling back-up begins; Kirby-c/a(p) thru #5 3.00
6,7 2.00

NOTE: ***Neal Adams** c-1i. **Kirby** c/a-1-5p. **Miller** c-7.*

DESTRUCTOR, THE
Atlas/Seaboard: February, 1975 - No. 4, Aug, 1975

1-Origin; Ditko/Wood-a; Wood-c(i) 5.00
2-4: 2-Ditko/Wood-a. 3,4-Ditko-a(p) 4.00

DETECTIVE COMICS (Also see other Batman titles)
National Periodical Publications/DC Comics: Mar, 1937 - Present

GD2.0 FN6.0 VF8.0

1-(Scarce)-Slam Bradley & Spy by Siegel & Shuster, Speed Saunders by Guardineer, Flat Foot Flannigan by Gustavson, Cosmo, the Phantom of Disguise, Buck Marshall, Bruce Nelson begin; Chin Lung in 'Claws of the Red Dragon' serial begins; Vincent Sullivan-c. 8,333.00 25,000.00 50,000.00
2 (Rare)-Creig Flessel-c begin; new logo 2333.00 6999.00 14,300.00
3 (Rare) 1666.00 5000.00 10,200.00

GD2.0 FN6.0 NM9.4

4,5: 5-Larry Steele begins 1033.00 3099.00 6500.00
6,7,9,10 750.00 2250.00 4700.00
8-Mister Chang-c; classic-c 1133.00 3399.00 7200.00
11-17,19: 17-1st app. Fu Manchu in Det. 566.00 1700.00 3600.00
18-Fu Manchu-c; last Flessel-c 950.00 2850.00 6000.00
20-The Crimson Avenger begins (1st app.) 866.00 2600.00 5500.00
21,23-25 450.00 1350.00 2800.00
22-1st Crimson Avenger-c by Chambers (12/38) 583.00 1749.00 3700.00
26 400.00 1200.00 2500.00

GD2.0 FN6.0 VF8.0 NM9.4

27-The Bat-Man & Commissioner Gordon begin (1st app.), created by Bill Finger & Bob Kane (5/39); Batman-c (1st)(by Kane). Bat-Man's secret identity revealed as Bruce Wayne in 6pg. sty. Signed Rob't Kane (also see Det. PIcture Stories #5) 25,000.00 65,000.00 105,000.00 175,000.00

27-Reprint, Oversize 13-1/2x10". WARNING: This comic is an exact duplicate reprint of the original except for its size. DC published it in 1974 with a second cover titling it as Famous First Edition. There have been many reported cases of the outer cover being removed and the interior sold as the original edition. The reprint with the new outer cover removed is practically worthless; see Famous First Edition for value.

GD2.0 FN6.0 NM9.4

28-2nd app. The Batman (6 pg. story); non-Bat-Man-c; signed Rob't Kane 1400.00 4200.00 15,500.00

GD2.0 FN6.0 VF8.0 NM9.4

29-1st app. Doctor Death-c/story, Batman's 1st name villain. 1st 2 part story (10 pgs.). 2nd Batman-c by Kane 2333.00 7000.00 15,165.00 26,000.00

GD2.0 FN6.0 NM9.4

30-Dr. Death app. Story concludes from issue #29. Classic Batman splash panel by Kane. 580.00 1740.00 5800.00

GD2.0 FN6.0 VF8.0 NM9.4

31-Classic Batman over castle-c; 1st app. The Monk & 1st Julie Madison (Bruce Wayne's 1st love interest); 1st Batplane (Bat-Gyro) and Batarang; 2nd 2-part Batman adventure. Gardner Fox takes over script from Bill Finger. 1st mention of Locale (New York City) where Batman lives 2333.00 7000.00 15,165.00 26,000.00

GD2.0 FN6.0 NM9.4

32-Batman story concludes from issue #31. 1st app. Dala (Monk's assistant). Batman uses gun for 1st time to slay The Monk and Dala. This was the 1st time a costumed hero used a gun in comic books. 1st Batman head logo on cover 530.00 1590.00 5300.00

Detective Comics #35 © DC

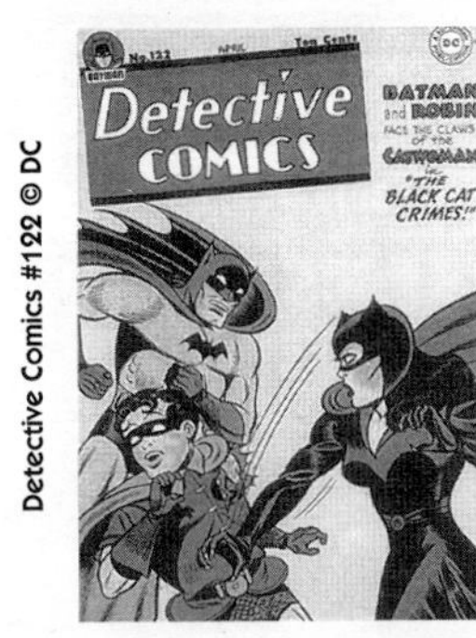

Detective Comics #122 © DC

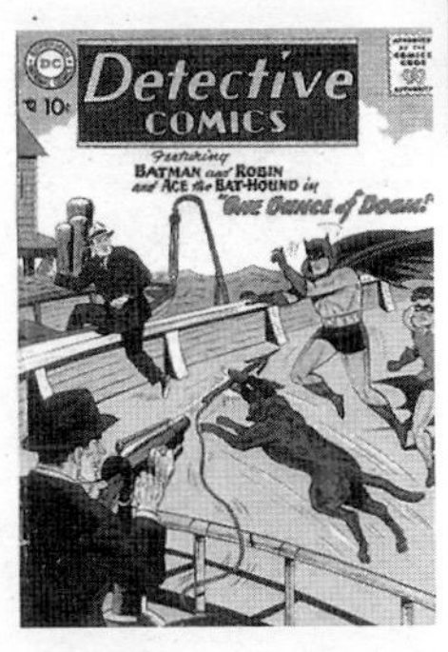

Detective Comics #254 © DC

GD2.0 FN6.0 VF8.0 NM9.4

33-Origin The Batman (2 pgs.)(1st told origin); Batman gun holster-c; Batman w/smoking gun panel at end of story. Batman story now 12 pgs. Classic Batman-c 3133.00 9400.00 20,365.00 36,000.00

GD2.0 FN6.0 NM9.4

34-2nd Crimson Avenger-c by Creig Flessel and last non Batman-c. Story from issue #32 x-over as Bruce Wayne sees Julie Madison off to America from Paris. Classic Batman splash panel used later in Batman #1 for origin story. Steve Malone begins 430.00 1290.00 4300.00

35-Classic Batman hypodermic needle-c that reflects story in issue #34. Classic Batman with smoking .45 automatic splash panel. Last time a costumed hero used a gun in comic books. Batman-c begin 800.00 2400.00 8000.00

36-Batman-c that reflects adventure in issue #35. Origin/1st app. of Dr. Hugo Strange (1st major villain, 2/40). 1st finned-gloves worn by Batman 570.00 1710.00 5700.00

37-Last solo Golden-Age Batman adventure in Detective Comics. Panel at end of story reflects solo Batman adventure in Batman #1 that was originally planned for Detective #38. Cliff Crosby begins 570.00 1710.00 5700.00

GD2.0 FN6.0 VF8.0 NM9.4

38-Origin/1st app. Robin the Boy Wonder (4/40); Batman and Robin-c begin; cover by Kane & Robinson taken from splash pg. 2766.00 8300.00 17,980.00 31,000.00

GD2.0 FN6.0 NM9.4

39-Opium story 500.00 1500.00 5000.00
40-Origin & 1st app. Clay Face (Basil Karlo); 1st Joker cover app. (6/40); Joker story intended for this issue was used in Batman #1 instead; cover is similar to splash pg. in 2nd Joker story in Batman #1 600.00 1800.00 6000.00
41-Robin's 1st solo 311.00 933.00 2800.00
42-44: 44-Crimson Avenger-new costume 225.00 675.00 1800.00
45-1st Joker story in Det. (3rd book app. & 4th story app. over all, 11/40) 311.00 933.00 2800.00
46-50: 46-Death of Hugo Strange. 48-1st time car called Batmobile (2/41); Gotham City 1st mention in Det. (1st mentioned in Wow #1; also see Batman #4). 49-Last Clay Face 200.00 600.00 1600.00
51-57 137.00 411.00 1100.00
58-1st Penguin app. (12/41); last Speed Saunders; Fred Ray-c 378.00 1134.00 3400.00
59,60: 59-Last Steve Malone; 2nd Penguin; Wing becomes Crimson Avenger's aide. 60-Intro. Air Wave; Joker app. (2nd in Det.) 162.00 486.00 1300.00
61,63: 63-Last Cliff Crosby; 1st app. Mr. Baffle 137.00 411.00 1100.00
62-Joker-c/story (2nd Joker-c, 4/42) 225.00 675.00 1800.00
64-Origin & 1st app. Boy Commandos by Simon & Kirby (6/42); Joker app. 378.00 1134.00 3400.00
65-1st Boy Commandos-c (S&K-a on Boy Commandos & Ray/Robinson-a on Batman & Robin on-c; 4 artists on one-c) 288.00 864.00 2400.00
66-Origin & 1st app. Two-Face 322.00 966.00 2900.00
67-1st Penguin-c (9/42) 212.00 636.00 1700.00
68-Two-Face-c/story; 1st Two-Face-c 162.00 486.00 1300.00
69-Joker-c/story 162.00 486.00 1300.00
70 112.00 336.00 900.00
71-Joker-c/story 131.00 393.00 1050.00
72,74,75: 74-1st Tweedledum & Tweedledee plus-c; S&K-a 100.00 300.00 800.00
73-Scarecrow-c/story (1st Scarecrow-c) 119.00 357.00 950.00
76-Newsboy Legion & The Sandman x-over in Boy Commandos; S&K-a; Joker-c/story 162.00 486.00 1300.00
77-79: All S&K-a 109.00 327.00 875.00
80-Two-Face app.; S&K-a 119.00 357.00 950.00
81,82,84,86-90: 81-1st Cavalier-c & app. 89-Last Crimson Avenger; 2nd Cavalier-c & app. 87.00 261.00 700.00
83-1st "skinny" Alfred (2/44)(see Batman #21; last S&K Boy Commandos. (also #92,128); most issues #84 on signed S&K are not by them 100.00 300.00 800.00
85-Joker-c/story; last Spy; Kirby/Klech Boy Commandos 115.00 345.00 920.00
91,102-Joker-c/story 109.00 327.00 870.00
92-98: 96-Alfred's last name 'Beagle' revealed, later changed to 'Pennyworth' in #214 72.00 216.00 575.00
99-Penguin-c 112.00 336.00 900.00
100 (6/45) 116.00 348.00 925.00
101,103-108,110-113,115-117,119: 108-1st Bat-signal-c (2/46). 114-1st small logo (8/46) 69.00 207.00 550.00
109,114,118-Joker-c/stories 97.00 291.00 775.00
120-Penguin-c (white-c, rare above fine) 145.00 435.00 1450.00
121,123,125,127,129,130 66.00 200.00 525.00
122-1st Catwoman-c (4/47) 125.00 375.00 1000.00
124,128-Joker-c/stories 92.00 276.00 735.00
126-Penguin-c 92.00 276.00 735.00
131-134,136,139 56.00 168.00 450.00
135-Frankenstein-c/story 63.00 189.00 500.00
137-Joker-c/story; last Air Wave 75.00 225.00 600.00
138-Origin Robotman (see Star Spangled #7 for 1st app.); series ends #202 106.00 318.00 850.00
140-The Riddler-c/story (1st app., 10/48) 400.00 1200.00 4000.00
141,143-148,150: 150-Last Boy Commandos 56.00 168.00 450.00
142-2nd Riddler-c/story 109.00 327.00 875.00
149-Joker-c/story 78.00 234.00 625.00
151-Origin & 1st app. Pow Wow Smith, Indian lawman (9/49) & begins series 69.00 207.00 550.00
152,154,155,157-160: 152-Last Slam Bradley 56.00 168.00 450.00
153-1st app. Roy Raymond TV Detective (11/49) ; origin The Human Fly 64.00 192.00 510.00
156(2/50)-The new classic Batmobile 80.00 240.00 640.00
161-167,169,170,172-176: Last 52 pg. issue 54.00 162.00 430.00
168-Origin the Joker 325.00 975.00 3100.00
171-Penguin-c 84.00 252.00 675.00
177-179,181-186,188,189,191,192,194-199,201,202,204,206-210,212,214-216: 184-1st app. Fire Fly. 185-Secret of Batman's utility belt. 187-Two-Face app. 202-Last Robotman & Pow Wow Smith. 215-1st app. of Batmen of all Nations. 216-Last precode (2/55) 47.00 141.00 380.00
180,193-Joker-c/story 53.00 159.00 425.00
187-Two-Face-c/story 53.00 159.00 425.00
190-Origin Batman retold 69.00 207.00 550.00
200(1/53),205: 205-Origin Batcave) 65.00 195.00 520.00
203,211-Catwoman-c/stories 53.00 159.00 425.00
213-Origin & 1st app. Mirror Man 56.00 168.00 450.00
217-224: 218-Batman Jr. & Robin Sr. app. 41.00 123.00 325.00

GD2.0 FN6.0 VF8.0 NM9.4

225-(11/55)-1st app. Martian Manhunter, John Jones; later changed to J'onn J'onzz; origin begins; also see Batman #78 329.00 988.00 2470.00 5600.00

GD2.0 FN6.0 NM9.4

226-Origin Martian Manhunter cont'd (2nd app.) 126.00 378.00 1260.00
227-229: Martian Manhunter stories in all 50.00 150.00 470.00
230-1st app. Mad Hatter; brief recap origin of Martian Manhunter 52.00 156.00 495.00
231-Brief origin recap Martian Manhunter 36.00 108.00 320.00
232,234,237-240: 232-Batwoman app. 239-Early DC grey tone-c 35.00 105.00 300.00
233-Origin & 1st app. Batwoman (7/56) 121.00 363.00 1150.00
235-Origin Batman & his costume; tells how Bruce Wayne's father (Thomas Wayne) wore Bat costume & fought crime (reprinted in Batman #255) 59.00 177.00 560.00
236-1st S.A. issue; J'onn J'onzz talks to parents and Mars-1st since being stranded on Earth; 1st app. Bat-Tank? 39.00 117.00 350.00
241-260: 246-Intro. Diane Meade, John Jones' girl. 249-Batwoman-c/app. 253-1st app. The Terrible Trio. 254-Bat-Hound-c/story. 257-Intro. & 1st app. Whirly Bats. 259-1st app. The Calendar Man 29.00 87.00 250.00
261-264,266,268-271: 261-J. Jones tie-in to sci/fi movie "Incredible Shrinking Man"; 1st app. Dr. Double X. 262-Origin Jackal. 268,271-Manhunter origin recap 22.00 66.00 185.00
265-Batman's origin retold with new facts 35.00 105.00 295.00

Detective Comics #484 © DC

Detective Comics #532 © DC

Detective Comics #730 © DC

GD2.0 FN6.0 NM9.4

267-Origin & 1st app. Bat-Mite (5/59) 32.00 96.00 270.00
272,274-280: 276-2nd app. Bat-Mite 17.00 51.00 145.00
273-J'onn J'onzz i.d. revealed for 1st time 18.00 54.00 155.00
281-292, 294-297: 285,286,292-Batwoman-c/app. 287-Origin J'onn J'onzz retold. 289-Bat-Mite-c/story. 292-Last Roy Raymond. 297-Last 10¢ issue (11/61) 14.00 43.00 115.00
293-(7/61)-Aquaman begins (pre #1); ends #300 15.00 45.00 120.00
298-(12/61)-1st modern Clayface (Matt Hagen) 22.00 66.00 220.00
299,300: 300-(2/62)-Aquaman ends 9.50 28.50 90.00
301-(3/62)-J'onn J'onzz returns to Mars (1st time since stranded on Earth six years before) 8.50 25.50 85.00
302-326,329,330: 302,307,311,318,321,325-Batwoman-c/app. 311-Intro. Zook in John Jones; 1st app. Cat-Man. 318,325-Cat-Man-c/story (2nd & 3rd app.); also 1st & 2nd app. Batwoman as the Cat-Woman. 321-2nd Terrible Trio. 322-Bat-Girl's 1st/only app. in Det. (6th in all); Batman cameo in J'onn J'onzz (only hero to app. in series). 326-Last J'onn J'onzz, story cont'd in H.O.M. #143; intro. Idol-Head of Diabolu 6.50 19.50 65.00
327-(5/64)-Elongated Man begins, ends #383; 1st new look Batman with new costume; Infantino/Giella new look-a begins; Batman with gun 10.50 32.00 105.00
328-Death of Alfred; Bob Kane biog, 2 pgs. 9.00 27.00 90.00
331,333-340,342-358,360-364,366-368,370: 334-1st app. The Outsider. 345-Intro Block Buster. 347-"What If" theme story (1/66). 351-Elongated Man new costume. 355-Zatanna x-over in Elongated Man. 356-Alfred brought back in Batman, 1st SA app.? 362,364-S.A. Riddler app. (early). 363-2nd app. new Batgirl. 370-1st Neal Adams-a on Batman (cover only, 12/67) 4.00 12.00 40.00
332,341,365-Joker-c/stories 4.80 14.40 48.00
359-Intro/origin Batgirl (Barbara Gordon)-c/story (1/67); 1st app. Killer Moth. 10.00 30.00 100.00
369(11/67)-N. Adams-a (Elongated Man); 3rd app. S.A. Catwoman (cameo; leads into Batman #197); 4th app. new Batgirl 5.50 16.50 55.00
371-1st new Batmobile from TV show (1/68) 4.50 13.50 45.00
372-386,389,390: 375-New Batmobile-c. 377-S.A. Riddler app. 3.50 10.50 35.00
387-r/1st Batman story from #27 (30th anniversary, 5/69); Joker-c; 4.00 12.00 40.00
388-Joker-c/story; last 12¢ issue 3.80 11.40 38.00
391-394,396,398,399,401,403,405,406,409: 392-1st app. Jason Bard. 401-2nd Batgirl/Robin team-up 2.60 7.80 26.00
395,397,402,404,407,408,410-Neal Adams-a. 404-Tribute to Enemy Ace 3.20 9.60 32.00
400-(6/70)-Origin & 1st app. Man-Bat; 1st Batgirl/Robin team-up (cont'd in #401); Neal Adams-a 5.00 15.00 55.00
411-413: 413-Last 15¢ issue 2.50 7.50 20.00
414-424: All-25¢, 52 pgs. 418-Creeper x-over. 424-Last Batgirl. 2.50 7.50 24.00
425-436: 426,430,436-Elongated Man app. 428,434-Hawkman begins, ends #467 1.75 5.25 14.00
437-New Manhunter begins (10-11/73, 1st app.) by Simonson, ends #443 2.50 7.50 24.00
438-445 (All 100 Page Super Spectaculars): 438-Kubert Hawkman-r. 439-Origin Manhunter. 440-G.A. Manhunter(Adv. #79) by S&K, Hawkman, Dollman, Gr. Lantern; Toth-a. 441-G.A. Plastic Man, Batman, Ibis-r. 442-G.A. Newsboy Legion, Bl. Canary, Elongated Man, Dr. Fate-r. 443-Origin The Creeper-r; death of Manhunter; G.A. Green Lantern, Spectre-r; Batman-r/Batman #18. 444-G.A. Kid Eternity-r. 445-G.A. Dr. Midnite-r 3.40 10.20 34.00
446-460: 457-Origin retold & updated 1.50 4.50 12.00
461-465,469,470,480: 480-(44 pgs.). 463-1st app. Black Spider. 464-2nd app. Black Spider 1.25 3.75 10.00
466-468,471-474,478,479-Rogers-a in all: 466-1st app. Signalman since Batman #139. 469-Intro/origin Dr. Phosphorous. 470,471-1st modern app. Hugo Strange. 474-1st app. new Deadshot. 478-1st app. 3rd Clayface (Preston Payne). 479-(44 pgs.)-Clayface app. 2.25 6.75 18.00
475,476-Joker-c/stories; Rogers-a 3.00 9.00 30.00
477-Neal Adams-a(r); Rogers-a (3 pgs.) 2.25 6.75 18.00
481-(Combined with Batman Family, 12-1/78-79, begin $1.00, 68 pg. issues, ends #495); 481-495-Batgirl, Robin solo stories 1.50 4.50 12.00
482-Starlin/Russell, Golden-a; The Demon begins (origin-r), ends #485 (by Ditko #483-485) 1.10 3.30 9.00
483-40th Anniversary issue; origin retold; Newton Batman begins 1.50 4.50 12.00
484-495 (68 pgs): 484-Origin Robin. 485-Death of Batwoman. 487-The Odd Man by Ditko. 489-Robin/Batgirl team-up. 490-Black Lightning begins. 491-(#492 on inside) 1.00 2.80 7.00
496-499 2.40 6.00
500-($1.50, 52 pgs.)-Batman/Deadman team-up; new Hawkman story by Joe Kubert; incorrectly says 500th anniv. of Det. 1.40 4.15 11.00
501-503,505-523: 512-2nd app. new Dr. Death. 519-Last Batgirl. 521-Green Arrow series begins. 523-Solomon Grundy app. 2.40 6.00
504-Joker-c/story 1.00 2.80 7.00
524-2nd app. Jason Todd (cameo)(3/83) 5.00
525-3rd app. Jason Todd (See Batman #357) 5.00
526-Batman's 500th app. in Detective Comics ($1.50, 68 pgs.); Death of Jason Todd's parents, Joker-c/story (55 pgs.); Bob Kane pin-up 1.75 5.25 14.00
527-531,533,534,536-568,571,573: 538-Cat-Man-c/story cont'd from Batman #371. 542-Jason Todd quits as Robin (becomes Robin again #547). 549, 550-Alan Moore scripts (Green Arrow). 554-1st new Black Canary (9/85). 566-Batman villains profiled. 567-Harlan Ellison scripts. 3.50
532,569,570-Joker-c/stories 2.40 6.00
535-Intro new Robin (JasonTodd)-1st appeared in Batman. 4.00
572-(3/87, $1.25, 60 pgs.)-50th Anniv. of Det. Comics 4.00
574-Origin Batman & Jason Todd retold 4.00
575-Year 2 begins, ends #578 1.25 3.75 10.00
576-578: McFarlane-c/a. 578-Clay Face app. 1.00 3.00 8.00
579-597,601-610: 579-New bat wing logo. 583-1st app. villains Scarface & Ventriloquist. 589-595-(52 pgs.)-Each contain free 16 pg. Batman stories. 604-607-Mudpack storyline; 604,607-Contain Batman mini-posters. 610-Faked death of Penguin; artists names app. on tombstone on-c 2.50
598-($2.95, 84 pgs.)- "Blind Justice" storyline begins by Batman movie writer Sam Hamm, ends #600 4.00
599 2.50
600-(5/89, $2.95, 84 pgs.)-50th Anniv. of Batman in Det.; 1 pg. Neal Adams pin-up, among other artists 4.00
611-626,628-658: 612-1st new look Cat-Man; Catwoman app. 615- "The Penguin Affair" part 2 (See Batman #448,449). 617-Joker-c/story. 624-1st new Catwoman (w/death) & 1st new Batwoman. 626-Batman's 600th app. in Det. 642-Return of Scarface, part 2. 644-Last $1.00-c. 652,653-Huntress-c/story w/new costume plus Travis Charest-c on both 3.00
627-($2.95, 84 pgs.)-Batman's 601st app. in Det.; reprints 1st story/#27 plus 3 versions (2 new) of same story 4.00
659-664: 659-Knightfall part 2; Kelley Jones-c. 660-Knightfall part 4; Bane-c by Sam Kieth. 661-Knightfall part 6; brief Joker & Riddler app. 662-Knightfall part 8; Riddler app.; Sam Kieth-c. 663-Knightfall part 10; Kelley Jones-c. 664-Knightfall part 12; Bane-c/story; Joker app.; continued in Showcase 93 #7 & 8; Jones-c 3.00
665-675: 665,666-Knightfall parts 16 & 18; 666-Bane-c/story. 667-Knightquest: The Crusade & new Batman begins (1st app. inBatman #500). 669-Begin $1.50-c; Knightquest, cont'd in Robin #1. 671,673-Joker app. 2.00
675-($2.95)-Collectors edition w/foil-c 3.50
676-($2.50, 52 pgs.)-KnightsEnd Pt. 3 3.00
677,678: 677-KnightsEnd Pt. 9. 678-(9/94)-Zero Hour tie-in. 2.00
0,679-684: 0-(10/94). 679-(11/94). 682-Troika Pt. 3 2.00
682-($2.50) Embossed-c Troika Pt. 3 2.50
686-699,701-719: 686-Begin $1.95-c. 693,694-Poison Ivy-c/app. 695-Contagion Pt. 2; Catwoman, Penguin app. 696-Contagion Pt. 8. 698-Two-Face-c/app. 701-Legacy Pt. 6; Batman vs. Bane-c/app. 702-Legacy Epilogue. 703-Final Night x-over. 705-707-Riddler-app. 714,715-Martian Manhunter-app. 2.00
700-($4.95, Collectors Edition)-Legacy Pt. 1; Ra's Al Ghul-c/app; Talia & Bane app; book displayed at shops in envelope 5.00
700-($2.95, Regular Edition)-Different-c 3.00
720-739: 720,721-Cataclysm pts. 5,14. 723-Green Arrow app.. 730-739-No

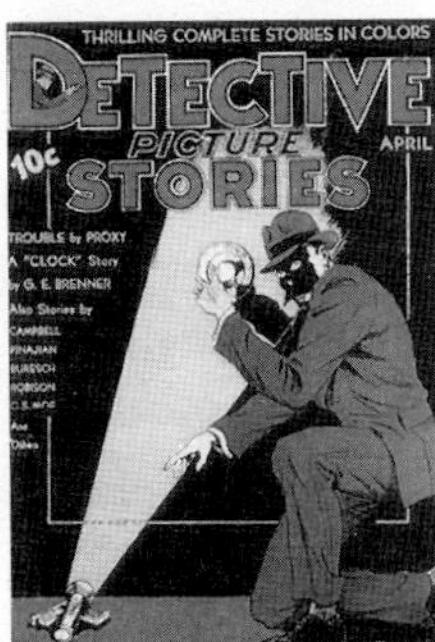

Detective Picture Stories #5 © Comics Mag. Co.

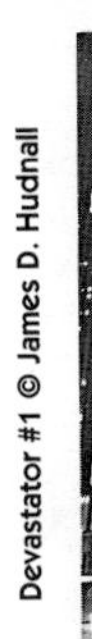

Devastator #1 © James D. Hudnall

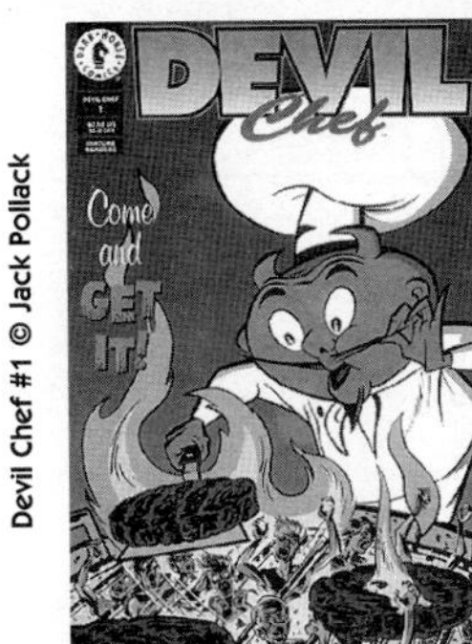

Devil Chef #1 © Jack Pollack

GD2.0 FN6.0 NM9.4

Man's Land stories 2.00
#1,000,000 (11/98) 853rd Century x-over 2.00
Annual 1 (1988, $1.50) 5.00
Annual 2-7,9 ('89-'94, '96, 68 pgs.)-4-Painted-c. 5-Joker-c/story (54 pgs.) continued in Robin Annual #1; Sam Kieth-c; Eclipso app. 6-Azrael as Batman in new costume; intro Geist the Twilight Man; Bloodlines storyline. 7-Elseworlds story. 9-Legends of the Dead Earth story 3.00
Annual 8 (1995, $3.95, 68 pgs.)-Year One story 4.00
Annual 10 (1997, $3.95)-Pulp Heroes story 4.00

NOTE: **Neal Adams** *c-370, 372, 383, 385, 389, 391, 392, 394-422, 439.* **Aparo** *a-437, 438, 444-446, 500, 625-632p, 638-643p; c-430, 437, 440-446, 448, 468-470, 480, 484(back), 492-502,508, 509, 515, 518-522, 641, 716, 719, 722, 724.* **Austin** *a(i)-450, 451, 463-468, 471-476; c(i)-474-476, 478.* **Baily** *a-443r.* **Buckler** *a-434, 446p, 479p; c(p)-467, 482, 505-507, 511, 513-516, 518.* **Burnley** *a(Batman)-65, 75, 78, 83, 100, 103, 125; c-62i, 63i, 64, 73i, 78, 83p, 96p, 103p, 105p, 106, 108, 121p, 123p, 125p.* **Chaykin** *a-441.* **Colan** *a(p)-510, 512, 517, 523, 528-538, 540-546, 555-567; c(p)-510, 512, 528, 530-535, 537, 538, 540, 541, 543-545, 556-558, 560-564.* **J. Craig** *a-488.* **Ditko** *a-443r, 483-485, 487.* **Golden** *a-482p; c-625, 626, 628-631, 633, 644-646.* **Alan Grant** *scripts-584-597, 601-621, 641, 642, Annual 5.* **Grell** *a-445, 455, 463p, 464p; c-455.* **Guardineer** *c-23, 24, 26, 28, 30, 32.* **Gustavson** *a-441r.* **Infantino** *a-442(2)r, 500, 572.* **Infantino/Anderson** *c-333, 337-340, 343, 344, 347, 351, 352, 359, 361-368, 371.* **Kelley Jones** *c-651, 657i, 658i, 659, 661, 663-675.* **Kaluta** *c-423, 424, 426-428, 431, 434, 438, 484, 486, 572.* **Bob Kane** *a-Most early issues #27 on, 297r, 356r, 438-440r, 442r, 443r.* **Kane/Robinson** *c-33.* **Gil Kane** *a(p)-368, 370-374, 384, 385, 388-407, 438r, 439r, 520.* **Kane/Anderson** *c-369.* **Sam Kieth** *c-654-656 (657, 658 w/***Kelley Jones***), 660, 662, Annual #5.* **Kubert** *a-438r, 439r, 500; c-348, 350.* **McFarlane** *c/a(p)-576-578.* **Meskin** *a-420r.* **Mignola** *c-583.* **Moldoff** *c-233-354, 259, 266, 267, 275, 287, 289, 290, 297, 300.* **Moldoff/Giella** *a-328, 330, 332, 334, 336, 338, 340, 342, 344, 346, 348, 350, 352, 354, 356.* **Mooney** *a-444r.* **Moreira** *a-153-300, 419r, 444r, 445r.* **Nasser/Netzer** *a-654, 655, 657, 658.* **Newton** *a(p)-480, 481, 483-499, 501-509, 511, 513-516, 518-520, 524, 526, 539; c-526p.* **Irv Novick** *c-375-377.* **Robbins** *a-426p, 429p.* **Robinson** *a-part: 66, 68, 71-73; all: 74-76, 79, 80; c-62, 64, 66, 68-74, 76, 79, 82, 86, 88, 442r, 443r.* **Rogers** *a-466-468, 471-479p, 481p; c-471p, 472p, 473, 474-479p.* **Roussos** *Airwave-76-105(most); c(i)-71, 72, 74-76, 79, 107.* **Russell** *a-481i, 482i.* **Simon/Kirby** *a-440r, 442r.* **Simonson** *a-437-443, 450, 469, 470, 500.* **Dick Sprang** *c-77, 82, 84, 85, 87, 89-93, 95-100, 102, 103i, 104i, 106, 108, 114, 117, 118, 122, 123, 128, 129, 131, 133, 135, 141, 148, 149, 168, 622-624.* **Starlin** *a-481p, 482p; c-503, 504, 567p.* **Starr** *a-444r.* **Toth** *a-442; r-414, 416, 418, 424, 440-441, 443, 444.* **Tuska** *a-486p, 490p.* **Matt Wagner** *c-647-649.* **Wrightson** *c-425.*

DETECTIVE DAN, SECRET OP. 48 (Also see Adventures of Detective Ace King and Bob Scully, The Two-Fisted Hick Detective)
Humor Publ. Co. (Norman Marsh): 1933 (10¢, 10x13", 36 pgs., B&W, one-shot) (3 color, cardboard-c)

nn-By Norman Marsh, 1st comic w/ original-a; 1st newsstand-c; Dick Tracy look-alike; forerunner of Dan Dunn. (Title and Wu Fang character inspired Detective #1 four years later.) GD2.0 FN6.0 VF8.0
(1st comic of a single theme) 1400.00 4200.00 6000.00

DETECTIVE EYE (See Keen Detective Funnies)
Centaur Publications: Nov, 1940 - No. 2, Dec, 1940

GD2.0 FN6.0 NM9.4
1-Air Man (see Keen Detective) & The Eye Sees begins; The Masked Marvel & Dean Denton app. 200.00 600.00 1600.00
2-Origin Don Rance and the Mysticape; Binder-a; Frank Thomas-c 125.00 375.00 1000.00

DETECTIVE PICTURE STORIES (Keen Detective Funnies No. 8 on?)
Comics Magazine Company: Dec, 1936 - No. 5, Apr, 1937
(1st comic of a single theme)

	GD2.0	FN6.0	NM9.4
1 (all issues are very scarce)	550.00	1650.00	3800.00
2-The Clock app. (1/37, early app.)	233.00	699.00	1600.00
3,4: 4-Eisner-a	150.00	450.00	1000.00
5-The Clock-c/story (4/37); 1st detective/adventure art by Bob Kane; Bruce Wayne prototype app.	166.00	500.00	1100.00

DETECTIVES, THE (TV)
Dell Publishing Co.: No. 1168, Mar-May, 1961 - No. 1240, Oct-Dec, 1961

	GD2.0	FN6.0	NM9.4
Four Color 1168 (#1)-Robert Taylor photo-c	9.00	27.00	100.00
Four Color 1219-Robert Taylor, Adam West photo-c	7.00	22.00	80.00
Four Color 1240-Tufts-a; Robert Taylor photo-c	7.00	22.00	80.00

DETECTIVES, INC. (See Eclipse Graphic Album Series)
Eclipse Comics: Apr, 1985 - No. 2, Apr, 1985 ($1.75, both w/April dates)

1,2: 2-Nudity 2.00

DETECTIVES, INC.: A TERROR OF DYING DREAMS
Eclipse Comics: Jun, 1987 - No. 3, Dec, 1987 ($1.75, B&W& sepia)

1-3: Colan-a 2.00
TPB ('99, $19.95) r/series 20.00

DETENTION COMICS
DC Comics: Oct, 1996 ($3.50, 56 pgs., one-shot)

1-Robin story by Dennis O'Neil & Norm Breyfogle; Superboy story by Ron Marz & Ron Lim; Warrior story by Ruben Diaz & Joe Phillips; Phillips-c 5.00

DETONATOR
Chaos! Comics: Dec, 1994 - No. 2, 1995 ($2.95, limited series)

1,2-Brian Pulido scripts; Steven Hughes-a 3.00

DEVASTATOR
Image Comics/Halloween: 1998 - No. 3 ($2.95, B&W, limited series)

1,2-Hudnall-s/Horn-c/a 3.00

DEVIL CHEF
Dark Horse Comics: July, 1994 ($2.50, B&W, one-shot)

nn 2.50

DEVIL DINOSAUR
Marvel Comics Group: Apr, 1978 - No. 9, Dec, 1978

	GD2.0	FN6.0	NM9.4
1-Kirby/Royer-a in all; all have Kirby-c	1.25	3.75	10.00
2-9: 4-7-UFO/sci. fic. 8-Dinoriders-c/sty		2.40	6.00

DEVIL DINOSAUR SPRING FLING
Marvel Comics: June, 1997 ($2.99. one-shot)

1-(48pgs.) Moon-Boy-c/app. 3.00

DEVIL-DOG DUGAN (Tales of the Marines No. 4 on)
Atlas Comics (OPI): July, 1956 - No. 3, Nov, 1956

	GD2.0	FN6.0	NM9.4
1-Severin-c	11.00	33.00	75.00
2-Iron Mike McGraw x-over; Severin-c	7.50	22.50	45.00
3	5.85	17.50	35.00

DEVIL DOGS
Street & Smith Publishers: 1942

	GD2.0	FN6.0	NM9.4
1-Boy Rangers, U.S. Marines	26.00	79.00	185.00

DEVLIN (See Avengelyne/Glory)
Maximum Press: Apr, 1996 ($2.50, one-shot)

1-Avengelyne app. 2.50

DEVILINA (Magazine)
Atlas/Seaboard: Feb, 1975 - No. 2, May, 1975 (B&W)

	GD2.0	FN6.0	NM9.4
1-Reese-a	1.75	5.25	14.00
2 (Low printing)	2.50	7.50	20.00

DEVIL KIDS STARRING HOT STUFF
Harvey Publications (Illustrated Humor): July, 1962 - No. 107, Oct, 1981 (Giant-Size #41-55)

	GD2.0	FN6.0	NM9.4
1 (12¢ cover price #1-#41-9/69)	14.00	42.00	140.00
2	7.00	21.00	70.00
3-10 (1/64)	5.00	15.00	50.00
11-20	2.60	7.80	26.00
21-30	2.50	7.50	20.00
31-40: 40-(6/69)	2.60	7.80	16.00
41-50: All 68 pg. Giants	2.50	7.50	20.00
51-55: All 52 pg. Giants	2.00	6.00	16.00
56-70	1.10	3.30	9.00
71-90		2.40	6.00
91-107			4.00

DEVILMAN
Verotik: June, 1995 -No. 3 ($2.95, mature)

1-3: Go Nagai story and art. 3-Bisley-c 3.00

DEXTER COMICS
Dearfield Publ.: Summer, 1948 - No. 5, July, 1949

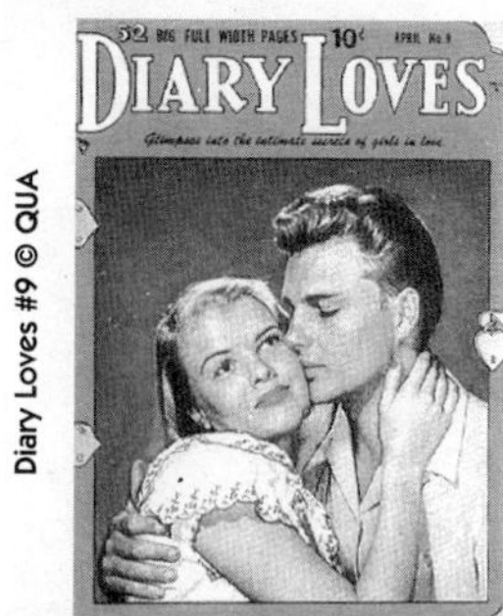

Diary Loves #9 © QUA

Dick Cole #5 © STAR

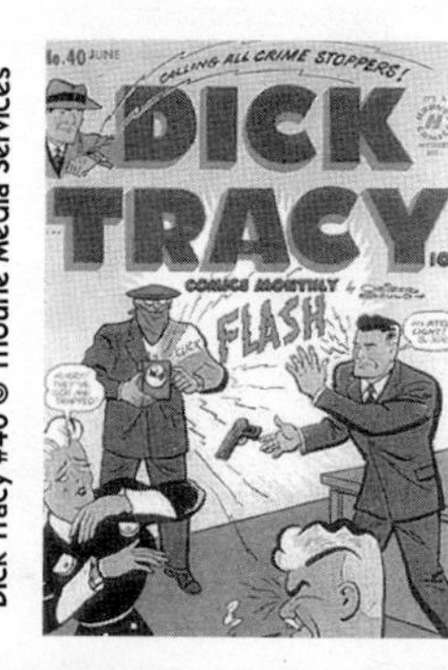

Dick Tracy #40 © Tribune Media Services

	GD2.0	FN6.0	NM9.4
1-Teen-age humor	8.35	25.00	50.00
2-Junie Prom app.	5.85	17.50	35.00
3-5	4.15	12.50	25.00

DEXTER'S LABORATORY (Cartoon Network)
DC Comics: Sept, 1999 - Present ($1.99)

	GD2.0	FN6.0	NM9.4
1-3: 2-McCracken-s			2.00

DEXTER THE DEMON (Formerly Melvin The Monster)(See Cartoon Kids & Peter the Little Pest)
Atlas Comics (HPC): No. 7, Sept, 1957

	GD2.0	FN6.0	NM9.4
7	5.00	15.00	30.00

DHAMPIRE: STILLBORN
DC Comics (Vertigo): 1996 ($5.95, one-shot, mature)

	GD2.0	FN6.0	NM9.4
1-Nancy Collins script; Paul Lee-c/a		2.40	6.00

DIARY CONFESSIONS (Formerly Ideal Romance)
Stanmor/Key Publ.(Medal Comics): No. 9, May, 1955 - No. 14, Apr, 1955

	GD2.0	FN6.0	NM9.4
9	6.35	19.00	38.00
10-14	4.25	13.00	28.00

DIARY LOVES (Formerly Love Diary #1; G. I. Sweethearts #32 on)
Quality Comics Group: No. 2, Nov, 1949 - No. 31, April, 1953

	GD2.0	FN6.0	NM9.4
2-Ward-c/a, 9 pgs.	16.00	47.00	110.00
3 (1/50)-Photo-c begin, end #27?	5.85	17.50	35.00
4-Crandall-a	8.00	24.00	48.00
5-7,10	4.25	13.00	28.00
8,9-Ward-a 6,8 pgs. 8-Gustavson-a	10.00	30.00	70.00
11,13,14,17-20	4.15	12.50	25.00
12,15,16-Ward-a 9,7,8 pgs.	10.00	30.00	65.00
21-Ward-a, 7 pgs.	8.35	25.00	50.00
22-31: 31-Whitney-a	3.60	9.00	18.00

NOTE: *Photo c-3-10, 12-27.*

DIARY OF HORROR
Avon Periodicals: December, 1952

	GD2.0	FN6.0	NM9.4
1-Hollingsworth-c/a; bondage-c	38.00	114.00	265.00

DIARY SECRETS (Formerly Teen-Age Diary Secrets)
St. John Publishing Co.: No. 10, Feb, 1952 - No. 30, Sept, 1955

	GD2.0	FN6.0	NM9.4
10-Baker-c/a most issues	16.00	47.00	110.00
11-16,18,19	11.50	34.00	80.00
17,20: Kubert-r/Hollywood Confessions #1. 17-r/Teen Age Romances #9	11.50	34.00	80.00
21-30: 22,27-Signed stories by Estrada. 28-Last precode (3/55)	8.35	25.00	50.00

(See Giant Comics Edition for Annual)

DIATOM
Photographics: Apr, 1995 ($4.95, unfinished limited series)

	GD2.0	FN6.0	NM9.4
1-Photo/computer-a			5.00

DICK COLE (Sport Thrills No. 11 on)(See Blue Bolt & Four Most #1)
Curtis Publ./Star Publications: Dec-Jan, 1948-49 - No. 10, June-July, 1950

	GD2.0	FN6.0	NM9.4
1-Sgt. Spook; L. B. Cole-c; McWilliams-a; Curt Swan's 1st work	29.00	86.00	200.00
2,5	13.00	39.00	90.00
3,4,6-10: All-L.B. Cole-c. 10-Joe Louis story	18.00	54.00	125.00
Accepted Reprint #7(V1#6 on-c)(1950's)-Reprints #7; L.B. Cole-c	7.50	22.50	45.00
Accepted Reprint #9(nd)-(Reprints #9 & #8-c)	7.50	22.50	45.00

NOTE: ***L. B. Cole** c-1, 3, 4, 6-10. **Al McWilliams** a-6. Dick Cole in 1-9. Baseball c-10. Basketball c-9. Football c-8.*

DICKIE DARE
Eastern Color Printing Co.: 1941 - No. 4, 1942 (#3 on sale 6/15/42)

	GD2.0	FN6.0	NM9.4
1-Caniff-a, Everett-c	40.00	120.00	320.00
2	26.00	77.00	180.00
3,4-Half Scorchy Smith by Noel Sickles who was very influential in Milton Caniff's development	29.00	86.00	200.00

DICK POWELL (Also see A-1 Comics)
Magazine Enterprises: No. 22, 1949 (one shot)

	GD2.0	FN6.0	NM9.4
A-1 22-Photo-c	25.00	75.00	175.00

DICK QUICK, ACE REPORTER (See Picture News #10)

DICKS
Caliber Comics: 1997 - No. 4, 1998 ($2.95, B&W)

	GD2.0	FN6.0	NM9.4
1-4-Ennis-s/McCrea-c/a; r/Fleetway			3.00
TPB ('98, $12.95) r/series			13.00

DICK'S ADVENTURES
Dell Publishing Co.: No. 245, Sept, 1949

	GD2.0	FN6.0	NM9.4
Four Color 245	4.50	13.50	50.00

DICK TRACY (See Famous Feature Stories, Harvey Comics Library, Limited Collectors' Ed., Mammoth Comics, Merry Christmas, The Original..., Popular Comics, Super Book No. 1, 7, 13, 25, Super Comics & Tastee-Freez)

DICK TRACY
David McKay Publications: May, 1937 - Jan, 1938

	GD2.0	FN6.0	NM9.4
Feature Books nn - 100 pgs., partially reprinted as 4-Color No. 1 (appeared before Large Feature Comics, 1st Dick Tracy comic book) (Very Rare-three known copies) Estimated Value....	600.00	1800.00	6000.00
Feature Books 4 - Reprints nn ish. w/new-c	110.00	330.00	1100.00
Feature Books 6,9	80.00	240.00	800.00

DICK TRACY (...Monthly #1-24)
Dell Publishing Co.: 1939 - No. 24, Dec, 1949

	GD2.0	FN6.0	NM9.4
Large Feature Comic 1 (1939) -Dick Tracy Meets The Blank	140.00	420.00	1400.00
Large Feature Comic 4,8	65.00	195.00	650.00
Large Feature Comic 11,13,15	75.00	225.00	750.00

	GD2.0	FN6.0	VF8.0	NM9.4
Four Color 1(1939)('35-r)	600.00	1800.00	3600.00	6600.00

	GD2.0	FN6.0	NM9.4
Four Color 6(1940)('37-r)-(Scarce)	145.00	435.00	1600.00
Four Color 8(1940)('38-'39-r)	73.00	219.00	800.00
Large Feature Comic 3(1941, Series II)	62.00	186.00	680.00
Four Color 21('41)('38-r)	60.00	180.00	665.00
Four Color 34('43)('39-'40-r)	41.00	123.00	450.00
Four Color 56('44)('40-r)	33.00	100.00	360.00
Four Color 96('46)('40-r)	24.00	72.00	260.00
Four Color 133('47)('40-'41-r)	20.00	60.00	220.00
Four Color 163('47)('41-r)	16.00	48.00	175.00
Four Color 215('48)-Titled "Sparkle Plenty", Tracy-r	9.50	29.00	105.00
1(1/48)('34-r)	38.00	114.00	420.00
2,3	21.00	63.00	230.00
4-10	20.00	60.00	220.00
11-18: 13-Bondage-c	14.00	42.00	150.00
19-1st app. Sparkle Plenty, B.O. Plenty & Gravel Gertie in a 3-pg. strip not by Gould	14.50	44.00	160.00
20-1st app. Sam Catchem; c/a not by Gould	11.00	33.00	120.00
21-24-Only 2 pg. Gould-a in each	11.00	33.00	120.00

NOTE: *No. 19-24 have a 2 pg. biography of a famous villain illustrated by **Gould**: 19-Little Face; 20-Flattop; 21-Breathless Mahoney; 22-Measles; 23-Itchy; 24-The Brow.*

DICK TRACY (Continued from Dell series)(...Comics Monthly #25-140)
Harvey Publications: No. 25, Mar, 1950 - No. 145, April, 1961

	GD2.0	FN6.0	NM9.4
25-Flat Top-c/story (also #26,27)	18.00	54.00	180.00
26-28,30: 28-Bondage-c. 28,29-The Brow-c/stories	13.00	38.00	125.00
29-1st app. Gravel Gertie in a Gould-r	17.00	51.00	170.00
31,32,34,35,37-40: 40-Intro/origin 2-way wrist radio (6/51)	11.50	34.00	115.00
33- "Measles the Teen-Age Dope Pusher"	13.00	38.00	125.00
36-1st app. B.O. Plenty in a Gould-r	13.00	38.00	125.00
41-50	9.50	28.50	95.00
51-56,58-80: 51-2pgs Powell-a	8.50	25.50	85.00
57-1st app. Sam Catchem in a Gould-r	10.50	32.00	105.00
81-99,101-140	6.50	19.50	65.00

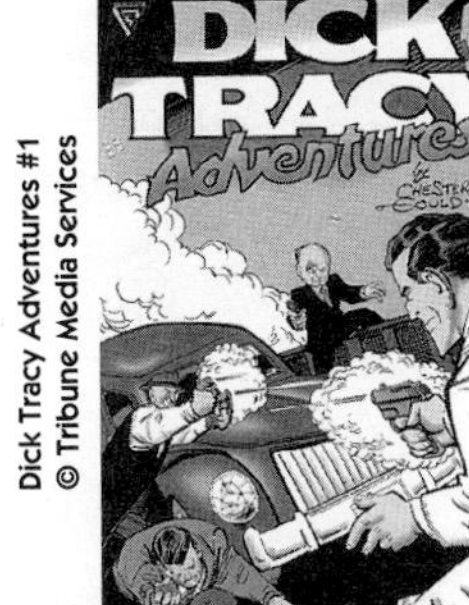

Dick Tracy Adventures #1 © Tribune Media Services

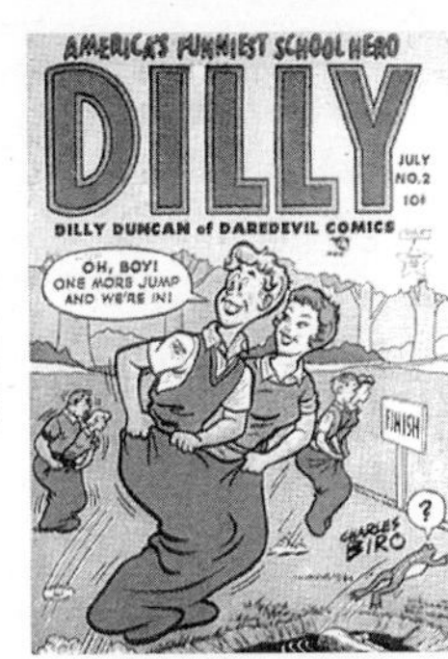

Dilly #2 © LEV

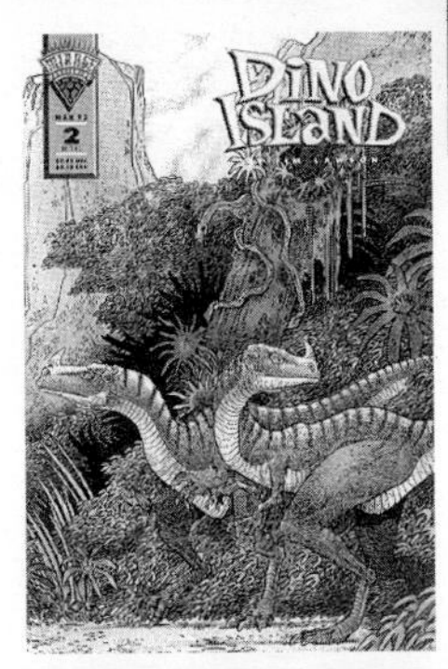

Dino Island #2 © Jim Lawson

GD2.0 FN6.0 NM9.4

100, 141-145 (25¢)(titled "Dick Tracy") 7.00 21.00 70.00
NOTE: ***Powell** a(1-2pgs.)-43, 44, 104, 108, 109, 145. No. 110-120, 141-145 are all reprints from earlier issues.*

DICK TRACY
Blackthorne Publishing: 12/84 - No. 24, 6/89 (1-12: $5.95; 13-24: $6.95, B&W, 76 pgs.)

1-8-1st printings; hard-c ed. ($14.95) 15.00
1-3-2nd printings, 1986; hard-c ed. 15.00
1-12-1st & 2nd printings; squarebound. thick-c 7.00
13-24 ($6.95): 21,22-Regular-c & stapled 7.00
NOTE: **Gould** daily & Sunday strip-r in all. 1-12 r-12/31/45-4/5/49; 13-24 r-7/13/41-2/20/44.

DICK TRACY (Disney)
WD Publications: 1990 - No. 3, 1990 (color) (Book 3 adapts 1990 movie)

Book One ($3.95, 52pgs.)-Kyle Baker-c/a 4.00
Book Two, Three ($5.95, 68pgs.)-Direct sale 6.00
Book Two, Three ($2.95, 68pgs.)-Newsstand 3.00

DICK TRACY ADVENTURES
Gladstone Publishing: May, 1991 ($4.95, 76 pgs.)

1-Reprints strips 2/1/42-4/18/42 5.00

DICK TRACY, EXPLOITS OF
Rosdon Books, Inc.: 1946 ($1.00, hard-c strip reprints)

1-Reprints the near complete case of "The Brow" from 6/12/44 to 9/24/44
(story starts a few weeks late) 25.00 75.00 175.00
with dust jacket... 40.00 120.00 300.00

DICK TRACY MONTHLY/WEEKLY
Blackthorne Publishing: May, 1986 - No. 99, 1989 ($2.00, B&W)
(Becomes Weekly #26 on)

1-99: Gould-r. 30,31-Mr. Crime app. 2.00
NOTE: *#1-10 reprint strips 3/10/40-7/13/41; #10(pg.8)-51 reprint strips 4/6/49-12/31/55; #52-99 reprint strips 12/26/56-4/26/64.*

DICK TRACY SPECIAL
Blackthorne Publ.: Jan, 1988 - No. 3, Aug. (no month), 1989 ($2.95, B&W)

1-3: 1-Origin D. Tracy; 4/strips 10/12/31-3/30/32 3.00

DICK TRACY: THE EARLY YEARS
Blackthorne Publishing: Aug, 1987 - No. 4, Aug (no month) 1989 ($6.95, B&W, 76 pgs.)

1-3: 1-4-r/strips 10/12/31(1st daily)-8/31/32 & Sunday strips 6/12/32-8/28/32;
Big Boy apps. in #1-3 1.00 2.80 7.00
4 ($2.95, 52pgs.) 3.00

DICK TRACY UNPRINTED STORIES
Blackthorne Publishing: Sept, 1987 - No. 4, June, 1988 ($2.95, B&W)

1-4: Reprints strips 1/1/56-12/25/56 3.00

DICK TURPIN (See Legend of Young...)

DIE-CUT
Marvel Comics UK, Ltd: Nov, 1993 - No. 4, Feb, 1994 ($1.75, limited series)

1-($2.50)-Die-cut-c; The Beast app. 2.50
2-4 2.00

DIE-CUT VS. G-FORCE
Marvel Comics UK, Ltd: Nov, 1993 - No. 2, Dec, 1993 ($2.75, limited series)

1,2-($2.75)-Gold foil-c on both 2.75

DIE, MONSTER, DIE (See Movie Classics)

DIESEL
Antarctic Press: Apr, 1997 - Present ($2.95)

1 3.00

DIGITEK
Marvel UK, Ltd: Dec, 1992 - No. 4, Mar, 1993 ($1.95/$2.25, mini-series)

1-4: 3-Deathlock-c/story 2.25

DILLY (Dilly Duncan from Daredevil Comics; see Boy Comics #57)
Lev Gleason Publications: May, 1953 - No. 3, Sept, 1953

1-Teenage; Biro-c 5.00 15.00 30.00
2,3-Biro-c 4.00 10.00 20.00

DILTON'S STRANGE SCIENCE (See Pep Comics #78)
Archie Comics: May, 1989 - No. 5, May, 1990 (75¢/$1.00)

1-5 2.00

DIME COMICS
Newsbook Publ. Corp.: 1945; 1951

1-Silver Streak-c/story; L. B. Cole-c 56.00 169.00 450.00
1(1951), 5 4.15 12.50 25.00

DINGBATS (See 1st Issue Special)

DING DONG
Compix/Magazine Enterprises: Summer?, 1946 - No. 5, 1947 (52 pgs.)

1-Funny animal 23.00 69.00 160.00
2 (9/46) 11.00 33.00 75.00
3 (Wint '46-'47) - 5 10.00 30.00 60.00

DINKY DUCK (Paul Terry's...) (See Blue Ribbon, Giant Comics Edition #5A & New Terrytoons)
St. John Publishing Co./Pines No. 16 on: Nov, 1951 - No. 16, Sept, 1955; No. 16, Fall, 1956; No. 17, May, 1957 - No. 19, Summer, 1958

1-Funny animal 11.00 33.00 75.00
2 6.35 19.00 38.00
3-10 4.00 12.00 24.00
11-16(9/55) 3.60 9.00 18.00
16(Fall,'56) - 19 2.80 7.00 14.00

DINKY DUCK & HASHIMOTO-SAN (See Deputy Dawg Presents...)

DINO (TV)(The Flintstones)
Charlton Publications: Aug, 1973 - No. 20, Jan, 1977 (Hanna-Barbera)

1 2.50 7.50 22.00
2-10 1.75 5.25 14.00
11-20 1.25 3.75 10.00

DINO ISLAND
Mirage Studios: Feb, 1994 - No. 2, Mar, 1994 ($2.75, limited series)

1,2-By Jim Lawson 2.75

DINO RIDERS
Marvel Comics: Feb, 1989 - No. 3, 1989 ($1.00)

1-3: Based on toys 2.00

DINOSAUR REX
Upshot Graphics (Fantagraphics): 1986 - No. 3, 1986 ($2.00, limited series)

1-3 2.00

DINOSAURS, A CELEBRATION
Marvel Comics (Epic): Oct, 1992 - No. 4, Oct, 1992 ($4.95, lim. series, 52 pgs.)

1-4: 2-Bolton painted-c 5.00

DINOSAURS ATTACK! THE GRAPHIC NOVEL
Eclipse Comics: 1991 ($3.95, coated stock, stiff-c)

Book One- Based on Topps trading cards 4.00

DINOSAURS FOR HIRE
Malibu Comics: Feb, 1993 - No. 12, Feb, 1994 ($1.95/$2.50)

1-12: 1,10-Flip bk. 8-Bagged w/Skycap; Staton-c. 10-Flip book 2.50

DINOSAURS GRAPHIC NOVEL (TV)
Disney Comics: 1992 - No. 2, 1993 ($2.95, 52 pgs.)

1,2-Staton-a; based on Dinosaurs TV show 3.00

DINOSAURUS
Dell Publishing Co.: No. 1120, Aug, 1960

Four Color 1120-Movie, painted-c 6.40 19.00 70.00

DIPPY DUCK
Atlas Comics (OPI): October, 1957

1-Maneely-a; code approved 8.35 25.00 50.00

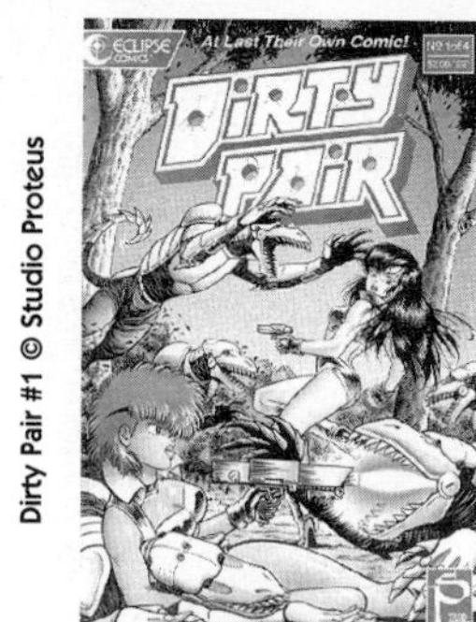

Dirty Pair #1 © Studio Proteus

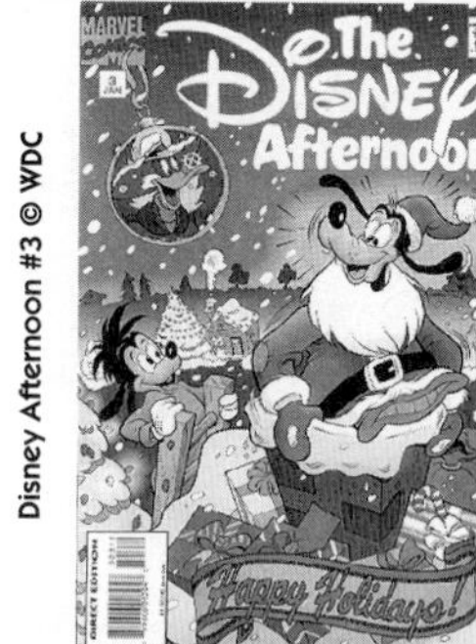

Disney Afternoon #3 © WDC

Disney's Tarzan #413 © ERB & WDC

GD2.0 FN6.0 NM9.4

DIRECTORY TO A NONEXISTENT UNIVERSE
Eclipse Comics: Dec, 1987 ($2.00, B&W)
1 — 2.00

DIRTY DOZEN (See Movie Classics)

DIRTY PAIR (Manga)
Eclipse Comics: Dec, 1988 - No. 4, Apr, 1989 ($2.00, B&W, limited series)
1-4: Japanese manga with original stories — 3.00

DIRTY PAIR: FATAL BUT NOT SERIOUS (Manga)
Dark Horse Comics: July, 1995 - No. 5, Nov, 1995 ($2.95, limited series)
1-5 — 3.00

DIRTY PAIR: SIM HELL (Manga)
Dark Horse Comics: May, 1993 - No. 4, Aug, 1993 ($2.50, B&W, limited series)
1-4 — 3.00

DIRTY PAIR II (Manga)
Eclipse Comics: June, 1989 - No. 5, Mar, 1990 ($2.00, B&W, limited series)
1-5: 3-Cover is misnumbered as #1 — 3.00

DIRTY PAIR III, THE (A Plague of Angels) (Manga)
Eclipse Comics: Aug, 1990 - No. 5, Aug, 1991 ($2.00, B&W, limited series)
1,2 — 3.00
3-5: ($2.25) — 2.25

DISHMAN
Eclipse Comics: Sept, 1988 ($2.50, B&W, 52 pgs.)
1 — 2.50

DISNEY AFTERNOON, THE (TV)
Marvel Comics: Nov, 1994 - No. 10?, Aug, 1995 ($1.50)
1-10: 3-w/bound-in Power Ranger Barcode Card — 2.50

DISNEY COMIC ALBUM
Disney Comics: 1990(no month, year) - No. 8, 1991 ($6.95/$7.95)
1,2 ($6.95): 1-Donald Duck and Gyro Gearloose by Barks(r). 2-Uncle Scrooge by Barks(r); Jr. Woodchucks app. — 8.00
3-8: 3-Donald Duck-r/F.C. 308 by Barks; begin $7.95-c. 4-Mickey Mouse Meets the Phantom Blot; r/M.M Club Parade(censored 1956 version of story). 5-Chip 'n' Dale Rescue Rangers; new-a. 6-Uncle Scrooge. 7-Donald Duck in Too Many Pets; Barks-r(4) including F.C. #29. 8-Super Goof; r/S.G. #1, D.D. #102 — 8.00

DISNEY COMIC HITS
Marvel Comics: Oct, 1995 - Present ($1.50/$2.50)
1-15: 4-Toy Story. 6-Aladdin. 7-Pocahontas. 10-The Hunchback of Notre Dame (Same story in Disney's The Hunchback of Notre Dame) 13-Aladdin and the Forty Thieves — 4.00

DISNEY COMICS
Disney Comics: June, 1990
Boxed set of #1 issues includes Donald Duck Advs., Ducktales, Chip 'n Dale Rescue Rangers, Roger Rabbit, Mickey Mouse Advs. & Goofy Advs.; limited to 10,000 sets — 1.85 — 5.50 — 15.00

DISNEYLAND BIRTHDAY PARTY (Also see Dell Giants)
Gladstone Publishing Co.: Aug, 1985 ($2.50)
1-Reprints Dell Giant with new-photo-c — 1.50 — 4.50 — 12.00
...Comics Digest #1-(Digest) — 1.75 — 5.25 — 14.00

DISNEYLAND MAGAZINE
Fawcett Publications: Feb. 15, 1972 - ? (10-1/4"x12-5/8", 20 pgs, weekly)
1-One or two page painted art features on Dumbo, Snow White, Lady & the Tramp, the Aristocats, Brer Rabbit, Peter Pan, Cinderella, Jungle Book, Alice & Pinocchio. Most standard characters app. — 2.50 — 7.50 — 20.00

DISNEYLAND, USA (See Dell Giant No. 30)

DISNEY MOVIE BOOK
Walt Disney Productions (Gladstone): 1990 ($7.95, 8-1/2"x11", 52 pgs.) (w/pull-out poster)
1-Roger Rabbit in Tummy Trouble; from the cartoon film strips adapted to the comic format. Ron Dias-c — 1.50 — 4.50 — 12.00

DISNEY'S ACTION CLUB
Acclaim Books: 1997 - Present ($4.50, digest size)
1-4: 1-Hercules. 4-Mighty Ducks — 4.50

DISNEY'S ALADDIN (Movie)
Marvel Comics: Oct, 1994 - No. 11, 1995 ($1.50)
1-11 — 3.00

DISNEY'S BEAUTY AND THE BEAST (Movie)
Marvel Comics: Sept, 1994 - No. 13, 1995 ($1.50)
1-13 — 3.00

DISNEY'S BEAUTY AND THE BEAST HOLIDAY SPECIAL
Acclaim Books: 1997 ($4.50, digest size, one-shot)
1-Based on The Enchanted Christmas video — 4.50

DISNEY'S COLOSSAL COMICS COLLECTION
Disney Comics: 1991 - No. 10, 1993 ($1.95, digest-size, 96/132 pgs.)
1-10: Ducktales, Talespin, Chip 'n Dale's Rescue Rangers. 4-r/Darkwing Duck #1-4. 6-Goofy begins. 8-Little Mermaid — 4.00

DISNEY'S COMICS IN 3-D
Disney Comics: 1992 ($2.95, w/glasses, polybagged)
1-Infinity-c; Barks, Rosa, Gottfredson-r — 5.00

DISNEY'S ENCHANTING STORIES
Acclaim Books: 1997 - Present ($4.50, digest size)
1-5: 1-Hercules. 2-Pocahontas — 4.50

DISNEY'S NEW ADVENTURES OF BEAUTY AND THE BEAST (Also see Beauty and the Beast & Disney's Beauty and the Beast)
Disney Comics: 1992 - No. 2, 1992 ($1.50, limited series)
1,2-New stories based on movie — 3.00

DISNEY'S POCAHONTAS (Movie)
Marvel Comics: 1995 ($4.95, one-shot)
1-Movie adaptation — 1.00 — 2.80 — 7.00

DISNEY'S TALESPIN LIMITED SERIES: "TAKE OFF" (TV) (See Talespin)
W. D. Publications (Disney Comics): Jan, 1991 - No. 4, Apr, 1991 ($1.50, limited series, 52 pgs.)
1-4: Based on animated series; 4 part origin — 2.50

DISNEY'S TARZAN (Movie)
Dark Horse Comics: June, 1999 - No. 2, July, 1999 ($2.95, limited series)
1,2: Movie adaptation — 3.00

DISNEY'S THE LION KING (Movie)
Marvel Comics: July, 1994 - No. 2, July, 1994 ($1.50, limited series)
1,2: 2-part movie adaptation — 3.00
1-($2.50, 52 pgs.)-Complete story — 4.00

DISNEY'S THE LITTLE MERMAID (Movie)
Marvel Comics: Sept, 1994 - No. 12, 1995 ($1.50)
1-12 — 3.00

DISNEY'S THE LITTLE MERMAID LIMITED SERIES (Movie)
Disney Comics: Feb, 1992 - No. 4, May, 1992 ($1.50, limited series)
1-4: Peter David scripts — 3.00

DISNEY'S THE LITTLE MERMAID: UNDERWATER ENGAGEMENTS
Acclaim Books: 1997 ($4.50, digest size)
1-Flip book — 4.50

DISNEY'S THE HUNCHBACK OF NOTRE DAME (Movie)(See Disney's Comic Hits #10)
Marvel Comics: July, 1996 ($4.95, squarebound, one-shot)
1-Movie adaptation. — 1.00 — 2.80 — 7.00
NOTE: *A different edition of this series was sold at Wal-Mart stores with new covers depicting scenes from the 1989 feature film. Inside contents and price were identical.*

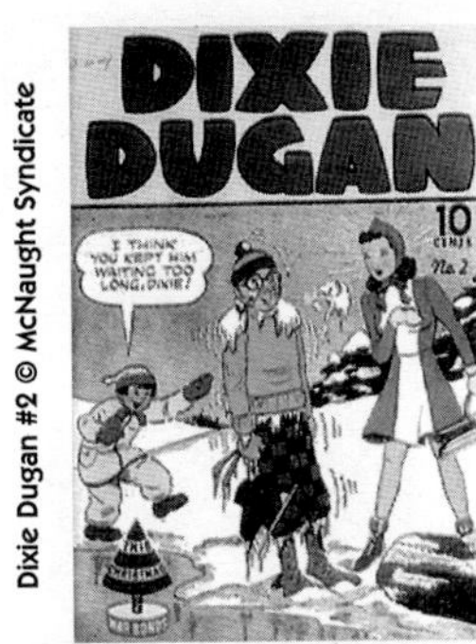

Dixie Dugan #2 © McNaught Syndicate

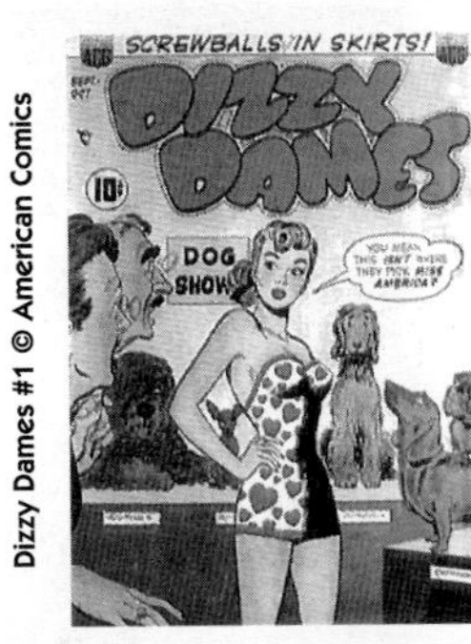

Dizzy Dames #1 © American Comics

Doc Savage #6 © Conde Nast

GD2.0 FN6.0 NM9.4

DISNEY'S THE THREE MUSKETEERS (Movie)
Marvel Comics: Jan, 1994 - No. 2, Feb, 1994 ($1.50, limited series)
1,2-Morrow-c; Spiegle-a; Movie adaptation 2.00

DISNEY'S TOY STORY (Movie)
Marvel Comics: Dec, 1995 ($4.95, one-shot)
nn-Adaptation of film 1.00 2.80 7.00

DISTANT SOIL, A (1st Series)
WaRP Graphics: Dec, 1983 - No. 9, Mar 1986 ($1.50, B&W)
1-9 3.00
NOTE: Second printings exist of #1, 2, 3 & 6.

DISTANT SOIL, A
Donning (Star Blaze): Mar, 1989 ($12.95, trade paperback)
nn-new material 13.00

DISTANT SOIL, A (2nd Series)
Aria Press/Image Comics (Highbrow Entertainment) #15 on: June, 1991 - Present ($1.75/$2.50/$2.95, B&W)
1-27: 13-$2.95-c begins. 14-Sketchbook. 15-(8/96)-1st Image issue 3.00
The Ascendant ('98, $18.95,TPB) r/#13-25 19.00
The Gathering ('97, $18.95,TPB) r/#1-13; intro. Neil Gaiman 19.00
NOTE: Four separate printings exist for #1 and are clearly marked. Second printings exist of #2-4 and are also clearly marked.

DISTANT SOIL, A: IMMIGRANT SONG
Donning (Star Blaze): Aug, 1987 ($6.95, trade paperback)
nn-new material 7.00

DIVER DAN (TV)
Dell Publishing Co.: Feb-Apr, 1962 - No. 2, June-Aug, 1962
Four Color 1254(#1), 2 4.50 13.50 50.00

DIVINE RIGHT
Image Comics (WildStorm Productions): Sept, 1997 - Present ($2.50)
Preview 6.00
1,2:1-Jim Lee-s/a(p)/c, 1-Variant-c by Charest 4.00
1-($3.50)-Voyager Pack w/Stormwatch preview 3.50
1-American Entertainment Ed. 8.00
2-Variant-c of Exotica & Blaze 6.00
3-5-Fairchild & Lynch app. 3.00
3-Chromium-c by Jim Lee 5.00
4,6-11: 4-American Entertainment Ed. 8-Two covers. 9-1st DC issue. 11-Divine Intervention pt. 1 3.00
5-Pacific Comicon Ed. 6.00
6-Glow in the dark variant-c, European Tour Edition 15.00
...Collected Edition #1-3 ($5.95, TPB) 1-r/#1,2. 2-r/#3,4. 3-r/#5,6 6.00
Divine Intervention/Gen 13 (11/99, $2.50) Part 3; D'Anda-a 2.50
Divine Intervention/Wildcats (11/99, $2.50) Part 2; D'Anda-a 2.50

DIVISION 13 (See Comic's Greatest World)
Dark Horse Comics: Sept, 1994 - Jan, 1995 ($2.50, color)
1-4: Giffen story in all. 1-Art Adams-c 2.50

DIXIE DUGAN (See Big Shot, Columbia Comics & Feature Funnies)
McNaught Syndicate/Columbia/Publication Ent.: July, 1942 - No. 13, 1949 (Strip reprints in all)
1-Joe Palooka x-over by Ham Fisher 28.00 84.00 195.00
2 15.00 45.00 105.00
3 11.00 33.00 75.00
4,5(1945-46)-Bo strip-r 8.35 25.00 50.00
6-13(1/47-49): 6-Paperdoll cut-outs 6.70 20.00 40.00

DIXIE DUGAN
Prize Publications (Headline): V3#1, Nov, 1951 - V4#4, Feb, 1954
V3#1 8.00 24.00 48.00
2-4 5.35 16.00 32.00
V4#1-4(#5-8) 4.25 13.00 26.00

DIZZY DAMES
American Comics Group (B&M Distr. Co.): Sept-Oct, 1952 - No. 6, Jul-Aug, 1953
1-Whitney-c 12.00 36.00 85.00
2 8.00 24.00 48.00
3-6 6.35 19.00 38.00

DIZZY DON COMICS
F. E. Howard Publications/Dizzy Don Ent. Ltd (Canada): 1942 - No. 22, Oct, 1946; No. 3, Apr, 1947 (Most B&W)
1 (B&W) 11.00 33.00 75.00
2 (B&W) 6.35 19.00 38.00
4-21 (B&W) 5.85 17.50 35.00
22-Full color, 52 pgs. 11.00 33.00 75.00
3 (4/47)-Full color, 52 pgs. 10.00 30.00 65.00

DIZZY DUCK (Formerly Barnyard Comics)
Standard Comics: No. 32, Nov, 1950 - No. 39, Mar, 1952
32-Funny animal 9.15 27.00 55.00
33-39 4.25 13.00 28.00

DNAGENTS (The New DNAgents V2/1 on)(Also see Surge)
Eclipse Comics: March, 1983 - No. 24, July, 1985 ($1.50, Baxter paper)
1-24: 1-Origin. 4-Amber app. 8-Infinity-c. 24-Dave Stevens-c 2.00

DOBERMAN (See Sgt. Bilko's Private...)

DOBIE GILLIS (See The Many Loves of...)

DOC CHAOS: THE STRANGE ATTRACTOR
Vortex Comics: Apr, 1990 - #3, 1990 ($3.00, 32 pgs.)
1-3: The Lust For Order 3.00

DOC SAMSON (Also see Incredible Hulk)
Marvel Comics: Jan, 1996 - No. 4, Apr, 1996 ($1.95, limited series)
1-4: 1-Hulk c/app. 2-She-Hulk-c/app. 3-Punisher-c/app. 4-Polaris-c/app. 2.00

DOC SAVAGE
Gold Key: Nov, 1966
1-Adaptation of the Thousand-Headed Man; James Bama c-r/1964 Doc Savage paperback 9.00 27.00 100.00

DOC SAVAGE (Also see Giant-Size...)
Marvel Comics Group: Oct, 1972 - No. 8, Jan, 1974
1 1.75 5.25 14.00
2,3-Steranko-c 1.10 3.30 9.00
4-8 1.00 2.80 7.00
NOTE: ***Gil Kane** c-5, 6. **Mooney** a-1i. No. 1, 2 adapts pulp story "The Man of Bronze"; No. 3, 4 adapts "Death in Silver"; No. 5, 6 adapts "The Monsters"; No. 7, 8 adapts "The Brand of The Werewolf".*

DOC SAVAGE (Magazine)
Marvel Comics Group: Aug, 1975 - No. 8, Spring, 1977 ($1.00, B&W)
1-Cover from movie poster; Ron Ely photo-c 1.25 3.75 10.00
2-5: 3-Buscema-a. 5-Adams-a(1 pg.), Rogers-a(1 pg) 2.40 6.00
6-8 1.00 2.80 7.00

DOC SAVAGE
DC Comics: Nov, 1987 - No. 4, Feb, 1988 ($1.75, limited series)
1-4 2.00

DOC SAVAGE
DC Comics: Nov, 1988 - No. 24, Oct, 1990 ($1.75/$2.00: #13-24)
1-24 2.00
Annual 1 (1989, $3.50, 68 pgs.) 3.50

DOC SAVAGE COMICS (Also see Shadow Comics)
Street & Smith Publications: May, 1940 - No. 20, Oct, 1943 (1st app. in Doc Savage pulp, 3/33)
1-Doc Savage, Cap Fury, Danny Garrett, Mark Mallory, The Whisperer, Captain Death, Billy the Kid, Sheriff Pete & Treasure Island begin; Norgil, the Magician app. 420.00 1260.00 4200.00
2-Origin & 1st app. Ajax, the Sun Man; Danny Garrett, The Whisperer end

Doc Savage V2 #5 © Conde Nast

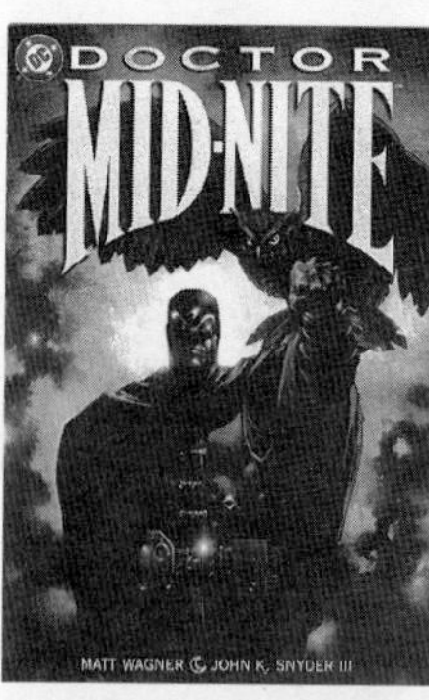

Dr. Mid-Nite #1 © DC

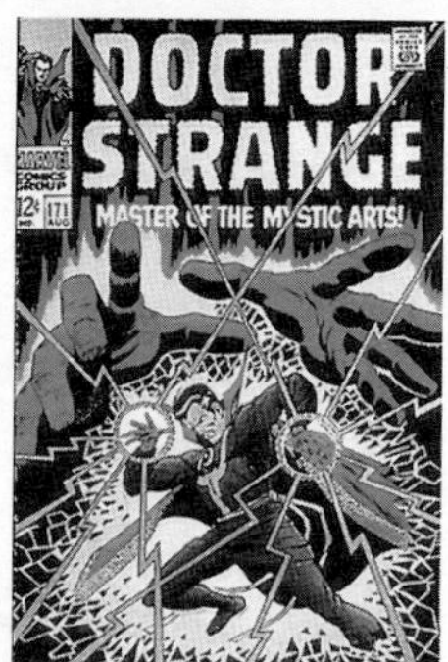

Doctor Strange #171 © MAR

	GD2.0	FN6.0	NM9.4
	150.00	450.00	1200.00
3	116.00	348.00	925.00
4-Treasure Island ends; Tuska-a	97.00	291.00	775.00
5-Origin & 1st app. Astron, the Crocodile Queen, not in #9 & 11; Norgi the Magician app.	75.00	225.00	600.00
6-10: 6-Cap Fury ends; origin & only app. Red Falcon in Astron story. 8-Mark Mallory ends; Charlie McCarthy app. on-c plus true life story. 9-Supersnipe app. 10-Origin & only app. The Thunderbolt	60.00	180.00	480.00
11,12	50.00	150.00	400.00
V2#1-8(#13-20): 16-The Pulp Hero, The Avenger app.; Fanny Brice story. 17-Sun Man ends; Nick Carter begins; Duffy's Tavern part photo-c & story. 18-Huckleberry Finn part-c/story. 19-Henny Youngman part photo-c & life story. 20-Only all funny-c w/Huckleberry Finn	50.00	150.00	400.00

DOC SAVAGE: CURSE OF THE FIRE GOD
Dark Horse Comics: Sept, 1995 - No, 4, Dec, 1995 ($2.95, limited series)

1-4 — 3.00

DOC SAVAGE: THE MAN OF BRONZE
Millennium Publications: 1991 - No. 4, 1991 ($2.50, limited series)

1-4: 1-Bronze logo — 2.50
...: The Manual of Bronze 1 ($2.50, B&W, color, one-shot)-Unpublished proposed Doc Savage strip in color, B&W strip-r — 2.50

DOC SAVAGE: THE MAN OF BRONZE, DOOM DYNASTY
Millennium Publ.: 1992 (Says 1991) - No. 2, 1992 ($2.50, limited series)

1,2 — 2.50

DOC SAVAGE: THE MAN OF BRONZE - REPEL
Innovation Publishing: 1992 ($2.50)

1-Dave Dorman painted-c — 2.50

DOC SAVAGE: THE MAN OF BRONZE THE DEVIL'S THOUGHTS
Millennium Publ.: 1992 (Says 1991) - No. 3, 1992 ($2.50, limited series)

1-3 — 2.50

DOC STEARN...MR. MONSTER (See Mr. Monster)

DR. ANTHONY KING, HOLLYWOOD LOVE DOCTOR
Minoan Publishing Corp./Harvey Publications No. 4: 1952(Jan) - No. 3, May, 1953; No. 4, May, 1954

	GD2.0	FN6.0	NM9.4
1	11.50	34.00	80.00
2-4: 4-Powell-a	7.50	22.50	45.00

DR. ANTHONY'S LOVE CLINIC (See Mr. Anthony's...)

DR. BOBBS
Dell Publishing Co.: No. 212, Jan, 1949

	GD2.0	FN6.0	NM9.4
Four Color 212	3.80	11.50	40.00

DOCTOR BOOGIE
Media Arts Publishing: 1987 ($1.75)

1-Airbrush wraparound-c; Nick Cuti-i — 2.00

DOCTOR CHAOS
Triumphant Comics: Nov, 1993 - No. 6, Mar, 1994 ($2.50)

1-6: 1,2-Triumphant Unleashed x-over. 2-1st app. War Dancer in pin-up. 3-Intro The Cry — 2.50

DOCTOR CYBORG
Attention! Publishing: 1996 - No. 5 ($2.95, B&W)

1-5 — 3.00
The Clone Conspiracy TPB (1998, $14.95) r/#1-5 — 15.00

DR. DOOM'S REVENGE
Marvel Comics: 1989 (Came w/computer game from Paragon Software)

V1#1-Spider-Man & Captain America fight Dr. Doom — 3.00

DR. FATE (See 1st Issue Special, The Immortal..., Justice League, More Fun #55, & Showcase)

DOCTOR FATE
DC Comics: July, 1987 - No. 4, Oct, 1987 ($1.50, limited series, Baxter paper)

1-4: Giffen-c/a in all — 2.50

DOCTOR FATE
DC Comics: Winter, 1988-'89 - No. 41, June, 1992 ($1.25/$1.50 #5 on)

1-41: 15-Justice League app. 25-1st new Dr. Fate. 36-Original Dr. returns — 2.00
Annual 1(1989, $2.95, 68 pgs.)-Sutton-a — 3.50

DR. FU MANCHU (See The Mask of...)
I.W. Enterprises: 1964

	GD2.0	FN6.0	NM9.4
1-r/Avon's "Mask of Dr. Fu Manchu"; Wood-a	7.50	22.50	75.00

DR. GIGGLES (See Dark Horse Presents #64-66)
Dark Horse Comics: Oct, 1992 - No. 2, Oct, 1992 ($2.50, limited series)

1,2-Based on movie — 2.50

DOCTOR GRAVES (Formerly The Many Ghosts of...)
Charlton Comics: No. 73, Sept, 1985 - No. 75, Jan, 1986

73-75-Low print run — 4.00

DR. JEKYLL AND MR. HYDE (See A Star Presentation & Supernatural Thrillers #4)

DR. KILDARE (TV)
Dell Publishing Co.: No. 1337, 4-6/62 - No. 9, 4-6/65 (All Richard Chamberlain photo-c)

	GD2.0	FN6.0	NM9.4
Four Color 1337(#1, 1962)	8.00	25.00	90.00
2-9	5.50	16.50	60.00

DR. MASTERS (See The Adventures of Young...)

DOCTOR MID-NITE
DC Comics: 1999 - No. 3, 1999 ($5.95, square-bound, limited series)

1-3-Matt Wagner-s/John K. Snyder III-painted art — 6.00

DOCTOR SOLAR, MAN OF THE ATOM (Also see The Occult Files of Dr. Spektor #14 & Solar)
Gold Key/Whitman No. 28 on: 10/62 - No. 27, 4/69; No. 28, 4/81 - No. 31, 3/82 (1-27 have painted-c)

	GD2.0	FN6.0	NM9.4
1-(#10000-210)-Origin/1st app. Dr. Solar (1st original Gold Key character)	18.00	55.00	200.00
2-Prof. Harbinger begins	7.00	20.00	75.00
3,4	4.50	13.50	50.00
5-Intro. Man of the Atom in costume	5.00	15.00	55.00
6-10	2.75	8.00	30.00
11-14,16-20	2.20	6.50	24.00
15-Origin retold	2.50	7.60	28.00
21-23: 23-Last 12¢ issue	2.00	6.00	20.00
24-27	1.80	5.40	18.00
28-31: 29-Magnus Robot Fighter begins. 31-The Sentinel app.	.90	2.70	8.00

NOTE: ***Frank Bolle** a-6-19, 29-31; c-29i, 30i. **Bob Fugitani** a-1-5. **Spiegle** a-29-31. **Al McWilliams** a-20-23.*

DOCTOR SOLAR, MAN OF THE ATOM
Valiant Comics: 1990 - No. 2, 1991 ($7.95, card stock-c, high quality, 96 pgs.)

	GD2.0	FN6.0	NM9.4
1,2: Reprints Gold Key series	.90	2.70	8.00

DOCTOR SPEKTOR (See The Occult Files of..., & Spine-Tingling Tales)

DOCTOR STRANGE (Formerly Strange Tales #1-168) (Also see The Defenders, Giant-Size..., Marvel Fanfare, Marvel Graphic Novel, Marvel Premiere, Marvel Treasury Edition & Strange Tales, 2nd Series)
Marvel Comics Group: No. 169, 6/68 - No. 183, 11/69; 6/74 - No. 81, 2/87

	GD2.0	FN6.0	NM9.4
169(#1)-Origin retold; panel swipe/M.D. #1-c	11.00	33.00	110.00
170-177: 177-New costume	3.20	9.60	32.00
178-183: 178-Black Knight app. 179-Spider-Man story-r. 180-Photo montage-c. 181-Brunner-c(part-i), last 12¢ issue	2.80	7.80	28.00
1(6/74, 2nd series)-Brunner-c/a	3.50	10.50	35.00
2	2.00	6.00	16.00
3-5	1.00	3.00	8.00
6-10			5.00
11-13,15-20: 13,15-17-(Regular 25¢ editions)			3.00

Doctor Strange V2 #1 © MAR

Doctor Who #3 © MAR

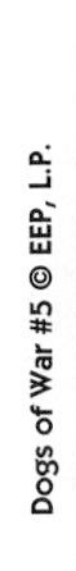

Dogs of War #5 © EEP, L.P.

GD2.0 FN6.0 NM9.4

13-17-(30¢-c variants, limited distribution).14(5/76) 1.50 4.50 12.00
14-Dracula app.; (regular 25¢ edition) 3.00
21-58,63-77,79-81: 21-Origin-r/Doctor Strange #169. 31-Sub-Mariner-c/story. 56-Origin retold. 58-Re-intro Hannibal King (cameo) 2.00
59-62: 59-Hannibal King full app. 59-62-Dracula app. (Darkhold storyline). 61,62-Doctor Strange, Blade, Hannibal King & Frank Drake team-up to battle Dracula. 62-Death of Dracula & Lilith 4.00
78-New costume 2.50
Annual 1(1976, 52 pgs.)-New Russell-a (35 pgs.) 5.00
.../Silver Dagger Special Edition 1 (3/83, $2.50)-r/#1,2,4,5; Wrightson-c 3.00
...What Is It That Disturbs You, Stephen? #1 (10/97, $5.99, 48 pgs.) Russell-a/Andreyko & Russell-s, retelling of Annual #1 story 2.40 6.00

NOTE: **Adkins** *a-169, 170, 171i; c-169-171, 172i, 173.* **Adams** *a-4i.* **Austin** *a(i)-48-60, 66, 68, 70, 73; c(i)-38, 47-53, 55, 58-60, 70.* **Brunner** *a-1-5p; c-1-6, 22, 28-30, 33.* **Colan** *a(p)-172-178, 180-183, 6-18, 36-45, 47; c(p)-172, 174-183, 11-21, 23, 27, 35, 36, 47.* **Ditko** *a-179r, 3r.* **Everett** *c-183i.* **Golden** *a-46p, 55p; c-42-44, 46, 55p.* **G. Kane** *c(p)-8-10.* **Miller** *c-46p.* **Nebres** *a-20, 22, 23, 24i, 26i, 32i; c-32i, 34.* **Rogers** *a-48-53p; c-47p-53p.* **Russell** *a-34i, 46i, Annual 1.* **B. Smith** *c-179.* **Paul Smith** *a-54p, 56p, 65, 66p, 68p, 69, 71-73; c-56, 65, 66, 68, 71.* **Starlin** *a-23p, 26; c-25, 26.* **Sutton** *a-27-29p, 31i, 33, 34p. Painted c-62, 63.*

DOCTOR STRANGE (Volume 2)
Marvel Comics: Feb, 1999 - No. 4, May, 1999 ($2.99, limited series)

1-4: 1,2-Tony Harris-a/painted cover. 3,4-Chadwick-a 3.00

DOCTOR STRANGE CLASSICS
Marvel Comics Group: Mar, 1984 - No. 4, June, 1984 ($1.50, Baxter paper)

1-4: Ditko-r; Byrne-c. 4-New Golden pin-up 2.00
NOTE: **Byrne** *c-1i, 2-4.*

DOCTOR STRANGEFATE (See Marvel Versus DC #3 & DC Versus Marvel #4)
DC Comics (Amalgam): Apr, 1996 ($1.95)

1-Ron Marz script w/Jose Garcia-Lopez-(p) & Kevin Nowlan-(i). Access & Charles Xavier app. 2.00

DOCTOR STRANGE MASTER OF THE MYSTIC ARTS (See Fireside Book Series)

DOCTOR STRANGE, SORCERER SUPREME
Marvel Comics (Midnight Sons imprint #60 on): Nov, 1988 - No. 90, June, 1996 ($1.25/$1.50/$1.75/$1.95, direct sales only, Mando paper)

1 ($1.25) 3.00
2-49,51-64: 3-New Defenders app. 5-Guice-96c/a begins. 14-18-Morbius story line. 26-Werewolf by Night app.10-Re-intro Morbius w/new costume (11/89) 11-Hobgoblin app.15-Unauthorized Amy Grant photo-c. 28-Ghost Rider story cont'd from G.R. #12; same book published at same time as Doctor Strange/Ghost Rider Special #1 (4/91). 31-36-Infinity Gauntlet x-overs: 31-Silver Surfer app. 33-Thanos-c & cameo. 36-Warlock app. 37-Silver Surfer app. 40-Daredevil x-over. 41-Wolverine-c/story. 42-47-Infinity War x-overs. 47-Gamora app. 52,53-Morbius-c/stories. 60,61-Siege of Darkness pt. 7 & 15. 60-Spot varnish-c. 61-New Doctor Strange begins (cameo, 1st app.). 62-Dr. Doom & Morbius app. 2.00
50-($2.95, 52 pgs.)-Holo-grafx foil-c; Hulk, Ghost Rider & Silver Surfer app.; leads into new Secret Defenders series 3.00
65-74, 76-90: 65-Begin $1.95-c; bound-in card sheet. 72-Silver ink-c. 80-82-Ellis-s. 84-DeMatteis story begins. 87-Death of Baron Mordo. 2.00
75 ($2.50) 2.50
75 ($3.50)-Foil-c 4.00
Annual 2-4 ('92-'94, 68 pgs.)-2-Defenders app. 3-Polybagged w/card 3.00
Ashcan (1995, 75¢) 2.00
.../Ghost Rider Special 1 (4/91, $1.50)-Same book as D.S.S.S. #28 2.00
...Vs. Dracula 1 (3/94, $1.75, 52 pgs.)-r/Tomb of Dracula #44 & Dr. Strange #14 2.00

NOTE: **Colan** *c/a-19.* **Golden** *c-28.* **Guice** *a-5-16, 18, 20-24; c-5-12, 20-24. See 1st series for Annual #1.*

DR. TOM BRENT, YOUNG INTERN
Charlton Publications: Feb, 1963 - No. 5, Oct, 1963

1 1.85 5.50 15.00
2-5 1.25 3.75 10.00

DR. TOMORROW
Acclaim Comics (Valiant): Sept, 1997 - No. 12 ($2.50)

GD2.0 FN6.0 NM9.4

1-12: 1-Mignola-c 2.50

DR. VOLTZ (See Mighty Midget Comics)

DR. WEIRD
Big Bang Comics: 1994 ($2.95, B&W)

1,2: 1-Frank Brunner-c 4.00

DR. WEIRD SPECIAL
Big Bang Comics: Feb, 1994 ($3.95, B&W, 68 pgs.)

1-Origin-r by Starlin; Starlin-c. 4.00

DOCTOR WHO (Also see Marvel Premiere #57-60)
Marvel Comics Group: Oct, 1984 - No. 23, Aug, 1986 ($1.50, color, direct sales, Baxter paper)

1-23-British-r. 3.00
Graphic Novel Voyager (1985, $8.95) color reprints of B&W comic pages from Doctor Who Magazine #88-99; Colin Baker afterword 12.00

DR. WHO & THE DALEKS (See Movie Classics)

DR. WONDER
Old Town Publishing: June, 1996 - Present ($2.95, B&W)

1-5: 1-Intro & origin of Dr. Wonder; Dick Ayers-c/a; Irwin Hasen-a; contains profiles of the artists 3.00

DOCTOR ZERO
Marvel Comics (Epic Comics): Apr, 1988 - No. 8, Aug, 1989 ($1.25/$1.50)

1-8: 1-Sienkiewicz-c. 6,7-Spiegle-a 2.00
NOTE: **Sienkiewicz** *a-3i, 4i; c-1.* **Spiegle** *a-6, 7.*

DO-DO (Funny Animal Circus Stories)
Nation-Wide Publishers: 1950 - No. 7, 1951 (5¢, 5x7-1/4" Miniature)

1 (52 pgs.) 23.00 69.00 160.00
2-7 11.50 34.00 80.00

DODO & THE FROG, THE (Formerly Funny Stuff; also see It's Game Time #2)
National Periodical Publications: No. 80, 9-10/54 - No. 88, 1-2/56; No. 89, 8-9/56; No. 90, 10-11/56; No. 91, 9/57; No. 92, 11/57 (See Comic Cavalcade)

80-1st app. Doodles Duck by Sheldon Mayer 20.00 60.00 140.00
81-91: Doodles Duck by Mayer in #81,83-90 13.00 39.00 90.00
92-(Scarce)-Doodles Duck by S. Mayer 17.00 51.00 120.00

DOGFACE DOOLEY
Magazine Enterprises: 1951 - No. 5, 1953

1(A-1 40) 5.85 17.50 35.00
2(A-1 43), 3(A-1 49), 4(A-1 53), 5(A-1 64) 4.25 13.00 26.00
I.W. Reprint #1('64), Super Reprint #17 2.40 6.00 12.00

DOG MOON
DC Comics (Vertigo): 1996 ($6.95, one-shot)

1-Robert Hunter-scripts; Tim Truman-c/a. 7.00

DOG OF FLANDERS, A
Dell Publishing Co.: No. 1088, Mar, 1960

Four Color 1088-Movie, photo-c 3.60 11.00 40.00

DOGPATCH (See Al Capp's... & Mammy Yokum)

DOGS OF WAR (Also see Warriors of Plasm)
Defiant: Apr, 1994 - No. 5, Aug, 1994 ($2.50)

1-5 2.50

DOGS-O-WAR
Crusade Comics: June, 1996 - No. 3, Jan, 1997 ($2.95, B&W, limited series)

1-3: 1,2-Photo-c 3.00

DOLLFACE & HER GANG (Betty Betz'...)
Dell Publishing Co.: No. 309, Jan, 1951

Four Color 309 4.50 13.50 50.00

DOLLMAN (Movie)
Eternity Comics: Sept, 1991 - No. 4, Dec, 1991 ($2.50, limited series)

1-4: Adaptation of film 2.50

Doll Man Quarterly #5 © QUA

Dominion #3 © ECL

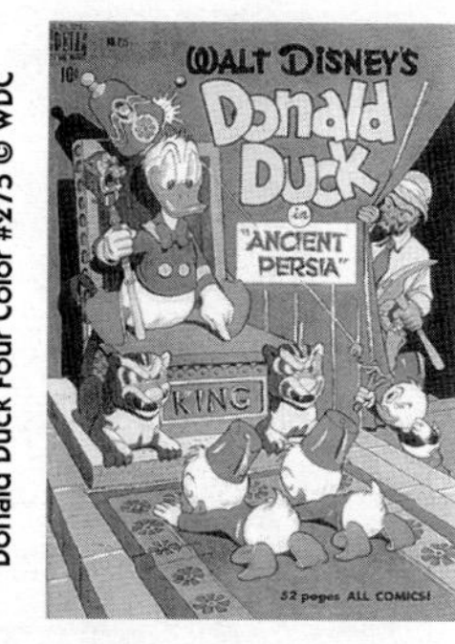

Donald Duck Four Color #275 © WDC

GD2.0 FN6.0 NM9.4

DOLL MAN QUARTERLY, THE (Doll Man #17 on; also see Feature Comics #27 & Freedom Fighters)
Quality Comics: Fall, 1941 - No. 7, Fall, '43; No. 8, Spr, '46 - No. 47, Oct, 1953

1-Dollman (by Cassone), Justin Wright begin 300.00 900.00 2700.00
2-The Dragon begins; Crandall-a(5) 125.00 375.00 1000.00
3,4 87.00 261.00 700.00
5-Crandall-a 69.00 207.00 550.00
6,7(1943) 52.00 156.00 420.00
8(1946)-1st app. Torchy by Bill Ward 150.00 450.00 1200.00
9 52.00 156.00 420.00
10-20 40.00 120.00 300.00
21-30: 28-Vs. The Flame 36.00 107.00 250.00
31-36,38,40: 31-(12/50)-Intro Elmo, the wonder dog (Dollman's faithful dog). 32-34-Jeb Rivers app.; 34 by Crandall(p) 29.00 86.00 200.00
37-Origin & 1st app. Dollgirl; Dollgirl bondage-c 40.00 120.00 300.00
39- "Narcotics...the Death Drug" c-/story 30.00 90.00 210.00
41-47 21.00 64.00 150.00
Super Reprint #11('64, r/#20),15(r/#23),17(r/#28): 15,17-Torchy app.; Andru/Esposito-c 3.00 9.00 30.00

NOTE: ***Ward*** *Torchy in 8, 9, 11, 12, 14-24, 26, 27; by Fox-#30, 35-47.* ***Crandall*** *a-2, 5, 10, 13 & Super #11, 17, 18.* ***Crandall/Cuidera*** *c-40-42.* ***Guardineer*** *a-3. Bondage c-27, 37, 38, 39.*

DOLLS
Sirius: June, 1996 ($2.95, B&W, one-shot)

1 3.00

DOLLY
Ziff-Davis Publ. Co.: No. 10, July-Aug, 1951 (Funny animal)

10-Painted-c 5.85 17.50 35.00

DOLLY DILL
Marvel Comics/Newsstand Publ.: 1945

1 15.00 45.00 105.00

DOMINION (Manga)
Eclipse Comics: Dec, 1990 - No. 6., July, 1990 ($2.00, B&W, limited series)

1-6 3.00

DOMINION: CONFLICT 1 (Manga)
Dark Horse Comics: Mar, 1996 - Present ($2.95, B&W, limited series)

1-5: Shirow-c/a/scripts 3.00

DOMINIQUE: KILLZONE
Caliber Comics: May, 1995 ($2.95, B&W)

1 3.00

DOMINO (See X-Force)
Marvel Comics: Jan, 1997 - No. 3, Mar, 1997 ($1.95, limited series)

1-3: 2-Deathstrike-c/app. 2.00

DOMINO CHANCE
Chance Enterprises: May-June, 1982 - No. 9, May, 1985 (B&W)

1-9: 7-1st app. Gizmo, 2 pgs. 8-1st full Gizmo story, 1-Reprint, May, 1985 2.50

DONALD AND MICKEY IN DISNEYLAND (See Dell Giants)

DONALD AND SCROOGE
Disney Comics: 1992 ($8.95, squarebound, 100 pgs.)

nn-Don Rosa reprint special; r/U.S., D.D. Advs. 1.25 3.75 10.00
1-3 (1992, $1.50)-r/D.D. Advs. (Disney) #1,22,24 & U.S. #261-263,269 2.00

DONALD AND THE WHEEL (Disney)
Dell Publishing Co.: No. 1190, Nov, 1961

Four Color 1190-Movie, Barks-c 6.40 19.00 70.00

DONALD DUCK (See Adventures of Mickey Mouse, Cheerios, Donald & Mickey, Ducktales, Dynabrite Comics, Gladstone Comic Album, Mickey & Donald, Mickey Mouse Mag., Story Hour Series, Uncle Scroogre, Walt Disney's Comics & Stories, W. D.'s Donald Duck, Wheaties & Whitman Comic Books, Wise Little Hen, The)

DONALD DUCK
Whitman Publishing Co./Grosset & Dunlap/K.K.: 1935, 1936 (All pages on heavy linen-like finish cover stock in color;1st book ever devoted to Donald Duck; see Advs. of Mickey Mouse for 1st app.) (9-1/2x13")

978(1935)-16 pgs.; Illustrated text story book 325.00 975.00 2300.00
nn(1936)-36 pgs.plus hard cover & dust jacket. Story completely rewritten with B&W illos added. Mickey appears and his nephews are named Morty & Monty
Book only 325.00 975.00 2300.00
Dust jacket only.... 85.00 255.00 600.00

DONALD DUCK (Walt Disney's) (10¢)
Whitman/K.K. Publications: 1938 (8-1/2x11-1/2", B&W, cardboard-c)
(Has D. Duck with bubble pipe on-c)

GD2.0 FN6.0 VF8.0 NM9.4

nn-The first Donald Duck & Walt Disney comic book; 1936 & 1937 Sunday strip-r(in B&W); same format as the Feature Books; 1st strips with Huey, Dewey & Louie from 10/17/37 300.00 900.00 1800.00 2400.00

DONALD DUCK (Walt Disney's...#262 on; see 4-Color listings for titles & Four Color No. 1109 for origin story)
Dell Publ. Co./Gold Key #85-216/Whitman #217-245/Gladstone #246 on: 1940 - No. 84, Sept-Nov, 1962; No. 85, Dec, 1962 - No. 245, 1984; No. 246, Oct, 1986 - No. 279, May, 1990; No. 280, Sept, 1993 - Present

GD2.0 FN6.0 VF8.0 NM9.4

Four Color 4(1940)-Daily 1939 strip-r by Al Taliaferro 846.00 2538.00 5922.00 11,000.00
Large Feature Comic 16(1/41?)-1940 Sunday strips-r in B&W 338.00 1014.00 2366.00 4400.00
Large Feature Comic 20('41)-Comic Paint Book, r-single panels from Large Feature #16 at top of each pg. to color; daily strip-r across bottom of each pg. 408.00 1224.00 2856.00 5300.00
Four Color 9('42)- "Finds Pirate Gold"; 64 pgs. by Carl Barks & Jack Hannah (pgs. 1,2,5,12-40 are by Barks, his 1st Donald Duck comic book art work; © 8/17/42) 615.00 1845.00 4300.00 8000.00
Four Color 29(9/43)- "Mummy's Ring" by Barks; reprinted in Uncle Scrooge & Donald Duck #1('65), W. D. Comics Digest #44('73) & Donald Duck Advs. #14 492.00 1476.00 3444.00 6400.00

GD2.0 FN6.0 NM9.4

Four Color 62(1/45)- "Frozen Gold"; 52 pgs. by Barks, reprinted in The Best of W.D. Comics & Donald Duck Advs. #4 154.00 462.00 2000.00
Four Color 108(1946)- "Terror of the River"; 52 pgs. by Carl Barks; reprinted in Gladstone Comic Album #2 112.00 335.00 1450.00
Four Color 147(5/47)-in "Volcano Valley" by Barks 77.00 231.00 1000.00
Four Color 159(8/47)-in "The Ghost of the Grotto";52 pgs. by Carl Barks; reprinted in Best of Uncle Scrooge & Donald Duck #1 ('66) & The Best of W.D. Comics & D.D. Advs. #9; two Barks stories 62.00 185.00 800.00
Four Color 178(12/47)-1st app. Uncle Scrooge by Carl Barks; reprinted in Gold Key Christmas Parade #3 & The Best of Walt Disney Comics 92.00 277.00 1200.00
Four Color 189(6/48)-by Carl Barks; reprinted in Best of Donald Duck & Uncle Scrooge #1('64) & D.D. Advs. #19 58.00 173.00 750.00
Four Color 199(10/48)-by Carl Barks; mentioned in Love and Death; r/in Gladstone Comic Album #5 64.00 190.00 825.00
Four Color 203(12/48)-by Barks; reprinted as Gold Key Christmas Parade #4 43.00 129.00 560.00
Four Color 223(4/49)-by Barks; reprinted as Best of Donald Duck #1 & Donald Duck Advs. #3 62.00 185.00 800.00
Four Color 238(8/49)-in "Voodoo Hoodoo" by Barks 43.00 129.00 560.00
Four Color 256(12/49)-by Barks; reprinted in Best of Donald Duck & Uncle Scrooge #2('67), Gladstone Comic Album #16 & W.D. Comics Digest 44('73) 33.00 99.00 425.00
Four Color 263(2/50)-Two Barks stories; r-in D.D. #278 31.00 92.00 400.00
Four Color 275(5/50), 282(7/50), 291(9/50), 300(11/50)-All by Carl Barks; 275, 282 reprinted in W.D. Comics Digest #44('73). #275 r/in Gladstone Comic Album #10. #291 r/in D. Duck Advs. #16 29.00 87.00 375.00
Four Color 308(1/51), 318(3/51)-by Barks; #318-reprinted in W.D. Comics Digest #34 & D.D. Advs. #2,19 25.00 75.00 325.00

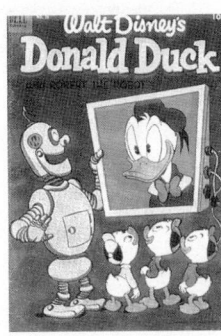

Donald Duck #28 © WDC

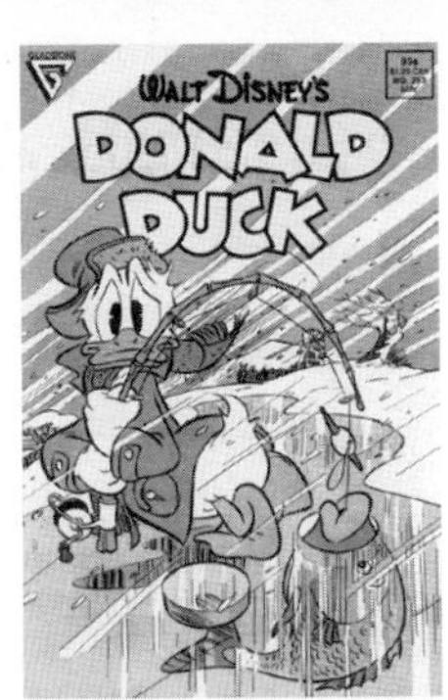

Donald Duck #253 © WDC

Don Fortune Magazine #1 © Don Fortune Publ.

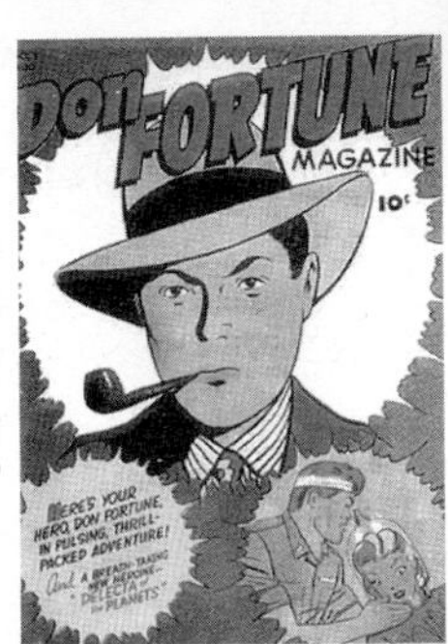

GD2.0 FN6.0 NM9.4

Four Color 328(5/51)-by Carl Barks 27.00 81.00 350.00

Four Color 339(7-8/51), 379-2nd Uncle Scrooge-c; art not by Barks. 6.00 18.00 60.00

Four Color 348(9-10/51), 356,394-Barks-c only 15.00 45.00 160.00

Four Color 367(1-2/52)-by Barks; reprinted as Gold Key Christmas Parade #2 & #8 25.00 75.00 320.00

Four Color 408(7-8/52), 422(9-10/52)-All by Carl Barks. #408-r-in Best of Donald Duck & Uncle Scrooge #1('64) & Gladstone Comic Album #13 25.00 75.00 320.00

26(11-12/52)-In "Trick or Treat" (Barks-a, 36pgs.) 1st story r-in Walt Disney Digest #16 & Gladstone C.A. #23 25.00 76.00 330.00

27-30-Barks-c only 10.00 30.00 110.00

31-44,47-50 4.50 13.50 50.00

45-Barks-a (6 pgs.) 11.00 34.00 125.00

46- "Secret of Hondorica" by Barks, 24 pgs.; reprinted in Donald Duck #98 & 154 18.00 55.00 200.00

51-Barks-a,1/2 pg. 5.00 15.00 55.00

52- "Lost Peg-Leg Mine" by Barks, 10 pgs. 12.35 37.00 135.00

53,55-59 4.00 12.00 45.00

54- "Forbidden Valley" by Barks, 26 pgs. (10¢ & 15¢ versions exist) 13.00 38.00 140.00

60- "Donald Duck & the Titanic Ants" by Barks, 20 pgs. plus 6 more pgs. 13.00 38.00 140.00

61-67,69,70 3.25 9.50 35.00

68-Barks-a, 5 pgs. 9.00 29.00 105.00

71-Barks-r, 1/2 pg. 3.25 9.50 35.00

72-78,80,82-97,99,100: 96-Donald Duck Album 3.25 9.50 35.00

79,81-Barks-a, 1pg. 3.25 9.50 35.00

98-Reprints #46 (Barks) 3.25 9.50 35.00

101-135: 102-Super Goof. 112-1st Moby Duck. 120-Last 12¢ issue. 134-Barks-r/#52 & WDC&S 194. 135-Barks-r/WDC&S 198, 19 pgs. 2.20 6.50 24.00

136-153,155,156,158 1.40 4.20 14.00

154-Barks-r(#46) 1.80 5.40 18.00

157,159,160,164: 157-Barks-r(#45). 159-Reprints/WDC&S #192 (10 pgs.). 160-Barks-r(#26). 164-Barks-r(#79) 1.40 4.20 14.00

161-163,165-173,175-187,189-191: 187-Barks r/#68. 1.00 3.00 10.00

174,188: 174-r/4-Color #394. 1.20 3.60 12.00

192-Barks-r(40 pgs.) from Donald Duck #60 & WDC&S #226,234 (52 pgs.) 1.50 4.50 15.00

193-200,202-207,209-211,213-216 1.00 2.80 7.00

201,208,212: 201-Barks-r/Christmas Parade #26, 16pgs. 208-Barks-r/#60 (6 pgs.). 212-Barks-r/WDC&S #130 1.00 2.80 7.00

217-219: 217 has 216 on-c. 219-Barks-r/WDC&S #106,107, 10 pgs. ea. 1.10 3.30 9.00

220,221,223,224 2.00 6.00 20.00

222-(8-12/80)-Only distr. in Whitman 3-pack 9.00 27.00 100.00

225-228: 228-Barks-r/F.C. #275. 1.20 3.60 12.00

229-240: 229-Barks-r/F.C. #282. 230-Barks-r/ #52 & WDC&S #194 1.00 3.00 8.00

241-245 1.40 4.20 14.00

246-(1st Gladstone issue)-Barks-r/FC #422 1.60 4.80 16.00

247-249,251: 248,249-Barks-r/DD #54 & 26. 251-Barks-r/1945 Firestone 1.00 3.00 10.00

250-($1.50, 68 pgs.)-Barks-r/4-Color #9 1.20 3.60 12.00

252-280. 286: 254-Barks-r/FC #328. 256-Barks-r/FC #147. 257-($1.50, 52 pgs.)-Barks-r/Vacaction Parade #1. 261-Barks-r/FC #300. 275-Kelly-r/FC #92. 278,279 ($1.95, 68 pgs.): 278-Rosa-a; Barks-r/FC #263. 279-Rosa-c; Barks-r/MOC #4. 280 (#1, 2nd Series). 286-Rosa-a 5.00

281,282,284 4.00

283-Don Rosa-a, part-c & scripts 5.00

285,287-304 2.00

286 ($2.95, 68 pgs.)-Happy Birthday, Donald 3.00

Mini-Comic #1(1976)-(3-1/4x6-1/2"); r/D.D. #150 6.00

NOTE: ***Carl Barks*** *wrote all issues he illustrated, but #117, 126, 138 contain his script only. Issues 4-Color #189, 199, 203, 223, 238, 256, 263, 275, 282, 308, 348, 356, 367, 394, 408, 422, 26-30, 35, 44, 46, 52, 55, 57, 60, 65, 70-73, 77-80, 83, 101, 103, 105, 106, 111, 126, 246r, 266r, 268r, 271r, 275r, 278r(F.C. 263) all have* ***Barks*** *covers.* ***Barks*** *r-263-267, 269-278-282, 284, 285. #96 titled "Comic Album", #99-"Christmas Album". New art issues (not reprints)-106-46, 148-63, 167, 169, 170, 172, 173, 175, 178, 179, 196, 209, 223, 225, 236.* ***Taliaferro*** *daily newspaper strips #258-260, 264, 284, 285; Sunday strips #247, 280-283.*

GD2.0 FN6.0 NM9.4

DONALD DUCK ALBUM (See Comic Album No. 1,3 & Duck Album)
Dell Publishing Co./Gold Key: 5-7/59 - F.C. No. 1239, 10-12/61; 1962; 8/63 - No. 2, Oct, 1963

Four Color 995 (#1) 5.00 15.00 55.00

Four Color 1182, 01204-207 (1962-Dell) 3.60 11.00 40.00

Four Color 1099,1140,1239-Barks-c 5.50 16.50 60.00

1(8/63-Gold Key)-Barks-c 5.00 15.00 55.00

2(10/63) 3.60 11.00 40.00

DONALD DUCK AND THE BOYS (Also see Story Hour Series)
Whitman Publishing Co.: 1948 (5-1/4x5-1/2", 100pgs., hard-c; art & text)

845-(49) new illos by Barks based on his Donald Duck 10-pager in WDC&S #74, Expanded text not written by Barks; Cover not by Barks 50.00 150.00 500.00

(Prices vary widely on this book)

DONALD DUCK AND THE CHRISTMAS CAROL
Whitman Publishing Co.: 1960 (A Little Golden Book, 6-3/8"x7-5/8", 28 pgs.)

nn-Story book pencilled by Carl Barks with the intended title "Uncle Scrooge's Christmas Carol." Finished art adapted by Norman McGary. (Rare)-Reprinted in Uncle Scrooge in Color. 100.00

DONALD DUCK BEACH PARTY (Also see Dell Giants)
Gold Key: Sept, 1965 (12¢)

1(#10158-509)-Barks-r/WDC&S #45; painted-c 5.50 16.50 60.00

DONALD DUCK BOOK (See Story Hour Series)

DONALD DUCK COMICS DIGEST
Gladstone Publishing: Nov, 1986 - No. 5, July, 1987 ($1.25/$1.50, 96 pgs.)

1,3: 1-Barks-c/a-r 1.00 3.00 8.00

2,4,5: 4,5-$1.50-c 5.00

DONALD DUCK FUN BOOK (See Dell Giants)

DONALD DUCK IN DISNEYLAND (See Dell Giants)

DONALD DUCK MARCH OF COMICS (See March of Comics #4,20,41,56,69,263)

DONALD DUCK MERRY CHRISTMAS (See Dell Giant No. 53)

DONALD DUCK PICNIC PARTY (See Picnic Party listed under Dell Giants)

DONALD DUCK TELLS ABOUT KITES (See Kite Fun Book)

DONALD DUCK, THIS IS YOUR LIFE (Disney, TV)
Dell Publishing Co.: No. 1109, Aug-Oct, 1960

Four Color 1109-Gyro flashback to WDC&S #141; origin Donald Duck (1st told) 14.00 41.00 150.00

DONALD DUCK XMAS ALBUM (See regular Donald Duck No. 99)

DONALD IN MATHMAGIC LAND (Disney)
Dell Publishing Co.: No. 1051, Oct-Dec, 1959 - No. 1198, May-July, 1961

Four Color 1051 (#1)-Movie 8.00 25.00 90.00

Four Color 1198-Reprint of above 5.50 16.50 60.00

DONATELLO, TEENAGE MUTANT NINJA TURTLE
Mirage Studios: Aug, 1986 ($1.50, B&W, one-shot, 44 pgs.)

1 2.40 6.00

DONDI
Dell Publishing Co.: No. 1176, Mar-May, 1961 - No. 1276, Dec, 1961

Four Color 1176 (#1)-Movie; origin, photo-c 3.60 11.00 40.00

Four Color 1276 1.80 5.50 20.00

DON FORTUNE MAGAZINE
Don Fortune Publishing Co.: Aug, 1946 - No. 6, Feb, 1947

1-Delecta of the Planets by C. C. Beck in all 21.00 64.00 150.00

2 12.00 36.00 85.00

Don Winslow of the Navy #25 © FAW

Doom Patrol (2nd series) #3 © DC

Doom 2099 #16 © MAR

GD2.0 FN6.0 NM9.4

3-6: 3-Bondage-c 10.00 30.00 70.00

DONKEY KONG (See Blip #1)

DONNA MATRIX
Reactor, Inc.: Aug, 1993 ($2.95, 52 pgs.)

1-Computer generated-c/a by Mike Saenz; 3-D effects 3.00

DONNA MIA
Dark Fantasy Productions: Oct, 1995 -No. 2, Sept, 1996 ($3.95/$4.95, limited series, mature)

1,2-($4.95): 1-Kaluta-c-red foil; fold-out centerfold. 2-Kaluta blue foil-c; nudity 5.00
1,2-($3.95): Kaluta-c on both. 2-Nudity 4.00

DON NEWCOMBE
Fawcett Publications: 1950 (Baseball)

nn-Photo-c 40.00 120.00 300.00

DON SIMPSON'S BIZARRE HEROES (Also see Megaton Man)
Fiasco Comics: May, 1990 - Present ($2.50/$2.95, B&W)

1-10,0,11-17: 0-Begin $2.95-c; r/Bizarre Heroes #1. 17-(9/96)-Indicia also reads Megaton Man #0; intro Megaton Man and the Fiascoverse to new readers 3.00

DON'T GIVE UP THE SHIP
Dell Publishing Co.: No. 1049, Aug, 1959

Four Color 1049-Movie, Jerry Lewis photo-c 6.40 19.00 70.00

DON WINSLOW OF THE NAVY
Merwil Publishing Co.: Apr, 1937 - No. 2, May, 1937 (96 pgs.)(A pulp/comic book cross; stapled spine)

GD2.0 FN6.0 VF8.0

V1#1-Has 16 pgs. comics in color. Captain Colorful & Jupiter Jones by Sheldon Mayer; complete Don Winslow novel 567.00 1700.00 3700.00
2-Sheldon Mayer-a 112.00 336.00 950.00

DON WINSLOW OF THE NAVY (See Crackajack Funnies, Famous Feature Stories, Popular Comics & Super Book #5,6)
Dell Publishing Co.: No. 2, Nov, 1939 - No. 22, 1941

Four Color 2 (#1)-Rare 127.00 381.00 1400.00
Four Color 22 30.00 89.00 325.00

DON WINSLOW OF THE NAVY (See TV Teens; Movie, Radio, TV) (Fightin' Navy No. 74 on)
Fawcett Publications/Charlton No. 70 on: 2/43 - #64, 12/48; #65, 1/51 - #69, 9/51; #70, 3/55 - #73, 9/55

GD2.0 FN6.0 NM9.4

1-(68 pgs.)-Captain Marvel on cover 103.00 309.00 825.00
2 50.00 150.00 400.00
3 40.00 120.00 290.00
4-6: 6-Flag-c 31.00 94.00 220.00
7-10: 8-Last 68 pg. issue? 23.00 69.00 160.00
11-20 18.00 54.00 125.00
21-40 11.50 34.00 80.00
41-64: 51,60-Singapore Sal (villain) app. 64-(12/48) 10.00 30.00 70.00
65(1/51)-Flying Saucer attack; photo-c 13.00 39.00 90.00
66 - 69(9/51): All photo-c. 66-sci-fi story 12.00 36.00 85.00
70(3/55)-73: 70-73 r-/#26,58 & 59 10.00 30.00 60.00

DOOM FORCE SPECIAL
DC Comics: July, 1992 ($2.95, 68 pgs., one-shot, mature) (X-Force parody)

1-Grant Morrison scripts; Simonson, Steacy, & others-a; Giffen/Mignola-c. 3.00

DOOM PATROL, THE (Formerly My Greatest Adventure No. 1-85; see Brave and the Bold, DC Special Blue Ribbon Digest 19, Official... Index & Showcase No. 94-96)
National Periodical Publications: No. 86, 3/64 - No. 121, 9-10/68; No. 122, 2/73 - No. 124, 6-7/73

86-1 pg. origin (#86-121 are 12¢ issues) 9.00 27.00 90.00
87-99: 88-Origin The Chief. 91-Intro. Mento. 99-Intro. Beast Boy (later becomes the Changeling in New Teen Titans 6.50 19.50 65.00

GD2.0 FN6.0 NM9.4

100-Origin Beast Boy; Robot-Maniac series begins (12/65) 7.00 21.00 70.00
101-110: 102-Challengers of the Unknown app. 105-Robot-Maniac series ends. 106-Negative Man begins (origin) 3.00 9.00 30.00
111-120 2.50 7.50 20.00
121-Death of Doom Patrol; Orlando-c. 7.00 21.00 70.00
122-124: All reprints 1.00 3.00 8.00

DOOM PATROL
DC Comics (Vertigo imprint #64 on): Oct, 1987 - No, 87, Feb, 1995 (75¢-$1.95, new format)

1 4.00
2-18: 3-1st app. Lodestone. 4-1st app. Karma. 8,15,16-Art Adams-c(i). 18-Invasion tie-in. 3.00
19-(2/89)-Grant Morrison scripts begin, ends #63; 1st app Crazy Jane; $1.50-c & new format begins. 6.00
20-30: 29-Superman app. 30-Night Breed fold-out 3.50
31-49,51-56,58-60: 35-1st app. of Flex Mentallo (cameo). 36-1st full app. of Flex Mentallo. 39-World Without End preview.42-Origin of Flex Mentallo 2.50
50,57 ($2.50, 52 pgs.) 2.50
61-87: 61,70-Photo-c. 73-Death cameo (2 panels) 2.00
...And Suicide Squad 1 (3/88, $1.50, 52 pgs.)-Wraparound-c 2.00
Annual 1 (1988, $1.50, 52 pgs.) 2.00
Annual 2 (1994, $3.95, 68 pgs.)-Children's Crusade tie-in. 4.00
NOTE: *Bisley painted c-26-48, 55-58. Bolland c-64, 75. Dringenberg a-42(p). Steacy a-53.*

DOOM PATROL (See Tangent Comics/ Doom Patrol)

DOOMSDAY
DC Comics: 1995 ($3.95, one-shot)

1-Year One story by Jurgens, L. Simonson, Ordway, and Gil Kane; Darkseid, Superman app. 4.00

DOOMSDAY + 1 (Also see Charlton Bullseye)
Charlton Comics: July, 1975 - No. 6, June, 1976; No. 7, June, 1978 - No. 12, May, 1979

1: #1-5 are 25¢ issues 1.50 4.50 12.00
2-6: 4-Intro Lor. 5-Ditko-a(1 pg.) 6-Begin 30¢ issues 1.00 2.80 7.00
V3#7-12 (reprints #1-6) 4.00
5 (Modern Comics reprint, 1977) 3.00
NOTE: *Byrne c/a-1-12; Painted covers-2-7.*

DOOMSDAY SQUAD, THE
Fantagraphics Books: Aug, 1986 - No. 7, 1987 ($2.00)

1-7: Byrne-a in all. 1-3-New Byrne-c. 3-Usagi Yojimbo app. (1st in color).4-N Adams-c. 5-7-Gil Kane-c 2.00

DOOM'S IV
Image Comics (Extreme): July, 1994 - No.4, Oct, 1994 ($2.50, limited series)

1-4-Liefeld story 2.50
1,2-Two alternate Liefeld-c each, 4 covers form 1 picture 5.00

DOOM 2099 (See Marvel Comics Presents #118 & 2099: World of Tomorrow)
Marvel Comics: Jan, 1993 - No. 44, Aug, 1996 ($1.25/$1.50/$1.95)

1 3.00
2-24,26-44: 1-Metallic foil stamped-c. 4-Ron Lim-c(p). 17-bound-in trading card sheet. 40-Namor & Doctor Strange app. 41-Daredevil app., Namor-c/app. 44-Intro The Emissary; story contin'd in 2099: World of Tomorrow 2.00
1-2nd printing 2.00
25 ($2.25, 52 pgs.) 2.25
25 ($2.95, 52pgs.) Foil embossed cover 3.00
29 ($3.50)-acetate-c. 3.50

DOORWAY TO NIGHTMARE (See Cancelled Comic Cavalcade)
DC Comics: Jan-Feb, 1978 - No. 5, Sept-Oct, 1978

1-5-Madame Xanadu in all. 4-Craig-a 5.00
NOTE: *Kaluta covers on all. Merged into The Unexpected with No. 190.*

DOPEY DUCK COMICS (Wacky Duck No. 3) (See Super Funnies)
Timely Comics (NPP): Fall, 1945 - No. 2, Apr, 1946

Dopey Duck #1 © MAR

Double Up #1 © Elliot Pub.

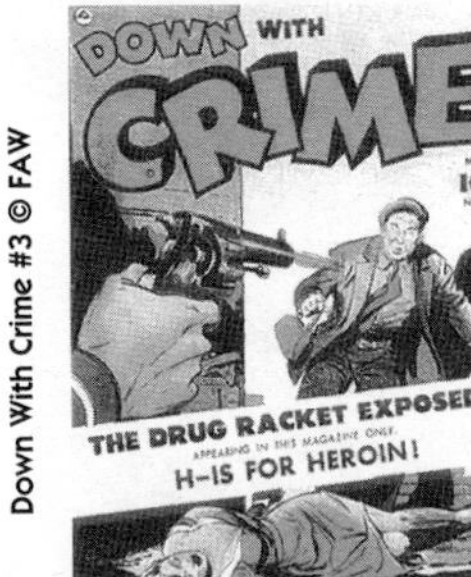

Down With Crime #3 © FAW

GD2.0 FN6.0 NM9.4

1,2-Casper Cat, Krazy Krow 19.00 58.00 135.00

DORK
Slave Labor: June, 1993 - Present ($2.50-$2.95, B&W, mature)

1-5: Evan Dorkin-c/a/scripts in all. 1(8/95),2(1/96)-(2nd printing): Reads 2nd Print on bottom inside-c 3.00

DOROTHY LAMOUR (Formerly Jungle Lil)(Stage, screen, radio)
Fox Features Syndicate: No. 2, June, 1950 - No. 3, Aug, 1950

2,3-Wood-a(3) each, photo-c 25.00 75.00 175.00

DOT DOTLAND (Formerly Little Dot Dotland)
Harvey Publications: No. 62, Sept, 1974 - No. 63, Nov, 1974

62,63 2.40 6.00

DOTTY (...& Her Boy Friends)(Formerly Four Teeners; Glamorous Romances No. 41 on)
Ace Magazines (A. A. Wyn): No. 35, June, 1948 - No. 40, May, 1949

35-Teen-age 6.35 19.00 38.00
36-40: 37-Transvestism story 4.00 10.00 20.00

DOTTY DRIPPLE (Horace & Dotty Dripple No. 25 on)
Magazine Ent.(Life's Romances)/Harvey No. 3 on: 1946 - No. 24, June, 1952
(Also see A-1 No. 3-8, 10)

A-1 #1 (1pg. D. Dripple; Mr. Ex, Bush Berry, Rocky, Lew Loyal (20 pgs.) 10.00 30.00 70.00
1 (nd) (10¢) 7.50 22.50 45.00
2 4.00 12.00 22.00
3-10: 3,4-Powell-a 2.80 7.00 14.00
11-24 1.80 4.50 9.00

DOTTY DRIPPLE AND TAFFY
Dell Publishing Co.: No. 646, Sept, 1955 - No. 903, May, 1958

Four Color 646 (#1) 2.75 8.00 30.00
Four Color 691,718,746,801,903 1.80 5.50 20.00

DOUBLE ACTION COMICS
National Periodical Publications: No. 2, Jan, 1940 (68 pgs., B&W)

2-Contains original stories(?); pre-hero DC contents; same cover as Adventure No. 37. (six known copies) (not an ashcan)
Estimated value.... 12,500.00

NOTE: *The cover to this book was probably reprinted from Adventure #37. #1 exists as an ash can copy with B&W cover; contains a coverless comic on inside with 1st & last page missing.*

DOUBLE COMICS
Elliot Publications: 1940 - 1944 (132 pgs.)

1940 issues; Masked Marvel-c & The Mad Mong vs. The White Flash covers known 212.00 636.00 1700.00
1941 issues; Tornado Tim-c, Nordac-c, & Green Light covers known 150.00 450.00 1200.00
1942 issues 112.00 336.00 900.00
1943,1944 issues 91.00 273.00 725.00

NOTE: *Double Comics consisted of an almost endless combination of pairs of remaindered, unsold issues of comics representing most publishers and usually mixed publishers in the same book; e.g., a Captain America with a Silver Streak, or a Feature with a Detective, etc., could appear inside the same cover. The actual contents would have to determine its price. Prices listed are for average contents. Any containing rare origin or first issues are worth much more. Covers also vary in same year. Value would be approximately 50 percent of contents.*

DOUBLE-CROSS (See The Crusaders)

DOUBLE-DARE ADVENTURES
Harvey Publications: Dec, 1966 - No. 2, Mar, 1967 (35¢/25¢, 68 pgs.)

1-Origin Bee-Man, Glowing Gladiator, & Magic-Master; Simon/Kirby-a (last S&K art as a team?) 5.00 15.00 50.00
2-Williamson/Crandall-a; r/Alarming Adv. #3('63) 4.00 12.00 40.00

NOTE: ***Powell** a-1. **Simon/Sparling** c-1, 2.*

DOUBLE DRAGON
Marvel Comics: July, 1991 - No. 6, Dec, 1991 ($1.00, limited series)

1-6: Based on video game. 2-Art Adams-c 2.00

DOUBLE EDGE
Marvel Comics: Alpha, 1995; Omega, 1995 ($4.95, limited series)

Alpha ($4.95)- Punisher story, Nick Fury app. 5.00
Omega ($4.95)-Punisher, Daredevil, Ghost Rider app. Death of Nick Fury 5.00

DOUBLE LIFE OF PRIVATE STRONG, THE
Archie Publications/Radio Comics: June, 1959 - No. 2, Aug, 1959

1-Origin & re-intro The Shield; Simon & Kirby-c/a, their re-entry into the super-hero genre; intro./1st app. The Fly; 1st S.A. super-hero for Archie Publ. 48.00 144.00 575.00
2-S&K-c/a; Tuska-a; The Fly app. (2nd or 3rd?) 32.00 96.00 320.00

DOUBLE TROUBLE
St. John Publishing Co.: Nov, 1957 - No. 2, Jan-Feb, 1958

1,2: Tuffy & Snuffy by Frank Johnson; dubbed "World's Funniest Kids" 5.00 15.00 30.00

DOUBLE TROUBLE WITH GOOBER
Dell Publishing Co.: No. 417, Aug, 1952 - No. 556, May, 1954

Four Color 417 2.25 6.75 25.00
Four Color 471,516,556 1.85 5.50 15.00

DOUBLE UP
Elliott Publications: 1941 (Pocket size, 200 pgs.)

1-Contains rebound copies of digest sized issues of Pocket Comics, Speed Comics, & Spitfire Comics 75.00 225.00 600.00

DOVER & CLOVER (See All Funny & More Fun Comics #93)

DOVER BOYS (See Adventures of the...)

DOVER THE BIRD
Famous Funnies Publishing Co.: Spring, 1955

1-Funny animal; code approved 5.35 16.00 32.00

DOWN WITH CRIME
Fawcett Publications: Nov, 1952 - No. 7, Nov, 1953

1 29.00 86.00 200.00
2,4,5: 2,4-Powell-a in each. 5-Bondage-c 14.00 43.00 100.00
3-Used in **POP**, pg. 106; "H is for Heroin" drug story 16.00 47.00 110.00
6,7: 6-Used in **POP**, pg. 80 12.00 36.00 85.00

DO YOU BELIEVE IN NIGHTMARES?
St. John Publishing Co.: Nov, 1957 - No. 2, Jan, 1958

1-Mostly Ditko-c/a 44.00 132.00 350.00
2-Ayers-a 24.00 73.00 170.00

D.P. 7
Marvel Comics Group (New Universe): Nov, 1986 - No. 32, June, 1989 (26 on: $1.50)

1-32, Annual #1 (11/87)-Intro. The Witness 2.00

NOTE: ***Williamson** a-9i, 11i; c-9i.*

DRACULA (See Bram Stoker's Dracula, Giant-Size..., Little Dracula, Marvel Graphic Novel, Requiem for Dracula, Spider-Man Vs...., Tomb of... & Wedding of...; also see Movie Classics under Universal Presents as well as Dracula)

DRACULA (See Movie Classics for #1)(Also see Frankenstein & Werewolf)
Dell Publ. Co.: No. 2, 11/66 - No. 4, 3/67; No. 6, 7/72 - No. 8, 7/73 (No #5)

2-Origin & 1st app. Dracula (11/66) (super hero) 2.80 8.40 28.00
3,4: 4-Intro. Fleeta ('67) 2.25 6.75 18.00
6-('72)-r/#2 w/origin 1.85 5.50 15.00
7,8-r/#3, #4 1.50 4.50 12.00

DRACULA (Magazine)
Warren Publishing Co.: 1979 (120 pgs., full color)

Book 1-Maroto art; Spanish material translated into English 4.20 12.60 42.00

DRACULA CHRONICLES
Topps Comics: Apr, 1995 - No. 3, June, 1995 ($2.50, limited series)

1-3-Linsner-c 2.50

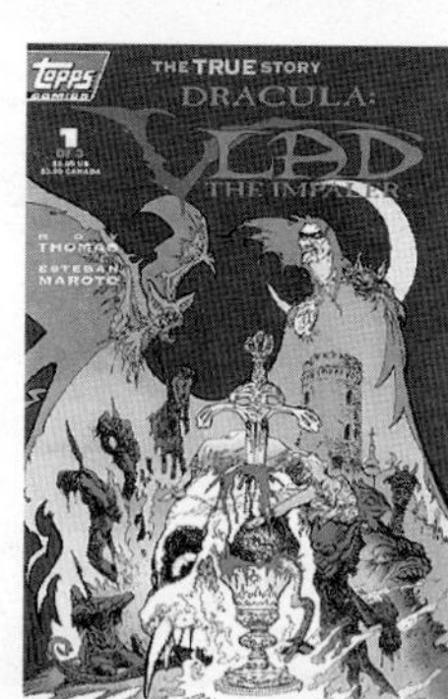

Dracula: Vlad the Impaler #1 © Topps

The Dragon #3 © Erik Larsen

Dragon Lines #4 © MAR

GD2.0 FN6.0 NM9.4

DRACULA LIVES! (Magazine)(Also see Tomb of Dracula)
Marvel Comics Group: 1973(no month) - No. 13, July, 1975 (75¢, B&W) (76 pgs.)

	GD2.0	FN6.0	NM9.4
1-Boris painted-c	3.80	11.40	38.00
2 (7/73)-1st time origin Dracula; Adams, Starlin-a	2.80	8.40	28.00
3-1st app. Robert E. Howard's Soloman Kane; Adams-c/a	2.80	8.40	28.00
4,5: 4-Ploog-a. 5(V2#1)-Bram Stoker's Classic Dracula adapt. begins	2.25	6.75	18.00
6-9: 6-8-Bram Stoker adapt. 9-Bondage-c	2.50	7.50	20.00
10 (1/75)-16 pg. Lilith solo (1st?)	2.80	8.40	28.00
11-13: 11-21 pg. Lilith solo sty. 12-31 pg. Dracula sty	2.50	7.50	20.00
Annual 1(Summer, 1975, $1.25, 92 pgs.)-Morrow painted-c; 6 Dracula stys. 25 pgs. Adams-a(r)	2.50	7.50	24.00

NOTE: ***N. Adams*** *a-2, 3i, 10i, Annual 1r(2, 3i).* ***Alcala*** *a-9.* ***Buscema*** *a-3p, 6p, Annual 1p.* ***Colan*** *a(p)-1, 2, 5, 6, 8.* ***Evans*** *a-7.* ***Gulacy*** *a-9.* ***Heath*** *a-1r, 13.* ***Pakula*** *a-6r. Sutton a-13.* ***Weiss*** *r-Annual 1p. 4* ***Dracula*** *stories each in 1, 609; 3* ***Dracula*** *stories each in 2, 4, 5,, 13.*

DRACULA: LORD OF THE UNDEAD
Marvel Comics: Dec, 1998 - No. 3, Dec, 1998 ($2.99, limited series)
1-3-Olliffe & Palmer-a 3.00

DRACULA: RETURN OF THE IMPALER
Slave Labor Graphics: July, 1993 - No. 4, Oct, 1994 ($2.95, limited series)
1-4 3.00

DRACULA VERSUS ZORRO
Topps Comics: Oct, 1993 - No. 2, Nov, 1993 ($2.95, limited series)
1,2: 1-Spot varnish & red foil-c. 2-Polybagged w/16 pg. Zorro #0 3.00

DRACULA VERSUS ZORRO
Dark Horse Comics: Sept, 1998 - No. 2, Oct, 1998 ($2.95, limited series)
1,2 3.00

DRACULA: VLAD THE IMPALER (Also see Bram Stoker's Dracula)
Topps Comics: Feb, 1993 - No. 3, Apr, 1993 ($2.95, limited series)
1-3-Polybagged with 3 trading cards each; Maroto-c/a 3.00

DRAFT, THE
Marvel Comics: 1988 ($3.50, one-shot, squarebound)
1-Sequel to "The Pitt" 3.50

DRAG 'N' WHEELS (Formerly Top Eliminator)
Charlton Comics: No. 30, Sept, 1968 - No. 59, May, 1973

	GD2.0	FN6.0	NM9.4
30	3.50	10.50	35.00
31-40-Scot Jackson begins	2.60	7.80	26.00
41-50	2.50	7.50	20.00
51-59: Scot Jackson	1.50	4.50	12.00
Modern Comics Reprint 58('78)			4.00

DRAGON, THE (Also see The Savage Dragon)
Image Comics (Highbrow Ent.): Mar, 1996 - No. 5, July, 1996 (99¢, lim. series)
1-5: Reprints Savage Dragon limited series w/new story & art. 5-Youngblood app; includes 5 pg. Savage Dragon story from 1984 2.00

DRAGON ARCHIVES, THE (Also see The Savage Dragon)
Image Comics: Aug, 1998 - Present ($2.95, B&W)
1-4: Reprints early Savage Dragon app. 3.00

DRAGON, THE: BLOOD & GUTS (Also see The Savage Dragon)
Image Comics (Highbrow Entertainment): Mar, 1995 - No. 3, May, 1995 ($2.50, limited series)
1-3: Jason Pearson-c/a/scripts 2.50

DRAGON CHIANG
Eclipse Books: 1991 ($3.95, B&W, squarebound, 52 pgs.)
nn -Timothy Truman-c/a(p) 4.00

DRAGONFLIGHT
Eclipse Books: Feb, 1991 - No. 3, 1991 ($4.95, 52 pgs.)
Book One - Three: Adapts 1968 novel 5.00

DRAGONFLY (See Americomics #4)
Americomics: Sum, 1985 - No. 8, 1986 ($1.75/$1.95)
1 3.00
2-8 2.00

DRAGONFORCE
Aircel Publishing: 1988 - No. 13, 1989 ($2.00)
1-Dale Keown-c/a/scripts in #1-12 3.00
2-13: 13-No Keown-a 2.00
...Chronicles Book 1-5 ($2.95, B&W, 60 pgs.): Dale Keown-r/Dragonring & Dragonforce 3.00

DRAGONHEART (Movie)
Topps Comics: May, 1996 - No. 2, June, 1996 ($2.95/$4.95, limited series)
1-($2.95, 24 pgs.)-Adaptation of the film; Hildebrandt Bros-c; Lim-a. 3.00
2-($4.95, 64 pgs.) 5.00

DRAGONLANCE (Also see TSR Worlds)
DC Comics: Dec, 1988 - No. 34, Sept, 1991 ($1.25/$1.50, Mando paper)
1, Annual 1 (1990, $2.95, 68 pgs.) 3.00
2-34: Based on TSR game. 30-32-Kaluta-c 2.00

DRAGON LINES
Marvel Comics (Epic Comics/Heavy Hitters): May, 1993 - No. 4, Aug, 1993 ($1.95, limited series)
1-($2.50)-Embossed-c; Ron Lim-c/a in all 2.50
2-4 2.00

DRAGON LINES: WAY OF THE WARRIOR
Marvel Comics (Epic Comics/ Heavy Hitters): Nov, 1993 - No. 2, Jan, 1994 ($2.25, limited series)
1,2-Ron Lim-c/a(p) 2.25

DRAGONQUEST
Silverwolf Comics: Dec, 1986 - No. 2, 1987 ($1.50, B&W, 28 pgs.)
1,2-Tim Vigil-c/a in all 2.00

DRAGONRING
Aircel Publishing: 1986 - V2#15, 1988 ($1.70/$2.00, B&W/color)
1-6: 6-Last B&W issue, V2#1-15($2.00, color) 2.00

DRAGON'S CLAWS
Marvel UK, Ltd.: July, 1988 - No. 10, Apr, 1989 ($1.25/$1.50/$1.75, British)
1-10: 3-Death's Head 1 pg. strip on back-c (1st app.). 4-Silhouette of Death's Head on last pg. 5-1st full app. new Death's Head 2.00

DRAGONSLAYER (Movie)
Marvel Comics Group: October, 1981 - No. 2, Nov, 1981
1,2-Paramount Disney movie adaptation 2.00

DRAGON'S STAR 2
Caliber Press: 1994 ($2.95, B&W)
1 3.00

DRAGON STRIKE
Marvel Comics: Feb, 1994 ($1.25)
1-Based on TSR role playing game 2.00

DRAGOON WELLS MASSACRE
Dell Publishing Co.: No. 815, June, 1957

	GD2.0	FN6.0	NM9.4
Four Color 815-Movie, photo-c	7.00	22.00	80.00

DRAGSTRIP HOTRODDERS (World of Wheels No. 17 on)
Charlton Comics: Sum, 1963; No. 2, Jan, 1965 - No. 16, Aug, 1967

	GD2.0	FN6.0	NM9.4
1	5.00	15.00	50.00
2-5	3.20	9.60	32.00
6-16	2.50	7.50	25.00

DRAKUUN
Dark Horse Comics: Feb, 1997 - Present ($2.95, B&W, manga)

Drakuun #19 © DH

Dreadstar #14 © MAR

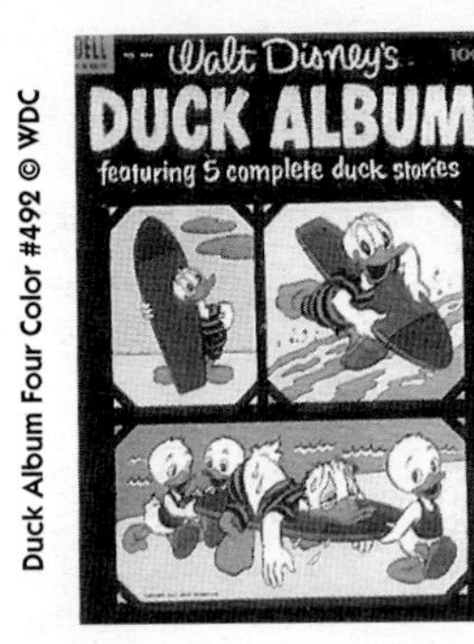

Duck Album Four Color #492 © WDC

GD2.0 FN6.0 NM9.4

1-25; 1-6- Johji Manabe-s/a in all. Rise of the Dragon Princess series. 7-12-Revenge of Gustav. 13-18-Shadow of the Warlock. 19-25-The Hidden War 3.00

DRAMA
Sirius: June, 1994 ($2.95, mature)

1-1st full color Dawn app. in comics 2.50 7.50 20.00
1-Limited edition (1400 copies); signed & numbered; fingerprint authenticity 4.50 13.50 50.00

NOTE: *Dawn's 1st full color app. was a pin-up in Amazing Heroes' Swimsuit Special #5.*

DRAMA OF AMERICA, THE
Action Text: 1973 ($1.95, 224 pgs.)

1- "Students' Supplement to History" 3.00

DREADLANDS (Also see Epic)
Marvel Comics (Epic Comics): 1992 - No. 4, 1992 ($3.95, lim. series, 52 pgs.)

1-4: Stiff-c 4.00

DREADSTAR
Marvel Comics (Epic Comics)/First Comics No. 27 on: Nov, 1982 - No. 64, Mar, 1991

1-64: 6,7-1st app. Interstellar Toybox; 8pgs. ea.; Wrightson-a 2.00
Annual 1 (12/83)-r/The Price 3.00

DREADSTAR
Malibu Comics (Bravura): Apr, 1994 - No.6, Jan, 1995 ($2.50, limited series)

1-6-Peter David scripts: 1,2-Starlin-c 2.50

NOTE: *Issues 1-6 contain Bravura stamps.*

DREADSTAR AND COMPANY
Marvel Comics (Epic Comics): July, 1985 - No. 6, Dec, 1985

1-6: 1,3,6-New Starlin-a: 2-New Wrightson-c; reprints of Dreadstar series. 2.00

DREAM BOOK OF LOVE (Also see A-1 Comics)
Magazine Enterprises: No. 106, June-July, 1954 - No. 123, Oct-Nov, 1954

A-1 106 (#1)-Powell, Bolle-a; Montgomery Clift, Donna Reed photo-c 11.00 33.00 75.00
A-1-114 (#2)-Guardineer, Bolle-a; Piper Laurie, Victor Mature photo-c 10.00 30.00 60.00
A-1 123 (#3)-Movie photo-c 8.35 25.00 50.00

DREAM BOOK OF ROMANCE (Also see A-1 Comics)
Magazine Enterprises: No. 92, 1954 - No. 124, Oct-Nov, 1954

A-1 92 (#5)-Guardineer-a; photo-c 10.00 30.00 65.00
A-1 101 (#6)(4-6/54)-Marlon Brando photo-c; Powell, Bolle, Guardineer-a 17.00 51.00 120.00
A-1 109,110,124: 109 (#7)(7-8/54)-Powell-a; movie photo-c. 110 (#8)(1/54)-Movie photo-c. 124 (#8)(10-11/54) 8.35 25.00 50.00

DREAMERY, THE
Eclipse Comics: Dec, 1986 - No. 14, Feb, 1989 ($2.00, B&W, Baxter paper)

1-14: 2-7-Alice In Wonderland adapt. 2.00

DREAMING, THE (See Sandman, 2nd Series)
DC Comics (Vertigo): June, 1996 - Present ($2.50)

1-McKean-c on all.; LaBan scripts & Snejbjerg-a 4.00
2-30,32-40: 2,3-LaBan scripts & Snejbjerg-a. 4-7-Hogan scripts; Parkhouse-a. 8-Zulli-a. 9-11-Talbot-s/Taylor-a(p) 2.50
31-($3.95) Art by various 4.00
...Beyond The Shores of Night TPB ('97, $19.95) r/#1-8 20.00
...Special (7/98, $5.95, one-shot) Trial of Cain 6.00
...Through The Gates of Horn and Ivory TPB ('99, $19.95) r/#15-19,22-25 20.00

DREAM OF LOVE
I. W. Enterprises: 1958 (Reprints)

1,2,8: 1-r/Dream Book of Love #1; Bob Powell-a. 2-r/Great Lover's Romances #10. 8-Great Lover's Romances #1; also contains 2 Jon Juan stories by Siegel & Schomburg; Kinstler-c. 1.50 4.50 12.00
9-Kinstler-c; 1pg. John Wayne interview & Frazetta illo from John Wayne Adv. Comics #2 1.50 4.50 12.00

GD2.0 FN6.0 NM9.4

DREAM TEAM (See Battlezones: Dream Team 2)
Malibu Comics (Ultraverse): July, 1995 ($4.95, one-shot)

1-Pin-ups teaming up Marvel & Ultraverse characters by various artists including Allred, Hamner, Romita, Darrow, Balent, Quesada & Palmiotti. 5.00

DREAMWALKER
Caliber Comics (Tapestry): Dec, 1996 - Present ($2.95, B&W)

1-5-Jenni Gregory-c/s/a 3.00

DRIFT FENCE (See Zane Grey 4-Color 270)

DRIFT MARLO
Dell Publishing Co.: May-July, 1962 - No. 2, Oct-Dec, 1962

01-232-207(#1), 2(12-232-212) 3.20 9.50 35.00

DRISCOLL'S BOOK OF PIRATES
David McKay Publ. (Not reprints): 1934 (B&W, hardcover; 124 pgs, 7x9")

nn-By Montford Amory 21.00 64.00 150.00

DROIDS (Also see Dark Horse Comics)
Marvel Comics (Star Comics): April, 1986 - No. 8, June, 1987
(Based on Saturday morning cartoon)

1-R2D2 & C-3PO from Star Wars app. in all 1.85 5.50 15.00
2-8: 2,5,7,8-Williamson-a(i) 1.40 4.15 11.00

NOTE: ***Romita** a-3p. **Sinnott** a-3i.*

DROOPY (see Tom & Jerry #60)

DROOPY (Tex Avery's...)
Dark Horse Comics: Oct, 1995 - No. 3, Dec, 1995 ($2.50, limited series)

1-3: Characters created by Tex Avery; painted-c 2.50

DROPSIE AVENUE: THE NEIGHBORHOOD
Kitchen Sink Press: June, 1995 ($15.95/$24.95, B&W)

nn-Will Eisner (softcover) 16.00
nn-Will Eisner (hardcover) 25.00

DROWNED GIRL, THE
DC Comics (Piranha Press): 1990 ($5.95, 52 pgs, mature)

nn 6.00

DRUG WARS
Pioneer Comics: 1989 ($1.95)

1-Grell-c 2.00

DRUID
Marvel Comics: May, 1995 - No. 4, Aug, 1995 ($2.50, limited series)

1-4: Warren Ellis scripts. 2.50

DRUM BEAT
Dell Publishing Co.: No. 610, Jan, 1955

Four Color 610-Movie, Alan Ladd photo-c 9.00 27.00 100.00

DRUMS OF DOOM
United Features Syndicate: 1937 (25¢)(Indian)(Text w/color illos.)

nn-By Lt. F.A. Methot; Golden Thunder app.; Tip Top Comics ad in comic; nice-c 33.00 99.00 230.00

DRUNKEN FIST
Jademan Comics: Aug, 1988 - No. 54, Jan, 1993 ($1.50/$1.95, 68 pgs.)

1-54 2.00

DUCK ALBUM (See Donald Duck Album)
Dell Publishing Co.: No. 353, Oct, 1951 - No. 840, Sept, 1957

Four Color 353 (#1)-Barks-c; 1st Uncle Scrooge-c (also appears on back-c). 8.25 25.00 90.00
Four Color 450-Barks-c 5.50 16.50 60.00
Four Color 492,531,560,586,611,649,686 4.50 13.50 50.00
Four Color 726,782,840 4.50 13.50 50.00

DUCKMAN

Dudley #1 © PRIZE

Durango Kid #8 © ME

DV8 #22 © WildStorm

GD2.0 FN6.0 NM9.4

Dark Horse Comics: Sept, 1990 ($1.95, B&W, one-shot)

1-Story & art by Everett Peck — 2.00

DUCKMAN
Topps Comics: Nov, 1994 - No. 5, May, 1995; No. 0, Feb, 1996 ($2.50)

0 (2/96, $2.95, B&W)-r/Duckman #1 from Dark Horse Comics — 4.00
1-5: 1-w/ coupon #A for Duckman trading card. 2-w/Duckman 1st season episode guide — 3.00

DUCKMAN: THE MOB FROG SAGA
Topps Comics: Nov, 1994 - No. 3, Feb, 1995 ($2.50, limited series)

1-3: 1-w/coupon #B for Duckman tradiing card, S. Shaw!-c — 2.50

DUCKTALES
Gladstone Publ.: Oct, 1988 - No. 13, May, 1990 (1,2,9-11: $1.50; 3-8: 95¢)

	GD2.0	FN6.0	NM9.4
1-Barks-r		2.40	6.00
2-11: Barks-r			4.00
12,13 ($1.95, 68 pgs.)-Barks-r; 12-r/F.C. #495			5.00

DUCKTALES (TV)
Disney Comics: June, 1990 - No. 18, Nov, 1991 ($1.50)

1-All new stories — 3.00
2-18 — 2.00
The Movie nn (1990, $7.95, 68 pgs.)-Graphic novel adapting animated movie — 9.00

DUDLEY (Teen-age)
Feature/Prize Publications: Nov-Dec, 1949 - No. 3, Mar-Apr, 1950

	GD2.0	FN6.0	NM9.4
1-By Boody Rogers	14.00	43.00	100.00
2,3	10.00	30.00	65.00

DUDLEY DO-RIGHT (TV)
Charlton Comics: Aug, 1970 - No. 7, Aug, 1971 (Jay Ward)

	GD2.0	FN6.0	NM9.4
1	8.00	23.00	85.00
2-7	5.50	16.50	60.00

DUKE OF THE K-9 PATROL
Gold Key: Apr, 1963

	GD2.0	FN6.0	NM9.4
1 (10052-304)	3.00	9.00	30.00

DUMBO (Disney; see Movie Comics, & Walt Disney Showcase #12)
Dell Publishing Co.: No. 17, 1941 - No. 668, Jan, 1958

	GD2.0	FN6.0	NM9.4
Four Color 17 (#1)-Mickey Mouse, Donald Duck, Pluto app.	173.00	519.00	1900.00
Large Feature Comic 19 ('41)-Part-r 4-Color 17	245.00	735.00	2700.00
Four Color 234 ('49)	9.00	27.00	100.00
Four Color 668 (12/55)-1st of two printings. Dumbo on-c with starry sky. Reprints Four Color 234? same-c as 234	7.00	22.00	80.00
Four Color 668 (1/58)-2nd printing. Same cover altered with Timothy Mouse added. Same contents as above	5.50	16.50	60.00

DUMBO COMIC PAINT BOOK (See Dumbo, Large Feature Comic No. 19)

DUNC AND LOO (#1-3 titled "Around the Block with Dunc and Loo")
Dell Publishing Co.: Oct-Dec, 1961 - No. 8, Oct-Dec, 1963

	GD2.0	FN6.0	NM9.4
1	8.75	26.50	95.00
2	5.50	16.50	60.00
3-8	4.00	12.00	45.00

NOTE: *Written by* ***John Stanley****;* ***Bill Williams*** *art.*

DUNCAN'S KINGDOM
Image Comics: 1999 - No. 2 ($2.95, B&W, limited series)

1-Gene Yang-s/Derek Kirk-a — 2.95

DUNE (Movie)
Marvel Comics: Apr, 1985 - No. 3, June, 1985

1-3-r/Marvel Super Special; movie adaptation — 2.00

DUNG BOYS, THE
Kitchen Sink Press: 1996 - No. 3, 1996 ($2.95, B&W, limited series)

1-3 — 3.00

DURANGO KID, THE (Also see Best of the West, Great Western & White Indian) (Charles Starrett starred in Columbia's Durango Kid movies)
Magazine Enterprises: Oct-Nov, 1949 - No. 41, Oct-Nov, 1955 (All 36 pgs.)

	GD2.0	FN6.0	NM9.4
1-Charles Starrett photo-c; Durango Kid & his horse Raider begin; Dan Brand & Tipi (origin) begin by Frazetta & continue through #16	71.00	212.00	565.00
2-Starrett photo-c.	37.00	111.00	260.00
3-5-All have Starrett photo-c.	35.00	105.00	245.00
6-10: 7-Atomic weapon-c/story	19.00	56.00	130.00
11-16-Last Frazetta issue	13.00	39.00	90.00
17-Origin Durango Kid	19.00	56.00	130.00
18-30: 18-Fred Meagher-a on Dan Brand begins.19-Guardineer-c/a(3) begins, end #41. 23-Intro. The Red Scorpion	10.00	30.00	70.00
31-Red Scorpion returns	10.00	30.00	65.00
32-41-Bolle/Frazettaish-a (Dan Brand; true in later issues?)	10.00	30.00	65.00

NOTE: *#6, 8, 14, 15 contain* ***Frazetta*** *art not reprinted in White Indian.* ***Ayers*** *c-18.* ***Guardineer*** *a(3)-19-41; c-19-41.* ***Fred Meagher*** *a-18-29 at least.*

DURANGO KID, THE
AC Comics: 1990 - #2, 1990 ($2.50,$2.75, half-color)

1,2: 1-Starrett photo front/back-c; Guardineer-r. 2-B&W)-Starrett photo-c; White Indian-r by Frazetta; Guardineer-r (50th anniversary of films) — 2.75

DUSTCOVERS: THE COLLECTED SANDMAN COVERS 1989-1997
DC Comics (Vertigo): 1997 ($39.95, Hardcover)

Reprints Dave McKean's Sandman covers with Gaiman text — 40.00
Softcover (1998, $24.95) — 30.00

DUSTY STAR
Image Comics (Desperado Studios): Apr, 1997 - Present ($2.95, B&W)

0,1-Pruett-s/Robinson-a — 3.00

DV8 (See Gen 13)
Image Comics (WildStorm Productions): Aug, 1996 - No. 25, Dec, 1998;
DC Comics (WildStorm Prod.): No. 0, Apr, 1999 - No. 32, Nov, 1999 ($2.50)

	GD2.0	FN6.0	NM9.4
1/2		2.40	6.00
1-Warren Ellis scripts & Humberto Ramos-c/a(p)			4.00
1-(7-variant covers, w/1 by Jim Lee...each			4.00
2-4: 3-No Ramos-a			3.00
5-30: 14-Regular-c, 14-Variant-c by Charest. 26-(5/99)-McGuinness-c			2.50
14-($3.50) Voyager Pack w/Danger Girl preview			5.00
0-(4/99, $2.95) Two covers (Rio and McGuinness)			3.00
Annual 1 (1/98, $2.95)			3.00
Annual 1999 ($3.50) Slipstream x-over with Gen13			3.50
Rave-(7/96, $1.75)-Ramos-c; pinups & interviews			3.00

DV8 VS. BLACK OPS
Image Comics (WildStorm): Oct, 1997 - No. 3, Dec, 1997 ($2.50, lim. series)

1-3-Bury-s/Norton-a — 3.00

DWIGHT D. EISENHOWER
Dell Publishing Co.: December, 1969

	GD2.0	FN6.0	NM9.4
01-237-912 - Life story	2.00	6.00	22.00

DYLAN DOG
Dark Horse (Bonelli Comics): Mar, 1999 - No. 6, Aug, 1999 ($4.95, B&W, digest size)

1-6-Reprints Italian series in English; Mignola-c — 5.00

DYNABRITE COMICS
Whitman Publishing Co.: 1978 - 1979 (69¢, 10x7-1/8", 48 pgs., cardboard-c) (Blank inside covers)

11350 - Walt Disney's Mickey Mouse & the Beanstalk (4-C 157). 11350-1 - Mickey Mouse Album (4-C 1057,1151,1246). 11351 - Mickey Mouse & His Sky Adventure (4-C 214, 343). 11352 - Donald Duck (4-C 408, Donald Duck 45,52)-Barks-a. 11352-1 - Donald Duck (4-C 318, 10 pg. Barks/WDC&S 125,128)-Barks-c(r). 11353 - Daisy Duck's Diary (4-C 1055,1150) Barks-a. 11354 - Goofy: A Gaggle of Giggles. 11354-1 - Super Goof Meets Super Thief. 11355 - Uncle Scrooge (Barks-a/U.S. 12,33). 11355-1 - Uncle Scrooge (Barks-a/U.S. 13,16) - Barks-c(r). 11356 - (?). 11357 - Star Trek (r/-Star Trek 33,41). 11358 - Star Trek (r/-Star Trek 34,36). 11359 - Bugs Bunny-r. 11360 - Winnie the Pooh Fun and Fantasy (Disney-r). 11361 - Gyro Gearloose & the

Dynamic Comics #8 © CHES

The Eagle #1 © FOX

Earth X #1 © MAR

GD2.0 FN6.0 NM9.4

Disney Ducks (r/4-C 1047,1184)-Barks-c(r)
each.... 5.00

DYNAMIC ADVENTURES
I. W. Enterprises: No. 8, 1964 - No. 9, 1964

8-Kayo Kirby-r by Baker?/Fight Comics 53. 2.50 7.50 20.00
9-Reprints Avon's "Escape From Devil's Island"; Kinstler-c 2.50 7.50 22.00
nn (no date)-Reprints Risks Unlimited with Rip Carson, Senorita Rio; r/Fight #53 2.50 7.50 20.00

DYNAMIC CLASSICS (See Cancelled Comic Cavalcade)
DC Comics: Sept-Oct, 1978 (44 pgs.)

1-Neal Adams Batman, Simonson Manhunter-r 5.00

DYNAMIC COMICS (No #4-7)
Harry 'A' Chesler: Oct, 1941 - No. 3, Feb, 1942; No. 8, Mar, 1944 - No. 25, May, 1948

1-Origin Major Victory by Charles Sultan (reprinted in Major Victory #1), Dynamic Man & Hale the Magician; The Black Cobra only app.; Major Victory & Dynamic Man begin 162.00 488.00 1300.00
2-Origin Dynamic Boy & Lady Satan; intro. The Green Knight & sidekick Lance Cooper 75.00 225.00 600.00
3-1st small logo, resumes with #10 62.00 186.00 500.00
8-Dan Hastings, The Echo, The Master Key, Yankee Boy begin; Yankee Doodle Jones app.; hypo story 62.00 186.00 500.00
9-Mr. E begins; Mac Raboy-c 66.00 198.00 525.00
10-Small logo begins 50.00 150.00 400.00
11-16: 15-The Sky Chief app. 16-Marijuana story 43.00 128.00 340.00
17(1/46)-Illustrated in **SOTI**, "The children told me what the man was going to do with the hot poker," but Wertham saw this in Crime Reporter #2 56.00 169.00 450.00
18,19,21,22,25: 21-Dinosaur-c; new logo 36.00 107.00 250.00
20-Bare-breasted woman-c 53.00 159.00 425.00
23,24-(68 pgs.): 23-Yankee Girl app. 39.00 116.00 270.00
I.W. Reprint #1,8('64): 1-r/#23. 8-Exist? 2.50 7.50 24.00
NOTE: ***Kinstler** c-IW #1. **Tuska** art in many issues, #3, 9, 11, 12, 16, 19. Bondage c-16.*

DYNAMITE (Becomes Johnny Dynamite No. 10 on)
Comic Media/Allen Hardy Publ.: May, 1953 - No. 9, Sept, 1954

1-Pete Morisi-a; Don Heck-c; r-as Danger #6 20.00 60.00 140.00
2 11.00 33.00 75.00
3-Marijuana story; Johnny Dynamite (1st app.) begins by Pete Morisi(c/a); Heck text-a; man shot in face at close range 13.50 41.00 95.00
4-Injury-to-eye, prostitution; Morisi-c/a 15.00 45.00 105.00
5-9-Morisi-c/a in all. 7-Prostitute story plus reprints 10.00 30.00 70.00

DYNAMO (Also see Tales of Thunder & T.H.U.N.D.E.R. Agents)
Tower Comics: Aug, 1966 - No. 4, June, 1967 (25¢)

1-Crandall/Wood, Ditko/Wood-a; Weed series begins; NoMan & Lightning cameos; Wood-c/a 6.00 18.00 60.00
2-4: Wood-c/a in all 4.00 12.00 40.00
NOTE: ***Adkins/Wood** a-2. **Ditko** a-4?. **Tuska** a-2, 3.*

DYNAMO JOE (Also see First Adventures & Mars)
First Comics: May, 1986 - No. 15, Jan, 1988 (#12-15: $1.75)

1-15: 4-Cargonauts begin, Special 1(1/87)-Mostly-r/Mars 2.00

DYNOMUTT (TV)(See Scooby-Doo (3rd series))
Marvel Comics Group: Nov, 1977 - No. 6, Sept, 1978 (Hanna-Barbera)

1-The Blue Falcon, Scooby Doo in all 1.85 5.50 15.00
2-6-All newsstand only 1.50 4.50 12.00

EAGLE, THE (1st Series) (See Science Comics & Weird Comics #8)
Fox Features Syndicate: July, 1941 - No. 4, Jan, 1942

1-The Eagle begins; Rex Dexter of Mars app. by Briefer; all issues feature German war covers 175.00 525.00 1400.00
2-The Spider Queen begins (origin) 81.00 243.00 650.00
3,4: 3-Joe Spook begins (origin) 66.00 200.00 525.00

EAGLE (2nd Series)
Rural Home Publ.: Feb-Mar, 1945 - No. 2, Apr-May, 1945

1-Aviation stories 37.00 111.00 260.00
2-Lucky Aces 23.00 69.00 160.00
NOTE: ***L. B. Cole** c/a in each.*

EAGLE
Crystal Comics/Apple Comics #17 on: Sept, 1986 - No. 23, 1989 ($1.50/1.75/1.95, B&W)

1-23: 12-Double size origin issue ($2.50) 2.00
1-Signed and limited 3.00

EAGLES DARE
Aager comics, Inc.: Aug, 1994 - Present? ($1.95, B&W, limited series)

1,2 2.00

EARTH MAN ON VENUS (An...) (Also see Strange Planets)
Avon Periodicals: 1951

nn-Wood-a (26 pgs.); Fawcette-c 119.00 356.00 950.00

EARTHWORM JIM (TV, cartoon)
Marvel Comics: Dec, 1995 - No. 3, Feb, 1996 ($2.25)

1-3: Based on video game and toys 2.25

EARTH X
Marvel Comics: No. 0, Mar, 1999 - No. 12 ($3.99/$2.99, limited series)

nn- (Wizard supplement) Alex Ross sketchbook; painted-c 5.00
Sketchbook (2/99) New sketches and previews 4.00
0-(3/99)-Prelude; Leon-a(p)/Ross-c, 1-(4/99)-Leon-a(p)/Ross-c 5.00
1-2nd printing, 2-7 3.00

EASTER BONNET SHOP (See March of Comics No. 29)

EASTER WITH MOTHER GOOSE
Dell Publishing Co.: No. 103, 1946 - No. 220, Mar, 1949

Four Color 103 (#1)-Walt Kelly-a 18.00 53.00 195.00
Four Color 140 ('47)-Kelly-a 14.50 44.00 160.00
Four Color 185 ('48),220-Kelly-a 12.30 37.00 135.00

EAST MEETS WEST
Innovation Publishing: Apr, 1990 - No. 2, 1990 ($2.50, limited series, mature)

1,2: 1-Stevens part-i; Redondo-c(i). 2-Stevens-c(i); 1st app. Cheech & Chong in comics 2.50

E. C. CLASSIC REPRINTS
East Coast Comix Co.: May, 1973 - No. 12, 1976 (E. C. Comics reprinted in color minus ads)

1-The Crypt of Terror #1 (Tales from the Crypt #46) 1.00 3.00 12.00
2-12: 2-Weird Science #15('52). 3-Shock SuspenStories #12. 4-Haunt of Fear #12. 5-Weird Fantasy #13('52). 6-Crime SuspenStories #25. 7-Vault of Horror #26. 8-Shock SuspenStories #6. 9-Two-Fisted Tales #34. 10-Haunt of Fear #23. 11-Weird Science #12(#1). 12-Shock SuspenStories #2 1.00 3.00 8.00

EC CLASSICS
Russ Cochran: Aug, 1985 - No. 12, 1986? (High quality paper; each-r 8 stories in color) (#2-12 were resolicited in 1990)($4.95, 56 pgs., 8x11")

1-12: 1-Tales From the Crypt. 2-Weird Science. 3-Two-Fisted Tales. 4-Shock SuspenStories. 5-Weird Fantasy. 6-Vault of Horror. 7-Weird Science-Fantasy (r/23,24). 8-Crime SuspensStories. 9-Haunt of Fear. 10-Panic (r/1,2). 11-Tales From the Crypt (r/23,24). 12-Weird Science (r/20,22) 2.40 6.00

ECHO OF FUTUREPAST
Pacific Comics/Continuity Com.: May, 1984 - No. 9, Jan, 1986 ($2.95, 52 pgs.)

1-9: Neal Adams-c/a in all? 4.00

NOTE: ***N. Adams** a-1-6,7i,9i; c-1-3, 5p,7i,8,9i. **Golden** a-1-6 (Bucky O'Hare); c-6. **Toth** a-6,7.*

ECLIPSE GRAPHIC ALBUM SERIES
Eclipse Comics: Oct, 1978 - 1989 (8-1/2x11") (B&W #1-5)

1-Sabre (10/78, B&W, 1st print.); Gulacy-a; 1st direct sale graphic novel 12.00

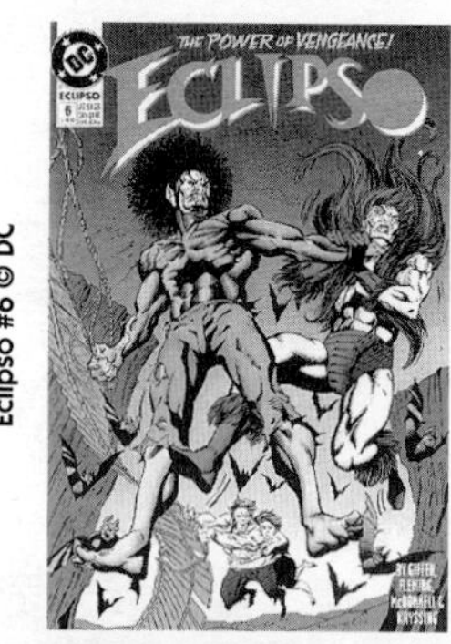

Eclipso #6 © DC

Eddie Campbell's Bacchus #31 © Eddie Campbell

Eerie #3 © AVON

GD2.0 FN6.0 NM9.4

1-Sabre (2nd printing, 1/79) 8.00
1-Sabre (3rd printing, $5.95) 6.00
3,4: 3-Detectives, Inc. (5/80, B&W, $6.95)-Rogers-a. 4-Stewart The Rat (1980, B&W)-G. Colan-a 8.00
5-The Price (10/81, B&W)-Starlin-a 14.00
2,6,7,13: 2-Night Music (11/79, B&W)-Russell-a. 6-I Am Coyote (11/84, color)-Rogers-c/a. 7-The Rocketeer (2nd print, $7.95). 7-The Rocketeer (3rd print, 1991, $8.95). 13-The Sisterhood of Steel ('87, $8.95, color) 9.00
7-The Rocketeer (9/85, color)-Dave Stevens-a (r/chapters 1-5)(see Pacific Presents & Starslayer); has 7 pgs. new-a 12.00
7-The Rocketeer, signed & limited HC 60.00
7-The Rocketeer, hard-c (1986, $19.95) 20.00
7-The Rocketeer, unsigned HC (3rd, $32.95) 33.00
8-Zorro In Old California ('86, color) 10.00
8,12-Hardcover 15.00
9,10: 9-Sacred And The Profane ('86)-Steacy-a. 10-Somerset Holmes ('86, $15.95)-Adults, soft-c 16.00
9,10,12-Hardcover ($24.95). 12-signed & #'d 25.00
11,14,16,18,20,23,24: 11-Floyd Farland, Citizen of the Future ('87, $3.95, B&W) 14-Samurai, Son of Death ('87, $4.95, B&W). 16,18,20,23-See Airfighters Classics #1-4. 24-Heartbreak ($4.95, B&W) 5.00
12,28,31,35,36: 12-Silverheels ('87, $7.95, color). 28-Miracleman Book I ($5.95) 31-Pigeons From Hell by R. E. Howard (11/88). 35-Rael: Into The Shadow of the Sun36-Dr. Watchstop: Adventures in Time and Space 8.00
14,17,21,14-Samurai, Son of Death ($3.95, 2nd printing). 17-Valkyrie, Prisoner of the Past SC ('88, $3.95, color). 21-XYR-Multiple ending comic ('88, $3.95, B&W) 4.00
15,22,27: 15-Twisted Tales (11/87, color)-Dave Stevens-c. 22-Alien Worlds #1 (5/88, $3.95, 52 pgs.)-Nudity. 27-Fast Fiction (She) ($5.95, B&W) 6.00
17-Valkyrie, Prisoner of the Past S&N Hardcover ('88, $19.95) 20.00
19-Scout: The Four Monsters ('88, $14.95, color)-r/Scout #1-7; soft-c 15.00
25,30,32-34: 25-Alex Toth's Zorro Vol. 1 ,2($10.95, B&W). 30-Brought To Light; Alan Moore scripts ('89). 32-Teenaged Dope Slaves and Reform School Girls. 33-Bogie. 34-Air Fighters Classics #5 11.00
29-Real Love: Best of Simon &Kirby Romance Comics(10/88, $12.95) 13.00
30,31: Limited hardcover ed. ($29.95). 31-signed 30.00

ECLIPSE MAGAZINE (Becomes Eclipse Monthly)
Eclipse Publishing: May, 1981 - No. 8, Jan, 1983 ($2.95, B&W, magazine)

1-8: 1-1st app. Cap'n Quick and a Foozle by Rogers, Ms. Tree by Beatty, and Dope by Trina Robbins. 2-1st app. I Am Coyote by Rogers. 7-1st app. Masked Man by Boyer 4.00

NOTE: ***Colan** a-3, 5, 8. **Golden** c/a-2. **Gulacy** a-6, c-1, 6. **Kaluta** c/a-5. **Mayerik** a-2, 3. **Rogers** a-1-8. **Starlin** a-1. **Sutton** a-6.*

ECLIPSE MONTHLY
Eclipse Comics: Aug, 1983 - No. 10, Jul, 1984 (Baxter paper, $2.00/$1.50/$1.75)

1-10: ($2.00, 52 pgs.)-Cap'n Quick and a Foozle by Rogers, Static by Ditko, Dope by Trina Robbins, Rio by Doug Wildey, The Masked Man by Boyer begin. 3-Ragamuffins begins 2.00

NOTE: ***Boyer** c-6. **Ditko** a-1-3. **Rogers** a-1-4; c-2, 4, 7. **Wildey** a-1, 2, 5, 9, 10; c-5, 10.*

ECLIPSO (See Brave and the Bold #64, House of Secrets #61 & Phantom Stranger, 1987)
DC Comics: Nov, 1992 - No. 18, Apr, 1994 ($1.25)

1-18: 1-Giffen plots/breakdowns begin. 10-Darkseid app. Creeper in #3-6,9,11-13. 18-Spectre-c/s 2.00
Annual 1 (1993, $2.50, 68 pgs.)-Intro Prism 2.50

ECLIPSO: THE DARKNESS WITHIN
DC Comics: July, 1992 - No. 2, Oct, 1992 ($2.50, 68 pgs.)

1-With purple gem attached to-c, 1-Without gem; Superman, Creeper app., 2-Concludes Eclipso storyline from annuals 2.50

E. C. 3-D CLASSICS (See Three Dimensional...)

ECTOKID (See Razorline)
Marvel Comics: Sept, 1993 - No. 9, May, 1994 ($1.75/$1.95)

1-($2.50)-Foil embossed-c; created by C. Barker 2.50
2-9: 2-Origin. 5-Saint Sinner x-over 2.00

GD2.0 FN6.0 NM9.4

...: Unleashed! 1 (10/94, $2.95, 52 pgs.) 3.00

ED "BIG DADDY" ROTH'S RATFINK COMIX (Also see Ratfink)
World of Fandom/ Ed Roth: 1991 - No. 3, 1991 ($2.50)

1-3: Regular Ed., 1-Limited double cover 1.25 3.75 10.00

EDDIE CAMPBELL'S BACCHUS
Eddie Campbell Comics: May, 1995 - Present ($2.95, B&W)

1-Cerebus app. 4.00
1-2nd printing (5/97) 3.00
2-47: 9-Alex Ross back-c. 3.00
Doing The Islands With Bacchus ('97, $17.95) 18.00
Earth, Water, Air & Fire ('98, $9.95) 10.00
King Bacchus ('99, $12.95) 13.00
The Eyeball Kid ('98, $8.50) 8.50

EDDIE STANKY (Baseball Hero)
Fawcett Publications: 1951 (New York Giants)

nn-Photo-c 33.00 99.00 230.00

EDEN MATRIX, THE
Adhesive Comics: 1994 ($2.95)

1,2-Two variant-c; alternate-c on inside back-c 3.00

EDGAR BERGEN PRESENTS CHARLIE McCARTHY
Whitman Publishing Co. (Charlie McCarthy Co.): No. 764, 1938 (36 pgs.; 15x10-1/2"; in color)

764 70.00 210.00 560.00

EDGAR RICE BURROUGHS' TARZAN: A TALE OF MUGAMBI
Dark Horse Comics: 1995 ($2.95, one-shot)

1 3.00

EDGAR RICE BURROUGHS' TARZAN: IN THE LAND THAT TIME FORGOT AND THE POOL OF TIME
Dark Horse Comics: 1996 ($12.95, trade paperback)

nn-r/Russ Manning-a 13.00

EDGAR RICE BURROUGHS' TARZAN: THE LOST ADVENTURE
Dark Horse Comics: Jan, 1995 - No. 4, Apr, 1995 ($2.95, B&W, limited series)

1-4: ERB's last Tarzan story, adapted by Joe Lansdale 3.00
Hardcover (12/95, $19.95) 20.00
Limited Edition Hardcover ($99.95)-signed & numbered 100.00

EDGAR RICE BURROUGHS' TARZAN: THE RETURN OF TARZAN
Dark Horse Comics: May, 1997 - No. 3, July, 1997 ($2.95, limited series)

1-3: 3.00

EDGE
Malibu Comics (Bravura): July, 1994 - No. 3, Apr, 1995 ($2.50, unfinished limited series)

1-3-S. Grant-story & Gil Kane-c/a; w/Bravura stamp 2.50

EDGE OF CHAOS
Pacific Comics: July, 1983 - No. 3, Jan, 1984 (Limited series)

1-3-Morrow c/a; all contain nudity 2.00

ED WHEELAN'S JOKE BOOK STARRING FAT & SLAT (See Fat & Slat)

EERIE (Strange Worlds No. 18 on)
Avon Per.: No. 1, Jan, 1947; No. 1, May-June, 1951 - No. 17, Aug-Sept, 1954

1(1947)-1st supernatural comic; Kubert, Fugitani-a; bondage-c 260.00 780.00 2600.00
1(1951)-Reprints story from 1947 #1 56.00 168.00 450.00
2-Wood-c/a; bondage-c 62.00 188.00 500.00
3-Wood-c; Kubert, Wood/Orlando-a 62.00 188.00 500.00
4,5-Wood-c 50.00 150.00 400.00
6,8,13,14: 8-Kinstler-a; bondage-c; Phantom Witch Doctor story 27.00 81.00 190.00
7-Wood/Orlando-c; Kubert-a 40.00 120.00 320.00
9-Kubert-a; Check-c 32.00 96.00 225.00
10,11: 10-Kinstler-a. 11-Kinstlerish-a by McCann 27.00 81.00 190.00

Eerie #16 © Warren

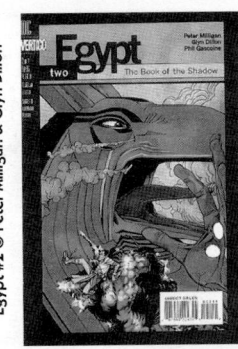

Egypt #2 © Peter Milligan & Glyn Dillon

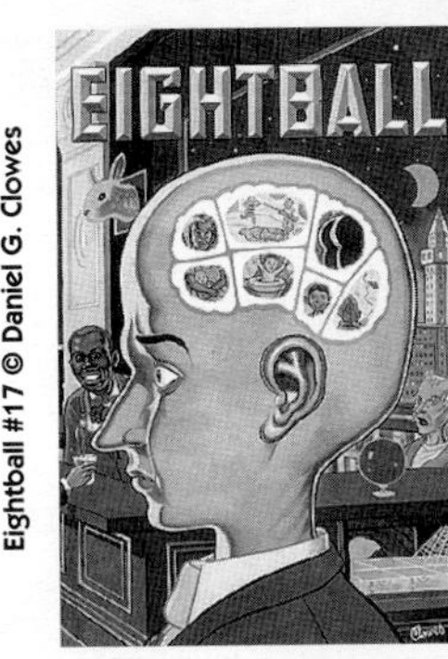

Eightball #17 © Daniel G. Clowes

	GD2.0	FN6.0	NM9.4
12-Dracula story from novel, 25 pgs.	34.00	103.00	240.00
15-Reprints No. 1('51) minus-c(bondage)	21.00	64.00	150.00
16-Wood-a r-/No. 2	21.00	64.00	150.00
17-Wood/Orlando & Kubert-a; reprints #3 minus inside & outside Wood-c	26.00	79.00	185.00

NOTE: ***Hollingsworth** a-9-11; c-10, 11.*

EERIE
I. W. Enterprises: 1964

	GD2.0	FN6.0	NM9.4
I.W. Reprint #1('64)-Wood-c(r); r-story/Spook #1	3.20	9.60	32.00
I.W. Reprint #2,6,8: 8-Dr. Drew by Grandenetti from Ghost #9	2.60	7.80	26.00
I.W. Reprint #9-r/Tales of Terror #1(Toby); Wood-c	3.50	10.50	35.00

EERIE (Magazine)(See Warren Presents)
Warren Publ. Co.: No. 1, Sept, 1965; No. 2, Mar, 1966 - No. 139, Feb, 1983

1-24 pgs., black & white, small size (5-1/4x7-1/4"), low distribution; cover from inside back cover of Creepy No. 2; stories reprinted from Creepy No. 7, 8. At least three different versions exist.
First Printing - B&W, 5-1/4" wide x 7-1/4" high, evenly trimmed. On page 18, panel 5, in the upper left-hand corner, the large rear view of a bald headed man blends into solid black and is unrecognizable. Overall printing quality is poor. 25.00 75.00 250.00
Second Printing - B&W, 5-1/4x7-1/4", with uneven, untrimmed edges (if one of these were trimmed evenly, the size would be less than as indicated). The figure of the bald headed man on page 18, panel 5 is clear and discernible. The staples have a 1/4" blue stripe. 9.50 28.50 95.00
Other unauthorized reproductions for comparison's sake would be practically worthless. One known version was probably shot off a first printing copy with some loss of detail; the finer lines tend to disappear in this version which can be determined by looking at the lower right-hand corner of page one, first story. The roof of the house is shaded with straight lines. These lines are sharp and distinct on original, but broken on this version.

NOTE: ***The Overstreet Comic Book Price Guide** recommends that, before buying a 1st issue, you consult an expert.*

	GD2.0	FN6.0	NM9.4
2-Frazetta-c (also #3,5,7,8)	6.00	18.00	60.00
3-Frazetta-c & half pg. ad (rerun in #4)	4.80	14.40	48.00
4-10: 4-Frazetta-a (1/2 pg. ad). 5,7,8-Frazetta-c. 9-Headlight-c	2.50	7.50	25.00
11-16,18-20,26-38,40,43-45	2.50	7.50	20.00
17 (scarce)	7.50	22.50	75.00
21,22,24,25: 25-Steranko-c	2.60	7.80	26.00
23-Frazetta-c	3.60	10.80	36.00
39,41: 39-1st Dax. 41 (scarce)	2.80	8.40	28.00
42,51-('73 & '74 Annuals). 51-Color poster insert	2.80	8.40	28.00
46-50,52,53: 46-Dracula series by Sutton begins	1.85	5.50	15.00
54,55-Color Spirit story by Eisner, reprints sections 12/21/47 & 6/16/46	2.25	6.75	18.00
56-60,62,68,69,72,77: All have an 8 pg. slick color insert., 60-Summer Giant (9/74, $1.25)	2.25	6.75	18.00
61,63-67,70,71,73-76,78: 78-The Mummy-r	1.50	4.50	12.00
79,80-Origin Darklon the Mystic by Starlin (1st app.)	1.85	5.50	15.00
81,83-94,96-129: 84-All sports issue	1.25	3.75	10.00
82-1st app. The Rook	2.50	7.50	20.00
95-The Rook & Vampirella team-up	1.75	5.25	14.00
130-Vampirella-c/story	1.75	5.25	14.00
131-139 (lower distr.)	1.50	4.50	12.00
Year Book '70, '71, '72-Reprints in both	3.00	9.00	30.00

NOTE: *The above books contain art by many good artists: **N. Adams, Brunner, Corben, Craig (Taycee), Crandall, Ditko, Eisner, Evans, Jeff Jones, Krenkel, McWilliams, Morrow, Orlando, Ploog, Severin, Starlin, Torres, Toth, Williamson, Wood,** and **Wrightson**; covers by **Bode', Corben, Davis, Frazetta, Morrow,** and **Orlando**. **Frazetta** c-2, 3, 7, 8, 23. Annuals from 1973-on are included in regular numbering. 1970-74 Annuals are complete reprints. Annuals from 1975-on are in the format of the regular issues.*

EERIE ADVENTURES (Also see Weird Adventures)
Ziff-Davis Publ. Co.: Winter, 1951 (Painted-c)

	GD2.0	FN6.0	NM9.4
1-Powell-a(2), McCann-a; used in **SOTI**; bondage-c; Krigstein back-c	39.00	116.00	270.00

NOTE: *Title dropped due to similarity to Avon's Eerie & legal action.*

EERIE TALES (Magazine)
Hastings Associates: 1959 (Black & White)

	GD2.0	FN6.0	NM9.4
1-Williamson, Torres, Tuska-a, Powell(2), & Morrow(2)-a	10.00	30.00	70.00

EERIE TALES
Super Comics: 1963-1964

	GD2.0	FN6.0	NM9.4
Super Reprint No. 10,11,12,18: 10('63)-r/Spook #27. Purple Claw in #11,12 ('63); #12-r/Avon's Eerie #1('51)-Kida-r	2.50	7.50	20.00
15-Wolverton-a, Spacehawk-r/Blue Bolt Weird Tales #113; Disbrow-a	4.50	13.50	45.00

EGBERT
Arnold Publications/Quality Comics Group: Spring, 1946 - No. 20, 1950

	GD2.0	FN6.0	NM9.4
1-Funny animal; intro Egbert & The Count	18.00	54.00	125.00
2	10.00	30.00	65.00
3-10	5.85	17.50	35.00
11-20	4.00	12.00	24.00

EGON
Dark Horse Comics: Jan, 1998 - No.2, Feb, 1998 ($2.95, limited series)

1,2-Horley-painted-c 3.00

EGYPT
DC Comics (Vertigo): Aug, 1995 - No.7, Feb, 1996 ($2.50, lim. series, mature)

1-7: Milligan scripts in all. 3.00

EH! (...Dig This Crazy Comic) (From Here to Insanity No. 8 on)
Charlton Comics: Dec, 1953 - No. 7, Nov-Dec, 1954 (Satire)

	GD2.0	FN6.0	NM9.4
1-Davisish-c/a by Ayers, Woodish-a by Giordano; Atomic Mouse app.	32.00	96.00	225.00
2-Ayers-c/a	20.00	60.00	140.00
3,5,7	17.00	51.00	120.00
4,6: Sexual innuendo-c. 6-Ayers-a	19.00	56.00	130.00

EIGHTBALL
Fantagraphics Books: Oct, 1989 - Present ($2.75/$2.95/$3.95, semi-annually, mature)

	GD2.0	FN6.0	NM9.4
1 (1st printing)	1.00	3.00	8.00
2-8			5.00
9-19: 17-(8/96)			4.00
20-($4.50)			4.50

EIGHTH WONDER, THE
Dark Horse Comics: Nov, 1997 ($2.95, one-shot)

nn-Reprints stories from Dark Horse Presents #85-87 3.00

EIGHT IS ENOUGH KITE FUN BOOK (See Kite Fun Book)

80 PAGE GIANT (...Magazine No. 2-15)
National Periodical Publications: 8/64 - No. 15, 10/65; No. 16, 11/65 - No. 89, 7/71 (25¢)(All reprints) (#1-56: 84 pgs.; #57-89: 68 pgs.)

	GD2.0	FN6.0	NM9.4
1-Superman Annual; originally planned as Superman Annual #9 (8/64)	35.00	105.00	470.00
2-Jimmy Olsen	19.25	58.00	280.00
3,4: 3-Lois Lane. 4-Flash-G.A.-r; Infantino-a	15.00	45.00	220.00
5-Batman; has Sunday newspaper strip; Catwoman-r; Batman's Life Story-r (25th anniversary special)	15.00	45.00	220.00
6-Superman	12.50	37.50	180.00
7-Sgt. Rock's Prize Battle Tales; Kubert-c/a	15.00	45.00	210.00
8-More Secret Origins-origins of JLA, Aquaman, Robin, Atom, & Superman; Infantino-a	28.00	85.00	400.00
9-15: 9-Flash (r/Flash #106,117,123 & Showcase #14); Infantino-a. 10-Superboy. 11-Superman; all Luthor issue. 12-Batman; has Sunday newspaper strip. 13-Jimmy Olsen. 14-Lois Lane. 15-Superman and Batman; Joker-c/story	11.75	35.00	165.00

Continued as part of regular series under each title in which that particular book came out, a Giant being published instead of the regular size. Issues No. 16 to No. 89 are listed for your information. See individual titles for prices.
16-JLA #39 (11/65), 17-Batman #176, 18-Superman #183, 19-Our Army at War #164, 20-Action #334, 21-Flash #160, 22-Superboy #129, 23-Superman #187, 24-Batman #182, 25-Jimmy Olsen #95, 26-Lois Lane #68, 27-Batman #185, 28-World's Finest #161, 29-JLA #48, 30-Batman #187, 31-Superman #193, 32-Our Army at War #177, 33-Action #347, 34-Flash #169, 35-Superboy

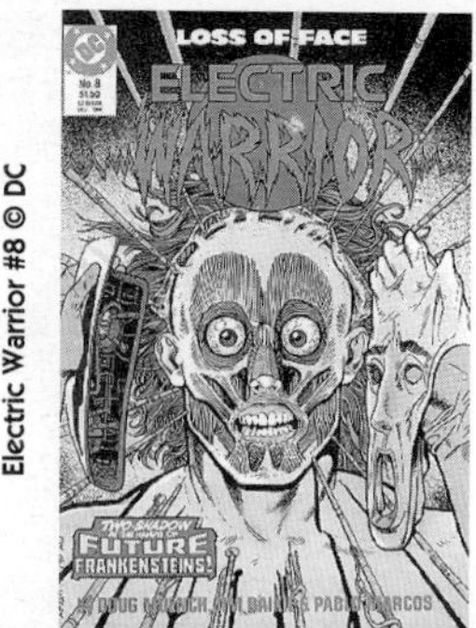

Electric Warrior #8 © DC

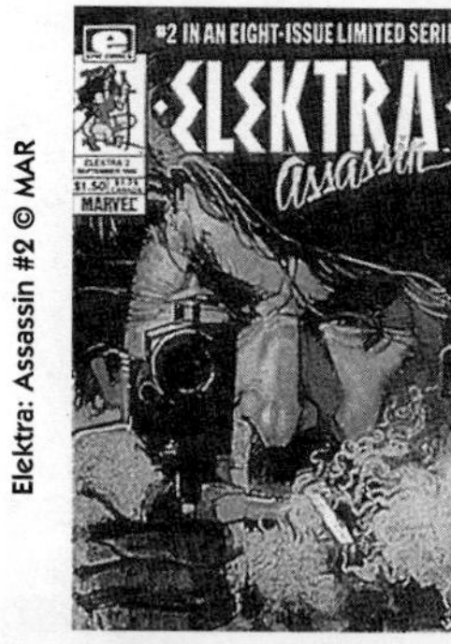

Elektra: Assassin #2 © MAR

Elementals #7 © Comico

#138, 36-Superman #197, 37-Batman #193, 38-Jimmy Olsen #104, 39-Lois Lane #77, 40-World's Finest #170, 41-JLA #58, 42-Superman #202, 43-Batman #198, 44-Our Army at War #190, 45-Action #360, 46-Flash #178, 47-Superboy #147, 48-Superman #207, 49-Batman #203, 50-Jimmy Olsen #113, 51-Lois Lane #86, 52-World's Finest #179, 53-JLA #67, 54-Superman #212, 55-Batman #208, 56-Our Army at War #203, 57-Action #373, 58-Flash #187, 59-Superboy #156, 60-Superman #217, 61-Batman #213, 62-Jimmy Olsen #122, 63-Lois Lane #95, 64-World's Finest #188, 65-JLA #76, 66-Superman #222, 67-Batman #218, 68-Our Army at War #216, 69-Adventure #390, 70-Flash #196, 71-Superboy #165, 72-Superman #227, 73-Batman #223, 74-Jimmy Olsen #131, 75-Lois Lane #104, 76-World's Finest #197, 77-JLA #85, 78-Superman #232, 79-Batman #228, 80-Our Army at War #229, 81-Adventure #403, 82-Flash #205, 83-Superboy #174, 84-Superman #239, 85-Batman #233, 86-Jimmy Olsen #140, 87-Lois Lane #113, 88-World's Finest #206, 89-JLA #93.

87TH PRECINCT (TV)
Dell Publishing Co.: Apr-June, 1962 - No. 2, July-Sept, 1962

Four Color 1309(#1)-Krigstein-a 9.00 27.00 100.00
2 7.00 22.00 80.00

EL BOMBO COMICS
Standard Comics/Frances M. McQueeny: 1946

nn(1946), 1(no date) 10.00 30.00 70.00

EL CID
Dell Publishing Co.: No. 1259, 1961

Four Color 1259-Movie, photo-c 6.40 19.00 70.00

EL DIABLO (See All-Star Western #2 & Weird Western Tales #12)
DC Comics: Aug, 1989 - No. 16, Jan, 1991 ($1.50-$1.75, color)

1 ($2.50, 52pgs.)-Masked hero 2.50
2-16 2.00

EL DORADO (See Movie Classics)

ELECTRIC UNDERTOW (See Strikeforce Morituri: Electric Undertow)

ELECTRIC WARRIOR
DC Comics: May, 1986 - No. 18, Oct, 1987 ($1.50, Baxter paper)

1-18 2.00

ELEKTRA (Also see Daredevil #319-325)
Marvel Comics: Mar, 1995 - No. 4, June, 1995 ($2.95, limited series)

1-4-Embossed-c; Scott McDaniel-a 3.00

ELEKTRA (Also see Daredevil)
Marvel Comics: Nov, 1996 - No. 19, Jun, 1998 ($1.95)

1-Peter Milligan scripts; Deodato-c/a 5.00
1-Variant-c 1.00 3.00 8.00
2- 3.00
9-19: 1(7/97): Dr. Strange-c/app. 0-Logan-c/app. 2.50
.../Cyblade (Image, 3/97,$2.95) Devil's Reign pt. 7 3.00

ELEKTRA: ASSASSIN (Also see Daredevil)
Marvel Comics (Epic Comics): Aug, 1986 - No. 8, June, 1987 (Limited series, mature)

1-Miller scripts in all; Sienkiewicz-c/a. 2.40 6.00
2-8 5.00
Signed & numbered hardcover (Graphitti Designs, $39.95, 2000 print run)-reprints 1-8 50.00

ELEKTRA LIVES AGAIN (Also see Daredevil)
Marvel Comics (Epic Comics): 1990 ($24.95, oversize, hardcover, 76 pgs.) (Produced by Graphitti Designs)

nn-Frank Miller-c/a/scripts; Lynn Varley painted-a; Matt Murdock & Bullseye app.; Elektra dies 25.00

ELEKTRA MEGAZINE
Marvel Comics: Nov, 1996 - No. 2, Dec, 1996 ($3.95, 96 pgs., reprints, limited series)

1,2: Reprints Frank Miller's Elektra stories in Daredevil 4.00

ELEKTRA SAGA, THE
Marvel Comics Group: Feb, 1984 - No. 4, June, 1984 ($2.00, limited series, Baxter paper)

1-4-r/Daredevil 168-190; Miller-c/a 3.00

GD2.0 FN6.0 NM9.4

ELEMENTALS, THE (See The Justice Machine & Morningstar Spec.)
Comico The Comic Co. : June, 1984 - No. 29, Sept, 1988; V2#1, Mar, 1989 - No. 28, 1994? ($1.50/$2.50, Baxter paper); V3#1, Dec, 1995 - No. 3 ($2.95)

1-Willingham-c/a, 1-8 3.00
2-29, V2#1-28: 9-Bissette-a(p). 10-Photo-c. V2#6-1st app. Strike Force America 18-Prelude to Avalon mini-series. 27-Prequel to Strike Force America series 2.50
V3#1-3: 1-Daniel-a(p), bagged w/gaming card 3.00
Lingerie (5/96, $2.95) 3.00
Special 1,2 (3/86, 1/89)-1-Willingham-a(p) 2.50

ELEMENTALS: (Title series), **Comico**

--GHOST OF A CHANCE, 12/95 ($5.95)-graphic nove, nn-Ross-c. 6.00
--HOW THE WAR WAS WON, 6/996 - No. 2, 8/96 ($2.95) 1,2-Tony Daniel-a, & 1-Variant-c; no logo 3.00
--SEX SPECIAL, 5/97 - No. 2, 6/97 ($2.95 1-Tony Daniel, Jeff Moy-a, 2-Robb Phipps, Adam McDaniel-a 3.00
--SWIMSUIT SPECTACULAR 1996, 6/96 ($2.95), 1-pin-ups, 1-Variant-c; no logo 3.00
--THE VAMPIRE'S REVENGE, 6/96 - No. 2 8/96 ($2.95) 1,2-Willingham-s, 1-Variant-c; no logo 3.00

1111 (ELEVEN ELEVEN)
Crusade Entertainment: Oct, 1996 ($2.95, B&W, one-shot)

1-Wrightson-c/a 3.00

ELEVEN OR ONE
Sirius: Apr, 1995 ($2.95)

1-Linsner-c/a 2.40 6.00
1-(6/96) 2nd printing 3.00

ELFLORD
Aircel Publ.: 1986 - No. 6, Oct, 1989 ($1.70, B&W); V2#1- V2#31, 1995 ($2.00)

1 3.00
2-4,V2#1-20,22-30: 4-6: Last B&W issue. V2#1-Color-a begin. 22-New cast. 25-Begin B&W 2.00
1,2-2nd printings 2.00
21-Double size ($4.95) 5.00

ELFLORD
Warp Graphics: Jan, 1997-No.4, Apr, 1997 ($2.95, B&W, mini-series)

1-4 3.00

ELFLORD (CUTS LOOSE) (Vol. 2)
Warp Graphics: Sept, 1997 - Present ($2.95, B&W, mini-series)

1-7 3.00

ELFLORD: DRAGON'S EYE
Night Wynd Enterprises: 1993 ($2.50, B&W)

1 2.50

ELFLORD: THE RETURN
Mad Monkey Press: 1996 ($6.95, magazine size)

1 7.00

ELFQUEST (Also see Fantasy Quarterly & Warp Graphics Annual)
Warp Graphics, Inc.: No. 2, Aug, 1978 - No. 21, Feb, 1985 (All magazine size) No. 1, Apr, 1979

NOTE: ***Elfquest*** was originally published as one of the stories in **Fantasy Quarterly** #1. When the publisher went out of business, the creative team, Wendy and Richard Pini, formed WaRP Graphics and continued the series, beginning with **Elfquest** #2. **Elfquest** #1, which reprinted the story from **Fantasy Quarterly**, was published about the same time **Elfquest** #4 was released. Thereafter, most issues were reprinted as demand warranted, until Marvel announced it would reprint the entire series under its Epic imprint (Aug., 1985).

1(4/79)-Reprints Elfquest story from Fantasy Quarterly No. 1
1st printing ($1.00-c) 2.50 7.50 22.00
2nd printing ($1.25-c) 1.10 3.30 9.00
3rd printings ($1.50-c) 3.00
4th printing; different-c ($1.50-c) 2.00

ELFQUEST
to hunt · to howl · to live free

Elfquest #23 © Richard & Wendy Pini

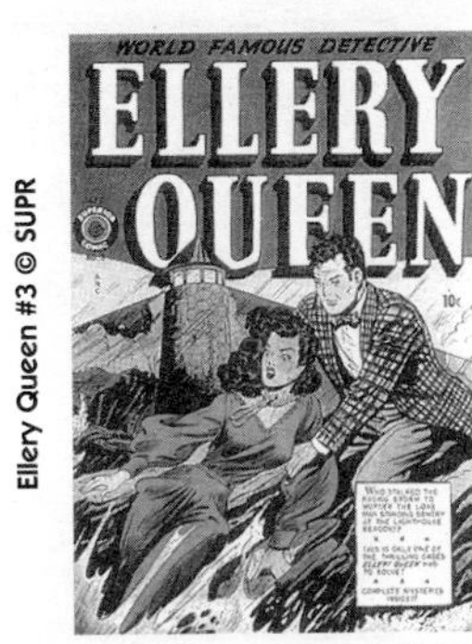

Ellery Queen #3 © SUPR

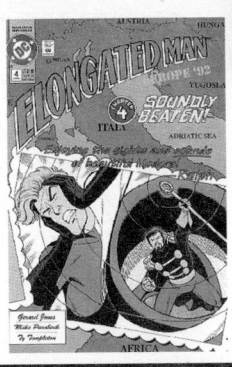

Elongated Man #4 © DC

GD2.0 FN6.0 NM9.4

2(8/78)-5: 1st printings ($1.00-c) 1.75 5.25 14.00
2nd printings ($1.25-c) 4.00
3rd & 4th printings ($1.50-c)(all 4th prints 1989) 2.50
6-9: 1st printings ($1.25-c) 2.40 6.00
2nd printings ($1.50-c) 3.50
3rd printings ($1.50-c) 2.00
10-21: ($1.50-c); 16-8pg. preview of A Distant Soil 4.00
10-14: 2nd printings ($1.50) 2.00

ELFQUEST
Marvel Comics (Epic Comics): Aug, 1985 - No. 32, Mar, 1988
1-Reprints in color the Elfquest epic by Warp Graphics 3.00
2-32 2.00

ELFQUEST (Title series), Warp Graphics
'89 - No. 4, '89 ($1.50, B&W) 1-4: R-original Elfquest series 2.00

ELFQUEST (Volume 2), **Warp Graphics:** V2#1, 5/96 - Present ($4.95, B&W)
V2#1-33: 1,3,5,8,10,12,13,18,21,23,25-Wendy Pini-c 5.00

--BLOOD OF TEN CHIEFS, 7/93 - No. 20, 9/95 ($2.00/$2.50) 1-20-By Richard & Wendy Pini 2.50

--HIDDEN YEARS, 5/92 - No. 29, 3/96 ($2.00/$2.25)1-29 2.50

--JINK, 11/94 - No. 12, 2/6 ($2.25/$2.50) 1-12-W. Pini/John Byrn-back-c 2.50

--KAHVI, 10/95 - No. 6,3/96 ($2.25, B&W) 1-6 2.50

--KINGS CROSS, 11/97 - No. 2, 12/97 ($2.95, B&W) 1,2 3.00

--KINGS OF THE BROKEN WHEEL, 6/90 - No. 9, 2/92 ($2.00, B&W) (3rd Elfquest saga) 1-9: By R. & W. Pini; 1-Color insert, 1-2nd printing 2.50

--METAMORPHOSIS, 4/96 ($2.95, B&W) 1 3.00

--NEW BLOOD (...Summer Special on-c #1 only), 8/92 - No. 35, 1/96 ($2.00-$2.50, color/B&W) 1-($3.95, 68 pgs.)-Byrne-a/scripts (16 pgs.) 4.00
2-34: Barry Blair-a in all 2.50

--SHARDS, 8/94 - No. 16, 3/96 ($2.25/$2.50) 1-16 2.50

--SIEGE AT BLUE MOUNTAIN, Waphics/Apple 3/87 - No. 8, 12/88 (1.75/$1.95, B&W) 1-Staton-a(i) in all; 2nd Elfquest saga 4.00
1-3-2nd printing, 3-8 2.50
2 3.00

--THE REBELS, 11/94 - No. 12, 3/96 ($2.25/$2.50, B&W/color) 1-12 2.50

--TWO-SPEAR, 10/95 - No. 5, 2/96 ($2.25, B&W) 1-5 2.50

--WAVE DANCERS, 12/93 - No. 6, 3/96, 1-6: 1-Foil-c & poster 2.50
Special 1 ($2.95) 3.00

--WORLDPOOL, 7/97 ($2.95, B&W) 1-Richard Pini-s/Barry Blair-a 3.00

ELF-THING
Eclipse Comics: March, 1987 ($1.50, B&W, one-shot)
1 2.00

ELIMINATOR (Also see The Solution #16 & The Night Man #16)
Malibu Comics (Ultraverse): Apr, 1995 - No. 3, Jul, 1995 ($2.95/$2.50, lim. series)
0-Mike Zeck-a in all 3.00
1-3-($2.50): 1-1st app. Siren 2.50
1-($3.95)-Black cover edition 4.00

ELIMINATOR FULL COLOR SPECIAL
Eternity Comics: Oct, 1991 ($2.95, one-shot)
1-Dave Dorman painted-c 3.00

ELLA CINDERS (See Comics On Parade, Comics Revue #1,4, Famous Comics Cartoon Book, Giant Comics Editions, Sparkler Comics, Tip Top & Treasury of Comics)

ELLA CINDERS
United Features Syndicate: 1938 - 1940
Single Series 3(1938) 40.00 120.00 300.00
Single Series 21(#2 on-c, #21 on inside), 28('40) 34.00 103.00 240.00

ELLA CINDERS
United Features Syndicate: Mar, 1948 - No. 5, Mar, 1949

GD2.0 FN6.0 NM9.4

1-(#2 on cover) 12.00 36.00 85.00
2 8.35 25.00 50.00
3-5 5.85 17.50 35.00

ELLERY QUEEN
Superior Comics Ltd.: May, 1949 - No. 4, Nov, 1949
1-Kamen-c; L.B. Cole-a; r-in Haunted Thrills 47.00 141.00 375.00
2-4: 3-Drug use stories(2) 37.00 111.00 260.00
NOTE: *Iger shop art in all issues.*

ELLERY QUEEN (TV)
Ziff-Davis Publishing Co.: 1-3/52 (Spring on-c) - No. 2, Summer/52 (Saunders painted-c)
1-Saunders-c 41.00 122.00 325.00
2-Saunders bondage, torture-c 37.00 111.00 260.00

ELLERY QUEEN (Also see Crackajack Funnies No. 23)
Dell Publishing Co.: No. 1165, Mar-May, 1961 - No.1289, Apr, 1962
Four Color 1165 (#1)- 10.50 31.50 115.00
Four Color 1243 (11-1/61-61), 1289 8.75 26.50 95.00

ELMER FUDD (Also see Camp Comics, Daffy, Looney Tunes #1 & Super Book #10, 22)
Dell Publishing Co.: No. 470, May, 1953 - No. 1293, Mar-May, 1962
Four Color 470 (#1) 4.50 13.50 50.00
Four Color 558,628,689('56) 3.20 9.50 35.00
Four Color 725,783,841,888,938,977,1032,1081,1131,1171,1222,1293('62) 2.20 6.50 24.00

ELMO COMICS
St. John Publishing Co.: Jan, 1948 (Daily strip-r)
1-By Cecil Jensen 10.00 30.00 60.00

ELONGATED MAN (See Flash #112 & Justice League of America #105)
DC Comics: Jan, 1992 - No. 4, Apr, 1992 ($1.00, limited series)
1-4: 3-The Flash app. 2.00

ELRIC (Of Melnibone)(See First Comics Graphic Novel #6 & Marvel Graphic Novel #2)
Pacific Comics: Apr, 1983 - No. 6, Apr, 1984 ($1.50, Baxter paper)
1-6: Russell-c/a(i) in all 2.00

ELRIC
Topps Comics: 1996 ($2.95, one-shot)
0--One Life: Russell-c/a; adapts Neil Gaiman's short story "One Life--Furnished in Early Moorcock." 3.00

ELRIC, SAILOR ON THE SEAS OF FATE
First Comics: June, 1985 - No. 7, June, 1986 ($1.75, limited series)
1-7: Adapts Michael Moorcock's novel 2.00

ELRIC, STORMBRINGER
Dark Horse Comics/Topps Comics: 1997 - No. 7, 1997($2.95, limited series)
1-7: Russell-c/s/a; adapts Michael Moorcock's novel 3.00

ELRIC: THE BANE OF THE BLACK SWORD
First Comics: Aug, 1988 - No. 6, June, 1989 ($1.75/$1.95, limited series)
1-6: Adapts Michael Moorcock's novel 2.00

ELRIC: THE VANISHING TOWER
First Comics: Aug, 1987 - No. 6, June, 1988 ($1.75, limited series)
1-6: Adapts Michael Moorcock's novel 2.00

ELRIC: WEIRD OF THE WHITE WOLF
First Comics: Oct, 1986 - No. 5, June, 1987 ($1.75, limited series)
1-5: Adapts Michael Moorcock's novel 2.00

EL SALVADOR - A HOUSE DIVIDED
Eclipse Comics: March, 1989 ($2.50, B&W, Baxter paper, stiff-c, 52 pgs.)
1-Gives history of El Salvador 2.50

ELSEWHERE PRINCE, THE (Moebius' Airtight Garage)

Elseworlds 80-Page Giant #1 © DC

Emergency #4 © CC

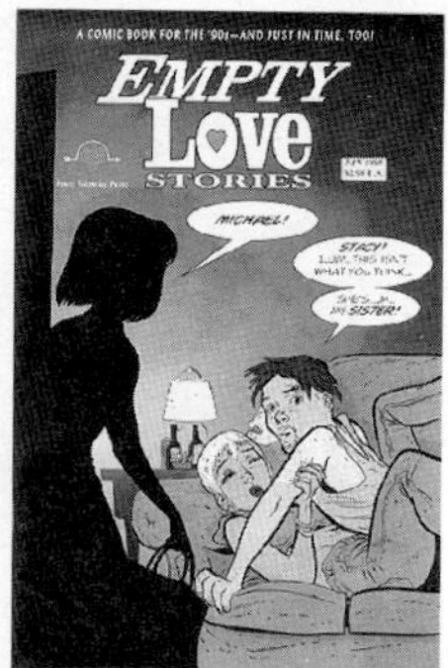

Empty Love Stories 1999 © Steve Darnall

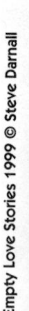

Marvel Comics (Epic): May, 1990 - No. 6, Oct, 1990 ($1.95, limited series)

1-6: Moebius scripts & back-up-a in all 2.00

ELSEWORLDS 80-PAGE GIANT
DC Comics: Aug, 1999 ($5.95, one-shot)

1-Most copies destroyed by DC over content of the "Superman's Babysitter" story; some UK shipments sold before recall 100.00

ELSEWORLD'S FINEST
DC Comics: 1997 - No. 2, 1997 ($4.95, limited series)

1,2: Elseworld's story-Superman & Batman in the 1920's 5.00

ELSEWORLD'S FINEST: SUPERGIRL & BATGIRL
DC Comics: 1998 ($5.95, one-shot)

1-Haley-a 6.00

ELSIE THE COW
D. S. Publishing Co.: Oct-Nov, 1949 - No. 3, July-Aug, 1950

	GD2.0	FN6.0	NM9.4
1-(36 pgs.)	23.00	69.00	160.00
2,3	17.00	51.00	120.00

ELSON'S PRESENTS
DC Comics: 1981 (100 pgs., no cover price)

Series 1-6: Repackaged 1981 DC comics; 1-DC Comics Presents #29, Flash #303, Batman #331. 2-Superman #335, Ghosts #96, Justice League of America #186. 3-New Teen Titans #3, Secrets of Haunted House #32, Wonder Woman #275. 4-Secrets of the LSH #1, Brave & the Bold #170, New Adv. of Superboy #13. 5-LSH #271, Green Lantern #136, Super Friends #40. 6-Action #515, Mystery in Space #115, Detective #498 6.00

ELVEN (Also see Prime)
Malibu Comics (Ultraverse): Oct, 1994 - No. 4, Feb, 1995 ($2.50, lim. series)

0 ($2.95)-Prime app. 3.00
1-4: 2,4-Prime app. 3-Primevil app. 2.50
1-Limited Foil Edition- no price on cover 3.00

ELVIRA MISTRESS OF THE DARK
Marvel Comics: Oct, 1988 ($2.00, B&W, magazine size)

1-Movie adaptation 4.00

ELVIRA MISTRESS OF THE DARK
Claypool Comics (Eclipse): May, 1993 - Present ($2.50, B&W)

1-Austin-a(i). Spiegle-a 5.00
2-6: Spiegle-a 3.00
7-73-Photo-c: 2.50

ELVIRA'S HOUSE OF MYSTERY
DC Comics: Jan, 1986 - No. 11, Jan, 1987

1,11: 11-Dave Stevens-c 3.00
2-10: 9-Photo-c, Special 1 (3/87, $1.25) 2.00

ELVIS MANDIBLE, THE
DC Comics (Piranha Press): 1990 ($3.50, 52 pgs., B&W, mature)

nn 3.50

ELVIS PRESLEY (See Career Girl Romances #32, Go-Go, Howard Chaykin's American Flagg #10, Humbug #8, I Love You #60 & Young Lovers #18)

E-MAN
Charlton Comics: Oct, 1973 - No. 10, Sept, 1975 (Painted-c No. 7-10)

	GD2.0	FN6.0	NM9.4
1-Origin & 1st app. E-Man; Staton c/a in all	2.00	6.00	16.00
2-4: 2,4-Ditko-a. 3-Howard-a	1.00	2.80	7.00
5-Miss Liberty Belle app. by Ditko		2.40	6.00
6-10: Early Byrne-a in all (#6 is 1/75). 6-Disney parody. 8-Full-length story; Nova begins as E-Man's partner	1.10	3.30	9.00
1-4,9,10(Modern Comics reprints, '77)			4.00

NOTE: *Killjoy app.-No. 2, 4. Liberty Belle app.-No. 5. Rog 2000 app.-No. 6, 7, 9, 10. Travis app.-No. 3.* ***Tom Sutton*** *a-1.*

E-MAN
Comico: Sept, 1989 ($2.75, one-shot, no ads, high quality paper)

1-Staton-c/a; Michael Mauser story 2.75

E-MAN
Comico: V4#1, Jan, 1990 - No. 3, Mar, 1990 ($2.50, limited series)

1-3: Staton-c/a 2.50

E-MAN
Alpha Productions: Oct, 1993 ($2.75)

V5#1-Staton-c/a; 20th anniversary issue 2.75

E-MAN COMICS (Also see Michael Mauser & The Original E-Man)
First Comics: Apr, 1983 - No. 25, Aug, 1985 ($1.00/$1.25, direct sales only)

1-25: 2-X-Men satire. 3-X-Men/Phoenix satire. 6-Origin retold. 8-Cutey Bunny app. 10-Origin Nova Kane. 24-Origin Michael Mauser 2.00

NOTE: ***Staton*** *a-1-5, 6-25p; c-1-25.*

E-MAN RETURNS
Alpha Productions: 1994 ($2.75, B&W)

1-Joe Staton-c/a(p) 2.75

EMBRACE
London Night Studios: Nov, 1996 ($3.00)

1-Photo-c(Carmen Electra) 3.00
1-($5.00)-NC-17 Edition 5.00

EMBRACE: HUNGER OF THE FLESH
London Night Studios: July, 1997 - No. 3 ($3.00, limited series)

1-3 3.00
1-3-($6.00)-Nude Edition 6.00

EMERALD DAWN
DC Comics: 1991 ($4.95, trade paperback)

nn-Reprints Green Lantern: Emerald Dawn #1-6 5.00

EMERALD DAWN II (See Green Lantern...)

EMERGENCY (Magazine)
Charlton Comics: June, 1976 - No. 4, Jan, 1977 (B&W)

	GD2.0	FN6.0	NM9.4
1-Neal Adams-c/a; Heath, Austin-a	2.50	7.50	25.00
2,3: 2-N. Adams-c. 3-N. Adams-a.	2.50	7.50	20.00
4-Alcala-a	1.85	5.50	15.00

EMERGENCY (TV)
Charlton Comics: June, 1976 - No. 4, Dec, 1976

	GD2.0	FN6.0	NM9.4
1-Staton-c; early Byrne-a (22 pages)	2.50	7.50	20.00
2-4: 2-Staton-c	1.50	4.50	12.00

EMERGENCY DOCTOR
Charlton Comics: Summer, 1963 (one-shot)

	GD2.0	FN6.0	NM9.4
1	2.50	7.50	24.00

EMIL & THE DETECTIVES (See Movie Comics)

EMMA PEEL & JOHN STEED (See The Avengers)

EMPEROR'S NEW CLOTHES, THE
Dell Publishing Co.: 1950 (10¢, 68 pgs., 1/2 size, oblong)

	GD2.0	FN6.0	NM9.4
nn - (Surprise Books series)	3.60	9.00	18.00

EMPIRE STRIKES BACK, THE (See Marvel Comics Super Special #16 & Marvel Special Edition)

EMPTY LOVE STORIES
Slave Labor #1 & 2/Funny Valentine Press: Nov, 1994 - Present ($2.95, B&W)

1,2: Steve Darnall scripts in all. 1-Alex Ross-c. 2-(8/96)-Mike Allred-c 4.00
1,2-2nd printing (Funny Valentine Press) 3.00
... 1999-Jeff Smith-c; Doran-a 3.00
..."Special" (2.95) Ty Templeton-c 3.00

ENCHANTED
Sirius Entertainment: 1997 - No. 3 ($2.50, B&W, limited series)

1-3-Robert Chang-s/a 2.50

ENCHANTED (Volume 2)
Sirius Entertainment: 1998 - No. 3 ($2.95, limited series)

1-Robert Chang-s/a 3.00

Enchanting Love #1 © Kirby Pub.

Enigma #8 © DC

ESPers #5 © James D. Hudnall

GD2.0 FN6.0 NM9.4

ENCHANTED APPLES OF OZ, THE (See First Comics Graphic Novel #5)

ENCHANTER
Eclipse Comics: Apr, 1987 - No. 3, Aug. 1987 ($2.00, B&W, limited series)

1-3 2.00

ENCHANTING LOVE
Kirby Publishing Co.: Oct, 1949 - No. 6, July, 1950 (All 52 pgs.)

	GD2.0	FN6.0	NM9.4
1-Photo-c	12.00	36.00	85.00
2-Photo-c; Powell-a	7.50	22.50	45.00
3,4,6: 3-Jimmy Stewart photo-c	6.70	20.00	40.00
5-Ingels-a, 9 pgs.; photo-c	13.50	41.00	95.00

ENCHANTMENT VISUALETTES (Magazine)
World Editions: Dec, 1949 - No. 5, Apr, 1950 (Painted c-1)

	GD2.0	FN6.0	NM9.4
1-Contains two romance comic strips each	13.50	41.00	95.00
2	10.00	30.00	70.00
3-5	10.00	30.00	60.00

ENEMY
Dark Horse Comics: May, 1994 - No. 5, Sept, 1994 ($2.50, limited series)

1-5 2.50

ENEMY ACE SPECIAL (Also see Our Army at War #151, Showcase #57, 58 & Star Spangled War Stories #138)
DC Comics: 1990 ($1.00, one-shot)

1-Kubert-r/Our Army #151,153; c-r/Showcase 57 3.00

ENIGMA
DC Comics (Vertigo): Mar, 1993 - No. 8, Oct, 1993 ($2.50, limited series)

1-8: Milligan scripts 2.50
Trade paperback ($19.95)-reprints 20.00

ENO AND PLUM (Also see Cud Comics)
Oni Press: Mar, 1998 ($2.95, B&W)

1-Terry LaBan-s/c/a 3.00

ENSIGN O'TOOLE (TV)
Dell Publishing Co.: Aug-Oct, 1963 - No. 2, 1964

	GD2.0	FN6.0	NM9.4
1,2	2.50	7.50	22.00

ENSIGN PULVER (See Movie Classics)

EPIC
Marvel Comics (Epic Comics): 1992 - Book 4, 1992 ($4.95, lim. series, 52 pgs.)

Book One-Four: 2-Dorman painted-c 5.00
NOTE: *Alien Legion in #3. Cholly & Flytrap by* ***Burden****(scripts) &* ***Suydam****(art) in 3, 4. Dinosaurs in #4. Dreadlands in #1. Hellraiser in #1. Nightbreed in #2. Sleeze Brothers in #2. Stalkers in #1-4. Wild Cards in #1-4.*

EPIC ILLUSTRATED (Magazine)
Marvel Comics Group: Spring, 1980 - No. 34, Feb, 1986 ($2.00/$2.50, B&W/color, mature)

1-Frazetta-c 4.50
2-18: 12-Wolverton Spacehawk-r edited & recolored w/article on him. 13-Blade Runner preview by Williamson. 14-Elric of Melnibone by Russell; Revenge of the Jedi preview. 15-Vallejo-c & interview; 1st Dreadstar story (cont'd in Dreadstar #1). 16-B. Smith-c/a(2). 4.50
19-30: 20-The Sacred & the Profane begins by Ken Steacy. 26-Galactus series begins; Cerebus the Aardvark story by Dave Sim. 27-Groo. 28-Cerebus app.

	GD2.0	FN6.0	NM9.4
	1.00	2.80	7.00
31-33	1.25	3.75	10.00
34	2.00	6.00	16.00

NOTE: ***N. Adams*** *a-7; c-6.* ***Austin*** *a-15-20i.* ***Bode*** *a-19, 23, 27r.* ***Bolton*** *a-7, 10-12, 15, 18, 22-25; c-10, 18, 22, 23.* ***Boris*** *c/a-15.* ***Brunner*** *c-12.* ***Buscema*** *a-1p, 9p, 11-13p.* ***Byrne/Austin*** *a-26-34.* ***Chaykin*** *a-2; c-8.* ***Conrad*** *a-2-5, 7-9, 25-34; c-17.* ***Corben*** *a-15; c-2.* ***Frazetta*** *c-1.* ***Golden*** *a-3r.* ***Gulacy*** *c/a-3.* ***Jeff Jones*** *c-25.* ***Kaluta*** *a-17r, 21, 24r, 26; c-4, 28.* ***Nebres*** *a-1.* ***Reese*** *a-12.* ***Russell*** *a-2-4, 9, 14, 33; c-14.* ***Simonson*** *a-17.* ***B. Smith*** *c/a-7, 16.* ***Starlin*** *a-1-9, 14, 15, 34.* ***Steranko*** *c-19.* ***Williamson*** *a-13, 27, 34.* ***Wrightson*** *a-13p, 22, 25, 27, 34; c-30.*

EPIC LITE
Marvel Comics (Epic Comics): Sept, 1991 ($3.95, 52 pgs., one-shot)

1-Bob the Alien, Normalman by Valentino 4.00

GD2.0 FN6.0 NM9.4

EPICURUS THE SAGE
DC Comics (Piranha Press): Vol. 1, 1991 - Vol. 2, 1991 ($9.95, 8-1/8x10-7/8")

Volume 1,2-Sam Kieth-c/a 10.00

EPSILON WAVE
Independent Comics/Elite Comics No. 5 on: Oct, 1985 - V2#2, 1987 ($1.50/$1.25/$1.75)

1-8,V2#1,2: 1-3,6-Seadragon app. V2 (B&W) 2.00

ERADICATOR
DC Comics: Aug, 1996 - No. 3, Oct, 1996 ($1.75, limited series)

1-3: Superman app. 3.00

ERNIE COMICS (Formerly Andy Comics #21; All Love Romances #26 on)
Current Books/Ace Periodicals: No. 22, Sept, 1948 - No. 25, Mar, 1949

	GD2.0	FN6.0	NM9.4
nn (9/48,11/48; #22,23)-Teenage humor	5.85	17.50	35.00
24,25	4.15	12.50	25.00

ESCAPADE IN FLORENCE (See Movie Comics)

ESCAPE FROM DEVIL'S ISLAND
Avon Periodicals: 1952

	GD2.0	FN6.0	NM9.4
1-Kinstler-c; r/as Dynamic Adventures #9	36.00	107.00	250.00

ESCAPE FROM THE PLANET OF THE APES (See Power Record Comics)

ESCAPE TO WITCH MOUNTAIN (See Walt Disney Showcase No. 29)

ESPERS (Also see Interface)
Eclipse Comics: July, 1986 - No. 5, Apr, 1987 ($1.25/$1.75, Mando paper)

1-5-James Hudnall story & David Lloyd-a. 2.00

ESPERS
Halloween Comics: V2#1, 1996 - No. 6, 1997 ($2.95, B&W) (1st Halloween Comics series)

V2#1-6: James D. Hudnall scripts 3.00
Undertow TPB ('98, $14.95) r/#1-6 15.00

ESPERS
Image Comics: V3#1, 1997 - Present ($2.95, B&W, limited series)

V3#1-7: James D. Hudnall scripts 3.00
Black Magic TPB ('98, $14.95) r/#1-4 15.00

ESPIONAGE (TV)
Dell Publishing Co.: May-July, 1964 - No. 2, Aug-Oct, 1964

	GD2.0	FN6.0	NM9.4
1,2	2.20	6.50	24.00

ESSENTIAL (Title series), **Marvel Comics**

--AVENGERS , '98 (B&W- r) V1-R-Avengers #1-24; new Immonen-c 15.00

--FANTASTIC FOUR, '98 - Present (B&W-r)
V1-Reprints FF #1-20, Annual #1; new Alan Davis-c 15.00
V2-Reprints FF #21-40, Annual #2; Davis and Farmer-c 15.00

--HULK, '99 (B&W-r) V1-R-Incred. Hulk #1-6, Tales to Astonish stories; new Timm-c 15.00

--SILVER SURFER, '98 (B&W-r) V1-R-material from SS#1-18 and Fantastic Four Annual #5 13.00

--SPIDER-MAN, '96 - Present (B&W-r)
V1-R-AF #15, Amaz. S-M #1-20, Ann. #1 (2 printings) 15.00
V2-R-Amaz. Spider-Man #21-43, Annual #2,3 13.00
V3-R-Amaz. Spider-Man #44-68 13.00

ESSENTIAL VERTIGO: THE SANDMAN
DC Comics (Vertigo): Aug, 1996 - No. 32, Mar, 1999 ($1.95/$2.25, reprints)

1-13,15-31: Reprints Sandman, 2nd series 3.00
14-($2.95) 3.50
32-($4.50) Reprints Sandman Special #1 4.50

ESSENTIAL UNCANNY X-MEN
Marvel Comics: 1999 - Present (B&W reprints)

V1-Reprints X-Men (1st series) #1-24; Timm-c 15.00

ESSENTIAL VERTIGO: SWAMP THING

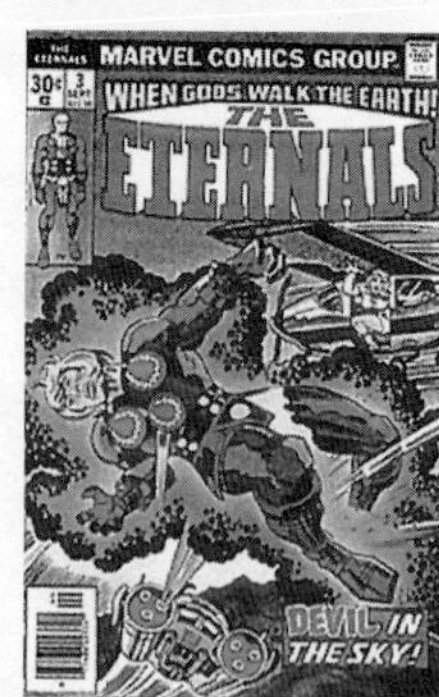

The Eternals (1st series) #3 © MAR

Evangeline V2 #10 © FC

Everything Happens to Harvey #6 © DC

GD2.0 FN6.0 NM9.4

DC Comics: Nov, 1996 - No. 24, Oct, 1998 ($1.95/$2.25,B&W, reprints)

1-11,13-24: 1-9-Reprints Alan Moore's Swamp Thing stories 3.00
12-($3.50) r/Annual #2 3.50

ESSENTIAL X-MEN
Marvel Comics: 1996 - Present (B&W reprints)

V1, V2-Reprints, V3--R-Uncanny X-Men #145-161, Ann. #3-5 15.00

ETC
DC Comics (Piranha Press): 1989 - No. 5, 1990 ($4.50, 60 pgs., mature)

Book 1-5: Conrad scripts/layouts in all 4.50

ETERNAL BIBLE, THE
Authentic Publications: 1946 (Large size) (16 pgs. in color)

1 13.50 41.00 95.00

ETERNALS, THE
Marvel Comics Group: July, 1976 - No. 19, Jan, 1978

1-(Regular 25¢ edition)-Origin & 1st app. Eternals 1.25 3.75 10.00
1-(30¢-c, limited distribution) 2.50 7.50 24.00
2-(Regular 25¢ edition)-1st app. Ajak & The Celestials 5.00
2-(30¢-c, limited distr.) 1.50 4.50 12.00
3-19: 14,15-Cosmic powered Hulk-c/story 5.00
Annual 1(10/77) 5.00
NOTE: *Kirby c/a(p) in all.*

ETERNALS, THE
Marvel Comics: Oct, 1985 - No. 12, Sept, 1986 (Maxi-series, mando paper)

1-12: 1,12 (52 pgs.): 12-Williamson-a(i) 2.00

ETERNALS: THE HEROD FACTOR
Marvel Comics: Nov, 1991 ($2.50, 68 pgs.)

1 2.50

ETERNAL WARRIOR (See Solar #10 & 11)
Valiant/Acclaim Comics (Valiant): Aug, 1992 - No. 50, Mar, 1996 ($2.25/$2.50)

1-Unity x-over; Miller-c; origin Eternal Warrior & Aram (Armstrong) 3.00
1-Gold logo 5.00
1-Gold foil logo 2.40 6.00
2-8: 2-Unity x-over; Simonson-c. 3-Archer & Armstrong x-over. 4-1st app. Bloodshot (last pg. cameo); see Rai #0 for 1st full app.; Cowan-c. 5-2nd full app. Bloodshot (12/92; see Rai #0). 6,7: 6-2nd app. Master Darque. 8-Flip book w/Archer & Armstrong #8 3.00
9-25,27-37: 9-1st Book of Geomancer. 14-16-Bloodshot app. 18-Doctor Mirage cameo. 19-Doctor Mirage app. 22-W/bound-in trading card. 25-Archer & Armstrong app.; cont'd from A&A #25 2.50
26-($2.75, 44 pgs.)-Flip book w/Archer & Armstrong 2.75
35-50: 35-Double-c; $2.50-c begins. 50-Geomancer app. 2.50
Special 1 (2/96, $2.50)-Art Holcomb script 2.50
Yearbook 1 (1993, $3.95), 2(1994, $3.95) 4.00

ETERNAL WARRIORS: BLACKWORKS
Acclaim Comics (Valiant Heroes): Mar, 1998 ($3.50, one-shot)

1 3.50

ETERNAL WARRIORS: DIGITAL ALCHEMY
Acclaim Comics (Valiant Heroes): Vol. 2, Sep, 1997 ($3.95, one-shot, 64 pgs.)

Vol. 2-Holcomb-s/Eaglesham-a(p) 4.00

ETERNAL WARRIORS: FIST AND STEEL
Acclaim Comics (Valiant): May, 1996 - No. 2, June, 1996 ($2.50, lim. series)

1,2: Geomancer app. in both. 1-Indicia reads "June." 2-Bo Hampton-a 2.50

ETERNAL WARRIORS: TIME AND TREACHERY
Acclaim Comics (Valiant Heroes): Vol. 1, Jun, 1997 ($3.95, one-shot, 48 pgs.)

Vol. 1-Reintro Aram, Archer, Ivar the Timewalker, & Gilad the Warmaster; 1st app. Shalla Redburn; Art Holcomb script 4.00

ETERNITY SMITH
Renegade Press: Sept, 1986 - No. 5, May, 1987 ($1.25/$1.50, 36 pgs.)

GD2.0 FN6.0 NM9.4

11-5: 1st app. Eternity Smith. 5-Death of Jasmine 2.00

ETERNITY SMITH
Hero Comics: Sept, 1987 - No. 9, 1988 ($1.95)

V2#1-9: 8-Indigo begins 2.00

ETTA KETT
King Features Syndicate/Standard: No. 11, Dec, 1948 - No. 14, Sept, 1949

11-Teenage 8.35 25.00 50.00
12-14 5.35 16.00 32.00

EUDAEMON, THE (See Dark Horse Presents #72-74)
Dark Horse Comics: Aug, 1993 - No. 3, Nov, 1993 ($2.50, limited series)

1-3: Nelson-a, painted-c & scripts 2.50

EUROPA AND THE PIRATE TWINS
Powder Monkey Productions: Oct, 1996 - No. 2, ($2.50, B&W, limited series)

1,2: Two covers 2.50

EVANGELINE (Also see Primer)
Comico/First Comics V2#1 on/Lodestone Publ.:
1984 - #2, 6/84; V2#1, 5/87 - V2#12, Mar, 1989 (Baxter paper)

1,2, V2#1 (5/87) - 12, Special #1 (1986, $2.00)-Lodestone Publ. 2.00

EVA THE IMP
Red Top Comic/Decker: 1957 - No. 2, Nov, 1957

1,2 3.60 9.00 18.00

EVERYBODY'S COMICS (See Fox Giants)

EVERYMAN, THE
Marvel Comics (Epic Comics): Nov, 1991 ($4.50, one-shot, 52 pgs.)

1-Mike Allred-a 1.00 2.80 7.00

EVERYTHING HAPPENS TO HARVEY
National Periodical Publications: Sept-Oct, 1953 - No. 7, Sept-Oct, 1954

1 24.00 73.00 170.00
2 13.50 41.00 95.00
3-7 11.00 33.00 75.00

EVERYTHING'S ARCHIE
Archie Publications: May, 1969 - No. 157, Sept, 1991 (Giant issues No. 1-20)

1-(68 pages) 7.00 21.00 70.00
2-(68 pages) 4.80 14.40 48.00
3-5-(68 pages) 3.50 10.50 35.00
6-13-(68 pages) 2.50 7.50 25.00
14-31-(52 pages) 1.85 5.50 15.00
32 (7/74)-50 (8/76) 1.10 3.30 9.00
51-80 (12/79),100 (4/82) 1.00 2.80 7.00
81-99 5.00
101-120 4.00
121-157: 142,148-Gene Colan-a 2.50

EVERYTHING'S DUCKY (Movie)
Dell Publishing Co.: No. 1251, 1961

Four Color 1251 3.60 11.00 40.00

EVIL ERNIE
Eternity Comics: Dec, 1991 - No. 5, 1992 ($2.50, B&W, limited series)

1-1st app. Lady Death by Steven Hughes (12,000 print run); Lady Death app. in all issues 4.00 12.00 40.00
2,3: 2-1st Lady Death-c. 2,3-(7,000 print run) 2.50 7.50 20.00
4-(8,000 print run) 1.85 5.50 15.00
5 1.50 4.50 12.00
Special Edition 1 2.50 7.50 20.00
Youth Gone Wild! ($9.95, trade paperback)-r/#1-5 1.25 3.75 10.00
Youth Gone Wild! Director's Cut ($4.95)-Limited to 15,000 copies, shows the making of the comic 5.00

EVIL ERNIE (Monthly series)
Chaos! Comics: July, 1998 - No. 10, Apr, 1999 ($2.95)

1-10-Pulido & Nutman-s/Brewer-a 3.00

Evil Eye #4 © Richard Sala

Excalibur #118 © MAR

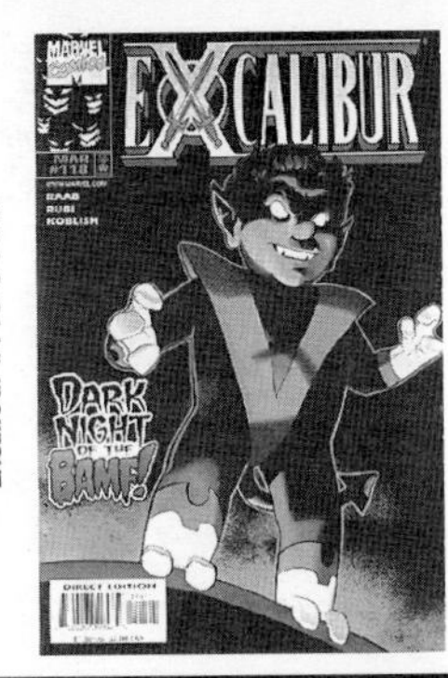

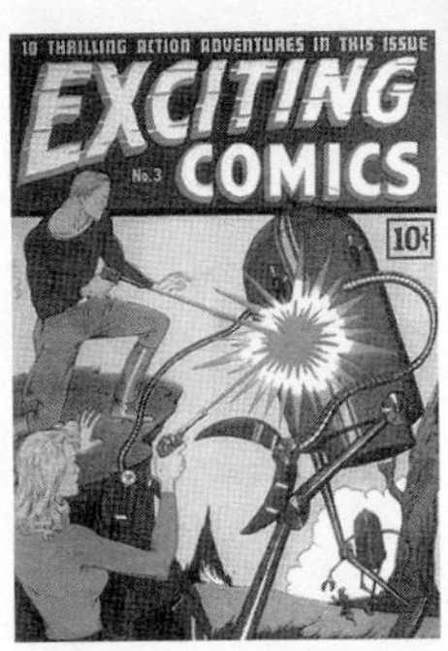

Exciting Comics #3 © STD

GD2.0 FN6.0 NM9.4

1-($10.00) Premium Ed. 10.00

EVIL ERNIE: BADDEST BATTLES
Chaos! Comics: Jan, 1997 ($1.50, one-shot)
1-Pin-ups, 1-Variant-c 2.00

EVIL ERNIE: DEPRAVED
Chaos! Comics: Jul, 1999 - No. 3, Sept, 1999 ($2.95, limited series)
1-3-Pulido-s/Brewer-a 3.00

EVIL ERNIE: DESTROYER
Chaos! Comics: Oct, 1997 - No. 9, Jun, 1998 ($2.95, limited series)
Preview ($2.50), 1-9-Flip cover 3.00

EVIL ERNIE: REVENGE
Chaos! Comics: Oct, 1994 - No.4, Feb, 1995 ($2.95, limited series)
1: 1-Glow-in-the-dark-c; Lady Death app. 1-3-flip book w. Kilzone Preview (series of 3) 5.00
1-Commemorative-(4000 print run) 1.25 3.75 10.00
2-4 4.00
Trade paperback (10/95, $12.95) 13.00

EVIL ERNIE: STRAIGHT TO HELL
Chaos! Comics: Oct, 1995 - No. 5, May, 1996 ($2.95, limited series)
1-5: 1-fold-out-c 3.00
1,3:1-($19.95) Chromium Ed. 3-Chastity Chase-c-(4000 printed) 20.00
Special Edition (10,000) 20.00

EVIL ERNIE: THE RESURRECTION
Chaos! Comics: 1993 - No. 4, 1994 (Limited series)
0 5.00
1 1.50 4.50 12.00
1A-Gold 3.00 9.00 30.00
2-4 1.00 3.00 8.00

EVIL ERNIE VS. THE MOVIE MONSTERS
Chaos! Comics: Mar, 1997 ($2.95, one-shot)
1 3.00
1-Variant-"Chaos-Scope•Terror Vision" card stock-c 5.00

EVIL ERNIE VS. THE SUPER HEROES
Chaos! Comics: Aug, 1995; Sept, 1998 ($2.95)
1-Lady Death poster 3.00
1-Foil-c variant (limited to 10,000) 2.50 7.50 20.00
1-Limited Edition (1000) 2.50 7.50 20.00
2-(9/98) Ernie vs. JLA and Marvel parodies 3.00

EVIL EYE
Fantagraphics Books: June, 1998 - Present ($2.95, B&W)
1-4-Richard Sala-s/a 3.00

EWOKS (Star Wars) (TV) (See Star Comics Magazine)
Marvel Comics (Star Comics): June, 1985 - No. 14, Jul, 1987 (75¢/$1.00)
1,10: 10-Williamson-a (From Star Wars) 1.25 3.75 10.00
2-9,11-14: 14-($1.00-c) 1.00 2.80 7.00

EXCALIBUR (Also see Marvel Comics Presents #31)
Marvel Comics: Apr, 1988; Oct, 1988 - No. 125, Oct, 1998 ($1.50/$1.75/$1.99)
Special Edition nn (The Sword is Drawn)(4/88, $3.25)-1st Excalibur comic 1.00 2.80 7.00
Special Edition nn (4/88)-no price on-c (scarce) 1.50 4.50 12.00
Special Edition nn (2nd & print, 10/88, 12/89) 4.50
...The Sword is Drawn (Apr, 1992, $4.95) 5.00
1($1.50, 10/88)-X-Men spin-off; Nightcrawler, Shadowcat(Kitty Pryde), Capt. Britain, Phoenix & Meggan begin 2.40 6.00
2-4 3.50
5-10 3.00
11-49,51-70,72-74,76: 10,11-Rogers/Austin-a; Austin-i. 21-Intro Crusader X. 22-Iron Man x-over. 24-John Byrne app. in story. 26-Ron Lim-c/a. 27-B. Smith-a(p). 37-Dr. Doom & Iron Man app. 41-X-Men (Wolverine) app.; Cable cameo 49-Neal Adams c-swipe. 52,57-X-Men(Cyclops, Wolverine) app. 53-Spider-Man-c/story. 58-X-Men (Wolverine, Gambit, Cyclops, etc.)-c/story. 61-Phoenix returns. 68-Starjammers-c/story 2.00
50-($2.75, 56 pgs.)-New logo 2.75
71-($3.95, 52 pgs.)-Hologram on-c; 30th anniversary 4.00
75-($3.50, 52 pgs.)-Holo-grafx foil-c 4.00
75-($2.25, 52 pgs.)-Regular edition 2.25
77-81,83-86: 77-Begin $1.95-c; bound-in trading card sheet. 83-86-Deluxe edition. 86-1st app. Pete Wisdom 2.00
82-($2.50)-Newsstand edition, 82-($3.50)-Enhanced edition 3.50
83-89,91-99,101-110, -1(7/97): 87-Return from Age of Apocalypse. 92-Colossus-c/app. 94-Days of Future Tense 95-X-Man-c/app. 96-Sebastian Shaw & the Hellfire Club app. 99-Onslaught app. 101-Onslaught tie-in. 102-w/card insert. 103-Last Warren Ellis scripts; Belasco app. 109-Spiral-c/app. 2.00
90,100-($2.95)-double-sized. 100-Onslaught tie-in; wraparound-c 3.50
111-124: 111-Begin $1.99-c, wraparound-c. 119-Calafiore-a 2.00
125-($2.99) Wedding of Capt. Britain and Meggan 4.00
Annual 1,,2 ('93, '94, 68pgs.)-1st app. Khaos.2-X-Men & Psylocke app. 3.00
...Air Apparent nn (12/91, $4.95)-Simonson-c 5.00
...Mojo Mayhem nn (12/89, $4.50)-Art Adams/Austin-c/a 4.50
...: The Possession nn (7/91, $2.95, 52 pgs.) 3.00
...: XX Crossing (7/92, 5/92-inside, $2.50)-vs. The X-Men 2.50

EXCITING COMICS
Nedor/Better Publications/Standard Comics: Apr, 1940 - No. 69, Sept, 1949
1-Origin & 1st app. The Mask, Jim Hatfield, Sgt. Bill King, Dan Williams begin; early Robot-c (see Smash #1) 355.00 1067.00 3200.00
2-The Sphinx begins; The Masked Rider app.; Son of the Gods begins, ends #8 156.00 468.00 1250.00
3-Robot-c 103.00 309.00 825.00
4-6 69.00 207.00 550.00
7,8 56.00 168.00 450.00
9-Origin/1st app. of The Black Terror & sidekick Tim, begin series (5/41) (Black Terror c-9-52,54,55) 720.00 2160.00 7200.00
10-2nd app. Black Terror 250.00 750.00 2000.00
11 125.00 375.00 1000.00
12,13 81.00 244.00 650.00
14-Last Sphinx, Dan Williams 56.00 168.00 450.00
15-The Liberator begins (origin) 59.00 177.00 475.00
16-20: 20-The Mask ends 47.00 141.00 375.00
21,23-25: 25-Robot-c 40.00 120.00 310.00
22-Origin The Eaglet; The American Eagle begins 47.00 141.00 375.00
26,27,29,30: 26-Schomburg-c begin 51.00 154.00 410.00
28-(Scarce) Crime Crusader begins, ends #58 62.00 187.00 500.00
31-38: 35-Liberator ends, not in 31-33 45.00 135.00 360.00
39-Origin Kara, Jungle Princess 55.00 165.00 440.00
40-50: 42-The Scarab begins. 45-Schomburg Robot-c. 49-Last Kara, Jungle Princess. 50-Last American Eagle 51.00 154.00 410.00
51-Miss Masque begins (1st app.) 57.00 172.00 460.00
52-54: Miss Masque ends. 53-Miss Masque-c 47.00 142.00 380.00
55-58: 55-Judy of the Jungle begins (origin), ends #69; 1 pg. Ingels-a; Judy of the Jungle c-56-66. 56-58: All airbrush-c 51.00 154.00 410.00
59-Frazetta art in Caniff style; signed Frank Frazeta (one t), 9 pgs. 51.00 154.00 410.00
60-66: 60-Rick Howard, the Mystery Rider begins. 66-Robinson/Meskin-a 45.00 135.00 360.00
67-69-All western covers 18.00 54.00 125.00
NOTE: ***Schomburg (Xela)*** *c-26-68; airbrush c-57-66. Black Terror by* ***R. Moreira****-#65.* ***Roussos*** *a-62. Bondage-c 9, 12, 13, 20, 23, 25, 30, 59.*

EXCITING ROMANCES
Fawcett Publications: 1949 (nd); No. 2, Spring, 1950 - No. 5, 10/50; No. 6 (1951, nd); No. 7, 9/51 -No. 14, 1/53
1,3: 1(1949). 3-Wood-a 13.00 39.00 90.00
2,4,5-(1950) 8.35 25.00 50.00
6-14 6.70 20.00 40.00
NOTE: ***Powell*** *a-8-10.* ***Marcus Swayze*** *a-5, 6, 9. Photo c-1-7, 10-12.*

EXCITING ROMANCE STORIES (See Fox Giants)

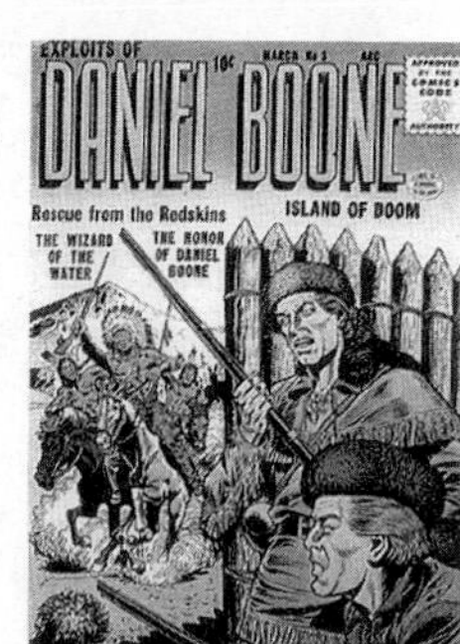

Exploits of Daniel Boone #3 © QUA

Extra! #2 © WMG

Extreme Justice #14 © DC

GD2.0 FN6.0 NM9.4

EXCITING WAR (Korean War)
Standard Comics (Better Publ.): No. 5, Sept, 1952 - No. 8, May, 1953; No. 9, Nov, 1953

	GD2.0	FN6.0	NM9.4
5	8.35	25.00	50.00
6,7,9	4.25	13.00	28.00
8-Toth-a	7.50	22.50	45.00

EXCITING X-PATROL
Marvel Comics (Amalgam): June, 1997 ($1.95, one-shot)

1-Barbara Kesel-s/ Bryan Hitch-a 2.00

EXILES (Also see Break-Thru)
Malibu Comics (Ultraverse): Aug, 1993 - No. 4, Nov, 1993 ($1.95)

	GD2.0	FN6.0	NM9.4
1,2,4: 1,2-Bagged copies of each exist. 2-Gustovich-c. 4-Team dies; story cont'd in Break-Thru #1			2.00
3-($2.50, 40 pgs.)-Rune flip-c/story by B. Smith (3 pgs.)			2.50
1-Holographic-c edition	1.00	3.00	8.00

EXILES (All New, The) (2nd Series) (Also see Black September)
Malibu Comics (Ultraverse): Sept, 1995 - V2#11, Aug, 1996 ($1.50)

	GD2.0	FN6.0	NM9.4
Infinity (9/95, $1.50)-Intro new team including Marvel's Juggernaut & Reaper.			2.00
Infinity (2000 signed), V2#1 (2000 signed)	1.25	3.75	10.00
V2#1-4,6-11: 1-(10/95, 64 pgs.)-Reprint of Ultraforce V2#1 follows lead story. 2-1st app. Hellblade. 8-Intro Maxis. 11-Vs. Maxis; Ripfire app.; cont'd in Ultraforce #12			2.00
V2#5-($2.50) Juggernaut returns to the Marvel Universe.			2.50

EXILES VS THE X-MEN
Malibu Comics (Ultraverse): Oct, 1995 (one-shot)

	GD2.0	FN6.0	NM9.4
0-Limited Super Premium Edition; signed w/certificate; gold foil logo, 0-Limited Premium Edition	1.25	3.75	10.00

EX-MUTANTS
Malibu Comics: Nov, 1992 - No. 18, Apr, 1994 ($1.95/$2.25/$2.50)

1-18: 1-Polybagged w/Skycap 2.50

EXORCISTS (See The Crusaders)

EXOSQUAD (TV)
Topps Comics: No. 0, Jan, 1994 ($1.25)

0-($1.00, 20 pgs.)-1st app.; Staton-a(p); wraparound-c 2.00

EXOTIC ROMANCES (Formerly True War Romances)
Quality Comics Group (Comic Magazines): No. 22, Oct, 1955-No. 31, Nov, 1956

	GD2.0	FN6.0	NM9.4
22	10.00	30.00	60.00
23-26,29	5.00	15.00	30.00
27,31-Baker-c/a	12.00	36.00	85.00
28,30-Baker-a	10.00	30.00	70.00

EXPLOITS OF DANIEL BOONE
Quality Comics Group: Nov, 1955 - No. 6, Oct, 1956

	GD2.0	FN6.0	NM9.4
1-All have Cuidera-c(i)	26.00	79.00	185.00
2	17.00	49.00	115.00
3-6	13.50	41.00	95.00

EXPLOITS OF DICK TRACY (See Dick Tracy)

EXPLORER JOE
Ziff-Davis Comic Group (Approved Comics): Win, 1951 - No. 2, Oct-Nov, 1952

	GD2.0	FN6.0	NM9.4
1-2: Saunders painted covers; 2-Krigstein-a	12.00	36.00	85.00

EXPLORERS OF THE UNKNOWN (See Archie Giant Series #587, 599)
Archie Comics: June, 1990 - No. 6, Apr, 1991 ($1.00)

1-6: Featuring Archie and the gang 3.00

EXPOSED (...True Crime Cases; ...Cases in the Crusade Against Crime #5-9)
D. S. Publishing Co.: Mar-Apr, 1948 - No. 9, July-Aug, 1949

	GD2.0	FN6.0	NM9.4
1	21.00	64.00	150.00
2-Giggling killer story with excessive blood; two injury-to-eye panels; electrocution panel	25.00	75.00	175.00
3,8,9	10.00	30.00	70.00
4-Orlando-a	11.00	33.00	75.00
5-Breeze Lawson, Sky Sheriff by E. Good	10.00	30.00	70.00
6,7: 6-Ingels-a; used in **SOTI**, illo. "How to prepare an alibi" 7-Illo. in **SOTI**, "Diagram for housebreakers;" used by N.Y. Legis. Committee	37.00	111.00	260.00

EXPOSURE
Image Comics: 1999 - Present ($2.50)

	GD2.0	FN6.0	NM9.4
1,2: Al Rio-a/David Campiti-s. 1-Wraparound & photo covers			2.50
Prelude ($5.00)			5.00

EXTRA!
E. C. Comics: Mar-Apr, 1955 - No. 5, Nov-Dec, 1955

	GD2.0	FN6.0	NM9.4
1-Not code approved	18.00	54.00	125.00
2-5	12.00	36.00	85.00

NOTE: *Craig, Crandall, Severin art in all.*

EXTRA COMICS
Magazine Enterprises: 1948 (25¢, 3 comics in one)

	GD2.0	FN6.0	NM9.4
1-Giant; consisting of rebound ME comics. Two versions known; (1)-Funnyman by Siegel & Shuster, Space Ace, Undercover Girl, Red Fox by L.B. Cole, Trail Colt & (2)-All Funnyman	50.00	150.00	400.00

EXTREME
Image Comics (Extreme Studios): Aug, 1993 (Giveaway)

0 3.00

EXTREME DESTROYER
Image Comics (Extreme Studios): Jan, 1996 ($2.50)

Prologue 1-Polybagged w/card; Liefeld-c, Epilogue 1-Liefeld-c 2.50

EXTREME JUSTICE
DC Comics: No. 0, Jan, 1995 - No. 18, July, 1996 ($1.50/$1.75)

0-18 3.00

EXTREMELY YOUNGBLOOD
Image Comics (Extreme Studios): Sept, 1996 ($3.50, one-shot)

1 3.50

EXTREME SACRIFICE
Image Comics (Extreme Studios): Jan, 1995 ($2.50, limited series)

	GD2.0	FN6.0	NM9.4
Prelude (#1)-Liefeld wraparound-c; polybagged w/ trading card			2.50
Epilogue (#2)-Liefeld wraparound-c; polybagged w/trading card			2.50
Trade paperback (6/95, $16.95)-Platt-a			17.00

EXTREME SUPER CHRISTMAS SPECIAL
Image Comics (Extreme Studios): Dec, 1994 ($2.95, one-shot)

1 3.00

EXTREMIST, THE
DC Comics (Vertigo): Sept, 1993 - No. 4, Dec, 1993 ($1.95, limited series)

	GD2.0	FN6.0	NM9.4
1-4-Peter Milligan scripts; McKeever-c/a			2.00
1-Platinum Edition			5.00

EYE OF THE STORM
Rival Productions: Dec, 1994 - No. 7, June, 1995? ($2.95)

1-7: Computer generated comic 3.00

FACE
DC Comics (Vertigo): Jan, 1995 ($4.95, one-shot)

1 5.00

FACE, THE (Tony Trent, the Face No. 3 on) (See Big Shot Comics)
Columbia Comics Group: 1941 - No. 2, 1941?

	GD2.0	FN6.0	NM9.4
1-The Face; Mart Bailey-c	87.00	262.00	700.00
2-Bailey-c	50.00	150.00	400.00

FACTOR X
Marvel Comics: Mar, 1995 - No. 4, July, 1995 ($1.95, limited series)

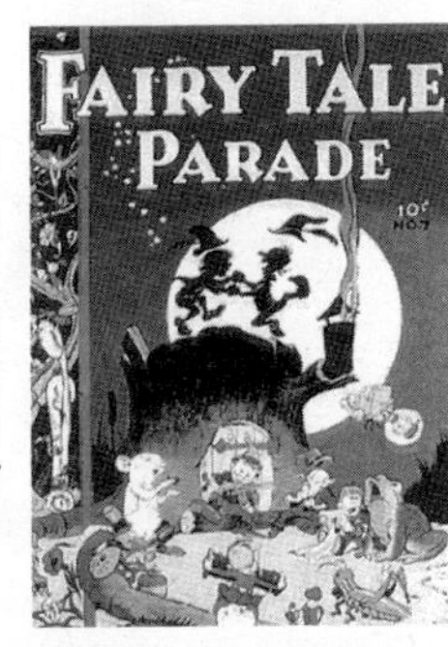

Fairy Tale Parade #7 © WEST

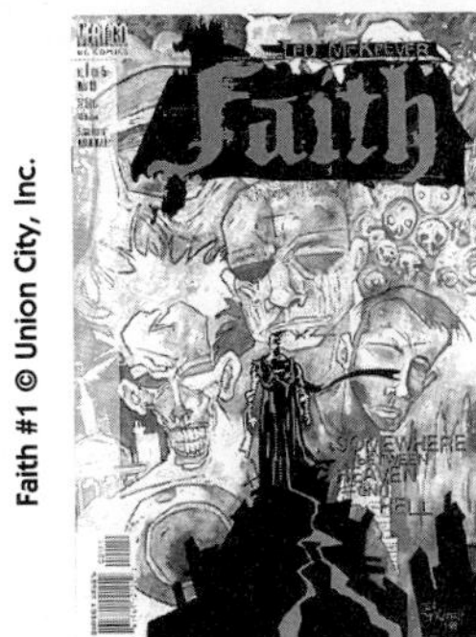

Faith #1 © Union City, Inc.

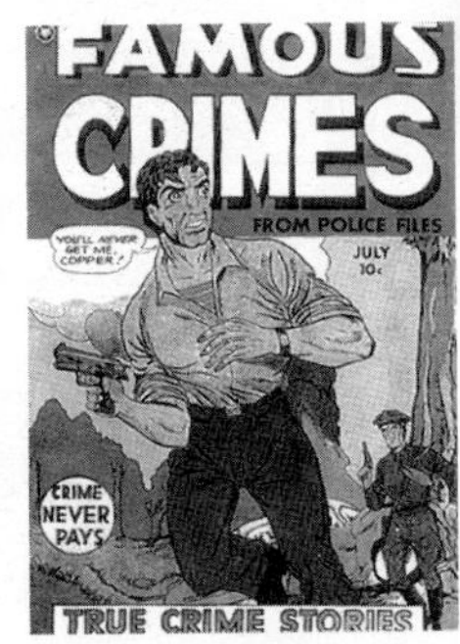

Famous Crimes #19 © FOX

GD2.0 FN6.0 NM9.4

1-Age of Apocalypse 3.00
2-4 2.00

FACULTY FUNNIES
Archie Comics: June, 1989 - No. 5, May, 1990 (75¢/95¢ #2 on)

1-5: 1,2-The Awesome Four app. 3.00

FAFHRD AND THE GREY MOUSER (Also see Sword of Sorcery & Wonder Woman #202)
Marvel Comics: Oct, 1990 - No. 4, 1991 ($4.50, 52 pgs., squarebound)

1-4: Mignola/Williamson-a; Chaykin scripts 4.50

FAIRY TALE PARADE (See Famous Fairy Tales)
Dell Publishing Co.: June-July, 1942 - No. 121, Oct, 1946 (Most by Walt Kelly)

1-Kelly-a begins 118.00 355.00 1300.00
2(8-9/42) 50.00 150.00 550.00
3-5 (10-11/42 - 2-4/43) 35.00 104.00 380.00
6-9 (5-7/43 - 11-1/43-44) 26.00 79.00 290.00
Four Color 50('44),69('45), 87('45) 25.00 74.00 270.00
Four Color 104,114('46)-Last Kelly issue 18.00 53.00 195.00
Four Color 121('46)-Not by Kelly 10.50 31.00 115.00
NOTE: *#1-9, 4-Color #50, 69 have **Kelly** c/a; 4-Color #87, 104, 114-**Kelly** art only. #9 has a redrawn version of The Reluctant Dragon. This series contains all the classic fairy tales from Jack In The Beanstalk to Cinderella.*

FAIRY TALES
Ziff-Davis Publ. Co. (Approved Comics): No. 10, Apr-May, 1951 - No. 11, June-July, 1951

10,11-Painted-c 18.00 54.00 125.00

FAITH
DC Comics (Vertigo): Nov, 1999 - No. 5 ($2.50, limited series)

1-Ted McKeever-s/c/a 2.50

FAITHFUL
Marvel Comics/Lovers' Magazine: Nov, 1949 - No. 2, Feb, 1950 (52 pgs.)

1,2-Photo-c 10.00 30.00 60.00

FALCON (See Marvel Premiere #49)(Also see Avengers #181 & Captain America #117 & 133)
Marvel Comics Group: Nov, 1983 - No. 4, Feb, 1984 (Mini-series)

1-4: 1-Paul Smith-c/a(p). 2-Paul Smith-c 2.00

FALLEN ANGEL ON THE WORLD OF MAGIC: THE GATHERING
Acclaim (Armada): May, 1996 ($5.95, one-shot)

1-Nancy Collins story. 6.00

FALLEN ANGELS
Marvel Comics Group: April, 1987 - No. 8, Nov, 1987 (Limited series)

1-8 2.00

FALLING IN LOVE
Arleigh Pub. Co./National Per. Pub.: Sept-Oct, 1955 - No. 143, Oct-Nov, 1973

1 37.00 111.00 260.00
2 18.00 54.00 125.00
3-10 11.00 33.00 75.00
11-20 9.15 27.00 55.00
21-40 6.35 19.00 38.00
41-47: 47-Last 10¢ issue? 4.25 13.00 28.00
48-70 2.50 7.50 20.00
71-99,108: 108-Wood-a (4 pgs., 7/69) 2.00 6.00 16.00
100 2.80 8.40 28.00
101-107,109-124 1.50 4.50 12.00
134-143 1.25 3.75 10.00
125-133: 52 pgs. 2.50 7.50 22.00
NOTE: ***Colan** c/a-75, 81. 52 pgs.-#125-133.*

FALLING MAN, THE
Image Comics: Feb, 1998 ($2.95)

1-McCorkindale-s/Hester-a 3.00

FALL OF THE HOUSE OF USHER, THE (See A Corben Special & Spirit section 8/22/48)

FALL OF THE ROMAN EMPIRE (See Movie Comics)

FAMILY AFFAIR (TV)
Gold Key: Feb, 1970 - No. 4, Oct, 1970 (25¢)

1-With pull-out poster; photo-c 5.00 15.00 50.00
1-With poster missing 2.50 7.50 22.00
2-4: 3,4-Photo-c 2.60 7.80 26.00

FAMILY FUNNIES
Parents' Magazine Institute: No. 9, Aug-Sept, 1946

9 4.00 11.00 24.00

FAMILY FUNNIES (Tiny Tot Funnies No. 9)
Harvey Publications: Sept, 1950 - No. 8, Apr, 1951

1-Mandrake (has over 30 King Feature strips) 9.15 27.00 55.00
2-Flash Gordon, 1 pg. 6.35 19.00 38.00
3-8: 4,5,7-Flash Gordon, 1 pg. 5.35 16.00 32.00
1(Black & white) 3.60 9.00 18.00

FAMILY MAN
DC Comics (Paradox Press): 1995 - No. 3, 1995 ($4.95, B&W, digest-size, limited series)

1-3 5.00

FAMOUS AUTHORS ILLUSTRATED (See Stories by...)

FAMOUS COMICS
King Features Synd. (Whitman Pub. Co.): 1934 (100 pgs., daily newspaper-r) (3-1/2x8-1/2"; paper cover) (came in a box)

684(#1)-Little Jimmy, Katzenjammer Kids, & Barney Google 34.00 103.00 240.00
684(#2)-Polly, Little Jimmy, Katzenjammer Kids 34.00 103.00 240.00
684(#3)-Little Annie Rooney, Polly and her Pals, Katzenjammer Kids 34.00 103.00 240.00
....Box price.... 32.00 96.00 225.00

FAMOUS COMICS CARTOON BOOKS
Whitman Publishing Co.: 1934 (8x7-1/4", 72 pgs., B&W hard-c, daily strip-r)

1200-The Captain & the Kids (1st app?); Dirks reprints credited to Bernard Dibble 29.00 86.00 200.00
1202-Captain Easy (1st app?) & Wash Tubbs by Roy Crane; 2 slightly different versions of cover exist 34.00 103.00 240.00
1203-Ella Cinders (1st app?) 28.00 84.00 195.00
1204-Freckles & His Friends (1st app?) 25.00 75.00 175.00
NOTE: *Called Famous Funnies Cartoon Books inside.*

FAMOUS CRIMES
Fox Features Syndicate/M.S. Dist. No. 51,52: June, 1948 - No. 19, Sept, 1950; No. 20, Aug, 1951; No. 51, 52, 1953

1-Blue Beetle app. & crime story-r/Phantom Lady #16 47.00 141.00 375.00
2-Has woman dissolved in acid; lingerie-c/panels 39.00 118.00 275.00
3-Injury-to-eye story used in **SOTI**, pg. 112; has two electrocution stories 44.00 132.00 350.00
4-6 20.00 60.00 140.00
7- "Tarzan, the Wyoming Killer" used in **SOTI**, pg. 44; drug trial/possession story 39.00 118.00 275.00
8-20: 17-Morisi-a. 20-Same cover as #15 15.00 45.00 105.00
51(nd, 1953) 15.00 45.00 105.00
52 8.35 25.00 50.00

FAMOUS FEATURE STORIES
Dell Publishing Co.: 1938 (7-1/2x11", 68 pgs.)

1-Tarzan, Terry & the Pirates, King of the Royal Mtd., Buck Jones, Dick Tracy, Smilin' Jack, Dan Dunn, Don Winslow, G-Man, Tailspin Tommy, Mutt & Jeff, Little Orphan Annie reprints - all illustrated text 67.00 202.00 540.00

FAMOUS FIRST EDITION (See Limited Collectors' Edition)
National Periodical Publications/DC Comics: ($1.00, 10x13-1/2", 72 pgs.) (No.6-8, 68 pgs.) 1974 - No. 8, Aug-Sept, 1975; C-61, 1979

GD2.0 FN6.0 NM9.4

Famous First Edition F-7 (All-Star Comics #3) © DC

Famous Funnies #1 © EAS

Famous Gangsters #3 © AVON

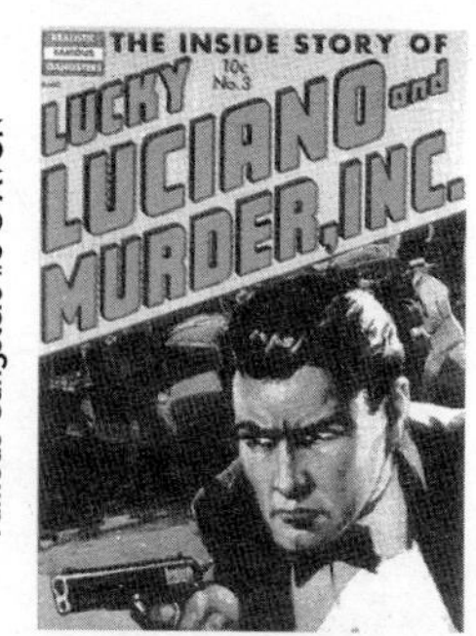

THE INSIDE STORY OF
LUCKY LUCIANO and MURDER, INC.

GD2.0 FN6.0 NM9.4

(Hardbound editions with dust jackets are from Lyle Stuart, Inc.)

C-26-Action Comics #1; gold ink outer-c 2.70 8.00 30.00
C-26-Hardbound edition w/dust jacket 16.00 48.00 160.00
C-28-Detective #27; silver ink outer-c 5.00 15.00 55.00
C-28-Hardbound edition w/dust jacket 21.00 63.00 210.00
C-30-Sensation #1(1974); bronze ink outer-c 2.70 8.00 30.00
C-30-Hardbound edition w/dust jacket 16.00 48.00 160.00
F-4-Whiz Comics #2(#1)(10-11/74)-Cover not identical to original (dropped "Gangway for Captain Marvel" from cover); gold ink on outer-c 2.70 8.00 30.00
F-4-Hardbound edition w/dust jacket 16.00 48.00 160.00
F-5-Batman #1(F-6 inside); silver ink on outer-c 4.00 12.00 45.00
F-5-Hardbound edition w/dust jacket 16.00 48.00 160.00
V2#F-6-Wonder Woman #1 2.70 8.00 30.00
F-7-All-Star Comics #3 2.20 6.60 22.00
F-8-Flash Comics #1(8-9/75) 2.20 6.60 22.00
V8#C-61-Superman #1(1979, $2.00) 1.80 5.40 18.00

Warning: The above books are almost **exact** reprints of the originals that they represent except for the Giant-Size format. None of the originals are Giant-Size. The first five issues and C-61 were printed with two covers. Reprint information can be found on the outside cover, but not on the inside cover which was reprinted exactly like the original (inside and out).

FAMOUS FUNNIES
Eastern Color: 1934; July, 1934 - No. 218, July, 1955

A Carnival of Comics (See Promotional Comics section)

GD2.0 FN6.0 VF8.0 NM9.4

Series 1-(Very rare)(nd-early 1934)(68 pgs.) No publisher given (Eastern Color PrintingCo.); sold in chain stores for 10¢. 35,000 print run. Contains Sunday strip reprints of Mutt & Jeff, Reg'lar Fellers, Nipper, Hairbreadth Harry, Strange As It Seems, Joe Palooka, Dixie Dugan, The Nebbs, Keeping Up With the Jones, and others. Inside front and back covers and pages 1-16 of Famous Funnies Series 1, #s 49-64 reprinted from **Famous Funnies, A Carnival of Comics**, and most of pages 17-48 reprinted from **Funnies on Parade**. This was the first comic book sold. 3000.00 9000.00 15,000.00 22,500.00

No. 1 (Rare)(7/34-on stands 5/34) - Eastern Color Printing Co. First monthly newsstand comic book. Contains Sunday strip reprints of Toonerville Folks, Mutt & Jeff, Hairbreadth Harry, S'Matter Pop, Nipper, Dixie Dugan, The Bungle Family, Connie, Ben Webster, Tailspin Tommy, The Nebbs, Joe Palooka, & others. 2215.00 6645.00 11,075.00 16,000.00

GD2.0 FN6.0 VF8.0

2 (Rare, 9/34) 450.00 1350.00 3100.00
3-Buck Rogers Sunday strip-r by Rick Yager begins, ends #218; not in #191-208; 1st comic book app. of Buck Rogers; the number of the 1st strip reprinted is pg. 190, Series No. 1 583.00 1750.00 4000.00
4 183.00 550.00 1250.00
5-1st Christmas-c on a newsstand comic 150.00 450.00 1050.00
6-10 108.00 324.00 725.00

GD2.0 FN6.0 NM9.4

11,12,18-Four pgs. of Buck Rogers in each issue, completes stories in Buck Rogers #1 which lacks these pages. 18-Two pgs. of Buck Rogers reprinted in Daisy Comics #1 95.00 287.00 650.00
13-17,19,20: 14-Has two Buck Rogers panels missing. 17-2nd Christmas-c on a newsstand comic (12/35) 73.00 219.00 500.00
21,23-30: 27-(10/36)-War on Crime begins (4 pgs.); 1st true crime in comics (reprints); part photo-c. 29-X-Mas-c (12/36) 52.00 157.00 360.00
22-Four pgs. of Buck Rogers needed to complete stories in Buck Rogers #1 56.00 170.00 390.00
31,33,34,36,37,39,40: 33-Careers of Baby Face Nelson & John Dillinger traced 40.00 120.00 270.00
32-(3/37) 1st app. the Phantom Magician (costume hero) in Advs. of Patsy 43.00 130.00 290.00
35-Two pgs. Buck Rogers omitted in Buck Rogers #2 43.00 130.00 290.00
38-Full color portrait of Buck Rogers 39.00 117.00 270.00
41-60: 41,53-X-Mas-c. 55-Last bottom panel, pg. 4 in Buck Rogers redrawn in Buck Rogers #3 28.00 84.00 190.00
61,63,64,66,67,69,70 21.00 62.00 145.00
62,65,68,73-78-Two pgs. Kirby-a "Lightnin' & the Lone Rider". 65,77-X-Mas-c 24.00 73.00 170.00
71,79,80: 80-(3/41)-Buck Rogers story continues from Buck Rogers #5 16.00 47.00 110.00

GD2.0 FN6.0 NM9.4

72-Speed Spaulding begins by Marvin Bradley (artist), ends #88. This series was written by Edwin Balmer & Philip Wylie (later appeared as film & book "When Worlds Collide") 17.00 49.00 105.00
81-Origin & 1st app. Invisible Scarlet O'Neil (4/41); strip begins #82, ends #167; 1st non-funny-c (Scarlet O'Neil) 13.00 39.00 90.00
82-Buck Rogers-c 16.00 47.00 110.00
83-87,90: 86-Connie vs. Monsters on the Moon-c (sci/fi). 87 has last Buck Rogers full page-r. 90-Bondage-c 12.00 36.00 85.00
88,89: 88-Buck Rogers in "Moon's End" by Calkins, 2 pgs.(not reprints). Beginning with #88, all Buck Rogers pgs. have rearranged panels. 89-Origin & 1st app. Fearless Flint, the Flint Man 13.00 39.00 90.00
91-93,95,96,98-99,101,103-110: 105-Series 2 begins (Strip Page #1) 11.50 34.00 80.00
94-Buck Rogers in "Solar Holocaust" by Calkins, 3 pgs.(not reprints) 12.00 36.00 85.00
97-War Bond promotion, Buck Rogers by Calkins, 2 pgs.(not reprints) 12.00 36.00 85.00
100-1st comic to reach #100; 100th Anniversary cover features 11 major Famous Funnies characters, including Buck Rogers 13.00 39.00 90.00
102-Chief Wahoo vs. Hitler,Tojo & Mussolini-c (1/43) 31.00 94.00 220.00
111-130 (5/45): 113-X-Mas-c 9.15 27.00 55.00
131-150 (1/47): 137-Strip page No. 110 omitted 6.70 20.00 40.00
151-162,164-168 5.85 17.50 35.00
163-St. Valentine's Day-c 7.00 21.00 42.00
169,170-Two text illos. by Williamson, his 1st comic book work 10.00 30.00 70.00
171-190: 171-Strip pgs. 227,229,230, Series 2 omitted. 172-Strip Pg. 232 omitted. 190-Buck Rogers ends with start of strip pg. 302, Series 2; Oaky Doaks-c/story 5.35 16.00 32.00
191-197,199,201,203,206-208: No Buck Rogers. 191-Barney Carr, Space detective begins, ends #192. 5.00 15.00 30.00
198,200,202,205-One pg. Frazetta ads; no B. Rogers 5.35 16.00 32.00
204-Used in **POP**, pg. 79,99; war-c begin, end #208 5.85 17.50 35.00
209-216: Frazetta-c. 209-Buck Rogers begins (12/53) with strip pg. 480, Series 2; 211-Buck Rogers ads by Anderson begins, ends #217. #215-Contains B. Rogers strip pg. 515-518, series 2 followed by pgs.179-181, Series 3 94.00 281.00 750.00
217,218-B. Rogers ends with pg. 199, Series 3. 218-Wee Three-c/story 5.35 16.00 32.00

NOTE: ***Rick Yager*** *did the Buck Rogers Sunday strips reprinted in Famous Funnies. The Sundays were formerly done by Russ Keaton and Lt. Dick Calkins did the dailies, but would sometimes assist Yager on a panel or two from time to time. Strip No. 169 is Yager's first full Buck Rogers page. Yager did the strip until 1958 when* ***Murphy Anderson*** *took over.* ***Tuska*** *art from 4/26/59 - 1965. Virtually every panel was rewritten for Famous Funnies. Not identical to the original Sunday page. The Buck Rogers reprints run continuously through Famous Funnies issue No. 190 (Strip No. 302) with no break in story line. The story line has no continuity after No. 190. The Buck Rogers newspaper strips came out in four series: Series 1, 3/30/30 - 9/21/41 (No. 1 - 600); Series 2, 9/28/41 -10/21/51 (No. 1 -525)(Strip No. 110-1/2 (1/2 pg.) published in only a few newspapers); Series 3, 10/28/51 -2/9/58 (No. 100-428)(No No.1-99); Series 4, 2/16/58 - 6/13/65 (No numbers, dates only).* ***Everett*** *c-85, 86.* ***Moulton*** *a-100. Chief Wahoo c-93, 97, 102, 116, 136, 139, 151. Dickie Dare c-83, 88. Fearless Flint c-89. Invisible Scarlet O'Neil c-81, 87, 95, 121(part), 132. Scorchy Smith c-84, 90.*

FAMOUS FUNNIES
Super Comics: 1964

Super Reprint Nos. 15-18:17-r/Double Trouble #1. 18-Space Comics #? 1.50 4.50 12.00

FAMOUS GANGSTERS (Crime on the Waterfront No. 4)
Avon Periodicals/Realistic No. 3: Apr, 1951 - No. 3, Feb, 1952

1-3: 1-Capone, Dillinger; c-/Avon paperback #329. 2-Dillinger Machine Gun Killer; Wood-c/a (1 pg.); r/Saint #7 & retitled "Mike Strong". 3-Lucky Luciano & Murder, Inc; c-/Avon paperback #66 35.00 105.00 245.00

FAMOUS INDIAN TRIBES
Dell Publishing Co.: July-Sept, 1962; No. 2, July, 1972

12-264-209(#1) (The Sioux) .90 1.80 10.00
2(7/72)-Reprints above 3.00

FAMOUS STARS
Ziff-Davis Publ. Co.: Nov-Dec, 1950 - No. 6, Spring, 1952 (All have photo-c)

Fantastic Comics #7 © FOX

Fantastic Fears #8 © AJAX

Fantastic Four #6 © MAR

GD2.0 FN6.0 NM9.4

1-Shelley Winters, Susan Peters, Ava Gardner, Shirley Temple; Jimmy Stewart & Shelley Winters photo-c; Whitney-a 30.00 90.00 210.00
2-Betty Hutton, Bing Crosby, Colleen Townsend, Gloria Swanson; Betty Hutton photo-c; Everett-a(2) 21.00 64.00 150.00
3-Farley Granger, Judy Garland's ordeal, Alan Ladd; Farley Granger & Judy Garland photo-c; Whitney-a 21.00 62.00 145.00
4-Al Jolson, Bob Mitchum, Ella Raines, Richard Conte, Vic Damone; Bob Mitchum photo-c; Crandall-a, 6pgs. 18.00 54.00 125.00
5-Liz Taylor, Betty Grable, Esther Williams, George Brent, Mario Lanza; Liz Taylor photo-c; Krigstein-a 24.00 73.00 170.00
6-Gene Kelly, Hedy Lamarr, June Allyson, William Boyd, Janet Leigh, Gary Cooper; Gene Kelly photo-c 16.00 47.00 110.00

FAMOUS STORIES (...Book No. 2)
Dell Publishing Co.: 1942 - No. 2, 1942

1,2: 1-Treasure Island. 2-Tom Sawyer 30.00 90.00 210.00

FAMOUS TV FUNDAY FUNNIES
Harvey Publications: Sept, 1961 (25¢ Giant)

1-Casper the Ghost, Baby Huey, Little Audrey 3.80 11.40 38.00

FAMOUS WESTERN BADMEN (Formerly Redskin)
Youthful Magazines: No. 13, Dec, 1952 - No. 15, Apr, 1953

13-Redskin story 11.50 34.00 80.00
14,15: 15-The Dalton Boys story 9.15 27.00 55.00

FAN BOY
DC Comics: Mar, 1999 - No. 6, Aug, 1999 ($2.50, limited series)

1-6: 1-Art by Aragonés and various in all. 2-Green Lantern-c/a by Gil Kane. 3-JLA. 4-Sgt. Rock. 5-Batman art by Sprang, Adams, Miller, Timm. 6-Wonder Woman; art by Rude, Grell 2.50

FANTASTIC (Formerly Captain Science; Beware No. 10 on)
Youthful Magazines: No. 8, Feb, 1952 - No. 9, Apr, 1952

8-Capt. Science by Harrison; decapitation, shrunken head panels 37.00 111.00 260.00
9-Harrison-a 26.00 77.00 180.00

FANTASTIC ADVENTURES
Super Comics: 1963 - 1964 (Reprints)

9,10,12,15,16,18: 9-r/? 10-r/He-Man #2(Toby). 11-Disbrow-a. 12-Unpublished Chesler material? 15-r/Spook #23. 16-r/Dark Shadows #2(Steinway); Briefer-a.18-r/Superior Stories #1 2.50 7.50 22.00
11-Wood-a; r/Blue Bolt #118 3.80 11.40 38.00
17-Baker-a(2) r/Seven Seas #6 3.80 11.40 38.00

FANTASTIC COMICS
Fox Features Syndicate: Dec, 1939 - No. 23, Nov, 1941

1-Intro/origin Samson; Stardust, The Super Wizard, Sub Saunders (by Kiefer), Space Smith, Capt. Kidd begin 400.00 1200.00 4000.00
2-Powell text illos 225.00 675.00 1800.00
3-Classic Lou Fine Robot-c; Powell text illos 800.00 2400.00 5200.00
4,5: Last Lou Fine-c 175.00 525.00 1400.00
6,7-Simon-c 131.00 393.00 1050.00
8-10: 10-Intro/origin David, Samson's aide 91.00 273.00 725.00
11-17,19,20,22: 16-Stardust ends. 22-Hitler-c 75.00 225.00 600.00
18-1st app. Black Fury & sidekick Chuck; ends #23 78.00 234.00 625.00
21,23: 21-The Banshee begins(origin); ends #23; Hitler-c. 22-Likeness of Hitler as furnace on cover. 23-Origin The Gladiator 78.00 234.00 625.00

NOTE: *Lou Fine c-1-5. Tuska a-3-5, 8. Bondage c-6, 8, 9. Issue #11 has indicia to Mystery Men Comics #15. All issues feature Samson covers.*

FANTASTIC COMICS (Fantastic Fears #1-9; Becomes Samson #12)
Ajax/Farrell Publ.: No. 10, Nov-Dec, 1954 - No. 11, Jan-Feb, 1955

10 (#1) 17.00 51.00 120.00
11-Robot-c 20.00 60.00 140.00

FANTASTIC FABLES
Silverwolf Comics: Feb, 1987 - No. 2, 1987 ($1.50, 28 pgs., B&W)

GD2.0 FN6.0 NM9.4

1,2: 1-Tim Vigil-a (6 pgs.). 2-Tim Vigil-a (7 pgs.) 2.00

FANTASTIC FEARS (Formerly Captain Jet) (Fantastic Comics #10 on)
Ajax/Farrell Publ.: No. 7, May, 1953 - No. 9, Sept-Oct, 1954

7(#1, 5/53)-Tales of Stalking Terror 40.00 120.00 280.00
8(#2, 7/53) 25.00 75.00 175.00
3,4 19.00 56.00 130.00
5-(1-2/54)-Ditko story (1st drawn) is written by Bruce Hamilton; r-in Weird V2#8 (1st pro work for Ditko but Daring Love #1 was published 1st) 75.00 225.00 600.00
6-Decapitation-girl's head w/paper cutter (classic) 44.00 132.00 350.00
7(5-6/54), 9(9-10/54) 19.00 56.00 130.00
8(7-8/54)-Contains story intended for Jo-Jo; name changed to Kaza; decapitation story 21.00 64.00 150.00

FANTASTIC FIVE
Marvel Comics: Oct, 1999 - No. 5, Feb, 2000 ($1.99)

1-M2 Universe; recaps origin; Ryan-a 2.00

FANTASTIC FORCE
Marvel Comics: Nov, 1994 - No. 18, Apr, 1996 ($1.75)

1-($2.50)-Foil wraparound-c; intro Fantastic Force w/Huntara, Delvor, Psi-Lord & Vibraxas 2.50
2-18: 13-She-Hulk app. 2.00

FANTASTIC FOUR (See America's Best TV..., Fireside Book Series, Giant-Size..., Giant Size Super-Stars, Marvel Collectors Item Classics, Marvel Milestone Edition, Marvel's Greatest, Marvel Treasury Edition, Marvel Triple Action, Official Marvel Index to... & Power Record Comics)

FANTASTIC FOUR
Marvel Comics Group: Nov, 1961 - No. 416, Sept, 1996 (Created by Stan Lee & Jack Kirby)

GD2.0 FN6.0 VF8.0 NM9.4

1-Origin & 1st app. The Fantastic Four (Reed Richards: Mr. Fantastic, Johnny Storm: The Human Torch, Sue Storm: The Invisible Girl, & Ben Grimm: The Thing–Marvel's 1st super-hero group since the G.A.; 1st app. S.A. Human Torch); origin/1st app. The Mole Man. 740.00 2220.00 7400.00 19,000.00

GD2.0 FN6.0 NM9.4

1-Golden Record Comic Set Reprint (1966)-cover not identical to original 12.00 36.00 120.00
with Golden Record 20.00 60.00 200.00
2-Vs. The Skrulls (last 10¢ issue) 240.00 720.00 3600.00
3-Fantastic Four don costumes & establish Headquarters; brief 1pg. origin; intro The Fantasti-Car; Human Torch drawn w/two left hands on-c 165.00 495.00 2300.00

GD2.0 FN6.0 VF8.0 NM9.4

4-1st S. A. Sub-Mariner app. (5/62) 200.00 600.00 1300.00 2800.00
5-Origin & 1st app. Doctor Doom 215.00 645.00 1400.00 3000.00

GD2.0 FN6.0 NM9.4

6-Sub-Mariner, Dr. Doom team up; 1st Marvel villain team-up (2nd S.A. Sub-Mariner app. 125.00 375.00 1500.00
7-10: 7-1st app. Kurrgo. 8-1st app. Puppet-Master & Alicia Masters. 9-3rd Sub-Mariner app. 10-Stan Lee & Jack Kirby app. in story 67.00 200.00 800.00
11-Origin/1st app. The Impossible Man (2/63) 54.00 162.00 650.00
12-Fantantic Four Vs. The Hulk (1st meeting); 1st Hulk x-over & ties w/Amazing Spider-Man #1 as 1st Marvel x-over; (3/63) 100.00 300.00 1200.00
13-Intro. The Watcher; 1st app. The Red Ghost 41.00 123.00 480.00
14-19: 14-Sub-Mariner x-over. 15-1st app. Mad Thinker. 16-1st Ant-Man x-over (7/63); Wasp cameo. 18-Origin/1st app. The Super Skrull. 19-Intro. Rama-Tut; Stan Lee & Jack Kirby cameo 29.00 87.00 290.00
20-Origin/1st app. The Molecule Man 31.00 93.00 310.00
21-Intro. The Hate Monger; 1st Sgt. Fury x-over (12/63) 21.00 63.00 210.00
22-24: 22-Sue Storm gains more powers 15.00 45.00 150.00
25,26-The Hulk vs. The Thing (their 1st battle). 25-3rd Avengers x-over (1st time w/Capt. America)(cameo, 4/64); 2nd S.A. app. Cap (takes place between Avengers #4 & 5. 26-4th Avengers x-over

Fantastic Four #116 © MAR

Fantastic Four #286 © MAR

Fantastic Four #389 © MAR

GD2.0 FN6.0 NM9.4

35.00 105.00 390.00
27-1st Doctor Strange x-over (6/64) 16.00 48.00 160.00
28-Early X-Men x-over (7/64); same date as X-Men #6
25.00 75.00 250.00
29,30: 30-Intro. Diablo 11.00 33.00 110.00
31-40: 31-Early Avengers x-over (10/64). 33-1st app. Attuma; part photo-c. 35-Intro/1st app. Dragon Man. 36-Intro/1st app. Madam Medusa & the Frightful Four (Sandman, Wizard, Paste Pot Pete). 39-Wood inks on Daredevil (early x-over) 9.50 28.50 95.00
41-44,47: 41-43-Frightful Four app. 44-Intro. Gorgon 6.50 19.50 65.00
45,46: 45-Intro/1st app. The Inhumans (c/story, 12/65); also see Incredible Hulk Special #1 & Thor #146, & 147. 46-1st Black Bolt-c (Kirby) & 1st full app.
8.00 24.00 80.00
48-Partial origin/1st app. The Silver Surfer & Galactus (3/66) by Lee & Kirby; Galactus cameo in last panel; 1st of 3 part story 71.00 213.00 850.00
49-2nd app./1st cover Silver Surfer & Galactus 25.00 75.00 250.00
50-Silver Surfer battles Galactus; full S.S.-c 27.00 81.00 270.00
51,54: 54-Inhumans cameo 5.00 15.00 50.00
52-1st app. The Black Panther (7/66) 12.00 36.00 120.00
53-Origin & 2nd app. The Black Panther 9.00 27.00 90.00
55-Thing battles Silver Surfer; 4th app. Silver Surfer 8.50 25.50 85.00
56-Silver Surfer cameo 5.50 16.50 55.00
57-60: Dr. Doom steals Silver Surfer's powers (See Silver Surfer: Loftier Than Mortals). 59,60-Inhumans cameos 5.50 16.50 55.00
61-65,68-70: 61-Silver Surfer cameo; Sandman-c/s 4.20 12.60 42.00
66-Begin 2 part origin of Him (Warlock); does not app. (9/67)
9.50 28.50 95.00
67-Origin/1st app. Him (Warlock); 1 pg. cameo; see Thor #165,166 for 1st full app. 10.50 32.00 105.00
71,73,78-80: 73-Spider-Man, D.D., Thor x-over; cont'd from Daredevil #38
3.50 10.50 35.00
72-Silver Surfer-c/story (pre-dates Silver Surfer #1) 4.20 12.60 42.00
74-77: Silver Surfer app.(#77 is same date/S.S. #1) 4.00 12.00 40.00
81-88: 81-Crystal joins & dons costume. 82,83-Inhumans app. 84-87-Dr. Doom app. 88-Last 12¢ issue 3.00 9.00 30.00
89-99,101: 94-Intro. Agatha Harkness. 2.50 7.50 24.00
100 (7/70) 7.25 22.00 80.00
102,103: Fantastic Four vs. Sub-Mariner 2.25 6.80 25.00
104-111: 104-Magneto-c/story; Sub-Mariner app. 108-Last Kirby issue (not in #103-107). 110-reg. version w/green faces 2.25 6.75 18.00
110-Variant-c w/flesh color faces and green Thing. Common version shows green faces. 2.70 8.00 27.00
112-Hulk Vs. Thing (7/71) 5.50 16.50 60.00
113-115: 115-Last 15¢ issue 1.85 5.50 15.00
116 (52 pgs.) 2.00 6.00 18.00
117-120 1.25 3.75 10.00
121-123-Silver Surfer-c/stories. 122,123-Galactus 1.85 5.50 15.00
124,125,127,129-149: 129-Intro. Thundra. 130-Sue leaves F.F. 131-Quicksilver app. 132-Medusa joins. 133-Thundra Vs. Thing. 142-Kirbyish-a by Buckler begins. 143-Dr. Doom-c/story. 147-Sub-Mariner 1.10 3.30 9.00
126-Origin F.F. retold; cover swipe of F.F. #1 1.50 4.50 12.00
128-Four pg. insert of F.F. Friends & Foes 1.50 4.50 12.00
150-Crystal & Quicksilver's wedding 1.50 4.50 12.00
151-154,158-160: 151-Origin Thundra. 159-Medusa leaves; Sue rejoins
1.00 2.80 7.00
155-157: Silver Surfer in all 1.10 3.30 9.00
161-165,168,174-180: 164-The Crusader (old Marvel Boy) revived (origin #165); 1st app.Frankie Raye. 168-170-Cage app. 176-Re-intro Impossible Man; Marvel artists app. 180-r/#101 by Kirby 5.00
166,167-vs. Hulk 2.40 6.00
169-173-(Regular 25¢ edition)(4-8/75) 3.50
169-173-(30¢-c, limited distribution) 2.50 7.50 20.00
181-199: 189-G.A. Human Torch app. & origin retold. 190,191-Fantastic Four break up 4.00
184-(35¢-c variant, limited dist.)(7/77) 2.00 6.00 16.00
200-(11/78, 52 pgs.)-F.F. re-united vs. Dr. Doom 2.40 6.00
201-208,219,222-231: 207-Human Torch vs. Spider-Man-c/story. 211-1st app. Terrax 4.00
209-216,218,220,221-Byrne-a. 209-1st Herbie the Robot. 220-Brief origin
4.00
217-Dazzler app. by Byrne 4.00
232-Byrne-a begins 4.00
233-235,237-249,251-260: All Byrne-a. 238-Origin Frankie Raye. 244-Frankie Raye becomes Nova, Herald of Galactus. 252-Reads sideways; Annihilus app.; contains skin "Tattooz" decals 3.50
236-20th Anniversary issue(11/81, 68 pgs., $1.00)-Brief origin F.F.; Byrne-c/a(p); new Kirby-a(p) 3.50
250-(52 pgs)-Spider-Man x-over; Byrne-a; Skrulls impersonate New X-Men
3.50
261-285: 261-Silver Surfer. 262-Origin Galactus; Byrne writes & draws himself into story. 264-Swipes-c of F.F. #1. 274-Spider-Man's alien costume app. (4th app., 1/85, 2 pgs.) 3.00
286-2nd app. X-Factor continued from Avengers #263; story continues in X-Factor #1 3.50
287-295: 292-Nick Fury app. 293-Last Byrne-a 2.50
296-($1.50)-Barry Smith-c/a; Thing rejoins 3.00
297-318,321-330: 300-Johnny Storm & Alicia Masters wed. 306-New team begins (9/87). 311-Re-intro The Black Panther. 312-X-Factor x-over. 327-Mr. Fantastic & Invisible Girl return 2.50
319,320: 319-Double size. 320-Thing vs. Hulk 3.00
331-346,351-357,359,360: 334-Simonson-c/scripts begin. 337-Simonson-a begins. 342-Spider-Man cameo. 356-F.F. vs. The New Warriors; Paul Ryan-c/a begins. 360-Last $1.00-c 2.00
347-Ghost Rider, Wolverine, Spider-Man, Hulk-c/stories thru #349; Arthur Adams-c/a(p) in each 3.00
347,348-Gold 2nd printing 2.00
348,349 2.25
350-($1.50, 52 pgs.)-Dr. Doom app. 3.00
358-(11/91, $2.25, 88 pgs.)-30th anniversary issue; gives history of F.F.; die cut-c; Art Adams back-up story-a 2.50
361-368,370,372-374,376-380,382-386: 362-Spider-Man app. 367-Wolverine app. (brief). 370-Infinity War x-over; Thanos & Magus app. 374-Secret Defenders (Ghost Rider, Hulk, Wolverine) x-over 2.00
369-Infinity War x-over; Thanos app. 2.50
371-All white embossed-c ($2.00) 4.00
371-All red 2nd printing ($2.00) 2.50
375-($2.95, 52 pgs.)-Holo-grafx foil-c; ann. issue 3.00
381-Death of Reed Richards (Mister Fantastic) & Dr. Doom 4.00
387-Newsstand ed. ($1.25) 2.00
387-($2.95)-Collector's Ed. w/Die-cut foil-c 3.00
388-393,395-397: 388-bound-in trading card sheet. 394-($1.50-c) 2.00
394,398,399: 394 ($2.95)-Collector's Edition-polybagged w/16 pg. Marvel Action Hour book and acetate print; pink logo. 398,399-Rainbow Foil-c 3.00
400-Rainbow-Foil-c 3.50
401-415: 401,402-Atlantis Rising. 407,408-Return of Reed Richards. 411-Inhumans app. 414-Galactus vs. Hyperstorm. 415-Onslaught tie-in; X-Men app. 2.00
416-($2.50)-Onslaught tie-in; Dr. Doom app.; wraparound-c 3.00
Annual 1('63)-Origin F.F.; Ditko-i; early Spidey app. 54.00 162.00 650.00
Annual 2('64)-Dr. Doom origin & c/story 31.00 93.00 350.00
Annual 3('65)-Reed & Sue wed; r/#6,11 13.00 39.00 130.00
Special 4(11/66)-G.A. Torch x-over (1st S.A. app.) & origin retold; r/#25,26 (Hulk vs. Thing); Torch vs. Torch battle 8.00 24.00 80.00
Special 5(11/67)-New art; Intro. Psycho-Man; early Black Panther, Inhumans & Silver Surfer (1st solo story) app. 9.00 27.00 90.00
Special 6(11/68)-Intro. Annihilus; birth of Franklin Richards; new 48 pg. movie length epic; last non-reprint annual 4.50 13.50 45.00
Special 7(11/69)-r/F.F. #1-5; Marvel staff photos 2.50 7.50 24.00
Special 8-10: All reprints. 8(12/70)-F.F. vs. Sub-Mariner plus gallery of F.F. foes. 9(12/71). 10('73) 2.00 6.00 16.00
Annual 11-14: 11(1976)-New art begins again. 12(1978). 13(1978). 14(1979)
2.40 6.00
Annual 15-27: 15('80-'94, 68 pgs.).17(1983)-Byrne-c/a. 21(1988)-Evolutionary War x-over. 22-Atlantis Attacks x-over; Sub-Mariner & The Avengers app.;

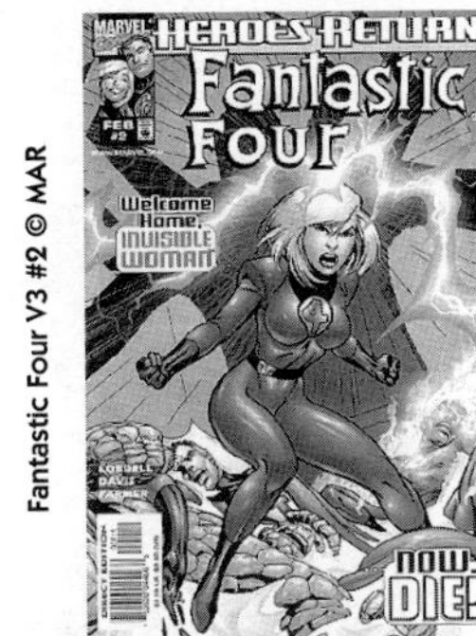

Fantastic Four V3 #2 © MAR

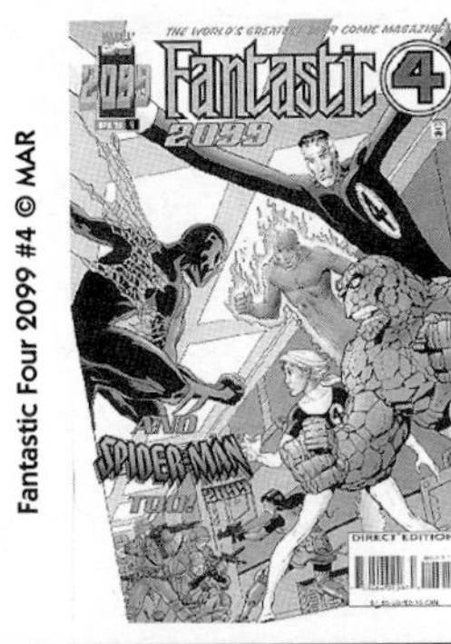

Fantastic Four 2099 #4 © MAR

Fantasy Masterpieces #9 © MAR

GD2.0 FN6.0 NM9.4

Buckler-a. 23-Byrne-c; Guice-p. 24-2 pg. origin recap of Fantastic Four; Guardians of the Galaxy x-over. 25-Moondragon story. 26-Bagged w/card 3.00
Special Edition 1(5/84)-r/Annual #1; Byrne-c/a 2.50
...: Monsters Unleashed nn (1992, $5.95)-r/F.F. #347-349 w/new Arthur Adams-c 2.40 6.00
...: Nobody Gets Out Alive (1994, $15.95) TPB r/ #387-392 16.00
Giveaway (nn, 1981, 32pgs., Young Model Builders Club) 4.00

NOTE: ***Arthur Adams*** *c/a-347-349p.* ***Austin*** *c(i)-232-236, 238, 240-242, 250i, 286i.* ***Buckler*** *c-168.* ***John Buscema*** *a(p)-107, 108(w/**Kirby** & **Romita**),109-130, 132, 134-141, 160, 173-175, 202, 296-309p, Annual 11, 13; c(p)-107-122, 124-129, 133-139, 202, Annual 12p, Special 10.* ***Byrne*** *a-209-218p, 220p, 221p, 232-265, 266i, 267-273, 274-293p, Annual 17, 19; c-211-214p, 220p, 232-236p, 237, 238p, 239, 240-242p, 243-249, 250p, 251-267, 269-277, 278-281p, 283p, 284, 285, 286p, 288-293, Annual 17, 18.* ***Ditko*** *a-13i, 14i(w/**Kirby**-p), Annual 16.* ***G. Kane*** *c-150p, 160p.* ***Kirby*** *a-1-102p, 108, 180r, 189r, 236p, Special 1-10; c-1-101, 164, 167, 171-177, 180, 181, 190, 200, Annual 11, Special 1-7, 9.* ***Marcos*** *a-Annual 14i.* ***Mooney*** *a-118i, 152i.* ***Perez*** *a(p)-164-167, 170-172, 176-178, 184-188, 191p, 192p. Annual 14p, 15p; c(p)-183-188, 191, 192, 194-197.* ***Simonson*** *a-337-341, 343, 344p, 345p, 346, 350p, 352-354; c-212, 334-341, 342p, 343-346, 350, 353, 354.* ***Steranko*** *c-130-132p.* ***Williamson*** *c-357i.*

FANTASTIC FOUR (Volume Two)
Marvel Comics: V2#1, Nov, 1996 - No. 13, Nov, 1997 ($2.95/$1.95/$1.99) (Produced by WildStorm Productions)

1-($2.95)-Reintro Fantastic Four; Jim Lee-c/a; Brandon Choi scripts; Mole Man app. 5.00
1-($2.95)-Variant-c 1.00 2.80 7.00
2-9,12: 2- Namor-c/app.. 3-Avengers-c/app. 4-2-covers; Dr. Doom cameo. 2-($2.99) "Heroes Reunited"-pt. 1 3.00
10,11,13: All $1.99-c. 13-"World War 3"-pt. 1, x-over w/Image 3.00

FANTASTIC FOUR (Volume Three)
Marvel Comics: V3#1, Jan, 1998 - Present ($2.99/$1.99)

1-($2.99)-Heroes Return; Lobdell-s/Davis & Farmer-a 5.00
1-Alternate Heroes Return-c 1.00 2.80 7.00
2-4,12: 2-2-covers. 4-Claremont-s/Larroca-a begin; Silver Surfer c/app.12-($2.99) Wraparound-c by Larroca 4.00
5-11,: 6-Heroes For Hire app. 9-Spider-Man-c/app. 3.00
13-22: 13,14-Ronan-c/app. 2.00
...'98 Annual ($3.50) Immonen-a 3.50
Wizard 1/2 -Lim-a 10.00

FANTASTIC FOUR: ATLANTIS RISING
Marvel Comics: June, 1995 - No. 2, July, 1995 ($3.95, limited series)

1,2: Acetate-c 4.00
Collector's Preview (5/95, $2.25, 52 pgs.) 2.50

FANTASTIC FOUR: FIREWORKS
Marvel Comics: Jan, 1999 - No. 3, Mar, 1999 ($2.99, limited series)

1-3-Remix; Jeff Johnson-a 3.00

FANTASTIC FOUR INDEX (See Official...)

FANTASTIC FOUR ROAST
Marvel Comics Group: May, 1982 (75¢, one-shot, direct sales)

1-Celebrates 20th anniversary of F.F.#1; X-Men, Ghost Rider & many others cameo; Golden, Miller, Buscema, Rogers, Byrne, Anderson art; Hembeck/Austin-c 4.00

FANTASTIC FOUR: THE LEGEND
Marvel Comics: Oct, 1996 ($3.95, one-shot)

1-Tribute issue 4.00

FANTASTIC FOUR 2099
Marvel Comics: Jan, 1996 - No. 8, Aug, 1996 ($3.95/$1.95)

1-($3.95)-Chromium-c; X-Nation preview 4.00
2-8: 4-Spider-Man 2099-c/app. 5-Doctor Strange app. 7-Thibert-c 2.00

NOTE: ***Williamson*** *a-1i; c-1i.*

FANTASTIC FOUR UNLIMITED
Marvel Comics: Mar, 1993 - No. 12, Dec, 1995 ($3.95, 68 pgs.)

1-12: 1-Black Panther app. 4-Thing vs. Hulk. 5-Vs. The Frightful Four. 6-Vs. Namor. 7, 9-12-Wraparound-c 4.00

GD2.0 FN6.0 NM9.4

FANTASTIC FOUR UNPLUGGED
Marvel Comics: Sept, 1995 - No. 6, Aug 1996 (99¢, bi-monthly)

1-6 2.00

FANTASTIC FOUR VS. X-MEN
Marvel Comics: Feb, 1987 - No. 4, June, 1987 (Limited series)

1-4: 4-Austin-a(i) 3.00

FANTASTIC GIANTS (Formerly Konga #1-23)
Charlton Comics: V2#24, Sept, 1966 (25¢, 68 pgs.)

V2#24-Special Ditko issue; origin Konga & Gorgo reprinted plus two new Ditko stories 6.00 18.00 60.00

FANTASTIC TALES
I. W. Enterprises: 1958 (no date) (Reprint, one-shot)

1-Reprints Avon's "City of the Living Dead" 3.00 9.00 30.00

FANTASTIC VOYAGE (See Movie Comics)
Gold Key: Aug, 1969 - No. 2, Dec, 1969

1 (TV) 4.50 13.50 45.00
2 3.50 10.50 35.00

FANTASTIC VOYAGES OF SINDBAD, THE
Gold Key: Oct, 1965 - No. 2, June, 1967

1-Painted-c on both 5.00 15.00 55.00
2 4.00 12.00 45.00

FANTASTIC WORLDS
Standard Comics: No. 5, Sept, 1952 - No. 7, Jan, 1953

5-Toth, Anderson-a 34.00 103.00 240.00
6-Toth-c/a 29.00 86.00 200.00
7 19.00 56.00 130.00

FANTASY FEATURES
Americomics: 1987 - No. 2, 1987 ($1.75)

1,2 2.00

FANTASY MASTERPIECES (Marvel Super Heroes No. 12 on)
Marvel Comics Group: Feb, 1966 - No. 11, Oct, 1967; V2#1, Dec, 1979 - No. 14, Jan, 1981

1-Photo of Stan Lee (12¢-c #1,2) 5.00 15.00 50.00
2-r/1st Fin Fang Foom from Strange Tales #89 2.50 7.50 25.00
3-8: 3-G.A. Capt. America-r begin, end #11; 1st 25¢ Giant; Colan-r. 3-6-Kirby-c (p). 4-Kirby-c(p)(i). 7-Begin G.A. Sub-Mariner, Torch-r/M. Mystery. 8-Torch battles the Sub-Mariner-r/Marvel Mystery #9 2.50 7.50 25.00
9-Origin Human Torch-r/Marvel Comics #1 3.00 9.00 30.00
10,11: 10-r/origin & 1st app. All Winners Squad from All Winners #19. 11-r/origin of Toro (H.T. #1) & Black Knight #1 2.50 7.50 25.00
V2#1(12/79, 75¢, 52 pgs.)-r/origin Silver Surfer from Silver Surfer #1 with editing plus reprints cover; J. Buscema-a 3.00
2-14-Reprints Silver Surfer #2-14 w/covers 2.00

NOTE: ***Buscema*** *c-V2#7-9(in part).* ***Ditko*** *r-1-3, 7, 9.* ***Everett*** *r-1,7-9.* ***Matt Fox*** *r-9i.* ***Kirby*** *r-1-11; c(p)-3, 4i, 5, 6.* ***Starlin*** *r-8-13. Some direct sale V2#14's had a 50¢ cover price. #3-11 contain Capt. America-r/Capt. America #3-10. #7-11 contain G.A.Human Torch & Sub-Mariner-r.*

FANTASY QUARTERLY (Also see Elfquest)
Independent Publishers Syndicate: Spring, 1978 (B&W) (2nd printing exist?)

1-1st app. Elfquest; Dave Sim-a (6 pgs.) 4.50 13.50 50.00

FANTOMAN (Formerly Amazing Adventure Funnies)
Centaur Publications: No. 2, Aug, 1940 - No. 4, Dec, 1940

2-The Fantom of the Fair, The Arrow, Little Dynamite-r begin; origin The Ermine by Filchock; Fantoman app. in 2-4; Burgos, J. Cole, Ernst, Gustavson-a 120.00 360.00 960.00
3,4: Gustavson-r. 4-Red Blaze story 100.00 300.00 800.00

FAREWELL MOONSHADOW (See Moonshadow)
DC Comics (Vertigo): Jan, 1997 ($7.95, one-shot)

nn-DeMatteis-s/Muth-c/a 8.00

FARGO KID (Formerly Justice Traps the Guilty)(See Feature Comics #47

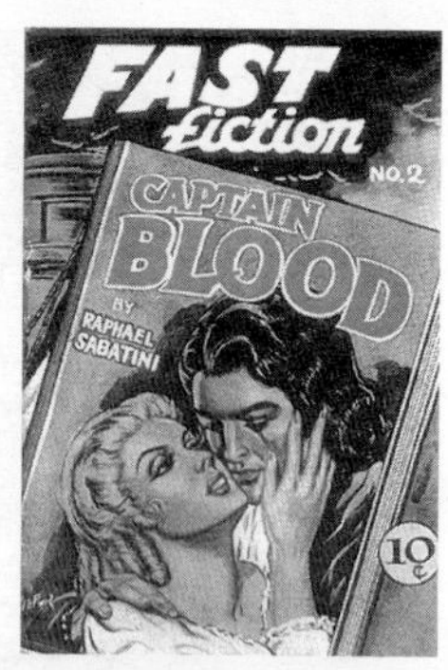

Fast Fiction #2 © Seaboard Pub.

Fathom #2 © Michael Turner

Fatman, The Human Flying Saucer #3 © Milson Pub.

GD2.0 FN6.0 NM9.4

Prize Publications: V11#3(#1), June-July, 1958 - V11#5, Oct-Nov, 1958

V11#3(#1)-Origin Fargo Kid, Severin-c/a; Williamson-a(2); Heath-a 18.00 54.00 125.00
V11#4,5-Severin-c/a 11.50 34.00 80.00

FARMER'S DAUGHTER, THE
Stanhall Publ./Trojan Magazines: Feb-Mar, 1954 - No. 3, June-July, 1954; No. 4, Oct, 1954

1-Lingerie, nudity panel 19.00 56.00 130.00
2-4(Stanhall) 12.00 36.00 85.00

FASHION IN ACTION
Eclipse Comics: Aug, 1986 - Feb, 1987 (Baxter paper)

Summer Special 1 , Winter Special 1, each Snyder III-c/a 2.00

FASTEST GUN ALIVE, THE (Movie)
Dell Publishing Co.: No. 741, Sept, 1956 (one-shot)

Four Color 741-Photo-c 6.40 19.00 70.00

FAST FICTION (...Action) (Stories by Famous Authors Illustrated #6 on)
Seaboard Publ./Famous Authors Ill.: Oct, 1949 - No. 5, Mar, 1950
(All have Kiefer-c)(48 pgs.)

1-Scarlet Pimpernel; Jim Lavery-c/a 37.00 111.00 260.00
2-Captain Blood; H. C. Kiefer-c/a 34.00 103.00 240.00
3-She, by Rider Haggard; Vincent Napoli-a 40.00 120.00 320.00
4-(1/50, 52 pgs.)-The 39 Steps; Lavery-c/a 26.00 79.00 185.00
5-Beau Geste; Kiefer-c/a 26.00 79.00 185.00
NOTE: ***Kiefer** a-2, 5; c-2, 3,5. **Lavery** c/a-1, 4. **Napoli** a-3.*

FAST FORWARD
DC Comics (Piranha Press): 1992 - No. 3, 1993 ($4.95, 68 pgs.)

1-3: 1-Morrison scripts; McKean-c/a. 3-Sam Kieth-a 5.00

FAST WILLIE JACKSON
Fitzgerald Periodicals, Inc.: Oct, 1976 - No. 7, 1977

1 1.00 3.00 8.00
2-7 4.00

FAT ALBERT (...& the Cosby Kids) (TV)
Gold Key: Mar, 1974 - No. 29, Feb, 1979

1 2.50 7.50 22.00
2-10 1.50 4.50 12.00
11-29 1.10 3.30 9.00

FATALE (Also see Powers That Be #1 & Shadow State #1,2)
Broadway Comics: Jan, 1996 - No. 6, Aug, 1996 ($2.50)

1-6: J.G. Jones-c/a in all, Preview Edition 1 (11/95, B&W) 2.50

FAT AND SLAT (Ed Wheelan) (Becomes Gunfighter No. 5 on)
E. C. Comics: Summer, 1947 - No. 4, Spring, 1948

1-Intro/origin Voltage, Man of Lightning; "Comics" McCormick, the World's No. 1 Comic Book Fan begins, ends #4 31.00 94.00 220.00
2-4: 4-Comics McCormick-c feature 23.00 69.00 160.00

FAT AND SLAT JOKE BOOK
All-American Comics (William H. Wise): Summer, 1944 (52 pgs., one-shot)

nn-by Ed Wheelan 25.00 75.00 175.00

FATE (See Hand of Fate & Thrill-O-Rama)

FATE
DC Comics: Oct, 1994 - No. 22, Sept, 1996 ($1.95/$2.25)

0,1-22: 8-Begin $2.25-c. 11-14-Alan Scott (Sentinel) app. 10,14-Zatanna app. 21-Phantom Stranger app. 22-Spectre app. 2.25

FATHER & SON
Kitchen Sink: July, 1995 ($2.75, B&W, limited series)

1-Jeff NIcholson-s/a 2.75

FATHOM
Comico: May, 1987 - No. 3, July, 1987 ($1.50, limited series)

1-3 2.00

GD2.0 FN6.0 NM9.4

FATHOM
Image Comics (Top Cow Prod.): Aug, 1998 - Present ($2.50)

Preview 10.00
0-Wizard supplement 8.00
1-Turner-s/a; three covers; alternate story pages 5.00
1-Wizard World Ed. 30.00
2-8 2.50
... Collected Edition 1 (3/99, $5.95) r/Preview & all three #1's 6.00
... Collected Edition 2 (3/99, $5.95) r/2,3 6.00
...Swimsuit Special (5/99, $2.95) Pin-ups by various 3.00

FATIMA...CHALLENGE TO THE WORLD
Catechetical Guild: 1951, 36 pgs. (15¢)

nn (not same as 'Challenge to the World') 2.80 7.00 14.00

FATMAN, THE HUMAN FLYING SAUCER
Lightning Comics(Milson Publ. Co.): April, 1967 - No. 3, Aug-Sept, 1967 (68 pgs.) (Written by Otto Binder)

1-Origin/1st app. Fatman & Tinman by Beck 5.00 15.00 50.00
2-C. C. Beck-a 3.20 9.60 32.00
3-(Scarce)-Beck-a 5.50 16.50 55.00

FAULTLINES
DC Comics (Vertigo): May, 1997 - No. 6, Oct, 1997 ($2.50, limited series)

1-6-Lee Marrs-s/Bill Koeb-a in all 2.50

FAUNTLEROY COMICS (Super Duck Presents...)
Close-Up/Archie Publications: 1950; No. 2, 1951; No. 3, 1952

1-Super Duck-c/stories by Al Fagaly in all 8.35 25.00 50.00
2,3 5.00 15.00 30.00

FAUST
Northstar Publishing/Rebel Studios #7 on: 1989 - No 11, 1997 ($2.00/$2.25, B&W, mature themes)

1-Decapitation-c; Tim Vigil-c/a in all; Begin $2.00-c 3.00 9.00 30.00
1-2nd printing 2.40 6.00
1-3rd & 4th printing 3.00
2 2.25 6.75 18.00
2-2nd & 3rd printings, 3,5-2nd printing 3.00
3-Begin $2.25-c 1.50 4.50 12.00
4-10: 7-Begin Rebel Studios series 5.00
11-($2.25) 2.25

FAWCETT MOTION PICTURE COMICS (See Motion Picture Comics)

FAWCETT MOVIE COMIC
Fawcett Publications: 1949 - No. 20, Dec, 1952 (All photo-c)

nn- "Dakota Lil"; George Montgomery & Rod Cameron (1949) 31.00 92.00 215.00
nn- "Copper Canyon"; Ray Milland & Hedy Lamarr (1950) 24.00 71.00 165.00
nn- "Destination Moon" (1950) 75.00 225.00 600.00
nn- "Montana"; Errol Flynn & Alexis Smith (1950) 24.00 71.00 165.00
nn- "Pioneer Marshal"; Monte Hale (1950) 24.00 71.00 165.00
nn- "Powder River Rustlers"; Rocky Lane (1950) 36.00 107.00 250.00
nn- "Singing Guns"; Vaughn Monroe, Ella Raines & Walter Brennan (1950) 21.00 62.00 145.00
7- "Gunmen of Abilene"; Rocky Lane; Bob Powell-a (1950) 26.00 79.00 185.00
8- "King of the Bullwhip"; Lash LaRue; Bob Powell-a (1950) 40.00 120.00 280.00
9- "The Old Frontier"; Monte Hale; Bob Powell-a(2/51; mis-dated 2/50) 25.00 75.00 175.00
10- "The Missourians"; Monte Hale (4/51) 25.00 75.00 175.00
11- "The Thundering Trail"; Lash LaRue (6/51) 33.00 99.00 230.00
12- "Rustlers on Horseback"; Rocky Lane (8/51) 26.00 79.00 185.00
13- "Warpath"; Edmond O'Brien & Forrest Tucker (10/51) 17.00 51.00 120.00
14- "Last Outpost"; Ronald Reagan (12/51) 40.00 120.00 290.00

Fawcett Movie Comic #19 © FAW

Fear #10 © MAR

Feature Books #11 © KING

GD2.0 FN6.0 NM9.4

15-(Scarce)- "The Man From Planet X"; Robert Clark; Schaffenberger-a (2/52) 206.00 619.00 1650.00
16- "10 Tall Men"; Burt Lancaster 13.50 41.00 95.00
17- "Rose of Cimarron"; Jack Buetel & Mala Powers 11.00 33.00 75.00
18- "The Brigand"; Anthony Dexter & Anthony Quinn; Schaffenberger-a 11.00 33.00 75.00
19- "Carbine Williams"; James Stewart; Costanza-a; James Stewart photo-c 12.00 36.00 85.00
20- "Ivanhoe"; Robert Taylor & Liz Taylor photo-c 18.00 54.00 125.00

FAWCETT'S FUNNY ANIMALS (No. 1-26, 80-on titled "Funny Animals"; becomes Li'l Tomboy No. 92 on?)
Fawcett Publications/Charlton Comics No. 84 on: 12/42 - #79, 4/53; #80, 6/53 - #83, 12?/53; #84, 4/54 - #91, 2/56

1-Capt. Marvel on cover; intro. Hoppy The Captain Marvel Bunny, cloned from Capt. Marvel; Billy the Kid & Willie the Worm begin 55.00 165.00 440.00
2-Xmas-c 31.00 94.00 220.00
3-5: 3(2/43)-Spirit of '43-c 19.00 58.00 135.00
6,7,9,10 13.00 39.00 90.00
8-Flag-c 13.50 41.00 95.00
11-20: 14-Cover is a 1944 calendar 10.00 30.00 70.00
21-40: 25-Xmas-c. 26-St. Valentines Day-c 7.00 21.00 42.00
41-86,90,91 5.35 16.00 32.00
87-89(10-54-2/55)-Merry Mailman ish (TV/Radio)-part photo-c 7.00 21.00 42.00

NOTE: *Marvel Bunny in all issues to at least No. 68 (not in 49-54).*

FAZE ONE FAZERS
Americomics (AC Comics): 1986 - No. 4, Sept, 1986 (Limited series)

1-4 2.00

F.B.I., THE
Dell Publishing Co.: Apr-June, 1965

1-Sinnott-a 2.50 7.50 20.00

F.B.I. STORY, THE (Movie)
Dell Publishing Co.: No. 1069, Jan-Mar, 1960

Four Color 1069-Toth-a; James Stewart photo-c 10.00 30.00 110.00

FEAR (Adventure into...)
Marvel Comics Group: Nov, 1970 - No. 31, Dec, 1975

1-Fantasy & Sci-Fi-r in early issues; Giant size; Kirby-a(r) 2.80 8.40 28.00
2-6: All Giant size. Kirby-a(r) 2.25 6.75 18.00
7-9-Kirby-a(r) 1.50 4.50 12.00
10-Man-Thing begins (10/72, 4th app.), ends #19; see Savage Tales #1 for 1st app.; 1st solo series; Chaykin/Morrow-c/a; 2.50 7.50 22.00
11,12: 11-N. Adams-c. 12-Starlin/Buckler-a 1.10 3.30 9.00
13,14,16-18: 17-Origin/1st app. Wundarr 1.00 2.80 7.00
15-1st full-length Man-Thing story (8/73) 1.10 3.30 9.00
19-Intro. Howard the Duck; Val Mayerik-a (12/73) 2.50 7.50 20.00
20-Morbius, the Living Vampire begins, ends #31; has history recap of Morbius with X-Men & Spider-Man 2.50 7.50 20.00
21-23,25 2.40 6.00
24-Blade-c/sty 2.15 6.50 17.00
26-31 5.00

NOTE: ***Bolle** a-13i. **Brunner** c-15-17. **Buckler** a-11p, 12i. **Chaykin** a-10i. **Colan** a-23r. **Craig** a-10p. **Ditko** a-6-8r. **Evans** a-30. **Everett** a-9, 10i, 21r. **Gulacy** a-20p. **Heath** a-12r. **Heck** a-8r, 13r. **Gil Kane** a-21p; c(p)-20, 21, 23-28, 31. **Kirby** a-1-9r. **Maneely** a-24r. **Mooney** a-11i, 26r. **Morrow** a-11i. **Paul Reinman** a-14r. **Robbins** a(p)-25-27, 31. **Russell** a-23p, 24p. **Severin** c-8. **Starlin** c-12p.*

FEARBOOK
Eclipse Comics: April, 1986 ($1.75, one-shot, mature)

1-Scholastic Mag- r; Bissette-a 2.00

FEAR IN THE NIGHT (See Complete Mystery No. 3)

FEARLESS FAGAN
Dell Publishing Co.: No. 441, Dec, 1952 (one-shot)

GD2.0 FN6.0 NM9.4

Four Color 441 3.00 9.00 35.00

FEATURE BOOK (Dell) (See Large Feature Comic)

FEATURE BOOKS (Newspaper-r, early issues)
David McKay Publications: May, 1937 - No. 57, 1948 (B&W)
(Full color, 68 pgs. begin #26 on)

Note: See individual alphabetical listings for prices

nn-Popeye & the Jeep (#1, 100 pgs.); reprinted as Feature Books #3(Very Rare; only 3 known copies, 1-VF, 2-in low grade)
nn-Dick Tracy (#1)-Reprinted as Feature Book #4 (100 pgs.) & in part as 4-Color #1 (Rare, less than 10 known copies)

NOTE: *Above books were advertised together with different covers from Feat. Books #3 & 4.*

1-King of the Royal Mtd. (#1)
3-Popeye (7/37) by Segar;
4-Dick Tracy (8/37)-Same as nn issue but a new cover added
6-Dick Tracy (10/37)
8-Secret Agent X-9 (12/37) -Not by Raymond
9-Dick Tracy (1/38)
11-Little Annie Rooney (#1, 3/38)
13-Inspector Wade (5/38)
15-Barney Baxter (#1) (7/38)
17-Gangbusters (#1, 9/38) (1st app.)
20-Phantom (#1, 12/38)
22-Phantom
24-Lone Ranger (1941)
26-Prince Valiant (1941)-Hal Foster -c/a; newspaper strips reprinted, pgs. 1-28,30-63; color & 68 pg. issues begin; Foster cover is only original comic book artwork by him
36('43),38,40('44),42,43, 45,47-Blondie
39-Phantom
46-Mandrake in the Fire World-(58 pgs.)
48-Maltese Falcon by Dashiell Hammett('46)
51,54-Rip Kirby; Raymond-c/s; origin-#51
53,56,57-Phantom
2-Popeye (6/37) by Segar same as nn issue but a new cover added
5-Popeye (9/37) by Segar
7-Little Orphan Annie (#1, 11/37) (Rare)-Reprints strips from 12/31/34 to 7/17/35
10-Popeye (2/38)
12-Blondie (#1) (4/38) (Rare)
14-Popeye (6/38) by Segar
16-Red Eagle (8/38)
18,19-Mandrake
21-Lone Ranger
23-Mandrake
25-Flash Gordon (#1)-Reprints not by Raymond
27-29,31,34-Blondie
30-Katzenjammer Kids (#1, 1942)
32,35,41,44-Katzenjammer Kids
33(nn)-Romance of Flying; World War II photos
37-Katzenjammer Kids; has photo & biog. of Harold H.Knerr(1883-1949) who took over strip from Rudolph Dirks in 1914
49,50-Perry Mason; based on Gardner novels
52,55-Mandrake

NOTE: *All Feature Books through #25 are over-sized 8-1/2x11-3/8" comics with color covers and black and white interiors. The covers are rough, heavy stock. The page counts, including covers, are as follows: nn, #3, 4-100 pgs.; #1, 2-52 pgs.; #5-25 are all 76 pgs. #33 was found in bound set from publisher.*

FEATURE COMICS (Formerly Feature Funnies)
Quality Comics Group: No. 21, June, 1939 - No. 144, May, 1950

21-The Clock, Jane Arden & Mickey Finn continue from Feature Funnies 58.00 174.00 465.00
22-26: 23-Charlie Chan begins (8/39, 1st app.) 40.00 120.00 325.00
26-(nn, nd)-Cover in one color, (10¢, 36 pgs.; issue No. blanked out. Two variations exist, each contain half of the regular #26) 13.50 41.00 95.00
27-(Rare)-Origin/1st app. Doll Man by Eisner (scripts) & Lou Fine (art); Doll Man begins, ends #139 355.00 1067.00 3200.00
28-2nd app. Doll Man by Lou Fine 156.00 468.00 1250.00
29,30: 30-1st Doll Man-c 91.00 273.00 700.00
31-Last Clock & Charlie Chan issue (4/40); Charlie Chan moves to Big Shot #1 following month (5/40) 72.00 216.00 575.00
32-37: 32-Rusty Ryan & Samar begin. 34-Captain Fortune app. 37-Last Fine Doll Man 52.00 156.00 420.00

Note: *A 15¢ Canadian version of Feature Comics #37, made in the US, exists.*

38-41: 38-Origin the Ace of Space. 39-Origin The Destroying Demon, ends #40; X-Mas-c. 40-Bruce Blackburn in costume 40.00 120.00 325.00
42,43,45-50: 42-USA, the Spirit of Old Glory begins. 46-Intro. Boyville Brigadiers in Rusty Ryan. 47-Fargo Kid begins. 48-USA ends 32.00 96.00 225.00
44-Doll Man by Crandall begins, ends #63; Crandall-a(2)

Feature Comics #35 © QUA

Federal Man Comics #2 © DC

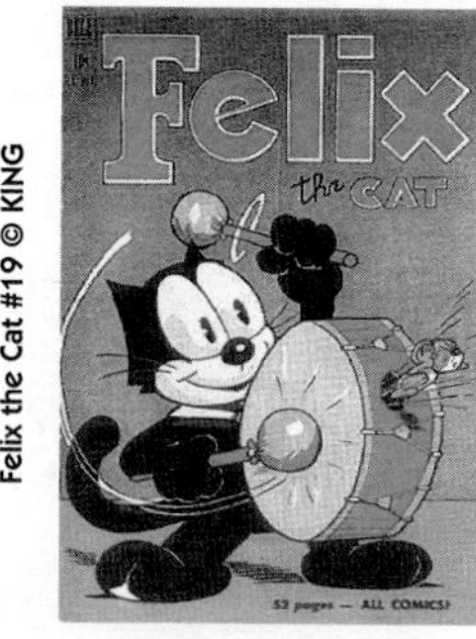

Felix the Cat #19 © KING

GD2.0 FN6.0 NM9.4

43.00 128.00 340.00
51-60: 56-Marijuana story in Swing Sisson strip. 57-Spider Widow begins. 60-Raven begins, ends #71 24.00 73.00 170.00
61-68 (5/43) 22.00 66.00 155.00
69,70-Phantom Lady x-over in Spider Widow 24.00 73.00 170.00
71-80,100: 71-Phantom Lady x-over. 72-Spider Widow ends 17.00 51.00 120.00
81-99 13.50 41.00 95.00
101-144: 139-Last Doll Man & last Doll Man-c. 140-Intro. Stuntman Stetson (Stuntman Stetson c-140-144) 11.50 34.00 80.00

NOTE: ***Celardo** a-37-43. **Crandall** a-44-60, 62, 63-on(most). **Gustavson** a-(Rusty Ryan)- 32-134. **Powell** a-34, 64-73. The Clock c-25, 28, 29. Doll Man c-30, 32, 34, 36, 38, 40, 42, 44, 46, 48, 50, 52, 54, 56, 58, 60, 62, 64, 66, 68, 70, 72, 74, 77-139. Joe Palooka c-21, 24, 27.*

FEATURE FILMS
National Periodical Publ.: Mar-Apr, 1950 - No. 4, Sept-Oct, 1950 (All photo-c)

1- "Captain China" with John Payne, Gail Russell, Lon Chaney & Edgar Bergen 62.00 187.00 500.00
2- "Riding High" with Bing Crosby 66.00 197.00 525.00
3- "The Eagle & the Hawk" with John Payne, Rhonda Fleming & D. O'Keefe 62.00 187.00 500.00
4- "Fancy Pants"; Bob Hope & Lucille Ball 66.00 197.00 525.00

FEATURE FUNNIES (Feature Comics No. 21 on)
Harry 'A' Chesler: Oct, 1937 - No. 20, May, 1939

1(V9#1-indicia)-Joe Palooka, Mickey Finn (1st app.), The Bungles, Jane Arden, Dixie Dugan (1st app.), Big Top, Ned Brant, Strange As It Seems, & Off the Record strip reprints begin 316.00 950.00 2200.00
2-The Hawk app. (11/37); Goldberg-c 145.00 437.00 975.00
3-Hawks of Seas begins by Eisner, ends #12; The Clock begins; Christmas-c 112.00 337.00 750.00
4,5 83.00 250.00 575.00
6-12: 11-Archie O'Toole by Bud Thomas begins, ends #22 62.00 187.00 425.00
13-Espionage, Starring Black X begins by Eisner, ends #20 70.00 210.00 480.00
14-20 50.00 150.00 350.00

NOTE: *Joe Palooka covers 1, 6, 9, 12, 15, 18.*

FEATURE PRESENTATION, A (Feature Presentations Magazine #6) (Formerly Women in Love) (Also see Startling Terror Tales #11)
Fox Features Syndicate: No. 5, April, 1950

5(#1)-Black Tarantula 40.00 120.00 310.00

FEATURE PRESENTATIONS MAGAZINE (Formerly A Feature Presentation #5; becomes Feature Stories Magazine #3 on)
Fox Features Syndicate: No. 6, July, 1950

6(#2)-Moby Dick; Wood-c 31.00 92.00 215.00

FEATURE STORIES MAGAZINE (Formerly Feature Presentations Mag. #6)
Fox Features Syndicate: No. 3, Aug, 1950 - No. 4, Oct, 1950

3-Jungle Lil, Zegra stories; bondage-c 32.00 96.00 225.00
4 25.00 75.00 175.00

FEDERAL MEN COMICS (See Adventure Comics #32, The Comics Magazine, New Adventure Comics, New Book of Comics, New Comics & Star Spangled Comics #91)
Gerard Publ. Co.: No. 2, 1945 (DC reprints from 1930's)

2-Siegel/Shuster-a; cover redrawn from Det. #9 37.00 11.00 260.00

FELICIA HARDY: THE BLACK CAT
Marvel Comics: July, 1994 - No. 4, Oct, 1994 ($1.50, limited series)

1-4: 1,4-Spider-Man app. 2.00

FELIX'S NEPHEWS INKY & DINKY
Harvey Publications: Sept, 1957 - No. 7, Oct, 1958

1-Cover shows Inky's left eye with 2 pupils 10.00 30.00 60.00
2-7 5.00 15.00 30.00

NOTE: ***Messmer** art in 1-6. **Oriolo** a-1-7.*

FELIX THE CAT (See Cat Tales 3-D, The Funnies, March of Comics #24,36, 51, New Funnies & Popular Comics)
Dell Publ. No. 1-19/Toby No. 20-61/Harvey No. 62-118/Dell No. 1-12: 1943 - No. 118, Nov, 1961; Sept-Nov, 1962 - No. 12, July-Sept, 1965

GD2.0 FN6.0 NM9.4

Four Color 15 67.00 202.00 740.00
Four Color 46('44) 40.00 120.00 440.00
Four Color 77('45) 37.00 112.00 410.00
Four Color 119('46)-All new stories begin 31.00 91.00 335.00
Four Color 135('46) 23.00 68.00 250.00
Four Color 162(9/47) 17.00 52.00 190.00
1(2-3/48)(Dell) 25.00 75.00 275.00
2 14.00 42.00 150.00
3-5 11.00 33.00 120.00
6-19(2-3/51-Dell) 8.00 23.00 85.00
20-30,32,33,36,38-61(6/55)-All Messmer issues.(Toby): 28-(2/52)-Some copies have #29 on cover, #28 on inside (Rare in high grade) 21.00 61.00 225.00
31,34,35-No Messmer-a; Messmer-c only 31,34 7.25 22.00 80.00
37-(100 pgs., 25 ¢, 1/15/53, X-Mas-c, Toby; daily & Sunday-r (rare) 43.00 130.00 475.00
62(8/55)-80,100 (Harvey) 3.80 11.50 40.00
81-99 3.20 9.50 34.00
101-118(11/61): 101-117-Reprints. 118-All new-a 2.20 6.50 24.00
12-269-211(#1, 9-11/62)(Dell)-No Messmer 3.50 10.50 38.00
2-12(7-9/65)(Dell, TV)-No Messmer 2.50 7.50 28.00
3-D Comic Book 1(1953-One Shot, 25¢)-w/glasses 34.00 103.00 290.00
Summer Annual nn ('53, 25¢, 100 pgs., Toby)-Daily & Sunday-r 38.00 113.00 390.00
Winter Annual 2 ('54, 25¢, 100 pgs., Toby)-Daily & Sunday-r 38.00 113.00 390.00

(Special note: Despite the covers on Toby 37 and the Summer Annual above proclaiming "all new stories," they were actually reformatted newspaper strips)

NOTE: ***Otto Messmer** went to work for Universal Film as an animator in 1915 and then worked for the Pat Sullivan animation studio in 1916. He created a black cat in the cartoon short, Feline Follies in 1919 that became known as Felix in the early 1920s. The Felix Sunday strip began Aug. 14, 1923 and continued until Sept. 19, 1943 whjen **Messmer** took the character to Dell (Western Publishing) and began doing Felix comic books, first adapting strips to the comic format. The first all new Felix comic was Four Color #119 in 1946 (#4 in the Dell run). The daily Felix was begun on May 9, 1927 by another artist, but by the following year, **Messmer** did it too. King Features took the daily away from **Messmer** in 1954 and he began to do some of his most dynamic art for Toby Press. The daily was continued by **Joe Oriolo** who drew it until it was discontinued Jan. 9, 1967. **Oriolo** was **Messmer's** assistant for many years and inked some of **Messmer's** pencils through the Toby run, as well as doing some of the stories by himself. Though **Messmer** continued to work for Harvey, his contirubitons were limited, and no all **Messmer** stories appeared after the Toby run until some early Toby reprints were published in the 1990s Harvey revival of the title. 4-Color No. 15, 46, 77 and the Toby Annuals are all daily or Sunday newspaper reprints from the 1930's-1940's drawn by **Otto Messmer**. #101-r/#64; 102-r/#65; 103-r/#67; 104-117-r/#68-81. **Messmer**-a in all Dell/Toby/Harvey issues except #31, 34, 35, 97, 98, 100, 118. **Oriolo** a-20, 31-on.*

FELIX THE CAT (Also see The Nine Lives of...)
Harvey Comics/Gladstone: Sept, 1991 - No. 7, Jan, 1993 ($1.25/$1.50, bi-monthly)

1: 1950s-r/Toby issues by Messmer begins. 1-Inky and Dinky back-up story (produced by Gladstone) 3.00
2-7, Big Book , V2#1 (9/92, $1.95, 52 pgs.) 2.00

FELIX THE CAT AND FRIENDS
Felix Comics: 1992 - No. 4, 1992 ($1.95)

1-Contains Felix trading cards 3.00
2-4 2.00

FELIX THE CAT & HIS FRIENDS (Pat Sullivan's...)
Toby Press: Dec, 1953 - No. 3, 1954 (Indicia title for #2&3 as listed)

1 (Indicia title, "Felix and His Friends," #1 only) 29.00 86.00 200.00
2-3 18.00 54.00 125.00

FELIX THE CAT DIGEST MAGAZINE
Harvey Comics: July, 1992 ($1.75, digest-size, 98 pgs.)

1-Felix, Richie Rich stories 4.00

FELIX THE CAT KEEPS ON WALKIN'
Hamilton Comics: 1991 ($15.95, 8-1/2"x11", 132 pgs.)

Femforce #92 © AC Comics

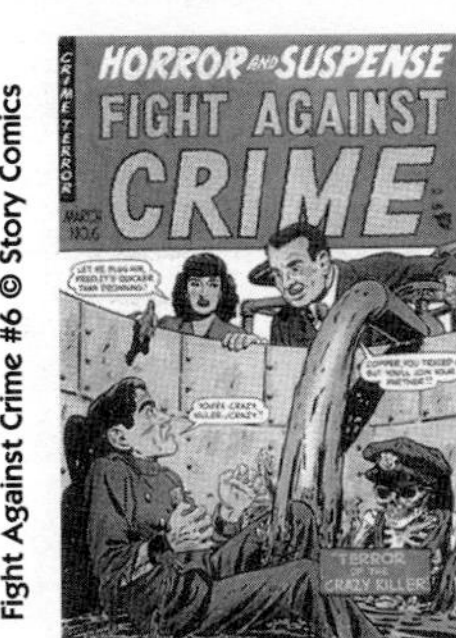

Fight Against Crime #6 © Story Comics

Fight Comics #49 © FH

GD2.0 FN6.0 NM9.4

nn-Reprints 15 Toby Press Felix the Cat and Felix and His Friends stories in new computer color 16.00

FEM FANTASTIQUE
AC Comics: Aug, 1988 ($1.95, B&W)

V2#1-By Bill Black; Betty Page pin-up 2.50

FEMFORCE (Also see Untold Origin of the Femforce)
Americomics: Apr, 1985 - No. 109 (1.75-/2.95, B&W #16-56)

1-Black-a in most; Nightveil, Ms. Victory begin 1.00 3.00 8.00
2 3.00
3-99:125-Origin/1st app. new Ms. Victory. 28-Colt leaves. 29,30-Camilla-r by Mayo from Jungle Comics. 51-Photo-c from movie. 57-Begin color issues. 64-Re-intro Black Phantom. 36 (2.95, 52 pgs.). 44-Contains mini-comic insert, Catman & Kitten #0. 50 (2.95, 52 pgs.)-Contains flexi-disc; origin retold; most AC characters app. 95-Photo-c 3.00
100-($3.95) 4.00
100-($6.90)-Polybagged 7.00
101-109-($4.95) 5.00
Special 1 (Fall, '84)(B&W, 52pgs.)-1st app. Ms. Victory, She-Cat, Blue Bulleteer, Rio Rita & Lady Luger 3.00
Bad Girl Backlash-(12/95, $5.00) 5.00
Frightbook 1 ('92, $2.95, B&W)-Halloween special, In the House of Horror 1 ('89, 2.50, B&W), Night of the Demon 1 ('90, 2.75, B&W), Out of the Asylum Special 1 ('87, B&W, $1.95), Pin-Up Portfolio 3.00

FEMFORCE UP CLOSE
AC Comics: Apr, 1992 - No. 4, 1993 ($2.75, quarterly)

1-4: 1-Stars Nightveil; inside f/c photo from Femforce movie. 2-Stars Stardust. 3-Stars Dragonfly. 4-Stars She-Cat 2.75

FERDINAND THE BULL (See Mickey Mouse Magazine V4#3)
Dell Publishing Co.: 1938 (10¢, large size, some color w/rest B&W)

nn 18.00 54.00 125.00

FERRET
Malibu Comics: Sept, 1992; May, 1993 - No. 10, Feb, 1994 ($1.95)

1-(1992, one-shot) 2.50
1-10: 1-Die-cut-c. 2-4-Collector's Ed. w/poster. 5-Polybagged w/Skycap 2.50
2-4-($1.95)-Newsstand Edition w/different-c 2.00

FEUD
Marvel Comics (Epic Comics/Heavy Hitters): July, 1993 - No. 4, Oct, 1993 ($1.95, limited series)

1-($2.50)-Embossed-c 2.50
2-4 2.00

FIBBER McGEE & MOLLY (Radio)(Also see A-1 Comics)
Magazine Enterprises: No. 25, 1949 (one-shot)

A-1 25 10.00 30.00 65.00

55 DAYS AT PEKING (See Movie Comics)

FICTION ILLUSTRATED
Byron Press Publ.: 1976

1-3: 1-Schlomo Raven; Sutton-a. 2 (128 pgs.)-Starfawn; Stephen Fabian-a. 3-Chandler; new Steranko-a 1.50 4.50 12.00

FIGHT AGAINST CRIME (Fight Against the Guilty #22, 23)
Story Comics: May, 1951 - No. 21, Sept, 1954

1-True crime stories #1-4 32.00 96.00 225.00
2 17.00 51.00 120.00
3,5: 5-Frazetta-a, 1 pg.; content change to horror & suspense 13.00 39.00 90.00
4-Drug story "Hopped Up Killers" 13.50 41.00 95.00
6,7: 6-Used in **POP**, pgs. 83,84 11.50 34.00 80.00
8-Last crime format issue 11.00 33.00 75.00
NOTE: *No. 9-21 contain violent, gruesome stories with blood, dismemberment, decapitation, E.C. style plot twists and several E.C. swipes. Bondage c-4, 6, 18, 19.*
9-11,13 30.00 90.00 210.00
12-Morphine drug story "The Big Dope" 31.00 94.00 220.00
14-Tothish art by Ross Andru; electrocution-c 30.00 90.00 210.00
15-B&W & color illos in **POP** 29.00 86.00 200.00
16-E.C. story swipe/Haunt of Fear #19; Tothish-a by Ross Andru; bondage-c 32.00 96.00 225.00
17-Wildey E.C. swipe/Shock SuspenStories #9; knife through neck-c (1/54) 33.00 99.00 230.00
18,19: 19-Bondage/torture-c 30.00 90.00 210.00
20-Decapitation cover; contains hanging, ax murder, blood & violence 47.00 141.00 375.00
21-E.C. swipe 25.00 75.00 175.00
NOTE: ***Cameron** a-4, 5, 8. **Hollingsworth** a-3-7, 9, 10, 13. **Wildey** a-6, 15, 16.*

FIGHT AGAINST THE GUILTY (Formerly Fight Against Crime)
Story Comics: No. 22, Dec, 1954 - No. 23, Mar, 1955

22-Tothish-a by Ross Andru; Ditko-a; E.C. story swipe; electrocution-c (Last pre-code) 25.00 75.00 175.00
23-Hollingsworth-a 19.00 58.00 135.00

FIGHT COMICS
Fiction House Magazines: Jan, 1940 - No. 83, 11/52; No. 84, Wint, 1952-53; No. 85, Spring, 1953; No. 86, Summer, 1954

1-Origin Spy Fighter, Starring Saber; Jack Dempsey life story; Shark Brodie & Chip Collins begin; Fine-c; Eisner-a 275.00 825.00 2200.00
2-Joe Louis life story; Fine/Eisner-c 109.00 327.00 875.00
3-Rip Regan, the Power Man begins (3/40) 78.00 234.00 625.00
4,5: 4-Fine-c 62.00 186.00 500.00
6-10: 6,7-Powell-c 47.00 141.00 375.00
11-14: Rip Regan ends 41.00 123.00 325.00
15-1st app. Super American plus-c (10/41) 56.00 169.00 450.00
16-Captain Fight begins (12/41); Spy Fighter ends 56.00 169.00 450.00
17,18: Super American ends 44.00 132.00 350.00
19-Captain Fight ends; Senorita Rio begins (6/42, origin & 1st app.); Rip Carson, Chute Trooper begins 44.00 132.00 350.00
20 40.00 120.00 280.00
21-31: 31-Decapitation-c 29.00 86.00 200.00
32-Tiger Girl begins (6/44, 1st app.?) 26.00 77.00 180.00
33-50: 44-Capt. Fight returns. 48-Used in Love and Death by Legman. 49-Jungle-c begin, end #81 23.00 69.00 160.00
51-Origin Tiger Girl; Patsy Pin-Up app. 39.00 116.00 270.00
52-60,62-64-Last Baker issue 19.00 56.00 130.00
61-Origin Tiger Girl retold 23.00 69.00 160.00
65-78: 78-Used in **POP**, pg. 99 17.00 51.00 120.00
79-The Space Rangers app. 17.00 51.00 120.00
80-85: 81-Last jungle-c. 82-85-War-c/stories 15.00 45.00 105.00
86-Two Tigerman stories by Evans-r/Rangers Comics #40,41; Moreira-r/ Rangers Comics #45 15.00 45.00 105.00
NOTE: *Bondage covers, Lingerie, headlights panels are common. Captain Fight by **Kamen**-51-66. Kayo Kirby by **Baker**-#43-64, 67(not by Baker). Senorita Rio by **Kamen**-#57-64; by **Grandenetti**-#65, 66. Tiger Girl by **Baker**-#36-60, 62-64; **Eisner** c-1-3, 5, 10, 11. **Kamen** a-54?, 57? **Tuska** a-1, 5, 8, 10, 21, 29, 34. **Whitman** c-73-84. **Zolnerwich** c-16, 17, 22. Power Man c-5, 6, 9. Super American c-15-17. Tiger Girl c-49-81.*

FIGHT FOR LOVE
United Features Syndicate: 1952 (no month)

nn-Abbie & Slats newspaper-r 10.00 30.00 60.00

FIGHTING AIR FORCE (See United States Fighting Air Force)

FIGHTIN' AIR FORCE (Formerly Sherlock Holmes?; Never Again? War and Attack #54 on)
Charlton Comics: No. 3, Feb, 1956 - No. 53, Feb-Mar, 1966

V1#3 6.70 20.00 40.00
4-10 4.00 12.00 24.00
11(3/58, 68 pgs.) 5.85 17.50 35.00
12 (100 pgs.) 8.35 25.00 50.00
13-30: 13,24-Glanzman-a. 24-Glanzman-c 2.50 7.50 20.00
31-50: 50-American Eagle begins 2.00 6.00 16.00
51-53 1.50 4.50 12.00

FIGHTIN' ARMY (Formerly Soldier and Marine Comics) (See Captain Willy Schultz)

Fighting American #2 © PRIZE

Fighting Leathernecks #2 © TOBY

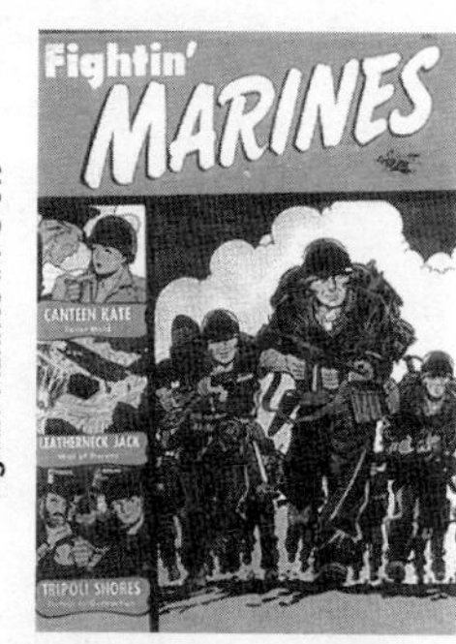

Fightin' Marines #4 © STJ

Charlton Comics: No. 16, 1/56 - No. 127, 12/76; No. 128, 9/77 - No. 172, 11/84

	GD2.0	FN6.0	NM9.4
16	7.70	23.00	45.00
17-19,21-23,25-30	4.00	12.00	24.00
20-Ditko-a	5.85	17.50	35.00
24 (3/58, 68 pgs.)	5.35	16.00	32.00
31-45	2.25	6.75	18.00
46-60	1.75	5.25	14.00
61-74	1.25	3.75	10.00
75-1st The Lonely War of Willy Schultz	1.50	4.50	12.00
76-80: 76-92-The Lonely War of Willy Schultz. 79-Devil Brigade	1.25	3.75	10.00
81-88,91,93-99: 82,83-Devil Brigade	1.10	3.30	9.00
89,90,92-Ditko-a	1.50	4.50	12.00
100	1.50	4.50	12.00
101-127	1.00	2.80	7.00
128-140			5.00
141-165			3.00
166-172-Low print run			4.00
108(Modern Comics-1977)-Reprint			4.00

NOTE: *Aparo c-154. Glanzman a-77-88.* ***Montes/Bache*** *a-48, 49, 51, 69, 75, 76, 170r.*

FIGHTING AMERICAN
Headline Publ./Prize (Crestwood): Apr-May, 1954 - No. 7, Apr-May, 1955

	GD2.0	FN6.0	NM9.4
1-Origin & 1st app. Fighting American & Speedboy (Capt. America & Bucky clones); S&K-c/a(3); 1st super hero satire series	162.00	487.00	1300.00
2-S&K-a(3)	78.00	234.00	625.00
3-5: 3,4-S&K-a(3). 5-S&K-a(2); Kirby/?-a	61.00	184.00	490.00
6-Origin-r (4 pgs.) plus 2 pgs. by S&K	59.00	176.00	470.00
7-Kirby-a	52.00	157.00	420.00

NOTE: ***Simon & Kirby*** *covers on all. 6 is last pre-code issue.*

FIGHTING AMERICAN
Harvey Publications: Oct, 1966 (25¢)

	GD2.0	FN6.0	NM9.4
1-Origin Fighting American & Speedboy by S&K-r; S&K-c/a(3); 1 pg. Neal Adams ad	4.00	12.00	40.00

FIGHTING AMERICAN
DC Comics: Feb, 1994 - No. 6, 1994 ($1.50, limited series)

	GD2.0	FN6.0	NM9.4
1-6			2.00

FIGHTING AMERICAN (Vol. 3)
Awesome Entertainment: Aug, 1997 - No. 2, Oct, 1997 ($2.50)

	GD2.0	FN6.0	NM9.4
Preview-Agent America (pre-lawsuit)	1.00	2.80	7.00
1-Four covers by Liefeld, Churchill, Platt, McGuiness			2.50
1-Platinum Edition, 1-Gold foil Edition			10.00
1-Comic Cavalcade Edition, 2-American Ent. Spice Ed.			4.00
2-Platt-c, 2-Liefeld variant-c			2.50

FIGHTING AMERICAN: DOGS OF WAR
Awesome-Hyperwerks: Sept, 1998 - No. 3 ($2.50)

	GD2.0	FN6.0	NM9.4
Limited Convention Special (7/98, B&W) Platt-a			2.50
1-3-Starlin-s/Platt-a/c			2.50

FIGHTING AMERICAN: RULES OF THE GAME
Awesome Entertainment: Nov, 1997 - No. 3, Mar, 1998 ($2.50, lim. series)

	GD2.0	FN6.0	NM9.4
1-3: 1-Loeb-s/McGuinness-a/c. 2-Flip book with Swat! preview			2.50
1-Liefeld SPICE variant-c, 1-Dynamic Forces Ed.; McGuinness-c			2.50
1-Liefeld Fighting American & cast variant-c			2.50

FIGHTING CARAVANS (See Zane Grey 4-Color 632)

FIGHTING DANIEL BOONE
Avon Periodicals: 1953

	GD2.0	FN6.0	NM9.4
nn-Kinstler-c/a, 22 pgs.	19.00	56.00	130.00
I.W. Reprint #1-Reprints #1 above; Kinstler-c/a; Lawrence/Alascia-a	2.25	6.75	18.00

FIGHTING DAVY CROCKETT (Formerly Kit Carson)
Avon Periodicals: No. 9, Oct-Nov, 1955

	GD2.0	FN6.0	NM9.4
9-Kinstler-c	10.00	30.00	65.00

FIGHTIN' FIVE, THE (Formerly Space War) (Also see The Peacemaker)
Charlton Comics: July, 1964 - No. 41, Jan, 1967; No. 42, Oct, 1981 - No. 49, Dec, 1982

	GD2.0	FN6.0	NM9.4
V2#28-Origin/1st app. Fightin' Five; Montes/Bache-a	4.20	12.60	42.00
29-39,41-Montes/Bache-a in all	2.50	7.50	20.00
40-Peacemaker begins (1st app.)	4.20	12.60	42.00
41-Peacemaker (2nd app.)	2.80	8.40	28.00
42-49: Reprints			4.00

FIGHTING FRONTS!
Harvey Publications: Aug, 1952 - No. 5, Jan, 1953

	GD2.0	FN6.0	NM9.4
1	8.35	25.00	50.00
2-Extreme violence; Nostrand/Powell-a	10.00	30.00	65.00
3-5: 3-Powell-a	5.00	15.00	30.00

FIGHTING INDIAN STORIES (See Midget Comics)

FIGHTING INDIANS OF THE WILD WEST!
Avon Periodicals: Mar, 1952 - No. 2, Nov, 1952

	GD2.0	FN6.0	NM9.4
1-Geronimo, Chief Crazy Horse, Chief Victorio, Black Hawk begin; Larsen-a; McCann-a(2)	15.00	45.00	105.00
2-Kinstler-c & inside-c only; Larsen, McCann-a	10.00	30.00	70.00
100 Pg. Annual (1952, 25¢)-Contains three comics rebound; Geronimo, Chief Crazy Horse, Chief Victorio; Kinstler-c	30.00	90.00	210.00

FIGHTING LEATHERNECKS
Toby Press: Feb, 1952 - No. 6, Dec, 1952

	GD2.0	FN6.0	NM9.4
1- "Duke's Diary"; full pg. pin-ups by Sparling	13.00	39.00	90.00
2-5: 2- "Duke's Diary". 3-5- "Gil's Gals"; full pg. pin-ups	10.00	30.00	65.00
6-(Same as No. 3-5?)	8.35	25.00	50.00

FIGHTING MAN, THE (War)
Ajax/Farrell Publications(Excellent Publ.): May, 1952 - No. 8, July, 1953

	GD2.0	FN6.0	NM9.4
1	11.50	34.00	80.00
2	5.85	17.50	35.00
3-8	5.00	15.00	30.00
Annual 1 (1952, 25¢, 100 pgs.)	21.00	64.00	150.00

FIGHTIN' MARINES (Formerly The Texan; also see Approved Comics)
St. John(Approved Comics)/Charlton Comics No. 14 on:
No. 15, 8/51 - No. 12, 3/53; No. 14, 5/55 - No. 132, 11/76; No. 133, 10/77 - No. 176, 9/84 (No #13?) (Korean war #1-3)

	GD2.0	FN6.0	NM9.4
15(#1)-Matt Baker c/a "Leatherneck Jack"; slightly large size; Fightin' Texan No. 16 & 17?	40.00	120.00	280.00
2-1st Canteen Kate by Baker; slightly large size; partial Baker-c	40.00	120.00	300.00
3-9,11-Canteen Kate by Baker; Baker c-#2,3,5-11; 4-Partial Baker-c	22.00	66.00	155.00
10-Matt Baker-c	10.00	30.00	60.00
12-No Baker-a; Last St. John issue?	4.15	12.50	25.00
14 (5/55; 1st Charlton issue; formerly?)-Canteen Kate by Baker; all stories reprinted from #2	17.00	51.00	120.00
15-Baker-c	8.35	25.00	50.00
16,18-20-Not Baker-c	4.00	11.00	22.00
17-Canteen Kate by Baker	12.00	36.00	85.00
21-24	4.00	11.00	22.00
25-(68 pgs.)(3/58)-Check-a?	7.50	22.50	45.00
26-(100 pgs.)(8/58)-Check-a(5)	10.00	30.00	70.00
27-50	2.80	7.00	14.00
51-81: 78-Shotgun Harker & the Chicken series begin	1.50	4.50	12.00
82-(100 pgs.)	2.80	8.40	28.00
83-85: 85-Last 12¢ issue	1.25	3.75	10.00
86-94: 94-Last 15¢ issue	1.10	3.30	9.00
95-100,122: 122-(1975) Pilot issue for "War" title (Fightin' Marines Presents War)	1.00	3.00	8.00
101-121			5.00
123-140			4.00

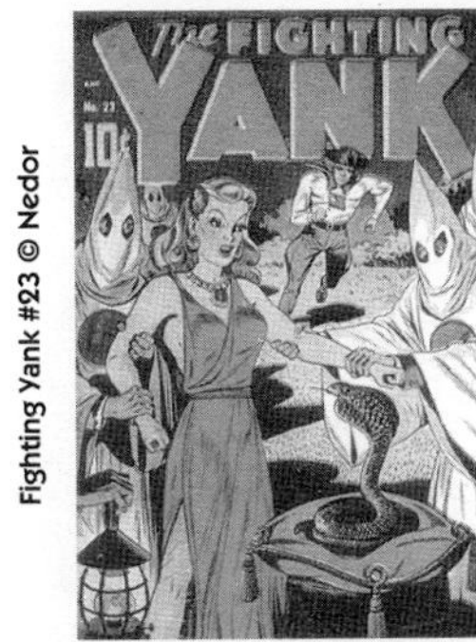

Fighting Yank #23 © Nedor

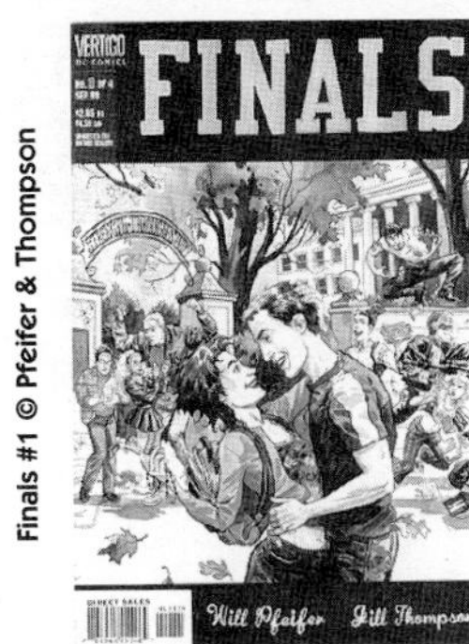

Finals #1 © Pfeifer & Thompson

Firehair Comics #1 © FH

GD2.0 FN6.0 NM9.4 | GD2.0 FN6.0 NM9.4

141-170 3.00
171-176-Low print run 4.00
120(Modern Comics reprint, 1977) 3.00
NOTE: *No. 14 & 16 (CC) reprint St. John issues; No. 16 reprints St. John insignia on cover.* ***Colan*** *a-3, 7.* ***Glanzman*** *c/a-92, 94.* ***Montes/Bache*** *a-48, 53, 55, 64, 65, 72-74, 77-83, 176r.*

FIGHTING MARSHAL OF THE WILD WEST (See The Hawk)

FIGHTIN' NAVY (Formerly Don Winslow)
Charlton Comics: No. 74, 1/56 - No. 125, 4-5/66; No. 126, 8/83 - No. 133, 10/84

	GD2.0	FN6.0	NM9.4
74	3.50	10.50	35.00
75-81	2.50	7.50	24.00
82-Sam Glanzman-a	2.50	7.50	20.00
83-(100 pgs.)	3.20	9.60	32.00
84-99,101: 101-UFO story	2.00	6.00	16.00
100	2.25	6.75	18.00
102-105,106-125('66)	1.50	4.50	12.00
126-133 (1984)-Low print run			4.00

NOTE: ***Montes/Bache*** *a-109.* ***Glanzman*** *a-82, 92, 96, 98, 100, 131r.*

FIGHTING PRINCE OF DONEGAL, THE (See Movie Comics)

FIGHTIN' TEXAN (Formerly The Texan & Fightin' Marines?)
St. John Publishing Co.: No. 16, Sept, 1952 - No. 17, Dec, 1952

	GD2.0	FN6.0	NM9.4
16,17: Tuska-a each. 17-Cameron-c/a	7.50	22.50	45.00

FIGHTING UNDERSEA COMMANDOS (See Undersea Fighting...)
Avon Periodicals: May, 1952 - No. 5, April, 1953 (U.S. Navy frogmen)

	GD2.0	FN6.0	NM9.4
1-Cover title is Undersea Fighting... #1 only	11.50	34.00	80.00
2	9.15	27.00	55.00
3-5: 1,3-Ravielli-c. 4-Kinstler-c	8.35	25.00	50.00

FIGHTING WAR STORIES
Men's Publications/Story Comics: Aug, 1952 - No. 5, 1953

	GD2.0	FN6.0	NM9.4
1	9.15	27.00	55.00
2-5	5.00	15.00	30.00

FIGHTING YANK (See America's Best Comics & Startling Comics)
Nedor/Better Publ./Standard: Sept, 1942 - No. 29, Aug, 1949

	GD2.0	FN6.0	NM9.4
1-The Fighting Yank begins; Mystico, the Wonder Man app; bondage-c	212.00	637.00	1700.00
2	94.00	281.00	750.00
3,4: 4-Schomburg-c begin	69.00	206.00	550.00
5-10: 7-Grim Reaper app. 8,10-Bondage/torture-c	53.00	159.00	425.00
11-20: 11-The Oracle app. 12-Hirohito bondage-c. 15-Bondage/torture-c. 18-The American Eagle app.	44.00	132.00	350.00
21,23,24: 21-Kara, Jungle Princess app. 24-Miss Masque app.	40.00	120.00	320.00
22-Miss Masque-c/story	47.00	141.00	380.00
25-Robinson/Meskin-a; strangulation, lingerie panel; The Cavalier app.	47.00	141.00	380.00
26-29: All-Robinson/Meskin-a. 28-One pg. Williamson-a	40.00	120.00	320.00

NOTE: ***Schomburg (Xela)*** *c-4-29; airbrush-c 28, 29. Bondage c-1, 4, 8, 10, 11, 12, 15, 17.*

FIGHTMAN
Marvel Comics: June, 1993 ($2.00, one-shot, 52 pgs.)
1 2.00

FIGHT THE ENEMY
Tower Comics: Aug, 1966 - No. 3, Mar, 1967 (25¢, 68 pgs.)

	GD2.0	FN6.0	NM9.4
1-Lucky 7 & Mike Manly begin	3.00	9.00	30.00
2-Boris Vallejo, McWilliams-a	2.50	7.50	25.00
3-Wood-a (1/2 pg.); McWilliams, Bolle-a	2.50	7.50	25.00

FILM FUNNIES
Marvel Comics (CPC): Nov, 1949 - No. 2, Feb, 1950 (52 pgs.)

	GD2.0	FN6.0	NM9.4
1-Krazy Krow, Wacky Duck	17.00	51.00	120.00
2-Wacky Duck	13.00	39.00	90.00

FILM STARS ROMANCES
Star Publications: Jan-Feb, 1950 - No. 3, May-June, 1950 (True life stories of movie stars)

	GD2.0	FN6.0	NM9.4
1-Rudy Valentino & Gregory Peck stories; L. B. Cole-c; lingerie panels	40.00	120.00	320.00
2-Liz Taylor/Robert Taylor photo-c & true life story	36.00	107.00	250.00
3-Douglas Fairbanks story; photo-c	24.00	73.00	170.00

FINAL CYCLE, THE
Dragon's Teeth Productions: July, 1987 - No. 4, 1988 (Limited series)
1-4 2.00

FINAL NIGHT, THE (See DC related titles and Parallax: Emerald Night)
DC Comics: Nov, 1996 - No. 4, Nov, 1996 ($1.95, weekly limited series)
1-4: Kesel-s/Immonen-a(p) in all. 4-Parallax's final acts 3.50
Preview 2.00
TPB-(1998, $12.95) r/#1-4, Parallax: Emerald Night #1, and preview 13.00

FINALS
DC Comics (Vertigo): Sept, 1999 - No. 4, Dec, 1999 ($2.95, limited series)
1-4-Will Pfeifer-s/Jill Thompson-a 3.00

FIRE
Caliber Press: 1993 - No. 2, 1993 ($2.95, B&W, limited series, 52 pgs.)
1,2-Brian Michael Bendis 3.00
TPB (1999, $9.95) Restored reprint of series 10.00

FIREARM (Also see Codename: Firearm, Freex #15, Night Man #4 & Prime #10)
Malibu Comics (Ultraverse): Sept, 1993 - No. 18, Mar, 1995 ($1.95/$2.50)
0 ($14.95)-Came w/ video containing 1st half of story (comic contains 2nd half); 1st app. Duet 15.00
1,3-6: 1-James Robinson scripts begin; Cully Hamner-a; Howard Chaykin-c; 1st app Alec Swan. 3-Intro The Sportsmen; Chaykin-c. 4-Break-Thru x-over; Chaykin-c. 5-1st app. Ellen (Swan's girlfriend);2 pg. origin of Prime. 6-Prime app. (story cont'd in Prime #10);Brereton-c 2.00
1-($2.50)-Newsstand edition polybagged w/card 2.50
1-Ultra Limited silver foil-c 5.00
2 ($2.50, 44 pgs.)-Hardcase app.;Chaykin-c; Rune flip-c/story by B. Smith (3 pgs.) 2.50
7-10,12-17: 12-The Rafferty Saga begins, ends #18; 1st app. Rafferty 15-Night Man & Freex app. 17-Swan marries Ellen 2.00
11-($3.50, 68 pgs.)-Flip book w/Ultraverse Premiere #5 3.50
18-Death of Rafferty; Chaykin-c 2.50
NOTE: ***Brereton*** *c-6.* ***Chaykin*** *c-1-4, 14, 16, 18.* ***Hamner*** *a-1-4.* ***Herrera*** *a-12.* ***James Robinson*** *scripts-0-18.*

FIRE BALL XL5 (See Steve Zodiac & The ...)

FIREBRAND (Also see Showcase '96 #4)
DC Comics: Feb, 1996 - No. 9, Oct, 1996 ($1.75)
1-9: Brian Augustyn scripts; Velluto-c/a in all. 9-Daredevil #319-c/swipe 2.00

FIRE CHIEF AND THE SAFE OL' FIREFLY, THE
National Board of Fire Underwriters: 1952 (16 pgs.) (Safety brochure given away at schools) (produced by American Visuals Corp.)(Eisner)

	GD2.0	FN6.0	NM9.4
nn-(Rare) Eisner-c/a	50.00	150.00	400.00

FIRE FROM HEAVEN
Image Comics (WildStorm Productions): Mar, 1996 ($2.50)
1,2-Moore-s 2.50

FIREHAIR COMICS (Formerly Pioneer West Romances #3-6; also see Rangers Comics)
Fiction House Magazines (Flying Stories): Winter/48-49; No. 2, Wint/49-50; No. 7, Spr/51 - No. 11, Spr/52

	GD2.0	FN6.0	NM9.4
1-Origin Firehair	55.00	165.00	440.00
2	27.00	81.00	190.00
7-11	18.00	54.00	125.00
I.W. Reprint 8-(nd)-Kinstler-c; reprints Rangers #57; Dr. Drew story by Grandenetti	2.50	7.50	25.00

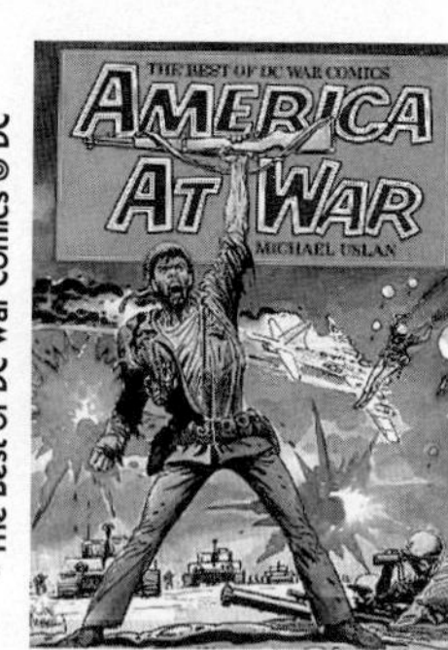

Fireside Book Series: America at War - The Best of DC War Comics © DC

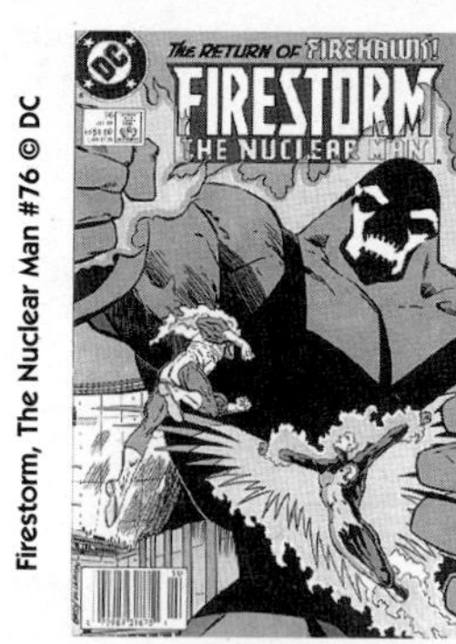

Firestorm, The Nuclear Man #76 © DC

First Love Illustrated #2 © HARV

		GD2.0	FN6.0	NM9.4

FIRESIDE BOOK SERIES (Hard and soft cover editions)
Simon and Schuster: 1974 - 1980 (130-260 pgs.), Square bound, color

		GD2.0	FN6.0	NM9.4
Amazing Spider-Man, The, 1979,	HC	7.00	21.00	75.00
130 pgs., $3.95, Bob Larkin-c	SC	4.50	13.50	45.00
America At War–The Best of DC War	HC	7.00	21.00	75.00
Comics, 1979, $6.95, 260 pgs, Kubert-c	SC	5.00	15.00	55.00
Bring On The Bad Guys (Origins of the	HC	6.50	19.50	70.00
Marvel Comics Villains) 1976, $6.95, 260 pgs.; Romita-c	SC	4.50	13.50	452.00
Captain America, Sentinel of Libertv,1979,	HC	5.50	16.50	60.00
130 pgs., $12.95, Cockrum-c	SC	3.50	10.50	35.00
Doctor Strange Master of the Mystic	HC	6.50	19.50	70.00
Arts, 1980, 130 pgs.	SC	4.50	13.50	45.00
Fantastic Four, The, 1979, 130 pgs.	HC	5.50	16.50	60.00
	SC	3.50	10.50	35.00
Heart Throbs–The Best of DC Romance	HC	13.00	40.00	145.00
Comics, 1979, 260 pgs., $6.,95	SC	8.50	26.00	95.00
Incredible Hulk, The, 1978, 260 pgs.	HC	5.50	16.50	60.00
(8 1/4" x 11")	SC	3.50	10.50	35.00
Marvel's Greatest Superhero Battles,	HC	9.00	27.00	100.00
1978, 260 pgs., $6.95, Romita-c	SC	5.00	15.00	55.00
Mysteries in Space, 1980, $7,95, Anderson-c. r-DC sci/fi stories	SC	4.50	13.50	50.00

Origins of Marvel Comics, 1974, 260 pgs., $5.95. r-covers & origins of Fantastic

Four, Hulk, Spider-Man, Thor,	HC	5.50	16.50	60.00
& Doctor Strange	SC	3.50	10.50	35.00
Silver Surfer, The, 1978, 130 pgs.,	HC	6.50	19.50	70.00
$4.95, Norem-c	SC	4.50	13.50	45.00

Son of Origins of Marvel Comics, 1975, 260 pgs., $6.95, Romita-c. Reprints

covers & origins of X-Men, Iron Man,	HC	5.50	16.50	60.00
Avengers, Daredevil, Silver Surfer	SC	3.50	8.70	35.00
Superhero Women, The–Featuring the	HC	7.50	23.00	85.00
Fabulous Females of Marvel Comics, 1977, 260 pgs., $6.95, Romita-c	SC	5.50	16.50	55.00

Note: Prices listed are for 1st printings. Later printings are worth 30% less.

FIRESTAR
Marvel Comics Group: Mar, 1986 - No. 4, June, 1986 (75¢)(From Spider-Man TV series)

1,2: 1-X-Men & New Mutants app. 2-Wolverine-c (not real Wolverine?); Art Adams-a(p) 3.00
3,4: 3-Art Adams/Sienkiewicz-c. 4-B. Smith-c 2.00

FIRESTONE (See Donald And Mickey Merry Christmas)

FIRESTORM (See Cancelled Comic Cavalcade, DC Comics Presents, Flash #289, The Fury of... & Justice League of America #179)
DC Comics: March, 1978 - No. 5, Oct-Nov, 1978

1,5: 1-Origin & 1st app. 2.40 6.00
2-4: 2-Origin Multiplex. 3-Origin & 1st app. Killer Frost. 4-1st app. Hyena 4.00

FIRESTORM, THE NUCLEAR MAN (Formerly Fury of Firestorm)
DC Comics: No. 65, Nov, 1987 - No. 100, Aug, 1990

65-99: 66-1st app. Zuggernaut; Firestorm vs. Green Lantern. 71-Death of Capt. X. 67,68-Millennium tie-ins. 83-1st new look 2.00
100-($2.95, 68 pgs.) 3.00
Annual 5 (10/87)-1st app. new Firestorm 2.00

FIRST ADVENTURES
First Comics: Dec, 1985 - No. 5, Apr, 1986 ($1.25)

1-5: Blaze Barlow, Whisper & Dynamo Joe in all 2.00

FIRST AMERICANS, THE
Dell Publishing Co.: No. 843, Sept, 1957

Four Color 843-Marsh-a 8.00 25.00 90.00

FIRST CHRISTMAS, THE (3-D)
Fiction House Magazines (Real Adv. Publ. Co.): 1953 (25¢, 8-1/4x10-1/4", oversize)(Came w/glasses)

nn-(Scarce)-Kelly Freas painted-c; Biblical theme, birth of Christ; Nativity-c 32.00 96.00 225.00

FIRST COMICS GRAPHIC NOVEL
First Comics: Jan, 1984 - No. 21? (52pgs./176 pgs., high quality paper)

1,2: 1-Beowulf ($5.95)(both printings). 2-Time Beavers 7.00
3($11.95, 100 pgs.)-American Flagg! Hard Times (2nd printing exists) 14.00
4-Nexus ($6.95)-r/B&W 1-3 10.00
5,7: 5-The Enchanted Apples of Oz ($7.95, 52 pgs.)-Intro by Harlan Ellison (1986). 7-The Secret Island Of Oz ($7.95) 9.00
6-Elric of Melnibone ($14.95, 176 pgs.)-Reprints with new color 16.00
8,10,14,18: Teenage Mutant Ninja Turtles Book I -IV ($9.95, 132 pgs.)-8-r/ TMNT #1-3 in color w/12 pgs. new-a; origin. 10-r/TMNT #4-6 in color. 14-r/ TMNT #7,8 in color plus new 12 pg. story. 18-r/TMNT #10,11 plus 3 pg. fold-out 10.00
9-Time 2: The Epiphany by Chaykin (11/86, $7.95, 52pgs. - indicia says #8) 8.00
11-Sailor On The Sea of Fate ($14.95) 15.00
nn-Time 2: The Satisfaction of Black Mariah (9/87) 8.00
12-American Flagg! Southern Comfort (10/87, $11.95) 12.00
13,15-17,19,21: 13-The Ice King Of Oz. 15-Hex Breaker: Badger ($7.95). 16-The Forgotten Forest of Oz ($8.95). 17-Mazinger (68 pgs., $8.95).19-The Original Nexus Graphic Novel ($7.95, 104 pgs.)-Reprints First Comics Graphic Novel #4 ($7.95). 21-Elric, The Weird of the White Wolf; r/#1-5 9.00
20-American Flagg!: State of the Union ($11.95, 96 pgs.); r/A.F. 7-9 14.00
NOTE: *Most or all issues have been reprinted.*

1ST FOLIO (The Joe Kubert School Presents...)
Pacific Comics: Mar, 1984 ($1.50, one-shot)

1-Joe Kubert-c/a(2 pgs.); Adam & Andy Kubert-a 2.00

1ST ISSUE SPECIAL
National Periodical Publications: Apr, 1975 - No. 13, Apr, 1976 (Tryout series)

1,5,6: 1-Intro. Atlas; Kirby-c/a/script. 5-Manhunter; Kirby-c/a/script. 6-Dingbats 2.40 6.00
2,7,9,12: 2-Green Team (see Cancelled.Comic Cavalcade). 7-The Creeper by Ditko (c/a). 9-Dr. Fate; Kubert-c. 12-Origin/1st app. "Blue" Starman (2nd app. in Starman, 2nd Series #3); Kubert-c. 2.40 6.00
3,4,10,11: 3-Metamorpho by Ramona Fradon. 4-Lady Cop. 10-The Outsiders. 11-Code Name: Assassin; Grell-c. 5.00
8,13: 8-Origin/1st app. The Warlord; Grell-c/a (11/75). 13-Return of the New Gods; Darkseid app.; 1st new costume Orion; predates New Gods #12 by more than a year 1.50 4.50 12.00

FIRST KISS
Charlton Comics: Dec, 1957 - No. 40, Jan, 1965

V1#1	3.50	10.50	35.00
V1#2-10	2.50	7.50	22.00
11-40	1.50	4.50	12.00

FIRST LOVE ILLUSTRATED
Harvey Publications(Home Comics)(True Love): 2/49 - No. 9, 6/50; No. 10, 1/51 - No. 86, 3/58; No. 87, 9/58 - No. 88, 11/58; No. 89, 11/62, No. 90, 2/63

1-Powell-a(2)	17.00	51.00	120.00
2-Powell-a	10.00	30.00	60.00
3-"Was I Too Fat To Be Loved" story	10.00	30.00	60.00
4-10	5.85	17.50	35.00
11-30: 13-"I Joined a Teen-age Sex Club" story. 30-Lingerie panel	4.25	13.00	26.00
31-34,37,39-49: 49-Last pre-code (2/55)	4.00	10.00	20.00
35-Used in **SOTI**, illo "The title of this comic book is First Love"	18.00	54.00	125.00
36-Communism story, "Love Slaves"	5.85	17.50	35.00

First Romance Magazine #2 © HARV

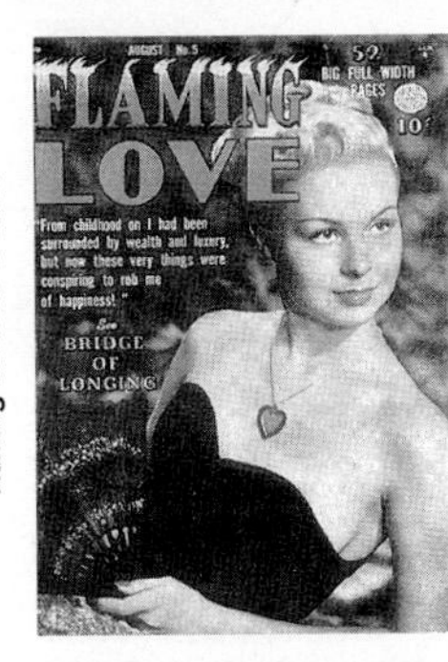

Flaming Love #5 © QUA

The Flash #137 © DC

GD2.0 FN6.0 NM9.4

	GD2.0	FN6.0	NM9.4
38-Nostrand-a	5.85	17.50	35.00
50-66,71-90	3.60	9.00	18.00
67-70-Kirby-c	4.00	12.00	24.00

NOTE: ***Disbrow*** *a-13.* ***Orlando*** *c-87.* ***Powell*** *a-1, 3-5, 7, 10, 11, 13-17, 19-24, 26-29, 33,35-41, 43, 45, 46, 50, 54, 55, 57, 58, 61-63, 65, 71-73, 76, 79r, 82, 84, 88.*

FIRSTMAN
Image Comics: June, 1997 ($2.50)

1 Snyder-s/ Andy Smith-a 2.50

FIRST MEN IN THE MOON (See Movie Comics)

FIRST ROMANCE MAGAZINE
Home Comics(Harvey Publ.)/True Love: 8/49 - #6, 6/50; #7, 6/51 - #50, 2/58; #51, 9/58 - #52, 11/58

	GD2.0	FN6.0	NM9.4
1	14.00	43.00	100.00
2	8.35	25.00	50.00
3-5	6.70	20.00	40.00
6-10,28: 28-Nostrand-a(Powell swipe)	5.35	16.00	32.00
11-20	4.00	12.00	24.00
21-27,29-32: 32-Last pre-code issue (2/55)	4.00	12.00	20.00
33-40,44-52	3.20	8.00	16.00
41-43-Kirby-c	4.00	12.00	24.00

NOTE: ***Powell*** *a-1-5, 8-10, 14, 18, 20-22, 24, 25, 28, 36, 46, 48, 51.*

FIRST TRIP TO THE MOON (See Space Adventures No. 20)

FISH POLICE (Inspector Gill of the...#2, 3)
Fishwrap Productions/Comico V2#5-17/Apple Comics #18 on: Dec, 1985 - No. 11, Nov, 1987 ($1.50, B&W); V2#5, April, 1988 - V2#17, May, 1989 ($1.75, color) No. 18, Aug, 1989 - No. 26, Dec, 1990 ($2.25, B&W)

1-11, 1(5/86),2-2nd print, V2#5-17-(Color): V2#5-11. 12-17, new-a, 18-26 ($2.25-c, B&W) 18-Origin Inspector Gill 2.50
Special 1($2.50, 7/87, Comico) 2.50
Graphic Novel: Hairballs (1987, $9.95, TPB) r/#1-4 in color 10.00

FISH POLICE
Marvel Comics: V2#1, Oct, 1992 - No. 6, Mar, 1993 ($1.25)

V2#1-6: 1-Hairballs Saga begins; r/#1 (1985) 2.00

5 CENT COMICS (Also see Whiz Comics)
Fawcett Publ.: Feb, 1940 (8 pgs., reg. size, B&W)

1 (nn-on c) 1st app. Dan Dare 500.00 1500.00 4800.00

NOTE: Only 2 known copies, in GD and NM condition. The NM copy sold in 1995 for $3000 and again in 2000 for $4800. A promo comic, same as ***Flash*** & ***Thrill Comics***.

5-STAR SUPER-HERO SPECTACULAR (See DC Special Series No. 1)

FLAME, THE (See Big 3 & Wonderworld Comics)
Fox Features Synd.: Sum, 1940 - No. 8, Jan, 1942 (#1,2: 68 pgs; #3-8: 44 pgs.)

	GD2.0	FN6.0	NM9.4
1-Flame stories reprinted from Wonderworld #5-9; origin The Flame; Lou Fine-a (36 pgs.), r/Wonderworld #3,10	306.00	918.00	2700.00
2-Fine-a(2); Wing Turner by Tuska	131.00	394.00	1050.00
3-8: 3-Powell-a	87.00	262.00	700.00

FLAME, THE (Formerly Lone Eagle)
Ajax/Farrell Publications (Excellent Publ.): No. 5, Dec-Jan, 1954-55 - No. 3, April-May, 1955

	GD2.0	FN6.0	NM9.4
5(#1)-1st app. new Flame	40.00	120.00	320.00
2,3	29.00	86.00	200.00

FLAMING CARROT (...Comics #6? on; see Anything Goes, Cerebus, Teenage Mutant Ninja Turtles/Flaming Carrot Crossover & Visions)
Aardvark-Vanaheim/Renegade Press #6-17/Dark Horse #18 on: 5/84 - No. 5, 1/85; No. 6, 3/85 - Present? ($1.70/$2.00, B&W)

	GD2.0	FN6.0	NM9.4
1-Bob Burden story/art	4.00	12.00	40.00
2	2.50	7.50	20.00
3	1.75	5.25	14.00
4-6	1.25	3.75	10.00
7-9	1.00	2.80	7.00
10-12			5.00
13-15			3.00
15-Variant without cover price			5.00
16-(6/87) 1st app. Mystery Men			5.00
17-20: 18-1st Dark Horse issue			3.50
21-23,25: 25-Contains trading cards; TMNT app.			2.50
24-(2.50, 52 pgs.)-10th anniversary issue			2.75
26-28: 26-Begin $2.25-c. 26,27-Teenage Mutant Ninja Turtles x-over. 27-Todd McFarlane-c			2.50
29-31-(2.50-c)			2.75
Annual 1(1/97, $5.00)			5.00
... :The Wild Shall Wild Remain (1997, $17.95, TPB) r/#4-11			18.00

FLAMING CARROT COMICS (Also see Junior Carrot Patrol)
Killian Barracks Press: Summer-Fall, 1981 ($1.95, one shot) (Lg size, 8-1/2x11")

1-Bob Burden-c/a/scripts; serially numbered to 6500 4.50 13.50 50.00

FLAMING LOVE
Quality Comics Group (Comic Magazines): Dec, 1949 - No. 6, Oct, 1950 (Photo covers #2-6) (52 pgs.)

	GD2.0	FN6.0	NM9.4
1-Ward-c/a (9 pgs.)	37.00	111.00	260.00
2	16.00	47.00	110.00
3-Ward-a (9 pgs.); Crandall-a	25.00	75.00	175.00
4-6: 4-Gustavson-a	13.50	41.00	95.00

FLAMING WESTERN ROMANCES (Formerly Target Western Romances)
Star Publications: No. 3, Mar-Apr, 1950

3-Robert Taylor, Arlene Dahl photo on-c with biographies inside; L. B. Cole-c 39.00 116.00 270.00

FLARE (Also see Champions for 1st app. & League of Champions)
Hero Comics/Hero Graphics Vol. 2 on: Nov, 1988 - No. 3, Jan, 1989 ($2.75, color, 52 pgs); V2#1, Nov, 1990 - No. 7, Nov, 1991 ($2.95/$3.50, color, mature, 52 pgs.);V2#8, Oct, 1992 - No. 16, Feb, 1994 ($3.50/$3.95, B&W, 36 pgs.)

V1#1-3, V2#1-16: 5-Eternity Smith returns. 6-Intro The Tigress 4.00
Annual 1(1992, $4.50, B&W, 52 pgs.)-Champions-r 4.50

FLARE ADVENTURES
Hero Graphics: Feb, 1992 - No. 12, 1993? ($3.50/$3.95)

1 (90¢, color, 20 pgs.) 2.00
2-12-Flip books w/Champions Classics 4.00

FLASH, THE (See Adventure, The Brave and the Bold, Crisis On Infinite Earths, DC Comics Presents, DC Special, DC Special Series, DC Super-Stars, The Greatest Flash Stories Ever Told, Green Lantern, Impulse, JLA, Justice League of America, Showcase, Spped Force, Super Team Family, Titans & World's Finest)

FLASH, THE (1st Series)(Formerly Flash Comics)(See Showcase #4,8,13,14)
National Periodical Publ./DC: No. 105, Feb-Mar, 1959 - No. 350, Oct, 1985

	GD2.0	FN6.0	VF8.0	NM9.4
105-(2-3/59)-Origin Flash(retold), & Mirror Master (1st app.)	311.00	933.00	2490.00	5600.00

	GD2.0	FN6.0	NM9.4
106-Origin Grodd & Pied Piper; Flash's 1st visit to Gorilla City; begin Grodd the Super Gorilla trilogy (Scarce)	125.00	375.00	1500.00
107-Grodd trilogy, part 2	67.00	200.00	800.00
108-Grodd trilogy ends	56.00	169.00	675.00
109-2nd app. Mirror Master	41.00	123.00	500.00
110-Intro/origin The Weather Wizard & Kid Flash who later becomes Flash in Crisis On Infinite Earths #12; begin Kid Flash trilogy, ends #112 (also in #114,116,118)	104.00	312.00	1250.00
111-2nd Kid Flash tryout; Cloud Creatures	33.00	100.00	365.00
112-Origin & 1st app. Elongated Man (4-5/60); also apps. in #115,119,130	39.00	117.00	430.00
113-Origin & 1st app. Trickster	33.00	100.00	365.00
114-Captain Cold app. (see Showcase #8)	27.00	81.00	270.00
115,116,118-120: 119-Elongated Man marries Sue Dearborn. 120-Flash & Kid Flash team-up for 1st time	21.50	65.00	215.00

117-Origin & 1st app. Capt. Boomerang; 1st & only S.A. app. Winky Blinky &

The Flash #165 © DC

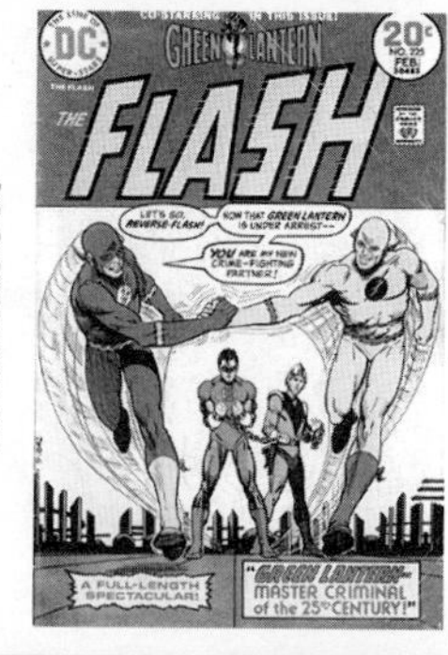

The Flash #225 © DC

The Flash (2nd series) #150 © DC

GD2.0 FN6.0 NM9.4

Noddy 28.00 84.00 280.00

121,122: 122-Origin & 1st app. The Top 16.00 48.00 160.00

123-(9/61)-Re-intro. Golden Age Flash; origins of both Flashes; 1st mention of an Earth II where DC G. A. heroes live 100.00 300.00 1200.00

124-Last 10¢ issue 13.00 39.00 130.00

125-128,130: 127-Return of Grodd-c/story. 128-Origin & 1st app. Abra Kadabra 13.00 39.00 130.00

129-2nd G.A. Flash x-over; J.S.A. cameo in flashback (1st S.A. app. G.A. Green Lantern, Hawkman, Atom, Black Canary & Dr. Mid-Nite) 29.00 87.00 290.00

131-136,138,140: 130-(7/62)-1st Gauntlet of Super-Villains (Mirror Master, Capt. Cold, The Top, Capt. Boomerang & Trickster). 131-Early Green Lantern x-over (9/62). 135-1st app. of Kid Flash's yellow costume (3/63). 136-1st Dexter Miles. 140-Origin & 1st app. Heat Wave 10.50 32.00 105.00

137-G.A. Flash x-over; J.S.A. cameo (1st S.A. app.)(1st real app. since 2-3/51); 1st S.A. app. Vandal Savage & Johnny Thunder; JSA team decides to re-form 40.00 120.00 415.00

139-Origin & 1st app. Prof. Zoom 11.50 34.00 115.00

141-150: 142-Trickster app. 9.00 27.00 90.00

151-Engagement of Barry Allen & Iris West; G.A. Flash vs. The Shade. 11.50 34.00 115.00

152-159 6.50 19.50 65.00

160-(80-Pg. Giant G-21); G.A. Flash & Johnny Quick-r 9.00 27.00 90.00

161-168,170: 165-Barry Allen weds Iris West. 167-New facts about Flash's origin. 168-Green Lantern-c/story. 170-Dr. Mid-Nite, Dr. Fate, G.A. Flash x-over 6.00 18.00 60.00

169-(80-Pg. Giant G-34)-New facts about origin 9.00 27.00 90.00

171-174,176,177,179,180: 171-JLA, Green Lantern, Atom flashbacks. 173-G.A. Flash x-over. 174-Barry Allen reveals I.D. to wife. 179-(5/68)-Flash travels to Earth-Prime and meets DC editor Julie Schwartz; 1st unnamed app. Earth-Prime (See Justice League of America #123 for 1st named app. & 3rd app. overall) 5.50 16.50 55.00

175-2nd Superman/Flash race (12/67) (See Superman #199 & World's Finest #198,199); JLA cameo; gold kryptonite used (on J'onn J'onzz impersonating Superman) 15.00 45.00 150.00

178-(80-Pg. Giant G-46) 7.50 22.50 75.00

181-186,188,189: 186-Re-intro. Sargon. 189-Last 12¢-c 3.20 9.60 32.00

187,196: (68-Pg. Giants G-58, G-70) 5.00 15.00 50.00

190-195,197-199 3.20 9.60 32.00

200 3.80 11.40 38.00

201-204,206,207: 201-New G.A. Flash story. 206-Elongated Man begins 207-Last 15¢ issue 2.50 7.50 20.00

205-(68-Pg. Giant G-82) 3.80 11.40 38.00

208-213-(52 pg.): 211-G.A. Flash origin-r/#104. 213-Reprints #137 2.50 7.50 22.00

214-DC 100 Page Super Spectacular DC-11; origin Metal Men-r/Showcase #37; never before published G.A. Flash story.
(see DC 100 pg. Super Spec. #11 for price)

215 (52 pgs.)-Flash-r/Showcase #4; G.A. Flash x-over, continued in #216 3.00 9.00 30.00

216,220: 220-1st app. Turtle since Showcase #4 2.25 6.75 18.00

217-219: Neal Adams-a in all. 217-Green Lantern/Green Arrow series begins (9/72); 2nd G.L. & G.A. team-up series (see Green Lantern #76). 219-Last Green Arrow 2.60 7.80 26.00

221-225,227,228,230,231,233: 222-G. Lantern x-over. 228-(7-8/74)-Flash writer Cary Bates travels to Earth-One & meets Flash, Iris Allen & Trickster; 2nd unnamed app. Earth-Prime (See Justice League of America #123 for 1st named app. & 3rd app. overall) 1.50 4.50 12.00

226-Neal Adams-p 1.75 5.25 14.00

229,232-(100 pg. issues)-G.A. Flash-r & new-a 3.00 9.00 30.00

234-250: 235-Green Lantern x-over. 243-Death of The Top. 245-Origin The Floronic Man in Green Lantern back-up, ends #246. 246-Last Green Lantern. 250-Intro Golden Glider 1.00 3.00 8.00

251-288,290: 256-Death of The Top retold. 265-267-(44 pgs.). 267-Origin of Flash's uniform. 270-Intro The Clown. 275,276-Iris West Allen dies. 286-Intro/origin Rainbow Raider 5.00

289-1st Perez DC art (Firestorm); new Firestorm back-up series begins (9/80), ends #304 1.00 2.80 7.00

291-299,301-305: 291-1st app. Saber-Tooth (villain). 295-Gorilla Grodd-c/story. 298-Intro/origin new Shade. 301-Atomic bomb-c. 303-The Top returns. 304-Intro/origin Colonel Computron; 305-G.A. Flash x-over 4.00

300-(52 pgs.)-Origin Flash retold; 25th ann. issue 5.00

306-349: 306-Dr. Fate by Giffen in all. 309-Origin Flash retold. 318-323-Creeper back-ups. 323,324-Two part Flash vs. Flash story. 324-Death of Reverse Flash (Professor Zoom). 328-Iris West Allen's death retold. 344-Origin Kid Flash 3.00

350-Double size ($1.25) Final issue 5.00

Annual 1(10-12/63, 84 pgs.)-Origin Elongated Man & Kid Flash-r; origin Grodd; G.A. Flash-r 36.00 108.00 395.00

The Life Story of the Flash (1997, $19.95, Hardcover) "Iris Allen's" chronicle of Barry Allen's life; comic panels w/additional text; Waid & Augustyn-s/ Kane & Staton-a/Orbik painted-c 20.00

The Life Story of the Flash (1998, $12.95, Softcover) New Orbik-c 13.00

NOTE: ***N. Adams*** *c-194, 195, 203, 204, 206-208, 211, 213, 215, 226p, 246.* ***M. Anderson*** *c-165, a(i)-195, 200-204, 206-208.* ***Austin*** *a-233i, 234i, 246i.* ***Buckler*** *a-271p, 272p; c(p)-247-250, 252, 253p, 255, 256p, 258, 262, 265-267, 269-271.* ***Giffen*** *a-306-313p; c-310p, 315.* ***Giordano*** *a-226i.* ***Sid Greene*** *a-167-174i, 229i(r).* ***Grell*** *a-237p, 238p, 240-243p; c-236.* ***Heck*** *a-198p.* ***Infantino/Anderson*** *a-135. c-135, 170-174, 192, 200, 201, 328-330.* ***Infantino/Giella*** *c-105-112, 163, 164, 166-168.* ***G. Kane*** *a-195p, 197-199p, 229r, 232r; c-197-199, 312p.* ***Kubert*** *a-108p, 215i(r); c-189-191.* ***Lopez*** *c-272.* ***Meskin*** *a-229r, 232r.* ***Perez*** *a-289-293p; c-293.* ***Starlin*** *a-294-296p.* ***Staton*** *c-263p, 264p. Green Lantern x-over-131, 143, 168, 171, 191.*

FLASH (2nd Series)(See Crisis on Infinite Earths #12 and Justice League Europe)
DC Comics: June, 1987 - Present (75¢-$1.99)

1-Guice-c/a begins; New Teen Titans app. 1.25 3.75 10.00

2-10: 3-Intro. Kilgore. 5-Intro. Speed McGee. 7-1st app. Blue Trinity. 8,9-Millennium tie-ins. 9-1st app. The Chunk 4.00

11-61: 12-Free extra 16 pg. Dr. Light story. 19-Free extra 16 pg. Flash story. 28-Capt. Cold app. 29-New Phantom Lady app. 40-Dr. Alchemy app. 50-($1.75, 52 pgs.) 2.50

62-78,80: 62-Flash: Year One begins, ends #65. 65-Last $1.00-c. 66-Aquaman app. 69,70-Green Lantern app. 70-Gorilla Grodd story ends. 73-Re-intro Barry Allen & begin saga ("Barry Allen's" true ID revealed in #78). 76-Re-intro of Max Mercury (Quality Comics' Quicksilver), not in uniform until #77. 80-($1.25-c) Regular Edition 4.00

79,80 ($2.50): 79-(68 pgs.) Barry Allen saga ends. 80-Foil-c 5.00

81-91,93,94,0,95-99,101: 81,82-Nightwing & Starfire app. 84-Razer app. 94-Zero Hour. 0-(10/94). 95-"Terminal Velocity" begins, ends #100. 96,98,99-Kobra app. 97-Origin Max Mercury; Chillblaine app. 4.00

92-1st Impulse 1.25 3.75 10.00

100 ($2.50)-Newstand edition; Kobra & JLA app. 4.00

100 ($3.50)-Foil-c edition; Kobra & JLA app. 5.00

102-131: 102-Mongul app.; begin-$1.75-c. 105-Mirror Master app. 107-Shazam app. 108-"Dead Heat" begins; 1st app. Savitar. 109-"Dead Heat" Pt. 2 (cont'd in Impulse #10). 110-"Dead Heat" Pt. 4 (cont'd in Impulse #11). 11-"Dead Heat" finale; Savitar disappears into the Speed Force; John Fox cameo (2nd app.). 112-"Race Against Time" begins, ends #118; re-intro John Fox; intro new Chillblaine. 113-Tornado Twins app. 119-Final Night x-over 127-129-Rogue's Gallery & Neron. 128,129-JLA-app.130-Morrison & Millar-s begin 2.00

132-150: 135-GL & GA app. 142-Wally marries Linda; Waid-s return. 144-Cobalt Blue origin. 145-Chain Lightning begins.147-Professor Zoom-c/app. 149-Barry Allen app. 150-($2.95) Final showdown with Cobalt Blue 3.00

151-154: 151-Casey-s. 152-New Flash-c 2.00

#1,000,000 (11/98) 853rd Century x-over 2.00

Annual 1-7,9: 2-('87-'94,'96, 68 pgs), 3-Gives history of G.A.,S.A., & Modern Age Flash in text. 4-Armaggedon 2001. 5-Eclipso-c/story. 7-Elseworlds story. 9-Legends of the Dead Earth story; J.H. Williams-a(p); Mick Gray-a(i) 3.00

Annual 8 (1995, $3.50)-Year One story 3.50

Annual 10 (1997, $3.95)-Pulp Heroes stories 4.00

Annual 11,12 ('98, '99)-11-Ghosts; Wrightson-c. 12-JLApe; Art Adams-c 3.00

...80-Page Giant (8/98, $4.95) Flash family stories by Waid, Byrne, Millar, and others; Mhan-c 5.00

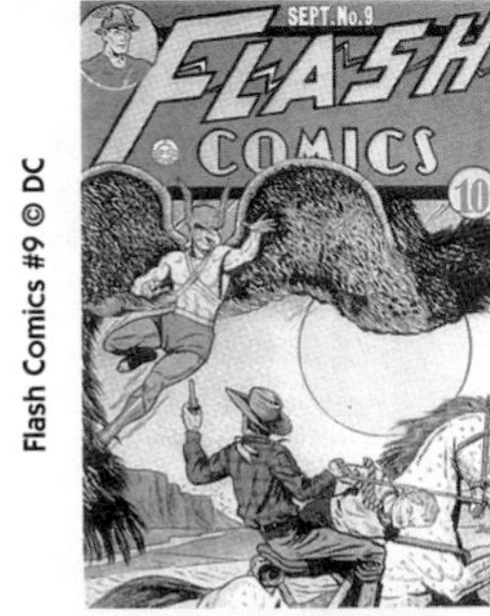

Flash Comics #9 © DC

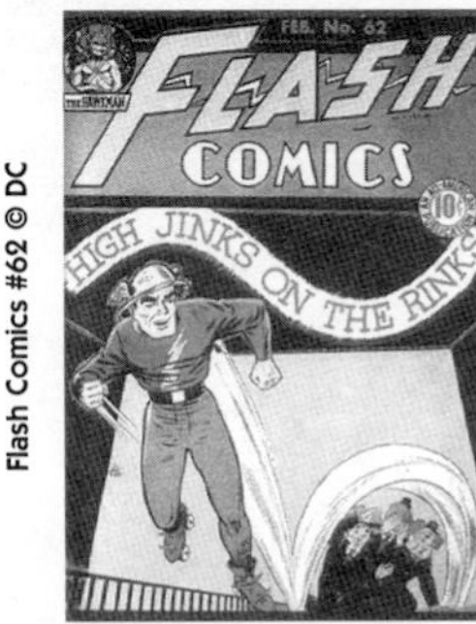

Flash Comics #62 © DC

Flash Gordon (Harvey Pub.) #3 © KING

GD2.0 FN6.0 NM9.4

...80-Page Giant 2 (4/99, $4.95) Stories of Flash family, future Kid Flash, original Teen Titans, XS — 5.00
...Plus 1 (1/1997, $2.95)-Nightwing-c/app. — 3.00
...Secret Files 1 (11/97, $4.95, one-shot) Origin-s & pin-ups — 5.00
Special 1 (1990, $2.95, 84 pgs.)-50th anniversary issue; Kubert-c; 1st Flash story by Mark Waid; 1st app. John Fox (27th Century Flash) — 3.00
TV Special 1 (1991, $3.95, 76 pgs.)-Photo-c plus behind the scenes photos of TV show; Saltares-a, Byrne scripts — 4.00
Terminal Velocity (1996, $12.95, TPB)-r/#95-100. — 13.00
The Return of Barry Allen (1996, $12.95, TPB)-r/#74-79. — 13.00

NOTE: ***Guice*** *a-1-9p, 11p, Annual 1p; c-1-9p, Annual 1p.* ***Perez*** *c-15-17, Annual 2i.* ***Travest Charest*** *c/a-Annual 5p.*

FLASH, THE (See Tangent Comics/ The Flash)

FLASH/ GREEN LANTERN: FASTER FRIENDS (See Green Lantern/Flash...)
DC Comics: No. 2, 1997 ($4.95, continuation of Green Lantern/Flash: Faster Friends #1)

2-Waid/Augustyn-s — 5.00

FLASH SPECTACULAR, THE (See DC Special Series No. 11)

FLASH COMICS (Whiz Comics No. 2 on)
Fawcett Publications: Jan, 1940 (12 pgs., B&W, regular size)
(Not distributed to newsstands; printed for in-house use)

NOTE: ***Whiz Comics*** *#2 was preceded by two books,* ***Flash Comics*** *and* ***Thrill Comics****, both dated Jan, 1940, (12 pgs, B&W, regular size) and were not distributed. These two books are identical except for the title, and were sent out to major distributors as ad copies to promote sales. It is believed that the complete 68 page issue of Fawcett's* ***Flash*** *and* ***Thrill Comics*** *#1 was finished and ready for publication with the January date. Since DC Comics was also about to publish a book with the same date and title, Fawcett hurriedly printed up the black and white version of* ***Flash Comics*** *to secure copyright before DC. The inside covers are blank, with the covers and inside pages printed on a high quality uncoated paper stock.The eight page origin story of Captain Thunder is composed of pages 1-7 and 13 of the Captain Marvel story essentially as they appeared in the first issue of* ***Whiz Comics****. The balloon dialogue on page thirteen was relettered to tie the story into the end of page seven in* ***Flash*** *and* ***Thrill Comics*** *to produce a shorter version of the origin story for copyright purposes. Obviously, DC acquired the copyright and Fawcett dropped* ***Flash*** *as well as* ***Thrill*** *and came out with* ***Whiz Comics*** *a month later. Fawcett never used the cover to* ***Flash*** *and* ***Thrill*** *#1, designing a new cover for* ***Whiz Comics****. Fawcett also must have discovered that Captain Thunder had already been used by another publisher (Captain Terry Thunder by Fiction House). All references to Captain Thunder were relettered to Captain Marvel before appearing in* ***Whiz****.*

1 (nn on-c, #1 on inside)-Origin & 1st app. Captain Thunder. Eight copies of Flash and three copies of Thrill exist. All 3 copies of Thrill sold in 1986 for between $4,000-$10,000 each. A NM copy of Thrill sold in 1987 for $12,000. A vg copy of Thrill sold in 1987 for $9000 cash; another copy sold in 1987 for $2000 cash, $10,000 trade; cover by Leo O'Mealia

FLASH COMICS (The Flash No. 105 on) (Also see All-Flash)
National Periodical Publ./All-American: Jan, 1940 - No. 104, Feb, 1949

	GD2.0	FN6.0	VF8.0	NM9.4
1-The Flash (origin/1st app.) by Harry Lampert, Hawkman (origin/1st app.) by Gardner Fox, The Whip, & Johnny Thunder (origin/1st app.) by Stan Asch; Cliff Cornwall by Moldoff, Flash Picture Novelets (later Minute Movies w/#12) begin; Moldoff (Shelly) cover; 1st app. Shiera Sanders who later becomes Hawkgirl, #24; reprinted in Famous First Edition (on sale 11/10/39); The Flash-c	5500.00	16,500.00	33,000.00	60,000.00

1-Reprint, Oversize 13-1/2x10". **WARNING:** This comic is an exact reprint of the original except for its size. DC published it in 1974 with a second cover titling it as a Famous First Edition. There have been many reported cases of the outer cover being removed and the interior sold as the original edition. The reprint with the new outer cover removed is practically worthless. See Famous First Edition for value.

	GD2.0	FN6.0	NM9.4
2-Rod Rian begins, ends #11; Hawkman-c	650.00	1950.00	6200.00
3-King Standish begins (1st app.), ends #41 (called The King #16-37,39-41); E.E. Hibbard-a begins on Flash	485.00	1455.00	4600.00
4-Moldoff (Shelly) Hawkman begins; The Whip-c	390.00	1170.00	3700.00
5-The King-c	316.00	948.00	3000.00
6-2nd Flash-c (alternates w/Hawkman #6 on)	440.00	1320.00	4200.00
7-2nd Hawkman-c; 1st Moldoff Hawkman-c	390.00	1170.00	3700.00
8-New logo begins; classic Moldoff Flash-c	287.00	861.00	2300.00
9,10: 9-Moldoff Hawkman-c; 10-Classic Moldoff Flash-c	300.00	900.00	2700.00
11-13,15-20: 12-Les Watts begins; "Sparks" #16 on. 17-Last Cliff Cornwall	188.00	562.00	1500.00
14-World War II cover	225.00	675.00	1800.00
21-23: 21-Classic Hawkman-c	162.00	486.00	1300.00
24-Shiera becomes Hawkgirl (12/41); see All-Star Comics #5 for 1st app.	194.00	582.00	1550.00
25-28,30: 28-Last Les Sparks.	112.00	337.00	875.00
29-Ghost Patrol begins (origin/1st app.), ends #104.	125.00	375.00	1000.00
31,33-Classic Hawkman-c. 33-Origin Shade	103.00	309.00	825.00
32,34-40	100.00	300.00	800.00
41-50	91.00	272.00	725.00
51-61: 52-1st computer in comics, c/s (4/44). 59-Last Minute Movies. 61-Last Moldoff Hawkman	80.00	240.00	640.00
62-Hawkman by Kubert begins	97.00	291.00	775.00
63-85: 66-68-Hop Harrigan in all. 70-Mutt & Jeff app. 80-Atom begins, ends #104	72.00	216.00	575.00
86-Intro. The Black Canary in Johnny Thunder (8/47); see All-Star #38.	250.00	750.00	2000.00
87,88,90: 87-Intro. The Foil. 88-Origin Ghost.	112.00	338.00	900.00
89-Intro villain The Thorn	150.00	450.00	1200.00
91,93-99: 98-Atom & Hawkman don new costumes	125.00	375.00	1000.00
92-1st solo Black Canary plus-c; rare in Mint due to black ink smearing on white-c	311.00	933.00	2800.00
100 (10/48),103(Scarce)-52 pgs. each	278.00	834.00	2500.00
101,102(Scarce)	237.00	711.00	1900.00
104-Origin The Flash retold (Scarce)	600.00	1800.00	6000.00

NOTE: ***Irwin Hasen*** *a-Wheaties Giveaway. c-97, Wheaties Giveaway.* ***E.E. Hibbard*** *c-6, 12, 20, 24, 26, 28, 30, 44, 46, 48, 50, 62, 66, 68, 69, 72, 74, 76, 78, 80, 82.* ***Infantino*** *a-86p, 90, 93-95, 99-104; c-90, 92, 93, 97, 99, 101, 103.* ***Kinstler*** *a-87, 89(Hawkman); c-87.* ***Chet Kozlak*** *c-77, 79, 81.* ***Krigstein*** *a-94.* ***Kubert*** *a-62-76, 83, 85, 86, 88-104; c-63, 65, 67, 70, 71, 73, 75, 83, 85, 86, 88, 89, 91, 94, 96, 98, 100, 104.* ***Moldoff*** *a-3; c-3, 7-11, 13-17, plus odd #'s 19-61.* ***Martin Naydell*** *c-52, 54, 56, 58, 60, 64, 84.*

FLASH DIGEST, THE (See DC Special Series #24)

FLASH GORDON (See Defenders Of The Earth, Eat Right to Work..., Giant Comic Album, King Classics, King Comics, March of Comics #118, 133, 142, The Phantom #18, Street Comix & Wow Comics, 1st series)

FLASH GORDON
Dell Publishing Co.: No. 25, 1941; No. 10, 1943 - No. 512, Nov, 1953

	GD2.0	FN6.0	NM9.4
Feature Books 25 (#1)(1941))-r-not by Raymond	73.00	218.00	800.00
Four Color 10(1943)-by Alex Raymond; reprints "The Ice Kingdom"	77.00	231.00	850.00
Four Color 84(1945)-by Alex Raymond; reprints "The Fiery Desert"	36.00	109.00	400.00
Four Color 173	13.00	38.00	140.00
Four Color 190-Bondage-c; "The Adventures of the Flying Saucers"; 5th Flying Saucer story (6/48)- see The Spirit 9/28/47(1st), Shadow Comics V7#10 (2nd, 1/48), Captain Midnight #60 (3rd, 2/48) & Boy Commandos #26 (4th, 3-4/48)	14.50	44.00	160.00
Four Color 204,247	10.00	30.00	110.00
Four Color 424-Painted-c	8.00	23.00	85.00
2(5-7/53-Dell)-Painted-c; Evans-a?	4.50	13.50	50.00
Four Color 512-Painted-c	4.50	13.50	50.00

FLASH GORDON (See Tiny Tot Funnies)
Harvey Publications: Oct, 1950 - No. 4, April, 1951

	GD2.0	FN6.0	NM9.4
1-Alex Raymond-a; bondage-c; reprints strips from 7/14/40 to 12/8/40	31.00	93.00	220.00
2-Alex Raymond-a; r/strips 12/15/40-4/27/41	21.00	64.00	150.00
3,4-Alex Raymond-a; 3-bondage-c; r/strips 5/4/41-9/21/41. 4-r/strips 10/24/37-3/27/38	20.00	60.00	140.00

5-(Rare)-Small size-5-1/2x8-1/2"; B&W; 32 pgs.; Distributed to some mail subscribers only. Estimated value — $200.00-$300.00
(Also see All-New No. 15, Boy Explorers No. 2, and Stuntman No. 3)

FLASH GORDON
Gold Key: June, 1965

Flinch #1 © DC

Flintstones and the Jetsons #19 © H-B

Flip #2 © HARV

1 (1947 reprint)-Painted-c 4.20 12.60 42.00

FLASH GORDON (Also see Comics Reading Libraries)
King #1-11/Charlton #12-18/Gold Key #19-23/Whitman #28 on: 9/66 - #11, 12/67; #12, 2/69 - #18, 1/70; #19, 9/78 - #37, 3/82 (Painted covers No. 19-30, 34)

1-1st S.A. app Flash Gordon; Williamson c/a(2); E.C. swipe/Incredible S.F. #32; Mandrake story 4.00 12.00 40.00
1-8: 1-Army giveaway(1968)("Complimentary" on cover)(Same as regular #1 minus Mandrake story & back-c). 2-Bolle, Gil Kane-c; Mandrake story. 3-Williamson-c. 4-Secret Agent X-9 begins, Williamson-c/a(3). 5-Williamson-c/a(2). 6,8-Crandall-a. 7-Raboy-a (last in comics?). 8-Secret Agent X-9-r 2.50 7.50 22.00
9-13: 9,10-Raymond-r. 10-Buckler's 1st pro work (11/67). 1-Crandall-a. 12-Crandall-c/a. 13-Jeff Jones-a (15 pgs.) 2.50 7.50 20.00
14,15: 15-Last 12¢ issue 1.75 5.25 14.00
16,17: 17-Brick Bradford story 1.50 4.50 12.00
18-Kaluta-a (3rd pro work?)(see Teen Confessions) 2.00 6.00 16.00
19(9/78, G.K.), 20-26 4.00
27-29.34-37: 34-37-Movie adaptation 2.40 6.00
30 (10/80) (scarce) 1.75 5.25 14.00
30 (7/81; re-issue), 31-33-single issues 4.00
31-33 (Bagged 3-pack): Movie adaptation; Williamson-a. 12.00
NOTE: *Aparo a-8.* ***Bolle*** *a-21, 22.* ***Boyette*** *a-14-18.* ***Briggs*** *c-10.* ***Buckler*** *a-10.* ***Crandall*** *c-6.* ***Estrada*** *a-3.* ***Gene Fawcette*** *a-29, 30, 34, 37.* ***McWilliams*** *a-31-33, 36.*

FLASH GORDON
DC Comics: June, 1988 - No. 9, Holiday, 1988-'89 ($1.25, mini-series)

1-9: 1,5-Painted-c 2.00

FLASH GORDON
Marvel Comics: June, 1995 - No. 2, July, 1995 ($2.95, limited series)

1,2: Schultz scripts; Williamson-a 3.00

FLASH GORDON THE MOVIE
Western Publishing Co.: 1980 (8-1/4 x 11", $1.95, 68 pgs.)

11294-Williamson-c/a; adapts movie 1.25 3.75 10.00
13743-Hardback edition 1.85 5.50 15.00

FLAT-TOP
Mazie Comics/Harvey Publ.(Magazine Publ.) No. 4 on: 11/53 - No. 3, 5/54; No. 4, 3/55 - No. 7, 9/55

1-Teenage; Flat-Top, Mazie, Mortie & Stevie begin 5.85 17.50 35.00
2,3 4.00 10.00 20.00
4-7 3.20 8.00 16.00

FLESH & BLOOD
Brainstorm Comics: Dec, 1995 ($2.95, B&W, mature)

1-Balent-c; foil-c. 3.00

FLESH AND BONES
Upshot Graphics (Fantagraphics Books): June, 1986 - No. 4, Dec, 1986 (Limited series)

1-4: Alan Moore scripts (r) & Dalgoda by Fujitake 2.00

FLESH CRAWLERS
Kitchen Sink Press: Aug, 1993 - No. 3, 1995 ($2.50, B&W, limited series, mature)

1-3 2.50

FLEX MENTALLO (Man of Muscle Mystery) (See Doom Patrol, 2nd Series)
DC Comics (Vertigo): Jun, 1996 - No. 4, Sept, 1996 ($2.50, lim. series, mature)

1-4: Grant Morrison scripts & Frank Quitely-c/a. in all 3.00

FLINCH (Horror anthology)
DC Comics (Vertigo): Jun, 1999 - Present ($2.50)

1-4: 1-Art by Jim Lee, Quitely, and Corben 2.50

FLINTSTONE KIDS, THE (TV) (See Star Comics Digest)
Star Comics/Marvel Comics #5 on: Aug, 1987 - No. 11, Apr, 1989

1-11 2.50

FLINTSTONES, THE (TV)(See Dell Giant #48 for No. 1)
Dell Publ. Co./Gold Key No. 7 (10/62) on: No. 2, Nov-Dec, 1961 - No. 60, Sept, 1970 (Hanna-Barbera)

2-2nd app. (TV show debuted on 9/30/60); 1st app. of Cave Kids; 15¢-c thru #5 9.00 27.00 100.00
3-6(7-8/62): 3-Perry Gunnite begins. 6-1st 12¢-c 6.00 18.00 65.00
7 (10/62; 1st GK) 6.00 18.00 65.00
8-10 4.50 13.50 50.00
11-1st app. Pebbles (6/63) 7.75 23.50 85.00
12-15,17-20 3.80 11.40 38.00
16-1st app. Bamm-Bamm (1/64) 6.75 20.50 75.00
21-23,25-30,33: 33-Meet Frankenstein & Dracula 3.20 9.60 32.00
24-1st app. The Grusomes 5.00 15.00 55.00
31,32,35-40: 31-Xmas-c. 39-Reprints 3.00 9.00 30.00
34-1st app. The Great Gazoo 5.00 15.00 55.00
41-60: 45-Last 12¢ issue 2.80 8.40 28.00
At N. Y. World's Fair ('64)-J.W. Books(25¢)-1st printing; no date on-c (29¢ version exists, 2nd print?) Most H-B characters app.; including Yogi Bear, Top Cat, Snagglepuss and the Jetsons 4.00 12.00 45.00
At N. Y. World's Fair (1965 on-c; re-issue). NOTE: Warehouse find in 1984 1.50 4.50 12.00
Bigger & Boulder 1(#30013-211) (Gold Key Giant, 11/62, 25¢, 84 pgs.) 7.25 22.00 80.00
Bigger & Boulder 2-(1966, 25¢)-Reprints B&B No. 1 6.00 18.00 65.00
...With Pebbles & Bamm Bamm (100 pgs., G.K.)-30028-511 (paper-c, 25¢) (11/65) 6.50 20.00 80.00
NOTE: *(See Comic Album #16, Bamm-Bamm & Pebbles Flintstone, Dell Giant 48, Golden Comics Digest, March of Comics #229, 243, 271, 289, 299, 317, 327, 341, Pebbles Flintstone, Top Comics #2-4, and Whitman Comic Book.)*

FLINTSTONES, THE (TV)(...& Pebbles)
Charlton Comics: Nov, 1970 - No. 50, Feb, 1977 (Hanna-Barbera)

1 5.00 15.00 55.00
2 3.00 9.00 30.00
3-7,9,10 2.50 7.50 22.00
8- "Flintstones Summer Vacation" (Summer, 1971, 52 pgs.) 5.00 15.00 55.00
11-20,36: 36-Mike Zeck illos (early work) 2.50 7.50 20.00
21-35,38-41,43-45: 45-Last 12¢ issue 1.85 5.50 15.00
37,42: 37-Byrne text illos (early work; see Nightmare #20). 42-Byrne-a (2 pgs.) 2.50 7.50 22.00
46-50 1.85 5.50 15.00
(Also see Barney & Betty Rubble, Dino, The Great Gazoo, & Pebbles & Bamm-Bamm)

FLINTSTONES, THE (TV)(See Yogi Bear, 3rd series) (Newsstand sales only)
Marvel Comics Group: October, 1977 - No. 9, Feb, 1979 (Hanna-Barbera)

1 1.85 5.50 15.00
2,3,5-9: Yogi Bear app. 1.50 4.50 12.00
4-The Jetsons app. 2.25 6.75 18.00

FLINTSTONES, THE (TV)
Harvey Comics: Sept, 1992 - No. 13, Jun, 1994 ($1.25/$1.50) (Hanna-Barbera)

V2#1-13, ...Big Book 1,2 (11/92, 3/93; both $1.95, 52 pgs.), ...Giant Size 1-3 (10/92, 4/93, 11/93; $2.25, 68 pgs.) 3.00

FLINTSTONES, THE (TV)
Archie Publications: Sept, 1995 - No. 22, June, 1997 ($1.50)

1-22 2.00

FLINTSTONES AND THE JETSONS, THE (TV)
DC Comics: Aug, 1997 - No. 21, May, 1999 ($1.75/$1.95)

1-21-($1.99): 19-Bizarro Elroy-c 2.00

FLINTSTONES CHRISTMAS PARTY, THE (See The Funtastic World of Hanna-Barbera No. 1)

FLIP
Harvey Publications: April, 1954 - No. 2, June, 1954 (Satire)

1,2-Nostrand-a each. 2-Powell-a 21.00 64.00 150.00

FLIPPER (TV)

Flippity & Flop #3 © DC

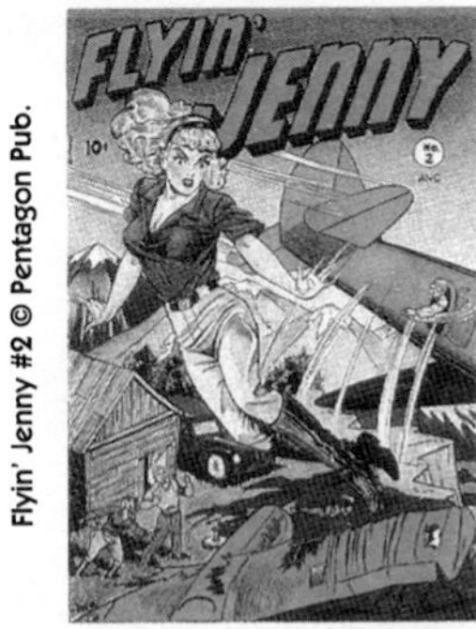

Flyin' Jenny #2 © Pentagon Pub.

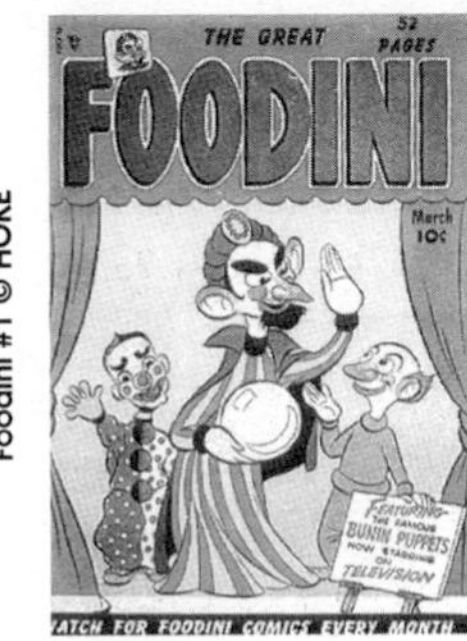

Foodini #1 © HOKE

Gold Key: Apr, 1966 - No. 3, Nov, 1967 (All have photo-c)
1 5.00 15.00 55.00
2,3 3.80 11.40 38.00

FLIPPITY & FLOP
National Per. Publ. (Signal Publ. Co.): 12-1/51-52 - No. 46, 8-10/59; No. 47, 9-11/60
1-Sam dog & his pets Flippity The Bird and Flop The Cat begin; Twiddle and Twaddle begin 26.00 77.00 180.00
2 14.00 43.00 100.00
3-5 11.50 34.00 80.00
6-10 10.00 30.00 70.00
11-20: 20-Last precode (3/55) 9.70 29.00 58.00
21-47 8.00 24.00 48.00

FLOATERS
Dark Horse Comics: Sept, 1993 - No. 5, Jan, 1994 ($2.50, B&W, lim. series)
1-5 2.50

FLOOD RELIEF
Malibu Comics (Ultraverse): Jan, 1994 (36 pgs.)(Ordered thru mail w/$5.00 to Red Cross)
1-Hardcase, Prime & Prototype app. 5.00

FLOYD FARLAND (See Eclipse Graphic Album Series #11)

FLY, THE (Also see Adventures of..., Blue Ribbon Comics & Flyman)
Archie Enterprises, Inc.: May, 1983 - No. 9, Oct, 1984
1-Mr. Justice app; origin Shield; Kirby-a; Steranko-c 3.00
2-9: 2-Flygirl app. 2.50
NOTE: ***Buckler*** *a-1, 2.* ***Ditko*** *a-2-9; c-4-8p.* ***Kirby*** *a-1.* ***Nebres*** *c-3, 4, 5i, 6, 7i.* ***Steranko*** *c-1, 2.*

FLY, THE
Impact Comics (DC): Aug, 1991 - No. 17, Dec, 1992 ($1.00)
1-17: 4-Vs. The Black Hood. 9-Trading card inside 2.00
Annual 1 ('92, $2.50, 68 pgs.)-Impact trading card 2.50

FLYBOY (Flying Cadets)(Also see Approved Comics)
Ziff-Davis Publ. Co. (Approved): Spring, 1952 - No. 4, 1953
1-Saunders painted-c 19.00 56.00 130.00
2-(10-11/52)-Saunders painted-c 13.00 39.00 90.00
3,4-Saunders painted-c 10.00 30.00 70.00

FLYING ACES (Aviation stories)
Key Publications: July, 1955 - No. 5, Mar, 1956
1 5.00 15.00 30.00
2-5: 2-Trapani-a 4.00 10.00 20.00

FLYING A'S RANGE RIDER, THE (TV)(See Western Roundup under Dell Giants)
Dell Publishing Co.: #404, 6-7/52; #2, June-Aug, 1953 - #24, Aug, 1959 (All photo-c)
Four Color 404(#1)-Titled "The Range Rider" 10.00 30.00 110.00
2 6.00 18.00 65.00
3-10 4.50 13.50 50.00
11-16,18-24 4.00 12.00 45.00
17-Toth-a 5.25 16.00 58.00

FLYING CADET (WW II Plane Photos)
Flying Cadet Publ. Co.; Jan, 1943 - V2#8, 1947 (Half photos, half comics)
V1#1-Painted-c 13.00 39.00 90.00
2 7.50 22.50 45.00
3-9 (Two #6's, Sept. & Oct.): 5,6a,6b-Photo-c 6.70 20.00 40.00
V2#1-7(#10-16) 5.35 16.00 32.00
8(#17)-Bare-breasted woman-c 17.00 51.00 120.00

FLYING COLORS 10th ANNIVERSARY SPECIAL
Flying Colors Comics: Fall 1998 ($2.95, one-shot)
1-Dan Brereton-c; pin-ups by Jim Lee and Jeff Johnson 3.00

FLYIN' JENNY
Pentagon Publ. Co./Leader Enterprises #2: 1946 - No. 2, 1947 (1945 strip-r)
nn-Marcus Swayze strip-r (entire insides) 13.00 39.00 90.00
2-Baker-c; Swayze strip reprints 15.00 45.00 105.00

FLYING MODELS
H-K Publ. (Health-Knowledge Publs.): V61#3, May, 1954 (5¢, 16 pgs.)
V61#3 (Rare) 8.35 25.00 50.00

FLYING NUN (TV)
Dell Publishing Co.: Feb, 1968 - No. 4, Nov, 1968
1-Sally Field photo-c 4.00 12.00 45.00
2-4: 2-Sally Field photo-c 2.75 8.25 30.00

FLYING NURSES (See Sue & Sally Smith...)

FLYING SAUCERS (See The Spirit 9/28/47(1st app.), Shadow Comics V7#10 (2nd, 1/48), Captain Midnight #60 (3rd, 2/48), Boy Commandos #26 (4th, 3-4/48) & Flash Gordon Four Color 190 (5th, 6/48))

FLYING SAUCERS
Avon Periodicals/Realistic: 1950; 1952; 1953
1(1950)-Wood-a, 21 pgs.; Fawcette-c 75.00 225.00 600.00
nn(1952)-Cover altered plus 2 pgs. of Wood-a not in original 43.00 128.00 340.00
nn(1953)-Reprints above 34.00 103.00 240.00

FLYING SAUCERS (Comics)
Dell Publishing Co.: April, 1967 - No. 4, Nov, 1967; No. 5, Oct, 1969
1 2.80 8.40 28.00
2-5 2.50 7.50 20.00

FLY MAN (Formerly Adventures of The Fly; Mighty Comics #40 on)
Mighty Comics Group (Radio Comics) (Archie):
No. 32, July, 1965 - No. 39, Sept, 1966 (Also see Mighty Crusaders)
32,33-Comet, Shield, Black Hood, The Fly & Flygirl x-over. 33-Re-intro Wizard, Hangman (1st S.A. appearances) 3.50 10.50 35.00
34-39: 34-Shield begins. 35-Origin Black Hood. 36-Hangman x-over in Shield; re-intro. & origin of Web (1st S.A. app.). 37-Hangman, Wizard x-over in Flyman; last Shield issue. 38-Web story. 39-Steel Sterling story (1st S.A. app.) 2.50 7.50 24.00

FOES
Ram Comics: 1989 - No. 3, 1989 ($1.95, limited series)
1-3 2.00

FOLLOW THE SUN (TV)
Dell Publishing Co.: May-July, 1962 - No. 2, Sept-Nov, 1962 (Photo-c)
01-280-207(No.1), 12-280-211(No.2) 3.60 11.00 40.00

FOODANG
Continum Comics: July, 1994 ($1.95, B&W, bi-monthly)
1 2.00

FOODINI (TV)(The Great...; see Jingle Dingle & Pinhead &...)
Continental Publ. (Holyoke): March, 1950 - No. 5, 1950 (All have 52 pgs.)
1-Based on TV puppet show (very early TV comic) 19.00 56.00 130.00
2-Jingle Dingle begins 10.00 30.00 75.00
3-5: 4-(8/50) 9.15 27.00 55.00

FOOEY (Magazine) (Satire)
Scoff Publishing Co.: Feb, 1961 - No. 4, May, 1961
1 4.20 12.60 42.00
2-4 2.80 8.40 28.00

FOOFUR (TV)
Marvel Comics (Star Comics)/Marvel No. 5 on: Aug, 1987 - No. 6, Jun, 1988
1-6 2.00

FOOLKILLER (Also see The Amazing Spider-Man #225, The Defenders #73 Man-Thing #3 & Omega the Unknown #8)
Marvel Comics: Oct, 1990 - No. 10, Oct, 1991 ($1.75, limited series)
1-10: 1-Origin 3rd Foolkiller; Greg Salinger app; DeZuniga-a(i) in 1-4. 8-Spider-Man x-over 2.00

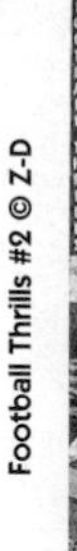
Football Thrills #2 © Z-D

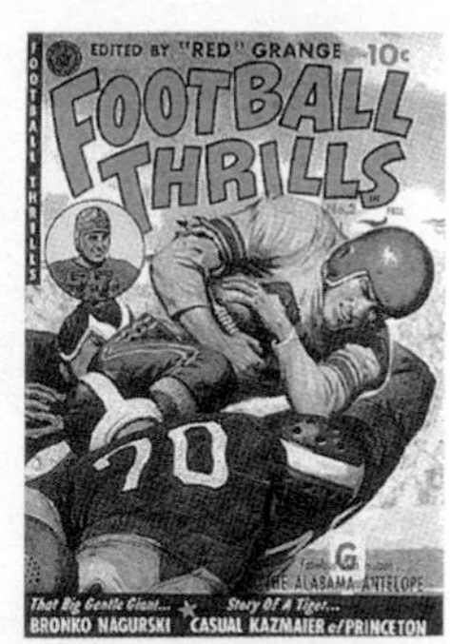

Forbidden Worlds #20 © ACG

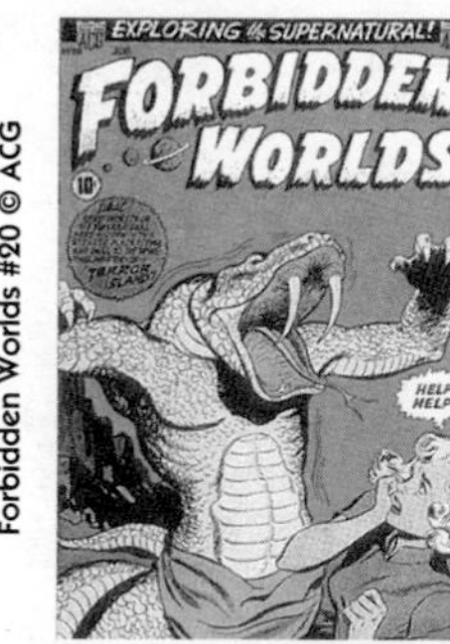

Force Works #21 © MAR

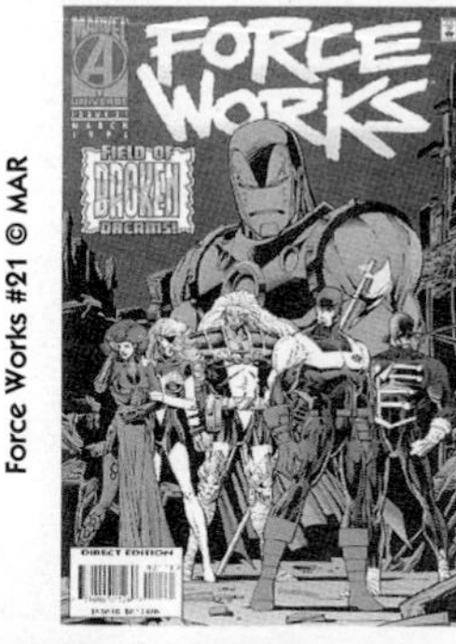

GD2.0 FN6.0 NM9.4

FOOTBALL THRILLS (See Tops In Adventure)
Ziff-Davis Publ. Co.: Fall-Winter, 1951-52 - No. 2, Fall, 1952
(Edited by "Red" Grange)

1-Powell a(2); Saunders painted-c; Red Grange, Jim Thorpe stories 28.00 84.00 195.00
2-Saunders painted-c 18.00 54.00 125.00

FOOT SOLDIERS, THE
Dark Horse Comics: Jan, 1996 - No. 4, Apr, 1996 ($2.95, limited series)

1-4: Jim Krueger story & Michael Avon Oeming-a. in all. 1-Alex Ross-c. 4-John K. Snyder, III-c. 3.00

FOOT SOLDIERS, THE (Volume Two)
Image Comics: Sept, 1997 - No. 5, May, 1998 ($2.95, limited series)

1-5: 1-Yeowell-a. 2-McDaniel, Hester, Sienkiewicz, Giffen-a 3.00

FOR A NIGHT OF LOVE
Avon Periodicals: 1951

nn-Two stories adapted from the works of Emile Zola; Astarita, Ravielli-a; Kinstler-c 29.00 86.00 200.00

FORBIDDEN KNOWLEDGE: ADVENTURE BEYOND THE DOORWAY TO SOULS WITH RADICAL DREAMER (Also see Radical Dreamer)
Mark's Giant Economy Size Comics: 1996 ($3.50, B&W, one-shot, 48 pgs.)

nn-Max Wrighter app.; Wheatley-c/a/script; painted infinity-c 3.50

FORBIDDEN LOVE
Quality Comics Group: Mar, 1950 - No. 4, Sept, 1950 (52 pgs.)

1-(Scarce)-Classic photo-c; Crandall-a 69.00 206.00 550.00
2-Classic photo-c 40.00 120.00 325.00
3-(Scarce)-Photo-c 36.00 107.00 250.00
4-(Scarce)-Ward/Cuidera-a; photo-c 40.00 120.00 280.00

FORBIDDEN LOVE (See Dark Mansion of...)

FORBIDDEN PLANET
Innovation Publishing: May, 1992 - No. 4, 1992 ($2.50, limited series)

1-4: Adapts movie; painted-c 2.50

FORBIDDEN TALES OF DARK MANSION (Formerly Dark Mansion of Forbidden Love #1-4)
National Periodical Publ.: No. 5, May-June, 1972 - No. 15, Feb-Mar, 1974

5-(52 pgs.) 3.00 9.00 30.00
6-15: 13-Kane/Howard-a 1.85 5.50 15.00

NOTE: ***N. Adams*** *c-9.* ***Alcala*** *a-9-11, 13.* ***Chaykin*** *a-7,15.* ***Evans*** *a-14.* ***Heck*** *a-5.* ***Kaluta*** *a-7i, 8-12; c-7, 8, 13.* ***G. Kane*** *a-13.* ***Kirby*** *a-6.* ***Nino*** *a-8, 12, 15.* ***Redondo*** *a-14.*

FORBIDDEN WORLDS
American Comics Group: 7-8/51 - No. 34, 10-11/54; No. 35, 8/55 - No. 145, 8/67 (No. 1-5: 52 pgs.; No. 6-8: 44 pgs.)

1-Williamson/Frazetta-a (10 pgs.) 131.00 393.00 1050.00
2 62.00 186.00 500.00
3-Williamson/Orlando-a (7 pgs.); Wood (2 panels); Frazetta (1 panel) 64.00 192.00 510.00
4 36.00 107.00 250.00
5-Krenkel/Williamson-a (8 pgs.) 50.00 150.00 400.00
6-Harrison/Williamson-a (8 pgs.) 43.00 128.00 340.00
7,8,10: 7-1st monthly issue 27.00 81.00 190.00
9-A-Bomb explosion story 30.00 90.00 210.00
11-20 19.00 56.00 130.00
21-33: 24-E.C. swipe by Landau 13.00 39.00 90.00
34(10-11/54)(Scarce)(becomes Young Heroes #35 on)-Last pre-code issue; A-Bomb explosion story 14.00 43.00 100.00
35(8/55)-Scarce 13.00 39.00 90.00
36-62 9.15 27.00 55.00
63,69,76,78-Williamson-a in all; w/Krenkel #69 10.00 30.00 60.00
64,66-68,70-72,74,75,77,79-85,87-90 7.50 22.50 45.00
65- "There's a New Moon Tonight" listed in #114 as holding 1st record fan mail response 9.15 27.00 55.00
73-1st app. Herbie by Ogden Whitney 36.00 107.00 250.00
86-Flying saucer-c by Schaffenberger 8.35 25.00 50.00
91-93,95-100 3.20 9.60 32.00
94-Herbie (2nd app.) 6.50 19.50 65.00
101-109,111-113,115,117-120 2.60 7.80 26.00
110,114,116-Herbie app. 114-1st Herbie-c; contains list of editor's top 20 ACG stories. 116-Herbie goes to Hell 4.50 13.50 45.00
121-123 2.50 7.50 24.00
124,126-130: 24-Magic Agent app. 2.80 8.40 28.00
125-Magic Agent app.; intro. & origin Magicman series, ends #141 3.80 11.40 38.00
131-139: 133-Origin/1st app. Dragonia in Magicman (1-2/66); returns in #138. 136-Nemesis x-over in Magicman 2.50 7.50 24.00
140-Mark Midnight app. by Ditko 3.00 9.00 30.00
141-145 2.50 7.50 20.00

NOTE: ***Buscema*** *a-75, 79, 81, 82, 140r.* ***Cameron*** *a-5.* ***Disbrow*** *a-10.* ***Ditko*** *a-137p, 138, 140.* ***Landau*** *a-24, 27-29, 31-34, 48, 86r, 96, 143-45.* ***Lazarus*** *a-18, 23, 24, 57.* ***Moldoff*** *a-27, 31, 139r.* ***Reinman*** *a-93.* ***Whitney*** *a-115, 116, 137; c-40, 46, 57, 60, 68, 78, 79, 90, 93, 94, 100, 102, 103, 106-108, 114, 129.*

FORCE, THE (See The Crusaders)

FORCE OF BUDDHA'S PALM THE
Jademan Comics: Aug, 1988 - No. 55, Feb, 1993 ($1.50/$1.95, 68 pgs.)

1-55-Kung Fu stories 2.00

FORCE WORKS
Marvel Comics: July, 1994 - No. 22, Apr, 1996 ($1.50)

1-($3.95)-Fold-out pop-up-c; Iron Man, Wonder Man, Spider-Woman,U.S. Agent & Scarlet Witch (new costume) 4.00
2-11, 13-22: 5-Blue logo version & pink logo version. 9-Intro Dreamguard. 13-Avengers app. 2.00
5-Pink logo ($2.95)-polybagged w/ 16pg. Marvel Action Hour Preview & acetate print 3.00
12 ($2.50)-Flip book w/War Machine. 2.50

FORD ROTUNDA CHRISTMAS BOOK (See Christmas at the Rotunda)

FOREIGN INTRIGUES (Formerly Johnny Dynamite; becomes Battlefield Action #16 on)
Charlton Comics: No. 13, 1956 - No. 15, Aug, 1956

13-15-Johnny Dynamite continues 5.35 16.00 32.00

FOREMOST BOYS (See 4Most)

FOR ETERNITY
Antarctic Press: July, 1997 - No. 4, Jan, 1998 ($2.95, B&W)

1-4 3.00

FOREVER AMBER
Image Comics: July, 1999 - Present ($2.95, B&W)

1-3-Don Hudson-s/a 3.00

FOREVER DARLING (Movie)
Dell Publishing Co.: No. 681, Feb, 1956

Four Color 681-w/Lucille Ball & Desi Arnaz; photo-c 10.00 30.00 110.00

FOREVER PEOPLE, THE
National Periodical Publications: Feb-Mar, 1971 - No. 11, Oct-Nov, 1972 (Fourth World) (#1-3, 10-11 are 36pgs; #4-9 are 52pgs.)

1-1st app. Forever People; Superman x-over; Kirby-c/a begins; 1st full app. Darkseid (3rd anywhere, 3 weeks before New Gods #1); Darkseid storyline begins, ends #8(app. in 1-4,6,8; cameos in 5,11) 4.00 12.00 40.00
2-9: 4-G.A. reprints thru #9. 9,10-Deadman app. 2.50 7.50 24.00
10,11: 1.50 4.50 12.00
Jack Kirby's Forever People TPB ('99, $14.95, B&W&Grey) r/#1-11 plus cover gallery of original series 15.00

NOTE: ***Kirby*** *c/a(p)-1-11; #4-9 contain Sandman reprints from Adventure #85, 84, 75, 80, 77, 74 in that order.*

FOREVER PEOPLE
DC Comics: Feb, 1988 - No. 6, July, 1988 ($1.25, limited series)

1-6 2.00

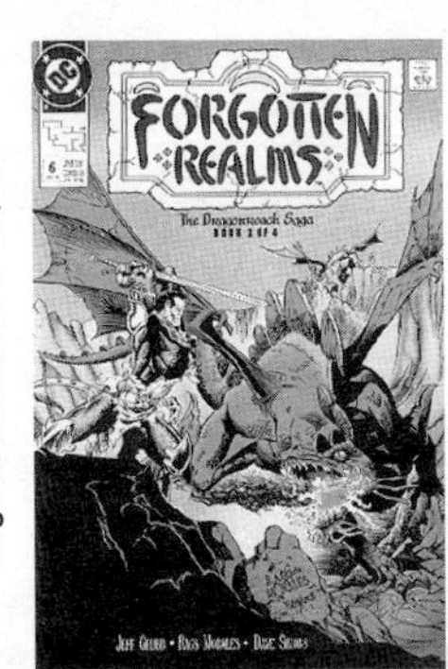

Forgotten Realms #6 © TSR, Inc.

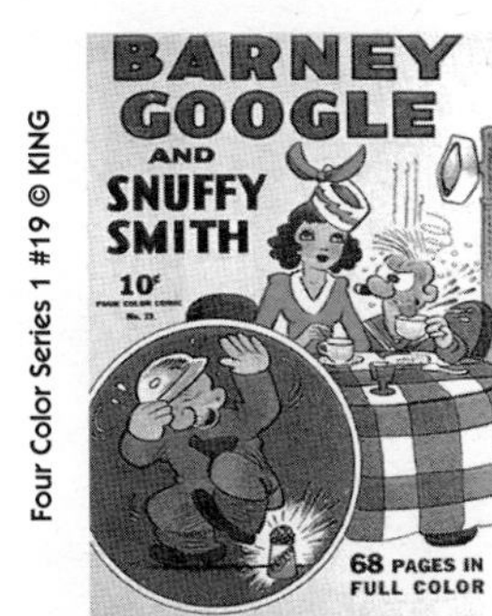

Four Color Series 1 #19 © KING

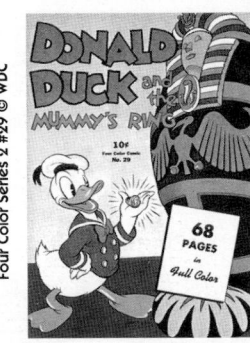

Four Color Series 2 #29 © WDC

	GD2.0	FN6.0	NM9.4

FOR GIRLS ONLY
Bernard Bailey Enterprises: 11/53 - No. 2, 6/54 (100 pgs., digest size, 25¢)

	GD2.0	FN6.0	NM9.4
1-25% comic book, 75% articles, illos, games	11.50	34.00	85.00
2-Eddie Fisher photo & story.	10.00	30.00	60.00

FORGOTTEN FOREST OF OZ, THE (See First Comics Graphic Novel #16)

FORGOTTEN REALMS (Also see Avatar & TSR Worlds)
DC Comics: Sept, 1989 - No. 25, Sept, 1991 ($1.50/$1.75)

	NM9.4
1, Annual 1 (1990, $2.95, 68 pgs.)	3.00
2-25: Based on TSR role-playing game. 18-Avatar story	2.00

FORLORN RIVER (See Zane Grey Four Color 395)

FOR LOVERS ONLY (Formerly Hollywood Romances)
Charlton Comics: No. 60, Aug, 1971 - No. 87, Nov, 1976

	GD2.0	FN6.0	NM9.4
60	2.80	8.40	28.00
61-72,74-87	1.50	4.50	12.00
73-Spanking scene-c/story	1.50	4.50	15.00

40 BIG PAGES OF MICKEY MOUSE
Whitman Publ. Co.: No. 945, Jan, 1936 (10-1/4x12-1/2", 44 pgs., cardboard-c)

	GD2.0	FN6.0	NM9.4
945-Reprints Mickey Mouse Magazine #1, but with a different cover; ads were eliminated and some illustrated stories had expanded text. The book is 3/4" shorter than Mickey Mouse Mag. #1, but the reprints are the same size (Rare)	150.00	450.00	1200.00

FOR YOUR EYES ONLY (See James Bond...)

FOUR COLOR
Dell Publishing Co.: Sept?, 1939 - No. 1354, Apr-June, 1962
(Series I are all 68 pgs.)

NOTE: *Four Color only appears on issues #19-25, 1-99,101. Dell Publishing Co. filed these as Series I, #1-25, and Series II, #1-1354. Issues beginning with #710? were printed with and without ads on back cover. Issues without ads are worth more.*

SERIES I:

	GD2.0	FN6.0	VF8.0	NM9.4
1(nn)-Dick Tracy	600.00	1800.00	3600.00	6600.00

	GD2.0	FN6.0	NM9.4
2(nn)-Don Winslow of the Navy (#1) (Rare) (11/39?)	127.00	381.00	1400.00
3(nn)-Myra North (1/40?)	73.00	218.00	800.00
4-Donald Duck by Al Taliaferro (1940)(Disney)(3/40?)	846.00	2538.00	11,000.00
(Prices vary widely on this book)			
5-Smilin' Jack (#1) (5/40?)	57.00	170.00	625.00
6-Dick Tracy (Scarce)	145.00	435.00	1600.00
7-Gang Busters	34.00	102.00	375.00
8-Dick Tracy	73.00	219.00	800.00
9-Terry and the Pirates-r/Super #9-29	56.00	168.00	615.00
10-Smilin' Jack	50.00	150.00	550.00
11-Smitty (#1)	35.00	105.00	385.00
12-Little Orphan Annie; reprints strips from 12/19/37 to 6/4/38	47.00	140.00	515.00
13-Walt Disney's Reluctant Dragon('41)-Contains 2 pgs. of photos from film; 2 pg. foreword to Fantasia by Leopold Stokowski; Donald Duck, Goofy, Baby Weems & Mickey Mouse (as the Sorcerer's Apprentice) app. (Disney)	155.00	464.00	1700.00
14-Moon Mullins (#1)	34.00	102.00	375.00
15-Tillie the Toiler (#1)	34.00	102.00	375.00

	GD2.0	FN6.0	VF8.0
16-Mickey Mouse (#1) (Disney) by Gottfredson	714.00	2143.00	10,000.00

	GD2.0	FN6.0	NM9.4
17-Walt Disney's Dumbo, the Flying Elephant (#1)(1941)-Mickey Mouse, Donald Duck, & Pluto app. (Disney)	173.00	519.00	1900.00
18-Jiggs and Maggie (#1)(1936-38-r)	38.00	115.00	420.00
19-Barney Google and Snuffy Smith (#1)-(1st issue with Four Color on the cover)	38.00	113.00	415.00
20-Tiny Tim	28.00	85.00	310.00
21-Dick Tracy	60.00	180.00	665.00
22-Don Winslow	30.00	89.00	325.00
23-Gang Busters	26.00	79.00	290.00
24-Captain Easy	41.00	123.00	450.00
25-Popeye (1942)	68.00	205.00	750.00

SERIES II:

	GD2.0	FN6.0	NM9.4
1-Little Joe (1942)	43.00	130.00	475.00
2-Harold Teen	25.50	76.00	280.00
3-Alley Oop (#1)	47.00	141.00	525.00
4-Smilin' Jack	42.00	127.00	465.00
5-Raggedy Ann and Andy (#1)	49.00	146.00	535.00
6-Smitty	21.00	63.00	230.00
7-Smokey Stover (#1)	31.00	93.00	340.00
8-Tillie the Toiler	22.00	65.00	240.00

	GD2.0	FN6.0	VF8.0	NM9.4
9-Donald Duck Finds Pirate Gold, by Carl Barks & Jack Hannah (Disney) (© 8/17/42)	615.00	1845.00	4300.00	8000.00

	GD2.0	FN6.0	NM9.4
10-Flash Gordon by Alex Raymond; reprinted from "The Ice Kingdom"	77.00	231.00	850.00
11-Wash Tubbs	28.65	86.00	315.00
12-Walt Disney's Bambi (#1)	52.00	157.00	575.00
13-Mr. District Attorney (#1)-See The Funnies #35 for 1st app.	29.00	86.00	315.00
14-Smilin' Jack	34.00	102.00	375.00
15-Felix the Cat (#1)	67.00	202.00	740.00
16-Porky Pig (#1)(1942)- "Secret of the Haunted House"	75.00	225.00	825.00
17-Popeye	50.00	150.00	550.00
18-Little Orphan Annie's Junior Commandos; Flag-c; reprints strips from 6/14/42 to 11/21/42	37.00	112.00	410.00
19-Walt Disney's Thumper Meets the Seven Dwarfs (Disney); reprinted in Silly Symphonies	52.00	157.00	575.00
20-Barney Baxter	26.00	78.00	285.00
21-Oswald the Rabbit (#1)(1943)	48.00	145.00	530.00
22-Tillie the Toiler	17.00	52.00	190.00
23-Raggedy Ann and Andy	36.00	108.00	395.00
24-Gang Busters	26.00	79.00	290.00
25-Andy Panda (#1) (Walter Lantz)	48.00	143.00	525.00
26-Popeye	50.00	150.00	550.00
27-Walt Disney's Mickey Mouse and the Seven Colored Terror	79.00	239.00	875.00
28-Wash Tubbs	20.50	61.00	225.00

	GD2.0	FN6.0	VF8.0	NM9.4
29-Donald Duck and the Mummy's Ring, by Carl Barks (Disney) (9/43)	492.00	1477.00	3446.00	6400.00

	GD2.0	FN6.0	NM9.4
30-Bambi's Children (1943)-Disney	52.00	157.00	575.00
31-Moon Mullins	18.00	53.00	195.00
32-Smitty	15.50	46.00	170.00
33-Bugs Bunny "Public Nuisance #1"	109.00	327.00	1200.00
34-Dick Tracy	41.00	123.00	450.00
35-Smokey Stover	16.50	49.00	180.00
36-Smilin' Jack	23.00	68.00	250.00
37-Bringing Up Father	19.00	57.00	210.00
38-Roy Rogers (#1, © 4/44)-1st western comic with photo-c	200.00	600.00	2200.00
39-Oswald the Rabbit (1944)	34.00	102.00	375.00
40-Barney Google and Snuffy Smith	22.00	66.00	240.00
41-Mother Goose and Nursery Rhyme Comics (#1)-All by Walt Kelly	21.00	63.00	230.00
42-Tiny Tim (1934-r)	16.35	49.00	180.00
43-Popeye (1938-'42-r)	31.00	93.00	340.00
44-Terry and the Pirates (1938-r)	39.00	117.00	430.00
45-Raggedy Ann	29.00	89.00	325.00
46-Felix the Cat and the Haunted Castle	40.00	120.00	440.00
47-Gene Autry (copyright 6/16/44)	40.00	120.00	440.00

Four Color #103 © Walt Kelly

Four Color #125 © Lone Ranger, Inc.

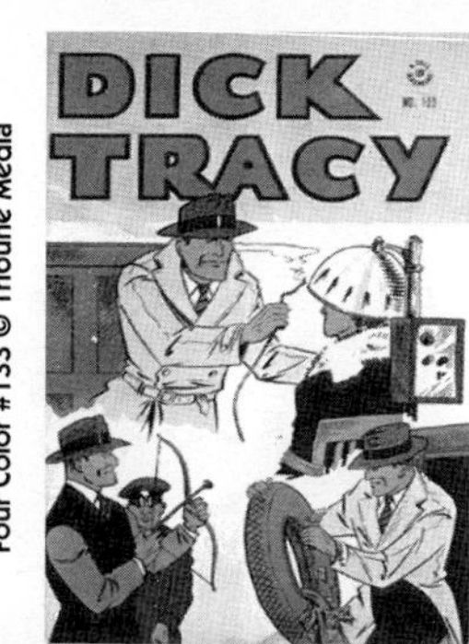

Four Color #133 © Tribune Media

	GD2.0	FN6.0	NM9.4
48-Porky Pig of the Mounties by Carl Barks (7/44)	95.00	286.00	1050.00
49-Snow White and the Seven Dwarfs (Disney)	59.00	176.00	645.00
50-Fairy Tale Parade-Walt Kelly art (1944)	25.00	74.00	270.00
51-Bugs Bunny Finds the Lost Treasure	35.00	105.00	385.00
52-Little Orphan Annie; reprints strips from 6/18/38 to 11/19/38	29.00	87.00	320.00
53-Wash Tubbs	15.00	46.00	170.00
54-Andy Panda	30.00	89.00	325.00
55-Tillie the Toiler	13.00	39.00	145.00
56-Dick Tracy	33.00	100.00	360.00
57-Gene Autry	38.00	115.00	420.00
58-Smilin' Jack	23.00	68.00	250.00
59-Mother Goose and Nursery Rhyme Comics-Kelly-c/a	19.00	56.00	205.00
60-Tiny Folks Funnies	13.00	40.00	150.00
61-Santa Claus Funnies(11/44)-Kelly art	23.00	68.00	250.00
62-Donald Duck in Frozen Gold, by Carl Barks (Disney) (1/45)	154.00	462.00	2000.00
63-Roy Rogers; color photo-all 4 covers	46.00	139.00	510.00
64-Smokey Stover	12.00	35.00	130.00
65-Smitty	12.00	35.00	130.00
66-Gene Autry	38.00	115.00	420.00
67-Oswald the Rabbit	17.00	50.00	185.00
68-Mother Goose and Nursery Rhyme Comics, by Walt Kelly	19.00	56.00	205.00
69-Fairy Tale Parade, by Walt Kelly	25.00	74.00	270.00
70-Popeye and Wimpy	25.00	75.00	275.00
71-Walt Disney's Three Caballeros, by Walt Kelly (© 4/45)-(Disney)	77.00	232.00	850.00
72-Raggedy Ann	24.00	74.00	270.00
73-The Gumps (#1)	11.35	34.00	125.00
74-Marge's Little Lulu (#1)	95.00	286.00	1050.00
75-Gene Autry and the Wildcat	30.00	89.00	325.00
76-Little Orphan Annie; reprints strips from 2/28/40 to 6/24/40	24.00	72.00	265.00
77-Felix the Cat	37.00	112.00	410.00
78-Porky Pig and the Bandit Twins	23.00	68.00	250.00
79-Walt Disney's Mickey Mouse in The Riddle of the Red Hat by Carl Barks (8/45)	100.00	300.00	1100.00
80-Smilin' Jack	15.00	45.00	165.00
81-Moon Mullins	9.50	29.00	105.00
82-Lone Ranger	41.00	123.00	450.00
83-Gene Autry in Outlaw Trail	30.00	89.00	325.00
84-Flash Gordon by Alex Raymond-Reprints from "The Fiery Desert"	36.00	109.00	400.00
85-Andy Panda and the Mad Dog Mystery	15.50	46.00	170.00
86-Roy Rogers; photo-c	34.00	102.00	375.00
87-Fairy Tale Parade by Walt Kelly; Dan Noonan-c	25.00	74.00	270.00
88-Bugs Bunny's Great Adventure (Sci/fi)	20.00	60.00	220.00
89-Tillie the Toiler	13.00	39.00	145.00
90-Christmas with Mother Goose by Walt Kelly (11/45)	17.00	52.00	190.00
91-Santa Claus Funnies by Walt Kelly (11/45)	17.00	50.00	185.00
92-Walt Disney's The Wonderful Adventures Of Pinocchio (1945); Donald Duck by Kelly, 16 pgs. (Disney)	57.00	170.00	625.00
93-Gene Autry in The Bandit of Black Rock	26.00	78.00	285.00
94-Winnie Winkle (1945)	11.30	34.00	125.00
95-Roy Rogers Comics; photo-c	34.00	102.00	375.00
96-Dick Tracy	24.00	72.00	260.00
97-Marge's Little Lulu (1946)	45.00	136.00	500.00
98-Lone Ranger, The	30.00	88.00	325.00
99-Smitty	10.00	30.00	110.00
100-Gene Autry Comics; photo-c	26.00	78.00	285.00
101-Terry and the Pirates	25.30	76.00	280.00

NOTE: No. 101 is last issue to carry "Four Color" logo on cover; all issues beginning with No. 100 are marked "...O. S." (One Shot) which can be found in the bottom left-hand panel on the first page; the numbers following "O. S." relate to the year/month issued.

	GD2.0	FN6.0	NM9.4
102-Oswald the Rabbit-Walt Kelly art, 1 pg.	14.50	43.50	160.00
103-Easter with Mother Goose by Walt Kelly	18.00	53.00	195.00
104-Fairy Tale Parade by Walt Kelly	18.00	53.00	195.00
105-Albert the Alligator and Pogo Possum (#1) by Kelly (4/46)	66.00	198.00	725.00
106-Tillie the Toiler	9.50	29.00	105.00
107-Little Orphan Annie; reprints strips from 11/16/42 to 3/24/43	20.00	61.00	225.00
108-Donald Duck in The Terror of the River, by Carl Barks (Disney) (© 4/16/46)	112.00	335.00	1450.00
109-Roy Rogers Comics; photo-c	25.00	75.00	275.00
110-Marge's Little Lulu	32.00	97.00	355.00
111-Captain Easy	14.00	41.00	150.00
112-Porky Pig's Adventure in Gopher Gulch	14.00	41.00	150.00
113-Popeye; all new Popeye stories begin	12.30	37.00	135.00
114-Fairy Tale Parade by Walt Kelly	18.00	53.00	195.00
115-Marge's Little Lulu	32.00	97.00	355.00
116-Mickey Mouse and the House of Many Mysteries (Disney)	22.00	67.00	245.00
117-Roy Rogers Comics; photo-c	18.00	53.00	195.00
118-Lone Ranger, The	30.00	88.00	325.00
119-Felix the Cat; all new Felix stories begin	31.00	91.00	335.00
120-Marge's Little Lulu	28.00	84.00	310.00
121-Fairy Tale Parade-(not Kelly)	10.50	31.00	115.00
122-Henry (#1) (10/46)	12.30	37.00	135.00
123-Bugs Bunny's Dangerous Venture	15.00	45.00	165.00
124-Roy Rogers Comics; photo-c	18.00	53.00	195.00
125-Lone Ranger, The	20.50	61.00	225.00
126-Christmas with Mother Goose by Walt Kelly (1946)	13.00	39.00	145.00
127-Popeye	12.30	37.00	135.00
128-Santa Claus Funnies- "Santa & the Angel" by Gollub; "A Mouse in the House" by Kelly	13.00	39.00	145.00
129-Walt Disney's Uncle Remus and His Tales of Brer Rabbit (#1) (1946)-Adapted from Disney movie "Song of the South"	27.00	82.00	300.00
130-Andy Panda (Walter Lantz)	9.50	29.00	105.00
131-Marge's Little Lulu	28.00	84.00	310.00
132-Tillie the Toiler (1947)	9.50	29.00	105.00
133-Dick Tracy	20.00	60.00	220.00
134-Tarzan and the Devil Ogre; Marsh-c/a	61.00	184.00	675.00
135-Felix the Cat	23.00	68.00	250.00
136-Lone Ranger, The	20.50	61.00	225.00
137-Roy Rogers Comics; photo-c	18.00	53.00	195.00
138-Smitty	8.65	26.00	95.00
139-Marge's Little Lulu (1947)	26.00	79.00	290.00
140-Easter with Mother Goose by Walt Kelly	14.50	44.00	160.00
141-Mickey Mouse and the Submarine Pirates (Disney)	19.00	57.00	210.00
142-Bugs Bunny and the Haunted Mountain	15.00	45.00	165.00
143-Oswald the Rabbit & the Prehistoric Egg	8.65	26.00	95.00
144-Roy Rogers Comics (1947)-Photo-c	18.00	53.00	195.00
145-Popeye	12.30	37.00	135.00
146-Marge's Little Lulu	26.00	79.00	290.00
147-Donald Duck in Volcano Valley, by Carl Barks (Disney) (5/47)	77.00	231.00	1000.00
148-Albert the Alligator and Pogo Possum by Walt Kelly (5/47)	58.00	175.00	640.00
149-Smilin' Jack	9.50	29.00	105.00
150-Tillie the Toiler (6/47)	8.65	26.00	95.00
151-Lone Ranger, The	17.00	50.00	185.00
152-Little Orphan Annie; reprints strips from 1/2/44 to 5/6/44	13.00	39.00	145.00
153-Roy Rogers Comics; photo-c	15.50	46.50	170.00
154-Walter Lantz Andy Panda	9.50	29.00	105.00
155-Henry (7/47)	8.00	23.00	85.00
156-Porky Pig and the Phantom	9.50	29.00	105.00
157-Mickey Mouse & the Beanstalk (Disney)	19.00	57.00	210.00

Four Color #170 © WDC

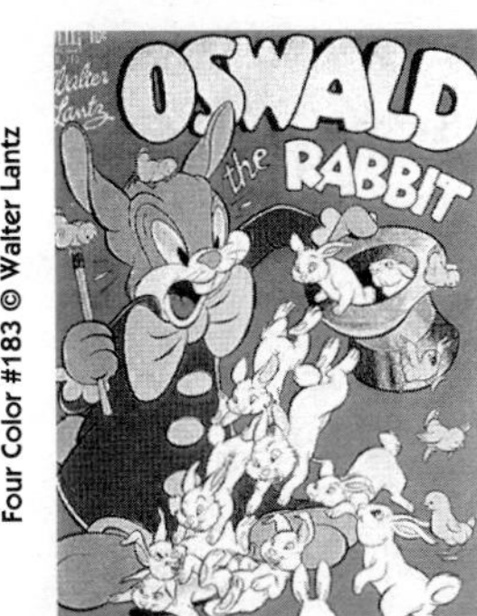

Four Color #183 © Walter Lantz

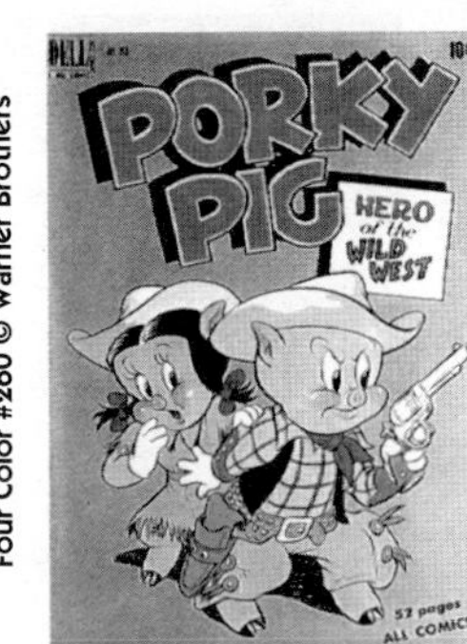

Four Color #260 © Warner Brothers

	GD2.0	FN6.0	NM9.4
158-Marge's Little Lulu	26.00	79.00	290.00
159-Donald Duck in the Ghost of the Grotto, by Carl Barks (Disney) (8/47)	62.00	185.00	800.00
160-Roy Rogers Comics; photo-c	15.50	46.50	170.00
161-Tarzan and the Fires Of Tohr; Marsh-c/a	52.00	157.00	575.00
162-Felix the Cat (9/47)	17.00	52.00	190.00
163-Dick Tracy	16.00	48.00	175.00
164-Bugs Bunny Finds the Frozen Kingdom	15.00	45.00	165.00
165-Marge's Little Lulu	26.00	79.00	290.00
166-Roy Rogers Comics (52 pgs.)-Photo-c	15.50	46.50	170.00
167-Lone Ranger, The	17.00	50.00	185.00
168-Popeye (10/47)	12.30	37.00	135.00
169-Woody Woodpecker (#1)- "Manhunter in the North"; drug use story	14.00	42.00	155.00
170-Mickey Mouse on Spook's Island (11/47)(Disney)-reprinted in Mickey Mouse #103	15.50	46.00	170.00
171-Charlie McCarthy (#1) and the Twenty Thieves	24.00	71.00	260.00
172-Christmas with Mother Goose by Walt Kelly (11/47)	13.00	39.00	145.00
173-Flash Gordon	13.00	38.00	140.00
174-Winnie Winkle	6.70	20.00	75.00
175-Santa Claus Funnies by Walt Kelly (1947)	13.00	39.00	145.00
176-Tillie the Toiler (12/47)	8.65	26.00	95.00
177-Roy Rogers Comics-(36 pgs.); Photo-c	15.50	46.50	170.00
178-Donald Duck "Christmas on Bear Mountain" by Carl Barks; 1st app. Uncle Scrooge (Disney)(12/47)	92.00	277.00	1200.00
179-Uncle Wiggily (#1)-Walt Kelly-c	15.00	45.00	165.00
180-Ozark Ike (#1)	9.50	29.00	105.00
181-Walt Disney's Mickey Mouse in Jungle Magic	15.50	46.00	170.00
182-Porky Pig in Never-Never Land (2/48)	9.50	29.00	105.00
183-Oswald the Rabbit (Lantz)	8.65	26.00	95.00
184-Tillie the Toiler	8.65	26.00	95.00
185-Easter with Mother Goose by Walt Kelly (1948)	12.30	37.00	135.00
186-Walt Disney's Bambi (4/48)-Reprinted as Movie Classic Bambi #3 (1956)	16.00	47.00	175.00
187-Bugs Bunny and the Dreadful Dragon	10.00	30.00	110.00
188-Woody Woodpecker (Lantz, 5/48)	9.50	29.00	105.00
189-Donald Duck in The Old Castle's Secret, by Carl Barks (Disney) (6/48)	58.00	173.00	750.00
190-Flash Gordon (6/48); bondage-c; "The Adventures of the Flying Saucers"; 5th Flying Saucer story- see The Spirit 9/28/47(1st), Shadow Comics V7#10 (2nd, 1/48),Captain Midnight #60 (3rd, 2/48) & Boy Commandos #26 (4th, 3-4/48)	14.50	44.00	160.00
191-Porky Pig to the Rescue	9.50	29.00	105.00
192-The Brownies (#1)-by Walt Kelly (7/48)	11.50	34.00	125.00
193-M.G.M. Presents Tom and Jerry (#1)(1948)	14.00	41.00	150.00
194-Mickey Mouse in The World Under the Sea (Disney)-Reprinted in Mickey Mouse #101	15.50	46.00	170.00
195-Tillie the Toiler	6.00	18.00	65.00
196-Charlie McCarthy in The Haunted Hide-Out; part photo-c	16.50	49.00	180.00
197-Spirit of the Border (#1) (Zane Grey) (1948)	11.00	32.00	115.00
198-Andy Panda	9.50	29.00	105.00
199-Donald Duck in Sheriff of Bullet Valley, by Carl Barks; Barks draws himself on wanted poster, last page; used in Love & Death (Disney) (10/48)	64.00	190.00	825.00
200-Bugs Bunny, Super Sleuth (10/48)	10.00	30.00	110.00
201-Christmas with Mother Goose by W. Kelly	11.25	34.00	125.00
202-Woody Woodpecker	5.75	17.00	63.00
203-Donald Duck in the Golden Christmas Tree, by Carl Barks (Disney) (12/48)	43.00	129.00	560.00
204-Flash Gordon (12/48)	10.00	30.00	110.00
205-Santa Claus Funnies by Walt Kelly	12.00	35.00	130.00
206-Little Orphan Annie; reprints strips from 11/10/40 to 1/11/41	7.00	20.00	75.00
207-King of the Royal Mounted (#1) (12/48)	14.00	41.00	150.00
208-Brer Rabbit Does It Again (Disney) (1/49)	11.00	32.00	120.00
209-Harold Teen	3.80	11.50	42.00
210-Tippie and Cap Stubbs	3.60	11.00	40.00
211-Little Beaver (#1)	7.00	20.00	75.00
212-Dr. Bobbs	3.60	10.80	40.00
213-Tillie the Toiler	6.00	18.00	65.00
214-Mickey Mouse and His Sky Adventure (2/49)(Disney)-Reprinted in Mickey Mouse #105	13.00	40.00	145.00
215-Sparkle Plenty (Dick Tracy-r by Gould)	9.50	29.00	105.00
216-Andy Panda and the Police Pup (Lantz)	6.25	18.50	68.00
217-Bugs Bunny in Court Jester	10.00	30.00	110.00
218-3 Little Pigs and the Wonderful Magic Lamp (Disney) (3/49)(#1)	11.00	33.00	120.00
219-Swee'pe	8.00	25.00	90.00
220-Easter with Mother Goose by Walt Kelly	12.30	37.00	135.00
221-Uncle Wiggily-Walt Kelly cover in part	9.00	27.00	100.00
222-West of the Pecos (Zane Grey)	5.50	16.50	60.00
223-Donald Duck "Lost in the Andes" by Carl Barks (Disney-4/49) (square egg story)	62.00	185.00	800.00
224-Little Iodine (#1), by Hatlo (4/49)	8.00	25.00	90.00
225-Oswald the Rabbit (Lantz)	5.00	15.00	55.00
226-Porky Pig and Spoofy, the Spook	7.00	22.00	80.00
227-Seven Dwarfs (Disney)	10.00	30.00	110.00
228-Mark of Zorro, The (#1) (1949)	20.00	60.00	220.00
229-Smokey Stover	4.50	13.50	50.00
230-Sunset Pass (Zane Grey)	5.50	16.50	60.00
231-Mickey Mouse and the Rajah's Treasure (Disney)	13.00	40.00	145.00
232-Woody Woodpecker (Lantz, 6/49)	5.75	17.00	63.00
233-Bugs Bunny, Sleepwalking Sleuth	10.00	30.00	110.00
234-Dumbo in Sky Voyage (Disney)	9.00	27.00	100.00
235-Tiny Tim	3.60	11.00	40.00
236-Heritage of the Desert (Zane Grey) (1949)	5.50	16.50	60.00
237-Tillie the Toiler	6.00	18.00	65.00
238-Donald Duck in Voodoo Hoodoo, by Carl Barks (Disney) (8/49)	43.00	129.00	560.00
239-Adventure Bound (8/49)	4.25	13.00	48.00
240-Andy Panda (Lantz)	6.25	18.50	68.00
241-Porky Pig, Mighty Hunter	7.00	22.00	80.00
242-Tippie and Cap Stubbs	2.75	8.00	30.00
243-Thumper Follows His Nose (Disney)	9.50	28.50	105.00
244-The Brownies by Walt Kelly	10.00	30.00	110.00
245-Dick's Adventures (9/49)	4.50	13.50	50.00
246-Thunder Mountain (Zane Grey)	3.60	11.00	40.00
247-Flash Gordon	10.00	30.00	110.00
248-Mickey Mouse and the Black Sorcerer (Disney)	13.00	40.00	145.00
249-Woody Woodpecker in the "Globetrotter" (10/49)	5.75	17.00	63.00
250-Bugs Bunny in Diamond Daze; used in **SOTI**, pg. 309	11.00	33.00	120.00
251-Hubert at Camp Moonbeam	3.60	11.00	40.00
252-Pinocchio (Disney)-not by Kelly; origin	9.50	29.00	105.00
253-Christmas with Mother Goose by W. Kelly	11.25	34.00	125.00
254-Santa Claus Funnies by Walt Kelly; Pogo & Albert story by Kelly (11/49)	12.00	35.00	130.00
255-The Ranger (Zane Grey) (1949)	3.60	11.00	40.00
256-Donald Duck in "Luck of the North" by Carl Barks (Disney) (12/49)-Shows #257 on inside	33.00	99.00	425.00
257-Little Iodine	6.40	19.00	70.00
258-Andy Panda and the Balloon Race (Lantz)	6.25	18.50	68.00
259-Santa and the Angel (Gollub art-condensed from #128) & Santa at the Zoo (12/49)-two books in one	3.60	11.00	40.00
260-Porky Pig, Hero of the Wild West (12/49)	7.00	22.00	80.00
261-Mickey Mouse and the Missing Key (Disney)	13.00	40.00	145.00
262-Raggedy Ann and Andy	6.40	19.00	70.00
263-Donald Duck in "Land of the Totem Poles" by Carl Barks (Disney) (2/50)-Has two Barks stories	31.00	92.00	400.00
264-Woody Woodpecker in the Magic Lantern (Lantz)			

Four Color #283 © KING

Four Color #319 © Gene Autry

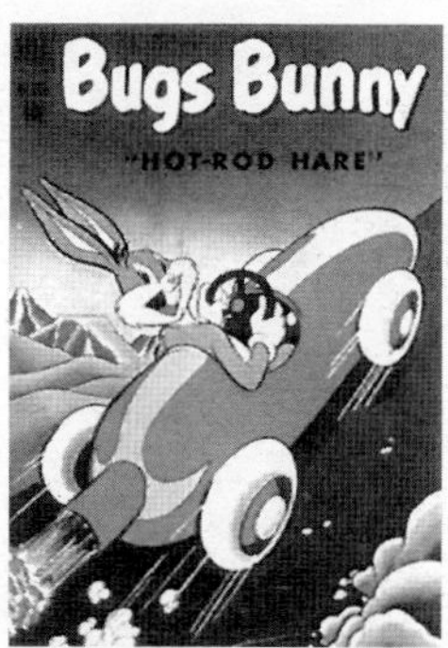

Four Color #355 © Warner Brothers

	GD2.0	FN6.0	NM9.4
	5.75	17.00	63.00
265-King of the Royal Mounted (Zane Grey)	7.00	22.00	80.00
266-Bugs Bunny on the "Isle of Hercules" (2/50)-Reprinted in Best of Bugs			
Bunny #1	8.00	25.00	90.00
267-Little Beaver; Harmon-c/a	3.50	11.00	38.00
268-Mickey Mouse's Surprise Visitor (1950) (Disney)			
	12.00	35.00	130.00
269-Johnny Mack Brown (#1)-Photo-c	22.00	65.00	240.00
270-Drift Fence (Zane Grey) (3/50)	3.60	11.00	40.00
271-Porky Pig in Phantom of the Plains	7.00	22.00	80.00
272-Cinderella (Disney) (4/50)	9.00	27.00	100.00
273-Oswald the Rabbit (Lantz)	5.00	15.00	55.00
274-Bugs Bunny, Hare-brained Reporter	8.00	25.00	90.00
275-Donald Duck in "Ancient Persia" by Carl Barks (Disney) (5/50)			
	29.00	87.00	375.00
276-Uncle Wiggily	7.00	22.00	80.00
277-Porky Pig in Desert Adventure (5/50)	7.00	22.00	80.00
278-Bill Elliott Comics (#1)-Photo-c	12.00	35.00	130.00
279-Mickey Mouse and Pluto Battle the Giant Ants (Disney); reprinted in			
Mickey Mouse #102 & 245	9.00	27.00	100.00
280-Andy Panda in The Isle Of Mechanical Men (Lantz)			
	6.25	18.50	
68.00281-Bugs Bunny in The Great Circus Mystery	8.00	25.00	90.00
282-Donald Duck and the Pixilated Parrot by Carl Barks (Disney)			
(© 5/23/50)	29.00	87.00	375.00
283-King of the Royal Mounted (7/50)	7.00	22.00	80.00
284-Porky Pig in The Kingdom of Nowhere	7.00	22.00	80.00
285-Bozo the Clown & His Minikin Circus (#1) (TV)	17.00	51.00	190.00
286-Mickey Mouse in The Uninvited Guest (Disney	9.00	27.00	100.00
287-Gene Autry's Champion in The Ghost Of Black Mountain; photo-c			
	8.50	25.50	95.00
288-Woody Woodpecker in Klondike Gold (Lantz)	5.75	17.00	63.00
289-Bugs Bunny in "Indian Trouble"	8.00	25.00	90.00
290-The Chief (#1) (8/50)	4.50	13.50	50.00
291-Donald Duck in "The Magic Hourglass" by Carl Barks (Disney) (9/50)			
	29.00	87.00	375.00
292-The Cisco Kid Comics (#1)	22.00	66.00	240.00
293-The Brownies-Kelly-c/a	10.00	30.00	110.00
294-Little Beaver	3.50	11.00	38.00
295-Porky Pig in President Porky (9/50)	7.00	22.00	80.00
296-Mickey Mouse in Private Eye for Hire (Disney)	9.00	27.00	100.00
297-Andy Panda in The Haunted Inn (Lantz, 10/50)	6.25	18.50	68.00
298-Bugs Bunny in Sheik for a Day	8.00	25.00	90.00
299-Buck Jones & the Iron Horse Trail (#1)	11.00	34.00	125.00
300-Donald Duck in "Big-Top Bedlam" by Carl Barks (Disney) (11/50)			
	29.00	87.00	375.00
301-The Mysterious Rider (Zane Grey)	3.60	11.00	40.00
302-Santa Claus Funnies (11/50)	3.60	11.00	40.00
303-Porky Pig in The Land of the Monstrous Flies	4.50	13.50	50.00
304-Mickey Mouse in Tom-Tom Island (Disney) (12/50)			
	7.00	22.00	80.00
305-Woody Woodpecker (Lantz)	3.00	10.00	36.00
306-Raggedy Ann	4.50	13.50	50.00
307-Bugs Bunny in Lumber Jack Rabbit	7.00	20.00	75.00
308-Donald Duck in "Dangerous Disguise" by Carl Barks (Disney) (1/51)			
	25.00	75.00	325.00
309-Betty Betz' Dollface and Her Gang (1951)	4.50	13.50	50.00
310-King of the Royal Mounted (1/51)	5.50	16.50	60.00
311-Porky Pig in Midget Horses of Hidden Valley	4.50	13.50	50.00
312-Tonto (#1)	9.00	27.00	100.00
313-Mickey Mouse in The Mystery of the Double-Cross Ranch (#1)			
(Disney) (2/51)	7.00	22.00	80.00

Note: Beginning with the above comic in 1951 Dell/Western began adding #1 in small print on the covers of several long running titles with the evident intention of switching these titles to their own monthly numbers, but when the conversions were made, there was no connection. It is thought that the post office may have stepped in and decreed the sequences should commence as though the first four colors printed had each begun with number one, or the first issues sold by subscription. Since the regular series' numbers don't correctly match to the numbers of earlier issues published, it's not known whether or not the numbering was in error.

	GD2.0	FN6.0	NM9.4
314-Ambush (Zane Grey)	3.60	11.00	40.00
315-Oswald the Rabbit (Lantz)	4.00	12.00	45.00
316-Rex Allen (#1)-Photo-c; Marsh-a	13.00	38.00	140.00
317-Bugs Bunny in Hair Today Gone Tomorrow (#1)	7.00	20.00	75.00
318-Donald Duck in "No Such Varmint" by Carl Barks (#1)-Indicia shows #317			
(Disney, © 1/23/51)	25.00	75.00	325.00
319-Gene Autry's Champion; painted-c	3.60	11.00	40.00
320-Uncle Wiggily (#1)	7.00	22.00	80.00
321-Little Scouts (#1) (3/51)	2.75	8.00	30.00
322-Porky Pig in Roaring Rockets (#1 on-c)	4.50	13.50	50.00
323-Susie Q. Smith (#1) (3/51)	3.00	9.00	35.00
324-I Met a Handsome Cowboy (3/51)	8.00	25.00	90.00
325-Mickey Mouse in The Haunted Castle (#2) (Disney) (4/51)			
	7.00	22.00	80.00
326-Andy Panda (#1) (Lantz)	3.75	11.50	40.00
327-Bugs Bunny and the Rajah's Treasure (#2)	7.00	20.00	75.00
328-Donald Duck in Old California (#2) by Carl Barks-Peyote drug use issue			
(Disney) (5/51)	27.00	81.00	350.00
329-Roy Roger's Trigger (#1)(5/51)-Photo-c	11.00	32.00	120.00
330-Porky Pig Meets the Bristled Bruiser (#2)	4.50	13.50	50.00
331-Alice in Wonderland (Disney) (1951)	13.75	41.50	150.00
332-Little Beaver	3.50	11.00	38.00
333-Wilderness Trek (Zane Grey) (5/51)	3.60	11.00	40.00
334-Mickey Mouse and Yukon Gold (Disney) (6/51)	7.00	22.00	80.00
335-Francis the Famous Talking Mule (#1, 6/51)-1st Dell non animated movie			
comic (all issues based on movie)	7.00	22.00	80.00
336-Woody Woodpecker (Lantz)	3.00	10.00	36.00
337-The Brownies-not by Walt Kelly	3.00	10.00	36.00
338-Bugs Bunny and the Rocking Horse Thieves	7.00	20.00	75.00
339-Donald Duck and the Magic Fountain-not by Carl Barks (Disney) (7-8/51)			
	6.00	18.00	60.00
340-King of the Royal Mounted (7/51)	5.50	16.50	60.00
341-Unbirthday Party with Alice in Wonderland (Disney) (7/51)			
	13.75	41.50	150.00
342-Porky Pig the Lucky Peppermint Mine; r/in Porky Pig #3			
	3.60	11.00	40.00
343-Mickey Mouse in The Ruby Eye of Homar-Guy-Am (Disney)-Reprinted in			
Mickey Mouse #104	5.50	16.50	60.00
344-Sergeant Preston from Challenge of The Yukon (#1) (TV)			
	11.00	33.00	120.00
345-Andy Panda in Scotland Yard (8-10/51) (Lantz)	3.75	11.50	40.00
346-Hideout (Zane Grey)	3.60	11.00	40.00
347-Bugs Bunny the Frigid Hare (8-9/51)	7.00	20.00	75.00
348-Donald Duck "The Crocodile Collector"; Barks-c only (Disney) (9-10/51)			
	15.00	45.00	160.00
349-Uncle Wiggily	5.50	16.50	60.00
350-Woody Woodpecker (Lantz)	3.00	10.00	36.00
351-Porky Pig & the Grand Canyon Giant (9-10/51)	3.60	11.00	40.00
352-Mickey Mouse in The Mystery of Painted Valley (Disney)			
	5.50	16.50	60.00
353-Duck Album (#1)-Barks-c (Disney)	8.00	24.00	90.00
354-Raggedy Ann & Andy	4.50	13.50	50.00
355-Bugs Bunny Hot-Rod Hare	7.00	20.00	75.00
356-Donald Duck in "Rags to Riches"; Barks-c only	15.00	45.00	160.00
357-Comeback (Zane Grey)	2.75	8.00	30.00
358-Andy Panda (Lantz) (11-1/52)	3.75	11.50	40.00
359-Frosty the Snowman (#1)	7.00	22.00	80.00
360-Porky Pig in Tree of Fortune (11-12/51)	3.60	11.00	40.00
361-Santa Claus Funnies	3.60	11.00	40.00
362-Mickey Mouse and the Smuggled Diamonds (Disney)			
	5.50	16.50	60.00
363-King of the Royal Mounted	4.50	13.50	50.00
364-Woody Woodpecker (Lantz)	3.00	9.00	34.00

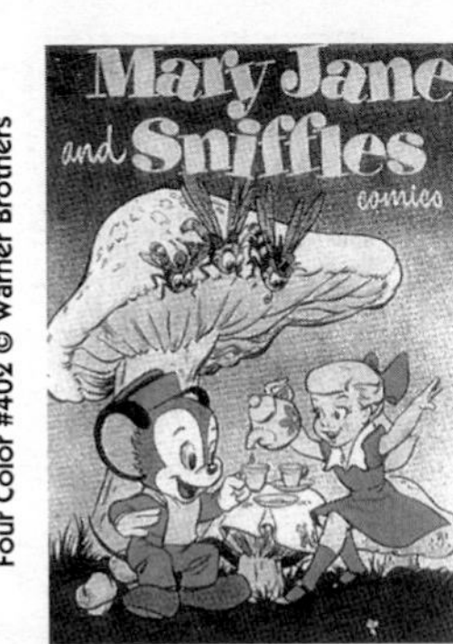

Four Color #402 © Warner Brothers

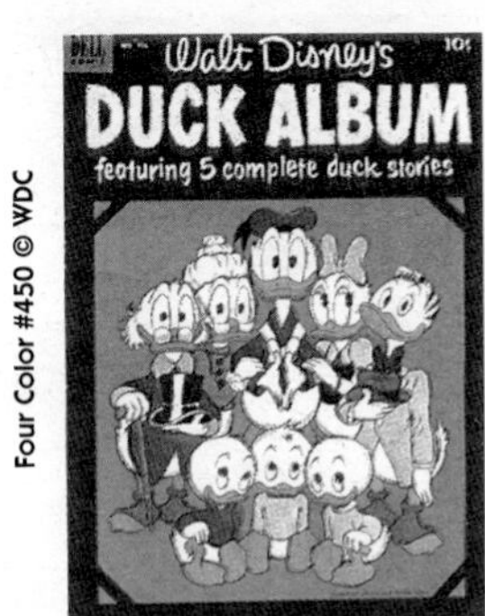

Four Color #450 © WDC

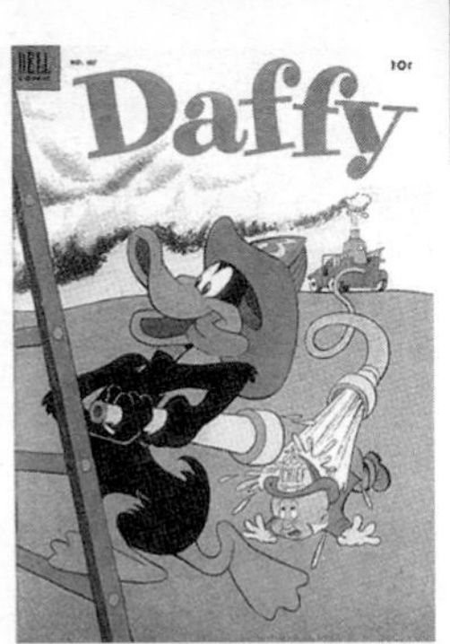

Four Color #457 © Warner Brothers

	GD2.0	FN6.0	NM9.4
365-The Brownies-not by Kelly	3.00	10.00	36.00
366-Bugs Bunny Uncle Buckskin Comes to Town (12-1/52)	7.00	20.00	75.00
367-Donald Duck in "A Christmas for Shacktown" by Carl Barks (Disney) (1-2/52)	25.00	75.00	320.00
368-Bob Clampett's Beany and Cecil (#1)	25.00	75.00	275.00
369-The Lone Ranger's Famous Horse Hi-Yo Silver (#1); Silver's origin	8.00	25.00	90.00
370-Porky Pig in Trouble in the Big Trees	3.60	11.00	40.00
371-Mickey Mouse in The Inca Idol Case (1952) (Disney)	5.50	16.50	60.00
372-Riders of the Purple Sage (Zane Grey)	2.75	8.00	30.00
373-Sergeant Preston (TV)	6.40	19.00	70.00
374-Woody Woodpecker (Lantz)	3.00	9.00	34.00
375-John Carter of Mars (E. R. Burroughs)-Jesse Marsh-a; origin	23.00	68.00	250.00
376-Bugs Bunny, "The Magic Sneeze"	7.00	20.00	75.00
377-Susie Q. Smith	2.75	8.00	30.00
378-Tom Corbett, Space Cadet (#1) (TV)-McWilliams-a	16.00	48.00	175.00
379-Donald Duck in "Southern Hospitality"; Not by Barks (Disney)	6.00	18.00	60.00
380-Raggedy Ann & Andy	4.50	13.50	50.00
381-Marge's Tubby (#1)	19.00	57.00	210.00
382-Snow White and the Seven Dwarfs (Disney)-origin; partial reprint of 4-Color #49 (Movie)	10.00	30.00	110.00
383-Andy Panda (Lantz)	3.00	9.00	32.00
384-King of the Royal Mounted (3/52)(Zane Grey)	4.50	13.50	50.00
385-Porky Pig in The Isle of Missing Ships (3-4/52)	3.60	11.00	40.00
386-Uncle Scrooge (#1)-by Carl Barks (Disney) in "Only a Poor Old Man" (3/52)	86.00	259.00	950.00
387-Mickey Mouse in High Tibet (Disney) (4-5/52)	5.50	16.50	60.00
388-Oswald the Rabbit (Lantz)	4.00	12.00	45.00
389-Andy Hardy Comics (#1)	2.75	8.00	30.00
390-Woody Woodpecker (Lantz)	3.00	9.00	34.00
391-Uncle Wiggily	5.50	16.50	60.00
392-Hi-Yo Silver	4.00	12.00	45.00
393-Bugs Bunny	7.00	20.00	75.00
394-Donald Duck in Malayalaya-Barks-c only (Disney)	15.00	45.00	160.00
395-Forlorn River(Zane Grey)-First Nevada (5/52)	2.75	8.00	30.00
396-Tales of the Texas Rangers(#1)(TV)-Photo-c	10.00	30.00	110.00
397-Sergeant Preston of the Yukon (TV) (5/52)	6.40	19.00	70.00
398-The Brownies-not by Kelly	3.00	10.00	36.00
399-Porky Pig in The Lost Gold Mine	3.60	11.00	40.00
400-Tom Corbett, Space Cadet (TV)-McWilliams-c/a	9.00	27.00	100.00
401-Mickey Mouse and Goofy's Mechanical Wizard (Disney) (6-7/52)	3.60	11.00	40.00
402-Mary Jane and Sniffles	7.00	22.00	80.00
403-Li'l Bad Wolf (Disney) (6/52)(#1)	6.40	19.00	70.00
404-The Range Rider (#1) (TV)-Photo-c	10.00	30.00	110.00
405-Woody Woodpecker (Lantz) (6-7/52)	3.00	9.00	34.00
406-Tweety and Sylvester (#1)	7.00	22.00	80.00
407-Bugs Bunny, Foreign-Legion Hare	5.50	16.50	60.00
408-Donald Duck and the Golden Helmet by Carl Barks (Disney) (7-8/52)	25.00	75.00	320.00
409-Andy Panda (7-9/52)	3.00	9.00	32.00
410-Porky Pig in The Water Wizard (7/52)	3.60	11.00	40.00
411-Mickey Mouse and the Old Sea Dog (Disney) (8-9/52)	3.60	11.00	40.00
412-Nevada (Zane Grey)	2.75	8.00	30.00
413-Robin Hood (Disney-Movie) (8/52)-Photo-c (1st Disney movie four color book)	10.00	30.00	110.00
414-Bob Clampett's Beany and Cecil (TV)	16.00	47.00	170.00
415-Rootie Kazootie (#1) (TV)	10.00	30.00	110.00
416-Woody Woodpecker (Lantz)	3.00	9.00	34.00

	GD2.0	FN6.0	NM9.4
417-Double Trouble with Goober (#1) (8/52)	2.25	6.75	25.00
418-Rusty Riley, a Boy, a Horse, and a Dog (#1)-Frank Godwin-a (strip reprints) (8/52)	3.60	11.00	40.00
419-Sergeant Preston (TV)	6.40	19.00	70.00
420-Bugs Bunny in The Mysterious Buckaroo (8-9/52)	5.50	16.50	60.00
421-Tom Corbett, Space Cadet(TV)-McWilliams-a	9.00	27.00	100.00
422-Donald Duck and the Gilded Man, by Carl Barks (Disney) (9-10/52) (#423 on inside)	25.00	75.00	320.00
423-Rhubarb, Owner of the Brooklyn Ball Club (The Millionaire Cat) (#1)-Painted cover	4.50	13.50	50.00
424-Flash Gordon-Test Flight in Space (9/52)	8.00	23.00	85.00
425-Zorro, the Return of	11.00	34.00	125.00
426-Porky Pig in The Scalawag Leprechaun	3.60	11.00	40.00
427-Mickey Mouse and the Wonderful Whizzix (Disney) (10-11/52)-Reprinted in Mickey Mouse #100	3.60	11.00	40.00
428-Uncle Wiggily	3.60	11.00	40.00
429-Pluto in "Why Dogs Leave Home" (Disney) (10/52)(#1)	8.00	23.00	85.00
430-Marge's Tubby, the Shadow of a Man-Eater	11.00	33.00	120.00
431-Woody Woodpecker (10/52) (Lantz)	3.00	9.00	34.00
432-Bugs Bunny and the Rabbit Olympics	5.50	16.50	60.00
433-Wildfire (Zane Grey) (11-1/52-53)	2.75	8.00	30.00
434-Rin Tin Tin "In Dark Danger" (#1) (TV) (11/52)-Photo-c	14.00	41.00	150.00
435-Frosty the Snowman (11/52)	3.60	11.00	40.00
436-The Brownies-not by Kelly (11/52)	3.00	9.00	32.00
437-John Carter of Mars (E. R. Burroughs)-Marsh-a	14.00	44.00	160.00
438-Annie Oakley (#1) (TV)	14.00	41.00	150.00
439-Little Hiawatha (Disney) (12/52)j(#1)	4.50	13.50	50.00
440-Black Beauty (12/52)	2.75	8.00	30.00
441-Fearless Fagan	3.00	9.00	35.00
442-Peter Pan (Disney) (Movie)	8.00	25.00	90.00
443-Ben Bowie and His Mountain Men (#1)	5.50	16.50	60.00
444-Marge's Tubby	11.00	33.00	120.00
445-Charlie McCarthy	4.50	13.50	50.00
446-Captain Hook and Peter Pan (Disney)(Movie)(1/53)	8.00	25.00	90.00
447-Andy Hardy Comics	2.25	6.75	25.00
448-Bob Clampett's Beany and Cecil (TV)	16.00	47.00	170.00
449-Tappan's Burro (Zane Grey) (2-4/53)	2.75	8.00	30.00
450-Duck Album; Barks-c (Disney)	5.50	16.50	60.00
451-Rusty Riley-Frank Godwin-a (strip-r) (2/53)	2.75	8.00	30.00
452-Raggedy Ann & Andy (1953)	4.50	13.50	50.00
453-Susie Q. Smith (2/53)	2.75	8.00	30.00
454-Krazy Kat Comics; not by Herriman	3.00	9.00	35.00
455-Johnny Mack Brown Comics(3/53)-Photo-c	5.00	15.00	55.00
456-Uncle Scrooge Back to the Klondike (#2) by Barks (3/53) (Disney)	57.00	170.00	625.00
457-Daffy (#1)	8.00	25.00	90.00
458-Oswald the Rabbit (Lantz)	2.90	8.70	32.00
459-Rootie Kazootie (TV)	6.40	19.00	70.00
460-Buck Jones (4/53)	4.50	13.50	50.00
461-Marge's Tubby	9.50	29.00	105.00
462-Little Scouts	1.35	4.00	15.00
463-Petunia (4/53)	3.00	9.00	35.00
464-Bozo (4/53)	8.00	25.00	90.00
465-Francis the Famous Talking Mule	4.50	13.50	50.00
466-Rhubarb, the Millionaire Cat; painted-c	3.60	11.00	40.00
467-Desert Gold (Zane Grey) (5-7/53)	2.75	8.00	30.00
468-Goofy (#1) (Disney)	11.00	34.00	125.00
469-Beetle Bailey (#1) (5/53	9.00	27.00	100.00
470-Elmer Fudd	4.50	13.50	50.00
471-Double Trouble with Goober	1.85	5.50	15.00
472-Wild Bill Elliott (6/53)-Photo-c	3.60	11.00	40.00
473-Li'l Bad Wolf (Disney) (6/53)(#2)	3.60	11.00	40.00
474-Mary Jane and Sniffles	6.40	19.00	70.00

Four Color #517 © WDC

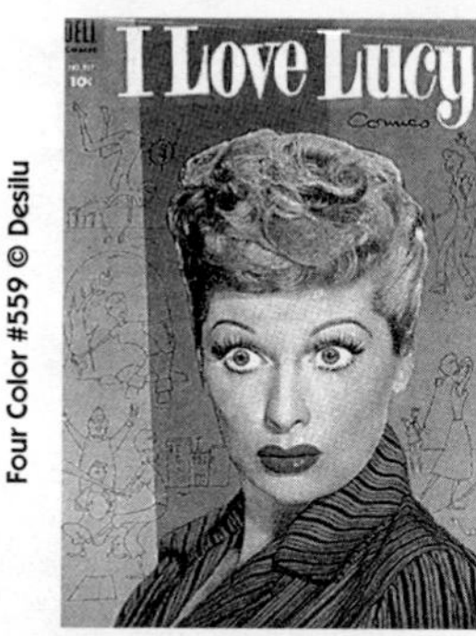

Four Color #559 © Desilu

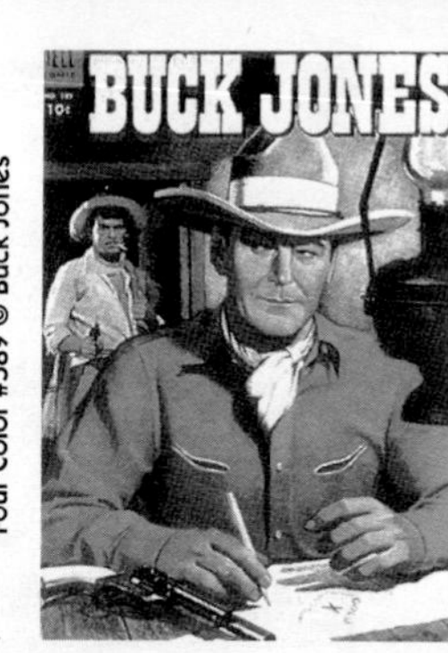

Four Color #589 © Buck Jones

	GD2.0	FN6.0	NM9.4
475-M.G.M.'s The Two Mouseketeers (#1)	6.40	19.00	70.00
476-Rin Tin Tin (TV)-Photo-c	7.00	22.00	80.00
477-Bob Clampett's Beany and Cecil (TV)	16.00	47.00	170.00
478-Charlie McCarthy	4.50	13.50	50.00
479-Queen of the West Dale Evans (#1)-Photo-c	21.00	63.00	230.00
480-Andy Hardy Comics	2.25	6.75	25.00
481-Annie Oakley And Tagg (TV)	8.00	23.00	85.00
482-Brownies-not by Kelly	3.00	9.00	32.00
483-Little Beaver (7/53)	2.75	8.00	30.00
484-River Feud (Zane Grey) (8-10/53)	2.75	8.00	30.00
485-The Little People-Walt Scott (#1)	5.50	16.50	60.00
486-Rusty Riley-Frank Godwin strip-r	2.75	8.00	30.00
487-Mowgli, the Jungle Book (Rudyard Kipling's)	5.00	15.00	55.00
488-John Carter of Mars (Burroughs)-Marsh-a; painted-c	14.00	48.00	160.00
489-Tweety and Sylvester	3.50	10.50	38.00
490-Jungle Jim (#1)	5.50	16.50	60.00
491-Silvertip (#1) (Max Brand)-Kinstler-a (8/53)	7.00	22.00	80.00
492-Duck Album (Disney)	4.50	13.50	50.00
493-Johnny Mack Brown; photo-c	5.00	15.00	55.00
494-The Little King (#1)	9.00	27.00	100.00
495-Uncle Scrooge (#3) (Disney)-by Carl Barks (9/53)	43.00	130.00	475.00
496-The Green Hornet; painted-c	23.00	68.00	250.00
497-Zorro (Sword of...)-Kinstler-a	12.00	37.00	135.00
498-Bugs Bunny's Album (9/53)	4.50	13.50	50.00
499-M.G.M.'s Spike and Tyke (#1) (9/53)	2.75	8.00	30.00
500-Buck Jones	4.50	13.50	50.00
501-Francis the Famous Talking Mule	3.60	11.00	40.00
502-Rootie Kazootie (TV)	6.40	19.00	70.00
503-Uncle Wiggily (10/53)	3.60	11.00	40.00
504-Krazy Kat; not by Herriman	3.00	9.00	35.00
505-The Sword and the Rose (Disney) (10/53)(Movie)-Photo-c	8.00	25.00	90.00
506-The Little Scouts	1.35	4.00	15.00
507-Oswald the Rabbit (Lantz)	3.00	9.00	32.00
508-Bozo (10/53)	8.00	25.00	90.00
509-Pluto (Disney) (10/53)	4.50	13.50	50.00
510-Son of Black Beauty	2.75	8.00	30.00
511-Outlaw Trail (Zane Grey)-Kinstler-a	3.60	11.00	40.00
512-Flash Gordon (11/53)	4.50	13.50	50.00
513-Ben Bowie and His Mountain Men	2.75	8.00	30.00
514-Frosty the Snowman (11/53)	3.60	11.00	40.00
515-Andy Hardy	2.25	6.75	25.00
516-Double Trouble With Goober	1.85	5.50	15.00
517-Chip 'N' Dale (#1) (Disney)	7.00	22.00	80.00
518-Rivets (11/53)	2.25	6.75	25.00
519-Steve Canyon (#1)-Not by Milton Caniff	8.00	25.00	90.00
520-Wild Bill Elliott-Photo-c	3.60	11.00	40.00
521-Beetle Bailey (12/53)	4.50	13.50	50.00
522-The Brownies	3.00	9.00	32.00
523-Rin Tin Tin (TV)-Photo-c (12/53)	7.00	22.00	80.00
524-Tweety and Sylvester	3.50	10.50	38.00
525-Santa Claus Funnies	3.60	11.00	40.00
526-Napoleon	1.80	5.50	20.00
527-Charlie McCarthy	4.50	13.50	50.00
528-Queen of the West Dale Evans; photo-c	9.50	28.50	105.00
529-Little Beaver	2.75	8.00	30.00
530-Bob Clampett's Beany and Cecil (TV) (1/54)	16.00	51.00	170.00
531-Duck Album (Disney)	4.50	13.50	50.00
532-The Rustlers (Zane Grey) (2-4/54)	2.75	8.00	30.00
533-Raggedy Ann and Andy	4.50	13.50	50.00
534-Western Marshal(Ernest Haycox's)-Kinstler-a	4.50	13.50	50.00
535-I Love Lucy (#1) (TV) (2/54)-Photo-c	48.00	143.00	525.00
536-Daffy (3/54)	4.00	12.00	45.00
537-Stormy, the Thoroughbred... (Disney-Movie) on top 2/3 of each page; Pluto story on bottom 1/3 of each page (2/54)	2.75	8.00	30.00
538-The Mask of Zorro; Kinstler-a	12.00	37.00	135.00
539-Ben and Me (Disney) (3/54)	3.00	9.00	32.00
540-Knights of the Round Table (3/54) (Movie)-Photo-c	6.40	19.00	70.00
541-Johnny Mack Brown; photo-c	5.00	15.00	55.00
542-Super Circus Featuring Mary Hartline (TV) (3/54)	6.40	19.00	70.00
543-Uncle Wiggily (3/54)	3.60	11.00	40.00
544-Rob Roy (Disney-Movie)-Manning-a; photo-c	7.00	22.00	80.00
545-The Wonderful Adventures of Pinocchio-Partial reprint of 4-Color #92 (Disney-Movie)	6.40	19.00	70.00
546-Buck Jones	4.50	13.50	50.00
547-Francis the Famous Talking Mule	3.60	11.00	40.00
548-Krazy Kat; not by Herriman (4/54)	2.75	8.00	30.00
549-Oswald the Rabbit (Lantz)	3.00	9.00	32.00
550-The Little Scouts	1.35	4.00	15.00
551-Bozo (4/54)	8.00	25.00	90.00
552-Beetle Bailey	4.50	13.50	50.00
553-Susie Q. Smith	2.75	8.00	30.00
554-Rusty Riley (Frank Godwin strip-r)	2.75	8.00	30.00
555-Range War (Zane Grey)	2.75	8.00	30.00
556-Double Trouble With Goober (5/54)	1.85	5.50	15.00
557-Ben Bowie and His Mountain Men	2.75	8.00	30.00
558-Elmer Fudd (5/54)	3.20	9.50	35.00
559-I Love Lucy (#2) (TV)-Photo-c	30.00	89.00	325.00
560-Duck Album (Disney) (5/54)	4.50	13.50	50.00
561-Mr. Magoo (5/54)	11.00	33.00	120.00
562-Goofy (Disney)(#2)	6.40	19.00	70.00
563-Rhubarb, the Millionaire Cat (6/54)	3.60	11.00	40.00
564-Li'l Bad Wolf (Disney)(#3)	3.60	11.00	40.00
565-Jungle Jim	2.75	8.00	30.00
566-Son of Black Beauty	2.75	8.00	30.00
567-Prince Valiant (#1)-By Bob Fuje (Movie)-Photo-c	10.00	30.00	110.00
568-Gypsy Colt (Movie) (6/54)	3.60	11.00	40.00
569-Priscilla's Pop	2.75	8.00	30.00
570-Bob Clampett's Beany and Cecil (TV)	16.00	47.00	170.00
571-Charlie McCarthy	4.50	13.50	50.00
572-Silvertip (Max Brand) (7/54); Kinstler-a	3.60	11.00	40.00
573-The Little People by Walt Scott	3.00	9.00	35.00
574-The Hand of Zorro; Kinstler-a	12.00	38.00	135.00
575-Annie Oakley and Tagg (TV)-Photo-c	8.00	23.00	85.00
576-Angel (#1) (8/54)	2.25	6.75	25.00
577-M.G.M.'s Spike and Tyke	1.80	5.50	20.00
578-Steve Canyon (8/54)	4.50	13.50	50.00
579-Francis the Famous Talking Mule	3.60	11.00	40.00
580-Six Gun Ranch (Luke Short-8/54)	2.75	8.00	30.00
581-Chip 'N' Dale (#2) (Disney)	4.50	13.50	50.00
582-Mowgli Jungle Book (Kipling) (8/54)	3.60	11.00	40.00
583-The Lost Wagon Train (Zane Grey)	2.75	8.00	30.00
584-Johnny Mack Brown-Photo-c	5.00	15.00	55.00
585-Bugs Bunny's Album	4.50	13.50	50.00
586-Duck Album (Disney)	4.50	13.50	50.00
587-The Little Scouts	1.35	4.00	15.00
588-King Richard and the Crusaders (Movie) (10/54) Matt Baker-a; photo-c	9.00	27.00	100.00
589-Buck Jones	4.50	13.50	50.00
590-Hansel and Gretel; partial photo-c	5.50	16.50	60.00
591-Western Marshal(Ernest Haycox's)-Kinstler-a	4.50	13.50	50.00
592-Super Circus (TV)	5.50	16.50	60.00
593-Oswald the Rabbit (Lantz)	3.00	9.00	32.00
594-Bozo (10/54)	8.00	25.00	90.00
595-Pluto (Disney)	2.75	8.00	30.00
596-Turok, Son of Stone (#1)	55.00	164.00	600.00
597-The Little King	4.50	13.50	50.00
598-Captain Davy Jones	3.60	11.00	40.00
599-Ben Bowie and His Mountain Men	2.75	8.00	30.00

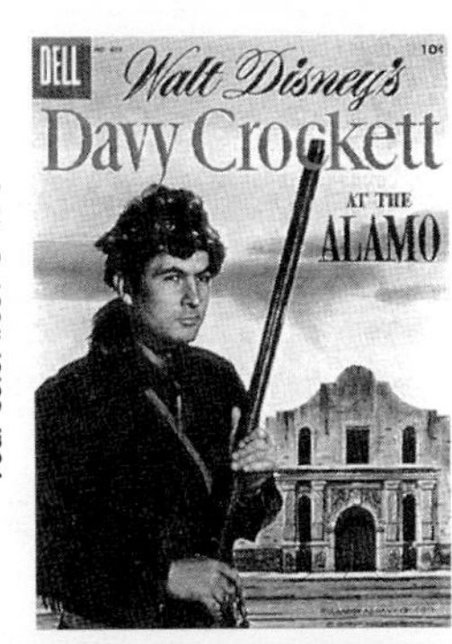

Four Color #639 © WDC

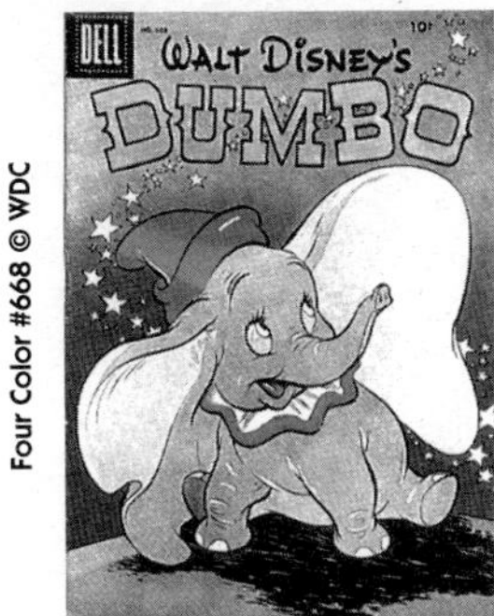

Four Color #668 © WDC

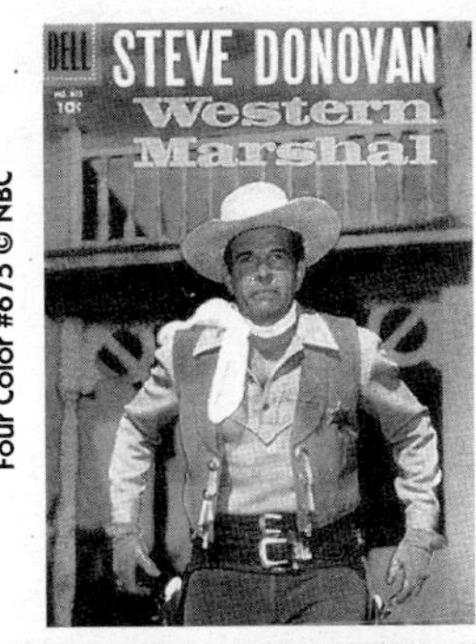

Four Color #675 © NBC

	GD2.0	FN6.0	NM9.4
600-Daisy Duck's Diary (#1) (Disney) (11/54)	6.00	18.00	65.00
601-Frosty the Snowman	3.60	11.00	40.00
602-Mr. Magoo and Gerald McBoing-Boing	11.00	33.00	120.00
603-M.G.M.'s The Two Mouseketeers	3.60	11.00	40.00
604-Shadow on the Trail (Zane Grey)	2.75	8.00	30.00
605-The Brownies-not by Kelly (12/54)	3.00	9.00	32.00
606-Sir Lancelot (not TV)	6.40	19.00	70.00
607-Santa Claus Funnies	3.60	11.00	40.00
608-Silvertip- "Valley of Vanishing Men" (Max Brand)-Kinstler-a	3.60	11.00	40.00
609-The Littlest Outlaw (Disney-Movie) (1/55)-Photo-c	5.50	16.50	60.00
610-Drum Beat (Movie); Alan Ladd photo-c	9.00	27.00	100.00
611-Duck Album (Disney)	4.50	13.50	50.00
612-Little Beaver (1/55)	2.75	8.00	30.00
613-Western Marshal (Ernest Haycox's) (2/55)-Kinstler-a	4.50	13.50	50.00
614-20,000 Leagues Under the Sea (Disney) (Movie) (2/55)-Painted-c	9.00	27.00	100.00
615-Daffy	4.00	12.00	45.00
616-To the Last Man (Zane Grey)	2.75	8.00	30.00
617-The Quest of Zorro	11.00	34.00	125.00
618-Johnny Mack Brown; photo-c	5.00	15.00	55.00
619-Krazy Kat; not by Herriman	2.75	8.00	30.00
620-Mowgli Jungle Book (Kipling)	3.60	11.00	40.00
621-Francis the Famous Talking Mule (4/55)	2.75	8.00	30.00
622-Beetle Bailey	4.50	13.50	50.00
623-Oswald the Rabbit (Lantz)	2.00	6.00	22.00
624-Treasure Island(Disney-Movie)(4/55)-Photo-c	9.00	27.00	90.00
625-Beaver Valley (Disney-Movie)	5.50	16.50	60.00
626-Ben Bowie and His Mountain Men	2.75	8.00	30.00
627-Goofy (Disney) (5/55)	6.40	19.00	70.00
628-Elmer Fudd	3.20	9.50	35.00
629-Lady and the Tramp with Jock (Disney)	6.00	18.00	65.00
630-Priscilla's Pop	2.75	8.00	30.00
631-Davy Crockett, Indian Fighter (#1) (Disney) (5/55) (TV)-Fess Parker photo-c	17.00	51.00	185.00
632-Fighting Caravans (Zane Grey)	2.75	8.00	30.00
633-The Little People by Walt Scott (6/55)	3.00	9.00	35.00
634-Lady and the Tramp Album (Disney) (6/55)	3.65	11.00	40.00
635-Bob Clampett's Beany and Cecil (TV)	16.00	47.00	170.00
636-Chip 'N' Dale (Disney)	4.50	13.50	50.00
637-Silvertip (Max Brand)-Kinstler-a	3.60	11.00	40.00
638-M.G.M.'s Spike and Tyke (8/55)	1.80	5.50	20.00
639-Davy Crockett at the Alamo (Disney) (7/55) (TV)-Fess Parker photo-c	13.00	40.00	145.00
640-Western Marshal(Ernest Haycox's)-Kinstler-a	4.50	13.50	50.00
641-Steve Canyon (1955)-by Caniff	4.50	13.50	50.00
642-M.G.M.'s The Two Mouseketeers	3.60	11.00	40.00
643-Wild Bill Elliott; photo-c	2.75	8.00	30.00
644-Sir Walter Raleigh (5/55)-Based on movie "The Virgin Queen"; photo-c	5.50	16.50	60.00
645-Johnny Mack Brown; photo-c	5.00	15.00	55.00
646-Dotty Dripple and Taffy (#1)	2.75	8.00	30.00
647-Bugs Bunny's Album (9/55)	4.50	13.50	50.00
648-Jace Pearson of the Texas Rangers (TV)-Photo-c	4.50	13.50	50.00
649-Duck Album (Disney)	4.50	13.50	50.00
650-Prince Valiant; by Bob Fuje	5.50	16.50	60.00
651-King Colt (Luke Short) (9/55)-Kinstler-a	2.75	8.00	30.00
652-Buck Jones	2.75	8.00	30.00
653-Smokey the Bear (#1) (10/55)	9.00	27.00	100.00
654-Pluto (Disney)	2.75	8.00	30.00
655-Francis the Famous Talking Mule	2.75	8.00	30.00
656-Turok, Son of Stone (#2) (10/55)	32.00	96.00	350.00
657-Ben Bowie and His Mountain Men	2.75	8.00	30.00
658-Goofy (Disney)	6.40	19.00	70.00

	GD2.0	FN6.0	NM9.4
659-Daisy Duck's Diary (Disney)(#2)	5.00	15.00	55.00
660-Little Beaver	2.75	8.00	30.00
661-Frosty the Snowman	3.60	11.00	40.00
662-Zoo Parade (TV)-Marlin Perkins (11/55)	4.00	12.00	45.00
663-Winky Dink (TV)	7.00	22.00	80.00
664-Davy Crockett in the Great Keelboat Race (TV) (Disney) (11/55)-Fess Parker photo-c	12.00	37.00	135.00
665-The African Lion (Disney-Movie) (11/55)	4.50	13.50	50.00
666-Santa Claus Funnies	3.60	11.00	40.00
667-Silvertip and the Stolen Stallion (Max Brand) (12/55)-Kinstler-a	3.60	11.00	40.00
668-Dumbo (Disney) (12/55)-First of two printings. Dumbo on cover with starry sky. Reprints 4-Color #234?; same-c as #234	7.00	22.00	80.00
668-Dumbo (Disney) (1/58)-Second printing. Same cover altered, with Timothy Mouse added. Same contents as above	5.50	16.50	60.00
669-Robin Hood (Disney-Movie) (12/55)-Reprints #413 plus-c; photo-c	4.50	13.50	50.00
670-M.G.M's Mouse Musketeers (#1) (1/56)-Formerly the Two Mouseketeers	2.75	8.00	30.00
671-Davy Crockett and the River Pirates (TV) (Disney) (12/55)-Jesse Marsh-a; Fess Parker photo-c	12.00	37.00	135.00
672-Quentin Durward (1/56) (Movie)-Photo-c	5.50	16.50	60.00
673-Buffalo Bill, Jr. (#1) (TV)-James Arness photo-c	5.75	17.00	63.00
674-The Little Rascals (#1) (TV)	6.40	19.00	70.00
675-Steve Donovan, Western Marshal (#1) (TV)-Kinstler-a; photo-c	7.00	22.00	80.00
676-Will-Yum!	1.80	5.50	20.00
677-Little King	4.50	13.50	50.00
678-The Last Hunt (Movie)-Photo-c	6.40	19.00	70.00
679-Gunsmoke (#1) (TV)-Photo-c	14.00	44.00	160.00
680-Out Our Way with the Worry Wart (2/56)	1.80	5.50	20.00
681-Forever Darling (Movie) with Lucille Ball & Desi Arnaz (2/56)-; photo-c	10.00	30.00	110.00
682-When Knighthood Was in Flower (Disney-Movie)-Reprint of #505; Renamed the Sword & the Rose for the novel; photo-c	6.40	19.00	70.00
683-Hi and Lois (3/56)	2.25	6.75	25.00
684-Helen of Troy (Movie)-Buscema-a; photo-c	10.00	30.00	110.00
685-Johnny Mack Brown; photo-c	5.00	15.00	55.00
686-Duck Album (Disney)	4.50	13.50	50.00
687-The Indian Fighter (Movie)-Kirk Douglas photo-c	7.00	22.00	80.00
688-Alexander the Great (Movie) (5/56)-Buscema-a; photo-c	6.00	19.00	68.00
689-Elmer Fudd (3/56)	3.20	9.50	35.00
690-The Conqueror (Movie) - John Wayne photo-c	14.00	44.00	160.00
691-Dotty Dripple and Taffy	1.80	5.50	20.00
692-The Little People-Walt Scott	3.00	9.00	35.00
693-Song of the South (Disney) (1956)-Partial reprint of #129	8.00	25.00	90.00
694-Super Circus (TV)-Photo-c	5.50	16.50	60.00
695-Little Beaver	2.75	8.00	30.00
696-Krazy Kat; not by Herriman (4/56)	2.75	8.00	30.00
697-Oswald the Rabbit (Lantz)	2.00	6.00	22.00
698-Francis the Famous Talking Mule (4/56)	2.75	8.00	30.00
699-Prince Valiant-by Bob Fuje	5.50	16.50	60.00
700-Water Birds and the Olympic Elk (Disney-Movie) (4/56)	4.50	13.50	50.00
701-Jiminy Cricket (#1) (Disney) (5/56)	8.00	25.00	90.00
702-The Goofy Success Story (Disney)	6.40	19.00	70.00
703-Scamp (#1) (Disney)	8.00	25.00	90.00
704-Priscilla's Pop (5/56)	2.75	8.00	30.00
705-Brave Eagle (#1) (TV)-Photo-c	5.50	16.50	60.00
706-Bongo and Lumpjaw (Disney) (6/56)	4.50	13.50	50.00
707-Corky and White Shadow (Disney) (5/56)-Mickey Mouse Club (TV); photo-c	6.40	19.00	70.00
708-Smokey the Bear	4.50	13.50	50.00
709-The Searchers (Movie) - John Wayne photo-c	24.00	71.00	260.00
710-Francis the Famous Talking Mule	2.75	8.00	30.00

Four Color #760 © WDC

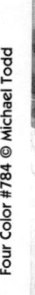

Four Color #784 © Michael Todd

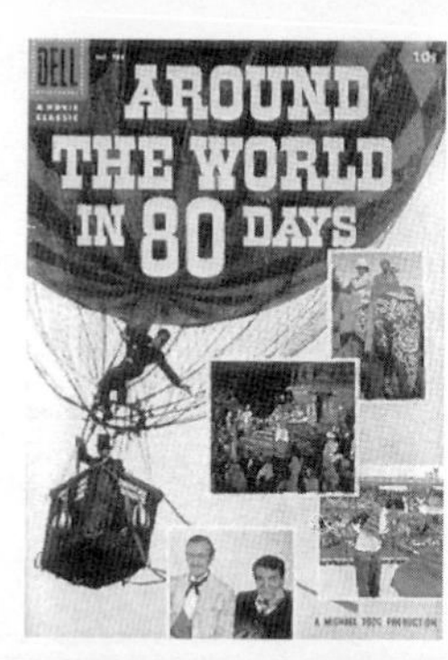

Four Color #791 © Screen Gems

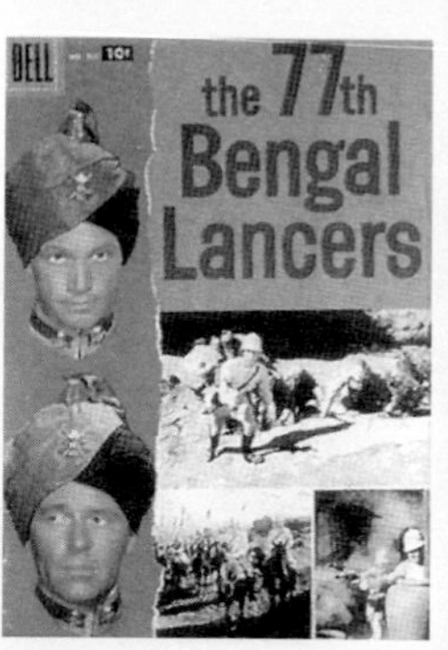

	GD2.0	FN6.0	NM9.4
711-M.G.M's Mouse Musketeers	1.80	5.50	20.00
712-The Great Locomotive Chase (Disney-Movie) (9/56)-Photo-c	6.40	19.00	70.00
713-The Animal World (Movie) (8/56)	2.75	8.00	30.00
714-Spin and Marty (#1) (TV) (Disney)-Mickey Mouse Club (6/56); photo-c	11.00	33.00	120.00
715-Timmy (8/56)	2.75	8.00	30.00
716-Man in Space (Disney)(A science feature from Tomorrowland)	8.00	25.00	90.00
717-Moby Dick (Movie)-Gregory Peck photo-c	8.00	25.00	90.00
718-Dotty Dripple and Taffy	1.80	5.50	20.00
719-Prince Valiant; by Bob Fuje (8/56)	5.50	16.50	60.00
720-Gunsmoke (TV)-James Arness photo-c	7.00	20.00	75.00
721-Captain Kangaroo (TV)-Photo-c	13.00	40.00	145.00
722-Johnny Mack Brown-Photo-c	5.00	15.00	55.00
723-Santiago (Movie)-Kinstler-a (9/56); Alan Ladd photo-c	10.00	30.00	110.00
724-Bugs Bunny's Album	3.60	11.00	40.00
725-Elmer Fudd (9/56)	2.20	6.50	24.00
726-Duck Album (Disney) (9/56)	4.50	13.50	50.00
727-The Nature of Things (TV) (Disney)-Jesse Marsh-a	4.50	13.50	50.00
728-M.G.M's Mouse Musketeers	1.80	5.50	20.00
729-Bob Son of Battle (11/56)	2.75	8.00	30.00
730-Smokey Stover	3.50	11.00	38.00
731-Silvertip and The Fighting Four (Max Brand)-Kinstler-a	3.60	11.00	40.00
732-Zorro, the Challenge of (10/56)	11.00	34.00	125.00
733-Buck Jones	2.75	8.00	30.00
734-Cheyenne (#1) (TV) (10/56)-Clint Walker photo-c	16.00	47.00	170.00
735-Crusader Rabbit (#1) (TV)	31.00	93.00	340.00
736-Pluto (Disney)	2.75	8.00	30.00
737-Steve Canyon-Caniff-a	4.50	13.50	50.00
738-Westward Ho, the Wagons (Disney-Movie)-Fess Parker photo-c	7.00	22.00	80.00
739-Bounty Guns (Luke Short)-Drucker-a	2.75	8.00	30.00
740-Chilly Willy (#1) (Walter Lantz)	3.60	11.00	40.00
741-The Fastest Gun Alive (Movie)(9/56)-Photo-c	6.40	19.00	70.00
742-Buffalo Bill, Jr. (TV)-Photo-c	4.00	12.00	45.00
743-Daisy Duck's Diary (Disney) (11/56)	5.00	15.00	55.00
744-Little Beaver	2.75	8.00	30.00
745-Francis the Famous Talking Mule	2.75	8.00	30.00
746-Dotty Dripple and Taffy	1.80	5.50	20.00
747-Goofy (Disney)	6.40	19.00	70.00
748-Frosty the Snowman (11/56)	3.00	9.00	35.00
749-Secrets of Life (Disney-Movie)-Photo-c	3.60	11.00	40.00
750-The Great Cat Family (Disney-TV/Movie)-Pinocchio & Alice app.	5.50	16.50	60.00
751-Our Miss Brooks (TV)-Photo-c	7.00	22.00	80.00
752-Mandrake, the Magician	9.00	27.00	100.00
753-Walt Scott's Little People (11/56)	3.00	9.00	35.00
754-Smokey the Bear	4.50	13.50	50.00
755-The Littlest Snowman (12/56)	3.00	10.00	36.00
756-Santa Claus Funnies	3.60	11.00	40.00
757-The True Story of Jesse James (Movie)-Photo-c	9.00	27.00	100.00
758-Bear Country (Disney-Movie)	4.50	13.50	50.00
759-Circus Boy (TV)-The Monkees' Mickey Dolenz photo-c (12/56)	10.00	32.00	115.00
760-The Hardy Boys (#1) (TV) (Disney)-Mickey Mouse Club; photo-c	10.00	30.00	110.00
761-Howdy Doody (TV) (1/57)	9.00	27.00	100.00
762-The Sharkfighters (Movie) (1/57); Buscema-a; photo-c	7.00	22.00	80.00
763-Grandma Duck's Farm Friends (#1) (Disney)	6.40	19.00	70.00
764-M.G.M's Mouse Musketeers	1.80	5.50	20.00

	GD2.0	FN6.0	NM9.4
765-Will-Yum!	1.80	5.50	20.00
766-Buffalo Bill, Jr. (TV)-Photo-c	4.00	12.00	45.00
767-Spin and Marty (TV) (Disney)-Mickey Mouse Club (2/57)	9.00	27.00	100.00
768-Steve Donovan, Western Marshal (TV)-Kinstler-a; photo-c	5.50	16.50	60.00
769-Gunsmoke (TV)-James Arness photo-c	7.00	20.00	75.00
770-Brave Eagle (TV)-Photo-c	2.75	8.00	30.00
771-Brand of Empire (Luke Short)(3/57)-Drucker-a	2.75	8.00	30.00
772-Cheyenne (TV)-Clint Walker photo-c	7.00	20.00	75.00
773-The Brave One (Movie)-Photo-c	4.50	13.50	50.00
774-Hi and Lois (3/57)	1.80	5.50	20.00
775-Sir Lancelot and Brian (TV)-Buscema-a; photo-c	7.00	22.00	80.00
776-Johnny Mack Brown; photo-c	5.00	15.00	55.00
777-Scamp (Disney) (3/57)	5.50	16.50	60.00
778-The Little Rascals (TV)	3.80	11.50	42.00
779-Lee Hunter, Indian Fighter (3/57)	3.60	11.00	40.00
780-Captain Kangaroo (TV)-Photo-c	11.00	34.00	125.00
781-Fury (#1) (TV) (3/57)-Photo-c	7.00	22.00	80.00
782-Duck Album (Disney)	4.50	13.50	50.00
783-Elmer Fudd	2.20	6.50	24.00
784-Around the World in 80 Days (Movie) (2/57)-Photo-c	5.75	17.00	63.00
785-Circus Boy (TV) (4/57)-The Monkees' Mickey Dolenz photo-c	10.00	30.00	110.00
786-Cinderella (Disney) (3/57)-Partial-r of #272	5.50	16.50	60.00
787-Little Hiawatha (Disney) (4/57)(#2)	3.60	11.00	40.00
788-Prince Valiant; by Bob Fuje	5.50	16.50	60.00
789-Silvertip-Valley Thieves (Max Brand) (4/57)-Kinstler-a	3.60	11.00	40.00
790-The Wings of Eagles (Movie) (John Wayne)-Toth-a; John Wayne photo-c; 10 & 15¢ editions exist	14.00	44.00	160.00
791-The 77th Bengal Lancers (TV)-Photo-c	6.40	19.00	70.00
792-Oswald the Rabbit (Lantz)	2.00	6.00	22.00
793-Morty Meekle	1.80	5.50	20.00
794-The Count of Monte Cristo (5/57) (Movie)-Buscema-a	8.00	25.00	90.00
795-Jiminy Cricket (Disney)(#2)	5.50	16.50	60.00
796-Ludwig Bemelman's Madeleine and Genevieve	2.75	8.00	30.00
797-Gunsmoke (TV)-Photo-c	7.00	20.00	75.00
798-Buffalo Bill, Jr. (TV)-Photo-c	4.00	12.00	45.00
799-Priscilla's Pop	2.75	8.00	30.00
800-The Buccaneers (TV)-Photo-c	6.40	19.00	70.00
801-Dotty Dripple and Taffy	1.80	5.50	20.00
802-Goofy (Disney) (5/57)	6.40	19.00	70.00
803-Cheyenne (TV)-Clint Walker photo-c	7.00	20.00	75.00
804-Steve Canyon-Caniff-a (1957)	4.50	13.50	50.00
805-Crusader Rabbit (TV)	24.00	72.00	260.00
806-Scamp (Disney) (6/57)	5.50	16.50	60.00
807-Savage Range (Luke Short)-Drucker-a	2.75	8.00	30.00
808-Spin and Marty (TV)(Disney)-Mickey Mouse Club; photo-c	9.00	27.00	100.00
809-The Little People (Walt Scott)	3.00	9.00	35.00
810-Francis the Famous Talking Mule	2.25	6.75	25.00
811-Howdy Doody (TV) (7/57)	9.00	27.00	100.00
812-The Big Land (Movie); Alan Ladd photo-c	9.00	27.00	100.00
813-Circus Boy (TV)-The Monkees' Mickey Dolenz photo-c	10.00	30.00	110.00
814-Covered Wagons, Ho! (Disney)-Donald Duck (TV) (6/57); Mickey Mouse app.	4.50	13.50	50.00
815-Dragoon Wells Massacre (Movie)-photo-c	7.00	22.00	80.00
816-Brave Eagle (TV)-photo-c	2.75	8.00	30.00
817-Little Beaver	2.75	8.00	30.00
818-Smokey the Bear (6/57)	4.50	13.50	50.00
819-Mickey Mouse in Magicland (Disney) (7/57)	3.00	9.00	35.00
820-The Oklahoman (Movie)-Photo-c	9.00	27.00	100.00

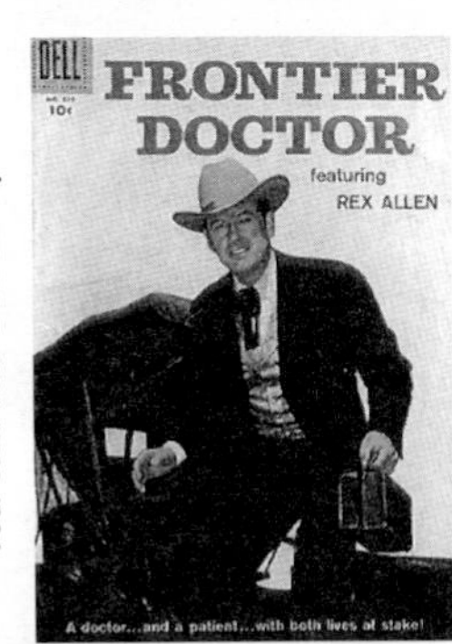

DELL
FRONTIER DOCTOR
featuring
REX ALLEN
A doctor...and a patient...with both lives at stake!

Four Color #877 © Studio City TV

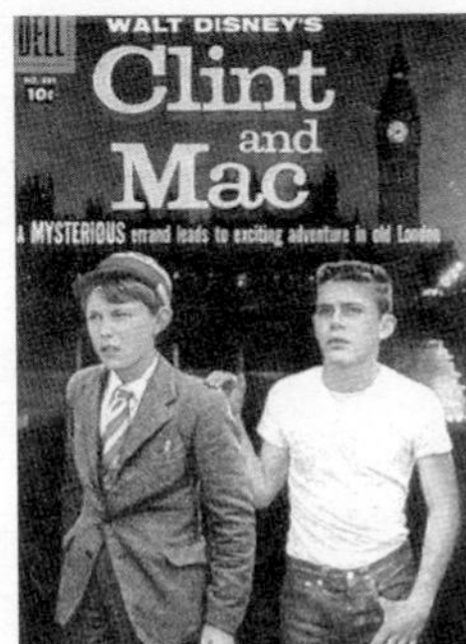

DELL
WALT DISNEY'S
Clint and Mac
A MYSTERIOUS errand leads to exciting adventure in old London

Four Color #889 © WDC

DELL
Will Hutchins as
SUGARFOOT
Can a Sugarfoot fill "Brannigan's Boots"?

Four Color #907 © Warner Brothers

	GD2.0	FN6.0	NM9.4
821-Wringle Wrangle (Disney)-Based on movie "Westward Ho, the Wagons"; Marsh-a; Fess Parker photo-c	7.00	22.00	80.00
822-Paul Revere's Ride with Johnny Tremain (TV) (Disney)-Toth-a	9.00	27.00	100.00
823-Timmy	1.80	5.50	20.00
824-The Pride and the Passion (Movie) (8/57)-Frank Sinatra & Cary Grant photo-c	8.00	25.00	90.00
825-The Little Rascals (TV)	3.80	11.50	42.00
826-Spin and Marty and Annette (TV) (Disney)-Mickey Mouse Club; Annette Funicello photo-c	23.00	68.00	250.00
827-Smokey Stover (8/57)	3.50	11.00	38.00
828-Buffalo Bill, Jr. (TV)-Photo-c	4.00	12.00	45.00
829-Tales of the Pony Express (TV) (8/57)-Painted-c	3.60	11.00	40.00
830-The Hardy Boys (TV) (Disney)-Mickey Mouse Club (8/57); photo-c	9.00	27.00	100.00
831-No Sleep 'Til Dawn (Movie)-Karl Malden photo-c	5.50	16.50	60.00
832-Lolly and Pepper (#1)	2.75	8.00	30.00
833-Scamp (Disney) (9/57)	5.50	16.50	60.00
834-Johnny Mack Brown; photo-c	5.00	15.00	55.00
835-Silvertip-The False Rider (Max Brand)	3.60	11.00	40.00
836-Man in Flight (Disney) (TV) (9/57)	6.40	19.00	70.00
837-All-American Athlete Cotton Woods	2.75	8.00	30.00
838-Bugs Bunny's Life Story Album (9/57)	3.60	11.00	40.00
839-The Vigilantes (Movie)	6.40	19.00	70.00
840-Duck Album (Disney) (9/57)	4.50	13.50	50.00
841-Elmer Fudd	2.20	6.50	24.00
842-The Nature of Things (Disney-Movie) ('57)-Jesse Marsh-a (TV series)	4.50	13.50	50.00
843-The First Americans (Disney) (TV)-Marsh-a	8.00	25.00	90.00
844-Gunsmoke (TV)-Photo-c	7.00	21.00	75.00
845-The Land Unknown (Movie)-Alex Toth-a	11.00	34.00	125.00
846-Gun Glory (Movie)-by Alex Toth; photo-c	9.00	27.00	100.00
847-Perri (squirrels) (Disney-Movie)-Two different covers published	4.50	13.50	50.00
848-Marauder's Moon (Luke Short)	3.60	11.00	40.00
849-Prince Valiant; by Bob Fuje	5.50	16.50	60.00
850-Buck Jones	2.75	8.00	30.00
851-The Story of Mankind (Movie) (1/58)-Hedy Lamarr & Vincent Price photo-c	6.40	19.00	70.00
852-Chilly Willy (2/58) (Lantz)	2.75	8.00	30.00
853-Pluto (Disney) (10/57)	2.75	8.00	30.00
854-The Hunchback of Notre Dame (Movie)-Photo-c	12.00	35.00	130.00
855-Broken Arrow (TV)-Photo-c	5.00	15.00	54.00
856-Buffalo Bill, Jr. (TV)-Photo-c	4.00	12.00	45.00
857-The Goofy Adventure Story (Disney) (11/57)	6.40	19.00	70.00
858-Daisy Duck's Diary (Disney) (11/57)	4.00	12.00	45.00
859-Topper and Neil (TV) (11/57)	3.60	11.00	40.00
860-Wyatt Earp (#1) (TV)-Manning-a; photo-c	10.00	30.00	110.00
861-Frosty the Snowman	3.00	9.00	35.00
862-The Truth About Mother Goose (Disney-Movie) (11/57)	6.40	19.00	70.00
863-Francis the Famous Talking Mule	2.25	6.75	25.00
864-The Littlest Snowman	3.00	10.00	36.00
865-Andy Burnett (TV) (Disney) (12/57)-Photo-c	9.00	27.00	100.00
866-Mars and Beyond (Disney-TV)(A science feature from Tomorrowland)	8.00	25.00	90.00
867-Santa Claus Funnies	3.60	11.00	40.00
868-The Little People (12/57)	3.00	9.00	35.00
869-Old Yeller (Disney-Movie)-Photo-c	4.50	13.50	50.00
870-Little Beaver (1/58)	2.75	8.00	30.00
871-Curly Kayoe	1.80	5.50	20.00
872-Captain Kangaroo (TV)-Photo-c	11.00	34.00	125.00
873-Grandma Duck's Farm Friends (Disney)	4.50	13.50	50.00
874-Old Ironsides (Disney-Movie with Johnny Tremain) (1/58)	5.50	16.50	60.00
875-Trumpets West (Luke Short) (2/58)	2.75	8.00	30.00
876-Tales of Wells Fargo (#1)(TV)(2/58)-Photo-c	9.00	27.00	100.00

	GD2.0	FN6.0	NM9.4
877-Frontier Doctor with Rex Allen (TV)-Alex Toth-a; Rex Allen photo-c	9.00	27.00	100.00
878-Peanuts (#1)-Schulz-c only (2/58)	14.00	41.00	150.00
879-Brave Eagle (TV) (2/58)-Photo-c	2.75	8.00	30.00
880-Steve Donovan, Western Marshal-Drucker-a (TV)-Photo-c	3.60	11.00	40.00
881-The Captain and the Kids (2/58)	2.75	8.00	30.00
882-Zorro (Disney)-1st Disney issue; by Alex Toth (TV) (2/58); photo-c	16.00	49.00	180.00
883-The Little Rascals (TV)	3.80	11.50	42.00
884-Hawkeye and the Last of the Mohicans (TV) (3/58); photo-c	6.40	19.00	70.00
885-Fury (TV) (3/58)-Photo-c	5.50	16.50	60.00
886-Bongo and Lumpjaw (Disney) (3/58)	3.80	11.50	40.00
887-The Hardy Boys (Disney) (TV)-Mickey Mouse Club (1/58)-Photo-c	9.00	27.00	100.00
888-Elmer Fudd (3/58)	2.20	6.50	24.00
889-Clint and Mac (Disney) (TV) (3/58)-Alex Toth-a; photo-c	12.00	37.00	135.00
890-Wyatt Earp (TV)-by Russ Manning; photo-c	7.00	20.00	75.00
891-Light in the Forest (Disney-Movie) (3/58)-Fess Parker photo-c	7.30	22.00	80.00
892-Maverick (#1) (TV) (4/58)-James Garner photo-c	25.00	75.00	275.00
893-Jim Bowie (TV)-Photo-c	4.50	13.50	50.00
894-Oswald the Rabbit (Lantz)	2.00	6.00	22.00
895-Wagon Train (#1) (TV) (3/58)-Photo-c	11.00	33.00	120.00
896-The Adventures of Tinker Bell (Disney)	8.00	24.00	85.00
897-Jiminy Cricket (Disney)	5.50	16.50	60.00
898-Silvertip (Max Brand)-Kinstler-a (5/58)	3.60	11.00	40.00
899-Goofy (Disney) (5/58)	3.60	11.00	40.00
900-Prince Valiant; by Bob Fuje	5.50	16.50	60.00
901-Little Hiawatha (Disney)	3.60	11.00	40.00
902-Will-Yum!	1.80	5.50	20.00
903-Dotty Dripple and Taffy	1.80	5.50	20.00
904-Lee Hunter, Indian Fighter	2.75	8.00	30.00
905-Annette (Disney) (TV) (5/58)-Mickey Mouse Club; Annette Funicello photo-c	26.00	78.00	285.00
906-Francis the Famous Talking Mule	2.25	6.75	25.00
907-Sugarfoot (#1) (TV)Toth-a; photo-c	12.00	37.00	135.00
908-The Little People and the Giant-Walt Scott (5/58)	3.00	9.00	35.00
909-Smitty	1.80	5.50	20.00
910-The Vikings (Movie)-Buscema-a; Kirk Douglas photo-c	8.00	25.00	90.00
911-The Gray Ghost (TV)-Photo-c	8.00	25.00	90.00
912-Leave It to Beaver (#1) (TV)-Photo-c	17.00	52.00	190.00
913-The Left-Handed Gun (Movie) (7/58); Paul Newman photo-c	10.00	30.00	110.00
914-No Time for Sergeants (Movie)-Andy Griffith photo-c; Toth-a	9.00	27.00	100.00
915-Casey Jones (TV)-Alan Hale photo-c	4.50	13.50	50.00
916-Red Ryder Ranch Comics (7/58)	2.75	8.00	30.00
917-The Life of Riley (TV)-Photo-c	11.00	33.00	120.00
918-Beep Beep, the Roadrunner (#1) (7/58)-Published with two different back covers	9.00	27.00	95.00
919-Boots and Saddles (#1) (TV)-Photo-c	7.00	22.00	80.00
920-Zorro (Disney) (TV) (6/58)Toth-a; photo-c	11.00	34.00	125.00
921-Wyatt Earp (TV)-Manning-a; photo-c	7.00	20.00	75.00
922-Johnny Mack Brown by Russ Manning; photo-c	6.00	18.00	65.00
923-Timmy	1.80	5.50	20.00
924-Colt .45 (#1) (TV) (8/58)-W. Preston photo-c	9.00	27.00	100.00
925-Last of the Fast Guns (Movie) (8/58)-Photo-c	6.40	19.00	70.00
926-Peter Pan (Disney)-Reprint of #442	3.60	11.00	40.00
927-Top Gun (Luke Short) Buscema-a	2.75	8.00	30.00
928-Sea Hunt (#1) (9/58) (TV)-Lloyd Bridges photo-c	11.00	33.00	120.00

Four Color #934 © Window Glen

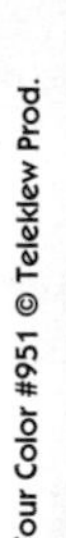
Four Color #951 © Teleklew Prod.

Four Color #976 © WDC

	GD2.0	FN6.0	NM9.4
929-Brave Eagle (TV)-Photo-c	2.75	8.00	30.00
930-Maverick (TV) (7/58)-James Garner photo-c	10.00	30.00	110.00
931-Have Gun, Will Travel (#1) (TV)-Photo-c	14.00	41.00	150.00
932-Smokey the Bear (His Life Story)	4.50	13.50	50.00
933-Zorro (Disney, 9/58) (TV)-Alex Toth-a; photo-c	11.00	34.00	125.00
934-Restless Gun (#1) (TV)-Photo-c	11.00	32.00	120.00
935-King of the Royal Mounted	2.75	8.00	30.00
936-The Little Rascals (TV)	3.80	11.50	42.00
937-Ruff and Reddy (#1) (9/58) (TV) (1st Hanna-Barbera comic book)	12.00	36.00	130.00
938-Elmer Fudd (9/58)	2.20	6.50	24.00
939-Steve Canyon - not by Caniff	4.50	13.50	50.00
940-Lolly and Pepper (10/58)	1.80	5.50	20.00
941-Pluto (Disney) (10/58)	2.75	8.00	30.00
942-Pony Express (TV)	3.60	11.00	40.00
943-White Wilderness (Disney-Movie) (10/58)	5.50	16.50	60.00
944-The 7th Voyage of Sinbad (Movie) (9/58)-Buscema-a; photo-c	12.00	35.00	130.00
945-Maverick (TV)-James Garner/Jack Kelly photo-c	10.00	30.00	110.00
946-The Big Country (Movie)-Photo-c	6.40	19.00	70.00
947-Broken Arrow (TV)-Photo-c (11/58)	4.00	12.00	45.00
948-Daisy Duck's Diary (Disney) (11/58)	4.00	12.00	45.00
949-High Adventure(Lowell Thomas')(TV)-Photo-c	5.50	13.50	50.00
950-Frosty the Snowman	3.00	9.00	35.00
951-The Lennon Sisters Life Story (TV)-Toth-a, 32 pgs.; photo-c	13.00	40.00	145.00
952-Goofy (Disney) (11/58)	3.60	11.00	40.00
953-Francis the Famous Talking Mule	2.25	6.75	25.00
954-Man in Space-Satellites (TV)	6.40	19.00	70.00
955-Hi and Lois (11/58)	1.80	5.50	20.00
956-Ricky Nelson (#1) (TV)-Photo-c	18.00	55.00	200.00
957-Buffalo Bee (#1) (TV)	9.00	27.00	100.00
958-Santa Claus Funnies	3.00	9.00	35.00
959-Christmas Stories-(Walt Scott's Little People) (1951-56 strip reprints)	3.00	9.00	35.00
960-Zorro (Disney) (TV) (12/58)-Toth art; photo-c	11.00	34.00	125.00
961-Jace Pearson's Tales of the Texas Rangers (TV)-Spiegle-a; photo-c	4.00	12.00	45.00
962-Maverick (TV) (1/59)-James Garner/Jack Kelly photo-c	10.00	30.00	110.00
963-Johnny Mack Brown; photo-c	5.00	15.00	55.00
964-The Hardy Boys (TV) (Disney) (1/59)-Mickey Mouse Club; photo-c	9.00	27.00	100.00
965-Grandma Duck's Farm Friends (Disney)(1/59)	3.60	11.00	40.00
966-Tonka (starring Sal Mineo; Disney-Movie)-Photo-c	7.00	22.00	80.00
967-Chilly Willy (2/59) (Lantz)	2.75	8.00	30.00
968-Tales of Wells Fargo (TV)-Photo-c	8.00	25.00	90.00
969-Peanuts (2/59)	10.00	30.00	110.00
970-Lawman (#1) (TV)-Photo-c	12.00	36.00	130.00
971-Wagon Train (TV)-Photo-c	6.00	18.00	65.00
972-Tom Thumb (Movie)-George Pal (1/59)	9.00	27.00	100.00
973-Sleeping Beauty and the Prince(Disney)(5/59)	11.00	33.00	120.00
974-The Little Rascals (TV) (3/59)	3.80	11.50	42.00
975-Fury (TV)-Photo-c	5.50	16.50	60.00
976-Zorro (Disney) (TV)-Toth-a; photo-c	11.00	34.00	125.00
977-Elmer Fudd (3/59)	2.20	6.50	24.00
978-Lolly and Pepper	1.80	5.50	20.00
979-Oswald the Rabbit (Lantz)	2.00	6.00	22.00
980-Maverick (TV) (4-6/59)-James Garner/Jack Kelly photo-c	10.00	30.00	110.00
981-Ruff and Reddy (TV) (Hanna-Barbera)	8.00	24.00	85.00
982-The New Adventures of Tinker Bell (TV) (Disney)	7.00	22.00	80.00
983-Have Gun, Will Travel (TV) (4-6/59)-Photo-c	9.00	27.00	95.00
984-Sleeping Beauty's Fairy Godmothers (Disney)	8.00	25.00	90.00

	GD2.0	FN6.0	NM9.4
985-Shaggy Dog (Disney-Movie)-Photo-all four covers; Annette on back-c(5/59)	6.40	19.00	70.00
986-Restless Gun (TV)-Photo-c	8.00	24.00	85.00
987-Goofy (Disney) (7/59)	3.60	11.00	40.00
988-Little Hiawatha (Disney)	3.60	11.00	40.00
989-Jiminy Cricket (Disney) (5-7/59)	5.50	16.50	60.00
990-Huckleberry Hound (#1)(TV)(Hanna-Barbera); 1st app. Huck, Yogi Bear, & Pixie & Dixie & Mr. Jinks	11.00	33.00	120.00
991-Francis the Famous Talking Mule	2.25	6.75	25.00
992-Sugarfoot (TV)-Toth-a; photo-c	11.00	34.00	125.00
993-Jim Bowie (TV)-Photo-c	4.50	13.50	50.00
994-Sea Hunt (TV)-Lloyd Bridges photo-c	8.00	25.00	85.00
995-Donald Duck Album (Disney) (5-7/59)(#1)	5.00	15.00	55.00
996-Nevada (Zane Grey)	2.75	8.00	30.00
997-Walt Disney Presents-Tales of Texas John Slaughter (#1) (TV) (Disney)-Photo-c; photo of W. Disney inside-c	6.40	19.00	70.00
998-Ricky Nelson (TV)-Photo-c	18.00	55.00	200.00
999-Leave It to Beaver (TV)-Photo-c	14.00	44.00	160.00
1000-The Gray Ghost (TV) (6-8/59)-Photo-c	8.00	25.00	90.00
1001-Lowell Thomas' High Adventure (TV) (8-10/59)-Photo-c	4.50	13.50	50.00
1002-Buffalo Bee (TV)	6.00	18.00	65.00
1003-Zorro (TV) (Disney)-Toth-a; photo-c	11.00	34.00	125.00
1004-Colt .45 (TV) (6-8/59)-Photo-c	7.00	20.00	75.00
1005-Maverick (TV)-James Garner/Jack Kelly photo-c	10.00	30.00	110.00
1006-Hercules (Movie)-Buscema-a; photo-c	9.00	27.00	100.00
1007-John Paul Jones (Movie)-Robert Stack photo-c	5.00	15.00	50.00
1008-Beep Beep, the Road Runner (7-9/59)	4.40	13.00	48.00
1009-The Rifleman (#1) (TV)-Photo-c	22.00	65.00	240.00
1010-Grandma Duck's Farm Friends (Disney)-by Carl Barks	12.00	37.00	135.00
1011-Buckskin (#1) (TV)-Photo-c	6.40	19.00	70.00
1012-Last Train from Gun Hill (Movie) (7/59)-Photo-c	8.00	24.00	90.00
1013-Bat Masterson (#1) (TV) (8/59)-Gene Barry photo-c	11.00	34.00	125.00
1014-The Lennon Sisters (TV)-Toth-a; photo-c	13.00	40.00	145.00
1015-Peanuts-Schulz-c	10.00	30.00	110.00
1016-Smokey the Bear Nature Stories	2.75	8.00	30.00
1017-Chilly Willy (Lantz)	2.75	8.00	30.00
1018-Rio Bravo (Movie)(6/59)-John Wayne; Toth-a; John Wayne, Dean Martin & Ricky Nelson photo-c	18.00	55.00	200.00
1019-Wagon Train (TV)-Photo-c	6.00	18.00	65.00
1020-Jungle Jim-McWilliams-a	2.25	6.75	25.00
1021-Jace Pearson's Tales of the Texas Rangers (TV)-Photo-c	4.00	12.00	45.00
1022-Timmy	1.80	5.50	20.00
1023-Tales of Wells Fargo (TV)-Photo-c	8.00	25.00	90.00
1024-Darby O'Gill and the Little People (Disney-Movie)-Toth-a; photo-c	9.00	27.00	100.00
1025-Vacation in Disneyland (8-10/59)-Carl Barks-a(24pgs.) (Disney)	18.00	55.00	200.00
1026-Spin and Marty (TV) (Disney) (9-11/59)-Mickey Mouse Club; photo-c	7.00	22.00	80.00
1027-The Texan (#1)(TV)-Photo-c	8.00	25.00	90.00
1028-Rawhide (#1) (TV) (9-11/59)-Clint Eastwood photo-c; Tufts-a	22.00	65.00	240.00
1029-Boots and Saddles (TV) (9/59)-Photo-c	4.50	13.50	50.00
1030-Spanky and Alfalfa, the Little Rascals (TV)	3.80	11.50	42.00
1031-Fury (TV)-Photo-c	5.50	16.50	60.00
1032-Elmer Fudd	2.20	6.50	24.00
1033-Steve Canyon-not by Caniff; photo-c	4.50	13.50	50.00
1034-Nancy and Sluggo Summer Camp (9-11/59)	3.25	10.00	36.00
1035-Lawman (TV)-Photo-c	6.40	19.00	70.00
1036-The Big Circus (Movie)-Photo-c	5.50	16.50	60.00
1037-Zorro (Disney) (TV)-Tufts-a; Annette Funicello photo-c	14.00	44.00	160.00

Four Color #1071 © Brennan-Westgate

Four Color #1100 © WDC

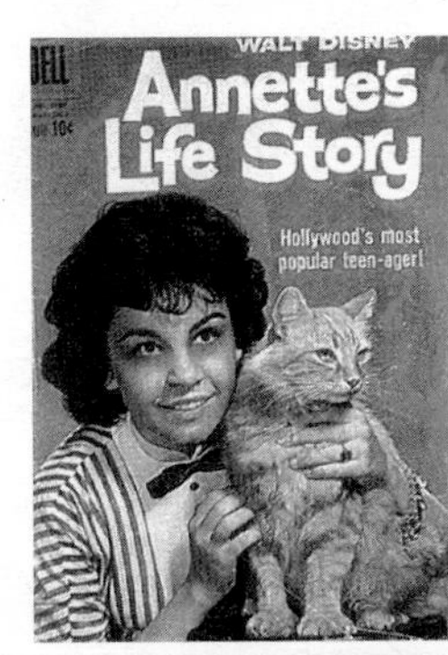

Four Color #1115 © Ozzie Nelson

	GD2.0	FN6.0	NM9.4
1038-Ruff and Reddy (TV)(Hanna-Barbera)(1959)	8.00	24.00	85.00
1039-Pluto (Disney) (11-1/60)	2.75	8.00	30.00
1040-Quick Draw McGraw (#1) (TV) (Hanna-Barbera) (12-2/60)	13.00	39.00	140.00
1041-Sea Hunt (TV) (10-12/59)-Toth-a; Lloyd Bridges photo-c	8.00	25.00	90.00
1042-The Three Chipmunks (Alvin, Simon & Theodore) (#1) (TV) (10-12/59)	5.00	15.00	55.00
1043-The Three Stooges (#1)-Photo-c	18.00	55.00	200.00
1044-Have Gun, Will Travel (TV)-Photo-c	9.00	27.00	95.00
1045-Restless Gun (TV)-Photo-c	8.00	24.00	85.00
1046-Beep Beep, the Road Runner (11-1/60)	4.40	13.00	48.00
1047-Gyro Gearloose (#1) (Disney)-All Barks-c/a	18.00	55.00	200.00
1048-The Horse Soldiers (Movie) (John Wayne)-Sekowsky-a; painted cover featuring John Wayne	13.00	38.00	140.00
1049-Don't Give Up the Ship (Movie) (8/59)-Jerry Lewis photo-c	6.40	19.00	70.00
1050-Huckleberry Hound (TV) (Hanna-Barbera) (10-12/59)	8.00	24.00	85.00
1051-Donald in Mathmagic Land (Disney-Movie)	8.00	25.00	90.00
1052-Ben-Hur (Movie) (11/59)-Manning-a	9.00	27.00	100.00
1053-Goofy (Disney) (11-1/60)	3.60	11.00	40.00
1054-Huckleberry Hound Winter Fun (TV) (Hanna-Barbera) (12/59)	8.00	24.00	85.00
1055-Daisy Duck's Diary (Disney)-by Carl Barks (11-1/60)	9.00	27.00	100.00
1056-Yellowstone Kelly (Movie)-Clint Walker photo-c	5.00	15.00	54.00
1057-Mickey Mouse Album (Disney)	2.75	8.00	30.00
1058-Colt .45 (TV)-Photo-c	7.00	20.00	75.00
1059-Sugarfoot (TV)-Photo-c	8.00	25.00	90.00
1060-Journey to the Center of the Earth (Movie)-Pat Boone & James Mason photo-c	11.00	33.00	120.00
1061-Buffalo Bee (TV)	6.00	18.00	65.00
1062-Christmas Stories (Walt Scott's Little People strip-r)	3.00	9.00	35.00
1063-Santa Claus Funnies	3.00	9.00	35.00
1064-Bugs Bunny's Merry Christmas (12/59)	3.60	11.00	40.00
1065-Frosty the Snowman	3.00	9.00	35.00
1066-77 Sunset Strip (#1) (TV)-Toth-a (1-3/60)-Efrem Zimbalist, Jr. & Edd "Kookie" Byrnes photo-c	11.00	33.00	120.00
1067-Yogi Bear (#1) (TV) (Hanna-Barbera)	11.00	32.00	115.00
1068-Francis the Famous Talking Mule	2.25	6.75	25.00
1069-The FBI Story (Movie)-Toth-a; James Stewart photo on-c	10.00	30.00	110.00
1070-Solomon and Sheba (Movie)-Sekowsky-a; photo-c	9.00	27.00	100.00
1071-The Real McCoys (#1) (TV) (1-3/60)-Toth-a; Walter Brennan photo-c	9.00	27.00	100.00
1072-Blythe (Marge's)	4.50	13.50	50.00
1073-Grandma Duck's Farm Friends-Barks-c/a (Disney)	12.00	37.00	135.00
1074-Chilly Willy (Lantz)	2.75	8.00	30.00
1075-Tales of Wells Fargo (TV)-Photo-c	8.00	25.00	90.00
1076-The Rebel (#1) (TV)-Sekowsky-a; photo-c	10.00	30.00	110.00
1077-The Deputy (#1) (TV)-Buscema-a; Henry Fonda photo-c	12.00	35.00	130.00
1078-The Three Stooges (2-4/60)-Photo-c	10.00	30.00	110.00
1079-The Little Rascals (TV) (Spanky & Alfalfa)	3.80	11.50	42.00
1080-Fury (TV) (2-4/60)-Photo-c	5.50	16.50	60.00
1081-Elmer Fudd	2.20	6.50	24.00
1082-Spin and Marty (Disney) (TV)-Photo-c	7.00	22.00	80.00
1083-Men into Space (TV)-Anderson-a; photo-c	4.50	13.50	50.00
1084-Speedy Gonzales	3.60	11.00	40.00
1085-The Time Machine (H.G. Wells) (Movie) (3/60)-Alex Toth-a; Rod Taylor photo-c	14.00	44.00	160.00
1086-Lolly and Pepper	1.80	5.50	20.00
1087-Peter Gunn (TV)-Photo-c	9.00	27.00	100.00

	GD2.0	FN6.0	NM9.4
1088-A Dog of Flanders (Movie)-Photo-c	3.60	11.00	40.00
1089-Restless Gun (TV)-Photo-c	8.00	23.00	85.00
1090-Francis the Famous Talking Mule	2.25	6.75	25.00
1091-Jacky's Diary (4-6/60)	3.60	11.00	40.00
1092-Toby Tyler (Disney-Movie)-Photo-c	5.50	16.50	60.00
1093-MacKenzie's Raiders (Movie/TV)-Richard Carlson photo-c from TV show	5.50	16.50	60.00
1094-Goofy (Disney)	3.60	11.00	40.00
1095-Gyro Gearloose (Disney)-All Barks-c/a	10.00	30.00	110.00
1096-The Texan (TV)-Rory Calhoun photo-c	7.00	22.00	80.00
1097-Rawhide (TV)-Manning-a; Clint Eastwood photo-c	14.00	41.00	150.00
1098-Sugarfoot (TV)-Photo-c	8.00	25.00	90.00
1099-Donald Duck Album (Disney) (5-7/60)-Barks-c	5.50	16.50	60.00
1100-Annette's Life Story (Disney-Movie) (5/60)-Annette Funicello photo-c	21.00	63.00	230.00
1101-Robert Louis Stevenson's Kidnapped (Disney-Movie) (5/60); photo-c	5.50	16.50	60.00
1102-Wanted: Dead or Alive (#1) (TV) (5-7/60); Steve McQueen photo-c	12.00	37.00	125.00
1103-Leave It to Beaver (TV)-Photo-c	14.00	44.00	160.00
1104-Yogi Bear Goes to College (TV) (Hanna-Barbera) (6-8/60)	7.00	20.00	75.00
1105-Gale Storm (Oh! Susanna) (TV)-Toth-a; photo-c	12.00	35.00	130.00
1106-77 Sunset Strip(TV)(6-8/60)-Toth-a; photo-c	9.00	27.00	100.00
1107-Buckskin (TV)-Photo-c	5.50	16.50	60.00
1108-The Troubleshooters (TV)-Keenan Wynn photo-c	4.50	13.50	50.00
1109-This Is Your Life, Donald Duck (Disney) (TV) (8-10/60)-Gyro flashback to WDC&S #141; origin Donald Duck (1st told)	14.00	41.00	150.00
1110-Bonanza (#1) (TV) (6-8/60)-Photo-c	34.00	102.00	375.00
1111-Shotgun Slade (TV)-Photo-c	5.50	16.50	60.00
1112-Pixie and Dixie and Mr. Jinks (#1) (TV) (Hanna-Barbera) (7-9/60)	7.00	20.00	75.00
1113-Tales of Wells Fargo (TV)-Photo-c	8.00	25.00	90.00
1114-Huckleberry Finn (Movie) (7/60)-Photo-c	4.50	13.50	50.00
1115-Ricky Nelson (TV)-Manning-a; photo-c	14.00	41.00	150.00
1116-Boots and Saddles (TV) (8/60)-Photo-c	4.50	13.50	50.00
1117-Boy and the Pirates (Movie)-Photo-c	5.50	16.50	60.00
1118-The Sword and the Dragon (Movie) (6/60)-Photo-c	7.00	22.00	80.00
1119-Smokey the Bear Nature Stories	2.75	8.00	30.00
1120-Dinosaurus (Movie)-Painted-c	6.40	19.00	70.00
1121-Hercules Unchained (Movie) (8/60)-Crandall/Evans-a	9.00	27.00	100.00
1122-Chilly Willy (Lantz)	2.75	8.00	30.00
1123-Tombstone Territory (TV)-Photo-c	9.00	27.00	100.00
1124-Whirlybirds (#1) (TV)-Photo-c	8.00	25.00	90.00
1125-Laramie (#1) (TV)-Photo-c; G. Kane/Heath-a	9.00	27.00	100.00
1126-Sundance (TV) (8-10/60)-Earl Holliman photo-c	5.50	16.50	60.00
1127-The Three Stooges-Photo-c (8-10/60)	10.00	30.00	110.00
1128-Rocky and His Friends (#1) (TV) (Jay Ward) (8-10/60)	36.00	109.00	400.00
1129-Pollyanna (Disney-Movie)-Hayley Mills photo-c	7.00	22.00	80.00
1130-The Deputy (TV)-Buscema-a; Henry Fonda photo-c	9.00	27.00	100.00
1131-Elmer Fudd (9-11/60)	2.20	6.50	24.00
1132-Space Mouse (Lantz) (8-10/60)	3.60	11.00	40.00
1133-Fury (TV)-Photo-c	5.50	16.50	60.00
1134-Real McCoys (TV)-Toth-a; photo-c	9.00	27.00	100.00
1135-M.G.M.'s Mouse Musketeers (9-11/60)	1.80	5.50	20.00
1136-Jungle Cat (Disney-Movie)-Photo-c	5.50	16.50	60.00
1137-The Little Rascals (TV)	3.80	11.50	42.00
1138-The Rebel (TV)-Photo-c	8.00	25.00	90.00

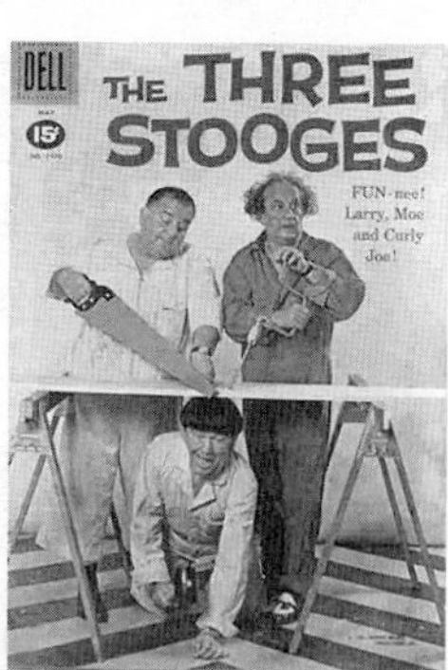

Four Color #1170 © DELL

Four Color #1180 © Danny Thomas

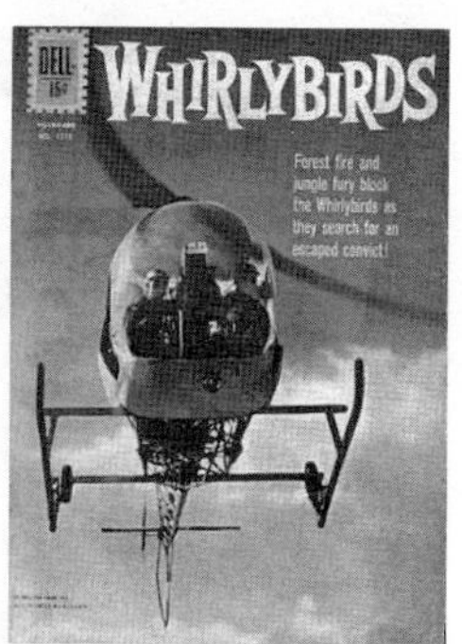

Four Color #1216 © DELL

	GD2.0	FN6.0	NM9.4
1139-Spartacus (Movie) (11/60)-Buscema-a; Kirk Douglas photo-c	12.00	35.00	130.00
1140-Donald Duck Album (Disney)-Barks-c	5.50	16.50	60.00
1141-Huckleberry Hound for President (TV) (Hanna-Barbera) (10/60)	7.00	22.00	80.00
1142-Johnny Ringo (TV)-Photo-c	6.40	19.00	70.00
1143-Pluto (Disney) (11-1/61)	2.75	8.00	30.00
1144-The Story of Ruth (Movie)-Photo-c	9.00	27.00	100.00
1145-The Lost World (Movie)-Gil Kane-a; photo-c; 1 pg. Conan Doyle biography by Torres	10.00	30.00	110.00
1146-Restless Gun (TV)-Photo-c; Wildey-a	8.00	24.00	85.00
1147-Sugarfoot (TV)-Photo-c	8.00	25.00	90.00
1148-I Aim at the Stars-the Wernher Von Braun Story (Movie) (11-1/61)-Photo-c	6.40	19.00	70.00
1149-Goofy (Disney) (11-1/61)	3.60	11.00	40.00
1150-Daisy Duck's Diary (Disney) (12-1/61) by Carl Barks	9.00	27.00	100.00
1151-Mickey Mouse Album (Disney) (11-1/61)	2.75	8.00	30.00
1152-Rocky and His Friends (TV) (Jay Ward) (12-2/61)	23.00	68.00	250.00
1153-Frosty the Snowman	3.00	9.00	35.00
1154-Santa Claus Funnies	3.00	9.00	35.00
1155-North to Alaska (Movie)-John Wayne photo-c	16.00	47.00	170.00
1156-Walt Disney Swiss Family Robinson (Movie) (12/60)-Photo-c	6.40	19.00	70.00
1157-Master of the World (Movie) (7/61)	4.50	13.50	50.00
1158-Three Worlds of Gulliver (2 issues exist with different covers) (Movie)-Photo-c	6.00	18.00	65.00
1159-77 Sunset Strip (TV)-Toth-a; photo-c	9.00	27.00	100.00
1160-Rawhide (TV)-Clint Eastwood photo-c	14.00	41.00	150.00
1161-Grandma Duck's Farm Friends (Disney) by Carl Barks (2-4/61)	12.00	37.00	135.00
1162-Yogi Bear Joins the Marines (TV) (Hanna-Barbera) (5-7/61)	7.00	20.00	75.00
1163-Daniel Boone (3-5/61); Marsh-a	4.50	13.50	50.00
1164-Wanted: Dead or Alive (TV)-Steve McQueen photo-c	9.00	27.00	100.00
1165-Ellery Queen (#1) (3-5/61)	10.00	32.00	115.00
1166-Rocky and His Friends (TV) (Jay Ward)	23.00	68.00	250.00
1167-Tales of Wells Fargo (TV)-Photo-c	7.00	22.00	80.00
1168-The Detectives (TV)-Robert Taylor photo-c	9.00	27.00	100.00
1169-New Adventures of Sherlock Holmes	14.00	44.00	160.00
1170-The Three Stooges (3-5/61)-Photo-c	10.00	30.00	110.00
1171-Elmer Fudd	2.20	6.50	24.00
1172-Fury (TV)-Photo-c	5.50	16.50	60.00
1173-The Twilight Zone (#1) (TV) (5/61)-Crandall/Evans-c/a; Crandall tribute to Ingles	18.00	55.00	200.00
1174-The Little Rascals (TV)	2.90	8.70	32.00
1175-M.G.M.'s Mouse Musketeers (3-5/61)	1.80	5.50	20.00
1176-Dondi (Movie)-Origin; photo-c	3.60	11.00	40.00
1177-Chilly Willy (Lantz) (4-6/61)	2.75	8.00	30.00
1178-Ten Who Dared (Disney-Movie) (12/60)-Painted-c; cast member photo on back-c	6.40	19.00	70.00
1179-The Swamp Fox (TV) (Disney)-Leslie Nielson photo-c	8.00	25.00	90.00
1180-The Danny Thomas Show (TV)-Toth-a; photo-c	14.00	44.00	160.00
1181-Texas John Slaughter (TV) (Disney) (4-6/61)-Photo-c	6.40	19.00	70.00
1182-Donald Duck Album (Disney) (5-7/61)	3.60	11.00	40.00
1183-101 Dalmatians (Disney-Movie) (3/61)	9.00	27.00	100.00
1184-Gyro Gearloose; All Barks-c/a (Disney) (5-7/61) Two variations exist	10.00	30.00	110.00
1185-Sweetie Pie	2.75	8.00	30.00
1186-Yak Yak (#1) by Jack Davis (2 versions - one minus 3-pg. Davis-c/a)	7.00	22.00	80.00
1187-The Three Stooges (6-8/61)-Photo-c	10.00	30.00	110.00

	GD2.0	FN6.0	NM9.4
1188-Atlantis, the Lost Continent (Movie) (5/61)-Photo-c	9.00	27.00	100.00
1189-Greyfriars Bobby (Disney-Movie) (11/61)-Photo-c (scarce)	6.40	19.00	70.00
1190-Donald and the Wheel (Disney-Movie) (11/61); Barks-c	6.40	19.00	70.00
1191-Leave It to Beaver (TV)-Photo-c	14.00	44.00	160.00
1192-Ricky Nelson (TV)-Manning-a; photo-c	14.00	41.00	150.00
1193-The Real McCoys (TV) (6-8/61)-Photo-c	8.00	25.00	90.00
1194-Pepe (Movie) (4/61)-Photo-c	1.80	5.50	20.00
1195-National Velvet (#1) (TV)-Photo-c	5.50	16.50	60.00
1196-Pixie and Dixie and Mr. Jinks (TV) (Hanna-Barbera) (7-9/61)	5.00	15.00	55.00
1197-The Aquanauts (TV) (5-7/61)-Photo-c	6.25	19.00	70.00
1198-Donald in Mathmagic Land (Disney-Movie)-Reprint of #1051	5.50	16.50	60.00
1199-The Absent-Minded Professor (Disney-Movie) (4/61)-Photo-c	6.40	19.00	70.00
1200-Hennessey (TV) (8-10/61)-Gil Kane-a; photo-c	5.50	16.50	60.00
1201-Goofy (Disney) (8-10/61)	3.60	11.00	40.00
1202-Rawhide (TV)-Clint Eastwood photo-c	14.00	41.00	150.00
1203-Pinocchio (Disney) (3/62)	4.50	13.50	50.00
1204-Scamp (Disney)	3.00	9.00	35.00
1205-David and Goliath (Movie) (7/61)-Photo-c	5.50	16.50	60.00
1206-Lolly and Pepper (9-11/61)	1.80	5.50	20.00
1207-The Rebel (TV)-Sekowsky-a; photo-c	8.00	25.00	90.00
1208-Rocky and His Friends (Jay Ward) (TV)	23.00	68.00	250.00
1209-Sugarfoot (TV)-Photo-c (10-12/61)	8.00	25.00	90.00
1210-The Parent Trap (Disney-Movie) (8/61)-Hayley Mills photo-c	8.00	25.00	90.00
1211-77 Sunset Strip (TV)-Manning-a; photo-c	8.00	25.00	90.00
1212-Chilly Willy (Lantz) (7-9/61)	2.75	8.00	30.00
1213-Mysterious Island (Movie)-Photo-c	8.00	25.00	90.00
1214-Smokey the Bear	2.75	8.00	30.00
1215-Tales of Wells Fargo (TV) (10-12/61)-Photo-c	7.00	22.00	80.00
1216-Whirlybirds (TV)-Photo-c	7.00	22.00	80.00
1218-Fury (TV)-Photo-c	5.50	16.50	60.00
1219-The Detectives (TV)-Robert Taylor & Adam West photo-c	7.00	22.00	80.00
1220-Gunslinger (TV)-Photo-c	8.00	25.00	90.00
1221-Bonanza (TV) (9-11/61)-Photo-c	16.00	49.00	180.00
1222-Elmer Fudd (9-11/61)	2.20	6.50	24.00
1223-Laramie (TV)-Gil Kane-a; photo-c	5.50	16.50	60.00
1224-The Little Rascals (TV) (10-12/61)	2.90	8.70	32.00
1225-The Deputy (TV)-Henry Fonda photo-c	9.00	27.00	100.00
1226-Nikki, Wild Dog of the North (Disney-Movie) (9/61)-Photo-c	4.50	13.50	50.00
1227-Morgan the Pirate (Movie)-Photo-c	7.00	22.00	80.00
1229-Thief of Baghdad (Movie)-Crandall/Evans-a; photo-c	6.00	18.00	65.00
1230-Voyage to the Bottom of the Sea (#1) (Movie)-Photo insert on-c	9.00	27.00	100.00
1231-Danger Man (TV) (9-11/61)-Patrick McGoohan photo-c	10.00	30.00	110.00
1232-On the Double (Movie)	3.60	11.00	40.00
1233-Tammy Tell Me True (Movie) (1961)	5.50	16.50	60.00
1234-The Phantom Planet (Movie) (1961)	6.40	19.00	70.00
1235-Mister Magoo (#1) (12-2/62)	9.00	27.00	100.00
1235-Mister Magoo (3-5/65) 2nd printing; reprint of 12-2/62 issue	5.50	16.50	60.00
1236-King of Kings (Movie)-Photo-c	7.00	22.00	80.00
1237-The Untouchables (#1) (TV)-Not by Toth; photo-c	22.00	65.00	240.00
1238-Deputy Dawg (TV)	10.00	30.00	110.00
1239-Donald Duck Album (Disney) (10-12/61)-Barks-c	5.50	16.50	60.00
1240-The Detectives (TV)-Tufts-a; Robert Taylor photo-c			

Four Color #1289 © DELL

	GD2.0	FN6.0	NM9.4
	7.00	22.00	80.00
1241-Sweetie Pie	2.75	8.00	30.00
1242-King Leonardo and His Short Subjects (#1) (TV) (11-1/62)	13.00	38.00	140.00
1243-Ellery Queen	9.00	27.00	95.00
1244-Space Mouse (Lantz) (11-1/62)	3.60	11.00	40.00
1245-New Adventures of Sherlock Holmes	14.00	44.00	160.00
1246-Mickey Mouse Album (Disney)	2.75	8.00	30.00
1247-Daisy Duck's Diary (Disney) (12-2/62)	4.00	12.00	45.00
1248-Pluto (Disney)	2.75	8.00	30.00
1249-The Danny Thomas Show (TV)-Manning-a; photo-c	14.00	44.00	160.00
1250-The Four Horsemen of the Apocalypse (Movie)-Photo-c	6.40	19.00	70.00
1251-Everything's Ducky (Movie) (1961)	3.60	11.00	40.00
1252-The Andy Griffith Show (TV)-Photo-c; 1st show aired 10/3/60	32.00	95.00	350.00
1253-Space Man (#1) (1-3/62)	6.40	19.00	70.00
1254- "Diver Dan" (#1) (TV) (2-4/62)-Photo-c	4.50	13.50	50.00
1255-The Wonders of Aladdin (Movie) (1961)	5.75	17.00	63.00
1256-Kona, Monarch of Monster Isle (#1) (2-4/62)-Glanzman-a	5.50	16.50	60.00
1257-Car 54, Where Are You? (#1) (TV) (3-5/62)-Photo-c	6.40	19.00	70.00
1258-The Frogmen (#1)-Evans-a	6.40	19.00	70.00
1259-El Cid (Movie) (1961)-Photo-c	6.40	19.00	70.00
1260-The Horsemasters (TV, Movie) (Disney) (12-2/62)-Annette Funicello photo-c	11.00	33.00	120.00
1261-Rawhide (TV)-Clint Eastwood photo-c	14.00	41.00	150.00
1262-The Rebel (TV)-Photo-c	8.00	25.00	90.00
1263-77 Sunset Strip (TV) (12-2/62)-Manning-a; photo-c	8.00	25.00	90.00
1264-Pixie and Dixie and Mr. Jinks (TV) (Hanna-Barbera)	5.00	15.00	55.00
1265-The Real McCoys (TV)-Photo-c	8.00	25.00	90.00
1266-M.G.M.'s Spike and Tyke (12-2/62)	1.65	5.00	18.00
1267-Gyro Gearloose; Barks-c/a, 4 pgs. (Disney) (12-2/62)	7.00	20.00	75.00
1268-Oswald the Rabbit (Lantz)	2.00	6.00	22.00
1269-Rawhide (TV)-Clint Eastwood photo-c	14.00	41.00	150.00
1270-Bullwinkle and Rocky (#1) (TV) (Jay Ward) (3-5/62)	18.00	55.00	200.00
1271-Yogi Bear Birthday Party (TV) (Hanna-Barbera) (11/61)	4.50	13.50	50.00
1272-Frosty the Snowman	3.00	9.00	35.00
1273-Hans Brinker (Disney-Movie)-Photo-c (2/62)	5.50	16.50	60.00
1274-Santa Claus Funnies (12/61)	3.00	9.00	35.00
1275-Rocky and His Friends (TV) (Jay Ward)	23.00	68.00	250.00
1276-Dondi	1.80	5.50	20.00
1278-King Leonardo and His Short Subjects (TV)	13.00	38.00	140.00
1279-Grandma Duck's Farm Friends (Disney)	3.60	11.00	40.00
1280-Hennessey (TV)-Photo-c	5.50	16.50	60.00
1281-Chilly Willy (Lantz) (4-6/62)	2.75	8.00	30.00
1282-Babes in Toyland (Disney-Movie) (1/62); Annette Funicello photo-c	11.00	34.00	125.00
1283-Bonanza (TV) (2-4/62)-Photo-c	16.00	49.00	180.00
1284-Laramie (TV)-Heath-a; photo-c	5.50	16.50	60.00
1285-Leave It to Beaver (TV)-Photo-c	14.00	44.00	160.00
1286-The Untouchables (TV)-Photo-c	16.00	47.00	170.00
1287-Man from Wells Fargo (TV)-Photo-c	5.00	15.00	55.00
1288-Twilight Zone (TV) (4/62)-Crandall/Evans-c/a	11.00	32.00	115.00
1289-Ellery Queen	9.00	27.00	95.00
1290-M.G.M.'s Mouse Musketeers	1.80	5.50	20.00
1291-77 Sunset Strip (TV)-Manning-a; photo-c	8.00	25.00	90.00
1293-Elmer Fudd (3-5/62)	2.20	6.50	24.00
1294-Ripcord (TV)	6.40	19.00	70.00
1295-Mister Ed, the Talking Horse (#1) (TV) (3-5/62)-Photo-c	12.00	35.00	130.00
1296-Fury (TV) (3-5/62)-Photo-c	5.50	16.50	60.00
1297-Spanky, Alfalfa and the Little Rascals (TV)	2.75	8.00	30.00
1298-The Hathaways (TV)-Photo-c	3.60	11.00	40.00
1299-Deputy Dawg (TV)	10.00	30.00	110.00
1300-The Comancheros (Movie) (1961)-John Wayne photo-c	14.00	44.00	160.00
1301-Adventures in Paradise (TV) (2-4/62)	3.60	11.00	40.00
1302-Johnny Jason, Teen Reporter (2-4/62)	2.75	8.00	30.00
1303-Lad: A Dog (Movie)-Photo-c	2.75	8.00	30.00
1304-Nellie the Nurse (3-5/62)-Stanley-a	6.40	19.00	70.00
1305-Mister Magoo (3-5/62)	9.00	27.00	100.00
1306-Target: The Corruptors (#1) (TV) (3-5/62)-Photo-c	5.00	15.00	55.00
1307-Margie (TV) (3-5/62)	3.60	11.00	40.00
1308-Tales of the Wizard of Oz (TV) (3-5/62)	11.00	32.00	115.00
1309-87th Precinct (#1) (TV) (4-6/62)-Krigstein-a; photo-c	9.00	27.00	100.00
1310-Huck and Yogi Winter Sports (TV) (Hanna-Barbera) (3/62)	8.00	24.00	85.00
1311-Rocky and His Friends (TV) (Jay Ward)	23.00	68.00	250.00
1312-National Velvet (TV)-Photo-c	2.75	8.00	30.00
1313-Moon Pilot (Disney-Movie)-Photo-c	6.40	19.00	70.00
1328-The Underwater City (Movie) (1961)-Evans-a; photo-c	6.40	19.00	70.00
1329-See Gyro Gearloose #01329-207			
1330-Brain Boy (#1)-Gil Kane-a	12.00	37.00	135.00
1332-Bachelor Father (TV)	7.00	22.00	80.00
1333-Short Ribs (4-6/62)	4.50	13.50	50.00
1335-Aggie Mack (4-6/62)	2.75	8.00	30.00
1336-On Stage; not by Leonard Starr	3.60	11.00	40.00
1337-Dr. Kildare (#1) (TV) (4-6/62)-Photo-c	8.00	25.00	90.00
1341-The Andy Griffith Show (TV) (4-6/62)-Photo-c	32.00	95.00	350.00
1348-Yak Yak (#2)-Jack Davis-c/a	7.00	22.00	80.00
1349-Yogi Bear Visits the U.N. (TV) (Hanna-Barbera) (1/62)-Photo-c	9.00	27.00	100.00
1350-Comanche (Disney-Movie)(1962)-Reprints 4-Color #966 (title change from "Tonka" to "Comanche") (4-6/62)-Sal Mineo photo-c	4.50	13.50	50.00
1354-Calvin & the Colonel (#1) (TV) (4-6/62)	7.00	22.00	80.00

NOTE: *Missing numbers probably do not exist.*

4-D MONKEY, THE (Adventures of... #? on)
Leung's Publications: 1988 - No. 11, 1990 ($1.80/$2.00, 52 pgs.)

	GD2.0	FN6.0	NM9.4
1-11: 1-Karate Pig, Ninja Flounder & 4-D Monkey (48 pgs., centerfold is a Christmas card). 2-4 (52pgs.)			2.00

FOUR FAVORITES (Crime Must Pay the Penalty No. 33 on)
Ace Magazines: Sept, 1941 - No. 32, Dec, 1947

	GD2.0	FN6.0	NM9.4
1-Vulcan, Lash Lightning (formerly Flash Lightning in Sure-Fire), Magno the Magnetic Man & The Raven begin; flag-c	137.00	412.00	1100.00
2-The Black Ace only app.	53.00	159.00	425.00
3-Last Vulcan	45.00	135.00	360.00
4,5: 4-The Raven & Vulcan end; Unknown Soldier begins (see Our Flag), ends #28. 5-Captain Courageous begins (5/42), ends #28 (moves over from Captain Courageous #6); not in #6	40.00	120.00	320.00
6-8: 6-The Flag app.; Mr. Risk begins (7/42)	39.00	118.00	275.00
9-Kurtzman-a (Lash Lightning); robot-c	40.00	120.00	320.00
10-Classic Kurtzman-c/a (Magno & Davey)	47.00	141.00	375.00
11-Kurtzman-a; Hitler, Mussolini, Hirohito-c; L.B. Cole-a; Unknown Soldier by Kurtzman	47.00	141.00	375.00
12-L.B. Cole-a	33.00	99.00	230.00
13-20: 18,20-Palais-c/a	26.00	77.00	180.00
21-No Unknown Soldier; The Unknown app.	19.00	58.00	135.00
22-26: 22-Captain Courageous drops costume. 23-Unknown Soldier drops costume. 25-29-HapHazard app. 26-Last Magno	19.00	58.00	135.00
27-32: 30-Funny-c begin (teen humor), end #32	13.00	39.00	90.00

NOTE: ***Dave Berg** c-5. **Jim Mooney** a-6; c-1-3. **Palais** a-18-20; c-18-25. Torture chamber c-5.*

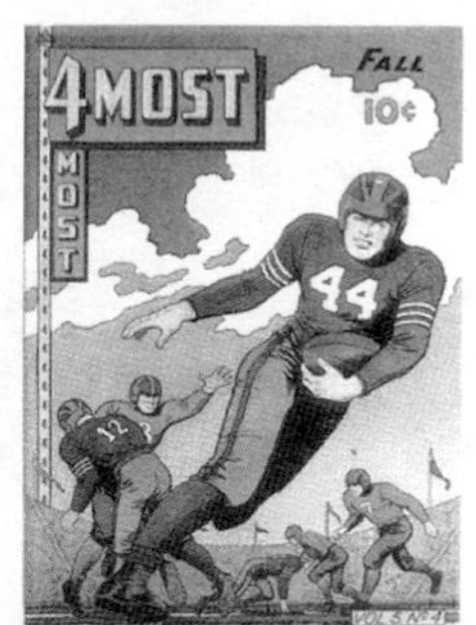

4Most V5 #4 © Premium Service

Fox and the Crow #9 © DC

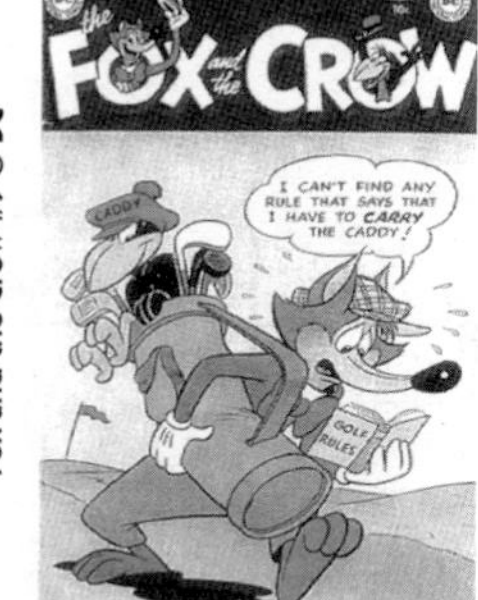

Fox Giants - Throbbing Love © FOX

GD2.0 FN6.0 NM9.4

FOUR HORSEMEN, THE (See The Crusaders)

FOUR HORSEMEN OF THE APOCALYPSE, THE (Movie)
Dell Publishing Co.: No. 1250, Jan-Mar, 1962 (one-shot)

Four Color 1250-Photo-c 6.40 19.00 70.00

4MOST (Foremost Boys No. 32-40; becomes Thrilling Crime Cases #41 on)
Novelty Publications/Star Publications No. 37-on:
Winter, 1941-42 - V8#5(#36), 9-10/49; #37, 11-12/49 - #40, 4-5/50

V1#1-The Target by Sid Greene, The Cadet & Dick Cole begin with origins retold; produced by Funnies Inc.; quarterly issues begin, end V6#3 119.00 356.00 950.00
2-Last Target (Spr/42) 49.00 146.00 390.00
3-Dan'l Flannel begins; flag-c 40.00 120.00 320.00
4-1pg. Dr. Seuss (signed) (Aut/42) 37.00 111.00 260.00
V2#1-3 12.00 36.00 85.00
4-Hitler, Tojo & Mussolini app. as pumpkins on-c 19.00 56.00 130.00
V3#1-4 11.50 34.00 80.00
V4#1-4: 2-Walter Johnson-c 10.00 30.00 60.00
V5#1-4: 1-The Target & Targeteers app. 9.15 27.00 55.00
V6#1-4 8.35 25.00 50.00
5-L. B. Cole-c 17.00 51.00 120.00
V7#1,3,5, V8#1, 37 8.35 25.00 50.00
2,4,6-L. B. Cole-c. 6-Last Dick Cole 17.00 51.00 120.00
V8#2,3,5-L. B. Cole-c/a 19.00 56.00 130.00
4-L. B. Cole-a 11.50 34.00 80.00
38-40: 38-Johnny Weismuller (Tarzan) life story & Jim Braddock (boxer) life story. 38-40-L.B. Cole-c. 40-Last White Rider 16.00 47.00 110.00
Accepted Reprint 38-40 (nd): 40-r/Johnny Weismuller life story; all have L.B. Cole-c 9.15 27.00 55.00

FOUR-STAR BATTLE TALES
National Periodical Publications: Feb-Mar, 1973 - No. 5, Nov-Dec, 1973

1-reprints begin 2.50 7.50 22.00
2-5 1.60 4.85 13.00
NOTE: ***Drucker** r-1, 3-5. **Heath** r-2, 5; c-1. **Krigstein** r-5. **Kubert** r-4; c-2.*

FOUR STAR SPECTACULAR
National Periodical Publications: Mar-Apr, 1976 - No. 6, Jan-Feb, 1977

1 1.25 3.75 10.00
2-6: Reprints in all. 2-Infinity cover 2.40 6.00
NOTE: *All contain DC Superhero reprints. #1 has 68 pgs.; #2-6, 52 pgs.. #1, 4-Hawkman app.; #2-Kid Flash app.; #3-Green Lantern app; #2, 4, 5-Wonder Woman, Superboy app; #5-Green Arrow, Vigilante app; #6-Blackhawk G.A.-r.*

FOUR TEENERS (Formerly Crime Must Pay The Penalty; Dotty No. 35 on)
A. A. Wyn: No. 34, April, 1948 (52 pgs.)

34-Teen-age comic; Dotty app.; Curly & Jerry continue from Four Favorites 5.00 15.00 30.00

FOURTH WORLD GALLERY, THE (Jack Kirby's...)
DC Comics: 1996 (9/96) ($3.50, one-shot)

nn-Pin-ups of Jack Kirby's Fourth World characters (New Gods, Forever People & Mister Miracle) by John Byrne, Rick Burchett, Dan Jurgens, Walt Simonson & others 3.50

FOX AND THE CROW (Stanley & His Monster No. 109 on) (See Comic Cavalcade & Real Screen Comics)
National Periodical Publications: Dec-Jan, 1951-52 - No. 108, Feb-Mar, 1968

1 100.00 300.00 800.00
2(Scarce) 47.00 142.00 380.00
3-5 34.00 103.00 240.00
6-10 24.00 73.00 170.00
11-20 17.00 51.00 120.00
21-30: 22-Last precode issue (2/55) 11.50 34.00 80.00
31-40 10.00 30.00 65.00
41-60 5.50 16.50 55.00
61-80 3.40 10.20 34.00
81-94: 94-(11/65)-The Brat Finks begin 2.50 7.50 25.00
95-Stanley & His Monster begins (origin & 1st app) 3.20 9.60 32.00

GD2.0 FN6.0 NM9.4

96-99,101-108 1.75 5.25 14.00
100 (10-11/66) 2.25 6.75 18.00
NOTE: *Many covers by **Mort Drucker.***

FOX AND THE HOUND, THE (Disney)(Movie)
Whitman Publishing Co.: Aug, 1981 - No. 3, Oct, 1981

11292(#1),2,3-Based on animated movie 5.00

FOXFIRE (See The Phoenix Resurrection)
Malibu Comics (Ultraverse): Feb, 1996 - No. 4, May, 1996 ($1.50)

1-4: Sludge, Ultraforce app. 4-Punisher app. 2.00

FOX GIANTS (Also see Giant Comics Edition)
Fox Features Syndicate: 1944 - 1950 (25¢, 132 - 196 pgs.)

Album of Crime nn(1949, 132p) 40.00 120.00 310.00
Album of Love nn(1949, 132p) 39.00 118.00 275.00
All Famous Crime Stories nn('49, 132p) 40.00 120.00 310.00
All Good Comics 1(1944, 132p)(R.W. Voigt)-The Bouncer, Purple Tigress, Rick Evans, Puppeteer, Green Mask; Infinity-c 39.00 116.00 270.00
All Great nn(1944, 132p)-Capt. Jack Terry, Rick Evans, Jaguar Man 39.00 116.00 270.00
All Great nn(Chicago Nite Life News)(1945, 132p)-Green Mask, Bouncer, Puppeteer, Rick Evans, Rocket Kelly 40.00 120.00 290.00
All-Great Confessions nn(1949, 132p) 36.00 109.00 255.00
All Great Crime Stories nn('49, 132p) 40.00 120.00 310.00
All Great Jungle Adventures nn('49, 132p) 46.00 137.00 365.00
All Real Confession Magazine 3 (3/49, 132p) 36.00 109.00 255.00
All Real Confession Magazine 4 (4/49, 132p) 36.00 109.00 255.00
All Your Comics 1(1944, 132p)-The Puppeteer, Red Robbins, & Merciless the Sorcerer 40.00 120.00 280.00
Almanac Of Crime nn(1948, 148p)-Phantom Lady 44.00 133.00 355.00
Almanac Of Crime 1(1950, 132p) 40.00 120.00 310.00
Book Of Love nn(1950, 132p) 35.00 105.00 245.00
Burning Romances 1(1949, 132p) 40.00 120.00 300.00
Crimes Incorporated nn(1950, 132p) 40.00 120.00 280.00
Daring Love Stories nn(1950, 132p) 35.00 105.00 245.00
Everybody's Comics 1(1944, 50¢, 196p)-The Green Mask, The Puppeteer, The Bouncer, Rocket Kelly, Rick Evans 40.00 120.00 310.00
Everybody's Comics 1(1946, 196p)-Green Lama, The Puppeteer 34.00 103.00 240.00
Everybody's Comics 1(1946, 196p)-Same as 1945 Ribtickler 26.00 79.00 185.00
Everybody's Comics nn(1947, 132p)-Jo-Jo, Purple Tigress, Cosmo Cat, Bronze Man 34.00 101.00 235.00
Exciting Romance Stories nn(1949, 132p) 35.00 105.00 245.00
Famous Love nn(1950, 132p) 35.00 105.00 245.00
Intimate Confessions nn(1950, 132p) 36.00 107.00 250.00
Journal Of Crime nn(1949, 132p) 40.00 120.00 310.00
Love Problems nn(1949, 132p) 36.00 109.00 255.00
Love Thrills nn(1950, 132p) 36.00 109.00 255.00
March of Crime nn('48, 132p)-Female w/rifle-c 40.00 120.00 280.00
March of Crime nn('49, 132p)-Cop w/pistol-c 40.00 120.00 280.00
March of Crime nn(1949, 132p)-Coffin & man w/machine-gun-c 40.00 120.00 280.00
Revealing Love Stories nn(1950, 132p) 36.00 107.00 250.00
Ribtickler nn(1945, 50¢, 196p)-Chicago Nite Life News; Marvel Mutt, Cosmo Cat, Flash Rabbit, The Nebbs app. 32.00 96.00 225.00
Romantic Thrills nn(1950, 132p) 35.00 105.00 245.00
Secret Love nn(1949, 132p) 35.00 105.00 245.00
Secret Love Stories nn(1949, 132p) 35.00 105.00 245.00
Strange Love nn(1950, 132p)-Photo-c 40.00 120.00 295.00
Sweetheart Scandals nn(1950, 132p) 35.00 105.00 245.00
Teen-Age Love nn(1950, 132p) 35.00 105.00 245.00
Throbbing Love nn(1950, 132p)-Photo-c; used in **POP**, pg. 107 40.00 120.00 290.00
Truth About Crime nn(1949, 132p) 40.00 120.00 310.00
Variety Comics 1(1946, 132p)-Blue Beetle, Jungle Jo 36.00 107.00 250.00

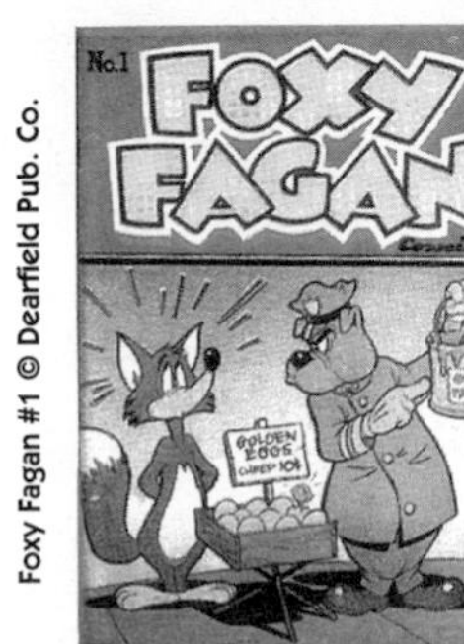

Foxy Fagan #1 © Dearfield Pub. Co.

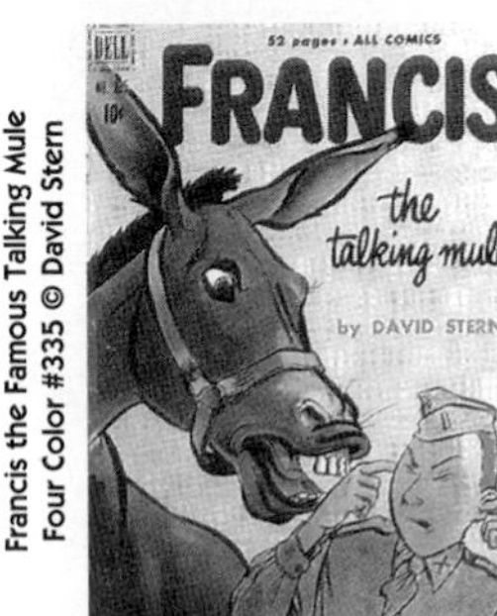

Francis the Famous Talking Mule Four Color #335 © David Stern

Frankenstein #8 © MAR

Variety Comics nn(1950, 132p)-Jungle Jo, My Secret Affair(w/Harrison/ Wood-a), Crimes by Women & My Story 35.00 105.00 245.00
Western Roundup nn('50, 132p)-Hoot Gibson; Cody of the Pony Express app. 39.00 116.00 270.00

NOTE: *Each of the above usually contain four remaindered Fox books minus covers. Since these missing covers often had the first page of the first story, most Giants therefore are incomplete. Approximate values are listed. Books with appearances of Phantom Lady, Rulah, Jo-Jo, etc. could bring more.*

FOXHOLE (Becomes Never Again #8?)
Mainline/Charlton No. 5 on: 9-10/54 - No. 4, 3-4/55; No. 5, 7/55 - No. 7, 3/56

1-Classic Kirby-c 40.00 120.00 300.00
2-Kirby-c/a(2); Kirby scripts based on his war time experiences 27.00 81.00 190.00
3-5-Kirby-c only 15.00 45.00 105.00
6-Kirby-c/a(2) 24.00 71.00 165.00
7 6.70 20.00 40.00
Super Reprints #10,15-17: 10-r/? 15,16-r/United States Marines #5,8. 17-r/Monty Hall #? 1.85 5.50 15.00
11,12,18-r/Foxhole #1,2,3; Kirby-c 2.25 6.75 18.00

NOTE: ***Kirby** a(r)-Super #11, 12. **Powell** a(r)-Super #15, 16. Stories by actual veterans.*

FOX KIDS FUNHOUSE (TV)
Acclaim Books: 1997 ($4.50, digest size)

1-The TIck 4.50

FOXY FAGAN COMICS (Funny Animal)
Dearfield Publishing Co.: Dec, 1946 - No. 7, Summer, 1948

1-Foxy Fagan & Little Buck begin 11.50 34.00 80.00
2 6.70 20.00 40.00
3-7: 6-Rocket ship-c 5.35 16.00 32.00

FRACTURED FAIRY TALES (TV)
Gold Key: Oct, 1962 (Jay Ward)

1 (10022-210)-From Bullwinkle TV show 15.00 31.00 115.00

FRAGGLE ROCK (TV)
Marvel Comics (Star Comics)/Marvel V2#1 on: Apr, 1985 - No. 8, Sept, 1986; V2#1, Apr, 1988 - No. 6, Sept, 1988

1-8 (75¢) 4.00
V2#1-6-($1.00): Reprints 1st series 2.00

FRANCIS, BROTHER OF THE UNIVERSE
Marvel Comics Group: 1980 (75¢, 52 pgs., one-shot)

nn-Buscema/Marie Severin-a; story of Francis Bernadone celebrating his 800th birthday in 1982 3.00

FRANCIS THE FAMOUS TALKING MULE (All based on movie)
Dell Publishing Co.: No. 335 (#1), June, 1951 - No. 1090, March, 1960

Four Color 335 (#1) 7.00 22.00 80.00
Four Color 465 4.50 13.50 50.00
Four Color 501,547,579 3.60 11.00 40.00
Four Color 621,655,698,710,745 2.75 8.00 30.00
Four Color 810,863,906,953,991,1068,1090 2.25 6.75 25.00

FRANK
Nemesis Comics (Harvey): Apr (Mar inside), 1994 - No. 4, 1994 ($1.75/$2.50, limited series)

1-4-($2.50, direct sale): 1-Foil-c Edition 2.50
1-4-($1.75)-Newsstand Editions; Cowan-a in all 2.00

FRANK
Fantagraphics Books: Sept, 1996 ($2.95, B&W)

1-Woodring-c/a/scripts 3.00

FRANK BUCK (Formerly My True Love)
Fox Features Syndicate: No. 70, May, 1950 - No. 3, Sept, 1950

70-Wood a(p)(3 stories)-Photo-c 32.00 96.00 225.00
71-Wood-a (9 pgs.); photo/painted-c 17.00 49.00 115.00
3: 3-Photo/painted-c 13.00 39.00 90.00

NOTE: *Based on "Bring 'Em Back Alive" TV show.*

FRANKENSTEIN (See Dracula, Movie Classics & Werewolf)
Dell Publishing Co.: Aug-Oct, 1964; No. 2, Sept, 1966 - No. 4, Mar, 1967

1(12-283-410)(1964) 4.00 12.00 45.00
2-Intro. & origin super-hero character (9/66) 2.50 7.50 28.00
3,4 1.50 4.50 16.00

FRANKENSTEIN (The Monster of...; also see Monsters Unleashed #2, Power Record Comics, Psycho & Silver Surfer #7)
Marvel Comics Group: Jan, 1973 - No. 18, Sept, 1975

1-Ploog-c/a begins, ends #6 3.50 10.50 35.00
2 2.50 7.50 22.00
3-5 2.00 6.00 16.00
6,7,10: 7-Dracula cameo 1.50 4.50 12.00
8,9-Dracula c/sty. 9-Death of Dracula 2.60 7.80 26.00
11-17 1.00 3.00 8.00
18-Wrightson-c(i) 1.25 3.75 10.00

NOTE: ***Adkins** c-17i. **Buscema** a-7-10p. **Ditko** a-12r. **G. Kane** c-15p. **Orlando** a-8r. **Ploog** a-1-3, 4p, 5p, 6; c-1-6. **Wrightson** c-18i.*

FRANKENSTEIN COMICS (Also See Prize Comics)
Prize Publ. (Crestwood/Feature): Sum, 1945 - V5#5(#33), Oct-Nov, 1954

1-Frankenstein begins by Dick Briefer (origin); Frank Sinatra parody 100.00 300.00 800.00
2 50.00 150.00 400.00
3-5 40.00 120.00 280.00
6-10: 7-S&K a(r)/Headline Comics. 8(7-8/47)-Superman satire 34.00 103.00 240.00
11-17(1-2/49)-11-Boris Karloff parody-c/story. 17-Last humor issue 29.00 86.00 200.00
18(3/52)-New origin, horror series begins 40.00 120.00 290.00
19,20(V3#4, 8-9/52) 25.00 75.00 175.00
21(V3#5), 22(V3#6), 23(V4#1) - #28(V4#6) 22.00 66.00 155.00
29(V5#1) - #33(V5#5) 22.00 66.00 155.00

NOTE: ***Briefer** c/a-all. **Meskin** a-21, 29.*

FRANKENSTEIN/DRACULA WAR, THE
Topps Comics: Feb, 1995 - No. 3, May, 1995 ($2.50, limited series)

1-3 2.50

FRANKENSTEIN, JR. (...& the Impossibles) (TV)
Gold Key: Jan, 1966 (Hanna-Barbera)

1-Super hero (scarce) 9.50 29.00 105.00

FRANKENSTEIN: OR THE MODERN PROMETHEUS
Caliber Press: 1994 ($2.95, one-shot)

1 3.00

FRANK FRAZETTA FANTASY ILLUSTRATED (Magazine)
Quantum Cat Entertainment: Spring 1998 - Present ($5.95, quarterly)

1-Anthology; art by Corben, Horley, Jusko 6.00
1-Linsner variant-c 8.00
2-Battle Chasers by Madureira; Harris-a 8.00
2-Madureira Battle Chasers variant-c 12.00
3-8-Frazetta-c 6.00
3-Tony Daniel variant-c 15.00
5,6-Portacio variant-c, 7,8-Alex Nino variant-c 10.00
8-Alex Ross Chicago Comicon variant-c 10.00

FRANK FRAZETTA'S THUN'DA TALES
Fantagraphics Books: 1987 ($2.00, one-shot)

1-Frazetta-r 2.00

FRANK FRAZETTA'S UNTAMED LOVE (Also see Untamed Love)
Fantagraphics Books: Nov, 1987 ($2.00, one-shot)

1-Frazetta-r from 1950's romance comics 2.00

FRANKIE COMICS (...& Lana No. 13-15) (Formerly Movie Tunes; becomes Frankie Fuddle No. 16 on)
Marvel Comics (MgPC): No. 4, Wint, 1946-47 - No. 15, June, 1949

4-Mitzi, Margie, Daisy app. 11.50 34.00 80.00
5-9 7.50 22.50 45.00

Freckles and his Friends #8 © STD

Freedom Fighters #8 © DC

The Friendly Ghost, Casper #4 © HARV

GD2.0 FN6.0 NM9.4

10-15: 13-Anti-Wertham editorial 5.85 17.50 35.00

FRANKIE DOODLE (See Sparkler, both series)
United Features Syndicate: No. 7, 1939

Single Series 7 31.00 92.00 215.00

FRANKIE FUDDLE (Formerly Frankie & Lana)
Marvel Comics: No. 16, Aug, 1949 - No. 17, Nov, 1949

16,17 5.85 17.50 35.00

FRANK LUTHER'S SILLY PILLY COMICS (See Jingle Dingle...)
Children's Comics (Maltex Cereal): 1950 (10¢)

1-Characters from radio, records, & TV 5.85 17.50 35.00

FRANK MERRIWELL AT YALE (Speed Demons No. 5 on?)
Charlton Comics: June, 1955 - No. 4, Jan, 1956 (Also see Shadow Comics)

1 5.35 16.00 32.00
2-4 4.25 13.00 26.00

FRANTIC (Magazine) (See Ratfink & Zany)
Pierce Publishing Co.: Oct, 1958 - V2#2, Apr, 1959 (Satire)

V1#1 9.15 27.00 55.00
2 7.00 21.00 42.00
V2#1,2: 1-Burgos-a, Severin-c/a; Powell-a? 5.35 16.00 32.00

FREAK FORCE (Also see Savage Dragon)
Image Comics (Highbrow Ent.): Dec, 1993 - No. 18, July, 1995 ($1.95/$2.50)

1-7-Superpatriot & Mighty Man in all; Erik Larsen scripts in all. 4-Vanguard app. 2.00
8-18: 8-Begin $2.50-c. 9-Cyberforce-c & app. 13-Variant-c 2.50

FREAK FORCE (Also see Savage Dragon)
Image Comics: Apr, 1997 - No. 3, July, 1997 ($2.95)

1-3-Larsen-s 3.00

FRECKLES AND HIS FRIENDS (See Crackajack Funnies, Famous Comics Cartoon Book, Honeybee Birdwhistle... & Red Ryder)

FRECKLES AND HIS FRIENDS
Standard Comics/Argo: No. 5, 11/47 - No. 12, 8/49; 11/55 - No. 4, 6/56

5-Reprints 6.70 20.00 40.00
6-12-Reprints. 7-9-Airbrush-c (by Schomburg?). 11-Lingerie panels 4.25 13.00 26.00

NOTE: *Some copies of No. 8 & 9 contain a printing oddity. The negatives were elongated in the engraving process, probably to conform to page dimensions on the filler pages. Those pages only look normal when viewed at a 45 degree angle.*

1(Argo,'55)-Reprints (NEA Service) 4.25 13.00 28.00
2-4 4.00 10.00 20.00

FREDDY (Formerly My Little Margie's Boy Friends) (Also see Blue Bird)
Charlton Comics: V2#12, June, 1958 - No. 47, Feb, 1965

V2#12 2.60 7.80 26.00
13-15 2.25 6.75 18.00
16-47 1.50 4.50 12.00

FREDDY
Dell Publishing Co.: May-July, 1963 - No. 3, Oct-Dec, 1964

1 2.50 7.50 22.00
2,3 1.75 5.25 14.00

FREDDY KRUEGER'S A NIGHTMARE ON ELM STREET
Marvel Comics: Oct, 1989 - No. 2, Dec, 1989 ($2.25, B&W, movie adaptation)

1,2: Origin Freddy Krueger; Buckler/Alcala-a 2.50

FREDDY'S DEAD: THE FINAL NIGHTMARE
Innovation Publishing: Oct, 1991 - No. 3, Dec 1991 ($2.50, color mini-series, adapts movie)

1-3: Dismukes (film poster artist) painted-c 2.50

FRED HEMBECK DESTROYS THE MARVEL UNIVERSE
Marvel Comics: July, 1989 ($1.50, one-shot)

1-Punisher app.; Staton-i (5 pgs.) 2.00

FRED HEMBECK SELLS THE MARVEL UNIVERSE
Marvel Comics: Oct, 1990 ($1.25, one-shot)

1-Punisher, Wolverine parodies; Hembeck/Austin-c 2.00

FREEDOM AGENT (Also see John Steele)
Gold Key: Apr, 1963 (12¢)

1 (10054-304)-Painted-c 3.00 9.00 30.00

FREEDOM FIGHTERS (See Justice League of America #107,108)
National Periodical Publ./DC Comics: Mar-Apr, 1976 - No. 15, July-Aug, 1978

1-Uncle Sam, The Ray, Black Condor, Doll Man, Human Bomb, & Phantom Lady begin (all former Quality characters) 1.25 3.75 10.00
2-9: 4,5-Wonder Woman x-over. 7-1st app. Crusaders 2.40 6.00
10-15: 10-Origin Doll Man; Cat-Man-c/story (4th app; 1st revival since Det. #325). 11-Origin The Ray. 12-Origin Firebrand. 13-Origin Black Condor. 14-Batgirl & Batwoman app. 15-Batgirl & Batwoman app.; origin Phantom Lady 2.40 6.00

NOTE: ***Buckler** c-5-11p, 13p, 14p.*

FREE SPEECHES
Oni Press: Aug, 1998 ($2.95, one-shot)

1-Speeches against comic censorship; Frank Miller-c 3.00

FREEX
Malibu Comics (Ultraverse): July, 1993 - No. 18, Mar, 1995 ($1.95)

1-3,5-14,16-18: 1-Polybagged w/trading card. 2-Some were polybagged w/card. 6-Nightman-c/story. 7-2 pg. origin Hardcase by Zeck. 17-Rune app. 2.00
1-Holographic-c edition 1.00 3.00 8.00
1-Ultra 5,000 limited silver ink-c 5.00
4-($2.50, 48 pgs.)-Rune flip-c/story by B. Smith (3 pgs.); 3 pg. Night Man preview 2.50
15 ($3.50)-w/Ultraverse Premiere #9 flip book; Alec Swan & Rafferty app. 3.50
Giant Size 1 (1994, $2.50)-Prime app. 2.50

NOTE: ***Simonson** c-1.*

FRENZY (Magazine) (Satire)
Picture Magazine: Apr, 1958 - No. 6, Mar, 1959

1 9.15 27.00 55.00
2-6 6.00 18.00 36.00

FRIDAY FOSTER
Dell Publishing Co.: October, 1972

1 2.20 6.50 24.00

FRIENDLY GHOST, CASPER, THE (Becomes Casper... #254 on)
Harvey Publications: Aug, 1958 - No. 224, Oct, 1982; No. 225, Oct, 1986 - No. 253, June, 1990

1-Infinity-c 26.00 72.00 260.00
2 12.00 36.00 120.00
3-10: 6-X-Mas-c 6.00 18.00 60.00
11-20: 18-X-Mas-c 4.00 12.00 40.00
21-30 2.40 7.20 24.00
31-50 2.25 6.75 18.00
51-70,100: 54-X-Mas-c 2.00 6.00 16.00
71-99 1.75 5.25 14.00
101-131: 131-Last 12¢ issue 1.50 4.50 12.00
132-159 1.25 3.75 10.00
160-163: All 52 pg. Giants 1.75 5.25 14.00
164-199: 173,179,185-Cub Scout Specials 2.40 6.00
200 1.00 2.80 7.00
201-224 5.00
225-237: 230-X-mas-c. 232-Valentine's-c 4.00
238-253: 238-Begin $1.00-c. 238,244-Halloween-c. 243-Last new material 2.00

FRIENDS OF MAXX (Also see Maxx)
Image Comics (I Before E): Apr, 1996 ($2.95)

1-Featuring Dude Japan; Sam Kieth-c/a/scripts 3.00

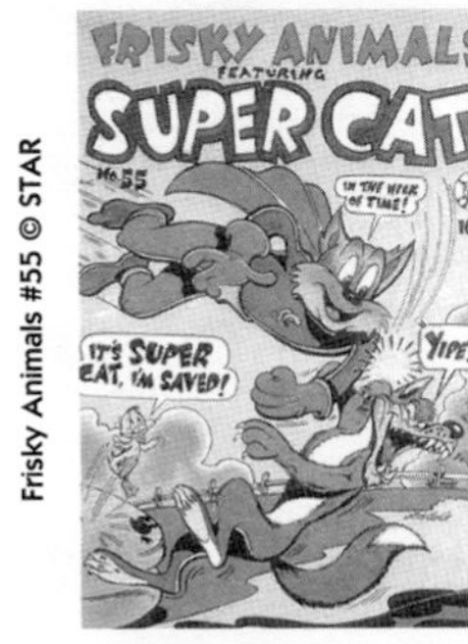

Frisky Animals #55 © STAR

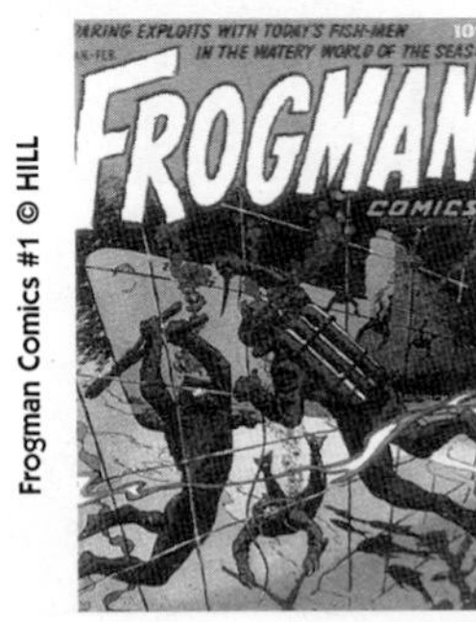

Frogman Comics #1 © HILL

Frontier Romances #2 © AVON

GD2.0 FN6.0 NM9.4

FRIGHT
Atlas/Seaboard Periodicals: June, 1975 (Aug on inside)
1-Origin The Son of Dracula; Frank Thorne-c/a 4.00

FRIGHT NIGHT
Now Comics: Oct, 1988 - No. 22, 1990 ($1.75)
1-22: 1,2 Adapts movie. 8, 9-Evil Ed horror photo-c from movie 2.00

FRIGHT NIGHT II
Now Comics: 1989 ($3.95, 52 pgs.)
1-Adapts movie sequel 4.00

FRISKY ANIMALS (Formerly Frisky Fables; Super Cat #56 on)
Star Publications: No. 44, Jan, 1951 - No. 55, Sept, 1953
44-Super Cat; L.B. Cole 21.00 64.00 150.00
45-Classic L. B. Cole-c 30.00 90.00 210.00
46-51,53-55: Super Cat. 54-Super Cat-c begin 20.00 60.00 140.00
52-L. B. Cole-c/a, 3 1/2 pgs.; X-Mas-c 21.00 64.00 150.00
NOTE: *All have* **L. B. Cole**-*c. No. 47-No Super Cat.* **Disbrow** *a-49, 52.* **Fago** *a-51.*

FRISKY ANIMALS ON PARADE (Formerly Parade Comics; becomes Superspook)
Ajax-Farrell Publ. (Four Star Comic Corp.): Sept, 1957 - No. 3, Dec-Jan, 1957-1958
1-L. B. Cole-c 19.00 56.00 130.00
2-No L. B. Cole-c 8.35 25.00 50.00
3-L. B. Cole-c 16.00 47.00 110.00

FRISKY FABLES (Frisky Animals No. 44 on)
Premium Group/Novelty Publ./Star Publ. V5#4 on: Spring, 1945 - No. 43, Oct, 1950
V1#1-Funny animal; Al Fago-c/a #1-38 20.00 60.00 140.00
2,3(Fall & Winter, 1945) 10.00 30.00 65.00
V2#1(#4, 4/46) - 9,11,12(#15, 3/47): 4-Flag-c 7.50 22.50 45.00
10-Christmas-c 8.35 25.00 50.00
V3#1(#16, 4/47) - 12(#27, 3/48): 4-Flag-c. 7,9-Infinity-c. 10-X-Mas-c 6.35 19.00 38.00
V4#1(#28, 4/48) - 7(#34, 2-3/49) 6.35 19.00 38.00
V5#1(#35, 4-5/49) - 4(#38, 10-11/49) 6.35 19.00 38.00
39-43-L. B. Cole-c; 40-X-mas-c 21.00 64.00 150.00
Accepted Reprint No. 43 (nd); L.B. Cole-c 8.350 25.00 50.00

FRITZI RITZ (See Comics On Parade, Single Series #5, 1(reprint), Tip Top & United Comics)

FRITZI RITZ (United Comics No. 8-26)
United Features Synd./St. John No. 37?-55/Dell No. 56 on: Fall, 1948 - No. 7, 1949; No. 27, 3-4/53 - No. 36, 9-10/54; No. 42, 1/55; No. 43, 6/56 - No. 55, 9-11/57; No. 56, 12-2/57-58 - No. 59, 9-11/58
nn(1948)-Special Fall issue; by Ernie Bushmiller 14.00 43.00 100.00
2 8.35 25.00 50.00
3-7(1949): 6-Abbie & Slats app. 6.70 20.00 40.00
27-29(1953): 29-Five pg. Abbie & Slats; 1 pg. Mamie by Russell Patterson 5.00 15.00 30.00
30-59: 31-Peanuts by Schulz (1st app.?, 11-12/53). 36-1 pg. Mamie by Patterson 4.25 13.00 28.00
NOTE: *Abbie & Slats in #6,7, 27-31. Li'l Abner in #33, 35, 36. Peanuts in #31, 43, 58, 59.*

FROGMAN COMICS
Hillman Periodicals: Jan-Feb, 1952 - No. 11, May, 1953
1 12.00 36.00 85.00
2 7.50 22.50 45.00
3,4,6-11: 4-Meskin-a 5.85 17.50 35.00
5-Krigstein-a 7.00 21.00 42.00

FROGMEN, THE
Dell Publishing Co.: No. 1258, Feb-Apr, 1962 - No. 11, Nov-Jan, 1964-65 (Painted-c)
Four Color 1258(#1)-Evans-a 6.40 19.00 70.00
2,3-Evans-a; part Frazetta inks in #2,3 5.00 15.00 55.00
4,6-11 2.25 6.75 25.00
5-Toth-a 3.00 9.00 35.00

FROM BEYOND THE UNKNOWN
National Periodical Publications: 10-11/69 - No. 25, 11-12/73
1 4.00 12.00 40.00
2-6 2.25 6.75 18.00
7-11: (64 pgs.) 7-Intro Col. Glenn Merrit 2.50 7.50 22.00
12-17: (52 pgs.) 13-Wood-a(i)(r) 2.25 6.75 18.00
18-25: Star Rovers-r begin #18,19. Space Museum in #23-25 1.50 4.50 12.00
NOTE: **N. Adams** *c-3, 6, 8, 9.* **Anderson** *c-2, 4, 5, 10, 11i, 15-17, 22; reprints-3, 4, 6-8, 10, 11, 13-16, 24, 25.* **Infantino** *r-1-5, 7-19, 23-25; c-11p.* **Kaluta** *c-18, 19.* **Gil Kane** *a-9r.* **Kubert** *c-1, 7, 12-14.* **Toth** *a-2r.* **Wood** *a-13i. Photo c-22.*

FROM DUSK TILL DAWN (Movie)
Big Entertainment: 1996 ($4.95, one-shot)
nn-Adaptation of the film; Brereton-c 5.00
nn-($9.95)Deluxe Ed. w/ new material 10.00

FROM HERE TO INSANITY (Satire) (Formerly Eh! #1-7) (See Frantic & Frenzy)
Charlton Comics: No. 8, Feb, 1955 - V3#1, 1956
8 15.00 45.00 105.00
9 13.00 39.00 90.00
10-Ditko-c/a (3 pgs.) 21.00 64.00 150.00
11,12-All Kirby except 4 pgs. 29.00 86.00 200.00
V3#1(1956)-Ward-c/a(2) (signed McCartney); 5 pgs. Wolverton-a; 3 pgs. Ditko-a; magazine format (cover says "Crazy, Man, Crazy" and becomes Crazy, Man, Crazy with V2#2) 40.00 120.00 290.00

FROM THE PIT
Fantagor Press: 1994 ($4.95, one-shot, mature)
1-R. Corben-a; HP Lovecraft back-up story 5.00

FRONTIER DOCTOR (TV)
Dell Publishing Co.: No. 877, Feb, 1958 (one-shot)
Four Color 877-Toth-a, Rex Allen photo-c 9.00 27.00 100.00

FRONTIER FIGHTERS
National Periodical Publications: Sept-Oct, 1955 - No. 8, Nov-Dec, 1956
1-Davy Crockett, Buffalo Bill (by Kubert), Kit Carson begin (Scarce) 56.00 169.00 450.00
2 40.00 120.00 320.00
3-8 39.00 118.00 275.00
NOTE: *Buffalo Bill by* **Kubert** *in all.*

FRONTIER ROMANCES
Avon Periodicals/I. W.: Nov-Dec, 1949 - No. 2, Feb-Mar, 1950 (Painted-c)
1-Used in **SOTI**, pg. 180(General reference) & illo. "Erotic spanking in a western comic book" 45.00 135.00 360.00
2 (Scarce)-Woodish-a by Stallman 36.00 107.00 250.00
I.W. Reprint #1-Reprints Avon's #1 3.50 10.50 35.00
I.W. Reprint #9-Reprints ? 2.50 7.50 22.00

FRONTIER SCOUT: DAN'L BOONE (Formerly Death Valley; The Masked Raider No. 14 on)
Charlton Comics: No. 10, Jan, 1956 - No. 13, Aug, 1956; V2#14, Mar, 1965
10 8.50 26.00 60.00
11-13(1956) 5.35 16.00 32.00
V2#14(3/65) 4.00 10.00 20.00

FRONTIER TRAIL (The Rider No. 1-5)
Ajax/Farrell Publ.: No. 6, May, 1958
6 4.25 13.00 28.00

FRONTIER WESTERN
Atlas Comics (PrPI): Feb, 1956 - No. 10, Aug, 1957
1 19.00 56.00 130.00
2,3,6-Williamson-a, 4 pgs. each 13.00 39.00 90.00
4,7,9,10: 10-Check-a 8.35 25.00 50.00
5-Crandall, Baker, Davis-a; Williamson text illos 11.50 34.00 80.00

Frontline Combat #6 © WMG

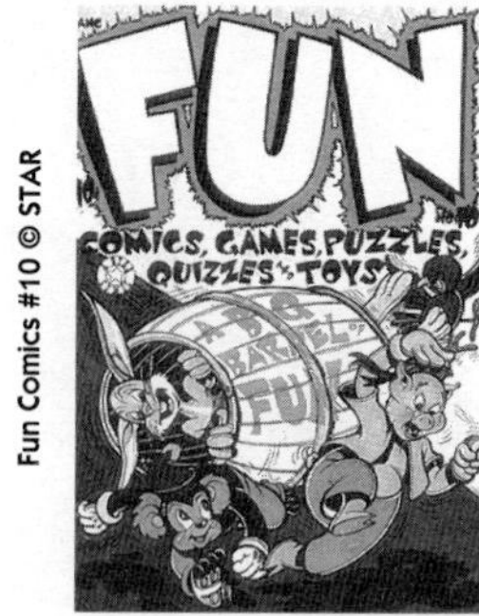

Fun Comics #10 © STAR

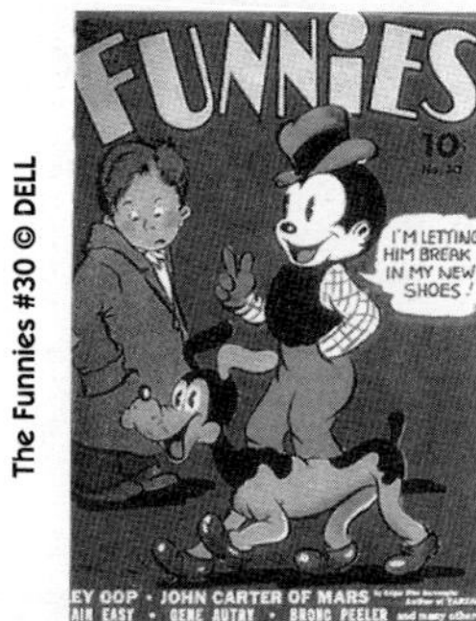

The Funnies #30 © DELL

	GD2.0	FN6.0	NM9.4
8-Crandall, Morrow, & Wildey-a	8.35	25.00	50.00

NOTE: ***Baker** a-9. **Colan** a-2, 6. **Drucker** a-3, 4. **Heath** c-5. **Maneely** c/a-2, 7, 9. **Maurera** a-2. **Romita** a-7. **Severin** c-6, 8, 10. **Tuska** a-2. **Wildey** a-5, 8. Ringo Kid in No. 4.*

FRONTLINE COMBAT
E. C. Comics: July-Aug, 1951 - No. 15, Jan, 1954

	GD2.0	FN6.0	NM9.4
1-Severin/Kurtzman-a	51.00	153.00	510.00
2	32.00	95.00	285.00
3	23.00	70.00	210.00
4-Used in **SOTI**, pg. 257; contains "Airburst" by Kurtzman which is his personal all-time favorite story	21.00	63.00	190.00
5	18.00	55.00	165.00
6-10	15.00	45.00	135.00
11-15	11.00	33.00	100.00

NOTE: ***Davis** a-in all; c-11, 12. **Evans** a-10-15. **Heath** a-1. **Kubert** a-14. **Kurtzman** a-1-5; c-1-9. **Severin** a-5-7, 9, 13, 15. **Severin/Elder** a-2-11; c-10. **Toth** a-8, 12. **Wood** a-1-4, 6-10, 12-15; c-13-15. Special issues: No. 7 (Iwo Jima), No. 9 (Civil War), No. 12 (Air Force).*
(Canadian reprints known; see Table of Contents.)

FRONTLINE COMBAT
Russ Cochran/Gemstone Publishing: Aug, 1995 - Present ($2.00/$2.50)

	GD2.0	FN6.0	NM9.4
1-14-E.C. reprints in all			2.50

FRONT PAGE COMIC BOOK
Front Page Comics (Harvey): 1945

	GD2.0	FN6.0	NM9.4
1-Kubert-a; intro. & 1st app. Man in Black by Powell; Fuje-c	39.00	117.00	270.00

FROST AND FIRE (See DC Science Fiction Graphic Novel)

FROSTY THE SNOWMAN
Dell Publishing Co.: No. 359, Nov, 1951 - No. 1272, Dec-Feb?/1961-62

	GD2.0	FN6.0	NM9.4
Four Color 359 (#1)	7.00	22.00	80.00
Four Color 435,514,601,661	3.60	11.00	40.00
Four Color 748,861,950,1065,1153,1272	3.00	9.00	35.00

FRUITMAN SPECIAL
Harvey Publications: Dec, 1969 (68 pgs.)

	GD2.0	FN6.0	NM9.4
1-Funny super hero	2.50	7.50	22.00

F-TROOP (TV)
Dell Publishing Co.: Aug, 1966 - No. 7, Aug, 1967 (All have photo-c)

	GD2.0	FN6.0	NM9.4
1	8.00	25.00	90.00
2-7	5.00	15.00	55.00

FUGITIVES FROM JUSTICE
St. John Publishing Co.: Feb, 1952 - No. 5, Oct, 1952

	GD2.0	FN6.0	NM9.4
1	19.00	56.00	130.00
2-Matt Baker-r/Northwest Mounties #2; Vic Flint strip reprints begin	19.00	58.00	135.00
3-Reprints panel from Authentic Police Cases that was used in **SOTI** with changes; Tuska-a	19.00	58.00	135.00
4	9.15	27.00	55.00
5-Last Vic Flint-r; bondage-c	10.00	30.00	72.00

FUGITOID
Mirage Studios: 1985 (B&W, magazine size, one-shot)

	GD2.0	FN6.0	NM9.4
1-Ties into Teenage Mutant Ninja Turtles #5			3.00

FULL COLOR COMICS
Fox Features Syndicate: 1946

	GD2.0	FN6.0	NM9.4
nn	11.50	34.00	80.00

FULL METAL FICTION
London Night Studios: Mar, 1997 - Present ($3.95, B&W, mature)

	GD2.0	FN6.0	NM9.4
1-8-Anthology: 1-Razor			4.00

FULL OF FUN
Red Top (Decker Publ.)(Farrell)/I. W. Enterprises: Aug, 1957 - No. 2, Nov, 1957; 1964

	GD2.0	FN6.0	NM9.4
1(1957)-Funny animal; Dave Berg-a	5.85	17.50	35.00
2-Reprints Bingo, the Monkey Doodle Boy	4.00	11.00	22.00
8-I.W. Reprint('64)	1.50	4.50	12.00

FUN AT CHRISTMAS (See March of Comics No. 138)

FUN CLUB COMICS (See Interstate Theatres...)

FUN COMICS (Formerly Holiday Comics #1-8; Mighty Bear #13 on)
Star Publications: No. 9, Jan, 1953 - No. 12, Oct, 1953

	GD2.0	FN6.0	NM9.4
9-(25¢ Giant)-L. B. Cole X-Mas-c; X-Mas issue	21.00	64.00	150.00
10-12-L. B. Cole-c. 12-Mighty Bear-c/story	18.00	54.00	125.00

FUNDAY FUNNIES (See Famous TV..., and Harvey Hits No. 35,40)

FUN-IN (TV)(Hanna-Barbera)
Gold Key: Feb, 1970 - No. 10, Jan, 1972; No. 11, 4/74 - No. 15, 12/74

	GD2.0	FN6.0	NM9.4
1-Dastardly & Muttley in Their Flying Machines; Perils of Penelope Pitstop in #1-4; It's the Wolf in all	5.00	15.00	55.00
2-4,6-Cattanooga Cats in 2-4	2.80	8.40	28.00
5,7-Motormouse & Autocat, Dastardly & Muttley in both; It's the Wolf in #7	3.20	9.60	32.00
8,10-The Harlem Globetrotters, Dastardly & Muttley in #10	2.60	7.80	26.00
9-Where's Huddles?, Dastardly & Muttley, Motormouse & Autocat app.	3.20	9.60	32.00
11-15: 11-Butch Cassidy. 12,15-Speed Buggy. 13-Hair Bear Bunch. 14-Inch High Private Eye	2.50	7.50	20.00

FUNKY PHANTOM, THE (TV)
Gold Key: Mar, 1972 - No. 13, Mar, 1975 (Hanna-Barbera)

	GD2.0	FN6.0	NM9.4
1	4.20	12.60	42.00
2-5	2.50	7.50	22.00
6-13	2.00	6.00	16.00

FUNLAND
Ziff-Davis (Approved Comics): No date (1940s) (25¢)

	GD2.0	FN6.0	NM9.4
nn-Contains games, puzzles, cut-outs, etc.	15.00	45.00	105.00

FUNLAND COMICS
Croyden Publishers: 1945

	GD2.0	FN6.0	NM9.4
1-Funny animal	15.00	45.00	105.00

FUNNIES, THE (New Funnies No. 65 on)
Dell Publishing Co.: Oct, 1936 - No. 64, May, 1942

	GD2.0	FN6.0	NM9.4
1-Tailspin Tommy, Mutt & Jeff, Alley Oop (1st app?), Capt. Easy (1st app.), Don Dixon begin	340.00	1020.00	2400.00
2 (11/36)-Scribbly by Mayer begins (see Poplar #6 for 1st app.)	140.00	420.00	975.00
3	110.00	330.00	750.00
4,5: 4(1/37)-Christmas-c	85.00	255.00	600.00
6-10	65.00	195.00	450.00
11-20: 16-Christmas-c	57.00	171.00	400.00
21-29: 25-Crime Busters by McWilliams(4pgs.)	45.00	135.00	310.00
30-John Carter of Mars (origin/1st app.) begins by Edgar Rice Burroughs; Warner Bros.' Bosko-c (4/39)	119.00	357.00	950.00
31-44: 33-John Coleman Burroughs art begins on John Carter. 34-Last funny-c. 35-(9/39)-Mr. District Attorney begins; based on radio show	72.00	216.00	575.00
45-Origin/1st app. Phantasmo, the Master of the World (Dell's 1st super-hero, 7/40) & his sidekick Whizzer McGee	69.00	207.00	550.00
46-50: 46-The Black Knight begins, ends #62	47.00	142.00	380.00
51-56-Last ERB John Carter of Mars	44.00	132.00	350.00
57-Intro. & origin Captain Midnight (7/41)	225.00	675.00	1800.00
58-60: 58-Captain Midnight-c begin, end #63	81.00	244.00	650.00
61-Andy Panda begins by Walter Lantz	62.00	187.00	500.00
62,63: 63-Last Captain Midnight-c; bondage-c	62.00	187.00	500.00
64-Format change; Oswald the Rabbit, Felix the Cat, Li'l Eight Ball app.; origin & 1st app. Woody Woodpecker in Oswald; last Capt. Midnight; Oswald, Andy Panda, Li'l Eight Ball-c	100.00	300.00	800.00

NOTE: ***Mayer** c-26, 48. **McWilliams** art in many issues on "Rex King of the Deep". Alley Oop c-17, 20. Captain Midnight c-57(i/2), 58-63. John Carter c-35-37, 40. Phantasmo c-45-56, 57(1/2), 58-61(part). Rex King c-38, 39, 42. Tailspin Tommy c-41.*

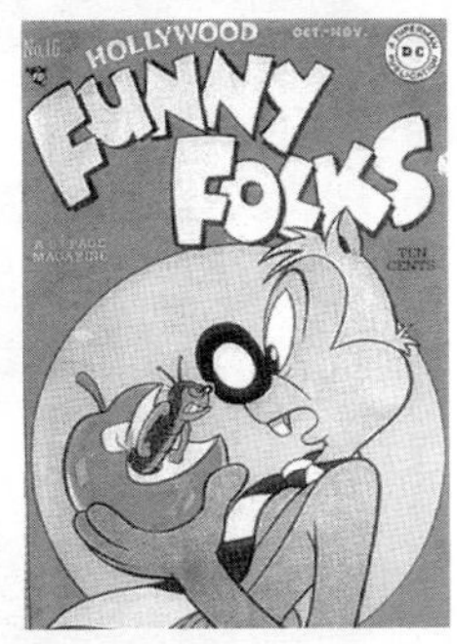

Funny Folks #16 © DC

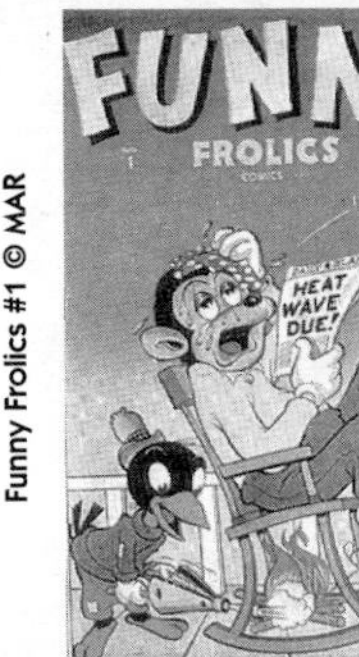

Funny Frolics #1 © MAR

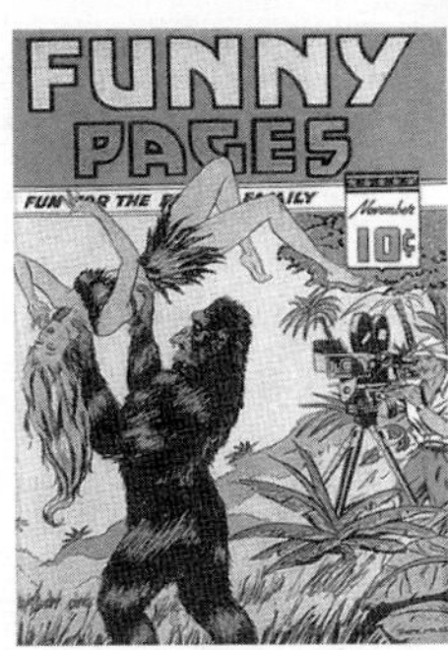

Funny Pages V3 #9 © CEN

GD2.0 FN6.0 NM9.4

FUNNIES ANNUAL, THE
Avon Periodicals: 1959 ($1.00, approx. 7x10", B&W; tabloid-size)

1-(Rare)-Features the best newspaper comic strips of the year: Archie, Snuffy Smith, Beetle Bailey, Henry, Blondie, Steve Canyon, Buz Sawyer, The Little King, Hi & Lois, Popeye, & others. Also has a chronological history of the comics from 2000 B.C. to 1959. 41.00 122.00 325.00

FUNNY ANIMALS (See Fàwcett's Funny Animals)
Charlton Comics: Sept, 1984 - No. 2, Nov, 1984

1,2-Atomic Mouse-r 4.00

FUNNYBONE (... The Laugh-Book of Comical Comics)
La Salle Publishing Co.: 1944 (25¢, 132 pgs.)

nn 27.00 81.00 190.00

FUNNY BOOK (...Magazine for Young Folks) (Hocus Pocus No. 9)
Parents' Magazine Press (Funny Book Publishing Corp.):
Dec, 1942 - No. 9, Aug-Sept, 1946 (Comics, stories, puzzles, games)

1-Funny animal; Alice In Wonderland app. 13.50 41.00 95.00
2-Gulliver in Giant-Land 8.00 24.00 48.00
3-9: 4-Advs. of Robin Hood. 9-Hocus-Pocus strip 5.85 17.50 35.00

FUNNY COMICS
Modern Store Publ.: 1955 (7¢, 5x7", 36 pgs.)

1-Funny animal 2.40 6.00 12.00

FUNNY COMIC TUNES (See Funny Tunes)

FUNNY FABLES
Decker Publications (Red Top Comics): Aug, 1957 - V2#2, Nov, 1957

V1#1 4.25 13.00 28.00
V1#2,V2#1,2: V1#2 (11/57)-Reissue of V1#1 3.60 9.00 18.00

FUNNY FILMS (Features funny animal characters from films)
American Comics Group(Michel Publ./Titan Publ.): Sept-Oct, 1949 - No. 29, May-June, 1954 (No. 1-4: 52 pgs.)

1-Puss An' Boots, Blunderbunny begin 18.00 54.00 125.00
2 10.00 30.00 65.00
3-10: 3-X-Mas-c 6.70 20.00 40.00
11-20 5.00 15.00 30.00
21-29 4.00 10.50 21.00

FUNNY FOLKS (Hollywood... on cover only No. 16-26; becomes Hollywood Funny Folks No. 27 on)
National Periodical Publications: April-May, 1946 - No. 26, June-July, 1950 (52 pgs., #16 on)

1-Nutsy Squirrel begins (1st app.) by Rube Grossman 40.00 120.00 290.00
2 19.00 56.00 130.00
3-5: 4-1st Nutsy Squirrel-c 13.50 41.00 95.00
6-10: 6,9-Nutsy Squirrel-c begin 10.00 30.00 70.00
11-26: 16-Begin 52 pg. issues (10-11/48) 10.00 30.00 60.00

NOTE: ***Sheldon Mayer** a-in some issues.* ***Post** a-18. Christmas c-12.*

FUNNY FROLICS
Timely/Marvel Comics (SPI): Summer, 1945 - No. 5, Dec, 1946

1-Sharpy Fox, Puffy Pig, Krazy Krow 21.00 64.00 150.00
2 11.50 34.00 80.00
3,4 10.00 30.00 60.00
5-Kurtzman-a 10.00 30.00 70.00

FUNNY FUNNIES
Nedor Publishing Co.: April, 1943 (68 pgs.)

1-Funny animals; Peter Porker app. 19.00 56.00 130.00

FUNNYMAN (Also see Cisco Kid Comics & Extra Comics)
Magazine Enterprises: Dec, 1947; No. 1, Jan, 1948 - No. 6, Aug, 1948

nn(12/47)-Prepublication B&W undistributed copy by Siegel & Shuster-(5-3/4x8"), 16 pgs.; Sold at auction in 1997 for $575.00
1-Siegel & Shuster-a in all; Dick Ayers 1st pro work (as assistant) on 1st few issues 40.00 120.00 320.00
2 27.00 81.00 190.00
3-6 23.00 69.00 160.00

FUNNY MOVIES (See 3-D Funny Movies)

FUNNY PAGES (Formerly The Comics Magazine)
Comics Magazine Co./Ultem Publ.(Chesler)/Centaur Publications:
No. 6, Nov, 1936 - No. 42, Oct, 1940

V1#6 (nn, nd)-The Clock begins (2 pgs., 1st app.), ends #11; The Clock is the 1st masked comic book hero 187.00 561.00 1500.00
7-11 75.00 225.00 600.00
V2#1-V2#3: V2#1 (9/37)(V2#2 on-c; V2#1 in indicia). V2#2 (10/37)(V2#3 on-c; V2#2 in indicia). V2#3(11/37)-5 52.00 157.00 420.00
6(1st Centaur, 3/38) 84.00 253.00 675.00
7-9 56.00 169.00 450.00
10(Scarce, 9/38)-1st app. of The Arrow by Gustavson (Blue costume) 288.00 864.00 2300.00
11,12 106.00 319.00 850.00
V3#1-6: 6,8-Last funny covers 100.00 300.00 800.00
7-1st Arrow-c (9/39) 200.00 600.00 1600.00
8,9: 9-Tarpe Mills jungle-c 103.00 309.00 825.00
10-2nd Arrow-c 162.00 487.00 1300.00
V4#1(1/40, Arrow-c)-(Rare)-The Owl & The Phantom Rider app.; origin Mantoka, Maker of Magic by Jack Cole. Mad Ming begins, ends #42; Tarpe Mills-a 200.00 600.00 1600.00
35-Classic Arrow-c 200.00 600.00 1600.00
36-38-Mad Ming-c 100.00 300.00 800.00
39-41-Arrow-c 150.00 450.00 1200.00
42 (Scarce,10/40)-Last Arrow; Arrow-c 156.00 468.00 1250.00

NOTE: ***Biro** c-V2#9.* ***Burgos** c-V3#10.* ***Jack Cole** a-V2#3, 7, 8, 10, 11, V3#2, 6, 9, 10, V4#1, 37; c-V3#2, 4.* ***Eisner** a-V1#7, 8?, 10.* ***Ken Ernst** a-V1#7, 8.* ***Everett** a-V2#11 (illos).* ***Filchock** c-V2#10, V3#6.* ***Gill Fox** a-V2#11.* ***Sid Greene** a-39.* ***Guardineer** a-V2#2, 3, 5.* ***Gustavson** a-V2#5, 11, 12, V3#1-10, 35, 38-42; c-V3#7, 35, 39-42.* ***Bob Kane** a-V3#1.* ***McWilliams** a-V2#12, V3#1, 3-6.* ***Tarpe Mills** a-V3#8-10, V4#1; c-V3#9.* ***Ed Moore Jr.** a-V2#12.* ***Schwab** c-V3#1.* ***Bob Wood** a-V2#2, 3, 8, 11, V3#6, 9, 10; c-V2#6, 7. Arrow c-V3#7, 10, V4#1, 35, 40-42.*

FUNNY PICTURE STORIES (Comic Pages V3#4 on)
Comics Magazine Co./Centaur Publications: Nov, 1936 - V3#3, May, 1939

V1#1-The Clock begins (c-feature)(see Funny Pages for 1st app.) 300.00 900.00 2700.00
2 106.00 319.00 850.00
3-9: 4-Eisner-a; X-Mas-c. 7-Racial humor-c 75.00 225.00 600.00
V2#1 (9/37; V1#10 on-c; V2#1 in indicia)-Jack Strand begins 52.00 156.00 420.00
2 (10/37; V1#11 on-c; V2#2 in indicia) 52.00 156.00 320.00
3-5,7-11: 4-Xmas-c 44.00 132.00 350.00
6-(1st Centaur, 3/38) 75.00 225.00 600.00
V3#1-3 40.00 120.00 325.00

NOTE: ***Biro** c-V2#1, 8, 9, 11.* ***Guardineer** a-V1#11; c-V2#6, V3#5.* ***Bob Wood** c/a-V1#11, V2#2; c-V2#3, 5.*

FUNNY STUFF (Becomes The Dodo & the Frog No. 80)
All-American/National Periodical Publications No. 7 on: Summer, 1944 - No. 79, July-Aug, 1954 (#1-7 are quarterly)

1-The Three Mouseketeers (ends #28) & The "Terrific Whatzit" begin; Sheldon Mayer-a 87.00 262.00 700.00
2-Sheldon Mayer-a 41.00 124.00 330.00
3-5: 3-Flash parody. 5-All Mayer-a/scripts issue 30.00 90.00 210.00
6-10 10-(6/46) 20.00 60.00 140.00
11-17,19,20: 20-1st Dodo & the Frog-c (4/47) 15.00 45.00 105.00
18-The Dodo & the Frog (2/47, 1st app?) begin?; X-Mas-c 26.00 79.00 185.00
21,23-30: 24-Infinity-c 10.00 30.00 70.00
22-Superman cameo 40.00 120.00 300.00
31-79: 70-1st Bo Bunny by Mayer & begins 8.70 26.00 52.00

NOTE: ***Mayer** a-1-8, 55, ,57, 58, 61, 62, 64, 65, 68, 70, 72, 74-79; c-2, 5, 6, 8.*

FUNNY STUFF STOCKING STUFFER
DC Comics: Mar, 1985 ($1.25, 52 pgs.)

1-Almost every DC funny animal featured 2.00

Funny Tunes #3 © AVON

The Further Adventures of Indiana Jones #10 © Lucasfilm

Future World Comics #1 © G.W. Dougherty

GD2.0 FN6.0 NM9.4

FUNNY 3-D
Harvey Publications: December, 1953 (25¢, came with 2 pair of glasses)
1-Shows cover in 3-D on inside 11.00 33.00 75.00

FUNNY TUNES (Animated Funny Comic Tunes No. 16-22; Funny Comic Tunes No. 23, on covers only; formerly Krazy Komics #15; Oscar No. 24 on)
U.S.A. Comics Magazine Corp. (Timely): No. 16, Summer, 1944 - No. 23, Fall, 1946
16-Silly Seal, Ziggy Pig, Krazy Krow begin 13.00 39.00 90.00
17 (Fall/44)-Becomes Gay Comics #18 on? 10.00 30.00 70.00
18-22: 21-Super Rabbit app. 9.15 27.00 55.00
23-Kurtzman-a 10.00 30.00 70.00

FUNNY TUNES (Becomes Space Comics #4 on)
Avon Periodicals: July, 1953 - No. 3, Dec-Jan, 1953-54
1-Space Mouse, Peter Rabbit, Merry Mouse, Spotty the Pup, Cicero the Cat begin; all continue in Space Comics 10.00 30.00 65.00
2,3 6.70 20.00 40.00

FUNNY WORLD
Marbak Press: 1947 - No. 3, 1948
1-The Berrys, The Toodles & other strip-r begin 7.50 22.50 45.00
2,3 5.85 17.50 35.00

FUNTASTIC WORLD OF HANNA-BARBERA, THE (TV)
Marvel Comics Group: Dec, 1977 - No. 3, June, 1978 ($1.25, oversized)
1-3: 1-The Flintstones Christmas Party(12/77). 2-Yogi Bear's Easter Parade(3/78). 3-Laff-a-lympics(6/78) 3.50 10.50 35.00

FUN TIME
Ace Periodicals: Spring, 1953; No. 2, Sum, 1953; No. 3(nn), Fall, 1953; No. 4, Wint, 1953-54
1-(25¢, 100 pgs.)-Funny animal 10.00 30.00 65.00
2-4 (All 25¢, 100 pgs.) 13.00 39.00 90.00

FUN WITH SANTA CLAUS (See March of Comics No. 11, 108, 325)

FURTHER ADVENTURES OF CYCLOPS AND PHOENIX (Also see Adventures of Cyclops and Phoenix, Uncanny X-Men & X-Men)
Marvel Comics: June, 1996 - No. 4, Sept, 1996 ($1.95, limited series)
1-4: Origin of Mr. Sinister; Peter Milligan scripts; John Paul Leon-c/a(p). 2-4-Apocalypse app. 3.00
Trade Paperback (1997, $14.99) r/1-4 15.00

FURTHER ADVENTURES OF INDIANA JONES, THE (Movie) (Also see Indiana Jones and the Last Crusade & Indiana Jones and the Temple of Doom)
Marvel Comics Group: Jan, 1983 - No. 34, Mar, 1986
1-34: 1-Byrne/Austin-a; Austin-c. 2-Byrne/Austin-c/a 2.00
NOTE: ***Austin*** *a-1i, 2i, 6i, 9i; c-1, 2i, 6i, 9i.* ***Byrne*** *a-1p, 2p; c-2p.* ***Chaykin*** *a-6p; c-6p, 8p-10p.* ***Ditko*** *a-21p, 25-28, 34.* ***Golden*** *c-24, 25.* ***Simonson*** *c-9. Painted c-14.*

FURTHER ADVENTURES OF NYOKA, THE JUNGLE GIRL, THE (See Nyoka)
AC Comics: 1988 - No. 5, 1989 ($1.95, color; $2.25/$2.50, B&W)
1-5 : 1,2-Bill Black-a plus reprints. 3-Photo-c. 4-Krigstein-r. 5-(B&W)-Reprints plus movie photos 2.50

FURY (Straight Arrow's Horse...) (See A-1 No. 119)

FURY (TV) (See March Of Comics #200)
Dell Publishing Co./Gold Key: No. 781, Mar, 1957 - Nov, 1962 (All photo-c)
Four Color 781 7.00 22.00 80.00
Four Color 885,975,1031,1080,1133,1172,1218,1296, 01292-208(#1-'62), 10020-211(11/62-G.K.) 5.50 16.50 60.00

FURY
Marvel Comics: May, 1994 ($2.95, one-shot)
1-Ironman, Red Skull, FF, Hatemonger, Logan, Scorpio app.; Origin Nick Fury 3.00

FURY/ AGENT 13
Marvel Comics: June, 1998 - No. 2, July, 1998 ($2.99, limited series)
1,2-Nick Fury returns 3.00

GD2.0 FN6.0 NM9.4

FURY OF FIRESTORM, THE (Becomes Firestorm The Nuclear Man #65 on) (Also see Firestorm)
DC Comics: June, 1982 - No. 64, Oct, 1987 (75¢ on)
1-Intro The Black Bison; brief origin 3.00
2-64: 4-JLA x-over. 17-1st app. Firehawk. 21-Death of Killer Frost. 22-Origin. 23-Intro. Byte. 24-(6/84)-1st app. Blue Devil & Bug (origin); origin Byte. 34-1st app./origin Killer Frost II. 39-Weasel's ID revealed 41,42-Crisis x-over. 48-Intro. Moonbow. 53-Origin/1st app. Silver Shade. 55,56-Legends x-over. 58-1st app./origin Parasite 2.00
61-Test cover variant; Superman logo 2.50 7.50 25.00
Annual 1-4: 1(1983), 2(1984), 3(1985), 4(1986) 2.00
NOTE: ***Colan*** *a-19p, Annual 4p.* ***Giffen*** *a-Annual 4p.* ***Gil Kane*** *c-30.* ***Nino*** *a-37.* ***Tuska*** *a-(p)-17, 18, 32, 45.*

FURY OF HELLINA (Also see Hellina)
Lightning Comics: Jan, 1995 ($2.75, B&W)
1 2.75

FURY OF SHIELD
Marvel Comics: Apr, 1995 - No. 4, July, 1995 ($2.50/$1.95, limited series)
1 ($2.50)-Foil-c 3.00
2-4: 4-Bagged w/ decoder 2.50

FUSION
Eclipse Comics: Jan, 1987 - No. 17, Oct, 1989 ($2.00, B&W, Baxter paper)
1-17: 11-The Weasel Patrol begins (1st app.?) 2.00

FUTURE COMICS
David McKay Publications: June, 1940 - No. 4, Sept, 1940
1-(6/40, 64 pgs.)-Origin The Phantom (4 pgs.); The Lone Ranger (8 pgs.) & Saturn Against the Earth (4 pgs.) begin 250.00 750.00 2000.00
2 119.00 356.00 950.00
3,4 97.00 291.00 775.00

FUTURETECH
Mushroom Comics: Jan, 1996 ($2.50, limited series)
1-Flipbook w/SWARM 2.50

FUTURE WORLD COMICS
George W. Dougherty: Summer, 1946 - No. 2, Fall, 1946
1,2: H. C. Kiefer-c; preview of the World of Tomorrow 30.00 90.00 210.00

FUTURE WORLD COMIX (Warren Presents...)
Warren Publications: Sept, 1978
1-Corben, Morrow, Nino, Sutton-a; Todd-c 1.25 3.75 10.00

FUTURIANS, THE (See Marvel Graphic Novel #9)
Lodestone Publishing/Eternity Comics: Sept, 1985 - No. 3, 1985 ($1.50)
1-3: Indicia title "Dave Cockrum's..." 2.00
Graphic Novel 1 ($9.95, Eternity)-r/#1-3, plus never published #4 issue 10.00

G-8 (See G-Eight)

GABBY (Formerly Ken Shannon) (Teen humor)
Quality Comics Group: No. 11, Jul, 1953; No. 2, Sep, 1953 - No. 9, Sep, 1954
11(#1)(7/53) 7.50 22.50 45.00
2 4.25 13.00 28.00
3-9 4.00 10.00 20.00

GABBY GOB (See Harvey Hits No. 85, 90, 94, 97, 100, 103, 106, 109)

GABBY HAYES ADVENTURE COMICS
Toby Press: Dec, 1953
1-Photo-c 15.00 45.00 105.00

GABBY HAYES WESTERN (Movie star) (See Monte Hale, Real Western Hero & Western Hero)
Fawcett Publications/Charlton Comics No. 51 on: Nov, 1948 - No. 50, Jan, 1953; No. 51, Dec, 1954 - No. 59, Jan, 1957
1-Gabby & his horse Corker begin; photo front/back-c begin

Gabby Hayes Western #4 © FAW

Galactus the Devourer #1 © MAR

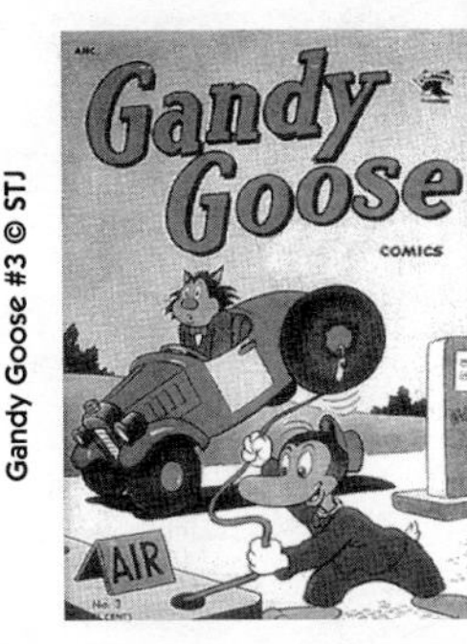

Gandy Goose #3 © STJ

GD2.0 FN6.0 NM9.4

50.00 150.00 400.00
2 24.00 73.00 170.00
3-5 17.00 49.00 115.00
6-10: 9-Young Falcon begins 13.50 41.00 95.00
11-20: 19-Last photo back-c 11.00 33.00 75.00
21-49: 20,22,24,26,28,29-(52 pgs.) 9.15 27.00 55.00
50-(1/53)-Last Fawcett issue; last photo-c? 10.00 30.00 65.00
51-(12/54)-1st Charlton issue; photo-c 10.00 30.00 70.00
52-59(1955-57): 53,55-Photo-c. 58-Swayze-a 5.85 17.50 35.00

GAGS
United Features Synd./Triangle Publ. No. 9 on: July, 1937 - V3#10, Oct, 1944 (13-3/4x10-3/4")
1(7/37)-52 pgs.; 20 pgs. Grin & Bear It, Fellow Citizen 6.35 19.00 38.00
V1#9 (36 pgs.) (7/42) 4.00 12.00 24.00
V3#10 4.00 10.00 20.00

GALACTIC GUARDIANS
Marvel Comics: July, 1994 - No. 4, Oct, 1994 ($1.50, limited series)
1-4 2.00

GALACTIC WAR COMIX (Warren Presents... on cover)
Warren Publications: December, 1978
nn-Wood, Williamson-r 1.25 3.75 10.00

GALACTUS THE DEVOURER
Marvel Comics: Sept, 1999 - No. 6 ($3.50/$2.50, limited series)
1-L. Simonson-s/Muth & Sienkiewicz-a 3.50
2-($2.50) Buscema & Sienkiewicz-a 2.50

GALLANT MEN, THE (TV)
Gold Key: Oct, 1963 (Photo-c)
1(1008-310)-Manning-a 2.50 7.50 22.00

GALLEGHER, BOY REPORTER (Disney, TV)
Gold Key: May, 1965
1(10149-505)-Photo-c 2.25 6.75 18.00

GAMBIT (See X-Men #266 & X-Men Annual #14)
Marvel Comics: Dec, 1993 - No. 4, Mar, 1994 ($2.00, limited series)
1-($2.50)-Lee Weeks-c/a in all; gold foil stamped-c. 5.00
1 (Gold) 1.85 5.50 15.00
2-4 3.00

GAMBIT
Marvel Comics: Sept, 1997 - No. 4, Dec, 1997 ($2.50, limited series)
1-4-Janson-a/ Mackie & Kavanagh-s 3.00

GAMBIT
Marvel Comics: Feb, 1999 - Present ($2.99/$1.99)
1-($2.99) Five covers; Nicieza-a/Skroce-a 3.00
2-8-($1.99): 2-Two covers (Skroce & Adam Kubert) 2.00
...1999 Annual ($3.50) Nicieza-s/McDaniel-a 3.50

GAMBIT AND THE X-TERNALS
Marvel Comics: Mar, 1995 - No. 4, July, 1995 ($1.95, limited series)
1-Age of Apocalyse 3.00
2-4 2.00

GAMEBOY (Super Mario covers on all)
Valiant: 1990 - No. 5 ($1.95, coated-c)
1-5: 3,4-Layton-c. 4-Morrow-a. 5-Layton-c(i) 4.00

GAMERA
Dark Horse Comics: Aug, 1996 - No. 4, Nov, 1996 ($2.95, limited series)
1-4 3.00

GAMMARAUDERS
DC Comics: Jan, 1989 - No. 10, Dec, 1989 ($1.25/$1.50/$2.00)
1-10-Based on TSR game 2.00

GD2.0 FN6.0 NM9.4

GAMORRA SWIMSUIT SPECIAL
Image Comics (WildStorm Productions): June, 1996 ($2.50, one-shot)
1-Campbell wraparound-c; pinups 2.50

GANDY GOOSE (Movies/TV)(See All Surprise, Giant Comics Edition #5A &10, Paul Terry's Comics & Terry-Toons)
St. John Publ. Co./Pines No. 5,6: Mar, 1953 - No. 5, Nov, 1953; No. 5, Fall, 1956 - No. 6, Sum/58
1-All St. John issues are pre-code 10.00 30.00 60.00
2 4.25 13.00 28.00
3-5(1953)(St. John) 4.00 12.00 24.00
5,6(1956-58)(Pines)-CBS Televison Presents... 3.60 9.00 18.00

GANG BUSTERS (See Popular Comics #38)
David McKay/Dell Publishing Co.: 1938 - 1943
Feature Books 17(McKay)('38)-1st app. 50.00 150.00 550.00
Large Feature Comic 10('39)-(Scarce) 50.00 150.00 550.00
Large Feature Comic 17('41) 31.00 93.00 340.00
Four Color 7(1940) 34.00 102.00 375.00
Four Color 23,24('42-43) 26.00 79.00 290.00

GANG BUSTERS (Radio/TV)(Gangbusters #14 on)
National Periodical Publications: Dec-Jan, 1947-48 - No. 67, Dec-Jan, 1958-59 (No. 1-23: 52 pgs.)
1 81.00 244.00 650.00
2 40.00 120.00 290.00
3-5 29.00 86.00 200.00
6-10: 9-Dan Barry-a. 9,10-Photo-c 23.00 69.00 160.00
11-13-Photo-c 19.00 58.00 135.00
14,17-Frazetta-a, 8 pgs. each. 14-Photo-c 40.00 120.00 280.00
15,16,18-20,26: 26-Kirby-a 13.50 41.00 95.00
21-25,27-30 12.00 36.00 85.00
31-44: 44-Last Pre-code (2-3/55) 11.00 33.00 75.00
45-67 10.00 30.00 60.00
NOTE: ***Barry** a-6, 8, 10. **Drucker** a-51. **Moreira** a-48, 50, 59. **Roussos** a-8.*

GANGLAND
DC Comics (Vertigo): Jun, 1998 - No. 4, Sept, 1998 ($2.95, limited series)
1-4:Crime anthology by various. 2-Corben-a 3.00

GANGSTERS AND GUN MOLLS
Avon Per./Realistic Comics: Sept, 1951 - No. 4, June, 1952 (Painted c-1-3)
1-Wood-a, 1 pg; c-/Avon paperback #292 43.00 128.00 340.00
2-Check-a, 8 pgs.; Kamen-a; Bonnie Parker story 36.00 107.00 250.00
3-Marijuana mentioned; used in **POP**, pg. 84,85 31.00 94.00 220.00
4-Syd Shores-c 26.00 77.00 180.00

GANGSTERS CAN'T WIN
D. S. Publishing Co.: Feb-Mar, 1948 - No. 9, June-July, 1949 (All 52 pgs?)
1-True crime stories 31.00 94.00 220.00
2 15.00 45.00 105.00
3-6: 4-Acid in face story 13.00 39.00 90.00
7-9 10.00 30.00 70.00
NOTE: ***Ingles** a-5, 6. **McWilliams** a-5, 7. **Reinman** c-6.*

GANG WORLD
Standard Comics: No. 5, Nov, 1952 - No. 6, Jan, 1953
5-Bondage-c 18.00 54.00 125.00
6 13.50 41.00 95.00

GARGOYLE (See The Defenders #94)
Marvel Comics Group: June, 1985 - No. 4, Sept, 1985 (75¢, limited series)
1-Wrightson-c; character from Defenders 3.00
2-4 2.00

GARGOYLES (TV cartoon)
Marvel Comics: Feb, 1995 - No. 17, June, 1996 ($2.50)
1-17: Based on animated series 3.00

GARRISON'S GORILLAS (TV)
Dell Publishing Co.: Jan, 1968 - No. 4, Oct, 1968; No. 5, Oct, 1969 (Photo-c)

Gay Comics #32 © MAR

Geisha #4 © Andi Watson

Gene Autry Comics #9 © Gene Autry

GD2.0 FN6.0 NM9.4

1 — 3.50 10.50 38.00
2-5: 5-Reprints #1 — 2.25 6.75 25.00

GARY GIANNI'S THE MONSTERMEN
Dark Horse Comics: Aug, 1999 ($2.95, one-shot)
1-Gianni-s/c/a; back-up Hellboy story by Mignola — 3.00

GASM
Stories, Layouts & Press, Inc.: Nov, 1977 - nn(No. 4), Jun, 1978 (B&W/color)
1-Mark Wheatley-s/a; Gene Day-s/a; Workman-a — 2.25 6.75 18.00
nn(#2, 2/78) Day-s/a; Wheatley-a; Workman-a — 1.50 4.50 12.00
nn(#3, 4/78) Day-s/a; Wheatley-a; Corben-a — 2.25 6.75 18.00
nn(#4, 6/78) Hempel-a; Howarth-a; Corben-a — 2.50 7.50 20.00

GASOLINE ALLEY (Top Love Stories No. 3 on?)
Star Publications: Sept-Oct, 1950 - No. 2, Dec, 1950 (Newspaper-r)
1-Contains 1 pg. intro. history of the strip (The Life of Skeezix); reprints 15 scenes of highlights from 1921-1935, plus an adventure from 1935 and 1936 strips; a 2-pg. filler is included on the life of the creator Frank King, with photo of the cartoonist. — 21.00 62.00 145.00
2-(1936-37 reprints)-L. B. Cole-c — 25.00 75.00 175.00
(See Super Book No. 21)

GASP!
American Comics Group: Mar, 1967 - No. 4, Aug, 1967 (12¢)
1 — 3.00 9.00 30.00
2-4 — 2.25 6.75 18.00

GAY COMICS (Honeymoon No. 41)
Timely Comics/USA Comic Mag. Co. No. 18-24: Mar, 1944 (no month); No. 18, Fall, 1944 - No. 40, Oct, 1949
1-Wolverton's Powerhouse Pepper; Tessie the Typist begins; 1st app. Willie (one shot) — 44.00 132.00 350.00
18-(Formerly Funny Tunes #17?)-Wolverton-a — 27.00 81.00 190.00
19-29: Wolverton-a in all. 21,24-6 pg., 7 pg. Powerhouse Pepper; additional 2 pg. story in 24). 23-7 pg Wolverton story & 2 two pg stories(total of 11pgs.). 24,29-Kurtzman-a (24-"Hey Look"(2)) — 21.00 62.00 145.00
30,33,36,37-Kurtzman's "Hey Look" — 10.00 30.00 60.00
31-Kurtzman's "Hey Look" (1), Giggles 'N' Grins (1-1/2) — 10.00 30.00 60.00
32,35,38-40: 35-Nellie The Nurse begins? — 8.35 25.00 50.00
34-Three Kurtzman's "Hey Look" — 10.00 30.00 65.00

GAY COMICS (Also see Smile, Tickle, & Whee Comics)
Modern Store Publ.: 1955 (7¢, 5x7-1/4", 52 pgs.)
1 — 2.00 5.00 10.00

GAY PURR-EE (See Movie Comics)

GAZILLION
Image Comics: Nov, 1998 ($2.50, one-shot)
1-Howard Shum-s/ Keron Grant-a — 2.50

GEEK, THE (See Brother Power... & Vertigo Visions)

GEEKSVILLE (Also see 3 Geeks, The)
3 Finger Prints: Aug, 1999 - Present ($2.75, B&W)
1,2-The 3 Geeks by Koslowski; Innocent Bystander by Sassaman — 2.75

G-8 AND HIS BATTLE ACES
Gold Key: Oct, 1966
1 (10184-610)-Painted-c — 3.20 9.60 32.00

G-8 AND HIS BATTLE ACES
Blazing Comics: 1991 ($1.50, one-shot)
1-Glanzman-a; Truman-c — 2.00
NOTE: *Flip book format with "The Spider's Web" #1 on other side w/***Glanzman***-a,* ***Truman***-c.*

GEISHA
Oni Press: Sept, 1998 - No. 4, Dec, 1998 ($2.95, limited series)
1-4-Andi Watson-s/a. 2-Adam Warren-c — 3.00

GEM COMICS
Spotlight Publishers: Apr, 1945 (52 pgs)
1-Little Mohee, Steve Strong app.; Jungle bondage-c — 32.00 96.00 225.00

GEMINI BLOOD
DC Comics (Helix): Sept, 1996 - No. 9, May, 1997 ($2.25, limited series)
1-9:5-Simonson-c — 2.25

GENE AUTRY (See March of Comics No. 25, 28, 39, 54, 78, 90, 104, 120, 135, 150 & Western Roundup under Dell Giants)

GENE AUTRY COMICS (Movie, Radio star; singing cowboy)
Fawcett Publications: 1941 (On sale 12/31/41) - No. 10, 1943 (68 pgs.) (Dell takes over with No. 11)
1 (Rare)-Gene Autry & his horse Champion begin — 720.00 2160.00 7200.00
2-(1942) — 137.00 411.00 1100.00
3-5: 3-(11/1/42) — 94.00 282.00 750.00
6-10 — 78.00 234.00 625.00

GENE AUTRY COMICS (...& Champion No. 102 on)
Dell Publishing Co.: No. 11, 1943 - No. 121, Jan-Mar, 1959 (TV - later issues)
11 (1943, 60 pgs.)-Continuation of Fawcett series; photo back-c — 55.00 164.00 600.00
12 (2/44, 60 pgs.) — 50.00 150.00 550.00
Four Color 47(1944, 60 pgs.) — 40.00 120.00 440.00
Four Color 57(11/44),66('45)(52 pgs. each) — 38.00 115.00 420.00
Four Color 75,83('45, 36 pgs. each) — 30.00 89.00 325.00
Four Color 93,100('45-46, 36 pgs. each): 100-Photo-c — 26.00 78.00 285.00
1(5-6/46, 52 pgs.) — 40.00 120.00 440.00
2(7-8/46)-Photo-c begin, end #111 — 22.00 66.00 240.00
3-5: 4-Intro Flapjack Hobbs — 16.00 48.00 175.00
6-10 — 13.00 38.00 140.00
11-20: 20-Panhandle Pete begins — 11.00 33.00 120.00
21-29(36pgs.) — 8.00 24.00 90.00
30-40(52pgs.) — 6.75 20.50 75.00
41-56(52pgs.) — 5.50 16.50 60.00
57-66(36pgs.): 58-X-mas-c — 4.00 12.00 45.00
67-80(52pgs.) — 4.00 12.00 45.00
81-90(52pgs.): 82-X-mas-c. 87-Blank inside-c — 3.20 9.60 35.00
91-99(36pgs. No. 91-on). 94-X-mas-c — 2.50 7.50 28.00
100 — 2.90 8.70 32.00
101-111-Last Gene Autry photo-c — 2.40 7.00 26.00
112-121-All Champion painted-c, most by Savitt — 2.00 6.00 22.00
NOTE: *Photo back covers 4-18, 20-45, 48-65.* ***Manning*** *a-118.* ***Jesse Marsh*** *art: 4-Color No. 66, 75, 93, 100, No. 1-25, 27-37, 39, 40.*

GENE AUTRY'S CHAMPION (TV)
Dell Publ. Co.: No. 287, 8/50; No. 319, 2/51; No. 3, 8-10/51 - No. 19, 8-10/55
Four Color 287(#1)('50, 52pgs.)-Photo-c — 8.50 26.50 95.00
Four Color 319(#2, '51), 3: 2-Painted-c begin, most by Sam Savitt — 3.60 11.00 40.00
4-19: 19-Last painted-c — 2.75 8.00 30.00

GENE DOGS
Marvel Comics UK: Oct, 1993 - No. 4, Jan, 1994 ($1.75, limited series)
1-($2.75)-Polybagged w/4 trading cards — 2.75
2-4: 2-Vs. Genetix — 2.00

GENERAL DOUGLAS MACARTHUR
Fox Features Syndicate: 1951
nn-True life story — 19.00 58.00 135.00

GENERIC COMIC, THE
Marvel Comics Group: Apr, 1984 (one-shot)
1 — 2.00

GENERATION HEX
DC Comics (Amalgam): June, 1997 ($1.95, one-shot)

Generation X #45 © MAR

Gen 13 #35 © WildStorm

Gen 13 Bootleg #18 © WildStorm

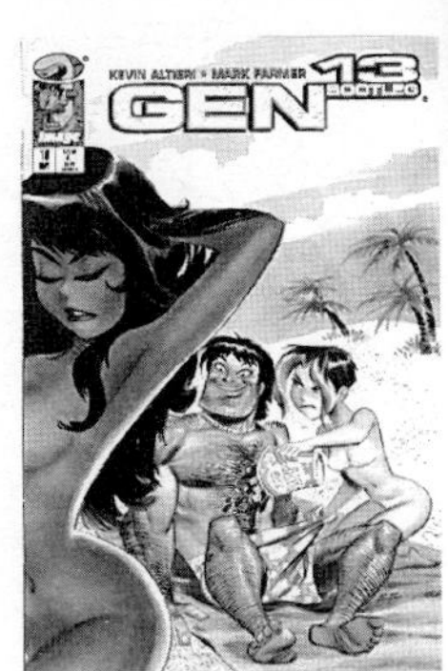

GD2.0 FN6.0 NM9.4

1-Milligan-s/ Pollina & Morales-a 2.00

GENERATION NEXT
Marvel Comics: Mar, 1995 - No. 4, June, 1995 ($1.95, limited series)

1-Age of Apocalypse; Scott Lobdell scripts & Chris Bachalo-c/a 5.00
2-4 3.00

GENERATION X (See Gen 13/ Generation X)
Marvel Comics: Oct, 1994 - Present ($1.50/$1.95/$1.99)

Collectors Preview ($1.75), "Ashcan" Edition 2.00
-1(7/97) Flashback story 3.00
1/2 (San Diego giveaway) 1.00 3.00 8.00
1-($3.95)-Wraparound chromium-c; Scott Lobdell scripts & Chris Bachalo-a begins. 1.00 3.00 8.00
2-($1.95)-Deluxe edition, Bachalo-a 4.00
3,4-($1.95)-Deluxe Edition; Bachalo-a 4.00
2-4-Standard Edition; Bachalo-a 2.50
5-24, 26-28: 5-Returns from "Age of Apocalypse," begin $1.95-c. 6-Bachalo-a(p) ends, returns #17. 7-Roger Cruz-a(p). 10-Omega Red-c/app. 13,14-Bishop-app. 17-Stan Lee app. (Stan Lee scripts own dialogue); Bachalo/Buckingham-a; Onslaught update. 18-Toad cameo. 20-Franklin Richards app; Howard the Duck cameo. 21-Howard the Duck app. 22-Nightmare app. 3.00
25-($2.99)-Wraparound-c. Black Tom, Howard the Duck app. 3.50
29-37: 29-Begin $1.99-c, "Operation Zero Tolerance". 33-Hama-s 2.50
38-49: 38-Dodson-a begins. 40-Penance ID revealed. 49-Maggott app. 2.50
50-($2.99) Crossover w/X-Man #50 3.00
51-56 2.00
'95 Special-($3.95) 4.00
'96 Special-($2.95)-Wraparound-c; Jeff Johnson-c/a 3.00
'97 Special-($2.99)-Wraparound-c; 3.00
'98 Annual-($3.50)-vs. Dracula 3.50
...Holiday Special 1 (2/99, $3.50) Pollina-a 3.50
...Underground Special 1 (5/98, $2.50, B&W) Mahfood-a 2.50

GENERATION X/ GEN 13 (Also see Gen 13/ Generation X)
Marvel Comics: 1997 ($3.99, one-shot)

1-Robinson-s/Larroca-a(p) 4.00

GENE RODDENBERRY'S LOST UNIVERSE
Tekno Comix: Apr, 1995 - No. 6, Dec, 1995 ($1.95)

0,1-6: 0 (11/95). 1-3-w/ bound-in game piece & trading card. 4-bound-in trading card 2.25

GENE RODDENBERRY'S XANDER IN LOST UNIVERSE
Tekno Comix: Dec, 1995 - No. 8, July, 1996 ($2.25)

1-8: 1-5-Jae Lee-c. 4-Polybagged. 8-Pt. 5 of The Big Bang x-over 2.25

GENESIS (See DC related titles)
DC Comics: Oct, 1997 - No. 4, Oct, 1997 ($1.95, weekly limited series)

1-4: Byrne-s/Wagner-a(p) in all. 3.00

GENESIS: THE #1 COLLECTION (WildStorm Archives)
WildStorm Productions: 1998 ($9.99, TPB, B&W)

nn-Reprints #1 issues of WildStorm titles and pin-ups 10.00

GENETIX
Marvel Comics UK: Oct, 1993 - No. 6, Mar, 1994 ($1.75, limited series)

1-($2.75)-Polybagged w/4 cards; Dark Guard app. 2.75
2-6: 2-Intro Tektos. 4-Vs. Gene Dogs 2.00

GEN 12 (Also see Gen 13 and Team 7)
Image Comics (WildStorm Productions): Feb, 1998 - No. 5, June, 1998 ($2.50, limited series)

1-5: 1-Team 7 & Gen 13 app.; wraparound-c 3.00

GEN 13 (Also see Wild C.A.T.S. #1 & Deathmate Black #2)
Image Comics (WildStorm Productions): Feb, 1994 - No. 5, July 1994 ($1.95, limited series)

0 (8/95, $2.50)-Ch. 1 w/Jim Lee-p; Ch.4 w/Charest-p 4.00

GD2.0 FN6.0 NM9.4

1/2 1.50 4.50 12.00
1-($2.50)-Created by Jim Lee 2.25 6.75 18.00
1-2nd printing 3.00
1-"3-D" Edition (9/97, $4.95)-w/glasses 5.00
2-($2.50) 1.60 4.85 13.00
3-Pitt-c & story 1.00 3.00 8.00
4-Pitt-c & story; wraparound-c 2.40 6.00
5 5.00
5-Alternate Portacio-c; see Deathblow #5 1.00 3.00 8.00
...Collected Edition ('94, $12.95)-r/#1-5 13.00
...Rave ($1.50, 3/95)-wraparound-c 2.00

NOTE: *Issues 1-4 contain coupons redeemable for the ashcan edition of Gen 13 #0. Price listed is for a complete book.*

GEN 13
Image Comics (WildStorm Productions): Mar, 1995 - No. 36, Dec, 1998;
DC Comics (WildStorm Prod.): No. 37, Mar, 1999 - Present ($2.95/$2.50)

1-A (Charge)-Campbell/Gardner-c 5.00
1-B (Thumbs Up)-Campbell/Gardner-c 5.00
1-C-1-K,1-M: 1-C (Lil' GEN 13)-Art Adams-c. 1-D (Barbari-GEN)-Simon Bisley-c 1-E (Your Friendly Neighborhood Grunge)-John Cleary-c. 1-F (GEN 13 Goes Madison Ave.)-Michael Golden-c. 1-G (Lin-GEN-re)-Michael Lopez-c. 1-H (GEN-et Jackson)-Jason Pearson-c. 1-I (That's the way we became GEN 13)-Campbell/Gibson-c. 1-J (All Dolled Up)-Campbell/McWeeney-c. 1-K (Verti-GEN)-Joe Dunn-c. 1-L (Picto-Fiction). 1-M (Do it Yourself Cover) 1.00 3.00 8.00
1-"3-D" Edition (2/98, $4.95)-w/glasses 5.00
2 ($1.95, Newsstand)-WildStorm Rising Pt. 4; bound-in card 2.00
2-12: 2-($2.50, Direct Market)-WildStorm Rising Pt. 4, bound-in card. 6,7-Jim Lee-c/a(p). 9-Ramos-a. 10,11-Fire From Heaven Pt. 3. & Pt.9 3.00
11-($4.95)-Special European Tour Edition; chromium-c 15.00
13A,13B,13C-($1.30, 13 pgs.): 13A-Archie & Friends app. 13B-Bone-c/app.; Teenage Mutant Ninja Turtles, Madman, Spawn & Jim Lee app. 2.00
14-24: 20-Last Campbell-a 2.50
25-($3.50)-Two covers by Campbell and Charest 3.50
25-($3.50)-Voyager Pack w/Danger Girl preview 3.50
26-34: 26-Arcudi-s/Frank-a begins. 33-Flip book w/Planetary preview 34-Back-up story by Art Adams 2.50
35-43: 36,38,40-Two covers. 37-First DC issue. 41-Last Frank-a 2.50
Annual 1 (1997, $2.95) Ellis-s/ Dillon-c/a. 3.00
Annual 1999 ($3.50, DC) Slipstream x-over w/ DV8 3.50
...Archives (4/98, $12.99) B&W reprints of mini-series, #0,1/2,1-13ABC; includes cover gallery and sourcebook 13.00
...European Vacation TPB($6.95) r/#6,7 7.00
...: Going West (6/99, $2.50, one-shot) Pruett-s 2.50
...: Grunge Saves the World (5/99, $5.95, one-shot) Altieri-c/a 6.00
...Lost in Paradise ($6.95, trade paperback) r/3-5 7.00
.../ Maxx (12/95, $3.50, one-shot) Messner-Loebs-s, 1st Coker-c/a. 3.50
...Starting Over TPB ($14.95) r/#1-7 15.00
...#13 A,B&C Collected Edition ($6.95, TPB) r/#13A,B&C 7.00
... 3-D Special (1997, $4.95, one-shot) Art Adams-s/a(p) 5.00
...: The Unreal World (7/96, $2.95, one-shot) Humberto Ramos-c/a 3.00
...: Wired (4/99, $2.50, one-shot) Richard Bennett-c/a 2.50
...: 'Zine (12/96, $1.95, B&W, digest size) Campbell/Garner-c 2.00
Variant Collection-Four editions (all 13 variants w/Chromium variant-limited, signed) 18.00 55.00 200.00

GEN 13 BOOTLEG
Image Comics (WildStorm): Nov, 1996 - No. 20, Jul, 1998 ($2.50)

1-Alan Davis-a; alternate costumes-c 3.00
1-Team falling variant-c 4.00
2-7: 2-Alan Davis-a. 5,6-Terry Moore-s. 7-Robinson-s/Scott Hampton-a. 2.50
8-10-Adam Warren-s/a 5.00
11-20: 11,12-Lopresti-s/a & Simonson-s. 13-Wieringo-s/a. 14-Mariotte-s/Phillips-a. 15,16-Strnad-s/Shaw-a. 18-Altieri-s/a(p)/c, 18-Variant-c by Bruce Timm 2.50
Annual 1 (2/98, $2.95) Ellis-s/Dillon-c/a 3.00
... Grunge: The Movie (12/97, $9.95) r/#8-10, Warren-c 10.00

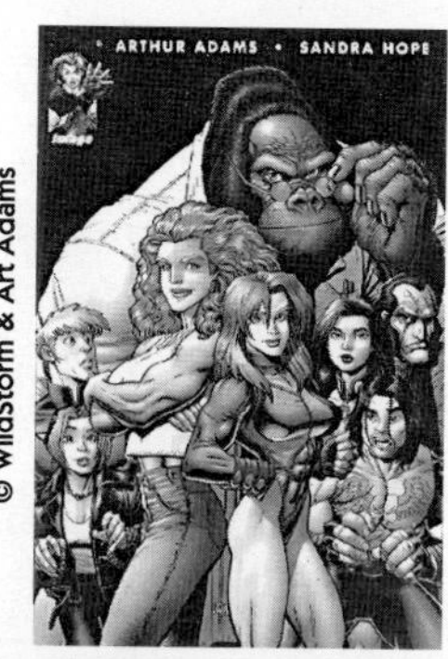

Gen 13 / Monkeyman & O'Brien #1 © WildStorm & Art Adams

George Pal's Puppetoons #1 © George Pal

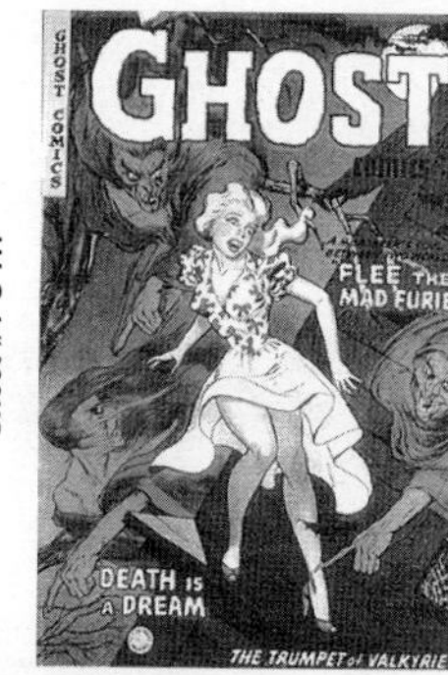

Ghost #4 © FH

...Vol. 1 TPB (10/98, $11.95) r/#1-4 12.00

GEN [13]/ GENERATION X (Also see Generation X / Gen [13])
Image Comics (WildStorm Publications): July, 1997 ($2.95, one-shot)
1-Choi-s/ Art Adams-p/Garner-i. Variant covers by Adams/Garner and Campbell/McWeeney 3.00
1-($4.95) 3-D Edition w/glasses; Campbell-c 5.00

GEN [13] INTERACTIVE
Image Comics (WildStorm): Oct, 1997 - No. 3, Dec, 1997 ($2.50, lim. series)
1-3-Internet voting used to determine storyline 2.50

GEN [13] : MAGICAL DRAMA QUEEN ROXY
Image Comics (WildStorm): Oct, 1998 - No. 3, Dec, 1998 ($3.50, lim. series)
1-3-Adam Warren-s/c/a; manga style, 2-Variant-c by Hiroyuki Utatane 3.50
1-($6.95) Dynamic Forces Ed. w/Variant Warren-c 7.00

GEN [13] /MONKEYMAN & O'BRIEN
Image Comics (WildStorm): Jun, 1998 - No. 2, July, 1998 ($2.50, lim. series)
1,2-Art Adams-s/a(p); 1-Two covers 2.50
1-($4.95) Chromium-c, 1-($6.95) Dynamic Forces Ed. 8.00

GEN [13]: ORDINARY HEROES
Image Comics (WildStorm Publications): Feb, 1996 - No. 2, July, 1996 ($2.50, limited series)
1,2-Adam Hughes-c/a/scripts 3.00

GENTLE BEN (TV)
Dell Publishing Co.: Feb, 1968 - No. 5, Oct, 1969 (All photo-c)
1 2.50 7.50 28.00
2-5: 5-Reprints #1 1.40 4.20 16.00

GEOMANCER (Also see Eternal Warrior: Fist & Steel)
Valiant: Nov, 1994 - No. 8, June, 1995 ($3.75/$2.25)
1 ($3.75)-Chromium wraparound-c; Eternal Warrior app. 3.75
2-8 2.25

GEORGE OF THE JUNGLE (TV)(See America's Best TV Comics)
Gold Key: Feb, 1969 - No. 2, Oct, 1969 (Jay Ward)
1 11.25 34.00 125.00
2 8.00 24.00 85.00

GEORGE PAL'S PUPPETOONS (Funny animal puppets)
Fawcett Publications: Dec, 1945 - No. 18, Dec, 1947; No. 19, 1950
1-Captain Marvel-c 40.00 120.00 300.00
2 21.00 64.00 150.00
3-10 13.00 39.00 90.00
11-19 11.00 33.00 75.00

GEORGIE COMICS (...& Judy Comics #20-35?; see All Teen & Teen Comics)
Timely Comics/GPI No. 1-34: Spr, 1945 - No. 39, Oct, 1952 (#1-3 are quarterly)
1-Dave Berg-a 23.00 69.00 160.00
2 11.00 33.00 75.00
3-5,7,8 10.00 30.00 60.00
6-Georgie visits Timely Comics 11.50 34.00 80.00
9,10-Kurtzman's "Hey Look" (1 & ?); Margie app. 10.00 30.00 65.00
11,12: 11-Margie, Millie app. 7.00 21.00 42.00
13-Kurtzman's "Hey Look", 3 pgs. 8.35 25.00 50.00
14-Wolverton-a(1 pg.); Kurtzman's "Hey Look" 10.00 30.00 60.00
15,16,18-20 5.85 17.50 35.00
17,29-Kurtzman's "Hey Look", 1 pg. 7.50 22.50 45.00
21-24,27,28,30-39: 21-Anti-Wertham editorial 5.00 15.00 30.00
25-Painted-c by classic pin-up artist Peter Driben 9.15 27.00 55.00
26-Logo design swipe from Archie Comics 5.85 17.50 35.00

GERALD McBOING-BOING AND THE NEARSIGHTED MR. MAGOO (TV) (Mr. Magoo No. 6 on)
Dell Publishing Co.: Aug-Oct, 1952 - No. 5, Aug-Oct, 1953
1 8.00 25.00 90.00
2-5 6.40 19.00 70.00

GERONIMO (See Fighting Indians of the Wild West!)
Avon Periodicals: 1950 - No. 4, Feb, 1952
1-Indian Fighter; Maneely-a; Texas Rangers-r/Cowpuncher #1; Fawcette-c 17.00 51.00 120.00
2-On the Warpath; Kit West app.; Kinstler-c/a 10.00 30.00 70.00
3-And His Apache Murderers; Kinstler-c/a(2); Kit West-r/Cowpuncher #6 10.00 30.00 70.00
4-Savage Raids of; Kinstler-c & inside front-c; Kinstlerish-a by McCann(3) 10.00 30.00 60.00

GERONIMO JONES
Charlton Comics: Sept, 1971 - No. 9, Jan, 1973
1 1.75 5.25 14.00
2-9 1.00 2.80 7.00
Modern Comics Reprint #7('78) 3.50

GETALONG GANG, THE (TV)
Marvel Comics (Star Comics): May, 1985 - No. 6, Mar, 1986
1-6: Saturday morning TV stars 2.00

GET LOST
Mikeross Publications/New Comics: Feb-Mar, 1954 - No. 3, June-July, 1954 (Satire)
1-Andru/Esposito-a in all? 29.00 86.00 200.00
2-Andru/Esposito-c; has 4 pg. E.C. parody featuring "The Sewer Keeper" 20.00 60.00 140.00
3-John Wayne 'Hondo' parody 16.00 47.00 110.00
1,2 (10,12/87-New Comics)-B&W r-original 2.00

GET SMART (TV)
Dell Publ. Co.: June, 1966 - No. 8, Sept, 1967 (All have Don Adams photo-c)
1 8.50 26.50 95.00
2,3-Ditko-a 6.00 18.00 65.00
4-8: 8-Reprints #1 (cover and insides) 5.00 15.00 55.00

GHOST (...Comics #9)
Fiction House Magazines: 1951(Winter) - No. 11, Summer, 1954
1-Most covers by Whitman 64.00 193.00 515.00
2-Ghost Gallery & Werewolf Hunter stories 34.00 103.00 240.00
3-9: 3,6,7,9-Bondage-c. 9-Abel, Discount-a 29.00 86.00 200.00
10,11-Dr. Drew by Grandenetti in each, reprinted from Rangers; 11-Evans-r/ Rangers #39; Grandenetti-r/Rangers #49 26.00 77.00 180.00

GHOST (See Comic's Greatest World)
Dark Horse Comics: Apr, 1995 - No. 36, Apr, 1998 ($2.50/$2.95)
1-Adam Hughes-a 1.00 3.00 8.00
2,3-Hughes-a 4.00
4-24: 4-Barb Wire app. 5,6-Hughes-c. 12-Ghost/Hellboy preview. 15,21-X app. 18,19-Barb Wire app. 2.50
25-($3.50)-48 pgs. special 3.50
26-36: 26-Begin $2.95-c. 29-Flip book w/Timecop. 33-36-Jade Cathedral; Harris painted-c 3.00
Special 1 (7/94, $3.95, 48 pgs.) 1.00 2.80 7.00
Special 2 (6/98, $3.95) Barb Wire app. 4.00
...Nocturnes (1996, $9.95, trade paperback)-r/#1-3 & 5 10.00
...Stories (1995, $9.95, trade paperback)-r/Early Ghost app. 10.00

GHOST (Volume 2)
Dark Horse Comics: Sept, 1998 - Present ($2.95)
1-11: 1-4-Ryan Benjamin-c/Zanier-a 3.00
Special 3 (12/98, $3.95) 4.00

GHOST AND THE SHADOW
Dark Horse Comics: Dec, 1995 ($2.95, one-shot)
1-Moench scripts 3.00

GHOST/HELLBOY
Dark Horse Comics: May, 1996 - No. 2, June, 1996 ($2.50, limited series)
1,2: Mike Mignola-c/scripts & breakdowns; Scott Benefiel finished-a 3.00

GHOST BREAKERS (Also see Racket Squad in Action, Red Dragon & (CC)

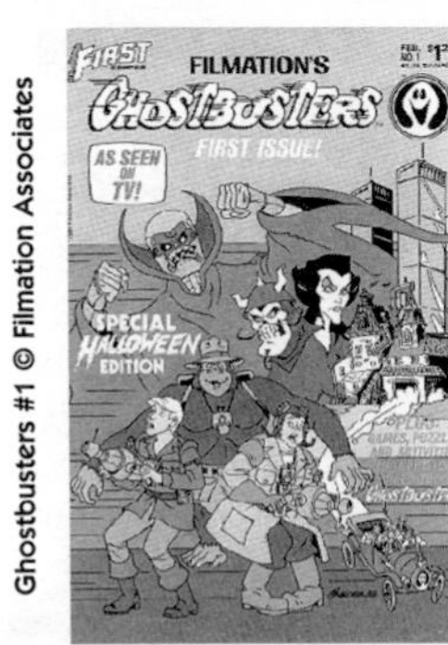

Ghostbusters #1 © Filmation Associates

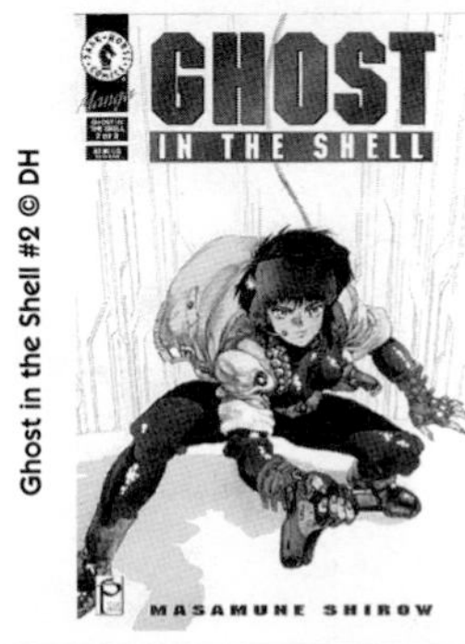

Ghost in the Shell #2 © DH

Ghost Rider ('73) #2 © MAR

GD2.0 FN6.0 NM9.4

Sherlock Holmes Comics)
Street & Smith Publications: Sept, 1948 - No. 2, Dec, 1948 (52 pgs.)

1-Powell-c/a(3); Dr. Neff (magician) app. 40.00 120.00 300.00
2-Powell-c/a(2); Maneely-a 34.00 101.00 235.00

GHOSTBUSTERS (TV) (Also, see Real...and Slimer)
First Comics: Feb, 1987 - No. 6, Aug, 1987 ($1.25)

1-6: Based on new animated TV series 2.00

GHOSTBUSTERS II
Now Comics: Oct, 1989 - No. 3, Dec, 1989 ($1.95, mini-series)

1-3: Movie Adaptation 2.00

GHOST CASTLE (See Tales of...)

GHOSTDANCING
DC Comics (Vertigo): Mar, 1995 - No. 6, Sept, 1995 ($1.95, limited series)

1-6: Case-c/a 2.00

GHOST IN THE SHELL (Manga)
Dark Horse: Mar, 1995 - No. 8, Oct, 1995 ($3.95, B&W/color, lim. series)

1 2.50 7.50 25.00
2 2.80 8.40 28.00
3 1.85 5.50 15.00
4-8 1.25 3.75 10.00

GHOSTLY HAUNTS (Formerly Ghost Manor)
Charlton Comics: #20, 9/71 - #53, 12/76; #54, 9/77 - #55, 10/77; #56, 1/78 - #58, 4/78

20 1.75 5.25 14.00
21-40: 27-Dr. Graves x-over. 32-New logo. 33-Back to old logo. 39-Origin & 1st app. Destiny Fox 1.25 3.75 10.00
41-58: 1.00 3.00 8.00
40,41(Modern Comics-r, 1977, 1978) 3.00

NOTE: ***Ditko** a-22-25, 27, 28, 31-34, 36-41, 43-48, 50, 52, 54, 56r; c-22-27, 29, 30, 33-37, 47, 54, 56. **Glanzman** a-20. **Howard** a-27, 30, 35, 40-43, 48, 54, 57. **Kim** a-38, 41, 57. **Larson** a-48, 50. **Newton** c/a-42. **Staton** a-32, 35; c-28, 46. **Sutton** c-33, 37, 39, 41.*

GHOSTLY TALES (Formerly Blue Beetle No. 50-54)
Charlton Comics: No. 55, 4-5/66 - No. 124, 12/76; No. 125, 9/77 - No. 169, 10/84

55-Intro. & origin Dr. Graves 3.20 9.60 32.00
56-71: 70-Dr. Graves ends. 71-Last 12¢ issue 2.00 6.00 16.00
72-100 1.25 3.75 10.00
101-124: 107-Sutton, Wood-a. 114-Newton-a 1.00 3.00 8.00
125-160 5.00
161-169-Lower print run 2.40 6.00

NOTE: ***Aparo** a-65, 66, 68, 72, 141r, 142r; c-71, 72, 74-76, 81, 146r. **Ditko** a-55-58, 60, 61, 67, 69-73, 75-90, 92-95, 97, 99-118, 120-122, 125r, 126r, 131-133r, 136-141r, 143r, 144r, 152, 155, 161, 163; c-67, 69, 73, 77, 78, 83, 84, 86-90, 92-97, 99, 102, 109, 111, 118, 120-122, 125, 131-133, 163. **Glanzman** a-167. **Howard** a-95, 98, 99, 108, 117, 129; c-98, 107, 120, 121, 161. **Larson** a-117, 119. **Morisi** a-83, 84, 86. **Newton** a-114; c-115(painted). **Palais** a-61. **Staton** a-161; c-117. **Sutton** a-106, 107, 111-114, 127, 130; c-100, 106, 110, 113(painted). **Wood** a-107.*

GHOSTLY WEIRD STORIES (Formerly Blue Bolt Weird)
Star Publications: No. 120, Sept, 1953 - No. 124, Sept, 1954

120-Jo-Jo-r 36.00 107.00 250.00
121-124: 121-Jo-Jo-r. 122-The Mask-r/Capt. Flight #5; Rulah-r; has 1pg. story 'Death and the Devil Pills'-r/Western Outlaws #17. 123-Jo-Jo; Disbrow-a(2). 124-Torpedo Man 30.00 90.00 210.00

NOTE: ***Disbrow** a-120-124. **L. B. Cole** covers-all issues (#122 is a sci-fi cover).*

GHOST MANOR (Ghostly Haunts No. 20 on)
Charlton Comics: July, 1968 - No. 19, July, 1971

1 2.60 7.80 26.00
2-6: 6-Last 12¢ issue 2.00 6.00 16.00
7-12,17: 17-Morisi-a 1.50 4.50 12.00
13-16,18,19-Ditko-a; c-15,18,19 1.85 5.50 15.00

GHOST MANOR (2nd Series)
Charlton Comics: Oct, 1971-No. 32, Dec, 1976; No. 33, Sept, 1977-No. 77, 11/84

1 2.50 7.50 24.00
2-7,9,10 1.50 4.50 12.00
8-Wood-a 1.75 5.25 14.00
11-17 1.00 3.00 8.00
18-Newton's 1st pro art 1.50 4.50 12.00
19-30: 19,20,22-Newton-a. 19,28-Nudity panels. 21-E-Man, Blue Beetle, Capt. Atom cameos. 1.25 3.75 10.00
31-39 1.00 2.80 7.00
40-Torture & drug use. 1.10 3.30 9.00
41-56 1.00 2.80 7.00
57-Wood, Ditko, Howard-a 1.10 3.30 9.00
58-70 5.00
71-77: 77-Aparo-r/Space Adventures V3#60 (Paul Mann) 2.40 6.00
19 (Modern Comics reprint, 1977) 3.00

NOTE: ***Ditko** a-4, 8, 10, 11(2), 13, 14, 18, 20-22, 24-26, 28, 29, 31, 37r, 38r, 40r, 42-44r, 46r, 47, 51r, 52r, 54r, 57, 60, 62(4), 64r, 71; c-2-7, 9-11, 14-16, 28, 31, 37, 38, 42, 43, 46, 47, 51, 52, 60, 62, 64. **Howard** a-4, 8, 12, 17, 19-21, 31, 41, 45, 57. **Newton** a-18-20, 22, 64; c-22. **Staton** a-13, 38, 44, 45. **Sutton** a-19, 23, 25, 45;c-8, 18.*

GHOST RIDER (See A-1 Comics, Best of the West, Black Phantom, Bobby Benson, Great Western, Red Mask & Tim Holt)
Magazine Enterprises: 1950 - No. 14, 1954

NOTE: *The character was inspired by Vaughn Monroe's "Ghost Riders in the Sky", and Disney's movie "The Headless Horseman".*

1(A-1 #27)-Origin Ghost Rider 69.00 206.00 550.00
2-5: 2(A-1 #29), 3(A-1 #31), 4(A-1 #34), 5(A-1 #37)-All Frazetta-c only 59.00 178.00 475.00
6,7: 6(A-1 #44)-Loco weed story, 7(A-1 #51) 26.00 79.00 185.00
8,9: 8(A-1 #57)-Drug use story, 9(A-1 #69) 24.00 71.00 165.00
10(A-1 #71)-Vs. Frankenstein 24.00 73.00 170.00
11-14: 11(A-1 #75). 12(A-1 #80)-Bondage-c; one-eyed Devil-c. 13(A-1 #84). 14(A-1 #112) 20.00 60.00 140.00

NOTE: ***Dick Ayers** art in all; c-1, 6-14.*

GHOST RIDER, THE (See Night Rider & Western Gunfighters)
Marvel Comics Group: Feb, 1967 - No. 7, Nov, 1967 (Western hero)(12¢)

1-Origin & 1st app. Ghost Rider; Kid Colt-reprints begin 5.50 16.50 55.00
2 3.20 9.60 32.00
3-7: 6-Last Kid Colt-r; All Ayers-c/a(p) 2.50 7.50 24.00

GHOST RIDER (See The Champions, Marvel Spotlight #5, Marvel Team-Up #15, 58, Marvel Treasury Edition #18, Marvel Two-In-One #8, The Original Ghost Rider & The Original Ghost Rider Rides Again)
Marvel Comics Group: Sept, 1973 - No. 81, June, 1983 (Super-hero)

1-Johnny Blaze, the Ghost Rider begins; 1st app. Daimon Hellstrom (Son of Satan) in cameo 5.00 15.00 55.00
2-1st full app. Daimon Hellstrom; gives glimpse of costume (1 panel); story continues in Marvel Spotlight #12 2.50 7.50 20.00
3-5: 3-Ghost Rider gets new cycle; Son of Satan app. 1.85 5.50 15.00
6-10: 10-Reprints origin/1st app. from Marvel Spotlight #5; Ploog-a 1.50 4.50 12.00
11-16 1.00 3.00 8.00
17,19-(Reg. 25¢ editions)(4,8/76) 1.00 3.00 8.00
17,19-(30¢-c variants, limited distribution) 3.20 9.60 32.00
18-(Reg. 25¢ edition)(6/76). Spider-Man-c & app. 1.00 3.00 8.00
18-(30¢-c variant, limited distribution) 3.20 9.60 32.00
20-Daredevil x-over; ties into D.D. #138; Byrne-a 1.50 4.50 12.00
21-30: 22-1st app. Enforcer. 29,30-Vs. Dr. Strange 2.40 6.00
31-34,36-49 5.00
35-Death Race classic; Starlin-c/a/sty 1.00 3.00 8.00
50-Double size 1.00 2.80 7.00
51-76,78-80: 80-Brief origin recap. 68,77-Origin retold 4.00
81-Death of Ghost Rider (Demon leaves Blaze) 1.00 3.00 8.00

NOTE: ***Anderson** c-64p. **Infantino** a(p)-43, 44, 51. **G. Kane** a-21p; c(p)-1, 2, 4, 5, 8, 9, 11-13, 19, 20, 24, 25. **Kirby** c-21-23. **Mooney** a-2-9p, 30i. **Nebres** c-26i. **Newton** a-23i. **Perez** c-26p. **Shores** a-2i. J. **Sparling** a-62p, 64p, 65p. **Starlin** a(p)-35. **Sutton** a-1p, 44i, 64i, 65i, 66, 67i. **Tuska** a-13p, 14p, 16p.*

GHOST RIDER (Volume 2) (Also see Doctor Strange/Ghost Rider Special,

Ghost Rider ('90) #93 © MAR

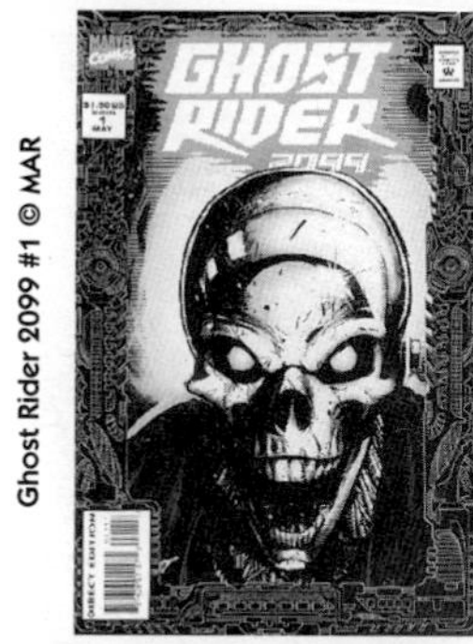

Ghost Rider 2099 #1 © MAR

Ghosts #80 © DC

GD2.0 FN6.0 NM9.4 **GD2.0 FN6.0 NM9.4**

Marvel Comics Presents & Midnight Sons Unlimited)
Marvel Comics (Midnight Sons imprint #44 on): V2#1, May, 1990 - No. 93, Feb, 1998 ($1.50/$1.75/$1.95)

1-($1.95, 52 pgs.)-Origin/1st app. new Ghost Rider; Kingpin app. 2.40 6.00
1-2nd printing (not gold) 2.00
2-5: 3-Kingpin app. 5-Punisher app.; Jim Lee-c 3.00
5-Gold background 2nd printing 2.00
6-14,16-24,29,30,32-39: 6-Punisher app. 9-X-Factor app. 10-Reintro Johnny Blaze on the last pg. 11-Stroman-c/a(p). 12,13-Dr. Strange x-over cont'd in D.S. #28. 13-Painted-c. 14-Johnny Blaze vs. Ghost Rider; origin recap 1st Ghost Rider (Blaze). . 5-Gold background 2nd printing. 6,17-Spider-Man/ Hobgoblin-c/story18-Painted-c by Nelson. 29-Wolverine-c/story. 32-Dr. Strange x-over; Johnny Blaze app. 34-Williamson-a(i). 36-Daredevil app. 37-Archangel app. 2.00
15-Glow in the dark-c 3.00
25-27: 25-($2.75)-Contains pop-up scene insert. 26,27-X-Men x-over; Lee/Williams-c on both 2.75
28,31-($2.50, 52 pgs.)-Polybagged w/poster; part 1 & part 6 of Rise of the Midnight Sons storyline (see Ghost Rider/Blaze #1) 2.50
40-Outer-c is Darkhold envelope made of black parchment w/gold ink; Midnight Massacre; Demogoblin app. 2.50
41-48: 41-Lilith & Centurious app.; begin $1.75-c. 41-43-Neon ink-c. 43-Has free extra 16 pg. insert on Siege of Darkness. 44,45-Siege of Darkness parts 2 & 10. 44-Spot varnish-c. 46-Intro new Ghost Rider. 48-Spider-Man app. 2.00
49,51-60,62-78: 49-Begin $1.95-c; bound-in trading card sheet; Hulk app. 55-Werewolf by Night app. 65-Punisher app. 67,68-Gambit app. 68-Wolverine app. 73,74-Blaze, Vengeance app. 78-New costume. 2.00
50,61: 50-($2.50, 52 pgs.)-Regular edition 2.50
50-($2.95, 52 pgs.)-Collectors ed. die cut foil-c 3.00
75-92,94: 6-Vs. Vengeance. 77-Dr. Strange-c/app. 78-Dr. Strange app. 94-Final issue 2.00
93-($2.99)-Saltares & Texeira-a 3.00
Annual 1,2 ('93, '94, $2.95, 68 pgs.)-1-Bagged w/card 3.00
...And Cable 1 (9/92, $3.95, stiff-c, 68 pgs.)-Reprints Marvel Comics Presents #90-98 w/new Kieth-c 4.00

NOTE: ***Andy & Joe Kubert*** *c/a-28-31.* ***Quesada*** *c-21.* ***Williamson*** *a(i)-33-35; c-33i.*

GHOST RIDER/BALLISTIC
Marvel Comics: Feb, 1997 ($2.95, one-shot)

1-Devil's Reign pt. 3 3.00

GHOST RIDER/BLAZE: SPIRITS OF VENGEANCE (Also see Blaze)
Marvel Comics (Midnight Sons imprint #17 on): Aug, 1992 - No. 23, June, 1994 ($1.75)

1-($2.75, 52 pgs.)-Polybagged w/poster; part 2 of Rise of the Midnight Sons storyline; Adam Kubert-c/a begins 3.00
2-11,14-21: 4-Art Adams & Joe Kubert-p. 5,6-Spirits of Venom parts 2 & 4 cont'd from Web of Spider-Man #95,96 w/Demogoblin. 14-17-Neon ink-c. 15-Intro Blaze's new costume & power. 17,18-Siege of Darkness parts 8 & 13. 17-Spot varnish-c 2.00
12-($2.95)-Glow-in-the-dark-c 3.00
13-($2.25)-Outer-c is Darkhold envelope made of black parchment w/gold ink; Midnight Massacre x-over 2.25
22,23: 22-Begin $1.95-c; bound-in trading card sheet 2.00

NOTE: ***Adam & Joe Kubert*** *c-7, 8.* ***Adam Kubert/Steacy*** *c-6.* ***J. Kubert*** *a-13p(6 pgs.)*

GHOST RIDER/CAPTAIN AMERICA: FEAR
Marvel Comics: Oct, 1992 ($5.95, 52 pgs.)

nn-Wraparound gatefold-c; Williamson inks 2.40 6.00

GHOST RIDER 2099
Marvel Comics: May, 1994 - No. 25, May, 1996 ($1.50/$1.95)

1 ($2.25)-Collector's Edition w/prismatic foil-c 3.00
1 ($1.50)-Regular Edition; bound-in trading card sheet 2.00
2-24: 7-Spider-Man 2099 app. 2.00
25 ($2.95) 3.00

GHOST RIDER, WOLVERINE, PUNISHER: THE DARK DESIGN
Marvel Comics: Dec, 1994 ($5.95, one-shot)

nn-Gatefold-c 2.40 6.00

GHOST RIDER; WOLVERINE; PUNISHER: HEARTS OF DARKNESS
Marvel Comics: Dec, 1991 ($4.95, one-shot, 52 pgs.)

1-Double gatefold-c; John Romita, Jr.-c/a(p) 5.00

GHOSTS (Ghost No. 1)
National Periodical Publications/DC Comics: Sept-Oct, 1971 - No. 112, May, 1982 (No. 1-5: 52 pgs.)

1-Aparo-a 7.25 22.00 80.00
2-Wood-a(i) 4.00 12.00 40.00
3-5 3.00 9.00 30.00
6-10 2.25 6.75 18.00
11-20 1.50 4.50 12.00
21-39 1.10 3.30 9.00
40-(68 pgs.) 2.00 6.00 16.00
41-60 2.40 6.00
61-96 5.00
97-99-The Spectre vs. Dr. 13 by Aparo. 97,98-Spectre-c by Aparo. 1.00 3.00 8.00
100-Infinity-c 5.00
101-112 4.00

NOTE: ***B. Baily*** *a-77.* ***Buckler*** *c-99, 100.* ***J. Craig*** *a-108.* ***Ditko*** *a-77, 111.* ***Giffen*** *a-104p, 106p, 111p.* ***Glanzman*** *a-2.* ***Golden*** *a-88.* ***Infantino*** *a-8.* ***Kaluta*** *c-7, 93, 101.* ***Kubert*** *a-8; c-89, 105-108, 111.* ***Mayer*** *a-111.* ***McWilliams*** *a-99.* ***Win Mortimer*** *a-89, 91, 94.* ***Nasser/Netzer*** *a-97.* ***Newton*** *a-92p, 94p.* ***Nino*** *a-35, 37, 57.* ***Orlando*** *a-74i; c-80.* ***Redondo*** *a-8, 13, 45.* ***Sparling*** *a(p)-90, 93, 94.* ***Spiegle*** *a-103, 105.* ***Tuska*** *a-2i. Dr. 13, the Ghostbreaker back-ups in 95-99, 101.*

GHOSTS SPECIAL (See DC Special Series No. 7)

GHOST STORIES (See Amazing Ghost Stories)

GHOST STORIES
Dell Publ. Co.: Sept-Nov, 1962; No. 2, Apr-June, 1963 - No. 37, Oct, 1973

12-295-211(#1)-Written by John Stanley 4.00 12.00 40.00
2 2.50 7.50 22.00
3-10: Two No. 6's exist with different c/a(12-295-406 & 12-295-503) #12-295-503 is actually #9 with indicia to #6 2.25 6.75 18.00
11-21: 21-Last 12¢ issue 1.75 5.25 14.00
22-37 1.25 3.75 10.00

NOTE: *#21-34, 36, 37 all reprint earlier issues.*

GHOUL TALES (Magazine)
Stanley Publications: Nov, 1970 - No. 5, July, 1971 (52 pgs.) (B&W)

1-Aragon pre-code reprints; Mr. Mystery as host; bondage-c 5.00 15.00 55.00
2,3: 2-(1/71)Reprint/Climax #1. 3-(3/71) 2.60 7.80 26.00
4-(5/71)Reprints story "The Way to a Man's Heart" used in **SOTI** 3.80 11.40 38.00
5-ACG reprints 2.50 7.50 20.00

NOTE: *No. 1-4 contain pre-code Aragon reprints.*

GIANT BOY BOOK OF COMICS (Also see Boy Comics)
Newsbook Publications (Gleason): 1945 (240 pgs., hard-c)

1-Crimebuster & Young Robin Hood; Biro-c 87.00 262.00 700.00

GIANT COMIC ALBUM
King Features Syndicate: 1972 (59¢, 11x14", 52 pgs., B&W, cardboard-c)

Newspaper reprints: Barney Google, Little Iodine, Katzenjammer Kids, Henry, Beetle Bailey, Blondie, & Snuffy Smith each... 2.60 7.80 26.00
Flash Gordon ('68-69 Dan Barry) 3.50 10.50 35.00
Mandrake the Magician ('59 Falk), Popeye 3.00 9.00 30.00

GIANT COMICS
Charlton Comics: Summer, 1957 - No. 3, Winter, 1957 (25¢, 100 pgs.)

1-Atomic Mouse, Hoppy app. 20.00 60.00 140.00
2,3: 2-Romance. 3-Christmas Book; Atomic Mouse, Atomic Rabbit, Li'l Genius, Li'l Tomboy & Atom the Cat stories 14.00 43.00 100.00

Giant Comics Edition #17 © STJ

Giantkiller #1 © Dan Brereton

Giant-Size Daredevil #1 © MAR

GD2.0 FN6.0 NM9.4

NOTE: *The above may be rebound comics; contents could vary.*

GIANT COMICS (See Wham-O Giant Comics)

GIANT COMICS EDITION (See Terry-Toons) (Also see Fox Giants)
St. John Publishing Co.: 1947 - No. 17, 1950 (25¢, 100-164 pgs.)

1-Mighty Mouse 43.00 127.00 425.00
2-Abbie & Slats 19.50 58.00 195.00
3-Terry-Toons Album; 100 pgs. 32.00 96.00 320.00
4-Crime comics; contains Red Seal No. 16, used & illo. in **SOTI** 49.00 147.00 490.00
5-Police Case Book (4/49, 132 pgs.)-Contents varies; contains remaindered St. John books - some volumes contain 5 copies rather than 4, with 160 pages; Matt Baker-c 47.00 141.00 470.00
5A-Terry-Toons Album (132 pgs.)-Mighty Mouse, Heckle & Jeckle, Gandy Goose & Dinky stories 29.00 87.00 290.00
6-Western Picture Stories; Baker-c/a(3); Tuska-a; The Sky Chief, Blue Monk, Ventrilo app., 132 pgs. 45.00 135.00 450.00
7-Contains a teen-age romance plus 3 Mopsy comics 26.00 78.00 260.00
8-The Adventures of Mighty Mouse (10/49) 29.00 87.00 290.00
9-Romance and Confession Stories; Kubert-a(4); Baker-a; photo-c (132 pgs.) 48.00 144.00 480.00
10-Terry-Toons Album (132 pgs.)-Mighty Mouse, Heckle & Jeckle, Gandy Goose stories 29.00 87.00 290.00
11-Western Picture Stories-Baker-c/a(4); The Sky Chief, Desperado, & Blue Monk app.; another version with Son of Sinbad by Kubert (132 pgs.) 43.00 127.00 425.00
12-Diary Secrets; Baker prostitute-c; 4 St. John romance comics; Baker-a 82.00 246.00 825.00
13-Romances; Baker, Kubert-a 42.00 126.00 420.00
14-Mighty Mouse Album (132 pgs.) 29.00 87.00 290.00
15-Romances (4 love comics)-Baker-c 45.00 135.00 450.00
16-Little Audrey; Abbott & Costello, Casper 30.00 90.00 300.00
17(nn)-Mighty Mouse Album (nn, no date, but did follow No. 16); 100 pgs. on cover but has 148 pgs. 29.00 87.00 290.00

NOTE: *The above books contain remaindered comics and contents could vary with each issue. No. 11, 12 have part photo magazine insides.*

GIANT COMICS EDITIONS
United Features Syndicate: 1940's (132 pgs.)

1-Abbie & Slats, Abbott & Costello, Jim Hardy, Ella Cinders, Iron Vic, Gordo, & Bill Bumlin 39.00 116.00 270.00
2-Jim Hardy, Ella Cinders, Elmo & Gordo 29.00 86.00 200.00

NOTE: *Above books contain rebound copies; contents can vary.*

GIANT GRAB BAG OF COMICS (See Archie All-Star Specials under Archie Comics)

GIANTKILLER
DC Comics: Aug, 1999 - No. 6 ($2.50, limited series)

1,2-Story and painted art by Dan Brereton 2.50
...A to Z: A Field Guide to Big Monsters (8/99) 2.50

GIANTS (See Thrilling True Story of the Baseball...)

GIANT-SIZE...
Marvel Comics Group: May, 1974 - Dec, 1975 (35/50¢, 52/68 pgs.)
(Some titles quarterly) (Scarce in strict NM or better due to defective cutting, gluing and binding; warping, splitting and off-center pages are common)

Avengers 1(8/74)-New-a plus G.A. H. Torch-r; 1st modern app. The Whizzer; 1st & only modern app. Miss America 1.25 4.00 16.00
Avengers 2,3,5: 2(11/74)-Death of the Swordsman. 3(2/75). 5(12/75)-Reprints Avengers Special #1 .75 2.50 10.00
Avengers 4 (6/75)-Vision marries Scarlet Witch. 1.00 3.00 12.00
Captain America 1(12/75)-r/stories T.O.S. 59-63 by Kirby (#63 reprints origin) 1.25 4.00 16.00
Captain Marvel 1(12/75)-r/Capt. Marvel #17, 20, 21 by Gil Kane (p) 1.00 3.00 12.00
Chillers 1(6/74, 52 pgs)-Curse of Dracula; origin/1st app. Lilith, Dracula's daughter; Heath-r, Colan-c/a(p); becomes Giant-Size Dracula #2 on 2.00 6.00 24.00

GD2.0 FN6.0 NM9.4

Chillers 1(2/75, 50¢, 68 pgs.)-Alacala-a 1.25 4.00 14.00
Chillers 2(5/75)-All-r; Everett-r from Advs. into Weird Worlds .75 2.50 10.00
Chillers 3(8/75)-Wrightson-c(new)/a(r); Colan, Kirby, Smith-r 1.00 3.00 12.00
Conan 1(9/74)-B. Smith-r/#3; start adaptation of Howard's "Hour of the Dragon" (ends #4); 1st app. Belit; new-a begins 1.25 4.00 15.00
Conan 2(12/74)-B. Smith-r/#5; Sutton-a(i)(#1 also); Buscema-c 1.00 3.00 12.00
Conan 3-5: 3(4/75)-B. Smith-r/#6; Sutton-a(i). 4(6/75)-B. Smith-r/#7. 5(1975)-B. Smith-r/#14,15; Kirby-c .75 2.50 10.00
Creatures 1(5/74, 52 pgs.)-Werewolf app; 1st app. Tigra (formerly Cat); Crandall-r; becomes Giant-Size Werewolf w/#2 1.50 4.50 18.00
Daredevil 1(1975)-Reprints Daredevil Annual #1 1.00 3.00 12.00
Defenders 1(7/74)-Silver Surfer app.; Starlin-a; Ditko, Everett & Kirby reprints 1.75 5.50 22.00
Defenders 2(10/74, 68 pgs.)-New G. Kane-c/a(p); Son of Satan app.; Sub-Mariner-r by Everett; Ditko-r/Strange Tales #119 (Dr. Strange); Maneely-r. 1.00 3.00 12.00
Defenders 3-5: 3(1/75)-1st app. Korvac.; Newton, Starlin-a; Ditko, Everett-r. 4(4/75)-Ditko, Everett-r; G. Kane-c. 5-(7/75)-Guardians app. .75 2.50 10.00
Doc Savage 1(1975, 68 pgs.)-r/#1,2; Mooney-r .75 2.50 10.00
Doctor Strange 1(11/75)-Reprints stories from Strange Tales #164-168; Lawrence, Tuska-r 1.00 3.00 12.00
Dracula 2(9/74, 50¢)-Formerly Giant-Size Chillers 1.00 3.00 12.00
Dracula 3(12/74)-Fox-r/Uncanny Tales #6 .75 2.50 10.00
Dracula 4(3/75)-Ditko-r(2) .75 2.50 10.00
Dracula 5(6/75)-1st Byrne art at Marvel 2.00 6.00 24.00
Fantastic Four 2-4: 2(8/74)-Formerly Giant-Size Super-Stars; Ditko-r. 3(11/74). 4(2/75)-1st Madrox; 2-4-All have Buscema-a 1.25 4.00 15.00
Fantastic Four 5,6: 5(5/75)-All-r; Kirby, G. Kane-r. 6(10/75)-All-r; Kirby-r 1.00 3.00 12.00
Hulk 1(1975) r/Hulk Special #1 1.75 5.50 20.00
Invaders 1(6/75, 50¢, 68 pgs.)-Origin; G.A. Sub-Mariner-r/Sub-Mariner #1; intro Master Man 1.25 4.00 15.00
Iron Man 1(1975)-Ditko reprint 1.25 4.00 16.00
Kid Colt 1-3: 1(1/75). 2(4/75). 3(7/75)-new Ayers-a 3.00 9.00 36.00
Man-Thing 1(8/74)-New Ploog-c/a (25 pgs.); Ditko-r/Amazing Adv. #11; Kirby-r/ Strange Tales Ann. #2 & T.O.S. #15; (#1-5 all have new Man-Thing stories, pre-hero-r & are 68 pgs.) 1.25 4.00 16.00
Man-Thing 2,3: 2(11/74)-Buscema-c/a(p); Kirby, Powell-r. 3(2/75)-Alcala-a; Ditko, Kirby, Sutton-r; Gil Kane-c .75 2.50 10.00
Man-Thing 4,5: 4(5/75)-Howard the Duck by Brunner-c/a; Ditko-r. 5(8/75)-Howard the Duck by Brunner (p); Dracaula cameo in Howard the Duck; Buscema-a(p); Sutton-a(i); G. Kane-c 1.25 4.00 16.00
Marvel Triple Action 1,2: 1(5/75). 2(7/75) 1.00 3.00 12.00
Master of Kung Fu 1(9/74)-Russell-a; Yellow Claw-r in #1-4; Gulacy-a in #1,2 1.25 4.00 16.00
Master of Kung Fu 2-4: 2-(12/74)-r/Yellow Claw #1. 3(3/75)-Gulacy-a; Kirby-a. 4(6/75)-Kirby-a .75 2.50 10.00
Power Man 1(1975) .75 2.50 10.00
Spider-Man 1(7/74)-Kirby/Ditko, Byrne-r plus new-a (Dracula-c/story) 3.25 10.00 40.00
Spider-Man 2,3: 2(10/74). 3(1/75)-Byrne-r 2.00 6.00 24.00
Spider-Man 4(4/75)-3rd Punisher app.; Byrne, Ditko-r 6.00 18.00 72.00
Spider-Man 5,6: 5(7/75)-Byrne-r. 6(9/75) 1.25 4.00 16.00
Super-Heroes Featuring Spider-Man 1(6/74, 35¢, 52 pgs.)-Spider-Man vs. Man-Wolf; Morbius, the Living Vampire app.; Ditko-r; G. Kane-a(p); Spidey villains app. 4.00 12.00 48.00
Super-Stars 1(5/74, 35¢, 52 pgs.)-Fantastic Four; Thing vs. Hulk; Kirbyish-c/a by Buckler/Sinnott; F.F. villains profiled; becomes Giant-Size Fantastic Four #2 on 1.75 5.50 22.00
Super-Villain Team-Up 1(3/75, 68 pgs.)-Craig-r(i) (Also see Fantastic Four #6 for 1st super-villain team-up) 1.00 3.00 12.00
Super-Villain Team-Up 2(6/75, 68 pgs.)-Dr. Doom, Sub-Mariner app.;

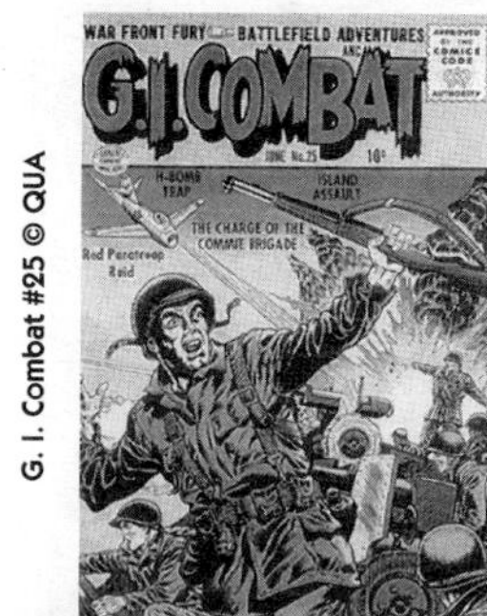

G. I. Combat #25 © QUA

Gifts of the Night #2 © John Bolton & Paul Chadwick

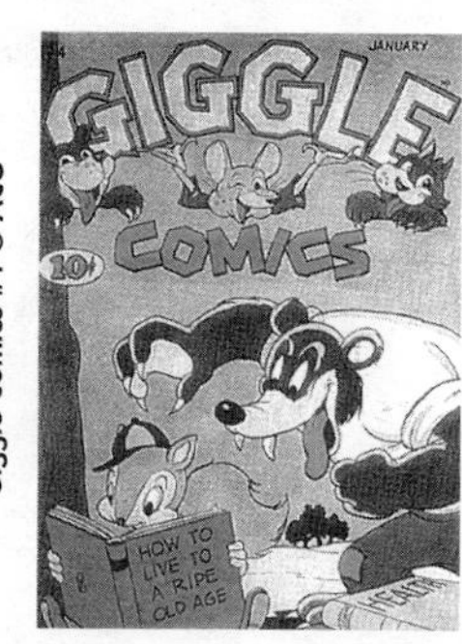

Giggle Comics #4 © ACG

GD2.0 FN6.0 NM9.4

Spider-Man-r/Amazing Spider-Man #8 by Ditko; Sekowsky-a(p) .75 2.50 10.00
Thor 1(7/75) 1.00 3.00 12.00
Werewolf 2(10/74, 68 pgs.)-Formerly Giant-Size Creatures; Ditko-r; Frankenstein app. 1.00 3.00 12.00
Werewolf 3,5: 3(1/75, 68 pgs.). 5(7/75, 68 pgs.) 1.00 3.00 12.00
Werewolf 4(4/75, 68 pgs.)-Morbius the Living Vampire app. 1.25 4.00 16.00
X-Men 1(Summer, 1975, 50¢, 68 pgs.)-1st app. new X-Men; intro Nightcrawler, Storm, Colossus & Thunderbird; 2nd full app. Wolverine after Incredible Hulk #181 41.00 122.00 490.00
X-Men 2 (11/75)-N. Adams-r (51 pgs) 4.60 14.00 55.00

GIANT SPECTACULAR COMICS (See Archie All-Star Special under Archie Comics)

GIANT SUMMER FUN BOOK (See Terry-Toons...)

G. I. COMBAT
Quality Comics Group: Oct, 1952 - No. 43, Dec, 1956

	GD2.0	FN6.0	NM9.4
1-Crandall-c; Cuidera a-1-43i	60.00	180.00	480.00
2	30.00	90.00	210.00
3-5,10-Crandall-c/a	27.00	81.00	190.00
6-Crandall-a	24.00	73.00	170.00
7-9	20.00	60.00	140.00
11-20	15.00	45.00	105.00
21-31,33,35-43: 41-1st S.A. issue	12.00	36.00	85.00
32-Nuclear attack-c/story "Atomic Rocket Assault"	15.00	45.00	105.00
34-Crandall-a	13.00	39.00	90.00

G. I. COMBAT (See DC Special Series #22)
National Periodical Publ./DC Comics: No. 44, Jan, 1957 - No. 288, Mar, 1987

	GD2.0	FN6.0	NM9.4
44-Grey tone-c	44.00	132.00	460.00
45	25.00	75.00	250.00
46-50	18.50	55.00	185.00
51-Grey tone-c	17.50	52.00	175.00
52-54,59,60	15.00	45.00	150.00
55-minor Sgt. Rock prototype by Finger	16.00	48.00	160.00
56-Sgt. Rock prototype by Kanigher/Kubert	17.00	51.00	170.00
57,58-Pre-Sgt. Rock Easy Co. stories	16.50	50.00	165.00
61-65,69-74	10.50	32.00	105.00
66-Pre-Sgt. Rock Easy Co. story	14.00	42.00	140.00
67-1st Tank Killer	15.00	45.00	150.00
68-(1/59) Introduces "The Rock", Sgt. Rock prototype by Kanigher/Kubert; once considered his actual 1st app. (see Our Army at War #82,83)	31.00	93.00	320.00
75-80: 75-Greytone-c begin, end #109	11.00	33.00	110.00
81,82,84-86	8.00	24.00	80.00
83-1st Big Al, Little Al, & Charlie Cigar	10.50	32.00	105.00
87-1st Haunted Tank; series begins	43.00	128.00	470.00
88-2nd Haunted Tank	16.00	48.00	160.00
89-91: 90-Last 10¢ issue. 91-1st Haunted Tank-c	9.00	27.00	90.00
92-99	7.00	21.00	70.00
100,108: 108-1st Sgt. Rock x-over	8.00	24.00	80.00
101-107,109: 109-Grey tone-c	6.00	18.00	60.00
110-113,115-120: 113-Grey tone-c	4.50	13.50	45.00
114-Origin Haunted Tank	10.50	32.00	105.00
121-136: 121-1st app. Sgt. Rock's father. 136-Last 12¢ issue	2.80	8.40	28.00
137,139,140	2.50	7.50	25.00
138-Intro. The Losers (Capt. Storm, Gunner/Sarge, Johnny Cloud) in Haunted Tank (10-11/69)	7.00	21.00	70.00
141-143	1.50	4.50	12.00
144-148 (68pgs.)	2.50	7.50	20.00
149,151-154 (52 pgs.): 151-Capt. Storm story. 151,153-Medal of Honor series by Maurer	1.50	4.50	12.00
150- (52 pgs.) Ice Cream Soldier story (tells how he got his name); Death of Haunted Tank-c/s	2.50	7.50	20.00
155-170,200	1.10	3.30	9.00
171-199	1.00	3.00	8.00
201-210 ($1.00 size)	1.10	3.30	9.00
211-230 ($1.00 size)		2.40	6.00
231-259 ($1.00 size).232-Origin Kana the Ninja. 244-Death of Slim Stryker; 1st app. The Mercenaries. 246-(76 pgs., $1.50)-30th Anniversary issue. 257-Intro. Stuart's Raiders			5.00
260-281: 260-Begin $1.25, 52 pg. issues, end #281. 264-Intro Sgt. Bullet; origin Kana. 269-Intro. The Bravos of Vietnam			4.00
282-288 (75¢): 282-New advs. begin			4.00

NOTE: ***N. Adams*** *c-168, 201, 202.* ***Check*** *a-168, 173.* ***Drucker*** *a-48, 61, 63, 66, 71, 72, 76, 134, 140, 141, 144, 147, 148, 153.* ***Evans*** *a-135, 138, 158, 164, 166, 201, 202, 204, 205, 215, 256. Giffen a-267.* ***Glanzman*** *a-most issues.* ***Kubert/Heath*** *a-most issues;* ***Kubert*** *covers most issues.* ***Morrow*** *a-159-161(2 pgs.).* ***Redondo*** *a-189, 240i, 243i.* ***Sekowsky*** *a-162p.* ***Severin*** *a-147, 152, 154.* ***Simonson*** *c-169.* ***Thorne*** *a-152, 156.* ***Wildey*** *a-153. Johnny Cloud app.-112, 115, 120. Mlle. Marie app.-123, 132, 200. Sgt. Rock app.-111-113, 115, 120, 125, 141, 146, 147, 149, 200. USS Stevens by* ***Glanzman****-145, 150-153, 157.* ***Grandenetti*** *c-44-48.*

GIDGET (TV)
Dell Publishing Co.: Apr, 1966 - No. 2, Dec, 1966

	GD2.0	FN6.0	NM9.4
1-Sally Field photo-c	8.00	24.00	90.00
2	5.50	16.50	60.00

GIFT (See The Crusaders)

GIFT COMICS
Fawcett Publications: 1942 - No. 4, 1949 (50¢/25¢, 324 pgs./152 pgs.)

	GD2.0	FN6.0	NM9.4
1-Captain Marvel, Bulletman, Golden Arrow, Ibis the Invincible, Mr. Scarlet, & Spy Smasher begin; not rebound, remaindered comics, printed at same time as originals; 50¢-c & 324 pgs. begin, end #3.	230.00	690.00	2300.00
2-Commando Yank, Phantom Eagle, others app.	150.00	450.00	1500.00
3	100.00	300.00	1000.00
4-(25¢, 152 pgs.)-The Marvel Family, Captain Marvel, etc.; each issue can vary in contents	62.50	187.50	625.00

GIFTS FROM SANTA (See March of Comics No. 137)

GIFTS OF THE NIGHT
DC Comics (Vertigo): Feb, 1999 - No. 4, May, 1999 ($2.95, limited series)

1-4-Bolton-c/a; Chadwick-s 3.00

GIGGLE COMICS (Spencer Spook No. 100) (Also see Ha Ha Comics)
Creston No.1-63/American Comics Group No. 64 on; Oct, 1943 - No. 99, Jan-Feb, 1955

	GD2.0	FN6.0	NM9.4
1-Funny animal	30.00	90.00	210.00
2	14.00	43.00	100.00
3-5: Ken Hultgren-a begins?	11.00	33.00	75.00
6-10: 9-1st Superkatt (6/44)	10.00	30.00	60.00
11-20	7.00	21.00	42.00
21-40: 32-Patriotic-c. 37,61-X-Mas-c. 39-St. Valentine's Day-c	5.85	17.50	35.00
41-54,56-59,61-99: 95-Spencer Spook begins?	5.00	15.00	30.00
55,60-Milt Gross-a	6.35	19.00	38.00

G-I IN BATTLE (G-I No. 1 only)
Ajax-Farrell Publ./Four Star: Aug, 1952 - No. 9, July, 1953; Mar, 1957 - No. 6, May, 1958

	GD2.0	FN6.0	NM9.4
1	10.00	30.00	65.00
2	5.35	16.00	32.00
3-9	4.25	13.00	28.00
Annual 1(1952, 25¢, 100 pgs.)	23.00	69.00	160.00
1(1957-Ajax)	6.35	19.00	38.00
2-6	4.00	12.00	24.00

G. I. JANE
Stanhall/Merit No. 11: May, 1953 - No. 11, Mar, 1955 (Misdated 3/54)

	GD2.0	FN6.0	NM9.4
1-PX Pete begins; Bill Williams-c/a	11.50	34.00	80.00
2-7(5/54)	6.70	12.00	40.00
8-10(12/54, Stanhall)	5.35	16.00	32.00
11 (3/55, Merit)	4.25	13.00	28.00

G. I. JOE (Also see Advs. of..., Showcase #53, 54 & The Yardbirds)
Ziff-Davis Publ. Co. (Korean War): No. 10, 1950; No. 11, 4-5/51 - No. 51, 6/57

G.I. Joe #17 © Z-D

Ginger #8 © AP

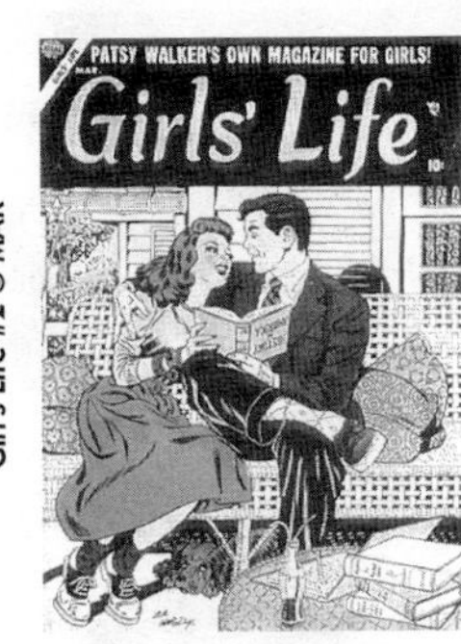

Girl's Life #2 © MAR

	GD2.0	FN6.0	NM9.4
(52pgs.: 10-14,6-17?)			
10(#1, 1950)-Saunders painted-c begin	13.00	39.00	90.00
11-14(#2-5, 10/51): 11-New logo. 12-New logo	10.00	30.00	60.00
V2#6(12/51)-17-(11/52; Last 52 pgs.?)	9.15	27.00	55.00
18-(25¢, 100 pg. Giant, 12-1/52-53)	20.00	60.00	140.00
19-30: 20-22,24,28-31-The Yardbirds app.	7.00	21.00	42.00
31-47,49-51	6.35	19.00	38.00
48-Atom bomb story	7.00	21.00	42.00

NOTE: ***Powell** a-V2#7, 8, 11. **Norman Saunders** painted c-10-14, V2#6-14, 26, 30, 31, 35, 38, 39. **Tuska** a-7. Bondage c-29, 35, 38.*

G. I. JOE (America's Movable Fighting Man)
Custom Comics: 1967 (5-1/8x8-3/8", 36 pgs.)

nn-Schaffenberger-a; based on Hasbro toy	2.50	7.50	20.00

G.I. JOE
Dark Horse Comics: Dec, 1995 - No. 4, Apr, 1996 ($1.95, limited series)

1-4: Mike W. Barr scripts. 1,2-Miller-c. 3-Simonson-c — 2.50

G.I. JOE
Dark Horse Comics: V2#1, June, 1996 - V2#4, Sept, 1996 ($2.50)

V2#1-4: Mike W. Barr scripts. 4-Painted-c — 2.50

G. I. JOE AND THE TRANSFORMERS
Marvel Comics Group: Jan, 1987 - No. 4, Apr, 1987 (Limited series)

1-4 — 3.00

G. I. JOE, A REAL AMERICAN HERO (...Starring Snake-Eyes on-c #135 on)
Marvel Comics Group: June, 1982 - No. 155, Dec, 1994

1-Printed on Baxter paper; based on Hasbro toy	1.25	3.75	10.00
2-Printed on reg. paper	1.25	3.75	10.00
3-10	1.00	3.00	7.00
11-20: 11-Intro Airborne		2.40	6.00
21,22,26,27: 26,27-Origin Snake-Eyes parts 1 & 2			5.00
23-25,28-30,60: 60-Todd McFarlane-a			4.00
31-59,61-138,143-155: 33-New headquarters. 110-1st Ron Garney-a. 135-138-($1.75)-Polybagged w/trading card.. 144-Origin Snake-Eyes			3.00
139-142-New Transformers app.			4.00
All 2nd printings			2.00
Special Treasury Edition (1982)-r/#1	1.50	4.50	12.00
Yearbook 1-4: (3/85-3/88)-r/#1; Golden-c. 2-Golden-c/a			3.00

NOTE: ***Garney** a(p)-110. **Golden** c-23, 29, 34, 36. **Heath** a-24. **Rogers** a(p)-75, 77-82, 84, 86; c-77.*

G. I. JOE COMICS MAGAZINE
Marvel Comics Group: Dec, 1986 - No. 13, 1988 ($1.50, digest-size)

1-13: G.I. Joe-r — 5.00

G.I. JOE EUROPEAN MISSIONS (Action Force in indicia)
Marvel Comics Ltd. (British): Jun, 1988 - No. 15, Dec, 1989 ($1.50/$1.75)

1-15: Reprints Action Force — 2.50

G. I. JOE ORDER OF BATTLE, THE
Marvel Comics Group: Dec, 1986 - No. 4, Mar, 1987 (limited series)

1-4 — 2.00

G. I. JOE SPECIAL MISSIONS (Indicia title: Special Missions)
Marvel Comics Group: Oct, 1986 - No. 28, Dec, 1989 ($1.00)

1-28 — 2.00

G. I. JUNIORS (See Harvey Hits No. 86,91,95,98,101,104,107,110,112,114,116,118,120,122)

GILGAMESH II
DC Comics: 1989 - No. 4, 1989 ($3.95, limited series, prestige format, mature)

1-4: Starlin-c/a/scripts — 4.00

GIL THORP
Dell Publishing Co.: May-July, 1963

1-Caniffish-a	2.70	8.00	30.00

GINGER
Archie Publications: 1951 - No. 10, Summer, 1954

	GD2.0	FN6.0	NM9.4
1-Teenage humor	10.00	30.00	100.00
2-(1952)	5.50	16.50	55.00
3-6: 6-(Sum/53)	4.00	12.00	40.00
7-10-Katy Keene app.	6.00	18.00	60.00

GINGER FOX (Also see The World of Ginger Fox)
Comico: Sept, 1988 - No. 4, Dec, 1988 ($1.75, limited series)

1-4: 1-4-part photo-c — 2.00

G.I. R.A.M.B.O.T.
Wonder Color Comics/Pied Piper #2: Apr, 1987 - No. 2? ($1.95)

1,2: 2-Exist? — 2.00

GIRL
DC Comics (Vertigo Verite): Jul, 1996 - No. 3, 1996 ($2.50, lim. series, mature)

1-3: Peter Milligan scripts; Fegredo-c/a — 2.50

GIRL COMICS (Becomes Girl Confessions No. 13 on)
Marvel/Atlas Comics(CnPC): Oct, 1949 - No. 12, Jan, 1952 (#1-4: 52 pgs.)

1-Photo-c	19.00	58.00	135.00
2-Kubert-a; photo-c	11.50	34.00	80.00
3-Everett-a; Liz Taylor photo-c	16.00	47.00	110.00
4-11: 4-Photo-c. 10-12-Sol Brodsky-c	10.00	30.00	60.00
12-Krigstein-a; Al Hartley-c	10.00	30.00	65.00

GIRL CONFESSIONS (Formerly Girl Comics)
Atlas Comics (CnPC/ZPC): No. 13, Mar, 1952 - No. 35, Aug, 1954

13-Everett-a	11.00	33.00	75.00
14,15,19,20	7.50	22.50	45.00
16-18-Everett-a	9.15	27.00	55.00
21-35: Robinson-a	5.00	15.00	30.00

GIRL CRAZY
Dark Horse Comics: May, 1996 - No. 3, July, 1996 ($2.95, B&W, limited series)

1-3: Gilbert Hernandez-a/scripts. — 3.00

GIRL FROM U.N.C.L.E., THE (TV) (Also see The Man From...)
Gold Key: Jan, 1967 - No. 5, Oct, 1967

1-McWilliams-a; Stephanie Powers photo front/back-c & pin-ups (no ads, 12¢)	8.20	24.60	90.00
2-5-Leonard Swift-Courier No. 5	5.50	16.50	60.00

GIRLS' FUN & FASHION MAGAZINE (Formerly Polly Pigtails)
Parents' Magazine Institute: V5#44, Jan, 1950 - V5#48, Sept., 1950

V5#44	4.25	13.00	28.00
45-48	3.60	9.00	18.00

GIRLS IN LOVE
Fawcett Publications: May, 1950 - No. 2, July, 1950

1,2-Photo-c	10.00	30.00	65.00

GIRLS IN LOVE (Formerly G. I. Sweethearts No. 45)
Quality Comics Group: No. 46, Sept, 1955 - No. 57, Dec, 1956

46	7.00	21.00	42.00
47-53,55,56	4.25	13.00	28.00
54- 'Commie' story	5.35	16.00	32.00
57-Matt Baker-c/a	8.35	25.00	50.00

GIRLS IN WHITE (See Harvey Comics Hits No. 58)

GIRLS' LIFE (Patsy Walker's Own Magazine For Girls!)
Atlas Comics (BFP): Jan, 1954 - No. 6, Nov, 1954

1	10.00	30.00	60.00
2-Al Hartley-c	5.85	17.50	35.00
3-6	4.25	13.00	28.00

GIRLS' LOVE STORIES
National Comics(Signal Publ. No. 9-65/Arleigh No. 83-117): Aug-Sept, 1949 - No. 180, Nov-Dec, 1973 (No. 1-13: 52 pgs.)

1-Toth, Kinstler-a, 8 pgs. each; photo-c	52.00	157.00	420.00
2-Kinstler-a?	31.00	94.00	220.00
3-10: 1-9-Photo-c. 7-Infantino-c(p)	21.00	62.00	145.00

The Girl Who Would Be Death #3 © DC

Glamorous Romances #45 © ACE

Gloom Cookie #1 © Valentino & Naifeh

GD2.0 FN6.0 NM9.4

	GD2.0	FN6.0	NM9.4
11-20	16.00	47.00	110.00
21-33: 21-Kinstler-a. 33-Last pre-code (1-2/55)	10.00	30.00	65.00
34-50	8.35	25.00	50.00
51-70	4.80	14.40	48.00
71-99: 83-Last 10¢ issue	3.20	9.60	32.00
100	3.80	11.40	38.00
101-146: 113-117-April O'Day app.	2.50	7.50	24.00
147-151- "Confessions" serial. 150-Wood-a	2.50	7.50	20.00
152-160,171-179	1.75	5.25	14.00
161-170 (52 pgs.)	2.60	7.80	26.00
180 Last issue	2.50	7.50	22.00

GIRLS' ROMANCES
National Periodical Publ.(Signal Publ. No. 7-79/Arleigh No. 84): Feb-Mar, 1950 - No. 160, Oct, 1971 (No. 1-11: 52 pgs.)

	GD2.0	FN6.0	NM9.4
1-Photo-c	51.00	154.00	410.00
2-Photo-c; Toth-a	30.00	90.00	210.00
3-10: 3-6-Photo-c	21.00	62.00	145.00
11,12,14-20	14.00	43.00	100.00
13-Toth-c	15.00	45.00	105.00
21-31: 31-Last pre-code (2-3/55)	10.00	30.00	60.00
32-50	4.80	14.40	48.00
51-99: 80-Last 10¢ issue	3.20	9.60	32.00
100	3.80	11.40	38.00
101-108,110-120	2.50	7.50	22.00
109-Beatles-c/story	11.00	33.00	110.00
121-133,135-140	2.25	6.75	18.00
134-Neal Adams-c (splash pg. is same as-c)	3.00	9.00	30.00
141-158	1.75	5.25	14.00
159,160-52 pgs.	2.50	7.50	24.00

GIRL WHO WOULD BE DEATH, THE
DC Comics (Vertigo): Dec, 1998 - No. 4, March, 1999 ($2.50, lim. series)

1-4-Kiernan-s/Ormston-a — 2.50

G. I. SWEETHEARTS (Formerly Diary Loves; Girls In Love #46 on)
Quality Comics Group: No. 32, June, 1953 - No. 45, May, 1955

	GD2.0	FN6.0	NM9.4
32	7.00	21.00	42.00
33-45: 44-Last pre-code (3/55)	4.25	13.00	28.00

G.I. TALES (Formerly Sgt. Barney Barker No. 1-3)
Atlas Comics (MCI): No. 4, Feb, 1957 - No. 6, July, 1957

	GD2.0	FN6.0	NM9.4
4-Severin-a(4)	7.50	22.50	45.00
5	5.35	16.00	32.00
6-Orlando, Powell, & Woodbridge-a	5.85	17.50	35.00

GIVE ME LIBERTY (Also see Dark Horse Presents Fifth Anniversary Special, Dark Horse Presents #100-4, Happy Birthday Martha Washington, Martha Washington Goes to War, Martha Washington Stranded In Space & San Diego Comicon Comics #2)
Dark Horse Comics: June, 1990 - No. 4, 1991 ($4.95, limited series, 52 pgs.)

1-4: 1st app. Martha Washington; Frank Miller scripts, Dave Gibbons-c/a in all. — 5.00

G. I. WAR BRIDES
Superior Publishers Ltd.: Apr, 1954 - No. 8, June, 1955

	GD2.0	FN6.0	NM9.4
1	7.50	22.50	45.00
2	4.25	13.00	26.00
3-8: 4-Kamenesque-a; lingerie panels	4.00	11.00	22.00

G. I. WAR TALES
National Periodical Publications: Mar-Apr, 1973 - No. 4, Oct-Nov, 1973

	GD2.0	FN6.0	NM9.4
1-Reprints in all; dinosaur-c/s	2.25	6.75	18.00
2-N. Adams-a(r)	2.00	6.00	16.00
3,4: 4-Krigstein-a(r)	1.75	5.25	14.00

NOTE: ***Drucker*** *a-3r, 4r.* ***Heath*** *a-4r.* ***Kubert*** *a-2, 3; c-4r.*

GIZMO (Also see Domino Chance)
Chance Ent.: May-June, 1985 (B&W, one-shot)

1 — 4.00

GD2.0 FN6.0 NM9.4

GIZMO
Mirage Studios: 1986 - No. 6, July, 1987 ($1.50, B&W)

1-6 — 2.00

GLADSTONE COMIC ALBUM
Gladstone: 1987 - No. 28, 1990 ($5.95/$9.95, 8-1/2x11")(All Mickey Mouse albums are by Gottfredson)

	GD2.0	FN6.0	NM9.4
1-10: 1-Uncle Scrooge; Barks-r; Beck-c. 2-Donald Duck; r/F.C. #108 by Barks. 3-Mickey Mouse-r by Gottfredson. 4-Uncle Scrooge; r/F.C. #456 by Barks w/ unedited story. 5-Donald Duck Advs.; r/F.C. #199. 6-Uncle Scrooge-r by Barks. 7-Donald Duck-r by Barks. 8-Mickey Mouse-r. 9-Bambi; r/F.C. #186? 10-Donald Duck Advs.; r/F.C. #275	1.25	3.75	10.00
11-20: 11-Uncle Scrooge; r/U.S. #4. 12-Donald And Daisy; r/F.C. #1055, WDC&S. 13-Donald Duck Advs.; r/F.C. #408. 14-Uncle Scrooge; Barks-r/ U.S #21. 15-Donald And Gladstone; Barks-r. 16-Donald Duck Advs.; r/F.C. #238. 17-Mickey Mouse strip-r (The World of Tomorrow, The Pirate Ghost Ship). 18-Donald Duck and the Junior Woodchucks; Barks-r. 19-Uncle Scrooge; r/U.S. #12; Rosa-c. 20-Uncle Scrooge; r/F.C. #386; Barks-c/a(r)	1.25	3.75	10.00
21-25: 21-Donald Duck Family; Barks-c/a(r). 22-Mickey Mouse strip-r. 23-Donald Duck; Barks-r/D.D. #26 w/unedited story. 24-Uncle Scrooge; Barks-r; Rosa-c. 25-D. Duck; Barks-c/a-r/F.C. #367	1.25	3.75	10.00
26-28: All have $9.95-c. 26-Mickey and Donald; Gottfredson-c/a(r). 27-Donald Duck; r/WDC&S by Barks; Barks painted-c. 28-Uncle Scrooge & Donald Duck; Rosa-c/a (4 stories)	1.25	3.75	10.00
Special 1-7: 1 ('89-'90, $9.95/13.95)-1-Donald Duck Finds Pirate Gold; r/F.C. #9 2 ('89, $8.95)-Uncle Scrooge and Donald Duck; Barks-r/Uncle Scrooge #5; Rosa-c. 3 ('89, $8.95)-Mickey Mouse strip-r. 4 ('89, $11.95)-Uncle Scrooge; Rosa-c/a-r/Son of the Sun from U.S. #219 plus Barks-r/U.S. 5 ('90, $11.95)-Donald Duck Advs.; Barks-r/F.C. #282 & 422 plusBarks painted-c. 6 ('90, $12.95)-Uncle Scrooge; Barks-c/a-r/Uncle Scrooge. 7 ('90, $13.95)-Mickey Mouse; Gottfredson strip-r	1.75	5.25	14.00

GLADSTONE COMIC ALBUM (2nd Series)(Also see The Original Dick Tracy)
Gladstone Publishing: 1990 ($5.95, 8-1/2 x 11," stiff-c, 52 pgs.)

	GD2.0	FN6.0	NM9.4
1,2-The Original Dick Tracy. 2-Origin of the 2-way wrist radio		2.40	6.00
3-D Tracy Meets the Mole-r by Gould ($6.95).	1.00	3.00	8.00

GLAMOROUS ROMANCES (Formerly Dotty)
Ace Magazines (A. A. Wyn): No. 41, July, 1949 - No. 90, Oct, 1956 (Photo-c 68-90)

	GD2.0	FN6.0	NM9.4
41-Dotty app.	7.50	22.50	45.00
42-72,74-80: 44-Begin 52 pg. issues. 45,50-61-Painted-c. 80-Last pre-code (2/55)	4.25	13.00	28.00
73-L.B. Cole-r/All Love #27	5.35	16.00	32.00
81-90	4.00	12.00	24.00

GLOBAL FORCE
Silverline Comics: 1987 - No. 2 ($1.95)

1,2 — 2.00

GLOOM COOKIE
SLG Publishing: June, 1999 - Present ($2.95, B&W)

1,2-Serena Valentino-s/Ted Naifeh-a — 3.00

GLORY
Image Comics (Extreme Studios)/Maximum Press: Mar, 1995 - No. 22, Apr, 1997 ($2.50)

	NM9.4
0-Deodato-c/a, 1-(3/95)-Deodato-a	2.50
1A-Variant-c	4.00
2-11,13-22: 4-Variant-c by Quesada & Palmiotti. 5-Bagged w/Youngblood gaming card. 7,8-Deodato-c/a(p). 8-Babewatch x-over. 9-Cruz-c; Extreme Destroyer Pt. 5; polybagged w/card. 10-Angela-c/app. 11-Deodato-c.	2.50
12-($3.50)-Photo-c	3.50
Trade Paperback (1995, $9.95)-r/#1-4	10.00

GLORY
Awesome Comics: Mar, 1999 - Present ($2.50)

Gods and Tulips © CBLDF

Godzilla #16 © MAR

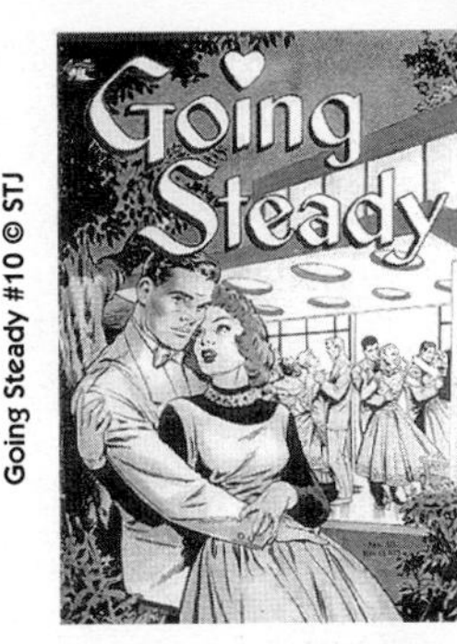

Going Steady #10 © STJ

0-Liefeld-c; story and sketch pages 2.50

GLORY & FRIENDS BIKINI FEST
Image Comics (Extreme): Sept, 1995 - No. 2, Oct, 1995 ($2.50, limited series)

1,2: 1-Photo-c; centerfold photo; pin-ups 2.50

GLORY & FRIENDS CHRISTMAS SPECIAL
Image Comics (Extreme Studios): Dec, 1995 ($2.50, one-shot)

1-Deodato-c 2.50

GLORY & FRIENDS LINGIRIE SPECIAL
Image Comics (Extreme Studios): Sept, 1995 ($2.95, one-shot)

1-Pin-ups w/photos; photo-c; varant-c exists 3.00

GLORY/ANGELA: ANGELS IN HELL (See Angela/Glory: Rage of Angels)
Image Comics (Extreme Studios): Apr, 1996 ($2.50, one-shot)

1-Flip book w/Darkchylde #1 2.50

GLORY/AVENGELYNE
Image Comics (Extreme Studios): Oct, 1995 ($3.95, one-shot)

1-Chromium-c, 1-Regular-c 4.00

GLORY/CELESTINE: DARK ANGEL
Image Comics/Maximum Press (Extreme Studios): Sept, 1996 - No. 3, Nov, 1996 ($2.50, limited series)

1-3 2.50

GNOME MOBILE, THE (See Movie Comics)

GOBBLEDYGOOK
Mirage Studios: 1984 - No. 2, 1984 (B&W)(1st Mirage comics, published at same time)

1,2-(24 pgs.)-1st Teenage Mutant Ninja Turtles 19.00 57.00 210.00

GOBBLEDYGOOK
Mirage Studios: Dec, 1986 ($3.50, B&W, one-shot, 100 pgs.)

1-New 8 pg. TMNT story plus a Donatello/Michaelangelo 7 pg. story & a Gizmo story; Corben-i(r)/TMNT #7 4.00

GOBLIN, THE
Warren Publishing Co.: June, 1982 - No. 4, Dec, 1982 (Magazine, $2.25)

1-The Gremlin app; Golden-a(p) 2.00 6.00 16.00
2-4: 2-1st Hobgoblin 1.25 3.75 10.00

GODDESS
DC Comics (Vertigo): June, 1995 - No. 8, Jan, 1996 ($2.95, limited series)

1-Garth Ennis scripts; Phil Winslade-c/a in all 5.00
2-8 4.00

GODFATHERS, THE (See The Crusaders)

GOD IS
Spire Christian Comics (Fleming H. Revell Co.): 1973, 1975 (35-49¢)

nn-By Al Hartley 5.00

GODS AND TULIPS
Westhampton House: Aug, 1999 ($3.00, B&W, one-shot for the CBLDF)

nn-Neil Gaiman speeches; Kaluta-c 3.00

GOD'S COUNTRY (Also see Marvel Comics Presents)
Marvel Comics: 1994 ($6.95)

nn-P. Craig Russell-a; Colossus story; r/Marvel Comics Presents #10-17 7.00

GODS FOR HIRE
Hot Comics: Dec, 1986 - No. 3 ($1.50)

1-3: Barry Crain-c/a(p) 2.00

GOD'S HEROES IN AMERICA
Catechetical Guild Educational Society: 1956 (nn) (25¢/35¢, 68 pgs.)

307 2.80 7.00 14.00

GOD'S SMUGGLER (Religious)
Spire Christian Comics/Fleming H. Revell Co.: 1972 (39¢/40¢)

1-Two variations exist 5.00

GODWHEEL
Malibu Comics (Ultraverse): No. 0, Jan, 1995 - No. 3, Feb, 1995 ($2.50, limited series)

0-3: 0-Flip-c. 1-1st app. of Primevil; Thor cameo (1 panel). 3-Perez-a in Chapter 3, Thor app. 2.50

GODZILLA (Movie)
Marvel Comics : August, 1977 - No. 24, July, 1979 (Based on movie series)

1-(Regular 30¢ edition)-Mooney-i 1.10 3.30 9.00
1-(35¢-c variant, limited distribution) 3.50 10.50 35.00
2-(Regular 30¢ edition)-Tuska-i. 2.40 6.00
2-(35¢-c variant, limited distribution) 2.50 7.50 24.00
3- Champions app.(w/o Ghost Rider) 1.10 3.30 9.00
4-10: 4,5-Sutton-a 2.40 6.00
11-23: 14-Shield app. 20-F.F. app. 21,22-Devil Dinosaur app. 5.00
24-Last issue 2.40 6.00

GODZILLA (Movie)
Dark Horse Comics: May, 1988 - No. 6, 1988 ($1.95, B&W, limited series) (Based on movie series)

1 5.00
2-6 3.00
...Collection (1990, $10.95)-r/1-6 with new-c 11.00
...Color Special 1 (Sum, 1992, $3.50, color, 44 pgs.)-Arthur Adams wrap-around-c/a & part scripts 4.00
...King Of The Monsters Special (8/87, $1.50)-Origin; Bissette-c/a 3.00
...Vs. Barkley nn (12/93, $2.95, color)-Dorman painted-c 3.00

GODZILLA (King of the Monsters) (Movie)
Dark Horse Comics: May, 1995 - No. 16, Sept, 1996 ($2.50) (Based on movies)

0-16: 0-r/Dark Horse Comics #10,11. 1-3-Kevin Maguire scripts. 3-8-Art Adams-c 4.00
...Vs. Hero Zero ($2.50) 2.50

GOG (VILLAINS) (See Kingdom Come)
DC Comics: Feb, 1998 ($1.95, one-shot)

1-Waid-s/Ordway-a(p)/Pearson-c 3.00

GO-GO
Charlton Comics: June, 1966 - No. 9, Oct, 1967

1-Miss Bikini Luv begins w/Jim Aparo's 1st published work; Rolling Stones, Beatles, Elvis, Sonny & Cher, Bob Dylan, Sinatra, parody; Herman's Hermits pin-ups; D'Agostino-c/a in #1-8 6.00 18.00 60.00
2-Ringo Starr, David McCallum & Beatles photos on cover; Beatles story and photos 6.00 18.00 60.00
3,4: 3-Blooperman begins, ends #6; 1 pg. Batman & Robin satire; full pg. photo pin-ups Lovin' Spoonful & The Byrds 3.20 9.60 32.00
5-7,9: 5 (2/67)-Super Hero & TV satire by Jim Aparo & Grass Green begins. 6-8-Aparo-a. 6-Petula Clark photo-c. 7-Photo of Brian Wilson of Beach Boys on-c & Beach Boys photo inside f/b-c. 9-Aparo-c/a 3.20 9.60 32.00
8-Monkees photo on-c & photo inside f/b-c 3.60 10.80 36.00

GO-GO AND ANIMAL (See Tippy's Friends...)

GOING STEADY (Formerly Teen-Age Temptations)
St. John Publ. Co.: No. 10, Dec, 1954 - No. 13, June, 1955; No. 14, Oct, 1955

10(1954)-Matt Baker-c/a 20.00 60.00 140.00
11(2/55, last precode), 12(4/55)-Baker-c 11.00 33.00 75.00
13(6/55)-Baker-c/a 13.50 41.00 95.00
14(10/55)-Matt Baker-c/a, 25 pgs. 16.00 47.00 110.00

GOING STEADY (Formerly Personal Love)
Prize Publications/Headline: V3#3, Feb, 1960 - V3#6, Aug, 1960; V4#1, Sept-Oct, 1960

V3#3-6, V4#1 2.25 6.75 18.00

GOING STEADY WITH BETTY (Becomes Betty & Her Steady No. 2)
Avon Periodicals: Nov-Dec, 1949

1 13.50 41.00 95.00

GOLDEN AGE, THE

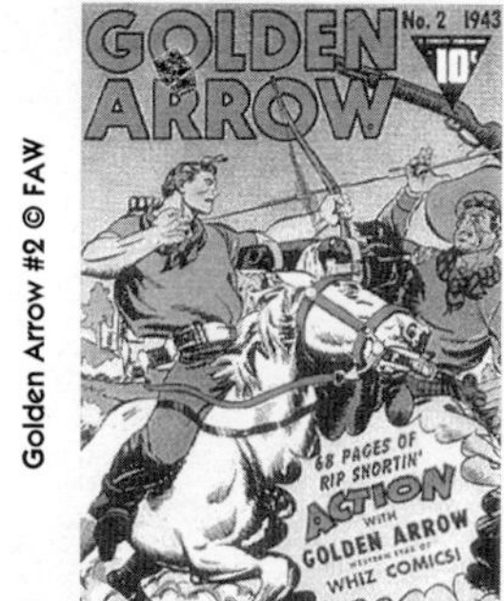

Golden Arrow #2 © FAW

Golden Digest Comics #32 © Walter Lantz

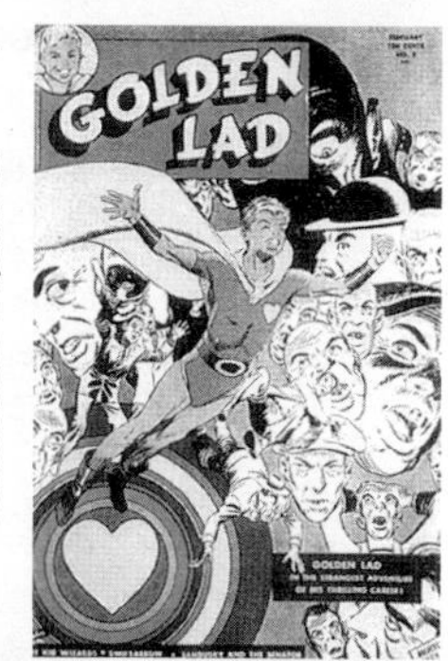

Golden Lad #3 © Spark Pub.

GD2.0 FN6.0 NM9.4

DC Comics (Elseworlds): 1993 - No. 4, 1994 ($4.95, limited series)

	GD2.0	FN6.0	NM9.4
1-4: James Robinson scripts; Paul Smith-c/a; gold foil embossed-c			6.00
Trade Paperback (1995, $19.95)			20.00

GOLDEN ARROW (See Fawcett Miniatures, Mighty Midget & Whiz Comics)

GOLDEN ARROW (...Western No. 6)
Fawcett Publications: Spring, 1942 - No. 6, Spring, 1947 (68 pgs.)

	GD2.0	FN6.0	NM9.4
1-Golden Arrow begins	82.00	247.00	700.00
2-(1943)	40.00	120.00	320.00
3-5: 3-(Win/45-46). 4-(Spr/46). 5-(Fall/46)	33.00	99.00	230.00
6-Krigstein-a	36.00	107.00	250.00

GOLDEN COMICS DIGEST
Gold Key: May, 1969 - No. 48, Jan, 1976
NOTE: *Whitman editions exist of many titles and are generally valued the same.*

	GD2.0	FN6.0	NM9.4
1-Tom & Jerry, Woody Woodpecker, Bugs Bunny	3.80	11.40	38.00
2-Hanna-Barbera TV Fun Favorites; Space Ghost, Flintstones, Atom Ant, Jetsons, Yogi Bear, Banana Splits, others app.	4.50	13.50	45.00
3-Tom & Jerry, Woody Woodpecker	2.25	6.75	18.00
4-Tarzan; Manning & Marsh-a	3.50	10.50	35.00
5,8-Tom & Jerry, W. Woodpecker, Bugs Bunny	1.85	5.50	15.00
6-Bugs Bunny	1.85	5.50	15.00
7-Hanna-Barbera TV Fun Favorites	3.00	9.00	30.00
9-Tarzan	3.50	10.50	35.00
10,12-17: 10-Bugs Bunny. 12-Tom & Jerry, Bugs Bunny, W. Woodpecker Journey to the Sun. 13-Tom & Jerry. 14-Bugs Bunny Fun Packed Funnies. 15-Tom & Jerry, Woody Woodpecker, Bugs Bunny. 16-Woody Woodpecker Cartoon Special. 17-Bugs Bunny	1.85	5.50	15.00
11-Hanna-Barbera TV Fun Favorites	3.00	9.00	30.00
18-Tom & Jerry; Barney Bear-r by Barks	2.25	6.75	18.00
19-Little Lulu	3.00	9.00	30.00
20-22: 20-Woody Woodpecker Falltime Funtime. 21-Bugs Bunny Showtime. 22-Tom & Jerry Winter Wingding	1.85	5.50	15.00
23-Little Lulu & Tubby Fun Fling	3.00	9.00	30.00
24-26,28: 24-Woody Woodpecker Fun Festival. 25-Tom & Jerry. 26-Bugs Bunny Halloween Hulla-Boo-Loo; Dr. Spektor article, also #25. 28-Tom & Jerry	1.75	5.25	14.00
27-Little Lulu & Tubby in Hawaii	2.60	7.80	26.00
29-Little Lulu & Tubby	2.60	7.80	26.00
30-Bugs Bunny Vacation Funnies	1.75	5.25	14.00
31-Turok, Son of Stone; r/4-Color #596,656; c-r/#9	2.70	8.00	30.00
32-Woody Woodpecker Summer Fun	1.75	5.25	14.00
33,36: 33-Little Lulu & Tubby Halloween Fun; Dr. Spektor app. 36-Little Lulu & Her Friends	3.00	9.00	30.00
34,35,37-39: 34-Bugs Bunny Winter Funnies. 35-Tom & Jerry Snowtime Funtime. 37-Woody Woodpecker County Fair. 39-Bugs Bunny Summer Fun	1.75	5.25	14.00
38-The Pink Panther	2.25	6.75	18.00
40,43: 40-Little Lulu & Tubby Trick or Treat; all by Stanley. 43-Little Lulu in Paris	3.20	9.60	32.00
41,42,44,47: 41-Tom & Jerry Winter Carnival. 42-Bugs Bunny. 44-Woody Woodpecker Family Fun Festival. 47-Bugs Bunny	1.50	4.50	12.00
45-The Pink Panther	2.25	6.75	18.00
46-Little Lulu & Tubby	2.50	7.50	25.00
48-The Lone Ranger	2.25	6.75	18.00

NOTE: *#1-30, 164 pgs.; #31 on, 132 pgs..*

GOLDEN LAD
Spark/Fact & Fiction Publ.: July, 1945 - No. 5, June, 1946 (#4, 5: 52 pgs.)

	GD2.0	FN6.0	NM9.4
1-Origin & 1st app. Golden Lad & Swift Arrow; Sandusky and the Senator begins	69.00	206.00	550.00
2-Mort Meskin-c/a	36.00	107.00	250.00
3,4-Mort Meskin-c/a	31.00	94.00	220.00
5-Origin/1st Golden Girl; Shaman & Flame app.	37.00	111.00	260.00

NOTE: *All have* ***Robinson,*** *and* ***Roussos*** *art plus* ***Meskin*** *covers and art.*

GOLDEN LEGACY
Fitzgerald Publishing Co.: 1966 - 1972 (Black History) (25¢)

GD2.0 FN6.0 NM9.4

1-Toussaint L'Ouverture (1966), 2-Harriet Tubman (1967), 3-Crispus Attucks & the Minutemen (1967), 4-Benjamin Banneker (1968), 5-Matthew Henson (1969), 6-Alexander Dumas & Family (1969), 7-Frederick Douglass, Part 1 (1969), 8-Frederick Douglass, Part 2 (1970), 9-Robert Smalls (1970), 10-J. Cinque & the Amistad Mutiny (1970), 11-Men in Action: White, Marshall J. Wilkins (1970), 12-Black Cowboys (1972), 13-The Life of Martin Luther King, Jr. (1972), 14-The Life of Alexander Pushkin (1971), 15-Ancient African Kingdoms (1972), 16-Black Inventors (1972)

	GD2.0	FN6.0	NM9.4
each....	1.25	3.75	10.00
1-10,12,13,15,16(1976)-Reprints		2.40	6.00

GOLDEN LOVE STORIES (Formerly Golden West Love)
Kirby Publishing Co.: No. 4, April, 1950

	GD2.0	FN6.0	NM9.4
4-Powell-a; Glenn Ford/Janet Leigh photo-c	15.00	45.00	105.00

GOLDEN PICTURE CLASSIC, A
Western Printing Co. (Simon & Shuster): 1956-1957 (Text stories w/illustrations in color; 100 pgs. each)

	GD2.0	FN6.0	NM9.4
CL-401: Treasure Island	9.15	27.00	55.00
CL-402,403: 402: Tom Sawyer. 403: Black Beauty	7.50	22.50	45.00
CL-404, 405: CL-404: Little Women. CL-405: Heidi	7.50	22.50	45.00
CL-406: Ben Hur	5.00	15.00	30.00
CL-407: Around the World in 80 Days	5.00	15.00	30.00
CL-408: Sherlock Holmes	6.35	19.00	38.00
CL-409: The Three Musketeers	5.00	15.00	30.00
CL-410: The Merry Advs. of Robin Hood	5.00	15.00	30.00
CL-411,412: 411: Hans Brinker. 412: The Count of Monte Cristo	6.35	19.00	38.00

(Both soft & hardcover editions are valued the same)

NOTE: *Recent research has uncovered new information. Apparently #s 1-6 were issued in 1956 and #7-12 in 1957. But they can be found in five different series listings: CL-1 to CL-12 (softbound); CL-401 to CL-412 (also softbound); CL-101 to CL-112 (hardbound); plus two new series discoveries: A Golden Reading Adventure, publ. by Golden Press; edited down to 60 pages and reduced in size to 6x9"; only #s discovered so far are #381 (CL-4), #382 (CL-6) & #387 (CL-3). They have no reorder list and some have covers different from GPC. There have also been found British hardbound editions of GPC with dust jackets. Copies of all five listed series vary from scarce to very rare. Some editions of some series have not yet been found at all.*

GOLDEN PICTURE STORY BOOK
Racine Press (Western): Dec, 1961 (50¢, Treasury size, 52 pgs.)
(All are scarce)

	GD2.0	FN6.0	NM9.4
ST-1-Huckleberry Hound (TV); Hokey Wolf, Pixie & Dixie, Quick Draw McGraw, Snooper and Blabber, Augie Doggie app.	20.00	60.00	200.00
ST-2-Yogi Bear (TV); Snagglepuss, Yakky Doodle, Quick Draw McGraw, Snooper and Blabber, Augie Doggie app.	20.00	60.00	200.00
ST-3-Babes in Toyland (Walt Disney's...)-Annette Funicello photo-c	23.00	69.00	230.00
ST-4-(...of Disney Ducks)-Walt Disney's Wonderful World of Ducks (Donald Duck, Uncle Scrooge, Donald's Nephews, Grandma Duck, Ludwig Von Drake, & Gyro Gearloose stories)	23.00	69.00	230.00

GOLDEN RECORD COMIC (See Amazing Spider-Man #1, Avengers #4, Fantastic Four #1, Journey Into Mystery #83)

GOLDEN STORY BOOKS
Western Printing Co. (Simon & Shuster): 1949 (Heavy covers, digest size, 128 pgs.) (Illustrated text in color)

	GD2.0	FN6.0	NM9.4
7-Walt Disney's Mystery in Disneyville, a book-length adventure starring Donald and Nephews, Mickey and Nephews, and with Minnie, Daisy and Goofy. Art by Dick Moores & Manuel Gonzales (scarce)	28.00	84.00	195.00
10-Bugs Bunny's Treasure Hunt, a book-length adventure starring Bugs & Porky Pig, with Petunia Pig & Nephew, Cicero. Art by Tom McKimson (scarce)	18.00	54.00	125.00

GOLDEN WEST LOVE (Golden Love Stories No. 4)
Kirby Publishing Co.: Sept-Oct, 1949 - No. 3, Feb, 1950 (All 52 pgs.)

	GD2.0	FN6.0	NM9.4
1-Powell-a in all; Roussos-a; painted-c	21.00	62.00	145.00
2,3: Photo-c	15.00	45.00	105.00

GOLDEN WEST RODEO TREASURY (See Dell Giants)

GOLDILOCKS (See March of Comics No. 1)

GOLD KEY CHAMPION
Gold Key: Mar, 1978 - No. 2, May, 1978 (50¢, 52pgs.)

Gold Medal Comics nn © Cambridge House

Goofy Comics #3 © STD

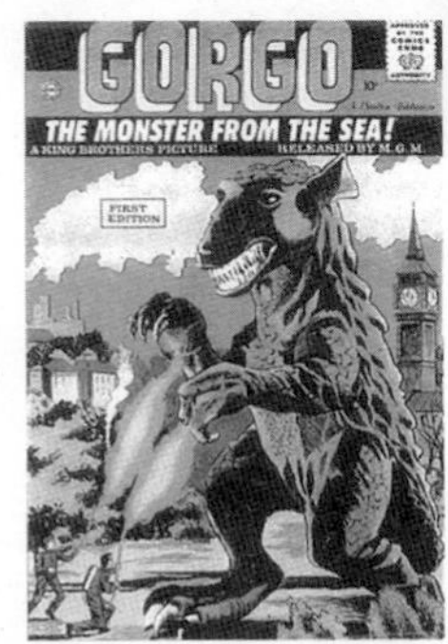

Gorgo #1 © CC

GD2.0 FN6.0 NM9.4

1,2: 1-Space Family Robinson; half-r. 2-Mighty Samson; half-r 1.00 2.80 7.00

GOLD KEY SPOTLIGHT
Gold Key: May, 1976 - No. 11, Feb, 1978

1-Tom, Dick & Harriet 1.00 2.80 7.00
2-11: 2-Wacky Advs. of Cracky. 3-Wacky Witch. 4-Tom, Dick & Harriet. 5-Wacky Advs. of Cracky. 6-Dagar the Invincible; Santos-a; origin Demonomicon. 7-Wacky Witch & Greta Ghost 10-O. G. Whiz.11-Tom, Dick & Harriet. 8-The Occult Files of Dr. Spektor, Simbar, Lu-sai; Santos-a. 9-Tragg 5.00

GOLD MEDAL COMICS
Cambridge House: 1945 (25¢, one-shot, 132 pgs.)

nn-Captain Truth by Fugitani, Crime Detector, The Witch of Salem, Luckyman, others app. 26.00 79.00 185.00

GOMER PYLE (TV)
Gold Key: July, 1966 - No. 3, Jan, 1967

1-Photo front/back-c 6.80 20.00 75.00
2,3 5.00 15.00 55.00

GON
DC Comics (Paradox Press): July, 1996 - No. 4, Oct, 1996 ($5.95, B&W, digest-size, limited series)

1-4: Misadventures of baby dinosaur; Tanaka-c/a/scripts in all 6.00

GON COLOR SPECTACULAR
DC Comics (Paradox Press): 1998 ($5.95, square-bound)

nn-Tanaka-c/a/scripts 6.00

GON SWIMMIN'
DC Comics (Paradox Press): 1997 ($6.95, B&W, digest-size)

nn-Tanaka-c/a/scripts in all 7.00

GOODBYE, MR. CHIPS (See Movie Comics)

GOOD GIRL ART QUARTERLY
AC Comics: Summer, 1990 - No. 16, 1992? (B&W/color, 52 pgs.)

1,3-16 ($3.50)-All have one new story (often FemForce) & rest reprints by Baker, Ward & other "good girl" artists 4.00
2 ($3.95) 4.00

GOOD GUYS, THE
Defiant: Nov, 1993 - No. 9, July, 1994 ($2.50/$3.25/$3.50)

1-($3.50, 52 pgs.)-Glory x-over from Plasm 3.50
2,3,5-9: 9-Pre-Schism issue 2.50
4-($3.25, 52 pgs.) 3.25

GOOFY (Disney)(See Dynabrite Comics, Mickey Mouse Magazine V4#7, Walt Disney Showcase #35 & Wheaties)
Dell Publishing Co.: No. 468, May, 1953 - Sept-Nov, 1962

Four Color 468 (#1) 11.00 34.00 125.00
Four Color 562,627,658,702,747,802,857 6.40 19.00 70.00
Four Color 899,952,987,1053,1094,1149,1201 3.60 11.00 40.00
12-308-211(Dell, 9-11/62) 3.60 11.00 40.00

GOOFY ADVENTURES
Disney Comics: June, 1990 - No. 17, 1991 ($1.50)

1-17: Most new stories. 2-Joshua Quagmire-a w/free poster. 7-WDC&S-r plus new-a. 9-Gottfredson-r. 14-Super Goof story. 15-All Super Goof issue. 17-Gene Colan-a(p) 2.00

GOOFY ADVENTURE STORY (See Goofy No. 857)

GOOFY COMICS (Companion to Happy Comics)(Not Disney)
Nedor Publ. Co. No. 1-14/Standard No. 14-48: June, 1943 - No. 48, 1953 (Animated Cartoons)

1-Funny animal; Oriolo-c 27.00 81.00 190.00
2 13.50 41.00 95.00
3-10 11.00 33.00 75.00
11-19 9.15 27.00 55.00
20-35-Frazetta text illos in all 10.00 30.00 70.00
36-48 6.70 20.00 40.00

GOOFY SUCCESS STORY (See Goofy No. 702)

GOOSE (Humor magazine)
Cousins Publ. (Fawcett): Sept, 1976 - No. 3, 1976 (75¢, 52 pgs., B&W)

1-Nudity in all 2.25 6.75 18.00
2,3: 2-(10/76) Fonz-c/s; Lone Ranger story. 3-Wonder Woman, King Kong, Six Million Dollar Man stories 1.50 4.50 12.00

GORDO (See Comics Revue No. 5 & Giant Comics Edition)

GORGO (Based on M.G.M. movie) (See Return of...)
Charlton Comics: May, 1961 - No. 23, Sept, 1965

1-Ditko-a, 22 pgs. 22.00 66.00 220.00
2,3-Ditko-c/a 11.00 33.00 110.00
4-Ditko-c 6.50 19.50 65.00
5-11,13-16: 11,13-16-Ditko-a 6.00 18.00 60.00
12,17-23: 12-Reptisaurus x-over; Montes/Bache-a-No. 17-23. 20-Giordano-c 3.00 9.00 30.00
Gorgo's Revenge('62)-Becomes Return of... 4.50 13.50 45.00

GOSPEL BLIMP, THE
Spire Christian Comics (Fleming H. Revell Co.): 1973,1974 (35¢/39¢, 36 pgs.)

nn 2.40 6.00

G.O.T.H.
Verotik: Dec, 1995 - No. 3, June, 1996 ($2.95, limited series, mature)

1-3: Danzig scripts; Liam Sharpe-a. 3.00

GOTHAM BY GASLIGHT (A Tale of the Batman)(See Batman: Master of...)
DC Comics: 1989 ($3.95, one-shot, squarebound, 52 pgs.)

nn-Mignola/Russell-a; intro by Robert Bloch 4.00

GOTHAM NIGHTS (See Batman: Gotham Nights II)
DC Comics: Mar, 1992 - No. 4, June, 1992 ($1.25, limited series)

1-4: Featuring Batman 2.00

GOTHIC ROMANCES
Atlas/Seaboard Publ.: Dec, 1974 (75¢, B&W, magazine, 76 pgs.)

1-Text w/ illos by N. Adams, Chaykin, Heath (2 pgs. ea.); painted cover 4.50 13.50 50.00

GOTHIC TALES OF LOVE (Magazine)
Marvel Comics: Apr, 1975 - No. 2, Jun, 1975 (B&W, 76 pgs.)

1,2-painted-c/a 4.00 12.00 40.00

GOVERNOR & J. J., THE (TV)
Gold Key: Feb, 1970 - No. 3, Aug, 1970 (Photo-c)

1 3.50 10.50 35.00
2,3 2.50 7.50 24.00

GRACKLE, THE
Acclaim Comics: Jan, 1997 - No. 4, Apr, 1997 ($2.95, B&W)

1-4: Mike Baron scripts & Paul Gulacy-c/a. 1-4-Doublecross 3.00

GRAFIK MUSIK
Caliber Press: Nov, 1990 - No. 4, Aug, 1991 ($3.50/$2.50)

1-($3.50, 48 pgs., color) Mike Allred-c/a/scripts-1st app. in color of Frank Einstein (Madman) 20.00
2-($2.50, 24 pgs., color) 10.00
3,4-($2.50, 24 pgs., B&W) 8.00

GRANDMA DUCK'S FARM FRIENDS(See Walt Disney's C&S 293 & Wheaties)
Dell Publishing Co.: No. 763, Jan, 1957 - No. 1279, Feb, 1962 (Disney)

Four Color 763 (#1) 6.40 19.00 70.00
Four Color 873 4.50 13.50 50.00
Four Color 965,1279 3.60 11.00 40.00
Four Color 1010,1073,1161-Barks-a; 1073,1161-Barks c/a 12.00 37.00 135.00

GRAND PRIX (Formerly Hot Rod Racers)
Charlton Comics: No. 16, Sept, 1967 - No. 31, May, 1970

Great Action Comics #9 © I.W. Enterprises

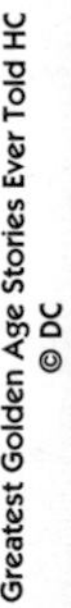

The Greatest Golden Age Stories Ever Told HC © DC

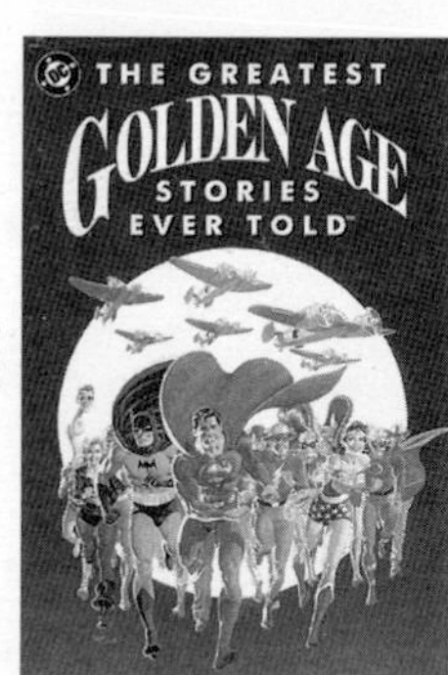

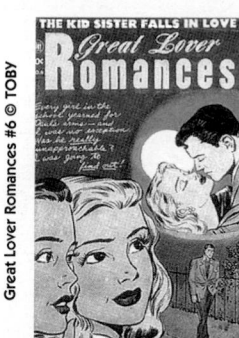

Great Lover Romances #6 © TOBY

GD2.0 FN6.0 NM9.4

16-Features Rick Roberts 2.60 7.80 26.00
17-20 2.50 7.50 20.00
21-31 2.00 6.00 16.00

GRAPHIQUE MUSIQUE
Slave Labor Graphics: Dec, 1989 - No. 3, May, 1990 ($2.95, 52 pgs.)
1-Mike Allred-c/a/scripts 4.00 12.00 40.00
2,3 3.00 9.00 30.00

GRAVEDIGGERS
Acclaim Comics: Nov, 1996 - No. 4, Feb, 1997 ($2.95, B&W)
1-4: Moretti scripts 3.00

GRAVESTONE
Malibu Comics: July, 1993 - No. 7, Feb, 1994 ($2.25)
1-6: 3-Polybagged w/Skycap 2.25
7-($2.50) 2.50

GRAVE TALES
Hamilton Comics: Oct, 1991 - No. 3, Feb, 1992 ($3.95, B&W, mag., 52 pgs.)
1-Staton-c/a 1.00 3.00 8.00
2,3: 2-Staton-a; Morrow-c 2.40 6.00

GRAY GHOST, THE
Dell Publishing Co.: No. 911, July, 1958; No. 1000, June-Aug, 1959
Four Color 911 (#1), 1000-Photo-c each 8.00 25.00 90.00

GREASE MONKEY
Image Comics: Jan, 1998 - Present ($2.95, B&W)
1,2-Tim Eldred-s/a 3.00

GREAT ACTION COMICS
I. W. Enterprises: 1958 (Reprints with new covers)
1-Captain Truth reprinted from Gold Medal #1 2.50 7.50 22.00
8,9-Reprints Phantom Lady #15 & 23 8.50 25.50 85.00

GREAT AMERICAN COMICS PRESENTS - THE SECRET VOICE
Peter George 4-Star Publ./American Features Syndicate: 1945 (10¢)
1-Anti-Nazi; "What Really Happened to Hitler" 29.00 86.00 200.00

GREAT AMERICAN WESTERN, THE
AC Comics: 1987 - No. 4, 1990? ($1.75/$2.95/$3.50, B&W with some color)
1-4: 1-Western-r plus Bill Black-a. 2-Tribute to ME comics; Durango Kid photo-c 3-Tribute to Tom Mix plus Roy Rogers, Durango Kid; Billy the Kid-r by Severin; photo-c. 4- ($3.50, 52 pgs., 16 pgs. color)-Tribute to Lash LaRue; photo-c & interior photos; Fawcett-r 3.50
...Presents 1 (1991, $5.00) New Sunset Carson; film history 5.00

GREAT CAT FAMILY, THE (Disney-TV/Movie)
Dell Publishing Co.: No. 750, Nov, 1956 (one-shot)
Four Color 750-Pinocchio & Alice app. 5.50 16.50 60.00

GREAT COMICS
Great Comics Publications: Nov, 1941 - No. 3, Jan, 1942
1-Origin/1st app. The Great Zarro; Madame Strange & Guy Gorham, Wizard of Science & The Great Zarro begin 125.00 375.00 1000.00
2-Buck Johnson, Jungle Explorer app.; X-Mas-c 62.00 187.00 500.00
3-Futuro Takes Hitler to Hell-c/s; "The Lost City" movie story (starring William Boyd); continues in Choice Comics #3 187.00 562.00 1500.00

GREAT COMICS
Novack Publishing Co./Jubilee Comics/Barrel O' Fun: 1945
1-(Novack)-The Defenders, Capt. Power app.; L. B. Cole-c 40.00 120.00 300.00
1-(Jubilee)-Same cover; Boogey Man, Satanas, & The Sorcerer & His Apprentice 29.00 86.00 200.00
1-(Barrel O' Fun)-L. B. Cole-c; Barrel O' Fun overprinted in indicia; Li'l Cactus, Cuckoo Sheriff (humorous) 19.00 56.00 130.00

GREAT DOGPATCH MYSTERY (See Mammy Yokum & the...)

GREATEST BATMAN STORIES EVER TOLD, THE

GD2.0 FN6.0 NM9.4

DC Comics:
Hardcover ($24.95) 40.00
Softcover ($15.95) "Greatest DC Stories Vol. 2" on spine 16.00
Vol. 2 softcover (1992, $16.95)"Greatest DC Stories Vol. 7" on spine 17.00

GREATEST FLASH STORIES EVER TOLD, THE
DC Comics: 1991 ($29.95, hardcover)
nn-Infantino-c 30.00

GREATEST GOLDEN AGE STORIES EVER TOLD, THE
DC Comics: 1990 ($24.95, hardcover)
nn-Ordway-c 40.00

GREATEST JOKER STORIES EVER TOLD, THE (See Batman)
DC Comics: 1983
Hardcover ($19.95)-Kyle Baker painted-c 30.00
Softcover ($14.95) 15.00
Stacked Deck...Expanded Edition (1992, $29.95)-Longmeadow Press Publ. 30.00

GREATEST 1950s STORIES EVER TOLD, THE
DC Comics: 1990
Hardcover ($29.95)-Kubert-c 40.00
Softcover ($14.95) "Greatest DC Stories Vol. 5" on spine 15.00

GREATEST TEAM-UP STORIES EVER TOLD, THE
DC Comics: 1989
Hardcover ($24.95)-DeVries and Infantino painted-c 40.00
Softcover ($14.95) "Greatest DC Stories Vol. 4" on spine; Adams-c 15.00

GREATEST SUPERMAN STORIES EVER TOLD, THE
DC Comics: 1987
Hardcover ($24.95) 40.00
Softcover ($15.95) 16.00

GREAT EXPLOITS
Decker Publ./Red Top: Oct, 1957
1-Krigstein-a(2) (re-issue on cover); reprints Daring Advs. #6 by Approved Comics 7.50 22.50 45.00

GREAT FOODINI, THE (See Foodini)

GREAT GAZOO, THE (The Flintstones)(TV)
Charlton Comics: Aug, 1973 - No. 20, Jan, 1977 (Hanna-Barbera)
1 2.50 7.50 24.00
2-10 1.75 5.25 14.00
11-20 1.10 3.30 9.00

GREAT GRAPE APE, THE (TV)(See TV Stars #1)
Charlton Comics: Sept, 1976 - No. 2, Nov, 1976 (Hanna-Barbera)
1 1.85 5.50 15.00
2 1.25 3.75 10.00

GREAT LOCOMOTIVE CHASE, THE (Disney)
Dell Publishing Co.: No. 712, Sept, 1956 (one-shot)
Four Color 712-Movie, photo-c 6.40 19.00 70.00

GREAT LOVER ROMANCES (Young Lover Romances #4,5)
Toby Press: 3/51; #2, 1951(nd); #3, 1952 (nd); #6, Oct?, 1952 - No. 22, May, 1955 (Photo-c #1-5, 10 ,13, 15, 17) (no #4, 5)
1-Jon Juan story-r/Jon Juan #1 by Schomburg; Dr. Anthony King app. 16.00 47.00 110.00
2-Jon Juan, Dr. Anthony King app. 9.15 27.00 55.00
3,7,9-14,16-22: 10-Rita Hayworth photo-c. 17-Rita Hayworth & Aldo Ray photo-c 5.35 16.00 32.00
6-Kurtzman-a (10/52) 9.15 27.00 55.00
8-Five pgs. of "Pin-Up Pete" by Sparling 10.00 30.00 60.00
15-Liz Taylor photo-c 10.00 30.00 70.00

GREAT RACE, THE (See Movie Classics)

GREAT SCOTT SHOE STORE (See Bulls-Eye)

Gold Medal Comics nn © Cambridge House

Goofy Comics #3 © STD

Gorgo #1 © CC

GD2.0 FN6.0 NM9.4

1,2: 1-Space Family Robinson; half-r. 2-Mighty Samson; half-r 1.00 2.80 7.00

GOLD KEY SPOTLIGHT
Gold Key: May, 1976 - No. 11, Feb, 1978

1-Tom, Dick & Harriet 1.00 2.80 7.00
2-11: 2-Wacky Advs. of Cracky. 3-Wacky Witch. 4-Tom, Dick & Harriet. 5-Wacky Advs. of Cracky. 6-Dagar the Invincible; Santos-a; origin Demonomicon. 7-Wacky Witch & Greta Ghost 10-O. G. Whiz.11-Tom, Dick & Harriet. 8-The Occult Files of Dr. Spektor, Simbar, Lu-sai; Santos-a. 9-Tragg 5.00

GOLD MEDAL COMICS
Cambridge House: 1945 (25¢, one-shot, 132 pgs.)

nn-Captain Truth by Fugitani, Crime Detector, The Witch of Salem, Luckyman, others app. 26.00 79.00 185.00

GOMER PYLE (TV)
Gold Key: July, 1966 - No. 3, Jan, 1967

1-Photo front/back-c 6.80 20.00 75.00
2,3 5.00 15.00 55.00

GON
DC Comics (Paradox Press): July, 1996 - No. 4, Oct, 1996 ($5.95, B&W, digest-size, limited series)

1-4: Misadventures of baby dinosaur; Tanaka-c/a/scripts in all 6.00

GON COLOR SPECTACULAR
DC Comics (Paradox Press): 1998 ($5.95, square-bound)

nn-Tanaka-c/a/scripts 6.00

GON SWIMMIN'
DC Comics (Paradox Press): 1997 ($6.95, B&W, digest-size)

nn-Tanaka-c/a/scripts in all 7.00

GOODBYE, MR. CHIPS (See Movie Comics)

GOOD GIRL ART QUARTERLY
AC Comics: Summer, 1990 - No. 16, 1992? (B&W/color, 52 pgs.)

1,3-16 ($3.50)-All have one new story (often FemForce) & rest reprints by Baker, Ward & other "good girl" artists 4.00
2 ($3.95) 4.00

GOOD GUYS, THE
Defiant: Nov, 1993 - No. 9, July, 1994 ($2.50/$3.25/$3.50)

1-($3.50, 52 pgs.)-Glory x-over from Plasm 3.50
2,3,5-9: 9-Pre-Schism issue 2.50
4-($3.25, 52 pgs.) 3.25

GOOFY (Disney)(See Dynabrite Comics, Mickey Mouse Magazine V4#7, Walt Disney Showcase #35 & Wheaties)
Dell Publishing Co.: No. 468, May, 1953 - Sept-Nov, 1962

Four Color 468 (#1) 11.00 34.00 125.00
Four Color 562,627,658,702,747,802,857 6.40 19.00 70.00
Four Color 899,952,987,1053,1094,1149,1201 3.60 11.00 40.00
12-308-211(Dell, 9-11/62) 3.60 11.00 40.00

GOOFY ADVENTURES
Disney Comics: June, 1990 - No. 17, 1991 ($1.50)

1-17: Most new stories. 2-Joshua Quagmire-a w/free poster. 7-WDC&S-r plus new-a. 9-Gottfredson-r. 14-Super Goof story. 15-All Super Goof issue. 17-Gene Colan-a(p) 2.00

GOOFY ADVENTURE STORY (See Goofy No. 857)

GOOFY COMICS (Companion to Happy Comics)(Not Disney)
Nedor Publ. Co. No. 1-14/Standard No. 14-48: June, 1943 - No. 48, 1953 (Animated Cartoons)

1-Funny animal; Oriolo-c 27.00 81.00 190.00
2 13.50 41.00 95.00
3-10 11.00 33.00 75.00
11-19 9.15 27.00 55.00
20-35-Frazetta text illos in all 10.00 30.00 70.00
36-48 6.70 20.00 40.00

GOOFY SUCCESS STORY (See Goofy No. 702)

GOOSE (Humor magazine)
Cousins Publ. (Fawcett): Sept, 1976 - No. 3, 1976 (75¢, 52 pgs., B&W)

1-Nudity in all 2.25 6.75 18.00
2,3: 2-(10/76) Fonz-c/s; Lone Ranger story. 3-Wonder Woman, King Kong, Six Million Dollar Man stories 1.50 4.50 12.00

GORDO (See Comics Revue No. 5 & Giant Comics Edition)

GORGO (Based on M.G.M. movie) (See Return of...)
Charlton Comics: May, 1961 - No. 23, Sept, 1965

1-Ditko-a, 22 pgs. 22.00 66.00 220.00
2,3-Ditko-c/a 11.00 33.00 110.00
4-Ditko-c 6.50 19.50 65.00
5-11,13-16: 11,13-16-Ditko-a 6.00 18.00 60.00
12,17-23: 12-Reptisaurus x-over; Montes/Bache-a-No. 17-23. 20-Giordano-c 3.00 9.00 30.00
Gorgo's Revenge('62)-Becomes Return of... 4.50 13.50 45.00

GOSPEL BLIMP, THE
Spire Christian Comics (Fleming H. Revell Co.): 1973,1974 (35¢/39¢, 36 pgs.)

nn 2.40 6.00

G.O.T.H.
Verotik: Dec, 1995 - No. 3, June, 1996 ($2.95, limited series, mature)

1-3: Danzig scripts; Liam Sharpe-a. 3.00

GOTHAM BY GASLIGHT (A Tale of the Batman)(See Batman: Master of...)
DC Comics: 1989 ($3.95, one-shot, squarebound, 52 pgs.)

nn-Mignola/Russell-a; intro by Robert Bloch 4.00

GOTHAM NIGHTS (See Batman: Gotham Nights II)
DC Comics: Mar, 1992 - No. 4, June, 1992 ($1.25, limited series)

1-4: Featuring Batman 2.00

GOTHIC ROMANCES
Atlas/Seaboard Publ.: Dec, 1974 (75¢, B&W, magazine, 76 pgs.)

1-Text w/ illos by N. Adams, Chaykin, Heath (2 pgs. ea.); painted cover 4.50 13.50 50.00

GOTHIC TALES OF LOVE (Magazine)
Marvel Comics: Apr, 1975 - No. 2, Jun, 1975 (B&W, 76 pgs.)

1,2-painted-c/a 4.00 12.00 40.00

GOVERNOR & J. J., THE (TV)
Gold Key: Feb, 1970 - No. 3, Aug, 1970 (Photo-c)

1 3.50 10.50 35.00
2,3 2.50 7.50 24.00

GRACKLE, THE
Acclaim Comics: Jan, 1997 - No. 4, Apr, 1997 ($2.95, B&W)

1-4: Mike Baron scripts & Paul Gulacy-c/a. 1-4-Doublecross 3.00

GRAFIK MUSIK
Caliber Press: Nov, 1990 - No. 4, Aug, 1991 ($3.50/$2.50)

1-($3.50, 48 pgs., color) Mike Allred-c/a/scripts-1st app. in color of Frank Einstein (Madman) 20.00
2-($2.50, 24 pgs., color) 10.00
3,4-($2.50, 24 pgs., B&W) 8.00

GRANDMA DUCK'S FARM FRIENDS(See Walt Disney's C&S 293 & Wheaties)
Dell Publishing Co.: No. 763, Jan, 1957 - No. 1279, Feb, 1962 (Disney)

Four Color 763 (#1) 6.40 19.00 70.00
Four Color 873 4.50 13.50 50.00
Four Color 965,1279 3.60 11.00 40.00
Four Color 1010,1073,1161-Barks-a; 1073,1161-Barks c/a 12.00 37.00 135.00

GRAND PRIX (Formerly Hot Rod Racers)
Charlton Comics: No. 16, Sept, 1967 - No. 31, May, 1970

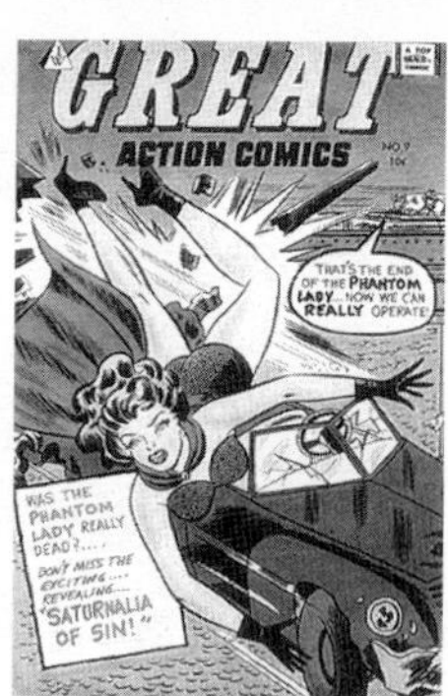

Great Action Comics #9 © I.W. Enterprises

The Greatest Golden Age Stories Ever Told HC © DC

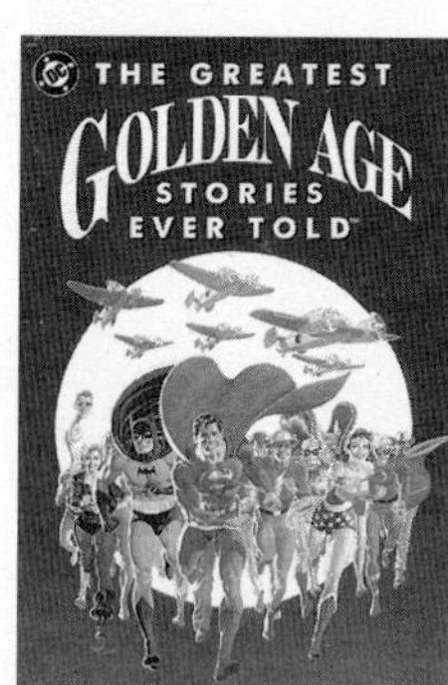

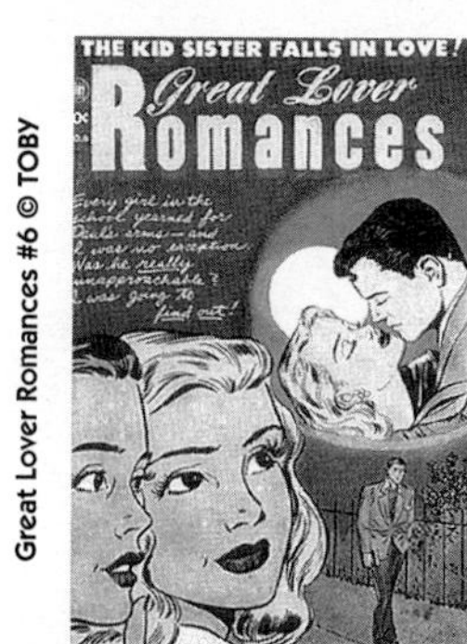

Great Lover Romances #6 © TOBY

GD2.0 FN6.0 NM9.4

16-Features Rick Roberts 2.60 7.80 26.00
17-20 2.50 7.50 20.00
21-31 2.00 6.00 16.00

GRAPHIQUE MUSIQUE
Slave Labor Graphics: Dec, 1989 - No. 3, May, 1990 ($2.95, 52 pgs.)
1-Mike Allred-c/a/scripts 4.00 12.00 40.00
2,3 3.00 9.00 30.00

GRAVEDIGGERS
Acclaim Comics: Nov, 1996 - No. 4, Feb, 1997 ($2.95, B&W)
1-4: Moretti scripts 3.00

GRAVESTONE
Malibu Comics: July, 1993 - No. 7, Feb, 1994 ($2.25)
1-6: 3-Polybagged w/Skycap 2.25
7-($2.50) 2.50

GRAVE TALES
Hamilton Comics: Oct, 1991 - No. 3, Feb, 1992 ($3.95, B&W, mag., 52 pgs.)
1-Staton-c/a 1.00 3.00 8.00
2,3: 2-Staton-a; Morrow-c 2.40 6.00

GRAY GHOST, THE
Dell Publishing Co.: No. 911, July, 1958; No. 1000, June-Aug, 1959
Four Color 911 (#1), 1000-Photo-c each 8.00 25.00 90.00

GREASE MONKEY
Image Comics: Jan, 1998 - Present ($2.95, B&W)
1,2-Tim Eldred-s/a 3.00

GREAT ACTION COMICS
I. W. Enterprises: 1958 (Reprints with new covers)
1-Captain Truth reprinted from Gold Medal #1 2.50 7.50 22.00
8,9-Reprints Phantom Lady #15 & 23 8.50 25.50 85.00

GREAT AMERICAN COMICS PRESENTS - THE SECRET VOICE
Peter George 4-Star Publ./American Features Syndicate: 1945 (10¢)
1-Anti-Nazi; "What Really Happened to Hitler" 29.00 86.00 200.00

GREAT AMERICAN WESTERN, THE
AC Comics: 1987 - No. 4, 1990? ($1.75/$2.95/$3.50, B&W with some color)
1-4: 1-Western-r plus Bill Black-a. 2-Tribute to ME comics; Durango Kid photo-c 3-Tribute to Tom Mix plus Roy Rogers, Durango Kid; Billy the Kid-r by Severin; photo-c. 4- ($3.50, 52 pgs., 16 pgs. color)-Tribute to Lash LaRue; photo-c & interior photos; Fawcett-r 3.50
...Presents 1 (1991, $5.00) New Sunset Carson; film history 5.00

GREAT CAT FAMILY, THE (Disney-TV/Movie)
Dell Publishing Co.: No. 750, Nov, 1956 (one-shot)
Four Color 750-Pinocchio & Alice app. 5.50 16.50 60.00

GREAT COMICS
Great Comics Publications: Nov, 1941 - No. 3, Jan, 1942
1-Origin/1st app. The Great Zarro; Madame Strange & Guy Gorham, Wizard of Science & The Great Zarro begin 125.00 375.00 1000.00
2-Buck Johnson, Jungle Explorer app.; X-Mas-c 62.00 187.00 500.00
3-Futuro Takes Hitler to Hell-c/s; "The Lost City" movie story (starring William Boyd); continues in Choice Comics #3 187.00 562.00 1500.00

GREAT COMICS
Novack Publishing Co./Jubilee Comics/Barrel O' Fun: 1945
1-(Novack)-The Defenders, Capt. Power app.; L. B. Cole-c 40.00 120.00 300.00
1-(Jubilee)-Same cover; Boogey Man, Satanas, & The Sorcerer & His Apprentice 29.00 86.00 200.00
1-(Barrel O' Fun)-L. B. Cole-c; Barrel O' Fun overprinted in indicia; Li'l Cactus, Cuckoo Sheriff (humorous) 19.00 56.00 130.00

GREAT DOGPATCH MYSTERY (See Mammy Yokum & the...)

GREATEST BATMAN STORIES EVER TOLD, THE
DC Comics:
Hardcover ($24.95) 40.00
Softcover ($15.95) "Greatest DC Stories Vol. 2" on spine 16.00
Vol. 2 softcover (1992, $16.95)"Greatest DC Stories Vol. 7" on spine 17.00

GREATEST FLASH STORIES EVER TOLD, THE
DC Comics: 1991 ($29.95, hardcover)
nn-Infantino-c 30.00

GREATEST GOLDEN AGE STORIES EVER TOLD, THE
DC Comics: 1990 ($24.95, hardcover)
nn-Ordway-c 40.00

GREATEST JOKER STORIES EVER TOLD, THE (See Batman)
DC Comics: 1983
Hardcover ($19.95)-Kyle Baker painted-c 30.00
Softcover ($14.95) 15.00
Stacked Deck...Expanded Edition (1992, $29.95)-Longmeadow Press Publ. 30.00

GREATEST 1950s STORIES EVER TOLD, THE
DC Comics: 1990
Hardcover ($29.95)-Kubert-c 40.00
Softcover ($14.95) "Greatest DC Stories Vol. 5" on spine 15.00

GREATEST TEAM-UP STORIES EVER TOLD, THE
DC Comics: 1989
Hardcover ($24.95)-DeVries and Infantino painted-c 40.00
Softcover ($14.95) "Greatest DC Stories Vol. 4" on spine; Adams-c 15.00

GREATEST SUPERMAN STORIES EVER TOLD, THE
DC Comics: 1987
Hardcover ($24.95) 40.00
Softcover ($15.95) 16.00

GREAT EXPLOITS
Decker Publ./Red Top: Oct, 1957
1-Krigstein-a(2) (re-issue on cover); reprints Daring Advs. #6 by Approved Comics 7.50 22.50 45.00

GREAT FOODINI, THE (See Foodini)

GREAT GAZOO, THE (The Flintstones)(TV)
Charlton Comics: Aug, 1973 - No. 20, Jan, 1977 (Hanna-Barbera)
1 2.50 7.50 24.00
2-10 1.75 5.25 14.00
11-20 1.10 3.30 9.00

GREAT GRAPE APE, THE (TV)(See TV Stars #1)
Charlton Comics: Sept, 1976 - No. 2, Nov, 1976 (Hanna-Barbera)
1 1.85 5.50 15.00
2 1.25 3.75 10.00

GREAT LOCOMOTIVE CHASE, THE (Disney)
Dell Publishing Co.: No. 712, Sept, 1956 (one-shot)
Four Color 712-Movie, photo-c 6.40 19.00 70.00

GREAT LOVER ROMANCES (Young Lover Romances #4,5)
Toby Press: 3/51; #2, 1951(nd); #3, 1952 (nd); #6, Oct?, 1952 - No. 22, May, 1955 (Photo-c #1-5, 10 ,13, 15, 17) (no #4, 5)
1-Jon Juan story-r/Jon Juan #1 by Schomburg; Dr. Anthony King app. 16.00 47.00 110.00
2-Jon Juan, Dr. Anthony King app. 9.15 27.00 55.00
3,7,9-14,16-22: 10-Rita Hayworth photo-c. 17-Rita Hayworth & Aldo Ray photo-c 5.35 16.00 32.00
6-Kurtzman-a (10/52) 9.15 27.00 55.00
8-Five pgs. of "Pin-Up Pete" by Sparling 10.00 30.00 60.00
15-Liz Taylor photo-c 10.00 30.00 70.00

GREAT RACE, THE (See Movie Classics)

GREAT SCOTT SHOE STORE (See Bulls-Eye)

Green Arrow #55 © DC

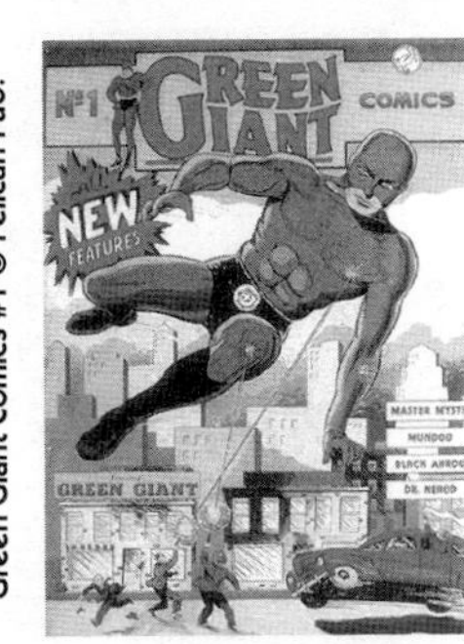

Green Giant Comics #1 © Pelican Pub.

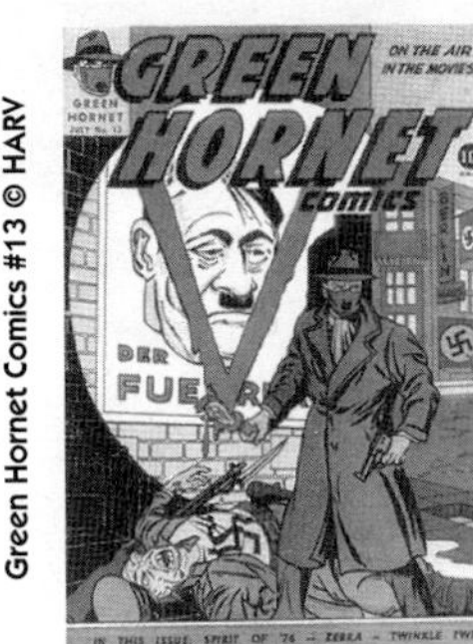

Green Hornet Comics #13 © HARV

GD2.0 FN6.0 NM9.4

GREAT WEST (Magazine)
M. F. Enterprises: 1969 (B&W, 52 pgs.)

V1#1 1.50 4.50 12.00

GREAT WESTERN
Magazine Enterprises: No. 8, Jan-Mar, 1954 - No. 11, Oct-Dec, 1954

8(A-1 93)-Trail Colt by Guardineer; Powell Red Hawk-r/Straight Arrow begins, ends #11; Durango Kid story 21.00 62.00 145.00
9(A-1 105), 11(A-1 127)-Ghost Rider, Durango Kid app. in each. 9-Red Mask-c, but no app. 12.00 36.00 85.00
10(A-1 113)-The Calico Kid by Guardineer-r/Tim Holt #8; Straight Arrow, Durango Kid app. 12.00 36.00 85.00
I.W. Reprint #1,2 9: 1,2-r/Straight Arrow #36,42. 9-r/Straight Arrow #? 2.50 7.50 20.00
I.W. Reprint #8-Origin Ghost Rider(r/Tim Holt #11); Tim Holt app.; Bolle-a 2.50 7.50 24.00
NOTE: *Guardineer c-8. Powell a(r)-8-11 (from Straight Arrow).*

GREEN ARROW (See Action #440, Adventure, Brave & the Bold, DC Super Stars #17, Detective #521, Flash #217, Green Lantern #76, Justice League of America #4, Leading, More Fun #73 (1st app.), Showcase '95 #9 & World's Finest Comics)

GREEN ARROW
DC Comics: May, 1983 - No. 4, Aug, 1983 (limited series)

1-Origin; Speedy cameo; Mike W. Barr scripts, Trevor Von Eeden-c/a 5.00
2-4 4.00

GREEN ARROW
DC Comics: Feb, 1988 - No. 137, Oct, 1998 ($1.00-$2.50) (Painted-c #1-3)

1-Mike Grell scripts begin, ends #80 5.00
2-49,51-74,76-86: 27,28-Warlord app. 35-38-Co-stars Black Canary; Bill Wray-i. 40-Grell-a. 47-Begin $1.50-c. 63-No longer has mature readers on-c. 63-66-Shado app. 81-Aparo-a begins, ends #100; Nuklon app. 82-Intro & death of Rival. 83-Huntress-c/story. 84-Deathstroke cameo. 85-Deathstroke-c/app. 86-Catwoman-c/story w/Jim Balent layouts 2.50
50,75-($2.50, 52 pgs.): Anniversary issues. 75-Arsenal (Roy Harper) & Shado app. 3.00
0,87-96: 87-$1.95-c begins. 88-Guy Gardner, Martian Manhunter, & Wonder Woman-c/app.; Flash-c. 89-Anarky app. 90-(9/94)-Zero Hour tie-in. 0-(10/94)-1st app. Connor Hawke; Aparo-a(p). 91-(11/94). 93-1st app. Camorouge. 95-Hal Jordan cameo. 96-Intro new Force of July; Hal Jordan (Parallax) app; Oliver Queen learns that Connor Hawke is his son 2.50
97-99,102-109: 97-Begin $2.25-c; no Aparo-a. 97-99-Arsenal app. 102,103-Underworld Unleashed x-over. 104-GL(Kyle Rayner)-c/app. 105-Robin-c/app. 107-109-Thorn app. 109-Lois Lane cameo; Weeks-c. 2.50
100-($3.95)-Foil-c; Superman app. 4.00
101-Apparent death of Oliver Queen; Superman app. 2.40 6.00
110,111-124: 110,111-GL x-over. 110-Intro Hatchet. 114-Final Night. 115-117-Black Canary & Oracle app. 2.50
125-($3.50, 48 pgs)-GL x-over cont. in GL #92 3.50
126-137: 126-Begin $2.50-c. 130-GL & Flash x-over. 132,133-JLA app. 134,135-Brotherhood of the Fist pts. 1,5. 136-Hal Jordan-c/app. 137-Last issue; Superman app. 2.50
#1,000,000 (11/98) 853rd Century x-over 2.50
Annual 1-6 ('88-'94, 68 pgs.)-1-No Grell scripts. 2-No Grell scripts; recaps origin Green Arrow,Speedy, Black Canary & others. 3-Bill Wray-a. 4-50th anniversary issue. 5-Batman, Eclipso app. 6-Bloodlines; Hook app. 3.50
7-('95, $3.95)-Year One story 4.00
NOTE: ***Aparo** a-0, 81-85, 86 (partial),87p, 88p, 91-95, 96i, 98-100p, 109p; c-81,98-100p. **Austin** c-96i. **Balent** layouts-86. **Burchett** c-91-95. **Campanella** a-100-108i, 110-113i; c-99i, 101-108i,110-113i. **Denys Cowan** a-39p, 41-43p, 47p, 48p, 60p; c-41-43. **Damaggio** a(p)-97p, 100-108p, 110-112p; c-97-99p, 101-108p, 110-113p. **Mike Grell** c-1-4, 10p, 11, 39, 40, 44, 45, 47-80, Annual 4, 5. **Nasser/Netzer** a-89, 96. **Sienkiewicz** a-109i. **Springer** a-67, 68. **Weeks** c-109.*

GREEN ARROW: THE LONG BOW HUNTERS
DC Comics: Aug, 1987 - No. 3, Oct, 1987 ($2.95, limited series, mature)

1-Grell-c/a in all 5.00
1,2-2nd printings 3.00
2,3 4.00
Trade paperback (1989, $12.95)-r/#1-3 13.00

GD2.0 FN6.0 NM9.4

GREEN ARROW: THE WONDER YEAR
DC Comics: Feb, 1993 - No. 4, May, 1993 ($1.75, limited series)

1-4: Mike Grell-a(p)/scripts & Gray Morrow-a(i) 2.00

GREEN BERET, THE (See Tales of...)

GREEN CANDLES
DC Comics (Paradox Press): Sept, 1995 - No. 3, Dec, 1995 ($5.95, B&W, limited series, digest size)

1-3 2.40 6.00

GREEN GIANT COMICS (Also see Colossus Comics)
Pelican Publ. (Funnies, Inc.): 1940 (No price on cover; distributed in New York City only)

GD2.0 FN6.0 VF8.0 NM9.4
1-Dr. Nerod, Green Giant, Black Arrow, Mundoo & Master Mystic app.; origin Colossus (Rare) 926.00 2780.00 5560.00 8800.00
NOTE: *The idea for this book came from George Kapitan. Printed by Moreau Publ. of Orange, N.J. as an experiment to see if they could profitably use the idle time of their 40-page Hoe color press. The experiment failed due to the difficulty of obtaining good quality color registration and Mr. Moreau believes the book never reached the stands. The book has no price or date which lends credence to this. Contains five pages reprinted from Motion Picture Funnies Weekly.*

GREEN GOBLIN
Marvel Comics: Oct, 1995 - No. 13, Oct, 1996 ($2.95/$1.95)

GD2.0 FN6.0 NM9.4
1-($2.95)-Scott McDaniel-c/a begins, ends #7; foil-c 3.00
2-13: 2-Begin $1.95-c. 4-Hobgoblin-c/app; Thing app. 6-Daredevil-c/app. 8-Darrick Robertson-a; McDaniel-c. 10-Arcade app. 12,13-Onslaught x-over. 13-Green Goblin quits; Spider-Man app. 2.00

GREENHAVEN
Aircel Publishing: 1988 - No. 3, 1988 ($2.00, limited series, 28 pgs.)

1-3 2.00

GREEN HORNET, THE (TV)
Dell Publishing Co./Gold Key: Sept, 1953; Feb, 1967 - No. 3, Aug, 1967

Four Color 496-Painted-c. 23.00 68.00 250.00
1-All have Bruce Lee photo-c 19.00 57.00 210.00
2,3 13.00 40.00 145.00

GREEN HORNET, THE (Also see Kato of the... & Tales of the...)
Now Comics: Nov, 1989 - No. 14, Feb, 1991 ($1.75)
V2#1, Sept, 1991 - V2#39, Dec, 1994 ($1.95)

1 ($2.95, double-size)-Steranko painted-c; G.A. Green Hornet 2.40 6.00
1,2: 1-2nd printing ('90, $3.95)-New Butler-c 4.00
3-14: 5-Death of original ('30s) Green Hornet. 6-Dave Dorman painted-c. 11-Snyder-c 3.00
V2#1-11,13-21,24-26,28-30,32-37,39: 1-Butler painted-c. 9-Mayerik-c 2.50
12-($2.50)-Color Green Hornet button polybagged inside 3.00
22,23-($2.95)-Bagged w/color hologravure card 3.00
27-($2.95)-Newsstand ed. polybagged w/multi-dimensional card (1993 Anniversary Special on cover), 27-($2.95)-Direct Sale ed. polybagged w/multi-dimensional card; cover variations 3.00
31,38: 31-($2.50)-Polybagged w/trading card 2.50
1-($2.50)-Polybagged w/button (same as #12) 2.50
2,3-($1.95)-Same as #13 & 14 2.00
Annual 1 (12/92, $2.50), Annual 1994 (10/94, $2.95) 3.00

GREEN HORNET: SOLITARY SENTINEL, THE
Now Comics: Dec, 1992 - No. 3, 1993 ($2.50, limited series)

1-3 2.50

GREEN HORNET COMICS (...Racket Buster #44) (Radio, movies)
Helnit Publ. Co.(Holyoke) No. 1-6/Family Comics(Harvey) No. 7-on:
Dec, 1940 - No. 47, Sept, 1949 (See All New #13,14)(Early issues: 68 pgs.)

1-1st app. Green Hornet & Kato; origin of Green Hornet on inside front-c; intro the Black Beauty (Green Hornet's car); painted-c 420.00 1260.00 4200.00
2-Early issues based on radio adventures 162.00 487.00 1300.00
3 131.00 394.00 1050.00

Green Lama #6 © Spark Pub.

THE GREEN LAMA
SMASHES A PLOT AGAINST AMERICA!

Green Lantern (1st series) #31 © DC

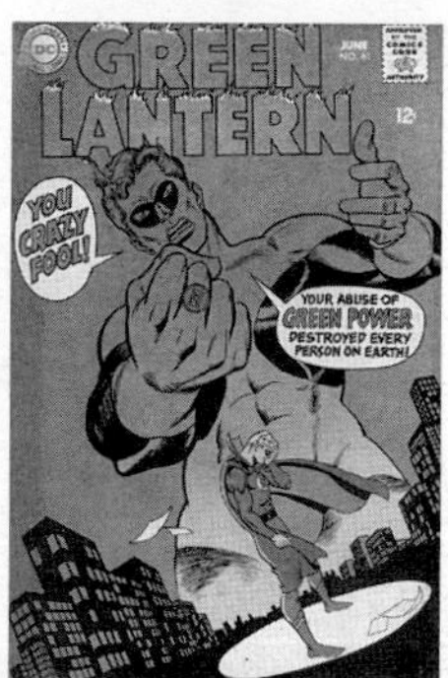

Green Lantern (2nd series) #61 © DC

4-6: 6-(8/41) 100.00 300.00 800.00
7 (6/42)-Origin The Zebra & begins; Robin Hood, Spirit of '76, Blonde Bomber & Mighty Midgets begin; new logo 87.00 262.00 700.00
8,10 75.00 225.00 600.00
9-Kirby-c 94.00 281.00 740.00
11,12-Mr. Q in both 75.00 225.00 600.00
13-1st Nazi-c; shows Hitler poster on-c 81.00 244.00 650.00
14-19 56.00 169.00 450.00
20-Classic-c 59.00 178.00 475.00
21-23,25-30 45.00 135.00 360.00
24-Sci-Fi-c 47.00 142.00 380.00
31-The Man in Black Called Fate begins (11-12/45, early app.) 46.00 139.00 370.00
32-36 40.00 120.00 300.00
37,38: Shock Gibson app. by Powell. 37-S&K Kid Adonis reprinted from Stuntman #3. 38-Kid Adonis app. 40.00 120.00 300.00
39-Stuntman story by S&K 47.00 141.00 375.00
40-47: 42-47-Kerry Drake in all. 45-Boy Explorers on-c only. 46- "Case of the Marijuana Racket" cover/story; Kerry Drake app. 32.00 96.00 225.00
NOTE: ***Fuje*** *a-23, 24, 26.* ***Henkle*** *c-7-9.* ***Kubert*** *a-20, 30.* ***Powell*** *a-7-10, 12, 14, 16-21, 30, 31(2), 32(3), 33, 34(3), 35, 36, 37(2), 38.* ***Robinson*** *a-27.* ***Schomburg*** *c-15, 17-23. Kirbyish c-7, 15. Bondage c-8, 14, 18, 26, 36.*

GREEN JET COMICS, THE (See Comic Books, Series 1)

GREEN LAMA (Also see Comic Books, Series 1, Daring Adventures #17 & Prize Comics #7)
Spark Publications/Prize No. 7 on: Dec, 1944 - No. 8, Mar, 1946
1-Intro. Lt. Hercules & The Boy Champions; Mac Raboy-c/a #1-8 125.00 375.00 1000.00
2-Lt. Hercules borrows the Human Torch's powers for one panel 72.00 216.00 575.00
3-6,8: 4-Dick Tracy take-off in Lt. Hercules story by H. L. Gold (sci-fiction writer).
5-Lt. Hercules story; Little Orphan Annie, Smilin' Jack & Snuffy Smith take-off (5/45) 59.00 178.00 475.00
7-X-mas-c; Raboy craft tint-c/a (note: a small quantity of NM copies surfaced) 41.00 124.00 330.00
NOTE: ***Robinson*** *a-3-5, 8. Roussos a-8. Formerly a pulp hero who began in 1940.*

GREEN LANTERN (1st Series) (See All-American, All Flash Quarterly, All Star Comics, The Big All-American & Comic Cavalcade)
National Periodical Publications/All-American: Fall, 1941 - No. 38, May-June, 1949 (#1-18 are quarterly)

	GD2.0	FN6.0	VF8.0	NM9.4
1-Origin retold; classic Purcell-c	2,333.00	7,000.00	14,000.00	28,000.00

	GD2.0	FN6.0	NM9.4
2-1st book-length story	600.00	1800.00	6000.00
3-Classic German war-c by Mart Nodell	430.00	1290.00	4300.00
4-Green Lantern & Doiby Dickles join the Army	355.00	10650.00	3200.00
5	250.00	750.00	2000.00
6,8: 8-Hop Harrigan begins; classic-c	200.00	600.00	1600.00
7-Robot-c.	219.00	657.00	1750.00
9,10: 10-Origin/1st app. Vandal Savage	181.00	543.00	1450.00
11-17,19,20: 12-Origin/1st app. Gambler	126.00	378.00	1070.00
18-Christmas-c	138.00	414.00	1175.00
21-26,28-30: 30-Origin/1st app. Streak the Wonder Dog by Toth (2-3/48)	115.00	345.00	975.00
27-Origin/1st app. Sky Pirate	118.00	354.00	1000.00
31-35: 35-Kubert-c. 35-38-New logo	97.00	291.00	825.00
36-38: 37-Sargon the Sorcerer app.	118.00	354.00	1000.00

NOTE: *Book-length stories #2-7.* ***Mayer/Moldoff*** *c-9.* ***Mayer/Purcell*** *c-8.* ***Purcell*** *c-1.* ***Mart Nodell*** *c-2, 3, 7.* ***Paul Reinman*** *c-11, 12, 15-22.* ***Toth*** *a-28, 30, 31, 34-38; c-28, 30, 34p, 36-38p. Cover to #8 says Fall while the indicia says Summer Issue. Streak the Wonder Dog c-30 (w/Green Lantern), 34, 36, 38.*

GREEN LANTERN (See Action Comics Weekly, Adventure Comics, Brave & the Bold, DC Special, DC Special Series, Flash, Guy Gardner, Guy Gardner Reborn, Justice League of America, Parallax: Emerald Night, Showcase, Showcase '93 #12 & Tales of The...Corps)

GREEN LANTERN (2nd Series)(Green Lantern Corps #206 on)
(See Showcase #22-24)
National Periodical Publ./DC Comics: 7-8/60 - No. 89, 4-5/72; No. 90, 8-9/76 - No. 205, 10/86

	GD2.0	FN6.0	VF8.0	NM9.4
1-(7-8/60)-Origin retold; Gil Kane-c/a continues; 1st app. Guardians of the Universe	200.00	600.00	1300.00	2800.00

	GD2.0	FN6.0	NM9.4
2-1st Pieface	58.00	174.00	700.00
3-Contains readers poll	36.00	108.00	400.00
4,5: 5-Origin/1st app. Hector Hammond	31.00	93.00	310.00
6-Intro Tomar-Re the alien G.L.	29.00	87.00	290.00
7-Origin/1st app. Sinestro (7-8/61)	25.00	75.00	250.00
8-10: 8-1st 5700 A.D. story; grey tone-c. 9-1st Jordan Brothers; last 10¢ issue	22.00	66.00	220.00
11,12	15.00	45.00	150.00
13-Flash x-over	18.00	54.00	180.00
14-20: 14-Origin/1st app. Sonar. 16-Origin & 1st app. Star Sapphire. 20-Flash x-over	13.00	39.00	130.00
21-30: 21-Origin & 1st app. Dr. Polaris. 23-1st Tattooed Man. 24-Origin & 1st app. Shark. 29-JLA cameo; 1st Blackhand	11.00	33.00	110.00
31-39: 37-1st app. Evil Star (villain)	9.00	27.00	90.00
40-1st app. Crisis (10/65); 2nd solo G.A. Green Lantern in Silver Age (see Showcase #55); origin The Guardians; Doiby Dickles app.	41.00	123.00	500.00
41-44,46-50: 42-Zatanna x-over. 43-Flash x-over	7.00	21.00	70.00
45-2nd S.A. app. G.A. Green Lantern in title (6/66)	13.00	39.00	130.00
51,53-58	5.25	15.75	52.00
52-G.A. Green Lantern x-over	7.50	22.50	75.00
59-1st app. Guy Gardner (3/68)	19.00	57.00	190.00
60,62-69: 69-Wood inks; last 12¢ issue	3.50	10.50	35.00
61-G.A. Green Lantern x-over	5.00	15.00	50.00
70-75	2.20	6.60	24.00
76-(4/70)-Begin Green Lantern/Green Arrow series (by Neal Adams #76-89) ends #122 (see Flash #217 for 2nd series)	16.00	48.00	175.00
77	4.75	14.00	52.00
78-80	3.80	11.50	42.00
81-84: 82-Wrightson-i(1 pg.). 83-G.L. reveals i.d. to Carol Ferris. 84-N. Adams/Wrightson-a(22 pgs.); last 15¢-c; partial photo-c	3.50	10.50	38.00
85,86-(52 pgs.)-Anti-drug issues. 86-G.A. Green Lantern-r; Toth-a	4.75	14.00	52.00
87-(52 pgs.): 2nd app. Guy Gardner (cameo); 1st app. John Stewart (12-1/71-72) (becomes 3rd Green Lantern in #182)	2.90	8.70	32.00
88-(2-3/72, 52 pgs.)-Unpubbed G.A. Green Lantern story; Green Lantern-r/Showcase #23. N. Adams-c/a (1 pg.)	1.40	4.20	14.00
89-(4-5/72, 52 pgs.)-G.A. Green Lantern-r; Green Lantern & Green Arrow move to Flash #217 (2nd team-up series)	2.00	6.00	20.00
90 (8-9/76)-Begin 3rd Green Lantern/Green Arrow team-up series; Mike Grell-c/a begins, ends #111	1.10	3.30	11.00
91-99		2.00	6.00
100-(1/78, Giant)-1st app. Air Wave II	1.20	3.60	12.00
101-107,111,113-115,117-119: 107-1st Tales of the G.L. Corps story			5.00
108-110-(44 pgs)-G.A. Green Lantern back-ups in each. 111-Origin retold; G.A. Green Lantern app.			5.00
112-G.A. Green Lantern origin retold	1.10	3.30	11.00
116-1st app. Guy Gardner as a G.L. (5/79)	2.50	7.40	27.00
120-122,124-150: 22-Last Green Lantern/Green Arrow team-up. 130-132-Tales of the G.L. Corps. 132-Adam Strange series begins, ends147. 136,137-1st app. Citadel; Space Ranger app. 141-1st app. Omega Men (6/81). 142,143-Omega Men app.;Perez-c. 144-Omega Men cameo. 148-Tales of the G.L. Corps begins, ends #173. 150-Anniversary issue, 52 pgs.; no G.L. Corps			3.00
123-Green Lantern back to solo action; 2nd app. Guy Gardner as Green Lantern			4.00
151-180,183,184,186,187: 159-Origin Evil Star. 160,161-Omega Men app.			2.50
181,182,185,188: 181-Hal Jordan resigns as G.L. 182-John Stewart becomes new G.L.; origin recap of Hal Jordan as G.L. 185-Origin new G.L. (John Stewart).188-I.D. revealed; Alan Moore back-up scripts.			2.50

189-193,196-199,201-205: 191-Re-intro Star Sapphire (cameo). 192-Re-intro Star Sapphire (1st full app.). 194,198-Crisis x-over. 199-Hal Jordan returns

Green Lantern (3rd series) #53 © DC

Green Lantern (3rd series) #119 © DC

Green Mask #7 © FOX

as a member of G.L. Corps (3 G.L.s now). 201-Green Lantern Corps begins (is cover title, says premiere issue) 2.50
194-Hal Jordan/Guy Gardner battle; Guardians choose Guy Gardner to become new Green Lantern 4.00
195-Guy Gardner becomes Green Lantern; Crisis x-over 1.10 3.30 9.00
200-Double-size 4.00
Annual 1 (Listed as Tales Of The Green Lantern Corps Annual 1)
Annual 2,3 (See Green Lantern Corps Annual #2,3) 3.00
Special 1 (1988), 2 (1989)-(Both $1.50, 52 pgs.) 2.50
NOTE: ***N. Adams*** *a-76, 77-87p, 89; c-63, 76-89.* ***M. Anderson*** *a-137i.* ***Austin*** *a-93i, 94i, 171i.* ***Chaykin*** *c-196.* ***Greene*** *a-39-49i, 58-63i; c-54-58i.* ***Grell*** *a-90-106, 108-111; c-90-106, 108-112.* ***Heck*** *a-120-122p.* ***Infantino*** *a-137p, 145-147p, 151, 152p.* ***Gil Kane*** *a-1-49p, 50-57, 58-61p, 68-75p, 85p(r), 87p(r), 88p(r), 156, 177, 184p; c-1-52, 54-61p, 67-75, 123, 154, 156, 165-171, 177, 184.* ***Newton*** *a-148p, 149p, 181.* ***Perez*** *c-132p, 141-144.* ***Sekowsky*** *a-65p, 170p.* ***Simonson*** *c-200.* ***Sparling*** *a-63p.* ***Starlin*** *c-129, 133.* ***Staton*** *a-117p, 123-127p, 128, 129-131p, 132-139, 140p, 141-146, 147p, 148-150, 151-155p; c-107p, 117p, 135(i), 136p, 145p, 146, 147, 148-152p, 155p.* ***Toth*** *a-86r, 171p.* ***Tuska*** *a-166-168p, 170p.*

GREEN LANTERN (3rd Series)
DC Comics: June, 1990 - Present ($1.00/$1.25/$1.50/$1.75/$1.95/$1.99)

1-Hal Jordan, John Stewart & Guy Gardner return; Batman app. 5.00
2-26: 9-12-Guy Gardner solo story. 13-(52 pgs.). 18-Guy Gardner solo story. 19-($1.75, 52 pgs.)-50th anniversary issue; Mart Nodell (original G.A. artist) part-p on G.A. Gr. Lantern; G. Kane-c. 25-($1.75, 52 pgs.)-Hal Jordan/Guy Gardner battle 4.00
27-45,47: 30,31-Gorilla Grodd-c/story(see Flash #69). 38,39-Adam Strange-c/story. 42-Deathstroke-c/s. 47-Green Arrow x-over 3.00
46,48,49,50: 46-Superman app. cont'd in Superman #82. 48-Emerald Twilight part 1. 50-($2.95, 52 pgs.)-Glow-in-the-dark-c 2.40 6.00
0, 51-62: 51-1st app. New Green Lantern (Kyle Rayner) with new costume. 53-Superman-c/story. 55-(9/94)-Zero Hour. 0-(10/94). 56-(11/94) 4.00
63,64-Kyle Rayner vs. Hal Jordan. 4.00
65-80,82-92: 63-Begin $1.75-c. 65-New Titans app. 66,67-Flash app. 71-Batman & Robin app. 72-Shazam!-c/app. 73-Wonder Woman-c/app. 73-75-Adam Strange app. 76,77-Green Arrow x-over. 80-Final Night x-over. 87-JLA app. 91-Genesis x-over. 92-Green Arrow x-over. 3.00
81-(Regular Ed.)-Memorial for Hal Jordan (Parallax); most DC heroes app. 5.00
81-($3.95, Deluxe Edition)-Embossed prism-c 2.40 6.00
93-99: 93-Begin $1.95-c; Deadman app. 94-Superboy app. 95-Starlin-a(p). 98,99-Legion of Super-Heroes-c/app. 2.50
100-($2.95) Two covers (Jordan & Rayner); vs. Sinestro 5.00
101-119: Hal Jordan-c/app. 103-JLA-c/app. 104-Green Arrow app. 3.00
#1,000,000 (11/98) 853rd Century x-over 2.00
Annual 1-3: ('92-'94, 68 pgs.)-1-Eclipso app. 2 -Intro Nightblade. 3-Elseworlds story 3.50
Annual 4 (1995, $3.50)-Year One story 4.00
Annual 5,7,8: ('96, '98, '99,$2.95)-5-Legends of the Dead Earth. 7-Ghosts; Wrightson-c. 9-JLApe; Art Adams-c 3.00
Annual 6 (1997, $3.95)-Pulp Heroes story 5.00
...80 Page Giant (12/98, $4.95) Stories by various 5.00
...80 Page Giant 2 (6/99, $4.95) Team-ups 5.00
...3-D #1 (12/98, $3.95) Jeanty-a 4.00
...: A New Dawn TPB (1998, $9.95)-r/#50-55 10.00
...: Baptism of Fire TPB (1999, $12.95)-r/#59,66,67,70-75 13.00
...: Emerald Knights TPB (1998, $12.95)-r/Hal Jordan's return 13.00
...: Emerald Twilight nn (1994, $5.95)-r/#48-50 6.00
...: Ganthet's Tale nn (1992, $5.95, 68 pgs.)-Silver foil stamped logo; Larry Niven scripts; Byrne-c/a 6.00
.../Green Arrow Collection, Vol. 2-r/Gl #84-87,89 & Flash #217-219 & GL/GA #5-7 by O'Neil/Adams/Wrightson 13.00
...Plus 1 (12/1996, $2.95)-The Ray & Polaris-c/app. 3.00
...Secret Files 1,2- (7/98-6/99, $4.95)1- Origin stories & profiles. 2-Grell-c 5.00
...The Road Back nn (1992, $8.95)-r/1-8 w/covers 9.00
NOTE: ***Staton*** *a(p)-9-12; c-9-12.*

GREEN LANTERN (See Tangent Comics/ Green Lantern)

GREEN LANTERN ANNUAL NO. 1, 1963
DC Comics: 1998 ($4.95, one-shot)

1-Reprints Golden Age & Silver Age stories in 1963-style 80 pg. Giant format; new Gil Kane sketch art 5.00

GREEN LANTERN CORPS, THE (Formerly Green Lantern; see Tales of...)
DC Comics: No. 206, Nov, 1986 - No. 224, May, 1988

206-223: 220,221-Millennium tie-ins 2.50
224-Double-size last issue 3.00
...Corps Annual 2,3- (12/86,8/87) 1-Formerly Tales of ...Annual #1; Alan Moore scripts. 3-Indicia says Green Lantern Annual #3; Moore scripts;Byrne-a 2.50
NOTE: ***Austin*** *a-Annual 3i.* ***Gil Kane*** *a-223, 224p; c-223, 224, Annual 2.* ***Russell*** *a-Annual 3i.* ***Staton*** *a-207-213p, 217p, 221p, 222p, Annual 3; c-207-213p, 217p, 221p, 222p.* ***Willingham*** *a-213p, 219p, 220p, 218p, 219p, Annual 2, 3p; c-218p, 219p.*

GREEN LANTERN CORPS QUARTERLY
DC Comics: Summer, 1992 - No. 8, Spring, 1994 ($2.50/$2.95, 68 pgs.)

1-8: 1-G.A. Green Lantern story; Staton-a(p). 2-G.A. G.L.-c/story; Austin-c(i); Gulacy-a(p). 3-G.A. G.L. story. 4-Austin-i. 7-Painted-c; Tim Vigil-a. 8-Lobo-c/s 3.00

GREEN LANTERN: EMERALD DAWN (Also see Emerald Dawn)
DC Comics: Dec, 1989 - No. 6, May, 1990 ($1.00, limited series)

1-Origin retold; Giffen plots in all 5.00
2-6 4.00

GREEN LANTERN: EMERALD DAWN II (Emerald Dawn II #1 & 2)
DC Comics: Apr, 1991 - No. 6, Sept, 1991 ($1.00, limited series)

1-6 2.00

GREEN LANTERN/FLASH: FASTER FRIENDS (See Flash/Green Lantern...)
DC Comics: 1997 ($4.95, limited series)

1-Marz-s 5.00

GREEN LANTERN GALLERY
DC Comics: Dec, 1996 ($3.50, one-shot)

1-Wraparound-c; pin-ups by various 3.50

GREEN LANTERN/GREEN ARROW (Also see The Flash #217)
DC Comics: Oct, 1983 - No. 7, April, 1984 (52-60 pgs.)

1-7- r- Green Lantern #7689 4.00
NOTE: ***Neal Adams*** *r-1-7; c-1-4.* ***Wrightson*** *r-4, 5.*

GREEN LANTERN: MOSAIC (Also see Cosmic Odyssey #2)
DC Comics: June, 1992 - No. 18, Nov, 1993 ($1.25)

1-18: Featuring John Stewart. 1-Painted-c by Cully Hamner 2.00

GREEN LANTERN/SENTINEL: HEART OF DARKNESS
DC Comics: Mar, 1998 - No. 3, May, 1998 ($1.95, limited series)

1-3-Marz-s/Pelletier-a 3.00

GREEN LANTERN/SILVER SURFER: UNHOLY ALLIANCES
DC Comics: 1995 ($4.95, one-shot)(Prelude to DC Versus Marvel)

nn-Hal Jordan app. 5.00

GREEN LANTERN: THE NEW CORPS
DC Comics:1999 - No. 2, 1999 ($4.95, limited series)

1,2-Kyle recruits new GL's; Eaton-a 5.00

GREEN MASK, THE (See Mystery Men)
Summer, 1940 - No. 9, 2/42; No. 10, 8/44 - No. 11, 11/44;
Fox Features Syndicate: V2#1, Spring, 1945 - No. 6, 10-11/46

V1#1-Origin The Green Mask & Domino; reprints/Mystery Men #1-3,5-7; Lou Fine-c 355.00 1067.00 3200.00
2-Zanzibar The Magician by Tuska 131.00 393.00 1050.00
3-Powell-a; Marijuana story 81.00 243.00 650.00
4-Navy Jones begins, ends #6 66.00 198.00 525.00
5 52.00 156.00 420.00
6-The Nightbird begins, ends #9; bondage/torture-c 43.00 128.00 340.00
7-9: 9(2/42)-Becomes The Bouncer #10(nn) on? & Green Mask #10 on 39.00 118.00 275.00
10,11: 10-Origin One Round Hogan & Rocket Kelly

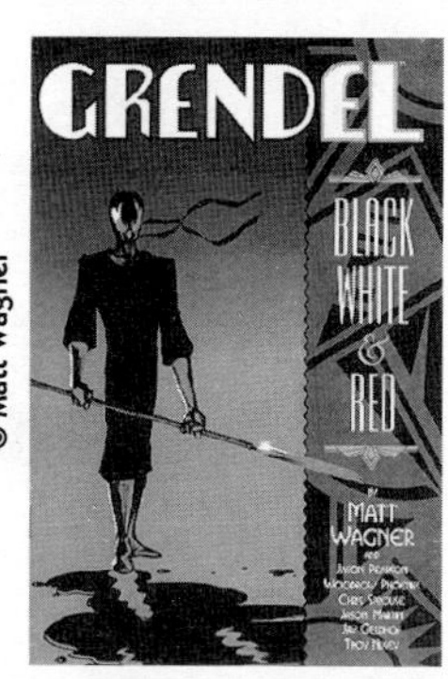

Grendel: Black, White and Red #4 © Matt Wagner

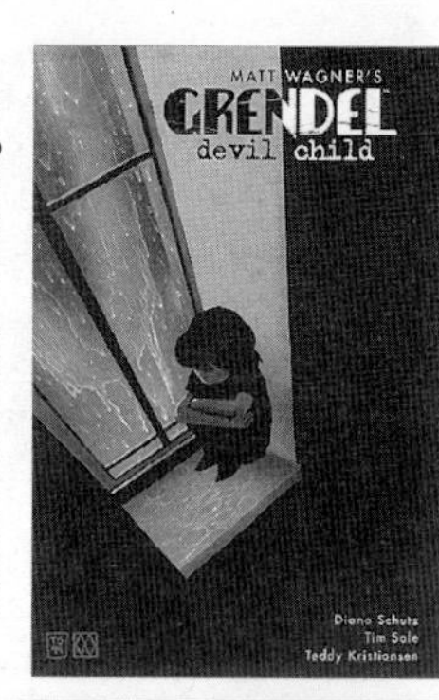

Grendel: Devil's Child #1 © Matt Wagner

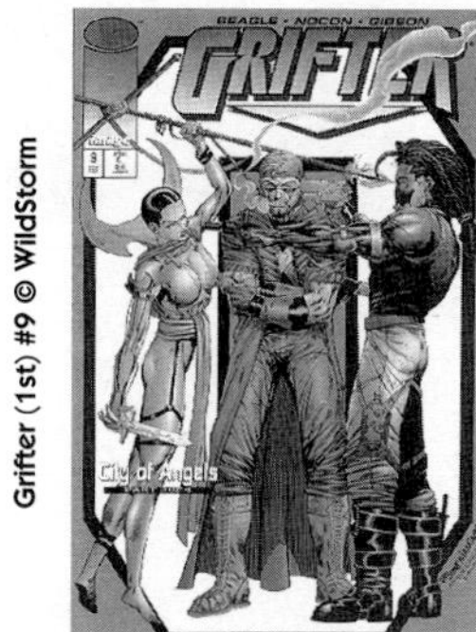

Grifter (1st) #9 © WildStorm

GD2.0 FN6.0 NM9.4

	30.00	90.00	210.00
V2#1	23.00	69.00	160.00
2-6	20.00	60.00	140.00

GREEN PLANET, THE
Charlton Comics: 1962 (one-shot) (12¢)

nn-Giordano-c; sci-fi 6.00 18.00 60.00

GREEN TEAM (See Cancelled Comic Cavalcade & 1st Issue Special)

GREETINGS FROM SANTA (See March of Comics No. 48)

GRENDEL (Also see Primer #2 and Mage)
Comico: Mar, 1983 - No. 3, Feb, 1984 ($1.50, B&W)(#1 has indicia to Skrog #1)

1-Origin Hunter Rose 9.00 27.00 100.00
2,3: 2-Origin Argent 7.25 22.00 80.00

GRENDEL
Comico: Oct, 1986 - No. 40, Feb, 1991 ($1.50/$1.95/$2.50, mature)

1 2.40 6.00
1,2: 2nd printings 2.00
2-40: 4-Dave Stevens-c(i). 13-15-Ken Steacy-c. 16-Re-intro Mage (series begins, ends #19). 24-25, 27-28,30-31-Snyder-c/a; 26,29-Snyder-i 3.00
Devil by the Deed (Graphic Novel, 10/86, $5.95, 52 pgs.)-r/Grendel back-ups/ Mage 6-14; Alan Moore intro. 1.00 2.80 7.00
Devil's Legacy ($14.95, 1988, Graphic Novel) 1.85 5.50 15.00
Devil's Vagary (10/87, B&W & red)-No price; included in Comico Collection 1.50 4.50 12.00

GRENDEL (Title series): **Dark Horse Comics**

--BLACK, WHITE, AND RED, 11/98 - No. 4, 2/99 ($3.95, anthology)
1-Wagner-s in all. Art by Sale, Leon and others 5.00
2-4: 2-Mack, Chadwick-a. 3-Allred, Kristensen-a. 4-Pearson, Sprouse-a 4.00

--CLASSICS, 7/95 - 8/95 ($3.95,mature) 1,2-reprints; new Wagner-c 4.00

--CYCLE, 10/95 ($5.95) 1-nn-history of Grendel by M. Wagner & others 6.00

--DEVIL BY THE DEED, 7/93 ($3.95, varnish-c) 1-nn-M. Wagner-c/a/scripts; r/Grendel back-ups from Mage #6-14 4.00
Reprint (12/97, $3.95) w/pin-ups by various 4.00

--DEVIL CHILD, 6/99 - No. 2, 7/99 ($2.95, mature) 1,2-Sale & Kristiansen-a/ Diane Schutz-s 3.00

--DEVIL QUEST, 11/95 ($4.95) 1-nn-Prequel to Batman/Grendel II; M. Wagner story & art; r/back-up story from Grendel Tales series. 5.00

--DEVILS AND DEATHS, 10/94 - 11/94 ($2.95, mature) 1,2 3.00

--TALES: DEVIL'S CHOICES, 3/95 - 6/95 ($2.95, mature) 1-4 3.00

--TALES: FOUR DEVILS, ONE HELL, 8/93 - 1/94 ($2.95, mature)
1-6-Wagner painted-c 3.00
TPB (12/94, $17.95) r/#1-6 18.00

--TALES: HOMECOMING, 12/94 - 2/95 ($2.95, mature) 1-3 3.00

--TALES: THE DEVIL IN OUR MIDST, 5/94 - 9/5 ($2.95, mature) 1-5-Wagner painted-c. in all 3.00

--TALES: THE DEVIL MAY CARE, 12/95 - '96 ($2.95, mature) 1-6-Terry LaBan scripts. 5-Batman/Grendel II preview 3.00

--TALES: THE DEVIL'S APPRENTICE, 9/97 - No. 3, 11/97 ($2.95, mature) 1-3 3.00

--TALES: THE DEVIL'S HAMMER, 2/94 - 4/94 ($2.95, mature) 1-3 3.00

GRENDEL: WAR CHILD
Dark Horse Comics: Aug, 1992 - No. 10, 1993 ($2.50, limited series, mature)

1-9: 1-4-Bisley painted-c; Wagner-i & scripts in all 2.50
10-($3.50, 52 pgs.) Wagner-c 3.50
Limited Edition Hardcover ($99.95) 100.00

GREYFRIARS BOBBY (Disney)(Movie)
Dell Publishing Co.: No. 1189, Nov, 1961 (one-shot)

Four Color 1189-Photo-c (scarce) 6.40 19.20 70.00

GREYLORE

GD2.0 FN6.0 NM9.4

Sirius: 12/85 - No. 5, Sept, 1986 ($1.50/$1.75, high quality paper)

1-5: Bo Hampton-a in all 2.00

GRIFFIN, THE
DC Comics: 1991 - No. 6, 1992 ($4.95, limited series, 52 pgs.)

Book 1-6: Matt Wagner painted-c 5.00

GRIFTER (Also see Team 7 & WildC.A.T.S)
Image Comics (WildStorm Prod.): May, 1995 - No. 10, Mar, 1996 ($1.95)

1 ($1.95, Newsstand)-WildStorm Rising Pt. 5 3.00
1-10:1 ($2.50, Direct)-WildStorm Rising Pt. 5, bound-in trading card 3.00

GRIFTER
Image Comics (WildStorm Prod.): V2#1, July, 1996 - No. 14, Aug, 1997 ($2.50)

V2#1-14: Steven Grant scripts 3.00

GRIFTER AND THE MASK
Dark Horse Comics: Sept, 1996 - No. 2, Oct, 1996 ($2.50, limited series) (1st Dark Horse Comics/Image x-over)

1,2: Steve Seagle scripts 2.50

GRIFTER/BADROCK (Also see WildC.A.T.S & Youngblood)
Image Comics (Extreme Studios): Oct, 1995 - No.2, Nov, 1995 ($2.50, unfinished limited series)

1,2: 2-Flip book w/Badrock #2 2.50

GRIFTER: ONE SHOT
Image Comics (WildStorm Productions): Jan, 1995 ($4.95, one-shot)

1-Flip-c 5.00

GRIFTER/SHI
Image Comics (WildStorm Productions): Apr, 1996 - No. 2, May, 1996 ($2.95, limited series)

1,2: 1-Jim Lee-c/a(p); Travis Charest-a(p). 2-Billy Tucci-c/a(p); Travis Charest-a(p) 3.00

GRIM GHOST, THE
Atlas/Seaboard Publ.: Jan, 1975 - No. 3, July, 1975

1-3: 1-Origin. 3-Heath-c 4.00

GRIMJACK (Also see Demon Knight & Starslayer)
First Comics: Aug, 1984 - No. 81, Apr, 1991 ($1.00/$1.95/$2.25)

1-John Ostrander scripts & Tim Truman-c/a begins. 3.00
2-25: 20-Sutton-c/a begins. 22-Bolland-a. 2.25
26-2nd color Teenage Mutant Ninja Turtles 2.25
27-74,76-81 (Later issues $1.95, $2.25): 30-Dynamo Joe x-over; 31-Mandrake-c/a begins. 73,74-Kelley Jones-a 2.25
75-($5.95, 52 pgs.)-Fold-out map; coated stock 2.40 6.00
NOTE: ***Truman** c/a-1-17.*

GRIMJACK CASEFILES
First Comics: Nov, 1990 - No. 5, Mar, 1991 ($1.95, limited series)

1-5 Reprints 1st stories from Starslayer #10 on 2.00

GRIMM'S GHOST STORIES (See Dan Curtis)
Gold Key/Whitman No. 55 on: Jan, 1972 - No. 60, June, 1982 (Painted-c #1-42,44,46-56)

1	2.50	7.50	22.00
2-5,8: 5,8-Williamson-a	1.50	4.50	12.00
6,7,9,10	1.10	3.30	7.00
11-20	1.00	2.80	7.00
21-42,45-54: 32,34-Reprints. 45-Photo-c			5.00
43,44,55-60: 43,44-(52 pgs.). 43-Photo-c. 59-Williamson-a(r/#8)	1.00	2.80	7.00
Mini-Comic No. 1 (3-1/4x6-1/2", 1976)			5.00

NOTE: *Reprints-#32?, 34?, 39, 43, 44, 47?, 53; 56-60(1/3).* ***Bolle*** *a-8, 17, 22-25, 27, 29(2), 33, 35, 41, 43r, 45(2), 48(2), 50, 52.* ***Celardo*** *a-17, 26, 28p, 30, 31, 43(2), 45.* ***Lopez*** *a-24, 25.* ***McWilliams*** *a-33, 44r, 48, 54(2), 57, 58.* ***Win Mortimer*** *a-31, 33, 49, 51, 55, 56, 58(2), 59, 60.* ***Roussos*** *a-25, 30.* ***Sparling*** *a-23, 24, 28, 30, 31, 33, 43r, 44, 45, 51(2), 52, 56, 58, 59(2), 60.* ***Spiegle*** *a-44.*

GRIN (The American Funny Book) (Satire)

Groo the Wanderer #117 © Sergio Aragonés

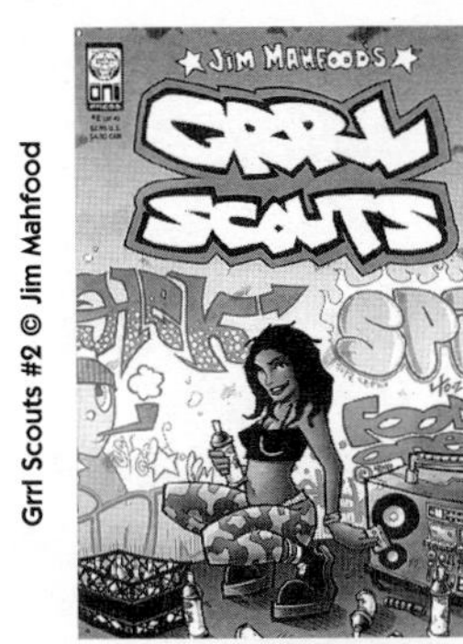

Grrl Scouts #2 © Jim Mahfood

Gunfighter #8 © WMG

GD2.0 FN6.0 NM9.4

APAG House Pubs: Nov, 1972 - No. 3, April, 1973 (Magazine, 52 pgs.)
1-Parodies-Godfather, All in the Family 2.50 7.50 20.00
2,3 1.75 5.25 14.00

GRIN & BEAR IT (See Gags)
Dell Publishing Co.: No. 28, 1941
Large Feature Comic 28 9.50 29.00 105.00

GRIPS (Extreme violence)
Silverwolf Comics: Sept, 1986 - No. 4, Dec, 1986 ($1.50, B&W, mature)
1-Tim Vigil-c/a in all 4.00
2-4 3.00

GRIT GRADY (See Holyoke One-Shot No. 1)

GROO (Sergio Aragones'...)
Image Comics: Dec, 1994 - No. 12, Dec, 1995 ($1.95)
1-12: 2-Indicia reads #1, Jan, 1995; Aragones-c/a in all 3.00

GROO (Sergio Aragones'...)
Dark Horse Comics: Jan, 1998 - No. 4, Apr, 1998 ($2.95)
1-4: Aragones-c/a in all 4.00

GROO CARNIVAL, THE
Marvel Comics (Epic Comics): Dec, 1991 ($8.95, trade paperback)
nn-Reprints Groo #9-12 by Aragones 1.10 3.30 9.00

GROO CHRONICLES, THE (Sergio Aragones)
Marvel Comics (Epic Comics): June, 1989 - No. 6, Feb, 1990 ($3.50)
Book 1-6: Reprints early Pacific issues 3.50

GROO SPECIAL
Eclipse Comics: Oct, 1984 ($2.00, 52 pgs., Baxter paper)
1-Aragones-c/a 1.75 5.25 14.00

GROO THE WANDERER (See Destroyer Duck #1, Marvel Graphic Novel #32 & & Starslayer #5)
Pacific Comics: Dec, 1982 - No. 8, Apr, 1984
1-Aragones-c/a(p) in all; Aragones biog., photo 2.25 6.75 18.00
2-8: 5-Deluxe paper (1.00-c) 1.50 4.50 12.00

GROO THE WANDERER (Sergio Aragones'...)
Marvel Comics (Epic Comics): March, 1985 - No. 120, Jan, 1995
1-Aragones-c/a in all 1.00 3.00 8.00
2 5.00
3-10 4.00
11-20,50-($1.50, double size) 3.00
21-49,51-99,101-120: 87-direct sale only, high quality paper 2.50
100-($2.95, 52 pgs.) 4.00
Marvel Graphic Novel 32: Death of Groo 1.50 4.50 12.00
Death of Groo 2nd printing ($5.95) 6.00
Groo Garden, The (4/94, $10.95)-r/25-28 11.00

GROOVY (Cartoon Comics - not CCA approved)
Marvel Comics Group: March, 1968 - No. 3, July, 1968
1-Monkees, Ringo Starr, Sonny & Cher, Mamas & Papas photos 7.00 21.00 70.00
2,3 4.80 14.40 48.00

GROSS POINT
DC Comics: Aug, 1997 - No. 14, Aug, 1998 ($2.50)
1-14: 1-Waid/Augustyn-s 2.50

GROUP LARUE, THE
Innovation Publishing: 1989 - No. 4, 1990 ($1.95, mini-series)
1-4-By Mike Baron 2.00

GRRL SCOUTS (Jim Mahfood's...)
Oni Press: Mar,1999 - No. 4, ($2.95, B&W, limited series)
1,2-Mahfood-s/c/a 3.00

GUADALCANAL DIARY (See American Library)

GD2.0 FN6.0 NM9.4

GUARDIANS OF JUSTICE & THE O-FORCE
Shadow Comics: 1990 (no date) ($1.50, 7-1/2 x10-1/4)
1-Super-hero group 2.00

GUARDIANS OF METROPOLIS
DC Comics: Nov, 1995 - Feb, 1995 ($1.50, limited series)
1-4: 1-Superman & Granny Goodness app. 2.00

GUARDIANS OF THE GALAXY (Also see The Defenders #26, Marvel Presents #3, Marvel Super-Heroes #18, Marvel Two-In-One #5)
Marvel Comics: June, 1990 - No. 62, July, 1995 ($1.00/$1.25)
1-Valentino-c/a(p) begin. 3.00
2-16: 2-Zeck-c(i). 5-McFarlane-c(i). 7-Intro Malevolence (Mephisto's daughter); Perez-c(i). 8-Intro Rancor (descendant of Wolverine) in cameo. 9-1st full app. Rancor; Rob Liefeld-c(i). 10-Jim Lee-c(i). 13,14-1st app. Spirit of Vengeance (futuristic Ghost Rider). 14-Spirit of Vengeance vs. The Guardians. 15-Starlin-c(i). 16-($1.50, 52 pgs.)-Starlin-c(i) 2.00
17-24,26-38,40-47: 17-20-31st century Punishers storyline. 20-Last $1.00-c. 21-Rancor app. 22-Reintro Starhawk. 24-Silver Surfer-c/story; Ron Lim-c. 26-Origin retold. 27-28-Infinity War x-over; 27-Inhumans app. 43-Intro Wooden (son of Thor) 2.00
25-($2.50)-Prism foil-c; Silver Surfer/Galactus-c/s 2.50
25-($2.50)-Without foil-c; newsstand edition 2.50
39-($2.95, 52 pgs.)-Embossed & holo-grafx foil-c; Dr. Doom vs. Rancor 3.00
48,49,51-62: 48-bound-in trading card sheet 2.00
50-($2.00, 52 pgs.)-Newsstand edition 3.00
50-($2.95, 52 pgs.)-Collectors ed. w/foil embossed-c 3.00
Annual 1-4: ('91-'94, 68 pgs.)-1-2 pg. origin. 2-Spirit of Vengeance-c/story. 3-Bagged w/card 3.00

GUERRILLA WAR (Formerly Jungle War Stories)
Dell Publishing Co.: No. 12, July-Sept, 1965 - No. 14, Mar, 1966
12-14 1.85 5.50 15.00

GUFF
Dark Horse Comics: Apr, 1998 ($1.95, B&W)
1-Flip book; Aragonés-c 2.00

GUILTY (See Justice Traps the Guilty)

GULLIVER'S TRAVELS (See Dell Jr. Treasury No. 3)
Dell Publishing Co.: Sept-Nov, 1965 - No. 3, May, 1966
1 4.35 13.00 48.00
2,3 3.20 9.50 35.00

GUMBY'S SUMMER FUN SPECIAL
Comico: July, 1987 ($2.50)
1-Art Adams-c/a; B. Burden scripts 3.00

GUMBY'S WINTER FUN SPECIAL
Comico: Dec, 1988 ($2.50, 44 pgs.)
1-Art Adams-c/a 3.00

GUMPS, THE (See Merry Christmas..., Popular & Super Comics)
Dell Publ. Co./Bridgeport Herald Corp.: No. 73, 1945; Mar-Apr, 1947 - No. 5, Nov-Dec, 1947
Four Color 73 (Dell)(1945) 11.35 34.00 125.00
1 (3-4/47) 15.00 45.00 105.00
2-5 10.00 30.00 65.00

GUNFIGHTER (Fat & Slat #1-4) (Becomes Haunt of Fear #15 on)
E. C. Comics (Fables Publ. Co.): No. 5, Sum, 1948 - No. 14, Mar-Apr, 1950
5,6-Moon Girl in each 47.00 141.00 375.00
7-14: 14-Bondage-c 37.00 111.00 260.00
NOTE: ***Craig & H. C. Kiefer*** *art in most issues.* ***Craig*** *c-5, 6, 13, 14.* ***Feldstein/Craig*** *a-10.* ***Feldstein*** *a-7-11.* ***Harrison/Wood*** *a-13, 14.* ***Ingels*** *a-5-14; c-7-12.*

GUNFIGHTERS, THE
Super Comics (Reprints): 1963 - 1964
10-12,15,16,18: 10,11-r/Billy the Kid #s? 12-r/The Rider #5(Swift Arrow). 15-r/Straight Arrow #42; Powell-r. 16-r/Billy the Kid #?(Toby). 18-r/

Guns Against Gangsters #1 © NOVP

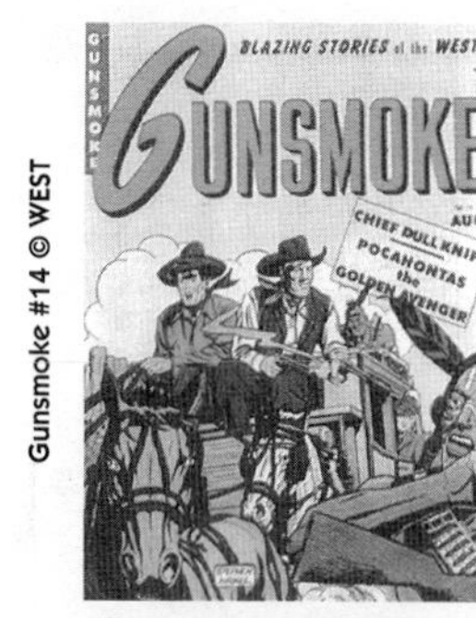

Gunsmoke #14 © WEST

Guy Gardner #8 © DC

GD2.0 FN6.0 NM9.4

The Rider #3; Severin-c 1.50 4.50 12.00

GUNFIGHTERS, THE (Formerly Kid Montana)
Charlton Comics: No. 51, 10/66 - No. 52, 10/67; No. 53, 6/79 - No. 85, 7/84

51,52 2.25 6.75 18.00
53,54,56:53,54-Williamson/Torres-r/Six Gun Heroes #47,49. 56-Williamson/Severin-c; Severin-r/Sheriff of Tombstone #1 2.40 6.00
55,57-80 4.00
81-84-Lower print run 5.00
85-S&K-r/1955 Bullseye 2.40 6.00

GUNFIRE (See Deathstroke Annual #2 & Showcase 94 #1,2)
DC Comics: May, 1994 - No. 13, June, 1995 ($1.75/$2.25)

1-5,0,6-13: 2-Ricochet-c/story. 5-(9/94). 0-(10/94). 6-(11/94) 2.25

GUN GLORY (Movie)
Dell Publishing Co.: No. 846, Oct, 1957 (one-shot)

Four Color 846-Toth-a, photo-c. 9.00 27.00 100.00

GUNHAWK, THE (Formerly Whip Wilson)(See Wild Western)
Marvel Comics/Atlas (MCI): No. 12, Nov, 1950 - No. 18, Dec, 1951
(Also see Two-Gun Western #5)

12 18.00 54.00 125.00
13-18: 13-Tuska-a. 16-Colan-a. 18-Maneely-c 13.00 39.00 90.00

GUNHAWKS (Gunhawk No. 7)
Marvel Comics Group: Oct, 1972 - No. 7, October, 1973

1,6: 1-Reno Jones, Kid Cassidy; Shores-c/a(p). 6-Kid Cassidy dies 1.75 5.25 14.00
2-5,7: 7-Reno Jones solo 1.25 3.75 10.00

GUNHED
Vix Comics: 1990 - No. 3, 1991? ($4.95, 7-1/8 x 9-1/8, 52 pgs., bi-monthly)

1-3: Japanese sci-fi based on 1991 movie 5.00

GUNMASTER (Becomes Judo Master #89 on)
Charlton Comics: 9/64 - No. 4, 1965; No. 84, 7/65 - No. 88, 3-4/66; No. 89, 10/67

V1#1 2.60 7.80 26.00
2,4, V5#84-86: 84-Formerly Six-Gun Heroes 2.25 6.75 18.00
V5#87-89 1.50 4.50 12.00
NOTE: *Vol. 5 was originally cancelled with #88 (3-4/66). #89 on, became Judo Master, then later in 1967, Charlton issued #89 as a Gunmaster one-shot.*

GUN RUNNER
Marvel Comics UK: Oct, 1993 - No. 6, Mar, 1994 ($1.75, limited series)

1-($2.75)-Polybagged w/4 trading cards; Spirits of Vengeance app. 2.75
2-6: 2-Ghost Rider & Blaze app. 2.00

GUNS AGAINST GANGSTERS (True-To-Life Romances #8 on)
Curtis Publications/Novelty Press: Sept-Oct, 1948 - No. 6, July-Aug, 1949; V2#1, Sept-Oct, 1949 - No. 2, 11-12/49

1-Toni & Greg Gayle begins by Schomburg; L.B. Cole-c 34.00 103.00 240.00
2-L.B. Cole-c 25.00 75.00 175.00
3-6, V2#1,2: 6-Toni Gayle-c 22.00 66.00 155.00
NOTE: ***L. B. Cole** c-1-6, V2#1, 2; a-1, 2, 3(2), 4-6.*

GUNSLINGER
Dell Publishing Co.: No. 1220, Oct-Dec, 1961 (one-shot)

Four Color 1220-Photo-c 8.00 25.00 90.00

GUNSLINGER (Formerly Tex Dawson...)
Marvel Comics Group: No. 2, Apr, 1973 - No. 3, June, 1973

2,3 1.75 5.25 14.00

GUNSMITH CATS: (Title series), **Dark Horse Comics**

--BAD TRIP (Manga), 6/98 - No. 6, 11/98 ($2.95, B&W) 1-6 3.00
--BEAN BANDIT (Manga), 1/99 - No. 9 ($2.95, B&W, limited series) 1-9 3.00
--GOLDIE VS. MISTY (Manga), 11/97 - No. 7, 5/98 ($2.95, B&W) 1-7 3.00

GD2.0 FN6.0 NM9.4

--THE RETURN OF GRAY (Manga), 8/96 - No. 7, 2/97 ($2.95, B&W) 1-7 3.00
--SHADES OF GRAY (Manga), 5/97 - No. 5, 9/97 ($2.95, B&W) 1-5 3.00

GUNSMOKE (Blazing Stories of the West)
Western Comics (Youthful Magazines): Apr-May, 1949 - No. 16, Jan, 1952

1-Gunsmoke & Masked Marvel begin by Ingels; Ingels bondage-c 40.00 120.00 310.00
2-Ingels-c/a(2) 28.00 84.00 195.00
3-Ingels bondage-c/a 22.00 66.00 155.00
4-6: Ingels-c 17.00 51.00 120.00
7-10 10.00 30.00 70.00
11-16: 15,16-Western/horror stories 9.15 27.00 55.00
NOTE: ***Stallman** a-11, 14. **Wildey** a-15, 16.*

GUNSMOKE (TV)
Dell Publishing Co./Gold Key (All have James Arness photo-c): No. 679, Feb, 1956 - No. 27, June-July, 1961; Feb, 1969 - No. 6, Feb, 1970

Four Color 679(#1) 15.00 45.00 160.00
Four Color 720,769,797,844 (#2-5),6(11-1/57-58),7 6.80 21.00 75.00
8,9,11,12-Williamson-a in all, 4 pgs. each 7.50 23.50 85.00
10-Williamson/Crandall-a, 4 pgs. 7.50 23.50 85.00
13-27 6.00 18.00 65.00
Gunsmoke Film Story (11/62-G.K. Giant) No. 30008-211 (scarce) 18.00 55.00 200.00
1 (Gold Key) 4.50 13.50 50.00
2-6('69-70) 2.60 7.80 26.00

GUNSMOKE TRAIL
Ajax-Farrell Publ./Four Star Comic Corp.: June, 1957 - No. 4, Dec, 1957

1 10.00 30.00 60.00
2-4 5.85 17.50 35.00

GUNSMOKE WESTERN (Formerly Western Tales of Black Rider)
Atlas Comics No. 32-35(CPS/NPI); Marvel No. 36 on: No. 32, Dec, 1955 - No. 77, July, 1963

32-Baker & Drucker-a 16.00 47.00 110.00
33,35,36-Williamson-a in each: 5,6 & 4 pgs. plus Drucker-a #33. 33-Kinstler-a? 13.00 39.00 90.00
34-Baker-a, 4 pgs.; Kirby-c 11.00 33.00 75.00
37-Davis-a(2); Williamson text illo 10.00 30.00 70.00
38,39: 39-Williamson text illo (unsigned) 8.35 25.00 50.00
40-Williamson/Mayo-a (4 pgs.) 10.00 30.00 60.00
41,42,45,46,48,49,52-54,57,58,60: 49,52-Kid from Texas story. 57-1st Two Gun Kid by Severin. 60-Sam Hawk app. in Kid Colt 5.85 17.50 35.00
43,44-Torres-a 5.85 17.50 35.00
47,51,59,61: 47,51,59-Kirby-a. 61-Crandall-a 7.00 21.00 42.00
50-Kirby, Crandall-a 8.00 24.00 48.00
55,56-Matt Baker-a 7.50 22.50 45.00
62-67,69,71-73,77-Kirby-a. 72-Origin Kid Colt 3.50 10.50 35.00
68,70,74-76 3.00 9.00 30.00
NOTE: ***Colan** a-35-37, 39, 72, 76. **Davis** a-37, 52, 54, 55; c-50, 54. **Ditko** a-66; c-56p. **Drucker** a-.32-34. **Heath** c-33. **Jack Keller** a-35, 40, 60, 72; c-72. **Kirby** a-47, 50, 51, 59, 62(3), 63-67, 69, 71, 73, 77; c-56(w/**Ditko**),57, 58, 60, 61(w/**Ayers**), 62, 63, 66, 68, 69, 71-77. **Robinson** a-35. **Severin** a-35, 59-61; c-34, 35, 39, 42, 43. **Tuska** a-34. **Wildey** a-10, 37, 42, 56, 57. Kid Colt in all. Two-Gun Kid in No. 57, 59, 60-63. Wyatt Earp in No. 45, 48, 49, 52, 54, 55, 58.*

GUNS OF FACT & FICTION (Also see A-1 Comics)
Magazine Enterprises: No. 13, 1948 (one-shot)

A-1 13-Used in **SOTI**, pg. 19; Ingels & J. Craig-a 29.00 86.00 200.00

GUNS OF THE DRAGON
DC Comics: Oct, 1998 - No. 4, Jan, 1999 ($2.50, limited series)

1-4-DCU in the 1920's; Enemy Ace & Bat Lash app. 2.50

GUY GARDNER (Guy Gardner: Warrior #17 on)(Also see Green Lantern #59)
DC Comics: Oct, 1992 - No. 44, July, 1996 ($1.25/$1.50/$1.75)

1-24,0,26-30: 1-Staton-c/a(p) begins. 6-Guy vs. Hal Jordan. 8-Vs. Lobo-c/story. 5-JLA x-over, begin $1.50-c. 18-Begin 4-part Emerald Fallout story; splash page x-over GL #50. 18-21-Vs. Hal Jordan. 24-(9/94)-Zero Hour.

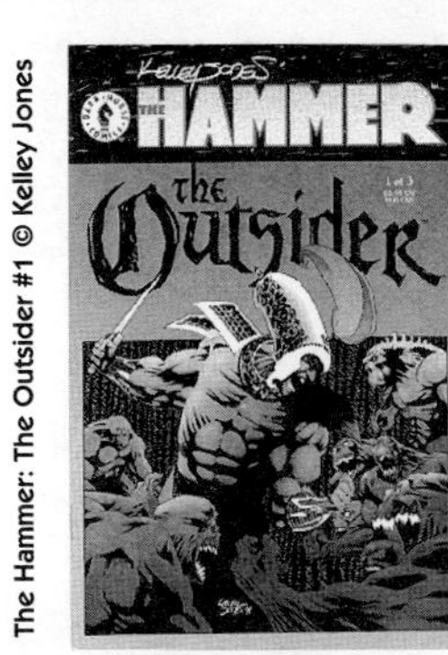

The Hammer: The Outsider #1 © Kelley Jones

Hand of Fate #9 © ACE

Hangman Comics #2 © MLJ Magazines

GD2.0 FN6.0 NM9.4

0-(10/94) 2.50
25 (11/94, $2.50, 52 pgs.) 3.00
29 ($2.95)-Gatefold-c 3.50
29-Variant-c (Edward Hopper's Nighthawks) 2.50
31-44: 31-$1.75-c begins. 40-Gorilla Grodd-c/app. 44-Parallax-app. (1 pg.) 2.50
Annual 1 (1995, $3.50)-Year One story 4.00
Annual 2 (1996, $2.95)-Legends of the Dead Earth story 3.00

GUY GARDNER REBORN
DC Comics: 1992 - Book 3, 1992 ($4.95, limited series)
1-3: Staton-c/a(p). 1-Lobo-c/cameo. 2,3-Lobo-c/s 5.00

GYPSY COLT
Dell Publishing Co.: No. 568, June, 1954 (one-shot)
Four Color 568--Movie 3.60 11.00 40.00

GYRO GEARLOOSE (See Dynabrite Comics, Walt Disney's C&S #140 & Walt Disney Showcase #18)
Dell Publishing Co.: No. 1047, Nov-Jan/1959-60 - May-July, 1962 (Disney)
Four Color 1047 (No. 1)-All Barks-c/a 18.00 55.00 200.00
Four Color 1095,1184-All by Carl Barks 10.00 30.00 110.00
Four Color 1267-Barks c/a, 4 pgs. 7.00 20.00 75.00
01329-207 (#1, 5-7/62)-Barks-c only (intended as 4-Color 1329?) 5.00 15.00 55.00

HACKER FILES, THE
DC Comics: Aug, 1992 - No. 12, July, 1993 ($1.95)
1-12: 1-Sutton-a(p) begins; computer generated-c 2.00

HAGAR THE HORRIBLE (See Comics Reading Libraries)

HA HA COMICS (Teepee Tim No. 100 on; also see Giggle Comics)
Scope Mag.(Creston Publ.) No. 1-80/American Comics Group: Oct, 1943 - No. 99, Jan, 1955
1-Funny animal 30.00 90.00 210.00
2 14.00 43.00 100.00
3-5: Ken Hultgren-a begins? 11.00 33.00 75.00
6-10 10.00 30.00 60.00
11-20: 14-Infinity-c 7.00 21.00 42.00
21-40 5.85 17.50 35.00
41-94,96-99: 49-X-Mas-c 5.00 15.00 30.00
95-3-D effect-c 13.50 41.00 95.00

HAIR BEAR BUNCH, THE (TV) (See Fun-In No. 13)
Gold Key: Feb, 1972 - No. 9, Feb, 1974 (Hanna-Barbera)
1 3.20 9.60 32.00
2-9 2.25 6.75 18.00

HALLELUJAH TRAIL, THE (See Movie Classics)

HALL OF FAME FEATURING THE T.H.U.N.D.E.R. AGENTS
JC Productions(Archie Comics Group): May, 1983 - No. 3, Dec, 1983
1-3: Thunder Agents-r(Crandall, Tuska, Wood-a) 2.00

HALLOWEEN HORROR
Eclipse Comics: Oct, 1987 (Seduction of the Innocent #7)($1.75)
1-Pre-code horror-r 2.00

HALLOWEEN MEGAZINE
Marvel Comics: Dec, 1996 ($3.95, one-shot, 96 pgs.)
1-Reprints Tomb of Dracula 4.00

HALO, AN ANGEL'S STORY
Sirius Entertainment: Apr, 1996 - No. 4, Sept, 1996 ($2.95, limited series)
1-4: Knowles-c/a/scripts 3.00
TPB ($12.95) r/#1-4 13.00

HALO JONES (See The Ballad of...)

HAMMER, THE
Dark Horse Comics: Oct, 1997 - No. 4, Jan, 1998 ($2.95, limited series)
1-4-Kelley Jones-s/c/a, ...: Uncle Alex (8/98, $2.95) 3.00

HAMMER, THE: THE OUTSIDER
Dark Horse Comics: Feb, 1999 - No. 3, Apr, 1999 ($2.95, limited series)
1-3-Kelley Jones-s/c/a 3.00

HAMMERLOCKE
DC Comics: Sept, 1992 - No. 9, May, 1993 ($1.75, limited series)
1-($2.50, 52 pgs.)-Chris Sprouse-c/a in all 2.50
2-9 2.00

HAMMER OF GOD (Also see Nexus)
First Comics: Feb, 1990 - No. 4, May, 1990 ($1.95, limited series)
1-4 2.00

HAMMER OF GOD: BUTCH
Dark Horse Comics: May, 1994 - No. 4, Aug, 1994 ($2.50, limited series)
1-3 2.50

HAMMER OF GOD: PENTATHLON
Dark Horse Comics: Jan, 1994 ($2.50, one shot)
1-character from Nexus 2.50

HAMMER OF GOD: SWORD OF JUSTICE
First Comics: Feb 1991 - Mar 1991 ($4.95, lim. series, squarebound, 52 pgs.)
V2#1,2 5.00

HANDBOOK OF THE CONAN UNIVERSE, THE
Marvel Comics: June, 1985 ($1.25, one-shot)
1-Kaluta-c. 2.00

HAND OF FATE (Formerly Men Against Crime)
Ace Magazines: No. 8, Dec, 1951 - No. 26, March, 1955 (Weird/horror stories) (Two #25's)
8-Surrealistic text story 36.00 109.00 255.00
9,10,21-Necronomicon sty; drug belladonna used 21.00 62.00 145.00
11-18,20,22,23 17.00 49.00 115.00
19-Bondage, hypo needle scenes 18.00 54.00 125.00
24-Electric chair-c 26.00 79.00 185.00
25a(11/54), 25b(12/54)-Both have Cameron-a 13.00 39.00 90.00
26-Nostrand-a; exist? 15.00 45.00 105.00
NOTE: ***Cameron*** *a-9, 10, 19-25a, 25b; c-13.* ***Sekowsky*** *a-8, 9, 13, 14.*

HAND OF FATE
Eclipse Comics: Feb, 1988 - No. 3, Apr, 1988 ($1.75/$2.00, Baxter paper)
1-3; 3-B&W 2.00

HANDS OF THE DRAGON
Seaboard Periodicals (Atlas): June, 1975
1-Origin; Mooney inks 5.00

HANGMAN COMICS (Special Comics No. 1; Black Hood No. 9 on) (Also see Flyman, Mighty Comics, Mighty Crusaders & Pep Comics)
MLJ Magazines: No. 2, Spring, 1942 - No. 8, Fall, 1943
2-The Hangman, Boy Buddies begin 181.00 545.00 1450.00
3-Beheading splash pg.; 1st Nazi war-c 119.00 356.00 950.00
4-8: 5-1st Jap war-c. 8-2nd app. Super Duck (ties w/Jolly Jingles #11) 103.00 309.00 825.00
NOTE: ***Fuje*** *a-7(3), 8(3); c-3.* ***Reinman*** *c/a-3. Bondage c-3.* ***Sahle*** *c-6.*

HANK
Pentagon Publishing Co.: 1946
nn-Coulton Waugh's newspaper reprint 7.00 21.00 42.00

HANNA-BARBERA (See Golden Comics Digest No. 2, 7, 11)

HANNA-BARBERA ALL-STARS
Archie Publications: Oct, 1995 - No. 6, Sept, 1996 ($1.50, bi-monthly)
1-6 2.00

HANNA-BARBERA BANDWAGON (TV)
Gold Key: Oct, 1962 - No. 3, Apr, 1963
1-Giant, 84 pgs. 1-Augie Doggie app.; 1st app. Lippy the Lion, Touché Turtle &

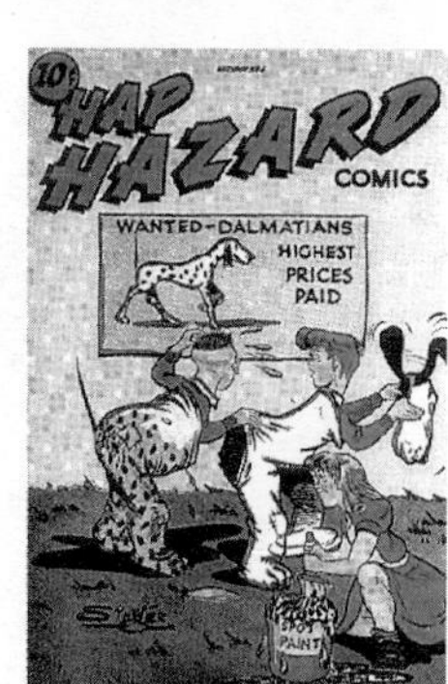

Hap Hazard Comics #6 © ACE

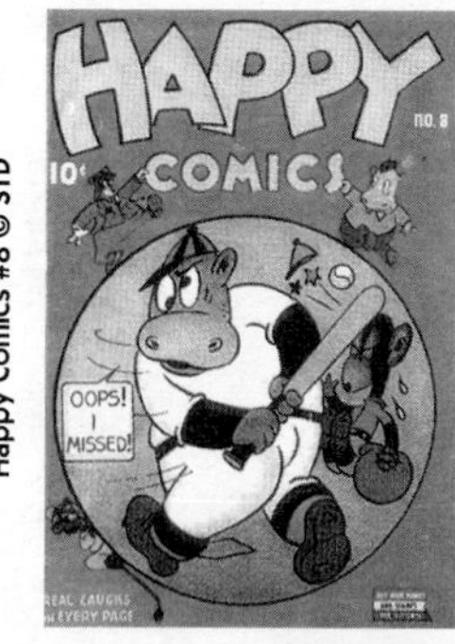

Happy Comics #8 © STD

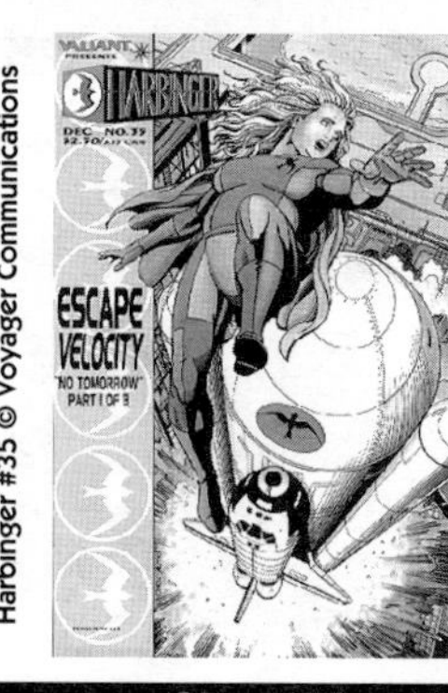

Harbinger #35 © Voyager Communications

Dum Dum, Wally Gator, Loopy de Loop, 11.25 34.00 125.00
2-Giant, 84 pgs.; Mr. & Mrs. J. Evil Scientist (1st app.) in Snagglepuss story; Yakky Doodle, Ruff and Ready and others app. 8.75 26.50 95.00
3-Regular size; Mr. & Mrs. J. Evil Scientist app. (pre-#1), Snagglepuss, Wally Gator and others app. 6.00 18.00 65.00

HANNA-BARBERA GIANT SIZE
Harvey Comics: Oct, 1992 - No. 3 ($2.25, 68 pgs.)
V2#1-3:Flintstones, Yogi Bear, Magilla Gorilla, Huckleberry Hound, Quick Draw McGraw, Yakky Doodle & Chopper, Jetsons & others 3.00

HANNA-BARBERA HI-ADVENTURE HEROES (See Hi-Adventure...)

HANNA-BARBERA PARADE (TV)
Charlton Comics: Sept, 1971 - No. 10, Dec, 1972
1 6.00 18.00 70.00
2,4-10 3.50 10.50 35.00
3-(52 pgs.)- "Summer Picnic" 5.50 16.50 55.00
NOTE: *No. 4 (1/72) went on sale late in 1972 with the January 1973 issues.*

HANNA-BARBERA PRESENTS
Archie Publications: Nov, 1995 - No. 6 ($1.50, bi-monthly)
1-6: 2-Wacky Races. 4-Quick Draw McGraw & Magilla Gorilla. 5-A Pup Named Scooby-Doo 2.00

HANNA-BARBERA SPOTLIGHT (See Spotlight)

HANNA-BARBERA SUPER TV HEROES (TV)
Gold Key: Apr, 1968 - No. 7, Oct, 1969 (Hanna-Barbera)
1-The Birdman, The Herculoids(ends #6; not in #2), Moby Dick, Young Samson & Goliath(ends #2,4), and The Mighty Mightor begin; Spiegle-a in all 15.50 46.00 170.00
2-The Galaxy Trio app.; Shazzan begins; 12¢ & 15¢ versions exist 10.50 31.00 115.00
3,6,7-The Space Ghost app. 10.00 30.00 110.00
4,5 9.00 27.00 100.00

HANNA-BARBERA TV FUN FAVORITES (See Golden Comics Digest #2,7,11)

HANNA-BARBERA (TV STARS) (See TV Stars)

HANS BRINKER (Disney)
Dell Publishing Co.: No. 1273, Feb, 1962 (one-shot)
Four Color 1273-Movie, photo-c 5.50 16.50 60.00

HANS CHRISTIAN ANDERSEN
Ziff-Davis Publ. Co.: 1953 (100 pgs., Special Issue)
nn-Danny Kaye (movie)-Photo-c; fairy tales 16.00 47.00 110.00

HANSEL & GRETEL
Dell Publishing Co.: No. 590, Oct, 1954 (one-shot)
Four Color 590-Partial photo-c 5.50 16.50 60.00

HANSI, THE GIRL WHO LOVED THE SWASTIKA
Spire Christian Comics (Fleming H. Revell Co.): 1973, 1976 (39¢/49¢)
nn 1.10 3.30 9.00

HAP HAZARD COMICS (Real Love No. 25 on)
Ace Magazines (Readers' Research): Summer, 1944 - No. 24, Feb, 1949 (#1-6 are quarterly issues)
1 13.00 39.00 90.00
2 7.50 22.50 45.00
3-10 5.35 16.00 32.00
11-13,15-24 4.25 13.00 26.00
14-Feldstein-c (4/47) 8.35 25.00 50.00

HAP HOPPER (See Comics Revue No. 2)

HAPPIEST MILLIONAIRE, THE (See Movie Comics)

HAPPI TIM (See March of Comics No. 182)

HAPPY BIRTHDAY MARTHA WASHINGTON (Also see Give Me Liberty, Martha Washington Goes To War, & Martha Washington Stranded In Space)
Dark Horse Comics: Mar, 1995 ($2.95, one-shot)
1-Miller script; Gibbons-c/a 3.00

HAPPY COMICS (Happy Rabbit No. 41 on)
Nedor Publ./Standard Comics (Animated Cartoons): Aug, 1943 - No. 40, Dec, 1950 (Companion to Goofy Comics)
1-Funny animal 26.00 77.00 180.00
2 13.00 39.00 90.00
3-10 10.00 30.00 60.00
11-19 7.00 21.00 42.00
20-31,34-37-Frazetta text illos in all (2 in #34&35, 3 in #27,28,30). 27-Al Fago-a 9.70 29.00 58.00
32-Frazetta-a, 7 pgs. plus 2 text illos; Roussos-a 19.00 58.00 135.00
33-Frazetta-a(2), 6 pgs. each (Scarce) 26.00 79.00 185.00
38-40 4.25 13.00 28.00

HAPPYDALE: DEVILS IN THE DESERT
DC Comics (Vertigo): 1999 - No. 2, 1999 ($6.95, limited series)
1,2-Andrew Dabb-s/Seth Fisher-a 7.00

HAPPY DAYS (TV)(See Kite Fun Book)
Gold Key: Mar, 1979 - No. 6, Feb, 1980
1-Photo-c of TV cast 1.25 3.75 10.00
2-6 2.40 6.00

HAPPY HOLIDAY (See March of Comics No. 181)

HAPPY HOULIHANS (Saddle Justice No. 3 on; see Blackstone, The Magician Detective)
E. C. Comics: Fall, 1947 - No. 2, Winter, 1947-48
1-Origin Moon Girl (same date as Moon Girl #1) 43.00 128.00 340.00
2 26.00 77.00 180.00

HAPPY JACK
Red Top (Decker): Aug, 1957 - No. 2, Nov, 1957
V1#1,2 4.00 10.00 20.00

HAPPY JACK HOWARD
Red Top (Farrell)/Decker: 1957
nn-Reprints Handy Andy story from E. C. Dandy Comics #5, renamed "Happy Jack" 4.00 12.00 24.00

HAPPY RABBIT (Formerly Happy Comics)
Standard Comics (Animated Cartoons): No. 41, Feb, 1951 - No. 48, Apr, 1952
41-Funny animal 5.00 15.00 30.00
42-48 4.00 10.00 20.00

HARBINGER (Also see Unity)
Valiant: Jan, 1992 - No. 41, June, 1995 ($1.95/$2.50)
0-(Advance), 1-1st app. 5.00
2-4: 4-Low print run 4.00
5-24,26-41: 8,9-Unity x-overs. 8-Miller-c. 9-Simonson-c. 10-1st app. H.A.R.D Corps 10/92). 14-1st app. Stronghold18-Intro Screen. 19-1st app. Stunner. 22-Archer & Armstrong app. 24-Cover similar to #1. 26-Intro New Harbingers. 29-Bound-in trading card. 30-H.A.R.D. Corps app. 32-Eternal Warrior app. 33-Dr. Eclipse app. 2.50
25-($3.50, 52 pgs.)-Harada vs. Sting 3.50
...Files 1,2 (8/94,2/95 $2.50) 2.50
Trade paperback nn (11/92, $9.95)-Reprints #1-4 & comes polybagged with a copy of Harbinger #0 w/new-c. 10.00
NOTE: *Issues 1-6 have coupons with origin of Harada and are redeemable for Harbinger #0.*

HARD BOILED
Dark Horse Comics: Sept, 1990 - No. 3, 1992 ($4.95/$5.95, 8 1/2x11", lim. ser.)
1-3-Miller-s; Darrow-c/a; sexually explicit & violent 1.00 2.80 7.00
TPB (5/93, $15.95) 16.00
Big Damn Hard Boiled (12/97, $29.95, B&W) r/#1-3 30.00

HARDCASE (See Break Thru, Flood Relief & Ultraforce, 1st Series)
Malibu Comics (Ultraverse): June, 1993 - No. 26, Aug, 1995 ($1.95/$2.50)
1-Intro Hardcase; Dave Gibbons-c; has coupon for Ultraverse Premiere #0; Jim Callahan-a(p) begin, ends #3 3.00

Hardcore Station #3 © Jim Starlin

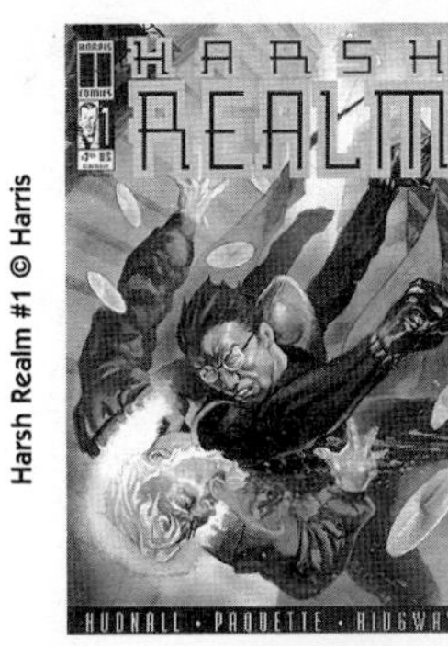

Harsh Realm #1 © Harris

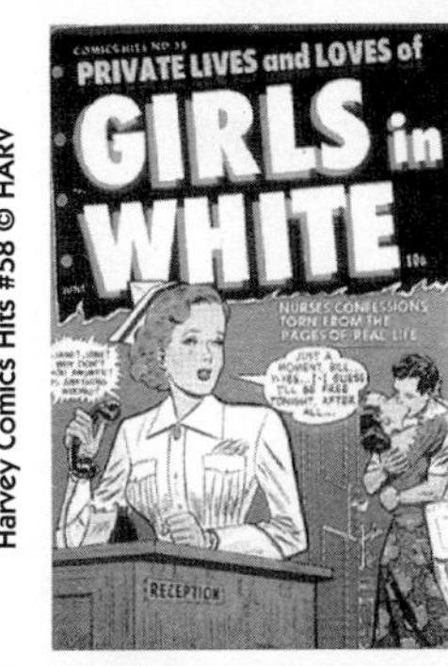

Harvey Comics Hits #58 © HARV

GD2.0 FN6.0 NM9.4

1-With coupon missing 2.00
1-Platinum Edition 4.00
1-Holographic Cover Edition; 1st full-c holograph tied w/Prime 1 & Strangers 1 7.00
1-Ultra Limited silver foil-c 4.00
2,3-Callahan-a, 2-($2.50)-Newsstand edition bagged w/trading card 2.50
4,6-15, 17-19: 4-Strangers app. 7-Break-Thru x-over. 8-Solution app. 9-Vs. Turf. 12-Silver foil logo, wraparound-c. 17-Prime app. 2.00
5-($2.50, 48 pgs.)-Rune flip-c/story by B. Smith (3 pgs.) 2.50
16 ($3.50, 68 pgs.)-Rune pin-up 3.50
20-26: 23-Loki app. 2.50
NOTE: ***Perez** a-8(2); c-20i.*

HARDCORE STATION
DC Comics: July, 1998 - No. 6, Dec, 1998 ($2.50, limited series)

1-6-Starlin-s/a(p). 3-Green Lantern-c/app. 5,6-JLA-c/app. 3.00

H.A.R.D. CORPS, THE (See Harbinger #10)
Valiant: Dec, 1992 - No. 30, Feb, 1995 ($2.25) (Harbinger spin-off)

1-(Advance) 3.00
1-($2.50)-Gatefold-c by Jim Lee & Bob Layton 2.50
1-Gold variant 4.00
2-30: 5-Bloodshot-c/story cont'd from Bloodshot #3. 5-Variant edition; came w/Comic Defense System. 10-Turok app. 17-vs. Armorines. 18-Bound-in trad ing card. 20-Harbinger app. 2.25

HARDWARE
DC Comics (Milestone): Apr, 1993 - No. 50, Apr, 1997 ($1.50/$1.75/$2.50)

1-($2.95)-Collector's Edition polybagged w/poster & trading card (direct sale only) 3.00
1-Platinum Edition 4.00
1-15,17-19: 11-Shadow War x-over. 11,14-Simonson-c. 12-Buckler-a(p). 17-Worlds Collide Pt. 2. 18-Simonson-c; Worlds Collide Pt. 9. 15-1st Humberto Ramos DC work 2.50
16,50-($3.95, 52 pgs.)-16-Collector's Edition w/gatefold 2nd cover by Byrne; new armor; Icon app. 4.00
16,20-24,26-49: 16-($2.50, 52 pgs.)-Newsstand Ed. 49-Moebius-c 2.50
25-($2.95, 52 pgs.) 3.00

HARDY BOYS, THE (Disney
Dell Publ. Co.: No. 760, Dec, 1956 - No. 964, Jan, 1959 (Mickey Mouse Club)

Four Color 760 (#1)-Photo-c 10.00 30.00 110.00
Four Color 830(8/57), 887(1/58), 964-Photo-c 9.00 27.00 100.00

HARDY BOYS, THE (TV)
Gold Key: Apr, 1970 - No. 4, Jan, 1971

1 3.50 10.50 35.00
2-4 2.50 7.50 24.00

HARLAN ELLISON'S DREAM CORRIDOR
Dark Horse Comics: Mar, 1995 - No. 5, July, 1995 ($2.95, anthology)

1-5: Adaptation of Ellison stories. 1-4-Byrne-a. 3.00
Special (1/95, $4.95) 5.00
Trade paperback-(1996, $18.95, 192 pgs)-r/#1-5 & Special #1 19.00

HARLAN ELLISON'S DREAM CORRIDOR QUARTERLY
Dark Horse Comics: V2#1, Aug, 1996 ($5.95, anthology, squarebound)

V2#1-Adaptations of Ellison's stories w/new material; Neal Adams-a 6.00

HARLEM GLOBETROTTERS (TV) (See Fun-In No. 8, 10)
Gold Key: Apr, 1972 - No. 12, Jan, 1975 (Hanna-Barbera)

1 2.50 7.50 24.00
2-5 2.00 6.00 16.00
6-12 1.50 4.50 12.00
NOTE: *#4, 8, and 12 contain 16 extra pages of advertising.*

HAROLD TEEN (See Popular Comics, & Super Comics)
Dell Publishing Co.: No. 2, 1942 - No. 209, Jan, 1949

Four Color 2 25.50 76.00 280.00
Four Color 209 3.80 11.50 42.00

GD2.0 FN6.0 NM9.4

HARRIERS
Entity Comics: June, 1995 - No. 3, 1995 ($2.50)

1-Foil-c; polybagged w/PC game, 1-3 ($2.50) 3.00

HARROWERS, THE (See Clive Barker's...)

HARSH REALM (Inspired 1999 TV series)
Harris Comics: 1993- No. 4, 1994 ($2.95, limited series)

1-4: Painted-c. Hudnall-s/Paquette & Ridgway-a 3.50

HARVEY
Marvel Comics: Oct, 1970; No. 2, 12/70; No. 3, 6/72 - No. 6, 12/72

1 6.35 19.00 70.00
2-6 4.50 13.50 45.00

HARVEY COLLECTORS COMICS (Richie Rich Collectors Comics #10 on, cover title only)
Harvey Publ.: Sept, 1975 - No. 15, Jan, 1978; No. 16, Oct, 1979 (52 pgs.)

1-Reprints Richie Rich #1,2 1.50 4.50 12.00
2-10: 7-Splash pg. shows-c to Friendly Ghost Casper #1 1.00 2.80 7.00
11-16: 16-Sad Sack-r 5.00
NOTE: *All reprints: Casper-#2, 7, Richie Rich-#1, 3, 5, 6, 8-15, Sad Sack-#16. Wendy-#4. #6 titled 'Richie Rich...'on inside.*

HARVEY COMICS HITS (Formerly Joe Palooka #50)
Harvey Publications: No. 51, Oct, 1951 - No. 62, Apr, 1953

51-The Phantom 29.00 86.00 200.00
52-Steve Canyon's Air Power(Air Force sponsored) 11.50 34.00 80.00
53-Mandrake the Magician 21.00 62.00 145.00
54-Tim Tyler's Tales of Jungle Terror 11.00 33.00 75.00
55-Love Stories of Mary Worth 6.35 19.00 38.00
56-The Phantom; bondage-c 24.00 71.00 165.00
57-Rip Kirby Exposes the Kidnap Racket; entire book by Alex Raymond 14.00 43.00 100.00
58-Girls in White (nurses stories) 5.85 17.50 35.00
59-Tales of the Invisible featuring Scarlet O'Neil 10.00 30.00 65.00
60-Paramount Animated Comics #1 (9/52) (3rd app. Baby Huey); 2nd Harvey app. Baby Huey & Casper the Friendly Ghost (1st in Little Audrey #25 (8/52)); 1st app. Herman & Catnip (c/story) & Buzzy the Crow 40.00 120.00 280.00
61-Casper the Friendly Ghost #6 (3rd Harvey Casper, 10/52)-Casper-c 40.00 120.00 300.00
62-Paramount Animated Comics #2; Herman & Catnip, Baby Huey & Buzzy the Crow 13.00 39.00 90.00

HARVEY COMICS LIBRARY
Harvey Publications: Apr, 1952 - No. 2, 1952

1-Teen-Age Dope Slaves as exposed by Rex Morgan, M.D.; drug propaganda story; used in **SOTI**, pg. 27 87.00 262.00 700.00
2-Dick Tracy Presents Sparkle Plenty in "Blackmail Terror" 20.00 60.00 140.00

HARVEY COMICS SPOTLIGHT
Harvey Comics: Sept, 1987 - No. 4, Mar, 1988 (75¢/$1.00)

1-New material; begin 75ç, ends #3; Sand Sack 3.00
2-4: 2,4-All new material. 2-Baby Huey. 3-Little Dot; contains reprints w/5 pg. new story. 4-$1.00-c; Little Audrey 2.00
NOTE: No. 5 was advertised but not published.

HARVEY HITS
Harvey Publications: Sept, 1957 - No. 122, Nov, 1967

1-The Phantom 24.00 72.00 240.00
2-Rags Rabbit (10/57) 2.60 7.80 26.00
3-Richie Rich (11/57)-r/Little Dot; 1st book devoted to Richie Rich; see Little Dot for 1st app. 67.00 200.00 800.00
4-Little Dot's Uncles (12/57) 13.50 42.00 135.00
5-Stevie Mazie's Boy Friend (1/58) 2.50 7.50 20.00
6-The Phantom (2/58); Kirby-c; 2pg. Powell-a 17.00 51.00 170.00
7-Wendy the Good Little Witch (3/58, pre-dates Wendy #1; 1st book devoted

Harvey Hits #14 © HARV

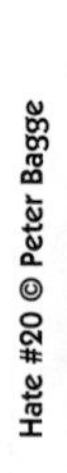

	GD2.0	FN6.0	NM9.4
to Wendy)	17.00	51.00	170.00
8-Sad Sack's Army Life; George Baker-c	5.50	16.50	55.00
9-Richie Rich's Golden Deeds; reprints (2nd book devoted to Richie Rich)	34.00	102.00	375.00
10-Little Lotta's Lunch Box	9.00	27.00	90.00
11-Little Audrey Summer Fun (7/58)	7.00	21.00	70.00
12-The Phantom; Kirby-c; 2pg. Powell-a (8/58)	13.50	41.00	135.00
13-Little Dot's Uncles (9/58); Richie Rich 1pg.	9.00	27.00	90.00
14-Herman & Katnip (10/58, TV/movies)	2.50	7.50	22.00
15-The Phantom (12/58)-1 pg. origin	13.50	41.00	135.00
16-Wendy the Good Little Witch (1/59); Casper app.	9.00	27.00	90.00
17-Sad Sack's Army Life (2/59)	4.50	13.50	45.00
18-Buzzy & the Crow	2.50	7.50	24.00
19-Little Audrey (4/59)	4.00	12.00	40.00
20-Casper & Spooky	5.50	16.50	55.00
21-Wendy the Witch	5.50	16.50	55.00
22-Sad Sack's Army Life	3.50	10.50	35.00
23-Wendy the Witch (8/59)	5.50	16.50	55.00
24-Little Dot's Uncles (9/59); Richie Rich 1pg.	7.00	21.00	70.00
25-Herman & Katnip (10/59)	2.25	6.75	18.00
26-The Phantom (11/59)	11.00	33.00	110.00
27-Wendy the Good Little Witch (12/59)	5.00	15.00	50.00
28-Sad Sack's Army Life (1/60)	2.50	7.50	22.00
29-Harvey-Toon (No.1)('60); Casper, Buzzy	3.50	10.50	35.00
30-Wendy the Witch (3/60)	5.50	16.50	55.00
31-Herman & Katnip (4/60)	1.75	5.25	14.00
32-Sad Sack's Army Life (5/60)	2.25	6.75	18.00
33-Wendy the Witch (6/60)	5.50	16.50	55.00
34-Harvey-Toon (7/60)	2.50	7.50	20.00
35-Funday Funnies (8/60)	1.75	5.25	14.00
36-The Phantom (1960)	9.50	28.50	95.00
37-Casper & Nightmare	3.80	11.40	38.00
38-Harvey-Toon	2.50	7.50	20.00
39-Sad Sack's Army Life (12/60)	2.25	6.75	18.00
40-Funday Funnies (1/61)	1.50	4.50	12.00
41-Herman & Katnip	1.75	5.25	14.00
42-Harvey-Toon (3/61)	2.00	6.00	16.00
43-Sad Sack's Army Life (4/61)	2.00	6.00	16.00
44-The Phantom (5/61)	9.00	27.00	90.00
45-Casper & Nightmare	3.20	9.60	32.00
46-Harvey-Toon (7/61)	1.75	5.25	14.00
47-Sad Sack's Army Life (8/61)	2.00	6.00	16.00
48-The Phantom (9/61)	9.00	27.00	90.00
49-Stumbo the Giant (1st app. in Hot Stuff)	8.00	24.00	80.00
50-Harvey-Toon (11/61)	1.75	5.25	14.00
51-Sad Sack's Army Life (12/61)	2.00	6.00	16.00
52-Casper & Nightmare	3.20	9.60	32.00
53-Harvey-Toons (2/62)	1.50	4.50	12.00
54-Stumbo the Giant	3.80	11.40	38.00
55-Sad Sack's Army Life (4/62)	2.00	6.00	16.00
56-Casper & Nightmare	2.80	8.40	28.00
57-Stumbo the Giant	3.80	11.40	38.00
58-Sad Sack's Army Life	2.00	6.00	16.00
59-Casper & Nightmare (7/62)	2.80	8.40	28.00
60-Stumbo the Giant (9/62)	3.80	11.40	38.00
61-Sad Sack's Army Life	1.75	5.25	14.00
62-Casper & Nightmare	2.50	7.50	24.00
63-Stumbo the Giant	3.20	9.60	32.00
64-Sad Sack's Army Life (1/63)	1.75	5.25	14.00
65-Casper & Nightmare	2.50	7.50	24.00
66-Stumbo The Giant (3/63)	3.20	9.60	32.00
67-Sad Sack's Army Life (4/63)	1.75	5.25	14.00
68-Casper & Nightmare	2.50	7.50	24.00
69-Stumbo the Giant (6/63)	3.20	9.60	32.00
70-Sad Sack's Army Life (7/63)	1.75	5.25	14.00
71-Casper & Nightmare (8/63)	2.25	6.75	18.00
72-Stumbo the Giant	3.20	9.60	32.00
73-Little Sad Sack (10/63)	1.75	5.25	14.00
74-Sad Sack's Muttsy... (11/63)	1.75	5.25	14.00
75-Casper & Nightmare	2.25	6.75	18.00
76-Little Sad Sack	1.75	5.25	14.00
77-Sad Sack's Muttsy...	1.75	5.25	14.00
78-Stumbo the Giant (3/64); JFK caricature	3.20	9.60	32.00
79-87: 79-Little Sad Sack (4/64). 80-Sad Sack's Muttsy... (5/64). 81-Little Sad Sack. 82-Sad Sack's Muttsy... 83-Little Sad Sack(8/64). 84-Sad Sack's Muttsy... 85-Gabby Gob (#1)(10/64). 86-G. I. Juniors (#1)(11/64). 87-Sad Sack's Muttsy... (12/64)	1.75	5.25	14.00
88-Stumbo the Giant (1/65)	3.20	9.60	32.00
89-122: 89-Sad Sack's Muttsy... 90-Gabby Gob. 91-G. I. Juniors. 92-Sad Sack's Muttsy... (5/65). 93-Sadie Sack (6/65). 94-Gabby Gob. 95-G. I. Juniors (8/65). 96-Sad Sack's Muttsy... (9/65). 97-Gabby Gob (10/65). 98-G. I. Juniors (11/65). 99-Sad Sack's Muttsy... (12/65). 100-Gabby Gob(1/66). 101-G. I. Juniors (2/66). 102-Sad Sack's Muttsy... (3/66). 103-Gabby Gob. 104- G. I. Juniors. 105-Sad Sack's Muttsy... 106-Gabby Gob (7/66). 107-G. I. Juniors (8/66). 108-Sad Sack's Muttsy... 109-Gabby Gob. 110-G. I. Juniors (11/66). 111-Sad Sack's Muttsy... (12/66). 112-G. I. Juniors. 113-Sad Sack's Muttsy... 114-G. I. Juniors. 115-Sad Sack's Muttsy... 116-G. I. Juniors (5/67). 117-Sad Sack's Muttsy... 118-G. I. Juniors. 119-Sad Sack's Muttsy... (8/67). 120-G. I. Juniors (9/67). 121-Sad Sack's Muttsy... (10/67). 122-G. I. Juniors (11/67)	1.00	3.00	8.00

HARVEY HITS COMICS
Harvey Publications: Nov, 1986 - No. 6, Oct, 1987

	GD2.0	FN6.0	NM9.4
1-Little Lotta, Little Dot, Wendy & Baby Huey			3.00
2-6: 3-Xmas-c			2.00

HARVEY POP COMICS (Teen Humor)
Harvey Publications: Oct, 1968 - No. 2, Nov, 1969 (Both are 68 pg. Giants)

	GD2.0	FN6.0	NM9.4
1-The Cowsills	4.50	13.50	45.00
2-Bunny	4.00	12.00	40.00

HARVEY 3-D HITS (See Sad Sack)

HARVEY-TOON (...S) (See Harvey Hits No. 29, 34, 38, 42, 46, 50, 53)

HARVEY WISEGUYS (...Digest #? on)
Harvey Comics: Nov, 1987; #2, Nov, 1988; #3, Apr, 1989 - No. 4, Nov, 1989 (98 pgs., digest-size, $1.25/$1.75)

	GD2.0	FN6.0	NM9.4
1-Hot Stuff, Spooky, etc.			5.00
2-4: 2 (68 pgs.)			4.00

HATARI (See Movie Classics)

HATE
Fantagraphics Books: Spr, 1990 - No. 30, 1998 ($2.50/$2.95, B&W/color)

	GD2.0	FN6.0	NM9.4
1	1.85	5.50	15.00
2-3	1.00	3.00	8.00
4-10			5.00
11-29: 16- color begins			3.00
30-($3.95) Last issue			4.00
Buddy Go Home! (1997, $16.95) r/Buddy stories in color			17.00
Hate-Ball Special Edition ($3.95, giveaway)-reprints			4.00
Hate Jamboree (10/98, $4.50) old & new cartoons			4.50

HATHAWAYS, THE (TV)
Dell Publishing Co.: No. 1298, Feb-Apr, 1962 (one-shot)

	GD2.0	FN6.0	NM9.4
Four Color 1298-Photo-c	3.60	11.00	40.00

HAUNTED (See This Magazine Is Haunted)

HAUNTED (Baron Weirwulf's Haunted Library on-c #21 on)
Charlton Comics: 9/71 - No. 30, 11/76; No. 31, 9/77 - No. 75, 9/84

	GD2.0	FN6.0	NM9.4
1-All Ditko issue	2.50	7.50	22.00
2-5	1.75	5.25	14.00
6-20	1.25	3.75	10.00
21-1st Baron Weirwulf; Newton-c/a	1.75	5.25	14.00
22-40	1.00	3.00	8.00
41-60: 51-Reprints #1		2.40	6.00
61-70: 64-Reprints			4.00

Haunted Thrills #1 © AJAX

Haunt of Fear #15 © WMG

The Hawk #3 © Z-D

GD2.0 FN6.0 NM9.4

71-75: 75-Reprints (Low printing) 5.00
NOTE: *Aparo c-45.* ***Ditko*** *a-1-8, 11-16, 18, 23, 24, 28, 30, 34r, 36r, 39-42r, 47r, 49-51r, 57, 60, 74. c-1-7, 11, 13, 14, 16, 30, 41, 47, 49-51, 74.* ***Howard*** *a-6, 9, 18, 22, 25, 32.* ***Kim*** *a-9, 19.* ***Morisi*** *a-13.* ***Newton*** *a-17, 21, 59r; c-21, 22(painted).* ***Staton*** *a-11, 12, 18, 21, 22, 30, 33, 35, 38; c-18, 33.* ***Sutton*** *a-10, 17, 20-22, 31, 35, 37, 38; c-15, 17, 18, 23(painted), 24(painted), 64r. #49 reprints Tales of the Mysterious Traveler #4.*

HAUNTED LOVE
Charlton Comics: Apr, 1973 - No. 11, Sept, 1975

	GD2.0	FN6.0	NM9.4
1-Tom Sutton-a (16 pgs.)	4.00	12.00	40.00
2,3, 6-11	2.25	6.75	18.00
4,5-Ditko-a	2.50	7.50	20.00
Modern Comics #1(1978)	1.25	3.75	10.00

NOTE: ***Howard*** *a-8i.* ***Kim*** *a-7-9.* ***Newton*** *c-8, 9.* ***Staton*** *a-1-6.* ***Sutton*** *a-1, 3-5, 10, 11.*

HAUNTED THRILLS (Tales of Horror and Terror)
Ajax/Farrell Publications: June, 1952 - No. 18, Nov-Dec, 1954

	GD2.0	FN6.0	NM9.4
1-r/Ellery Queen #1	40.00	120.00	300.00
2-L. B. Cole-a r-/Ellery Queen #1	28.00	84.00	195.00
3-5: 3-Drug use story	24.00	73.00	170.00
6-10,12: 7-Hitler story.	20.00	60.00	140.00
11-Nazi death camp story	21.00	64.00	150.00
13-18: 18-Lingerie panels. 14-Jesus Christ apps. in story by Webb. 15-Jo-Jo-r	17.00	51.00	120.00

NOTE: ***Kamenish*** *art in most issues.* ***Webb*** *a-12.*

HAUNT OF FEAR (Formerly Gunfighter)
E. C. Comics: No. 15, May-June, 1950 - No. 28, Nov-Dec, 1954

	GD2.0	FN6.0	NM9.4
15(#1, 1950)(Scarce)-1st app. Old Witch	235.00	705.00	2350.00
16	95.00	285.00	900.00
17-Origin of Crypt of Terror, Vault of Horror, & Haunt of Fear; used in **SOTI**, pg. 43; last pg. Ingels-a used by N.Y. Legis. Comm.; story "Monster Maker" based on Frankenstein	95.00	285.00	900.00
4	63.00	189.00	600.00
5-Injury-to-eye panel, pg. 4 of Wood story	47.00	141.00	450.00
6-10: 8-Shrunken head cover. 10-Ingels biog.	35.00	105.00	310.00
11-13,15-18: 11-Kamen biog. 12-Feldstein biog. 16,18-Ray Bradbury adaptations. 18-Ray Bradbury biography	26.00	78.00	235.00
14-Origin Old Witch by Ingels	38.00	114.00	345.00
19-Used in **SOTI**, ill. "A comic book baseball game" & Senate investigation on juvenile delinq. bondage/decapitation-c	35.00	105.00	310.00
20-Feldstein-r/Vault of Horror #12	24.00	72.00	215.00
21-27: 23-Used in **SOTI**, pg. 241. 24-Used in Senate Investigative Report, pg.8. 26-Contains anti-censorship editorial, 'Are you a Red Dupe?' 27-Cannibalism story; Wertham cameo	17.00	50.00	150.00
28-Low distribution	18.00	53.00	160.00

NOTE: *(Canadian reprints known; see Table of Contents).* ***Craig*** *a-15-17, 5, 7, 10, 12, 13; c-15-17, 5-7.* ***Crandall*** *a-20, 21, 26, 27.* ***Davis*** *a-4-26, 28.* ***Evans*** *a-15-19, 22-25, 27.* ***Feldstein*** *a-15-17, 20; c-4, 8-10.* ***Ingels*** *a-16, 17, 4-28; c-11-28.* ***Kamen*** *a-16, 4, 6, 7, 9-11, 13-19, 21-28.* ***Krigstein*** *a-28.* ***Kurtzman*** *a-15(#1), 17(#3).* ***Orlando*** *a-9, 12.* ***Wood*** *a-15, 16, 4-6.*

HAUNT OF FEAR, THE
Gladstone Publishing: May, 1991 - No. 2, July, 1991 ($2.00, 68 pgs.)

1,2: 1-Ghastly Ingels-c(r); 2-Craig-c(r) 2.50

HAUNT OF FEAR
Russ Cochran/Gemstone Publ.: Sept, 1991 - No. 5, 1992 ($2.00, 68 pgs.); Nov, 1992 - Present ($1.50/$2.00/$2.50)

1-25: 1-Ingels-c(r). 1-3-r/HOF #15-17 with original-c. 4,5-r/HOF #4,5 with original-c 2.50
Annual 1-5: 1- r/#1-5. 2- r/#6-10. 3- r/#11-15. 4- r/#16-20. 5- r/#21-25 14.00
Annual 6-r/#26-28 8.95

HAUNT OF HORROR, THE (Digest)
Marvel Comics: Jun, 1973 - No. 2, Aug, 1973 (164 pgs.; text and art)

	GD2.0	FN6.0	NM9.4
1-Morrow painted skull-c; stories by Ellison, Howard, and Leiber; Brunner-a	2.50	7.50	24.00
2-Kelly Freas painted bondage-c; stories by McCaffrey, Goulart,Leiber, Ellison; art by Simonson, Brunner, and Buscema	2.25	6.75	18.00

HAUNT OF HORROR, THE (Magazine)
Cadence Comics Publ. (Marvel): May, 1974 - No. 5, Jan, 1975 (75¢) (B&W)

	GD2.0	FN6.0	NM9.4
1	1.75	5.25	14.00
2,4: 2-Origin & 1st app. Gabriel the Devil Hunter; Satana begins. 4-Neal Adams-a	1.25	3.75	10.00
3,5: 5-Evans-a(2)	1.00	3.000	8.00

NOTE: ***Alcala*** *a-2.* ***Colan*** *a-2p.* ***Heath*** *r-1.* ***Krigstein*** *r-3.* ***Reese*** *a-1.* ***Simonson*** *a-1.*

HAVE GUN, WILL TRAVEL (TV)
Dell Publishing Co.: No. 931, 8/58 - No. 14, 7-9/62 (All Richard Boone photo-c)

	GD2.0	FN6.0	NM9.4
Four Color 931 (#1)	14.00	42.00	150.00
Four Color 983,1044 (#2,3)	8.50	25.50	95.00
4 (1-3/60) - 10	7.00	21.00	75.00
11-14	8.00	23.00	85.00

HAVOK & WOLVERINE - MELTDOWN (See Marvel Comics Presents #24)
Marvel Comics (Epic Comics): Mar, 1989 - No. 4, Oct, 1989 ($3.50, mini-series, squarebound, mature)

1-4: Violent content 4.00

HAWAIIAN EYE (TV)
Gold Key: July, 1963 (Troy Donahue, Connie Stevens photo-c)

	GD2.0	FN6.0	NM9.4
1 (10073-307)	4.00	12.00	45.00

HAWAIIAN ILLUSTRATED LEGENDS SERIES
Hogarth Press: 1975 (B&W)(Cover printed w/blue, yellow, and green)

1-Kalelealuaka, the Mysterious Warrior 2/00

HAWK, THE (Also see Approved Comics #1, 7 & Tops In Adventure)
Ziff-Davis/St. John Publ. Co. No. 4 on: Wint/51 - No. 3, 11-12/52; No. 4, 1953 - No. 12, 5/55 (Painted c-1-4)

	GD2.0	FN6.0	NM9.4
1-Anderson-a	20.00	60.00	140.00
2 (Sum, '52)-Kubert, Infantino-a	11.00	33.00	75.00
3-7,11: 11-Buckskin Belle & The Texan app.	10.00	30.00	60.00
8-10,12: 8-Reprints #3 w/different-c by Baker. 9-Baker-c/a; Kubert-a(r)/#2. 10-Baker-c/a; r/one story from #2. 12-Baker-c/a; Buckskin Belle app.	11.50	34.00	80.00
3-D 1(11/53, 25¢)-Came w/glasses; Baker-c	34.00	101.00	235.00

NOTE: ***Baker*** *c-8-12.* ***Larsen*** *a-10.* ***Tuska*** *a-1, 9, 12. Painted c-1, 4, 7.*

HAWK AND THE DOVE, THE (See Showcase #75 & Teen Titans) (1st series)
National Periodical Publications: Aug-Sept, 1968 - No. 6, June-July, 1969

	GD2.0	FN6.0	NM9.4
1-Ditko-c/a	6.00	18.00	60.00
2-6: 5-Teen Titans cameo	4.00	12.00	40.00

NOTE: ***Ditko*** *c/a-1, 2.* ***Gil Kane*** *a-3p, 4p, 5, 6p; c-3-6.*

HAWK AND DOVE (2nd Series)
DC Comics: Oct, 1988 - No. 5, Feb, 1989 ($1.00, limited series)

1-Rob Liefeld-c/a(p) in all 3.00
2-5 2.50
Trade paperback ('93, $9.95)-Reprints #1-5 10.00

HAWK AND DOVE
DC Comics: June, 1989 - No. 28, Oct, 1991 ($1.00)

1-28 2.00
Annual 1,2 ('90, '91; $2.00) 1-Liefeld pin-up. 2-Armageddon 2001 x-over 2.50

HAWK AND DOVE
DC Comics: Nov, 1997 - No.5, Mar, 1998 ($2.50, limited series)

1-5-Baron-s/Zachary & Giordano-a 3.50

HAWK AND WINDBLADE (See Elflord)
Warp Graphics: Aug, 1997 - No.2, Sept, 1997 ($2.95, limited series)

1,2-Blair-s/Chan-c/a 3.00

HAWKEYE (See The Avengers #16 & Tales Of Suspense #57)
Marvel Comics Group: Sept, 1983 - No. 4, Dec, 1983 (limited series)

1-4: Mark Gruenwald-a/scripts. 1-Origin Hawkeye. 3-Origin Mockingbird. 4-Hawkeye & Mockingbird elope 2.50

HAWKEYE
Marvel Comics: Jan, 1994 - No. 4, Apr, 1994 ($1.75, limited series)

Hawkman (4th series) #13 © DC

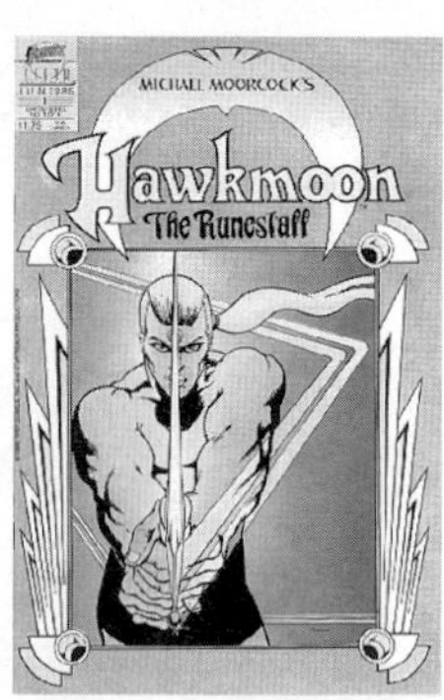

Hawkmoon: The Runestaff #1 © FC

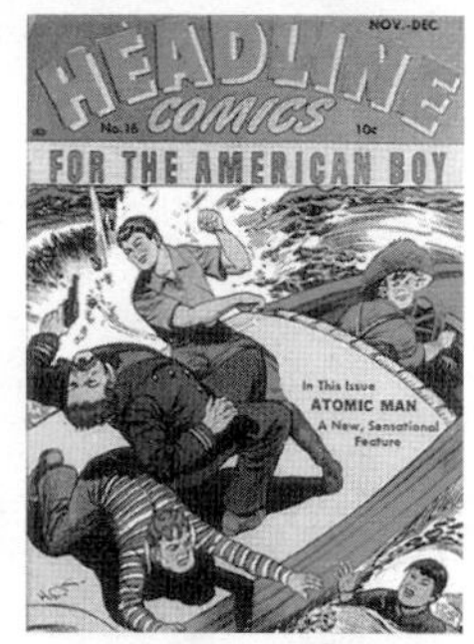

Headline Comics #16 © PRIZE

1-4 2.00

HAWKEYE & THE LAST OF THE MOHICANS (TV)
Dell Publishing Co.: No. 884, Mar, 1958 (one-shot)

Four Color 884-Photo-c 6.40 19.00 70.00

HAWKEYE: EARTH'S MIGHTIEST MARKSMAN
Marvel Comics: Oct, 1998 ($2.99, one-shot)

1-Justice and Firestar app.; DeFalco-s 3.00

HAWKMAN (See Atom & Hawkman, The Brave & the Bold, DC Comics Presents, Detective, Flash Comics, Hawkworld, Justice League of America #31, Mystery in Space, Shadow War Of..., Showcase, & World's Finest #256)

HAWKMAN (1st Series) (Also see The Atom #7 & Brave & the Bold #34-36, 42-44, 51)
National Periodical Publications: Apr-May, 1964 - No. 27, Aug-Sept, 1968

1-(4-5/64)-Anderson-c/a begins, ends #21 41.00 123.00 500.00
2 17.50 52.00 175.00
3,5 10.00 30.00 100.00
4-Origin & 1st app. Zatanna (10-11/64) 14.00 42.00 140.00
6 9.00 27.00 90.00
7 8.00 24.00 80.00
8-10: 9-Atom cameo; Hawkman & Atom learn each other's I.D.; 2nd app. Shadow Thief 7.00 21.00 70.00
11-15 5.00 15.00 50.00
16-27: 18-Adam Strange x-over (cameo #19). 25-G.A. Hawkman-r by Moldoff. 26-Kirby-a(r). 27-Kubert-c 4.00 12.00 40.00

HAWKMAN (2nd Series)
DC Comics: Aug, 1986 - No. 17, Dec, 1987

1-17: 10-Byrne-c, Special #1 (1986, $1.25) 2.00
Trade paperback (1989, $19.95)-r/Brave and the Bold #34-36,42-44 by Kubert; Kubert-c 20.00

HAWKMAN (4th Series)(See both Hawkworld limited & ongoing series)
DC Comics: Sept, 1993 - No. 33, July, 1996 ($1.75/$1.95/$2.25)

1-($2.50)-Gold foil embossed-c; storyline cont'd from Hawkworld ongoing series; new costume & powers. 3.00
2-13,0,14-33: 2-Green Lantern x-over. 3-Airstryke app. 4,6-Won. Woman app. 13-(9/94)-Zero Hour. 0-(10/94). 14-(11/94). 15-Aquaman-c & app. 23-Wonder Woman app. 25-Kent Williams-c. 29,30-Chaykin-c. 32-Breyfogle-c 3.00
Annual 1 (1993, $2.50, 68 pgs.)-Bloodlines Earthplague 3.00
Annual 2 (1995, $3.95)-Year One story 4.00

HAWKMOON: THE JEWEL IN THE SKULL
First Comics: May, 1986 - No. 4, Nov, 1986 ($1.75, limited series, Baxter paper)

1-4: Adapts novel by Michael Moorcock 2.00

HAWKMOON: THE MAD GOD'S AMULET
First Comics: Jan, 1987 - No. 4, July, 1987 ($1.75, limited series, Baxter paper)

1-4: Adapts novel by Michael Moorcock 2.00

HAWKMOON: THE RUNESTAFF
First Comics: Jun, 1988 -No. 4, Dec, 1988 ($1.75-$1.95, lim. series, Baxter paper)

1-4: ($1.75) Adapts novel by Michael Moorcock. 3,4 ($1.95) 2.00

HAWKMOON: THE SWORD OF DAWN
First Comics : Sept, 1987 - No. 4, Mar, 1988 ($1.75, lim. series, Baxter paper)

1-4: Dorman painted-c; adapts Moorcock novel 2.00

HAWKWORLD
DC Comics: 1989 - No. 3, 1989 ($3.95, prestige format, limited series)

Book 1-3: 1-Tim Truman story & art in all; Hawkman dons new costume; reintro Byth. 4.00
TPB (1991, $16.95) r/#1-3 17.00

HAWKWORLD (3rd Series)
DC Comics: June, 1990 - No. 32, Mar, 1993 ($1.50/$1.75)

1-Hawkman spin-off; story cont'd from limited series. 2.50
2-32: 15,16-War of the Gods x-over. 22-J'onn J'onzz app. 2.00

GD2.0 FN6.0 NM9.4

Annual 1-3 ('90-'92, $2.95, 68 pgs.), 2-2nd printing with silver ink-c 3.00
NOTE: ***Truman*** *a-30-32; c-27-32, Annual 1.*

HAYWIRE
DC Comics: Oct, 1988 - No. 13, Sept, 1989 ($1.25, mature)

1-13 2.00

HAZARD
Image Comics (WildStorm Prod.): June, 1996 - No. 7, Nov, 1996 ($1.75)

1-7: 1-Intro Hazard; Jeff Mariotte scripts begin; Jim Lee-c(p) 3.00

HEADBUSTERS
Antarctic Press: Oct, 1998 ($2.95, B&W)

1-Mallette-s 3.00

HEADHUNTERS
Image Comics: Apr, 1997 - No. 3, June, 1997 ($2.95, B&W)

1-3: Chris Marrinan-s/a 3.00

HEADLINE COMICS (...For the American Boy) (...Crime No. 32-39)
Prize Publ./American Boys' Comics: Feb, 1943 - No. 22, Nov-Dec, 1946; No. 23, 1947 - No. 77, Oct, 1956

1-Junior Rangers-c/stories begin; Yank & Doodle x-over in Junior Rangers (Junior Rangers are Uncle Sam's nephews) 43.00 128.00 340.00
2 21.00 64.00 150.00
3-Used in **POP**, pg. 84 17.00 51.00 120.00
4-7,9,10: 4,9,10-Hitler stories in each 15.00 45.00 105.00
8-Classic Hitler-c 40.00 120.00 280.00
11,12 12.00 36.00 85.00
13-15-Blue Streak in all 13.50 41.00 95.00
16-Origin & 1st app. Atomic Man (11-12/45) 24.00 73.00 170.00
17,18,20,21: 21-Atomic Man ends (9-10/46) 12.00 36.00 85.00
19-S&K-a 27.00 81.00 190.00
22-Last Junior Rangers; Kiefer-c 10.00 30.00 60.00
23,24: (All S&K-a). 23-Valentine's Day Massacre story; content changes to true crime. 24-Dope-crazy killer story 26.00 77.00 180.00
25-35-S&K-c/a. 25-Powell-a 24.00 73.00 170.00
36-S&K-a; photo-c begin 18.00 54.00 125.00
37-1 pg. S&K, Severin-a; rare Kirby photo-c app. 18.00 54.00 125.00
38,40-Meskin-a 7.00 21.00 42.00
39,41-43,46-50,52-55: 41-J. Edgar Hoover 26th Anniversary Issue with photo on-c. 43,49-Meskin-a 5.35 16.00 32.00
44-S&K-c; Severin/Elder, Meskin-a 11.00 33.00 75.00
45-Kirby-a 10.00 30.00 60.00
51-Kirby-c 5.85 17.50 35.00
56-S&K-a 11.00 33.00 75.00
57-77: 72-Meskin-c/a(i) 4.00 12.00 24.00
NOTE: ***Hollingsworth*** *a-30. Photo c-36-43.* ***H. C. Kiefer*** *c-12-16, 22. Atomic Man c-17-19.*

HEADMAN
Innovation Publishing: 1990 ($2.50, mature)

1-Sci/fi 2.50

HEAP, THE
Skywald Publications: Sept, 1971 (52 pgs.)

1-Kinstler-r/Strange Worlds #8 2.25 6.75 18.00

HEART AND SOUL
Mikeross Publications: April-May, 1954 - No. 2, June-July, 1954

1,2 6.35 19.00 38.00

HEARTBREAKERS (Also see Dark Horse Presents)
Dark Horse Comics: Apr, 1996 - No. 4, July, 1996 ($2.95, limited series)

1-4: 1-W/paper doll & pin-up. 2-Ross pin-up. 3-Evan Dorkin pin-ups. 4-Brereton-c; Matt Wagner pin-up 3.00
...Superdigest (7/98, $9.95, digest-size) new stories 10.00

HEARTLAND (See Hellblazer)
DC Comics (Vertigo): Mar, 1997 ($4.95, one-shot, mature)

1-Garth Ennis-s/Steve Dillon-c/a 5.00

Heart Throbs #9 © QUA

Heavy Liquid #1 © Paul Pope

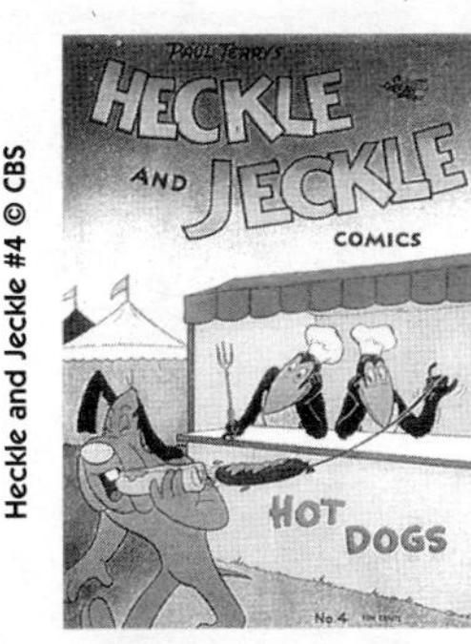

Heckle and Jeckle #4 © CBS

GD2.0 FN6.0 NM9.4 | GD2.0 FN6.0 NM9.4

HEART OF DARKNESS
Hardline Studios: 1994 ($2.95)
1-Brereton-c 3.00

HEART OF EMPIRE
Dark Horse Comics: Apr, 1999 - No. 9 ($2.95, limited series)
1-5-Bryan Talbot-s/a 3.00

HEART OF THE BEAST, THE
DC Comics (Vertigo): 1994 ($19.95, hardcover, mature)
1-Dean Motter scripts 20.00

HEARTS OF DARKNESS (See Ghost Rider; Wolverine; Punisher: Hearts of...)

HEART THROBS (Love Stories No. 147 on)
Quality Comics/National Periodical #47(4-5/57) on (Arleigh #48-101):
8/49 - No. 8, 10/50; No. 9, 3/52 - No. 146, Oct, 1972

	GD2.0	FN6.0	NM9.4
1-Classic Ward-c, Gustavson-a, 9 pgs.	40.00	120.00	290.00
2-Ward-c/a (9 pgs); Gustavson-a	24.00	73.00	170.00
3-Gustavson-a	9.15	27.00	55.00
4,6,8-Ward-a, 8-9 pgs.	12.00	36.00	85.00
5,7	5.85	17.50	35.00
9-Robert Mitchum, Jane Russell photo-c	9.15	27.00	55.00
10,15-Ward-a	10.00	30.00	65.00
11-14,16-20: 12 (7/52)	4.25	13.00	28.00
21-Ward-c	9.15	27.00	55.00
22,23-Ward-a(p)	6.35	19.00	38.00
24-33: 33-Last pre-code (3/55)	4.15	12.50	25.00
34-39,41-46 (12/56; last Quality issue)	4.00	11.00	22.00
40-Ward-a; r-7 pgs./#21	5.85	17.50	35.00
47-(4-5/57; 1st DC issue)	22.50	68.00	225.00
48-60, 100	8.00	24.00	80.00
61-70	5.50	16.50	55.00
71-99: 74-Last 10 cent issue	4.20	12.60	42.00
101-The Beatles app. on-c	12.50	38.00	125.00
102-120: 102-123-(Serial)-Three Girls, Their Lives, Their Loves	2.50	7.50	22.00
121-132,143-146	2.00	6.00	16.00
133-142-(52 pgs.)	2.50	7.50	24.00

NOTE: ***Gustavson** a-8. **Tuska** a-128. Photo c-4, 5, 8-10, 15, 17.*

HEART THROBS - THE BEST OF DC ROMANCE COMICS (See Fireside Book Series)

HEART THROBS
DC Comics (Vertigo): Jan, 1999 - No. 4, Apr, 1999 ($2.95, lim. series)
1-4-Romance anthology. 1-Timm-c. 3-Corben-a 3.00

HEATHCLIFF (See Star Comics Magazine)
Marvel Comics (Star Comics)/Marvel Comics No. 23 on: Apr, 1985 - No. 56, Feb, 1991 (#16-on, $1.00)
1-56: Post-a most issues. 43-X-Mas issue. 47-Batman parody (Catman vs. the Soaker), Annual 1 ('87) 2.00

HEATHCLIFF'S FUNHOUSE
Marvel Comics (Star Comics)/Marvel No. 6 on: May, 1987 - No. 10, 1988
1-10 2.00

HEAVY HITTERS
Marvel Comics (Epic Comics): 1993 ($3.75, 68 pgs.)
1-Bound w/trading card; Lawdog, Feud, Alien Legion, Trouble With Girls, & Spyke 3.75

HEAVY LIQUID
DC Comics (Vertigo): Oct, 1999 - No. 5 ($5.95, limited series)
1,2-Paul Pope-s/a; flip covers 6.00

HECKLE AND JECKLE (See Blue Ribbon, Giant Comics Edition #5A & 10, Paul Terry's, Terry-Toons Comics)
St. John Publ. Co. No. 1-24/Pines No. 25 on: 10/51 - No. 24, 10/55; No. 25, Fall/56 - No. 34, 6/59

	GD2.0	FN6.0	NM9.4
1-Funny animal	25.00	75.00	175.00
2	13.00	39.00	90.00
3-5	10.00	30.00	70.00
6-10	7.50	22.50	45.00
11-20	5.85	17.50	35.00
21-34: 25-Begin CBS Television Presents on-c	4.25	13.00	26.00

HECKLE AND JECKLE (TV) (See New Terrytoons)
Gold Key/Dell Publ. Co.: 11/62 - No. 4, 8/63; 5/66; No. 2, 10/66; No. 3, 8/67

	GD2.0	FN6.0	NM9.4
1 (11/62; Gold Key)	5.50	16.50	60.00
2-4	2.80	8.40	28.00
1 (5/66; Dell)	3.50	10.50	35.00
2,3	2.50	7.50	25.00

(See March of Comics No. 379, 472, 484)

HECKLE AND JECKLE 3-D
Spotlight Comics: 1987 - No. 2?, 1987 ($2.50)
1,2 3.00

HECKLER, THE
DC Comics: Sept, 1992 - No. 6, Feb, 1993 ($1.25)
1-6-T&M Bierbaum-s/Keith Giffen-c/a 1.00

HECTIC PLANET
Slave Labor Graphics 1998 ($12.95/$14.95)
Book 1,2-r-Dorkin-s/a from Pirate Corp$ Vol. 1 & 2 15.00

HECTOR COMICS (The Keenest Teen in Town)
Key Publications: Nov, 1953 - No. 3, 1954

	GD2.0	FN6.0	NM9.4
1-Teen humor	4.00	11.00	22.00
2,3	2.80	7.00	14.00

HECTOR HEATHCOTE (TV)
Gold Key: Mar, 1964

	GD2.0	FN6.0	NM9.4
1 (10111-403)	6.35	19.00	70.00

HECTOR THE INSPECTOR (See Top Flight Comics)

HEDY DEVINE COMICS (Formerly All Winners #21? or Teen #22?(6/47); Hedy of Hollywood #36 on; also see Annie Oakley, Comedy & Venus)
Marvel Comics (RCM)/Atlas #50: No. 22, Aug, 1947 - No. 50, Sept, 1952

	GD2.0	FN6.0	NM9.4
22-1st app. Hedy Devine (also see Joker #32)	17.00	51.00	120.00
23,24,27-30: 23-Wolverton-a, 1 pg; Kurtzman's "Hey Look", 2 pgs. 24,27-30-"Hey Look" by Kurtzman, 1-3 pgs.	16.00	47.00	110.00
25-Classic "Hey Look" by Kurtzman, "Optical Illusion"	17.00	51.00	120.00
26- "Giggles 'n' Grins" by Kurtzman	10.00	30.00	70.00
31-34,36-50: 32-Anti-Wertham editorial	9.15	27.00	55.00
35-Four pgs. "Rusty" by Kurtzman	13.00	39.00	90.00

HEDY-MILLIE-TESSIE COMEDY (See Comedy Comics)

HEDY WOLFE (Also see Patsy & Hedy & Miss America Magazine V1#2)
Atlas Publishing Co. (Emgee): Aug, 1957

	GD2.0	FN6.0	NM9.4
1-Patsy Walker's rival; Al Hartley-c	10.00	30.00	70.00

HEE HAW (TV)
Charlton Press: July, 1970 - No. 7, Aug, 1971

	GD2.0	FN6.0	NM9.4
1	2.80	8.40	28.00
2-7	2.50	7.50	20.00

HEIDI (See Dell Jr. Treasury No. 6)

HELEN OF TROY (Movie)
Dell Publishing Co.: No. 684, Mar, 1956 (one-shot)

	GD2.0	FN6.0	NM9.4
Four Color 684-Buscema-a, photo-c	10.00	30.00	110.00

HELLBLAZER (John Constantine) (See Saga of Swamp Thing #37) (Also see Books of Magic limited series)
DC Comics (Vertigo #63 on): Jan, 1988 - Present ($1.25/$1.50/$1.95/$2.25)

	GD2.0	FN6.0	NM9.4
1-(44 pgs.)-John Constantine; McKean-c thru #21	1.50	4.50	12.00
2-5	1.00	3.00	8.00

Hellblazer #128 © DC

Hellcop #1 © Brian Haberlin

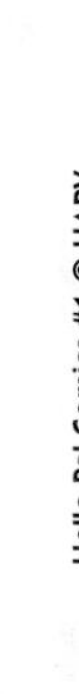
Hello Pal Comics #1 © HARV

GD2.0 FN6.0 NM9.4

6-10: 9-X-over w/Swamp Thing #76. 9,10-Swamp Thing cameo 5.00
11-20: 19-Sandman app. 5.00
21-26,28-30: 22-Williams-c. 24-Contains bound-in Shocker movie poster. 25,26-Grant Morrison scripts. 5.00
27,41: 27-Neil Gaiman scripts; Dave McKean-a; fold-out guide to Nightbreed. 41-Ennis scripts begin; ends #83 5.00
31-39: 36-Preview of World Without End. 4.00
40-($2.25, 52 pgs.)-Dave McKean-a & colors; preview of Kid Eternity 4.00
42-120: 44,45-Sutton-a(i). 50-($3.00, 52 pgs.). 52-Glenn Fabry painted-c begin. 62-Special Death insert by McKean. 63-Silver metallic ink on-c. 77-Totleben-c. 84-Sean Phillips-c/a begins; Delano story. 85-88-Eddie Campbell story. 75-($2.95, 52 pgs.). 89-Paul Jenkins scripts begin;108-Adlard-a. 100,120 ($3.50,48 pgs.) 3.50
Annual 1 (1989, $2.95, 68 pgs.)-Bryan Talbot's 1st work in American comics 2.40 6.00
Special 1 (1993, $3.95, 68 pgs.)-Ennis story; w/pin-ups. 2.40 6.00
...Damnation's Flame (1999, $16.95, TPB) r/#72-77, ...Dangerous Habits (1997, $14.95, TPB) r/#41-46, ...Fear and Loathing (1997, $14.95, TPB) r/#62-67, ...Tainted Love (1998, $16.95, TPB) r/#68-71, Vertigo Jam #1 and Hellblazer Special #1 17.00

NOTE: ***Alcala** a-8i, 9i, 18-22i. **Gaiman** scripts-27. **McKean** a-27,40; c-1-21. **Sutton** a-44i, 45i. **Talbot** a-Annual 1.*

HELLBLAZER/THE BOOKS OF MAGIC
DC Comics (Vertigo): Dec, 1997 - No. 2, Jan, 1998 ($2.50, mini-series)

1,2-John Constantine and Tim Hunter 2.50

HELLBOY (Also see Dark Horse Presents, John Byrne's Next Men. San Diego Comic Con #2, Danger Unlimited #4, Gen13 #13B, Ghost/Hellboy, & Savage Dragon)

HELLBOY: ALMOST COLOSSUS
Dark Horse Comics (Legend): Jun, 1997 - No. 2, Jul, 1997 ($2.95, lim. series)

1,2-Mignola-s/a 3.00

HELLBOY: BOX FULL OF EVIL
Dark Horse Comics: Aug, 1999 - No. 2, Sept, 1999 ($2.95, lim. series)

1,2-Mignola-s/a; back-up story w/ Matt Smith-a 3.00

HELLBOY CHRISTMAS SPECIAL
Dark Horse Comics: Dec, 1997 ($3.95, one-shot)

nn-Christmas stories by Mignola, Gianni, Darrow, Purcell 4.00

HELLBOY, JR., HALLOWEEN SPECIAL
Dark Horse Comics: Oct, 1997 ($3.95, one-shot)

nn-"Harvey" style renditions of Hellboy characters; Bill Wray, Mike Mignola & various-s/a; wraparound-c by Wray 4.00

HELLBOY: SEED OF DESTRUCTION
Dark Horse Comics (Legend): Mar, 1994 - No. 4, Jun, 1994 ($2.50, lim. series)

1-4-Mignola-c/a w/Byrne scripts; Monkeyman & O'Brien back-up story (origin) by Art Adams. 3.00
Trade paperback (1994, $17.95)-collects all four issues plus r/Hellboy's 1st app. in San Diego Comic Con #2 & pin-ups 18.00
Limited edition hardcover (1995, $99.95)-includes everything in trade paperback plus additional material. 100.00

HELLBOY: THE CORPSE AND THE IRON SHOES
Dark Horse Comics (Legend): Jan, 1996 ($2.95, one-shot)

nn-Mignola-c/a/scripts; reprints "The Corpse" serial from Capitol City's Advance Comics catalog w/new story 3.00

HELLBOY: THE WOLVES OF ST. AUGUST
Dark Horse Comics (Legend): 1995 ($4.95, squarebound, one-shot)

nn-Mignola--c/a/scripts; r/Dark Horse Presents #88-91 with additional story. 5.00

HELLBOY: WAKE THE DEVIL (Sequel to Seed of Destruction)
Dark Horse Comics (Legend): Jun, 1996 - No. 5, Oct, 1996 ($2.95, lim. series)

1-5: Mignola-c/a & scripts; The Monstermen back-up story by Gary Gianni 3.00
TPB (1997, $17.95) r/#1-5 18.00

HELLCOP

GD2.0 FN6.0 NM9.4

Image Comics (Avalon Studios): Aug, 1998 - Present ($2.50)

1-4: 1-(Oct. on-c) Casey-s 2.50

HELL ETERNAL
DC Comics (Vertigo Verité): 1998 ($6.95, squarebound, one-shot)

1-Delano-s/Phillips-a 7.00

HELLHOLE
Image Comics: July, 1999 - No. 2, Oct, 1999 ($2.50)

1,2-Lobdell-s/Polina-a 2.50

HELLHOUNDS (...: Panzer Cops #3-6)
Dark Horse Comics: 1994 - No. 6, July, 1994 ($2.50, B&W, limited series)

1-6: 1-Hamner-c. 3-(4/94). 2-Joe Phillips-c 3.00

HELLHOUND, THE REDEMPTION QUEST
Marvel Comics (Epic Comics): Dec, 1993 - No. 4, Mar, 1994 ($2.25, limited series, coated stock)

1-4 2.25

HELLO, I'M JOHNNY CASH
Spire Christian Comics (Fleming H. Revell Co.): 1976 (39/49¢)

nn 5.00

HELL ON EARTH (See DC Science Fiction Graphic Novel)

HELLO PAL COMICS (Short Story Comics)
Harvey Publications: Jan, 1943 - No. 3, May, 1943 (Photo-c)

1-Rocketman & Rocketgirl begin; Yankee Doodle Jones app.; Mickey Rooney photo-c 60.00 180.00 480.00
2-Charlie McCarthy photo-c (scarce) 50.00 150.00 400.00
3-Bob Hope photo-c 49.00 146.00 390.00

HELLRAISER/NIGHTBREED – JIHAD (Also see Clive Barker's...)
Epic Comics (Marvel Comics): 1991 - Book 2, 1991 ($4.50, 52 pgs.)

Book 1,2 4.50

HELL-RIDER (Magazine)
Skywald Publications: Aug, 1971 - No. 2, Oct, 1971 (B&W)

1-Origin & 1st app.; Butterfly & Wildbunch begins 4.00 12.00 40.00
2 2.80 8.40 28.00

NOTE: *#3 advertised in Psycho #5 but did not come out. **Buckler** a-1, 2. **Morrow** c-3.*

HELL'S ANGEL (Becomes Dark Angel #6 on)
Marvel Comics UK: July, 1992 - No. 5, Nov, 1993 ($1.75)

1-5: X-Men (Wolverine, Cyclops)-c/stories. 1-Origin. 3-Jim Lee cover swipe 2.00

HELLSHOCK
Image Comics: July, 1994 - No. 4, Nov, 1994 ($1.95, limited series)

1-4-Jae Lee-c/a & scripts. 4-variant-c. 2.00

HELLSHOCK
Image Comics: Jan, 1997 - No.2, Feb, 1997 ($2.95/$2.50, limited series)

1-($2.95)-Jae Lee-c/s/a, Villarrubia-painted-a 5.00
2-($2.50) 3.00

HELLSHOCK BOOK THREE: THE SCIENCE OF FAITH
Image Comics: Jan, 1998 ($2.50)

1-Jae Lee-c/s/a, Villarrubia-painted-a 2.50

HELLSTORM: PRINCE OF LIES (See Ghost Rider #1 & Marvel Spotlight #12)
Marvel Comics: Apr, 1993 - No. 21, Dec, 1994 ($2.00)

1-($2.95)-Parchment-c w/red thermographic ink 3.00
2-21: 14-Bound-in trading card sheet. 18-P. Craig Russell-c 2.00

HE-MAN (See Masters Of The Universe)

HE-MAN (Also see Tops In Adventure)
Ziff-Davis Publ. Co. (Approved Comics): Fall, 1952

1-Kinstler painted-c; Powell-a 15.00 45.00 105.00

HE-MAN

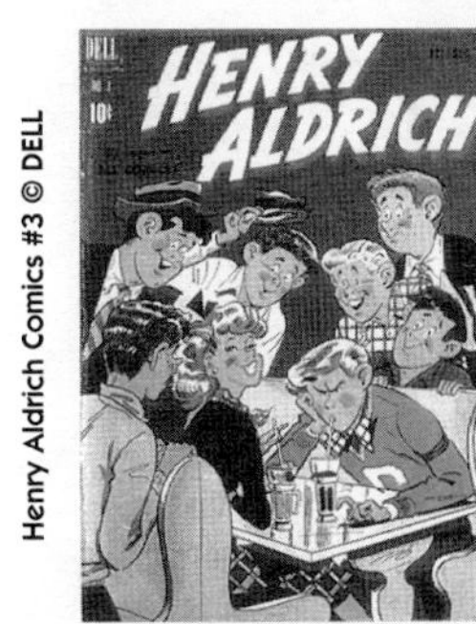

Henry Aldrich Comics #3 © DELL

Hercules #8 © CC

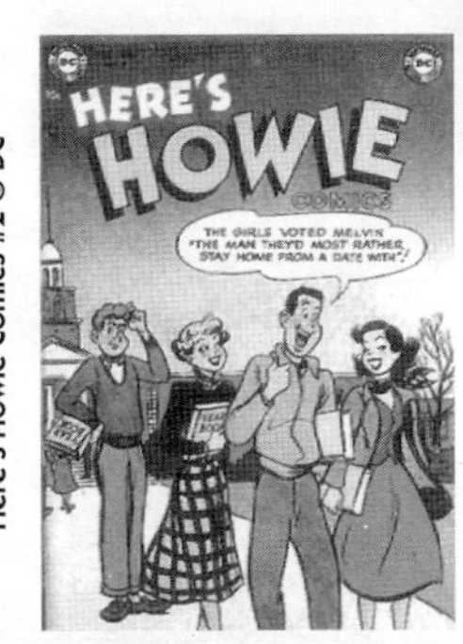

Here's Howie Comics #2 © DC

GD2.0 FN6.0 NM9.4

Toby Press: May, 1954 - No. 2, July, 1954 (Painted-c by B. Safran)
1 13.50 41.00 95.00
2 11.00 33.00 75.00

HENNESSEY (TV)
Dell Publishing Co.: No. 1200, Aug-Oct, 1961 - No. 1280, Mar-May, 1962
Four Color 1200-Gil Kane-a, photo-c 5.50 16.50 60.00
Four Color 1280-Photo-c 5.50 16.50 60.00

HENRY (Also see Little Annie Rooney)
David McKay Publications: 1935 (52 pgs.) (Daily B&W strip reprints)(10"x10" cardboard-c)
1-By Carl Anderson 39.00 116.00 270.00

HENRY (See King Comics & Magic Comics)
Dell Publishing Co.: No. 122, Oct, 1946 - No. 65, Apr-June, 1961
Four Color 122-All new stories begin 12.30 37.00 135.00
Four Color 155 (7/47), 1 (1-3/48)-All new stories 8.00 23.00 85.00
2 3.65 11.00 40.00
3-10 3.20 9.50 35.00
11-20: 20-Infinity-c 2.00 6.00 22.00
21-30 1.65 5.00 18.00
31-40 1.25 3.75 12.00
41-65 1.10 3.30 9.00

HENRY (See Giant Comic Album and March of Comics No. 43, 58, 84, 101, 112, 129, 147, 162, 178, 189)

HENRY ALDRICH COMICS (TV)
Dell Publishing Co.: Aug-Sept, 1950 - No. 22, Sept-Nov, 1954
1-Part series written by John Stanley; Bill Williams-a
7.00 22.00 80.00
2 3.60 11.00 40.00
3-5 3.00 9.00 35.00
6-10 2.50 7.50 28.00
11-22 1.80 5.50 20.00

HENRY BREWSTER
Country Wide (M.F. Ent.): Feb, 1966 - V2#7, Sept, 1967 (All 25¢ Giants)
1 2.25 6.75 18.00
2-6(12/66), V2#7-Powell-a in most 1.25 3.75 10.00

HEPCATS
Antarctic Press: Nov, 1996 - Present ($2.95, B&W)
0-12-Martin Wagner-c/s/a: 0-color 3.00
0-($9.95) CD Edition 10.00

HERBIE (See Forbidden Worlds & Unknown Worlds)
American Comics Group: April-May, 1964 - No. 23, Feb, 1967 (All 12¢)
1-Whitney-c/a in most issues 15.00 45.00 150.00
2-4 8.00 24.00 80.00
5-Beatles, Dean Martin, F. Sinatra app. 9.50 28.50 95.00
6,7,9,10 6.00 18.00 60.00
8-Origin & 1st app. The Fat Fury 7.50 22.50 75.00
11-23: 14-Nemesis & Magicman app. 17-r/2nd Herbie from Forbidden Worlds #94. 23-r/1st Herbie from F.W. #73 4.50 13.50 45.00

HERBIE
Dark Horse Comics: Oct, 1992 - No. 12, 1993 ($2.50, limited series)
1-6: Whitney-r plus new-c/a. 1-Byrne-c/a & scripts. 3-Bob Burden-c/a. 4-Art Adams-c 2.50

HERBIE GOES TO MONTE CARLO, HERBIE RIDES AGAIN (See Walt Disney Showcase No. 24, 41)

HERCULES (See Hit Comics #1-21, Journey Into Mystery Annual, Marvel Graphic Novel #37, Marvel Premiere #26 & The Mighty...)

HERCULES
Charlton Comics: Oct, 1967 - No. 13, Sept, 1969; Dec, 1968
1-Thane of Bagarth begins; Glanzman-a in all 2.50 7.50 20.00
2-13: 1-5,7-10-Aparo-a. 8-(12¢-c) 1.75 5.25 14.00

GD2.0 FN6.0 NM9.4

8-(Low distribution)(12/68, 35¢, B&W); magazine format; new Hercules story plus-r story/#1; Thane-r/#1-3 4.20 12.60 42.00
Modern Comics reprint 10('77), 11('78) 5.00

HERCULES (Prince of Power) (Also see The Champions)
Marvel Comics Group: V1#1, 9/82 - V1#4, 12/82; V2#1, 3/84 - V2#4, 6/84 (color, both limited series)
1-4, V2#1-4: Layton-c/a. 4-Death of Zeus. 2.00
NOTE: *Layton a-1, 2, 3p, 4p, V2#1-4; c-1-4, V2#1-4.*

HERCULES: HEART OF CHAOS
Marvel Comics: Aug, 1997 - No. 3, Oct, 1997 ($2.50, limited series)
1-3-DeFalco-s, Frenz-a 2.50

HERCULES: OFFICIAL COMICS MOVIE ADAPTION
Acclaim Books: 1997 ($4.50, digest size)
nn-Adaption of the Disney animated movie 4.50

HERCULES: THE LEGENDARY JOURNEYS (TV)
Topps Comics: June, 1996 - No. 5, Oct, 1996 ($2.95)
1-2: 1-Golden-c. 3.00
3-Xena-c/app. 1.00 2.80 7.00
3-Variant-c 1.85 5.50 15.00
4,5: Xena-c/app. 5.00

HERCULES UNBOUND
National Periodical Publications: Oct-Nov, 1975 - No. 12, Aug-Sept, 1977
1-Wood-i begins 2.40 6.00
2-12: 7-Adams ad. 10-Atomic Knights x-over 3.50
NOTE: ***Buckler*** *c-7p.* ***Layton*** *inks-No. 9, 10.* ***Simonson*** *a-7-10p, 11, 12; c- 8p, 9-12.* ***Wood*** *a-1-8i; c-7i, 8i.*

HERCULES (...Unchained #1121) (Movie)
Dell Publishing Co.: No. 1006, June-Aug, 1959 - No.1121, Aug, 1960
Four Color 1006-Buscema-a, photo-c 9.00 27.00 100.00
Four Color 1121-Crandall/Evans-a 9.00 27.00 100.00

HERE COMES SANTA (See March of Comics No. 30, 213, 340)

HERE COME THE BIG PEOPLE
Event Comics: Oct, 1997 ($2.95, one-shot)
1-Trace Beaulieu-s/Conner & Palmiotti-c/a; variant-c by Darrow 3.00

HERE'S HOWIE COMICS
National Periodical Publications: Jan-Feb, 1952 - No. 18, Nov-Dec, 1954
1 23.00 69.00 160.00
2 11.50 34.00 80.00
3-5: 5-Howie in the Army issues begin (9-10/52) 9.15 27.00 55.00
6-10 7.50 22.50 45.00
11-18 5.85 17.50 35.00

HERETIC, THE
Dark Horse Comics (Blanc Noir): Nov, 1996 - No. 4, Mar, 1997 ($2.95, limited series)
1-4:-w/back-up story 3.00

HERITAGE OF THE DESERT (See Zane Grey, 4-Color 236)

HERMAN & KATNIP (See Harvey Comics Hits #60 & 62, Harvey Hits #14,25,31,41 & Paramount Animated Comics #1)

HERMES VS. THE EYEBALL KID
Dark Horse Comics: Dec, 1994 - No. 3,Feb, 1995 ($2.95, B&W, limited series)
1-3: Eddie Campbell-c/a/scripts 3.00

HERO (Warrior of the Mystic Realms)
Marvel Comics: May, 1990 - No. 6, Oct, 1990 ($1.50, limited series)
1-6: 1-Portacio-i 2.00

HERO ALLIANCE, THE
Sirius Comics: Dec, 1985 - No. 2, Sept, 1986 (B&W)
1,2: 2-($1.50), Special Edition 1 (7/86, color) 2.00

HERO ALLIANCE

Heroes For Hire #9 © MAR

Hero For Hire #10 © MAR

Heroic Comics #16 © EAS

GD2.0 FN6.0 NM9.4

Wonder Color Comics: May, 1987 ($1.95)
1-Ron Lim-a 2.00

HERO ALLIANCE
Innovation Publishing: V2#1, Sept, 1989 - V2#17, Nov, 1991 ($1.95, 28 pgs.)
V2#1-17: 1,2-Ron Lim-a 2.00
Annual 1 (1990, $2.75, 36 pgs.)-Paul Smith-c/a 2.75
Special 1 (1992, $2.50, 32 pgs.)-Stuart Immonen-a (10 pgs.) 2.50

HERO ALLIANCE: END OF THE GOLDEN AGE
Innovation Publishing: July, 1989 - No. 3, Aug, 1989 ($1.75, bi-weekly limited series)
1-3: Bart Sears & Ron Lim-c/a; reprints & new-a 2.00

HEROES (Also see Shadow Cabinet & Static)
DC Comics (Milestone): May, 1996 - No. 6, Nov, 1996 ($2.50, limited series)
1-6: 1-Intro Heroes (Iota, Donner, Blitzen, Starlight, Payback & Static) 2.50

HEROES AGAINST HUNGER
DC Comics: 1986 ($1.50; one-shot for famine relief)
1-Superman, Batman app.; Neal Adams-c(p); includes many artists work; Jeff Jones assist (2 pg.) on B. Smith-a; Kirby-a 3.00

HEROES ALL CATHOLIC ACTION ILLUSTRATED
Heroes All Co.: 1943 - V6#5, Mar 10, 1948 (paper covers)
V1#1,2-(16 pgs., 8x11") 18.00 54.00 125.00
V2#1(1/44)-3(3/44)-(16 pgs., 8x11") 15.00 45.00 105.00
V3#1(1/45)-10(12/45)-(16 pgs., 8x11") 13.00 39.00 90.00
V4#1-35 (12/20/46)-(16 pgs.) 11.00 33.00 75.00
V5#1(1/10/47)-8(2/28/47)-(16 pgs.), V5#9(3/7/47)-20(11/25/47)-(32 pgs.), V6#1(1/10/48)-5(3/10/48)-(32 pgs.) 10.00 30.00 60.00

HEROES FOR HIRE
Marvel Comics: July, 1997 - No. 19, Jan, 1999 ($2.99/$1.99)
1-($2.99)-Wraparound cover 5.00
2-19: 2-Variant cover. 7-Thunderbolts app. 9-Punisher-c/app. 10,11 Deadpool-c/app. 18,19-Wolverine-c/app. 3.00
.../Quicksilver '98 Annual ($2.99) Siege of Wundagore pt.5 3.00

HEROES FOR HOPE STARRING THE X-MEN
Marvel Comics Group: Dec, 1985 ($1.50, one-shot, 52pgs., proceeds donated to famine relief)
1-Stephen King scripts; Byrne, Miller, Corben-a; Wrightson/J. Jones-a (3 pgs.); Art Adams-c; Starlin back-c 4.00

HEROES, INC. PRESENTS CANNON
Wally Wood/CPL/Gang Publ. No. 2: 1969 - No. 2, 1976 (Sold at Army PX's)
nn-Ditko, Wood-a; Wood-c; Reese-a(p) 1.50 4.50 12.00
2-Wood-c; Ditko, Byrne, Wood-a; 8-1/2x10-1/2"; B&W; $2.00 2.25 6.75 18.00
NOTE: *First issue not distributed by publisher; 1,800 copies were stored and 900 copies were stolen from warehouse. Many copies have surfaced in recent years.*

HEROES OF THE WILD FRONTIER (Formerly Baffling Mysteries)
Ace Periodicals: No. 27, Jan, 1956 - No. 2, Apr, 1956
27(#1),2-Davy Crockett, Daniel Boone, Buffalo Bill 4.25 13.00 26.00

HEROES REBORN: THE RETURN
Marvel Comics: Dec, 1997 - No. 4 ($2.50, weekly mini-series)
1-4-Avengers, Fantastic Four, Iron Man & Captain America rejoin regular Marvel Universe; Peter David-s/Larocca-c/a 4.00
1-4-Variant-c for each 2.40 6.00
Wizard 1/2 1.10 3.30 9.00
Return of the Heroes TPB ('98, $14.95) r/#1-4 15.00

HERO FOR HIRE (Power Man No. 17 on; also see Cage)
Marvel Comics Group: June, 1972 - No. 16, Dec, 1973
1-Origin & 1st app. Luke Cage; Tuska-a(p) 4.00 12.00 40.00
2-Tuska-a(p) 1.75 5.25 14.00
3-5: 3-1st app. Mace. 4-1st app. Phil Fox of the Bugle 1.25 3.75 10.00

GD2.0 FN6.0 NM9.4

6-10: 8,9-Dr. Doom app. 9-F.F. app. 1.00 2.80 7.00
11-16: 14-Origin retold. 15-Everett Subby-r('53). 16-Origin Stilletto; death of Rackham 2.40 6.00

HERO HOTLINE (1st app. in Action Comics Weekly #637)
DC Comics: April, 1989 - No. 6, Sept, 1989 ($1.75, limited series)
1-6: Super-hero humor; Schaffenberger-i 2.00

HEROIC ADVENTURES (See Adventures)

HEROIC COMICS (Reg'lar Fellers...#1-15; New Heroic #41 on)
Eastern Color Printing Co./Famous Funnies(Funnies, Inc. No. 1): Aug, 1940 - No. 97, June, 1955
1-Hydroman (origin) by Bill Everett, The Purple Zombie (origin) & Mann of India by Tarpe Mills begins (all 1st apps.) 150.00 450.00 1200.00
2 70.00 210.00 560.00
3,4 45.00 135.00 360.00
5,6 40.00 120.00 290.00
7-Origin & 1st app. Man O'Metal (1 pg.) 40.00 120.00 325.00
8-10: 10-Lingerie panels 30.00 90.00 210.00
11,13: 13-Crandall/Fine-a 29.00 86.00 200.00
12-Music Master (origin/1st app.) begins by Everett, ends No. 31; last Purple Zombie & Mann of India 31.00 94.00 220.00
14,15-Hydroman x-over in Rainbow Boy. 14-Origin & 1st app. Rainbow Boy (super hero). 15-1st app. Downbeat 30.00 90.00 210.00
16-20: 16-New logo. 17-Rainbow Boy x-over in Hydroman. 19-Rainbow Boy x-over in Hydroman & vice versa 21.00 64.00 150.00
21-30:25-Rainbow Boy x-over in Hydroman. 28-Last Man O'Metal. 29-Last Hydroman 13.50 41.00 95.00
31,34,38 4.25 13.00 28.00
32,36,37-Toth-a (3-4 pgs. each) 7.00 21.00 42.00
33,35-Toth-a (8 & 9 pgs.) 7.50 22.50 45.00
39-42-Toth, Ingels-a 7.50 22.50 45.00
43,46,47,49-Toth-a (2-4 pgs.). 47-Ingels-a 5.85 17.50 35.00
44,45,50-Toth-a (6-9 pgs.) 6.70 20.00 40.00
48,53,54 4.25 13.00 26.00
51-Williamson-a 7.00 21.00 42.00
52-Williamson-a (3 pg. story) 5.35 16.00 32.00
55-Toth-c/a 5.85 17.50 35.00
56-60-Toth-c. 60-Everett-a 5.35 16.00 32.00
61-Everett-a 4.25 13.00 26.00
62,64-Everett-c/a 4.25 13.00 28.00
63-Everett-c 4.00 11.00 22.00
65-Williamson/Frazetta-a; Evans-a (2 pgs.) 8.35 25.00 50.00
66,75,94-Frazetta-a (2 pgs. each) 4.25 13.00 28.00
67,73-Frazetta-a (4 pgs. each) 5.85 17.50 35.00
68,74,76-80,84,85,88-93,95-97: 95-Last pre-code 4.00 11.00 22.00
69,72-Frazetta-a (6 & 8 pgs. each); 1st (?) app. Frazetta Red Cross ad 8.35 25.00 50.00
70,71,86,87-Frazetta, 3-4 pgs. each; 1 pg. ad by Frazetta in #70 5.00 15.00 30.00
81,82-Frazetta art (1 pg. each): 81-1st (?) app. Frazetta Boy Scout ad (tied w/ Buster Crabbe #9 4.00 11.00 22.00
83-Frazetta-a (1/2 pg.) 4.00 11.00 22.00
NOTE: ***Evans*** *a-64, 65.* ***Everett*** *a-(Hydroman-c/a-No. 1-9), 44, 60-64; c-1-9, 62-64.* ***Harvey Fuller*** *c-28-35.* ***Sid Greene*** *a-38-43, 46.* ***Guardineer*** *a-42(3), 43, 44, 45(2), 49(3), 50, 60, 61(2), 65, 67(2) 70-72.* ***Ingels*** *c-41.* ***Kiefer*** *a-46, 48; c-19-22, 24, 44, 46, 48, 51-53, 65, 67-69, 71-74, 76, 77, 79, 80, 82, 85, 86, 88, 89, 94, 95.* ***Mort Lawrence*** *a-45.* ***Tarpe Mills*** *a-2(2), 3(2), 10.* ***Ed Moore*** *a-49, 52-54, 56-63, 65-69, 72-74, 76, 77.* ***H.G. Peter*** *a-58-74, 76, 77, 87.* ***Paul Reinman*** *a-49.* ***Rico*** *a-31. Captain Tootsie by* ***Beck****-31, 32. Painted-c #16 on. Hydroman c-1-11. Music Master c-12, 13, 15. Rainbow Boy c-14.*

HERO ZERO (Also see Comics' Greatest World & Godzilla Versus Hero Zero)
Dark Horse Comics: Sept, 1994 ($2.50)
0 2.50

HEX (Replaces Jonah Hex)
DC Comics: Sept, 1985 - No. 18, Feb, 1987 (Story cont'd from Jonah Hex # 92)
1-18: 1-Hex in post-atomic war world; origin. 6-Origin Stiletta. 11-13: All contain future Batman storyline. 13-Intro The Dogs of War (origin #15) 2.50

Hi-Ho Comics #1 © Four Star Pub.

Hi-School Romance #3 © HARV

Hit Comics #25 © QUA

	GD2.0	FN6.0	NM9.4

NOTE: ***Giffen*** *a(p)-15-18; c(p)-15,17,18.* ***Texeira*** *a-1, 2p, 3p, 5-7p, 9p, 11-14p; c(p)-1, 2, 4-7, 12.*

HEXBREAKER (See First Comics Graphic Novel #15)

HEY THERE, IT'S YOGI BEAR (See Movie Comics)

HI-ADVENTURE HEROES (TV)
Gold Key: May, 1969 - No. 2, Aug, 1969 (Hanna-Barbera)

	GD2.0	FN6.0	NM9.4
1-Three Musketeers, Gulliver, Arabian Knights	4.50	13.50	45.00
2-Three Musketeers, Micro-Venture, Arabian Knights	3.50	10.50	35.00

HI AND LOIS
Dell Publishing Co.: No. 683, Mar, 1956 - No. 955, Nov, 1958

	GD2.0	FN6.0	NM9.4
Four Color 683 (#1)	2.25	6.75	25.00
Four Color 774(3/57),955	1.80	5.50	20.00

HI AND LOIS
Charlton Comics: Nov, 1969 - No. 11, July, 1971

	GD2.0	FN6.0	NM9.4
1	2.25	6.75	18.00
2-11	1.25	3.75	10.00

HICKORY (See All Humor Comics)
Quality Comics Group: Oct, 1949 - No. 6, Aug, 1950

	GD2.0	FN6.0	NM9.4
1-Sahl-c/a in all; Feldstein?-a	15.00	45.00	105.00
2	9.15	27.00	55.00
3-6	8.00	24.00	48.00

HIDDEN CREW, THE (See The United States Air Force Presents:...)

HIDE-OUT (See Zane Grey, Four Color No. 346)

HIDING PLACE, THE
Spire Christian Comics (Fleming H. Revell Co.): 1973 (39¢/49¢)

	GD2.0	FN6.0	NM9.4
nn			5.00

HIGH ADVENTURE
Red Top(Decker) Comics (Farrell): Oct, 1957

	GD2.0	FN6.0	NM9.4
1-Krigstein-r from Explorer Joe (re-issue on-c)	4.25	13.00	26.00

HIGH ADVENTURE (TV)
Dell Publishing Co.: No. 949, Nov, 1958 - No. 1001, Aug-Oct, 1959 (Lowell Thomas)

	GD2.0	FN6.0	NM9.4
Four Color 949 (#1)-Photo-c	4.50	13.50	50.00
Four Color 1001-Lowell Thomas'...(#2)	4.50	13.50	50.00

HIGH CHAPPARAL (TV)
Gold Key: Aug, 1968 (Photo-c)

	GD2.0	FN6.0	NM9.4
1 (10226-808)-Tufts-a	4.50	13.50	45.00

HIGH SCHOOL CONFIDENTIAL DIARY (Confidential Diary #12 on)
Charlton Comics: June, 1960 - No. 11, Mar, 1962

	GD2.0	FN6.0	NM9.4
1	3.50	10.50	35.00
2-11	2.50	7.50	20.00

HIGH VOLTAGE
Blackout Comics: 1996 ($2.95)

	GD2.0	FN6.0	NM9.4
0-Mike Baron-s			3.00

HI-HO COMICS
Four Star Publications: nd (2/46?) - No. 3, 1946

	GD2.0	FN6.0	NM9.4
1-Funny Animal; L. B. Cole-c	36.00	107.00	250.00
2,3: 2-L. B. Cole-c	20.00	60.00	140.00

HI-JINX (Teen-age Animal Funnies)
La Salle Publ. Co./B&I Publ. Co. (American Comics Group)/Creston: 1945; July-Aug, 1947 - No. 7, July-Aug, 1948

	GD2.0	FN6.0	NM9.4
nn-(© 1945, 25 cents, 132 Pgs.)(La Salle)	20.00	60.00	140.00
1-Teen-age, funny animal	15.00	45.00	105.00
2,3	10.00	30.00	65.00
4-7-Milt Gross. 4-X-Mas-c	12.00	36.00	85.00

HI-LITE COMICS
E. R. Ross Publishing Co.: Fall, 1945

	GD2.0	FN6.0	NM9.4
1-Miss Shady	17.00	51.00	120.00

HILLBILLY COMICS
Charlton Comics: Aug, 1955 - No. 4, July, 1956 (Satire)

	GD2.0	FN6.0	NM9.4
1-By Art Gates	8.35	25.00	50.00
2-4	5.00	15.00	30.00

HILLY ROSE'S SPACE ADVENTURES
Astro Comics: May, 1995 - Present ($2.95, B&W)

	GD2.0	FN6.0	NM9.4
1		2.40	6.00
2-9			3.00
Trade Paperback (1996, $12.95)-r/#1-5			13.00

HIP-IT-TY HOP (See March of Comics No. 15)

HI-SCHOOL ROMANCE (...Romances No. 41 on)
Harvey Publ./True Love(Home Comics): Oct, 1949 - No. 5, June, 1950; No. 6, Dec, 1950 - No. 73, Mar, 1958; No. 74, Sept, 1958 - No. 75, Nov, 1958

	GD2.0	FN6.0	NM9.4
1-Photo-c	13.50	41.00	95.00
2-Photo-c	8.35	25.00	50.00
3-9: 3,5-Photo-c	5.85	17.50	35.00
10-Rape story	8.35	25.00	50.00
11-20	4.00	11.00	22.00
21-31	3.60	9.00	18.00
32- "Unholy passion" story	5.85	17.50	35.00
33-36: 36-Last pre-code (2/55)	3.20	8.00	16.00
37-75: 54-58,73-Kirby-c	2.40	6.00	12.00

NOTE: ***Powell*** *a-1-3, 5, 8, 12-16, 18, 21-23, 25-27, 30-34, 36, 37, 39, 45-48, 50-52, 57, 58, 60, 64, 65, 67, 69.*

HI-SCHOOL ROMANCE DATE BOOK
Harvey Publications: Nov, 1962 - No. 3, Mar, 1963 (25¢ Giants)

	GD2.0	FN6.0	NM9.4
1-Powell, Baker-a	3.20	9.60	32.00
2,3	2.25	6.75	18.00

HIS NAME IS SAVAGE (Magazine format)
Adventure House Press: June, 1968 (35¢, 52 pgs.)

	GD2.0	FN6.0	NM9.4
1-Gil Kane-a	3.50	10.50	35.00

HI-SPOT COMICS (Red Ryder No. 1 & No. 3 on)
Hawley Publications: No. 2, Nov, 1940

	GD2.0	FN6.0	NM9.4
2-David Innes of Pellucidar; art by J. C. Burroughs; written by Edgar Rice Burroughs	112.00	337.00	900.00

HISTORY OF THE DC UNIVERSE (Also see Crisis on Infinite Earths)
DC Comics: Sept, 1986 - No. 2, Nov, 1986 ($2.95, limited series)

	GD2.0	FN6.0	NM9.4
1,2: 1-Perez-c/a			3.00
Limited Edition hardcover	4.00	12.00	40.00

HITCHHIKERS GUIDE TO THE GALAXY (See Life, the Universe and Everything & Restaraunt at the End of the Universe)
DC Comics: 1993 - No. 3, 1993 ($4.95, limited series)

	GD2.0	FN6.0	NM9.4
1-3: Adaptation of Douglas Adams book			5.00
TPB (1997, $14.95) r/#1-3			15.00

HIT COMICS
Quality Comics Group: July, 1940 - No. 65, July, 1950

	GD2.0	FN6.0	NM9.4
1-Origin/1st app. Neon, the Unknown & Hercules; intro. The Red Bee; Bob & Swab, Blaze Barton, the Strange Twins, X-5 Super Agent, Casey Jones & Jack & Jill (ends #7) begin	567.00	1700.00	5400.00
2-The Old Witch begins, ends #14	250.00	750.00	2000.00
3-Casey Jones ends; transvestism story "Jack & Jill"	225.00	675.00	1800.00
4-Super Agent (ends #17), & Betty Bates (ends #65) begin; X-5 ends	200.00	600.00	1600.00
5-Classic Lou Fine cover	500.00	1500.00	4500.00
6-10: 10-Old Witch by Crandall (4 pgs.); 1st work in comics (4/41)	181.00	544.00	1450.00
11-Classic cover	156.00	469.00	1250.00
12-17: 13-Blaze Barton ends. 17-Last Neon; Crandall Hercules in all; Last Lou Fine-c	112.00	338.00	900.00

Hitman #16 © DC

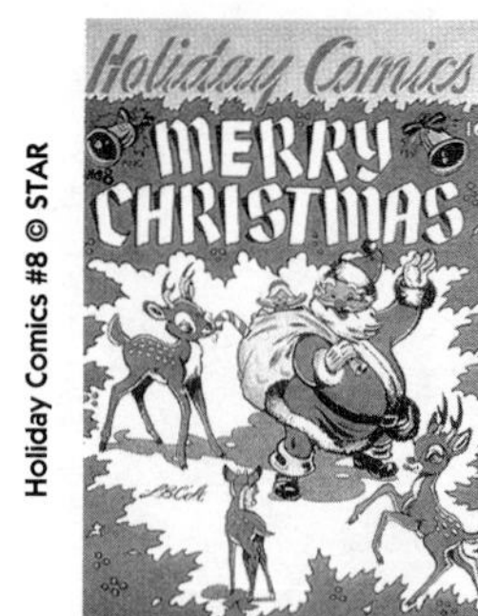

Holiday Comics #8 © STAR

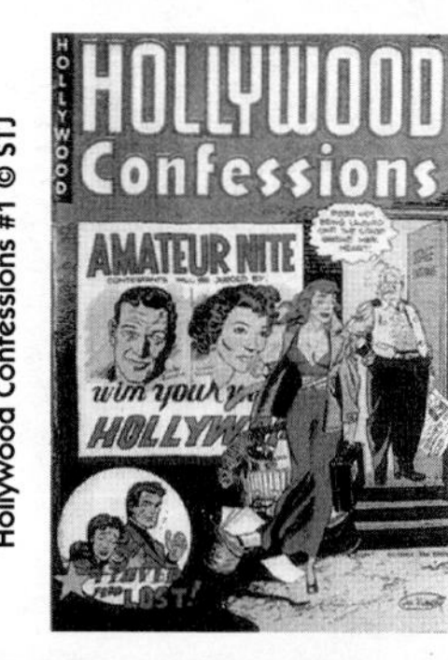

Hollywood Confessions #1 © STJ

GD2.0 FN6.0 NM9.4

18-Origin & 1st app. Stormy Foster, the Great Defender (12/41); The Ghost of Flanders begins; Crandall-c 122.00 366.00 975.00
19,20 100.00 300.00 800.00
21-24: 21-Last Hercules. 24-Last Red Bee & Strange Twins 94.00 281.00 750.00
25-Origin & 1st app. Kid Eternity and begins by Moldoff (12/42); 1st app. The Keeper (Kid Eternity's aide) 175.00 525.00 1400.00
26-Blackhawk x-over in Kid Eternity 100.00 300.00 800.00
27-29 47.00 141.00 375.00
30,31- "Bill the Magnificent" by Kurtzman, 11 pgs. in each 43.00 128.00 340.00
32-40: 32-Plastic Man x-over. 34-Last Stormy Foster 26.00 77.00 180.00
41-50 18.00 54.00 125.00
51-60-Last Kid Eternity 17.00 49.00 115.00
61-63-Crandall-c/a; 61-Jeb Rivers begins 17.00 51.00 120.00
64,65-Crandall-a 17.00 49.00 115.00

NOTE: ***Crandall*** *a-11-17(Hercules), 23, 24(Stormy Foster); c-18-20, 23, 24.* ***Fine*** *c-1-14, 16, 17(most).* ***Ward*** *c-33. Bondage c-7, 64. Hercules c-3, 10-17. Jeb Rivers c-61-65. Kid Eternity c-25-60 (w/Keeper-28-34, 36, 39-43, 45-55). Neon the Unknown c-2, 4, 8, 9. Red Bee c-1, 5-7. Stormy Foster c-18-24.*

HITLER'S ASTROLOGER (See Marvel Graphic Novel #35)

HITMAN (Also see Bloodbath #2, Batman Chronicles #4, Demon #43-45 & Demon Annual #2)
DC Comics: May, 1996 - Present ($2.25/$2.50)

1-Garth Ennis-s & John McCrea-c/a begin; Batman app. 1.50 4.50 12.00
2-Joker-c;Two Face, Mad Hatter, Batman app. 1.00 3.00 8.00
3-5: 3-Batman-c/app.; Joker app. 4-1st app. Nightfist 1.00 2.80 7.00
6-20: 8-Final Night x-over. 10-GL cameo. 11-20: 11,12-GL-c/app. 15-20-"Ace of Killers". 16-18-Catwoman app. 17-19-Demon-app 4.00
21-41: 34-Superman-c/app. 3.00
#1,000,000 (11/98) Hitman goes to the 853rd Century 2.50
Annual 1 (1997, $3.95) Pulp Heroes 5.00
TPB-(1997, $9.95) r/#1-3, Demon Ann. #2, Batman Chronicles #4 10.00
Local Heroes TPB ('99, $17.95) r/#9-14 & Annual #1 18.00
10,000 Bullets TPB ('98, $9.95) r/#4-8 10.00

HI-YO SILVER (See Lone Ranger's Famous Horse... and also see The Lone Ranger and March of Comics No. 215)

HOBBIT, THE
Eclipse Comics: 1989 - No. 3, 1990 ($4.95, squarebound, 52 pgs.)

Book 1-3: Adapts novel (#1has a 2nd printing) 5.00

HOCUS POCUS (Formerly Funny Book)
Parents' Magazine Press: No. 9, Aug-Sept, 1946

9 5.00 15.00 30.00

HOGAN'S HEROES (TV)
Dell Publishing Co.: June, 1966 - No. 8, Sept, 1967; No. 9, Oct, 1969

1: #1-7 photo-c 6.75 20.50 75.00
2,3-Ditko-a(p) 4.25 13.00 48.00
4-9: 9-Reprints #1 2.90 8.70 32.00

HOKUM & HEX (See Razorline)
Marvel Comics (Razorline): Sept, 1993 - No. 9, May, 1994 ($1.75/$1.95)

1-($2.50)-Foil embossed-c; by Clive Barker 2.50
2-9: 5-Hyperkind x-over 2.00

HOLIDAY COMICS
Fawcett Publications: 1942 (25¢, 196 pgs.)

1-Contains three Fawcett comics plus two page portrait of Captain Marvel; Capt. Marvel, Nyoka #1, & Whiz. Not rebound, remaindered comics; printed at the same time as originals 140.00 420.00 1400.00

HOLIDAY COMICS (Becomes Fun Comics #9-12)
Star Publications: Jan, 1951 - No. 8, Oct, 1952

GD2.0 FN6.0 NM9.4

1-Funny animal contents (Frisky Fables) in all; L. B. Cole X-Mas-c 34.00 103.00 240.00
2-Classic L. B. Cole-c 37.00 111.00 260.00
3-8: 5,8-X-Mas-c; all L.B. Cole-c 23.00 69.00 160.00
Accepted Reprint 4 (nd)-L.B. Cole-c 10.00 30.00 65.00

HOLIDAY DIGEST
Harvey Comics: 1988 ($1.25, digest-size)

1 2.40 6.00

HOLIDAY PARADE (Walt Disney's...)
W. D. Publications (Disney): Winter, 1990-91(no yr. given) - No. 2, Winter, 1990-91 ($2.95, 68 pgs.)

1-Reprints 1947 Firestone by Barks plus new-a 3.00
2-Barks-r plus other stories 3.00

HOLI-DAY SURPRISE (Formerly Summer Fun)
Charlton Comics: V2#55, Mar, 1967 (25¢ Giant)

V2#55 2.50 7.50 25.00

HOLLYWOOD COMICS
New Age Publishers: Winter, 1944 (52 pgs.)

1-Funny animal 17.00 51.00 120.00

HOLLYWOOD CONFESSIONS
St. John Publishing Co.: Oct, 1949 - No. 2, Dec, 1949

1-Kubert-c/a (entire book) 25.00 75.00 175.00
2-Kubert-c/a (entire book) (Scarce) 34.00 103.00 240.00

HOLLYWOOD DIARY
Quality Comics Group: Dec, 1949 - No. 5, July-Aug, 1950

1-No photo-c 18.00 54.00 125.00
2-Photo-c 11.50 34.00 80.00
3-5-Photo-c. 5-June Allyson/Peter Lawford photo-c 10.00 30.00 65.00

HOLLYWOOD FILM STORIES
Feature Publications/Prize: April, 1950 - No. 4, Oct, 1950 (All photo-c; "Fumetti" type movie comic)

1-June Allyson photo-c 18.00 54.00 125.00
2-4: 2-Lizabeth Scott photo-c. 3-Barbara Stanwick photo-c. 4-Betty Hutton photo-c 13.50 41.00 95.00

HOLLYWOOD FUNNY FOLKS (Formerly Funny Folks; Becomes Nutsy Squirrel #61 on)
National Periodical Publ.: No. 27, Aug-Sept, 1950 - No. 60, July-Aug, 1954

27 13.00 39.00 90.00
28-40 10.00 30.00 60.00
41-60 8.35 25.00 50.00

NOTE: ***Sheldon Mayer*** *a-27-35, 37-40, 43-46, 48-51, 53, 56, 57, 60.*

HOLLYWOOD LOVE DOCTOR (See Doctor Anthony King...)

HOLLYWOOD PICTORIAL (...Romances on cover)
St. John Publishing Co.: No. 3, Jan, 1950

3-Matt Baker-a; photo-c 23.00 69.00 160.00
(Becomes a movie magazine - Hollywood Pictorial Western with No. 4.)

HOLLYWOOD ROMANCES (Formerly Brides In Love; becomes For Lovers Only #60 on)
Charlton Comics: V2#46, 11/66; #47, 10/67; #48, 11/68;V3#49,11/69-V3#59, 6/71

V2#46-Rolling Stones-c/story 7.50 22.50 75.00
V2#47-V3#59: 56- "Born to Heart Break" begins 1.10 3.30 9.00

HOLLYWOOD SECRETS
Quality Comics Group: Nov, 1949 - No. 6, Sept, 1950

1-Ward-c/a (9 pgs.) 31.00 94.00 220.00
2-Crandall-a, Ward-c/a (9 pgs.) 21.00 64.00 150.00
3-6: All photo-c. 5-Lex Barker (Tarzan)-c 11.00 33.00 75.00
...of Romance, I.W. Reprint #9; r/#2 above w/Kinstler-c 1.75 5.25 14.00

HOLLYWOOD SUPERSTARS

Hoyoke One-Shot #9 © HOKE

Honeymoon Romance #2 © Artful Pub.

Hopalong Cassidy #8 © FAW

GD2.0 FN6.0 NM9.4

Marvel Comics (Epic Comics): Nov, 1990 - No. 5, Apr, 1991 ($2.25)
1-($2.95, 52 pgs.)-Spiegle-c/a in all; Aragones-a, inside front-c plus 2-4 pgs. 3.00
2-5 ($2.25) 2.25

HOLO-MAN (See Power Record Comics)

HOLYOKE ONE-SHOT
Holyoke Publishing Co. (Tem Publ.): 1944 - No. 10, 1945 (All reprints)
1,2: 1-Grit Grady (on cover only), Miss Victory, Alias X (origin)-All reprints from Captain Fearless. 2-Rusty Dugan (Corporal); Capt. Fearless (origin), Mr. Miracle (origin) app. 10.00 30.00 70.00
3-Miss Victory; r/Crash #4; Cat Man (origin), Solar Legion by Kirby app.; Miss Victory on cover only (1945) 23.00 69.00 160.00
4,6,8: 4-Mr. Miracle; The Blue Streak app. 6-Capt. Fearless, Alias X, Capt. Stone (splash used as-c to #10); Diamond Jim & Rusty Dugan (splash from cover of #2). 8-Blue Streak, Strong Man (story matches cover to #7)-Crash reprints 10.00 30.00 60.00
5,7: 5-U.S. Border Patrol Comics (Sgt. Dick Carter of the...), Miss Victory (story matches cover to #3), Citizen Smith, & Mr. Miracle app. 7-Secret Agent Z-2, Strong Man, Blue Streak (story matches cover to #8); Reprints from Crash #2 10.00 30.00 70.00
9-Citizen Smith, The Blue Streak, Solar Legion by Kirby & Strongman, the Perfect Human app.; reprints from Crash #4 & 5; Citizen Smith on cover only-from story in #5 (1944-before #3) 15.00 45.00 105.00
10-Captain Stone; r/Crash; Solar Legion by S&K 15.00 45.00 105.00

HOMER COBB (See Adventures of...)

HOMER HOOPER
Atlas Comics: July, 1953 - No. 4, Dec, 1953
1-Teenage humor 9.15 27.00 55.00
2-4 5.85 17.50 35.00

HOMER, THE HAPPY GHOST (See Adventures of...)
Atlas(ACI/PPI/WPI)/Marvel: 3/55 - No. 22, 11/58; V2#1, 11/69 - V2#4, 5/70
V1#1-Dan DeCarlo-c/a begins, ends #22 15.00 45.00 105.00
2-1st code approved issue 9.15 27.00 55.00
3-10 7.00 21.00 42.00
11-22 5.85 17.50 35.00
V2#1 (11/69) 8.00 24.00 80.00
2-4 4.00 12.00 40.00

HOME RUN (Also see A-1 Comics)
Magazine Enterprises: No. 89, 1953 (one-shot)
A-1 89 (#3)-Powell-a; Stan Musial photo-c 11.50 34.00 80.00

HOMICIDE (Also see Dark Horse Presents)
Dark Horse Comics: Apr, 1990 ($1.95, B&W, one-shot)
1-Detective story 2.00

HOMICIDE: TEARS OF THE DEAD
Chaos! Comics: Apr, 1997 ($2.95, one-shot)
1-Brom-c, 1-Premium Ltd. Ed. w/wraparound-c 3.00

HONEYMOON (Formerly Gay Comics)
A Lover's Magazine(USA) (Marvel): No. 41, Jan, 1950
41-Photo-c; article by Betty Grable 10.00 30.00 60.00

HONEYMOONERS, THE (TV)
Lodestone: Oct, 1986 ($1.50)
1-Photo-c 3.00

HONEYMOONERS, THE (TV)
Triad Publications: Sept, 1987 - No. 13? ($2.00)
1-13 3.00

HONEYMOON ROMANCE
Artful Publications (Canadian): Apr, 1950 - No. 2, July, 1950 (25¢, digest size)
1,2-(Rare) 36.00 107.00 250.00

HONEY WEST (TV)

GD2.0 FN6.0 NM9.4

Gold Key: Sept, 1966 (Photo-c)
1 (10186-609) 9.50 28.50 105.00

HONG KONG PHOOEY (TV)
Charlton Comics: June, 1975 - No. 9, Nov, 1976 (Hanna-Barbera)
1 4.00 12.00 40.00
2 2.50 7.50 20.00
3-9 1.85 5.50 15.00

HONG ON THE RANGE
Image/Flypaper Press: Dec, 1997 - No. 3, Feb, 1998 ($2.50, lim. series)
1-3: Wu-s/Lafferty-a 2.50

HOODED HORSEMAN, THE (Also see Blazing West)
American Comics Group (Michel Publ.): No. 21, 1-2/52 - No. 27, 1-2/53; No. 18, 12-1/54-55 - No. 27, 6-7/56
21(1-2/52)-Hooded Horseman, Injun Jones continue 13.50 41.00 95.00
22 10.00 30.00 60.00
23-25,27(1-2/53) 7.50 22.50 45.00
26-Origin/1st app. Cowboy Sahib by L. Starr 10.00 30.00 70.00
18(11-12/54)(Formerly Out of the Night) 10.00 30.00 60.00
19,21-24,26,27(6-7/56): 19-Last precode (1-2/55) 6.70 20.00 40.00
20-Origin Johnny Injun 8.35 25.00 50.00
25-Cowboy Sahib on cover only; Hooded Horseman i.d. revealed 7.50 22.50 45.00
NOTE: *Whitney c/a-21('52), 20-22.*

HOODED MENACE, THE (Also see Daring Adventures)
Realistic/Avon Periodicals: 1951 (one-shot)
nn-Based on a band of hooded outlaws in the Pacific Northwest, 1900-1906; reprinted in Daring Advs. #15 45.00 135.00 360.00

HOODS UP
Fram Corp.: 1953 (15¢, distributed to service station owners, 16 pgs.)
1-(Very Rare; only 2 known); Eisner-c/a in all. 47.00 141.00 375.00
2-6-(Very Rare; only 1 known of #3, 4, 2 known of #2) 47.00 141.00 375.00
NOTE: *Convertible Connie gives tips for service stations, selling Fram oil filters.*

HOOK (Movie)
Marvel Comics: Early Feb, 1992 - No. 4, Late Mar, 1992 ($1.00, limited series)
1-4: Adapts movie; Vess-c; 1-Morrow-a(p) 2.00
nn (1991, $5.95, 84 pgs.)-Contains #1-4; Vess-c 2.40 6.00
1 (1991, $2.95, magazine, 84 pgs.)-Contains #1-4; Vess-c (same cover as nn issue) 3.00

HOOT GIBSON'S WESTERN ROUNDUP (See Western Roundup under Fox Giants)

HOOT GIBSON WESTERN (Formerly My Love Story)
Fox Features Syndicate: No. 5, May, 1950 - No. 3, Sept, 1950
5,6(#1,2): 5-Photo-c. 6-Photo/painted-c 26.00 79.00 185.00
3-Wood-a; painted-c 29.00 86.00 200.00

HOPALONG CASSIDY (Also see Bill Boyd Western, Master Comics, Real Western Hero, Six Gun Heroes & Western Hero; Bill Boyd starred as H. Cassidy in the movies; H. Cassidy in movies, radio & TV)
Fawcett Publications: Feb, 1943; No. 2, Summer, 1946 - No. 85, Nov, 1953
1 (1943, 68 pgs.)-H. Cassidy & his horse Topper begin (on sale 1/8/43)-Captain Marvel app. on-c 436.00 1308.00 4800.00
2-(Sum, '46) 74.00 222.00 670.00
3,4: 3-(Fall, '46, 52 pgs. begin) 33.00 99.00 300.00
5- "Mad Barber" story mentioned in **SOTI**, pgs. 308,309; photo-c 27.00 80.00 240.00
6-10: 8-Photo-c 22.00 63.00 200.00
11-19: 11,13-19-Photo-c 17.00 50.00 150.00
20-29 (52 pgs.)-Painted/photo-c 13.00 39.00 115.00
30,31,33,34,37-39,41 (52 pgs.)-Painted-c 11.00 33.00 75.00
32,40 (36pgs.)-Painted-c 10.00 30.00 65.00
35,42,43,45-47,49-51,43,43,56 (52 pgs.)-Photo-c 10.00 30.00 70.00

Horrific #12 © Comic Media

The Horrors #14 © STAR

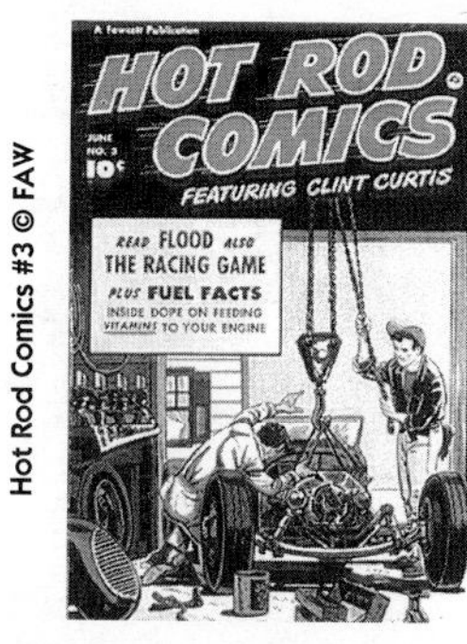

Hot Rod Comics #3 © FAW

	GD2.0	FN6.0	NM9.4
36,44,48 (36 pgs.)-Photo-c	10.00	30.00	60.00
52,55,57-70 (36 pgs.)-Photo-c	8.35	25.00	50.00
71-84-Photo-c	6.35	19.00	38.00
85-Last Fawcett issue; photo-c	8.35	25.00	50.00

NOTE: *Line-drawn c-1-4, 6, 7, 9, 10, 12.*

... & The 5 Men of Evil (AC Comics, 1991, $12.95) r/newspaper strips and Fawcett story "Signature of Death" 13.00

HOPALONG CASSIDY (TV)
National Periodical Publications: No. 86, Feb, 1954 - No. 135, May-June, 1959 (All-36 pgs.)

	GD2.0	FN6.0	NM9.4
86-Gene Colan-a begins, ends #117; photo covers continue	38.00	114.00	265.00
87	21.00	64.00	150.00
88-91: 91-1 pg. Superboy-sty (6/54)	14.00	43.00	100.00
92-99 (98 has #93 on-c; last precode issue, 2/55). 95-Reversed photo-c to #52. 98-Reversed photo-c to #61. 99-Reversed photo-c to #60	12.00	36.00	85.00
100-Same cover as #50	13.50	41.00	95.00
101-108: 105-Same photo-c as #54. 107-Same photo-c as #51. 108-Last photo-c	6.50	19.50	65.00
109-130: 118-Gil Kane-a begins. 123-Kubert-a (2 pgs.). 124-Painted-c	5.50	16.50	55.00
131-135	6.00	18.00	60.00

HOPE SHIP
Dell Publishing Co.: June-Aug, 1963

	GD2.0	FN6.0	NM9.4
1	1.50	4.50	12.00

HOPPY THE MARVEL BUNNY (See Fawcett's Funny Animals)
Fawcett Publications: Dec, 1945 - No. 15, Sept, 1947

	GD2.0	FN6.0	NM9.4
1	29.00	86.00	200.00
2	13.50	41.00	95.00
3-15: 7-Xmas-c	11.50	34.00	80.00

HORACE & DOTTY DRIPPLE (Dotty Dripple No. 1-24)
Harvey Publications: No. 25, Aug, 1952 - No. 43, Oct, 1955

	GD2.0	FN6.0	NM9.4
25-43	2.00	5.00	10.00

HORIZONTAL LIEUTENANT, THE (See Movie Classics)

HOROBI
Viz Premiere Comics: 1990 - No. 8, 1990 ($3.75, B&W, mature readers, 84 pgs.) V2#1, 1990 - No. 7, 1991 ($4.25, B&W, 68 pgs.)

1-8: Japanese manga, Part Two, #1-7 4.50

HORRIFIC (Terrific No. 14 on)
Artful/Comic Media/Harwell/Mystery: Sept, 1952 - No. 13, Sept, 1954

	GD2.0	FN6.0	NM9.4
1	40.00	120.00	280.00
2	21.00	64.00	150.00
3-Bullet in head-c	39.00	116.00	270.00
4,5,7,9,10: 4-Shrunken head-c. 7-Guillotine-c	17.00	51.00	125.00
6-Jack The Ripper story	18.00	54.00	105.00
8-Origin & 1st app. The Teller (E.C. parody)	21.00	64.00	150.00
11-13: 11-Swipe/Witches Tales #6,27; Devil-c	14.00	43.00	100.00

NOTE: ***Don Heck** a-8; c-3-13. **Hollingsworth** a-4. **Morisi** a-8. **Palais** a-5, 7-12.*

HORROR FROM THE TOMB (Mysterious Stories No. 2 on)
Premier Magazine Co.: Sept, 1954

	GD2.0	FN6.0	NM9.4
1-Woodbridge/Torres, Check-a; The Keeper of the Graveyard is host	39.00	116.00	270.00

HORRORIST, THE (Also see Hellblazer)
DC Comics (Vertigo): Dec, 1995 - No. 2, Jan, 1996 ($5.95, lim. series, mature)

	GD2.0	FN6.0	NM9.4
1,2: Jamie Delano scripts, David Lloyd-c/a; John Constantine (Hellblazer) app.		2.40	6.00

HORRORS, THE (Formerly Startling Terror Tales #10)
Star Publications: No. 11, Jan, 1953 - No. 15, Apr, 1954

	GD2.0	FN6.0	NM9.4
11-Horrors of War; Disbrow-a(2)	26.00	79.00	185.00
12-Horrors of War; color illo in **POP**	25.00	75.00	175.00
13-Horrors of Mystery; crime stories	24.00	71.00	165.00
14,15-Horrors of the Underworld; crime stories	25.00	75.00	175.00

NOTE: *All have **L. B. Cole** covers; a-12. **Hollingsworth** a-13. **Palais** a-13r.*

HORROR TALES (Magazine)
Eerie Publications: V1#7, 6/69 - V6#6, 12/74; V7#1, 2/75; V7#2, 5/76 - V8#5, 1977; V9#3, 8/78; (V1-V6: 52 pgs.; V7, V8#2: 112 pgs.; V8#4 on: 68 pgs.) (No V5#3, V8#1,3)

	GD2.0	FN6.0	NM9.4
V1#7	3.80	11.40	38.00
V1#8,9	2.60	7.80	26.00
V2#1-6('70), V3#1-6('71), V4#1-3,5-7('72)	2.50	7.50	22.00
V4#4-LSD story reprint/Weird V3#5	3.20	9.60	32.00
V5#1,2,4,5(6/73),5(10/73),6(12/73),V6#1-6('74),V7#1,2,4('76),V7#3('76)-Giant issue,V8#2,4,5('77)	2.20	6.50	24.00
V9#1-3(11/78, $1.50)	2.50	7.60	28.00

NOTE: *Bondage-c-V6#1, 3, V7#2.*

HORSE FEATHERS COMICS
Lev Gleason Publ.: Nov, 1945 - No. 4, July(Summer on-c), 1948 (52 pgs.)

	GD2.0	FN6.0	NM9.4
1-Wolverton's Scoop Scuttle, 2 pgs.	18.00	54.00	125.00
2	10.00	30.00	60.00
3,4: 3-(5/48)	6.70	20.00	40.00

HORSEMAN
Crusade Comics/Kevlar Studios: Mar, 1996 - No. 3, Nov, 1997 ($2.95)

0-1st Kevlar Studios issue, 1-(3/96)-Crusade issue; Shi-c/app., 1-(11/96)-3-(11/97)-Kevlar Studios 3.00

HORSEMASTERS, THE (Disney)(TV, Movie)
Dell Publishing Co.: No. 1260, Dec-Feb, 1961/62

	GD2.0	FN6.0	NM9.4
Four Color 1260-Annette Funicello photo-c	11.00	33.00	120.00

HORSE SOLDIERS, THE
Dell Publishing Co.: No. 1048, Nov-Jan, 1959/60 (John Wayne movie)

	GD2.0	FN6.0	NM9.4
Four Color 1048-Painted-c, Sekowsky-a	13.00	38.00	140.00

HORSE WITHOUT A HEAD, THE (See Movie Comics)

HOT DOG
Magazine Enterprises: June-July, 1954 - No. 4, Dec-Jan, 1954-55

	GD2.0	FN6.0	NM9.4
1(A-1 #107)	7.00	21.00	42.00
2,3(A-1 #115),4(A-1 #136)	5.00	15.00	30.00

HOT DOG (See Jughead's Pal, Hotdog)

HOTEL DEPAREE - SUNDANCE (TV)
Dell Publishing Co.: No. 1126, Aug-Oct, 1960 (one-shot)

	GD2.0	FN6.0	NM9.4
Four Color 1126-Earl Holliman photo-c	5.50	16.50	60.00

HOT ROD AND SPEEDWAY COMICS
Hillman Periodicals: Feb-Mar, 1952 - No. 5, Apr-May, 1953

	GD2.0	FN6.0	NM9.4
1	26.00	77.00	180.00
2-Krigstein-a	18.00	54.00	125.00
3-5	10.00	30.00	70.00

HOT ROD COMICS (...Featuring Clint Curtis) (See XMas Comics)
Fawcett Publications: Nov, 1951 (no month given) - V2#7, Feb, 1953

	GD2.0	FN6.0	NM9.4
nn (V1#1)-Powell-c/a in all	30.00	90.00	210.00
2 (4/52)	17.00	51.00	120.00
3-6, V2#7	12.00	36.00	85.00

HOT ROD KING (Also see Speed Smith the Hot Rod King)
Ziff-Davis Publ. Co.: Fall, 1952

	GD2.0	FN6.0	NM9.4
1-Giacoia-a; Saunders painted-c	25.00	75.00	175.00

HOT ROD RACERS (Grand Prix No. 16 on)
Charlton Comics: Dec, 1964 - No. 15, July, 1967

	GD2.0	FN6.0	NM9.4
1	7.00	21.00	70.00
2-5	4.20	12.60	42.00
6-15	3.00	9.00	30.00

HOT RODS AND RACING CARS
Charlton Comics (Motor Mag. No. 1): Nov, 1951 - No. 120, June, 1973

Hot Stuff, The Little Devil #4 © HARV

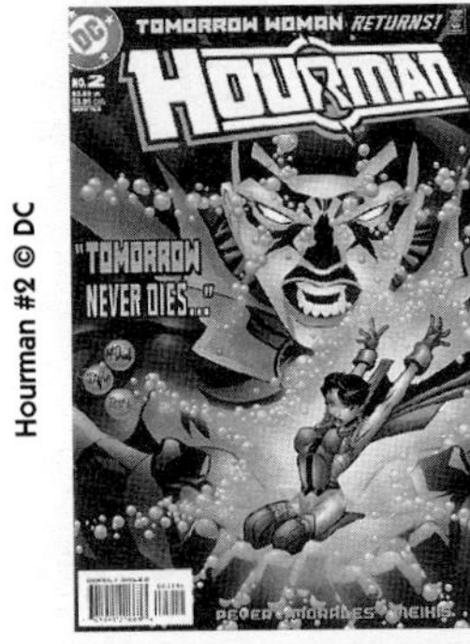

Hourman #2 © DC

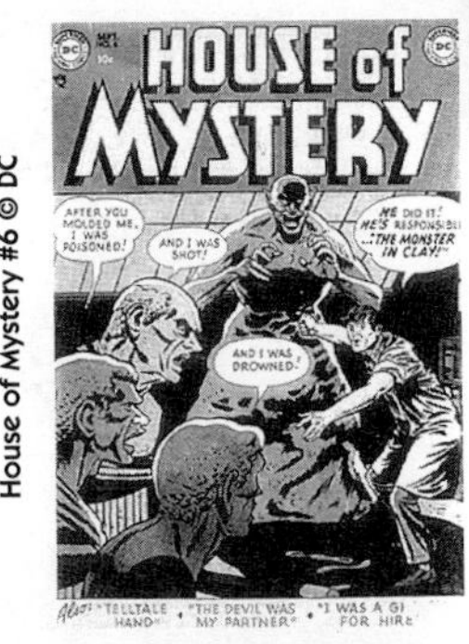

House of Mystery #6 © DC

	GD2.0	FN6.0	NM9.4
1-Speed Davis begins; Indianapolis 500 story	27.00	81.00	190.00
2	13.50	41.00	95.00
3-10	10.00	30.00	65.00
11-20	8.00	24.00	48.00
21-34,36-40	6.35	19.00	38.00
35 (6/58, 68 pgs.)	10.00	30.00	60.00
41-60	5.00	15.00	30.00
61-80	2.50	7.50	22.00
81-100	2.00	6.00	16.00
101-120	1.50	4.50	12.00

HOT SHOT CHARLIE
Hillman Periodicals: 1947 (Lee Elias)

1	9.15	27.00	55.00

HOT SHOTS: AVENGERS
Marvel Comics: Oct, 1995 ($2.95, one-shot)

nn-pin-ups 3.00

HOTSPUR
Eclipse Comics: Jun, 1987 - No. 3, Sep, 1987 ($1.75, lim. series, Baxter paper)

1-3 2.00

HOT STUFF (See Stumbo Tinytown)
Harvey Comics: V2#1, Sept, 1991 - No. 12, June, 1994 ($1.00)

V2#1-Stumbo back-up story 3.00
2-12 ($1.50) 2.00
...Big Book 1 (11/92), 2 (6/93) (Both $1.95, 52 pgs.) 3.00

HOT STUFF CREEPY CAVES
Harvey Publications: Nov, 1974 - No. 7, Nov, 1975

1	2.50	7.50	24.00
2-7	1.75	5.25	14.00

HOT STUFF DIGEST
Harvey Comics: July, 1992 - No. 5, Nov, 1993 ($1.75, digest-size)

V2#1-Hot Stuff, Stumbo, Richie Rich stories 3.50
2-5 2.00

HOT STUFF GIANT SIZE
Harvey Comics: Oct, 1992 - No. 3, Oct, 1993 ($2.25, 68 pgs.)

V2#1-Hot Stuff & Stumbo stories 3.50
2,3 2.50

HOT STUFF SIZZLERS
Harvey Publications: July, 1960 - No. 59, Mar, 1974; V2#1, Aug, 1992

1: 84 pgs. begin, ends #5; Hot Stuff, Stumbo begin	12.00	36.00	120.00
2-5	5.00	15.00	50.00
6-10: 6-68 pgs. begin, ends #45	3.20	9.60	32.00
11-20	2.60	7.80	26.00
21-45	1.80	5.40	18.00
46-52: 52 pgs. begin	1.40	4.20	14.00
53-59	1.10	3.30	9.00
V2#1-(8/92, $1.25)-Stumbo back-up			3.00

HOT STUFF, THE LITTLE DEVIL (Also see Devil Kids & Harvey Hits)
Harvey Publications (Illustrated Humor): 10/57 - No. 141, 7/77; No. 142, 2/78 - No. 164, 8/82; No. 165, 10/86 - No. 171, 11/87; No. 172, 11/88; No. 173, Sept, 1990 - No. 177, 1/91

1	34.00	102.00	340.00
2-1st app. Stumbo the Giant (12/57)	17.00	51.00	170.00
3-5	12.50	38.00	125.00
6-10	7.50	22.50	75.00
11-20	5.50	16.50	55.00
21-40	3.20	9.60	32.00
41-60	2.00	6.00	20.00
61-80	1.60	4.80	16.00
81-105	1.20	3.60	12.00
106-112: All 52 pg. Giants	1.60	4.80	16.00
113-125		2.40	6.00
126-141			4.00
142-177: 172-177-($1.00)			3.00

HOT WHEELS (TV)
National Periodical Publications: Mar-Apr, 1970 - No. 6, Jan-Feb, 1971

1	7.70	23.00	85.00
2,4,5	3.50	10.50	38.00
3-Neal Adams-c	3.80	11.50	42.00
6-Neal Adams-c/a	5.50	16.50	60.00

NOTE: ***Toth*** *a-1p, 2-5; c-1p, 5.*

HOURMAN (Justice Society member, see Adventure Comics #48)

HOURMAN (See JLA and DC One Million)
DC Comics: Apr, 1999 - Present ($2.50)

1-JLA app.; McDaniel-c 3.00
2-7: 2-Tomorrow Woman-c/app. 6,7-Amazo app. 2.50

HOUSE OF MYSTERY (See Brave and the Bold #93, Elvira's House of Mystery, Limited Collectors' Edition & Super DC Giant)

HOUSE OF MYSTERY, THE
National Periodical Publications/DC Comics: Dec-Jan, 1951-52 - No. 321, Oct, 1983 (No. 194-203: 52 pgs.)

1-DC's first horror comic	193.00	581.00	1700.00
2	84.00	253.00	750.00
3	62.00	187.00	550.00
4,5	47.00	141.00	420.00
6-10	40.00	120.00	320.00
11-15	34.00	101.00	260.00
16(7/53)-25	25.00	75.00	200.00
26-35(2/55)-Last pre-code issue; 30-Woodish-a	19.00	56.00	150.00
36-50: 50-Text story of Orson Welles' War of the Worlds broadcast	12.50	38.00	125.00
51-60: 55-1st S.A. issue	10.50	32.00	105.00
61,63,65,66,70,72,76,85-Kirby-a	10.50	32.00	105.00
62,64,67-69,71,73-75,77-83,86-99	8.50	25.50	85.00
84-Prototype of Negative Man (Doom Patrol)	12.50	38.00	125.00
100 (7/60)	9.50	28.50	95.00
101-116: 109-Toth, Kubert-a. 116-Last 10¢ issue	7.50	22.50	75.00
117-130: 117-Swipes-c to HOS #20. 120-Toth-a	7.00	21.00	70.00
131-142	5.50	16.50	55.00
143-J'onn J'onzz, Manhunter begins (6/64), ends #173; story continues from Detective #326	21.00	63.00	210.00
144	10.00	30.00	100.00
145-155,157-159: 149-Toth-a. 155-The Human Hurricane app. (12/65), Red Tornado prototype. 158-Origin/1st app. Diabolu Idol-Head in J'onn J'onzz	6.00	18.00	60.00
156-Robby Reed begins (origin/1st app.), ends #173	8.50	25.50	85.00
160-(7/66)-Robby Reed becomes Plastic Man in this issue only; 1st S.A. app. Plastic Man; intro Marco Xavier (Martian Manhunter) & Vulture Crime Organization; ends #173	11.00	33.00	110.00
161-173: 169-Origin/1st app. Gem Girl	4.50	13.50	45.00
174-Mystery format begins.	4.50	13.50	45.00
175-177: 175-1st app. Cain (HOM host)	3.00	9.00	30.00
178-Neal Adams-a (2/68)	3.80	11.40	38.00
179-N. Adams/Orlando, Wrightson-a (1st pro work, 3 pgs.)	7.00	21.00	70.00
180,181,183: Wrightson-a (3,10, & 3 pgs.). 180-Last 12¢ issue; Kane/Wood-a(2). 183-Wood-a	3.00	9.00	30.00
182,184: 182-Toth-a. 184-Kane/Wood, Toth-a	2.50	7.50	20.00
185-Williamson/Kaluta-a; Howard-a (3 pgs.)	2.60	7.80	26.00
186-N. Adams-c/a; Wrightson-a (10 pgs.)	2.80	8.40	28.00
187,190: Adams-c. 187-Toth-a. 190-Toth-a(r)	2.00	6.00	16.00
188-Wrightson-a (8 & 3pgs.); Adams-c	2.60	7.80	26.00
189,192,197: Adams-c on all. 189-Wood-a(i). 192-Last 15¢-c	2.00	6.00	16.00
191-Wrightson-a (8 & 3pgs.); Adams-c	2.50	7.50	22.00
193-Wrightson-c	2.25	6.75	18.00

House of Mystery #313 © DC

House of Secrets #7 © DC

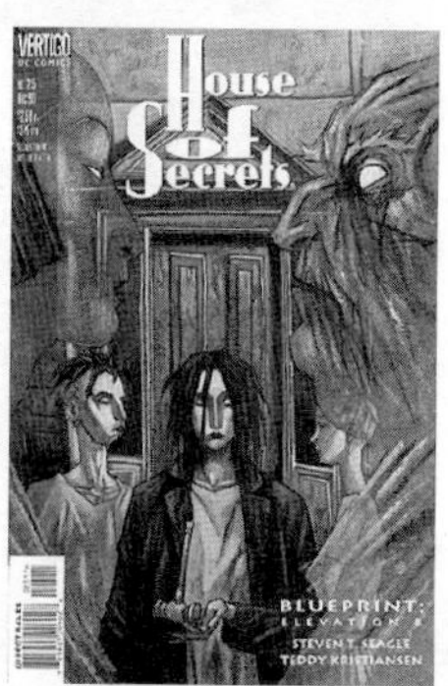

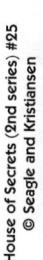

House of Secrets (2nd series) #25 © Seagle and Kristiansen

	GD2.0	FN6.0	NM9.4
194-Wrightson-c; 52 pgs begin, end #203; Toth,Kirby-a	2.50	7.50	22.00
195: Wrightson-c. Swamp creature story by Wrightson similar to Swamp Thing (10 pgs.)(10/71)	2.80	8.40	28.00
196,198	2.25	6.75	18.00
199-Adams-c; Wood-a(8pgs.); Kirby-a	2.50	7.50	20.00
200-(25¢, 52 pgs.)-One third-r (3/72)	2.50	7.50	22.00
201-203-(25¢, 52 pgs.)-One third-r	2.50	7.50	20.00
204-Wrightson-c/a, 9 pgs.	2.25	6.75	18.00
205,206,208,210,212,215,216,218	1.25	3.75	10.00
207-Wrightson c/a; Starlin, Redondo-a	2.00	6.00	16.00
209,211,213,214,217,219-Wrightson-c	1.50	4.50	12.00
220,222,223	1.00	3.00	8.00
221-Wrightson/Kaluta-a(8 pgs.)	1.75	5.25	14.00
224-229: 224-Wrightson-r from Spectre #9; Dillin/Adams-r from House of Secrets #82; begin 100 pg. issues; Phantom Stranger-r. 225,227-(100 pgs.): 225-Spectre app. 226-Wrightson/Redondo-a Phantom Stranger-r. 228-N. Adams inks; Wrightson-r. 229-Wrightson-a(r); Toth-r; last 100 pg. issue.	3.00	9.00	30.00
230,232-235,237-250		2.40	6.00
231,236-Wrightson-c. 236Ditko-a(p); N. Adams-i	1.10	3.30	9.00
251-254-(84 pgs.)-Adams-c. 251-Wood-a	1.10	3.30	9.00
255,256-(84 pgs.)-Wrightson-c	1.25	3.75	10.00
257-259-(84 pgs.)	1.10	3.30	9.00
260-289,291-299: 282-(68 pgs.)-Has extra story "The Computers That Saved Metropolis" Radio Shack giveaway by Jim Starlin			5.00
290-1st "I, Vampire"	1.25	3.75	10.00
300,319,321: Death of "I, Vampire"	1.00	3.00	8.00
301-318,320: 301-318-"I, Vampire"			5.00
Welcome to the House of Mystery (7/98, $5.95) reprints stories with new framing story by Gaiman and Aragonés		2.40	6.00

NOTE: ***Neal Adams*** *a-236i; c-175-192, 197, 199, 251-254.* ***Alcala*** *a-209, 217, 219, 224, 227.* ***M. Anderson*** *a-212; c/a-37.* ***Aparo*** *a-209.* ***Aragones*** *a-185, 186, 194, 196, 200, 202, 229, 251.* ***Baily*** *a-279p.* ***Cameron*** *a-76, 79.* ***Colan*** *a-202r.* ***Craig*** *a-263, 275, 295, 300.* ***Dillin/Adams*** *r-224.* ***Ditko*** *a-236p, 247, 254, 258, 276; c-277.* ***Drucker*** *a-37.* ***Evans*** *c-218.* ***Fraden*** *a-251.* ***Giffen*** *a-284.* ***Giunta*** *a-199, 227r.* ***Golden*** *a-257, 259.* ***Heath*** *a-194r; c-203.* ***Howard*** *a-182, 185, 187, 196, 229r, 247i, 254, 279i.* ***Kaluta*** *a-195, 200, 250r; c-200-202, 210, 212, 233, 260, 261, 263, 265, 267, 268, 273, 276, 284, 287, 288, 293-295, 300, 302, 304, 305, 309-319, 321.* ***Bob Kane*** *a-84.* ***Gil Kane*** *a-196p, 253p, 300p.* ***Kirby*** *a-194r, 199r; c-65, 76, 78, 79, 85.* ***Kubert*** *c-282, 283, 285, 286, 289-292, 297-299, 301, 303, 306-308.* ***Maneely*** *a-68, 227r.* ***Mayer*** *a-317p.* ***Meskin*** *a-52-144 (most), 195r, 224r, 229r; c-63, 66, 124, 127.* ***Mooney*** *a-24, 159, 160.* ***Moreira*** *a-3, 4, 20-50, 58, 59, 62, 68, 77, 79, 90, 108, 113, 123, 201r, 228; c-4-28, 44, 47, 50, 54, 59, 62, 64, 68, 70, 73.* ***Morrow*** *a-192, 196, 255, 320i.* ***Mortimer*** *a-204(3 pgs.).* ***Nasser*** *a-276.* ***Newton*** *a-259, 272.* ***Nino*** *a-204, 212, 213, 220, 224, 225, 245, 250, 252-256, 283.* ***Orlando*** *a-175(2 pgs.), 178, 240i; c-240, 258p, 262, 264p, 270p, 271, 272, 274, 275, 278, 296i.* ***Redondo*** *a-194, 195, 197, 202, 203, 207, 211, 214, 217, 219, 226, 227, 229, 235, 241, 287(layout), 302p, 303i, 308; c-229.* ***Reese*** *a-195, 200, 205i.* ***Rogers*** *a-254, 274, 277.* ***Roussos*** *a-65, 84, 224i.* ***Sekowsky*** *a-282p.* ***Sparling*** *a-203.* ***Starlin*** *a-207(2 pgs.), 282p; c-281.* ***Leonard Starr*** *a-9.* ***Staton*** *a-300p.* ***Sutton*** *a-189, 271, 290, 291, 293, 295, 297-299, 302, 303, 306-309, 310-313i, 314.* ***Tuska*** *a-293p, 294p, 316p.* ***Wrightson*** *c-193-195, 204, 207, 209, 211, 213, 214, 217, 219, 221, 231, 236, 255, 256; r-224.*

HOUSE OF SECRETS (Combined with The Unexpected after #154)
National Periodical Publications/DC Comics: 11-12/56 - No. 80, 9-10/66; No. 81, 8-9/69 - No. 140, 2-3/76; No. 141, 8-9/76 - No. 154, 10-11/78

	GD2.0	FN6.0	NM9.4
1-Drucker-a; Moreira-c	104.00	312.00	1250.00
2-Moreira-a	40.00	120.00	450.00
3-Kirby-c/a	34.00	102.00	375.00
4-Kirby-a	28.00	84.00	280.00
5-7	18.00	54.00	180.00
8-Kirby-a	22.00	66.00	220.00
9-11: 11-Lou Cameron-a (unsigned)	16.00	48.00	160.00
12-Kirby-c/a; Lou Cameron-a	17.50	52.00	175.00
13-15: 14-Flying saucer-c	12.00	36.00	120.00
16-20	10.50	32.00	105.00
21,22,24-30	9.50	28.50	95.00
23-1st app. Mark Merlin & begin series (8/59)	10.50	32.00	105.00
31-50: 48-Toth-a. 50-Last 10¢ issue	8.00	24.00	80:00
51-60: 58-Origin Mark Merlin	7.00	21.00	70.00
61-First Eclipso (7-8/63) and begin series	16.50	50.00	165.00
62	8.00	24.00	80.00
63-65,67-Toth-a on Eclipso (see Brave and the Bold #64)	6.50	19.50	65.00
66-1st Eclipso-c (also #67,70,78,79); Toth-a	8.50	25.50	85.00
68-80: 73-Mark Merlin becomes Prince Ra-Man (1st app.). 76-Prince Ra-Man vs. Eclipso. 80-Eclipso, Prince Ra-Man end	6.50	19.50	65.00
81-Mystery format begins; 1st app. Abel (House Of Secrets host); (cameo in DC Special #4)	4.50	13.50	45.00
82-84: 82-Neal Adams-c(i)	2.50	7.50	22.00
85,87,90: 85-N. Adams-a(i). 87-Wrightson & Kaluta-a. 90-Buckler (early work)/ N. Adams-a(i)	3.00	9.00	33.00
86,88,89,91	2.20	6.25	22.00
92-1st app. Swamp Thing-c/story (8 pgs.)(6-7/71) by Berni Wrightson(p) w/JeffJones/Kaluta/Weiss ink assists; classic-c.	45.00	134.00	490.00
93,95,97,98-(52 pgs.)-Wrightson-c	2.50	7.50	20.00
94,96-Wrightson-c. 94-Wrightson-a(i);96-Wood-a	2.00	6.00	20.00
99-Wrightson splash pg.	1.60	4.80	16.00
100-Wrightson-c	2.50	7.50	24.00
101,102,104,105,108-120	1.00	3.00	10.00
103,106,107-Wrightson-c	1.40	4.20	14.00
121-133	1.00	3.00	8.00
134-136,139-Wrightson-a	1.10	3.30	9.00
137,138,141-154		2.40	6.00
140-1st solo origin of the Patchworkman (see Swamp Thing #3)	2.25	6.75	18.00

NOTE: ***Neal Adams*** *c-81, 82, 84-88, 90, 91.* ***Alcala*** *a-104-107.* ***Anderson*** *a-91. Aparo a-93, 97, 105.* ***B. Bailey*** *a-107.* ***Cameron*** *a-13, 15.* ***Colan*** *a-63.* ***Ditko*** *a-139p, 148.* ***Elias*** *a-58.* ***Evans*** *a-118.* ***Finlay*** *a-7r(Real Fact?).* ***Glanzman*** *a-91.* ***Golden*** *a-151.* ***Heath*** *a-31.* ***Heck*** *a-85.* ***Kaluta*** *a-87, 98, 99; c-98, 99, 101, 102, 105, 149, 151, 154.* ***Bob Kane*** *a-18, 21.* ***G. Kane*** *a-85p.* ***Kirby*** *c-3, 11, 12.* ***Kubert*** *a-39.* ***Meskin*** *a-2-68 (most), 94r; c-55-60.* ***Moreira*** *a-7, 8, 51, 54, 102-104, 106, 108, 113, 116, 118, 121, 123, 127; c-1, 2, 4-10, 13-20.* ***Morrow*** *a-86, 89, 90; c-89, 146-148.* ***Nino*** *a-101, 103, 106, 109, 115, 117, 126, 128, 131, 147, 153.* ***Redondo*** *a-95, 99, 102, 104p, 113, 116, 134, 136, 139, 140.* ***Reese*** *a-85.* ***Severin*** *a-91.* ***Starlin*** *c-150.* ***Sutton*** *a-154.* ***Toth*** *a-63-67, 83, 93r, 94r, 96r-98r, 123.* ***Tuska*** *a-90, 104.* ***Wrightson*** *a-134; c-92-94, 96, 100, 103, 106, 107, 135, 136, 139.*

HOUSE OF SECRETS
DC Comics (Vertigo): Oct, 1996 - No. 25, Dec, 1998 ($2.50) (Creator-owned series)

	GD2.0	FN6.0	NM9.4
1-Steven Seagle-s/Kristiansen-c/a.			3.50
2-25: 5,7-Kristiansen-c/a. 6-Fegrado-a			3.00
TPB-(1997, $14.95) r/1-5			15.00

HOUSE OF TERROR (3-D)
St. John Publishing Co.: Oct, 1953 (25¢, came w/glasses)

	GD2.0	FN6.0	NM9.4
1-Kubert, Baker-a	33.00	99.00	230.00

HOUSE OF YANG, THE (See Yang)
Charlton Comics: July, 1975 - No. 6, June, 1976; 1978

	GD2.0	FN6.0	NM9.4
1-Sanho Kim-a in all	1.00	3.00	8.00
2-6			5.00
Modern Comics #1,2(1978)			3.00

HOUSE II: THE SECOND STORY
Marvel Comics: Oct, 1987 (One-shot)

	GD2.0	FN6.0	NM9.4
1-Adapts movie			2.00

HOWARD CHAYKIN'S AMERICAN FLAGG (See American Flagg!)
First Comics: V2#1, May, 1988 - V2#12, Apr, 1989 ($1.75/$1.95, Baxter paper)

	GD2.0	FN6.0	NM9.4
V2#1-9,11,12-Chaykin-c(p) in all			2.00
10-Elvis Presley photo-c			3.00

HOWARD THE DUCK (See Bizarre Adventures #34, Crazy Magazine, Fear, Man-Thing, Marvel Treasury Edition & Sensational She-Hulk #14-17)
Marvel Comics Group: Jan, 1976 - No. 31, May, 1979; No. 32, Jan, 1986; No. 33, Sept, 1986

	GD2.0	FN6.0	NM9.4
1-Brunner-c/a; Spider-Man x-over (low distr.)	1.50	4.50	12.00
2-Brunner-c/a (low distr.)			5.00
3,4-(Regular 25¢ edition). 3-Buscema-a(p), (7/76)			4.00
3,4-(30¢-c, limited distribution)	1.50	4.50	12.00
5			4.00

6-11: 8-Howard The Duck for president. 9-1st Sgt. Preston Dudley of RCMP.

Howard the Duck #29 © MAR

Howdy Doody #12 © California National Prod.

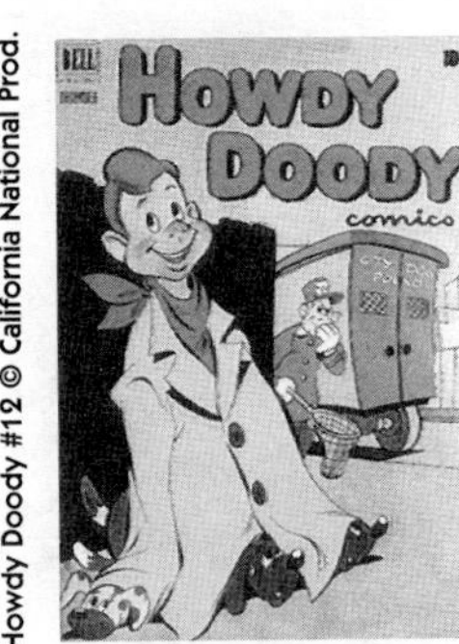

How to Draw for the Comics nn © Conde Nast

GD2.0 FN6.0 NM9.4

10-Spider-Man-c/sty 3.00
12-1st app. Kiss (cameo, 3/77) 1.25 3.75 10.00
13-Kiss app. (1st full story, 6/77); Daimon Hellstrom app. plus cameo of Howard as Son of Satan 1.85 5.50 15.00
14-33: 14-Howard as Son of Satan-c/story; Son of Satan app. 16-Album issue; 3 pgs. comics. 22,23-Man-Thing-c/stories; Star Wars parody. 30,32-P. Smith-a 3.00
Annual 1(1977, 52 pgs.)-Mayerik-a 4.00
NOTE: ***Austin** c-29i. **Bolland** c-33. **Brunner** a-1p, 2p; c-1, 2. **Buckler** c-3p. **Buscema** a-3p. **Colan** a(p)-4-15, 17-20, 24-27, 30, 31; c(p)-4-31, Annual 1p. **Leialoha** a-1-13i; c(i)-3-5, 8-11. **Mayerik** a-22, 23, 33. **Paul Smith** a-30p, 32. Man-Thing app. in #22, 23.*

HOWARD THE DUCK (Magazine)
Marvel Comics Group: Oct, 1979 - No. 9, Mar, 1981 (B&W, 68 pgs.)
1 2.40 6.00
2,3,5-9: 3-Xmas issue. 7-Has poster by Byrne 4.00
4-Beatles, John Lennon, Elvis, Kiss & Devo cameos; Hitler app. 2.40 6.00
NOTE: ***Buscema** a-4p. **Colan** a-1-5p, 7-9p. **Jack Davis** c-3. **Golden** a(p)-1, 5, 6(51pgs.). **Rogers** a-7, 8. **Simonson** a-7.*

HOWARD THE DUCK HOLIDAY SPECIAL
Marvel Comics: Feb, 1997 ($2.50, one-shot)
1-Wraparound-c; Hama-s 2.50

HOWARD THE DUCK: THE MOVIE
Marvel Comics Group: Dec, 1986 - No. 3, Feb, 1987 (Limited series)
1-3: Movie adaptation; r/Marvel Super Special 2.00

HOW BOYS AND GIRLS CAN HELP WIN THE WAR
The Parents' Magazine Institute: 1942 (10¢, one-shot)
1-All proceeds used to buy war bonds 24.00 73.00 170.00

HOWDY DOODY (TV)(See Jackpot of Fun-- & Poll Parrot)
Dell Publishing Co.: 1/50 - No. 38, 7-9/56; No. 761, 1/57; No. 811, 7/57
1-(Scarce)-Photo-c; 1st TV comic 82.00 246.00 900.00
2-Photo-c 35.00 104.00 380.00
3-5: All photo-c 19.00 57.00 210.00
6-Used in **SOTI**, pg. 309; painted-c begin 16.00 48.00 175.00
7-10 13.00 40.00 145.00
11-20: 13-X-Mas-c 10.50 31.00 115.00
21-38, Four Color 761,811 9.00 27.00 100.00

HOW IT BEGAN
United Features Syndicate: No. 15, 1939 (one-shot)
Single Series 15 32.00 96.00 225.00

HOW SANTA GOT HIS RED SUIT (See March of Comics No. 2)

HOW THE WEST WAS WON (See Movie Comics)

HOW TO DRAW FOR THE COMICS
Street and Smith: No date (1942?) (10¢, 64 pgs., B&W & color, no ads)
nn-Art by Winsor McCay, George Marcoux (Supersnipe artist), Vernon Greene (The Shadow artist), Jack Binder(with biog.), Thorton Fisher, Jon Small, & Jack Farr; has biographies of each artist 26.00 79.00 185.00

H. P. LOVECRAFT'S CTHULHU
Millennium Publications: Dec, 1991 - No. 3, May, 1992 ($2.50, limited series)
1-3: 1-Contains trading cards on thin stock 2.50

H. R. PUFNSTUF (TV) (See March of Comics #360)
Gold Key: Oct, 1970 - No. 8, July, 1972
1-Photo-c (all have photo-c?) 18.00 55.00 200.00
2-8 9.00 27.00 100.00

HUBERT AT CAMP MOONBEAM
Dell Publishing Co.: No. 251, Oct, 1949 (one shot)
Four Color 251 3.60 11.00 40.00

HUCK & YOGI JAMBOREE (TV)
Dell Publishing Co.: Mar, 1961 ($1.00, 6-1/4x9", 116 pgs., cardboard-c, high quality paper) (B&W original material)
nn 8.30 25.00 100.00

GD2.0 FN6.0 NM9.4

HUCK & YOGI WINTER SPORTS (TV)
Dell Publishing Co.: No. 1310, Mar, 1962 (Hanna-Barbara) (one-shot)
Four Color 1310 8.50 25.50 85.00

HUCK FINN (See The New Adventures of... & Power Record Comics)

HUCKLEBERRY FINN (Movie)
Dell Publishing Co.: No. 1114, July, 1960
Four Color 1114-Photo-c 4.50 13.50 50.00

HUCKLEBERRY HOUND (See Dell Giant #31,44, Golden Picture Story Book, Kite Fun Book, March of Comics #199, 214, 235, Spotlight #1 & Whitman Comic Books)

HUCKLEBERRY HOUND (TV)
Dell/Gold Key No. 18 (10/62) on: No. 990, 5-7/59 - No. 43, 10/70 (Hanna-Barbera)
Four Color 990(#1)-1st app. Huckleberry Hound, Yogi Bear, & Pixie & Dixie & Mr. Jinks 11.00 33.00 120.00
Four Color 1050,1054 (12/59) 7.75 23.50 85.00
3(1-2/60) - 7 (9-10/60), Four Color 1141 (10/60) 7.30 22.00 80.00
8-10 5.25 16.00 58.00
11,13-17 (6-8/62) 3.60 11.00 40.00
12-1st Hokey Wolf & Ding-a-Ling 4.50 13.50 50.00
18,19 (84pgs.; 18-20 titled ...Chuckleberry Tales) 7.25 22.00 80.00
20-Titled Chuckleberry Tales 2.75 8.00 35.00
21-30 2.75 8.00 30.00
31-43: 37-Reprints 2.00 6.00 22.00

HUCKLEBERRY HOUND (TV)
Charlton Comics: Nov, 1970 - No. 8, Jan, 1972 (Hanna-Barbera)
1 3.80 11.40 38.00
2-8 2.50 7.50 22.00

HUEY, DEWEY, & LOUIE (See Donald Duck, 1938 for 1st app. Also see Mickey Mouse Magazine V4#2, V5#7 & Walt Disney's Junior Woodchucks Limited Series)

HUEY, DEWEY, & LOUIE BACK TO SCHOOL (See Dell Giant #22, 35, 49 & Dell Giants)

HUEY, DEWEY, AND LOUIE JUNIOR WOODCHUCKS (Disney)
Gold Key No. 1-61/Whitman No. 62 on: Aug, 1966 - No. 81, 1984 (See Walt Disney's Comics & Stories #125)
1 4.50 13.50 50.00
2,3(12/68) 2.70 8.00 30.00
4,5(4/70)-r/two WDC&S D.Duck stys by Barks 2.50 7.50 28.00
6-17 2.25 6.75 25.00
18,27-30 1.50 4.50 16.00
19-23,25-New storyboarded scripts by Barks, 13-25 pgs. per issue 2.30 7.00 26.00
24,26: 26-r/Barks Donald Duck WDC&S stories 1.50 4.50 16.00
31-57,60,61: 35,41-r/Barks J.W. scripts .80 2.40 8.00
58,59: 58-r/Barks Donald Duck WDC&S stories 1.00 3.00 10.00
62-64 (Whitman) .90 2.70 9.00
65-(9/80), 66 (Pre-pack? scarce) 1.40 4.20 15.00
67 (1/81),68 1.10 3.30 12.00
69-74 1.00 3.00 10.00
75-81 (all #90183; pre-pack?; nd, nd code; scarce) 1.10 3.30 12.00

HUGGA BUNCH (TV)
Marvel Comics (Star Comics): Oct, 1986 - No. 6, Aug, 1987
1-6 2.00

HULK (Magazine)(Formerly The Rampaging Hulk)(Also see The Incredible Hulk)
Marvel Comics: No. 10, Aug., 1978 - No. 27, June, 1981 ($1.50)
10,11: 10-Bill Bixby interview. 11-Moon Knight begins, ends 20 2.40 6.00
12-23: Moon Knight stories. 12-Lou Ferrigno interview. 24-Part color, Lou Ferrigno interview. 25-Part color. 17,18,20: Moon Knight stories. 26,27-are B&W. 23-Last full color issue; Banner is attacked 4.00
NOTE: ***Alcala** a(i)-15, 17-20, 22, 24-27. **Buscema** a-23; c-26. **Chaykin** a-21-25. **Colan** a(p)-11, 19, 24-27. **Jusko** painted c-12. **Nebres** a-16. **Severin** a-19i. Moon Knight by **Sienkiewicz** in 13-15, 17, 18, 20. **Simonson** a-27; c-23. Dominic Fortune appears in #21-24.*

HULK (Becomes Incredible Hulk Vol. 2 with issue #12)

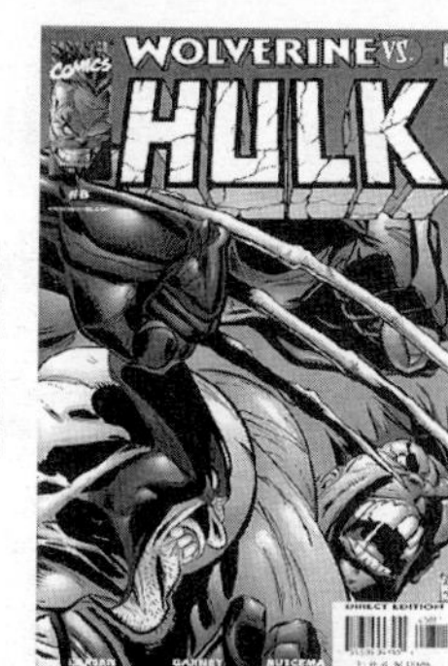

Hulk #8 © MAR

Human Fly #3 © MAR

Human Torch #10 © MAR

GD2.0 FN6.0 NM9.4

Marvel Comics: Apr, 1999 - No. 11, Feb, 2000 ($2.99/$1.99)

1-($2.99) Byrne-s/Garney-a 3.00
1-Variant-c 10.00
1-Gold foil variant 10.00
2-11-($1.99): 2-Two covers. 5-Art by Jurgens, Buscema & Texeira. 7-Avengers app. 11-She-Hulk app. 2.00
1999 Annual ($3.50) Chapter One story; Byrne-s/Weeks-a 3.50

HULK: FUTURE IMPERFECT
Marvel Comics: Jan, 1993 - No. 2, Dec, 1992 (In error) ($5.95, 52 pgs., square-bound, limited series)

1,2: Embossed-c; Peter David story & George Perez-c/a. 1-1st app. Maestro. 1.00 3.00 8.00

HULK/ PITT
Marvel Comics: 1997 ($5.99, one-shot)

1 David-s/Keown-c/a 2.00 6.00

HULK 2099
Marvel Comics: Dec, 1994 - No. 10, Sept, 1995 ($1.50/$1.95)

1 ($2.50)-Green foil-c 2.50
2-10: 2-A. Kubert-c 2.00

HUMAN FLY
I.W. Enterprises/Super: 1963 - 1964 (Reprints)

I.W. Reprint #1-Reprints Blue Beetle #44('46) 1.75 5.25 14.00
Super Reprint #10-R/Blue Beetle #46('47) 1.75 5.25 14.00

HUMAN FLY, THE
Marvel Comics Group: Sept, 1977 - No. 19, Mar, 1979

1,2: 1-Origin; Spider-Man x-over. 2-Ghost Rider app. 4.00
3-19: 9-Daredevil x-over; Byrne-c(p) 2.00
NOTE: ***Austin*** *c-4i, 9i.* ***Elias*** *a-1, 3p, 4p, 7p, 10-12p, 15p, 18p, 19p.* ***Layton*** *c-19.*

HUMAN TARGET
DC Comics (Vertigo): Apr, 1999 - No. 4, July, 1999 ($2.95, limited series)

1-4-Milligan-s/Bradstreet-c 3.00

HUMAN TARGET SPECIAL (TV)
DC Comics: Nov, 1991 ($2.00, 52 pgs., one-shot)

1 2.00

HUMAN TORCH, THE (Red Raven #1)(See All-Select, All Winners, Marvel Mystery, Men's Adventures, Mystic Comics (2nd series), Sub-Mariner, USA & Young Men)
Timely/Marvel Comics (TP 2,3/TCI 4-9/SePI 10/SnPC 11-25/CnPC 26-35/Atlas Comics (CPC 36-38)): No. 2, Fall, 1940 - No. 15, Spring, 1944; No. 16, Fall, 1944 - No. 35, Mar, 1949 (Becomes Love Tales #36 on); No. 36, April, 1954 - No. 38, Aug, 1954

GD2.0 FN6.0 VF8.0 NM9.4
2(#1)-Intro & Origin Toro; The Falcon, The Fiery Mask, Mantor the Magician, & Microman only app.; Human Torch by Burgos, Sub-Mariner by Everett begin (origin of each in text) 2000.00 6000.00 12,000.00 22,000.00

GD2.0 FN6.0 NM9.4
3(#2)-40pg. H.T. story; H.T. & S.M. battle over who is best artist in text-Everett or Burgos 440.00 1320.00 4400.00
4(#3)-Origin The Patriot in text; last Everett Sub-Mariner; Sid Greene-a 367.00 1100.00 3300.00
5(#4)-The Patriot app; Angel x-over in Sub-Mariner (Summer, 1941); 1st Nazi war-c this title 278.00 834.00 2500.00
5-Human Torch battles Sub-Mariner (Fall, '41); 60 pg. story 422.00 1266.00 3800.00
6,9 194.00 582.00 1550.00
7-1st Japanese war-c 206.00 618.00 1650.00
8-Human Torch battles Sub-Mariner; 52 pg. story; Wolverton-a, 1 pg. 300.00 900.00 2700.00
10-Human Torch battles Sub-Mariner, 45 pg. story; Wolverton-a, 1 pg. 262.00 786.00 2100.00
11,13-15: 14-1st Atlas Globe logo (Winter, 1943-44; see All Winners #11 also) 156.00 468.00 1250.00
12-classic-c 250.00 750.00 2000.00
16-20: 20-Last War issue 109.00 327.00 875.00
21,22,24-30: 103.00 309.00 825.00
23 (Sum/46)-Becomes Junior Miss 24? Classic Schomburg Robot-c 119.00 357.00 950.00
31,32: 31-Namora x-over in Sub-Mariner (also #30); last Toro. 32-Sungirl, Namora app.; Sungirl-c 87.00 261.00 700.00
33-Capt. America x-over 91.00 273.00 725.00
34-Sungirl solo 81.00 243.00 650.00
35-Captain America & Sungirl app. (1949) 87.00 261.00 700.00
36-38(1954)-Sub-Mariner in all 84.00 252.00 675.00
NOTE: ***Ayers*** *Human Torch in 36(3).* ***Brodsky*** *c-25, 31-33?, 37, 38,* ***Burgos*** *c-36.* ***Everett*** *a-1-3, 27, 28, 30, 37, 38.* ***Powell*** *a-36(Sub-Mariner).* ***Schomburg*** *c-1-3, 5-8, 10-23.* ***Sekowsky*** *c-28, 34?, 35?* ***Shores*** *c-24, 26, 27, 29, 30.* ***Mickey Spillane*** *text 4-6. Bondage c-2, 12, 19.*

HUMAN TORCH, THE (Also see Avengers West Coast, Fantastic Four, The Invaders, Saga of the Original... & Strange Tales #101)
Marvel Comics Group: Sept, 1974 - No. 8, Nov, 1975

1: 1-8-r/stories from Strange Tales #101-108 1.50 4.50 12.00
2-8: 1st H.T. title since G.A. 7-vs. Sub-Mariner 1.00 2.80 7.00
NOTE: *Golden Age & Silver Age Human Torch-r #1-8.* ***Ayers*** *r-6, 7.* ***Kirby/Ayers*** *r-1-5, 8.*

HUMBUG (Satire by Harvey Kurtzman)
Humbug Publications: Aug, 1957 - No. 9, May, 1958; No. 10, June, 1958; No. 11, Oct, 1958

1-Wood-a (intro pgs. only) 27.00 81.00 190.00
2 13.00 39.00 90.00
3-9: 8-Elvis in Jailbreak Rock 11.00 33.00 75.00
10,11-Magazine format. 10-Photo-c 14.00 43.00 100.00
Bound Volume(#1-9)(extremely rare) 62.00 188.00 500.00
NOTE: ***Davis*** *a-1-11.* ***Elder*** *a-2-4, 6-9, 11.* ***Heath*** *a-2, 4-8, 10.* ***Jaffee*** *a-2, 4-9.* ***Kurtzman*** *a-11.*

HUMDINGER (Becomes White Rider and Super Horse #3 on?)
Novelty Press/Premium Group: May-June, 1946 - V2#2, July-Aug, 1947

1-Jerkwater Line, Mickey Starlight by Don Rico, Dink begin 33.00 99.00 230.00
2 14.00 43.00 100.00
3-6, V2#1,2 10.00 30.00 65.00

HUMONGOUS MAN
Alternative Press (Ikon Press): Sept, 1997 -Present ($2.25, B&W)

1-3-Stepp & Harrison-c/s/a. 2.25

HUMOR (See All Humor Comics)

HUMPHREY COMICS (Joe Palooka Presents...; also see Joe Palooka)
Harvey Publications: Oct, 1948 - No. 22, Apr, 1952

1-Joe Palooka's pal (r); (52 pgs.)-Powell-a 11.00 33.00 75.00
2,3: Powell-a 5.85 17.50 35.00
4-Boy Heroes app.; Powell-a 6.70 20.00 40.00
5-8,10: 5,6-Powell-a. 7-Little Dot app. 4.25 13.00 26.00
9-Origin Humphrey 5.85 17.50 35.00
11-22 4.00 10.00 20.00

HUNCHBACK OF NOTRE DAME, THE
Dell Publishing Co.: No. 854, Oct, 1957 (one shot)

Four Color 854-Movie, photo-c 12.00 35.00 130.00

HUNK
Charlton Comics: Aug, 1961 - No. 11, 1963

1 2.80 8.40 28.00
2-11 1.75 5.25 14.00

HUNTED (Formerly My Love Memoirs)
Fox Features Syndicate: No. 13, July, 1950 - No. 2, Sept, 1950

13(#1)-Used in **SOTI**, pg. 42 & illo. "Treating police contemptuously" (lower left); Hollingsworth bondage-c 33.00 99.00 230.00
2 14.00 43.00 100.00

HUNTER'S HEART
DC Comics: June, 1995 - No. 3, Aug, 1995 ($5.95, B&W, limited series)

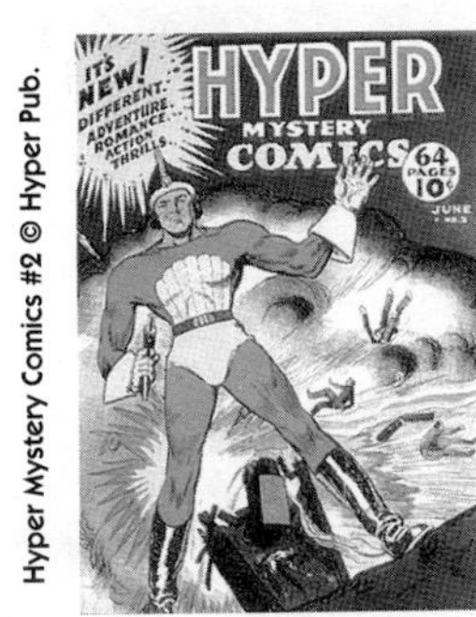

Hyper Mystery Comics #2 © Hyper Pub.

Ibis, the Invincible #3 © FAW

I Feel Sick #1 © Jhonen Vasquez

GD2.0 FN6.0 NM9.4

1-3 2.40 6.00

HUNTRESS, THE (See All-Star Comics #69, Batman Family, Brave & the Bold #62, DC Super Stars #17, Detective #652, Infinity, Inc. #1, Sensation Comics #68 & Wonder Woman #271)
DC Comics: Apr, 1989 - No. 19, Oct, 1990 ($1.00, mature)

1-19: Staton-c/a(p) in all. 17-19-Batman-c/stories 2.00

HUNTRESS, THE
DC Comics: June, 1994 - No. 4, Sept, 1994 ($1.50, limited series)

1-4-Netzer-c/a: 2-Batman app. 2.00

HURRICANE COMICS
Cambridge House: 1945 (52 pgs.)

1-(Humor, funny animal) 21.00 64.00 150.00

HYBRIDS
Continunity Comics: Jan, 1994 ($2.50, one-shot)

1-Neal Adams-c(p) & part-a(i); embossed-c. 2.50

HYBRIDS DEATHWATCH 2000
Continuity Comics: Apr, 1993 - No. 5, Aug, 1993 ($2.50)

0-(Giveaway)-Foil-c; Neal Adams-c(i) & plots (also #1,2) 2.50
1-5: 1-Polybagged w/card; die-cut-c. 2-Thermal-c. 3-Polybagged w/card; indestructible-c; Adams plot. 4,5-Valeria She-Bat; origin Hybrids; Adams-c(p) 2.50

HYBRIDS ORIGIN
Continunity Comics: 1993 - No. 5, 1994? ($2.50)

1-5: 2,3-Neal Adams-c. 4,5-Valeria the She-Bat app. Adams-c(i) 2.50

HYDE-25
Harris Publications: Apr, 1995 ($2.95, one-shot)

0-coupon for poster; r/Vampirella's 1st app. 3.00

HYDROMAN (See Heroic Comics)

HYPERKIND (See Razorline)
Marvel Comics: Sept, 1993 - No. 9, May, 1994 ($1.75/$1.95)

1-($2.50)-Foil embossed-c; by Clive Barker 2.50
2-9 2.00

HYPERKIND UNLEASED
Marvel Comics: Aug, 1994 ($2.95, 52 pgs., one-shot)

1 3.00

HYPER MYSTERY COMICS
Hyper Publications: May, 1940 - No. 2, June, 1940 (68 pgs.)

1-Hyper, the Phenomenal begins; Calkins-a 194.00 581.00 1550.00
2 103.00 309.00 825.00

HYPERSONIC
Dark Horse Comics: Nov, 1997 - No. 4, Feb, 1998 ($2.95, limited series)

1-4: Abnett & White/Erskine-a 3.00

I AIM AT THE STARS (Movie)
Dell Publishing Co.: No. 1148, Nov-Jan/1960-61 (one-shot)

Four Color 1148-The Werner Von Braun Sty-photo-c 6.40 19.00 70.00

I AM COYOTE (See Eclipse Graphic Album Series & Eclipse Magazine #2)

I AM LEGEND
Eclipse Books: 1991 - No. 4, 1991 ($5.95, B&W, squarebound, 68 pgs.)

1-4: Based on 1954 novel 2.40 6.00

IBIS, THE INVINCIBLE (See Fawcett Miniatures, Mighty Midget & Whiz)
Fawcett Publications: 1942 (Fall?); #2, Mar.,1943; #3, Wint, 1945 - #5, Fall, 1946; #6, Spring, 1948

1-Origin Ibis; Raboy-c; on sale 1/2/43 175.00 525.00 1400.00
2-Bondage-c (on sale 2/5/43) 87.00 262.00 700.00
3-Wolverton-a #3-6 (4 pgs. each) 69.00 206.00 550.00
4-6: 5-Bondage-c 47.00 141.00 375.00

NOTE: ***Mac Raboy** c(p)-3-5. **Shaffenberger** c-6.*

GD2.0 FN6.0 NM9.4

I-BOTS (See Isaac Asimov's I-BOTS)

ICE AGE ON THE WORLD OF MAGIC: THE GATHERING (See Magic The Gathering)

ICE KING OF OZ, THE (See First Comics Graphic Novel #13)

ICEMAN (Also see The Champions & X-Men #94)
Marvel Comics Group: Dec, 1984 - No. 4, June, 1985 (Limited series)

1-4: 3-The Defenders, Champions (Ghost Rider) & the original X-Men x-over. Zeck covers 2.00

ICON
DC Comics (Milestone): May, 1993 - No. 42, Feb, 1997($1.50/$1.75/$2.50)

1-($2.95)-Collector's Edition polybagged w/poster & trading card (direct sale only) 3.00
1-24,30-42: 9-Simonson-c. 15,16-Worlds Collide Pt. 4 & 11. 15-Superboy app. 16-Superman-c/story. 40-Vs. Blood Syndicate 2.50
25-($2.95, 52 pgs.) 3.00

IDAHO
Dell Publishing Co.: June-Aug, 1963 - No. 8, July-Sept, 1965

1 2.25 6.75 18.00
2-8: 5-7-Painted-c 1.25 3.75 10.00

IDEAL (... a Classical Comic) (2nd Series) (Love Romances No. 6 on)
Timely Comics: July, 1948 - No. 5, March, 1949 (Feature length stories)

1-Antony & Cleopatra 34.00 103.00 240.00
2-The Corpses of Dr. Sacotti 30.00 90.00 210.00
3-Joan of Arc; used in **SOTI,** pg. 308 'Boer War' 26.00 79.00 185.00
4-Richard the Lion-hearted; titled "...the World's Greatest Comics"; The Witness app. 40.00 120.00 320.00
5-Ideal Love & Romance; change to love; photo-c 17.00 49.00 115.00

IDEAL COMICS (1st Series) (Willie Comics No. 5 on)
Timely Comics (MgPC): Fall, 1944 - No. 4, Spring, 1946

1-Funny animal; Super Rabbit in all 20.00 60.00 140.00
2 12.00 36.00 85.00
3,4 11.50 34.00 80.00

IDEAL LOVE & ROMANCE (See Ideal, A Classical Comic)

IDEAL ROMANCE (Formerly Tender Romance)
Key Publ.: No. 3, April, 1954 - No. 8, Feb, 1955 (Diary Confessions No. 9 on)

3-Bernard Baily-c 8.35 25.00 50.00
4-8: 4,5-B. Baily-c 5.00 15.00 30.00

IDOL
Marvel Comics (Epic Comics): 1992 - No. 3, 1992 ($2.95, mini-series, 52 pgs.)

Book 1-3 3.00

I DREAM OF JEANNIE (TV)
Dell Publishing Co.: Apr, 1965 - No. 2, Dec, 1966 (Photo-c)

1-Barbara Eden photo-c, each 14.50 44.00 160.00
2 11.00 33.00 120.00

I FEEL SICK
Slave Labor Graphics: Aug, 1999 - No. 2 ($3.95, limited series)

1-Jhonen Vasquez-s/a 4.00

ILLUMINATOR
Marvel Comics/Nelson Publ.: 1993 - No. 4, 1993 ($4.99/$2.95, 52 pgs.)

1,2-($4.99) Religious themed 5.00
3,4 3.00

ILLUSTRATED GAGS
United Features Syndicate: No. 16, 1940

Single Series 16 16.00 47.00 110.00

ILLUSTRATED LIBRARY OF..., AN (See Classics Illustrated Giants)

ILLUSTRATED STORIES OF THE OPERAS
Baily (Bernard) Publ. Co.: 1943 (16 pgs.; B&W) (25 cents) (cover-B&W & red)

nn-(Rare)(4 diff. issues)-Faust (part-r in Cisco Kid #1), nn-Aida, nn-Carmen;

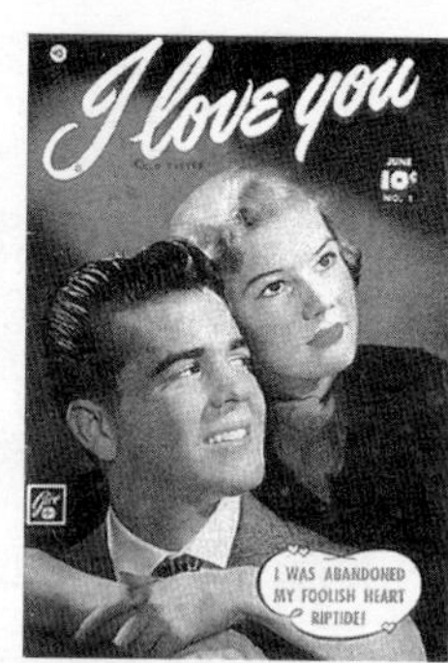

I Love You #1 © FAW

Impact #2 © WMG

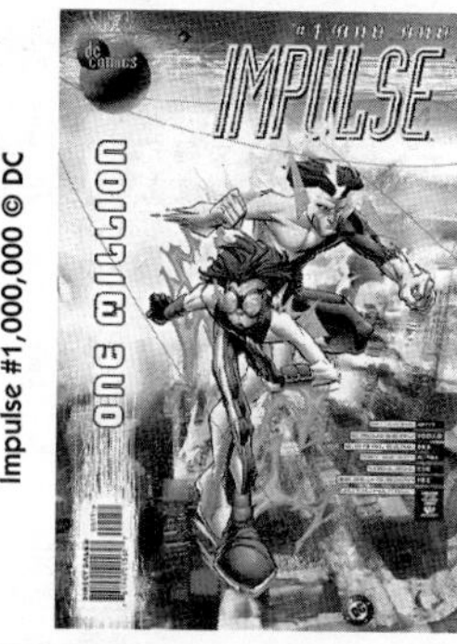

Impulse #1,000,000 © DC

	GD2.0	FN6.0	NM9.4
Baily-a, nn-Rigoleito	55.00	165.00	440.00

ILLUSTRATED STORY OF ROBIN HOOD & HIS MERRY MEN, THE
(See Classics Giveaways, 12/44)

ILLUSTRATED TARZAN BOOK, THE (See Tarzan Book)

I LOVED (Formerly Rulah; Colossal Features Magazine No. 33 on)
Fox Features Syndicate: No. 28, July, 1949 - No. 32, Mar, 1950

	GD2.0	FN6.0	NM9.4
28	10.00	30.00	60.00
29-32	6.70	20.00	40.00

I LOVE LUCY
Eternity Comics : 6/90 - No. 6, 1990;V2#1, 11/90 - No. 6, 1991 ($2.95, B&W, mini-series)

1-6: Reprints 1950s comic strip; photo-c 3.00
Book II #1-6: Reprints comic strip; photo-c 3.00
...In Full Color 1 (1991, $5.95, 52 pgs.)-Reprints I Love Lucy Comics #4,5,8,16; photo-c with embossed logo (2 versions exist, one with pgs. 18 & 19 reversed, the other corrected) 2.40 6.00
...In 3-D 1 (1991, $3.95, w/glasses)-Reprints I Love Lucy Comics; photo-c sealed in plastic bag 4.00

I LOVE LUCY COMICS (TV) (Also see The Lucy Show)
Dell Publishing Co.: No. 535, Feb, 1954 - No. 35, Apr-June, 1962 (All have Lucille Ball photo-c)

	GD2.0	FN6.0	NM9.4
Four Color 535(#1)	48.00	143.00	525.00
Four Color 559(#2, 5/54)	30.00	89.00	325.00
3 (8-10/54) - 5	17.00	52.00	190.00
6-10	14.00	41.00	150.00
11-20	10.00	30.00	110.00
21-35	8.00	23.00	85.00

I LOVE YOU
Fawcett Publications: June, 1950 (one-shot)

	GD2.0	FN6.0	NM9.4
1-Photo-c	13.50	41.00	95.00

I LOVE YOU (Formerly In Love)
Charlton Comics: No. 7, 9/55 - No. 121, 12/76; No. 122, 3/79 - No. 130, 5/80

	GD2.0	FN6.0	NM9.4
7-Kirby-c; Powell-a	8.00	24.00	80.00
8-10	3.00	9.00	30.00
11-16,18-20	2.50	7.50	24.00
17-(68 pg. Giant)	5.50	16.50	55.00
21-25,27-50	2.50	7.50	22.00
26-No Torres-a	2.25	6.75	18.00
51-59	1.75	5.25	14.00
60-(1/66)-Elvis Presley line drawn c/story	12.50	38.00	125.00
61-85	1.10	3.30	9.00
86-110		2.40	6.00
111-130			4.00

I, LUSIPHER (Becomes Poison Elves, 1st series #8 on)
Mulehide Graphics: 1991 - No. 7, 1992 (B&W, magazine size)

	GD2.0	FN6.0	NM9.4
1-Drew Hayes-c/a/scripts	6.50	19.00	70.00
2,4,5	4.00	12.00	40.00
3-Low print run	8.00	24.00	90.00
6,7	3.00	9.00	30.00

Poison Elves: Requiem For An Elf (Sirius Ent., 6/96, $14.95, trade paperback)-Reprints I, Lusiphur #1,2 as text, and 3-6 15.00

I'M A COP
Magazine Enterprises: 1954 - No. 3, 1954?

	GD2.0	FN6.0	NM9.4
1(A-1 #111)-Powell-c/a in all	15.00	45.00	105.00
2(A-1 #126), 3(A-1 #128)	9.15	27.00	55.00

IMAGE GRAPHIC NOVEL
Image Int.: 1984 ($6.95)(Advertised as Pacific Comics Graphic Novel #1)

1-The Seven Samuroid; Brunner-c/a 7.00

IMAGES OF A DISTANT SOIL
Image Comics: Feb, 1997 ($2.95, B&W, one-shot)

1-Sketches by various 3.00

IMAGES OF SHADOWHAWK (Also see Shadowhawk)
Image Comics: Sept, 1993 - No. 3, 1994 ($1.95, limited series)

1-3: Keith Giffen-c/a; Trencher app. 2.00

IMAGE ZERO
Image Comics: 1993 (Received through mail w/coupons from Image books)

0-Savage Dragon, StormWatch, Shadowhawk, Strykeforce; 1st app. Troll; 1st app. McFarlane's Freak, Blotch, Sweat and Bludd 5.00

I'M DICKENS - HE'S FENSTER (TV)
Dell Publishing Co.: May-July, 1963 - No. 2, Aug-Oct, 1963 (Photo-c)

	GD2.0	FN6.0	NM9.4
1	4.50	13.50	50.00
2	4.00	12.00	45.00

I MET A HANDSOME COWBOY
Dell Publishing Co.: No. 324, Mar, 1951

	GD2.0	FN6.0	NM9.4
Four Color 324	8.00	25.00	90.00

IMMORTAL DOCTOR FATE, THE
DC Comics: Jan, 1985 - No. 3, Mar, 1985 ($1.25, limited series)

1-3: 1-Simonson-c/a. 2-Giffen-c/a(p) 2.00

IMMORTALIS (See Mortigan Goth: Immortalis)

IMMORTAL II
Image Comics: Apr, 1997 - No. 5, Feb, 1998 ($2.50, B&W&Grey, lim. series)

1-5: 1-B&W w/ color pull-out poster 2.50

IMPACT
E. C. Comics: Mar-Apr, 1955 - No. 5, Nov-Dec, 1955

	GD2.0	FN6.0	NM9.4
1-Not code approved	13.00	40.00	125.00
2	8.50	26.00	80.00
3-5: 4-Crandall-a	7.00	21.00	65.00

NOTE: ***Crandall** a-1-4. **Davis** a-2-4; c-1-5. **Evans** a-1, 4, 5. **Ingels** a-in all. **Kamen** a-3. **Krigstein** a-1, 5. **Orlando** a-2, 5.*

IMPACT
Gemstone Publishing: Apr, 1999 - No. 5 ($2.50)

1-3-Reprints E.C. series 2.50

IMPACT CHRISTMAS SPECIAL
DC Comics (Impact Comics): 1991 ($2.50, 68 pgs.)

1-Gift of the Magi by Infantino/Rogers; The Black Hood, The Fly, The Jaguar, & The Shield stories 2.50

IMPOSSIBLE MAN SUMMER VACATION SPECTACULAR, THE
Marvel Comics: Aug, 1990; No. 2, Sept, 1991 ($2.00, 68 pgs.) (See Fantastic Four#11)

1-Spider Man, Quasar, Dr. Strange, She-Hulk, Punisher & Dr. Doom stories; Barry Crain, Guice-a; Art Adams-c(i) 2.00
2-Ka Zar & Thor app.; Cable Wolverine-c app. 2.00

IMPERIAL GUARD
Marvel Comics: Jan, 1997 - No. 3, Mar, 1997 ($1.95, limited series)

1-3: Augustyn-s in all; 1-Wraparound-c 2.00

IMPULSE (See Flash #92, 2nd Series for 1st app.) (Also see Young Justice)
DC Comics: Apr, 1995 - Present ($1.50/$1.75/$1.95/$2.25)

1-Mark Waid scripts & Humberto Ramos-c/a(p) begin; brief retelling of origin 1.25 3.75 10.00
2-12: 9-XS from Legion (Impulse's cousin) comes to the 20th Century, returns to the 30th Century in #12. 10-Dead Heat Pt. 3 (cont'd in Flash #110). 11-Dead Heat Pt. 4 (cont'd in Flash #111); Johnny Quick dies. 5.00
13-53: 14-Trickster app. 17-Zatanna-c/app. 21-Legion-c/app. 22-Jesse Quick-c/app. 24-Origin; Flash app. 25-Last Ramos-a. 26-Rousseau-a(p) begins. 28-1st new Arrowette (see World's Finest #113). 30-Genesis x-over.41-Arrowette-c/app. 47-Superman-c/app. 50-53: 50-Batman & Joker-c/app. Van Sciver-a begins. 52,53-Simonson art pages 3.00
#1,000,000 (11/98) John Fox app. 2.25
Annual 1 (1996, $2.95)-Legends of the Dead Earth; Parobeck-a 4.00

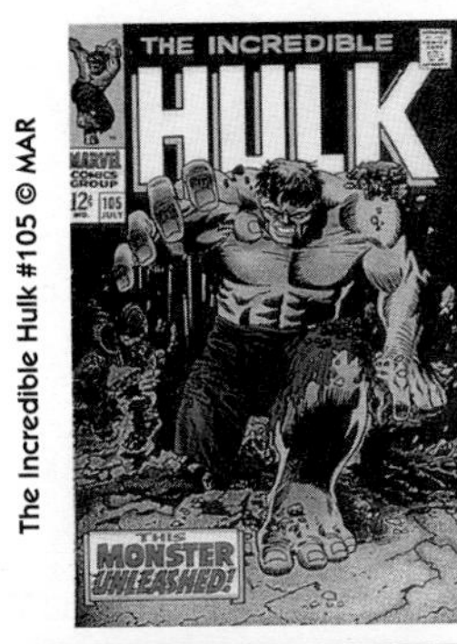

The Incredible Hulk #105 © MAR

The Incredible Hulk #287 © MAR

The Incredible Hulk #467 © MAR

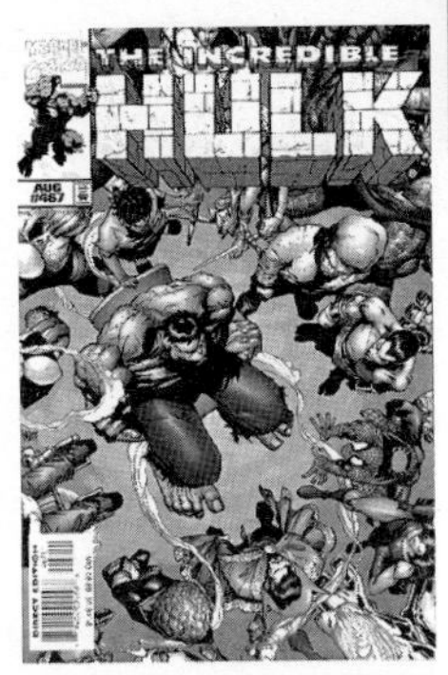

GD2.0 FN6.0 NM9.4

Annual 2 (1997, $3.95)-Pulp Heroes stories; Orbik painted-c 4.00
.../Atom Double-Shot 1(2/98, $1.95) Jurgens-s/Mhan-a 3.00
...: Bart Saves the Universe (4/99, $5.95) JSA app. 6.00
...Plus(9/97, $2.95) w/Gross Out (Scare Tactics)-c/app. 3.00
...Reckless Youth (1997, $14.95, TPB) r/Flash #92-94, Impulse #1-6 15.00

INCAL, THE
Marvel Comics (Epic): Nov, 1988 - No. 3, Jan, 1989 ($10.95/$12.95, mature)
1-3: Moebius-c/a in all; sexual content 13.00

INCOMPLETE DEATH'S HEAD (Also see Death's Head)
Marvel Comics UK: Jan, 1993 - No. 12, Dec, 1993 ($1.75, limited series)
1-($2.95, 56 pgs.)-Die-cut cover 3.00
2-11: 2-Re-intro original Death's Head. 3-Original Death's Head vs. Dragon's Claws 2.00
12-($2.50, 52 pgs.)-She Hulk app. 2.50

INCREDIBLE HULK, THE (See Aurora, The Avengers #1, The Defenders #1, Giant-Size..., Hulk, Marvel Collectors Item Classics, Marvel Comics Presents #26, Marvel Fanfare, Marvel Treasury Edition, Power Record Comics, Rampaging Hulk, She-Hulk & 2099 Unlimited)

INCREDIBLE HULK, THE
Marvel Comics: May, 1962 - No. 6, Mar, 1963; No. 102, Apr, 1968 - No. 474, Mar, 1999

GD2.0 FN6.0 VF8.0 NM9.4
1-Origin & 1st app. (skin is grey colored); Kirby pencils begin, end #5 545.00 1635.00 4900.00 12,000.00
2-1st green skinned Hulk; Kirby/Ditko-a 145.00 435.00 1085.00 2300.00
3-Origin retold; 1st app. Ringmaster & Hercules (9/62) 95.00 285.00 665.00 1400.00
4,5: 4-Brief origin retold 85.00 255.00 595.00 1300.00
6-Intro. Teen Brigade; all Ditko-a 125.00 375.00 875.00 1900.00

GD2.0 FN6.0 NM9.4
102 (Formerly Tales to Astonish)-Origin retold; story continued from Tales to Astonish #101 12.50 37.50 150.00
103 7.00 21.00 70.00
104-Rhino app. 6.50 19.50 65.00
105-108: 105-1st Missing Link. 107-Mandarin app.(9/68). 108-Mandarin & Nick Fury app. (10/68). 5.50 16.50 55.00
109,110: 109-Ka-Zar app. 3.80 11.40 38.00
111-117: 117-Last 12¢ issue 3.00 9.00 30.00
118-Hulk vs. Sub-Mariner 2.60 7.80 26.00
119-121,123-125 2.50 7.50 22.00
122-Hulk battles Thing (12/69) 4.00 12.00 40.00
126-1st Barbara Norriss (Valkyrie) 2.50 7.50 24.00
127-139: 131-Hulk vs. Iron Man; 1st Jim Wilson, Hulk's new sidekick. 136-1st Xeron, The Star-Slayer 1.75 5.25 14.00
140-Written by Harlan Ellison; 1st Jarella, Hulk's love 2.15 6.50 17.00
141-1st app. Doc Samson (7/71) 3.20 9.60 32.00
142-144: 144-Last 15¢ issue 1.25 3.75 10.00
145-(52 pgs.)-Origin retold 1.50 4.50 12.00
146-160: 149-1st app. The Inheritor. 155-1st app. Shaper. 158-Warlock cameo(12/72) 1.00 3.00 8.00
161-The Mimic dies; Beast app. 1.25 3.75 10.00
162-1st app. The Wendigo (4/73); Beast app. 1.25 3.75 10.00
163-171,173-176: 163-1st app. The Gremlin. 164-1st Capt. Omen & Colonel John D. Armbruster. 166-1st Zzzax. 168-1st The Harpy; nudity panels of Betty Brant. 169-1st app. Bi-Beast.176-Warlock cameo (2 panels only); same date as Strange Tales #178 (6/74) 1.00 2.80 7.00
172-X-Men cameo; origin Juggernaut retold 1.75 5.25 14.00
177-1st actual death of Warlock (last panel only) 1.25 3.75 10.00
178-Rebirth of Warlock 1.50 4.50 12.00
179-No Warlock 2.40 6.00
180-(10/74)-1st app. Wolverine (cameo last pg.) 6.00 18.00 65.00
181-(11/74)-1st full Wolverine story; Trimpe-a 43.00 131.00 480.00
182-Wolverine cameo; see Giant-Size X-Men #1 for next app.; 1st Crackajack Jackson 5.50 16.50 60.00
183-199: 185-Death of Col. Armbruster 2.40 6.00
198,199, 201-203-(30¢-c variants, lim. distribution) 1.20 3.60 12.00
200-(25¢-c) Silver Surfer app.; anniversary issue 2.00 6.00 20.00
200-(30¢-c variant, limited distribution)(6/76) 7.50 22.50 80.00
201-240: 201-Conan swipe-c/sty. 212-1st app. The Constrictor. 227-Original Avengers app. 232-Capt. America x-over from C.A. #230. 233-Marvel Man app. 234-(4/79)-1st app. Quasar (formerly Marvel Man & changes name to Quasar) 4.00
241-249: 243-Cage app. 3.50
250-Giant size; Silver Surfer app. 1.00 3.00 8.00
251-299: 271-Rocket Raccoon app. 272-Sasquatch & Wendigo app.; Wolverine & Alpha Flight cameo in flashback. 278,279-Most Marvel characters app. (Wolverine in both). 279-X-Men & Alpha Flight cameos. 282-284-She-Hulk app. 293-F.F. app. 3.50
300-(11/84, 52 pgs.)-Spider-Man app in new black costume on-c & 2 pg. cameo 5.00
301-313: 312-Origin Hulk retold 3.00
314-Byrne-c/a begins, ends #319 4.00
315-319: 319-Bruce Banner & Betty Talbot wed 2.50
320-323,325,327-329 2.50
324-1st app. Grey Hulk since #1 (c-swipe of #1) 1.00 3.00 8.00
326-Grey vs. Green Hulk 2.50
330,331: 330-1st McFarlane ish (4/87); Thunderbolt Ross dies. 331-Grey Hulk series begins 1.25 3.75 10.00
332-334,336-339: 336,337-X-Factor app. 1.00 3.00 8.00
335-No McFarlane-a 3.00
340-Hulk battles Wolverine by McFarlane 2.25 6.75 18.00
341-346: 345-($1.50, 52 pgs.). 346-Last McFarlane issue 4.00
347-349,351-358,360-366: 347-1st app. Marlo 2.00
350-Hulk/Thing battle 5.00
359-Wolverine app. (illusion only) 2.00
367,372,377: 367-1st Dale Keown-a on Hulk (3/90). 372-Green Hulk app.;Keown -c/a. 377-1st all new Hulk; fluorescent-c; Keown-c/a .85 2.60 7.00
368-371,373-376: 368-Sam Kieth-c/a, 1st app. Pantheon. 369,370-Dale Keown-c/a. 370,371-Original Defenders app. 371,373-376: Keown-c/a. 376-Green vs. Grey Hulk 3.50
377-Fluorescent green logo 2nd printing 3.00
378,380,389: No Keown-a. 380-Doc Samson app. 2.00
379,381-388,390-393-Keown-a. 385-Infinity Gauntlet x-over. 389-Last $1.00-c. 392-X-Factor app. 393-($2.50, 72 pgs.)-30th anniversary issue; green foil stamped-c; swipes-c to #1; has pin-ups of classic battles; Keown-c/a 3.50
393-2nd printing 2.50
394-399: 394-No Keown-c/a; intro Trauma. 395,396-Punisher-c/stories; Keown-c/a. 397-Begin "Ghost of the Past" 4-part sty; Keown c/a. 398-Last Keown-c/a 2.00
400-($2.50, 68 pgs.)-Holo-grafx foil-c & r/TTA #63 3.00
400-416: 400-2nd print-Diff. color foil-c. 402-Return of Doc Samson 2.00
417-424: 417-Begin $1.50-c; Rick Jones' bachelor party; Hulk returns from "Future Imperfect"; bound-in trading card sheet. 418-(Regular edition)-Rick Jones marries Marlo; includes cameo apps of various Marvel characters as well as DC's Death & Peter David. 420-Death of Jim Wilson 2.00
418-($2.50)-Collector's Edition w/gatefold die-cut-c 2.50
425 ($2.25, 52 pgs.) 2.25
425 ($3.50, 52 pgs.)-Holographic-c 3.50
426-434, 436-442: 426-Begin $1.95-c. 427, 428-Man-Thing app. 431,432-Abomination app. 434-Funeral for Nick Fury. 436-Ghosts of the Future begins, ends #440. 439-Hulk becomes Maestro, Avengers app. 440-Thor-c/app. 441,442-She-Hulk-c/app. 442-Molecule Man app. 2.00
435 ($2.50)-Rhino-app; excerpt from "What Savage Beast" 2.50
443-448: 443-Begin $1.50-c; re-app. of Hulk. 444-Cable-c/app.; "Onslaught". 445-"Onslaught". 446-w/card insert. 447-Begin Deodato-c/a(p) 2.00
447,449: 447-Variant cover. 449-Thunderbolts-c/app. 4.00
450-($2.95)-Thunderbolts app.; 2 stories; Heroes Reborn-c/app. 5.00
451-473: 455-X-Men-c/app. 460-Bruce Banner returns. 464-Silver Surfer-c/app. 466,467: Betty dies. 467-Last Peter David-s/Kubert-a. 468-Casey-s/Pulido-a begin 2.50
474-($2.99) Last issue; Abomination app. 3.50

The Incredible Hulk Vs. Superman #1 © MAR/DC

Indiana Jones and the Arms of Gold #3 © Lucasfilm

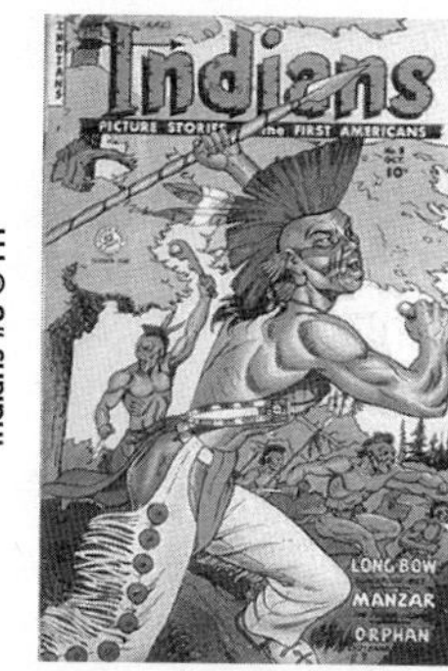

Indians #8 © FH

GD2.0 FN6.0 NM9.4

Special 1 (10/68, 25¢, 68 pg.)-New 51 pg. story, Hulk battles The Inhumans (early app.); Steranko-c. 7.50 22.50 75.00
Special 2 (10/69, 25¢, 68 pg.)-Origin retold 4.50 13.50 45.00
Special 3,4 (1/71, 1/72, 25¢, 68 pg.) 1.85 5.50 15.00
Annual 5 (1976) 1.00 3.00 8.00
Annual 68 ('77-79)-7-Byrne/Layton-c/a; Iceman & Angel app. in book-length story. 8-Book-length Sasquatch-c/sty 5.00
Annual 9,12-17: 9('80). 12 ('83). 13('84). 14('85). 15('86). 16('90, $2.00, 68 pgs.)-She-Hulk app. 17(1991, $2.00)-Origin retold 3.00
Annual 10,11: 10 ('81). 11('82)-Doc Samson back-up by Miller(p)(5 pgs.); Spider-Man & Avengers app. Buckler-a(p) 3.50
Annual 18-20 ('92-'94 68 pgs.)-18-Return of the Defenders, Pt. I; no Keown-c/a 19-Bagged w/card 3.00
...'97 ($2.99) Pollina-c 3.00
...And Wolverine 1 (10/86, $2.50)-r/1st app. #180-181 1.25 3.75 10.00
...: Beauty and the Behemoth ('98, $19.95, TPB) r/Bruce & Betty stories 20.00
...Ground Zero ('95, $12.95) r/#340-346 13.00
...Hercules Unleashed (10/96, $2.50) David-s/Deodato-c/a 2.50
.../Sub-Mariner "98 Annual ($2.99) 3.00
...Versus Quasimodo 1 (3/83, one-shot)-Based on Saturday morning cartoon 3.00
...Vs. Superman 1 (7/99, $5.95, one-shot)-painted-c by Rude 6.00
...Versus Venom 1 (4/94, $2.50, one-shot)-Embossed-c; red foil logo 2.75
(Also see titles listed under **Hulk**)

NOTE: ***Adkins*** *a-111-116i.* ***Austin*** *a(i)-350, 351, 353, 354; c-302i, 350i.* ***Ayers*** *a-3-5i.* ***Buckler*** *a-Annual 5; c-252.* ***John Buscema*** *c-202p.* ***Byrne*** *a-314-319p; c-314-316, 318, 319, 359, Annual 14i.* ***Colan*** *c-363.* ***Ditko*** *a-2i, 6, 249, Annual 2r(5), 3r, 9p; c-2i, 6, 235, 249.* ***Everett*** *c-133i.* ***Golden*** *c-248; 251.* ***Kane*** *c(p)-193, 194, 196, 198.* ***Dale Keown*** *a(p)-367, 369-377, 379, 381-388, 390-393, 395-398; c-369-377p, 381, 382p, 384, 385, 386, 387p, 388, 390p, 391-393, 395p, 396, 397p, 398.* ***Kirby*** *a-1-5p, Special 2, 3p, Annual 5p; c-1-5, Annual 5.* ***McFarlane*** *a-330-334p, 336-339p, 340-343, 344-346p; c-330p, 340p, 341-343, 344p, 345, 346p.* ***Mignola*** *c-302, 305, 313.* ***Miller*** *c-258p, 261, 264, 268.* ***Mooney*** *a-230p, 287i, 288i.* ***Powell*** *a-Special 3r(2).* ***Romita*** *a-Annual 17p.* ***Severin*** *a(i)-108-110, 131-133, 141-151, 153-155; c(i)-109, 110, 132, 142, 144-155.* ***Simonson*** *c-283, 364-367.* ***Starlin*** *a-222p; c-217.* ***Staton*** *a(i)-187-189, 191-209.* ***Tuska*** *a-102i, 105i, 106i, 218p.* ***Williamson*** *a-310i; c-310i, 311i.* ***Wrightson*** *c-197.*

INCREDIBLE HULK (Vol. 2) (Formerly Hulk #1-11)
Marvel Comics: No. 12, Mar, 2000 - Present ($2.99, $1.99)

12-Jenkins-s/Garney & McKone-a 2.99

INCREDIBLE MR. LIMPET, THE (See Movie Classics)

INCREDIBLE SCIENCE FICTION (Formerly Weird Science-Fantasy)
E. C. Comics: No. 30, July-Aug, 1955 - No. 33, Jan-Feb, 1956

30,33: 33-Story-r/Weird Fantasy #18 32.00 96.00 285.00
31-Williamson/Krenkel-a, Wood-a(2) 33.00 99.00 300.00
32-Williamson/Krenkel-a 33.00 99.00 300.00

NOTE: ***Davis*** *a-30, 32, 33; c-30-32.* ***Krigstein*** *a-in all.* ***Orlando*** *a-30, 32, 33("Judgement Day" reprint).* ***Wood*** *a-30, 31, 33; c-33.*

INCREDIBLE SCIENCE FICTION (Formerly Weird Science-Fantasy)
Russ Cochran/Gemstone Publ.: No. 8, Aug, 1994 - No. 11, May, 1995 ($2.00)

8-11: Reprints #30-33 of E.C. series 2.50

INDEPENDENCE DAY (Movie)
Marvel Comics: No. 0, June, 1996 - No. 2, Aug, 1996 ($1.95, limited series)

0-Special Edition; photo-c 5.00
0-2 2.00

INDEPENDENT VOICES
Peregrine Entertainment: Sept, 1998 ($1.95, B&W)

1-Sampler of Indy titles for CBLDF 2.00

INDIANA JONES (Title series), **Dark Horse Comics**
--AND THE ARMS OF GOLD, 2/94 - 5/94 ($2.50) 1-4 2.50
--AND THE FATE OF ATLANTIS, 3/91 - 9/91 ($2.50) 1-4-Dorman painted-c on all; contain trading cards (#1 has a 2nd printing, 10/91) 2.50
--AND THE GOLDEN FLEECE, 6/94 - 7/94 ($2.50) 1,2 2.50
--AND THE IRON PHOENIX, 12/94 - 3/95 ($2.50) 1-4 2.50

INDIANA JONES AND THE LAST CRUSADE
Marvel Comics: 1989 - No. 4, 1989 ($1.00, limited series, movie adaptation)

1-4: Williamson-i assist 2.50
1-(1989, $2.95, B&W mag., 80 pgs.) 4.00

--AND THE SHRINE OF THE SEA DEVIL: Dark Horse, 9/94 ($2.50, one shot)
1-Gary Gianni-a 2.50
--AND THE SPEAR OF DESTINY: Dark Horse, 4/95 - 8/95 ($2.50) 1-4 2.50
--THUNDER IN THE ORIENT: Dark Horse, 9/93 - '94 ($2.50)
1-6: Dan Barry story & art in all; 1-Dorman painted-c 2.50

INDIANA JONES AND THE TEMPLE OF DOOM
Marvel Comics Group: Sept, 1984 - No. 3, Nov, 1984 (Movie adaptation)

1-3-r/Marvel Super Special; Guice-a 2.50

INDIAN BRAVES (Baffling Mysteries No. 5 on)
Ace Magazines: March, 1951 - No. 4, Sept, 1951

1-Green Arrowhead begins, ends #3 11.00 33.00 75.00
2 6.35 19.00 38.00
3,4 5.00 15.00 30.00
I.W. Reprint #1 (nd)-r/Indian Braves #4 1.50 4.50 12.00

INDIAN CHIEF (White Eagle...) (Formerly The Chief, Four Color 290)
Dell Publ. Co.: No. 3, July-Sept, 1951 - No. 33, Jan-Mar, 1959 (All painted-c)

3 3.00 9.00 35.00
4-11: 6-White Eagle app. 2.50 7.50 28.00
12-1st White Eagle(10-12/53)-Not same as earlier character 3.00 9.00 35.00
13-29 1.80 5.50 20.00
30-33-Buscema-a 2.00 6.00 22.00

INDIAN CHIEF (See March of Comics No. 94, 110, 127, 140, 159, 170, 187)

INDIAN FIGHTER, THE (Movie)
Dell Publishing Co.: No. 687, May, 1956 (one-shot)

Four Color 687-Kirk Douglas photo-c 7.00 22.00 80.00

INDIAN FIGHTER
Youthful Magazines: May, 1950 - No. 11, Jan, 1952

1 11.50 34.00 80.00
2-Wildey-a/c(bondage) 8.00 24.00 48.00
3-11: 3,4-Wildey-a 5.35 16.00 32.00

NOTE: ***Walter Johnson*** *c-1, 3, 4, 6.* ***Palais*** *a-10.* ***Stallman*** *a-7.* ***Wildey*** *a-2-4; c-2, 5.*

INDIAN LEGENDS OF THE NIAGARA (See American Graphics)

INDIANS
Fiction House Magazines (Wings Publ. Co.): Spring, 1950 - No. 17, Spring, 1953 (1-8: 52 pgs.)

1-Manzar The White Indian, Long Bow & Orphan of the Storm begin 27.00 81.00 190.00
2-Starlight begins 13.50 41.00 95.00
3-5: 5-17-Most-c by Whitman 11.50 34.00 80.00
6-10 10.00 30.00 65.00
11-17 9.15 27.00 55.00

INDIANS OF THE WILD WEST
I. W. Enterprises: Circa 1958? (no date) (Reprints)

9-Kinstler-c; Whitman-a; r/Indians #? 1.75 5.25 14.00

INDIANS ON THE WARPATH
St. John Publishing Co.: No date (Late 40s, early 50s) (132 pgs.)

nn-Matt Baker-c; contains St. John comics rebound. Many combinations possible 30.00 90.00 210.00

INDIAN TRIBES (See Famous Indian Tribes)

INDIAN WARRIORS (Formerly White Rider and Super Horse; becomes Western Crime Cases #9)
Star Publications: No. 7, June, 1951 - No. 8, Sept, 1951

7-White Rider & Superhorse continue; "Last of the Mohicans" serial begins; L.B. Cole-c 17.00 51.00 120.00
8-L. B. Cole-c 16.00 47.00 110.00
3-D 1(12/53, 25¢)-Came w/glasses; L. B. Cole-c 40.00 120.00 290.00

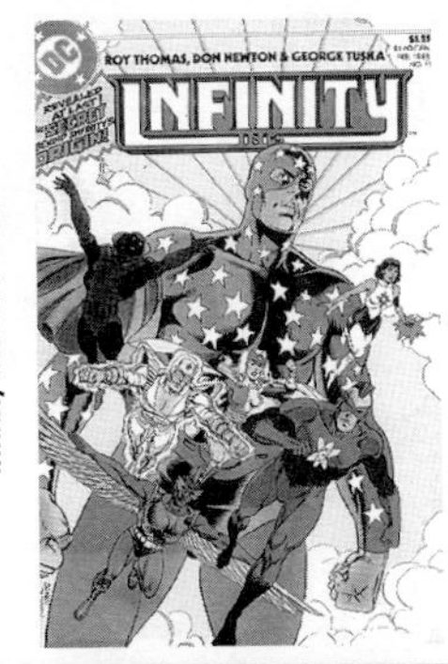

Infinity Inc. #11 © DC

Inhumans V2 #3 © MAR

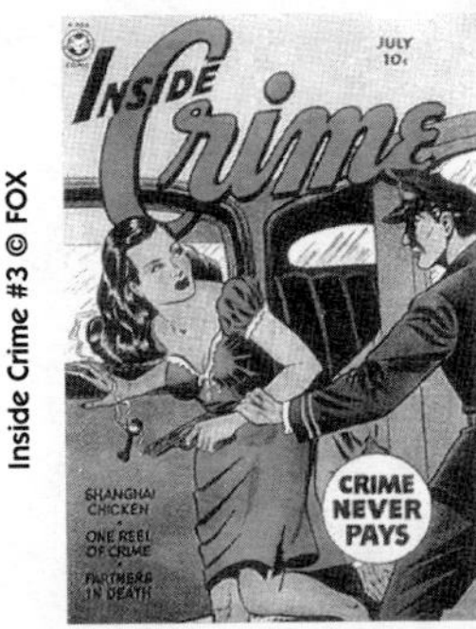

Inside Crime #3 © FOX

GD2.0 FN6.0 NM9.4

Accepted Reprint(nn)(inside cover shows White Rider & Superhorse #11)-r/ cover to #7; origin White Rider &...;. L. B. Cole-c 5.85 17.50 35.00
Accepted Reprint #8 (nd); L.B. Cole-c (r-cover to #8) 5.85 17.50 35.00

INDOORS-OUTDOORS (See Wisco)

INDOOR SPORTS
National Specials Co.: nd (6x9", 64 pgs., B&W-r, hard-c)
nn-By Tad 5.00 15.00 30.00

INDUSTRIAL GOTHIC
DC Comics (Vertigo): Dec, 1995 - No. 5, Apr, 1996 ($2.50, limited series)
1-5: Ted McKeever-c/a/scripts 2.50

INFERIOR FIVE, THE (Inferior 5 #11, 12) (See Showcase #62, 63, 65)
National Periodical Publications (#1-10: 12¢): 3-4/67 - No. 10, 9-10/68; No. 11, 8-9/72 - No. 12, 10-11/72
1-(3-4/67)-Sekowsky-a(p); 4th app. 3.80 11.40 38.00
2-5: 2-Plastic Man, F.F. app. 4-Thor app. 2.50 7.50 22.00
6-9: 6-Stars DC staff 2.00 6.00 16.00
10-Superman x-over; F.F., Spider-Man & Sub-Mariner app. 2.50 7.50 20.00
11,12: Orlando-c/a; both r/Showcase #62,63 2.00 6.00 16.00

INFERNO
Caliber Comics: 1995 - No. 5 ($2.95, B&W)
1-5 3.00

INFERNO (See Legion of Super-Heroes)
DC Comics: Oct, 1997 - No. 4, Feb, 1998 ($2.50, limited series)
1-Immonen-s/c/a in all 4.00
2-4 3.00

INFINITY CRUSADE
Marvel Comics: June, 1993 - No. 6, Nov, 1993 ($2.50, limited series, 52 pgs.)
1-6: By Jim Starlin & Ron Lim 2.50

INFINITY GAUNTLET (The... #2 on; see Infinity Crusade, The Infinity War & Warlock & the Infinity Watch)
Marvel Comics: July, 1991 - No. 6, Dec, 1991 ($2.50, limited series)
1-6:Thanos-c/stories in all; Starlin scripts in all; 5,6-Ron Lim-c/a 2.50
NOTE: ***Lim*** *a-3p(part), 5p, 6p; c-5i, 6i.* ***Perez*** *a-1-3p, 4p(part); c-1(painted), 2-4, 5i, 6i.*

INFINITY, INC. (See All-Star Squadron #25)
DC Comics: Mar, 1984 - No. 53, Aug, 1988 ($1.25, Baxter paper, 36 pgs.)
1-Brainwave, Jr., Fury, The Huntress, Jade, Northwind, Nuklon, Obsidian, Power Girl, Silver Scarab & Star Spangled Kid begin 3.00
2-13,38-49,51-53: 2-Dr. Midnite, G.A. Flash, W. Woman, Dr. Fate, Hourman, Gr/Lantern, Wildcat app. 5-Nudity panels. 46,47-Millennium tie-ins 2.00
14-Todd McFarlane-a (5/85, 2nd full story) 1.00 3.00 8.00
15-37-McFarlane-a (20,23,24: 5 pgs. only; 33: 2 pgs.); 18-24-Crisis x-over. 21-Intro new Hourman & Dr. Midnight. 26-New Wildcat app. 31-Star Spangled Kid becomes Skyman.. 32-Green Fury becomes Green Flame. 33-Origin Obsidian. 35-1st modern app. G.A. Fury 2.50
50 ($2.50, 52 pgs.) 2.50
Annual 1,2: 1(12/85)-Crisis x-over. 2('88, $2.00), Special 1 ('87, $1.50) 2.50
NOTE: ***Kubert*** *r-4.* ***McFarlane*** *a-14-37p, Annual 1p; c(p)-14-19, 22, 25, 26, 31-33, 37, Annual 1.* ***Newton*** *a-12p, 13p(last work 4/85).* ***Tuska*** *a-11p. JSA app. 3-10.*

INFINITY WAR, THE (Also see Infinity Gauntlet & Warlock and the Infinity...)
Marvel Comics: June, 1992 - No. 6, Nov, 1992 ($2.50, mini-series)
1-Starlin scripts, Lim-c/a(p), Thanos app. in all 2.50
2-6: All have wraparound gatefold covers 2.50

INFORMER, THE
Feature Television Productions: April, 1954 - No. 5, Dec, 1954
1-Sekowsky-a begins 10.00 30.00 70.00
2 7.50 22.50 45.00
3-5 6.70 20.00 40.00

IN HIS STEPS
Spire Christian Comics (Fleming H. Revell Co.): 1973, 1977 (39/49¢)
nn 2.40 6.00

INHUMANOIDS, THE (TV)
Marvel Comics (Star Comics): Jan, 1987 - No. 4, July 1987
1-4: Based on Hasbro toys 2.00

INHUMANS, THE (See Amazing Adventures, Fantastic Four #54 & Special #5, Incredible Hulk Special #1, Marvel Graphic Novel & Thor #146)
Marvel Comics Group: Oct, 1975 - No. 12, Aug, 1977
1: #1-4,6 are 25¢ issues 1.25 3.75 10.00
2-12: 9-Reprints Amazing Adventures #1,2('70). 12-Hulk app. 5.00
4,6-(30¢-c variants, limited distribution)(4,8/76) 1.85 5.50 15.00
Special 1(4/90, $1.50, 52 pgs.)-F.F. cameo 3.00
NOTE: ***Buckler*** *c-2-4p, 5.* ***Gil Kane*** *a-5-7p; c-1p, 7p, 8p.* ***Kirby*** *a-9r.* ***Mooney*** *a-11i.* ***Perez*** *a-1-4p, 8p.*

INHUMANS (Marvel Knights)
Marvel Comics: Nov, 1998 - No. 12, ($2.99, limited series)
1-Jae Lee-c/a; Paul Jenkins-s 10.00
1-($6.95) DF Edition; Jae Lee variant-c 7.00
2-Two covers by Lee and Darrow 4.00
3-10 3.00

INHUMANS: THE GREAT REFUGE
Marvel Comics: May, 1995 ($2.95, one-shot)
1 3.00

INKY & DINKY (See Felix's Nephews...)

IN LOVE (...Magazine on-c; I Love You No. 7 on)
Mainline/Charlton No. 5 (5/55)-on: Aug-Sept, 1954 - No. 6, July, 1955 ('Adult Reading' on-c)
1-Simon & Kirby-a; book-length novel in all issues 34.00 103.00 240.00
2,3-S&K-a. 3-Last pre-code (12-1/54-55) 20.00 60.00 140.00
4-S&K-a.(Rare) 17.00 51.00 120.00
5-S&K-c only 10.00 30.00 60.00
6-No S&K-a 5.85 17.50 35.00

INNOVATION SPECTACULAR
Innovation Publishing: 1991 - No. 2, 1991 ($2.95, squarebound, 100 pgs.)
1,2: Contains rebound comics w/o covers 3.00

INNOVATION SUMMER FUN SPECIAL
Innovation Publishing: 1991 ($3.50, B&W/color, squarebound)
1-Contains rebound comics (Power Factory) 3.50

INSANE
Dark Horse Comics: Feb, 1988 - No. 2? ($1.75, B&W)
1,2: 1-X-Men, Godzilla parodies. 2-Concrete 2.00

INSANE CLOWN POSSE
Chaos Comics: June, 1999 - Present ($2.95)
1-McCann-s 4.00

IN SEARCH OF THE CASTAWAYS (See Movie Comics)

INSIDE CRIME (Formerly My Intimate Affair)
Fox Features Syndicate (Hero Books): No. 3, July, 1950 - No. 2, Sept, 1950
3-Wood-a (10 pgs.); L. B. Cole-c 26.00 79.00 185.00
2-Used in **SOTI**, pg. 182,183; r/Spook #24 21.00 62.00 145.00
nn(no publ. listed, nd) 9.15 27.00 55.00

INSPECTOR, THE (TV) (Also see The Pink Panther)
Gold Key: July, 1974 - No. 19, Feb, 1978
1 2.50 7.50 22.00
2-5 1.75 5.25 14.00
6-9 1.25 3.75 10.00
10-19: 11-Reprints 2.40 6.00

INSPECTOR GILL OF THE FISH POLICE (See Fish Police)

INSPECTOR WADE
David McKay Publications: No. 13, May, 1938

Intimate Confessions #1 © REAL

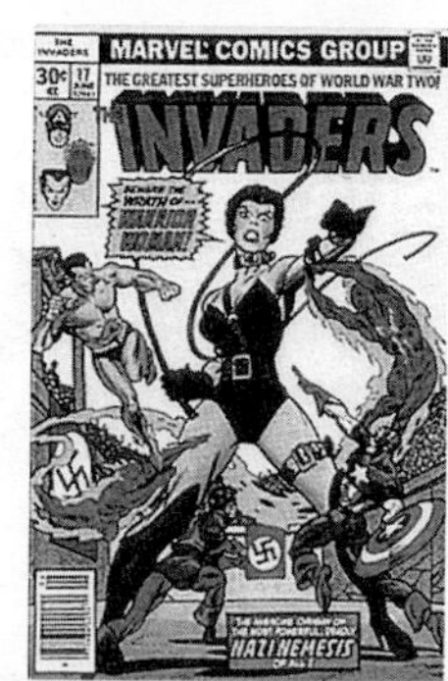

The Invaders #17 © MAR

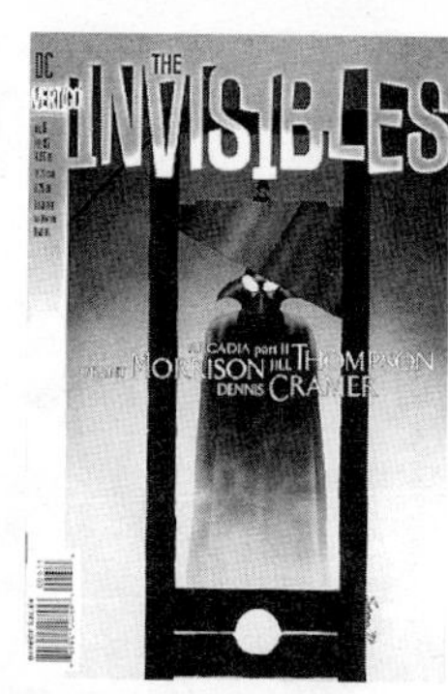

The Invisibles (1st series) #6 © Grant Morrison

GD2.0 FN6.0 NM9.4

Feature Books 13 19.00 57.00 190.00

INSTANT PIANO
Dark Horse Comics: Aug, 1994 - No. 4, Feb, 1995 ($3.95, B&W, bimonthly, mature)
1-4 4.00

INTERFACE
Marvel Comics (Epic Comics): Dec, 1989 - No. 8, Dec, 1990 ($1.95, mature, coated paper)
1-8: Cont. from 1st ESPers series; painted-c/a 2.25
Espers: Interface TPB ('98, $16.95) r/#1-6 17.00

INTERNATIONAL COMICS (...Crime Patrol No. 6)
E. C. Comics: Spring, 1947 - No. 5, Nov-Dec, 1947
1-Schaffenberger-a begins, ends #4 47.00 142.00 450.00
2 35.00 105.00 320.00
3-5 30.00 90.00 270.00

INTERNATIONAL CRIME PATROL (Formerly International Comics #1-5; becomes Crime Patrol No. 7 on)
E. C. Comics: No. 6, Spring, 1948
6-Moon Girl app. 48.00 145.00 460.00

IN THE DAYS OF THE MOB (Magazine)
Hampshire Dist. Ltd. (National): Fall, 1971 (B&W)
1-Kirby-a; John Dillinger wanted poster inside 7.00 21.00 75.00

IN THE PRESENCE OF MINE ENEMIES
Spire Christian Comics/Fleming H. Revell Co.: 1973 (35/49¢)
nn 5.00

INTIMATE
Charlton Comics: Dec, 1957 - No. 3, May, 1958
1 4.00 11.00 22.00
2,3 3.20 8.00 16.00

INTIMATE CONFESSIONS (See Fox Giants)

INTIMATE CONFESSIONS
Realistic Comics: July-Aug, 1951 - No. 7, Aug, 1952; No. 8, Mar, 1953 (All painted-c)
1-Kinstler-c/a; c/Avon paperback #222 70.00 210.00 560.00
2 19.00 56.00 130.00
3-c/Avon paperback #250; Kinstler-c/a 21.00 64.00 150.00
4-6,8: 4-c/Avon paperback #304; Kinstler-c. 6-c/Avon paperback #120. 8-c/Avon paperback #375; Kinstler-a 19.00 56.00 130.00
7-Spanking panel 19.00 56.00 130.00

INTIMATE CONFESSIONS
I. W. Enterprises/Super Comics: 1964
I.W. Reprint #9,10, Super Reprint #10,12,18 1.75 5.25 14.00

INTIMATE LOVE
Standard Comics: No. 5, 1950 - No. 28, Aug, 1954
5-8: 6-8-Severin/Elder-a 7.50 22.50 45.00
9 4.00 12.00 24.00
10-Jane Russell, Robert Mitchum photo-c 8.35 25.00 50.00
11-18,20,23,25,27,28 3.60 9.00 18.00
19,21,22,24,26-Toth-a 5.35 16.00 32.00
NOTE: ***Celardo*** *a-8, 10.* ***Colletta*** *a-23.* ***Moreira*** *a-13(2). Photo-c-6, 7, 10, 12, 14, 15, 18-20, 24, 26, 27.*

INTIMATE SECRETS OF ROMANCE
Star Publications: Sept, 1953 - No. 2, Apr, 1954
1,2-L. B. Cole-c 17.00 51.00 120.00

INTRIGUE
Quality Comics Group: Jan, 1955
1-Horror; Jack Cole reprint/Web of Evil 30.00 90.00 210.00

INTRIGUE
Image Comics: Aug, 1999 - Present ($2.50)

GD2.0 FN6.0 NM9.4

1-Two covers (Andrews, Wieringo); Shum-s/Andrews-a 2.50

INTRUDER
TSR, Inc.: 1990 - No. 10, 1991 ($2.95, 44 pgs.)
1-10 3.00

INVADERS, THE (TV)
Gold Key: Oct, 1967 - No. 4, Oct, 1968 (All have photo-c)
1-Spiegle-a in all 9.00 27.00 100.00
2-4 6.40 19.00 70.00

INVADERS, THE (Also see The Avengers #71 & Giant-Size Invaders)
Marvel Comics Group: August, 1975 - No. 40, May, 1979; No. 41, Sept, 1979
1-Captain America & Bucky, Human Torch & Toro, & Sub-Mariner begin; cont'd. from Giant Size Invaders #1; #1-7 are 25¢ issues 2.50 7.50 20.00
2-5,8-10: 2-1st app. Brain-Drain. 3-Battle issue; Cap vs. Namor vs. Torch; intro U-Man. 8-Union Jack-c/story. 9-Origin Baron Blood. 10-G.A. Capt. America-r/C.A #22 1.00 3.00 8.00
6,7-(Regular 25¢ edition). 6-(7/76) Liberty Legion app. 7-Intro Baron Blood & intro/1st app. Union Jack; Human Torch origin retold. 1.00 3.00 8.00
6,7-(30¢-c variant, limited distribution) 2.50 7.50 24.00
11-19: 11-Origin Spitfire; intro The Blue Bullet. 14-1st app. The Crusaders. 16-Re-intro The Destroyer. 17-Intro Warrior Woman. 18-Re-intro The Destroyer w/new origin. 19-Hitler-c/story 5.00
20-Reprints origin/1st app. Sub-Mariner from Motion Picture Funnies Weekly with color added & brief write-up about MPFW; 1st app. new Union Jack II 1.00 3.00 8.00
21-(Regular 30¢ edition)-r/Marvel Mystery #10 (battle issue) 4.00
21-(35¢-c variant, limited distribution) 2.50 7.50 20.00
22-30,34-40: 22-New origin Toro. 24-r/Marvel Mystery #17 (team-up issue; all-r). 25-All new-a begins. 28-Intro new Human Top & Golden Girl. 29-Intro Teutonic Knight. 34-Mighty Destroyer joins. 35-The Whizzer app. 4.00
31-33: 31-Frankenstein-c/sty. 32,33-Thor app. 2.40 6.00
41-Double size last issue 1.00 3.00 8.00
Annual 1 (9/77)-Schomburg, Rico stories (new); Schomburg-c/a (1st for Marvel in 30 years); Avengers app.; re-intro The Shark & The Hyena 1.50 4.50 12.00
NOTE: ***Buckler*** *a-5.* ***Everett*** *r-20('39), 21(1940), 24, Annual 1.* ***Gil Kane*** *c(p)-13, 17, 18, 20-27.* ***Kirby*** *c(p)-3-12, 14-16, 32, 33.* ***Mooney*** *a-5i, 16, 22.* ***Robbins*** *a-1-4, 6-9, 10(3 pg.), 11-15, 17-21, 23, 25-28; c-28.*

INVADERS (See Namor, the Sub-Mariner #12)
Marvel Comics Group: May, 1993 - No. 4, Aug, 1993 ($1.75, limited series)
1-4 2.00

INVADERS FROM HOME
DC Comics (Piranha Press): 1990 - No. 6, 1990 ($2.50, mature)
1-6 2.50

INVASION
DC Comics: Holiday, 1988-'89 - No. 3, Jan, 1989 ($2.95, lim. series, 84 pgs.)
1-3:1-McFarlane/Russell-a. 2-McFarlane/Russell & Giffen/Gordon-a 3.00

INVINCIBLE FOUR OF KUNG FU & NINJA
Leung Publications: April, 1988 - No. 6, 1989 ($2.00)
1-($2.75) 2.75
2-6: 2-Begin $2.00-c 2.00

INVISIBLE BOY (See Approved Comics)

INVISIBLE MAN, THE (See Superior Stories #1 & Supernatural Thrillers #2)

INVISIBLES, THE (1st Series)
DC Comics (Vertigo): Sept, 1994 - No. 25, Oct, 1996 ($1.95/$2.50, mature)
1-($2.95, 52 pgs.)-Intro King Mob, Ragged Robin, Boy, Lord Fanny & Dane (Jack Frost); Grant Morrison scripts in all 6.00
2-8: 4-Includes bound-in trading cards. 5-1st app. Orlando; brown paper-c 4.00
9-25: 10-Intro Jim Crow. 13-15-Origin Lord Fanny. 19-Origin King Mob; polybagged. 20-Origin Boy. 21-Mister Six revealed. 25-Intro Division X 2.50

Iron Fist (3rd series) #3 © MAR

Iron Man #21 © MAR

Iron Man #100 © MAR

GD2.0 FN6.0 NM9.4

Say You Want A Revolution (1996, $17.50, TPB)-r/#1-8 18.00

NOTE: *Buckingham a-25p. Rian Hughes c-1, 5. Phil Jimenez a-17p-19p. Paul Johnson a-16, 21. Sean Phillips c-2-4, 6-25. Weston a-10p. Yeowell a-1p-4p, 22p-24p.*

INVISIBLES, THE (2nd Series)
DC Comics (Vertigo): V2#1, Feb, 1997 - No. 22, Feb, 1999 ($2.50, mature)

1-Intro Jolly Roger; Grant Morrison scripts, Phil Jimenez-a, & Brian Bolland-c begins 4.00
2-22: 9,14-Weston-a 2.50
Bloody Hell in America TPB ('98, $12.95) r/#1-4 13.00
Counting to None TPB ('99, $19.95) r/#5-13 20.00

INVISIBLES, THE (3rd Series) (Issue #'s go in reverse from #12 to #1)
DC Comics (Vertigo): V3#12, Apr, 1999 - No. 1 ($2.95, mature)

12-7-Bolland-c; Morrison-s/Phillip Bond-a 3.00

INVISIBLE SCARLET O'NEIL (Also see Famous Funnies #81 & Harvey Comics Hits #59)
Famous Funnies (Harvey): Dec, 1950 - No. 3, Apr, 1951
(2-3 pgs. of Powell-a in each issue.)

1 13.00 39.00 90.00
2,3 10.00 30.00 70.00

IRON CORPORAL, THE (See Army War Heroes #22)
Charlton Comics: No. 23, Oct, 1985 - No. 25, Feb, 1986

23-25: Glanzman-a(r) 3.00

IRON FIST (See Deadly Hands of Kung Fu, Marvel Premiere & Power Man)
Marvel Comics: Nov, 1975 - No. 15, Sept, 1977

1-Iron Fist battles Iron Man (#1-6: 25¢) 3.00 9.00 30.00
2 2.50 7.50 20.00
3-10: 4-6-(Regular 25¢ edition)(4-6/76). 8-Origin retold 1.75 5.25 14.00
4-6-(30¢-c variant, limited distribution) 4.80 14.40 48.00
11-13: 12-Capt. America app. 1.10 3.30 9.00
14-1st app. Sabretooth (8/77)(see Power Man) 8.50 26.00 95.00
15-(Regular 30¢ ed.) X-Men app., Byrne-a 3.80 11.40 38.00
15-(35¢-c variant, limited distribution) 9.00 27.00 100.00

NOTE: *Adkins a-8p, 10i, 13i; c-8i. Byrne a-1-15p; c-8p, 15p. G. Kane c-4-6p. McWilliams a-1i.*

IRON FIST
Marvel Comics: Sept, 1996 - No. 2, Oct, 1996 ($1.50, limited series)

1,2 3.00

IRON FIST
Marvel Comics: Jul, 1998 - No. 3, Sept, 1998 ($2.50, limited series)

1-3: Jurgens-s/Guice-a 2.50

IRONHAND OF ALMURIC (Robert E. Howard's...)
Dark Horse Comics: Aug, 1991 - No. 4, 1991 ($2.00, B&W, mini-series)

1-4: 1-Conrad painted-c 2.00

IRON HORSE (TV)
Dell Publishing Co.: March, 1967 - No. 2, June, 1967

1,2-Dale Robertson photo covers on both 1.75 5.25 14.00

IRONJAW (Also see The Barbarians)
Atlas/Seaboard Publ.: Jan, 1975 - No. 4, July, 1975

1-1st app. Iron Jaw; Neal Adams-c; Sekowsky-a(p) 4.00
2-4: 2-Neal Adams-c. 4-Origin 3.00

IRON LANTERN
Marvel Comics (Amalgam): June, 1997 ($1.95, one-shot)

1-Kurt Busiek-s/Paul Smith & Al Williamson-a 2.00

IRON MAN (Also see The Avengers #1, Giant-Size..., Marvel Collectors Item Classics, Marvel Double Feature, Marvel Fanfare & Tales of Suspense #39)
Marvel Comics: May, 1968 - No. 332, Sept, 1996

1-Origin; Colan-c/a(p); story continued from Iron Man & Sub-Mariner #1 31.00 93.00 350.00
2 11.00 33.00 110.00

GD2.0 FN6.0 NM9.4

3 6.00 18.00 60.00
4,5 5.00 15.00 50.00
6-10: 9-Iron Man battles green Hulk-like android 4.00 12.00 40.00
11-15: 15-Last 12¢ issue 2.60 7.80 26.00
16-20 2.50 7.50 20.00
21-24,26-30: 22-Death of Janice Cord. 27-Intro Fire Brand 1.85 5.50 15.00
25-Iron Man battles Sub-Mariner 2.25 6.75 18.00
31-42: 33-1st app. Spymaster. 35-Nick Fury & Daredevil x-over. 42-Last 15¢ issue 1.85 5.50 15.00
43-Intro The Guardsman; 25¢ giant 1.85 5.50 15.00
44-46,48-50: 43-Giant-Man back-up by Ayers. 44-Ant-Man by Tuska. 46-The Guardsman dies. 50-Princess Python app. 1.50 4.50 12.00
47-Origin retold; Barry Smith-a(p) 1.85 5.50 15.00
51-53: 53-Starlin part pencils 1.10 3.30 9.00
54-Iron Man battles Sub-Mariner; 1st app. Moondragon (1/73) as Madame MacEvil; Everett part-c 2.25 6.75 18.00
55-1st app. Thanos (cameo), Drax the Destroyer, Mentor, Starfox & Kronos (2/73); Starlin-c/a 7.00 21.00 75.00
56-Starlin-a 1.85 5.50 15.00
57-67,69,70: 59-Firebrand returns. 65-Origin Dr. Spectrum. 66-Iron Man vs. Thor. 67-Last 20¢ issue 1.00 3.00 8.00
68-Sunfire & Unicorn app.; origin retold; Starlin-c 1.10 3.30 9.00
71-84,89-99: 72-Cameo portraits of N. Adams, 73-Rename Stark Industries to Stark International; Brunner. 76-r/#9. 89-Daredevil app.; last 25¢ issue. 96-1st app. new Guardsman 2.40 6.00
85-88-(Regular 25¢ editions): 86-1st app. Blizzard. 87-Origin Blizzard. 88-Thanos app. 2.40 6.00
85-88-(30¢-c variants, limited distribution)(4-8/76) 2.25 6.75 18.00
100-(7/77)-Starlin-c 1.50 4.50 12.00
101-117: 101-Intro DreadKnight. 109-1st app. new Crimson Dynamo; 1st app. Vanguard. 110-Origin Jack of Hearts retold; death of Count Nefaria. 114-Avengers app. 5.00
102-(35¢-c variant, limited dist.)(9/77) 2.50 7.50 20.00
118-Byrne-a(p); 1st app. Jim Rhodes 1.00 2.80 7.00
119-128: 120,121-Sub-Mariner x-over. 122-Origin. 123-128-Tony Stark treated for alcohol problem. 125-Ant-Man app. 4.50
129-149: 131,132-Hulk x-over 3.50
150-Double size 5.00
151-168: 152-New armor. 161-Moon Knight app. 167-Tony Stark alcohol problem starts again 3.00
169-New Iron Man (Jim Rhodes replaces Tony Stark) 5.00
170,171 3.00
172-199: 172-Captain America x-over. 186-Intro Vibro. 190-Scarlet Witch app. 191-198-Tony Stark returns as original Iron Man. 192-Both Iron Men battle 2.50
200-(11/85, $1.25, 52 pgs.)-Tony Stark returns as new Iron Man (red & white armor) thru #230 3.50
201-224: 213-Intro new Dominic Fortune. 214-Spider-Woman apps. in new black costume (1/87) 2.00
225-Double size ($1.25) 3.00
226-243,245-249: 228-vs. Capt. America. 231-Intro new Iron Man. 233-Ant-Man app. 234-Spider-Man x-over. 243-Tony Stark loses use of legs. 247-Hulk x-over 2.00
244-($1.50, 52 pgs.)-New Armor makes him walk 3.00
250-($1.50, 52 pgs.)-Dr. Doom-c/story 3.00
251-274,276-281,283,285-287,289,291-299: 258-277-Byrne scripts. 271-Fin Fang Foom app. 276-Black Widow-c/story; last $1.00-c. 281-1st app. ;War Machine (cameo). 283-2nd full app. War Machine 2.00
275-($1.50, 52 pgs.) 3.00
282-1st full app. War Machine (7/92) 4.00
284-Death of Iron Man (Tony Stark) 4.00
288-($2.50, 52pg.)-Silver foil stamped-c; Iron Man's 350th app. in comics 3.00
290-($2.95, 52pg.)-Gold foil stamped-c; 30th ann. 3.00
300-($3.95, 68 pgs.)-Collector's Edition w/embossed foil-c; anniversary issue; War Machine-c/story 4.00
300-($2.50, 68 pgs.)-Newsstand Edition 2.50

Iron Man V3 #17 © MAR

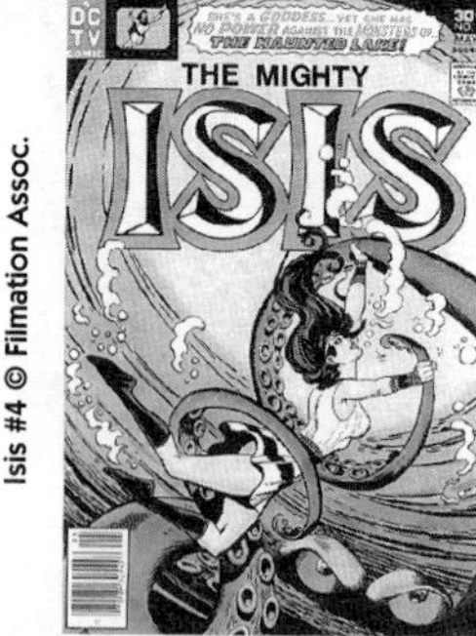

Isis #4 © Filmation Assoc.

I Spy #3 © GK

GD2.0 FN6.0 NM9.4

301-303: 302-Venom-c/story (cameo #301) 2.00
304-316,318-324,326-331: 304-Begin $1.50-c; bound-in trading card sheet; Thunderstrike-c/story. 310-Orange logo. 312-w/bound-in Power Ranger Card. 319-Prologue to "The Crossing." 326-New Tony Stark; Pratt-c. 330-War Machine & Stockpile app; return of Morgan Stark 2.00
310,325,332: 310 ($2.95)-Polybagged w/ 16 pg. Marvel Action Hour preview & acetate print; white logo. 325-($2.95)-Wraparound-c. 332-Onsalught x-over 3.00
317 ($2.50)-Flip book 2.50
Special 1 (8/70)-Sub-Mariner x-over; Everett-c 2.50 7.50 24.00
Special 2 (11/71)-r/TOS #81,82,91 (all-r) 1.50 4.50 12.00
Annual 3 (1976)-Man-Thing app. 5.00
King Size 4 (8/77)-The Champions (w/Ghost Rider) app.; Newton-a(i) 4.00
Annual 5-15: ('82-'94)-5-New-a. 6 -New Iron Man (J. Rhodes) app. 8-X-Factor app. 10-Atlantis Attacks x-over; P. Smith-a; Layton/Guice-a; Sub-Mariner app. 11-(1990)-Origin of Mrs. Arbogast by Ditko (p&i). 12-1 pg. origin recap; Ant-Man back-up story. 13-Darkhawk & Avengers West Coast app.; Colan/Williamson-a. 14-Bagged w/card 3.00
Manual 1 (1993, $1.75)-Operations handbook 2.00
Graphic Novel: Crash (1988, $12.95, Adults, 72 pgs)-Computer generated art & color; violence & nudity 13.00
...Collector's Preview 1(11/94, $1.95)-wraparound-c; text & illos-no comics 2.00
...Vs. Dr. Doom (12/94, $12.95)-r/#149-150, 249,250. Julie Bell-c 13.00

NOTE: ***Austin*** *c-105i, 109-111i, 151i.* ***Byrne*** *a-118p; c-109p, 197, 253.* ***Colan*** *a-1p, 253, Special 1p(3); c-1p.* ***Craig*** *a-1i, 2-4, 5-13i, 14, 15-19i, 24p, 25p, 26-28i; c-2-4.* ***Ditko*** *a-160p.* ***Everett*** *c-29.* ***Guice*** *a-233-241p.* ***G. Kane*** *c(p)-52-54, 63, 67, 72-75, 77-79, 88, 98.* ***Kirby*** *a-Special 1p; c-13, 80p, 90, 92-95.* ***Mooney*** *a-40i, 43i, 47i.* ***Perez*** *c-103p.* ***Simonson*** *c-Annual 8.* ***B. Smith*** *a-232p, 243i; c-232.* ***P. Smith*** *a-159p, 245p, Annual 10p; c-159.* ***Starlin*** *a-53p(part), 55p, 56p; c-55p, 160, 163.* ***Tuska*** *a-5-13p, 15-23p, 24i, 32p, 38-46p, 48-54p, 57-61p, 63-69p, 70-72p, 78p, 86-92p, 95-106p, Annual 4p.* ***Wood*** *a-Special 1i.*

IRON MAN (The Invincible...) (Volume Two)
Marvel Comics: Nov, 1996 - No. 13, Nov, 1997 ($2.95/$1.95/$1.99) (Produced by WildStorm Productions)

V2#1-3-Heroes Reborn begins; Scott Lobdell scripts & Whilce Portacio-c/a begin; new origin Iron Man & Hulk. 2-Hulk app. 3-Fantastic Four app. 4.00
1-Variant-c 5.00
4-11: 4-Two covers. 6-Fantastic Four app.; Industrial Revolution; Hulk app. 7-Return of Rebel. 11-($1.99) Dr. Doom-c/app. 3.00
12-($2.99) "Heroes Reunited"-pt. 3; Hulk-c/app. 3.50
13-($1.99) "World War 3"-pt. 3, x-over w/Image 3.00

IRON MAN (The Invincible...) (Volume Three)
Marvel Comics: Feb, 1998 - Present ($2.99/$1.99)

V3#1-($2.99)-Follows Heroes Return; Busiek scripts & Chen-c/a begin; Deathsquad app. 5.00
1-Alternate Ed. 1.00 3.00 8.00
2-12: 2-Two covers. 6-Black Widow-c/app. 7-Warbird-c/app. 8-Black Widow app. 9-Mandarin returns 2.00
13-($2.99) battles the Controller 3.50
14-21: 14-Fantastic Four-c/app. 2.50
.../Captain America '98 Annual ($3.50) vs. Modok 3.50
1999 Annual ($3.50) 3.50

IRON MAN & SUB-MARINER
Marvel Comics Group: Apr, 1968 (12¢, one-shot) (Pre-dates Iron Man #1 & Sub-Mariner #1)

1-Iron Man story by Colan/Craig continued from Tales of Suspense #99 & continued in Iron Man #1; Sub-Mariner story by Colan continued from Tales to Astonish #101 & continued in Sub-Mariner #1; Colan/Everett-c 10.00 30.00 100.00

IRON MAN: THE IRON AGE
Marvel Comics: Aug, 1998 - No. 2, Sept, 1998 ($5.99, limited series)

1,2-Busiek-s; flashback story from gold armor days 2.40 6.00

IRON MAN: THE LEGEND
Marvel Comics: Sept, 1996 ($3.95, one-shot)

1-Tribute issue 4.50

GD2.0 FN6.0 NM9.4

IRON MAN 2020 (Also see Machine Man limited series)
Marvel Comics: June, 1994 ($5.95, one-shot)

nn 2.40 6.00

IRON MAN/X-O MANOWAR: HEAVY METAL (See X-O Manowar/Iron Man: In Heavy Metal)
Marvel Comics: Sept, 1996 ($2.50, one-shot) (1st Marvel/Valiant x-over)

1-Pt. II of Iron Man/X-O Manowar x-over; Fabian Nicieza scripts; 1st app. Rand Banion 2.50

IRON MARSHALL
Jademan Comics: July, 1990 - No. 32, Feb, 1993 ($1.75, plastic coated-c)

1-32: Kung Fu stories. 1-Poster centerfold 2.00

IRON VIC (See Comics Revue No. 3 & Giant Comics Editions)
United Features Syndicate/St. John Publ. Co.: 1940; Aug, 1947 - No. 3, 1947

Single Series 22 32.00 96.00 225.00
2,3(St. John) 8.35 25.00 50.00

IRONWOLF
DC Comics: 1986 ($2.00, one shot)

1-r/Weird Worlds 8-10; Chaykin story & art 2.00

IRONWOLF: FIRES OF THE REVOLUTION (See Weird Worlds #8-10)
DC Comics: 1992 ($29.95, hardcover)

nn-Chaykin/Moore story, Mignola-a w/Russell inks. 30.00

ISAAC ASIMOV'S I-BOTS
Tekno Comix: Dec, 1995 - No. 7, May, 1996 ($1.95)

1-7: 1-6-Perez-c/a. 2-Chaykin variant-c exists. 3-Polybagged. 7-Lady Justice-c/app. 2.25

ISAAC ASIMOV'S I-BOTS
BIG Entertainment: V2#1, June, 1996 - Present ($2.25)

V2#1-9: 1-Lady Justice-c/app. 6-Gil Kane-c 2.25

ISIS (TV) (Also see Shazam)
National Per.l Publ./DC Comics: Oct-Nov, 1976 - No. 8, Dec-Jan, 1977-78

1-Wood inks 1.10 3.30 9.00
2-8: 5-Isis new look. 7-Origin 5.00

ISLAND AT THE TOP OF THE WORLD (See Walt Disney Showcase #27)

ISLAND OF DR. MOREAU, THE (Movie)
Marvel Comics Group: Oct, 1977 (52 pgs.)

1-Gil Kane-c 4.00

I SPY (TV)
Gold Key: Aug, 1966 - No. 6, Sept, 1968 (All have photo-c)

1-Bill Cosby, Robert Culp photo covers 22.00 66.00 240.00
2-6: 3,4-McWilliams-a 13.00 39.00 140.00

IT! (See Astonishing Tales No. 21-24 & Supernatural Thrillers No. 1)

ITCHY & SCRATCHY COMICS (The Simpsons TV show)
Bongo Comics: 1993 - No. 3, 1993 ($1.95)

1-3: 1-Bound-in jumbo poster. 3-w/decoder screen trading card 2.50
Holiday Special ('94, $1.95) 2.50

IT REALLY HAPPENED
William H. Wise No. 1,2/Standard (Visual Editions): 1944 - No. 11, Oct, 1947

1-Kit Carson & Ben Franklin stories 19.00 56.00 130.00
2 10.00 30.00 70.00
3,4,6,9,11: 6-Joan of Arc story. 9-Captain Kidd & Frank Buck stories 9.15 27.00 55.00
5-Lou Gehrig & Lewis Carroll stories 14.00 43.00 100.00
7-Teddy Roosevelt story 9.15 27.00 55.00
8-Story of Roy Rogers 16.00 47.00 110.00
10-Honus Wagner & Mark Twain stories 11.50 34.00 80.00

NOTE: ***Guardineer*** *a-7(2), 8(2), 11.* ***Schomburg*** *c-1-7, 9-11.*

IT RHYMES WITH LUST (Also see Bold Stories & Candid Tales)
St. John Publishing Co.: 1950 (Digest size, 128 pgs.)

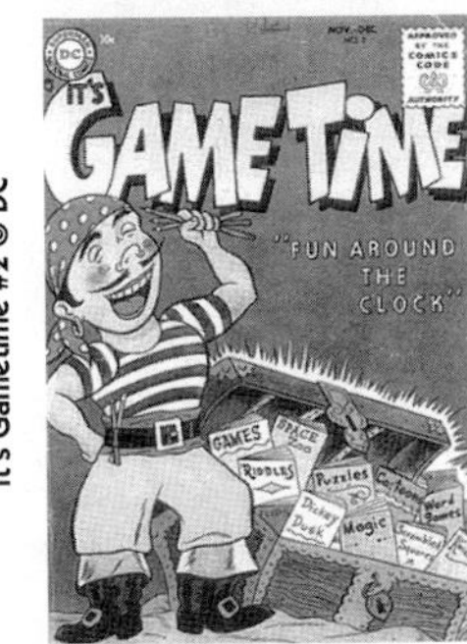

It's Gametime #2 © DC

Jackie Gleason and the Honeymooners #1 © DC

Jack Kirby's Fourth World #14 © DC

	GD2.0	FN6.0	NM9.4
nn (Rare)-Matt Baker & Ray Osrin-a	56.00	169.00	450.00

IT'S ABOUT TIME (TV)
Gold Key: Jan, 1967

	GD2.0	FN6.0	NM9.4
1 (10195-701)-Photo-c	3.80	11.40	38.00

IT'S A DUCK'S LIFE
Marvel Comics/Atlas(MMC): Feb, 1950 - No. 11, Feb, 1952

	GD2.0	FN6.0	NM9.4
1-Buck Duck, Super Rabbit begin	13.50	41.00	95.00
2	7.00	21.00	42.00
3-11	5.85	17.50	35.00

IT'S GAMETIME
National Periodical Publications: Sept-Oct, 1955 - No. 4, Mar-Apr, 1956

	GD2.0	FN6.0	NM9.4
1-(Scarce)-Infinity-c; Davy Crockett app. in puzzle	72.00	216.00	575.00
2,3 (Scarce): 2-Dodo & The Frog	56.00	169.00	450.00
4 (Rare)	59.00	178.00	475.00

IT'S LOVE, LOVE, LOVE
St. John Publishing Co.: Nov, 1957 - No. 2, Jan, 1958 (10¢)

	GD2.0	FN6.0	NM9.4
1,2	4.25	13.00	28.00

IVANHOE (See Fawcett Movie Comics No. 20)

IVANHOE
Dell Publishing Co.: July-Sept, 1963

	GD2.0	FN6.0	NM9.4
1 (12-373-309)	2.50	7.50	28.00

IWO JIMA (See Spectacular Features Magazine)

JACE PEARSON OF THE TEXAS RANGERS (Radio/TV)(4-Color #396 is titled Tales of the Texas Rangers; ...'s Tales of ... #11-on)(See Western Roundup under Dell Giants)
Dell Publishing Co.: No. 396, 5/52 - No. 1021, 8-10/59 (No #10) (All-Photo-c)

	GD2.0	FN6.0	NM9.4
Four Color 396 (#1)	10.00	30.00	110.00
2(5-7/53) - 9(2-4/55)	5.50	16.50	60.00
Four Color 648(#10, 9/55)	4.50	13.50	50.00
11(11-2/55-56) - 14,17-20(6-8/58)	4.00	12.00	45.00
15,16-Toth-a	4.50	13.50	50.00
Four Color 961, 1021: 961--Spiegle-a	4.00	12.00	45.00

NOTE: *Joel McCrea photo c-1-9, F.C. 648 (starred on radio show only); Willard Parker photo c-11-on (starred on TV series).*

JACK ARMSTRONG (Radio)(See True Comics)
Parents' Institute: Nov, 1947 - No. 9, Sept, 1948; No. 10, Mar, 1949 - No. 13, Sept, 1949

	GD2.0	FN6.0	NM9.4
1-(Scarce) (odd size)	40.00	120.00	325.00
2	19.00	58.00	135.00
3-5	13.50	41.00	95.00
6-13: 7-Vic Hardy's Crime Lab begins?	11.00	33.00	75.00

JACK HUNTER
Blackthorne Publishing: July, 1987 - No. 3 ($1.25)

	GD2.0	FN6.0	NM9.4
1-3			2.00

JACKIE CHAN'S SPARTAN X
Topps Comics: May, 1997 - No. 3 ($2.95, limited series)

	GD2.0	FN6.0	NM9.4
1-3-Michael Golden-s/a; variant photo-c			3.00

JACKIE CHAN'S SPARTAN X: HELL BENT HERO FOR HIRE
Image Comics (Little Eva Ink): Mar, 1998 - No. 3 ($2.95, B&W)

	GD2.0	FN6.0	NM9.4
1-3-Michael Golden-s/a: 1-variant photo-c			3.00

JACKIE GLEASON (TV) (Also see The Honeymooners)
St. John Publishing Co.: 1948 - No. 2, 1948; Sept, 1955 - No. 4, Dec, 1955?

	GD2.0	FN6.0	NM9.4
1(1948)	69.00	206.00	550.00
2(1948)	52.00	157.00	420.00
1(1955)(TV)-Photo-c	56.00	169.00	450.00
2-4	40.00	120.00	300.00

JACKIE GLEASON AND THE HONEYMOONERS (TV)
National Periodical Publications: June-July, 1956 - No. 12, Apr-May, 1958

	GD2.0	FN6.0	NM9.4
1-1st app. Ralph Kramden	81.00	244.00	650.00
2	52.00	157.00	420.00
3-11	40.00	120.00	315.00
12 (Scarce)	57.00	172.00	460.00

JACKIE JOKERS (Became Richie Rich &...)
Harvey Publications: March, 1973 - No. 4, Sept, 1973 (#5 was advertised, but not published)

	GD2.0	FN6.0	NM9.4
1-1st app.	2.50	7.50	20.00
2-4: 2-President Nixon app.	1.10	3.30	9.00

JACKIE ROBINSON (Famous Plays of...) (Also see Negro Heroes #2 & Picture News #4)
Fawcett Publications: May, 1950 - No. 6, 1952 (Baseball hero) (All photo-c)

	GD2.0	FN6.0	NM9.4
nn	87.00	262.00	700.00
2	53.00	159.00	425.00
3-6	43.00	128.00	340.00

JACK IN THE BOX (Formerly Yellowjacket Comics #1-10; becomes Cowboy Western Comics #17 on)
Frank Comunale/Charlton Comics No. 11 on: Feb, 1946; No. 11, Oct, 1946 - No. 16, Nov-Dec, 1947

	GD2.0	FN6.0	NM9.4
1-Stitches, Marty Mouse & Nutsy McKrow	13.00	39.00	90.00
11-Yellowjacket (early Charlton comic)	17.00	51.00	120.00
12,14,15	7.50	22.50	45.00
13-Wolverton-a	20.00	60.00	140.00
16-12 pg. adapt. of Silas Marner; Kiefer-a	10.00	30.00	70.00

JACK KIRBY'S FOURTH WORLD (See New Gods, 3rd Series)
DC Comics: Mar, 1997 - No. 20, Oct, 1998 ($1.95/$2.25)

	GD2.0	FN6.0	NM9.4
1-20: 1-Byrne-a/scripts & Simonson-c begin; story cont'd from New Gods, 3rd Series #15; retells "The Pact" (New Gods, 1st Series #7); 1st DC app. Thor (cameo). 2-Thor vs. Big Barda; "Apokolips Then" back-up begins; Kirby-c/swipe (Thor #126) 8-Genesis x-over. 10-Simonson-s/a 13-Simonson back-up story. 20-Superman-c/app.			2.25

JACK KIRBY'S SECRET CITY SAGA
Topps Comics (Kirbyverse): No. 0, Apr, 1993; No. 1, May, 1993 - No. 4, Aug, 1993 ($2.95, limited series)

	GD2.0	FN6.0	NM9.4
0-(No cover price, 20 pgs.)-Simonson-c/a			3.00
1-4-Bagged w/3 trading cards; Ditko-c/a: 1-Ditko/Art Adams-c. 2-Ditko/Byrne-c; has coupon for Pres. Clinton holo-foil trading card. 3-Dorman poster; has coupon for Gore holo-foil trading card. 4-Ditko/Perez-c			3.00

NOTE: *Issues #1-4 contain coupons redeemable for Kirbychrome version of #1*

JACK KIRBY'S SILVER STAR (Also see Silver Star)
Topps Comics (Kirbyverse): Oct, 1993 ($2.95)(Intended as a 4-issue limited series)

	GD2.0	FN6.0	NM9.4
1-Silver ink-c; Austin-c/a(i); polybagged w/3 cards			3.00

JACK KIRBY'S TEENAGENTS (See Satan's Six)
Topps Comics (Kirbyverse): Aug, 1993 - No. 3, Oct, 1993 ($2.95)(Intended as a 4-issue limited series)

	GD2.0	FN6.0	NM9.4
1-3: Polybagged with/3 trading cards; 1-3-Austin-c(i): 3-Liberty Project app.			3.00

JACK OF HEARTS (Also see The Deadly Hands of Kung Fu #22 & Marvel Premiere #44)
Marvel Comics Group: Jan, 1984 - No. 4, Apr, 1984 (60¢, limited series)

	GD2.0	FN6.0	NM9.4
1-4			2.00

JACKPOT COMICS (Jolly Jingles #10 on)
MLJ Magazines: Spring, 1941 - No. 9, Spring, 1943

	GD2.0	FN6.0	NM9.4
1-The Black Hood, Mr. Justice, Steel Sterling & Sgt. Boyle begin; Biro-c	288.00	862.00	2300.00
2-S. Cooper-c	125.00	375.00	1000.00
3-Hubbell-c	94.00	281.00	750.00
4-Archie begins (Win/41; on sale 12/41)-(also see Pep Comics #22); 1st app. Mrs. Grundy, the principal; Novick-c	325.00	975.00	3100.00
5-Hitler-c by Montana; 1st definitive Mr. Weatherbee; 1st app. Reggie in 1 panel cameo	144.00	431.00	1150.00

Jackpot Comics #6 © MLJ

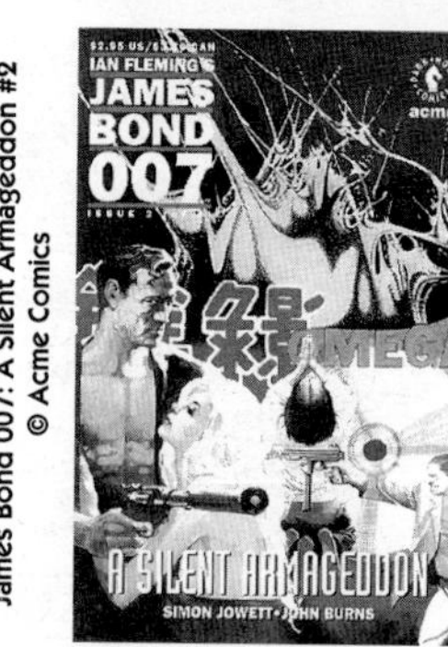

James Bond 007: A Silent Armageddon #2 © Acme Comics

Jeanie Comics #15 © MAR

	GD2.0	FN6.0	NM9.4
6-9: 6,7-Bondage-c by Novick. 8,9-Sahle-c	100.00	300.00	800.00

JACK Q FROST (See Unearthly Spectaculars)

JACK THE GIANT KILLER (See Movie Classics)

JACK THE GIANT KILLER (New Adventures of...)
Bimfort & Co.: Aug-Sept, 1953

	GD2.0	FN6.0	NM9.4
V1#1-H. C. Kiefer-c/a	21.00	64.00	150.00

JACKY'S DIARY
Dell Publishing Co.: No. 1091, Apr-June, 1960 (one-shot)

	GD2.0	FN6.0	NM9.4
Four Color 1091	3.60	11.00	40.00

JADEMAN COLLECTION
Jademan Comics: Dec, 1989 - No. 3, 1990 ($2.50, plastic coated-c, 68 pgs.)

1-3: 1-Wraparound-c w/fold-out poster 2.50

JADEMAN KUNG FU SPECIAL
Jademan Comics: 1988 ($1.50, 64 pgs.)

1 2.00

JAGUAR, THE (Also see The Adventures of...)
Impact Comics (DC): Aug, 1991 - No. 14, Oct, 1992 ($1.00)

1-14: 4-The Black Hood x-over. 7-Sienkiewicz-c. 9-Contains Crusaders trading card 2.00
Annual 1 (1992, $2.50, 68 pgs.)-With trading card 2.50

JAGUAR GOD
Verotik: Mar, 1995 - Present ($2.95, mature)

	GD2.0	FN6.0	NM9.4
0 (2/96, $3.50)-Embossed Frazetta-c; Bisley-a; w/pin-ups.		2.40	6.00
1-Frazetta-c.		2.40	6.00
2-7: 2-Frazetta-c. 3-Bisley-c. 4-Emond-c. 7-($2.95)-Frazetta-c			5.00

JAKE THRASH
Aircel Publishing: 1988 - No. 3, 1988 ($2.00)

1-3 2.00

JAM, THE (...Urban Adventure)
Slave Labor Nos. 1-5/Dark Horse Comics Nos. 6-8/Caliber Comics No. 9 on: Nov, 1989 - Present ($1.95/$2.50/$2.95, B&W)

1-13: Bernie Mireault-c/a/scripts. 6-1st Dark Horse issue. 9-1st Caliber issue 3.00

JAMBOREE
Round Publishing Co.: Feb, 1946(no mo. given) - No. 3, Apr, 1946

	GD2.0	FN6.0	NM9.4
1-Funny animal	24.00	73.00	170.00
2,3	14.00	43.00	100.00

JAMES BOND 007: A SILENT ARMAGEDDON
Dark Horse Comics/Acme Press: Mar, 1993 - Apr 1993 (limited series)

1,2 3.50

JAMES BOND 007: GOLDENEYE (Movie)
Topps Comics: Jan, 1996 ($2.95, unfinished limited series of 3)

1-Movie adaptation; Stelfreeze-c 3.00

JAMES BOND 007: SERPENT'S TOOTH
Dark Horse Comics/Acme Press: July 1992 - Aug 1992 ($4.95, limited series)

1-3-Paul Gulacy-c/a 5.00

JAMES BOND 007: SHATTERED HELIX
Dark Horse Comics: Jun 1994 - July 1994 ($2.50, limited series)

1,2 3.00

JAMES BOND 007: THE QUASIMODO GAMBIT
Dark Horse Comics: Jan 1995 - May 1995 ($3.95, limited series)

1-3 4.50

JAMES BOND FOR YOUR EYES ONLY
Marvel Comics Group: Oct, 1981 - No. 2, Nov, 1981

1,2-Movie adapt.; r/Marvel Super Special #19 2.00

JAMES BOND JR. (TV)
Marvel Comics: Jan, 1992 - No. 12, Dec, 1992 (#1: $1.00, #2-on: $1.25)

1-12: Based on animated TV show 2.00

JAMES BOND: LICENCE TO KILL (See Licence To Kill)

JAMES BOND: PERMISSION TO DIE
Eclipse Comics/ACME Press: 1989 - No. 3, 1991 ($3.95, limited series, squarebound, 52 pgs.)

1-3: Mike Grell-c/a/scripts in all. 3-($4.95) 5.00

JAM, THE: SUPER COOL COLOR INJECTED TURBO ADVENTURE #1 FROM HELL!
Comico: May, 1988 ($2.50, 44 pgs., one-shot)

1 2.50

JANE ARDEN (See Feature Funnies & Pageant of Comics)
St. John (United Features Syndicate): Mar, 1948 - No. 2, June, 1948

	GD2.0	FN6.0	NM9.4
1-Newspaper reprints	15.00	45.00	105.00
2	11.00	33.00	75.00

JANN OF THE JUNGLE (Jungle Tales No. 1-7)
Atlas Comics (CSI): No. 8, Nov, 1955 - No. 17, June, 1957

	GD2.0	FN6.0	NM9.4
8(#1)	30.00	90.00	210.00
9,11-15	17.00	49.00	115.00
10-Williamson/Colletta-c	17.00	51.00	120.00
16,17-Williamson/Mayo-a(3), 5 pgs. each	19.00	56.00	130.00

NOTE: ***Everett** c-15-17. **Heck** a-8, 15, 17. **Maneely** c-11. **Shores** a-8.*

JAR OF FOOLS
Penny Dreadful Press: 1994 ($5.95, B&W)

1-Jason Lutes-c/a/scripts 6.00

JAR OF FOOLS
Black Eye Productions: 1994 - No. 2, 1994 ($6.95, B&W)

1,2: 1-Reprints of earlier ed. Jason Lutes-c/a/scripts 7.00

JASON & THE ARGONAUTS (See Movie Classics)

JASON GOES TO HELL: THE FINAL FRIDAY (Movie)
Topps Comics: July, 1993 - No. 3, Sept, 1993 ($2.95, limited series)

1-3: Adaptation of film. 1-Glow-in-the-dark-c 3.00

JASON'S QUEST (See Showcase #88-90)

JASON VS. LEATHERFACE
Topps Comics: Oct, 1995 - No. 3, Jan, 1996 ($2.95, limited series)

1-3: Collins scripts; Bisley-c 3.00

JAWS 2 (See Marvel Comics Super Special, A)

JAY & SILENT BOB (See Clerks & Oni Double Feature)
Oni Press: July, 1998 - No. 4, Oct, 1999 ($2.95, B&W, limited series)

1-Kevin Smith-s/Fegredo-a; photo-c & Quesada/Palmiotti-c 8.00
1-San Diego Comic Con variant covers (2 different covers, came packaged with action figures) 10.00
1-2nd & 3rd printings, 2-4: 2-Allred-c. 3-Flip-c by Jaime Hernandez 3.00
Chasing Dogma TPB (1999, $11.95) r/#1-4; Alanis Morissette intro. 12.00

JCP FEATURES
J.C. Productions (Archie): Feb, 1982-c; Dec, 1981-indicia ($2.00, one-shot, B&W)

	GD2.0	FN6.0	NM9.4
1-T.H.U.N.D.E.R. Agents; Black Hood by Morrow & Neal Adams; 2 pgs. S&K-a from Fly #1		2.40	6.00

JEANIE COMICS (Formerly All Surprise; Cowgirl Romances #28)
Marvel Comics/Atlas(CPC): No. 13, April, 1947 - No. 27, Oct, 1949

	GD2.0	FN6.0	NM9.4
13-Mitzi, Willie begin	16.00	47.00	110.00
14,15	11.50	34.00	80.00
16-Used in Love and Death by Legman; Kurtzman's "Hey Look"	14.00	43.00	100.00
17-19,22-Kurtzman's "Hey Look", (1-3 pgs. each)	10.00	30.00	70.00
20,21,23-27	9.15	27.00	55.00

JEEP COMICS (Also see G.I. Comics and Overseas Comics)

Jesse James #6 © AVON

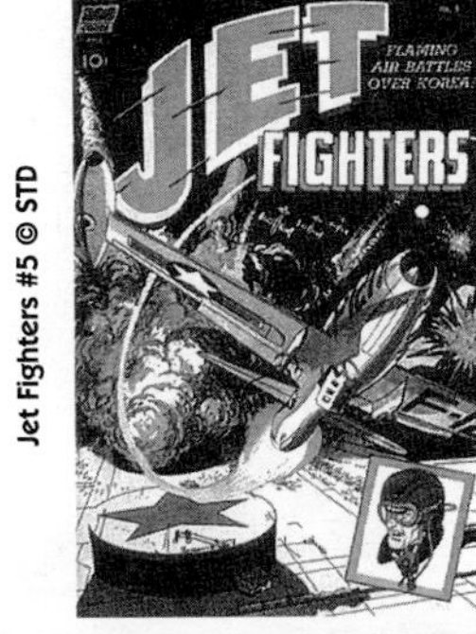

Jet Fighters #5 © STD

Jet Power #1 © I.W. Enterprises

GD2.0 FN6.0 NM9.4

R. B. Leffingwell & Co.: Winter, 1944 - No. 3, Mar-Apr, 1948
1-Capt. Power, Criss Cross & Jeep & Peep (costumed) begin
43.00 128.00 340.00
2 30.00 90.00 210.00
3-L. B. Cole dinosaur-c 40.00 120.00 320.00

JEFF JORDAN, U.S. AGENT
D. S. Publishing Co.: Dec, 1947 - Jan, 1948
1 12.00 36.00 85.00

JEMM, SON OF SATURN
DC Comics: Sept, 1984 - No. 12, Aug, 1985 (Maxi-series, mando paper)
1-12: 3-Origin 2.00
NOTE: ***Colan*** *a-1-12p; c-1-5, 7-12p.*

JENNY FINN
Oni Press: June, 1999 - No. 2, Sept, 1999 ($2.95, B&W, unfinished lim. series)
1,2-Mignola & Nixey-s/Nixey-a/Mignola-c 3.00

JERRY DRUMMER (Formerly Soldier & Marine V2#9)
Charlton Comics: V2#10, Apr, 1957 - V3#12, Oct, 1957
V2#10, V3#11,12: 11-Whitman-c/a 5.00 15.00 30.00

JERRY IGER'S... (All titles, Blackthorne/First)(Value: cover or less)

JERRY LEWIS (See The Adventures of...)

JESSE JAMES (The True Story Of..., also seeThe Legend of...)
Dell Publishing Co.: No. 757, Dec, 1956 (one shot)
Four Color 757-Movie, photo-c 9.00 27.00 100.00

JESSE JAMES (See Badmen of the West & Blazing Sixguns)
Avon Periodicals: 8/50 - No. 9, 11/52; No. 15, 10/53 - No. 29, 8-9/56
1-Kubert Alabam-r/Cowpuncher #1 16.00 47.00 110.00
2-Kubert-a(3) 13.00 39.00 90.00
3-Kubert Alabam-r/Cowpuncher #2 11.50 34.00 80.00
4,9-No Kubert 5.35 16.00 32.00
5,6-Kubert Jesse James-a(3); 5-Wood-a(1pg.) 11.50 34.00 80.00
7-Kubert Jesse James-a(2) 10.00 30.00 65.00
8-Kinstler-a(3) 7.00 21.00 42.00
15-Kinstler-r/#3 4.25 13.00 28.00
16-Kinstler-r/#3 & story-r/Butch Cassidy #1 5.00 15.00 30.00
17-19,21: 17-Jesse James-r/#4; Kinstler-c idea from Kubert splash in #6. 18-Kubert Jesse James-r/#5. 19-Kubert Jesse James-r/#6. 21-Two Jesse James-r/#4, Kinstler-r/#4 4.00 12.00 24.00
20-Williamson/Frazetta-a; r/Chief Vic. Apache Massacre; Kubert Jesse James-r/#6; Kit West story by Larsen 12.00 36.00 85.00
22-29: 22,23-No Kubert. 24-New McCarty strip by Kinstler; Kinstler-r. 25-New McCarty Jesse James strip by Kinstler; Jesse James-r/#7,9. 26,27-New McCarty Jesse James strip plus a Kinstler/McCann Jesse James-r. 28-Reprints most of Red Mountain, Featuring Quantrells Raiders
4.00 12.00 24.00
Annual nn (1952; 25¢, 100 pgs.)- "...Brings Six-Gun Justice to the West"- 3 earlier issues rebound; Kubert, Kinstler-a(3) 26.00 79.00 185.00
NOTE: *Mostly reprints #10 on.* ***Fawcette*** *c-1, 2.* ***Kida*** *a-5.* ***Kinstler*** *a-3, 4, 7-9, 15r, 16r(2), 21-27; c-3, 4, 9, 17-27. Painted c-5-8. 22 has 2 stories r/Sheriff Bob Dixon's Chuck Wagon #1 with name changed to Sheriff Bob Trent.*

JESSE JAMES
Realistic Publications: July, 1953
nn-Reprints Avon's #1; same-c, colors different 10.00 30.00 60.00

JEST (Formerly Snap; becomes Kayo #12)
Harry 'A' Chesler: No. 10, 1944; No. 11, 1944
10-Johnny Rebel & Yankee Boy app. in text 15.00 45.00 105.00
11-Little Nemo in Adventure Land 15.00 45.00 105.00

JESTER
Harry 'A' Chesler: No. 10, 1945
10 13.00 39.00 90.00

JESUS
Spire Christian Comics (Fleming H. Revell Co.): 1979 (49¢)
nn 5.00

JET (See Jet Powers)

JET ACES
Fiction House Magazines: 1952 - No. 4, 1953
1 11.50 34.00 80.00
2-4 8.35 25.00 50.00

JET DREAM (...and Her Stunt-Girl Counterspies)(See The Man from Uncle #7)
Gold Key: June, 1968 (12¢)
1-Painted-c 3.00 9.00 30.00

JET FIGHTERS (Korean War)
Standard Magazines: No. 5, Nov, 1952 - No. 7, Mar, 1953
5,7-Toth-a. 5-Toth-c 11.00 33.00 75.00
6-Celardo-a 5.00 15.00 30.00

JET POWER
I.W. Enterprises: 1963
I.W. Reprint 1,2-r/Jet Powers #1,2 2.60 7.80 26.00

JET POWERS (American Air Forces No. 5 on)
Magazine Enterprises: 1950 - No. 4, 1951
1(A-1 #30)-Powell-c/a begins 32.00 96.00 225.00
2(A-1 #32) 23.00 69.00 160.00
3(A-1 #35)-Williamson/Evans-a 38.00 114.00 265.00
4(A-1 #38)-Williamson/Wood-a; "The Rain of Sleep" drug story
38.00 114.00 265.00

JET PUP (See 3-D Features)

JETSONS, THE (TV) (See March of Comics #276, 330, 348 & Spotlight #3)
Gold Key: Jan, 1963 - No. 36, Oct, 1970 (Hanna-Barbera)
1-1st comic book app. 21.00 62.00 225.00
2 10.50 31.50 115.00
3-10 8.20 24.60 90.00
11-20 5.40 16.20 60.00
21-36 4.50 13.50 50.00

JETSONS, THE (TV) (Also see Golden Comics Digest)
Charlton Comics: Nov, 1970 - No. 20, Dec, 1973 (Hanna-Barbera)
1 6.00 17.50 65.00
2 3.20 9.60 32.00
3-10 2.60 7.80 26.00
11-20 2.00 6.00 16.00

JETSONS, THE (TV)
Harvey Comics: V2#1, Sept, 1992 - No. 5, Nov, 1993 ($1.25/$1.50) (Hanna-Barbera)
V2#1-5 3.00
...Big Book V2#1,2,3 ($1.95, 52 pgs.): 1-(11/92). 2-(4/93). 3-(7/93) 3.00
...Giant Size 1,2,3 ($2.25, 68 pgs): 1-(10/92). 2-(4/93). 3-(10/93) 3.00

JETSONS, THE (TV)
Archie Comics: Sept, 1995 - No. 17, Aug, 1996 ($1.50)
1-17 2.00

JETTA OF THE 21ST CENTURY
Standard Comics: No. 5, Dec, 1952 - No. 7, Apr, 1953 (Teen-age Archie type)
5 21.00 64.00 150.00
6,7: 6-Robot-c 12.00 36.00 85.00

JEZEBEL JADE (Hanna-Barbara)
Comico: Oct, 1988 - No. 3, Dec, 1988 ($2.00, mini-series)
1-3: Johnny Quest spin-off 2.00

JIGGS & MAGGIE
Dell Publishing Co.: No. 18, 1941 (one shot)
Four Color 18 (#1)-(1936-38-r) 38.00 115.00 420.00

JIGGS & MAGGIE

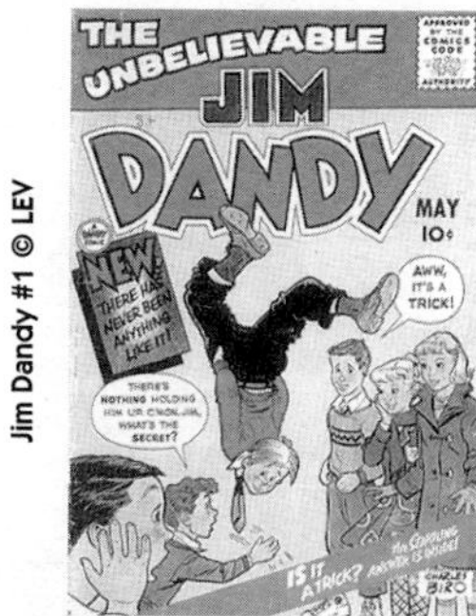

Jim Dandy #1 © LEV

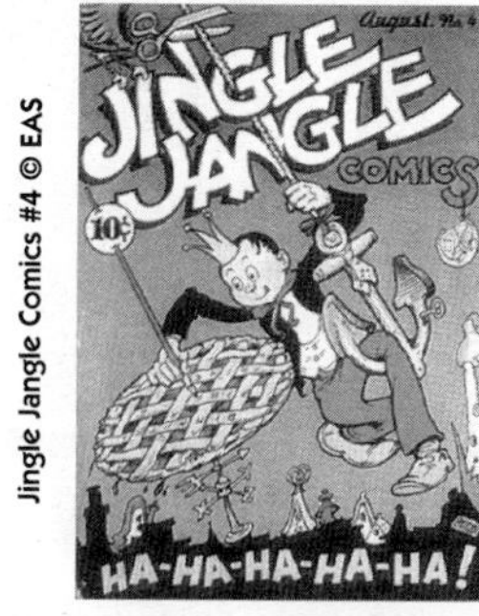

Jingle Jangle Comics #4 © EAS

JLA #29 © DC

GD2.0 FN6.0 NM9.4

Standard Comics/Harvey Publications No. 22 on: No. 11, 1949(June) - No. 21, 2/53; No. 22, 4/53 - No. 27, 2-3/54

	GD2.0	FN6.0	NM9.4
11	10.00	30.00	70.00
12-15,17-21	5.85	17.50	35.00
16-Wood text illos.	7.50	22.50	45.00
22-24-Little Dot app.	5.00	15.00	30.00
25,27	4.25	13.00	28.00
26-Four pgs. partially in 3-D	13.00	39.00	90.00

NOTE: *Sunday page reprints by McManus loosely blended into story continuity. Based on Bringing Up Father strip. Advertised on covers as "All New."*

JIGSAW (Big Hero Adventures)
Harvey Publ. (Funday Funnies): Sept, 1966 - No. 2, Dec, 1966 (36 pgs.)

1-Origin & 1st app.; Crandall-a (5 pgs.)	2.00	6.00	16.00
2-Man From S.R.A.M.	1.50	4.50	12.00

JIGSAW OF DOOM (See Complete Mystery No. 2)

JIM BOWIE (Formerly Danger; Black Jack No. 20 on)
Charlton Comics: No. 15, 1955? - No. 19, Apr, 1957

15	6.70	20.00	40.00
16-19	4.25	13.00	28.00

JIM BOWIE (TV, see Western Tales)
Dell Publishing Co.: No. 893, Mar, 1958 - No. 993, May-July, 1959

Four Color 893 (#1), 993-Photo-c	4.50	13.50	50.00

JIM DANDY
Dandy Magazine (Lev Gleason): May, 1956 - No. 3, Sept, 1956 (Charles Biro)

1-Biro-c	7.00	21.00	42.00
2,3	4.25	13.00	26.00

JIM HARDY (See Giant Comics Eds., Sparkler & Treasury of Comics #2 & 5)
United Features Syndicate/Spotlight Publ.: 1939; 1942; 1947 - No. 2, 1947

Single Series 6 ('39)	40.00	120.00	300.00
Single Series 27('42)	34.00	103.00	240.00
1('47)-Spotlight Publ.	13.00	39.00	90.00
2	8.35	25.00	50.00

JIM HARDY
Spotlight/United Features Synd.: 1944 (25¢, 132 pgs.) (Tip Top, Sparkler-r)

nn-Origin Mirror Man; Triple Terror app.	40.00	120.00	290.00

JIMINY CRICKET (Disney,, see Mickey Mouse Mag. V5#3 & Walt Disney Showcase #37)
Dell Publishing Co.: No. 701, May, 1956 - No. 989, May-July, 1959

Four Color 701	8.00	25.00	90.00
Four Color 795, 897, 989	5.50	16.50	60.00

JIMMY DURANTE (Also see A-1 Comics)
Magazine Enterprises: No. 18, 1949 - No. 20, 1949

A-1 18,20-Photo-c	40.00	120.00	320.00

JIMMY OLSEN (See Superman's Pal...)

JIMMY WAKELY (Cowboy movie star)
National Per. Publ.: Sept-Oct, 1949 - No. 18, July-Aug, 1952 (1-13: 52pgs.)

1-Photo-c, 52 pgs. begin; Alex Toth-a; Kit Colby Girl Sheriff begins	106.00	318.00	850.00
2-Toth-a	45.00	135.00	360.00
3,4,6,7-Frazetta-a in all, 3 pgs. each; Toth-a in all. 7-Last photo-c. 4-Kurtzman "Pot-Shot Pete", 1 pg; Toth-a	46.00	138.00	370.00
5,8-15,18-Toth-a; 12,14-Kubert-a (3 & 2 pgs.)	39.00	117.00	270.00
16,17	31.00	94.00	220.00

NOTE: ***Gil Kane** c-10-19p.*

JIM RAY'S AVIATION SKETCH BOOK
Vital Publishers: Mar-Apr, 1946 - No. 2, May-June, 1946

1,2-Picture stories about planes and pilots	25.00	75.00	175.00

JIM SOLAR (See Wisco/Klarer)

JINGLE BELLS (See March of Comics No. 65)

GD2.0 FN6.0 NM9.4

JINGLE DINGLE CHRISTMAS STOCKING COMICS (See Foodini #2)
Stanhall Publications: V2#1, 1951 (no date listed) (25¢, 100 pgs.; giant-size) (Publ. annually)

V2#1-Foodini & Pinhead, Silly Pilly plus games & puzzles	16.00	47.00	110.00

JINGLE JANGLE COMICS (Also see Puzzle Fun Comics)
Eastern Color Printing Co.: Feb, 1942 - No. 42, Dec, 1949

1-Pie-Face Prince of Old Pretzleburg, Jingle Jangle Tales by George Carlson, Hortense, & Benny Bear begin	40.00	120.00	300.00
2-4: 2,3-No Pie-Face Prince. 4-Pie-Face Prince-c	19.00	58.00	135.00
5	17.00	51.00	120.00
6-10: 8-No Pie-Face Prince	14.00	43.00	100.00
11-15	11.00	33.00	75.00
16-30: 17,18-No Pie-Face Prince. 30-XMas-c	10.00	30.00	60.00
31-42: 36,42-Xmas-c	8.35	25.00	50.00

NOTE: ***George Carlson** a-(2) in all except No. 2, 3, 8; c-1-6. **Carlson** 1 pg. puzzles in 9, 10, 12-15, 18, 20. **Carlson** illustrated a series of Uncle Wiggily books in 1930's.*

JING PALS
Victory Publishing Corp.: Feb, 1946 - No. 4, Aug?, 1946 (Funny animal)

1-Wishing Willie, Puggy Panda & Johnny Rabbit begin	13.00	39.00	90.00
2-4	7.50	22.50	45.00

JINKS, PIXIE, AND DIXIE (See Kite Fun Book & Whitman Comic Books)

JINX
Caliber Press: 1996 - No. 7, 1996 ($2.95, B&W, 32 pgs.)

1-7: Brian Michael Bendis-c/a/scripts. 2-Photo-c			3.00

JINX (Volume 2)
Image Comics: 1997 - Present ($2.95, B&W, bi-monthly)

1-4: Brian Michael Bendis-c/a/scripts.			3.00
5-($3.95) Brereton-c			4.00
...Buried Treasures ('98, $3.95) short stories, ...Confessions ('98, $3.95) short stories, ...Pop Culture Hoo-hah ('98, $3.95) humor shorts			4.00
TPB (1997, $10.95) r/Vol 1,#1-4			11.00

JINX: TORSO
Image Comics: 1998 - Present ($3.95/$4.95, B&W)

1,2-Brian Michael Bendis & Marc Andreyko-s/Bendis-a			4.00
3-6-($4.95)			5.00

JLA (See Justice League of America)
DC Comics: Jan, 1997 - Present ($1.95/$1.99)

1-Morrison-s/Porter & Dell-a. The Hyperclan app.	1.85	5.50	15.00
2	1.25	3.75	10.00
3,4	1.00	3.00	8.00
5-Membership drive; Tomorrow Woman app.		2.40	6.00
6-9: 8-Green Arrow joins.		2.40	6.00
10-21: 10-Rock of Ages begins. 11-Joker and Luthor-c/app. 15-($2.95) Rock of Ages concludes. 16-New members join; Prometheus app. 17,20-Jorgensen-a. 18-21-Waid-s. 20,21-Adam Strange c/app.			5.00
22-35: 22-Begin $1.99-c; Sandman (Daniel) app. 27-Amazo app. 28-31-JSA app.			2.00
#1,000,000 (11/98)853rd Century x-over			2.00
Annual 1 (1997, $3.95) Pulp Heroes; Augustyn-s/Olivetti & Ha-a			4.00
Annual 2 (1998, $2.95) Ghosts; Wrightson-c			4.00
Annual 3 (1999, $2.95) JLApe; Art Adams-c			3.00
...80-Page Giant 1 (7/98, $4.95) stories & art by various			5.00
...Foreign Bodies (1999, $5.95) Kobra app.; Semeiks-a			6.00
...Gallery (1997, $2.95) pin-ups by various; Quitely-c			3.00
...In Crisis Secret Files 1 (11/98, $4.95) recap of JLA in DC x-overs			5.00
American Dreams (1998, $7.95, TPB) r/#5-9			8.00
New World Order (1997, $5.95, TPB) r/#1-4			6.00
Rock of Ages (1998, $9.95, TPB) r/#10-15			10.00
Strength in Numbers (1998, $12.95, TPB) r/#16-23, Secret Files #2 and Prometheus #1			13.00

JLA: Year One #6 © DC

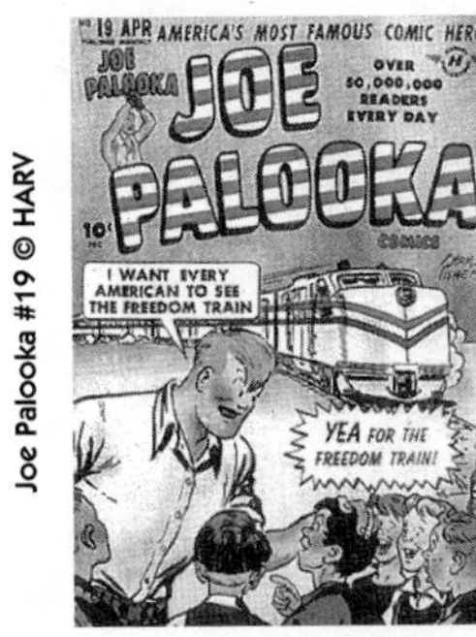

Joe Palooka #19 © HARV

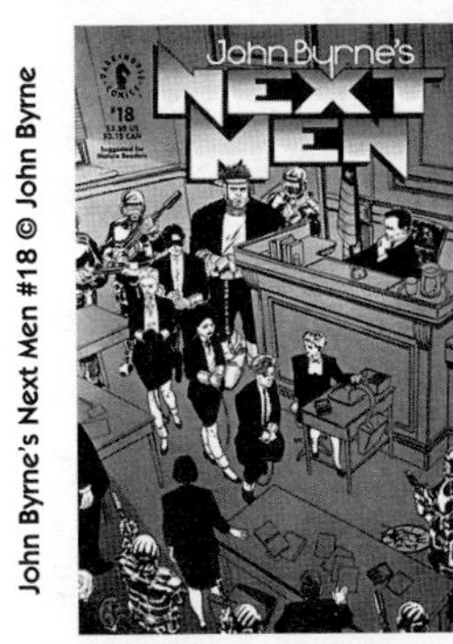

John Byrne's Next Men #18 © John Byrne

GD2.0 FN6.0 NM9.4

JLA PARADISE LOST
DC Comics: Jan, 1998 - No. 3, Mar, 1998 ($1.95, limited series)
1-3-Millar-s/Olivetti-a — 2.00

JLA SECRET FILES
DC Comics: Sept, 1997 - Present ($4.95)
1-Standard Ed. w/origin-s & pin-ups — 5.00
1-Collector's Ed. w/origin-s & pin-ups; cardstock-c — 2.40 — 6.00
2-(8/98) origin-s of JLA #16's newer members — 5.00

JLA: THE NAIL (Elseworlds)
DC Comics: Aug, 1998 - No. 3, Oct, 1998 ($4.95, prestige format)
1-3-JLA in a world without Superman; Alan Davis-s/a(p) — 5.00
TPB ('98, $12.95) r/series w/new Davis-c — 13.00

JLA / TITANS
DC Comics: Dec, 1998 - No. 3, Feb, 1999 ($2.95, limited series)
1-3-Grayson-s; P. Jimenez-c/a — 3.00

JLA: TOMORROW WOMAN (Girlfrenzy)
DC Comics: June, 1998 ($1.95, one-shot)
1-Peyer-s; story takes place during JLA #5 — 2.50

JLA/ WILDC.A.T.S
DC Comics: 1997 ($5.95, one-shot, prestige format)
1-Morrison-s/Semeiks & Conrad-a — 2.40 — 6.00

JLA/ WORLD WITHOUT GROWN-UPS (See Young Justice)
DC Comics: Aug, 1998 - No. 2, Sept, 1998 ($4.95, prestige format)
1,2-JLA, Robin, Impulse & Superboy app.; Ramos & McKone-a — 6.00
TPB ('98, $9.95) r/series & Young Justice: The Secret #1 — 10.00

JLA: YEAR ONE
DC Comics: Jan, 1998 - No. 12, Dec, 1998 ($2.95/$1.95, limited series)
1-($2.95)-Waid & Augustyn-s/Kitson-a — 4.00
1-Platinum Edition — 15.00
2-8-($1.95): 5-Doom Patrol-c/app. 7-Superman app. — 4.00
9-12 — 3.00
TPB ('99, $19.95) r/#1-12; Busiek intro. — 20.00

JLX
DC Comics (Amalgam): Apr, 1996 ($1.95, one-shot)
1-Mark Waid scripts — 2.00

JLX UNLEASHED
DC Comics (Amalgam): June, 1997 ($1.95, one-shot)
1-Priest-s/ Oscar Jimenez & Rodriquez/a — 2.00

JOAN OF ARC (Also see A-1 Comics & Ideal a Classical Comic)
Magazine Enterprises: No. 21, 1949 (one shot)
A-1 21-Movie adaptation; Ingrid Bergman photo-covers & interior photos; Whitney-a — 26.00 — 79.00 — 185.00

JOE COLLEGE
Hillman Periodicals: Fall, 1949 - No. 2, Wint, 1950 (Teen-age humor, 52 pgs.)
1,2: Powell-a; 1-Briefer-a — 10.00 — 30.00 — 65.00

JOE JINKS
United Features Syndicate: No. 12, 1939
Single Series 12 — 29.00 — 86.00 — 200.00

JOE LOUIS (See Fight Comics #2, Picture News #6 & True Comics #5)
Fawcett Publications: Sept, 1950 - No. 2, Nov, 1950 (Photo-c) (Boxing champ) (See Dick Cole #10)
1-Photo-c; life story — 53.00 — 159.00 — 425.00
2-Photo-c — 39.00 — 118.00 — 275.00

JOE PALOOKA (1st Series)(Also see Big Shot Comics, Columbia Comics & Feature Funnies)
Columbia Comic Corp. (Publication Enterprises): 1942 - No. 4, 1944
1-1st to portray American president; gov't permission required — 75.00 — 225.00 — 600.00
2 (1943)-Hitler-c — 45.00 — 135.00 — 360.00
3,4: 3-Nazi Sub-c — 32.00 — 96.00 — 225.00

JOE PALOOKA (2nd Series) (Battle Adv. #68-74; ...Advs. #75, 77-81, 83-85, 87; Champ of the Comics #76, 82, 86, 89-93) (See All-New)
Harvey Publications: Nov, 1945 - No. 118, Mar, 1961
1 — 42.00 — 126.00 — 335.00
2 — 21.00 — 64.00 — 150.00
3,4,6,7-1st Flyin' Fool, ends #25 — 13.00 — 39.00 — 90.00
5-Boy Explorers by S&K (7-8/46) — 19.00 — 58.00 — 135.00
8-10 — 10.00 — 30.00 — 70.00
11-14,16-20: 19-Freedom Train-c — 9.15 — 27.00 — 55.00
15-Origin & 1st app. Humphrey (12/47); Super heroine Atoma app. by Powell — 13.00 — 39.00 — 90.00
21-26,28-30: 30-Nude female painting — 6.70 — 20.00 — 40.00
27-1st app. Little Max? (12/48) — 8.35 — 25.00 — 50.00
31-61: 35-Little Max-c/story. 36-Humphrey story. 39-Humphrey & Little Max begin (12/49). 41-Bing Crosby photo on-c. 44-Palooka marries Ann Howe. 50-(11/51)-Becomes Harvey Comics Hits #51 — 5.35 — 16.00 — 32.00
62-S&K Boy Explorers-r — 6.70 — 20.00 — 40.00
63-80,100: 66,67-'Commie' torture story — 4.25 — 13.00 — 28.00
81-99,101-115 — 4.00 — 12.00 — 24.00
116-S&K Boy Explorers-r (Giant, '60) — 6.70 — 20.00 — 40.00
117,118-Giants — 5.85 — 17.50 — 35.00
...**Visits the Lost City** nn (1945)(One Shot)(50¢)-164 page continuous story strip reprint. Has biography & photo of Ham Fisher; possibly the single longest comic book story published (159 pgs.?) — 135.00 — 405.00 — 1350.00
NOTE: *Nostrand/Powell a-73. Powell a-7, 8, 10, 12, 14, 17, 19, 26-45, 47-53, 70, 73 at least. Black Cat text stories #8, 12, 13, 19.*

JOE PSYCHO & MOO FROG
Goblin Studios: 1996 - Present ($2.50, B&W)
1-5: 4-Two covers — 2.50
...Full Color Extravagarbonzo ($2.95, color) — 3.00

JOE YANK (Korean War)
Standard Comics (Visual Editions): No. 5, Mar, 1952 - No. 16, 1954
5-Toth, Celardo, Tuska-a — 6.70 — 20.00 — 40.00
6-Toth, Severin/Elder-a — 8.35 — 25.00 — 50.00
7 — 4.15 — 12.50 — 25.00
8-Toth-c — 6.35 — 19.00 — 38.00
9-16: 9-Andru-c. 12-Andru-a — 4.00 — 12.00 — 24.00

JOHN BOLTON'S HALLS OF HORROR
Eclipse Comics: June, 1985 - No. 2, June, 1985 ($1.75, limited series)
1,2-British-r; Bolton-c/a — 2.00

JOHN BOLTON'S STRANGE WINK
Dark Horse Comics: Mar, 1998 - No. 3, May, 1998 ($2.95, B&W, limited series)
1-3-Anthology; Bolton-s/c/a — 3.00

JOHN BYRNE'S NEXT MEN (See Dark Horse Presents #54)
Dark Horse Comics (Legend imprint #19 on): Jan, 1992 - No. 30, Dec, 1994 ($2.50, mature)
1-Silver foil embossed-c; Byrne-c/a/scripts in all — 4.00
1-4: 1-2nd printing with gold ink logo — 2.50
0-(2/92)-r/chapters 1-4 from DHP w/new Byrne-c — 2.50
5-20,22-30: 7-10-MA #1-4 mini-series on flip side. 16-Origin of Mark IV. 17-Miller-c. 19-22-Faith storyline. 23-26-Power storyline. 27-30-Lies storyline Pt. 1-4. — 2.50
21-1st Hellboy — 4.00
...Parallel, Book 2 ($16.95)-TPB; r/#7-12 — 17.00
...Fame, Book 3($16.95)-TPB r/#13-18 — 17.00
...Faith, Book 4($14.95)-TPB r/#19-22 — 15.00
NOTE: *Issues 1 through 6 contain certificates redeemable for an exclusive Next Men trading card set by Byrne. Prices are for complete books.* **Cody** *painted c-23-26.* **Mignola** *a-21(part); c-21.*

JOHN BYRNE'S 2112
Dark Horse Comics (Legend): Oct, 1994 ($9.95, TPB)

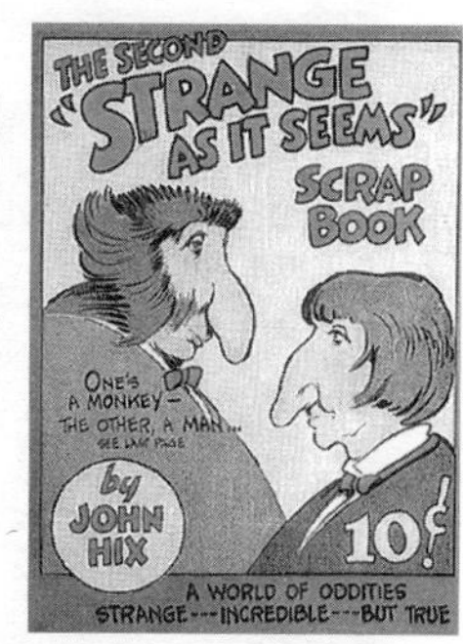

The John Hix Scrap Book #2 © EAS

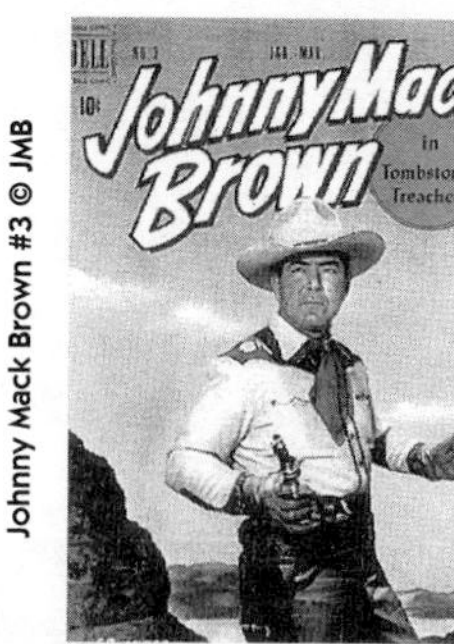

Johnny Mack Brown #3 © JMB

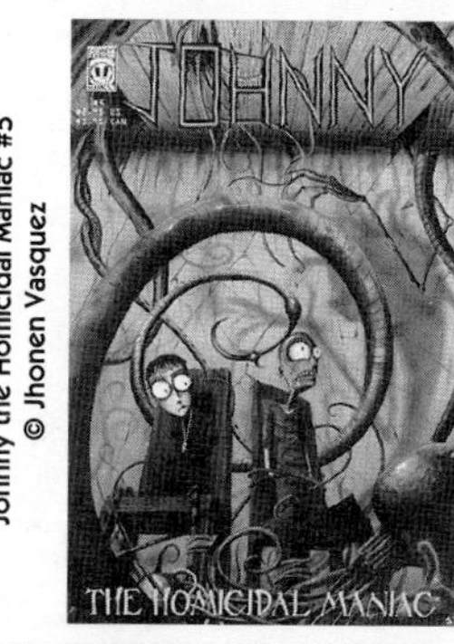

Johnny the Homicidal Maniac #5 © Jhonen Vasquez

GD2.0 FN6.0 NM9.4

1-Byrne-c/a/s 10.00

JOHN CARTER OF MARS (See The Funnies & Tarzan #207)
Dell Publishing Co.: No. 375, Mar-May, 1952 - No. 488, Aug-Oct, 1953 (Edgar Rice Burroughs)

Four Color 375 (#1)-Origin; Jesse Marsh-a 23.00 68.00 250.00
Four Color 437, 488-Painted-c 14.00 44.00 160.00

JOHN CARTER OF MARS
Gold Key: Apr, 1964 - No. 3, Oct, 1964

1(10104-404)-r/4-Color #375; Jesse Marsh-a 4.50 13.50 50.00
2(407), 3(410)-r/4-Color #437 & 488; Marsh-a 3.20 9.50 35.00

JOHN CARTER OF MARS
House of Greystroke: 1970 (10-1/2x16-1/2", 72 pgs., B&W, paper-c)

1941-42 Sunday strip-r; John Coleman Burroughs-a 2.50 7.50 20.00

JOHN CARTER, WARLORD OF MARS (Also see Weird Worlds)
Marvel Comics: June, 1977 - No. 28, Oct, 1979

1,18: 18-Frank Miller-a(p)(1st publ. Marvel work) 4.00
2-17,19-28: 1-Origin. 11-Origin Dejah Thoris 2.50
Annuals 1-3: 1(1977). 2(1978). 3(1979)-All 52 pgs. with new book-length stories 2.50

NOTE: ***Austin** c-24i. **Gil Kane** a-1-10p; c-1p, 2p, 3, 4-9p, 10, 15p, Annual 1p. **Layton** a-17i. **Miller** c-25, 26p. **Nebres** a-2-4i, 8-16i; c(i)-6-9, 11-22, 25, Annual 1. **Perez** c-24p. **Simonson** a-15p. **Sutton** a-7i.*

JOHN F. KENNEDY, CHAMPION OF FREEDOM
Worden & Childs: 1964 (no month) (25¢)

nn-Photo-c 5.00 15.00 50.00

JOHN F. KENNEDY LIFE STORY
Dell Publishing Co.: Aug-Oct, 1964; Nov, 1965; June, 1966 (12¢)

12-378-410-Photo-c 3.50 10.50 35.00
12-378-511 (reprint, 11/65) 2.50 7.50 22.00
12-378-606 (reprint, 6/66) 2.50 7.50 20.00

JOHN FORCE (See Magic Agent)

JOHN HIX SCRAP BOOK, THE
Eastern Color Printing Co. (McNaught Synd.): Late 1930's (no date) (10¢, 68 pgs., regular size)

1-Strange As It Seems (resembles Single Series books) 36.00 107.00 250.00
2-Strange As It Seems 26.00 77.00 180.00

JOHN JAKES' MULLKON EMPIRE
Tekno Comix: Sept, 1995 - No. 6, Feb, 1996 ($1.95)

1-6 2.00

JOHN LAW DETECTIVE(See Smash Comics #3)
Eclipse Comics: April, 1983 ($1.50, Baxter paper)

1-Three Eisner stories originally drawn in 1948 for the never published John Law #1; original cover pencilled in 1948 & inked in 1982 by Eisner 2.00

JOHNNY APPLESEED (See Story Hour Series)

JOHNNY CASH (See Hello, I'm...)

JOHNNY DANGER (See Movie Comics, 1946)
Toby Press: 1950 (Based on movie serial)

1-Photo-c; Sparling-a 17.00 49.00 115.00

JOHNNY DANGER PRIVATE DETECTIVE
Toby Press: Aug, 1954 (Reprinted in Danger #11 by Super)

1-Photo-c; Opium den story 13.00 39.00 90.00

JOHNNY DYNAMITE (Formerly Dynamite #1-9; Foreign Intrigues #13 on)
Charlton Comics: No. 10, June, 1955 - No. 12, Oct, 1955

10-12 8.00 24.00 48.00

JOHNNY DYNAMITE
Dark Horse Comics: Sept, 1994 - Dec, 1994 ($2.95, B&W & red, limited series)

GD2.0 FN6.0 NM9.4

1-4: Max Allan Collins scripts in all. 3.00

JOHNNY HAZARD
Best Books (Standard Comics) (King Features): No. 5, Aug, 1948 - No. 8, May, 1949; No. 35, date?

5-Strip reprints by Frank Robbins (c/a) 17.00 51.00 120.00
6,8-Strip reprints by Frank Robbins 14.00 43.00 100.00
7,35: 7-New art, not Robbins 10.00 30.00 60.00

JOHNNY JASON (...Teen Reporter)
Dell Publishing Co.: Feb-Apr, 1962 - No. 2, June-Aug, 1962

Four Color 1302, 2(01380-208) 2.75 8.00 30.00

JOHNNY LAW, SKY RANGER
Good Comics (Lev Gleason): Apr, 1955 - No. 3, Aug, 1955; No. 4, Nov, 1955

1-Edmond Good-c/a 9.15 27.00 55.00
2-4 5.35 16.00 32.00

JOHNNY MACK BROWN (TV western star; see Western Roundup under Dell Giants)
Dell Publishing Co.: No. 269, Mar, 1950 - No. 963, Feb, 1959 (All Photo-c)

Four Color 269(#1)(3/50, 52pgs.)-Johnny Mack Brown & his horse Rebel begin; photo front/back-c begin; Marsh-a in #1-9 22.00 65.00 240.00
2(10-12/50, 52pgs.) 11.00 33.00 120.00
3(1-3/51, 52pgs.) 8.50 26.00 95.00
4-10 (9-11/52)(36pgs.), Four Color 455,493,541,584,618,645,685,722,776, 834,963 5.50 16.50 60.00
Four Color 922-Manning-a 6.00 18.00 65.00

JOHNNY NEMO
Eclipse Comics: Sept, 1985 - No. 3, Feb, 1986 (Mini-series)

1-3 2.00

JOHNNY PERIL (See Comic Cavalcade #15, Danger Trail #5, Sensation Comics #107 & Sensation Mystery)

JOHNNY RINGO (TV)
Dell Publishing Co.: No. 1142, Nov-Jan, 1960/61 (one shot)

Four Color 1142-Photo-c 6.40 19.00 70.00

JOHNNY STARBOARD (See Wisco)

JOHNNY THE HOMICIDAL MANIAC
Slave Labor Graphics: Aug, 1995 - No. 7, Jan, 1997 ($2.95, B&W, lim. series)

1-Jhonen Vasquez-c/s/a 1.85 5.50 15.00
1-Signed & numbered edition 2.50 7.50 20.00
2,3: 2-(11/95). 3-(2/96) 1.00 3.00 8.00
4-7: 4-(5-96). 5-(8/96) 4.00
Hardcover-($29.95) r/#1-7 30.00
TPB-($19.95) 20.00

JOHNNY THUNDER
National Periodical Publications: Feb-Mar, 1973 - No. 3, July-Aug, 1973

1-Johnny Thunder & Nighthawk-r. in all 1.50 4.50 12.00
2,3: 2-Trigger Twins app. 1.00 3.00 8.00

NOTE: *All contain 1950s DC reprints from All-American Western. **Drucker** r-2, 3. **G. Kane** r-2, 3. **Moriera** r-1. **Toth** r-1, 3; c-1r, 3r. Also see All-American, All-Star Western, Flash Comics, Western Comics, World's Best & World's Finest.*

JOHN PAUL JONES
Dell Publishing Co.: No. 1007, July-Sept, 1959 (one-shot)

Four Color 1007-Movie, Robert Stack photo-c 4.50 13.50 50.00

JOHN STEED & EMMA PEEL (See The Avengers, Gold Key series)

JOHN STEELE SECRET AGENT (Also see Freedom Agent)
Gold Key: Dec, 1964

1-Freedom Agent 8.00 23.00 85.00

JOHN WAYNE ADVENTURE COMICS (Movie star; See Big Tex, Oxydol-Dreft, Tim McCoy, & With The Marines...#1)
Toby Press: Winter, 1949-50 - No. 31, May, 1955 (Photo-c: 1-12,17,25-on)

1 (36pgs.)-Photo-c begin (1st time in comics on-c) 147.00 441.00 1175.00

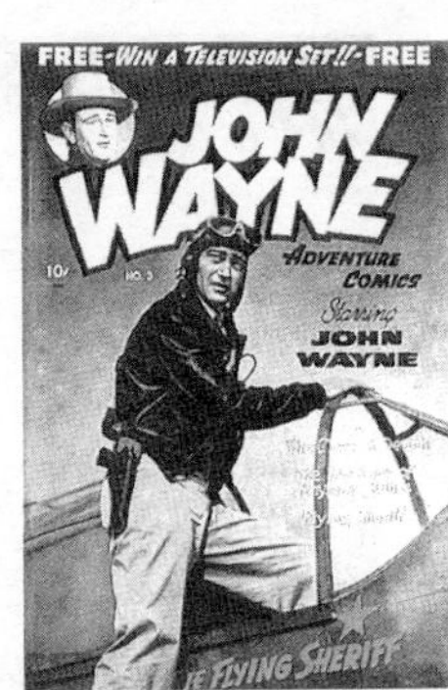

John Wayne Adventure Comics #3 © TOBY

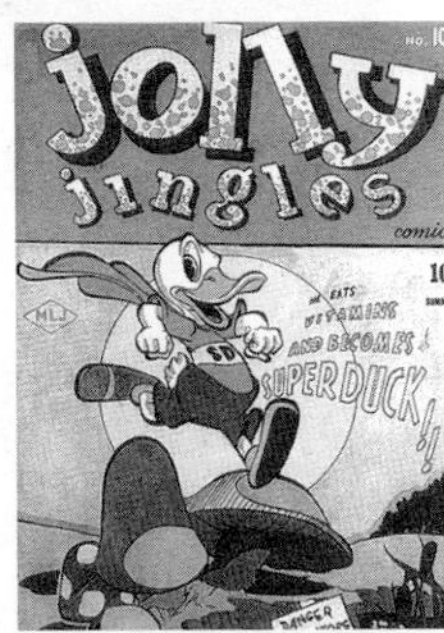

Jolly Jingles #10 © MLJ

Jonah Hex: Shadows West #1 © DC

GD2.0 FN6.0 NM9.4

2-4: 2 (4/50, 36pgs.)-Williamson/Frazetta-a(2) 6 & 2 pgs. (one story-r/Billy the Kid #1); photo back-c. 3 (36pgs.)-Williamson/Frazetta-a(2), 16 pgs. total; photo back-c. 4 (52pgs.)-Williamson/Frazetta-a(2), 16 pgs. total 61.00 184.00 490.00
5 (52pgs.)-Kurtzman-a-(Alfred "L" Newman in Potshot Pete) 45.00 135.00 360.00
6 (52pgs.)-Williamson/Frazetta-a (10 pgs.); Kurtzman-a "Pot-Shot Pete", (5 pgs.); & "Genius Jones", (1 pg.) 57.00 172.00 460.00
7 (52pgs.)-Williamson/Frazetta-a (10 pgs.) 45.00 135.00 360.00
8 (36pgs.)-Williamson/Frazetta-a(2) (12 & 9 pgs.) 57.00 172.00 460.00
9-11: Photo western-c 36.00 107.00 250.00
12,14-Photo war-c. 12-Kurtzman-a(2 pg.) "Genius" 36.00 107.00 250.00
13,15: 13,15-Line-drawn-c begin, end #24 32.00 96.00 225.00
16-Williamson/Frazetta-r/Billy the Kid #1 35.00 105.00 245.00
17-Photo-c 35.00 105.00 245.00
18-Williamson/Frazetta-a (r/#4 & 8, 19 pgs.) 40.00 120.00 280.00
19-24: 23-Evans-a? 29.00 86.00 200.00
25-Photo-c resume; end #31; Williamson/Frazetta-r/Billy the Kid #3 38.00 114.00 265.00
26-28,30-Photo-c 33.00 99.00 230.00
29,31-Williamson/Frazetta-a in each (r/#4, 2) 36.00 109.00 255.00
NOTE: *Williamsonish art in later issues by* ***Gerald McCann.***

JO-JO COMICS (...Congo King #7-29; My Desire #30 on)
(Also see Fantastic Fears and Jungle Jo)
Fox Feature Syndicate: 1945 - No. 29, July, 1949 (Two No.7's; no #13)

nn(1945)-Funny animal, humor 16.00 47.00 110.00
2(Sum,'46)-6(4-5/47): Funny animal. 2-Ten pg. Electro story (Fall/46) 9.15 27.00 55.00
7(7/47)-Jo-Jo, Congo King begins (1st app.); Bronze Man & Purple Tigress app. 84.00 253.00 675.00
7(#8) (9/47) 59.00 178.00 475.00
8-10(#9-11): 8-Tanee begins 47.00 141.00 375.00
11,12(#12,13),14,16: 11,16-Kamen bondage-c 43.00 128.00 340.00
15,17: 15-Cited by Dr. Wertham in 5/47 Saturday Review of Literature. 17-Kamen bondage-c 44.00 132.00 350.00
18-20 43.00 128.00 340.00
21-29: 21-Hollingsworth-a(4 pgs.; 23-1 pg.) 40.00 120.00 280.00
NOTE: *Many bondage-c/a by* ***Baker/Kamen/Feldstein/Good.*** *No. 7's have Princesses Gwenna, Geesa, Yolda, & Safra before settling down on Tanee.*

JOKEBOOK COMICS DIGEST ANNUAL (...Magazine No. 5 on)
Archie Publications: Oct, 1977 - No. 13, Oct, 1983 (Digest Size)

1(10/77)-Reprints; Neal Adams-a 1.40 4.20 14.00
2(4/78)-5 1.10 3.30 9.00
6-11 1.00 2.80 7.00

JOKER, THE (See Batman #1, Batman: The Killing Joke, Brave & the Bold, Detective, Greatest Joker Stories & Justice League Annual #2)
National Periodical Publications: May, 1975 - No. 9, Sept-Oct, 1976

1-Two-Face app. 2.50 7.50 25.00
2,3: 3-The Creeper app. 1.50 4.50 12.00
4-9: 4-Green Arrow-c/sty. 6-Sherlock Holmes-c/sty. 7-Lex Luthor-c/story. 8-Scarecrow-c/story. 9-Catwoman-c/story 1.25 3.75 10.00

JOKER, THE (See Tangent Comics/ The Joker)

JOKER COMICS (Adventures Into Terror No. 43 on)
Timely/Marvel Comics No. 36 on (TCI/CDS): Apr, 1942 - No. 42, Aug, 1950

1-(Rare)-Powerhouse Pepper (1st app.) begins by Wolverton; Stuporman app. from Daring Comics 225.00 675.00 1800.00
2-Wolverton-a; 1st app. Tessie the Typist & begin series 81.00 244.00 650.00
3-5-Wolverton-a 52.00 157.00 420.00
6-10-Wolverton-a. 6-Tessie-c begin 40.00 120.00 285.00
11-20-Wolverton-a 32.00 96.00 225.00
21,22,24-27,29,30-Wolverton cont'd. & Kurtzman's "Hey Look" in #23-27 27.00 81.00 190.00
23-1st "Hey Look" by Kurtzman; Wolverton-a 30.00 90.00 210.00

GD2.0 FN6.0 NM9.4

28,32,34,37-41: 28-Millie the Model begins. 32-Hedy begins. 41-Nellie the Nurse app. 9.15 27.00 55.00
31-Last Powerhouse Pepper; not in #28 19.00 58.00 135.00
33,35,36-Kurtzman's "Hey Look" 10.00 30.00 70.00
42-Only app. 'Patty Pinup,' clone of Millie the Model 10.00 30.00 60.00

JOKER: DEVIL'S ADVOCATE
DC Comics: 1996 ($24.95/$12.95, one-shot)

nn-(Hardcover)-Dixon scripts/Nolan & Hanna-a 25.00
nn-(Softcover) 13.00

JOLLY CHRISTMAS, A (See March of Comics No. 269)

JOLLY COMICS
Four Star Publishing Co.: 1947

1 10.00 30.00 60.00

JOLLY JINGLES (Formerly Jackpot Comics)
MLJ Magazines: No. 10, Sum, 1943 - No. 16, Wint, 1944/45

10-Super Duck begins (origin & 1st app.); Woody The Woodpecker begins (not same as Lantz character) 36.00 107.00 250.00
11 (Fall, '43)-2nd Super Duck(see Hangman #8) 18.00 54.00 125.00
12-Hitler-c 18.00 54.00 125.00
13-16: 13-Sahle-c. 15-Vigoda-c 11.50 34.00 80.00

JONAH HEX (See All-Star Western, Hex and Weird Western Tales)
National Periodical Pub./DC Comics: Mar-Apr, 1977 - No. 92, Aug, 1985

1 4.50 13.50 45.00
2-4,9: 9-Wrightson-c. 2.25 6.75 18.00
5,6,10: 5-Rep 1st app. from All-Star Western #10 1.75 5.25 14.00
7,8-Explains Hex's face disfigurement (origin) 2.50 7.50 20.00
11-20: 12-Starlin-c 1.00 3.00 8.00
21-50: 31,32-Origin retold 5.00
51-91: 89-Mark Texeira-a. 92-Story contd in Hex #1 4.00
92 1.50 4.50 12.00
NOTE: ***Ayers*** *a(p)-35-37, 40, 41, 44-53, 56, 58-82.* ***Buckler*** *a-11; c-11, 13-16.* ***Kubert*** *c-43-46.* ***Morrow*** *a-90-92; c-10.* ***Spiegle(Tothish)*** *a-34, 38, 40, 49, 52.* ***Texeira*** *a-89p. Batlash back-ups in 49, 52. El Diablo back-ups in 48, 56-60, 73-75. Scalphunter back-ups in 40, 41, 45-47.*

JONAH HEX AND OTHER WESTERN TALES (Blue Ribbon Digest)
DC Comics: Sept-Oct, 1979 - No. 3, Jan-Feb, 1980 (100 pgs.)

1-3: 1-Origin Scalphunter-r, Ayers/Evans, Neal Adams-a.; painted-c. 2-Weird Western Tales-r; Neal Adams, Toth, Aragones-a. 3-Outlaw-r, Scalphunter-r; Gil Kane, Wildey-a 1.00 3.00 8.00

JONAH HEX: RIDERS OF THE WORM AND SUCH
DC Comics (Vertigo): Mar, 1995 - No. 5, July, 1995 ($2.95, limited series)

1-5-Lansdale story, Truman -a 3.00

JONAH HEX: SHADOWS WEST
DC Comics (Vertigo): Feb, 1999 - No. 3, Apr, 1999 ($2.95, limited series)

1-3-Lansdale-s/Truman -a 3.00

JONAH HEX SPECTACULAR (See DC Special Series No. 16)

JONAH HEX: TWO-GUN MOJO
DC Comics (Vertigo): Aug, 1993 - No. 5, Dec, 1993 ($2.95, limited series)

1-Lansdale scripts in all;Truman/Glanzman-a in all w/Truman-c 5.00
1-Platinum edition with no price on cover 20.00
2-5 3.00
TPB-(1994, $12.95) r/#1-5 13.00

JONESY (Formerly Crack Western)
Comic Favorite/Quality Comics Group: No. 85, Aug, 1953; No. 2, Oct, 1953 - No. 8, Oct, 1954

85(#1)-Teen-age humor 5.85 17.50 35.00
2 4.00 12.00 24.00
3-8 3.20 8.00 16.00

JON JUAN (Also see Great Lover Romances)
Toby Press: Spring, 1950

1-All Schomburg-a (signed Al Reid on-c); written by Siegel; used in **SOTI**,

Jon Juan #1 © TOBY

Journey into Fear #20 © SUPR

Journey into Mystery #95 © MAR

GD2.0 FN6.0 NM9.4

pg. 38 (Scarce) 57.00 172.00 460.00

JONNI THUNDER (...A.K.A. Thunderbolt)
DC Comics: Feb, 1985 - No. 4, Aug, 1985 (75¢, limited series)

1-4: 1-Origin & 1st app. 2.00

JONNY DEMON
Dark Horse Comics: May, 1994 - No. 3, July, 1994 ($2.50, limited series)

1-3 2.50

JONNY DOUBLE
DC Comics (Vertigo): Sept, 1998 - No. 4, Dec, 1998 ($2.95, limited series)

1-4-Azzarello-s 3.00

JONNY QUEST (TV)
Gold Key: Dec, 1964 (Hanna-Barbera)

1 (10139-412) 33.00 100.00 360.00

JONNY QUEST (TV)
Comico: June 1986 - No. 31, Dec, 1988 ($1.50/$1.75)(Hanna-Barbera)

1 3.00
2,3,5: 3,5-Dave Stevens-c 3.00
4,6-31: 30-Adapts TV episode 2.00
Special 1(9/88, $1.75), 2(10/88, $1.75) 2.00

*NOTE: **M. Anderson** a-9. **Mooney** a-Special 1. **Pini** a-2. **Quagmire** a-31p. **Rude** a-1; c-2i. **Sienkiewicz** c-11. **Spiegle** a-7, 12, 21; c-21 **Staton** a-2i, 11p. **Steacy** c-8. **Stevens** a-4i; c-3,5. **Wildey** a-1, c-1, 7, 12. **Williamson** a-4i; c-4i.*

JONNY QUEST CLASSICS (TV)
Comico: May, 1987 - No. 3, July, 1987 ($2.00) (Hanna-Barbera)

1-3: Wildey-c/a; 3-Based on TV episode 2.00

JON SABLE, FREELANCE (Also see Mike Grell's Sable & Sable)
First Comics: 6/83 - No. 56, 2/88 (#1-17, $1; #18-33, $1.25, #34-on, $1.75)

1-Mike Grell-c/a/scripts 3.00
2-56: 3-5-Origin, parts 1-3. 6-Origin, part 4. 11-1st app. of Maggie the Cat. 14-Mando paper begins. 16-Maggie the Cat. app. 25-30-Shatter app. 34-Deluxe format begins ($1.75) 2.00

*NOTE: **Aragones** a-33; c-33(part). **Grell** a-1-43;c-1-52, 53p, 54-56.*

JOSEPH & HIS BRETHREN (See The Living Bible)

JOSIE (She's... #1-16) (...& the Pussycats #45 on) (See Archie Giant Series Magazine #528, 540, 551, 562, 571, 584, 597, 610, 622)
Archie Publications/Radio Comics: Feb, 1963; No. 2, Aug, 1963 - No. 106, Oct, 1982

1 16.00 48.00 160.00
2 8.00 24.00 80.00
3-5 5.00 15.00 50.00
6-10 3.50 10.50 35.00
11-20 2.50 7.50 24.00
21, 23-30 2.25 6.75 18.00
22 (9/66)-Mighty Man & Mighty (Josie Girl) app. 3.00 9.00 30.00
31-44 2.00 6.00 16.00
45 (12/69)-Josie and the Pussycats begins (Hanna Barbera TV cartoon); 1st app. of the Pussycats 5.00 15.00 50.00
46-2nd app./1st cover Pussycats 3.00 9.00 30.00
47-3rd app. of the Pussycats 2.50 7.50 20.00
48,49 Pussycats band-c/s 2.50 7.50 22.00
50-J&P-c; go to Hollywood, meet Hanna & Barbera 3.50 10.50 35.00
51-54 2.25 6.75 18.00
55-74 (2/74)(52pg. issues) 1.85 5.50 15.00
75-90(8/76) 1.10 3.30 9.00
91-99,101-106 1.00 2.80 7.00
100 (10/79) 1.25 3.75 10.00

JOSIE & THE PUSSYCATS (TV)
Archie Comics: 1993 - No. 2, 1994 ($2.00, 52 pgs.)(Published annually)

1,2-Bound-in pull-out poster in each. 2-(Spr/94) 3.00

JOURNAL OF CRIME (See Fox Giants)

GD2.0 FN6.0 NM9.4

JOURNEY
Aardvark-Vanaheim #1-14/Fantagraphics Books #15-on: 1983 - No. 14, 9/84; No. 15, 4/85 - No. 27, 7/86 (B&W)

1 3.00
2-27: 20-Sam Kieth-a 2.00

JOURNEY INTO FEAR
Superior-Dynamic Publications: May, 1951 - No. 21, Sept, 1954

1-Baker-r(2) 56.00 169.00 450.00
2 40.00 120.00 280.00
3,4 34.00 103.00 240.00
5-10,15: 15-Used in **SOTI**, pg. 389 23.00 69.00 160.00
11-14,16-21 21.00 64.00 150.00

*NOTE: Kamenish 'headlight'-a most issues. **Robinson** a-10.*

JOURNEY INTO MYSTERY (1st Series) (Thor Nos. 126-502)
Atlas(CPS No. 1-48/AMI No. 49-68/Marvel No. 69 (6/61) on): 6/52 - No. 48, 8/57; No. 49, 11/58 - No. 125, 2/66; 503, 11/96 - No. 521, June, 1998

1-Weird/horror stories begin 280.00 840.00 2800.00
2 95.00 285.00 850.00
3,4 75.00 225.00 640.00
5-11 52.00 156.00 420.00
12-20,22: 15-Atomic explosion panel. 22-Davisesque-a; last pre-code issue (2/55) 40.00 120.00 320.00
21-Kubert-a; Tothish-a by Andru 40.00 120.00 325.00
23-32,35-38,40: 24-Torres?-a. 38-Ditko-a 25.00 75.00 200.00
33-Williamson-a; Ditko-a (his 1st for Atlas?) 28.00 84.00 225.00
34,39: 34-Krigstein-a. 39-1st S.A. issue; Wood-a 26.00 78.00 210.00
41-Crandall-a; Frazettaesque-a by Morrow 18.00 54.00 180.00
42,46,48: 42,48-Torres-a. 46-Torres & Krigstein-a 18.00 54.00 180.00
43,44-Williamson/Mayo-a in both 19.00 57.00 190.00
45,47,50,52-54: 50-Davis-a. 54-Williamson-a 17.00 51.00 170.00
49-Matt Fox, Check-a 18.00 55.00 185.00
51-Kirby/Wood-a 20.00 60.00 200.00
55-61,63-65,67-69,71,72,74,75: 74-Contents change to Fantasy. 75-Last 10¢ issue 17.00 52.00 175.00
62-Prototype ish. (The Hulk); 1st app. Xemnu (Titan) called "The Hulk" 25.00 75.00 250.00
66-Prototype ish. (The Hulk)-Return of Xemnu "The Hulk" 24.00 72.00 240.00
70-Prototype ish. (The Sandman)(7/61); similar to Spidey villain 23.00 69.00 230.00
73-Story titled "The Spider" where a spider is exposed to radiation & gets powers of a human and shoots webbing; a reverse prototype of Spider-Man's origin 34.00 102.00 340.00
76,77,80-82: 80-Anti-communist propaganda story 14.00 42.00 140.00
76-(10¢ cover price blacked out, 12¢ printed on) 30.00 90.00 300.00
78-The Sorceror (Dr. Strange prototype) app. (3/62) 23.00 69.00 230.00
79-Prototype issue. (Mr. Hyde) 20.00 60.00 200.00

GD2.0 FN6.0 VF8.0 NM9.4

83-Origin & 1st app. The Mighty Thor by Kirby (8/62) and begin series; Thor-c also begin 300.00 900.00 2100.00 4500.00

GD2.0 FN6.0 NM9.4

83-Reprint from the Golden Record Comic Set 9.00 27.00 90.00
with the record (1966) 16.00 48.00 160.00
84-2nd app. Thor 81.00 244.00 975.00
85-1st app. Loki & Heimdall; Odin cameo (1 panel) 50.00 150.00 600.00
86-1st full app. Odin 36.00 108.00 400.00
87-89: 89-Origin Thor retold 28.00 84.00 280.00
90-No Kirby-a 16.00 48.00 160.00
91,92,94,96-Sinnott-a 13.50 41.00 135.00
93,97-Kirby-a; Tales of Asgard series begins #97 (origin which concludes in #99) 16.00 48.00 160.00
95-Sinnott-a (scarce in VF/NM) 14.50 44.00 145.00
98-100-Kirby/Heck-a. 98-Origin/1st app. The Human Cobra. 99-1st app. Surtur & Mr. Hyde 12.00 36.00 120.00

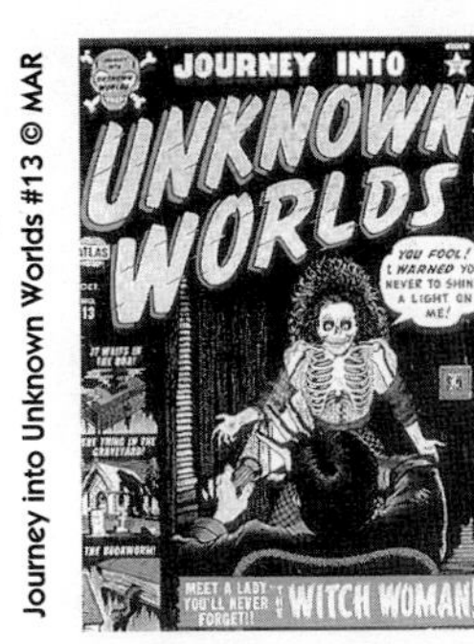

Journey into Unknown Worlds #13 © MAR

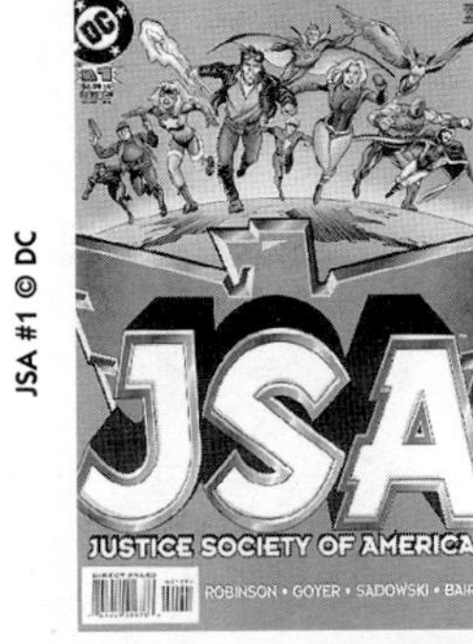

JSA #1 © DC

J2 #10 © MAR

GD2.0 FN6.0 NM9.4

101-108,110: 101-(2/64)-2nd Avengers x-over (w/o Capt. America); see Tales Of Suspense #49 for 1st x-over. 102-Intro Sif. 103-1st app. Enchantress. 105-109-Ten extra pgs. Kirby-a in each. 107-1st app. Grey Gargoyle. 108-(9/64)-Early Dr. Strange & Avengers x-over 8.00 24.00 80.00
109-Magneto-c & app. (1st x-over, 10/64) 11.00 33.00 110.00
111,113,114,116-125: 113-Origin Loki. 114-Origin/1st app. Absorbing Man. 118-1st app. Destroyer. 119-Intro Hogun, Fandrall, Volstagg. 124-Hercules-c/story 7.00 21.00 70.00
112-Thor Vs. Hulk (1/65). 112-Origin Loki 19.00 57.00 190.00
115-Origin Loki 9.00 27.00 90.00
503-521: 503-(11/96, $1.50)-The Lost Gods begin; Tom DeFalco scripts & Deodato Studios-c/a. 505-Spider-Man-c/app. 509-Loki-c/app. 514-516-Shang-Chi 2.00
Annual 1(1965, 25¢, 72 pgs.)-New Thor vs. Hercules(1st app.)-c/story (see Incredible Hulk #3); Kirby-c/a; r/#85,93,95,97 16.00 48.00 160.00

NOTE: ***Ayers*** *a-14, 39, 64i, 71i, 74i, 80i.* ***Bailey*** *a-43.* ***Briefer*** *a-5, 12.* ***Cameron*** *a-35.* ***Check*** *a-17.* ***Colan*** *a-23, 81; c-14.* ***Ditko*** *a-33, 38, 50-96; c-58, 67, 71, 88i.* ***Kirby/Ditko*** *a-50-83.* ***Everett*** *a-20, 48; c-4-7, 9, 36, 37, 39-42, 44, 45, 47.* ***Forte*** *a-19, 35, 40, 53.* ***Heath*** *a-4-6, 11, 14; c-1, 8, 11, 15, 51.* ***Heck*** *a-53, 73.* ***Kirby*** *a(p)-51, 52, 56, 57, 60, 62, 64, 66, 69, 71-74, 76, 79, 80-89, 93, 97, 98, 100(w/****Heck****), 101-125; c-50-57, 59-66, 68-70, 72-82, 88(w/****Ditko****), 83 & 84(w/****Sinnott****), 85-96(w/****Ayers****), 97-125p.* ***Leiber/Fox*** *a-93, 98-102.* ***Maneely*** *c-20-22.* ***Morisi*** *a-42.* ***Morrow*** *a-41, 42.* ***Orlando*** *a-30, 45, 57.* ***Mac Pakula*** *(Tothish) a-9, 35, 41.* ***Powell*** *a-20, 27, 34.* ***Reinman*** *a-39, 87, 92, 96i.* ***Robinson*** *a-9.* ***Roussos*** *a-39.* ***Robert Sale*** *a-14.* ***Severin*** *a-27; c-30.* ***Sinnott*** *a-41; c-50.* ***Tuska*** *a-11.* ***Wildey*** *a-16.*

JOURNEY INTO MYSTERY (2nd Series)
Marvel Comics: Oct, 1972 - No. 19, Oct, 1975

1-Robert Howard adaptation; Starlin/Ploog-a 1.85 5.50 15.00
2-5: 2,3,5-Bloch adapt. 4-H. P. Lovecraft adapt. 1.25 3.75 10.00
6-19: Reprints 2.40 6.00

NOTE: ***N. Adams*** *a-2i.* ***Ditko*** *r-7, 10, 12, 14, 15, 19; c-10.* ***Everett*** *r-9, 14.* ***G. Kane*** *a-1p, 2p; c-1-3p.* ***Kirby*** *r-7, 13, 15, 18, 19; c-7.* ***Mort Lawrence*** *r-2.* ***Maneely*** *r-3.* ***Orlando*** *r-16.* ***Reese*** *a-1, 2i.* ***Starlin*** *a-1p, 3p.* ***Torres*** *r-16.* ***Wildey*** *r-9, 14.*

JOURNEY INTO UNKNOWN WORLDS (Formerly Teen)
Atlas Comics (WFP): No. 36, 9/50 - No. 38, 2/51; No. 4, 4/51 - No. 59, 8/57

36(#1)-Science fiction/weird; "End Of The Earth" c/story 212.00 636.00 1700.00
37(#2)-Science fiction; "When Worlds Collide" c/story; Everett-c/a; Hitler story 97.00 291.00 775.00
38(#3)-Science fiction 80.00 240.00 640.00
4-6,8,10-Science fiction/weird 50.00 150.00 400.00
7-Wolverton-a "Planet of Terror", 6 pgs; electric chair c-inset/story 84.00 252.00 675.00
9-Giant eyeball story 60.00 180.00 480.00
11,12-Krigstein-a 40.00 120.00 300.00
13,16,17,20 32.00 96.00 225.00
14-Wolverton-a "One of Our Graveyards Is Missing", 4 pgs; Tuska-a 62.00 186.00 500.00
15-Wolverton-a "They Crawl by Night", 5 pgs.; 2 pg. Maneely s/f story 62.00 186.00 500.00
18,19-Matt Fox-a 37.00 111.00 260.00
21-33: 21-Decapitation-c. 24-Sci/fic story. 26-Atom bomb panel. 27-Sid Check-a. 33-Last pre-code (2/55) 25.00 75.00 175.00
34-Kubert, Torres-a 18.00 54.00 125.00
35-Torres-a 17.00 49.00 115.00
36-45,48,50,53,55,59: 43-Krigstein-a. 44-Davis-a. 45,55,59-Williamson-a in all; with Mayo #55,59. 55-Crandall-a. 48,53-Crandall-a (4 pgs. #48). 48-Check-a. 50-Davis, Crandall-a 16.00 47.00 110.00
46,47,49,52,54,56-58: 54-Torres-a 13.50 41.00 95.00
51-Ditko, Wood-a 17.00 51.00 120.00

NOTE: ***Ayers*** *a-24, 43,* ***Berg*** *a-38(#3), 43.* ***Lou Cameron*** *a-33.* ***Colan*** *a-37(#2), 6, 17, 19, 20, 23, 39.* ***Ditko*** *a-45, 51.* ***Drucker*** *a-35, 58.* ***Everett*** *a-37(#2), 11, 14, 41, 55, 56; c-37(#2), 11, 13, 14, 17, 22, 47, 48, 50, 53-55, 59.* ***Forte*** *a-49.* ***Fox*** *a-21i.* ***Heath*** *a-36(#1), 4, 6-8, 17, 20, 22, 36i; c-18.* ***Keller*** *a-15.* ***Mort Lawrence*** *a-38, 39.* ***Maneely*** *a-7, 8, 15, 16, 22, 49, 58; c-19, 25, 52.* ***Morrow*** *a-48.* ***Orlando*** *a-44, 57.* ***Pakula*** *a-36.* ***Powell*** *a-42, 53, 54.* ***Reinman*** *a-8.* ***Rico*** *a-21.* ***Robert Sale*** *a-24, 49.* ***Sekowsky*** *a-4, 5, 9.* ***Severin*** *a-38, 51; c-38, 48i, 56.* ***Sinnott*** *a-9, 21, 24.* ***Tuska*** *a-38(#3), 14.* ***Wildey*** *a-25, 43, 44.*

JOURNEYMAN
Image Comics: Aug, 1999 - Present ($2.95, B&W, limited series)

1,2-Brandon McKinney-s/a 3.00

JOURNEY OF DISCOVERY WITH MARK STEEL (See Mark Steel)

JOURNEY TO THE CENTER OF THE EARTH (Movie)
Dell Publishing Co.: No. 1060, Nov-Jan, 1959/60 (one-shot)

Four Color 1060-Pat Boone & James Madson photo-c 11.00 33.00 120.00

JSA (Justice Society of America) (Also see All Star Comics)
DC Comics: Aug, 1999 - Present ($2.50)

1-Robinson and Goyer-s; funeral of Wesley Dodds 2.50
2-4: 4-Return of Dr. Fate 2.50
... Secret Files 1 (8/99, $4.95) Origin stories and pin-ups 5.00

J2 (Also see A-Next and Juggernaut)
Marvel Comics: Oct, 1998 - No. 12 ($1.99)

1-Juggernaut's son; Lim-a 2.00
2-12: 2-Two covers; X-People app. 3-J2 battles the Hulk 2.00

JUDE, THE FORGOTTEN SAINT
Catechetical Guild Education Soc.: 1954 (16 pgs.; 8x11"; full color; paper-c)

nn 2.40 6.00 12.00

JUDGE COLT
Gold Key: Oct, 1969 - No. 4, Sept, 1970

1 1.85 5.50 15.00
2-4 1.00 3.00 8.00

JUDGE DREDD (...Classics #62 on; also see Batman - Judge Dredd, Dredd Rules, The Law of Dredd & 2000 A.D. Monthly)
Eagle Comics/IPC Magazines Ltd./Quality Comics #34-35, V2#1-37/ Fleetway #38 on: Nov, 1983 - No. 35, 1986; V2#1, Oct, 1986 - No. 77, 1993

1-Bolland-c/a 2.40 6.00
2-35 2.50
V2#1-77: 1-('86)-New look begins. 20-Begin $1.50-c. 21/22, 23/24-Two issue numbers in one. 28-1st app. Megaman (super-hero). 39-Begin $1.75-c. 51-Begin $1.95-c. 53-Bolland-a. 57-Reprints 1st published Judge Dredd story 2.50
Special 1 2.50

NOTE: ***Bolland*** *a-1-6, 8, 10; c-1-10, 15.* ***Guice*** *c-V2#23/24, 26, 27.*

JUDGE DREDD (3rd Series)
DC Comics: Aug, 1994 - No. 18, Jan, 1996 ($1.95)

1-18: 12-Begin $2.25-c 2.50
nn ($5.95)-Movie adaptation, Sienkiewicz-c 2.40 6.00

JUDGE DREDD'S CRIME FILE
Eagle Comics: Aug, 1989 - No. 6, Feb, 1986 ($1.25, limited series)

1-6: 1-Byrne-a 2.50

JUDGE DREDD: LEGENDS OF THE LAW
DC Comics: Dec, 1994 - No. 13, Dec, 1995 ($1.95)

1-13: 1-5-Dorman-c 2.50

JUDGE DREDD: THE EARLY CASES
Eagle Comics: Feb, 1986 - No. 6, Jul, 1986 ($1.25, Mega-series, Mando paper)

1-6: 2000 A.D.-r 2.50

JUDGE DREDD: THE JUDGE CHILD QUEST (Judge Child in indicia)
Eagle Comics: Aug, 1984 - No. 5, Oct, 1984 ($1.25, Lim. series, Baxter paper)

1-5: 2000A.D.-r; Bolland-c/a 2.50

JUDGE DREDD: THE MEGAZINE
Fleetway/Quality: 1991 - Present ($4.95, stiff-c, squarebound, 52 pgs.)

1-3 5.00

JUDGE PARKER
Argo: Feb, 1956 - No. 2, 1956

1-Newspaper strip reprints 5.35 16.00 32.00
2 4.00 11.00 22.00

JUDGMENT DAY
Awesome Entertainment: June, 1997 - No. 3, Oct, 1997 ($2.50, limited series)

Judo Joe #1 © Jay-Jay Corp.

Juggernaut #1 © MAR

Jughead's Double Digest #62 © AP

	GD2.0	FN6.0	NM9.4
1-3: 1 Alpha-Moore-s/Liefeld-c/a(p) flashback art by various in all. 2 Omega. 3 Final Judgment,			2.50
1-3-Variant cover by Dave Gibbons			2.50
...Aftermath-($3.50) Moore-s/Kane-a; Youngblood, Glory, New Men, Maximage Allies and Spacehunter short stoiries			3.50
...Aftermath-Variant cover by Dave Gibbons			3.50

JUDGMENT PAWNS
Antarctic Press: Feb, 1997 ($2.95, one-shot)

	GD2.0	FN6.0	NM9.4
1			3.00

JUDO JOE
Jay-Jay Corp.: Aug, 1953 - No. 3, Dec, 1953 (Judo lessons in each issue)

	GD2.0	FN6.0	NM9.4
1-Drug ring story	8.35	25.00	50.00
2,3: 3-Hypo needle story	5.85	17.50	35.00

JUDOMASTER (Gun Master #84-89) (Also see Crisis on Infinite Earths, Sarge Steel #6 & Special War Series)
Charlton Comics: No. 89, May-June, 1966 - No. 98, Dec, 1967 (Two No. 89's)

	GD2.0	FN6.0	NM9.4
89-3rd app. Judomaster	3.00	9.00	30.00
90,92-98: 93-Intro. Tiger	2.50	7.50	24.00
91-Sarge Steel begins	2.80	8.40	28.00
93,94,96,98 (Modern Comics reprint, 1977)			4.00

NOTE: ***Morisi*** *Thunderbolt #90. #91 has 1 pg. biography on writer/artist Frank McLaughlin.*

JUDY CANOVA (Formerly My Experience) (Stage, screen, radio)
Fox Features Syndicate: No. 23, May, 1950 - No. 3, Sept, 1950

	GD2.0	FN6.0	NM9.4
23(#1)-Wood-c,a(p)?	19.00	58.00	135.00
24-Wood-a(p)	20.00	60.00	140.00
3-Wood-c; Wood/Orlando-a	23.00	69.00	160.00

JUDY GARLAND (See Famous Stars)

JUDY JOINS THE WAVES
Toby Press: 1951 (For U.S. Navy)

	GD2.0	FN6.0	NM9.4
nn	5.35	16.00	32.00

JUGGERNAUT (See X-Men)
Marvel Comics: Apr, 1997, Nov, 1999 ($2.99, one-shots)

	GD2.0	FN6.0	NM9.4
1-(4/97) Kelly-s/ Rouleau-a			3.00
1-(11/99) Casey-s; Eighth Day x-over; Thor, Iron Man, Spidey app.			3.00

JUGHEAD (Formerly Archie's Pal...)
Archie Publications: No. 127, Dec, 1965 - No. 352, June, 1987

	GD2.0	FN6.0	NM9.4
127-130	2.50	7.50	22.00
131,133,135-160(9/68)	2.25	6.75	18.00
132,134: 132-Shield-c; The Fly & Black Hood app.; Shield cameo. 134-Shield-c	2.50	7.50	24.00
161-180	1.75	5.25	14.00
181-199	1.00	3.00	10.00
200(1/'72)	1.20	3.60	12.00
201-240(5/75)	.85	2.60	7.00
241-270(11/77)			5.00
271-299			4.00
300(5/80)			5.00
301-320(1/82): 300-Anniversary issue; infinity-c			3.00
321-352			2.00

JUGHEAD (2nd Series)(Becomes Archie's Pal Jughead Comics #46 on)
Archie Enterprises: Aug, 1987 - No. 45, May, 1993 (.75/$1.00/$1.25)

	GD2.0	FN6.0	NM9.4
1			4.00
2-10			3.00
11-45: 4-X-Mas issue. 17-Colan-c/a			2.00

JUGHEAD AS CAPTAIN HERO (See Archie as Purehear the Powerful, Archie Giant Series Magazine #142 & Life With Archie)
Archie Publications: Oct, 1966 - No. 7, Nov, 1967

	GD2.0	FN6.0	NM9.4
1-Super hero parody	5.00	15.00	50.00
2	3.50	10.50	35.00
3-7	2.50	7.50	24.00

JUGHEAD JONES COMICS DIGEST, THE (...Magazine No. 10-64; Jughead Jones Digest Magazine #65)
Archie Publ.: June, 1977 - No. 100, May, 1996 ($1.35/$1.50/$1.75, digest-size, 128 pgs.)

	GD2.0	FN6.0	NM9.4
1-Neal Adams-a; Capt. Hero-r	2.20	6.50	22.00
2(9/77)-Neal Adams-a	1.80	5.40	18.00
3-6,8-10	1.20	3.60	12.00
7-Origin Jaguar-r; N. Adams-a.	1.50	4.50	15.00
11-20: 13-r/1957 Jughead's Folly	1.00	3.00	8.00
21-50		2.40	6.00
51-70			4.00
71-100			2.00

JUGHEAD'S BABY TALES
Archie Comics: Spring, 1994 - No. 2, Wint. 1994 ($2.00, 52 pgs.)

	GD2.0	FN6.0	NM9.4
1,2: 1-Bound-in pull-out poster			3.00

JUGHEAD'S DINER
Archie Comics: Apr, 1990 - No. 7, Apr, 1991 ($1.00)

	GD2.0	FN6.0	NM9.4
1			3.00
2-7			2.00

JUGHEAD'S DOUBLE DIGEST (...Magazine #5)
Archie Comics: Oct, 1989 - Present ($2.25/$2.50/$2.75/$2.79/$2.95/$2.99)

	GD2.0	FN6.0	NM9.4
1	1.10	3.30	9.00
2-10: 2,5-Capt. Hero stories	1.00	2.60	6.50
11-25			4.00
26-65: 58-Begin $2.99-c			3.00

JUGHEAD'S EAT-OUT COMIC BOOK MAGAZINE (See Archie Giant Series Magazine No. 170)

JUGHEAD'S FANTASY
Archie Publications: Aug, 1960 - No. 3, Dec, 1960

	GD2.0	FN6.0	NM9.4
1	17.00	51.00	170.00
2	11.00	33.00	110.00
3	10.00	30.00	100.00

JUGHEAD'S FOLLY
Archie Publications (Close-Up): 1957 (36 pgs.)(one-shot)

	GD2.0	FN6.0	NM9.4
1-Jughead a la Elvis (Rare) (1st reference to Elvis in comics?)	49.00	146.00	390.00

JUGHEAD'S JOKES
Archie Publications: Aug, 1967 - No. 78, Sept, 1982
(No. 1-8, 38 on: reg. size; No. 9-23: 68 pgs.; No. 24-37: 52 pgs.)

	GD2.0	FN6.0	NM9.4
1	6.00	18.00	60.00
2	3.20	9.60	32.00
3-8	2.50	7.50	22.00
9,10 (68 pgs.)	2.50	7.50	24.00
11-23(4/71) (68 pgs.)	1.80	5.40	18.00
24-37(1/74) (52 pgs.)	1.50	4.50	15.00
38-50(9/76)	1.00	2.80	7.00
51-78			3.50

JUGHEAD'S PAL HOT DOG (See Laugh #14 for 1st app.)
Archie Comics: Jan, 1990 - No. 5, Oct, 1990 ($1.00)

	GD2.0	FN6.0	NM9.4
1			3.00
2-5			2.00

JUGHEAD'S SOUL FOOD
Spire Christian Comics (Fleming H. Revell Co.): 1979 (49 cents)

	GD2.0	FN6.0	NM9.4
nn	1.00	3.00	8.00

JUGHEAD'S TIME POLICE
Archie Comics: July, 1990 - No. 6, May, 1991 ($1.00, bi-monthly)

	GD2.0	FN6.0	NM9.4
1			3.00
2-6: Colan a-3-6p; c-3-6			2.00

JUGHEAD WITH ARCHIE DIGEST (...Plus Betty & Veronica & Reggie Too No. 1,2; ...Magazine #33-?, 101-on; ...Comics Digest Mag.)

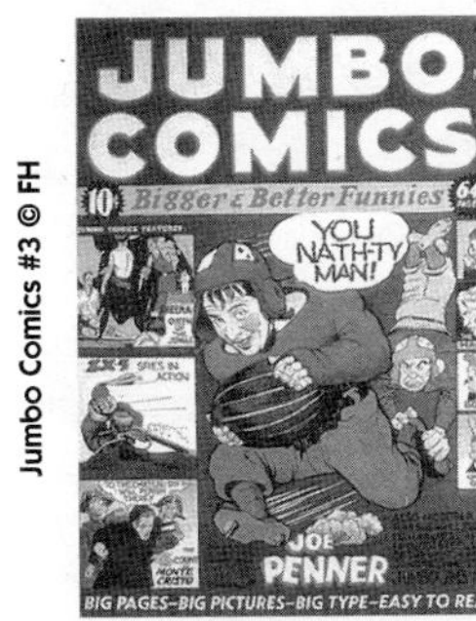

Jumbo Comics #3 © FH

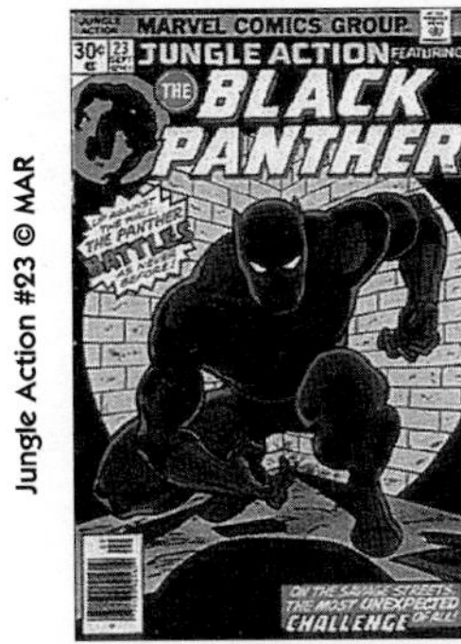

Jungle Action #23 © MAR

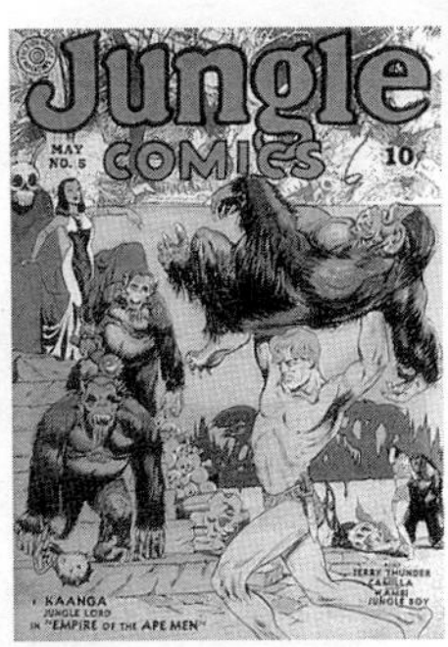

Jungle Comics #5 © FH

GD2.0 FN6.0 NM9.4

Archie Pub.: Mar, 1974 - Present ($1.00/$1.25/$1.35/$1.50/$1.75/$1.95/$1.99)

1 4.00 12.25 45.00
2 2.50 7.60 28.00
3-10 1.80 5.40 18.00
11-13,15-17,19,20: Capt. Hero-r in #14-16; Capt. Pureheart #17,19
1.20 3.60 12.00
14,18,21,22-Pureheart the Powerful in #18,21,22 1.40 4.20 14.00
23-30: 29-The Shield-r. 30-The Fly-r 1.10 3.30 9.00
31-50,100 1.00 2.80 7.00
51-99 2.40 6.00
101-121 3.00
122-154 2.00

JUKE BOX COMICS
Famous Funnies: Mar, 1948 - No. 6, Jan, 1949

1-Toth-c/a; Hollingsworth-a 40.00 120.00 300.00
2-Transvestism story 26.00 77.00 180.00
3-6: 3-Peggy Lee story. 4-Jimmy Durante line drawn-c. 6-Features Desi Arnaz plus Arnaz line drawn-c 19.00 58.00 135.00

JUMBO COMICS (Created by S.M. Iger)
Fiction House Magazines (Real Adv. Publ. Co.): Sept, 1938 - No. 167, Mar, 1953 (No. 1-3: 68 pgs.; No. 4-8: 52 pgs.)(No. 1-8 oversized-10-1/2x14-1/2"; black & white)

GD2.0 FN6.0 VF8.0

1-(Rare)-Sheena Queen of the Jungle(1st app.) by Meskin, Hawks of the Seas (The Hawk #10 on; see Feature Funnies #3) by Eisner, The Hunchback by Dick Briefer (ends #8), Wilton of the West (ends #24), Inspector Dayton (ends #67) & ZX-5 (ends #140) begin; 1st comic art by Jack Kirby (Count of Monte Cristo & Wilton of the West); Mickey Mouse appears (1 panel) with brief biography of Walt Disney; 1st app. Peter Pupp by Bob Kane. Note: Sheena was created by Iger for publication in England as a newspaper strip. The early issues of Jumbo contain Sheena strip-r; mutiple panel-c 1,2,7
1550.00 4650.00 17,000.00
2-(Rare)-Origin Sheena. Diary of Dr. Hayward by Kirby (also #3) plus 2 other stories; contains strip from Universal Film featuring Edgar Bergen & Charlie McCarthy plus-c (preview of film) 550.00 1650.00 5500.00
3-Last Kirby issue 380.00 1140.00 3800.00
4-(Scarce)-Origin The Hawk by Eisner; Wilton of the West by Fine (ends #14)(1st comic work); Count of Monte Cristo by Fine (ends #15); The Diary of Dr. Hayward by Fine (cont'd #8,9) 360.00 1080.00 3600.00
5-Christmas-c 316.00 948.00 3100.00
6-8-Last B&W issue. #8 was a 1939 N. Y. World's Fair Special Edition; Frank Buck's Jungleland story 274.00 822.00 2700.00
9-Stuart Taylor begins by Fine (ends #140); Fine-c; 1st color issue (8-9/39)-1st Sheena (jungle) cover; 8-1/4x10-1/4" (oversized in width only)
256.00 768.00 2400.00

GD2.0 FN6.0 NM9.4

10-Regular size 68 pg. issues begin; Sheena dons new costume w/ origin costume; Stuart Taylor sci/fi-c; classic Lou Fine-c.
175.00 525.00 1400.00
11-13: 12-The Hawk-c by Eisner. 13-Eisner-c 120.00 360.00 960.00
14-Intro. Lightning (super-hero) on-c only 125.00 375.00 1000.00
15,17-20: 15-1st Lightning story and begins, ends #41. 17-Lightning part-c
75.00 225.00 600.00
16-Lightning-c 94.00 281.00 750.00
21-30: 22-1st Tom, Dick & Harry; origin The Hawk retold. 25-Midnight the Black Stallion begins, ends #65 59.00 178.00 475.00
31-40: 31-(9/41)-1st app. Mars God of War in Stuart Taylor story (see Planet Comics #15. 35-Shows V2#11 (correct number does not appear)
47.00 141.00 375.00
41-50: 42-Ghost Gallery begins, ends #167 40.00 120.00 300.00
51-60: 52-Last Tom, Dick & Harry 34.00 103.00 240.00
61-70: 68-Sky Girl begins, ends #130; not in #79 26.00 79.00 185.00
71-93,95-99: 89-ZX5 becomes a private eye. 20.00 60.00 140.00
94-Used in Love and Death by Legman 21.00 64.00 150.00
100 21.00 62.00 145.00
101-140,150-158: 155-Used in **POP**, pg. 98 16.00 48.00 110.00
141-149-Two Sheena stories. 141-Long Bow, Indian Boy begins, ends #160
16.00 48.00 110.00
159-163: Space Scouts serial in all. 160-Last jungle-c (6/52). 161-Ghost Gallery covers begin, end #167. 163-Suicide Smith app. 14.00 43.00 100.00
164-The Star Pirate begins, ends #165 14.00 43.00 100.00
165-167: 165,167-Space Rangers app. 14.00 43.00 100.00

NOTE: *Bondage covers, negligee panels, torture, etc. are common in this series. Hawks of the Seas, Inspector Dayton, Spies in Action, Sports Shorts, & Uncle Otto by Eisner, #1-7. Hawk by* ***Eisner****-#10-15.* ***Eisner*** *c-1-8, 12-14. 1pg. Patsy pin-ups in 92-97, 99-101. Sheena by* ***Meskin****-#1, 4; by* ***Powell****-#2, 3, 5-28;* ***Powell*** *c-14, 16, 17, 19.* ***Powell/Eisner*** *c-15. Sky Girl by* ***Matt Baker****-#69-78, 80-130. ZX-5 & Ghost Gallery by* ***Kamen****-#90-130.* ***Bailey*** *a-3-8.* ***Briefer*** *a-1-8, 10.* ***Fine*** *a-14; c-9-11.* ***Kamen*** *a-101, 105, 123, 132; c-105, 121-145.* ***Bob Kane*** *a-1-8.* ***Whitman*** *c-146-167(most). Jungle c-9, 13, 15, 17 on.*

JUNGLE ACTION
Atlas Comics (IPC): Oct, 1954 - No. 6, Aug, 1955

1-Leopard Girl begins by Al Hartley (#1,3); Jungle Boy by Forte; Maneely-a in all 36.00 107.00 250.00
2-(3-D effect cover) 37.00 111.00 260.00
3-6: 3-Last precode (2/55) 23.00 69.00 160.00

NOTE: ***Maneely*** *c-1, 2, 5, 6.* ***Romita*** *a-3, 6.* ***Shores*** *a-3, 6; c-3, 4?.*

JUNGLE ACTION (...& Black Panther #18-21?)
Marvel Comics Group: Oct, 1972 - No. 24, Nov, 1976

1-Lorna, Jann-r (All reprints in 1-4) 2.00 6.00 16.00
2-4 1.25 3.75 10.00
5-Black Panther begins (r/Avengers #62) 2.00 6.00 16.00
6,8: 6-New stories begin. 8-Origin Black Panther 1.25 3.75 10.00
7,9,10: 9-Contains pull-out centerfold ad by Mark Jewelers
1.00 3.00 8.00
11-20,23,24: 19-23-KKK x-over. 23-r/#22. 24-1st Wind Eagle; sty contd in Marvel Premiere #51-#53 5.00
21,22-(Regular 25¢ edition)(5,7/76) 4.00
21,22-(30¢-c variant, limited distribution) 2.50 7.50 20.00

NOTE: ***Buckler*** *a-6-9p, 22; c-8p, 12p.* ***Buscema*** *a-5p; c-22.* ***Byrne*** *c-23.* ***Gil Kane*** *a-8p; c-2, 4, 10p, 11p, 13-17, 19, 24.* ***Kirby*** *c-18.* ***Maneely*** *r-1.* ***Russell*** *a-13i.* ***Starlin*** *c-3p.*

JUNGLE ADVENTURES
Super Comics: 1963 - 1964 (Reprints)

10,12,15,17,18: 10-r/Terrors of the Jungle #4 & #10(Rulah). 12-r/Zoot #14 (Rulah).15-r/Kaanga from Jungle #152 & Tiger Girl . 17-All Jo-Jo-r. 18-Reprints/White Princess of the Jungle #1; no Kinstler-a; origin of both White Princess & Cap'n Courage 3.20 9.60 32.00

JUNGLE ADVENTURES
Skywald Comics: Mar, 1971 - No. 3, June, 1971 (25¢, 52 pgs.)

1-Zangar origin; reprints of Jo-Jo, Blue Gorilla(origin)/White Princess #3, Kinstler-r/White Princess #2 2.00 6.00 16.00
2,3: 2-Zangar, Sheena-r/Sheena #17 & Jumbo #162, Jo-Jo, origin Slave Girl-r. 3-Zangar, Jo-Jo, White Princess, Rulah-r 1.25 3.75 10.00

JUNGLE BOOK (See King Louie and Mowgli, Movie Comics, Mowgli..., Walt Disney Showcase #45 & Walt Disney's The Jungle Book)

JUNGLE CAT (Disney)
Dell Publishing Co.: No. 1136, Sept-Nov, 1960 (one shot)

Four Color 1136-Movie, photo-c 5.50 16.50 60.00

JUNGLE COMICS
Fiction House Magazines: 1/40 - No. 157, 3/53; No. 158, Spr, 1953 - No. 163, Summer, 1954

1-Origin The White Panther, Kaanga, Lord of the Jungle, Tabu, Wizard of the Jungle; Wambi, the Jungle Boy, Camilla & Capt. Terry Thunder begin (all 1st app.). Lou Fine-c 360.00 1080.00 3600.00
2-Fantomah, Mystery Woman of the Jungle begins, ends #51; The Red Panther begins, ends #26 150.00 450.00 1200.00
3,4 125.00 375.00 1000.00
5-Classic Eisner-c 137.00 411.00 1100.00
6-10: 7,8-Powell-c 72.00 216.00 575.00
11-20: 13-Tuska-c 50.00 150.00 400.00
21-30: 25-Shows V2#1 (correct number does not appear). #27-New origin

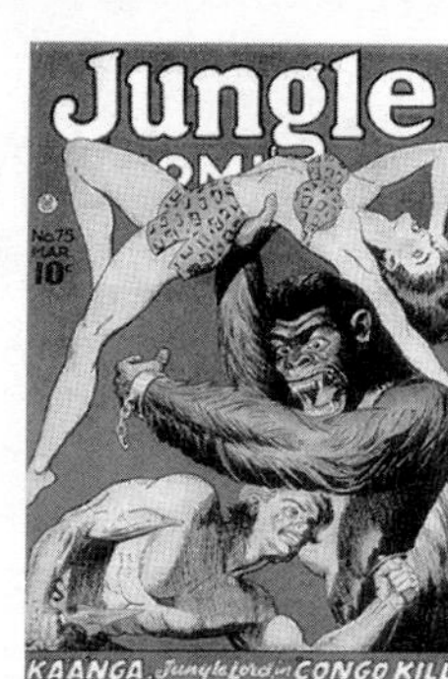

Jungle Comics #75 © FH

Jungle Jim #11 © STD

Junior Comics #13 © FOX

GD2.0 FN6.0 NM9.4

Fantomah, Daughter of the Pharoahs; Camilla dons new costume
41.00 124.00 330.00
31-40 33.00 99.00 230.00
41,43-50 29.00 86.00 200.00
42-Kaanga by Crandall, 12 pgs. 31.00 94.00 220.00
51-60 26.00 79.00 185.00
61-70: 67-Cover swipes Crandall splash pg. in #42 21.00 64.00 150.00
71-80: 79-New origin Tabu 19.00 58.00 135.00
81-97,99,101-110 17.00 51.00 120.00
98-Used in **SOTI**, pg. 185 & illo "In ordinary comic books, there are pictures within pictures for children who know how to look;" used by N.Y. Legis. Comm. 31.00 92.00 215.00
100 21.00 64.00 150.00
111-163: 104-In Camilla story villain is Dr. Wertham. 118-Clyde Beatty app. 135-Desert Panther begins in Terry Thunder (origin), not in #137; ends (dies) #138. 139-Last 52 pg. issue. 141-Last Tabu. 143,145-Used in **POP**, pg. 99. 151-Last Camilla & Terry Thunder. 152-Tiger Girl begins. 158-Last Wambi; Sheena app. 16.00 47.00 110.00
I.W. Reprint #1,9: 1-r/? 9-r/#151 2.60 7.80 26.00

NOTE: *Bondage covers, negligee panels, torture, etc. are common to this series. Camilla by* ***Fran Hopper****-#70-92; by* ***Baker****-#69, 100-113, 115, 116; by* ***Lubbers****-#97-99 by* ***Tuska****-#63, 65. Kaanga by* ***John Celardo****-#80-113; by* ***Larsen****-#71, 75-79; by* ***Moreira****-#58, 60, 61, 63-70, 72-74; by* ***Tuska****-#37, 62; by* ***Whitman****-#114-163. Tabu by* ***Larsen****-#59-75, 82-92; by* ***Whitman****-#93-115. Terry Thunder by* ***Hopper****-#71, 72; by* ***Celardo****-#78, 79; by* ***Lubbers****-#80-85. Tiger Girl-r by* ***Baker****-#152, 153, 155-157, 159. Wambi by* ***Baker****-#62-67, 74.* ***Astarita*** *c-45, 46.* ***Celardo*** *a-78; c-98-113.* ***Crandall*** *c-67 from splash pg.* ***Eisner*** *c-2, 5, 6.* ***Fine*** *c-1.* ***Larsen*** *a-65, 66, 71, 72, 74, 75, 79, 83, 84, 87-90.* ***Moriera*** *c-43, 44.* ***Morisi*** *a-51.* ***Powell*** *c-7, 8.* ***Sultan*** *c-3, 4.* ***Tuska*** *c-13.* ***Whitman*** *c-132-163(most).* ***Zolnerowich*** *c-11, 12, 18-41.*

JUNGLE COMICS
Blackthorne Publishing: May, 1988 - No.4 ($2.00, B&W/color)
1-4: 1-Dave Stevens-c; B. Jones scripts in all. 2-B&W-a begins 2.00

JUNGLE GIRL (See Lorna, the...)

JUNGLE GIRL (Nyoka, Jungle Girl No. 2 on)
Fawcett Publications: Fall, 1942 (one-shot)(No month listed)
1-Bondage-c; photo of Kay Aldridge who played Nyoka in movie serial app. on-c. Adaptation of the classic Republic movie serial Perils of Nyoka. 1st comic to devote entire contents to a movie serial adaptation 122.00 366.00 975.00

JUNGLE GIRLS
AC Comics: 1989 - No. 16, 1993 (B&W)
1-16: 1-4,10,13-16-New story & "good girl" reprints. 5-9,11,12-All g.g. reprints (Baker, Powell, Lubbers, others) 2.50

JUNGLE JIM (Also see Ace Comics)
Standard Comics (Best Books): No. 11, Jan, 1949 - No. 20, Apr, 1951
11 9.15 27.00 55.00
12-20 5.35 156.00 32.00

JUNGLE JIM
Dell Publishing Co.: No. 490, 8/53 - No. 1020, 8-10/59 (Painted-c)
Four Color 490(#1) 5.50 16.50 60.00
Four Color 565(#2, 6/54) 2.75 8.00 30.00
3(10-12/54)-5 2.50 7.50 28.00
6-19(1-3/59), Four Color 1020(#20) 2.25 6.75 25.00

JUNGLE JIM
King Features Syndicate: No. 5, Dec, 1967
5-Reprints Dell #5; Wood-c 1.50 4.50 12.00

JUNGLE JIM (Continued from Dell series)
Charlton Comics: No. 22, Feb, 1969 - No. 28, Feb, 1970 (#21 was an overseas edition only)
22-Dan Flagg begins; Ditko/Wood-a 2.50 7.50 25.00
23-26: 23-Last Dan Flagg; Howard-c. 24-Jungle People begin 2.00 6.00 16.00
27,28: 27-Ditko/Howard-a. 28-Ditko-a 2.50 7.50 20.00

GD2.0 FN6.0 NM9.4

NOTE: *Ditko cover of #22 reprints story panels*

JUNGLE JO
Fox Feature Syndicate (Hero Books): Mar, 1950 - No. 6, Mar, 1951
nn-Jo-Jo blanked out, leaving Congo King; came out after Jo-Jo #29 (intended as Jo-Jo #30?) 40.00 120.00 280.00
1-Tangi begins; part Wood-a 43.00 128.00 340.00
2-6 34.00 103.00 240.00

JUNGLE LIL (Dorothy Lamour #2 on; also see Feature Stories Magazine)
Fox Feature Syndicate (Hero Books): April, 1950
1 37.00 111.00 260.00

JUNGLE TALES (Jann of the Jungle No. 8 on)
Atlas Comics (CSI): Sept, 1954 - No. 7, Sept, 1955
1-Jann of the Jungle 36.00 107.00 250.00
2-7: 3-Last precode (1/55) 24.00 73.00 170.00
NOTE: ***Heath*** *c-5.* ***Heck*** *a-6, 7.* ***Maneely*** *a-2; c-1, 3.* ***Shores*** *a-5-7; c-4, 6.* ***Tuska*** *a-2.*

JUNGLE TALES OF CAVEWOMAN
Basement Comics: 1998 ($2.95, B&W)
1-Budd Root-s/a 3.00

JUNGLE TALES OF TARZAN
Charlton Comics: Dec, 1964 - No. 4, July, 1965
1 4.20 12.60 42.00
2-4 3.20 9.60 32.00
NOTE: ***Giordano*** *c-3p.* ***Glanzman*** *a-1-3.* ***Montes/Bache*** *a-4.*

JUNGLE TERROR (See Harvey Comics Hits No. 54)

JUNGLE THRILLS (Formerly Sports Thrills; Terrors of the Jungle #17 on)
Star Publications: No. 16, Feb, 1952; Dec, 1953; No. 7, 1954
16-Phantom Lady & Rulah story-reprint/All Top No. 15; used in **POP**, pg. 98,99; L. B. Cole-c 47.00 142.00 380.00
3-D 1(12/53, 25¢)-Came w/glasses; Jungle Lil & Jungle Jo appear; L. B. Cole-c 50.00 150.00 400.00
7-Titled 'Picture Scope Jungle Adventures;' (1954, 36 pgs, 15¢)-3-D effect c/stories; story & coloring book; Disbrow-a/script; L.B. Cole-c 46.00 139.00 370.00

JUNGLE TWINS, THE (Tono & Kono)
Gold Key/Whitman No. 18: Apr, 1972 - No. 17, Nov, 1975; No. 18, May, 1982
1 1.75 5.25 14.00
2-5 1.00 3.00 8.00
6-18: 18-Reprints 5.00
NOTE: *UFO c/story No. 13. Painted-c No. 1-17.* ***Spiegle*** *c-18.*

JUNGLE WAR STORIES (Guerrilla War No. 12 on)
Dell Publishing Co.: July-Sept, 1962 - No. 11, Apr-June, 1965 (Painted-c)
01-384-209 (#1) 2.50 7.50 24.00
2-11 2.25 6.75 18.00

JUNIE PROM (Also see Dexter Comics)
Dearfield Publishing Co.: Winter, 1947-48 - No. 7, Aug, 1949
1-Teen-age 11.50 34.00 80.00
2 7.00 21.00 42.00
3-7 5.00 15.00 30.00

JUNIOR CARROT PATROL (Jr. Carrot Patrol #2)
Dark Horse Comics: May, 1989; No. 2, Nov, 1990 ($2.00, B&W)
1,2-Flaming Carrot spin-off. 1-Bob Burden-c(i) 2.00

JUNIOR COMICS (Formerly Li'l Pan; becomes Western Outlaws with #17)
Fox Feature Syndicate: No. 9, Sept, 1947 - No. 16, July, 1948
9-Feldstein-c/a; headlights-c 75.00 225.00 600.00
10-16-Feldstein-c/a; headlights-c on all 66.00 197.00 525.00

JUNIOR FUNNIES (Formerly Tiny Tot Funnies No. 9)
Harvey Publ. (King Features Synd.): No. 10, Aug, 1951 - No. 13, Feb, 1952
10-Partial reprints in all; Blondie, Dagwood, Daisy, Henry, Popeye, Felix, Katzenjammer Kids 4.00 10.00 20.00

Jurassic Park #4 © Universal City Studios

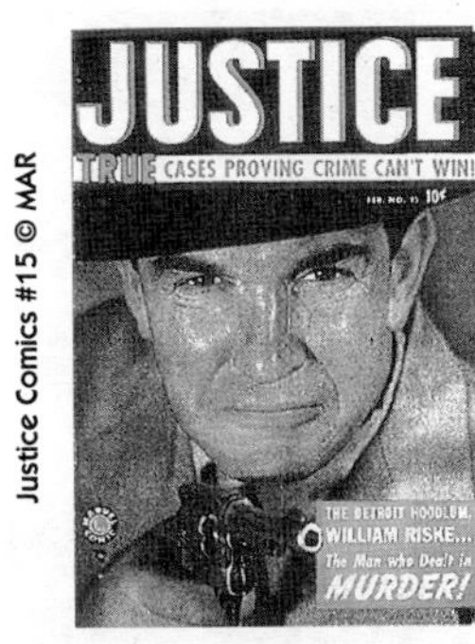

Justice Comics #15 © MAR

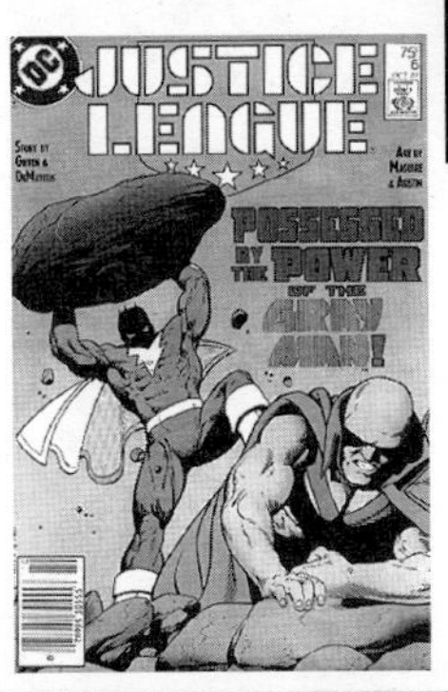

Justice League #6 © DC

	GD2.0	FN6.0	NM9.4
11-13	3.60	9.00	18.00

JUNIOR HOPP COMICS
Stanmor Publ.: Feb, 1952 - No. 3, July, 1952

1-Teenage humor	9.15	27.00	55.00
2,3: 3-Dave Berg-a	5.00	15.00	30.00

JUNIOR MEDICS OF AMERICA, THE
E. R. Squire & Sons: No. 1359, 1957 (15¢)

1359	2.80	7.00	14.00

JUNIOR MISS
Timely/Marvel (CnPC): Wint, 1944; No. 24, Apr, 1947 - No. 39, Aug, 1950

1-Frank Sinatra & June Allyson life story	26.00	77.00	180.00
24-Formerly The Human Torch #23?	11.50	34.00	80.00
25-38: 29,31,34-Cindy-c/stories (others?)	6.70	20.00	40.00
39-Kurtzman-a	9.15	27.00	55.00

NOTE: *Painted-c 35-37. 35, 37-all romance. 36, 38-mostly teen humor.*

JUNIOR PARTNERS (Formerly Oral Roberts' True Stories)
Oral Roberts Evangelistic Assn.: No. 120, Aug, 1959 - V3#12, Dec, 1961

120(#1)	3.20	9.60	32.00
2(9/59)	2.50	7.50	22.00
3-12(7/60)	1.75	5.25	14.00
V2#1(8/60)-5(12/60)	1.10	3.30	9.00
V3#1(1/61)-12	1.00	2.80	7.00

JUNIOR TREASURY (See Dell Junior...)

JUNIOR WOODCHUCKS GUIDE (Walt Disney's...)
Danbury Press: 1973 (8-3/4"x5-3/4", 214 pgs., hardcover)

nn-Illustrated text based on the long-standing J.W. Guide used by Donald Duck's nephews Huey, Dewey & Louie by Carl Barks. The guidebook was a popular plot devise to enable the nephews to solve problems facing their uncle or Scrooge McDuck (scarce) 3.80 11.40 38.00

JUNIOR WOODCHUCKS LIMITED SERIES (Walt Disney's...)
W. D. Publications (Disney): July, 1991 - No. 4, Oct, 1991 ($1.50, limited series; new & reprint-a)

1-4: 1-The Beagle Boys app.; Barks-r 2.00

JUNIOR WOODCHUCKS (See Huey, Dewey & Louie...)

JUNK CULTURE
DC Comics (Vertigo): July, 1997 - No. 2, Aug, 1997 ($2.50, limited series)

1,2: Ted McKeever-s/a in all 2.50

JURASSIC JANE
London Night Studios: Apr, 1997 - No. 7 ($3.00, B&W)

1-7			3.00
1-7-($6.00)-Variant nude-c		2.40	6.00

JURASSIC PARK
Topps Comics: 6/93 - No. 4, 8/93; #5, 10/94 - #10, 2/95

1-($2.50)-Newsstand Edition; Kane/Perez-a in all; 1-4: movie adaptation			2.50
1-($2.95)-Collector's Ed.; polybagged w/3 cards			4.00
1-Amberchrome Edition w/no price or ads	1.00	2.80	7.00
2-4-($2.50)-Newsstand Edition			2.50
2,3-($2.95)-Collector's Ed.; polybagged w/3 cards			3.00
4-10: 4-($2.95)-Collector's Ed.; polybagged w/1 of 4 different action hologram trading card; Gil Kane/Perez-a. 5-becomes Advs. of			3.00
Annual 1 ($3.95, 5/95)			4.00
Trade paperback (1993, $9.95)-r/#1-4; bagged w/#0			10.00

JURASSIC PARK: RAPTOR
Topps Comics: Nov, 1993 - No. 2, Dec, 1993 ($2.95, limited series)

1,2: 1-Bagged w/3 trading cards & Zorro #0; Golden c-1,2 3.00

JURASSIC PARK: RAPTORS ATTACK
Topps Comics: Mar, 1994 - No. 4, June, 1994 ($2.50, limited series)

1-4-Michael Golden-c/frontispiece 2.50

JURASSIC PARK: RAPTORS HIJACK
Topps Comics: July, 1994 - No. 4, Oct, 1994 ($2.50, limited series)

1-4: Michael Golden-c/front piece 2.50

JUSTICE
Marvel Comics Group (New Universe): Nov, 1986 - No. 32, June, 1989

1-32: 26-32-$1.50-c 2.00

JUSTICE COMICS (Formerly Wacky Duck; Tales of Justice #53 on)
Marvel/Atlas Comics (NPP 7-9,4-19/CnPC 20-23/MjMC 24-38/Male 39-52: No. 7, Fall/47 - No. 9, 6/48; No. 4, 8/48 - No. 52, 3/55

	GD2.0	FN6.0	NM9.4
7(#1, 1947)	26.00	79.00	185.00
8(#2)-Kurtzman-a "Giggles 'n' Grins" (3)	18.00	54.00	125.00
9(#3, 6/48)	17.00	49.00	115.00
4	15.00	45.00	105.00
5(9/48)-9: 8-Anti-Wertham editorial	13.00	39.00	90.00
10-15-Photo-c	10.00	30.00	70.00
16-30	9.15	27.00	55.00
31-40,42-52: 35-Gene Colan-a. 48-Last precode; Pakula & Tuska-a.	8.35	25.00	50.00
41-Electrocution-c	15.00	45.00	105.00

NOTE: ***Heath** a-24. **Maneely** c-44, 52. **Pakula** a-43, 45, 48. **Louis Ravielli** a-39. **Robinson** a-22, 25, 41. **Shores** c-7(#1), 8(#2)? **Tuska** a-48. **Wildey** a-52.*

JUSTICE: FOUR BALANCE
Marvel Comics: Sept, 1994 - No. 4, Dec, 1994 ($1.75, limited series)

1-4: 1-Thing & Firestar app. 2.00

JUSTICE, INC. (The Avenger) (Pulp)
National Periodical Publications: May-June, 1975 - No. 4, Nov-Dec, 1975

1-McWilliams-a, Kubert-c; origin	7.00
2-4: 2-4-Kirby-a(p), c-2,3p. 4-Kubert-c	5.00

NOTE: *Adapted from Kenneth Robeson novel, creator of Doc Savage.*

JUSTICE, INC. (Pulp)
DC Comics: 1989 - No. 2, 1989 ($3.95, 52 pgs., squarebound, mature)

1,2: Re-intro The Avenger; Andrew Helfer scripts & Kyle Baker-c/a 4.00

JUSTICE LEAGUE (...International #7-25; ...America #26 on)
DC Comics: May, 1987 - No. 113, Aug, 1996 (Also see Legends #6)

1-Batman, Green Lantern (Guy Gardner), Blue Beetle, Mr. Miracle, Capt. Marvel & Martian Manhunter begin			5.00
2,3: 3-Regular-c (white background)			3.00
3-Limited-c (yellow background, Superman logo)	3.00	9.00	30.00
4-10: 4-Booster Gold joins. 5-Origin Gray Man; Batman vs. Guy Gardner; Creeper app. 7-($1.25, 52 pgs.)-Capt. Marvel & Dr. Fate resign; Capt. Atom & Rocket Red join. 9,10-Millennium x-over			3.00
11-68,72-82: 16-Bruce Wayne-c/story. 18-21-Lobo app. 24-($1.50)-1st app. Justice League Europe. 31,32-Justice League Europe x-over. 58-Lobo app. 61-New team begins; swipes-c to JLA #1(10-11/60). 50-($1.75, 52 pgs.) 80-Intro new Booster Gold. 82,83-Guy Gardner-c/stories			2.00
69-Doomsday tie-in; takes place between Superman: The Man of Steel #18 & Superman #74			4.00
69,70-2nd printings			2.00
70-Funeral for a Friend part 1; red 3/4 outer-c			3.00
70-92,0,93-99,101-113: 70-Newsstand version w/o outer-c. 71-Direct sales version w/black outer-c. 71-Newsstand version w/o outer-c. 92-(9/94)-Zero Hour x-over; Triumph app. 0-(10/94)-New team begins (Hawkman, Wonder Woman, Metamorpho, Flash, Nuklon, Crimson Fox, Obsidian & Fire). 93-(11/94). 113-Flash, Green Lantern & Hawkman app.			2.00
100 ($3.95)-Foil-c; 52 pgs.			4.00
100 ($2.95)-Newstand			3.00
Annual 1-8,10 ('87-'94, '96, 68 pgs.): 2-Joker-c/story; Batman cameo. 5-Armageddon 2001 x-over; Silver ink 2nd print. 7-Bloodlines x-over. 8-Elseworlds story. 10-Legends of the Dead Earth			3.00
Annual 9 (1995, $3.50)-Year One story			3.50
Special 1,2('90, '9152 pgs.)-1-Giffen plots. 2-Staton-a(p)			3.00
Spectacular 1 (1992, $1.50, 52 pgs.)-Intro new JLI & JLE teams; ties into JLI #61 & JLE #37			3.00
A New Beginning Trade Paperback (1989, $12.95)-r/#1-7			13.00

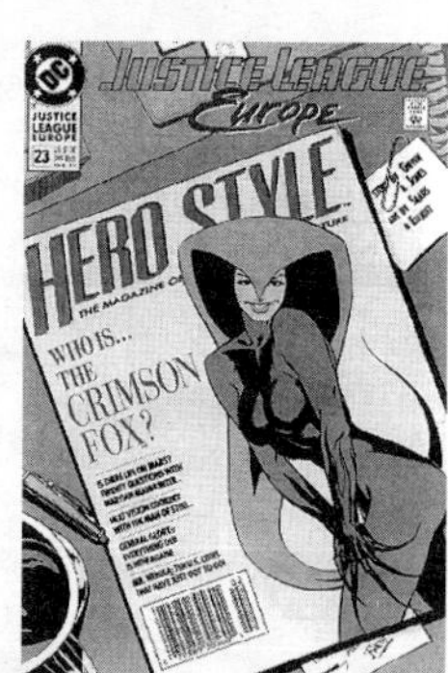

Justice League Europe #23 © DC

Justice League of America #55 © DC

Justice League of America #111 © DC

NOTE: ***Anderson** c-61i. **Austin** a-1i, 60i; c-1i. **Giffen** a-13; c-21p. **Guice** a-62i. **Maguire** a-1-12, 16-19, 22, 23. **Russell** a-Annual 1i; c-54i. **Willingham** a-30p, Annual 2.*

JUSTICE LEAGUE: A MIDSUMMER'S NIGHTMARE
DC Comics: Sept, 1996 - No. 3, Nov, 1996 ($2.95, limited series, 38 pgs.)

1-3: Re-establishes Superman, Batman, Green Lantern, The Martian Manhunter, Flash, Aquaman & Wonder Woman as the Justice League; Mark Waid & Fabian Nicieza co-scripts; Jeff Johnson & Darick Robertson-a(p); Kevin Maguire-c. 5.00
TPB-(1997, $8.95) r/1-3 9.00

JUSTICE LEAGUE EUROPE (Justice League International #51 on)
DC Comics: Apr, 1989 - No. 68, Sept., 1994 (75¢/ $1.00/$1.25/$1.50)

1-Giffen plots in all, breakdowns in #1-8,13-30; Justice League #1-c/swipe 3.00
2-49: 7-9-Batman app. 7,8-JLA x-over. 8,9-Superman app. 12-Metal Men app. 20-22-Rogers-c/a(p). 33,34-Lobo vs. Despero. 37-New team begins; swipes-c to JLA #9; see JLA Spectacular 2.00
50-($2.50, 68 pgs.)-Battles Sonar 2.50
51-68: 68-Zero Hour x-over; Triumph joins Justice League Task Force (See JLTF #17) 2.00
Annual 1-5 ('90-'94, 68 pgs.)-1-Return of the Global Guardians; Giffen plots/ breakdowns. 2-Armageddon 2001; Giffen-a(p); Rogers-a(p); Golden-a(i) 3-Eclipso app. 4-Intro Lionheart. 5-Elseworlds story 3.00

NOTE: ***Phil Jimenez** a-68p. **Rogers** c/a-20-22. **Sears** a-1-12, 14-19, 23-29; c-1-10, 12, 14-19, 23-29.*

JUSTICE LEAGUE INTERNATIONAL (See Justice League Europe)

JUSTICE LEAGUE OF AMERICA (See Brave & the Bold #28-30, Mystery In Space #75 & Official... Index)
National Periodical Publ./DC Comics: Oct-Nov, 1960 - No. 261, Apr, 1987 (#91-99,139-157: 52 pgs.)

	GD2.0	FN6.0	VF8.0	NM9.4
1-(10-11/60)-Origin & 1st app. Despero; Aquaman, Batman, Flash, Green Lantern, J'onn J'onzz, Superman & Wonder Woman continue from Brave and the Bold	240.00	720.00	1560.00	3600.00

	GD2.0	FN6.0	NM9.4
2	58.00	174.00	700.00
3-Origin/1st app. Kanjar Ro (see Mystery in Space #75)(scarce in high grade due to black-c)	48.00	144.00	575.00
4-Green Arrow joins JLA	35.00	105.00	390.00
5-Origin & 1st app. Dr. Destiny	30.00	90.00	300.00
6-8,10: 6-Origin & 1st app. Prof. Amos Fortune. 7-(10-11/61)-Last 10¢ issue. 10-(3/62)-Origin & 1st app. Felix Faust; 1st app. Lord of Time.	26.00	78.00	260.00
9-(2/62)-Origin JLA (1st origin)	36.00	108.00	400.00
11-15: 12-(6/62)-Origin & 1st app. Dr. Light. 13-(8/62)-Speedy app. 14-(9/62)-Atom joins JLA.	18.00	54.00	180.00
16-20: 17-Adam Strange flashback	15.50	47.00	155.00
21-(8/63)-"Crisis on Earth-One"; re-intro. of JSA in this title (see Flash #129) (1st S.A. app. Hourman & Dr. Fate)	30.00	90.00	300.00
22- "Crisis on Earth-Two"; JSA x-over (story continued from #21)	27.00	81.00	270.00
23-28: 24-Adam Strange app. 27-Robin app.	10.50	32.00	105.00
29-JSA x-over; 1st S.A. app. Starman; "Crisis on Earth-Three"	14.00	42.00	140.00
30-JSA x-over	12.00	36.00	120.00
31-Hawkman joins JLA, Hawkgirl cameo (11/64)	9.50	28.50	95.00
32,34: 32-Intro & Origin Brain Storm. 34-Joker-c/sty	6.50	19.50	65.00
33,35,36,40,41: 40-3rd S.A. Penguin app. 41-Intro & origin The Key	6.00	18.00	60.00
37-39: 37,38-JSA x-over (1st S.A. app. Mr. Terrific #37). 37-1st S.A. app. Mr. Terrific; Batman cameo. 38-"Crisis on Earth-A". 39-Giant G-16; r/B&B #28,30 & JLA #5	9.50	28.50	95.00
42-45: 42-Metamorpho app. 43-Intro. Royal Flush Gang	5.00	15.00	50.00
46-JSA x-over; 1st S.A. app. Sandman; 3rd S.A. app. of G.A. Spectre (8/66)	10.00	30.00	100.00
47-JSA x-over; 4th S.A. app of G.A. Spectre.	6.00	18.00	60.00
48-Giant G-29; r/JLA #2,3 & B&B #29	6.00	18.00	60.00
49-54,57,59,60	4.50	13.50	45.00
55-Intro. Earth 2 Robin (1st G.A. Robin in S.A.)	6.00	18.00	60.00
56-JLA vs. JSA (1st G.A. Wonder Woman in S.A.)	5.00	15.00	50.00
58-Giant G-41; r/JLA #6,8,1	5.50	16.50	55.00
61-63,66,68-72: 69-Wonder Woman quits. 71-Manhunter leaves. 72-Last 12¢ issue	3.20	9.60	32.00
64,65-JSA story. 64-(8/68)-Origin/1st app. S.A. Red Tornado	3.50	10.50	35.00
67-Giant G-53; r/JLA #4,14,31	4.50	13.50	45.00
73-1st S.A. app. of G.A. Superman; 1st app. of S. A. Black Canary	3.50	10.50	35.00
74-Black Canary joins; 1st meeting of G.A. & S.A. Superman.	2.80	8.40	28.00
75-2nd app. Green Arrow in new costume (see Brave & the Bold #85)	2.50	7.50	24.00
76-Giant G-65	3.80	11.40	38.00
77-80: 78-Re-intro Vigilante (1st S.A. app?)	2.50	7.50	20.00
81-84,86-90: 82-1st S.A. app. of G.A. Batman (cameo). 83-Death of Spectre. 90-Last 15¢ issue	2.50	7.50	20.00
85,93-(Giant G-77,G-89; 68 pgs.)	3.00	9.00	30.00
91,92: 91-1st meeting of the G.A. & S.A. Robin; begin 25¢, 52 pgs. issues, ends #99. 92-S.A. Robin tries on costume that is similar to that of G.A. Robin in All Star Comics #58.	2.50	7.50	22.00
94-Reprints 1st Sandman story (Adv. #40) & origin/1st app. Starman (Adv. #61); Deadman x-over; N. Adams-a (4 pgs.)	7.00	21.00	70.00
95,96: 95-Origin Dr. Fate & Dr. Midnight -r/ More Fun #67, All-American #25). 96-Origin Hourman (Adv. #48); Wildcat-r	2.70	8.00	27.00
97-99: 97-Origin JLA retold; Sargon, Starman-r. 98-G.A. Sargon, Starman-r. 99-G.A. Sandman, Atom-r; last 52 pg. issue	2.50	7.50	22.00
100-(8/72)-1st meeting of G.A. & S.A. W. Woman	3.20	9.60	32.00
101,102: JSA x-overs. 102-Red Tornado dies	2.00	6.00	16.00
103-106,109: 103-Phantom Stranger joins. 105-Elongated Man joins. 106-New Red Tornado joins. 109-Hawkman resigns	1.50	4.50	12.00
107,108-G.A. Uncle Sam, Black Condor, The Ray, Dollman, Phantom Lady & The Human Bomb (JSA) x-over, 1st S.A. app.	1.75	5.25	14.00
110-116: All 100 pgs. 111-JLA vs. Injustice Gang; Shining Knight, Green Arrow-r. 112-Amazo app; Crimson Avenger, Vigilante-r; origin Starman-r/Adv. #81. 115-Martian Manhunter app.	2.50	7.50	22.00
117-134: 117-Hawkman rejoins. 120,121-Adam Strange app.123-(10/75)-1st named app. Earth-Prime (3rd app. overall) (See Flash; 1st Series #179 & 228); DC editor Julie Schwartz & JLA writers Cary Bates & Elliot S! Maggin appear in story as themselves. 123,124-JLA/JSA app. 125-Two-Face-c/story. 126-Two-Face app. 128-Wonder Woman rejoins. 129-Destruction of Red Tornado	1.00	3.00	8.00
135-136: 135-137-G.A. Bulletman, Bulletgirl, Spy Smasher, Mr. Scarlet, Pinky & Ibis x-over, 1st S.A. appearances	1.25	3.75	10.00
137-Superman battles G.A. Capt. Marvel	1.50	4.50	12.00
138,139-157: 138-Adam Strange app. w/c by Neal Adams; 1st app. Green Lanternof the 73rd Century. 139-157-(52 pgs.): 139-Adam Strange app. 144-Origin retold; origin J'onn J'onzz. 145-Red Tornado resurrected. 147,148-Legion x-over	1.00	3.00	8.00
158-182: 158-160-(44 pgs.). 161-Zatanna joins & new costume. 171-Mr. Terrific murdered. 178-Cover similar to #1; J'onn J'onzz app. 179-Firestorm joins. 181-Green Arrow leaves JLA			4.00
183-185-JSA/New Gods/Darkseid/Mr.Miracle x-over			5.00
186-199: 192,193-Real origin Red Tornado. 193-1st app. All-Star Squadron as free 16 pg. insert			3.00
200 ($1.50, Anniversary issue, 76pgs.)-JLA origin retold; Green Arrow rejoins; Bolland, Broderick, Aparo, Giordano, Gil Kane, Infantino, Kubert-a; Perez-c/a.			4.00
201-259: 203-Intro/origin new Royal Flush Gang. 207,208-JSA, JLA, & All-Star Squadron team-up. 219,220-True origin Black Canary. 228-Re-intro Martian Manhunter. 228-230-War of the Worlds storyline; JLA Satellite destroyed by Martians. 233-Story cont'd from Annual #2. 243-Aquaman leaves. 244,245-Crisis x-over. 250-Batman rejoins. 253-Origin Despero. 258-Death of Vibe. 258-261-Legends x-over			2.00

Justice Society of America (2nd series) #6 © DC

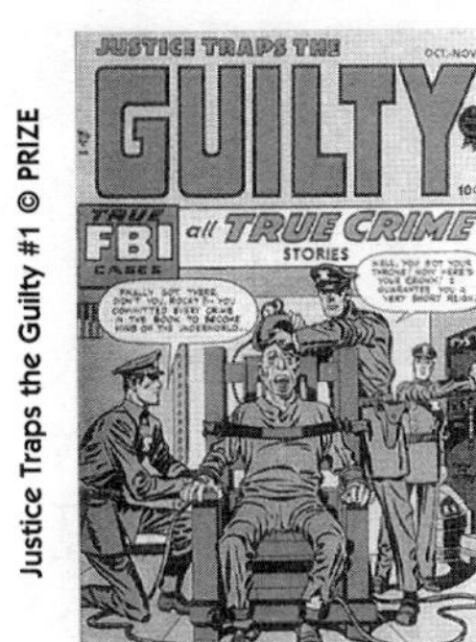

Justice Traps the Guilty #1 © PRIZE

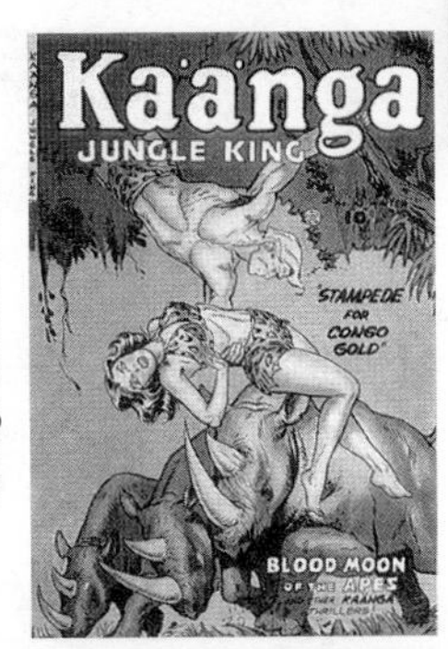

Ka'a'nga Comics #10 © FH

GD2.0 FN6.0 NM9.4

260-Death of Steel 4.00
261-Last issue 2.40 6.00
Annual 1-3 ('83-'85), 2-Intro new J.L.A. (Aquaman, Martian Manhunter, Steel, Gypsy,Vixen, Vibe, Elongated Man, & Zatanna). 3-Crisis x-over 3.00

NOTE: ***Neal Adams*** *c-63, 66, 67, 70, 74, 79, 81, 82, 86-89, 91, 92, 94, 96-98, 138, 139.* ***M. Anderson*** *c-1-4, 6, 7, 10, 12-14.* ***Aparo*** *a-200.* ***Austin*** *a-200i.* ***Baily*** *a-96r.* ***Bolland*** *a-200.* ***Buckler*** *c-158, 163, 164.* ***Burnley*** *r-94, 98, 99.* ***Greene*** *a-46-61i, 64-73i, 110i(r).* ***Grell*** *c-117, 122.* ***Kaluta*** *c-154p.* ***Gil Kane*** *a-200.* ***Krigstein*** *a-96(r/Sensation #84).* ***Kubert*** *a-200; c-72, 73.* ***Nino*** *a-228i, 230i.* ***Orlando*** *c-151i.* ***Perez*** *a-184-186p, 192-197p, 200p; c-184p, 186, 192-195, 196p, 197p, 199, 200, 201p, 202, 203-205p, 207-209, 212-215, 217, 219, 220.* ***Reinman*** *r-97.* ***Roussos*** *a-62i.* ***Sekowsky*** *a-37, 38, 44-63p, 110-112p(r); c-46-48p, 51p.* ***Sekowsky/Anderson*** *c-5, 8, 9, 11, 15.* ***B. Smith*** *c-185i.* ***Starlin*** *c-178-180, 183, 185p.* ***Staton*** *a-244p; c-157p, 244p.* ***Toth*** *r-110.* ***Tuska*** *a-153, 228p, 241-243p. JSA x-overs-21, 22, 29, 30, 37, 38, 46, 47, 55, 56, 64, 65, 73, 74, 82, 83, 91, 92, 100, 101, 102, 107, 108, 110, 113, 115, 123, 124, 135-137, 147, 148, 159, 160, 171, 172, 183-185, 195-197, 207-209, 219, 220, 231, 232, 244.*

JUSTICE LEAGUE OF AMERICA SUPER SPECTACULAR
DC Comics: 1999 ($5.95, mimics format of DC 100 Page Super Spectaculars)

1-Reprints Silver Age JLA and Golden Age JSA 6.00

JUSTICE LEAGUE QUARTERLY (...International Quarterly #6 on)
DC Comics: Winter, 1990-91 - No. 17, Winter, 1994 ($2.95/$3.50, 84 pgs.)

1-12,14-17: 1-Intro The Conglomerate (Booster Gold, Praxis, Gypsy, Vapor, Echo, Maxi-Man, & Reverb); Justice League #1-c/swipe. 1,2-Giffen plots/ breakdowns. 3-Giffen plot; 72 pg. story. 4-Rogers/Russell-a in back-up. 5,6-Waid scripts. 8,17-Global Guardians app. 12-Waid script 3.50
13-Linsner-c 5.00

NOTE: ***Phil Jimenez*** *a-17p.* ***Sprouse*** *a-1p.*

JUSTICE LEAGUE TASK FORCE
DC Comics: June, 1993 - No. 37, Aug, 1996 ($1.25/$1.50/$1.75)

1-16,0,17-37: Aquaman, Nightwing, Flash, J'onn J'onzz, & Gypsy form team. 5,6-Knight-quest tie-ins (new Batman cameo #5, 1 pg.). 15-Triumph cameo. 16-(9/94)-Zero Hour x-over;Triumph app. 0-(10/94). 17-(11/94)-Triumph becomes part of Justice League Task Force (See JLE #68). 26-Impulse app. 35-Warlord app. 37-Triumph quits team 2.00

JUSTICE MACHINE, THE
Noble Comics: June, 1981 - No. 5, Nov, 1983 ($2.00, nos. 1-3 are mag. size)

1-Byrne-c(p) 2.50 7.50 20.00
2-Austinpc(i) 1.50 4.50 12.00
3 1.00 3.00 8.00
4,5, Annual 1 (1/84, 68 pgs.)(published by Texas Comics); 1st app. The Elementals; Golden-c(p) 5.00

JUSTICE MACHINE (Also see The New Justice Machine)
Comico/Innovation Publishing: Jan, 1987 - No. 29, May 1989 ($1.50/$1.75)

1-29 2.25
Annual 1(6/89, $2.50, 36 pgs.)-Last Comico ish. 3.00
Summer Spectacular 1 ('89, $2.75)-Innovation Publ.; Byrne/Gustovich cover 3.00

JUSTICE MACHINE, THE
Innovation Publishing: 1990 - No. 4, 1990 ($1.95/$2.25, deluxe format, mature)

1-4: Gustovich-c/a in all 2.25

JUSTICE MACHINE FEATURING THE ELEMENTALS
Comico: May, 1986 - No. 4, Aug, 1986 ($1.50, limited series)

1-4 2.25

JUSTICE RIDERS
DC Comics: 1997 ($5.95, one-shot, prestige format)

1-Elseworlds; Dixon-s/Williams & Gray-a 2.40 6.00

JUSTICE SOCIETY OF AMERICA (See Adventure #461 & All-Star #3)
DC Comics: April, 1991 - No. 8, Nov, 1991 ($1.00, limited series)

1-8: 1-Flash. 2-Black Canary. 3-Green Lantern. 4-Hawkman. 5-Flash/ Hawkman. 6-Green Lantern/Black Canary. 7-JSA 2.00

JUSTICE SOCIETY OF AMERICA (Also see Last Days of the... Special)
DC Comics: Aug, 1992 - No. 10, May, 1993 ($1.25)

1-10 2.00

GD2.0 FN6.0 NM9.4

JUSTICE TRAPS THE GUILTY (Fargo Kid V11#3 on)
Prize/Headline Publications: Oct-Nov, 1947 - V11#2(#92), Apr-May, 1958 (True FBI Cases)

V2#1-S&K-c/a; electrocution-c 52.00 157.00 420.00
2-S&K-c/a 33.00 99.00 230.00
3-5-S&K-c/a 30.00 90.00 210.00
6-S&K-c/a; Feldstein-a 32.00 96.00 225.00
7,9-S&K-c/a. 7-9-V2#1-3 in indicia; #7-9 on-c 26.00 79.00 185.00
8,10-Krigstein-a; S&K-c. 10-S&K-a 28.00 84.00 195.00
11,18,19-S&K-c 12.00 36.00 85.00
12,14-17,20-No S&K. 14-Severin/Elder-a (8pg.) 6.70 20.00 40.00
13-Used in **SOTI**, pg. 110-111 9.15 27.00 55.00
21,30-S&K-c/a 11.00 33.00 75.00
22,23,27-S&K-c 8.35 25.00 50.00
24-26,28,29,31-50: 28-Kirby-c. 32-Meskin story 5.35 16.00 32.00
51-55,57,59-70 5.00 15.00 30.00
56-Ben Oda, Joe Simon, Joe Genola, Mort Meskin & Jack Kirby app. in police line-up on classic-c 8.35 25.00 50.00
58-Illo. in **SOTI**, "Treating police contemptuously" (top left); text on heroin 26.00 77.00 180.00
71-92: 76-Orlando-a 4.15 12.50 25.00

NOTE: ***Bailey*** *a-12, 13.* ***Elder*** *a-8.* ***Kirby*** *a-19p.* ***Meskin*** *a-22, 27, 63, 64; c-45, 46.* ***Robinson/ Meskin*** *a-5, 19.* ***Severin*** *a-8, 11p. Photo c-12, 15-17.*

JUST MARRIED
Charlton Comics: January, 1958 - No. 114, Dec, 1976

1 5.50 16.50 55.00
2 3.20 9.60 32.00
3-10 2.50 7.50 22.00
11-30 2.00 6.00 16.00
31-50 1.50 4.50 12.00
51-70 1.10 3.30 9.00
71-90 2.40 6.00
91-114 5.00

JUSTY
Viz Comics: Dec 6, 1988 - No. 9, 1989 ($1.75, B&W, bi-weekly mini-series)

1-9: Japanese manga 2.00

KA'A'NGA COMICS (...Jungle King)(See Jungle Comics)
Fiction House Magazines (Glen-Kel Publ. Co.): Spring, 1949 - No. 20, Summer, 1954

1-Ka'a'nga, Lord of the Jungle begins 50.00 150.00 400.00
2 (Winter, '49-'50) 29.00 86.00 200.00
3,4 20.00 60.00 140.00
5-Camilla app. 15.00 45.00 105.00
6-10: 7-Tuska-a. 9-Tabu, Wizard of the Jungle app. 10-Used in **POP**, pg. 99 13.00 39.00 90.00
11-15: 15-Camilla-r by Baker/Jungle #106 11.00 33.00 75.00
16-Sheena app. 11.50 34.00 80.00
17-20 10.00 30.00 70.00
I.W. Reprint #1,8: 1-r/#18; Kinstler-c. 8-r/#10 2.50 7.50 20.00

NOTE: ***Celardo*** *c-1.* ***Whitman*** *c-8-20(most).*

KABOOM
Awesome Entertainment: Sept, 1997 - No. 3, Nov, 1997 ($2.50)

1-3: 1-Matsuda-a/Loeb-s; 4 covers exist (Matsuda, Sale, Pollina and McGuinness), 1-Dynamic Forces Edition, 2-Regular, 2-Alicia Watcher variant-c, 2-Gold logo variant -c, 3-Two covers by Liefeld & Matsuda, 3-Dynamic Forces Ed., Prelude ED. 2.50
Prelude Gold Edition 4.00

KABOOM (2nd series)
Awesome Entertainment: July, 1999 - Present ($2.50)

1,2: 1-Grant-a(p); at least 4 variant covers 2.50

KABUKI
Caliber: Nov, 1994 ($3.50, B&W, one-shot)

nn-(Fear The Reaper) 1st app.; David Mack-c/a/scripts 5.00

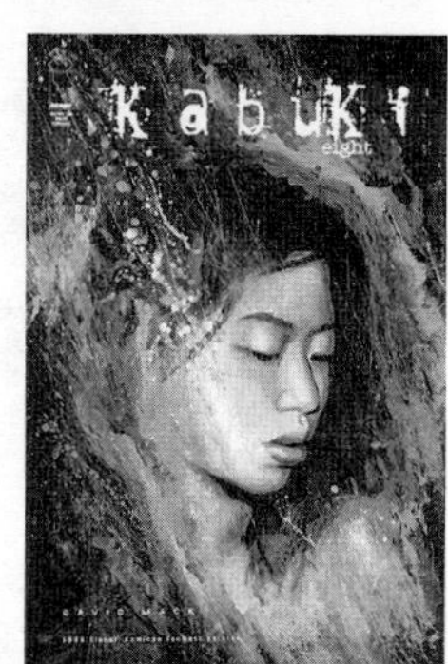

Kabuki #8 © David Mack

Kaos Moon #3 © David Boller

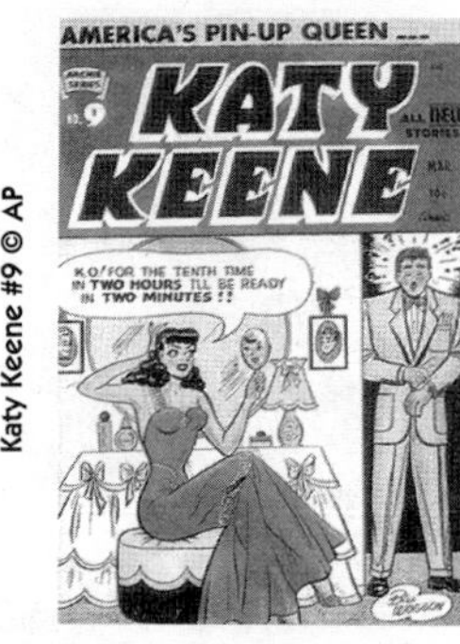

Katy Keene #9 © AP

GD2.0 FN6.0 NM9.4

Color Special (1/96, $2.95)-Mack-c/a/scripts; pin-ups by Tucci, Harris & Quesada 4.00
Gallery (8/95, $2.95)- pinups from Mack, Bradstreet, Paul Pope & others 3.00

KABUKI
Image Comics: Oct, 1997 - Present ($2.95, color)
1-David Mack-c/s/a 4.00
1-($10.00)-Dynamic Forces Edition 10.00
2-8 3.00
...Classics (2/99, $3.95) Reprints Fear the Reaper 4.00
...Classics 2 (3/99, $3.95) Reprints Dance of Dance 4.00
...Classics 3-5 (3-6/99, $4.95) Reprints Circle of Blood-Acts 1-3 5.00
...Classics 6,7 (7,8/99, $3.25) Reprints Circle of Blood-Acts 4,5 3.25
...Images (6/98, $4.95) r/#1 with new pin-ups 5.00
...Images 2 (1/99, $4.95) r/#1 with new pin-ups 5.00
...Reflections 1,2 (7/98, 12/98; $4.95) new story plus art techniques 5.00

KABUKI AGENTS (SCARAB)
Image Comics: Aug, 1999 - Present ($2.95, B&W)
1-David Mack-s/Rick Mays-a 3.00

KABUKI: CIRCLE OF BLOOD
Caliber Press: Jan, 1995 - No. 6, Nov, 1995 ($2.95, B&W)
1-David Mack story/a in all 5.00
2-6: 3-#1on inside indicia. 3.00
6-Variant-c 3.00
TPB ($16.95) r/#1-6, intro. by Steranko 17.00
TPB (1997, $17.95) Image Edition-r/#1-6, intro. by Steranko 18.00
TPB ($24.95) Deluxe Edition 25.00

KABUKI: DANCE OF DEATH
London Night Studios: Jan, 1995 ($3.00, B&W, one-shot)
1-David Mack-c/a/scripts 5.00

KABUKI: DREAMS
Image Comics: Jan, 1998 ($4.95, TPB)
nn-Reprints Color Special & Dreams of the Dead 5.00

KABUKI: DREAMS OF THE DEAD
Caliber: July, 1996 ($2.95, one-shot)
nn-David Mack-c/a/scripts 3.00

KABUKI FAN EDITION
Gemstone Publ./Caliber: Feb, 1997 (mail-in offer, one-shot)
nn-David Mack-c/a/scripts 4.00

KABUKI: MASKS OF THE NOH
Caliber: May, 1996 - No. 4, Feb, 1997 ($2.95, limited series)
1-4: 1-Three-c (1A-Quesada, 1B-Buzz, &1C-Mack). 3-Terry Moore pin-up 3.00
TPB-(4/98, $10.95) r/#1-4; intro by Terry Moore 11.00

KABUKI: SKIN DEEP
Caliber Comics: Oct, 1996 - No. 3, May, 1997 ($2.95)
1-3:David Mack-c/a/scripts. 2-Two-c (1-Mack, 1-Ross) 3.00
TPB-(5/98, $9.95) r/#1-3; intro by Alex Ross 10.00

KAMANDI: AT EARTH'S END
DC Comics: June, 1993 - No. 6, Nov, 1993 ($1.75, limited series)
1-6: Elseworlds storyline 2.50

KAMANDI, THE LAST BOY ON EARTH (Also see Alarming Tales #1, Brave and the Bold #120 & 157 & Cancelled Comic Cavalcade)
National Periodical Publ./DC Comics: Oct-Nov, 1972 - 59, Sept-Oct, 1978
1-Origin & 1st app. Kamandi 3.50 10.50 35.00
2 2.25 6.75 18.00
3-5: 4-Intro. Prince Tuftan of the Tigers 1.25 3.75 10.00
6-10 1.00 3.00 8.00
11-20 1.00 2.80 7.00
21-28,30,31,33-40: 24-Last 20¢ issue. 31-Intro Pyra. 5.00
29,32: 29-Superman x-over. 32-(68 pgs.)-r/origin from #1 plus one new story; 4 pg. biog. of Jack Kirby with B&W photos 1.00 3.00 8.00
41-57 4.00
58-(44 pgs.)-Karate Kid x-over from LSH 1.00 3.00 8.00
59-(44 pgs.)-Cont'd in B&B #157; The Return of Omac back-up by Starlin-c/a(p) 1.00 3.00 8.00
NOTE: ***Ayers*** *a(p)-48-59 (most).* ***Giffen*** *a-44p, 45p.* ***Kirby*** *a-1-40p; c-1-33.* ***Kubert*** *c-34-41.* ***Nasser*** *a-45p, 46p.* ***Starlin*** *a-59p; c-57, 59p.*

KAMUI (Legend Of...#2 on)
Eclipse Comics/Viz Comics: May 12, 1987 - No. 37, Nov. 15, 1988 ($1.50, B&W, bi-weekly)
1-37: 1-3 have 2nd printings 2.00

KAOS MOON (Also see Negative Burn #34)
Caliber Comics: 1996 - No. 4, 1997 ($2.95, B&W)
1-4-David Boller-s/a 3.00
3,4-Limited Alternate-c 4.00
3,4-Gold Alternate-c, Full Circle TPB ($5.95) r/#1,2 2.40 6.00

KARATE KID (See Action, Adventure, Legion of Super-Heroes, & Superboy)
National Periodical Publications/DC Comics: Mar-Apr, 1976 - No. 15, July-Aug, 1978 (Legion spin-off)
1,15: 1-Meets Iris Jacobs; Estrada/Staton-a. 15-Continued into Kamandi #58 1.00 3.00 8.00
2-14: 2-Major Disaster app. 14-Robin x-over 5.00
NOTE: ***Grell*** *c-1-4, 5p, 6p, 7, 8.* ***Staton*** *a-1-9i. Legion x-over-No. 1, 2, 4, 6, 10, 12, 13. Princess Projectra x-over-#8, 9.*

KATHY
Standard Comics: Sept, 1949 - No. 17, Sept, 1955
1-Teen-age 10.00 30.00 60.00
2-Schomburg-c 6.35 19.00 38.00
3-5 4.00 12.00 24.00
6-17: 17-Code approved 3.20 8.00 16.00

KATHY (The Teenage Tornado)
Atlas Comics/Marvel (ZPC): Oct, 1959 - No. 27, Feb, 1964
1-Teen-age 5.50 16.50 55.00
2 2.80 8.40 28.00
3-15 2.25 6.75 18.00
16-27 1.25 3.75 10.00

KAT KARSON
I. W. Enterprises: No date (Reprint)
1-Funny animals 1.50 4.50 12.00

KATO OF THE GREEN HORNET (Also see The Green Hornet)
Now Comics: Nov, 1991 - No. 4, Feb, 1992 ($2.50, mini-series)
1-4: Brent Anderson-c/a 2.50

KATY KEENE (Also see Kasco Komics, Laugh, Pep, Suzie, & Wilbur)
Archie Publ./Close-Up/Radio Comics: 1949 - No. 4, 1951; No. 5, 3/52 - No. 62, Oct, 1961 (50-53-Adventures of...on-c)
1-Bill Woggon-c/a begins; swipes-c to Mopsy #1 94.00 281.00 750.00
2-(1950) 47.00 141.00 375.00
3-5: 3-(1951). 4-(1951) 40.00 120.00 280.00
6-10 33.00 99.00 230.00
11,13-21: 21-Last pre-code issue (3/55) 28.00 84.00 195.00
12-(Scarce) 31.00 94.00 220.00
22-40 20.00 60.00 140.00
41-62: 54-Wedding Album plus wedding pin-up. 62-Robot-c 16.00 47.00 110.00
Annual 1('54, 25¢)-All new stories; last pre-code 44.00 132.00 350.00
Annual 2-6('55-59, 25¢)-All new stories 28.00 84.00 195.00
3-D 1(1953, 25¢, large size)-Came w/glasses 40.00 120.00 285.00
Charm 1(9/58)-Woggon-c/a; new stories, and cut-outs 26.00 79.00 185.00
Glamour 1(1957)-Puzzles, games, cut-outs 26.00 79.00 185.00
Spectacular 1('56) 26.00 79.00 185.00
NOTE: *Debby's Diary in #45, 47-49, 52, 57.*

Katzenjammer Kids #5 © KING

Ka-Zar V1 #12 © MAR

Keen Detective Funnies V2 #9 © CEN

GD2.0 FN6.0 NM9.4

KATY KEENE COMICS DIGEST MAGAZINE
Close-Up, Inc. (Archie Ent.): 1987 - No. 10, July, 1990 ($1.25/$1.35/$1.50, digest size)

1 1.00 2.80 7.00
2-10 4.00

KATY KEENE FASHION BOOK MAGAZINE
Radio Comics/Archie Publications: 1955 - No. 13, Sum, '56 - N. 23, Wint, '58-59 (nn 3-10)

1-Bill Woggon-c/a 44.00 132.00 350.00
2 28.00 84.00 195.00
11-18: 18-Photo Bill Woggon 20.00 60.00 140.00
19-23 16.00 48.00 110.00

KATY KEENE HOLIDAY FUN (See Archie Giant Series Magazine No. 7, 12)

KATY KEENE PINUP PARADE
Radio Comics/Archie Publications: 1955 - No. 15, Summer, 1961 (25¢)
(Cut-out & missing pages are common)

1-Cut-outs in all?; last pre-code issue 44.00 132.00 350.00
2-(1956) 25.00 75.00 175.00
3-5: 3-(1957) 22.00 66.00 155.00
6-10,12-14: 8-Mad parody. 10-Bill Woggon photo 19.00 56.00 130.00
11-Story of how comics get CCA approved, narrated by Katy 24.00 73.00 170.00
15(Rare)-Photo artist & family 40.00 120.00 320.00

KATY KEENE SPECIAL (Katy Keene #7 on; see Laugh Comics Digest)
Archie Ent.: Sept, 1983 - No. 33, 1990 (Later issues published quarterly)

1-Woggon-r; new Woggon-c 4.00
2-33: 3-Woggon-r 2.00

KATZENJAMMER KIDS, THE (See Captain & the Kids & Giant Comic Album)
David McKay Publ./Standard No. 12-21(Spring/'50 - 53)/Harvey No. 22, 4/53 on: 1945-1946; Summer, 1947 - No. 27, Feb-Mar, 1954

Feature Books 30 17.00 51.00 120.00
Feature Books 32,35('45),41,44('46) 16.00 47.00 110.00
Feature Book 37-Has photos & biography of Harold Knerr 17.00 51.00 120.00
1(1947)-All new stories begin 17.00 51.00 120.00
2 10.00 30.00 60.00
3-11 6.35 19.00 38.00
12-14(Standard) 4.35 13.00 28.00
15-21(Standard) 4.00 12.00 24.00
22-25,27(Harvey): 22-24-Henry app. 4.00 11.00 22.00
26-Half in 3-D 19.00 56.00 130.00

KAYO (Formerly Bullseye & Jest; becomes Carnival Comics)
Harry 'A' Chesler: No. 12, Mar, 1945

12-Green Knight, Capt. Glory, Little Nemo (not by McCay) 15.00 45.00 105.00

KA-ZAR (Also see Marvel Comics #1, Savage Tales #6 & X-Men #10)
Marvel Comics Group: Aug, 1970 - No. 3, Mar, 1971 (Giant-Size, 68 pgs.)

1-Reprints earlier Ka-Zar stories; Avengers x-over in Hercules; Daredevil, X-Men app.; hidden profanity-c 2.50 7.50 24.00
2,3-Daredevil-r. 2-r/Daredevil #13 w/Kirby layouts; Ka-Zar origin, Angel-r from X-Men by Tuska. 3-Romita & Heck-a (no Kirby) 2.25 6.75 18.00

NOTE: ***Buscema** r-2. **Colan** a-1p(r). **Kirby** c/a-1, 2. #1-Reprints X-Men #10 & Daredevil #24*

KA-ZAR
Marvel Comics Group: Jan, 1974 - No. 20, Feb, 1977 (Regular Size)

1 1.50 4.50 12.00
2,3-new X-Men Angel; w/death of parents (see Marvel Tales #30) 1.00 3.00 8.00
4-10 2.40 6.00
11-14,16,18-20 4.00
15,17-(Regular 25¢ edition)(8/76) 4.00
15,17-(30¢-c, limited distribution) 1.85 5.50 15.00

NOTE: ***Alcala** a-6i, 8i. **Brunner** c-4. **J. Buscema** a-6-10p; c-1, 5, 7. **Heath** a-12. **G. Kane** c(p)-3, 5, 8-11, 15, 20. **Kirby** c-12p. **Reinman** a-1p.*

KA-ZAR (Volume 2)
Marvel Comics: May, 1997 - No. 20, Dec, 1998 ($1.95/$1.99)

1-Waid-s/Andy Kubert-c/a. thru #4 3.00
1-2nd printing; new cover 2.00
2,4: 2-Two-c 2.00
3-Alpha Flight #1 preview 3.00
5-13,15-20: 8-Includes Spider-Man Cybercomic CD-ROM. 9-11-Thanos app. 15-Priest-s/Martinez & Rodriguez-a begin; Punisher app. 2.00
14-($2.99) Last Waid/Kubert issue; flip book with 2nd story previewing new creative team of Priest-s/Martinez & Rodriguez-a 3.00
'97 Annual ($2.99)-Wraparound-c 3.00

KA-ZAR OF THE SAVAGE LAND
Marvel Comics: Feb, 1997 ($2.50, one-shot)

1-Wraparound-c 2.50

KA-ZAR: SIBLING RIVALRY
Marvel Comics: July, 1997 ($1.95, one-shot)

(# -1)-Flashback story w/Alpha Flight #1 preview 2.00

KA-ZAR THE SAVAGE (See Marvel Fanfare)
Marvel Comics Group: Apr, 1981 - No. 34, Oct, 1984 (Regular size)
(Mando paper #10 on)

1 3.00
2-28,30-34: 11-Origin Zabu. 12-One of two versions with panel missing on pg. 10. 20-Kraven the Hunter-c/story (also apps. in #21). 21-23, 25,26-Spider-Man app. 26-Photo-c. 2.00
12-Version with panel on pg. 10 (1600 printed) 4.00
29-Double size; Ka-Zar & Shanna wed 3.00

NOTE: ***B. Anderson** a-1-15p, 18, 19; c-1-17, 18p, 20(back). **G. Kane** a(back-up)-11, 12, 14.*

KEEN DETECTIVE FUNNIES (Formerly Detective Picture Stories?)
Centaur Publications: No. 8, July, 1938 - No. 24, Sept, 1940

V1#8-The Clock continues-r/Funny Picture Stories #1; Roy Crane-a (1st?) 200.00 600.00 1600.00
9-Tex Martin by Eisner; The Gang Buster app. 81.00 244.00 650.00
10,11: 11-Dean Denton story (begins?) 72.00 216.00 575.00
V2#1,2-The Eye Sees by Frank Thomas begins; ends #23(Not in V2#3&5). 2-Jack Cole-a 66.00 197.00 525.00
3-6: 3-TNT Todd begins. 4-Gabby Flynn begins. 5,6-Dean Denton story 62.00 187.00 500.00
7-The Masked Marvel by Ben Thompson begins (7/39, 1st app.)(scarce) 225.00 675.00 1800.00
8-Nudist ranch panel w/four girls 81.00 244.00 650.00
9-11 69.00 206.00 550.00
12(12/39)-Origin The Eye Sees by Frank Thomas; death of Masked Marvel's sidekick ZL 87.00 262.00 700.00
V3#1,2 66.00 197.00 525.00
18,19,21,22: 18-Bondage/torture-c 66.00 197.00 525.00
20-Classic Eye Sees-c by Thomas 92.00 277.00 740.00
23-Air Man begins (intro); Air Man-c 87.00 262.00 700.00
24-(scarce) Air Man-c 94.00 282.00 750.00

NOTE: ***Burgos** a-V2#2. **Jack Cole** a-V2#2. **Eisner** a-10, V2#6r. **Ken Ernst** a-V2#4-7, 9, 10, 19, 21; c-V2#4. **Everett** a-V2#6, 7, 9, 11, 12, 20. **Guardineer** a-V2#5, 66. **Gustavson** a-V2#4-6. **Simon** c-V3#1. **Thompson** c-V2#7, 9, 10, 22.*

KEEN KOMICS
Centaur Publications: V2#1, May, 1939 - V2#3, Nov, 1939

V2#1(Large size)-Dan Hastings (s/f), The Big Top, Bob Phantom the Magician, The Mad Goddess app. 94.00 281.00 750.00
V2#2(Reg. size)-The Forbidden Idol of Machu Picchu; Cut Carson by Burgos begins 59.00 178.00 475.00
V2#3-Saddle Sniffl by Jack Cole, Circus Pays, Kings Revenge app. 59.00 178.00 475.00

NOTE: ***Binder** a-V2#2. **Burgos** a-V2#2, 3. **Ken Ernst** a-V2#3. **Gustavson** a-V2#2. **Jack Cole** a-V2#3.*

KEEN TEENS (Girls magazine)
Life's Romances Publ./Leader/Magazine Ent.: 1945 - No. 6, Aug-Sept, 1947

Ken Shannon #6 © QUA

Key Comics #3 © Consolidated Magazines

Kid Colt Outlaw #130 © MAR

GD2.0 FN6.0 NM9.4

nn (#1)-14 pgs. Claire Voyant (cont'd. in other nn issue) movie photos, Dotty Dripple, Gertie O'Grady & Sissy; Van Johnson, Frank Sinatra photo-c 26.00 77.00 180.00
nn (#2, 1946)-16 pgs. Claire Voyant & 16 pgs. movie photos 26.00 77.00 180.00
3-6: 4-Glenn Ford photo-c. 5-Perry Como-c 9.15 27.00 55.00

KEIF LLAMA
Oni Press: Mar, 1999 ($2.95, B&W, one-shot)

1-Matt Howarth-s/a 3.00

KELLYS, THE (Formerly Rusty Comics; Spy Cases No. 26 on)
Marvel Comics (HPC): No. 23, Jan, 1950 - No. 25, June, 1950 (52 pgs.)

23-Teenage 11.00 33.00 75.00
24,25: 24-Margie app. 7.50 22.50 45.00

KELVIN MACE
Vortex Publications: 1986 - No. 2, 1986 ($2.00, B&W)

1,2: 1-(B&W). 1-2nd print (1/87, $1.75). 2-(Color) 2.00

KEN MAYNARD WESTERN (Movie star)(See Wow Comics, 1936)
Fawcett Publ.: Sept, 1950 - No. 8, Feb, 1952 (All 36 pgs; photo front/back-c)

1-Ken Maynard & his horse Tarzan begin 56.00 169.00 450.00
2 37.00 111.00 260.00
3-8: 6-Atomic bomb explosion panel 29.00 86.00 200.00

KEN SHANNON (Becomes Gabby #11 on) (Also see Police Comics #103)
Quality Comics Group: Oct, 1951 - No. 10, Apr, 1953 (A private eye)

1-Crandall-a 35.00 105.00 245.00
2-Crandall c/a(2) 29.00 86.00 200.00
3-5-Crandall-a. 3-Horror-c 19.00 58.00 135.00
6-Crandall-c/a; "The Weird Vampire Mob"-c/s 21.00 64.00 150.00
7,10: 7-Crandall-a. 10-Crandall-c 16.00 47.00 110.00
8,9: 8-Opium den drug use story 15.00 45.00 105.00

NOTE: ***Crandall/Cuidera** c-1-10. **Jack Cole** a-1-9. #1-15 published after title change to Gabby.*

KEN STUART
Publication Enterprises: Jan, 1949 (Sea Adventures)

1-Frank Borth-c/a 10.00 30.00 60.00

KENT BLAKE OF THE SECRET SERVICE (Spy)
Marvel/Atlas Comics(20CC): May, 1951 - No. 14, July, 1953

1-Injury to eye, bondage, torture; Brodsky-c 19.00 56.00 130.00
2-Drug use w/hypo scenes; Brodsky-c 13.00 39.00 90.00
3-14: 8-R.Q. Sale-a (2 pgs.) 8.35 25.00 50.00

NOTE: ***Heath** c-5, 7, 8. **Infantino** c-12. **Maneely** c-3. **Sinnott** a-2(3). **Tuska** a-8(3pg.).*

KENTS, THE
DC Comics: Aug, 1997 - No. 12, July, 1998 ($2.50, limited series)

1-12-Ostrander-s/art by Truman and Bair (#1-8), Mandrake (#9-12) 3.00
TPB ($19.95) r/#1-12 19.95

KERRY DRAKE (Also see A-1 Comics)
Argo: Jan, 1956 - No. 2, March, 1956

1,2-Newspaper-r 7.500 22.50 45.00

KERRY DRAKE DETECTIVE CASES (...Racket Buster No. 32,33)
(Also see Chamber of Clues & Green Hornet Comics #42-47)
Life's Romances/Com/Magazine Ent. No.1-5/Harvey No.6 on: 1944 - No. 5, 1944; No. 6, Jan, 1948 - No. 33, Aug, 1952

nn(1944)(A-1 Comics)(slightly over-size) 27.00 81.00 190.00
2 17.00 51.00 120.00
3-5(1944) 14.00 43.00 100.00
6,8(1948): Lady Crime by Powell. 8-Bondage-c 10.00 30.00 60.00
7-Kubert-a; biog of Andriola (artist) 11.00 33.00 75.00
9,10-Two-part marijuana story; Kerry smokes marijuana in #10 14.00 43.00 100.00
11-15 9.15 27.00 55.00
16-30 6.70 20.00 40.00
31-33 7.00 21.00 42.00

NOTE: ***Andiola** c-6-9. **Berg** a-5. **Powell** a-10-23, 28, 29.*

GD2.0 FN6.0 NM9.4

KEWPIES
Will Eisner Publications: Spring, 1949

1-Feiffer-a; Kewpie Doll ad on back cover 43.00 128.00 340.00

KEY COMICS
Consolidated Magazines: Jan, 1944 - No. 5, Aug, 1946

1-The Key, Will-O-The-Wisp begin 40.00 120.00 280.00
2 (3/44) 20.00 60.00 140.00
3,4: 4-(5/46)-Origin John Quincy The Atom (begins); Walter Johnson c-3-5 17.00 51.00 120.00
5-4pg. Faust Opera adaptation; Kiefer-a; back-c advertises "Masterpieces Illustrated" by Lloyd Jacquet after he left Classic Comics (no copies of Masterpieces Illustrated known) 23.00 69.00 160.00

KEY RING COMICS
Dell Publishing Co.: 1941 (16 pgs.; two colors) (sold 5 for 10¢)

1-Sky Hawk, 1-Viking Carter, 1-Features Sleepy Samson, 1-Origin Greg Gilday-r/War Comics #2, 1-Radior (Super hero) 5.00 15.00 30.00

NOTE: *Each book has two holes in spine to put in binder.*

KICKERS, INC.
Marvel Comics Group: Nov, 1986 - No. 12, Oct, 1987

1-12 2.00

KID CARROTS
St. John Publishing Co.: September, 1953

1-Funny animal 5.85 17.50 35.00

KID COLT OUTLAW (Kid Colt #1-4; ...Outlaw #5-on)(Also see All Western Winners, Best Western, Black Rider, Giant-Size..., Two-Gun Kid, Two-Gun Western, Western Winners, Wild Western, Wisco)
Marvel Comics(LCC) 1-16; Atlas(LMC) 17-102; Marvel 103-on: 8/48 - No. 139, 3/68; No. 140, 11/69 - No. 229, 4/79

1-Kid Colt & his horse Steel begin. 94.00 281.00 750.00
2 42.00 127.00 340.00
3-5: 4-Anti-Wertham editorial; Tex Taylor app. 5-Blaze Carson app. 37.00 111.00 260.00
6-8: 6-Tex Taylor app; 7-Nimo the Lion begins, ends #10 24.00 73.00 170.00
9,10 (52 pgs.) 24.00 73.00 170.00
11-Origin 29.00 86.00 200.00
12-20 19.00 56.00 130.00
21-32 15.00 45.00 105.00
33-45: Black Rider in all 11.50 34.00 80.00
46,47,49,50 10.00 30.00 65.00
48-Kubert-a 10.00 30.00 70.00
51-53,55,56 8.35 25.00 50.00
54-Williamson/Maneely-c 10.00 30.00 60.00
57-60,66: 4-pg. Williamson-a in all 6.50 19.50 65.00
61-63,67-78,80-86: 70-Severin-c. 73-Maneely-c. 86-Kirby-a(r). 3.80 11.40 38.00
64,65-Crandall-a 4.20 12.60 42.00
79,87: 79-Origin retold. 87-Davis-a(r) 4.20 12.60 42.00
88,89-Williamson-a in both (4 pgs.). 89-Redrawn Matt Slade #2 4.80 14.40 48.00
90-99,101: 91-Kirby/Ayers-c. 95-Kirby/Ayers-c/story. 101-Last 10¢ issue 2.80 8.40 28.00
100 3.50 10.50 35.00
101-109,111-120: 107-Only Kirby sci-fi cover of title; Kirby -a. 114-(1/64)-2nd app. Iron Mask 2.50 7.50 24.00
110-(5/63)-1st app. Iron Mask (Iron Man type villain) 2.80 8.40 28.00
121-129,133-139: 121-Rawhide Kid x-over. 125-Two-Gun Kid x-over 139-Last 12¢ issue 2.00 6.00 16.00
130-132 (68 pgs.)-one new story each. 130-Origin 2.50 7.50 24.00
140-155: 140-Reprints begin (later issues all-r). 155-Last 15¢ issue 1.50 4.50 12.00
156-Giant; reprints 2.25 6.75 18.00
157-180,200: 170-Origin retold. 1.50 4.50 12.00

Kid Cowboy #10 © Z-D

Kid Eternity #11 © QUA

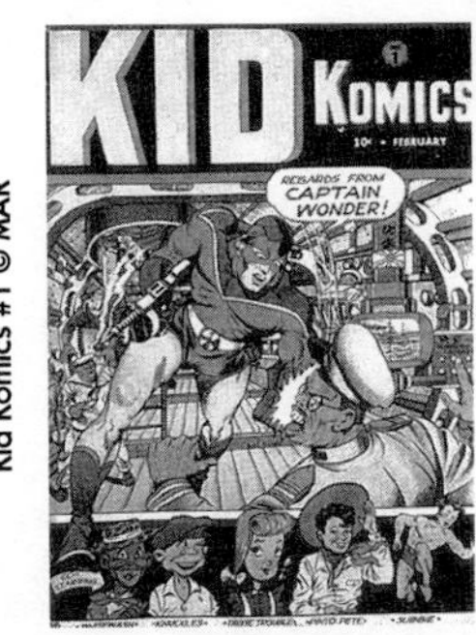

Kid Komics #1 © MAR

GD2.0 FN6.0 NM9.4

181-199 1.25 3.75 10.00
201-229: 229-Rawhide Kid-r 1.00 2.80 7.00
...Album (no date; 1950's; Atlas Comics)-132 pgs.; random binding, cardboard cover, B&W stories; contents can vary (Rare) 75.00 225.00 600.00

*NOTE: **Ayers** a-many. **Colan** a-52, 53; c(p)-223, 228, 229. **Crandall** a-140r, 167r. **Everett** a-90, 137i, 225i(r). **Heath** a-8(2); c-34, 35, 39, 44, 46, 48, 49, 57, 64. **Heck** a-135, 139. **Jack Keller** a-25(2), 26-68(3-4), 78, 94p, 98, 99, 108, 110, 130, 132, 140-150r. **Kirby** a-86r, 93, 96, 107, 119, 176(part); c-87, 92-95, 97, 99-112, 114-117, 121-123, 197r; w/**Ditko** c-89. **Maneely** a-12, 68, 81; c-17, 19, 40-43, 47, 52, 53, 62, 65, 68, 78, 81, 142r, 150r. **Morrow** a-173r, 216r. **Rico** a-13, 18. **Severin** c-58, 59, 143, 148, 149i. **Shores** a-39, 41-43, 143r; c-1-10(most), 24. **Sutton** a-136, 137p, 225p(r). **Wildey** a-47, 54, 82, 144r. **Williamson** r-147, 170, 172, 216. **Woodbridge** a-64, 81. Black Rider in #33-45, 74, 86. Iron Mask in #110, 114, 121, 127. Sam Hawk in #84, 101, 111, 121, 146, 174, 181, 188.*

KID COWBOY (Also see Approved Comics #4 & Boy Cowboy)
Ziff-Davis Publ./St. John (Approved Comics): 1950 - No. 14, 1954 (Painted covers #1-10, 14)

1-Lucy Belle & Red Feather begin 14.00 43.00 100.00
2-Maneely-c 10.00 30.00 60.00
3-14: 5-Berg-a. 14-Code approved 8.35 25.00 50.00

KID DEATH & FLUFFY HALLOWEEN SPECIAL
Event Comics: Oct, 1997 ($2.95, B&W, one-shot)

1-Variant-c by Cebollero & Quesada/Palmiotti 3.00

KID DEATH & FLUFFY SPRING BREAK SPECIAL
Event Comics: July, 1996 ($2.50, B&W, one-shot)

1-Quesada & Palmiotti-c/scripts 2.50

KIDDIE KAPERS
Kiddie Kapers Co., 1945/Decker Publ. (Red Top-Farrell): 1945?(nd); Oct, 1957; 1963 - 1964

1(nd, 1945-46?, 36 pgs.)-Infinity-c; funny animal 7.50 22.50 45.00
1(10/57)(Decker)-Little Bit-r from Kiddie Karnival 4.00 12.00 24.00
Super Reprint #7, 10('63), 12, 14('63), 15,17('64), 18('64): 10, 14-r/Animal Adventures #1. 15-Animal Adventures #? 17-Cowboys 'N' Injuns #? 1.25 3.75 10.00

KIDDIE KARNIVAL
Ziff-Davis Publ. Co. (Approved Comics): 1952 (25¢, 100 pgs.) (One Shot)

nn-Rebound Little Bit #1,2; painted-c 36.00 107.00 250.00

KID ETERNITY (Becomes Buccaneers) (See Hit Comics)
Quality Comics Group: Spring, 1946 - No. 18, Nov, 1949

1 81.00 244.00 650.00
2 40.00 120.00 280.00
3-Mac Raboy-a 40.00 120.00 300.00
4-10 24.00 71.00 165.00
11-18 18.00 54.00 125.00

KID ETERNITY
DC Comics: 1991 - No. 3, Nov, 1991 ($4.95, limited series)

1-3: Grant Morrison scripts 6.00

KID ETERNITY
DC Comics (Vertigo): May, 1993 - No. 16, Sept, 1994 ($1.95, mature)

1-16: 1-Gold ink-c. 6-Photo-c. All Sean Phillips-c/a except #15 (Phillips-c/i only) 2.00

KID FROM DODGE CITY, THE
Atlas Comics (MMC): July, 1957 - No. 2, Sept, 1957

1-Don Heck-c 10.00 30.00 60.00
2-Everett-c 5.85 17.50 35.00

KID FROM TEXAS, THE (A Texas Ranger)
Atlas Comics (CSI): June, 1957 - No. 2, Aug, 1957

1-Powell-a; Severin-c 10.00 30.00 65.00
2 5.85 17.50 35.00

KID KOKO
I. W. Enterprises: 1958

Reprint #1,2-(r/M.E.'s Koko & Kola #4, 1947) 1.25 3.75 10.00

GD2.0 FN6.0 NM9.4

KID KOMICS (Kid Movie Komics No. 11)
Timely Comics (USA 1,2/FCI 3-10): Feb, 1943 - No. 10, Spring, 1946

1-Origin Captain Wonder & sidekick Tim Mullrooney, & Subbie; intro the Sea-Going Lad, Pinto Pete, & Trixie Trouble; Knuckles & Whitewash Jones (from Young Allies) app.; Wolverton-a (7 pgs.) 355.00 1067.00 3200.00
2-The Young Allies, Red Hawk, & Tommy Tyme begin; last Captain Wonder & Subbie 162.00 487.00 1300.00
3-The Vision, Daredevils & Red Hawk app. 125.00 375.00 1000.00
4-The Destroyer begins; Sub-Mariner app.; Red Hawk & Tommy Tyme end 106.00 319.00 850.00
5,6: 5-Tommy Tyme begins, ends #10 81.00 244.00 650.00
7-10: 7,10-The Whizzer app. Destroyer not in #7,8. 10-Last Destroyer, Young Allies & Whizzer 75.00 225.00 600.00

*NOTE: **Brodsky** c-5. **Schomburg** c-2-4, 6-10. **Shores** c-1. Captain Wonder c-1, 2. The Young Allies c-3-10.*

KID MONTANA (Formerly Davy Crockett Frontier Fighter; The Gunfighters No. 51 on)
Charlton Comics: V2#9, Nov, 1957 - No. 50, Mar, 1965

V2#9 4.00 12.00 40.00
10 3.00 9.00 30.00
11,12,14-20 2.50 7.50 20.00
13-Williamson-a 3.00 9.00 30.00
21-35 1.75 5.25 14.00
36-50 1.10 3.30 9.00

NOTE: Title change to Montana Kid on cover only #44 & 45; remained Kid Montana on inside.

KID MOVIE KOMICS (Formerly Kid Komics; Rusty Comics #12 on)
Timely Comics: No. 11, Summer, 1946

11-Silly Seal & Ziggy Pig; 2 pgs. Kurtzman "Hey Look" plus 6 pg. "Pigtales" story 25.00 75.00 175.00

KIDNAPPED (Robert Louis Stevenson's...also see Movie Comics)(Disney)
Dell Publishing Co.: No. 1101, May, 1960

Four Color 1101-Movie, photo-c 5.50 16.50 60.00

KIDNAP RACKET (See Harvey Comics Hits No. 57)

KID SLADE GUNFIGHTER (Formerly Matt Slade...)
Atlas Comics (SPI): No. 5, Jan, 1957 - No. 8, July, 1957

5-Maneely, Roth, Severin-a in all; Maneely-c 11.50 34.00 80.00
6,8-Severin-c 6.70 20.00 40.00
7-Williamson/Mayo-a, 4 pgs. 10.00 30.00 65.00

KID SUPREME (See Supreme)
Image Comics (Extreme Studios): Mar, 1996 - No. 3, July, 1996 ($2.50)

1-3: Fraga-a/scripts. 3-Glory-c/app. 2.50

KID TERRIFIC
Image Comics: Nov, 1998 ($2.95, B&W)

1-Snyder & Diliberto-s/a 3.00

KID ZOO COMICS
Street & Smith Publications: July, 1948 (52 pgs.)

1-Funny Animal 26.00 77.00 180.00

KILLER (...Tales By Timothy Truman)
Eclipse Comics: March, 1985 ($1.75, one-shot, Baxter paper)

1-Timothy Truman-c/a 2.00

KILLER INSTINCT (Video game)
Acclaim Comics: June, 1996 - Present ($2.50, limited series)

1-6: 1-Bart Sears-a(p). 4-Special #1. 5-Special #2. 6-Special #3 3.00

KILLERS, THE
Magazine Enterprises: 1947 - No. 2, 1948 (No month)

1-Mr. Zin, the Hatchet Killer; mentioned in **SOTI**, pgs. 179,180; used by N.Y. Legis. Comm.; L. B. Cole-c 94.00 281.00 750.00
2-(Scarce)-Hashish smoking story; "Dying, Dying, Dead" drug story; Whitney, Ingels-a; Whitney hanging-c 81.00 244.00 650.00

KILLING JOKE, THE (See Batman: The Killing Joke under Batman one-shots)

King Comics #39 © KING

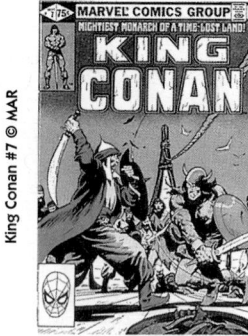

King Conan #7 © MAR

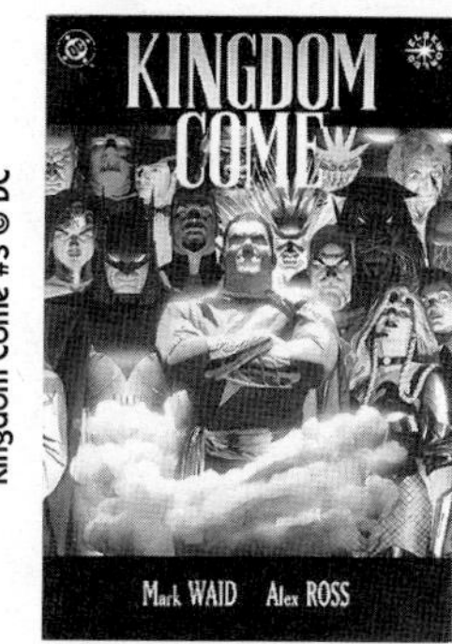

Kingdom Come #3 © DC

GD2.0 FN6.0 NM9.4

KILLPOWER: THE EARLY YEARS
Marvel Comics UK: Sept, 1993 - No. 4, Dec, 1993 ($1.75, mini-series)

	GD2.0	FN6.0	NM9.4
1-($2.95)-Foil embossed-c			3.00
2-4: 2-Genetix app. 3-Punisher app.			2.00

KILLRAZOR
Image Comics (Top Cow Productions): Aug, 1995 ($2.50, one-shot)

	GD2.0	FN6.0	NM9.4
1			2.50

KILL YOUR BOYFRIEND
DC Comics (Vertigo): June, 1995 ($4.95, one-shot)

	GD2.0	FN6.0	NM9.4
1-Grant Morrison story		2.40	6.00
1($5.95, 1998) 2nd printing			6.00

KILROY (Volume 2)
Caliber Press: 1998 ($2.95, B&W)

	GD2.0	FN6.0	NM9.4
1-Pruett-s			3.00

KILROY IS HERE
Caliber Press: 1995 ($2.95, B&W)

	GD2.0	FN6.0	NM9.4
1-10			3.00

KILROYS, THE
B&I Publ. Co. No. 1-19/American Comics Group: June-July, 1947 - No. 54, June-July, 1955

	GD2.0	FN6.0	NM9.4
1	21.00	64.00	150.00
2	11.00	33.00	75.00
3-5: 5-Gross-a	9.15	27.00	55.00
6-10: 8-Milt Gross's Moronica	6.70	20.00	40.00
11-20: 14-Gross-a	5.85	17.50	35.00
21-30	4.25	13.00	26.00
31-47,50-54	4.00	12.00	24.00
48,49-(3-D effect-c/stories)	17.00	49.00	115.00

KILROY: THE SHORT STORIES
Caliber Press: 1995 ($2.95, B&W)

	GD2.0	FN6.0	NM9.4
1			3.00

KINDRED, THE
Image Comics (WildStorm Productions): Mar, 1994 - No. 4, July, 1995 ($1.95, limited series)

	GD2.0	FN6.0	NM9.4
1-($2.50)-Grifter & Backlash app. in all; bound-in trading card			2.50
2-4			2.50
2,3: 2-Variant-c. 3-Alternate-c by Portacio, see Deathblow #5			4.00
Trade paperback (2/95, $9.95)			10.00

NOTE: ***Booth** c/a-1-4. The first four issues contain coupons redeemable for a Jim Lee Grifter/Backlash print.*

KING ARTHUR AND THE KNIGHTS OF JUSTICE
Marvel Comics UK: Dec, 1993 - No. 3, Feb, 1994 ($1.25, limited series)

	GD2.0	FN6.0	NM9.4
1-3: TV adaptation			2.00

KING CLASSICS
King Features : 1977 (36 pgs., cardboard-c)
(Printed in Spain for U.S. distr.)

1-Connecticut Yankee, 2-Last of the Mohicans, 3-Moby Dick, 4-Robin Hood, 5-Swiss Family Robinson, 6-Robinson Crusoe, 7-Treasure Island, 8-20,000 Leagues, 9-Christmas Carol, 10-Huck Finn, 11-Around the World in 80 Days, 12-Davy Crockett, 13-Don Quixote, 14-Gold Bug, 15-Ivanhoe, 16-Three Musketeers, 17-Baron Munchausen, 18-Alice in Wonderland, 19-Black Arrow, 20-Five Weeks in a Balloon, 21-Great Expectations, 22-Gulliver's Travels, 23-Prince & Pauper, 24-Lawrence of Arabia (Originals, 1977-78)

	GD2.0	FN6.0	NM9.4
each....	1.25	3.75	10.00
Reprints (1979; HRN-24)	1.00	2.80	7.00

NOTE: *The first eight issues were not numbered. Issues No. 25-32 were advertised but not published. The 1977 originals have HRN 32a; the 1978 originals have HRN 32b.*

KING COLT (See Luke Short's Western Stories)

KING COMICS (Strip reprints)
David McKay Publications/Standard #156-on: 4/36 - No. 155, 11-12/49; No. 156, Spr/50 - No. 159, 2/52 (Winter on-c)

	GD2.0	FN6.0	VF8.0
1-1st app. Flash Gordon by Alex Raymond; Brick Bradford (1st app.), Popeye, Henry (1st app.) & Mandrake the Magician (1st app.) begin; Popeye-c begin	1125.00	3375.00	7500.00

	GD2.0	FN6.0	NM9.4
2	329.00	987.00	2350.00
3	214.00	642.00	1550.00
4	164.00	492.00	1200.00
5	121.00	363.00	875.00
6-10: 9-X-Mas-c	86.00	258.00	625.00
11-20	67.00	200.00	480.00
21-30: 21-X-Mas-c	49.00	147.00	350.00
31-40: 33-Last Segar Popeye	39.00	117.00	280.00
41-50: 46-Text illos by Marge Buell contain characters similar to Lulu, Alvin & Tubby. 50-The Lone Ranger begins	31.00	92.00	240.00
51-60: 52-Barney Baxter begins?	21.00	64.00	160.00
61-The Phantom begins	19.00	58.00	150.00
62-80: 76-Flag-c. 79-Blondie begins	16.00	48.00	120.00
81-99	13.00	38.00	95.00
100	15.00	46.00	115.00
101-114: 114-Last Raymond issue (1 pg.); Flash Gordon by Austin Briggs begins, ends #155	11.00	34.00	85.00
115-145: 117-Phantom origin retold	9.30	28.00	65.00
146,147-Prince Valiant in both	7.15	21.50	50.00
148-155: 155-Flash Gordon ends (11-12/49)	7.15	21.50	50.00
156-159: 156-New logo begins (Standard)	6.50	19.50	45.00

NOTE: *Marge Buell text illos in No. 24-46 at least.*

KING CONAN (Conan The King No. 20 on)
Marvel Comics Group: Mar, 1980 - No. 19, Nov, 1983 (52 pgs.)

	GD2.0	FN6.0	NM9.4
1			4.00
2-19: 4-Death of Thoth Amon. 7-1st Paul Smith-a, 1 pg. pin-up (9/81)			2.00

NOTE: ***J. Buscema** a-1-9p, 17p; c(p)-1-5, 7-9, 14, 17. **Kaluta** c-19. **Nebres** a-17i, 18, 19i. **Severin** c-18. **Simonson** c-6.*

KINGDOM, THE
DC Comics: Feb, 1999 - No. 2, Feb, 1999 ($2.95, limited series)

	GD2.0	FN6.0	NM9.4
1,2-Waid-s; sequel to Kingdom Come; introduces Hypertime			4.00
...: Kid Flash 1 (2/99, $1.99) Waid-s/Pararillo-a, ...: Nightstar 1 (2/99, $1.99) Waid-s/Haley-a, ...: Offspring 1 (2/99, $1.99) Waid-s/Quitely-a, ...: Planet Krypton 1 (2/99, $1.99) Waid-s/Kitson-a, ...: Son of the Bat 1 (2/99, $1.99) Waid-s/Apthorp-a			2.00

KINGDOM COME
DC Comics: 1996 - No. 4, 1996 ($4.95, painted limited series)

	GD2.0	FN6.0	NM9.4
1- Mark Waid scripts & Alex Ross-painted c/a in all; tells the last days of the DC Universe; 1st app. Magog	1.25	3.75	10.00
2-Superman forms new Justice League	1.25	3.75	10.00
3-Return of Capt. Marvel	1.00	3.00	8.00
4-Final battle of Superman and Capt. Marvel	1.00	3.00	8.00
Deluxe Slipcase Edition-($89.95) w/Revelations companion book, 12 new story pages, foil stamped covers, signed and numbered			150.00
Hardcover Edition-($29.95)-Includes 12 new story pages and artwork from Revelations, new cover artwork with gold foil inlay			35.00
Hardcover 2nd printing			30.00
Softcover Ed.-($14.95)-Includes 12 new story pgs. & artwork from Revelations, new c-artwork			15.00

KING KONG (See Movie Comics)

KING LEONARDO & HIS SHORT SUBJECTS (TV)
Dell Publishing Co./Gold Key: Nov-Jan, 1961-62 - No. 4, Sept, 1963

	GD2.0	FN6.0	NM9.4
Four Color 1242,1278	13.00	38.00	140.00
01390-207(5-7/62)(Dell)	10.00	30.00	110.00
1 (10/62)	10.50	32.00	115.00
2-4	8.25	25.00	90.00

KING LOUIE & MOWGLI (See Jungle Book under Movie Comics)
Gold Key: May, 1968 (Disney)

	GD2.0	FN6.0	NM9.4
1 (#10223-805)-Characters from Jungle Book	2.50	7.50	22.00

KING OF DIAMONDS (TV)

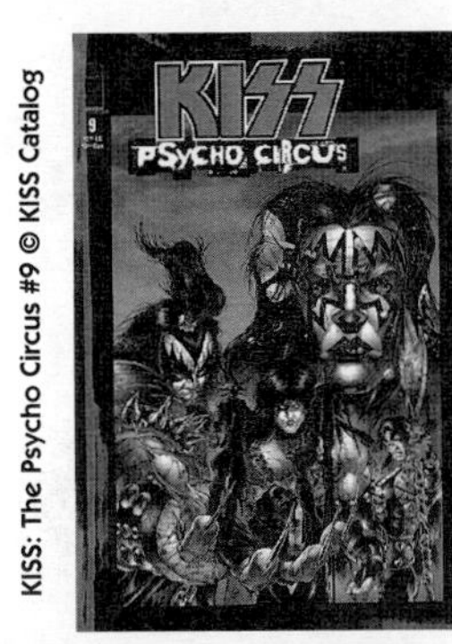

KISS: The Psycho Circus #9 © KISS Catalog

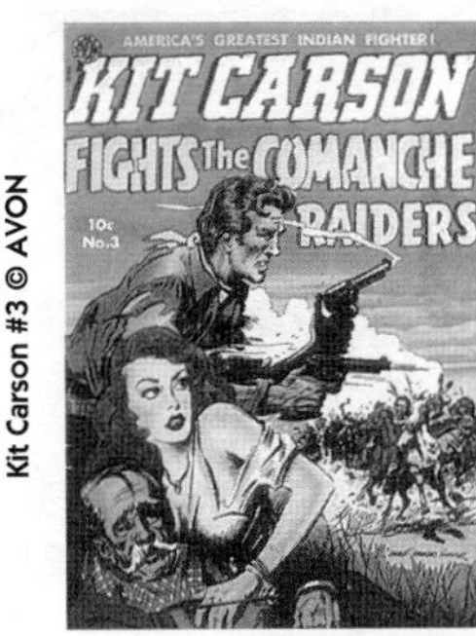

Kit Carson #3 © AVON

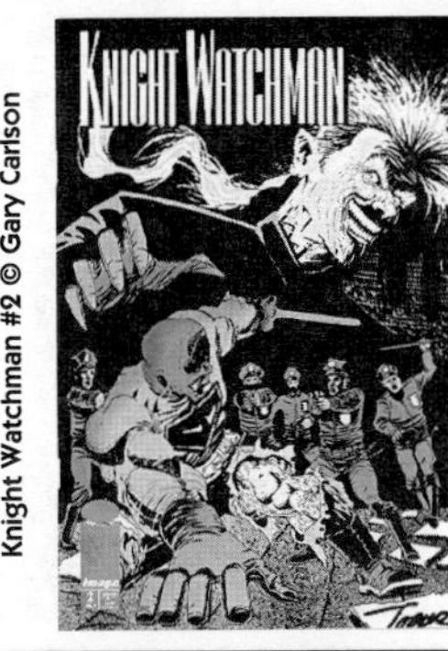

Knight Watchman #2 © Gary Carlson

Dell Publishing Co.: July-Sept, 1962

01-391-209-Photo-c 3.20 9.50 35.00

KING OF KINGS (Movie)
Dell Publishing Co.: No. 1236, Oct-Nov, 1961

Four Color 1236-Photo-c 7.00 22.00 80.00

KING OF THE BAD MEN OF DEADWOOD
Avon Periodicals: 1950 (See Wild Bill Hickok #16)

nn-Kinstler-c; Kamen/Feldstein-r/Cowpuncher #2 15.00 45.00 105.00

KING OF THE ROYAL MOUNTED (See Famous Feature Stories, King Comics, Red Ryder #3 & Super Book #2, 6)

KING OF THE ROYAL MOUNTED (Zane Grey's...)
David McKay/Dell Publishing Co.: No. 1, May, 1937; No. 9, 1940; No. 207, Dec, 1948 - No. 935, Sept-Nov, 1958

Feature Books 1 (5/37)(McKay) 68.00 205.00 750.00
Large Feature Comic 9 (1940) 36.00 109.00 400.00
Four Color 207(#1, 12/48) 14.00 41.00 150.00
Four Color 265,283 7.00 22.00 80.00
Four Color 310,340 5.50 16.50 60.00
Four Color 363,384, 8(6-8/52)-10 4.50 13.50 50.00
11-20 3.00 9.00 35.00
21-28(3-5/58), Four Color 935(9-11/58) 2.75 8.00 30.00
NOTE: *4-Color No. 207, 265, 283, 310, 340, 363, 384 are all newspaper reprints with* ***Jim Gary*** *art. No. 8 on are all Dell originals. Painted c-No. 9-on.*

KINGPIN
Marvel Comics: Nov, 1997 ($5.99, squarebound, one-shot)

nn-Spider-Man & Daredevil vs. Kingpin; Stan Lee-s/ John Romita Sr.-a 2.40 6.00

KING RICHARD & THE CRUSADERS
Dell Publishing Co.: No. 588, Oct, 1954

Four Color 588-Movie, Matt Baker-a, photo-c 9.00 27.00 100.00

KINGS OF THE NIGHT
Dark Horse Comics: 1990 - No. 2, 1990 ($2.25, limited series)

1,2-Robert E. Howard adaptation; Bolton-c 2.25

KING SOLOMON'S MINES (Movie)
Avon Periodicals: 1951

nn (#1 on 1st page) 39.00 116.00 270.00

KING TIGER & MOTORHEAD
Dark Horse Comics: Aug, 1996 - No. 2, Sept, 1996 ($2.95, limited series)

1,2: Chichester scripts 3.00

KIPLING, RUDYARD (See Mowgli, The Jungle Book)

KISS (See Crazy Magazine, Howard the Duck #12, 13, Marvel Comics Super Special #1, 5, Rock Fantasy Comics #10 & Rock N' Roll Comics #9)

KISS: THE PSYCHO CIRCUS
Image Comics: Aug, 1997 - Present ($1.95/$2.25)

1-Holguin-s/Medina-a(p) 1.50 4.50 12.00
1-2nd & 3rd printings 2.50
2 1.00 2.80 7.00
3,4: 4-Photo-c 5.00
5-8: 5-Begin $2.25-c 4.00
9-23 3.00
Book 1 TPB ('98, $12.95) r/#1-6 13.00
Book 2 Destroyer TPB (8/99, $9.95) r/#10-13 10.00
...Magazine 1 ($6.95) r/#1-3 plus interviews 7.00
...Magazine 2,3 ($4.95) 2-r/#4,5 plus interviews. 3-r/#6,7 5.00

KISSYFUR (TV)
DC Comics: 1989 (Sept.) ($2.00, 52 pgs., one-shot)

1-Based on Saturday morning cartoon 2.50

KIT CARSON (Formerly All True Detective Cases No. 4; Fighting Davy Crockett No. 9; see Blazing Sixguns & Frontier Fighters)
Avon Periodicals: 1950; No. 2, 8/51 - No. 3, 12/51; No. 5, 11-12/54 - No. 8, 9/55 (No #4)

nn(#1) (1950)- "...Indian Scout" ; r-Cowboys 'N' Injuns #? 13.00 39.00 90.00
2(8/51) 9.15 27.00 55.00
3(12/51)- "...Fights the Comanche Raiders" 7.50 22.50 45.00
5-6,8(11-12/54-9/55): 5-Formerly All True Detective Cases (last pre-code); titled "...and the Trail of Doom" 7.00 21.00 42.00
7-McCann-a? 7.50 22.50 45.00
I.W. Reprint #10('63)-r/Kit Carson #1; Severin-c 1.75 5.25 14.00
NOTE: ***Kinstler*** *c-1-3, 5-8.*

KIT CARSON & THE BLACKFEET WARRIORS
Realistic: 1953

nn-Reprint; Kinstler-c 9.15 27.00 55.00

KIT KARTER
Dell Publishing Co.: May-July, 1962

1 2.00 6.00 22.00

KITTY
St. John Publishing Co.: Oct, 1948

1-Teenage; Lily Renee-c/a 6.70 20.00 40.00

KITTY PRYDE, AGENT OF S.H.I.E.L.D. (Also see Excalibur)
Marvel Comics: Dec, 1997 - No. 3, Feb, 1998 ($2.50, limited series)

1-3-Hama-s 2.50

KITTY PRYDE AND WOLVERINE (Also see Uncanny X-Men & X-Men)
Marvel Comics Group: Nov, 1984 - No. 6, Apr, 1985 (Limited series)

1-6: Characters from X-Men 3.00

KLARER GIVEAWAYS (See Wisco)

KNIGHTHAWK
Acclaim Comics (Windjammer): Sept, 1995 - No. 6, Nov, 1995 ($2.50, lim. series)
1-6: 6-origin 2.50

KNIGHTMARE
Antarctic Press: July, 1994 - May, 1995 ($2.75, B&W, mature readers)

1-6 2.75

KNIGHTMARE
Image Comics (Extreme Studios): Feb, 1995 - No. 5, June, 1995 ($2.50)

0 ($3.50) 3.50
1-5: 4-Quesada & Palmiotti variant-c, 5-Flip book w/Warcry 2.50

KNIGHTS OF PENDRAGON, THE (Also see Pendragon)
Marvel Comics Ltd.: July, 1990 - No. 18, Dec, 1991 ($1.95)

1-18: 1-Capt. Britain app. 2,8-Free poster inside. 9,10-Bolton-c. 11,18-Iron Man app. 2.00

KNIGHTS OF THE ROUND TABLE
Dell Publishing Co.: No. 540, Mar, 1954

Four Color 540-Movie, photo-c 6.40 19.00 70.00

KNIGHTS OF THE ROUND TABLE
Pines Comics: No. 10, April, 1957

10 4.00 12.00 24.00

KNIGHTS OF THE ROUND TABLE
Dell Publishing Co.: Nov-Jan, 1963-64

1 (12-397-401)-Painted-c 2.50 7.50 28.00

KNIGHTSTRIKE (Also see Operation: Knightstrike)
Image Comics (Extreme Studios): Jan, 1996 ($2.50)

1-Rob Liefeld & Eric Stephenson story; Extreme Destroyer Part 6. 2.50

KNIGHT WATCHMAN (See Big Bang & Dr. Weird)
Image Comics: June, 1998 - No. 4, Oct, 1998 ($2.95, B&W, limited series)

1-4-Ben Torres-c/a 3.00

KNIGHT WATCHMAN: GRAVEYARD SHIFT

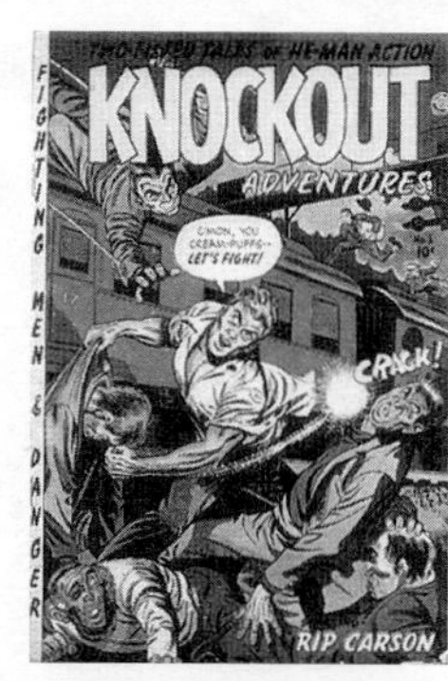

Knockout Adventures #1 © FH

Koko and Kola #2 © ME

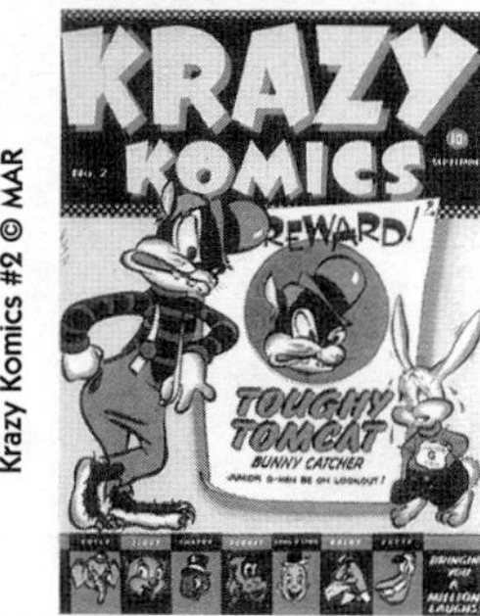

Krazy Komics #2 © MAR

GD2.0 FN6.0 NM9.4

Caliber Press: 1994 ($2.95, B&W)
1,2-Ben Torres-a 3.00

KNOCK KNOCK (...Who's There?)
Whitman Publ./Gerona Publications: No. 801, 1936 (52 pgs.) (8x9", B&W)
801-Joke book; Bob Dunn-a 6.70 20.00 40.00

KNOCKOUT ADVENTURES
Fiction House Magazines: Winter, 1953-54
1-Reprints Fight Comics #53 w/Rip Carson-c/s 13.00 39.00 90.00

KNUCKLES
Archie Publications: Apr, 1997 - Present ($1.50/$1.75/$1.79)
1-29 2.00

KNUCKLES' CHAOTIX
Archie Publications: Jan, 1996 ($2.00, annual)
1 2.00

KOBALT
DC Comics (Milestone): June, 1994 - No. 16, Sept, 1995 ($1.75/$2.50)
1-16: 1-Byrne-c. 4-Intro Page. 16-Kent Williams-c 2.50

KOBRA (See DC Special Series No. 1)
National Periodical Publications: Feb-Mar, 1976 - No. 7, Mar-Apr, 1977
1-1st app.; Kirby-a redrawn by Marcos; only 25¢ issue 2.40 6.00
2-7: (All 30¢ issues) 3-Giffen-a 4.00
NOTE: ***Austin** a-3i. **Buckler** a-5p; c-5p. **Kubert** c-4. **Nasser** a-6p, 7; c-7.*

KOKEY KOALA (...and the Magic Button)
Toby Press: May, 1952
1 10.00 30.00 70.00

KOKO AND KOLA (Also see A-1 Comics #16 & Tick Tock Tales)
Com/Magazine Enterprises: Fall, 1946 - No. 5, May, 1947; No. 6, 1950
1-Funny animal 10.00 30.00 70.00
2-X-Mas-c 6.35 19.00 38.00
3-6: 6(A-1 28) 5.00 15.00 30.00

KO KOMICS
Gerona Publications: Oct, 1945
1-The Duke of Darkness & The Menace (hero) 62.00 187.00 500.00

KOMIC KARTOONS
Timely Comics (EPC): Fall, 1945 - No. 2, Winter, 1945
1,2-Andy Wolf, Bertie Mouse 19.00 56.00 130.00

KOMIK PAGES (Formerly Snap; becomes Bullseye #11)
Harry 'A' Chesler, Jr. (Our Army, Inc.): Apr, 1945 (All reprints)
10(#1 on inside)-Land O' Nod by Rick Yager (2 pgs.), Animal Crackers, Foxy GrandPa, Tom, Dick & Mary, Cheerio Minstrels, Red Starr plus other 1-2 pg. strips; Cole-a 23.00 69.00 160.00

KONA (...Monarch of Monster Isle)
Dell Publishing Co.: Feb-Apr, 1962 - No. 21, Jan-Mar, 1967 (Painted-c)
Four Color 1256 (#1) 5.50 16.50 60.00
2-10: 4-Anak begins 2.50 7.50 28.00
11-21 1.80 5.50 20.00
NOTE: ***Glanzman** a-all issues.*

KONGA (Fantastic Giants No. 24) (See Return of...)
Charlton Comics: 1960; No. 2, Aug, 1961 - No. 23, Nov, 1965
1(1960)-Based on movie; Giordano-c 23.00 69.00 230.00
2-5: 2-Giordano-c; no Ditko-a 9.50 28.50 95.00
6-15 7.00 21.00 70.00
16-23 4.50 13.50 45.00
NOTE: ***Ditko** a-1, 3-15; c-4, 6-9. **Glanzman** a-12. **Montes** & **Bache** a-16-23.*

KONGA'S REVENGE (Formerly Return of...)
Charlton Comics: No. 2, Summer, 1963 - No. 3, Fall, 1964; Dec, 1968
2,3: 2-Ditko-c/a 5.00 15.00 50.00
1(12/68)-Reprints Konga's Revenge #3 2.50 7.50 25.00

KONG THE UNTAMED
National Periodical Publications: June-July, 1975 - V2#5, Feb-Mar, 1976
1-1st app. Kong; Wrightson-c; Alcala-a 2.40 6.00
2-5: 2-Wrightson-c. 2,3-Alcala-a 4.00

KOOKIE
Dell Publishing Co.: Feb-Apr, 1962 - No. 2, May-July, 1962 (15 cents)
1,2: 1- Written by John Stanley; Bill Williams-a 7.00 21.00 70.00

KOOSH KINS
Archie Comics: Oct, 1991 - No. 3, Feb, 1992 ($1.00, bi-monthly, limited series)
1-3 2.00
NOTE: *No. 4 was planned, but cancelled.*

KORAK, SON OF TARZAN (Edgar Rice Burroughs)(See Tarzan #139)
Gold Key: Jan, 1964 - No. 45, Jan, 1972 (Painted-c No. 1-?)
1-Russ Manning-a 5.50 16.50 60.00
2-11-Russ Manning-a 3.20 9.60 32.00
12-23: 12,13-Warren Tufts-a. 14-Jon of the Kalahari ends. 15-Mabu, Jungle Boy begins. 21-Manning-a. 23-Last 12¢ issue 2.50 7.50 22.00
24-30 2.00 6.00 16.00
31-45 1.25 3.75 10.00

KORAK, SON OF TARZAN (Tarzan Family #60 on; see Tarzan #230)
National Periodical Publications: V9#46, May-June, 1972 - V12#56, Feb-Mar, 1974; No. 57, May-June, 1975 - No. 59, Sept-Oct, 1975 (Edgar Rice Burroughs)
46-(52 pgs.)-Carson of Venus begins (origin), ends #56; Pellucidar feature; Weiss-a 1.50 4.50 12.00
47-59: 49-Origin Korak retold 5.00
NOTE: *All have covers by **Joe Kubert**. **Manning** strip reprints-No. 57-59. **Murphy Anderson** a-52. **Michael Kaluta** a-46-56. **Frank Thorne** a-46-51.*

KORG: 70,000 B. C. (TV)
Charlton Publications: May, 1975 - No. 9, Nov, 1976 (Hanna-Barbera)
1,2: 1-Boyette-c/a. 2-Painted-c; Byrne text illos 1.50 4.50 12.00
3-9 1.00 3.00 8.00

KORNER KID COMICS
Four Star Publications: 1947
1 7.00 21.00 42.00

KOSMIC KAT ACTIVITY BOOK (See Deity)
Image Comics: Aug, 1999 ($2.95, one-shot)
1-Stories and games by various 3.00

KRAZY KAT
Holt: 1946 (Hardcover)
Reprints daily & Sunday strips by Herriman 56.00 169.00 450.00
dust jacket only 44.00 131.00 350.00

KRAZY KAT (See Ace Comics & March of Comics No. 72, 87)

KRAZY KAT COMICS (...& Ignatz the Mouse early issues)
Dell Publ. Co./Gold Key: May-June, 1951 - F.C. #696, Apr, 1956; Jan, 1964 (None by Herriman)
1(1951) 6.40 19.00 70.00
2-5 (#5, 8-10/52) 3.60 11.00 40.00
Four Color 454,504 3.00 9.00 35.00
Four Color 548,619,696 (4/56) 2.75 8.00 30.00
1(10098-401)(1/64-Gold Key)(TV) 2.75 8.00 30.00

KRAZY KOMICS (1st Series) (Cindy Comics No. 27 on)
Timely Comics (USA No. 1-21/JPC No. 22-26): July, 1942 - No. 26, Spr, 1947 (Also see Ziggy Pig)
1-Toughy Tomcat, Ziggy Pig (by Jaffee) & Silly Seal begin 52.00 156.00 415.00
2 26.00 77.00 180.00
3-8,10 19.00 56.00 130.00
9-Hitler parody 20.00 60.00 140.00
11,13,14 12.00 36.00 85.00

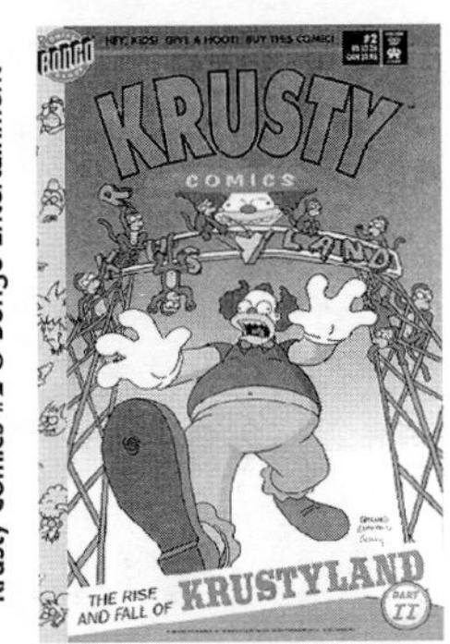

Krusty Comics #2 © Bongo Entertainment

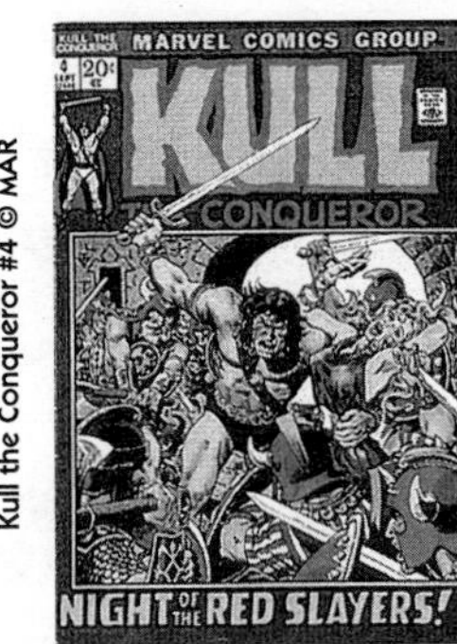

Kull the Conqueror #4 © MAR

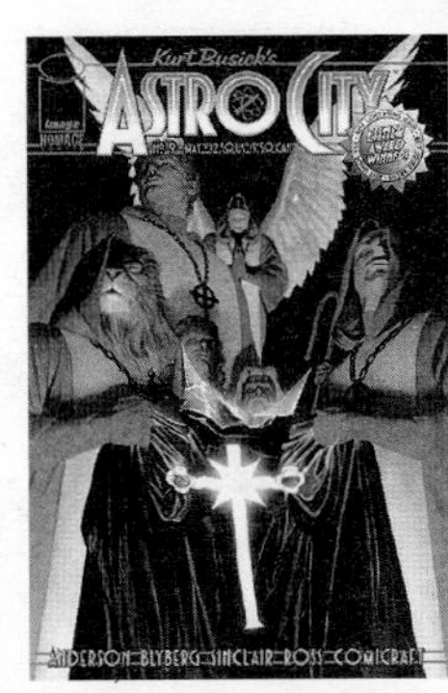

Kurt Busiek's Astro City #9 © Juke Box Prod.

12-Timely's entire art staff drew themselves into a Creeper story 24.00 73.00 170.00
15-(8-9/44)-Becomes Funny Tunes #16; has "Super Soldier" by Pfc. Stan Lee 12.00 36.00 85.00
16-24,26: 16-(10-11/44). 26-Super Rabbit-c/story 10.00 30.00 70.00
25-Wacky Duck-c/story & begin; Kurtzman-a (6pgs.) 12.00 36.00 85.00

KRAZY KOMICS (2nd Series)
Timely/Marvel Comics: Aug, 1948 - No. 2, Nov, 1948

1-Wolverton (10 pgs.) & Kurtzman (8 pgs.)-a; Eustice Hayseed begins (Li'l Abner swipe) 40.00 120.00 290.00
2-Wolverton-a (10 pgs.); Powerhouse Pepper cameo 30.00 90.00 210.00

KRAZY KROW (Also see Dopey Duck, Film Funnies, Funny Frolics & Movie Tunes)
Marvel Comics (ZPC): Summer, 1945 - No. 3, Wint, 1945/46

1 17.00 51.00 120.00
2,3 11.50 34.00 80.00
I.W. Reprint #1('57), 2('58), 7 2.00 6.00 16.00

KRAZYLIFE (Becomes Nutty Life #2)
Fox Feature Syndicate: 1945 (no month)

1-Funny animal 13.50 41.00 95.00

KREE/SKRULL WAR STARRING THE AVENGERS, THE
Marvel Comics: Sept, 1983 - No. 2, Oct, 1983 ($2.50, 68 pgs., Baxter paper)

1,2 2.50
*NOTE: **Neal Adams** p-1r, 2. **Buscema** a-1r, 2r. **Simonson** a-1p; c-1p.*

KROFFT SUPERSHOW (TV)
Gold Key: Apr, 1978 - No. 6, Jan, 1979

1-Photo-c 1.50 4.50 12.00
2-6: 6-Photo-c 1.25 3.75 10.00

KRULL
Marvel Comics Group: Nov, 1983 - No. 2, Dec, 1983

1,2-Adaptation of film; r/Marvel Super Special. 1-Photo-c from movie 2.00

KRUSTY COMICS (TV)(See Simpsons Comics)
Bongo Comics: 1995 - No. 3, 1995 ($2.25, limited series)

1-3 2.50

KRYPTON CHRONICLES
DC Comics: Sept, 1981 - No. 3, Nov, 1981

1-3: 1-Buckler-c(p) 2.00

KULL AND THE BARBARIANS
Marvel Comics: May, 1975 - No. 3, Sept, 1975 ($1.00, B&W, magazine, 84 pgs.)

1-Andru/Wood-r/Kull #1; 2 pgs. Neal Adams; Gil Kane(p), Marie & John Severin-a(r); Krenkel text illo. 1.10 3.30 9.00
2,3: 2-Red Sonja by Chaykin begins; Soloman Kane by Weiss/N. Adams; Gil Kane-a. 3-Origin Red Sonja by Chaykin; Adams-a; Solomon Kane app. 2.40 6.00

KULL THE CONQUEROR (...the Destroyer #11 on; see Conan #1, Creatures on the Loose #10, Marvel Preview, Monsters on the Prowl)
Marvel Comics Group: June, 1971 - No. 2, Sept, 1971; No. 3, July, 1972 - No. 15, Aug, 1974; No. 16, Aug, 1976 - No. 29, Oct, 1978

1-Andru/Wood-a; 2nd app. & origin Kull; 15¢ issue 2.50 7.50 24.00
2-5: 2-3rd Kull app. Last 15¢ iss. 3-13: 20¢ issues 1.25 3.75 10.00
6-10 1.00 2.80 7.00
11-15: 11-15-Ploog-a. 14,15: 25¢ issues 5.00
16-(Regular 25¢ edition)(8/76) 5.00
16-(30¢-c variant, limited distribution) 2.50 7.50 20.00
17-29 4.00
*NOTE: No. 1, 2, 7-9, 11 are based on Robert E. Howard stories. **Alcala** a-17p, 18-20i; c-24. **Ditko** a-12r, 15r. **Gil Kane** c-15p, 21. **Nebres** a-22i-27i; c-25i, 27i. **Ploog** c-11, 12p, 13. **Severin** a-2-9i; c-2-10i, 19. **Starlin** c-14.*

KULL THE CONQUEROR
Marvel Comics Group: Dec, 1982 - No. 2, Mar, 1983 (52 pgs., Baxter paper)

1,2: 1-Buscema-a(p) 3.00

KULL THE CONQUEROR (No. 9,10 titled "Kull")
Marvel Comics Group: 5/83 - No. 10, 6/85 (52 pgs., Baxter paper)

V3#1-10: Buscema-a in #1-3,5-10 2.00
NOTE: Bolton a-4. Golden painted c-3-8. Guice a-4p. Sienkiewicz a-4; c-2.

KUNG FU (See Deadly Hands of..., & Master of...)

KUNG FU FIGHTER (See Richard Dragon...)

KURT BUSIEK'S ASTRO CITY (Limited series)
Image Comics (Juke Box Productions): Aug, 1995 - No. 6, Jan, 1996 ($2.25)

1-Kurt Busiek scripts, Brent Anderson-a & Alex Ross front & back-c begins; 1st app. Samaritan & Honor Guard (Cleopatra, MHP, Beautie, The Black Rapier, Quarrel & N-Forcer) 1.50 4.50 12.00
2-6: 2-1st app. The Silver Agent, The Old Soldier, & the "original" Honor Guard (Max O'Millions, Starwoman, the "original" Cleopatra, the "original" N-Forcer, the Bouncing Beatnik, Leopardman & Kitkat). 3-1st app. Jack-in-the-Box & The Deacon. 4-1st app. Winged Victory (cameo), The Hanged Man & The First Family. 5-1st app. Crackerjack, The Astro City Irregulars, Nightingale & Sunbird. 6-Origin Samaritan; 1st full app Winged Victory 1.25 3.75 10.00
Life In The Big City-(8/96, $19.95, trade paperback)-r/Image Comics limited series w/sketchbook & cover gallery; Ross-c 20.00
Life In The Big City-(8/96, $49.95, hardcover, 1000 print run)-r/Image Comics limited series w/sketchbook & cover gallery; Ross-c 50.00

KURT BUSIEK'S ASTRO CITY (1st Homage Comics series)
Image Comics (Homage Comics): V2#1, Sept, 1996 - No. 15, Dec, 1998;
DC Comics (Homage Comics): No. 16, Mar, 1999 - Present ($2.50)

1/2-(10/96)-The Hanged Man story; 1st app. The All-American & Slugger, The Lamplighter, The Time-Keeper & Eterneon 1.25 3.75 10.00
1/2-(1/98) 2nd printing w/new cover 2.50
1- Kurt Busiek scripts, Alex Ross-c, Brent Anderson-p & Will Blyberg-i begin; intro The Gentleman, Thunderhead & Helia. 1.00 3.00 8.00
1-(12/97, $4.95) "3-D Edition" w/glasses 5.00
2-Origin The First Family; Astra story 1.00 2.80 7.00
3-5: 4-1st app. The Crossbreed, Ironhorse, Glue Gun & The Confessor (cameo) 2.40 6.00
6-10 5.00
11-19: 16-(3/99) First DC issue 2.50
TPB-($19.95) Ross-c, r/#4-9, #1/2 w/sketchbook 20.00
Family Album TPB ($19.95) r/#1-3,10-13 20.00

LABMAN
Image Comics: Nov, 1996 ($3.50, one-shot)

1-Allred-c 4.00

LABYRINTH
Marvel Comics Group: Nov, 1986 - No. 3, Jan, 1987 (Limited series)

1-3: David Bowie movie adaptation; r/Marvel Super Special #40 2.00

LA COSA NOSTROID (See Scud: The Disposible Assassin)
Fireman Press: Mar, 1996 - Present ($2.95, B&W)

1-9-Dan Harmon-s/Rob Schrab-c/a 3.00

LAD: A DOG (Movie)
Dell Publishing Co.: 1961 - No. 2, July-Sept, 1962

Four Color 1303, 2 2.75 8.00 30.00

LADY AND THE TRAMP (Disney, See Dell Giants & Movie Comics)
Dell Publishing Co.: No. 629, May, 1955 - No. 634, June, 1955

Four Color 629 (#1)-..with Jock 6.00 18.00 65.00
Four Color 634-...Album 3.65 11.00 40.00

LADY COP (See 1st Issue Special)

LADY DEATH (See Evil Ernie)
Chaos! Comics: Jan, 1994 - No. 3, Mar, 1994 ($2.75, limited series)

1/2-S. Hughes-c/a in all, 1/2 Velvet 1.25 3.75 10.00

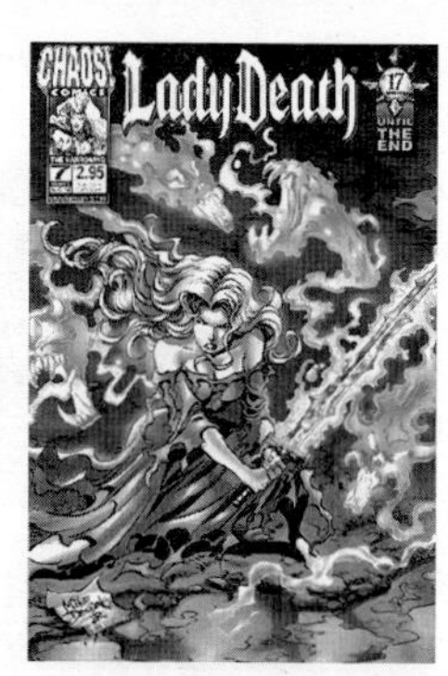

Lady Death #7 © Chaos!

Lady Pendragon #3 © Matt Hawkins

Lance O'Casey #1 © FAW

	GD2.0	FN6.0	NM9.4
1/2 Gold	1.85	5.50	15.00
1/2 Signed Limited Edition	2.00	6.00	16.00
1-($3.50)-Chromium-c	2.50	7.50	25.00
1-Commemorative	2.50	7.50	20.00
1-(9/96, $2.95) "Encore Presentation"; r/#1			3.00
2	1.50	4.50	12.00
3	1.00	3.00	8.00
...And The Women of Chaos! Gallery #1 (11/96, $2.25) pin-ups by various			2.25
...Death Becomes Her #0 (11/97, $2.95) Hughes-c/a			3.00
...FAN Edition: All Hallow's Eve #1 (1/97, mail-in)		2.40	6.00
...In Lingerie #1 (8/95, $2.95) pin-ups, wraparound-c			3.00
...In Lingerie #1-Leather Edition (10,000)	2.00	6.00	16.00
...In Lingerie #1-Micro Premium Edition; Lady Demon-c (2,000)	4.50	13.50	45.00
...Swimsuit Special #1-($2.50)-Wraparound-c			3.00
...Swimsuit Special #1-Red velvet-c	2.00	6.00	16.00
...: The Reckoning (7/94, $6.95)-r/#1-3			7.00
...: The Reckoning (8/95, $12.95)- new printing including Lady Death 1/2 & Swimsuit Special #1			13.00
.../Vampirella (3/99, $3.50) Hughes-c/a			3.50

LADY DEATH (Ongoing series)
Chaos! Comics: Feb, 1998 - No. 16, May, 1999 ($2.95)

	GD2.0	FN6.0	NM9.4
1-16: 1-4: Pulido-s/Hughes-c/a. 5-8,13-16-Deodato-a. 9-11-Hughes-a			3.00
...Retribution (8/98, $2.95) Jadsen-a			3.00
...Retribution Premium Ed.			10.00

LADY DEATH: JUDGEMENT WAR
Chaos! Comics: Nov, 1999 - No. 3 ($2.95, limited series)

	GD2.0	FN6.0	NM9.4
Prelude (10/99) two covers			
1-Ivan Reis-a			3.00

LADY DEATH: THE CRUCIBLE
Chaos! Comics: Nov, 1996 - No. 6, Oct, 1997 ($3.50/$2.95, limited series)

	GD2.0	FN6.0	NM9.4
1/2			4.00
1/2 Cloth Edition	1.00	3.00	8.00
1-Wraparound silver foil embossed-c			4.00
1-($19.95)-Leather Edition			20.00
2-6-($2.95)			3.00

LADY DEATH: THE ODYSSEY
Chaos! Comics: Apr, 1996 - No. 4, Aug, 1996 ($3.50/$2.95)

	GD2.0	FN6.0	NM9.4
1-($1.50)-Sneak Peek Preview			2.00
1-($1.50)-Sneak Peek Preview Micro Premium Edition (2500 print run)	1.85	5.50	15.00
1-($3.50)-Embossed, wraparound goil foil-c		2.40	6.00
1-Black Onyx Edition (200 print run)	8.00	24.00	90.00
1-($19.95)-Premium Edition (10,000 print run)			20.00
2-4-($2.95)			3.00

LADY DEATH: THE RAPTURE
Chaos! Comics: Jun, 1999 - No. 4, Sept, 1999 ($2.95, limited series)

	GD2.0	FN6.0	NM9.4
1-4-Ivan Reis-c/a; Pulido-s			3.00

LADY DEATH II: BETWEEN HEAVEN & HELL
Chaos! Comics: Mar, 1995 - No. 4, July, 1995 ($3.50, limited series)

	GD2.0	FN6.0	NM9.4
1-Chromium wraparound-c; Evil Ernie cameo		2.40	6.00
1-Commemorative (4,000, 1-Black Velvet-c	2.50	7.50	20.00
1-Gold	1.50	4.50	12.00
1-"Refractor" edition (5,000)	2.50	7.50	25.00
2-4			3.00
4-Lady Demon variant-c	1.00	3.00	8.00
Trade paperback-($12.95)-r/#1-4			13.00

LADY FOR A NIGHT (See Cinema Comics Herald)

LADY JUSTICE (See Neil Gaiman's...)

LADY LUCK (Formerly Smash #1-85) (Also see Spirit Sections #1)
Quality Comics Group: No. 86, Dec, 1949 - No. 90, Aug, 1950

	GD2.0	FN6.0	NM9.4
86(#1)	81.00	244.00	650.00
87-90	62.00	187.00	500.00

LADY PENDRAGON
Maximum Press: Mar, 1996 ($2.50)

	GD2.0	FN6.0	NM9.4
1-Matt Hawkins script			2.50

LADY PENDRAGON
Image Comics: Nov, 1998 - No. 3, Jan, 1999 ($2.50, mini-series)

	GD2.0	FN6.0	NM9.4
Preview (6/98) Flip book w/ Deity preview			3.00
1-3: 1-Matt Hawkins-s/Stinsman-a			3.00
1-($6.95) DF Ed. with variant-c by Jusko			7.00
2-($4.95)Variant edition			5.00
0-(3/99) Origin; flip book			2.50

LADY PENDRAGON (Volume 3)
Image Comics: Apr, 1999 - Present ($2.50, mini-series)

	GD2.0	FN6.0	NM9.4
1,2,4,5: 1-Matt Hawkins-s/Stinsman-a. 2-Peterson-c			2.50
3-Flip book w/Alley Cat preview (1st app.)			3.00
Gallery Edition (10/99, $2.95) pin-ups			3.00

LADY PENDRAGON/ MORE THAN MORTAL
Image Comics: May, 1999 ($2.50, one-shot)

	GD2.0	FN6.0	NM9.4
Preview (2/99) Diamond Dateline suppl.			2.00
1-Scott-s/Norton-a; 2 covers by Norton & Finch			2.50

LADY RAWHIDE
Topps Comics: July, 1995 - No. 5, Mar, 1996 ($2.95, bi-monthly, limited series)

	GD2.0	FN6.0	NM9.4
1-5: Don McGregor scripts & Mayhew-a. in all. 2-Stelfreeze-c. 3-Hughes-c. 4-Golden-c. 5-Julie Bell-c.			3.00
It Can't Happen Here TPB (8/99, $16.95) r/#1-5			17.00
Special Edition 1 (6/95, $3.95)-Reprints			4.00

LADY RAWHIDE (Volume 2)
Topps Comics: Oct, 1996 -No. 5, June, 1997 ($2.95, limited series)

	GD2.0	FN6.0	NM9.4
1-5: 1-Julie Bell-c.			3.00

LADY RAWHIDE OTHER PEOPLE'S BLOOD (ZORRO'S ...)
Image Comics: Mar, 1999 - No. 5, July, 1999 ($2.95, B&W)

	GD2.0	FN6.0	NM9.4
1-5-Reprints Lady Rawhide series in B&W			3.00

LADY SUPREME (See Asylum)(Also see Supreme & Kid Supreme)
Image Comics (Extreme): May, 1996 - No. 2, June, 1996 ($2.50, limited series)

	GD2.0	FN6.0	NM9.4
1,2-Terry Moore -s: 1-Terry Moore-c. 2-Flip book w/Newmen preview			2.50

LAFF-A-LYMPICS (TV)(See The Funtastic World of Hanna-Barbera)
Marvel Comics: Mar, 1978 - No. 13, Mar, 1979 (Newsstand sales only)

	GD2.0	FN6.0	NM9.4
1-Yogi Bear, Scooby Doo, Pixie & Dixie, etc.	1.75	5.25	14.00
2-8	1.50	4.50	12.00
9-13: 11-Jetsons x-over; 1 pg. illustrated bio of Mighty Mightor, Herculoids, Shazzan, Galaxy Trio & Space Ghost	2.00	6.00	16.00

LAFFY-DAFFY COMICS
Rural Home Publ. Co.: Feb, 1945 - No. 2, Mar, 1945

	GD2.0	FN6.0	NM9.4
1,2-Funny animal	9.15	27.00	55.00

LANA (Little Lana No. 8 on)
Marvel Comics (MjMC): Aug, 1948 - No. 7, Aug, 1949 (Also see Annie Oakley)

	GD2.0	FN6.0	NM9.4
1-Rusty, Millie begin	17.00	51.00	120.00
2-Kurtzman's "Hey Look" (1); last Rusty	11.00	33.00	75.00
3-7: 3-Nellie begins	8.35	25.00	50.00

LANCELOT & GUINEVERE (See Movie Classics)

LANCELOT LINK, SECRET CHIMP (TV)
Gold Key: Apr, 1971 - No. 8, Feb, 1973

	GD2.0	FN6.0	NM9.4
1-Photo-c	4.00	12.00	40.00
2-8: 2-Photo-c	2.50	7.50	24.00

LANCELOT STRONG (See The Shield)

LANCE O'CASEY (See Mighty Midget & Whiz Comics)
Fawcett Publications: Spring, 1946 - No. 3, Fall, 1946; No. 4, Summer, 1948

	GD2.0	FN6.0	NM9.4
1-Captain Marvel app. on-c	34.00	103.00	240.00

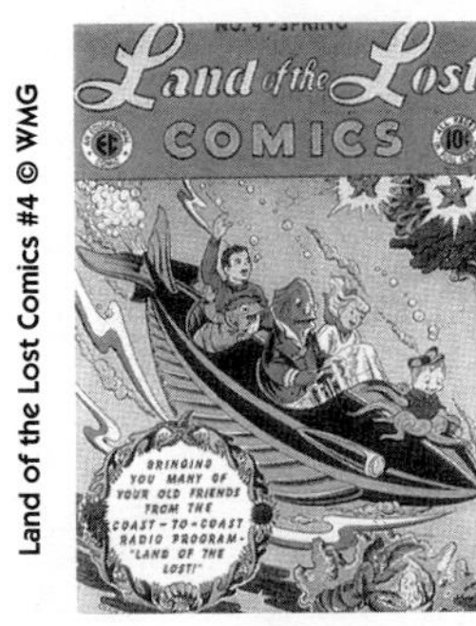

Land of the Lost Comics #4 © WMG

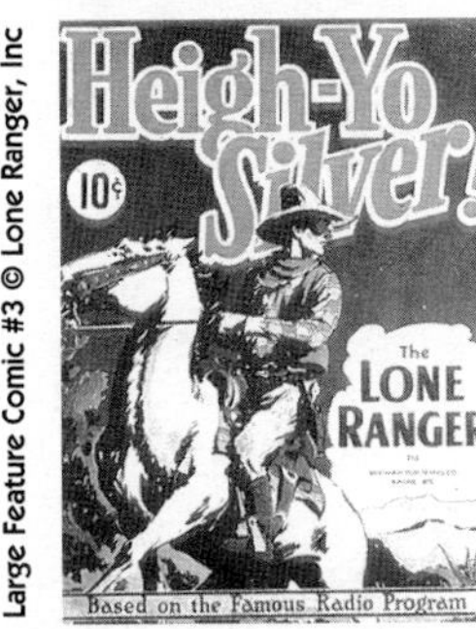

Large Feature Comic #3 © Lone Ranger, Inc

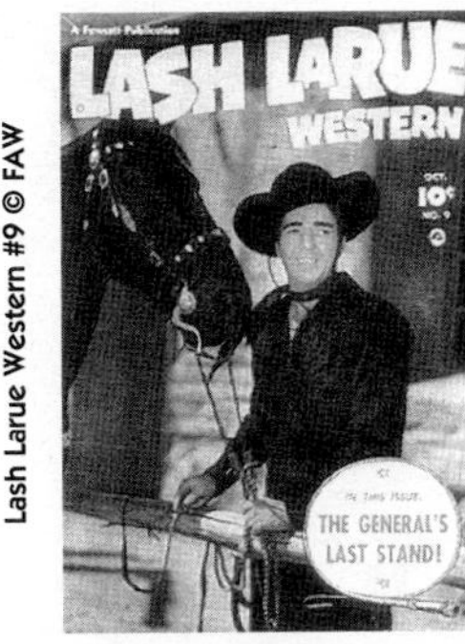

Lash Larue Western #9 © FAW

GD2.0 FN6.0 NM9.4

2 21.00 64.00 150.00
3,4 16.00 47.00 110.00
NOTE: *The cover for the 1st issue was done in 1942 but was not published until 1946. The cover shows 68 pages but actually has only 36 pages.*

LANCER (TV)(Western)
Gold Key: Feb, 1969 - No. 3, Sept, 1969 (All photo-c)
1 3.00 9.00 30.00
2,3 2.50 7.50 22.00

LAND OF NOD, THE
Dark Horse Comics: July, 1997 - Present ($2.95, B&W)
1-3-Jetcat; Jay Stephens-s/a 3.00

LAND OF OZ
Arrow Comics: 1998 - Present ($2.95, B&W)
1-Bishop-s/Bryan-s/a 3.00

LAND OF THE GIANTS (TV)
Gold Key: Nov, 1968 - No. 5, Sept, 1969 (All have photo-c)
1 5.00 15.00 55.00
2-5 3.20 9.60 32.00

LAND OF THE LOST COMICS (Radio)
E. C. Comics: July-Aug, 1946 - No. 9, Spring, 1948
1 32.00 96.00 225.00
2 21.00 64.00 150.00
3-9 17.00 51.00 120.00

LAND UNKNOWN, THE (Movie)
Dell Publishing Co.: No. 845, Sept, 1957
Four Color 845-Alex Toth-a 11.00 34.00 125.00

LA PACIFICA
DC Comics (Paradox Press): 1994/1995 ($4.95, B&W, limited series, digest size, mature readers)
1-3 5.00

LARAMIE (TV)
Dell Publishing Co.: Aug, 1960 - July, 1962 (All photo-c)
Four Color 1125-Gil Kane/Heath-a 9.00 27.00 100.00
Four Color 1223,1284, 01-418-207 (7/62) 5.50 16.50 60.00

LAREDO (TV)
Gold Key: June, 1966
1 (10179-606)-Photo-c 3.20 9.60 32.00

LARGE FEATURE COMIC (Formerly called Black & White in previous guides)
Dell Publishing Co.: 1939 - No. 13, 1943

Note: See individual alphabetical listings for prices

1 (Series I)-Dick Tracy Meets the Blank
2-Terry and the Pirates (#1)
3-Heigh-Yo Silver! The Lone Ranger (text & ill.)(76 pgs.); also exists as a Whitman #710; based on radio
4-Dick Tracy Gets His Man
5-Tarzan of the Apes (#1) by Harold Foster (origin); reprints 1st Tarzan dailies from 1929
6-Terry & the Pirates & The Dragon Lady; reprints dailies from 1936
7-(Scarce, 52 pgs.)-Hi-Yo Silver the Lone Ranger to the Rescue; also exists as a Whitman #715, based on radio program
8-Dick Tracy the Racket Buster
9-King of the Royal Mounted (Zane Grey's...)
10-(Scarce)-Gang Busters (No. appears on inside front cover); first slick cover (based on radio program)
11-Dick Tracy Foils the Mad Doc Hump
12-Smilin' Jack; no number on-c
13-Dick Tracy and Scottie of Scotland Yard
14-Smilin' Jack Helps G-Men Solve a Case!
15-Dick Tracy and the Kidnapped Princes
16-Donald Duck; 1st app. Daisy Duck on back cover (6/41-Disney)
17-Gang Busters (1941)
18-Phantasmo (see The Funnies #45)
19-Dumbo Comic Paint Book (Disney); partial-r from 4-Color #17
20-Donald Duck Comic Paint Book (rarer than #16) (Disney)
21,22: 21-Private Buck. 22-Nuts & Jolts
23-The Nebbs
24-Popeye in "Thimble Theatre" by Segar
25-Smilin' Jack-1st issue to show title on-c
26-Smitty
27-Terry and the Pirates; Caniff-c/a
28-Grin and Bear It
29-Moon Mullins
30-Tillie the Toiler
1 (Series II)-Peter Rabbit by Harrison Cady; arrival date-3/27/42
2-Winnie Winkle (#1)
3-Dick Tracy
4-Tiny Tim (#1)
5-Toots and Casper
6-Terry and the Pirates; Caniff-a
7-Pluto Saves the Ship (#1) (Disney)-Written by Carl Barks, Jack Hannah, & Nick George (Barks' 1st comic book work)
8-Bugs Bunny (#1)('42)
9-Bringing Up Father
10-Popeye (Thimble Theatre)
11-Barney Google and Snuffy Smith
12-Private Buck
13-(nn)-1001 Hours Of Fun; puzzles & games; by A. W. Nugent. This book was bound as #13 with Large Feature Comics in publisher's files

NOTE: *The Black & White Feature Books are oversized 8-1/2x11-3/8" comics with color covers and black and white interiors. The first nine issues all have rough, heavy stock covers and, except for #7, all have 76 pages, including covers. #7 and #10-on all have 52 pages. Beginning with #10 the covers are slick and thin and, because of their size, are difficult to handle without damaging. For this reason, they are seldom found in fine to mint condition. The paper stock, unlike Wow #1 and Capt. Marvel #1, is itself not unstable ...just thin.*

LARRY DOBY, BASEBALL HERO
Fawcett Publications: 1950 (Cleveland Indians)
nn-Bill Ward-a; photo-c 72.00 217.00 580.00

LARRY HARMON'S LAUREL AND HARDY (...Comics)
National Periodical Publ.: July-Aug, 1972 (Digest advertised, not published)
1 6.00 18.00 65.00

LARS OF MARS
Ziff-Davis Publishing Co.: No. 10, Apr-May, 1951 - No. 11, July-Aug, 1951 (Painted-c) (Created by Jerry Siegel, editor)
10-Origin; Anderson-a(3) in each; classic robot-c 77.00 231.00 615.00
11-Gene Colan-a; classic-c 61.00 182.00 485.00

LARS OF MARS 3-D
Eclipse Comics: Apr, 1987 ($2.50)
1-r/Lars of Mars #10,11 in 3-D plus new story 3.00
2-D limited edition (B&W, 100 copies) 5.00

LASER ERASER & PRESSBUTTON (See Axel Pressbutton & Miracle Man 9)
Eclipse Comics: Nov, 1985 - No. 6, 1987 (95¢/$2.50, limited series)
1-6: 5,6-(95¢) 2.00
...In 3-D 1 (8/86, $2.50) 2.50
2-D 1 (B&W, limited to 100 copies signed & numbered) 4.00

LASH LARUE WESTERN (Movie star; king of the bullwhip)(See Fawcett Movie Comic, Motion Picture Comics & Six-Gun Heroes)
Fawcett Publications: Sum, 1949 - No. 46, Jan, 1954 (36pgs., 1-7,9,13,16-on)
1-Lash & his horse Black Diamond begin; photo front/back-c begin 103.00 309.00 825.00
2(11/49) 43.00 128.00 340.00
3-5 40.00 120.00 285.00
6,7,9: 6-Last photo back-c; intro. Frontier Phantom (Lash's twin brother) 31.00 94.00 220.00
8,10 (52pgs.) 33.00 99.00 230.00
11,12,14,15 (52pgs.) 22.00 66.00 155.00
13,16-20 (36pgs.) 19.00 56.00 130.00
21-30: 21-The Frontier Phantom app. 17.00 49.00 115.00
31-45 14.00 43.00 100.00
46-Last Fawcett issue & photo-c 15.00 45.00 105.00

LASH LARUE WESTERN (Continues from Fawcett series)
Charlton Comics: No. 47, Mar-Apr, 1954 - No. 84, June, 1961
47-Photo-c 19.00 56.00 130.00

Lassie #2 © MGM

Last One #5 © JM DeMatteis & Dan Sweetman

Laugh Comics #21 © AP

GD2.0 FN6.0 NM9.4

48 13.50 41.00 95.00
49-60, 67,68-(68 pgs.). 68-Check-a 10.00 30.00 70.00
61-66,69,70: 52-r/#8; 53-r/#22 10.00 30.00 65.00
71-83 7.00 21.00 42.00
84-Last issue 9.15 27.00 55.00

LASH LARUE WESTERN
AC Comics: 1990 ($3.50, 44 pgs) (24 pgs. of color, 16 pgs. of B&W)
1-Photo covers; r/Lash #6; r/old movie posters 3.50
Annual 1 (1990, $2.95, B&W, 44 pgs.)-Photo covers 3.00

LASSIE (TV)(M-G-M's... #1-36; see Kite Fun Book)
Dell Publ. Co./Gold Key No. 59 (10/62) on: June, 1950 - No. 70, July, 1969
1 (52 pgs.)-Photo-c; inside lists One Shot #282 in error 13.00 39.00 140.00
2-Painted-c begin 5.50 16.50 60.00
3-10 3.65 11.00 40.00
11-19: 12-Rocky Langford (Lassie's master) marries Gerry Lawrence. 15-1st app. Timbu 2.70 8.00 30.00
20-22-Matt Baker-a 3.00 9.00 34.00
23-38,40: 33-Robinson-a. 2.20 6.50 24.00
39-1st app. Timmy as Lassie picks up her TV family 4.00 12.00 45.00
41-50 2.20 6.50 24.00
51-58 2.00 6.00 22.00
59 (10/62)-1st Gold Key 3.25 9.75 36.00
60-70: 63-Last Timmy (10/63). 64-r/#19. 65-Forest Ranger Corey Stuart begins, ends #69. 70-Forest Rangers Bob Ericson & Scott Turner app. (Lassie's new masters) 2.20 6.50 24.00
11193(1978, $1.95, 224 pgs., Golden Press)-Baker-r (92 pgs.) 1.80 5.50 20.00
NOTE: *Photo c-57, 63. (See March of Comics #210, 217, 230, 254, 266, 278, 296, 308, 324, 334, 346, 358, 370, 381, 394, 411, 432)*

LAST AMERICAN, THE
Marvel Comics (Epic): Dec, 1990 - No. 4, March, 1991 ($2.25, mini-series)
1-4: Alan Grant scripts 2.25

LAST AVENGERS STORY, THE (Last Avengers #1)
Marvel Comics: Nov, 1995 - No. 2, Dec, 1995 ($5.95, painted, limited series) (Alterniverse)
1,2: Peter David story; acetate-c in all. 1-New team (Hank Pym, Wasp, Human Torch, Cannonball, She-Hulk, Hotshot, Bombshell, Tommy Maximoff, Hawkeye, & Mockingbird) forms to battle Ultron 59, Kang the Conqueror, The Grim Reaper & Oddball 2.40 6.00

LAST DAYS OF THE JUSTICE SOCIETY SPECIAL
DC Comics: 1986 ($2.50, one-shot, 68 pgs.)
1-62 pg. JSA story plus unpubbed G.A. pg. 4.00

LAST GENERATION, THE
Black Tie Studios: 1986 - No. 5, 1989 ($1.95, B&W, high quality paper)
1-5 2.00
Book 1 (1989, $6.95)-By Caliber Press 7.00

LAST HUNT, THE
Dell Publishing Co.: No. 678, Feb, 1956
Four Color 678-Movie, photo-c 6.40 19.00 70.00

LAST KISS
ACME Press (Eclipse): 1988 ($3.95, B&W, squarebound, 52 pgs.)
1-One story adapts E.A. Poe's The Black Cat 4.00

LAST OF THE COMANCHES (Movie) (See Wild Bill Hickok #28)
Avon Periodicals: 1953
nn-Kinstler-c/a, 21pgs.; Ravielli-a 14.00 43.00 100.00

LAST OF THE ERIES, THE (See American Graphics)

LAST OF THE FAST GUNS, THE
Dell Publishing Co.: No. 925, Aug, 1958
Four Color 925-Movie, photo-c 6.40 19.00 70.00

LAST OF THE MOHICANS (See King Classics & White Rider and...)

LAST OF THE VIKING HEROES, THE (Also see Silver Star #1)
Genesis West Comics: Mar, 1987 - No. 12 ($1.50/$1.95)
1-4,5A,5B,6-12: 4-Intro The Phantom Force, 1-Signed edition ($1.50), 5A-Kirby/Stevens-c. 5B,6 ($1.95). 7-Art Adams-c. 8-Kirby back-c. 2.50
Summer Special 1-3: 1-(1988)-Frazetta-c & illos. 2 (1990, $2.50)-A TMNT app. 3 (1991, $2.50)-Teenage Mutant Ninja Turtles 2.50
Summer Special 1-Signed edition (sold for $1.95) 2.50
NOTE: ***Art Adams** c-7. **Byrne** c-3. **Kirby** c-1p, 5p. **Perez** c-2i. **Stevens** c-5Ai.*

LAST ONE, THE
DC Comics (Vertigo): July, 1993 - No. 6, Dec, 1993 ($2.50, lim. series, mature)
1-6 2.50

LAST STARFIGHTER, THE
Marvel Comics Group: Oct, 1984 - No. 3, Dec, 1984 (75¢, movie adaptation)
1-3: r/Marvel Super Special; Guice-c 2.00

LAST TEMPTATION, THE
Marvel Comics: 1994 - No. 3, 1994 ($4.95, limited series)
1-3-Alice Cooper story; Neil Gaiman scripts; McKean-c; Zulli-a: 1-Two covers. 5.00

LAST TRAIN FROM GUN HILL
Dell Publishing Co.: No. 1012, July, 1959
Four Color 1012-Movie, photo-c 8.00 25.00 90.00

LATEST ADVENTURES OF FOXY GRANDPA (See Foxy Grandpa)

LATEST COMICS (Super Duper No. 3?)
Spotlight Publ./Palace Promotions (Jubilee): Mar, 1945 - No. 2, 1945?
1-Super Duper 15.00 45.00 105.00
2-Bee-29 (nd); Jubilee in indicia blacked out 11.50 34.00 80.00

LAUGH
Archie Enterprises: June, 1987 - No. 29, Aug, 1991 (75¢/$1.00)
V2#1 4.00
2-10,14,24: 5-X-Mas issue. 14-1st app. Hot Dog. 24-Re-intro Super Duck 3.00
11-13,15-23,25-29: 19-X-Mas issue 2.00

LAUGH COMICS (Teenage) (Formerly Black Hood #9-19) (Laugh #226 on)
Archie Publications (Close-Up): No. 20, Fall, 1946 - No. 400, Apr, 1987
20-Archie begins; Katy Keene & Taffy begin by Woggon; Suzie & Wilbur also begin; Archie covers begin 59.00 178.00 475.00
21-23,25 33.00 99.00 230.00
24- "Pipsy" by Kirby (6 pgs.) 34.00 103.00 240.00
26-30 17.00 51.00 120.00
31-40 13.00 39.00 90.00
41-60: 41,54-Debbi by Woggon 9.15 27.00 55.00
61-80: 67-Debbi by Woggon 6.70 20.00 40.00
81-99 3.20 9.60 32.00
100 3.80 11.40 38.00
101-126,145-156,158-160: 125-Debbi app. 2.50 7.50 22.00
127-144: Super-hero app. in all (see note) 3.00 9.00 30.00
157-Josie app.(4/64) 2.80 8.40 28.00
161-165,167-180, 200 (12/67) 2.25 6.75 18.00
166-Beatles-c (1/65) 3.40 10.20 34.00
181-199 1.75 5.25 14.00
201-240(3/71) 1.40 4.15 11.00
241-280(7/74) 1.00 3.00 8.00
281-299 2.40 6.00
300(3/76) 1.00 2.80 7.00
301-340 (7/79) 4.00
341-370 (1/82) 3.00
371-380,385-399 2.50
381-384,400: 381-384-Katy Keene app.; by Woggon-381,382 3.00
NOTE: *The Fly app. in 128, 129, 132, 134, 138, 139. Flygirl app. in 136, 137, 143. Flyman app. in 137. The Jaguar app. in 127, 130, 131, 133, 135, 140-142, 144. Josie app. in 145, 160, 164. Katy Keene app. in 20-125, 129, 130, 133. Many issues contain paper dolls.* ***Al Fagaly***

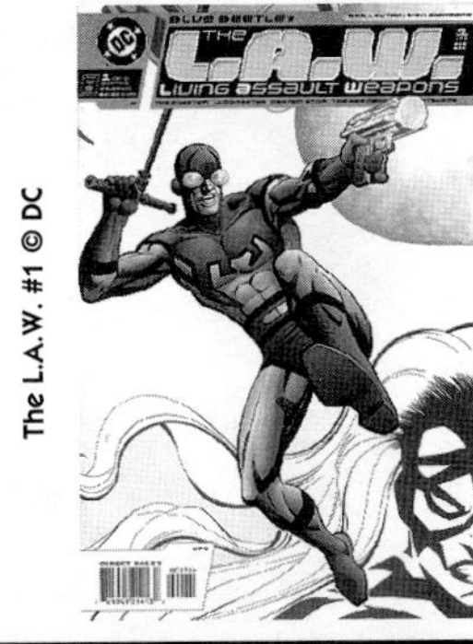

The L.A.W. #1 © DC

Law Against Crime #1 © Essenkay Pub.

Leading Comics #3 © DC

c-20-29. ***Montana*** *c-33, 36, 37, 42.* ***BillVigoda*** *c-30, 50.*

LAUGH COMICS DIGEST (...Magazine #23-89; Laugh Digest Mag. #90 on)
Archie Publ. (Close-Up No. 1, 3 on): 8/74; No. 2, 9/75; No. 3, 3/76 - Present (Digest-size)

	GD2.0	FN6.0	NM9.4
1-Neal Adams-a	3.20	9.60	35.00
2,7,8,19-Neal Adams-a	2.00	6.00	20.00
3-6,9,10	1.40	4.20	14.00
11-18,20	1.20	3.60	12.00
21-40	1.10	3.30	9.00
41-80		2.40	6.00
81-99			5.00
100			5.50
101-138			2.50
139-155: 139-Begin $1.95-c. 148-Begin $1.99-c			2.00

NOTE: *Katy Keene in 23, 25, 27, 32-38, 40, 45-48, 50. The Fly-r in 19, 20. The Jaguar-r in 25, 27. Mr. Justice-r in 21. The Web-r in 23.*

LAUGH COMIX (Formerly Top Notch Laugh; Suzie Comics No. 49 on)
MLJ Magazines: No. 46, Summer, 1944 - No. 48, Winter, 1944-45

	GD2.0	FN6.0	NM9.4
46-Wilbur & Suzie in all; Harry Sahle-c	21.00	64.00	150.00
47,48: 47-Sahle-c. 48-Bill Vigoda-c	15.00	45.00	105.00

LAUGH-IN MAGAZINE (TV)(Magazine)
Laufer Publ. Co.: Oct, 1968 - No. 12, Oct, 1969 (50¢) (Satire)

	GD2.0	FN6.0	NM9.4
V1#1	3.80	11.40	38.00
2-12	2.80	8.40	28.00

LAUREL & HARDY (See Larry Harmon's... & March of Comics No. 302, 314)

LAUREL AND HARDY (...Comics)
St. John Publ. Co.: 3/49 - No. 3, 9/49; No. 26, 11/55 - No. 28, 3/56 (No #4-25)

	GD2.0	FN6.0	NM9.4
1	66.00	197.00	525.00
2	40.00	120.00	300.00
3	29.00	86.00	200.00
26-28 (Reprints)	16.00	47.00	110.00

LAUREL AND HARDY (TV)
Dell Publishing Co.: Oct, 1962 - No. 4, Sept-Nov, 1963

	GD2.0	FN6.0	NM9.4
12-423-210 (8-10/62)	4.50	13.50	50.00
2-4 (Dell)	3.20	9.50	35.00

LAUREL AND HARDY (Larry Harmon's...)
Gold Key: Jan, 1967 - No. 2, Oct, 1967

	GD2.0	FN6.0	NM9.4
1-Photo back-c	4.50	13.50	45.00
2	3.50	10.50	35.00

L.A.W., THE (LIVING ASSAULT WEAPONS)
DC Comics: Sept, 1999 - No. 6 ($2.50, limited series)

	GD2.0	FN6.0	NM9.4
1-3-Blue Beetle, Question, Judomaster, Capt. Atom app.; Giordano-a			2.50

LAW AGAINST CRIME (Law-Crime on cover)
Essenkay Publishing Co.: April, 1948 - No. 3, Aug, 1948 (Real Stories from Police Files)

	GD2.0	FN6.0	NM9.4
1-(#1-3 are half funny animal, half crime stories)-L. B. Cole-c/a in all; electrocution-c	66.00	197.00	525.00
2-L. B. Cole-c/a	50.00	150.00	400.00
3-Used in **SOTI**, pg. 180,181 & illo "The wish to hurt or kill couples in lovers' lanes;" reprinted in All-Famous Crime #9	62.00	187.00	500.00

LAW AND ORDER
Maximum Press: Sept, 1995 - No. 2, 1995 ($2.50, unfinished limited series)

	GD2.0	FN6.0	NM9.4
1,2			2.50

LAWBREAKERS (...Suspense Stories No. 10 on)
Law and Order Magazines (Charlton): Mar, 1951 - No. 9, Oct-Nov, 1952

	GD2.0	FN6.0	NM9.4
1	31.00	94.00	220.00
2	17.00	51.00	120.00
3,5,6,8,9	13.00	39.00	90.00
4- "White Death" junkie story	16.00	47.00	110.00
7- "The Deadly Dopesters" drug story	16.00	47.00	110.00

LAWBREAKERS ALWAYS LOSE!
Marvel Comics (CBS): Spring, 1948 - No. 10, Oct, 1949

	GD2.0	FN6.0	NM9.4
1-2pg. Kurtzman-a, "Giggles 'n' Grins"	31.00	94.00	220.00
2	16.00	47.00	110.00
3-5: 4-Vampire story	12.00	36.00	85.00
6(2/49)-Has editorial defense against charges of Dr. Wertham	13.00	39.00	90.00
7-Used in **SOTI**, illo "Comic-book philosophy"	29.00	86.00	200.00
8-10: 9,10-Photo-c	11.50	34.00	80.00

NOTE: ***Brodsky*** *c-4, 5.* ***Shores*** *c-1-3, 6-8.*

LAWBREAKERS SUSPENSE STORIES (Formerly Lawbreakers; Strange Suspense Stories No. 16 on)
Capitol Stories/Charlton Comics: No. 10, Jan, 1953 - No. 15, Nov, 1953

	GD2.0	FN6.0	NM9.4
10	30.00	90.00	210.00
11 (3/53)-Severed tongues-c/story & woman negligee scene	78.00	234.00	625.00
12-14: 13-Giordano-c begin, end #15	17.00	51.00	120.00
15-Acid-in-face-c/story; hands dissolved in acid sty	40.00	120.00	320.00

LAW-CRIME (See Law Against Crime)

LAWDOG
Marvel Comics (Epic Comics): May, 1993 - No. 10, Feb, 1993

	GD2.0	FN6.0	NM9.4
1-10			2.00

LAWDOG/GRIMROD: TERROR AT THE CROSSROADS
Marvel Comics (Epic Comics): Sept, 1993 ($3.50)

	GD2.0	FN6.0	NM9.4
1			3.50

LAWMAN (TV)
Dell Publishing Co.: No. 970, Feb, 1959 - No. 11, Apr-June, 1962 (All photo-c)

	GD2.0	FN6.0	NM9.4
Four Color 970(#1)	12.00	36.00	130.00
Four Color 1035('60), 3(2-4/60)-Toth-a	6.40	19.00	70.00
4-11	4.50	13.50	50.00

LAW OF DREDD, THE (Also see Judge Dredd)
Quality Comics/Fleetway #8 on: 1989 - No. 33, 1992 ($1.50/$1.75)

	GD2.0	FN6.0	NM9.4
1-33: Bolland a-1-6,8,10-12,14(2 pg),15,19			2.00

LAWRENCE (See Movie Classics)

LAZARUS CHURCHYARD
Tundra Publishing: June, 1992 - No. 3, 1992 ($3.95, 44 pgs., coated stock)

	GD2.0	FN6.0	NM9.4
1-3			4.00

LEADING COMICS (...Screen Comics No. 42 on)
National Periodical Publications: Winter, 1941-42 - No. 41, Feb-Mar, 1950

	GD2.0	FN6.0	NM9.4
1-Origin The Seven Soldiers of Victory; Crimson Avenger, Green Arrow & Speedy, Shining Knight, The Vigilante, Star Spangled Kid & Stripesy begin; The Dummy (Vigilante villain) 1st app.	389.00	1167.00	3500.00
2-Meskin-a; Fred Ray-c	150.00	450.00	1200.00
3	122.00	366.00	975.00
4,5	87.00	261.00	700.00
6-10	78.00	234.00	625.00
11-14(Spring, 1945): 13-Robot-c	54.00	162.00	435.00
15-(Sum,'45)-Contents change to funny animal	26.00	79.00	185.00
16-22,24-30: 16-Nero Fox-c begin, end #22	11.50	34.00	80.00
23-1st app. Peter Porkchops by Otto Feur & begins	26.00	77.00	180.00
31,32,34-41: 34-41-Leading Screen... on-c only	10.00	30.00	65.00
33-(Scarce)	20.00	60.00	140.00

NOTE: ***Rube Grossman****-a(Peter Porkchops)-most #15-on; c-15-41.* ***Post*** *a-23-37, 39, 41.*

LEADING SCREEN COMICS (Formerly Leading Comics)
National Periodical Publ.: No. 42, Apr-May, 1950 - No. 77, Aug-Sept, 1955

	GD2.0	FN6.0	NM9.4
42-Peter Porkchops-c/stories continue	10.00	30.00	65.00
43-77	9.15	27.00	55.00

NOTE: ***Grossman*** *a-most.* ***Mayer*** *a-45-48, 50, 54-57, 60, 62-74, 75(3), 76, 77.*

LEAGUE OF CHAMPIONS, THE (Also see The Champions)
Hero Graphics: Dec, 1990 - No. 12, 1992 ($2.95, 52 pgs.)

League of Extraordinary Gentlemen #1
© Alan Moore & Kevin O'Neill

Leave It to Binky #3 © DC

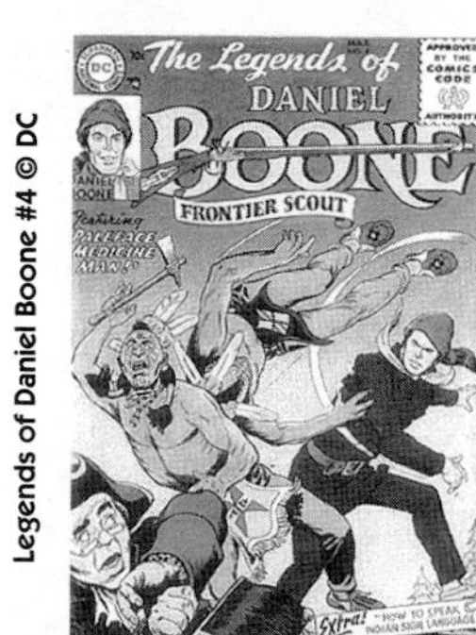

Legends of Daniel Boone #4 © DC

GD2.0 FN6.0 NM9.4

1-12: 1-Flare app. 2-Origin Malice 3.00

LEAGUE OF EXTRAORDINARY GENTLEMEN, THE
America's Best Comics: Mar, 1999 - No. 6 ($2.95, limited series)

1-Alan Moore-s/Kevin O'Neill-a 3.00
1-DF Edition ($10.00) O'Neill-c 10.00
2,4 3.00

LEAGUE OF JUSTICE
DC Comics (Elseworlds): 1996 - No. 2, 1996 ($5.95, 48 pgs., squarebound)

1,2: Magic-based alternate DC Universe story; Giordano-i 2.40 6.00

LEATHERFACE
Arpad Publishing: May (April on-c), 1991 - No. 4, May, 1992 ($2.75, painted-c)

1-4-Based on Texas Chainsaw movie; Dorman-c 3.00

LEATHERNECK THE MARINE (See Mighty Midget Comics)

LEAVE IT TO BEAVER (TV)
Dell Publishing Co.: No. 912, June, 1958; May-July, 1962 (All photo-c)

	GD2.0	FN6.0	NM9.4
Four Color 912	17.00	52.00	190.00
Four Color 999,1103,1191,1285, 01-428-207	14.00	44.00	160.00

LEAVE IT TO BINKY (Binky No. 72 on) (Super DC Giant) (No. 1-22: 52 pgs.)
National Periodical Publications: 2-3/48 - #60, 10/58; #61, 6-7/68 - #71, 2-3/70 (Teen-age humor)

	GD2.0	FN6.0	NM9.4
1-Lucy wears Superman costume	34.00	103.00	240.00
2	17.00	51.00	120.00
3,4	10.00	30.00	65.00
5-Superman cameo	17.00	49.00	115.00
6-10	9.15	27.00	55.00
11-14,16-22: Last 52pg. issue	7.50	22.50	45.00
15-Scribbly story by Mayer	10.00	30.00	65.00
23-28,30-45: 45-Last pre-code (2/55)	4.25	13.00	28.00
29-Used in **POP**, pg. 78	5.00	15.00	30.00
46-60: 60-(10/58)	2.50	7.50	22.00
61 (6-7/68)	4.00	12.00	40.00
62-69	2.50	7.50	22.00
70-7pg. app. Bus Driver who looks like Ralph from Honeymooners	3.20	9.00	32.00
71-Last issue	2.60	7.80	26.00

NOTE: ***Aragones**-a-61, 62, 67. **Drucker** a-28. **Mayer** a-1, 2, 15. Created by **Mayer**.*

LEAVE IT TO CHANCE
Image Comics (Homage Comics): Sept, 1996 - No. 11, Sept, 1998;
DC Comics (Homage Comics): No. 12, Jun, 1999 - Present ($2.50/$2.95)

1-3: 1-Intro Chance Falconer & St. George; James Robinson scripts & Paul Smith-c/a begins 5.00
4-12 3.00
Shaman's Rain TPB (1997, $9.95) r/#1-4 10.00
Trick or Threat TPB (1997, $12.95) r/#5-8 13.00

LEE HUNTER, INDIAN FIGHTER
Dell Publishing Co.: No. 779, Mar, 1957; No. 904, May, 1958

	GD2.0	FN6.0	NM9.4
Four Color 779 (#1)	3.60	11.00	40.00
Four Color 904	2.75	8.00	30.00

LEFT-HANDED GUN, THE (Movie)
Dell Publishing Co.: No. 913, July, 1958

Four Color 913-Paul Newman photo-c 10.00 30.00 110.00

LEGACY
Majestic Entertainment: Oct, 1993 - No. 2, Nov, 1993; No. 0, 1994 ($2.25)

1-2,0: 1-Glow-in-the-dark-c. 0-Platinum 2.25

LEGEND OF CUSTER, THE (TV)
Dell Publishing Co.: Jan, 1968

1-Wayne Maunder photo-c 2.50 7.50 24.00

LEGEND OF JESSE JAMES, THE (TV)
Gold Key: Feb, 1966

10172-602-Photo-c 2.50 7.50 24.00

LEGEND OF KAMUI, THE (See Kamui)

LEGEND OF LOBO, THE (See Movie Comics)

LEGEND OF MOTHER SARAH (Manga)
Dark Horse Comics: Apr, 1995 - No. 8, Nov, 1995 ($2.50, limited series)

1-8: Katsuhiro Otomo scripts 4.00

LEGEND OF MOTHER SARAH: CITY OF THE ANGELS (Manga)
Dark Horse Comics: Oct, 1996 - Present ($3.95, B&W, limited series)

1(10/96), 2(12/97),3-9: Otomo scripts 4.00

LEGEND OF MOTHER SARAH: CITY OF THE CHILDREN (Manga)
Dark Horse Comics: Jan, 1996 - No. 7, July, 1996 ($3.95, B&W, limited series)

1-7: Otomo scripts 4.00

LEGEND OF SUPREME
Image Comics (Extreme): Dec, 1994 - No. 3, Feb, 1995 ($2.50, limited series)

1-3 2.50

LEGEND OF THE ELFLORD
DavDez Arts: July, 1998 ($2.95)

1-Barry Blair & Colin Chin-s/a 3.00

LEGEND OF THE SHIELD, THE
DC Comics (Impact Comics): July, 1991 - No. 16, Oct, 1992 ($1.00)

1-16: 6,7-The Fly x-over. 12-Contains trading card 2.00
Annual 1 (1992, $2.50, 68 pgs.)-Snyder-a; w/trading card 2.50

LEGEND OF WONDER WOMAN, THE
DC Comics: May, 1986 - No. 4, Aug, 1986 (75¢, limited series)

1-4 2.50

LEGEND OF YOUNG DICK TURPIN, THE (Disney)(TV)
Gold Key: May, 1966

1 (10176-605)-Photo/painted-c 2.50 7.50 24.00

LEGEND OF ZELDA, THE (Link: The Legend... in indicia)
Valiant Comics: 1990 - No. 4, 1990 ($1.95, coated stiff-c)
V2#1, 1990 - No. 5, 1990 ($1.50)

1-4: 4-Layton-c(i) 3.00
V2#1-5 3.00

LEGENDS
DC Comics: Nov, 1986 - No. 6, Apr, 1987 (75¢, limited series)

1-6: 1-Byrne-c/a(p) in all; 1st app. new Capt. Marvel. 3-1st app. new Suicide Squad; death of Blockbuster. 6-1st app. new Justice League 3.00

LEGENDS OF DANIEL BOONE, THE (...Frontier Scout)
National Periodical Publications: Oct-Nov, 1955 - No. 8, Dec-Jan, 1956-57

	GD2.0	FN6.0	NM9.4
1 (Scarce)-Nick Cardy c-1-8	59.00	176.00	470.00
2 (Scarce)	43.00	128.00	340.00
3-8 (Scarce)	40.00	120.00	300.00

LEGENDS OF KID DEATH AND FLUFFY
Event Comics: Feb, 1997 ($2.95, B&W, one-shot)

1-Five covers 3.00

LEGENDS OF NASCAR, THE
Vortex Comics: Nov, 1990 - No. 14, 1992? (#1 3rd printing (1/91) says 2nd printing inside)

1-Bill Elliott biog.; Trimpe-a ($1.50) 5.00
1-2nd printing (11/90, $2.00) 2.00
1-3rd print; contains Maxx racecards ($3.00) 3.00
($2.00) 4.00
2-14: 2-Richard Petty. 3-Ken Schrader (7/91). 4-Bobby Allison; Spiegle-a(p); Adkins part-i. 5-Sterling Marlin. 6-Bill Elliott. 7-Junior Johnson; Spiegle-c/a. 8-Benny Parsons; Heck-a 3.00
1-13-Hologram cover versions. 2-Hologram shows Bill Elliott's car by mistake (all are numbered & limited) 5.00
2-Hologram corrected version 5.00

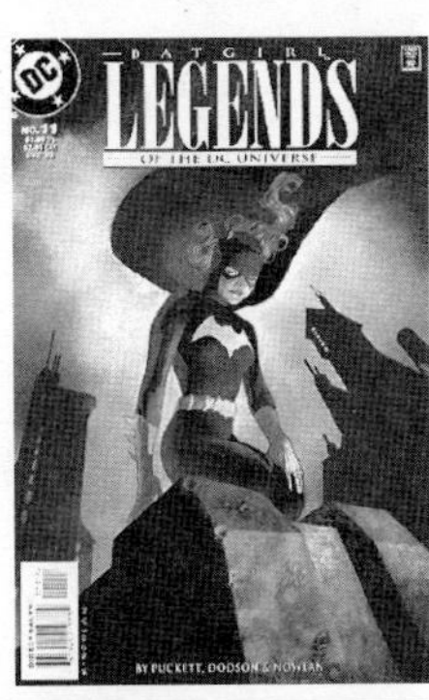

Legends of the DC Universe #11 © DC

Legionnaires #14 © DC

Legion of Super-Heroes (3rd series) #45 © DC

GD2.0 FN6.0 NM9.4

Christmas Special ($5.95) 2.40 6.00

LEGENDS OF THE DARK CLAW
DC Comics (Amalgam): Apr, 1996 ($1.95)

1-Jim Balent-c/a 3.00

LEGENDS OF THE DARK KNIGHT (See Batman: ...)

LEGENDS OF THE DC UNIVERSE
DC Comics: Feb, 1998 - Present ($1.95/$1.99)

1-13,15-21: 1-3-Superman; Robinson-s/Semeiks-a/Orbik-painted-c. 4,5-Wonder Woman; Deodato-a/Rude painted-c. 8-GL/GA, O'Neil-s. 10,11-Batgirl; Dodson-a. 12,13-Justice League. 15-17-Flash. 18-Kid Flash; Guice-a. 19-Impulse; prelude to JLApe Annuals. 20,21-Abin Sur 3.00
14-($3.95) Jimmy Olsen; Kirby-esque-c by Rude 4.00
22-Superman; Rude-c/Ladronn-a 2.00
... Crisis on Infinite Earths 1 (2/99, $4.95) Untold story during and after Crisis on I.E. #4; Wolfman-s/Ryan-a/Orbik-c 5.00
... 80 Page Giant 1 (9/98, $4.95) Stories and art by various incl. Ditko, Perez, Gibbons, Mumy; Joe Kubert-c 5.00
... 3-D Gallery (12/98, $2.95) Pin-ups w/glasses 3.00

LEGENDS OF THE LEGION (See Legion of Super-Heroes)
DC Comics: Feb, 1998 - No. 4, May, 1998 ($2.25, limited series)

1-4:1-Origin-s of Ultra Boy. 2-Spark. 3-Umbra. 4-Star Boy 3.00

LEGENDS OF THE STARGRAZERS (See Vanguard Illustrated #2)
Innovation Publishing: Aug, 1989 - No. 6, 1990 ($1.95, limited series, mature)

1-6: 1-Redondo part inks 2.00

LEGENDS OF THE WORLD'S FINEST (See World's Finest)
DC Comics: 1994 - No. 3, 1994 ($4.95, squarebound, limited series)

1-3: Simonson scripts; Brereton-c/a; embossed foil logos 2.40 6.00
TPB-(1995, $14.95) r/#1-3 15.00

L.E.G.I.O.N. (The # to right of title represents year of print)(Also see Lobo & R.E.B.E.L.S.)
DC Comics: Feb, 1989 - No. 70, Sept, 1994 ($1.50/$1.75)

1-Giffen plots/breakdowns in #1-12,28 5.00
2-22,24-47: 3-Lobo app. #3 on. 4-1st Lobo-c this title. 5-Lobo joins L.E.G.I.O.N. 13-Lar Gand app. 16-Lar Gand joins L.E.G.I.O.N., leaves #19. 31-Capt. Marvel app. 35-L.E.G.I.O.N. '92 begins 3.00
23,70-($2.50, 52 pgs.)-L.E.G.I.O.N. '91 begins. 70-Zero Hour 4.00
48,49,51-69: 48-Begin $1.75-c. 63-L.E.G.I.O.N. '94 begins; Superman x-over 3.00
50-($3.50, 68 pgs.) 4.00
Annual 1-5 ('90-94, 68 pgs.): 1-Lobo, Superman app. 2-Alan Grant scripts. 5-Elseworlds story; Lobo app. 4.00
NOTE: ***Alan Grant*** *scripts in #1-39, 51, Annual 1, 2.*

LEGIONNAIRES (See Legion of Super-Heroes #40, 41 & Showcase 95 #6)
DC Comics: Apr, 1992 - No. 81, Mar, 2000($1.25/$1.50/$2.25)

1-18,0,19-49,51-77: 1-Chris Sprouse-c/a; polybagged w/SkyBox trading card. 11-Kid Quantum joins. 18-(9/94)-Zero Hour. 0-(10/94)-Restart of Legion conti nuity. 19(11/94). 37-Valor (Lar Gand) becomes M'onel (5/96). 43-Legion try outs; reintro Princess Projectra, Shadow Lass & others. 47-Forms one cover image with LSH #91. 52-Shrinking Violet becomes LeViathan. 60-Karate Kid & Kid Quantum join. 61-Silver Age & 70's Legion app. 76-Return of Wildfire 2.50
50-($3.95) Pullout poster by Davis/Farmer 4.00
#1,000,000 (11/98) Sean Phillips-a 2.50
Annual 1,3 ('94,'96 $2.95)-1-Elseworlds-s. 3-Legends of the Dead Earth-s 3.00
Annual 2 (1995, $3.95)-Year One-s 4.50

LEGIONNAIRES THREE
DC Comics: Jan, 1986 - No. 4, May, 1986 (75¢, limited series)

1-4 2.00

LEGION OF MONSTERS (Also see Marvel Premiere #28 & Marvel Preview #8)
Marvel Comics Group: Sept, 1975 ($1.00, B&W, magazine, 76 pgs.)

1-Origin & 1st app. Legion of Monsters; Neal Adams-c; Morrow-a; origin & only app. The Manphibian; Frankenstein by Mayerik; Bram Stoker's Dracula adaptation; Reese-a; painted-c (#2 was advertised with Morbius & Satana, but was never published) 2.50 7.50 20.00

LEGION OF NIGHT, THE
Marvel Comics: Oct, 1991 - No. 2, Oct, 1991 ($4.95, 52 pgs.)

1,2-Whilce Portacio-c/a(p) 5.00

LEGION OF SUBSTITUTE HEROES SPECIAL (See Adventure Comics #306)
DC Comics: July, 1985 ($1.25, one-shot, 52 pgs.)

1-Giffen-c/a(p) 2.00

LEGION OF SUPER-HEROES (See Action, Adventure, All New Collectors Edition, Legionnaires, Legends of the Legion, Limited Collectors Edition, Secrets of the..., Superboy & Superman)
National Periodical Publications: Feb, 1973 - No. 4, July-Aug, 1973

1-Legion & Tommy Tomorrow reprints begin 2.25 6.75 18.00
2-4: 2-Forte-r. 3-r/Adv. #340. Action #240. 4-r/Adv. #341, Action #233; Mooney-r 1.25 3.75 10.00

LEGION OF SUPER-HEROES, THE (Formerly Superboy and...; Tales of The Legion No. 314 on)
DC Comics: No. 259, Jan, 1980 - No. 313, July, 1984

259(#1)-Superboy leaves Legion 2.40 6.00
260-270,285-290,294: 265-Contains 28 pg. insert "Superman & the TRS-80 computer"; origin Tyroc; Tyroc leaves Legion. 290-294-Great Darkness saga. 294-Double size (52 pgs.) 4.00
271-284,291-293: 272-Blok joins; origin; 20 pg. insert-Dial 'H' For Hero. 277-Intro Reflecto. 280-Superboy re-joins Legion. 282-Origin Reflecto. 283-Origin Wildfire 3.00
295-299,301-313: 297-Origin retold. 298-Free 16pg. Amethyst preview. 306-Brief origin Star Boy 2.00
300-(68 pgs., Mando paper)-Anniversary issue; has c/a by almost everyone at DC 4.00
Annual 1-3(82-84, 52 pgs.)-1-Giffen-c/a; 1st app./origin new Invisible Kid who joins Legion. Karate Kid & Princess Projectra wed & resign 2.50
...The Great Darkness Saga (1989, $17.95, 196 pgs.)-r/LSH #287,290-294 & Annual #3; Giffen-c/a 1.80 5.40 18.00
NOTE: ***Aparo*** *c-282, 283, 300(part).* ***Austin*** *c-268i.* ***Buckler*** *c-273p, 274p, 276p.* ***Colan*** *a-311p.* ***Ditko*** *a(p)-267, 268, 272, 274, 276, 281.* ***Giffen*** *a-285-313p, Annual 1p; c-287p, 288p, 289, 290p, 291p, 292, 293, 294-299p, 300, 301-313p, Annual 1p, 2p.* ***Perez*** *c-268p, 277-280, 281p.* ***Starlin*** *a-265.* ***Staton*** *a-259p, 260p, 280.* ***Tuska*** *a-308p.*

LEGION OF SUPER-HEROES (3rd Series) (Reprinted in Tales of the Legion)
DC Comics: Aug, 1984 - No. 63, Aug, 1989 ($1.25/$1.75, deluxe format)

1-Silver ink logo 4.00
2-36,39-44,46-49,51-62: 4-Death of Karate Kid. 5-Death of Nemesis Kid. 12-Cosmic Boy, Lightning Lad, & Saturn Girl resign. 14-Intro new members: Tellus, Sensor Girl, Quislet. 15-17-Crisis tie-ins. 18-Crisis x-over. 25-Sensor Girl i.d. revealed as Princess Projectra. 35-Saturn Girl rejoins. 42,43-Millennium tie-ins. 44-Origin Quislet 2.50
37,38-Death of Superboy 1.50 4.50 12.00
45,50: 45 ($2.95, 68 pgs.)-Anniversary ish. 50-Double size ($2.50-c) 4.00
63-Final issue 2.00
Annual 1-4 (10/85-'88, 52 pgs.)-1-Crisis tie-in 2.50
NOTE: ***Byrne*** *c-36p.* ***Giffen*** *a(p)-1, 2, 50-55, 57-63, Annual 1p, 2; c-1-5p, 54p, Annual 1.* ***Orlando*** *a-6p.* ***Steacy*** *c-45-50, Annual 3.*

LEGION OF SUPER-HEROES (4th Series)
DC Comics: Nov, 1989 - No. 125, Mar, 2000 ($1.75/$1.95/$2.25)

1-Giffen-c/a(p)/scripts begin (4 pg.-a only #18) 4.00
2-49,51-53,55-58: 4-Mon-El (Lar Gand) destroys Time Trapper, changes reality. 5-Alt. reality story where Mordru rules all; Ferro Lad app. 6-1st app. of Laurel Gand (Lar Gand's cousin). 8-Origin. 13-Free poster by Giffen show ing new costumes. 15-(2/91)-1st reference of Lar Gand as Valor. 21-24-Lobo & Darkseid storyline. 26-New map of headquarters. 34-Six pg. preview of Timber Wolf mini-series. 40-Minor Legionnaires app. 41-(3/93)-Intro SW6 Legionnaires 3.00
50-($3.50, 68 pgs.) 3.50
54-($2.95)-Die-cut & foil stamped-c 4.00

Legion of Super-Heroes (4th series) #114 © DC

Lenore #4 © Roman Dirge

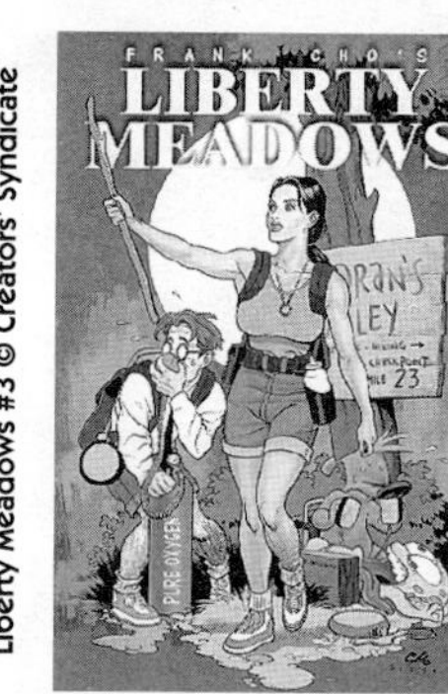

Liberty Meadows #3 © Creators' Syndicate

59-61,0,61-69-99: 61-(9/94)-Zero Hour. 0-(10/94). 762-(11/94). 5-XS travels back to the 20th Century (cont'd in Impulse #9). 77-Origin of Brainiac 5. 81-Reintro Sun Boy. 85-Half of the Legion sent to the 20th century, Superman-c/app. 86-Final Night. 87-Deadman-c/app. 88-Impulse-c/app. Adventure Comics #247 cover swipe. 91-Forms one cover image with Legionnaires #47. 96-Wedding of Ultra Boy and Apparition. 99-Robin, Impulse, Superboy app. 2.50
100-($5.95, 96 pgs.)-Legionnaires return to the 30th Century; gatefold-c; 5 stories-art by Simonson, Davis and others 1.00 2.80 7.00
101-115: 101-Armstrong-a(p) begins. 105-Legion past & present vs. Time Trapper. 109-Moder-a. 110-Thunder joins. 114,115-Bizarro Legion. 120,121-Fatal Five 2.50
#1,000,000 (11/98) Giffen-a 2.50
Annual 1-5 (1990-1994, $3.50, 68 pgs.): 4-Bloodlines. 5-Elseworlds story 3.50
Annual 6 (1995,$3.95)-Year One story 4.00
Annual 7 (1996, $3.50, 48 pgs.)-Legends of the Dead Earth story; intro 75th Century Legion of Super-Heroes; Wildfire app. 3.50
Legion: Secret Files 1 (1/98, $4.95) Retold origin & pin-ups 5.00
Legion: Secret Files 2 (6/99, $4.95) Story and profile pages 5.00
The Beginning of Tomorrow TPB ('99, $17.95) r/post-Zero Hour reboot 18.00
NOTE: **Giffen** a-1-24; breakdowns-26-32, 34-36; c-1-7, 8(part), 9-24. **Brandon Peterson** a(p)-15(1st for DC), 16, 18, Annual 2(54 pgs.); c-Annual 2p. **Swan/Anderson** c-8(part).

LEGION: SCIENCE POLICE (See Legion of Super-Heroes)
DC Comics: Aug, 1998 - No. 4, Nov, 1998 ($2.25, limited series)
1-4-Ryan-a 2.50

LEMONADE KID, THE (See Bobby Benson's B-Bar-B Riders)
AC Comics: 1990 ($2.50, 28 pgs.)
1-Powell-c(r); Red Hawk-r by Powell; Lemonade Kid-r/Bobby Benson by Powell (2 stories) 2.50

LENNON SISTERS LIFE STORY, THE
Dell Publishing Co.: No. 951, Nov, 1958 - No. 1014, Aug, 1959
Four Color 951 (#1)-Toth-a, 32pgs, photo-c 13.00 40.00 145.00
Four Color 1014-Toth-a, photo-c 13.00 40.00 145.00

LENORE
Slave Labor Graphics: Feb, 1998 - Present ($2.95, B&W)
1-6: 1-Roman Dirge-s/a, 1,2-2nd printing 3.00
...: Noogies TPB ($11.95) r/#1-4 12.00

LEONARD NIMOY'S PRIMORTALS
Tekno Comix: Mar, 1995 - No. 15, May, 1996 ($1.95)
1-15: Concept by Leonard Nimoy & Isaac Asimov 1-3-w/bound-in game piece & trading card. 4-w/Teknophage Steel Edition coupon. 13,14-Art Adams-c. 15-Simonson-c 2.25

LEONARD NIMOY'S PRIMORTALS
BIG Entertainment: V2#0, June, 1996 - No. 8, Feb, 1997 ($2.25)
V2#0-8: 0-Includes Pt. 9 of "The Big Bang" x-over. 0,1-Simonson-c. 3-Kelley Jones-c 2.25

LEONARD NIMOY'S PRIMORTALS ORIGINS
Tekno Comix: Nov, 1995 - No. 2, Dec, 1995 ($2.95, limited series)
1,2: Nimoy scripts; Art Adams-c; polybagged 3.00

LEONARDO (Also see Teenage Mutant Ninja Turtles)
Mirage Studios: Dec, 1986 ($1.50, B&W, one-shot)
1 3.00

LEO THE LION
I. W. Enterprises: No date(1960s) (10¢)
1-Reprint 1.25 3.75 10.00

LEROY (Teen-age)
Standard Comics: Nov, 1949 - No. 6, Nov, 1950
1 6.70 20.00 40.00
2-Frazetta text illo. 5.00 15.00 30.00
3-6: 3-Lubbers-a 4.00 12.00 24.00

GD2.0 FN6.0 NM9.4

LETHAL (Also see Brigade)
Image Comics (Extreme Studios): Feb, 1996 ($2.50, unfinished limited series)
1-Marat Mychaels-c/a. 2.50

LETHAL FOES OF SPIDER-MAN (Sequel to Deadly Foes of Spider-Man)
Marvel Comics: Sept, 1993 - No. 4, Dec, 1993 ($1.75, limited series)
1-4 2.00

LETHAL STRYKE
London Night Studios: June, 1995 - No. 3, 1995 ($3.00)
0-(8/95, $5.95)-Collector's ed. 2.40 6.00
1/2, 1-3: 1-polybagged w/card 3.00
Annual 1-(1996, $3.00) 3.00
Annual 1-Platinum Edition 10.00
Trade paperback-(1996, $12.95)-r/#(1/2)-3 13.00

LETHAL STRYKE/DOUBLE IMPACT: LETHAL IMPACT
London Night Studios: May, 1996 ($3.00, one-shot)
1-Hartsoe/Lyon-a(p) 3.00
1-Natural Born Killers Edition 5.00

LETHARGIC LAD
Crusade Ent.: June, 1996 - No. 3, Sept, 1996 ($2.95, B&W, limited series)
1,2 3.00
3-Alex Ross-c/swipe (Kingdom Come) 4.00

LETHARGIC LAD ADVENTURES
Crusade Ent./Destination Ent.#3 on: Oct, 1997 - Present ($2.95, B&W)
1-11-Hyland-s/a. 9-Alex Ross sketch page & back-c 3.00

LET'S PRETEND (CBS radio)
D. S. Publishing Co.: May-June, 1950 - No. 3, Sept-Oct, 1950
1 15.00 45.00 105.00
2,3 11.50 34.00 80.00

LET'S READ THE NEWSPAPER
Charlton Press: 1974
nn-Features Quincy by Ted Sheares 1.00 2.80 7.00

LET'S TAKE A TRIP (TV) (CBS Television Presents)
Pines Comics: Spring, 1958
1-Marv Levy-c/a 4.00 12.00 24.00

LETTERS TO SANTA (See March of Comics No. 228)

LEX LUTHOR: THE UNAUTHORIZED BIOGRAPHY
DC Comics: 1989 ($3.95, 52 pgs., one-shot, squarebound)
1-Painted-c; Clark Kent app. 4.00

LIBERTY COMICS (Miss Liberty No. 1)
Green Publishing Co.: No. 4, 1945 - No. 15, July, 1946 (MLJ & other reprints)
4 14.00 43.00 100.00
5 (5/46)-The Prankster app; Starr-a 13.00 39.00 90.00
10-Hangman & Boy Buddies app.; Suzie & Wilbur begin; reprints Hangman story from Hangman #8 17.00 51.00 120.00
11(V2#2, 1/46)-Wilbur in women's clothes 14.00 43.00 100.00
12-Black Hood & Suzie app. 15.00 45.00 105.00
14,15-Patty of Airliner; Starr-a in both 10.00 30.00 65.00

LIBERTY GUARDS
Chicago Mail Order: No date (1946?)
nn-Reprints Man of War #1 with cover of Liberty Scouts #1; Gustavson-c 36.00 107.00 250.00

LIBERTY MEADOWS
Insight Studios Group: 1999 - Present ($2.95, B&W)
1-3-Frank Cho-s/a; reprints newspaper strips 2.95

LIBERTY PROJECT, THE
Eclipse Comics: June, 1987 - No. 8, May, 1988 ($1.75, color, Baxter paper)
1-8: 6-Valkyrie app. 2.00

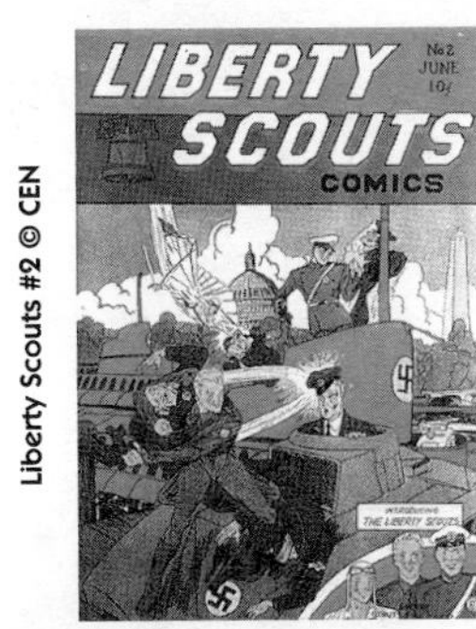

Liberty Scouts #2 © CEN

Life of Captain Marvel #1 © MAR

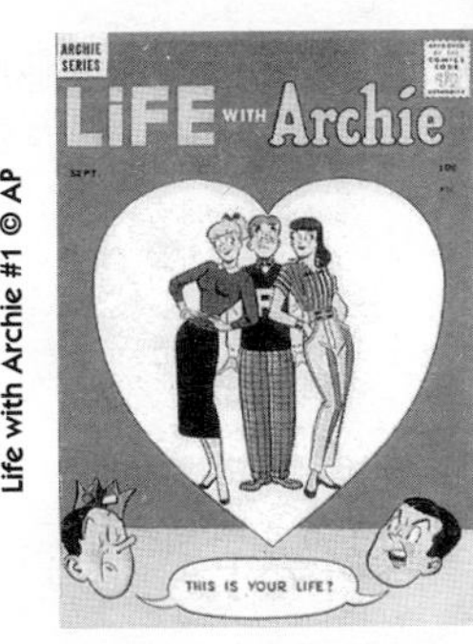

Life with Archie #1 © AP

	GD2.0	FN6.0	NM9.4
LIBERTY SCOUTS (See Liberty Guards & Man of War)			
Centaur Publications: No. 2, June, 1941 - No. 3, Aug, 1941			
2(#1)-Origin The Fire-Man, Man of War; Vapo-Man & Liberty Scouts begin; intro Liberty Scouts; Gustavson-c/a in both	122.00	366.00	975.00
3(#2)-Origin & 1st app. The Sentinel	91.00	272.00	725.00
LICENCE TO KILL (James Bond 007) (Movie)			
Eclipse Comics: 1989 ($7.95, slick paper, 52 pgs.)			
nn-Movie adaptation; Timothy Dalton photo-c	1.00	3.00	8.00
Limited Hardcover ($24.95)			25.00
LIDSVILLE (TV)			
Gold Key: Oct, 1972 - No. 5, Oct, 1973			
1-Photo-c	3.50	10.50	35.00
2-5	2.50	7.50	22.00
LIEUTENANT, THE (TV)			
Dell Publishing Co.: April-June, 1964			
1-Photo-c	2.50	7.50	24.00
LIEUTENANT BLUEBERRY (Also see Blueberry)			
Marvel Comics (Epic Comics): 1991 - No. 3, 1991 (Graphic novel)			
1,2 ($8.95)-Moebius-a in all			9.00
3 ($14.95)			15.00
LT. ROBIN CRUSOE, U.S.N. (See Movie Comics & Walt Disney Showcase #26)			
LIFE OF CAPTAIN MARVEL, THE			
Marvel Comics Group: Aug, 1985 - No. 5, Dec, 1985 ($2.00, Baxter paper)			
1-5: 1-All reprint Starlin issues of Iron Man #55, Capt. Marvel #25-34 plus Marvel Feature #12 (all with Thanos). 4-New Thanos back-c by Starlin			2.00
LIFE OF CHRIST, THE			
Catechetical Guild Educational Society: No. 301, 1949 (35¢, 100 pgs.)			
301-Reprints from Topix(1949)-V5#11,12	8.35	25.00	50.00
LIFE OF CHRIST: THE CHRISTMAS STORY, THE			
Marvel Comics/Nelson: Feb, 1993 ($2.99, slick stock)			
nn			4.00
LIFE OF CHRIST: THE EASTER STORY, THE			
Marvel Comics/Nelson: 1993 ($2.99, slick stock)			
nn			3.00
LIFE OF CHRIST VISUALIZED			
Standard Publishers: 1942 - No. 3, 1943			
1-3: All came in cardboard case	5.85	17.50	35.00
With case.....	10.00	30.00	60.00
LIFE OF CHRIST VISUALIZED			
The Standard Publ. Co.: 1946? (48 pgs. in color)			
nn	3.20	8.00	16.00
LIFE OF ESTHER VISUALIZED			
The Standard Publ. Co.: No. 2062, 1947 (48 pgs. in color)			
2062	3.60	9.00	18.00
LIFE OF JOSEPH VISUALIZED			
The Standard Publ. Co.: No. 1054, 1946 (48 pgs. in color)			
1054	3.20	8.00	16.00
LIFE OF PAUL (See The Living Bible)			
LIFE OF POPE JOHN PAUL II, THE			
Marvel Comics Group: Jan, 1983 ($1.50/$1.75)			
1			4.00
LIFE OF RILEY, THE (TV)			
Dell Publishing Co.: No. 917, July, 1958			
Four Color 917-Photo-c	11.00	33.00	120.00
LIFE'S LIKE THAT			
Croyden Publ. Co.: 1945 (25¢, B&W, 68 pgs.)			
nn-Newspaper Sunday strip-r by Neher	5.85	17.50	35.00
LIFE STORIES OF AMERICAN PRESIDENTS (See Dell Giants)			
LIFE STORY			
Fawcett Publications: Apr, 1949 - V8#46, Jan, 1953; V8#47, Apr, 1953 (All have photo-c?)			
V1#1	12.00	36.00	85.00
2	5.85	17.50	35.00
3-6, V2#7-12	5.00	15.00	30.00
V3#13-Wood-a	13.00	39.00	90.00
V3#14-18, V4#19-24, V5#25-30, V6#31-35	4.25	13.00	26.00
V6#36- "I sold drugs" on-c	5.35	16.00	32.00
V7#37,40-42, V8#44,45	3.60	9.00	18.00
V7#38, V8#43-Evans-a	5.00	15.00	30.00
V7#39-Drug Smuggling & Junkie story	4.25	13.00	28.00
V8#46,47 (Scarce)	4.25	13.00	28.00
NOTE: ***Powell*** *a-13, 23, 24, 26, 28, 30, 32, 39.* ***Marcus Swayze*** *a-1-3, 10-12, 15, 16, 20, 21, 23-25, 31, 35, 37, 40, 44, 46.*			
LIFE, THE UNIVERSE AND EVERYTHING (See Hitchhikers Guide to the Galaxy & Restaurant at the End of the Universe)			
DC Comics: 1996 - No. 3, 1996 ($6.95, squarebound, limited series)			
1-3: Adaptation of novel by Douglas Adams.	.85	2.60	7.00
LIFE WITH ARCHIE			
Archie Publications: Sept, 1958 - No. 285, July, 1991			
1	27.00	81.00	270.00
2-(9/59)	13.00	39.00	130.00
3-5: 3-(7/60)	9.00	27.00	90.00
6-10	6.00	18.00	60.00
11-20	4.50	13.50	45.00
21(7/63)-30	3.20	9.60	32.00
31-41	2.50	7.50	24.00
42-Pureheart begins (1st app.-c/s, 10/65)	5.50	16.50	55.00
43,44	3.20	9.60	32.00
45(1/66) 1st Man From R.I.V.E.R.D.A.L.E.	4.20	12.60	42.00
46-Origin Pureheart	2.60	7.80	26.00
47-49	2.50	7.50	22.00
50-United Three begin: Pureheart (Archie), Superteen (Betty), Captain Hero (Jughead)	2.80	8.40	28.00
51-59: 59-Pureheart ends	2.50	7.50	25.00
60-Archie band begins, ends #66	3.20	9.60	32.00
61-66: 61-Man From R.I.V.E.R.D.A.L.E.-c/s	2.50	7.50	20.00
67-80	1.40	4.20	14.00
81-99	1.20	3.60	12.00
100 (8/70), 113-Sabrina & Salem app.	1.80	5.40	18.00
101-112, 114-130(2/73), 139(11/73)-Archie Band c/s	1.10	3.30	9.00
131,134-138,140-146,148-161,164-170(6/76)	1.00	2.80	7.00
132,133,147,163-all horror-c/s	1.10	3.30	9.00
162-UFO c/s	1.25	3.75	10.00
171,173-175,177-184,186,189,191-194,196			5.00
172,185,197 : 172-(9/77)-Bi-Cent. spec. ish, 185-2nd 24th cent.-c/s, 197-Time machine/SF-c/s		2.40	6.00
176(12/76)-1st app. Capt. Archie of Starship Rivda, in 24th century c/s; 1st app. Stella the Robot	1.10	3.30	9.00
187,188,195,198,199-all horror-c/s		2.40	6.00
190-1st Dr. Doom-c/s		2.40	6.00
200 (12/78) Maltese Pigeon-s	1.00	2.80	7.00
201-203,205-237,239,240(1/84): 208-Reintro Veronica.			3.00
204-Flying saucer-c/s			5.00
238-(9/83)-25th anniversary issue; Ol' Betsy (jalopy) replaced			3.00
241-278,280-284: 250-Comic book convention-s			2.00
279,285: 279-Intro Mustang Sally ($1.00, 7/90)			3.00
NOTE: ***Gene Colan*** *a-272-279, 285, 286.*			
LIFE WITH MILLIE (Formerly A Date With Millie) (Modeling With Millie #21 on)			
Atlas/Marvel Comics Group: No. 8, Dec, 1960 - No. 20, Dec, 1962			
8-Teenage	6.50	19.50	65.00

Limited Collectors' Edition C-22 © ERB

Linda #4 © AJAX

Lionheart #1 © Awesome Entertainment

GD2.0 FN6.0 NM9.4

9-11 4.20 13.20 42.00
12-20 3.20 9.60 32.00

LIFE WITH SNARKY PARKER (TV)
Fox Feature Syndicate: Aug, 1950

1-Early TV comic; photo-c from TV puppet show 26.00 77.00 180.00

LIGHT AND DARKNESS WAR, THE
Marvel Comics (Epic Comics): Oct, 1988 - No. 6, Dec, 1989 ($1.95, lim. series)

1-6 2.00

LIGHT FANTASTIC, THE (Terry Pratchett's)
Innovation Publishing: June, 1992 - No. 4, Sept, 1992 ($2.50, mini-series)

1-4: Adapts 2nd novel in Discworld series 2.50

LIGHT IN THE FOREST (Disney)
Dell Publishing Co.: No. 891, Mar, 1958

Four Color 891-Movie, Fess Parker photo-c 7.30 22.00 80.00

LIGHTNING COMICS (Formerly Sure-Fire No. 1-3)
Ace Magazines: No. 4, Dec, 1940 - No. 13(V3#1), June, 1942

4-Characters continue from Sure-Fire 97.00 291.00 775.00
5,6: 6-Dr. Nemesis begins 64.00 191.00 510.00
V2#1-6: 2- "Flash Lightning" becomes "Lash..." 51.00 154.00 410.00
V3#1-Intro. Lightning Girl & The Sword 51.00 154.00 410.00
NOTE: ***Anderson*** *a-V2#6.* ***Mooney*** *c-V1#5, 6, V2#1-6, V3#1. Bondage c-V2#6. Lightning-c on all.*

LIGHTNING COMICS PRESENTS
Lightning Comics: May, 1994 ($3.50)

1-Red foil-c distr. by Diamond Distr., 1-Black/yellow/blue-c distrib. by Capital Distr., 1-Red/yellow-c distributed by H. World, 1-Platinum 3.50

LI'L ... (See Little ...)

LILLITH (See Warrior Nun...)
Antarctic Press: Sept, 1996 - No. 3, Feb, 1997 ($2.95, limited series)

1-3: 1-Variant-c 3.00

LIMITED COLLECTORS' EDITION (See Famous First Edition, Marvel Treasury #28, Rudolph The Red-Nosed Reindeer, & Superman Vs. The Amazing Spider-Man; becomes All-New Collectors' Edition)
National Periodical Publications/DC Comics:
(#21-34,51-59: 84 pgs.; #35-41: 68 pgs.; #42-50: 60 pgs.)
C-21, Summer, 1973 - No. C-59, 1978 ($1.00) (10x13-1/2")

(Rudolph...C-20 (implied), 12/72)-See Rudolph The Red-Nosed Reindeer
C-21: Shazam (TV); r/Captain Marvel Jr. #11 by Raboy; C.C. Beck-c, biog. & photo 2.50 7.50 28.00
C-22: Tarzan; complete origin reprinted from #207-210; all Kubert-c/a; Joe Kubert biography & photo inside 2.20 6.60 22.00
C-23: House of Mystery; Wrightson, N. Adams/Orlando, G. Kane/Wood, Toth, Aragones, Sparling reprints 2.90 8.70 32.00
C-24: Rudolph The Red-Nosed Reindeer 7.00 21.00 70.00
C-25: Batman; Neal Adams-c/a(r); G.A. Joker-r; Batman/Enemy Ace-r; has photos from TV show 3.50 10.50 38.00
C-26: See Famous First Edition C-26 (same contents)
C-27,C-29,C-31: C-27: Shazam (TV); G.A. Capt. Marvel & Mary Marvel-r; Beck-r. C-29: Tarzan; reprints "Return of Tarzan" from #219-223 by Kubert; Kubert-c. C-31: Superman; origin-r; N. Adams-a; photos of George Reeves from 1950s TV show on inside b/c; Burnley, Boring-r 2.00 6.00 22.00
C-32: Ghosts (new-a) 2.90 8.70 32.00
C-33: Rudolph The Red-Nosed Reindeer(new-a) 5.50 16.50 60.00
C-34: Christmas with the Super-Heroes; unpublished Angel & Ape story by Oksner & Wood; Batman & Teen Titans-r 2.00 6.00 20.00
C-35: Shazam (TV); photo cover features TV's Captain Marvel, Jackson Bostwick; Beck-r; TV photos inside b/c 1.80 5.40 18.00
C-36: The Bible; all new adaptation beginning with Genesis by Kubert, Redondo & Mayer; Kubert-c 1.80 5.40 18.00
C-37: Batman; r-1946 Sundays; inside b/c photos of Batman TV show villains (all villain issue; r/G.A. Joker, Catwoman, Penguin, Two-Face, & Scarecrow stories plus 1946 Sundays-r) 2.20 6.60 24.00

GD2.0 FN6.0 NM9.4

C-38: Superman; 1 pg. N. Adams; part photo-c; photos from TV show on inside back-c 1.80 5.40 18.00
C-39: Secret Origins of Super-Villains; N. Adams-i(r); collection reprints 1950's Joker origin, Luthor origin from Adv. Comics #271, Capt. Cold origin from Showcase #8 among others; G.A. Batman-r; Beck-r. 1.80 5.40 18.00
C-40: Dick Tracy by Gould featuring Flattop; newspaper-r from 12/21/43 - 5/17/44; biog. of Chester Gould 1.80 5.40 18.00
C-41: Super Friends (TV); JLA-r(1965); Toth-c/a 2.00 6.00 20.00
C-42: Rudolph 4.00 12.25 45.00
C-43-C-47: C-43: Christmas with the Super-Heroes; Wrightson, S&K, Neal Adams-a. C-44: Batman; N. Adams-p(r) & G.A.-r; painted-c. C-45: More Secret Origins of Super-Villains; Flash-r/#105; G.A. Wonder Woman & Batman/Catwoman-r. C-46: Justice League of America(1963-r); 3 pgs. Toth-a C-47: Superman Salutes the Bicentennial (Tomahawk interior); 2 pgs. new-a 1.80 5.40 18.00
C-48,C-49: C-48: Superman Vs. The Flash (Superman/Flash race); swipes-c to Superman #199; r/Superman #199 & Flash #175; 6 pgs. Neal Adams-a. C-49: Superboy & the Legion of Super-Heroes 2.00 6.00 20.00
C-50: Rudolph The Red-Nosed Reindeer 4.00 12.25 45.00
C-51: Batman; Neal Adams-c/a 2.00 6.00 22.00
C-52,C-57: C-52: The Best of DC; Neal Adams-c/a; Toth, Kubert-a. C-57: Welcome Back, Kotter-r(TV)(5/78) 2.00 6.00 20.00
C-59: Batman's Strangest Cases; N. Adams-r; Wrightson-r/Swamp Thing #7; N. Adams/Wrightson-c 1.80 5.40 18.00
NOTE: *All-r with exception of some special features and covers.* ***Aparo*** *a-52r; c-37.* ***Grell*** *c-49.* ***Infantino*** *a-25, 39, 44, 45, 52.* ***Bob Kane*** *r-25.* ***Robinson*** *r-25, 44.* ***Sprang*** *r-44. Issues #21-31, 35-39, 45, 48 have back cover cut-outs.*

LINDA (Everybody Loves...) (Phantom Lady No. 5 on)
Ajax-Farrell Publ. Co.: Apr-May, 1954 - No. 4, Oct-Nov, 1954

1-Kamenish-a 14.00 43.00 100.00
2-Lingerie panel 11.50 34.00 80.00
3,4 10.00 30.00 60.00

LINDA CARTER, STUDENT NURSE
Atlas Comics (AMI): Sept, 1961 - No. 9, Jan, 1963

1-Al Hartley-c 3.80 11.40 38.00
2-9 2.80 8.40 28.00

LINDA LARK
Dell Publishing Co.: Oct-Dec, 1961 - No. 8, Aug-Oct, 1963

1 2.50 7.50 24.00
2-8 1.75 5.25 14.00

LINUS, THE LIONHEARTED (TV)
Gold Key: Sept, 1965

1 (10155-509) 7.70 23.00 85.00

LION, THE (See Movie Comics)

LIONHEART
Awesome Comics: Sept, 1999 - Present ($2.99)

1-Ian Churchill-story/a, Jeph Loeb-s; Coven app. 3.00

LION OF SPARTA (See Movie Classics)

LIPPY THE LION AND HARDY HAR HAR (TV)
Gold Key: Mar, 1963 (12¢) (See Hanna-Barbera Band Wagon #1)

1 (10049-303) 9.00 27.00 100.00

LISA COMICS (TV)(See Simpsons Comics)
Bongo Comics: 1995 ($2.25)

1-Lisa in Wonderland 2.25

LI'L ABNER (See Comics on Parade, Sparkle, Sparkler Comics, Tip Top Comics & Tip Topper)
United Features Syndicate: 1939 - 1940

Single Series 4 ('39) 69.00 206.00 550.00
Single Series 18 ('40) (#18 on inside, #2 on-c) 56.00 169.00 450.00

LI'L ABNER (Al Capp's; continued from Comics on Parade #58)

Li'l Abner #62 © TOBY

Little Al of the Secret Service #10 (#1) © Z-D

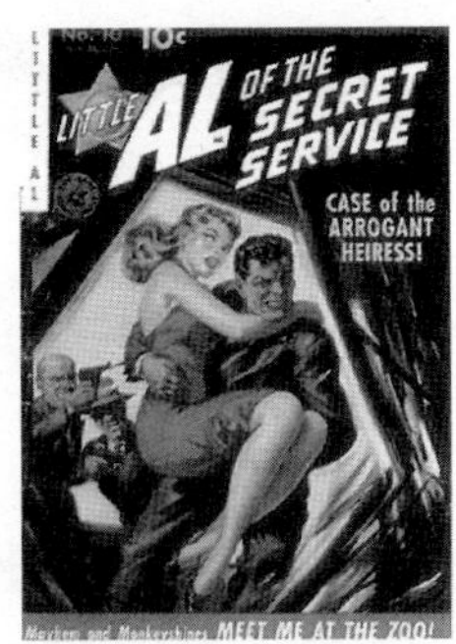

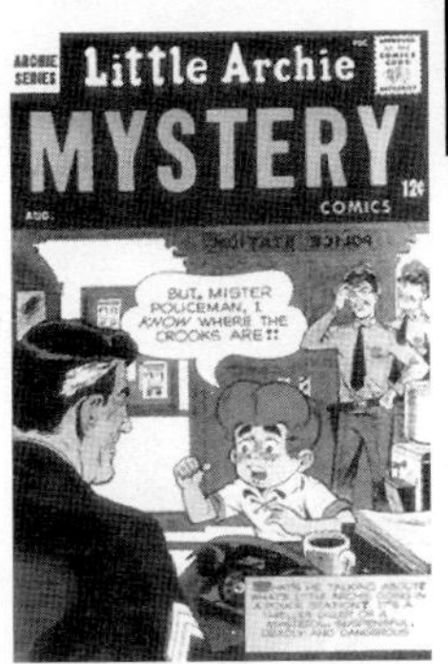

Little Archie Mystery #1 © AP

Harvey Publ. No. 61-69 (2/49)/Toby Press No. 70 on: No. 61, Dec, 1947 - No. 97, Jan, 1955 (See Oxydol-Dreft)

	GD2.0	FN6.0	NM9.4
61(#1)-Wolverton & Powell-a	34.00	101.00	235.00
62-65: 63-The Wolf Girl app. 65-Powell-a	20.00	60.00	140.00
66,67,69,70	17.00	51.00	120.00
68-Full length Fearless Fosdick-c/story	19.00	56.00	130.00
71-74,76,80	13.50	41.00	95.00
75,77-79,86,91-All with Kurtzman art; 91-r/#77	17.00	51.00	120.00
81-85,87-90,92-94,96,97: 93-reprints #71	12.00	36.00	85.00
95-Full length Fearless Fosdick story	15.00	45.00	105.00

LI'L ABNER
Toby Press: 1951

	GD2.0	FN6.0	NM9.4
1	17.00	51.00	120.00

LI'L ABNER'S DOGPATCH (See Al Capp's...)

LITTLE AL OF THE F.B.I.
Ziff-Davis Publications: No. 10, 1950 (no month) - No. 11, Apr-May, 1951 (Saunders painted-c)

	GD2.0	FN6.0	NM9.4
10(1950)	15.00	45.00	105.00
11(1951)	12.00	36.00	85.00

LITTLE AL OF THE SECRET SERVICE
Ziff-Davis Publications: No. 10, 7-8/51; No, 2, 9-10/51; No. 3, Winter, 1951 (Saunders painted-c)

	GD2.0	FN6.0	NM9.4
10(#1)-Spanking panels (2)	16.00	47.00	110.00
2,3	12.00	36.00	85.00

LITTLE AMBROSE
Archie Publications: September, 1958

	GD2.0	FN6.0	NM9.4
1-Bob Bolling-c	14.00	43.00	100.00

LITTLE ANGEL
Standard (Visual Editions)/Pines: No. 5, Sept, 1954; No. 6, Sept, 1955 - No. 16, Sept, 1959

	GD2.0	FN6.0	NM9.4
5-Last pre-code issue	6.35	19.00	38.00
6-16	4.00	12.00	24.00

LITTLE ANNIE ROONEY (Also see Henry)
David McKay Publ.: 1935 (25¢, B&W dailies, 48 pgs.)(10"x10", cardboard-c)

	GD2.0	FN6.0	NM9.4
Book 1-Daily strip-r by Darrell McClure	37.00	111.00	260.00

LITTLE ANNIE ROONEY (See King Comics & Treasury of Comics)
David McKay/St. John/Standard: 1938; Aug, 1948 - No. 3, Oct, 1948

	GD2.0	FN6.0	NM9.4
Feature Books 11 (McKay, 1938)	37.00	111.00	260.00
1 (St. John)	12.00	36.00	85.00
2,3	8.35	25.00	50.00

LITTLE ARCHIE (The Adventures of... #13-on) (See Archie Giant Series Mag. #527, 534, 538, 545, 549, 556, 560, 566, 570, 583, 594, 596, 607, 609, 619)
Archie Publications: 1956 - No. 180, Feb, 1983 (Giants No. 3-84)

	GD2.0	FN6.0	NM9.4
1-(Scarce)	52.00	156.00	625.00
2 (1957)	24.00	72.00	240.00
3-5: 3-(1958)-Bob Bolling-c & giant issues begin	13.00	39.00	130.00
6-10	10.00	30.00	100.00
11-22 (84 pgs.)	6.00	18.00	60.00
23-39 (68 pgs.)	4.00	12.00	40.00
40 (Fall/66)-Intro. Little Pureheart-c/s (68 pgs.)	4.50	13.50	45.00
41,44-Little Pureheart (68 pgs.)	3.50	10.50	35.00
42-Intro The Little Archies Band, ends #66 (68 pgs.)	4.50	13.50	45.00
43-1st Boy From R.I.V.E.R.D.A.L.E. (68 pgs.)	4.00	12.00	40.00
45-58 (68pgs.)	2.50	7.50	25.00
59 (68pgs.)-Little Sabrina begins	6.50	16.50	65.00
60-66 (68 pgs.)	2.50	7.50	25.00
67(9/71)-84: 84-Last 52pg. Giant-Size (2/74)	1.40	4.20	14.00
85-99	1.10	3.30	9.00
100	1.20	3.60	12.00
101-112,114-116,118-129		2.40	6.00
113,117,130: 113-Halloween Special issue(12/76). 117-Donny Osmond-c cameo			
130-UFO cover (5/78)	1.00	3.00	8.00
131-150(1/80), 180(Last issue, 2/83)			5.00
151-179			3.50
...In Animal Land 1 (1957)	12.00	36.00	120.00
...In Animal Land 17 (Winter, 1957-58)-19 (Summer,1958)-Formerly Li'l Jinx	6.50	19.50	65.00

NOTE: *Little Archie Band app. 42-66. Little Sabrina in 59-78,80-180*

LITTLE ARCHIE CHRISTMAS SPECIAL (See Archie Giant Series #581)

LITTLE ARCHIE COMICS DIGEST ANNUAL (...Magazine #5 on)
Archie Publications: 10/77 - No. 48, 5/91 (Digest-size, 128 pgs., later issues $1.35-$1.50)

	GD2.0	FN6.0	NM9.4
1(10/77)-Reprints	1.80	5.40	18.00
2(4/78,3(11/78)-Neal Adams-a. 3-The Fly-r by S&K	1.60	4.80	16.00
4(4/79) - 10	1.20	3.60	12.00
11-20	1.00	3.00	8.00
21-30: 28-Christmas-c		2.40	6.00
31-48: 40,46-Christmas-c			4.00

NOTE: *Little Archie, Little Jinx, Little Jughead & Little Sabrina in most issues.*

LITTLE ARCHIE DIGEST MAGAZINE
Archie Comics: July, 1991 - No. 25 ($1.50/$1.79/$1.89, digest size, bi-annual)

	GD2.0	FN6.0	NM9.4
V2#1			5.00
2-10			3.00
11-25			2.00

LITTLE ARCHIE MYSTERY
Archie Publications: Aug, 1963 - No. 2, Oct, 1963 (12¢ issues)

	GD2.0	FN6.0	NM9.4
1	10.50	32.00	105.00
2	5.50	16.50	55.00

LITTLE ASPIRIN (See Little Lenny & Wisco)
Marvel Comics (CnPC): July, 1949 - No. 3, Dec, 1949 (52 pgs.)

	GD2.0	FN6.0	NM9.4
1-Oscar app.; Kurtzman-a (4 pgs.)	15.00	45.00	105.00
2-Kurtzman-a (4 pgs.)	10.00	30.00	60.00
3-No Kurtzman-a	5.35	16.00	32.00

LITTLE AUDREY (Also see Playful...)
St. John Publ.: Apr, 1948 - No. 24, May, 1952

	GD2.0	FN6.0	NM9.4
1-1st app. Little Audrey	40.00	120.00	300.00
2	21.00	62.00	145.00
3-5	13.50	41.00	95.00
6-10	10.00	30.00	65.00
11-20: 16-X-Mas-c	7.50	22.50	45.00
21-24	5.85	17.50	35.00

LITTLE AUDREY (See Harvey Hits #11, 19)
Harvey Publications: No. 25, Aug, 1952 - No. 53, April, 1957

	GD2.0	FN6.0	NM9.4
25-(Paramount Pictures Famous Star... on-c); 1st Harvey Casper and Baby Huey (1 month earlier than Harvey Comic Hits #60(9/52))	10.50	31.50	105.00
26-30: 26-28-Casper app.	5.50	16.50	55.00
31-40: 32-35-Casper app.	4.50	13.50	45.00
41-53	2.80	8.40	28.00
...Clubhouse 1 (9/61, 68 pg. Giant)-New stories & reprints	7.50	22.50	75.00

LITTLE AUDREY
Harvey Comics: Aug, 1992 - No. 8, July, 1993 ($1.25/$1.50)

	GD2.0	FN6.0	NM9.4
V2#1			3.00
2-8			2.00

LITTLE AUDREY (...Yearbook)
St. John Publishing Co.: 1950 (50¢, 260 pgs.)

	GD2.0	FN6.0	NM9.4
Contains 8 complete 1949 comics rebound; Casper, Alice in Wonderland, Little Audrey, Abbott & Costello, Pinocchio, Moon Mullins, Three Stooges (from Jubilee), Little Annie Rooney app. (Rare)	60.00	180.00	600.00

(Also see All Good & Treasury of Comics)

NOTE: *This book contains remaindered St. John comics; many variations possible.*

LITTLE AUDREY & MELVIN (Audrey & Melvin No. 62)

Little Dot Dotland #1 © HARV

Little Eva #3 © STJ

Little Giant Comics #3 © CEN

	GD2.0	FN6.0	NM9.4

Harvey Publications: May, 1962 - No. 61, Dec, 1973

	GD2.0	FN6.0	NM9.4
1	8.00	24.00	80.00
2-5	4.00	12.00	40.00
6-10	3.00	9.00	30.00
11-20	2.00	6.00	20.00
21-40: 22-Richie Rich app.	1.50	4.50	15.00
41-50,55-61	1.00	3.00	10.00
51-54: All 52 pg. Giants	1.50	4.50	15.00

LITTLE AUDREY TV FUNTIME
Harvey Publ.: Sept, 1962 - No. 33, Oct, 1971 (#1-31: 68 pgs.; #32,33: 52 pgs.)

	GD2.0	FN6.0	NM9.4
1-Richie Rich app.	7.50	22.50	75.00
2,3: Richie Rich app.	5.00	15.00	50.00
4,5: 5-25¢ & 35¢ issues exist	4.00	12.00	40.00
6-10	2.50	7.50	25.00
11-20	1.50	4.50	15.00
21-33	1.20	3.60	12.00

LITTLE BAD WOLF (Disney; seeWalt Disney's C&S #52, Walt Disney Showcase #21 & Wheaties)
Dell Publishing Co.: No. 403, June, 1952 - No. 564, June, 1954

	GD2.0	FN6.0	NM9.4
Four Color 403 (#1)	6.40	19.00	70.00
Four Color 473 (6/53), 564	3.60	11.00	40.00

LITTLE BEAVER
Dell Publishing Co.: No. 211, Jan, 1949 - No. 870, Jan, 1958 (All painted-c)

	GD2.0	FN6.0	NM9.4
Four Color 211('49)-All Harman-a	7.00	20.00	75.00
Four Color 267,294,332(5/51)	3.50	11.00	38.00
3(10-12/51)-8(1-3/53)	3.00	9.00	35.00
Four Color 483(8-10/53),529	2.75	8.00	30.00
Four Color 612,660,695,744,817,870	2.75	8.00	30.00

LITTLE BIT
Jubilee/St. John Publishing Co.: Mar, 1949 - No. 2, June, 1949

	GD2.0	FN6.0	NM9.4
1,2	5.00	15.00	32.00

LITTLE DOT (See Humphrey, Li'l Max, Sad Sack, and Tastee-Freez Comics)
Harvey Publications: Sept, 1953 - No. 164, Apr, 1976

	GD2.0	FN6.0	NM9.4
1-Intro./1st app. Richie Rich & Little Lotta	94.00	282.00	940.00
2-1st app. Freckles & Pee Wee (Richie Rich's poor friends)	38.00	114.00	380.00
3	24.00	72.00	240.00
4	17.50	52.00	175.00
5-Origin dots on Little Dot's dress	24.00	72.00	245.00
6-Richie Rich, Little Lotta, & Little Dot all on cover; 1st Richie Rich cover featured	22.00	66.00	225.00
7-10: 9-Last pre-code issue (1/55)	13.00	39.00	130.00
11-20	8.50	25.50	85.00
21-40	4.50	13.50	45.00
41-60	2.40	7.20	24.00
61-80	1.80	5.40	18.00
81-100	1.40	4.20	14.00
101-141	1.00	3.00	10.00
142-145: All 52 pg. Giants	1.60	4.80	16.00
146-164		2.40	6.00

NOTE: *Richie Rich & Little Lotta in all.*

LITTLE DOT
Harvey Comics: Sept, 1992 - No. 7, June, 1994 ($1.25/$1.50)

	GD2.0	FN6.0	NM9.4
V2#1-Little Dot, Little Lotta, Richie Rich in all			3.00
2-7 ($1.50)			2.00

LITTLE DOT DOTLAND (Dot Dotland No. 62, 63)
Harvey Publications: July, 1962 - No. 61, Dec, 1973

	GD2.0	FN6.0	NM9.4
1-Richie Rich begins	9.00	27.00	90.00
2,3	4.50	13.50	45.00
4,5	3.80	11.40	38.00
6-10	2.60	7.80	26.00
11-20	2.00	6.00	20.00
21-30	1.40	4.20	14.00
31-50	1.20	3.60	12.00
51-54: All 52 pg. Giants	1.60	4.80	16.00
55-61	.90	2.70	9.00

LITTLE DOT'S UNCLES & AUNTS (See Harvey Hits No. 4, 13, 24)
Harvey Enterprises: Oct, 1961; No. 2, Aug, 1962 - No. 52, Apr, 1974

	GD2.0	FN6.0	NM9.4
1-Richie Rich begins; 68 pgs. begin	11.00	33.00	110.00
2,3	6.00	18.00	60.00
4,5	4.00	12.00	40.00
6-10	3.00	9.00	30.00
11-20	2.50	7.50	25.00
21-37: Last 68 pg. issue	1.80	5.40	18.00
38-52: All 52 pg. Giants	1.60	4.80	16.00

LITTLE DRACULA
Harvey Comics: Jan, 1992 - No. 3, May, 1992 ($1.25, quarterly, mini-series)

	GD2.0	FN6.0	NM9.4
1-3			2.00

LITTLE EVA
St. John Publishing Co.: May, 1952 - No. 31, Nov, 1956

	GD2.0	FN6.0	NM9.4
1	13.00	39.00	90.00
2	7.50	22.50	45.00
3-5	5.00	15.00	30.00
6-10	4.00	11.00	22.00
11-31	4.00	10.00	20.00
3-D 1,2(10/53, 11/53, 25¢)-Both came w/glasses. 1-Infinity-c	20.00	60.00	140.00
I.W. Reprint #1-3,6-8: 1-r/Little Eva #28. 2-r/Little Eva #29. 3-r/Little Eva #24	1.00	3.00	8.00
Super Reprint #10,12('63),14,16,18('64): 18-r/Little Eva #25.	1.00	3.00	8.00

LI'L GENIUS (Summer Fun No. 54) (See Blue Bird & Giant Comics #3)
Charlton Comics: 1954 - No. 52, 1/65; No. 53, 10/65; No. 54, 10/85 - No. 55, 1/86

	GD2.0	FN6.0	NM9.4
1	10.00	30.00	60.00
2	5.00	15.00	30.00
3-15,19,20	4.00	11.00	22.00
16,17-(68 pgs.)	6.35	19.00	38.00
18-(100 pgs., 10/58)	9.15	27.00	55.00
21-35	2.50	7.50	20.00
36-53	1.75	5.25	14.00
54,55 (Low print)			4.00

LI'L GHOST
St. John Publ. Co./Fago No. 1 on: Feb, 1958; Nov?, 1958 - No. 3, Mar, 1959

	GD2.0	FN6.0	NM9.4
1(St. John)	8.35	25.00	50.00
1(Fago)-Al Fago-c/a begins	5.35	16.00	32.00
2,3: 2-(1/59)	4.00	12.00	24.00

LITTLE GIANT COMICS
Centaur Publications: 7/38 - No. 3, 10/38; No. 4, 2/39 (132 pgs.) (6-3/4x4-1/2")

	GD2.0	FN6.0	NM9.4
1-B&W with color-c; stories, puzzles, magic	60.00	180.00	480.00
2,3-B&W with color-c	52.00	157.00	420.00
4 (6-5/8x9-3/8")(68 pgs., B&W inside)	52.00	157.00	420.00

NOTE: ***Filchock** c-2, 4. **Gustavson** a-1. **Pinajian** a-4. **Bob Wood** a-1.*

LITTLE GIANT DETECTIVE FUNNIES
Centaur Publ.: Oct, 1938 - No. 4, Jan, 1939 (6-3/4x4-1/2", 132 pgs., B&W)

	GD2.0	FN6.0	NM9.4
1-B&W with color-c	69.00	206.00	550.00
2,3	52.00	157.00	420.00
4(1/39, B&W; color-c; 68 pgs., 6-1/2x9-1/2")-Eisner-r	55.00	165.00	440.00

LITTLE GIANT MOVIE FUNNIES
Centaur Publ.: Aug, 1938 - No. 2, Oct, 1938 (6-3/4x4-1/2", 132 pgs., B&W)

	GD2.0	FN6.0	NM9.4
1-Ed Wheelan's "Minute Movies" reprints	69.00	206.00	550.00
2-Ed Wheelan's "Minute Movies" reprints	52.00	157.00	420.00

LITTLE GROUCHO (...the Red-Headed Tornado; ...Grouchy No. 2)

Little Ike #3 © STJ

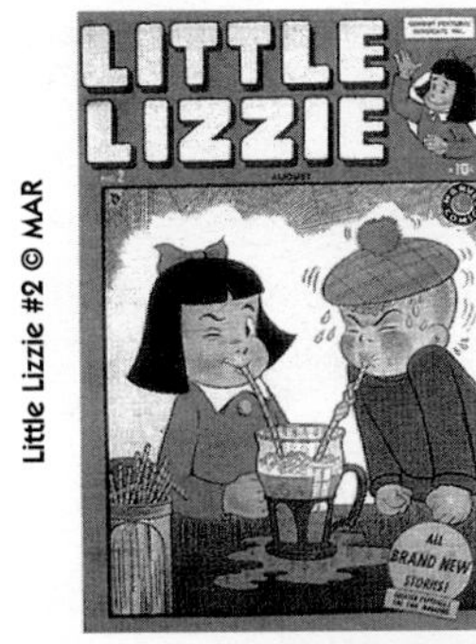

Little Lizzie #2 © MAR

Little Lotta #3 © HARV

Reston Publ. Co.: No. 16; Feb-Mar, 1955 - No. 2, June-July, 1955
(See Tippy Terry)

	GD2.0	FN6.0	NM9.4
16, 1 (2-3/55)	7.50	22.50	45.00
2(6-7/55)	5.00	15.00	30.00

LITTLE HIAWATHA (Disney; see Walt Disney's C&S #143)
Dell Publishing Co.: No. 439, Dec, 1952 - No. 988, May-July, 1959

	GD2.0	FN6.0	NM9.4
Four Color 439 (#1)	4.50	13.50	50.00
Four Color 787 (4/57), 901 (5/58), 988	3.60	11.00	40.00

LITTLE IKE
St. John Publishing Co.: April, 1953 - No. 4, Oct, 1953

	GD2.0	FN6.0	NM9.4
1	9.15	27.00	55.00
2	5.00	15.00	30.00
3,4	4.00	12.00	24.00

LITTLE IODINE (See Giant Comic Album)
Dell Publ. Co.: No. 224, 4/49 - No. 257, 1949: 3-5/50 - No. 56, 4-6/62 (1-4-52pgs.)

	GD2.0	FN6.0	NM9.4
Four Color 224-By Jimmy Hatlo	8.00	25.00	90.00
Four Color 257	6.40	19.00	70.00
1(3-5/50)	8.00	25.00	90.00
2-5	3.00	10.00	36.00
6-10	2.50	7.50	27.00
11-20	1.65	5.00	18.00
21-30: 27-Xmas-c	1.50	4.50	16.00
31-40	1.40	4.20	12.00
41-56	1.25	3.75	10.00

LITTLE JACK FROST
Avon Periodicals: 1951

	GD2.0	FN6.0	NM9.4
1	9.15	27.00	55.00

LI'L JINX (Little Archie in Animal Land #17) (Also see Pep Comics #62)
Archie Publications: No. 11, Nov, 1956 - No. 16, Sept, 1957

	GD2.0	FN6.0	NM9.4
11-By Joe Edwards	11.50	34.00	80.00
12(1/57)-16	9.15	27.00	55.00

LI'L JINX (See Archie Giant Series Magazine No. 223)

LI'L JINX CHRISTMAS BAG (See Archie Giant Series Mag. No. 195, 206, 219)

LI'L JINX GIANT LAUGH-OUT (See Archie Giant Series Mag. No. 176, 185)
Archie Publications: No. 33, Sept, 1971 - No. 43, Nov, 1973 (52 pgs.)

	GD2.0	FN6.0	NM9.4
33-43 (52 pgs.)	1.75	5.25	14.00

LITTLE JOE (See Popular Comics & Super Comics)
Dell Publishing Co.: No. 1, 1942

	GD2.0	FN6.0	NM9.4
Four Color 1	43.00	130.00	475.00

LITTLE JOE
St. John Publishing Co.: Apr, 1953

	GD2.0	FN6.0	NM9.4
1	4.00	10.00	20.00

LI'L KIDS (Also see Li'l Pals)
Marvel Comics Group: 8/70 - No. 2, 10/70; No. 3, 11/71 - No. 12, 6/73

	GD2.0	FN6.0	NM9.4
1	4.50	13.50	45.00
2-9	2.50	7.50	25.00
10-12-Calvin app.	3.00	9.00	30.00

LITTLE KING
Dell Publishing Co.: No. 494, Aug, 1953 - No. 677, Feb, 1956

	GD2.0	FN6.0	NM9.4
Four Color 494 (#1)	9.00	27.00	100.00
Four Color 597, 677	4.50	13.50	50.00

LITTLE LANA (Formerly Lana)
Marvel Comics (MjMC): No. 8, Nov, 1949; No. 9, Mar, 1950

	GD2.0	FN6.0	NM9.4
8,9	7.50	22.50	45.00

LITTLE LENNY
Marvel Comics (CDS): June, 1949 - No. 3, Nov, 1949

	GD2.0	FN6.0	NM9.4
1-Little Aspirin app.	10.00	30.00	70.00
2,3	5.85	17.50	35.00

LITTLE LIZZIE
Marvel Comics (PrPl)/Atlas (OMC): 6/49 - No. 5, 4/50; 9/53 - No. 3, Jan, 1954

	GD2.0	FN6.0	NM9.4
1	11.50	34.00	80.00
2-5	7.50	22.50	45.00
1 (9/53, 2nd series by Atlas)-Howie Post-c	8.35	25.00	50.00
2,3	5.85	17.50	35.00

LITTLE LOTTA (See Harvey Hits No. 10)
Harvey Publications: 11/55 - No. 110, 11/73; No. 111, 9/74 - No. 120, 5/76
V2#1, Oct, 1992 - No. 4, July, 1993 ($1.25)

	GD2.0	FN6.0	NM9.4
1-Richie Rich (r) & Little Dot begin	30.00	90.00	300.00
2,3	13.00	39.00	130.00
4,5	7.50	22.50	75.00
6-10	6.50	19.50	65.00
11-20	4.00	12.00	40.00
21-40	2.60	7.80	26.00
41-60	2.20	6.60	22.00
61-80: 62-1st app. Nurse Jenny	1.80	5.40	18.00
81-99	1.20	3.60	12.00
100-103: All 52 pg. Giants	1.60	4.80	16.00
104-120	1.00	3.00	8.00
V2#1-4 (1992-93)			2.00

NOTE: *No. 121 was advertised, but never released.*

LITTLE LOTTA FOODLAND
Harvey Publications: 9/63 - No. 14, 10/67; No. 15, 10/68 - No. 29, Oct, 1972

	GD2.0	FN6.0	NM9.4
1-Little Lotta, Little Dot, Richie Rich, 68 pgs. begin	11.00	33.00	110.00
2,3	7.00	21.00	70.00
4,5	5.00	15.00	50.00
6-10	3.50	10.50	35.00
11-20	2.50	7.50	25.00
21-26: 26-Last 68 pg. issue	2.00	6.00	20.00
27,28: Both 52 pgs.	1.80	5.40	18.00
29-(36 pgs.)	1.00	3.00	10.00

LITTLE LULU (Formerly Marge's...)
Gold Key 207-257/Whitman 258 on: No. 207, Sept, 1972 - No. 268, April, 1984

	GD2.0	FN6.0	NM9.4
207,209,220-Stanley-r. 207-1st app. Henrietta	1.10	3.30	9.00
208,210-219: 208-1st app. Snobbly, Wilbur's butler	1.00	2.80	7.00
221-240,242-249, 250(r/#166), 251-254(r/#206)			5.00
241,263-Stanley-r		2.40	6.00
255-257(Gold Key): 256-r/#212			4.00
258,259,262,264,265 (Whitman)	1.00	2.80	7.00
260,261	1.10	3.30	9.00
266-268 (All #90028 on-c; no date, no date code; 3-pack?): 268-Stanley-r	1.50	4.50	12.00

LITTLE MARY MIXUP (See Comics On Parade)
United Features Syndicate: No. 10, 1939, - No. 26, 1940

	GD2.0	FN6.0	NM9.4
Single Series 10, 26	34.00	103.00	240.00

LITTLE MAX COMICS (Joe Palooka's Pal; see Joe Palooka)
Harvey Publications: Oct, 1949 - No. 73, Nov, 1961

	GD2.0	FN6.0	NM9.4
1-Infinity-c; Little Dot begins; Joe Palooka on-c	18.00	54.00	125.00
2-Little Dot app.; Joe Palooka on-c	10.00	30.00	65.00
3-Little Dot app.; Joe Palooka on-c	7.50	22.50	45.00
4-10: 5-Little Dot app., 1pg.	5.00	15.00	30.00
11-20	4.00	12.00	24.00
21-40: 23-Little Dot app. 38-r/#20	3.60	10.80	22.00
41-73: 63-65,67-73-Include new five pg. Richie Rich stories. 70-73-Little Lotta app.	1.80	5.40	18.00

LI'L MENACE
Fago Magazine Co.: Dec, 1958 - No. 3, May, 1959

	GD2.0	FN6.0	NM9.4
1-Peter Rabbit app.	7.00	21.00	42.00
2-Peter Rabbit (Vincent Fago's)	5.35	16.00	32.00
3	4.25	13.00	28.00

LITTLE MERMAID, THE (Walt Disney's...; also see Disney's...)

Little Miss Muffet #13 © STD

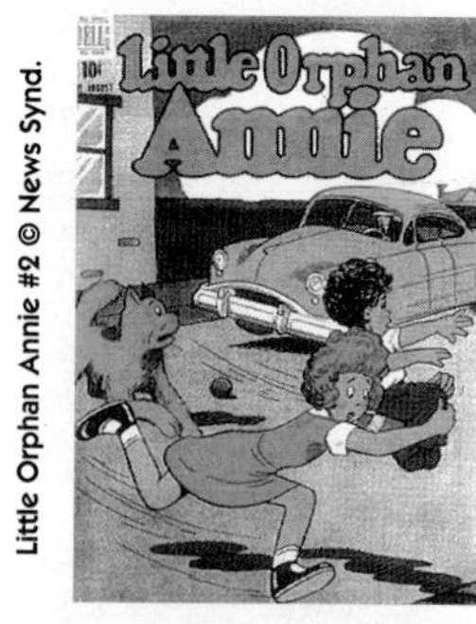

Little Orphan Annie #2 © News Synd.

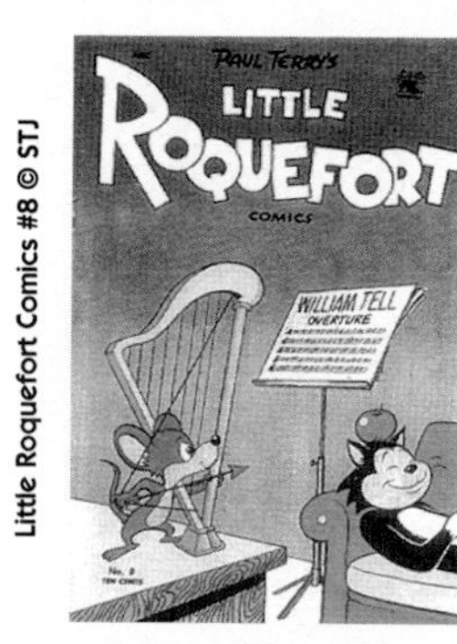

Little Roquefort Comics #8 © STJ

W. D. Publications (Disney): 1990 (no date given)($5.95, no ads, 52 pgs.)
nn-Adapts animated movie 1.00 2.80 7.00
nn-Comic version ($2.50) 3.00

LITTLE MERMAID, THE
Disney Comics: 1992 - No. 4, 1992 ($1.50, mini-series)
1-4: Based on movie 3.00
1-4: 2nd printings sold at Wal-Mart w/different-c 2.00

LITTLE MISS MUFFET
Best Books (Standard Comics)/King Features Synd.: No. 11, Dec, 1948 - No. 13, March, 1949
11-Strip reprints; Fanny Cory-c/a 7.50 22.50 45.00
12,13-Strip reprints; Fanny Cory-c/a 5.00 15.00 30.00

LITTLE MISS SUNBEAM COMICS
Magazine Enterprises/Quality Bakers of America: June-July, 1950 - No. 4, Dec-Jan, 1950-51
1 15.00 45.00 105.00
2-4 9.15 27.00 55.00
...Advs. In Space ('55) 5.35 16.00 32.00

LITTLE MONSTERS, THE (See March of Comics #423, Three Stooges #17)
Gold Key: Nov, 1964 - No. 44, Feb, 1978
1 4.80 14.40 48.00
2 2.50 7.50 24.00
3-10 2.50 7.50 20.00
11-20 2.00 6.00 16.00
21-30 1.50 4.50 12.00
31-44: 20,34-39,43-Reprints 1.00 3.00 8.00

LITTLE MONSTERS (Movie)
Now Comics: 1989 - No. 6, June, 1990 ($1.75)
1-6: Photo-c from movie 2.00

LITTLE NEMO (See Cocomalt, Future Comics, Help, Jest, Kayo, Punch, Red Seal, & Superworld; most by Winsor McCay Jr., son of famous artist) (Other McCay books: see Little Sammy Sneeze & Dreams of the Rarebit Fiend)

LITTLE NEMO (...in Slumberland)
McCay Features/Nostalgia Press('69): 1945 (11x7-1/4", 28 pgs., B&W)
1905 & 1911 reprints by Winsor McCay 10.00 30.00 60.00
1969-70 (Exact reprint) 2.00 5.00 10.00

LITTLE ORPHAN ANNIE (See Annie, Famous Feature Stories, Marvel Super Special, Merry Christmas..., Popular Comics, Super Book #7, 11, 23 & Super Comics)

LITTLE ORPHAN ANNIE
David McKay Publ./Dell Publishing Co.: No. 7, 1937 - No. 3, Sept-Nov, 1948; No. 206, Dec, 1948
Feature Books(McKay) 7-(1937) (Rare) 79.00 238.00 875.00
Four Color 12(1941) 47.00 140.00 515.00
Four Color 18(1943)-Flag-c 37.00 112.00 410.00
Four Color 52(1944) 29.00 87.00 320.00
Four Color 76(1945) 24.00 72.00 265.00
Four Color 107(1946) 20.00 61.00 225.00
Four Color 152(1947) 13.00 39.00 145.00
1(3-5/48)-r/strips from 5/7/44 to 7/30/44 13.00 39.00 145.00
2-r/strips from 7/21/40 to 9/9/40 9.00 26.00 95.00
3-r/strips from 9/10/40 to 11/9/40 9.00 26.00 95.00
Four Color 206(12/48) 7.00 20.00 75.00

LI'L PALS (Also see Li'l Kids)
Marvel Comics Group: Sept, 1972 - No. 5, May, 1973
1 4.00 12.00 40.00
2-5 2.50 7.50 24.00

LI'L PAN (Formerly Rocket Kelly; becomes Junior Comics with #9)
Fox Features Syndicate: No. 6, Dec-Jan, 1946-47 - No. 8, Apr-May, 1947 (Also see Wotalife Comics)
6 9.15 27.00 55.00
7,8: 7-Atomic bomb story; robot-c 6.35 19.00 38.00

LITTLE PEOPLE
Dell Publishing Co.: No. 485, Aug-Oct, 1953 - No. 1062, Dec, 1959 (Walt Scott's)
Four Color 485 (#1) 5.50 16.50 60.00
Four Color 573(7/54), 633(6/55) 3.00 9.00 35.00
Four Color 692(3/56),753(11/56),809(7/57),868(12/57),908(5/58), 959(12/58), 1062 3.00 9.00 35.00
Four Color 1024-Darby O'Gill &...-Movie, Toth-a, photo-c 9.00 27.00 100.00

LITTLE RASCALS
Dell Publishing Co.: No. 674, Jan, 1956 - No. 1297, Mar-May, 1962
Four Color 674 (#1) 6.40 19.00 70.00
Four Color 778(3/57),825(8/57) 3.75 11.50 42.00
Four Color 883(3/58),936(9/58),974(3/59),1030(9/59),1079(2-4/60),1137 (9-11/60) 3.75 11.50 42.00
Four Color 1174(3-5/61),1224(10-12/61),1297 3.00 9.00 32.00

LI'L RASCAL TWINS (Formerly Nature Boy)
Charlton Comics: No. 6, 1957 - No. 18, Jan, 1960
6-Li'l Genius & Tomboy in all 5.00 15.00 30.00
7-18: 7-Timmy the Timid Ghost app. 3.60 9.00 18.00

LITTLE RED HOT: (CHANE OF FOOLS)
Image Comics: Feb, 1999 - No. 3, Apr, 1999 ($2.95/$3.50, B&W, limited series)
1-Dawn Brown-s/a 3.00
2,3-($3.50) 3.50

LITTLE ROQUEFORT COMICS (See Paul Terry's Comics #105)
St. John Publishing Co.(all pre-code)/Pines No. 10: June, 1952 - No. 9, Oct, 1953; No. 10, Summer, 1958
1-By Paul Terry 10.00 30.00 60.00
2 4.25 13.00 28.00
3-10: 10-CBS Television Presents on-c 4.00 11.00 22.00

LITTLE SAD SACK (See Harvey Hits No. 73, 76, 79, 81, 83)
Harvey Publications: Oct, 1964 - No. 19, Nov, 1967
1-Richie Rich app. on cover only 4.00 12.00 40.00
2-10 2.50 7.50 22.00
11-19 2.25 6.75 18.00

LITTLE SCOUTS
Dell Publishing Co.: No. 321, Mar, 1951 - No. 587, Oct, 1954
Four Color #321 (#1, 3/51) 2.75 8.00 30.00
2(10-12/51) - 6(10-12/52) 1.35 4.00 15.00
Four Color #462,506,550,587 1.35 4.00 15.00

LITTLE SHOP OF HORRORS SPECIAL (Movie)
DC Comics: Feb, 1987 ($2.00, 68 pgs.)
1-Colan-c/a 2.00

LITTLE SPUNKY
I. W. Enterprises: No date (1963?) (10¢)
1-r/Frisky Fables #1 1.25 3.75 10.00

LITTLE STOOGES, THE (The Three Stooges' Sons)
Gold Key: Sept, 1972 - No. 7, Mar, 1974
1-Norman Maurer cover/stories in all 2.50 7.50 24.00
2-7 1.75 5.25 14.00

LITTLEST OUTLAW (Disney)
Dell Publishing Co.: No. 609, Jan, 1955
Four Color 609-Movie, photo-c 5.50 16.50 60.00

LITTLEST SNOWMAN, THE
Dell Publishing Co.: No. 755, 12/56; No. 864, 12/57; 12-2/1963-64
Four Color #755,864, 1(1964) 3.00 10.00 36.00

LI'L TOMBOY (Formerly Fawcett's Funny Animals; see Giant Comics #3)
Charlton Comics: V14#92, Oct, 1956; No. 93, Mar, 1957 - No. 107, Feb, 1960

Living Bible #3 © Living Bible Corp.

Lobo #17 © DC

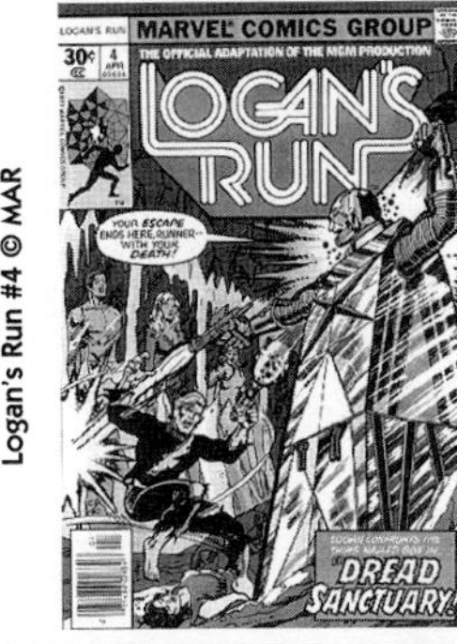

Logan's Run #4 © MAR

GD2.0 FN6.0 NM9.4

V14#92 4.25 13.00 28.00
93-107: 97-Atomic Bunny app. 4.00 11.00 22.00

LI'L WILLIE COMICS (Formerly & becomes Willie Comics #22 on)
Marvel Comics (MgPC): No. 20, July, 1949 - No. 21, Sept, 1949
20,21: 20-Little Aspirin app. 7.50 22.50 45.00

LITTLE WOMEN (See Power Record Comics)

LIVE IT UP
Spire Christian Comics (Fleming H. Revell Co.): 1973, 1976 (39-49 cents)
nn 5.00

LIVING BIBLE, THE
Living Bible Corp.: Fall, 1945 - No. 3, Spring, 1946
1-The Life of Paul; all have L. B. Cole-c 40.00 120.00 280.00
2-Joseph & His Brethren; Jonah & the Whale 25.00 75.00 175.00
3-Chaplains At War (classic-c) 40.00 120.00 280.00

LOBO
Dell Publishing Co.: Dec, 1965; No. 2, Oct, 1966
1,2-1st black character to have his own title. 2.25 6.75 18.00

LOBO (Also see Action #650, Adventures of Superman, Demon (2nd series), Justice League, L.E.G.I.O.N., Mister Miracle, Omega Men #3 & Superman #41)
DC Comics: Nov, 1990 - No. 4, Feb, 1991 ($1.50, color, limited series)
1-(99¢)-Giffen plots/Breakdowns in all 4.00
1-2nd printing 2.50
2-4: 2-Legion '89 spin-off. 1-4 have Bisley painted covers & art 2.50
...: Blazing Chain of Love 1 (9/92, $1.50)-Denys Cowan-c/a; Alan Grant scripts, ...Convention Special 1 (1993, $1.75), ...Paramilitary Christmas Special 1 (1991, $2.39, 52 pgs.)-Bisley-c/a, ...: Portrait of a Victim 1 (1993, $1.75) 2.50

LOBO (Also see Showcase '95 #9)
DC Comics: Dec, 1993 - No. 64, Jul, 1999 ($1.75/$1.95/$2.25/$2.50, mature)
1 ($2.95)-Foil enhanced-c; Alan Grant scripts begin 3.00
2-9,0,10-64: 2-7-Alan Grant scripts. 9-(9/94). 0-(10/94)-Origin retold. 50-Lobo vs. the DCU. 58-Giffen-a 2.50
#1,000,000 (11/98) 853rd Century x-over 2.50
Annual 1 (1993, $3.50, 68 pgs.)-Bloodlines x-over 3.50
Annual 2 (1994, $3.50)-21 artists (20 listed on-c); Alan Grant script; Elseworlds story 3.50
Annual 3 (1995, $3.95)-Year One story 4.00
...Big Babe Spring Break Special (Spr, '95, $1.95)-Balent-a 2.50
...Bounty Hunting for Fun and Profit ('95)-Bisley-c 5.00
... Chained (5/97, $2.50)-Alan Grant story 2.50
.../Deadman: The Brave And The Bald (2/95, $3.50) 3.50
.../Demon: Helloween (12/96, $2.25)-Giarrano-a 2.50
...Fragtastic Voyage 1 ('97, $5.95)-Mejia painted-c/a 6.00
...Gallery (9/95, $3.50)-pin-ups. 3.50
...In the Chair 1 (8/94, $1.95, 36 pgs.), ...I Quit-(12/95, $2.25) 2.50
.../Judge Dredd ('95, $4.95). 5.00
...Lobocop 1 (2/94, $1.95)-Alan Grant scripts; painted-c 2.50

LOBO: (Title Series), DC Comics
--A CONTRACT ON GAWD, 4/94 - 7/94 (mature) 1-4: Alan Grant scripts. 3-Groo cameo 2.50
--DEATH AND TAXES, 10/96 - No. 4, 1/97, 1-4-Giffen/Grant scripts 2.50
--GOES TO HOLLYWOOD, 8/96 ($2.25), 1-Grant scripts 2.50
--INFANTICIDE, 10/92 - 1/93 ($1.50, mature), 1-4-Giffen-c/a; Alan Grant scripts 2.50
--/ MASK, 2/97 - No.2, 3/97 ($5.95), 1,2 6.00
--'S BACK, 5/92 - No. 4, 11/92 ($1.50, mature), 1-4: 1-Has 3 outer covers. Bisley painted-c 1,2; a-1-3. 3-Sam Kieth-c; all have Giffen plots/breakdown & Grant scripts 2.50
Trade paperback (1993, $9.95)-r/1-4 10.00
--THE DUCK, 6/97 ($1.95), 1-A. Grant-s/V. Semeiks & R. Kryssing-a 2.00
--UNAMERICAN GLADIATORS, 6/93 - 9/93 ($1.75, mature), 1-4-Mignola-c; Grant/Wagner scripts 2.50

LOCKE!
Blackthorne Publishing: 1987 - No. 3, ($1.25, limited series)
1-3 2.00

LOCO (Magazine) (Satire)
Satire Publications: Aug, 1958 - V1#3, Jan, 1959
V1#1-Chic Stone-a 7.50 22.50 45.00
V1#2,3-Severin-a, 2 pgs. Davis; 3-Heath-a 5.85 17.50 35.00

LOGAN: PATH OF THE WARLORD
Marvel Comics: Feb, 1996 ($5.95, one-shot)
1-John Paul Leon-a 6.00

LOGAN: SHADOW SOCIETY
Marvel Comics: 1996 ($5.95, one-shot)
1 6.00

LOGAN'S RUN
Marvel Comics Group: Jan, 1977 - No. 7, July, 1977
1: 1-5-Based on novel & movie 5.00
2-5,7: 6,7-New stories adapted from novel 4.00
6-1st Thanos (also see Iron Man #55) solo story (back-up) by Zeck (6/77) 1.25 3.75 10.00
NOTE: ***Austin*** *a-6i.* ***Gulacy*** *c-6.* ***Kane*** *c-7p.* ***Perez*** *a-1-5p; c-1-5p.* ***Sutton*** *a-6p, 7p.*

LOIS & CLARK, THE NEW ADVENTURES OF SUPERMAN
DC Comics: 1994 ($9.95, one-shot)
1-r/Man of Steel #2, Superman Annual 1, Superman #9 & 11, Action #600 & 655, Adventures of Superman #445, 462 & 466 1.00 3.00 10.00

LOIS LANE (Also see Daring New Adventures of Supergirl, Showcase #9,10 & Superman's Girlfriend...)
DC Comics: Aug, 1986 - No. 2, Sept, 1986 ($1.50, 52 pgs.)
1,2-Morrow-c/a in each 3.00

LOLLY AND PEPPER
Dell Publishing Co.: No. 832, Sept, 1957 - July, 1962
Four Color 832(#1) 2.75 8.00 30.00
Four Color 940,978,1086,1206 1.80 5.50 20.00
01-459-207 (7/62) 1.80 5.50 20.00

LOMAX (See Police Action)

LONDON'S DARK
Escape/Titan: 1989 ($8.95, B&W, graphic novel)
nn-James Robinson script; Paul Johnson-c/a .90 2.70 9.00

LONE EAGLE (The Flame No. 5 on)
Ajax/Farrell Publications: Apr-May, 1954 - No. 4, Oct-Nov, 1954
1 11.50 34.00 80.00
2-4: 3-Bondage-c 8.35 25.00 50.00

LONELY HEART (Formerly Dear Lonely Hearts; Dear Heart #15 on)
Ajax/Farrell Publ. (Excellent Publ.): No. 9, Mar, 1955 - No. 14, Feb, 1956
9-Kamenesque-a; (Last precode) 9.15 27.00 55.00
10-14 5.35 16.00 32.00

LONE RANGER, THE (See Ace Comics, Aurora, Dell Giants,Future Comics, Golden Comics Digest #48, King Comics, Magic Comics & March of Comics #165, 174, 193, 208, 225, 238, 310, 322, 338, 350)

LONE RANGER, THE
Dell Publishing Co.: No. 3, 1939 - No. 167, Feb, 1947
Large Feature Comic 3(1939)-Heigh-Yo Silver; text with illus. by Robert Weisman; also exists as a Whitman #710 105.00 315.00 1050.00
Large Feature Comic 7(1939)-Illustr. by Henry Vallely; Hi-Yo Silver the Lone Ranger to the Rescue; also exists as a Whitman #715 100.00 300.00 1000.00
Feature Book 21(1940), 24(1941) 70.00 210.00 700.00
Four Color 82(1945) 41.00 123.00 450.00

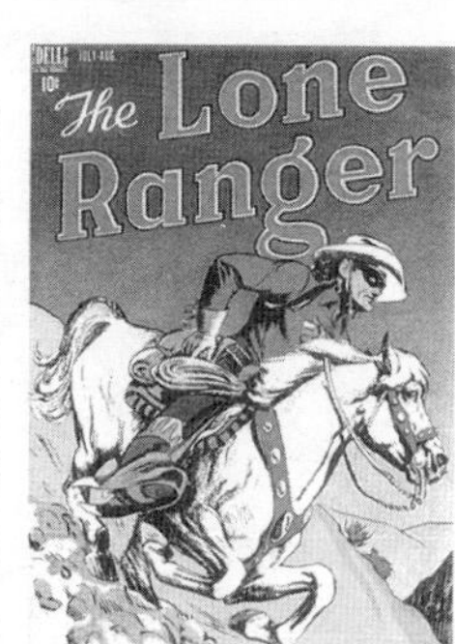

Lone Ranger #4 © Lone Ranger, Inc

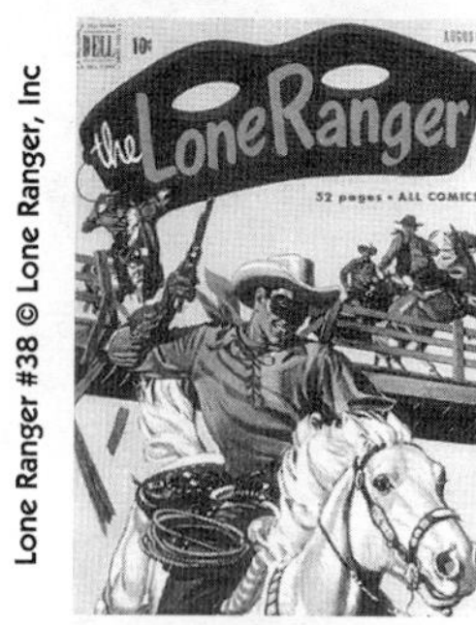

Lone Ranger #38 © Lone Ranger, Inc

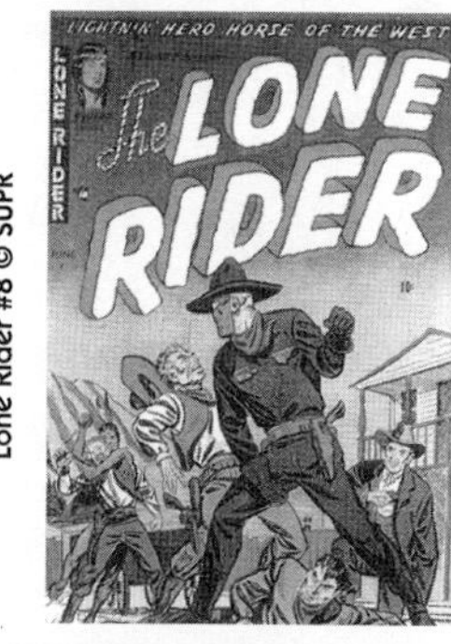

Lone Rider #8 © SUPR

GD2.0 FN6.0 NM9.4

Four Color 98(1945),118(1946) 30.00 88.00 325.00
Four Color 125(1946),136(1947) 20.50 61.00 225.00
Four Color 151,167(1947) 17.00 50.00 185.00

LONE RANGER, THE (Movie, radio & TV; Clayton Moore starred as Lone Ranger in the movies; No. 1-37: strip reprints)(See Dell Giants)
Dell Publishing Co.: Jan-Feb, 1948 - No. 145, May-July, 1962

1 (36 pgs.)-The Lone Ranger, his horse Silver, companion Tonto & his horse Scout begin 59.00 177.00 650.00
2 (52 pgs. begin, end #41) 27.00 82.00 300.00
3-5 20.00 60.00 220.00
6,7,9,10 17.00 51.00 185.00
8-Origin retold; Indian back-c begin, end #35 20.50 61.00 225.00
11-20: 11- "Young Hawk" Indian boy serial begins, ends #145 10.50 31.00 115.00
21,22,24-31: 51-Reprint. 31-1st Mask logo 9.00 27.00 100.00
23-Origin retold 11.30 34.00 125.00
32-37: 32-Painted-c begin. 36-Animal photo back-c begin, end #49. 37-Last newspaper-r issue; new outfit 7.30 22.00 80.00
38-41 (All 52 pgs.) 38-Paul S. Newman-s (wrote most of the stories #38-on) 6.30 19.00 70.00
42-50 (36 pgs.) 5.00 15.00 55.00
51-74 (52 pgs.): 56-One pg. origin story of Lone Ranger & Tonto. 71-Blank inside-c 5.00 15.00 55.00
75,77-99: 79-X-mas-c 4.00 12.00 45.00
76-Classic flag-c 5.00 15.00 55.00
100 6.00 18.00 65.00
101-111: Last painted-c 4.50 13.50 50.00
112-Clayton Moore photo-c begin, end #145 15.50 46.00 170.00
113-117 8.50 26.50 95.00
118-Origin Lone Ranger, Tonto, & Silver retold; Special anniversary issue 22.00 66.00 240.00
119-140: 139-Fran Striker-s 7.65 23.00 85.00
141-145 8.50 26.50 95.00
NOTE: ***Hank Hartman*** *painted c(signed)-65, 66, 70, 75, 82; unsigned-64?, 67-69?, 71, 72, 73?, 74?, 76-78, 80, 81, 83-91, 92?, 93-111.* ***Ernest Nordli*** *painted c(signed)-42, 50, 52, 53, 56, 59, 60; unsigned-39-41, 44-49, 51, 54, 55, 57, 58, 61-63?*

LONE RANGER, THE
Gold Key (Reprints in #13-20): 9/64 - No. 16, 12/69; No. 17, 11/72; No. 18, 9/74 - No. 28, 3/77

1-Retells origin 5.00 15.00 50.00
2 2.50 7.50 25.00
3-10: Small Bear-r in #6-12. 10-Last 12¢ issue 2.50 7.50 20.00
11-17 1.75 5.25 14.00
18-28 1.00 3.00 8.00
Golden West 1(30029-610, 10/66)-Giant; r/most Golden West #3 including Clayton Moore photo front/back-c 6.00 18.00 65.00

LONE RANGER AND TONTO, THE
Topps Comics: Aug, 1994 - No. 4, Nov, 1994 ($2.50, limited series)

1-4: 3-Origin of Lone Ranger; Tonto leaves; Lansdale story, Truman-c/a in all. 2.50
1-4: Silver logo. 1-Signed by Lansdale and Truman 6.00
Trade paperback (1/95, $9.95) 10.00

LONE RANGER'S COMPANION TONTO, THE (TV)
Dell Publishing Co.: No. 312, Jan, 1951 - No. 33, Nov-Jan/58-59 (All painted-c)

Four Color 312(#1, 1/51) 9.00 27.00 100.00
2(8-10/51),3: (#2 titled "Tonto") 4.50 13.50 50.00
4-10 4.00 12.00 45.00
11-20 3.00 9.00 32.00
21-33 2.00 6.00 22.00
NOTE: ***Ernest Nordli*** *painted c(signed)-2, 7; unsigned-3-6, 8-11, 12?, 13, 14, 18?, 22-24? See Aurora Comic Booklets.*

LONE RANGER'S FAMOUS HORSE HI-YO SILVER, THE (TV)
Dell Publishing Co.: No. 369, Jan, 1952 - No. 36, Oct-Dec, 1960 (All painted-c, most by Sam Savitt)

GD2.0 FN6.0 NM9.4

Four Color 369(#1)-Silver's origin as told by The Lone Ranger 8.00 25.00 90.00
Four Color 392(#2, 4/52) 4.00 12.00 45.00
3(7-9/52)-10(4-6/52) 3.00 10.00 36.00
11-36 2.50 7.50 27.00

LONE RIDER (Also see The Rider)
Superior Comics(Farrell Publ.): Apr, 1951 - No. 26, Jul, 1955 (#3-on: 36 pgs.)

1 (52 pgs.)-The Lone Rider & his horse Lightnin' begin; Kamenish-a begins 19.00 58.00 135.00
2 (52 pgs.)-The Golden Arrow begins (origin) 10.00 30.00 70.00
3-6: 6-Last Golden Arrow 10.00 30.00 60.00
7-Golden Arrow becomes Swift Arrow; origin of his shield 10.00 30.00 70.00
8-Origin Swift Arrow 11.50 34.00 80.00
9,10 8.35 25.00 50.00
11-14 6.35 19.00 38.00
15-Golden Arrow origin-r from #2, changing name to Swift Arrow 8.00 24.00 48.00
16-20,22-26: 23-Apache Kid app. 6.35 19.00 38.00
21-3-D effect-c 13.00 39.00 90.00

LONE WOLF AND CUB
First Comics: May, 1987 - No. 45, Apr, 1991 ($1.95-$3.25, B&W, deluxe size)

1 4.00
1-2nd print, 3rd print, 2-2nd print 3.25
2-38,40,42-45: 6-72 pgs. origin ish. 40,42-Ploog-c 3.25
39-($5.95, 120 pgs.)-Ploog-c 6.00
41-($3.95, 84 pgs.)-Ploog-c 4.00
Deluxe Edition ($19.95, B&W) 20.00
NOTE: ***Miller*** *c-1-12p; intro 1-12.* ***Sienkiewicz*** *c-13-24.* ***Matt Wagner*** *c-25-30.*

LONG BOW (...Indian Boy)(See Indians & Jumbo Comics #141)
Fiction House Mag. (Real Adventures Publ.): 1951 - No. 9, Wint, 1952/53

1-Most covers by Maurice Whitman 14.00 43.00 100.00
2 10.00 30.00 65.00
3-9 8.35 25.00 50.00

LONG HOT SUMMER, THE
DC Comics (Milestone): Jul, 1995 - No. 3, Sept, 1995 ($2.95/$2.50, lim. series)

1 ($2.95) 3.00
2,3 ($2.50) 2.50

LONG JOHN SILVER & THE PIRATES (Formerly Terry & the Pirates)
Charlton Comics: No. 30, Aug, 1956 - No. 32, March, 1957 (TV)

30-32: Whitman-c 9.15 27.00 55.00

LONGSHOT (Also see X-Men, 2nd Series #10)
Marvel Comics: Sept, 1985 - No. 6, Feb, 1986 (60¢, limited series)

1-6: 1-Art Adams/Whilce Portacio-c/a in all. 4-Spider-Man app. 6-Double size 2.40 6.00
Trade Paperback (1989, $16.95)-r/#1-6 17.00

LONGSHOT
Marvel Comics: Feb, 1998 ($3.99, one-shot)

1-DeMatteis-s/Zulli-a 4.00

LOONEY TUNES (2nd Series) (TV)
Gold Key/Whitman: April, 1975 - No. 47, July, 1984

1 -Reprints 2.50 7.50 24.00
2-10: 2,4-reprints 1.75 5.25 14.00
11-20: 16-reprints 1.10 3.30 9.00
21-30 2.40 6.00
31,32,36-42 4.00
33-35('80) (Whitman, scarce) 1.50 4.50 12.00
43,44 (low distribution) 1.00 2.80 7.00
45-47 (All #90296 on-c; nd, nd code, pre-pack?) 1.25 3.75 10.00

LOONEY TUNES (3rd Series) (TV)
DC Comics: Apr, 1994 - Present ($1.50/$1.75/$1.95/$1.99)

Looney Tunes #27 © WB

Lorna the Jungle Queen #7 © MAR

Lost in Space #2 © New Line

GD2.0 FN6.0 NM9.4

1-22: 1-Marvin Martian-c/sty; Bugs Bunny, Roadrunner, Daffy begin 2.00
23-59: 23-34-($1.75-c). 35-43-($1.95-c). 44-59-($1.99-c) 2.00

LOONEY TUNES AND MERRIE MELODIES COMICS ("Looney Tunes" #166 (8/55) on)(Also see Porky's Duck Hunt)
Dell Publishing Co.: 1941 - No. 246, July-Sept, 1962

	GD2.0	FN6.0	VF8.0	NM9.4
1-Porky Pig, Bugs Bunny, Daffy Duck, Elmer Fudd, Mary Jane & Sniffles, Pat Patsy and Pete begin (1st comic book app. of each). Bugs Bunny story by Win Smith (early Mickey Mouse artist)	900.00	2700.00	5400.00	10,500.00

	GD2.0	FN6.0	NM9.4
2 (11/41)	140.00	420.00	1400.00
3-Kandi the Cave Kid begins by Walt Kelly; also in #4-6,8,11,15	120.00	360.00	1200.00
4-Kelly-a	120.00	360.00	1200.00
5-Bugs Bunny The Super-Duper Rabbit story (1st funny animal super hero, 3/42; also see Coo Coo); Kelly-a	90.00	270.00	900.00
6,8-Kelly-a	67.00	202.00	675.00
7,9,10: 9-Painted-c. 10-Flag-c	50.00	150.00	500.00
11,15-Kelly-a; 15-X-Mas-c	50.00	150.00	500.00
12-14,16-19	35.00	105.00	350.00
20-25: Pat, Patsy & Pete by Walt Kelly in all	31.00	93.00	310.00
26-30	22.00	67.00	225.00
31-40: 33-War bond-c. 39-X-Mas-c	18.00	54.00	180.00
41-50	14.00	43.00	145.00
51-60	9.50	29.00	105.00
61-80	6.30	19.00	70.00
81-99: 87-X-Mas-c	4.50	13.50	50.00
100	5.50	16.50	60.00
101-120	3.50	10.50	38.00
121-150	2.90	9.00	32.00
151-200: 159-X-Mas-c	2.00	6.00	22.00
201-240	1.65	5.00	18.00
241-246	1.80	5.50	20.00

LOONY SPORTS (Magazine)
3-Strikes Publishing Co.: Spring, 1975 (68 pgs.)

1-Sports satire 1.00 3.00 8.00

LOOSE CANNON (Also see Action Comics Annual #5 & Showcase '94 #5)
DC Comics: June, 1995 - No. 4, Sept, 1995 ($1.75, limited series)

1-4: Adam Pollina-a. 1-Superman app. 2.50

LOOY DOT DOPE
United Features Syndicate: No. 13, 1939

Single Series 13 29.00 86.00 200.00

LORD JIM (See Movie Comics)

LORD PUMPKIN
Malibu Comics (Ultraverse): Oct, 1994 ($2.50, one-shot)

0-Two covers 2.50

LORD PUMPKIN/NECROMANTRA
Malibu Comics (Ultraverse): Apr, 1995 - No. 4, July, 1995 ($2.95, limited series, flip book)

1-4 3.00

LORDS OF MISRULE
Dark Horse Comics: Jan, 1997 - No. 6, Jun, 1997 ($2.95, B&W, limited series)

1-6: 1-Wraparound-c 3.00

LORDS OF THE ULTRA-REALM
DC Comics: June, 1986 - No. 6, Nov, 1986 (Mini-series)

1-6, Special 1(12/87, $2.25) 2.25

LORNA THE JUNGLE GIRL (...Jungle Queen #1-5)
Atlas Comics (NPI 1/OMC 2-11/NPI 12-26): July, 1953 - No. 26, Aug, 1957

	GD2.0	FN6.0	NM9.4
1-Origin & 1st app.	36.00	107.00	250.00
2-Intro. & 1st app. Greg Knight	18.00	54.00	125.00
3-5	15.00	45.00	105.00
6-11: 11-Last pre-code (1/55)	12.00	36.00	85.00
12-17,19-26: 14-Colletta & Maneely-c	10.00	30.00	65.00
18-Williamson/Colletta-c	11.00	33.00	75.00

NOTE: ***Brodsky*** *c-1-3, 5, 9.* ***Everett*** *c-21, 23-26.* ***Heath*** *c-6, 7.* ***Maneely*** *c-12, 15.* ***Romita*** *a-20, 22, 24, 26.* ***Shores*** *a-14-16, 24, 26; c-11, 13, 16.* ***Tuska*** *a-6.*

LOSERS SPECIAL (See Our Fighting Forces #123)(Also see G.I. Combat & Our Fighting Forces)
DC Comics: Sept, 1985 ($1.25, one-shot)

1-Capt. Storm, Gunner & Sarge; Crisis x-over 3.00

LOST, THE
Chaos! Comics: Dec, 1997 - No. 3 ($2.95, B&W, unfinished limited series)

1-3-Andreyko-script: 1-Russell back-c 3.00

LOST CONTINENT
Eclipse Int'l: Sept, 1990 - No. 6, 1991 ($3.50, B&W, squarebound, 60 pgs.)

1-6: Japanese story translated to English 3.50

LOST HEROES
Davdez Arts: Mar, 1998 - Present ($2.95)

0-3-Rob Prior-s/painted-a 3.00

LOST IN SPACE (TV)(Also see Space Family Robinson)
Innovation Publishing: Aug, 1991 - No. 12, Jan, 1993 ($2.50, limited series)

1-12: Bill Mumy (Will Robinson) scripts in #1-9. 9-Perez-c 2.50
1,2-Special Ed.; r/#1,2 plus new art & new-c 2.50
Annual 1,2 (1991, 1992, $2.95, 52 pgs.) 3.00

LOST IN SPACE (Movie)
Dark Horse Comics: Apr, 1998 - No. 3, July, 1998 ($2.95, limited series)

1-3-Continuation of movie; Erskine-c 3.00

LOST IN SPACE: PROJECT ROBINSON (TV)
Innovation Publishing: Nov, 1993 ($2.50, limited series intended)

1-Takes place after #12 2.50

LOST IN SPACE: VOYAGE TO THE BOTTOM OF THE SOUL
Innovation Publishing: No. 13, Aug, 1993 - No. 18, 1994 ($2.50, limited series)

13(V1#1, $2.95)-Embossed silver logo edition; Bill Mumy scripts begin; painted-c 3.00
13(V1#1, $4.95)-Embossed gold logo edition bagged w/poster 5.00
14-18: Painted-c 2.50

NOTE: *Originally intended to be a 12 issue limited series.*

LOST PLANET
Eclipse Comics: 5/87 - No. 5, 2/88; No. 6, 3/89 (Mini-series, Baxter paper)

1-6-Bo Hampton-c/a in all 2.00

LOST WAGON TRAIN, THE (See Zane Grey Fou r Color 583)

LOST WORLD, THE
Dell Publishing Co.: No. 1145, Nov-Jan, 1960-61

Four Color 1145-Movie, Gil Kane-a, photo-c; 1pg. Conan Doyle biography by Torres 10.00 30.00 110.00

LOST WORLD, THE (See Jurassic Park)
Topps Comics: May, 1997 - No. 4, Aug, 1997 ($2.95, limited series)

1-4-Movie adaption 3.00

LOST WORLDS (Weird Tales of the Past and Future)
Standard Comics: No. 5, Oct, 1952 - No. 6, Dec, 1952

	GD2.0	FN6.0	NM9.4
5- "Alice in Terrorland" by Alex Toth; J. Katz-a	40.00	120.00	295.00
6-Toth-a	35.00	105.00	245.00

LOTS 'O' FUN COMICS
Robert Allen Co.: 1940's? (5¢, heavy stock, blue covers)

nn-Contents can vary; Felix, Planet Comics known; contents would determine value. Similar to Up-To-Date Comics. Remainders - re-packaged.

LOU GEHRIG (See The Pride of the Yankees)

LOVE ADVENTURES (Actual Confessions #13)

Love Confessions #1 © QUA

Love Diary #1 © QUA

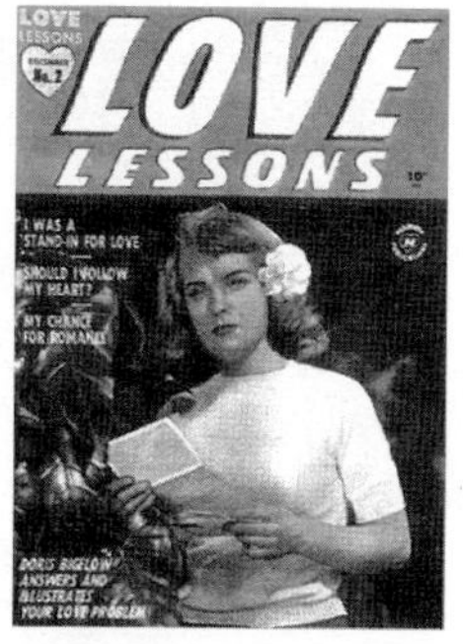

Love Lessons #2 © HARV

Marvel (IPS)/Atlas Comics (MPI): Oct, 1949; No. 2, Jan, 1950; No. 3, Feb, 1951 - No. 12, Aug, 1952

	GD2.0	FN6.0	NM9.4
1-Photo-c	13.50	41.00	95.00
2-Powell-a; Tyrone Power, Gene Tierney photo-c	13.50	41.00	95.00
3-8,10-12: 8-Robinson-a	7.50	22.50	45.00
9-Everett-a	8.35	25.00	50.00

LOVE AND MARRIAGE
Superior Comics Ltd.: Mar, 1952 - No. 16, Sept, 1954

	GD2.0	FN6.0	NM9.4
1	11.50	34.00	80.00
2	6.70	20.00	40.00
3-10	4.25	13.00	28.00
11-16	4.00	12.00	24.00
I.W. Reprint #1,2,8,11,14: 8-r/Love and Marriage #3. 11-r/Love and Marriage #11.	1.25	3.75	10.00
Super Reprint #10('63),15,17('64):15-Love and Marriage #?	1.25	3.75	10.00

NOTE: *All issues have **Kamenish** art.*

LOVE AND ROCKETS
Fantagraphics Books: July, 1982 - No. 50, May, 1996 ($2.95/$2.50/$4.95, B&W, mature)

	GD2.0	FN6.0	NM9.4
1-B&W-c (6/82, $2.95; small size, publ. by Hernandez Bros.)(800 printed)	2.50	7.50	20.00
1 (Fall, '82; color-c)	2.25	6.75	78.00
1-2nd & 3rd printing, 2-11,29-31: 2nd printings			3.00
2		2.40	6.00
3-10			4.00
11-49: 30 ($2.95, 52 pgs.)			3.00
50-($4.95)			5.00

LOVE AND ROMANCE
Charlton Comics: Sept, 1971 - No. 24, Sept, 1975

	GD2.0	FN6.0	NM9.4
1	2.50	7.50	20.00
2-10	1.40	4.15	11.00
11-24	1.00	2.80	7.00

LOVE AT FIRST SIGHT
Ace Magazines (RAR Publ. Co./Periodical House): Oct, 1949 - No. 43, Nov, 1956 (Photo-c: 21-42)

	GD2.0	FN6.0	NM9.4
1-Painted-c	12.00	36.00	85.00
2-Painted-c	7.00	21.00	42.00
3-10: 4-Painted-c	4.25	13.00	28.00
11-20	4.15	12.50	25.00
21-33: 33-Last pre-code	4.00	10.00	20.00
34-43	3.00	7.50	15.00

LOVE BUG, THE (See Movie Comics)

LOVE CLASSICS
A Lover's Magazine/Marvel: Nov, 1949 - No. 2, Feb, 1950 (Photo-c, 52 pgs.)

	GD2.0	FN6.0	NM9.4
1,2: 2-Virginia Mayo photo-c; 30 pg. story "I Was a Small Town Flirt"	12.00	36.00	85.00

LOVE CONFESSIONS
Quality Comics: Oct, 1949 - No. 54, Dec, 1956 (Photo-c: 3,4,6,7,9,11-18,21)

	GD2.0	FN6.0	NM9.4
1-Ward-c/a, 9 pgs; Gustavson-a	29.00	86.00	200.00
2-Gustavson-a; Ward-c	12.00	36.00	85.00
3	7.50	22.50	45.00
4-Crandall-a	10.00	30.00	60.00
5-Ward-a, 7 pgs.	11.00	33.00	75.00
6,7,9,11-13,15,16,18: 7-Van Johnson photo-c. 8-Robert Mitchum & Jane Russell photo-c	5.00	15.00	30.00
8,10-Ward-a(2 stories in #10)	11.00	33.00	75.00
14,17,19,22-Ward-a; 17-Faith Domerque photo-c	10.00	30.00	65.00
20-Ward-a(2)	11.00	33.00	75.00
21,23-28,30-38,40-42: Last precode, 4/55	4.00	10.00	20.00
29-Ward-a	10.00	30.00	60.00
39-Matt Baker-a	6.35	19.00	38.00
43,44,46-48,50-54: 47-Ward-c?	3.60	9.00	18.00
45-Ward-a	5.35	16.00	32.00
49-Baker-c/a	7.50	22.50	45.00

LOVE DIARY
Our Publishing Co./Toytown/Patches: July, 1949 - No. 48, Oct, 1955 (Photo-c: 1-24,27-29) (52 pgs. #1-11?)

	GD2.0	FN6.0	NM9.4
1-Krigstein-a	16.00	47.00	110.00
2,3-Krigstein & Mort Leav-a in each	10.00	30.00	70.00
4-8	5.00	15.00	30.00
9,10-Everett-a	5.85	17.50	35.00
11-20: 16- Mort Leav-a, 3 pg. Baker-sty. Leav-a	4.25	13.00	26.00
21-30,32-48: 45-Leav-a. 47-Last precode(12/54)	4.00	11.00	22.00
31-John Buscema headlights-c	4.25	13.00	28.00

LOVE DIARY (Diary Loves #2 on; title change due to previously published title)
Quality Comics Group: Sept, 1949

	GD2.0	FN6.0	NM9.4
1-Ward-c/a, 9 pgs.	30.00	90.00	210.00

LOVE DIARY
Charlton Comics: July, 1958 - No. 102, Dec, 1976

	GD2.0	FN6.0	NM9.4
1	8.35	25.00	50.00
2	5.35	16.00	32.00
3-5,7-10: 10-Photo-c	4.00	11.00	22.00
6-Torres-a	5.35	16.00	32.00
11-20: 20-Photo-c	2.25	6.75	18.00
21-40	1.85	5.50	15.00
41-60	1.25	3.75	10.00
61-80,100-102	1.00	3.00	8.00
81-99		2.40	6.00

LOVE DOCTOR (See Dr. Anthony King...)

LOVE DRAMAS (True Secrets No. 3 on?)
Marvel Comics (IPS): Oct, 1949 - No. 2, Jan, 1950

	GD2.0	FN6.0	NM9.4
1-Jack Kamen-a; photo-c	16.00	47.00	110.00
2	11.50	34.00	80.00

LOVE EXPERIENCES (Challenge of the Unknown No. 6)
Ace Periodicals (A.A. Wyn/Periodical House): Oct, 1949 - No. 5, June, 1950; No. 6, Apr, 1951 - No. 38, June, 1956

	GD2.0	FN6.0	NM9.4
1-Painted-c	11.00	33.00	75.00
2	5.35	16.00	32.00
3-5: 5-Painted-c	4.00	12.00	24.00
6-10	4.00	10.00	20.00
11-30: 30-Last pre-code (2/55)	3.20	8.00	16.00
31-38: 38-Indicia date-6/56; c-date-8/56	2.80	7.00	14.00

NOTE: ***Anne Brewster** a-15. Photo c-4, 15-35, 38.*

LOVE JOURNAL
Our Publishing Co.: No. 10, Oct, 1951 - No. 25, July, 1954

	GD2.0	FN6.0	NM9.4
10	10.00	30.00	65.00
11-25: 19-Mort Leav-a	5.35	16.00	32.00

LOVELAND
Mutual Mag./Eye Publ. (Marvel): Nov, 1949 - No. 2, Feb, 1950 (52 pgs.)

	GD2.0	FN6.0	NM9.4
1,2-Photo-c	10.00	30.00	60.00

LOVE LESSONS
Harvey Comics/Key Publ. No. 5: Oct, 1949 - No. 5, June, 1950

	GD2.0	FN6.0	NM9.4
1-Metallic silver-c printed over the cancelled covers of Love Letters #1; indicia title is "Love Letters"	12.00	36.00	85.00
2-Powell-a; photo-c	5.85	17.50	35.00
3-5: 3-Photo-c	4.25	13.00	28.00

LOVE LETTERS (10/49, Harvey; advertised but never published; covers were printed before cancellation and were used as the cover to Love Lessons #1)

LOVE LETTERS (Love Secrets No. 32 on)
Quality Comics: 11/49 - #6, 9/50; #7, 3/51 - #31, 6/53; #32, 2/54 - #51, 12/56

	GD2.0	FN6.0	NM9.4
1-Ward-c, Gustavson-a	23.00	69.00	160.00
2-Ward-c, Gustavson-a	18.00	54.00	125.00

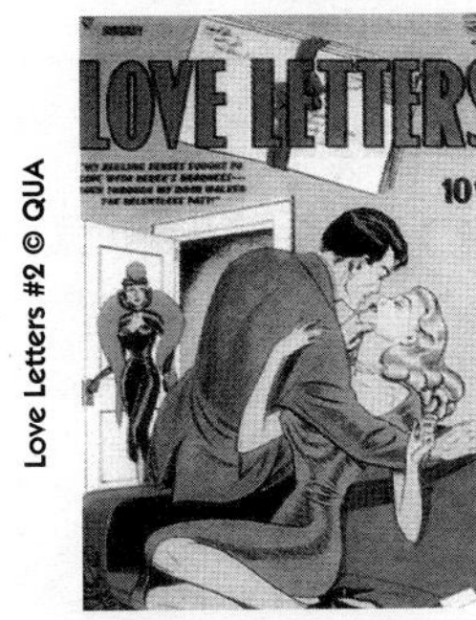

Love Letters #2 © QUA

Lovers' Lane #3 © LEV

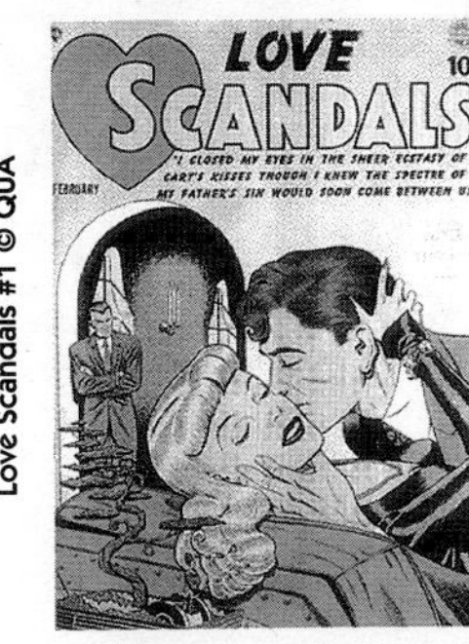

Love Scandals #1 © QUA

	GD2.0	FN6.0	NM9.4
3-Gustavson-a	12.00	36.00	85.00
4-Ward-a, 9 pgs.	17.00	51.00	120.00
5-8,10	5.35	16.00	32.00
9-One pg. Ward "Be Popular with the Opposite Sex"; Robert Mitchum photo-c	7.50	22.50	45.00
11-Ward-r/Broadway Romances #2 & retitled	7.50	22.50	45.00
12-15,18-20	4.25	13.00	28.00
16,17-Ward-a; 16-Anthony Quinn photo-c. 17-Jane Russell photo-c	10.00	30.00	70.00
21-29	4.25	13.00	26.00
30,31(6/53)-Ward-a	6.70	20.00	40.00
32(2/54)-39: 38-Crandall-a. 39-Last precode (4/55)	4.00	10.00	20.00
40-48	3.20	8.00	16.00
49,50-Baker-a	7.50	22.50	45.00
51-Baker-c	5.85	17.50	35.00

NOTE: *Photo-c on most 3-28.*

LOVE LIFE
P. L. Publishing Co.: Nov, 1951

	GD2.0	FN6.0	NM9.4
1	9.15	27.00	55.00

LOVELORN (Confessions of the Lovelorn #52 on)
American Comics Group (Michel Publ./Regis Publ.): Aug-Sept, 1949 - No. 51, July, 1954 (No. 1-26: 52 pgs.)

	GD2.0	FN6.0	NM9.4
1	13.50	41.00	95.00
2	8.00	24.00	48.00
3-10	5.35	16.00	32.00
11-20,22-48: 18-Drucker-a(2 pgs.). 46-Lazarus-a	4.25	13.00	26.00
21-Prostitution story	6.35	19.00	38.00
49-51-Has 3-D effect-c/stories	15.00	45.00	105.00

LOVE MEMORIES
Fawcett Publications: 1949 (no month) - No. 4, July, 1950 (All photo-c)

	GD2.0	FN6.0	NM9.4
1	12.00	36.00	85.00
2-4: 2-(Win/49-50)	7.50	22.50	45.00

LOVE MYSTERY
Fawcett Publications: June, 1950 - No. 3, Oct, 1950 (All photo-c)

	GD2.0	FN6.0	NM9.4
1-George Evans-a	20.00	60.00	140.00
2,3-Evans-a. 3-Powell-a	16.00	47.00	110.00

LOVE PROBLEMS (See Fox Giants)

LOVE PROBLEMS AND ADVICE ILLUSTRATED (see True Love...)

LOVE ROMANCES (Formerly Ideal #5)
Timely/Marvel/Atlas(TCI No. 7-71/Male No. 72-106): No. 6, May, 1949 - No. 106, July, 1963

	GD2.0	FN6.0	NM9.4
6-Photo-c	12.00	36.00	85.00
7-Photo-c; Kamen-a	8.35	25.00	50.00
8-Kubert-a; photo-c	8.35	25.00	50.00
9-20: 9-12-Photo-c	5.85	17.50	35.00
21,24-Krigstein-a	7.50	22.50	45.00
22,23,25-35,37,39,40	5.35	16.00	32.00
36,38-Krigstein-a	6.70	20.00	40.00
41-44,46,47: Last precode (2/55)	5.00	15.00	30.00
45,57-Matt Baker-a	7.50	22.50	45.00
48,50-52,54-56,58-74	2.50	7.50	24.00
49,53-Toth-a, 6 & ? pgs.	4.00	12.00	40.00
75,77,82-Matt Baker-a	4.20	12.60	42.00
76,78-81,86,88-90,92-95: 80-Heath-c. 95-Last 10¢-c?	2.50	7.50	24.00
83,84,87,91-Kirby-c. 83-Severin-a	4.00	12.00	40.00
85,96,97,99-105-Kirby-c/a	5.50	16.50	55.00
98-Kirby-c/a	6.50	19.50	65.00

NOTE: ***Anne Brewster** a-67, 72. **Colletta** a-37, 40, 42, 44, 67(2); c-42, 44, 49, 54, 80. **Everett** c-70. **Heath** a-87. **Kirby** c-80, 85, 88. **Robinson** a-29.*

LOVERS (Formerly Blonde Phantom)
Marvel Comics No. 23,24/Atlas No. 25 on (ANC): No. 23, May, 1949 - No. 86, Aug?, 1957

	GD2.0	FN6.0	NM9.4
23-Photo-c begin, end #28	12.00	36.00	85.00
24-Tothish plus Robinson-a	6.70	20.00	40.00
25,30-Kubert-a; 7, 10 pgs.	7.50	22.50	45.00
26-29,31-36,39,40	5.00	15.00	30.00
37,38-Krigstein-a	7.50	22.50	45.00
41-Everett-a(2)	6.70	20.00	40.00
42,44-65: 65-Last pre-code (1/55)	4.25	13.00	28.00
43-Frazetta 1 pg. ad	5.00	15.00	30.00
66,68-86	4.00	12.00	24.00
67-Toth-a	5.35	16.00	32.00

NOTE: ***Anne Brewster** a-86. **Colletta** a-54, 59, 62, 64, 65, 69, 85; c-61, 64, 65, 75. **Heath** a-61. **Maneely** a-57. **Powell** a-27, 30. **Robinson** a-54, 56.*

LOVERS' LANE
Lev Gleason Publications: Oct, 1949 - No. 41, June, 1954 (No. 1-18: 52 pgs.)

	GD2.0	FN6.0	NM9.4
1-Biro-c	10.00	30.00	60.00
2-Biro-c	5.35	16.00	32.00
3-20: 3,4-Painted-c. 20-Frazetta 1 pg. ad	4.00	12.00	24.00
21-38,40,41	3.20	8.00	16.00
39-Story narrated by Frank Sinatra	5.35	16.00	32.00

NOTE: ***Briefer** a-6, 21. **Fuje** a-4, 16; c-many. **Guardineer** a-1. **Kinstler** c-41. **Tuska** a-6. Painted c-3-18. Photo c-19-22, 26-28.*

LOVE SCANDALS
Quality Comics: Feb, 1950 - No. 5, Oct, 1950 (Photo-c #2-5) (All 52 pgs.)

	GD2.0	FN6.0	NM9.4
1-Ward-c/a, 9 pgs.	25.00	75.00	175.00
2,3: 2-Gustavson-a	10.00	30.00	60.00
4-Ward-a, 18 pgs; Gil Fox-a	20.00	60.00	140.00
5-C. Cuidera-a; tomboy story "I Hated Being a Woman"	10.00	30.00	60.00

LOVE SECRETS
Marvel Comics(IPC): Oct, 1949 - No. 2, Jan, 1950 (52 pgs., photo-c)

	GD2.0	FN6.0	NM9.4
1	12.00	36.00	85.00
2	8.35	25.00	50.00

LOVE SECRETS (Formerly Love Letters #31)
Quality Comics Group: No. 32, Aug, 1953 - No. 56, Dec, 1956

	GD2.0	FN6.0	NM9.4
32	9.15	27.00	55.00
33,35-39	4.25	13.00	28.00
34-Ward-a	9.15	27.00	55.00
40-Matt Baker-c	6.70	20.00	40.00
41-43: 43-Last precode (3/55)	4.25	13.00	26.00
44,47-50,53,54	3.60	9.00	18.00
45,46-Ward-a. 46-Baker-a	7.50	22.50	45.00
51,52-Ward(r). 52-r/Love Confessions #17	5.00	15.00	30.00
55,56: 55-Baker-a. 56-Baker-c	5.85	17.50	35.00

LOVE STORIES (Formerly My Love Affair #5)
Fox Feature Syndicate: No. 6, 1950 - No. 12, 1951

	GD2.0	FN6.0	NM9.4
6,8-Wood-a	19.00	56.00	130.00
7,9-12	9.15	27.00	55.00

LOVE STORIES (Formerly Heart Throbs)
National Periodical Publ.: No. 147, Nov, 1972 - No. 152, Oct-Nov, 1973

	GD2.0	FN6.0	NM9.4
147-152	1.75	5.25	14.00

LOVE STORIES OF MARY WORTH (See Harvey Comics Hits #55 & Mary Worth)
Harvey Publications: Sept, 1949 - No. 5, May, 1950

	GD2.0	FN6.0	NM9.4
1-1940's newspaper reprints-#1-4	6.70	20.00	40.00
2-5: 3-Kamen/Baker-a?	5.00	15.00	30.00

LOVE SUCKS
Ace Comics: 1995; Oct, 1996 - Present ($2.95, B&W)

	GD2.0	FN6.0	NM9.4
1-5: 1-(1995) Hynes-s/Juch-a, 1-(10/96) Santiago-s/Juch-a			3.00

LOVE TALES (Formerly The Human Torch #35)
Marvel/Atlas Comics (ZPC No. 36-50/MMC No. 67-75): No. 36, 5/49 - No. 58, 8/52; No. 59, date? - No. 75, Sept, 1957

	GD2.0	FN6.0	NM9.4
36-Photo-c	12.00	36.00	85.00
37	7.50	22.50	45.00

Lucky Comics #2 © Consolidated Mags.

Lucky Star #3 © Nationwide Publ.

Machine Man #1 © MAR

GD2.0 FN6.0 NM9.4

38-44,46-50: 39-41-Photo-c 5.35 16.00 32.00
45,51,52,69: 45-Powell-a. 51,69-Everett-a. 52-Krigstein-a
6.00 18.00 36.00
53-60: 60-Last pre-code (2/55) 4.15 12.50 25.00
61-68,70-75: 75-Brewster, Cameron, Colletta-a 3.60 9.00 18.00

LOVE THRILLS (See Fox Giants)

LOVE TRAILS (Western romance)
A Lover's Magazine (CDS)(Marvel): Dec, 1949 - No. 2, Mar, 1950 (52 pgs.)
1,2: 1-Photo-c 12.00 36.00 85.00

LOWELL THOMAS' HIGH ADVENTURE (See High Adventure)

LT. (See Lieutenant)

LUBA
Fantographics Books: Feb, 1998 - Present ($2.95, B&W, mature)
1-3-Gilbert Hernandez-s/a 3.00

LUCIFER'S HAMMER (Larry Niven & Jerry Pournelle's...)
Innovation Publishing: Nov, 1993 - No. 6, 1994 ($2.50, painted, limited series)
1-6: Adaptatin of novel, painted-c & art 2.50

LUCKY COMICS
Consolidated Magazines: Jan, 1944; No. 2, Sum, 1945 - No. 5, Sum, 1946
1-Lucky Starr & Bobbie begin 19.00 58.00 135.00
2-5: 5-Devil-c by Walter Johnson 11.00 33.00 75.00

LUCKY DUCK
Standard Comics (Literary Ent.): No. 5, Jan, 1953 - No. 8, Sept, 1953
5-Funny animal; Irving Spector-a 10.00 30.00 70.00
6-8-Irving Spector-a 9.15 27.00 55.00
NOTE: Harvey Kurtzman tried to hire Spector for Mad #1.

LUCKY "7" COMICS
Howard Publishers Ltd.: 1944 (No date listed)
1-Pioneer, Sir Gallagher, Dick Royce, Congo Raider, Punch Powers; bondage-c 34.00 103.00 240.00

LUCKY STAR (Western)
Nation Wide Publ. Co.: 1950 - No. 7, 1951; No. 8, 1953 - No. 14, 1955 (5x7-1/4"; full color, 5¢)
nn (#1)-(5¢, 52 pgs.)-Davis-a 11.50 34.00 80.00
2,3-(5¢, 52 pgs.)-Davis-a 8.35 25.00 50.00
4-7-(5¢, 52 pgs.)-Davis-a 7.50 22.50 45.00
8-14-(36 pgs.) 5.85 17.50 35.00
Given away with Lucky Star Western Wear by the Juvenile Mfg. Co.
4.00 10.00 20.00

LUCY SHOW, THE (TV) (Also see I Love Lucy)
Gold Key: June, 1963 - No. 5, June, 1964 (Photo-c: 1,2)
1 12.25 37.00 135.00
2 6.25 19.00 70.00
3-5: Photo back c-1,2,4,5 5.50 16.50 60.00

LUCY, THE REAL GONE GAL (Meet Miss Pepper #5 on)
St. John Publishing Co.: June, 1953 - No. 4, Dec, 1953
1-Negligee panels 11.00 33.00 75.00
2 6.70 20.00 40.00
3,4: 3-Drucker-a 5.35 16.00 32.00

LUDWIG BEMELMAN'S MADELEINE & GENEVIEVE
Dell Publishing Co.: No. 796, May, 1957
Four Color 796 2.75 8.00 30.00

LUDWIG VON DRAKE (TV)(Disney)(See Walt Disney's C&S #256)
Dell Publishing Co.: Nov-Dec, 1961 - No. 4, June-Aug, 1962
1 6.00 18.00 65.00
2-4 4.00 12.00 45.00

LUFTWAFFE: 1946 (Volume 1)
Antarctic Press: July, 1996 - No.4, Jan, 1997 ($2.95, B&W, limited series)
1-4-Ben Dunn & Ted Nomura-s/a, ...Special Ed. 3.00

LUFTWAFFE: 1946 (Volume 2)
Antarctic Press: Mar, 1997 - Present ($2.95/$2.99, B&W, limited series)
1-16: 8-Reviews Tigers of Terra series 3.00
Annual 1 (4/98, $2.95)-Reprints early Nomura pages 3.00
...Color Special (4/98) 3.00
...Technical Manual 1,2 (2/98, 4/99) 4.00

LUGER
Eclipse Comics: Oct, 1986 - No. 3, Feb, 1987 ($1.75, miniseries, Baxter paper)
1-3: Bruce Jones scripts; Yeates-c/a 2.00

LUKE CAGE (See Cage & Hero for Hire)

LUKE SHORT'S WESTERN STORIES
Dell Publishing Co.: No. 580, Aug, 1954 - No. 927, Aug, 1958
Four Color 580(8/54), 651(9/55)-Kinstler-a 2.75 8.00 30.00
Four Color 739,771,807,875,927 2.75 8.00 30.00
Four Color 848 3.60 11.00 40.00

LUNATIC FRINGE, THE
Innovation Publishing: July, 1989 - No. 2, 1989 ($1.75, deluxe format)
1,2 2.00

LUNATICKLE (Magazine) (Satire)
Whitstone Publ.: Feb, 1956 - No. 2, Apr, 1956
1,2-Kubert-a (scarce) 4.00 10.00 20.00

LUNATIK
Marvel Comics: Dec, 1995 - No. 3, Feb, 1996 ($1.95, limited series)
1-3 2.00

LUST FOR LIFE
Slave Labor Graphics: Feb, 1997 - No. 4, Jan, 1998 ($2.95, B&W)
1-4: 1-Jeff Levin-s/a 3.00

LYCANTHROPE LEO
Viz Communications: 1994 - No. 7($2.95, B&W, limited series, 44 pgs.)
1-7 3.00

LYNCH (See Gen 13)
Image Comics (WildStorm Productions): May, 1997 ($2.50, one-shot)
1-Helmut-c/app. 2.50

LYNCH MOB
Chaos! Comics: June, 1994 - No. 4, Sept, 1994 ($2.50, limited series)
1-4 2.50
1-Special edition full foil-c 5.00

LYNDON B. JOHNSON
Dell Publishing Co.: Mar, 1965
12-445-503-Photo-c 2.50 7.50 20.00

M
Eclipse Books: 1990 - No. 4, 1991 ($4.95, painted, 52 pgs.)
1-Adapts movie; contains flexi-disc ($5.95) 6.00
2-4 5.00

MACHINE, THE
Dark Horse Comics: Nov, 1994 - Feb, 1995 ($2.50, color)
1-4 2.50

MACHINE MAN (Also see 2001, A Space Odyssey)
Marvel Comics Group: Apr, 1978 - No. 9, Dec, 1978; No. 10, Aug, 1979 - No. 19, Feb, 1981
1-Jack Kirby-c/a/scripts begin; end #9 1.00 3.00 8.00
2-17: 10-Marv Wolfman scripts & Ditko-a begins 4.00
18-Wendigo, Alpha Flight-ties into X-Men #140 1.25 3.75 10.00
19-Intro/1st app. Jack O'Lantern (Macendale), later becomes 2nd Hobgoblin
1.25 3.75 10.00
NOTE: ***Austin*** *c-7i, 19i.* ***Buckler*** *c-17p, 18p.* ***Byrne*** *c-14p.* ***Ditko*** *a-10-19; c-10-13, 14i, 15, 16.* ***Kirby*** *a-1-9p; c-1-5, 7-9p.* ***Layton*** *c-7i.* ***Miller*** *c-19p.* ***Simonson*** *c-6.*

Machine Man/ Bastion 1998 Annual © MAR

Mad #22 © EC Publ.

Mad #189 © EC Publ.

GD2.0 FN6.0 NM9.4 GD2.0 FN6.0 NM9.4

MACHINE MAN (Also see X-51)
Marvel Comics Group: Oct, 1984 - No. 4, Jan, 1985 (Limited-series)

1-4-Barry Smith-c/a(i) & colors in all 3.00
TPB (1988, $6.95) r/ #1-4; Barry Smith-c 7.00
.../Bastion '98 Annual ($2.99) wraparound-c 3.00

MACHINE MAN 2020
Marvel Comics: Aug, 1994 - Nov, 1994 ($2.00, 52 pgs., limited series)

1-4: Reprints Machine Man limited series; Barry Windsor-Smith-c/i(r) 2.00

MACK BOLAN: THE EXECUTIONER (Don Pendleton's...)
Innovation Publishing: July, 1993 ($2.50)

1-3-($2.50) 2.50
1-($3.95)-Indestructible Cover Edition 4.00
1-($2.95)-Collector's Gold Edition; foil stamped 3.00
1-($3.50)-Double Cover Edition; red foil outer-c 3.50

MACKENZIE'S RAIDERS (Movie, TV)
Dell Publishing Co.: No. 1093, Apr-June, 1960

Four Color 1093-Richard Carlson photo-c from TV show 5.50 16.50 60.00

MACROSS (Becomes Robotech: The Macross Saga #2 on)
Comico: Dec, 1984 ($1.50)(Low print run)

1-Early manga app. 2.00 6.00 20.00

MACROSS II
Viz Select Comics: 1992 - No. 10, 1993 ($2.75, B&W, limited series)

1-10: Based on video series 2.75

MAD (Tales Calculated to Drive You...)
E. C. Comics (Educational Comics): Oct-Nov, 1952 - Present (No. 24 on are magazine format) (Kurtzman editor No. 1-28, Feldstein No. 29 - No. ?)

1-Wood, Davis, Elder start as regulars 513.00 1540.00 5900.00
2-Dick Tracy cameo 130.00 390.00 1300.00
3,4: 3-Stan Lee mentioned. 4-Reefer mention story "Flob Was a Slob" by Davis; Superman parody 75.00 225.00 750.00
5-Low distr.; W.M. Gaines biog. 130.00 390.00 1300.00
6-11: 6-Popeye cameo. 7,8- "Hey Look" reprints by Kurtzman. 11-Wolverton-a; Davis story was-r/Crime Suspenstories #12 w/new Kurtzman dialogue 56.00 168.00 560.00
12-15: 15,18-Pot Shot Pete-r by Kurtzman 44.00 132.00 440.00
16-23(5/55): 18-Alice in Wonderland by Jack Davis. 21-1st app. Alfred E. Neuman on-c in fake ad. 22-All by Elder plus photo-montages by Kurtzman. 23-Special cancel announcement 37.00 111.00 335.00
24(7/55)-1st magazine issue (25¢); Kurtzman logo & border on-c; 1st "What? Me Worry?" on-c; 2nd printing exists 88.00 264.00 825.00
25-Jaffee starts as regular writer 37.00 111.00 330.00
26,27: 27-Jaffee starts as story artist; new logo 34.00 102.00 270.00
28-Last issue edited by Kurtzman; (three cover variations exist with different wording on contents banner on lower right of cover; value of each the same) 31.00 93.00 250.00
29-Kamen-a; Don Martin starts as regular; Feldstein editing begins 31.00 93.00 250.00
30-1st A. E. Neuman cover by Mingo; last Elder-a; Bob Clarke starts as regular; Disneyland & Elvis Presley spoof 43.00 130.00 390.00
31-Freas starts as regular; last Davis-a until #99 25.00 75.00 200.00
32,33: 32-Orlando, Drucker, Woodbridge start as regulars; Wood back-c. 33-Orlando back-c 23.00 70.00 180.00
34-Berg starts as regular 19.00 56.00 150.00
35-Mingo wraparound-c; Crandall-a 19.00 56.00 150.00
36-40 (7/58) 14.00 43.00 100.00
41-50: 42-Danny Kaye-s. 44-Xmas-c. 47-49-Sid Caesar-s. 48-Uncle Sam-c. 50 (10/59)-Peter Gunn-s 10.00 30.00 80.00
51-59: 52-Xmas-c; 77 Sunset Strip. 53-Rifleman-s. 55-Sid Caesar-s. 59-Strips of Superman, Flash Gordon, Donald Duck & others. 59-Halloween/Headless Horseman-c 10.00 30.00 70.00
60 (1/61)-JFK/Nixon flip-c; 1st Spy vs. Spy by Prohias, who starts as regular 11.50 34.00 80.00
61-70: 64-Rickard starts as regular. 65-JFK-s. 66-JFK-c. 68-Xmas-c by Martin. 70-Route 66-s 6.00 18.00 55.00
71-75,77-80 (7/63): 72-10th Anniv. special; 1/3 pg. strips of Superman, Tarzan & others. 73-Bonanza-s. 74-Dr. Kildare-s 4.00 12.00 45.00
76-Aragonés starts as regular 4.50 13.50 55.00
81-85: 81-Superman strip. 82-Castro-c. 85-Lincoln-c 3.50 10.50 40.00
86-1st Fold-in; commonly creased back covers makes these and later issues scarcer in NM 3.75 11.25 45.00
87,88 3.50 10.50 42.00
89,90: 89-One strip by Walt Kelly; Frankenstein-c; Fugitive-s. 90-Ringo back-c by Frazetta; Beatles app. 3.75 11.25 45.00
91,94,96,100: 91-Jaffee starts as story artist. 94-King Kong-c. 96-Man From U.N.C.L.E. 100-(1/66)-Anniversary issue 3.00 9.00 36.00
92,93,95,97-99: 99-Davis-a resumes 3.00 9.00 36.00
101,104,106,108,114,115,119,121: 101-Infinity-c; Voyage to the Bottom of the Sea-s. 104-Lost in Space-s. 106-Tarzan back-c by Frazetta; 2 pg. Batman by Aragonés. 108-Hogan's Heroes by Davis. 114-Rat Patrol-s. 115-Star Trek. 119-Invaders (TV). 121-Beatles-c; Ringo pin-up; flip-c of Sik-Teen; Flying Nun-s 3.00 9.00 30.00
102,103,107,109-113,116-118,120(7/68): 118-Beatles cameo 2.70 8.00 27.00
105-Batman-c/s, TV show parody (9/66) 3.80 11.40 38.00
122,124,126,128,129,131-134,136,137,139,140: 122-Ronald Reagan photo inside; Drucker & Mingo-c. 126-Family Affair-s. 128-Last Orlando. 131-Reagan photo back-c. 132-Xmas-c. 133-John Wayne/True Grit. 136-Room 222 2.25 6.75 18.00
123-Three different covers 2.50 7.50 20.00
125,127,130,135,138: 125-2001 Space Odyssey; Hitler back-c. 127-Mod Squad-c/s. 130-Land of the Giants-s; Torres begins as reg. 135-Easy Rider-c by Davis. 138-Snoopy-c; MASH-s 2.50 7.50 24.00
141-149,151-156,158-170: 141-Hawaii Five-0. 147-All in the Family-s. 153-Dirty Harry-s. 155-Godfather-c/s. 156-Columbo-s. 159-Clockwork Orange-c/s. 161-Tarzan-s. 164-Kung Fu (TV)-s. 165-James Bond-s; Dean Martin-c. 169-Drucker-c; McCloud-s. 170-Exorcist-s 2.00 6.00 16.00
150-(4/72) Partridge Family-s 2.25 6.75 18.00
157-(4/72) Planet of the Apes-c/s 2.50 7.50 22.00
171-185,187,189-192,194,195,198,199: 172-Six Million Dollar Man-s; Hitler back-c. 178-Godfather II-c/s. 180-Jaws-c/s (1/76). 182-Bob Jones starts as regular.185-Starsky & Hutch-s. 187-Fonz/Happy Days-c/s; Harry North starts as regular. 189-Travolta/Kotter-c/s. 190-John Wayne-c/s. 192-King Kong-c/s. 194-Rocky-c/s; Laverne & Shirley-s. 199-James Bond-s. 1.75 5.25 14.00
186,188,197,200: 186-Star Trek-c/s. 188-Six Million Dollar Man/ Bionic Woman. 197-Spock-s; Star Wars-s. 200-Close Encounters 2.25 6.75 18.00
193,196: 193-Farrah/Charlie's Angels-c/s. 196-Star Wars-c/s 2.50 7.50 20.00
201,203,205,220: 201-Sat. Night Fever-c/s. 203-Star Wars. 205-Travolta/Grease. 220-Yoda-c, Empire Strikes Back-s 1.75 5.25 14.00
202,204,206,207,209-219,221-227,229,230: 204-Hulk TV show. 206-Tarzan. 208-Superman movie. 209-Mork & Mindy. 210-Lord of the Rings. 212-Spider-Man-s; Alien (movie)-s. 213-James Bond, Dracula, Rocky II-s 216-Star Trek. 219-Martin-c. 221-Shining-s. 223-Dallas-c/s. 225-Popeye. 226-Superman II. 229-James Bond. 230-Star Wars 1.00 3.00 8.00
208,228: 208-Superman movie-c/s; Battlestar Galactica-s. 228-Raiders of the Lost Ark-c/s 1.50 4.50 12.00
231-235,237-241,243-249,251-260: 233-Pac-Man-c. 234-MASH-c/s. 235-Flip-c with Rocky III & Conan; Boris-a. 239-Mickey Mouse-c. 241-Knight Rider-s. 243-Superman III. 245- Last Rickard-a. 247-Seven Dwarfs-c. 253-Supergirl movie-s; Prince/Purple Rain-s. 254-Rock stars-s. 255-Reagan-c; Cosby-s. 256-Last issue edited by Feldstein; Dynasty, Bev. Hills Cop. 259-Rambo. 260-Back to the Future-c/s; Honeymooners-s 1.00 2.80 7.00
236,242,250: 236-E.T.-c/s;Star Trek II-s. 242-Star Wars/A-Team-c/s. 250-Temple of Doom-c/s; Tarzan-s 1.00 3.00 8.00
261-267,269-276,278-288,290-297: 261-Miami Vice. 262-Rocky IV-c/s, Leave It To Beaver-s. 263-Young Sherlock Holmes-s. 264-Hulk Hogan-c; Rambo-s. 267-Top Gun. 271-Star Trek IV-c/s. 272-ALF-c; Get Smart-s. 273-Pee Wee Herman-c/s. 274-Last Martin-a. 281-California Raisins-c.

Mad #344 © EC Publ.

Madballs #3 © MAR

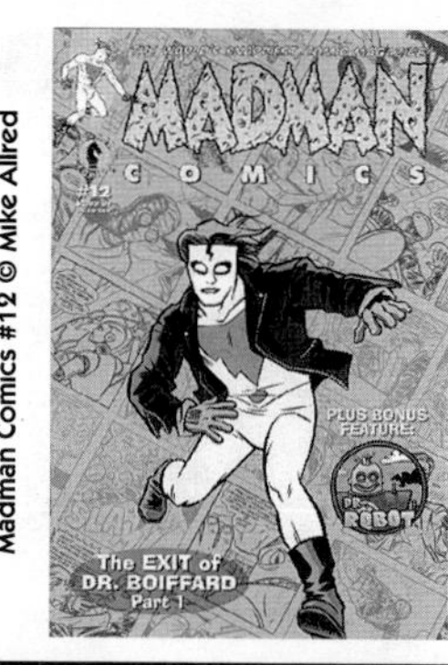

Madman Comics #12 © Mike Allred

282-Star Trek:TNG-s; ALF-s. 283-Rambo III-c/s. 284-Roger Rabbit-c/s. 285-Hulk Hogan-c. 287-3 pgs. Eisner-a. 291-TMNT-c; Indiana Jones-s. 292-Super Mario Bros.-c; Married with Children-s. 295-Back to the Future II. 297-Mike Tyson-c — 5.00

268,277,289,298-300: 268-Aliens-c/s. 277-Michael Jackson-c/s; Robocop-s. 289-Batman movie parody. 298-Gremlins II-c/s; Robocop II. Batman-s. 299-Simpsons-c/story; Total Recall-s. 300(1/91) Casablanca-s, Dick Tracy-s, Wizard of Oz-s, Gone With The Wind-s — 1.00 2.80 7.00

300-303 (1/91-6/91)-Special Hussein Asylum Editions; only distributed to the troops in the Middle East (see Mad Super Spec.) — 5.00

301-310,312,313,315-320,322,324,326-334,337-349: 303-Home Alone-c/s. 305-Simpsons-s. 306-TMNT II movie. 308-Terminator II. 315-Tribute to William Gaines. 316-Photo-c. 319-Dracula-c/s. 320-Disney's Aladdin-s. 322-Batman Animated series. 327-Seinfeld-s; X-Men-s. 331-Flintstones-c/s. 332-O.J. Simpson-c/s; Simpsons app. in Lion King. 334-Frankenstein-c/s. 338-Judge Dredd-c by Frazetta. 341-Pocahontas-s. 345-Beatles app. (1 pg.) 347-Broken Arrow & Mission Impossible — 3.00

311,314,321,323,325,335,336,350,354,358: 311-Addams Family-c/story, Home Improvement-s. 314-Batman Returns-c/story. 321-Star Trek DS9-c/s. 323-Jurassic Park-c/s. 325,336-Beavis & Butthead-c/s. 335-X-Files-s; Pulp Fiction-s; Interview with the Vampire-s. 336-Lois & Clark-s. 350-Polybagged w/CD Rom. 354-Star Wars; Beavis & Butthead-s. 358-X-Files — 4.00

351-353,355-357,359-388 — 2.50

NOTE: ***Aragones*** *c-210, 293.* ***Davis*** *c-2, 27, 135, 139, 173, 178, 212, 213, 219, 246, 260, 296, 308.* ***Drucker*** *c-122, 169, 176, 225, 234, 264, 266, 274, 280, 285, 297, 299, 303, 314, 315, 321.* ***Elder*** *c-5, 259, 261, 268.* ***Elder/Kurtzman*** *a-258-274.* ***Jules Feiffer*** *a(r)-42.* ***Freas*** *c-39-59, 62-67, 69-70, 72, 74.* ***Heath*** *a-14, 27.* ***Jaffee*** *c-199, 217, 224, 258.* ***Kamen*** *a-29.* ***Krigstein*** *a-12, 17, 24, 26.* ***Kurtzman*** *c-1, 3, 4, 6-10, 13, 16, 18.* ***Martin*** *c-68, 165, 229.* ***Mingo*** *c-30-37, 61, 71, 75-80, 82-114, 117-124, 126, 129, 131, 133, 134, 136, 140, 143-148, 150-162, 164, 166-168, 171, 172, 174, 175, 177, 179, 181, 183, 185, 198, 206, 209, 211, 214, 218, 221, 222, 300.* ***John Severin*** *a-1-6, 9, 10.* ***Wolverton*** *c-11; a-11, 17, 29, 31, 36, 40, 82, 137.* ***Wood*** *a-24-45, 59; c-26, 28, 29.* ***Woodbridge*** *a-43. Issues 1-23 are 36 pgs.; 24-28 are 58 pgs.; 29 on are 52 pgs.*

MAD (See Mad Follies, ...Special, More Trash from..., and The Worst from...)

MAD ABOUT MILLIE (Also see Millie the Model)
Marvel Comics Group: April, 1969 - No. 17, Dec, 1970

	GD2.0	FN6.0	NM9.4
1-Giant issue	5.50	16.50	55.00
2,3 (Giants)	3.80	11.40	38.00
4-10	2.50	7.50	22.00
11-16: 16-r	2.25	6.75	18.00
17 (Exist?)	4.00	12.00	40.00
Annual 1(11/71)	2.50	7.50	22.00

MADAME XANADU
DC Comics: July, 1981 ($1.00, no ads, 36 pgs.)

1-Marshall Rogers-a(25 pgs.); Kaluta-c/a(2pgs.); pin-up of Madame Xanadu — 3.00

MADBALLS
Star Comics/Marvel Comics #9 on: Sept, 1986 - No. 3, Nov, 1986; No. 4, June, 1987 - No. 10, June, 1988

1-10: Based on toys. 9-Post-a — 3.00

MAD DISCO
E.C. Comics: 1980 (one-shot, 36 pgs.)

	GD2.0	FN6.0	NM9.4
1-Includes 30 minute flexi-disc of Mad disco music	2.00	6.00	16.00

MAD DOGS
Eclipse Comics: Feb, 1992 - No. 3, July, 1992 ($2.50, B&W, limited series)

1-3 — 2.50

MAD 84 (Mad Extra)
E.C. Comics: 1984 (84 pgs.)

	GD2.0	FN6.0	NM9.4
1		2.40	6.00

MAD FOLLIES (Special)
E. C. Comics: 1963 - No. 7, 1969

	GD2.0	FN6.0	NM9.4
nn(1963)-Paperback book covers	23.00	70.00	255.00
2(1964)-Calendar	17.00	50.00	190.00
3(1965)-Mischief Stickers	13.00	40.00	140.00
4(1966)-Mobile; Frazetta-r/back-c Mad #90	10.00	30.00	110.00
5,6: 5(1967)-Stencils. 6(1968)-Mischief Stickers	6.80	20.00	75.00
7(1969)-Nasty Cards	6.80	20.00	75.00

(If bonus is missing, issue is half price)
NOTE: ***Clarke*** *c-4.* ***Frazetta*** *r-4, 6 (1 pg. ea.).* ***Mingo*** *c-1-3.* ***Orlando*** *a-5.*

MAD HATTER, THE (Costumed Hero)
O. W. Comics Corp.: Jan-Feb, 1946; No. 2, Sept-Oct, 1946

	GD2.0	FN6.0	NM9.4
1-Freddy the Firefly begins; Giunta-c/a	80.00	240.00	640.00
2-Has ad for E.C.'s Animal Fables #1	40.00	120.00	300.00

MADHOUSE
Ajax/Farrell Publ. (Excellent Publ./4-Star): 3-4/54 - No. 4, 9-10/54; 6/57 - No. 4, Dec?, 1957

	GD2.0	FN6.0	NM9.4
1(1954)	29.00	86.00	200.00
2,3	16.00	47.00	110.00
4-Surrealistic-c	25.00	75.00	175.00
1(1957, 2nd series)	12.00	36.00	85.00
2-4	9.15	27.00	55.00

MAD HOUSE (Formerly Madhouse Glads; ...Comics #104? on)
Red Circle Productions/Archie Publications: No. 95, 9/74 - No. 97, 1/75; No. 98, 8/75 - No. 130, 10/82

	GD2.0	FN6.0	NM9.4
95,96-Horror stories through #97	1.25	3.75	10.00
97-Intro. Henry Hobson; Morrow, Thorne-a	1.00	2.80	7.00
98,99,101-130-Satire/humor stories. 110-Sabrina app.,1pg.		2.40	6.00
100	1.00	2.80	7.00
Annual 8(1970-71)-Formerly Madhouse Ma-ad Annual;Sabrina app. (6 pgs.)	2.50	7.50	24.00
Annual 9- 12(1974-75): 11-Wood-a(r)	1.75	5.25	14.00
...Comics Digest 1('75-76)	1.85	5.50	15.00
2- 8(8/82)(...Mag. #5 on)-Sabrina in many	1.50	4.50	12.00

NOTE: ***B. Jones*** *a-96.* ***McWilliams*** *a-97.* ***Morrow*** *a-96, 97; c-95-97.* ***Wildey*** *a-95, 96. See Archie Comics Digest #1, 13.*

MADHOUSE GLADS (Formerly ...Ma-ad; Madhouse #95 on)
Archie Publ.: No. 73, May, 1970 - No. 94, Aug, 1974 (No. 78-92: 52 pgs.)

	GD2.0	FN6.0	NM9.4
73-77,93,94: 74-1 pg. Sabrina	1.25	3.75	10.00
78-92 (52 pgs.)	1.75	5.25	14.00

MADHOUSE MA-AD (...Jokes #67-70; ...Freak-Out #71-74)
(Formerly Archie's Madhouse) (Becomes Madhouse Glads #73 on)
Archie Publications: No. 67, April, 1969 - No. 72, Jan, 1970

	GD2.0	FN6.0	NM9.4
67-71: 70-1 pg. Sabrina	1.50	4.50	12.00
72-6 pgs. Sabrina	2.25	6.75	18.00
...Annual 7(1969-70)-Formerly Archie's Madhouse Annual; becomes Madhouse Annual; 6 pgs. Sabrina	2.50	7.50	24.00

MADMAN (See Creatures of the Id #1)
Tundra Publishing: Mar, 1992 - No. 3, 1992 ($3.95, duotone, high quality, limited series, 52 pgs.)

	GD2.0	FN6.0	NM9.4
1-Mike Allred-c/a in all	1.75	5.25	14.00
1-2nd printing			5.00
2,3	1.25	3.75	10.00

MADMAN ADVENTURES
Tundra Publishing: 1992 - No. 3, 1993 ($2.95, limited series)

	GD2.0	FN6.0	NM9.4
1-Mike Allred-c/a in all	1.25	3.75	10.00
2,3	1.00	2.80	7.00

MADMAN COMICS
Dark Horse Comics (Legend No. 2 on): Apr, 1994 - Present ($2.95, bi-monthly)

1-Allred-c/a; F. Miller back-c. — 5.00

2-3: 3-Alex Toth back-c. — 5.00

4-11: 4-Dave Stevens back-c. 6,7-Miller/Darrow's Big Guy app. 6-Bruce Timm back-c. 7-Darrow back-c. 8-Origin?; Bagge back-c. 10-Allred/Ross-c; Ross back-c. 11-Frazetta back-c — 4.00

12(4/99)-15 — 3.00

Ltd. Ed. Slipcover (1997, $99.95, signed and numbered) w/Vol.1 & Vol. 2.

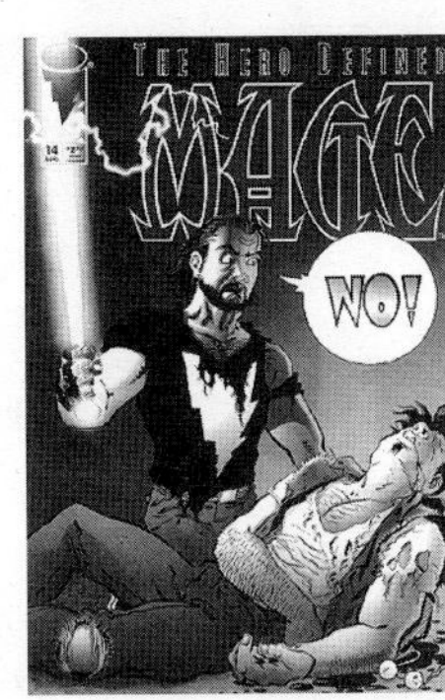

Mad Super Special #114 © EC Publ.

Mage (The Hero Defined) #14 © Matt Wagner

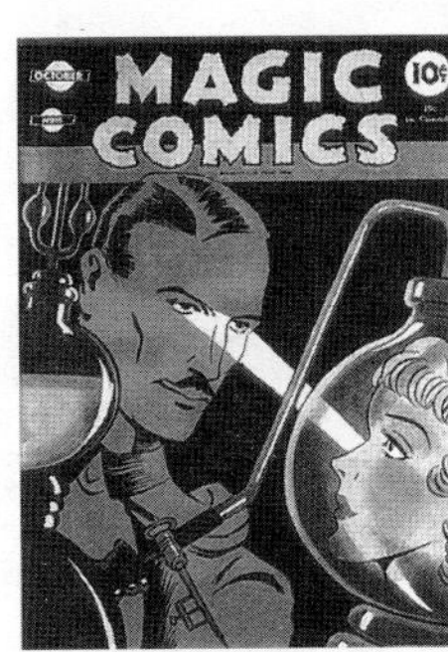

Magic Comics #15 © KING

GD2.0 FN6.0 NM9.4

Vol.1- reprints #1-5; Vol. 2- reprints #6-10 — 100.00
Yearbook '95 (1996, $17.95, TPB)-r/#1-5, intro by Teller — 18.00
Volume 2 ($17.95, TPB) r/#6-10 — 18.00

MADMAN / THE JAM
Dark Horse Comics: Jul, 1998 - No. 2, Aug, 1998 ($2.95, mini-series)
1,2-Allred & Mireault-s/a — 3.00

MAD MONSTER PARTY (See Movie Classics)

MADNESS IN MURDERWORLD
Marvel Comics: 1989 (Came with computer game from Paragon Software)
V1#1-Starring The X-Men — 2.00

MADRAVEN HALLOWEEN SPECIAL
Hamilton Comics: Oct, 1995 ($2.95, one-shot)
nn-Morrow-a — 3.00

MAD SPECIAL (...Super Special)
E. C. Publications, Inc.: Fall, 1970 - Present (84 - 116 pgs.)
(If bonus is missing, issue is half price)

	GD2.0	FN6.0	NM9.4
Fall 1970(#1)-Bonus-Voodoo Doll; contains 17 pgs. new material	7.50	22.50	75.00
Spring 1971(#2)-Wall Nuts; 17 pgs. new material	4.50	13.50	45.00
3-Protest Stickers	4.50	13.50	45.00
4-8: 4-Mini Posters. 5-Mad Flag. 6-Mad Mischief Stickers. 7-Presidential candidate posters, Wild Shocking Message posters. 8-TV Guise	3.80	11.40	38.00
9(1972)-Contains Nostalgic Mad #1 (28 pgs.)	2.80	8.40	28.00
10-13: 10-Nonsense Stickers (Don Martin). 13-Sickie Stickers; 3 pgs. Wolverton-r/Mad #137. 11-Contains 33-1/3 RPM record . 12-Contains Nostalgic Mad #2 (36 pgs.); Davis, Wolverton-a	2.50	7.50	25.00
14,16-21,24: 4-Vital Message posters & Art Depreciation paintings. 16-Mad-hesive Stickers. 17-Don Martin posters. 20-Martin Stickers. 18-Contains Nostalgic Mad #4 (36 pgs.). 21,24-Contains Nostalgic Mad #5 (28 pgs.) & #6 (28 pgs.)	1.60	4.80	16.00
15-Contains Nostalgic Mad #3 (28 pgs.)	1.80	5.40	18.00
22,23,25,27-29,30: 22-Diplomas. 23-Martin Stickers. 25-Martin Posters.27-Mad Shock-Sticks. 28-Contains Nostalgic Mad #7 (36 pgs.). 29-Mad Collectable-Correctables Posters. 30-The Movies	1.00	3.00	10.00
26-Has 33-1/3 RPM record	1.40	4.20	14.00
31-50: 32-Contains Nostalgic Mad #8. 36-Has 96 pgs. of comic book & comic strip spoofs: titles "The Comics" on-c	1.00	3.00	10.00
51-70	1.00	3.00	8.00
71-88,90-100: 71-Batman parodies-r by Wood, Drucker. 72-Wolverton-c r-from 1st panel in Mad #11; Wolverton-s r/new dialogue. 83-All Star Trek spoof issue		2.40	6.00
76-(Fall, 1991)-Special Hussein Asylum Edition; distributed only to the troops in the Middle East (see Mad #300-303)		2.40	6.00
89-($3.95)-Polybaged w/1st of 3 Spy vs. Spy hologram trading cards (direct sale only issue)(other cards came w/card set)		2.40	6.00
101-135: 117-Sci-Fi parodies-r.			4.00

NOTE: *#28-30 have no number on cover.* ***Freas*** *c-76.* ***Mingo*** *c-9, 11, 15, 19, 23.*

MAGE (The Hero Discovered...; also see Grendel #16)
Comico: Feb, 1984 (no month) - No. 15, Dec, 1986 ($1.50, Mando paper)

	GD2.0	FN6.0	NM9.4
1-Comico's 1st color comic	1.25	3.75	10.00
2-5: 3-Intro Edsel			4.00
6-Grendel begins (1st in color)	2.50	7.50	25.00
7-1st new Grendel story	1.50	4.50	12.00
8-14: 13-Grendel dies. 14-Grendel story ends		2.40	6.00
15-$2.95, Double size w/pullout poster		2.40	6.00
Volume 1 TPB (10/98, $5.95) r/#1,2			6.00

MAGE (The Hero Defined)
Image Comics: July, 1997 - Present ($2.50)
1-14:Matt Wagner-c/s/a in all. 13-Three covers — 2.50
1-"3-D Editon" (2/98, $4.95) w/glasses — 5.00
0-(7/97, $5.00) American Ent. Ed. — 5.00
Volume 1 TPB ('98, $9.95) r/#1-4 — 10.00

MAGGIE AND HOPEY COLOR SPECIAL (See Love and Rockets)
Fantagraphics Books: May, 1997 ($3.50, one-shot)
1 — 3.50

MAGGIE THE CAT (Also see Jon Sable, Freelance #11 & Shaman's Tears #12)
Image Comics (Creative Fire Studio): Jan, 1996 - No. 2, Feb, 1996 ($2.50, unfinished limited series)
1,2: Mike Grell-c/a/scripts — 2.50

MAGIC AGENT (See Forbidden Worlds & Unknown Worlds)
American Comics Group: Jan-Feb, 1962 - No. 3, May-June, 1962

	GD2.0	FN6.0	NM9.4
1-Origin & 1st app. John Force	3.00	9.00	30.00
2,3	2.50	7.50	24.00

MAGIC COMICS
David McKay Publications: Aug, 1939 - No. 123, Nov-Dec, 1949

	GD2.0	FN6.0	NM9.4
1-Mandrake the Magician, Henry, Popeye , Blondie, Barney Baxter, Secret Agent X-9 (not by Raymond), Bunky by Billy DeBeck & Thornton Burgess text stories illustrated by Harrison Cady begin; Henry covers begin	300.00	900.00	2200.00
2	100.00	300.00	750.00
3	77.00	232.00	575.00
4	66.00	200.00	475.00
5	50.00	150.00	360.00
6-10: 8-11,21-Mandrake/Henry-c	41.00	125.00	300.00
11-16,18,20: 12-Mandrake-c begin.	36.00	108.00	260.00
17-The Lone Ranger begins	39.00	116.00	270.00
19-Robot-c	41.00	125.00	310.00
21-30: 25-Only Blondie-c. 26-Dagwood-c begin	22.00	66.00	165.00
31-40: 36-Flag-c	16.00	48.00	120.00
41-50	12.00	36.00	95.00
51-60	11.00	33.00	85.00
61-70	9.00	27.00	60.00
71-99, 107,108-Flash Gordon app; not by Raymond	7.00	21.00	45.00
100	8.00	24.00	55.00
101-106,109-123: 123-Last Dagwood-c	6.00	18.00	40.00

MAGICA DE SPELL (See Walt Disney Showcase #30)

MAGIC FLUTE, THE (See Night Music #9-11)

MAGIC PRIEST (See Warrior Nun)
Antarctic Press: June, 1998 ($2.95, B&W)
1-Lyga-s — 3.00

MAGIC SWORD, THE (See Movie Classics)

MAGIC THE GATHERING (Title Series), **Acclaim Comics (Armada)**
...ANTIQUITIES WAR,11/95 - 2/96 ($2.50), 1-4-Paul Smith-a(p) — 2.50
...ARABIAN NIGHTS, 12/95 - 1/96 ($2.50), 1,2 — 2.50
...COLLECTION ,'95 ($4.95), 1,2-polybagged — 5.00
...CONVOCATIONS, '95 ($2.50), 1-nn-pin-ups — 2.50
...ELDER DRAGONS ,'95 ($2.50), 1,2-Doug Wheatley-a — 2.50
...FALLEN ANGEL ,'95 ($5.95), nn — 6.00
...FALLEN EMPIRES ,9/95 - 10/95 ($2.75), 1,2 — 2.75
...Collection ($4.95)-polybagged — 5.00
...HOMELANDS ,'95 ($5.95), nn-polybagged w/card; Hildebrandts-c — 6.00
... ICE AGE (On The World of...) ,7/5 -11/95 ($2.50), 1-4: 1,2-bound-in Magic Card. 3,4-bound-in insert — 2.50
...LEGEND OF JEDIT OJANEN, '96 ($2.50), 1,2 — 2.50
...NIGHTMARE, '95 ($2.50, one shot), 1 — 2.50
...THE SHADOW MAGE, 7/95 - 10/95 ($2.50), 1-4--polybagged w/Magic The Gathering card — 2.50
...Collection 1,2 (1995, $4.95)-Trade paperback; polybagged — 5.00
...SHANDALAR ,'96 ($2.50), 1,2 — 2.50
...WAYFARER ,11/95 - 2/96 ($2.50), 1-5 — 2.50

Magneto Rex #1 © MAR

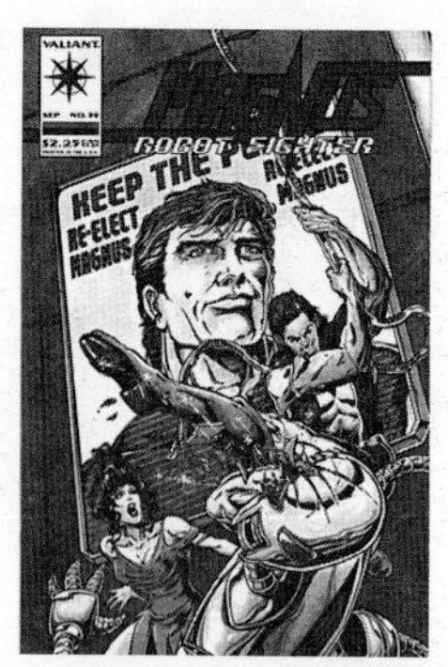

Magnus Robot Fighter #39 © VAL

Major Victory Comics #1 © CHES

GD2.0 FN6.0 NM9.4

MAGIC: THE GATHERING: GERRARD'S QUEST
Dark Horse Comics: Mar, 1998 - No. 4, June, 1998 ($2.95, limited series)

1-4: Grell-s/Mhan-a 3.00

MAGIK (Illyana and Storm Limited Series)
Marvel Comics Group: Dec, 1983 - No. 4, Mar, 1984 (60¢, limited series)

1-4: 1-Characters from X-Men; Inferno begins; X-Men cameo (Buscema pencils in #1,2; c-1p. 2-4: 2-Nightcrawler app. & X-Men cameo 2.50

MAGILLA GORILLA (TV) (See Kite Fun Book)
Gold Key: May, 1964 - No. 10, Dec, 1968 (Hanna-Barbera)

1-1st comic app. 8.00 24.50 90.00
2,4-10: 4-1st Punkin Puss & Mushmouth, Ricochet Rabbit & Droop-a-Long 5.00 15.00 55.00
3-Vs. Yogi Bear for President 6.00 18.00 65.00

MAGILLA GORILLA (TV)(See Spotlight #4)
Charlton Comics: Nov, 1970 - No. 5, July, 1971 (Hanna-Barbera)

1 3.80 11.40 38.00
2-5 2.50 7.50 24.00

MAGNETIC MEN FEATURING MAGNETO
Marvel Comics (Amalgam): June, 1997 ($1.95, one-shot)

1-Tom Peyer-s/Barry Kitson & Dan Panosian-a 2.00

MAGNETO (See X-Men #1)
Marvel Comics: nd (Sept, 1993) (Giveaway) (one-shot)

0-Embossed foil-c by Sienkiewicz; r/Classic X-Men #19 & 12 by Bolton 5.00

MAGNETO
Marvel Comics: Nov, 1996 - No. 4, Feb, 1997 ($1.95, limited series)

1-4: Peter Milligan scripts & Kelley Jones-a(p) 2.00

MAGNETO AND THE MAGNETIC MEN
Marvel Comics (Amalgam): Apr, 1996 ($1.95, one-shot)

1-Jeff Matsuda-a(p) 2.00

MAGNETO ASCENDANT
Marvel Comics: May, 1999 ($3.99, squarebound one-shot)

1-Reprints early Magneto appearances 4.00

MAGNETO REX
Marvel Comics: Apr, 1999 - No. 3, July, 1999 ($2.50, limited series)

1-3-Rogue, Quicksilver app.; Peterson-a(p) 2.50

MAGNUS, ROBOT FIGHTER (...4000 A.D.)(See Doctor Solar)
Gold Key: Feb, 1963 - No. 46, Jan, 1977 (All painted covers except #5)

1-Origin & 1st app. Magnus; Aliens (1st app.) series begins 20.00 60.00 220.00
2,3 9.00 27.00 100.00
4-10: 10-Simonson fan club illo (5/65, 1st-a?) 5.00 15.00 55.00
11-20 2.90 8.70 32.00
21,24-28: 28-Aliens ends 2.00 6.00 22.00
22,23: 22-Origin-r/#1; last 12¢ issue 2.20 6.60 24.00
29-46-Mostly reprints 1.00 3.00 10.00

NOTE: ***Manning** a-1-22, 28-43(r). **Spiegle** a-23, 44r.*

MAGNUS ROBOT FIGHTER (Also see Vintage Magnus)
Valiant/Acclaim Comics: May, 1991 - No. 64, Feb, 1996 ($1.75/$1.95/$2.25/$2.50)

1-Nichols/Layton-c/a; 1-8 have trading cards 4.00
2-8: 4-Rai cameo. 5-Origin & 1st full app. Rai (10/91); 5-8 are in flip book format and back-c & half of book are Rai #1-4 mini-series. 6-1st Solar x-over. 7-Magnus vs. Rai-c/story; 1st X-O Armor 2.50
0-Origin issue; Layton-a; ordered through mail w/coupons from 1st 8 issues plus 50¢; B. Smith trading card 4.00
0-Sold thru comic shops without trading card 2.50
9-11 2.50
12-(3.25, 44 pgs.)-Turok-c/story (1st app. in Valiant universe, 5/92); has 8 pg. Magnus story insert 5.00
13-24,26-48, 50-63: 14-1st app. Isak. 15,16-Unity x-overs. 15-Miller-c. 16-Birth of Magnus. 24-Story cont'd in Rai & the Future Force #9. 33-Timewalker app.36-Bound-in trading cards. 37-Rai & Starwatchers app. 44-Bound-in sneak peek card. 21-New direction & new logo; Reese inks. 21-Gold ink variant 2.50
25-($2.95)-Embossed silver foil-c; new costume 3.00
49, 64 ($2.50): 64-Magnus dies? 2.50
...Invasion (1994, $9.95)-r/Rai #1-4 & Magnus #5-8 10.00
Yearbook (1994, $3.95, 52 pgs.) 4.00

NOTE: ***Ditko/Reese** a-18. **Layton** a(i)-5; c-6-9i, 25; back(i)-5-8. **Reese** a(i)-22, 25, 28; c(i)-22, 24, 28. **Simonson** c-16. Prices for issues 1-8 are for trading cards and coupons intact.*

MAGNUS ROBOT FIGHTER
Acclaim Comics (Valiant Heroes): V2#1, May, 1997 - No. 17 ($2.50)

1-17: 1-Reintro Magnus; Donavon Wylie (X-O Manowar) cameo; Tom Peyer scripts & Mike McKone-c/a begin; painted variant-c exists 2.50

MAGNUS ROBOT FIGHTER 4000 A.D.
Valiant: 1990 - No. 2?, 1991 ($7.95, high quality paper, card stock-c, 96 pgs.)

1,2: Russ Manning-r in all. 1-Origin 8.00

MAGNUS ROBOT FIGHTER/NEXUS
Valiant/Dark Horse Comics: Dec, 1993 - No. 2, Apr, 1994 ($2.95, lim. series)

1,2: Steve Rude painted-c & pencils in all 3.00

MAID OF THE MIST (See American Graphics)

MAI, THE PSYCHIC GIRL
Eclipse Comics: May, 1987 - No. 28, July, 1989 ($1.50, B&W, bi-weekly, 44pgs.)

1-28, 1,2-2nd print 2.00

MAJOR BUMMER
DC Comics: Aug, 1997 - No. 15, Oct, 1998 ($2.50)

1-15: 1-Origin and 1st app. Major Bummer 2.50

MAJOR HOOPLE COMICS (See Crackajack Funnies)
Nedor Publications: nd (Jan, 1943)

1-Mary Worth, Phantom Soldier app. by Moldoff 40.00 120.00 280.00

MAJOR VICTORY COMICS (Also see Dynamic Comics)
H. Clay Glover/Service Publ./Harry 'A' Chesler: 1944 - No. 3, Summer, 1945

1-Origin Major Victory (patriotic hero) by C. Sultan (reprint from Dynamic #1); 1st app. Spider Woman 56.00 169.00 450.00
2-Dynamic Boy app. 40.00 120.00 290.00
3-Rocket Boy app. 36.00 107.00 250.00

MALIBU ASHCAN: RAFFERTY (See Firearm #12)
Malibu Comics (Ultraverse): Nov, 1994 (99¢, B&W w/color-c; one-shot)

1-Previews "The Rafferty Saga" storyline in Firearm; Chaykin-c. 2.00

MALTESE FALCON
David McKay Publications: No. 48, 1946

Feature Books 48-by Dashiell Hammett 70.00 210.00 560.00

MALU IN THE LAND OF ADVENTURE
I. W. Enterprises: 1964 (See White Princess of Jungle #2)

1-r/Avon's Slave Girl Comics #1; Severin-c 4.50 13.50 45.00

MAMMOTH COMICS
Whitman Publishing Co.(K. K. Publ.): 1938 (84 pgs.) (B&W, 8-1/2x11-1/2")

1-Alley Oop, Terry & the Pirates, Dick Tracy, Little Orphan Annie, Wash Tubbs, Moon Mullins, Smilin' Jack, Tailspin Tommy, Don Winslow, Dan Dunn, Smokey Stover & other reprints 175.00 525.00 1400.00

MAN AGAINST TIME
Image Comics (Motown Machineworks): May, 1996 - No. 3, June, 1996 ($2.25, limited series)

1-3: 1-Simonson-c. 2,3,-Leon-c. 2.25

MAN-BAT (See Batman Family, Brave & the Bold, & Detective #400)
National Periodical Publications/DC Comics: Dec-Jan, 1975-76 - No. 2, Feb-

Man Comics #15 © MAR

Manhunt! #3 © ME

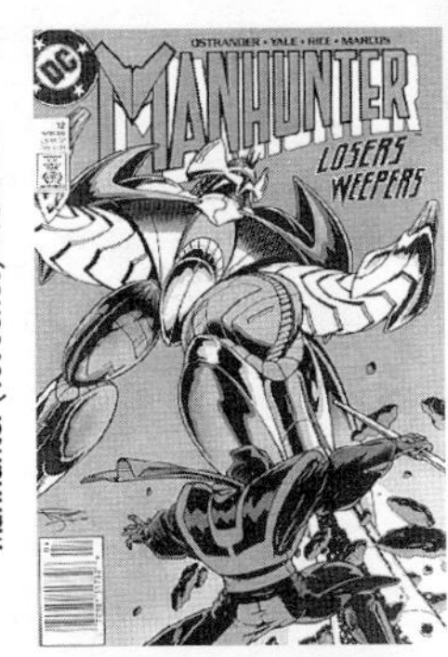

Manhunter (1st series) #12 © DC

GD2.0 FN6.0 NM9.4

Mar, 1976; Dec, 1984
1-Ditko-a(p); Aparo-c; Batman app.; 1st app. She-Bat? 1.25 3.75 10.00
2-Aparo-c 2.40 6.00
1 (12/84)-N. Adams-r(3)/Det.(Vs. Batman on-c) 4.00

MAN-BAT
DC Comics: Feb, 1996 - No. 3, Apr, 1996 ($2.25, limited series)
1-3: Dixon scripts in all. 2-Killer Croc-c/app. 2.25

MAN CALLED A-X, THE
Malibu Comics (Bravura): Nov, 1994 - No. 4, Jun, 1995 ($2.95, limited series)
0-4: Marv Wolfman scripts & Shawn McManus-c/a. 0-(2/95). 1-"1A" on cover 3.00

MAN CALLED A-X, THE
DC Comics: Oct, 1997 - No. 8, May, 1998 ($2.50)
1-8: Marv Wolfman scripts & Shawn McManus-c/a. 2.50

MAN COMICS
Marvel/Atlas Comics (NPI): Dec, 1949 - No. 28, Sept, 1953 (#1-6: 52 pgs.)
1-Tuska-a 20.00 60.00 140.00
2-Tuska-a 11.00 33.00 75.00
3-6 10.00 30.00 60.00
7,8 9.15 27.00 55.00
9-13,15: 9-Format changes to war 5.85 17.50 35.00
14-Henkel (3 pgs.); Pakula-a 7.50 22.50 45.00
16-21,23-28: 28-Crime issue (Bob Brant) 5.00 15.00 30.00
22-Krigstein-a, 5 pgs. 7.50 22.50 45.00
NOTE: ***Berg** a-14, 15, 19. **Colan** a-9, 21. **Everett** a-8, 22; c-22, 25. **Heath** a-11, 17, 21. Kubertish a-by **Bob Brown**-3. **Maneely** a-11; c-10, 11. **Reinman** a-11. **Robinson** a-7, 10, 14. **Robert Sale** a-9, 11. **Sinnott** a-22, 23. **Tuska** a-14, 23.*

MANDRAKE THE MAGICIAN (See Defenders Of The Earth, 123, 46, 52, 55, Giant Comic Album, King Comics, Magic Comics, The Phantom #21, Tiny Tot Funnies & Wow Comics, '36)

MANDRAKE THE MAGICIAN (See Harvey Comics Hits #53)
David McKay Publ./Dell/King Comics (All 12¢): 1938 - 1948; Sept, 1966 - No. 10, Nov, 1967 (Also see Four Color #752)
Feature Books 18,19,25 (1938) 45.00 135.00 450.00
Feature Books 46 40.00 120.00 300.00
Feature Books 52,55 34.00 103.00 240.00
Four Color 752 (11/56) 10.00 30.00 100.00
1-Begin S.O.S. Phantom, ends #3 3.50 10.50 35.00
2-7,9: 4-Girl Phantom app. 5-Flying Saucer-c/story. 5,6-Brick Bradford app. 7-Origin Lothar. 9-Brick Bradford app. 2.00 6.00 20.00
8-Jeff Jones-a (4 pgs.) 2.80 8.40 28.00
10-Rip Kirby app.; Raymond-a (14 pgs.) 3.00 9.00 30.00

MANDRAKE THE MAGICIAN
Marvel Comics: Apr, 1995 - No. 2, May, 1995 ($2.95, unfinished limited series)
1,2: Mike Barr scripts 3.00

MAN-EATING COW (See Tick #7,8)
New England Comics: July, 1992 - No. 10, 1994? ($2.75, B&W, limited series)
1-10 3.00
Man-Eating Cow Bonanza (6/96, $4.95, 128 pgs.)-r/#1-4. 5.00

MAN FROM ATLANTIS (TV)
Marvel Comics: Feb, 1978 - No. 7, Aug, 1978
1-(84 pgs.)-Sutton-a(p), Buscema-c; origin & cast photos 4.00
2-7 2.50

MAN FROM PLANET X, THE
Planet X Productions: 1987 (no price;probably unlicensed)
1-Reprints Fawcett Movie Comic 2.00

MAN FROM U.N.C.L.E., THE (TV) (Also see The Girl From Uncle)
Gold Key: Feb, 1965 - No. 22, Apr, 1969 (All photo-c)
1 14.00 42.00 155.00
2-Photo back c-2-8 8.00 23.00 85.00
3-10: 7-Jet Dream begins (1st app., also see Jet Dream) (all new stories) 5.00 15.00 55.00
11-22: 19-Last 12¢ issue. 21,22-Reprint #10 & 7 4.00 12.00 45.00

MAN FROM U.N.C.L.E., THE (TV)
Entertainment Publishing: 1987 - No. 11 ($1.50/$1.75, B&W)
1-7 ($1.50), 8-11 ($1.75) 2.00

MAN FROM WELLS FARGO (TV)
Dell Publishing Co.: No. 1287, Feb-Apr, 1962 - May-July, 1962 (Photo-c)
Four Color 1287, #01-495-207 5.00 15.00 55.00

MANGA SHI (See Tomoe)
Crusade Entertainment: Aug, 1996 ($2.95)
1-Printed backwards (manga-style) 3.00

MANGA SHI 2000
Crusade Entertainment: Feb, 1997 - No. 3, June, 1997 ($2.95, mini-series)
1-3: 1-Two covers 3.00

MANGA ZEN (Also see Zen Intergalactic Ninja)
Zen Comics (Fusion Studios): 1996 - No. 3, 1996 ($2.50, B&W)
1-3 2.50

MANGAZINE
Antarctic Press: Aug, 1985 - No. 4, Sept, 1986 (B&W)
1-Soft paper-c 1.25 3.75 10.00
2-4 2.40 6.00

MANGLE TANGLE TALES
Innovation Publishing: 1990 ($2.95, deluxe format)
1-Intro by Harlan Ellison 3.00

MANHUNT! (Becomes Red Fox #15 on)
Magazine Enterprises: Oct, 1947 - No. 14, 1953
1-Red Fox by L. B. Cole, Undercover Girl by Whitney, Space Ace begin (1st app.); negligee panels 45.00 135.00 360.00
2-Electrocution-c 38.00 114.00 265.00
3-6 32.00 96.00 225.00
7-10: 7-Space Ace ends. 8-Trail Colt begins (intro/1st app., 5/48) by Guardineer; Trail Colt-c. 10-G. Ingels-a 29.00 86.00 200.00
11(8/48)-Frazetta-a, 7 pgs.; The Duke, Scotland Yard begin 40.00 120.00 290.00
12 21.00 64.00 150.00
13(A-1 #63)-Frazetta, r-/Trail Colt #1, 7 pgs. 39.00 116.00 270.00
14(A-1 #77)-Bondage/hypo-c; last L. B. Cole Red Fox; Ingels-a 30.00 90.00 210.00
NOTE: ***Guardineer** a-1-5; c-8. **Whitney** a-2-14; c-1-6, 10. Red Fox by **L. B. Cole**-#1-14. #15 was advertised but came out as Red Fox #15. Bondage c-6.*

MANHUNTER (See Adventure #58, 73, Brave & the Bold, Detective Comics, 1st Issue Special, House of Mystery #143 and Justice League of America)
DC Comics: 1984 ($2.50, 76 pgs; high quality paper)
1-Simonson-c/a(r)/Detective; Batman app. 2.50

MANHUNTER
DC Comics: July, 1988 - No. 24, Apr, 1990 ($1.00)
1-24: 8,9-Flash app. 9-Invasion. 17-Batman-c/sty 2.25

MANHUNTER
DC Comics: No. 0, Nov, 1994 - No. 12, Nov, 1995 ($1.95/$2.25)
0-12 2.25

MANHUNTER: THE SPECIAL EDITION
DC Comics: 1999 ($9.95)
TPB-Reprints Detective Comics stories by Goodwin and Simonson 10.00

MAN IN BLACK (See Thrill-O-Rama) (Also see All New Comics, Front Page, Green Hornet #31, Strange Story & Tally-Ho Comics)
Harvey Publications: Sept, 1957 - No. 4, Mar, 1958
1-Bob Powell-c/a 15.00 45.00 105.00
2-4: Powell-c/a 12.00 36.00 85.00

Man O' Mars #1 © FH

Man-Thing V1 #1 © MAR

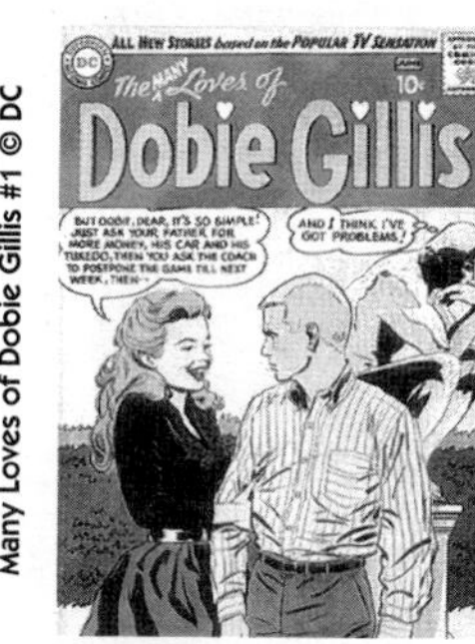

Many Loves of Dobie Gillis #1 © DC

MAN IN BLACK
Lorne-Harvey Publications (Recollections): 1990 - No. 2, July, 1991 (B&W)
1,2 — 2.00

MAN IN FLIGHT (Disney, TV)
Dell Publishing Co.: No. 836, Sept, 1957
Four Color 836 — 6.40 19.00 70.00

MAN IN SPACE (Disney, TV, see Dell Giant #27)
Dell Publishing Co.: No. 716, Aug, 1956 - No. 954, Nov, 1958
Four Color 716-A science feat. from Tomorrowland — 8.00 25.00 90.00
Four Color 954-Satellites — 6.40 19.00 70.00

MANKIND (WWF Wrestling)
Chaos Comics: Sept, 1999 ($2.95, one-shot)
1-Regular and photo-c — 3.00
1-Premium Edition ($10.00) Dwayne Turner & Danny Miki-c — 10.00

MAN OF STEEL, THE (Also see Superman: The Man of Steel)
DC Comics: 1986 (June release) - No. 6, 1986 (75¢, limited series)
1-6: 1-Silver logo; Byrne-c/a/scripts in all; origin, 1-Alternate-c for newsstand sales,1-Distr. to toy stores by So Much Fun, 2-6: 2-Intro. Lois Lane, Jimmy Olsen. 3-Intro/origin Magpie; Batman-c/story. 4-Intro. new Lex Luthor — 3.00
1-6-Silver Editions (1993, $1.95)-r/1-6 — 3.00
...The Complete Saga nn-Contains #1-6, given away in contest — 3.00
Limited Edition, softcover — 4.00 12.00 40.00
NOTE: *Issues 1-6 were released between Action #583 (9/86) & Action #584 (1/87) plus Superman #423 (9/86) & Advs. of Superman #424 (1/87).*

MAN OF THE ATOM (See Solar, Man of the Atom Vol. 2)

MAN OF WAR (See Liberty Guards & Liberty Scouts)
Centaur Publications: Nov, 1941 - No. 2, Jan, 1942
1-The Fire-Man, Man of War, The Sentinel, Liberty Guards, & Vapo-Man begin; Gustavson-c/a; Flag-c — 156.00 469.00 1250.00
2-Intro The Ferret; Gustavson-c/a — 119.00 356.00 950.00

MAN OF WAR
Eclipse Comics: Aug, 1987 - No. 3, Feb, 1988 ($1.75, Baxter paper)
1-3: Bruce Jones scripts — 2.00

MAN OF WAR (See The Protectors)
Malibu Comics: 1993 - No, 8, Feb, 1994 ($1.95/$2.50/$2.25)
1-5 ($1.95)-Newsstand Editions w/different-c — 2.00
1-8-1-5-Collector's Edi. w/poste.r. 6-8 ($2.25): 6-Polybagged w/Skycap. 8-Vs. Rocket Rangers — 2.50

MAN O' MARS
Fiction House Magazines: 1953; 1964
1-Space Rangers; Whitman-c — 40.00 120.00 290.00
I.W. Reprint #1-r/Man O'Mars #1 & Star Pirate; Murphy Anderson-a — 4.50 13.50 45.00

MANTECH ROBOT WARRIORS
Archie Enterprises, Inc.: Sept, 1984 - No. 4, Apr, 1985 (75¢)
1-4: Ayers-c/a(p). 1-Buckler-c(i) — 2.00

MAN-THING (See Fear, Giant-Size..., Marvel Comics Presents, Marvel Fanfare, Monsters Unleashed, Power Record Comics & Savage Tales)
Marvel Comics Group: Jan, 1974 - No. 22, Oct, 1975; V2#1, Nov, 1979 - V2#11, July, 1981
1-Howard the Duck(2nd app.) cont'd/Fear #19 — 2.25 6.75 18.00
2 — 1.25 3.75 10.00
3-1st app. original Foolkiller — 1.00 3.00 8.00
4-Origin Foolkiller; last app. 1st Foolkiller — 2.40 6.00
5-11-Ploog-a. 11-Foolkiller cameo (flashback) — 5.00
12-22: 19-1st app. Scavenger. 20-Spidey cameo. 21-Origin Scavenger, Man-Thing. 22-Howard the Duck cameo — 4.00
V2#1(1979) - 11 — 3.00
NOTE: ***Alcala** a-14. **Brunner** c-1. J. **Buscema** a-12p, 13p, 16p. **Gil Kane** c-4p, 10p, 12-20p, 21. **Mooney** a-17, 18, 19p, 20-22, V2#1-3p. **Ploog** Man-Thing-5p, 6p, 7, 8, 9-11p; c-5, 6, 8, 9, 11. **Sutton** a-13i. No. 19 says #10 in indicia.*

MAN-THING (Volume Three, continues in Strange Tales #1 (9/98))
Marvel Comics: Dec, 1997 - No. 8, July, 1998 ($2.99)
1-8-DeMatteis-s/Sharp-a. 2-Two covers. 6-Howard the Duck-c/app. — 3.00

MANTRA
Malibu Comics (Ultraverse): July, 1993 - No. 24, Aug, 1995 ($1.95/$2.50)
1-Polybagged w/trading card & coupon — 2.50
1-Newsstand edition w/o trading card or coupon — 2.00
1-Full cover holographic edition — 1.25 3.75 10.00
1-Ultra-limited silver foil-c — 5.00
2-9,11-24: 3-Intro Warstrike & Kismet. 6-Break-Thru x-over. 2-($2.50-Newsstand edition bagged w/card. 4-($2.50, 48 pgs.)-Rune flip-c/story by B. Smith (3 pgs.). 7-Prime app.; origin Prototype by Jurgens/Austin (2 pgs.). 11-New costume. 17-Intro NecroMantra & Pinnacle; prelude to Godwheel — 2.50
10-($3.50, 68 pgs.)-Flip-c w/Ultraverse Premiere #2 — 3.50
Giant Size 1 (7/94, $2.50, 44 pgs.) — 2.50
...Spear of Destiny 1,2 (4/95, $2.50, 36pgs.) — 2.50

MANTRA (2nd Series) (Also See Black September)
Malibu Comics (Ultraverse): Infinity, Sept, 1995 - No. 7, Apr, 1996 ($1.50)
Infinity (9/95, $1.50)-Black September x-over, Intro new Mantra. — 2.00
1-7: 1-(10/95). 5-Return of Eden (original Mantra). 6,7-Rush app. — 2.00

MAN WITH THE X-RAY EYES, THE (See X,... under Movie Comics)

MANY GHOSTS OF DR. GRAVES, THE (Doctor Graves #73 on)
Charlton Comics: 5/67 - No. 60, 12/76; No. 61, 9/77 - No. 62, 10/77; No. 63, 2/78 - No. 65, 4/78; No. 66, 6/81 - No. 72, 5/82
1-Palais-a; early issues 12¢-c — 2.80 8.40 28.00
2-10 — 1.75 5.25 14.00
11-20 — 1.25 3.75 10.00
21-44 — 1.00 2.80 7.00
46-72: 47,49-Newton-a — 2.40 6.00
45-1st Newton comic work (8 pgs.); new logo — 1.25 3.75 10.00
Modern Comics Reprint 12,25 (1978) — 4.00
NOTE: ***Aparo** a-4, 5, 7, 8, 66r, 69r; c-8, 14, 19, 66r, 67r. **Byrne** c-54. **Ditko** a-1, 7, 9, 11-13, 15-18, 20-22, 24, 26, 27, 29, 30-35, 37, 38, 40-44, 47, 48, 51-54, 58, 60r-65r, 70, 72; c-11-13, 16-18, 22, 24, 26-35, 38, 40, 55, 58, 62-65. **Howard** a-38, 39, 45i, 65; c-48. **Kim** a-36, 46, 52. **Larson** a-58. **Morisi** a-13, 14, 23, 26. **Newton** a-45, 47p, 49p; c-49, 52. **Staton** a-36, 37, 41, 43. **Sutton** a-39, 42, 47-50, 55, 65; c-42, 44, 45; painted c-53. **Zeck** a-56, 59.*

MANY LOVES OF DOBIE GILLIS (TV)
National Periodical Publications: May-June, 1960 - No. 26, Oct, 1964
1-Most covers by Bob Oskner — 23.00 69.00 230.00
2-5 — 12.50 38.00 125.00
6-10 — 8.50 25.50 85.00
11-26: 20-Drucker-a — 7.50 22.50 75.00

MARAUDER'S MOON (See Luke Short, Four Color #848)

MARCH OF COMICS (See Promotional Comics section)

MARCH OF CRIME (Formerly My Love Affair #1-6) (See Fox Giants)
Fox Features Synd.: No. 7, July, 1950 - No. 2, Sept, 1950; No. 3, Sept, 1951
7(#1)(7/50)-True crime stories; Wood-a — 39.00 118.00 275.00
2(9/50)-Wood-a (exceptional) — 37.00 111.00 260.00
3(9/51) — 17.00 49.00 115.00

MARCO POLO
Charlton Comics Group: 1962 (Movie classic)
nn (Scarce)-Glanzman-c/a (25 pgs.) — 10.50 32.00 105.00

MARC SPECTOR: MOON KNIGHT (Also see Moon Knight)
Marvel Comics: June, 1989 - No. 60, Mar, 1994 ($1.50/$1.75, direct sales)
1-24,26-49,51-60: 4-Intro new Midnight. 8,9-Punisher app. 15-Silver Sable app. 19-21-Spider-Man & Punisher app. 32,33-Hobgoblin II (Macendale) & Spider-Man (in black costume) app. 35-38-Punisher story. 42-44-Infinity War x-over. 46-Demogoblin app. 51,53-Gambit app. 55-New look. 25-(52 pgs.)-Ghost Rider app. . 57-Spider-Man-c/story. 60-Moon Knight dies — 2.50
50-(56 pgs.)-Special die-cut-c — 3.00
...: Divided We Fall ($4.95, 52 pgs.) — 5.00

Marge's Little Lulu #4 © Marjorie H. Buell

Marines in Battle #3 © MAR

The Mark #1 © DH

GD2.0 FN6.0 NM9.4

Special 1 (1992, $2.50) 2.50
NOTE: *Cowan c(p) 20-23. Guice c-20. Heath c/a-4. Platt c-a. Platt -a 55-57,60; c-55-60.*

MARGARET O'BRIEN (See The Adventures of...)

MARGE'S LITTLE LULU (Little Lulu #207 on)
Dell Publishing Co./Gold Key #165-206: No. 74, 6/45 - No. 164, 7-9/62; No. 165, 10/62 - No. 206, 8/72

Marjorie Henderson Buell, born in Philadelphia, Pa., in 1904, created Little Lulu, a cartoon character that appeared weekly in the Saturday Evening Post from Feb. 23, 1935 through Dec. 30, 1944. She was not responsible for any of the comic books. **John Stanley** did pencils only on all Little Lulu comics through at least #135 (1959). He did pencils and inks on Four Color #74 & 97. **Irving Tripp** began inking stories from #1 on, and remained the comic's illustrator throughout its entire run. **Stanley** did storyboards (layouts), pencils, and scripts in all cases and inking only on covers. His word balloons were written in cursive. **Tripp** and occasionally other artists at Western Publ. in Poughkeepsie, N.Y. blew up the pencilled pages, inked the blowups, and lettered them. **Arnold Drake** did storyboards, pencils and scripts starting with #197 (1970) on, amidst reprinted issues. **Buell** sold her rights exclusively to Western Publ. in Dec., 1971. The earlier issues had to be approved by **Buell** prior to publication.

Four Color 74('45)-Intro Lulu, Tubby & Alvin 95.00 286.00 1050.00
Four Color 97(2/46) 45.00 136.00 500.00
(Above two books are all John Stanley - cover, pencils, and inks.)
Four Color 110('46)-1st Alvin Story Telling Time; 1st app. Willy; variant cover may exist 32.00 97.00 355.00
Four Color 115-1st app. Boys' Clubhouse 32.00 97.00 355.00
Four Color 120, 131: 120-1st app. Eddie 28.00 84.00 310.00
Four Color 139('47),146,158 26.00 79.00 290.00
Four Color 165 (10/47)-Smokes doll hair & has wild hallucinations. 1st Tubby detective story 26.00 79.00 290.00
1(1-2/48)-Lulu's Diary feature begins 54.00 164.00 600.00
2-1st app. Gloria; 1st Tubby story in a L.L. comic; 1st app. Miss Feeny 27.00 82.00 300.00
3-5 25.00 75.00 275.00
6-10: 7-1st app. Annie; Xmas-c 19.00 56.00 205.00
11-20: 18-X-Mas-c. 19-1st app. Wilbur. 20-1st app. Mr. McNabbem 16.00 48.00 175.00
21-30: 26-r/F.C. 110. 30-Xmas-c 13.00 38.00 140.00
31-38,40: 35-1st Mumday story 11.30 34.00 125.00
39-Intro. Witch Hazel in "That Awful Witch Hazel" 12.30 37.00 135.00
41-60: 42-Xmas-c. 45-2nd Witch Hazel app. 49-Gives Stanley & others credit 10.50 31.00 115.00
61-80: 63-1st app. Chubby (Tubby's cousin). 68-1st app. Prof. Cleff. 78-Xmas-c. 80-Intro. Little Itch (2/55) 7.30 22.00 80.00
81-99: 90-Xmas-c 5.50 16.50 60.00
100 6.00 18.00 65.00
101-130: 123-1st app. Fifi 5.00 15.00 55.00
131-164: 135-Last Stanley-p 4.00 12.00 45.00
165-Giant; ...in Paris ('62) 11.00 33.00 120.00
166-Giant; ...Christmas Diary (1962 - '63) 11.00 33.00 120.00
167-169 3.50 10.50 38.00
170,172,175,176,178-196,198-200-Stanley-r. 182-1st app. Little Scarecrow Boy 1.80 5.40 18.00
171,173,174,177,197 1.20 3.60 12.00
201,203,206-Last issue to carry Marge's name .90 2.70 9.00
202,204,205-Stanley-r 1.40 4.20 14.00
...& Tubby in Japan (12¢)(5-7/62) 01476-207 6.00 18.00 65.00
...Summer Camp 1(8/67-G.K.-Giant) '57-58-r 4.00 12.00 45.00
...Trick 'N' Treat 1(12¢)(12/62-Gold Key) 5.00 15.00 55.00
NOTE: *See Dell Giant Comics #23, 29, 36, 42, 50, & Dell Giants for annuals. All Giants not by Stanley from L.L. on Vacation (7/54) on. Irving Tripp a-#1-on. Christmas c-7, 18, 30, 42, 78, 90, 126, 166, 250. Summer Camp issues #173, 177, 181, 189, 197, 201, 206.*

MARGE'S LITTLE LULU (See Golden Comics Digest #19, 23, 27, 29, 33, 36, 40, 43, 46, & March of Comics #251, 267, 275, 293, 307, 323, 335, 349, 355, 369, 385, 406, 417, 427, 439, 456, 468, 475, 488)

MARGE'S TUBBY (Little Lulu)(See Dell Giants)
Dell Publishing Co./Gold Key: No. 381, Aug, 1952 - No. 49, Dec-Feb, 1961-62

Four Color 381(#1)-Stanley script; Irving Tripp-a 19.00 57.00 210.00
Four Color 430,444-Stanley-a 11.00 33.00 120.00
Four Color 461 (4/53)-1st Tubby & Men From Mars story; Stanley-a 9.50 29.00 105.00
5 (7-9/53)-Stanley-a 8.00 23.00 85.00
6-10 6.00 18.00 65.00
11-20 4.00 12.00 45.00
21-30 3.00 9.00 32.00
31-49 2.60 7.65 28.00
...& the Little Men From Mars No. 30020-410(10/64-G.K.)-25¢, 68 pgs. 7.00 21.00 75.00
NOTE: ***John Stanley** did all storyboards & scripts through at least #35 (1959). **Lloyd White** did all art except F.C. 381, 430, 444, 461 & #5.*

MARGIE (See My Little...)

MARGIE (TV)
Dell Publ. Co.: No. 1307, Mar-May, 1962 - No. 2, July-Sept, 1962 (Photo-c)

Four Color 1307(#1) 4.50 13.50 50.00
2 3.60 11.00 40.00

MARGIE COMICS (Formerly Comedy Comics; Reno Browne #50 on)
(Also see Cindy Comics & Teen Comics)
Marvel Comics (ACI): No. 35, Winter, 1946-47 - No. 49, Dec, 1949

35 13.00 39.00 90.00
36-38,42,45,47-49 8.35 25.00 50.00
39,41,43(2),44,46-Kurtzman's "Hey Look" 10.00 30.00 65.00
40-Three "Hey Looks", three "Giggles 'n' Grins" by Kurtzman 11.00 33.00 75.00

MARINES (See Tell It to the...)

MARINES ATTACK
Charlton Comics: Aug, 1964 - No. 9, Feb-Mar, 1966

1-Glanzman-a begins 2.50 7.50 22.00
2-9 1.75 5.25 14.00

MARINES AT WAR (Formerly Tales of the Marines #4)
Atlas Comics (OPI): No. 5, Apr, 1957 - No. 7, Aug, 1957

5-7 6.70 20.00 40.00
NOTE: ***Colan** a-5. **Drucker** a-5. **Everett** a-5. **Maneely** a-5. **Orlando** a-7. **Severin** c-5.*

MARINES IN ACTION
Atlas News Co.: June, 1955 - No. 14, Sept, 1957

1-Rock Murdock, Boot Camp Brady begin 10.00 30.00 65.00
2-14 6.70 20.00 40.00
NOTE: ***Berg** a-2, 8, 9, 11, 14. **Heath** c-2, 9. **Maneely** c-1. **Severin** a-4; c-7-11, 14.*

MARINES IN BATTLE
Atlas Comics (ACI No. 1-12/WPI No. 13-25): Aug, 1954 - No. 25, Sept, 1958

1-Heath-c; Iron Mike McGraw by Heath; history of U.S. Marine Corps. begins 17.00 51.00 120.00
2-Heath-c 10.00 30.00 65.00
3-6,8-10: 4-Last precode (2/55) 7.50 22.50 45.00
7-Kubert/Moskowitz-a (6 pgs.) 8.35 25.00 50.00
11-16,18-21,24 6.70 20.00 40.00
17-Williamson-a (3 pgs.) 10.00 30.00 60.00
22,25-Torres-a 7.50 22.50 45.00
23-Crandall-a; Mark Murdock app. 8.35 25.00 50.00
NOTE: ***Berg** a-22. **G. Colan** a-22, 23. **Drucker** a-6. **Everett** a-4, 15; c-21. **Heath** c-1, 2, 4. **Maneely** c-23, 24. **Orlando** a-14. **Pakula** a-6, 23. **Powell** a-16. **Severin** a-22; c-12. **Sinnott** a-23. **Tuska** a-15.*

MARINE WAR HEROES (Charlton Premiere #19 on)
Charlton Comics: Jan, 1964 - No. 18, Mar, 1967

1-Montes/Bache-c/a 2.50 7.50 22.00
2-18: 14,18-Montes/Bache-a 1.75 5.25 14.00

MARK, THE (Also see Mayhem)
Dark Horse Comics: Dec, 1993 - No. 4, Mar, 1994 ($2.50, limited series)

1-4 2.50

MARK HAZZARD: MERC
Marvel Comics Group: Nov, 1986 - No. 12, Oct, 1987 (75¢)

1-12: Morrow-a, Annual 1 (11/87, $1.25) 2.00

MARK OF ZORRO (See Zorro, Four Color #228)

Marmaduke Mouse #10 © QUA

Married... with Children 1994 Annual © ELP Communications

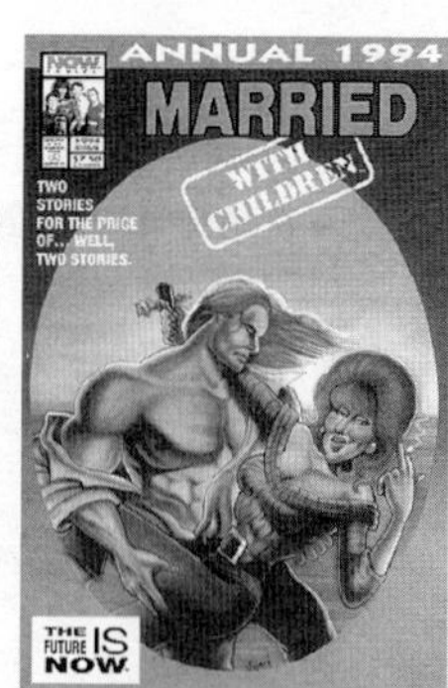

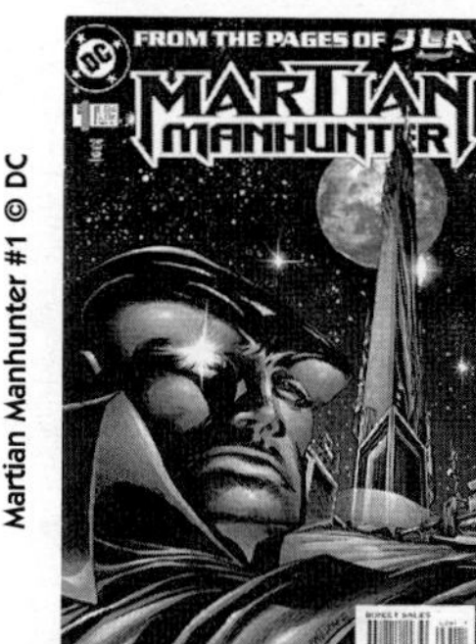

Martian Manhunter #1 © DC

GD2.0 FN6.0 NM9.4

MARK 1 COMICS (Also see Shaloman)
Mark 1 Comics: Apr, 1988 - No. 3, Mar, 1989 ($1.50)
1-3: Early Shaloman app. 2-Origin 2.00

MARKSMAN, THE (Also see Champions)
Hero Comics: Jan, 1988 - No. 5, 1988 ($1.95)
1-5: 1-Rose begins. 1-3-Origin The Marksman 2.00
Annual 1 ('88, $2.75, 52pgs)-Champions app. 2.75

MARK TRAIL
Standard Magazines (Hall Syndicate)/Fawcett Publ. No. 5: Oct, 1955; No. 5, Summer, 1959
1(1955)-Sunday strip-r 5.85 17.50 35.00
5(1959) 4.00 10.00 20.00
...Adventure Book of Nature 1 (Summer, 1958, 25¢, Pines)-100 pg. Giant; Special Camp Issue; contains 78 Sunday strip-r 9.15 27.00 55.00

MARMADUKE MONK
I. W. Enterprises/Super Comics: No date; 1963 (10¢)
I.W. Reprint 1 (nd) 1.25 3.75 10.00
Super Reprint 14 (1963)-r/Monkeyshines Comics #? 1.25 3.75 10.00

MARMADUKE MOUSE
Quality Comics Group (Arnold Publ.): Spring, 1946 - No. 65, Dec, 1956 (Early issues: 52 pgs.)
1-Funny animal 16.00 47.00 110.00
2 9.15 27.00 55.00
3-10 6.70 20.00 40.00
11-30 5.00 15.00 30.00
31-65: Later issues are 36 pgs. 4.00 12.00 24.00
Super Reprint #14(1963) 1.50 4.50 12.00

MARRIAGE OF HERCULES AND XENA, THE
Topps Comics: July, 1998 ($2.95, one-shot)
1-Photo-c; Lopresti-a; Alex Ross pin-up, 1-Alex Ross painted-c 3.00
1-Gold foil logo-c 5.00

MARRIED ... WITH CHILDREN (TV)(Based on Fox TV show)
Now Comics: June, 1990 - No. 7, Feb, 1991(12/90 inside) ($1.75)
V2#1, Sept, 1991 - No. 12, 1992 ($1.95)
1-7: 2-Photo-c, 1,2-2nd printing, V2#1-12: 1,4,5,9-Photo-c 2.00
...Buck's Tale (6/94, $1.95) 2.00
...1994 Annual nn (2/94, $2.50, 52 pgs.)-Flip book format 2.50
Special 1 (7/92, $1.95)-Kelly Bundy photo-c/poster 2.00

MARRIED ... WITH CHILDREN: KELLY BUNDY
Now Comics: Aug, 1992 - No. 3, Oct, 1992 ($1.95, limited series)
1-3: Kelly Bundy photo-c & poster in each 2.00

MARRIED ... WITH CHILDREN: QUANTUM QUARTET
Now Comics: Oct, 1993 - No. 4, 1994, ($1.95, limited series)
1-4: Fantastic Four parody 2.00

MARRIED ... WITH CHILDREN: 2099
Now Comics: June, 1993 - No. 3, Aug, 1993 ($1.95, limited series)
1-3 2.00

MARS
First Comics: Jan, 1984 - No. 12, Jan, 1985 ($1.00, Mando paper)
nn: 1-12: Marc Hempel & Mark Wheatley story & art. 2-The Black Flame begins. 10-Dynamo Joe begins 2.00

MARS & BEYOND (Disney, TV)
Dell Publishing Co.: No. 866, Dec, 1957
Four Color 866-A Science feat. from Tomorrowland 8.00 25.00 90.00

MARS ATTACKS
Topps Comics: May, 1994 - No. 5, Sept, 1994 ($2.95, limited series)
1-5-Giffen story; flip books 4.00
Special Edition 1.50 4.50 12.00
Trade paperback (12/94, $12.95)-r/limited series plus new 8 pg. story 13.00

MARS ATTACKS
Topps Comics: V2#1, 8/95 - V2#3, 10/95; V2#4, 1/96 - No. 7, 5/96($2.95, bi-monthly #6 on)
V2#1-7: 1-Counterstrike storyline begins. 4-(1/96). 5-(1/96). 5,7-Brereton-c. 6-(3/96)-Simonson-c. 7-Story leads into Baseball Special #1 3.00
Baseball Special 1 (6/96, $2.95)-Bisley-c. 3.00

MARS ATTACKS HIGH SCHOOL
Topps Comics: May, 1997 - No. 2, Sept, 1997 ($2.95, B&W, limited series)
1,2-Stelfreeze-c 3.00

MARS ATTACKS IMAGE
Topps Comics: Dec, 1996 - No. 4, Mar, 1997 ($2.50, limited series)
1-4-Giffen-s/Smith/Sienkiewicz-a 3.00

MARS ATTACKS THE SAVAGE DRAGON
Topps Comics: Dec, 1996 - No. 4, Mar, 1997 ($2.95, limited series)
1-4: 1--w/bound-in card 3.00

MARSHAL BLUEBERRY (See Blueberry)
Marvel Comics (Epic Comics): 1991 (14.95, graphic novel)
1-Moebius-a 15.00

MARSHAL LAW (Also see Crime And Punishment: Marshall Law...)
Marvel Comics (Epic Comics): Oct, 1987 - No. 6, May, 1989 ($1.95, mature)
1-6 2.00

M.A.R.S. PATROL TOTAL WAR (Formerly Total War #1,2)
Gold Key: No. 3, Sept, 1966 - No. 10, Aug, 1969 (All-Painted-c except #7)
3-Wood-a; aliens invade USA 4.80 14.40 48.00
4-10 2.60 7.80 26.00

MARTHA WASHINGTON (Also see Dark Horse Presents Fifth Anniversary Special, Dark Horse Presents #100-4, Give Me Liberty, Happy Birthday Martha Washington & San Diego Comicon Comics #2)

MARTHA WASHINGTON GOES TO WAR
Dark Horse Comics (Legend): May, 1994 - No. 5, Sep, 1994 ($2.95, lim. series)
1-5-Miller scripts; Gibbons-c/a 3.00
TPB ($17.95) r/#1-5 18.00

MARTHA WASHINGTON SAVES THE WORLD
Dark Horse Comics: Dec, 1997 - No. 3, Feb, 1998 ($2.95/$3.95, lim. series)
1,2-Miller scripts; Gibbons-c/a in all 3.00
3-($3.95) 4.00

MARTHA WASHINGTON STRANDED IN SPACE
Dark Horse Comics (Legend): Nov, 1995 ($2.95, one-shot)
nn-Miller-s/Gibbons-a; Big Guy app. 3.00

MARTHA WAYNE (See The Story of...)

MARTIAN MANHUNTER (See Detective Comics & Showcase '95 #9)
DC Comics: May, 1988 - No. 4, Aug,. 1988 ($1.25, limited series)
1-4: 1,4-Batman app. 2-Batman cameo 2.00
Special 1-(1996, $3.50) 3.50

MARTIAN MANHUNTER (See JLA)
DC Comics: No. 0, Oct, 1998 - Present ($1.99)
0-Origin retold; Ostrander-s/Mandrake-c/a 3.00
1-13: 1-(12/98). 6,7-JLA app. 2.50
#1,000,000 (11/98) 853rd Century x-over 2.50
Annual 1,2 (1998,1999; $2.95) 1-Ghosts; Wrightson-c. 2-JLApe 3.00

MARTIAN MANHUNTER: AMERICAN SECRETS
DC Comics: 1992 - Book Three, 1992 ($4.95, limited series, prestige format)
1-3: Barreto-a 5.00

MARTIN KANE (William Gargan as... Private Eye)(Stage/Screen/Radio/TV)
Fox Features Syndicate (Hero Books): No. 4, June, 1950 - No. 2, Aug, 1950 (Formerly My Secret Affair)

Marvel Adventures #15 © MAR

Marvel Adventures Starring Daredevil #6 © MAR

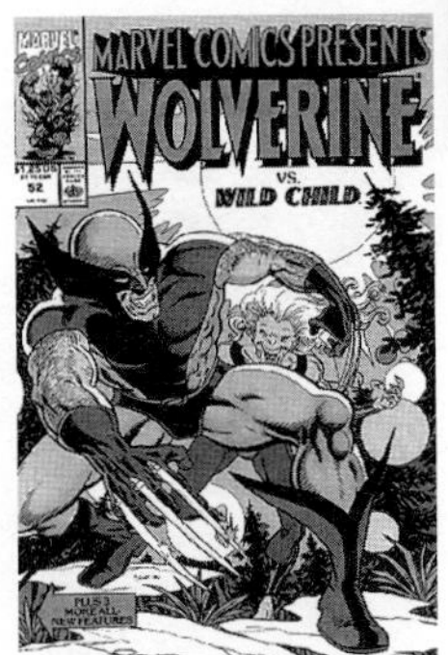

Marvel Comics Presents #52 © MAR

GD2.0 FN6.0 NM9.4

4(#1)-True crime stories; Wood-c/a(2); used in **SOTI**, pg. 160; photo back-c 29.00 86.00 200.00
2-Wood/Orlando story, 5 pgs; Wood-a(2) 23.00 69.00 160.00

MARTIN MYSTERY
Dark Horse (Bonelli Comics): Mar, 1999 - No. 6, Aug, 1999 ($4.95, B&W, digest size)

1-6-Reprints Italian series in English; Gibbons-c on #1-3 5.00

MARTY MOUSE
I. W. Enterprises: No date (1958?) (10¢)

1-Reprint 1.25 3.75 10.00

MARVEL ACTION HOUR FEATURING IRON MAN (TV cartoon)
Marvel Comics: Nov, 1994 - No. 8, June, 1995 ($1.50/$2.95)

1-8: Based on cartoon series 2.00
1 ($2.95)-Polybagged w/16 pg Marvel Action Hour Preview & acetate print 3.00

MARVEL ACTION HOUR FEATURING THE FANTASTIC FOUR (TV cartoon)
Marvel Comics: Nov, 1994 - No. 8, June, 1995 ($1.50/$2.95)

1-8: Based on cartoon series 2.00
1-($2.95)-Polybagged w/ 16 pg. Marvel Action Hour Preview & acetate print 3.00

MARVEL ACTION UNIVERSE (TV cartoon)
Marvel Comics: Jan, 1989 ($1.00, one-shot)

1-r/Spider-Man And His Amazing Friends 2.00

MARVEL ADVENTURES
Marvel Comics: Apr, 1997 - No. 18, Sept, 1998 ($1.50)

1-18-"Animated style": 1,4,7-Hulk-c/app. 2,11-Spider-Man. 3,8,15-X-Men. 5-Spider-Man & X-Men. 6-Spider-Man & Human Torch. 9,12-Fantastic Four. 10,16-Silver Surfer. 13-Spider-Man & Silver Surfer. 14-Hulk & Dr. Strange 18-Capt. America 2.00

MARVEL ADVENTURES STARRING DAREDEVIL (...Adventure #3 on)
Marvel Comics Group: Dec, 1975 - No. 6, Oct, 1976

1 1.10 3.30 9.00
2-6-r/Daredevil #22-27 by Colan. 3-5-(25¢-c) 5.00
3-5-(30¢-c variants, limited distribution)(4,6,8/76) 1.85 5.50 15.00

MARVEL AND DC PRESENT FEATURING THE UNCANNY X-MEN AND THE NEW TEEN TITANS
Marvel Comics/DC Comics: 1982 ($2.00, 68 pgs., one-shot, Baxter paper)

1-3rd app. Deathstroke the Terminator; Darkseid app.; Simonson/Austin-c/a 1.50 4.50 15.00

MARVEL BOY (Astonishing #3 on; see Marvel Super Action #4)
Marvel Comics (MPC): Dec, 1950 - No. 2, Feb, 1951

1-Origin Marvel Boy by Russ Heath 91.00 272.00 725.00
2-Everett-a 70.00 210.00 560.00

MARVEL CHILLERS (Also see Giant-Size Chillers)
Marvel Comics Group: Oct, 1975 - No. 7, Oct, 1976 (All 25¢ issues)

1-Intro. Modred the Mystic, ends #2; Kane-c(p) 1.00 3.00 8.00
2,4,5,7: 4-Kraven app. 5,6-Red Wolf app. 7-Kirby-c; Tuska-p 5.00
3-Tigra, the Were-Woman begins (origin), ends #7 (see Giant-Size Creatures #1). Chaykin/Wrightson-c. 1.50 4.50 12.00
4-6-(30¢-c variants, limited distribution)(4-8/76) 2.50 7.50 20.00
6-Byrne-a(p); Buckler-c(p) 2.40 6.00
NOTE: ***Bolle** a-1. **Buckler** c-2. **Kirby** c-7.*

MARVEL CLASSICS COMICS SERIES FEATURING... (Also see Pendulum Illustrated Classics)
Marvel Comics Group: 1976 - No. 36, Dec, 1978 (52 pgs., no ads)

1-Dr. Jekyll and Mr. Hyde 1.75 5.25 14.00
2-10,28: 28-1st Golden-c/a; Pit and the Pendulum 1.25 3.75 10.00
11-27,29-36 1.00 3.00 8.00
NOTE: ***Adkins** c-1i, 4i, 12i. **Alcala** a-34i; c-34. **Bolle** a-35. **Buscema** c-17p, 19p, 26p. **Golden** c/a-28. **Gil Kane** c-1-16p, 21p, 22p, 24p, 32p. **Nebres** a-5; c-24i. **Nino** a-2, 8, 12. **Redondo** a-1, 9. No. 1-12 were reprinted from Pendulum Illustrated Classics.*

MARVEL COLLECTIBLE CLASSICS: AVENGERS
Marvel Comics: 1998 ($10.00, reprints with chromium wraparound-c)

1-Reprints Avengers Vol.3, #1; Perez-c 10.00

MARVEL COLLECTIBLE CLASSICS: SPIDER-MAN
Marvel Comics: 1998 ($10.00, reprints with chromium wraparound-c)

1-Reprints Amazing Spider-Man #300; McFarlane-c 10.00
2-Reprints Spider-Man #1; McFarlane-c 10.00

MARVEL COLLECTIBLE CLASSICS: X-MEN
Marvel Comics: 1998 ($10.00, reprints with chromium wraparound-c)

1-6: 1-Reprints (Uncanny) X-Men #1 & 2; Adam Kubert-c. 2-Reprints Uncanny X-Men #141 & 142; Byrne-c. 3-Reprints (Uncanny) X-Men #137; Larroca-c. 4-Reprints X-Men #25; Andy Kubert-c. 5-Reprints Giant Size X-Men #1; Gary Frank-c. 6-Reprints X-Men V2#1; Ramos-c 10.00

MARVEL COLLECTOR'S EDITION
Marvel Comics: 1992 (Ordered thru mail with Charleston Chew candy wrapper)

1-Flip-book format; Spider-Man, Silver Surfer, Wolverine (by Sam Kieth), & Ghost Rider stories; Wolverine back-c by Kieth 3.00

MARVEL COLLECTORS' ITEM CLASSICS (Marvel's Greatest #23 on)
Marvel Comics Group(ATF): Feb, 1965 - No. 22, Aug, 1969 (25¢, 68 pgs.)

1-Fantastic Four, Spider-Man, Thor, Hulk, Iron Man-r begin 7.50 22.50 75.00
2 (4/66) 3.80 11.40 38.00
3,4 3.00 9.00 30.00
5-10 2.50 7.50 24.00
11-22: 22-r/The Man in the Ant Hill/TTA #27 2.25 6.75 18.00
NOTE: *All reprints; **Ditko, Kirby** art in all.*

MARVEL COMICS (Marvel Mystery Comics #2 on)
Timely Comics (Funnies, Inc.): Oct, Nov, 1939

NOTE: The first issue was originally dated October 1939. Most copies have a black circle stamped over the date (on cover and inside) with "November" printed over it. However, some copies do not have the November overprint and could have a higher value. Most No. 1's have printing defects, i.e., tilted pages which caused trimming into the panels usually on right side and bottom. Covers exist with and without gloss finish.

GD2.0 FN6.0 VF8.0 NM9.4

1-Origin Sub-Mariner by Bill Everett(1st newsstand app.); 1st 8 pgs. were produced for Motion Picture Funnies Weekly #1 which was probably not distributed outside of advance copies; intro Human Torch by Carl Burgos, Kazar the Great (1st Tarzan clone), & Jungle Terror(only app.); intro. The Angel by Gustavson, The Masked Raider & his horse Lightning (ends #12); cover by sci/fi pulp illustrator Frank R. Paul 11,000.00 33,000.00 66,000.00 125,000.00

MARVEL COMICS PRESENTS
Marvel Comics (Midnight Sons imprint #143 on): Early Sept, 1988 - No. 175, Feb, 1995 ($1.25/$1.50/$1.75, bi-weekly)

GD2.0 FN6.0 NM9.4

1-Wolverine by Buscema in #1-10 2.40 6.00
2-5 4.00
6-10: 6-Sub-Mariner app. 10-Colossus begins 3.00
11-47,51-71: 17-Cyclops begins. 19-1st app. Damage Control. 24-Havok begins. 25-Origin/1st app. Nth Man. 26-Hulk begins by Rogers. 29-Quasar app. 31-Excalibur begins by Austin (i). 32-McFarlane-a(p). 37-Devil-Slayer app. 33-Capt. America; Jim Lee-a. 38-Wolverine begins by Buscema; Hulk app. 39-Spider-Man app. 46-Liefeld Wolverine-c. 51-53-Wolverine by Rob Liefeld. 54-61-Wolverine/Hulk story: 54-Werewolf by Night begins; The Shroud by Ditko. 58-Iron Man by Ditko. 59-Punisher. 62-Deathlok & Wolverine stories 63-Wolverine. 64-71-Wolverine/Ghost Rider 8-part story. 70-Liefeld Ghost Rider/Wolverine-c 2.50
48-50-Wolverine & Spider-Man team-up by Erik Larsen-c/a. 48-Wasp app. 49, 50-Savage Dragon prototype app. by Larsen. 50-Silver Surfer. 50-53-Comet Man; Bill Mumy scripts 4.00
72-Begin13-part Weapon-X story (Wolverine origin) by B. Windsor-Smith (prologue) 5.00
73-Weapon-X part 1; Black Knight, Sub-Mariner 4.00

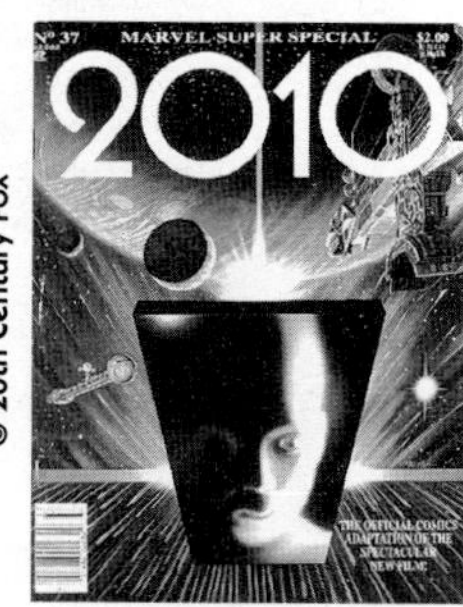

Marvel Comics Super Special #37 © 20th Century Fox

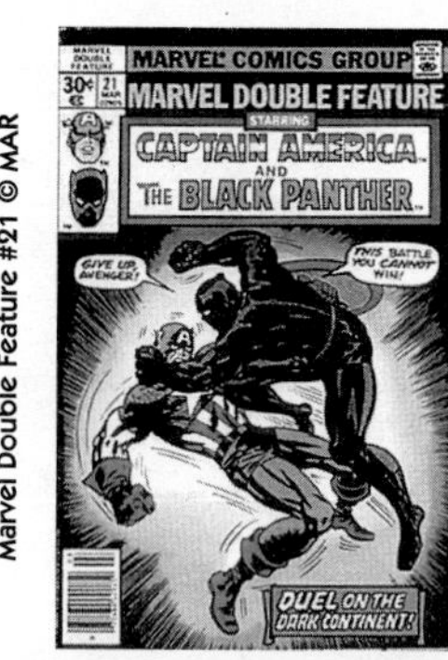

Marvel Double Feature #21 © MAR

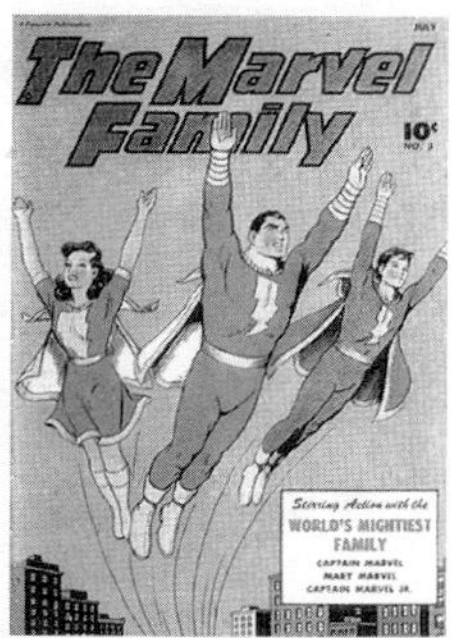

Marvel Family #3 © FAW

74-84: 74-Weapon-X part 2; Black Knight, Sub-Mariner. 76-Death's Head story. 77-Mr. Fantastic story. 78-Iron Man by Steacy. 80,81-Capt. America by Ditko/Austin. 81-Daredevil by Rogers/Williamson. 82-Power Man. 83-Human Torch by Ditko(a&scripts); $1.00-c direct, $1.25 newsstand. 84-Last Weapon-X(24 pg. conclusion) 3.00
85-Begin 8-part Wolverine story by Sam Keith (c/a); 1st Kieth-a on Wolverine; begin 8-part Beast story by Jae Lee(p) with Liefeld part pencils #85,86; 1st Jae Lee-a (assisted w/Liefeld, 1991) 4.00
86-90: 86-89-Wolverine, Beast stories continue. 90-Begin 8-part Ghost Rider & Cable story, ends #97; begin flip book format w/two-c 3.00
91-175: 93-Begin 6-part Wolverine story, ends #98. 98-Begin 2-part Ghost Rider story. 99-Spider-Man story. 101-Begin 6-part Ghost Rider/Dr. Strange story & begin 8-part Wolverine/Nightcrawler story by Colan/Williamson; Punisher story. 107-Begin 6-part Ghost Rider/Werewolf by Night story. 112-Demogoblin story by Colan/Williamson; Pip the Troll story w/Starlin scripts & Gamora cameo. 113-Begin 6-part Giant-Man & begin 6-part Ghost Rider/Iron Fist sto ries. 100-Full-length Ghost Rider/Wolverine story by Sam Keith w/Tim Vigil assists; anniversary issue, non flip-book. 108-Begin 4 part Thanos story; Starlin scripts. 109-Begin 8 part Wolverine/Typhoid Mary story. 111-Iron Fist. 117-Preview of Ravage 2099 (1st app.); begin 6 part Wolverine/Venom story w/Kieth-a. 118-Preview of Doom 2099 (1st app.). 119-Begin Ghost Rider/Cloak & Dagger story by Colan. 120,136,138-Spider-Man. 123-Begin 8-part Ghost Rider/Typhoid Mary story; begin 4-part She Hulk story; begin 8-part Wolverine/Lynx story. 125-Begin 6-part Iron Fist story. 129-Jae Lee back-c. 130-Begin 6-part Ghost Rider/ Cage story. 131-Begin 6-part Ghost Rider/ Cage story. 132-Begin 5-part Wolverine story. 133-136-Iron Fist vs. Sabretooth. 136-Daredevil. 137-Begin 6-part Wolverine story & 6-part Ghost Rider story. 147-Begin 2-part Vengeance-c/story w/new Ghost Rider. 149-Vengeance-c/story w/new Ghost Rider. 150-Silver ink-c; begin 2-part Bloody Mary story w/Typhoid Mary,Wolverine, Daredevil, new Ghost Rider; intro Steel Raven. 152-Begin 4-part Wolverine, 4-part War Machine, 4-part Vengeance, 3-part Moon Knight stories; same date as War Machine #1. 143-146: Siege of Darkness parts 3,6,11,14; all have spot-varnished-c. 143-Ghost Rider/ Scarlet Witch; intro new Werewolf. 144-Begin 2-part Morbius story. 145-Begin 2-part Nightstalkers story. 153-155-Bound-in Spider-Man trading card sheet 2.00
...Colossus: God's Country (1994, $6.95) r/#10-17 1.00 2.80 7.00

NOTE: ***Austin*** *a-31-37i; c(i)-48, 50, 99, 122.* ***Buscema*** *a-1-10, 38-47; c-6.* ***Byrne*** *a-79; c-71.* ***Colan*** *a(p)-36, 37.* ***Colan/Williamson*** *a-101-108.* ***Ditko*** *a-7p, 10, 56p, 58, 80, 81, 83.* ***Guice*** *a-62.* ***Sam Kieth*** *a-85-92, 117-122; c-85-98, 99, 100-108, 117, 118, 120-122; back c-109-113, 117.* ***Jae Lee*** *c-129(back).* ***Liefeld*** *a-51, 52, 53p(2), 85p; c-46, 70.* ***McFarlane*** *c-32.* ***Mooney*** *a-73.* ***Rogers*** *a-26, 38, 46i, 81p.* ***Russell*** *a-10-14,16,17i; c-4,19, 30,31i.* ***Saltares*** *a-8p(early), 38-45p.* ***Simonson*** *c-1.* ***B. Smith*** *a-72-84; c-72-84.* ***P. Smith*** *c-34.* ***Sparling*** *a-33.* ***Starlin*** *a-89i.* ***Staton*** *a-74.* ***Steacy*** *a-78.* ***Sutton*** *a-101-105.* ***Williamson*** *c-62i. Two Gun Kid by* ***Gil Kane*** *in #116, 122.*

MARVEL COMICS SUPER SPECIAL, A (Marvel Super Special #5 on)
Marvel Comics: Sept, 1977 - No. 41(?), Nov, 1986 (nn 7) ($1.50, magazine)

1-Kiss, 40 pgs. comics plus photos & features; Simonson-a(p); also see Howard the Duck #12; ink contains real KISS blood 9.00 27.00 100.00
2-Conan (1978) 1.50 4.50 12.00
3-Close Encounters of the Third Kind (1978); Simonson-a 1.00 3.00 8.00
4-The Beatles Story (1978)-Perez/Janson-a; has photos & articles 3.00 9.00 30.00
5-Kiss (1978)-Includes poster 9.00 27.00 100.00
6-Jaws II (1978) 1.00 3.00 8.00
7-Sgt. Pepper; Beatles movie adaptation; withdrawn from U.S. distribution
8-Battlestar Galactica; tabloid size ($1.50, 1978); adapts TV show 2.00 6.00 16.00
8-Modern-r of tabloid size; scarce 2.80 8.40 28.00
8-Battlestar Galactica; publ. in regular magazine format; low distribution ($1.50, 8-1/2x11") 1.75 5.25 14.00
9-Conan 1.00 3.00 8.00
10-Star-Lord 2.40 6.00
11-13-Weirdworld begins #11; 25 copy special press run of each with gold seal and signed by artists (Proof quality), Spring-June, 1979 7.25 22.00 80.00
11-15: 11-13-Weirdworld (regular issues): 11-Fold-out centerfold. 14-Miller-c(p); adapts movie "Meteor." 15-Star Trek with photos & pin-ups($1.50) 5.00
15-With $2.00 price (scarce); the price was changed at tail end of a 200,000 press run 1.00 3.00 8.00
16-Empire Strikes Back adaption; Williamson-a 1.00 2.80 7.00
17-20 (Movie adaptations):17-Xanadu. 18-Raiders of the Lost Ark. 19-For Your Eyes Only (James Bond). 20-Dragonslayer 5.00
21-26,28-30 (Movie adaptations): 21-Conan. 22-Blade Runner; Williamson-a; Steranko-c. 23-Annie. 24-The Dark Crystal. 25-Rock and Rule-w/photos; artwork is from movie. 26-Octopussy (James Bond). 28-Krull; photo-c. 29-Tarzan of the Apes (Greystoke movie). 30-Indiana Jones and the Temple of Doom 2.40 6.00
27,31-41: 27-Return of the Jedi. 31-The Last Star Fighter. 32-The Muppets Take Manhattan. 33-Buckaroo Banzai. 34-Sheena. 35-Conan The Destroyer. 36-Dune. 37-2010. 38-Red Sonja. 39-Santa Claus:The Movie. 40-Labyrinth. 41-Howard The Duck 1.00 2.80 7.00

NOTE: ***J. Buscema*** *a-1, 2, 9, 11-13, 18p, 21, 35, 40; c-11(part), 12.* ***Chaykin*** *a-9, 19p; c-18, 19.* ***Colan*** *a(p)-6, 10, 14.* ***Morrow*** *a-34; c-1i, 34.* ***Nebres*** *a-11.* ***Spiegle*** *a-29.* ***Stevens*** *a-27.* ***Williamson*** *a-27. #22-28 contain photos from movies.*

MARVEL DOUBLE FEATURE
Marvel Comics Group: Dec, 1973 - No. 21, Mar, 1977

1-Capt. America, Iron Man-r/T.O.S. begin 1.25 3.75 10.00
2-10: 3-Last 20¢ issue 2.40 6.00
11-17,20,21:17-Story-r/Iron Man & Sub-Mariner #1; last 25¢ issue 4.00
15-17-(30¢-c variants, limited distribution)(4,6,8/76) 1.50 4.50 12.00
18,19-Colan/Craig-r from Iron Man #1 in both 5.00

NOTE: ***Colan*** *r-1-19p.* ***Craig*** *r-17-19i.* ***G. Kane*** *r-15p; c-15p.* ***Kirby*** *r-1-16p, 20, 21; c-17-20.*

MARVEL FAMILY (Also see Captain Marvel Adventures No. 18)
Fawcett Publications: Dec, 1945 - No. 89, Jan, 1954

1-Origin Captain Marvel, Captain Marvel Jr., Mary Marvel, & Uncle Marvel retold; origin/1st app. Black Adam 150.00 450.00 1200.00
2-The 3 Lt. Marvels & Uncle Marvel app. 70.00 210.00 560.00
3 49.00 146.00 390.00
4,5 40.00 120.00 320.00
6-10: 7-Shazam app. 37.00 111.00 260.00
11-20 27.00 81.00 190.00
21-30 21.00 64.00 150.00
31-40 19.00 56.00 130.00
41-46,48-50 14.00 43.00 100.00
47-Flying Saucer-c/story (5/50) 20.00 60.00 140.00
51-76,79,80,82-89: 79-Horror satire-c 13.50 41.00 95.00
77-Communist Threat-c 21.00 64.00 150.00
78,81-Used in **POP**, pg. 92,93. 15.00 45.00 105.00

MARVEL FANFARE (1st Series)
Marvel Comics Group: March, 1982 - No. 60, Jan, 1992 ($1.25/$2.25, slick paper, direct sales)

1-Spider-Man/Angel team-up; 1st Paul Smith-a (1st full story; see King Conan #7); Daredevil app. 2.40 6.00
2-Spider-Man, Ka-Zar, The Angel. F.F. origin retold 5.00
3,4-X-Men & Ka-Zar. 4-Deathlok, Spidey app. 4.00
5-32,34-50: 5-Dr. Strange, Capt. America. 6-Spider-Man, Scarlet Witch. 7-Incredible Hulk; D.D. back-up(also 15). 8-Dr. Strange; Wolf Boy begins. 9-Man-Thing. 10-13-Black Widow. 14-The Vision. 15-The Thing by Barry Smith, c/a. 16,17-Skywolf. 16-Sub-Mariner back-up. 17-Hulk back-up. 18-Capt. America by Miller. 19-Cloak and Dagger. 20-Thing/Dr. Strange. 21-Thing/Dr. Strange /Hulk. 22,23-Iron Man vs. Dr. Octopus. 24-26-Weirdworld. 24-Wolverine back-up. 27-Daredevil/Spider-Man. 28-Alpha Flight. 29-Hulk. 30-Moon Knight. 31,32-Captain America. 34-37-Warriors Three. 38-Moon Knight/Dazzler. 39-Moon Knight/Hawkeye. 40-Angel/Rogue & Storm. 41-Dr. Strange. 42-Spider-Man. 43-Sub-Mariner/Human Torch. 44-Iron Man vs. Dr. Doom by Ken Steacy. 45-All pin-up issue by Steacy, Art Adams & others. 46-Fantastic Four. 47-Hulk. 48-She-Hulk/Vision. 49-Dr. Strange/Nick Fury. 50-X-Factor; begin. 33-X-Men, Wolverine app.; Punisher pin-up 2.50
51-($2.95, 52 pgs.)-Silver Surfer; Fantastic Four & Capt. Marvel app.; 51,52-Colan/Williamson back-up (Dr. Strange) 3.00
52-60: 52-54-Black Knight; 53-Iron Man back up. 54,55-Wolverine back-ups. 55-Power Pack. 56-60: 56-59-Shanna the She-Devil. 58-Vision & Scarlet Witch

Marvel Fanfare (2nd series) #4 © MAR

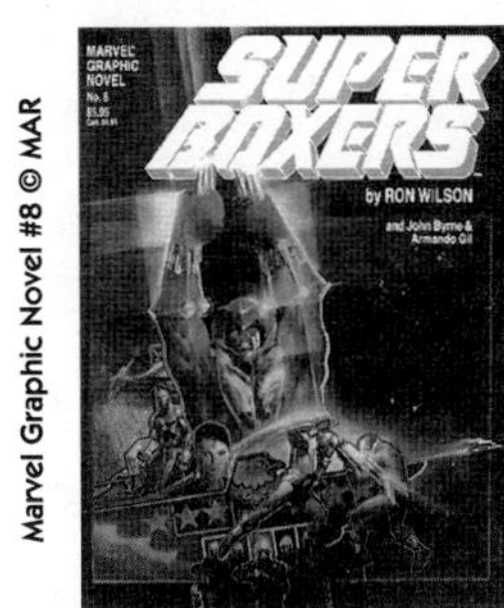

Marvel Graphic Novel #8 © MAR

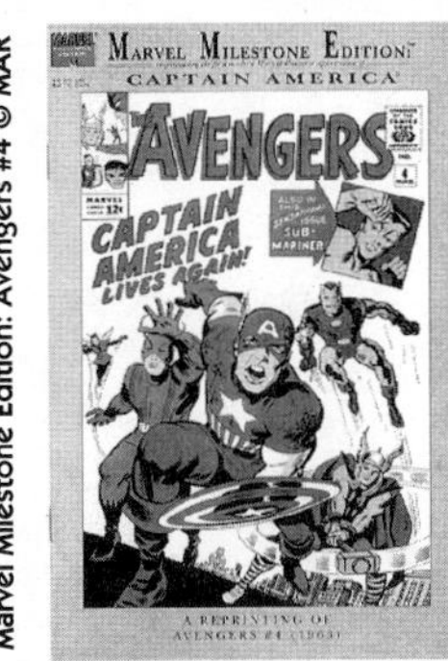

Marvel Milestone Edition: Avengers #4 © MAR

GD2.0 FN6.0 NM9.4

back-up. 60-Black Panther/Rogue/Daredevil stories 2.50

NOTE: ***Art Adams** c-13. **Austin** a-1i, 4i, 33i, 38i; c-8i, 33i. **Buscema** a-51p. **Byrne** a-1p, 29, 48; c-29. **Chiodo** painted c-56-59. **Colan** a-51p. **Cowan/Simonson** c/a-60. **Golden** a-1, 2, 4p, 47; c-1, 2, 47. **Infantino** c/a(p)-8. **Gil Kane** a-8-11p. **Miller** a-18; c-1(Back-c), 18. **Perez** a-10, 11p, 12, 13p; c-10-13p. **Rogers** a-5p; c-5p. **Russell** a-5i, 6i, 8-11i, 43i; c-5i, 6. **Paul Smith** a-1p, 4p, 32, 60; c-4p. Staton c/a-50(p). **Williamson** a-30i, 51i.*

MARVEL FANFARE (2nd Series)
Marvel Comics: Sept, 1996 - No. 6, Feb, 1997 (99¢)

1-6: 1-Capt. America & The Falcon-c/story; Deathlok app. 2-Wolverine & Hulk-c/app. 3-Ghost Rider & Spider-Man-c/app. 5-Longshot-c/app. 6-Sabretooth, Power Man, & Iron Fist-c/app 2.00

MARVEL FEATURE (See Marvel Two-In-One)
Marvel Comics Group: Dec, 1971 - No. 12, Nov, 1973 (1,2: 25¢ giants)(#1-3: quarterly)

1-Origin/1st app. The Defenders (Sub-Mariner, Hulk & Dr. Strange); see Sub-Mariner #34,35 for prequel; Dr. Strange solo story (predates D.S. #1) plus 1950s Sub-Mariner-r; Neal Adams-c 9.50 29.00 105.00
2-2nd app. Defenders; 1950s Sub-Mariner-r 5.00 15.00 55.00
3-Defenders ends 4.00 12.00 40.00
4-Re-intro Antman (1st app. since 1960s), begin series; brief origin; Spider-Man app. 2.25 6.75 18.00
5-7,9,10: 6-Wasp app. & begins team-ups. 9-Iron Man app. 10-Last Antman 1.00 3.00 8.00
8-Origin Antman & Wasp-r/TTA #44; Kirby-a 1.50 4.50 12.00
11-Thing vs. Hulk; 1st Thing solo book (9/73); origin Fantastic Four retold 3.00 9.00 30.00
12-Thing/Iron Man; early Thanos app.; occurs after Capt. Marvel #33; Starlin-a(p) 1.85 5.50 15.00

NOTE: ***Bolle** a-9i. **Everett** a-1i, 3i. **Hartley** r-10. **Kane** c-3p, 7p. **Russell** a-7-10p. **Starlin** a-8, 11, 12; c-8.*

MARVEL FEATURE (Also see Red Sonja)
Marvel Comics: Nov, 1975 - No. 7, Nov, 1976 (Story cont'd in Conan #68)

1,7: 1-Red Sonja begins (pre-dates Red Sonja #1); adapts Howard short story; Adams-r/Savage Sword of Conan #1. 7-Battles Conan 5.00
2-6: Thorne-c/a in #2-7. 4,5-(Regular 25¢ edition)(5,7/76) 3.00
4,5-(30¢-c variant, limited distribution) 1.50 4.50 12.00

MARVEL FRONTIER COMICS UNLIMITED
Marvel Frontier Comics: Jan, 1994 ($2.95, 68 pgs.)

1-Dances with Demons, Immortalis, Children of the Voyager, Evil Eye, The Fallen stories 3.00

MARVEL FUMETTI BOOK
Marvel Comics Group: Apr, 1984 ($1.00, one-shot)

1-All photos; Stan Lee photo-c; Art Adams touch-ups 3.00

MARVEL FUN & GAMES
Marvel Comics Group: 1979/80 (color comic for kids)

1,11: 1-Games, puzzles, etc. 11-X-Men-c 2.40 6.00
2-10,12,13: (beware marked pages) 4.00

MARVEL GRAPHIC NOVEL
Marvel Comics Group (Epic Comics): 1982 - No. 38, 1990? ($5.95/$6.95)

1-Death of Captain Marvel (2nd Marvel graphic novel); Capt. Marvel battles Thanos by Jim Starlin (c/a/scripts) 2.00 6.00 16.00
1 (2nd & 3rd printings) 1.00 2.80 7.00
2-Elric: The Dreaming City 1.25 3.75 10.00
3-Dreadstar; Starlin-c/a, 52 pgs. 1.25 3.75 10.00
4-Origin/1st app. The New Mutants (1982) 1.50 4.50 12.00
4,5-2nd printings 1.00 2.80 7.00
5-X-Men; book-length story (1982) 2.00 6.00 16.00
6-21,23-31: 6-The Star Slammers. 7-Killraven. 8-Super Boxers; Byrne scripts. 9-The Futurians. 10-Heartburst. 11-Void Indigo. 12-The Dazzler. 13-Starstruck. 14-The Swords Of The Swashbucklers. 15-The Raven Banner (Asgard). 16-The Aladdin Effect. 17-Revenge Of The Living Monolith. 18-She Hulk. 19-The Witch Queen of Acheron (Conan). 20-Greenberg the Vampire. 21-Marada the She-Wolf. 23-Dr. Strange. 25-Alien Legion. 24-Love and War (Daredevil); Miller scripts. 26-Dracula. 27-Avengers (Emperor Doom). 28-Conan the Reaver. 29-The Big Chance (Thing vs. Hulk). 30-A Sailor's Story. 31-Wolfpack 1.00 3.00 8.00
22-Amaz. Spider-Man in Hooky by Wrightson 1.50 4.50 12.00
32-Death of Groo 1.50 4.50 12.00
32-2nd printing ($5.95) 1.00 2.80 7.00
33,34,36,37: 33-Thor. 34-Predator & Prey (Cloak & Dagger). 36-Willow (movie adapt.). 37-Hercules 1.00 3.00 8.00
35-Hitler's Astrologer (The Shadow, $12.95, hard-c) 1.75 5.25 14.00
35-Soft-c reprint (1990, $10.95) 1.40 4.15 11.00
38-Silver Surfer (Judgement Day)($14.95) 1.85 5.50 15.00
nn-Arena by Bruce Jones ($5.95) 1.00 2.80 7.00
nn-Black Widow Coldest War (4/90, $9.95) 1.25 3.75 10.00
nn-Inhumans (1988, $7.95)-Williamson-i 1.10 3.30 9.00
nn-Last of the Dragons (1988, $6.95) 1.00 2.80 7.00
nn-Squadron Supreme: Death of a Universe (1989, $9.95) Gruenwald-s; Ryan & Williamson-a 1.25 3.75 10.00
nn-Who Framed Roger Rabbit (1989, $6.95) 1.25 3.75 10.00
nn-Roger Rabbit In The Resurrection Of Doom (1989, $8.95) 1.25 3.75 10.00

NOTE: ***Aragones** a-27, 32. **Buscema** a-38. **Byrne** c/a-18. **Heath** a-35i. **Kaluta** a-13, 35p; c-13. **Miller** a-24p. **Simonson** a-6; c-6. **Starlin** c/a-1,3. **Williamson** a-34. **Wrightson** c-29i.*

MARVEL-HEROES & LEGENDS
Marvel Comics: Oct, 1996; 1997 ($2.95)

nn-Wraparound-c, ...1997 ($2.99) -Original Avengers story 3.00

MARVEL HOLIDAY SPECIAL
Marvel Comics: No. 1, 1991 ($2.25, 84 pgs.); nn, Jan, 1993 ($2.95, 68 pgs.)

1-X-Men, Fantastic Four, Punisher, Thor, Capt. America, Ghost Rider, Capt. Ultra, Spidey stories; Art Adams-c/a 3.00
nn (1/93)-Wolverine, Thanos (by Starlin/Lim/Austin) 3.00
nn (1994)-Capt. America, X-Men, Silver Surfer 3.00
...1996-Spider-Man by Waid & Olliffe; X-Men, Silver Surfer 3.00

NOTE: ***Art Adams** c-'93. **Golden** a-'93. **Perez** c-'94.*

MARVEL ILLUSTRATED: SWIMSUIT ISSUE (See Marvel Swimsuit Spec.)
Marvel Comics: 1991 ($3.95, magazine, 52 pgs.)

V1#1-Parody of Sports Illustrated swimsuit issue; Mary Jane Parker centerfold pin-up by Jusko; 2nd print exists 5.00

MARVEL KNIGHTS (See Black Panther, Daredevil, Inhumans, & Punisher)
Marvel Comics: 1998 (Previews for upcoming series)

Sketchbook-Wizard suppl.; Quesada & Palmiotti-c 3.00
Tourbook-($2.99) Interviews and art previews 3.00

MARVEL MASTERPIECES COLLECTION, THE
Marvel Comics: May, 1993 - No. 4, Aug, 1993 ($2.95, coated paper, lim. series)

1-4-Reprints Marvel Masterpieces trading cards w/ new Jusko paintings in in each; Jusko painted-c/a 3.00

MARVEL MASTERPIECES 2 COLLECTION, THE
Marvel Comics: July, 1994 - No. 3, Sept, 1994 ($2.95, limited series)

1-3: 1-Kaluta-c; r/trading cards; new Steranko centerfold 3.00

MARVEL MILESTONE EDITION
Marvel Comics: 1991 - Present ($2.95, coated stock)(r/originals with original ads w/silver ink-c)

...: X-Men #1-Reprints X-Men #1 (1991) 3.00
...: Giant Size X-Men #1-(1991, $3.95, 68 pgs.) 4.00
...: Fantastic Four #1 (11/91), ...: Incredible Hulk #1 (3/92, says 3/91 by error), ...: Amazing Fantasy #15 (3/92), ...: Fantastic Four #5 (11/92), ...: Amazing Spider-Man #129 (11/92), ...: Iron Man #55 (11/92), ...: Iron Fist #14 (11/92) ...: Amazing Spider-Man #1 (1/93), ...: Amazing Spider-Man #1 (1/93) variation- no price on-c, ...: Tales of Suspense #39 (3/93), ...: Avengers #1 (9/93) ...: X-Men #9 (10/93), ...: Avengers #16 (10/93), ...:Amazing Spider-Man #149 (11/94, $2.95), ...:X-Men #28 (11/94, $2.95) 3.00
...:Captain America #1 (3/95, $3.95) 4.00
...:Amazing Spider-Man #3 (3/95, $2.95), ...:Avengers #4 (3/95, $2.95), ...:Strange Tales-r/Dr. Strange stories from #110, 111, 114, & 115 3.00

Marvel Mystery Comics #9 © MAR

Marvel Mystery Comics #82 © MAR

Marvel Premiere #15 © MAR

....:Hulk #181 (8/99, $2.99) 2.99

MARVEL MINI-BOOKS (See Promotional Comics section)

MARVEL MOVIE PREMIERE (Magazine)
Marvel Comics Group: Sept, 1975 (B&W, one-shot)

1-Burroughs' "The Land That Time Forgot" adapt. 1.10 3.30 9.00

MARVEL MOVIE SHOWCASE FEATURING STAR WARS
Marvel Comics Group: Nov, 1982 - No. 2, Dec, 1982 ($1.25, 68 pgs.)

1,2-Star Wars movie adaptation; reprints Star Wars #1-6 by Chaykin; 1-Reprints-c to Star Wars #1. 2-Stevens-r 3.00

MARVEL MOVIE SPOTLIGHT FEATURING RAIDERS OF THE LOST ARK
Marvel Comics Group: Nov, 1982 ($1.25, 68 pgs.)

1-Edited-r/Raiders of the Lost Ark #1-3; Buscema-c/a(p); movie adaptation 2.00

MARVEL MYSTERY COMICS (Formerly Marvel Comics) (Becomes Marvel Tales No. 93 on)
Timely /Marvel Comics (TP #2-17/TCI #18-54/MCI #55-92): No. 2, Dec, 1939 - No. 92, June, 1949

GD2.0 FN6.0 VF8.0 NM9.4

2-(Rare)-American Ace begins, ends #3; Human Torch (blue costume) by Burgos, Sub-Mariner by Everett continue; 2 pg. origin recap of Human Torch 1818.00 5455.00 11,817.00 20,000.00
3-New logo from Marvel pulp begins 900.00 2700.00 5400.00 9000.00
4-Intro. Electro, the Marvel of the Age (ends #19), The Ferret, Mystery Detective (ends #9); 1st Sub-Mariner-c by Schomburg; 1st Nazi war-c on a comic book & 1st German flag (Swastika) on-c of a comic (2/40) 720.00 2160.00 4320.00 7200.00
5 Classic Schomburg-c (Scarce) 1475.00 4425.00 8850.00 15,500.00
6,7: 6-Gustavson Angel story 490.00 1470.00 2940.00 4900.00
8-1st Human Torch & Sub-Mariner battle(6/40) 750.00 2250.00 4500.00 7500.00
9-(Scarce)-Human Torch & Sub-Mariner battle (cover/story); 1st Television in comics?; classic-c 1600.00 4800.00 9600.00 18,500.00

GD2.0 FN6.0 NM9.4

10-Human Torch & Sub-Mariner battle, conclusion; Terry Vance, the Schoolboy Sleuth begins, ends #57 520.00 1560.00 5200.00
11 300.00 900.00 2700.00
12-Classic Kirby-c 355.00 1065.00 3200.00
13-Intro. & 1st app. The Vision by S&K (11/40); Sub-Mariner dons new costume, ends #15 400.00 1200.00 3800.00
14-16: 14-Shows-c to Human Torch #1 on-c (12/40). 15-S&K Vision, Gustavson Angel story 225.00 675.00 1800.00
17-Human Torch/Sub-Mariner team-up by Burgos/Everett; pin-up on back-c; shows-c to Human Torch #2 on-c 250.00 750.00 2000.00
18 200.00 600.00 1600.00
19,20: 19-Origin Toro in text; shows-c to Sub-Mariner #1 on-c. 20-Origin The Angel in text 219.00 657.00 1750.00
21-Intro. & 1st app. The Patriot (7/41); not in #46-48; pin-up on back-c 206.00 618.00 1650.00
22-25: 23-Last Gustavson Angel; origin The Vision in text. 24-Injury-to-eye story 175.00 525.00 1400.00
26-30: 27-Ka-Zar ends; last S&K Vision who battles Satan. 28-Jimmy Jupiter in the Land of Nowhere begins, ends #48; Sub-Mariner vs. The Flying Dutchman. 30-1st Japanese war-c 162.00 486.00 1300.00
31-33,35,36,38,39: 31-Sub-Mariner by Everett ends, resumes #84. 32-1st app. The Boboes 144.00 432.00 1150.00
34-Everett, Burgos, Martin Goodman, Funnies, Inc. office appear in story & battles Hitler; last Burgos Human Torch 162.00 486.00 1300.00
37-Classic Hitler-c 150.00 450.00 1200.00
40-Classic Zeppelin-c 150.00 450.00 1200.00
41-43,45,47,48: 48-Last Vision; flag-c 119.00 357.00 950.00
44-Classic Super Plane-c 125.00 375.00 1000.00
46-Classic Hitler-c 125.00 375.00 1000.00
49-Origin Miss America 162.00 486.00 1300.00
50-Mary becomes Miss Patriot (origin) 125.00 375.00 1000.00
51-60: 53-Bondage-c. 60-Last Japanese war-c 112.00 336.00 900.00
61,62,64-Last German war-c 106.00 308.00 850.00
63-Classic Hitler War-c; The Villainess Cat-Woman only app. 116.00 348.00 925.00
65,66-Last Japanese War-c 106.00 318.00 850.00
67-78: 74-Last Patriot. 75-Young Allies begin. 76-Ten Chapter Miss America serial begins, ends #85 94.00 282.00 750.00
79-New cover format; Super Villains begin on cover; last Angel 100.00 300.00 800.00
80-1st app. Capt. America in Marvel Comics 122.00 366.00 975.00
81-Captain America app. 94.00 282.00 750.00
82-Origin & 1st app. Namora (5/47); 1st Sub-Mariner/Namora team-up; Captain America app. 237.00 711.00 1900.00
83,85: 83-Last Young Allies. 85-Last Miss America; Blonde Phantom app. 87.00 261.00 700.00
84-Blonde Phantom begins (on-c of #84,88,89); Sub-Mariner by Everett begins; Captain America app. 122.00 366.00 975.00
86-Blonde Phantom i.d. revealed; Captain America app.; last Bucky app. 97.00 291.00 775.00
87-1st Capt. America/Golden Girl team-up 103.00 309.00 825.00
88-Golden Girl, Namora, & Sun Girl (1st in Marvel Comics) x-over; Captain America, Blonde Phantom app.; last Toro 97.00 291.00 775.00
89-1st Human Torch/Sun Girl team-up; 1st Captain America solo; Blonde Phantom app. 97.00 291.00 775.00
90,91: 90-Blonde Phantom un-masked; Captain America app. 91-Capt. America app.; Blonde Phantom & Sub-Mariner end; early Venus app. (4/49) 106.00 318.00 850.00
92-Feature story on the birth of the Human Torch and the death of Professor Horton (his creator); 1st app. The Witness in Marvel Comics; Captain America app. 250.00 750.00 2000.00
132 Pg. issue, B&W, 25¢ (1943-44)-printed in N. Y.; square binding, blank inside covers; has Marvel No. 33-c in color; contains Capt. America #18 & Marvel Mystery Comics #33; same contents as Captain America Annual

GD2.0 FN6.0 VF8.0

(Less than 5 copies known to exist) 2667.00 8000.00 16,000.00

NOTE: ***Brodsky*** *c-49, 72, 86, 88-92.* ***Crandall*** *a-26i.* ***Everett*** *c-7-9, 27, 84.* ***Gabrielle*** *c-30-32.* ***Schomburg*** *c-3-11, 13-29, 33-36, 39-48, 50-59, 63-69, 74, 76, 132 pg. issue.* ***Shores*** *c-37, 38, 75p, 77, 78p, 79p, 80, 81p, 82-84, 85p, 87p.* ***Sekowsky*** *c-73. Bondage covers-3, 4, 7, 12, 28, 29, 49, 50, 52, 56, 57, 58, 59, 65. Angel c-2, 3, 8, 12. Remember Pearl Harbor issues-#30-32.*

MARVEL MYSTERY COMICS
Marvel Comics: Dec, 1999 ($3.95, reprints)

GD2.0 FN6.0 NM9.4

1-Reprints original 1940s stories; Schomburg-c from #74 4.00

MARVEL NO-PRIZE BOOK, THE (The Official... on-c)
Marvel Comics Group: Jan, 1983 (one-shot, direct sales only)

1-Golden-c; Kirby-a 3.00

MARVEL PREMIERE
Marvel Comics Group: April, 1972 - No. 61, Aug, 1981 (A tryout book for new characters)

1-Origin Warlock (pre-#1) by Gil Kane/Adkins; origin Counter-Earth; Hulk & Thor cameo (#1-14 are 20¢-c) 3.50 10.50 35.00
2-Warlock ends; Kirby Yellow Claw-r 2.25 6.75 18.00
3-Dr. Strange series begins (pre #1, 7/72), B. Smith-c/a(p) 2.60 7.80 26.00
4-Smith/Brunner-a 1.50 4.50 12.00
5-9: 8-Starlin-c/a(p) 1.00 2.80 7.00
10-Death of the Ancient One 1.25 3.75 10.00
11-14: 11-Dr. Strange origin-r by Ditko. 14-Last Dr. Strange (3/74), gets own title 3 months later 5.00
15-Origin/1st app. Iron Fist (5/74), ends #25 5.00 15.00 50.00
16,25: 16-2nd app. Iron Fist; origin cont'd from #15; Hama's 1st Marvel-a. 25-1st Byrne Iron Fist (moves to own title next) 2.25 6.75 18.00
17-24: Iron Fist in all 1.50 4.50 12.00
26-Hercules. 5.00
27-Satana 1.00 2.80 7.00
28-Legion of Monsters (Ghost Rider, Man-Thing, Morbius, Werewolf)

Marvel Presents #3 © MAR

Marvels of Science #1 © CC

Marvel Spotlight #19 © MAR

GD2.0 FN6.0 NM9.4

1.50 4.50 12.00
29-49,51-56,58-61: 29,30-The Liberty Legion. 29-1st modern app. Patriot. 31-1st app. Woodgod; last 25¢ issue. 32-1st app. Monark Starstalker. 33,34-1st color app. Solomon Kane (Robert E. Howard adaptation "Red Shadows".) 35-Origin/1st app. 3-D Man. 36,37-3-D Man. 38-1st Weirdworld. 39,40-Torpedo. 41-1st Seeker 3000! 42-Tigra. 43-Paladin. 44-Jack of Hearts (1st solo book, 10/78). 45,46-Man-Wolf. 47-Origin/1st app. new Ant-Man. 48-Ant-Man. 49-The Falcon (1st solo book, 8/79). 51-53-Black Panther. 54-1st Caleb Hammer. 55-Wonder Man. 56-1st color app. Dominic Fortune. 58-60-Dr. Who. 61-Star Lord 2.50
29-31-(30¢-c variants, limited distribution)(4-8/76) 1.25 3.75 10.00
50-1st app. Alice Cooper; co-plotted by Alice 1.25 3.75 10.00
57-Dr. Who (2nd U.S. app.-see Movie Classics) 4.00
NOTE: ***N. Adams*** *(Crusty Bunkers) part inks-10, 12, 13.* ***Austin*** *a-50i, 56i; c-46i, 50i, 56i, 58.* ***Brunner*** *a-4i, 6p, 9-14p; c-9-14.* ***Byrne*** *a-47p, 48p.* ***Chaykin*** *a-32-34; c-32, 33, 56.* ***Giffen*** *a-31p, 44p; c-44.* ***Gil Kane*** *a(p)-1, 2, 15; c(p)-1, 2, 15, 16, 22-24, 27, 36, 37.* ***Kirby*** *c-26, 29-31, 35.* ***Layton*** *a-47i, 48i; c-47.* ***McWilliams*** *a-25i.* ***Miller*** *c-49p, 53p, 58p.* ***Nebres*** *a-44i; c-38i.* ***Nino*** *a-38i.* ***Perez*** *c/a-38p, 45p, 46p.* ***Ploog*** *a-38; c-5-7.* ***Russell*** *a-7p.* ***Simonson*** *a-60(2pgs.); c-57.* ***Starlin*** *a-8p; c-8.* ***Sutton*** *a-41, 43, 50p, 61; c-50p, 61. #57-60 publ'd w/two different prices on-c.*

MARVEL PRESENTS
Marvel Comics: October, 1975 - No. 12, Aug, 1977 (#1-6 are 25¢ issues)

1-Origin & 1st app. Bloodstone 1.00 2.80 7.00
2-Origin Bloodstone continued; Kirby-c 5.00
3-Guardians of the Galaxy (1st solo book, 2/76) begins, ends #12
1.00 3.00 8.00
4-7,9-12: 9,10-Origin Starhawk 5.00
4-6-(30¢-c variants, limited distribution)(4-8/76) 2.50 7.50 20.00
8-r/story from Silver Surfer #2 plus 4 pgs. new-a 5.00
NOTE: ***Austin*** *a-6i.* ***Buscema*** *r-8p.* ***Chaykin*** *a-5p.* ***Kane*** *c-1p.* ***Starlin*** *layouts-10.*

MARVEL PREVIEW (Magazine) (Bizarre Adventures #25 on)
Marvel Comics: Feb (no month), 1975 - No. 24, Winter, 1980 (B&W) ($1.00)

1-Man-Gods From Beyond the Stars; Crusty Bunkers (Neal Adams)-a(i) & cover; Nino-a 1.10 3.30 9.00
2-1st origin The Punisher (see Amaz. Spider-Man #129 & Classic Punisher); 1st app. Dominic Fortune; Morrow-c 5.50 16.50 60.00
3,8,10: 3-Blade the Vampire Slayer. 8-Legion of Monsters; Morbius app. 10-Thor the Mighty; Starlin frontispiece 1.25 3.75 10.00
4,5: 4-Star-Lord & Sword in the Star (origins & 1st app.). 5,6-Sherlock Holmes. 1.00 3.00 8.00
6,9: 6-Sherlock Holmes; N. Adams frontispiece. 9-Man-God; origin Star Hawk, ends #20 5.00
7-Satana, Sword in the Star app. 1.00 2.80 7.00
11,16,19: 11-Star-Lord; Byrne-a; Starlin frontispiece. 16-Masters of Terror. 19-Kull 4.00
12-15,17,18,20-24: 12-Haunt of Horror. 14,15-Star-Lord. 14-Starlin painted-c. 16-Masters of Terror. 17-Blackmark by G. Kane (see SSOC #1-3). 18-Star-Lord. 20-Bizarre Advs. 21-Moon Knight (Spr/80)-Predates Moon Knight #1; The Shroud by Ditko. 22-King Arthur. 23-Bizarre Advs.; Miller-a. 24-Debut Paradox 3.00
NOTE: ***N. Adams*** *(C. Bunkers) r-20i.* ***Buscema*** *a-22, 23.* ***Byrne*** *a-11.* ***Chaykin*** *a-20r; c-20 (new).* ***Colan*** *a-8, 16p(3), 18p, 23p; c-16p.* ***Elias*** *a-18.* ***Giffen*** *a-7.* ***Infantino*** *a-14p.* ***Kaluta*** *a-12; c-15.* ***Miller*** *a-23.* ***Morrow*** *a-8i; c-2-4.* ***Perez*** *a-20p.* ***Ploog*** *a-8.* ***Starlin*** *c-13, 14. Nudity in some issues*

MARVEL RIOT
Marvel Comics: Dec, 1995 ($1.95, one-shot)

1-"Age of Apocalypse" spoof; Lobdell script 2.00

MARVELS
Marvel Comics: Jan, 1994 - No. 4, Apr, 1994 ($5.95, painted lim. series)
No. 1 (2nd Printing), Apr, 1996 - No. 4 (2nd Printing), July, 1996 ($2.95)

1-4: Kurt Busiek scripts & Alex Ross painted-c/a in all; double-c w/acetate overlay 1.00 3.00 8.00
Marvel Classic Collectors Pack ($11.90)-Issues #1 & 2 boxed (1st printings). 2.00 6.00 16.00
0-(8/94, $2.95)-no acetate overlay. 4.00
1-4-(2nd printing): r/original limited series w/o acetate overlay 3.00
Hardcover (1994, $59.95)-r/#0-4; w/intros by Stan Lee, John Romita, Sr., Kurt Busiek & Scott McCloud. 60.00
Trade paperback ($19.95) 20.00

MARVEL SAGA, THE
Marvel Comics Group: Dec, 1985 - No. 25, Dec, 1987

1-25 2.00
NOTE: ***Williamson*** *a(i)-9, 10; c(i)-7, 10-12, 14, 16.*

MARVEL'S GREATEST COMICS (Marvel Collectors' Item Classics #1-22)
Marvel Comics Group: No. 23, Oct, 1969 - No. 96, Jan, 1981

23-34 (Giants). Begin Fantastic Four-r/#30s?-116 2.00 6.00 16.00
35-37-Silver Surfer-r/Fantastic Four #48-50 1.00 3.00 8.00
38-50: 42-Silver Surfer-r/F.F.(others?) 5.00
51-70: 63,63-(25¢ editions) 3.00
63,64-(30¢-c variants, limited distribution)(5,7/76) 1.50 4.50 12.00
71-96 2.50
NOTE: *Dr. Strange, Fantastic Four, Iron Man, Watcher-#23, 24. Capt. America, Dr. Strange, Iron Man, Fantastic Four-#25-28. Fantastic Four-#38-96.* ***Buscema*** *r-85-92; c-87-92r.* ***Ditko*** *r-23-28.* ***Kirby*** *r-23-82; c-75, 77p, 80p. #81 reprints Fantastic Four #100.*

MARVEL'S GREATEST SUPERHERO BATTLES (See Fireside Book Series)

MARVEL: SHADOWS AND LIGHT
Marvel Comics: Feb, 1997 ($2.95, B&W, one-shot)

1-Tony Daniel-c 3.00

MARVELS OF SCIENCE
Charlton Comics: March, 1946 - No. 4, June, 1946

1-A-Bomb story 21.00 64.00 150.00
2-4 13.00 39.00 90.00

MARVEL SPECIAL EDITION FEATURING... (Also see Special Collectors' Ed.)
Marvel Comics Group: 1975 - 1978 (84 pgs.) (Oversized)

1-The Spectacular Spider-Man ($1.50); r/Amazing Spider-Man #6,35, Annual 1; Ditko-a(r) 1.75 5.25 14.00
1,2-Star Wars ('77,'78; r/Star Wars #1-3 & #4-6 1.50 4.50 12.00
3-Star Wars ('78, $2.50, 116pgs.); r/S. Wars #1-6 1.75 5.25 14.00
3-Close Encounters of the Third Kind (1978, $1.50, 56 pgs.)-Movie adaptation; Simonson-a(p) 1.50 4.50 12.00
V2#2(Spring, 1980, $2.00, oversized)- "Star Wars: The Empire Strikes Back"; r/Marvel Comics Super Special #16 2.50 7.50 22.00
NOTE: ***Chaykin*** *c/a(r)-1(1977), 2, 3.* ***Stevens*** *a(r)-2i, 3i.* ***Williamson*** *a(r)-V2#2.*

MARVEL SPECTACULAR
Marvel Comics Group: Aug, 1973 - No. 19, Nov, 1975

1-Thor-r from mid-sixties begin by Kirby 1.00 3.00 8.00
2-19 4.00

MARVELS: PORTRAITS
Marvel Comics: Mar, 1995 - No. 4, June, 1995 ($2.95, limited series)

1-4:Different artists renditions of Marvel characters 3.00

MARVEL SPOTLIGHT (...& Son of Satan #19, 20, 23, 24)
Marvel Comics Group: Nov, 1971 - No. 33, Apr, 1977; V2#1, July, 1979 - V2#11, Mar, 1981 (A try-out book for new characters)

1-Origin Red Wolf (western hero)(1st solo book, pre-#1); Wood inks, Neal Adams-c; only 15¢ issue 2.50 7.50 24.00
2-(25¢, 52 pgs.)-Venus-r by Everett; origin/1st app. Werewolf By Night (begins) by Ploog; N. Adams-c 10.50 31.00 115.00
3,4: 4-Werewolf By Night ends (6/72); gets own title 9/72
3.50 10.50 35.00
5-Origin/1st app. Ghost Rider (8/72) & begins 7.00 21.00 75.00
6-8: 6-Origin G.R. retold. 8-Last Ploog issue 3.20 9.60 32.00
9-11-Last Ghost Rider (gets own title next mo.) 2.50 7.50 22.00
12-Origin & 2nd full app. The Son of Satan (10/73); story cont'd from Ghost Rider #2 & into #3; series begins, ends #24 2.50 7.50 22.00
13-24: 13-Partial origin Son of Satan. 14-Last 20¢ issue. 22-Ghost Rider-c & cameo (5 panels)24-Last Son of Satan (10/75); gets own title 12/75
1.00 2.80 7.00
25,27,30,31: 27-(Regular 25¢-c), Sub-Mariner app. 30-The Warriors Three. 31-Nick Fury 4.00

Marvel Super Hero Contest of Champions #1 © MAR

Marvel Super-Heroes #20 © MAR

Marvel Tales (1st series) #124 © MAR

26-Scarecrow 2.40 6.00
27-29-(30¢-c variants, limited distribution) 4.80 14.40 48.00
28,29,32: 28-(Regular 25¢-c) 1st solo Moon Knight app. 29-(Regular 25¢-c) (8/76) Moon Knight app.; last 25¢ issue. 32-1st app./partial origin Spider-Woman (2/77); Nick Fury app. 2.00 6.00 16.00
33-Deathlok; 1st app. Devil-Slayer 6.00
V2#1-7,9-11: 1-4-Capt. Marvel. 5-Dragon Lord. 6,7-StarLord; origin #6. 9-11-Capt. Universe (see Micronauts #8) 2.00
8-Capt. Marvel; Miller-c/a(p) 3.00

NOTE: ***Austin*** *c-V2#2i, 8.* ***J. Buscema*** *c/a-30p.* ***Chaykin*** *a-31; c-26, 31.* ***Colan*** *a-18p, 19p.* ***Ditko*** *a-V2#4, 5, 9-11; c-V2#4, 9-11.* ***Kane*** *c-21p, 32p.* ***Kirby*** *c-29p.* ***McWilliams*** *a-20i.* ***Miller*** *a-V2#8p; c(p)-V2#2, 5, 7, 8.* ***Mooney*** *a-8i, 10i, 14p, 15, 16p, 17p, 24p, 27, 32i.* ***Nasser*** *a-33p.* ***Ploog*** *a-2-5, 6-8p; c-3-9.* ***Romita*** *c-13.* ***Sutton*** *a-9-11p, V2#6, 7. #29-25¢ & 30¢ issues exist.*

MARVEL SUPER ACTION (Magazine)
Marvel Comics Group: Jan, 1976 (B&W, 76 pgs.)

1-Origin/2nd app. Dominic Fortune(see Marv. Preview); early Punisher app.; Weird World & The Huntress; Evans, Ploog-a 4.00 12.00 40.00

MARVEL SUPER ACTION
Marvel Comics Group: May, 1977 - No. 37, Nov, 1981

1-Reprints Capt. America #100 by Kirby 1.00 3.00 8.00
2-13: 2,3,5-13 r/Capt. America #101,102,103-111. 11-Origin-r. 12,13-Classic Steranko-c/a(r). 4-Marvel Boy-r(origin)/M. Boy #1 4.00
14-20: r/Avengers #55,56, Annual 2, others 3.00
21-37: 30-r/Hulk #6 from U.K. 2.00

NOTE: ***Buscema*** *a(r)-14p, 15p; c-18-20, 22, 35r-37.* ***Everett*** *a-4.* ***Heath*** *a-4r.* ***Kirby*** *r-1-3, 5-11.* ***B. Smith*** *a-27r, 28r.* ***Steranko*** *a(r)-12p, 13p; c-12r, 13r.*

MARVEL SUPER HERO CONTEST OF CHAMPIONS
Marvel Comics Group: June, 1982 - No. 3, Aug, 1982 (Limited series)

1-3: Features nearly all Marvel characters currently appearing in their comics; 1st Marvel limited series 4.00

MARVEL SUPER HEROES
Marvel Comics Group: October, 1966 (25¢, 68 pgs.) (1st Marvel one-shot)

1-r/origin Daredevil from D.D. #1; r/Avengers #2; G.A. Sub-Mariner-r/Marvel Mystery #8 (Human Torch app.). Kirby-a 5.80 17.40 70.00

MARVEL SUPER-HEROES (Formerly Fantasy Masterpieces #1-11)
(Also see Giant-Size Super Heroes) (#12-20: 25¢, 68 pgs.)
Marvel Comics: No. 12, 12/67 - No. 31, 11/71; No. 32, 9/72 - No. 105, 1/82

12-Origin & 1st app. Capt. Marvel of the Kree; G.A. Human Torch, Destroyer, Capt. America, Black Knight, Sub-Mariner-r (#12-20 all contain new stories and reprints) 5.00 15.00 60.00
13-2nd app. Capt. Marvel; G.A. Black Knight, Torch, Vision, Capt. America, Sub-Mariner-r 2.70 8.00 30.00
14-Amazing Spider-Man (5/68, new-a by Andru/Everett); G.A. Sub-Mariner, Torch, Mercury (1st Kirby-a at Marvel), Black Knight, Capt. America reprints 5.50 16.50 60.00
15-17: 15-Black Bolt cameo in Medusa (new-a); Black Knight, Sub-Mariner, Black Marvel, Capt. America-r. 16-Origin & 1st app. S. A. Phantom Eagle; G.A. Torch, Capt. America, Black Knight, Patriot, Sub-Mariner-r. 17-Origin Black Knight (new-a); G.A. Torch, Sub-Mariner-r; reprint from All- Winners Squad #21 (cover & story) 2.25 6.80 25.00
18-Origin/1st app. Guardians of the Galaxy (1/69); G.A. Sub-Mariner, All-Winners Squad-r 2.50 7.50 30.00
19-Ka-Zar (new-a); G.A. Torch, Marvel Boy, Black Knight, Sub-Mariner reprints; Smith-c(p); Tuska-a(r) 1.20 3.60 12.00
20-Doctor Doom (5/69); r/Young Men #24 w/-c 1.80 5.40 20.00
21-31: All-r issues. 21-X-Men, Daredevil, Iron Man-r begin, end #31. 31-Last Giant issue 1.20 3.60 10.00
32-50: 32-Hulk/Sub-Mariner-r begin from TTA. 4.00
51-105: 56-r/origin Hulk/Inc. Hulk #102; Hulk-r begin 2.50
57,58-(30¢-c variants, limited distribution)(5,7/76) .90 2.70 9.00

NOTE: ***Austin*** *a-104.* ***Colan*** *a(p)-12, 13, 15, 18; c-12, 13, 15, 18.* ***Everett*** *a-14i(new); r-14, 15i, 18, 19, 33; c-85(r). New* ***Kirby*** *c-22, 27, 54.* ***Maneely*** *r-14, 15, 19.* ***Severin*** *r-83-85i, 100-102; c-100-102r.* ***Starlin*** *c-47.* ***Tuska*** *a-19p. Black Knight-r by* ***Maneely*** *in 12-16, 19. Sub-Mariner-r by* ***Everett*** *in 12-20.*

MARVEL SUPER-HEROES
Marvel Comics: May, 1990 - V2#15, Oct, 1993 ($2.95/$2.50, quart., 68-84 pgs.)

1-Moon Knight, Hercules, Black Panther, Magik, Brother Voodoo, Speedball (by Ditko) & Hellcat; Hembeck-a 3.00
2,4,5,V2#3,6-15: 2-Summer Special(7/90); Rogue, Speedball (by Ditko), Iron Man, Falcon,Tigra & Daredevil. 4-Spider-Man/Nick Fury, Daredevil,Speedball, Wonder Man, Spitfire & Black Knight; Byrne-c. 5-Thor, Dr. Strange, Thing & She-Hulk; Speedball by Ditko(p). V2#3-Retells origin Capt. America w/new facts; Blue Shield, Capt. Marvel,Speedball, Wasp; Hulk by Ditko/Rogers V2#6-9: 6-8-$2.25-c. 6,7-X-Men, Cloak & Dagger, The Shroud (by Ditko) & Marvel Boy in each. 8-X-Men, Namor & Iron Man (by Ditko); Larsen-c. 9-W.C Avengers, Iron Man app.; Kieth-c(p). V2#10-Ms. Marvel/Sabretooth-c/story (intended for Ms. Marvel #24; shows-c to #24); Namor, Vision, Scarlet Witch stories. V2#11,12 :11-Original Ghost Rider-c/story; Giant-Man, Ms. Marvel stories. 12-Dr. Strange, Falcon, Iron Man. V2#13-15 ($2.75, 84 pgs.): 13-All Iron Man 30th anniversary. 15-Iron Man/Thor/Volstagg/Dr. Druid 2.75

MARVEL SUPER-HEROES MEGAZINE
Marvel Comics: Oct, 1994 - No. 6, Mar, 1995 ($2.95, 100 pgs.)

1-6: 1-r/FF #232, DD #159, Iron Man #115, Incred. Hulk #314 3.00

MARVEL SUPER-HEROES SECRET WARS (See Secret Wars II)
Marvel Comics Group: May, 1984 - No. 12, Apr, 1985 (limited series)

1 5.00
1-3-2nd printings (sold in multi-packs) 2.00
2-7,9-12: 6-The Wasp dies. 7-Intro. new Spider-Woman. 12-($1.00, 52 pgs.) 4.00
8-Spider-Man's new black costume explained as alien costume (1st app. Venom as alien costume) 2.25 6.75 18.00

NOTE: ***Zeck*** *a-1-12; c-1,3,8-12.*

MARVEL SUPER SPECIAL, A (See Marvel Comics Super...)

MARVEL SWIMSUIT SPECIAL (Also see Marvel Illustrated...)
Marvel Comics: 1992 - No. 4, 1995 ($3.95/$4.50, magazine, 52 pgs.)

1-4-Silvestri-c; pin-ups by diff. artists. 2-Jusko painted-c. 3-Hughes-c 4.50

MARVEL TAILS STARRING PETER PORKER THE SPECTACULAR SPIDER-HAM (Also see Peter Porker...)
Marvel Comics Group: Nov, 1983 (one-shot)

1-Peter Porker, the Spectacular Spider-Ham, Captain Americat, Goose Rider, Hulk Bunny app. 2.00

MARVEL TALES (Formerly Marvel Mystery Comics #1-92)
Marvel/Atlas Comics (MCI): No. 93, Aug, 1949 - No. 159, Aug, 1957

93-Horror/weird stories begin 131.00 393.00 1050.00
94-Everett-a 90.00 270.00 720.00
95,96,99,101,103,105: 95-New logo 59.00 177.00 475.00
97-Sun Girl, 2 pgs; Kirbyish-a; one story used in N.Y. State Legislative document 72.00 216.00 575.00
98,,100: 98-Krigstein-a 62.00 186.00 500.00
102-Wolverton-a "The End of the World", (6 pgs.) 87.00 261.00 700.00
104-Wolverton-a "Gateway to Horror", (6 pgs.) 84.00 252.00 675.00
106,107-Krigstein-a. 106-Decapitation story 50.00 150.00 400.00
108-120: 118-Hypo-c/panels in End of World story. 120-Jack Katz-a 39.00 116.00 270.00
121,123-131: 128-Flying Saucer-c. 131-Last precode (2/55) 31.00 92.00 215.00
122-Kubert-a 31.00 94.00 220.00
132,133,135-141,143,145 19.00 58.00 135.00
134-Krigstein, Kubert-a; flying saucer-c 21.00 62.00 145.00
142-Krigstein-a 19.00 58.00 135.00
144-Williamson/Krenkel-a, 3 pgs. 19.00 58.00 135.00
146,148-151,154-156,158: 150-1st S.A. issue. 156-Torres-a 15.00 45.00 105.00
147,152: 147-Ditko-a. 152-Wood, Morrow-a 18.00 54.00 125.00
153-Everett End of World c/story 19.00 58.00 135.00
157,159-Krigstein-a 16.00 47.00 110.00

NOTE: ***Andru*** *a-103.* ***Briefer*** *a-118.* ***Check*** *a-147.* ***Colan*** *a-105, 107, 118, 120, 121, 127, 131.* ***Drucker*** *a-127, 135, 141, 146, 150.* ***Everett*** *a-98, 104, 106(2), 108(2), 131, 148, 151, 153, 155; c-107, 109, 111, 112, 114, 117, 127, 143, 147-151, 153, 155, 156.* ***Forte*** *a-119, 125, 130.* ***Heath***

Marvel Tales (2nd series) #31 © MAR

Marvel Tales (1st series) #63 © MAR

Marvel Team-Up (1st series) #11 © MAR

GD2.0 FN6.0 NM9.4

a-110, 113, 118, 119; c-104-106, 110, 130. ***Gil Kane*** *a-117.* ***Lawrence*** *a-130.* ***Maneely*** *a-111, 126, 129; c-108, 116, 120, 129, 152.* ***Mooney*** *a-114.* ***Morisi*** *a-153.* ***Morrow*** *a-150, 152, 156.* ***Orlando*** *a-149, 151, 157.* ***Pakula*** *a-119, 121, 135, 144, 150, 152, 156.* ***Powell*** *a-136, 137, 150, 154.* ***Ravielli*** *a-117.* ***Rico*** *a-97, 99.* ***Romita*** *a-108.* ***Sekowsky*** *a-96-98.* ***Shores*** *a-110; c-96.* ***Sinnott*** *a-105, 116.* ***Tuska*** *a-114.* ***Whitney*** *a-107.* ***Wildey*** *a-126, 138.*

MARVEL TALES (...Annual #1,2; ...Starring Spider-Man #123 on)
Marvel Comics Group (NPP earlier issues): 1964 - No. 291, Nov, 1994 (No. 1-32: 72 pgs.)

1-Reprints origins of Spider-Man/Amazing Fantasy #15, Hulk/Inc. Hulk#1, Ant-Man/T.T.A. #35, Giant Man/T.T.A. #49, Iron Man/T.O.S. #39,48, Thor/J.I.M. #83 & r/Sgt. Fury #1 — 27.00 81.00 270.00
2 ('65)-r/X-Men #1(origin), Avengers #1(origin), origin Dr. Strange-r/Strange Tales #115 & origin Hulk(Hulk #3) — 9.00 27.00 90.00
3 (7/66)-Spider-Man, Strange Tales (H. Torch), Journey into Mystery (Thor), Tales to Astonish (Ant-Man)-r begin (r/Strange Tales #101) — 4.00 12.00 40.00
4,5 — 2.80 8.40 28.00
6-8,10: 10-Reprints 1st Kraven/Amaz. S-M #15 — 2.25 6.75 18.00
9-r/Amazing Spider-Man #14 w/cover — 2.50 7.50 22.00
11-33: 11-Spider-Man battles Daredevil-r/Amaz. Spider-Man #16. 13-Origin Marvel Boy-r/M. Boy #1. 22-Green Goblin-c/story-r/Amaz. Spider-Man #27. 30-New Angel story (x-over w/Ka-Zar #2,3). 32-Last 72 pg. iss. 33-(52 pgs.) Kraven-r — 2.00 6.00 16.00
34-50: 34-Begin regular size issues — 5.00
51-65 — 3.00
66-70-(Regular 25¢ editions)(4-8/76) — 3.00
66-70-(30¢-c variants, limited distribution) — 1.85 5.50 15.00
71-105: 75-Origin Spider-Man-r. 77-79-Drug issues-r/Amaz. Spider-Man #96-98. 98-Death of Gwen Stacy-r/Amaz. Spider-Man #121 (Green Goblin). 99-Death Green Goblin-r/Amaz. Spider-Man #122. 100-(52 pgs.)-New Hawkeye/Two Gun Kid story. 101-105-All Spider-Man-r — 3.00
106-r/1st Punisher-Amazing Spider-Man #129 — 4.00
107-136: 107-133-All Spider-Man-r. 111,112-r/Spider-Man #134,135 (Punisher). 113,114-r/Spider-Man #136,137(Green Goblin). 126-128-r/clone story from Amazing Spider-Man #149-151. 134-136-Dr. Strange-r begin; SpM stories continue. 134-Dr. Strange-r/Strange Tales #110 — 2.50
137-Origin-r Dr. Strange; shows original unprinted-c & origin Spider-Man/Amazing Fantasy #15 — 4.00
137-Nabisco giveaway — 2.40 6.00
138-Reprints all Amazing Spider-Man #1; begin reprints of Spider-Man with covers similar to originals — 3.00
139-144: r/Amazing Spider-Man #2-7 — 2.50
145-200: Spider-Man-r continue w/#8 on. 149-Contains skin "Tattooz" decals. 150-($1.00, 52pgs.)-r/Spider-Man Annual 1(Kraven app.). 153-r/1st Kraven/Spider-Man #15. 155-r/2nd Green Goblin/Spider-Man #17. 161,164,165-Gr. Goblin-c/stories-r/Spider-Man #23,26,27. 178,179-Green Goblin-c/story-r/Spider-Man #39,40. 187,189-Kraven-r. 191-($1.50, 68 pgs.)-r/Spider-Man #96-98. 193-Byrne-r/Marvel Team-Up begin w/scripts. 192-($1.25, 52 pgs.)-r/Spider-Man #121,122. 200-Double size ($1.25)-Miller-c & r/Annual #14 — 2.00
201-257: 208-Last Byrne-r. 210,211-r/Spidey #134,135. 212,213-r/Giant-Size Spidey #4. 213-r/1st solo Silver Surfer story/F.F. Annual #5. 214,215-r/Spidey #161,162. 222-Reprints origin Punisher/Spectacular Spider-Man #83; last Punisher reprint. 209-Reprints 1st app. The Punisher/Amazing Spider-Man #129; Punisher reprints begin, end #222. 223-McFarlane-c begins, end #239. 233-Spider-Man/X-Men team-ups begin; r/X-Men #35. 234-r/Marvel Team-Up #4. 235,236-r/M. Team-Up Annual #1. 237,238-r/M. Team-Up #150. 239,240-r/M. Team-Up #38,90(Beast). 242-r/M.Team-Up #89. 243-r/M. Team-Up #117(Wolverine). 250-($1.50, 52pgs.)-r/1st Karma/M. Team-Up #100. 251-r/Spider-Man #100 (Green Goblin-c/story). 252-r/1st app. Morbius/Amaz. Spider-Man #101. 253-($1.50, 52 pgs.)-r/Amaz. S-M #102254-r/M. Team-Up #15(Ghost Rider); new painted-c. 255,256-Spider-Man & Ghost Rider-r/Marvel Team-Up #58,91. 257-Hobgoblin-r begin(r/Amazing Spider-Man #238). — 2.00
258-291: 258-261-r/A. Spider-Man #239,249-251(Hobgoblin). 262,263-r/Marv. Team-Up #53,54. 262-New X-Men vs. Sunstroke story. 263-New Woodgod origin story. 264,265-r/A. Spider-Man Annual 5. 266-273-Reprints alien costume stories/A. S-M 252-259. 277-r/1st Silver Sable/A. S-M 265. 283-r/A. S-M 275 (Hobgoblin). 284-r/A. S-M 276 (Hobgoblin) — 2.00
285-variant w/Wonder-Con logo on c-no price-giveaway — 2.00
286-($2.95)-p/bagged w/16 page insert & animation print — 3.00

NOTE: *All contain reprints; some have new art. #89-97-r/Amazing Spider-Man #110-118; #98-136-r/#121-159; #137-150-r/Amazing Fantasy #15, #1-12 & Annual 1; #151-167-r/#13-28 & Annual 2; #168-186-r/#29-46.* ***Austin*** *a-100i; c-272i, 273i.* ***Byrne*** *a(r)-193-198p, 201-208p.* ***Ditko*** *a-1-30, 83, 100, 137-155.* ***G. Kane*** *a-71, 81, 98-101p, 249r; c-125-127p, 130p, 137-155.* ***Sam Kieth*** *c-255, 262, 263.* ***Ron Lim*** *c-266p-281p, 283p-285p.* ***McFarlane*** *c-223-239.* ***Mooney*** *a-63, 95-97i, 103(i).* ***Nasser*** *a-100p.* ***Nebres*** *a-242i.* ***Perez*** *c-259-261.* ***Rogers*** *c-240, 241, 243-252.*

MARVEL TEAM-UP (See Marvel Treasury Edition #18 & Official Marvel Index To...) (Replaced by Web of Spider-Man)
Marvel Comics Group: March, 1972 - No. 150, Feb, 1985
NOTE: *Spider-Man team-ups in all but Nos. 18, 23, 26, 29, 32, 35, 97, 104, 105, 137.*

1-Human Torch — 9.00 27.00 100.00
2-Human Torch — 3.20 9.60 32.00
3-Spider-Man/Human Torch vs. Morbius (part 1); 3rd app. of Morbius (7/72) — 3.50 10.50 35.00
4-Spider-Man/X-Men vs. Morbius (part 2 of story); 4th app. of Morbius — 4.00 12.00 40.00
5-10: 5-Vision. 6-Thing. 7-Thor. 8-The Cat (4/73, came out between The Cat #3 & 4). 9-Iron Man. 10-H-T — 1.85 5.50 15.00
11,13,14,16-20: 11-Inhumans. 13-Capt. America. 14-Sub-Mariner. 16-Capt. Marvel. 17-Mr. Fantastic. 18-H-T/Hulk. 19-Ka-Zar. 20-Black Panther; last 20¢ issue — 1.10 3.30 9.00
12-Werewolf (8/73, 1 month before Werewolf #1). — 2.50 7.50 20.00
15-1st Spider-Man/Ghost Rider team-up (11/73) — 2.50 7.50 20.00
21-30: 21-Dr. Strange. 22-Hawkeye. 23-H-T/Iceman (X-Men cameo). 24-Brother Voodoo. 25-Daredevil. 26-H-T/Thor. 27-Hulk. 28-Hercules. 29-H-T/Iron Man. 30-Falcon — 5.00
31-45,47-50: 31-Iron Fist. 32-H-T/Son of Satan. 33-Nighthawk. 34-Valkyrie. 35-H-T/Dr. Strange. 36-Frankenstein. 37-Man-Wolf. 38-Beast. 39-H-T. 40-Sons of the Tiger/H-T. 41-Scarlet Witch. 42-The Vision. 43-Dr. Doom; retells origin. 44-Moondragon. 45-Killraven. 47-Thing. 48-Iron Man; last 25¢ issue. 49-Dr. Strange; Iron Man app. 50-Iron Man; Dr. Strange app. — 4.00
44-48-(30¢-c variants, limited distribution)(4-8/76) — 2.00 6.00 16.00
46-Spider-Man/Deathlok team-up — 5.00
51,52,56,57: 51-Iron Man; Dr. Strange app. 52-Capt. America. 56-Daredevil. 57-Black Widow — 3.00
53-Hulk; Woodgod & X-Men app., 1st Byrne-a on X-Men (1/77) — 2.50 7.50 20.00
54,55,58-60: 54,59,60: 54-Hulk; Woodgod app. 59-Yellowjacket/The Wasp. 60-The Wasp (Byrne-a in all). 55-Warlock-c/story; Byrne-a. 58-Ghost Rider — 5.00
61-70: All Byrne-a; 61-H-T. 62-Ms. Marvel; last 30¢ issue. 63-Iron Fist. 64-Daughters of the Dragon. 65-Capt. Britain (1st U.S. app.). 66-Capt. Britain; 1st app. Arcade. 67-Tigra; Kraven the Hunter app. 68-Man-Thing. 69-Havok (from X-Men). 70-Thor — 4.00
71-74,76-78,80: 71-Falcon. 72-Iron Man. 73-Daredevil. 74-Not Ready for Prime Time Players (Belushi). 76-Dr. Strange. 77-Ms. Marvel. 78-Wonder Man. 80-Dr. Strange/Clea; last 35¢ issue — 3.00
75,79,81: Byrne-a(p). 75-Power Man; Cage app. 79-Mary Jane Watson as Red Sonja; Clark Kent cameo (1 panel, 3/79). 81-Death of Satana — 4.00
82-99: 82-Black Widow. 83-Nick Fury. 84-Shang-Chi. 86-Guardians of the Galaxy. 89-Nightcrawler (from X-Men). 91-Ghost Rider. 92-Hawkeye. 93-Werewolf by Night. 94-Spider-Man vs. The Shroud. 95-Mockingbird (intro.); Nick Fury app. 96-Howard the Duck; last 40¢ issue. 97-Spider-Woman/ Hulk. 98-Black Widow. 99-Machine Man. 85-Shang-Chi/Black Widow/Nick Fury. 87-Black Panther. 88-Invisible Girl. 90-Beast — 2.50
100-(Double-size)-Fantastic Four/Storm/Black Panther; origin/1st app. Karma, one of the New Mutants; origin Storm; X-Men x-over; Miller-c/a(p); Byrne-a (on X-Men app. only) — 5.00
101-116: 101-Nighthawk(Ditko-a). 102-Doc Samson. 103-Ant-Man. 104-Hulk/Ka-Zar. 105-Hulk/Powerman/Iron Fist. 106-Capt. America. 107-She-Hulk. 108-Paladin; Dazzler cameo. 109-Dazzler; Paladin app. 110-Iron Man. 111-Devil-Slayer. 112-King Kull; last 50¢ issue. 113-Quasar. 114-Falcon.

Marvel Team-Up (1st series) #94 © MAR

Marvel Treasury #10 © MAR

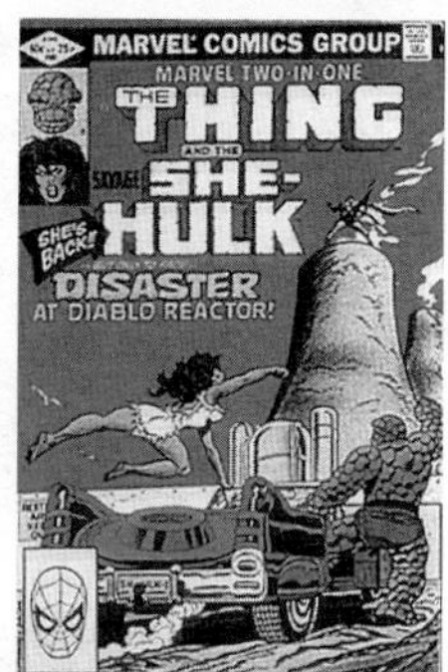

Marvel Two-In-One #88 © MAR

115-Thor. 116-Valkyrie 2.00
117-Wolverine-c/story 1.00 3.00 8.00
118-140,142-149: 118-Professor X; Wolverine app. (4 pgs.); X-Men cameo. 119-Gargoyle. 120-Dominic Fortune. 121-Human Torch. 122-Man-Thing. 123-Daredevil. 124-The Beast. 125-Tigra. 126-Hulk & Powerman/Son of Satan. 127-The Watcher. 128-Capt. America; Spider-Man/Capt. America photo-c. 129-The Vision. 130-Scarlet Witch. 131-Frogman. 132-Mr. Fantastic. 133-Fantastic Four. 134-Jack of Hearts. 135-Kitty Pryde; X-Men cameo. 136-Wonder Man. 137-Aunt May/Franklin Richards. 138-Sandman. 139-Nick Fury. 140-Black Widow. 142-Capt. Marvel. 143-Starfox. 144-Moon Knight. 145-Iron Man. 146-Nomad. 147-Human Torch; SpM back to old costume. 148-Thor. 149-Cannonball 2.00
141-Daredevil; SpM/Black Widow app. (Spidey in new black costume; ties w/ Amaz. S-M #252 for 1st black costume) 3.00
150-X-Men ($1.00, double-size); B. Smith-c 4.00
Annual 1 (1976)-Spider-Man/X-Men (early app.) 1.85 5.50 15.00
Annual 2 (1979)-Spider-Man/Hulk 5.00
Annuals 3-7: 3 (1980)-Hulk/Power Man/Machine Man/Iron Fist; Miller-c(p). 4 (1981)-SpM/Daredevil/Moon Knight/Power Man/Iron Fist; brief origins of each; Miller-c; Miller scripts on Daredevil. 5 (1982)-SpM/The Thing/Scarlet Witch/Dr. Strange/Quasar. 6 (1983)-SpM/New Mutants (early app.), Cloak & Dagger. 7(1984)-Alpha Flight; Byrne-c(i) 2.50

NOTE: ***Art Adams*** *c-141p.* ***Austin*** *a-79i; c-76i, 79i, 96i, 101i, 112i, 130i.* ***Bolle*** *a-9i.* ***Byrne*** *a(p)-53-55, 59-70, 75, 79, 100; c-68p, 70p, 72p, 75, 76p, 79p, 129i, 133i.* ***Colan*** *a-87p.* ***Ditko*** *a-101.* ***Kane*** *a(p)-4-6, 13, 14, 16-19, 23; c(p)-4, 13, 14, 17-19, 23, 25, 26, 32-35, 37, 41, 44, 45, 47, 53, 54.* ***Miller*** *a-100p; c-95p, 99p, 100p, 102p, 106.* ***Mooney*** *a-2i, 7i, 8, 10p, 11p, 16i, 24-31p, 72, 93i, Annual 5i.* ***Nasser*** *a-89p; c-101p.* ***Simonson*** *c-99i, 148.* ***Paul Smith*** *c-131, 132.* ***Starlin*** *c-27.* ***Sutton*** *a-93p. "H-T" means Human Torch; "SpM" means Spider-Man; "S-M" means Sub-Mariner.*

MARVEL TEAM-UP (2nd Series)
Marvel Comics: Sept, 1997 - No. 11, July, 1998 ($1.99)

1-11: 1-Spider-Man team-ups begin, Generation x-app. 2-Hercules-c/app.; two covers. 3-Sandman. 4-Man-Thing. 7-Blade. 8-Namor team-ups begin, Dr. Strange app. 9-Capt. America.10-Thing. 11-Iron Man 2.00

MARVEL TREASURY EDITION
Marvel Comics Group: 1974; #2, Dec, 1974 - #28, 1981 ($1.50/$2.50, 100 pgs., oversized, new-a &-r)(Also see Amazing Spider-Man, The, Marvel Spec. Ed. Feat.--, Savage Fists of Kung Fu, Superman Vs. , & 2001, A Space Odyssey)

1-Spectacular Spider-Man; story-r/Marvel Super-Heroes #14; Romita-c/a(r); G. Kane, Ditko-r; Green Goblin/Hulk-r 4.00 12.00 40.00
1-1,000 numbered copies signed by Stan Lee & John Romita on front-c & sold thru mail for $5.00; these were the1st 1,000 copies off the press 10.00 30.00 110.00
2-10: 2-Fantastic Four-r/F.F. 6,11,48-50(Silver Surfer). 3-The Mighty Thor-r/Thor #125-130. 4-Conan the Barbarian; Barry Smith-c/a(r)/Conan #11. 5-The Hulk (origin-r/Hulk #3). 6-Dr. Strange. 7-Mighty Avengers. 8-Giant Superhero Holiday Grab-Bag; Spider-Man, Hulk, Nick Fury. 9-Giant; Super-hero Team-up. 10-Thor; r/Thor #154-157 2.00 6.00 16.00
11-25,27: 11-Fantastic Four. 12-Howard the Duck (r/#H. the Duck #1 & G.S. Man-Thing #4,5) plus new Defenders story. 13-Giant Super-Hero Holiday Grab-Bag. 14-The Sensational Spider-Man; r/1st Morbius from Amazing S-M #101,102 plus #100 & r/Not Brand Echh #6. 15-Conan; B. Smith, Neal Adams-i; r/Conan #24. 16-The Defenders (origin) & Valkyrie; r/Defenders #1,4,13,14. 17-The Hulk. 18-The Astonishing Spider-Man; r/Spider-Man's 1st team-ups with Iron Fist, The X-Men, Ghost Rider & Werewolf by Night; inside back-c has photos from 1978 Spider-Man TV show. 19-Conan the Barbarian. 20-Hulk. 21-Fantastic Four. 22-Spider-Man. 23-Conan. 24-Rampaging Hulk. 25-Spider-Man vs. The Hulk. 27-Spider-Man 1.50 4.50 12.00
26-The Hulk; 6 pg. new Wolverine/Hercules-s 1.85 5.50 15.00
28-Spider-Man/Superman; (origin of each) 2.50 7.50 24.00

NOTE: *Reprints-2, 3, 5, 7-9, 13, 14, 16, 17.* ***Neal Adams*** *a(i)-6, 15.* ***Brunner*** *a-6, 12; c-6.* ***Buscema*** *a-15, 19, 28; c-28.* ***Colan*** *a-6r; c-12p.* ***Ditko*** *a-1, 6.* ***Gil Kane*** *c-16p.* ***Kirby*** *a-1-3, 5, 7, 9-11; c-7.* ***Perez*** *a-26.* ***Romita*** *c-1, 5.* ***B. Smith*** *a-4, 15, 19; c-4, 19.*

MARVEL TREASURY OF OZ FEATURING THE MARVELOUS LAND OF OZ
Marvel Comics Group: 1975 ($1.50, oversized) (See MGM's Marvelous...)

1-Buscema-a; Romita-c 2.00 6.00 16.00

GD2.0 FN6.0 NM9.4

MARVEL TREASURY SPECIAL (Also see 2001: A Space Odyssey)
Marvel Comics Group: 1974; 1976 ($1.50, oversized, 84 pgs.)

Vol. 1-Spider-Man, Torch, Sub-Mariner, Avengers "Giant Superhero Holiday Grab-Bag"; Wood, Colan/Everett, plus 2 Kirby-r; reprints Hulk vs. Thing from Fantastic Four #25,26 2.00 6.00 16.00
Vol. 1-... Featuring Captain America's Bicentennial Battles (6/76)-Kirby-a; B. Smith inks, 11 pgs. 2.50 7.50 20.00

MARVEL TRIPLE ACTION (See Giant-Size...)
Marvel Comics Group: Feb, 1972 - No. 24, Mar, 1975; No. 25, Aug, 1975 - No. 47, Apr, 1979

1-(25¢ giant, 52 pgs.)-Dr. Doom, Silver Surfer, The Thing begin, end #4 ('66 reprints from Fantastic Four) 1.85 45.50 15.00
2-5 1.00 3.00 8.00
6-10 5.00
11-47: 45-r/X-Men #45. 46-r/Avengers #53(X-Men) 3.00
29,30-(30¢-c variants, limited distribution)(5,7/76) 1.50 4.50 12.00

NOTE: *#5-44, 46, 47 reprint Avengers #11 thru ?. #40-r/Avengers #48(1st Black Knight).* ***Buscema*** *a(r)-35p, 36p, 38p, 39p, 41, 42, 43p, 44p, 46p, 47p.* ***Ditko*** *a-2r; c-47.* ***Kirby*** *a(r)-1-4p; c-1-4, 9-19, 22, 24, 29.* ***Starlin*** *c-7.* ***Tuska*** *a(r)-40p, 43i, 46i, 47i. #2 through #17 are 20¢-c.*

MARVEL TWO-IN-ONE (...Featuring ... #82? on; also see The Thing)
Marvel Comics Group: January, 1974 - No. 100, June, 1983

1-Thing team-ups begin; Man-Thing 4.00 12.00 40.00
2-6: 2-Sub-Mariner; last 20¢ issue. 3-Daredevil. 4-Capt. America. 5-Guardians of the Galaxy (9/74, 2nd app.?). 6-Dr. Strange (11/74) 1.50 4.50 12.00
7,9,10 1.00 3.00 8.00
8-Early Ghost Rider app. (3/75) 1.25 3.75 10.00
11-14,18-20: 13-Power Man. 14-Son of Satan (early app.). 18-Last 25¢ issue 5.00
15-17-(Regular 25¢ editions)(5-7/76) 17-Spider-Man. 5.00
15-17-(30¢-c variants, limited distribution) 2.00 6.00 16.00
21-27,29,31-40: 27-Deathlok. 9-Master of Kung Fu; Spider-Woman cameo. 31-33-Spider-Woman. 39-Vision 4.00
28-(Regular 30¢ edition)(6/77) 4.00
28-(35¢-c variant, limited distribution) 1.50 4.50 12.00
30-2nd full app. Spider-Woman (see Marvel Spotlight #32 for 1st app.) 2.40 6.00
41,42,44,45,47-49: 42-Capt. America. 45-Capt. Marvel 3.00
43,50,53,55-Byrne-a(p). 53-Quasar(7/79, 2nd app.) 4.00
46-Thing battles Hulk-c/story 2.40 6.00
51-The Beast, Nick Fury, Ms. Marvel; Miller-p 4.00
52-Moon Knight app. 3.00
54-Death of Deathlok; Byrne-a 1.00 3.00 8.00
56-74,76-79,81,82: 60-Intro. Impossible Woman. 68-Angel. 71-1st app. Maelstrom. 76-Iceman. 61-63: 61-Starhawk (from Guardians); "The Coming of Her" storyline begins,ends #63; cover similar to F.F. #67 (Him-c). 62-Moondragon; Thanos & Warlock cameo in flashback; Starhawk app. 63-Warlock; Warlock revived shortly; Starhawk & Moondragon app. 69-Guardians of the Galaxy 2.00
75-Avengers (52 pgs.) 3.00
80,83-100: 80-Ghost Rider. 83-Sasquatch. 84-Alpha Flight app. 90-Spider-Man. 93-Jocasta dies. 96-X-Men-c & cameo. 100-Double size, Byrne scripts 2.00
Annual 1 (1976, 52 pgs.)-Thing/Liberty Legion; Kirby-c 4.00
Annual 2(1977, 52 pgs.)-Thing/Spider-Man; 2nd death of Thanos; end of Thanos saga; Warlock app.; Starlin-c/a 1.75 5.25 14.00
Annual 3,4 (1978-79, 52 pgs.): 3-Nova. 4-Black Bolt 2.50
Annual 5-7 (1980-82, 52 pgs.): 5-Hulk. 6-1st app. American Eagle. 7-The Thing/Champion; Sasquatch, Colossus app.; X-Men cameo (1 pg.) 2.50

NOTE: ***Austin*** *c(i)-42, 54, 56, 58, 61, 63, 66.* ***John Buscema*** *a-30p, 45; c-30p.* ***Byrne*** *(p)-43, 50, 53-55; c-43, 53p, 56p, 98i, 99i.* ***Gil Kane*** *a-1p, 2p; c(p)-1-3, 9, 11, 14, 28.* ***Kirby*** *c-10, 12, 19p, 20, 25, 27.* ***Mooney*** *a-18i, 38i, 90i.* ***Nasser*** *a-70p.* ***Perez*** *a(p)-56-58, 60, 64, 65; c(p)-32, 33, 42, 50-52, 54, 55, 57, 58, 61-66, 70.* ***Roussos*** *a-Annual 1i.* ***Simonson*** *c-43i, 97p, Annual 6i.* ***Starlin*** *c-6, Annual 1.* ***Tuska*** *a-6p.*

MARVEL UNIVERSE (See Official Handbook Of The...)

MARVEL UNIVERSE
Marvel Comics: June, 1998 - No. 7, Dec, 1998 ($2.99/$1.99)

Mary Marvel Comics #28 © FAW

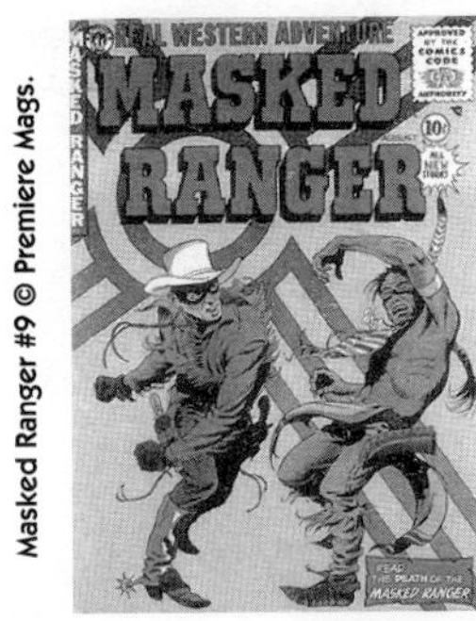

Masked Ranger #9 © Premiere Mags.

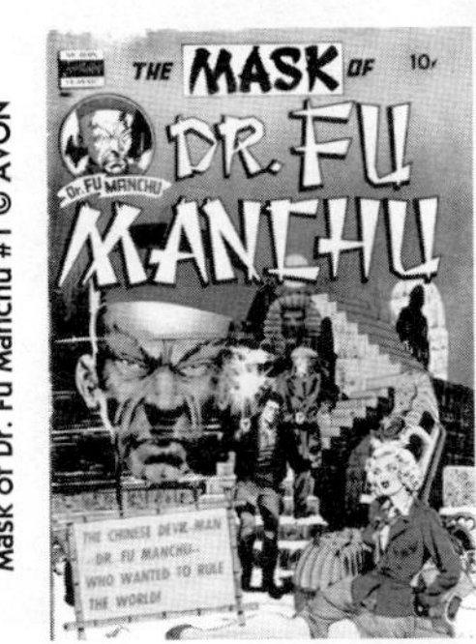

Mask of Dr. Fu Manchu #1 © AVON

GD2.0 FN6.0 NM9.4

1-($2.99)-Invaders stories from WW2; Stern-s 3.00
2-7-($1.99): 2-Two covers. 4-7-Monster Hunters; Manley-a/Stern-s 2.00

MARVEL VERSUS DC (See DC Versus Marvel) (Also see Amazon, Assassins, Bruce Wayne: Agent of S.H.I.E.L.D., Bullets & Bracelets, Doctor Strangefate, JLX, Legend of the Dark Claw, Magneto & The Magnetic Men, Speed Demon, Spider-Boy, Super Soldier, & X-Patrol)
Marvel Comics: No. 2, 1996 - No. 3, 1996 ($3.95, limited series)

2,3: 2-Peter David script. 3-Ron Marz script; Dan Jurgens-a(p). 1st app. of Super Soldier, Spider-Boy, Dr. Doomsday, Doctor Strangefate, The Dark Claw, Nightcreeper, Amazon, Wraith & others. Storyline continues in Amalgam books. 4.00

MARVEL X-MEN COLLECTION, THE
Marvel Comics: Jan, 1994 - No. 3, Mar, 1994 ($2.95, limited series)

1-3-r/X-Men trading cards by Jim Lee 3.00

MARVEL - YEAR IN REVIEW (Magazine)
Marvel Comics: 1989 - No. 3, 1991 (52 pgs.)

1-3: 1-Spider-Man-c by McFarlane. 2-Capt. America-c. 3-X-Men/Wolverine-c 5.00

MARVIN MOUSE
Atlas Comics (BPC): September, 1957

1-Everett-c/a; Maneely-a 11.00 34.00 80.00

MARY JANE & SNIFFLES (See Looney Tunes)
Dell Publishing Co.: No. 402, June, 1952 - No. 474, June, 1953

Four Color 402 (#1) 7.00 22.00 80.00
Four Color 474 6.40 19.00 70.00

MARY MARVEL COMICS (Monte Hale #29 on) (Also see Captain Marvel #18, Marvel Family, Shazam, & Wow Comics)
Fawcett Publications: Dec, 1945 - No. 28, Sept, 1948

1-Captain Marvel introduces Mary on-c; intro/origin Georgia Sivana 181.00 544.00 1450.00
2 71.00 214.00 570.00
3,4: 3-New logo 46.00 139.00 370.00
5-8: 8-Bulletgirl x-over in Mary Marvel; X-Mas-c 37.00 111.00 260.00
9,10 33.00 99.00 230.00
11-20 21.00 64.00 150.00
21-28: 28-Western-c 19.00 56.00 130.00

MARY POPPINS (See Movie Comics & Walt Disney Showcase No. 17)

MARY SHELLEY'S FRANKENSTEIN
Topps Comics: Oct, 1994 - Jan, 1995 ($2.95, limited series)

1-4-polybagged w/3 trading cards 3.00
1-4 ($2.50)-Newstand ed. 2.50

MARY WORTH (See Harvey Comics Hits #55 & Love Stories of...)
Argo: March, 1956 (Also see Romantic Picture Novelettes)

1 7.00 21.00 42.00

MASK (TV)
DC Comics: Dec, 1985 - No. 4, Mar, 1986; Feb, 1987 - No. 9, Oct, 1987

1-4; 1-9 (2nd series)-Sat. morning TV show. 2.00

MASK, THE (Also see Mayhem)
Dark Horse Comics: Aug, 1991 - No. 4, Oct, 1991; No. 0, Dec, 1991 ($2.50, 36 pgs., limited series)

1-4: 1-1st app. Lt. Kellaway as The Mask (see Dark Horse Presents #10 for 1st app.) 5.00
0-(12/91, B&W, 56 pgs.)-r/Mayhem #1-4 4.00

...: HUNT FOR GREEN OCTOBER July, 1995 - Oct, 1995 ($2.50, lim. series)
1-4-Evan Dorkin scripts 2.50

.../ MARSHALL LAW Feb, 1998 - No. 2, Mar, 1998 ($2.95, lim. series)
1,2-Mills-s/O'Neill-a 3.00

...: OFFICIAL MOVIE ADAPTATION July, 1994 - Aug, 1994 ($2.50, lim. series)
1,2 2.50

GD2.0 FN6.0 NM9.4

... RETURNS Oct, 1992 - No. 4, Mar, 1993 ($2.50, limited series)
1-4 4.00

... SOUTHERN DISCOMFORT Mar, 1996 - No. 4, July, 1996 ($2.50, lim. series)
1-4 2.50

... STRIKES BACK Feb, 1995 - No. 5, Jun, 1995 ($2.50, limited series)
1-5 2.50

... SUMMER VACATION July, 1995 ($10.95, one shot, hard-c)
1-nn-Rick Geary-c/a 11.00

... TOYS IN THE ATTIC Aug, 1998 - No. 4, Nov, 1998 ($2.95, limited series)
1-4-Fingerman-s 3.00

... VIRTUAL SURREALITY July, 1997 ($2.95, one shot)
nn-Mignola, Aragonés, and others-s/a 3.00

... WORLD TOUR Dec, 1995 - No. 4, Mar, 1996 ($2.50, limited series)
1-4: 3-X & Ghost-c/app. 2.50

MASK COMICS
Rural Home Publ.: Feb-Mar, 1945 - No. 2, Apr-May, 1945; No. 2, Fall, 1945

1-Classic L. B. Cole Satan-c/a; Palais-a 250.00 750.00 2000.00
2-(Scarce)-Classic L. B. Cole Satan-c; Black Rider, The Boy Magician, & The Collector app. 162.00 487.00 1300.00
2-(Fall, 1945)-No publ.-same as regular #2; L. B. Cole-c 125.00 375.00 1000.00

MASKED BANDIT, THE
Avon Periodicals: 1952

nn-Kinstler-a 15.00 45.00 105.00

MASKED MAN, THE
Eclipse Comics: 12/84 - #10, 4/86; #11, 10/87; #12, 4/88 ($1.75/$2.00, color/B&W #9 on, Baxter paper)

1-12: 1-Origin retold. 3-Origin Aphid-Man; begin $2.00-c 2.00

MASKED MARVEL (See Keen Detective Funnies)
Centaur Publications: Sept, 1940 - No. 3, Dec, 1940

1-The Masked Marvel begins 159.00 478.00 1275.00
2,3: 2-Gustavson, Tarpe Mills-a 106.00 319.00 850.00

MASKED RAIDER, THE (Billy The Kid #9 on; Frontier Scout, Daniel Boone #10-13) (Also see Blue Bird)
Charlton Comics: June, 1955 - No. 8, July, 1957; No. 14, Aug, 1958 - No. 30, June, 1961

1-Masked Raider & Talon the Golden Eagle begin; painted-c 11.00 33.00 75.00
2 7.00 21.00 42.00
3-8,15: 8-Billy The Kid app. 15-Williamson-a, 7 pgs. 5.00 15.00 30.00
14,16-30: 22-Rocky Lane app. 4.00 12.00 24.00

MASKED RANGER
Premier Magazines: Apr, 1954 - No. 9, Aug, 1955

1-The Masked Ranger, his horse Streak, & The Crimson Avenger (origin) begin, end #9; Woodbridge/Frazetta-a 40.00 120.00 290.00
2,3 12.00 36.00 85.00
4-8-All Woodbridge-a. 5-Jesse James by Woodbridge. 6-Billy The Kid by Woodbridge. 7-Wild Bill Hickok by Woodbridge. 8-Jim Bowie's Life Story 13.50 41.00 95.00
9-Torres-a; Wyatt Earp by Woodbridge; Says Death of Masked Ranger on-c 14.00 43.00 100.00

NOTE: *Check a-1. Woodbridge c/a-1, 4-9.*

MASK OF DR. FU MANCHU, THE (See Dr. Fu Manchu)
Avon Periodicals: 1951

1-Sax Rohmer adapt.; Wood-c/a (26 pgs.); Hollingsworth-a 87.00 262.00 700.00

MASK OF ZORRO, THE
Image Comics: Aug, 1998 - No. 4, Dec, 1998 ($2.95, limited series)

1-4-Movie adapt. Photo variant-c 3.00

MASQUE OF THE RED DEATH (See Movie Classics)

Master Comics #23 © FAW

Master Comics #107 © FAW

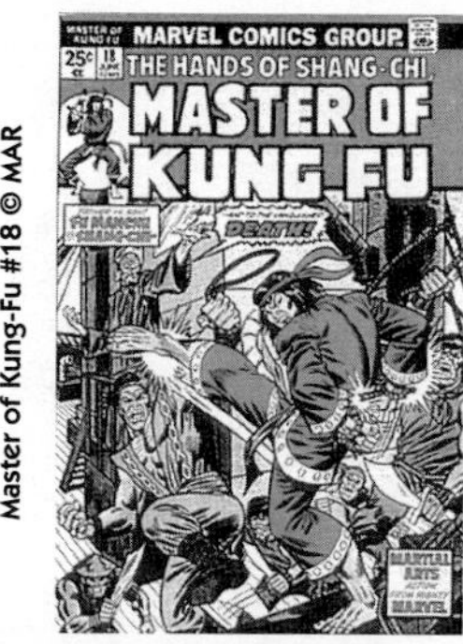

Master of Kung-Fu #18 © MAR

MASTER COMICS (Combined with Slam Bang Comics #7 on)
Fawcett Publications: Mar, 1940 - No. 133, Apr, 1953 (No. 1-6: oversized issues) (#1-3: 15¢, 52 pgs.; #4-6: 10¢, 36 pgs.; #7-Begin 68 pg. issues)

GD2.0 FN6.0 VF8.0 NM9.4

1-Origin & 1st app. Master Man; The Devil's Dagger, El Carim, Master of Magic, Rick O'Say, Morton Murch, White Rajah, Shipwreck Roberts, Frontier Marshal, Streak Sloan, Mr. Clue begin (all features end #6) 700.00 2100.00 4200.00 7000.00

GD2.0 FN6.0 NM9.4

2 206.00 318.00 1650.00
3-6: 6-Last Master Man 159.00 477.00 1275.00
NOTE: *#1-6 rarely found in near mint to mint condition due to large-size format.*
7-(10/40)-Bulletman, Zoro, the Mystery Man (ends #22), Lee Granger, Jungle King, & Buck Jones begin; only app. The War Bird & Mark Swift & the Time Retarder; Zoro, Lee Granger, Jungle King & Mark Swift all continue from Slam Bang; Bulletman moves from Nickel 275.00 825.00 2200.00
8-The Red Gaucho (ends #13), Captain Venture (ends #22) & The Planet Princess begin 144.00 432.00 1150.00
9,10: 10-Lee Granger ends 112.00 336.00 900.00
11-Origin & 1st app. Minute-Man (2/41) 250.00 750.00 2000.00
12 125.00 375.00 1000.00
13-Origin & 1st app. Bulletgirl; Hitler-c 194.00 582.00 1550.00
14-16: 14-Companions Three begins, ends #31 103.00 309.00 825.00
17-20: 17-Raboy-a on Bulletman begins. 20-Captain Marvel cameo app. in Bulletman 97.00 291.00 775.00

GD2.0 FN6.0 VF8.0 NM9.4

21-(12/41; Scarce)-Captain Marvel & Bulletman team up against Capt. Nazi; origin & 1st app. Capt. Marvel Jr's most famous nemesis Captain Nazi who will cause creation of Capt. Marvel Jr. in Whiz #25. Part I of trilogy origin of Capt. Marvel Jr.; 1st Mac Raboy-c for Fawcett; Capt. Nazi-c 460.00 1380.00 2760.00 4600.00
22-(1/42)-Captain Marvel Jr. moves over from Whiz #25 & teams up with Bulletman against Captain Nazi; part III of trilogy origin of Capt. Marvel Jr. & his 1st cover and adventure 420.00 1260.00 2520.00 4200.00

GD2.0 FN6.0 NM9.4

23-Capt. Marvel Jr. c/stories begin (1st solo story); fights Capt. Nazi by himself. 275.00 825.00 2200.00
24,25 94.00 282.00 750.00
26-28,30-Captain Marvel Jr. vs. Capt. Nazi. 30-Flag-c 84.00 252.00 675.00
29-Hitler & Hirohito-c 97.00 291.00 775.00
31-33,35: 32-Last El Carim & Buck Jones; intro Balbo, the Boy Magician in El Carim story; classic Eagle-c by Raboy. 33-Balbo, the Boy Magician (ends #47), Hopalong Cassidy (ends #49) begins 62.00 186.00 500.00
34-Capt. Marvel Jr. vs. Capt. Nazi-c/story 69.00 207.00 550.00
36-40: 40-Flag-c 56.00 168.00 450.00
41-(8/43)-Bulletman, Capt. Marvel Jr. & Bulletgirl x-over in Minute-Man; only app.Crime Crusaders Club (Capt. Marvel Jr., Minute-Man, Bulletman & Bulletgirl) 62.00 186.00 500.00
42-47,49: 47-Hitler becomes Corpl. Hitler Jr. 49-Last Minute-Man 40.00 120.00 280.00
48-Intro. Bulletboy; Capt. Marvel cameo in Minute-Man 40.00 120.00 325.00
50-Intro Radar & Nyoka the Jungle Girl & begin series (5/44); Radar also intro in Captain Marvel #35 (same date); Capt. Marvel x-over in Radar; origin Radar; Capt. Marvel & Capt. Marvel, Jr. introduce Radar on-c 40.00 120.00 290.00
51-58 21.00 62.00 145.00
59-62: Nyoka serial "Terrible Tiara" in all; 61-Capt. Marvel Jr. 1st meets Uncle Marvel 24.00 71.00 165.00
63-80 17.00 49.00 115.00
81,83-87,89-91,95-99: 88-Hopalong Cassidy begins (ends #94). 95-Tom Mix begins (ends #133) 14.00 43.00 100.00
82,88,92-94-Krigstein-a 16.00 47.00 110.00
100 15.00 45.00 105.00
101-106-Last Bulletman 13.50 41.00 95.00
107-131 12.00 36.00 85.00
132-B&W and color illos in **POP** 13.00 39.00 90.00
133-Bill Battle app. 18.00 54.00 125.00
NOTE: ***Mac Raboy*** *a-15-39, 40(part), 42, 58. c-21-49, 51, 52, 54, 56, 58, 68(part), 69(part). Bulletman c-7-11, 13(half), 15, 18(part), 19, 20, 21(w/Capt. Marvel & Capt. Nazi), 22(w/Capt. Marvel, Jr.). Capt. Marvel, Jr. c-23-133. Master Man c-1-6. Minute Man c-12, 13(half), 14, 16, 17, 18(part).*

MASTER DARQUE
Acclaim Comics (Valiant): Feb, 1998 ($3.95)

1-Manco-a/Christina Z.-s 4.00

MASTER DETECTIVE
Super Comics: 1964 (Reprints)

17-r/Criminals on the Loose V4 #2; r/Young King Cole #?; McWilliams-r 1.25 3.75 10.00

MASTER OF KUNG FU (Formerly Special Marvel Edition; see Deadly Hands of Kung Fu & Giant-Size...)
Marvel Comics Group: No. 17, April, 1974 - No. 125, June, 1983

17-Starlin-a; intro Black Jack Tarr; 3rd Shang-Chi (ties w/Deadly Hands #1) 2.25 6.75 18.00
18-20: 19-Man-Thing-c/story 1.25 3.75 10.00
21-23,25-30 2.40 6.00
24-Starlin, Simonson-a 1.00 3.00 8.00
31-50: 33-1st Leiko Wu. 43-Last 25¢ issue 4.00
40-42-(30¢-c variants, limited distribution)(5-7/76) 1.50 4.50 12.00
51-99 3.50
100118,125-Double size 4.00
101-117,119-124 3.00
Annual 1(4/76)-Iron Fist app. 1.10 3.30 9.00
NOTE: ***Austin*** *c-63i, 74i.* ***Buscema*** *c-44p.* ***Gulacy*** *a(p)-18-20, 22, 25, 29-31, 33-35, 38, 39, 40(p&i), 42-50, 53r(#20); c-51, 55, 64, 67.* ***Gil Kane*** *c(p)-20, 38, 39, 42, 45, 59, 63.* ***Nebres*** *c-73i.* ***Starlin*** *a-17p, 24; c-54.* ***Sutton*** *a-42i. #53 reprints #20.*

MASTER OF KUNG-FU: BLEEDING BLACK
Marvel Comics: Feb, 1991 ($2.95, 84 pgs., one-shot)

1-The Return of Shang-Chi 3.00

MASTER OF THE WORLD
Dell Publishing Co.: No. 1157, July, 1961

Four Color 1157-Movie 4.50 13.50 50.00

MASTERS OF TERROR (Magazine)
Marvel Comics Group: July, 1975 - No. 2, Sept, 1975 (B&W) (All reprints)

1-Brunner, Barry Smith-a; Morrow/Steranko-c; Starlin-a(p); Gil Kane-a 1.50 4.50 12.00
2-Reese, Kane, Mayerik-a; Adkins/Steranko-c 1.25 3.75 10.00

MASTERS OF THE UNIVERSE (See DC Comics Presents #47 for 1st app.)
DC Comics: Dec, 1982 - No. 3, Feb, 1983 (Mini-series)

1-3: 2-Origin He-Man & Ceril 2.00
NOTE: ***Alcala*** *a-1i,, 2i.* ***Tuska*** *a-1-3p; c-1-3p. #2 has 75 & 95 cent cover price.*

MASTERS OF THE UNIVERSE (Comic Album)
Western Publishing Co.: 1984 (8-1/2x11", $2.95, 64 pgs.)

11362-Based on Mattel toy & cartoon 1.00 3.00 8.00

MASTERS OF THE UNIVERSE
Star Comics/Marvel #7 on: May 1986 - No. 13, May, 1988 (75¢/$1.00)

1-11: 8-Begin $1.00-c 3.00
12-Death of He-Man (1st Marvel app.) 4.00
13-Return of He-Man & death of Skeletor 4.00
The Motion Picture (11/87, $2.00)-Tuska-p 2.00

MASTERWORKS SERIES OF GREAT COMIC BOOK ARTISTS, THE
Sea Gate Dist./DC Comics: May, 1983 - No. 3, Dec, 1983 (Baxter paper)

1-3: 1,2-Shining Knight by Frazetta r-/Adventure. 2-Tomahawk by Frazetta-r. 3-Wrightson-c/a(r) 3.00

MATT SLADE GUNFIGHTER (Kid Slade Gunfighter #5 on; See Western Gunfighters)
Atlas Comics (SPI): May, 1956 - No. 4, Nov, 1956

Maverick #8 © MAR

Maze Agency #3 © Mike W. Barr

MD #3 © WMG

GD2.0 FN6.0 NM9.4

1-Intro Matt & horse Eagle; Williamson/Torres-a 19.00 56.00 130.00
2-Williamson-a 11.00 33.00 75.00
3,4 10.00 30.00 60.00
NOTE: ***Maneely*** *a-1, 3, 4; c-1, 2, 4.* ***Roth*** *a-2-4.* ***Severin*** *a-1, 3, 4.* ***Maneely*** *c/a-1.*

MAVERICK (TV)
Dell Publishing Co.: No. 892, 4/58 - No. 19, 4-6/62 (All have photo-c)
Four Color 892 (#1)-James Garner photo-c begin 25.00 75.00 275.00
Four Color 930,945,962,980,1005 (6-8/59): 945-James Garner/Jack Kelly photo-c begin 10.00 30.00 110.00
7 (10-12/59) - 14: Last Garner/Kelly-c 8.00 23.00 85.00
15-18: Jack Kelly/Roger Moore photo-c 6.50 19.50 72.00
19-Jack Kelly photo-c 6.50 19.50 72.00

MAVERICK (See X-Men)
Marvel Comics: Jan, 1997 ($2.95, one-shot)
1-Hama-s 3.00

MAVERICK (See X-Men)
Marvel Comics: Sept, 1997 - No. 12, Aug, 1998 ($2.99/$1.99)
1-12: 1-($2.99)-Wraparound-c. 2-Two covers. 4-Wolverine. 6,7-Sabretooth app. 12-($2.99) Battles Omega Red 3.00

MAVERICK MARSHAL
Charlton Comics: Nov, 1958 - No. 7, May, 1960
1 5.35 16.00 32.00
2-7 4.00 11.00 22.00

MAVERICKS
Daggar Comics Group: Jan, 1994 - No. 5, 1994 (#1-$2.75, #2-5-$2.50)
1-5: 1-Bronze. 1-Gold. 1-Silver 2.75

MAX BRAND (See Silvertip)

MAXIMAGE
Image Comics (Extreme Studios): Dec, 1995 - No. 7, June 1996 ($2.50)
1-7: 1-Liefeld-c. 2-Extreme Destroyer Pt. 2; polybagged w/card. 4-Angela & Glory-c/app. 2.50

MAXX (Also see Darker Image, Primer #5, & Friends of Maxx)
Image Comics (I Before E): Mar, 1993 - Present ($1.95)
1/2 1.25 3.75 10.00
1/2 (Gold) 20.00
1-Sam Kieth-c/a/scripts 4.00
1-Glow-in-the-dark variant 1.50 4.50 12.00
1-"3-D Edition" (1/98, $4.95) plus new back-up story 5.00
2-12: 6-Savage Dragon cameo(1 pg.). 7,8-Pitt-c & story 2.50
13-16 2.50
17-35: 21-Alan Moore-s 2.00

MAYA (See Movie Classics)
Gold Key: Mar, 1968
1 (10218-803)(TV) 2.50 7.50 20.00

MAYHEM
Dark Horse Comics: May, 1989 - No. 4, Sept, 1989 ($2.50, B&W, 52 pgs.)
1- 4-part Stanley Ipkiss/Mask story begins; Mask-c 1.25 3.75 10.00
2-4: 2-Mask 1/2 back-c. 4-Mask-c 1.10 3.30 9.00

MAZE AGENCY, THE
Comico/Innovation Publ. #8 on: Dec, 1988 - No. 20, 1991 ($1.95-$2.50, color)
1-20: 9-Ellery Queen app. 7 ($2.50)-Last Comico issue 2.50
Annual 1 (1990, $2.75)-Ploog-c; Spirit tribute ish 2.75
Special 1 (1989, $2.75)-Staton-p (Innovation) 2.75

MAZE AGENCY, THE (Vol. 2)
Caliber Comics: July, 1997 - Present ($2.95, B&W)
1-3: 1-Barr-s/Gonzales-a(p). 3-Hughes-c 3.00

MAZIE (...& Her Friends) (See Flat-Top, Mortie, Stevie & Tastee-Freez)
Mazie Comics(Magazine Publ.)/Harvey Publ. No. 13-on: 1953 - #12, 1954; #13, 12/54 - #22, 9/56; #23, 9/57 - #28, 8/58

GD2.0 FN6.0 NM9.4

1-(Teen-age)-Stevie's girlfriend 7.50 22.50 45.00
2 4.00 11.00 22.00
3-10 3.60 9.00 18.00
11-28 2.40 6.00 12.00

MAZIE
Nation Wide Publishers: 1950 - No. 7, 1951 (5¢) (5x7-1/4"-miniature)(52 pgs.)
1-Teen-age 14.00 43.00 100.00
2-7 8.35 25.00 50.00

MAZINGER (See First Comics Graphic Novel #17)

'MAZING MAN
DC Comics: Jan, 1986 - No. 12, Dec, 1986
1-12: 7,8-Hembeck-a. 12-Dark Knight part-c by Miller 2.00
Special 1 ('87), 2 (4/88), 3 ('90)-All $2.00, 52pgs. 2.00

McHALE'S NAVY (TV) (See Movie Classics)
Dell Publ. Co.: May-July, 1963 - No. 3, Nov-Jan, 1963-64 (All have photo-c)
1 5.00 15.00 55.00
2,3 4.00 12.00 45.00

McKEEVER & THE COLONEL (TV)
Dell Publishing Co.: Feb-Apr, 1963 - No. 3, Aug-Oct, 1963
1-Photo-c 5.00 15.00 55.00
2,3 3.80 11.50 40.00

McLINTOCK (See Movie Comics)

MD
E. C. Comics: Apr-May, 1955 - No. 5, Dec-Jan, 1955-56
1-Not approved by code; Craig-c 10.00 30.00 100.00
2-5 7.50 22.50 75.00
NOTE: ***Crandall, Evans, Ingels, Orlando*** *art in all issues;* ***Craig*** *c-1-5.*

MD
Russ Cochran/Gemstone Publishing: Sept, 1999 - No. 5 ($2.50)
1-3-Reprints original EC series 2.50

M.D. GEIST
CPM Comics: 1995 - No. 3, 1995 (Limited series)
1-3 3.00

M.D. GEIST DATA ALBUM
CPM Comics: June, 1996 ($9.95, trade paperback)
1 10.00

M.D. GEIST: GROUND ZERO
CPM Comics: Mar, 1996 - No. 3, May, 1996 ($2.95, limited series)
1-3 3.00

MEASLES
Fantagraphics Books: Christmas 1998 - Present ($2.95, B&W, quarterly)
1-4-Anthology: 1-Venus-s by Hernandez 3.00

MEAT CAKE
Iconographix: 1992 (B&W)
1 2.00

MEAT CAKE
Fantagraphics Books: No. 1, Oct, 1993 - Present (B&W)
0-8: 3-Sal Buscema-a. 0-(1996)-r/Meat Cake #1 from Iconographix. 2.50
9-($3.95) Alan Moore-s 4.00

MECHA (Also see Mayhem)
Dark Horse Comics: June, 1987 - No. 6, 1988 ($1.50/$1.95, color/B&W)
1-6: 1,2 ($1.95, color), 3,4-($1.75, B&W), 5,6-($1.50, B&W) 2.00

MECHANIC, THE
Image Comics: 1998 ($5.95, one-shot, squarebound)
1-Chiodo-painted art; Peterson-s 2.40 6.00
1-($10.00) DF Alternate Cover Ed. 10.00

MECHA SPECIAL

Meet Miss Bliss #1 © MAR

Mega Dragon & Tiger #1 © Jade Dynasty

Menace #7 © ATL

GD2.0 FN6.0 NM9.4 | GD2.0 FN6.0 NM9.4

Dark Horse Comics: May, 1995 ($2.95, one-shot)
1 — 3.00

MEDAL FOR BOWZER, A
American Visuals: 1966 (8 pgs.)
nn-Eisner-c/script — 25.00 65.00 215.00

MEDAL OF HONOR COMICS
A. S. Curtis: Spring, 1946
1-War stories — 11.00 33.00 75.00

MEDAL OF HONOR SPECIAL
Dark Horse Comics: 1994 ($2.50, one-shot)
1-Kubert-c/a (first story) — 2.50

MEDIA STARR
Innovation Publ.: July, 1989 - No. 3, Sept, 1989 ($1.95, mini-series, 28pgs.)
1-3: Deluxe format — 2.00

MEDIEVAL SPAWN/WITCHBLADE
Image Comics (Top Cow Productions): May, 1996 - No. 3, June, 1996 ($2.95, limited series)
1-3-Garth Ennis scripts in all — 2.40 6.00
1-Platinum foil-c (500 copies from Pittsburgh Con) — 35.00
1-Gold — 10.00
1-ETM Exclusive Edition; gold foil logo — 7.00
TPB ($9.95) r/#1-3 — 10.00

MEET ANGEL (Formerly Angel & the Ape)
National Periodical Publications: No. 7, Nov-Dec, 1969
7-Wood-a(i) — 2.25 6.75 18.00

MEET CORLISS ARCHER (Radio/Movie)(My Life #4 on)
Fox Features Syndicate: Mar, 1948 - No. 3, July, 1948
1-(Teen-age)-Feldstein-c/a; headlight-c — 65.00 195.00 520.00
2-Feldstein-c only — 50.00 150.00 400.00
3-Part Feldstein-c only — 45.00 135.00 360.00
NOTE: *No. 1-3 used in Seduction of the Innocent, pg. 39.*

MEET HERCULES (See Three Stooges)

MEET MERTON
Toby Press: Dec, 1953 - No. 4, June, 1954
1-(Teen-age)-Dave Berg-c/a — 7.50 22.50 45.00
2-Dave Berg-c/a — 4.25 13.00 28.00
3,4-Dave Berg-c/a — 4.25 13.00 26.00
I.W. Reprint #9, Super Reprint #11('63), 18 — 1.10 3.30 9.00

MEET MISS BLISS (Becomes Stories Of Romance #5 on)
Atlas Comics (LMC): May, 1955 - No. 4, Nov, 1955
1-Al Hartley-c/a — 12.00 36.00 85.00
2-4 — 8.35 25.00 50.00

MEET MISS PEPPER (Formerly Lucy, The Real Gone Gal)
St. John Publishing Co.: No. 5, April, 1954 - No. 6, June, 1954
5-Kubert/Maurer-a — 20.00 60.00 140.00
6-Kubert/Maurer-a; Kubert-c — 16.00 47.00 110.00

MEGA DRAGON & TIGER
Image Comics: Mar, 1999 - Present ($2.95)
1-5-Tony Wong-s/a — 3.00

MEGAHURTZ
Image Comics: Aug, 1997 - No. 3, Oct, 1997 ($2.95, B&W)
1-3-St. Pierre-s — 3.00

MEGALITH DEATHWATCH 2000 (Megalith #3 on)
Continuity: Apr, 1993 - No. 9, Mar, 1994 ($2.50)
0-Foil-c; no c-price, giveaway; Adams plot — 3.00
1-9: 1-3-Bagged w/card: 1-Gatefold-c by Nebres; Adams plot. 2-Fold-out-c; Adamsplot. 3-Indestructible-c. 4-9-Embossed-c: 4-Adams/Nebres-c; Adams part-i. 5-Sienkiewicz-i. 6-Adams part-i. 7-Adams-c(p); Adams plot — 3.00

MEGATON (A super hero)
Megaton Publ.: Nov, 1983; No. 2, Oct, 1985 - No. 8, Aug, 1987 (B&W)
1-($2.00, 68 pgs.)-Erik Larsen's 1st pro work; Vanguard by Larsen begins (1st app.), ends #4; 1st app. Megaton, Berzerker, & Ethrian; Guice-c/a(p); Gustovich-a(p) in #1,2 — 1.00 3.00 8.00
2-($2.00, 68 pgs.)-The Dragon cameo (1 pg.) by Larsen (later The Savage Dragon in Image Comics); Guice-c/a(p) — 5.00
3-(44 pgs.)-1st full app. Savage Dragon-c/story by Larsen; 1st comic book work by Angel Medina (pin-up) — 1.50 4.50 12.00
4-(52 pgs.)-2nd full app. Savage Dragon by Larsen; 4,5-Wildman by Grass Green — 1.10 3.30 9.00
5-1st Liefeld published-a (inside f/c, 6/86) — 5.00
6,7: 6-Larsen-c — 3.00
8-1st Liefeld story-a (7 pg. super hero story) plus 1 pg. Youngblood ad — 5.00
...Explosion (6/87, 16 pg. color giveaway)-1st app. Youngblood by Rob Liefeld (2 pg. spread); shows Megaton heroes — 1.85 5.50 15.00
...Holiday Special 1 (1994, $2.95, color, 40 pgs., publ. by Entity Comics)-Gold foil logo; bagged w/Kelley Jones card; Vanguard, Megaton plus shows unpublished-c to 1987 Youngblood #1 by Liefeld/Ordway — 3.00
NOTE: *Copies of Megaton Explosion were also released in early 1992 all signed by Rob Liefeld and were made available to retailers.*

MEGATON MAN (See Don Simpson's Bizarre Heroes)
Kitchen Sink Enterprises: Nov, 1984 - No. 10, 1986
1-10, 1-2nd printing (1989) — 2.00
...Meets The Uncategorizable X-Thems 1 (4/89, $2.00) — 2.00

MEGATON MAN: BOMB SHELL
Image Comics: Jul, 1999 - No. 2 ($2.95, B&W, mini-series)
1-Reprints stories from Megaton Man internet site — 3.00

MEGATON MAN: HARD COPY
Image Comics: Feb, 1999 - No. 2, Apr, 1999 ($2.95, B&W, mini-series)
1,2-Reprints stories from Megaton Man internet site — 3.00

MEGATON MAN VS. FORBIDDEN FRANKENSTEIN
Fiasco Comics: Apr, 1996 ($2.95, B&W, one-shot)
1-Intro The Tomb Team (Forbidden Frankenstein, Drekula, Bride of the Monster, & Moon Wolf). — 3.00

MEL ALLEN SPORTS COMICS (The Voice of the Yankees)
Standard Comics: No. 5, Nov, 1949; No. 6, June, 1950
5(#1 on inside)-Tuska-a — 21.00 64.00 150.00
6(#2)-Lou Gehrig story — 14.00 43.00 100.00

MELTING POT
Kitchen Sink Press: Dec, 1993 - No. 4, Sept, 1994 ($2.95)
1-4: Bisley-painted-c — 3.00

MELVIN MONSTER
Dell Publishing Co.: Apr-June, 1965 - No. 10, Oct, 1969
1-By John Stanley — 10.00 30.00 110.00
2-10-All by Stanley. #10-r/#1 — 7.00 20.00 75.00

MELVIN THE MONSTER (See Peter, the Little Pest & Dexter The Demon #7)
Atlas Comics (HPC): July, 1956 - No. 6, July, 1957
1-Maneely-c/a — 12.00 36.00 85.00
2-6: 4-Maneely-c/a — 9.15 27.00 55.00

MENACE
Atlas Comics (HPC): Mar, 1953 - No. 11, May, 1954
1-Horror & sci/fi stories begin; Everett-c/a — 60.00 180.00 480.00
2-Post-atom bomb disaster by Everett; anti-Communist propaganda/torture scenes; Sinnott sci/fi story "Rocket to the Moon" — 40.00 120.00 325.00
3,4,6-Everett-a. 4-Sci/fi story "Escape to the Moon". 6-Romita sci/fi story "Science Fiction" — 36.00 107.00 250.00
5-Origin & 1st app. The Zombie by Everett (reprinted in Tales of the Zombie #1)(7/53); 5-Sci/fi story "Rocket Ship" — 47.00 141.00 375.00
7,8,10,11: 7-Frankenstein story. 8-End of world story; Heath 3-D art(3 pgs.). 10-H-Bomb panels — 26.00 79.00 185.00

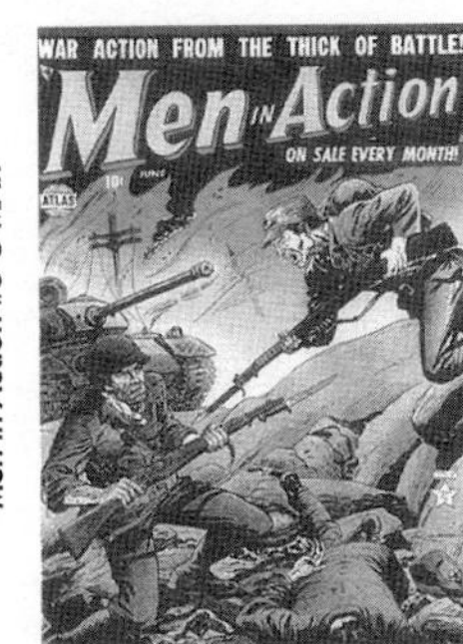

Men in Action #3 © MAR

Men's Adventures #28 © MAR

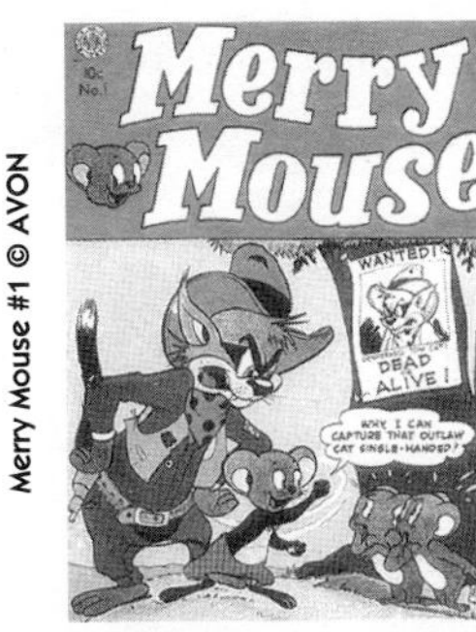

Merry Mouse #1 © AVON

GD2.0 FN6.0 NM9.4

9-Everett-a r-in Vampire Tales #1 30.00 90.00 210.00
NOTE: **Brodsky** *c-7, 8, 11.* **Colan** *a-6; c-9.* **Everett** *a-1-6, 9; c-1-6.* **Heath** *a-1-8; c-10.* **Katz** *a-11.* **Maneely** *a-3, 5, 7-9.* **Powell** *a-11.* **Romita** *a-3, 6, 8, 11.* **Shelly** *a-10.* **Shores** *a-7.* **Sinnott** *a-2, 7.* **Tuska** *a-1, 2, 5.*

MENACE
Awesome-Hyperwerks: Nov, 1998 ($2.50)
1-Jada Pinkett Smith-s/Fraga-a 2.50

MEN AGAINST CRIME (Formerly Mr. Risk; Hand of Fate #8 on)
Ace Magazines: No. 3, Feb, 1951 - No. 7, Oct, 1951
3-Mr. Risk app. 10.00 30.00 65.00
4-7: 4-Colan-a; entire book-r as Trapped! #4. 5-Meskin-a 6.35 19.00 38.00

MEN, GUNS, & CATTLE (See Classics Illustrated Special Issue)

MEN IN ACTION (Battle Brady #10 on)
Atlas Comics (IPS): April, 1952 - No. 9, Dec, 1952 (War stories)
1-Berg, Reinman-a 14.00 43.00 100.00
2 10.00 30.00 60.00
3-6,8,9: 3-Heath-c/a 7.50 22.50 45.00
7-Krigstein-a; Heath-c 10.00 30.00 65.00
NOTE: **Brodsky** *c-1, 4-6.* **Maneely** *c-5.* **Pakula** *a-1, 6.* **Robinson** *c-8.* **Shores** *c-9.*

MEN IN ACTION
Ajax/Farrell Publications: April, 1957 - No. 9, 1958
1 8.35 25.00 50.00
2 4.25 13.00 28.00
3-9 4.00 12.00 24.00

MEN IN BLACK, THE (1st series)
Aircel Comics (Malibu): Jan, 1990 - No. 3 Mar, 1990 ($2.25, B&W, lim. series)
1-Cunningham-s/a in all 4.00 12.00 40.00
2,3 2.50 7.50 25.00
Graphic Novel (Jan, 1991) r/#1-3 2.50 7.50 20.00

MEN IN BLACK (2nd series)
Aircel Comics (Malibu): May, 1991 - No. 3, Jul, 1991 ($2.50, B&W, lim. series)
1-Cunningham-s/a in all 2.50 7.50 20.00
2,3 1.00 3.00 8.00

MEN IN BLACK: FAR CRY
Marvel Comics: Aug, 1997 ($3.99, color, one-shot)
1-Cunningham-s 4.00

MEN IN BLACK: RETRIBUTION
Marvel Comics: Dec, 1997 ($3.99, color, one-shot)
1-Cunningham-s; continuation of the movie 4.00

MEN IN BLACK: THE MOVIE
Marvel Comics: Oct, 1997 ($3.99, one-shot, movie adaption)
1-Cunningham-s 4.00

MEN INTO SPACE
Dell Publishing Co.: No. 1083, Feb-Apr, 1960
Four Color 1083-Anderson-a, photo-c 4.50 13.50 50.00

MEN OF BATTLE (Also see New Men of Battle)
Catechetical Guild: V1#5, March, 1943 (Hardcover)
V1#5-Topix reprints 4.00 11.00 22.00

MEN OF WAR
DC Comics, Inc.: August, 1977 - No. 26, March, 1980 (#9,10: 44 pgs.)
1-Enemy Ace, Gravedigger (origin #1,2) begin 1.00 3.00 8.00
2-4,8-10,12-14,19,20: All Enemy Ace stories. 4-1st Dateline Frontline. 9-Unknown Soldier app. 5.00
5-7,11,15-18,21-25: 17-1st app. Rosa 4.00
26-Sgt. Rock & Easy Co.-c/s 1.00 3.00 8.00
NOTE: **Chaykin** *a-9, 10, 12-14, 19, 20.* **Evans** *c-25.* **Kubert** *c-2-23, 24p, 26.*

MEN'S ADVENTURES (Formerly True Adventures)
Marvel/Atlas Comics (CCC): No. 4, Aug, 1950 - No. 28, July, 1954
4(#1)(52 pgs.) 30.00 90.00 210.00
5-Flying Saucer story 19.00 58.00 135.00
6-8: 7-Buried alive story. 8-Sci/fic story 17.00 49.00 115.00
9-20: All war format 11.00 33.00 75.00
21,22,24-26: All horror format. 25-Shrunken head-c 17.00 51.00 120.00
23-Crandall-a; Fox-a(i); horror format 19.00 58.00 135.00
27,28-Human Torch & Toro-c/stories; Captain America & Sub-Mariner stories in each (also see Young Men #24-28) 95.00 285.00 760.00
NOTE: **Ayers** *a-27(H. Torch).* **Berg** *a-15, 16.* **Brodsky** *c-4-9, 11, 12, 16-18, 24.* **Burgos** *c-27, 28(Human Torch).* **Colan** *a-14, 19.* **Everett** *a-10, 14, 22, 25, 28; c-14, 21-23.* **Heath** *a-8, 11, 24; c-13, 20, 26.* **Lawrence** *a-23; 27(Captain America).* **Maneely** *a-24; c-10, 15.* **Mac Pakula** *a-15, 25.* **Post** *a-23.* **Powell** *a-27(Sub-Mariner).* **Reinman** *a-11, 12.* **Robinson** *c-19.* **Romita** *a-22.* **Shores** *c-25.* **Sinnott** *a-21.* **Tuska** *a-24. Adventure-#4-8; War-#9-20; Weird/Horror-#21-26.*

MENZ INSANA
DC Comics (Vertigo): 1997 ($7.95, one-shot)
nn-Fowler-s/Bolton painted art 1.00 3.00 8.00

MEPHISTO VS... (See Silver Surfer #3)
Marvel Comics Group: Apr, 1987 - No. 4, July, 1987 ($1.50, mini-series)
1-4: 1-Fantastic Four; Austin-i. 2-X-Factor. 3-X-Men. 4-Avengers 2.50

MERC (See Mark Hazzard: Merc)

MERCHANTS OF DEATH
Acme Press (Eclipse): Jul, 1988 - No. 4, Nov, 1988 ($3.50, B&W/16 pgs. color, 44pg. mag.)
1-4: 4-Toth-c 3.50

MERCY
DC Comics (Vertigo): 1993 ($5.95, 68 pgs., mature)
nn 2.40 6.00

MERLIN JONES AS THE MONKEY'S UNCLE (See Movie Comics and The Misadventures of... under Movie Comics)

MERRILL'S MARAUDERS (See Movie Classics)

MERRY CHRISTMAS (See A Christmas Adventure, Donald Duck..., Dell Giant #39, & March of Comics #153)

MERRY COMICS
Carlton Publishing Co.: Dec, 1945 (No cover price)
nn-Boogeyman app. 19.00 58.00 135.00

MERRY COMICS
Four Star Publications: 1947
1 13.00 39.00 90.00

MERRY-GO-ROUND COMICS
LaSalle Publ. Co./Croyden Publ./Rotary Litho.: 1944 (25¢, 132 pgs.); 1946; 9-10/47 - No. 2, 1948
nn(1944)(LaSalle)-Funny animal; 29 new features 17.00 51.00 120.00
21 6.70 20.00 40.00
1(1946)(Croyden)-Al Fago-c; funny animal 10.00 30.00 60.00
V1#1,2(1947-48; 52 pgs.)(Rotary Litho. Co. Ltd., Canada); Ken Hultgren-a 6.70 20.00 40.00

MERRY MAILMAN (See Fawcett's Funny Animals #87-89)

MERRY MOUSE (Also see Funny Tunes & Space Comics)
Avon Periodicals: June, 1953 - No. 4, Jan-Feb, 1954
1-1st app.; funny animal; Frank Carin-c/a 9.15 27.00 55.00
2-4 5.35 16.00 32.00

META-4
First Comics: Feb, 1991 - No. 4, 1991 ($2.25)
1-($3.95, 52pgs.) 4.00
2-4 2.25

METAL MEN (See Brave & the Bold, DC Comics Presents, and Showcase #37-40)
National Periodical Publications/DC Comics: 4-5/63 - No. 41, 12-1/69-70; No. 42, 2-3/73 - No. 44, 7-8/73; No. 45, 4-5/76 - No. 56, 2-3/78
1-(4-5/63)-5th app. Metal Men 41.00 123.00 500.00

Meteor Comics #1 © Croyden

Mickey Finn #1 © McNaught Syndicate

Mickey Mouse Four Color #79 © WDC

	GD2.0	FN6.0	NM9.4
2	16.00	48.00	160.00
3-5	9.00	27.00	90.00
6-10	6.00	18.00	60.00
11-20: 12-Beatles cameo (12/65)	4.50	13.50	45.00
21-26,28-30: 21-Batman, Robin & Flash x-over	3.50	10.50	32.00
27-Origin Metal Men retold	4.50	13.50	45.00
31-41(1968-70): 38-Last 12¢ issue. 41-Last 15¢	2.50	7.50	20.00
42-44(1973)-Reprints	1.25	3.75	10.00
45('76)-49-Simonson-a in all: 48,49-Re-intro Eclipso		2.40	6.00
50-56: 50-Part-r. 54,55-Green Lantern x-over		2.40	6.00

NOTE: ***Andru/Esposito** c-1-29. **Aparo** c-53-56. **Giordano** c-45, 46. **Kane** a-30, 31p; c-31. **Simonson** a-45-49; c-47-52. **Staton** a-50-56.*

METAL MEN
DC Comics: Oct, 1993 - No. 4, Jan, 1994 ($1.25, mini-series)

1-($2.50)-Multi-colored foil-c	3.00
2-4: 2-Origin	2.00

METAL MEN (See Tangent Comics/ Metal Men)

METAMORPHO (See Action Comics #413, Brave & the Bold #57,58, 1st Issue Special,& World's Finest #217)
National Periodical Publications: July-Aug, 1965 - No. 17, Mar-Apr, 1968 (All 12¢ issues)

1-(7-8/65)-3rd app. Metamorpho	9.50	28.50	95.00
2,3	5.00	15.00	50.00
4-6,10:10-Origin & 1st app. Element Girl (1-2/67)	3.50	10.50	35.00
7-9	3.00	9.00	30.00
11-17	2.50	7.50	20.00

NOTE: ***Ramona Fraden** a-B&B 57, 58, 1-4. **Orlando** a-5, 6; c-5-9, 11. **Sal Trapani** a-7-16.*

METAMORPHO
DC Comics: Aug, 1993 - No. 4, Nov, 1993 ($1.50, mini-series)

1-4	2.00

METAPHYSIQUE
Malibu Comics (Bravura): Apr, 1995 - No. 6, Oct, 1995 ($2.95, limited series)

1-6: Norm Breyfogle-c/a/scripts	3.00

METEOR COMICS
L. L. Baird (Croyden): Nov, 1945

1-Captain Wizard, Impossible Man, Race Wilkins app.; origin Baldy Bean, Capt. Wizard's sidekick; bare-breasted mermaids story	40.00	120.00	280.00

METEOR MAN
Marvel Comics: Aug, 1993 - No. 6, Jan, 1994 ($1.25, limited series)

1-6: 1-Polybagged w/button & rap newspaper. 4-Night Thrasher-c/story. 6-Terry Austin-c(i)	2.00

METROPOL (See Ted McKeever's...)

METROPOL A.D. (See Ted McKeever's...)

METROPOLIS S.C.U. (Also see Showcase '96 #1)
DC Comics: Nov, 1995 - No. 4, Feb, 1996 ($1.50, limited series)

1-4:1-Superman-c & app.	2.00

MEZZ: GALACTIC TOUR 2494 (Also See Nexus)
Dark Horse Comics: May, 1994 ($2.50, one-shot)

1	2.50

MGM'S MARVELOUS WIZARD OF OZ (See Marvel Treasury of Oz)
Marvel Comics Group/National Periodical Publications: 1975 ($1.50, 84 pgs.; oversize)

1-Adaptation of MGM's movie; J. Buscema-a	1.50	4.50	12.00

M.G.M'S MOUSE MUSKETEERS (Formerly M.G.M.'s The Two Mouseketeers)
Dell Publishing Co.: No. 670, Jan, 1956 - No. 1290, Mar-May, 1962

Four Color 670 (#4)	2.75	8.00	30.00
Four Color 711,728,764	1.80	5.50	20.00
8 (4-6/57) - 21 (3-5/60)	1.65	5.00	18.00
Four Color 1135,1175,1290	1.80	5.50	20.00

M.G.M.'S SPIKE AND TYKE (also see Tom & Jerry #79)
Dell Publishing Co.: No. 499, Sept, 1953 - No. 1266, Dec-Feb, 1961-62

	GD2.0	FN6.0	NM9.4
Four Color 499 (#1)	2.75	8.00	30.00
Four Color 577,638	1.80	5.50	20.00
4(12-2/55-56)-10	1.65	5.00	18.00
11-24(12-2/60-61)	1.50	4.50	15.00
Four Color 1266	1.65	5.00	18.00

M.G.M.'S THE TWO MOUSKETEERS
Dell Publishing Co.: No. 475, June, 1953 - No. 642, July, 1955

Four Color 475 (#1)	6.40	19.00	70.00
Four Color 603 (11/54), 642	3.60	11.00	40.00

MICHAELANGELO CHRISTMAS SPECIAL (See Teenage Mutant Ninja Turtles Christmas Special)

MICHAELANGELO, TEENAGE MUTANT NINJA TURTLE
Mirage Studios: 1986 (One shot) ($1.50, B&W)

1	3.00
1-2nd printing ('89, $1.75)-Reprint plus new-a	2.00

MICHAEL MOORCOCK'S MULTIVERSE
DC Comics (Helix): Nov, 1997 - No. 12, Oct, 1998 ($2.50, limited series)

1-12: Simonson, Reeve & Ridgway-a	2.50
TPB (1999, $19.95) r/#1-12	20.00

MICKEY AND DONALD (See Walt Disney's...)

MICKEY AND DONALD IN VACATIONLAND (See Dell Giant No. 47)

MICKEY & THE BEANSTALK (See Story Hour Series)

MICKEY & THE SLEUTH (See Walt Disney Showcase #38, 39, 42)

MICKEY FINN (Also see Big Shot Comics #74 & Feature Funnies)
Eastern Color 1-4/McNaught Synd. #5 on (Columbia)/Headline V3#2: Nov?, 1942 - V3#2, May, 1952

1	29.00	88.00	205.00
2	14.00	43.00	100.00
3-Charlie Chan story	10.00	30.00	70.00
4	8.35	25.00	50.00
5-10	6.35	19.00	38.00
11-15(1949): 12-Sparky Watts app.	4.25	13.00	28.00
V3#1,2(1952)	4.00	11.00	22.00

MICKEY MALONE
Hale Nass Corp.: 1936 (Color, punchout-c) (B&W-a on back)

	GD2.0	FN6.0	VF8.0
nn-1pg. of comics	125.00	250.00	400.00

MICKEY MANTLE (See Baseball's Greatest Heroes #1)

MICKEY MOUSE (See Adventures of Mickey Mouse, The Best of Walt Disney Comics, Cheerios giveaways, Donald and ..., Dynabrite Comics, 40 Big Pages..., Gladstone Comic Album, Merry Christmas From..., Walt Disney's Mickey and Donald, Walt Disney's Comics & Stories, Walt Disney's..., & Wheaties)

MICKEY MOUSE (...Secret Agent #107-109; Walt Disney's... #148-205?) (See Dell Giants for annuals) (#204 exists from both G.K. & Whitman)
Dell Publ. Co./Gold Key #85-204/Whitman #204-218/Gladstone #219 on: #16, 1941 - #84, 7-9/62; #85, 11/62 - #218, 7/84; #219, 10/86 - #256, 4/90

	GD2.0	FN6.0	VF8.0
Four Color 16(1941)-1st Mickey Mouse comic book; "...vs. the Phantom Blot" by Gottfredson	714.00	2143.00	10,000.00
	GD2.0	**FN6.0**	**NM9.4**
Four Color 27(1943)- "7 Colored Terror"	79.00	239.00	875.00
Four Color 79(1945)-By Carl Barks (1 story)	100.00	300.00	1100.00
Four Color 116(1946)	22.00	67.00	245.00
Four Color 141,157(1947)	19.00	57.00	210.00
Four Color 170,181,194('48)	15.50	46.00	170.00
Four Color 214('49),231,248,261	13.00	40.00	145.00
Four Color 268-Reprints/WDC&S #22-24 by Gottfredson ("Surprise Visitor")	12.00	35.00	130.00
Four Color 279,286,296	9.00	27.00	100.00

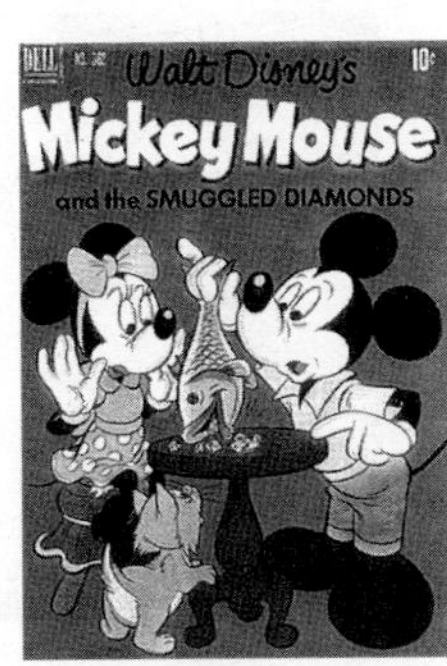

Mickey Mouse Four Color #362 © WDC

Mickey Mouse Magazine #3 © WDC

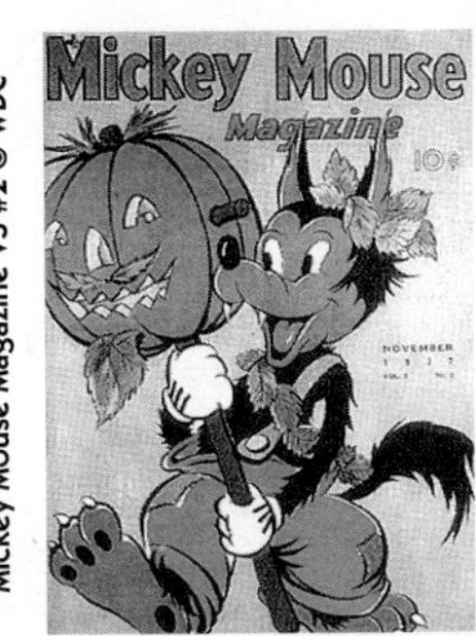

Mickey Mouse Magazine V3 #2 © WDC

GD2.0 FN6.0 NM9.4

Four Color 304,313(#1),325(#2),334 7.00 22.00 80.00
Four Color 343,352,362,371,387 5.50 16.50 60.00
Four Color 401,411,427(10-11/52) 3.60 11.00 40.00
Four Color 819-Mickey Mouse in Magicland 3.00 9.00 35.00
Four Color 1057,1151,1246(1959-61)-Album 2.75 8.00 30.00
28(12-1/52-53)-32,34 2.50 7.50 28.00
33-(Exists with 2 dates, 10-11/53 & 12-1/54) 2.50 7.50 28.00
35-50 2.20 6.50 24.00
51-73,75-80 2.00 6.00 16.00
74-Story swipe "The Rare Stamp Search" from 4-Color #422- "The Gilded Man" 1.80 5.40 20.00
81-105: 93,95-titled "Mickey Mouse Club Album". 100-105: Reprint 4-Color #427,194,279,170,343,214 in that order 1.65 5.00 18.00
106-120 1.40 4.20 14.00
121-130 1.20 3.60 12.00
131-146 1.00 3.00 10.00
147,148: 147-Reprints "The Phantom Fires" from WDC&S #200-202.148-Reprints "The Mystery of Lonely Valley" from WDC&S #208-210 1.10 3.30 9.00
149-158 5.00
159-Reprints "The Sunken City" from WDC&S #205-207 1.00 2.80 8.00
160-178,180-203: 162-170-r. 200-r/Four Color #371 5.00
179-(52 pgs.) 2.40 6.00
204-(Whitman or G.K.), 205,206 1.00 3.00 8.00
207(8/80), 209(pre-pack?) 1.75 5.25 14.00
208-(8-12/80)-Only distr. in Whitman 3-pack 3.25 9.80 36.00
210(2/81),211-214 1.00 2.80 7.00
215-218 1.10 3.30 9.00
219-1st Gladstone issue; The Seven Ghosts serial-r begins by Gottfredson 1.85 5.50 15.00
220,221 1.00 3.00 8.00
222-225: 222-Editor-in Grief strip-r 3.00
226-230 3.00
231-243,246-254: 240-r/March of Comics #27. 245-r/F.C. #279. 250-r/F.C. #248 3.00
244 (1/89, $2.95, 100 pgs.)-Squarebound 60th anniversary issue; gives history of Mickey 4.00
245, 256: 245-r/F.C. #279. 256-$1.95, 68 pgs. 4.00
255 ($1.95, 68 pgs.) 2.00

NOTE: *Reprints #195-197, 198(2/3), 199(1/3), 200-208, 211(1/2), 212, 213, 215(1/3), 216-on.* ***Gottfredson*** *Mickey Mouse serials in #219-239, 241-244, 246-249, 251-253, 255.*

Album 01-518-210(Dell), 1(10082-309)(9/63-Gold Key) 2.00 6.00 16.00
...Club 1(1/64-Gold Key)(TV) 2.60 7.80 26.00
Mini Comic 1(1976)(3-1/4x6-1/2")-Reprints 158 2.40 6.00
New Mickey Mouse Club Fun Book 11190 (Golden Press, 1977, $1.95, 224 pgs.) 2.00 6.00 16.00
Surprise Party 1(30037-901, G.K.)(1/69)-40th Anniversary (see Walt Disney Showcase #47) 2.50 7.50 24.00
Surprise Party 1(1979)-r/1969 issue 5.00

MICKEY MOUSE
Whitman Publishing Co.: c. 1933-1934 (10"x8-3/4", 34 pgs., cardboard-c)

948-1932 & 1933 Sunday strips in color, printed from the same plates as Mickey Mouse Book #3 by David McKay, but only pages 5-17 & 32-48 (including all of the "Wolf Barker" continuity) 137.00 412.00 1100.00

NOTE: Some copies bound with back cover upside down. Variance doesn't affect value. Same art appears on front and back covers of all copies. Height of Whitman reissue of McKay book trimmed 1/2 inch.

MICKEY MOUSE ADVENTURES
Disney Comics: June, 1990 - No. 18, Nov, 1991 ($1.50)

1-18: 1-Bradbury, Murry-r/M.M. #45,73 plus new-a. 2-Begin all new stories. 8-Byrne-c. 9-Fantasia 50th ann. issue w/new adapt. of movie. 10-r/F.C. #214 2.50

MICKEY MOUSE CLUB MAGAZINE (See Walt Disney...)

MICKEY MOUSE COMICS DIGEST
Gladstone: 1986 - No. 5, 1987 (96 pgs.)

1 ($1.25-c) 1.00 3.00 8.00
2-5: 3-5 ($1.50-c) 5.00

MICKEY MOUSE IN COLOR
Another Rainbow/Pantheon: 1988 (Deluxe, 13"x17", hard-c, $250.00) (Trade, 9-7/8"x11-1/2", hard-c, $39.95)

Deluxe limited edition of 3,000 copies signed by Floyd Gottfredson and Carl Barks, designated as the "Official Mickey Mouse 60th Anniversary" book. Mickey Sunday and daily reprints, plus Barks "Riddle of the Red Hat" from Four Color #79. Comes with 45 r.p.m. record interview with Gottfredson and Barks. 240 pgs. 23.00 68.00 250.00
Deluxe, limited to 100 copies, as above, but with a unique colored pencil original drawing of Mickey Mouse by Carl Barks. Add value of art to book price. 750.00
Pantheon trade edition, edited down & without Barks, 192 pgs. 3.80 11.50 40.00

MICKEY MOUSE MAGAZINE (Becomes Walt Disney's Comics & Stories)
K. K. Publ./Western Publishing Co.: Summer, 1935 (June-Aug, indicia) - V5#12, Sept, 1940; V1#1-5, V3#11,12, V4#1-3 are 44 pgs; V2#3-100 pgs; V5#12-68 pgs; rest are 36 pgs.(No V3#1, V4#6)

GD2.0 FN6.0 VF8.0 NM9.4

V1#1 (Large size, 13-1/4x10-1/4"; 25¢)-Contains puzzles, games, cels, stories & comics of Disney characters. Promotional magazine for Disney cartoon movies and paraphernalia 1100.00 3300.00 7150.00 11000.00

Note: *Some copies were autographed by the editors & given away with all early one year subscriptions.*

GD2.0 FN6.0 VF8.0

2 (Size change, 11-1/2x8-1/2"; 10/35; 10¢)-High quality paper begins; Messmer-a 131.00 395.00 1100.00
3,4: 3-Messmer-a 72.00 216.00 575.00
5-1st Donald Duck solo-c; 2nd cover app. ever; last 44 pg. & high quality paper issue 81.00 244.00 650.00
6-9: 6-36 pg. issues begin; Donald becomes editor. 8-2nd Donald solo-c. 9-1st Mickey/Minnie-c 64.00 193.00 525.00
10-12, V2#1,2: 11-1st Pluto/Mickey-c; Donald fires himself and appoints Mickey as editor 61.00 182.00 475.00
V2#3-Special 100 pg. Christmas issue (25¢); Messmer-a; Donald becomes editor of Wise Quacks 287.00 862.00 2300.00
4-Mickey Mouse Comics & Roy Ranger (adventure strip) begin; both end V2#9; Messmer-a 54.00 160.00 420.00

GD2.0 FN6.0 NM9.4

5-9: 5-Ted True (adventure strip, ends V2#9) & Silly Symphony Comics (ends V3#3) begin. 6-1st solo Minnie-c. 6-9-Mickey Mouse Movies cut-out in each 43.00 130.00 330.00
10-1st full color issue; Mickey Mouse (by Gottfredson; ends V3#12) & Silly Symphony (ends V3#3) full color Sunday-r, Peter The Farm Detective (ends V5#8) & Ole Of The North (ends V3#3) begins 67.00 200.00 550.00
11-13: 12-Hiawatha-c & feature story 43.00 130.00 330.00
V3#2-Big Bad Wolf Halloween-c 52.00 155.00 420.00
3 (12/37)-1st app. Snow White & The Seven Dwarfs (before release of movie)(possibly 1st in print); Mickey X-Mas-c 90.00 270.00 675.00
4 (1/38)-Snow White & The Seven Dwarfs serial begins (on stands before release of movie); Ducky Symphony (ends V3#11) begins 72.00 215.00 550.00
5-1st Snow White & Seven Dwarfs-c (St. Valentine's Day) 93.00 280.00 700.00
6-Snow White serial ends; Lonesome Ghosts app. (2 pp.) 50.00 150.00 390.00
7-Seven Dwarfs Easter-c 49.00 145.00 375.00
8-10: 9-Dopey-c. 10-1st solo Goofy-c 40.00 120.00 310.00
11,12 (44 pgs; 8 more pgs. color added). 11-Mickey the Sheriff serial (ends V4#3) & Donald Duck strip-r (ends V3#12) begin. Color feature on Snow White's Forest Friends 43.00 130.00 330.00
V4#1 (10/38; 44 pgs.)-Brave Little Tailor-c/feature story, nominated for Academy Award; Bobby & Chip by Otto Messmer (ends V4#2) &

Mickey Mouse Magazine V4 #5 © WDC

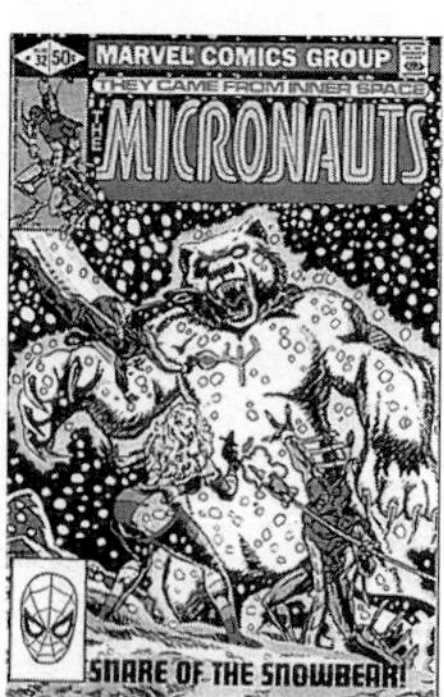

Micronauts #32 © MAR

Midnight Sons Unlimited #5 © MAR

	GD2.0	FN6.0	NM9.4
The Practical Pig (ends V4#2) begin	43.00	130.00	330.00
2 (44 pgs.)-1st Huey, Dewey & Louie-c	44.00	132.00	340.00
3 (12/38, 44 pgs.)-Ferdinand The Bull-c/feature story, Academy Award winner; Mickey Mouse & The Whalers serial begins, ends V4#12	43.00	130.00	330.00
4-Spotty, Mother Pluto strip-r begin, end V4#8	40.00	120.00	310.00
5-St. Valentine's day-c. 1st Pluto solo-c	47.00	141.00	360.00
7 (3/39)-The Ugly Duckling-c/feature story, Academy Award winner	43.00	130.00	330.00
7 (4/39)-Goofy & Wilbur The Grasshopper classic-c/feature story from 1st Goofy solo cartoon movie; Timid Elmer begins, ends V5#5	43.00	130.00	330.00
8-Big Bad Wolf-c from Practical Pig movie poster; Practical Pig feature story	43.00	130.00	330.00
9-Donald Duck & Mickey Mouse Sunday-r begin; The Pointer feature story, nominated for Academy Award	43.00	130.00	330.00
10-Classic July 4th drum & fife-c; last Donald Sunday-r	54.00	160.00	440.00
11-1st slick-c; last over-sized issue	40.00	120.00	310.00
12 (9/39; format change, 10-1/4x8-1/4")-1st full color, cover to cover issue; Donald's Penguin-c/feature story	48.00	145.00	390.00
V5#1-Black Pete-c; Officer Duck-c/feature story; Autograph Hound feature story; Robinson Crusoe serial begins	48.00	145.00	375.00
2-Goofy-c; 1st app. Pinocchio (cameo)	64.00	195.00	500.00
3 (12/39)-Pinocchio Christmas-c (Before movie release). 1st app. Jiminy Cricket; Pinocchio serial begins	72.00	215.00	560.00
4,5: 5-Jiminy Cricket-c; Pinocchio serial ends; Donald's Dog Laundry feature story	48.00	145.00	375.00
6,7: 6-Tugboat Mickey feature story; Rip Van Winkle feature begins, ends V5#8. 7-2nd Huey, Dewey & Louie-c	47.00	140.00	360.00
8-Last magazine size issue; 2nd solo Pluto-c; Figaro & Cleo feature story	48.00	144.00	370.00
9-11: 9 (6/40; change to comic book size)-Jiminy Cricket feature story; Donald-c & Sunday-r begin. 10-Special Independence Day issue. 11-Hawaiian Holiday & Mickey's Trailer feature stories; last 36 pg. issue	52.00	155.00	400.00
12 (Format change)-The transition issue (68 pgs.) becoming a comic book. With only a title change to follow, becomes Walt Disney's Comics & Stories #1 with the next issue	411.00	1233.00	3700.00

NOTE: ***Otto Messmer**-a is in many issues of the first two-three years. The following story titles and issues have gags created by **Carl Barks:** V4#3(12/38)-'Donald's Better Self' & 'Donald's Golf Game;' V4#4(1/39)-'Donald's Lucky Day;' V4#7(3/39)-'Hockey Champ;' V4#7(4/39)-'Donald's Cousin Gus;' V4#9(6/39)-'Sea Scouts;' V4#12(9/39)-'Donald's Penguin;' V5#9 (6/40)-'Donald's Vacation;' V5#10(7/40)-'Bone Trouble;' V5#12(9/40)-'Window Cleaners.'*

MICKEY MOUSE MARCH OF COMICS (See March of Comics #8,27,45,60,74)

MICKEY MOUSE'S SUMMER VACATION (See Story Hour Series)

MICKEY MOUSE SUMMER FUN (See Dell Giants)

MICKEY SPILLANE'S MIKE DANGER
Tekno Comix: Sept, 1995 - No. 11, May, 1996 ($1.95)

	GD2.0	FN6.0	NM9.4
1-11: 1-Frank Miller-c. 7-polybagged; Simonson-c. 8,9-Simonson-c.			2.00

MICKEY SPILLANE'S MIKE DANGER
Big Entertainment: V2#1, June, 1996 - No. 10, Apr, 1997 ($2.25)

	GD2.0	FN6.0	NM9.4
V2#1-10: Max Allan Collins scripts			2.25

MICROBOTS, THE
Gold Key: Dec, 1971 (one-shot)

	GD2.0	FN6.0	NM9.4
1 (10271-112)	2.00	6.00	16.00

MICRONAUTS (Toys)
Marvel Comics Group: Jan, 1979 - No. 59, Aug, 1984 (Mando paper #53 on)

	GD2.0	FN6.0	NM9.4
1-Intro/1st app. Baron Karza			3.00
2-59: 7-Man-Thing app. 8-1st app. Capt. Universe (8/79). 9-1st app. Cilicia. 13-1st app. Jasmine. 15-Death of Microtron. 15-17-Fantastic Four app. 17-Death of Jasmine. 20-Ant-Man app. 21-Microverse series begins. 25-Origin Baron Karza. 25-29-Nick Fury app. 27-Death of Biotron. 34,35-Dr. Strange app. 35-Double size; origin Microverse; intro Death Squad. 37-Nightcrawler app.; X-Men cameo (2 pgs.). 38-First direct sale. 40-Fantastic Four app. 57-(52 pgs.). 59-Golden painted-c			2.00
nn-Reprints #1-3; blank UPC; diamond on top			2.00
Annual 1,2 (12/79,10/80)-Ditko-c/a			2.50

NOTE: *#38-on distributed only through comic shops. **N. Adams** c-7i. **Chaykin** a-13-18p. **Ditko** a-39p. **Giffen** a-36p, 37p(part). **Golden** a-1-12p; c-2-7p, 8-23, 24p, 38, 39, 59. **Guice** a-48-58p; c-49-58. **Gil Kane** a-38, 40-45p; c-40-45. **Layton** c-33-37. **Miller** c-31.*

GD2.0 FN6.0 NM9.4

MICRONAUTS (Toys)
Marvel Comics Group: Oct, 1984 - No. 20, May, 1986

	GD2.0	FN6.0	NM9.4
V2#1-20			2.00

NOTE: ***Kelley Jones** a-1; c-1, 6. **Guice** a-4p; c-2p.*

MICRONAUTS SPECIAL EDITION
Marvel Comics Group: Dec, 1983 - No. 5, Apr, 1984 ($2.00, limited series, Baxter paper)

	GD2.0	FN6.0	NM9.4
1-5: r-/original series 1-12; Guice-c(p)-all			2.00

MIDGET COMICS (Fighting Indian Stories)
St. John Publishng Co.: Feb, 1950 - No. 2, Apr, 1950 (5-3/8x7-3/8", 68 pgs.)

	GD2.0	FN6.0	NM9.4
1-Fighting Indian Stories; Matt Baker-c	19.00	56.00	130.00
2-Tex West, Cowboy Marshal (also in #1)	10.00	30.00	60.00

MIDNIGHT (See Smash Comics #18)

MIDNIGHT
Ajax/Farrell Publ. (Four Star Comic Corp.): Apr, 1957 - No. 6, June, 1958

	GD2.0	FN6.0	NM9.4
1-Reprints from Voodoo & Strange Fantasy with some changes	13.00	39.00	90.00
2-6	8.35	25.00	50.00

MIDNIGHT EYE
Viz Premiere Comics: 1991 - No. 6, 1992 ($4.95, 44 pgs., mature)

	GD2.0	FN6.0	NM9.4
1-6: Japanese stories translated into English			5.00

MIDNIGHT MEN
Marvel Comics (Epic Comics/Heavy Hitters): June, 1993 - No. 4, Sept, 1993 ($2.50/$1.95, limited series)

	GD2.0	FN6.0	NM9.4
1-($2.50)-Embossed-c; Chaykin-c/a & scripts in all.			2.50
2-4			2.00

MIDNIGHT MYSTERY
American Comics Group: Jan-Feb, 1961 - No. 7, Oct, 1961

	GD2.0	FN6.0	NM9.4
1-Sci/Fi story	8.00	24.00	80.00
2-7: 7-Gustavson-a	4.20	12.60	42.00

NOTE: ***Reinman** a-1, 3. **Whitney** a-1, 4-6; c-1-3, 5, 7.*

MIDNIGHT SONS UNLIMITED
Marvel Comics (Midnight Sons imprint #4 on): Apr, 1993 - No. 9, May, 1995 ($3.95, 68 pgs.)

	GD2.0	FN6.0	NM9.4
1-9: Blaze, Darkhold (by Quesada #1), Ghost Rider, Morbius & Nightstalkers in all. 1-Painted-c. 3-Spider-Man app. 4-Siege of Darkness part 17; new Dr. Strange & new Ghost Rider app.; spot varnish-c			4.00

NOTE: ***Sears** a-2.*

MIDNIGHT TALES
Charlton Press: Dec, 1972 - No. 18, May, 1976

	GD2.0	FN6.0	NM9.4
V1#1	2.00	6.00	16.00
2-10	1.10	3.30	9.00
11-18: 11-14-Newton-a(p)	1.00	2.80	7.00
12,17(Modern Comics reprint, 1977)			4.00

NOTE: ***Adkins** a-12i, 13i. **Ditko** a-12. **Howard** (Wood imitator) a-1-15, 17, 18; c-1-18. **Don Newton** a-11-14p. **Staton** a-1, 3-11, 13. **Sutton** a-3-10.*

MIGHTY ATOM, THE (...& the Pixies #6) (Formerly The Pixies #1-5)
Magazine Enterprises: No. 6, 1949; Nov, 1957 - No. 6, Aug-Sept, 1958

	GD2.0	FN6.0	NM9.4
6(1949-M.E.)-no month (1st Series)	5.00	15.00	30.00
1-6(2nd Series)-Pixies-r	3.60	9.00	18.00
I.W. Reprint #1(nd)	1.00	3.00	8.00

MIGHTY BEAR (Formerly Fun Comics; becomes Unsane #15)
Star Publ. No. 13,14/Ajax-Farrell (Four Star): No. 13, Jan, 1954 - No. 14, Mar,

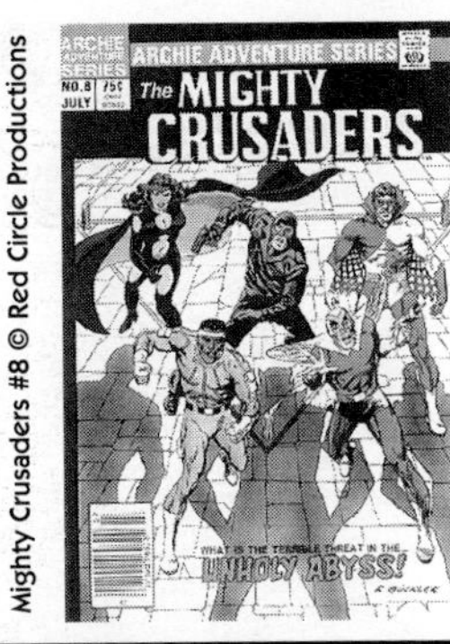

Mighty Crusaders #8 © Red Circle Productions

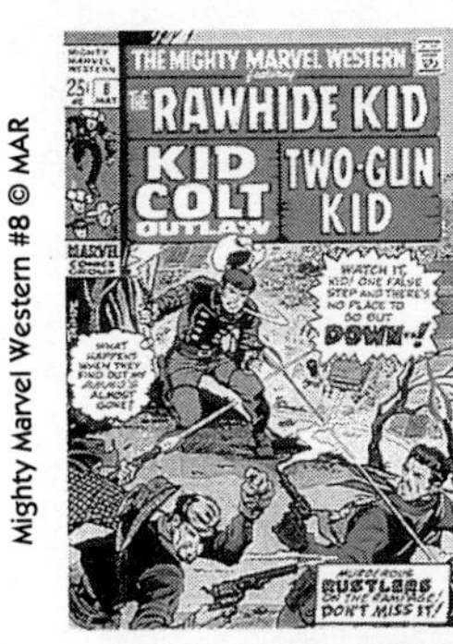

Mighty Marvel Western #8 © MAR

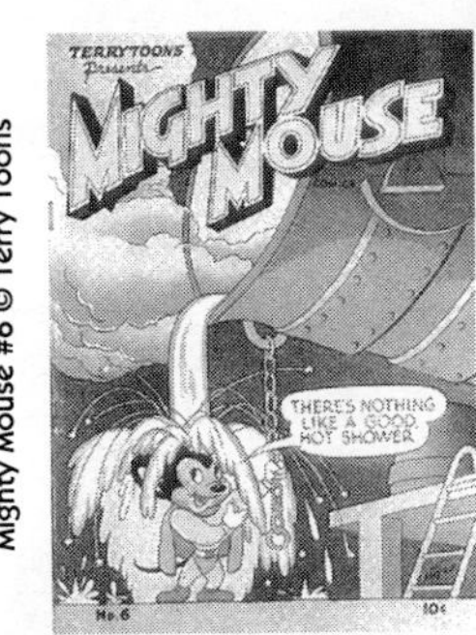

Mighty Mouse #6 © Terry Toons

1954; 9/57 - No. 3, 2/58

13,14-L. B. Cole-c 17.00 51.00 120.00
1-3('57-58)Four Star; becomes Mighty Ghost #4 4.25 13.00 28.00

MIGHTY COMICS (...Presents) (Formerly Flyman)
Radio Comics (Archie): No. 40, Nov, 1966 - No. 50, Oct, 1967 (All 12¢ issues)

40-Web 2.60 7.80 26.00
41-50: 41-Shield, Black Hood. 42-Black Hood. 43-Shield, Web & Black Hood. 44-Black Hood, Steel Sterling & The Shield. 45-Shield & Hangman; origin Web retold. 46-Steel Sterling, Web & Black Hood. 47-Black Hood & Mr. Justice. 48-Shield & Hangman; Wizard x-over in Shield. 49-Steel Sterling & Fox; Black Hood x-over in Steel Sterling. 50-Black Hood & Web; Inferno x-over in Web 2.50 7.50 22.00
NOTE: ***Paul Reinman*** *a-40-50.*

MIGHTY CRUSADERS, THE (Also see Adventures of the Fly, The Crusaders & Fly Man)
Mighty Comics Group (Radio Comics): Nov, 1965 - No. 7, Oct, 1966 (All 12¢)

1-Origin The Shield 4.50 13.50 45.00
2-Origin Comet 2.60 7.80 26.00
3,5-7: 3-Origin Fly-Man. 5-Intro. Ultra-Men (Fox, Web, Capt. Flag) & Terrific Three (Jaguar, Mr. Justice, Steel Sterling). 7-Steel Sterling feature; origin Fly-Girl 2.50 7.50 22.00
4-1st S.A. app. Fireball, Inferno & Fox; Firefly, Web, Bob Phantom, Blackjack, Hangman, Zambini, Kardak, Steel Sterling, Mr. Justice, Wizard, Capt. Flag, Jaguar x-over 2.50 7.50 24.00
NOTE: ***Reinman*** *a-6.*

MIGHTY CRUSADERS, THE (All New Advs. of...#2)
Red Circle Prod./Archie Ent. No. 6 on: Mar, 1983 - No. 13, Sept, 1985 ($1.00, 36 pgs, Mando paper)

1-Origin Black Hood, The Fly, Fly Girl, The Shield, The Wizard, The Jaguar, Pvt. Strong & The Web. 3.00
2-13: 2-Mister Midnight begins. 4-Darkling replaces Shield. 5-Origin Jaguar, Shield begins. 7-Untold origin Jaguar 2.00
NOTE: ***Buckler*** *a-1-3, 4i, 5p, 7p, 8i, 9i; c-1-10p.*

MIGHTY GHOST (Formerly Mighty Bear #1-3)
Ajax/Farrell Publ.: No. 4, June, 1958

4 4.00 12.00 24.00

MIGHTY HERCULES, THE (TV)
Gold Key: July, 1963 - No. 2, Nov, 1963

1 (10072-307), 2 (10072-311) 14.00 41.00 150.00

MIGHTY HEROES, THE (TV) (Funny)
Dell Publishing Co.: Mar, 1967 - No. 4, July, 1967

1-Also has a 1957 Heckle & Jeckle-r 13.50 41.00 150.00
2-4: 4-Has two 1958 Mighty Mouse-r 9.50 29.00 105.00

MIGHTY HEROES
Spotlight Comics: 1987 (B&W, one-shot)

1-Heckle & Jeckle backup 2.00

MIGHTY HEROES
Marvel Comics: Jan, 1998 ($2.99, one-shot)

1-Origin of the Mighty Heroes 3.00

MIGHTY MARVEL WESTERN, THE
Marvel Comics Group (LMC earlier issues): Oct, 1968 - No. 46, Sept, 1976 (#1-14: 68 pgs.; #15,16: 52 pgs.)

1-Begin Kid Colt, Rawhide Kid, Two-Gun Kid-r 3.50 10.50 35.00
2-16: (2-14-68 pgs./ 15,16-52 pgs.) 2.50 7.50 22.00
17-20 1.50 4.50 12.00
21-30,32,37: 24-Kid Colt-r end. 25-Matt Slade-r begin. 32-Origin-r/Rawhide Kid #23; Williamson-r/Kid Slade #7. 37-Williamson, Kirby-r/Two-Gun Kid 51 1.25 3.75 10.00
31,33-36,38-46: 31-Baker-r. 1.00 3.00 8.00
44-46-(30¢-c variants, limited distribution)(4-8/76) 2.80 8.40 28.00
NOTE: ***Jack Davis*** *a(r)-21-24.* ***Keller*** *r-1-13, 22.* ***Kirby*** *a(r)-1-3, 6, 9, 12-14, 16, 25-29, 32-38, 40, 41, 43-46; c-29.* ***Maneely*** *a(r)-22.* ***Severin*** *c-3i, 9. No Matt Slade-#43.*

MIGHTY MIDGET COMICS, THE (Miniature)
Samuel E. Lowe & Co.: No date; circa 1942-1943 (Sold 2 for 5¢, B&W and red, 36 pgs, approx. 5x4")

Bulletman #11(1943)-r/cover/Bulletman #3 19.00 58.00 135.00
Captain Marvel Adventures #11 19.00 58.00 135.00
Captain Marvel #11 (Same as above except for full color ad on back cover; this issue was glued to cover of Captain Marvel #20 and is not found in fine-mint condition) 250.00 750.00 –
Captain Marvel Jr. #11 (Same-c as Master #27 19.00 58.00 135.00
Captain Marvel Jr. #11 (Same as above except for full color ad on back-c; this issue was glued to cover of Captain Marvel #21 and is not found in fine-mint condition) 250.00 750.00 –
Golden Arrow #11 18.00 54.00 125.00
Ibis the Invincible #11(1942)-Origin; reprints cover to Ibis #1 (Predates Fawcett's Ibis the Invincible #1). 19.00 58.00 135.00
Spy Smasher #11(1942) 19.00 58.00 135.00
NOTE: *The above books came in a box called "box full of books" and was distributed with other Samuel Lowe puzzles, paper dolls, coloring books, etc. They are not titled Mighty Midget Comics. All have a war bond seal on back cover which is otherwise blank. These books came in a "Mighty Midget" flat cardboard counter display rack.*
Balbo, the Boy Magician #12 (1943)-1st book devoted entirely to character. 9.15 27.00 55.00
Bulletman #12 13.50 41.00 95.00
Commando Yank #12 (1943)-Only comic devoted entirely to character. 10.00 30.00 70.00
Dr. Voltz the Human Generator (1943)-Only comic devoted entirely to character. 9.15 27.00 55.00
Lance O'Casey #12 (1943)-1st comic devoted entirely to character (Predates Fawcett's Lance O'Casey #1). 9.15 27.00 55.00
Leatherneck the Marine (1943)-Only comic devoted entirely to character. 9.15 27.00 55.00
Minute Man #12 13.50 41.00 95.00
Mister "Q" (1943)-Only comic devoted entirely to character. 9.15 27.00 55.00
Mr. Scarlet and Pinky #12 (1943)-Only comic devoted entirely to character. 11.50 34.00 80.00
Pat Wilton and His Flying Fortress (1943)-1st comic devoted entirely to character. 9.15 27.00 55.00
The Phantom Eagle #12 (1943)-Only comic devoted entirely to character. 10.00 30.00 60.00
State Trooper Stops Crime (1943)-Only comic devoted entirely to character. 9.15 27.00 55.00
Tornado Tom (1943)-Origin, r/from Cyclone #1-3; only comic devoted entirely to character. 9.15 27.00 55.00

MIGHTY MORPHIN' POWER RANGERS: THE MOVIE (Also see Saban's Mighty Morphin' Power Rangers)
Marvel Comics: Sept, 1995 ($3.95, one-shot)

nn-adaptation of movie 4.00

MIGHTY MOUSE (See Adventures of..., Dell Giant #43, Giant Comics Edition, March of Comics #205, 237, 247, 257, 447, 459, 471, 483, Oxydol-Dreft, Paul Terry's, & Terry-Toons Comics)

MIGHTY MOUSE (1st Series)
Timely/Marvel Comics (20th Century Fox): Fall, 1946 - No. 4, Summer, 1947

1 116.00 347.00 925.00
2 53.00 159.00 425.00
3,4 40.00 120.00 280.00

MIGHTY MOUSE (2nd Series) (Paul Terry's... #62-71)
St. John Publishing Co./Pines No. 68 (3/56) on (TV issues #72 on): Aug, 1947 - No. 67, 11/55; No. 68, 3/56 - No. 83, 6/59

5(#1) 37.00 111.00 260.00
6-10 19.00 56.00 130.00
11-19 11.50 34.00 80.00
20 (11/50) - 25-(52 pg. editions) 10.00 30.00 60.00
20-25-(36 pg. editions) 8.35 25.00 50.00

Mike Barnett, Man Against Crime #6 © FAW

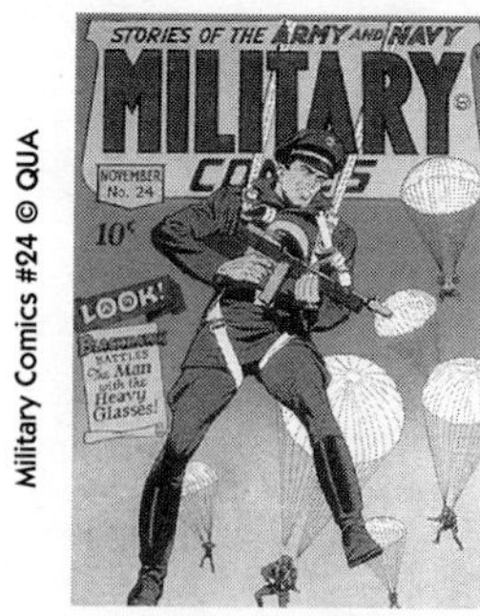

Military Comics #24 © QUA

Millennium #1 © DC

GD2.0 FN6.0 NM9.4

26-37: 35-Flying saucer-c 6.70 20.00 40.00
38-45-(100 pgs.) 17.00 51.00 120.00
46-83: 62-64,67-Painted-c. 82-Infinity-c 6.35 19.00 38.00
Album 1(10/52, 25¢, 100 pgs., St. John)-Gandy Goose app. 27.00 81.00 190.00
Album 2,3(11/52 & 12/52, St. John) (100 pgs.) 21.00 64.00 150.00
Fun Club Magazine 1(Fall, 1957-Pines, 25¢, 100 pgs.) (CBS TV)-Tom Terrific, Heckle & Jeckle, Dinky Duck, Gandy Goose 15.00 45.00 105.00
Fun Club Magazine 2-6(Winter, 1958-Pines) 10.00 30.00 65.00
3-D 1-(1st printing-9/53, 25¢)(St. John)-Came w/glasses; stiff covers; says World's First! on-c; 1st 3-D comic 29.00 86.00 200.00
3-D 1-(2nd printing-10/53, 25¢)-Came w/glasses; slick, glossy covers, slightly smaller 26.00 77.00 180.00
3-D 2,3(11/53, 12/53, 25¢)-(St. John)-With glasses 24.00 73.00 170.00

MIGHTY MOUSE (TV)(3rd Series)(Formerly Adventures of Mighty Mouse)
Gold Key/Dell Publ. Co. No. 166-on: No. 161, Oct, 1964 - No. 172, Oct, 1968
161(10/64)-165(9/65)-(Becomes Adventures of... No. 166 on) 4.00 12.00 40.00
166(3/66), 167(6/66)-172 2.80 8.40 28.00

MIGHTY MOUSE (TV)
Spotlight Comics: 1987 - No. 2, 1987 ($1.50, color)
1,2-New stories 2.00
...And Friends Holiday Special (11/87, $1.75) 2.00

MIGHTY MOUSE (TV)
Marvel Comics: Oct, 1990 - No. 10, July, 1991 ($1.00)(Based on Sat. cartoon)
1-10: 1-Dark Knight-c parody. 2-10: 3-Intro Bat-Bat; Byrne-c. 4,5-Crisis-c/story parodies w/Perez-c. 6-Spider-Man-c parody. 7-Origin Bat-Bat 2.00

MIGHTY MOUSE ADVENTURE MAGAZINE
Spotlight Comics: 1987 ($2.00, B&W, 52 pgs., magazine size, one-shot)
1-Deputy Dawg, Heckle & Jeckle backup stories 4.00

MIGHTY MOUSE ADVENTURES (Adventures of... #2 on)
St. John Publishing Co.: November, 1951
1 33.00 99.00 230.00

MIGHTY MOUSE ADVENTURE STORIES (Paul Terry's... on-c only)
St. John Publishing Co.: 1953 (50¢, 384 pgs.)
nn-Rebound issues 41.00 124.00 330.00

MIGHTY MUTANIMALS (See Teenage Mutant Ninja Turtles Adventures #19)
May, 1991 - No. 3, July, 1991 ($1.00, limited series)
Archie Comics: Apr, 1992 - Present ($1.25)
1-3: 1-Story cont'd from TMNT Advs. #19. 2.00
1-8 (1992): 7-1st app. Merdude 2.00

MIGHTY SAMSON (Also see Gold Key Champion)
Gold Key: 7/64 - #20, 11/69; #21, 8/72; #22, 12/73 - #31, 3/76; #32, 8/82 (Painted c-1-31)
1-Origin/1st app.; Thorne-a begins 7.25 22.00 80.00
2-5 4.00 12.00 40.00
6-10: 7-Tom Morrow begins, ends #20 2.50 7.50 24.00
11-20 2.25 6.75 18.00
21-31: 21,22-r 1.50 4.50 12.00
32-r 1.00 3.00 8.00

MIGHTY THOR (See Thor)

MIKE BARNETT, MAN AGAINST CRIME (TV)
Fawcett Publications: Dec, 1951 - No. 6, Oct, 1952
1 19.00 56.00 130.00
2 11.00 33.00 75.00
3,4,6 10.00 30.00 65.00
5- "Market for Morphine" cover/story 11.50 34.00 80.00

MIKE DANGER (See Mickey Spillane's...)

MIKE DEODATO'S...
Caliber Comics: 1996, ($2.95, B&W)
...FALLOUT 3000 #1, ...JONAS (mag. size) #1,...PRIME CUTS (mag. size) #1, ...PROTHEUS #1,2, ...RAMTHAR #1,...RAZOR NIGHTS #1 3.00

MIKE GRELL'S SABLE (Also see Jon Sable & Sable)
First Comics: Mar, 1990 - No. 10, Dec, 1990 ($1.75)
1-10: r/Jon Sable Freelance #1-10 by Grell 2.00

MIKE MIST MINUTE MIST-ERIES (See Ms. Tree/Mike Mist in 3-D)
Eclipse Comics: April, 1981 ($1.25, B&W, one-shot)
1 2.00

MIKE SHAYNE PRIVATE EYE
Dell Publishing Co.: Nov-Jan, 1962 - No. 3, Sept-Nov, 1962
1 2.40 7.00 26.00
2,3 1.60 4.80 16.00

MILITARY COMICS (Becomes Modern Comics #44 on)
Quality Comics Group: Aug, 1941 - No. 43, Oct, 1945

GD2.0 FN6.0 VF8.0 NM9.4

1-Origin/1st app. Blackhawk by C. Cuidera (Eisner scripts); Miss America, The Death Patrol by Jack Cole (also #2-7,27-30), & The Blue Tracer by Guardineer; X of the Underground, The Yankee Eagle, Q-Boat & Shot & Shell, Archie Atkins, Loops & Banks by Bud Ernest (Bob Powell)(ends #13) begin 800.00 2400.00 4800.00 8000.00

GD2.0 FN6.0 NM9.4

2-Secret War News begins (by McWilliams #2-16); Cole-a; new uniform with yellow circle & hawk's head for Blackhawk 250.00 750.00 2000.00
3-Origin/1st app. Chop Chop 212.00 636.00 1700.00
4 169.00 507.00 1350.00
5-The Sniper begins; Miss America in costume #4-7 144.00 432.00 1150.00
6-9: 8-X of the Underground begins (ends #13). 9-The Phantom Clipper begins (ends #16) 106.00 318.00 850.00
10-Classic Eisner-c 109.00 327.00 875.00
11-Flag-c 84.00 252.00 675.00
12-Blackhawk by Crandall begins, ends #22 109.00 327.00 875.00
13-15: 14-Private Dogtag begins (ends #83) 81.00 243.00 650.00
16-20: 16-Blue Tracer ends. 17-P.T. Boat begins 70.00 210.00 560.00
21-31: 22-Last Crandall Blackhawk. 23-Shrunken head-c. 27-Death Patrol revived 60.00 180.00 480.00
32-43 52.00 157.00 420.00

NOTE: ***Berg** a-6. **Al Bryant** c-31-34, 38, 40-43. **J. Cole** a-1-3, 27-32. **Crandall** a-12-22; c-13-20. **Cuidera** c-2-9. **Eisner** c-1, 2(part), 9, 10. **Kotsky** c-21-29, 35, 37, 39. **McWilliams** a-2-16. **Powell** a-1-13. **Ward** Blackhawk-30, 31(15 pgs. each); c-30.*

MILK AND CHEESE (Also see Cerebus Bi-Weekly #20)
Slave Labor: 1991 - Present ($2.50, B&W)
1-Evan Dorkin story & art in all. 4.50 13.50 50.00
1-2nd-6th printings 4.00
2-"Other #1" 3.00 9.00 30.00
2-reprint 3.00
3-"Third #1" 2.50 7.50 20.00
4-"Fourth #1", 5-"First Second Issue" 1.25 3.75 10.00
6,7:6-"#666" 5.00

NOTE: *Multiple printings of all issues exist and are worth cover price unless listed here.*

MILLENNIUM
DC Comics: Jan, 1988 - No. 8, Feb, 1988 (Weekly limited series)
1-Staton c/a(p) begins 3.00
2-8 2.00

MILLENNIUM FEVER
DC Comics (Vertigo): Oct, 1995 - No.4, Jan, 1996 ($2.50, limited series)
1-4: Duncan Fegredo-c/a 2.50

MILLENNIUM INDEX
Independent Comics Group: Mar, 1988 - No. 2, Mar, 1988 ($2.00)
1,2 2.00

MILLIE, THE LOVABLE MONSTER
Dell Publishing Co.: Sept-Nov, 1962 - No. 6, Jan, 1973

Millie the Model #129 © MAR

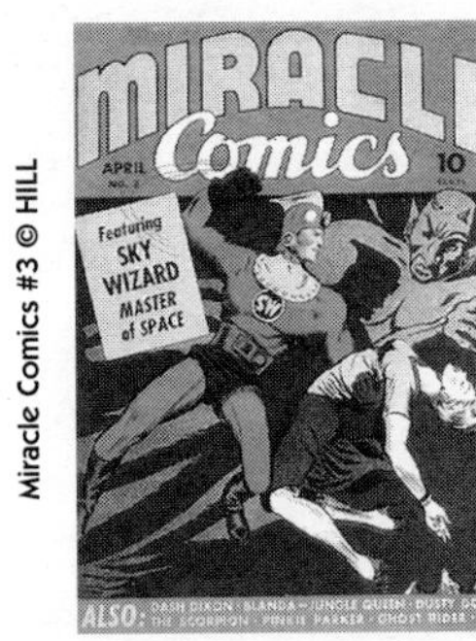

Miracle Comics #3 © HILL

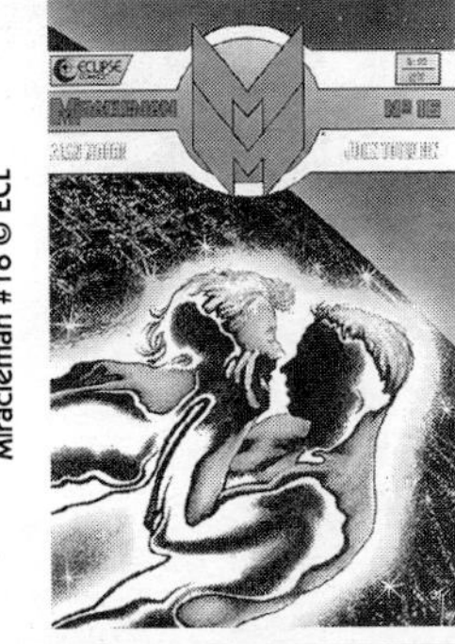

Miracleman #16 © ECL

GD2.0 FN6.0 NM9.4

12-523-211 3.50 10.50 38.00
2(8-10/63)-Bill Woggon c/a 3.00 9.00 35.00
3(8-10/64) 2.50 7.50 28.00
4(7/72), 5(10/72), 6(1/73) 1.40 4.20 14.00
NOTE: ***Woggon** a-3-6; c-3-6. 4 reprints 1; 5 reprints 2; 6 reprints 3.*

MILLIE THE MODEL (See Comedy Comics, A Date With..., Joker Comics #28, Life With..., Mad About..., Marvel Mini-Books, Misty & Modeling With...)
Marvel/Atlas/Marvel Comics(CnPC #1)(SPI/Male/VPI):1945 - No. 207, Dec, 1973

1-Origin 75.00 225.00 600.00
2 (10/46)-Millie becomes The Blonde Phantom to sell Blonde Phantom perfume; a pre-Blonde Phantom app. (see All-Select #11, Fall, 1946) 40.00 120.00 300.00
3-8,10: 4-7-Willie app. 7-Willie smokes extra strong tobacco. 8,10-Kurtzman's "Hey Look". 8-Willie & Rusty app. 26.00 77.00 180.00
9-Powerhouse Pepper by Wolverton, 4 pgs. 30.00 90.00 210.00
11-Kurtzman-a, "Giggles 'n' Grins" 18.00 54.00 125.00
12,15,17-20: 12-Rusty & Hedy Devine app. 12.00 36.00 85.00
13,14,16-Kurtzman's "Hey Look". 13-Hedy Devine app. 13.50 41.00 95.00
21-30 10.00 30.00 60.00
31-60 4.50 13.50 45.00
61-99 3.20 9.60 32.00
100 3.80 11.40 38.00
101-130: 107-Jack Kirby app. in story 2.80 8.40 28.00
131-153: 141-Groovy Gears-c/s 2.50 7.50 22.00
154-New Millie begins (10/67) 3.20 9.60 32.00
155-190,192: 192-52 pgs. 2.50 7.50 20.00
191,193-199,201-206 2.25 6.75 18.00
200,207(Last issue) 2.50 7.50 24.00
(Beware: cut-up pages are common in all Annuals)
Annual 1(1962)-Early Marvel annual (2nd?) 17.00 51.00 170.00
Annual 2(1963) 12.50 38.00 125.00
Annual 3-5 (1964-1966) 7.00 21.00 70.00
Annual 6-10(1967-11/71) 5.50 16.50 55.00
Queen-Size 11(9/74), 12(1975) 4.50 13.50 45.00
NOTE: ***Dan DeCarlo** a-18-93.*

MILLION DOLLAR DIGEST (Richie Rich... #23 on; also see Richie Rich...)
Harvey Publications: 11/86 - No. 7, 11/87; No. 8, 4/88 - No. 34, Nov, 1994 ($1.25/$1.75, digest size)

1-8: 8-(68 pgs.) 3.00
9-34: 9-Begin $1.75-c. 14-May not exist 2.00

MILT GROSS FUNNIES (Also see Picture News #1)
Milt Gross, Inc. (ACG?): Aug, 1947 - No. 2, Sept, 1947

1,2 11.50 34.00 80.00

MILTON THE MONSTER & FEARLESS FLY (TV)
Gold Key: May, 1966

1 (10175-605) 9.50 28.50 105.00

MINIMUM WAGE
Fantagraphics Books: V1#1, July, 1995 ($9.95, B&W, graphic novel, mature)
V2#1, 1995 - Present ($2.95, B&W, mature)

V1#1-Bob Fingerman story & art 1.25 3.75 10.00
V2#1-9($2.95): Bob Fingerman story & art. 2-Kevin Nowlan back-c. 4-w/pin-ups. 5-Mignola back-c 3.00
Book Two TPB ('97, $12.95) r/V2#1-5 13.00

MINUTE MAN (See Master Comics & Mighty Midget Comics)
Fawcett Publications: Summer, 1941 - No. 3, Spring, 1942 (68 pgs.)

1 162.00 487.00 1300.00
2,3 104.00 311.00 830.00

MINX, THE
DC Comics (Vertigo): Oct, 1998 - No. 8, May, 1999 ($2.50, limited series)

1-8-Milligan-s/Phillips-c/a 3.00

MIRACLE COMICS
Hillman Periodicals: Feb, 1940 - No. 4, Mar, 1941

1-Sky Wizard Master of Space, Dash Dixon, Man of Might, Pinkie Parker, Dusty Doyle, The Kid Cop, K-7, Secret Agent, The Scorpion, & Blandu, Jungle Queen begin; Masked Angel only app. (all 1st app.) 175.00 525.00 1400.00
2 87.00 262.00 700.00
3,4: 3-Bill Colt, the Ghost Rider begins. 4-The Veiled Prophet & Bullet Bob (by Burnley) app. 75.00 225.00 600.00

MIRACLEMAN
Eclipse Comics: Aug, 1985 - No. 15, Nov, 1988; No. 16, Dec, 1989 - No. 24, 1994

1-r/British Marvelman series; Alan Moore scripts in #1-16 3.00
1-Gold & Silver editions 3.00
2-12: 8-Airboy preview. 9,10-Origin Miracleman. 9-Shows graphic scenes of childbirth. 10-Snyder-c 3.00
13,14,16: 16-Last Alan Moore-s; 1st $1.95-c 2.40 6.00
15-($1.75-c) end of Kid Miracleman 1.00 3.00 8.00
17,18-($1.95): 17-"The Golden Age" begins, ends #22. Dave McKean-c begins, end #22; Neil Gaiman scripts in #17-24 3.00
19-24-($2.50); 23-"The Silver Age" begins. 23,24-B. Smith-c. 3.00
3-D 1 (12/85) 3.00
Book One: A Dream of Flying (1988, $10.95, TPB) r/#1-5 20.00
Book Two: The Red King Syndrome (1990, $14.95, TPB) r/#6-10 20.00
Book Three: Olympus (1990, $12.95, TPB) r/#11-16 40.00
Book Four: The Golden Age (1992, $14.95, TPB) r/#17-22 20.00
Book Four: The Golden Age (1993, $12.99, TPB) new McKean-c 13.00
NOTE: ***Chaykin** c-3. **Gulacy** c-7. **McKean** c-17-22. **B. Smith** c-23, 24. **Starlin** c-4. **Totleben** a-11-13; c-9, 11-13. **Truman** c-6.*

MIRACLEMAN: APOCRYPHA
Eclipse Comics: Nov, 1991 - No. 3, Feb, 1992 ($2.50, limited series)

1-3: 1-Stories by Neil Gaiman, Mark Buckingham, Alex Ross & others. 3-Stories by James Robinson, Kelley Jones, Matt Wagner, Neil Gaiman, Mark Buckingham & others 2.50
TPB (12/92, $15.95) r/#1-3; Buckingham-c 20.00

MIRACLEMAN FAMILY
Eclipse Comics: May, 1988 - No. 2, Sept, 1988 ($1.95, lim. series, Baxter paper)

1,2: 2-Gulacy-c 2.00

MIRACLE OF THE WHITE STALLIONS, THE (See Movie Comics)

MIRACLE SQUAD, THE
Upshot Graphics (Fantagraphics Books): Aug, 1986 - No. 4, 1987 ($2.00)

1-4 2.00

MIRACLE SQUAD: BLOOD AND DUST, THE
Apple Comics: Jan, 1989 - No. 4, July, 1989 ($1.95, B&W, limited series)

1-4 2.00

MIRRORWORLD: RAIN
NetCo Partners (Big Ent.): Feb, 1997 - No. 0, Apr, 1997 ($3.25, limited series)

0,1-Tad Williams-s 3.25

MISADVENTURES OF MERLIN JONES, THE (See Movie Comics & Merlin Jones as the Monkey's Uncle under Movie Comics)

MISS AMERICA COMICS (Miss America Magazine #2 on; also see Blonde Phantom & Marvel Mystery Comics)
Marvel Comics (20CC): 1944 (one-shot)

1-2 pgs. pin-ups 150.00 450.00 1200.00

MISS AMERICA MAGAZINE (Formerly Miss America; Miss America #51 on)
Miss America Publ. Corp./Marvel/Atlas (MAP): V1#2, Nov, 1944 - No. 93, Nov, 1958

V1#2-Photo-c of teenage girl in Miss America costume; Miss America, Patsy Walker (intro.) comic stories plus movie reviews & stories; intro. Buzz Baxter & Hedy Wolfe; 1 pg. origin Miss America 120.00 360.00 960.00
3-5-Miss America & Patsy Walker stories 45.00 135.00 360.00
6-Patsy Walker only 11.00 33.00 75.00

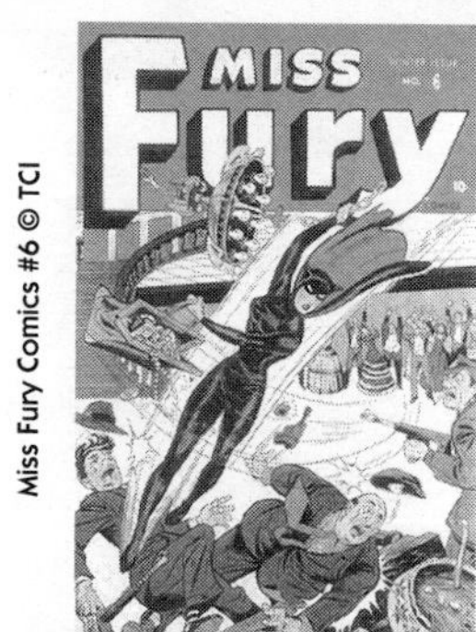

Miss Fury Comics #6 © TCI

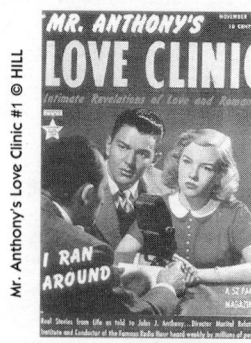

Mr. Anthony's Love Clinic #1 © HILL

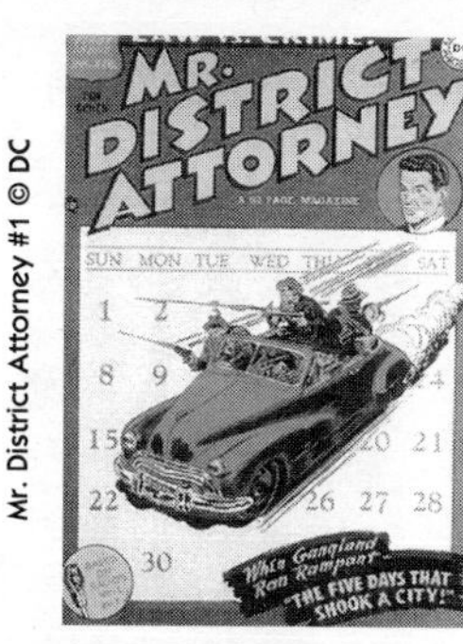

Mr. District Attorney #1 © DC

	GD2.0	FN6.0	NM9.4
V2#1(4/45)-6(9/45)-Patsy Walker continues	6.70	20.00	40.00
V3#1(10/45)-6(4/46)	6.70	20.00	40.00
V4#1(5/46),2,5(9/46)	5.85	17.50	35.00
V4#3(7/46)-Liz Taylor photo-c	10.00	30.00	60.00
V4#4 (8/46; 68 pgs.), V4#6 (10/46; 92 pgs.)	5.35	16.00	32.00
V5#1(11/46)-6(4/47), V6#1(5/47)-3(7/47)	5.35	16.00	32.00
V7#1(8/47)-14,16-23(#56, 6/49)	4.25	13.00	28.00
V7#15-All comics	5.85	17.50	35.00
V7#24(#57, 7/49)-Kamen-a (becomes Best Western #58 on?)	5.35	16.00	32.00
V7#25(8/49), 27-44(3/52), VII,nn(5/52)	4.25	13.00	26.00
V7#26(9/49)-All comics	5.35	16.00	32.00
V1,nn(7/52)-V1,nn(1/53)(#46-49), V7#50(Spring '53), V1#51-V7?#54(7/53), 55-93	4.25	13.00	26.00

NOTE: *Photo-c #1, 4, V2#1, 4, 5, V3#5, V4#3, 4, 6, V7#15, 16, 24, 26, 34, 37, 38. Painted c-3.* ***Powell*** *a-V7#31.*

MISS BEVERLY HILLS OF HOLLYWOOD (See Adventures of Bob Hope)
National Periodical Publ.: Mar-Apr, 1949 - No. 9, July-Aug, 1950 (52 pgs.)

1 (Meets Alan Ladd)	57.00	172.00	460.00
2-William Holden photo on-c	40.00	120.00	325.00
3-5: 2-9-Part photo-c. 5-Bob Hope photo on-c	37.00	111.00	260.00
6,7,9: 6-Lucille Ball photo on-c	35.00	105.00	245.00
8-Reagan photo on-c	40.00	120.00	300.00

NOTE: *Beverly meets Alan Ladd in #1, Eve Arden #2, Betty Hutton #4, Bob Hope #5.*

MISS CAIRO JONES
Croyden Publishers: 1945

1-Bob Oksner daily newspaper-r (1st strip story); lingerie panels	20.00	60.00	140.00

MISS FURY COMICS (Newspaper strip reprints)
Timely Comics (NPI 1/CmPI 2/MPC 3-8): Winter, 1942-43 - No. 8, Winter, 1946 (Published quarterly)

1-Origin Miss Fury by Tarpe' Mills (68 pgs.) in costume w/pin-ups	311.00	933.00	2800.00
2-(60 pgs.)-In costume w/pin-ups	162.00	487.00	1300.00
3-(60 pgs.)-In costume w/pin-ups; Hitler-c	131.00	394.00	1050.00
4-(52 pgs.)-In costume, 2 pgs. w/pin-ups	100.00	300.00	800.00
5-(52 pgs.)-In costume w/pin-ups	87.00	262.00	700.00
6-(52 pgs.)-Not in costume in inside stories, w/pin-ups	81.00	244.00	650.00
7,8-(36 pgs.)-In costume 1 pg. each; no pin-ups	75.00	225.00	600.00

NOTE: ***Schomburg*** *c-1, 5, 6.*

MISS FURY
Adventure Comics: 1991 - No. 4, 1991 ($2.50, limited series)

1-4: 1-Origin; granddaughter of original Miss Fury			2.50
1-Limited ed. ($4.95)			5.00

MISSION IMPOSSIBLE (TV)
Dell Publ. Co.: May, 1967 - No. 4, Oct, 1968; No. 5, Oct, 1969 (All have photo-c)

1	7.50	22.50	90.00
2-5: 5-Reprints #1	5.00	15.00	60.00

MISSION IMPOSSIBLE (Movie)
Marvel Comics (Paramount Comics): May, 1996 ($2.95, one-shot) (1st Paramount Comics book)

1-Liefeld-c & back-up story			3.00

MISS LIBERTY (Becomes Liberty Comics)
Burten Publishing Co.: 1945 (MLJ reprints)

1-The Shield & Dusty, The Wizard, & Roy, the Super Boy app.; r/Shield-Wizard #13	29.00	86.00	200.00

MISS MELODY LANE OF BROADWAY (See The Adventures of Bob Hope)
National Periodical Publ.: Feb-Mar, 1950 - No. 3, June-July, 1950 (52 pgs.)

1-Movie stars photos app. on all-c.	57.00	172.00	460.00
2,3: 3-Ed Sullivan photo on-c.	40.00	120.00	290.00

MISS PEACH
Dell Publishing Co.: Oct-Dec, 1963; 1969

	GD2.0	FN6.0	NM9.4
1-Jack Mendelsohn-a/script	6.40	19.00	70.00
...Tells You How to Grow (1969; 25¢)-Mel Lazarus-a; also given away (36 pgs.)	3.60	11.00	40.00

MISS PEPPER (See Meet Miss Pepper)

MISS SUNBEAM (See Little Miss...)

MISS VICTORY (See Captain Fearless #1,2, Holyoke One-Shot #3, Veri Best Sure Fire & Veri Best Sure Shot Comics)

MISTER AMERICA
Endeavor Comics: Apr, 1994 - No. 2, May, 1994 ($2.95, limited series)

1,2			3.00

MR. & MRS. BEANS
United Features Syndicate: No. 11, 1939

Single Series 11	34.00	103.00	240.00

MR. & MRS. J. EVIL SCIENTIST (TV)(See The Flintstones & Hanna-Barbera Band Wagon #3)
Gold Key: Nov, 1963 - No. 4, Sept, 1966 (Hanna-Barbera, all 12¢)

1	7.00	22.00	80.00
2-4	4.50	13.50	50.00

MR. ANTHONY'S LOVE CLINIC (Based on radio show)
Hillman Periodicals: Nov, 1949 - No. 5, Apr-May, 1950 (52 pgs.)

1-Photo-c	12.00	36.00	85.00
2	8.35	25.00	50.00
3-5: 5-Photo-c	6.70	20.00	40.00

MISTER BLANK
Amaze Ink: No. 0, Jan, 1996 - Present ($1.75/$2.95, B&W)

0-($1.75, 16 pgs.) Origin of Mr. Blank			2.00
1-7-($2.95) Chris Hicks-s/a			3.00

MR. DISTRICT ATTORNEY (Radio/TV)
National Per. Publ.: Jan-Feb, 1948 - No. 67, Jan-Feb, 1959 (1-23: 52 pgs.)

1-Howard Purcell c-5-23 (most)	100.00	300.00	800.00
2	44.00	132.00	350.00
3-5	34.00	103.00	240.00
6-10	26.00	79.00	185.00
11-20	21.00	62.00	145.00
21-43: 43-Last pre-code (1-2/55)	13.50	41.00	95.00
44-67	11.00	33.00	75.00

MR. DISTRICT ATTORNEY (SeeThe Funnies #35)
Dell Publishing Co.: No. 13, 1942

Four Color 13-See The Funnies #35 for 1st app.	29.00	86.00	315.00

MISTER E (Also see Books of Magic limited series)
DC Comics: Jun, 1991- No. 4, Sept, 1991($1.75, limited series)

1-4-Snyder III-c/a; follow-up to Books of Magic limited series			2.00

MISTER ED, THE TALKING HORSE (TV)
Dell Publishing Co./Gold Key: Mar-May, 1962 - No. 6, Feb, 1964 (All photo-c; photo back-c: 1-6)

Four Color 1295	12.00	35.00	130.00
1(11/62) (Gold Key)-Photo-c	9.00	27.00	100.00
2-6: Photo-c	5.00	15.00	55.00

(See March of Comics #244, 260, 282, 290)

MR. HERO, THE NEWMATIC MAN (See Neil Gaiman's...)

MR. MAGOO (TV) (The Nearsighted..., ...& Gerald McBoing Boing 1954 issues; formerly Gerald McBoing-Boing And ...)
Dell Publishing Co.: No. 6, Nov-Jan, 1953-54; 5/54 - 3-5/62; 9-11/63 - 3-5/65

6	11.00	33.00	120.00
Four Color 561(5/54),602(11/54)	11.00	33.00	120.00
Four Color 1235(#1, 12-2/62),1305(#2, 3-5/62)	9.00	27.00	100.00
3(9-11/63) - 5	8.00	23.00	85.00
Four Color 1235(12-536-505)(3-5/65)-2nd Printing	5.50	16.50	60.00

Mr. Majestic #1 © WildStorm

Mister Mystery #2 © Media Pub.

Mr. Punch SC © Neil Gaiman & Dave McKean

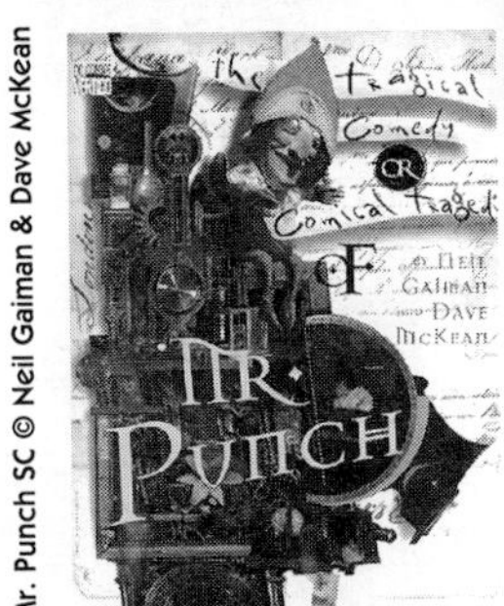

GD2.0 FN6.0 NM9.4

MR. MAJESTIC (See WildC.A.T.S.)
DC Comics (WildStorm): Sept, 1999 - Present ($2.50)

1-3: 1-McGuinness-a/Casey & Holguin-s. 2-Two covers 2.50

MISTER MIRACLE (1st series) (See Cancelled Comic Cavalcade)
National Periodical Publications/DC Comics: 3-4/71 - V4#18, 2-3/74; V5#19, 9/77 - V6#25, 8-9/78; 1987 (Fourth World)

1-1st app. Mr. Miracle (#1-3 are 15¢) 3.50 10.50 35.00
2,3: 3-Last 15¢ issue 2.25 6.75 18.00
4-8: 4-Boy Commandos-r begin; all 52 pgs. 2.50 7.50 22.00
9-18: 9-Origin Mr. Miracle; Darkseid cameo. 15-Intro/1st app. Shilo Norman. 18-Barda & Scott Free wed; New Gods app. & Darkseid cameo; Last Kirby issue. 1.50 4.50 12.00
19-25 (1977-78) 2.40 6.00
Special 1(1987, $1.25, 52 pgs.) 3.00
Jack Kirby's Mister Miracle TPB ('98, $12.95) B&W&Grey-toned reprint of #1-10; David Copperfield intro. 13.00
NOTE: ***Austin** a-19i.* ***Ditko** a-6r.* ***Golden** a-23-25p; c-25p.* ***Heath** a-24i, 25i; c-25i.* ***Kirby** a(p)/c-1-18.* ***Nasser** a-19i.* ***Rogers** a-19-22p; c-19, 20p, 21p, 22-24. 4-8 contain* ***Simon & Kirby** Boy Commandos reprints from Detective 82,76, Boy Commandos 1, 3 & Detective 64 in that order.*

MISTER MIRACLE (2nd Series) (See Justice League)
DC Comics: Jan, 1989 - No. 28, June, 1991 ($1.00)

1-28: 13,14-Lobo app. 22-1st new Mr. Miracle w/new costume 2.00

MISTER MIRACLE (3rd Series)
DC Comics: Apr, 1996 - No. 7, Oct, 1996 ($1.95)

1-7: 2-Vs. JLA. 6-Simonson-c 2.00

MR. MIRACLE (See Capt. Fearless #1 & Holyoke One-Shot #4)

MR. MONSTER (1st Series)(Doc Stearn... #7 on; See Airboy-Mr. Monster Special, Dark Horse Presents, Super Duper Comics & Vanguard Illustrated #7)
Eclipse Comics: Jan, 1985 - No. 10, June, 1987 ($1.75, Baxter paper)

1-1st story-r from Vanguard Ill. #7(1st app.) 3.00
2-10: 2-Dave Stevens-c. 3-Alan Moore scripts; Wolverton-r/Weird Mysteries #5. 6-Ditko-r/Fantastic Fears #5 plus new Giffen-a 10 6-D issue 2.00

MR. MONSTER
Dark Horse Comics: Feb, 1988 - No. 8, July, 1991 ($1.75, B&W)

1-7 2.00
8-($4.95, 60 pgs.)-Origins conclusion 5.00

MR. MONSTER ATTACKS! (Doc Stearn...)
Tundra Publ.: Aug, 1992 - No. 3, Oct, 1992 ($3.95, limited series, 32 pgs.)

1-3: Michael T. Gilbert-a/scripts; Gilbert/Dorman painted-c 4.00

MR. MONSTER PRESENTS (CRACK-A-BOOM!)
Caliber Comics: 1997 - No. 3, 1997 ($2.95, B&W&Red, limited series)

1-3: Michael T. Gilbert-a/scripts: 1-Wraparound-c 3.00

MR. MONSTER'S SUPER-DUPER SPECIAL
Eclipse Comics: May, 1986 - No. 8, July, 1987

1-(5/86)...3-D High Octane Horror #1 3.00
1-(5/86)...2-D version, 100 copies 1.50 4.50 12.00
2-(8/86)...High Octane Horror #1, 3-(9/86)...True Crime #1, 4-(11/86)...True Crime #2, 5-(1/87)...Hi-Voltage Super Science #1, 6-(3/87)...High Shock Schlock #1, 7-(5/87)...High Shock Schlock #2, 8-(7/87)...Weird Tales Of The Future #1 3.00
NOTE: ***Jack Cole** r-3, 4.* ***Evans** a-2r.* ***Kubert** a-1r.* ***Powell** a-5r.* ***Wolverton** a-2r, 7r, 8r.*

MR. MONSTER VS. GORZILLA
Image Comics: July, 1998 ($2.95, one-shot)

1- Michael T. Gilbert-a 3.00

MR. MUSCLES (Formerly Blue Beetle #18-21)
Charlton Comics: No. 22, Mar, 1956; No. 23, Aug, 1956

22,23 7.00 21.00 42.00

MR. MXYZPTLK (VILLAINS)
DC Comics: Feb, 1998 ($1.95, one-shot)

1-Grant-s/Morgan-a/Pearson-c 2.00

GD2.0 FN6.0 NM9.4

MISTER MYSTERY (Tales of Horror and Suspense)
Mr. Publ. (Media Publ.) No. 1-3/SPM Publ./Stanmore (Aragon): Sept, 1951 - No. 19, Oct, 1954

1-Kurtzmanesque horror story 78.00 234.00 625.00
2,3-Kurtzmanesque story. 3-Anti-Wertham edit. 51.00 154.00 410.00
4,6: Bondage-c; 6-Torture 51.00 154.00 410.00
5,8,10 46.00 139.00 370.00
7- "The Brain Bats of Venus" by Wolverton; partially re-used in Weird Tales of the Future #7 103.00 309.00 825.00
9-Nostrand-a 46.00 139.00 370.00
11-Wolverton "Robot Woman" story/Weird Mysteries #2, cut up, rewritten & partially redrawn 72.00 261.00 575.00
12-Classic injury to eye-c 103.00 309.00 825.00
13-17,19: 15- "Living Dead" junkie story. 17-Severed heads-c. 19-Reprints 34.00 103.00 240.00
18- "Robot Woman" by Wolverton reprinted from Weird Mysteries #2; decapitation, bondage-c 55.00 165.00 440.00
NOTE: ***Andru** a-1, 2p, 3p.* ***Andru/Esposito** c-1-3.* ***Baily** c-10-18(most).* ***Mortellaro** c-5-7. Bondage c-7. Some issues have graphic dismemberment scenes.*

MR. PUNCH
DC Comics (Vertigo): 1994 ($24.95, one-shot)

nn (Hard-c)-Gaiman scripts; McKean-c/a 40.00
nn (Soft-c) 15.00

MISTER Q (See Mighty Midget Comics & Our Flag Comics #5)

MR. RISK (Formerly All Romances; Men Against Crime #3 on)(Also see Our Flag Comics & Super-Mystery Comics)
Ace Magazines: No. 7, Oct, 1950 - No. 2, Dec, 1950

7,2 8.00 24.00 48.00

MR. SCARLET & PINKY (See Mighty Midget Comics)

MR. T AND THE T-FORCE
Now Comics: June, 1993 - No. 10, May, 1994 ($1.95, color)

1-10-Newsstand editions: 1-7-polybagged with photo trading card in each. 1,2-Neal Adams-c/a(p). 3-Dave Dorman painted-c 2.00
1-10-Direct Sale editions polybagged w/line drawn trading cards. 1-Contains gold foil trading card by Neal Adams 2.00

MISTER UNIVERSE (Professional wrestler)
Mr. Publications Media Publ. (Stanmor, Aragon): July, 1951; No. 2, Oct, 1951 - No. 5, April, 1952

1 21.00 62.00 145.00
2- "Jungle That Time Forgot", (24 pg. story); Andru/Esposito-c 13.00 39.00 90.00
3-Marijuana story 13.00 39.00 90.00
4,5- "Goes to War" cover/stories 10.00 30.00 65.00

MISTER X (See Vortex)
6/84 - No. 14, 8/88 ($1.50/$2.25, direct sales, coated paper)
Mr. Publications/Vortex Comics/Caliber V3#1 on: V2#1, Apr, 1989 - V2#12, Mar, 1990 ($2.00/$2.50, B&W, newsprint) V3#1, 1996 - Present ($2.95, B&W)

1-14,V2#1-12,V3#1-3: 11-Dave McKean story & art (6 pgs.), V2#1-11 (Second Coming, B&W): 1-Four diff.-c. 10-Photo-c 3.00
Return of... ($11.95, graphic novel)-r/1-4 12.00
Return of... ($34.95, hardcover limited edition)-r/1-4 35.00
Special (no date, 1990?) 3.00

MISTY
Marvel Comics (Star Comics): Dec, 1985 - No. 6, May, 1986 (Limited series)

1-6: Millie The Model's niece 2.50

MITZI COMICS (Becomes Mitzi's Boy Friend #2-7)(See All Teen)
Timely Comics: Spring, 1948 (one-shot)

1-Kurtzman's "Hey Look" plus 3 pgs. "Giggles 'n' Grins" 20.00 60.00 140.00

MITZI'S BOY FRIEND (Formerly Mitzi Comics; becomes Mitzi's Romances)
Marvel Comics (TCI): No. 2, June, 1948 - No. 7, April, 1949

Modeling with Millie #48 © MAR

Modern Comics #65 © QUA

Modern Love #5 © WMG

	GD2.0	FN6.0	NM9.4
2	10.00	30.00	70.00
3-7	8.35	25.00	50.00

MITZI'S ROMANCES (Formerly Mitzi's Boy Friend)
Timely/Marvel Comics (TCI): No. 8, June, 1949 - No. 10, Dec, 1949

	GD2.0	FN6.0	NM9.4
8-Becomes True Life Tales #8 (10/49) on?	10.00	30.00	70.00
9,10: 10-Painted-c	8.35	25.00	50.00

MOBFIRE
DC Comics (Vertigo): Dec, 1994 - No. 6, May, 1995 ($2.50, limited series)

	GD2.0	FN6.0	NM9.4
1-6			2.50

MOBY DICK (See Feature Presentations #6, and King Classics)
Dell Publishing Co.: No. 717, Aug, 1956

	GD2.0	FN6.0	NM9.4
Four Color 717-Movie, Gregory Peck photo-c	8.00	25.00	90.00

MOBY DUCK (See Donald Duck #112 & Walt Disney Showcase #2,11)
Gold Key (Disney): Oct, 1967 - No. 11, Oct, 1970; No. 12, Jan, 1974 - No. 30, Feb, 1978

	GD2.0	FN6.0	NM9.4
1	2.50	7.50	20.00
2-5	1.50	4.50	12.00
6-11	1.00	3.00	8.00
12-30: 21,30-r			5.00

MODEL FUN (With Bobby Benson)
Harle Publications: No. 3, Winter, 1954-55 - No. 5, July, 1955

	GD2.0	FN6.0	NM9.4
3-Bobby Benson	4.35	19.00	38.00
4,5-Bobby Benson	4.00	12.00	24.00

MODELING WITH MILLIE (Formerly Life With Millie)
Atlas/Marvel Comics (Male Publ.): No. 21, Feb, 1963 - No. 54, June, 1967

	GD2.0	FN6.0	NM9.4
21	7.50	22.50	75.00
22-30	4.20	12.60	42.00
31-54	3.00	9.00	30.00

MODERN COMICS (Formerly Military Comics #1-43)
Quality Comics Group: No. 44, Nov, 1945 - No. 102, Oct, 1950

	GD2.0	FN6.0	NM9.4
44-Blackhawk continues	52.00	157.00	420.00
45-52: 49-1st app. Fear, Lady Adventuress	40.00	120.00	300.00
53-Torchy by Ward begins (9/46)	40.00	120.00	325.00
54-60: 55-J. Cole-a	35.00	105.00	245.00
61-77,79,80: 73-J. Cole-a	31.00	94.00	220.00
78-1st app. Madame Butterfly	35.00	105.00	245.00
81-99,101: 82,83-One pg. J. Cole-a. 83-The Spirit app.; last 52 pg. issue? 99-Blackhawks on the moon-c/story	31.00	94.00	220.00
100	31.00	94.00	220.00
102-(Scarce)-J. Cole-a; Spirit by Eisner app.	37.00	111.00	260.00

NOTE: ***Al Bryant*** *c-44-51, 54, 55, 66, 69.* ***Jack Cole*** *a-55, 73.* ***Crandall*** *Blackhawk-#46, 47, 50, 51, 54, 56, 58-60, 64, 67-70, 73, 74, 76-78, 80-83; c-60-65, 67, 68, 70-95.* ***Crandall/Cuidera*** *c-56-59, 96-102.* ***Gustavson*** *a-47.* ***Ward*** *Blackhawk-#52, 53, 55 (15 pgs. each). Torchy in #53-102; by* ***Ward*** *only in #53-89(9/49); by* ***Gil Fox*** *#93, 102.*

MODERN LOVE
E. C. Comics: June-July, 1949 - No. 8, Aug-Sept, 1950

	GD2.0	FN6.0	NM9.4
1	51.00	153.00	460.00
2-Craig/Feldstein-c	37.00	110.00	330.00
3-Spanking panel	33.00	99.00	280.00
4-6 (Scarce): 4-Bra/panties panels	47.00	140.00	420.00
7,8	35.00	106.00	300.00

NOTE: ***Craig*** *a-3.* ***Feldstein*** *a-in most issues; c-1, 2i, 3-8.* ***Harrison*** *a-4.* ***Iger*** *a-6-8.* ***Ingels*** *a-1, 2, 4-7.* ***Palais*** *a-5.* ***Wood*** *a-7.* ***Wood/Harrison*** *a-5-7. (Canadian reprints known; see Table of Contents.)*

MOD LOVE
Western Publishing Co.: 1967 (50¢, 36 pgs.)

	GD2.0	FN6.0	NM9.4
1	2.80	8.40	28.00

MODNIKS, THE
Gold Key: Aug, 1967 - No. 2, Aug, 1970

	GD2.0	FN6.0	NM9.4
10206-708(#1)	2.50	7.50	24.00
2	2.00	6.00	16.00

MOD SQUAD (TV)
Dell Publishing Co.: Jan, 1969 - No. 3, Oct, 1969 - No. 8, April, 1971

	GD2.0	FN6.0	NM9.4
1-Photo-c	4.50	13.50	50.00
2-4: 2-4-Photo-c	2.90	8.70	32.00
5-8: 8-Photo-c; Reprints #2	2.40	7.00	26.00

MOD WHEELS
Gold Key: Mar, 1971 - No. 19, Jan, 1976

	GD2.0	FN6.0	NM9.4
1	2.50	7.50	24.00
2-9	2.00	6.00	16.00
10-19: 11,15-Extra 16 pgs. ads	1.50	4.50	12.00

MOE & SHMOE COMICS
O. S. Publ. Co.: Spring, 1948 - No. 2, Summer, 1948

	GD2.0	FN6.0	NM9.4
1	7.50	22.50	45.00
2	5.35	16.00	32.00

MOEBIUS (Graphic novel)
Marvel Comics (Epic Comics): Oct, 1987 - No. 6, 1988; No. 7, 1990; No. 8, 1991 ($9.95, 8x11", mature)

	GD2.0	FN6.0	NM9.4
1,2,4-6,8: (#2, 2nd printing, $9.95)			10.00
3,7,0: 3-(1st & 2nd printings, $12.95). 0 (1990, $12.95)			13.00
Moebius I-Signed & numbered hard-c ($45.95, Graphitti Designs, 1,500 copies printed)-r/#1-3			46.00

MOEBIUS COMICS
Caliber: May, 1996 - No. 6 ($2.95, B&W)

	GD2.0	FN6.0	NM9.4
1-6: Moebius-c/a. 1-William Stout-a			3.00

MOEBIUS: THE MAN FROM CIGURI
Dark Horse Comics: 1996 ($7.95, digest-size)

	GD2.0	FN6.0	NM9.4
nn-Moebius-c/a			8.00

MOLLY MANTON'S ROMANCES (Romantic Affairs #3)
Marvel Comics (SePI): Sept, 1949 - No. 2, Dec, 1949 (52 pgs.)

	GD2.0	FN6.0	NM9.4
1-Photo-c (becomes Blaze the Wonder Collie #2 (10/49) on? & Molly Manton's Romances #2	12.00	36.00	85.00
2-Titled "Romances of..."; photo-c	10.00	30.00	60.00

MOLLY O'DAY (Super Sleuth)
Avon Periodicals: February, 1945 (1st Avon comic)

	GD2.0	FN6.0	NM9.4
1-Molly O'Day, The Enchanted Dagger by Tuska (r/Yankee #1), Capt'n Courage, Corporal Grant app.	45.00	135.00	360.00

MONA
Kitchen Sink Press: 1999 ($4.95, B&W, one-shot)

	GD2.0	FN6.0	NM9.4
1-Cartoons by Kurtzman and various; Hernandez-c			5.00

MONKEES, THE (TV)(Also see Circus Boy, Groovy, Not Brand Echh #3, Teen-Age Talk, Teen Beam & Teen Beat)
Dell Publishing Co.: March, 1967 - No. 17, Oct, 1969 (#1-4,6,7,9,10,12,15,16 have photo-c)

	GD2.0	FN6.0	NM9.4
1-Photo-c	8.00	25.00	90.00
2-6,7,9,10,12,15,16: All photo-c	5.00	15.00	55.00
8,11,13,14,17-No photo-c: 17-Reprints #1	3.50	11.00	38.00

MONKEY AND THE BEAR, THE
Atlas Comics (ZPC): Sept, 1953 - No. 3, Jan, 1954

	GD2.0	FN6.0	NM9.4
1-Howie Post-c/a in all; funny animal	7.50	22.50	45.00
2,3	4.25	13.00	28.00

MONKEYMAN AND O'BRIEN (Also see Dark Horse Presents #80, 100-5, Gen[13]/..., Hellboy: Seed of Destruction, & San Diego Comic Con #2)
Dark Horse Comics (Legend): Jul, 1996 - No. 3, Sept, 1996 ($2.95, lim. series)

	GD2.0	FN6.0	NM9.4
1-3: New stories; Art Adams-c/a/scripts			3.50
nn-(2/96, $2.95)-r/back-up stories from Hellboy: Seed of Destruction; Adams-c/a/scripts			3.50

MONKEYSHINES COMICS
Ace Periodicals/Publishers Specialists/Current Books/Unity Publ.: Summer, 1944 - No. 27, July, 1949

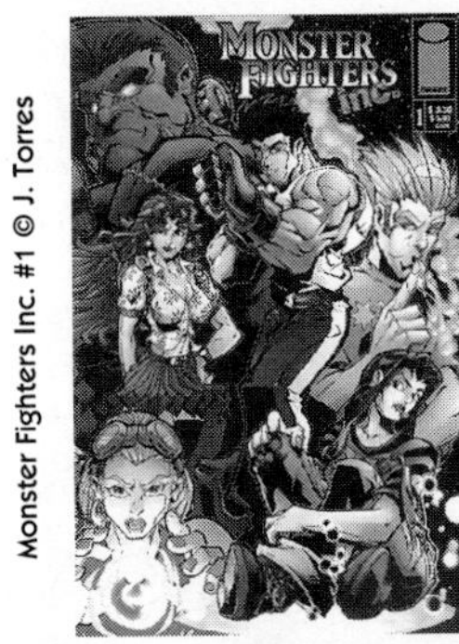

Monster Fighters Inc. #1 © J. Torres

Monte Hale Western #33 © FAW

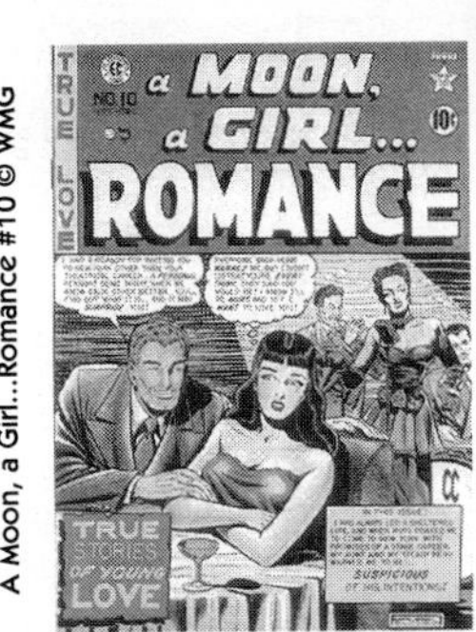

A Moon, a Girl...Romance #10 © WMG

	GD2.0	FN6.0	NM9.4
1-Funny animal	10.00	30.00	70.00
2-(Aut/44)	5.85	17.50	35.00
3-10: 3-(Win/44)	4.25	13.00	28.00
11-17,19-27: 23,24-Fago-c/a	4.00	12.00	24.00
18-Frazetta-a	5.85	17.50	35.00

MONKEY'S UNCLE, THE (See Merlin Jones As... under Movie Comics)

MONROES, THE (TV)
Dell Publishing Co.: Apr, 1967

1-Photo-c 2.20 6.50 24.00

MONSTER
Fiction House Magazines: 1953 - No. 2, 1953

1-Dr. Drew by Grandenetti; reprint from Rangers Comics #48; Whitman-c 45.00 135.00 360.00
2-Whitman-c 37.00 111.00 260.00

MONSTER CRIME COMICS (Also see Crime Must Stop)
Hillman Periodicals: Oct, 1952 (15¢, 52 pgs.)

1 (Scarce) 94.00 281.00 750.00

MONSTER FIGHTERS INC.
Image Comics (Bright Anvil Studios): Apr, 1999 - Present ($3.50)

1-Torres-s/Lubera & Yeung-a 3.50

MONSTER HOWLS (Magazine)
Humor-Vision: December, 1966 (Satire) (35¢, 68 pgs.)

1 4.50 13.50 45.00

MONSTER HUNTERS
Charlton Comics: Aug, 1975 - No. 9, Jan, 1977; No. 10, Oct, 1977 - No. 18, Feb, 1979

1-Howard-a; Newton-c.	2.25	6.75	18.00
2-Ditko-a	1.75	5.25	14.00
3-10	1.25	3.75	10.00
11-13,15-18	1.00	2.80	7.00
14-Special all-Ditko issue	1.75	5.25	14.00
1,2 (Modern Comics reprints, 1977)			3.00

NOTE: ***Ditko*** *a-2, 6, 8, 10, 13-15r, 18r; c-13-15, 18.* ***Howard*** *a-1, 3, 17; r-13.* ***Morisi*** *a-1.* ***Staton*** *a-1, 13.* ***Sutton*** *a-2, 4; c-2, 4; r-16-18.* ***Zeck*** *a-4-9. Reprints in #12-18.*

MONSTER MADNESS (Magazine)
Marvel Comics: 1972 - #3, 1973 (60¢, B&W)

1-3: Stories by "Sinister" Stan Lee 2.50 7.50 24.00

MONSTER MAN
Image Comics (Action Planet): Sept, 1997 ($2.95, B&W)

1-Mike Manley-c/s/a 3.00

MONSTER MASTERWORKS
Marvel Comics: 1989 ($12.95, TPB)

nn-Reprints 1960's monster stories; art by Kirby, Ditko, Ayers, Everett 13.00

MONSTER MATINEE
Chaos! Comics: Oct, 1997 - No. 3, Oct, 1997 ($2.50, limited series)

1-3: pin-ups 2.50

MONSTER MENACE
Marvel Comics: Dec, 1993 - No. 4, Mar, 1994 ($1.25, limited series)

1-4: Pre-code Atlas horror reprints. 3.00

NOTE: ***Ditko-r*** *&* ***Kirby-r*** *in all.*

MONSTER OF FRANKENSTEIN (See Frankenstein)

MONSTERS ON THE PROWL (Chamber of Darkness #1-8)
Marvel Comics Group (No. 13,14: 52 pgs.): No. 9, 2/71 - No. 27, 11/73; No. 28, 6/74 - No. 30, 10/74

9-Barry Smith inks	2.50	7.50	22.00
10-12,15: 12-Last 15¢ issue	1.50	4.50	12.00
13,14-(52 pgs.)	2.25	6.75	18.00
16-(4/72)-King Kull 4th app.; Severin-c	1.75	5.25	14.00
17-30	1.25	3.75	10.00

NOTE: ***Ditko*** *r-9, 14, 16.* ***Kirby*** *r-10-17, 21, 23, 25, 27, 28, 30; c-9, 25.* ***Kirby/Ditko*** *r-14, 17-20, 22, 24, 26, 29.* ***Marie/John Severin*** *a-16(Kull). 9-13, 15 contain one new story. Woodish art by* ***Reese****-11. King Kull created by Robert E. Howard.*

MONSTERS TO LAUGH WITH (Magazine) (Becomes Monsters Unlimited #4)
Marvel Comics Group: 1964 - No. 3, 1965 (B&W)

1-Humor by Stan Lee	5.50	16.50	55.00
2,3	3.20	9.60	32.00

MONSTERS UNLEASHED (Magazine)
Marvel Comics Group: July, 1973 - No. 11, Apr, 1975; Summer, 1975 (B&W)

1-Soloman Kane sty; Werewolf app. 2.80 8.40 28.00
2-4: 2-The Frankenstein Monster begins, ends #10. 3-Neal Adams-c/a; The Man-Thing begins (origin-r); Son of Satan preview. 4-Werewolf app. 2.50 7.50 24.00
5-7: Werewolf in all. 5-Man-Thing. 7-Williamson-a(r) 1.75 5.25 14.00
8-11: 8-Man-Thing; N. Adams-r. 9-Man-Thing; Wendigo app. 10-Origin Tigra 2.25 6.75 18.00
Annual 1 (Summer,1975, 92 pgs.)-Kane-a 2.00 6.00 16.00

NOTE: ***Boris*** *c-2, 6.* ***Brunner*** *a-2; c-11.* ***J. Buscema*** *a-2p, 4p, 5p.* ***Colan*** *a-1, 4r.* ***Davis*** *a-3r.* ***Everett*** *a-2r.* ***G. Kane*** *a-3.* ***Krigstein*** *r-4.* ***Morrow*** *a-3; c-1.* ***Perez*** *a-8.* ***Ploog*** *a-6.* ***Reese*** *a-1, 2.* ***Tuska*** *a-3p.* ***Wildey*** *a-1r.*

MONSTERS UNLIMITED (Magazine) (Formerly Monsters To Laugh With)
Marvel Comics Group: No. 4, 1965 - No. 7, 1966 (B&W)

4-7 2.80 8.40 28.00

MONTANA KID, THE (See Kid Montana)

MONTE HALE WESTERN (Movie star; Formerly Mary Marvel #1-28; also see Fawcett Movie Comic, Motion Picture Comics, Picture News #8, Real Western Hero, Six-Gun Heroes, Western Hero & XMas Comics)
Fawcett Publ./Charlton No. 83 on: No. 29, Oct, 1948 - No. 88, Jan, 1956

29-(#1, 52 pgs.)-Photo-c begin, end #82; Monte Hale & his horse Pardner begin 47.00 142.00 380.00
30-(52 pgs.)-Big Bow and Little Arrow begin, end #34; Captain Tootsie by Beck 25.00 75.00 175.00
31-36,38-40-(52 pgs.): 34-Gabby Hayes begins, ends #80. 39-Captain Tootsie by Beck 19.00 56.00 130.00
37,41,45,49-(36 pgs.) 13.00 39.00 90.00
42-44,46-48,50-(52 pgs.): 47-Big Bow & Little Arrow app. 13.50 41.00 95.00
51,52,54-56,58,59-(52 pgs.) 11.00 33.00 75.00
53,57-(36 pgs.): 53-Slim Pickens app. 9.70 29.00 58.00
60-81: 36 pgs. #60-on. 80-Gabby Hayes ends 9.70 29.00 58.00
82-Last Fawcett issue (6/53) 11.00 33.00 75.00
83-1st Charlton issue (2/55); B&W photo back-c begin. Gabby Hayes returns, ends #86 12.00 36.00 85.00
84 (4/55) 10.00 30.00 65.00
85-86 9.70 29.00 58.00
87,88: 87-Wolverton-r, 1/2 pg. 88-Last issue 10.00 30.00 65.00

NOTE: ***Gil Kane*** *a-33?, 34? Rocky Lane -1 pg. (Carnation ad)-38, 40, 41, 43, 44, 46, 55.*

MONTY HALL OF THE U.S. MARINES (See With the Marines...)
Toby Press: Aug, 1951 - No. 11, Apr, 1953

1	10.00	30.00	70.00
2	6.35	19.00	38.00
3-5	5.70	17.00	34.00
6-11	5.00	15.00	30.00

NOTE: *Full page pin-ups (Pin-Up Pete) by* ***Jack Sparling*** *in #1-9.*

MOON, A GIRL...ROMANCE, A (Becomes Weird Fantasy #13 on; formerly Moon Girl #1-8)
E. C. Comics: No. 9, Sept-Oct, 1949 - No. 12, Mar-Apr, 1950

9-Moon Girl cameo; spanking panel	59.00	176.00	500.00
10,11	45.00	134.00	380.00
12-(Scarce)	60.00	180.00	510.00

NOTE: ***Feldstein, Ingels*** *art in all.* ***Feldstein*** *c-9-12.* ***Wood/Harrison*** *a-10-12. Canadian reprints known; see Table of Contents.*

MOON GIRL AND THE PRINCE (#1) (Moon Girl #2-6; Moon Girl Fights Crime #7, 8; becomes A Moon, A Girl, Romance #9 on)(Also see Animal

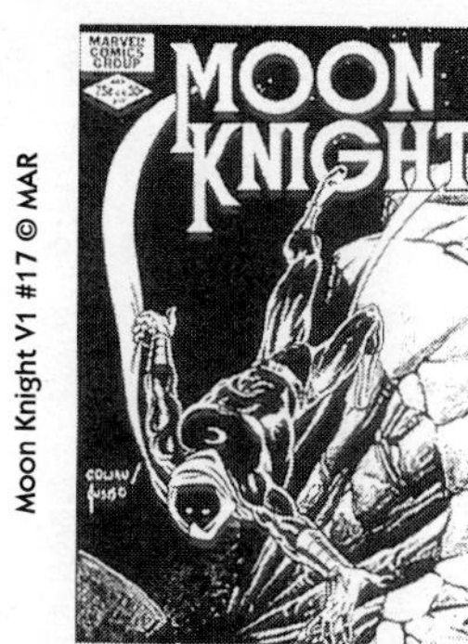

Moon Knight V1 #17 © MAR

Mopsy #3 © STJ

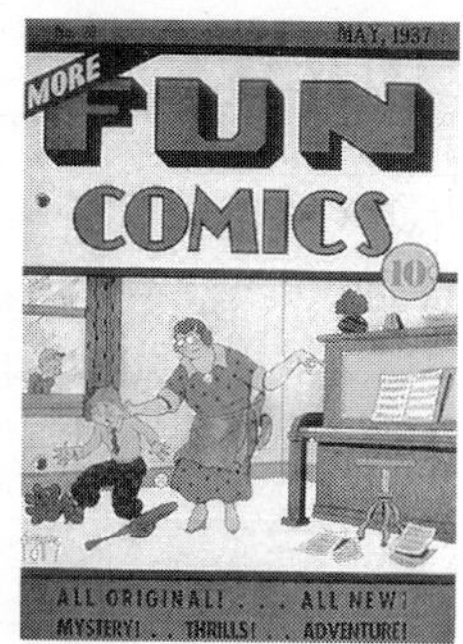

More Fun Comics #20 © DC

Fables #7 and Happy Houlihans)
E. C. Comics: Fall, 1947 - No. 8, Summer, 1949

1-Origin Moon Girl (see Happy Houlihans #1) 75.00 225.00 750.00
2 38.00 114.00 380.00
3,4: 4-Moon Girl vs. a vampire 32.00 96.00 325.00
5-E.C.'s 1st horror story, "Zombie Terror" 82.00 246.00 825.00
6-8 (Scarce): 7-Origin Star (Moongirl's sidekick) 41.00 123.00 410.00
NOTE: ***Craig*** *a-2, 5.* ***Moldoff*** *a-1-8; c-2-6.* ***Wheelan's*** *Fat and Slat app. in #3, 4, 6. #2 & #3 are 52 pgs., #4 on, 36 pgs. Canadian reprints known; (see Table of Contents.)*

MOON KNIGHT (Also see The Hulk, Marc Spector..., Marvel Preview #21, Marvel Spotlight & Werewolf by Night #32)
Marvel Comics Group: Nov, 1980 - No. 38, Jul, 1984 (Mando paper #33 on)

1-Origin resumed in #4 3.00
2-38: 4-Intro Midnight Man. 16-The Thing app. 25-Double size. 35-($1.00, 52 pgs.)-X-men app.; F.F. cameo 2.00
NOTE: ***Austin*** *c-27i, 31i.* ***Cowan*** *a-16; c-16, 17.* ***Kaluta*** *c-36-38; back c-35.* ***Miller*** *c-9, 12p, 13p, 15p, 27p.* ***Ploog*** *back c-35.* ***Sienkiewicz*** *a-1-15, 17-20, 22-26, 28-30, 33i, 36(4), 37; c-1-5, 7, 8, 10, 11, 14-16, 18-26, 28-30, 31p, 33, 34.*

MOON KNIGHT
Marvel Comics Group: June, 1985 - V2#6, Dec, 1985

V2#1-6: 1-Double size; new costume. 6-Sienkiewicz painted-c. 2.00

MOON KNIGHT
Marvel Comics: Jan, 1998 - No. 4, Apr, 1998 ($2.50, limited series)

1-4-Moench-s/Edwards-c/a 2.50

MOON KNIGHT (Volume 3)
Marvel Comics: Jan, 1999 - No. 4, Feb, 1999 ($2.99, limited series)

1-4-Moench-s/Texeira-a(p) 3.00

MOON KNIGHT: DIVIDED WE FALL
Marvel Comics: 1992 ($4.95, 52 pgs.)

nn-Denys Cowan-c/a(p) 5.00

MOON KNIGHT SPECIAL
Marvel Comics: Oct, 1992 ($2.50, 52 pgs.)

1-Shang Chi, Master of Kung Fu-c/story 2.50

MOON KNIGHT SPECIAL EDITION
Marvel Comics Group: Nov, 1983 - No. 3, Jan, 1984 ($2.00, limited series, Baxter paper)

1-3: Reprints from Hulk mag. by Sienkiewicz 2.00

MOON MULLINS (See Popular Comics, Super Book #3 & Super Comics)
Dell Publishing Co.: 1941 - 1945

Four Color 14(1941) 34.00 102.00 375.00
Large Feature Comic 29(1941) 25.00 74.00 270.00
Four Color 31(1943) 18.00 53.00 195.00
Four Color 81(1945) 9.50 29.00 105.00

MOON MULLINS
Michel Publ. (American Comics Group)#1-6/St. John #7,8: Dec-Jan, 1947-48 - No. 8, 1949 (52 pgs)

1-Alternating Sunday & daily strip-r 20.00 60.00 140.00
2 10.00 30.00 70.00
3-8: 7,8-St. John Publ. 8-...Featuring Kayo on-c 9.15 27.00 55.00
NOTE: ***Milt Gross*** *a-2-6, 8.* ***Frank Willard*** *r-all.*

MOON PILOT
Dell Publishing Co.: No. 1313, Mar-May, 1962

Four Color 1313-Movie, photo-c 6.40 19.00 70.00

MOONSHADOW (Also see Farewell, Moonshadow)
Marvel Comics (Epic Comics): 5/85 - #12, 2/87 ($1.50/$1.75, mature) (1st fully painted comic book)

1-Origin; J. M. DeMatteis scripts & Jon J. Muth painted-c/a. 5.00
2-12: 11-Origin 3.00
Trade paperback (1987?)-r/#1-12 14.00
Signed & numbered hard-c ($39.95, 1,200 copies)-r/#1-12 6.00 18.00 60.00

MOONSHADOW
DC Comics (Vertigo): Oct, 1994 - No. 12, Aug, 1995 ($2.25/$2.95)

1-11: Reprints Epic series. 2.50
12 ($2.95)-w/expanded ending 3.00
The Complete Moonshadow TPB ('98, $39.95) r/#1-12 and Farewell Moonshadow; new Muth painted-c 40.00

MOON-SPINNERS, THE (See Movie Comics)

MOPSY (See Pageant of Comics & TV Teens)
St. John Publ. Co.: Feb, 1948 - No. 19, Sept, 1953

1-Part-r; reprints "Some Punkins" by Neher 17.00 51.00 120.00
2 10.00 30.00 65.00
3-10(1953): 8-Lingerie panels 8.35 25.00 50.00
11-19: 19-Lingerie-c 6.70 20.00 40.00
NOTE: *#1, 3-6, 13, 18, 19 have paper dolls.*

MORBID ANGEL
London Night Studios: Oct, 1995 ($3.00, B&W)

1-Hartsoe-c 3.00

MORBID ANGEL
London Night Studios: July, 1996 - No. 3, Jan, 1997 ($3.00, limited series)

1/2-($9.95)-Angel Tear Edition; foil logo 10.00
1-3, 1-Penance-c, ...-To Hell and Back-(10/96, $3.00, B&W) 3.00

MORBIUS REVISITED
Marvel Comic: Aug, 1993 - No. 5, Dec, 1993 ($1.95, mini-series)

1-5-Reprints Fear #27-31 2.00

MORBIUS: THE LIVING VAMPIRE (Also see Amazing Spider-Man #101, 102, Fear #20, Marvel Team-Up #3, 4, Midnight Sons Unl. & Vampire Tales)
Marvel Comics (Midnight Sons imprint #16 on): Sept, 1992 - No. 32, Apr, 1995 ($1.75/$1.95)

1-($2.75, 52 pgs.)-Polybagged w/poster; Ghost Rider & Johnny Blaze x-over (part 3 of Rise of the Midnight Sons) 3.00
2-11,3-24,26-32: 3,4-Vs. Spider-Man-c/s.15-Ghost Rider app. 16-Spot varnish-c. 16,17-Siege of Darkness,parts 5 &13. 18-Deathlok app. 21-Bound-in Spider-Man trading card sheet; S-M app. 2.00
12-($2.25)-Outer-c is a Darkhold envelope made of black parchment w/gold ink; Midnight Massacre x-over 2.50
25-($2.50, 52 pgs.)-Gold foil logo 2.50

MORE FUN COMICS (Formerly New Fun Comics #1-6)
National Periodical Publications: No. 7, Jan, 1936 - No. 127, Nov-Dec, 1947 (No. 7,9-11: paper-c)

	GD2.0	FN6.0	VF8.0
7(1/36)-Oversized, paper-c; 1 pg. Kelly-a	723.00	2170.00	4700.00
8(2/36)-Oversized (10x12"), slick-c; 1 pg. Kelly-a	723.00	2170.00	4700.00
9(3-4/36)(Very rare, 1st comic-sized issue)-Last multiple panel-c	892.00	2675.00	5800.00
10,11(7/36): 10-Last Henri Duval by Siegel & Shuster. 11-1st "Calling All Cars" by Siegel & Shuster; new classic logo begins	508.00	1525.00	3300.00
12(8/36)-Slick-c begin	400.00	1200.00	2600.00
V2#1(9/36, #13)	370.00	1110.00	2400.00
2(10/36, #14)-Dr. Occult in costume (1st in color)(Superman proto-type; 1st DC appearance) continues from The Comics Magazine, ends #17	1770.00	5300.00	11,500.00
V2#3(11/36, #15), 16(V2#4), 17(V2#5): 16-Cover numbering begins; Xmas-c; last Superman tryout issue	708.00	2123.00	4600.00
18-20(V2#8, 5/37)	277.00	831.00	1800.00

	GD2.0	FN6.0	NM9.4
21(V2#9)-24(V2#12, 9/37)	275.00	825.00	1900.00
25(V3#1, 10/37)-27(V3#3, 12/37): 27-Xmas-c	275.00	825.00	1900.00
28-30: 30-1st non-funny cover	245.00	735.00	1750.00
31-Has ad for Action #1	261.00	785.00	1800.00
32-35: 32-Last Dr. Occult	245.00	735.00	1700.00
36-40: 36-(10/38)-The Masked Ranger & sidekick Pedro begins; Ginger Snap by Bob Kane (2 pgs.; 1st-a?). 39-Xmas-c	245.00	735.00	1700.00

More Fun Comics #65 © DC

More Fun Comics #117 © DC

More Than Mortal: Otherworlds #2 © Sharon Scott

GD2.0 FN6.0 NM9.4

41-50: 41-Last Masked Ranger 187.00 560.00 1300.00
51-The Spectre app. (in costume) in one panel ad at end of Buccaneer story 723.00 2170.00 4700.00

GD2.0 FN6.0 VF8.0 NM9.4

52-(2/40)-Origin/1st app. The Spectre (in costume splash panel only), part 1 by Bernard Baily (parts 1 & 2 written by Jerry Siegel; Spectre's costume changes color from purple & blue to green & grey; last Wing Brady; Spectre-c 4166.00 12,500.00 25,000.00 50,000.00
53-Origin The Spectre (in costume at end of story), part 2; Capt. Desmo begins;Spectre-c 2200.00 6,600.00 15,000.00 30,000.00
54-The Spectre in costume; last King Carter; classic-Spectre-c 820.00 2460.00 4920.00 8400.00
55-(Scarce, 5/40)-Dr. Fate begins (Intro & 1st app.); last Bulldog Martin; Spectre-c 1046.00 3138.00 6800.00 11,500.00

GD2.0 FN6.0 NM9.4

56-1st Dr. Fate-c (classic), origin continues. Congo Bill begins (6/40), 1st app.; 430.00 1290.00 4300.00
57-60-All Spectre-c 311.00 933.00 2800.00
61,65: 61-Classic Dr. Fate-c. 65-Classic Spectre-c 289.00 867.00 2600.00
62-64,66: 63-Last St. Bob Neal. 64-Lance Larkin begins; all Spectre-c 287.00 825.00 2300.00

GD2.0 FN6.0 VF8.0 NM9.4

67-(5/41)-Origin (1st) Dr. Fate; last Congo Bill & Biff Bronson (C.B. cont. in Action Comics #37, 6/41)-Spectre-c 600.00 1800.00 3600.00 6000.00

GD2.0 FN6.0 NM9.4

68-70: 68-Clip Carson begins. 70-Last Lance Larkin; all Dr. Fate-c 225.00 675.00 1800.00

GD2.0 FN6.0 VF8.0 NM9.4

71-Origin & 1st app. Johnny Quick by Mort Weisinger (9/41); classic sci/fi Dr. Fate-c 490.00 1470.00 2940.00 4900.00

GD2.0 FN6.0 NM9.4

72-Dr. Fate's new helmet; last Sgt. Carey, Sgt. O'Malley & Captain Desmo; German submarine-c (only German war-c) 212.00 636.00 1700.00

GD2.0 FN6.0 VF8.0 NM9.4

73-Origin & 1st app. Aquaman (11/41) by Paul Norris; intro. Green Arrow & Speedy; Dr. Fate-c 1000.00 3000.00 6000.00 11,000.00

GD2.0 FN6.0 NM9.4

74-2nd Aquaman; 1st Percival Popp, Supercop; Dr. Fate-c 250.00 750.00 1900.00
75,76: 75-New origin Spectre; Nazi spy ring cover w/Hitler's photo. 76-Last Dr. Fate-c; Johnny Quick (by Meskin #76-97) begins, ends #107; Last Clip Carson 225.00 675.00 1800.00
77-80: 77-Green Arrow-c begin 212.00 637.00 1700.00
81-83,85,88,90: 81-Last large logo. 82-1st small logo. 106.00 318.00 950.00
84-Green Arrow Japanese war-c 117.00 350.00 1050.00
86,87-Johnny Quick-c. 87-Last Radio Squad 106.00 318.00 950.00
89-Origin Green Arrow & Speedy Team-up 122.00 366.00 1100.00
91-99: 91-1st bi-monthly issue. 93-Dover & Clover begin (1st app., 9-10/43). 97-Kubert-a. 98-Last Dr. Fate 75.00 225.00 675.00
100 (11-12/44)-Johnny Quick-c 106.00 318.00 950.00

GD2.0 FN6.0 VF8.0 NM9.4

101-Origin & 1st app. Superboy (1-2/45)(not by Siegel & Shuster); last Spectre issue; Green Arrow-c 720.00 2160.00 4320.00 7200.00

GD2.0 FN6.0 NM9.4

102-2nd Superboy app; 1st Dover & Clover-c 122.00 366.00 975.00
103-3rd Superboy app; last Green Arrow-c 94.00 282.00 750.00
104-1st Superboy-c w/Dover & Clover 81.00 243.00 650.00
105,106-Superboy-c 78.00 234.00 625.00
107-Last Johnny Quick & Superboy 78.00 234.00 625.00
108-120: 108-Genius Jones begins; 1st c-app. (3-4/46; cont'd from Adventure Comics #102) 21.00 64.00 150.00
121-124,126: 121-123,126-Post funny animal(Jimminy & the Magic Book)-c 16.00 47.00 110.00
125-Superman c-app.w/Jimminy 72.00 216.00 575.00
127-(Scarce)-Post-c/a 33.00 99.00 230.00

GD2.0 FN6.0 NM9.4

NOTE: *All issues are scarce to rare. Cover features: The Spectre-#52-55, 57-60, 62-67. Dr. Fate-#56, 61, 68-76. The Green Arrow & Speedy-#77-85, 88-97, 99, 101 (w/Dover & Clover-#98, 103). Johnny Quick-#86, 87, 100. Dover & Clover-#102, (104, 106 w/Superboy), 107, 108(w/Genius Jones), 110, 112, 114, 117, 119. Genius Jones-#109, 111, 113, 115, 118, 120.* ***Baily*** *a-45, 52-on; c-52-55, 57-60, 62-67.* ***Al Capp*** *a-45(signed Koppy).* ***Ellsworth*** *c-7.* ***Creig Flessel*** *c-30, 31, 35-48(most).* ***Guardineer*** *c-47, 49, 50.* ***Kiefer*** *a-20.* ***Meskin*** *c-86, 87, 100?* ***Moldoff*** *c-51.* ***George Papp*** *c-77-85.* ***Post*** *c-121-127.* ***Vincent Sullivan*** *c-8-28, 32-34.*

MORE SEYMOUR (See Seymour My Son)
Archie Publications: Oct, 1963

1 2.25 6.75 18.00

MORE THAN MORTAL (Also see Lady Pendragon/...)
Liar Comics: June, 1997 - No. 4, Apr, 1998 ($2.95, limited series)

1-Blue forest background-c, 1-Variant-c 4.00
1-White-c 2.40 6.00
1-2nd printing; purple sky cover 3.00
2-4: 3-Silvestri-c, 4-Two-c, one by Randy Queen 3.00

MORE THAN MORTAL: OTHERWORLDS
Image Comics: July, 1999 - No. 4 ($2.95, limited series)

1,2-Firchow-a. 1-Two covers 3.00

MORE THAN MORTAL SAGAS
Liar Comics: Jun, 1998 - No. 3, Dec, 1998 ($2.95, limited series)

1,2-Painted art by Romano. 2-Two-c, one by Firchow 3.00
1-Variant-c by Linsner 5.00

MORE THAN MORTAL TRUTHS AND LEGENDS
Liar Comics: Aug, 1998 - No. 6, Apr, 1999 ($2.95)

1-6-Firchow-a(p) 3.00
1-Variant-c by Dan Norton 4.50

MORE TRASH FROM MAD (Annual)
E. C. Comics: 1958 - No. 12, 1969
(Note: Bonus missing = half price)

nn(1958)-8 pgs. color Mad reprint from #20 17.50 52.00 185.00
2(1959)-Market Product Labels 12.00 36.00 130.00
3(1960)-Text book covers 11.00 33.00 120.00
4(1961)-Sing Along with Mad booklet 11.00 33.00 120.00
5(1962)-Window Stickers; r/from Mad #39 7.50 22.50 80.00
6(1963)-TV Guise booklet 8.50 25.50 90.00
7(1964)-Alfred E. Neuman commemorative stamps 6.00 18.00 65.00
8(1965)-Life size poster-Alfred E. Neuman 4.00 12.00 45.00
9-12: 9,10(1966-67)-Mischief Sticker. 11(1968)-Campaign poster & bumper sticker. 12(1969)-Pocket medals 3.50 10.50 38.00

NOTE: ***Kelly Freas*** *c-1, 2, 4.* ***Mingo*** *c-3, 5-9, 12.*

MORGAN THE PIRATE (Movie)
Dell Publishing Co.: No. 1227, Sept-Nov, 1961

Four Color 1227-Photo-c 7.00 22.00 80.00

MORLOCK 2001
Atlas/Seaboard Publ.: Feb, 1975 - No. 3, July, 1975

1,2: 1-(Super-hero)-Origin & 1st app. 4.00
3-Ditko/Wrightson-a; origin The Midnight Man & The Midnight Men 5.00

MORNINGSTAR SPECIAL
Comico: Apr, 1990 ($2.50)

1-From the Elementals; Willingham-c/a/scripts 3.00

MORRIGAN
Dimension X: Aug, 1993 ($2.75, B&W)

1-Foil stamped-c 3.00

MORRIGAN
Sirius Entertainment: 1997 ($2.95, limited series)

1-Tenuta-c/a 3.00

MORTAL KOMBAT
Malibu Comics: July, 1994 - No. 6, Dec, 1994 ($2.95)

1-6: 1-Two diff. covers exist 3.00

Mortie #1 © Magazine Publ.

Motion Picture Comics #109 © FAW

Movie Classics - Lawrence © DELL

1-Limited edition gold foil embossed-c 4.00
0 (12/94), Special Edition 1 (11/94) 3.00
Tournament Edition I12/94, $3.95), II('95)($3.95) 4.00
...: **BARAKA** ,June, 1995 ($2.95, one-shot) #1; ...**BATTLEWAVE** ,2/95 - No. 6, 7/95 , #1-6; ...**GORO, PRINCE OF PAIN** ,9/94 - No. 3, 11/94, #1-3; ... **KITANA AND MILEENA** ,8/95 , #1; ...**KUNG LAO** ,7/95 , #1; ... **RAYDON & KANO** ,3/95 - No. 3, 5/95, #1-3: ...(all $2.95) 3.00
U.S. SPECIAL FORCES ,1/95 - No. 2, ($3.50), #1,2 3.50

MORTIE (Mazie's Friend; also see Flat-Top)
Magazine Publishers: Dec, 1952 - No. 4, June, 1953?

1 7.50 22.50 45.00
2-4 4.15 12.50 25.00

MORTIGAN GOTH: IMMORTALIS (See Marvel Frontier Comics Unlimited)
Marvel Comics: Sept, 1993 - No. 4, Mar, 1994 ($1.95, mini-series)

1-($2.95)-Foil-c 3.00
2-4 2.00

MORT THE DEAD TEENAGER
Marvel Comics: Nov, 1993 - No. 4, Mar, 1994 ($1.75, mini-series)

1-4 2.00

MORTY MEEKLE
Dell Publishing Co.: No. 793, May, 1957

Four Color 793 1.80 5.50 20.00

MOSES & THE TEN COMMANDMENTS (See Dell Giants)

MOTHER GOOSE AND NURSERY RHYME COMICS (See Christmas With Mother Goose)
Dell Publishing Co.: No. 41, 1944 - No. 862, Nov, 1957

Four Color 41-Walt Kelly-c/a 21.00 63.00 230.00
Four Color 59, 68-Kelly c/a 19.00 56.00 205.00
Four Color 862-The Truth About..., Movie (Disney) 6.40 19.00 70.00

MOTHER TERESA OF CALCUTTA
Marvel Comics Group: 1984

1-(52 pgs.) No ads 2.50

MOTION PICTURE COMICS (See Fawcett Movie Comics)
Fawcett Publications: No. 101, 1950 - No. 114, Jan, 1953 (All-photo-c)

101- "Vanishing Westerner"; Monte Hale (1950) 30.00 90.00 210.00
102- "Code of the Silver Sage"; Rocky Lane (1/51) 28.00 84.00 195.00
103- "Covered Wagon Raid"; Rocky Lane (3/51) 28.00 84.00 195.00
104- "Vigilante Hideout"; Rocky Lane (5/51)-Book length Powell-a 28.00 84.00 195.00
105- "Red Badge of Courage"; Audie Murphy; Bob Powell-a (7/51) 34.00 101.00 235.00
106- "The Texas Rangers"; George Montgomery (9/51) 29.00 86.00 200.00
107- "Frisco Tornado"; Rocky Lane (11/51) 25.00 75.00 175.00
108- "Mask of the Avenger"; John Derek 18.00 54.00 125.00
109- "Rough Rider of Durango"; Rocky Lane 26.00 77.00 180.00
110- "When Worlds Collide"; George Evans-a (5/52); Williamson & Evans drew themselves in story; (also see Famous Funnies No. 72-88) 94.00 281.00 750.00
111- "The Vanishing Outpost"; Lash LaRue 31.00 92.00 215.00
112- "Brave Warrior"; Jon Hall & Jay Silverheels 17.00 51.00 120.00
113- "Walk East on Beacon"; George Murphy; Schaffenberger-a 12.00 36.00 85.00
114- "Cripple Creek"; George Montgomery (1/53) 13.50 41.00 95.00

MOTION PICTURE FUNNIES WEEKLY (See Promotional Comics section)

MOTORHEAD (See Comic's Greatest World)
Dark Horse Comics: Aug, 1995 - No. 6, Jan, 1996 ($2.50)

1-6: Bisley-c on all. 1-Predator app. 2.50
Special 1 (3/94, $3.95, 52pgs.)-Jae Lee-c; Barb Wire, The Machine & Wolf Gang app. 4.00

MOTORMOUTH (... & Killpower #7? on)
Marvel Comics UK: June, 1992 - No. 12, May, 1993 ($1.75)

1-13: 1,2-Nick Fury app. 3-Punisher-c/story. 5,6-Nick Fury & Punisher app. 6-Cable cameo. 7-9-Cable app. 2.00

MOUNTAIN MEN (See Ben Bowie)

MOUSE MUSKETEERS (See M.G.M.'s...)

MOUSE ON THE MOON, THE (See Movie Classics)

MOVIE CLASSICS
Dell Publishing Co.: Jan, 1963 - Dec, 1969

(Before 1963, most movie adaptations were part of the 4-Color series)
(Disney movie adaptations after 1970 are in Walt Disney Showcase)

Around the World Under the Sea 12-030-612 (12/66) 2.50 7.50 25.00
Bambi 3(4/56)-Disney; r/4-Color #186 3.20 9.60 32.00
Battle of the Bulge 12-056-606 (6/66) 2.80 8.40 28.00
Beach Blanket Bingo 12-058-509 5.50 16.50 55.00
Bon Voyage 01-068-212 (12/62)-Disney; photo-c 3.00 9.00 30.00
Castilian, The 12-110-401 2.80 8.40 28.00
Cat, The 12-109-612 (12/66) 2.40 7.20 24.00
Cheyenne Autumn 12-112-506 (4-6/65) 5.00 15.00 50.00
Circus World, Samuel Bronston's 12-115-411; John Wayne app.; John Wayne photo-c 9.00 27.00 90.00
Countdown 12-150-710 (10/67)-James Caan photo-c 2.80 8.40 28.00
Creature, The 1 (12-142-302) (12-2/62-63) 5.50 16.50 55.00
Creature, The 12-142-410 (10/64) 3.50 10.50 35.00
David Ladd's Life Story 12-173-212 (10-12/62)-Photo-c 6.50 19.50 65.00
Die, Monster, Die 12-175-603 (3/66)-Photo-c 4.00 12.00 40.00
Dirty Dozen 12-180-710 (10/67) 3.80 11.40 38.00
Dr. Who & the Daleks 12-190-612 (12/66)-Peter Cushing photo-c; 1st U.S. app. of Dr. Who 9.50 28.00 95.00
Dracula 12-231-212 (10-12/62) 4.50 13.50 45.00
El Dorado 12-240-710 (10/67)-John Wayne; photo-c 11.50 34.00 115.00
Ensign Pulver 12-257-410 (8-10/64) 2.40 7.20 24.00
Frankenstein 12-283-305 (3-5/63) 5.00 15.00 50.00
Great Race, The 12-299-603 (3/66)-Natallie Wood, Tony Curtis photo-c 3.80 11.40 38.00
Hallelujah Trail, The 12-307-602 (2/66) (Shows 1/66 inside); Burt Lancaster, Lee Remick photo-c 4.00 12.00 40.00
Hatari 12-340-301 (1/63)-John Wayne 7.00 21.00 70.00
Horizontal Lieutenant, The 01-348-210 (10/62) 2.40 7.20 24.00
Incredible Mr. Limpet, The 12-370-408; Don Knotts photo-c 3.20 9.60 32.00
Jack the Giant Killer 12-374-301 (1/63) 7.50 22.50 75.00
Jason & the Argonauts 12-376-310 (8-10/63)-Photo-c 9.00 27.00 90.00
Lancelot & Guinevere 12-416-310 (10/63) 4.50 13.50 45.00
Lawrence 12-426-308 (8/63)-Story of Lawrence of Arabia; movie ad on back-c; not exactly like movie 4.50 13.50 45.00
Lion of Sparta 12-439-301 (1/63) 3.00 9.00 30.00
Mad Monster Party 12-460-801 (9/67)-Based on Kurtzman's screenplay 5.00 15.00 50.00
Magic Sword, The 01-496-209 (9/62) 4.80 14.40 48.00
Masque of the Red Death 12-490-410 (8-10/64)-Vincent Price photo-c 4.80 14.40 48.00
Maya 12-495-612 (12/66)-Clint Walker & Jay North part photo-c 3.50 10.50 35.00
McHale's Navy 12-500-412 (10-12/64) 3.50 10.50 35.00
Merrill's Marauders 12-510-301 (1/63)-Photo-c 2.40 7.20 24.00
Mouse on the Moon, The 12-530-312 (10/12/63)-Photo-c 3.20 9.60 32.00
Mummy, The 12-537-211 (9-11/62) 2 versions with different back-c 5.50 16.50 55.00
Music Man, The 12-538-301 (1/63) 2.40 7.20 24.00
Naked Prey, The 12-545-612 (12/66)-Photo-c 5.00 15.00 50.00
Night of the Grizzly, The 12-558-612 (12/66)-Photo-c 3.00 9.00 30.00

Movie Comics #2 © DC

Movie Comics #3 © FH

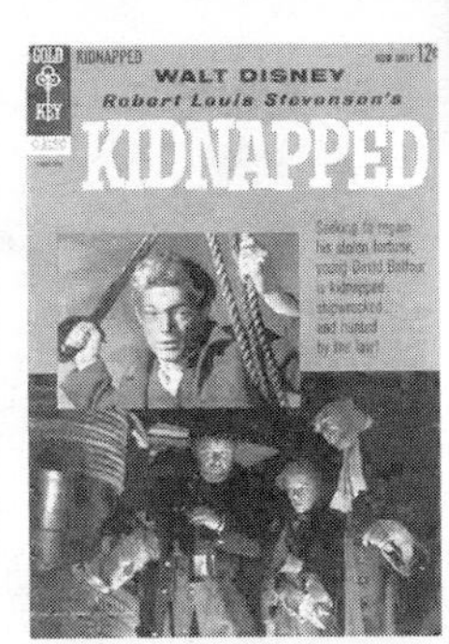

Movie Comics - Kidnapped © WDC

GD2.0 FN6.0 NM9.4

None But the Brave 12-565-506 (4-6/65) 5.00 15.00 50.00
Operation Bikini 12-597-310 (10/63)-Photo-c 2.80 8.40 28.00
Operation Crossbow 12-590-512 (10-12/65) 2.80 8.40 28.00
Prince & the Pauper, The 01-654-207 (5-7/62)-Disney 3.20 9.60 32.00
Raven, The 12-680-309 (9/63)-Vincent Price photo-c 4.50 13.50 45.00
Ring of Bright Water 01-701-910 (10/69) (inside shows #12-701-909) 3.00 9.00 30.00
Runaway, The 12-707-412 (10-12/64) 2.50 7.50 25.00
Santa Claus Conquers the Martians #? (1964)-Photo-c 6.50 19.50 65.00
Santa Claus Conquers the Martians 12-725-603 (3/66, 12¢)-Reprints 1964 issue; photo-c 5.50 16.50 55.00
Another version given away with a Golden Record, SLP 170, nn, no price (3/66)-Complete with record 13.00 39.00 130.00
Six Black Horses 12-750-301 (1/63)-Photo-c 2.80 8.40 28.00
Ski Party 12-743-511 (9-11/65)-Frankie Avalon photo-c 4.00 12.00 40.00
Smoky 12-746-702 (2/67) 2.50 7.50 25.00
Sons of Katie Elder 12-748-511 (9-11/65); John Wayne app.; photo-c 12.00 36.00 120.00
Tales of Terror 12-793-302 (2/63)-Evans-a 3.50 10.50 35.00
Three Stooges Meet Hercules 01-828-208 (8/62)-Photo-c 7.50 22.50 75.00
Tomb of Ligeia 12-830-506 (4-6/65) 3.50 10.50 35.00
Treasure Island 01-845-211 (7-9/62)-Disney; r/4-Color #624 2.80 8.40 28.00
Twice Told Tales (Nathaniel Hawthorne) 12-840-401 (11-1/63-64); Vincent Price photo-c 4.00 12.00 40.00
Two on a Guillotine 12-850-506 (4-6/65) 2.80 8.40 28.00
Valley of Gwangi 01-880-912 (12/69) 8.00 24.00 80.00
War Gods of the Deep 12-900-509 (7-9/65) 2.80 8.40 28.00
War Wagon, The 12-533-709 (9/67); John Wayne app. 7.50 22.50 75.00
Who's Minding the Mint? 12-924-708 (8/67) 2.40 7.20 24.00
Wolfman, The 12-922-308 (6-8/63) 4.00 12.00 40.00
Wolfman, The 1(12-922-410)(8-10/64)-2nd printing; r/#12-922-308 3.20 9.60 32.00
Zulu 12-950-410 (8-10/64)-Photo-c 7.00 21.00 70.00

MOVIE COMICS (See Cinema Comics Herald & Fawcett Movie Comics)

MOVIE COMICS
National Periodical Publications/Picture Comics: April, 1939 - No. 6, Sept-Oct, 1939 (Most all photo-c)

1- "Gunga Din", "Son of Frankenstein", "The Great Man Votes", "Fisherman's Wharf", & "Scouts to the Rescue" part 1; Wheelan "Minute Movies" begin 311.00 933.00 2800.00
2- "Stagecoach", "The Saint Strikes Back", "King of the Turf","Scouts to the Rescue" part 2, "Arizona Legion", Andy Devine photo-c 219.00 656.00 1750.00
3- "East Side of Heaven", "Mystery in the White Room", "Four Feathers", "Mexican Rose" with Gene Autry, "Spirit of Culver", "Many Secrets", "The Mikado" 156.00 469.00 1250.00
4- "Captain Fury", Gene Autry in "Blue Montana Skies", "Streets of N.Y." with Jackie Cooper, "Oregon Trail" part 1 with Johnny Mack Brown, "Big Town Czar" with Barton MacLane, & "Star Reporter" with Warren Hull 122.00 366.00 975.00
5- "The Man in the Iron Mask", "Five Came Back", "Wolf Call", "The Girl & the Gambler", "The House of Fear", "The Family Next Door", "Oregon Trail" part 2 137.00 412.00 1100.00
6- "The Phantom Creeps", "Chumps at Oxford", & "The Oregon Trail" part 3; 2nd Robot-c 181.00 544.00 1450.00

NOTE: *Above books contain many original movie stills with dialogue from movie scripts. All issues are scarce.*

MOVIE COMICS
Fiction House Magazines: Dec, 1946 - No. 4, 1947

1-Big Town (by Lubbers), Johnny Danger begin; Celardo-a; Mitzi of the Movies by Fran Hopper 52.00 157.00 420.00
2-(2/47)- "White Tie & Tails" with William Bendix; Mitzi of the Movies begins by Matt Baker, ends #4 40.00 120.00 315.00
3-(6/47)-Andy Hardy starring Mickey Rooney 40.00 120.00 315.00
4-Mitzi In Hollywood by Matt Baker; Merton of the Movies with Red Skelton; Yvonne DeCarlo & George Brent in "Slave Girl" 47.00 141.00 375.00

MOVIE COMICS
Gold Key/Whitman: Oct, 1962 - 1984

Alice in Wonderland 10144-503 (3/65)-Disney; partial reprint of 4-Color #331 3.40 10.20 34.00
Aristocats, The 1 (30045-103)(3/71)-Disney; with pull-out poster (25¢) (No poster = half price) 6.50 19.50 65.00
Bambi 1 (10087-309)(9/63)-Disney; r/4-C #186 3.20 9.60 32.00
Bambi 2 (10087-607)(7/66)-Disney; r/4-C #186 2.40 7.20 24.00
Beneath the Planet of the Apes 30044-012 (12/70)-with pull-out poster; photo-c (No poster = half price) 8.00 24.00 80.00
Big Red 10026-211 (11/62)-Disney; photo-c 2.80 8.40 28.00
Big Red 10026-503 (3/65)-Disney; reprints 10026-211; photo-c 2.40 7.20 24.00
Blackbeard's Ghost 10222-806 (6/68)-Disney 2.60 7.80 26.00
Bullwhip Griffin 10181-706 (6/67)-Disney; Manning-a; photo-c 3.20 9.60 32.00
Captain Sindbad 10077-309 (9/63)-Manning-a; photo-c 5.00 15.00 50.00
Chitty Chitty Bang Bang 1 (30038-902)(2/69)-with pull-out poster; Disney; photo-c (No poster = half price) 6.00 18.00 60.00
Cinderella 10152-508 (8/65)-Disney; r/4-C #786 3.00 9.00 30.00
Darby O'Gill & the Little People 10251-001(1/70)-Disney; reprints 4-Color #1024 (Toth-a); photo-c 4.50 13.50 45.00
Dumbo 1 (10090-310)(10/63)-Disney; r/4-C #668 3.00 9.00 30.00
Emil & the Detectives 10120-502 (2/65)-Disney; photo-c 2.80 8.40 28.00
Escapade in Florence 1 (10043-301)(1/63)-Disney; starring Annette Funicello 7.50 22.50 75.00
Fall of the Roman Empire 10118-407 (7/64); Sophia Loren photo-c 3.20 9.60 32.00
Fantastic Voyage 10178-702 (2/67)-Wood/Adkins-a; photo-c 4.80 14.40 48.00
55 Days at Peking 10081-309 (9/63)-Photo-c 2.80 8.40 28.00
Fighting Prince of Donegal, The 10193-701 (1/67)-Disney 2.60 7.80 26.00
First Men in the Moon 10132-503 (3/65)-Fred Fredericks-a; photo-c 2.80 8.40 28.00
Gay Purr-ee 30017-301(1/63, 84 pgs.) 4.50 13.50 45.00
Gnome Mobile, The 10207-710 (10/67)-Disney 3.00 9.00 30.00
Goodbye, Mr. Chips 10246-006 (6/70)-Peter O'Toole photo-c 2.80 8.40 28.00
Happiest Millionaire, The 10221-804 (4/68)-Disney 3.00 9.00 30.00
Hey There, It's Yogi Bear 10122-409 (9/64)-Hanna-Barbera 5.50 16.50 55.00
Horse Without a Head, The 10109-401 (1/64)-Disney 2.60 7.80 26.00
How the West Was Won 10074-307 (7/63)-Tufts-a 3.00 9.00 30.00
In Search of the Castaways 10048-303 (3/63)-Disney; Hayley Mills photo-c 6.00 18.00 60.00
Jungle Book, The 1 (6022-801)(1/68-Whitman)-Disney; large size (10x13-1/2"); 59¢ 5.50 16.50 55.00
Jungle Book, The 1 (30033-803)(3/68, 68 pgs.)-Disney; same contents as Whitman #1 3.50 10.50 35.00
Jungle Book, The 1 (6/78, $1.00 tabloid) 1.80 5.40 18.00
Jungle Book (1984)-r/Giant 2.40 6.00
Kidnapped 10080-306 (6/63)-Disney; reprints 4-Color #1101; photo-c 2.80 8.40 28.00
King Kong 30036-809(9/68-68 pgs.)-painted-c 2.80 8.40 28.00
King Kong nn-Whitman Treasury($1.00, 68 pgs.,1968), same cover as Gold Key issue 4.00 12.00 40.00
King Kong 11299(#1-786, 10x13-1/4", 68 pgs., $1.00, 1978)

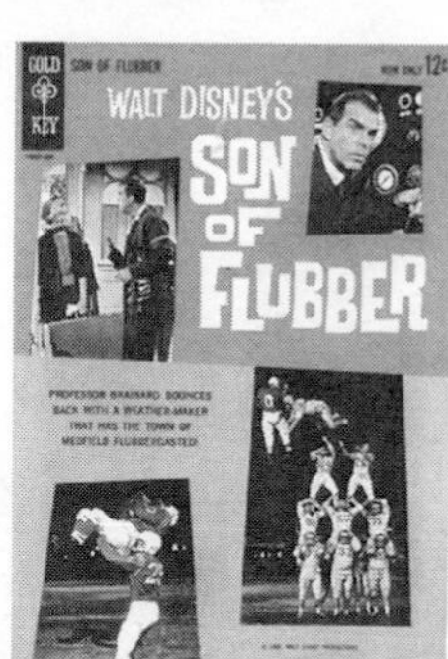
Movie Comics - Son of Flubber © WDC

Movie Love #2 © FF

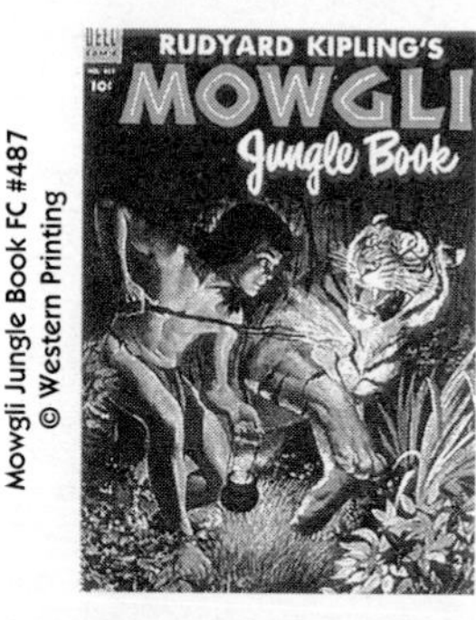
Mowgli Jungle Book FC #487 © Western Printing

GD2.0 FN6.0 NM9.4

2.00 6.00 20.00
Lady and the Tramp 10042-301 (1/63)-Disney; r/4-Color #629
3.20 9.60 32.00
Lady and the Tramp 1 (1967-Giant; 25¢)-Disney; reprints part of Dell #1
4.80 14.40 48.00
Lady and the Tramp 2 (10042-203)(3/72)-Disney; r/4-Color #629
1.90 5.70 19.00
Legend of Lobo, The 1 (10059-303)(3/63)-Disney; photo-c
2.20 6.60 22.00
Lt. Robin Crusoe, U.S.N. 10191-610 (10/66)-Disney; Dick Van Dyke photo-c
2.00 6.00 20.00
Lion, The 10035-301 (1/63)-Photo-c 2.00 6.00 20.00
Lord Jim 10156-509 (9/65)-Photo-c 2.20 6.60 22.00
Love Bug, The 10237-906 (6/69)-Disney; Buddy Hackett photo-c
2.40 7.20 24.00
Mary Poppins 10136-501 (1/65)-Disney; photo-c 3.80 11.40 38.00
Mary Poppins 30023-501 (1/65-68 pgs.)-Disney; photo-c
6.00 18.00 60.00
McLintock 10110-403 (3/64); John Wayne app.; John Wayne & Maureen O'Hara photo-c 11.00 33.00 110.00
Merlin Jones as the Monkey's Uncle 10115-510 (10/65)-Disney; Annette Funicello front/back photo-c 4.20 12.60 42.00
Miracle of the White Stallions, The 10065-306 (6/63)-Disney
2.60 7.80 26.00
Misadventures of Merlin Jones, The 10115-405 (5/64)-Disney; Annette Funicello photo front/back-c 4.50 13.50 45.00
Moon-Spinners, The 10124-410 (10/64)-Disney; Haley Mills photo-c
6.00 18.00 60.00
Mutiny on the Bounty 1 (10040-302)(2/63)-Marlon Brando photo-c
2.80 8.40 28.00
Nikki, Wild Dog of the North 10141-412 (12/64)-Disney; reprints 4-Color #1226
2.20 6.60 22.00
Old Yeller 10168-601 (1/66)-Disney; reprints 4-Color #869; photo-c
2.40 7.20 24.00
One Hundred & One Dalmations 1 (10247-002) (2/70)-Disney; reprints Four Color #1183 2.60 7.80 26.00
Peter Pan 1 (10086-309)(9/63)-Disney; reprints Four Color #442
3.00 9.00 30.00
Peter Pan 2 (10086-909)(9/69)-Disney; reprints Four Color #442
2.20 6.60 22.00
Peter Pan 1 ('83)-r/4-Color #442 3.00
P.T. 109 10123-409 (9/64)-John F. Kennedy 3.50 10.50 35.00
Rio Conchos 10143-503(3/65) 3.20 9.60 32.00
Robin Hood 10163-506 (6/65)-Disney; reprints Four Color #413
2.60 7.80 26.00
Shaggy Dog & the Absent-Minded Professor 30032-708 (8/67-Giant, 68 pgs.) Disney; reprints 4-Color #985,1199 4.80 14.40 48.00
Sleeping Beauty 1 (30042-009)(9/70)-Disney; reprints Four Color #973; with pull-out poster (No poster = half price) 5.80 17.40 58.00
Snow White & the Seven Dwarfs 1 (10091-310)(10/63)-Disney; reprints Four Color #382 2.60 7.80 26.00
Snow White & the Seven Dwarfs 10091-709 (9/67)-Disney; reprints Four Color #382 2.20 6.60 22.00
Snow White & the Seven Dwarfs 90091-204 (2/84)-Reprints Four Color #382
3.00
Son of Flubber 1 (10057-304)(4/63)-Disney; sequel to "The Absent-Minded Professor" 2.60 7.80 26.00
Summer Magic 10076-309 (9/63)-Disney; Hayley Mills photo-c; Manning-a
6.00 18.00 60.00
Swiss Family Robinson 10236-904 (4/69)-Disney; reprints Four Color #1156; photo-c 2.60 7.80 26.00
Sword in the Stone, The 30019-402 (2/64-Giant, 68 pgs.)-Disney (see March of Comics #258 & Wart and the Wizard 5.50 16.50 55.00
That Darn Cat 10171-602 (2/66)-Disney; Hayley Mills photo-c
5.50 16.50 55.00
Those Magnificent Men in Their Flying Machines 10162-510 (10/65); photo-c
2.80 8.40 28.00

GD2.0 FN6.0 NM9.4

Three Stooges in Orbit 30016-211 (11/62-Giant, 32 pgs.)-All photos from movie; stiff-photo-c 9.00 27.00 90.00
Tiger Walks, A 10117-406 (6/64)-Disney; Torres?, Tufts-a; photo-c
3.60 10.80 36.00
Toby Tyler 10142-502 (2/65)-Disney; reprints Four Color #1092; photo-c
2.60 7.80 26.00
Treasure Island 1 (10200-703)(3/67)-Disney; reprints Four Color #624; photo-c
2.40 7.20 24.00
20,000 Leagues Under the Sea 1 (10095-312)(12/63)-Disney; reprints Four Color #614 2.60 7.80 26.00
Wonderful Adventures of Pinocchio, The 1 (10089-310)(10/63)-Disney; reprints Four Color #545 (see Wonderful Advs. of...) 3.00 9.00 30.00
Wonderful Adventures of Pinocchio, The 10089-109 (9/71)-Disney; reprints Four Color #545 2.40 7.20 24.00
Wonderful World of the Brothers Grimm 1 (10008-210)(10/62)
3.80 11.40 38.00
X, the Man with the X-Ray Eyes 10083-309 (9/63)-Ray Milland photo on-c
6.20 18.60 62.00
Yellow Submarine 35000-902 (2/69-Giant, 68 pgs.)-With pull-out poster; The Beatles cartoon movie; Paul S. Newman-s 22.00 66.00 220.00
Without poster 6.50 19.50 65.00

MOVIE LOVE (Also see Personal Love)
Famous Funnies: Feb, 1950 - No. 22, Aug, 1953 (All photo-c)

1-Dick Powell, Evelyn Keyes, & Mickey Rooney photo-c
13.00 39.00 90.00
2-Myrna Loy photo-c 7.50 22.50 45.00
3-7,9: 6-Ricardo Montalban photo-c. 9-Gene Tierney, John Lund, Glenn Ford, & Rhonda Fleming photo-c. 6.35 19.00 38.00
8-Williamson/Frazetta-a, 6 pgs. 37.00 111.00 260.00
10-Frazetta-a, 6 pgs. 40.00 120.00 290.00
11,14-16: 14-Janet Leigh photo-c 5.35 16.00 32.00
12-Dean Martin & Jerry Lewis photo-c (12/51, pre-dates Advs. of Dean Martin & Jerry Lewis comic) 7.50 22.50 45.00
13-Ronald Reagan photo-c with 1 pg. biog. 20.00 60.00 140.00
17-Leslie Caron & Ralph Meeker photo-c; 1 pg. Frazetta ad
5.35 16.00 32.00
18-22: 19-John Derek photo-c. 21-Paul Henreid & Patricia Medina photo-c. 22-John Payne & Coleen Gray photo-c 5.00 15.00 30.00
NOTE: *Each issue has a full-length movie adaptation with photo covers.*

MOVIE THRILLERS (Movie)
Magazine Enterprises: 1949

1-Adaptation of "Rope of Sand" w/Burt Lancaster; Burt Lancaster photo-c
30.00 90.00 210.00

MOVIE TOWN ANIMAL ANTICS (Formerly Animal Antics; becomes Raccoon Kids #52 on)
National Periodical Publ.: No. 24, Jan-Feb, 1950 - No. 51, July-Aug, 1954

24-Raccoon Kids continue 11.00 33.00 75.00
25-51 10.00 30.00 65.00
NOTE: ***Sheldon Mayer** a-28-33, 35, 37-41, 43, 44, 47, 49-51.*

MOVIE TUNES COMICS (Formerly Animated...; Frankie No. 4 on)
Marvel Comics (MgPC): No. 3, Fall, 1946

3-Super Rabbit, Krazy Krow, Silly Seal & Ziggy Pig 11.50 34.00 80.00

MOWGLI JUNGLE BOOK (Rudyard Kipling's...)
Dell Publ. Co.: No. 487, Aug-Oct, 1953 - No. 620, Apr, 1955

Four Color 487 (#1) 5.00 15.00 55.00
Four Color 582 (8/54), 620 3.60 11.00 40.00

MR. (See Mister)

MS. CYANIDE & ICE
Blackout Comics: June, 1995 - No. 1, 1995 ($2.95, B&W)

0,1 3.00

MS. FORTUNE
Image Comics: Jan, 1998 ($2.95, B&W, one-shot)

Ms. Marvel #22 © MAR

Murder Incorporated #2 © FOX

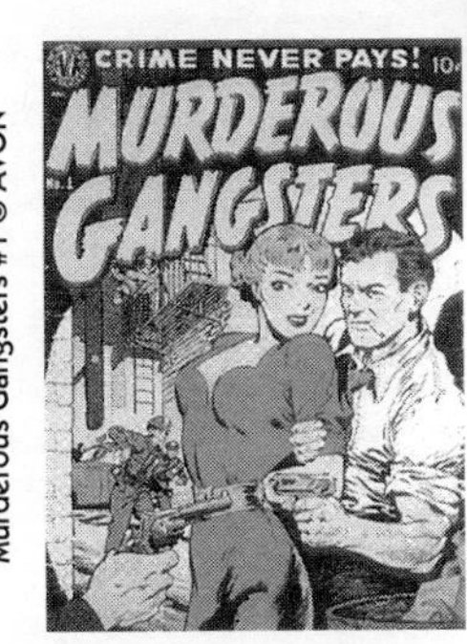

Murderous Gangsters #1 © AVON

GD2.0 FN6.0 NM9.4

1-Chris Marrinan-s/a 3.00

MS. MARVEL (Also see The Avengers #183)
Marvel Comics Group: Jan, 1977 - No. 23, Apr, 1979

1-1st app. Ms. Marvel; Scorpion app. in #1,2 5.00
2-10: 2-Origin. 5-Vision app. 6-(Reg. 30¢-c). 10-Last 30¢ issue 3.00
6-(35¢-c variant, limited dist.)(6/77) 1.50 4.50 12.00
11-15,19-23: 19-Capt. Marvel app. 20-New costume. 23-Vance Astro (leader of the Guardians) app. 2.50
16,17-Mystique cameo 1.00 3.00 8.00
18-1st full Mystique; Avengers x-over 1.50 4.50 12.00
NOTE: ***Austin*** *c-14i, 16i, 17i, 22i.* ***Buscema*** *a-1-3p; c(p)-2, 4, 6, 7, 15.* ***Infantino*** *a-14p, 19p.* ***Gil Kane*** *c-8.* ***Mooney*** *a-4-8p, 13p, 15-18p.* ***Starlin*** *c-12.*

MS. MYSTIC
Pacific Comics: Oct, 1982 - No. 2, Feb, 1984 ($1.00/$1.50)

1,2: Neal Adams-c/a/script. 1-Origin; intro Erth, Ayre, Fyre & Watr 3.00

MS. MYSTIC
Continunity Comics: V2#1, Oct, 1993 - V2#9, 1994 ($2.50)

V2#1-9: 1-Adams-c(i)/part-i. 2-4-Embossed-c. 2-Nebres part-i. 3-Adams-c(i)/plot. 4-Adams-c(p)/plot 2.50

MS. MYSTIC DEATHWATCH 2000 (Ms. Mystic #3)
Continuity: May, 1993 - No. 3, Aug, 1993 ($2.50)

1-3-Bagged w/card; Adams plots 2.50

MS. TREE QUARTERLY / SPECIAL
DC Comics: Summer, 1990 -No. 10, 1992 ($3.95/$3.50, 84 pgs, mature)

1-10: 1-Midnight story; Batman text story, Grell-a. 2,3-Midnight stories; The Butcher text stories 4.00
NOTE: ***Cowan*** *c-2.* ***Grell*** *c-1, 6.* ***Infantino*** *a-8.*

MS. TREE'S THRILLING DETECTIVE ADVS (Ms. Tree #4 on; also see The Best of Ms. Tree)(Baxter paper #4-9)
Eclipse Comics/Aardvark-Vanaheim 10-18/Renegade Press 19 on: 2/83 - #9, 7/84; #10, 8/84 - #18, 5/85; #19, 6/85 - #50, 6/89

1 3.00
2-49: 2-Schythe begins. 9-Last Eclipse & last color issue. 10,11-2-tone 2.00
50-Contains flexi-disc ($3.95, 52pgs.) 4.00
Summer Special 1 (8/86) 3.00
1950s 3-D Crime (7/87, no glasses)-Johnny Dynamite in 3-D 3.00
Mike Mist in 3-D (8/85)-With glasses 3.00
NOTE; ***Miller*** *pin-up 1-4. Johnny Dynamite-r begin #36 by* ***Morisi.***

MS. VICTORY SPECIAL(Also see Capt. Paragon & Femforce)
Americomics: Jan, 1985 (nd)

1 2.00

MUGGSY MOUSE (Also see Tick Tock Tales)
Magazine Enterprises: 1951 - No. 3, 1951; No. 4, 1954 - No. 5, 1954; 1963

1(A-1 #33) 5.85 17.50 35.00
2(A-1 #36)-Racist-c 8.35 25.00 50.00
3(A-1 #39), 4(A-1 #95), 5(A-1 #99) 4.00 10.00 20.00
Super Reprint #14(1963), I.W. Reprint #1,2 (nd) 1.00 3.00 8.00

MUGGY-DOO, BOY CAT
Stanhall Publ.: July, 1953 - No. 4, Jan, 1954

1-Funny animal; Irving Spector-a 6.70 20.00 40.00
2-4 4.25 13.00 28.00
Super Reprint #12('63), 16('64) 1.00 3.00 8.00

MUKTUK WOLFSBREATH: HARD-BOILED SHAMAN
DC Comics (Vertigo): Aug, 1998 - No. 3, Oct, 1998 ($2.50)

1-3-Terry LaBan-s/Steve Parkhouse-a 2.50

MULLKON EMPIRE (See John Jake's...)

MUMMY, THE (See Universal Presents... under Dell Giants & Movie Classics)

MUNDEN'S BAR ANNUAL
First Comics: Apr, 1988; 1989 ($2.95/$5.95)

1-($2.95)-r/from Grimjack; Fish Police story 3.00
2-($5.95)-Teenage Mutant Ninja Turtles app. 2.40 6.00

MUNSTERS, THE (TV)
Gold Key: Jan, 1965 - No. 16, Jan, 1968 (All photo-c)

1 (10134-501) 17.00 52.00 200.00
2 8.00 25.00 95.00
3-5 6.40 19.00 75.00
6-16 5.50 16.50 65.00

MUNSTERS, THE (TV)
TV Comics!: Aug, 1997 - Present ($2.95, B&W)

1-4-All have photo-c 3.00
1,4-($7.95)-Variant-c 8.00
2-Variant-c w/Beverly Owens as Marilyn 3.00
Special Comic Con Ed. (7/97, $9.95) 10.00

MUPPET BABIES, THE (TV)(See Star Comics Magazine)
Marvel Comics (Star Comics)/Marvel #18 on: Aug, 1985 - No. 26, July, 1989 (Children's book)

1-26 2.00

MUPPETS TAKE MANHATTAN, THE
Marvel Comics (Star Comics): Nov, 1984 - No. 3, Jan, 1985

1-3-Movie adapt. r-/Marvel Super Special 2.00

MURCIELAGA, SHE-BAT
Heroic Publishing: Jan, 1993 - No. 2, 1993 (B&W)

1-($1.50, 28 pgs.) 2.00
2-($2.95, 36 pgs.)-Coated-c 3.00

MURDER CAN BE FUN
Slave Labor Graphics: Feb, 1996 - Present ($2.95, B&W)

1-12: 1-Dorkin-c. 2-Vasquez-c. 3.00

MURDER INCORPORATED (My Private Life #16 on)
Fox Feature Syndicate: 1/48 - No. 15, 12/49; (2 No.9's); 6/50 - No. 3, 8/51

1 (1st Series); 1,2 have 'For Adults Only' on-c 47.00 141.00 375.00
2-Electrocution story 39.00 118.00 275.00
3-7,9(4/49),10(5/49),11-15 21.00 64.00 150.00
8-Used in **SOTI**, pg. 160 23.00 69.00 160.00
9(3/49)-Possible use in **SOTI**, pg. 145; r/Blue Beetle #56('48) 21.00 64.00 150.00
5(#1, 6/50)(2nd Series)-Formerly My Desire #4; bondage-c. 16.00 47.00 110.00
2(8/50)-Morisi-a 13.50 41.00 95.00
3(8/51)-Used in **POP**, pg. 81; Rico-a; lingerie-c/panels 15.00 45.00 105.00

MURDEROUS GANGSTERS
Avon Per./Realistic No. 3 on: Jul, 1951; No. 2, Dec, 1951 - No. 4, Jun, 1952

1-Pretty Boy Floyd, Leggs Diamond; 1 pg. Wood-a 40.00 120.00 300.00
2-Baby-Face Nelson; 1 pg. Wood-a; painted-c 26.00 79.00 185.00
3-Painted-c 21.00 62.00 145.00
4- "Murder by Needle" drug story; Mort Lawrence-a; Kinstler-c 26.00 79.00 185.00

MURDER TALES (Magazine)
World Famous Publications: V1#10, Nov, 1970 - V1#11, Jan, 1971 (52 pgs.)

V1#10-One pg. Frazetta ad 3.00 9.00 30.00
11-Guardineer-r; bondage-c 2.50 7.50 20.00

MUSHMOUSE AND PUNKIN PUSS (TV)
Gold Key: September, 1965 (Hanna-Barbera)

1 (10153-509) 8.65 26.00 95.00

MUSIC MAN, THE (See Movie Classics)

MUTANT CHRONICLES (Video game)
Acclaim Comics (Armada): May, 1996 - No. 4, Aug, 1996 ($2.95, lim. series)

1-4: Simon Bisley-c on all, Sourcebook (#5) 3.00

MUTANT MISADVENTURES OF CLOAK AND DAGGER, THE (Becomes

Mutant X #8 © MAR

Mutt and Jeff #30 © DC

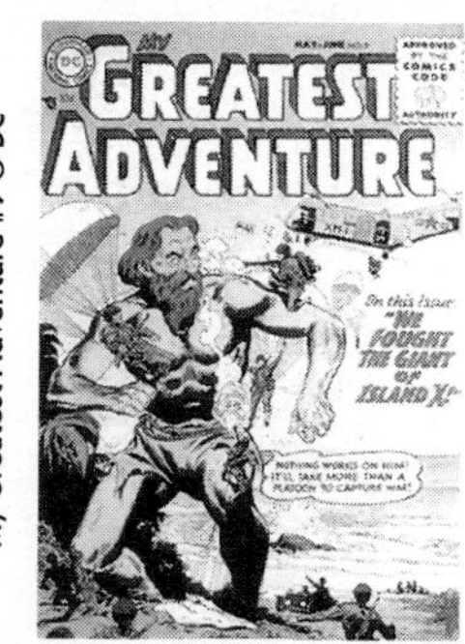

My Greatest Adventure #9 © DC

Cloak and Dagger #14 on)
Marvel Comics: Oct, 1988 - No. 19, Aug, 1991 ($1.25/$1.50)

1-8,10-18: 1-X-Factor app. 9,10-Painted-c. 12-Dr. Doom app. 14-Begin new direction. 16-18-Spider-Man x-over. 18-Infinity Gauntlet x-over; Thanos cameo; Ghost Rider app. 2.00
9,19: (52 pgs.)-9-The Avengers x-over. 19-Origin Cloak & Dagger 2.50
NOTE: *Austin a-12i; c(i)-4, 12, 13; scripts-all. Russell a-2i. Williamson a-14i-16i; c-15i.*

MUTANTS & MISFITS
Silverline Comics (Solson): 1987 - No. 3, 1987 ($1.95)

1-3 2.00

MUTANTS VS. ULTRAS
Malibu Comics (Ultraverse): Nov, 1995 ($6.95, one-shot)

1-r/Exiles vs. X-Men, Night Man vs. Wolverine, Prime vs. Hulk 7.00

MUTANT X (See X-Factor)
Marvel Comics: Nov, 1998 - Present ($2.99/$1.99)

1-($2.99) Alex Summers with alternate world's X-Men 3.00
2-11,13-15-($1.99): 2-Two covers. 5-Man-Spider-c/app. 2.00
12-($2.99) Pin-up gallery by Kaluta, Romita, Byrne 3.00
Annual '99 (5/99, $3.50) 3.50

MUTATIS
Marvel Comics (Epic Comics): 1992 - No. 3, 1992 ($2.25, mini-series)

1-3: Painted-c 2.25

MUTINY (Stormy Tales of the Seven Seas)
Aragon Magazines: Oct, 1954 - No. 3, Feb, 1955

1 16.00 47.00 110.00
2,3: 2-Capt. Mutiny. 3-Bondage-c 12.00 36.00 85.00

MUTINY ON THE BOUNTY (See Classics Illustrated #100 & Movie Comics)

MUTT AND JEFF (See All-American, All-Flash #18, Cicero's Cat, Comic Cavalcade, Famous Feature Stories, The Funnies, Popular & Xmas Comics)
All American/National 1-103(6/58)/Dell 104(10/58)-115 (10-12/59)/ Harvey 116(2/60)-148: Summer, 1939 (nd) - No. 148, Nov, 1965

1(nn)-Lost Wheels 121.00 363.00 1150.00
2(nn)-Charging Bull (Summer, 1940, nd; on sale 6/20/40) 66.00 200.00 625.00
3(nn)-Bucking Broncos (Summer, 1941, nd) 47.00 141.00 450.00
4(Winter, '41), 5(Summer, '42) 42.00 126.00 400.00
6-10 20.00 60.00 185.00
11-20: 20-X-Mas-c 13.00 39.00 115.00
21-30 9.00 27.00 85.00
31-50: 32-X-Mas-c 7.00 21.00 60.00
51-75-Last Fisher issue. 53-Last 52 pgs. 6.00 18.00 45.00
76-99,101-103: 76-Last pre-code issue(1/55) 3.20 10.00 32.00
100 3.80 11.40 38.00
104-148: 116-131-Richie Rich app. 2.20 6.60 22.00
...Jokes 1-3(8/60-61, Harvey)-84 pgs.; Richie Rich in all; Little Dot in #2,3 Lotta in #2 3.00 9.00 30.00
...New Jokes 1-4(10/63-11/65, Harvey)-68 pgs.; Richie Rich in #1-3; Stumbo in #1 2.00 6.00 20.00
NOTE: *Most all issues by **Al Smith**. Issues from 1963 on have **Fisher** reprints. Clarification: early issues signed by Fisher are mostly drawn by Smith.*

MY BROTHERS' KEEPER
Spire Christian Comics (Fleming H. Revell Co.): 1973 (35/49¢, 36 pgs.)

nn 5.00

MY CONFESSIONS (My Confession #7&8; formerly Western True Crime; A Spectacular Feature Magazine #11)
Fox Feature Syndicate: No. 7, Aug, 1949 - No. 10, Jan-Feb, 1950

7-Wood-a (10 pgs.) 21.00 64.00 150.00
8,9: 8-Harrison/Wood-a (19 pgs.). 9-Wood-a 19.00 58.00 135.00
10 10.00 30.00 60.00

MY DATE COMICS (Teen-age)
Hillman Periodicals: July, 1947 - V1#4, Jan, 1948 (2nd Romance comic; see Young Romance)

1-S&K-c/a 34.00 103.00 240.00
2-4-S&K-c/a; Dan Barry-a 23.00 69.00 160.00

MY DESIRE (Formerly Jo-Jo Comics; becomes Murder, Inc. #5 on)
Fox Feature Syndicate: No. 30, Aug, 1949 - No. 4, April, 1950

30(#1) 13.00 39.00 90.00
31 (#2, 10/49),3(2/50),4 10.00 30.00 60.00
31 (Canadian edition) 5.85 17.50 35.00
32(12/49)-Wood-a 18.00 54.00 125.00

MY DIARY (Becomes My Friend Irma #3 on?)
Marvel Comics (A Lovers Mag.): Dec, 1949 - No. 2, Mar, 1950

1,2-Photo-c 13.00 39.00 90.00

MY EXPERIENCE (Formerly All Top; becomes Judy Canova #23 on)
Fox Feature Syndicate: No. 19, Sept, 1949 - No. 22, Mar, 1950

19,21: 19-Wood-a. 21-Wood-a(2) 23.00 69.00 160.00
20 10.00 30.00 60.00
22-Wood-a (9 pgs.) 19.00 56.00 130.00

MY FAVORITE MARTIAN (TV)
Gold Key: 1/64; No.2, 7/64 - No. 9, 10/66 (No. 1,3-9 have photo-c)

1-Russ Manning-a 12.00 37.00 135.00
2 6.00 18.00 65.00
3-9 5.00 15.00 55.00

MY FRIEND IRMA (Radio/TV) (Formerly My Diary? and/or Western Life Romances?)
Marvel/Atlas Comics (BFP): No. 3, June, 1950 - No. 47, Dec, 1954; No. 48, Feb, 1955

3-Dan DeCarlo-a in all; 52 pgs. begin, end ? 13.00 39.00 90.00
4-Kurtzman-a (10 pgs.) 17.00 49.00 115.00
5- "Egghead Doodle" by Kurtzman (4 pgs.) 12.00 36.00 85.00
6,8-10: 9-paper dolls, 1 pg; Millie app. (5 pgs.) 9.15 27.00 55.00
7-One pg. Kurtzman-a 9.15 27.00 55.00
11-23: 23-One pg. Frazetta-a 5.35 16.00 32.00
24-48: 41,48-Stan Lee & Dan DeCarlo app. 4.25 13.00 28.00

MY GIRL PEARL
Atlas Comics: 4/55 - #4, 10/55; #5, 7/57 - #6, 9/57; #7, 8/60 - #11, ?/61

1-Dan DeCarlo-c/a in #1-6 12.00 36.00 85.00
2 7.00 21.00 42.00
3-6 4.25 13.00 28.00
7-11 2.50 7.50 22.00

MY GREATEST ADVENTURE (Doom Patrol #86 on)
National Periodical Publications: Jan-Feb, 1955 - No. 85, Feb, 1964

1-Before CCA 120.00 360.00 1200.00
2 45.00 135.00 550.00
3-5 32.00 96.00 355.00
6-10: 6-Science fiction format begins 31.00 93.00 310.00
11-14: 12-1st S.A. issue 21.00 63.00 210.00
15-18: Kirby-a in all. 18-Kirby-c 23.00 69.00 230.00
19,22-25 18.00 54.00 180.00
20,21,28-Kirby-a 21.00 63.00 210.00
26,27,29,30 13.00 39.00 130.00
31-40 10.50 32.00 105.00
41,42,44-57,59 8.00 24.00 80.00
43-Kirby-c/a 8.50 25.50 85.00
58,60,61-Toth-a; Last 10¢ issue 8.00 24.00 80.00
62-76,78,79: 79-Promotes "Legion of the Strange" for next issue; renamed Doom Patrol for #80 4.50 13.50 45.00
77-Toth-a; Robotman prototype 5.00 15.00 50.00
80-(6/63)-Intro/origin Doom Patrol and begin series; origin & 1st app. Negative Man, Elasti-Girl & S.A. Robotman 33.00 100.00 370.00
81-85: 81,85-Toth-a 15.00 45.00 150.00
NOTE: ***Anderson** a-42. **Cameron** a-24. **Colan** a-77. **Meskin** a-25, 26, 32, 39, 45, 50, 56, 57, 61, 64, 70, 73, 74, 76, 79; c-76. **Moreira** a-11, 12, 15, 17, 20, 23, 25, 27, 37, 40-43, 46, 48, 55-57, 59,*

My Life #7 © FOX

My Love Affair #5 © FOX

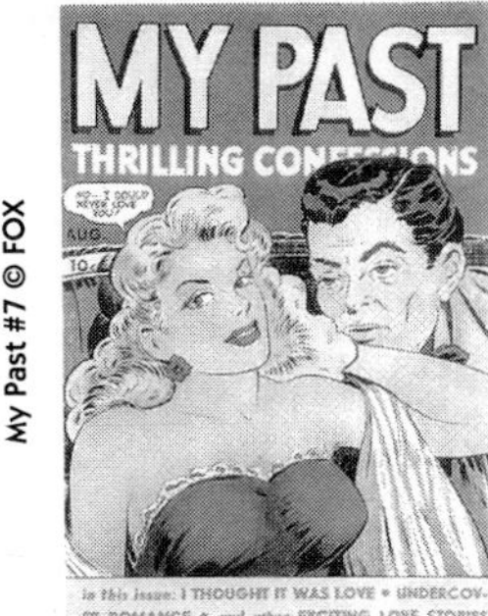

My Past #7 © FOX

	GD2.0	FN6.0	NM9.4

60, 62-65, 67, 69, 70; c-1-4, 7-10. ***Roussos*** *c/a-71-73.* ***Wildey*** *a-32.*

MY GREAT LOVE (Becomes Will Rogers Western #5)
Fox Feature Syndicate: Oct, 1949 - No. 4, Apr, 1950

	GD2.0	FN6.0	NM9.4
1	13.00	39.00	90.00
2-4	8.00	24.00	48.00

MY INTIMATE AFFAIR (Inside Crime #3)
Fox Feature Syndicate: Mar, 1950 - No. 2, May, 1950

	GD2.0	FN6.0	NM9.4
1	13.00	39.00	90.00
2	8.00	24.00	48.00

MY LIFE (Formerly Meet Corliss Archer)
Fox Feature Syndicate: No. 4, Sept, 1948 - No. 15, July, 1950

	GD2.0	FN6.0	NM9.4
4-Used in **SOTI**, pg. 39; Kamen/Feldstein-a	39.00	116.00	270.00
5-Kamen-a	20.00	60.00	140.00
6-Kamen/Feldstein-a	21.00	62.00	145.00
7-Wood-a; wash cover	19.00	56.00	130.00
8,9,11-15	9.15	27.00	55.00
10-Wood-a	17.00	51.00	120.00

MY LITTLE MARGIE (TV)
Charlton Comics: July, 1954 - No. 54, Nov, 1964

	GD2.0	FN6.0	NM9.4
1-Photo front/back-c	31.00	94.00	220.00
2-Photo front/back-c	14.00	43.00	100.00
3-7,10	9.15	27.00	55.00
8,9-Infinity-c	10.00	30.00	60.00
11-14: Part-photo-c (#13, 8/56)	8.35	25.00	50.00
15-19	3.80	11.40	38.00
20-(25¢, 100 pg. issue)	8.00	24.00	80.00
21-39-Last 10¢ issue?	3.20	9.60	32.00
40-53	2.60	7.80	26.00
54-Beatles on cover; lead story spoofs the Beatle haircut craze of the 1960's	13.50	41.00	135.00

NOTE: *Doll cut-outs in 32, 33, 40, 45, 50.*

MY LITTLE MARGIE'S BOY FRIENDS (TV) (Freddy V2#12 on)
Charlton Comics: Aug, 1955 - No. 11, Apr?, 1958

	GD2.0	FN6.0	NM9.4
1-Has several Archie swipes	13.00	39.00	90.00
2	8.35	25.00	50.00
3-11	5.85	17.50	35.00

MY LITTLE MARGIE'S FASHIONS (TV)
Charlton Comics: Feb, 1959 - No. 5, Nov, 1959

	GD2.0	FN6.0	NM9.4
1	11.50	34.00	80.00
2-5	7.00	21.00	42.00

MY LOVE (Becomes Two Gun Western #5 (11/50) on?)
Marvel Comics (CLDS): July, 1949 - No. 4, Apr, 1950 (All photo-c)

	GD2.0	FN6.0	NM9.4
1	12.00	36.00	85.00
2,3	8.35	25.00	50.00
4-Betty Page photo-c (see Cupid #2)	29.00	86.00	200.00

MY LOVE
Marvel Comics Group: Sept, 1969 - No. 39, Mar, 1976

	GD2.0	FN6.0	NM9.4
1	3.50	10.50	35.00
2-9: 4-6-Colan-a	2.25	6.75	18.00
10-Williamson-r/My Own Romance #71; Kirby-a	2.50	7.50	22.00
11-13,15-20	2.00	6.00	16.00
14-(52 pgs.)-Woodstock-c/sty; Morrow-c/a; Kirby/Colletta-r	2.80	8.40	28.00
21,22,24-27,29-38: 38-Reprints	1.50	4.50	12.00
23-Steranko-r/Our Love Story #5	2.25	6.75	18.00
28-Kirby-a	1.75	5.25	14.00
39-Last issue; reprints	2.00	6.00	16.00
Special(12/71)(52 pgs.)	2.80	8.40	28.00

NOTE: ***John Buscema*** *a-1-7, 10, 22r(2), 24r, 25r, 29r, 34r, 36r, 37r, Spec. (r)(4); c-13, 15, 25, 27, Spec.* ***Colan*** *a-16,22,24r,35r,39r.* ***Colan/Everett*** *a-13, 15, 16, 27(r/#13).* ***Kirby*** *a-(r)-14,28.*

MY LOVE AFFAIR (March of Crime #7 on)
Fox Feature Syndicate: July, 1949 - No. 6, May, 1950

	GD2.0	FN6.0	NM9.4
1	13.00	39.00	90.00
2	8.35	25.00	50.00
3-6-Wood-a. 5-(3/50)-Becomes Love Stories #6	17.00	51.00	120.00

MY LOVE LIFE (Formerly Zegra)
Fox Feature Synd.: No. 6, June, 1949 - No. 13, Aug, 1950; No. 13, Sept, 1951

	GD2.0	FN6.0	NM9.4
6-Kamenish-a	14.00	43.00	100.00
7-13	8.35	25.00	50.00
13 (9/51)	7.50	22.50	45.00

MY LOVE MEMOIRS (Formerly Women Outlaws; Hunted #13 on)
Fox Feature Syndicate: No. 9, Nov, 1949 - No. 12, May, 1950

	GD2.0	FN6.0	NM9.4
9,11,12-Wood-a	16.00	47.00	110.00
10	8.35	25.00	50.00

MY LOVE SECRET (Formerly Phantom Lady; Animal Crackers #31)
Fox Feature Syndicate/M. S. Distr.: No. 24, June, 1949 - No. 30, June, 1950; No. 53, 1954

	GD2.0	FN6.0	NM9.4
24-Kamen/Feldstein-a	16.00	47.00	110.00
25-Possible caricature of Wood on-c?	10.00	30.00	60.00
26,28-Wood-a	16.00	47.00	110.00
27,29,30: 30-Photo-c	8.00	24.00	48.00
53-(Reprint, M.S. Distr.) 1954? nd given; formerly Western Thrillers; becomes Crimes by Women #54; photo-c	4.25	13.00	28.00

MY LOVE STORY (Hoot Gibson Western #5 on)
Fox Feature Syndicate: Sept, 1949 - No. 4, Mar, 1950

	GD2.0	FN6.0	NM9.4
1	13.00	39.00	90.00
2	8.35	25.00	50.00
3,4-Wood-a	17.00	51.00	120.00

MY LOVE STORY
Atlas Comics (GPS): April, 1956 - No. 9, Aug, 1957

	GD2.0	FN6.0	NM9.4
1	10.00	30.00	70.00
2	5.35	16.00	32.00
3,7: Matt Baker-a. 7-Toth-a	8.35	25.00	50.00
4-6,8,9	5.00	15.00	30.00

NOTE: ***Brewster*** *a-3.* ***Colletta*** *a-1(2), 3, 4(2), 5; c-3.*

MY NAME IS CHAOS
DC Comics: 1992 - No. 4, 1992 ($4.95, limited series, 52 pgs.)

	GD2.0	FN6.0	NM9.4
Book 1-4: Tom Veitch scripts; painted-c			5.00

MY NAME IS HOLOCAUST
DC Comics: May, 1995 - No. 5, Sept, 1995 ($2.50, limited series)

	GD2.0	FN6.0	NM9.4
1-5			2.50

MY ONLY LOVE
Charlton Comics: July, 1975 - No. 9, Nov, 1976

	GD2.0	FN6.0	NM9.4
1	1.75	5.25	14.00
2,4-9	1.10	3.30	9.00
3-Toth-a	1.40	4.15	11.00

MY OWN ROMANCE (Formerly My Romance; Teen-Age Romance #77 on)
Marvel/Atlas (MjPC/RCM No. 4-59/ZPC No. 60-76): No. 4, Mar, 1949 - No. 76, July, 1960

	GD2.0	FN6.0	NM9.4
4-Photo-c	13.00	39.00	90.00
5-10: 5,6,8-10-Photo-c	7.00	21.00	42.00
11-20: 14-Powell-a	5.85	17.50	35.00
21-42,55: 42-Last precode (2/55). 55-Toth-a	5.35	16.00	32.00
43-54,56-60	2.50	7.50	24.00
61-70,72,73,75,76	2.50	7.50	20.00
71-Williamson-a	3.50	10.50	35.00
74-Kirby-a	2.50	7.50	25.00

NOTE: ***Brewster*** *a-59.* ***Colletta*** *a-45(2), 48, 50, 55, 57(2), 59; c-58i, 59, 61.* ***Everett*** *a-25; c-58p.* ***Kirby*** *c-71, 75, 76.* ***Morisi*** *a-18.* ***Orlando*** *a-61.* ***Romita*** *a-36.* ***Tuska*** *a-10.*

MY PAL DIZZY (See Comic Books, Series I)

MY PAST (...Confessions) (Formerly Western Thrillers)
Fox Feature Syndicate: No. 7, Aug, 1949 - No. 11, Apr, 1950 (Crimes Inc. #12)

My Private Life #17 © FOX

Mysteries (Weird and Strange) #7 © SUPR

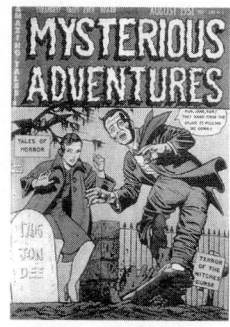

Mysterious Adventures #3 © Story Comics

	GD2.0	FN6.0	NM9.4
7	13.00	39.00	90.00
8-10	8.35	25.00	50.00
11-Wood-a	16.00	47.00	110.00

MY PERSONAL PROBLEM
Ajax/Farrell/Steinway Comic: 11/55; No. 2, 2/56; No. 3, 9/56 - No. 4, 11/56; 10/57 - No. 3, 5/58

	GD2.0	FN6.0	NM9.4
1	8.35	25.00	50.00
2-4	5.35	16.00	32.00
1-3('57-'58)-Steinway	4.25	13.00	28.00

MY PRIVATE LIFE (Formerly Murder, Inc.; becomes Pedro #18)
Fox Feature Syndicate: No. 16, Feb, 1950 - No. 17, April, 1950

	GD2.0	FN6.0	NM9.4
16,17	11.00	33.00	75.00

MYRA NORTH (See The Comics, Crackajack Funnies & Red Ryder)
Dell Publishing Co.: No. 3, Jan, 1940

	GD2.0	FN6.0	NM9.4
Four Color 3	73.00	218.00	800.00

MY REAL LOVE
Standard Comics: No. 5, June, 1952 (Photo-c)

	GD2.0	FN6.0	NM9.4
5-Toth-a, 3 pgs.; Tuska, Cardy, Vern Greene-a	12.00	36.00	85.00

MY ROMANCE (Becomes My Own Romance #4 on)
Marvel Comics (RCM): Sept, 1948 - No. 3, Jan, 1949

	GD2.0	FN6.0	NM9.4
1	13.00	39.00	90.00
2,3: 2-Anti-Wertham editorial (11/48)	8.35	25.00	50.00

MY ROMANTIC ADVENTURES (Formerly Romantic Adventures)
American Comics Group: No. 68, 8/56 - No. 115, 12/60; No. 116, 7/61 - No. 138, 3/64

	GD2.0	FN6.0	NM9.4
68	8.00	24.00	48.00
69-85	4.25	13.00	26.00
86-Three pg. Williamson-a (2/58)	6.70	20.00	40.00
87-100	2.25	6.75	18.00
101-138	1.50	4.50	12.00

NOTE: ***Whitney** art in most issues.*

MY SECRET (Becomes Our Secret #4 on)
Superior Comics, Ltd.: Aug, 1949 - No. 3, Oct, 1949

	GD2.0	FN6.0	NM9.4
1	12.00	36.00	85.00
2,3	8.35	25.00	50.00

MY SECRET AFFAIR (Becomes Martin Kane #4)
Hero Book (Fox Feature Syndicate): Dec, 1949 - No. 3, April, 1950

	GD2.0	FN6.0	NM9.4
1-Harrison/Wood-a (10 pgs.)	19.00	56.00	130.00
2-Wood-a (poor)	12.00	36.00	85.00
3-Wood-a	16.00	47.00	110.00

MY SECRET CONFESSION
Sterling Comics: September, 1955

	GD2.0	FN6.0	NM9.4
1-Sekowsky-a	8.35	25.00	50.00

MY SECRET LIFE (Formerly Western Outlaws; Romeo Tubbs #26 on)
Fox Feature Syndicate: No. 22, July, 1949 - No. 27, May, 1950

	GD2.0	FN6.0	NM9.4
22	10.00	30.00	70.00
23,26-Wood-a, 6 pgs.	16.00	47.00	110.00
24,25,27	7.50	22.50	45.00

NOTE: *The title was changed to Romeo Tubbs after #25 even though #26 & 27 did come out.*

MY SECRET LIFE (Formerly Young Lovers; Sue & Sally Smith #48)
Charlton Comics: No. 19, Aug, 1957 - No. 47, Sept, 1962

	GD2.0	FN6.0	NM9.4
19	2.50	7.50	24.00
20-35	1.50	4.50	12.00
36-47: 44-Last 10¢ issue	1.25	3.75	10.00

MY SECRET MARRIAGE
Superior Comics, Ltd.: May, 1953 - No. 24, July, 1956

	GD2.0	FN6.0	NM9.4
1	10.00	30.00	70.00
2	5.35	16.00	32.00
3-24	4.00	12.00	24.00

	GD2.0	FN6.0	NM9.4
I.W. Reprint #9	1.00	3.00	8.00

NOTE: *Many issues contain **Kamenish** art.*

MY SECRET ROMANCE (Becomes A Star Presentation #3)
Hero Book (Fox Feature Syndicate): Jan, 1950 - No. 2, March, 1950

	GD2.0	FN6.0	NM9.4
1	12.00	36.00	85.00
2-Wood-a	16.00	47.00	110.00

MY SECRET STORY (Formerly Captain Kidd #25; Sabu #30 on)
Fox Feature Syndicate: No. 26, Oct, 1949 - No. 29, April, 1950

	GD2.0	FN6.0	NM9.4
26	13.00	39.00	90.00
27-29	8.35	25.00	50.00

MYS-TECH WARS
Marvel Comics UK: Mar, 1993 - No. 4, June, 1993 ($1.75, mini-series)

	GD2.0	FN6.0	NM9.4
1-4: 1-Gatefold-c			2.00

MYSTERIES (...Weird & Strange)
Superior/Dynamic Publ. (Randall Publ. Ltd.): May, 1953 - No. 11, Jan, 1955

	GD2.0	FN6.0	NM9.4
1	34.00	103.00	240.00
2-A-Bomb blast story	19.00	56.00	130.00
3-11: 10-Kamenish-c/a reprinted from Strange Mysteries #2; cover is from a panel in Strange Mysteries #2	17.00	49.00	115.00

MYSTERIES IN SPACE (See Fireside Book Series)

MYSTERIES OF SCOTLAND YARD (Also see A-1 Comics)
Magazine Enterprises: No. 121, 1954 (one shot)

	GD2.0	FN6.0	NM9.4
A-1 121-Reprinted from Manhunt (5 stories)	16.00	47.00	110.00

MYSTERIES OF UNEXPLORED WORLDS (See Blue Bird) (Becomes Son of Vulcan V2#49 on)
Charlton Comics: Aug, 1956; No. 2, Jan, 1957 - No. 48, Sept, 1965

	GD2.0	FN6.0	NM9.4
1	34.00	103.00	240.00
2-No Ditko	13.00	39.00	90.00
3,4,8,9 Ditko-a. 3-Diko c/a (4). 4-Ditko c/a (2).	25.00	75.00	175.00
5-7,10,11: 5,6-Ditko-c/a (all). 7-(2/58, 68 pgs.); Ditko-a(4). 10-Ditko-c/a(4). 11-Ditko-c/a(3); signed J. Kotdi	27.00	81.00	190.00
12,19,21-24,26-Ditko-a. 12-Ditko sty (3); Baker story "The Charm Bracelet."	19.00	56.00	130.00
13-18,20,	5.85	17.50	35.00
25,27-30	2.50	7.50	24.00
31-45	2.25	6.75	18.00
46(5/65)-Son of Vulcan begins (origin/1st app.)	3.50	10.50	35.00
47,48	2.25	6.75	18.00

NOTE: ***Ditko** c-3-6, 10, 11, 19, 21-24. Covers to #19, 21-24 reprint story panels.*

MYSTERIOUS ADVENTURES
Story Comics: Mar, 1951 - No. 24, Mar, 1955; No. 25, Aug, 1955

	GD2.0	FN6.0	NM9.4
1-All horror stories	45.00	135.00	360.00
2	27.00	81.00	190.00
3,4,6,10	24.00	71.00	165.00
5-Bondage-c	27.00	81.00	190.00
7-Daggar in eye panel	37.00	111.00	260.00
8-Eyeball story	40.00	120.00	280.00
9-Extreme violence	31.00	94.00	220.00
11(12/52)-Used in **SOTI**, pg. 84	31.00	94.00	220.00
12,13	26.00	79.00	185.00
14-E.C. Old Witch swipe	26.00	79.00	185.00
15-21: 18-Used in Senate Investigative report, pgs. 5,6; E.C. swipe/TFTC #35; The Coffin-Keeper & Corpse (hosts). 20-Used by Wertham in the Senate hearings. 21-Bondage/beheading-c	34.00	103.00	240.00
22- "Cinderella" parody	26.00	77.00	180.00
23-Disbrow-a (6 pgs.); E.C. swipe "The Mystery Keeper's Tale" (host) and "Mother Ghoul's Nursery Tale"	26.00	77.00	180.00
24,25	20.00	60.00	140.00

NOTE: ***Tothish** art by **Ross Andru**-#22, 23. **Bache** a-8. **Cameron** a-5-7. **Harrison** a-12. **Hollingsworth** a-3-8, 12. **Schaffenberger** a-24, 25. **Wildey** a-15, 17.*

MYSTERIOUS ISLAND
Dell Publishing Co.: No. 1213, July-Sept, 1961

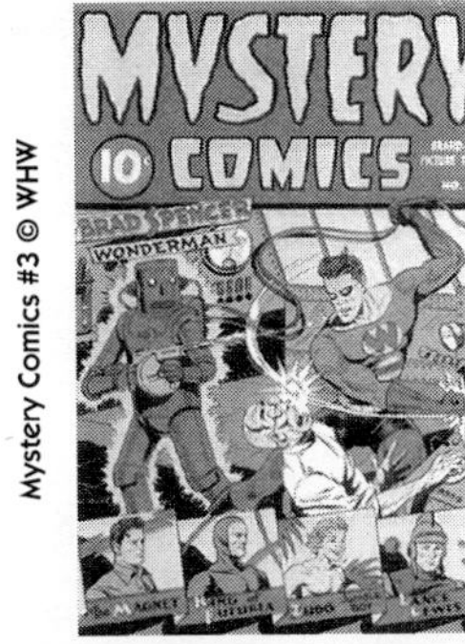

Mystery Comics #3 © WHW

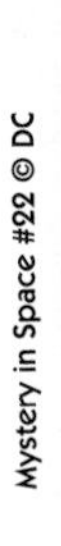

Mystery in Space #22 © DC

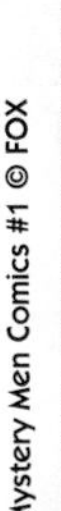

Mystery Men Comics #1 © FOX

GD2.0 FN6.0 NM9.4

Four Color 1213-Movie, photo-c 8.00 25.00 90.00

MYSTERIOUS ISLE
Dell Publishing Co.: Nov-Jan, 1963/64 (Jules Verne)

1 2.50 7.50 20.00

MYSTERIOUS RIDER, THE (See Zane Grey, 4-Color 301)

MYSTERIOUS STORIES (Formerly Horror From the Tomb #1)
Premier Magazines: No. 2, Dec-Jan, 1954-1955 - No. 7, Dec, 1955

2-Woodbridge-c; last pre-code issue 39.00 116.00 270.00
3-Woodbridge-c/a 26.00 77.00 180.00
4-7: 5-Cinderella parody. 6-Woodbridge-c 24.00 73.00 170.00
NOTE: *Hollingsworth a-2, 4.*

MYSTERIOUS SUSPENSE
Charlton Comics: Oct, 1968 (12¢)

1-Return of the Question by Ditko (c/a) 5.50 16.50 55.00

MYSTERIOUS TRAVELER (See Tales of the...)

MYSTERIOUS TRAVELER COMICS (Radio)
Trans-World Publications: Nov, 1948

1-Powell-c/a(2); Poe adaptation, "Tell Tale Heart" 55.00 165.00 440.00

MYSTERY COMICS
William H. Wise & Co.: 1944 - No. 4, 1944 (No months given)

1-The Magnet, The Silver Knight, Brad Spencer, Wonderman, Dick Devins, King of Futuria, & Zudo the Jungle Boy begin (all 1st app.); Schomburg-c on all 100.00 300.00 800.00
2-Bondage-c 66.00 197.00 525.00
3,4: 3-Lance Lewis, Space Detective begins (1st app.); Robot-c. 4(V2#1 inside) 59.00 178.00 475.00

MYSTERY COMICS DIGEST
Gold Key/Whitman?: Mar, 1972 - No. 26, Oct, 1975

1-Ripley's Believe It or Not; reprint of Ripley's #1 origin Ra-Ka-Tep the Mummy; Wood-a 3.20 9.50 35.00
2-9: 2-Boris Karloff Tales of Mystery; Wood-a; 1st app. Werewolf Count Wulfstein 3-Twilight Zone (TV); Crandall, Toth & George Evans-a; 1st app. Tragg & Simbar the Lion Lord; (2) Crandall/Frazetta-r/Twilight Zone #1 4-Ripley's Believe It or Not; 1st app. Baron Tibor, the Vampire. 5-Boris Karloff Tales of Mystery; 1st app. Dr. Spektor. 6-Twilight Zone (TV); 1st app. U.S. Marshal Reid & Sir Duane; Evans-r. 7-Ripley's Believe It or Not; origin The Lurker in the Swamp; 1st app. Duroc. 8-Boris Karloff Tales of Mystery; McWilliams-r; Orlando-r. 9-Twilight Zone (TV); Williamson, Crandall, McWilliams-a; 2nd Tragg app.;Torres, Evans, Heck/Tuska-r 2.20 6.60 22.00
10-26: 10,13-Ripley's Believe It or Not: 13-Orlando-r. 11,14-Boris Karloff Tales of Mystery. 14-1st app. Xorkon. 12,15-Twilight Zone (TV). 16,19,22,25-Ripley's Believe It or Not. 17-Boris Karloff Tales of Mystery; Williamson-r; Orlando-r. 18,21,24-Twilight Zone (TV). 20,23,26-Boris Karloff Tales of Mystery 1.60 4.80 16.00
NOTE: *Dr. Spektor app.-#5, 10-12, 21. Durak app.-#15. Duroc app.-#14 (later called Durak). King George 1st app.-#8.*

MYSTERY IN SPACE (Also see Fireside Book Series and Pulp Fiction Library)
National Periodical Publ.: 4-5/51 - No. 110, 9/66; No. 111, 9/80 - No. 117, 3/81 (#1-3: 52 pgs.)

1-Frazetta-a, 8 pgs.; Knights of the Galaxy begins, ends #8 200.00 600.00 2600.00
2 83.00 250.00 1000.00
3 67.00 200.00 800.00
4,5 54.00 162.00 650.00
6-10: 7-Toth-a 45.00 135.00 540.00
11-15: 13-Toth-a 34.00 102.00 380.00
16-18,20-25: Interplanetary Insurance feature by Infantino in all. 21-1st app. Space Cabbie. 24-Last pre-code issue 31.00 93.00 340.00
19-Virgil Finlay-a 33.00 100.00 370.00
26-40: 26-Space Cabbie feature begins. 34-1st S.A. issue 28.00 84.00 280.00

GD2.0 FN6.0 NM9.4

41-52: 47-Space Cabbie feature ends 21.00 63.00 210.00

GD2.0 FN6.0 VF8.0 NM9.4

53-Adam Strange begins (8/59, 10pg. sty); robot-c 133.00 400.00 800.00 1600.00

GD2.0 FN6.0 NM9.4

54 37.00 111.00 410.00
55-Grey tone-c 28.00 84.00 280.00
56-60: 59-Kane/Anderson-a 20.00 60.00 200.00
61-71: 61-1st app. Adam Strange foe Ulthoon. 62-1st app. A.S. foe Mortan. 63-Origin Vandor. 66-Star Rovers begin (1st app.). 68-1st app. Dust Devils (6/61). 69-1st Mailbag. 70-2nd app. Dust Devils. 71-Last 10¢ issue 15.50 47.00 155.00
72-74,76-80 11.00 33.00 110.00
75-JLA x-over in Adam Strange (5/62)(sequel to JLA #3) 23.50 70.00 235.00
81-86 7.50 22.50 75.00
87-(11/63)-Adam Strange/Hawkman double feat begins; 3rd Hawkman tryout series 18.50 55.00 185.00
88-Adam Strange & Hawkman stories 16.50 50.00 165.00
89-Adam Strange & Hawkman stories 15.50 47.00 155.00
90-Adam Strange & Hawkman team-up for 1st time (3/64); Hawkman moves to own title next month 17.50 52.00 175.00
91-103: 91-End Infantino art on Adam Strange; double-length Adam Strange story. 92-Space Ranger begins (6/64), ends #103. 92-94,96,98-Space Ranger-c. 94,98-Adam Strange/Space Ranger team-up. 102-Adam Strange ends (no Space Ranger). 103-Origin Ultra, the Multi-Alien; last Space Ranger 3.50 10.50 35.00
104-110: 110-(9/66)-Last 12¢ issue 2.50 7.50 22.00
V17#111(9/80)-117: 117-Newton-a(3 pgs.) 5.00
NOTE: ***Anderson** a-2, 4, 8-10, 12-17, 19, 45-48, 51, 57, 59i, 61-64, 70, 76, 87-91; c-9, 10, 15-25, 87, 89, 105-108, 110. **Aparo** a-111. **Austin** a-112i. **Bolland** a-115. **Craig** a-114, 116. **Ditko** a-111, 114-116. **Drucker** a-13, 14. **Elias** a-98, 102, 103. **Golden** a-113p. **Sid Greene** a-78, 91. **Infantino** a-1-8, 11, 14-25, 27-46, 48, 49, 51, 53-91, 103, 117; c-60-86, 88, 90, 91, 105, 107. **Gil Kane** a-14p, 15p, 18p, 19p, 26p, 29-59p(most), 100-102; c-52, 101. **Kubert** a-113; c-111-115. **Moriera** c-27, 28. **Rogers** a-111. **Sekowsky** a-52. **Simon & Kirby** a-4(2 pgs.). **Spiegle** a-111, 114. **Starlin** c-116. **Sutton** a-112. **Tuska** a-115p, 117p.*

MYSTERY MEN COMICS
Fox Features Syndicate: Aug, 1939 - No. 31, Feb, 1942

1-Intro. & 1st app. The Blue Beetle, The Green Mask, Rex Dexter of Mars by Briefer, Zanzibar by Tuska, Lt. Drake, D-13-Secret Agent by Powell, Chen Chang, Wing Turner, & Captain Denny Scott 950.00 2850.00 9500.00
2-Robot & sci/fi-c (2nd Robot-c w/Movie #6) 300.00 900.00 2700.00
3 (10/39)-Classic Lou Fine-c 378.00 1133.00 3400.00
4,5: 4-Capt. Savage begins (11/39) 237.00 712.00 1900.00
6-Tuska-c 200.00 600.00 1600.00
7-1st Blue Beetle-c app. 237.00 712.00 1900.00
8-Lou Fine-c 212.00 637.00 1700.00
9-The Moth begins; Lou Fine-c 106.00 319.00 850.00
10-12: All Joe Simon-c. 10-Wing Turner by Kirby; Simon-c. 11-Intro. Domino 94.00 281.00 750.00
13-Intro. Lynx & sidekick Blackie (8/40) 62.00 187.00 500.00
14-18 60.00 180.00 480.00
19-Intro. & 1st app. Miss X (ends #21) 62.00 187.00 500.00
20-24 55.00 165.00 440.00
25 -31: 26-The Wraith begins 56.00 169.00 450.00
NOTE: ***Briefer** a-1-15, 20, 24; c-9. **Cuidera** a-22. **Lou Fine** c-1-5,8,9. **Powell** a-1-15, 24. **Simon** c-10-12. **Tuska** a-1-16, 22, 24, 27; c-6. Bondage-c 1, 3, 7, 8, 25, 27-29, 31. Blue Beetle c-7, 8, 10-31. D-13 Secret Agent c-6. Green Mask c-1, 3-5. Rex Dexter of Mars c-2, 9.*

MYSTERY MEN MOVIE ADAPTION
Dark Horse Comics: July, 1999 - No. 2, Aug, 1999 ($2.95, mini-series)

1,2-Fingerman-s; photo-c 3.00

MYSTERY PLAY, THE
DC Comics (Vertigo): 1994 ($19.95, one-shot)

nn-Hardcover-Morrison-s/Muth-painted art 25.00
Softcover ($9.95)-New Muth cover 10.00

MYSTERY TALES

Mystery Tales #4 © MAR

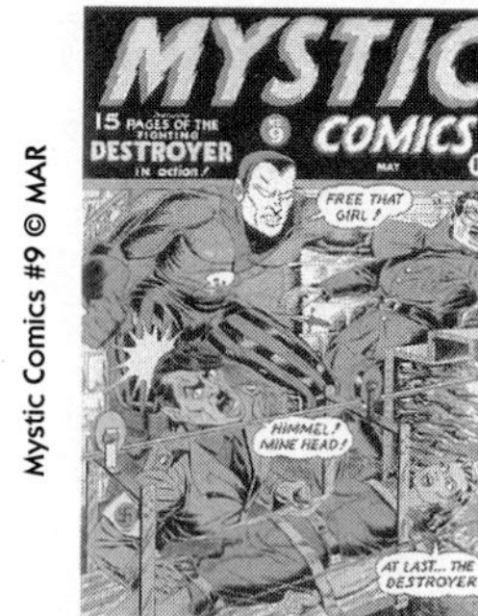

Mystic Comics #9 © MAR

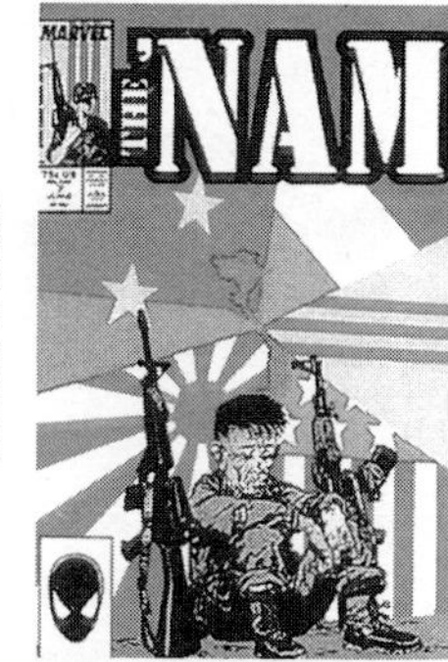

The 'Nam #7 © MAR

GD2.0 FN6.0 NM9.4

Atlas Comics (20CC): Mar, 1952 - No. 54, Aug, 1957
1-Horror/weird stories in all 78.00 234.00 625.00
2-Krigstein-a 40.00 120.00 325.00
3-10: 6-A-Bomb panel. 10-Story similar to "The Assassin" from Shock SuspenStories 36.00 107.00 250.00
11,13-21: 14-Maneely s/f story. 20-Electric chair issue. 21-Matt Fox-a; decapitation story 26.00 79.00 185.00
12,22: 12-Matt Fox-a. 22-Forte/Matt Fox-c; a(i) 29.00 86.00 200.00
23-26 (2/55)-Last precode issue 21.00 62.00 145.00
27,29-35,37,38,41-43,48,49: 43-Morisi story contains Frazetta art swipes from Untamed Love 16.00 47.00 110.00
28,36,39,40,45: 28-Jack Katz-a. 36,39-Krigstein-a. 40,45-Ditko-a (#45 is 3 pgs. only) 17.00 49.00 115.00
44,51-Williamson/Krenkel-a 18.00 54.00 125.00
46-Williamson/Krenkel-a; Crandall text illos 18.00 54.00 125.00
47-Crandall, Ditko, Powell-a 18.00 54.00 125.00
50,52,53: 50-Torres, Morrow-a 16.00 47.00 110.00
54-Crandall, Check-a 17.00 49.00 115.00
NOTE: ***Ayers*** *a-18, 49, 52.* ***Berg*** *a-17, 51.* ***Colan*** *a-1, 3, 18, 35, 43.* ***Colletta*** *a-18.* ***Drucker*** *a-41.* ***Everett*** *a-2, 29, 33, 35, 41; c-8-11, 14, 38, 39, 41, 43, 44, 46, 48-51, 53.* ***Fass*** *a-16.* ***Forte*** *a-21, 22, 45, 46.* ***Matt Fox*** *a-12?, 21, 22; c-22.* ***Heath*** *a-3; c-3, 15, 17, 26.* ***Heck*** *a-25.* ***Kinstler*** *a-15.* ***Mort Lawrence*** *a-26, 32, 34.* ***Maneely*** *a-1, 9, 14, 22; c-12, 23, 24, 27.* ***Mooney*** *a-3, 40.* ***Morisi*** *a-43, 49, 52.* ***Morrow*** *a-50.* ***Orlando*** *a-51.* ***Pakula*** *a-16.* ***Powell*** *a-21, 29, 37, 38, 47.* ***Reinman*** *a-1, 14, 17.* ***Robinson*** *a-7p, 42.* ***Romita*** *a-37.* ***Roussos*** *a-4, 44.* ***R.Q. Sale*** *a-45, 46, 49.* ***Severin*** *c-52.* ***Shores*** *a-17, 45.* ***Tuska*** *a-10, 12, 14.* ***Whitney*** *a-2.* ***Wildey*** *a-37.*

MYSTERY TALES
Super Comics: 1964
Super Reprint #16,17('64): 16-r/Tales of Horror #2. 17-r/Eerie #14(Avon), 18-Kubert-r/Strange Terrors #4 2.25 6.75 18.00

MYSTIC (3rd Series)
Marvel/Atlas Comics (CLDS 1/CSI 2-21/OMC 22-35/CSI 35-61): March, 1951 - No. 61, Aug, 1957
1-Atom bomb panels; horror/weird stories in all 84.00 253.00 675.00
2 46.00 139.00 370.00
3-Eyes torn out 40.00 120.00 290.00
4- "The Devil Birds" by Wolverton (6 pgs.) 72.00 216.00 575.00
5,7-10 30.00 90.00 210.00
6- "The Eye of Doom" by Wolverton (7 pgs.) 72.00 216.00 575.00
11-20: 16-Bondage/torture c/story 26.00 79.00 185.00
21-25,27-36-Last precode (3/55). 25-E.C. swipe 21.00 62.00 145.00
26-Atomic War, severed head stories 23.00 69.00 160.00
37-51,53-57,61: 57-Story "Trapped in the Ant-Hill" (1957) is very similar to "The Man in the Ant Hill" in TTA #27 17.00 49.00 115.00
52-Wood-a; Crandall-a? 19.00 56.00 130.00
58,59-Krigstein-a 17.00 51.00 120.00
60-Williamson/Mayo-a (4 pgs.) 17.00 51.00 120.00
NOTE: ***Andru*** *a-23, 25.* ***Ayers*** *a-35, 53; c-8.* ***Berg*** *a-49.* ***Cameron*** *a-49, 51.* ***Check*** *a-31, 60.* ***Colan*** *a-3, 7, 12, 21, 37, 60.* ***Colletta*** *a-29.* ***Drucker*** *a-46, 52, 56.* ***Everett*** *a-8, 9, 17, 40, 44, 57; c-13, 18, 21, 42, 47, 49, 51-55, 57-59, 61.* ***Forte*** *a-35, 52, 58.* ***Fox*** *a-24i.* ***Al Hartley*** *a-35.* ***Heath*** *a-10; c-10, 20, 22, 23, 25, 30.* ***Infantino*** *a-12.* ***Kane*** *a-8, 24p.* ***Jack Katz*** *a-31, 33.* ***Mort Law.rence*** *a-19, 37.* ***Maneely*** *a-22, 24, 58; c-7, 15, 28, 29, 31.* ***Moldoff*** *a-29.* ***Morisi*** *a-48, 49, 52.* ***Morrow*** *a-51.* ***Orlando*** *a-57, 61.* ***Pakula*** *a-52, 57, 59.* ***Powell*** *a-52, 54-56.* ***Robinson*** *a-5.* ***Romita*** *a-11, 15.* ***R.Q. Sale*** *a-35, 53, 58.* ***Sekowsky*** *a-1, 2, 4, 5.* ***Severin*** *c-56, 60.* ***Tuska*** *a-15.* ***Whitney*** *a-33.* ***Wildey*** *a-28, 30.* ***Ed Win*** *a-17, 20. Canadian reprints known-title 'Startling.'*

MYSTICAL TALES
Atlas Comics (CCC 1/EPI 2-8): June, 1956 - No. 8, Aug, 1957
1-Everett-c/a 43.00 128.00 340.00
2,4: 2-Berg-a 24.00 73.00 170.00
3,5: 3,4-Crandall-a. 5-Williamson-a (4 pgs.) 25.00 75.00 175.00
6-Torres, Krigstein-a 24.00 71.00 165.00
7-Bolle, Forte, Torres, Orlando-a 24.00 71.00 165.00
8-Krigstein, Check-a 21.00 64.00 150.00
NOTE: ***Everett*** *a-1; c-1-4, 6, 7.* ***Orlando*** *a-1, 2, 7.* ***Pakula*** *a-3.* ***Powell*** *a-1, 4.*

MYSTIC COMICS (1st Series)
Timely Comics (TPI 1-5/TCI 8-10): March, 1940 - No. 10, Aug, 1942
GD2.0 FN6.0 VF8.0 NM9.4
1-Origin The Blue Blaze, The Dynamic Man, & Flexo the Rubber Robot; Zephyr Jones, 3X's & Deep Sea Demon app.; The Magician begins (all 1st app.); c-from Spider pulp V18#1, 6/39 1136.00 3400.00 6800.00 12,500.00
GD2.0 FN6.0 NM9.4
2-The Invisible Man & Master Mind Excello begin; Space Rangers, Zara of the Jungle, Taxi Taylor app. 367.00 1100.00 3300.00
3-Origin Hercules, who last appears in #4 278.00 834.00 2500.00
4-Origin The Thin Man & The Black Widow; Merzak the Mystic app.; last Flexo, Dynamic Man, Invisible Man & Blue Blaze (some issues have date sticker on cover; others have July w/August overprint in silver color); Roosevelt assassination-c 300.00 900.00 2700.00
5-(3/41)-Origin The Black Marvel, The Blazing Skull, The Sub-Earth Man, Super Slave & The Terror; The Moon Man & Black Widow app.; 5-German war-c begin, end #10 278.00 834.00 2500.00
6-(10/41)-Origin The Challenger & The Destroyer (1st app.?; also see All-Winners #2, Fall, 1941) 310.00 930.00 2800.00
7-The Witness begins (12/41, origin & 1st app.); origin Davey & the Demon; last Black Widow; Hitler opens his trunk of terror-c by Simon & Kirby (classic-c) 333.00 1000.00 3000.00
8,9: 9-Gary Gaunt app.; last Black Marvel, Mystic & Blazing Skull; Hitler-c 188.00 562.00 1500.00
10-Father Time, World of Wonder, & Red Skeleton app.; last Challenger & Terror 188.00 562.00 1500.00
NOTE: ***Gabrielle*** *c-8-10.* ***Kirby/Schomburg*** *c-6.* ***Rico*** *a-9(2).* ***Schomburg*** *a-1-4; c-1-5.* ***Sekowsky*** *a-9.* ***Sekowsky/Klein*** *a-8(Challenger). Bondage c-1, 2, 9.*

MYSTIC COMICS (2nd Series)
Timely Comics (ANC): Oct, 1944 - No. 3, Win, 1944-45; No. 4, Mar, 1945
1-The Angel, The Destroyer, The Human Torch, Terry Vance the Schoolboy Sleuth, & Tommy Tyme begin 212.00 636.00 1700.00
2-(Fall/44)-Last Human Torch & Terry Vance; bondage/hypo-c 112.00 338.00 900.00
3-Last Angel (two stories) & Tommy Tyme 106.00 318.00 850.00
4-The Young Allies-c & app.; Schomburg-c 100.00 300.00 800.00

MYSTIC EDGE (Manga)
Antarctic Press: Oct, 1998 ($2.95, one-shot)
1-Ryan Kinnaird-s/a/c 3.00

MYSTIQUE & SABRETOOTH (Sabretooth and Mystique on-c)
Marvel Comics: Dec, 1996 - No. 4, Mar, 1997 ($1.95, limited series)
1-4: Characters from X-Men 3.00

MY STORY (...True Romances in Pictures #5,6) (Formerly Zago)
Hero Books (Fox Features Syndicate): No. 5, May, 1949 - No. 12, Aug, 1950
5-Kamen/Feldstein-a 19.00 56.00 130.00
6-8,11,12: 12-Photo-c 10.00 30.00 60.00
9,10-Wood-a 17.00 51.00 120.00

MYTHOGRAPHY
Bardic Press: Sept, 1996 - Present ($3.95/$4.25, B&W, anthology)
1-3: 1-Drew Hayes-s/a 5.00
4-8 4.25

MYTHOS: THE FINAL TOUR
DC Comics/Vertigo: Dec, 1996 - No. 3, Feb, 1997 ($5.95, limited series)
1-3: 1-Ney Rieber-s/Amaro-a. 2-Snejbjerg-a; Constantine-app. 3-Kristiansen-a; Black Orchid-app. 6.00

MY TRUE LOVE (Formerly Western Killers #64; Frank Buck #70 on)
Fox Features Syndicate: No. 65, July, 1949 - No. 69, March, 1950
65 13.00 39.00 90.00
66,68,69: 69-Morisi-a 9.15 27.00 55.00
67-Wood-a 17.00 51.00 120.00

NAKED PREY, THE (See Movie Classics)

'NAM, THE (See Savage Tales #1, 2nd series & Punisher Invades...)
Marvel Comics Group: Dec, 1986 - No. 84, Sept, 1993
1-Golden a(p)/c begins, ends #13 3.00
1 (2nd printing) 2.00
2-74,76-84: 7-Golden-a (2 pgs.). 32-Death R. Kennedy. 52,53-Frank Castle

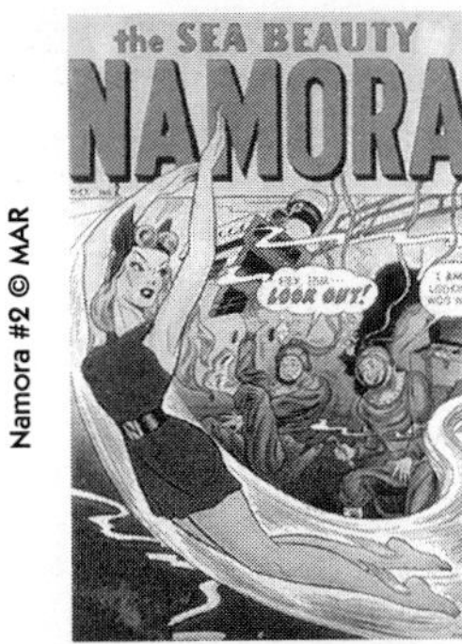

Namora #2 © MAR

Nash #2 © Kevin Nash

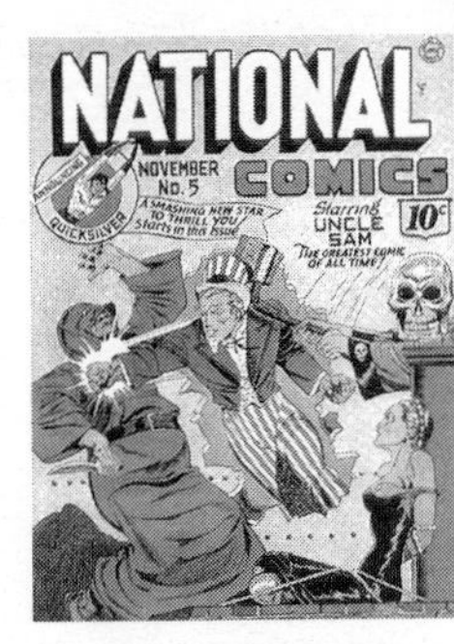

National Comics #5 © QUA

GD2.0 FN6.0 NM9.4

(The Punisher) app. 52,53-Gold 2nd printings. 58-Silver logo. 65-Heath-c/a. 67-69-Punisher 3 part story. 70-Lomax scripts begin 2.00
75-($2.25, 52 pgs.) 2.25
Trade Paperback 1,2: 1-r/#1-4. 2-r/#5-8 4.50
TPB ('99, $14.95) r/#1-4; recolored 15.00

'NAM MAGAZINE, THE
Marvel Comics: Aug, 1988 - No. 10, May, 1989 ($2.00, B&W, 52pgs.)
1-10: Each issue reprints 2 of the comic 2.00

NAMELESS, THE
Image Comics: May, 1997 - No. 5, Sept, 1997 ($2.95, B&W)
1-5: Pruett/Hester-s/a 3.00

NAMORA (See Marvel Mystery Comics #82 & Sub-Mariner Comics)
Marvel Comics (PrPl): Fall, 1948 - No. 3, Dec, 1948
1-Sub-Mariner x-over in Namora; Namora by Everett(2), Sub-Mariner by Rico (10 pgs.) 212.00 635.00 1700.00
2-The Blonde Phantom & Sub-Mariner story; Everett-a 120.00 360.00 960.00
3-(Scarce)-Sub-Mariner app.; Everett-a 120.00 360.00 960.00

NAMOR, THE SUB-MARINER (See Prince Namor & Sub-Mariner)
Marvel Comics: Apr, 1990 - No. 62, May, 1995 ($1.00/$1.25/$1.50)
1-Byrne-c/a/scripts in 1-25 (scripts only #26-32) 4.00
2-5: 5-Iron Man app. 3.00
6-25,27-49,51-62: 16-Re-intro Iron Fist (8-cameo only). 12-(52pgs.)-Re-intro. The Invaders. 18-Punisher cameo (1 panel); 21-23,25-Wolverine cameos. 22,23-Iron Fist app. 24-Namor vs. Wolverine. 28-Iron Fist-c/story. 31-Dr. Doom-c/story. 33,34-Iron Fist cameo. 35-New Tiger Shark-c/story. 37-Aqua holografx foil-c48-The Thing app. 2.00
26-Namor w/new costume; 1st Jae Lee-c/a this title (5/92) & begins 3.00
50-($1.75, 52 pgs.)-Newsstand edition; w/bound-in S-M trading card sheet (both versions) 2.00
50-($2.95, 52 pgs.)-Collector edition w/foil-c 3.00
Annual 1-4 ('91-94, 68 pgs.): 1-3 pg. origin recap. 2-Return/Defenders. 3-Bagged w/card. 4-Painted-c 3.00
NOTE: ***Jae Lee** a-26-30p, 31-37, 38p, 39, 40; c-26-40.*

NANCY AND SLUGGO (See Comics On Parade & Sparkle Comics)
United Features Syndicate: No. 16, 1949 - No. 23, 1954
16(#1) 8.00 24.00 48.00
17-23 5.00 15.00 30.00

NANCY & SLUGGO (Nancy #146-173; formerly Sparkler Comics)
St. John/Dell #146-187/Gold Key #188 on: No. 121, Apr, 1955-No. 192, Oct, 1963
121(4/55)(St. John) 6.35 19.00 38.00
122-145(7/57)(St. John) 4.25 13.00 28.00
146(9/57)-Peanuts begins, ends #192 (Dell) 3.65 11.00 40.00
147-161 (Dell) 2.75 8.00 30.00
162-165,177-180-John Stanley-a 6.40 19.00 70.00
166-176-Oona & Her Haunted House series; Stanley-a 7.00 22.00 80.00
181-187(3-5/62)(Dell) 2.90 8.70 32.00
188(10/62)-192 (Gold Key) 3.25 10.00 36.00
Four Color 1034(9-11/59)-Summer Camp 3.25 10.00 36.00
(See Dell Giant #34, 45 & Dell Giants)

NANNY AND THE PROFESSOR (TV)
Dell Publishing Co.: Aug, 1970 - No. 2, Oct, 1970 (Photo-c)
1,2: 1 (01-546-008) 2.75 8.00 30.00

NAPOLEON
Dell Publishing Co.: No. 526, Dec, 1953
Four Color 526 1.80 5.50 20.00

NAPOLEON & SAMANTHA (See Walt Disney Showcase No. 10)

NAPOLEON & UNCLE ELBY (See Clifford McBride's...)
Eastern Color Printing Co.: July, 1942 (68 pgs.) (One Shot)
1 40.00 120.00 280.00

GD2.0 FN6.0 NM9.4

1945-American Book-Strafford Press (128 pgs.) (8x10-1/2"; B&W reprints; hardcover) 13.00 39.00 90.00

NARRATIVE ILLUSTRATION, THE STORY OF THE COMICS
M.C. Gaines: Summer, 1942 (32 pgs., 7-1/4"x10", B&W w/color inserts)
nn-16pgs. text with illustrations of ancient art, strips and comic covers; 4 pg. WWII War Bond promo, "The Minute Man Answers the Call" color comic drawn by Shelly and a special 8-page color comic insert of "The Story of Saul" from Picture Stories from the Bible #1 or soon to appear in PS #1. Insert has special title page indicating it was No. 10 of a Sunday newspaper supplement insert series that had already run in a New England "Sunday Herald." (very rare; only two known copies.) Estimated value... 1,100.00

NASH (WCW Wrestling)
Image Comics: Aug, 1999 - Present ($2.95)
1,2-Regular and photo-c 3.00
1-($6.95) Photo-split-cover Edition 7.00

NATHANIEL DUSK
DC Comics: Feb, 1984 - No. 4, May, 1984 ($1.25, mini-series, direct sales, Baxter paper)
1-4: 1-Intro/origin; Gene Colan-c/a in all 2.00

NATHANIEL DUSK II
DC Comics: Oct, 1985 - No. 4, Jan, 1986 ($2.00, mini-series, Baxter paper)
1-4: Gene Colan-c/a in all 2.00

NATHAN NEVER
Dark Horse (Bonelli Comics): Mar, 1999 - No. 6, Aug, 1999 ($4.95, B&W, digest size)
1-6-Reprints Italian series in English. 1-4-Art Adams-c 5.00

NATIONAL COMICS
Quality Comics Group: July, 1940 - No. 75, Nov, 1949
1-Uncle Sam begins (1st app.); origin sidekick Buddy by Eisner; origin Wonder Boy & Kid Dixon; Merlin the Magician (ends #45); Cyclone, Kid Patrol, Sally O'Neil Policewoman, Pen Miller (by Klaus Nordling; ends #22), Prop Powers (ends #26), & Paul Bunyan (ends #22) begin 475.00 1425.00 4750.00
2 225.00 675.00 1800.00
3-Last Eisner Uncle Sam 156.00 468.00 1250.00
4-Last Cyclone 125.00 375.00 1000.00
5-(11/40)-Quicksilver begins (1st app.; 3rd w/lightning speed?; re-intro'd by DC in 1993 as Max Mercury in Flash #76, 2nd series); origin Uncle Sam; bondage-c 144.00 432.00 1150.00
6,8-11: 8-Jack & Jill begins (ends #22). 9-Flag-c 125.00 375.00 1000.00
7-Classic Lou Fine-c 200.00 600.00 1600.00
12 94.00 282.00 750.00
13-16-Lou Fine-a 84.00 252.00 675.00
17,19-22: 22-Last Pen Miller (moves to Crack #23) 62.00 186.00 500.00
18-(12/41)-Shows orientals attacking Pearl Harbor; on stands one month before actual event 112.00 336.00 900.00
23-The Unknown & Destroyer 171 begin 65.00 195.00 520.00
24-Japanese War-c 62.00 186.00 500.00
25-30: 26-Wonder Boy ends. 27- G-2 the Unknown begins (ends #46). 29-Origin The Unknown 44.00 132.00 350.00
31-33: 33-Chic Carter begins (ends #47) 40.00 120.00 320.00
34-40: 35-Last Kid Patrol. 39-Hitler-c 36.00 107.00 250.00
41-50: 42-The Barker begins (1st app?, 5/44); The Barker covers begin. 48-Origin The Whistler 21.00 64.00 150.00
51-Sally O'Neil by Ward, 8 pgs. (12/45) 28.00 84.00 195.00
52-60 17.00 51.00 120.00
61-67: 67-Format change; Quicksilver app. 13.00 39.00 90.00
68-75: The Barker ends 10.00 30.00 70.00
NOTE: ***Cole** Quicksilver-13; Barker-43; c-43, 46, 47, 49-51. **Crandall** Uncle Sam-11-13 (with **Fine**), 25, 26; c-24-26, 30-33, 43. **Crandall** Paul Bunyan-10-13. **Fine** Uncle Sam-13 (w/**Crandall**), 17, 18; c-1-14, 16, 18, 21. **Gill Fox** c-69-74. **Guardineer** Quicksilver-27, 35. **Gustavson** Quicksilver-14-26. **McWilliams** a-23-28, 55, 57. Uncle Sam c-1-41. Barker c-42-75.*

NATIONAL COMICS (Also see All Star Comics 1999 crossover titles)

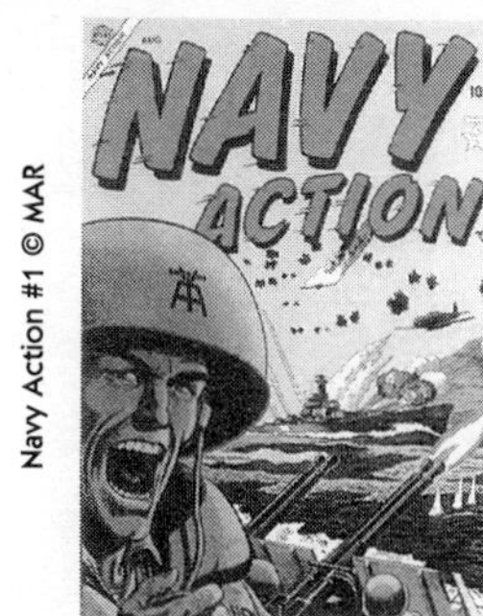

Navy Action #1 © MAR

Negative Burn #14 © Caliber

Neil Gaiman & Charles Vess' Stardust #1 © Neil Gaiman & Charles Vess

GD2.0 FN6.0 NM9.4

DC Comics: May, 1999 ($1.99, one-shot)

1-Golden Age Flash and Mr. Terrific; Waid-s/Lopresti-a 2.00

NATIONAL CRUMB, THE (Magazine-Size)
Mayfair Publications: August, 1975 (52 pgs., B&W) (Satire)

1-Grandenetti-c/a, Ayers-a 1.50 4.50 12.00

NATIONAL VELVET (TV)
Dell Publishing Co./Gold Key: May-July, 1961 - No. 2, Mar, 1963 (All photo-c)

Four Color 1195 (#1) 5.50 16.50 60.00
Four Color 1312, 01-556-207, 12-556-210 (Dell) 2.75 8.00 30.00
1,2: 1(12/62) (Gold Key). 2(3/63) 3.20 9.50 35.00

NATION OF SNITCHES
Piranha Press (DC): 1990 ($4.95, color, 52 pgs.)

nn 5.00

NATURE BOY (Formerly Danny Blaze; Li'l Rascal Twins #6 on)
Charlton Comics: No. 3, March, 1956 - No. 5, Feb, 1957

3-Origin; Blue Beetle story; Buscema-c/a 21.00 64.00 150.00
4,5 16.00 47.00 110.00
NOTE: ***John Buscema*** *a-3, 4p, 5; c-3.* ***Powell*** *a-4.*

NATURE OF THINGS (Disney, TV/Movie)
Dell Publishing Co.: No. 727, Sept, 1956 - No. 842, Sept, 1957

Four Color 727 (#1), 842-Jesse Marsh-a 4.50 13.50 50.00

NAUSICAA OF THE VALLEY OF WIND
Viz Comics: 1988 - No. 7, 1989; 1989 - No. 4, 1990 ($2.50, B&W, 68pgs.)

Book 1-7: 1-Contains Moebius poster 3.25
Part II, Book 1-4 ($2.95) 3.25

NAVY ACTION (Sailor Sweeney #12-14)
Atlas Comics (CDS): Aug, 1954 - No. 11, Apr, 1956; No. 15, 1/57 - No. 18, 8/57

1-Powell-a 17.00 49.00 115.00
2-Lawrence-a 10.00 30.00 60.00
3-11: 4-Last precode (2/55) 6.70 20.00 40.00
15-18 5.85 17.50 35.00
NOTE: ***Berg*** *a-7, 9.* ***Colan*** *a-8.* ***Drucker*** *a-7, 17.* ***Everett*** *a-3, 7, 16; c-16, 17.* ***Heath*** *c-1, 2, 6.* ***Maneely*** *a-7, 8, 18; c-9, 11.* ***Pakula*** *a-2, 3, 9.* ***Reinman*** *a-17.*

NAVY COMBAT
Atlas Comics (MPI): June, 1955 - No. 20, Oct, 1958

1-Torpedo Taylor begins by Don Heck 17.00 49.00 115.00
2 10.00 30.00 60.00
3-10 6.70 20.00 40.00
11,13,15,16,18-20 6.35 19.00 38.00
12-Crandall-a 10.00 30.00 60.00
14-Torres-a 7.00 21.00 42.00
17-Williamson-a, 4 pgs.; Torres-a 7.50 22.50 45.00
NOTE: ***Berg*** *a-10, 11.* ***Colan*** *a-11.* ***Drucker*** *a-7.* ***Everett*** *a-3, 20; c-8 & 9 w/****Tuska****, 10, 13-16.* ***Heck*** *a-11(2).* ***Maneely*** *c-1, 6, 11, 17.* ***Morisi*** *a-8.* ***Pakula*** *a-7.* ***Powell*** *a-20.*

NAVY HEROES
Almanac Publishing Co.: 1945

1-Heavy in propaganda 11.00 33.00 75.00

NAVY PATROL
Key Publications: May, 1955 - No. 4, Nov, 1955

1 6.35 19.00 38.00
2-4 4.00 11.00 22.00

NAVY TALES
Atlas Comics (CDS): Jan, 1957 - No. 4, July, 1957

1-Everett-c; Berg, Powell-a 14.00 43.00 100.00
2-Williamson/Mayo-a(5 pgs); Crandall-a 12.00 36.00 85.00
3,4-Reinman-a; Severin-c. 4-Crandall-a 11.00 33.00 75.00
NOTE: ***Colan*** *a-4.* ***Maneely*** *c-2.* ***Sinnott*** *a-4.*

NAVY TASK FORCE
Stanmor Publications/Aragon Mag. No. 4-8: Feb, 1954 - No. 8, April, 1956

GD2.0 FN6.0 NM9.4

1 7.50 22.50 45.00
2 4.00 12.00 24.00
3-8: #8-r/Navy Patrol #1 4.00 10.00 20.00

NAVY WAR HEROES
Charlton Comics: Jan, 1964 - No. 7, Mar-Apr, 1965

1 2.50 7.50 24.00
2-7 2.00 6.00 16.00

NAZA (Stone Age Warrior)
Dell Publishing Co.: Nov-Jan, 1963-64 - No. 9, March, 1966

12-555-401 (#1)-Painted-c 3.20 9.60 35.00
2-9: 2-4-Painted-c 2.50 7.50 24.00

NAZZ, THE
DC Comics: 1990 - No. 4, 1991 ($4.95, 52 pgs., mature)

1-4 5.00

NEBBS, THE (Also see Crackajack Funnies)
Dell Publishing Co./Croydon Publishing Co.: 1941; 1945

Large Feature Comic 23(1941) 14.00 41.00 150.00
1(1945, 36 pgs.)-Reprints 11.00 33.00 75.00

NECROMANCER: THE GRAPHIC NOVEL
Marvel Comics (Epic Comics): 1989 ($8.95)

nn 9.00

NEGATIVE BURN
Caliber : 1993 - No. 50, 1997 ($2.95, B&W, anthology)

1,2,4-12,14-47: Anthology by various including Bolland, Burden, Doran, Gaiman, Moebius, Moore, & Pope 4.00
3,13: 3-Bone story. 13-Strangers in Paradise story 1.50 4.50 12.00
48,49-($4.95) 5.00
50-($6.95, 96 pgs.)-Gaiman, Robinson, Bolland 7.00

NEGRO (See All-Negro)

NEGRO HEROES (Calling All Girls, Real Heroes, & True Comics reprints)
Parents' Magazine Institute: Spring, 1947 - No. 2, Summer, 1948

1 81.00 244.00 650.00
2-Jackie Robinson-c/story 87.00 262.00 700.00

NEGRO ROMANCE (Negro Romances #4)
Fawcett Publications: June, 1950 - No. 3, Oct, 1950 (All photo-c)

1-Evans-a 106.00 320.00 850.00
2,3 84.00 253.00 675.00

NEGRO ROMANCES (Formerly Negro Romance; Romantic Secrets #5 on)
Charlton Comics: No. 4, May, 1955

4-Reprints Fawcett #2 66.00 197.00 525.00

NEIL GAIMAN AND CHARLES VESS' STARDUST
DC Comics (Vertigo): 1997 - No. 4, 1998 ($5.95/$6.95, square-bound, lim. series)

1-4: Gaiman text with Vess paintings in all 7.00
Hardcover (1998, $29.95) r/series with new sketches 35.00
Softcover (1999, $19.95) oversized; new Vess-c 20.00

NEIL GAIMAN'S LADY JUSTICE
Tekno Comix: Sept, 1995 - No. 11, May, 1996 ($1.95/$2.25)

1-11: 1-Sienkiewicz-c; pin-ups. 1-5-Brereton-c. 7-polybagged. 11-Includes The Big Bang Pt. 7 2.25

NEIL GAIMAN'S LADY JUSTICE
BIG Entertainment: V2#1, June, 1996 - No. 9, Feb, 1997 ($2.25)

V2#1-9: Dan Brereton-c on all. 6-8-Dan Brereton script 2.25

NEIL GAIMAN'S MR. HERO-THE NEWMATIC MAN
Tekno Comix: Mar, 1995 - No. 17, May, 1996 ($1.95/$2.25)

1-17: 1-Intro Mr. Hero & Teknophage; bound-in game piece and trading card 4-w/Steel edition Neil Gaiman's Teknophage #1 coupon. 13-polybagged. 2.25

NEIL GAIMAN'S MR. HERO-THE NEWMATIC MAN

Nevada #4 © Steve Gerber & DC

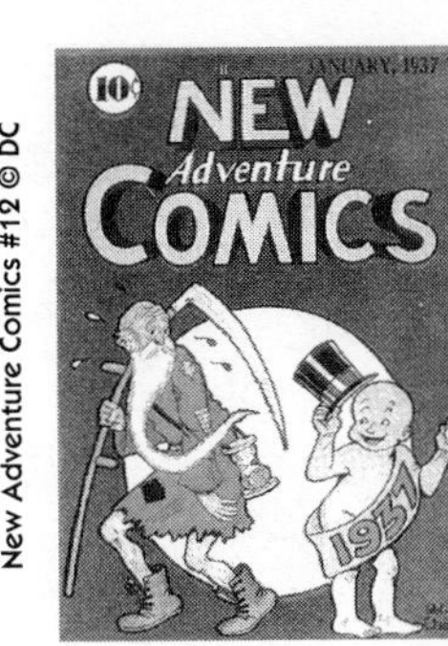

New Adventure Comics #12 © DC

New Adventures of Charlie Chan #2 © DC

GD2.0 FN6.0 NM9.4

BIG Entertainment: V2#1, June, 1996 ($2.25)

	GD2.0	FN6.0	NM9.4
V2#1-Teknophage destroys Mr. Hero; includes The Big Bang Pt. 10			2.25

NEIL GAIMAN'S PHAGE-SHADOWDEATH
BIG Entertainment: June, 1996 - No. 6, Nov, 1996 ($2.25, limited series)

	GD2.0	FN6.0	NM9.4
1-6: Bryan Talbot-c & scripts in all. 1-1st app. Orlando Holmes			2.25

NEIL GAIMAN'S TEKNOPHAGE
Tekno Comix: Aug, 1995 - No. 10, Mar, 1996 ($1.95/$2.25)

	GD2.0	FN6.0	NM9.4
1-6-Rick Veitch scripts & Bryan Talbot-c/a.			2.25
1-Steel Edition			4.00
7-10: Paul Jenkins scripts in all. 8-polybagged			2.25

NEIL GAIMAN'S WHEEL OF WORLDS
Tekno Comix: Apr, 1995 - No. 1, May, 1996 ($2.95/$3.25)

	GD2.0	FN6.0	NM9.4
0-1st app. Lady Justice; 48 pgs.; bound-in poster			3.25
0-Regular edition			2.00
1 ($3.25, 5/96)-Bruce Jones scripts; Lady Justice & Teknophage app.; computer-generated photo-c.			3.25

NEIL THE HORSE (See Charlton Bullseye #2)
Aardvark-Vanaheim #1-10/Renegade Press #11 on: 2/83 - No. 10, 12/84; No. 11, 4/85 - #15, 1985 (B&W)

	GD2.0	FN6.0	NM9.4
1($1.40)			4.00
1-2nd print			2.00
2-13: 13-Double size; 11,13-w/paperdolls			2.00
14,15: Double size ($3.00). 15 is a flip book(2-c)			3.00

NELLIE THE NURSE (Also see Gay Comics & Joker Comics)
Marvel/Atlas Comics (SPI/LMC): 1945 - No. 36, Oct, 1952; 1957

	GD2.0	FN6.0	NM9.4
1-(1945)	39.00	116.00	270.00
2-(Spring/46)	19.00	56.00	130.00
3,4: 3-New logo (9/46)	13.50	41.00	95.00
5-Kurtzman's "Hey Look" (3); Georgie app.	16.00	47.00	110.00
6-8,10: 7,8-Georgie app. 10-Millie app.	12.00	36.00	85.00
9-Wolverton-a (1 pg.); Mille the Model app.	13.00	39.00	90.00
11,14-16,18-Kurtzman's "Hey Look"	13.50	41.00	95.00
12- "Giggles 'n' Grins" by Kurtzman	12.00	36.00	85.00
13,17,19,20: 17-Annie Oakley app.	10.00	30.00	60.00
21-27,29,30	8.00	24.00	48.00
28-Mr. Nexdoor-r (3 pgs.) by Kurtzman/Rusty #22	8.35	25.00	50.00
31-36: 36-Post-c	6.70	20.00	40.00
1('57)-Leading Mag. (Atlas)-Everett-a, 20 pgs	8.35	25.00	50.00

NELLIE THE NURSE
Dell Publishing Co.: No. 1304, Mar-May, 1962

	GD2.0	FN6.0	NM9.4
Four Color 1304-Stanley-a	6.40	19.00	70.00

NEMESIS THE WARLOCK (Also see Spellbinders)
Eagle Comics: Sept, 1984 - No. 7, Mar, 1985 (limited series, Baxter paper)

	GD2.0	FN6.0	NM9.4
1-7: 2000 A.D. reprints			2.00

NEMESIS THE WARLOCK
Quality Comics/Fleetway Quality #2 on: 1989 - No. 19, 1991 ($1.95, B&W)

	GD2.0	FN6.0	NM9.4
1-19			2.00

NEON CYBER
Image Comics (Dreamwave Prod.): Jul, 1999 - Present ($2.50)

	GD2.0	FN6.0	NM9.4
1,2-Adrian Tsang-s			2.50

NEUTRO
Dell Publishing Co.: Jan, 1967

	GD2.0	FN6.0	NM9.4
1-Jack Sparling-c/a (super hero)	2.80	8.40	28.00

NEVADA (See Zane Grey's Four Color 412, 996 & Zane Grey's Stories of the West #1)

NEVADA (Also see Vertigo Winter's Edge #1)
DC Comics (Vertigo): May, 1998 - No. 6, Oct, 1998 ($2.50, limited series)

	GD2.0	FN6.0	NM9.4
1-6-Gerber-s/Winslade-c/a			2.50
TPB-(1999, $14.95) r/#1-6 & Vertigo Winter's Edge preview			15.00

NEVER AGAIN (War stories; becomes Soldier & Marine V2#9)
Charlton Comics: Aug, 1955 - No. 2, Oct?, 1955; No. 8, July, 1956 (No #3-7)

	GD2.0	FN6.0	NM9.4
1	8.35	25.00	50.00
2-(Becomes Fightin' Air Force #3), 8-(Formerly Foxhole?)	4.25	13.00	28.00

NEW ADVENTURE COMICS (Formerly New Comics; becomes Adventure Comics #32 on; V1#12 indicia says NEW COMICS #12)
National Periodical Publications: V1#12, Jan, 1937 - No. 31, Oct, 1938

	GD2.0	FN6.0	VF8.0	NM9.4
V1#12-Federal Men by Siegel & Shuster continues; Jor-L mentioned; Whitney Ellsworth-c begin, end #14	483.00	1450.00	3100.00	-
V2#1(2/37, #13)-(Rare)	450.00	1350.00	2900.00	-
V2#2 (#14)	400.00	1200.00	2600.00	-

	GD2.0	FN6.0	NM9.4
15(V2#3)-20(V2#8): 15-1st Adventure logo; Creig Flessel-c begin, end #31. 16-1st non-funny cover. 17-Nadir, Master of Magic begins, ends #30	355.00	1065.00	1775.00	2500.00
21(V2#9),22(V2#10, 2/37): 22-X-Mas-c	325.00	975.00	1625.00	2300.00
23-31	275.00	825.00	1375.00	1950.00

NEW ADVENTURES OF ABRAHAM LINCOLN, THE
Image Comics (Homage): 1998 ($19.95, one-shot)

	GD2.0	FN6.0	NM9.4
1-Scott McCloud-s/computer art			20.00

NEW ADVENTURES OF CHARLIE CHAN, THE (TV)
National Periodical Publications: May-June, 1958 - No. 6, Mar-Apr, 1959

	GD2.0	FN6.0	NM9.4
1 (Scarce)-Gil Kane/Sid Greene-a in all	65.00	195.00	520.00
2 (Scarce)	44.00	132.00	350.00
3-6 (Scarce)-Greene/Giella-a	40.00	120.00	290.00

NEW ADVENTURES OF HUCK FINN, THE (TV)
Gold Key: December, 1968 (Hanna-Barbera)

	GD2.0	FN6.0	NM9.4
1- "The Curse of Thut"; part photo-c	3.40	10.20	34.00

NEW ADVENTURES OF PINOCCHIO (TV)
Dell Publishing Co.: Oct-Dec, 1962 - No. 3, Sept-Nov, 1963

	GD2.0	FN6.0	NM9.4
12-562-212(#1)	8.65	26.00	95.00
2,3	6.00	18.00	65.00

NEW ADVENTURES OF ROBIN HOOD (See Robin Hood)

NEW ADVENTURES OF SHERLOCK HOLMES (Also see Sherlock Holmes)
Dell Publishing Co.: No. 1169, Mar-May, 1961 - No. 1245, Nov-Jan, 1961/62

	GD2.0	FN6.0	NM9.4
Four Color 1169(#1), 1245	14.00	44.00	160.00

NEW ADVENTURES OF SPEED RACER
Now Comics: Dec, 1993 - No. 7, 1994? ($1.95)

	GD2.0	FN6.0	NM9.4
1-7			2.00
0-(Premiere)-3-D cover			3.00

NEW ADVENTURES OF SUPERBOY, THE (Also see Superboy)
DC Comics: Jan, 1980 - No. 54, June, 1984

	GD2.0	FN6.0	NM9.4
1,7,50: 7-Has extra story "The Computers That Saved Metropolis" by Starlin (Radio Shack giveaway w/indicia). 50-Legion app.			3.00
2-6,8-49,51-54: 11-Superboy gets new power. 14-Lex Luthor app. 15-Superboy gets new parents. 28-Dial "H" For Hero begins, ends #49. 45-47-1st app. Sunburst. 48-Begin 75¢-c.			2.00

NOTE: ***Buckler** a-9p; c-36p. **Giffen** a-50; c-50. 40i. **Gil Kane** c-32p, 33p, 35, 39, 41-49. **Miller** c-51. **Starlin** a-7. Krypto back-ups in 17, 22. Superbaby in 11, 14, 19, 24.*

NEW ADVENTURES OF THE PHANTOM BLOT, THE (See The Phantom Blot)

NEW AMERICA
Eclipse Comics: Nov, 1987 - No. 4, Feb, 1988 ($1.75, Baxter paper)

	GD2.0	FN6.0	NM9.4
1-4: Scout limited series			2.00

NEW ARCHIES, THE (TV)
Archie Comic Publications: Oct, 1987 - No. 22, May, 1990 (75¢)

	GD2.0	FN6.0	NM9.4
1			4.00
2-10: 3-Xmas issue			3.00

New Book of Comics #1 © DC

New Funnies #66 © DELL

Nw Gods (2nd series) #7 © DC

11-22: 17-22 (95¢-$1.00): 21-Xmas issue 2.00

NEW ARCHIES DIGEST (TV)(...Comics Digest Magazine #4?-10; ...Digest Magazine #11 on)
Archie Comics: May, 1988 - No. 14, July, 1991 ($1.35/$1.50, quarterly)

1 2.40 6.00
2-14: 6-Begin $1.50-c 3.50

NEW BOOK OF COMICS (Also see Big Book Of Fun)
National Periodical Publ.: 1937; No. 2, Spring, 1938 (100 pgs. each) (Reprints)

GD2.0 FN6.0 VF8.0 NM9.4
1(Rare)-1st regular size comic annual; 2nd DC annual; contains r/New Comics #1-4 & More Fun #9; r/Federal Men (8 pgs.), Henri Duval (1 pg.), & Dr. Occult in costume (1 pg.) by Siegel & Shuster; Moldoff, Sheldon Mayer (15 pgs.)-a 1900.00 5700.00 12,500.00 –
GD2.0 FN6.0 VF8.0 NM9.4
2-Contains-r/More Fun #15 & 16; r/Dr. Occult in costume (a Superman prototype), & Calling All Cars (4 pgs.) by Siegel & Shuster 950.00 2850.00 6200.00 –

NEW COMICS (New Adventure #12 on)
National Periodical Publ.: 12/35 - No. 11, 12/36 (No. 1-6: paper cover) (No. 1-5: 84 pgs.)

GD2.0 FN6.0 VF8.0 NM9.4
V1#1-Billy the Kid, Sagebrush 'n' Cactus, Jibby Jones, Needles, The Vikings, Sir Loin of Beef, Now-When I Was a Boy, & other 1-2 pg. strips; 2 pgs. Kelly art(1st)-(Gulliver's Travels); Sheldon Mayer-a(1st)(2 2pg. strips); Vincent Sullivan-c(1st) 2550.00 7650.00 17,000.00 –
2-1st app. Federal Men by Siegel & Shuster & begins (also see The Comics Magazine #2); Mayer, Kelly-a (Rare)(1/36) 950.00 2850.00 6200.00 –
3-6: 3,4-Sheldon Mayer-a which continues in The Comics Magazine #1. 3-Vincent Sullivan-c. 4-Dickens' "A Tale of Two Cities" adaptation begins. 5-Junior Federal Men Club; Kiefer-a. 6- "She" adaptation begins 550.00 1650.00 3600.00 –
7-11: 11-Christmas-c 450.00 1350.00 2900.00 –

NOTE: *#1-6 rarely occur in mint condition.* ***Whitney Ellsworth*** *c-4-11.*

NEW DEFENDERS (See Defenders)

NEW DNAGENTS, THE (Formerly DNAgents)
Eclipse Comics: V2#1, Oct, 1985 - V2#17, Mar, 1987 (Whole #s 25-40; Mando paper)

V2#1-17: 1-Origin recap. 7-Begin 95 cent-c. 9,10-Airboy preview 2.00
3-D 1 (1/86, $2.25) 2.25
2-D 1 (1/86)-Limited ed. (100 copies) 4.00

NEWFORCE (Also see Newmen)
Image Comics (Extreme Studios): Jan, 1996-No. 4, Apr, 1996 ($2.50, lim. series)

1-4: 1-"Extreme Destroyer" Pt. 8; polybagged w/gaming card. 4-Newforce disbands. 2.50

NEW FUN COMICS (More Fun #7 on; see Big Book of Fun Comics)
National Periodical Publications: Feb, 1935 - No. 6, Oct, 1935 (10x15", No. 1-4,: slick-c) (No. 1-5: 36 pgs; 40 pgs. No. 6)

GD2.0 FN6.0 VF8.0 NM9.4
V1#1 (1st DC comic); 1st app. Oswald The Rabbit; Jack Woods (cowboy) begins 6170.00 18,500.00 39,000.00 –
2(3/35)-(Very Rare) 2590.00 7750.00 17,000.00 –
3-5(8/35): 3-Don Drake on the Planet Soro-c/story (sci/fi, 4/35). 5-Soft-c 1300.00 3900.00 8200.00 –
6(10/35)-1st Dr. Occult by Siegel & Shuster (Leger & Reuths); last "New Fun" title. "New Comics" #1 begins in Dec. which is reason for title change to More Fun; Henri Duval (ends #10) by Siegel & Shuster begins; paper-c 2917.00 8750.00 19,000.00 –

NEW FUNNIES (The Funnies #1-64; Walter Lantz...#109 on; New TV... #259, 260, 272, 273; TV Funnies #261-271)
Dell Publishing Co.: No. 65, July, 1942 - No. 288, Mar-Apr, 1962

GD2.0 FN6.0 NM9.4
65(#1)-Andy Panda in a world of real people, Raggedy Ann & Andy, Oswald the Rabbit (with Woody Woodpecker x-overs), Li'l Eight Ball & Peter Rabbit begin 64.00 191.00 700.00
66-70: 66-Felix the Cat begins. 67-Billy & Bonnie Bee by Frank Thomas begins. 69-Kelly-a (2 pgs.); The Brownies begin (not by Kelly) 29.00 89.00 325.00
71-75: 72-Kelly illos. 75-Brownies by Kelly? 18.00 54.00 200.00
76-Andy Panda (Carl Barks & Pabian-a); Woody Woodpecker x-over in Oswald ends 91.00 273.00 1000.00
77,78: 77-Kelly-c. 78-Andy Panda in a world with real people ends 18.00 54.00 200.00
79-81 13.00 39.00 145.00
82-Brownies by Kelly begins; Homer Pigeon begins 14.00 42.00 155.00
83-85-Brownies by Kelly in ea. 83-X-mas-c. 85-Woody Woodpecker, 1 pg. strip begins 14.00 42.00 155.00
86-90: 87-Woody Woodpecker stories begin 10.00 30.00 110.00
91-99 6.35 19.00 70.00
100 (6/45) 7.00 20.00 75.00
101-120: 119-X-Mas-c 4.00 12.00 45.00
121-150: 131,143-X-Mas-c 3.25 9.50 35.00
151-200: 155-X-Mas-c. 168-X-Mas-c. 182-Origin & 1st app. Knothead & Splinter. 191-X-Mas-c 2.25 6.80 25.00
201-240 1.80 5.40 18.00
241-288: 270,271-Walter Lantz c-app. 281-1st story swipes/WDC&S #100 1.40 4.20 14.00

NOTE: *Early issues written by* ***John Stanley.***

NEW GODS, THE (1st Series)(New Gods #12 on)(See Adventure #459, DC Graphic Novel #4, 1st Issue Special #13 & Super-Team Family)
National Periodical Publications/DC Comics: 2-3/71 - V2#11, 10-11/72; V3#12, 7/77 - V3#19, 7-8/78 (Fourth World)

1-Intro/1st app. Orion; 4th app. Darkseid (cameo; 3 weeks after Forever People #1) (#1-3 are 15¢ issues) 5.50 16.50 55.00
2-Darkseid-c/story (2nd full app., 4-5/71) 3.00 9.00 30.00
3-1st app. Black Racer; last 15¢ issue 2.50 7.50 22.00
4-9: (25¢, 52 pg. giants): 4-Darkseid cameo; origin Manhunter-r. 5,7,8-Young Gods feature. 7-Darkseid app. (2-3/72); origin Orion; 1st origin of all New Gods as a group. 9-1st app. Forager 2.25 6.75 18.00
10,11: 11-Last Kirby issue. 1.25 3.75 10.00
12-19: Darkseid storyline w/minor apps. 12-New costume Orion (see 1st Issue Special #13 for 1st new costume). 19-Story continued in Adventure Comics #459,460 2.40 6.00
Jack Kirby's New Gods TPB ('98, $11.95, B&W&Grey) r/#1-11 plus cover gallery of original series and "84 reprints 12.00

NOTE: *#4-9(25¢, 52 pgs.) contain Manhunter-r by* ***Simon*** *&* ***Kirby*** *from Adventure #73, 74, 75, 76, 77, 78 with covers in that order.* ***Adkins*** *i-12-14, 17-19.* ***Buckler*** *a(p)-15.* ***Kirby*** *c/a-1-11p.* ***Newton*** *a(p)-12-14, 16-19.* ***Starlin*** *c-17.* ***Staton*** *c-19p.*

NEW GODS (Also see DC Graphic Novel #4)
DC Comics: June, 1984 - No. 6, Nov, 1984 ($2.00, Baxter paper)

1-5: New Kirby-c; r/New Gods #1-10. 2.50
6-Reprints New Gods #11 w/48 pgs of new Kirby story & art; leads into DC Graphic Novel #4 2.40 6.00

NEW GODS (2nd Series)
DC Comics: Feb, 1989 - No. 28, Aug, 1991 ($1.50)

1-28 2.00

NEW GODS (3rd Series) (Becomes Jack Kirby's Fourth World) (Also see Showcase '94 #1 & Showcase '95 #7)
DC Comics: Oct, 1995 - No. 15, Feb, 1997 ($1.95)

1-11,13-15: 9-Giffen-a(p). 10,11-Superman app. 13-Takion, Mr. Miracle & Big Barda app. 13-15-Byrne-a(p)/scripts & Simonson-c. 15-Apokolips merged w/ New Genesis; story cont'd in Jack Kirby's Fourth World 2.50
12-(11/96, 99¢)-Byrne-a(p)/scripts & Simonson-c begin; Takion cameo; indicia reads October 1996 2.00
...Secret Files 1 (9/98, $4.95) Origin-s 5.00

NEW GUARDIANS, THE
DC Comics: Sept, 1988 - No. 12, Sept, 1989 ($1.25)

New Kids on the Block Chillin' #1 © Big Step Prod.

New Mutants #23 © MAR

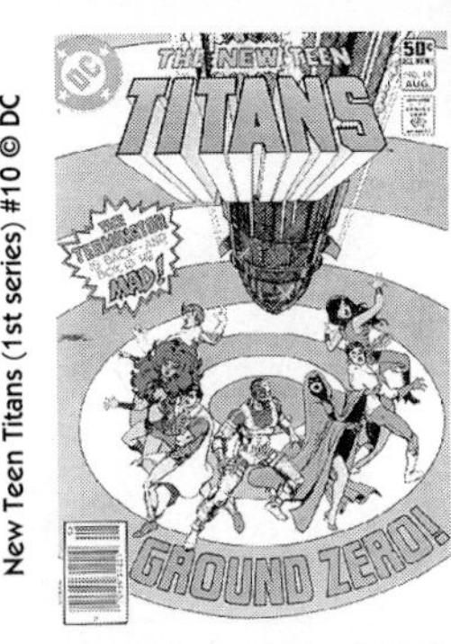

New Teen Titans (1st series) #10 © DC

GD2.0 FN6.0 NM9.4

1-($2.00, 52pgs)-Staton-c/a in #1-9 3.00
2-12 2.00

NEW HEROIC (See Heroic)

NEW JUSTICE MACHINE, THE (Also see The Justice Machine)
Innovation Publishing: 1989 - No. 3, 1989 ($1.95, limited series)

1-3 2.00

NEW KIDS ON THE BLOCK, THE (Also see Richie Rich and...)
Harvey Comics: Dec, 1990 -1991 ($1.25)

1-5 2.00
...**Backstage Pass** 1(12/90) - 5 **Chillin'** 1(12/90) - 5: 1-Photo-c...**Comics Tour** '90/91 1 (12/90) - 5 **Hanging Tough** 1 (2/91) - 3 **Live** 1 (2/91) - 3 **Magic Summer Tour** 1 (Fall/90, one-shot) **Step By Step** 1 (Fall/90, one-shot) **Valentine Girl** 1 (Fall/90, one-shot)-Photo-c 2.00

NEW LOVE (See Love & Rockets)
Fantagraphics Books: Aug, 1996 - No. 6, Dec, 1997 ($2.95, B&W, lim. series)

1-6: Gilbert Hernandez-s/a 3.00

NEWMAN
Image Comics (Extreme Studios): Jan, 1996 - No. 4, Apr, 1996 ($2.50, lim. series)

1-4: 1-Extreme Destroyer Pt. 3; polybagged w/card. 4-Shadowhunt tie-in; Eddie Collins becomes new Shadowhawk 2.50

NEWMEN (becomes The Adventures Of The...#22)
Image Comics (Extreme Studios): Apr, 1994 - No. 20, Nov, 1995; No. 21, Nov, 1996 ($1.95/$2.50)

1-21: 1-5: Matsuda-c/a. 1-Liefeld/Matsuda plot. 10-Polybagged w/trading card. 11-Polybagged. 20-Has a variant-c; Babewatch! x-over. 21-(11/96)-Series relaunch; ChrisSprouse-a begins; pin-up. 16-Has a variant-c by Quesada & Palmiotti 2.50
TPB-(1996, $12.95) r/#1-4 w/pin-ups 13.00

NEW MEN OF BATTLE, THE
Catechetical Guild: 1949 (nn) (Carboard-c)

nn(V8#1-3,5,6)-192 pgs.; contains 5 issues of Topix rebound 6.35 19.00 38.00
nn(V8#7-V8#11)-160 pgs.; contains 5 iss. of Topix 6.35 19.00 38.00

NEW MUTANTS, THE (See Marvel Graphic Novel #4 for 1st app.)(Also see X-Force & Uncanny X-Men #167)
Marvel Comics Group: Mar, 1983 - No. 100, Apr, 1991

1 5.00
2-10: 3,4-Ties into X-Men #167. 10-1st app. Magma 3.00
11-17,19,20: 13-Kitty Pryde app. 16-1st app. Warpath (w/out costume); see X-Men #193 2.50
18,21: 18-Intro. new Warlock. 21-Double size; origin new Warlock; newsstand version has cover price written in by Sienkiewicz 3.00
22-24,27-30: 23-25-Cloak & Dagger app. 2.50
25,26: 25-Legion app. (cameo). 26-1st full Legion app. 4.00
31-58: 35-Magneto intro'd as new headmaster. 43-Portacio-i. 50-Double size. 58-Contains pull-out mutant registration form 2.00
59-61: Fall of The Mutants series. 60(52 pgs.) 3.00
62-85: 68-Intro Spyder. 63-X-Men & Wolverine clones app. 73-(52 pgs.). 76-X-Factor & X-Terminator app. 85-Liefeld-c begin 2.00
86-Rob Liefeld-a begins; McFarlane-c(i) swiped from Ditko splash pg.; Cable cameo (last page teaser) 5.00
87-1st full app. Cable (3/90) 1.50 4.50 12.00
87-2nd printing; gold metallic ink-c ($1.00) 2.00
88-2nd app. Cable 2.40 6.00
92-No Liefeld-a; Liefeld-c 3.00
89,90,91,93-100: 89-3rd app. Cable. 90-New costumes. 90,91-Sabretooth app.. 93,94-Cable vs. Wolverine. 95-97-X-Tinction Agenda x-over. 95-Death of new Warlock. 97-Wolverine & Cable-c, but no app. 98-1st app. Deadpool, Gideon & Domino (2/91);2nd Shatterstar (cameo). 99-1st app. of Feral (of X-Force); Byrne-c/swipe (X-Men, 1st Series #138). 100-(52 pgs.)-1st app. X-Force (cameo) 4.00
95,100-Gold 2nd printing. 100-Silver ink 3rd printing 2.00
Annual 1 (1984) 3.00
Annual 2 (1986, $1.25)-1st Psylocke 1.00 2.80 7.00
Annual 3,4,6,7 ('87, '88,'90,'91, 68 pgs.): 4-Evolutionary War x-over. 6-1st new costumes by Liefeld (3 pgs.); 1st app. (cameo) Shatterstar (of X-Force). 7-Liefeld pin-up only; X-Terminators back-up story; 2nd app. X-Force (continued in New Warriors Annual #1) 2.50
Annual 5 (1989, $2.00, 68 pgs.)-Atlantis Attacks; 1st Liefeld-a on New Mutants 4.00
Special 1-Special Edition ('85, 68 pgs.)-Ties in w/X-Men Alpha Flight limited series; cont'd in X-Men Annual #9; Art Adams/Austin-a 5.00
Summer Special 1(Sum/90, $2.95, 84 pgs.) 3.00
NOTE: ***Art Adams** c-38, 39. **Austin** c-57i. **Byrne** c/a-75p. **Liefeld** a-86-91p, 93-96p, 98-100, Annual 5p, 6(3 pgs.); c-85-91p, 92, 93p, 94, 95, 96p, 97-100, Annual 5, 6p. **McFarlane** c-85-89i, 93i. **Portacio** a(i)-43. **Russell** a-48i. **Sienkiewicz** a-18-31, 35-38i; c-17-31, 35i, 37i, Annual 1. **Simonson** c-11p. **B. Smith** c-36, 40-48. **Williamson** a(i)-69, 71-73, 78-80, 82, 83; c(i)-69, 72, 73, 78i.*

NEW MUTANTS, THE: TRUTH OR DEATH
Marvel Comics: Nov, 1997 - No. 3, Jan, 1998 ($2.50, limited series)

1-3-Raab-s/Chang-a(p) 2.50

NEW ORDER, THE
CFD Publishing: Nov, 1994 ($2.95)

1 3.00

NEW PEOPLE, THE (TV)
Dell Publishing Co.: Jan, 1970 - No. 2, May, 1970

1,2 1.45 4.35 16.00

NEW ROMANCES
Standard Comics: No. 5, May, 1951 - No. 21, May, 1954

5-Photo-c 11.00 33.00 75.00
6-9: 6-Barbara Bel Geddes, Richard Basehart "Fourteen Hours" photo-c. 7-Ray Milland & Joan Fontaine photo-c. 9-Photo-c from '50s movie 6.35 19.00 38.00
10,14,16,17-Toth-a 7.50 22.50 45.00
11-Toth-a; Liz Taylor, Montgomery Cliff photo-c 13.00 39.00 90.00
12,13,15,18-21 4.25 13.00 28.00
NOTE: ***Celardo** a-9. **Moreira** a-6. **Tuska** a-7, 20. Photo c-5-16.*

NEW SHADOWHAWK, THE (Also see Shadowhawk & Shadowhunt)
Image Comics (Shadowline Ink): June, 1995 - No. 7, Mar, 1996 ($2.50)

1-7: Kurt Busiek scripts in all 3.00

NEW STATESMEN, THE
Fleetway Publications (Quality Comics): 1989 - No. 5, 1990 ($3.95, limited series, mature readers, 52pgs.)

1-5: Futuristic; squarebound; 3-Photo-c 4.00

NEWSTRALIA
Innovation Publ.: July, 1989 - No. 5, 1989 ($1.75, color)(#2 on, $2.25, B&W)

1-5: 1,2: Timothy Truman-c/a; Gustovich-i 2.25

NEW TALENT SHOWCASE (Talent Showcase #16 on)
DC Comics: Jan, 1984 - No. 19, Oct, 1985 (Direct sales only)

1-19: Features new strips & artists. 18-Williamson-c(i) 2.00

NEW TEEN TITANS, THE (See DC Comics Presents 26, Marvel and DC Present & Teen Titans; Tales of the Teen Titans #41 on)
DC Comics: Nov, 1980 - No. 40, Mar, 1984

1-Robin, Kid Flash, Wonder Girl, The Changeling (1st app.), Starfire, The Raven, Cyborg begin; partial origin 1.00 2.80 7.00
2-1st app. Deathstroke the Terminator 2.40 6.00
3-10: 3-Origin Starfire; Intro The Fearsome Five. 4-Origin continues; J.L.A. app. 6-Origin Raven. 7-Cyborg origin. 8-Origin Kid Flash retold. 9-Minor cameo Deathstroke on last pg. 10-2nd app. Deathstroke the Terminator (see Marvel & DC Present for 3rd app.); origin Changeling retold 4.00
11-40: 13-Return of Madame Rouge & Capt. Zahl; Robotman revived. 14-Return of Mento; origin Doom Patrol. 15-Death of Madame Rouge & Capt. Zahl; intro. new Brotherhood of Evil. 16-1st app. Captain Carrot (free 16 pg. preview). 18-Return of Starfire. 19-Hawkman teams-up. 21-Intro Night Force

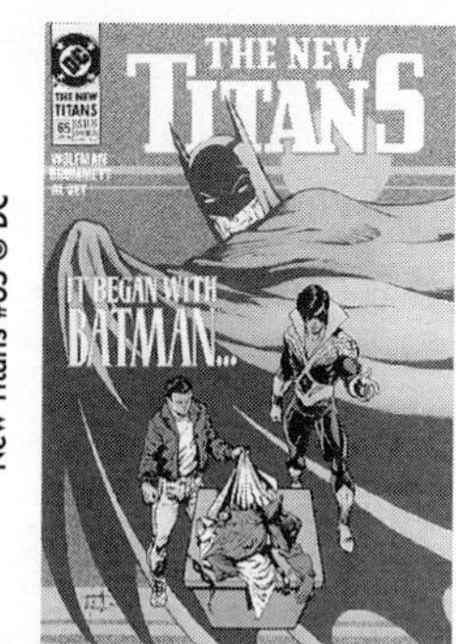

New Titans #65 © DC

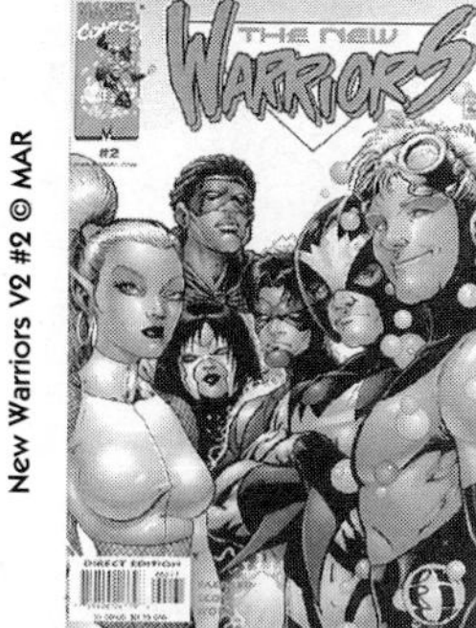

New Warriors V2 #2 © MAR

New York World's Fair #2 © DC

in free 16 pg. insert; intro Brother Blood. 23-1st app. Vigilante (not in costume), & Blackfire. 24-Omega Men app. 25-Omega Men cameo; free 16 pg. preview Masters of the Universe. 26-1st app. Terra. 27-Free 16 pg. preview Atari Force. 29-The New Brotherhood of Evil & Speedy app. 30-Terra joins the Titans. 37-Batman & The Outsiders x-over. 38-Origin Wonder Girl. 34-4th app. Deathstroke the Terminator. 39-Last Dick Grayson as Robin; Kid Flash quits 2.25

Annual 1(11/82)-Omega Men app. 2.50

Annual V2#2(9/83)-1st app. Vigilante in costume 2.50

Annual 3 (See Tales of the Teen Titans Annual #3)

NOTE: *Perez a-1-4p, 6-34p, 37-40p, Annual 1p, 2p; c-1-12, 13-17p, 18-21, 22p, 23p, 24-37, 38, 39(painted), 40, Annual 1, 2.*

NEW TEEN TITANS, THE (Becomes The New Titans #50 on)
DC Comics: Aug, 1984 - No. 49, Nov, 1988 ($1.25/$1.75; deluxe format)

1-New storyline; Perez-c/a begins 4.00

2,3: 2-Re-intro Lilith 3.00

4-10: 5-Death of Trigon. 7-9-Origin Lilith. 8-Intro Kole. 10-Kole joins 3.00

11-49: 13,14-Crisis x-over. 20-Robin (Jason Todd) joins; original Teen Titans return. 38-Infinity, Inc. x-over. 47-Origin of all Titans; Titans (East & West) pin-up by George Perez. 2.25

Annual 1-4 (9/85-'88): 1-Intro. Vanguard. 2-Byrne c/a(p); origin Brother Blood; intro new Dr. Light. 3-Intro. Danny Chase. 4-Perez-c 2.50

NOTE: ***Buckler** c-10. **Kelley Jones** a-47, Annual 4. **Erik Larsen** a-33. **Orlando** c-33p. **Perez** a-1-5; c-1-7, 19-23, 43. **Steacy** c-47.*

NEW TERRYTOONS (TV)
Dell Publishing Co./Gold Key: 6-8/60 - No. 8, 3-5/62; 10/62 - No. 54, 1/79

	GD2.0	FN6.0	NM9.4
1(1960-Dell)-Deputy Dawg, Dinky Duck & Hashimoto-San begin (1st app. of each)	4.50	13.50	50.00
2-8(1962)	2.50	7.60	28.00
1(30010-210)(10/62-Gold Key, 84 pgs.)-Heckle & Jeckle begins	6.35	19.00	70.00
2(30010-301)-84 pgs.	5.50	16.50	60.00
3-5	2.00	6.00	20.00
6-10	1.80	5.40	18.00
11-20	1.40	4.20	14.00
21-30	1.10	3.30	9.00
31-43		2.40	6.00
44-54: Mighty Mouse-c/s in all	1.00	2.80	7.00

NOTE: *Reprints: #4-12, 38, 40, 47. (See March of Comics #379, 393, 412, 435)*

NEW TESTAMENT STORIES VISUALIZED
Standard Publishing Co.: 1946 - 1947

"New Testament Heroes–Acts of Apostles Visualized, Book I"
"New Testament Heroes–Acts of Apostles Visualized, Book II"

	GD2.0	FN6.0	NM9.4
"Parables Jesus Told" Set....	11.50	34.00	80.00

NOTE: *All three are contained in a cardboard case, illustrated on front and info about the set.*

NEW TITANS, THE (Formerly The New Teen Titans)
DC Comics: No. 50, Dec, 1988 - No. 130, Feb, 1996 ($1.75/$2.25)

50-Perez-c/a begins; new origin Wonder Girl 3.00

51-59: 50-55-Painted-c. 55-Nightwing (Dick Grayson) forces Danny Chase to resign; Batman app. in flashback, Wonder Girl becomes Troia 2.25

60,61: 60-A Lonely Place of Dying Part 2 continues from Batman #440; new Robin tie-in; Timothy Drake app. 61-A Lonely Place of Dying Part 4 3.00

62-99,101-114,0,115-124,126-130: 62-65: Deathstroke the Terminator app. 65-Timothy Drake (Robin) app. 70-1st Deathstroke solo cover/sty. 71-(44 pgs.)-10th anniversary issue; Deathstroke cameo. 72-79-Deathstroke in all: 74-Intro. Pantha. 79-Terra brought back to life;1 panel cameo Team Titans (1st app.). Deathstroke in #80-84,86. 80-2nd full app. Team Titans. 83,84-Deathstroke kills his son, Jericho. 85-Team Titans app. 86-Deathstroke vs. Nightwing-c/story; last Deathstroke app. 87-New costume Nightwing. 90-92-Parts 2,5,8 Total Chaos (Team Titans). 0-(10/94); Zero Hour. 115-(11/94) 2.25

100-($3.50, 52 pgs.)-Holo-grafx foil-c 3.50

125 (3.50)-wraparound-c 3.50

Annual 5-10 ('89-'94, 68 pgs.. 7-Armaggedon 2001 x-over; 1st full app. Teen (Team) Titans (new group). 8-Deathstroke app.; Eclipso app. (minor). 10-Elseworlds story 3.50

Annual 11 (1995, $3.95)-Year One story 4.00

NOTE: ***Perez** a-50-55p, 57,60p, 58,59,61(layouts); c-50-61, 62-67i, Annual 5i; co-plots-66.*

NEW TV FUNNIES (See New Funnies)

NEW TWO-FISTED TALES, THE
Dark Horse Comics/Byron Preiss: 1993 ($4.95, limited series, 52 pgs.)

1-Kurtzman-r & new-a 5.00

NOTE: ***Eisner** c-1i. **Kurtzman** c-1p, 2.*

NEW WARRIORS, THE (See Thor #411,412)
Marvel Comics: July, 1990 - No. 75, 1996 ($1.00/$1.25/$1.50)

1-Williamson-i; Bagley-c/a(p) in 1-13, Annual 1 4.00

1-Gold 2nd printing (7/91) 2.00

2-5: 1,3-Guice-c(i). 2-Williamson-c/a(i). 3.00

6-24,26-49,51-59: 7-Punisher cameo (last pg.). 8,9-Punisher app. 14-Darkhawk & Namor x-over. 17-Fantastic Four & Silver Surfer x-over. 19-Gideon (of X-Force) app. 28-Intro Turbo & Cardinal. 31-Cannonball & Warpath app. 42-Nova vs. Firelord. 46-Photo-c. 47-Bound-in S-M trading card sheet. 52-12 pg. ad insert. 62-Scarlet Spider-c/app. 70-Spider-Man-c/app. 72-Avengers-c/app. 2.00

25-($2.50, 52 pgs.)-Die-cut cover 2.50

40,60: 40-($2.25)-Gold foil collector's edition 2.50

50-($2.95, 52 pgs.)-Glow in the dark-c 3.00

Annual 1-4('91-'94,68 pgs.)-1-Origins all members; 3rd app. X-Force (cont'd from New Mutants Ann. #7 & cont'd in X-Men Ann. #15); x-over before X-Force #1. 3-Bagged w/card 3.00

NEW WARRIORS, THE
Marvel Comics: Oct, 1999 - Present ($2.99/$2.50)

0-Wizard supplement; short story and preview sketchbook 1.00

1-($2.99) 3.00

2,3: 2-Two covers 2.50

NEW WAVE, THE
Eclipse Comics: 6/10/86 - No. 13, 3/87 (#1-8: bi-weekly, 20pgs; #9-13: monthly)

1-13:1-Origin, concludes #5. 6-Origin Megabyte. 8,9-The Heap returns. 13-Snyder-c 2.00

Versus the Volunteers 3-D #1,2(4/87): 1-Snyder-c 2.50

NEW WORLD (See Comic Books, series I)

NEW WORLDS
Caliber: 1996 - No. 6 ($2.95, 80 pgs., B&W, anthology)

1-6: 1-Mister X & other stories 3.00

NEW YORK GIANTS (See Thrilling True Story of the Baseball Giants)

NEW YORK STATE JOINT LEGISLATIVE COMMITTEE TO STUDY THE PUBLICATION OF COMICS, THE
N.Y. State Legislative Document: 1951, 1955

This document was referenced by Wertham for **Seduction of the Innocent.** Contains numerous repros from comics showing violence, sadism, torture, and sex.
1955 version (196p, No. 37, 2/23/55)-Sold for $180 in 1986.

NEW YORK WORLD'S FAIR (Also see Big Book of Fun & New Book of Fun)
National Periodical Publ.: 1939, 1940 (100 pgs.; cardboard covers)
(DC's 4th & 5th annuals)

	GD2.0	FN6.0	VF8.0	NM9.4
1939-Scoop Scanlon, Superman (blond haired Superman on-c), Sandman, Zatara, Slam Bradley, Ginger Snap by Bob Kane begin; 1st published app. The Sandman (see Adventure #40 for his 1st drawn story); Vincent Sullivan-c; cover background by Guardineer	2000.00	6000.00	13,000.00	24,000.00
1940-Batman, Hourman, Johnny Thunderbolt, Red, White & Blue & Hanko (by Creig Flessel) app.; Superman, Batman & Robin-c (1st time they all appear together); early Robin app.; 1st Burnley-c/a (per Burnley)	1080.00	3240.00	7020.00	13,000.00

NOTE: *The 1939 edition was published 4/29/39 and released 4/30/39, the day the fair opened, at 25¢, and was first sold only at the fair. Since all other comics were 10¢, it didn't sell. Remaining copies were advertised beginning in the August issues of most DC comics for 25¢, but soon the price was dropped to 15¢. Everyone that sent a quarter through the mail for it received a free Superman #1 or a #2 to make up the dime difference. 15¢ stickers were placed over the 25¢*

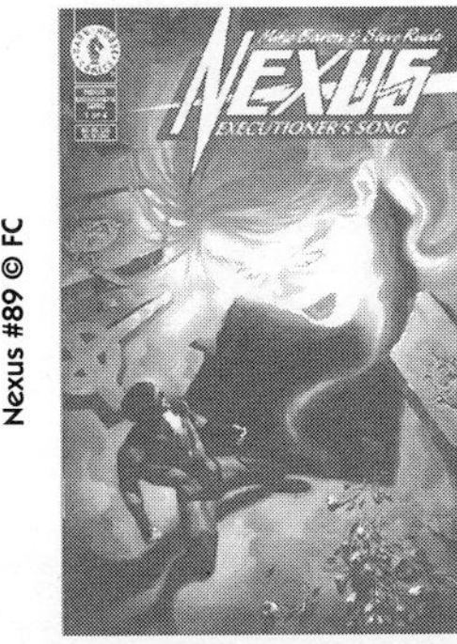

Nexus #89 © FC

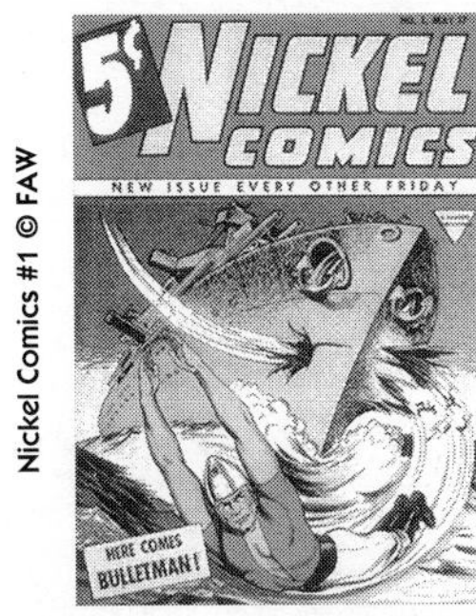

Nickel Comics #1 © FAW

Nick Fury, Agent of S.H.I.E.L.D. #7 © MAR

GD2.0 FN6.0 NM9.4

price. Four variations on the 15¢ stickers are known. The 1940 edition was published 5/11/40 and was priced at 15¢. It was a precursor to World's Best #1.

NEW YORK: YEAR ZERO
Eclipse Comics: July, 1988 - No. 4, Oct, 1988 ($2.00, B&W, limited series)
1-4 2.00

NEXT MAN
Comico: Mar, 1985 - No. 5, Oct, 1985 ($1.50, color, Baxter paper)
1-5 2.00

NEXT MEN (See John Byrne's...)

NEXT NEXUS, THE
First Comics: Jan, 1989 - No. 4, April, 1989 ($1.95, limited series, Baxter paper)
1-4: Mike Baron scripts & Steve Rude-c/a. 2.00

NEXUS (See First Comics Graphic Novel #4, 19 & The Next Nexus)
Capital Comics/First Comics No. 7 on: June, 1981 - No. 6, Mar, 1984; No. 7, Apr, 1985 - No. 80?, May, 1991
(Direct sales only, 36 pgs.; V2#1('83)-printed on Baxter paper

	GD2.0	FN6.0	NM9.4
1-B&W version; mag. size; w/double size poster	1.85	5.50	15.00
1-B&W 1981 limited edition; 500 copies printed and signed; same as above except this version has a 2-pg. poster & a pencil sketch on paperboard by Rude	2.50	7.50	20.00
2-B&W, magazine size	1.50	4.50	12.00
3-B&W, magazine size; contains 33-1/3 rpm record ($2.95 price)	1.00	3.00	8.00
V2#1-Color version			4.00
2-49,51-80: 2-Nexus' origin begins. 67-Snyder-c/a			2.25
50-($3.50, 52 pgs.)			3.50

NOTE: ***Bissette** c-V2#29. **Giffen** c/a-V2#23. **Gulacy** c-1 (B&W), 2(B&W). **Mignola** c/a-V2#28. **Rude** c-3(B&W), V2#1-22, 24-27, 33-36, 39-42, 45-48, 50, 58-60, 75; a-1-3, V2#1-7, 8-16p, 18-22p, 24-27p, 33-36p, 39-42p, 45-48p, 50, 58, 59p, 60. **Paul Smith** a-V2#37, 38, 43, 44, 51-55p; c-V2#37, 38, 43, 44, 51-55.*

NEXUS: ALIEN JUSTICE
Dark Horse Comics: Dec, 1992 - No. 3, Feb, 1993 ($3.95, limited series)
1-3: Mike Baron scripts & Steve Rude-c/a 4.00

NEXUS: EXECUTIONER'S SONG
Dark Horse Comics: June, 1996 - No. 4, Sept, 1996 ($2.95, limited series)
1-4: Mike Baron scripts & Steve Rude-c/a 3.00

NEXUS FILES
First Comics: 1989 ($4.50, color/16pgs. B&W, one-shot, squarebound, 52pgs.)
1-New Rude-a; info on Nexus 4.50

NEXUS: GOD CON
Dark Horse Comics: Apr, 1997 - No. 2, May, 1997 ($2.95, limited series)
1,2-Baron-s/Rude-c/a 3.00

NEXUS LEGENDS
First Comics: May, 1989 - No. 23, Mar, 1991 ($1.50, Baxter paper)\
1-23: R/1-3(Capital) & early First Comics issues w/new Rude covers #1-6,9,10 2.00

NEXUS MEETS MADMAN (...Special)
Dark Horse Comics: May, 1996 ($2.95, one-shot)
nn-Mike Baron & Mike Allred scripts, Steve Rude-c/a. 3.00

NEXUS: NIGHTMARE IN BLUE
Dark Horse Comics: July, 1997 - No. 4, Oct, 1997 ($2.95, limited series)
1-4: 1,2,4-Adam Hughes-c 3.00

NEXUS: THE LIBERATOR
Dark Horse Comics: Aug, 1992 - No. 4, Nov, 1992 ($2.95, limited series)
1-4 3.00

NEXUS: THE ORIGIN
Dark Horse Comics: July, 1996 ($3.95, one-shot)
nn-Mike Baron- scripts, Steve Rude-c/a. 4.00

GD2.0 FN6.0 NM9.4

NEXUS: THE WAGES OF SIN
Dark Horse Comics: Mar, 1995 - No. 4, June, 1995 ($2.95, limited series)
1-4 3.00

NICKEL COMICS
Dell Publishing Co.: 1938 (Pocket size - 7-1/2x5-1/2")(132 pgs.)

	GD2.0	FN6.0	NM9.4
1- "Bobby & Chip" by Otto Messmer, Felix the Cat artist. Contains some English reprints	66.00	197.00	525.00

NICKEL COMICS
Fawcett Publications: May, 1940 - No. 8, Aug, 1940 (36 pgs.; Bi-Weekly; 5¢)

	GD2.0	FN6.0	NM9.4
1-Origin/1st app. Bulletman	367.00	1101.00	3300.00
2	122.00	366.00	975.00
3	91.00	272.00	725.00
4-The Red Gaucho begins	78.00	234.00	625.00
5-8: 8-World's Fair-c; Bulletman moved to Master Comics #7 in October	72.00	216.00	575.00

NOTE: ***Beck** c-5-8. **Jack Binder** c-1-4. Bondage c-5. Bulletman c-1-8.*

NICK FURY, AGENT OF SHIELD (See Fury, Marvel Spotlight #31 & Shield)
Marvel Comics Group: 6/68 - No. 15, 11/69; No. 16, 11/70 - No. 18, 3/71

	GD2.0	FN6.0	NM9.4
1	7.00	21.00	70.00
2-4: 4-Origin retold	3.80	11.40	38.00
5-Classic-c	4.50	13.50	45.00
6,7: 7-Salvador Dali painting swipe	2.60	7.80	26.00
8-11,13: 9-Hate Monger begins, ends #11. 10-Smith layouts/pencil. 11-Smith-c. 13-1st app. Super-Patriot; last 12¢ issue	1.75	5.25	14.00
12-Smith-c/a	2.25	6.75	18.00
14-Begin 15¢ issues	1.50	4.50	12.00
15-1st app. & death of Bullseye-c/story(11/69); Nick Fury shot & killed; last 15¢ issue	4.50	13.50	45.00
16-18-(25¢, 52 pgs.)-r/Str. Tales #135-143	1.00	3.00	15.00

NOTE: ***Adkins** a-3i. **Craig** a-10i. **Sid Greene** a-12i. **Kirby** a-16-18r. **Springer** a-4, 6, 7, 8p, 9, 10p, 11; c-8, 9. **Steranko** a(p)-1-3, 5; c-1-7.*

NICK FURY AGENT OF SHIELD (Also see Strange Tales #135)
Marvel Comics: Dec, 1983 - No. 2, Jan, 1984 (2.00, 52 pgs., Baxter paper)
1,2-r/Nick Fury #1-4; new Steranko-c 2.00

NICK FURY, AGENT OF S.H.I.E.L.D.
Marvel Comics: Sept, 1989 - No. 47, May, 1993 ($1.50/$1.75)
V2#1-47: 10-Capt. America app. 13-Return of The Yellow Claw. 15-Fantastic Four app. 27-29-Wolverine-c/stories. 30,31-Deathlok app. 36-Cage app. 37-Woodgod c/story. 38-41-Flashes back to pre-Shield days after WWII. 44-Capt. America-c/s. 45-Viper-c/s. 46-Gideon x-over 2.00

NOTE: ***Alan Grant** scripts-11. **Guice** a(p)-20-23, 25, 26; c-20-28.*

NICK FURY VS. S.H.I.E.L.D.
Marvel Comics: June, 1988 - No. 6, Nov, 1988 ($3.50, 52 pgs, deluxe format)
1,2: 1-Steranko-c. 2-(Low print run) Sienkiewicz-c 5.00
3-6 4.00

NICK HALIDAY (Thrill of the Sea)
Argo: May, 1956

	GD2.0	FN6.0	NM9.4
1-Daily & Sunday strip-r by Petree	7.50	22.50	45.00

NIGHT AND THE ENEMY (Graphic Novel)
Comico: 1988 (8-1/2x11") ($11.95, color, 80 pgs.)
1-Harlan Ellison scripts/Ken Steacy-c/a; r/Epic Illustrated & new-a (1st and 2nd printings) 12.00
1-Limited edition ($39.95) 40.00

NIGHT BEFORE CHRISTMAS, THE (See March of Comics No. 152)

NIGHT BEFORE CHRISTMASK, THE
Dark Horse Comics: Nov, 1994 ($9.95, one-shot)
nn-Hardcover book; Rick Geary -c/a 10.00

NIGHTBREED (See Clive Barker's Nightbreed)

NIGHTCRAWLER
Marvel Comics Group: Nov, 1985 - No. 4, Feb, 1986 (Mini-series from X-Men)

Night Man #12 © MAL

Nightmare #3 © STJ

Nightmask #4 © MAR

1-4: 1-Cockrum-c/a 2.50

NIGHTFALL: THE BLACK CHRONICLES
DC Comics (Homage): Dec, 1999 - No. 3 ($2.95, limited series)
1-Coker-a/Gilmore-s 2.95

NIGHT FORCE, THE (See New Teen Titans #21)
DC Comics: Aug, 1982 - No. 14, Sept, 1983 (60¢)
1 3.00
2-14: 13-Origin Baron Winter. 14-Nudity panels 2.25
NOTE: ***Colan** c/a-1-14p.* ***Giordano** c-1i, 2i, 4i, 5i, 7i, 12i.*

NIGHT FORCE
DC Comics: Dec, 1996 - No. 12, Nov, 1997 ($2.25)
1-12: 1-3-Wolfman-s/Anderson-a(p). 8-"Convergence" part 2 2.25

NIGHT GLIDER
Topps Comics (Kirbyverse): April, 1993 ($2.95, one-shot)
1-Kirby c-1, Heck-a; polybagged w/Kirbychrome trading card 3.00

NIGHTHAWK
Marvel Comics: Sept, 1998 - No. 3, Nov, 1998 ($2.99, mini-series)
1-3-Krueger-s; Daredevil app. 3.00

NIGHTINGALE, THE
Henry H. Stansbury Once-Upon-A-Time Press, Inc.: 1948 (10¢, 7-1/4x10-1/4", 14 pgs., 1/2 B&W)
(Very Rare)-Low distribution; distributed to Westchester County & Bronx, N.Y. only; used in **Seduction of the Innocent**, pg. 312,313 as the 1st and only "good" comic book ever published. Ill. by Dong Kingman; 1,500 words of text, printed on high quality paper & no word balloons. Copyright registered 10/22/48, distributed week of 12/5/48. (By Hans Christian Andersen)
Estimated value........ $200

NIGHT MAN, THE (See Sludge #1)
Malibu Comics (Ultraverse): Oct, 1993 - No. 23, Aug, 1995 ($1.95/$2.50)
1-($2.50, 48 pgs.)-Rune flip-c/story by B. Smith (3 pgs.) 2.50
1-Ultra-Limited silver foil-c 2.40 6.00
2-15, 17: 3-Break-Thru x-over; Freex app. 4-Origin Firearm (2 pgs.) by Chaykin. 6-TNTNT app. 8-1st app. Teknight 2.50
16 ($3.50)-flip book (Ultraverse Premiere #11) 3.50
...:The Pilgrim Conundrum Saga (1/95, $3.95, 68 pgs.)-Strangers app. 4.00
18-23: 22-Loki-c/a 2.50
Infinity ($1.50) 2.50
...Vs. Wolverine #0-Kelley Jones-c; mail in offer 1.25 3.75 10.00
NOTE: ***Zeck** a-16.*

NIGHT MAN, THE
Malibu Comics (Ultraverse): Sept, 1995 - No.4, Dec, 1995 ($1.50, lim. series)
1-4: Post Black September storyline 2.00

NIGHT MAN, THE /GAMBIT
Malibu Comics (Ultraverse): Mar, 1996 - No. 3, May, 1996 ($1.95, lim. series)
0-Limited Premium Edition 4.00
1-3: David Quinn scripts in all. 3-Rhiannon discovered to be The Night Man's mother 2.00

NIGHTMARE
Ziff-Davis (Approved Comics)/St. John No. 3,4: Summer, 1952 - No. 3, Winter, 1952, 53 (Painted-c)
1-1 pg. Kinstler-a; Tuska-a(2) 51.00 154.00 410.00
2-Kinstler-a-Poe's "Pit & the Pendulum" 40.00 120.00 280.00
3-Kinstler-a 32.00 96.00 225.00

NIGHTMARE (Weird Horrors #1-9) (Amazing Ghost Stories #14 on)
St. John Publishing Co.: No. 10, Dec, 1953 - No. 13, Aug, 1954
10-Reprints Ziff-Davis Weird Thrillers #2 w/new Kubert-c plus 2 pgs. Kinstler-a; Anderson, Colan & Toth-a 51.00 154.00 410.00
11-Krigstein-a; painted-c; Poe adapt., "Hop Frog" 40.00 120.00 280.00
12-Kubert bondage-c; adaptation of Poe's "The Black Cat"; Cannibalism story 34.00 103.00 240.00
13-Reprints Z-D Weird Thrillers #3 with new cover; Powell-a(2), Tuska-a; Baker-c 26.00 79.00 185.00

NIGHTMARE (Magazine)
Skywald Publishing Corp.: Dec, 1970 - No. 23, Feb, 1975 (B&W, 68 pgs.)
1-Everett-a 5.00 15.00 55.00
2-6,8,9: 4-Decapitation story. 6-Kaluta-a; Jeff Jones photo & interview. 8-Features E. C. movie "Tales From the Crypt"; reprints some E.C. comics panels. 9-Wrightson-a 2.80 8.40 28.00
7,10 2.50 7.50 22.00
11-19: 12-Excessive gore, severed heads 2.50 7.50 20.00
20-Byrne's 1st artwork (8/74); severed head-c 2.50 7.50 20.00
21-23: 21-(1974 Summer Special)-Kaluta-a. 22-Tomb of Horror issue. 23-(1975 Winter Special) 2.50 7.50 24.00
Annual 1(1972)-B. Jones-a 2.80 8.40 28.00
Winter Special 1(1973) 2.50 7.50 22.00
Yearbook nn(1974)-B. Jones, Reese, Wildey-a 2.50 7.50 22.00
NOTE: ***Adkins** a-5.* ***Boris** c-2, 3, 5 (#4 is not by Boris).* ***Buckler** a-3, 15.* ***Byrne** a-20p.* ***Everett** a-4, 5, 12.* ***Jeff Jones** a-6, 21r(Psycho #6); c-6.* ***Katz** a-5.* ***Reese** a-4, 5.* ***Wildey** a-4, 5, 6, 21, '74 Yearbook.*

NIGHTMARE (Alex Nino's)
Innovation Publishing: 1989 ($1.95)
1-Alex Nino-a 2.00

NIGHTMARE
Marvel Comics: Dec, 1994 - No. 4, Mar, 1995 ($1.95, limited series)
1-4 2.00

NIGHTMARE & CASPER (See Harvey Hits #71) (Casper & Nightmare #6 on) (See Casper The Friendly Ghost #19)
Harvey Publications: Aug, 1963 - No. 5, Aug, 1964 (25¢)
1-All reprints? 6.00 18.00 60.00
2-5: All reprints? 3.50 10.50 35.00

NIGHTMARE ON ELM STREET, A (See Freddy Krueger's...)

NIGHTMARES (See Do You Believe in Nightmares)

NIGHTMARES
Eclipse Comics: May, 1985 - No. 2, May, 1985 ($1.75, Baxter paper)
1,2 2.00

NIGHTMARE THEATER
Chaos! Comics: Nov, 1997 - No. 4, Nov, 1997 ($2.50, mini-series)
1-4-Horror stories by various; Wrightson-a 2.50

NIGHTMARK: BLOOD & HONOR
Alpha Productions: 1994 - No. 3, 1994 ($2.50, B&W, mini-series)
1,2 2.50

NIGHTMARK MYSTERY SPECIAL
Alpha Productions: Jan, 1994 ($2.50, B&W)
1 2.50

NIGHTMASK
Marvel Comics Group: Nov, 1986 - No. 12, Oct, 1987
1-12 2.00

NIGHT MASTER
Silverwolf: Feb, 1987 ($1.50, B&W)
1-Tim Vigil-c/a 2.00

NIGHT MUSIC (See Eclipse Graphic Album Series, The Magic Flute)
Eclipse Comics: Dec, 1984 - No. 11, 1990 ($1.75/$3.95/$4.95, Baxter paper)
1-7: 3-Russell's Jungle Book adapt. 4,5-Pelleas And Melisande (double titled) 6-Salome' (double titled). 7-Red Dog #1 2.00
8-($3.95) Ariane and Bluebeard 4.00
9-11-($4.95) The Magic Flute; Russell adapt. 5.00

NIGHT NURSE
Marvel Comics Group: Nov, 1972 - No. 4, May, 1973
1 8.65 26.00 95.00
2-4 6.00 18.00 65.00

NIGHT OF MYSTERY

Nightwatch #6 © MAR

Nightwing #32 © DC

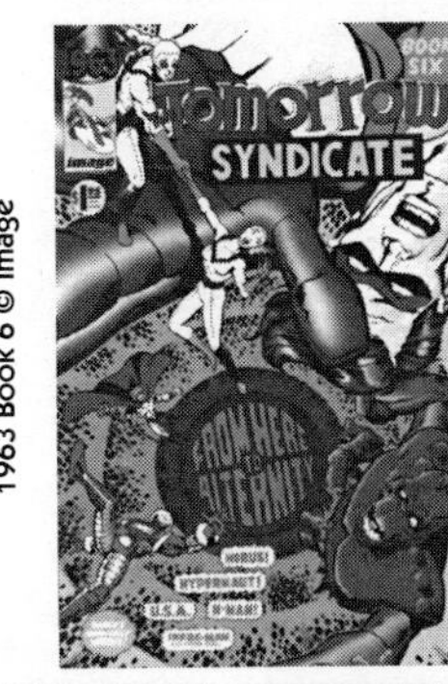

1963 Book 6 © Image

GD2.0 FN6.0 NM9.4

Avon Periodicals: 1953 (no month) (one-shot)
nn-1 pg. Kinstler-a, Hollingsworth-c 40.00 120.00 300.00

NIGHT OF THE GRIZZLY, THE (See Movie Classics)

NIGHTRAVEN: THE COLLECTED STORIES
Marvel Comics UK, Ltd.: 1991 ($9.95, graphic novel)
nn-Bolton-r/British Hulk mag.; David Lloyd-c/a 10.00

NIGHT RIDER (Western)
Marvel Comics Group: Oct, 1974 - No. 6, Aug, 1975
1: 1-6 reprint Ghost Rider #1-6 (#1-origin) 1.50 4.50 12.00
2-6 1.00 3.00 8.00

NIGHT'S CHILDREN: THE VAMPIRE
Millenium: July, 1995 - No. 2, Aug, 1995 ($2.95, B&W)
1,2: Wendy Snow-Lang story & art 3.00

NIGHTSHADE
No Mercy Comics: Aug, 1997 ($2.50)
1-Mark Williams-s/a 2.50

NIGHTS INTO DREAMS (Based on video game)
Archie Comics: Feb, 1998 -No. 6, Oct, 1998 ($1.75, limited series)
1-6 2.00

NIGHTSTALKERS (Also see Midnight Sons Unlimited)
Marvel Comics (Midnight Sons #14 on): Nov, 1992 - No. 18, Apr, 1994 ($1.75)
1-($2.75, 52 pgs.)-Polybagged w/poster; part 5 of Rise of the Midnight Sons storyline; Garney/Palmer-c/a begins; Hannibal King, Blade & Frank Drake begin (see Tomb of Dracula for & Dr. Strange) 2.75
2-9,11-18: 5-Punisher app. 7-Ghost Rider app. 8,9-Morbius app. 14-Spot varnish-c. 14,15-Sioege of Darkness Pts 1 & 9 2.00
10-($2.25)-Outer-c is a Darkhold envelope made of black parchment w/gold ink; Midnight Massacre part 1 2.25

NIGHT THRASHER (Also see The New Warriors)
Marvel Comics: Aug, 1993 - No. 21, Apr, 1995 ($1.75/$1.95)
1-($2.95, 52 pgs.)-Red holo-grafx foil-c; origin 3.00
2-21: 2-Intro Tantrum. 3-Gideon (of X-Force) app. 10-Bound-in trading card sheet; Iron Man app. 15-Hulk app. 2.00

NIGHT THRASHER: FOUR CONTROL
Marvel Comics: Oct, 1992 - No. 4, Jan, 1993 ($2.00, limited series)
1-4: 1-Hero from New Warriors. 2-Intro Tantrum. 3-Gideon (of X-Force) app. 2.00

NIGHT TRIBES
DC Comics (WildStorm): July, 1999 ($4.95, one-shot)
1-Golden & Sniegoski-s/Chin-a 5.00

NIGHTVEIL (Also see Femforce)
Americomics/AC Comics: Nov, 1984 - No. 7, 1985 ($1.75)
1-7 2.00
...'s Cauldron Of Horror 1 (1989, B&W)-Kubert, Powell, Wood-r plus new Nightveil story 3.00
...'s Cauldron Of Horror 2 (1990, $2.95, B&W, 44pgs)-Pre-code horror-r by Kubert & Powell 3.00
Special 1 ('88, $1.95)-Kaluta-c 2.00
One Shot ('96, $5.95)-Flip book w/ Colt 6.00

NIGHTWATCH
Marvel Comics: Apr, 1994 - No. 12, Mar, 1995 ($1.50)
1-($2.95)-Collectors edition; foil-c; Ron Lim-c/a begins; Spider-Man app. 3.00
1-12-Regular edition. 2-Bound-in S-M trading card sheet; 5,6-Venom-c & app. 7,11-Cardiac app. 2.00

NIGHTWING (Also see New Teen Titans, New Titans, Showcase '93 #11,12, Tales of the New Teen Titans & Teen Titans Spotlight)
DC Comics: Sept, 1995 - No. 4, Dec, 1995 ($2.25, limited series)
1-Dennis O'Neil story/Greg Land-a in all 5.00
2-4 4.00
...: Alfred's Return (7/95, $3.50) Giordano-a 4.00
...Ties That Bind (1997, $12.95, TPB) r/mini-series & Alfred's Return 13.00

NIGHTWING
DC Comics: Oct, 1996 - Present ($1.95/$1.99)
1-Chuck Dixon scripts & Scott McDaniel-c/a 1.25 3.75 10.00
2,3 2.40 6.00
4-10: 6-Robin-c/app. 4.00
11-38: 13-15-Batman app. 19,20-Cataclysm pts. 2,11. 23-Green Arrow app. 26-29-Huntress-c/app. 30-Superman-c/app. 35-38-No Man's Land 2.00
#1,000,000 (11/98) teams with future Batman 2.00
Annual 1(1997, $3.95) Pulp Heroes 4.00
...: A Knight in Blüdhaven (1998, $14.95, TPB) r/#1-8 15.00
...: Rough Justice (1999, $17.95, TPB) r/#9-18 18.00
Secret Files 1 (10/99, $4.95) Origin-s and pin-ups 5.00
Wizard 1/2 (Mail offer) 5.00

NIGHTWING (See Tangent Comics/ Nightwing)

NIGHTWING AND HUNTRESS
DC Comics: May, 1998 - No. 4, Aug, 1998 ($1.95, limited series)
1-4-Grayson-s/Land & Sienkiewicz-a 2.50

NIGHTWINGS (See DC Science Fiction Graphic Novel)

NIKKI, WILD DOG OF THE NORTH (Disney, see Movie Comics)
Dell Publishing Co.: No. 1226, Sept, 1961
Four Color 1226-Movie, photo-c 4.50 13.50 50.00

1963
Image Comics (Shadowline Ink): Apr, 1993 - No. 6, Oct, 1993 ($1.95, lim. series)
1-6: Alan Moore scripts; Veitch, Bissette & Gibbons-a(p) 2.00
1-Gold 3.00
NOTE: ***Bissette*** *a-2-4;* ***Gibbons*** *a-1i, 2i, 6i; c-2.*

1984 (Magazine) (1994 #11 on)
Warren Publishing Co.: June, 1978 - No. 10, Jan, 1980 ($1.50)
1-Nino-a in all 1.85 5.50 15.00
2-10 1.25 3.75 10.00
NOTE: ***Alacla*** *a-1-3, 5i.* ***Corben*** *a-1-8; c-1, 2.* ***Thorne*** *a-7-10.* ***Wood*** *a-1, 2, 5i.*

1994 (Formerly 1984) (Magazine)
Warren Publishing Co.: No. 11, Feb, 1980 - No. 29, Feb, 1983
11-29: 27-The Warhawks return 1.00 3.00 8.00
NOTE: ***Corben*** *c-26.* ***Nino*** *a-11-19, 20(2), 21, 25, 26, 28; c-21.* ***Redondo*** *c-20.* ***Thorne*** *a-11-14, 17-21, 25, 26, 28, 29.*

NINE VOLT
Image Comics (Top Cow Productions): July, 1997 - No. 4, Oct, 1997 ($2.50)
1-4 2.50

NINJA HIGH SCHOOL (1st series)
Antarctic Press: 1986 - No. 3, Aug, 1987 (B&W)
1-Ben Dunn-s/c/a; early Manga series 1.50 4.50 12.00
2,3 1.00 3.00 8.00

NINJAK (See Bloodshot #6, 7 & Deathmate)
Valiant/Acclaim Comics (Valiant) No. 16 on: Feb, 1994 - No. 26, Nov. 1995 ($2.25/$2.50)
1 ($3.50)-Chromium-c; Quesada-c/a(p) in #1-3 3.50
1-Gold 5.00
2-13: 3-Batman, Spawn & Random (from X-Factor) app. as costumes at party (cameo). 4-w/bound-in trading card. 5,6-X-O app. 2.50
0,00,14-26: 14-(4/95)-Begin $2.50-c. 0-(6/95, $2.50). 00-(6/95, $2.50) 2.50
Yearbook 1 (1994, $3.95) 4.00

NINJAK
Acclaim Comics (Valiant Heroes): V2#1, Mar, 1997 -No. 12, Feb, 1998 ($2.50)
V2#1-12: 1-Intro new Ninjak; 1st app. Brutakon; Kurt Busiek scripts begin; painted variant-c exists. 2-1st app. Karnivor & Zeer. 3-1st app. Gigantik,

Nocturnals: The Witching Hour #1 © Dan Brereton

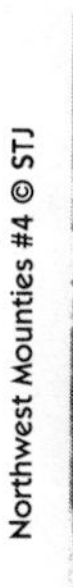

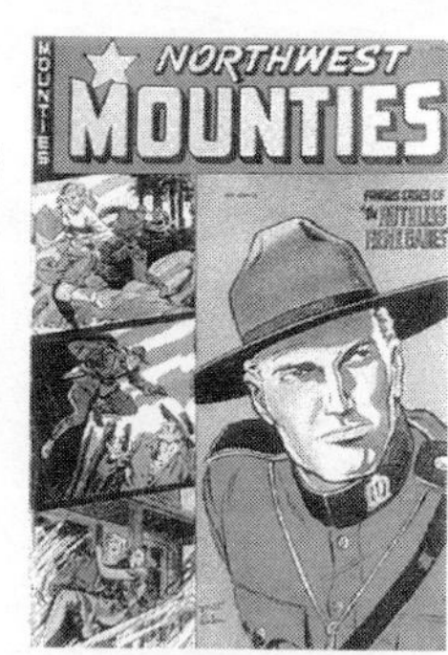

Northwest Mounties #4 © STJ

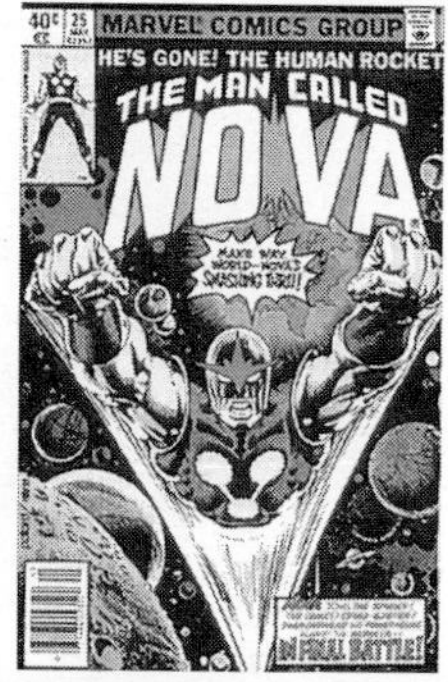

Nova #25 © MAR

Shurikai, & Nixie. 4-Origin; 1st app. Yasuiti Motomiya; intro The Dark Dozen; Colin King (original Ninjak) cameo. 9-Copycat-c 2.50

NINTENDO COMICS SYSTEM (Also see Adv. of Super Mario Brothers)
Valiant Comics: Feb, 1990 - No. 9, Oct, 1991 ($4.95, card stock-c, 68pgs.)

1-9: 1-Featuring Game Boy, Super Mario, Clappwall. 3-Layton-c. 5-8-Super Mario Bros. 9-Dr. Mario 1st app. 5.00

N.I.O.
Acclaim Comics: Nov, 1998 - No. 4, Feb, 1999 ($2.50, limited series)

1-3-Bury-s 2.50

NOAH'S ARK
Spire Christian Comics/Fleming H. Revell Co.: 1973 (35/49¢)

nn-By Al Hartley 5.00

NOBODY (Amado, Cho & Adlard's...)
Oni Press: Nov, 1998 - No. 4, Feb, 1999 ($2.95. B&W, mini-series)

1-4 3.00

NOCTURNALS, THE
Malibu Comics (Bravura): Jan, 1995 - No. 6, Aug, 1995 ($2.95, limited series)

1-6: Dan Brereton painted-c/a & scripts 3.00
1-Glow-in-the-Dark premium edition 5.00
Black Planet TPB ('98, $19.95, Oni Press) r/#1-6 20.00

NOCTURNALS, THE :WITCHING HOUR
Dark Horse Comics: May 1998 ($4.95, one-shot)

1-Brereton-s/painted-a; reprints DHP stories + 8 new pgs. 5.00

NOCTURNE
Marvel Comics: June, 1995 - No. 4, Sept. 1995 ($1.50, limited series)

1-4 2.00

NO ESCAPE (Movie)
Marvel Comics: June, 1994 - No. 3, Aug, 1994 ($1.50)

1-3: Based on movie 2.00

NOMAD (See Captain America #180)
Marvel Comics: Nov, 1990 - No. 4, Feb, 1991 ($1.50, limited series)

1-4: 1,4-Captain America app. 2.00

NOMAD
Marvel Comics: V2#1, May, 1992 - No. 25, May, 1994 ($1.75)

V2#1-25: 1-Has gatefold-c w/map/wanted poster. 4-Deadpool x-over. 5-Punisher vs. Nomad-c/story. 6-Punisher & Daredevil-c/story cont'd in Punisher War Journal #48. 7-Gambit-c/story. 10-Red Wolf app. 21-Man-Thing-c/story. 25-Bound-in trading card sheet 2.00

NOMAN (See Thunder Agents)
Tower Comics: Nov, 1966 - No. 2, March, 1967 (25¢, 68 pgs.)

1-Wood/Williamson-c; Lightning begins; Dynamo cameo; Kane-a(p) & Whitney-a 6.50 19.50 65.00
2-Wood-c only; Dynamo x-over; Whitney-a 4.50 13.50 45.00

NONE BUT THE BRAVE (See Movie Classics)

NOODNIK COMICS (See Pinky the Egghead)
Comic Media/Mystery/Biltmore: Dec, 1953; No. 2, Feb, 1954 - No. 5, Aug, 1954

3-D(1953, 25¢; Comic Media)(#1)-Came w/glasses 33.00 99.00 230.00
2-5 6.35 19.00 38.00

NORMALMAN (See Cerebus the Aardvark #55, 56)
Aardvark-Vanaheim/Renegade Press #6 on: Jan, 1984 - No. 12, Dec, 1985 ($1.70/$2.00)

1-12: 1-Jim Valentino-c/a in all. 6-12 ($2.00, B&W): 10-Cerebus cameo; Sim-a (2 pgs.) 2.25
...3-D 1 (Annual, 1986, $2.25) 2.25

NORMALMAN-MEGATON MAN SPECIAL
Image Comics: Aug, 1994 ($2.50, color)

1 2.50

NORTH AVENUE IRREGULARS (See Walt Disney Showcase #49)

NORTHSTAR
Marvel Comics: Apr, 1994 - No. 4, July, 1994 ($1.75, mini-series)

1-4: Character from Alpha Flight 2.00

NORTH TO ALASKA
Dell Publishing Co.: No. 1155, Dec, 1960

Four Color 1155-Movie, John Wayne photo-c 16.00 47.00 170.00

NORTHWEST MOUNTIES (Also see Approved Comics #12)
Jubilee Publications/St. John: Oct, 1948 - No. 4, July, 1949

1-Rose of the Yukon by Matt Baker; Walter Johnson-a; Lubbers-c 44.00 132.00 350.00
2-Baker-a; Lubbers-c. Ventrilo app. 38.00 114.00 265.00
3-Bondage-c, Baker-a; Sky Chief, K-9 app. 39.00 116.00 270.00
4-Baker-c/a(2 pgs.); Blue Monk & The Desperado app. 39.00 116.00 270.00

NO SLEEP 'TIL DAWN
Dell Publishing Co.: No. 831, Aug, 1957

Four Color 831-Movie, Karl Malden photo-c 5.50 16.50 60.00

NOSTALGIA ILLUSTRATED
Marvel Comics: Nov, 1974 - V2#8, Aug, 1975 (B&W, 76 pgs.)

V1#1 2.50 7.50 25.00
V1#2, V2#1-8 1.50 4.50 12.00

NOT BRAND ECHH (Brand Echh #1-4; See Crazy, 1973)
Marvel Comics Group (LMC): Aug, 1967 - No. 13, May, 1969
(1st Marvel parody book)

1: 1-8 are 12¢ issues 3.50 10.50 35.00
2-8: 3-Origin Thor, Hulk & Capt. America; Monkees, Alfred E. Neuman cameo. 4-X-Men app. 5-Origin/intro. Forbush Man. 7-Origin Fantastical-4 & Stupor-man. Beatles cameo; X-Men satire; last 12¢ish. 2.50 7.50 22.00
9-13 (25¢, 68 pgs., all Giants) 9-Beatles cameo. 10-All-r; The Old Witch, Crypt Keeper & Vault Keeper cameos. 12,13-Beatles cameo 2.80 8.40 28.00

NOTE: ***Colan*** *a(p)-4, 5, 8, 9, 13.* ***Everett*** *a-1i.* ***Kirby*** *a(p)-1, 3, 5-7, 10r; c-1p.* ***J. Severin*** *a-1; c-3, 6-8, 11.* ***M. Severin*** *a-1-13; c-2, 9, 10, 12, 13.* ***Sutton*** *a-3, 4, 5i, 6i, 8, 9, 10r, 11-13; c-5. Archie satire in #9. Avengers satire in #8, 12.*

NOTHING CAN STOP THE JUGGERNAUT
Marvel Comics: 1989 ($3.95)

1-r/Amazing Spider-Man #229 & 230 4.00

NO TIME FOR SERGEANTS (TV)
Dell Publ. Co.: No. 914, July, 1958; Feb-Apr, 1965 - No. 3, Aug-Oct, 1965

Four Color 914 (Movie)-Toth-a; Andy Griffith photo-c 9.00 27.00 100.00
1(2-4/65) (TV): Photo-c 4.50 13.50 50.00
2,3 (TV): Photo-c 3.60 11.00 40.00

NOVA (The Man Called... No. 22-25)(See New Warriors)
Marvel Comics Group: Sept, 1976 - No. 25, May, 1979

1-Origin/1st app. Nova 1.00 3.00 8.00
2-4,12: 4-Thor x-over. 12-Spider-Man x-over 5.00
5-11 4.00
13-(Regular 30¢ edition)(9/77) Intro Crime-Buster. 3.00
13-(35¢-c variant, limited distribution) 1.50 4.50 12.00
14-25: 14-Last 30¢ issue. 18-Yellow Claw app. 19-Wally West (Kid Flash) cameo. 25-Last issue 3.00

NOTE: ***Austin*** *c-21i, 23i.* ***John Buscema*** *a(p)-1-3, 8, 21; c-1p, 2, 15.* ***Infantino*** *a(p)-15-20, 22-25; c-17-20, 21p, 23p, 24p.* ***Kirby*** *c-4p, 5, 7.* ***Nebres*** *c-25i.* ***Simonson*** *a-23i.*

NOVA
Marvel Comics: Jan, 1994 - June, 1995 ($1.75/$1.95)
(Started as 4-part mini-series)

1-($2.95, 52 pgs.)-Collector's Edition w/gold foil-c; new Nova costume 3.00
1-($2.25, 52 pgs.)-Newsstand Edition w/o foil-c 2.25
2-18: 3-Spider-Man-c/story. 5-Stan Lee app. 5-Bound-in card sheet. 13-Firestar

Nova V2 #1 © MAR

Nuts! #3 © PG

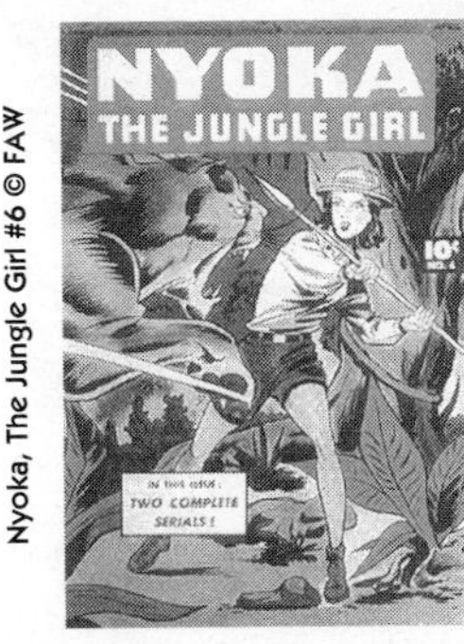

Nyoka, The Jungle Girl #6 © FAW

GD2.0 FN6.0 NM9.4

& Night Thrasher app.14-Darkhawk 2.00

NOVA
Marvel Comics: May, 1999 - No. 7, Nov, 1999 ($2.99/$1.99)

1-($2.99) Larsen-s/Bennett-a; wraparound-c by Larsen 3.00
2-7-($1.99): 2-Two covers; Capt. America app. 5-Spider-Man. 7-Venom 2.00

NOW AGE ILLUSTRATED (See Pendulum Illustrated Classics)

NOW AGE BOOKS ILLUSTRATED (See Pendulum Illustrated Classics)

NTH MAN THE ULTIMATE NINJA (See Marvel Comics Presents 25)
Marvel Comics: Aug, 1989 - No. 16, Sept, 1990 ($1.00)

1-16-Ninja mercenary. 8-Dale Keown's 1st Marvel work (1/90, pencils) 2.00

NUCLEUS (Also see Cerebus)
Heiro-Graphic Publications: May, 1979 ($1.50, B&W, adult fanzine)

1-Contains "Demonhorn" by Dave Sim; early app. of Cerebus The Aardvark (4 pg. story) 3.40 10.20 34.00

NUKLA
Dell Publishing Co.: Oct-Dec, 1965 - No. 4, Sept, 1966

1-Origin & 1st app. Nukla (super hero) 3.20 9.60 32.00
2,3 2.50 7.50 20.00
4-Ditko-a, c(p) 3.00 9.00 30.00

NURSE BETSY CRANE (Formerly Teen Secret Diary)
Charlton Comics: V2#12, Aug, 1961 - V2#27, Mar, 1964 (See Soap Opera Romances)

V2#12-27 1.75 5.25 14.00

NURSE HELEN GRANT (See The Romances of...)

NURSE LINDA LARK (See Linda Lark)

NURSERY RHYMES
Ziff-Davis Publ. Co. (Approved Comics): No. 10, July-Aug, 1951 - No. 2, Winter, 1951 (Painted-c)

10 (#1), 2: 10-Howie Post-a 15.00 45.00 105.00

NURSES, THE (TV)
Gold Key: April, 1963 - No. 3, Oct, 1963 (Photo-c: #1,2)

1 3.00 9.00 30.00
2,3 2.50 7.50 20.00

NUTS! (Satire)
Premiere Comics Group: March, 1954 - No. 5, Nov, 1954

1-Hollingsworth-a 29.00 86.00 200.00
2,4,5: 5-Capt. Marvel parody 20.00 60.00 140.00
3-Drug "reefers" mentioned 20.00 60.00 140.00

NUTS (Magazine) (Satire)
Health Knowledge: Feb, 1958 - No. 2, April, 1958

1 8.00 24.00 48.00
2 5.85 17.50 35.00

NUTS & JOLTS
Dell Publishing Co.: No. 22, 1941

Large Feature Comic 22 9.50 28.50 105.00

NUTSY SQUIRREL (Formerly Hollywood Funny Folks)(See Comic Cavalcade)
National Periodical Publications: #61, 9-10/54 - #69, 1-2/56; #70, 8-9/56 - #71, 10-11/56; #72, 11/57

61-Mayer-a; Grossman-a in all 13.00 39.00 90.00
62-72: Mayer a-62,65,67-72 10.00 30.00 60.00

NUTTY COMICS
Fawcett Publications: Winter, 1946 (Funny animal)

1-Capt. Kidd story; 1 pg. Wolverton-a 12.00 36.00 85.00

NUTTY COMICS
Home Comics (Harvey Publications): 1945 - No. 8, June-July, 1947

nn-Helpful Hank, Bozo Bear & others (funny animal) 7.50 22.50 45.00
2-4 4.25 13.00 28.00

GD2.0 FN6.0 NM9.4

5-8: 5-Rags Rabbit begins(1st app.); infinity-c 4.00 11.00 22.00

NUTTY LIFE (Formerly Krazy Life #1; becomes Wotalife Comics #3 on)
Fox Features Syndicate: No. 2, Summer, 1946

2 10.00 30.00 60.00

NYOKA, THE JUNGLE GIRL (Formerly Jungle Girl; see The Further Adventures of..., Master Comics #50 & XMas Comics)
Fawcett Publications: No. 2, Winter, 1945 - No. 77, June, 1953 (Movie serial)

2 55.00 165.00 440.00
3 31.00 94.00 220.00
4,5 27.00 81.00 190.00
6-11,13,14,16-18-Krigstein-a: 17-Sam Spade ad by Lou Fine 19.00 58.00 135.00
12,15,19,20 17.00 51.00 120.00
21-30: 25-Clayton Moore photo-c? 11.00 33.00 75.00
31-40 10.00 30.00 60.00
41-50 7.50 22.50 45.00
51-60 5.85 17.50 35.00
61-77 5.00 15.00 30.00

NOTE: *Photo-c from movies 25, 30-70, 72, 75-77. Bondage c-4, 5, 7, 8, 14, 24.*

NYOKA, THE JUNGLE GIRL (Formerly Zoo Funnies; Space Adventures #23 on)
Charlton Comics: No. 14, Nov, 1955 - No. 22, Nov, 1957

14 10.00 30.00 65.00
15-22 7.50 22.50 45.00

OAKLAND PRESS FUNNYBOOK, THE
The Oakland Press: 9/17/78 - 4/13/80 (16 pgs.) (Weekly)
Full color in comic book form; changes to tabloid size 4/20/80-on

Contains Tarzan by Manning, Marmaduke, Bugs Bunny, etc. (low distribution); 9/23/79 - 4/13/80 contain Buck Rogers by Gray Morrow & Jim Lawrence 2.00

OAKY DOAKS (See Famous Funnies #190)
Eastern Color Printing Co.: July, 1942 (One Shot)

1 32.00 96.00 225.00

OBIE
Store Comics: 1953 (6¢)

1 5.00

OBLIVION
Comico: Aug, 1995 - No. 3, May, 1996 ($2.50)

1-3: 1-Art Adams-c. 2-(1/96)-Polybagged w/gaming card. 3-(5/96)-Darrow-c 2.50

OBNOXIO THE CLOWN (Character from Crazy Magazine)
Marvel Comics Group: April, 1983 (one-shot)

1-Vs. the X-Men 2.00

OCCULT FILES OF DR. SPEKTOR, THE
Gold Key/Whitman No. 25: Apr, 1973 - No. 24, Feb, 1977; No. 25, May, 1982 (Painted-c #1-24)

1-1st app. Lakota; Baron Tibor begins 2.50 7.50 24.00
2-5: 3-Mummy-c/s. 5-Jekyll & Hyde-c/s 1.25 3.75 10.00
6-10: 6,9-Frankenstein. 8,9-Dracula c/s. 9.-Jekyll & Hyde c/s. 9,10-Mummy-c/s 1.00 3.00 8.00
11-13,15-17,19-22,24,25: 11-1st app. Spektor as Werewolf. 11-13-Werewolf-c/s. 12,16-Frankenstein c/s. 17-Zombie/Voodoo-c. 19-Sea monster-c/s. 20-mummy-s. 21-Swamp monster c/s. 24-Dragon c/s.25-R/ #1 with line drawn-c 2.40 6.00
14-Dr. Solar app. 1.50 4.50 12.00
18,23-Dr. Solar cameo 1.00 3.00 8.00
22-Return of the Owl c/s 1.25 3.75 10.00
9(Modern Comics reprint, 1977)(exist?) 4.00

NOTE: *Also see Dan Curtis, Golden Comics Digest 33, Gold Key Spotlight, Mystery Comics Digest 5, & Spine Tingling Tales.*

ODELL'S ADVENTURES IN 3-D (See Adventures in 3-D)

Official Handbook of the Marvel Universe #7 © MAR

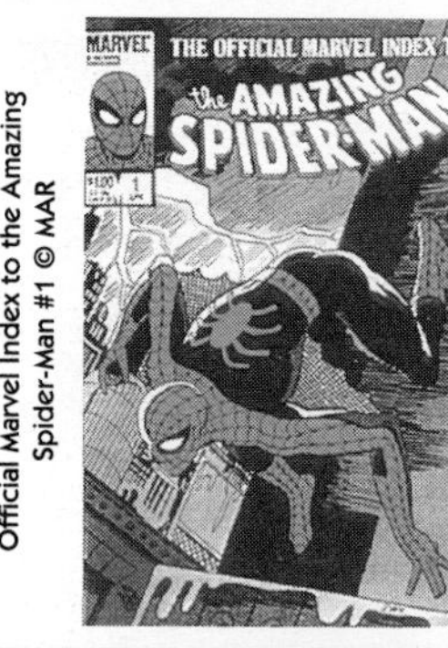

Official Marvel Index to the Amazing Spider-Man #1 © MAR

Oh My Goddess Part 4 #2 © Kosuke Fujishima

OFFCASTES
Marvel Comics (Epic Comics/Heavy Hitters): July, 1993 - No. 3, Sept, 1993 ($1.95, limited series)
1-3: Mike Vosburg-c/a/scripts in all 2.00

OFFICIAL CRISIS ON INFINITE EARTHS INDEX, THE
Independent Comics Group (Eclipse): Mar, 1986 ($1.75)
1 2.00

OFFICIAL CRISIS ON INFINITE EARTHS CROSSOVER INDEX, THE
Independent Comics Group (Eclipse): July, 1986 ($1.75)
1-Perez-c. 2.00

OFFICIAL DOOM PATROL INDEX, THE
Independent Comics Group (Eclipse): Feb, 1986 - No. 2, Mar, 1986 ($1.50, limited series)
1,2: Byrne-c. 2.00

OFFICIAL HANDBOOK OF THE CONAN UNIVERSE (See Handbook of...)

OFFICIAL HANDBOOK OF THE MARVEL UNIVERSE, THE
Marvel Comics Group: Jan, 1983 - No. 15, May, 1984 (Limited series)
1-Lists Marvel heroes & villains (letter A) 4.00
2-15: 2 (B-C, 3-(C-D). 4-(D-G). 5-(H-J), 6-(K-L). 7-(M). 8-(N-P); Punisher-c. 9-(Q-S), 10-(S). 11-(S-U). 12-(V-Z); Wolverine-c. 13,14-Book of the Dead. 15-Weaponry catalogue 3.00
NOTE: ***Bolland*** *a-8.* ***Byrne*** *c/a(p)-1-14; c-15p.* ***Grell*** *a-6, 9.* ***Kirby*** *a-1, 3.* ***Layton*** *a-2, 5, 7.* ***Mignola*** *a-3, 4, 5, 6, 8, 12.* ***Miller*** *a-4-6, 8, 10.* ***Nebres*** *a-3, 4, 8.* ***Redondo*** *a-3, 4, 8, 13, 14.* ***Simonson*** *a-1, 4, 6-13.* ***Paul Smith*** *a-1-12.* ***Starlin*** *a-5, 7, 8, 10, 13, 14.* ***Steranko*** *a-8p.* ***Zeck****-2-14.*

OFFICIAL HANDBOOK OF THE MARVEL UNIVERSE, THE
Marvel Comics Group: Dec, 1985 - No. 20, Feb, 1988 ($1.50, maxi-series)
V2#1-Byrne-c 3.00
2-20: 2,3-Byrne-c 2.50
Trade paperback Vol. 1-10 ($6.95) 7.00
NOTE: ***Art Adams*** *a-7, 8, 11, 12, 14.* ***Bolland*** *a-8, 10, 13.* ***Buckler*** *a-1, 3, 5, 10.* ***Buscema*** *a-1, 5, 8, 9, 10, 13, 14.* ***Byrne*** *a-1-14; c-1-11.* ***Ditko*** *a-1, 2, 4, 6, 7, 11, 13. a-7, 11.* ***Mignola*** *a-2, 4, 9, 11, 13.* ***Miller*** *a-2, 4, 12.* ***Simonson*** *a-1, 2, 4-13, 15.* ***Paul Smith*** *a-1-5, 7-12, 14.* ***Starlin*** *a-6, 8, 9, 12, 16.* ***Zeck*** *a-1-4, 6, 7, 9-14, 16.*

OFFICIAL HANDBOOK OF THE MARVEL UNIVERSE, THE
Marvel Comics: July, 1989 - No. 8, Mid-Dec, 1990 ($1.50, lim. series, 52 pgs.)
V3#1-8: 1-McFarlane-a(2 pgs.) 2.50

OFFICIAL HAWKMAN INDEX, THE
Independent Comics Group: Nov, 1986 - No. 2, Dec, 1986 ($2.00)
1,2 3.00

OFFICIAL JUSTICE LEAGUE OF AMERICA INDEX, THE
Independent Comics Group (Eclipse): April, 1986 - No. 8, Mar, 1987 ($2.00, Baxter paper)
1-8: 1,2-Perez-c. 4.00

OFFICIAL LEGION OF SUPER-HEROES INDEX, THE
Independent Comics Group (Eclipse): Dec, 1986 - No. 5, 1987 ($2.00, limited series)(No Official in Title #2 on)
1-5: 4-Mooney-c 4.00

OFFICIAL MARVEL INDEX TO MARVEL TEAM-UP
Marvel Comics Group: Jan, 1986 - No. 6, 1986 ($1.25, limited series)
1-6 2.00

OFFICIAL MARVEL INDEX TO THE AMAZING SPIDER-MAN
Marvel Comics Group: Apr, 1985 - No. 9, Dec, 1985 ($1.25, limited series)
1 ($1.00)-Byrne-c. 3.00
2-9: 5,6,8,9-Punisher-c. 2.00

OFFICIAL MARVEL INDEX TO THE AVENGERS, THE
Marvel Comics: Jun, 1987 - No. 7, Aug, 1988 ($2.95, limited series)
1-7 4.00

OFFICIAL MARVEL INDEX TO THE AVENGERS, THE
Marvel Comics: V2#1, Oct, 1994 - V2#6, 1995 ($1.95, limited series)
V2#1-#6 2.00

OFFICIAL MARVEL INDEX TO THE FANTASTIC FOUR
Marvel Comics Group: Dec, 1985 - No. 12, Jan, 1987 ($1.25, limited series)
1-12: 1-Byrne-c. 1,2-Kirby back-c (unpub. art) 2.00

OFFICIAL MARVEL INDEX TO THE X-MEN, THE
Marvel Comics: May, 1987 - No. 7, July, 1988 ($2.95, limited series)
1-7 4.00

OFFICIAL MARVEL INDEX TO THE X-MEN, THE
Marvel Comics: V2#1, Apr, 1994 - V2#5, 1994 ($1.95, limited series)
V2#1-5: 1-Covers X-Men #1-51. 2-Covers #52-122,Special #1,2,Giant-Size #1,2. 3-Byrne-c; covers #123-177, Annuals 3-7, Spec. Ed. #1. 4-Covers Uncanny X-Men #178-234, Annuals 8-12. 5-Covers #235-287, Annuals 13-15 2.00

OFFICIAL SOUPY SALES COMIC (See Soupy Sales)

OFFICIAL TEEN TITANS INDEX, THE
Indep. Comics Group (Eclipse): Aug, 1985 - No. 5, 1986 ($1.50, lim. series)
1-5 3.00

OFFICIAL TRUE CRIME CASES (Formerly Sub-Mariner #23; All-True Crime Cases #26 on)
Marvel Comics (OCI): No. 24, Fall, 1947 - No. 25, Winter, 1947-48

	GD2.0	FN6.0	NM9.4
24(#1)-Burgos-a; Syd Shores-c	20.00	60.00	150.00
25-Syd Shores-c; Kurtzman's "Hey Look"	16.00	48.00	120.00

OF SUCH IS THE KINGDOM
George A. Pflaum: 1955 (15¢, 36 pgs.)

	GD2.0	FN6.0	NM9.4
nn-Reprints from 1951 Treasure Chest	2.80	7.00	14.00

O.G. WHIZ (See Gold Key Spotlight #10)
Gold Key: 2/71 - No. 6, 5/72; No. 7, 5/78 - No. 11, 1/79 (No. 7: 52 pgs.)

	GD2.0	FN6.0	NM9.4
1,2-John Stanley scripts	5.00	15.00	55.00
3-6(1972)	2.50	7.50	28.00
7-11(1978-79)-Part-r: 9-Tubby issue	1.50	4.50	12.00

OH, BROTHER! (Teen Comedy)
Stanhall Publ.: Jan, 1953 - No. 5, Oct, 1953

	GD2.0	FN6.0	NM9.4
1-By Bill Williams	6.35	19.00	38.00
2-5	4.00	12.00	24.00

OH MY GODDESS! (Manga)
Dark Horse Comics: Aug, 1994 - No. 6, Jan, 1995 ($2.50, B&W, limited series)
1-6 3.00
... **PART II** 2/95 - No. 9, 9/95 ($2.50, B&W, lim.series) #1-9 3.00
... **PART III** 11/95 - No. 11, 9/96 ($2.95, B&W, lim. series) #1-11 3.00
... **PART IV** 12/96 - No. 8, 7/97 ($2.95, B&W, lim. series) #1-8 3.00
... **PART V** 9/97 - Np. 12, 8/98 ($2.95, B&W, lim. series)
1,2,5,8: 5-Ninja Master pt. 1 3.00
3,4,6,7,10-12-($3.95, 48 pgs.) 10-Fallen Angel. 11-Play The Game 4.00
9-($3.50) "It's Lonely At The Top" 3.50
... **PART VI** 10/98 - No. 5, 3/99 ($3.50/$2.95, B&W, lim. series)
1-($3.50) 3.50
2-6-($2.95)-6-Super Urd one-shot 3.00
... **PART VII** 5/9 - No. 8 ($2.95, B&W, lim. series) #1-3 3.00
4,5-($3.50) 3.50

OH MY GOTH
Sirius Entertainment (Dog Star Press): 1998 - No. 4, 1999 ($2.95, B&W)
1-4-Voltaire-s/a 3.00

OH SUSANNA (TV)
Dell Publishing Co.: No. 1105, June-Aug, 1960 (Gale Storm)

	GD2.0	FN6.0	NM9.4
Four Color 1105-Toth-a, photo-c	12.00	35.00	130.00

OINK: BLOOD AND CIRCUS
Kitchen Sink: 1998 - No. 4, July, 1998 ($4.95, limited series)

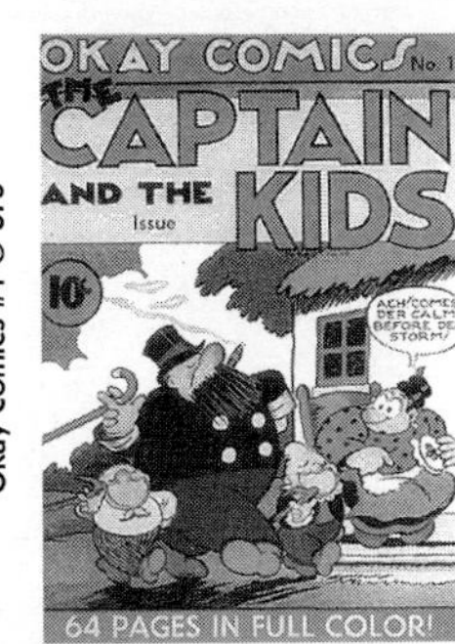

Okay Comics #1 © UFS

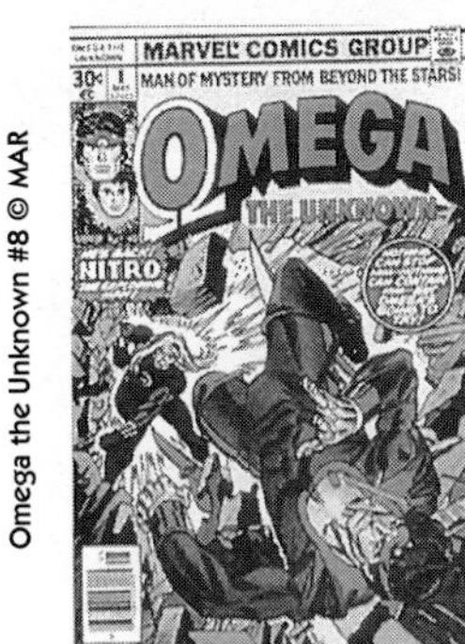

Omega the Unknown #8 © MAR

Omen #5 © Chaos!

GD2.0 FN6.0 NM9.4

1-4-John Mueller-s/a 5.00

OKAY COMICS
United Features Syndicate: July, 1940

1-Captain & the Kids & Hawkshaw the Detective reprints 40.00 120.00 320.00

O.K. COMICS
United Features Syndicate/Hit Publications: July, 1940 - No. 2, Oct, 1940

1-Little Giant (w/super powers), Phantom Knight, Sunset Smith, & The Teller Twins begin 75.00 225.00 600.00
2 (Rare)-Origin Mister Mist by Chas. Quinlan 75.00 225.00 600.00

OKLAHOMA KID
Ajax/Farrell Publ.: June, 1957 - No. 4, 1958

1 10.00 30.00 65.00
2-4 6.35 19.00 38.00

OKLAHOMAN, THE
Dell Publishing Co.: No. 820, July, 1957

Four Color 820-Movie, photo-c 9.00 27.00 100.00

OKTANE
Dark Horse Comics: Aug, 1995 - Nov, 1995($2.50, color, limited series)

1-4-Gene Ha-a 2.50

OLD IRONSIDES (Disney)
Dell Publishing Co.: No. 874, Jan, 1958

Four Color 874-Movie w/Johnny Tremain 5.50 16.50 60.00

OLD YELLER (Disney, see Movie Comics, and Walt Disney Showcase #25)
Dell Publishing Co.: No. 869, Jan, 1958

Four Color 869-Movie, photo-c 4.50 13.50 50.00

OMAC (One Man Army; ...Corps. #4 on; also see Kamandi #59 & Warlord) (See Cancelled Comic Cavalcade)
National Periodical Publications: Sept-Oct, 1974 - No. 8, Nov-Dec, 1975

1-Origin 1.50 4.50 12.00
2-8: 8-2 pg. Neal Adams ad 2.40 6.00
NOTE: *Kirby a-1-8p; c-1-7p.* ***Kubert*** *c-8.*

OMAC: ONE MAN ARMY CORPS
DC Comics: 1991 - No. 4, 1991 ($3.95, B&W, mini-series, mature, 52 pgs.)

Book One - Four: John Byrne-c/a & scripts 4.00

O'MALLEY AND THE ALLEY CATS
Gold Key: April, 1971 - No. 9, Jan, 1974 (Disney)

1 2.25 6.75 18.00
2-9 1.50 4.50 12.00

OMEGA ELITE
Blackthorne Publishing: 1987 ($1.25)

1-Starlin-c 2.00

OMEGA MEN, THE (See Green Lantern #141)
DC Comics: Dec, 1982 - No. 38, May, 1986 ($1.00/$1.50; Baxter paper)

1,20: 20-2nd full Lobo story 3.00
2-9,11-19,21-36,38: 2-Origin Broot. 5,9-2nd & 3rd app. Lobo (cameo, 2 pgs. each). 7-Origin The Citadel. 19-Lobo cameo. 26,27-Alan Moore scripts. 30-Intro new Primus. 31-Crisis x-over. 34,35-Teen Titans x-over 2.00
3-1st app. Lobo (5 pgs.)(6/83); Lobo-c 2.40 6.00
10-1st full Lobo story 4.00
37-1st solo Lobo story (8 pg. back-up by Giffen) 3.00
Annual 1(11/84, 52 pgs.), 2(11/85) 2.50
NOTE: ***Giffen*** *c/a-1-6p.* ***Morrow*** *a-24r.* ***Nino*** *c/a-16, 21; a-Annual 1i.*

OMEGA THE UNKNOWN
Marvel Comics Group: March, 1976 - No. 10, Oct, 1977

1-1st app. Omega 6.00
2,3-(Regular 25¢ editions). 2-Hulk-c/story. 3-Electro-c/story. 4.00
2,3-(30¢-c variants, limited distribution) 1.60 4.80 16.00
4-10: 8-1st app. 2nd Foolkiller (Greg Salinger), 1 panel only (cameo). 9-Regular 30¢ edition)(7/77)-1st full app. 2nd Foolkiller 4.00
9-(35¢-c variant, limited distribution) 1.60 4.80 16.00
NOTE: ***Kane*** *c(p)-3, 5, 8, 9.* ***Mooney*** *a-1-3, 4p, 5, 6p, 7, 8i, 9, 10.*

GD2.0 FN6.0 NM9.4

OMEN
Northstar Publishing: 1989 - No. 3, 1989 ($2.00, B&W, mature)

1-Tim Vigil-c/a in all 2.40 6.00
1, (2nd printing) 2.00
2,3 4.00

OMEN, THE
Chaos! Comics: May, 1998 - No. 5, Sept, 1998 ($2.95, limited series)

1-5: 1-Six covers, ...: Vexed (10/98, $2.95) Chaos! characters appear 3.00

OMNI MEN
Blackthorne Publishing: 1987 - No. 3, 1987 ($1.25)

1-3 2.00

ONE, THE
Marvel Comics (Epic Comics): July, 1985 - No. 6, Feb, 1986 (Limited series, mature)

1-6: Post nuclear holocaust super-hero. 2-Intro The Other 2.00

ONE-ARM SWORDSMAN, THE
Victory Prod./Lueng's Publ. #4 on: 1987 - No. 12, 1990 ($2.75/$1.80, 52pgs.)

1-3 ($2.75) 2.75
4-12: 4-6-$1.80-c. 7-12-$2.00-c 2.00

ONE HUNDRED AND ONE DALMATIANS (Disney, see Cartoon Tales, Movie Comics, and Walt Disney Showcase #9, 51)
Dell Publishing Co.: No. 1183, Mar, 1961

Four Color 1183-Movie 9.00 27.00 100.00

101 DALMATIONS (Movie)
Disney Comics: 1991 (52 pgs., graphic novel)

nn-($4.95, direct sales)-r/movie adaptation & more 5.00
1-($2.95, newsstand edition) 3.00

101 WAYS TO END THE CLONE SAGA (See Spider-Man)
Marvel Comics: Jan, 1997 ($2.50, one-shot)

1 2.50

100 BULLETS
DC Comics (Vertigo): Aug, 1999 - Present ($2.50)

1-5-Azzarello-s/Risso-a/Dave Johnson-c 2.50

100 PAGES OF COMICS
Dell Publishing Co.: 1937 (Stiff covers, square binding)

101(Found on back cover)-Alley Oop, Wash Tubbs, Capt. Easy, Og Son of Fire, Apple Mary, Tom Mix, Dan Dunn, Tailspin Tommy, Doctor Doom 150.00 450.00 1200.00

100 PAGE SUPER SPECTACULAR (See DC 100 Page...)

100% TRUE?
DC Comics (Paradox Press): Summer 1996 - Present ($4.95, B&W)

1,2-Reprints stories from various Paradox Press books. 5.00

$1,000,000 DUCK (See Walt Disney Showcase #5)

ONE MILLION YEARS AGO (Tor #2 on)
St. John Publishing Co.: Sept, 1953

1-Origin & 1st app. Tor; Kubert-c/a; Kubert photo inside front cover 19.00 58.00 135.00

ONE SHOT (See Four Color...)

1001 HOURS OF FUN
Dell Publishing Co.: No. 13, 1943

Large Feature Comic 13 (nn)-Puzzles & games; by A.W. Nugent. This book was bound as #13 w/Large Feature Comics in publisher's files 27.00 81.00 190.00

ONE TRICK RIP OFF, THE (See Dark Horse Presents)

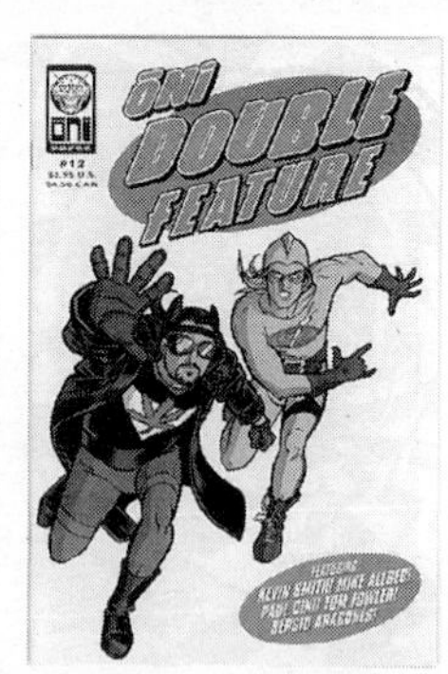

Oni Double Feature #12 © Oni Press

Operation Peril #5 © ACG

Original E-Man and Michael Mauser #4 © CC

GD2.0 FN6.0 NM9.4

ONI DOUBLE FEATURE (See Clerks: The Comic Book and Jay & Silent Bob)
Oni Press: Jan, 1998 - No. 13, Sept, 1999 ($2.95, B&W)

1-Jay & Silent Bob; Kevin Smith-s/Matt Wagner-a 1.25 3.75 10.00
1-2nd printing 3.00
2-11,13: 2,3-Paul Pope-s/a. 3,4-Nixey-s/a. 4,5-Sienkewicz-s/a. 6,7-Gaiman-s. 9-Bagge-c. 13-All Paul Dini-s; Jingle Belle 3.00
12-Jay & Silent Bob as Bluntman & Chronic; Smith-s/Allred-a 4.00

ONIGAMI (See Warrior Nun Areala: Black & White)
Antarctic Press: Apr, 1998 - No. 3, July, 1998 ($2.95, B&W, limited series)

1-3-Michel Lacombe-s/a 3.00

ONSLAUGHT: EPILOGUE
Marvel Comics: Feb, 1997 ($2.95, one-shot)

1-Hama-s/Green-a; Xavier-c; Bastion-app. 3.00

ONSLAUGHT: MARVEL
Marvel Comics: Oct, 1996 ($3.95, one-shot)

1-Conclusion to Onslaught x-over; wraparound-c 1.00 2.80 7.00

ONSLAUGHT: X-MEN
Marvel Comics: Aug, 1996 ($3.95, one-shot)

1-Mark Waid & Scott Lobdell script; Fantastic Four & Avengers app.; Xavier as Onslaught 5.00
1-Variant-c 1.50 4.50 12.00

ON STAGE
Dell Publishing Co.: No. 1336, Apr-June, 1962

Four Color 1336-Not by Leonard Starr 3.60 11.00 40.00

ON THE DOUBLE (Movie)
Dell Publishing Co.: No. 1232, Sept-Nov, 1961

Four Color 1232 3.60 11.00 40.00

ON THE ROAD WITH ANDRAE CROUCH
Spire Christian Comics (Fleming H. Revell): 1973, 1977 (39¢)

nn 5.00

ON THE SPOT (Pretty Boy Floyd...)
Fawcett Publications: Fall, 1948

nn-Pretty Boy Floyd photo on-c; bondage-c 32.00 96.00 225.00

ONYX OVERLORD
Marvel Comics (Epic): Oct, 1992 - No. 4, Jan, 1993 ($2.75, mini-series)

1-4: Moebius scripts 2.75

OPEN SPACE
Marvel Comics: Mid-Dec, 1989 - No. 4, Aug, 1990 ($4.95, bi-monthly, 68 pgs.)

1-4: 1-Bill Wray-a; Freas-c 5.00
0-(1999) Wizard supplement; unpubl. early Alex Ross-a; new Ross-c 1.00

OPERATION BIKINI (See Movie Classics)
OPERATION BUCHAREST (See The Crusaders)
OPERATION CROSSBOW (See Movie Classics)

OPERATION: KNIGHTSTRIKE (See Knightstrike)
Image Comics (Extreme Studios): May, 1995 - No.3, July, 1995 ($2.50)

1-3 2.50

OPERATION PERIL
American Comics Group (Michel Publ.): Oct-Nov, 1950 - No. 16, Apr-May, 1953 (#1-5: 52 pgs.)

1-Time Travelers, Danny Danger (by Leonard Starr) & Typhoon Tyler (by Ogden Whitney) begin 37.00 111.00 260.00
2-War-c 22.00 66.00 155.00
3-War-c; horror story 19.00 58.00 135.00
4,5-Sci/fi-c/story 21.00 64.00 150.00
6-10: 6,8,9,10-Sci/fi-c. 6-Dinosaur-c. 7-Sabretooth-c 17.00 51.00 120.00
11,12-War-c; last Time Travelers 12.00 36.00 85.00
13-16: All war format 9.15 27.00 55.00

NOTE: ***Starr** a-2, 5. **Whitney** a-1, 2, 5-10, 12; c-1, 3, 5, 8, 9.*

GD2.0 FN6.0 NM9.4

OPERATION: STORMBREAKER
Acclaim Comics (Valiant Heroes): Aug, 1997 ($3.95, one-shot)

1-Waid/Augustyn-s, Braithwaite-a 4.00

OPTIC NERVE
Drawn and Quarterly: Apr, 1995 - Present ($2.95, bi-annual)

1-5: Adrian Tomine-c/a/scripts in all 3.00
32 Stories-($9.95, trade paperback)-r/Optic Nerve mini-comics 10.00
32 Stories-($29.95, hardcover)-r/Optic Nerve mini-comics; signed & numbered 30.00

ORAL ROBERTS' TRUE STORIES (Junior Partners #120 on)
TelePix Publ. (Oral Roberts' Evangelistic Assoc./Healing Waters): 1956 (no month) - No. 119, 7/59 (15¢)(No. 102: 25¢)

V1#1(1956)-(Not code approved)- "The Miracle Touch" 19.00 58.00 135.00
102-(Only issue approved by code, 10/56) "Now I See" 11.50 34.00 80.00
103-119: 115-(114 on inside) 8.35 25.00 50.00

NOTE: *Also see Happiness & Healing For You.*

ORANGE BIRD, THE
Walt Disney Educational Media Co.: No date (1980) (36 pgs.; in color; slick cover)

nn-Included with educational kit on foods, ...in Nutrition Adventures nn (1980) ...and the Nutrition Know-How Revue nn (1983) 2.00

ORBIT
Eclipse Books:1990 - No. 3, 1990 ($4.95, 52 pgs., squarebound)

1-3: Reprints from Isaac Asimov's Science Fiction Magazine; 1-Dave Stevens-c, Bolton-a. 3-Bolton-c/a, Yeates-a 5.00

ORIENTAL HEROES
Jademan Comics: Aug, 1988 - No. 55, Feb, 1993 ($1.50/$1.95, 68pgs.)

1-55 2.00

ORIGINAL ASTRO BOY, THE
Now Comics: Sept, 1987 - No. 19, 1989 ($1.50/$1.75)

1-All have Ken Steacy painted-c/a 3.00
2-19 2.00

ORIGINAL BLACK CAT, THE
Recollections: Oct. 6, 1988 - No. 9, 1992 ($2.00, limited series)

1-9: Elias-r; 1-Bondage-c. 2-M. Anderson-c 3.00

ORIGINAL DICK TRACY, THE
Gladstone Publishing: Sept, 1990 - No. 5, 1991 ($1.95, bi-monthly, 68pgs.)

1-5: 1-Vs. Pruneface. 2-& the Evil influence; begin $2.00-c 2.00

NOTE: *#1 reprints strips 7/16/43 - 9/30/43. #2 reprints strips 12/1/46 - 2/2/47. #3 reprints 8/31/46 - 11/14/46. #4 reprints 9/17/45 - 12/23/45. #5 reprints 6/10/46 - 8/28/46.*

ORIGINAL DOCTOR SOLAR, MAN OF THE ATOM, THE
Valiant: Apr, 1995 ($2.95, one-shot)

1-Reprints Doctor Solar, Man of the Atom #1,5; Bob Fugitani-r; Paul Smith-c; afterword by Seaborn Adamson 3.00

ORIGINAL E-MAN AND MICHAEL MAUSER, THE
First Comics: Oct, 1985 - No. 7, April, 1986 ($1.75, Baxter paper)

1-7: 1-Has r/Charlton's E-Man, Vengeance Squad. 2-Shows #4 in indicia by mistake. 7 ($2.00, 44pgs.)-Staton-a 2.00

ORIGINAL GHOST RIDER, THE
Marvel Comics: July, 1992 - No. 20, Feb, 1994 ($1.75)

1-20: 1-7-r/Marvel Spotlight #5-11 by Ploog w/new-c. 3-New Phantom Rider (former Night Rider) back-ups begin by Ayers. 4-Quesada-c(p). 8-Ploog-c. 8,9-r/Ghost Rider #1,2. 10-r/Marvel Spotlight #12. 11-18,20-r/Ghost Rider #3-12. 19-r/Marvel Two-in-One #8 2.00

ORIGINAL GHOST RIDER RIDES AGAIN, THE
Marvel Comics: July, 1991 - No. 7, Jan, 1992, ($1.50, limited series, 52 pgs.)

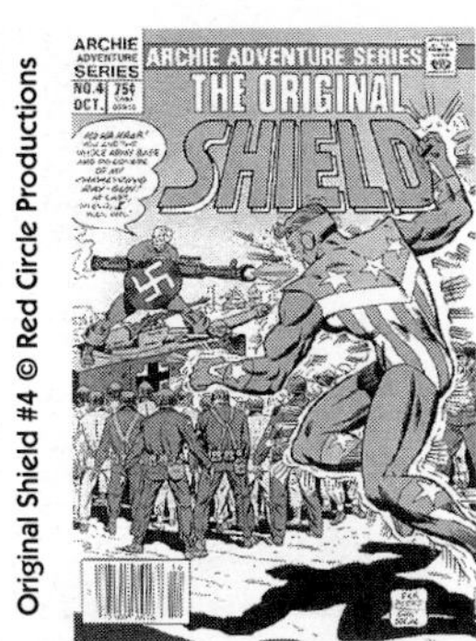

Original Shield #4 © Red Circle Productions

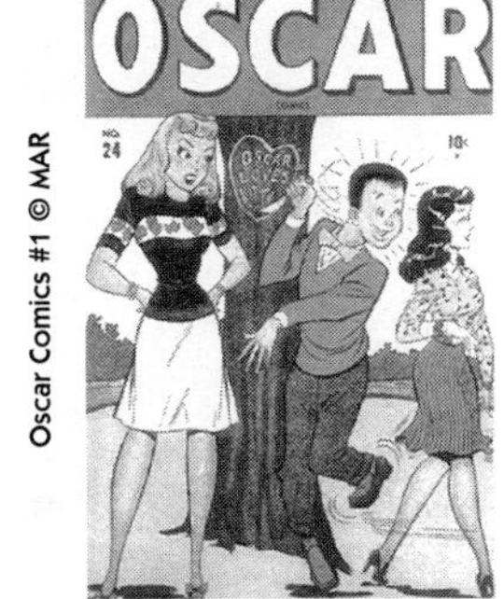

Oscar Comics #1 © MAR

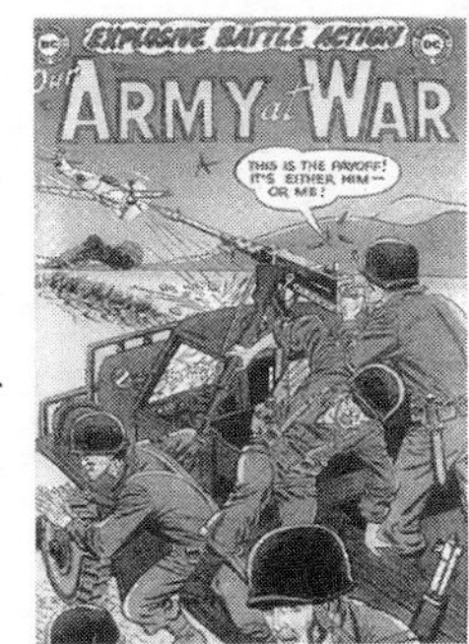

Our Army at War #3 © DC

GD2.0 FN6.0 NM9.4 | GD2.0 FN6.0 NM9.4

1-7: 1-R/Ghost Rider #68(origin),69 w/covers. 2-7: R/ G.R. #70-81 w/covers 2.00

ORIGINAL MAGNUS ROBOT FIGHTER, THE
Valiant: Apr, 1995 ($2.95, one-shot)

1-Reprints Magnus, Robot Fighter 4000 #2; Russ Manning-r; Rick Leonardi-c; afterword by Seaborn Adamson 3.00

ORIGINAL NEXUS GRAPHIC NOVEL (See First Comics Graphic Novel #19)

ORIGINAL SHIELD, THE
Archie Enterprises, Inc.: Apr, 1984 - No. 4, Oct, 1984

1-4: 1,2-Origin Shield; Ayers p-1-4, Nebres c-1,2 3.00

ORIGINAL SWAMP THING SAGA, THE (See DC Special Series #2, 14, 17, 20)

ORIGINAL TUROK, SON OF STONE, THE
Valiant: Apr, 1995 - No. 2, May, 1995 ($2.95, limited series)

1,2: 1-Reprints Turok, Son of Stone #24,25,42; Alberto Gioletti-r; Rags Morales-c; afterword by Seaborn Adamson. 2-Reprints Turok, Son of Stone #24,33; Gioletti-r; Mike McKone-c 3.00

ORIGIN OF GALACTUS (See Fantastic Four #48-50)
Marvel Comics: Feb, 1996 ($2.50, one-shot)

1-Lee & Kirby reprints w/pin-ups 2.50

ORIGIN OF THE DEFIANT UNIVERSE, THE
Defiant Comics: Feb, 1994 ($1.50, 20 pgs., one-shot)

1-David Lapham, Adam Pollina & Alan Weiss-a; Weiss-c 5.00
NOTE: *The comic was originally published as Defiant Genesis and was distributed at the 1994 Philadelphia ComicCon.*

ORIGINS OF MARVEL COMICS (See Fireside Book Series)

ORION (Manga)
Dark Horse Comics: Sept, 1992 - No. 6, July, 1993 ($2.95/$3.95, B&W, bimonthly, limited series)

1-6:1,2,6-Squarebound): 1-Masamune Shirow-c/a/s in all 4.00

OSBORNE JOURNALS (See Spider-Man titles)
Marvel Comics: Feb, 1997 ($2.95, one-shot)

1-Hotz-c/a 3.00

OSCAR COMICS (Formerly Funny Tunes; Awful...#11 & 12)
(Also see Cindy Comics)
Marvel Comics: No. 24, Spring, 1947 - No. 10, Apr, 1949; No. 13, Oct, 1949

	GD2.0	FN6.0	NM9.4
24(#1, Spring, 1947)	14.00	43.00	100.00
25(#2, Sum, 1947)-Wolverton-a plus Kurtzman's "Hey Look"	17.00	51.00	120.00
26(#3)-Same as regular #3 except #26 was printed over in black ink with #3 appearing on-c below the over print	10.00	30.00	70.00
3-9,13: 8-Margie app.	10.00	30.00	70.00
10-Kurtzman's "Hey Look"	11.50	34.00	80.00

OSWALD THE RABBIT (Also see New Fun Comics #1)
Dell Publishing Co.: No. 21, 1943 - No. 1268, 12-2/61-62 (Walter Lantz)

	GD2.0	FN6.0	NM9.4
Four Color 21(1943)	48.00	145.00	530.00
Four Color 39(1943)	34.00	102.00	375.00
Four Color 67(1944)	17.00	50.00	185.00
Four Color 102(1946)-Kelly-a, 1 pg.	14.50	43.50	160.00
Four Color 143,183	8.65	26.00	95.00
Four Color 225,273	5.00	15.00	55.00
Four Color 315,388	4.00	12.00	45.00
Four Color 458,507,549,593	2.90	8.70	32.00
Four Color 623,697,792,894,979,1268	2.00	6.00	22.00

OSWALD THE RABBIT (See The Funnies, March of Comics #7, 38, 53, 67, 81, 95, 111, 126, 141, 156, 171, 186, New Funnies & Super Book #8, 20)

OTHERS, THE
Image Comics (Shadowline Ink): 1995 - No. 3, 1995 ($2.50)

0 ($1.00)-16 pg. preview 2.00
1-3 2.50

OTIS GOES TO HOLLYWOOD
Dark Horse Comics: Apr, 1997 - No.2, May, 1997 ($2.95, B&W, mini-series)

1,2-Fingerman-c/s/a 3.00

OUTCAST, THE
Valiant: Dec, 1995 ($2.50, one-shot)

1-Breyfogle-a. 2.50

OUR ARMY AT WAR (Becomes Sgt. Rock #302 on; also see Army At War)
National Periodical Publications: Aug, 1952 - No. 301, Feb, 1977

	GD2.0	FN6.0	NM9.4
1	121.00	362.00	1450.00
2	56.00	168.00	675.00
3,4: 4-Krigstein-a	45.00	134.00	490.00
5-7	36.00	108.00	400.00
8-11,14-Krigstein-a	33.00	100.00	370.00
12,15-20	29.00	87.00	290.00
13-Krigstein-c/a; flag-c	35.00	103.00	380.00
21-31: Last precode (2/55)	20.00	60.00	200.00
32-40	16.50	50.00	165.00
41-60: 51-1st S.A. issue	14.00	42.00	140.00
61-70: 67-Minor Sgt. Rock prototype	12.00	36.00	120.00
71-80	10.00	30.00	100.00

	GD2.0	FN6.0	VF8.0	NM9.4
81- (4/59)-Sgt. Rocky of Easy Co. app. by Andru & Esposito-a/ Haney-s; (the last Sgt. Rock prototype)	177.00	531.00	900.00	2300.00
82-1st Sgt. Rock app., in name only, in Easy Co. story (6 panels) by Kanigher & Drucker	41.00	123.00	246.00	500.00
83-(6/59)-1st true Sgt. Rock app. in "The Rock and the Wall" by Kubert & Kanigher; (most similar to prototype in G.I. Combat #68)	117.00	350.00	700.00	1400.00

	GD2.0	FN6.0	NM9.4
84-Kubert-c	24.00	72.00	240.00
85-Origin & 1st app. Ice Cream Soldier	32.00	96.00	330.00
86,87-Early Sgt. Rock; Kubert-a	23.00	69.00	230.00
88-1st Sgt. Rock-c; Kubert-c/a	26.00	78.00	260.00
89	21.00	63.00	210.00
90-Kubert-c/a; How Rock got his stripes	28.00	84.00	280.00
91-All-Sgt. Rock issue; Grandenetti-c/Kubert-a	48.00	144.00	575.00
92,94,96-99: 97-Regular Kubert-c begin	14.50	44.00	145.00
93-1st Zack Nolan	15.00	45.00	150.00
95,100: 95-1st app. Bulldozer	15.50	47.00	155.00
101,105,108,113,115: 101-1st app. Buster. 105-1st app. Junior. 113-1st app. Wildman & Jackie Johnson. 115-Rock revealed as orphan; 1st x-over Mlle. Marie. 1st Sgt. Rock's battle family	10.50	32.00	105.00
102-104,106,107,109,110,114,116-120: 104-Nurse Jane-c/s. 109-Pre Easy Co. Sgt. Rock-s. 118-Sunny injured	9.50	28.50	95.00
111-1st app. Wee Willie & Sunny	10.50	32.00	105.00
112-Classic Easy Co. roster-c	12.00	36.00	120.00
121-125,130-133,135-139,141-150: 138-1st Sparrow. 141-1st Shaker. 147,148-Rock becomes a General	6.00	18.00	60.00
126,129,134: 126-1st app. Canary; grey tone-c	6.50	19.50	65.00
127-2nd all-Sgt. Rock issue; 1st app. Little Sure	7.50	22.50	75.00
128-Training & origin Sgt. Rock; 1st Sgt. Krupp	21.00	63.00	210.00
140-3rd all-Sgt. Rock issue	6.50	19.50	65.00
151-Intro. Enemy Ace by Kubert (2/65)	32.00	99.00	320.00
152-4th all-Sgt. Rock issue	5.50	16.50	55.00
153-2nd app. Enemy Ace (4/65)	14.50	44.00	145.00
154,156,157,159-161,165-167: 157-2 pg. pin-up: 159-1st Nurse Wendy Winston-c/s. 165-2nd Iron Major	5.00	15.00	50.00
155-3rd app. Enemy Ace (6/65)(see Showcase)	10.00	30.00	100.00
158-Origin & 1st app. Iron Major(9/65), formerly Iron Captain	6.00	18.00	60.00
162,163-Viking Prince x-over in Sgt. Rock	5.50	16.50	55.00
164-Giant G-19	9.50	28.50	95.00
168-1st Unknown Soldier app.; referenced in Star-Spangled War Stories #157; (Sgt. Rock x-over) (6/66)	9.00	27.00	90.00
169,170	4.50	13.50	45.00

Our Fighting Forces #6 © DC

Our Flag Comics #2 © ACE

Our Gang Comics #25 © Loew's Inc.

	GD2.0	FN6.0	NM9.4
171-176,178-181: 171-1st Mad Emperor	3.50	10.50	35.00
177-(80 pg. Giant G-32)	6.00	18.00	60.00
182,183,186-Neal Adams-a. 186-Origin retold	4.50	13.50	45.00
184,185,187,188,193-195,197-199: 184-Wee Willie dies	3.20	9.60	32.00
189,191,192,196: 189-Intro. The Teen-age Underground Fighters of Unit 3. 196-Hitler cameo	3.20	9.60	32.00
190-(80 pg. Giant G-44)	5.00	15.00	50.00
200-12 pg. Rock story told in verse; Evans-a	3.80	11.40	38.00
2.50	7.50	20.00	
201,202,204-207: 201-Krigstein-r/#14. 204,205-All reprints; no Sgt. Rock. 207-Last 12¢ cover	2.50	7.50	20.00
203-(80 pg. Giant G-56)-All-r, Sgt. Rock story	4.50	13.50	45.00
208-216,229-(80 pg. Giants G-68, G-80): 216-Has G-58 on-c by mistake	4.50	13.50	45.00
217-219: 218-1st U.S.S. Stevens	2.00	6.00	16.00
220-Classic dinosaur/Sgt. Rock-c/s	2.50	7.50	20.00
221-228,230-234: 231-Intro/death Rock's brother. 234-Last 15¢ issue	1.75	5.25	14.00
235-239,241: 52 pg. Giants	2.25	6.75	18.00
240-Neal Adams-a; 52 pg. Giant	2.60	7.80	26.00
242-Also listed as **DC 100 Page Super Spectacular #9**; see for price			-
243-246: 244-(52 pgs.) no Adams-a	2.00	6.00	16.00
247-250,254-268,270: 247-Joan of Arc	1.50	4.50	12.00
251-253-Return of Iron Major	1.50	4.50	12.00
269,275-(100 pgs.)	2.80	8.40	28.00
271-274,276-279: 273-Crucifixion-c	1.40	4.15	11.00
280-(68 pgs.)-200th app. Sgt. Rock; reprints Our Army at War #81,83	2.50	7.50	20.00
281-299,301: 295-Bicentennial cover	1.25	3.75	10.00
300-Sgt. Rock-s by Kubert (2/77)	1.50	4.50	12.00

NOTE **Alcala** *a-251.* **Drucker** *a-27, 67, 68, 79, 82, 83, 96, 164, 177, 203, 212, 243r, 244, 269r, 275r, 280r.* **Evans** *a-165-175, 200, 266, 269, 270, 274, 276, 278, 280.* **Glanzman** *a-218, 220, 222, 223, 225, 227, 230-232, 238-241, 244, 247, 248, 256-259, 261, 265-267, 271, 282, 283, 298.* **Grandenetti** *c-91.* **Grell** *a-287.* **Heath** *a-50, 164, & most 176-281.* **Kubert** *a-38, 59, 67, 68 & most issues from 83-165, 233, 236, 267, 275, 300; c-84, 280.* **Maurer** *a-233, 237, 239, 240, 45, 280, 284, 288, 290, 291, 295.* **Severin** *a-236, 252, 265, 267, 269r, 272.* **Toth** *a-235, 241, 254.* **Wildey** *a-283-285, 287p.* **Wood** *a-249.*

OUR FIGHTING FORCES

National Per. Publ./DC Comics: Oct-Nov, 1954 - No. 181, Sept-Oct, 1978

	GD2.0	FN6.0	NM9.4
1-Grandenetti-c/a	75.00	225.00	825.00
2	35.00	105.00	390.00
3-Kubert-c; last precode issue (3/55)	31.00	93.00	325.00
4,5	25.00	75.00	250.00
6-9: 7-1st S.A. issue	21.50	65.00	215.00
10-Wood-a	22.50	68.00	225.00
11-20: 20-Grey tone-c (4/57)	17.00	51.00	170.00
21-30	12.00	36.00	120.00
31-40	11.00	33.00	110.00
41-Unknown Soldier tryout	13.50	41.00	135.00
42-44	9.50	28.50	95.00
45-Gunner & Sarge begins, end #94	32.00	96.00	320.00
46	13.50	41.00	135.00
47	9.50	28.50	95.00
48,50	7.50	22.50	75.00
49-1st Pooch	10.50	32.00	105.00
51-64: 51-Grey tone-c. 64-Last 10¢ issue	7.00	21.00	70.00
65-70	5.00	15.00	50.00
71-80: 71-Grey tone-c	3.00	9.00	30.00
81-90	2.80	8.40	28.00
91-98: 95-Devil-Dog begins, ends #98.	2.25	6.75	18.00
99-Capt. Hunter begins, ends #106	2.50	7.50	24.00
100	2.50	7.50	22.00
101-105,107-120: 116-Mlle. Marie app. 120-Last 12¢ issue	2.00	6.00	16.00
106-Hunters Hellcats begin	2.25	6.75	18.00
121,122: 121-Intro. Heller	1.60	4.80	16.00
123-Losers (Capt. Storm, Gunner & Sarge, Johnny Cloud) begin	3.50	10.50	35.00
124-132: 132-Last 15¢ issue	1.75	5.25	14.00
133-137 (Giants). 134-Toth-a	2.00	6.00	16.00
138-150: 146-Toth-a	1.25	3.75	10.00
151-162-Kirby a(p)	1.75	5.25	14.00
163-180	1.00	3.00	8.00
181-Last issue	1.25	3.75	10.00

NOTE: **N. Adams** *c-147.* **Drucker** *a-28, 37, 39, 42-44, 49, 53, 133r.* **Evans** *a-149, 164-174, 177-181.* **Glanzman** *a-125-128, 132, 134, 138-141, 143, 144.* **Heath** *a-2, 16, 18, 28, 41, 44, 49, 114, 135-138r; c-51.* **Kirby** *a-151-162p; c-152-159.* **Kubert** *c/a in many issues.* **Maurer** *a-135.* **Redondo** *a-166.* **Severin** *a-123-130, 131i, 132-150.*

OUR FIGHTING MEN IN ACTION (See Men In Action)

OUR FLAG COMICS

Ace Magazines: Aug, 1941 - No. 5, April, 1942

	GD2.0	FN6.0	NM9.4
1-Captain Victory, The Unknown Soldier (intro.) & The Three Cheers begin	250.00	750.00	2000.00
2-Origin The Flag (patriotic hero); 1st app?	112.00	338.00	900.00
3-5: 5-Intro & 1st app. Mr. Risk	87.00	262.00	700.00

NOTE: **Anderson** *a-1, 4.* **Mooney** *a-1, 2; c-2.*

OUR GANG COMICS (With Tom & Jerry #39-59; becomes Tom & Jerry #60 on; based on film characters)

Dell Publishing Co.: Sept-Oct, 1942 - No. 59, June, 1949

	GD2.0	FN6.0	NM9.4
1-Our Gang & Barney Bear by Kelly, Tom & Jerry, Pete Smith, Flip & Dip, The Milky Way begin (all 1st app.)	82.00	246.00	900.00
2-Benny Burro begins (#2 by Kelly)	41.00	123.00	450.00
3-5	27.00	82.00	300.00
6-Bumbazine & Albert only app. by Kelly	41.00	123.00	450.00
7-No Kelly story	21.00	63.00	230.00
8-Benny Burro begins by Barks	52.00	157.00	575.00
9-Barks-a(2): Benny Burro & Happy Hound; no Kelly story	47.00	142.00	520.00
10-Benny Burro by Barks	34.00	101.00	370.00
11-1st Barney Bear & Benny Burro by Barks (5-6/44); Happy Hound by Barks	47.00	142.00	520.00
12-20	21.00	63.00	230.00
21-30: 30-X-Mas-c	14.00	41.00	150.00
31-36-Last Barks issue	10.00	30.00	110.00
37-40	6.00	18.00	65.00
41-50	4.35	13.00	48.00
51-57	3.50	10.50	38.00
58,59-No Kelly art or Our Gang stories	2.90	9.00	32.00

NOTE: **Barks** *art in part only.* **Barks** *did not write Barney Bear stories #30-34. (See March of Comics #3, 26). Early issues have photo back-c.*

OUR LADY OF FATIMA

Catechetical Guild Educational Society: 3/11/55 (15¢) (36 pgs.)

	GD2.0	FN6.0	NM9.4
395	4.00	11.00	22.00

OUR LOVE (True Secrets #3 on? or Romantic Affairs #3 on?)

Marvel Comics (SPC): Sept, 1949 - No. 2, Jan, 1950

	GD2.0	FN6.0	NM9.4
1-Photo-c	12.00	36.00	85.00
2-Photo-c	8.35	25.00	50.00

OUR LOVE STORY

Marvel Comics Group: Oct, 1969 - No. 38, Feb, 1976

	GD2.0	FN6.0	NM9.4
1	3.50	10.50	35.00
2-4,6-8,10,11	2.25	6.75	18.00
5-Steranko-a	5.50	16.50	60.00
9,12-Kirby-a	2.50	7.50	20.00
13-(10/71, 52 pgs.)	2.80	8.40	28.00
14-New story by Gary Fredrich & Tarpe' Mills	2.50	7.50	20.00
15-20,27:27-Colan/Everett-a(r?); Kirby/Colletta-r	1.75	5.25	14.00
21-26,28-37:	1.50	4.50	12.00
38-Last issue	2.00	6.00	16.00

NOTE: **J. Buscema** *a-1-3, 5-7, 9, 13r, 16r, 19r(2), 21r, 22r(2), 23r, 34r, 35r; c-11, 13, 16, 22, 23, 24, 27, 35.* **Colan** *a-3-6, 21r(#6), 22r, 23r(#3), 24r(#4), 27; c-19.* **Katz** *a-17.* **Maneely** *a-13r.* **Romita** *a-13r.* **Weiss** *a-16, 17, 29r(#17).*

Outlanders #27 © Studio Proteus

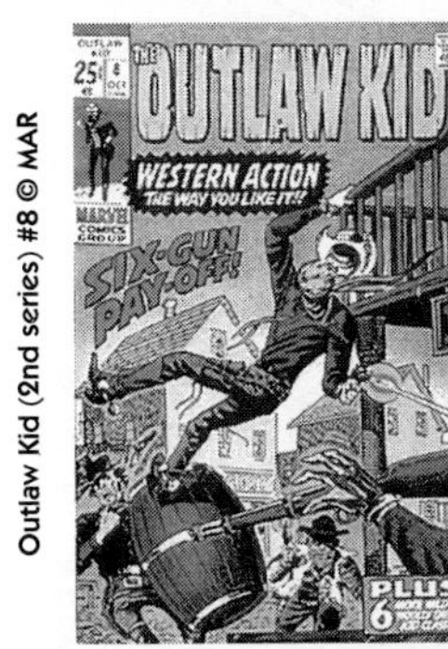

Outlaw Kid (2nd series) #8 © MAR

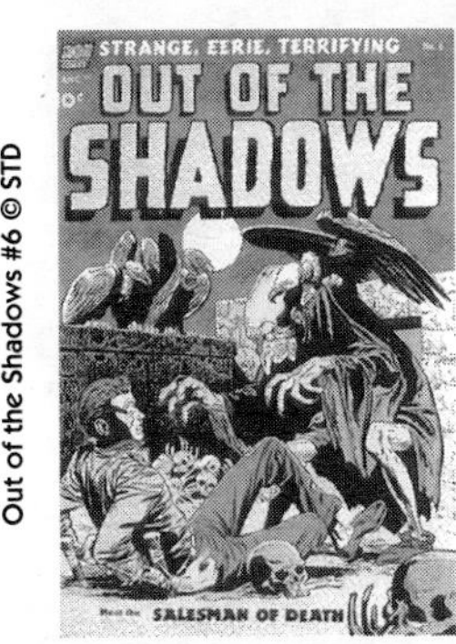

Out of the Shadows #6 © STD

GD2.0 FN6.0 NM9.4

OUR MISS BROOKS
Dell Publishing Co.: No. 751, Nov, 1956

Four Color 751-Photo-c 7.00 22.00 80.00

OUR SECRET (Exciting Love Stories)(Formerly My Secret)
Superior Comics Ltd.: No. 4, Nov, 1949 - No. 8, Jun, 1950

4-Kamen-a; spanking scene 17.00 51.00 120.00
5,6,8 10.00 30.00 60.00
7-Contains 9 pg. story intended for unpublished Ellery Queen #5; lingerie panels 10.00 30.00 70.00

OUTBREED 999
Blackout Comics: May, 1994 - No. 6, 1994 ($2.95)

1-6: 4-1st app. of Extreme Violet in 7 pg. backup story 3.00

OUTCASTS
DC Comics: Oct, 1987 - No. 12, Sept, 1988 ($1.75, limited series)

1-12: John Wagner & Alan Grant scripts in all 2.00

OUTER LIMITS, THE (TV)
Dell Publishing Co.: Jan-Mar, 1964 - No. 18, Oct, 1969 (Most painted-c)

1 10.50 32.00 105.00
2-5 6.00 18.00 60.00
6-10 5.00 15.00 50.00
11-18: 17-Reprints #1. 18-r/#2 3.50 10.50 35.00

OUTER SPACE (Formerly This Magazine Is Haunted, 2nd Series)
Charlton Comics: No. 17, May, 1958 - No. 25, Dec, 1959; Nov, 1968

17-Williamson/Wood style art; not by them (Sid Check?) 12.00 36.00 90.00
18-20-Ditko-a 20.00 60.00 140.00
21-25: 21-Ditko-c 11.50 34.00 80.00
V2#1(11/68)-Ditko-a, Boyette-c 3.80 11.40 38.00

OUTER SPACE BABES, THE
Silhouette Studios: Feb, 1994 ($2.95)

V3#1 3.00

OUTLANDERS (Manga)
Dark Horse Comics: Dec, 1988 - No. 33, Sep,1991 ($2.00-$2.50, B&W, 44pgs.)

1-33: Japanese Sci-fi manga 2.50

OUTLAW (See Return of the...)

OUTLAW FIGHTERS
Atlas Comics (IPC): Aug, 1954 - No. 5, Apr, 1955

1-Tuska-a 12.00 36.00 85.00
2-5: 5-Heath-c/a, 7 pgs. 8.35 25.00 50.00
NOTE: ***Heath*** *c/a-5.* ***Maneely*** *c-2.* ***Pakula*** *a-2.* ***Reinman*** *a-2.* ***Tuska*** *a-1, 2.*

OUTLAW KID, THE (1st Series; see Wild Western)
Atlas Comics (CCC No. 1-11/EPI No. 12-29): Sept, 1954 - No. 19, Sept, 1957

1-Origin; The Outlaw Kid & his horse Thunder begin; Black Rider app. 25.00 75.00 175.00
2-Black Rider app. 12.00 36.00 85.00
3-7,9: 3-Wildey-a(3) 11.00 33.00 75.00
8-Williamson/Woodbridge-a, 4 pgs. 11.50 34.00 80.00
10-Williamson-a 11.00 33.00 75.00
11-17,19: 13-Baker text illo. 15-Williamson text illo (unsigned) 8.35 25.00 50.00
18-Williamson/Mayo-a 10.00 30.00 60.00
NOTE: ***Berg*** *a-4, 7, 13.* ***Maneely*** *c-1-3, 5-8, 11-13, 15, 16, 18.* ***Pakula*** *a-3.* ***Severin*** *c-10, 17, 19.* ***Shores*** *a-1.* ***Wildey*** *a-1(3), 2-8, 10, 11, 12(4), 13(4), 15-19(4 each); c-4.*

OUTLAW KID, THE (2nd Series)
Marvel Comics Group: Aug, 1970 - No. 30, Oct, 1975

1-Reprints; 1-Orlando-r, Wildey-r(3) 2.50 7.50 20.00
2,3,9: 2-Reps. 3,9-Williamson-a(r) 2.00 6.00 16.00
4-7: 7-Last 15¢ issue 1.75 5.25 14.00
8-Double size; Crandall-r 2.25 6.75 18.00
10-Origin 2.50 7.50 20.00
11-20: new-a in #10-16 1.50 4.50 12.00
21-30: 27-Origin-r/#10 1.00 3.00 8.00
NOTE: ***Ayers*** *a-10, 27r.* ***Berg*** *a-7, 25r.* ***Everett*** *a-2(2 pgs.).* ***Gil Kane*** *c-10, 11, 15, 27r, 28.* ***Roussos*** *a-10i, 27i(r).* ***Severin*** *c-1, 9, 20, 25.* ***Wildey*** *r-1-4, 6-9, 19-22, 25, 26.* ***Williamson*** *a-28r.* ***Woodbridge/Williamson*** *a-9r.*

OUTLAWS
D. S. Publishing Co.: Feb-Mar, 1948 - No. 9, June-July, 1949

1-Violent & suggestive stories 31.00 94.00 220.00
2-Ingels-a; Baker-a 31.00 94.00 220.00
3,5,6: 3-Not Frazetta. 5-Sky Sheriff by Good app. 6-McWilliams-a 13.50 41.00 95.00
4-Orlando-a 16.00 47.00 110.00
7,8-Ingels-a in each 24.00 73.00 170.00
9-(Scarce)-Frazetta-a (7 pgs.) 45.00 135.00 360.00
NOTE: *Another #3 was printed in Canada with* ***Frazetta*** *art "Prairie Jinx," 7 pgs.*

OUTLAWS, THE (Formerly Western Crime Cases)
Star Publishing Co.: No. 10, May, 1952 - No. 13, Sep, 1953; No. 14, Apr, 1954

10-L. B. Cole-c 19.00 56.00 130.00
11-14-L. B. Cole-c. 14-Reprints Western Thrillers #4 (Fox) w/new L.B. Cole-c; Kamen, Feldstein-r 1400 43.00 100.00

OUTLAWS
DC Comics: Sept, 1991 - No. 8, Apr, 1992 ($1.95, limited series)

1-8: Post-apocalyptic Robin Hood. 2.00

OUTLAWS OF THE WEST (Formerly Cody of the Pony Express #10)
Charlton Comics: No. 11, 7/57 - No. 81, 5/70; No. 82, 7/79 - No. 88, 4/80

11 7.50 22.50 45.00
12,13,15-17,19,20 4.25 13.00 26.00
14-(68 pgs., 2/58) 8.00 24.00 48.00
18-Ditko-a 10.00 30.00 60.00
21-30 2.50 7.50 20.00
31-50: 34-Gunmaster app. 2.00 6.00 16.00
51-70: 54-Kid Montana app. 64-Captain Doom begins (1st app.). 68-Kid Montana series begins 1.50 4.50 12.00
71-79: 73-Origin & 1st app. The Sharp Shooter, last app. #74. 75-Last Capt. Doom 1.25 3.75 10.00
80,81-Ditko-a 1.75 5.25 14.00
82-88 3.50
64,79(Modern Comics-r, 1977, '78) 3.00

OUTLAWS OF THE WILD WEST
Avon Periodicals: 1952 (25¢, 132 pgs.) (4 rebound comics)

1-Wood back-c; Kubert-a (3 Jesse James-r) 31.00 94.00 220.00

OUTLAW TRAIL (See Zane Grey 4-Color 511)

OUT OF SANTA'S BAG (See March of Comics #10)

OUT OF THE NIGHT (The Hooded Horseman #18 on)
Amer. Comics Group (Creston/Scope): Feb-Mar, 1952 - No. 17, Oct-Nov, 1954

1-Williamson/LeDoux-a (9 pgs.) 59.00 176.00 470.00
2-Williamson-a (5 pgs.) 46.00 137.00 365.00
3,5-10: 9-Sci/Fic story 25.00 75.00 175.00
4-Williamson-a (7 pgs.) 40.00 120.00 300.00
11-17: 13-Nostrand-a? 17-E.C. Wood swipe 19.00 58.00 135.00
NOTE: ***Landau*** *a-14, 16, 17.* ***Shelly*** *a-12.*

OUT OF THE SHADOWS
Standard Comics/Visual Editions: No. 5, July, 1952 - No. 14, Aug, 1954

5-Toth-p; Moreira, Tuska-a; Roussos-c 46.00 139.00 370.00
6-Toth/Celardo-a; Katz-a(2) 36.00 107.00 250.00
7,9: 7-Jack Katz-c/a(2). 9-Crandall-a(2) 26.00 77.00 180.00
8-Katz shrunken head-c 34.00 103.00 240.00
10-Spider-c; Sekowsky-a 23.00 69.00 160.00
11-Toth-a, 2 pgs.; Katz-a; Andru-c 26.00 77.00 180.00
12-Toth/Peppe-a(2); Katz-a 34.00 103.00 240.00
13-Cannabalism story; Sekowsky-a; Roussos-c 29.00 86.00 200.00

Out of This World #8 © CC

Ozark Ike #12 © KING

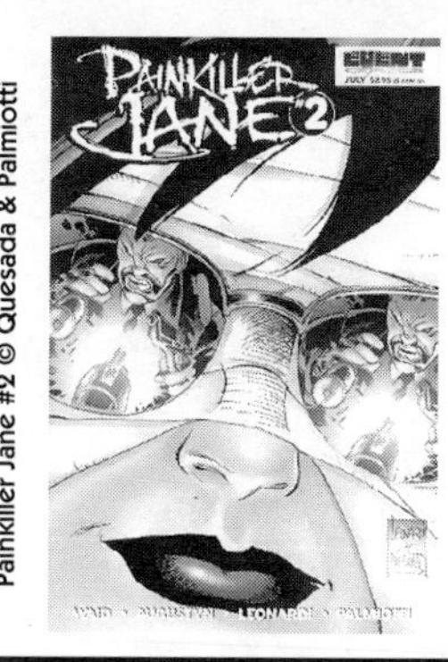

Painkiller Jane #2 © Quesada & Palmiotti

GD2.0 FN6.0 NM9.4

14-Toth-a 26.00 77.00 180.00

OUT OF THE VORTEX (Comics' Greatest World:... #1-4)
Dark Horse Comics: Oct., 1993 - No. 12, Oct, 1994 ($2.00, limited series)

1-11: 1-Foil logo. 4-Dorman-c(p). 6-Hero Zero x-over 2.00
12 ($2.50) 2.50

NOTE: ***Art Adams*** *c-7.* ***Golden*** *c-8.* ***Mignola*** *c-2.* ***Simonson*** *c-3.* ***Zeck*** *c-10.*

OUT OF THIS WORLD
Charlton Comics: Aug, 1956 - No. 16, Dec, 1959

1 23.00 69.00 160.00
2 11.50 34.00 80.00
3-6-Ditko-c/a (3) each 29.00 86.00 200.00
7-(2/58, 15¢, 68 pgs.)-Ditko-c/a(4) 29.00 86.00 200.00
8-(5/58, 15¢, 68 pgs.)-Ditko-a(2) 24.00 73.00 170.00
9,10,12,16-Ditko-a 20.00 60.00 140.00
11-Ditko c/a (3) 23.00 69.00 160.00
13-15 9.15 27.00 55.00

NOTE: ***Ditko*** *c-3-12, 16.* ***Reinman*** *a-10.*

OUT OF THIS WORLD (...Adventures #2)
Avon Periodicals: June, 1950; No. 2, Dec, 1950 (25¢ pulp)

1-Kubert-a(2) (one reprinted/Eerie #1, 1947) plus Crom the Barbarian by Gardner Fox & John Giunta (origin); Fawcette-c 59.00 176.00 470.00
2-Kubert-a plus The Spider God of Akka by Gardner Fox & John Giunta. pulp magazine w/comic insert 43.00 129.00 345.00

NOTE: *Out of This World Adventures is a sci-fi pulp magazine w/32 pgs. of color comics.*

OUT OUR WAY WITH WORRY WART
Dell Publishing Co.: No. 680, Feb, 1956

Four Color 680 1.80 5.50 20.00

OUTPOSTS
Blackthorne Publishing: June, 1987 - No. 4, 1987 ($1.25)

1-4: 1-Kaluta-c(p) 2.00

OUTSIDERS, THE
DC Comics: Nov, 1985 - No. 28, Feb, 1988

1 3.00
2-28: 18-26-Batman returns. 21-Intro. Strike Force Kobra; 1st app. Clayface IV 22-E.C. parody; Orlando-a. 21- 25-Atomic Knight app. 27,28-Millennium tie-ins. 2.25
Annual 1 (12/86, $2.50), Special 1 (7/87, $1.50) 2.50

NOTE: ***Aparo*** *a-1-7, 9-14, 17-22, 25, 26; c-1-7, 9-14, 17, 19-26.* ***Byrne*** *a-11.* ***Bolland*** *a-6, 18; c-16.* ***Ditko*** *a-13p.* ***Erik Larsen*** *a-24, 27 28; c-27, 28.* ***Morrow*** *a-12.*

OUTSIDERS
DC Comics: Nov, 1993 - No. 24, Nov, 1995 ($1.75/$1.95/$2.25)

1-11,0,12-24: 1-Alpha; Travis Charest-c. 1-Omega; Travis Charest-c. 5-Atomic Knight app. 8-New Batman-c/story. 11-(9/94)-Zero Hour. 0-(10/94).12-(11/94). 21-Darkseid cameo. 22-New Gods app. 2.25

OVER THE EDGE
Marvel Comics: Nov, 1995 - No. 10, Aug, 1996 (99¢)

1-10: 1,6,10-Daredevil-c/story. 2,7-Dr. Strange-c/story. 3-Hulk-c/story. 4,9-Ghost Rider-c/story. 5-Punisher-c/story. 8-Elektra-c/story 2.00

OWL, THE (See Crackajack Funnies #25, Popular Comics #72 and Occult Files of Dr. Spektor #22)
Gold Key: April, 1967; No. 2, April, 1968

1,2-Written by Jerry Siegel; '40s super hero 3.80 11.40 38.00

OZ (See First Comics Graphic Novel, Marvel Treaury Of Oz & MGM's Marvelous...)

OZ
Caliber Press: 1994 - 1997 ($2.95, B&W)

0-22 3.00
1 ($5.95)-Limited Edition; double-c 6.00
...Specials: Freedom Fighters. Lion. Scarecrow. Tin Man 3.00

OZARK IKE
Dell Publishing Co./Standard Comics B11 on: Feb, 1948; Nov, 1948 - No. 24, Dec, 1951; No. 25, Sept, 1952

Four Color 180(1948-Dell) 9.50 29.00 105.00
B11, B12, 13-15 8.35 25.00 50.00
16-25 6.35 19.00 38.00

OZ: DAEMONSTORM
Caliber Press: 1997 ($3.95, B&W, one-shot)

1 4.00

OZ: ROMANCE IN RAGS
Caliber Press: 1996 ($2.95, B&W, limited series)

1-3, ..Special 3.00

OZ SQUAD
Brave New Worlds/Patchwork Press: 1992 - No. 4, 1994 ($2.50/$2.75, B&W)

1-4-Patchwork Press 2.75

OZ SQUAD
Patchwork Press: Dec, 1995 - No. 10, 1996 ($2.95, B&W)

1 ($3.95)-10 3.00

OZ: STRAW AND SORCERY
Caliber Press: 1997 ($2.95, B&W, limited series)

1-3 3.00

OZ-WONDERLAND WARS, THE
DC Comics: Jan, 1986 - No. 3, March, 1986 (Mini-series)

1-3-Capt Carrot app. 3.00

OZZIE & BABS (TV Teens #14 on)
Fawcett Publications: Dec, 1947 - No. 13, Fall, 1949

1-Teen-age 8.35 25.00 50.00
2 4.25 13.00 26.00
3-13 4.00 10.00 20.00

OZZIE AND HARRIET (The Adventures of... on cover) (Radio)
National Periodical Publications: Oct-Nov, 1949 - No. 5, June-July, 1950

1-Photo-c 90.00 270.00 720.00
2 45.00 135.00 360.00
3-5 40.00 120.00 290.00

PACIFIC COMICS GRAPHIC NOVEL (See Image Graphic Novel)

PACIFIC PRESENTS (Also see Starslayer #2, 3)
Pacific Comics: Oct, 1982 - No. 2, Apr, 1983; No. 3, Mar, 1984 - No. 4, Jun, 1984

1-Chapter 3 of The Rocketeer; Stevens-c/a; Bettie Page model 2.40 6.00
2-Chapter 4 of The Rocketeer (4th app.); nudity; Stevens-c/a 2.40 6.00
3,4: 3-1st app. Vanity 2.00

NOTE: ***Conrad*** *a-3, 4; c-3.* ***Ditko*** *a-1-3; c-1(1/2).* ***Dave Stevens*** *a-1, 2; c-1(1/2), 2.*

PACT, THE
Image Comics: Feb, 1994 - No. 3, June, 1994 ($1.95, limited series)

1-3: Valentino co-scripts & layouts 2.00

PAGEANT OF COMICS (See Jane Arden & Mopsy)
Archer St. John: Sept, 1947 - No. 2, Oct, 1947

1,2: 1-Mopsy strip-r. 2-Jane Arden strip-r 9.15 27.00 55.00

PAINKILLER JANE
Event Comics: June, 1997 - Present ($3.95/$2.95)

1-Augustyn/Waid-s/Leonardi/Palmiotti-a, variant-c 4.00
2-5: Two covers (Quesada, Leonardi) 3.00
0-(1/99, $3.95) Retells origin; two covers 4.00

PAINKILLER JANE / DARKCHYLDE
Event Comics: Oct, 1998 ($2.95, one-shot)

Preview-($6.95) DF Edition, 1-($6.95) DF Edition 7.00
1-Three covers; J.G. Jones-a 3.00

PAINKILLER JANE / HELLBOY
Event Comics: Aug, 1998 ($2.95, one-shot)

1-Leonardi & Palmiotti-a 3.00

PAINKILLER JANE VS. THE DARKNESS

Pakkin's Land: Forgotten Dreams #1 © Gary adn Rhoda Shipman

Pandemonium #1 © Chaos!

Panic #5 © WMG

Event Comics: Apr, 1997 ($2.95, one-shot)

1-Ennis-s; four variant-c (Conner, Hildebrandts, Quesada, Silvestri) 3.50

PAKKIN'S LAND
Caliber Comics (Tapestry): 1996 - No. 6 ($2.95, B&W)

1-Gary and Rhoda Shipman-s/a 1.25 3.75 10.00
2,3 2.40 6.00
1-3-2nd printing 3.00
4-6,0 4.00

PAKKIN'S LAND: FORGOTTEN DREAMS
Caliber Comics: Apr, 1998 - No. 4 ($2.95, B&W)

1-4-Gary and Rhoda Shipman-s/a 3.00

PAKKIN'S LAND: QUEST FOR KINGS
Caliber Comics: Aug, 1997 - No. 6, Mar, 1998 ($2.95, B&W)

1-6: 1-Gary and Rhoda Shipman-s/a; Jeff Smith var-c 3.00

PANCHO VILLA
Avon Periodicals: 1950

nn-Kinstler-c 24.00 71.00 165.00

PANDEMONIUM
Chaos! Comics: Sept, 1998 ($2.95, one-shot)

1-Al Rio-c 3.00

PANDORA
Avatar Press: Jan, 1997 - No. 2, Feb, 1997 ($3.00, B&W, limited series)

0,1,2: 1-Lindo-c 3.00
...Demonography (5/97, $3.00) 3.00

PANHANDLE PETE AND JENNIFER (TV) (See Gene Autry #20)
J. Charles Laue Publishing Co.: July, 1951 - No. 3, Nov, 1951

1 10.00 30.00 60.00
2,3 6.70 20.00 40.00

PANIC (Companion to Mad)
E. C. Comics (Tiny Tot Comics): Feb-Mar, 1954 - No. 12, Dec-Jan, 1955-56

1-Used in Senate Investigation hearings; Elder draws entire E. C. staff; Santa Claus & Mickey Spillane parody 22.00 66.00 220.00
2 10.00 30.00 100.00
3,4: 3-Senate Subcommittee parody; Davis draws Gaines, Feldstein & Kelly, 1 pg.; Old King Cole smokes marijuana. 4-Infinity-c; John Wayne parody 9.00 27.00 90.00
5-11: 8-Last pre-code issue (5/55). 9-Superman, Smilin' Jack & Dick Tracy app. on-c; has photo of Walter Winchell on-c. 11-Wheedies cereal box-c 8.00 24.00 80.00
12 (Low distribution; thousands were destroyed) 10.00 30.00 100.00

NOTE: *Davis a-1-12; c-12. Elder a-1-12. Feldstein c-1-3, 5. Kamen a-1. Orlando a-1-9. Wolverton c-4, panel-3. Wood a-2-9, 11, 12.*

PANIC (Magazine) (Satire)
Panic Publ.: July, 1958 - No. 6, July, 1959; V2#10, Dec, 1965 - V2#12, 1966

1 10.00 30.00 70.00
2-6 6.35 19.00 38.00
V2#10-12: Reprints earlier issues 2.60 7.80 26.00

NOTE: *Davis a-3(2 pgs.), 4, 5, 10; c-10. Elder a-5. Powell a-V2#10, 11. Torres a-1-5. Tuska a-V2#11.*

PANIC
Gemstone Publishing: March, 1997 - Present ($2.50, quarterly)

1-11: E.C. reprints 2.50

PANTHA (See Vampirella-The New Monthly #16,17)

PANTHA: HAUNTED PASSION (Also see Vampirella Monthly #0)
Harris Comics: May, 1997 ($2.95, B&W, one-shot)

1-r/Vampirella #30,31 3.00

PARADAX (Also see Strange Days)
Eclipse Comics: 1986 (one-shot)

1 2.00

PARADAX
Vortex Comics: April, 1987 - No. 2, Aug, 1987 ($1.75, mature)

1,2-Nudity, adult language 2.00

PARADE (See Hanna-Barbera...)

PARADE COMICS (Frisky Animals on Parade #2 on)
Ajax/Farrell Publ. (World Famous Publ.): Sept, 1957

1 6.35 19.00 38.00

NOTE: *Cover title: Frisky Animals on Parade.*

PARADE OF PLEASURE
Derric Verschoyle Ltd., London, England: 1954 (192 pgs.) (Hardback book)

By Geoffrey Wagner. Contains section devoted to the censorship of American comic books with illustrations in color and black and white. (Also see **Seduction of the Innocent**). Distributed in USA by Library Publishers, N. Y. 40.00 120.00 285.00
with dust jacket.... 75.00 225.00 600.00

PARADOX
Dark Visions Publ: June, 1994 - No. 2, Aug, 1994 ($2.95, B&W, mature)

1,2: 1-Linsner-c. 2-Boris-c. 3.00

PARALLAX: EMERALD NIGHT (See Final Night)
DC Comics: Nov, 1996 ($2.95, one-shot, 48 pgs.)

1-Final Night tie-in; Green Lantern (Kyle Rayner) app. 4.00

PARAMOUNT ANIMATED COMICS (See Harvey Comics Hits #60, 62)
Harvey Publications: No. 3, Feb, 1953 - No. 22, July, 1956

3-Baby Huey, Herman & Katnip, Buzzy the Crow begin 20.00 60.00 140.00
4-6 10.00 30.00 60.00
7-Baby Huey becomes permanent cover feature; cover title becomes Baby Huey with #9 19.00 58.00 135.00
8-10: 9-Infinity-c 9.15 27.00 55.00
11-22 6.70 20.00 40.00

PARENT TRAP, THE (Disney)
Dell Publishing Co.: No. 1210, Oct-Dec, 1961

Four Color 1210-Movie, Haley Mills photo-c 8.00 25.00 90.00

PARODY
Armour Publishing: Mar, 1977 - No. 3, Aug, 1977 (B&W humor magazine)

1 2.00 6.00 16.00
2,3: 2-King Kong, Happy Days. 3-Charlie's Angels, Rocky 1.50 4.50 12.00

PAROLE BREAKERS
Avon Periodicals/Realistic #2 on: Dec, 1951 - No. 3, July, 1952

1(#2 on inside)-r-c/Avon paperback #283 (painted) 40.00 120.00 300.00
2-Kubert-a; r-c/Avon paperback #114 (photo-c) 30.00 90.00 210.00
3-Kinstler-c 27.00 81.00 190.00

PARTRIDGE FAMILY, THE (TV)(Also see David Cassidy)
Charlton Comics: Mar, 1971 - No. 21, Dec, 1973

1 5.00 15.00 50.00
2-4,6-10 2.50 7.50 22.00
5-Partridge Family Summer Special (52 pgs.); The Shadow, Lone Ranger, Charlie McCarthy, Flash Gordon, Hopalong Cassidy, Gene Autry & others app. 5.50 16.50 60.00
11-21 2.25 6.75 18.00

PARTS UNKNOWN
Eclipse Comics/FX: July, 1992 - No. 4, Oct, 1992 ($2.50, B&W, mature)

1-4: All contain FX gaming cards 2.50

PASSION, THE
Catechetical Guild: No. 394, 1955

394 4.00 10.00 20.00

PASSOVER (See Avengelyne)
Maximum Press: Dec, 1996 ($2.99, one-shot)

Pat Boone #2 © DC

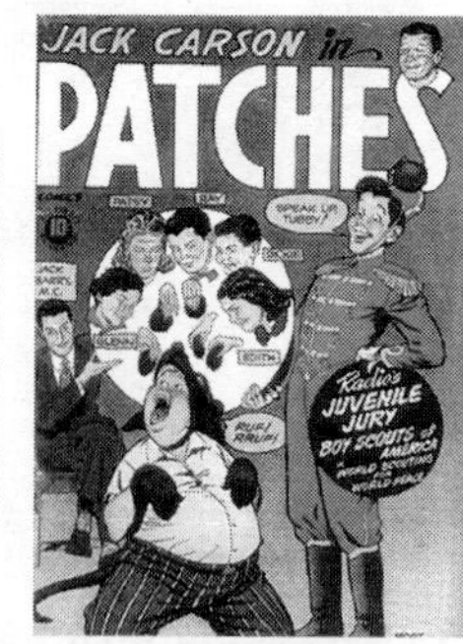

Patches #10 © Patches Publ.

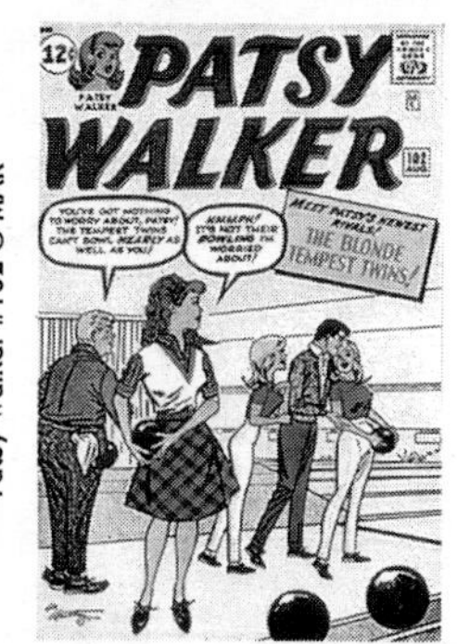

Patsy Walker #102 © MAR

GD2.0 FN6.0 NM9.4

1 3.00

PAT BOONE (TV)(Also see Superman's Girlfriend Lois Lane #9)
National Per. Publ.: Sept-Oct, 1959 - No. 5, May-Jun, 1960 (All have photo-c)

1 41.00 122.00 320.00
2-5: 3-Fabian, Connie Francis & Paul Anka photos on-c. 4-Previews "Journey To The Center Of The Earth". 4-Johnny Mathis & Bobbie Darin photos on-c. 5-Dick Clark & Frankie Avalon photos on-c 36.00 107.00 250.00

PATCHES
Rural Home/Patches Publ. (Orbit): Mar-Apr, 1945 - No. 11, Nov, 1947

1-L. B. Cole-c 36.00 107.00 250.00
2 13.00 39.00 90.00
3,4,6,8-11: 6-Henry Aldrich story. 8-Smiley Burnette-c/s (6/47); pre-dates Smiley Burnette #1. 9-Mr. District Attorney story (radio). Leav/Keigstein-a (16 pgs.). 9-11-Leav-c. 10-Jack Carson (radio) c/story; Leav-c. 11-Red Skelton story 12.00 36.00 85.00
5-Danny Kaye-c/story; L.B. Cole-c. 19.00 56.00 130.00
7-Hopalong Cassidy-c/story 15.00 45.00 105.00

PATHWAYS TO FANTASY
Pacific Comics: July, 1984

1-Barry Smith-c/a; Jeff Jones-a (4 pgs.) 3.00

PATORUZU (See Adventures of...)

PATSY & HEDY (Teenage)(Also see Hedy Wolfe)
Atlas Comics/Marvel (GPI/Male): Feb, 1952 - No. 110, Feb, 1967

1-Patsy Walker & Hedy Wolfe; Al Jaffee-c 20.00 60.00 140.00
2 11.00 33.00 75.00
3-10: 3,8-Al Jaffee-c 9.15 27.00 55.00
11-20 6.70 20.00 40.00
21-40 5.35 16.00 32.00
41-60 2.50 7.50 24.00
61-80,100: 88-Lingerie panel 2.25 6.75 18.00
81-87,89-99,101-110 2.00 6.00 16.00
Annual 1(1963)-Early Marvel annual 8.50 25.50 85.00

PATSY & HER PALS (Teenage)
Atlas Comics (PPI): May, 1953 - No. 29, Aug, 1957

1-Patsy Walker 17.00 51.00 120.00
2 10.00 30.00 60.00
3-10 8.35 25.00 50.00
11-29: 24-Everett-c 5.85 17.50 35.00

PATSY WALKER (See All Teen, A Date With Patsy, Girls' Life, Miss America Magazine, Patsy & Hedy, Patsy & Her Pals & Teen Comics)
Marvel/Atlas Comics (BPC): 1945 (no month) - No. 124, Dec, 1965

1-Teenage 45.00 135.00 360.00
2 23.00 69.00 160.00
3,4,6-10 18.00 54.00 125.00
5-Injury-to-eye-c; spanking panel 21.00 62.00 145.00
11,12,15,16,18 11.50 34.00 80.00
13,14,17,19-22-Kurtzman's "Hey Look" 12.00 36.00 85.00
23,24 10.00 30.00 60.00
25-Rusty by Kurtzman; painted-c 12.00 36.00 85.00
26-29,31: 26-31: 52 pgs. 8.35 25.00 50.00
30(52 pgs.)-Egghead Doodle by Kurtzman (1 pg.) 9.15 27.00 55.00
32-57: Last precode (3/55) 5.00 15.00 30.00
58-80,100 2.50 7.50 24.00
81-99: 92,98-Millie x-over 2.25 6.75 18.00
101-124 2.00 6.00 16.00
Fashion Parade 1(1966, 68 pgs.) (Beware cut-out & marked pages) 6.50 19.50 65.00

NOTE: *Painted c-25-28. Anti-Wertham editorial in #21. Georgie app. in #8, 11. Millie app. in #10, 92, 98. Mitzi app. in #11. Rusty app. in #12, 25. Willie app. in #12.* ***Al Jaffee*** *c-57, 58.*

PAT THE BRAT (Adventures of Pipsqueak #34 on)
Archie Publications (Radio): June, 1953; Summer, 1955 - No. 4, 5/56; No. 15, 7/56 - No. 33, 7/59

nn(6/53) 12.00 36.00 85.00
1(Summer, 1955) 9.15 27.00 55.00
2-4-(5/56) (#5-14 not published) 5.35 16.00 32.00
15-(7/56)-33 2.50 7.50 20.00

PAT THE BRAT COMICS DIGEST MAGAZINE
Archie Publications: October, 1980

1-Li'l Jinx & Super Duck app. 1.75 5.25 14.00

PATTY CAKE
Permanent Press: Mar, 1995 - No. 9, Jul, 1996 ($2.95, B&W)

1-9: Scott Roberts-s/a 3.00

PATTY CAKE
Caliber Press (Tapestry): Oct, 1996 - No. 3, Apr, 1997 ($2.95, B&W)

1-3: Scott Roberts-s/a, ...Christmas (12/96) 3.00

PATTY CAKE & FRIENDS
Slave Labor Graphics: Nov, 1997 - Present ($2.95, B&W)

Here There Be Monsters (10/97), 1-14: Scott Roberts-s/a 3.00

PATTY POWERS (Formerly Della Vision #3)
Atlas Comics: No. 4, Oct, 1955 - No. 7, Oct, 1956

4 9.15 27.00 55.00
5-7 4.25 13.00 28.00

PAT WILTON (See Mighty Midget Comics)

PAUL
Spire Christian Comics (Fleming H. Revell Co.): 1978 (49¢)

nn 5.00

PAULINE PERIL (See The Close Shaves of...)

PAUL REVERE'S RIDE (TV, Disney, see Walt Disney Showcase #34)
Dell Publishing Co.: No. 822, July, 1957

Four Color 822-w/Johnny Tremain, Toth-a 9.00 27.00 100.00

PAUL TERRY'S ADVENTURES OF MIGHTY MOUSE (See Adventures of...)

PAUL TERRY'S COMICS (Formerly Terry-Toons Comics; becomes Adventures of Mighty Mouse No. 126 on)
St. John Publishing Co.: No. 85, Mar, 1951 - No. 125, May, 1955

85,86-Same as Terry-Toons #85, & 86 with only a title change; published at same time?; Mighty Mouse, Heckle & Jeckle & Gandy Goose continue from Terry-Toons 10.00 30.00 70.00
87-99 7.00 21.00 42.00
100 8.35 25.00 50.00
101-104,107-125: 121,122,125-Painted-c 6.70 20.00 40.00
105,106-Giant Comics Edition (25¢, 100 pgs.) (9/53 & ?). 105-Little Roquefort-c/story 17.00 51.00 120.00

PAUL TERRY'S MIGHTY MOUSE (See Mighty Mouse)

PAUL TERRY'S MIGHTY MOUSE ADVENTURE STORIES (See Mighty Mouse Adventure Stories)

PAUL THE SAMURAI (See The Tick #4)
New England Comics: July, 1992 - No. 6, July, 1993 ($2.75, B&W)

1-6 2.75

PAWNEE BILL
Story Comics (Youthful Magazines?): Feb, 1951 - No. 3, July, 1951

1-Bat Masterson, Wyatt Earp app. 11.50 34.00 80.00
2,3: 3-Origin Golden Warrior; Cameron-a 7.50 22.50 45.00

PAY-OFF (This Is the..., ...Crime, ...Detective Stories)
D. S. Publishing Co.: July-Aug, 1948 - No. 5, Mar-Apr, 1949 (52 pgs.)

1-True Crime Cases #1,2 23.00 69.00 160.00
2 13.50 41.00 95.00
3-5-Thrilling Detective Stories 12.00 36.00 85.00

PEACEMAKER, THE (Also see Fightin' Five)
Charlton Comics: V3#1, Mar, 1967 - No. 5, Nov, 1967 (All 12¢ cover price)

Peanuts #1 © UFS

Penny #6 © AVON

Penny Century #5 © Jaime Hernandez

	GD2.0	FN6.0	NM9.4
1-Fightin' Five begins	3.50	10.50	35.00
2,3,5	2.50	7.50	20.00
4-Origin The Peacemaker	3.20	9.60	32.00
1,2(Modern Comics reprint, 1978)			3.00

PEACEMAKER (Also see Crisis On Infinite Earths & Showcase '93 #7,9,10)
DC Comics: Jan, 1988 - No. 4, Apr, 1988 ($1.25, limited series)

1-4 2.00

PEANUTS (Charlie Brown) (See Fritzi Ritz, Nancy & Sluggo, Tip Top, Tip Topper & United Comics)
Dell Publishing Co./Gold Key: 1953-54; No. 878, 2/58 - No. 13, 5-7/62; 5/63 - No. 4, 2/64

	GD2.0	FN6.0	NM9.4
1(1953-54)-Reprints United Features' Strange As It Seems, Willie, Ferdnand	11.00	33.00	120.00
Four Color 878(#1)	14.00	41.00	150.00
Four Color 969,1015('59)	10.00	30.00	110.00
4(2-4/60)	8.00	23.00	85.00
5-13	5.50	16.50	60.00
1(Gold Key, 5/63)	10.50	31.00	115.00
2-4	6.25	18.50	70.00

PEBBLES & BAMM BAMM (TV) (See Cave Kids #7, 12)
Charlton Comics: Jan, 1972 - No. 36, Dec, 1976 (Hanna-Barbera)

	GD2.0	FN6.0	NM9.4
1-From the Flintstones; "Teen Age..." on cover	4.00	12.00	45.00
2-10	2.50	7.50	22.00
11-20	2.00	6.00	16.00
21-36	1.50	4.50	12.00

PEBBLES & BAMM BAMM (TV)
Harvey Comics: Nov, 1993 - No. 3, Mar, 1994 ($1.50) (Hanna-Barbera)

V2#1-3 3.00
...Giant Size 1 (10/93, $2.25, 68 pgs.)("Summer Special" on-c) 3.00

PEBBLES FLINTSTONE (TV) (See The Flintstones #11)
Gold Key: Sept, 1963 (Hanna-Barbera)

	GD2.0	FN6.0	NM9.4
1 (10088-309)-Early Pebbles app.	9.00	27.00	100.00

PEDRO (Formerly My Private Life #17; also see Romeo Tubbs)
Fox Features Syndicate: No. 18, June, 1950 - No. 2, Aug, 1950?

	GD2.0	FN6.0	NM9.4
18(#1)-Wood-c/a(p)	21.00	64.00	150.00
2-Wood-a?	16.00	47.00	110.00

PEE-WEE PIXIES (See The Pixies)

PELLEAS AND MELISANDE (See Night Music #4, 5)

PENALTY (See Crime Must Pay the...)

PENDRAGON (Knights of... #5 on; also see Knights of...)
Marvel Comics UK, Ltd.: July, 1992 - No. 15, Sept, 1993 ($1.75)

1-15: 1-4-Iron Man app. 6-8-Spider-Man app. 2.00

PENDULUM ILLUSTRATED BIOGRAPHIES
Pendulum Press: 1979 (B&W)

19-355x-George Washington/Thomas Jefferson, 19-3495-Charles Lindbergh/Amelia Earhart, 19-3509-Harry Houdini/Walt Disney, 19-3517-Davy Crockett/Daniel Boone-Redondo-a, 19-3525-Elvis Presley/Beatles, 19-3533-Benjamin Franklin/Martin Luther King Jr, 19-3541-Abraham Lincoln/Franklin D. Roosevelt, 19-3568-Marie Curie/Albert Einstein-Redondo-a, 19-3576-Thomas Edison/Alexander Graham Bell-Redondo-a, 19-3584-Vince Lombardi/Pele, 19-3592-Babe Ruth/Jackie Robinson, 19-3606-Jim Thorpe/Althea Gibson

Softback 2.00
Hardback 4.50

NOTE: *Above books still available from publisher.*

PENDULUM ILLUSTRATED CLASSICS (Now Age Illustrated)
Pendulum Press: 1973 - 1978 (75¢, 62pp, B&W, 5-3/8x8")
(Also see Marvel Classics)

64-100x(1973)-Dracula-Redondo art, 64-131x-The Invisible Man-Nino art, 64-0968-Dr. Jekyll and Mr. Hyde-Redondo art, 64-1005-Black Beauty, 64-1010-Call of the Wild, 64-1020-Frankenstein, 64-1025-Hucklebury Finn, 64-1030-Moby Dick-Nino-a, 64-1040-Red Badge of Courage, 64-1045-The Time Machine-Nino-a, 64-1050-Tom Sawyer, 64-1055-Twenty Thousand Leagues Under the Sea, 64-1069-Treasure Island, 64-1328(1974)-Kidnapped, 64-1336-Three Musketeers-Nino art, 64-1344-A Tale of Two Cities, 64-1352-Journey to the Center of the Earth, 64-1360-The War of the Worlds-Nino-a, 64-1379-The Greatest Advs. of Sherlock Holmes-Redondo art, 64-1387-Mysterious Island, 64-1395-Hunchback of Notre Dame, 64-1409-Helen Keller-story of my life, 64-1417-Scarlet Letter, 64-1425-Gulliver's Travels, 64-2618(1977)-Around the World in Eighty Days, 64-2626-Captains Courageous, 64-2634-Connecticut Yankee, 64-2642-The Hound of the Baskervilles, 64-2650-The House of Seven Gables, 64-2669-Jane Eyre, 64-2677-The Last of the Mohicans, 64-2685-The Best of O'Henry, 64-2693-The Best of Poe-Redondo-a, 64-2707-Two Years Before the Mast, 64-2715-White Fang, 64-2723-Wuthering Heights, 64-3126(1978)-Ben Hur-Redondo art, 64-3134-A Christmas Carol, 64-3142-The Food of the Gods, 64-3150-Ivanhoe, 64-3169-The Man in the Iron Mask, 64-3177-The Prince and the Pauper, 64-3185-The Prisoner of Zenda, 64-3193-The Return of the Native, 64-3207-Robinson Crusoe, 64-3215-The Scarlet Pimpernel, 64-3223-The Sea Wolf, 64-3231-The Swiss Family Robinson, 64-3851-Billy Budd, 64-386x-Crime and Punishment, 64-3878-Don Quixote, 64-3886-Great Expectations, 64-3894-Heidi, 64-3908-The Iliad, 64-3916-Lord Jim, 64-3924-The Mutiny on Board H.M.S. Bounty, 64-3932-The Odyssey, 64-3940-Oliver Twist, 64-3959-Pride and Prejudice, 64-3967-The Turn of the Screw

Softback 2.00
Hardback 4.50

NOTE: *All of the above books can be ordered from the publisher; some were reprinted as Marvel Classic Comics #1-12. In 1972 there was another brief series of 12 titles which contained Classics Ill. artwork. They were entitled* **Now Age Books** *Illustrated, but can be easily distinguished from later series by the small Classics Illustrated logo at the top of the front cover. The format is the same as the later series. The 48 pg. C.I. art was stretched out to make 62 pgs. After Twin Circle Publ. terminated the Classics Ill. series in 1971, they made a one year contract with Pendulum Press to print these twelve titles of C.I. art. Pendulum was unhappy with the contract, and at the end of 1972 began their own art series, utilizing the talents of the Filipino artist group. One detail which makes this rather confusing is that when they redid the art in 1973, they gave it the same identifying no. as the 1972 series. All 12 of the 1972 C.I. editions have new covers, taken from internal art panels. In spite of their recent age, all of the 1972 C.I. series are very rare. Mint copies would fetch at least $50. Here is a list of the 1972 series, with C.I. title no. counterpart:*

64-1005 (CI#60-A2) 64-1010 (CI#91) 64-1015 (CI-Jr #503) 64-1020 (CI#26)
64-1025 (CI#19-A2) 64-1030 (CI#5-A2) 64-1035 (CI#169) 64-1040 (CI#98)
64-1045 (CI#133) 64-1050 (CI#50-A2) 64-1055 (CI#47) 64-1060 (CI-Jr#535)

PENDULUM ILLUSTRATED ORIGINALS
Pendulum Press: 1979 (In color)

94-4254-Solarman: The Beginning (See Solarman) 3.00

PENDULUM'S ILLUSTRATED STORIES
Pendulum Press: 1990 - No. 72, 1990? (No cover price ($4.95), squarebound, 68 pgs.)

1-72: Reprints Pendulum Ill. Classics series 5.00

PENNY
Avon Comics: 1947 - No. 6, Sept-Oct, 1949 (Newspaper reprints)

	GD2.0	FN6.0	NM9.4
1-Photo & biography of creator	11.00	33.00	75.00
2-5	7.50	22.50	45.00
6-Perry Como photo on-c	8.35	25.00	50.00

PENNY CENTURY (See Love and Rockets)
Fantagraphics Books: Dec, 1997 - Present ($2.95, B&W, mini-series)

1-5-Jaime Hernandez-s/a 3.00

PENTHOUSE COMIX
General Media Int.: 1994 - No. 33, July, 1998 ($4.95, bimonthly, magazine, mature)

	GD2.0	FN6.0	NM9.4
1	1.00	3.00	8.00
2-5		2.40	6.00
6-33: 15-Corben-c. 16-Dorman-c. 17-Manara-c. 20-Chiodo-c. 21,23-Boris-c 24-Scott Hampton-c. 26-33-Comic-sized			5.00

PENTHOUSE MAX
General Media International: July, 1996 - No. 3 ($4.95, magazine, mature)

1-3: 1-Giffen, Sears, Maguire-a. 2-Political satire. 3-Mr. Monster-c/app.; Dorman-c 5.00

PENTHOUSE MEN'S ADVENTURE COMIX
General Media International: 1995 - No. 7, 1996 ($4.95, magazine, mature)

1-7 (Magazine Size): 1-Boris-c, 1-5 (Comic Size): 1-Boris-c 5.00

PEP COMICS (See Archie Giant Series #576, 589, 601, 614, 624)
MLJ Magazines/Archie Publications No. 56 (3/46) on: Jan, 1940 - No. 411, Mar, 1987

Pep Comics #8 © AP

Pep Comics #41 © AP

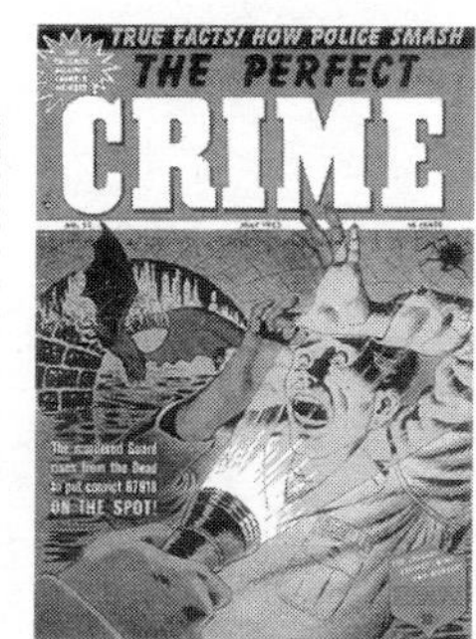

Perfect Crime #33 © Cross Publ.

GD2.0 FN6.0 NM9.4

	GD2.0	FN6.0	VF8.0	NM9.4
1-Intro. The Shield (1st patriotic hero) by Irving Novick; origin & 1st app. The Comet by Jack Cole, The Queen of Diamonds & Kayo Ward; The Rocket, The Press Guardian (The Falcon #1 only), Sergeant Boyle, Fu Chang, & Bentley of of Scotland Yard; Robot-c; Shield-c begin	700.00	2100.00	4200.00	7200.00

	GD2.0	FN6.0	NM9.4
2-Origin The Rocket	212.00	637.00	1700.00
3	156.00	469.00	1250.00
4-Wizard cameo	125.00	375.00	1000.00
5-Wizard cameo in Shield story	125.00	375.00	1000.00
6-10: 8-Last Cole Comet; no Cole-a in #6,7	97.00	291.00	775.00
11-Dusty, Shield's sidekick begins (1st app.); last Press Guardian, Fu Chang	103.00	309.00	825.00
12-Origin & 1st app. Fireball (2/41); last Rocket & Queen of Diamonds; Danny in Wonderland begins	125.00	375.00	1000.00
13-15	78.00	234.00	625.00
16-Origin Madam Satan; blood drainage-c	125.00	375.00	1000.00
17-Origin/1st app. The Hangman (7/41); death of The Comet; Comet is revealed as Hangman's brother	300.00	900.00	2700.00
18-21: 20-Last Fireball. 21-Last Madam Satan	78.00	234.00	625.00

	GD2.0	FN6.0	VF8.0	NM9.4
22-Intro. & 1st app. Archie, Betty, & Jughead(12/41); (also see Jackpot)	1000.00	3000.00	6000.00	11,000.00

	GD2.0	FN6.0	NM9.4
23	137.00	412.00	1100.00
24,25: 24-Coach Kleets app. (unnamed until Archie #94); bondage/torture-c. 25-1st app. Archie's jalopy; 1st skinny Mr. Weatherbee prototype	106.00	319.00	850.00
26-1st app. Veronica Lodge (4/42)	150.00	450.00	1200.00
27-30: 29-Origin Shield retold; 30-Capt. Commando begins; bondage/torture-c; 1st Miss Grundy (definitive version); see Jackpot #4	87.00	262.00	700.00
31-35: 31-MLJ offices & artists are visited in Sgt. Boyle story; 1st app. Mr. Lodge. 32-Shield dons new costume. 34-Bondage/Hypo-c. 33-Pre-Moose tryout (see Jughead #1)	69.00	206.00	550.00
36-1st Archie-c (2/43) w/Shield & Hangman	162.00	487.00	1300.00
37-40	50.00	150.00	400.00
41-50: 41-Archie-c begin. 47-Last Hangman issue; infinity-c. 48-Black Hood begins (5/44); ends #51,59,60	37.00	111.00	260.00
51-60: 52-Suzie begins. 56-Last Capt. Commando. 59-Black Hood not in costume; spanking & lingerie panels; Archie dresses as his aunt; Suzie ends. 60-Katy Keene begins(3/47), ends #154	25.00	75.00	175.00
61-65-Last Shield. 62-1st app. Li'l Jinx (7/47)	21.00	62.00	145.00
66-80: 66-G-Man Club becomes Archie Club (2/48); Nevada Jones by Bill Woggon. 78-1st app. Dilton	13.00	39.00	90.00
81-99	10.00	30.00	70.00
100	12.00	36.00	85.00
101-130	5.85	17.50	35.00
131(2/59)-149(9/61)	2.50	7.50	24.00
150-160-Super-heroes app. in each (see note). 150 (10/61?)-2nd or 3rd app. The Jaguar? 152-157-Sci/Fi-c. 157-Li'l Jinx story	3.20	9.60	32.00
161(3/63)-167,169-180	2.25	6.75	18.00
168.200: 168-.(1/64)-Jaguar app. 200 (12/66)	2.50	7.50	22.00
181(5/65)-199: 192-UFO-c. 198-Giantman-c(only)	2.00	6.00	16.00
201-217,219-226,228-240(4/70)	1.50	4.50	12.00
218,227-Archies Band-c only	1.75	5.25	14.00
241-270(10/72)	1.50	4.50	12.00
271-299: 298-Josie and the Pussycats-c	1.00	3.00	8.00
300(4/75)	1.25	3.75	10.00
301-340(8/78)			4.00
341-382			3.00
383(4/82),393(3/84): 383-Marvelous Maureen begins (Sci/fi). 393-Thunder-bunny begins			4.00
384-392,394-399,401-410			2.50
400(5/85),411: 400-Story featuring Archie staff (DeCarlo-a)			4.00

NOTE: ***Biro*** *a-2, 4, 5.* ***Jack Cole*** *a-1-5, 8.* ***Al Fagaly*** *c-55-72.* ***Fuje*** *a-39, 45, 47; c-34.* ***Meskin*** *a-2, 4, 5, 11(2).* ***Montana*** *c-30, 32, 33, 36, 73-87(most).* ***Novick*** *c-1-28, 29(w/****Schomburg****), 31i.* ***Harry Sahle*** *c-35, 39-50.* ***Schomburg*** *c-38.* ***Bob Wood*** *a-2, 4-6, 11. The Fly app. in 151, 154, 160. Flygirl app. in 153, 155, 156, 158. Jaguar app. in 150, 152, 157, 159, 168. Katy Keene by* ***Bill Woggon*** *in many later issues. Bondage c-7, 12, 13, 15, 18, 21, 31, 32. Cover features: Shield #1-16; Shield/Hangman #17-27, 29-41; Hangman #28. Archie #36, 41-on.*

PEPE
Dell Publishing Co.: No. 1194, Apr, 1961

	GD2.0	FN6.0	NM9.4
Four Color 1194-Movie, photo-c	1.80	5.50	20.00

PERFECT CRIME, THE
Cross Publications: Oct, 1949 - No. 33, May, 1953 (#2-12, 52 pgs.)

	GD2.0	FN6.0	NM9.4
1-Powell-a(2)	29.00	86.00	200.00
2 (4/50)	16.00	47.00	110.00
3-10: 7-Steve Duncan begins, ends #30. 10-Flag-c	13.50	41.00	95.00
11-Used in **SOTI**, pg. 159	15.00	45.00	105.00
12-14	12.00	36.00	85.00
15- "The Most Terrible Menace" 2 pg. drug editorial	13.00	39.00	90.00
16,17,19-25,27-29,31-33	10.00	30.00	65.00
18-Drug cover, heroin drug propaganda story, plus 2 pg. anti-drug editorial	21.00	62.00	145.00
26-Drug-c with hypodermic; drug propaganda story	21.00	64.00	150.00
30-Strangulation cover	21.00	64.00	150.00

NOTE: ***Powell*** *a-No. 1, 2, 4.* ***Wildey*** *a-1, 5. Bondage c-11.*

PERFECT LOVE
Ziff-Davis(Approved Comics)/St. John No. 9 on: #10, 8-9/51 (cover date; 5-6/51 indicia date); #2, 10-11/51 - #10, 12/53

	GD2.0	FN6.0	NM9.4
10(#1)(8-9/51)-Painted-c	18.00	54.00	125.00
2(10-11/51)	12.00	36.00	85.00
3,5-7: 3-Painted-c. 5-Photo-c	10.00	30.00	60.00
4,8 (Fall, 1952)-Kinstler-a; last Z-D issue	10.00	30.00	65.00
9,10 (10/53, 12/53, St. John): 9-Painted-c. 10-Photo-c	9.15	27.00	55.00

PERG (Also see Hellina)
Lightning Comics: Oct, 1993 - No. 8, May, 1994 ($2.95)

	GD2.0	FN6.0	NM9.4
1-($3.50)-Flip-c is glow-in-the-dark by Saltares			3.50
1-4: Platinum Editions			3.00
2-8: 4-Origin Perg. 7-Blue & Pink cover versions			3.00

PERRI (Disney)
Dell Publishing Co.: No. 847, Jan, 1958

	GD2.0	FN6.0	NM9.4
Four Color 847-Movie, w/2 diff-c publ.	4.50	13.50	50.00

PERRY MASON
David McKay Publications: No. 49, 1946 - No. 50, 1946

	GD2.0	FN6.0	NM9.4
Feature Books 49, 59-Based on Gardner novels	26.00	77.00	180.00

PERRY MASON MYSTERY MAGAZINE (TV)
Dell Publishing Co.: June-Aug, 1964 - No. 2, Oct-Dec, 1964

	GD2.0	FN6.0	NM9.4
1,2: 2-Raymond Burr photo-c	3.00	9.00	30.00

PERSONAL LOVE (Also see Movie Love)
Famous Funnies: Jan, 1950 - No. 33, June, 1955

	GD2.0	FN6.0	NM9.4
1-Photo-c	16.00	47.00	110.00
2-Kathryn Grayson & Mario Lanza photo-c	10.00	30.00	60.00
3-7,10: 7-Robert Walker & Joanne Dru photo-c. 10-Loretta Young & Joseph Cotton photo-c	7.50	22.50	45.00
8,9: 8-Esther Williams & Howard Keel photo-c. 9-Debra Paget & Louis Jourdan photo-c	8.00	24.00	48.00
11-Toth-a; Glenn Ford & Gene Tierney photo-c	10.00	30.00	65.00
12,16,17-One pg. Frazetta each. 17-Rock Hudson & Yvonne DeCarlo photo-c	7.50	22.50	45.00
13-15,18-23: 12-Jane Greer & William Lundigan photo-c. 14-Kirk Douglas photo-c. 15-Dale Robertson & Joanne Dru photo-c. 18-Gregory Peck & Susan Hayworth photo-c. 19-Anthony Quinn & Suzan Ball photo-c. 20-Robert Wagner & Kathleen Crowley photo-c. 21-Roberta Peters & Byron Palmer photo-c. 22-Dale Robertson photo-c. 23-Rhonda Fleming-c	6.35	19.00	38.00

Personal Love #9 © FF

Peter Parker: Spider-Man #2 © MAR

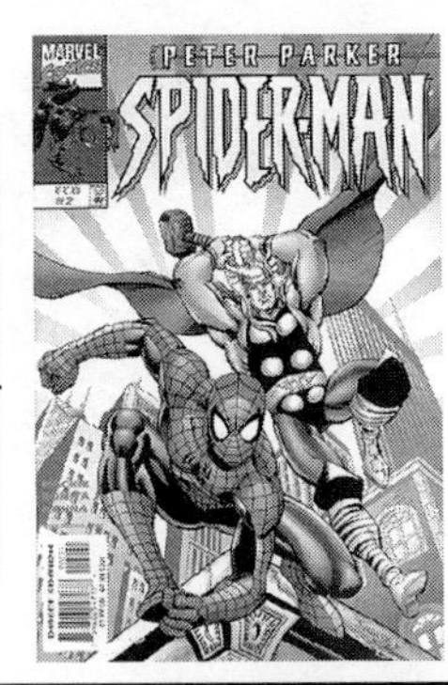

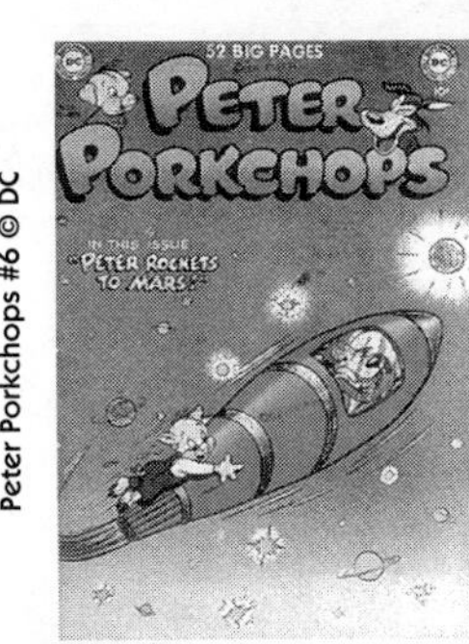

Peter Porkchops #6 © DC

GD2.0 FN6.0 NM9.4

24,27,28-Frazetta-a in each (8,8&6 pgs.). 27-Rhonda Fleming & Fernando Lamas photo-c. 28,30-Mitzi Gaynor photo-c 38.00 114.00 265.00
25-Frazetta-a (tribute to Betty Page, 7 pg. story); Tyrone Power/Terry Moore photo-c from "King of the Khyber Rifles" 39.00 118.00 275.00
26,29,30,33: 26-Constance Smith & Byron Palmer photo-c. 29-Charlton Heston & Nicol Morey photo-c. 30-Johnny Ray & Mitzi Gaynor photo-c. 33-Dana Andrews & Piper Laurie photo-c 5.85 17.50 35.00
31-Marlon Brando & Jean Simmons photo-c; last pre-code (2/55) 10.00 30.00 60.00
32-Classic Frazetta-a (8 pgs.); Kirk Douglas & Bella Darvi photo-c 48.00 144.00 385.00
NOTE: *All have photo-c. Many feature movie stars.* ***Everett*** *a-5, 9, 10, 24.*

PERSONAL LOVE (Going Steady V3#3 on)
Prize Publ. (Headline): V1#1, Sept, 1957 - V3#2, Nov-Dec, 1959
V1#1 8.35 25.00 50.00
2 4.25 13.00 28.00
3-6(7-8/58) 4.25 13.00 26.00
V2#1(9-10/58)-V2#6(7-8/59) 4.00 11.00 22.00
V3#1-Wood?/Orlando-a 5.00 15.00 30.00
2 4.00 10.00 20.00

PETER CANNON - THUNDERBOLT (See Crisis on Infinite Earths)(Also see Thunderbolt)
DC Comics: Sept, 1992 - No. 12, Aug, 1993 ($1.25)
1-12 2.00

PETER COTTONTAIL
Key Publications: Jan, 1954; Feb, 1954 - No. 2, Mar, 1954 (Says 3/53 in error)
1(1/54)-Not 3-D 7.50 22.50 45.00
1(2/54)-(3-D, 25¢)-Came w/glasses; written by Bruce Hamilton 21.00 64.00 150.00
2-Reprints 3-D #1 but not in 3-D 5.35 16.00 32.00

PETER GUNN (TV)
Dell Publishing Co.: No. 1087, Apr-June, 1960
Four Color 1087-Photo-c 9.00 27.00 100.00

PETER PAN (Disney) (See Hook, Movie Classics & Comics, New Adventures of... & Walt Disney Showcase #36)
Dell Publishing Co.: No. 442, Dec, 1952 - No. 926, Aug, 1958
Four Color 442 (#1)-Movie 8.00 25.00 90.00
Four Color 926-Reprint of 442 3.60 11.00 40.00

PETER PAN
Disney Comics: 1991 ($5.95, graphic novel, 68 pgs.)(Celebrates video release)
nn-r/Peter Pan Treasure Chest from 1953 7.00

PETER PANDA
National Periodical Publications: Aug-Sept, 1953 - No. 31, Aug-Sept, 1958
1-Grossman-c/a in all 40.00 120.00 300.00
2 20.00 60.00 140.00
3-10: 9-Robot-c 15.00 45.00 105.00
11-31 10.00 30.00 70.00

PETER PAN TREASURE CHEST (See Dell Giants)

PETER PARKER (See The Spectacular Spider-Man)

PETER PARKER: SPIDER-MAN
Marvel Comics: Jan, 1999 - Present ($2.99/$1.99)
1-Mackie-s/Romita Jr.-a; wraparound-c 3.00
1-($6.95) DF Edition w/variant cover by the Romitas 7.00
2-11-($1.99): 2-Two covers; Thor app. 3-Iceman-c/app. 4-Marrow-c/app. 5-Spider-Woman app. 7,8-Blade app. 9,10-Venom app. 11-Iron Man & Thor-c/app. 2.00
...'99 Annual (8/99, $3.50) Man-Thing app. 3.50

PETER PAT
United Features Syndicate: No. 8, 1939
Single Series 8 33.00 99.00 230.00

GD2.0 FN6.0 NM9.4

PETER PAUL'S 4 IN 1 JUMBO COMIC BOOK
Capitol Stories (Charlton): No date (1953)
1-Contains 4 comics bound; Space Adventures, Space Western, Crime & Justice, Racket Squad in Action 40.00 120.00 280.00

PETER PIG
Standard Comics: No. 5, May, 1953 - No. 6, Aug, 1953
5,6 5.35 16.00 32.00

PETER PORKCHOPS (See Leading Comics #23)
National Periodical Publications: 11-12/49 - No. 61, 9-11/59; No. 62, 10-12/60 (1-11: 52 pgs.)
1 32.00 96.00 225.00
2 16.00 47.00 110.00
3-10: 6- "Peter Rockets to Mars!" c/story 11.50 34.00 80.00
11-30 10.00 30.00 60.00
31-62 8.35 25.00 50.00
NOTE: ***Otto Feur*** *a-all.* ***Sheldon Mayer*** *a-30-38, 40-44, 46-52, 61.*

PETER PORKER, THE SPECTACULAR SPIDER-HAM
Star Comics (Marvel): May, 1985 - No. 17, Sept, 1987 (Also see Marvel Tails)
1-Michael Golden-c 3.00
2-17: 12-Origin/1st app. Bizarro Phil. 13-Halloween issue 2.50
NOTE: *Back-up features: 2-X-Bugs. 3-Iron Mouse. 4-Croctor Strange. 5-Thrr, Dog of Thunder.*

PETER POTAMUS (TV)
Gold Key: Jan, 1965 (Hanna-Barbera)
1-1st app. Peter Potamus & So-So, Breezly & Sneezly 8.20 24.50 90.00

PETER RABBIT (See New Funnies #65 & Space Comics)
Dell Publishing Co.: No. 1, 1942
Large Feature Comic 1 38.00 115.00 420.00

PETER RABBIT (Adventures of...; New Advs. of... #9 on)(Also see Funny Tunes & Space Comics)
Avon Periodicals: 1947 - No. 34, Aug-Sept, 1956
1(1947)-Reprints 1943-44 Sunday strips; contains a biography & drawing of Cady 34.00 103.00 240.00
2 (4/48) 25.00 75.00 175.00
3 ('48) - 6(7/49)-Last Cady issue 21.00 64.00 150.00
7-10(1950-8/51): 9-New logo 6.70 20.00 40.00
11(11/51)-34('56)-Avon's character 4.25 13.00 28.00
...Easter Parade (1952, 25¢, 132 pgs.) 16.00 47.00 110.00
...Jumbo Book (1954-Giant Size, 25¢)-Jesse James by Kinstler (6 pgs.); space ship-c 21.00 64.00 150.00

PETER RABBIT
Fago Magazine Co.: 1958
1 7.00 21.00 42.00

PETER RABBIT 3-D
Eternity Comics: April, 1990 ($2.95, with glasses; sealed in plastic bag)
1-By Harrison Cady (reprints) 3.00

PETER, THE LITTLE PEST (#4 titled Petey)
Marvel Comics Group: Nov, 1969 - No. 4, May, 1970
1 4.50 13.50 45.00
2-4-r-Dexter the Demon & Melvin the Monster 3.20 9.60 32.00

PETE'S DRAGON (See Walt Disney Showcase #43)

PETE THE PANIC
Stanmor Publications: November, 1955
nn-Code approved 4.00 11.00 22.00

PETEY (See Peter, the Little Pest)

PETTICOAT JUNCTION (TV)
Dell Publ. Co.: Oct-Dec, 1964 - No. 5, Oct-Dec, 1965 (#1-3, 5 have photo-c)
1 5.50 16.50 60.00
2-5 4.00 12.25 45.00

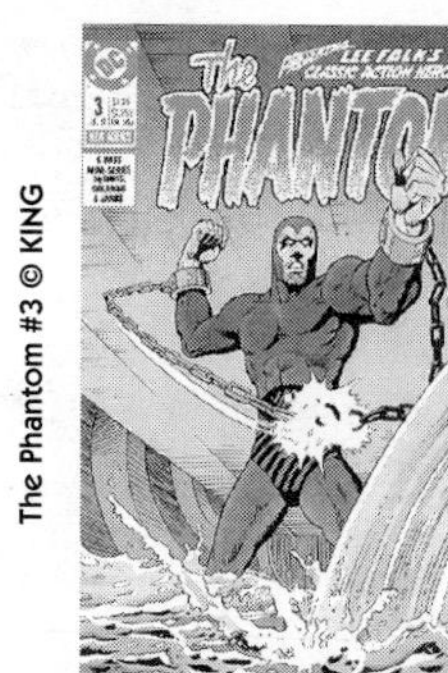

The Phantom #3 © KING

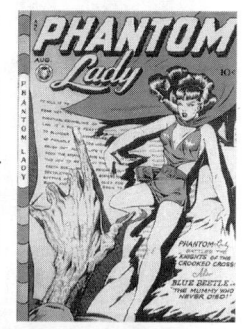

Phantom Lady #13 © FOX

Phantom Stranger #4 © DC

GD2.0 FN6.0 NM9.4

PETUNIA (Also see Looney Tunes and Porky Pig)
Dell Publishing Co.: No. 463, Apr, 1953

Four Color 463 3.00 9.00 35.00

PHAGE (See Neil Gaiman's Teknophage & Neil Gaiman's Phage-Shadowdeath)

PHANTACEA
McPherson Publishing Co.: Sept, 1977 - No. 6, Summer, 1980 (B&W)

1-Early Dave Sim-a (32 pgs.) 2.80 8.40 28.00
2-Dave Sim-a(10 pgs.) 1.75 5.25 14.00
3,5: 3-Flip-c w/Damnation Bridge 1.00 3.00 8.00
4,6: 4-Gene Day-a 1.00 3.00 8.00

PHANTASMO (See The Funnies #45)
Dell Publishing Co.: No. 18, 1941

Large Feature Comic 18 24.50 74.00 270.00

PHANTOM, THE
David McKay Publishing Co.: 1939 - 1949

Feature Books 20 64.00 191.00 700.00
Feature Books 22 53.00 158.00 580.00
Feature Books 39 49.00 146.00 390.00
Feature Books 53,56,57 40.00 120.00 300.00

PHANTOM, THE (See Ace Comics, Defenders Of The Earth, Eat Right to Work and Win, Future Comics, Harvey Comics Hits #51,56, Harvey Hits #1, 6, 12, 15, 26, 36, 44, 48, & King Comics)

PHANTOM, THE (nn 29-Published overseas only) (Also see Comics Reading Library)
Gold Key(#1-17)/King(#18-28)/Charlton(#30 on): Nov, 1962 - No. 17, Jul, 1966; No. 18, Sept, 1966 - No. 28, Dec, 1967; No. 30, Feb, 1969 - No. 74, Jan, 1977

1-Manning-a; origin revealed on inside-c. & back-c 14.00 42.00 140.00
2-King, Queen & Jack begins, ends #11 7.00 21.00 70.00
3-10 5.50 16.50 55.00
11-17: 12-Track Hunter begins 4.50 13.50 45.00
18-Flash Gordon begins; Wood-a 4.00 12.00 40.00
19-27: 20-Flash Gordon ends (both by Gil Kane). 21-Mandrake begins. 20,24-Girl Phantom app. 26-Brick Bradford app. 25-Jeff Jones-a(4 pgs.); 1 pg. Williamson ad 3.00 9.00 30.00
28(nn)-Brick Bradford app. 2.50 7.50 24.00
30-33: 33-Last 12¢ issue 2.50 7.50 20.00
34-40,67: 36,39-Ditko-a. 67-Origin retold 2.25 6.75 18.00
41-66: 46-Intro. The Piranha. 62-Bolle-c 2.00 6.00 16.00
68-73-Newton-c/a 1.25 3.75 10.00
74-Classic flag-c by Newton; Newton-a; 2.00 6.00 16.00
NOTE: ***Aparo*** *a-31-34, 36-38; c-31-38, 60, 61. Painted c-1-17.*

PHANTOM, THE
DC Comics: May, 1988 - No. 4, Aug, 1988 ($1.25, mini-series)

1-4: Orlando-c/a in all 2.00

PHANTOM, THE
DC Comics: Mar, 1989 - No. 13, Mar, 1990 ($1.50)

1-13: 1-Brief origin 2.00

PHANTOM, THE
Wolf Publishing: 1992 - No. 8, 1993 ($2.25)

1-8 2.25

PHANTOM BLOT, THE (#1 titled New Adventures of...)
Gold Key: Oct, 1964 - No. 7, Nov, 1966 (Disney)

1 (Meets The Beagle Boys) 5.00 15.00 50.00
2-1st Super Goof 4.50 13.50 45.00
3-7 2.60 7.80 26.00

PHANTOM EAGLE (See Mighty Midget, Marvel Super Heroes #16 & Wow #6)

PHANTOM FORCE
Image Comics/Genesis West #0, 3-7: 12/93 - #2, 1994; #0, 3/94; #3, 5/94 - #8, 10/94 ($2.50/$3.50, limited series)

0 (3/94, $2.50)-Kirby/Jim Lee-c; Kirby-p pgs. 1,5,24-29. 3.00
1 (12/93, $2.50)-Polybagged w/trading card; Kirby Liefeld-c; Kirby plots/pencils w/inks by Liefeld, McFarlane, Jim Lee, Silvestri, Larsen, Williams, Ordway & Miki. 3.00
2 ($3.50)-Kirby-a(p); Kirby/Larson-c 3.50
3-8: 3-(5/94, $2.50)-Kirby/McFarlane-c 4-(5/94)-Kirby-c(p). 5-(6/94) 3.00

PHANTOM GUARD
Image Comics (WildStorm Productions): Oct, 1997 - No. 6, Mar, 1998 ($2.50)

1-6: 1-Two covers 3.00
1-($3.50)-Voyager Pack w/Wildcore preview 3.50

PHANTOM LADY (1st Series) (My Love Secret #24 on) (Also see All Top, Daring Adventures, Freedom Fighters, Jungle Thrills, & Wonder Boy)
Fox Features Syndicate: No. 13, Aug, 1947 - No. 23 Apr, 1949

13(#1)-Phantom Lady by Matt Baker begins (1st app.); The Blue Beetle story 355.00 1067.00 3200.00
14-16: 14(#2)-Not Baker-c. 15-P.L. injected with experimental drug. 16-Negligee-c, panels; true crime stories begin 231.00 694.00 1850.00
17-Classic bondage cover; used in **SOTI**, illo "Sexual stimulation by combining 'headlights' with the sadist's dream of tying up a woman" 489.00 1467.00 4400.00
18,19 162.00 487.00 1300.00
20-22 125.00 375.00 1000.00
23-Bondage-c 137.00 412.00 1100.00
NOTE: ***Matt Baker*** *a-in all; c-13, 15-21.* ***Kamen*** *a-22, 23.*

PHANTOM LADY (2nd Series) (See Terrific Comics) (Formerly Linda)
Ajax/Farrell Publ.: V1#5, Dec-Jan, 1954/1955 - No. 4, June, 1955

V1#5(#1)-By Matt Baker 106.00 319.00 850.00
V1#2-Last pre-code 81.00 244.00 650.00
3,4-Red Rocket. 3-Heroin story 65.00 195.00 520.00

PHANTOM LADY
Verotik Publications: 1994 ($9.95)

1-Reprints G. A. stories from Phantom Lady and All Top Comics; Adam Hughes-c 10.00

PHANTOM PLANET, THE
Dell Publishing Co.: No. 1234, 1961

Four Color 1234-Movie 6.40 19.00 70.00

PHANTOM STRANGER, THE (1st Series)(See Saga of Swamp Thing)
National Periodical Publications: Aug-Sept, 1952 - No. 6, June-July, 1953

1(Scarce)-1st app. 187.00 562.00 1500.00
2 (Scarce) 103.00 309.00 825.00
3-6 (Scarce) 91.00 272.00 725.00

PHANTOM STRANGER, THE (2nd Series) (See Showcase #80)
National Periodical Publications: May-June, 1969 - No. 41, Feb-Mar, 1976

1-2nd S.A. app. P. Stranger; only 12¢ issue 8.00 24.00 80.00
2,3 3.20 9.60 32.00
4-1st new look Phantom Stranger; N. Adams-a 3.80 11.40 38.00
5-7 2.50 7.50 24.00
8-14: 14-Last 15¢ issue 2.50 7.50 20.00
15-19: All 25¢ giants (52 pgs.) 2.50 7.50 20.00
20-Dark Circle begins, ends #24. 2.00 6.00 16.00
21,22 1.25 3.75 10.00
23-Spawn of Frankenstein begins by Kaluta 2.50 7.50 20.00
24,25,27-30-Last Spawn of Frankenstein 1.75 5.25 14.00
26- Book-length story featuring Phantom Stranger, Dr.13 & Spawn of Frankenstein 2.00 6.00 16.00
31-The Black Orchid begins (6-7/74). 2.50 7.50 20.00
32,34-38: 34-Last 20¢ issue (#35 on are 25¢) 1.25 3.75 10.00
33,39-41: 33-Deadman-c/story. 39-41-Deadman ap. 1.75 5.25 14.00
NOTE: ***N. Adams*** *a-4; c-3-19.* ***Anderson*** *a-4, 5i.* ***Aparo*** *a-7-17, 19-26; c-20-24, 33-41.* ***B. Bailey*** *a-27-30.* ***DeZuniga*** *a-12-16, 18, 19, 21, 22, 31, 34.* ***Grell*** *a-33.* ***Kaluta*** *a-23-25; c-26.* ***Meskin*** *r-15, 16, 18, 19.* ***Redondo*** *a-32, 35, 36.* ***Sparling*** *a-20.* ***Starr*** *a-17r.* ***Toth*** *a-15r. Black Orchid by* ***Carrillo****-38-41. Dr. 13 solo in-13, 18, 19, 20, 21, 34. Frankenstein by* ***Kaluta****-23-25; by* ***Baily****-27-30. No Black Orchid-33, 34, 37.*

PHANTOM STRANGER (See Justice League of America #103)

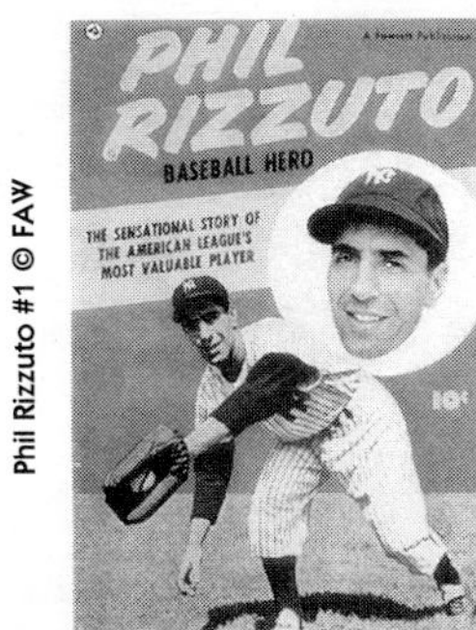

Phil Rizzuto #1 © FAW

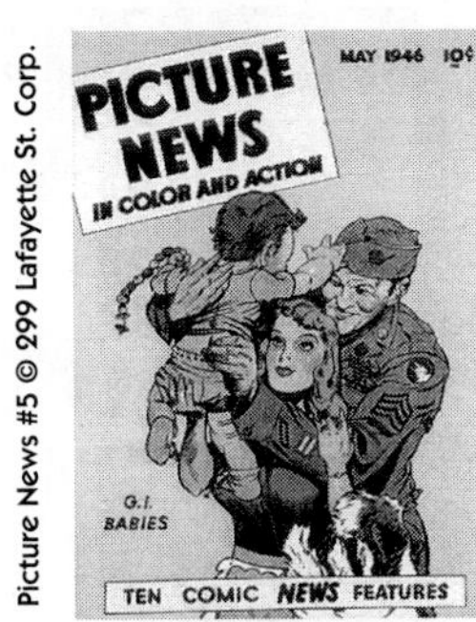

Picture News #5 © 299 Lafayette St. Corp.

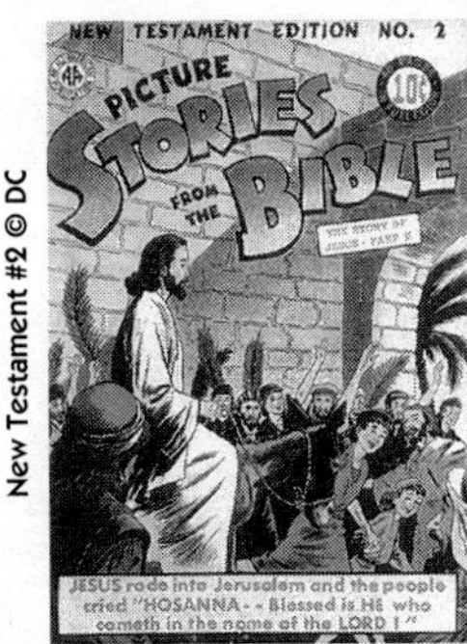

Picture Stories from the Bible - New Testament #2 © DC

GD2.0 FN6.0 NM9.4

DC Comics: Oct, 1987 - No. 4, Jan, 1988 (75¢, limited series)

1-Mignola/Russell-c/a & Eclipso app. in all 3.00
2-4: 3,4-Eclipso-c 2.00

PHANTOM STRANGER (See Vertigo Visions-The Phantom Stranger)

PHANTOM: THE GHOST WHO WALKS
Marvel Comics: Feb, 1995 - No. 3, Apr, 1995 ($2.95, limited series)

1-3 3.00

PHANTOM 2040 (TV cartoon)
Marvel Comics: May, 1995 - No. 4, Aug, 1995 ($1.50)

1-4-Based on animated series 2.00

PHANTOM WITCH DOCTOR (Also see Durango Kid #8 & Eerie #8)
Avon Periodicals: 1952

1-Kinstler-c/a (7 pgs.) 43.00 128.00 340.00

PHANTOM ZONE, THE (See Adventure #283 & Superboy #100, 104)
DC Comics: January, 1982 - No. 4, April, 1982

1-4-Superman app. in all. 2-4: Batman, Green Lantern app. 2.00
NOTE: ***Colan*** *a-1-4p; c-1-4p.* ***Giordano*** *c-1-4i.*

PHAZE
Eclipse Comics: Apr, 1988 - No. 2, Oct, 1988 ($2.25)

1,2: 1-Sienkiewicz-c. 2-Gulacy painted-c 2.25

PHIL RIZZUTO (Baseball Hero)(See Sport Thrills, Accepted reprint)
Fawcett Publications: 1951 (New York Yankees)

nn-Photo-c 62.00 187.00 500.00

PHOENIX
Atlas/Seaboard Publ.: Jan, 1975 - No. 4, Oct, 1975

1-Origin 5.00
2-4: 3-Origin & only app. The Dark Avenger. 4-New origin/costume The Protector (formerly Phoenix) 4.00
NOTE: ***Infantino*** *appears in #1, 2.* ***Austin*** *a-3i.* ***Thorne*** *c-3.*

PHOENIX (...The Untold Story)
Marvel Comics Group: April, 1984 ($2.00, one-shot)

1-Byrne/Austin-r/X-Men #137 with original unpublished ending 1.10 3.30 9.00

PHOENIX RESURRECTION, THE
Malibu Comics (Ultraverse): 1995 - 1996 ($3.95)

Genesis #1 (12/95)-X-Men app; wraparound-c, Revelations #1 (12/95)-X-Men app; wraparound-c, Aftermath #1 (1/96)-X-Men app. 4.00
0-($1.95)-r/series 2.00
0-American Entertainment Ed. 4.00

PICNIC PARTY (See Dell Giants)

PICTORIAL CONFESSIONS (Pictorial Romances #4 on)
St. John Publishing Co.: Sept, 1949 - No. 3, Dec, 1949

1-Baker-c/a(3) 28.00 84.00 195.00
2-Baker-a; photo-c 18.00 54.00 125.00
3-Kubert, Baker-a; part Kubert-c 18.00 54.00 125.00

PICTORIAL LOVE STORIES (Formerly Tim McCoy)
Charlton Comics: No. 22, Oct, 1949 - No. 26, July, 1950 (all photo-c)

22-26: All have "Me-Dan Cupid". 25-Fred Astaire-c 19.00 56.00 130.00

PICTORIAL LOVE STORIES
St. John Publishing Co.: October, 1952

1-Baker-c 26.00 79.00 185.00

PICTORIAL ROMANCES (Formerly Pictorial Confessions)
St. John Publ. Co.: No. 4, Jan, 1950; No. 5, Jan, 1951 - No. 24, Mar, 1954

4-Baker-a; photo-c 27.00 81.00 190.00
5,10-All Matt Baker issues. 5-Reprints all stories from #4 w/new Baker-c 20.00 60.00 140.00
6-9,12,13,15,16-Baker-c, 2-3 stories 15.00 45.00 105.00

GD2.0 FN6.0 NM9.4

11-Baker-c/a(3); Kubert-r/Hollywood Confessions #1 16.00 47.00 110.00
14,21-24: Baker-c/a each. 21,24-Each has signed story by Estrada 13.00 39.00 90.00
17-20(7/53, 25¢, 100 pgs.): Baker-c/a; each has two signed stories by Estrada 26.00 79.00 185.00
NOTE: ***Matt Baker*** *art in most issues.* ***Estrada*** *a-17-20(2), 21, 24.*

PICTURE NEWS
Lafayette Street Corp.: Jan, 1946 - No. 10, Jan-Feb, 1947

1-Milt Gross begins, ends No. 6; 4 pg. Kirby-a; A-Bomb-c/story 40.00 120.00 280.00
2-Atomic explosion panels; Frank Sinatra/Perry Como story 20.00 60.00 140.00
3-Atomic explosion panels; Frank Sinatra, June Allyson, Benny Goodman stories 17.00 49.00 115.00
4-Atomic explosion panels; "Caesar and Cleopatra" movie adapt. w/Claude Raines & Vivian Leigh; Jackie Robinson story 20.00 60.00 140.00
5-7: 5-Hank Greenberg story. 6-Joe Louis-c/story 13.00 39.00 90.00
8-10: 8-Monte Hale story (9-10/46; 1st?). 9-A-Bomb story; "Crooked Mile" movie adaptation; Joe DiMaggio story. 10-Dick Quick; A-Bomb story; Krigstein, Gross-a 14.00 43.00 100.00

PICTURE PARADE (Picture Progress #5 on)
Gilberton Company (Also see A Christmas Adventure): Sept, 1953 - V1#4, Dec, 1953 (28 pgs.)

V1#1-Andy's Atomic Adventures; A-bomb blast-c; (Teachers version distributed to schools exists) 18.00 54.00 125.00
2-Around the World with the United Nations 11.00 33.00 75.00
3-Adventures of the Lost One(The American Indian), 4-A Christmas Adventure (r-under same title in 1969) 11.00 33.00 75.00

PICTURE PROGRESS (Formerly Picture Parade)
Gilberton Corp.: V1#5, Jan, 1954 - V3#2, Oct, 1955 (28-36 pgs.)

V1#5-9,V2#1-9: 5-News in Review 1953. 6-The Birth of America. 7-The Four Seasons. 8-Paul Revere's Ride. 9-The Hawaiian Islands(5/54). V2#1-The Story of Flight(9/54). 2-Vote for Crazy River(The Meaning of Elections). 3-Louis Pasteur. 4-The Star Spangled Banner. 5-News in Review 1954. 6-Alaska: The Great Land. 7-Life in the Circus. 8-The Time of the Cave Man. 9-Summer Fun(5/55) 5.85 17.50 35.00
V3#1,2: 1-The Man Who Discovered America. 2-The Lewis & Clark Expedition 5.85 17.50 35.00

PICTURE SCOPE JUNGLE ADVENTURES (See Jungle Thrills)

PICTURE STORIES FROM AMERICAN HISTORY
National/All-American/E. C. Comics: 1945 - No. 4, Sum, 1947 (#1,2: 10¢, 56 pgs.; #3,4: 15¢, 52 pgs.)

1 29.00 86.00 200.00
2-4 24.00 73.00 170.00

PICTURE STORIES FROM SCIENCE
E.C. Comics: Spring, 1947 - No. 2, Fall, 1947

1-(15¢) 29.00 86.00 200.00
2-(10¢) 26.00 77.00 180.00

PICTURE STORIES FROM THE BIBLE (See Narrative Illustration, the Story of the Comics by M.C. Gaines)
National/All-American/E.C. Comics: 1942 - No. 4, Fall, 1943; 1944-46

1-4('42-Fall, '43)-Old Testament (DC) 22.00 66.00 155.00
Complete Old Testament Edition, (12/43-DC, 50¢, 232 pgs.);-1st printing; contains #1-4; 2nd - 8th (1/47) printings exist; later printings by E.C. 26.00 79.00 185.00
Complete Old Testament Edition (1945-publ. by Bible Pictures Ltd.)-232 pgs., hardbound, in color with dust jacket 26.00 79.00 185.00
NOTE: *Both Old and New Testaments published in England by Bible Pictures Ltd. in hardback, 1943, in color, 376 pgs. (2 vols.: O.T. 232 pgs. & N.T. 144 pgs.), and were also published by Scarf Press in 1979 (Old Test., $9.95) and in 1980 (New Test., $7.95)*

1-3(New Test.; 1944-46, DC)-52 pgs. ea. 17.00 49.00 115.00
The Complete Life of Christ Edition (1945, 25¢, 96 pgs.)-Contains #1&2 of the

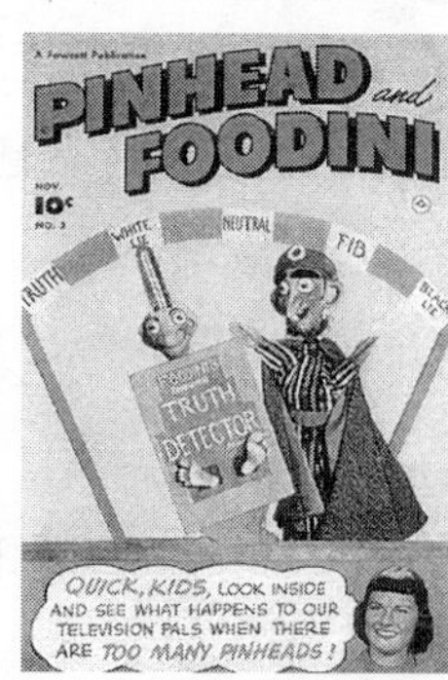

Pinhead & Foodini #3 © FAW

Pinky and the Brain #20 © Warner Bros.

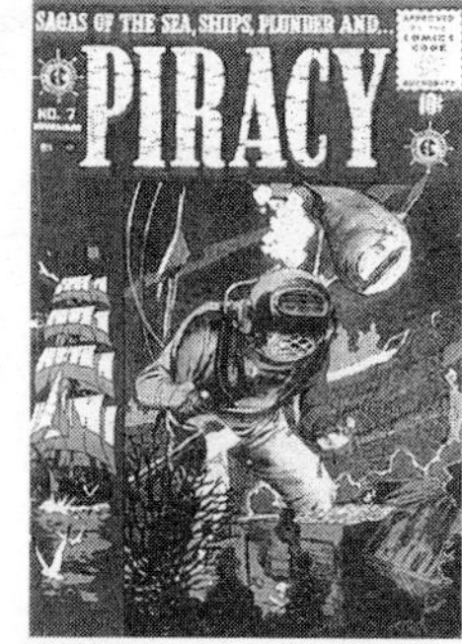

Piracy #7 © WMG

GD2.0 FN6.0 NM9.4

New Testament Edition 22.00 66.00 155.00
1,2(Old Testament-r in comic book form)(E.C., 1946; 52 pgs.) 17.00 49.00 115.00
1(DC),2(AA),3(EC)(New Testament-r in comic book form)(E.C., 1946; 52 pgs.) 17.00 49.00 115.00
Complete New Testament Edition (1946-E.C., 50¢, 144 pgs.)-Contains #1-3 22.00 66.00 155.00

NOTE: *Another British series entitled* ***The Bible Illustrated*** *from 1947 has recently been discovered, with the same internal artwork. This eight edition series (5-OT, 3-NT) is of particular interest to Classics Ill. collectors because it exactly copied the C.I. logo format. The British publisher was Thorpe & Porter, who in 1951 began publishing the British Classics Ill. series. All editions of The Bible Ill. have new British painted covers. While this market is still new, and not all editions have as yet been found, current market value is about the same as the first U.S. editions of Picture Stories From The Bible.*

PICTURE STORIES FROM WORLD HISTORY
E.C. Comics: Spring, 1947 - No. 2, Summer, 1947 (52, 48 pgs.)
1-(15¢) 29.00 86.00 200.00
2-(10¢) 26.00 77.00 180.00

PINHEAD
Marvel Comics (Epic Comics): Dec, 1993 - No. 6, May, 1994 ($2.50)
1-($2.95)-Embossed foil-c by Kelley Jones; Intro Pinhead & Disciples (Snakeoil, Hangman, Fan Dancer & Dixie) 3.00
2-6 2.50

PINHEAD & FOODINI (TV)(Also see Foodini & Jingle Dingle Christmas...)
Fawcett Publications: July, 1951 - No. 4, Jan, 1952 (Early TV comic)
1-(52 pgs.)-Photo-c; based on TV puppet show 31.00 94.00 220.00
2,3-Photo-c 15.00 45.00 105.00
4 12.00 36.00 85.00

PINHEAD VS. MARSHALL LAW (Law in Hell)
Marvel Comics (Epic): Nov, 1993 - No. 2, Dec, 1993 ($2.95, lim. series)
1,2: 1-Embossed red foil-c. 2-Embossed silver foil-c 3.00

PINK DUST
Kitchen Sink Press: 1998 ($3.50, B&W, mature)
1-J. O'Barr-s/a 3.50

PINK PANTHER, THE (TV)(See The Inspector & Kite Fun Book)
Gold Key #1-70/Whitman #71-87: April, 1971 - No. 87, 1984
1-The Inspector begins 4.00 12.00 40.00
2-5 2.25 6.75 18.00
6-10 1.75 5.25 14.00
11-30: Warren Tufts-a #16-on 1.25 3.75 10.00
31-60 1.00 3.00 8.00
61-70 5.00
71-74,81-83 1.00 2.80 7.00
75(8/80),76-80(pre-pack?) 1.50 4.50 12.00
84-87(All #90266 on-c, no date or date code) 1.25 3.75 10.00
Mini-comic No. 1(1976)(3-1/4x6-1/2") 1.00 3.00 8.00

NOTE: *Pink Panther began as a movie cartoon. (See Golden Comics Digest #38, 45 and March of Comics #376, 384, 390, 409, 418, 429, 441, 449, 461, 473, 486); #37, 72, 80-85 contain reprints.*

PINK PANTHER SUPER SPECIAL (TV)
Harvey Comics: Oct, 1993 ($2.25, 68 pgs.)
V2#1-The Inspector & Wendy Witch stories also 3.00

PINK PANTHER, THE
Harvey Comics: Nov, 1993 - No. 9, July, 1994 ($1.50)
V2#1-9 2.00

PINKY & THE BRAIN (See Animaniacs)
DC Comics: July, 1996 - No. 27, Nov, 1998 ($1.75/$1.95/$1.99)
1-27, ...Christmas Special (1/96, $1.50) 2.50

PINKY LEE (See Adventures of...)

PINKY THE EGGHEAD
I.W./Super Comics: 1963 (Reprints from Noodnik)
I.W. Reprint #1,2(nd) 1.10 3.30 9.00
Super Reprint #14-r/Noodnik Comics #4 1.10 3.30 9.00

PINOCCHIO (See 4-Color #92, 252, 545, 1203, Mickey Mouse Mag. V5#3, Movie Comics under Wonderful Advs. of..., New Advs. of..., Thrilling Comics #2, Walt Disney Showcase, Walt Disney's..., Wonderful Advs. of..., & World's Greatest Stories #2)
Dell Publishing Co.: No. 92, 1945 - No. 1203, Mar, 1962 (Disney)
Four Color 92-The Wonderful Adventures of...; 16 pg. Donald Duck story; entire book by Kelly 57.00 170.00 625.00
Four Color 252 (10/49)-Origin, not by Kelly 9.50 29.00 105.00
Four Color 545 (3/54)-The Wonderful Advs. of...; part-r of 4-Color #92; Disney-movie 6.40 19.00 70.00
Four Color 1203 (3/62) 4.50 13.50 50.00

PINOCCHIO AND THE EMPEROR OF THE NIGHT
Marvel Comics: Mar, 1988 ($1.25, 52 pgs.)
1-Adapts film 2.50

PINOCCHIO LEARNS ABOUT KITES (See Kite Fun Book)

PIN-UP PETE (Also see Great Lover Romances & Monty Hall...)
Toby Press: 1952
1-Jack Sparling pin-ups 18.00 54.00 125.00

PIONEER MARSHAL (See Fawcett Movie Comics)

PIONEER PICTURE STORIES
Street & Smith Publications: Dec, 1941 - No. 9, Dec, 1943
1-The Legless Air Ace begins 29.00 86.00 200.00
2 -True life story of Errol Flynn 14.00 43.00 100.00
3-9 12.00 36.00 85.00

PIONEER WEST ROMANCES (Firehair #1,2,7-11)
Fiction House Magazines: No. 3, Spring, 1950 - No. 6, Winter, 1950-51
3-(52 pgs.)-Firehair continues 19.00 58.00 135.00
4-6 19.00 58.00 135.00

PIPSQUEAK (See The Adventures of...)

PIRACY
E. C. Comics: Oct-Nov, 1954 - No. 7, Oct-Nov, 1955
1-Williamson/Torres-a 22.00 66.00 200.00
2-Williamson/Torres-a 13.00 40.00 125.00
3-7 11.00 33.00 105.00

NOTE: ***Crandall*** *a-in all; c-2-4.* ***Davis*** *a-1, 2, 6.* ***Evans*** *a-3-7; c-7.* ***Ingels*** *a-3-7.* ***Krigstein*** *a-3-5, 7; c-5, 6.* ***Wood*** *a-1, 2; c-1.*

PIRACY
Gemstone Publishing: March, 1998 - No. 7, Sept, 1998 ($2.50)
1-7: E.C. reprints 2.50
Annual 1 ($10.95) Collects #1-4 11.00
Annual 2 ($7.95) Collects #5-7 8.00

PIRANA (See The Phantom #46 & Thrill-O-Rama #2, 3)

PIRATE CORP$, THE (See Hectic Planet)
Eternity Comics/Slave Labor Graphics: 1987 - No. 5, 1988 ($1.95)
1-5: 3-Color begins, Special 1 ('89,B&W)-Slave Labor Publ. 2.00

PIRATE CORP$, THE (Volume 2)
Slave Labor Graphics: 1989 - No. 4, 1992 ($1.95)
1-4-Dorkin-s/a 2.00

PIRATE OF THE GULF, THE (See Superior Stories #2)

PIRATES COMICS
Hillman Periodicals: Feb-Mar, 1950 - No. 4, Aug-Sept, 1950 (All 52 pgs.)
1 24.00 71.00 165.00
2-Dave Berg-a 17.00 49.00 115.00
3,4-Berg-a 16.00 47.00 110.00

PIRATES OF DARK WATER, THE (Hanna Barbera)
Marvel Comics: Nov, 1991 - No. 9, Aug, 1992 ($1.95)
1-9: 9-Vess-c 2.00

Planetary #5 © WildStorm

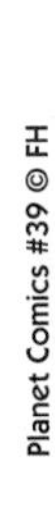

Planet Comics #39 © FH

Planet of the Apes #17 © MAR

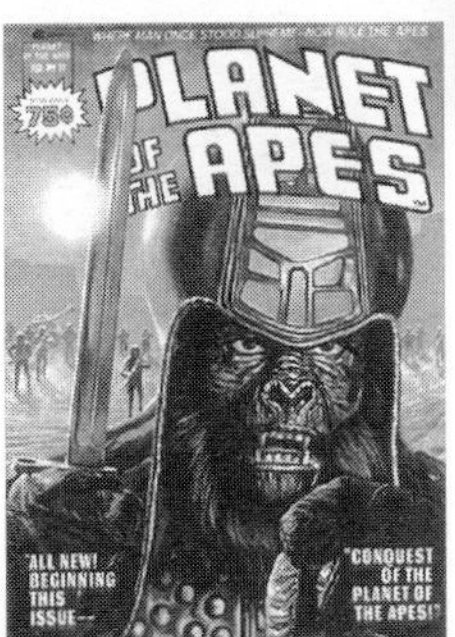

GD2.0 FN6.0 NM9.4

P.I.'S: MICHAEL MAUSER AND MS. TREE, THE
First Comics: Jan, 1985 - No. 3, May, 1985 ($1.25, limited series)

1-3: Staton-c/a(p) 2.00

PITT, THE (Also see The Draft & The War)
Marvel Comics: Mar, 1988 ($3.25, 52 pgs., one-shot)

1-Ties into Starbrand, D.P.7 3.50

PITT (See Youngblood #4 & Gen 13 #3,#4)
Image Comics #1-9/Full Bleed #1/2,10-on: Jan, 1993 - Present ($1.95, intended as a four part limited series)

1/2-(12/95)-1st Full Bleed issue 4.00
1-Dale Keown-c/a. 1-1st app. The Pitt 4.00
2-13: All Dale Keown-c/a. 3 (Low distribution). 10 (1/96)-Indicia reads "January 1995" 3.00
14-20: 14-Begin $2.50-c, pullout poster 2.50
TPB-(1997, $9.95) r/#1/2, 1-4 10.00
TPB 2-(1999, $11.95) r/#5-9 12.00

PITT CREW
Full Bleed Studios: Aug, 1998 - Present ($2.50)

1-4: 1-Richard Pace-s/Ken Lashley-a. 2-4-Scott Lee-a 2.50

PITT IN THE BLOOD
Full Bleed Studios: Aug, 1996 ($2.50, one-shot)

nn-Richard Pace-a/script 2.50

PIXIE & DIXIE & MR. JINKS (TV)(See Jinks, Pixie, and Dixie & Whitman Comic Books)
Dell Publishing Co./Gold Key: July-Sept, 1960 - Feb, 1963 (Hanna-Barbera)

Four Color 1112 6.75 21.00 75.00
Four Color 1196,1264, 01-631-207 (Dell, 7/62) 5.00 15.00 55.00
1(2/63-Gold Key) 5.50 16.50 60.00

PIXIE PUZZLE ROCKET TO ADVENTURELAND
Avon Periodicals: Nov, 1952

1 12.00 36.00 85.00

PIXIES, THE (Advs. of...)(The Mighty Atom and ...#6 on)(See A-1 Comics #16)
Magazine Enterprises: Winter, 1946 - No. 4, Fall?, 1947; No. 5, 1948

1-Mighty Atom 7.50 22.50 45.00
2-5-Mighty Atom 4.00 12.00 24.00
I.W. Reprint #1(1958), 8-(Pee-Wee Pixies), 10-I.W. on cover, Super on inside 1.25 3.75 10.00

PIZZAZZ
Marvel Comics: Oct, 1977 - No. 16, Jan, 1979 (slick-color kids mag. w/puzzles, games, comics)

1-Star Wars photo-c/article; origin Tarzan; KISS photos/article; Iron-On bonus; 2 pg. pin-up calendars thru #8 2.50 7.50 22.00
2-Spider-Man-c; Beatles pin-up calendar 1.60 4.85 13.00
3-8: 3-Close Encounters-s; Bradbury-s. 4-Alice Cooper, Travolta; Charlie's Angels/Fonz/Hulk/Spider-Man-c. 5-Star Trek quiz. 6-Asimov-s. 7-James Bond; Spock/Darth Vader-c. 8-TV Spider-Man photo-c/article 1.60 4.85 13.00
9-14: 9-Shaun Cassidy-c. 10-Sgt. Pepper-c/s. 12-Battlestar Galactica-s; Spider-Man app. 13-TV Hulk-c/s. 14-Meatloaf-c/s 1.10 3.30 9.00
15,16: 15-Battlestar Galactica-s. 16-Movie Superman photo-c/s, Hulk. 1.40 4.15 11.00

*NOTE: **Star Wars** comics in all (1-6:Chaykin-a, 7-9: DeZuniga-a, 10-13:Simonson/Janson-a. 14-16:Cockrum-a). **Tarzan** comics, 1pg.-#1-8. 1pg. "Hey Look" by Kurtzman #12-16.*

PLANETARY
DC Comics (WildStorm Prod.): Apr, 1999 - Present ($2.50)

1,2-Ellis-s/Cassaday-a/c 3.00

PLANET COMICS
Fiction House Magazines: 1/40 - No. 62, 9/49; No. 63, Wint, 1949-50; No. 64, Spring, 1950; No. 65, 1951(nd); No. 66-68, 1952(nd); No. 69, Wint, 1952-53; No. 70-72, 1953(nd); No. 73, Winter, 1953-54

GD2.0 FN6.0 NM9.4

GD2.0 FN6.0 VF8.0 NM9.4
1-Origin Auro, Lord of Jupiter by Briefer (ends #61); Flint Baker & The Red Comet begin; Eisner/Fine-c 950.00 2850.00 5700.00 9500.00

GD2.0 FN6.0 NM9.4
2-Lou Fine-c (Scarce) 400.00 1200.00 3600.00
3-Eisner-c 278.00 833.00 2500.00
4-Gale Allen and the Girl Squadron begins 250.00 750.00 2000.00
5,6-(Scarce): 5-Eisner/Fine-c 237.00 712.00 1900.00
7-12: 8-Robot-c. 12-The Star Pirate begins 200.00 600.00 1600.00
13,14: 13-Reff Ryan begins 144.00 431.00 1150.00
15-(Scarce)-Mars, God of War begins (11/41); see Jumbo Comics #31 for 1st app. 288.00 862.00 2300.00
16-20,22 131.00 394.00 1050.00
21-The Lost World & Hunt Bowman begin 137.00 412.00 1100.00
23-26: 26-Space Rangers begin (9/43), end #71 125.00 375.00 1000.00
27-30 100.00 300.00 800.00
31-35: 33-Origin Star Pirates Wonder Boots, reprinted in #52. 35-Mysta of the Moon begins, ends #62 84.00 253.00 675.00
36-45: 38-1st Mysta of the Moon-c. 41-New origin of "Auro, Lord of Jupiter". 42-Last Gale Allen. 43-Futura begins 75.00 225.00 600.00
46-60: 48-Robot-c. 53-Used in **SOTI**, pg. 32 59.00 178.00 475.00
61-68,70: 61-Last 68 pg. issue. 64,70-Robot-c. 65-70-All partial-r of earlier issues. 70-r/stories from #41 44.00 132.00 350.00
69-Used in **POP**, pgs. 101,102 44.00 132.00 350.00
71-73-No series stories. 71-Space Rangers strip 36.00 107.00 250.00
I.W. Reprint 1,8,9: 1(nd)-r/#70; cover-r from Attack on Planet Mars. 8 (r/#72), 9-r/#73 6.50 19.50 65.00

*NOTE: **Anderson** a-33-38, 40-51 (Star Pirate). **Matt Baker** a-53-59 (Mysta of the Moon). **Celardo** c-12. **Bill Discount** a-71 (Space Rangers). **Elias** c-70. **Evans** a-46-49 (Auro, Lord of Jupiter), 50-64 (Lost World). **Fine** c-2, 5. **Hopper** a-31, 35 (Gale Allen), 41, 42, 48, 49 (Mysta of the Moon). **Ingels** a-24-31 (Lost World), 56-61 (Auro, Lord of Jupiter). **Lubbers** a-44-47 (Space Rangers); c-40, 41. **Moriera** a-43, 44 (Mysta of the Moon. **Renee** a-40-49 (Lost World); c-33, 35, 39. **Tuska** a-30 (Star Pirate). **M. Whitman** a-50-52 (Mysta of the Moon), 53-58 (Star Pirate); c-71-73. **Starr** a-59. **Zolnerwich** c-10. 13-25. Bondage c-53.*

PLANET COMICS
Blackthorne Publishing: Apr, 1988 - No. 3 (2.00, color/B&W #3)

1-3: New stories. 1-Dave Stevens-c 2.00

PLANET OF THE APES (Magazine) (Also see Adventures on the... & Power Record Comics)
Marvel Comics Group: Aug, 1974 - No. 29, Feb, 1977 (B&W) (Based on movies)

1-Ploog-a 2.60 7.80 26.00
2-Ploog-a 1.75 5.25 14.00
3-10 1.25 3.75 10.00
11-20 (uncommon) 1.50 4.50 12.00
21-28 (low distribution) 2.00 6.00 16.00
29 (scarce) 2.50 7.50 20.00

*NOTE: **Alcala** a-7-11, 17-22, 24. **Ploog** a-1-4, 6, 8, 11, 13, 14, 19. **Sutton** a-11, 12, 15, 17, 19, 20, 23, 24, 29. **Tuska** a-1-6.*

PLANET OF THE APES
Adventure Comics: Apr, 1990 - No. 24, 1992 ($2.50, B&W)

1-New movie tie-in; comes w/outer-c (3 colors) 4.00
1-Limited serial numbered edition ($5.00) 5.00
1-2nd printing (no outer-c, $2.50) 2.50
2-24 2.50
Annual 1 ($3.50) 3.50
...Urchak's Folly 1-4 ($2.50, mini-series) 2.50

PLANET OF VAMPIRES
Seaboard Publications (Atlas): Feb, 1975 - No. 3, July, 1975

1-Neal Adams-c(i); 1st Broderick c/a(p) 5.00
2,3: 2-Neal Adams-c. 3-Heath-c/a 4.00

PLANET TERRY
Marvel Comics (Star Comics)/Marvel: April, 1985 - No. 12, March, 1986 (Children's comic)

1-12 2.00

PLASM (See Warriors of Plasm)

Plastic Man #38 © QUA

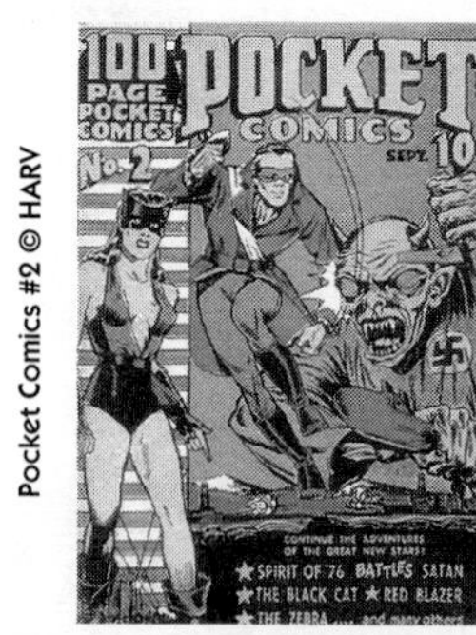

Pocket Comics #2 © HARV

Poe V2 #8 © Jason Asala

GD2.0 FN6.0 NM9.4

Defiant Comics: June, 1993

0-Came bound into Diamond Previews V3#6 (6/93); price is for complete Previews with comic still attached 3.00
0-Comic only removed from Previews 2.00

PLASMER
Marvel Comics UK: Nov, 1993 - No. 4, Feb, 1994 ($1.95, limited series)

1-($2.50)-Polybagged w/4 trading cards 2.50
2-4: Capt. America & Silver Surfer app. 2.00

PLASTIC FORKS
Marvel Comis (Epic Comics): 1990 - No. 5, 1990 ($4.95, 68 pgs., limited series, mature)

Book 1-5: Squarebound 5.00

PLASTIC MAN (Also see Police Comics & Smash Comics #17)
Vital Publ. No. 1,2/Quality Comics No. 3 on: Sum, 1943 - No. 64, Nov, 1956

nn(#1)- "In The Game of Death"; Skull-c; Jack Cole-c/a begins; ends-#64? 355.00 1065.00 3200.00
nn(#2, 2/44)- "The Gay Nineties Nightmare" 162.00 487.00 1300.00
3 (Spr, '46) 100.00 300.00 800.00
4 (Sum, '46) 81.00 244.00 650.00
5 (Aut, '46) 69.00 206.00 550.00
6-10 56.00 169.00 450.00
11-20 50.00 150.00 400.00
21-30: 26-Last non-r issue? 40.00 120.00 320.00
31-40: 40-Used in POP, pg. 91 34.00 103.00 240.00
41-64: 53-Last precode issue. 54-Robot-c 29.00 86.00 200.00
Super Reprint 11,16,18: 11('63)-r/#16. 16-r/#18 & #21; Cole-a. 18('64)-Spirit-r by Eisner from Police #95 4.20 12.60 42.00
NOTE: *Cole r-44, 49, 56, 58, 59 at least. Cuidera c-32-64i.*

PLASTIC MAN (See DC Special #15 & House of Mystery #160)
National Periodical Publications/DC Comics: 11-12/66 - No. 10, 5-6/68; V4#11, 2-3/76 - No. 20, 10-11/77

1-Real 1st app. Silver Age Plastic Man (House of Mystery #160 is actually tryout); Gil Kane-c/a; 12¢ issues begin 7.00 21.00 70.00
2-5: 4-Infantino-c; Mortimer-a 3.20 9.60 32.00
6-10('68): 7-G.A. Plastic Man & Woozy Winks (1st S.A. app.) app.; origin retold. 10-Sparling-a; last 12¢ issue 2.50 7.50 20.00
V4#11('76)-20: 11-20-Fradon-p. 17-Origin retold 2.40 6.00

PLASTIC MAN
DC Comics: Nov, 1988 - No. 4, Feb, 1989 ($1.00, mini-series)

1-4: 1-Origin; Woozy Winks app. 2.00

PLASTRON CAFE
Mirage Studios: Dec, 1992 - No. 4, July, 1993 ($2.25, B&W)

1-4: 1-Teenage Mutant Ninja Turtles app.; Kelly Freas-c. 2-Hildebrandt painted-c. 4-Spaced & Alien Fire stories 2.25

PLAYFUL LITTLE AUDREY (TV)(Also see Little Audrey #25)
Harvey Publications: 6/57 - No. 110, 11/73; No. 111, 8/74 - No. 121, 4/76

1 20.00 60.00 200.00
2 10.50 32.00 105.00
3-5 7.50 22.50 75.00
6-10 4.80 14.40 48.00
11-20 3.20 9.60 32.00
21-40 2.20 6.60 22.00
41-60 1.80 5.40 18.00
61-84: 84-Last 12¢ issue 1.40 4.20 14.00
85-99 1.00 3.00 10.00
100-52 pg. Giant 1.60 4.80 16.00
101-103: 52 pg. Giants 1.40 4.20 14.00
104-121 1.00 2.80 7.00
...In 3-D (Spring, 1988, $2.25, Blackthorne #66) 4.00

PLOP! (Also see The Best of DC #60)
National Periodical Publications: Sept-Oct, 1973 - No. 24, Nov-Dec, 1976

GD2.0 FN6.0 NM9.4

1-Sergio Aragonés-a begins; Wrightson-a 2.50 7.50 20.00
2-20: 5-Wrightson-a 1.25 3.75 10.00
21-24 (52 pgs.). 23-No Aragonés-a (52 pgs.) 1.85 5.50 15.00
NOTE: *Alcala a-1-3. Anderson a-5. Aragonés a-1-22, 24. Ditko a-16p. Evans a-1. Mayer a-1. Orlando a-21, 22; c-21. Sekowsky a-5, 6p. Toth a-11. Wolverton r-4, 22-24(1 pg.ea.); c-1-12, 14, 17, 18. Wood a-14, 16i, 18-24; c-13, 15, 16, 19.*

PLUTO (See Cheerios Premiums, Four Color #537, Mickey Mouse Magazine, Walt Disney Showcase #4, 7, 13, 20, 23, 33 & Wheaties)
Dell Publ. Co.: No. 7, 1942; No. 429, 10/52 - No. 1248, 11-1/61-62 (Disney)

Large Feature Comic 7(1942)-Written by Carl Barks, Jack Hannah, & Nick George (Barks' 1st comic book work) 109.00 327.00 1200.00
Four Color 429 (#1) 8.00 23.00 85.00
Four Color 509 4.50 13.50 50.00
Four Color 595,654,736,853 2.75 8.00 30.00
Four Color 941,1039,1143,1248 2.75 8.00 30.00

POCKET COMICS (Becomes Super Duper #5?; also see Double Up)
Harvey Publications: Aug, 1941 - No. 4, Jan, 1942 (Pocket size; 100 pgs.) (1st Harvey comic)

1-Origin & 1st app. The Black Cat, Cadet Blakey the Spirit of '76, The Red Blazer, The Phantom, Sphinx, & The Zebra; Phantom Ranger, British Agent #99, Spin Hawkins, Satan, Lord of Evil begin (1st app. of each); Simon-c/a in #1-3 94.00 281.00 750.00
2 (9/41)-Black Cat on-c #2-4 62.00 187.00 500.00
3,4 47.00 141.00 375.00

POE
Cheese Comics: Sept, 1996 - No. 6, Apr, 1997 ($2.00, B&W)

1-6-Jason Asala-s/a 2.50

POE
Sirius Entertainment (Dogstar Press): Oct, 1997 - Present ($2.50, B&W)

1-19-Jason Asala-s/a 2.50
... Color Special (12/98, $2.95) Linsner-c 3.00

POGO PARADE (See Dell Giants)

POGO POSSUM (Also see Animal Comics & Special Delivery)
Dell Publishing Co.: No. 105, 4/46 - No. 148, 5/47; 10-12/49 - No. 16, 4-6/54

Four Color 105(1946)-Kelly-c/a 66.00 198.00 725.00
Four Color 148-Kelly-c/a 58.00 175.00 640.00
1-(10-12/49)-Kelly-c/a in all 48.00 143.00 525.00
2 38.00 115.00 420.00
3-5 26.00 78.00 285.00
6-10: 10-Infinity-c 22.00 65.00 240.00
11-16: 11-X-Mas-c 17.00 52.00 190.00
NOTE: *#1-4, 9-13: 52 pgs.; #5-8, 14-16: 36 pgs.*

POINT BLANK
Acme Press (Eclipse): May, 1989 - No. 2, 1989 ($2.95, B&W, magazine)

1,2-European-r 3.00

POISON ELVES (Formerly I, Lusiphur)
Mulehide Graphics: No. 8, 1993- No. 20, 1995 (B&W, magazine/comic size, mature readers)

8-Drew Hayes-c/a/scripts. 2.50 7.50 20.00
9-11: 11-1st comic size issue 2.50 7.50 20.00
12,14,16,20 1.50 4.50 12.00
13,15-scarce 2.50 7.50 25.00
15-2nd print 4.00
17-19 1.50 4.50 12.00
...Desert of the Third Sin-(1997, $14.95, TPB)-r/#13-18 15.00
...Patrons-($4.95, TPB)-r/#19,20 5.00
...Traumatic Dogs-(1996, $14.95,TPB)-Reprints I, Lusiphur #7, Poison Elves #8-12 15.00

POISON ELVES (See I, Lusiphur)
Sirius Entertainment: June, 1995 - Present ($2.50, B&W, mature readers)

1-Linsner-c; Drew Hayes-a/scripts in all. 1.00 3.00 8.00
1-2nd print 2.50

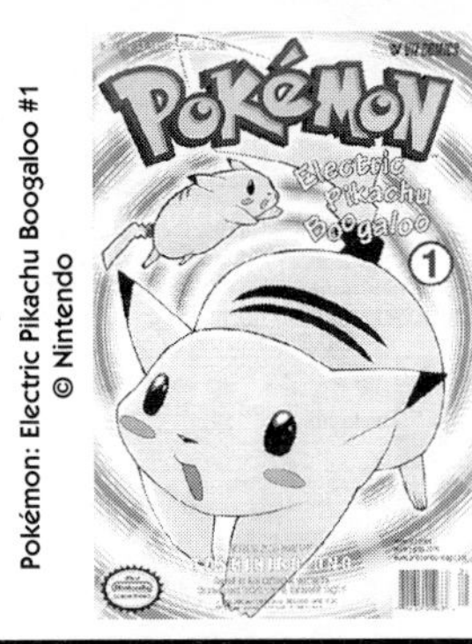
Pokémon: Electric Pikachu Boogaloo #1 © Nintendo

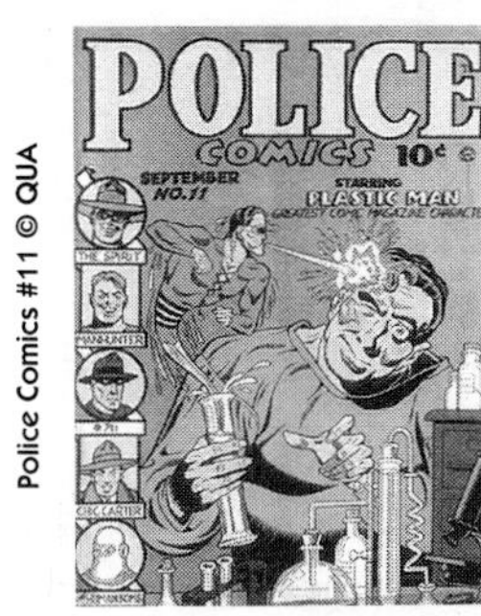
Police Comics #11 © QUA

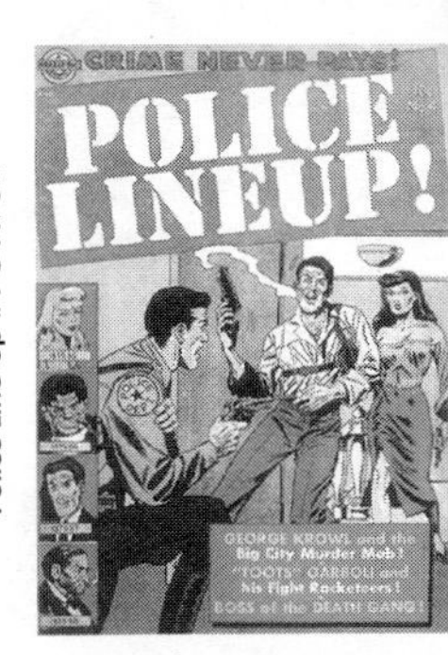
Police Line-Up #4 © AVON

	GD2.0	FN6.0	NM9.4
2-25,46: 12-Purple Marauder-c/app.			3.00
26-45, 47-49			2.50
... Color Special #1 (12/98, $2.95)	1.00	3.00	8.00
... FAN Edition #1 mail-in offer; Drew Hayes-c/s/a	1.00	3.00	8.00
...Sanctuary-(1999, $14.95, TPB)-r/#1-12			15.00

POKÉMON: THE ELECTRIC TALE OF PIKACHU (TV)
Viz Comics: Nov, 1998 - No. 4, Feb, 1999 ($3.25/$3.50, B&W)

	GD2.0	FN6.0	NM9.4
1-Toshiro Ono-s/a	1.85	5.50	15.00
1-4 (2nd through current printings)			5.00
2	1.00	3.00	8.00
3,4			5.00
TPB ($12.95)			13.00
...Part 2: Pikachu Strikes Back			
1	1.00	3.00	8.00
2-4			4.00
...Part 3: Electric Pikachu Boogaloo			
1			3.50
2,3 ($2.95)			3.00
...Part 4: Surf's Up Pikachu			
1			3.50

NOTE: Multiple printings exist for most issues

POLICE ACADEMY (TV)
Marvel Comics: Nov, 1989 - No. 6, Feb, 1990 ($1.00)

	GD2.0	FN6.0	NM9.4
1-6: Based on TV cartoon; Post-c/a(p) in all			2.00

POLICE ACTION
Atlas News Co.: Jan, 1954 - No. 7, Nov, 1954

	GD2.0	FN6.0	NM9.4
1-Violent-a by Robert Q. Sale	20.00	60.00	140.00
2	10.00	30.00	70.00
3-7: 7-Powell-a	10.00	30.00	60.00

NOTE: ***Ayers** a-4, 5. **Colan** a-1. **Forte** a-1, 2. **Mort Lawrence** a-5. **Maneely** a-3; c-1, 5. **Reinman** a-6, 7.*

POLICE ACTION
Atlas/Seaboard Publ.: Feb, 1975 - No. 3, June, 1975

	GD2.0	FN6.0	NM9.4
1-3: 1-Lomax, N.Y.P.D., Luke Malone begin; McWilliams-a. 2-Origin Luke Malone, Manhunter			4.00

NOTE: ***Ploog** art in all. **Sekowsky/McWilliams** a-1-3. **Thorne** c-3.*

POLICE AGAINST CRIME
Premiere Magazines: April, 1954 - No. 9, Aug, 1955

	GD2.0	FN6.0	NM9.4
1-Disbrow-a; extreme violence (man's face slashed with knife); Hollingsworth-a	23.00	69.00	160.00
2-Hollingsworth-a	12.00	36.00	85.00
3-9	10.00	30.00	70.00

POLICE BADGE #479 (Formerly Spy Thrillers #1-4)
Atlas Comics (PrPl): No. 5, Sept, 1955

	GD2.0	FN6.0	NM9.4
5-Maneely-c/a (6 pgs.)	10.00	30.00	70.00

POLICE CASE BOOK (See Giant Comics Editions)

POLICE CASES (See Authentic... & Record Book of...)

POLICE COMICS
Quality Comics Group (Comic Magazines): Aug, 1941 - No. 127, Oct, 1953

	GD2.0	FN6.0	NM9.4
1-Origin/1st app. Plastic Man by Jack Cole (r-in DC Special #15), The Human Bomb by Gustavson, & No. 711; intro. Chic Carter by Eisner, The Firebrand by Reed Crandall, The Mouthpiece by Guardineer, Phantom Lady, & The Sword; Firebrand-c 1-4	650.00	1950.00	6500.00
2-Plastic Man smuggles opium	288.00	862.00	2400.00
3	200.00	500.00	1600.00
4	188.00	562.00	1500.00
5-Plastic Man-c begin; Plastic Man forced to smoke marijuana; Plastic Man covers begin, end #102	175.00	525.00	1400.00
6,7	156.00	469.00	1250.00
8-Manhunter begins (origin/1st app.) (3/42)	181.00	544.00	1450.00
9,10	125.00	375.00	1000.00
11-The Spirit strip reprints begin by Eisner (origin-strip #1); 1st comic book app. The Spirit & 1st cover app. (9/42)	206.00	619.00	1650.00
12-Intro. Ebony	131.00	394.00	1050.00
13-Intro. Woozy Winks; last Firebrand	125.00	375.00	1000.00
14-19: 15-Last No. 711; Destiny begins	91.00	272.00	725.00
20-The Raven x-over in Phantom Lady; features Jack Cole himself	91.00	272.00	725.00
21,22: 21-Raven & Spider Widow x-over in Phantom Lady (cameo in #22)	75.00	225.00	600.00
23-30: 23-Last Phantom Lady. 24-26-Flatfoot Burns by Kurtzman in all	69.00	206.00	550.00
31-41: 37-1st app. Candy by Sahle & begins (12/44). 41-Last Spirit-r by Eisner	47.00	141.00	375.00
42,43-Spirit-r by Eisner/Fine	40.00	120.00	300.00
44-Fine Spirit-r begin, end #88,90,92	37.00	111.00	260.00
45-50: 50-(#50 on-c, #49 on inside, 1/46)	37.00	111.00	260.00
51-60: 58-Last Human Bomb	31.00	94.00	220.00
61-88: 63-(Some issues have #65 printed on cover, but #63 on inside) Kurtzman-a, 6 pgs.	24.00	73.00	170.00
89,91,93-No Spirit stories	21.00	64.00	150.00
90,92-Spirit by Fine	26.00	79.00	185.00
94-99,101,102: Spirit by Eisner in all; 101-Last Manhunter. 102-Last Spirit & Plastic Man by Jack Cole	33.00	99.00	230.00
100	40.00	120.00	280.00
103-Content change to crime; Ken Shannon & T-Man begin (1st app. of each, 12/50)	24.00	73.00	170.00
104-112,114-127: Crandall-a most issues (not in 104,105,122,125-127). 109-Atomic bomb story. 112-Crandall-a	19.00	56.00	130.00
113-Crandall-c/a(2), 9 pgs. each	19.00	58.00	135.00

NOTE: *Most Spirit stories signed by Eisner are not by him; all are reprints. **Cole** c-17, 19-21, 24-26, 28-31, 36-38, 40-42, 45-48, 65-68, 69, 73, 75. **Crandall** Firebrand-1-8. Spirit by **Eisner** 1-41, 94-102; by **Eisner/Fine**-42, 43; by **Fine**-44-88, 90, 92. 103, 109. **Al Bryant** c-33, 34. **Cole** c-17-32, 35-102(most). **Crandall** c-13, 14. **Crandall/Cuidera** c-105-127. **Eisner** c-4i. **Gill Fox** c-1-3, 4p, 5-12, 15. Bondage c-103, 109, 125.*

POLICE LINE-UP
Avon Periodicals/Realistic Comics #3,4: Aug, 1951 - No. 4, July, 1952 (Painted-c #1-3)

	GD2.0	FN6.0	NM9.4
1-Wood-a, 1 pg. plus part-c; spanking panel-r/Saint #5	39.00	116.00	270.00
2-Classic story "The Religious Murder Cult", drugs, perversion; r/Saint #5; c-r/Avon paperback #329	27.00	81.00	190.00
3,4: 3-Kubert-a(r?)/part-c; Kinstler-a (inside-c only)	20.00	60.00	140.00

POLICE TRAP (Public Defender In Action #7 on)
Mainline #1-4/Charlton #5,6: 8-9/54 - No. 4, 2-3/55; No. 5, 7/55 - No. 6, 9/55

	GD2.0	FN6.0	NM9.4
1-S&K covers-all issues; Meskin-a; Kirby scripts	29.00	86.00	200.00
2-4	17.00	51.00	120.00
5,6-S&K-c/a	24.00	71.00	165.00

POLICE TRAP
Super Comics: No. 11, 1963; No. 16-18, 1964

	GD2.0	FN6.0	NM9.4
Reprint #11,16-18: 11-r/Police Trap #3. 16-r/Justice Traps the Guilty #? 17-r/Inside Crime #3 & r/Justice Traps The Guilty #83; 18-r/Inside Crime #3	1.25	3.75	10.00

POLLY & HER PALS (See Comic Monthly #1)

POLLYANNA (Disney)
Dell Publishing Co.: No. 1129, Aug-Oct, 1960

	GD2.0	FN6.0	NM9.4
Four Color 1129-Movie, Haley Mills photo-c	7.00	22.00	80.00

POLLY PIGTAILS (Girls' Fun & Fashion Magazine #44 on)
Parents' Magazine Institute/Polly Pigtails: Jan, 1946 - V4#43, Oct-Nov, 1949

	GD2.0	FN6.0	NM9.4
1-Infinity-c; photo-c	10.00	30.00	70.00
2-Photo-c	5.85	17.50	35.00
3-5: 3,4-Photo-c	4.25	13.00	26.00
6-10: 7-Photo-c	4.00	11.00	22.00
11-30: 22-Photo-c	3.20	8.00	16.00
31-43	2.80	7.00	14.00

PONY EXPRESS (See Tales of the...)

Popeye Four Color #145 © KING

Popeye #3 © KING

Popular Comics #47 © DELL

	GD2.0	FN6.0	NM9.4

PONYTAIL
Dell Publishing Co./Charlton No. 13 on: 7-9/62 - No. 12, 10-12/65; No. 13, 11/69 - No. 20, 1/71

	GD2.0	FN6.0	NM9.4
12-641-209(#1)	2.35	7.00	26.00
2-12	1.60	4.80	16.00
13-20	1.00	3.00	10.00

POP COMICS
Modern Store Publ.: 1955 (36 pgs.; 5x7"; in color) (7¢)

	GD2.0	FN6.0	NM9.4
1-Funny animal	1.00	3.00	8.00

POPEYE (See Comic Album #7, 11, 15, Comics Reading Libraries, Eat Right to Work and Win, Giant Comic Album, King Comics, Kite Fun Book, Magic Comics, March of Comics #37, 52, 66, 80, 96, 117, 134, 148, 157, 169, 194, 246, 264, 274, 294, 453, 465, 477 & Wow Comics, 1st series)

POPEYE (See Thimble Theatre in the Platinum Age section)
David McKay Publications: 1935 (25¢; 52 pgs.; B&W) (By Segar)

	GD2.0	FN6.0	NM9.4
1-Daily strip serial reprints- "The Gold Mine Thieves"	63.00	187.00	625.00
2-Daily strip-r	47.00	142.00	475.00

NOTE: *Popeye first entered Thimble Theatre in 1929.*

POPEYE
David McKay Publications: 1937 - 1939 (All by Segar)

	GD2.0	FN6.0	NM9.4
Feature Books nn (100 pgs.) (Very Rare)	564.00	1691.00	6200.00
Feature Books 2 (52 pgs.)	64.00	191.00	700.00
Feature Books 3 (100 pgs.)-r/nn issue with a new-c	59.00	177.00	650.00
Feature Books 5,10 (76 pgs.)	55.00	164.00	600.00
Feature Books 14 (76 pgs.) (Scarce)	64.00	191.00	700.00

POPEYE (Strip reprints through 4-Color #70)
Dell #1-65/Gold Key #66-80/King #81-92/Charlton #94-138/Gold Key #139-155/Whitman #156 on: 1941 - 1947; #1, 2-4/48 - #65, 7-9/62; #66, 10/62 - #80, 5/66; #81, 8/66 - #92, 12/67; #94, 2/69 - #138, 1/77; #139, 5/78 - #171, 7/84 (no #93,160,161)

	GD2.0	FN6.0	NM9.4
Large Feature Comic 24('41)-Half by Segar	52.00	157.00	575.00
Four Color 25('41)-by Segar	68.00	205.00	750.00
Large Feature Comic 10('43)	43.00	130.00	475.00
Four Color 17('43),26('43)-by Segar	50.00	150.00	550.00
Four Color 43('44)	31.00	93.00	340.00
Four Color 70('45)-Title: ...& Wimpy	25.00	75.00	275.00
Four Color 113('46-original strips begin),127,145('47),168	12.30	37.00	135.00
1(2-4/48)(Dell)-All new stories continue	26.00	79.00	290.00
2	13.00	39.00	145.00
3-10: 5-Popeye on moon w/rocket-c	11.00	32.00	120.00
11-20	9.00	27.00	100.00
21-40,46: 46-Origin Swee' Pee	7.00	22.00	80.00
41-45,47-50	5.50	16.50	60.00
51-60	5.00	15.00	55.00
61-65 (Last Dell issue)	4.00	12.00	45.00
66,67-Both 84 pgs. (Gold Key)	5.50	16.50	60.00
68-80	2.20	6.60	24.00
81-92,94-97 (no #93): 97-Last 12¢ issue	1.80	5.40	18.00
98,99,101-130	1.20	3.60	12.00
100	2.00	6.00	22.00
131-155: 144-50th Anniversary issue		2.40	6.00
156,157,162-167(Whitman) (no #160,161,168)	1.10	3.30	9.00
158(9/80),159(11/80)-pre-pack?	1.50	4.50	15.00
169-171: 169(#168 on-c). All #90069 on-c; pre-pack?	1.20	3.60	12.00

NOTE: *Reprints-#145, 147, 149, 151, 153, 155, 157, 163-68(1/3), 170.*

POPEYE
Harvey Comics: Nov, 1993 - No. 7, Aug, 1994 ($1.50)

	GD2.0	FN6.0	NM9.4
V2#1-7			2.00
...Summer Special V2#1-(10/93, $2.25, 68 pgs.)-Sagendorf-r & others			2.25

POPEYE CARTOON BOOK
The Saalfield Publ. Co.: 1934 (8-1/2x13", 40 pgs., cardboard-c)

	GD2.0	FN6.0	NM9.4
2095-(Rare)-1933 strip reprints in color by Segar; each page contains a vertical half of a Sunday strip, so the continuity reads row by row completely across each double page spread. If each page is read by itself, the continuity makes no sense. Each double page spread reprints one complete Sunday page (from 1933)	250.00	750.00	2000.00
12 Page Version	100.00	300.00	800.00

POPEYE SPECIAL
Ocean Comics: Summer, 1987 - No. 2, Sept, 1988 ($1.75/$2.00)

	GD2.0	FN6.0	NM9.4
1,2: 1-Origin			2.00

POPPLES (TV, movie)
Star Comics (Marvel): Dec, 1986 - No. 5, Aug, 1987

	GD2.0	FN6.0	NM9.4
1-5-Based on toys			2.00

POPPO OF THE POPCORN THEATRE
Fuller Publishing Co. (Publishers Weekly): 10/29/55 - No. 13, 1956 (weekly)

	GD2.0	FN6.0	NM9.4
1	8.35	25.00	50.00
2-5	5.35	16.00	32.00
6-13	4.25	13.00	26.00

NOTE: *By **Charles Biro.** 10¢ cover, given away by supermarkets such as IGA.*

POP-POP COMICS
R. B. Leffingwell Co.: No date (Circa 1945) (52 pgs.)

	GD2.0	FN6.0	NM9.4
1-Funny animal	10.00	30.00	70.00

POPULAR COMICS
Dell Publishing Co.: Feb, 1936 - No. 145, July-Sept, 1948

	GD2.0	FN6.0	VF8.0
1-Dick Tracy (1st comic book app.), Little Orphan Annie, Terry & the Pirates, Gasoline Alley, Don Winslow (1st app.), Harold Teen, Little Joe, Skippy, Moon Mullins, Mutt & Jeff, Tailspin Tommy, Smitty, Smokey Stover, Winnie Winkle & The Gumps begin (all strip-r)	566.00	1700.00	3800.00
2	183.00	550.00	1275.00
3	145.00	437.00	950.00
4-6(7/36): 5-Tom Mix begins. 6-1st app. Scribbly	119.00	357.00	800.00
7-10: 8,9-Scribbly & Reglar Fellers app.	91.00	275.00	600.00

	GD2.0	FN6.0	NM9.4
11-20: 12-X-Mas-c	78.00	234.00	500.00
21-27: 27-Last Terry & the Pirates, Little Orphan Annie, & Dick Tracy	54.00	162.00	360.00
28-37: 28-Gene Autry app. 31,32-Tim McCoy app. 35-Christmas-c; Tex Ritter app.	45.00	137.00	310.00
38-43: Tarzan in text only. 38-(4/39)-Gang Busters (Radio, 2nd app.) & Zane Grey's Tex Thorne begins? 43-The Masked Pilot app.; 1st non-funny-c?	40.00	120.00	320.00
44,45: 45-Hurricane Kid-c	31.00	94.00	220.00
46-Origin/1st app. Martan, the Marvel Man(12/39)	40.00	120.00	300.00
47-50	30.00	90.00	210.00
51-Origin The Voice (The Invisible Detective) strip begins (5/40)	31.00	94.00	220.00
52-59: 52-Robot-c. 55-End of World story	24.00	73.00	170.00
60-Origin/1st app. Professor Supermind and Son (2/41)	25.00	75.00	175.00
61-71: 63-Smilin' Jack begins	19.00	58.00	135.00
72-The Owl & Terry & the Pirates begin (2/42); Smokey Stover reprints begin	40.00	120.00	300.00
73-75	26.00	77.00	180.00
76-78-Capt. Midnight in all (see The Funnies #57)	37.00	111.00	260.00
79-85-Last Owl	23.00	69.00	160.00
86-99: 98-Felix the Cat, Smokey Stover-r begin	17.00	49.00	115.00
100	18.00	54.00	125.00
101-130	10.00	30.00	70.00
131-145: 142-Last Terry & the Pirates	10.00	30.00	65.00

NOTE: *Martan, the Marvel Man c-47-49, 52, 57-59. Professor Supermind c-60-63, 64(1/2), 65, 66. The Voice c-53.*

POPULAR FAIRY TALES (See March of Comics #6, 18)

POPULAR ROMANCE

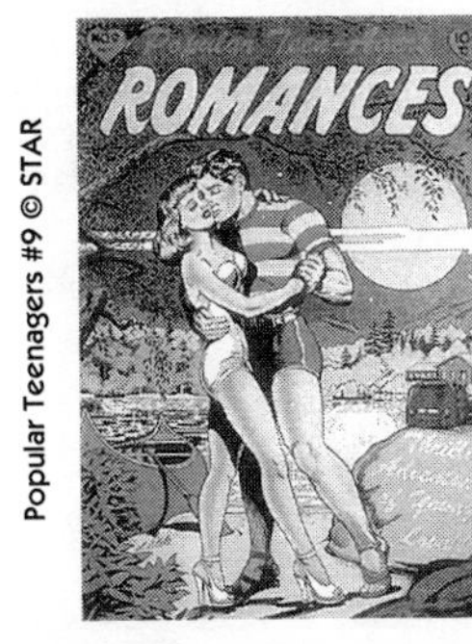

Popular Teenagers #9 © STAR

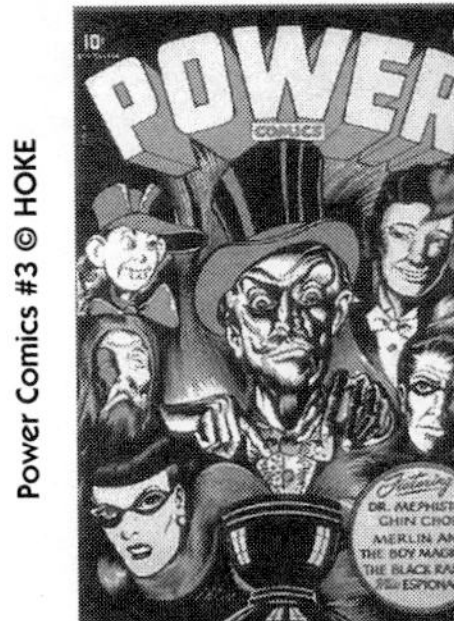

Power Comics #3 © HOKE

Power and Glory #1a © MAL

	GD2.0	FN6.0	NM9.4

Better-Standard Publications: No. 5, Dec, 1949 - No. 29, July, 1954

	GD2.0	FN6.0	NM9.4
5	10.00	30.00	60.00
6-9: 7-Palais-a; lingerie panels	5.85	17.50	35.00
10-Wood-a (2 pgs.)	8.35	25.00	50.00
11,12,14-16,18-21,28,29	5.00	15.00	30.00
13,17-Severin/Elder-a (3&8 pgs.)	5.85	17.50	35.00
22-27-Toth-a	8.35	25.00	50.00

NOTE: *All have photo-c.* ***Tuska*** *art in most issues.*

POPULAR TEEN-AGERS (Secrets of Love) (School Day Romances #1-4)
Star Publications: No. 5, Sept, 1950 - No. 23, Nov, 1954

	GD2.0	FN6.0	NM9.4
5-Toni Gay, Midge Martin & Eve Adams continue from School Day Romances; Ginger Bunn (formerly Ginger Snapp & becomes Honey Bunn #6 on) begins; all features end #8	32.00	96.00	225.00
6-8 (7/51)-Honey Bunn begins; all have L. B. Cole-c; 6-Negligee panels	29.00	86.00	200.00
9-(...Romances; 1st romance issue, 10/51)	18.00	54.00	125.00
10-(...Secrets of Love thru #23)	17.00	51.00	120.00
11,16,18,19,22,23	13.50	41.00	95.00
12,13,17,20,21-Disbrow-a	15.00	45.00	105.00
14-Harrison/Wood-a; 2 spanking scenes	20.00	60.00	140.00
15-Wood?, Disbrow-a	17.00	51.00	120.00
Accepted Reprint 5,6 (nd); L.B. Cole-c	7.50	22.50	45.00

NOTE: *All have* ***L. B. Cole*** *covers.*

PORKY PIG (See Bugs Bunny &..., Kite Fun Book, Looney Tunes, March of Comics #42, 57, 71, 89, 99, 113, 130, 143, 164, 175, 192, 209, 218, 367, and Super Book #6, 18, 30)

PORKY PIG (...& Bugs Bunny #40-69)
Dell Publishing Co./Gold Key No. 1-93/Whitman No. 94 on: No. 16, 1942 - No. 81, Mar-Apr, 1962; Jan, 1965 - No. 109, July, 1984

	GD2.0	FN6.0	NM9.4
Four Color 16(#1, 1942)	75.00	225.00	825.00
Four Color 48(1944)-Carl Barks-a	95.00	286.00	1050.00
Four Color 78(1945)	23.00	68.00	250.00
Four Color 112(7/46)	14.00	41.00	150.00
Four Color 156,182,191('49)	9.50	29.00	105.00
Four Color 226,241('49),260,271,277,284,295	7.00	22.00	80.00
Four Color 303,311,322,330: 322-Sci/fi-c/story	4.50	13.50	50.00
Four Color 342,351,360,370,385,399,410,426	3.60	11.00	40.00
25 (11-12/52)-30	2.75	8.00	30.00
31-40	1.50	4.50	16.00
41-60	1.40	4.20	15.00
61-81(3-4/62)	1.30	3.90	14.00
1(1/65-Gold Key)(2nd Series)	3.80	11.40	38.00
2,4,5-r/4-Color 226,284 & 271 in that order	2.40	7.20	24.00
3,6-10: 3-r/Four Color #342	1.60	4.80	16.00
11-30	1.20	3.60	12.00
31-54	1.10	3.30	9.00
55-70		2.40	6.00
71-93(Gold Key)			4.00
94-96			5.00
97(9/80),98,99-pre-pack?	1.00	3.00	10.00
100	1.00	2.80	7.00
101-105			5.00
106-109 (All #90140 on-c, no date or date code)	1.10	3.30	9.00

NOTE: *Reprints-#1-8, 9-35(2/3); 36-46, 58, 67, 69-74, 76, 78, 102-109(1/3-1/2).*

PORKY PIG'S DUCK HUNT
Saalfield Publishing Co.: 1938 (12pgs.)(large size)(heavy linen-like paper)

	GD2.0	FN6.0	NM9.4
2178-1st app. Porky Pig & Daffy Duck by Leon Schlesinger. Illustrated text story book written in verse. 1st book ever devoted to these characters. (see Looney Tunes #1 for their 1st comic book app.)	66.00	197.00	525.00

PORTIA PRINZ OF THE GLAMAZONS
Eclipse Comics: Dec, 1986 - No. 6, Oct, 1987 ($2.00, B&W, Baxter paper)

	GD2.0	FN6.0	NM9.4
1-6			2.00

POST GAZETTE (See Meet the New...)

POWDER RIVER RUSTLERS (See Fawcett Movie Comics)

POWER & GLORY (See American Flagg! & Howard Chaykin's American Flagg!
Malibu Comics (Bravura): Feb, 1994 - No. 4, May, 1994 ($2.50, limited series, mature)

	GD2.0	FN6.0	NM9.4
1A, 1B-By Howard Chaykin; w/Bravura stamp			2.50
1-Newsstand ed. (polybagged w/children's warning on bag), Gold ed., Silver-foil ed., Blue-foil ed.(print run of 10,000), Serigraph ed. (print run of 3,000)($2.95)-Howard Chaykin-c/a begin			3.00
2-4-Contains Bravura stamp			2.50
Holiday Special (Win '94, $2.95)			3.00

POWER COMICS
Holyoke Publ. Co./Narrative Publ.: 1944 - No. 4, 1945

	GD2.0	FN6.0	NM9.4
1-L. B. Cole-c	137.00	412.00	1100.00
2-Hitler, Hirohito-c (scarce)	137.00	412.00	1100.00
3-Classic L.B. Cole-c; Dr. Mephisto begins?	150.00	450.00	1200.00
4-L.B. Cole-c; Miss Espionage app. #3,4; Leav-a	137.00	412.00	1100.00

POWER COMICS
Power Comics Co.: 1977 - No. 5, Dec, 1977 (B&W)

	GD2.0	FN6.0	NM9.4
1- "A Boy And His Aardvark" by Dave Sim; first Dave Sim aardvark (not Cerebus)	1.25	3.75	10.00
1-Reprint (3/77, black-c)			4.00
2-Cobalt Blue by Gustovich			5.00
3-5: 3-Nightwitch. 4-Northern Light. 5-Bluebird			5.00

POWER COMICS
Eclipse Comics (Acme Press): Mar, 1988 - No. 4, Sept, 1988 ($2.00, B&W, mini-series)

	GD2.0	FN6.0	NM9.4
1-4: Bolland, Gibbons-r in all			2.00

POWER FACTOR
Wonder Color Comics: May, 1987 - No. 2, 1987 ($1.95)

	GD2.0	FN6.0	NM9.4
1,2: Super team. 2-Infantino-c			2.00

POWER FACTOR
Innovation Publishing: Oct, 1990 - No. 3, 1991 ($1.95/$2.25)

	GD2.0	FN6.0	NM9.4
1-3: 1-R-/1st story + new-a, 2-r/2nd story + new-a. 3-Infantino-a			2.25

POWER GIRL (See All-Star #58, Infinity, Inc., Showcase #97-99)
DC Comics: June, 1988 - No. 4, Sept, 1988 ($1.00, color, limited series)

	GD2.0	FN6.0	NM9.4
1-4			2.00

POWERHOUSE PEPPER COMICS (See Gay Comics, Joker Comics & Tessie the Typist)
Marvel Comics (20CC): No. 1, 1943; No. 2, May, 1948 - No. 5, Nov, 1948

	GD2.0	FN6.0	NM9.4
1-(60 pgs.)-Wolverton-a in all; c-2,3	150.00	450.00	1200.00
2	81.00	244.00	650.00
3,4	75.00	225.00	600.00
5-(Scarce)	87.00	262.00	700.00

POWER LINE
Marvel Comics (Epic Comics): May, 1988 - No. 8, Sept, 1989 ($1.25/$1.50)

	GD2.0	FN6.0	NM9.4
1-8: 2-Williamson-i. 3- Dr. Zero app. 4-7-Morrow-a. 8-Williamson-i			2.00

POWER LORDS
DC Comics: Dec, 1983 - No. 3, Feb, 1984 (Limited series, Mando paper)

	GD2.0	FN6.0	NM9.4
1-3: Based on Revell toys			2.00

POWER MAN (Formerly Hero for Hire; ...& Iron Fist #68 on; see Cage & Giant-Size...)
Marvel Comics Group: No. 17, Feb, 1974 - No. 125, Sept, 1986

	GD2.0	FN6.0	NM9.4
17-Luke Cage continues; Iron Man app.	1.00	3.00	8.00
18-20,31: 18-Last 20¢ issue. 31-Part Neal Adams-i			5.00
21-30			4.00
30-(30¢-c variant, limited distribution)(4/76)	2.00	6.00	16.00
31-(30¢-c variant, limited distribution)(5/76)	2.50	7.50	24.00
32-46: 34-Last 25¢ issue. 36-r/Hero For Hire #12. 41-1st app. Thunderbolt. 45-Starlin-c.			3.00
32-34-(30¢-c variants, limited distribution)(6-8/76)	1.50	4.50	12.00
47-Barry Smith-a			5.00

Power of Shazam! #42 © DC

Power Pack #15 © MAR

Preacher #50 © Garth Ennis & Steve Dillon

GD2.0 FN6.0 NM9.4

48-50-Byrne-a(p); 48-Power Man/Iron Fist 1st meet. 50-Iron Fist joins Cage 1.00 3.00 8.00
57-New X-Men app. (6/79) 1.25 3.75 10.00
51-56,58-65,67-77,79-83,85-125: 758-Intro El Aguila. 5-Double size. 77-Daredevil app. 87-MoonKnight app. 90-Unus app. 109-The Reaper app. 100-Double size; origin K'un L'un. 125-Double size; death of Iron Fist 2.00
66,78,84: 66-2nd app. Sabretooth (see Iron Fist #14) . 78-3rd app. Sabretooth (cameo under cloak). 84-4th app. Sabretooth 1.00 3.00 8.00
Annual 1(1976)-Punisher cameo in flashback 1.00 3.00 8.00
NOTE: ***Austin*** *c-102i.* ***Byrne*** *a-48-50; c-102, 104, 106, 107, 112-116.* ***Kane*** *c(p)-24, 25, 28, 48.* ***Miller*** *a-68, 76(2 pgs.); c-66-68, 70-74, 80i.* ***Mooney*** *a-38i, 53i, 55i.* ***Nebres*** *a-76p.* ***Nino*** *a-42i, 43i.* ***Perez*** *a-27.* ***B. Smith*** *a-47i.* ***Tuska*** *a(p)-17, 20, 24, 26, 28, 29, 36, 47. Painted c-75, 100.*

POWER OF PRIME
Malibu Comics (Ultraverse): July, 1995 - No. 4, Nov, 1995 ($2.50, lim. series)
1-4 2.50

POWER OF SHAZAM!, THE (See SHAZAM!)
DC Comics: 1994 (Painted graphic novel) (Prequel to new series)
Hardcover-($19.95)-New origin of Shazam!; Ordway painted-c/a & script 2.50 7.50 25.00
Softcover-($7.50), Softcover-($9.95)-New-c. 1.50 4.50 12.00

POWER OF SHAZAM!, THE
DC Comics: Mar, 1995 - No. 47, Mar, 1999 ($1.50/$1.75/$1.95/$2.50)
1-Jerry Ordway scripts begin 3.00
2-47: 4-Begin $1.75-c. 6:Re-intro of Capt. Nazi. 8-Re-intro of Spy Smasher, Bulletman & Minuteman; Swan-a (7 pgs.). 11-Re-intro of Ibis,Swan-a(2 pgs.). 14-Gil Kane-a(p). 20-Superman-c/app.; "Final Night". 21-Plastic Man-c/app. 22-Batman-c/app. 35,36-Crossover w/Starman #39,40. 38-41-Mr. Mind. 43-Bulletman app. 45-JLA-c/app. 2.50
#1,000,000 (11/98) 853rd Century x-over; Ordway-c/s/a 3.00
Annual 1 (1996, $2.95)-Legends of the Dead Earth story; Jerry Ordway-c; Mike Manley-a 4.00

POWER OF STRONGMAN, THE (Also see Strongman)
AC Comics: 1989 ($2.95)
1-Powell G.A.-r 3.00

POWER OF THE ATOM (See Secret Origins #29)
DC Comics: Aug, 1988 - No. 18, Nov, 1989 ($1.00)
1-18: 6-Chronos returns; Byrne-p. 9-JLI app. 2.00

POWER PACHYDERMS
Marvel Comics: Sept, 1989 ($1.25, one-shot)
1-Elephant super-heroes; parody of X-Men, Elektra, & 3 Stooges 2.00

POWER PACK
Marvel Comics Group: Aug, 1984 - No. 62, Feb, 1991
1-($1.00, 52 pgs.)-Origin & 1st app. Power Pack 3.00
2-26,28,30-45,47-62: 19-(52 pgs.)-Cloak & Dagger, Wolverine app. 2.00
27-Mutant massacre; Wolverine & Sabretooth app. 4.00
29,46: 29-Spider-Man & Hobgoblin app. 46-Punisher app. 2.00
...Holiday Special 1 (2/92, $2.25, 68 pgs.) 2.25
NOTE: ***Austin*** *scripts-53.* ***Mignola*** *c-20.* ***Morrow*** *a-51.* ***Spiegle*** *a-55i.* ***Williamson*** *a(i)-43, 50, 52.*

POWER RANGERS ZEO (TV)(Saban's...)(Also see Saban's Mighty Morphin Power Rangers)
Image Comics (Extreme Studios): Aug, 1996 ($2.50)
1-Based on TV show 2.50

POWERS THAT BE (Becomes Star Seed No.7 on)
Broadway Comics: Nov, 1995 - No. 6, June, 1996 ($2.50)
1-6: 1-Intro of Fatale & Star Seed. 6-Begin $2.95-c. 3.00
Preview Editions 1-3 (9/95 - 11/95, B&W) 2.50

POW MAGAZINE (Bob Sproul's) (Satire Magazine)
Humor-Vision: Aug, 1966 - No. 3, Feb, 1967 (30¢)
1-3: 2-Jones-a. 3-Wrightson-a 3.20 9.60 32.00

PREACHER

GD2.0 FN6.0 NM9.4

DC Comics (Vertigo): Apr, 1995 - Present ($2.50, mature)
nn-Preview 3.00 9.00 30.00
1 ($2.95)-Ennis scripts, Dillon-a & Fabry-c in all; 1st app. Jesse, Tulip, & Cassidy 2.25 6.75 18.00
2,3: 2-1st app. Saint of Killers. 1.85 5.50 15.00
4,5 1.25 3.75 10.00
6-10 1.00 2.80 7.00
11-20: 12-Polybagged w/videogame w/Ennis text. 13-Hunters storyline begins; ends #17. 19-Saint of Killers app.; begin "Crusaders", ends #24 2.40 6.00
21-25: 21-24-Saint of Killers app. 25-Origin of Cassidy. 4.00
26-40 3.00
41-49,51-56: 51,52-Tulip origin 2.50
50-($3.75) Pin-ups by Jim Lee, Bradstreet, Quesada and Palmiotti 3.75
Dixie Fried (1998, $14.95, TPB)-r/#27-33, Special: Cassidy 15.00
Gone To Texas (1996, $14.95, TPB)-r/#1-7; Fabry-c 15.00
Proud Americans (1997, $14.95, TPB)-r/#18-26; Fabry-c 15.00
Salvation (1999, $14.95, TPB)-r/#41-50; Fabry-c 15.00
Until the End of the World (1996, $14.95, TPB)-r/#8-17; Fabry-c 15.00
War in the Sun (1999, $14.95, TPB)-r/#34-40 15.00

PREACHER SPECIAL: CASSIDY: BLOOD & WHISKEY
DC Comics (Vertigo): 1998 ($5.95, one-shot)
1-Ennis-scripts/Fabry-c /Dillon-a 6.00

PREACHER SPECIAL: ONE MAN'S WAR
DC Comics (Vertigo): Mar, 1998 ($4.95, one-shot)
1-Ennis-scripts/Fabry-c /Snejbjerg-a 5.00

PREACHER SPECIAL: SAINT OF KILLERS
DC Comics (Vertigo): Aug, 1996 - No. 4, Nov, 1996 ($2.50, lim. series, mature)
1-4: Ennis-scripts/Fabry-c. 1,2-Pugh-a. 3,4-Ezquerra-a 3.00
1-Signed & numbered 20.00

PREACHER SPECIAL: THE GOOD OLD BOYS
DC Comics (Vertigo): Aug, 1997 ($4.95, one-shot, mature)
1-Ennis-scripts/Fabry-c /Esquerra-a 5.00

PREACHER SPECIAL: THE STORY OF YOU-KNOW-WHO
DC Comics (Vertigo): Dec, 1996 ($4.95, one-shot, mature)
1-Ennis-scripts/Fabry-c/Case-a 5.00

PREDATOR (Also see Aliens Vs. ..., Batman vs. ..., Dark Horse Comics, & Dark Horse Presents)
Dark Horse Comics: June, 1989 - No. 4, Mar, 1990 ($2.25, limited series)
1-Based on movie; 1st app. Predator 2.40 6.00
1-2nd printing 3.00
2 5.00
3,4 4.00
Trade paperback (1990, $12.95)-r/#1-4 13.00

PREDATOR: (title series) **Dark Horse Comics**
--BAD BLOOD, 12/93 - No. 4, 1994 ($2.50) 1-4 3.00
--BIG GAME, 3/91 - No. 4, 6/91 ($2.50) 1-4: 1-3-Contain 2 Dark Horse trading cards 3.00
--BLOODY SANDS OF TIME, 2/92 - No. 2, 2/92 ($2.50\)
1,2-Dan Barry-c/a(p)/scripts 3.00
--CAPTIVE, 4/98 ($2.95, one-shot) 1 3.00
--COLD WAR, 9/91 - No. 4, 12/91 ($2.50) 1-4: All have painted-c 3.00
--DARK RIVER, 7/96 - No.4, 10/96 ($2.95)1-4: Miran Kim-c 3.00
--HELL & HOT WATER, 4/97 - No. 3, 6/97 ($2.95) 1-3 3.00
--HELL COME A WALKIN', 2/98 - No. 2, 3/98 ($2.95) 1,2-In the Civil War 3.00
--HOMEWORLD, 3/99 - No. 4 ($2.95) 1-4 3.00
--INVADERS FROM THE FOURTH DIMENSION, 7/94 ($3.95, one-shot, 52 pgs.) 1 4.00
--JUNGLE TALES. 3/95 ($2.95t) 1-r/Dark Horse Comics 3.00

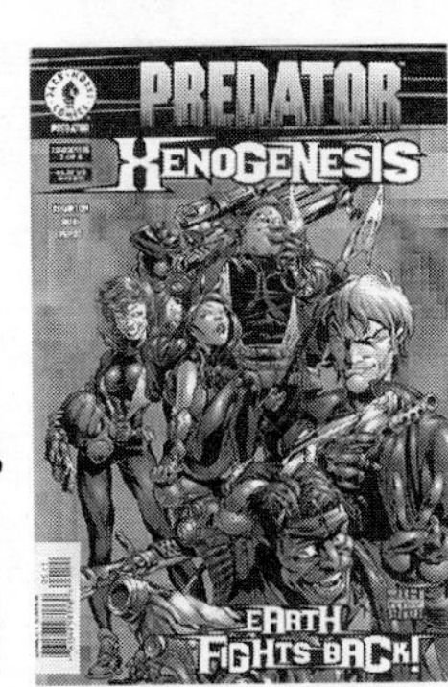

Predator: Xenogenesis #1 © 20th Century Fox

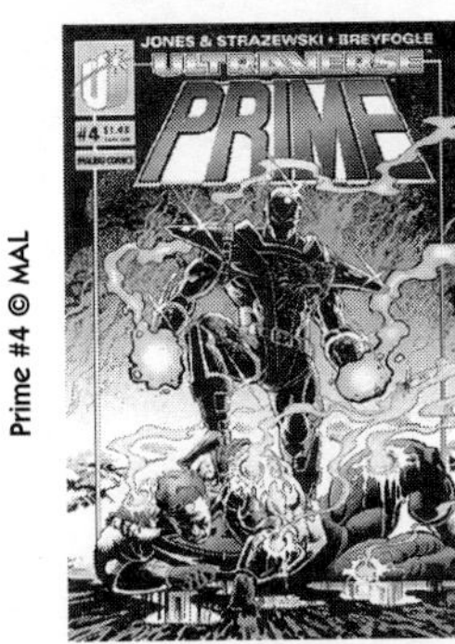

Prime #4 © MAL

Prince Valiant Four Color #650 © KING

--**KINDRED,** 12/96 - No. 4, 3/97 ($2.50) 1-4 3.00
--**NEMESIS,** 12/97 - No. 2, 1/98 ($2.95) 1,2-Predator in Victorian England; Taggart-c 3.00
--**PRIMAL,** 7/97 - No. 2, 8/97 ($2.95) 1,2 3.00
--**RACE WAR** (See Dark Horse Presents #67), 2/93 - No. 4,10/93 ($2.50, color)
1-4,0: 1-4-Dorman painted-c #1-4, 0(4/930 3.00
--**STRANGE ROUX,** 11/96 ($2.95, one-shot) 1 3.00
--**XENOGENESIS** (Also see Aliens Xenogenesis), 8/99 - No. 4 ($2.95)
1,2-Edginton-s 3.00

PREDATOR 2
Dark Horse Comics: Feb, 1991 - No. 2, June, 1991 ($2.50, limited series)
1,2: 1-Adapts movie; both w/trading cards & photo-c 3.00

PREDATOR VS. JUDGE DREDD
Dark Horse Comics: Oct, 1997 - No. 3 ($2.50, limited series)
1-3-Wagner-s/Alcatena-a/Bolland-c 3.00

PREDATOR VS. MAGNUS ROBOT FIGHTER
Dark Horse/Valiant: Oct, 1992 - No. 2, 1993 ($2.95, limited series)
(1st Dark Horse/Valiant x-over)
1,2: (Reg.)-Barry Smith-c; Lee Weeks-a. 2-w/trading cards 3.00
1 (Platinum edition, 11/92)-Barry Smith-c 5.00

PREHISTORIC WORLD (See Classics Illustrated Special Issue)

PREMIERE (See Charlton Premiere)

PRESTO KID, THE (See Red Mask)

PRETTY BOY FLOYD (See On the Spot)

PREZ (See Cancelled Comic Cavalcade & Supergirl #10)
National Periodical Publications: Aug-Sept, 1973 - No. 4, Feb-Mar, 1974
1-Origin; Joe Simon scripts 2.00 6.00 16.00
2-4 1.25 3.75 10.00

PRICE, THE (See Eclipse Graphic Album Series)

PRIDE & JOY
DC Comics (Vertigo): July, 1997 - No. 4, Oct, 1997 (2.50, limited series)
1-4-Ennis-s 2.50

PRIDE AND THE PASSION, THE
Dell Publishing Co.: No. 824, Aug, 1957
Four Color 824-Movie, Frank Sinatra & Cary Grant photo-c 8.00 25.00 90.00

PRIDE OF THE YANKEES, THE (See Real Heroes & Sport Comics)
Magazine Enterprises: 1949 (The Life of Lou Gehrig)
nn-Photo-c; Ogden Whitney-a 78.00 234.00 625.00

PRIEST (Also see Asylum)
Maximum Press: Aug, 1996 - No. 2, Oct, 1996 ($2.99)
1,2 3.00

PRIMAL FORCE
DC Comics: No. 0, Oct, 1994 - No. 14, Dec, 1995 ($1.95/$2.25)
0-14: 0- Teams Red Tornado, Golem, Jack O'Lantern, Meridian & Silver Dragon. 9-begin $2.25-c 2.25

PRIMAL MAN (See The Crusaders)

PRIMAL RAGE
Sirius Entertainment: 1996 ($2.95)
1-Dark One-c; based of video game 3.00

PRIME (See Break-Thru, Flood Relief & Ultraforce)
Malibu Comics (Ultraverse): June, 1993 - No. 26, Aug, 1995 ($1.95/$2.50)
1-1st app. Prime; has coupon for Ultraverse Premiere #0 3.00
1-With coupon missing 2.00
1-Full cover holographic edition; 1st of kind w/Hardcase #1 & Strangers #1 2.40 6.00
1-Ultra 5,000 edition w/silver ink-c 4.00
2-11,14-26: 2-Polybagged w/card & coupon for U. Premiere #0. 3,4-Prototype app. 4-Direct sale w/o card.4-($2.50)-Newsstand ed. polybagged w/card 5-($2.50, 48 pgs.)-Rune flip-c/story part B by Barry Smith; see Sludge #1 for 1st app. Rune; 3-pg. Night Man preview. 6-Bill & Chelsea Clinton app. 7-Break-Thru x-over. 8-Mantra app.; 2-pg. origin Freex by Simonson. 10-Firearm app.15-Intro Papa Verite; Perez-c/a. 16-Intro Turbo Charge 2.50
12-($3.50, 68 pgs.)-Flip book w/Ultraverse Premiere #3; silver foil logo 3.50
13-($2.95, 52 pgs.)-Variant covers 3.00
...: Gross and Disgusting 1 (10/94, $3.95)-Boris-c; "Annual" on cover, published monthly in indicia 4.00
...Month "Ashcan" (8/94, 75¢)-Boris-c 2.00
... Time: A Prime Collection (1994, $9.95)-r/1-4 10.00
...Vs. The Incredible Hulk (1995)-mail away limited edition 10.00
...Vs. The Incredible Hulk Premium edition 10.00
...Vs. The Incredible Hulk Super Premium edition 15.00
NOTE: *Perez a-15; c-15, 16.*

PRIME (Also see Black September)
Malibu Comics (Ultraverse): Infinity, Sept, 1995 - V2#15, Dec, 1996 ($1.50)
Infinity, V2#1-8: Post Black September storyline. 6-8-Solitaire app. 9-Breyfogle-c/a. 10-12-Ramos-c. 15-Lord Pumpkin app. 2.00
Infinity Signed Edition (2,000 printed) 5.00

PRIME/CAPTAIN AMERICA
Malibu Comics: Mar, 1996 ($3.95, one-shot)
1-Norm Breyfogle-a 4.00

PRIMER (Comico...)
Comico: Oct (no month), 1982 - No. 6, Feb, 1984 (B&W)
1 (52 pgs.) 1.00 2.80 7.00
2-1st app. Grendel & Argent by Wagner 9.00 27.00 100.00
3,4 2.40 6.00
5-1st Sam Kieth art in comics ('83) & 1st The Maxx 3.00 9.00 30.00
6-Intro & 1st app. Evangeline 5.00

PRIMORTALS (Leonard Nimoy's...)

PRIMUS (TV)
Charlton Comics: Feb, 1972 - No. 7, Oct, 1972
1-Staton-a in all 1.75 5.25 14.00
2-7: 6-Drug propaganda story 1.10 3.30 9.00

PRINCE NAMOR, THE SUB-MARINER (Also see Namor ...)
Marvel Comics Group: Sept, 1984 - No. 4, Dec, 1984 (Limited-series)
1-4 2.50

PRINCE VALIANT (See Ace Comics, Comics Reading Libraries, & King Comics #146, 147)
David McKay Publ./Dell: No. 26, 1941; No. 67, June, 1954 - No. 900, May, 1958
Feature Books 26 ('41)-Harold Foster-c/a; newspaper strips reprinted, pgs. 1-28,30-63; color & 68 pgs; Foster cover is only original comic book artwork by him 68.00 205.00 750.00
Four Color 567 ((6/54)(#1)-By Bob Fuje-Movie, photo-c 10.00 30.00 110.00
Four Color 650 (9;55), 699 (4/56), 719 (8/56),-Fuje-a 5.50 16.50 60.00
Four Color 788 (4/57), 849 (1/58), 900-Fuje-a 5.50 16.50 60.00

PRINCE VALIANT
Marvel Comics: Dec, 1994 - No. 4, Mar, 1995 ($3.95, limited series)
1-4; Kaluta-c in all. 4.00

PRINCE VANDAL
Triumphant Comics: Nov, 1993 - Apr?, 1994 ($2.50)
1-6: 1,2-Triumphant Unleashed x-over 2.50

PRINCESS SALLY (Video game)
Archie Publications: Apr, 1995 - No. 3, June, 1995 ($1.50, limited series)
1-3: Spin-off from Sonic the Hedgehog 3.00

PRIORITY: WHITE HEAT
AC Comics: 1986 - No. 2, 1986 ($1.75, mini-series)

Prison Break #2 © AVON

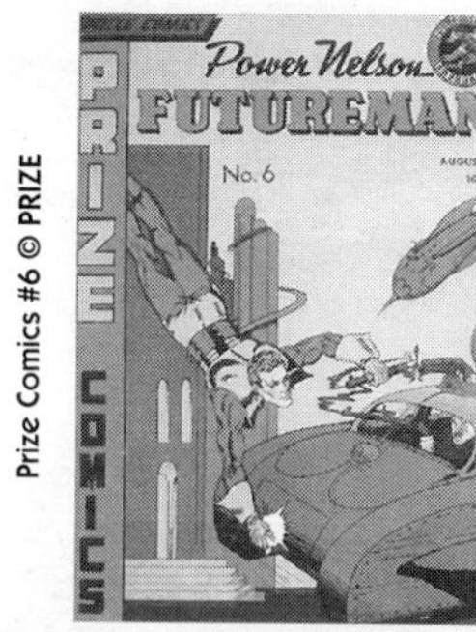

Prize Comics #6 © PRIZE

Project A-Ko #1 © Central Park Media Corp.

GD2.0 FN6.0 NM9.4

1,2-Bill Black-a 2.00

PRISCILLA'S POP
Dell Publishing Co.: No. 569, June, 1954 - No. 799, May, 1957

Four Color 569 (#1), 630 (5/55), 704 (5/56),799 2.75 8.00 30.00

PRISON BARS (See Behind...)

PRISON BREAK!
Avon Per./Realistic No. 3 on: Sept, 1951 - No. 5, Sept, 1952 (Painted c-3)

1-Wood-c & 1 pg.; has-r/Saint #7 retitled Michael Strong Private Eye 40.00 120.00 300.00
2-Wood-c; Kubert-a; Kinstler inside front-c 29.00 86.00 200.00
3-Orlando, Check-a; c-/Avon paperback 179 25.00 75.00 175.00
4,5: 4-Kinstler-c & inside f/c; Lawrence, Lazarus-a. 5-Kinstler-c; Infantino-a 21.00 64.00 150.00

PRISONER, THE (TV)
DC Comics: 1988 - No. 4, 1989 ($3.50, squarebound, mini-series)

1-4 (Books a-d) 3.50

PRISON RIOT
Avon Periodicals: 1952

1-Marijuana Murders-1 pg. text; Kinstler-c; 2 Kubert illos on text pages 27.00 81.00 190.00

PRISON TO PRAISE
Logos International: 1974 (35¢)

nn-True Story of Merlin R. Carothers 2.40 6.00

PRIVATE BUCK
Dell Publishing Co.: No. 21, 1941 - No. 12, 1942

Large Feature Comic 21 (#1)(1941)(Series I), 22 (1941)(Series I), 12 (1942)(Series II) 9.00 27.00 100.00

PRIVATEERS
Vanguard Graphics: Aug, 1987 - No. 2, 1987 ($1.50)

1,2 2.00

PRIVATE EYE (Cover title: Rocky Jorden...#6-8)
Atlas Comics (MCI): Jan, 1951 - No. 8, March, 1952

1-Cover title: Crime Cases... #1-5 21.00 62.00 145.00
2,3-Tuska c/a(3) 12.00 36.00 85.00
4-8 10.00 30.00 70.00

NOTE: ***Henkel*** *a-6(3), 7; c-7.* ***Sinnott*** *a-6.*

PRIVATE EYE (See Mike Shayne...)

PRIVATE SECRETARY
Dell Publishing Co.: Dec-Feb, 1962-63 - No. 2, Mar-May, 1963

1,2 2.50 7.50 22.00

PRIVATE STRONG (See The Double Life of...)

PRIZE COMICS (...Western #69 on) (Also see Treasure Comics)
Prize Publications: March, 1940 - No. 68, Feb-Mar, 1948

1-Origin Power Nelson, The Futureman & Jupiter, Master Magician; Ted O'Neil, Secret Agent M-11, Jaxon of the Jungle, Bucky Brady & Storm Curtis begin (1st app. of each) 225.00 675.00 1800.00
2-The Black Owl begins (1st app.) 103.00 309.00 825.00
3,4: 4-Robot-c 87.00 262.00 700.00
5,6: Dr. Dekkar, Master of Monsters app. in each 81.00 244.00 650.00
7-(Scarce)-Black Owl by S&K; origin/1st app. Dr. Frost & Frankenstein; The Green Lama, Capt. Gallant, The Great Voodini & Twist Turner begin; 1st app. The Green Lama (12/40) 175.00 525.00 1400.00
8,9-Black Owl & Ted O'Neil by S&K 91.00 272.00 725.00
10-12,14-20: 11-Origin Bulldog Denny. 16-Spike Mason begins 62.00 187.00 500.00
13-Yank & Doodle begin (8/41, origin/1st app.) 70.00 210.00 560.00
21-24 44.00 131.00 350.00
25-30 29.00 86.00 200.00
31-33 24.00 71.00 165.00
34-Origin Airmale, Yank & Doodle; The Black Owl joins army, Yank & Doodle's father assumes Black Owl's role 27.00 81.00 190.00
35-36,38-40: 35-Flying Fist & Bingo begin 19.00 58.00 135.00
37-Intro. Stampy, Airmale's sidekick; Hitler-c 29.00 86.00 200.00
41-50: 45-Yank & Doodle learn Black Owl's I.D. (their father). 48-Prince Ra begins 15.00 45.00 105.00
51-62,64,67,68: 53-Transvestism story. 55-No Frankenstein. 57-X-Mas-c. 64-Black Owl retires 13.00 39.00 90.00
63-Simon & Kirby c/a 16.00 47.00 110.00
65,66-Frankenstein-c by Briefer 13.50 41.00 95.00

NOTE: ***Briefer*** *a 7-on; c-65, 66.* ***J. Binder*** *a-16; c-21-29.* ***Guardineer*** *a-62.* ***Kiefer*** *c-62.* ***Palais*** *c-68.* ***Simon & Kirby*** *c-63, 75, 83.*

PRIZE COMICS WESTERN (Formerly Prize Comics #1-68)
Prize Publications (Feature): No. 69(V7#2), Apr-May, 1948 - No. 119, Nov-Dec, 1956 (No. 69-84: 52 pgs.)

69(V7#2) 13.50 41.00 95.00
70-75: 74-Kurtzman-a (8 pgs.) 11.50 34.00 80.00
76-Randolph Scott photo-c; "Canadian Pacific" movie adaptation 13.00 39.00 90.00
77-Photo-c; Severin/Elder, Mart Bailey-a; "Streets of Laredo" movie adaptation 11.50 34.00 80.00
78-Photo-c; S&K-a, 10 pgs.; Severin, Mart Bailey-a; "Bullet Code", & "Roughshod" movie adaptations 17.00 51.00 120.00
79-Photo-c; Kurtzman-a, 8 pgs.; Severin/Elder, Severin, Mart Bailey-a; "Stage To Chino" movie adaptation w/George O'Brien 17.00 51.00 120.00
80-82-Photo-c; 80,81-Severin/Elder-a(2). 82-1st app. The Preacher by Mart Bailey; Severin/Elder-a(3) 12.00 36.00 85.00
83,84 10.00 30.00 70.00
85-1st app. American Eagle by John Severin & begins (V9#6, 1-2/51) 24.00 73.00 170.00
86,101-105, 109-Severin/Williamson-a 11.50 34.00 80.00
87-99,110,111-Severin/Elder-a(2-3) each 12.00 36.00 85.00
100 13.50 41.00 95.00
106-108,112 10.00 30.00 60.00
113-Williamson/Severin-a(2)/Frazetta? 12.00 36.00 85.00
114-119: Drifter series in all; by Mort Meskin #114-118 8.35 25.00 50.00

NOTE: ***Fass*** *a-81.* ***Severin & Elder*** *c-84-99.* ***Severin*** *a-72, 75, 77-79, 83-86, 96, 97, 100-105; c-92,100-109(most), 110-119.* ***Simon & Kirby*** *c-75, 83.*

PRIZE MYSTERY
Key Publications: May, 1955 - No. 3, Sept, 1955

1 10.00 30.00 60.00
2,3 7.50 22.50 45.00

PROFESSIONAL FOOTBALL (See Charlton Sport Library)

PROFESSOR COFFIN
Charlton Comics: No. 19, Oct, 1985 - No. 21, Feb, 1986

19-21: Wayne Howard-a(r) 4.00

PROFESSOR OM
Innovation Publishing: May, 1990 - No. 2, 1990 ($2.50, limited series)

1,2-East Meets West spin-off 2.50

PROFESSOR XAVIER AND THE X-MEN (Also see X-Men, 1st series)
Marvel Comics: Nov, 1995 - No. 18 (99¢)

1-18: Stories featuring the Original X-Men. 2-vs. The Blob. 5-Vs. the Original Brotherhood of Evil Mutants. 10-Vs The Avengers 2.00

PROJECT A-KO (Manga)
Malibu Comics: Mar, 1994 - No. 4, June, 1994 ($2.95)

1-4-Based on anime film 3.00

PROJECT A-KO 2 (Manga)
CPM Comics: May, 1995 - No. 3, Aug, 1995 ($2.95, limited series)

1-3 3.00

PROJECT A-KO VERSUS THE UNIVERSE (Manga)
CPM Comics: Oct, 1995 - No. 5, June, 1996 ($2.95, limited series, bi-monthly)

Promethea #1 © America's Best Comics

Prowler #2 © ECL

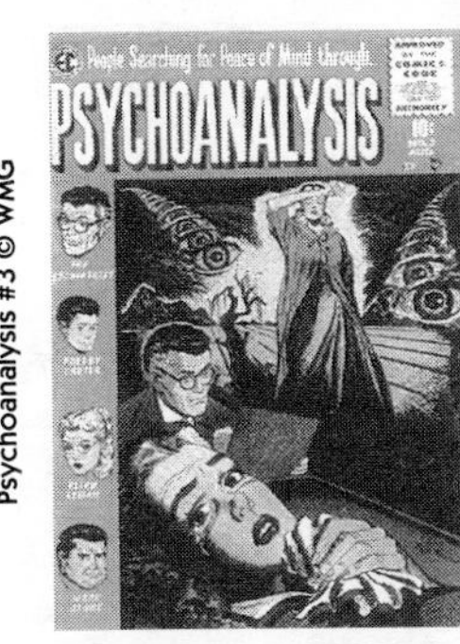

Psychoanalysis #3 © WMG

	GD2.0	FN6.0	NM9.4

1-5 3.00

PROJECT: HERO
Vanguard Graphics (Canadian): Aug, 1987 ($1.50)

1 2.00

PROMETHEA
America's Best Comics: Aug, 1999 - Present ($3.50/$2.95)

1-Moore-s/Williams III & Gray-a; Alex Ross painted-c 3.50
1-Variant-c by Williams III & Gray 3.50
2,3-($2.95) 3.00

PROMETHEUS (VILLAINS) (Leads into JLA #16,17)
DC Comics: Feb, 1998 ($1.95, one-shot)

1-Origin & 1st app.; Morrison-s/Pearson-c 3.00

PROPELLERMAN
Dark Horse Comics: Jan, 1993 - No. 8, Mar, 1994 ($2.95, limited series)

1-8: 2,4,8-Contain 2 trading cards 3.00

PROPHET (See Youngblood #2)
Image Comics (Extreme Studios): Oct, 1993 - No. 10, 1995 ($1.95)

1-($2.50)-Liefeld/Panosian-c/a; 1st app. Mary McCormick; Liefeld scripts in 1-4; #1-3 contain coupons for Prophet #0 2.50
1-Gold foil embossed-c edition rationed to dealers 4.00
2-10: 2-Liefeld-c(p). 3-1st app. Judas. 4-1st app. Omen; Black and White Pt. 3 by Thibert. 4-Alternate-c by Stephen Platt. 5,6-Platt-c/a. 7-(9/94, $2.50)-Platt-c/a. 8-Bloodstrike app. 10-Polybagged w/trading card; Platt-c. 2.50
0-(7/94, $2.50)-San Diego Comic Con ed. (2200 copies) 3.00

PROPHET
Image Comics (Extreme Studios): V2#1, Aug, 1995 - No. 8 ($3.50)

V2#1-8: Dixon scripts in all. 1-4-Platt-a. 1-Boris-c; F. Miller variant-c. 4-Newmen app. 5,6-Wraparound-c 2.50
Annual 1 (9/95, $2.50)-Bagged w/Youngblood gaming card; Quesada-c 2.50
Babewatch Special 1 (12/95, $2.50)-Babewatch tie-in 2.50
1995 San Diego Edition-B&W preview of V2#1. 3.00
TPB-(1996, $12.95) r/#1-7 13.00

PROPHET/CABLE
Image Comics (Extreme): Jan, 1997 - No. 2, Mar, 1997 ($3.50, limited series)

1,2-Liefeld-c/a: 2-#1 listed on cover 3.50

PROPHET/CHAPEL: SUPER SOLDIERS
Image Comics (Extreme): May, 1996 - No. 2, June, 1996 ($2.50, limited series)

1,2: 1-Two covers exist 2.50
1-San Diego Edition; B&W-c 2.50

PROTECTORS (Also see The Ferret)
Malibu Comics: Sept, 1992 - No. 20, May, 1994 ($1.95-$2.95)

1-20 ($2.50, direct sale)-With poster & diff-c: 1-Origin; has 3/4 outer-c. 3-Polybagged w/Skycap 2.50
1-12 ($1.95, newsstand)-Without poster 2.00

PROTOTYPE (Also see Flood Relief & Ultraforce)
Malibu Comics (Ultraverse): Aug, 1993 - No. 18, Feb, 1995 ($1.95/$2.50)

1-Holo-c 6.00
1-Ultra Limited silver foil-c 4.00
1-12,0,14-18: 3-($2.50, 48 pgs.)-Rune flip-c/story by B. Smith (3 pgs.). 4-Intro Wrath. 5-Break-Thru & Strangers x-over. 6-Arena cameo. 7,8-Arena-c/story. 12-(7/94). 0-(8/94,$ 2.50, 44 pgs.), 14(10/94) 2.50
13 (8/94, $3.50)-Flip book(Ultraverse Premiere #6) 3.50
Giant Size 1 (10/94, $2.50, 44 pgs.) 2.50

PROWLER (Also see Revenge of the...)
Eclipse Comics: July, 1987 - No. 4, Oct, 1987 ($1.75)

1-4: Snyder-c/a. 3,4-Origin 2.00

PROWLER, THE
Marvel Comics: Nov, 1994 ($1.75)

1-4: 1-Spider-Man app. 2.00

	GD2.0	FN6.0	NM9.4

PROWLER IN "WHITE ZOMBIE", THE
Eclipse Comics: Oct, 1988 ($2.00, B&W, Baxter paper)

1-Adapts Bela Lugosi movie White Zombie 2.00

PRUDENCE & CAUTION (Also see Dogs of War & Warriors of Plasm)
Defiant: May, 1994 - No. 2, June, 1994 ($3.50/$2.50)(Spanish versions exist)

1-($3.50, 52 pgs.)-Chris Claremont scripts in all 3.50
2-($2.50) 2.50

PRYDE AND WISDOM (Also see Excalibur)
Marvel Comics: Sept, 1996 - No. 3, Nov, 1996 ($1.95, limited series)

1-3: Warren Ellis scripts; Terry Dodson & Karl Story-c/a 2.00

PSI-FORCE
Marvel Comics Group: Nov, 1986 - No. 32, June, 1989 (75¢/$1.50)

1-32: 11-13-Williamson-i 2.00
Annual 1 (10/87) 2.00

PSI-JUDGE ANDERSON
Fleetway Publications (Quality): 1989 - No. 15, 1990 ($1.95, B&W)

1-15 2.50

PSI-LORDS
Valiant: Sept, 1994 - No. 10, June, 1995 ($2.25)

1-($3.50)-Chromium wraparound-c 3.50
1-Gold 5.00
2-10: 3-Chaos Effect Epsilon Pt. 2 2.25

PSYBA-RATS (Also see Showcase '94 #3,4)
DC Comics: Apr, 1995-No. 3, June, 1995 ($2.50, limited series)

1-3 2.50

PSYCHO (Magazine)
Skywald Publ. Corp.: Jan, 1971 - No. 24, Mar, 1975 (68 pgs.; B&W) (No #22?)

	GD2.0	FN6.0	NM9.4
1-All reprints	5.00	15.00	50.00
2-Origin & 1st app. The Heap, & Frankenstein series by Adkins	3.50	10.50	35.00
3-10	2.50	7.50	24.00
11-20: 13-Cannabalism; 3 pgs of Christopher Lee as Dracula photos. 18-Injury to eye-c. 20-Severed Head-c	2.25	6.75	18.00
21-24: 24-1975 Winter Special	2.50	7.50	22.00
Annual 1(1972)(68 pgs.)	2.80	8.40	28.00
Fall Special (1974)-Reese, Wildey-a(r)	2.50	7.50	22.00
Winter Special 1 (1975)-Dave Sim scripts	2.50	7.50	22.00
Yearbook(1974-nn)-Everett, Reese-a	2.50	7.50	22.00

NOTE: ***Boris** c-3, 5. **Buckler** a-2, 4, 5. **Gene Day** a-24. **Everett** a-3-6. **B. Jones** a-4. **Jeff Jones** a-6, 7, 9; c-12. **Kaluta** a-13. **Katz/Buckler** a-3. **Kim** a-24. **Morrow** a-1. **Reese** a-5. **Dave Sim** a-24. **Sutton** a-3. **Wildey** a-5.*

PSYCHOANALYSIS
E. C. Comics: Mar-Apr, 1955 - No. 4, Sept-Oct, 1955

	GD2.0	FN6.0	NM9.4
1-All Kamen-c/a; not approved by code	15.00	45.00	140.00
2-4-Kamen-c/a in all	11.00	33.00	110.00

PSYCHOANALYSIS
Gemstone Publishing: Oct, 1999 - No. 4 ($2.50)

1,2-Reprints E.C. series 2.50

PSYCHOBLAST
First Comics: Nov, 1987 - No. 9, July, 19898 ($1.75)

1-9 2.00

PSYCHONAUTS
Marvel Comics (Epic Comics): Oct, 1993 - No. 4, Jan, 1994 ($4.95, lim. series)

1-4: American/Japanese co-produced comic 5.00

PSYLOCKE & ARCHANGEL CRIMSON DAWN
Marvel Comics: Aug, 1997 - No. 4, Nov, 1997 ($2.50, limited series)

1-4-Raab-s/Larroca-a(p) 2.50

P.T. 109 (See Movie Comics)

Punch Comics #12 © CHES

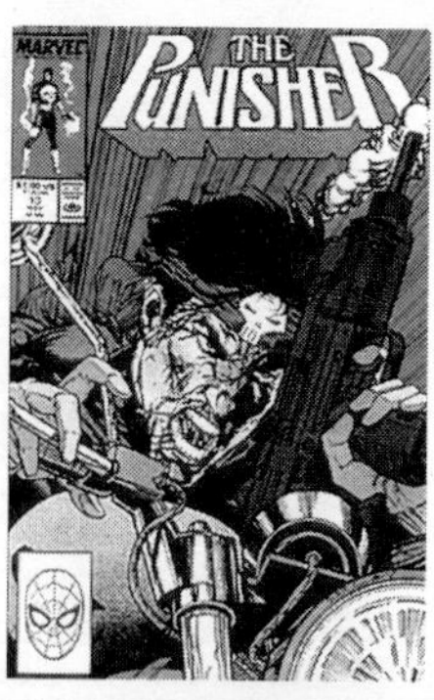

Punisher #13 © MAR

Punisher #1 (DF Edition) © MAR

PUBLIC DEFENDER IN ACTION (Formerly Police Trap)
Charlton Comics: No. 7, Mar, 1956 - No. 12, Oct, 1957

7 10.00 30.00 60.00
8-12 6.35 19.00 38.00

PUBLIC ENEMIES
D. S. Publishing Co.: 1948 - No. 9, June-July, 1949

1-True Crime Stories 23.00 69.00 160.00
2-Used in **SOTI**, pg. 95 20.00 60.00 140.00
3-5: 5-Arrival date of 10/1/48 12.00 36.00 85.00
6,8,9 11.50 34.00 80.00
7-McWilliams-a; injury to eye panel 12.00 36.00 85.00

PUDGY PIG
Charlton Comics: Sept, 1958 - No. 2, Nov, 1958

1,2 2.50 7.50 22.00

PULP FICTION LIBRARY: MYSTERY IN SPACE
DC Comics: 1999 ($19.95, TPB)

nn-Reprints classic sci-fi stories from Mystery in Space, Strange Adventures, Real Fact Comics and My Greatest Adventure 19.95

PUMA BLUES
Aardvark One International/Mirage Studios #21 on: 1986 - No. 26, 1990 ($1.70-$1.75, B&W)

1-19, 21-26: 1-1st & 2nd printings. 25,26-$1.75-c 2.00
20 ($2.25)-By Alan Moore, Miller, Grell, others 2.50
Trade Paperback (12/88, $14.95) 15.00

PUMPKINHEAD: THE RITES OF EXORCISM (Movie)
Dark Horse Comics: 1993 - No. 2, 1993 ($2.50, limited series)

1,2: Based on movie; painted-c by McManus 2.50

PUNCH & JUDY COMICS
Hillman Per.: 1944; No. 2, Fall, 1944 - V3#2, 12/47; V3#3, 6/51 - V3#9, 12/51

V1#1-(60 pgs.) 20.00 60.00 140.00
2 11.50 34.00 80.00
3-12(7/46) 10.00 30.00 60.00
V2#1(8/49),3-9 5.85 17.50 35.00
V2#2,10-12, V3#1-Kirby-a(2) each 21.00 64.00 150.00
V3#2-Kirby-a 20.00 60.00 140.00
3-9 5.85 17.50 35.00

PUNCH COMICS
Harry 'A' Chesler: 12/41; #2, 2/42; #9, 7/44 - #19, 10/46; #20, 7/47 - #23, 1/48

1-Mr. E, The Sky Chief, Hale the Magician, Kitty Kelly begin 125.00 375.00 1000.00
2-Captain Glory app. 84.00 253.00 675.00
9-Rocketman & Rocket Girl & The Master Key begin 75.00 225.00 600.00
10-Sky Chief app.; J. Cole-a; Master Key-r/Scoop #3 58.00 174.00 465.00
11-Origin Master Key-r/Scoop #1; Sky Chief, Little Nemo app.; Jack Cole-a; Fineish art by Sultan 55.00 165.00 440.00
12-Rocket Boy & Capt. Glory app; classic Skull-c 119.00 356.00 950.00
13-Cover has list of 4 Chesler artists' names on tombstone 59.00 178.00 475.00
14-17,19: 51.00 154.00 410.00
18-Bondage-c; hypodermic panels 66.00 197.00 525.00
20-Unique cover with bare-breasted women 91.00 272.00 725.00
21-Hypo needle story 51.00 154.00 410.00
22,23-Little Nemo-not by McCay. 22-Intro Baxter (teenage) 27.00 81.00 190.00

PUNCHY AND THE BLACK CROW
Charlton Comics: No. 10, Oct, 1985 - No. 12, Feb, 1986

10-12: Al Fago funny animal-r 2.00

PUNISHER (See Amazing Spider-Man #129, Blood and Glory, Captain America #241, Classic Punisher, Daredevil #182-184, 257, Daredevil and the..., Ghost Rider V2#5, 6, Marc Spector #8 & 9, Marvel Preview #2, Marvel Super Action, Marvel Tales, Power Pack #46, Spectacular Spider-Man #81-83, 140, 141, 143 & new Strange Tales #13 & 14)

PUNISHER (The...)
Marvel Comics Group: Jan, 1986 - No. 5, May, 1986 (Limited series)

1-Double size 1.00 3.00 8.00
2-5 4.00
Trade Paperback (1988)-r/#1-5 11.00
NOTE: ***Zeck*** *a-1-4; c-1-5.*

PUNISHER (The...)
Marvel Comics: July, 1987 - No. 104, July, 1995

V2#1 5.00
2-9,11-74,76-85,87-89: 8-Portacio/Williams-c/a begins, ends #18. 9-Scarcer, low distri. 13-18-Kingpin app. 19-Stroman-c/a. 20-Portacio-c(p). 24-1st app. Shadowmasters. 25,50:($1.50,52 pgs.). 25-Shadowmasters app. 57-Photo-c; came w/outer-c (newsstand ed. w/o outer-c). 59-Punisher is severely cut & has skin grafts (has black skin). 60-62-Luke Cage app. 62-Punisher back to white skin. 68-Tarantula- c/story. 85-Prequel to Suicide Run Pt. 0. 87,88-Suicide Run Pt. 6 & 9 3.00
10-Daredevil app; ties in w/Daredevil #257 4.00
75-($2.75, 52 pgs.)-Embossed silver foil-c 3.00
86-($2.95, 52 pgs.)-Embossed & foil stamped-c; Suicide Run part 3 3.00
90-99, 101-103: 90-bound-in cards. 99-Cringe app. 102-Bullseye. 2.00
100,104: 100-($2.95, 68 pgs.). 104-Last issue 3.00
100-($3.95, 68 pgs.)-Foil cover 4.00
"Ashcan" edition (75¢)-Joe Kubert-c 2.00
Annual 1-7 ('88-'94, 68 pgs.)-1-Evolutionary War x-over. 2 -Atlantis Attacks x-over; Jim Lee-a(p) (back-up story, 6 pgs.); Moon Knight app. 4-Golden-c(p). 6-Bagged w/card. 7-Rapido app. 3.00
...: A Man Named Frank (1994, $6.95, TPB) 7.00
...and Wolverine in African Saga nn (1989, $5.95, 52 pgs.)-Reprints Punisher War Journal #6 & 7; Jim Lee-c/a(r) 6.00
Back to School Special 1-3 (11/92-10/94, $2.95, 68 pgs.) 3.00
.../Batman: Deadly Knights (10/94, $4.95) 5.00
...Bloodlines nn (1991, $5.95, 68 pgs.) 6.00
...: Die Hard in the Big Easy nn ('92, $4.95, 52 pgs.) 5.00
...: Empty Quarter nn ('94, $6.95) 7.00
...G-Force nn (1992, $4.95, 52 pgs.)-Painted-c 5.00
...Holiday Special 1-3 (1/93-1/95,, 52 pgs.,68pgs.)-1-Foil-c 3.00
...Invades the 'Nam: Final Invasion nn (2/94, $6.95)-J. Kubert-c & chapter break art; reprints The 'Nam #84 & unpublished #85,86 7.00
...Meets Archie (8/94, $3.95, 52 pgs.)-Die cut-c; no ads; same contents as Archie Meets The Punisher 4.00
...Movie Special 1 (6/90, $5.95, 68 pgs.) 6.00
...: No Escape nn (1990, $4.95, 52 pgs.)-New-a 5.00
...The Prize nn (1990, $4.95, 68 pgs.)-New-a 5.00
Summer Special 1 -4(8/9-7/94 52 pgs.)-1-No ads. 2-Bisley painted-c; Austin-a(i). 3-No ads 3.00
NOTE: ***Austin*** *c(i)-47, 48.* ***Cowan*** *c-39.* ***Golden*** *c-50, 85, 86, 100.* ***Heath*** *a-26, 27, 89, 90; c-26, 27.* ***Quesada*** *c-56p, 62p.* ***Sienkiewicz*** *c-Back to School 1.* ***Stroman*** *a-76p(9 pgs.).* ***Williamson*** *a(i)-25, 60-62i, 64-70, 74, Annual 5; c(i)-62, 65-68.*

PUNISHER (Also see Double Edge)
Marvel Comics: Nov, 1995 - No. 18, Apr, 1997 ($2.95/$1.95/$1.50)

1 ($2.95)-Ostrander scripts begin; foil-c. 3.00
2-18: 7-Vs. S.H.I.E.L.D. 11-"Onslaught." 12-17-X-Cutioner-c/app. 17-Daredevil, Spider-Man-c/app. 2.00

PUNISHER (Marvel Knights)
Marvel Comics: Nov, 1998 - No. 4, Feb, 1999 ($2.99, limited series)

1-4: 1-Wrightson-a; Wrightson & Jusko-c 3.00
1-($6.95) DF Edition; Jae Lee variant-c 7.00

PUNISHER AND WOLVERINE: DAMAGING EVIDENCE (See Wolverine and...)

PUNISHER ARMORY, THE
Marvel Comics: 7/90 ($1.50); No. 2, 6/91; No. 3, 4/92 - 10/94($1.75/$2.00)

1-10: 1-r/weapons pgs. from War Journal. 1,2-Jim Lee-c. 3-10- All new material. 3-Jusko painted-c 2.00

Punisher War Journal #11 © MAR

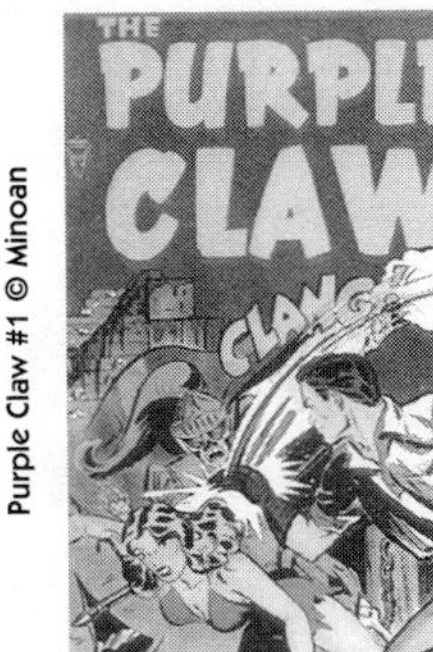

Purple Claw #1 © Minoan

Quantum & Woody #1 © Acclaim

GD2.0 FN6.0 NM9.4

PUNISHER KILLS THE MARVEL UNIVERSE
Marvel Comics: Nov, 1995 ($5.95, one-shot)

1-Garth Ennis script 6.00

PUNISHER MAGAZINE, THE
Marvel Comics: Oct, 1989 - No. 16, Nov, 1990 ($2.25, B&W, Magazine, 52 pgs.)

1-16: 1-r/Punisher #1('86). 2,3-r/Punisher 2-5. 4-16: 4-7-r/Punisher V2#1-8. 4-Chiodo-c. 8-r/Punisher #10 & Daredevil #257; Portacio & Lee-r. 14-r/Punisher War Journal #1,2 w/new Lee-c. 16-r/Punisher W. J. #3,8 2.25

NOTE: ***Chiodo*** *painted c-4, 7, 16.* ***Jusko*** *painted c-6, 8.* ***Jim Lee*** *r-8, 14-16; c-14.* ***Portacio/ Williams*** *r-7-12.*

PUNISHER MOVIE COMIC
Marvel Comics: Nov, 1989 - No. 3, Dec, 1989 ($1.00, limited series)

1-3: Movie adaptation 2.00
1 (1989, $4.95, squarebound)-contains #1-3 5.00

PUNISHER: ORIGIN OF MICRO CHIP, THE
Marvel Comics: July, 1993 - No. 2, Aug, 1993 ($1.75, limited series)

1,2 2.00

PUNISHER: P.O.V.
Marvel Comics: 1991 - No. 4, 1991 ($4.95, painted, limited series, 52 pgs.)

1-4: Starlin scripts & Wrightson painted-c/a in all. 2-Nick Fury app. 5.00

PUNISHER: THE GHOSTS OF INNOCENTS
Marvel Comics: Jan, 1993 - No. 2, Jan, 1993 ($5.95, 52 pgs.)

1,2-Starlin scripts 6.00

PUNISHER 2099 (See Punisher War Journal #50)
Marvel Comics: Feb, 1993 - No. 34, Nov, 1995 ($1.25/$1.50/$1.95)

1-24,26-34: 1-Foil stamped-c. 1-Second printing. 13-Spider-Man 2099 x-over; Ron Lim-c(p). 16-bound-in card sheet 2.00
25 ($2.95, 52 pgs.)-Deluxe edition; embossed foil-cover 3.00
25 ($2.25, 52 pgs.) 2.25

PUNISHER WAR JOURNAL, THE
Marvel Comics: Nov, 1988 - No. 80, July, 1995 ($1.50/$1.75/$1.95)

1-Origin The Punisher; Matt Murdock cameo; Jim Lee inks begin 4.00
2-7: 2,3-Daredevil x-over; Jim Lee-c(i). 4-Jim Lee c/a begins. 6-Two part Wolverine story begins. 7-Wolverine-c, story ends 3.00
8-49,51-60,62,63,65: 13-16,20-22: No Jim Lee-a. 13-Lee-c only. 13-15-Heath-i. 14,15-Spider-Man x-over. 19-Last Jim Lee-c/a.29,30-Ghost Rider app. 31-Andy & Joe Kubert art. 36-Photo-c. 47,48-Nomad/Daredevil-c/stories; see Nomad. 57,58-Daredevil & Ghost Rider-c/stories. 62,63-Suicide Run Pt. 4 & 7. 2.00
50,61,64($2.95, 52 pgs.): 50-Preview of Punisher 2099 (1st app.); embossed-c. 61-Embossed foil cover; Suicide Run Pt. 1. 64-Die-cut-c; Suicide Run Pt. 10 3.00
64-($2.25, 52 pgs.)-Regular cover edition 2.25
66-74,76-80: 66-Bound-in card sheet 2.00
75 ($2.50, 52 pgs.) 2.50

NOTE: ***Golden*** *c-25-30, 40, 61, 62.* ***Jusko*** *painted c-31, 32.* ***Jim Lee*** *a-1i-3i, 4p-13p, 17p-19p; c-2i, 3i, 4p-15p, 17p, 18p, 19p. Painted c-40.*

PUNISHER: WAR ZONE, THE
Marvel Comics: Mar, 1992 - No. 41, July, 1995 ($1.75/$1.95)

1-($2.25, 40 pgs.)-Die cut-c; Romita, Jr.-c/a begins 3.00
2-22,24,26,27-41: 8-Last Romita, Jr.-c/a. 19-Wolverine app. 24-Suicide Run Pt. 5. 27-Bound-in card sheet 2.00
23-($2.95, 52 pgs.)-Enbossed foil-c; Suicide Run part 2; Buscema-a(part) 3.00
25-($2.25, 52 pgs.)-Suicide Run part 8; painted-c 2.25
Annual 1,2 ('93, 94, $2.95, 68 pgs.)-1-Bagged w/card; John Buscema-a 3.00

NOTE: ***Golden*** *c-23.* ***Romita, Jr.*** *c/a-1-8.*

PUNISHER: YEAR ONE
Marvel Comics: Dec, 1994 - No. 4, Apr, 1995 ($2.50, limited series)

1-4 2.50

PUNX
Acclaim (Valiant): Nov, 1995 - No. 3, Jan, 1996 ($2.50, unfinished lim. series)

1-3: Giffen story & art in all. 2-Satirizes Scott McCloud's Understanding Comics 2.50
(Manga) Special 1 (3/96, $2.50)-Giffen scripts 2.50

PUPPET COMICS
George W. Dougherty Co.: Spring, 1946 - No. 2, Summer, 1946

1,2-Funny animal 10.00 30.00 70.00

PUPPETOONS (See George Pal's...)

PURGATORI
Chaos! Comics: Prelude #-1, 5/96 ($1.50, 16 pgs.); 1996 - No. 3 Dec, 1996 ($3.50/$2.95, limited series)

Prelude #-1-Brian Pulido story; Jim Balent-c/a; contains sketches & interviews. 2.00
1-($3.50)-Wraparound cover; red foil embossed-c; Jim Balent-a 5.00
1-($19.95)-Premium Edition (1000 print run) 20.00
2-($3.00)-Wraparound-c 3.00
2-Variant-c 5.00
...The Dracula Gambit-($2.95) 3.00
...The Dracula Gambit Sketchbook-($2.95) 3.00
...The Vampire's Myth 1-($19.95) Premium ed. (10,000) 20.00

PURGATORI
Chaos! Comics: Oct, 1998 - No. 7, Apr, 1999 ($2.95)

1-7-Quinn-s/Rio-c/a. 2-Lady Death-c 3.00

PURGATORI: GODDESS RISING
Chaos! Comics: July, 1999 - No. 4, Oct, 1999 ($2.95, limited series)

1-4-Deodato-c/a 3.00

PURGE
ANIA/U.P. Comics: Aug, 1993 ($1.95, unfinished limited series)

1 2.00

PURPLE CLAW, THE (Also see Tales of Horror)
Minoan Publishing Co./Toby Press: Jan, 1953 - No. 3, May, 1953

	GD2.0	FN6.0	NM9.4
1-Origin; horror/weird stories in all	29.00	86.00	200.00
2,3: 1-3 r-in Tales of Horror #9-11	21.00	64.00	150.00
I.W. Reprint #8-Reprints #1	2.50	7.50	24.00

PUSSYCAT (Magazine)
Marvel Comics Group: Oct, 1968 (B&W reprints from Men's magazines)

1-(Scarce)-Ward, Everett, Wood-a; Everett-c 16.00 48.00 160.00

PUZZLE FUN COMICS (Also see Jingle Jangle)
George W. Dougherty Co.: Spring, 1946 - No. 2, Summer, 1946 (52 pgs.)

	GD2.0	FN6.0	NM9.4
1-Gustavson-a	21.00	64.00	150.00
2	14.00	43.00	100.00

NOTE: *#1 & 2('46) each contain a* ***George Carlson*** *cover plus a 6 pg. story "Alec in Fumbleland"; also many puzzles in each.*

QUACK!
Star Reach Productions: July, 1976 - No. 6, 1977? ($1.25, B&W)

1-Brunner-c/a on Duckaneer (Howard the Duck clone); Dave Stevens, Gilbert, Shaw-a 1.25 3.75 10.00
1-2nd printing (10/76) 2.00
2-6: 2-Newton the Rabbit Wonder by Aragones/Leialoha; Gilbert, Shaw-a; Leialoha-c. 3-The Beavers by Dave Sim begin, end #5; Gilbert, Shaw-a; Sim/Leialoha-c6-Brunner-a (Duckeneer); Gilbert-a 5.00

QUADRANT
Quadrant Publications: 1983 - No. 8, 1986 (B&W, nudity, adults)

1-Peter Hsu-c/a in all 3.00
2-8 2.00

QUANTUM & WOODY
Acclaim Comics: June, 1997 - No. 17, No. 32 - Present ($2.50)

1-17: 1-1st app.; two covers. 6-Copycat-c. 9-Troublemakers app. 2.50
32-(9/99)(No #18-31) 2.50

Quicksilver #5 © MAR

Quick-Trigger Western #13 © MAR

Q-Unit #1 © HARV

GD2.0 FN6.0 NM9.4

The Director's Cut TPB ('97, $7.95) r/#1-4 plus extra pages 8.00

QUANTUM LEAP (TV) (See A Nightmare on Elm Street)
Innovation Publishing: Sept, 1991 - No. 12, Jun, 1993 ($2.50, painted-c)

1-12: Based on TV show; all have painted-c. 8-Has photo gallery 3.00
Special Edition 1 (10/92)-r/#1 w/8 extra pgs. of photos & articles 3.00
Time and Space Special 1 (#13) ($2.95)-Foil logo 3.00

QUASAR (See Avengers #302, Captain America #217, Incredible Hulk #234, Marvel Team-Up #113 & Marvel Two-in-One #53)
Marvel Comics: Oct, 1989 - No. 60, Jul, 1994 ($1.00/$1.25, Direct sales #17 on)

1-Origin; formerly Marvel Boy/Marvel Man 2.00
2-49,51-60: 3-Human Torch app. 6-Venom cameo (2 pgs.). 7-Cosmic Spidey. 11-Excalibur x-over. 14-McFarlane-c. 16-($1.50, 52 pgs.). 17-Flash parody (Buried Alien). 20-Fantastic Four app. 23-Ghost Rider x-over. 25-($1.50, 52 pgs.)-New costume Quasar. 26-Infinity Gauntlet x-over; Thanos-c/story. 27-Infinity Gauntlet x-over. 30-Thanos cameo in flashback; last $1.00-c. 31-Begin $1.25-c; D.P. 7 guest stars. 38-40-Infinity War x-overs. 38-Battles Warlock. 39-Thanos-c & cameo. 40-Thanos app. 42-Punisher-c/story. 53-Warlock & Moondragon app. 58-w/bound-in card sheet 2.00
50-($2.95, 52 pgs.)-Holo-grafx foil-c; Silver Surfer, Man-Thing, Ren & Stimpy app. 3.00
Special #1-3 ($1.25, newsstand)-Same as #32-34 1.25

QUEEN OF THE WEST, DALE EVANS (TV)(See Dale Evans Comics, Roy Rogers & Western Roundup under Dell Giants)
Dell Publ. Co.: No. 479, 7/53 - No. 22, 1-3/59 (All photo-c; photo back c-4-8,15)

Four Color 479(#1, '53) 21.00 63.00 230.00
Four Color 528(#2, '54) 9.00 28.00 105.00
3,4: 3(4-6/54)-Toth-a. 4-Toth, Manning-a 8.00 23.00 85.00
5-10-Manning-a. 5-Marsh-a 6.00 18.00 65.00
11,19,21-No Manning 21-Tufts-a 4.40 13.00 48.00
12-18,20,22-Manning-a 5.25 16.00 58.00

QUENTIN DURWARD
Dell Publishing Co.: No. 672, Jan, 1956

Four Color 672-Movie, photo-c 5.50 16.50 60.00

QUESTAR ILLUSTRATED SCIENCE FICTION CLASSICS
Golden Press: 1977 (224 pgs.) ($1.95)

11197-Stories by Asimov, Sturgeon, Silverberg & Niven; Starstream-r 2.20 6.25 22.00

QUEST FOR CAMELOT
DC Comics: July, 1998 ($4.95)

1-Movie adaption 5.00

QUEST FOR DREAMS LOST (Also see Word Warriors)
Literacy Volunteers of Chicago: July 4, 1987 ($2.00, B&W, 52 pgs.)(Proceeds donated to help illiteracy)

1-Teenage Mutant Ninja Turtles by Eastman/Laird, Trollords, Silent Invasion, The Realm, Wordsmith, Reacto Man, Eb'nn, Aniverse 2.00

QUESTION, THE (See Americomics, Blue Beetle (1967), Charlton Bullseye & Mysterious Suspense)

QUESTION, THE (Also see Showcase '95 #3)
DC Comics: Feb, 1987 - No. 36, Mar, 1990 ($1.50)

1-36: Denny O'Neil scripts in all 2.00
Annual 1 (1988, $2.50) 2.50
Annual 2 (1989, $3.50) 3.50

QUESTION QUARTERLY, THE
DC Comics: Summer, 1990 - No. 5, Spring, 1992 ($2.50, 52pgs.)

1-5 2.50
NOTE: **Cowan** *a-1, 2, 4, 5; c-1-3, 5.* **Mignola** *a-5i.* **Quesada** *a-3-5.*

QUESTION RETURNS, THE
DC Comics: Feb, 1997 ($3.50, one-shot)

1-Brereton-c 3.50

QUESTPROBE
Marvel Comics: 8/84; No. 2, 1/85; No. 3, 11/85 (lim. series)

1-3: 1-The Hulk app. by Romita. 2-Spider-Man; Mooney-a(i). 3-Human Torch & Thing 2.00

QUICK DRAW McGRAW (TV) (Hanna-Barbera)(See Whitman Comic Books)
Dell Publishing Co./Gold Key No. 12 on: No. 1040, 12-2/59-60 - No. 11, 7-9/62; No. 12, 11/62; No. 13, 2/63; No. 14, 4/63; No. 15, 6/69
(1st show aired 9/29/59)

Four Color 1040(#1) 1st app. Quick Draw & Baba Looey, Augie Doggie & Doggie Daddy and Snooper & Blabber 13.00 39.00 140.00
2(4-6/60)-4,6: 2-Augie Doggie & Snooper & Blabber stories (8 pgs. each); pre-dates both of their #1 issues. 4-Augie Doggie & Snooper & Blabber stories. 7.00 21.00 75.00
5-1st Snagglepuss app.; last 10¢ issue 8.00 23.00 85.00
7-11 5.00 15.00 55.00
12,13-Title change to ...Fun-Type Roundup (84pgs.) 8.00 23.00 85.00
14,15 4.00 12.00 45.00

QUICK DRAW McGRAW (TV)(See Spotlight #2)
Charlton Comics: Nov, 1970 - No. 8, Jan, 1972 (Hanna-Barbera)

1 4.50 13.50 45.00
2-8 2.60 7.80 26.00

QUICKSILVER (See Avengers)
Marvel Comics: Nov, 1997 - No. 13, Nov, 1998 ($2.99/$1.99)

1-($2.99)-Peyer-s/Casey Jones-a; wraparound-c 3.00
2-11: 2-Two covers-variant by Golden. 4-6-Inhumans app. 2.00
12-($2.99) Siege of Wundagore pt. 4 3.00
13-Magneto-c/app.; last issue 2.00

QUICK-TRIGGER WESTERN (...Action #12; Cowboy Action #5-11)
Atlas Comics (ACI #12/WPI #13-19): No. 12, May, 1956 - No. 19, Sept, 1957

12-Baker-a 15.00 45.00 105.00
13-Williamson-a, 5 pgs. 14.00 43.00 100.00
14-Everett, Crandall, Torres-a; Heath-c 13.00 39.00 90.00
15,16: 15-Torres, Crandall-a. 16-Orlando, Kirby-a 10.00 30.00 70.00
17,18: 18-Baker-a 10.00 30.00 65.00
19 8.35 25.00 50.00
NOTE: **Ayers** *a-17.* **Colan** *a-16.* **Maneely** *a-15, 17; c-15, 18.* **Morrow** *a-18.* **Powell** *a-14.* **Severin** *a-19; c-12, 13, 16, 17, 19.* **Shores** *a-16.* **Tuska** *a-17.*

QUINCY (See Comics Reading Libraries)

Q-UNIT
Harris Comics: Dec, 1993 ($2.95)

1-($2.95)-Polybagged w/trading card version 1.2 3.00

RABID
FantaCo Enterprises: 1994 ($5.95, B&W)

1 6.00

RACCOON KIDS, THE (Formerly Movietown Animal Antics)
National Periodical Publications (Arleigh No. 63,64): No. 52, Sept-Oct, 1954 - No. 62, Oct-Nov, 1956; No. 63, Sept, 1957; No. 64, Nov, 1957

52-Doodles Duck by Mayer 14.00 43.00 100.00
53-64: 53-62-Doodles Duck by Mayer 10.00 30.00 70.00

RACE FOR THE MOON
Harvey Publications: Mar, 1958 - No. 3, Nov, 1958

1-Powell-a(5); 1/2-pg. S&K-a; cover redrawn from Galaxy Science Fiction pulp (5/53) 13.00 39.00 90.00
2-Kirby/Williamson-c(r)/a(3); Kirby-p 7 more stys 25.00 75.00 175.00
3-Kirby/Williamson-c/a(4); Kirby-p 6 more stys 26.00 79.00 185.00

RACE OF SCORPIONS
Dark Horse Comics: 1990 - No. 2, 1990 ($4.50/$4.95, 52pgs.)

1,2: 1-r/stories from Dark Horse Presents #23-27. 2-($4.95-c) 5.00

RACER-X
Now Comics: 8/88 - No. 11, 8/89; V2#1, 9/89 - V2#10, 1990 ($1.75)

0-Deluxe ($3.50) 3.50

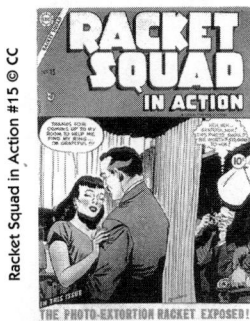

Racket Squad in Action #15 © CC

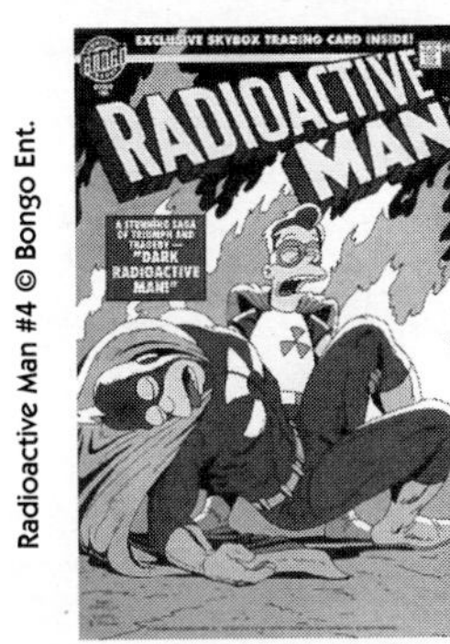

Radioactive Man #4 © Bongo Ent.

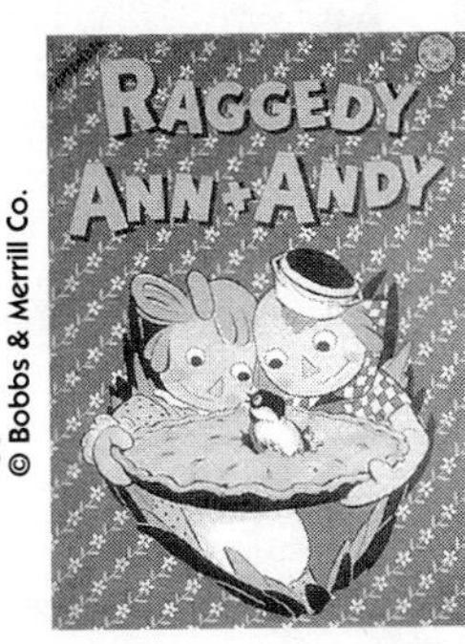

Raggedy Ann & Andy #4 © Bobbs & Merrill Co.

	GD2.0	FN6.0	NM9.4
1 (9/88) - 11, V2#1-10			2.00

RACK & PAIN
Dark Horse Comics: Mar, 1994 - No. 4, June, 1994 ($2.50, limited series)

1-4: Brian Pulido scripts in all. 1-Greg Capullo-c — 3.00

RACK & PAIN: KILLERS
Chaos! Comics: Sept, 1996 - No. 4, Jan, 1997 ($2.95, limited series)

1-4: Reprints Dark Horse series; Jae Lee-c — 3.00

RACKET SQUAD IN ACTION
Capitol Stories/Charlton Comics: May-June, 1952 - No. 29, Mar, 1958

	GD2.0	FN6.0	NM9.4
1	27.00	81.00	190.00
2-4,6: 3,4,6-Dr. Neff, Ghost Breaker app.	13.50	41.00	95.00
5-Dr. Neff, Ghost Breaker app; headlights-c	21.00	64.00	150.00
7-10: 10-Explosion-c	12.00	36.00	85.00
11-Ditko-c/a	29.00	86.00	200.00
12-Ditko explosion-c (classic); Shuster-a(2)	44.00	132.00	350.00
13-Shuster-c(p)/a.	10.00	30.00	70.00
14-Marijuana story "Shakedown"	12.00	36.00	85.00
15-28	10.00	30.00	65.00
29-(15¢, 68 pgs.)	10.00	30.00	70.00

RADIANT LOVE (Formerly Daring Love #1)
Gilmor Magazines: No. 2, Dec, 1953 - No. 6, Aug, 1954

	GD2.0	FN6.0	NM9.4
2	7.50	22.50	45.00
3-6	4.25	13.00	28.00

RADICAL DREAMER
Blackball Comics: No. 0, May, 1994 - No. 4, Nov, 1994 ($1.99, bi-monthly) (1st poster format comic)

0-4: 0-2-($1.99, poster format): 0-1st app. Max Wrighter. 3,4-($2.50-c) — 3.00

RADICAL DREAMER
Mark's Giant Economy Size Comics: V2#1, June, 1995 - V2#6, Feb, 1996 ($2.95, B&W, limited series)

V2#1-6 — 3.00
Prime (5/96, $2.95) — 3.00
Dreams Cannot Die!-(1996, $20.00, softcover)-Collects V1#0-4 & V2#1-6; intro by Kurt Busiek; afterward by Mark Waid — 20.00
Dreams Cannot Die!-(1996, $60.00, hardcover)-Signed & limited edition; collects V1#0-4 & V2#1-6; intro by Kurt Busiek; afterward by Mark Waid — 60.00

RADIOACTIVE MAN (Simpsons TV show)
Bongo Comics: 1993 - No. 6, 1994 ($1.95/$2.25, limited series)

1-($2.95)-Glow-in-the-dark-c; bound-in jumbo poster; origin Radioactive Man; (cover dated Nov. 1952) — 3.25
2-6: 2-Says #88 on-c & inside & dated May 1962; cover parody of Atlas Kirby monster-c; Superior Squad app.; origin Fallout Boy. 3-($1.95)-Cover "dated" Aug 1972 #216. 4-($2.25)-Cover "dated" Oct 1980 #412; w/trading card. 5-Cover "dated" Jan 1986 #679; w/trading card. 6-(Jan 1995 #1000) — 2.25
Colossal #1-($4.95) — 5.00

RAGAMUFFINS
Eclipse Comics: Jan, 1985 ($1.75, one shot)

1-Eclipse Magazine-r, w/color — 2.00

RAGGEDY ANN AND ANDY (See Dell Giants, March of Comics #23 & New Funnies)
Dell Publishing Co.: No. 5, 1942 - No. 533, 2/54; 10-12/64 - No. 4, 3/66

	GD2.0	FN6.0	NM9.4
Four Color 5(1942)	49.00	146.00	535.00
Four Color 23(1943)	36.00	108.00	395.00
Four Color 45(1943)	29.00	89.00	325.00
Four Color 72(1945)	24.00	74.00	270.00
1(6/46)-Billy & Bonnie Bee by Frank Thomas	25.00	75.00	275.00
2,3: 3-Egbert Elephant by Dan Noonan begins	13.00	38.00	140.00
4-Kelly-a, 16 pgs.	14.00	41.00	150.00
5-10: 7-Little Black Sambo, Black Mumbo & Black Jumbo only app; Christmas-c	10.00	30.00	110.00
11-21: 21-Alice In Wonderland cover/story	8.00	25.00	90.00
22-27,29-39(8/49), Four Color 262(1/50): 34-"...In Candyland"	6.40	19.00	70.00
28-Kelly-c	7.00	22.00	80.00
Four Color 306,354,380,452,533	4.50	13.50	50.00
1(10-12/64-Dell)	2.90	8.70	32.00
2,3(10-12/65), 4(3/66)	2.00	6.00	20.00

NOTE: **Kelly** art ("Animal Mother Goose")-#1-34, 36, 37; c-28. Peterkin Pottle by **John Stanley** in 32-38.

RAGGEDY ANN AND ANDY
Gold Key: Dec, 1971 - No. 6, Sept, 1973

	GD2.0	FN6.0	NM9.4
1	2.50	7.50	24.00
2-6	1.75	5.25	14.00

RAGGEDY ANN & THE CAMEL WITH THE WRINKLED KNEES (See Dell Jr. Treasury #8)

RAGMAN (See Batman Family #20, The Brave & The Bold #196 & Cancelled Comic Cavalcade)
National Per. Publ./DC Comics No. 5: Aug-Sept, 1976 - No. 5, Jun-Jul, 1977

	GD2.0	FN6.0	NM9.4
1-Origin & 1st app.	1.00	3.00	8.00
2-5: 2-Origin ends; Kubert-c. 4-Drug use story			5.00

NOTE: **Kubert** a-4, 5; c-1-5. **Redondo** studios a-1-4.

RAGMAN (2nd Series)
DC Comics: Oct, 1991 - No. 8, May, 1992 ($1.50, limited series)

1-8: 1-Giffen plots/breakdowns. 3-Origin. 8-Batman-c/story — 2.00

RAGMAN: CRY OF THE DEAD
DC Comics: Aug, 1993 - No. 6, Jan, 1994 ($1.75, limited series)

1-6: Joe Kubert-c — 3.00

RAGMOP
Image Comics: Sept, 1997 - Present ($2.95, B&W)

1,2-Rob Walton-c/s/a — 3.00

RAGS RABBIT (Formerly Babe Ruth Sports #10 or Little Max #10?; also see Harvey Hits #2, Harvey Wiseguys & Tastee Freez)
Harvey Publications: No. 11, June, 1951 - No. 18, March, 1954 (Written & drawn for little folks)

	GD2.0	FN6.0	NM9.4
11-(See Nutty Comics #5 for 1st app.)	4.25	13.00	26.00
12-18	4.00	10.00	20.00

RAI (Rai and the Future Force #9-23) (See Magnus #5-8)
Valiant: Mar, 1992 - No. 0, Oct, 1992; No. 9, May, 1993 - No. 33, Jun, 1995 ($1.95/$2.25)

1,2-Valiant's 1st original character — 4.00
3-8,0,9-33: 4-Low print run. 6,7-Unity x-overs. 7-Death of Rai. 0-(11/92)-Origin/1st app. new Rai (Rising Spirit) & 1st full app. & partial originBloodshot; also see Eternal Warrior #4; tells future of all characters. 9-($2.50)-Gatefold-c; story cont'd from Magnus #24; Magnus, Eternal Warrior & X-O app. 15-Manowar Armor app. 17-19-Magnus x-over. 21-1st app. The Starwatchers (cameo); trading card. 22-Death of Rai. 26-Chaos Effect Epsilon Pt. 3 — 2.50

NOTE: **Layton** c-2i, 9i. **Miller** c-6. **Simonson** c-7.

RAIDERS OF THE LOST ARK (Movie)
Marvel Comics Group: Sept, 1981 - No. 3, Nov, 1981 (Movie adaptation)

1-3: 1-r/Marvel Comics Super Special #18 — 2.50

NOTE: **Buscema** a(p)-1-3; c(p)-1. **Simonson** a-3i; scripts-1-3.

RAINBOW BRITE AND THE STAR STEALER
DC Comics: 1985

nn-Movie adaptation — 5.00

RALPH KINER, HOME RUN KING
Fawcett Publications: 1950 (Pittsburgh Pirates)

	GD2.0	FN6.0	NM9.4
nn-Photo-c; life story	56.00	169.00	450.00

RALPH SNART ADVENTURES
Now Comics: June, 1986 - V2#9, 1987; V3#1 - #26, Feb, 1991; V4#1, 1992 - #4, 1992

1-3, V2#1-7,V3#1-23,25,26:1-($1.00, B&W)-1(B&W),V2#1(11/86), B&W), 8,9-

Rampaging Hulk #1 © MAR

Rangeland Love #2 © MAR

Rangers Comics #22 © FH

GD2.0 FN6.0 NM9.4

color. V3#1(9/88)-Color begins 2.50
V3#24-($2.50)-3-D issue, V4#1-3-Direct sale versions w/cards 2.50
V4#1-3-Newsstand versions w/random cards 2.50
Book 1 1.00 3.00 8.00
3-D Special (11/92, $3.50)-Complete 12-card set w/3-D glasses 3.50

RAMAR OF THE JUNGLE (TV)
Toby Press No. 1/Charlton No. 2 on: 1954 (no month); No. 2, Sept, 1955 - No. 5, Sept, 1956

1-Jon Hall photo-c; last pre-code issue 20.00 60.00 140.00
2-5: 2-Jon Hall photo-c 13.50 41.00 95.00

RAMM
Megaton Comics: May, 1987 - No. 2, Sept, 1987 ($1.50, B&W)

1,2-Both have 1 pg. Youngblood ad by Liefeld 2.00

RAMPAGING HULK (The Hulk #10 on; see Marvel Treasury Edition)
Marvel Comics Group: Jan, 1977 - No. 9, June, 1978 ($1.00, B&W magazine)

1-Bloodstone story 1.50 4.50 12.00
2-Old X-Men app; origin old & new X-Men in text w/Cockrum illos 1.25 3.75 10.00
3-9: 7-Man-Thing story. 9-Thor vs. Hulk battle; Shanna the She-Devil story 1.00 2.80 7.00

NOTE: **Alcala** *a-1-3i, 5i, 8i.* **Buscema** *a-1.* **Giffen** *a-4.* **Nino** *a-4i.* **Simonson** *a-1-3p.* **Starlin** *a-4(w/***Nino***), 7; c-4, 5, 7.*

RAMPAGING HULK
Marvel Comics: Aug, 1998 - No. 6, Jan, 1999 ($2.99/$1.99)

1-($2.99) Flashback stories of Savage Hulk; Leonardi-a 3.00
2-6-($1.99): 2-Two covers 2.00

RANDOLPH SCOTT (Movie star)(See Crack Western #67, Prize Comics Western #76, Western Hearts #8, Western Love #1 & Western Winners #7)

RANGE BUSTERS
Fox Features Syndicate: Sept, 1950 - No. 8, 1951

1 19.00 56.00 130.00
2 11.50 34.00 80.00
3-8 10.00 30.00 65.00

RANGE BUSTERS (Formerly Cowboy Love?; Wyatt Earp, Frontier Marshall #11 on)
Charlton Comics: No. 8, May, 1955 - No. 10, Sept, 1955

8 7.50 22.50 45.00
9,10 5.00 15.00 30.00

RANGELAND LOVE
Atlas Comics (CDS): Dec, 1949 - No. 2, Mar, 1950 (52 pgs.)

1-Robert Taylor & Arlene Dahl photo-c 16.00 47.00 110.00
2-Photo-c 13.00 39.00 90.00

RANGER, THE (See Zane Grey, Four Color #255)

RANGE RIDER, THE (TV)(See Flying A's...)

RANGE ROMANCES
Comic Magazines (Quality Comics): Dec, 1949 - No. 5, Aug, 1950 (#5: 52 pg)

1-Gustavson-c/a 25.00 75.00 175.00
2-Crandall-c/a; "spanking" scene 31.00 92.00 215.00
3-Crandall, Gustavson-a; photo-c 21.00 64.00 150.00
4-Crandall-a; photo-c 19.00 56.00 130.00
5-Gustavson-a; Crandall-a(p); photo-c 19.00 56.00 130.00

RANGERS COMICS (...of Freedom #1-7)
Fiction House Magazines: 10/41 - No. 67, 10/52; No. 68, Fall, 1952; No. 69, Winter, 1952-53 (Flying stories)

1-Intro. Ranger Girl & The Rangers of Freedom; ends #7, cover app. only #5 206.00 619.00 1650.00
2 75.00 225.00 600.00
3 62.00 187.00 500.00
4,5 56.00 169.00 450.00
6-10: 8-U.S. Rangers begin 44.00 132.00 350.00
11,12-Commando Rangers app. 41.00 122.00 325.00
13-Commando Ranger begins-not same as Commando Rangers 40.00 120.00 300.00
14-20 36.00 107.00 250.00
21-Intro/origin Firehair (begins, 2/45) 39.00 118.00 275.00
22-30: 23-Kazanda begins, ends #28. 28-Tiger Man begins (origin/1st app., 4/46), ends #46. 30-Crusoe Island begins, ends #40 27.00 81.00 190.00
31-40: 33-Hypodermic panels 23.00 69.00 160.00
41-46: 41-Last Werewolf Hunter 18.00 54.00 125.00
47-56- "Eisnerish" Dr. Drew by Grandenetti. 48-Last Glory Forbes. 53-Last 52 pg. issue. 55-Last Sky Rangers 18.00 54.00 125.00
57-60-Straight Dr. Drew by Grandenetti 13.50 41.00 95.00
61-69: 64-Suicide Smith begins. 63-Used in **POP**, pgs. 85, 99. 67-Space Rangers begin, end #69 12.00 36.00 85.00

NOTE: *Bondage, discipline covers, lingerie panels are common. Crusoe Island by* **Larsen***-#30-36. Firehair by* **Lubbers***-#30-49. Glory Forbes by* **Baker***-#36-45, 47; by* **Whitman***-#34, 35. I Confess in #41-53. Jan of the Jungle in #42-58. King of the Congo in #49-53. Tiger Man by* **Celardo***-#30-39.* **M. Anderson** *a-30?* **Baker** *a-36-38, 42, 44.* **John Celardo** *a-34, 36-39.* **Lee Elias** *a-21-28.* **Evans** *a-19, 38-46, 48-52.* **Hopper** *a-25, 26.* **Ingels** *a-13-16.* **Larsen** *a-34.* **Bob Lubbers** *a-30-38, 40-44; c-40-45.* **Moreira** *a-41-47.* **Tuska** *a-16, 17, 19, 22.* **M. Whitman** *c-61-66.* **Zolnerwich** *c-1-17.*

RANGO (TV)
Dell Publishing Co.: Aug, 1967

1-Tim Conway photo-c 2.50 7.50 20.00

RAPHAEL (See Teenage Mutant Ninja Turtles)
Mirage Studios: 1985 ($1.50, 7-1/2x11", B&W w/2 color cover, one-shot)

1-1st Turtles one-shot spin-off; contains 1st drawing of the Turtles as a group from 1983 3.00
1-2nd printing (11/87); new-c & 8 pgs. art 2.00

RASCALS IN PARADISE
Dark Horse Comics: Aug, 1994 - No. 3, Dec, 1994 ($3.95, magazine size)

1-3-Jim Silke-a/story 4.00
Trade paperback-($16.95)-r/#1-3 17.00

RATFINK (See Frantic, Zany, & Ed "Big Daddy" Roth's Ratfink Comix)
Canrom, Inc.: Oct, 1964

1-Woodbridge-a 3.50 10.50 35.00

RAT PATROL, THE (TV)
Dell Publishing Co.: Mar, 1967 - No. 5, Nov, 1967; No. 6, Oct, 1969

1-Christopher George photo-c 6.00 18.00 60.00
2-6: 3-6-Photo-c 3.50 10.50 35.00

RAVAGE 2099 (See Marvel Comics Presents #117)
Marvel Comics: Dec, 1992 - No. 33, Aug, 1995($1.25/$1.50)

1-($1.75)-Gold foil stamped-c; Stan Lee scripts 3.00
1-($1.75)-2nd printing 2.00
2-24,26-33: 5-Last Ryan-c. 6-Last Ryan-a. 14-Punisher 2099 x-over. 15-Ron Lim-c(p). 18-Bound-in card sheet 2.00
25 ($2.25, 52 pgs.) 2.25
25 ($2.95, 52 pgs.)-Silver foil embossed-c 3.00

RAVEN, THE (See Movie Classics)

RAVEN CHRONICLES
Caliber (New Worlds): 1995 - Present ($2.95, B&W)

1-15: 10-Flip book w/Wordsmith #6. 15-Flip book w/High Caliber #4 3.00

RAVENING, THE
Avatar Press: June, 1997 - No. 2 ($3.00, B&W, limited series)

1,2 3.00

RAVENS AND RAINBOWS
Pacific Comics: Dec, 1983 (Baxter paper)(Reprints fanzine work in color)

1-Jeff Jones-c/a(r); nudity scenes 2.00

RAWHIDE (TV)
Dell Publishing Co./Gold Key: Sept-Nov, 1959 - June-Aug, 1962; July, 1963 -

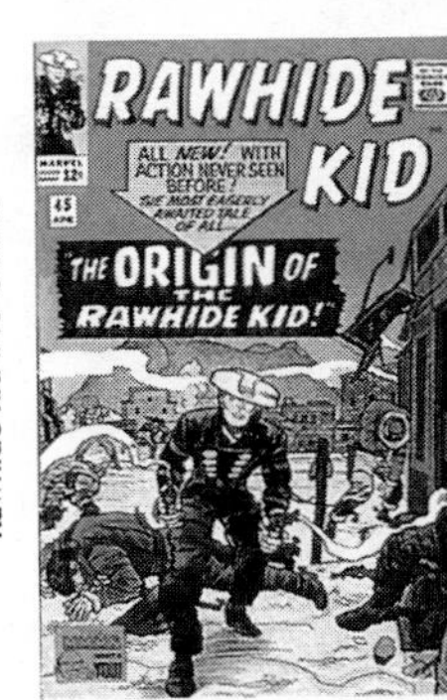

Rawhide Kid #45 © MAR

The Ray #5 © DC

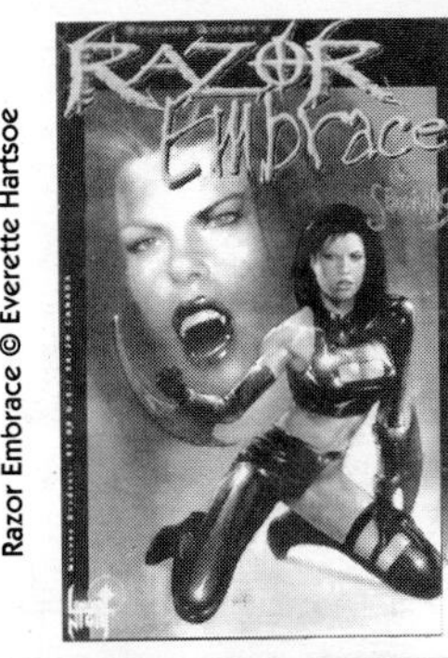

Razor Embrace © Everette Hartsoe

	GD2.0	FN6.0	NM9.4
No. 2, Jan, 1964			
Four Color 1028 (#1)	22.00	65.00	240.00
Four Color 1097,1160,1202,1261,1269	14.00	41.00	150.00
01-684-208(8/62-Dell)	12.00	35.00	130.00
1,2: 1(10071-307, Gold Key). 2-(12¢)	11.00	32.00	120.00

NOTE: *All have Clint Eastwood photo-c.* **Tufts** *a-1028.*

RAWHIDE KID
Atlas/Marvel Comics (CnPC No. 1-16/AMI No. 17-30): 3/55 - No. 16, 9/57; No. 17, 8/60 - No. 151, 5/79

	GD2.0	FN6.0	NM9.4
1-Rawhide Kid, his horse Apache & sidekick Randy begin; Wyatt Earp app.; #1 was not code approved; Maneely splash pg.	81.00	244.00	650.00
2	37.00	111.00	260.00
3-5	26.00	77.00	180.00
6-10: 7-Williamson-a (4 pgs.)	20.00	60.00	140.00
11-16: 16-Torres-a	16.00	47.00	110.00
17-Origin by Jack Kirby; Kirby-a begins	22.00	66.00	220.00
18-21,24-30	11.00	33.00	110.00
22-Monster-c/story by Kirby/Ayers	13.00	39.00	130.00
23-Origin retold by Jack Kirby	16.00	48.00	160.00
31-35,40: 31,32-Kirby-a. 33-35-Davis-a. 34-Kirby-a. 35-Intro & death of The Raven. 40-Two-Gun Kid x-over.	8.50	25.50	85.00
36,37,39,41,42-No Kirby. 42-1st Larry Lieber issue	7.50	22.50	75.00
38-Red Raven-c/story; Kirby-c (2/64).	9.50	28.50	95.00
43-Kirby-a (beware: pin-up often missing)	9.00	27.00	90.00
44,46: 46-Toth-a. 46-Doc Holliday-c/s	6.50	19.50	65.00
45-Origin retold, 17 pgs.	9.00	27.00	90.00
47-49,51-60	3.50	10.50	35.00
50-Kid Colt x-over; vs. Rawhide Kid	4.00	12.00	40.00
61-70: 64-Kid Colt story. 66-Two-Gun Kid story. 67-Kid Colt story. 70-Last 12¢ issue	3.00	9.00	30.00
71-78,80-83,85	2.25	6.75	18.00
79,84,86,95: 79-Williamson-a(r). 84,86: Kirby-a. 86-Origin-r; Williamson-r/Ringo Kid #13 (4 pgs.)	2.50	7.50	20.00
87-91: 90-Kid Colt app. 91-Last 15¢ issue	2.00	6.00	16.00
92,93 (52 pg.Giants). 92-Kirby-a	2.60	7.80	26.00
94,96-99	2.00	6.00	16.00
100 (6/72)-Origin retold & expanded	2.50	7.50	20.00
101-120: 115-Last new story	1.50	4.50	12.00
121-151	1.10	3.30	9.00
Special 1(9/71, 25¢, 68 pgs.)-All Kirby/Ayers-r	2.60	7.80	26.00

NOTE: **Ayers** *a-13, 14, 16.* **Colan** *a-5, 35, 37; c-145p, 148p, 149p.* **Davis** *a-125r.* **Everett** *a-54i, 65, 66, 88, 96i, 148i(r).* **Gulacy** *c-147.* **Heath** *c-4.* **G. Kane** *c-101, 144.* **Keller** *a-5, 144r.* **Kirby** *a-17-32, 34, 42, 43, 84, 86, 92, 109r, 112r, 137r, Spec. 1; c-17-35, 37, 38, 40, 41, 43-47, 137r.* **Maneely** *c-1, 2, 5, 6, 14.* **Morisi** *a-13.* **Morrow/Williamson** *r-111.* **Roussos** *r-146i, 147i, 149-151i.* **Severin** *a-16; c-8, 13.* **Sutton** *a-93.* **Torres** *a-99r.* **Tuska** *a-14.* **Wildey** *r-146-151(Outlaw Kid).* **Williamson** *r-79, 86, 95.*

RAWHIDE KID
Marvel Comics Group: Aug, 1985 - No. 4, Nov, 1985 (Mini-series)

	GD2.0	FN6.0	NM9.4
1-4			3.00

RAY, THE (See Freedom Fighters & Smash Comics #14)
DC Comics: Feb, 1992 - No. 6, July, 1992 ($1.00, mini-series)

	GD2.0	FN6.0	NM9.4
1-Sienkiewicz-c; Joe Quesada-a(p) in 1-5			5.00
2-6: 3-6-Quesada-c(p). 6-Quesada layouts only			3.00
...In a Blaze of Power (1994, $12.95)-r/#1-6 w/new Quesada-c			13.00

RAY, THE
DC Comics: May, 1994 - No. 28, Oct, 1996 ($1.75/$1.95/$2.25)

	GD2.0	FN6.0	NM9.4
1-Quesada-c(p); Superboy app.			3.00
1-($2.95)-Collectors Edition w/diff. Quesada-c; embossed foil-c			4.00
2-5,0,6-24,26-28: 2-Quesada-c(p); Superboy app. 5-(9/94). 0-(10/94)			2.25
25-($3.50)-Future Flash (Bart Allen)-c/app; double size			3.50
Annual 1 ($3.95, 68 pgs.)-Superman app.			4.00

RAY BRADBURY COMICS
Topps Comics: Feb, 1993 - V4#1, June, 1994 ($2.95)

	GD2.0	FN6.0	NM9.4
1-5-Polybagged w/3 trading cards each. 1-All dinosaur issue; Corben-a; Williamson/Torres/Krenkel-r/Weird Science-Fantasy #25. 3-All dinosaur issue; Steacy painted-c; Stout-a			3.00
Special Edition 1 (1994, $2.95)-The Illustrated Man			3.00
...Special: Tales of Horror #1 ($2.50), ...Trilogy of Terror V3#1 (5/94, $2.50), ...Martian Chronicles V4#1 (6/94, $2.50)-Steranko-c			2.50

NOTE: **Kelley Jones** *a-Trilogy of Terror V3#1.* **Kaluta** *a-Martian Chronicles V4#1.* **Kurtzman/Matt Wagner** *c-2.* **McKean** *c-4.* **Mignola** *a-4.* **Wood** *a-Trilogy of Terror V3#1r.*

RAZOR
London Night Studios: May, 1992 - No. 51, Apr, 1999 ($3.95/$3.00, B&W)

	GD2.0	FN6.0	NM9.4
0 (5/92, $3.95)-Direct market	1.50	4.50	12.00
0 (4/95, $3.00)-London Night edition			3.50
1/2 (4/95, mail-in offer)-1st Poizon; Linsner-c			5.00
1 (8/92, $2.50)-Fathom Press	1.50	4.50	12.00
1-2nd printing			3.50
2 ($2.95)-J. O'Barr-c	1.25	3.75	10.00
2-Limited edi. in red & blue, 2-Platinum; no c-price	1.50	4.50	12.00
3-($3.95)-Jim Balent-c			5.00
3-w/poster insert		2.40	6.00
4-Vigil-c			4.00
4-w/poster insert			5.00
5-Linsner-c		2.40	6.00
5-Platinum	1.25	3.75	10.00
6-31,33,34:10-1st app. Stryke. 1,12 -Rituals Pt. 1 & 2. 21-Rose & Gunn app. 25-Photo-c			3.00
25-Uncut ($10.00)-Nude Edition; double-c			10.00
32-($3.50)			3.50
32-($5.00)-Nude Edition; Nude-c			5.00
35-49,51			3.00
40-Uncut ($6.00)-Nude Edition			6.00
50-Uncut-Four covers incl. Tony Dainel			3.00
Annual 1 (1993, $2.95)-1st app. Shi	2.50	7.50	20.00
Annual 1-Gold (1200 printed)	2.50	7.50	25.00
Annual 2 (Late 1994, $3.00)			3.00
.../Cry No More 1-($3.95)-Origin Razor; variant-c exists			4.00
.../Embrace nn-($3.00)-Variant photo-c(Carmen Electra)			3.00
...Pictorial 1-(10/97, $5.00)			5.00
.../Shi Special 1 (7/94, $3.00)		2.40	6.00
.../Switchblade Symphony 1-($3.95)-Hartsoe-s			4.00
...: Swimsuit Special-painted-c			3.00
...: The Darkest Night 1,2 ($4.95)-painted-c			5.00
.../Warrior Nun Areala-Faith-(5/96, $3.95)			4.00
.../Warrior Nun Areala-Faith-(5/96, $3.95)-Virgin-c			5.00

RAZOR AND THE LADIES OF LONDON NIGHT
London Night Studios: March, 1997 ($3.95, one-shot, mature)

	GD2.0	FN6.0	NM9.4
1-Photo-c & insides			4.00

RAZOR: ARCHIVES
London Night Studios: May, 1997 - Present ($3.95/$5.00, mature)

	GD2.0	FN6.0	NM9.4
1-($3.95). 2-5-($5.00)			5.00

RAZOR: BURN
London Night Studios: 1994 - No. 5, 1994 ($3.00, limited series, mature)

	GD2.0	FN6.0	NM9.4
1-5			3.00
TPB-($14.95) r/ #1-5			15.00

RAZOR/DARK ANGEL: THE FINAL NAIL
Boneyard Press #1/London Night Studios #2: June, 1994 -No. 2, June, 1994 ($2.95, B&W, limited series, mature)

	GD2.0	FN6.0	NM9.4
1,2			3.00

RAZOR• DEEP CUTS
London Night Studios: Sept, 1997 ($5.00, one-shot, mature)

	GD2.0	FN6.0	NM9.4
1-Photo-c & insides			5.00
1-($10.00)-Nude Edition; Photo-c & insides			10.00

RAZOR/MORBID ANGEL: SOUL SEARCH
London Night Studios: Sept, 1996 - No. 3, 1997 ($3.00, limited series, mature)

	GD2.0	FN6.0	NM9.4
1-3			3.00

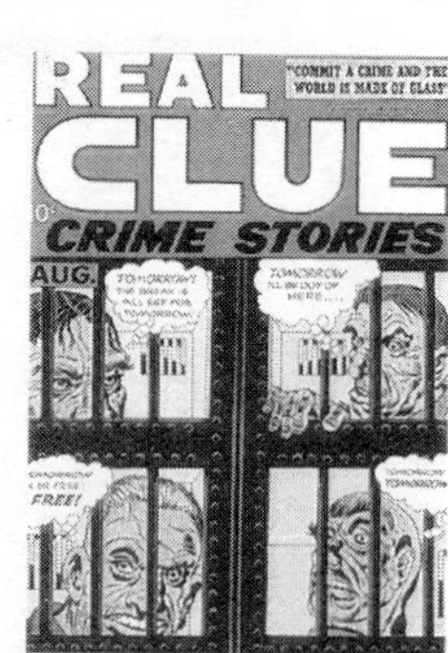

Real Clue Crime Stories V2 #6 © HILL

Real Fact Comics #3 © DC

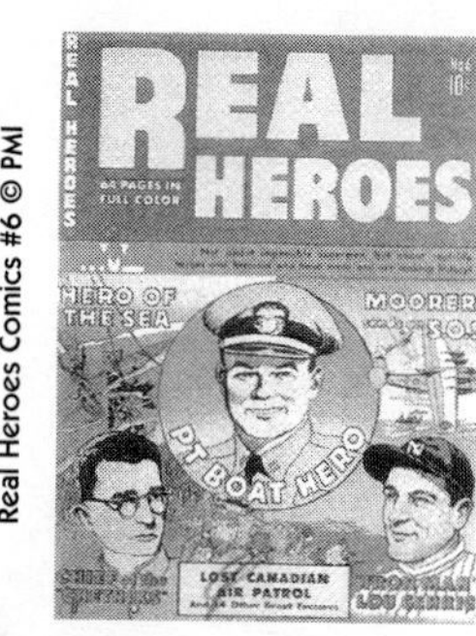

Real Heroes Comics #6 © PMI

GD2.0 FN6.0 NM9.4

RAZOR: THE SUFFERING
London Night Studios: 1994 - No. 3, 1995 ($2.95, limited series, mature)
1-3 ($2.95): 2-(9/94), 1-($3.00)-Director's Cut 3.00
1-Platinum 5.00
Trade paperback-($12.95) 13.00

RAZOR: TORTURE
London Night Studios: 1995 - No. 6, 1995 ($3.00, limited series, mature)
0-($3.95)-Wraparound, chromium-c; polybagged w/card; alternate-c exists? 4.00
1-6 ($3.00): 3-Error & corrected issues exist 3.00

RAZOR: VOLUME TWO
London Night Studios: Oct, 1996 - Present ($3.95/$3.00, mature)
1-Wraparound foil-c; Quinn-s 4.00
2-7-($3.00):3-Error & corrected issues exist 3.00

RAZORLINE
Marvel Comics: Sept, 1993 (75¢, one-shot)
1-Clive Barker super-heroes: Ectokid, Hokum & Hex, Hyperkind & Saint Sinner (all 1st app.) 2.00

REAL ADVENTURE COMICS (Action Adventure #2 on)
Gillmor Magazines: Apr, 1955
1 5.00 15.00 30.00

REAL ADVENTURES OF JONNY QUEST, THE
Dark Horse Comics: Sept, 1996 - No. 12, Sept, 1997 ($2.95)
1-12 3.00

REAL CLUE CRIME STORIES (Formerly Clue Comics)
Hillman Periodicals: V2#4, June, 1947 - V8#3, May, 1953
V2#4(#1)-S&K c/a(3); Dan Barry-a 43.00 128.00 340.00
5-7-S&K c/a(3-4). 7-Iron Lady app. 36.00 107.00 250.00
8-12 10.00 30.00 65.00
V3#1-8,10-12, V4#1-3,5-8,11,12 9.15 27.00 55.00
V3#9-Used in **SOTI**, pg. 102 11.50 34.00 80.00
V4#4-S&K-a 12.00 36.00 85.00
V4#9,10-Krigstein-a 10.00 30.00 65.00
V5#1-5,7,8,10,12 6.70 20.00 40.00
6,9,11(1/54)-Krigstein-a 10.00 30.00 60.00
V6#1-5,8,9,11 5.85 17.50 35.00
6,7,10,12-Krigstein-a. 10-Bondage-c 9.15 27.00 55.00
V7#1-3,5-11, V8#1-3: V7#6-1 pg. Frazetta ad "Prayer" - 1st app.? 5.85 17.50 35.00
4,12-Krigstein-a 9.15 27.00 55.00
NOTE: ***Barry** a-9, 10; c-V2#8. **Briefer** a-V6#6. **Fuje** a- V2#7(2), 8, 11. **Infantino** a-V2#8; c-V2#11. **Lawrence** a-V3#8, V5#7. **Powell** a-V4#11, 12. V5#4, 5, 7 are 68 pgs.*

REAL EXPERIENCES (Formerly Tiny Tessie)
Atlas Comics (20CC): No. 25, Jan, 1950
25-Virginia Mayo photo-c from movie "Red Light" 6.70 20.00 40.00

REAL FACT COMICS
National Periodical Publications: Mar-Apr, 1946 - No. 21, July-Aug, 1949
1-S&K-c/a; Harry Houdini story; Just Imagine begins (not by Finlay); Fred Ray-a 56.00 167.00 450.00
2-S&K-a; Rin-Tin-Tin & P. T. Barnum stories 40.00 120.00 300.00
3-H.G. Wells, Lon Chaney stories; 1st DC letter column 36.00 107.00 250.00
4-Virgil Finlay-a on 'Just Imagine' begins, ends #12 (2 pgs. each); Jimmy Stewart & Jack London stories; Joe DiMaggio 1 pg. biography 40.00 120.00 300.00
5-Batman/Robin-c taken from cover of Batman #9; 5 pg. story about creation of Batman & Robin; Tom Mix story 175.00 525.00 1400.00
6-Origin & 1st app. Tommy Tomorrow by Finlay (1-2/47); Flag-c; 1st writing by Harlan Ellison (letter column, non-professional); "First Man to Reach Mars" epic-c/story 109.00 328.00 875.00
7-(No. 6 on inside)-Roussos-a; D. Fairbanks sty. 18.00 54.00 125.00
8-2nd app. Tommy Tomorrow by Finlay (5-6/47) 59.00 178.00 475.00
9-S&K-a; Glenn Miller, Indianapolis 500 stories 29.00 86.00 200.00
10-Vigilante by Meskin (based on movie serial); 4 pg. Finlay s/f story 26.00 79.00 185.00
11,12: 11-Annie Oakley, G-Men stories; Kinstler-a 15.00 45.00 105.00
13-Dale Evans and Tommy Tomorrow-c/stories 50.00 150.00 400.00
14,17,18: 14-Will Rogers story 13.50 41.00 95.00
15-Nuclear explosion part-c ("Last War on Earth" story); Clyde Beatty story 18.00 54.00 125.00
16-Tommy Tomorrow app.; 1st Planeteers? 44.00 132.00 350.00
19-Sir Arthur Conan Doyle story 16.00 47.00 110.00
20-Kubert-a, 4 pgs; Daniel Boone story 17.00 51.00 120.00
21-Kubert-a, 2 pgs; Kit Carson story 13.50 41.00 95.00
NOTE: ***Barry** c-16. **Virgil Finlay** c-6, 8. **Meskin** c-10. **Roussos** a-1-4, 6.*

REAL FUNNIES
Nedor Publishing Co.: Jan, 1943 - No. 3, June, 1943
1-Funny animal, humor; Black Terrier app. (clone of The Black Terror) 32.00 96.00 225.00
2,3 16.00 47.00 110.00

REAL GHOSTBUSTERS, THE (Also see Slimer)
Now Comics: Aug, 1988 - No. 32, 1991 ($1.75/$1.95)
1-32: 1-Based on Ghostbusters movie. 30-Begin $1.95-c 2.00

REAL HEROES COMICS
Parents' Magazine Institute: Sept, 1941 - No. 16, Oct, 1946
1-Roosevelt-c/story 31.00 94.00 220.00
2-J. Edgar Hoover-c/story 13.50 41.00 95.00
3-5,7-10: 4-Churchill, Roosevelt stories 11.50 34.00 80.00
6-Lou Gehrig-c/story 19.00 58.00 135.00
11-16: 13-Kiefer-a 8.35 25.00 50.00

REALISTIC ROMANCES
Realistic Comics/Avon Periodicals: July-Aug, 1951 - No. 17, Aug-Sept, 1954 (No #9-14)
1-Kinstler-a; c-/Avon paperback #211 21.00 62.00 145.00
2 10.00 30.00 65.00
3,4 9.15 27.00 55.00
5,8-Kinstler-a 10.00 30.00 60.00
6-c-/Diversey Prize Novels #6; Kinstler-a 10.00 30.00 65.00
7-Evans-a?; c-/Avon paperback #360 10.00 30.00 65.00
15,17: 17-Kinstler-c 9.15 27.00 50.00
16-Kinstler marijuana story-r/Romantic Love #6 10.00 30.00 65.00
I.W. Reprint #1,8,9: #1-r/Realistic Romances #4; Astarita-a. 9-r/Women To Love #1 1.25 3.75 10.00
NOTE: ***Astarita** a-2-4, 7, 8, 17. Photo c-1, 2. Painted c-3, 4.*

REAL LIFE COMICS
Nedor/Better/Standard Publ./Pictorial Magazine No. 13: Sept, 1941 - No. 59, Sept, 1952
1-Uncle Sam-c/story; Daniel Boone story 47.00 141.00 375.00
2 23.00 69.00 160.00
3-Hitler cover 56.00 169.00 450.00
4,5: 4-Story of American flag "Old Glory" 14.00 43.00 100.00
6-10: 6-Wild Bill Hickok story 13.50 41.00 95.00
11-20: 17-Albert Einstein story 11.50 34.00 80.00
21-23,25,26,28-30: 29-A-Bomb story 10.00 30.00 65.00
24-Story of Baseball (Babe Ruth) 16.00 47.00 110.00
27-Schomburg A-Bomb-c; story of A-Bomb 16.00 47.00 110.00
31-33,35,36,42-44,48,49: 49-Baseball issue 8.35 25.00 50.00
34,37-41,45-47: 34-Jimmy Stewart story. 37-Story of motion pictures; Bing Crosby story. 38-Jane Froman story. 39- "1,000,000 A.D." story. 40-Bob Feller story. 41-Jimmie Foxx story; "Home Run" Baker story. 45-Story of Olympic games; Burl Ives & Kit Carson story. 46-Douglas Fairbanks Jr. & Sr. story. 47-George Gershwin story 10.00 30.00 65.00
50-Frazetta-a (5 pgs.) 26.00 77.00 180.00
51-Jules Verne "Journey to the Moon" by Evans 18.00 54.00 125.00
52-Frazetta-a (4 pgs.); Severin/Elder-a(2); Evans-a 28.00 84.00 195.00
53-57-Severin/Elder-a. 54-Bat Masterson-c/story 11.50 34.00 80.00

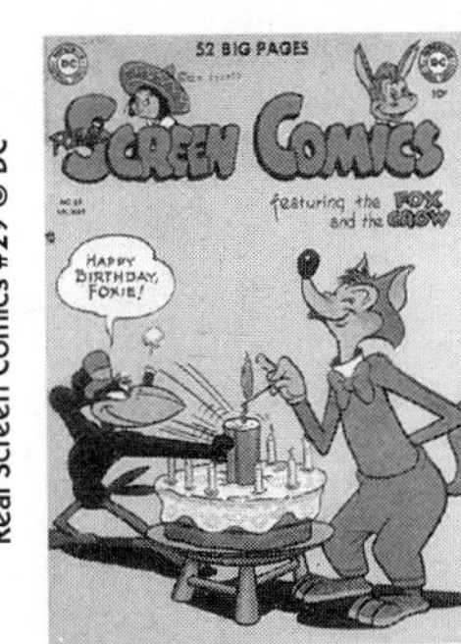

Real Screen Comics #29 © DC

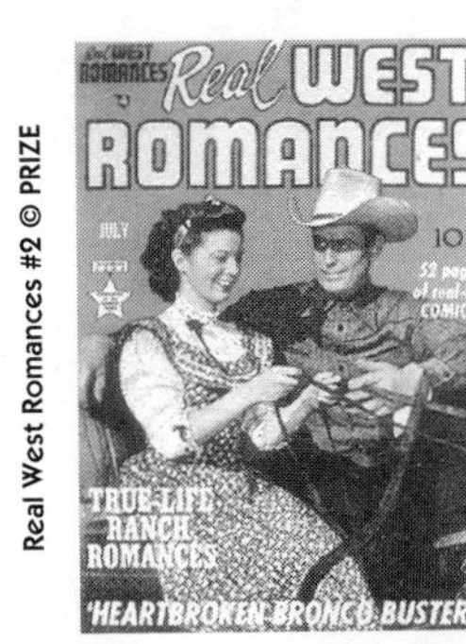

Real West Romances #2 © PRIZE

R.E.B.E.L.S. '95 #11 © DC

GD2.0 FN6.0 NM9.4

58-Severin/Elder-a(2) 12.00 36.00 85.00
59-1 pg. Frazetta; Severin/Elder-a 11.00 33.00 75.00
NOTE: *Some issues had two titles.* **Guardineer** *a-40(2), 44.* **Meskin** *a-52.* **Roussos** *a-50.* **Schomburg** *c-1, 2, 4, 5, 7, 11, 13-21, 23, 24, 26, 28, 30-32, 34-40, 42, 44-47, 55.* **Tuska** *a-53. Photo-c 5, 6.*

REAL LIFE SECRETS (Real Secrets #2 on)
Ace Periodicals: Sept, 1949 (one-shot)
1-Painted-c 10.00 30.00 60.00

REAL LIFE STORY OF FESS PARKER (Magazine)
Dell Publishing Co.: 1955
1 9.00 27.00 90.00

REAL LIFE TALES OF SUSPENSE (See Suspense)

REAL LOVE (Formerly Hap Hazard)
Ace Periodicals (A. A. Wyn): No. 25, April, 1949 - No. 76, Nov, 1956
25 11.00 33.00 75.00
26 6.70 20.00 40.00
27-L. B. Cole-a 10.00 30.00 70.00
28-35 5.00 15.00 30.00
36-66: 66-Last pre-code (2/55) 4.25 13.00 28.00
67-76 3.60 9.00 18.00
NOTE: *Photo c-50-76. Painted c-46.*

REALM, THE
Arrow Comics/WeeBee Comics #13/Caliber Press #14 on: Feb, 1986 - No. 21, 1991 ($1.50/$1.95/$2.50, B&W)
1-21: 4-1st app. Deadworld (9/86) 2.50
Book 1 ($4.95, B&W) 5.00

REAL McCOYS, THE (TV)
Dell Publ. Co.: No. 1071, 1-3/60 - 5-7/1962 (All have Walter Brennan photo-c)
Four Color 1071,1134-Toth-a in both 9.00 27.00 100.00
Four Color 1193,1265 8.00 25.00 90.00
01-689-207 (5-7/62) 7.00 22.00 80.00

REAL SCREEN COMICS (#1 titled Real Screen Funnies; TV Screen Cartoons #129-138)
National Periodical Publications: Spring, 1945 - No. 128, May-June, 1959 (#1-40: 52 pgs.)
1-The Fox & the Crow, Flippity & Flop, Tito & His Burrito begin
100.00 300.00 800.00
2 47.00 141.00 375.00
3-5 31.00 94.00 220.00
6-10 (2-3/47) 21.00 62.00 145.00
11-20 (10-11/48): 13-The Crow x-over in Flippity & Flop
16.00 47.00 110.00
21-30 (6-7/50) 11.50 34.00 80.00
31-50 10.00 30.00 70.00
51-99 9.15 27.00 55.00
100 10.00 30.00 60.00
101-128 6.70 20.00 40.00

REAL SECRETS (Formerly Real Life Secrets)
Ace Periodicals: No. 2, Nov, 1950 - No. 5, May, 1950
2-Painted-c 9.15 27.00 55.00
3-5: 3-Photo-c 5.85 17.50 35.00

REAL SPORTS COMICS (All Sports Comics #2 on)
Hillman Periodicals: Oct-Nov, 1948 (52 pgs.)
1-Powell-a (12 pgs.) 39.00 116.00 270.00

REAL WAR STORIES
Eclipse Comics: July, 1987; No. 2, Jan, 1991 ($2.00, 52 pgs.)
1-Bolland-a(p), Bissette-a, Totleben-a(i); Alan Moore scripts (2nd printing exists, 2/88) 2.00
2-($4.95) 5.00

REAL WESTERN HERO (Formerly Wow #1-69; Western Hero #76 on)
Fawcett Publications: No. 70, Sept, 1948 - No. 75, Feb, 1949 (All 52 pgs.)
70(#1)-Tom Mix, Monte Hale, Hopalong Cassidy, Young Falcon begin
34.00 103.00 240.00
71-75: 71-Gabby Hayes begins. 71,72-Captain Tootsie by Beck. 75-Big Bow and Little Arrow app. 21.00 64.00 150.00
NOTE: *Painted/photo c-70-73; painted c-74, 75.*

REAL WEST ROMANCES
Crestwood Publishing Co./Prize Publ.: 4-5/49 - V1#6, 3/50; V2#1, Apr-May, 1950 (All 52 pgs. & photo-c)
V1#1-S&K-a(p) 23.00 69.00 160.00
2-Spanking panel 11.50 34.00 80.00
3-Kirby-a(p) only 12.00 36.00 85.00
4-S&K-a; Whip Wilson, Reno Browne photo-c 18.00 54.00 125.00
5-Audie Murphy, Gale Storm photo-c; S&K-a 17.00 49.00 115.00
6-Produced by S&K, no S&K-a; Robert Preston & Cathy Downs photo-c
12.00 36.00 85.00
V2#1-Kirby-a(p) 10.00 30.00 70.00
NOTE: **Meskin** *a-V1#5, 6.* **Severin/Elder** *a-V1#3-6, V2#1.* **Meskin** *a-V1#6.* **Leonard Starr** *a-1-3. Photo-c V1#1-6, V2#1.*

RE-ANIMATOR IN FULL COLOR
Adventure Comics: Oct, 1991 - No. 3, 1992 ($2.95, mini-series)
1-3: Adapts horror movie. 1-Dorman painted-c 3.00

REAP THE WILD WIND (See Cinema Comics Herald)

REBEL, THE (TV)
Dell Publishing Co.: No. 1076, Feb-Apr, 1960 - No. 1262, Dec-Feb, 1961-62
Four Color 1076 (#1)-Sekowsky-a, photo-c 10.00 30.00 110.00
Four Color 1138 (9-11/60), 1207 (9-11/61), 1262-Photo-c
8.00 25.00 90.00

R.E.B.E.L.S. '94 (Becomes R.E.B.E.L.S. '95 & R.E.B.E.L.S. '96)
DC Comics: No. 0, Oct, 1994 - No. 17, Mar, 1996 ($1.95/$2.25)
0-17: 8-$2.25-c begins. 15-R.E.B.E.L.S '96 begins. 2.25

REBEL SWORD (Manga)
Dark Horse Comics: Oct, 1994 - No. 6, Feb, 1995 ($2.50, B&W)
1-6 2.50

RECORD BOOK OF FAMOUS POLICE CASES
St. John Publishing Co.: 1949 (25¢, 132 pgs.)
nn-Kubert-a(3); r/Son of Sinbad; Baker-c 37.00 111.00 260.00

RED ARROW
P. L. Publishing Co.: May-June, 1951 - No. 3, Oct, 1951
1 10.00 30.00 65.00
2,3 8.00 24.00 48.00

RED BAND COMICS
Enwil Associates: Feb, 1945 - No. 4, May, 1945
1 36.00 107.00 250.00
2-Origin Bogeyman & Santanas; c-reprint/#1 26.00 79.00 185.00
3,4-Captain Wizard app. in both (1st app.); each has identical contents/cover
24.00 73.00 170.00

REDBLADE
Dark Horse Comics: Apr, 1993 - No. 3, July, 1993 ($2.50, mini-series)
1-3: 1-Double gatefold-c 3.00

RED CIRCLE COMICS
Rural Home Publications (Enwil): Jan, 1945 - No. 4, April, 1945
1-The Prankster & Red Riot begin 34.00 103.00 240.00
2-Starr-a; The Judge (costumed hero) app. 27.00 81.00 190.00
3,4-Starr-c/a. 3-The Prankster not in costume 21.00 62.00 145.00
4-(Dated 4/45)-Leftover covers to #4 were later restapled over early 1950s coverless comics; variations in the coverless comics used are endless; Woman Outlaws, Dorothy Lamour, Crime Does Not Pay, Sabu, Diary Loves, Love Confessions & Young Love V3#3 known 13.00 39.00 90.00

RED CIRCLE SORCERY (Chilling Adventures in Sorcery #1-5)
Red Circle Prod. (Archie): No. 6, Apr, 1974 - No. 11, Feb, 1975 (All 25¢ iss.)

Red Dragon Comics (2nd series) #3 © Conde Nast

"Red" Rabbit Comics #1 © Dearfield Publ.

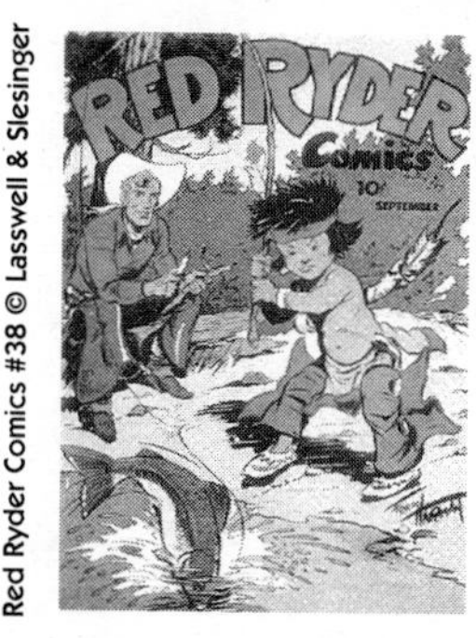

Red Ryder Comics #38 © Lasswell & Slesinger

GD2.0 FN6.0 NM9.4

6,8,9,11: 8-Only app. The Cobra 2.40 6.00
7-Bruce Jones-a with Wrightson, Kaluta, Jeff Jones 1.00 3.00 8.00
10-Wood-a(i) 1.00 2.80 7.00
NOTE: *Chaykin a-6, 10. McWilliams a-10(2 & 3 pgs.). Mooney a-11p. Morrow a-6-8, 9(text illos), 10, 11i; c-6-11. Thorne a-8, 10. Toth a-8, 9.*

RED DOG (See Night Music #7)

RED DRAGON
Comico: June, 1996 ($2.95)
1-Bisley-c 3.00

RED DRAGON COMICS (1st Series) (Formerly Trail Blazers; see Super Magician V5#7, 8)
Street & Smith Publications: No. 5, Jan, 1943 - No. 9, Jan, 1944
5-Origin Red Rover, the Crimson Crimebuster; Rex King, Man of Adventure, Captain Jack Commando, & The Minute Man begin; text origin Red Dragon; Binder-c 100.00 300.00 800.00
6-Origin The Black Crusader & Red Dragon (3/43); 1st story app. Red Dragon & 1st cover (classic-c) 200.00 600.00 1600.00
7-Classic-c 137.00 412.00 1100.00
8-The Red Knight app. 70.00 280.00 560.00
9-Origin Chuck Magnon, Immortal Man 70.00 280.00 560.00

RED DRAGON COMICS (2nd Series)(See Super Magician V2#8)
Street & Smith Publications: Nov, 1947 - No. 6, Jan, 1949; No. 7, July, 1949
1-Red Dragon begins; Elliman, Nigel app.; Edd Cartier-c/a 87.00 262.00 700.00
2-Cartier-c 62.00 187.00 500.00
3-1st app. Dr. Neff Ghost Breaker by Powell; Elliman, Nigel app. 53.00 159.00 425.00
4-Cartier c/a 69.00 206.00 550.00
5-7 40.00 120.00 300.00
NOTE: *Maneely a-5, 7. Powell a-2-7; c-3, 5, 7.*

RED EAGLE
David McKay Publications: No. 16, Aug, 1938
Feature Books 16 16.00 48.00 1750.00

REDEYE (See Comics Reading Libraries)

RED FOX (Formerly Manhunt! #1-14; also see Extra Comics)
Magazine Enterprises: No. 15, 1954
15(A-1 #108)-Undercover Girl story; L.B. Cole-c/a (Red Fox); r-from Manhunt; Powell-a 18.00 54.00 125.00

RED FURY
High Impact Entertainment: 1997 ($2.95, B&W)
1 3.00

RED GOOSE COMIC SELECTIONS (See Comic Selections)

RED HAWK (See A-1 Comics, Bobby Benson's ..#14-16 & Straight Arrow #2)
Magazine Enterprises: No. 90, 1953
A-1 90-Powell-c/a 11.50 34.00 80.00

RED MASK (Formerly Tim Holt; see Best Comics, Blazing Six-Guns)
Magazine Enterprises No. 42-53/Sussex No. 54 (M.E. on-c): No. 42, June-July, 1954 - No. 53, May, 1956; No. 54, Sept, 1957
42-Ghost Rider by Ayers continues, ends #50; Black Phantom continues; 3-D effect c/stories begin 21.00 62.00 145.00
43-3-D effect-c/stories 18.00 55.00 128.00
44-52: 3-D effect stories only. 47-Last pre-code issue. 50-Last Ghost Rider. 51-The Presto Kid begins by Ayers (1st app.); Presto Kid-c begins; last 3-D effect story. 52-Origin The Presto Kid 17.00 51.00 118.00
53,54-Last Black Phantom; last Presto Kid-c 13.00 39.00 90.00
I.W. Reprint #1 (r-/#52). 2 (nd, r/#51 w/diff.-c). 3, 8 (nd; Kinstler-c); 8-r/Red Mask #52 2.50 7.50 20.00
NOTE: *Ayers art on Ghost Rider & Presto Kid. Bolle art in all (Red Mask); c-43, 44, 49. Guardineer a-52. Black Phantom in #42-44, 47-50, 53, 54.*

REDMASK OF THE RIO GRANDE
AC Comics: 1990 ($2.50, 28pgs.)(Has photos of movie posters)
1-Bolle-c/a(r); photo inside-c 2.50

RED MOUNTAIN FEATURING QUANTRELL'S RAIDERS (Movie)(Also see Jesse James #28)
Avon Periodicals: 1952
nn-Alan Ladd; Kinstler-c 26.00 79.00 185.00

"RED" RABBIT COMICS
Dearfield Comic/J. Charles Laue Publ. Co.: Jan, 1947 - No. 22, Aug-Sep, 1951
1 11.50 34.00 80.00
2 7.00 21.00 42.00
3-10 5.35 16.00 32.00
11-17,19-22 4.25 13.00 28.00
18-Flying Saucer-c (1/51) 7.00 21.00 42.00

RED RAVEN COMICS (Human Torch #2 on)(Also see X-Men #44 & Sub-Mariner #26, 2nd series)
Timely Comics: August, 1940 **GD2.0 FN6.0 VF8.0 NM9.4**
1-Origin & 1st app. Red Raven; Comet Pierce & Mercury by Kirby, The Human Top & The Eternal Brain; intro. Magar, the Mystic & only app.; Kirby-c (his 1st signed work) 1000.00 3000.00 6000.00 10,000.00

RED ROCKET 7
Dark Horse Comics: Aug, 1997 - No. 7, June, 1998 ($3.95, square format, limited series)
1-7-Mike Allred-c/s/a 4.00

RED RYDER COMICS (Hi Spot #2)(Movies, radio)(See Crackajack Funnies & Super Book of Comics)
Hawley Publ. No. 1/Dell Publishing Co.(K.K.) No. 3 on: 9/40; No. 3, 8/41 - No. 5, 12/41; No. 6, 4/42 - No. 151, 4-6/57 **GD2.0 FN6.0 NM9.4**
1-Red Ryder, his horse Thunder, Little Beaver & his horse Papoose strip reprints begin by Fred Harman; 1st meeting of Red & Little Beaver; Harman line-drawn-c #1-85 260.00 780.00 2600.00
3-(Scarce)-Alley Oop, King of the Royal Mtd., Capt. Easy, Freckles & His Friends, Myra North, Dan Dunn strip-r begin 86.00 259.00 950.00
4-6: 6-1st Dell issue (4/42) 41.00 123.00 450.00
7-10 33.00 98.00 360.00
11-20 23.00 68.00 250.00
21-32-Last Alley Oop, Dan Dunn, Capt. Easy, Freckles 14.00 44.00 160.00
33-40 (52 pgs.) 9.00 27.00 100.00
41 (52 pgs.)-Rocky Lane photo back-c; photo back-c begin, end #57 9.00 29.00 105.00
42-46 (52 pgs.): 46-Last Red Ryder strip-r 8.00 23.00 85.00
47-53 (52 pgs.): 47-New stories on Red Ryder begin. 49,52-Harmon photo back-c 6.40 19.00 70.00
54-92: 54-73 (36 pgs.). 59-Harmon photo back-c. 73-Last King of the Royal Mtd; strip-r by Jim Gary. 74-85,93 (52 pgs.)-Harman line-drawn-c. 86-92 (52 pgs.)-Harman painted-c 5.00 15.00 54.00
94-99,101-106: 94-96 (36 pgs.)-Harman painted-c. 97,98,107,108 (36 pgs.)-Harman line-drawn-c. 99,101-106 (36 pgs.)-Jim Bannon Photo-c 3.60 11.00 40.00
100 (36 pgs.)-Bannon photo-c 4.00 12.00 45.00
109-118 (52 pgs.)-Harman line-drawn-c 3.20 9.50 35.00
119-129 (52 pgs.): 119-Painted-c begin, not by Harman, end #151 2.90 8.70 32.00
130-144 (#130 on have 36 pgs.) 2.70 8.00 30.00
145-151: 145-148: 145-Title change to Red Ryder Ranch Mag. with photos. 149-151: 149-Title changed to R.R. Ranch Comics 2.40 7.00 26.00
Four Color 916 (7/58) 2.75 8.00 30.00
NOTE: *Fred Harman a-1-99; c-1-98, 107-118. Don Red Barry, Allan Rocky Lane, Wild Bill Elliott & Jim Bannon starred as Red Ryder in the movies. Robert Blake starred as Little Beaver.*

RED RYDER PAINT BOOK
Whitman Publishing Co.: 1941 (8-1/2x11-1/2", 148 pgs.)
nn-Reprints 1940 daily strips 75.00 225.00 600.00

RED SEAL COMICS (Formerly Carnival Comics, and/or Spotlight Comics?)
Harry 'A' Chesler/Superior Publ. No. 19 on: No. 14, 10/45 - No. 18, 10/46; No.

Real Screen Comics #29 © DC

Real West Romances #2 © PRIZE

R.E.B.E.L.S. '95 #11 © DC

GD2.0 FN6.0 NM9.4

58-Severin/Elder-a(2) 12.00 36.00 85.00
59-1 pg. Frazetta; Severin/Elder-a 11.00 33.00 75.00
NOTE: *Some issues had two titles.* ***Guardineer*** *a-40(2), 44.* ***Meskin*** *a-52.* ***Roussos*** *a-50.* ***Schomburg*** *c-1, 2, 4, 5, 7, 11, 13-21, 23, 24, 26, 28, 30-32, 34-40, 42, 44-47, 55.* ***Tuska*** *a-53. Photo-c 5, 6.*

REAL LIFE SECRETS (Real Secrets #2 on)
Ace Periodicals: Sept, 1949 (one-shot)
1-Painted-c 10.00 30.00 60.00

REAL LIFE STORY OF FESS PARKER (Magazine)
Dell Publishing Co.: 1955
1 9.00 27.00 90.00

REAL LIFE TALES OF SUSPENSE (See Suspense)

REAL LOVE (Formerly Hap Hazard)
Ace Periodicals (A. A. Wyn): No. 25, April, 1949 - No. 76, Nov, 1956
25 11.00 33.00 75.00
26 6.70 20.00 40.00
27-L. B. Cole-a 10.00 30.00 70.00
28-35 5.00 15.00 30.00
36-66: 66-Last pre-code (2/55) 4.25 13.00 28.00
67-76 3.60 9.00 18.00
NOTE: *Photo c-50-76. Painted c-46.*

REALM, THE
Arrow Comics/WeeBee Comics #13/Caliber Press #14 on: Feb, 1986 - No. 21, 1991 ($1.50/$1.95/$2.50, B&W)
1-21: 4-1st app. Deadworld (9/86) 2.50
Book 1 ($4.95, B&W) 5.00

REAL McCOYS, THE (TV)
Dell Publ. Co.: No. 1071, 1-3/60 - 5-7/1962 (All have Walter Brennan photo-c)
Four Color 1071,1134-Toth-a in both 9.00 27.00 100.00
Four Color 1193,1265 8.00 25.00 90.00
01-689-207 (5-7/62) 7.00 22.00 80.00

REAL SCREEN COMICS (#1 titled Real Screen Funnies; TV Screen Cartoons #129-138)
National Periodical Publications: Spring, 1945 - No. 128, May-June, 1959 (#1-40: 52 pgs.)
1-The Fox & the Crow, Flippity & Flop, Tito & His Burrito begin
100.00 300.00 800.00
2 47.00 141.00 375.00
3-5 31.00 94.00 220.00
6-10 (2-3/47) 21.00 62.00 145.00
11-20 (10-11/48): 13-The Crow x-over in Flippity & Flop
16.00 47.00 110.00
21-30 (6-7/50) 11.50 34.00 80.00
31-50 10.00 30.00 70.00
51-99 9.15 27.00 55.00
100 10.00 30.00 60.00
101-128 6.70 20.00 40.00

REAL SECRETS (Formerly Real Life Secrets)
Ace Periodicals: No. 2, Nov, 1950 - No. 5, May, 1950
2-Painted-c 9.15 27.00 55.00
3-5: 3-Photo-c 5.85 17.50 35.00

REAL SPORTS COMICS (All Sports Comics #2 on)
Hillman Periodicals: Oct-Nov, 1948 (52 pgs.)
1-Powell-a (12 pgs.) 39.00 116.00 270.00

REAL WAR STORIES
Eclipse Comics: July, 1987; No. 2, Jan, 1991 ($2.00, 52 pgs.)
1-Bolland-a(p), Bissette-a, Totleben-a(i); Alan Moore scripts (2nd printing exists, 2/88) 2.00
2-($4.95) 5.00

REAL WESTERN HERO (Formerly Wow #1-69; Western Hero #76 on)
Fawcett Publications: No. 70, Sept, 1948 - No. 75, Feb, 1949 (All 52 pgs.)
70(#1)-Tom Mix, Monte Hale, Hopalong Cassidy, Young Falcon begin
34.00 103.00 240.00
71-75: 71-Gabby Hayes begins. 71,72-Captain Tootsie by Beck. 75-Big Bow and Little Arrow app. 21.00 64.00 150.00
NOTE: *Painted/photo c-70-73; painted c-74, 75.*

REAL WEST ROMANCES
Crestwood Publishing Co./Prize Publ.: 4-5/49 - V1#6, 3/50; V2#1, Apr-May, 1950 (All 52 pgs. & photo-c)
V1#1-S&K-a(p) 23.00 69.00 160.00
2-Spanking panel 11.50 34.00 80.00
3-Kirby-a(p) only 12.00 36.00 85.00
4-S&K-a; Whip Wilson, Reno Browne photo-c 18.00 54.00 125.00
5-Audie Murphy, Gale Storm photo-c; S&K-a 17.00 49.00 115.00
6-Produced by S&K, no S&K-a; Robert Preston & Cathy Downs photo-c
12.00 36.00 85.00
V2#1-Kirby-a(p) 10.00 30.00 70.00
NOTE: ***Meskin*** *a-V1#5, 6.* ***Severin/Elder*** *a-V1#3-6, V2#1.* ***Meskin*** *a-V1#6.* ***Leonard Starr*** *a-1-3. Photo-c V1#1-6, V2#1.*

RE-ANIMATOR IN FULL COLOR
Adventure Comics: Oct, 1991 - No. 3, 1992 ($2.95, mini-series)
1-3: Adapts horror movie. 1-Dorman painted-c 3.00

REAP THE WILD WIND (See Cinema Comics Herald)

REBEL, THE (TV)
Dell Publishing Co.: No. 1076, Feb-Apr, 1960 - No. 1262, Dec-Feb, 1961-62
Four Color 1076 (#1)-Sekowsky-a, photo-c 10.00 30.00 110.00
Four Color 1138 (9-11/60), 1207 (9-11/61), 1262-Photo-c
8.00 25.00 90.00

R.E.B.E.L.S. '94 (Becomes R.E.B.E.L.S. '95 & R.E.B.E.L.S. '96)
DC Comics: No. 0, Oct, 1994 - No. 17, Mar, 1996 ($1.95/$2.25)
0-17: 8-$2.25-c begins. 15-R.E.B.E.L.S '96 begins. 2.25

REBEL SWORD (Manga)
Dark Horse Comics: Oct, 1994 - No. 6, Feb, 1995 ($2.50, B&W)
1-6 2.50

RECORD BOOK OF FAMOUS POLICE CASES
St. John Publishing Co.: 1949 (25¢, 132 pgs.)
nn-Kubert-a(3); r/Son of Sinbad; Baker-c 37.00 111.00 260.00

RED ARROW
P. L. Publishing Co.: May-June, 1951 - No. 3, Oct, 1951
1 10.00 30.00 65.00
2,3 8.00 24.00 48.00

RED BAND COMICS
Enwil Associates: Feb, 1945 - No. 4, May, 1945
1 36.00 107.00 250.00
2-Origin Bogeyman & Santanas; c-reprint/#1 26.00 79.00 185.00
3,4-Captain Wizard app. in both (1st app.); each has identical contents/cover
24.00 73.00 170.00

REDBLADE
Dark Horse Comics: Apr, 1993 - No. 3, July, 1993 ($2.50, mini-series)
1-3: 1-Double gatefold-c 3.00

RED CIRCLE COMICS
Rural Home Publications (Enwil): Jan, 1945 - No. 4, April, 1945
1-The Prankster & Red Riot begin 34.00 103.00 240.00
2-Starr-a; The Judge (costumed hero) app. 27.00 81.00 190.00
3,4-Starr-c/a. 3-The Prankster not in costume 21.00 62.00 145.00
4-(Dated 4/45)-Leftover covers to #4 were later restapled over early 1950s coverless comics; variations in the coverless comics used are endless; Woman Outlaws, Dorothy Lamour, Crime Does Not Pay, Sabu, Diary Loves, Love Confessions & Young Love V3#3 known 13.00 39.00 90.00

RED CIRCLE SORCERY (Chilling Adventures in Sorcery #1-5)
Red Circle Prod. (Archie): No. 6, Apr, 1974 - No. 11, Feb, 1975 (All 25¢ iss.)

RED DRAGON
10¢
THE WORLD'S WEIRDEST TRICKS AND MOST FANTASTIC COMICS
FEATURING DR. NEFF GHOST BREAKER

Red Dragon Comics (2nd series) #3 © Conde Nast

"Red" Rabbit Comics #1 © Dearfield Publ.

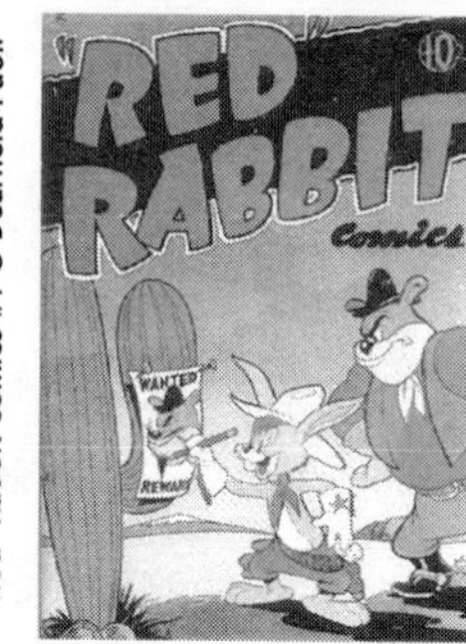

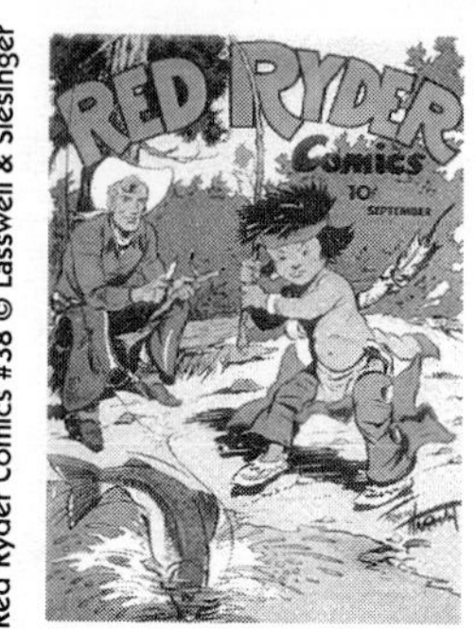

Red Ryder Comics #38 © Lasswell & Slesinger

	GD2.0	FN6.0	NM9.4
6,8,9,11: 8-Only app. The Cobra		2.40	6.00
7-Bruce Jones-a with Wrightson, Kaluta, Jeff Jones	1.00	3.00	8.00
10-Wood-a(i)	1.00	2.80	7.00

NOTE: ***Chaykin** a-6, 10. **McWilliams** a-10(2 & 3 pgs.). **Mooney** a-11p. **Morrow** a-6-8, 9(text illos), 10, 11i; c-6-11. **Thorne** a-8, 10. **Toth** a-8, 9.*

RED DOG (See Night Music #7)

RED DRAGON
Comico: June, 1996 ($2.95)

1-Bisley-c — 3.00

RED DRAGON COMICS (1st Series) (Formerly Trail Blazers; see Super Magician V5#7, 8)
Street & Smith Publications: No. 5, Jan, 1943 - No. 9, Jan, 1944

	GD2.0	FN6.0	NM9.4
5-Origin Red Rover, the Crimson Crimebuster; Rex King, Man of Adventure, Captain Jack Commando, & The Minute Man begin; text origin Red Dragon; Binder-c	100.00	300.00	800.00
6-Origin The Black Crusader & Red Dragon (3/43); 1st story app. Red Dragon & 1st cover (classic-c)	200.00	600.00	1600.00
7-Classic-c	137.00	412.00	1100.00
8-The Red Knight app.	70.00	280.00	560.00
9-Origin Chuck Magnon, Immortal Man	70.00	280.00	560.00

RED DRAGON COMICS (2nd Series)(See Super Magician V2#8)
Street & Smith Publications: Nov, 1947 - No. 6, Jan, 1949; No. 7, July, 1949

	GD2.0	FN6.0	NM9.4
1-Red Dragon begins; Elliman, Nigel app.; Edd Cartier-c/a	87.00	262.00	700.00
2-Cartier-c	62.00	187.00	500.00
3-1st app. Dr. Neff Ghost Breaker by Powell; Elliman, Nigel app.	53.00	159.00	425.00
4-Cartier c/a	69.00	206.00	550.00
5-7	40.00	120.00	300.00

NOTE: ***Maneely** a-5, 7. **Powell** a-2-7; c-3, 5, 7.*

RED EAGLE
David McKay Publications: No. 16, Aug, 1938

	GD2.0	FN6.0	NM9.4
Feature Books 16	16.00	48.00	1750.00

REDEYE (See Comics Reading Libraries)

RED FOX (Formerly Manhunt! #1-14; also see Extra Comics)
Magazine Enterprises: No. 15, 1954

	GD2.0	FN6.0	NM9.4
15(A-1 #108)-Undercover Girl story; L.B. Cole-c/a (Red Fox); r-from Manhunt; Powell-a	18.00	54.00	125.00

RED FURY
High Impact Entertainment: 1997 ($2.95, B&W)

1 — 3.00

RED GOOSE COMIC SELECTIONS (See Comic Selections)

RED HAWK (See A-1 Comics, Bobby Benson's ..#14-16 & Straight Arrow #2)
Magazine Enterprises: No. 90, 1953

	GD2.0	FN6.0	NM9.4
A-1 90-Powell-c/a	11.50	34.00	80.00

RED MASK (Formerly Tim Holt; see Best Comics, Blazing Six-Guns)
Magazine Enterprises No. 42-53/Sussex No. 54 (M.E. on-c): No. 42, June-July, 1954 - No. 53, May, 1956; No. 54, Sept, 1957

	GD2.0	FN6.0	NM9.4
42-Ghost Rider by Ayers continues, ends #50; Black Phantom continues; 3-D effect c/stories begin	21.00	62.00	145.00
43-3-D effect-c/stories	18.00	55.00	128.00
44-52: 3-D effect stories only. 47-Last pre-code issue. 50-Last Ghost Rider. 51-The Presto Kid begins by Ayers (1st app.); Presto Kid-c begins; last 3-D effect story. 52-Origin The Presto Kid	17.00	51.00	118.00
53,54-Last Black Phantom; last Presto Kid-c	13.00	39.00	90.00
I.W. Reprint #1 (r-/#52). 2 (nd, r/#51 w/diff.-c). 3, 8 (nd; Kinstler-c); 8-r/Red Mask #52	2.50	7.50	20.00

NOTE: ***Ayers** art on Ghost Rider & Presto Kid. **Bolle** art in all (Red Mask); c-43, 44, 49. **Guardineer** a-52. Black Phantom in #42-44, 47-50, 53, 54.*

REDMASK OF THE RIO GRANDE
AC Comics: 1990 ($2.50, 28pgs.)(Has photos of movie posters)

1-Bolle-c/a(r); photo inside-c — 2.50

RED MOUNTAIN FEATURING QUANTRELL'S RAIDERS (Movie)(Also see Jesse James #28)
Avon Periodicals: 1952

	GD2.0	FN6.0	NM9.4
nn-Alan Ladd; Kinstler-c	26.00	79.00	185.00

"RED" RABBIT COMICS
Dearfield Comic/J. Charles Laue Publ. Co.: Jan, 1947 - No. 22, Aug-Sep, 1951

	GD2.0	FN6.0	NM9.4
1	11.50	34.00	80.00
2	7.00	21.00	42.00
3-10	5.35	16.00	32.00
11-17,19-22	4.25	13.00	28.00
18-Flying Saucer-c (1/51)	7.00	21.00	42.00

RED RAVEN COMICS (Human Torch #2 on)(Also see X-Men #44 & Sub-Mariner #26, 2nd series)
Timely Comics: August, 1940

	GD2.0	FN6.0	VF8.0	NM9.4
1-Origin & 1st app. Red Raven; Comet Pierce & Mercury by Kirby, The Human Top & The Eternal Brain; intro. Magar, the Mystic & only app.; Kirby-c (his 1st signed work)	1000.00	3000.00	6000.00	10,000.00

RED ROCKET 7
Dark Horse Comics: Aug, 1997 - No. 7, June, 1998 ($3.95, square format, limited series)

1-7-Mike Allred-c/s/a — 4.00

RED RYDER COMICS (Hi Spot #2)(Movies, radio)(See Crackajack Funnies & Super Book of Comics)
Hawley Publ. No. 1/Dell Publishing Co.(K.K.) No. 3 on: 9/40; No. 3, 8/41 - No. 5, 12/41; No. 6, 4/42 - No. 151, 4-6/57

	GD2.0	FN6.0	NM9.4
1-Red Ryder, his horse Thunder, Little Beaver & his horse Papoose strip reprints begin by Fred Harman; 1st meeting of Red & Little Beaver; Harman line-drawn-c #1-85	260.00	780.00	2600.00
3-(Scarce)-Alley Oop, King of the Royal Mtd., Capt. Easy, Freckles & His Friends, Myra North, Dan Dunn strip-r begin	86.00	259.00	950.00
4-6: 6-1st Dell issue (4/42)	41.00	123.00	450.00
7-10	33.00	98.00	360.00
11-20	23.00	68.00	250.00
21-32-Last Alley Oop, Dan Dunn, Capt. Easy, Freckles	14.00	44.00	160.00
33-40 (52 pgs.)	9.00	27.00	100.00
41 (52 pgs.)-Rocky Lane photo back-c; photo back-c begin, end #57	9.00	29.00	105.00
42-46 (52 pgs.): 46-Last Red Ryder strip-r	8.00	23.00	85.00
47-53 (52 pgs.): 47-New stories on Red Ryder begin. 49,52-Harmon photo back-c	6.40	19.00	70.00
54-92: 54-73 (36 pgs.). 59-Harmon photo back-c. 73-Last King of the Royal Mtd; strip-r by Jim Gary. 74-85,93 (52 pgs.)-Harman line-drawn-c. 86-92 (52 pgs.)-Harman painted-c	5.00	15.00	54.00
94-99,101-106: 94-96 (36 pgs.)-Harman painted-c. 97,98,107,108 (36 pgs.)-Harman line-drawn-c. 99,101-106 (36 pgs.)-Jim Bannon Photo-c	3.60	11.00	40.00
100 (36 pgs.)-Bannon photo-c	4.00	12.00	45.00
109-118 (52 pgs.)-Harman line-drawn-c	3.20	9.50	35.00
119-129 (52 pgs.): 119-Painted-c begin, not by Harman, end #151	2.90	8.70	32.00
130-144 (#130 on have 36 pgs.)	2.70	8.00	30.00
145-151: 145-148: 145-Title change to Red Ryder Ranch Mag. with photos. 149-151: 149-Title changed to R.R. Ranch Comics	2.40	7.00	26.00
Four Color 916 (7/58)	2.75	8.00	30.00

NOTE: ***Fred Harman** a-1-99; c-1-98, 107-118. Don Red Barry, Allan Rocky Lane, Wild Bill Elliott & Jim Bannon starred as Red Ryder in the movies. Robert Blake starred as Little Beaver.*

RED RYDER PAINT BOOK
Whitman Publishing Co.: 1941 (8-1/2x11-1/2", 148 pgs.)

	GD2.0	FN6.0	NM9.4
nn-Reprints 1940 daily strips	75.00	225.00	600.00

RED SEAL COMICS (Formerly Carnival Comics, and/or Spotlight Comics?)
Harry 'A' Chesler/Superior Publ. No. 19 on: No. 14, 10/45 - No. 18, 10/46; No.

Red Seal Comics #20 © SUPR

Redskin #4 © YM

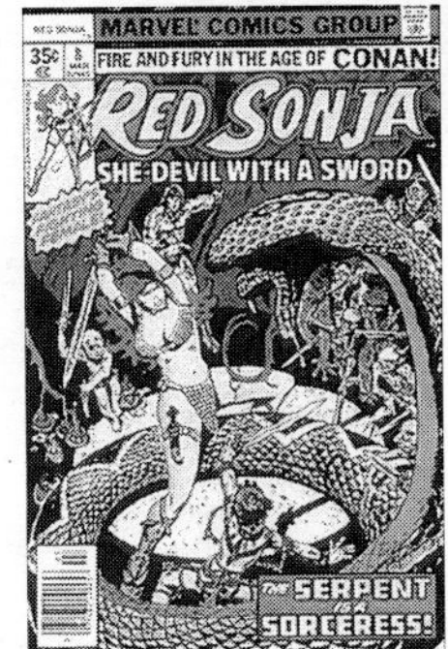

Red Sonja #8 © MAR

GD2.0 FN6.0 NM9.4

9, 6/47 - No. 22, 12/47

14-The Black Dwarf begins (continued from Spotlight?); Little Nemo app; bondage/hypo-c; Tuska-a 69.00 206.00 550.00
15-Torture story; funny-c 44.00 132.00 350.00
16-Used in **SOTI**, pg. 181, illo "Outside the forbidden pages of de Sade, you find draining a girl's blood only in children's comics;" drug club story r-later in Crime Reporter #1; Veiled Avenger & Barry Kuda app; Tuska-a; funny-c 59.00 178.00 475.00
17,18,20: Lady Satan, Yankee Girl & Sky Chief app; 17-Tuska-a 45.00 135.00 360.00
19-No Black Dwarf (on-c only); Zor, El Tigre app. 40.00 120.00 300.00
21-Lady Satan & Black Dwarf app. 34.00 103.00 240.00
22-Zor, Rocketman app. (68 pgs.) 34.00 103.00 240.00

REDSKIN (Thrilling Indian Stories)(Famous Western Badmen #13 on)
Youthful Magazines: Sept, 1950 - No. 12, Oct, 1952

1-Walter Johnson-a (7 pgs.) 14.00 43.00 100.00
2 10.00 30.00 65.00
3-12: 3-Daniel Boone story. 6-Geronimo story 9.15 27.00 55.00
NOTE: ***Walter Johnson** c-3, 4. **Palais** a-11. **Wildey** a-5, 11. Bondage c-6, 12.*

RED SONJA (Also see Conan #23, Kull & The Barbarians, Marvel Feature & Savage Sword Of Conan #1)
Marvel Comics Group: 1/77 - No. 15, 5/79; V1#1, 2/83 - V2#2, 3/83; V3#1, 8/83 - V3#4, 2/84; V3#5, 1/85 - V3#13, 5/86

1-Created by Robert E. Howard 2.40 6.00
2-10: 5-Last 30¢ issue 4.00
11-15, V1#1,V2#2: 14-Last 35¢ issue 3.00
V3#1-13: #1-4 ($1.00, 52 pgs.) 2.00
NOTE: ***Brunner** c-12-14. **J. Buscema** a(p)-12, 13, 15; c-V#1. **Nebres** a-V3#3i(part). **N. Redondo** a-8i, V3#2i, 3i. **Simonson** a-V3#1. **Thorne** c/a-1-11.*

RED SONJA: SCAVENGER HUNT
Marvel Comics: Dec, 1995 ($2.95, one-shot)

1 3.00

RED SONJA: THE MOVIE
Marvel Comics Group: Nov, 1985 - No. 2, Dec, 1985 (Limited series)

1,2-Movie adapt-r/Marvel Super Spec. #38 2.00

RED TORNADO (See All-American #20 & Justice League of America #64)
DC Comics: July, 1985 - No. 4, Oct, 1985 (Limited series)

1-4: Kurt Busiek scripts in all. 1-3-Superman cameos. 1,3-Batman cameos 2.00

RED WARRIOR
Marvel/Atlas Comics (TCI): Jan, 1951 - No. 6, Dec, 1951

1-Red Warrior & his horse White Wing; Tuska-a 16.00 47.00 110.00
2-Tuska-c 10.00 30.00 60.00
3-6: 4-Origin White Wing. 6-Maneely-c 8.35 25.00 50.00

RED WOLF (See Avengers #80 & Marvel Spotlight #1)
Marvel Comics Group: May, 1972 - No. 9, Sept, 1973

1-(Western hero); Gil Kane/Severin-c; Shores-a 1.85 5.50 15.00
2-9: 2-Kane-c; Shores-a. 6-Tuska-r in back-up. 7-Red Wolf as super hero begins. 9-Origin sidekick, Lobo (wolf) 1.10 3.30 9.00

REESE'S PIECES
Eclipse Comics: Oct, 1985 - No.2, Oct, 1985 ($1.75, Baxter paper)

1,2-B&W-r in color 2.00

REFORM SCHOOL GIRL!
Realistic Comics: 1951

nn-Used in **SOTI**, pg. 358, & cover ill. with caption "Comic books are supposed to be like fairy tales" 137.00 412.00 1100.00
(Prices vary widely on this book)
NOTE: *The cover and title originated from a digest-sized book published by Diversey Publishing Co. of Chicago in 1948. The original book "House of Fury", Doubleday, came out in 1941. The girl's real name which appears on the cover of the digest and comic is Marty Collins, Canadian model and ice skating star who posed for this special color photograph for the Diversey novel.*

REGENTS ILLUSTRATED CLASSICS
Prentice Hall Regents, Englewood Cliffs, NJ 07632: 1981 (Plus more recent reprintings) (48 pgs., B&W-a with 14 pgs. of teaching helps)
NOTE: *This series contains Classics Ill. art, and was produced from the same illegal source as **Cassette Books.** But when Twin Circle sued to stop the sale of the Cassette Books, they decided to permit this series to continue. This series was produced as a teaching aid. The 20 title series is divided into four levels based upon number of basic words used therein. There is also a teacher's manual for each level. All of the titles are still available from the publisher for about $5 each retail. The number to call for mail order purchases is (201)767-5937. Almost all of the issues have new covers taken from some interior art panel. Here is a list of the series by Regents ident. no. and the Classics Ill. counterpart.*

16770(CI#24-A2)18333(CI#3-A2)21668(CI#13-A2)32224(CI#21)33051(CI#26)
35788(CI#84)37153(CI#16)44460(CI#19-A2)44808(CI#18-A2)52395(CI#4-A2)
58627(CI#5-A2)60067(CI#30)68405(CI#23-A1)70302(CI#29)78192(CI#7-A2)
78193(CI#10-A2)79679(CI#85)92046(CI#1-A2)93062(CI#64)93512(CI#25)

RE: GEX
Awesome-Hyperwerks: Sept, 1998 - Present ($2.50)

Preview (7/98) Wizard Con Edition 3.00
0-(12/98) Loeb-s/Liefeld-a/Pat Lee-c, 1-Loeb-s/Liefeld-a/c 2.50

REGGIE (Formerly Archie's Rival...; Reggie & Me #19 on)
Archie Publications: No. 15, Sept, 1963 - No. 18, Nov, 1965

15(9/63), 16(10/64), 17(8/65), 18(11/65) 4.00 12.00 40.00
NOTE: *Cover title No. 15 & 16 is Archie's Rival Reggie.*

REGGIE AND ME (Formerly Reggie)
Archie Publ.: No. 19, Aug, 1966 - No. 126, Sept, 1980 (No. 50-68: 52 pgs.)

19-Evilheart app. 2.80 8.40 28.00
20-23-Evilheart app.; with Pureheart #22 2.00 6.00 20.00
24-40(3/70) 1.20 3.60 12.00
41-49(7/71) 1.00 3.00 10.00
50(9/71)-68 (1/74, 52 pgs.) 1.40 4.20 14.00
69-99 2.40 6.00
100(10/77) 1.10 3.30 9.00
101-126 5.00

REGGIE'S JOKES (See Reggie's Wise Guy Jokes)

REGGIE'S REVENGE!
Archie Comic Publications, Inc.: Spring, 1994 - No. 3 ($2.00, 52 pgs.) (Published semi-annually)

1-Bound-in pull-out poster 3.00
2,3 2.00

REGGIE'S WISE GUY JOKES
Archie Publications: Aug, 1968 - No. 60, Jan, 1982 (#5-28 are Giants)

1 3.80 11.40 38.00
2-4 2.00 6.00 16.00
5-16 (1/71)(68 pg. Giants) 2.20 6.60 22.00
17-28 (52 pg. Giants) 1.50 4.50 15.00
29-40(1/77) 1.00 2.80 7.00
41-60 4.00

REGISTERED NURSE
Charlton Comics: Summer, 1963

1-r/Nurse Betsy Crane & Cynthia Doyle 2.25 6.75 18.00

REG'LAR FELLERS
Visual Editions (Standard): No. 5, Nov, 1947 - No. 6, Mar, 1948

5,6 8.35 25.00 50.00

REG'LAR FELLERS HEROIC (See Heroic Comics)

REGULATORS
Image Comics: June, 1995 - No. 3, Aug, 1995 ($2.50)

1-3: Kurt Busiek scripts 2.50

REID FLEMING, WORLD'S TOUGHEST MILKMAN
Eclipse Comics/ Deep Sea Comics: 8/86; V2#1, 12/86 - V2#3, 12/88; V2#4, 11/89; V2#5, 11/90 (B&W)

1 (3rd print, large size, 8/86, $2.50), 1-4th & 5th printings ($2.50) 2.50
V2#1 (10/86, regular size, $2.00), 1-2nd print, 3rd print ($2.00, 2/89) 2.00
2-8 , V2#2-2nd & 3rd printings, V2#4-2nd printing, V2#5 ($2.00) 2.00

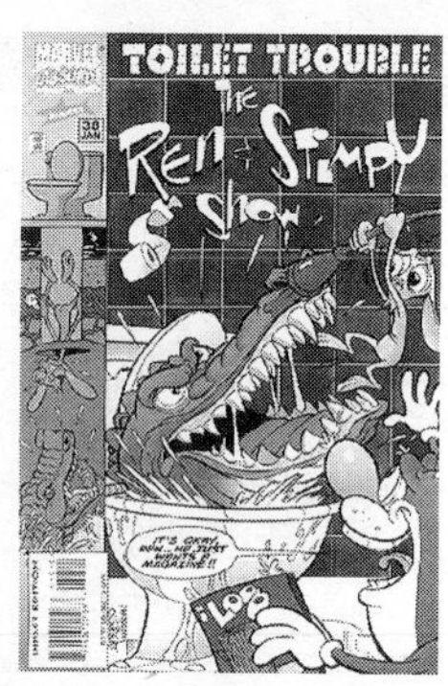

Ren & Stimpy Show #38 © Nickelodeon

Reptilicus #1 © CC

Resurrection Man #25 © DC

GD2.0 FN6.0 NM9.4

RELUCTANT DRAGON, THE (Walt Disney's...)
Dell Publishing Co.: No. 13, 1940

Four Color 13-Contains 2 pgs. of photos from film; 2 pg. foreword to Fantasia by Leopold Stokowski; Donald Duck, Goofy, Baby Weems & Mickey Mouse (as the Sorcerer's Apprentice) app. 155.00 464.00 1700.00

REMEMBER PEARL HARBOR
Street & Smith Publications: 1942 (68 pgs.) (Illustrated story of the battle)

nn-Uncle Sam-c; Jack Binder-a 43.00 128.00 340.00

REN & STIMPY SHOW, THE (TV) (Nicklodeon cartoon characters)
Marvel Comics: Dec, 1992 - No. 44, July, 1996 ($1.75/$1.95)

1-($2.25)-Polybagged w/scratch & sniff Ren or Stimpy air fowler (equal amounts of each were made) 2.40 6.00
1-2nd & 3rd printing; different dialogue on-c 2.00
2-6: 4-Muddy Mudskipper back-up. 5-Bill Wray painted-c. 6-Spider-Man vs. Powdered Toast Man 4.00
7-17: 12-1st solo back-up story w/Tank & Brenner 2.50
18-44: 18-Powered Toast Man app. 2.00
25 ($2.95) Deluxe edition w/die cut cover 3.00
...Don't Try This at Home (3/94, $12.95, TPB)-r/#9-12 13.00
...Eenteractive Special ('95, $2.95) 3.00
...Holiday Special 1994 (2/95, $2.95, 52 pgs.) 3.00
...Pick of the Litter nn (1993, $12.95, TPB)-r/#1-4 13.00
...Radio Daze (11/95, $1.95) 2.00
...Running Joke nn (1993, $12.95, TPB)-r/#1-4 plus new-a 13.00
...Seeck Little Monkeys (1/95, $12.95)-r/#17-20 13.00
...Special 2 (7/94, $2.95, 52 pgs.), ...Special 3 (10/94, $2.95, 52 pgs.)-Choose adventure, ...Special: Around the World in a Daze ($2.95), ...Special: Four Swerks (1/95, $2.95, 52 pgs.)-FF #1 cover swipe; cover reads "Four Swerks w/5 pg. coloring book.", ...Special: Powdered Toast Man 1 (4/94, $2.95, 52 pgs.), ...Special: Powdered Toast Man's Cereal Serial (4/95, $2.95), ...Special: Sports (10/95, $2.95) 3.00
...Tastes Like Chicken nn (11/93,$12.95,TPB)-r/#5-8 13.00
...Your Pals (1994, $12.95, TPB)-r/#13-16 13.00

RENFIELD
Caliber Press:1994 - No. 3, 1995 ($2.95, B&W, limited series)

1-3 3.00

RENO BROWNE, HOLLYWOOD'S GREATEST COWGIRL (Formerly Margie Comics; Apache Kid #53 on; also see Western Hearts, Western Life Romances & Western Love)
Marvel Comics (MPC): No. 50, April, 1950 - No. 52, Sept, 1950 (52 pgs.)

50-Reno Browne photo-c on all 32.00 96.00 225.00
51,52 26.00 79.00 185.00

REPLACEMENT GOD
Amaze Ink: June, 1995 - No. 8 ($2.95, B&W)

1-8-Zander Cannon-s/a 3.00

REPLACEMENT GOD
Image Comics: May, 1997 - No. 5 ($2.95, B&W)

1-5: 1-Flip book w/"Knute's Escapes", r/original series. 2-Flip book w/"Harris Thermidor". 3-5: 3-Flip book w/"Myth and Legend" 3.00

REPTILICUS (Becomes Reptisaurus #3 on)
Charlton Comics: Aug, 1961 - No. 2, Oct, 1961

1 (Movie) 14.00 42.00 140.00
2 8.00 24.00 80.00

REPTISAURUS (Reptilicus #1,2)
Charlton Comics: V2#3, Jan, 1962 - No. 8, Dec, 1962; Summer, 1963

V2#3-8: 8-Montes/Bache-c/a 5.50 16.50 55.00
Special Edition 1 (Summer, 1963) 5.00 15.00 50.00

REQUIEM FOR DRACULA
Marvel Comics: Feb, 1993 ($2.00, 52 pgs.)

nn-r/Tomb of Dracula #69,70 by Gene Colan 2.00

GD2.0 FN6.0 NM9.4

RESCUERS, THE (See Walt Disney Showcase #40)

RESIDENT EVIL (Based on video game)
Image Comics (WildStorm): Mar, 1998 - Present ($4.95, quarterly magazine)

1 7.00
2-5 5.00

RESTAURANT AT THE END OF THE UNIVERSE, THE (See Hitchhiker's Guide to the Galaxy & Life, the Universe & Everything)
DC Comics: 1994 - No. 3, 1994 ($6.95, limited series)

1-3 7.00

RESTLESS GUN (TV)
Dell Publishing Co.: No. 934, Sept, 1958 - No. 1146, Nov-Jan, 1960-61

Four Color 934 (#1)-Photo-c 11.00 33.00 120.00
Four Color 986 (5/59), 1045 (11-1/60), 1089 (3/60), 1146-Wildey-a; all photo-c 8.00 23.00 85.00

RESURRECTION MAN
DC Comics: May, 1997 - No. 27, Aug, 1999 ($2.50)

1-Lenticular disc on cover 2.40 6.00
2-JLA app. 1.00 3.00 8.00
3-5 4.00
6-10: 6-Genesis-x-over. 7-Batman app. 10-Hitman-c/app. 3.50
11-15 3.00
16,17-Supergirl x-over 3.00
18-27: 18-Deadman & Phantom Stranger-c/app. 21-JLA-c/app 2.50
#1,000,000 (11/98) 853rd Century x-over 2.50

RETIEF (Keith Laumer's)
Adventure Comics (Malibu): Dec, 1989 - Vol. 2, No.6, ($2.25, B&W)

1-6,Vol. 2, #1-6,Vol. 3 (...of The CDT) #1-6 2.50
...and The Warlords #1-6, ...: Diplomatic Immunity #1 (4/91)
...: Giant Killer #1 (9/91), ...: Crime & Punishment #1 (11/91) 2.50

RETURN FROM WITCH MOUNTAIN (See Walt Disney Showcase #44)

RETURN OF GORGO, THE (Formerly Gorgo's Revenge)
Charlton Comics: No. 2, Aug, 1963; No. 3, Fall, 1964 (12¢)

2,3-Ditko-c/a; based on M.G.M. movie 6.50 19.50 65.00

RETURN OF KONGA, THE (Konga's Revenge #2 on)
Charlton Comics: 1962

nn 6.00 18.00 60.00

RETURN OF MEGATON MAN
Kitchen Sink Press: July, 1988 - No. 3, 1988 ($2.00, limited series)

1-3: Simpson-c/a 2.00

RETURN OF THE OUTLAW
Toby Press (Minoan): Feb, 1953 - No. 11, 1955

1-Billy the Kid 10.00 30.00 60.00
2 5.35 16.00 32.00
3-11 4.25 13.00 26.00

RETURN TO JURASSIC PARK
Topps Comics: Apr, 1995 - No. 9, Feb, 1996 ($2.50/$2.95)

1-9: 3-Begin $2.95-c. 9-Artist's Jam issue 3.00

RETURN TO THE AMALGAM AGE OF COMICS: THE MARVEL COMICS COLLECTION
Marvel Comics: 1997 ($12.95, TPB)

nn-Reprints Amalgam one-shots: Challengers of the Fantastic #1, The Exciting X-Patrol #1, Iron Lantern# 1, The Magnetic Men Featuring Magneto #1, Spider-Boy Team-Up #1 & Thorion of the New Asgods #1 13.00

REVEALING LOVE STORIES (See Fox Giants)

REVEALING ROMANCES
Ace Magazines: Sept, 1949 - No. 6, Aug, 1950

1 10.00 30.00 60.00
2 5.00 15.00 30.00

Rex Allen Comics #10 © DELL

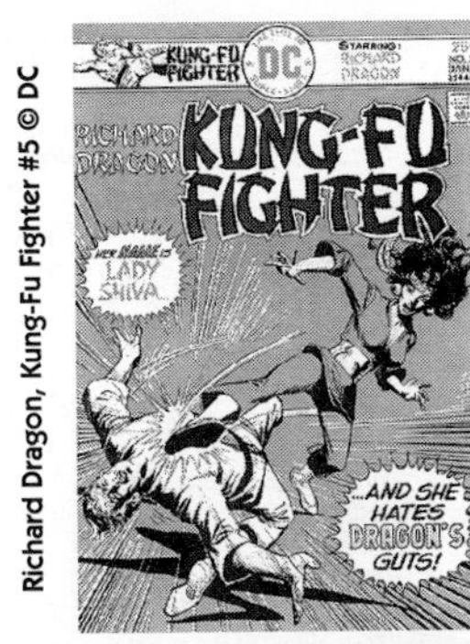

Richard Dragon, Kung-Fu Fighter #5 © DC

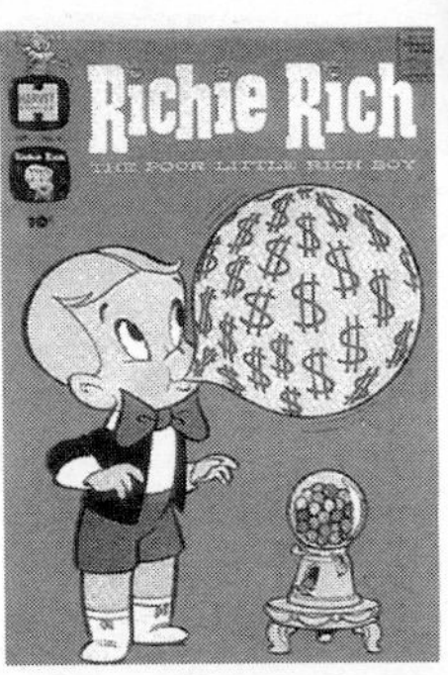

Richie Rich #6 © HARV

GD2.0 FN6.0 NM9.4

3-6 4.00 12.00 24.00

REVENGE OF THE PROWLER (Also see The Prowler)
Eclipse Comics: Feb, 1988 - No. 4, June, 1988 ($1.75/$1.95)

1,3,4: 1-$1.75. 3,4-$1.95-c; Snyder III-a(p) 2.00
2 ($2.50)-Contains flexi-disc 2.50

REVENGERS FEATURING MEGALITH
Continuity Comics: Sept, 1985; 1987 - No. 6, 1988 ($2.00, Baxter paper)

1 (1985)-Origin; Neal Adams-c/a, scripts, 1-6 ('87-'88, newsstand) 2.00

REX ALLEN COMICS (Movie star)(Also see Four Color #877 & Western Roundup under Dell Giants)
Dell Publ. Co.: No. 316, Feb, 1951 - No. 31, Dec-Feb, 1958-59 (All-photo-c)

Four Color 316(#1)(52 pgs.)-Rex Allen & his horse Koko begin; Marsh-a
13.00 38.00 140.00
2 (9-11/51, 36 pgs.) 8.00 23.00 85.00
3-10 5.50 16.50 60.00
11-20 4.50 13.50 50.00
21-23,25-31 4.00 12.00 45.00
24-Toth-a 5.00 15.00 55.00
NOTE: *Manning a-20, 27-30. Photo back-c F.C. #316, 2-12, 20, 21.*

REX DEXTER OF MARS (See Mystery Men Comics)
Fox Features Syndicate: Fall, 1940 (68 pgs.)

1-Rex Dexter, Patty O'Day, & Zanzibar (Tuska-a) app.; Briefer-c/a
187.00 562.00 1500.00

REX HART (Formerly Blaze Carson; Whip Wilson #9 on)
Timely/Marvel Comics (USA): No. 6, Aug, 1949 - No. 8, Feb, 1950 (All photo-c)

6-Rex Hart & his horse Warrior begin; Black Rider app; Captain Tootsie by Beck 27.00 81.00 190.00
7,8: 18 pg. Thriller in each. 8-Blaze the Wonder Collie app. in text
19.00 56.00 130.00

REX MORGAN, M.D. (Also see Harvey Comics Library)
Argo Publ.: Dec, 1955 - No. 3, Apr?, 1956

1-r/Rex Morgan daily newspaper strips & daily panel-r of "These Women" by D'Alessio & "Timeout" by Jeff Keate 11.50 34.00 80.00
2,3 9.15 27.00 55.00

REX THE WONDER DOG (See The Adventures of...)

RHUBARB, THE MILLIONAIRE CAT
Dell Publishing Co.: No. 423, Sept-Oct, 1952 - No. 563, June, 1954

Four Color 423 (#1) 4.50 13.50 50.00
Four Color 466(5/53),563 3.60 11.00 40.00

RIB
Dilemma Productions: Oct, 1995 - April, 1996 ($1.95, B&W)

Ashcan, 1 2.00

RIB
Bookmark Productions: 1996 ($2.95, B&W)

1-Sakai-c; Andrew Ford-s/a 3.00

RIB
Caliber Comics: May, 1997 - No. 5, 1998 ($2.95, B&W)

1-5: 1-"Beginnings" pts. 1 & 2 3.00

RIBIT!
Comico: Jan, 1989 - No. 4, April?, 1989 ($1.95, limited series)

1-4: Frank Thorne-c/a/scripts 2.00

RIBTICKLER (Also see Fox Giants)
Fox Feature Synd./Green Publ. (1957)/Norlen (1959): 1945 - No. 9, Aug, 1947; 1957; 1959

1-Funny animal 14.00 43.00 100.00
2-(1946) 8.35 25.00 50.00
3-9: 3,7-Cosmo Cat app. 6.70 20.00 40.00
3,7,8 (Green Publ.-1957), 3,7,8 (Norlen Mag.-1959) 2.25 6.75 18.00

GD2.0 FN6.0 NM9.4

RICHARD DRAGON, KUNG-FU FIGHTER (See The Batman Chronicles #5, Brave & the Bold, & The Question)
National Periodical Publ./DC Comics: Apr-May, 1975 - No. 18, Nov-Dec, 1977

1-3: 1-Intro Richard Dragon, Ben Stanley & O-Sensei; 1st app. Barney Ling; adaptation of Jim Dennis novel "Dragon's Fists" begins, ends #4. 2-Intro Carolyn Woosan; Starlin/Weiss-c/a; bondage-c. 3-Kirby-a(p); Giordano bondage-c 1.00 3.00 8.00
4-8-Wood inks. 4-Carolyn Woosan dies. 5-1st app. Lady Shiva 5.00
9-13,15-18: 9-Ben Stanley becomes Ben Turner; intro Preying Mantis. 16-1st app. Prof Ojo. 18-1st app. Ben Turner as The Bronze Tiger 5.00
14-"Spirit of Bruce Lee" 1.00 3.00 8.00
NOTE: ***Buckler** a-14. c-15, 18. **Chua** c-13. **Estrada** a-9, 13-18. **Estrada/Abel** a-10-12. **Estrada/Wood** a-4-8. **Giordano** c-1, 3-11. **Weiss** a-2(partial) c-2i.*

RICHARD THE LION-HEARTED (See Ideal a Classical Comic)

RICHIE RICH (See Harvey Collectors Comics, Harvey Hits, Little Dot, Little Lotta, Little Sad Sack, Million Dollar Digest, Mutt & Jeff, Super Richie, and 3-D Dolly)

RICHIE RICH (...the Poor Little Rich Boy) (See Harvey Hits #3, 9)
Harvey Publ.: Nov, 1960 - #218, Oct, 1982; #219, Oct, 1986 - #254, Jan, 1991

1-(See Little Dot for 1st app.) 140.00 420.00 1400.00
2 47.50 142.00 475.00
3-5 27.00 81.00 270.00
6-10: 8-Christmas-c 16.50 50.00 165.00
11-20 10.00 30.00 100.00
21-30 8.00 24.00 80.00
31-40 6.00 18.00 60.00
41-50: 42(10/67)-Flying saucer-c 5.00 15.00 50.00
51-55,57-60: 59-Buck, prototype of Dollar the Dog 3.50 10.50 35.00
56-1st app. Super Richie 4.50 13.50 45.00
61-64,66-80: 71-Nixon & Robert Kennedy caricatures 2.20 6.60 22.00
65-1st app. Dollar the Dog 2.80 8.40 28.00
81-99 1.60 4.80 16.00
100(12/70)-1st app. Irona the robot maid 2.00 6.00 20.00
101-111,117-120 1.20 3.60 12.00
112-116: All 52 pg. Giants 1.80 5.40 18.00
121-140: 137-1st app. Mr. Cheepers 1.00 3.00 8.00
141-160: 145-Infinity-c. 155-3rd app. The Money Monster 2.40 6.00
161-180 5.00
181-199 4.00
200 2.40 6.00
201-218: 210-Stone-Age Riches app 3.00
219-254: 237-Last original material 2.00

RICHIE RICH
Harvey Comics: Mar, 1991 - No. 28, Nov, 1994 ($1.00, bi-monthly)

1 , Giant Size 1-4 (10/91-10/93, $2.25, 68 pgs.) 3.00
2-28: Reprints best of Richie Rich 2.00

RICHIE RICH ADVENTURE DIGEST MAGAZINE
Harvey Comics: 1992 - No. 7, Sept, 1994 ($1.25, quarterly, digest-size)

1-7 4.00

RICHIE RICH AND...
Harvey Comics: Oct, 1987 - No. 11, May, 1990 ($1.00)

1-Professore Keenbean 4.00
2-11: 2-Casper. 3-Dollar the Dog. 4-Cadbury. 5 Mayda Munny. 6-Irona. 7-Little Dot. 8-Professor Keenbean. 9-Little Audrey. 10-Mayda Munny. 11-Cadbury.
2.00

RICHIE RICH AND BILLY BELLHOPS
Harvey Publications: Oct, 1977 (52 pgs., one-shot)

1 1.25 3.75 10.00

RICHIE RICH AND CADBURY
Harvey Publ.: 10/77; #2, 9/78 - #23, 7/82; #24, 7/90 - #29, 1/91 (1-10: 52pgs.)

1-(52 pg. Giant) 1.40 4.20 14.00
2-10-(52 pg. Giant) 1.10 3.30 9.00
11-23 5.00
24-29: 24-Begin $1.00-c 2.50

Richie Rich Bank Books #37 © HARV

Richie Rich Diamonds #1 © HARV

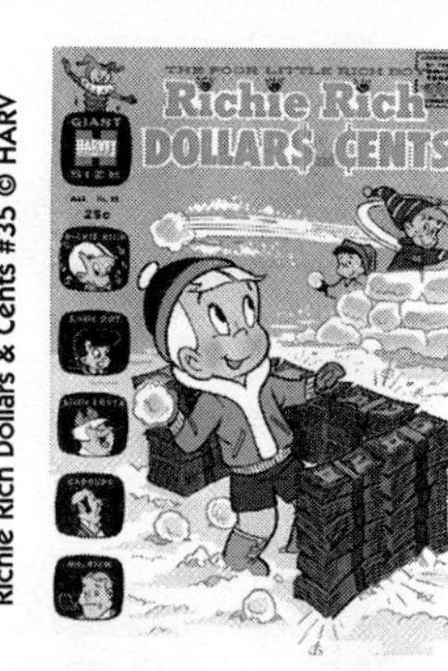

Richie Rich Dollars & Cents #35 © HARV

RICHIE RICH AND CASPER
Harvey Publications: Aug, 1974 - No. 45, Sept, 1982

	GD2.0	FN6.0	NM9.4
1	2.40	7.20	24.00
2-5	1.40	4.20	14.00
6-10: 10-Xmas-c	1.10	3.30	9.00
11-20		2.40	6.00
21-45: 22-Xmas-c			3.50

RICHIE RICH AND DOLLAR THE DOG (See Richie Rich #65)
Harvey Publications: Sept, 1977 - No. 24, Aug, 1982 (#1-10: 52 pgs.)

	GD2.0	FN6.0	NM9.4
1-(52 pg. Giant)	1.20	3.60	12.00
2-10-(52 pg. Giant)	1.00	3.00	8.00
11-24			3.50

RICHIE RICH AND DOT
Harvey Publications: Oct, 1974 (one-shot)

	GD2.0	FN6.0	NM9.4
1	1.80	5.40	18.00

RICHIE RICH AND GLORIA
Harvey Publications: Sept, 1977 - No. 25, Sept, 1982 (#1-11: 52 pgs.)

	GD2.0	FN6.0	NM9.4
1-(52 pg. Giant)	1.20	3.60	12.00
2-11-(52 pg. Giant)	1.00	3.00	8.00
12-25			3.50

RICHIE RICH AND HIS GIRLFRIENDS
Harvey Publications: April, 1979 - No. 16, Dec, 1982

	GD2.0	FN6.0	NM9.4
1-(52 pg. Giant)	1.20	3.60	12.00
2-(52 pg. Giant)	1.00	3.00	8.00
3-10			5.00
11-16			3.00

RICHIE RICH AND HIS MEAN COUSIN REGGIE
Harvey Publications: April, 1979 - No. 3, 1980 (50¢) (#1,2: 52 pgs.)

	GD2.0	FN6.0	NM9.4
1	1.00	3.00	10.00
2-3:		2.40	6.00

NOTE: *No. 4 was advertised, but never released.*

RICHIE RICH AND JACKIE JOKERS (Also see Jackie Jokers)
Harvey Publications: Nov, 1973 - No. 48, Dec, 1982

	GD2.0	FN6.0	NM9.4
1: 52 pg. Giant; contains material from unpublished Jackie Jokers #5	3.50	10.50	35.00
2,3-(52 pg. Giants). 2-R.R. & Jackie 1st meet	2.20	6.60	22.00
4,5	1.50	4.50	15.00
6-10	1.10	3.30	9.00
11-20,26: 11-1st app. Kool Katz. 26-Star Wars parody	1.00	2.80	7.00
21-25,27-40			5.00
41-48			3.50

RICHIE RICH AND PROFESSOR KEENBEAN
Harvey Comics: Sept, 1990 - No. 2, Nov, 1990 ($1.00)

	GD2.0	FN6.0	NM9.4
1,2			2.00

RICHIE RICH AND THE NEW KIDS ON THE BLOCK
Harvey Publications: Feb, 1991 - No. 3, June, 1991 ($1.25, bi-monthly)

	GD2.0	FN6.0	NM9.4
1-3: 1,2-New Richie Rich stories			2.00

RICHIE RICH AND TIMMY TIME
Harvey Publications: Sept, 1977 (50¢, 52 pgs, one-shot)

	GD2.0	FN6.0	NM9.4
1	1.10	3.30	9.00

RICHIE RICH BANK BOOKS
Harvey Publications: Oct, 1972 - No. 59, Sept, 1982

	GD2.0	FN6.0	NM9.4
1	4.00	12.00	40.00
2-5: 2-2nd app. The Money Monster	2.40	7.20	24.00
6-10	1.60	4.80	16.00
11-20: 18-Super Richie app.	1.00	3.00	10.00
21-30	1.00	2.80	7.00
31-40			5.00
41-59			3.50

RICHIE RICH BEST OF THE YEARS
Harvey Publications: Oct, 1977 - No. 6, June, 1980 (128 pgs., digest-size)

	GD2.0	FN6.0	NM9.4
1(10/77)-Reprints	1.20	3.60	12.00
2-6(11/79-6/80, 95¢). #2(10/78)-Rep.. #3(6/79, 75¢)	1.00	3.00	8.00

RICHIE RICH BIG BOOK
Harvey Publications: Nov, 1992 - No. 2, May, 1993 ($1.50, 52 pgs.)

	GD2.0	FN6.0	NM9.4
1,2			3.00

RICHIE RICH BIG BUCKS
Harvey Publications: Apr, 1991 - No. 8, July, 1992 ($1.00, bi-monthly)

	GD2.0	FN6.0	NM9.4
1-8			2.00

RICHIE RICH BILLIONS
Harvey Publications: Oct, 1974 - No. 48, Oct, 1982 (#1-33: 52 pgs.)

	GD2.0	FN6.0	NM9.4
1	3.20	9.60	32.00
2-5	1.80	5.40	18.00
6-10	1.20	3.60	12.00
11-20	1.10	3.30	9.00
21-33		2.40	6.00
34-48: 35-Onion app.			3.50

RICHIE RICH CASH
Harvey Publications: Sept, 1974 - No. 47, Aug, 1982

	GD2.0	FN6.0	NM9.4
1-1st app. Dr. N-R-Gee	3.20	9.60	32.00
2-5	1.80	5.40	18.00
6-10	1.40	4.20	14.00
11-20	1.10	3.30	9.00
21-30		2.40	6.00
31-47: 33-Dr. Blemish app.			3.50

RICHIE RICH CASH MONEY
Harvey Comics: May, 1992 - No. 2, Aug, 1992 ($1.25)

	GD2.0	FN6.0	NM9.4
1,2			2.00

RICHIE RICH, CASPER & WENDY NATIONAL LEAGUE
Harvey Publications: June, 1976 (52 pgs.)

	GD2.0	FN6.0	NM9.4
1 (Released-3/76 with 6/76 date)	1.20	3.60	12.00
1 (6/76)-2nd version w/San Francisco Giants & KTVU 2 logos; has "Compliments of Giants and Straw Hat Pizza" on-c	1.20	3.60	12.00
1-Variants for other 11 NL teams, similar to Giants version but with different ad on inside front-c	1.20	3.60	12.00

RICHIE RICH COLLECTORS COMICS (See Harvey Collectors Comics)

RICHIE RICH DIAMONDS
Harvey Publications: Aug, 1972 - No. 59, Aug, 1982 (#1, 23-45: 52 pgs.)

	GD2.0	FN6.0	NM9.4
1-(52 pg. Giant)	5.00	15.00	50.00
2-5	2.20	6.60	22.00
6-10	1.40	4.20	14.00
11-22	1.10	3.30	9.00
23-30-(52 pg. Giants)		2.40	6.00
31-45: 39-r/Origin Little Dot			5.00
46-50			4.00
51-59			3.00

RICHIE RICH DIGEST
Harvey Publications: Oct, 1986 - No. 42, Oct, 1994 ($1.25/$1.75, digest-size)

	GD2.0	FN6.0	NM9.4
1	1.00	3.00	8.00
2-10			5.00
11-20			4.00
21-42			3.00

RICHIE RICH DIGEST STORIES (...Magazine #?-on)
Harvey Publications: Oct, 1977 - No., 17, Oct, 1982 (75¢/95¢, digest-size)

	GD2.0	FN6.0	NM9.4
1-Reprints	1.20	3.60	12.00
2-10: Reprints	1.00	2.80	7.00
11-17: Reprints			4.50

RICHIE RICH DIGEST WINNERS
Harvey Publications: Dec, 1977 - No. 16, Sept, 1982 (75¢/95¢, 132 pgs., digest-size)

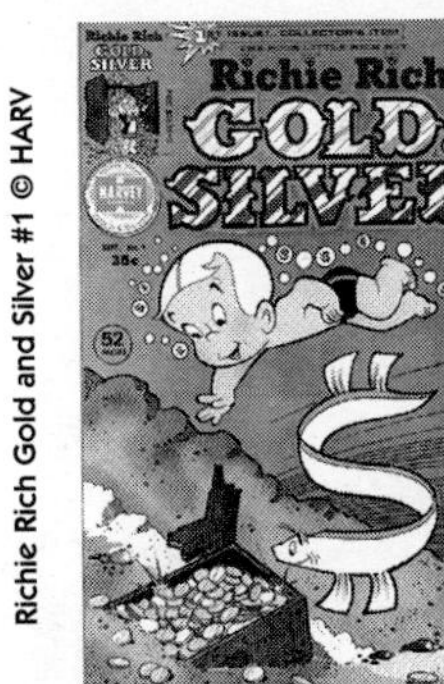
Richie Rich Gold and Silver #1 © HARV

Richie Rich Inventions #1 © HARV

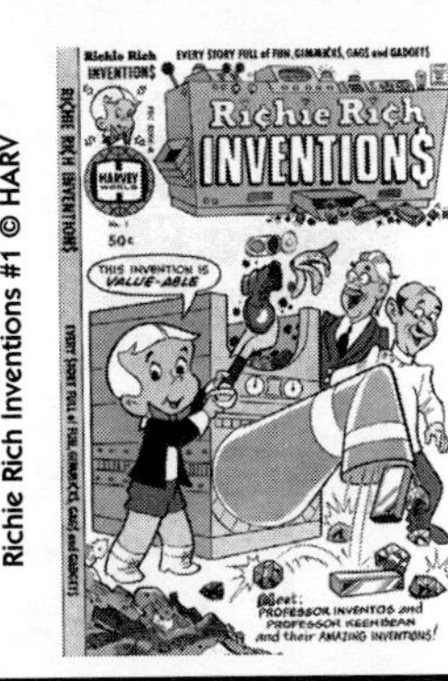

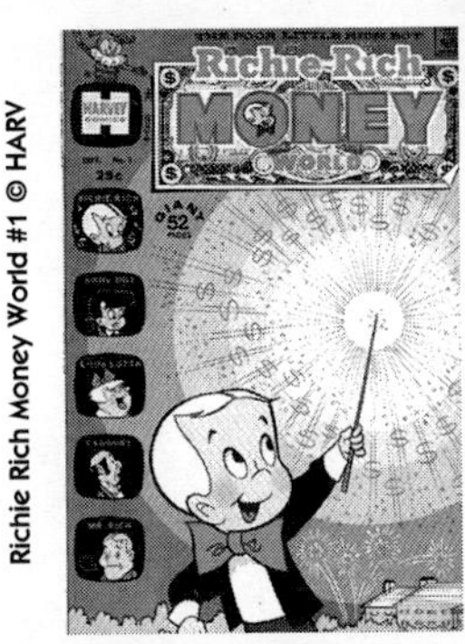

Richie Rich Money World #1 © HARV

	GD2.0	FN6.0	NM9.4
1	1.20	3.60	12.00
2-5	1.00	2.80	7.00
6-16			4.50

RICHIE RICH DOLLARS & CENTS
Harvey Publications: Aug, 1963 - No. 109, Aug, 1982 (#1-43: 68 pgs.; 44-60, 71-94: 52 pgs.)

	GD2.0	FN6.0	NM9.4
1: (#1-64 are all reprint issues)	16.00	46.00	155.00
2	7.50	22.50	75.00
3-5: 5-r/1st app. of R.R. from Little Dot #1	5.00	15.00	50.00
6-10	3.20	9.60	32.00
11-20	2.80	8.40	28.00
21-30: 25-r/1st app. Nurse Jenny (Little Lotta #62)	2.00	6.00	20.00
31-43: 43-Last 68 pg. issue	1.60	4.80	16.00
44-60: All 52 pgs.	1.40	4.20	14.00
61-71	1.00	2.80	7.00
72-94: All 52 pgs.	1.00	3.00	10.00
95-99,101-109			4.00
100-Anniversary issue		2.40	6.00

RICHIE RICH FORTUNES
Harvey Publications: Sept, 1971 - No. 63, July, 1982 (#1-15: 52 pgs.)

	GD2.0	FN6.0	NM9.4
1	5.00	15.00	50.00
2-5	2.60	7.80	26.00
6-10	1.60	4.80	16.00
11-15: 11-r/1st app. The Onion	1.20	3.60	12.00
16-30		2.40	6.00
31-40			4.00
41-63: 62-Onion app.			3.00

RICHIE RICH GEMS
Harvey Publications: Sept, 1974 - No. 43, Sept, 1982

	GD2.0	FN6.0	NM9.4
1	3.00	9.00	30.00
2-5	1.60	4.80	16.00
6-10	1.20	3.60	12.00
11-20	1.00	2.80	7.00
21-30			5.00
31-43: 36-Dr. Blemish, Onion app. 38-1st app. Stone-Age Riches			3.50

RICHIE RICH GOLD AND SILVER
Harvey Publications: Sept, 1975 - No. 42, Oct, 1982 (#1-27: 52 pgs.)

	GD2.0	FN6.0	NM9.4
1	2.40	7.20	24.00
2-5	1.40	4.20	14.00
6-10	1.00	3.00	10.00
11-27	1.00	3.00	8.00
28-42: 34-Stone-Age Riches app.			4.00

RICHIE RICH GOLD NUGGETS DIGEST
Harvey Publications: Feb., 1991 - No. 4, June, 1991 ($1.75, digest-size)

	GD2.0	FN6.0	NM9.4
1			3.00
2-4			2.00

RICHIE RICH HOLIDAY DIGEST MAGAZINE (...Digest #4)
Harvey Publications: Jan, 1980 - #3, Jan, 1982; #4, 3/88; #5, 2/89 (annual)

	GD2.0	FN6.0	NM9.4
1-X-Mas-c	1.00	3.00	10.00
2-5: 2,3: All X-Mas-c. 4-(3/88, $1.25), 5-(2/89, $1.75)	1.00	2.80	7.00

RICHIE RICH INVENTIONS
Harvey Publications: Oct, 1977 - No. 26, Oct, 1982 (#1-11: 52 pgs.)

	GD2.0	FN6.0	NM9.4
1	1.20	3.60	12.00
2-5	1.00	3.00	8.00
6-11		2.40	6.00
12-26			4.00

RICHIE RICH JACKPOTS
Harvey Publications: Oct, 1972 - No. 58, Aug, 1982 (#41-43: 52 pgs.)

	GD2.0	FN6.0	NM9.4
1	5.00	15.00	50.00
2-5	2.40	7.20	24.00
6-10	1.60	4.80	16.00
11-15,17-20	1.00	3.00	10.00
16-Super Richie app.	.90	2.70	9.00
21-30	1.00	2.80	7.00
31-40,44-50: 37-Caricatures of Frank Sinatra, Dean Martin, Sammy Davis, Jr. 45-Dr. Blemish app.		2.40	6.00
41-43 (52 pgs.)	1.00	3.00	8.00
51-58			4.00

RICHIE RICH MILLION DOLLAR DIGEST (...Magazine #?-on)(See Million Dollar Digest)
Harvey Publications: Oct, 1980 - No. 10, Oct, 1982 ($1.50)

	GD2.0	FN6.0	NM9.4
1	1.10	3.30	9.00
2-10			5.00

RICHIE RICH MILLIONS
Harvey Publ.: 9/61; #2, 9/62 - #113, 10/82 (#1-48: 68 pgs.; 49-64, 85-97: 52 pgs.)

	GD2.0	FN6.0	NM9.4
1: (#1-3 are all reprint issues)	19.00	57.00	190.00
2	10.00	30.00	100.00
3-10: All other giants are new & reprints. 5-1st 15 pg. Richie Rich story	8.00	24.00	80.00
11-20	4.00	12.00	40.00
21-30	3.00	9.00	30.00
31-48: 31-1st app. The Onion. 48-Last 68 pg. Giant	2.00	6.00	20.00
49-64: 52 pg. Giants	1.40	4.20	14.00
65-67,69-73,75-84	1.00	3.00	8.00
68-1st Super Richie-c (11/74)	1.60	4.80	16.00
74-1st app. Mr. Woody; Super Richie app.	1.00	3.00	8.00
85-97: 52 pg. Giants	1.00	3.00	10.00
98,99			5.00
100		2.40	6.00
101-113			3.00

RICHIE RICH MONEY WORLD
Harvey Publications: Sept, 1972 - No. 59, Sept, 1982

	GD2.0	FN6.0	NM9.4
1-(52 pg. Giant)-1st app. Mayda Munny	5.00	15.00	50.00
2-Super Richie app.	2.50	7.50	25.00
3-5	2.00	6.00	20.00
6-10: 9,10-Richie Rich mistakenly named Little Lotta on covers	1.40	4.20	14.00
11-20: 16,20-Dr. N-R-Gee	1.00	3.00	8.00
21-30		2.40	6.00
31-50			5.00
51-59			3.00
Digest 1 (2/91, $1.75)			4.00
2-8 (12/93, $1.75)			2.00

RICHIE RICH PROFITS
Harvey Publications: Oct, 1974 - No. 47, Sept, 1982

	GD2.0	FN6.0	NM9.4
1	3.50	10.50	35.00
2-5	1.60	4.80	16.00
6-10: 10-Origin of Dr. N-R-Gee	1.00	3.00	10.00
11-20: 15-Christmas-c	1.00	2.80	7.00
21-30			5.00
31-47			4.00

RICHIE RICH RELICS
Harvey Comics: Jan, 1988 - No.4, Feb, 1989 (75¢/$1.00, reprints)

	GD2.0	FN6.0	NM9.4
1-4			3.00

RICHIE RICH RICHES
Harvey Publications: July, 1972 - No. 59, Aug, 1982 (#1, 2, 41-45: 52 pgs.)

	GD2.0	FN6.0	NM9.4
1-(52 pg. Giant)-1st app. The Money Monster	5.00	15.00	50.00
2-(52 pg. Giant)	2.40	7.20	24.00
3-5	1.60	4.80	16.00
6-10	1.20	3.60	12.00
11-20: 17-Super Richie app. (3/75)	1.00	3.00	8.00
21-40		2.40	6.00
41-45: 52 pg. Giants	1.00	3.00	8.00
46-59: 56-Dr. Blemish app.			4.00

RICHIE RICH SUCCESS STORIES

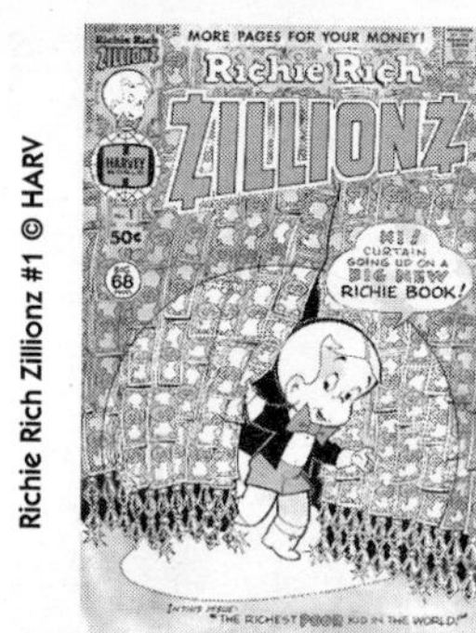

Richie Rich Zillionz #1 © HARV

Rima, The Jungle Girl #4 © DC

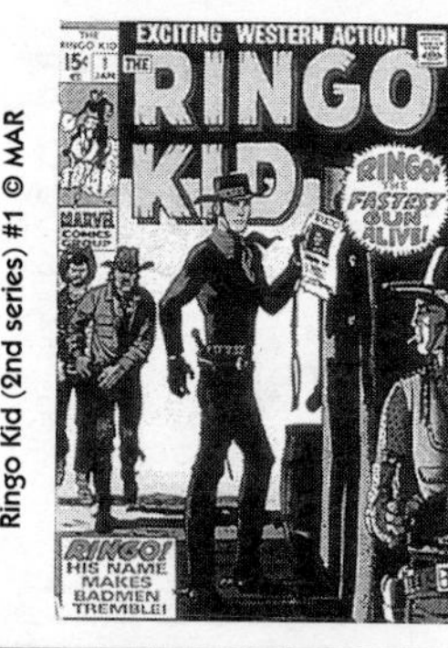

Ringo Kid (2nd series) #1 © MAR

GD2.0 FN6.0 NM9.4

Harvey Publications: Nov, 1964 - No. 105, Sept, 1982 (#1-38: 68 pgs., 39-55, 67-90: 52 pgs.)

1 17.00 51.00 170.00
2-5 8.00 24.00 80.00
6-10 4.50 13.50 45.00
11-20 3.80 11.40 38.00
21-30: 27-1st Penny Van Dough (8/69) 2.40 7.20 24.00
31-38: 38-Last 68 pg. Giant 2.00 6.00 20.00
39-55-(52 pgs.): 44-Super Richie app. 1.60 4.80 16.00
56-66 1.00 3.00 8.00
67-90: 52 pgs. 1.10 3.30 9.00
91-105: 91-Onion app. 101-Dr. Blemish app. 4.00

RICHIE RICH SUMMER BONANZA
Harvey Comics: Oct, 1991 ($1.95, one-shot, 68 pgs.)

1-Richie Rich, Little Dot, Little Lotta 3.00

RICHIE RICH TREASURE CHEST DIGEST (...Magazine #3)
Harvey Publications: Apr, 1982 - No. 3, Aug, 1982 (95¢, Digest Mag.) (#4 advertised but not publ.)

1 1.00 2.80 7.00
2,3 5.00

RICHIE RICH VACATION DIGEST
Harvey Comics: Oct, 1991; Oct, 1992; Oct, 1993 ($1.75, digest-size)

1-(10/91), 1-(10/92), 1-(10/93) 4.00

RICHIE RICH VACATIONS DIGEST
Harvey Publ.: 11/77; No. 2, 10/78 - No. 7, 10/81; No. 8, 8/82; (Digest, 132 pgs.)

1-Reprints 1.20 3.60 12.00
2-8 1.00 2.80 7.00

RICHIE RICH VAULT OF MYSTERY
Harvey Publications: Nov, 1974 - No. 47, Sept, 1982

1 2.40 7.20 24.00
2-10 1.40 4.20 14.00
11-20 1.00 3.00 8.00
21-30 5.00
31-47 3.50

RICHIE RICH ZILLIONZ
Harvey Publ.: Oct, 1976 - No. 33, Sept, 1982 (#1-4: 68 pgs.; #5-18: 52 pgs.)

1 2.20 6.60 22.00
2-4: 4-Last 68 pg. Giant 1.40 4.20 14.00
5-10 1.00 3.00 8.00
11-18: 18-Last 52 pg. Giant 2.40 6.00
19-33 3.00

RICK GEARY'S WONDERS AND ODDITIES
Dark Horse Comics: Dec, 1988 ($2.00, B&W, one-shot)

1 2.00

RICKY
Standard Comics (Visual Editions): No. 5, Sept, 1953

5-Teenage humor 4.00 12.00 24.00

RICKY NELSON (TV)(See Sweethearts V2#42)
Dell Publishing Co.: No. 956, Dec, 1958 - No. 1192, June, 1961 (All photo-c)

Four Color 956,998 18.00 55.00 200.00
Four Color 1115 14.00 41.00 150.00
Four Color 1192-Manning-a 14.00 41.00 150.00

RIDER, THE (Frontier Trail #6; also see Blazing Sixguns I.W. Reprint #10, 11)
Ajax/Farrell Publ. (Four Star Comic Corp.): Mar, 1957 - No. 5, 1958

1-Swift Arrow, Lone Rider begin 11.00 33.00 75.00
2-5 6.35 19.00 38.00

RIDERS OF THE PURPLE SAGE (See Zane Grey & Four Color #372)

RIFLEMAN, THE (TV)
Dell Publ. Co./Gold Key No. 13 on: No. 1009, 7-9/59 - No. 12, 7-9/62; No. 13, 11/62 - No. 20, 10/64

GD2.0 FN6.0 NM9.4

Four Color 1009 (#1) 22.00 65.00 240.00
2 (1-3/60) 11.00 33.00 120.00
3-Toth-a (4 pgs.) 12.00 35.00 130.00
4-10: 6-Toth-a (4 pgs.) 9.00 27.00 100.00
11-20 7.00 20.00 75.00

NOTE: ***Warren Tufts** a-2-9. All have Chuck Connors photo-c. Photo back c-13-15.*

RIMA, THE JUNGLE GIRL
National Periodical Publications: Apr-May, 1974 - No. 7, Apr-May, 1975

1-Origin, part 1 (#1-5: 20¢; 6,7: 25¢) 1.00 3.00 8.00
2-7: 2-4-Origin, parts 2-4. 7-Origin & only app. Space Marshal 5.00

NOTE: ***Kubert** c-1-7. **Nino** a-1-7. **Redondo** a-1-7.*

RING OF BRIGHT WATER (See Movie Classics)

RING OF THE NIBELUNG, THE
DC Comics: 1989 - No. 4, 1990 ($4.95, squarebound, 52 pgs., mature readers)

1-4: Adapts novel, Gil Kane-c/a 5.00

RINGO KID, THE (2nd Series)
Marvel Comics Group: Jan, 1970 - No. 23, Nov, 1973; No. 24, Nov, 1975 - No. 30, Nov, 1976

1-Williamson-a r-from #10, 1956. 2.50 7.50 22.00
2-11: 2-Severin-c. 11-Last 15¢ issue 1.75 5.25 14.00
12 (Giant) 2.50 7.50 20.00
13-20: 13-Wildey-r. 20-Williamson-r/#1 1.25 3.75 10.00
21-30 1.00 3.00 8.00
27,28-(30¢-c variant, limited distribution)(5,7/76) 3.00 9.00 30.00

RINGO KID WESTERN, THE (1st Series) (See Wild Western & Western Trails)
Atlas Comics (HPC)/Marvel Comics: Aug, 1954 - No. 21, Sept, 1957

1-Origin; The Ringo Kid begins 29.00 86.00 200.00
2-Black Rider app.; origin/1st app. Ringo's Horse Arab
14.00 43.00 100.00
3-5 10.00 30.00 65.00
6-8-Severin-a(3) each 11.00 33.00 75.00
9,11,12,14-21: 12-Orlando-a (4 pgs.) 8.35 25.00 50.00
10,13-Williamson-a (4 pgs.) 9.15 27.00 55.00

NOTE: ***Berg** a-8. **Maneely** a-1-5, 15, 16(text illos only), 17(4), 18, 20, 21; c-1-6, 8, 13, 15-18, 20. **J. Severin** c-10, 11. **Sinnott** a-1. **Wildey** a-16-18.*

RIN TIN TIN (See March of Comics #163,180,195)

RIN TIN TIN (TV) (...& Rusty #21 on; see Western Roundup under Dell Giants)
Dell Publishing Co./Gold Key: Nov, 1952 - No. 38, May-July, 1961; Nov, 1963 (All Photo-c)

Four Color 434 (#1) 14.00 41.00 150.00
Four Color 476,523 7.00 22.00 80.00
4(3-5/54)-10 5.50 16.50 60.00
11-20 5.00 15.00 55.00
21-38: 36-Toth-a (4 pgs.) 3.60 11.00 40.00
... & Rusty 1 (11/63-Gold Key) 5.00 15.00 55.00

RIO (Also see Eclipse Monthly)
Comico: June, 1987 ($8.95, 64 pgs.)

1-Wildey-c/a 9.00

RIO AT BAY
Dark Horse Comics: July, 1992 - No. 2, Aug, 1992 ($2.95, limited series)

1,2-Wildey-c/a 3.00

RIO BRAVO (Movie) (See 4-Color #1018)
Dell Publishing Co.: June, 1959

Four Color #1018-Toth-a; John Wayne, Dean Martin, & Ricky Nelson photo-c.
18.00 55.00 200.00

RIO CONCHOS (See Movie Comics)

RIOT (Satire)
Atlas Comics (ACI No. 1-5/WPI No. 6): Apr, 1954 - No. 3, Aug, 1954; No. 4, Feb, 1956 - No. 6, June, 1956

Riot #3 © MAR

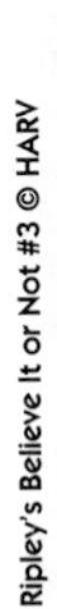

Ripley's Believe It or Not #3 © HARV

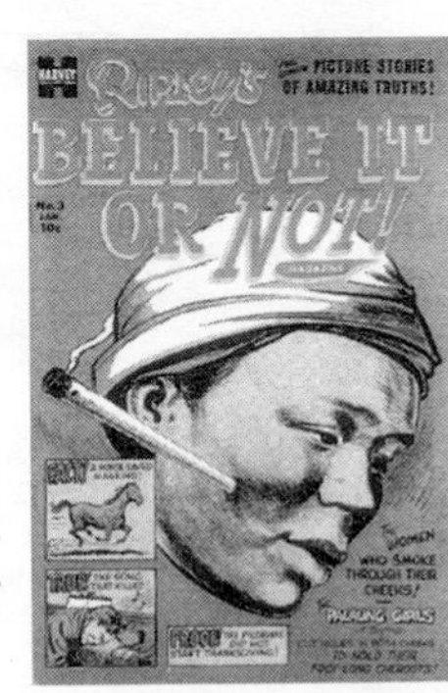

Rising Stars #1 © J. Michael Straczynski

GD2.0 FN6.0 NM9.4

1-Russ Heath-a 29.00 86.00 200.00
2-Li'l Abner satire by Post 21.00 64.00 150.00
3-Last precode (8/54) 19.00 56.00 130.00
4-Infinity-c; Marilyn Monroe "7 Year Itch" movie satire; Mad Rip-off ads 24.00 73.00 170.00
5-Marilyn Monroe, John Wayne parody; part photo-c 25.00 75.00 175.00
6-Lorna of the Jungle satire by Everett; Dennis the Menace satire-c/story; part photo-c 19.00 56.00 130.00

NOTE: ***Berg*** *a-3.* ***Burgos*** *c-1, 2.* ***Colan*** *a-1.* ***Everett*** *a-1, 4, 6.* ***Heath*** *a-1.* ***Maneely*** *a-1, 2, 4-6; c-3, 4, 6.* ***Post*** *a-1-4.* ***Reinman*** *a-2.* ***Severin*** *a-4-6.*

RIOT GEAR
Triumphant Comics: Sept, 1993 - No. 11, July, 1994 ($2.50, serially numbered)

1-11: 1-2nd app. Riot Gear. 2-1st app. Rabin. 3,4-Triumphant Unleashed x-over. 3-1st app. Surzar. 4-Death of Captain Tich 2.50
Violent Past 1,2: 1-(2/94, $2.50) 2.50

R.I.P.
TSR, Inc.:1990 - No. 8, 1991 ($2.95, 44 pgs.)

1-8-Based on TSR game 3.00

RIPCLAW (See Cyberforce)
Image Comics (Top Cow Prod.): Apr, 1995 - No. 3, June, 1995 (Limited series)

1/2-Gold, 1/2-San Diego ed., 1/2-Chicago ed. 1.25 3.75 10.00
1-3: Brandon Peterson-a(p) 3.00

RIPCLAW
Image Comics (Top Cow Prod.): V2#1, Dec, 1995 - No. 6, June, 1996 ($2.50)

V2#1-6: 5-Medieval Spawn/Witchblade Preview 2.50
Special (10/95, $2.50) 2.50

RIPCORD (TV)
Dell Publishing Co.: Mar-May, 1962

Four Color 1294 6.40 19.00 70.00

RIPFIRE
Malibu Comics (Ultraverse): No. 0, Apr, 1995 ($2.50, one-shot)

0 2.50

RIP HUNTER TIME MASTER (See Showcase #20, 21, 25, 26 & Time Masters)
National Periodical Publications: Mar-Apr, 1961 - No. 29, Nov-Dec, 1965

1-(3-4/61) 41.00 123.00 470.00
2 22.50 68.00 225.00
3-5: 5-Last 10¢ issue 13.00 39.00 130.00
6,7-Toth-a in each 9.00 27.00 90.00
8-15 6.50 19.50 65.00
16-20: 20-Hitler c/s 5.50 16.50 55.00
21-29: 29-Gil Kane-c 4.50 13.50 45.00

RIP IN TIME (Also see Teenage Mutant Ninja Turtles #5-7)
Fantagor Press: Aug, 1986 - No.5, 1987 ($1.50, B&W)

1-5: Corben-c/a in all 2.00

RIP KIRBY (Also see Harvey Comics Hits #57, & Street Comix)
David McKay Publications: 1948

Feature Books 51,54: Raymond-c; 51-Origin 33.00 99.00 230.00

RIPLEY'S BELIEVE IT OR NOT! (See Ace Comics, All-American Comics, Mystery Comics Digest #1, 4, 7, 10, 13, 16, 19, 22, 25)

RIPLEY'S BELIEVE IT OR NOT!
Harvey Publications: Sept, 1953 - No. 4, March, 1954

1-Powell-a 11.50 34.00 80.00
2-4 9.15 27.00 55.00

RIPLEY'S BELIEVE IT OR NOT! (Formerly ...True War Stories)
Gold Key: No. 4, April, 1967 - No. 94, Feb, 1980

4-Photo-c; McWilliams-a 2.60 7.80 26.00
5-Subtitled "True War Stories"; Evans-a; 1st Jeff Jones-a in comics? (2 pgs.) 2.60 7.80 26.00
6-10: 6-McWilliams-a. 10-Evans-a(2) 2.50 7.50 24.00
11-20: 15-Evans-a 2.25 6.75 18.00
21-30 1.75 5.25 14.00
31-38,40-60 1.25 3.75 10.00
39-Crandall-a 1.50 4.50 10.00
61-73 1.00 2.80 7.00
74,77-83-(52 pgs.) 1.25 3.75 10.00
75,76,84-94 5.00
Story Digest Mag. 1(6/70)-4-3/4x6-1/2", 148pp. 4.50 13.50 45.00

NOTE: ***Evanish*** *art by* ***Luiz Dominguez*** *#22-25, 27, 30, 31, 40.* ***Jeff Jones*** *a-5(2 pgs.).* ***McWilliams*** *a-65, 66, 70, 89.* ***Orlando*** *a-8.* ***Sparling*** *c-68. Reprints-74, 77-84, 87 (part); 91, 93 (all).* ***Williamson, Wood*** *a-80r/#1.*

RIPLEY'S BELIEVE IT OR NOT! TRUE GHOST STORIES (Becomes ...True War Stories) (See Dan Curtis)
Gold Key: June, 1965 - No. 2, Oct, 1966

1-Williamson, Wood & Evans-a; photo-c 5.00 15.00 50.00
2-Orlando, McWilliams-a; photo-c 3.20 9.60 32.00
Mini-Comic 1(1976-3-1/4x6-1/2") 1.00 2.80 7.00
11186(1977)-Golden Press; ($1.95, 224 pgs.)-All-r 2.50 7.50 24.00
11401(3/79)-Golden Press; ($1.00, 96 pgs.)-All-r 2.00 6.00 16.00

RIPLEY'S BELIEVE IT OR NOT! TRUE WAR STORIES (Formerly ...True Ghost Stories; becomes Ripley's Believe It or Not! #4 on)
Gold Key: Nov, 1966

1(#3)-No Williamson-a 2.80 8.40 28.00

RIPLEY'S BELIEVE IT OR NOT! TRUE WEIRD
Ripley Enterprises: June, 1966 - No. 2, Aug, 1966 (B&W Magazine)

1,2-Comic stories & text 2.50 7.50 20.00

RIPTIDE
Image Comics: Sep, 1995 - No. 2, Oct, 1995 ($2.50, limited series)

1,2: Rob Liefeld-c 2.50

RISE OF APOCALYPSE
Marvel Comics: Oct, 1996 - No. 4, Jan, 1997 ($1.95, limited series)

1-4: Adam Pollina-c/a 2.00

RISING STARS
Image Comics(Top Cow): Mar, 1999 - Present ($2.50)

Preview-(3/99, $5.00) Straczynski-s 5.00
0-(3/99) Wizard supplement; Straczynski-s 2.00
1-Four covers; Keu Cha-c/a 3.00
1-($10.00) Gold Editions-four covers 10.00
1-($50.00) Holofoil-c 50.00
2,3 2.50

RIVERDALE HIGH (Archie's... #7,8)
Archie Comics: Aug, 1990 - No. 8, Oct, 1991 ($1.00, bi-monthly)

1-8 2.00

RIVER FEUD (See Zane Grey & Four Color #484)

RIVETS
Dell Publishing Co.: No. 518, Nov, 1953

Four Color 518 2.25 6.75 25.00

RIVETS (A dog)
Argo Publ.: Jan, 1956 - No. 3, May, 1956

1-Reprints Sunday & daily newspaper strips 4.25 13.00 26.00
2,3 3.60 9.00 18.00

ROACHMILL
Blackthorne Publ.: Dec, 1986 - No. 6, Oct, 1987 ($1.75, B&W)

1-6 2.00

ROACHMILL
Dark Horse Comics: May, 1988 - No. 10, Dec, 1990 ($1.75, B&W)

1-10: 10-Contains trading cards 2.00

ROAD RUNNER (See Beep Beep, the...)

ROADWAYS

Robin #52 © DC

Robin Hood Tales #9 © DC

Robin II #1 © DC

GD2.0 FN6.0 NM9.4

Cult Press: May, 1994 ($2.75, B&W, limited series)
1 2.75

ROARIN' RICK'S RARE BIT FIENDS
King Hell Press: July, 1994 - Present ($2.95, B&W, mature)
1-21: Rick Veitch-c/a/scripts in all. 20-(5/96). 21-(8/96)-Reads Subtleman #1 on cover 3.00
Rabid Eye: The Dream Art of Rick Veitch ($14.95, B&W, TPB)-r/#1-8 & the appendix from #12 15.00
Pocket Universe (6/96, $14.95, B&W, TPB)-Reprints 15.00

ROBERT E. HOWARD'S CONAN THE BARBARIAN
Marvel Comics: 1983 ($2.50, 68 pgs., Baxter paper)
1-r/Savage Tales #2,3 by Smith, c-r/Conan #21 by Smith. 2.50

ROBERT LOUIS STEVENSON'S KIDNAPPED (See Kidnapped)

ROBIN (See Aurora, Detective Comics #38, New Teen Titans, Robin II, Robin III, Robin 3000, Star Spangled Comics #65, Teen Titans & Young Justice)

ROBIN (See Batman #457)
DC Comics: Jan, 1991 - No. 5, May, 1991 ($1.00, limited series)
1-Free poster by N. Adams; Bolland-c on all 4.00
1-2nd & 3rd printings (without poster) 2.00
2-5 2.50
2-2nd printing 2.00
Annual 1,2 (1992-93, $2.50, 68 pgs.): 1-Grant/Wagner scripts; Sam Kieth-c. 2-Intro Razorsharp; Jim Balent-c(p) 2.50

ROBIN (See Detective #668)
DC Comics: Nov, 1993 - Present ($1.50/$1.95/$1.99)
1-($2.95)-Collector's edition w/foil embossed-c; 1st app. Robin's car, The Redbird; Azrael as Batman app. 3.00
1-Newsstand ed. 2.00
0,2-49,51-66-Regular editions: 3-5-The Spoiler app. 6-The Huntress-c/story cont'd from Showcase '94 #5. 7-Knightquest: The Conclusion w/new Batman (Azrael) vs. Bruce Wayne. 8-KnightsEnd Pt. 5. 9-KnightsEnd Aftermath; Batman-c & app. 10-(9/94)-Zero Hour. 0-(10/94). 11-(11/94). 25-Green Arrow -c/app. 26-Batman app. 27-Contagion Pt. 3; Catwoman-c/app; Penguin & Azrael app. 28-Contagion Pt. 11. 29-Penguin app. 31-Wildcat-c/app. 32-Legacy Pt. 3. 33-Legacy Pt. 7. 35-Final Night. 46-Genesis. 52,53-Cataclysm pt. 7, conclusion. 55-Green Arrow app. 62-64-Flash-c/app. 2.00
14 ($2.50)-Embossed-c; Troika Pt. 4 2.50
50-($2.95)-Lady Shiva & King Snake app. 3.00
67-71-No Man's Land 2.00
#1,000,000 (11/98) 853rd Century x-over 2.00
Annual 3-5: 3-(1994, $2.95)-Elseworlds story. 4-(1995, $2.95)-Year One story. 5-(1996, $2.95)-Legends of the Dead Earth story 3.00
Annual 6 (1997, $3.95)-Pulp Heroes story. 4.00
.../Argent 1 (2/98, $1.95) Argent (Teen Titans) app. 2.00
...Plus 1 (12/96, $2.95) Impulse-c/app.; Waid-s 3.00
...Plus 2 (12/97, $2.95) Fang (Scare Tactics) app. 3.00

ROBIN: A HERO REBORN
DC Comics: 1991 ($4.95, squarebound, trade paperback)
nn-r/Batman #455-457 & Robin #1-5; Bolland-c 5.00

ROBIN HOOD (See The Advs. of..., Brave and the Bold, Four Color #413, 669, King Classics, Movie Comics & Power Record Comics)

ROBIN HOOD (...& His Merry Men, The Illustrated Story of...) (See Classic Comics #7 & Classics Giveaways, 12/44)

ROBIN HOOD (Adventures of... #7, 8)
Magazine Enterprises (Sussex Pub. Co.): No. 52, Nov, 1955 - No. 6, Jun, 1957
52 (#1)-Origin Robin Hood & Sir Gallant of the Round Table 16.00 47.00 110.00
53 (#2), 3-6: 6-Richard Greene photo-c (TV) 11.50 34.00 80.00
I.W. Reprint #1,2,9: 1-r/#3. 2-r/#4. 9-r/#52 (1963) 2.00 6.00 16.00
Super Reprint #10,15: 10-r/#53. 15-r/#5 2.00 6.00 16.00
NOTE: ***Bolle*** *a-in all; c-52.* ***Powell*** *a-6.*

ROBIN HOOD (Not Disney)
Dell Publishing Co.: May-July, 1963 (one-shot)
1 2.00 6.00 22.00

ROBIN HOOD (Disney)
Western Publishing Co.: 1973 ($1.50, 8-1/2x11", 52 pgs., cardboard-c)
96151- "Robin Hood", based on movie, 96152- "The Mystery of Sherwood Forest", 96153- "In King Richard's Service", 96154- "The Wizard's Ring" each.... 2.25 6.75 18.00

ROBIN HOOD
Eclipse Comics: July, 1991 - No. 3, 1991 ($2.50, limited series)
1-3: Timothy Truman layouts 2.50

ROBIN HOOD AND HIS MERRY MEN (Formerly Danger & Adventure)
Charlton Comics: No. 28, Apr, 1956 - No. 38, Aug, 1958
28 9.15 27.00 55.00
29-37 6.70 20.00 40.00
38-Ditko-a (5 pgs.); Rocke-c 12.00 36.00 85.00

ROBIN HOOD TALES (Published by National Periodical #7 on)
Quality Comics Group (Comic Magazines): Feb, 1956 - No. 6, Nov-Dec, 1956
1-All have Baker/Cuidera-c 33.00 99.00 230.00
2-6-Matt Baker-a 31.00 94.00 220.00

ROBIN HOOD TALES (Cont'd from Quality series)(See Brave & the Bold #5)
National Periodical Publ.: No. 7, Jan-Feb, 1957 - No. 14, Mar-Apr, 1958
7-All have Andru/Esposito-c 39.00 116.00 270.00
8-14 31.00 94.00 220.00

ROBINSON CRUSOE (See King Classics & Power Record Comics)
Dell Publishing Co.: Nov-Jan, 1963-64
1 1.50 4.50 12.00

ROBIN II (The Joker's Wild)
DC Comics: Oct, 1991 - No. 4, Dec, 1991 ($1.50, mini-series)
1-(Direct sales, $1.50)-With 4 diff.-c; same hologram on each 2.50
1-(Newsstand, $1.00)-No hologram; 1 version 2.00
1-Collector's set ($10.00)-Contains all 5 versions bagged with hologram trading card inside 10.00
2-(Direct sales, $1.50)-With 3 different-c 2.50
2-4-(Newsstand, $1.00)-1 version of each 2.00
2-Collector's set ($8.00)-Contains all 4 versions bagged with hologram trading card inside 8.00
3-(Direct sale, $1.50)-With 2 different-c 2.50
3-Collector's set ($6.00)-Contains all 3 versions bagged with hologram trading card inside 6.00
4-(Direct sales, $1.50)-Only one version 2.50
4-Collector's set ($4.00)-Contains both versions bagged with Bat-Signal hologram trading card 4.00
Multi-pack (All four issues w/hologram sticker) 4.00
Deluxe Complete Set ($30.00)-Contains all 14 versions of #1-4 plus a new hologram trading card; numbered & limited to 25,000; comes with slipcase & 2 acid free backing boards 30.00

ROBIN III: CRY OF THE HUNTRESS
DC Comics: Dec, 1992 - No. 6, Mar, 1993 (Limited series)
1-6 ($2.50, collector's ed.)-Polybagged w/movement enhanced-c plus mini-poster of newsstand-c by Zeck 2.50
1-6 ($1.25, newsstand ed.): All have Zeck-c 2.00

ROBIN 3000
DC Comics (Elseworlds): 1992 - No. 2, 1992 ($4.95, mini-series, 52 pgs.)
1,2-Foil logo; Russell-c/a 5.00

ROBOCOP
Marvel Comics: Oct, 1987 ($2.00, B&W, magazine, one-shot)
1-Movie adaptation 2.00

ROBOCOP (Also see Dark Horse Comics)
Marvel Comics: Mar, 1990 - No. 23, Jan, 1992 ($1.50)

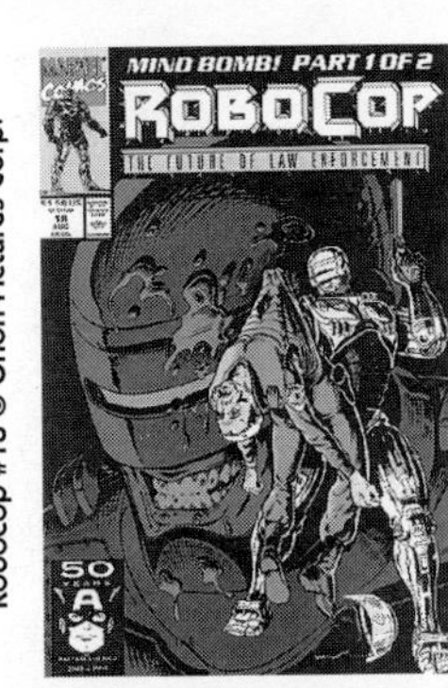

Robocop #18 © Orion Pictures Corp.

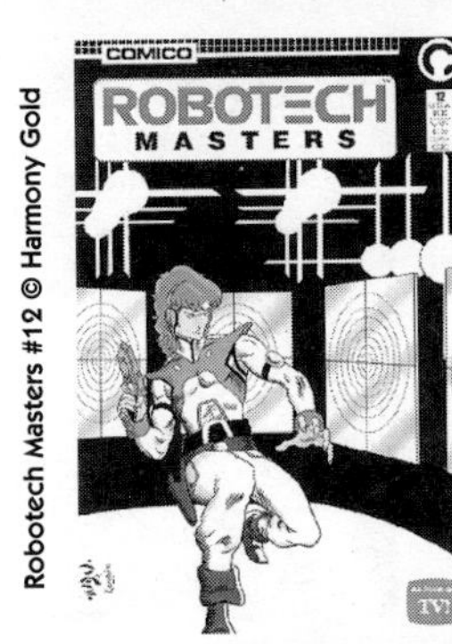

Robotech Masters #12 © Harmony Gold

Robotech Vermilion #1 © Harmony Gold

GD2.0 FN6.0 NM9.4

1-Based on movie 3.00
2-23 2.00
nn (7/90, $4.95, 52 pgs.)-r/B&W magazine in color; adapts 1st movie 5.00

ROBOCOP: MORTAL COILS
Dark Horse Comics: Sept, 1993 - No. 4, Dec, 1993 ($2.50, limited series)
1-4: 1,2-Cago painted-c 2.50

ROBOCOP: PRIME SUSPECT
Dark Horse Comics: Oct, 1992 - No. 4, Jan, 1993 ($2.50, limited series)
1-4: 1,3-Nelson painted-c. 2,4-Bolton painted-c 2.50

ROBOCOP: ROULETTE
Dark Horse Comics: Dec, 1993 - No. 4, 1994 ($2.50, limited series)
1-4: 1,3-Nelson painted-c. 2,4-Bolton painted-c 2.50

ROBOCOP 2
Marvel Comics: Aug, 1990 ($2.25, B&W, magazine, 68 pgs.)
1-Adapts movie sequel 2.25

ROBOCOP 2
Marvel Comics: Aug, 1990; Late Aug, 1990 - #3, Late Sept, 1990 ($1.00, limited series)
nn-(8/90, $4.95, 68 pgs., color)-Same contents as B&W magazine 5.00
1: #1-3 reprint no number issue 3.00
2,3: 2-Guice-c(i) 2.00

ROBOCOP 3
Dark Horse Comics: July, 1993 - No. 3, Nov, 1993 ($2.50, limited series)
1-3: Nelson painted-c; Nguyen-a(p) 2.50

ROBOCOP VERSUS THE TERMINATOR
Dark Horse Comics: Sept, 1992 - No. 4, 1992 (Dec.) ($2.50, limited series)
1-4: Miller scripts & Simonson-c/a in all 2.50
1-Platinum Edition 6.00
NOTE: *All contain a different Robocop cardboard cut-out stand-up.*

ROBO-HUNTER (Also see Sam Slade...)
Eagle Comics: Apr, 1984 - No. 5, 1984 ($1.00)
1-5-2000 A.D. 2.00

R.O.B.O.T. BATTALION 2050
Eclipse Comics: Mar, 1988 ($2.00, B&W, one-shot)
1 2.00

ROBOT COMICS
Renegade Press: No. 0, June, 1987 ($2.00, B&W, one-shot)
0-Bob Burden story & art 2.00

ROBOTECH
Antarctic Press: Mar, 1997 - Present ($2.95)
1-11, Annual 1 (4/98, $2.95) 3.00
...Class Reunion (12/98, $3.95, B&W) 4.00
...Escape (5/98, $2.95, B&W), ...Final Fire (12/98, $2.95, B&W) 3.00

ROBOTECH: COVERT-OPS
Antarctic Press: Aug, 1998 - No. 2, Sept, 1998 ($2.95, B&W, limited series)
1,2-Gregory Lane-s/a 3.00

ROBOTECH DEFENDERS
DC Comics: Mar, 1985 - No. 2, Apr, 1985 (Mini-series)
1,2 2.00

ROBOTECH IN 3-D (TV)
Comico: Aug, 1987 ($2.50)
1-Steacy painted-c 3.00

ROBOTECH MASTERS (TV)
Comico: July, 1985 - No. 23, Apr, 1988 ($1.50)
1-23 3.00

ROBOTECH: SENTINELS - RUBICON
Antarctic Press: July, 1998 - Present ($2.95, B&W)
1 3.00

ROBOTECH SPECIAL
Comico: May, 1988 ($2.50, one-shot, 44 pgs.)
1-Steacy wraparound-c; partial photo-c 3.00

ROBOTECH THE GRAPHIC NOVEL
Comico: Aug, 1986 ($5.95, 8-1/2x11", 52 pgs.)
1-Origin SDF-1; intro T.R. Edwards, Steacy-c/a; 2nd printing also exists (12/86). 6.00

ROBOTECH: THE MACROSS SAGA (TV)(Formerly Macross)
Comico: No. 2, Feb, 1985 - No. 36, Feb, 1989 ($1.50)
2-10 3.00
11-36: 12,17-Ken Steacy painted-c. 26-Begin $1.75-c. 35,36-($1.95) 3.00

ROBOTECH: THE NEW GENERATION
Comico: July, 1985 - No. 25, July, 1988
1-25 3.00

ROBOTECH: VERMILION
Antarctic Press: Mar, 1997 - No. 4, ($2.95, B&W, limited series)
1-4 3.00

ROBOTECH: WINGS OF GIBRALTAR
Antarctic Press: Aug, 1998 - No. 2, Sept, 1998 ($2.95, B&W, limited series)
1,2-Lee Duhig-s/a 3.00

ROBOTIX
Marvel Comics: Feb, 1986 (75¢, one-shot)
1-Based on toy 2.00

ROBOTMEN OF THE LOST PLANET (Also see Space Thrillers)
Avon Periodicals: 1952 (Also see Strange Worlds #19)
1-McCann-a (3 pgs.); Fawcette-a 95.00 285.00 760.00

ROB ROY
Dell Publishing Co.: 1954 (Disney-Movie)
Four Color 544-Manning-a, photo-c 7.00 22.00 80.00

ROBYN OF SHERWOOD
Caliber Comics: 1998 - Present ($2.95, B&W)
1-Two covers 3.00

ROCK & ROLL HIGH SCHOOL
Roger Corman's Cosmic Comics: Oct, 1995 ($2.50)
1-Bob Fingerman scripts 2.50

ROCK AND ROLLO (Formerly TV Teens)
Charlton Comics: V2#14, Oct, 1957 - No. 19, Sept, 1958
V2#14-19 4.25 13.00 28.00

ROCK COMICS
Landgraphic Publ.: Jul/Aug, 1979 ($1.25, tabloid size, 28 pgs.)
1-N. Adams-c; Thor(not Marvel's) story by Adams 1.75 5.25 14.00

ROCKET COMICS
Hillman Periodicals: Mar, 1940 - No. 3, May, 1940
1-Rocket Riley, Red Roberts the Electro Man (origin), The Phantom Ranger, The Steel Shark, The Defender, Buzzard Barnes and his Sky Devils, Lefty Larson, & The Defender, the Man with a Thousand Faces begin (1st app. of each); all have Rocket Riley-c 237.00 712.00 1900.00
2,3 120.00 360.00 960.00

ROCKETEER, THE (See Eclipse Graphic Album Series, Pacific Presents & Starslayer)

ROCKETEER ADVENTURE MAGAZINE, THE
Comico/Dark Horse Comics No. 3: July, 1988 ($2.00); No. 2, July, 1989 ($2.75); No. 3, Jan, 1995 ($2.95)
1-(7/88, $2.00)-Dave Stevens-c/a in all; Kaluta back-up-a; 1st app. Jonas (character based on The Shadow) 1.00 3.00 8.00
2-(6/88, $2.75)-Stevens/Dorman painted-c 5.00
3-(1/95, $2.95)-Includes pinups by Stevens, Gulacy, Plunkett, & Mignola 3.00

Rocketman #1 © AJAX

Rock Fantasy Comics #9
© Rock Fantasy Comics

Rocky Lane Western #20 © FAW

GD2.0 FN6.0 NM9.4

Volume 2-(9/96, $9.95, magazine size TPB)-Reprints #1-3 10.00

ROCKETEER SPECIAL EDITION, THE
Eclipse Comics: Nov, 1984 ($1.50, Baxter paper)(Chapter 5 of Rocketeer serial)

1-Stevens-c/a; Kaluta back-c; pin-ups inside 1.15 4.50 12.00
NOTE: *Originally intended to be published in Pacific Presents.*

ROCKETEER: THE OFFICIAL MOVIE ADAPTATION, THE
W. D. Publications (Disney): 1991

nn-($5.95, 68 pgs.)-Squarebound deluxe edition 6.00
nn-($2.95, 68 pgs.)-Stapled regular edition 3.00
3-D Comic Book (1991, $7.98, 52 pgs.) 8.00

ROCKET KELLY (See The Bouncer, Green Mask #10); becomes Li'l Pan #6)
Fox Feature Syndicate: 1944; Fall, 1945 - No. 5, Oct-Nov, 1946

nn (1944), 1 29.00 86.00 200.00
2-The Puppeteer app. (costumed hero) 23.00 69.00 160.00
3-5: 5-(#5 on cover, #4 inside) 20.00 60.00 140.00

ROCKETMAN (Strange Fantasy #2 on) (See Hello Pal & Scoop Comics)
Ajax/Farrell Publications: June, 1952 (Strange Stories of the Future)

1-Rocketman & Cosmo 40.00 120.00 300.00

ROCKET RACCOON
Marvel Comics: May, 1995 - No. 4, Aug, 1985 (color, limited series)

1-4: Mignola-a 2.00

ROCKET SHIP X
Fox Features Syndicate: September, 1951; 1952

1 59.00 178.00 475.00
1952 (nn, nd, no publ.)-Edited 1951-c 40.00 120.00 290.00

ROCKET TO ADVENTURE LAND (See Pixie Puzzle...)

ROCKET TO THE MOON
Avon Periodicals: 1951

nn-Orlando-c/a; adapts Otis Aldebert Kline's "Maza of the Moon"
98.00 294.00 785.00

ROCK FANTASY COMICS
Rock Fantasy Comics: Dec, 1989 - No. 16?, 1991 ($2.25/$3.00, B&W)(No cover price)

1-Pink Floyd part 1 3.00
1-2nd printing ($3.00-c) 3.00
2,3: 2-Rolling Stones #1. 3-Led Zeppelin #1 3.00
2,3: 2nd printings ($3.00-c, 1/90 & 2/90) 3.00
4-Stevie Nicks Not published
5-Monstrosities of Rock #1; photo back-c 3.00
5-2nd printing ($3.00, 3/90 indicia, 2/90-c) 3.00
6-9,11-15,17,18: 6-Guns n' Roses #1 (1st & 2nd printings, 3/90)-Begin $3.00-c. 7-Sex Pistols #1. 8-Alice Cooper; not published. 9-Van Halen #1; photo back-c. 11-Jimi Hendrix #1; wraparound-c 3.00
10-Kiss #1; photo back-c 2.40 6.00
16-($5.00, 68 pgs.)-The Great Gig in the Sky(Floyd) 5.00

ROCK HAPPENING (Harvey Pop Comics:...)(See Bunny)
Harvey Publications: Sept, 1969 - No. 2, Nov, 1969

1,2: Featuring Bunny 2.80 8.40 28.00

ROCK N' ROLL COMICS
Revolutionary Comics: Jun, 1989 - No. 24, 1992 ($1.50/$1.95, B&W/col. #15 on)

1-Guns N' Roses 1.00 3.00 8.00
1-2nd thru 7th printings. 7th printing (full color w/new-c/a) 2.00
2-Metallica 1.25 3.75 10.00
2-2nd thru 6th printings (6th in color) 2.00
3-Bon Jovi (no reprints) 1.00 3.00 8.00
4-8,10-24: 4-Motley Crue(2nd printing only, 1st destroyed). 5-Def Leppard (2 printings). 6-Rolling Stones(4 printings). 7-The Who(3 printings). 8-Skid Row; not published. 10-Warrant/Whitesnake(2 printings; 1st has 2 diff.-c). 11-Aerosmith (2 printings?). 12-New Kids on the Block(2 printings). 12-3rd printing; rewritten & titled NKOTB Hate Book. 13-Led Zeppelin. 14-Sex Pistols. 15-Poison; 1st color issue. 16-Van Halen. 17-Madonna. 18-Alice Cooper. 19-Public Enemy/2 Live Crew. 20-Queensryche/Tesla. 21-Prince? 22-AC/DC; begin $2.50-c. 23-Living Colour. 24-Anthrax 5.00
9-Kiss 1.50 4.50 12.00
9-2nd & 3rd printings 2.00
NOTE: *Most issues were reprinted except #3. Later reprints are in color. #8 was not released.*

ROCKO'S MODERN LIFE (TV)
Marvel Comics: June, 1994 - No. 7, Dec, 1994 ($1.95) (Nickelodeon cartoon)

1-7 2.00

ROCKY AND HIS FIENDISH FRIENDS (TV)(Bullwinkle)
Gold Key: Oct, 1962 - No. 5, Sept, 1963 (Jay Ward)

1 (25¢, 80 pgs.) 20.00 60.00 220.00
2,3 (25¢, 80 pgs.) 14.00 42.00 155.00
4,5 (Regular size, 12¢) 9.00 29.00 105.00

ROCKY AND HIS FRIENDS (See Kite Fun Book & March of Comics #216)

ROCKY AND HIS FRIENDS (TV)
Dell Publishing Co.: No. 1128, 8-10/60 - No.1311,1962 (Jay Ward)

Four Color #1128 (#1) (8-10/60) 36.00 109.00 400.00
Four Color #1152 (12-2/61), 1166, 1208, 1275, 1311('62)
23.00 68.00 250.00

ROCKY HORROR PICTURE SHOW THE COMIC BOOK, THE
Caliber Press: Jul, 1990 - No. 3, 1990 ($2.95, mini-series, 52 pgs.)(Photo-c #1)

1-3: 1-Adapts cult film plus photos, etc., 1-2nd printing 3.00
...Collection ($4.95) 5.00

ROCKY JONES SPACE RANGER (See Space Adventures #15-18)

ROCKY JORDEN PRIVATE EYE (See Private Eye)

ROCKY LANE WESTERN (Allan Rocky Lane starred in Republic movies & TV for a short time as Allan Lane, Red Ryder & Rocky Lane) (See Black Jack Fawcett Movie Comics, Motion Picture Comics & Six-Gun Heroes)
Fawcett Publications/Charlton No. 56 on: May, 1949 - No. 87, Nov, 1959

1 (36 pgs.)-Rocky, his stallion Black Jack, & Slim Pickens begin; photo-c begin, end #57; photo back-c 97.00 291.00 775.00
2 (36 pgs.)-Last photo back-c 40.00 120.00 310.00
3-5 (52 pgs.): 4-Captain Tootsie by Beck 29.00 86.00 200.00
6,10 (36 pgs.): 10-Complete western novelette "Badman's Reward"
21.00 62.00 145.00
7-9 (52 pgs.) 22.00 66.00 155.00
11-13,15-17 (52 pgs.): 15-Black Jack's Hitching Post begins, ends #25
17.00 49.00 115.00
14,18 (36 pgs.) 13.50 41.00 95.00
19-21,23,24 (52 pgs.): 20-Last Slim Pickens. 21-Dee Dickens begins, ends #55,57,65-68 13.50 41.00 95.00
22,25-28,30 (36 pgs. begin) 13.00 39.00 90.00
29-Classic complete novel "The Land of Missing Men" with hidden land of ancient temple ruins (r-in #65) 18.00 54.00 125.00
31-40 11.50 34.00 80.00
41-54 10.00 30.00 70.00
55-Last Fawcett issue (1/54) 11.00 33.00 75.00
56-1st Charlton issue (2/54)-Photo-c 18.00 54.00 125.00
57,60-Photo-c 11.00 33.00 75.00
58,59,61-64,66-78,80-86: 59-61-Young Falcon app. 64-Slim Pickens app. 66-68: Reprints #30,31,32 9.15 27.00 55.00
65-r/#29, "The Land of Missing Men" 10.00 30.00 65.00
79-Giant Edition (68 pgs.) 11.00 33.00 75.00
87-Last issue 10.00 30.00 70.00
NOTE: *Complete novels in #10, 14, 18, 22, 25, 30-32, 36, 38, 39, 49. Captain Tootsie in #4, 12, 20. Big Bow and Little Arrow in #11, 28, 63. Black Jack's Hitching Post in #15-25, 64, 73.*

ROCKY LANE WESTERN
AC Comics: 1989 ($2.50, B&W, one-shot?)

1-Photo-c; Giordano reprints 3.00
Annual 1 (1991, $2.95, B&W, 44 pgs.)-photo front/back & inside-c; reprints.
3.00

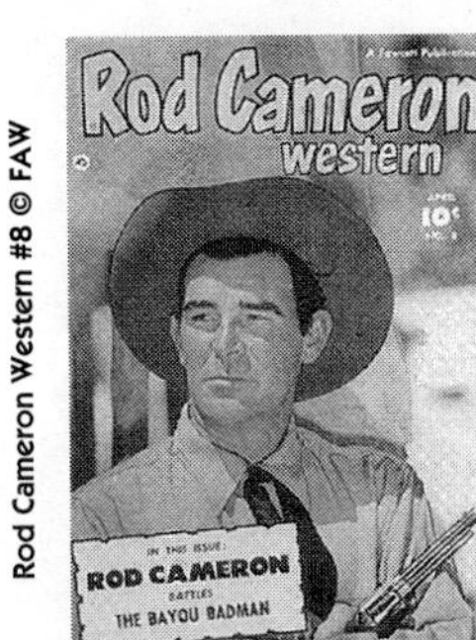

Rod Cameron Western #8 © FAW

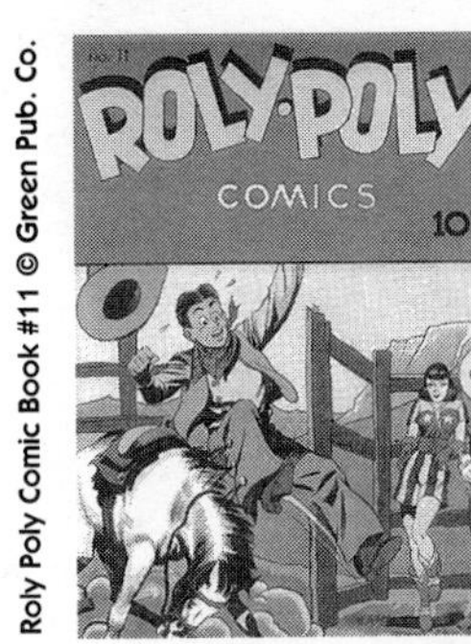

Roly Poly Comic Book #11 © Green Pub. Co.

ROM #39 © Parker Bros.

GD2.0 FN6.0 NM9.4 — GD2.0 FN6.0 NM9.4

ROD CAMERON WESTERN (Movie star)
Fawcett Publications: Feb, 1950 - No. 20, Apr, 1953

1-Rod Cameron, his horse War Paint, & Sam The Sheriff begin; photo front/back-c begin 52.00 157.00 420.00
2 26.00 79.00 185.00
3-Novel length story "The Mystery of the Seven Cities of Cibola" 22.00 66.00 155.00
4-10: 9-Last photo back-c 18.00 54.00 125.00
11-19 14.00 43.00 100.00
20-Last issue & photo-c 15.00 45.00 105.00
NOTE: *Novel length stories in No. 1-8, 12-14.*

RODEO RYAN (See A-1 Comics #8)

ROEL
Sirius: Feb, 1997 ($2.95, B&W, one-shot)

1 3.00

ROGAN GOSH
DC Comics (Vertigo): 1994 ($6.95, one-shot)

nn-Peter Milligan scripts 7.00

ROGER DODGER (Also in Exciting Comics #57 on)
Standard Comics: No. 5, Aug, 1952

5-Teen-age 4.15 12.50 25.00

ROGER RABBIT (Also see Marvel Graphic Novel)
Disney Comics: June, 1990 - No. 18, Nov, 1991 ($1.50)

1-18-All new stories 2.00
In 3-D 1 (1992, $2.50)-Sold at Wal-Mart?; w/glasses 2.50

ROGER RABBIT'S TOONTOWN
Disney Comics: Aug, 1991 - No. 5, Dec, 1991 ($1.50)

1-5 2.00

ROGER ZELAZNY'S AMBER: THE GUNS OF AVALON
DC Comics: 1996 - No. 3, 1996 ($6.95, limited series)

1-3: Based on novel 7.00

ROG 2000
Pacific Comics: June, 1982 ($2.95, 44 pgs., B&W, one-shot)

nn-Byrne-c/a (r) 1.00 3.00 8.00
2nd printing (7/82) 5.00

ROG 2000
Fantagraphics Books: 1987 - No. 2, 1987 ($2.00, limited series)

1,2-Byrne-r 2.00

ROGUE
Marvel Comics: Jan, 1995 - No. 4, Apr, 1995 ($2.95, limited series)

1-4: 1-Gold foil logo 4.00
TPB-($12.95) r/#1-4 13.00

ROGUES GALLERY
DC Comics: 1996 ($3.50, one-shot)

1-Pinups of DC villains by various artists 3.50

ROGUES, THE (VILLAINS) (See The Flash)
DC Comics: Feb, 1998 ($1.95, one-shot)

1-Augustyn-s/Pearson-c 2.00

ROGUE TROOPER
Quality Comics/Fleetway Quality #38-on : Oct, 1986 - No. 49, 1991 ($1.25/$1.50/$1.75)

1-49: 6-Double size. 21,22,25-27-Guice-c. 47,48-Alan Moore scripts 2.00

ROLLING STONES: VOODOO LOUNGE
Marvel Comics: 1995 ($6.95, Prestige format, one-shot)

nn-Dave McKean-script/design/art 7.00

ROLY POLY COMIC BOOK
Green Publishing Co.: 1945 - No. 15, 1946 (MLJ reprints)

1-Red Rube & Steel Sterling begin; Sahle-c 29.00 86.00 200.00
6-The Blue Circle & The Steel Fist app. 16.00 47.00 110.00
10-Origin Red Rube retold; Steel Sterling story (Zip #41) 16.00 47.00 110.00
11,12,14: The Black Hood app. in each. 14-Decapitation-c 17.00 51.00 120.00
15-The Blue Circle & The Steel Fist app.; cover exact swipe from Fox Blue Beetle #1 31.00 94.00 220.00

ROM (Based on the Parker Brothers toy)
Marvel Comics Group: Dec, 1979 - No. 75, Feb, 1986

1 5.00
2-16,19-23,28-30: 1-Origin/1st app.13-Saga of the Space Knights begins. 19-X-Men cameo 2.50
17,18-X-Men app. 5.00
24-27: 24-F.F. cameo; Skrulls, Nova & The New Champions app. 25-Double size. 26,27-Galactus app. 3.00
31-49,51-60: 31,32-Brotherhood of Evil Mutants app. 32-X-Men cameo. 34,35-Sub-Mariner app. 41,42-Dr. Strange app. 56,57-Alpha Flight app. 58,59-Ant-Man app. 2.50
50-Skrulls app. (52 pgs.) 4.00
61-74: 65-West Coast Avengers & Beta Ray Bill app. 65,66-X-Men app. 2.00
75-Last issue 4.00
Annual 1-4: (1982-85, 52 pgs.) 2.50
NOTE: ***Austin** c-3i, 18i, 61i. **Byrne** a-74i; c-56, 57, 74. **Ditko** a-59-75p, Annual 4. **Golden** c-7-12, 19. **Guice** a-61i; c-55, 58, 60p, 70p. **Layton** a-59i, 72i; c-15, 59i, 69. **Miller** c-2p?, 3p, 17p, 18p. **Russell** a(i)-64, 65, 67, 69, 71, 75; c-64, 65i, 66, 71i, 75. **Severin** c-41p. **Sienkiewicz** a-53i; c-46, 47, 52-54, 68, 71p, Annual 2. **Simonson** c-18. **P. Smith** c-59p. **Starlin** c-67. **Zeck** c-50.*

ROMANCE (See True Stories of...)

ROMANCE AND CONFESSION STORIES (See Giant Comics Edition)
St. John Publishing Co.: No date (1949) (25¢, 100 pgs.)

1-Baker-c/a; remaindered St. John love comics 40.00 120.00 295.00

ROMANCE DIARY
Marvel Comics (CDS)(CLDS): Dec, 1949 - No. 2, Mar, 1950

1,2 12.00 36.00 85.00

ROMANCE OF FLYING, THE
David McKay Publications: 1942

Feature Books 33 (nn)-WW II photos 13.50 41.00 95.00

ROMANCES OF MOLLY MANTON (See Molly Manton)

ROMANCES OF NURSE HELEN GRANT, THE
Atlas Comics (VPI): Aug, 1957

1 6.35 19.00 38.00

ROMANCES OF THE WEST (Becomes Romantic Affairs #3?)
Marvel Comics (SPC): Nov, 1949 - No. 2, Mar, 1950 (52 pgs.)

1-Movie photo-c of Yvonne DeCarlo & Howard Duff (Calamity Jane & Sam Bass) 21.00 64.00 150.00
2-Photo-c 14.00 43.00 100.00

ROMANCE STORIES OF TRUE LOVE (Formerly True Love Problems & Advice Illustrated)
Harvey Publications: No. 45, 5/57 - No. 50, 3/58; No. 51, 9/58 - No. 52, 11/58

45-51: 45,46,48-50-Powell-a 4.00 12.00 24.00
52-Matt Baker-a 7.50 22.50 45.00

ROMANCE TALES (Formerly Western Winners #6?)
Marvel Comics (CDS): No. 7, Oct, 1949 - No. 9, Mar, 1950 (7,8: photo-c)

7 12.00 36.00 85.00
8,9: 8-Everett-a 10.00 30.00 60.00

ROMANCE TRAIL
National Periodical Publications: July-Aug, 1949 - No. 6, May-June, 1950 (All photo-c & 52 pgs.)

1-Kinstler, Toth-a; Jimmy Wakely photo-c 56.00 169.00 450.00
2-Kinstler-a; Jim Bannon photo-c 30.00 90.00 210.00
3-Photo-c; Kinstler, Toth-a 33.00 99.00 230.00

Romantic Adventures #3 © ACG

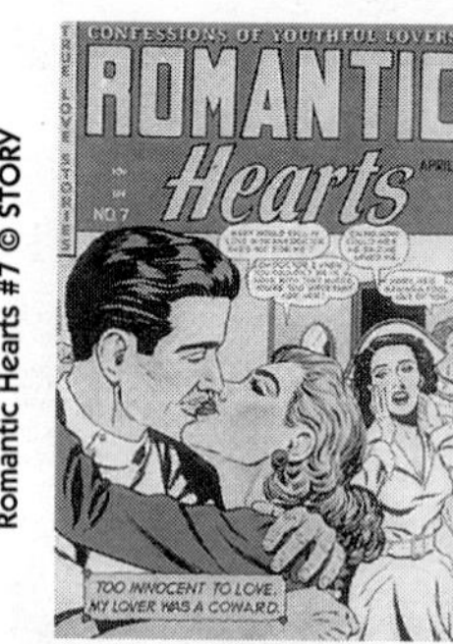

Romantic Hearts #7 © STORY

Romantic Story #1 © FAW

	GD2.0	FN6.0	NM9.4
4-Photo-c; Toth-a	24.00	73.00	170.00
5,6: Photo-c on both. 5-Kinstler-a	21.00	64.00	150.00

ROMAN HOLIDAYS, THE (TV)
Gold Key: Feb, 1973 - No. 4, Nov, 1973 (Hanna-Barbera)

	GD2.0	FN6.0	NM9.4
1	3.50	10.50	35.00
2-4	2.50	7.50	22.00

ROMANTIC ADVENTURES (My... #49-67, covers only)
American Comics Group (B&I Publ. Co.): Mar-Apr, 1949 - No. 67, July, 1956 (Becomes My... #68 on)

	GD2.0	FN6.0	NM9.4
1	16.00	47.00	110.00
2	9.15	27.00	55.00
3-10	5.85	17.50	35.00
11-20 (4/52)	4.25	13.00	28.00
21-45,49,51,52: 52-Last Pre-code (2/55)	4.00	12.00	24.00
46-48-3-D effect-c/stories (TrueVision)	10.00	30.00	70.00
50-Classic cover/story "Love of A Lunatic"	9.15	27.00	55.00
53-67	3.60	9.00	18.00

NOTE: *#1-23, 52 pgs.* ***Shelly*** *a-40. Whitney c/art in many issues.*

ROMANTIC AFFAIRS (Formerly Molly Manton's Romances #2 and/or Romances of the West #2 and/or Our Love #2?)
Marvel Comics (SPC): No. 3, Mar, 1950

	GD2.0	FN6.0	NM9.4
3-Photo-c from Molly Manton's Romances #2	8.35	25.00	50.00

ROMANTIC CONFESSIONS
Hillman Periodicals: Oct, 1949 - V3#1, Apr-May, 1953

	GD2.0	FN6.0	NM9.4
V1#1-McWilliams-a	14.00	43.00	100.00
2-Briefer-a; negligee panels	9.15	27.00	55.00
3-12	5.85	17.50	35.00
V2#1,2,4-8,10-12: 2-McWilliams-a	5.00	15.00	30.00
3-Krigstein-a	7.50	22.50	45.00
9-One pg. Frazetta ad	5.00	15.00	30.00
V3#1	4.25	13.00	28.00

ROMANTIC HEARTS
Story Comics/Master/Merit Pubs.: Mar, 1951 - No. 10, Oct, 1952; July, 1953 - No. 12, July, 1955

	GD2.0	FN6.0	NM9.4
1(3/51) (1st Series)	12.00	36.00	85.00
2	6.70	20.00	40.00
3-10: Cameron-a	5.35	16.00	32.00
1(7/53) (2nd Series)-Some say #11 on-c	8.35	25.00	50.00
2	4.25	13.00	28.00
3-12	4.00	12.00	24.00

ROMANTIC LOVE
Avon Periodicals/Realistic (No #14-19): 9-10/49 - #3, 1-2/50; #4, 2-3/51 - #13, 10/52; #20, 3-4/54 - #23, 9-10/54

	GD2.0	FN6.0	NM9.4
1-c-/Avon paperback #252	23.00	69.00	160.00
2-5: 3-c-/paperback Novel Library #12. 4-c-/paperback Diversey Prize Novel #5. 5-c-/paperback Novel Library #34	13.00	39.00	90.00
6- "Thrill Crazy" marijuana story; c-/Avon paperback #207; Kinstler-a	19.00	56.00	130.00
7,8: 8-Astarita-a(2)	11.50	34.00	80.00
9-12: 9-c-/paperback Novel Library #41; Kinstler-a. 10-c-/Avon paperback #212. 11-c-/paperback Novel Library #17; Kinstler-a. 12-c-/paperback Novel Library #13	13.00	39.00	90.00
13,21-23: 22,23-Kinstler-c	11.50	34.00	80.00
20-Kinstler-c/a	12.00	36.00	85.00
nn(1-3/53)(Realistic-r)	9.15	27.00	55.00

NOTE: ***Astarita*** *a-7, 10, 11, 21. Painted c-1-3, 5, 7-11, 13. Photo c-4, 6.*

ROMANTIC LOVE
Quality Comics Group: No. 4, June, 1950

	GD2.0	FN6.0	NM9.4
4 (6/50)(Exist?)	5.85	17.50	35.00
I.W. Reprint #2,3,8: 2-r/Romantic Love #2	1.10	3.30	9.00

ROMANTIC MARRIAGE (Cinderella Love #25 on)
Ziff-Davis/St. John No. 18 on (#1-8: 52 pgs.): #1-3 (1950, no months); #4, 5-6/51 - #17, 9/52; #18, 9/53 - #24, 9/54

	GD2.0	FN6.0	NM9.4
1-Photo-c; Cary Grant/Betsy Drake photo back-c.	19.00	56.00	130.00
2-Painted-c; Anderson-a (also #15)	11.50	34.00	80.00
3-9: 3,4,8,9-Painted-c; 5-7-Photo-c	10.00	30.00	60.00
10-Unusual format; front-c is a painted-c; back-c is a photo-c complete with logo, price, etc.	17.00	51.00	120.00
11-17 13-Photo-c. 15-Signed story by Anderson. 17-(9/52)-Last Z-D issue	9.15	27.00	55.00
18-22,24: 20-Photo-c	9.15	27.00	55.00
23-Baker-c; all stories are reprinted from #15	10.00	30.00	60.00

ROMANTIC PICTURE NOVELETTES
Magazine Enterprises: 1946

	GD2.0	FN6.0	NM9.4
1-Mary Worth-r; Creig Flessel-c	16.00	47.00	110.00

ROMANTIC SECRETS (Becomes Time For Love)
Fawcett/Charlton Comics No. 5 (10/55) on: Sept, 1949 - No. 39, 4/53; No. 5, 10/55 - No. 52, 11/64 (#1-5: photo-c)

	GD2.0	FN6.0	NM9.4
1-(52 pg. issues begin, end #?)	14.00	43.00	100.00
2,3	9.15	27.00	55.00
4,9-Evans-a	10.00	30.00	60.00
5-8,10	5.85	17.50	35.00
11-23	5.35	16.00	32.00
24-Evans-a	7.00	21.00	42.00
25-39('53)	4.25	13.00	28.00
5 (Charlton, 2nd Series)(10/55, formerly Negro Romances #4)	9.15	27.00	55.00
6-10	5.85	17.50	35.00
11-20	2.50	7.50	24.00
21-35: Last 10¢ issue?	2.25	6.75	18.00
36-52('64)	1.75	5.25	14.00

NOTE: ***Bailey*** *a-20.* ***Powell*** *a(1st series)-5, 7, 10, 12, 16, 17, 20, 26, 29, 33, 34, 36, 37.* ***Sekowsky*** *a-26. Photo c(1st series)-1-5, 16, 25, 27, 33.* ***Swayze*** *a(1st series)-16, 18, 19, 23, 26-28, 31, 32, 39.*

ROMANTIC STORY (Cowboy Love #28 on)
Fawcett/Charlton Comics No. 23 on: 11/49 - #22, Sum, 1953; #23, 5/54 - #27, 12/54; #28, 8/55 - #130, 11/73

	GD2.0	FN6.0	NM9.4
1-Photo-c begin, end #24; 52 pgs. begins	16.00	47.00	110.00
2	9.15	27.00	55.00
3-5	7.50	22.50	45.00
6-14	5.85	17.50	35.00
15-Evans-a	7.50	22.50	45.00
16-22(Sum, '53; last Fawcett issue). 21-Toth-a?	4.25	13.00	28.00
23-39: 26,29-Wood swipes	4.25	13.00	28.00
40-(100 pgs.)	10.00	30.00	60.00
41-50	2.50	7.50	20.00
51-80: 57-Hypo needle story	1.75	5.25	14.00
81-99	1.25	3.75	10.00
100	1.50	4.50	12.00
101-130	1.00	3.00	8.00

NOTE: ***Jim Aparo*** *a-94.* ***Powell*** *a-7, 8, 16, 20, 30.* ***Marcus Swayze*** *a-2, 12, 20, 32.*

ROMANTIC THRILLS (See Fox Giants)

ROMANTIC WESTERN
Fawcett Publications: Winter, 1949 - No. 3, June, 1950 (All Photo-c)

	GD2.0	FN6.0	NM9.4
1	20.00	60.00	140.00
2-(Spr/50)-Williamson, McWilliams-a	20.00	60.00	140.00
3	13.50	41.00	95.00

ROMEO TUBBS (...That Lovable Teenager; formerly My Secret Life)
Fox Feature Syndicate/Green Publ. Co. No. 27: No. 26, 5/50 - No. 28, 7/50; No. 1, 1950; No. 27, 12/52

	GD2.0	FN6.0	NM9.4
26-Teen-age	10.00	30.00	70.00
27-Contains Pedro on inside; Wood-a	15.00	45.00	105.00
28, 1	10.00	30.00	60.00

RONALD McDONALD (TV)
Charlton Press (King Features Synd.): Sept, 1970 - No. 4, March, 1971

Roswell: Little Green Man #3 © Bongo Ent.

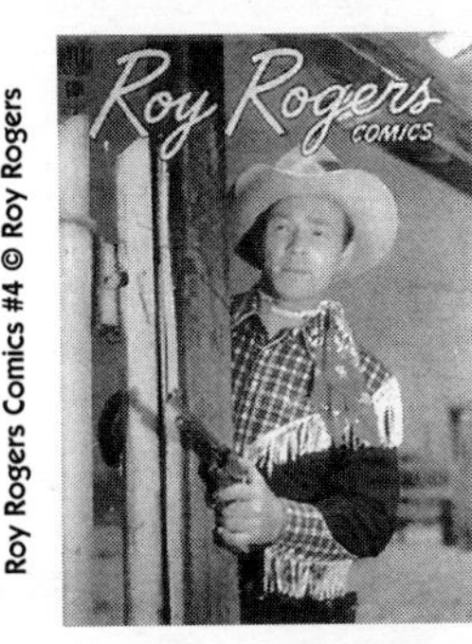

Roy Rogers Comics #4 © Roy Rogers

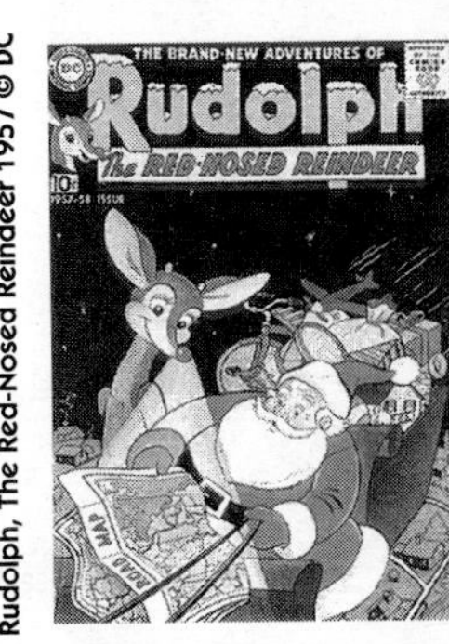

Rudolph, The Red-Nosed Reindeer 1957 © DC

GD2.0 FN6.0 NM9.4 GD2.0 FN6.0 NM9.4

1 5.50 16.50 60.00
2-4 3.50 10.50 35.00
V2#3-Special reprint for McDonald systems; "Not for resale" on cover 4.50 13.50 50.00

RONIN
DC Comics: July, 1983 - No. 6, Aug, 1984 ($2.50, limited series, 52 pgs.)
1-5-Frank Miller-c/a/scripts in all 5.00
6-Scarcer; has fold-out poster. .90 2.70 8.00
Trade paperback (1987, $12.95)-Reprints #1-6 13.00

RONNA
Knight Press: Apr, 1997 ($2.95, B&W, one-shot)
1-Beau Smith-s 3.00

ROOK (See Eerie Magazine & Warren Presents: The Rook)
Warren Publications: Nov, 1979 - No. 14, April, 1982
1-Nino-a 1.75 5.25 14.00
2-14: 3,4-Toth-a 1.10 3.30 9.00

ROOK
Harris Comics: No. 0, Jun, 1995 - No. 4, 1995 ($2.95)
0-4: 0-short stories (3) w/preview. 4-Brereton-c. 3.00

ROOKIE COP (Formerly Crime and Justice?)
Charlton Comics: No. 27, Nov, 1955 - No. 33, Aug, 1957
27 8.35 25.00 50.00
28-33 5.85 17.50 35.00

ROOM 222 (TV)
Dell Publishing Co.: Jan, 1970; No. 2, May, 1970 - No. 4, Jan, 1971
1 4.00 12.00 45.00
2-4: 2,4-Photo-c. 3-Marijuana story. 4 r/#1 2.50 7.50 28.00

ROOTIE KAZOOTIE (TV)(See 3-D-ell)
Dell Publishing Co.: No. 415, Aug, 1952 - No. 6, Oct-Dec, 1954
Four Color 415 (#1) 10.00 30.00 110.00
Four Color 459,502(#2,3), 4(4-6/54)-6 6.40 19.00 70.00

ROOTS OF THE SWAMP THING
DC Comics: July, 1986 - No.5, Nov, 1986 ($2.00, Baxter paper, 52 pgs.)
1-5: r/Swamp Thing #1-10 by Wrightson & House of Mystery-r. 1-new Wrightson-c (2-5 reprinted covers). 3.50

ROSE N' GUNN
Bishop Press: Jan, 1995 - No. 6, May, 1996 ($2.95, B&W, mature)
1-6, Creator's Choice ($2.95)-reprints w/pin-ups 3.00

ROSE N'GUNN
London Night Studios: June, 1996 - Aug, 1996 ($3.00, B&W, mature)
1,2 3.00
1-($6.00)-Blood & Glory Edition 6.00

ROSWELL: LITTLE GREEN MAN (See Simpsons Comics #19-22)
Bongo Comics: 1996 - Present ($2.95, quarterly)
1-6 3.50
...Walks Among Us ('97, $12.95, TPB) r/ #1-3 & Simpsons flip books 13.00

ROUNDUP (...Western Crime Stories)
D. S. Publishing Co.: July-Aug, 1948 - No. 5, Mar-Apr, 1949 (All 52 pgs.)
1-Kiefer-a 19.00 58.00 135.00
2-5: 2-Marijuana drug mention story 13.00 39.00 90.00

ROYAL ROY
Marvel Comics (Star Comics): May, 1985 - No.6, Mar, 1986 (Children's book)
1-6 2.00

ROY CAMPANELLA, BASEBALL HERO
Fawcett Publications: 1950 (Brooklyn Dodgers)
nn-Photo-c; life story 56.00 169.00 450.00

ROY ROGERS (See March of Comics #17, 35, 47, 62, 68, 73, 77, 86, 91, 100, 105, 116, 121, 131, 136, 146, 151, 161, 167, 176, 191, 206, 221, 236, 250)

ROY ROGERS AND TRIGGER
Gold Key: Apr, 1967
1-Photo-c; reprints 4.50 13.50 45.00

ROY ROGERS COMICS (See Western Roundup under Dell Giants)
Dell Publishing Co.: No. 38, 4/44 - No. 177, 12/47 (#38-166: 52 pgs.)
Four Color 38 (1944)-49 pg. story; photo front/back-c on all 4-Color issues (1st western comic with photo-c) 200.00 600.00 2200.00
Four Color 63 (1945)-Color photos on all four-c 46.00 139.00 510.00
Four Color 86,95 (1945) 34.00 102.00 375.00
Four Color 109 (1946) 25.00 75.00 275.00
Four Color 117,124,137,144 18.00 53.00 195.00
Four Color 153,160,166: 166-48 pg. story 15.50 46.50 170.00
Four Color 177 (36 pgs.)-32 pg. story 15.50 46.50 170.00

ROY ROGERS COMICS (...& Trigger #92(8/55)-on)(Roy starred in Republic movies, radio & TV) (Singing cowboy) (Also see Dale Evans, It Really Happened #8, Queen of the West Dale Evans, & Roy Rogers' Trigger)
Dell Publishing Co.: Jan, 1948 - No. 145, Sept-Oct, 1961 (#1-19: 36 pgs.)
1-Roy, his horse Trigger, & Chuck Wagon Charley's Tales begin; photo-c begin, end #145 75.00 225.00 825.00
2 24.00 74.00 270.00
3-5 17.00 52.00 190.00
6-10 13.00 40.00 145.00
11-19: 19-Chuck Wagon Charley's Tales ends 10.00 30.00 110.00
20 (52 pgs.)-Trigger feature begins, ends #46 10.00 30.00 110.00
21-30 (52 pgs.) 8.50 26.00 95.00
31-46 (52 pgs.): 37-X-Mas-c 6.70 20.00 75.00
47-56 (36 pgs.): 47-Chuck Wagon Charley's Tales returns, ends #133. 49-X-mas-c. 55-Last photo back-c 5.00 15.00 55.00
57 (52 pgs.)-Heroin drug propaganda story 5.50 16.50 60.00
58-70 (52 pgs.): 58-Heroin drug use/dealing story. 61-X-Mas-c 5.00 15.00 55.00
71-80 (52 pgs.): 73-X-Mas-c 4.00 12.00 45.00
81-91 (36 pgs. #81-on): 85-X-Mas-c 3.80 11.50 40.00
92-99,101-110,112-118: 92-Title changed to Roy Rogers and Trigger (8/55) 3.80 11.50 40.00
100-Trigger feature returns, ends #131 5.00 15.00 55.00
111,119-124-Toth-a 5.50 16.50 60.00
125-131: 125-Toth-a (1 pg.) 3.25 10.00 36.00
132-144-Manning-a. 132-1st Dale Evans-sty by Russ Manning. 138,144-Dale Evans featured 4.35 13.00 48.00
145-Last issue 5.50 16.50 60.00
NOTE: ***Buscema** a-74-108(2 stories each). **Manning** a-123, 124, 132-144. **Marsh** a-110. Photo back-c No. 1-9, 11-35, 38-55.*

ROY ROGERS' TRIGGER (TV)
Dell Publishing Co.: No. 329, May, 1951 - No. 17, June-Aug, 1955
Four Color 329 (#1)-Painted-c 11.00 33.00 120.00
2 (9-11/51)-Photo-c 9.50 29.00 105.00
3-5: 3-Painted-c begin, end #17, most by S. Savitt 4.00 12.00 45.00
6-17: Title merges with Roy Rogers after #17 2.90 8.75 32.00

ROY ROGERS WESTERN CLASSICS
AC Comics: 1989 -No. 4 ($2.95/$3.95, 44pgs.) (24 pgs. color, 16 pgs. B&W)
1-4: 1-Dale Evans-r by Manning, Trigger-r by Buscema; photo covers & interior photos by Roy & Dale. 2-Buscema-r (3); photo-c & B&W photos inside. 3-Dale Evans-r by Manning; Trigger-r by Buscema plus other Buscema-r; photo-c. 4.00

RUDOLPH, THE RED-NOSED REINDEER
National Per. Publ.: 1950 - No. 13, Winter, 1962-63 (Issues are not numbered)
1950 issue (#1); Grossman-c/a begins 20.00 60.00 140.00
1951-53 issues (3 total) 11.50 34.00 80.00
1954/55, 55/56, 56/57 10.00 30.00 65.00
1957/58, 58/59, 59/60, 60/61, 61/62 5.50 16.50 55.00
1962/63 (rare) 9.50 28.50 95.00
NOTE: *The 1962-63 issue is 84 pages. 9? total issues published. Has games & puzzles also.*

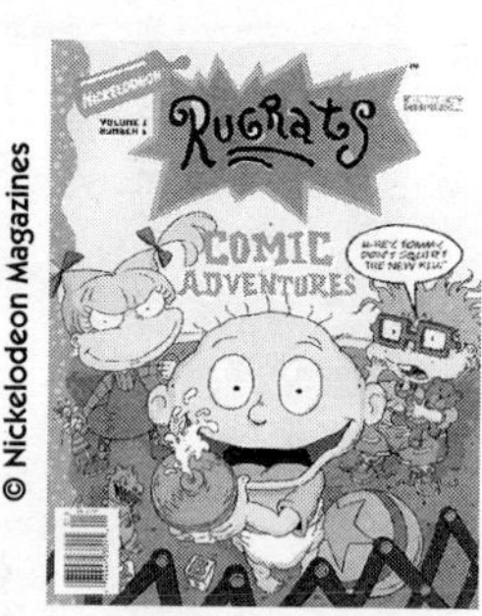
Rugrats Comic Adventures #1 © Nickelodeon Magazines

Rulah Jungle Goddess #18 © FOX

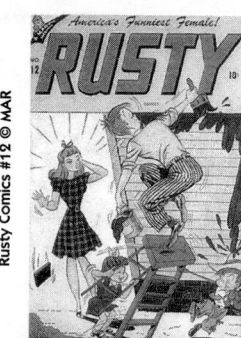

Rusty Comics #12 © MAR

GD2.0 FN6.0 NM9.4

RUDOLPH, THE RED-NOSED REINDEER (Also see Limited Collectors' Edition C-20, C-24, C-33, C-42, C-50; and All-New Collectors' Edition C-53 & C-60)
National Per. Publ.: Christmas 1972 (Treasury-size)

nn-Precursor to Limited Collectors' Edition title (scarce) (implied to be Lim. Coll .Ed.C-20) 25.00 75.00 250.00

RUFF AND REDDY (TV)
Dell Publ. Co.: No. 937, 9/58 - No. 12, 1-3/62 (Hanna-Barbera)(#9 on: 15¢)

Four Color 937(#1)(1st Hanna-Barbera comic book) 12.00 36.00 130.00
Four Color 981,1038 8.00 23.00 85.00
4(1-3/60)-12: 8-Last 10¢ issue 5.90 18.00 65.00

RUGGED ACTION (Strange Stories of Suspense #5 on)
Atlas Comics (CSI): Dec, 1954 - No. 4, June, 1955

1-Brodsky-c 12.00 36.00 85.00
2-4: 2-Last precode (2/55) 9.15 27.00 55.00
NOTE: ***Ayers** a-2, 3. **Maneely** c-2, 3. **Severin** a-2.*

RUGRATS COMIC ADVENTURES (TV)
Nickelodeon Magazines: 1999 - Present ($2.95, magazine size)

1,2 3.00

RUINS
Marvel Comics (Alterniverse): July, 1995 - No. 2, Sept, 1995 ($5.00, painted, limited series)

1,2: Phil Sheldon from Marvels; Warren Ellis scripts; acetate-c 5.00

RULAH JUNGLE GODDESS (Formerly Zoot; I Loved #28 on) (Also see All Top Comics & Terrors of the Jungle)
Fox Features Syndicate: No. 17, Aug, 1948 - No. 27, June, 1949

17 87.00 262.00 700.00
18-Classic girl-fight interior splash 62.00 187.00 500.00
19,20 59.00 178.00 475.00
21-Used in **SOTI**, pg. 388,389 62.00 187.00 500.00
22-Used in **SOTI**, pg. 22,23 59.00 178.00 475.00
23-27 45.00 135.00 360.00
NOTE: ***Kamen** c-17-19, 21, 22.*

RUNAWAY, THE (See Movie Classics)

RUN BABY RUN
Logos International: 1974 (39¢)

nn-By Tony Tallarico from Nicky Cruz's book 4.00

RUN, BUDDY, RUN (TV)
Gold Key: June, 1967 (Photo-c)

1 (10204-706) 2.50 7.50 22.00

RUNE (See Curse of Rune, Sludge & all other Ultraverse titles for previews)
Malibu Comics (Ultraverse): 1994 - No. 9, Apr, 1995 ($1.95)

0-Obtained by sending coupons from 11 comics; came w/Solution #0, poster, temporary tattoo, card 1.00 3.00 8.00
1,2,4-9: 1-Barry Windsor-Smith-c/a/stories begin, ends #6. 5-1st app. of Gemini. 6-Prime & Mantra app. 2.00
1-(1/94)-"Ashcan" edition flip book w/Wrath #1 2.00
1-Ultra 5000 Limited silver foil edition 4.00
3-(3/94, $3.50, 68 pgs.)-Flip book w/Ultraverse Premiere #1 3.50
Giant Size 1 ($2.50, 44 pgs.)-B.Smith story & art. 2.50

RUNE (2nd Series)(Formerly Curse of Rune)(See Ultraverse Unlimited #1)
Malibu Comics (Ultraverse): Infinity, Sept, 1995 - V2#7, Apr, 1996 ($1.50)

Infinity, V2#1-7: Infinity-Black September tie-in; black-c & painted-c exist. 1,3-7-Marvel's Adam Warlock app; regular & painted-c exist. 2-Flip book w/ "Phoenix Resurrection" Pt. 6. 2.00
...Vs. Venom 1 (12/95, $3.95) 4.00

RUNE: HEARTS OF DARKNESS
Malibu Comics (Ultraverse): Sept, 1996 - No. 3, Nov, 1996 ($1.50, lim. series)

1-3: Doug Moench scripts & Kyle Hotz-c/a; flip books w/6 pg. Rune story by the Pander Bros. 2.00

RUNE/SILVER SURFER
Marvel Comics/Malibu Comics (Ultraverse): Apr, 1995 ($5.95/$2.95, one-shot)

1 ($5.95, direct market)-BWS-c 6.00
1 ($2.95, newstand)-BWS-c 3.00
1-Collector's limited edition 6.00

RUST
Now Comics: 7/87 - No. 15, 11/88; V2#1, 2/89 - No. 7, 1989 ($1.50/$1.75)

1-15,V2#1-7: 12-(8/88)-5 pg. preview of The Terminator (1st app.) 2.00

RUST
Caliber Comics: 1996/1997 ($2.95, B&W)

1,2 3.00

RUSTLERS, THE (See Zane Grey Four Color 532)

RUSTY, BOY DETECTIVE
Good Comics/Lev Gleason: Mar-April, 1955 - No. 5, Nov, 1955

1-Bob Wood, Carl Hubbell-a begins 8.35 25.00 50.00
2-5 5.00 15.00 30.00

RUSTY COMICS (Formerly Kid Movie Comics; Rusty and Her Family #21, 22; The Kelleys #23 on; see Millie The Model)
Marvel Comics (HPC): No. 12, Apr, 1947 - No. 22, Sept, 1949

12-Mitzi app. 18.00 54.00 125.00
13 10.00 30.00 65.00
14-Wolverton's Powerhouse Pepper (4 pgs.) plus Kurtzman's "Hey Look" 20.00 60.00 140.00
15-17-Kurtzman's "Hey Look" 14.00 43.00 100.00
18,19 9.15 27.00 55.00
20-Kurtzman-a (5 pgs.) 15.00 45.00 105.00
21,22-Kurtzman-a (17 & 22 pgs.) 20.00 60.00 140.00

RUSTY DUGAN (See Holyoke One-Shot #2)

RUSTY RILEY
Dell Publishing Co.: No. 418, Aug, 1952 - No. 554, April, 1954 (Frank Godwin strip reprints)

Four Color 418 (...a Boy, a Horse, and a Dog #1 3.60 11.00 40.00
Four Color #451(2/53), 486 ('53), 554 2.75 8.00 30.00

SAARI ("The Jungle Goddess")
P. L. Publishing Co.: November, 1951

1 40.00 120.00 320.00

SABAN POWERHOUSE (TV)
Acclaim Books: 1997 - Present ($4.50, digest size)

1,2-Power Rangers, BeetleBorgs, and others 4.50

SABAN PRESENTS POWER RANGERS TURBO VS. BEETLEBORGS METALLIX (TV)
Acclaim Books: 1997 ($4.50, digest size, one-shot)

nn 4.50

SABAN'S MIGHTY MORPHIN POWER RANGERS
Hamilton Comics: Dec, 1994 - No. 6, May, 1995 ($1.95, limited series)

1-6: 1-w/bound-in Power Ranger Barcode Card 2.00

SABAN'S MIGHTY MORPHIN POWER RANGERS (TV)
Marvel Comics: 1995 - No. 8, 1996 ($1.75)

1-8 2.00

SABAN'S NINJA RANGERS
Hamilton Comics: Dec, 1995 - No. 4, Mar, 1995 ($1.95, limited series)

1-4: Flip book w/Saban's V.R. Troopers 2.00

SABAN'S V.R. TROOPERS (See Saban's Ninja Rangers)

SABLE (Formerly Jon Sable, Freelance; also see Mike Grell's...)
First Comics: Mar, 1988 - No. 27, May, 1990 ($1.75/$1.95)

1-27: 10-Begin $1.95-c 2.00

SABRE (See Eclipse Graphic Album Series)
Eclipse Comics: Aug, 1982 - No. 14, Aug, 1985 (Baxter paper #4 on)

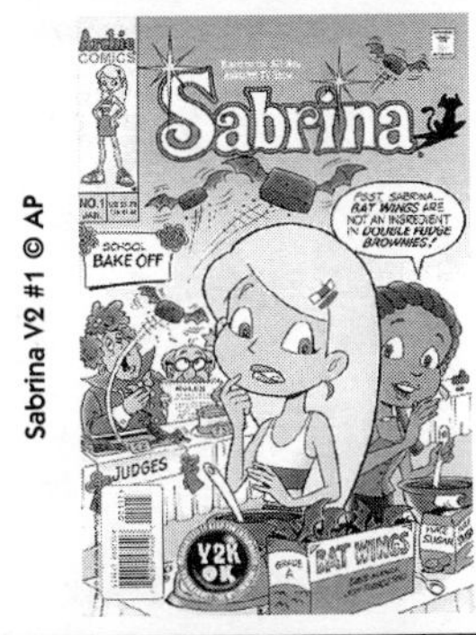

Sabrina V2 #1 © AP

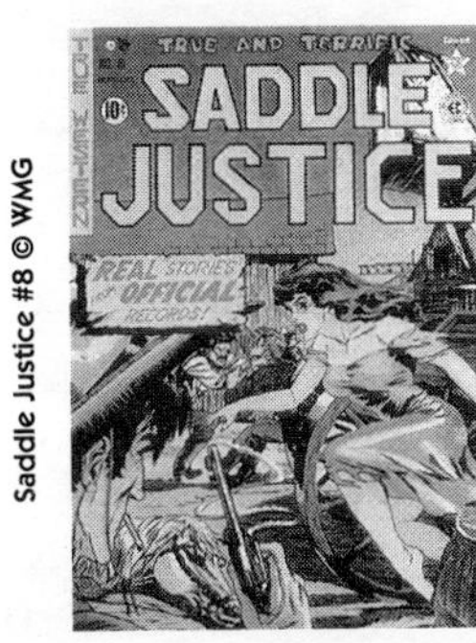

Saddle Justice #8 © WMG

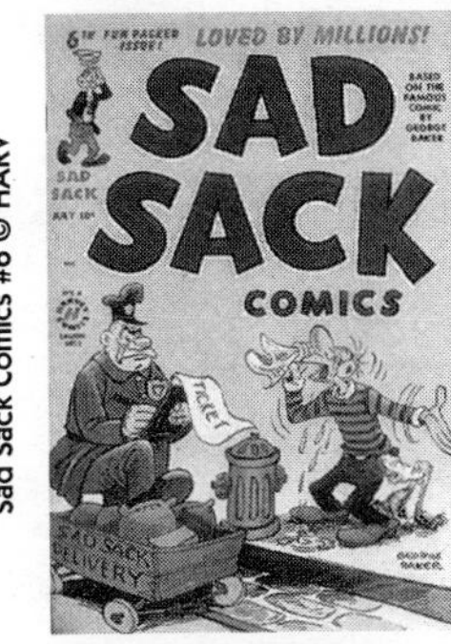

Sad Sack Comics #6 © HARV

GD2.0 FN6.0 NM9.4

1-14: 1-Sabre & Morrigan Tales begin. 4-6-Incredible Seven origin 2.00

SABRETOOTH (See Iron Fist, Power Man, X-Factor #10 & X-Men)
Marvel Comics: Aug, 1993 - No. 4, Nov, 1993 ($2.95, lim. series, coated paper)

1-4: 1-Die-cut-c. 3-Wolverine app. 4.00
...Special 1 "In the Red Zone"(1995, $4.95) Chromium wraparound-c 6.00
V2 #1 (1/98, $5.95, one-shot) Wildchild app. 6.00
Trade paperback (12/94, $12.95) r/#1-4 13.00

SABRETOOTH AND MYSTIQUE (See Mystique and Sabretooth)

SABRETOOTH CLASSIC
Marvel Comics: May, 1994 - No. 15, July, 1995 ($1.50)

1-15: 1-3-r/Power Man & Iron Fist #66,78,84. 4-r/Spec. S-M #116. 9-Uncanny X-Men #212, 10-r/Uncanny X-Men #213. 11-0r/ Daredevil #238. 12-r/Classic X-Men #10 3.00

SABRINA (Volume 2) (Based on animated series)
Archie Publications: Jan, 2000 - Present ($1.79)

1,2: 1-Teen-age Witch magically reverted to 12 years old 2.00

SABRINA'S CHRISTMAS MAGIC (See Archie Giant Series Magazine #196, 207, 220, 231, 243, 455, 467, 479, 491, 503, 515)

SABRINA'S HALLOWEEN SPOOOKTACULAR
Archie Publications: 1993 - 1995 ($2.00, 52 pgs.)

1-Neon orange ink-c; bound-in poster 4.00
2,3 3.00

SABRINA, THE TEEN-AGE WITCH (TV)(See Archie Giant Series, Archie's Madhouse 22, Archie's TV..., Chilling Advs. In Sorcery, Little Archie #59)
Archie Publications: April, 1971 - No. 77, Jan, 1983 (52 pg.Giants No. 1-17)

	GD2.0	FN6.0	NM9.4
1-52 pgs. begin, end #17	9.50	28.50	105.00
2-Archie's group x-over	5.00	15.00	50.00
3-5: 3,4-Archie's Group x-over	3.20	9.60	32.00
6-10	2.50	7.50	25.00
11-17(2/74)	2.50	7.50	20.00
18-30	1.85	5.50	15.00
31-40(8/77)	1.50	4.50	12.00
41-60(6/80)	1.00	3.00	8.00
61-77		2.40	6.00

SABRINA, THE TEEN-AGE WITCH
Archie Publications: 1996 ($1.50, 32 pgs., one-shot)

1-Updated origin 3.00

SABRINA, THE TEEN-AGE WITCH (Continues in Sabrina, Vol. 2)
Archie Publications: May, 1997 - No. 32, Dec, 1999 ($1.50/$1.75/$1.79)

1-Photo-c with Melissa Joan Hart 4.00
2-10: 9-Begin $1.75-c 3.00
11-32: 24-Begin $1.79-c. 28-Sonic the Hedgehog-c/app. 2.00

SABU, "ELEPHANT BOY" (Movie; formerly My Secret Story)
Fox Features Syndicate: No. 30, June, 1950 - No. 2, Aug, 1950

	GD2.0	FN6.0	NM9.4
30(#1)-Wood-a; photo-c from movie	25.00	75.00	175.00
2-Photo-c from movie; Kamen-a	18.00	54.00	125.00

SACHS & VIOLENS
Marvel Comics (Epic Comics): Nov, 1993 - No. 4, July, 1994 ($2.25, limited series, mature)

1-($2.75)-Embossed-c w/bound-in trading card 2.75
1-($3.50)-Platinum edition (1 for each 10 ordered) 4.00
2-4: Perez-c/a; bound-in trading card: 2-(5/94) 2.25

SACRAMENTS, THE
Catechetical Guild Educational Society: Oct, 1955 (25¢)

	GD2.0	FN6.0	NM9.4
304	3.20	8.00	16.00

SACRED AND THE PROFANE, THE (See Eclipse Graphic Album Series #9 & Epic Illustrated #20)

SADDLE JUSTICE (Happy Houlihans #1,2) (Saddle Romances #9 on)
E. C. Comics: No. 3, Spring, 1948 - No. 8, Sept-Oct, 1949

	GD2.0	FN6.0	NM9.4
3-The 1st E.C. by Bill Gaines to break away from M. C. Gaines' old Educational Comics format. Craig, Feldstein, H. C. Kiefer, & Stan Asch-a; mentioned in Love and Death	40.00	120.00	340.00
4-1st Graham Ingels-a for E.C.	37.00	113.00	320.00
5-8-Ingels-a in all	35.00	106.00	300.00

NOTE: ***Craig*** *and* ***Feldstein*** *art in most issues. Canadian reprints known; see Table of Contents.* ***Craig*** *c-3, 4.* ***Ingels*** *c-5-8. #4 contains a biography of* ***Craig.***

SADDLE ROMANCES (Saddle Justice #3-8; Weird Science #12 on)
E. C. Comics: No. 9, Nov-Dec, 1949 - No. 11, Mar-Apr, 1950

	GD2.0	FN6.0	NM9.4
9,11: 9-Ingels-c/a. 11-Ingels-a; Feldstein-c	37.00	110.00	310.00
10-Wood's 1st work at E. C.; Ingels-a; Feldstein-c	37.00	113.00	320.00

NOTE: *Canadian reprints known; see Table of Contents.* ***Wood/Harrison*** *a-10, 11.*

SADE
Bishop Press/London Night Studios: No. 0, May, 1995 - No. 2, 1996 ($2.95, B&W, mature)

0-2: All Bishop Press issues. 1-Razor app; w/pin-ups 3.00
1($3.00)-London Night Studio's Encore Edition. 3.00
Special 1-Razor app. 3.00
Special 1 ($4.95, limited edition)-Razor app. 5.00

SADE
London Night Studios: June, 1996 - No. 4 ($3.00, B&W, mature)

1-4, 1-Balance of Pain Edition 3.00

SADE AND ROSE & GUNN CONFEDERATE MISTS
Bishop Press: Mar, 1996 ($3.00, B&W, one-shot, mature)

1-w/pin-ups. 3.00

SADIE SACK (See Harvey Hits #93)

SAD SACK AND THE SARGE
Harvey Publications: Sept, 1957 - No. 155, June, 1982

	GD2.0	FN6.0	NM9.4
1	12.00	36.00	120.00
2	5.50	16.50	55.00
3-10	4.00	12.00	40.00
11-20	3.50	10.50	35.00
21-30	2.50	7.50	22.00
31-50	1.75	5.25	14.00
51-70	1.00	3.00	10.00
71-90,97-99	.85	2.60	7.00
91-96: All 52 pg. Giants	1.20	3.60	12.00
100	.90	2.70	9.00
101-120			5.00
121-155			4.00

SAD SACK COMICS (See Harvey Collector's Comics #16, Little Sad Sack, Tastee Freez Comics #4 & True Comics #55)
Harvey Publications/Lorne-Harvey Publications (Recollections) #288 On: Sept, 1949 - No. 287, Oct, 1982; No. 288, 1992 - No. 293?, 1993

	GD2.0	FN6.0	NM9.4
1-Infinity-c; Little Dot begins (1st app.); civilian issues begin, end #21; based on comic strip	40.00	120.00	400.00
2-Flying Fool by Powell	20.00	60.00	200.00
3	11.00	32.00	110.00
4-10	8.00	24.00	80.00
11-21	5.50	16.50	55.00
22-("Back In The Army Again" on covers #22-36); "The Specialist" story about Sad Sack's return to Army	3.50	10.50	35.00
23-50	2.50	7.50	22.00
51-80,100: 62-"The Specialist" reprinted	2.25	6.75	18.00
81-99	1.85	5.50	15.00
101-140	1.20	3.60	12.00
141-170,200	1.00	3.00	10.00
171-199	.90	2.70	9.00
201-207: 207-Last 12¢ issue	1.00	2.80	7.00
208-222		2.40	6.00
223-228 (25¢ Giants, 52 pgs.)	1.00	3.00	10.00
229-285			4.00
286,287-Limited distribution		2.40	6.00

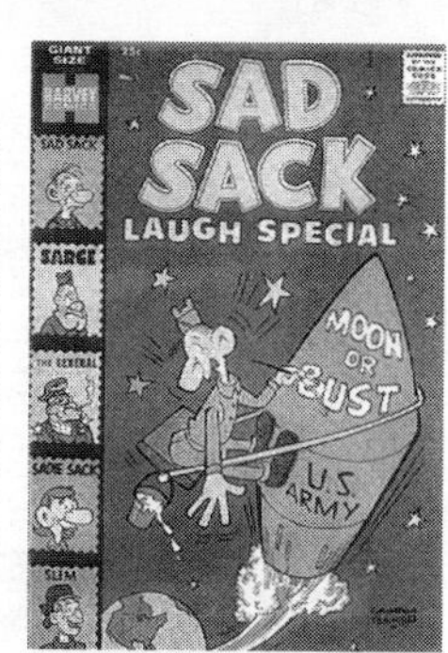

Sad Sack Laugh Special #1 © HARV

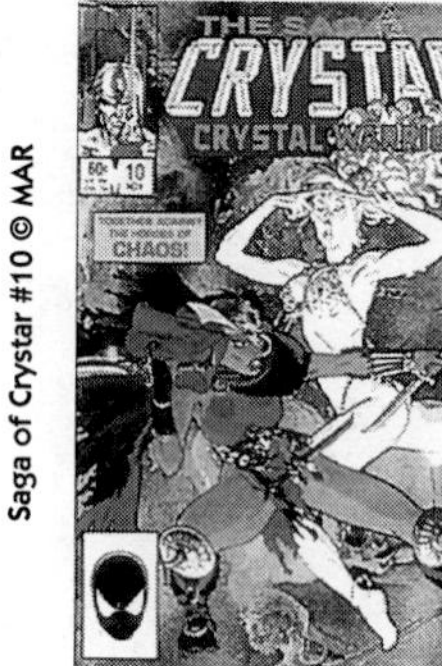

Saga of Crystar #10 © MAR

The Saint #4 © AVON

288,289 ($2.75, 1992): 289-50th anniversary issue — 5.00
290-293 ($1.00, 1993, B&W) — 3.00
3-D 1 (1/54, 25¢)-Came with 2 pairs of glasses; titled "Harvey 3-D Hits" — 16.50 50.00 165.00
...At Home for the Holidays 1 (1993, no-c price)-Publ. by Lorne-Harvey' X-Mas issue — 2.00

NOTE: *The Sad Sack Comics comic book was a spin-off from a Sunday Newspaper strip launched through John Wheeler's Bell Syndicate. The previous Sunday page and the first 21 comics depicted the Sad Sack in civvies. Unpopularity caused the Sunday page to be discontinued in the early '50s. Meanwhile Sad Sack returned to the Army, by popular demand, in issue No. 22, remaining there ever since. Incidentally, relatively few of the first 21 issues were ever collected and remain scarce due to this.*

SAD SACK FUN AROUND THE WORLD
Harvey Publications: 1974 (no month)

1-About Great Britain — 1.40 4.20 14.00

SAD SACK GOES HOME
Harvey Publications: 1951 (16 pgs. in color, no cover price)

nn-By George Baker — 4.50 13.50 45.00

SAD SACK LAUGH SPECIAL
Harvey Publications: Winter, 1958-59 - No. 93, Feb, 1977 (#1-9: 84 pgs.; #10-60: 68 pgs.; #61-76: 52 pgs.)

	GD2.0	FN6.0	NM9.4
1-Giant 25¢ issues begin	10.00	30.00	100.00
2	5.00	15.00	50.00
3-10	3.50	10.50	35.00
11-30	2.80	8.40	28.00
31-60: 31-1st app. Hi-Fi Tweeter. 60-Last 68 pg. Giant	2.00	6.00	16.00
61-76-(All 52 pg. issues)	1.20	3.60	12.00
77-93		2.40	6.00

SAD SACK NAVY, GOBS 'N' GALS
Harvey Publications: Aug, 1972 - No. 8, Oct, 1973

	GD2.0	FN6.0	NM9.4
1: 52 pg. Giant	1.80	5.40	18.00
2-8	1.00	3.00	10.00

SAD SACK'S ARMY LIFE (See Harvey Hits #8, 17, 22, 28, 32, 39, 43, 47, 51, 55, 58, 61, 64, 67, 70)

SAD SACK'S ARMY LIFE (...Parade #1-57, ...Today #58 on)
Harvey Publications: Oct, 1963 - No. 60, Nov, 1975; No. 61, May, 1976

	GD2.0	FN6.0	NM9.4
1-(68 pg. issues begin)	5.50	16.50	55.00
2-10	2.80	8.40	28.00
11-20	1.50	4.50	15.00
21-34: Last 68 pg. issue	1.20	3.60	12.00
35-51: All 52 pgs.	1.00	3.00	10.00
52-61		2.40	6.00

SAD SACK'S FUNNY FRIENDS (See Harvey Hits #75)
Harvey Publications: Dec, 1955 - No. 75, Oct, 1969

	GD2.0	FN6.0	NM9.4
1	9.00	27.00	90.00
2-10	4.50	13.50	45.00
11-20	2.50	7.50	22.00
21-30	1.40	4.20	14.00
31-50	1.20	3.60	12.00
51-75	1.00	3.00	10.00

SAD SACK'S MUTTSY (See Harvey Hits #74, 77, 80, 82, 84, 87, 89, 92, 96, 99, 102, 105, 108, 111, 113, 115, 117, 119, 121)

SAD SACK USA (...Vacation #8)
Harvey Publications: Nov, 1972 - No. 7, Nov, 1973; No. 8, Oct, 1974

	GD2.0	FN6.0	NM9.4
1	1.50	4.50	15.00
2-8	.90	2.70	8.00

SAD SACK WITH SARGE & SADIE
Harvey Publications: Sept, 1972 - No. 8, Nov, 1973

	GD2.0	FN6.0	NM9.4
1-(52 pg. Giant)	1.80	5.40	18.00
2-8	.90	2.70	8.00

SAD SAD SACK WORLD
Harvey Publ.: Oct, 1964 - No. 46, Dec, 1973 (#1-31: 68 pgs.; #32-38: 52 pgs.)

	GD2.0	FN6.0	NM9.4
1	5.00	15.00	50.00
2-10	2.50	7.50	25.00
11-20	2.00	6.00	20.00
21-31: 31-Last 68 pg. issue	1.80	5.40	18.00
32-39-(All 52 pgs)	1.20	3.60	12.00
40-46	.85	2.60	7.00

SAFEST PLACE IN THE WORLD, THE
Dark Horse Comics: 1993 ($2.50, one-shot)

1-Steve Ditko-c/a/scripts — 2.50

SAFETY-BELT MAN
Sirius Entertainment: June, 1994 - No. 6, 1995 ($2.50, B&W)

1-6: 1-Horan-s/Dark One-a/Sprouse-c. 2,3-Warren-c. 4-Linsner back-up story. 5,6-Crilley-a — 3.00

SAFETY-BELT MAN ALL HELL
Sirius Entertainment: June, 1996 - No. 6, Mar, 1997 ($2.95, color)

1-6-Horan-s/Fillbach Bros.-a — 3.00

SAGA OF BIG RED, THE
Omaha World-Herald: Sept, 1976 ($1.25) (In color)

nn-by Win Mumma; story of the Nebraska Cornhuskers (sports) — 3.00

SAGA OF CRYSTAR, CRYSTAL WARRIOR, THE
Marvel Comics: May, 1983 - No. 11, Feb, 1985 (Remco toy tie-in)

1 (Baxter paper) — 3.00
2-11: 3-Dr. Strange app. 3-11-Golden-c (painted-4,5). 6-Nightcrawler app; Golden-c.11-Alpha Flight app. — 2.00

SAGA OF RA'S AL GHUL, THE
DC Comics: Jan, 1988 - No. 4, Apr, 1988 ($2.50, limited series)

1-4-r/N. Adams Batman — 5.00

SAGA OF SABAN'S MIGHTY MORPHIN POWER RANGERS (Also see Saban's Mighty Morphin Power Rangers)
Hamilton Comics: 1995 - No. 4, 1995 ($1.95, limited series)

1-4 — 2.00

SAGA OF THE SWAMP THING, THE (See Swamp Thing)

SAGA OF THE ORIGINAL HUMAN TORCH
Marvel Comics: Apr, 1990 - No. 4, July, 1990 ($1.50, limited series)

1-4: 1-Origin; Buckler-c/a(p). 3-Hitler-c — 2.00

SAGA OF THE SUB-MARINER, THE
Marvel Comics: Nov, 1988 - No. 12, Oct, 1989 ($1.25/$1.50 #5 on)

1-12: 9-Original X-Men app. — 2.00

SAILOR MOON (Manga)
Mixx Entertainment Inc.: 1998 - Present ($2.95)

1 — 4.00
1-(San Diego edition) — 10.00
2-16 — 3.00
... Rini's Moon Stick 1 — 15.00

SAILOR ON THE SEA OF FATE (See First Comics Graphic Novel #11)

SAILOR SWEENEY (Navy Action #1-11, 15 on)
Atlas Comics (CDS): No. 12, July, 1956 - No. 14, Nov, 1956

12-14: 12-Shores-a. 13-Severin-c — 8.00 24.00 48.00

SAINT, THE (Also see Movie Comics(DC) #2 & Silver Streak #18)
Avon Periodicals: Aug, 1947 - No. 12, Mar, 1952

	GD2.0	FN6.0	NM9.4
1-Kamen bondage-c/a	69.00	206.00	550.00
2	40.00	120.00	300.00
3,4: 4-Lingerie panels	33.00	99.00	230.00
5-Spanking panel	39.00	116.00	270.00
6-Miss Fury app. by Tarpe Mills (14 pgs.)	41.00	123.00	325.00
7-c-/Avon paperback #118	26.00	77.00	180.00
8,9(12/50): Saint strip-r in #8-12; 9-Kinstler-c	23.00	69.00	160.00

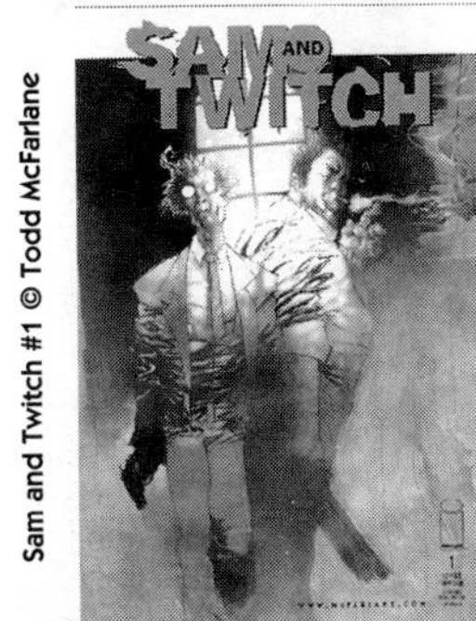

Sam and Twitch #1 © Todd McFarlane

Samson #3 © FOX

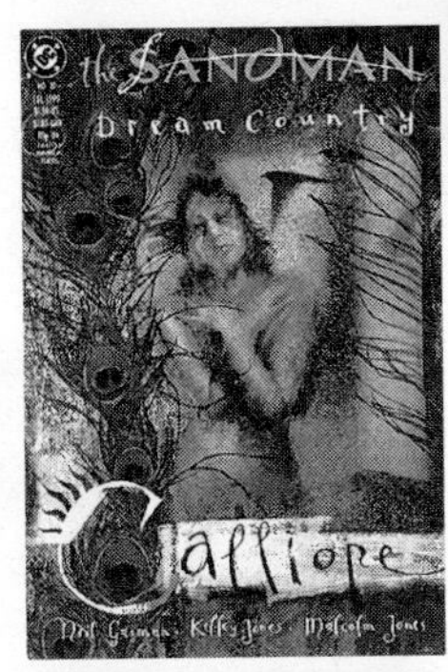

Sandman #17 © DC

GD2.0 FN6.0 NM9.4

10-Wood-a, 1 pg; c-/Avon paperback #289 23.00 69.00 160.00
11 16.00 47.00 110.00
12-c-/Avon paperback #123 19.00 56.00 130.00
NOTE: *Lucky Dale, Girl Detective in #1,2,4,6.* **Hollingsworth** *a-4, 6. Painted-c 7, 8, 10-12.*

ST. GEORGE
Marvel Comics (Epic Comics): June, 1988 - No.8, Oct, 1989 ($1.25,/$1.50)
1-8: Sienkiewicz-c 3-begin $1.50-c 2.00

SAINT GERMAINE
Caliber Comics: 1997 - Present ($2.95)
1-8: 1,5-Alternate covers 3.00

SAINT SINNER (See Razorline)
Marvel Comics (Razorline): Oct, 1993 - No. 7, Apr, 1994 ($1.75)
1-($2.50)-Foil embossed-c; created by Clive Barker 2.50
2-7: 5-Ectokid x-over 2.00

ST. SWITHIN'S DAY
Trident Comics: Apr, 1990 ($2.50, one-shot)
1-Grant Morrison scripts 3.00

ST. SWITHIN'S DAY
Oni Press: Mar, 1998 ($2.95, B&W, one-shot)
1-Grant Morrison-s/Paul Grist-a 3.00

SALOMÉ (See Night Music #6)

SAM AND MAX, FREELANCE POLICE SPECIAL
Fishwrap Prod./Comico: 1987 ($1.75, B&W); Jan, 1989 ($2.75, 44 pgs.)
1 ($1.75, B&W, Fishwrap) 2.00
2 ($2.75, color, Comico) 2.75

SAM AND TWITCH (See Spawn)
Image Comics (Todd McFarlane Prod.): Aug, 1999 - Present ($2.50)
1-3-Bendis-s/Medina-a 2.50

SAM HILL PRIVATE EYE
Close-Up (Archie): 1950 - No. 7, 1951
1 16.00 47.00 110.00
2 10.00 30.00 65.00
3-7 9.15 27.00 55.00

SAM SLADE ROBOHUNTER
Quality Comics: Oct, 1986 - No. 31, 1989 ($1.25/$1.50)
1-31 2.00

SAMSON (1st Series) (Captain Aero #7 on; see Big 3 Comics)
Fox Features Syndicate: Fall, 1940 - No. 6, Sept, 1941 (See Fantastic Comics)
1-Samson begins, ends #6; Powell-a, signed 'Rensie;' Wing Turner by Tuska app; Fine-c? 225.00 675.00 1800.00
2-Dr. Fung by Powell; Fine-c? 84.00 253.00 675.00
3-Navy Jones app.; Joe Simon-c 66.00 197.00 525.00
4-Yarko the Great, Master Magician begins 56.00 169.00 450.00
5,6: 6-Origin The Topper 44.00 132.00 350.00

SAMSON (2nd Series) (Formerly Fantastic Comics #10, 11)
Ajax/Farrell Publications (Four Star): No. 12, April, 1955 - No. 14, Aug, 1955
12-Wonder Boy 29.00 86.00 200.00
13,14: 13-Wonder Boy, Rocket Man 25.00 75.00 175.00

SAMSON (See Mighty Samson)

SAMSON & DELILAH (See A Spectacular Feature Magazine)

SAMUEL BRONSTON'S CIRCUS WORLD (See Circus World under Movie Comics)

SAMURAI (Also see Eclipse Graphic Album Series #14)
Aircel Publications: 1985 - No. 23, 1987 ($1.70, B&W)
1, 14-16-Dale Keown-a 3.00
1-12,17-23: 1,2 (reprintings) 2.00
13-Dale Keown's 1st published artwork (1987) 5.00

SAMURAI
Warp Graphics: May, 1997 - Present ($2.95, B&W)
1 3.00

SAMURAI CAT
Marvel Comics (Epic Comics): June, 1991 - No. 3, Sept, 1991 ($2.25, limited series)
1-3: 3-Darth Vader-c/story parody 2.25

SAMUREE
Continuity Comics: May, 1987 - No. 9, Jan, 1991
1-9 2.50

SAMUREE
Continuity Comics: V2#1, May, 1993 - V2#4, Jan,1994 ($2.50)
V2#1-4-Embossed-c: 2,4-Adams plot, Nebres-i. 3-Nino-c(i) 2.50

SAMUREE
Acclaim Comics (Windjammer): Oct, 1995 - No. 2, Nov,1995 ($2.50, lim. series)
1,2 2.50

SAN DIEGO COMIC CON COMICS
Dark Horse Comics: 1992 - No.4, 1995 (B&W, promo comic for the San Diego Comic Con)
1-(1992)-Includes various characters published from Dark Horse including Concrete, The Mask, RoboCop and others; 1st app. of Sprint from John Byrne's Next Men; art by Quesada, Byrne, Rude, Burden, Moebius & others; pin-ups by Rude, Dorkin, Allred & others; Chadwick-c. 4.00
2-(1993)-Intro of Legend imprint; 1st app. of John Byrne's Danger Unlimited, Mike Mignola's Hellboy, Art Adams' Monkeyman & O'Brien; contains stories featuring Concrete, Sin City, Martha Washington & others; Grendel, Madman, & Big Guy pin-ups; Don Martin-c. 5.00
3-(1994)-Contains stories featuring Barb Wire, The Mask, The Dirty Pair, & Grendel by Matt Wagner; contains pin-ups of Ghost, Predator & Rascals In Paradise; The Mask-c. 4.00
4-(1995)-Contains Sin City story by Miller (3pg.), Star Wars, The Mask, Tarzan, Foot Soldiers; Sin City & Star Wars flip-c 4.00

SANDMAN, THE (1st Series) (Also see Adventure Comics #40, New York World's Fair & World's Finest #3)
National Periodical Publications: Winter, 1974; No. 2, Apr-May, 1975 - No. 6, Dec-Jan, 1975-76
1-1st app. Bronze Age Sandman by Simon & Kirby (last S&K collaboration) . 2.50 7.50 20.00
2-6: 6-Kirby/Wood-c/a 1.10 3.30 9.00
NOTE: ***Kirby*** *a-1p, 4-6p; c-1-5, 6p.*

SANDMAN (2nd Series) (See Books of Magic, Vertigo Jam & Vertigo Preview)
DC Comics (Vertigo imprint #47 on): Jan, 1989 - No. 75, Mar, 1996 ($1.50/$1.75/$2.50, mature)
1 ($2.00, 52 pgs.)-1st app. Modern Age Sandman (Morpheus); Neil Gaiman scripts begin; Sam Kieth-a(p) in #1-5; Wesley Dodds (G.A. Sandman) cameo. 4.00 12.00 40.00
2-Cain & Abel app. (from HOM & HOS) 2.00 6.00 16.00
3-5: 3-John Constantine app. 1.75 5.25 14.00
6,7 1.10 3.30 9.00
8-Death-c/story (1st app.)-Regular ed. has Jeanette Kahn publishorial & American Cancer Society ad w/no indicia on inside front-c; 2.50 7.50 25.00
8-Limited ed. (600+ copies?); has Karen Berger editorial and next issue teaser on inside covers (has indicia) 6.00 17.50 65.00
9-14: 10-Has explaination about #8 mixup; has bound-in Shocker movie poster. 14-(52 pgs.)-Bound-in Nightbreed fold-out 1.00 3.00 8.00
15-20: 16-Photo-c. 17,18-Kelley Jones-a. 19-Vess-a. 2.40 6.00
18-Error version w/1st 3 panels on pg. 1 in blue ink 2.50 7.50 20.00
19-Error version w/pages 18 & 20 facing each other 2.50 7.50 20.00
21,23-27: Seasons of Mist storyline. 22-World Without End preview. 24-Kelley Jones/Russell-a 2.40 6.00
22-1st Daniel (Later becomes new Sandman) 1.50 4.50 12.00
28-30 5.00

Sandman Presents: Lucifer #1 © DC

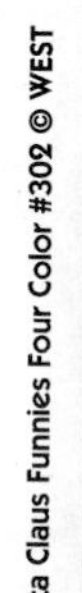
Santa Claus Funnies Four Color #302 © WEST

Sarge Steel #7 © CC

GD2.0 FN6.0 NM9.4

31-49,51-74: 41,44-48-Metallic ink on-c. 48-Cerebus appears as a doll. 36-(52 pgs.). 54-Re-intro Prez; Death app.; Belushi, Nixon & Wildcat cameos. 57-Metallic ink on c. 65-w/bound-in trading card. 69-Death of Sandman. 70-73-Zulli-a. 74-Jon J. Muth-a. 4.00
50-($2.95, 52 pgs.)-Black-c w/metallic ink by McKean; Russell-a; McFarlane pin-up. 5.00
50-($2.95)-Signed & limited (5,000) Treasury Edition with sketch of Neil Gaiman 1.25 3.75 10.00
50-Platinum 25.00
75-($3.95)-Vess-a. 6.00
Special 1 (1991, $3.50, 68 pgs.)-Glow-in-the-dark-c 5.00
...: A Gallery of Dreams ($2.95)-Intro by N. Gaiman 3.00
...: Preludes & Nocturnes ($29.95, HC)-r/#1-8. 40.00
...: The Doll's House (1990, $29.95, HC)-r/#8-16. 40.00
...: Dream Country ($29.95, HC)-r/#17-20. 30.00
...: Season of Mists ($29.95, Leatherbound HC)-r/#21-28. 60.00
...: A Game of You ($29.95, HC)-r/32-37, ...: Fables and Reflections ($29.95, HC)-r/Vertigo Preview #1, Sandman Special #1, #29-31, #38-40 & #50. ...: Brief Lives ($29.95, HC)-r/#41-49. ...: World's End ($29.95, HC)-r/#51-56. 30.00
...: The Kindly Ones (1996, $34.95, HC)-r/#57-69 & Vertigo Jam#1 35.00
...: The Wake ($29.95, HC)-r/#70-75. 30.00
NOTE: *A new set of hardcover printings with new covers was introduced in 1998-99. Multiple printings exist of softcover collections.* ***Bachalo*** *a-12;* ***Kelley Jones*** *a-17, 18, 22, 23, 26, 27.* ***Vess*** *a-19, 75.*

SANDMAN MIDNIGHT THEATRE
DC Comics (Vertigo): Sept, 1995 ($6.95, squarebound, one-shot)
nn-Modern Age Sandman (Morpheus) meets G.A. Sandman; Gaiman & Wagner story; McKean-c; Kristiansen-a 7.00

SANDMAN MYSTERY THEATRE (Also see Sandman (2nd Series) #1)
DC Comics (Vertigo): Apr, 1993 - No. 70, Feb, 1999 ($1.95/$2.25/$2.50)
1-G.A. Sandman advs. begin; Matt Wagner scripts begin 4.50
2-49: 5-Neon ink logo. 29-32-Hourman app. 38-Ted Knight (G.A. Starman) app. 42-Jim Corrigan (Spectre) app. 45-48-Blackhawk app. 3.50
50-($3.50, 48 pgs.) w/bonus story of S.A. Sandman, Torres-a 4.00
51-69 2.50
Annual 1 (10/94, $3.95, 68 pgs.)-Alex Ross, Bolton & others-a 5.00

SANDMAN PRESENTS: LOVE STREET
DC Comics (Vertigo): Jul, 1999 - No. 3, Sept, 1999 ($2.95, limited series)
1-3: Teenage Hellblazer in 1968 London; Zulli-a 3.00

SANDMAN PRESENTS: LUCIFER
DC Comics (Vertigo): Mar, 1999 - No. 3, May, 1999 ($2.95, limited series)
1-3: Scott Hampton painted-c/a 3.00

SANDMAN, THE: THE DREAM HUNTERS
DC Comics (Vertigo): Oct, 1999 ($29.95, one-shot, hardcover)
Hardcover-Neil Gaiman-s/Yoshitaka Amano-painted art 30.00

SANDS OF THE SOUTH PACIFIC
Toby Press: Jan, 1953
1 21.00 62.00 145.00

SANTA AND HIS REINDEER (See March of Comics #166)

SANTA AND THE ANGEL (See Dell Junior Treasury #7)
Dell Publishing Co.: Dec, 1949 (Combined w/Santa at the Zoo) (Gollub-a condensed from FC#128)
Four Color 259 3.60 11.00 40.00

SANTA AT THE ZOO (See Santa And The Angel)

SANTA CLAUS AROUND THE WORLD (See March of Comics #241 in Promotional Comics section)

SANTA CLAUS CONQUERS THE MARTIANS (See Movie Classics)

SANTA CLAUS FUNNIES (Also see Dell Giants)
Dell Publishing Co.: Dec?, 1942 - No. 1274, Dec, 1961
nn(#1)(1942)-Kelly-a 36.00 107.00 390.00

GD2.0 FN6.0 NM9.4

2(12/43)-Kelly-a 23.00 70.00 255.00
Four Color 61(1944)-Kelly-a 23.00 68.00 250.00
Four Color 91(1945)-Kelly-a 17.00 50.00 185.00
Four Color 128('46),175('47)-Kelly-a 13.00 39.00 145.00
Four Color 205,254-Kelly-a 12.00 35.00 130.00
Four Color 302,361,525,607,666,756,867 3.60 11.00 40.00
Four Color 958,1063,1154,1274 3.00 9.00 35.00
NOTE: *Most issues contain only one Kelly story.*

SANTA CLAUS PARADE
Ziff-Davis (Approved Comics)/St. John Publishing Co.: 1951; No. 2, Dec, 1952; No. 3, Jan, 1955 (25¢)
nn(1951-Ziff-Davis)-116 pgs. (Xmas Special 1,2) 28.00 84.00 195.00
2(12/52-Ziff-Davis)-100 pgs.; Dave Berg-a 21.00 64.00 150.00
V1#3(1/55-St. John)-100 pgs.; reprints-c/#1 18.00 54.00 125.00

SANTA CLAUS' WORKSHOP (See March of Comics #50,168 in Promotional Comics sect.)

SANTA IS COMING (See March of Comics #197 in Promotional Comics section)

SANTA IS HERE (See March of Comics #49 in Promotional Comics section)

SANTA'S BUSY CORNER (See March of Comics #31 in Promotional Comics section)

SANTA'S CANDY KITCHEN (See March of Comics #14 in Promotional Comics section)

SANTA'S CHRISTMAS BOOK (See March of Comics #123 in Promotional Comics sect.)

SANTA'S CHRISTMAS COMICS
Standard Comics (Best Books): Dec, 1952 (100 pgs.)
nn-Supermouse, Dizzy Duck, Happy Rabbit, etc. 17.00 49.00 115.00

SANTA'S CHRISTMAS LIST (See March of Comics #255 in Promotional Comics section)

SANTA'S HELPERS (See March of Comics #64, 106, 198 in Promotional Comics section)

SANTA'S LITTLE HELPERS (See March of Comics #270 in Promotional Comics section)

SANTA'S SHOW (See March of Comics #311 in Promotional Comics section)

SANTA'S SLEIGH (See March of Comics #298 in Promotional Comics section)

SANTA'S SURPRISE (See March of Comics #13 in Promotional Comics section)

SANTA'S TINKER TOTS
Charlton Comics: 1958
1-Based on "The Tinker Tots Keep Christmas" 2.15 7.50 20.00

SANTA'S TOYLAND (See March of Comics #242 in Promotional Comics section)

SANTA'S TOYS (See March of Comics #12 in Promotional Comics section)

SANTA'S VISIT (See March of Comics #283 in Promotional Comics section)

SANTA THE BARBARIAN
Maximum Press: Dec, 1996 ($2.99, one-shot)
1-Fraga/Mhan-s/a 3.00

SANTIAGO (Movie)
Dell Publishing Co.: Sept, 1956 (Alan Ladd photo-c)
Four Color 723-Kinstler-a 10.00 30.00 110.00

SARGE SNORKEL (Beetle Bailey)
Charlton Comics: Oct, 1973 - No. 17, Dec, 1976
1 1.75 5.25 14.00
2-10 1.10 3.30 9.00
11-17 1.00 2.80 7.00

SARGE STEEL (Becomes Secret Agent #9 on; also see Judomaster)
Charlton Comics: Dec, 1964 - No. 8, Mar-Apr, 1966 (All 12¢ issues)
1-Origin & 1st app. 2.60 7.80 26.00
2-5,7,8 2.00 6.00 16.00
6-2nd app. Judomaster 2.50 7.50 20.00

SATANIKA
Verotik: Jan, 1995 - No. 3, 1996 ($2.95, limited series, mature)
0-3: Danzig story in all. 0-(7/95)-Frazetta-c; 1-Bisley-c. 5.00
The Brimstone Trail (1996, $9.95, TPB)-r/#0-2. 10.00

SATANIKA
Verotik: Feb, 1996 - Present ($2.95, mature)

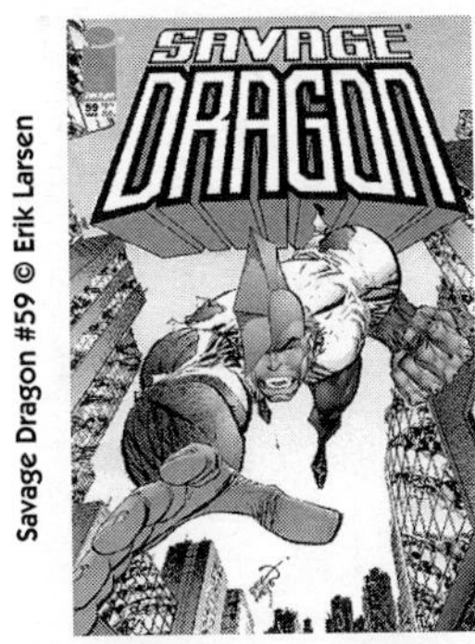

Savage Dragon #59 © Erik Larsen

Savage She-Hulk #6 © MAR

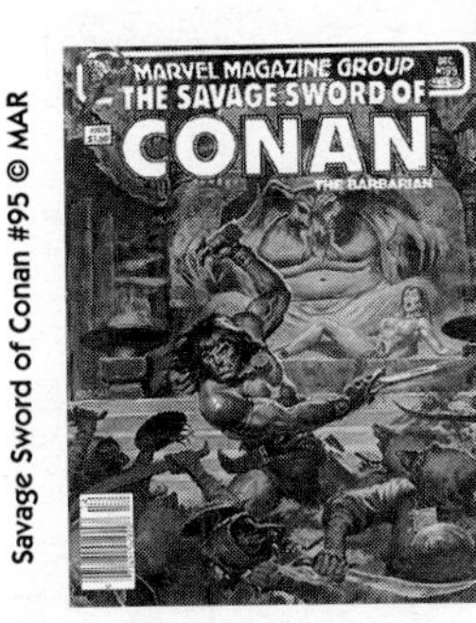

Savage Sword of Conan #95 © MAR

GD2.0 FN6.0 NM9.4

1-10: Danzig story in all. 2-Igrat cameo; indicia reads "Satanika #1." 4,5-nudity-c 3.00

SATANIKA X
Verotik: Feb, 1996 ($4.95, one-shot, mature)

1-Embossed-c. 5.00

SATAN'S SIX
Topps Comics (Kirbyverse): Apr, 1993 - No. 4, July, 1993 ($2.95, lim. series)

1-4: 1-Polybagged w/Kirbychrome trading card; Kirby/McFarlane-c plus 8 pgs. Kirby-a(p); has coupon for Kirbychrome ed. of Secret City Saga #0. 2-4-Polybagged w/3 cards. 4-Teenagents preview 3.00
NOTE: ***Ditko*** *a-1.* ***Miller*** *a-1.*

SATAN'S SIX: HELLSPAWN
Topps Comics (Kirbyverse): June, 1994 - No. 3, July, 1994 ($2.50, lim. series)

1-3: 1-(6/94)-Indicia incorrectly shows "Vol 1 #2". 2-(6/94) 2.50

SAVAGE COMBAT TALES
Atlas/Seaboard Publ.: Feb, 1975 - No. 3, July, 1975

1-3: 1-Sgt. Stryker's Death Squad begins (origin). 2-Only app. Warhawk 5.00
NOTE: ***Buckler*** *c-3.* ***McWilliams*** *a-1-3; c-1.* ***Sparling*** *a-1, 3.* ***Toth*** *a-2.*

SAVAGE DRAGON, THE (See Megaton #3 & 4)
Image Comics (Highbrow Entertainment): July, 1992 - No. 3, Dec, 1992 ($1.95, limited series)

1-Erik Larsen-c/a/scripts & bound-in poster in all; 4 cover color variations w/4 different posters; 1st Highbrow Entertainment title 3.00
2-Intro SuperPatriot-c/story (10/92) 3.00
3-Contains coupon for Image Comics #0 2.00
3-With coupon missing 2.00
...Vs. Savage Megaton Man 1 (3/93, $1.95)-Larsen & Simpson-c/a. 2.00
TPB-('93, $9.95) r/#1-3 10.00

SAVAGE DRAGON, THE
Image Comics (Highbrow Entertainment): June, 1993 - Present ($1.95/$2.50)

1-Erik Larsen-c/a/scripts 3.00
2-30: 2-(Wondercon Exclusive): 2-($2.95, 52 pgs.)-Teenage Mutant Ninja Turtles-c/story; flip book features Vanguard #0 (See Megaton for 1st app.). 27 (Wondercon Exclusive)-new-c. 3-7: Erik Larsen-c/a/scripts. 3-Mighty Man back-up story w/Austin-a(i). 4-Flip book w/Ricochet. 5-Mighty Man flip-c & back-up plus poster. 6-Jae Lee poster. 7-Vanguard poster. 8-Deadly Duo poster by Larsen. 13A (10/94)-Jim Lee-c/a; 1st app. Max Cash (Condition Red).13B (6/95)-Larsen story. 15-Dragon poster by Larsen. 22-TMNT-c/a; Bisley pin-up. 28-Maxx-c/app. 29-Wildstar-c/app. 30-Spawn app. 2.50
25 ($3.95)-variant-c exists. 4.00
27-"Wondercon Exclusive" new-c 3.00
31-49,51-66: 31-God vs. The Devil; alternate version exists w/o expletives (has "God Is Good" inside Image logo) 33-Birth of Dragon/Rapture's baby. 34,35-Hellboy-c/app. 51-Origin of She-Dragon. 58-Savage Dragon returns 2.50
50-($5.95, 100 pgs.) Kaboom and Mighty Man app.; Matsuda back-c; pin-ups by McFarlane, Simonson, Capullo and others 6.00
The Fallen (11/97, $12.95, TPB) r/#7-11, ...Possessed (9/98, $12.95, TPB) r/#12-16, ...Revenge (1998, $12.95, TPB) r/#17-21 13.00
...Team-Ups (10/98, $19.95, TPB) r/team-ups 20.00

SAVAGE DRAGON ARCHIVES (See Dragon Archives, The)

SAVAGE DRAGON/DESTROYER DUCK, THE
Image Comics/ Highbrow Entertainment: Nov, 1996 ($3.95, one-shot)

1 4.00

SAVAGE DRAGON/MARSHALL LAW
Image Comics: July, 1997 - No. 2, Aug, 1997 ($2.95, B&W, limited series)

1,2-Pat Mills-s, Kevin O'Neill-a 3.00

SAVAGE DRAGON: SEX & VIOLENCE
Image Comics: Aug, 1997 - No. 2, Sept, 1997 ($2.50, limited series)

1,2-T&M Bierbaum-s, Mays, Lupka, Adam Hughes-a 2.50

SAVAGE DRAGON/TEENAGE MUTANT NINJA TURTLES CROSSOVER
Mirage Studios: Sept, 1993 ($2.75, one-shot)

GD2.0 FN6.0 NM9.4

1-Erik Larsen-c(i) only 2.75

SAVAGE DRAGON: THE RED HORIZON
Image Comics/ Highbrow Entertainment: Feb, 1997 - No. 3 ($2.50, lim. series)

1-3 2.50

SAVAGE FISTS OF KUNG FU
Marvel Comics Group: 1975 (Marvel Treasury)

1-Iron Fist, Shang Chi, Sons of Tiger; Adams, Starlin-a 2.25 6.75 18.00

SAVAGE HENRY
Vortex Comics: Jan, 1987 - No. 16?, 1990 ($1.75/$2.00, B&W, mature)

1-16 2.50

SAVAGE HULK, THE (Also see Incredible Hulk)
Marvel Comics: Jan, 1996 ($6.95, one-shot)

1-Bisley-c; David, Lobdell, Wagner, Loeb, Gibbons, Messner-Loebs scripts; McKone, Kieth, Ramos & Sale-a. 7.00

SAVAGE RAIDS OF GERONIMO (See Geronimo #4)

SAVAGE RANGE (See Luke Short, Four Color 807)

SAVAGE RETURN OF DRACULA
Marvel Comics: 1992 ($2.00, 52 pgs.)

1-r/Tomb of Dracula #1,2 by Gene Colan 2.00

SAVAGE SHE-HULK, THE (See The Avengers, Marvel Graphic Novel #18 & The Sensational She-Hulk)
Marvel Comics Group: Feb, 1980 - No. 25, Feb, 1982

1-Origin & 1st app. She-Hulk 1.00 3.00 8.00
2-25: 25(52 pgs.) 3.00
NOTE: ***Austin*** *a-25i; c-23i-25i.* ***J. Buscema*** *a-1p; c-1, 2p.* ***Golden*** *c-8-11.*

SAVAGE SWORD OF CONAN (The... #41 on; ...The Barbarian #175 on)
Marvel Comics Group: Aug, 1974 - No. 235, July, 1995 ($1.00/$1.25/$2.25, B&W magazine, mature)

1-Smith-r; J. Buscema/N. Adams/Krenkel-a; origin Blackmark by Gil Kane (part 1, ends #3); Blackmark's 1st app. in magazine form-r/from paperback) & Red Sonja (3rd app.) 6.50 19.00 70.00
2-Neal Adams-c; Chaykin/N. Adams-a 2.80 8.40 28.00
3-Severin/B. Smith-a; N. Adams-a 2.25 6.75 18.00
4-Neal Adams/Kane-a(r) 2.00 6.00 16.00
5-10: 5-Jeff Jones frontispiece (r) 1.75 5.25 14.00
11-20 1.50 4.50 12.00
21-50: 34-3 pg. preview of Conan newspaper strip. 35-Cover similar to Savage Tales #1. 45-Red Sonja returns; begin $1.25-c 1.25 3.75 10.00
51-100: 63-Toth frontispiece. 65-Kane-a w/Chaykin/Miller/Simonson/Sherman finishes. 70-Article on movie. 83-Red Sonja-r by Neal Adams from #1 2.40 6.00
101-176: 163-Begin $2.25-c. 169-King Kull story. 171-Soloman Kane by Williamson (i). 172-Red Sonja story 4.00
177-235: 179,187,192-Red Sonja app. 190-193-4 part King Kull story. 196, 202-King Kull story. 200-New Buscema-a; Robert E. Howard app. with Conan in story. 204-60th anniversary (1932-92). 211-Rafael Kayanan's 1st Conan-a. 214-Sequel to Red Nails by Robert E. Howard 3.00
Special 1(1975, B&W)-B. Smith-r/Conan #10,13 2.00 6.00 16.00
NOTE: ***N. Adams*** *a-14p, 60, 83p(r).* ***Alcala*** *a-2 ,4, 7, 12, 15-20, 23, 24, 28, 59, 67, 69, 75, 76i, 80i, 82i, 83i, 89, 180i, 184i, 187i, 189i, 216p.* ***Austin*** *a-78i.* ***Boris*** *painted c-1, 4, 5, 7, 9, 10, 12, 15.* ***Brunner*** *a-30; c-8, 30.* ***Buscema*** *a-1-5, 7, 10-12, 15-24, 26-28, 31, 32, 36-43, 45, 47-58p, 60-67p, 70, 71-74p, 76-81p, 87-96p, 98, 99-101p, 190-204p; painted c-40.* ***Chaykin*** *c-31.* ***Chiodo*** *painted c-71, 76, 79, 81, 84, 85, 178.* ***Conrad*** *c-215, 217.* ***Corben*** *a-4, 16, 29.* ***Finlay*** *a-16.* ***Golden*** *a-98, 101; c-98, 101, 105, 106, 117, 124, 150.* ***Kaluta*** *a-11, 18; c-3, 91, 93.* ***Gil Kane*** *a-2, 3, 8, 13r, 29, 47, 64, 65, 67, 85p, 86p.* ***Rafael Kayanan*** *a-211-213, 215, 217.* ***Krenkel*** *a-9, 11, 14, 16, 24.* ***Morrow*** *a-7.* ***Nebres*** *a-93i, 101i, 107, 114.* ***Newton*** *a-6.* ***Nino*** *c/a-6.* ***Redondo*** *painted c-48-50, 52, 56, 57, 85i, 90, 96i.* ***Marie & John Severin*** *a-Special 1.* ***Simonson*** *a-7, 8, 12, 15-17.* ***Barry Smith*** *a-7, 16, 24, 82r, Special 1r.* ***Starlin*** *c-26.* ***Toth*** *a-64.* ***Williamson*** *a(i)-162, 171, 186. No. 8 , 10 & 16 contain a Robert E. Howard Conan adaptation.*

SAVAGE TALES (...Featuring Conan #4 on)(Magazine)
Marvel Comics Group: May, 1971; No. 2, 10/73; No. 3, 2/74 - No. 12, Summer, 1975 (B&W)

Scare Tactics #7 © DC

Scary Godmother Holiday Spooktacular #1 © Jill Thompson

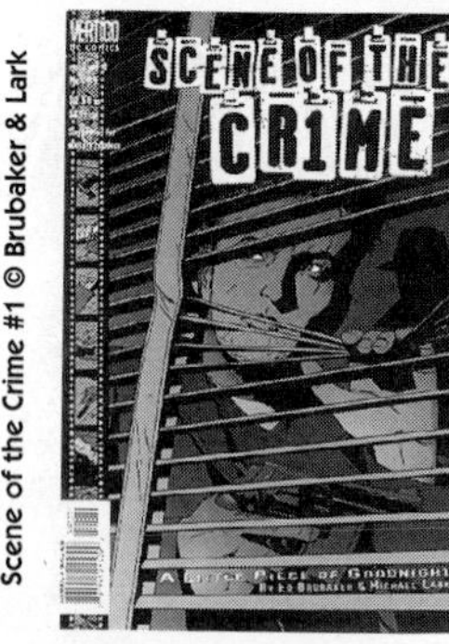

Scene of the Crime #1 © Brubaker & Lark

GD2.0 FN6.0 NM9.4

1-Origin/1st app. The Man-Thing by Morrow; Conan the Barbarian by Barry Smith (1st Conan x-over outside his own title); Femizons by Romita-r/in #3; Ka-Zar story by Buscema 11.00 34.00 125.00
2-B. Smith, Brunner, Morrow, Williamson-a; Wrightson King Kull reprint/ Creatures on the Loose #10 3.00 9.00 30.00
3-B. Smith, Brunner, Steranko, Williamson-a 2.50 7.50 20.00
4,5-N. Adams-c; last Conan (Smith-r/#4) plus Kane/N. Adams-a. 5-Brak the Barbarian begins, ends #8 2.00 6.00 16.00
6-Ka-Zar begins; Williamson-r; N. Adams-c 1.25 3.75 10.00
7-N. Adams-i 1.00 3.00 8.00
8-Shanna, the She-Devil app. thru #10; Williamson-r 1.00 2.80 7.00
9,11 1.00 2.80 7.00
10-Neal Adams-a(i), Williamson-r 1.10 3.30 9.00
...Featuring Ka-Zar Annual 1 (Summer, '75, B&W)(#12 on inside)-Ka-Zar origin by G. Kane; B. Smith-r/Astonishing Tales 1.20 3.60 12.00

NOTE: *Boris c-7, 10. Buscema a-5r, 6p, 8p; c-2. Colan a-1p. Fabian c-8. Golden a-1, 4; c-1. Heath a-10p, 11p. Kaluta c-9. Maneely r-2, 4(The Crusader in both). Morrow a-1, 2, Annual 1. Reese a-2. Severin a-1-7. Starlin a-5. Robert E. Howard adaptations-1-4.*

SAVAGE TALES
Marvel Comics Group: Nov, 1985 - No. 9, Mar, 1987 ($1.50, B&W, magazine, mature)

1-1st app. The Nam; Golden, Morrow-a 3.00
2-9: 2,7-Morrow-a. 4-2nd Nam story; Golden-a 2.00

SAVANT GARDE (Also see WildC.A.T.S...)
Image Comics/WildStorm Productions: Mar, 1997 - No. 7, Sept, 1997 ($2.50)

1-7 2.50

SAVED BY THE BELL (TV)
Harvey Comics: Mar, 1992 - No. 4, Aug, 1992? ($1.25, limited series)

1-4, Special 1 (9/92, $1.50)-photo-c 2.00

SCAMP (Walt Disney)(See Walt Disney's Comics & Stories #204)
Dell Publ. Co./Gold Key: No. 703, 5/56 - No. 1204, 8-10/61; 11/67 - No. 45, 1/79

Four Color 703(#1) 8.00 25.00 90.00
Four Color 777,806('57),833 5.50 16.50 60.00
5(3-5/58)-10(6-8/59) 4.50 13.50 50.00
11-16(12-2/60-61), Four Color 1204(1961) 3.00 9.00 35.00
1(12/67-Gold Key)-Reprints begin 3.20 9.50 35.00
2(3/69)-10 1.50 4.50 15.00
11-20 .90 2.70 9.00
21-45 2.40 6.00

NOTE: *New stories-#20(in part), 22-25, 27, 29-31, 34, 36-40, 42-45. New covers-#11, 12, 14, 15, 17-25, 27, 29-31, 34, 36-38.*

SCARAB
DC Comics (Vertigo): Nov, 1993 - No. 8, June, 1994 ($1.95, limited series)

1-8-Glenn Fabry painted-c: 1-Silver ink-c. 2-Phantom Stranger app. 2.00

SCAR FACE (See The Crusaders)

SCARECROW OF ROMNEY MARSH, THE (See W. Disney Showcase #53)
Gold Key: April, 1964 - No. 3, Oct, 1965 (Disney TV Show)

10112-404 (#1) 3.00 9.00 30.00
2,3 2.50 7.50 22.00

SCARECROW (VILLAINS) (See Batman)
DC Comics: Feb, 1998 ($1.95, one-shot)

1-Fegredo-a/Milligan-s/Pearson-c 2.00

SCARE TACTICS
DC Comics: Dec, 1996 - No. 12, Mar, 1998 ($2.25)

1-12: 1-1st app. 2.25

SCARLET O'NEIL (See Harvey Comics Hits #59 & Invisible...)

SCARLET CRUSH
Awesome Entertainment: Jan, 1998 - No. 2, Feb, 1998 ($2.50)

1-Five covers by Liefeld, Stinsman(wraparound), Churchill, Skroce, and Sprouse; Stinsman-s/a(p) 2.50
1-American Entertainment Ed.; Stinsman-c 5.00

GD2.0 FN6.0 NM9.4

2-Three covers by Stinsman, McGuinness & Peterson 2.50

SCARLET SPIDER
Marvel Comics: Nov, 1995 - No. 2, Jan, 1996 ($1.95)

1,2: Replaces Spider-Man 2.00

SCARLET SPIDER UNLIMITED
Marvel Comics: Nov, 1995 ($3.95, one-shot)

1-Replaces Spider-Man Unlimited 4.00

SCARLETT
DC Comics: Jan, 1993 - No. 14, Feb, 1994 (1.75)

1-($2.95) 3.00
2-14 2.00

SCARLET THUNDER
Amaze Ink: Nov, 1995, - Present ($1.50, B&W)

1-3: 3-(5/96) 2.00

SCARLET WITCH (See Avengers #16, Vision &... & X-Men #4)
Marvel Comics: Jan, 1994 - No. 4, Apr, 1994 ($1.75, limited series)

1-4 2.00

SCARY GODMOTHER: BLOODY VALENTINE SPECIAL
Sirius: Feb, 1998 ($3.95,B&W, one-shot)

1-Jill Thompson-s/a; pin-ups by Ross, Mignola, Russell 4.00

SCARY GODMOTHER: HOLIDAY SPOOKTAKULAR
Sirius: Nov, 1998 ($2.95,B&W, one-shot)

1-Thompson-s/a; pin-ups by Brereton, LaBan, Dorkin, Fingerman 3.00

SCARY TALES
Charlton Comics: 8/75 - #9, 1/77; #10, 9/77 - #20, 6/79; #21, 8/80 - #46, 10/84

1-Origin/1st app. Countess Von Bludd, not in #2 1.75 5.25 14.00
2-11: 3-Sutton painted-c 1.10 3.30 9.00
12-20 1.00 2.80 7.00
21-46: 39,46-reprints. 37,38,40-45-New-a. 38-Mr. Jigsaw app. 2.40 6.00
1(Modern Comics reprint, 1977) 4.00

NOTE: *Adkins a-31i; c-31i. Ditko a-3, 5, 7, 8(2), 11, 12, 14-16r, 18(3)r, 19r, 21r, 30r, 32, 39r; c-5, 11, 14, 18, 30, 32. Newton a-31p; c-31p. Powell a-18r. Staton a-1(2 pgs.), 4, 20r; c-1, 20. Sutton a-9; c-4, 9.*

SCATTERBRAIN
Dark Horse Comics: Jun, 1998 - Present ($2.95, limited series)

1-4-Humor anthology by Aragonés, Dorkin, Stevens and others 3.00

SCAVENGERS
Quality Comics: Feb, 1988 - No. 14, 1989 ($1.25/$1.50)

1-14: 9-13-Guice-c 2.00

SCAVENGERS
Triumphant Comics: 1993(nd, July) - No. 11, May, 1994 ($2.50, serially numbered)

1-9,0,10,11: 5,6-Triumphant Unleashed x-over. 9-(3/94). 0-Retail edition (3/94, $2.50, 36 pgs.). 0-Giveaway edition (3/94, 20 pgs.). 0-Coupon redemption edition. 10-(4/94) 2.50

SCENE OF THE CRIME
DC Comics (Vertigo): May, 1999 - No. 4, Aug, 1999 ($2.50, limited series)

1-4-Brubaker-s/Lark-a 2.50

SCHOOL DAY ROMANCES (...of Teen-Agers #4; Popular Teen-Agers #5 on)
Star Publications: Nov-Dec, 1949 - No. 4, May-June, 1950 (Teenage)

1-Toni Gayle (later Toni Gay), Ginger Snapp, Midge Martin & Eve Adams begin 26.00 77.00 180.00
2,3: 3-Jane Powell photo on-c & true life story 18.00 54.00 125.00
4-Ronald Reagan photo on-c; L.B. Cole-c 29.00 86.00 200.00

NOTE: *All have L. B. Cole covers.*

SCHWINN BICYCLE BOOK (...Bike Thrills, 1959)
Schwinn Bicycle Co.: 1949; 1952; 1959 (10¢)

1949 5.00 15.00 30.00

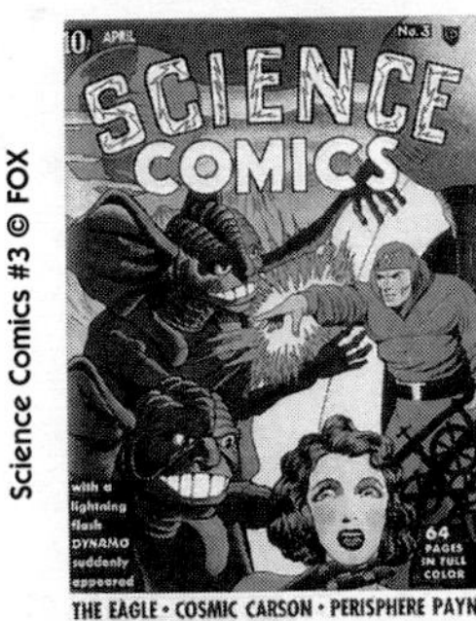

Science Comics #3 © FOX

Scooby-Doo (DC) #26 © H-B

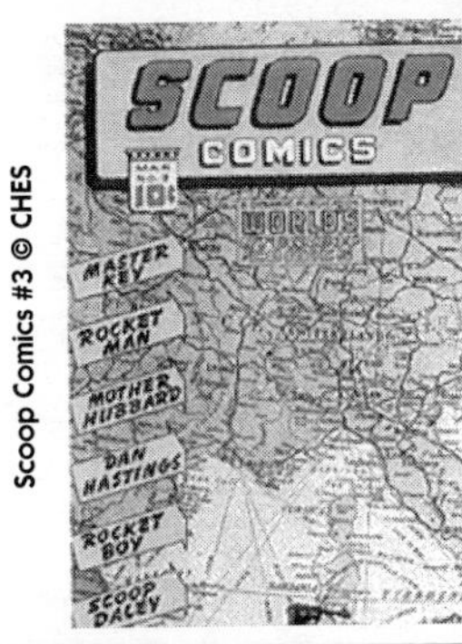

Scoop Comics #3 © CHES

GD2.0 FN6.0 NM9.4

1952-Believe It or Not facts; comic format; 36 pgs. 4.00 10.00 20.00
1959 2.00 5.00 10.00

SCIENCE COMICS (1st Series)
Fox Features Syndicate: Feb, 1940 - No. 8, Sept, 1940

1-Origin Dynamo (1st app., called Electro in #1), The Eagle (1st app.), & Navy Jones; Marga, The Panther Woman (1st app.), Cosmic Carson & Perisphere Payne, Dr. Doom begin; bondage/hypo-c; Electro-c 389.00 1167.00 3500.00
2-Classic Lou Fine Dynamo-c 200.00 600.00 1600.00
3-Classic Lou Fine Dynamo-c 169.00 506.00 1350.00
4-Kirby-a; Cosmic Carson-c by Joe Simon 150.00 450.00 1200.00
5-8: 5,8-Eagle-c. 6,7-Dynamo-c 87.00 262.00 700.00
NOTE: *Cosmic Carson by* ***Tuska****-#1-3; by* ***Kirby****-#4.* ***Lou Fine*** *c-1-3 only.*

SCIENCE COMICS (2nd Series)
Humor Publications (Ace Magazines?): Jan, 1946 - No. 5, 1946

1-Palais-c/a in #1-3; A-Bomb-c 16.00 47.00 110.00
2 9.15 27.00 55.00
3-Feldstein-a (6 pgs.) 14.00 43.00 100.00
4,5: 4-Palais-c 7.00 21.00 42.00

SCIENCE COMICS
Ziff-Davis Publ. Co.: May, 1947 (8 pgs. in color)

nn-Could be ordered by mail for 10¢; like the nn Amazing Adventures (1950) & Boy Cowboy (1950); used to test the market 36.00 107.00 250.00

SCIENCE COMICS (True Science Illustrated)
Export Publication Ent., Toronto, Canada: Mar, 1951
Distr. in U.S. by Kable News Co.

1-Science Adventure stories plus some true science features; man on moon story 9.15 27.00 55.00

SCIENCE FICTION SPACE ADVENTURES (See Space Adventures)

SCI-TECH
DC Comics (WildStorm): Sept, 1999 - No. 4 ($2.50, limited series)

1-3-Benes-a/Choi & Peterson-s 2.50

SCOOBY DOO (TV)(...Where are you? #1-16,26; ...Mystery Comics #17-25, 27 on)(See March Of Comics #356, 368, 382, 391)
Gold Key: Mar, 1970 - No. 30, Feb, 1975 (Hanna-Barbera)

1 7.00 20.00 75.00
2-5 4.50 13.50 50.00
6-10 3.80 11.40 38.00
11-20: 11-Tufts-a 2.60 7.80 26.00
21-30 2.50 7.50 20.00

SCOOBY DOO (TV)
Charlton Comics: Apr, 1975 - No. 11, Dec, 1976 (Hanna-Barbera)

1 3.60 10.80 36.00
2-5 2.50 7.50 22.00
6-11 2.00 6.00 16.00

SCOOBY-DOO (TV) (Newsstand sales only)
Marvel Comics Group: Oct, 1977 - No. 9, Feb, 1979 (Hanna-Barbera)

1,6-9: 1-Dyno-Mutt begins 1.75 5.25 14.00
2-5 1.25 3.75 10.00

SCOOBY-DOO (TV)
Harvey Comics: Sept, 1992 - No. 3, May, 1993 ($1.25)

V2#1,2 2.00
Big Book 1,2 (11/92, 4/93, $1.95, 52 pgs.) 3.00
Giant Size 1,2 (10/92, 3/93, $2.25, 68 pgs.) 3.00

SCOOBY DOO (TV)
Archie Comics: Oct, 1995 -No. 21, June, 1997 ($1.50)

1-21: 12-Cover by Scooby Doo creative designer Iwao Takamoto 2.00

SCOOBY DOO (TV)
DC Comics: Aug, 1997 - Present ($1.75/$1.95/$1.99)

GD2.0 FN6.0 NM9.4

1-28: 5-Begin-$1.95-c. 14-Begin $1.99-c 2.00
...Spooky Spectacular 1 (10/99, $3.95) Comic Convention story 4.00

SCOOP COMICS (Becomes Yankee Comics #4-7, a digest sized cartoon book not listed in this guide; becomes Snap #9)
Harry 'A' Chesler (Holyoke): November, 1941 - No. 3, Mar, 1943; No. 8, 1944

1-Intro. Rocketman & Rocketgirl & begins; origin The Master Key & begins; Dan Hastings begins; Charles Sultan-c/a 125.00 375.00 1000.00
2-Rocket Boy begins; injury to eye story (reprinted in Spotlight #3); classic-c 131.00 394.00 1050.00
3-Injury to eye story-r from #2; Rocket Boy 62.00 187.00 500.00
8-Formerly Yankee Comics; becomes Snap 40.00 120.00 320.00

SCOOTER (See Swing With...)

SCOOTER COMICS
Rucker Publ. Ltd. (Canadian): Apr, 1946

1-Teen-age/funny animal 10.00 30.00 65.00

SCORCHED EARTH
Tundra Publishing: Apr, 1991 - No. 6, 1991 ($2.95, stiff-c)

1-6 3.00

SCORE, THE
DC Comics (Piranha Press): 1989 - No. 4, 1990 ($4.95, 52 pgs, squarebound, mature)

Books One - Four 5.00

SCORPION
Atlas/Seaboard Publ.: Feb, 1975 - No. 3, July, 1975

1-Intro.; bondage-c by Chaykin 2.40 6.00
2-Chaykin-a w/Wrightson, Kaluta, Simonson assists(p) 2.40 6.00
3 4.00
NOTE: ***Chaykin*** *a-1, 2; c-1.* ***Colon*** *c-2.* ***Craig*** *c/a-3.*

SCORPION CORPS
Dagger Comics Group: Nov, 1993 - No. 7, May, 1994? ($2.75/$2.50)

1,2-($2.75): 1-Intro Angel Dust, Shellcase, Tork, Feedback & Magnon 2.75
2-Bronze, 2-Gold, 2-Silver 2.75
3-7-($2.50) 2.50

SCORPIO ROSE
Eclipse Comics: Jan, 1983 - No. 2, Oct, 1983 ($1.25, Baxter paper)

1,2: Dr. Orient back-up story begins. 2-origin. 2.00

SCOTLAND YARD (Inspector Farnsworth of)(Texas Rangers in Action #5 on?)
Charlton Comics Group: June, 1955 - No. 4, Mar, 1956

1-Tothish-a 13.50 41.00 95.00
2-4: 2-Tothish-a 10.00 30.00 65.00

SCOUT (See Eclipse Graphic Album #16, New America & Swords of Texas)(Becomes Scout: War Shaman)
Eclipse Comics: Dec, 1985 - No. 24, Oct, 1987($1.75/$1.25, Baxter paper)

1-15,17,18,20-24: 19-Airboy preview. 10-Bissette-a. 11-Monday, the Eliminator begins. 15-Swords of Texas 2.00
16,19: 16-Scout 3-D Special ($2.50), 16-Scout 2-D Limited Edition, 19-contains flexidisk ($2.50) 2.50
...Handbook 1 (8/87, $1.75, B&W) 2.00
Mount Fire (1989, $14.95, TPB) r/#8-14 15.00

SCOUT: WAR SHAMAN (Formerly Scout)
Eclipse Comics: Mar, 1988 - No. 16, Dec, 1989 ($1.95)

1-16 2.00

SCREAM (...Comics) (Andy Comics #20 on)
Humor Publications/Current Books(Ace Magazines): Autumn, 1944 - No. 19, Apr, 1948

1-Teenage humor 15.00 45.00 105.00
2 9.15 27.00 55.00
3-16: 11-Racist humor (Indians). 16-Intro. Lily-Belle 7.00 21.00 42.00

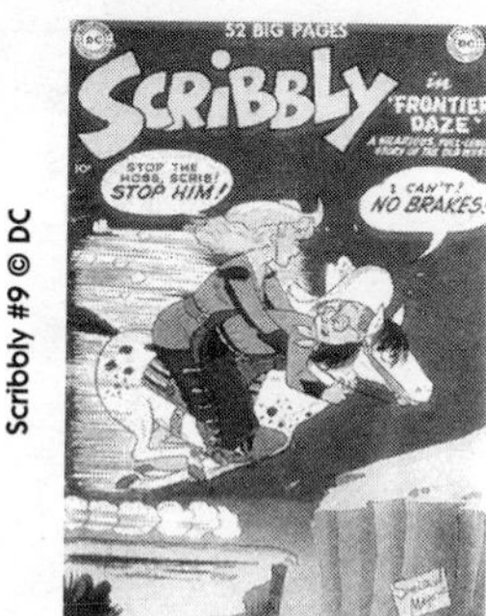

Scribbly #9 © DC

Sea Hound #4 © AVON

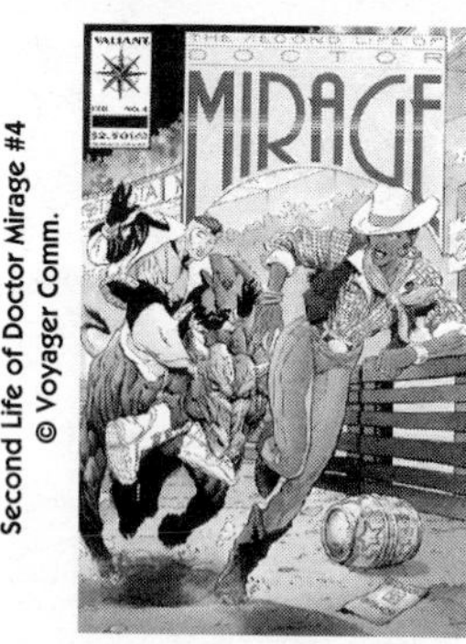

Second Life of Doctor Mirage #4 © Voyager Comm.

GD2.0 FN6.0 NM9.4

17,19 5.35 16.00 32.00
18-Hypo needle story 7.00 21.00 42.00

SCREAM
Skywald Publishing Corp.: Aug, 1973 - No. 11, Feb, 1975 (68 pgs., B&W, magazine)

1 3.20 9.60 32.00
2-5: 2-Origin Lady Satan. 3 (12/73)-#3 found on pg. 22 2.25 6.75 18.00
6-8: 6-Origin The Victims 1.75 5.25 14.00
9-11: 9-Severed head-c. 11- "Mr. Poe and the Raven" story 2.25 6.75 18.00

SCREWBALL SQUIRREL
Dark Horse Comics: July, 1995 - No. 3, Sept, 1995 ($2.50, limited series)

1-3: Characters created by Tex Avery 2.50

SCRIBBLY (See All-American Comics, Buzzy, The Funnies, Leave It To Binky & Popular Comics)
National Periodical Publications: 8-9/48 - No. 13, 8-9/50; No. 14, 10-11/51 - No. 15, 12-1/51-52

1-Sheldon Mayer-c/a in all; 52 pgs. begin 94.00 281.00 750.00
2 61.00 184.00 490.00
3-5 49.00 146.00 390.00
6-10 37.00 111.00 260.00
11-15: 13-Last 52 pgs. 33.00 99.00 230.00

SCUD: TALES FROM THE VENDING MACHINE
Fireman Press: 1998 - Present ($2.50, B&W)

1-5: 1-Kaniuga-a. 2-Ruben Martinez-a 2.50

SCUD: THE DISPOSABLE ASSASSIN
Fireman Press: Feb, 1994 - Present ($2.95, B&W)

1 1.00 3.00 8.00
1-2nd printing in color 3.00
2,3 5.00
4-9 4.00
10-19 3.00
Heavy 3PO ($12.95, TPB) r/#1-4 13.00
Programmed For Damage ($14.95, TPB) r/#5-9 15.00
Solid Gold Bomb ($17.95, TPB) r/#10-15 18.00

SEA DEVILS (See Limited Collectors' Edition #39,45, & Showcase #27-29)
National Periodical Publications: Sept-Oct, 1961 - No. 35, May-June, 1967

1-(9-10/61) 41.00 123.00 500.00
2-Last 10¢ issue 25.00 75.00 250.00
3-Begin 12¢ issues thru #35 16.00 48.00 160.00
4,5 14.50 44.00 145.00
6-10 8.50 25.50 85.00
11,12,14-20 6.00 18.00 60.00
13-Kubert, Colan-a; Joe Kubert app. in story 6.50 19.50 65.00
21-35: 22-Intro. International Sea Devils; origin & 1st app. Capt. X & Man Fish 4.00 12.00 40.00
NOTE: *Heath a-B&B 27-29, 1-10; c-B&B 27-29, 1-10, 14-16. Moldoff a-16i.*

SEA DEVILS (See Tangent Comics/ Sea Devils)

SEADRAGON (Also see the Epsilion Wave)
Elite Comics: May, 1986 - No. 8, 1987 ($1.75)

1-8: 1-1st & 2nd printings exist 2.00

SEA HOUND, THE (Captain Silver's Log Of The...)
Avon Periodicals: 1945 (no month) - No. 2, Sept-Oct, 1945

nn (#1)-29 pg. novel length sty-"The Esmeralda's Treasure" 16.00 47.00 110.00
2 11.50 34.00 80.00

SEA HOUND, THE (Radio)
Capt. Silver Syndicate: No. 3, July, 1949 - No. 4, Sept, 1949

3,4 9.70 29.00 58.00

GD2.0 FN6.0 NM9.4

SEA HUNT (TV)
Dell Publishing Co.: No. 928, 8/58 - No. 1041, 10-12/59; No. 4, 1-3/60 - No. 13, 4-6/62 (All have Lloyd Bridges photo-c)

Four Color 928(#1) 11.00 33.00 120.00
Four Color 994(#2), 4-13: Manning-a #4-6,8-11,13 8.00 23.00 85.00
Four Color 1041(#3)-Toth-a 8.00 25.00 90.00

SEAQUEST (TV)
Nemesis Comics: Mar, 1994 ($2.25)

1-Has 2 diff-c stocks (slick & cardboard); Alcala-i 2.25

SEARCH FOR LOVE
American Comics Group: Feb-Mar, 1950 - No. 2, Apr-May, 1950 (52 pgs.)

1 11.00 33.00 75.00
2,3(6-7/50): 3-Exist? 8.35 25.00 50.00

SEARCHERS, THE (Movie)
Dell Publishing Co.: No. 709, 1956

Four Color 709-John Wayne photo-c 24.00 71.00 260.00

SEARCHERS, THE
Caliber Comics: 1996 - No. 4, 1996 ($2.95, B&W)

1-4 3.00

SEARCHERS, THE : APOSTLE OF MERCY
Caliber Comics: 1997 - No. 2, 1997 ($2.95/$3.95, B&W)

1-($2.95) 3.00
2-($3.95) 4.00

SEARS (See Merry Christmas From...)

SEASON'S GREETINGS
Hallmark (King Features): 1935 (6-1/4x5-1/4", 32 pgs. in color)

nn-Cover features Mickey Mouse, Popeye, Jiggs & Skippy. "The Night Before Christmas" told one panel per page, each panel by a famous artist featuring their character. Art by Alex Raymond, Gottfredson, Swinnerton, Segar, Chic Young, Milt Gross, Sullivan (Messmer), Herriman, McManus, Percy Crosby & others (22 artists in all)
Estimated value... 600.00

SEBASTION O
DC Comics (Vertigo): May, 1993 - No. 3, July, 1993 ($1.95, limited series)

1-3-Grant Morrison scripts 2.00

SECOND LIFE OF DOCTOR MIRAGE, THE (See Shadowman #16)
Valiant: Nov, 1993 - No. 18, May, 1995 ($2.50)

1-18: 1-With bound-in poster. 5-Shadowman x-over. 7-Bound-in trading card 2.50
1-Gold ink logo edition; no price on-c 3.00

SECRET AGENT (Formerly Sarge Steel)
Charlton Comics: V2#9, Oct, 1966; V2#10, Oct, 1967

V2#9-Sarge Steel part-r begins 2.50 7.50 20.00
10-Tiffany Sinn, CIA app. (from Career Girl Romances #39); Aparo-a 1.75 5.25 14.00

SECRET AGENT (TV) (See Four Color #1231)
Gold Key: Nov, 1966; No. 2, Jan, 1968

1-Photo-c 11.00 33.00 115.00
2-Photo-c 7.00 20.00 75.00

SECRET AGENT X-9 (See Flash Gordon #4 by King)
David McKay Publ.: 1934 (Book 1: 84 pgs.; Book 2: 124 pgs.) (8x7-1/2")

Book 1-Contains reprints of the first 13 weeks of the strip by Alex Raymond; complete except for 2 dailies 40.00 120.00 325.00
Book 2-Contains reprints immediately following contents of Book 1, for 20 weeks by Alex Raymond; complete except for two dailies. Note: Raymond mis-dated the last five strips from 6/34, and while the dating sequence is confusing, the continuity is correct 40.00 120.00 280.00

SECRET AGENT X-9 (See Magic Comics)
Dell Publishing Co.: Dec, 1937 (Not by Raymond)

Secret Defenders #14 © MAR

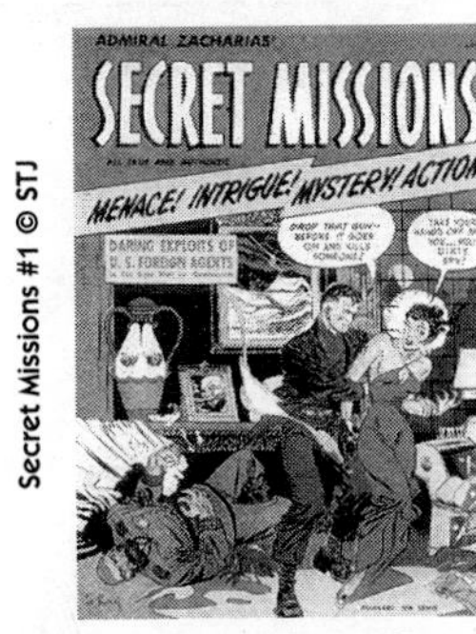

Secret Missions #1 © STJ

Secret Origins (2nd series) #3 © DC

GD2.0 FN6.0 NM9.4

Feature Books 8 35.00 106.00 390.00

SECRET AGENT Z-2 (See Holyoke One-Shot No. 7)

SECRET CITY SAGA (See Jack Kirby's Secret City Saga)

SECRET DEFENDERS (Also see The Defenders & Fantastic Four #374)
Marvel Comics: Mar, 1993 - No. 25, Mar, 1995 ($1.75/$1.95)

1-($2.50)-Red foil stamped-c; Dr. Strange, Nomad, Wolverine, Spider Woman & Darkhawk begin 2.50
2-11,13-24: 9-New team w/Silver Surfer, Thunderstrike, Dr. Strange & War Machine. 13-Thanos replaces Dr. Strange as leader; leads into Cosmic Powers limited series; 14-Dr. Druid. 15-Bound in card sheet. 8-Giant Man & Iron Fist app. 2.00
12,25: 12-($2.50)-Prismatic foil-c. 25 ($2.50, 52 pgs.) 2.50

SECRET DIARY OF EERIE ADVENTURES
Avon Periodicals: 1953 (25¢ giant, 100 pgs., one-shot)

nn-(Rare)-Kubert-a; Hollingsworth-c; Sid Check back-c 156.00 469.00 1250.00

SECRET HEARTS
National Periodical Publications (Beverly)(Arleigh No. 50-113):
9-10/49 - No. 6, 7-8/50; No. 7, 12-1/51-52 - No. 153, 7/71

1-Kinstler-a; photo-c begin, end #6 51.00 154.00 410.00
2-Toth-a (1 pg.); Kinstler-a 28.00 84.00 195.00
3,6 (1950) 24.00 73.00 170.00
4,5-Toth-a 25.00 75.00 175.00
7(12-1/51-52) (Rare) 40.00 120.00 300.00
8-10 (1952) 17.00 51.00 120.00
11-20 13.50 41.00 95.00
21-26: 26-Last precode (2-3/55) 11.50 34.00 80.00
27-40 6.00 18.00 60.00
41-50 4.00 12.00 40.00
51-60 3.20 9.60 32.00
61-75,100: 75-Last 10¢ issue 2.60 7.80 26.00
76-99,101-109 2.50 7.50 20.00
110- "Reach for Happiness" serial begins, ends #138 2.50 7.50 20.00
111-119,121-126 2.00 6.00 16.00
120,134-Neal Adams-c 2.50 7.50 24.00
127 (4/68)-Beatles cameo 2.50 7.50 24.00
128-133,135-142: 141,142- "20 Miles to Heartbreak", Chapter 2 & 3 (see Young Love for Chapters 1 & 4); Toth, Colletta-a 1.75 5.25 14.00
143-148,150-152: 144-Morrow-a 1.50 4.50 12.00
149,153: 149-Toth-a. 153-Kirby-i 1.75 5.25 14.00

SECRET ISLAND OF OZ, THE (See First Comics Graphic Novel)

SECRET LOVE (See Fox Giants & Sinister House of...)

SECRET LOVE
Ajax-Farrell/Four Star Comic Corp. No. 2 on: 12/55 - No. 3, 8/56; 4/57 - No. 5, 2/58; No. 6, 6/58

1(12/55-Ajax, 1st series) 10.00 30.00 60.00
2,3 5.85 17.50 35.00
1(4/57-Ajax, 2nd series) 7.50 22.50 45.00
2-6: 5-Bakerish-a 5.00 15.00 30.00

SECRET LOVES
Comic Magazines/Quality Comics Group: Nov, 1949 - No. 6, Sept, 1950

1-Ward-c 23.00 69.00 160.00
2-Ward-c 20.00 60.00 140.00
3-Crandall-a 12.00 36.00 85.00
4,6 9.15 27.00 55.00
5-Suggestive art "Boom Town Babe"; photo-c 12.00 36.00 85.00

SECRET LOVE STORIES (See Fox Giants)

SECRET MISSIONS (Admiral Zacharia's...)
St. John Publishing Co.: February, 1950

1-Joe Kubert-c; stories of U.S. foreign agents 20.00 60.00 140.00

SECRET MYSTERIES (Formerly Crime Mysteries & Crime Smashers)

GD2.0 FN6.0 NM9.4

Ribage/Merit Publications No. 17 on: No. 16, Nov, 1954 - No. 19, July, 1955

16-Horror, Palais-a; Myron Fass-c 24.00 73.00 170.00
17-19-Horror. 17-Fass-c; mis-dated 3/54? 16.00 47.00 110.00

SECRET ORIGINS (1st Series) (See 80 Page Giant #8)
National Periodical Publications: Aug-Oct, 1961 (Annual) (Reprints)

1-Origin Adam Strange (Showcase #17), Green Lantern (Green Lantern #1), Challengers (partial-r/Showcase #6, 6 pgs. Kirby-a), J'onn J'onzz (Det. #225), The Flash (Showcase #4), Green Arrow (1 pg. text), Superman-Batman team (W. Finest #94), Wonder Woman (Wonder Woman #105) 45.00 135.00 540.00
Replica Edition (1998, $4.95) r/entire book and house ads 5.00

SECRET ORIGINS (2nd Series)
National Periodical Publications: Feb-Mar, 1973 - No. 6, Jan-Feb, 1974; No. 7, Oct-Nov, 1974 (All 20¢ issues) (All origin reprints)

1-Superman(r/1 pg. origin/Action #1, 1st time since G.A.), Batman(Det. #33), Ghost(Flash #88), The Flash(Showcase #4) 2.80 8.40 28.00
2-7: 2-Green Lantern & The Atom(Showcase #22 & 34), Supergirl(Action #252). 3-Wonder Woman(W.W. #1), Wildcat(Sensation #1). 4-Vigilante (Action #42) by Meskin, Kid Eternity(Hit #25). 5-The Spectre by Baily (More Fun #52,53). 6-Blackhawk(Military #1) & Legion of Super-Heroes(Superboy #147). 7-Robin (Detective #38), Aquaman (More Fun #73) 1.75 5.25 14.00

NOTE: *Infantino a-1.* ***Kane*** *a-2.* ***Kubert*** *a-1.*

SECRET ORIGINS (3rd Series)
DC Comics: 4/86 - No. 50, 8/90 (All origins)(52 pgs. #6 on)(#27 on: $1.50)

1-Origin Superman 3.50
2-6: 2-Blue Beetle. 3-Shazam. 4-Firestorm. 5-Crimson Avenger. 6-Halo/G.A. Batman 2.00
7-12,14-26: 7-Green Lantern(Guy Gardner)/G.A. Sandman. 8-Shadow Lass/Doll Man. 9-G.A. Flash/Skyman. 10-Phantom Stranger w/Alan Moore scripts; Legends spin-off. 11-G.A. Hawkman/Power Girl. 12-Challengers of Unknown/G.A. Fury (2nd modern app.). 14-Suicide Squad; Legends spin-off. 15-Spectre/Deadman. 16-G.A. Hourman/Warlord. 17-Adam Strange story by Carmine infantino; Dr. Occult. 18-G.A. Gr. Lantern/The Creeper. 19-Uncle Sam/The Guardian. 20-Batgirl/G.A. Dr. Mid-Nite. 21-Jonah Hex/Black Condor. 22-Manhunters. 23-Floronic Man/Guardians of the Universe. 24-Blue Devil/Dr. Fate. 25-LSH/Atom. 26-Black Lightning/Miss America 2.00
13-Origin Nightwing; Johnny Thunder app. 2.00
27-49: 27-Zatara/Zatanna. 28-Midnight/Nightshade. 29-Power of the Atom/Mr. America; new 3 pg. Red Tornado story by Mayer (last app. of Scribbly, 8/88). 30-Plastic Man/Elongated Man. 31-JSA. 32-JLA. 33-35-JLI. 36-Poison Ivy by Neil Gaiman & Mark Buckingham/Green Lantern. 37-Legion Of Substitute Heroes/Doctor Light. 38-Green Arrow/Speedy; Grell scripts. 39-Animal Man-c/story continued in Animal Man #10; Grant Morrison scripts;Batman app.40-All Ape issue. 41-Rogues Gallery of Flash. 42-Phantom Girl/GrimGhost. 43-Original Hawk & Dove/Cave Carson/Chris KL-99. 44-Batman app.;story based on Det. #40. 45-Blackhawk/El Diablo. 46-JLA/LSH/New Titans. 47-LSH. 48-Ambush Bug/Stanley & His Monster/Rex the Wonder Dog/Trigger Twins. 49-Newsboy Legion/Silent Knight/brief origin Bouncing Boy 2.00
50-($3.95, 100 pgs.)-Batman & Robin in text, Flash of Two Worlds, Johnny Thunder, Dolphin, Black Canary & Space Museum 5.00
Annual 1 (8/87)-Capt. Comet/Doom Patrol 3.00
Annual 2 ('88, $2.00)-Origin Flash II & Flash III 3.00
Annual 3 ('89, $2.95, 84 pgs.)-Teen Titans; 1st app. new Flamebird who replaces original Bat-Girl 3.50
Special 1 (10/89, $2.00)-Batman villains: Penguin, Riddler, & Two-Face; Bolland-c; Sam Kieth-a; Neil Gaiman scripts(2) 3.00

NOTE: ***Art Adams*** *a-33i(part).* ***M. Anderson*** *8, 19, 21, 25i; c-19(part).* ***Aparo*** *c/a-10.* ***Bissette*** *c-23.* ***Bolland*** *c-7.* ***Byrne*** *c/a-Annual 1.* ***Colan*** *c/a-5p.* ***Forte*** *a-37.* ***Giffen*** *a-18p, 44p, 48.* ***Infantino*** *a-17, 50p.* ***Kaluta*** *c-39.* ***Gil Kane*** *a-2, 28; c-2p.* ***Kirby*** *c-19(part).* ***Erik Larsen*** *a-13.* ***Mayer*** *a-29.* ***Morrow*** *a-21.* ***Orlando*** *a-10.* ***Perez*** *a-50i, Annual 3i; c- Annual 3.* ***Rogers*** *a-6p.* ***Russell*** *a-27i.* ***Simonson*** *c-22.* ***Staton*** *a-36, 50p.* ***Steacy*** *a-35.* ***Tuska*** *a-4p, 9p.*

SECRET ORIGINS 80 PAGE GIANT (Young Justice)
DC Comics: Dec, 1998 ($4.95, one-shot)

1-Origin-s of Young Justice members; Ramos-a (Impulse) 5.00

Secret Society of Super-Villains #5 © DC

Secrets of Haunted House #19 © DC

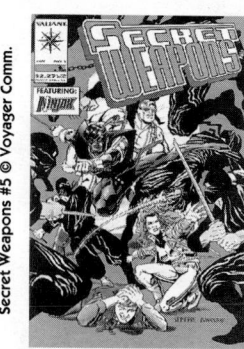

Secret Weapons #5 © Voyager Comm.

GD2.0 FN6.0 NM9.4

SECRET ORIGINS FEATURING THE JLA
DC Comics: 1999 ($14.95, TPB)

1-Reprints recent origin-s of JLA members; Cassaday-c 15.00

SECRET ORIGINS OF SUPER-HEROES (See DC Special Series #10, 19)

SECRET ORIGINS OF THE WORLD'S GREATEST SUPER-HEROES
DC Comics: 1989 ($4.95, 148 pgs.)

nn-Reprints Superman, JLA.origins; new Batman-o; Bolland-c. 6.00

SECRET ROMANCE
Charlton Comics: Oct, 1968 - No. 41, Nov, 1976; No. 42, Mar, 1979 - No. 48, Feb, 1980

1-Begin 12¢ issues, ends #? 1.50 4.50 12.00
2-10: 9-Reese-a 1.00 3.00 8.00
11-30 5.00
31-48 3.00
NOTE: *Beyond the Stars app.-No. 9, 11, 12, 14.*

SECRET ROMANCES (Exciting Love Stories)
Superior Publications Ltd.: Apr, 1951 - No. 27, July, 1955

1 12.00 36.00 85.00
2 8.35 25.00 50.00
3-10 6.00 18.00 36.00
11-13,15-18,20-27 4.25 13.00 28.00
14,19-Lingerie panels 5.85 17.50 35.00

SECRET SERVICE (See Kent Blake of the...)

SECRET SIX (See Action Comics Weekly)
National Periodical Publications: Apr-May, 1968 - No. 7, Apr-May, 1969 (12¢)

1-Origin/1st app. 4.80 14.40 48.00
2-7 2.80 8.40 28.00

SECRET SIX (See Tangent Comics/ Secret Six)

SECRET SOCIETY OF SUPER-VILLAINS
National Per. Publ./DC Comics: May-June, 1976 - No. 15, June-July, 1978

1-Origin; JLA cameo & Capt. Cold app. 1.25 3.75 10.00
2,4: 2-Re-intro/origin Capt. Comet; Green Lantern x-over 2.40 6.00
3,5: 5-Green Lantern, Hawkman x-over; Darkseid app. 2.40 6.00
6-14: 9,10-Creeper x-over. 11-Capt. Comet; Orlando-i. 15-G.A. Atom, Dr. Midnite, & JSA app. 5.00

SECRET SOCIETY OF SUPER-VILLAINS SPECIAL (See DC Special Series #6)

SECRETS OF HAUNTED HOUSE
National Periodical Publications/DC Comics: 4-5/75 - #5, 12-1/75-76; #6, 6-7/77 - #14, 10-11/78; #15, 8/79 - #46, 3/82

1 2.50 7.50 24.00
2-4 1.50 4.50 12.00
5-Wrightson-c 1.75 5.25 14.00
6-14 1.00 3.00 8.00
15-30 2.40 6.00
31,44: 31-Mr. E series begins, ends #41. 44-Wrightson-c 2.40 6.00
32-43,45,46 4.00
NOTE: ***Aparo** c-7. **Aragones** a-1. **B. Bailey** a-8. **Bissette** a-46. **Buckler** c-32-40p. **Ditko** a-9, 12, 41, 45. **Golden** a-10. **Howard** a-13i. **Kaluta** c-8, 10, 11, 14, 16, 29. **Kubert** c-41, 42. **Sheldon Mayer** a-43p. **McWilliams** a-35. **Nasser** a-24. **Newton** a-30p. **Nino** a-1, 13, 19. **Orlando** c-13, 30, 43, 45i. **N. Redondo** a-4, 5, 29. **Rogers** c-26. **Spiegle** a-31-41. **Wrightson** c-5, 44.*

SECRETS OF HAUNTED HOUSE SPECIAL (See DC Special Series #12)

SECRETS OF LIFE (Movie)
Dell Publishing Co.: 1956 (Disney)

Four Color 749-Photo-c 3.60 11.00 40.00

SECRETS OF LOVE (See Popular Teen-Agers...)

SECRETS OF LOVE AND MARRIAGE
Charlton Comics: V2#1, Aug, 1956 - V2#25, June, 1961

V2#1 3.50 10.50 35.00
V2#2-6 2.50 7.50 24.00
V2#7-9-(All 68 pgs.) 3.80 11.40 38.00
10-25 2.00 6.00 16.00

SECRETS OF MAGIC (See Wisco)

SECRETS OF SINISTER HOUSE (Sinister House of Secret Love #1-4)
National Periodical Publ.: No. 5, June-July, 1972 - No. 18, June-July, 1974

5-(52 pgs.). 3.20 9.60 32.00
6-9: 7-Redondo-a 2.00 6.00 16.00
10-Neal Adams-a(i) 2.50 7.50 22.00
11-18: 15-Redondo-a. 17-Barry-a; early Chaykin 1 pg. strip 1.25 3.75 10.00
NOTE: ***Alcala** a-6, 13, 14. **Glanzman** a-7. **Kaluta** c-6, 7. **Nino** a-8, 11-13. Ambrose Bierce adapt.-#14.*

SECRETS OF THE LEGION OF SUPER-HEROES
DC Comics: Jan, 1981 - No. 3, Mar, 1981 (Limited series)

1-3: 1-Origin of the Legion. 2-Retells origins of Brainiac 5, Shrinking Violet, Sun-Boy, Bouncing Boy, Ultra-Boy, Matter-Eater Lad, Mon-El, Karate Kid, & Dream Girl 3.00

SECRETS OF TRUE LOVE
St. John Publishing Co.: Feb, 1958

1 4.25 13.00 28.00

SECRETS OF YOUNG BRIDES
Charlton Comics: No. 5, Sept, 1957 - No. 44, Oct, 1964; July, 1975 - No. 9, Nov, 1976

5 3.50 10.50 35.00
6-10: 8-Negligee panel 2.50 7.50 24.00
11-20 2.50 7.50 20.00
21-30: Last 10¢ issue? 1.75 5.25 14.00
31-44(10/64) 1.25 3.75 10.00
1-(2nd series) (7/75) 1.50 4.50 12.00
2-9 2.40 6.00

SECRET SQUIRREL (TV)(See Kite Fun Book)
Gold Key: Oct, 1966 (12¢) (Hanna-Barbera)

1-1st Secret Squirrel and Moracco Mole, Squiddly Diddly, Winsome Witch 12.00 36.00 130.00

SECRET STORY ROMANCES (Becomes True Tales of Love)
Atlas Comics (TCI): Nov, 1953 - No. 21, Mar, 1956

1-Everett-a; Jay Scott Pike-c 13.00 39.00 90.00
2 7.50 22.50 45.00
3-11: 11-Last pre-code (2/55) 5.85 17.50 35.00
12-21 5.00 15.00 30.00
NOTE: ***Colletta** a-10, 14, 15, 17, 21; c-10, 14, 17.*

SECRET VOICE, THE (See Great American Comics Presents...)

SECRET WARS II (Also see Marvel Super Heroes...)
Marvel Comics Group: July, 1985 - No. 9, Mar, 1986 (Maxi-series)

1,9: 9-(52 pgs.) X-Men app., Spider-Man app. 3.00
2-8: 2,8-X-Men app. 5-1st app. Boom Boom. 5,8-Spider-Man app. 2.00

SECRET WEAPONS
Valiant: Sept, 1993 - No. 21, May, 1995 ($2.25)

1-10,12-21: 3-Reese-a(i). 5-Ninjak app. 9-Bound-in trading card. 12-Bloodshot app. 2.50
11-(Sept. on envelope, Aug on-c, $2.50)-Enclosed in manilla envelope; Bloodshot app; intro new team. 2.50

SECTAURS
Marvel Comics: June, 1985 - No. 10?, 1986 (75¢) (Based on Coleco Toys)

1-10, 1-Coleco giveaway; different-c 2.00

SEDUCTION OF THE INNOCENT (Also see New York State Joint Legislative Committee to Study...)
Rinehart & Co., Inc., N. Y.: 1953, 1954 (400 pgs.) (Hardback, $4.00)(Written by Fredric Wertham, M.D.)(Also printed in Canada by Clarke, Irwin & Co. Ltd.)

(1st Version)-with bibliographical note intact (pages 399 & 400)(several copies got out before the comic publishers forced the removal of this page)

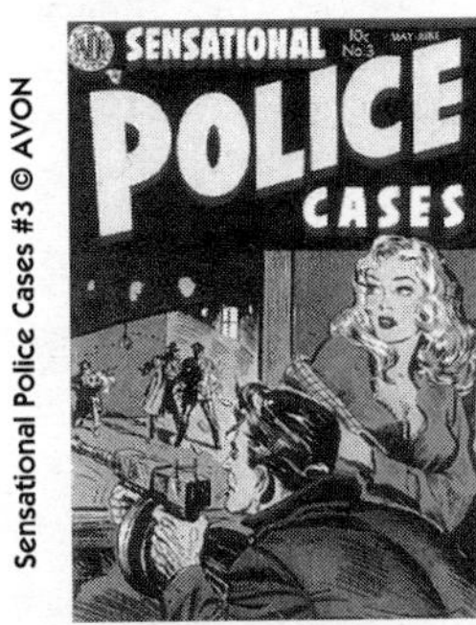

Sensational Police Cases #3 © AVON

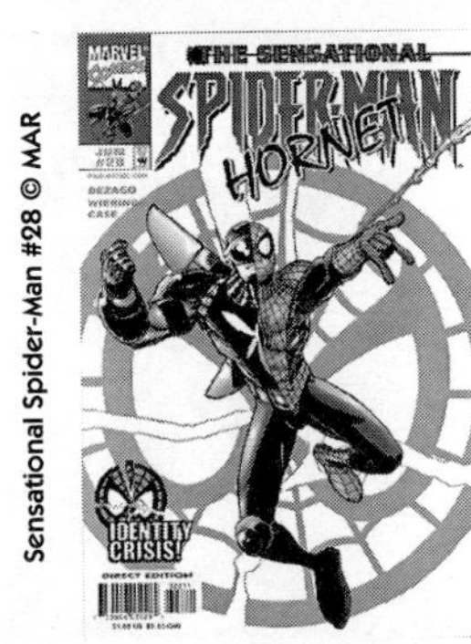

Sensational Spider-Man #28 © MAR

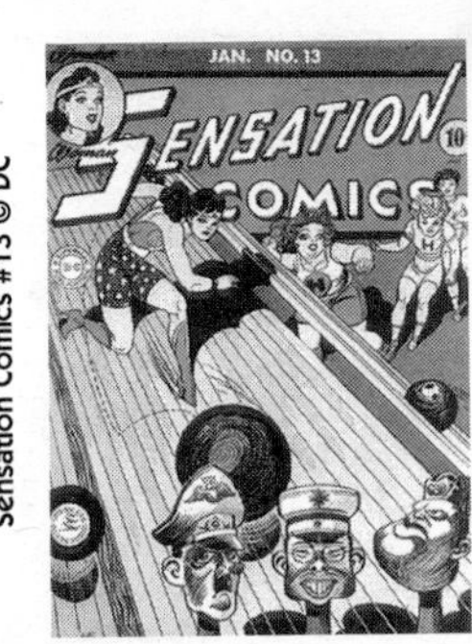

Sensation Comics #13 © DC

GD2.0 FN6.0 NM9.4

	GD2.0	FN6.0	NM9.4
	52.00	157.00	420.00
Dust jacket only	30.00	90.00	210.00
(1st Version)-without bibliographical note	30.00	90.00	210.00
Dust jacket only	13.50	41.00	95.00
(2nd Version)-Published in England by Kennikat Press, 1954, 399 pgs. has bibliographical page	10.00	30.00	70.00
1972 r-/of 2nd version; 400 pgs. w/bibliography page; Kennikat Press	2.50	7.50	24.00

NOTE: *Material from this book appeared in the November, 1953(Vol.70, pp50-53,214) issue of the* **Ladies' Home Journal** *under the title "What Parents Don't Know About Comic Books". With the release of this book, Dr. Wertham reveals seven years of research attempting to link juvenile delinquency to comic books. Many illustrations showing excessive violence, sex, sadism, and torture are shown. This book was used at the Kefauver Senate hearings which led to the Comics Code Authority. Because of the influence this book had on the comic industry and the collector's interest in it, we feel this listing is justified. Also see* **Parade of Pleasure.**

SEDUCTION OF THE INNOCENT! (Also see Halloween Horror)
Eclipse Comics: Nov, 1985 - 3-D#2, Apr, 1986 ($1.75)

1-6: Double listed under cover title from #7 on — 2.00
3-D 1 (10/85, $2.25, 36 pgs.)-contains unpublished Advs. Into Darkness #15 (pre-code);Dave Stevens-c — 3.00
2D 1 (100 copy limited signed & numbered edition)(B&W) — 5.00
3-D 2 (4/86)-Baker, Toth, Wrightson-c — 3.00
2-D 2 (100 copy limited signed & numbered edition)(B&W) — 5.00
NOTE: **Anderson** *r-2, 3.* **Crandall** *c/a(r)-1.* **Meskin** *c/a(r)-3, 3-D 1.* **Moreira** *r-2.* **Toth** *a-1-6r; c-4r.* **Tuska** *r-6.*

SEEKER
Sky Comics: Apr, 1994 ($2.50, one-shot)

1 — 2.50

SEEKERS INTO THE MYSTERY
DC Comics (Vertigo): Jan, 1996 - No. 15, Apr, 1997 ($2.50)

1-14: J.M. DeMatteis scripts in all. 1-4-Glenn Barr-a. 5,10-Muth-c/a. 6-9-Zulli-c/a. 11-14-Bolton-c; Jill Thompson-a — 2.50
15-($2.95)-Muth-c/a — 3.00

SEEKER 3000 (See Marvel Premiere #41)
Marvel Comics: Jun, 1998 - No. 4, Sept, 1998 ($2.99/$2.50, limited series)

1-($2.99)-Set 25 years after 1st app.; wraparound-c — 3.00
2-4-($2.50) — 2.50
...Premiere 1 (6/98, $1.50) Reprints 1st app. from Marvel Premiere #41; wraparound-c — 2.00

SELECT DETECTIVE (Exciting New Mystery Cases)
D. S. Publishing Co.: Aug-Sept, 1948 - No. 3, Dec-Jan, 1948-49

	GD2.0	FN6.0	NM9.4
1-Matt Baker-a	25.00	75.00	175.00
2-Baker, McWilliams-a	16.00	47.00	110.00
3	13.00	39.00	90.00

SELF-LOATHING COMICS
Fantagraphics Books: Feb, 1995 ($2.95, B&W)

1,2-Crumb — 3.00

SEMPER FI (Tales of the Marine Corp)
Marvel Comics: Dec, 1988- No.9, Aug, 1989 (75¢)

1-9: Severin-c/a — 2.00

SENSATIONAL POLICE CASES (Becomes Captain Steve Savage, 2nd Series)
Avon Periodicals: 1952; 1954 - No. 4, July-Aug, 1954

	GD2.0	FN6.0	NM9.4
nn-(1952, 25¢, 100 pgs.)-Kubert-a?; Check, Larsen, Lawrence & McCann-a; Kinstler-c	40.00	120.00	290.00
1 (1954)-Exists?	15.00	45.00	105.00
2-4: 2-Kirbyish-a (3-4/54). 4-Reprint/Saint #5; spanking panel	12.00	36.00	85.00
I.W. Reprint #5-(1963?, nd)-Reprints Prison Break #5(1952-Realistic); Infantino-a	2.50	7.50	24.00

SENSATIONAL SHE-HULK, THE (She-Hulk #21-23) (See Savage She-Hulk)
Marvel Comics: V2#1, 5/89 - No. 60, Feb, 1994 ($1.50/$1.75, deluxe format)

V2#1-Byrne-c/a(p)/scripts begin, end #8 — 3.00
2-8: 3-Spidey. 4-Reintro G.A. Blonde Phantom — 2.00
9-49,51-60: 14-17-Howard the Duck app. 21-23-Return of the Blonde Phantom. 22-All Winners Squad app. 25-Thor app. 26-Excalibur app.; Guice-c. 29-Wolverine app. (3 pgs.). 30-Hobgoblin-c & cameo. 31-Byrne-c/a/scripts begin again. 35-Last $1.50-c. 37-Wolverine/Punisher/Spidey-c, but no app. 39-Thing app. 56-War Zone app.; Hulk cameo. 57-Vs. Hulk-c/story. 58-Electro-c/story. 59-Jack O'Lantern app. — 2.00
50-($2.95, 52 pgs.)-Embossed green foil-c; Byrne app.; last Byrne-c/a; Austin, Chaykin, Simonson-a; Miller-a(2 pgs.) — 3.00
NOTE: **Dale Keown** *a(p)-13, 15-22.*

SENSATIONAL SHE-HULK IN CEREMONY, THE
Marvel Comics: 1989 - No. 2, 1989 ($3.95, squarebound, 52 pgs.)

nn-Part 1, nn-Part 2 — 4.00

SENSATIONAL SPIDER-MAN
Marvel Comics: Apr, 1989 ($5.95, squarebound, 80 pgs.)

1-r/Amazing Spider-Man Annual #14,15 by Miller & Annual #8 by Kirby & Ditko. — 6.00

SENSATIONAL SPIDER-MAN, THE
Marvel Comics: Jan, 1996 - No. 33, Nov, 1998 ($1.95/$1.99)

	GD2.0	FN6.0	NM9.4
0 ($4.95)-Lenticular-c; Jurgens-a/scripts			5.00
1-18: 2-Kaine & Rhino app. 3-Giant-Man app. 9-Onslaught tie-in; revealed that Peter & Mary Jane's unborn baby is a girl. 11-Revelations. 13-15-Ka-Zar app. 14,15-Hulk app.			4.00
1-($2.95) variant-c; polybagged w/cassette	1.00	3.00	8.00
19-24: Living Pharoah app. 22,23-Dr. Strange app.			3.00
25-($2.99) Spiderhunt pt. 1; Normie Osborne kidnapped			4.00
25-Variant-c	1.00	3.00	8.00
26-33: 26-Nauck-a. 27-Double-c with "The Sensational Hornet #1"; Vulture app. 28-Hornet vs. Vulture. 29,30-Black Cat-c/app. 33-Last issue; Gathering of Five concludes			4.00
'96 Annual ($2.95)			3.00

SENSATION COMICS (Sensation Mystery #110 on)
National Per. Publ./All-American: Jan, 1942 - No. 109, May-June, 1952

	GD2.0	FN6.0	VF8.0	NM9.4
1-Origin Mr. Terrific(1st app.), Wildcat(1st app.), The Gay Ghost, & Little Boy Blue; Wonder Woman(cont'd from All Star #8), The Black Pirate begin; intro. Justice & Fair Play Club	2000.00	6000.00	12,000.00	22,000.00

1-Reprint, Oversize 13-1/2x10". WARNING: This comic is an exact duplicate reprint of the original except for its size. DC published it in 1974 with a second cover titling it as a Famous First Edition. There have been many reported cases of the outer cover being removed and the interior sold as the original edition. The reprint with the new outer cover removed is practically worthless. See Famous First Edition for value.

	GD2.0	FN6.0	NM9.4
2-Etta Candy begins	400.00	1200.00	3600.00
3-W. Woman gets secretary's job	237.00	711.00	1900.00
4-1st app. Stretch Skinner in Wildcat	175.00	525.00	1400.00
5-Intro. Justin, Black Pirate's son	137.00	411.00	1100.00
6-Origin/1st app. Wonder Woman's magic lasso	137.00	411.00	1100.00
7-10	100.00	300.00	800.00
11,12,14-20	91.00	272.00	725.00
13-Hitler, Tojo, Mussolini-c (as bowling pins)	122.00	336.00	975.00
21-30	72.00	216.00	575.00
31-33	55.00	165.00	440.00
34-Sargon, the Sorcerer begins (10/44), ends #36; begins again #52	57.00	172.00	460.00
35-40: 38-X-Mas-c	47.00	141.00	375.00
41-50: 43-The Whip app.	40.00	120.00	325.00
51-67,69-80: 51-Last Black Pirate. 56,57-Sargon by Kubert. 63-Last Mr. Terrific. 66-Wildcat by Kubert	39.00	118.00	275.00
68-Origin & 1st app.Huntress (8/47)	40.00	120.00	290.00
81-Used in **SOTI**, pg. 33,34; Krigstein-a	40.00	120.00	290.00
82-93: 83-Last Sargon. 86-The Atom app. 90-Last Wildcat. 91-Streak begins by Alex Toth. 92-Toth-a (2 pgs.)	31.00	94.00	220.00
94-1st all girl issue	43.00	128.00	340.00

95-99,101-106: 95-Unmasking of Wonder Woman-c/story. 99-1st app. Astra, Girl of the Future, ends #106. 103-Robot-c. 105-Last 52 pgs. 106-Wonder

Sgt. Bilko #6 © DC

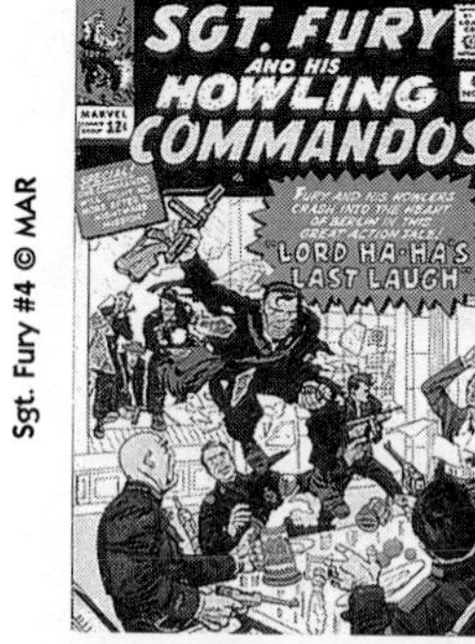

Sgt. Fury #4 © MAR

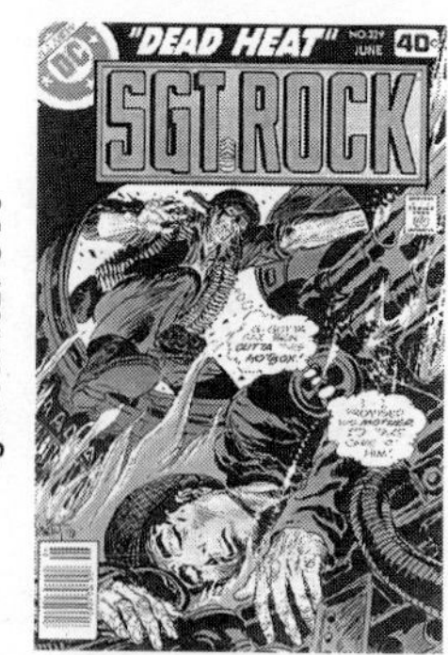

Sgt. Rock #329 © DC

GD2.0 FN6.0 NM9.4

Woman ends 40.00 120.00 310.00
100-(11-12/50) 55.00 165.00 440.00
107-(Scarce, 1-2/52)-1st mystery issue; Johnny Peril by Toth(p), 8 pgs. & begins; continues from Danger Trail #5 (3-4/51)(see Comic Cavalcade #15 for 1st app.) 66.00 197.00 525.00
108-(Scarce)-Johnny Peril by Toth(p) 53.00 159.00 425.00
109-(Scarce)-Johnny Peril by Toth(p) 66.00 197.00 525.00
NOTE: ***Krigstein** a-(Wildcat)-81, 83, 84.* ***Moldoff** Black Pirate-1-25; Black Pirate not in 34-36, 43-48.* ***Oskner** c(i)-89-91, 94-106. Wonder Woman by **H. G. Peter**, all issues except #8, 17-19, 21; c-4-7, 9-18, 20-88, 92, 93. **Toth** a-91, 98; c-107. Wonder Woman c-1-106.*

SENSATION COMICS (Also see All Star Comics 1999 crossover titles)
DC Comics: May, 1999 ($1.99, one-shot)

1-Golden Age Wonder Woman and Hawkgirl; Robinson-s 2.00

SENSATION MYSTERY (Formerly Sensation Comics #1-109)
National Periodical Publ.: No. 110, July-Aug, 1952 - No. 116, July-Aug, 1953

110-Johnny Peril continues 40.00 120.00 310.00
111-116-Johnny Peril in all. 116-M. Anderson-a 40.00 120.00 310.00
NOTE: ***M. Anderson** c-110. **Colan** a-114p. **Giunta** a-112. **G. Kane** c(p)-108, 109, 111-115.*

SENTINELS OF JUSTICE, THE (See Americomics & Captain Paragon &...)

SENTRY SPECIAL
Innovation Publishing: 1991 ($2.75, one-shot)(Hero Alliance spin-off)

1-Lost in Space preview (3 pgs.) 2.75

SERAPHIM
Innovation Publishing: May, 1990 ($2.50, mature readers)

1 2.50

SERGEANT BARNEY BARKER (Becomes G. I. Tales #4 on)
Atlas Comics (MCI): Aug, 1956 - No. 3, Dec, 1956

1-Severin-c/a(4) 19.00 56.00 130.00
2,3: 2-Severin-c/a(4). 3-Severin-c/a(5) 13.00 39.00 90.00

SERGEANT BILKO (Phil Silvers Starring as...) (TV)
National Periodical Publications: May-June, 1957 - No. 18, Mar-Apr, 1960

1-All have Bob Oskner-c 70.00 210.00 560.00
2 40.00 120.00 280.00
3-5 33.00 99.00 230.00
6-18: 11,12,15,17-Photo-c 27.00 81.00 190.00

SGT. BILKO'S PVT. DOBERMAN (TV)
National Periodical Publications: June-July, 1958 - No. 11, Feb-Mar, 1960

1-Bob Oskner c-1-4,7,11 33.00 100.00 320.00
2 20.00 60.00 190.00
3-5: 5-Photo-c 14.00 42.00 130.00
6-11: 6,9-Photo-c 10.00 30.00 95.00

SGT. DICK CARTER OF THE U.S. BORDER PATROL (See Holyoke One-Shot)

SGT. FURY (& His Howling Commandos)(See Fury & Special Marvel Edition)
Marvel Comics Group (BPC earlier issues): May, 1963 - No. 167, Dec, 1981

1-1st app. Sgt. Nick Fury (becomes agent of Shield in Strange Tales #135); Kirby/Ayers-c/a; 1st Dum-Dum Dugan & the Howlers 92.00 275.00 1100.00
2-Kirby-a 30.00 90.00 300.00
3-5: 3-Reed Richards x-over. 4-Death of Junior Juniper. 5-1st Baron Strucker app.; Kirby-a 17.50 52.00 175.00
6-10: 8-Baron Zemo, 1st Percival Pinkerton app. 9-Hitler-c & app. 10-1st app. Capt. Savage (the Skipper)(9/64) 11.00 33.00 110.00
11,12,14-20: 14-1st Blitz Squad. 18-Death of Pamela Hawley 5.50 16.50 55.00
13-Captain America & Bucky app.(12/64); 2nd solo Capt. America x-over outside The Avengers; Kirby-a 29.00 87.00 290.00
21-30: 25-Red Skull app. 27-1st app. Eric Koenig; origin Fury's eye patch 4.00 12.00 40.00
31-50: 34-Origin Howling Commandos. 35-Eric Koenig joins Howlers. 43-Bob Hope, Glen Miller app. 44-Flashback on Howlers' 1st mission 2.50 7.50 20.00
51-60 2.25 6.75 18.00

GD2.0 FN6.0 NM9.4

61-67: 64-Capt. Savage & Raiders x-over. 67-Last 12¢ issue 2.00 6.00 16.00
68-80: 76-Fury's Father app. in WWI story 1.85 5.50 15.00
81-91: 91-Last 15¢ issue 1.85 5.50 15.00
92,93-(52 pgs.) 2.00 6.00 16.00
94-99: 98-Deadly Dozen x-over 1.50 4.50 12.00
100-Capt. America, Fantastic 4 cameos; Stan Lee, Martin Goodman & others app. 2.00 6.00 16.00
101-120: 101-Origin retold 1.25 3.75 10.00
121-130: 121-123-r/#19-21 1.00 3.00 8.00
131-167: 167-Reprints (from 1963) 1.00 2.80 7.00
133,134-(30¢-c variants, limited distribution)(5,7/76) 2.80 8.40 28.00
Annual 1(1965, 25¢, 72 pgs.)-r/#4,5 & new-a 12.50 38.00 125.00
Special 2(1966) 4.00 12.00 40.00
Special 3(1967) 2.50 7.50 25.00
Special 4(1968) 2.25 6.75 18.00
Special 5-7(1969-11/71) 1.50 4.50 12.00
NOTE: ***Ayers** a-8, Annual 1. **Ditko** a-15i. **Gil Kane** c-37, 96. **Kirby** a-1-7, 13p, 167p(r). Special 5; c-1-20, 25, 167p. **Severin** a-44-46, 48, 162, 164; inks-49-79, Special 4, 6; c-4i, 5, 6, 44, 46, 110, 149i, 155i, 162-166. **Sutton** a-57p. Reprints in #80, 82, 85, 87, 89, 91, 93, 95, 99, 101, 103, 105, 107, 109, 111, 121-123, 145-155, 167.*

SGT. FURY AND HIS HOWLING DEFENDERS (See The Defenders #147)

SERGEANT PRESTON OF THE YUKON (TV)
Dell Publishing Co.: No. 344, Aug, 1951 - No. 29, Nov-Jan, 1958-59

Four Color 344(#1)-Sergeant Preston & his dog Yukon King begin; painted-c begin, end #18 11.00 33.00 120.00
Four Color 373,397,419('52) 6.40 19.00 70.00
5(11-1/52-53)-10(2-4/54): 6-Bondage-c. 4.50 13.50 50.00
11,12,14-17 3.60 11.00 40.00
13-Origin Sgt. Preston 4.50 13.50 50.00
18-Origin Yukon King; last painted-c 4.50 13.50 50.00
19-29: All photo-c 6.00 18.00 65.00

SGT. ROCK (Formerly Our Army at War; see Brave & the Bold #52 & Showcase #45)
National Periodical Publications/DC Comics: No. 302, Mar, 1977 - No. 422, July, 1988 (See G.I. Combat #108)

302 2.50 7.50 25.00
303-310 1.85 5.50 15.00
311-320: 318-Reprints 1.25 3.75 10.00
321-350 1.00 3.00 8.00
351-399,401-421 5.00
400,422: 422-1st Joe, Adam, Andy Kubert-a team 1.00 2.80 7.00
Annual 2-4: 2(1982)-Formerly Sgt. Rock's Prize Battle Tales #1. 3(1983). 4(1984) 5.00
NOTE: ***Estrada** a-322, 327, 331, 336, 337, 341, 342i. **Glanzman** a-384, 421. **Kubert** a-302, 303, 305r, 306, 328, 351, 356, 368, 373, 422; c-317, 318r, 319-323, 325-333-on, Annual 2, 3. **Severin** a-347. **Spiegle** a-382, Annual 2, 3. **Thorne** a-384. **Toth** a-385r. **Wildey** a-307, 311, 313, 314.*

SGT. ROCK SPECIAL (Sgt. Rock #14 on; see DC Special Series #3)
DC Comics: Oct, 1988 - No. 21, Feb, 1992; No. 1, 1992; No. 2, 1994 ($2.00, quarterly/monthly, 52 pgs)

1-Reprint begin 5.00
2-21: All-r; 5-r/early Sgt. Rock/Our Army at War #81. 7-Tomahawk-r by Thorne. 9-Enemy Ace-r by Kubert. 10-All Rock issue. 11-r/1st Haunted Tank story. 12-All Kubert issue;begins monthly. 13-Dinosaur story by Heath(r). 14-Enemy Ace-r (22 pgs.) by Adams/Kubert. 15-Enemy Ace (22 pgs.) by Kubert. 16-Iron Major-c/story. 16,17-Enemy Ace-r. 19-r/Batman/Sgt. Rock team-up/B&B #108 by Aparo 4.00
1 (1992, $2.95, 68 pgs.)-Simonson-c; unpubbed Kubert-a; Glanzman, Russell, Pratt, & Wagner-a 4.00
2 (1994, $2.95) Brereton painted-c 3.50
NOTE: ***Neal Adams** r-1, 8, 14p. **Chaykin** a-2; r-3, 9(2pgs.); c-3. **Drucker** r-6. **Glanzman** r-20. **Golden** a-1. **Heath** a-2; r-5, 9-13, 16, 19, 21. **Krigstein** r-4, 8. **Kubert** r-1-17, 20, 21; c-1p, 2, 8, 14-21. **Miller** r-6p. **Severin** r-3, 6, 10. **Simonson** r-2, 4; c-4. **Thorne** r-7. **Toth** r-2, 8, 11. **Wood** r-4.*

SGT. ROCK SPECTACULAR (See DC Special Series #13)

SGT. ROCK'S PRIZE BATTLE TALES (Becomes Sgt. Rock Annual #2 on;

Sergio Aragonés' Boogeyman #4
© Sergio Aragonés & Mark Evanier

Seven Seas Comics #6
© Universal Phoenix Features

Shade, The Changing Man #15 © DC

GD2.0 FN6.0 NM9.4

see DC Special Series #18 & 80 Page Giant #7)
National Periodical Publications: Winter, 1964 (Giant - 80 pgs., one-shot)
1-Kubert, Heath-r; new Kubert-c 31.00 93.00 310.00

SGT. STRYKER'S DEATH SQUAD (See Savage Combat Tales)

SERGIO ARAGONES' BOOGEYMAN
Dark Horse Comics: June, 1998 - No. 4, Sept, 1998 ($2.95, B&W, lim. series)
1-4-Aragonés-c/a 3.00

SERGIO ARAGONES DESTROYS DC
DC Comics: June, 1996 ($3.50, one-shot)
1-DC Superhero parody book; Aragonés-c/a; Evanier scripts 3.50

SERGIO ARAGONES' DIA DE LOS MUERTOS
Dark Horse Comics: Oct, 1998 ($2.95, one-shot)
1-Aragonés-c/a; Evanier scripts 3.00

SERGIO ARAGONES' GROO & RUFFERTO
Dark Horse Comics: Dec, 1998 - No. 4, Mar, 1999 ($2.95, lim. series)
1-3-Aragonés-c/a 3.00

SERGIO ARAGONES' GROO THE WANDERER (See Groo...)

SERGIO ARAGONES' LOUDER THAN WORDS
Dark Horse Comics: July, 1997 - No. 6, Dec, 1997 ($2.95, B&W, limited series)
1-6-Aragonés-c/a 3.00

SERGIO ARAGONES MASSACRES MARVEL
Marvel Comics: June, 1996 ($3.50, one-shot)
1-Marvel Superhero parody book; Aragonés-c/a; Evanier scripts 3.50

SERRA ANGEL ON THE WORLDS OF MAGIC THE GATHERING
Acclaim Comics (Armada): Aug, 1996 ($5.95, one-shot)
1 6.00

SERINA
Antarctic Press: Mar, 1996 - No. 3, July, 1996 ($2.95)
1-3: Warrior Nun app. 3.00

SEVEN BLOCK
Marvel Comics (Epic Comics): 1990 ($4.50, one-shot, 52 pgs.)
1 4.50

SEVEN DEAD MEN (See Complete Mystery #1)

SEVEN DWARFS (Also see Snow White)
Dell Publishing Co.: No. 227, 1949 (Disney-Movie)
Four Color #227 10.00 30.00 110.00

SEVEN MILES A SECOND
DC Comics (Vertigo Verité): 1996 ($7.95, one-shot)
nn-Wojnarowicz-s/Romberg-a 8.00

SEVEN SAMUROID, THE (See Image Graphic Novel)

SEVEN SEAS COMICS
Universal Phoenix Features/Leader No. 6: Apr, 1946 - No. 6, 1947(no month)
1-South Sea Girl by Matt Baker, Capt. Cutlass begin; Tugboat Tessie by Baker app. 81.00 244.00 650.00
2-Swashbuckler-c 69.00 206.00 550.00
3,5,6: 3-Six pg. Feldstein-a 62.00 187.00 500.00
4-Classic Baker-c 66.00 197.00 525.00
NOTE: ***Baker*** *a-1-6; c-3-6.*

1776 (See Charlton Classic Library)

7TH VOYAGE OF SINBAD, THE (Movie)
Dell Publishing Co.: Sept, 1958 (photo-c)
Four Color 944-Buscema-a 12.00 35.00 130.00

77 SUNSET STRIP (TV)
Dell Publ. Co./Gold Key: No. 1066, Jan-Mar, 1960 - No. 2, Feb, 1963 (All photo-c)
Four Color 1066-Toth-a 11.00 33.00 120.00

GD2.0 FN6.0 NM9.4

Four Color 1106,1159-Toth-a 9.00 27.00 100.00
Four Color 1211,1263,1291, 01-742-209(7-9/62)-Manning-a in all 8.00 25.00 90.00
1,2: Manning-a. 1(11/62-G.K.) 9.00 27.00 100.00

77TH BENGAL LANCERS, THE (TV)
Dell Publishing Co.: May, 1957
Four Color 791-Photo-c 6.40 19.00 70.00

SEYMOUR, MY SON (See More Seymour)
Archie Publications (Radio Comics): Sept, 1963
1 2.60 7.80 26.00

SHADE, THE (See Starman)
DC Comics: Apr, 1997 - No. 4, July, 1997 ($2.25, limited series)
1-4-Robinson-s/Harris-c: 1-Gene Ha-a. 2-Williams/Gray-a 3-Blevins-a. 4-Zulli-a 3.00

SHADE, THE CHANGING MAN (See Cancelled Comic Cavalcade)
National Per. Publ./DC Comics: June-July, 1977 - No. 8, Aug-Sept, 1978
1-1st app. Shade; Ditko-c/a in all 1.00 3.00 8.00
2-8 5.00

SHADE, THE CHANGING MAN (2nd series) (Also see Suicide Squad #16)
DC Comics (Vertigo imprint #33 on): July, 1990 - No.70, 1996 ($1.50/$1.75/$1.95/$2.25, mature)
1-($2.50, 52 pgs.)-Peter Milligan scripts in all 4.00
2-49,51-59: 6-Preview of World Without End. 17-Begin $1.75-c. 33-Metallic ink on-c. 41-Begin $1.95-c. 42-44-John Constantine app. 2.25
50-($2.95, 52 pgs.) 3.50
60-70: 60-begin $2.25-c 2.25
NOTE: ***Bachalo*** *a-1-9, 11-13, 15-21, 23-26, 33-39, 42-45, 47, 49, 50; c-30, 33-41.*

SHADO: SONG OF THE DRAGON (See Green Arrow #63-66)
DC Comics: 1992 - No. 4, 1992 ($4.95, limited series, 52 pgs.)
Book One - Four: Grell scripts; Morrow-a(i) 5.00

SHADOW, THE (See Batman #253, 259 & Marvel Graphic Novel #35)

SHADOW, THE (Pulp, radio)
Archie Comics (Radio Comics): Aug, 1964 - No. 8, Sept, 1965 (All 12¢)
1-Jerrry Siegel scripts in all; Shadow-c. 5.00 15.00 50.00
2-8: 2-App. in super-hero costume on-c only; Reinman-a(backup). 3-Superhero begins; Reinman-a (book-length novel). 3,4,6,7-The Fly 1 pg. strips. 4-8-Reinman-a. 5-8-Siegel scripts. 7-Shield app. 3.00 9.00 30.00

SHADOW, THE
National Periodical Publications: Oct-Nov, 1973 - No. 12, Aug-Sept, 1975
1-Kaluta-a begins 2.50 7.50 24.00
2 1.50 4.50 12.00
3-Kaluta/Wrightson-a 1.85 5.50 15.00
4,6-Kaluta-a ends. 4-Chaykin, Wrightson part-i 1.25 3.75 10.00
5,7-12: 11-The Avenger (pulp character) x-over 2.40 6.00
NOTE: ***Craig*** *a-10.* ***Cruz*** *a-10-12.* ***Kaluta*** *a-1, 2, 3p, 4, 6; c-1-4, 6, 10-12.* ***Kubert*** *c-9.* ***Robbins*** *a-5, 7-9; c-5, 7, 8.*

SHADOW, THE
DC Comics: May, 1986 - No. 4, Aug, 1986 (limited series)
1-4: Howard Chaykin art in all 2.50
Blood & Judgement ($12.95)-r/1-4 13.00

SHADOW, THE
DC Comics: Aug, 1987 - No. 19, Jan, 1989 ($1.50)
1-19: Andrew Helfer scripts in all. 2.50
Annual 1,2 (12/87, '88,)-2-The Shadow dies; origin retold (story inspired by the movie "Citizen Kane"). 2.50
NOTE: ***Kyle Baker*** *a-7i, 8-19, Annual 2.* ***Chaykin*** *c-Annual 1.* ***Helfer*** *scripts in all.* ***Orlando*** *a-Annual 1.* ***Rogers*** *c/a-7.* ***Sienkiewicz*** *c/a-1-6.*

SHADOW, THE (Movie)
Dark Horse Comics: June, 1994 - No. 2, July, 1994 ($2.50, limited series)
1,2-Adaptation from Universal Pictures film 3.00

Shadow Comics #2 © S&S

The Shadow: In the Coils of the Leviathan #3 © Conde Nast

Shadow Lady: Dangerous Love #3 © Studio Proteus

GD2.0 FN6.0 NM9.4

NOTE: *Kaluta c/a-1, 2.*

SHADOW AND DOC SAVAGE, THE
Dark Horse Comics: July, 1995 - No. 2, Aug, 1995 ($2.95, limited series)
1,2 3.50

SHADOW AND THE MYSTERIOUS 3, THE
Dark Horse Comics: Sept, 1994 ($2.95, one-shot)
1-Kaluta co-scripts. 3.00
NOTE: *Stevens c-1.*

SHADOW CABINET (See Heroes)
DC Comics (Milestone): Jan, 1994 - No. 17, Oct, 1995 ($1.75/$2.50)
0,1-17: 0-($2.50, 52 pgs.)-Silver ink-c; Simonson-c. 1-Byrne-c 2.50

SHADOW COMICS (Pulp, radio)
Street & Smith Publications: Mar, 1940 - V9#5, Aug-Sept, 1949
NOTE: *The Shadow first appeared on radio in 1929 and was featured in pulps beginning in April, 1931, written by Walter Gibson. The early covers of this series were reprinted from the pulp covers.*

V1#1-Shadow, Doc Savage, Bill Barnes, Nick Carter (radio), Frank Merriwell, Iron Munro, the Astonishing Man begin 400.00 1200.00 4000.00
2-The Avenger begins, ends #6; Capt. Fury only app. 175.00 525.00 1400.00
3(nn-5/40)-Norgil the Magician app.; cover is exact swipe of Shadow pulp from 1/33 121.00 364.00 970.00
4,5: 4-The Three Musketeers begins, ends #8. 5-Doc Savage ends 99.00 296.00 790.00
6,8,9: 9-Norgil the Magician app. 86.00 257.00 685.00
7-Origin/1st app. The Hooded Wasp & Wasplet (11/40); series ends V3#8; Hooded Wasp/Wasplet app. on-c thru #9 94.00 281.00 750.00
10-Origin The Iron Ghost, ends #11; The Dead End Kids begins, ends #14 86.00 257.00 685.00
11-Origin Hooded Wasp & Wasplet retold 86.00 257.00 685.00
12-Dead End Kids app. 67.00 200.00 535.00
V2#1,2(11/41): 2-Dead End Kids story 60.00 180.00 480.00
3-Origin & 1st app. Supersnipe (3/42); series begins; Little Nemo story 86.00 257.00 685.00
4,5: 4,8-Little Nemo story 54.00 163.00 435.00
6-9: 6-Blackstone the Magician story 47.00 141.00 375.00
10-12: 10-Supersnipe app. 47.00 141.00 375.00
V3#1-12: 10-Doc Savage begins, not in V5#5, V6#10-12, V8#4 44.00 132.00 350.00
V4#1-12 40.00 120.00 320.00
V5#1-12 40.00 120.00 285.00
V6#1-11: 9-Intro. Shadow, Jr. (12/46) 36.00 107.00 250.00
12-Powell-c/a; atom bomb panels 40.00 120.00 285.00
V7#1,2,5,7-9,12: 2,5-Shadow, Jr. app.; Powell-a 40.00 120.00 315.00
3,6,11-Powell-c/a 43.00 129.00 345.00
4-Powell-c/a; Atom bomb panels 46.00 139.00 370.00
10(1/48)-Flying Saucer-c/story (2nd of this theme; see The Spirit 9/28/47); Powell-c/a 52.00 157.00 420.00
V8#1-12-Powell-a. 8-Powell Spider-c/a 43.00 129.00 345.00
V9#1,5-Powell-a 40.00 120.00 310.00
2-4-Powell-c/a 43.00 129.00 345.00
NOTE: ***Binder** c-V3#1. **Powell** art in most issues beginning V6#12. Painted c-1-6.*

SHADOWDRAGON
DC Comics: 1995 ($3.50, annual)
Annual 1-Year One story 3.50

SHADOW EMPIRES: FAITH CONQUERS
Dark Horse Comics: Aug, 1994 - No. 4, Nov, 1994 ($2.95, limited series)
1-4 3.00

SHADOWHAWK (See Images of Shadowhawk, New Shadowhawk, Shadowhawk II, Shadowhawk III & Youngblood #2)
Image Comics (Shadowline Ink): Aug, 1992 - No. 4, Mar, 1993; No. 12, Aug, 1994 - No. 18, May, 1995 ($1.95/$2.50)
1-($2.50)-Embossed silver foil stamped-c; Valentino/Liefeld-c; Valentino-c/a/scripts in all; has coupon for Image #0; 1st Shadowline Ink title 4.00
1-With coupon missing 2.00
1-($1.95)-Newsstand version w/o foil stamp 2.00
2-13,0,1418: 2-Shadowhawk poster w/McFarlane-i; brief Spawn app.; wrap around-c w/silver ink highlights. 3-($2.50)-Glow-in-the-dark-c. 4-Savage Dragon-c/story; Valentino/Larsen-c. 5-11-(See Shadowhawk II and III). 12-Cont'd fromShadowhawk III; pull-out poster by Texeira.13-w/ShadowBone poster; WildC.A.T.s app. 0 (10/94)-Liefeld c/a/story; ShadowBart poster. 14-(10/94, $2.50)-The Others app. 16-Supreme app. 17-Spawn app.; story cont'd from Badrock & Co. #6. 18-Shadowhawk dies; Savage Dragon & Brigade app. 2.50
Special 1(12/94, $3.50, 52 pgs.)-Silver Age Shadowhawk flip book 3.50
Gallery (4/94, $1.95) 2.00
Out of the Shadows ($19.95)-r/Youngblood #2, Shadowhawk #1-4, Image Zero #0, Operation :Urban Storm (Never published) 20.00
.../Vampirella (2/95, $4.95)-Pt.2 of x-over (See Vampirella/Shadowhawk for Pt. 1) 5.00
NOTE: *Shadowhawk was originally a four issue limited series. The story continued in Shadowhawk II, Shadowhawk III & then became Shadowhawk again with issue #12.*

SHADOWHAWK II (Follows Shadowhawk #4)
Image Comics (Shadowline Ink): V2#1, May, 1993 - V2#3, Aug, 1993 ($3.50/$1.95/$2.95, limited series)
V2#1 ($3.50)-Cont'd from Shadowhawk #4; die-cut mirricard-c 3.50
2 ($1.95)-Foil embossed logo; reveals identity; gold-c variant exists 2.50
3 ($2.95)-Pop-up-c w/Pact ashcan insert 3.00

SHADOWHAWK III (Follows Shadowhawk II #3)
Image Comics (Shadowline Ink): V3#1, Nov, 1993 - V3#4, Mar, 1994 ($1.95, limited series);
V3#1-4: 1-Cont'd from Shadowhawk II; intro Valentine; gold foil & red foil stamped-c variations. 2-(52 pgs.)-Shadowhawk contracts HIV virus; U.S. Male by M. Anderson (p) in free 16 pg.insert. 4-Continues in Shadowhawk #12. 2.50

SHADOWHAWKS OF LEGEND
Image Comics (Shadowline Ink): Nov, 1995 ($4.95, one-shot)
nn-Stories of past Shadowhawks by Kurt Busiek, Beau Smith & Alan Moore. 5.00

SHADOW, THE: HELL'S HEAT WAVE (Movie, pulp, radio)
Dark Horse Comics: Apr, 1995 - No. 3, June, 1995 ($2.95, limited series)
1-3: Kaluta story 3.00

SHADOWHUNT SPECIAL
Image Comics (Extreme Studios): Apr, 1996 ($2.50)
1-Retells origin of past Shadowhawks; Valentino script; Chapel app. 2.50

SHADOW, THE: IN THE COILS OF THE LEVIATHAN (Movie, pulp, radio)
Dark Horse Comics: Oct, 1993 - No. 4, Apr, 1994 ($2.95, limited series)
1-4-Kaluta-c & co-scripter 3.00
Trade paperback (10/94, $13.95)-r/1-4 14.00

SHADOW LADY: DANGEROUS LOVE (Masakazu Katsura's...)
Dark Horse Comics: Oct, 1998 - No. 7, Apr, 1999 ($2.50, B&W, limited series)
1-7-Manga by Masakazu Katsura-s/a 2.50

SHADOW LADY: THE EYES OF A STRANGER (Masakazu Katsura's...)
Dark Horse Comics: May, 1999 - No. 5, Sept, 1999 ($2.50, B&W, limited series)
1-5-Manga by Masakazu Katsura-s/a 2.50

SHADOWLINE SAGA: CRITICAL MASS, A
Marvel Comics (Epic): Jan, 1990 - No. 7, July, 1990 ($4.95, lim. series, 68 pgs)
1-6: Dr. Zero, Powerline, St. George 5.00
7 ($5.95, 84 pgs.)-Morrow-a, Williamson-c(i) 6.00

SHADOWMAN (See X-O Manowar #4)
Valiant/Acclaim Comics (Valiant): May, 1992 - No. 43, Dec, 1995 ($2.50)
1-Partial origin 4.00
2-5: 3-1st app. Sousa the Soul Eater 3.00
6-43: 8-1st app. Master Darque. 16-1st app. Dr. Mirage (8/93). 15-Minor Turok

Shadowman V3 #1 © Acclaim

Shadows & Light #3 © MAR

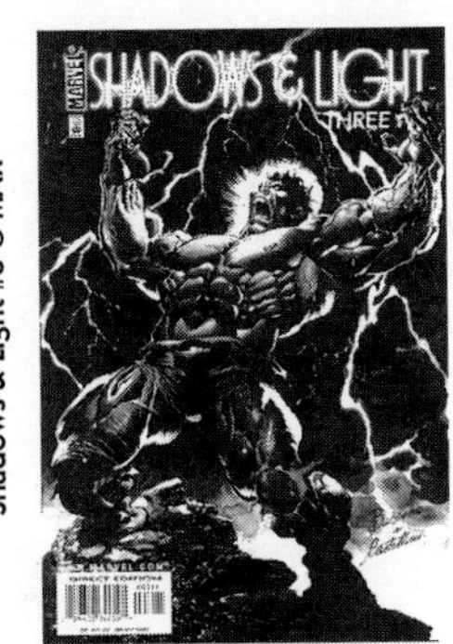

Shanna, the She-Devil #5 © MAR

app. 17,18-Archer & Armstrong x-over. 19-Aerosmith-c/story. 23-Dr. Mirage x-over. 24-(4/94). 25-Bound-in trading card. 29-Chaos Effect. 43-Shadowman jumps to his death 2.50
0-($2.50, 4/94)-Regular edition 2.50
0-($3.50)-Wraparound chromium-c edition 3.50
0-Gold 6.00
Yearbook 1 (12/94, $3.95) 4.00

SHADOWMAN (Volume 2)
Acclaim Comics (Valiant Heroes): Mar, 1997 - No. 20 ($2.50, mature)

1-20: 1-1st app. Zero; Garth Ennis scripts begin, end #4. 2-Zero becomes new Shadowman. 4-Origin; Jack Boniface (original Shadowman) rises from the grave. 5-Jamie Delano scripts begin. 9-Copycat-c 2.50
1-Variant painted cover 2.50

SHADOWMAN (Volume 3)
Acclaim Comics: July, 1999 - Present ($3.95/$2.50)

1-($3.95)-Abnett & Lanning-s/Broome & Benjamin-a 4.00
2,3-($2.50): 3-Flip book with Unity 2000 2.50

SHADOWMASTERS
Marvel Comics: Oct, 1989 - No.4, Jan, 1990 ($3.95, squarebound, 52 pgs.)

1-4: Heath-a(i). 1-Jim Lee-c; story cont'd from Punisher 4.00

SHADOW OF THE BATMAN
DC Comics: Dec, 1985 - No. 5, Apr, 1986 ($1.75, limited series)

1-Detective-r (all have wraparound-c) 1.00 2.80 7.00
2,3,5: 3-Penguin-c & cameo. 5-Clayface app. 5.00
4-Joker-c/story 2.40 6.00
NOTE: **Austin** a(new)-2i, 3i; r-2-4i. **Rogers** a(new)-1, 2p, 3p, 4, 5; r-1-5p; c-1-5. **Simonson** a-1r.

SHADOW OF THE TORTURER, THE
Innovation: July, 1991 - No. 3, 1992 ($2.50, limited series)

1-3: Based on Pocket Books novel 2.50

SHADOW ON THE TRAIL (See Zane Grey & Four Color #604)

SHADOW PLAY (Tales of the Supernatural)
Whitman Publications: June, 1982

1-Painted-c 4.00

SHADOW RIDERS
Marvel Comics UK, Ltd.: June, 1993 - No. 4, Sept, 1993 ($1.75, limited series)

1-($2.50)-Embossed-c; Cable-c/story 2.50
2-4-Cable app. 2-Ghost Rider app. 2.00

SHADOWS & LIGHT
Marvel Comics: Feb, 1998 - No. 3, July, 1998 ($2.99, B&W, quarterly)

1-3: 1-B&W anthology of Marvel characters; Black Widow art by Gene Ha, Hulk by Wrightson, Iron Man by Ditko & Daredevil by Stelfreeze; Stelfreeze painted-c. 2-Weeks, Sharp, Starlin, Thompson-a. 3-Buscema, Grindberg, Giffen, Layton-a 3.00

SHADOW'S FALL
DC Comics (Vertigo): Nov, 1994 - No. 6, Apr, 1995 ($2.95, limited series)

1-6: Van Fleet-c/a in all. 3.00

SHADOWS FROM BEYOND (Formerly Unusual Tales)
Charlton Comics: V2#50, October, 1966

V2#50-Ditko-c 2.50 7.50 22.00

SHADOW SLASHER
Pocket Change Comics: No. 0, 1994 - No. 6, 1995? ($2.50, B&W)

0-6 2.50

SHADOW STATE
Broadway Comics: Dec, 1995 - No. 5, Apr, 1996 ($2.50)

1-5: 1,2-Fatale back-up story; Cockrum-a(p) 2.50
Preview Edition 1,2 (10-11/95, $2.50, B&W) 2.50

SHADOW STRIKES!, THE (Pulp, radio)
DC Comics: Sept, 1989 - No.31, May, 1992 ($1.75)

1-31: 5,6-Doc Savage x-over. 31-Mignola-c. 2.50
Annual 1 (1989, $3.50, 68 pgs.)-Spiegle a; Kaluta-c 3.50

SHADOW WAR OF HAWKMAN
DC Comics: May, 1985 - No. 4, Aug, 1985 (limited series)

1-4 2.00

SHAGGY DOG & THE ABSENT-MINDED PROFESSOR (See Movie Comics & Walt Disney Showcase #46)(Disney-Movie)
Dell Publ. Co.: No. 985, May, 1959; No. 1199, Apr, 1961

Four Color #985,1199 6.40 19.00 70.00

SHALOMAN
Al Wiesner/ Mark 1 Comics: 1989 - Present (B&W)

V1#1-9-Al Wiesner-s/a in all 2.50
V2 #1(The New Adventures)-4,6-10, V3 (The Legend) #1-5 2.50
5 (Color)-Shows Vol 2, No. 4 in indicia 3.00

SHAMAN'S TEARS (Also see Maggie the Cat)
Image Comics (Creative Fire Studio): 5/93 - No. 2, 8/93; No. 3, 11/94 - No. 0, 1/96 ($2.50/$1.95)

0-2: 0-(DEC-c, 1/96)-Last Issue. 1-(5/93)-Embossed red foil stamped-c; Mike Grell-c/a & scripts in all. 2-Cover unfolds into poster (8/93-c, 7/93 inside). 2.50
3-12: 3-Begin $1.95-c. 5-Re-intro Jon Sable. 12-Re-intro Maggie the Cat (1 pg.) 2.00

SHANNA, THE SHE-DEVIL (See Savage Tales #8)
Marvel Comics Group: Dec, 1972 - No. 5, Aug, 1973 (All are 20¢ issues)

1-1st app. Shanna; Steranko-c; Tuska-a(p) 1.75 5.25 14.00
2-Steranko-c; heroin drug story 1.25 3.75 10.00
3-5 1.00 3.00 8.00

SHARDS
Ascension Comics: Apr, 1994 ($2.50, B&W, unfinished limited series)

1-Flip-c. 2.50

SHARK FIGHTERS, THE (Movie)
Dell Publishing Co.: Jan, 1957

Four Color 762-Buscema-a; photo-c 7.00 22.00 80.00

SHARKY
Image Comics: Feb, 1998 - No. 4, 1998 ($2.50, bi-monthly)

1-4: 1-Mask app.; Elliot-s/a. Horley painted-c. 3-Three covers by Horley, Bisley, & Horley/Elliot. 4-Two covers (swipe of Avengers #4 and wraparound) 2.50
1-($2.95) "$1,000,000" variant 3.00
2-($2.50) Savage Dragon variant-c 2.50

SHARP COMICS (Slightly large size)
H. C. Blackerby: Winter, 1945-46 - V1#2, Spring, 1946 (52 pgs.)

V1#1-Origin Dick Royce Planetarian 40.00 120.00 290.00
2-Origin The Pioneer; Michael Morgan, Dick Royce, Sir Gallagher, Planetarian, Steve Hagen, Weeny and Pop app. 36.00 107.00 250.00

SHARPY FOX (See Comic Capers & Funny Frolics)
I. W. Enterprises/Super Comics: 1958; 1963

1,2-I.W. Reprint (1958): 2-r/Kiddie Kapers #1 1.25 3.75 10.00
14-Super Reprint (1963) 1.25 3.75 10.00

SHATTER (See Jon Sable #25-30)
First Comics: June, 1985; Dec, 1985 - No. 14, Apr, 1988. ($1.75, Baxter paper/deluxe paper)

1 (6/85)-1st computer generated-a in a comic book (1st printing) 3.00
1-(2nd print.); 1(12/85)-14: computer generated-a & lettering in all 2.00

SHATTERED IMAGE
Image Comics (WildStorm Productions): Aug, 1996 - No. 4, Dec, 1996 ($2.50, limited series)

1-4: 1st Image company-wide x-over; Kurt Busiek scripts in all. 1-Tony Daniel-c/a(p). 2-Alex Ross-c/swipe (Kingdom Come) by Ryan Benjamin & Travis Charest 2.50

Shazam! #11 © DC

Sheena, Queen of the Jungle #5 © FH

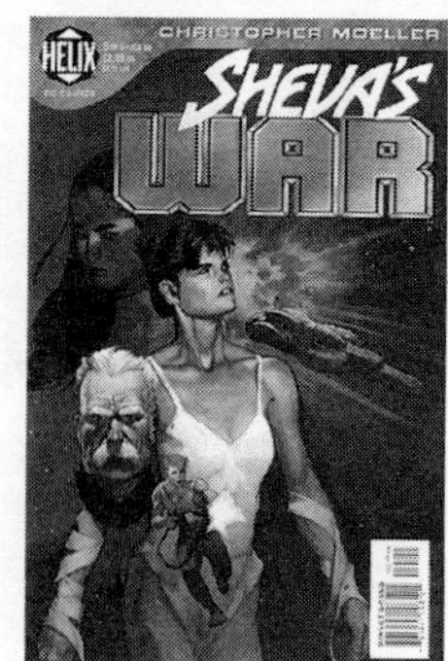

Sheva's War #5 © Christopher Moeller

GD2.0 FN6.0 NM9.4

SHAZAM (See Giant Comics to Color, Limited Collectors' Edition & The Power Of Shazam!)

SHAZAM! (TV)(See World's Finest #253)
National Periodical Publ./DC Comics: Feb, 1973 - No. 35, May-June, 1978

1-1st revival of original Captain Marvel since G.A. (origin retold), by Beck; Captain Marvel Jr. & Mary Marvel x-over; Superman-c. 1.25 3.75 10.00
2-5: 2-Infinity photo-c.; re-intro Mr. Mind & Tawny. 3-Capt. Marvel-r. (10/46). 4-Origin retold; Capt. Marvel-r. (1949). 5-Capt. Marvel Jr. origin retold; Capt. Marvel-r. (1948, 7 pgs.) 2.40 6.00
6,7,9-11: 6-photo-c; Capt. Marvel-r (1950, 6 pgs.). 9-Mr. Mind app. 10-Last C.C. Beck issue. 11-Schaffenberger-a begins. 4.00
8 (100 pgs.) 8-r/Capt. Marvel Jr. by Raboy; origin/C.M. #80; origin Mary Marvel/C.M. #18; origin Mr. Tawny/C.M. #79 2.80 8.40 28.00
12-17-(All 100 pgs.). 15-vs. Lex Luthor & Mr. Mind. 2.50 7.50 20.00
18-35: 21-24-All reprints. 25-1st app. Isis. 26-Sivana app. (10/76). 27-Kid Eternity teams up w/Capt. Marvel. 28-1st S.A. app. of Black Adam. 30-1st DC app. 3 Lt. Marvels. 31-1st DC app. Minuteman. 34-Origin Capt. Nazi & Capt. Marvel Jr. retold 2.40 6.00

NOTE: *Reprints in #1-8, 10, 12-17, 21-24.* ***Beck*** *a-1-10, 12-17r, 21-24r; c-1, 3-9.* ***Nasser*** *c-35p.* ***Newton*** *a-35p.* ***Raboy*** *a-5r, 8r, 17r.* ***Schaffenberger*** *a-11, 14-20, 25, 26, 27p, 28, 29-31p, 33i, 35i; c-20, 22, 23, 25, 26i, 27i, 28-33.*

SHAZAM: THE NEW BEGINNING
DC Comics: Apr, 1987 - No. 4, July, 1987 (Legends spin-off) (Limited series)

1-4: 1-New origin & 1st modern app. Captain Marvel; Marvel Family cameo. 2-4-Sivana & Black Adam app. 2.00

SHEA THEATRE COMICS
Shea Theatre: No date (1940's) (32 pgs.)

nn-Contains Rocket Comics; MLJ cover in one color 10.00 30.00 60.00

SHE-BAT (See Murcielaga, She-Bat & Valeria the She-Bat)

SHEENA (Movie)
Marvel Comics: Dec, 1984 - No. 2, Feb, 1985 (limited series)

1,2-r/Marvel Comics Super Special #34; Tanya Roberts movie 2.00

SHEENA, QUEEN OF THE JUNGLE (See Jerry Iger's Classic..., Jumbo Comics, & 3-D Sheena)
Fiction House Magazines: Spr, 1942; No. 2, Wint, 1942-43; No. 3, Spr, 1943; No. 4, Fall, 1948; No. 5, Sum, 1949; No. 6, Spr, 1950; No. 7-10, 1950(nd); No. 11, Spr, 1951 - No. 18, Wint, 1952-53 (#1-3: 68 pgs.; #4-7: 52 pgs.)

1-Sheena begins 225.00 675.00 1800.00
2 (Winter, 1942-43) 100.00 300.00 800.00
3 (Spring, 1943) 75.00 225.00 600.00
4,5 (Fall, 1948, Sum, 1949): 4-New logo; cover swipe from Jumbo #20 45.00 135.00 360.00
6,7 (Spring, 1950, 1950) 40.00 120.00 300.00
8-10(1950 - Win/50, 36 pgs.) 39.00 118.00 275.00
11-18: 15-Cover swipe from Jumbo #43. 18-Used in **POP**, pg. 98 31.00 94.00 220.00
I.W. Reprint #9-r/#18; c-r/White Princess #3 4.20 12.60 42.00

NOTE: ***Baker*** *c-5-10?* ***Whitman*** *c-11-18(most).*

SHEENA-QUEEN OF THE JUNGLE
London Night: Feb, 1998 - Present ($3.00)

0-($3.00)-Hartsoe-s/Sandoval-c 3.00
0-($5.00) Crocodile, Zebra, & Leopard editions 5.00
1-3-($3.00) 3.00
1-3-($5.00) Ministry Edition 5.00

SHEENA 3-D SPECIAL (Also see Blackthorne 3-D Series #1)
Eclipse Comics: Jan, 1985 ($2.00)

1-Dave Stevens-c 4.00

SHE-HULK (See The Savage She-Hulk & The Sensational She-Hulk)

SHERIFF BOB DIXON'S CHUCK WAGON (TV) (See Wild Bill Hickok #22)
Avon Periodicals: Nov, 1950

1-Kinstler-c/a(3) 13.00 39.00 90.00

GD2.0 FN6.0 NM9.4

SHERIFF OF TOMBSTONE
Charlton Comics: Nov, 1958 - No. 17, Sept, 1961

V1#1-Giordano-c; Severin-a 6.00 18.00 60.00
2 3.80 11.40 38.00
3-10 2.60 7.80 26.00
11-17 2.50 7.50 22.00

SHERLOCK HOLMES (See Marvel Preview, New Adventures of..., & Spectacular Stories)

SHERLOCK HOLMES (All New Baffling Adventures of...)(Young Eagle #3 on?)
Charlton Comics: Oct, 1955 - No. 2, Mar, 1956

1-Dr. Neff, Ghost Breaker app. 40.00 120.00 310.00
2 36.00 109.00 255.00

SHERLOCK HOLMES (Also see The Joker)
National Periodical Publications: Sept-Oct, 1975

1-Cruz-a; Simonson-c 2.50 7.50 20.00

SHERRY THE SHOWGIRL (Showgirls #4)
Atlas Comics: July, 1956 - No. 3, Dec, 1956; No. 5, Apr, 1957 - No. 7, Aug, 1957

1-Dan DeCarlo-c/a in all 13.00 39.00 90.00
2 10.00 30.00 65.00
3,5-7 7.50 22.50 45.00

SHE'S JOSIE (See Josie)

SHEVA'S WAR
DC Comics (Helix): Oct, 1998 - No. 5, Feb, 1999 ($2.95, mini-series)

1-5-Christopher Moeller-s/painted-a/c 3.00

SHI (See Razor Annual #1 for 1st app.)

SHI: BLACK, WHITE AND RED
Crusade Comics: Mar, 1998 - No. 2, May, 1998 ($2.95, B&W&Red, mini-series)

1,2-J.G. Jones-painted art 3.00

SHI/CYBLADE: THE BATTLE FOR THE INDEPENDENTS
Crusade Comics: Sept, 1995 ($2.95)

1-Tucci c; features Cerebus, Bone, Hellboy, as well as others 4.00
1-Silvestri variant-c 2.40 6.00

SHI/DAREDEVIL: HONOR THY MOTHER (See Daredevil/Shi..)
Crusade Comics: Jan, 1997 ($2.95, one-shot)

1-Flip book 3.00

SHI: EAST WIND RAIN
Crusade Comics: Nov, 1997 - No. 2, Feb, 1998 ($3.50, limited series)

1,2-Shi at WW2 Pearl Harbor 3.50

SHI: FAN EDITIONS
Crusade Comics: 1997

1-3-Two covers polybagged in FAN #19-21 4.00
1-3-Gold editions 6.00

SHI: HEAVEN AND EARTH
Crusade Comics: June, 1997 - No. 4, Apr, 1998 ($2.95)

1-4 3.00
4-($4.95) Pencil-c variant 5.00
Rising Sun Edition-signed by Tucci in FanClub Starter Pack 4.00
"Tora No Shi" variant-c 3.00

SHI: KAIDAN
Crusade Comics: Oct, 1996 ($2.95)

1-Two covers; Tucci-c; Jae Lee wraparound-c 3.00

SHI: MASQUERADE
Crusade Comics: Mar, 1998 ($3.50, one-shot)

1-Painted art by Lago, Texeira, and others 3.50

SHI: NIGHTSTALKERS
Crusade Comics: Sept, 1997 ($3.50, one-shot)

1-Painted art by Val Mayerik 3.50

Shi: The Series #7 © William Tucci

S.H.I.E.L.D. #2 © MAR

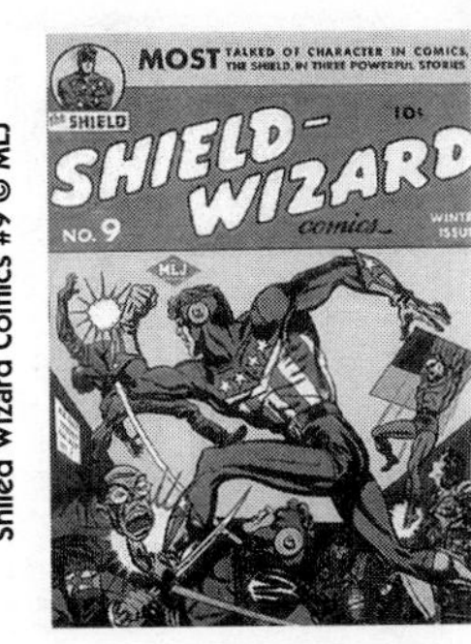
Shiled Wizard Comics #9 © MLJ

GD2.0 FN6.0 NM9.4

SHI: REKISHI
Crusade Comics: Jan, 1997 ($2.95)

1-Character bios and story summaries of Shi: The Way of the Warrior told in Detective Joe Labianca's point of view; Christopher Golden script; Tucci-c; J.G. Jones-a; flip book w/Shi: East Wind Rain preview 3.00

SHI: SENRYAKU
Crusade Comics: Aug, 1995 - No. 3, Nov, 1995 ($2.95, limited series)

1-3: 1-Tucci-c; Quesada, Darrow, Sim, Lee, Smith-a. 2-Tucci-c; Silvestri, Balent, Perez, Mack-a. 3-Jusko-c; Hughes, Ramos, Bell, Moore-a 4.00
1-variant-c (no logo) 2.40 6.00
Hardcover ($24.95)-r/#1-3; Frazetta-c. 25.00
Trade Paperback ($13.95)-r/#1-3; Frazetta-c. 14.00

SHI: THE ART OF WAR TOURBOOK
Crusade Comics: 1998 ($4.95, one-shot)

1-Blank cover for Convention sketches; early Tucci-a inside 5.00
1-Mexico Edition ($10.00) Mexican flag-c 10.00
1-U.K. Edition ($10.00) British flag-c 10.00

SHI: THE SERIES
Crusade Comics: Aug, 1997 - Present ($2.95, color #1-10, B&W #11)

1-10 3.00
11-13: 11-B&W. 12-Color; Lau-a 3.00

SHI: THE WAY OF THE WARRIOR
Crusade Comics: Mar, 1994 - No. 12, Apr, 1997 ($2.50/$2.95)

1/2 2.40 6.00
1 1.85 5.50 15.00
1-Commemorative ed., B&W, new-c; given out at 1994 San Diego Comic Con 3.00 9.00 30.00
1-Fan appreciation edition -r/#1 3.00
1-Fan appreciation edition (variant) 1.85 5.50 15.00
2 1.25 3.75 10.00
2-Commemorative edition (3,000) 3.00 9.00 30.00
2-Fan appreciation edition -r/#2 3.00
3 1.00 3.00 8.00
4-7: 4-Silvestri poster. 7-Tomoe app. 4.00
5,6: 5-Silvestri variant-c. 6-Tomoe #1 variant-c 1.00 3.00 8.00
5-Gold edition 40.00
6,8-12: 6-Fan appreciation edition 3.00
8-Signed Edition-(5000) 5.00
Trade paperback (1995, $12.95)-r/#1-4 13.00
Trade paperback (1995, $14.95)-r/#1-4 revised; Julie Bell-c 15.00

SHI/ VAMPIRELLA
Crusade Comics: Oct, 1997 ($2.95, one-shot)

1-Ellis-s/Lau-a 5.00

SHI VS. TOMOE
Crusade Comics: Aug, 1996 ($3.95, one-shot)

1-Tucci-a/scripts; wraparound foil-c 4.00
1-(6/96, $5.00. B&W)-Preview Ed.; sold at San Diego Comic Con 5.00

S.H.I.E.L.D. (Nick Fury & His Agents of…) (Also see Nick Fury)
Marvel Comics Group: Feb, 1973 - No. 5, Oct, 1973 (All 20¢ issues)

1-Steranko-c 1.50 4.50 12.00
2-5: 2-Steranko flag-c. 1-5 all contain-r from Str. Tales #146-155. 3-5-are cover-r; 3-Kirby/Steranko-c(r). 4-Steranko-c(r) 1.00 2.80 7.00
NOTE: ***Buscema*** *a-3p(r).* ***Kirby*** *layouts 1-5; c-3 (w/****Steranko****).* ***Steranko*** *a-3r, 4r(2).*

SHIELD, THE (Becomes Shield-Steel Sterling #3; #1 titled Lancelot Strong; also see Advs. of the Fly, Double Life of Private Strong, Fly Man, Mighty Comics, The Mighty Crusaders, The Original… & Pep Comics #1)
Archie Enterprises, Inc.: June, 1983 - No. 2, Aug, 1983

1,2: Steel Sterling app. 2.00

SHIELD-STEEL STERLING (Formerly The Shield)
Archie Enterprises, Inc.: No. 3, Dec, 1983 (Becomes Steel Sterling No. 4)

3-Nino-a 2.00

GD2.0 FN6.0 NM9.4

SHIELD WIZARD COMICS (Also see Pep Comics & Top-Notch Comics)
MLJ Magazines: Summer, 1940 - No. 13, Spring, 1944

1-(V1#5 on inside)-Origin The Shield by Irving Novick & The Wizard by Ed Ashe, Jr; Flag-c 400.00 1200.00 3600.00
2-(Winter/40)-Origin The Shield retold; Wizard's sidekick, Roy the Super Boy begins (see Top-Notch #8 for 1st app.) 187.00 562.00 1500.00
3,4 122.00 366.00 975.00
5-Dusty, the Boy Detective begins 109.00 328.00 875.00
6-8: 6-Roy the Super Boy begins. 7-Shield dons new costume (Summer, 1942); S & K-c? 100.00 300.00 800.00
9-13: 13-Bondage-c 81.00 244.00 650.00
NOTE: ***Bob Montana*** *c-13.* ***Novick*** *c-1-6,8-11.* ***Harry Sahle*** *c-12.*

SHINING KNIGHT (See Adventure Comics #66)

SHIP AHOY
Spotlight Publishers: Nov, 1944 (52 pgs.)

1-L. B. Cole-c 17.00 51.00 120.00

SHIP OF FOOLS
Image Comics: Aug, 1997 - Present ($2.95, B&W)

0-3-Glass-s/Oeming-a 3.00

SHIPWRECKED! (Disney-Movie)
Disney Comics: 1990 ($5.95, graphic novel, 68 pgs.)

nn-adaptation; Spiegle-a 6.00

SHMOO (See Al Capp's… & Washable Jones &…)

SHOCK (Magazine)
Stanley Publ.: May, 1969 - V3#4, Sept, 1971 (B&W reprints from horror comics)

V1#1-Cover-r/Weird Tales of the Future #7 by Bernard Baily; r/Weird Chills #1 3.50 10.50 35.00
2-Wolverton-r/Weird Mysteries 5; r-Weird Mysteries #7 used in **SOTI**; cover reprints cover to Weird Chills #1 3.20 9.60 32.00
3,5,6 2.50 7.50 20.00
4-Harrison/Williamson-r/Forbid. Worlds #6 2.50 7.50 24.00
V2#2, V1#8, V2#4-6(1/71), V3#1-4: V2#4-Cover swipe from Weird Mysteries #6 2.25 6.75 18.00
NOTE: ***Disbrow*** *r-V2#4; Bondage c-V1#4, V2#6, V3#1.*

SHOCK DETECTIVE CASES (Formerly Crime Fighting Detective) (Becomes Spook Detective Cases No. 22)
Star Publications: No. 20, Sept, 1952 - No. 21, Nov, 1952

20,21-L.B. Cole-c; based on true crime cases 21.00 62.00 145.00
NOTE: ***Palais*** *a-20. No. 21-Fox-r.*

SHOCK ILLUSTRATED (…Adult Crime Stories; Magazine format)
E. C. Comics: Sept-Oct, 1955 - No. 3, Spring, 1956 (Adult Entertainment on-c #1,2)(All 25¢)

1-All by Kamen; drugs, prostitution, wife swapping 8.35 25.00 50.00
2-Williamson-a redrawn from Crime SuspenStories #13 plus Ingels, Crandall, Evans & part Torres-i; painted-c 10.00 30.00 60.00
3-Only 100 known copies bound & given away at E.C. office; Crandall, Evans-a; painted-c; shows May, 1956 on-c 87.00 262.00 700.00

SHOCKING MYSTERY CASES (Formerly Thrilling Crime Cases)
Star Publications: No. 50, Sept, 1952 - No. 60, Oct, 1954 (All crime reprints?)

50-Disbrow "Frankenstein" story 40.00 120.00 290.00
51-Disbrow-a 24.00 71.00 165.00
52-60: 56-Drug use story 22.00 66.00 155.00
NOTE: ***L. B. Cole*** *covers on all; a-60(2 pgs.).* ***Hollingsworth*** *a-52.* ***Morisi*** *a-55.*

SHOCKING TALES DIGEST MAGAZINE
Harvey Publications: Oct, 1981 (95¢)

1-1957-58-r; Powell, Kirby, Nostrand-a 1.25 3.75 10.00

SHOCK SUSPENSTORIES
E. C. Comics: Feb-Mar, 1952 - No. 18, Dec-Jan, 1954-55

1-Classic Feldstein electrocution-c 65.00 195.00 640.00
2 38.00 114.00 360.00

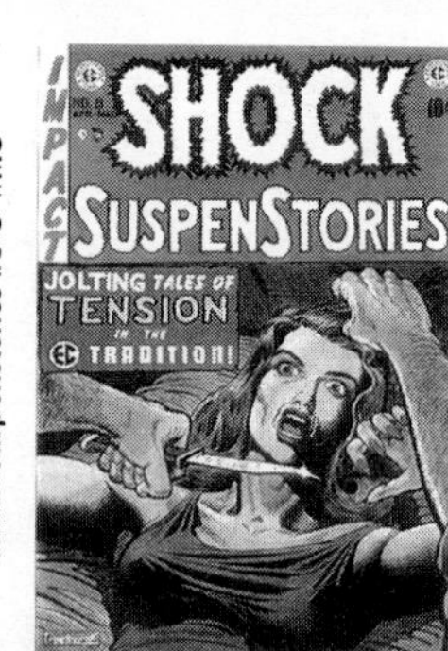

Shock Suspenstories #8 © WMG

Showcase #6 © DC

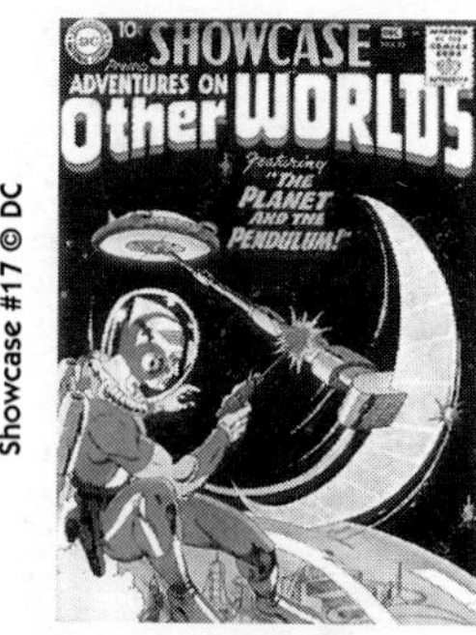

Showcase #17 © DC

GD2.0 FN6.0 NM9.4

3,4: 4-Used in **SOTI**, pg. 387,388 27.00 81.00 240.00
5-Hanging-c 27.00 81.00 240.00
6,7: 6-Classic bondage-c. 7-Classic face melting-c 32.00 96.00 285.00
8-Williamson-a 27.00 81.00 240.00
9-11: 9-Injury to eye panel. 10-Junkie story 22.00 66.00 200.00
12- "The Monkey" classic junkie cover/story; anti-drug propaganda issue 27.00 81.00 240.00
13-Frazetta's only solo story for E.C., 7 pgs. 32.00 96.00 290.00
14-Used in Senate Investigation hearings 17.00 50.00 150.00
15-Used in 1954 Reader's Digest article, "For the Kiddies to Read"; Bill Gaines stars in prose story "The EC Caper" 17.00 50.00 150.00
16-18: 16- "Red Dupe" editorial; rape story 15.00 45.00 135.00

NOTE: ***Ray Bradbury** adaptations-1, 7, 9. **Craig** a-11; c-11. **Crandall** a-9-13, 15-18. **Davis** a-1-5. **Evans** a-7, 8, 14-18; c-16-18. **Feldstein** c-1, 7-9, 12. **Ingels** a-1, 2, 6. **Kamen** a-in all; c-10, 13, 15. **Krigstein** a-14, 18. **Orlando** a-1, 3-7, 9, 10, 12, 16, 17. **Wood** a-2-15; c-2-6, 14.*

SHOCK SUSPENSTORIES
Russ Cochran/Gemstone Publishing: Sept, 1992 - No. 18, Dec, 1996 ($1.50/$2.00/$2.50, quarterly)

1-18: 1-3: Reprints with original-c. 17-r/HOF #17 2.50

SHOGUN WARRIORS
Marvel Comics Group: Feb, 1979 - No. 20, Sept, 1980 (Based on Mattel toys) (1-3: 35¢; 4-19: 40¢; 20: 50¢)

1-Raydeen, Combatra, & Dangard Ace begin 5.00
2-20: 11-Austin-c. 12-Simonson-c. 19,20-FF x-over 3.00
1-3: Reprints 3.00

SHOOK UP (Magazine) (Satire)
Dodsworth Publ. Co.: Nov, 1958

V1#1 3.00 9.00 30.00

SHORT RIBS
Dell Publishing Co.: No. 1333, Apr - June, 1962

Four Color 1333 4.50 13.50 50.00

SHORT STORY COMICS (See Hello Pal,...)

SHORTY SHINER (The Five-Foot Fighter in the Ten Gallon Hat)
Dandy Magazine (Charles Biro): June, 1956 - No. 3, Oct, 1956

1 5.35 16.00 32.00
2,3 4.00 11.00 22.00

SHOTGUN MARY
Antarctic Press: Sept, 1995 - No. 2; Mar, 1998 - No. 2, May, 1998 ($2.95)

1,2-w/pin-ups 3.00
1-($8.95)-Bagged w/CD 9.00
...Deviltown-(7/96, $2.95), ...Shooting Gallery-(6/96, $2.95), ...Son Of The Beast-(10/97, $2.95) Painted-a by Esad Ribic 3.00

SHOTGUN MARY: BLOOD LORE
Antarctic Press: Feb, 1997 - No.4, Aug, 1997 (2.95, mini-series)

1-4 3.00

SHOTGUN SLADE (TV)
Dell Publishing Co.: No. 1111, July-Sept, 1960

Four Color 1111-Photo-c 5.50 16.50 60.00

SHOWCASE (See Cancelled Comic Cavalcade & New Talent...)
National Per. Publ./DC Comics: 3-4/56 - No. 93, 9/70; No. 94, 8-9/77 - No. 104, 9/78

GD2.0 FN6.0 VF8.0 NM9.4
1-Fire Fighters; w/Fireman Farrell 221.00 664.00 1437.00 3100.00
GD2.0 FN6.0 NM9.4
2-Kings of the Wild; Kubert-a (animal stories) 71.00 212.00 850.00
3-The Frogmen by Russ Heath; Heath greytone-c (early DC example, 7-8/56) 69.00 206.00 825.00
GD2.0 FN6.0 VF8.0 NM9.4
4-Origin/1st app. The Flash (1st DC S.A. hero, Sept-Oct, 1956) & The Turtle; Kubert-a; r/in Secret Origins #1 ('61 & '73); Flash shown reading G.A. Flash #13; Infantino/Kubert-c 1100.00 3300.00 11,000.00 25,000.00
GD2.0 FN6.0 NM9.4
5-Manhunters 75.00 225.00 900.00
GD2.0 FN6.0 VF8.0 NM9.4
6-Origin/1st app. Challengers of the Unknown by Kirby, partly r/in Secret Origins #1 & Challengers #64,65 (1st S.A. hero team & 1st original concept S.A. series)(1-2/56) 250.00 750.00 1625.00 3500.00
GD2.0 FN6.0 NM9.4
7-Challengers of the Unknown by Kirby (2nd app.) reprinted in Challengers of the Unknown #75 123.00 369.00 1600.00
GD2.0 FN6.0 VF8.0 NM9.4
8-The Flash (5-6/57, 2nd app.); origin & 1st app. Capt. Cold 800.00 2400.00 5600.00 12,000.00
9-Lois Lane (Pre-#1, 7-8/57) (1st Showcase character to win own series) Superman app. on-c 558.00 1675.00 3625.00 6700.00
GD2.0 FN6.0 NM9.4
10-Lois Lane; Jor-el cameo; Superman app. on-c 179.00 536.00 2500.00
11-Challengers of the Unknown by Kirby (3rd) 115.00 345.00 1500.00
12-Challengers of the Unknown by Kirby (4th) 115.00 345.00 1500.00
GD2.0 FN6.0 VF8.0 NM9.4
13-The Flash (3rd app.); origin Mr. Element 286.00 857.00 1860.00 4000.00
14-The Flash (4th app.); origin Dr. Alchemy, former Mr. Element (rare in NM) 295.00 885.00 2200.00 5000.00
15-Space Ranger (7-8/58, 1st app.) 125.00 375.00 812.00 1750.00
GD2.0 FN6.0 NM9.4
16-Space Ranger (9-10/58, 2nd app.) 75.00 225.00 900.00
GD2.0 FN6.0 VF8.0 NM9.4
17-(11-12/58)-Adventures on Other Worlds; origin/1st app. Adam Strange by Gardner Fox & Mike Sekowsky. 150.00 450.00 975.00 2100.00
18-Adventures on Other Worlds (2nd A. Strange) 85.00 255.00 1100.00
19-Adam Strange; 1st Adam Strange logo 92.00 276.00 1200.00
20-Rip Hunter; origin & 1st app. (5-6/59); Moriera-a 71.00 212.00 850.00
21-Rip Hunter (7-8/59, 2nd app.); Sekowsky-c/a 42.00 126.00 460.00
GD2.0 FN6.0 VF8.0 NM9.4
22-Origin & 1st app. Silver Age Green Lantern by Gil Kane (9-10/59); reprinted in Secret Origins #2 300.00 900.00 2100.00 4500.00
23-Green Lantern (11-12/59, 2nd app.); nuclear explosion-c 113.00 339.00 735.00 1475.00
24-Green Lantern (1-2/60, 3rd app.) 113.00 339.00 735.00 1475.00
GD2.0 FN6.0 NM9.4
25,26-Rip Hunter by Kubert. 25-Grey tone-c 29.00 87.00 290.00
27-Sea Devils (7-8/60, 1st app.); Heath-c/a 61.00 182.00 730.00
28-Sea Devils (9-10/60, 2nd app.); Heath-c/a 34.00 102.00 375.00
29-Sea Devils; Heath-c/a; grey tone c-27-29 33.00 100.00 370.00
30-Origin Silver Age Aquaman (1-2/61) (see Adventure #260 for 1st S.A. origin) 58.00 174.00 700.00
31,32-Aquaman 34.00 102.00 375.00
33-Aquaman 38.00 114.00 420.00
GD2.0 FN6.0 VF8.0 NM9.4
34-Origin & 1st app. Silver Age Atom by Kane & Anderson (9-10/61); reprinted in Secret Origins #2 96.00 288.00 625.00 1250.00
GD2.0 FN6.0 NM9.4
35-The Atom by Gil Kane (2nd); last 10¢ issue 60.00 180.00 725.00
36-The Atom by Gil Kane (1-2/62, 3rd app.) 43.00 129.00 545.00
37-Metal Men (3-4/62, 1st app.) 47.00 142.00 570.00
38-Metal Men (5-6/62, 2nd app.) 38.00 114.00 420.00
39-Metal Men (7-8/62, 3rd app.) 31.00 93.00 320.00
40-Metal Men (9-10/62, 4th app.) 29.00 87.00 290.00
41,42-Tommy Tomorrow (parts 1 & 2). 42-Origin 16.00 48.00 160.00
43-Dr. No (James Bond); Nodel-a; originally published as British Classics Illustrated #158A & as #6 in a European Detective series, all with diff. painted-c. This Showcase #43 version is actually censored, deleting all racial skin color and dialogue thought to be racially demeaning (1st DC S.A. movie adaptation)(based on Ian Fleming novel & movie) 40.00 120.00 450.00
44-Tommy Tomorrow 11.00 33.00 110.00
45-Sgt. Rock (7-8/63); pre-dates B&B #52; origin retold; Heath-c 25.00 75.00 250.00
46,47-Tommy Tomorrow 9.00 27.00 90.00

Showcase #61 © DC

Showcase '93 #9 © DC

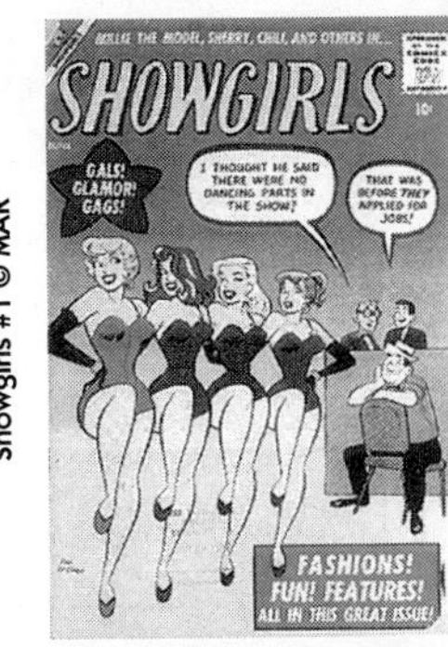

Showgirls #1 © MAR

GD2.0 FN6.0 NM9.4

48,49-Cave Carson (3rd tryout series; see B&B) 7.00 21.00 70.00
50,51-I Spy (Danger Trail-r by Infantino), King Farady story (#50 has new 4 pg. story) 7.00 21.00 70.00
52-Cave Carson 5.50 16.50 55.00
53,54-G.I. Joe (11-12/64, 1-2/65); Heath-a 10.00 30.00 100.00
55-Dr. Fate & Hourman (3-4/65); origin of each in text; 1st solo app. G.A. Green Lantern in Silver Age (pre-dates Gr. Lantern #40); 1st S.A. app. Solomon Grundy 22.50 68.00 225.00
56-Dr. Fate & Hourman 12.00 36.00 120.00
57-Enemy Ace by Kubert (7-8/65, 4th app. after Our Army at War #155) 18.00 54.00 180.00
58-Enemy Ace by Kubert (5th app.) 16.00 48.00 160.00
59-Teen Titans (11-12/65, 3rd app.) 9.50 28.50 95.00
60-1st S. A. app. The Spectre; Anderson-a (1-2/66); origin in text 25.00 75.00 250.00
61-The Spectre by Anderson (2nd app.) 13.00 39.00 130.00
62-Origin & 1st app. Inferior Five (5-6/66) 8.50 25.50 85.00
63,65-Inferior Five. 63-Hulk parody. 65-X-Men parody (11-12/66) 4.50 13.50 45.00
64-The Spectre by Anderson (5th app.) 12.50 38.00 125.00
66,67-B'wana Beast 3.00 9.00 30.00
68-Maniaks 3.00 9.00 30.00
69,71-Maniaks. 71-Woody Allen-c/app. 3.00 9.00 30.00
70-Binky (9-10/67)-Tryout issue 3.00 9.00 30.00
72-Top Gun (Johnny Thunder-r)-Toth-a 3.00 9.00 30.00
73-Origin/1st app. Creeper; Ditko-c/a (3-4/68) 10.50 32.00 105.00
74-Intro/1st app. Anthro; Post-c/a (5/68) 7.00 21.00 70.00
75-Origin/1st app. Hawk & the Dove; Ditko-c/a 9.00 27.00 90.00
76-1st app. Bat Lash (8/68) 5.00 15.00 50.00
77-1st app. Angel & The Ape (9/68) 5.00 15.00 50.00
78-1st app. Jonny Double (11/68) 2.80 8.40 28.00
79-1st app. Dolphin (12/68); Aqualad origin-r 4.50 13.50 45.00
80-1st S.A. app. Phantom Stranger (1/69); Neal Adams-c 4.00 12.00 40.00
81-Windy & Willy 3.00 9.00 30.00
82-1st app. Nightmaster (5/69) by Grandenetti & Giordano; Kubert-c 5.50 16.50 55.00
83,84-Nightmaster by Wrightson w/Jones/Kaluta ink assist in each; Kubert-c. 83-Last 12¢ issue 84-Origin retold; begin 15¢ 5.00 15.00 50.00
85-87-Firehair; Kubert-a 2.50 7.50 20.00
88-90-Jason's Quest: 90-Manhunter 2070 app. 1.75 5.25 14.00
91-93-Manhunter 2070: 92-Origin. 93-(9/70) Last 15¢ issue 1.75 5.25 14.00
94-Intro/origin new Doom Patrol & Robotman(8-9/77) 1.25 3.75 10.00
95,96-The Doom Patrol. 95-Origin Celsius 1.10 3.30 9.00
97-99-Power Girl; origin-97,98; JSA cameos 1.10 3.30 9.00
100-(52 pgs.)-Most Showcase characters featured 1.50 4.50 12.00
101-103-Hawkman; Adam Strange x-over 1.00 3.00 8.00
104-(52 pgs.)-O.S.S. Spies at War 1.00 3.00 8.00

NOTE: ***Anderson*** *a-22-24i, 34-36i, 55, 56, 60, 61, 64, 101-103i; c-50i, 51i, 55, 56, 60, 61, 64.* ***Aparo*** *c-94-96.* ***Boring*** *c-10.* ***Estrada*** *a-104.* ***Fraden*** *c(p)-30, 31, 33.* ***Heath*** *c-3, 27-29.* ***Infantino*** *c/a(p)-4, 8, 13, 14; c-50p, 51p.* ***Gil Kane*** *a-22-24p, 34-36p; c-17-19, 22-24p(w/* ***Giella****), 31.* ***Kane/Anderson*** *c-34-36.* ***Kirby*** *c-11, 12.* ***Kirby/Stein*** *c-6, 7.* ***Kubert*** *a-2, 4i, 25, 26, 45, 53, 54, 72; c-25, 26, 53, 54, 57, 58, 82-87, 101-104; c-2, 4i.* ***Moriera*** *c-5.* ***Orlando*** *a-62p, 63p, 97i; c-62, 63, 97i.* ***Sekowsky*** *a-65p.* ***Sparling*** *a-78.* ***Staton*** *a-94, 95-99p, 100; c-97-100p.*

SHOWCASE '93
DC Comics: Jan, 1993 - No. 12, Dec, 1993 ($1.95, limited series, 52 pgs.)

1-12: 1-Begin 4 part Catwoman story & 6 part Blue Devil story; begin Cyborg story; Art Adams/Austin-c. 3-Flash by Travis Charest (p). 6-Azrael in Bat-costume (2 pgs.). 7,8-Knightfall parts 13 & 14. 6-10-Deathstroke app. (6,10-cameo). 9,10-Austin-i. 10-Azrael as Batman in new costume app.; Gulacy-c. 11-Perez-c. 12-Creeper app.; Alan Grant scripts. 3.00

NOTE: ***Chaykin*** *c-9.* ***Fabry*** *c-8.* ***Giffen*** *a-12.* ***Golden*** *c-3.* ***Zeck*** *c-6.*

SHOWCASE '94
DC Comics: Jan, 1994 - No. 12, Dec, 1994 ($1.95, limited series, 52 pgs.)

1-12: 1,2-Joker & Gunfire stories. 1-New Gods. 4-Riddler story. 5-Huntress-c/story w/app. new Batman. 6-Huntress-c/story w/app. Robin; Atom story. 7-Penguin story.by Peter David, P. Craig Russell, & Michael T. Gilbert; Penguin-c by Jae Lee. 8,9-Scarface origin story by Alan Grant, John Wagner,& Teddy Kristiansen; Prelude to Zero Hour. 10-Zero Hour tie-in story. 11-Man-Bat. 3.00

NOTE: ***Alan Grant*** *scripts-3, 4.* ***Kelley Jones*** *c-12.* ***Mignola*** *c-3.* ***Nebres*** *a(i)-2.* ***Quesada*** *c-10.* ***Russell*** *a-7p.* ***Simonson*** *c-5.*

SHOWCASE '95
DC Comics: Jan, 1995 - No. 12, Dec, 1995 ($2.50/$2.95, limited series)

1-4-Supergirl story. 3-Eradicator-c.; The Question story. 4-Thorn c/story 3.00
5-12: 5-Thorn-c/story; begin $2.95-c. 8-Spectre story. 12-The Shade story by James Robinson & Wade Von Grawbadger; Maitresse story by Chris Claremont & Alan Davis. 3.00

SHOWCASE '96
DC Comics: Jan, 1996 - No. 12, Dec, 1996 ($2.95, limited series)

1-12: 1-Steve Geppi cameo. 3-Black Canary & Lois Lane-c/story; Deadman story by Jamie Delano & Wade Von Grawbadger, Gary Frank-c. 4-Firebrand & Guardian-c/story; The Shade & Dr. Fate "Times Past" story by James Robinson & Matt Smith begins, ends #5. 6-Superboy-c/app.; Atom app.; Capt. Marvel (Mary Marvel)-c/app. 8-Supergirl by David & Dodson. 11-Scare Tactics app. 11,12-Legion of Super-Heroes vs. Brainiac. 12-Jesse Quick app. 3.00

SHOWGIRLS (Formerly Sherry the Showgirl #3)
Atlas Comics (MPC No. 2): No. 4, 2/57; June, 1957 - No. 2, Aug, 1957

4-Dan DeCarlo-c/a begins 8.35 25.00 50.00
1-Millie, Sherry, Chili, Pearl & Hazel begin 11.00 33.00 75.00
2 8.35 25.00 50.00

SHROUD, THE (See Super-Villain Team-Up #5)
Marvel Comics: Mar, 1994 - No. 4, June, 1994 ($1.75, mini-series)

1-4: 1,2,4-Spider-Man & Scorpion app. 2.00

SHROUD OF MYSTERY
Whitman Publications: June, 1982

1 4.00

SHUT UP AND DIE
Image Comics/Halloween: 1998 - Present ($2.95,B&W, bi-monthly)

1-3: Hudnall-s 3.00

SICK (Sick Special #131) (Magazine) (Satire)
Feature Publ./Headline Publ./Crestwood Publ. Co./Hewfred Publ./ Pyramid Comm./Charlton Publ. No. 109 (4/76) on: Aug, 1960 - No. 134, Fall, 1980

V1#1-Jack Paar photo on-c; Torres-a 14.00 42.00 140.00
2-5-Torres-a in all 7.50 22.50 75.00
6, V2#1-8(#7-14) 5.50 16.50 55.00
V3#1-8(#15-22) 3.50 10.50 35.00
V4#1-5(#23-27) 2.80 8.40 28.00
28,30-32,34-40 2.50 7.50 20.00
29-Beatles-c by Jack Davis 2.80 8.40 28.00
33-Ringo Starr photo-c & spoof on "A Hard Day's Night"; inside-c has Beatles photos 4.00 12.00 40.00
41-60: 45 has #44 on-c & #45 on inside 2.25 6.75 18.00
61-80,100: 70-John & Yoko-c 2.00 6.00 16.00
81-99 1.50 4.50 12.00
101-120 1.25 3.75 10.00
121-130: 128-Superman-c/movie parody 1.75 5.25 14.00
131-133: 131-Superman parody 2.50 7.50 20.00
134 (scarce) 3.00 9.00 30.00
Annual 1969, 1970, 1971 2.50 7.50 24.00
Annual 2-4(1980) 1.25 3.75 10.00
Big Sick Laff-in (1968)-w/psychedelic posters 2.80 8.40 28.00
Birthday Annual (1967)-3 pg. Huckleberry Fink fold out 3.20 9.60 32.00
7th Annual Yearbook (1967)-Davis-c, 2 pg. glossy poster insert 2.50 7.50 25.00
Special 2 (1978) 1.10 3.30 9.00
Yearbook 14(1974), 15(1975, 84 pgs.) 1.50 4.50 12.00

Silly Tunes #2 © MAR

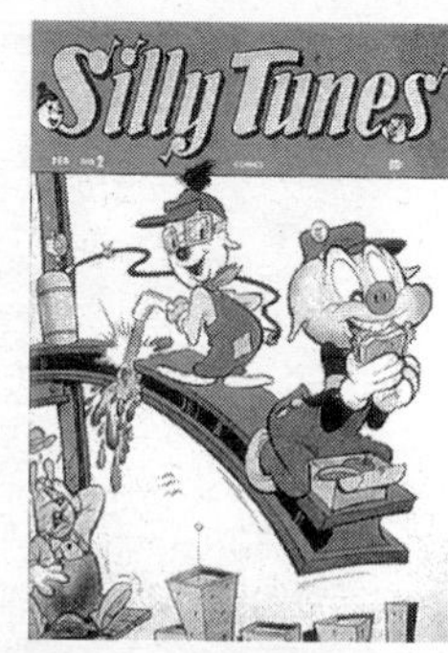

Silver Kid Western #2 © Stanmor

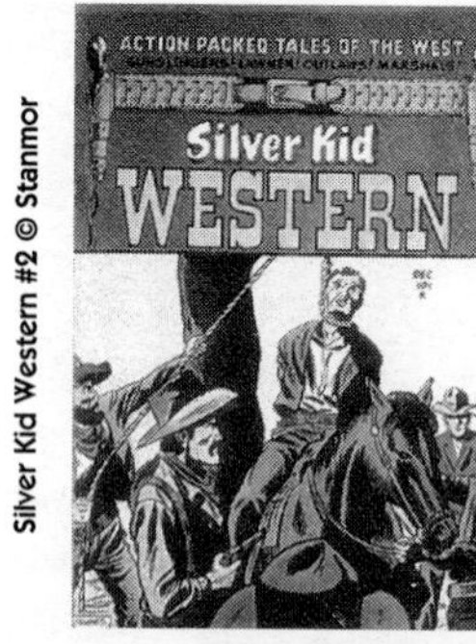

Silver Streak Comics #5 © LEV

GD2.0 FN6.0 NM9.4

NOTE: ***Davis*** *a-42, 87; c-22, 23, 25, 29, 31, 32.* ***Powell*** *a-7, 31, 57.* ***Simon*** *a-1-3, 10, 41, 42, 87, 99; c-1, 47, 57, 59, 69, 91, 95-97, 99, 100, 102, 107, 112.* ***Torres*** *a-1-3, 29, 31, 47, 49.* ***Tuska*** *a-14, 41-43. Civil War Blackouts-23, 24. #42 has biography of Bob Powell.*

SIDESHOW
Avon Periodicals: 1949 (one-shot)

1-(Rare)-Similar to Bachelor's Diary 30.00 90.00 210.00

SIEGE
Image Comics (WildStorm Prod.): Jan, 1997 - No. 4, Apr, 1997 ($2.50)

1-4 2.50

SIEGEL AND SHUSTER: DATELINE 1930s
Eclipse Comics: Nov, 1984 - No. 2, Sept, 1985 ($1.50/$1.75, Baxter paper #1)

1,2: 1-Unpublished samples of strips from the '30s; includes 'Interplanetary Police'; Shuster-c. 2 ($1.75, B&W)-unpublished strips; Shuster-c 2.00

SIGMA
Image Comics (WildStorm Productions): March, 1996 - No. 3, June, 1996 ($2.50, limited series)

1-3: 1-"Fire From Heaven" prelude #2; Coker-a
2-"Fire From Heaven" pt. 6. 3-"Fire From Heaven" pt. 14. 2.50

SILENT INVASION, THE
Rengade Press: Apr, 1986 - No.12, Mar, 1988 ($1.70/$2.00, B&W)

1-12-UFO sightings of the '50's 2.00
Book 1- reprints ($7.95) 8.00

SILENT MOBIUS
Viz Select Comics: 1991 - No. 5, 1992 ($4.95, color, squarebound, 44 pgs.)

1-5: Japanese stories translated to English 5.00

SILENT RAPTURE
Avatar Press: Jan, 1997 - No.2, Apr, 1997 ($3.00, B&W, limited series)

1,2 3.00

SILLY PILLY (See Frank Luther's...)

SILLY SYMPHONIES (See Dell Giants)

SILLY TUNES
Timely Comics: Fall, 1945 - No. 7, June, 1947

1-Silly Seal, Ziggy Pig begin 19.00 58.00 135.00
2-(2/46) 10.00 30.00 70.00
3-7: 6-New logo 9.15 27.00 55.00

SILVER (See Lone Ranger's Famous Horse...)

SILVERBACK
Comico: 1989 - No. 3, 1990 ($2.50, color, limited series, mature readers)

1-3: Character from Grendel: Matt Wagner-a 3.00

SILVERBLADE
DC Comics: Sept, 1987 - No. 12, Sept, 1988

1-12: Colan -c/a in all 2.00

SILVER CROSS (See Warrior Nun series)
Antarctic Press: Nov, 1997 - No. 3, Mar, 1998 ($2.95)

1-3-Ben Dunn-s/a 3.00

SILVERHAWKS
Star Comics/Marvel Comics #6: Aug, 1987 - No. 6, June, 1988 ($1.00)

1-6 2.00

SILVERHEELS
Pacific Comics: Dec, 1983 - No. 3, May, 1984 ($1.50)

1-3 2.00

SILVER KID WESTERN
Key/Stanmor Publications: Oct, 1954 - No. 5, July?, 1955

1 10.00 30.00 65.00
2 5.35 16.00 32.00
3-5 5.00 15.00 30.00
I.W. Reprint #1,2-Severin-c: 1-r/#? 2-r/#1 1.50 4.50 12.00

GD2.0 FN6.0 NM9.4

SILVER SABLE AND THE WILD PACK (See Amazing Spider-Man #265)
Marvel Comics: June, 1992 - No. 35, Apr, 1995 ($1.25/$1.50

1-($2.00)-Embossed & foil stamped-c; Spider-Man app. 3.00
2-26: 4,5-Dr. Doom-c/story. 6,7-Deathlok-c/story. 9-Origin Silver Sable. 10-Punisher-c/s. 15-Capt. America-c/s. 16,17-Intruders app. 18,19-Venom-c/s. 19-Siege of Darkness x-over. 23-Daredevil (in new costume) & Deadpool app. 24-Bound-in card sheet. Li'l Sylvie backup story. 25-($2.00, 52 pgs.)-Li'l Sylvie backup story 2.00

SILVER STAR (Also see Jack Kirby's...)
Pacific Comics: Feb, 1983 - No. Jan, 1984 ($1.00)

1-6: 1-1st app. Last of the Viking Heroes. 1-5-Kirby-c/a. 2-Ditko-a 3.00

SILVER STREAK COMICS (Crime Does Not Pay #22 on)
Your Guide Publs. No. 1-7/New Friday Publs. No. 8-17/Comic House Publ./Newsbook Publ.: Dec, 1939 - No. 21, May, 1942; No. 22-24, 1946 (Silver logo-#1-5)

GD2.0 FN6.0 VF8.0 NM9.4

1-(Scarce)-Intro The Claw by Cole (r-/in Daredevil #21), Red Reeves, Boy Magician, & Captain Fearless; The Wasp, Mister Midnight begin; Spirit Man app. Silver metallic-c begin, end #5; Claw c-1,2,6-8
955.00 2865.00 5730.00 11,000.00

GD2.0 FN6.0 NM9.4

2-The Claw by Cole; Simon-c/a 378.00 1133.00 3400.00
3-1st app. & origin Silver Streak (2nd with lightning speed); Dickie Dean the Boy Inventor, Lance Hale, Ace Powers, Bill Wayne, & The Planet Patrol begin 322.00 967.00 2900.00
4-Sky Wolf begins; Silver Streak by Jack Cole (new costume); 1st app. Jackie, Lance Hale's sidekick 162.00 486.00 1300.00
5-Jack Cole c/a(2) 194.00 581.00 1550.00

GD2.0 FN6.0 VF8.0 NM9.4

6-(Scarce, 9/40)-Origin & 1st app. Daredevil (blue & yellow costume) by Jack Binder; The Claw returns; classic Cole Claw-c
1083.00 3250.00 6500.00 13,000.00
7-Claw vs. Daredevil (new costume-blue & red) by Jack Cole & 3 other Cole stories (38 pgs.) 700.00 2100.00 4200.00 7200.00

GD2.0 FN6.0 NM9.4

8-Claw vs. Daredevil by Cole; last Cole Silver Streak
288.00 862.00 2600.00
9-Claw vs. Daredevil by Cole 188.00 562.00 1500.00
10-Origin & 1st app. Captain Battle (5/41); Claw vs. Daredevil by Cole; Robot-c 162.00 487.00 1300.00
11-Intro. Mercury by Bob Wood, Silver Streak's sidekick; conclusion Claw vs. Daredevil by Rico; in 'Presto Martin,' 2nd pg., newspaper says 'Roussos does it again' 112.00 338.00 900.00
12-14: 13-Origin Thun-Dohr 84.00 253.00 675.00
15, 17-Last Daredevil issue. 78.00 234.00 625.00
16-Hitler-c 87.00 262.00 700.00
18-The Saint begins (2/42, 1st app.) by Leslie Charteris (see Movie Comics #2 by DC); The Saint-c 66.00 197.00 525.00
19-21(1942): 20,21 have Wolverton's Scoop Scuttle. 21-Hitler app. in strip on cover 51.00 154.00 410.00
22-24(1946)-Reprints. 23-Bondage-c 31.00 94.00 220.00
nn(11/46)(Newsbook Publ.)-R-/S.S. story from #4-7 plus 2 Captain Fearless stories, all in color; bondage/torture-c 45.00 135.00 360.00

NOTE: ***Binder*** *c-3, 4, 13-15, 17.* ***Jack Cole*** *a-(Daredevil)-#6-10, (Dickie Dean)-#3-10, (Pirate Prince)-#7, (Silver Streak)-#4-8, nn; c-5 (Silver Streak), 6 (Claw), 7, 8 (Daredevil).* ***Everett*** *Red Reed begins #20.* ***Guardineer*** *a-#8-13.* ***Don Rico*** *a-11-17 (Daredevil); c-11, 12, 16.* ***Simon*** *a-3 (Silver Streak).* ***Bob Wood*** *a-9 (Silver Streak); c-9, 10. Captain Battle c-11, 13-15, 17. Claw c-#1, 2, 6-8. Daredevil c-7, 8, 12. Dickie Dean c-19. Ned of the Navy c-20 (war). The Saint c-18. Silver Streak c-5, 9, 10, 16, 23.*

SILVER SURFER (See Fantastic Four, Fantasy Masterpieces V2#1, Fireside Book Series, Marvel Graphic Novel, Marvel Presents #8, Marvel's Greatest Comics & Tales To Astonish #92)

SILVER SURFER, THE (Also see Essential Silver Surfer)
Marvel Comics Group: Aug, 1968 - No. 18, Sept, 1970; June, 1982

1-More detailed origin by John Buscema (p); The Watcher back-up stories begin (origin), end #7; (No. 1-7: 25¢, 68 pgs.) 39.00 117.00 435.00
2 17.50 52.00 175.00

Silver Surfer (1st series) #11 © MAR

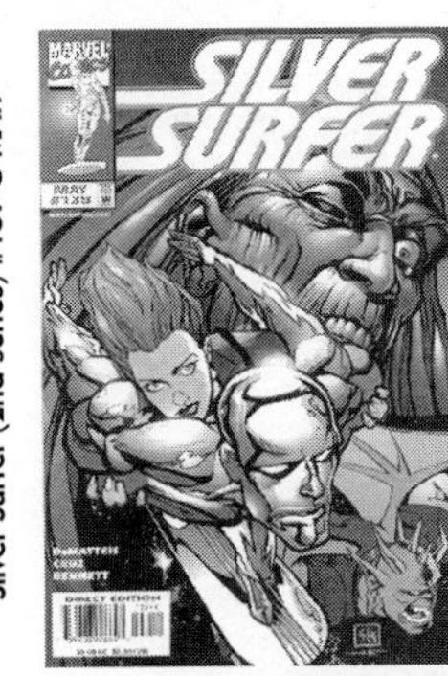

Silver Surfer (2nd series) #139 © MAR

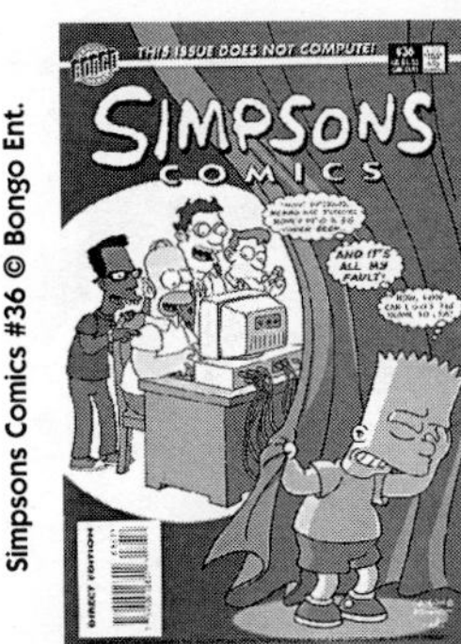

Simpsons Comics #36 © Bongo Ent.

GD2.0 FN6.0 NM9.4

3-1st app. Mephisto 13.50 41.00 135.00
4-Low distribution; Thor & Loki app. 36.00 108.00 400.00
5-7-Last giant size. 5-The Stranger app.; Fantastic Four app. 6-Brunner inks. 7-(8/69)-1st app. Frankenstein's monster (cameo) 8.50 25.50 85.00
8-10: 8-18-(15¢ issues) 6.50 19.50 65.00
11-13,15-18: 15-Silver Surfer vs. Human Torch; Fantastic Four app. 17-Nick Fury app. 18-Vs. The Inhumans; Kirby-c/a 5.00 15.00 50.00
14-Spider-Man x-over 7.00 21.00 70.00
V2#1 (6/82, 52 pgs.)-Byrne-c/a 1.10 3.30 9.00

NOTE: ***Adkins** a-8-15i. **Brunner** a-6i. **J. Buscema** a-1-17p. **Colan** a-1-3p. **Reinman** a-1-4i. #1-14 were reprinted in Fantasy Masterpieces V2#1-14.*

SILVER SURFER (Volume 3) (See Marvel Graphic Novel #38)
Marvel Comics Group: V3#1, July, 1987 - No. 146, Nov, 1998

1-Double size ($1.25) 1.10 3.30 9.00
2 4.00
3-17: 15-Ron Lim-c/a begins (9/88) 4.00
18-33,39-43: 25,31 ($1.50, 52 pgs.). 25-Skrulls app. 32,39-No Ron Lim-c/a. 39-Alan Grant scripts 3.00
34-Thanos returns (cameo); Starlin scripts begin 5.00
35-38: 35-1st full Thanos app. in Silver Surfer (3/90); reintro Drax the Destroyer on last pg. (cameo). 36-Recaps history of Thanos; Capt. Marvel & Warlock app. in recap. 37-1st full app. Drax the Destroyer; Drax-c. 38-Silver Surfer battles Thanos 2.40 6.00
44,45,49-Thanos stories (c-44,45) 4.00
46-48: 46-Return of Adam Warlock (2/91); re-intro Gamora & Pip the Troll. 47-Warlock battles Drax. 48-Last Starlin scripts (also #50) 4.00
50-($1.50, 52 pgs.)-Embossed & silver foil-c; Silver Surfer has brief battle w/Thanos; story cont'd in Infinity Gauntlet #1 1.00 2.80 7.00
50-2nd & 3rd printings 2.00
51-59: 51-53: Infinity Gauntlet x-over . 54-57: Infinity Gauntlet x-overs. 54-Rhino app. 55,56-Thanos-c & app. 57-Thanos-c & cameo. 58,59-Infinity Gauntlet x-overs; 58-Ron Lim-c only. 59-Thanos battles Silver Surfer-c/story; Thanos joins 3.00
60-74,76-99,101-124,126-139: 63-Capt. Marvel app. 67-69-Infinity War x-overs. 76-78-Jack of Hearts-c/s. 83-85-Infinity Crusade x-over; 83,84-Thanos cameo. 85-Storm, Wonder Man x-over. 86-Thor-c/s. 87-Dr. Strange & Warlock app. 88-Thanos-c/s. 82 (52 pgs.). 101-Bound in card sheet. 5-FF app. 96-Hulk & FF app. 97-Terrax & Nova app. 106-Doc Doom app. 121-Quasar & Beta Ray Bill app. 123-w/card insert; begin Garney-a. 126-Dr. Strange-c/app. 128-Spider-Man & Daredevil-c/app. 138-Thing-c 2.00
75-($2.50, 52 pgs.)-Embossed foil-c; Lim-c/a 3.00
100 ($2.25, 52 pgs.)-Wraparound-c 2.25
100 ($3.95, 52 pgs.)-Enhanced-c 4.00
125 ($2.95)-Wraparound-c; Vs. Hulk-c/app. 3.00
140-146: 140-142,144,145-Muth-c/a. 143,146-Cowan-a. 146-Last issue 2.00
Annual 1 (1988, $1.75)-Evolutionary War app.; 1st Ron Lim-a on Silver Surfer (20 pg. back-up story & pin-ups) 5.00
Annual 2-7 ('89-'94, 68 pgs.): 2-Atlantis Attacks. 4-3 pg. origin story; Silver Surfer battles Guardians of the Galaxy. 5-Return of the Defenders, part 3; Lim-c/a (3 pgs. of pin-ups only). 6-Polybagged w/trading card; 1st app. Legacy; card is by Lim/Austin 3.00
Annual '97 ($2.99), .../Thor Annual '98 ($2.99) 3.00
...Dangerous Artifacts-(1996, $3.95)-Ron Marz scripts; Galactus-c/app. 4.00
Graphic Novel (Hardcover, $14.95) 15.00
The Enslavers Graphic Novel (1990, $16.95) 17.00
Inner Demons TPB (4/98, $3.50)r/#123,125,126 3.50
...: The First Coming of Galactus nn (11/92, $5.95, 68 pgs.)-Reprints Fantastic Four #48-50 with new Lim-c 2.40 6.00
Wizard 1/2 1.85 5.50 15.00

NOTE: ***Austin** c(i)-7, 8, 71, 73, 74, 76, 79. Cowan a-143,146. **Cully Hamner** a-83p. **Ron Lim** a(p)-15-31, 33-38, 40-55, (56, 57-part-p), 60-65, 73-82, Annual 2, 4; c(p)-15-31, 32-38, 40-84, 86-92, Annual 2, 4-6. Muth c/a-140-142,144,145. **M. Rogers** a-1-10, 12, 19, 21; c-1-9, 11, 12, 21.*

SILVER SURFER, THE
Marvel Comics (Epic): Dec, 1988 - No. 2, Jan, 1989 ($1.00, lim. series)

1,2: By Stan Lee scripts & Moebius-c/a 3.00
...: Parable ('98, $5.99) r/#1&2 6.00

GD2.0 FN6.0 NM9.4

SILVER SURFER: LOFTIER THAN MORTALS
Marvel Comics: Oct, 1999 - No. 2, Oct, 1999 ($2.50, limited series)

1,2-Remix of Fantastic Four #57-60; Velluto-a 2.50

SILVER SURFER/SUPERMAN
Marvel Comics: 1996 ($5.95,one-shot)

1-Perez-s/Lim-c/a(p) 6.00

SILVER SURFER VS. DRACULA
Marvel Comics: Feb, 1994 ($1.75, one-shot)

1-r/Tomb of Dracula #50; Everett Vampire-r/Venus #19; Howard the Duck back-up by Brunner; Lim-c(p) 2.00

SILVER SURFER/WARLOCK: RESURRECTION
Marvel Comics: Mar, 1993 - No. 4, June, 1993 ($2.50, limited series)

1-4: Starlin-c/a & scripts 2.50

SILVER SURFER/WEAPON ZERO
Marvel Comics: Apr, 1997 ($2.95,one-shot)

1-"Devil's Reign" pt. 8 3.00

SILVERTIP (Max Brand)
Dell Publishing Co.: No. 491, Aug, 1953 - No. 898, May, 1958

Four Color 491 (#1); all painted-c 7.00 22.00 80.00
Four Color 572,608,637,667,731,789,898-Kinstler-a 3.60 11.00 40.00
Four Color 835 3.60 11.00 40.00

SIMPSONS COMICS (See Bartman, Itchy & Scratchy & Radioactive Man)
Bongo Comics Group: 1993 - Present ($1.95, color)

1-($2.25)-FF#1-c swipe; pull-out poster; flip book 3.00
2-40: 2-Patty & Selma on flip side. 3-Krusty, Agent of K.L.O.W.N. flip-c/story. 4-Infinity-c; flip-c of Busman #1; w/trading card. 5-Wraparound-c w/trading card. 6-40: All Flip books. 6-w/Chief Wiggum's "Crime Comics". 7-w/"McBain Comics". 8-w/"Edna, Queen of the Congo". 9-w/"Barney Gumble". 10-w/"Apu". 11-w/"Homer". 12-w/"White Knuckled War Stories". 13-w/"Jimbo Jones' Wedgie Comics". 14-w/"Grampa". 15-w/"Itchy & Scratchy". 16-w/"Bongo Grab Bag". 17-w/"Headlight Comics". 18-w/"Milhouse".19-22-w/"Roswell". 23-w/"Hellfire Comics". 24-w/"Lil' Homey" 36-39-Flip book w/Radioactive Man 2.25
41-44 ($2.50): 43-Flip book w/Poochie 2.50
...Big Bonanza (1998, $11.95)-r/#28-31, ...Extravaganza (1994, $10.00)-r/#1-4; infinity-c, ...On Parade (1998, $11.95)-r/#24-27, ...Simpsorama (1996, $10.95)-r/#11-14 12.00

SIMPSONS COMICS AND STORIES
Welsh Publishing Group: 1993 ($2.95, one-shot)

1-(Direct Sale)-Polybagged w/Bartman poster 5.00
1-(Newsstand Edition)-Without poster 3.00

SIMULATORS, THE
Neatly Chiseled Features: 1991 ($2.50, stiff-c)

1-Super hero group 2.50

SINBAD, JR (TV Cartoon)
Dell Publishing Co.: Sept-Nov, 1965 - No. 3, May, 1966

1 2.50 7.50 24.00
2,3 3.60 9.00 18.00

SIN CITY (See Dark Horse Presents, Decade of Dark Horse, A & San Diego Comic Con Comics #2,4)
Dark Horse Comics (Legend)
TPB ($15.00) Reprints early DHP stories 15.00

SIN CITY: A DAME TO KILL FOR
Dark Horse Comics (Legend): Nov, 1993 - No. 6, May, 1994 ($2.95, B&W, limited series)

1-6: Frank Miller-c/a & story in all. 1-1st app. Dwight. 5.00
Limited Edition Hardcover 100.00
Hardcover 25.00
TPB ($15.00) 15.00

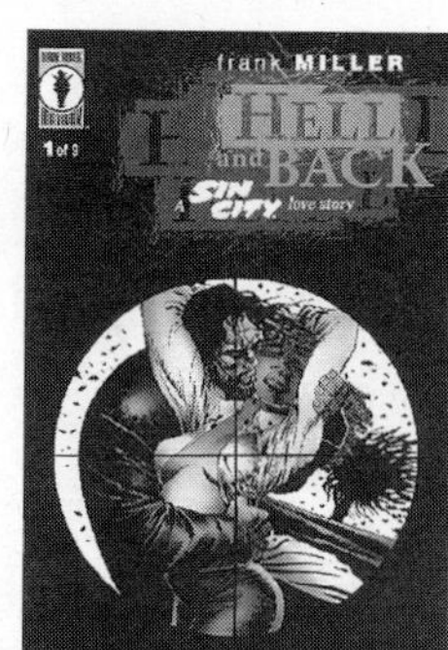

Sin City: Hell and Back #1 © Frank Miller

Single Series #11 © UFS

Six From Sirius #1 © Moench & Gulacy

GD2.0 FN6.0 NM9.4

SIN CITY: FAMILY VALUES
Dark Horse Comics (Legend): Oct, 1997 ($10.00, B&W, squarebound, one-shot)

nn-Miller-c/a & story — 10.00
Limited Edition Hardcover — 75.00

SIN CITY: HELL AND BACK
Dark Horse (Maverick): Jul, 1999 - No. 9 ($2.95, B&W, limited series)

1-3-Miller-c/a & story — 3.00

SIN CITY: JUST ANOTHER SATURDAY NIGHT
Dark Horse Comics (Legend): Aug, 1997 (Wizard 1/2 offer, B&W, one-shot)

1/2-Miller-c/a & story — 1.00 — 3.00 — 8.00
nn (10/98, $2.50) r/#1/2 — 2.50

SIN CITY: LOST, LONELY & LETHAL
Dark Horse Comics (Legend): Dec, 1996 ($2.95, B&W and blue, one-shot)

nn-Miller-c/s/a; w/pin-ups — 4.00

SIN CITY: SEX AND VIOLENCE
Dark Horse Comics (Legend): Mar, 1997 ($2.95, B&W and blue, one-shot)

nn-Miller-c/a & story — 4.00

SIN CITY: SILENT NIGHT
Dark Horse Comics (Legend): Dec, 1995 ($2.95, B&W, one-shot)

1-Miller-c/a & story; Marv app. — 4.00

SIN CITY: THAT YELLOW BASTARD
Dark Horse Comics (Legend): Feb, 1996 - No. 6, July, 1996 ($2.95/$3.50, B&W and yellow, limited series)

1-5: Miller-c/a & story in all. 1-1st app. Hartigan. — 5.00
6-($3.50) Error & corrected — 5.00
Limited Edition Hardcover — 25.00
TPB ($15.00) — 15.00

SIN CITY: THE BABE WORE RED AND OTHER STORIES
Dark Horse Comics (Legend): Nov, 1994 ($2.95, B&W and red, one-shot)

1-r/serial run in Previews as well as other stories; Miller-c/a & scripts; Dwight app. — 3.00

SIN CITY: THE BIG FAT KILL
Dark Horse Comics (Legend): Nov, 1994 - No. 5, Mar, 1995 ($2.95, B&W, limited series)

1-5-Miller story & art in all; Dwight app. — 4.00
Hardcover — 25.00
TPB ($15.00) — 15.00

SINDBAD (See Capt. Sindbad under Movie Comics, and Fantastic Voyages of Sindbad)

SINGING GUNS (See Fawcett Movie Comics)

SINGLE SERIES (Comics on Parade #30 on)(Also see John Hix...)
United Features Syndicate: 1938 - No. 28, 1942 (All 68 pgs.)

Note: See Individual Alphabetical Listings for prices

1-Captain and the Kids (#1)	2-Broncho Bill (1939) (#1)
3-Ella Cinders (1939)	4-Li'l Abner (1939) (#1)
5-Fritzi Ritz (#1)	6-Jim Hardy by Dick Moores (#1)
7-Frankie Doodle	8-Peter Pat (On sale 7/14/39)
9-Strange As It Seems	10-Little Mary Mixup
11-Mr. and Mrs. Beans	12-Joe Jinks
13-Looy Dot Dope	14-Billy Make Believe
15-How It Began (1939)	16-Illustrated Gags (1940)-Has ad for Captain and the Kids #1 reprint listed below
17-Danny Dingle	
18-Li'l Abner (#2 on-c)	
19-Broncho Bill (#2 on-c)	20-Tarzan by Hal Foster
21-Ella Cinders (#2 on-c; on sale 3/19/40)	22-Iron Vic
23-Tailspin Tommy by Hal Forrest (#1)	24-Alice in Wonderland (#1)
25-Abbie and Slats	26-Little Mary Mixup (#2 on-c, 1940)
27-Jim Hardy by Dick Moores (1942)	28-Ella Cinders & Abbie and Slats (1942)
1-Captain and the Kids (1939 reprint)-2nd Edition	1-Fritzi Ritz (1939 reprint)-2nd ed.

NOTE: *Some issues given away at the 1939-40 New York World's Fair (#6).*

GD2.0 FN6.0 NM9.4

SINISTER HOUSE OF SECRET LOVE, THE (Becomes Secrets of Sinister House No. 5 on)
National Periodical Publ.: Oct-Nov, 1971 - No. 4, Apr-May, 1972

1 (all 52 pgs.) — 12.00 — 36.00 — 120.00
2-4: 2-Jeff Jones-c. 3-Toth-a — 4.00 — 12.00 — 40.00

SIR CHARLES BARKLEY AND THE REFEREE MURDERS
Hamilton Comics: 1993 ($9.95, 8-1/2" x 11", 52 pgs.)

nn-Photo-c; Sports fantasy comic book fiction (uses real names of NBA super stars). Script by Alan Dean Foster, art by Joe Staton. Comes with bound-in sheet of 35 gummed "Moods of Charles Barkley" stamps. Photo/story on Barkley — 1.25 — 3.75 — 10.00
Special Edition of 100 copies for charity signed on an affixed book plate by Barkley, Foster & Staton — 150.00
Ashcan edition given away to dealers, distributors & promoters (low distribution). Four pages in color, balance of story in b&w — 1.25 — 3.75 — 10.00

SIREN (Also see Eliminator & Ultraforce)
Malibu Comics (Ultraverse): Sept, 1995 - No. 3, Dec, 1995 ($1.50)

Infinity, 1-3: Infinity-Black-c & painted-c exists. 1-Regular-c & painted-c; War Machine app. 2-Flip book w/Phoenix Resurrection Pt. 3 — 2.00
Special 1-(2/96, $1.95, 28 pgs.)-Origin Siren; Marvel Comic's Juggernaut-c/app. — 2.00

SIREN: SHAPES
Image Comics: May, 1998 - No. 3, Nov, 1998 ($2.95, B&W, limited series)

1-3-J. Torres -s — 3.00

SIR LANCELOT (TV)
Dell Publishing Co.: No. 606, Dec, 1954 - No. 775, Mar, 1957

Four Color 606 (not TV) — 6.40 — 19.00 — 70.00
Four Color 775(...and Brian)-Buscema-a; photo-c — 7.00 — 22.00 — 80.00

SIR WALTER RALEIGH (Movie)
Dell Publishing Co.: May, 1955 (Based on movie "The Virgin Queen")

Four Color 644-Photo-c — 5.50 — 16.50 — 60.00

SISTERHOOD OF STEEL (See Eclipse Graphic Adventure Novel #13)
Marvel Comics (Epic Comics): Dec, 1984 -No. 8, Feb, 1986 ($1.50, Baxter paper, mature)

1-8 — 2.00

SISTERS OF MERCY
Maximum Press/No Mercy Comics #3 on: Dec, 1995 - No. 5, Oct, 1996 ($2.50)

1-5: 1-Liefeld variant-c exists — 2.50
V2#0-(3/97, $1.50) Liefeld-c — 2.00

SISTERS OF MERCY: PARADISE LOST
London Night Studios/No Mercy Comics: Apr, 1997 - No. 4 ($2.50)

1-4 — 2.50

SISTERS OF MERCY: WHEN RAZORS CRY CRIMSON TEARS
No Mercy Comics: Oct, 1996 ($2.50, one-shot)

1 — 2.50

6, THE
Virtual Comics (Byron Preiss Multimedia): Oct, 1996 - No. 3, Dec, 1996 ($2.50, limited series)

1-3: L. Simonson-s — 2.50

6 BLACK HORSES (See Movie Classics)

SIX FROM SIRIUS
Marvel Comics (Epic Comics): July, 1984 - No. 4, Oct, 1984 ($1.50, limited series, mature)

1-4: Moench scripts; Gulacy-c/a in all — 2.00

SIX FROM SIRIUS II
Marvel Comics (Epic Comics): Feb, 1986 - No. 4, May, 1986 ($1.50, limited series, mature)

1-4: Moench scripts; Gulacy-c/a in all — 2.00

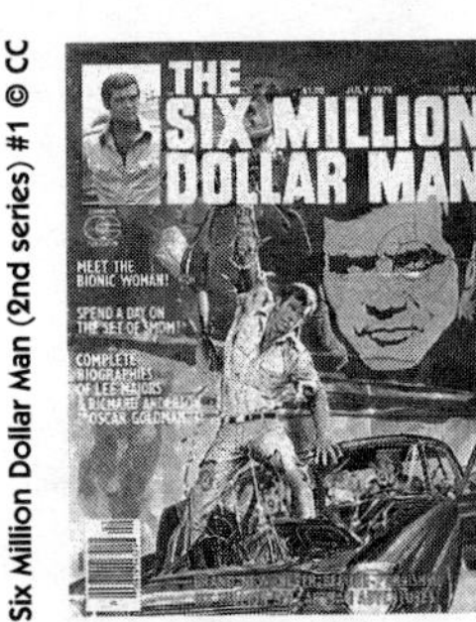

Six Million Dollar Man (2nd series) #1 © CC

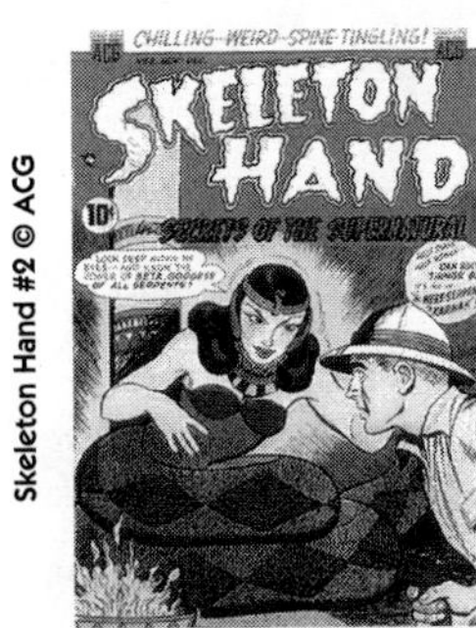

Skeleton Hand #2 © ACG

Skyman #4 © CCG

	GD2.0	FN6.0	NM9.4

SIX-GUN HEROES
Fawcett Publications: March, 1950 - No. 23, Nov, 1953 (Photo-c #1-23)

	GD2.0	FN6.0	NM9.4
1-Rocky Lane, Hopalong Cassidy, Smiley Burnette begin (same date as Smiley Burnette #1)	43.00	129.00	345.00
2	26.00	79.00	185.00
3-5: 5-Lash LaRue begins	18.00	54.00	125.00
6-15	13.50	41.00	95.00
16-22: 17-Last Smiley Burnette. 18-Monte Hale begins	11.50	34.00	80.00
23-Last Fawcett issue	13.00	39.00	90.00

NOTE: *Hopalong Cassidy photo c-1-3. Monte Hale photo c-18. Rocky Lane photo c-4, 5, 7, 9, 11, 13, 15, 17, 20, 21, 23. Lash LaRue photo c-6, 8, 10, 12, 14, 16, 19, 22.*

SIX-GUN HEROES (Cont'd from Fawcett; Gunmasters #84 on) (See Blue Bird)
Charlton Comics: No. 24, Jan, 1954 - No. 83, Mar-Apr, 1965 (All Vol. 4)

	GD2.0	FN6.0	NM9.4
24-Lash LaRue, Hopalong Cassidy, Rocky Lane & Tex Ritter begin; photo-c	20.00	60.00	140.00
25	10.00	30.00	65.00
26-30: 26-Rod Cameron story. 28-Tom Mix begins?	9.15	27.00	55.00
31-40: 38-Jingles & Wild Bill Hickok (TV)	8.35	25.00	50.00
41-46,48,50	7.50	22.50	45.00
47-Williamson-a, 2 pgs; Torres-a	8.35	25.00	50.00
49-Williamson-a (5 pgs.)	9.15	27.00	55.00
51-56,58-60: 58-Gunmaster app.	3.00	9.00	30.00
57-Origin & 1st app. Gunmaster	3.50	10.50	35.00
61,63-70	2.50	7.50	24.00
62-Origin Gunmaster	2.60	7.80	26.00
71-75,77,78,80-83	2.25	6.75	18.00
76,79: 76-Gunmaster begins. 79-1st app. & origin of Bullet, the Gun-Boy	2.50	7.50	20.00

SIXGUN RANCH (See Luke Short & Four Color #580)

SIX-GUN WESTERN
Atlas Comics (CDS): Jan, 1957 - No. 4, July, 1957

	GD2.0	FN6.0	NM9.4
1-Crandall-a; two Williamson text illos	19.00	58.00	135.00
2,3-Williamson-a in both	14.00	43.00	100.00
4-Woodbridge-a	10.00	30.00	60.00

NOTE: ***Ayers** a-2, 3. **Maneely** a-1; c-2, 3. **Orlando** a-2. **Pakula** a-2. **Powell** a-3. **Romita** a-1, 4. **Severin** c-1, 4. **Shores** a-2.*

SIX MILLION DOLLAR MAN, THE (TV)
Charlton Comics: 6/76 - No. 4, 12/76; No. 5, 10/77; No. 6, 2/78 - No. 9, 6/78

	GD2.0	FN6.0	NM9.4
1-Staton-c/a; Lee Majors photo on-c	1.25	3.75	10.00
2-9: 2-Neal Adams-c; Staton-a	1.00	2.80	7.00

SIX MILLION DOLLAR MAN, THE (TV)(Magazine)
Charlton Comics: July, 1976 - No. 7, Nov, 1977 (B&W)

	GD2.0	FN6.0	NM9.4
1-Neal Adams-c/a	2.00	6.00	16.00
2-Neal Adams-c	1.50	4.50	12.00
3-N. Adams part inks; Chaykin-a	1.50	4.50	12.00
4-7	1.10	3.30	9.00

SIX STRING SAMURAI
Awesome-Hyperwerks: Sept, 1998 ($2.95)

	GD2.0	FN6.0	NM9.4
1-Stinsman & Fraga-a			3.00

67 SECONDS
Marvel Comics (Epic Comics): 1992 ($15.95, 54 pgs., graphic novel)

	GD2.0	FN6.0	NM9.4
nn-James Robinson scripts; Steve Yeowell-c/a	2.25	6.75	18.00

SKATEMAN
Pacific Comics: Nov, 1983 (Baxter paper, one-shot)

	GD2.0	FN6.0	NM9.4
1-Adams-c/a			3.00

SKELETON HAND (...In Secrets of the Supernatural)
American Comics Gr. (B&M Dist. Co.): Sept-Oct, 1952 - No. 6, Jul-Aug, 1953

	GD2.0	FN6.0	NM9.4
1	40.00	120.00	310.00
2	30.00	90.00	210.00
3-6	25.00	75.00	175.00

SKELETON KEY
Amaze Ink: July, 1995 - No. 30, Jan, 1998 ($1.25/$1.50/$1.75, B&W)

	GD2.0	FN6.0	NM9.4
1-30			2.00
Special #1 (2/98, $4.95) Unpublished short stories			5.00
Sugar Kat Special (10/98, $2.95) Halloween stories			3.00
Beyond The Threshold TPB (6/96. $11.95)-r/#1-6			12.00
Cats and Dogs TPB ($12.95)-r/#25-30			13.00
The Celestial Calendar TPB ($19.95)-r/#7-18			20.00
Telling Tales TPB ($12.95)-r/#19-24			13.00

SKELETON KEY (Volume 2)
Amaze Ink: 1999 - No. 4, 1999 ($2.95, B&W)

	GD2.0	FN6.0	NM9.4
1-4-Andrew Watson-s/a			3.00

SKELETON WARRIORS
Marvel Comics: Apr, 1995 - No. 4, July, 1995 ($1.50)

	GD2.0	FN6.0	NM9.4
1-4: Based on animated series.			2.00

SKIN GRAFT: THE ADVENTURES OF A TATTOOED MAN
DC Comics (Vertigo): July, 1993 - No. 4, Oct, 1993 ($2.50, lim. series, mature)

	GD2.0	FN6.0	NM9.4
1-4			2.50

SKI PARTY (See Movie Classics)

SKREEMER
DC Comics: May, 1989 - No. 6, Oct, 1989 ($2.00, limited series, mature)

	GD2.0	FN6.0	NM9.4
1-6: Contains graphic violence			2.00

SKRULL KILL KREW
Marvel Comics: Sept, 1995 - No. 5, Dec, 1995 ($2.95, limited series)

	GD2.0	FN6.0	NM9.4
1-5: Grant Morrison scripts. 2,3-Cap America app.			3.00

SKUL, THE
Virtual Comics (Byron Preiss Multimedia): Oct, 1996 - No. 3, Dec, 1996 ($2.50, limited series)

	GD2.0	FN6.0	NM9.4
1-3: Ron Lim & Jimmy Palmiotti-a			2.50

SKULL & BONES
DC Comics: 1992 - No. 3, 1992 ($4.95, limited series, 52 pgs.)

	GD2.0	FN6.0	NM9.4
Book 1-3: 1-1st app.			5.00

SKULL, THE SLAYER
Marvel Comics Group: Aug, 1975 - No. 8, Nov, 1976 (20¢/25¢)

	GD2.0	FN6.0	NM9.4
1-Origin & 1st app.; Gil Kane-c	1.00	3.00	8.00
2-8: 2-Gil Kane-c. 5,6-(Regular 25¢-c). 8-Kirby-c			5.00
5,6-(30¢-c variants, limited distribution)(5,7/76)	2.50	7.50	20.00

SKY BLAZERS (CBS Radio)
Hawley Publications: Sept, 1940 - No. 2, Nov, 1940

	GD2.0	FN6.0	NM9.4
1-Sky Pirates, Ace Archer, Flying Aces begin	59.00	178.00	475.00
2-WWII aerial battle-c	40.00	120.00	290.00

SKYMAN (See Big Shot Comics & Sparky Watts)
Columbia Comics Gr.: Fall?, 1941 - No. 2, Fall?, 1942; No. 3, 1948 - No. 4, 1948

	GD2.0	FN6.0	NM9.4
1-Origin Skyman, The Face, Sparky Watts app.; Whitney-c/a; 3rd story-r from Big Shot #1; Whitney c-1-4	112.00	337.00	900.00
2 (1942)-Yankee Doodle	56.00	169.00	450.00
3,4 (1948)	39.00	118.00	275.00

SKYPILOT
Ziff-Davis Publ. Co.: No. 10, 1950(nd) - No. 11, Apr-May, 1951

	GD2.0	FN6.0	NM9.4
10,11-Frank Borth-a; Saunders painted-c	13.50	41.00	95.00

SKY RANGER (See Johnny Law...)

SKYROCKET
Harry 'A' Chesler: 1944

	GD2.0	FN6.0	NM9.4
nn-Alias the Dragon, Dr. Vampire, Skyrocket & The Desperado app.; WWII Jap zero-c	29.00	86.00	200.00

SKY SHERIFF (Breeze Lawson...) (Also see Exposed & Outlaws)
D. S. Publishing Co.: Summer, 1948

Slave Girl Comics #1 © AVON

Slingers #2 © DC

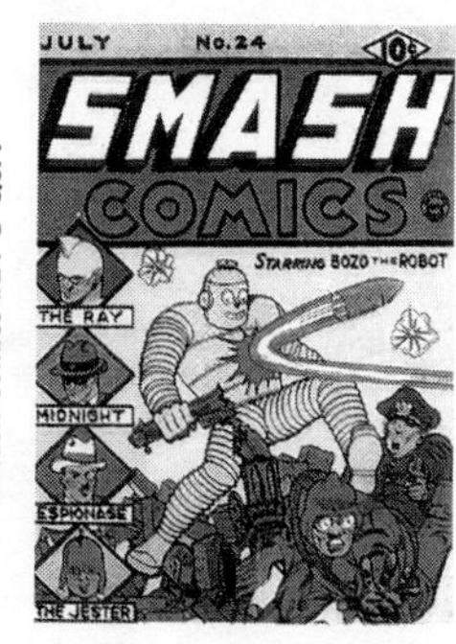

Smash Comics #24 © QUA

GD2.0 FN6.0 NM9.4

1-Edmond Good-c/a 12.00 36.00 85.00

SKY WOLF (Also see Airboy)
Eclipse Comics: Mar, 1988 - No. 3, Oct, 1988 ($1.25/$1.50/$1.95, lim. series)

1-3 2.00

SLACKER COMICS
Slave Labor Graphics: Aug, 1994 - Present ($2.95, B&W, quarterly)

1-18, 1 (2nd printing)-Reads "2nd print" in indicia 3.00

SLAINE, THE BERSERKER (Slaine the King #21 on)
Quality: July, 1987 - No. 28, 1989 ($1.25/$1.50)

1-28 2.00

SLAINE, THE HORNED GOD
Fleetway: 1998 - No. 3 ($6.99)

1-3-Reprints series from 2000 A.D.; Bisley-a 7.00

SLAM BANG COMICS (Western Desperado #8)
Fawcett Publications: Mar, 1940 - No. 7, Sept, 1940 (Combined with Master Comics #7)

1-Diamond Jack, Mark Swift & The Time Retarder, Lee Granger, Jungle King begin & continue in Master 200.00 600.00 1600.00
2 87.00 262.00 700.00
3-Classic-c 122.00 366.00 975.00
4-7: 6-Intro Zoro, the Mystery Man (also in #7) 69.00 206.00 550.00

SLAPSTICK
Marvel Comics: Nov, 1992 - No. 4, Feb, 1993 ($1.25, limited series)

1-4: Fry/Austin-c/a. 4-Ghost Rider, D.D., F.F. app. 2.00

SLAPSTICK COMICS
Comic Magazines Distributors: nd (1946?) (36 pgs.)

nn-Firetop feature; Post-a(2) 23.00 69.00 160.00

SLASH-D DOUBLECROSS
St. John Publishing Co.: 1950 (Pocket-size, 132 pgs.)

nn-Western comics 21.00 64.00 150.00

SLASH MARAUD
DC Comics: Nov, 1987 - No. 6, Apr, 1988 ($1.75, limited series)

1-6 2.00

SLAUGHTERMAN
Comico: Feb, 1983 - No. 2, 1983 ($1.50, B&W)

1,2 2.00

SLAVE GIRL COMICS (See Malu... & White Princess of the Jungle #2)
Avon Periodicals/Eternity Comics (1989): Feb, 1949 - No. 2, Apr, 1949 (52 pgs.); Mar, 1989 (B&W, 44 pgs)

1-Larsen-c/a 84.00 253.00 675.00
2-Larsen-a 62.00 187.00 500.00
1-(3/89, $2.25, B&W, 44 pgs.)-r/#1 2.25

SLEDGE HAMMER (TV)
Marvel Comics: Feb, 1988 - No. 2, Mar,1988 ($1.00, limited series)

1,2 2.00

SLEEPING BEAUTY (See Dell Giants & Movie Comics)
Dell Publishing Co.: No. 973, May, 1959 - No. 984, June, 1959 (Disney)

Four Color 973 (...and the Prince) 11.00 33.00 120.00
Four Color 984 (...Fairy Godmother's) 8.00 25.00 90.00

SLEEPWALKER
Marvel Comics: June, 1991 - No. 33, Feb, 1994 ($1.00/$1.25)

1-1st app. Sleepwalker 3.00
2-33: 4-Williamson-i. 5-Spider-Man-c/stor. 7-Infinity Gauntlet x-over. 8-Vs. Deathlok-c/story. 11-Ghost Rider-c/story. 12-Quesada-c/a(p) 14-Intro Spectra. 15-F.F.-c/story. 17-Darkhawk & Spider-Man x-over. 18-Infinity War x-over; Quesada/Williamson-c. 21,22-Hobgoblin app. 19-($2.00)-Die-cut Sleepwalker mask-c 2.00
25-($2.95, 52 pgs.)-Holo-grafx foil-c; origin 3.00

GD2.0 FN6.0 NM9.4

Holiday Special 1 (1/93, $2.00, 52 pgs.)-Quesada-c(p) 2.00

SLEEPWALKING
Hall of Heroes: Jan, 1996 ($2.50, B&W)

1-Kelley Jones-c 2.50

SLEEZE BROTHERS, THE
Marvel Comics (Epic Comics): Aug, 1989 - No. 6, Jan, 1990 ($1.75, mature)

1-6: 4-6 (9/89 - 11/89 indicia dates) 2.00
nn-(1991, $3.95, 52 pgs.) 4.00

SLICK CHICK COMICS
Leader Enterprises: 1947(nd) - No. 3, 1947(nd)

1-Teenage humor 11.00 33.00 75.00
2,3 8.35 25.00 50.00

SLIDERS (TV)
Acclaim Comics (Armada): June, 1996 - No. 2, July, 1996 ($2.50, lim. series)

1,2: D.G. Chichester scripts; Dick Giordano-a. 2.50

SLIDERS: DARKEST HOUR (TV)
Acclaim Comics (Armada): Oct, 1996 - No. 3, Dec, 1996 ($2.50, limited series)

1-3 2.50

SLIDERS SPECIAL
Acclaim Comics (Armada): Nov, 1996 - No 3, Mar, 1997 ($3.95, limited series)

1-3: 1-Narcotica-Jerry O'Connell-s. 2-Blood and Splendor. 3-Deadly Secrets 4.00

SLIDERS: ULTIMATUM (TV)
Acclaim Comics (Armada): Sept, 1996 - No. 2, Sept, 1996 ($2.50, lim. series)

1,2 2.50

SLIMER! (TV cartoon) (Also see the Real Ghostbusters)
Now Comics: 1989 - No. 19, Feb?, 1991 ($1.75)

1-19: Based on animated cartoon 2.00

SLIM MORGAN (See Wisco)

SLINGERS (See Spider-Man: Identity Crisis issues)
Marvel Comics: Dec, 1998 - No. 12, Nov, 1999 ($2.99/$1.99)

0-(Wizard #88 supplement) Prelude story 2.00
1-($2.99) Four editions w/different covers for each hero, 16 pages common to all, the other pages from each hero's perspective 3.00
2-12: 2-Two-c. 12-Saltares-a 2.00

SLUDGE
Malibu Comics (Ultraverse): Oct, 1993 - No. 12, Dec, 1994 ($2.50/$1.95)

1-($2.50, 48 pgs.)-Intro/1st app. Sludge; Rune flip-c/story Pt. 1 (1st app., 3 pgs.) by Barry Smith; The Night Man app. (3 pg. preview); The Mighty Magnor 1 pg strip begins by Aragones (cont. in other titles) 2.50
1-Ultra 5000 Limited silver foil 4.00
2-11: 3-Break-Thru x-over. 4-2 pg. Mantra origin. 8-Bloodstorm app. 2.00
12 ($3.50)-Ultraverse Premiere #8 flip book; Alex Ross poster 3.50
...:Red Xmas (12/94, $2.50, 44 pgs.) 2.50

SLUGGER (Little Wise Guys Starring...)(Also see Daredevil Comics)
Lev Gleason Publications: April, 1956

1-Biro-c 5.85 17.50 35.00

SMASH COMICS (Becomes Lady Luck #86 on)
Quality Comics Group: Aug, 1939 - No. 85, Oct, 1949

1-Origin Hugh Hazard & His Iron Man, Bozo the Robot, Espionage, Starring Black X by Eisner, & Hooded Justice (Invisible Justice #2 on); Chic Carter & Wings Wendall begin; 1st Robot on the cover of a comic book (Bozo) 275.00 825.00 2200.00
2-The Lone Star Rider app; Invisible Hood gains power of invisibility 97.00 291.00 775.00
3-Captain Cook & Eisner's John Law begin 62.00 187.00 500.00
4,5: 4-Flash Fulton begins 56.00 169.00 450.00
6-12: 12-One pg. Fine-a 47.00 142.00 380.00
13-Magno begins (8/40); last Eisner issue; The Ray app. in full page ad; The

Smash Comics #57 © QUA

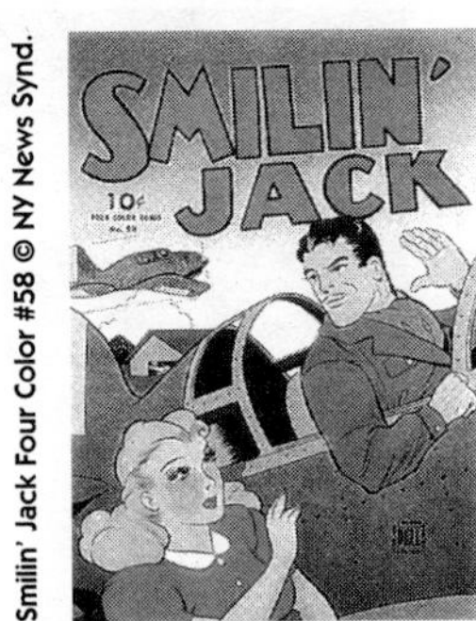

Smilin' Jack Four Color #58 © NY News Synd.

Smurfs #1 © MAR

	GD2.0	FN6.0	NM9.4
Purple Trio begins	50.00	150.00	400.00
14-Intro. The Ray (9/40) by Lou Fine & others	275.00	825.00	2200.00
15,16: 16-The Scarlet Seal begins	120.00	360.00	960.00
17-Wun Cloo becomes plastic super-hero by Jack Cole (9-months before Plastic Man)	125.00	375.00	1000.00
18-Midnight by Jack Cole begins (origin & 1st app., 1/41)	150.00	450.00	1200.00
19-22: Last Ray by Fine; The Jester begins-#22	81.00	244.00	650.00
23,24: 24-The Sword app.; last Chic Carter; Wings Wendall dons new costume #24,25	64.00	191.00	510.00
25-Origin/1st app. Wildfire; Rookie Rankin begins	72.00	216.00	575.00
26-30: 28-Midnight-c begin, end #85	61.00	184.00	490.00
31,32,34: Ray by Rudy Palais; also #33	47.00	141.00	375.00
33-Origin The Marksman	59.00	178.00	475.00
35-37	47.00	141.00	375.00
38-The Yankee Eagle begins; last Midnight by Jack Cole	62.00	187.00	500.00
39,40-Last Ray issue	45.00	135.00	360.00
41,44-50	33.00	99.00	230.00
42-Lady Luck begins by Klaus Nordling	84.00	253.00	675.00
43-Lady Luck-c (1st & only in Smash)	36.00	107.00	250.00
51-60	24.00	73.00	170.00
61-70	21.00	62.00	145.00
71-85: 79-Midnight battles the Men from Mars-c/s	19.00	58.00	135.00

*NOTE: **Al Bryant** c-54, 63-68. **Cole** a-17-38, 68, 69, 72, 73, 78, 80, 83, 85; c-38, 60-62, 69-84. **Crandall** a-(Ray)-23-29, 35-38; c-36, 39, 40, 42-44, 46. **Fine** a(Ray)-14, 15, 16(w/**Tuska**), 17-22. **Fox** c-24-35. **Fuje** Ray-30. **Gil Fox** a-6-7, 9, 11-13. **Guardineer** a-(The Marksman)-39-?, 49, 52. **Gustavson** a-4-7, 9, 11-13 (The Jester)-22-46; (Magno)-13-21; (Midnight)-39(Cole inks), 49, 52, 63-65. **Kotzky** a-(Espionage)-33-38; c-45, 47-53. **Nordling** a-49, 52, 63-65. **Powell** a-11, 12, (Abdul the Arab)-13-24. Black X c-2, 6, 9, 11, 13, 16. Bozo the Robot c-1, 3, 5, 8, 10, 12, 14, 18, 20, 22, 24, 26. Midnight c-28-85. The Ray c-15, 17, 19, 21, 23, 25, 27. Wings Wendall c-4, 7.*

SMASH COMICS (Also see All Star Comics 1999 crossover titles)
DC Comics: May, 1999 ($1.99, one-shot)

	GD2.0	FN6.0	NM9.4
1-Golden Age Doctor Mid-nite and Hourman			2.00

SMASH HIT SPORTS COMICS
Essankay Publications: V2#1, Jan, 1949

	GD2.0	FN6.0	NM9.4
V2#1-L.B. Cole-c/a	30.00	90.00	210.00

SMILE COMICS (Also see Gay Comics, Tickle, & Whee)
Modern Store Publ.: 1955 (52 pgs.; 5x7-1/4") (7¢)

	GD2.0	FN6.0	NM9.4
1	1.60	4.00	8.00

SMILEY BURNETTE WESTERN (Also see Patches #8 & Six-Gun Heroes)
Fawcett Publ.: March, 1950 - No. 4, Oct, 1950 (All photo front & back-c)

	GD2.0	FN6.0	NM9.4
1-Red Eagle begins	43.00	129.00	345.00
2-4	33.00	99.00	230.00

SMILEY (THE PSYCHOTIC BUTTON) (See Evil Ernie)
Chaos! Comics: July, 1998 - Present ($2.95, one-shots)

	GD2.0	FN6.0	NM9.4
1-Ivan Reis-a			3.00
... Holiday Special (1/99), ...'s Spring Break (4/99), ...Wrestling Special (5/99)			3.00

SMILIN' JACK (See Famous Feature Stories, Popular Comics, Super Book #1, 2, 7, 19 & Super Comics)
Dell Publishing Co.: No. 5, 1940 - No. 8, Oct-Dec, 1949

	GD2.0	FN6.0	NM9.4
Four Color 5	57.00	170.00	625.00
Four Color 10 (1940)	50.00	150.00	550.00
Large Feature Comic 12,14,25 (1941)	48.00	145.00	530.00
Four Color 4 (1942)	42.00	127.00	465.00
Four Color 14 (1943)	34.00	102.00	375.00
Four Color 36,58 (1943-44)	23.00	68.00	250.00
Four Color 80 (1945)	15.00	45.00	165.00
Four Color 149 (1947), 1 (1-3/48)	9.50	29.00	105.00
1 (1-3/48)	9.00	27.00	100.00
2	5.00	15.00	54.00
3-8 (10-12/49)	3.00	10.00	36.00

SMILING SPOOK SPUNKY (See Spunky)

SMITTY (See Popular Comics, Super Book #2, 4 & Super Comics)
Dell Publishing Co.: No. 11, 1940 - No. 7, Aug-Oct, 1949; No. 909, Apr, 1958

	GD2.0	FN6.0	NM9.4
Four Color 11 (1940)	35.00	105.00	385.00
Large Feature Comic 26 (1941)	25.00	75.00	275.00
Four Color 6 (1942)	21.00	63.00	230.00
Four Color 32 (1943)	15.50	46.00	170.00
Four Color 65 (1945)	12.00	35.00	130.00
Four Color 99 (1946)	10.00	30.00	110.00
Four Color 138 (1947)	8.65	26.00	95.00
1 (2-4/48)	8.00	25.00	90.00
2-(5-7/48)	4.00	12.00	45.00
3,4: 3-(8-10/48), 4-(11-1/48-49)	3.00	10.00	36.00
5-7, Four Color 909 (4/58)	1.80	5.50	20.00

SMOKEY BEAR (TV) (See March Of Comics #234, 362, 372, 383, 407)
Gold Key: Feb, 1970 - No. 13, Mar, 1973

	GD2.0	FN6.0	NM9.4
1	2.50	7.50	24.00
2-5	1.25	3.75	10.00
6-13	1.00	2.80	7.00

SMOKEY STOVER (See Popular Comics, Super Book #5,17,29 & Super Comics)
Dell Publishing Co.: No. 7, 1942 - No. 827, Aug, 1957

	GD2.0	FN6.0	NM9.4
Four Color 7 (1942)-Reprints	31.00	93.00	340.00
Four Color 35 (1943)	16.50	49.00	180.00
Four Color 64 (1944)	12.00	35.00	130.00
Four Color 229 (1949)	4.50	13.50	50.00
Four Color 730,827	3.50	11.00	38.00

SMOKEY THE BEAR (See Forest Fire for 1st app.)
Dell Publ. Co.: No. 653, 10/55 - No. 1214, 8/61 (See March of Comics #234)

	GD2.0	FN6.0	NM9.4
Four Color 653 (#1)	9.00	27.00	100.00
Four Color 708,754,818,932	4.50	13.50	50.00
Four Color 1016,1119,1214	2.75	8.00	30.00

SMOKY (See Movie Classics)

SMURFS (TV)
Marvel Comics: 1982 (Dec) - No. 3, 1983

	GD2.0	FN6.0	NM9.4
1-3			4.50
...Treasury Edition 1 (64 pgs.)-r/#1-3	2.50	7.50	24.00

SNAFU (Magazine)
Atlas Comics (RCM): Nov, 1955 - V2#2, Mar, 1956 (B&W)

	GD2.0	FN6.0	NM9.4
V1#1-Heath/Severin-a; Everett, Maneely-a	11.50	34.00	80.00
V2#1,2-Severin-a	10.00	30.00	60.00

SNAGGLEPUSS (TV)(See Hanna-Barbera Band Wagon, Quick Draw McGraw #5 & Spotlight #4)
Gold Key: Oct, 1962 - No. 4, Sept, 1963 (Hanna-Barbera)

	GD2.0	FN6.0	NM9.4
1	7.75	23.00	85.00
2-4	5.50	16.50	60.00

SNAP (Formerly Scoop #8; becomes Jest #10,11 & Komik Pages #10)
Harry 'A' Chesler: No. 9, 1944

	GD2.0	FN6.0	NM9.4
9-Manhunter, The Voice	19.00	56.00	130.00

SNAPPY COMICS
Cima Publ. Co. (Prize Publ.): 1945

	GD2.0	FN6.0	NM9.4
1-Airmale app.; 9 pg. Sorcerer's Apprentice adapt; Kiefer-a	30.00	90.00	210.00

SNARKY PARKER (See Life With...)

SNIFFY THE PUP
Standard Publ. (Animated Cartoons): No. 5, Nov, 1949 - No. 18, Sept, 1953

	GD2.0	FN6.0	NM9.4
5-Two Frazetta text illos	10.00	30.00	70.00
6-10	4.25	13.00	26.00
11-18	4.00	10.00	20.00

SNOOPER AND BLABBER DETECTIVES (TV) (See Whitman Comic Books)
Gold Key: Nov, 1962 - No. 3, May, 1963 (Hanna-Barbera)

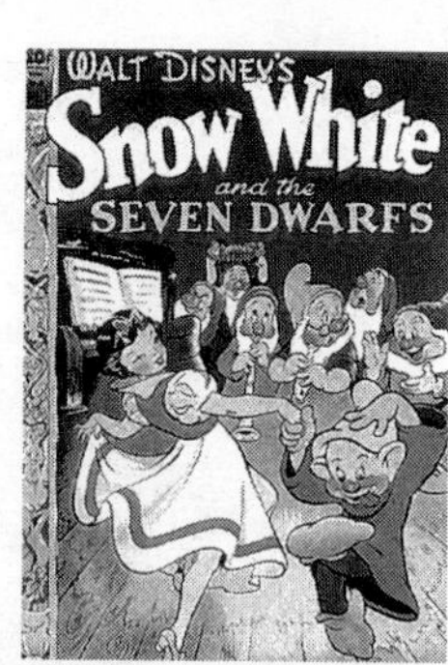

Snow White Four Color #49 © WDC

Solar Lord #1 © Jade Dynasty

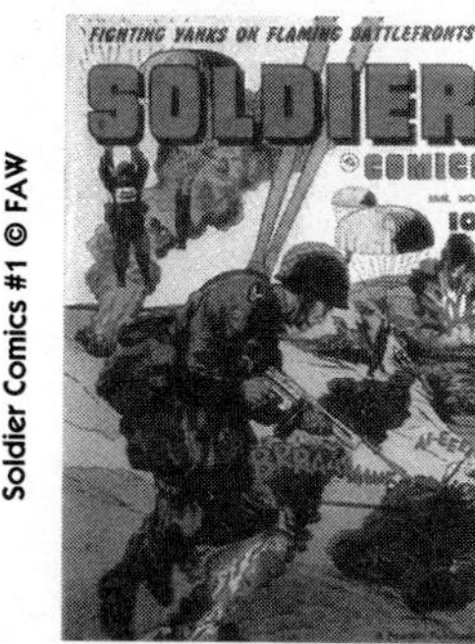

Soldier Comics #1 © FAW

GD2.0 FN6.0 NM9.4

1 7.75 23.00 85.00
2,3 6.00 18.00 65.00

SNOWMAN
Hall of Heroes/Avatar Press: 1996 - Present ($2.50, B&W)

1 1.25 3.75 10.00
1-Ltd. Ed. 1.85 5.50 15.00
2,3, 3-Chromium-c 4.00
2,3-Ltd. Ed. 2.40 6.00
0-(Avatar Press), 0-Alternate-c 4.00
0-Gold 8.00
0-Silver Foil 10.00
0-Black Leather 15.00
0-Blue Foil-c 30.00

SNOWMAN DEAD AND DYING
Avatar Press: Nov,1997 - No. 3, Apr, 1998 ($3.00, B&W, limited series)

1-3 3.50
1-($4.95) Ltd. Edition, 3-($4.95) variant-c 5.00
3-($25.00) White velvet variant-c 25.00

SNOWMAN HORROR SHOW
Avatar Press: Mar, 1998 ($3.00, B&W, one-shot)

1-Pin-ups by Matt Martin 3.00
1-($4.95) Frozen Fear Edition 5.00
1-Leather-c 25.00

SNOWMAN 1944
Entity Comics: Oct, 1996 - No. 4 ($2.75, B&W)

1 3.00
1-Ltd. Ed. 5.00
2-4 3.00
3-Ltd. Ed. 3.00
...Special 1 (10/97, $3.95) 4.00

SNOWMAN SQUARED
Avatar Press: Sept, 1998 - No. 2 ($3.00, B&W, limited series)

1-Matt Martin-s/a; Snowman vs. Snowman 1944 3.00
1-Commemorative Edition 5.00

SNOW WHITE (See Christmas With..., Mickey Mouse Mag., Movie Comics & Seven Dwarfs)
Dell Publishing Co.: No. 49, July, 1944 - No. 382, Mar, 1952 (Disney-Movie)

Four Color 49 (...& the Seven Dwarfs) 59.00 176.00 645.00
Four Color 382 (1952)-origin; partial reprint of Four Color 49
10.00 30.00 110.00

SNOW WHITE
Marvel Comics: Jan, 1995 ($1.95, one-shot)

1-r/1937 Sunday newspaper pages 2.00

SNOW WHITE AND THE SEVEN DWARFS
Whitman Publications: April, 1982 (60¢)

nn-r/Four Color 49 5.00

SNOW WHITE AND THE SEVEN DWARFS GOLDEN ANNIVERSARY
Gladstone: Fall, 1987 ($2.95, magazine size, 52 pgs.)

1-Contains poster 1.00 3.00 8.00

SOAP OPERA LOVE
Charlton Comics: Feb, 1983 - No. 3, June, 1983

1-3 1.25 3.75 10.00

SOAP OPERA ROMANCES
Charlton Comics: July, 1982 - No. 5, March, 1983

1-5-Nurse Betsy Crane-r 1.25 3.75 10.00

SOCK MONKEY
Dark Horse Comics: Sept, 1998 - No. 2, Oct, 1998 ($2.95, B&W)

1,2-Tony Millionaire-s/a 3.00
Vol.2 -(Tony Millionaire's Sock Monkey) July, 1999 - Present

GD2.0 FN6.0 NM9.4

1,2 3.00

SO DARK THE ROSE
CFD Productions: Oct, 1995 ($2.95)

1-Wrightson-c 3.00

SOJOURN
White Cliffs Publ. Co.: Sept, 1977 - No. 2, 1978 ($1.50, B&W & color, full tabloid size)

1,2: 1-Tor by Kubert, Eagle by Severin, E. V. Race, Private Investigator by Doug Wildey, T. C. Mars by Aragones begin plus other strips
1.00 3.00 8.00

NOTE: Most copies came folded. Unfolded copies are worth 50% more.

SOLAR (...Man of the Atom) (Also see Doctor Solar)
Valiant/Acclaim Comics (Valiant): Sept, 1991 - No. 60, Apr, 1996 ($1.75/$1.95/$2.50, 44 pgs.)

1-Layton-a(i) on Solar; Barry Windsor-Smith-c/a 5.00
2-9: 2-Layton-a(i) on Solar, B. Smith-a. 3-1st app. Harada (11/91). 7-vs. X-O Armor 3.00
10-(6/92, $3.95)-1st app. Eternal Warrior (6 pgs.); black embossed-c; origin & 1st app. Geoff McHenry (Geomancer) 2.40 6.00
10-($3.95)-2nd printing 4.00
11-15: 11-1st full app. Eternal Warrior. 12,13-Unity x-overs. 14-1st app. Fred Bender (becomes Dr. Eclipse). 15-2nd Dr. Eclipse 3.00
16-60: 17-X-O Manowar app. 23-Solar splits. 29-1st Valiant Vision book. 33-Valiant Vision; bound-in trading card. 38-Chaos Effect Epsilion Pt.1. 46-52-Dan Jurgens-a(p)/scripts w/Giordano-i. 53,54-Jurgens scripts only. 60-Giffen scripts; Jeff Johnson-a(p) 2.50
0-($9.95, trade paperback)-r/Alpha and Omega origin story; polybagged w/poster 10.00
...:Second Death (1994, $9.95)-r/issues #1-4. 10.00

NOTE: *#1-10 all have free 8 pg. insert "Alpha and Omega" which is a 10 chapter Solar origin story. All 10 centerfolds can pieced together to show climax of story.* ***Ditko*** *a-11p, 14p.* ***Giordano*** *a-46, 47, 48, 49, 50, 51, 52i.* ***Johnson*** *a-60p.* ***Jurgens*** *a-46, 47, 48, 49, 50 , 51, 52p.* ***Layton*** *a-1-3i; c-2i, 11i, 17i, 25i.* ***Miller*** *c-12.* ***Quesada*** *c-17p, 20-23p, 29p.* ***Simonson*** *c-13.* ***B. Smith*** *a-1-10; c-1, 3, 5, 7, 19i.* ***Thibert*** *c-22i, 23i.*

SOLAR LORD
Image Comics: Mar, 1999 - No. 7, Sept, 1999 ($2.50)

1-7-Khoo Fuk Lung-s/a 2.50

SOLARMAN (See Pendulum Ill. Originals)
Marvel Comics: Jan, 1989 - No. 2, May, 1990 ($1.00, limited series)

1,2 2.00

SOLAR, MAN OF THE ATOM (Man of the Atom on cover)
Acclaim Comics (Valiant Heroes): Vol. 2, May, 1997 ($3.95, one-shot, 46 pgs) (1st Valiant Heroes Special Event)

Vol. 2-Reintro Solar; Ninjak cameo; Warren Ellis scripts; Darick Robertson-a 4.00

SOLAR, MAN OF THE ATOM: HELL ON EARTH
Acclaim Comics (Valiant Heroes): Jan, 1998 - No. 4 ($2.50, limited series)

1-4-Priest-s/ Zircher-a(p) 2.50

SOLAR, MAN OF THE ATOM: REVELATIONS
Acclaim Comics (Valiant Heroes): Nov, 1997 ($3.95, one-shot, 46 pgs.)

1-Krueger-s/ Zircher-a(p) 4.00

SOLDIER & MARINE COMICS (Fightin' Army #16 on)
Charlton Comics (Toby Press of Conn. V1#11): No. 11, Dec, 1954 - No. 15, Aug, 1955; V2#9, Dec, 1956

V1#11 (12/54)-Bob Powell-a 7.50 22.50 45.00
V1#12(2/55)-15: 12-Photo-c 4.25 13.00 28.00
V2#9(Formerly Never Again; Jerry Drummer V2#10 on)
4.00 12.00 24.00

SOLDIER COMICS
Fawcett Publications: Jan, 1952 - No. 11, Sept, 1953

1 11.00 33.00 75.00

The Solution #7 © MAL

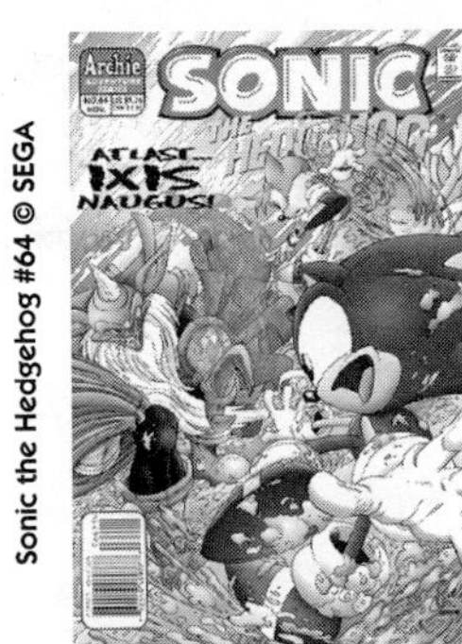

Sonic the Hedgehog #64 © SEGA

Son of Ambush Bug #5 © DC

GD2.0 FN6.0 NM9.4

2 6.35 19.00 38.00
3-5 5.00 15.00 30.00
6-11: 8-Illo. in **POP** 4.25 13.00 26.00

SOLDIERS OF FORTUNE
American Comics Group (Creston Publ. Corp.): Mar-Apr, 1951 - No. 13, Feb-Mar, 1953
1-Capt. Crossbones by Shelly, Ace Carter, Lance Larson begin 22.00 66.00 155.00
2 12.00 36.00 85.00
3-10: 6-Bondage-c 11.00 33.00 75.00
11-13 (War format) 5.85 17.50 35.00
NOTE: ***Shelly*** *a-1-3, 5.* ***Whitney*** *a-6, 8-11, 13; c-1-3, 5, 6.*

SOLDIERS OF FREEDOM
Americomics: 1987 - No. 2, 1987 ($1.75)
1,2 2.00

SOLITAIRE (Also See Prime V2#6-8)
Malibu Comics (Ultraverse): Nov, 1993 - No. 12, Dec, 1994 ($1.95)
1-($2.50)-Collector's edition bagged w/playing card 2.50
1-12: 1-Regular edition w/o playing card. 2,4-Break-Thru x-over. 3-2 pg. origin The Night Man. 4-Gatefold-c. 5-Two pg. origin the Strangers 2.00

SOLO
Marvel Comics: Sept, 1994 - No. 4, Dec, 1994 ($1.75, limited series)
1-4: Spider-Man app. 2.00

SOLO (Movie)
Dark Horse Comics: July, 1996 - No. 2, Aug, 1996 ($2.50, limited series)
1,2: Adaptation of film; photo-c 2.50

SOLO AVENGERS (Becomes Avenger Spotlight #21 on)
Marvel Comics: Dec, 1987 - No. 20, July, 1989 (75¢/$1.00)
1-Jim Lee-a on back-up story 3.00
2-20: 11-Intro Bobcat 2.00

SOLOMON AND SHEBA (Movie)
Dell Publishing Co.: No. 1070, Jan-Mar, 1960
Four Color 1070-Sekowsky-a; photo-c 9.00 27.00 100.00

SOLOMON KANE (Also see Blackthorne 3-D Series #60 & Marvel Premiere)
Marvel Comics: Sept, 1985 - No. 6, July, 1986 (Limited series)
1-6: 1-Double size. 3-6-Williamson-a(i) 2.00

SOLUTION, THE
Malibu Comics (Ultraverse): Sept, 1993 - No. 17, Feb, 1995 ($1.95)
1,3-15: 1-Intro Meathook, Deathdance, Black Tiger, Tech. 4-Break-Thru x-over; gatefold-c. 5-2 pg. origin The Strangers. 11-Brereton-c 2.00
1-($2.50)-Newsstand ed. polybagged w/trading card 2.50
1-Ultra 5000 Limited silver foil 4.00
0-Obtained w/Rune #0 by sending coupons from 11 comics 3.00
2-($2.50, 48 pgs.)-Rune flip-c/story by B. Smith; The Mighty Magnor 1 pg. strip by Aragones 2.50
16 ($3.50)-Flip-c Ultraverse Premiere #10 3.50
17 ($2.50) 2.50

SOMERSET HOLMES (See Eclipse Graphic Novel Series)
Pacific Comics/ Eclipse Comics No. 5, 6: Sept, 1983 - No. 6, Dec, 1984 ($1.50, Baxter paper)
1-6: 1-Brent Anderson-c/a. Cliff Hanger by Williams in all 2.00

SONG OF THE SOUTH (See Brer Rabbit)

SONIC & KNUCKLES
Archie Comics: Aug, 1995 ($2.00)
1 3.00

SONIC DISRUPTORS
DC Comics: Dec, 1987 - No. 7, July, 1988 ($1.75, limited series, mature)
1-7 2.00

SONIC'S FRIENDLY NEMESIS KNUCKLES
Archie Publications: July, 1996 - No. 3, Sept, 1996 ($1.50, limited series)
1-3 2.50

SONIC SUPER SPECIAL
Archie Publications: 1997 - Present ($2.00/$2.25/$2.29, 48 pgs)
1-3 3.00
4-6,8-11: 10-Sabrina-c/app. 2.50
7-(w/Image) Spawn, Maxx, Savage Dragon-c/app.; Valentino-a 2.50

SONIC THE HEDGEHOG (TV, video game)
Archie Comics: Feb, 1993 - No. 3, May, 1993 ($1.25, mini-series)
0(2/93),1: Shaw-a(p) & covers on all 2.00 6.00
2,3 2.00 6.00

SONIC THE HEDGEHOG (TV, video game)
Archie Comics: July, 1993 - Present ($1.25/$1.50/$1.75/$1.79)
1 1.00 3.00 8.00
2,3 2.40 6.00
4-10: 8-Neon ink-c. 5.00
11-20 4.00
21-50 ($1.50): 25-Silver ink-c 3.00
51-79 2.00
Triple Trouble Special (10/95, $2.00, 48 pgs.) 4.00

SONIC VS. KNUCKLES "BATTLE ROYAL" SPECIAL
Archie Publications: 1997 ($2.00, one-shot)
1 3.00

SON OF AMBUSH BUG (See Ambush Bug)
DC Comics: July, 1986 - No. 6, Dec, 1986 (75¢)
1-6: Giffen-c/a in all. 5-Bissette-a. 2.00

SON OF BLACK BEAUTY (Also see Black Beauty)
Dell Publishing Co.: No. 510, Oct, 1953 - No. 566, June, 1954
Four Color 510, 566 2.75 8.00 30.00

SON OF FLUBBER (See Movie Comics)

SON OF MUTANT WORLD
Fantagor Press: 1990 - No. 5, 1990? ($2.00, bi-monthly)
1-5: 1-3: Corben-c/a. 4,5 ($1.75, B&W) 2.00

SON OF ORIGINS OF MARVEL COMICS (See Fireside Book Series)

SON OF SATAN (Also see Ghost Rider #1 & Marvel Spotlight #12)
Marvel Comics Group: Dec, 1975 - No. 8, Feb, 1977 (25¢)
1-Mooney-a; Kane-c(p), Starlin splash(p) 2.25 6.75 18.00
2,6-8: 2-Origin The Possessor. 8-Heath-a 1.25 3.75 10.00
3-5-(Regular 25¢ editions)(4-8/76): 5-Russell-p 1.25 3.75 10.00
3-5-(30¢-c variants, limited distribution) 3.00 9.00 30.00

SON OF SINBAD (Also see Abbott & Costello & Daring Adventures)
St. John Publishing Co.: Feb, 1950
1-Kubert-c/a 40.00 120.00 290.00

SON OF TOMAHAWK (See Tomahawk)

SON OF VULCAN (Formerly Mysteries of Unexplored Worlds #1-48; Thunderbolt V3#51 on)
Charlton Comics: V2#49, Nov, 1965 - V2#50, Jan, 1966
V2#49,50: 50-Roy Thomas scripts (1st pro work) 2.50 7.50 20.00

SON OF YUPPIES FROM HELL (See Yuppies From Hell)
Marvel Comics: 1990 ($3.50, B&W, squarebound, 52 pgs.)
nn 3.50

SONS OF KATIE ELDER (See Movie Classics)

SORCERY (See Chilling Adventures in... & Red Circle...)

SORORITY SECRETS
Toby Press: July, 1954
1 8.35 25.00 50.00

SOULSEARCHERS AND COMPANY

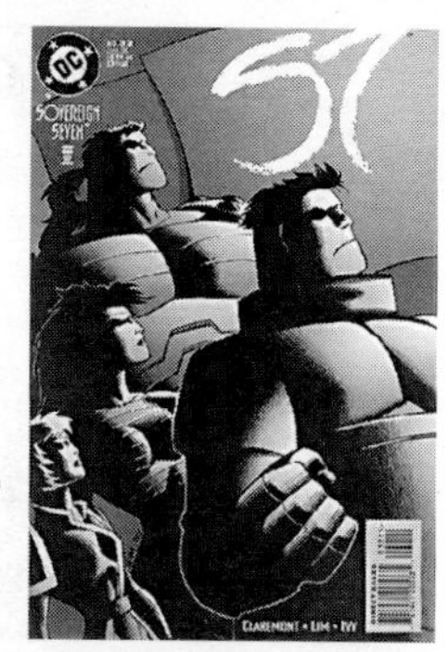

Sovereign Seven #32 © Chris Claremont

Space Action #3 © ACE

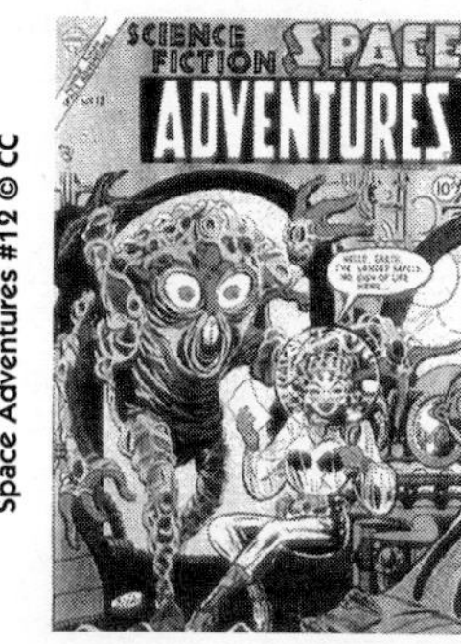

Space Adventures #12 © CC

GD2.0 FN6.0 NM9.4

Claypool Comics: June, 1995 - Present ($2.50, B&W)
1-10: Peter David scripts 2.50
11-36 2.50

SOULQUEST
Innovation: Apr, 1989 ($3.95, squarebound, 52 pgs.)
1-Blackshard app. 4.00

SOULWIND
Image Comics: Mar, 1997 - Present ($2.95, B&W, limited series)
1-8: 5-"The Day I Tried To Live" pt. 1 3.00
...The Kid From Planet Earth (1997, $9.95, TPB) 10.00

SOUPY SALES COMIC BOOK (TV)(The Official...)
Archie Publications: 1965
1 8.50 25.50 85.00

SOUTHERN KNIGHTS, THE (See Crusaders #1)
Guild Publ/Fictioneer Books: 1983 - No. 34? (B&W)
2-Magazine size 3.00
3-34 2.00
Dread Halloween Special 1, Special 1 (Spring, 1989, $2.25) 2.25
Graphic Novels #1-4 4.00

SOVEREIGN SEVEN (Also see Showcase '95 #12)
DC Comics: July, 1995 - No. 36, July, 1998 ($1.95) (1st creator-owned mainstream DC comic)
1-1st app. Sovereign Seven (Reflex, Indigo, Cascade, Finale, Cruiser, Network & Rampart); 1st app. Maitresse; Darkseid app.; Chris Claremont scripts & Dwayne Turner-c/a begins. 3.00
1-Gold 8.00
1-Platinum 40.00
2-25: 2-Wolverine cameo. 4-Neil Gaiman cameo. 5,8-Batman app. 7-Ramirez cameo (from the movie Highlander). 9-Humphrey Bogart cameo from Casablanca. 10-Impulse app; Manoli Wetherell & Neal Conan cameo from Uncanny X-Men #226. 11-Robin app. 16-Final Night. 24-Superman app. 25-Power Girl app. 2.25
26-36: 26-Begin $2.25-c. 28-Impulse-c/app. 2.25
Annual 1 (1995, $3.95)-Year One story; Big Barda & Lobo app.; Jeff Johnson-c/a. 4.00
Annual 2 (1996, $2.95)-Legends of the Dead Earth; Leonardi-c/a 3.50
...Plus 1(2/97, $2.95)-Legion-c/app. 3.50
TPB-($12.95) r/#1-5, Annual #1 & Showcase '95 #12 13.00

SPACE: ABOVE AND BEYOND (TV)
Topps Comics: Jan, 1996 - No. 3, Mar, 1996 ($2.95, limited series)
1-3: Adaptation of pilot episode; Steacy-c. 3.00

SPACE: ABOVE AND BEYOND--THE GAUNTLET (TV)
Topps Comics: May, 1996 -No. 2, June, 1996 ($2.95, limited series)
1,2 3.00

SPACE ACE (Also see Manhunt!)
Magazine Enterprises: No. 5, 1952
5(A-1 #61)-Guardineer-a 47.00 142.00 380.00

SPACE ACTION
Ace Magazines (Junior Books): June, 1952 - No. 3, Oct, 1952
1-Cameron-a in all (1 story) 67.00 202.00 540.00
2,3 52.00 157.00 420.00

SPACE ADVENTURES (War At Sea #22 on)
Capitol Stories/Charlton Comics: 7/52 - No. 21, 8/56; No. 23, 5/58 - No. 59, 11/64; V3#60, 10/67; V1#2, 7/68 - V1#8, 7/69; No. 9, 5/78 - No. 13, 3/79
1 43.00 128.00 340.00
2 24.00 73.00 170.00
3-5: 4,6-Flying saucer-c/stories 19.00 58.00 135.00
6-9: 7-Sex change story "Transformation". 8-Robot-c. 9-A-Bomb panel 17.00 51.00 120.00
10,11-Ditko-c/a. 10-Robot-c. 11-Two Ditko stories 43.00 128.00 340.00
12-Ditko-c (classic) 50.00 150.00 400.00
13-(Fox-r, 10-11/54); Blue Beetle-c/story 14.00 43.00 100.00
14-Blue Beetle-c/story; Fox-r (12-1/54-55, last pre-code) 18.00 54.00 125.00
15,17,18-Rocky Jones-c/s.(TV); 15-Part photo-c 19.00 56.00 130.00
16-Krigstein-a; Rocky Jones-c/story (TV) 21.00 62.00 145.00
19 12.00 36.00 85.00
20-Reprints Fawcett's "Destination Moon" 25.00 75.00 175.00
21-(8/56) (no #22)(Becomes War At Sea) 12.00 36.00 85.00
23-(5/58; formerly Nyoka, The Jungle Girl)-Reprints Fawcett's "Destination Moon" 21.00 64.00 150.00
24,25,31,32-Ditko-a. 24-Severin-a(signed "LePoer") 19.00 56.00 130.00
26,27-Ditko-a(4) each. 26,28-Flying saucer-c 20.00 60.00 140.00
28-30 8.35 25.00 50.00
33-Origin/1st app. Capt. Atom by Ditko (3/60) 34.00 102.00 375.00
34-40,42-All Captain Atom by Ditko 14.00 42.00 140.00
41,43,45-59: 45-Mercury Man app. 3.00 9.00 30.00
44-1st app. Mercury Man 3.00 9.00 30.00
V3#60(#1, 10/67)-Origin & 1st app. Paul Mann & The Saucers From the Future 3.50 10.50 35.00
2,5,6,8 (1968-69)-Ditko-a: 2-Aparo-c/a 2.50 7.50 20.00
3,4,7: 4-Aparo-c/a 2.00 6.00 16.00
9-13(1978-79)-Capt. Atom-r/Space Adventures by Ditko; 9-Reprints origin/1st app. Capt. Atom from #33 4.00
NOTE: ***Aparo** a-V3#60. c-V3#8. **Ditko** c-12, 31-42. **Giordano** c-3, 4, 7-9, 18p. **Krigstein** c-15. **Shuster** a-11. Issues 13 & 14 have Blue Beetle logos; #15-18 have Rocky Jones logos.*

SPACE ARK
Americomics (AC Comics)/ Apple Comics #3 on: June, 1985 - No. 5, Sept, 1987 ($1.75)
1-5: Funny animal (#1,2-color; #3-5-B&W) 2.00

SPACE BUSTERS
Ziff-Davis Publ. Co.: Spring, 1952 - No. 2, Fall, 1952
1-Krigstein-a(3); Painted-c by Norman Saunders 78.00 234.00 625.00
2-Kinstler-a(2 pgs.); Saunders painted-c 60.00 180.00 480.00
NOTE: ***Anderson** a-2. Bondage c-2.*

SPACE CADET (See Tom Corbett,...)

SPACE COMICS (Formerly Funny Tunes)
Avon Periodicals: No. 4, Mar-Apr, 1954 - No. 5, May-June, 1954
4,5-Space Mouse, Peter Rabbit, Super Pup (formerly Spotty the Pup), & Merry Mouse continue from Funny Tunes 5.85 17.50 35.00
I.W. Reprint #8 (nd)-Space Mouse-r 1.10 3.30 9.00

SPACED
Anthony Smith Publ. #1,2/Unbridled Ambition/Eclipse Comics #10 on: 1982 - No. 13, 1988 ($1.25/$1.50, B&W, quarterly)
1-($1.25-c) 3.00
2-13, Special Edition (1983, Mimeo) 2.00

SPACE DETECTIVE
Avon Periodicals: July, 1951 - No. 4, July, 1952
1-Rod Hathway, Space Detective begins, ends #4; Wood-c/a(3)-23 pgs.; "Opium Smugglers of Venus" drug story; Lucky Dale-r/Saint #4 100.00 300.00 800.00
2-Tales from the Shadow Squad story; Wood/Orlando-c; Wood inside layouts; "Slave Ship of Saturn" story 69.00 206.00 550.00
3,4: 3-Kinstler-c. 4-Kinstlerish-a by McCann 40.00 120.00 290.00
I.W. Reprint #1(Reprints #2), 8(Reprints cover #1 & part Famous Funnies #191) 3.50 10.50 35.00
I.W. Reprint #9-Exist? 3.50 10.50 35.00

SPACE EXPLORER (See March of Comics #202)

SPACE FAMILY ROBINSON (TV)(...Lost in Space #15-37, ...Lost in Space On Space Station One #38 on)(See Gold Key Champion)
Gold Key: Dec, 1962 - No. 36, Oct, 1969; No. 37, 10/73 - No. 54, 11/78; No. 55, 3/81 - No. 59, 5/82 (All painted covers)
1-(Low distribution); Spiegle-a in all 23.00 70.00 255.00

Spaceman #3 © MAR

Space Patrol #1 © Z-D

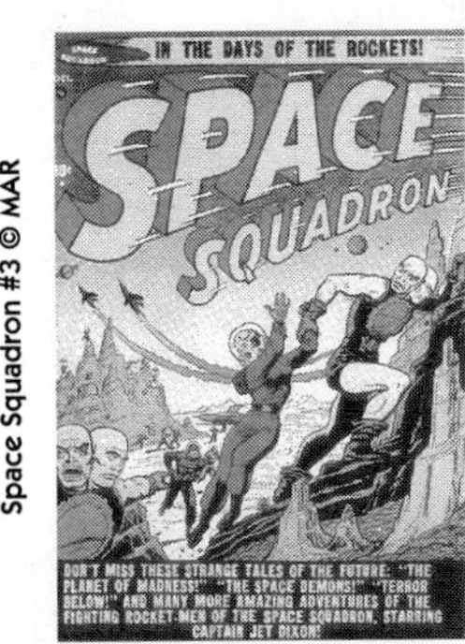

Space Squadron #3 © MAR

	GD2.0	FN6.0	NM9.4
2(3/63)-Family becomes lost in space	11.00	33.00	120.00
3-5	6.40	19.20	70.00
6-10: 6-Captain Venture back-up stories begin	5.50	16.50	60.00
11-20: 14-(10/65). 15-Title change (1/66)	3.65	11.00	40.00
21-36: 28-Last 12¢ issue. 36-Captain Venture ends	2.40	7.00	26.00
37-48: 37-Origin retold	1.10	3.30	9.00
49-59: Reprints #49,50,55-59			5.00

NOTE: *The TV show first aired on 9/15/65. Title changed after TV show debuted.*

SPACE FAMILY ROBINSON (See March of Comics #320, 328, 352, 404, 414)

SPACE GHOST (TV) (Also see Golden Comics Digest #2 & Hanna-Barbera Super TV Heroes #3-7)
Gold Key: March, 1967 (Hanna-Barbera) (TV debut was 9/10/66)

1 (10199-703)-Spiegle-a 33.00 98.00 360.00

SPACE GHOST (TV cartoon)
Comico: Mar, 1987 ($3.50, deluxe format, one-shot) (Hanna-Barbera)

1-Steve Rude-c/a 1.00 2.80 7.00

SPACE GIANTS, THE (TV cartoon)
FBN Publications: 1979 ($1.00, B&W, one-shots)

1-Based on Japanese TV series 1.00 3.00 8.00

SPACEHAWK
Dark Horse Comics: 1989 - No. 3, 1990 ($2.00, B&W)

1-3-Wolverton-c/a(r) plus new stories by others. 3.00

SPACE JAM
DC Comics: 1996 ($5.95, one-shot, movie adaption)

1-Wraparound photo cover of Michael Jordan 1.00 3.00 8.00

SPACE KAT-ETS (...in 3-D)
Power Publishing Co.: Dec, 1953 (25¢, came w/glasses)

1 32.00 96.00 225.00

SPACEMAN (Speed Carter...)
Atlas Comics (CnPC): Sept, 1953 - No. 6, July, 1954

1-Grey tone-c 61.00 182.00 485.00
2 40.00 120.00 310.00
3-6: 4-A-Bomb explosion-c 39.00 116.00 270.00

NOTE: ***Everett** c-1, 3. **Heath** a-1. **Maneely** a-1(3), 2(4), 3(3), 4-6; c-5, 6. **Romita** a-1. **Sekowsky** c-4. **Sekowsky/Abel** a-4(3). **Tuska** a-5(3).*

SPACE MAN
Dell Publ. Co.: No. 1253, 1-3/62 - No. 8, 3-5/64; No. 9, 7/72 - No. 10, 10/72

Four Color 1253 (#1)(1-3/62)(15¢-c) 6.40 19.00 70.00
2,3: 2-(15¢-c). 3-(12¢-c) 3.00 10.00 36.00
4-8-(12¢-c) 2.50 7.50 27.00
9,10-(15¢-c): 9-Reprints #1253. 10-Reprints #2 1.00 2.80 7.00

SPACE MOUSE (Also see Funny Tunes & Space Comics)
Avon Periodicals: April, 1953 - No. 5, Apr-May, 1954

1 9.15 27.00 55.00
2 5.85 17.50 35.00
3-5 4.00 12.00 24.00

SPACE MOUSE (Walter Lantz...#1; see Comic Album #17)
Dell Publishing Co./Gold Key: No. 1132, Aug-Oct, 1960 - No. 5, Nov, 1963 (Walter Lantz)

Four Color 1132,1244, 1(11/62)(G.K.) 3.60 11.00 40.00
2-5 2.75 8.00 30.00

SPACE MYSTERIES
I.W. Enterprises: 1964 (Reprints)

1-r/Journey Into Unknown Worlds #4 w/new-c 2.50 7.50 20.00
8,9: 9-r/Planet Comics #73 2.50 7.50 20.00

SPACE: 1999 (TV) (Also see Power Record Comics)
Charlton Comics: Nov, 1975 - No. 7, Nov, 1976

1-Origin Moonbase Alpha; Staton-c/a 1.10 3.30 9.00
2,7: 2-Staton-a 2.40 6.00

	GD2.0	FN6.0	NM9.4
3-6: All Byrne-a; c-3,5,6	1.25	3.75	10.00

SPACE: 1999 (TV)(Magazine)
Charlton Comics: Nov, 1975 - No. 8, Nov, 1976 (B&W) (#7 shows #6 inside)

1-Origin Moonbase Alpha; Morrow-c/a 1.50 4.50 12.00
2-8: 2,3-Morrow-c/a. 4-6-Morrow-c. 5,8-Morrow-a 1.00 3.00 8.00

SPACE PATROL (TV)
Ziff-Davis Publishing Co. (Approved Comics): Summer, 1952 - No. 2, Oct-Nov, 1952 (Painted-c by Norman Saunders)

1-Krigstein-a 84.00 253.00 675.00
2-Krigstein-a(3) 59.00 178.00 475.00

SPACE PIRATES (See Archie Giant Series #533)

SPACE RANGER (See Mystery in Space #92, Showcase #15 & Tales of the Unexpected)

SPACE SQUADRON (In the Days of the Rockets)(Becomes Space Worlds #6)
Marvel/Atlas Comics (ACI): June, 1951 - No. 5, Feb, 1952

1-Space team; Brodsky c-1,5 61.00 184.00 490.00
2: Tuska c-2-4 53.00 159.00 425.00
3-5: 3-Capt. Jet Dixon by Tuska(3). 4-Weird advs. begin
43.00 128.00 340.00

SPACE THRILLERS
Avon Periodicals: 1954 (25¢ Giant)

nn-(Scarce)-Robotmen of the Lost Planet; contains 3 rebound comics of The Saint & Strange Worlds. Contents could vary 106.00 319.00 850.00

SPACE TRIP TO THE MOON (See Space Adventures #23)

SPACE USAGI
Mirage Studios: June, 1992 - No. 3, 1992 ($2.00, B&W, mini-series)
V2#1, Nov, 1993 - V2#3, Jan, 1994 ($2.75)

1-3: Stan Sakai-c/a/scripts, V2#1-3 2.75

SPACE USAGI
Dark Horse Comics: Jan, 1996 - No. 3, Mar, 1996 ($2.00, B&W, limited series)

1-3: Stan Sakai-c/a/scripts 2.00

SPACE WAR (Fightin' Five #28 on)
Charlton Comics: Oct, 1959 - No. 27, Mar, 1964; No. 28, Mar, 1978 - No. 34, 3/79

V1#1-Giordano-c begin, end #3 13.00 39.00 130.00
2,3 6.50 19.50 65.00
4-6,8,10-Ditko-c/a 13.00 39.00 130.00
7,9,11-15: Last 10¢ issue? 3.50 10.50 35.00
16-27 (3/64): 18,19-Robot-c 3.20 9.60 32.00
28(3/78),29-31,33,34-Ditko-c/a(r): 30-Staton, Sutton/Wood-a. 31-Ditko-c/a(3); same-c as Strange Suspense Stories #2 (1968); atom blast-c
2.40 6.00
32-r/Charlton Premiere V2#2; Sutton-a 3.00

SPACE WESTERN (Formerly Cowboy Western Comics; becomes Cowboy Western Comics #46 on)
Charlton Comics (Capitol Stories): No. 40, Oct, 1952 - No. 45, Aug, 1953

40-Intro Spurs Jackson & His Space Vigilantes; flying saucer story
55.00 165.00 440.00
41,43-45: 41-Flying saucer-c. 45-Hitler app. 40.00 120.00 310.00
42-Atom bomb explosion-c 43.00 128.00 340.00

SPACE WORLDS (Formerly Space Squadron #1-5)
Atlas Comics (Male): No. 6, April, 1952

6-Sol Brodsky-c 40.00 120.00 310.00

SPANKY & ALFALFA & THE LITTLE RASCALS (See The Little Rascals)

SPANNER'S GALAXY
DC Comics: Dec, 1984 - No. 6, May, 1985 (limited series)

1-6: Mandrake-c/a in all. 2.00

SPARKIE, RADIO PIXIE (Radio)(Becomes Big Jon & Sparkie #4)
Ziff-Davis Publ. Co.: Winter, 1951 - No. 3, July-Aug, 1952 (Painted-c)(Sparkie #2,3; #1?)

Sparkle Comics #2 © UFS

Sparkler Comics #19 © UFS

Spawn #80 © Todd McFarlane Prod.

	GD2.0	FN6.0	NM9.4
1-Based on children's radio program	21.00	64.00	150.00
2,3: 3-Big Jon and Sparkie on-c only	16.00	47.00	110.00

SPARKLE COMICS
United Features Synd.: Oct-Nov, 1948 - No. 33, Dec-Jan, 1953-54

	GD2.0	FN6.0	NM9.4
1-Li'l Abner, Nancy, Captain & the Kids, Ella Cinders (#1-3: 52 pgs.)	13.00	39.00	90.00
2	7.50	22.50	45.00
3-10	5.85	17.50	35.00
11-20	5.00	15.00	30.00
21-33	4.00	12.00	24.00

SPARKLE PLENTY (See Harvey Comics Library #2 & Dick Tracy)

SPARKLER COMICS (1st series)
United Feature Comic Group: July, 1940 - No. 2, 1940

	GD2.0	FN6.0	NM9.4
1-Jim Hardy	40.00	120.00	280.00
2-Frankie Doodle	30.00	90.00	210.00

SPARKLER COMICS (2nd series)(Nancy & Sluggo #121 on)(Cover title becomes Nancy and Sluggo #101? on)
United Features Syndicate: July, 1941 - No. 120, Jan, 1955

	GD2.0	FN6.0	NM9.4
1-Origin 1st app. Sparkman; Tarzan (by Hogarth in all issues), Captain & the Kids, Ella Cinders, Danny Dingle, Dynamite Dunn, Nancy, Abbie & Slats, Broncho Bill, Frankie Doodle, begin; Spark Man c-1-9,11,12; Hap Hopper c-10,13	225.00	675.00	1800.00
2	78.00	234.00	625.00
3,4	61.00	184.00	490.00
5-9: 9-Spark Man's new costume	55.00	165.00	440.00
10-Origin Spark Man?	56.00	169.00	450.00
11,12-Spark Man war-c. 12-Spark Man's new costume (color change)	45.00	135.00	360.00
13-Hap Hopper war-c	40.00	120.00	320.00
14-Tarzan-c by Hogarth	51.00	154.00	410.00
15,17: 15-Capt & Kids-c. 17-Nancy & Sluggo-c	40.00	120.00	300.00
16,18-Spark Man war-c	41.00	124.00	330.00
19-1st Race Riley and the Commandos-c/s	40.00	120.00	320.00
20-Nancy war-c	40.00	120.00	310.00
21,25,28,31,34,37,39-Tarzan-c by Hogarth	43.00	128.00	340.00
22-24,26,27,29,30: 22-Race Riley & the Commandos strips begin, ends #44	34.00	101.00	235.00
32,33,35,36,38,40	18.00	54.00	125.00
41,43,45,46,48,49	13.50	41.00	95.00
42,44,47,50-Tarzan-c (42,47,50 by Hogarth)	27.00	81.00	190.00
51,52,54-70: 57-Li'l Abner begins (not in #58); Fearless Fosdick app. in #58	12.00	36.00	85.00
53-Tarzan-c by Hogarth	23.00	69.00	160.00
71-80	8.35	25.00	50.00
81,82,84-86: 86 Last Tarzan; lingerie panels	7.50	22.50	45.00
83-Tarzan-c; Li'l Abner ends	11.00	33.00	75.00
87-96,98-99	6.70	20.00	40.00
97-Origin Casey Ruggles by Warren Tufts	11.50	34.00	80.00
100	8.35	25.00	50.00
101-107,109-112,114-120	5.00	15.00	30.00
108,113-Toth-a	8.35	25.00	50.00

SPARKLING LOVE
Avon Periodicals/Realistic (1953): June, 1950; 1953

	GD2.0	FN6.0	NM9.4
1(Avon)-Kubert-a; photo-c	21.00	64.00	150.00
nn(1953)-Reprint; Kubert-a	8.35	25.00	50.00

SPARKLING STARS
Holyoke Publishing Co.: June, 1944 - No. 33, March, 1948

	GD2.0	FN6.0	NM9.4
1-Hell's Angels, FBI, Boxie Weaver, Petey & Pop, & Ali Baba begin	17.00	51.00	120.00
2-Speed Spaulding story	10.00	30.00	70.00
3-Actual FBI case photos & war photos	8.35	25.00	50.00
4-10: 7-X-Mas-c	7.00	21.00	42.00
11-19: 13-Origin/1st app. Jungo the Man-Beast-c/s	6.35	19.00	38.00
20-Intro Fangs the Wolf Boy	7.00	21.00	42.00
21-29,32,33: 29-Bondage-c	6.35	19.00	38.00
31-Sid Greene-a	6.70	20.00	40.00

SPARK MAN (See Sparkler Comics)
Frances M. McQueeny: 1945 (36 pgs., one-shot)

	GD2.0	FN6.0	NM9.4
1-Origin Spark Man r/Sparkler #1-3; female torture story; cover redrawn from Sparkler #1	31.00	94.00	220.00

SPARKY WATTS (Also see Big Shot Comics & Columbia Comics)
Columbia Comic Corp.: Nov?, 1942 - No. 10, 1949

	GD2.0	FN6.0	NM9.4
1(1942)-Skyman & The Face app; Hitler-c	45.00	135.00	360.00
2(1943)	26.00	77.00	180.00
3(1944)	19.00	56.00	130.00
4(1944)-Origin	17.00	51.00	120.00
5(1947)-Skyman app.; Boody Rogers-c/a	14.00	43.00	100.00
6,7,9,10: 6(1947),10(1949)	10.00	30.00	60.00
8(1948)-Surrealistic-c	13.00	39.00	90.00

NOTE: ***Boody Rogers** c-1-8.*

SPARTACUS (Movie)
Dell Publishing Co.: No. 1139, Nov, 1960 (Kirk Douglas photo-c)

	GD2.0	FN6.0	NM9.4
Four Color 1139-Buscema-a	12.00	35.00	130.00

SPARTAN: WARRIOR SPIRIT (Also see WildC.A.T.S: Covert Action Teams)
Image Comics (WildStorm Productions): July, 1995 - No. 4, Nov, 1995 ($2.50, limited series)

	GD2.0	FN6.0	NM9.4
1-4: Kurt Busiek scripts; Mike McKone-c/a			2.50

SPAWN (Also see Curse of the Spawn and Sam & Twitch)
Image Comics (Todd McFarlane Productions): May, 1992 - Present ($1.95)

	GD2.0	FN6.0	NM9.4
1-1st app. Spawn; McFarlane-c/a begins; McFarlane/Steacy-c; 1st Todd McFarlane Productions title.	1.85	5.50	15.00
1-Black & white edition			25.00
2,3: 2-1st app. Violator; McFarlane/Steacy-c	1.50	4.50	12.00
4-Contains coupon for Image Comics #0	1.50	4.50	12.00
4-With coupon missing			4.00
4-Newsstand edition w/o poster or coupon			4.00
5-Cerebus cameo (1 pg.) as stuffed animal; Spawn mobile poster #1	1.00	2.80	7.00
6-8,10: 7-Spawn Mobile poster #2. 8-Alan Moore scripts; Miller poster. 10-Cerebus app.; Dave Sim scripts; 1 pg. cameo app. by Superman.		2.40	6.00
9-Neil Gaiman scripts; Jim Lee poster; 1st Angela.	1.00	3.00	8.00
11-17,19,20,22-30: 11-Miller script; Darrow poster. 12-Bloodwulf poster by Liefeld. 14,15-Violator app. 16,17-Grant Morrison scripts; Capullo-c/a(p). 23,24-McFarlane-a/stories. 25-(10/94). 19-(10/94). 20-(11/94)			5.00
18-Grant Morrison script, Capullo-c/a(p); low distr.	1.25	3.75	10.00
21-low distribution	1.25	3.75	10.00
31-49, 51-66: 31-1st app. The Redeemer; new costume cameo. 32-1st full app new costume. 38-40,42,44,46,48-Tony Daniel-c/a(p). 38-1st app. Cy-Gor. 40,41-Cy-Gor & Curse app. 52-Savage Dragon app. 56-w/ Darkchylde preview. 57-Cy-Gor-c/app. 64-Polybagged w/McFarlane Toys catalog. 65-Photo-c of movie Spawn and McFarlane			3.00
50-($3.95, 48 pgs.)			4.00
67-87: 75-Spawn goes to the Greenworld. 81-Billy Kincaid returns			2.00
...Bible-(8/96, $1.95)-Character bios			3.50
Book 1 TPB($9.95) r/#1-5; Book 2-r/#6-9,11; Book 3 -r/#12-15, Book 4- r/#16-20; Book 5-r/#21-25' Book 6- r/#26-30' Book 7-r/#31-34; Book 8-r/#35-38 Book 9-r/#39-42			10.00

NOTE: ***Capullo** a-16p-18p; c-16p-18p. **Daniel** a-38-40, 42, 44, 46. **McFarlane** a-1-15; c-1-15p. **Thibert** a-16i(part). Posters come with issues 1, 4, 7-9, 11, 12. #25 was released before #19 & 20.*

SPAWN-BATMAN (Also see Batman/Spawn: War Devil under Batman: One-Shots)
Image Comics (Todd McFarlane Productions): 1994 ($3.95, one-shot)

	GD2.0	FN6.0	NM9.4
1-Miller scripts; McFarlane-c/a		2.40	6.00

SPAWN: BLOOD FEUD

Spawn: The Undead #1 © Todd McFarlane Prod.

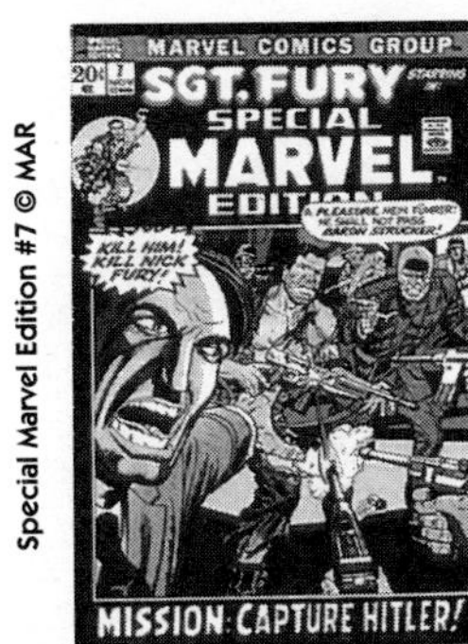

Special Marvel Edition #7 © MAR

Spectacular Spider-Man #15 © MAR

GD2.0 FN6.0 NM9.4

Image Comics (Todd McFarlane Productions): June, 1995 - No. 4, Sept, 1995 ($2.25, limited series)

1-4-Alan Moore scripts, Tony Daniel-a 3.50

SPAWN FAN EDITION
Image Comics (Todd McFarlane Productions): Aug, 1996 - No. 3, Oct, 1996 (Giveaway, 12 pgs.) (Polybagged w/Overstreet's FAN)

1-3: Beau Smith scripts; Brad Gorby-a(p). 1-1st app. Nordik, the Norse Hellspawn. 2-1st app. McFallon, the Dragon Master. 3-1st app. Mercy 1.00 3.00 8.00
1-3-(Gold): All retailer incentives 16.00
1-3-Variant-c 1.00 3.00 8.00
2-(Platinum)-Retailer incentive 25.00

SPAWN: THE DARK AGES
Image Comics (Todd McFarlane Productions): Mar, 1999 - Present ($2.50)

1-Fabry-c; Holguin-s/Sharp-a; variant-c by McFarlane 2.50
2-8 2.50

SPAWN THE IMPALER
Image Comics (Todd McFarlane Productions): Oct, 1996 - No. 3, Dec, 1996 ($2.95, limited series)

1-3-Mike Grell scripts, painted-a 3.00

SPAWN: THE UNDEAD
Image Comics (Todd McFarlane Productions): Jun, 1999 - Present ($2.50)

1-4-Dwayne Turner-c/a; Jenkins-s 2.50

SPAWN/WILDC.A.T.S
Image Comics (WildStorm Productions): Jan, 1996 - No. 4, Apr, 1996 ($2.50, limited series)

1-4: Alan Moore scripts in all. 3.00

SPECIAL AGENT (Steve Saunders...)(Also see True Comics #68)
Parents' Magazine Institute (Commended Comics No. 2): Dec, 1947 - No. 8, Sept, 1949 (Based on true FBI cases)

1-J. Edgar Hoover photo on-c 11.00 33.00 75.00
2 7.00 21.00 42.00
3-8 5.35 16.00 32.00

SPECIAL COLLECTORS' EDITION (See Savage Fists of Kung-Fu)

SPECIAL COMICS (Becomes Hangman #2 on)
MLJ Magazines: Winter, 1941-42

1-Origin The Boy Buddies (Shield & Wizard x-over); death of The Comet; origin The Hangman retold; Hangman-c 262.00 787.00 2100.00

SPECIAL EDITION (See Gorgo and Reptisaurus)

SPECIAL EDITION COMICS
Fawcett Publications: 1940 (August) (68 pgs., one-shot)

GD2.0 FN6.0 VF8.0 NM9.4

1-1st book devoted entirely to Captain Marvel; C.C. Beck-c/a; only app. of Capt. Marvel with belt buckle; Capt. Marvel appears with button-down flap; 1st story (came out before Captain Marvel #1) 800.00 2400.00 4800.00 8000.00

NOTE: *Prices vary widely on this book. Since this book is all Captain Marvel stories, it is actually a pre-Captain Marvel #1. There is speculation that this book almost became **Captain Marvel** #1. After **Special Edition** was published, there was an editor change at Fawcett. The new editor commissioned Kirby to do a nn **Captain Marvel** book early in 1941. This book was followed by a 2nd book several months later. This 2nd book was advertised as a #3 (making Special Edition the #1, & the nn issue the #2). However, the 2nd book did come out as a #2.*

SPECIAL EDITION: SPIDER-MAN VS. THE HULK (See listing under The Amazing Spider-Man)

SPECIAL EDITION X-MEN
Marvel Comics Group: Feb, 1983 ($2.00, one-shot, Baxter paper)

GD2.0 FN6.0 NM9.4

1-r/Giant-Size X-Men #1 plus one new story 1.25 3.75 10.00

SPECIAL MARVEL EDITION (Master of Kung Fu #17 on)
Marvel Comics Group: Jan, 1971 - No. 16, Feb, 1974 (#1-3: 25¢, 68 pgs.; #4: 52 pgs.; #5-16: 20¢, regular ed.)

1-Thor-r by Kirby; 68 pgs. 2.50 7.50 20.00
2-4: Thor-r by Kirby; 2,3-68 pg. Giant. 4-(52 pgs.) 1.75 5.25 14.00
5-14: Sgt. Fury-r; 11-r/Sgt. Fury #13 (Capt. America) 1.00 3.00 8.00
15-Master of Kung Fu (Shang-Chi) begins (1st app., 12/73); Starlin-a; origin/1st app. Nayland Smith & Dr. Petric 4.50 13.50 45.00
16-1st app. Midnight; Starlin-a (2nd Shang-Chi) 2.25 6.75 18.00

NOTE: ***Kirby** c-10-14.*

SPECIAL MISSIONS (See G.I. Joe...)

SPECIAL WAR SERIES (Attack V4#3 on?)
Charlton Comics: Aug, 1965 - No. 4, Nov, 1965

V4#1-D-Day (also see D-Day listing) 2.50 7.50 24.00
2-Attack! 2.00 6.00 16.00
3-War & Attack (also see War & Attack) 2.00 6.00 16.00
4-Judomaster (intro/1st app.; see Sarge Steel) 4.50 13.50 45.00

SPECIES (Movie)
Dark Horse Comics: June, 1995 - No. 4, Sept, 1995 ($2.50, limited series)

1-4: Adaptation of film 3.00

SPECIES: HUMAN RACE (Movie)
Dark Horse Comics: Nov, 1996 - No. 4, Feb, 1997 ($2.95, limited series)

1-4 3.00

SPECTACULAR ADVENTURES (See Adventures)

SPECTACULAR FEATURE MAGAZINE, A (Formerly My Confessions) (Spectacular Features Magazine #12)
Fox Feature Syndicate: No. 11, April, 1950

11 (#1)-Samson and Delilah 30.00 90.00 210.00

SPECTACULAR FEATURES MAGAZINE (Formerly A Spectacular Feature Magazine)
Fox Feature Syndicate: No. 12, June, 1950 - No. 3, Aug, 1950

12 (#2)-Iwo Jima; photo flag-c 30.00 90.00 210.00
3-True Crime Cases From Police Files 23.00 69.00 160.00

SPECTACULAR SCARLET SPIDER
Marvel Comics: Nov, 1995 - No. 2, Dec, 1995 ($1.95, limited series)

1,2: Replaces Spectacular Spider-Man 2.00

SPECTACULAR SPIDER-MAN, THE (See Marvel Special Edition and Marvel Treasury Edition)

SPECTACULAR SPIDER-MAN, THE (Magazine)
Marvel Comics Group: July, 1968 - No. 2, Nov, 1968 (35¢)

1-(B&W)-Romita/Mooney 52 pg. story plus updated origin story with Everett-a(i) 7.50 22.50 75.00
1-Variation w/single c-price of 40¢ 7.50 22.50 75.00
2-(Color)-Green Goblin-c & 58 pg. story; Romita painted-c (story reprinted in King Size Spider-Man #9); Romita/Mooney-a 9.50 28.50 95.00

SPECTACULAR SPIDER-MAN, THE (Peter Parker...#54-132, 134)
Marvel Comics Group: Dec, 1976 - No. 263, Nov, 1998

1-Origin recap in text; return of Tarantula 3.00 9.00 30.00
2-Kraven the Hunter app. 1.50 4.50 12.00
3-5: 3-Intro Lightmaster. 4-Vulture app. 1.10 3.30 9.00
6-8-Morbius app.; 6-r/Marvel Team-Up #3 w/Morbius 1.50 4.50 12.00
9-20: 9,10-White Tiger app. 11-Last 30¢-c. 17,18-Angel & Iceman app. (from Champions); Ghost Rider cameo in flashback 1.00 2.80 7.00
21,24-26: 21-Scorpion app. 26-Daredevil app. 2.40 6.00
22,23-Moon Knight app. 1.00 2.80 7.00
27-Miller's 1st art on Daredevil (2/79); also see Captain America #235 1.50 4.50 12.00
28-Miller Daredevil (p) 1.10 3.30 9.00
29-55,57,59: 33-Origin Iguana. 38-Morbius app. 5.00
56-2nd app. Jack O'Lantern (Macendale) & 1st Spidey/Jack O'Lantern battle (7/81) 2.40 6.00
58-Byrne-a(p) 5.00
60-Double size; origin retold with new facts revealed 2.40 6.00

Spectacular Spider-Man #258 © MAR

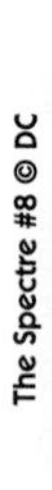
The Spectre #8 © DC

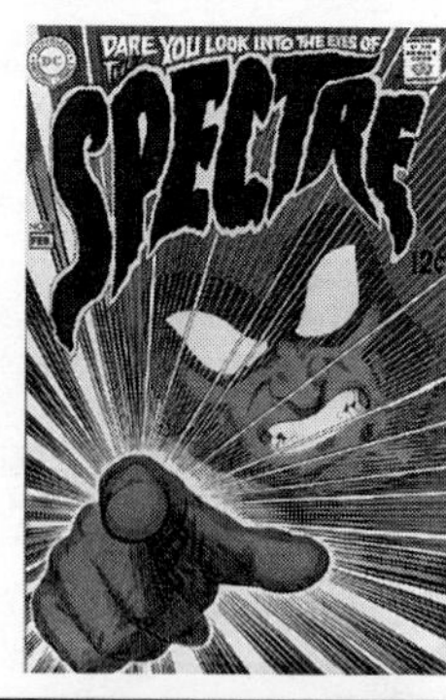

Speed Comics #10 © Brookwood Pub.

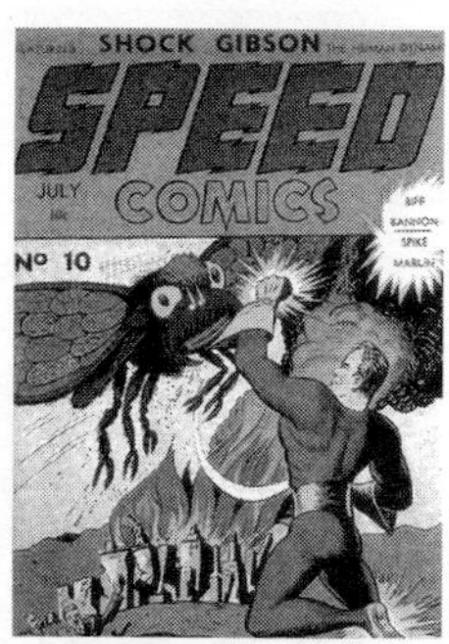

GD2.0 FN6.0 NM9.4

61-63,65-68,71-74: 65-Kraven the Hunter app. 4.00
64-1st app. Cloak & Dagger (3/82) 1.00 3.00 8.00
69,70-Cloak & Dagger app. 2.40 6.00
75-Double size 5.00
76-82: 78,79-Punisher cameo. 81,82-Punisher, Cloak & Dagger app. 4.00
83-Origin Punisher retold (10/83) 1.00 2.80 7.00
84,86-99: 90-Spider-man's new black costume, last panel(ties w/Amazing Spider-Man #252 & Marvel Team-Up #141 for 1st app.). 94-96-Cloak & Dagger app. 98-Intro The Spot 3.00
85-Hobgoblin (Ned Leeds) app. (12/83); gains powers of original Green Goblin (see Amazing Spider-Man #238) 1.00 2.80 7.00
100-(3/85)-Double size 4.00
101-115,117,118,120-129: 107-110-Death of Jean DeWolff. 111-Secret Wars II tie-in. 128-Black Cat new costume 2.50
116,119-Sabretooth-c/story 5.00
130-132: 30-Hobgoblin app. 131-Six part Kraven tie-in. 132-Kraven tie-in 5.00
133-140: 138-1st full app. Tombstone (origin #139). 140-Punisher cameo app. 2.50
141-143-Punisher app. 3.00
144-146,148-157: 151-Tombstone returns 2.50
147-1st app. new Hobgoblin (Macendale) in 1 pg. cameo; continued in Web of Spider-Man #48 1.25 3.75 10.00
158-Spider-Man gets new powers (1st Cosmic Spidey, cont'd in Web of Spider-Man #59) 5.00
159-Cosmic Spider-Man app. 5.00
160-170: 161-163-Hobgoblin app. 168-170-Avengers x-over. 169-1st app. The Outlaws 2.50
171-188,190-199: 180,181,183,184-Green Goblin app. 197-199-Original X-Men-c/story 2.00
189-($2.95, 52 pgs.)-Silver hologram on-c; battles Green Goblin; origin Spidey retold; Vess poster w/Spidey & Hobgoblin 4.00
189-(2nd printing)-Gold hologram on-c 3.00
195-(Deluxe ed.)-Polybagged w/audio cassette 3.00
200-($2.95)-Holo-grafx foil-c; Green Goblin-c/story 3.00
201-219,221,222,224,226-228,230-247,-1(7/97): 212-w/card sheet. 203-Maximum Carnage x-over. 204-Begin 4 part death of Tombstone story. 207,208-The Shroud-c/story. 208-Siege of Darkness x-over (#207 is a tie-in). 209-Black Cat back-up215,216-Scorpion app. 217-Power & Responsibility Pt. 4. 231-Returnof Kaine; Spider-Man corpse discovered. 232-New Doc Octopus app. 233-Carnage-c/app. 235-Dragon Man cameo. 236-Dragon Man-c/app; Lizard app.; Peter Parker regains powers. 238,239-Lizard app. 239-w/card insert. 240-Revelations storyline begins. 241-Flashback 2.00
213-Collectors ed. polybagged w/16 pg. preview & animation cel; foil-c; 1st meeting Spidey & Typhoid Mary 3.00
213-Version polybagged w/Gamepro #7; no-c date, price 2.00
217,219 ($2.95)-Deluxe edition foil-c: flip book 3.00
220 ($2.25, 52 pgs.)-Flip book, Mary Jane reveals pregnancy 3.00
223,229: ($2.50) 229-Spidey quits 3.00
223,225: ($2.95)-223-Die Cut-c. 225-Newsstand ed. 3.00
225,229: ($3.95) 225-Direct Market Holodisk-c (Green Goblin). 229-Acetate-c, Spidey quits 4.00
240-Variant-c 3.00
248,249,251-254,256: 249-Return of Norman Osborne 256-1st app. Prodigy 2.00
250-($3.25) Double gatefold-c 3.25
255-($2.99) Spiderhunt pt. 4 3.00
257-262: 257-Double cover with "Spectacular Prodigy #1"; battles Jack O'Lantern. 258-Spidey is cleared. 259,260-Green Goblin & Hobgoblin app. 262-Byrne-s 2.00
263-Final issue; Byrne-c; Aunt May returns 3.00
Annual 1 (1979)-Doc Octopus-c & 46 pg. story .85 2.60 7.00
Annual 2 (1980)-Origin/1st app. Rapier 4.00
Annual 3-14: 3('81-'94)-3-Last Man-Wolf. 8 ('88,$ 1.75)-Evolutionary War x-over; Daydreamer returns GwenStacy "clone" back to real self (not Gwen Stacy). 9 ('89, $2.00, 68 pgs.)-Atlantis Attacks. 10 ('90, $2.00, 68 pgs.)-McFarlane-a 11 ('91, $2.00, 68 pgs.)-Iron Man app. 12 ('92, $2.25, 68 pgs.)-Venom solo story cont'd from Amazing Spider-Man Annual #26. 13 ('93, $2.95, 68 pgs.)-Polybagged w/trading card; John Romita, Sr. back-up-a 3.00
Special 1 (1995, $3.95)-Flip book 4.00

NOTE: ***Austin*** *c-21i, Annual 11i.* ***Buckler*** *a-103, 107-111, 116, 117, 119, 122, Annual 1, Annual 10; c-103, 107-111, 113, 116-119, 122, Annual 1.* ***Buscema*** *a-121.* ***Byrne*** *c(p)-17, 43, 58, 101, 102.* ***Giffen*** *a-120p.* ***Hembeck*** *c/a-86p.* ***Larsen*** *c-Annual 11p.* ***Miller*** *c-46p, 48p, 50, 51p, 52p, 54p, 55, 56p, 57, 60.* ***Mooney*** *a-7i, 11i, 21p, 23p, 25p, 26p, 29-34p, 36p, 37p, 39i, 41, 42i, 49p, 50i, 51i, 53p, 54-57i, 59-66i, 68i, 71i, 73-79i, 81-83i, 85i, 87-99i, 102i, 125p, Annual 1i, 2p.* ***Nasser*** *c-37p.* ***Perez*** *c-10.* ***Simonson*** *c-54i.* ***Zeck*** *a-118, 131, 132; c-131, 132.*

SPECTACULAR STORIES MAGAZINE (Formerly A Star Presentation)
Fox Feature Syndicate (Hero Books): No. 4, July, 1950 - No. 3, Sept, 1950

4-Sherlock Holmes (true crime stories) 39.00 116.00 270.00
3-The St. Valentine's Day Massacre (true crime) 26.00 77.00 180.00

SPECTRE, THE (1st Series) (See Adventure Comics #431-440, More Fun & Showcase)
National Periodical Publ.: Nov-Dec, 1967 - No. 10, May-June, 1969 (All 12¢)

1-(11-12/67)-Anderson-c/a 9.00 27.00 90.00
2-5-Neal Adams-c/a; 3-Wildcat x-over 6.50 19.50 65.00
6-8,10: 6-8-Anderson inks. 7-Hourman app. 4.00 12.00 40.00
9-Wrightson-a 5.00 15.00 50.00

SPECTRE, THE (2nd Series) (See Saga of the Swamp Thing #58, Showcase '95 #8 & Wrath of the...)
DC Comics: Apr, 1987 - No. 31, Oct, 1989 ($1.00, new format)

1-31: 1-Colan-a begins. 9-Nudity panels. 10-Batman cameo. 10,11-Millenium tie-ins 2.50
Annual 1 (1988, $2.00)-Deadman app. 2.50

NOTE: ***Art Adams*** *c-Annual 1.* ***Colan*** *a-1-6.* ***Kaluta*** *c-1-3.* ***Mignola*** *c-7-9.* ***Morrow*** *a-9-15.* ***Sears*** *c/a-22.* ***Vess*** *c-13-15.*

SPECTRE, THE (3rd Series) (Also see Brave and the Bold #72, 75, 116, 180, 199 & Showcase '95 #8)
DC Comics: Dec, 1992 - No. 62, Feb, 1998 ($1.75/$1.95/$2.25/$2.50)

1-($1.95)-Glow-in-the-dark-c; Mandrake-a begins 5.00
2,3 3.00
4-7,9-12,14-20: 10-Kaluta-c. 11-Hildebrandt painted-c. 16-Aparo/K. Jones-a. 20-Sienkiewicz-c 2.50
8,13-($2.50)-Glow-in-the-dark-c 3.00
21,22,0,23-62: 22-(9/94)-Superman-c & app. 0-(10/94). 23-(11/94). 43-Kent Williams-c. 44-Kaluta-c. 47-Final Night x-over. 49-Begin-Bolton-c. 51-Batman-c/app. 52-Gianni-c. 54-Corben-c. 60-Harris-c 2.50
Annual 1 (1995, $3.95)-Year One story 4.00

NOTE: ***Bisley*** *c-27.* ***Fabry*** *c-2.* ***Kelley Jones*** *c-31.* ***Vess*** *c-5.*

SPEEDBALL (See Amazing Spider-Man Annual #12, Marvel Super-Heroes & The New Warriors)
Marvel Comics: Sept, 1988(10/88-inside) - No. 11, July, 1989 (75¢)

1-11: Ditko/Guice a-1-4, c-1; Ditko a-1-10; c-1-11p 2.00

SPEED BUGGY (TV)(Also see Fun-In #12, 15)
Charlton Comics: July, 1975 - No. 9, Nov, 1976 (Hanna-Barbera)

1 2.50 7.50 20.00
2-9 1.75 5.25 14.00

SPEED CARTER SPACEMAN (See Spaceman)

SPEED COMICS (New Speed)(Also see Double Up)
Brookwood Publ./Speed Publ./Harvey Publications No. 14 on:
10/39 - #11, 8/40; #12, 3/41 - #44, 1-2/47 (#14-16: pocket size, 100 pgs.)

1-Origin & 1st app. Shock Gibson; Ted Parrish, the Man with 1000 Faces begins; Powell-a; becomes Champion #2 on? 312.00 937.00 2500.00
2-Powell-a 100.00 300.00 800.00
3 59.00 176.00 470.00
4,5: 4-Powell-a?5-Dinosaur-c 50.00 150.00 400.00
6-11: 7-Mars Mason begins, ends #11 44.00 132.00 350.00
12 (3/41; shows #11 in indicia)-The Wasp begins; Major Colt app. (Capt. Colt #12) 50.00 150.00 400.00
13-Intro. Captain Freedom & Young Defenders; Girl Commandos, Pat Parker (costumed heroine), War Nurse begins; Major Colt app. 56.00 169.00 450.00

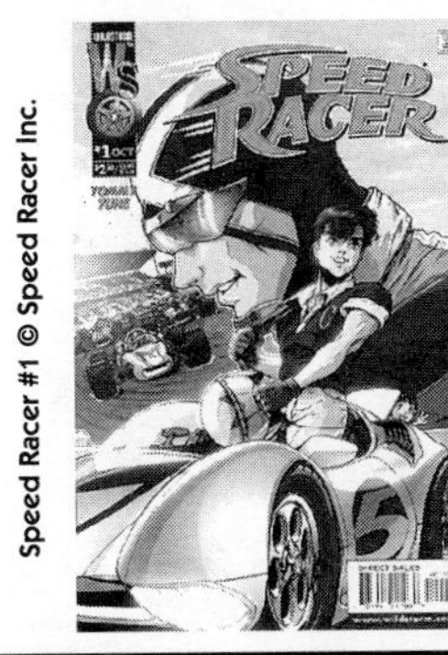

Speed Racer #1 © Speed Racer Inc.

Spellbound #1 © MAR

Spider-Girl #2 © MAR

14-16 (100 pg. pocket size, 1941): 14-2nd Harvey comic (See Pocket); Shock Gibson dons new costume. 15-Pat Parker dons costume, last in costume #23; no Girl Commandos 59.00 178.00 475.00
17-Black Cat begins (4/42, early app.; see Pocket #1); origin Black Cat-r/ Pocket #1; not in #40,41; S&K-c 69.00 206.00 550.00
18-20-S&K-c 50.00 150.00 400.00
21,22-Kirby-c. 21-Hitler, Tojo-c 50.00 150.00 400.00
23-Origin Girl Commandos; Kirby-c 53.00 159.00 425.00
24-Pat Parker team-up with Girl Commandos; Hitler, Tojo, & Mussolini-c 40.00 120.00 320.00
25-30: 26-Flag-c 40.00 120.00 300.00
31-Schomburg Hitler & Hirohito-c 50.00 150.00 400.00
32-36-Schomburg-c 45.00 135.00 360.00
37,39-42, 44 40.00 120.00 300.00
38-Iwo-Jima Flag-c 40.00 120.00 320.00
43-Robot-c 43.00 128.00 340.00

NOTE: ***Al Avison*** *c-14-16, 30, 43.* ***Briefer*** *a-6, 7.* ***Jon Henri*** *(Kirbyesque) c-17-20.* ***Kubert*** *a-7-11(Mars Mason), 37, 38, 42-44.* ***Kirby/Caseneuve*** *c-21-23.* ***Palais*** *c-37, 39-42.* ***Powell*** *a-1, 2, 4-7, 28, 31, 44.* ***Schomburg*** *c-31-36.* ***Tuska*** *a-3, 6, 7. Bondage c-18, 35. Captain Freedom c-16-24, 25(part), 26-44(w/Black Cat #27, 29, 31, 32-40). Shock Gibson c-1-15.*

SPEED DEMON (Also see Marvel Versus DC #3 & DC Versus Marvel #4)
Marvel Comics (Amalgam): Apr, 1996 ($1.95, one-shot)

1 2.00

SPEED DEMONS (Formerly Frank Merriwell at Yale #1-4?; Submarine Attack #11 on)
Charlton Comics: No. 5, Feb, 1957 - No. 10, 1958

5-10 5.50 16.00 32.00

SPEED FORCE (See The Flash 2nd Series #143-Cobalt Blue)
DC Comics: Nov, 1997 ($3.95, one-shot)

1-Flash & Kid Flash vs. Cobalt Blue; Waid-s/Aparo & Sienkiewicz-a; Flash family stories and pin-ups by various 5.00

SPEED RACER (Also see The New Adventures of...)
Now Comics: July, 1987 - No. 38, Nov, 1990 ($1.75)

1-38, 1-2nd printing 2.50
Special 1 (1988, $2.00) 2.50
Special 2 (1988, $3.50) 3.50

SPEED RACER (TV)
DC Comics (WildStorm): Oct, 1999 - No. 3, Dec, 1999 ($2.50, limited series)

1-3-Tommy Yune-s/a; origin of Racer X 2.50

SPEED RACER FEATURING NINJA HIGH SCHOOL
Now Comics: Aug, 1993 - No. 2, 1993 ($2.50, mini-series)

1,2: 1-Polybagged w/card. 2-Exists? 2.50

SPEED RACER: RETURN OF THE GRX
Now Comics: Mar, 1994 - No. 2, Apr, 1994 ($1.95, limited series)

1,2 2.50

SPEED SMITH-THE HOT ROD KING (Also see Hot Rod King)
Ziff-Davis Publishing Co.: Spring, 1952

1-Saunders painted-c 23.00 69.00 160.00

SPEEDY GONZALES
Dell Publishing Co.: No. 1084, Mar, 1960

Four Color 1084 3.65 11.00 40.00

SPEEDY RABBIT (See Television Puppet Show)
Realistic/I. W. Enterprises/Super Comics: nd (1953); 1963

nn (1953)-Realistic Reprint? 2.40 6.00 12.00
I.W. Reprint #1 (2 versions w/diff. c/stories exist)-Peter Cottontail #?
Super Reprint #14(1963) 1.00 3.00 8.00

SPELLBINDERS
Quality: Dec, 1986 - No. 12, Jan, 1988 ($1.25)

1-12: Nemesis the Warlock, Amadeus Wolf 2.00

SPELLBOUND (See The Crusaders)

SPELLBOUND (Tales to Hold You... #1, Stories to Hold You...)
Atlas Comics (ACI 1-15/Male 16-23/BPC 24-34): Mar, 1952 - #23, June, 1954; #24, Oct, 1955 - #34, June, 1957

1-Horror/weird stories in all 59.00 178.00 475.00
2-Edgar A. Poe app. 36.00 107.00 250.00
3-5: 3-Whitney-a; cannibalism story 30.00 90.00 210.00
6-Krigstein-a 30.00 90.00 210.00
7-10: 8-Ayers-a 25.00 75.00 175.00
11-16,18-20: 14-Ed Win-a 21.00 62.00 145.00
17-Krigstein-a 21.00 64.00 150.00
21-23: 23-Last precode (6/54) 18.00 54.00 125.00
24-28,30,31,34: 25-Orlando-a 16.00 47.00 110.00
29-Ditko-a (4 pgs.) 18.00 54.00 125.00
32,33-Torres-a 16.00 47.00 110.00

NOTE: ***Brodsky*** *a-5; c-1, 5-7, 10, 11, 13, 15, 25-27, 32.* ***Colan*** *a-17.* ***Everett*** *a-2, 5, 7, 10, 16, 28, 31; c-2, 8, 9, 14, 17-19, 28, 30.* ***Forgione/Abel*** *a-29.* ***Forte/Fox*** *a-16.* ***Al Hartley*** *a-2.* ***Heath*** *a-2, 4, 8, 9, 12, 14, 16; c-3, 4, 12, 16, 20, 21.* ***Infantino*** *a-15.* ***Keller*** *a-5.* ***Kida*** *a-2, 14.* ***Maneely*** *a-7, 14, 27; c-24, 29, 31.* ***Mooney*** *a-5, 13, 18.* ***Mac Pakula*** *a-22, 32.* ***Post*** *a-8.* ***Powell*** *a-19, 20, 32.* ***Robinson*** *a-1.* ***Romita*** *a-24, 26, 27.* ***R.Q. Sale*** *a-29.* ***Sekowsky*** *a-5.* ***Severin*** *c-29.* ***Sinnott*** *a-8, 16, 17.*

SPELLBOUND
Marvel Comics: Jan, 1988 - Apr, 1988 ($1.50, bi-weekly, Baxter paper)

1-5 2.00
6 ($2.25, 52 pgs.) 2.50

SPELLJAMMER (Also see TSR Worlds Comics Annual)
DC Comics: Sept, 1990 - No. 15, Nov, 1991 ($1.75)

1-15: Based on TSR game. 11-Heck-a. 2.00

SPENCER SPOOK (Formerly Giggle Comics; see Adventures of...)
American Comics Group: No. 100, Mar-Apr, 1955 - No. 101, May-June, 1955

100,101 6.35 19.00 38.00

SPIDER, THE
Eclipse Books: 1991 - Book 3, 1991 ($4.95, 52 pgs., limited series)

Book 1-3-Truman-c/a 5.00

SPIDER-BOY (Also see Marvel Versus DC #3)
Marvel Comics (Amalgam): Apr, 1996 ($1.95)

1-Mike Wieringo-c/a; Karl Kesel story; 1st app. of Bizarnage, Insect Queen, Challengers of the Fantastic, Sue Storm: Agent of S.H.I.E.L. D., & King Lizard. 2.00

SPIDER-BOY TEAM-UP
Marvel Comics (Amalgam): June, 1997 ($1.95, one-shot)

1-Karl Kesel & Roger Stern-s/Jo Ladronn-a(p) 2.00

SPIDER-GIRL (See What If #105)
Marvel Comics: Oct, 1998 - Present ($1.99)

0-($2.99)-r/1st app. Peter Parker's daughter from What If #105; previews reg. series, Avengers-Next and J2 1.00 2.80 7.00
1-DeFalco-s/Olliffe & Williamson-s 1.00 2.80 7.00
2-Two covers 4.00
3-15: 3-Fantastic Five-c/app. 10,11-Spider-Girl time travels to meet teenaged Spider-Man 3.00
1999 Annual ($3.99) 4.00
... A Fresh Start (1/99,$5.99, TPB) r/#1&2 6.00

SPIDER-MAN (See Amazing..., Giant-Size..., Marvel Tales, Marvel Team-Up, Spectacular..., Spidey Super Stories, Venom, & Web Of...)

SPIDER-MAN
Marvel Comics: Aug, 1990 - No. 98, Nov, 1998 ($1.75/$1.95/ $1.99)

1-Silver edition, direct sale only (unbagged) 2.40 6.00
1-Silver bagged edition; direct sale, no price on comic, but $2.00 on plastic bag (125,000 print run) 15.00
1-Regular edition w/Spidey face in UPC area (unbagged); green-c 5.00
1-Regular bagged edition w/Spidey face in UPC area; green cover (125,000) 10.00
1-Newsstand bagged w/UPC code 8.00

Spider-Man #93 © MAR

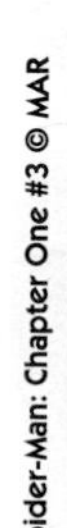

Spider-Man: Chapter One #3 © MAR

Spider-Man: Friends and Enemies #2 © MAR

1-Gold edition, 2nd printing (unbagged) with Spider-Man in box (400,000-450,000) 5.00
1-Gold 2nd printing w/UPC code; sold in Wal-Mart; not scarce 5.00
1-Platinum ed. mailed to retailers only (10,000 print run); has new McFarlane-a & editorial material instead of ads; stiff-c, no cover price 150.00
2-26: 2-McFarlane-c/a/scripts continue. 6,7-Ghost Rider & Hobgoblin app. 8-Wolverine cameo; Wolverine storyline begins. 12-Wolverine storyline ends. 13-Spidey's black costume returns; Morbius app. 14-Morbius app. 15-Erik Larsen-c/a; Beast c/s. 16-X-Force-c/story w/Liefeld assists; continues in X-Force #4; reads sideways; last McFarlane issue. 17-Thanos-c/story; Leonardi/Williamson-c/a. 13,14-Spidey in black costume. 18-Ghost Rider-c/story. 18-23-Sinister Six storyline w/Erik Larsen-c/a/scripts. 19-Hulk & Hobgoblin-c & app. 20-22-Deathlok app. 22,23-Ghost Rider, Hulk, Hobgoblin app. 23-Wrap-around gatefold-c. 24-Infinity War x-over w/Demogoblin & Hobgoblin-c/story. 24-Demogoblin dons new costume & battles Hobgoblin-c/story. 26-($3.50, 52 pgs.)-Silver hologram on-c w/gatefold poster by Ron Lim; Spidey retells his origin. 4.00
26-2nd printing; gold hologram on-c 3.50
27-45: 32-34-Punisher-c/story. 37-Maximum Carnage x-over. 39,40-Electro-c/s (cameo #38). 41-43-Iron Fist-c/stories w/Jae Lee-c/a. 42-Intro Platoon. 44-Hobgoblin app 2.50
46-49,51-53, 55, 56,58-74,76-81, -1(7/97): 46-Begin $1.95-c; bound-in card sheet. 51-Power & Responsibility Pt. 3. 52,53-Venom app. 60-Kaine revealed. 61-Origin Kaine. 65-Mysterio app. 66-Kaine-c/app.; Peter Parker app. 67-Carnage-c/app. 68,69-Hobgoblin-c/app. 72-Onslaught x-over; Spidey vs. Sentinels. 74-Daredevil-c/app. 77-80-Morbius-c/app. 2.50
46-($2.95)-Polybagged; silver ink-c w/16 pg. preview of cartoon series & animation style print; bound-in trading card sheet 3.00
50-($2.50)-Newsstand edition 2.50
50-($3.95)-Collectors edition w/holographic-c 4.00
51-($2.95)-Deluxe edition foil-c; flip book 3.00
54 ($2.75, 52 pgs.)-Flip book 2.75
57 ($2.50) 2.50
57 ($2.95)-Die cut-c 3.00
65-($2.95)-Variant-c; polybagged w/cassette 3.00
75-($2.95)-Wraparound-c; return of the Green Goblin;death of Ben Reilly (who was the clone) 4.00
82-97: 84-Juggernaut app. 91-Double cover with "Dusk #1"; battles the Shocker. 93-Ghost Rider app. 2.00
98-Double cover; final issue 3.00
Annual '97 ($2.99), '98 ($2.99)-Devil Dinosaur-c/app. 3.00
...: Carnage nn (6/93, $6.95, TPB)-r/Amazing S-M #344,345,359-363; spot varnish-c 7.00
.../Dr. Strange: "The Way to Dusty Death" nn (1992, $6.95, 68 pgs.) 7.00
.../Elektra '98-($2.99) vs. The Silencer 3.00
Giant-Sized Spider-Man (12/98, $3.99) r/team-ups 4.00
Identity Crisis (9/98, $19.95, TPB) 20.00
...Revelations ('97, $14.99, TPB) r/end of Clone Saga plus 14 new pages by Romita Jr. 15.00
Special Edition 1 (12/92-c, 11/92 inside)-The Trial of Venom; ordered thru mail with $5.00 donation or more to UNICEF; embossed metallic ink; came bagged w/bound-in poster; Daredevil app. 1.25 3.75 10.00
Super Special (7/95, $3.95)-Planet of the Symbiotes 4.00
The Death of Gwen Stacy ($14.95) r/AS-M#96-98,121,122 14.95
...Vs. Venom nn (1990, $8.95, TPB)-r/Amaz. S-M #300,315-317 w/new McFarlane-c 9.00
Wizard 1/2 ($10.00) Leonardi-a; Green Goblin app. 10.00
NOTE: ***Erik Larsen*** *c/a-15, 18-23.* ***M. Rogers/Keith Williams*** *c/a-27, 28.*

SPIDER-MAN ADVENTURES
Marvel Comics: Dec, 1994 - No. 15, Mar, 1996 ($1.50)

1-15 ($1.50)-Based on animated series 2.00
1-($2.95)-Foil embossed-c 3.00

SPIDER-MAN AND BATMAN
Marvel Comics: 1995 ($5.95, one-shot)

nn-DeMatteis-s; Joker, Carnage app. 6.00

SPIDER-MAN AND DAREDEVIL
Marvel Comics Group: Mar, 1984 ($2.00, one-shot, deluxe paper)

1-r/Spectacular Spider-Man #26-28 by Miller 3.00

SPIDER-MAN AND HIS AMAZING FRIENDS (See Marvel Action Universe)
Marvel Comics Group: Dec, 1981 (one-shot)

1-Adapted from NBC TV cartoon show; Green Goblin-c/story; 1st Spidey, Firestar, Iceman team-up; Spiegle-p 4.00

SPIDER-MAN AND THE INCREDIBLE HULK (See listing under Amazing...)

SPIDER-MAN AND THE UNCANNY X-MEN
Marvel Comics: Mar, 1996 ($16.95, trade paperback)

nn-r/Uncanny X-Men #27, Uncanny X-men #35, Amazing Spider-Man #92, Marvel Team-Up Annual #1, Marvel Team-Up #150, & Spectacular Spider-Man #197-199 17.00

SPIDER-MAN AND X-FACTOR
Marvel Comics: May, 1994 - No. 3, July, 1994 ($1.95, limited series)

1-3 2.00

SPIDER-MAN /BADROCK
Maximum Press: Mar, 1997 ($2.99, mini-series)

1A, 1B(#2)-Jurgens-s 3.00

SPIDER-MAN: CHAPTER ONE
Marvel Comics: Dec, 1998 - No. 12, Oct, 1999 ($2.50, limited series)

1-Retelling/updating of origin; John Byrne-s/c/a 2.50
1-($6.95) DF Edition w/variant-c by Jae Lee 7.00
2-11: 2-Two covers (one is swipe of ASM #1); Fantastic Four app. 9-Daredevil. 11-Giant-Man-c/app. 2.50
12-($3.50) Battles the Sandman 3.50
0-(5/99) Origins of Vulture, Lizard and Sandman 2.50

SPIDER-MAN CLASSICS
Marvel Comics: Apr, 1993 - No. 16, July, 1994 ($1.25)

1-14,16: 1-r/Amaz. Fantasy #15 & Strange Tales #115. 2-16-r/Amaz. Spider-Man #1-15. 6-Austin-c(i) 2.00
15-($2.95)-Polybagged w/16 pg. insert & animation style print; r/Amazing S-M #14 (1st Green Goblin) 3.00

SPIDER-MAN COLLECTOR'S PREVIEW
Marvel Comics: Dec, 1994 ($1.50, 100 pgs., one-shot)

1-wraparound-c; no comics 2.00

SPIDER-MAN COMICS MAGAZINE
Marvel Comics Group: Jan, 1987 - No. 13, 1988 ($1.50, digest-size)

1-13-Reprints 2.00

SPIDER-MAN: DEAD MAN'S HAND
Marvel Comics: Apr, 1997 ($2.99, one-shot)

1 3.00

SPIDER-MAN: FRIENDS AND ENEMIES
Marvel Comics: Jan, 1995 - No. 4, Apr, 1995 ($1.95, limited series)

1-4-Darkhawk, Nova & Speedball app. 2.00

SPIDER-MAN: FUNERAL FOR AN OCTOPUS
Marvel Comics: Mar, 1995 - No. 3, May, 1995 ($1.50, limited series)

1-3 2.00

SPIDER-MAN/ GEN 13
Marvel Comics: Nov, 1996 ($4.95, one-shot)

nn-Peter David-s/Stuart Immonen-a 5.00

SPIDER-MAN: HOBGOBLIN LIVES
Marvel Comics: Jan, 1997 - No. 3, Mar, 1997 ($2.50, limited series)

1-3-Wraparound-c 2.50
TPB (1/98, $14.99) r/#1-3 plus timeline 15.00

SPIDER-MAN: HOT SHOTS
Marvel Comics: Jan, 1996 ($2.95, one-shot)

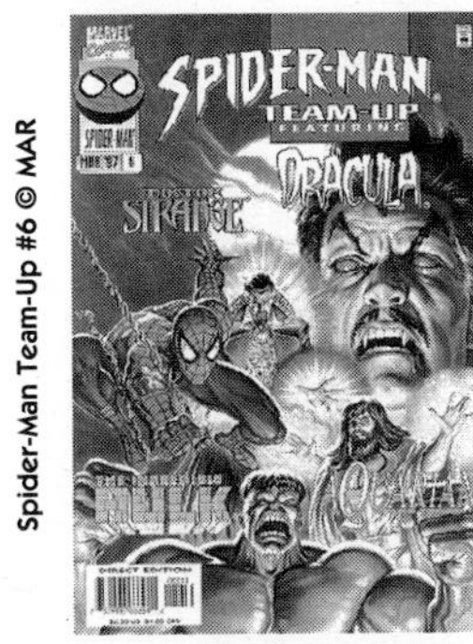

Spider-Man Team-Up #6 © MAR

Spider-Man: The Manga #28 © MAR

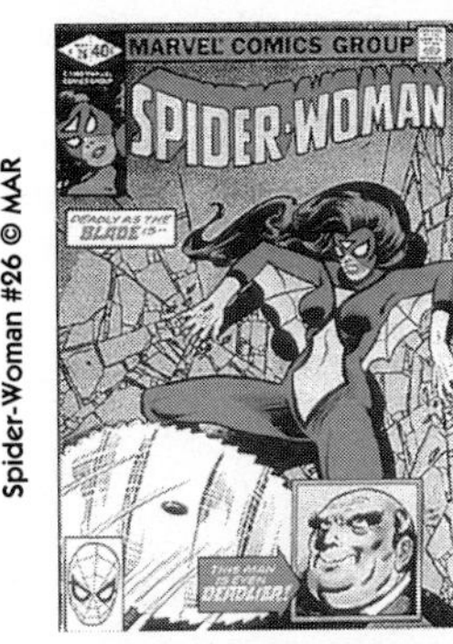

Spider-Woman #26 © MAR

GD2.0 FN6.0 NM9.4

nn-fold out posters by various, inc. Vess and Ross 3.00

SPIDER-MAN: LEGACY OF EVIL
Marvel Comics: June, 1996 ($3.95, one-shot)

1-Kurt Busiek script & Mark Texeira-c/a 4.00

SPIDER-MAN: MADE MEN
Marvel Comics: Aug, 1998 ($5.99, one-shot)

1-Spider-Man & Daredevil vs. Kingpin 6.00

SPIDER-MAN MAGAZINE
Marvel Comics: 1994 - No. 3, 1994 ($1.95, magazine)

1-3: 1-Contains 4 S-M promo cards & 4 X-Men Ultra Fleer cards; Spider-Man story by Romita, Sr.; X-Men story; puzzles & games. 2-Doc Octopus & X-Men stories 2.00

SPIDER-MAN: MAXIMUM CLONAGE
Marvel Comics: 1995 ($4.95)

Alpha #1-Acetate-c, Omega #1-Chromium-c. 5.00

SPIDER-MAN MEGAZINE
Marvel Comics: Oct, 1994 - No. 6, Mar, 1995 ($2.95, 100 pgs.)

1-6: 1-r/ASM #16,224,225, Marvel Team-Up #1 3.00

SPIDER-MAN: POWER OF TERROR
Marvel Comics: Jan, 1995 - No. 4, Apr, 1995 ($1.95, limited series)

1-4-Silvermane & Deathlok app. 2.00

SPIDER-MAN/PUNISHER: FAMILY PLOT
Marvel Comics: Feb, 1996 - No. 2, Mar, 1996 ($2.95, limited series)

1,2 3.00

SPIDER-MAN: REDEMPTION
Marvel Comics: Sept, 1996 - No. 4, Dec, 1996 ($1.50, limited series)

1-4: DeMatteis scripts; Zeck-a 2.00

SPIDER-MAN SAGA
Marvel Comics: Nov, 1991 - No. 4, Feb, 1992 ($2.95, limited series)

1-4: Gives history of Spider-Man: text & illustrations 3.00

SPIDER-MAN TEAM-UP
Marvel Comics: Dec, 1995 - No. 7, June, 1996 ($2.95)

1-7: 1-w/ X-Men. 2-w/ Silver Surfer. 3-w/Fantastic Four. 4-w/Avengers. 5-Gambit & Howard the Duck-c/app. 7-Thunderbolts-c/app. 3.00

SPIDER-MAN: THE ARACHNIS PROJECT
Marvel Comics: Aug, 1994 - No. 6, Jan, 1995 ($1.75, limited series)

1-6-Venom, Styx, Stone & Jury app. 2.00

SPIDER-MAN: THE CLONE JOURNAL
Marvel Comics: Mar, 1995 ($2.95, one-shot)

1 2.00

SPIDER-MAN: THE FINAL ADVENTURE
Marvel Comics: Nov, 1995 - No. 4, Feb, 1996 ($2.95, limited series)

1-4: 1-Nicieza scripts; foil-c 3.00

SPIDER-MAN: THE JACKAL FILES
Marvel Comics: Aug, 1995 ($1.95, one-shot)

1 2.00

SPIDER-MAN: THE LOST YEARS
Marvel Comics: Aug, 1995-No. 3, Oct, 1995; No. 0, 1996 ($2.95/$3.95,lim. series)

0-(1/96, $3.95)-Reprints. 4.00
1-3-DeMatteis scripts, Romita, Jr.-c/a 3.00
NOTE: ***Romita** c-0i. **Romita, Jr.** a-0r, 1-3p. c-0-3p. **Sharp** a-0r.*

SPIDER-MAN: THE MANGA
Marvel Comics: Dec, 1997 - No. 31, June, 1999 ($3.99/$2.99, B&W, bi-weekly)

1-($3.99)-English translation of Japanese Spider-Man 4.00
2-31-($2.99) 3.00

SPIDER-MAN: THE MUTANT AGENDA
Marvel Comics: No. 0, Feb, 1994; No. 1, Mar, 1994 - No. 3, May, 1994 ($1.75, limited series)

0-(2/94, $1.25, 52 pgs.)-Crosses over w/newspaper strip; has empty pages to paste in newspaper strips; gives origin of Spidey 2.00
1-3: Beast & Hobgoblin app. 1-X-Men app. 2.00

SPIDER-MAN: THE PARKER YEARS
Marvel Comics: Nov, 1995 ($2.50, one-shot)

1 2.50

SPIDER-MAN 2099 (See Amazing Spider-Man #365)
Marvel Comics: Nov, 1992 - No. 46, Aug, 1996 ($1.25/$1.50/$1.95)

1-(stiff-c)-Red foil stamped-c; begins origin of Miguel O'Hara (Spider-Man 2099); Leonardi/Williamson-c/a begins 3.00
1-2nd printing, 2-24,26-36: 2-Origin continued, ends #3. 4-Doom 2099 app. 13-Extra 16 pg. insert on Midnight Sons. 19-Bound-in trading card sheet. 35-Variant-c. 36-Ttwo-c; Jae Lee-a. 37,38-Two-c. 46-The Vulture app; Mike McKone-a(p) 2.00
25-($2.25, 52 pgs.)-Newsstand edition 2.25
25-($2.95, 52 pgs.)-Deluxe edition w/embossed foil-c 3.00
Annual 1 (1994, $2.95, 68 pgs.) 3.00
Special 1 (1995, $3.95) 4.00
NOTE: ***Chaykin** c-37. **Ron Lim** a(p)-18; c(p)-13, 16, 18. **Kelley Jones** c/a-9. **Leonardi/Williamson** a-1-8, 10-13, 15-17, 19, 20, 22-25; c-1-13, 15, 17-19, 20, 22-25, 35.*

SPIDER-MAN 2099 MEETS SPIDER-MAN
Marvel Comics: 1995 ($5.95, one-shot)

nn-Peter David script; Leonardi/Williamson-c/a. 6.00

SPIDER-MAN UNLIMITED
Marvel Comics: May, 1993 - No. 22, Nov, 1998 ($3.95, quarterly, 68 pgs.)

1-Begin Maximum Carnage storyline, ends; Carnage-c/story 5.00
2-12: 2-Venom & Carnage-c/story; Ron Lim-c/a(p) in #2-6. 10-Vulture app., McManus-a 4.00
13-22: 13-Begin $2.99-c; Scorpion-c/app. 15-Daniel-c; Puma-c/app. 19-Lizard-c/app. 20-Hannibal King and Lilith app. 21,22-Deodato-a 3.00

SPIDER-MAN UNMASKED
Marvel Comics: Nov, 1996 ($5.95, one-shot)

nn-Art w/text 6.00

SPIDER-MAN: VENOM AGENDA
Marvel Comics: Jan, 1998 ($2.99, one-shot)

1-Hama-s/Lyle-c/a 3.00

SPIDER-MAN VS. DRACULA
Marvel Comics: Jan, 1994 ($1.75, 52 pgs., one-shot)

1-r/Giant-Size Spider-Man #1 plus new Matt Fox-a 2.00

SPIDER-MAN VS. WOLVERINE
Marvel Comics Group: Feb, 1987; V2#1, 1990 (68 pgs.)

1-Williamson-c/a(i); intro Charlemagne; death of Ned Leeds (old Hobgoblin) 2.50 7.50 20.00
V2#1 (1990, $4.95)-Reprints #1 (2/87) 5.00

SPIDER-MAN: WEB OF DOOM
Marvel Comics: Aug, 1994 - No. 3, Oct, 1994 ($1.75, limited series)

1-3 2.00

SPIDER REIGN OF THE VAMPIRE KING, THE (Also see The Spider)
Eclipse Books: 1992 - No. 3, 1992 ($4.95, limited series, coated stock, 52 pgs.)

Book One - Three: Truman scripts & painted-c 5.00

SPIDER'S WEB, THE (See G-8 and His Battle Aces)

SPIDER-WOMAN (Also see The Avengers #240, Marvel Spotlight #32, Marvel Super Heroes Secret Wars #7 & Marvel Two-In-One #29)
Marvel Comics Group: April, 1978 - No. 50, June, 1983 (New logo #47 on)

1-New complete origin & mask added 1.00 3.00 8.00
2-5,7-18,21-27,30,31,33-36,: 13,15-The Shroud-c/s. 3.00
6,19,20,28,29,32,37,38: 6,19,32-Werewolf by Night-c/s. 20,28,29-Spider-Man

Spider-Woman #1 © MAR

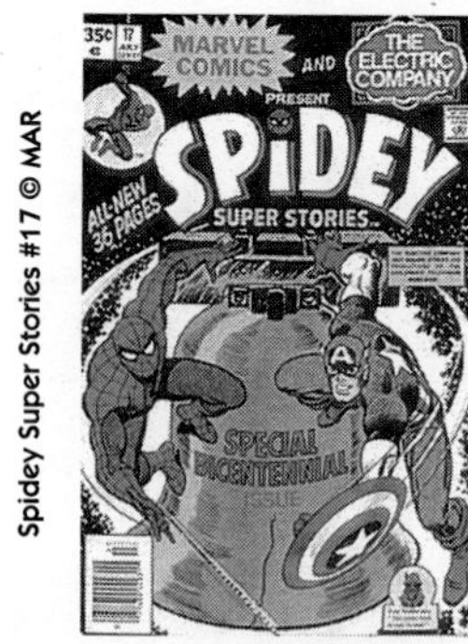

Spidey Super Stories #17 © MAR

The Spirit #10 © Will Eisner

GD2.0 FN6.0 NM9.4

app. 32-Miller-c. 37,38-X-Men x-over; 37-1st app. Siryn of X-Force; origin retold 4.00
39-49: 46-Kingpin app. 49-Tigra-c/story 3.00
50-(52 pgs.)-Death of Spider-Woman; photo-c 2.40 6.00
NOTE: ***Austin*** *a-37i.* ***Byrne*** *c-26p.* ***Layton*** *c-19.* ***Miller*** *c-32p.*

SPIDER-WOMAN
Marvel Comics: Nov, 1993 - No. 4, Feb, 1994 ($1.75, mini-series)
V2#1-4: 1,2-Origin; U.S. Agent app. 2.00

SPIDER-WOMAN
Marvel Comics: July, 1999 - Present ($2.99/$1.99)
1-($2.99) Byrne-s/Sears-a 3.00
2-6-($1.99): 2-Two covers 2.00

SPIDEY SUPER STORIES (Spider-Man)
Marvel/Children's TV Workshop: Oct, 1974 - No. 57, Mar, 1982 (35¢, no ads)

	GD2.0	FN6.0	NM9.4
1-Origin (stories simplified)	2.50	7.50	25.00
2-Kraven	1.85	5.50	15.00
3-10,15: 6-Iceman. 15-Storm-c/sty	1.50	4.50	12.00
11-14,16-20: 19,20-Kirby-c	1.10	3.30	9.00
21-57: 24-Kirby-c. 31-Moondragon-c/story; Dr. Doom app. 33-Hulk. 34-Sub-Mariner. 38-F.F. 44-Vision.39-Thanos-c/story. 45-Silver Surfer & Dr. Doom app. 56-BattlesJack O'Lantern-c/sty (exactly one year after 1st app. in Machine Man #19)	1.00	2.80	7.00

SPIKE AND TYKE (See M.G.M.'s...)

SPIN & MARTY (TV) (Walt Disney's)(See Walt Disney Showcase #32)
Dell Publishing Co. (Mickey Mouse Club): No. 714, June, 1956 - No. 1082, Mar-May, 1960 (All photo-c)

	GD2.0	FN6.0	NM9.4
Four Color 714 (#1)	11.00	32.00	120.00
Four Color 767,808 (#2,3)	9.00	27.00	100.00
Four Color 826 (#4)-Annette Funicello photo-c	23.00	68.00	250.00
5(3-5/58) - 9(6-8/59)	7.25	22.00	80.00
Four Color 1026,1082	7.25	22.00	80.00

SPINE-TINGLING TALES (Doctor Spektor Presents...)
Gold Key: May, 1975 - No. 4, Jan, 1976 (All 25¢ issues)
1-1st Tragg-r/Mystery Comics Digest #3 1.10 3.30 9.00
2-4: 2-Origin Ra-Ka-Tep-r/Mystery Comics Digest #1; Dr. Spektor #12. 3-All Durak-r issue; 4-Baron Tibor's 1st app.-r/Mystery Comics Digest #4; painted-c 2.40 6.00

SPINWORLD
Amaze Ink (Slave Labor Graphics): July, 1997 - No. 4, Jan, 1998 ($2.95/$3.95, B&W, mini-series)
1-3-Brent Anderson-a(p) 3.00
4-($3.95) 4.00

SPIRAL PATH, THE
Eclipse Comics: July, 1986 - No. 2 ($1.75, Baxter paper, limited series)
1,2 2.00

SPIRAL ZONE
DC Comics: Feb, 1988 - No. 4, May, 1988 ($1.00, mini-series)
1-4-Based on Tonka toys 2.00

SPIRIT, THE (Newspaper comics - see Promotional Comics section)

SPIRIT, THE (1st Series)(Also see Police Comics #11)
Quality Comics Group (Vital): 1944 - No. 22, Aug, 1950

	GD2.0	FN6.0	NM9.4
nn(#1)- "Wanted Dead or Alive"	72.00	216.00	575.00
nn(#2)- "Crime Doesn't Pay"	40.00	120.00	325.00
nn(#3)- "Murder Runs Wild"	36.00	107.00	250.00
4,5: 4-Flatfoot Burns begins, ends #22. 5-Wertham app.	29.00	86.00	200.00
6-10	24.00	73.00	170.00
11	21.00	64.00	150.00
12-17-Eisner-c. 19-Honeybun app.	34.00	103.00	240.00
18-21-Strip-r by Eisner; Eisner-c	40.00	120.00	310.00
22-Used by N.Y. Legis. Comm; classic Eisner-c	53.00	159.00	425.00
Super Reprint #11-r/Quality Spirit #19 by Eisner	2.80	8.40	28.00
Super Reprint #12-r/Spirit #17 by Fine; Sol Brodsky-c	2.80	8.40	28.00

GD2.0 FN6.0 NM9.4

SPIRIT, THE (2nd Series)
Fiction House Magazines: Spring, 1952 - No. 5, 1954

	GD2.0	FN6.0	NM9.4
1-Not Eisner	40.00	120.00	300.00
2-Eisner-c/a(2)	40.00	120.00	280.00
3-Eisner/Grandenetti-c	30.00	90.00	210.00
4-Eisner/Grandenetti-c; Eisner-a	31.00	94.00	220.00
5-Eisner-c/a(4)	36.00	107.00	250.00

SPIRIT, THE
Harvey Publications: Oct, 1966 - No. 2, Mar, 1967 (Giant Size, 25¢, 68 pgs.)
1-Eisner-r plus 9 new pgs.(origin Denny Colt, Take 3, plus 2 filler pgs.) (#3 was advertised, but never published) 6.00 18.00 60.00
2-Eisner-r plus 9 new pgs.(origin of the Octopus) 5.50 16.50 55.00

SPIRIT, THE (Underground)
Kitchen Sink Enterprises (Krupp Comics): Jan, 1973 - No. 2, Sept, 1973 (Black & White)
1-New Eisner-c & 4 pgs. new Eisner-a plus-r (titled Crime Convention) 1.85 5.50 15.00
2-New Eisner-c & 4 pgs. new Eisner-a plus-r (titled Meets P'Gell) 2.50 7.50 20.00

SPIRIT, THE (Magazine)
Warren Publ. Co./Krupp Comic Works No. 17 on: 4/74 - No. 16, 10/76; No. 17, Winter, 1977 - No. 41, 6/83 (B&W w/color)

	GD2.0	FN6.0	NM9.4
1-Eisner-r begin	2.80	8.40	28.00
2-5	2.25	6.75	18.00
6-9,11-15: 7-All Ebony issue. 8-Female Foes issue. 12-X-Mas issue	1.75	5.25	14.00
10-Giant Summer Special ($1.50)-Origin	2.50	7.50	22.00
16-Giant Summer Special ($1.50)	2.25	6.75	18.00
17,18(8/78): 17-Lady Luck-r	1.00	3.00	8.00
19-21-New Eisner-a. 20,21-Wood-r (#21-r/A DP on the Moon by Wood). 20-Outer Space-r	1.00	3.00	8.00
22-41: 22,23-Wood-r (#22-r/Mission the Moon by Wood). 28-r/last story (10/5/52). 30-(7/81)-Special Spirit Jam issue w/Caniff, Corben, Bolland, Byrne, Miller, Kurtzman, Rogers, Sienkiewicz-a & 40 others. 36-Begin Spirit Section-r; r/1st story (6/2/40) in color; new Eisner-c/a(18 pgs.)($2.95). 37-r/2nd story in color plus 18 pgs. new Eisner-a. 38-41: r/3rd - 6th stories in color. 41-Lady Luck Mr. Mystic in color	1.00	2.80	7.00
Special 1(1975)-All Eisner-a (mail only)	4.00	12.00	40.00

NOTE: *Covers pencilled/inked by* ***Eisner*** *only #1-9,12-16; painted by Eisner & Ken Kelly #10 & 11; painted by Eisner #17-up; one color story reprinted in #1-10.* ***Austin*** *a-30i.* ***Byrne*** *a-30p.* ***Miller*** *a-30p.*

SPIRIT, THE
Kitchen Sink Enterprises: Oct, 1983 - No. 87, Jan, 1992 ($2.00, Baxter paper)
1-11: 1-Origin-r/12/23/45 Spirit Section. 2-r/sections 1/20/46-2/10/46. 3-r/2/17/46-3/10/46. 4-r/3/17/46-4/7/46. 11-Last color issue 3.00
12-87: 54-r/section 2/19/50. 85-87-Reprint the Outer Space Spirit stories by Wood. 86-r/A DP on the Moon by Wood from 1952 2.00

SPIRIT JAM
Kitchen Sink Press: Aug, 1998 ($5.95, B&W, oversized, square-bound)
nn-Reprints Spirit (Magazine) #30 by Eisner & 50 others; and "Cerebus Vs. The Spirit" from Cerebus Jam #1 6.00

SPIRIT, THE: THE NEW ADVENTURES
Kitchen Sink Press: 1997 - No. 8, Nov, 1998 ($3.50, anthology)
1-Moore-s/Gibbons-c/a 4.00
2-8: 2-Gaiman-s/Eisner-c. 3-Moore-s/Bolland-c/Moebius back-c. 4-Allred-s/a; Busiek-s/Anderson-a. 5-Chadwick-s/c/a(p); Nyberg-i. 6-S.Hampton & Mandrake-a 3.50

SPIRIT: THE ORIGIN YEARS

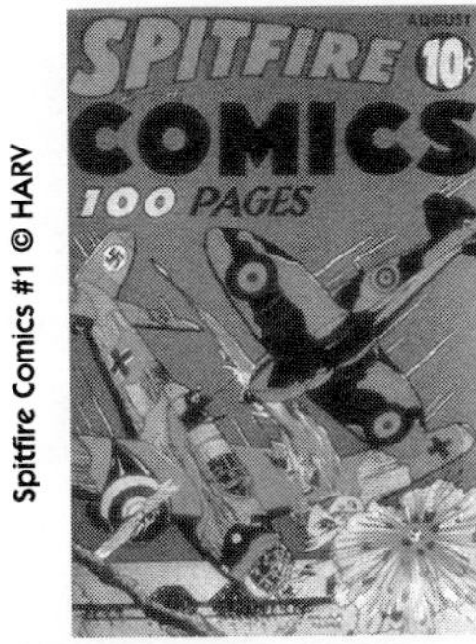

Spitfire Comics #1 © HARV

Spoof #1 © MAR

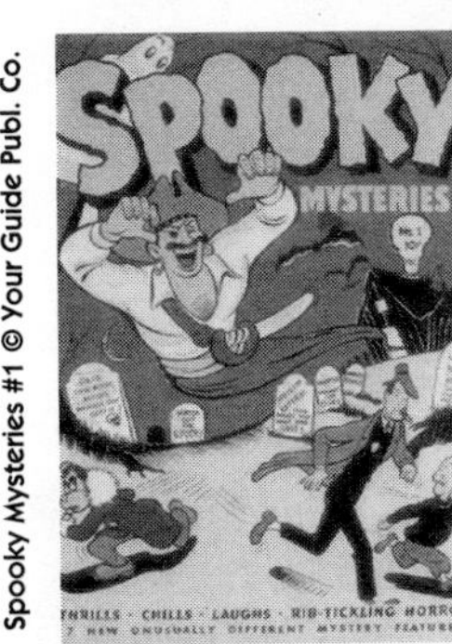

Spooky Mysteries #1 © Your Guide Publ. Co.

GD2.0 FN6.0 NM9.4

Kitchen Sink Press: May, 1992 - No. 10, Dec, 1993 ($2.95, B&W, high quality paper)

1-10: 1-r/sections 6/2/40(origin)-6/23/40 (all 1940s) 3.00

SPIRITMAN (Also see Three Comics)
No publisher listed: No date (1944) (10¢)
(Triangle Sales Co. ad on back cover)

1-Three 16pg. Spirit sections bound together, (1944, 10¢, 52 pgs.) 20.00 60.00 140.00
2-Two Spirit sections (3/26/44, 4/2/44) bound together; by Lou Fine 17.00 51.00 120.00

SPIRIT OF THE BORDER (See Zane Grey & Four Color #197)

SPIRIT OF THE TAO
Image Comics (Top Cow): Jun, 1998 - Present ($2.50)

Preview 5.00
1-8: 1-D-Tron-s/Tan & D-Tron-a 2.50

SPIRIT OF WONDER (Manga)
Dark Horse Comics: Apr, 1996 - No. 5, Aug, 1996 ($2.95, B&W, limited series)

1-5 3.00

SPIRIT WORLD (Magazine)
National Periodical Publications: Fall, 1971 (B&W)

1-New Kirby-a; Neal Adams-c; poster inside 5.00 15.00 55.00
(1/2 price without poster)

SPITFIRE
Malverne Herald (Elliot)(J. R. Mahon): No. 132, 1944 (Aug) - No. 133, 1945
(Female undercover agent)

132,133: Both have Classics Gift Box ads on b/c with checklist to #20 24.00 73.00 170.00

SPITFIRE AND THE TROUBLESHOOTERS
Marvel Comics: Oct, 1986 - No. 9, June, 1987 (Codename: Spitfire #10 on)

1-9: 4-McFarlane-a 2.00

SPITFIRE COMICS (Also see Double Up)
Harvey Publications: Aug, 1941 - No. 2, Oct, 1941 (Pocket size; 100 pgs.)

1-Origin The Clown, The Fly-Man, The Spitfire & The Magician From Bagdad 72.00 216.00 575.00
2 62.00 187.00 500.00

SPLITTING IMAGE
Image Comics: Mar, 1993 - No. 2, 1993 ($1.95)

1,2-Simpson-c/a; parody comic 2.00

SPOOF
Marvel Comics Group: Oct, 1970; No. 2, Nov, 1972 - No. 5, May, 1973

1-Infinity-c; Dark Shadows-c & parody 1.85 5.50 15.00
2-5: 3-Beatles, Osmond's, Jackson 5, David Cassidy, Nixon & Agnew-c. 5-Rod Serling, Woody Allen, Ted Kennedy-c 1.25 3.75 10.00

SPOOK (Formerly Shock Detective Cases)
Star Publications: No. 22, Jan, 1953 - No. 30, Oct, 1954

22-Sgt. Spook-r; acid in face story; hanging-c 36.00 107.00 250.00
23,25,27: 25-Jungle Lil-r. 27-Two Sgt. Spook-r 25.00 75.00 175.00
24-Used in **SOTI**, pgs. 182,183-r/Inside Crime #2; Transvestism story 27.00 81.00 190.00
26,28-30: 26-Disbrow-a. 28,29-Rulah app. 29-Jo-Jo app. 30-Disbrow-c/a(2); only Star-c 25.00 75.00 175.00

NOTE: *L. B. Cole covers-all issues; a-28(1 pg.). **Disbrow** a-26(2), 28, 29(2), 30(2); No. 30 r/Blue Bolt Weird Tales #114.*

SPOOK COMICS
Baily Publications/Star: 1946

1-Mr. Lucifer story 27.00 81.00 190.00

SPOOKY (The Tuff Little Ghost; see Casper The Friendly Ghost)
Harvey Publications: 11/55 - 139, 11/73; No. 140, 7/74 - No. 155, 3/77; No. 156, 12/77 - No. 158, 4/78; No. 159, 9/78; No. 160, 10/79; No. 161, 9/80

1-Nightmare begins (see Casper #19) 34.00 102.00 340.00
2 16.00 48.00 160.00
3-10(1956-57) 9.50 28.50 95.00
11-20(1957-58) 5.00 15.00 50.00
21-40(1958-59) 3.20 9.60 32.00
41-60 2.20 6.60 22.00
61-80,100 1.80 5.40 18.00
81-99 1.60 4.80 16.00
101-120 1.00 3.00 10.00
121-126,133-140 .90 2.70 8.00
127-132: All 52 pg. Giants 1.20 3.60 12.00
141-161 5.00

SPOOKY
Harvey Comics: Nov, 1991 - No. 4, Sept, 1992 ($1.00/$1.25)

1 3.00
2-4: 3-Begin $1.25-c 2.00
...Digest 1-3 (10/92, 6/93, 10/93, $1.75, 100 pgs.)-Casper, Wendy, etc. 4.00

SPOOKY HAUNTED HOUSE
Harvey Publications: Oct, 1972 - No. 15, Feb, 1975

1 2.60 7.80 26.00
2-5 1.40 4.20 14.00
6-10 1.10 3.30 9.00
11-15 1.00 2.80 7.00

SPOOKY MYSTERIES
Your Guide Publ. Co.: No date (1946) (10¢)

1-Mr. Spooky, Super Snooper, Pinky, Girl Detective app. 19.00 56.00 130.00

SPOOKY SPOOKTOWN
Harvey Publ.: 9/61; No. 2, 9/62 - No. 52, 12/73; No. 53, 10/74 - No. 66, 12/76

1-Casper, Spooky; 68 pgs. begin 15.00 45.00 150.00
2 7.50 22.50 75.00
3-5 5.00 15.00 50.00
6-10 3.50 10.50 35.00
11-20 2.50 7.50 25.00
21-39: 39-Last 68 pg. issue 2.00 6.00 20.00
40-45: All 52 pgs. 1.40 4.20 14.00
46-66: 61-Hot Stuff/Spooky team-up story 1.00 2.80 7.00

SPORT COMICS (Becomes True Sport Picture Stories #5 on)
Street & Smith Publications: Oct, 1940 (No mo.) - No. 4, Nov, 1941

1-Life story of Lou Gehrig 51.00 154.00 410.00
2 30.00 90.00 210.00
3,4 26.00 77.00 180.00

SPORT LIBRARY (See Charlton Sport Library)

SPORTS ACTION (Formerly Sport Stars)
Marvel/Atlas Comics (ACI No. 2,3/SAI No. 4-14): No. 2, Feb, 1950 - No. 14, Sept, 1952

2-Powell painted-c; George Gipp life story 34.00 103.00 240.00
1-(nd,no price, no publ., 52pgs, #1 on-c; has same-c as #2; blank inside-c (giveaway?) 19.00 58.00 135.00
3-Everett-a 21.00 64.00 150.00
4-11,14: Weiss-a 19.00 58.00 135.00
12,13: 12-Everett-c. 13-Krigstein-a 21.00 64.00 150.00

NOTE: *Title may have changed after No. 3, to Crime Must Lose No. 4 on, due to publisher change. **Sol Brodsky** c-4-7, 13, 14. **Maneely** c-3, 8-11.*

SPORT STARS
Parents' Magazine Institute (Sport Stars): Feb-Mar, 1946 - No. 4, Aug-Sept, 1946 (Half comic, half photo magazine)

1- "How Tarzan Got That Way" story of Johnny Weissmuller 39.00 116.00 270.00
2-Baseball greats 24.00 73.00 170.00
3,4 21.00 64.00 150.00

SPORT STARS (Becomes Sports Action #2 on)

Spotlight Comics #3 © CHES

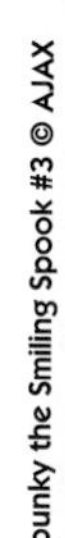
Spunky the Smiling Spook #3 © AJAX

Spy Smasher #4 © FAW

	GD2.0	FN6.0	NM9.4
Marvel Comics (ACI): Nov, 1949 (52 pgs.)			
1-Knute Rockne; painted-c	34.00	103.00	240.00
SPORT THRILLS (Formerly Dick Cole; becomes Jungle Thrills #16)			
Star Publications: No. 11, Nov, 1950 - No. 15, Nov, 1951			
11-Dick Cole begins, ends #13?; Ted Williams & Ty Cobb life stories	29.00	86.00	200.00
12-Joe DiMaggio, Phil Rizzuto stories & photos on-c; L.B. Cole-c/a	23.00	69.00	160.00
13-15-All L. B. Cole-c. 13-Jackie Robinson, Pee Wee Reese stories & photo on-c. 14-Johnny Weissmuler life story	23.00	69.00	160.00
Accepted Reprint #11 (#15 on-c, nd); L.B. Cole-c	7.50	22.50	45.00
Accepted Reprint #12 (nd); L.B. Cole-c; Joe DiMaggio & Phil Rizzuto life stories-r/#12	7.50	22.50	45.00
SPOTLIGHT (TV) (newsstand sales only)			
Marvel Comics Group: Sept, 1978 - No. 4, Mar, 1979 (Hanna-Barbera)			
1-Huckleberry Hound, Yogi Bear; Shaw-a	2.50	7.50	20.00
2,4: 2-Quick Draw McGraw, Augie Doggie, Snooper & Blabber. 4-Magilla Gorilla, Snagglepuss	1.75	5.25	14.00
3-The Jetsons; Yakky Doodle	2.50	7.50	20.00
SPOTLIGHT COMICS (Becomes Red Seal Comics #14 on?)			
Harry 'A' Chesler (Our Army, Inc.): Nov, 1944 - No. 3, 1945			
1-The Black Dwarf (cont'd in Red Seal?), The Veiled Avenger, & Barry Kuda begin; Tuska-c	59.00	178.00	475.00
2	50.00	150.00	400.00
3-Injury to eye story (reprinted from Scoop #3)	51.00	154.00	410.00
SPOTTY THE PUP (Becomes Super Pup #4, see Television Puppet Show)			
Avon Periodicals/Realistic Comics: No. 2, Oct-Nov, 1953 - No. 3, Dec-Jan, 1953-54 (Also see Funny Tunes)			
2,3	4.25	13.00	26.00
nn (1953, Realistic-r)	2.80	7.00	14.00
SPUNKY (...Junior Cowboy)(...Comics #2 on)			
Standard Comics: April, 1949 - No. 7, Nov, 1951			
1,2-Text illos by Frazetta	8.35	25.00	50.00
3-7	4.00	12.00	24.00
SPUNKY THE SMILING SPOOK			
Ajax/Farrell (World Famous Comics/Four Star Comic Corp.): Aug, 1957 - No. 4, May, 1958			
1-Reprints from Frisky Fables	8.35	25.00	50.00
2-4	5.00	15.00	30.00
SPY AND COUNTERSPY (Becomes Spy Hunters #3 on)			
American Comics Group: Aug-Sept, 1949 - No. 2, Oct-Nov, 1949 (52 pgs.)			
1-Origin, 1st app. Jonathan Kent, Counterspy	23.00	69.00	160.00
2	15.00	45.00	105.00
SPY CASES (Formerly The Kellys)			
Marvel/Atlas Comics (Hercules Publ.): No. 26, Sept, 1950 - No. 19, Oct, 1953			
26 (#1)	21.00	64.00	150.00
27(#2),28(#3, 2/51): 27-Everett-a; bondage-c	13.00	39.00	90.00
4(4/51) - 7,9,10	11.00	33.00	75.00
8-A-Bomb-c/story	12.00	36.00	85.00
11-19: 10-14-War format	10.00	30.00	60.00

NOTE: ***Sol Brodsky** c-1-5, 8, 9, 11-14, 17, 18. **Maneely** a-8; c-7, 10. **Tuska** a-7.*

	GD2.0	FN6.0	NM9.4
SPY FIGHTERS			
Marvel/Atlas Comics (CSI): March, 1951 - No. 15, July, 1953 (Cases from official records)			
1-Clark Mason begins; Tuska-a; Brodsky-c	23.00	69.00	160.00
2-Tuska-a	12.00	36.00	85.00
3-13: 3-5-Brodsky-c. 7-Heath-c	11.00	33.00	75.00
14,15-Pakula-a(3), Ed Win-a. 15-Brodsky-c	11.50	34.00	80.00
SPY-HUNTERS (Formerly Spy & Counterspy)			
American Comics Group: No. 3, Dec-Jan, 1949-50 - No. 24, June-July, 1953 (#3-14: 52 pgs.)			
3-Jonathan Kent continues, ends #10	22.00	66.00	155.00
4-10: 4,8,10-Starr-a	12.00	36.00	85.00
11-15,17-22,24: 18-War-c begin. 21-War-c/stories begin	10.00	30.00	65.00
16-Williamson-a (9 pgs.)	15.00	45.00	105.00
23-Graphic torture, injury to eye panel	20.00	60.00	140.00

NOTE: ***Drucker** a-12. **Whitney** a-many issues; c-7, 8, 10-12, 15, 16.*

	GD2.0	FN6.0	NM9.4
SPYMAN (Top Secret Adventures on cover)			
Harvey Publications (Illustrated Humor): Sept, 1966 - No. 3, Feb, 1967 (12¢)			
1-Origin and 1st app. of Spyman. Steranko-a(p)-1st pro work; 1 pg. Neal Adams ad; Tuska-c/a, Crandall-a(i)	5.00	15.00	50.00
2-Simon-c; Steranko-a(p)	3.50	10.50	35.00
3-Simon-c	3.20	9.60	32.00
SPY SMASHER (See Mighty Midget, Whiz & Xmas Comics) (Also see Crime Smasher)			
Fawcett Publications: Fall, 1941 - No. 11, Feb, 1943			
1-Spy Smasher begins; silver metallic-c	333.00	1000.00	3000.00
2-Raboy-c	162.00	487.00	1300.00
3,4: 3-Bondage-c. 4-Irvin Steinberg-c	106.00	319.00	850.00
5-7: Raboy-a; 6-Raboy-c/a. 7-Part photo-c (movie).	97.00	291.00	775.00
8,11	78.00	234.00	625.00
9-Hitler, Tojo, Mussolini-c.	87.00	262.00	700.00
10-Hitler-c	84.00	253.00	675.00
SPY THRILLERS (Police Badge No. 479 #5)			
Atlas Comics (PrPI): Nov, 1954 - No. 4, May, 1955			
1-Brodsky c-1,2	20.00	60.00	140.00
2-Last precode (1/55)	11.50	34.00	80.00
3,4	10.00	30.00	65.00
SQUADRON SUPREME (Also see Marvel Graphic Novel)			
Marvel Comics Group: Aug, 1985 - No. 12, Aug, 1986 (Maxi-series)			
1-Double size			3.00
2-12			2.00
TPB ($24.99) r/#1-12; Alex Ross painted-c; printing inks contain some of the cremated remains of late writer Mark Gruenwald			25.00
TPB-2nd printing ($24.99): Inks contain no ashes			25.00
SQUADRON SUPREME: NEW WORLD ORDER			
Marvel Comics: Sept, 1998 ($5.99, one-shot)			
1-Wraparound-c; Kaminski-s			6.00
SQUALOR			
First Comics: Dec, 1989 - Aug, 1990 ($2.75, limited series)			
1-4: Sutton-a			2.75
SQUEE			
Slave Labor Graphics: Apr, 1997 - No. 4, May, 1998 ($2.95, B&W)			
1-4: Jhonen Vasquez-s/a in all			3.00
SQUEEKS (Also see Boy Comics)			
Lev Gleason Publications: Oct, 1953 - No. 5, June, 1954			
1-Funny animal; Biro-c; Crimebuster's pet monkey "Squeeks" begins	7.50	22.50	45.00
2-Biro-c	4.00	12.00	24.00
3-5: 3-Biro-c	4.00	10.00	20.00
S.R. BISSETTE'S SPIDERBABY COMIX			
SpiderBaby Grafix: Aug, 1996 - No. 2 ($3.95, B&W, magazine size)			
Preview-(8/96, $3.95)-Graphic violence & nudity; Laurel & Hardy app.			4.00
1,2			4.00
S.R. BISSETTE'S TYRANT			
SpiderBaby Grafix: Sept, 1994 - No. 4 ($2.95, B&W)			
1-4			4.00

STAINLESS STEEL RAT

Stalker #1 © DC

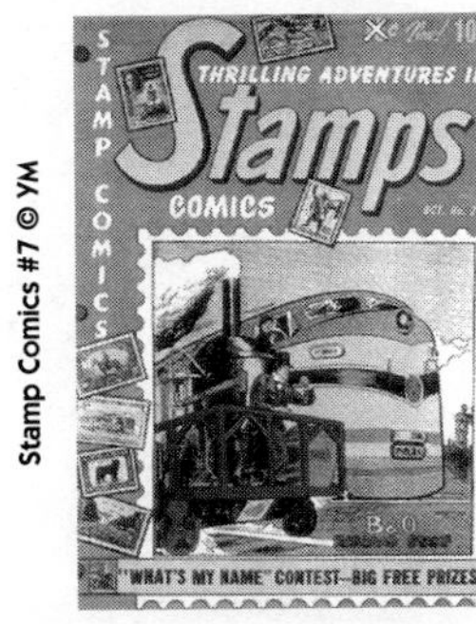

Stamp Comics #7 © YM

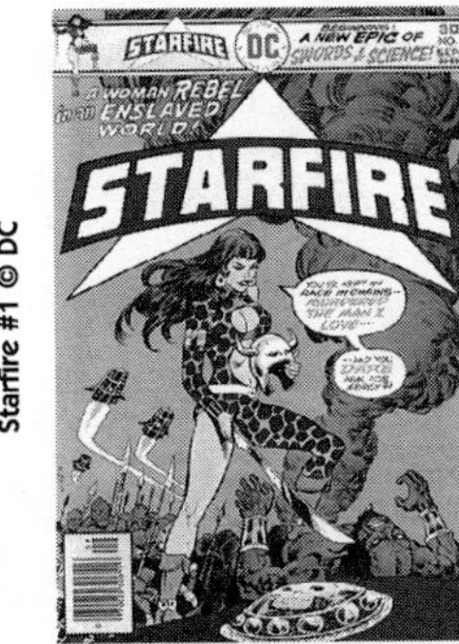

Starfire #1 © DC

	GD2.0	FN6.0	NM9.4

Eagle Comics: Oct, 1985 - No. 6, Mar, 1986 (Limited series)

1 (52 pgs.; $2.25-c)			2.50
2-6 ($1.50)			2.00

STALKER (Also see All Star Comics 1999 and crossover issues)
National Periodical Publications: June-July, 1975 - No. 4, Dec-Jan, 1975-76

1-Origin & 1st app; Ditko/Wood-c/a	1.00	3.00	8.00
2-4-Ditko/Wood-c/a			5.00

STALKERS
Marvel Comics (Epic Comics): Apr, 1990 - No. 12, Mar, 1991 ($1.50)

1-12: 1-Chadwick-c			2.00

STAMP COMICS (Stamps... on-c; Thrilling Adventures In...#8)
Youthful Magazines/Stamp Comics, Inc.: Oct, 1951 - No. 7, Oct, 1952

1-(15¢) ('Stamps' on indicia No. 1-3,5,7)	29.00	86.00	200.00
2	16.00	47.00	110.00
3-6: 3,4-Kiefer, Wildey-a	14.00	43.00	100.00
7-Roy Krenkel (4 pgs.)	17.00	51.00	120.00

NOTE: *Promotes stamp collecting; gives stories behind various commemorative stamps. No. 2, 10¢ printed over 15¢ c-price.* ***Kiefer*** *a-1-7.* ***Kirkel*** *a-1-6.* ***Napoli*** *a-2-7.* ***Palais*** *a-2-4, 7.*

STANLEY & HIS MONSTER (Formerly The Fox & the Crow)
National Periodical Publ.: No. 109, Apr-May, 1968 - No. 112, Oct-Nov, 1968

109-112	2.50	7.50	22.00

STANLEY & HIS MONSTER
DC Comics: Feb, 1993 - No. 4, May, 1993 ($1.50, limited series)

1-4			2.00

STAN SHAW'S BEAUTY & THE BEAST
Dark Horse Comics: Nov, 1993 ($4.95, one-shot)

1			5.00

STAR
Image Comics (Highbrow Entertainment): June, 1995 - No. 4, Oct, 1995 ($2.50, limited series)

1-4			2.50

STARBLAST
Marvel Comics: Jan, 1994 - No. 4, Apr, 1994 ($1.75, limited series)

1-4: 1-($2.00, 52 pgs.)-Nova, Quasar, Black Bolt; painted-c			2.00

STAR BLAZERS
Comico: Apr, 1987 - No. 4, July, 1987 ($1.75, limited series)

1-4			3.00

STAR BLAZERS
Comico: 1989 ($1.95/$2.50, limited series)

1-5- Steacy wraparound painted-c on all			3.00

STAR BLAZERS (The Magazine of Space Battleship Yamato)
Argo Press: No. 0, Aug, 1995 - No. 3, Dec, 1995 ($2.95)

0-3			3.00

STAR BRAND
Marvel Comics (New Universe): Oct, 1986 - No. 19, May, 1989 (75¢/$1.25)

1-19: 14-begin $1.25-c. 16-19-Byrne story & art.			2.00
Annual 1 (10/87)			2.00

STARCHILD
Tailspin Press: 1992 - No. 12($2.25/$2.50, B&W)

1,2-('92),0(4/93),3-12: 0-Illos by Chadwick, Eisner, Sim, M. Wagner. 3-(7/93). 4-(11/93). 6-(2/94)			3.00

STARCHILD: MYTHOPOLIS
Image Comics: July, 1997 - Present ($2.95, B&W, limited series)

0-2-James Owen-s/a			3.00

STAR COMICS
Ultem Publ. (Harry 'A' Chesler)/Centaur Publications: Feb, 1937 - V2#7 (No. 23), Aug, 1939 (#1-6: large size)

V1#1-Dan Hastings (s/f) begins	159.00	469.00	1250.00
2	75.00	225.00	600.00
3-6 (#6, 9/37): 4,5-Little Nemo-c/stories	67.00	202.00	540.00
7-9: 8-Severed head centerspread; Impy & Little Nemo by Winsor McCay Jr, Popeye app. by Bob Wood; Mickey Mouse & Popeye app. as toys in Santa's bag on-c; X-Mas-c	59.00	176.00	470.00
10 (1st Centaur; 3/38)-Impy by Winsor McCay Jr; Don Marlow by Guardineer begins	81.00	244.00	650.00
11-1st Jack Cole comic-a, 1 pg. (4/38)	59.00	176.00	470.00
12-15: 12-Riders of the Golden West begins; Little Nemo app. 15-Speed Silvers by Gustavson & The Last Pirate by Burgos begins	51.00	154.00	410.00
16 (12/38)-The Phantom Rider & his horse Thunder begins, ends V2#6	52.00	157.00	420.00
V2#1(#17, 2/39)-Phantom Rider-c (only non-funny-c)	52.00	157.00	420.00
2-7(#18-23): 2-Diana Deane by Tarpe Mills app. 3-Drama of Hollywood by Mills begins. 7-Jungle Queen app.	45.00	135.00	360.00

NOTE: ***Biro*** *c-6, 9, 10.* ***Burgos*** *a-15, 16, V2#1-7.* ***Ken Ernst*** *a-10, 12, 14.* ***Filchock*** *c-15, 18, 22.* ***Gill Fox*** *c-14, 19.* ***Guardineer*** *a-6, 8-14.* ***Gustavson*** *a-13-16, V2#1-7.* ***Winsor McCay*** *c-4, 5.* ***Tarpe Mills*** *a-15, V2#1-7.* ***Schwab*** *c-20, 23.* ***Bob Wood*** *a-10, 12, 13; c-7, 8.*

STAR COMICS MAGAZINE
Marvel Comics (Star Comics): Dec, 1986 - No. 13, 1988 ($1.50, digest-size)

1,9-Spider-Man-c/s	1.00	3.00	8.00
2-8-Heathcliff, Ewoks, Top Dog, Madballs-r in #1-13		2.40	6.00
10-13	1.00	2.80	7.00

S.T.A.R. CORPS
DC Comics: Nov, 1993 - No. 6, Apr, 1994 ($1.50, limited series)

1-6: 1,2-Austin-c(i). 1-Superman app.			2.00

STAR CROSSED
DC Comics (Helix): June, 1997 - No. 3, Aug, 1997 ($2.50, limited series)

1-3-Matt Howarth-s/a			2.50

STARDUST (See Neil Gaiman and Charles Vess' Stardust)

STAR FEATURE COMICS
I. W. Enterprises: 1963

Reprint #9-Stunt-Man Stetson-r/Feat. Comics #141	1.00	2.80	7.00

STARFIRE (Not the Teen Titans character)
National Periodical Publ./DC Comics: Aug-Sept, 1976 - No. 8, Oct-Nov, 1977

1-Origin (CCA stamp fell off cover art; so it was approved by code)	1.00	3.00	8.00
2-8			5.00

STARGATE (Movie)
Entity Comics: July, 1996 - No. 4, Oct, 1996 ($2.95, limited series)

1-4: Based on film			3.00
1-4-($3.50): Special Edition foil-c			3.50

STARGATE: DOOMSDAY WORLD (Movie)
Entity Comics: Nov, 1996 - No. 3, Jan, 1997 ($2.95, limited series)

1-3			3.00
1-3-($3.50)-Foil-c			3.50

STARGATE: ONE NATION UNDER RA (Movie)
Entity Comics: Apr, 1997 ($2.75, B&W, one-shot)

1-($2.75)			3.00
1-($3.50)-Foil-c			3.50

STARGATE: REBELLION (Movie)
Entity Comics: May/June, 1997 - No. 3, Nov, 1997 ($2.75, B&W, limited series)

1-3			3.00
1-3-($3.50)-Gold foil-c			3.50

STARGATE: THE NEW ADVENTURES COLLECTION (Movie)
Entity Comics: Dec, 1997 ($5.95, B&W)

1-Regular and photo-c			6.00

Starlet O'Hara #1 © STD

Starman (2nd series) #50 © DC

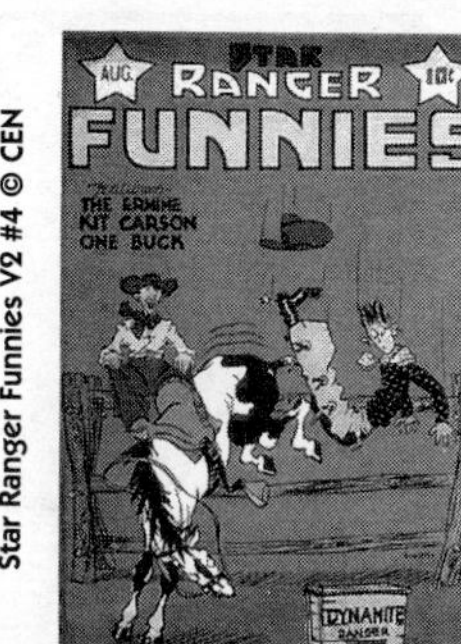

Star Ranger Funnies V2 #4 © CEN

GD2.0 FN6.0 NM9.4

STARGATE: UNDERWORLD (Movie)
Entity Comics: May, 1997 ($2.75, B&W, one-shot)

1 — 3.00

STAR HUNTERS (See DC Super Stars #16)
National Periodical Publ./DC Comics: Oct-Nov, 1977 - No. 7, Oct-Nov, 1978

1,7: 1-Newton-a(p). 7-44 pgs. — 6.00
2-6 — 4.00

NOTE: ***Buckler** a-4-7p; c-1-7p. **Layton** a-1-5i; c-1-6i. **Nasser** a-3p. **Sutton** a-6i.*

STARJAMMERS (See X-Men Spotlight on Starjammers)

STARJAMMERS (Also see Uncanny X-Men)
Marvel Comics: Oct, 1995 - No. 4, Jan, 1996 ($2.95, limited series)

1-4: Foil-c; Ellis scripts — 3.00

STARK TERROR
Stanley Publications: Dec, 1970 - No. 5, Aug, 1971 (B&W, magazine, 52 pgs.)

	GD2.0	FN6.0	NM9.4
1-Bondage, torture-c	4.00	12.00	40.00
2-4 (Gillmor/Aragon-r)	2.50	7.50	22.00
5 (ACG-r)	2.25	6.75	18.00

STARLET O'HARA IN HOLLYWOOD (Teen-age) (Also see Cookie)
Standard Comics: Dec, 1948 - No. 4, Sept, 1949

	GD2.0	FN6.0	NM9.4
1-Owen Fitzgerald-a in all	17.00	51.00	120.00
2	11.50	34.00	80.00
3,4	10.00	30.00	70.00

STAR-LORD THE SPECIAL EDITION (Also see Marvel Comics Super Special #10, Marvel Premiere & Preview & Marvel Spotlight V2#6,7)
Marvel Comics Group: Feb, 1982 (one-shot, direct sales)
(1st Baxter paper comic)

1-Byrne/Austin-a; Austin-c; 8 pgs. of new-a by Golden (p); Dr. Who story by Dave Gibbons; 1st deluxe format comic — 5.00

STARLORD
Marvel Comics: Dec, 1996 - No. 3, Feb, 1997 ($2.50, limited series)

1-3-Timothy Zahn-s — 2.50

STARLORD MEGAZINE
Marvel Comics: Nov, 1996 ($2.95, one-shot)

1-Reprints w/preview of new series — 3.00

STARMAN (1st Series) (Also see Justice League & War of the Gods)
DC Comics: Oct, 1988 - No. 45, Apr, 1992 ($1.00)

1-25,27-45: 1-Origin. 4-Intro The Power Elite. 9,10,34-Batman app. 14-Superman app. 17-Power Girl app. 27-Starman (David Knight) app. 28-Starman disguised as Superman; leads into Superman #50. 38-War of the Gods x-over. 42-Lobo cameo.42-45-Eclipso-c/stories (#43,44 with Lobo) — 2.50
26-Ist app. David Knight (G.A.Starman's son). — 5.00

STARMAN (2nd Series) (Also see The Golden Age, Showcase 95 #12, Showcase 96 #4,5)
DC Comics : No. 0, Oct, 1994 - Present ($1.95/$2.25/$2.50)

0,1: 0-James Robinson scripts, Tony Harris-c/a(p) & Wade Von Grawbadger-a(i) begins; Sins of the Father storyline begins, ends #3; 1st app. new Starman (Jack Knight); reintro of the G.A. Mist & G.A. Shade; 1st app. Nash; David Knight dies — 1.10 — 3.30 — 9.00
2-7: 2-Reintro Charity from Forbidden Tales of Dark Mansion. 3-Reintro/2nd app "Blue" Starman (1st app. in 1st Issue Special #12); Will Payton app. (both cameos). 5-David Knight app. 6-The Shade "Times Past" story; Teddy Kristiansen-a. 7-The Black Pirate cameo — 1.00 — 2.80 — 7.00
8-17: 8-Begin $2.25-c. 10-1st app. new Mist (Nash). 11-JSA "Times Past" story; Matt Smith-a. 12-Sins of the Child storyline begins, ends #16. 17-The Black Pirate app. — 4.00
18-37: 18-G.A. Starman "Times Past" story; Watkiss-a. 19-David Knight app. 20-23-G.A. Sandman app. 24-26-Demon Quest; all 3 covers make-up triptych. 33-36-Batman-c/app. 37-David Knight and deceased JSA members app. — 3.00
38-49,51-56: 38-Nash vs. Justice League Europe. 39,40-Crossover w/ Power of Shazam! #35,36; Bulletman app. 42-Demon-c/app. 43-JLA-c/app. 44-Phantom Lady-c/app. 46-Gena Ha-a. 51-Jor-el app. 52,53-Adam Strange-c/app. — 2.50
50-($3.95) Gold foil logo on-c; Star Boy (LSH) app. — 4.00
57-60: Painted covers by Harris and Alex Ross — 2.50
#1,000,000 (11/98) 853rd Century x-over; Snejbjerg-a — 2.50
Annual 1 (1996, $3.50)-Legends of the Dead Earth story; Prince Gavyn & G.A. Starman stories; J.H. Williams III, Bret Blevins, Craig Hamilton-c/a(p) — 4.00
Annual 2 (1997, $3.95)-Pulp Heroes story; — 4.00
...80 Page Giant (1/99, $4.95) Harris-c — 5.00
...Secret Files 1 (4/98, $4.95)-Origin stories and profile pages — 5.00
...The Mist (6/98, $1.95) Girlfrenzy; Mary Marvel app. — 2.00
Night and Day-($14.95, TPB)-r/#7-10,12-16 — 15.00
Sins of the Father-($12.95, TPB)-r/#0-5 — 13.00
Times Past-($17.95, TPB)-r/stories of other Starmen — 18.00

STARMASTERS
Americomics: Mar, 1984 ($1.50, one-shot)

1-Origin The Women of W.O.S.P. & Breed — 2.00

STAR PRESENTATION, A (Formerly My Secret Romance #1,2; Spectacular Stories #4 on) (Also see This Is Suspense)
Fox Features Syndicate (Hero Books): No. 3, May, 1950

3-Dr. Jekyll & Mr. Hyde by Wood & Harrison (reprinted in Startling Terror Tales #10); "The Repulsing Dwarf" by Wood; Wood-c — 51.00 — 154.00 — 410.00

STAR QUEST COMIX (Warren Presents... on cover)
Warren Publications: Oct, 1978

1-Corben, Maroto, Neary-a; Ken Kelly-c — 1.50 — 4.50 — 12.00

STAR RAIDERS (See DC Graphic Novel #1)

STAR RANGER (Cowboy Comics #13 on)
Ultem Publ./Centaur Publ.: Feb, 1937 - No. 12, May, 1938 (Large size: No. 1-6)

1-(1st Western comic)-Ace & Deuce, Air Plunder; Creig Flessel-a — 169.00 — 506.00 — 1350.00
2 — 78.00 — 234.00 — 625.00
3-6 — 69.00 — 206.00 — 550.00
7-9: 8(12/37)-Christmas-c; Air Patrol, Gold coast app.; Guardineer centerfold — 53.00 — 159.00 — 425.00
V2#10 (1st Centaur; 3/38) — 84.00 — 253.00 — 675.00
11,12 — 62.00 — 187.00 — 500.00

NOTE: ***J. Cole** a-10, 12; c-12. **Ken Ernst** a-11. **Gill Fox** a-8(illo), 9, 10. **Guardineer** a-1, 3, 6, 7, 8(illos), 9, 10, 12. **Gustavson** a-8-10, 12. **Fred Schwab** c-2-11. **Bob Wood** a-8-10.*

STAR RANGER FUNNIES (Formerly Cowboy Comics)
Centaur Publications: V1#15, Oct, 1938 - V2#5, Oct, 1939

V1#15-Lyin Lou, Ermine, Wild West Junior, The Law of Caribou County by Eisner, Cowboy Jake, The Plugged Dummy, Spurs by Gustavson, Red Coat, Two Buckaroos & Trouble Hunters begin — 97.00 — 291.00 — 775.00
V2#1 (1/39) — 70.00 — 210.00 — 560.00
2-5: 2-Night Hawk by Gustavson. 4-Kit Carson app. — 59.00 — 176.00 — 470.00

NOTE: ***Jack Cole** a-V2#1, 3; c-V2#1. **Filchock** c-V2#2, 3. **Guardineer** a-V2#3. **Gustavson** a-V2#2. **Pinajian** c/a-V2#5.*

STAR REACH
Star Reach Publ.: Apr, 1974 - No. 18 (B&W, #12-15 w/color)

	GD2.0	FN6.0	NM9.4
1-(52 pgs.) Art by Starlin, Simonson, Chaykin	1.50	4.50	12.00
1-2nd, 3th, and 4th printings			4.00
2-11: 2-Adams, Giordano-a. 6-Elric-c. 7-BWS-c		2.40	6.00
2-2nd printing			3.00
12-15 (44 pgs.), 16-18: 17,18-Magazine size	1.00	3.00	8.00

STAR REACH CLASSICS
Eclipse Comics: Mar, 1984 - No. 6, Aug, 1984 ($1.50, Baxter paper)

1-6: 1-Neal Adams-r/Star Reach #1 — 2.00

NOTE: ***Dave Sim** a-1. **Starlin** a-1.*

Stars and S.T.R.I.P.E. #1 © DC

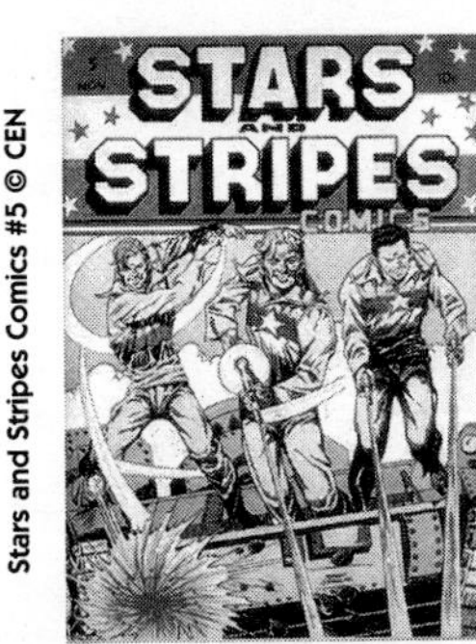

Stars and Stripes Comics #5 © CEN

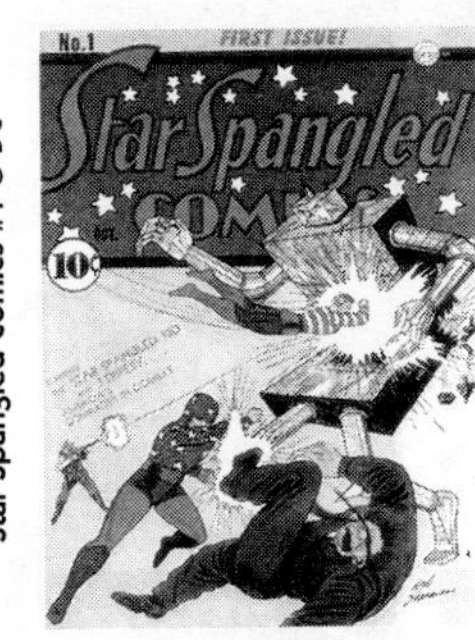

Star Spangled Comics #1 © DC

GD2.0 FN6.0 NM9.4

STARR FLAGG, UNDERCOVER GIRL (See Undercover...)

STARRIORS
Marvel Comics: Aug, 1984 - Feb, 1985 (Limited series) (Based on Tomy toys)

1-4 2.00

STARS AND S.T.R.I.P.E. (Also see JSA)
DC Comics: July, 1999 - Present ($2.95/$2.50)

0-($2.95) Moder and Weston-a; Starman app. 3.00
1-Johns and Robinson-s/Moder-a; origin new Star Spangled Kid 2.50
2-4: 4-Marvel Family app. 2.50

STARS AND STRIPES COMICS
Centaur Publications: No. 2, May, 1941 - No. 6, Dec, 1941

2(#1)-The Shark, The Iron Skull, A-Man, The Amazing Man, Mighty Man, Minimidget begin; The Voice & Dash Dartwell, the Human Meteor, Reef Kinkaid app.; Gustavson Flag-c 212.00 637.00 1700.00
3-Origin Dr. Synthe; The Black Panther app. 122.00 366.00 975.00
4-Origin/1st app. The Stars and Stripes; injury to eye-c 109.00 328.00 875.00
5(#5 on cover & inside) 75.00 225.00 600.00
5(#6)-(#5 on cover, #6 on inside) 75.00 225.00 600.00
NOTE: ***Gustavson** c/a-3. **Myron Strauss** c-4, 5(#5), 5(#6).*

STAR SEED (Formerly Powers That Be)
Broadway Comics: No. 7, 1996 - No. 9 ($2.95)

7-9 3.00

STARSHIP TROOPERS
Dark Horse Comics: 1997 - No. 2, 1997 ($2.95, limited series)

1,2-Movie adaption 3.00

STARSHIP TROOPERS: BRUTE CREATIONS
Dark Horse Comics: 1997 ($2.95, one-shot)

1 3.00

STARSHIP TROOPERS: DOMINANT SPECIES
Dark Horse Comics: Aug, 1998 - No. 4, Nov, 1998 ($2.95, limited series)

1-4-Strnad-s/Bolton-c 3.00

STARSHIP TROOPERS: INSECT TOUCH
Dark Horse Comics: 1997 - No. 3, 1997 ($2.95, limited series)

1-3 3.00

STAR SLAMMERS (See Marvel Graphic Novel #6)
Malibu Comics (Bravura): May, 1994 - No. 4, Aug, 1994 ($2.50, unfinished limited series)

1-4: W. Simonson-a/stories; contain Bravura stamps 2.50

STAR SLAMMERS SPECIAL
Dark Horse Comics (Legend): June, 1996 ($2.95, one-shot)

nn-Simonson-c/a/scripts; concludes Bravura limited series. 3.00

STARSLAYER
Pacific Comics/First Comics No. 7 on: Feb, 1982 - No. 6, Apr, 1983; No. 7, Aug, 1983 - No. 34, Nov, 1985

1-Origin & 1st app.; excessive blood & gore; 1 pg. Rocketeer cameo which continues in #2 5.00
2-Origin/1st full app. the Rocketeer (4/82) by Dave Stevens (Chapter 1 of Rocketeer saga; see Pacific Presents #1,2) 1.00 3.00 8.00
3-Chapter 2 of Rocketeer saga by Stevens 2.40 6.00
4,6,7: 7-Grell-a ends 3.00
5-2nd app. Groo the Wanderer by Aragones 2.40 6.00
8-34: 10-1st app. Grimjack (11/83, ends #17). 18-Starslayer meets Grimjack. 20-The Black Flame begins (9/84, 1st app.), ends #33. 27-Book length Black Flame story 2.00
NOTE: ***Grell** a-1-7; c-1-8. **Stevens** back c-2, 3. **Sutton** a-17p, 20-22p, 24-27p, 29-33p.*

STARSLAYER (The Director's Cut)
Acclaim Comics (Windjammer): June, 1994 - No. 8, Dec, 1995 ($2.50)

1-8: Mike Grell-c/a/scripts 2.50

GD2.0 FN6.0 NM9.4

STAR SPANGLED COMICS (Star Spangled War Stories #131 on)
National Periodical Publications: Oct, 1941 - No. 130, July, 1952

1-Origin/1st app. Tarantula; Captain X of the R.A.F., Star Spangled Kid (see Action #40), Armstrong of the Army begin; Robot-c 410.00 1230.00 4100.00
2 159.00 478.00 1275.00
3-5 100.00 300.00 800.00
6-Last Armstrong/Army; Penniless Palmer begins 62.00 187.00 500.00

GD2.0 FN6.0 VF8.0 NM9.4

7-(4/42)-Origin/1st app. The Guardian by S&K, & Robotman (by Paul Cassidy & created by Siegel);The Newsboy Legion (1st app.), Robotman & TNT begin; last Captain X 600.00 1800.00 3600.00 6300.00

GD2.0 FN6.0 NM9.4

8-Origin TNT & Dan the Dyna-Mite 212.00 637.00 1700.00
9,10 162.00 487.00 1300.00
11-17 119.00 356.00 950.00
18-Origin Star Spangled Kid 150.00 450.00 1200.00
19-Last Tarantula 117.00 351.00 935.00
20-Liberty Belle begins (5/43) 117.00 351.00 935.00
21-29-Last S&K issue; 23-Last TNT. 25-Robotman by Jimmy Thompson begins. 29-Intro Robbie the Robotdog 97.00 291.00 775.00
30-40: 31-S&K-c 50.00 150.00 400.00
41-50: 41,49-Kirby-c 45.00 135.00 360.00
51-64: Last Newsboy Legion & The Guardian; last Liberty Belle? 51-Robot-c by Kirby. 53 by S&K 45.00 135.00 360.00
65-Robin begins with c/app. (2/47); Batman cameo in 1 panel; Robin-c begins, end #95 137.00 412.00 1100.00
66-Batman cameo in Robin story 81.00 244.00 650.00
67,68,70-80: 72-Burnley Robin-c 66.00 197.00 525.00
69-Origin/1st app. Tomahawk by F. Ray; atom bomb story & splash (6/47) 100.00 300.00 800.00
81-Origin Merry, Girl of 1000 Gimmicks in Star Spangled Kid story 50.00 150.00 400.00
82,85: 82-Last Robotman? 50.00 150.00 400.00
83-Tomahawk enters the lost valley, a land of dinosaurs; Capt. Compass begins, ends #130 50.00 150.00 400.00
84,87 (Rare): 87-Batman cameo in Robin 78.00 234.00 625.00
86-Batman cameo in Robin story; last Star Spangled Kid 56.00 169.00 450.00
88(1/49)-94: Batman-c/stories in all. 91-Federal Men begin, end #93. 94-Manhunters Around the World begin, end #121 59.00 178.00 475.00
95-Batman story; last Robin-c 55.00 165.00 440.00
96,98-Batman cameo in Robin stories. 96-1st Tomahawk-c (also #97-121) 40.00 120.00 280.00
97,99 34.00 101.00 235.00
100 (1/50)-Pre-Bat-Hound tryout in Robin story (pre-dates Batman #92). 40.00 120.00 290.00
101-109,118,119,121: 121-Last Tomahawk-c 31.00 92.00 215.00
110,111,120-Batman cameo in Robin stories. 120-Last 52 pg. issue 32.00 96.00 225.00
112-Batman & Robin story 34.00 103.00 240.00
113-Frazetta-a (10 pgs.) 41.00 124.00 330.00
114-Retells Robin's origin (3/51); Batman & Robin story 43.00 128.00 340.00
115,117-Batman app. in Robin stories 34.00 103.00 240.00
116-Flag-c 34.00 101.00 235.00
122-(11/51)-Ghost Breaker-c/stories begin (origin/1st app.), ends #130 (Ghost Breaker covers #122-130) 39.00 116.00 270.00
123-126,128,129 27.00 81.00 190.00
127-Batman cameo 29.00 86.00 200.00
130-Batman cameo in Robin story 30.00 90.00 210.00
NOTE: *Most all issues after #29 signed by Simon & Kirby are not by them. **Bill Ely** c-122-130. **Mortimer** c-65-74(most), 76-95(most). **Fred Ray** c-96-106, 109, 110, 112, 113, 115-120. **S&K** c-7-31, 33, 34, 36, 37, 39, 40, 48, 49, 50-54, 56-58. **Hal Sherman** c-1-6. **Dick Sprang** c-75.*

STAR SPANGLED COMICS (Also see All Star Comics 1999 crossover titles)
DC Comics: May, 1999 ($1.99, one-shot)

Star Spangled War Stories #16 © DC

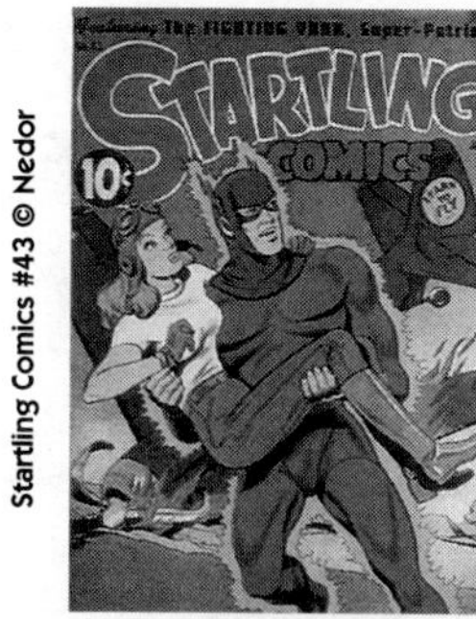

Startling Comics #43 © Nedor

Startling Terror Tales #13 © STAR

GD2.0 FN6.0 NM9.4

1-Golden Age Sandman and the Star Spangled Kid 2.00

STAR SPANGLED KID (See Action #40, Leading Comics & Star Spangled Comics)

STAR SPANGLED WAR STORIES (Formerly Star Spangled Comics #1-130; Becomes The Unknown Soldier #205 on) (See Showcase)
National Periodical Publications: No. 131, 8/52 - No. 133, 10/52; No. 3, 11/52 - No. 204, 2-3/77

	GD2.0	FN6.0	NM9.4
131(#1)	80.00	240.00	850.00
132	58.00	174.00	600.00
133-Used in **POP**, pg. 94	50.00	150.00	490.00
3-6: 4-Devil Dog Dugan app. 6-Evans-a	29.00	87.00	270.00
7-10	23.00	69.00	215.00
11-20	20.00	60.00	190.00
21-30: 30-Last precode (2/55)	17.00	51.00	160.00
31-33,35-40	11.50	34.00	115.00
34-Krigstein-a	12.00	36.00	120.00
41-50: 45-1st DC grey tone-c (5/56). 50-1st S.A. issue	11.00	33.00	110.00
51,52,54-63,65,66, 68-83	7.50	22.50	75.00
53-"Rock Sergeant," 3rd Sgt. Rock prototype; inspired "P.I. & The Sand Fleas" in G.I. Combat #56 (1/57)	12.00	36.00	120.00
64-Pre-Sgt. Rock Easy Co. story (12/57)	10.00	30.00	100.00
67-2 Easy Co. stories without Sgt. Rock	10.50	32.00	105.00
84-Origin Mlle. Marie	16.00	48.00	160.00
85-89-Mlle. Marie in all	9.00	27.00	90.00
90-1st app. "War That Time Forgot" series; dinosaur issue-c/story (4-5/60)	31.00	93.00	350.00
91,93-No dinosaur stories	7.00	21.00	70.00
92-2nd dinosaur-c/s	11.00	33.00	110.00
94 (12/60)- "Ghost Ace" story; Baron Von Richter as The Enemy Ace (pre-dates Our Army... #151)	16.00	48.00	160.00
95-99: Dinosaur-c/s	11.00	33.00	110.00
100-Dinosaur-c/story.	13.00	39.00	130.00
101-115: All dinosaur issues	9.00	27.00	90.00
116-125,127-133,135-137-Last dinosaur story; Heath Birdman-#129,131	8.00	24.00	80.00
126-No dinosaur story	5.50	16.50	55.00
134-Dinosaur story; Neal Adams-a	9.00	27.00	90.00
138-New Enemy Ace-c/stories begin by Joe Kubert (4-5/68), end #150 (also see Our Army at War #151 and Showcase #57)	10.00	30.00	100.00
139-Origin Enemy Ace (7/68)	8.00	24.00	80.00
140-143,145: 145-Last 12¢ issue (6-7/69)	5.00	15.00	50.00
144-Neal Adams/Kubert-a	6.50	19.50	65.00
146-Enemy Ace-c only	3.30	9.90	33.00
147,148-New Enemy Ace stories	4.00	12.00	40.00
149,150-Last new Enemy Ace by Kubert. Viking Prince by Kubert	3.50	10.50	35.00
151-1st solo app. Unknown Soldier (6-7/70); Enemy Ace-r begin (from Our Army at War, Showcase & SSWS); end #161	12.00	36.00	130.00
152,153,155-Enemy Ace reprints	2.50	7.50	20.00
154-Origin Unknown Soldier	9.00	27.00	100.00
156-1st Battle Album; Unknown Soldier story; Kubert-c/a	2.50	7.50	20.00
157-Sgt. Rock x-over in Unknown Soldier story.	2.25	6.75	18.00
158-163-(52 pgs.): New Unknown Soldier stories; Kubert-c/a. 161-Last Enemy Ace-r	1.50	4.50	12.00
164-183,200: 181-183-Enemy Ace vs. Balloon Buster serial app; Frank Thorne-a. 200-Enemy Ace back-up	1.00	3.00	10.00
184-199,201-204	.90	2.70	8.00

NOTE: ***Anderson*** *a-28.* ***Chaykin*** *a-167.* ***Drucker*** *a-59, 61, 64, 66, 67, 73-84.* ***Estrada*** *a-149.* ***John Giunta*** *a-72.* ***Glanzman*** *a-167, 171, 172, 174.* ***Heath*** *a-122, 132, 133; c-67, 122, 132-134.* ***Kaluta*** *a-197i; c-167.* ***G. Kane*** *a-169.* ***Kubert*** *a-6-163(most later issues), 200.* ***Maurer*** *a-160, 165.* ***Severin*** *a-65, 162.* ***S&K*** *c-7-31, 33, 34, 37, 40.* ***Simonson*** *a-170, 172, 174, 180.* ***Sutton*** *a-168.* ***Thorne*** *a-183.* ***Toth*** *a-164.* ***Wildey*** *a-161. Suicide Squad in 110, 116-118, 120, 121, 127.*

STARSTREAM (Adventures in Science Fiction)(See Questar illustrated)
Whitman/Western Publishing Co.: 1976 (79¢, 68 pgs, cardboard-c)

	GD2.0	FN6.0	NM9.4
1-4: 1-Bolle-a. 2-4-McWilliams & Bolle-a	1.25	3.75	10.00

STARSTRUCK
Marvel Comics (Epic Comics): Feb, 1985 - No. 6, Feb, 1986 ($1.50, mature)

1-6: Kaluta-a 3.00

STARSTRUCK
Dark Horse Comics: Aug, 1990 - No. 4, Nov?, 1990 ($2.95, B&W, 52pgs.)

1-3:Kaluta-r/Epic series plus new-c/a in all 3.00
4 (68, pgs.)-contains 2 trading cards 3.00

STAR STUDDED
Cambridge House/Superior Publishers: 1945 (25¢, 132 pgs.); 1945 (196 pgs.)

	GD2.0	FN6.0	NM9.4
nn-Captain Combat by Giunta, Ghost Woman, Commandette, & Red Rogue app.; Infantino-a	30.00	90.00	210.00
nn-The Cadet, Edison Bell, Hoot Gibson, Jungle Lil (196 pgs.); copies vary; Blue Beetle in some	25.00	75.00	175.00

STARTLING COMICS
Better Publications (Nedor): June, 1940 - No. 53, May, 1948

	GD2.0	FN6.0	NM9.4
1-Origin Captain Future-Man Of Tomorrow, Mystico (By Eisner/Fine), The Wonder Man; The Masked Rider & his horse Pinto begins; Masked Rider formerly in pulps; drug use story	225.00	675.00	1800.00
2 -Don Davis, Espionage Ace begins	87.00	262.00	700.00
3	75.00	225.00	600.00
4	56.00	169.00	450.00
5-9	45.00	135.00	360.00
10-The Fighting Yank begins (9/41, origin/1st app.)	311.00	933.00	2800.00
11-2nd app. Fighting Yank	103.00	309.00	825.00
12-Hitler, Hirohito, Mussolini-c	75.00	225.00	600.00
13-15	55.00	165.00	440.00
16-Origin The Four Comrades; not in #32,35	60.00	180.00	480.00
17-Last Masked Rider & Mystico	43.00	128.00	340.00
18-Pyroman begins (12/42, origin)(also see America's Best Comics #3 for 1st app., 11/42)	91.00	272.00	725.00
19	43.00	128.00	340.00
20,21: 20-The Oracle begins (3/43); not in issues 26,28,33,34. 21-Origin The Ape, Oracle's enemy	44.00	132.00	350.00
22-34: 34-Origin The Scarab & only app.	43.00	128.00	340.00
35-Hypodermic syringe attacks Fighting Yank in drug story	44.00	132.00	350.00
36-43: 36-Last Four Comrades. 38-Bondage/torture-c. 40-Last Capt. Future & Oracle. 41-Front Page Peggy begins; A-Bomb-c. 43-Last Pyroman	40.00	120.00	290.00
44,45: 44-Lance Lewis, Space Detective begins; Ingels-c; sci/fi-c begin. 45-Tygra begins (intro/origin, 5/47); Ingels-c/a (splash pg. & inside f/c B&W ad	56.00	169.00	450.00
46-Classic Ingels-c; Ingels-a	75.00	225.00	600.00
47,48,50-53: 50,51-Sea-Eagle app.	52.00	157.00	420.00
49-Classic Schomburg Robot-c; last Fighting Yank	288.00	862.00	2600.00

NOTE: ***Ingels*** *a-44, 45; c-44, 45, 46(wash).* ***Schomburg (Xela)*** *c-21-43; 47-53 (airbrush).* ***Tuska*** *c-45? Bondage c-16, 21, 37, 46-49. Captain Future c-1-9, 13, 14. Fighting Yank c-10-12, 15-17, 21, 22, 24, 26, 28, 30, 32, 34, 36, 38, 40, 42. Pyroman c-18-20, 23, 25, 27, 29, 31, 33, 35, 37, 39, 41, 43.*

STARTLING TERROR TALES
Star Publications: No. 10, May, 1952 - No. 14, Feb, 1953; No. 4, Apr, 1953 - No. 11, 1954

	GD2.0	FN6.0	NM9.4
10-(1st Series)-Wood/Harrison-a (r/A Star Presentation #3) Disbrow/Cole-c; becomes 4 different titles after #10; becomes Confessions of Love #11 on, The Horrors #11 on, Terrifying Tales #11 on, Terrors of the Jungle #11 on & continues w/Startling Terror #11	62.00	187.00	500.00
11-(8/52)-L. B. Cole Spider-c; r-Fox's "A Feature Presentation" #5 (blue-c)	66.00	197.00	525.00
11-Black-c (variant; believed to be a pressrun change) (Unique)	91.00	272.00	725.00
12,14	25.00	75.00	175.00
13-Jo-Jo-r; Disbrow-a	26.00	79.00	185.00
4-9,11(1953-54) (2nd Series): 11-New logo	21.00	64.00	150.00

Star Trek #28 © Paramount

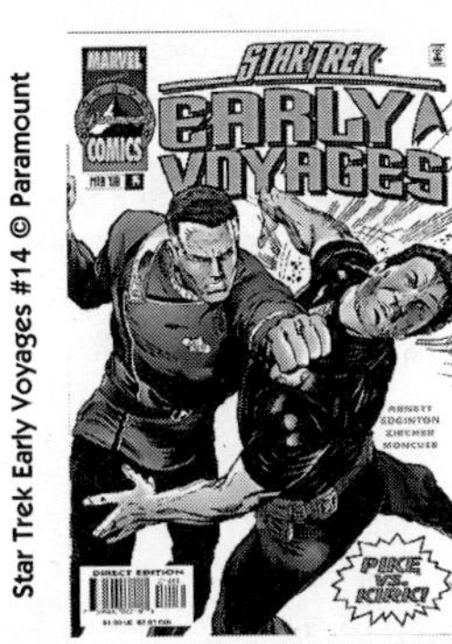

Star Trek Early Voyages #14 © Paramount

Star Trek: Deep Space Nine #4 © Paramount

	GD2.0	FN6.0	NM9.4
10-Disbrow-a	25.00	75.00	175.00

NOTE: *L. B. Cole covers-all issues.* ***Palais*** *a-V2#8r, V2#11r.*

STAR TREK (TV) (See Dan Curtis Giveaways, Dynabrite Comics & Power Record Comics)
Gold Key: 7/67; No. 2, 6/68; No. 3, 12/68; No. 4, 6/69 - No. 61, 3/79

	GD2.0	FN6.0	NM9.4
1-Photo-c begin, end #9	38.00	115.00	420.00
2	22.00	66.00	240.00
2 (rare variation w/photo back-c)	36.00	109.00	400.00
3-5	15.00	44.00	160.00
3 (rare variation w/photo back-c)	25.00	76.00	280.00
6-9	12.00	36.00	130.00
10-20	7.00	21.00	75.00
21-30	5.00	15.00	55.00
31-40	3.20	9.50	35.00
41-61: 52-Drug propaganda story	2.25	6.75	25.00
...the Enterprise Logs nn (8/76)-Golden Press, ($1.95, 224 pgs.)-r/#1-8 plus 7 pgs. by McWilliams (#11185)-Photo-c	2.80	8.40	28.00
...the Enterprise Logs Vol. 2 ('76)-r/#9-17 (#11187)-Photo-c	2.80	8.40	28.00
...the Enterprise Logs Vol. 3 ('77)-r/#18-26 (#11188); McWilliams-a (4 pgs.)-Photo-c	2.80	8.40	28.00
Star Trek Vol. 4 (Winter '77)-Reprints #27,28,30-34,36,38 (#11189) plus 3 pgs. new art	2.80	8.40	28.00

NOTE: ***McWilliams*** *a-38, 40-44, 46-61. #29 reprints #1; #35 reprints #4; #37 reprints #5; #45 reprints #7. The tabloids all have photo covers and blank inside covers. Painted covers #10-44, 46-59.*

STAR TREK
Marvel Comics Group: April, 1980 - No. 18, Feb, 1982

	GD2.0	FN6.0	NM9.4
1: 1-3-r/Marvel Super Special; movie adapt.	1.00	3.00	8.00
2-16: 5-Miller-c			5.00
17-Low print run	1.00	3.00	8.00
18-Last issue; low print run	1.85	5.50	15.00

NOTE: ***Austin*** *c-18i.* ***Buscema*** *a-13.* ***Gil Kane*** *a-15.* ***Nasser*** *c/a-7.* ***Simonson*** *c-17.*

STAR TREK (Also see Who's Who In Star Trek)
DC Comics: Feb, 1984 - No. 56, Nov, 1988 (75¢, Mando paper)

	GD2.0	FN6.0	NM9.4
1-Sutton-a(p) begins	1.25	3.75	10.00
2-5		2.40	6.00
6-10: 7-Origin Saavik			5.00
11-20: 19-Walter Koenig story			4.00
21-32			3.50
33-($1.25, 52 pgs.)-20th anniversary issue			4.00
34-49: 37-Painted-c			3.00
50-($1.50, 52 pgs.)			4.00
51-56, Annual 1-3: 1(1985). 2(1986). 3(1988, $1.50)			3.00

NOTE: ***Morrow*** *a-28, 35, 36, 56.* ***Orlando*** *c-8i.* ***Perez*** *c-1-3.* ***Spiegle*** *a-19.* ***Starlin*** *c-24, 25.* ***Sutton*** *a-1-6p, 8-18p, 20-27p, 29p, 31-34p, 39-52p, 55p; c-4-6p, 8-22p, 46p.*

STAR TREK
DC Comics: Oct, 1989 - No. 80, Jan, 1996 ($1.50/$1.75/$1.95/$2.50)

	GD2.0	FN6.0	NM9.4
1-Capt. Kirk and crew		2.40	6.00
2,3			4.00
4-23,25-30: 10-12-The Trial of James T. Kirk. 21-Begin $1.75-c			2.50
24-($2.95, 68 pgs.)-40 pg. epic w/pin-ups			3.50
31-49,51-60			2.50
50-($3.50, 68 pgs.)-Painted-c			3.50
61-74,76-80			2.50
75 ($3.95)			4.00
Annual 1-6('90-'95, 68 pgs.): 1-Morrow-a. 3-Painted-c			4.00
Special 1-3 ('9-'95, 68 pgs.)-1-Sutton-a.			4.00
...: The Ashes of Eden (1995, $14.95, 100 pgs.)-Shatner story			15.00
...Generations (1994, $3.95, 68 pgs.)-Movie adaptation			4.00
...Generations (1994, $5.95, 68 pgs.)-Squarebound			6.00

STAR TREK: DEEP SPACE NINE (TV)
Malibu Comics: Aug, 1993 - No. 32, Jan, 1996 ($2.50)

	GD2.0	FN6.0	NM9.4
1-Direct Sale Edition w/line drawn-c			2.50
1-Newsstand Edition with photo-c			2.50
0 (1/95, $2.95)-Terok Nor			3.00
2-30: 2-Polybagged w/trading card. 9-4 pg. prelude to Hearts & Minds			2.50
31-($3.95)			4.00
32-($3.50)			3.50
Annual 1 (1/95, $3.95, 68 pgs.)			4.00
Special 1 (1995, $3.50)			3.50
Ultimate Annual 1 (12/95, $5.95)			6.00
...:Lightstorm (12/94, $3.50)			3.50

STAR TREK: DEEP SPACE NINE (TV)
Marvel Comics (Paramount Comics): Nov, 1996 - No. 15, Mar, 1998 ($1.95/$1.99)

	GD2.0	FN6.0	NM9.4
1-15: 12,13-"Telepathy War" pt. 2,3			2.00

STAR TREK DEEP SPACE NINE-THE CELEBRITY SERIES
Malibu Comics: May, 1995 ($2.95)

	GD2.0	FN6.0	NM9.4
1-Blood and Honor; Mark Lenard script			3.00
1-Rules of Diplomacy; Aron Eisenberg script			3.00

STAR TREK: DEEP SPACE NINE HEARTS AND MINDS
Malibu Comics: June, 1994 - No. 4, Sept, 1994 ($2.50, limited series)

	GD2.0	FN6.0	NM9.4
1-4			2.50
1-Holographic-c			4.00

STAR TREK: DEEP SPACE NINE, THE MAQUIS
Malibu Comics: Feb, 1995 - No. 3, Apr, 1995 ($2.50, limited series)

	GD2.0	FN6.0	NM9.4
1-3-Newsstand-c, 1-Photo-c			2.50

STAR TREK: DEEP SPACE NINE/THE NEXT GENERATION
Malibu Comics: Oct, 1994 - No. 2, Nov, 1994 ($2.50, limited series)

	GD2.0	FN6.0	NM9.4
1,2: Parts 2 & 4 of "Prophet & Losses."			2.50

STAR TREK: DEEP SPACE NINE WORF SPECIAL
Malibu Comics: Dec, 1995 ($3.95, one-shot)

	GD2.0	FN6.0	NM9.4
1-Includes pinups			4.00

STAR TREK EARLY VOYAGES(TV)
Marvel Comics (Paramount Comics): Feb, 1997 - No. 17, Jun, 1998 ($2.95/$1.95/$1.99)

	GD2.0	FN6.0	NM9.4
1-($2.95)			3.00
2-17			2.00

STAR TREK: FIRST CONTACT (Movie)
Marvel Comics (Paramount Comics): Nov, 1996 ($5.95, one-shot)

	GD2.0	FN6.0	NM9.4
nn-Movie adaption			6.00

STAR TREK: MIRROR MIRROR
Marvel Comics (Paramount Comics): Feb, 1997 ($3.95, one-shot)

	GD2.0	FN6.0	NM9.4
1-DeFalco-s			4.00

STAR TREK MOVIE SPECIAL
DC Comics: 1984 (June) - No. 2, 1987 ($1.50); No. 1, 1989 ($2.00, 52 pgs)

	GD2.0	FN6.0	NM9.4
nn-(#1)-Adapts Star Trek III; Sutton-p (68 pgs.)			2.50
2-Adapts Star Trek IV; Sutton-a; Chaykin-c. (68 pgs.)			2.50
1 (1989)-Adapts Star Trek V; painted-c			2.50

STAR TREK: OPERATION ASSIMILATION
Marvel Comics (Paramount Comics): Dec, 1996 ($2.95, one-shot)

	GD2.0	FN6.0	NM9.4
1			3.00

STAR TREK VI: THE UNDISCOVERED COUNTRY (Movie)
DC Comics: 1992

	GD2.0	FN6.0	NM9.4
1-($2.95, regular edition, 68 pgs.)-Adaptation of film			3.00
nn-($5.95, prestige edition)-Has photos of movie not included in regular edition; painted-c by Palmer; photo back-c			6.00

STAR TREK: STARFLEET ACADEMY
Marvel Comics (Paramount Comics): Dec, 1996 - No. 19, Jun, 1998 ($1.95/$1.99)

	GD2.0	FN6.0	NM9.4
1-19: Begin new series. 12-"Telepathy War" pt. 1. 18-English and Klingon language editions			2.00

Star Trek: The Next Generation #50 © Paramount

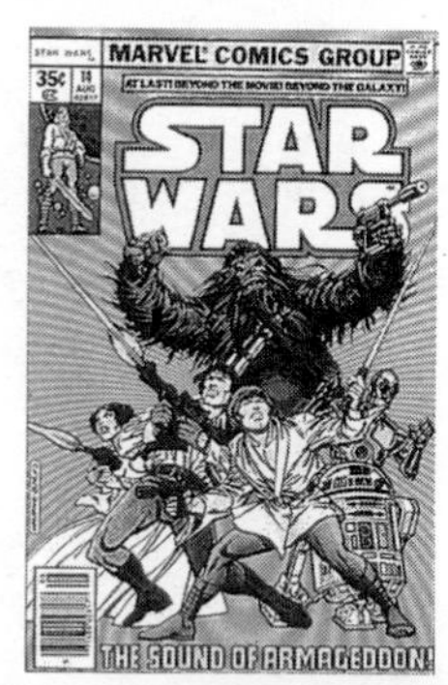

Star Wars #14 © Lucasfilm

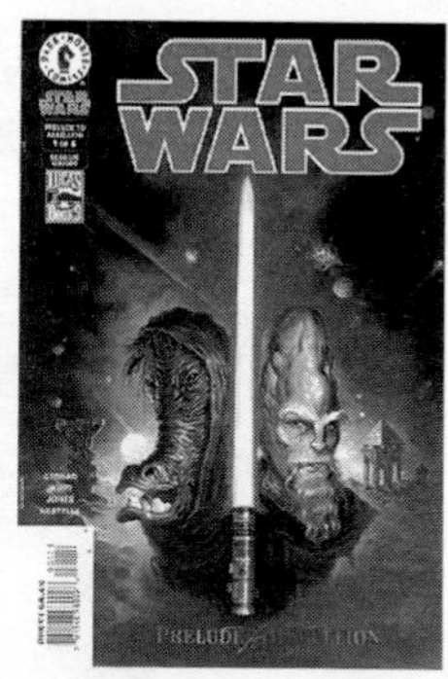

Star Wars (monthy series) #1 © Lucasfilm

GD2.0 FN6.0 NM9.4

STAR TREK: TELEPATHY WAR
Marvel Comics (Paramount Comics): Nov, 1997 ($2.99, 48 pgs., one-shot)
1-"Telepathy War" x-over pt. 6 — 3.00

STAR TREK - THE MODALA IMPERATIVE
DC Comics: Late July, 1991 - No. 4, Late Sept, 1991 ($1.75, limited series)
1-4 — 2.50

STAR TREK: THE NEXT GENERATION (TV)
DC Comics: Feb, 1988 - No. 6, July, 1988 (limited series)
1 ($1.50, 52 pgs.)-Sienkiewicz painted-c — 5.00
2-6 ($1.00) — 3.00

STAR TREK: THE NEXT GENERATION (TV)
DC Comics: Oct, 1989 -No. 80, 1995 ($1.50/$1.75/$1.95)
1-Capt. Picard and crew from TV show — 1.10 — 3.30 — 9.00
2,3 — 5.00
4-10 — 4.00
11-23,25-49,51-60 — 3.00
24,50: 24-($2.50, 52 pgs.). 50-($3.50, 68 pgs.)-Painted-c — 5.00
61-74,76-80 — 2.50
75-($3.95, 50 pgs.) — 4.00
Annual 1-6 ('90-'95, 68 pgs.) — 4.00
Special 1 -3('93-'95, 68 pgs.)-1-Contains 3 stories — 4.00
...-The Series Finale (1994, $3.95, 68 pgs.) — 4.00

STAR TREK: THE NEXT GENERATION/DEEP SPACE NINE (TV)
DC Comics: Dec, 1994 - No. 2, Jan, 1995 ($2.50, limited series)
1,2-Parts 1 & 3 of "Prophets & Losses" — 2.50

STAR TREK: THE NEXT GENERATION - ILL WIND
DC Comics: Nov, 1995 - No. 3, Feb, 1996 ($2.50, limited series)
1-3 — 2.50

STAR TREK: THE NEXT GENERATION - RIKER
Marvel Comics (Paramount Comics): July, 1998 ($3.50, one-shot)
1-Riker joins the Maquis — 3.50

STAR TREK: THE NEXT GENERATION - SHADOWHEART
DC Comics: Dec, 1994 - No. 4, Mar, 1995 ($1.95, limited series)
1-4 — 2.00

STAR TREK: THE NEXT GENERATION - THE MODALA IMPERATIVE
DC Comics: Early Sept, 1991 - No. 4, Late Oct, 1991 ($1.75, limited series)
1-4 — 2.50

STAR TREK UNLIMITED
Marvel Comics (Paramount Comics): Nov, 1996 - No. 10, July, 1998 ($2.95/$2.99)
1,2-Stories from original series and Next Generation — 4.00
3-10: 3-Begin $2.99-c. 6-"Telepathy War" pt. 4. 7-Q & Trelane swap Kirk & Picard — 3.50

STAR TREK UNTOLD VOYAGES
Marvel Comics (Paramount Comics): May, 1998 - No. 5, July, 1998 ($2.50)
1-5-Kirk's crew after the 1st movie — 2.50

STAR TREK: VOYAGER
Marvel Comics (Paramount Comics): Nov, 1996 - No. 15, Mar, 1998 ($1.95/$1.99)
1-15: 13-"Telepathy War" pt. 5. 14-Seven of Nine joins crew — 3.00

STAR TREK: VOYAGER SPLASHDOWN
Marvel Comics (Paramount Comics): Apr, 1998 - No. 4, July, 1998 ($2.50, limited series)
1-4-Voyager crashes on a water planet — 3.00

STAR TREK/ X-MEN
Marvel Comics (Paramount Comics): Dec, 1996 ($4.99, one-shot)
1-Kirk's crew & X-Men; art by Silvestri, Tan, Winn & Finch; Lobdell-s — 5.00

STAR TREK/ X-MEN: 2ND CONTACT
Marvel Comics (Paramount Comics): May, 1998 ($4.99, 64 pgs., one-shot)
1-Next Gen. crew & X-Men battle Kang, Sentinels & Borg following First Contact movie — 5.00
1-Painted wraparound variant cover — 5.00

STAR WARS (Movie) (See Classic..., Contemporary Motivators, Dark Horse Comics, The Droids, The Ewoks, Marvel Movie Showcase, Marvel Special Ed.)
Marvel Comics Group: July, 1977 - No. 107, Sept, 1986
1-(Regular 30¢ edition)-Price in square w/UPC code; #1-6 adapt first movie — 3.50 — 10.50 — 35.00
1-(35¢-c; limited distribution - 1500 copies?)- Price in square w/UPC code — 44.00 — 132.00 — 530.00
NOTE: *The rare 35¢ edition has the cover price in a square box, and the UPC box in the lower left hand corner has the UPC code lines running through it.*
2-6: 2-4-30¢ issues. 4-Battle with Darth Vader. 6-Dave Stevens-a(i). — 2.25 — 6.75 — 18.00
2-4-35¢ with UPC code; not reprints — 6.50 — 19.00 — 72.00
7-20 — 1.50 — 4.50 — 12.00
21-70: 39-44-The Empire Strikes Back-r by Al Williamson in all. 68-Reintro Boba Fett. — 1.10 — 3.30 — 9.00
71-80 — 1.25 — 3.75 — 10.00
81-90: 81-Boba Fett app. — 1.50 — 4.50 — 12.00
91,93-99: 98-Williamson-a. — 1.75 — 5.25 — 14.00
92,100-106: 92,100-($1.00, 52 pgs.). — 3.20 — 8.00 — 16.00
107 (scarce); Portacio-a(i) — 5.00 — 15.00 — 50.00
1-9: Reprints; has "reprint" in upper lefthand corner of cover or on inside or price and number inside a diamond with no date or UPC on cover; 30¢ and 35¢ issues published — 4.00
Annual 1 (12/79, 52 pgs.)-Simonson-c — 1.50 — 4.50 — 12.00
Annual 2 (11/82, 52 pgs.), 3(12/83, 52 pgs.) — 1.25 — 3.75 — 10.00
***Austin** a-11-15i, 21i, 38; c-12-15i, 21i. **Byrne** c-13p. **Chaykin** a-1-10p; c-1. **Golden** c/a-38. **Miller** c-47p; pin-up-43. **Nebres** c/a-Annual 2i. **Portacio** a-107i. **Sienkiewicz** c-92i, 98. **Simonson** a-16p, 49p, 51-63p, 65p, 66p; c-16, 49-51, 52p, 53-62, Annual 1. **Steacy** painted a-105i, 106i; c-105. **Williamson** a-39-44p, 50p, 98; c-39, 40, 41-44p. Painted c-81, 87, 92, 95, 98, 100, 105.*

STAR WARS (Monthly series)
Dark Horse Comics: Dec, 1998 - Present ($2.50, limited series)
1-9: 1-6-Prelude To Rebellion; Strnad-s. 4-Brereton-c. 7-9-Outlander — 2.50
#0 Another Universe.com Ed.($10.00) r/serialized pages from Pizzazz Magazine; new Dorman painted-c — 10.00

STAR WARS: A NEW HOPE- THE SPECIAL EDITION
Dark Horse Comics: Jan, 1997 - No. 4, Apr, 1997 ($2.95, limited series)
1-4-Dorman-c — 4.00

STAR WARS: BOBA FETT
Dark Horse Comics: Dec, 1995 - No. 3 ($3.95) (Originally intended as a one-shot)
1-Kennedy-c/a — 2.40 — 6.00
2,3 — 5.00
Death, Lies, & Treachery TPB (1/98, $12.95) r/#1-3 — 13.00
Twin Engines of Destruction (1/97, $2.95) — 3.00

STAR WARS: BOBA FETT: ENEMY OF THE EMPIRE
Dark Horse Comics: Jan, 1999 - No. 4, Apr, 1999 ($2.95, limited series)
1-4-Recalls 1st meeting of Fett and Vader — 3.00

STAR WARS: CRIMSON EMPIRE
Dark Horse Comics: Dec, 1997 - No. 6, May, 1998 ($2.95, limited series)
1-Richardson-s/Gulacy-a — 5.00
2-6 — 4.00

STAR WARS: CRIMSON EMPIRE II: COUNCIL OF BLOOD
Dark Horse Comics: Nov, 1998 - No. 6, Apr, 1999 ($2.95, limited series)
1-6-Richardson & Stradley-s/Gulacy-a — 3.00

STAR WARS: DARK EMPIRE
Dark Horse Comics: Dec, 1991 - No. 6, Oct, 1992 ($2.95, limited series)
Preview-(99¢) — 2.00
1-All have Dorman painted-c — 1.50 — 4.50 — 12.00
1-3-2nd printing — 4.00

GD2.0 FN6.0 NM9.4

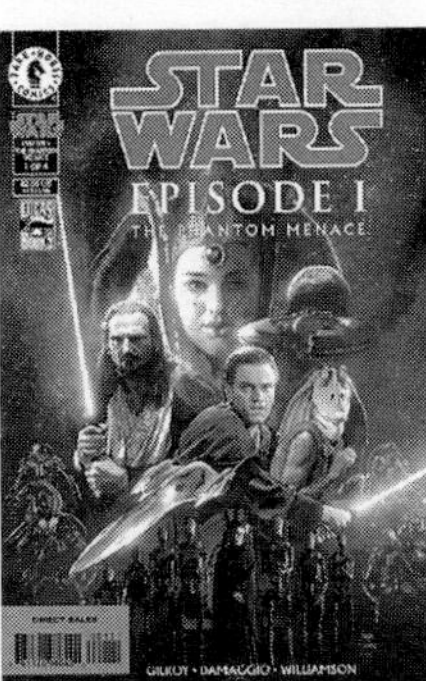

Star Wars: Episode 1 The Phantom Menace #1 © Lucasfilm

Star Wars: Mara Jade #4 © Lucasfilm

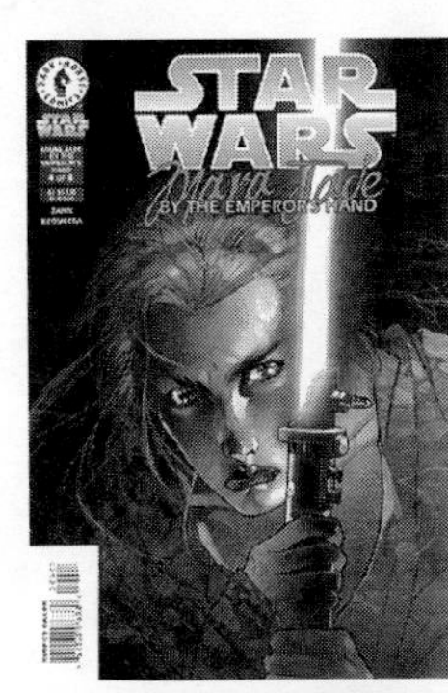

Star Wars: Vader's Quest #1 © Lucasfilm

GD2.0 FN6.0 NM9.4

2-Low print run 1.85 5.50 15.00
3 2.40 6.00
4-6 4.00
Gold Embossed Set (#1-6)-With gold embossed foil logo (price is for set) 80.00
Platinum Embossed Set (#1-6) 150.00
Trade paperback (4/93, 16.95) 17.00
Ltd. Ed. Hardcover ($99.95) Signed & numbered 125.00

STAR WARS: DARK EMPIRE II
Dark Horse Comics: Dec, 1994 - No. 6, May, 1995 ($2.95, limited series)

1-Dave Dorman painted-c 5.00
2-6: Dorman-c in all. 4.00
Platinum Embossed Set (#1-6) 35.00
Trade paperback ($17.95) 18.00

STAR WARS: DARK FORCE RISING
Dark Horse Comics: May, 1997 - No. 6, Oct, 1997 ($2.95, limited series)

1-6 4.00
TPB (2/98, $17.95) r/#1-6 18.00

STAR WARS: DROIDS (See Dark Horse Comics #17-19)
Dark Horse Comics: Apr, 1994 - #6, Sept, 1994; V2#1, Apr, 1995 - V2#8, Dec, 1995 ($2.50, limited series)

1-($2.95)-Embossed-c 4.00
2-6 , Special 1 (1/95, $2.50), V2#1-8 3.00

STAR WARS: EMPIRE'S END
Dark Horse Comics: Oct, 1995 - No. 2, Nov, 1995 ($2.95, limited series)

1,2-Dorman-c 3.00

STAR WARS: EPISODE 1 THE PHANTOM MENACE
Dark Horse Comics: May, 1999 - No. 4 ($2.95, movie adaption)

1-4-Regular and photo-c; Damaggio & Williamson-a 3.00
TPB ($12.95) r/#1-4 13.00
...Anakin Skywalker-Photo-c & Bradstreet-c, ...Obi-Wan Kenobi-Photo-c & Egeland-c, ...Queen Amidala-Photo-c & Bradstreet-c, ...Qui-Gon Jinn-Photo-c & Bradstreet-c 3.00
Gold foil covers; Wizard 1/2 10.00

STAR WARS HANDBOOK
Dark Horse Comics: July, 1998; July, 1999 ($2.95, one-shots)

...X-Wing Rogue Squadron (7/98)-Guidebook to characters and spacecraft 3.00
...Crimson Empire (7/99) Dorman-c 3.00

STAR WARS : HEIR TO THE EMPIRE
Dark Horse Comics: Oct, 1995 - No.6, Apr, 1996 ($2.95, limited series)

1-6: Adaptation of Zahn novel 3.00

STAR WARS: JABBA THE HUTT
Dark Horse Comics: Apr, 1995 ($2.50, one-shots)

nn, ...The Betrayal, ...The Dynasty Trap, ...The Hunger of Princess Nampi 3.00

STAR WARS: JEDI ACADEMY - LEVIATHAN
Dark Horse Comics: Oct, 1998 - No. 4, Jan, 1999 ($2.95, limited series)

1-Lago-c. 2-4-Chadwick-c 3.00

STAR WARS: MARA JADE
Dark Horse Comics: Aug, 1998 - No. 6, Jan, 1999 ($2.95, limited series)

1-6-Ezquerra-a 3.00

STAR WARS: RETURN OF THE JEDI (Movie)
Marvel Comics Group: Oct, 1983 - No. 4, Jan, 1984 (limited series)

1-4-Williamson-p in all; r/Marvel Super Special #27 5.00
Oversized issue (1983, $2.95, 10-3/4x8-1/4", 68 pgs., cardboard-c)-r/#1-4 1.10 3.30 9.00

STAR WARS: RIVER OF CHAOS
Dark Horse Comics: June, 1995 - No. 4, Sept, 1995 ($2.95, limited series)

1-4: Louise Simonson scripts 3.00

STAR WARS: SHADOWS OF THE EMPIRE
Dark Horse Comics: May, 1996 - No. 6, Oct, 1996 ($2.95, limited series)

1-6: Story details events between The Empire Strikes Back & Return of the Jedi; Russell-a(i). 3.00

STAR WARS: SHADOWS OF THE EMPIRE - EVOLUTION
Dark Horse Comics: Feb, 1998 - No. 5, June, 1998 ($2.95, limited series)

1-5: Perry-s/Fegredo-c. 3.00

STAR WARS: SHADOW STALKER
Dark Horse Comics: Sept, 1997 ($2.95, one-shot)

nn-Windham-a. 3.00

STAR WARS: SPLINTER OF THE MIND'S EYE
Dark Horse Comics: Dec, 1995 - No. 4, June, 1996 ($2.50, limited series)

1-4: Adaption of Alan Dean Foster novel 3.00

STAR WARS: TALES FROM MOS EISLEY
Dark Horse Comics: Mar, 1996 ($2.95, one-shot)

nn-Bret Blevins-a. 3.00

STAR WARS: TALES OF THE JEDI (See Dark Horse Comics #7)
Dark Horse Comics: Oct, 1993 - No. 5, Feb, 1994 ($2.50, limited series)

1-5: All have Dave Dorman painted-c. 3-r/Dark Horse Comics #7-9 w/new coloring & some panels redrawn 3.00
1-5-Gold foil embossed logo; limited # printed-7500 (set) 50.00

STAR WARS: TALES OF THE JEDI-DARK LORDS OF THE SITH
Dark Horse Comics: Oct, 1994 - No. 6, Mar, 1995 ($2.50, limited series)

1-6: 1-Polybagged w/trading card 3.00

STAR WARS: TALES OF THE JEDI-REDEMPTION
Dark Horse Comics: July, 1998 - No. 5, Nov, 1998 ($2.95, limited series)

1-5: 1-Kevin J. Anderson-s/Kordey-c 3.00

STAR WARS: TALES OF THE JEDI-THE FALL OF THE SITH
Dark Horse Comics: June, 1997 - No. 5, Oct, 1997 ($2.95, limited series)

1-5 3.00

STAR WARS: TALES OF THE JEDI-THE FREEDON NADD UPRISING
Dark Horse Comics: Aug, 1994 - No. 2, Nov, 1994 ($2.50, limited series)

1,2 3.00

STAR WARS: TALES OF THE JEDI-THE GOLDEN AGE OF THE SITH
Dark Horse Comics: July, 1996 - No. 5, Feb, 1997 (99¢/$2.95, limited series)

0-(99¢)-Anderson-s 2.00
1-5-Anderson-s 3.00

STAR WARS: TALES OF THE JEDI-THE SITH WAR
Dark Horse Comics: Aug, 1995 - No. 6, Jan, 1996 ($2.50, limited series)

1-6: Anderson scripts 3.00

STAR WARS: THE BOUNTY HUNTERS
Dark Horse Comics: July, 1999 - Present ($2.95, one-shots)

...Aurra Sing, ...Scoundrel's Wages (8/99) Lando Calrissian app. 3.00

STAR WARS: THE JABBA TAPE
Dark Horse Comics: Dec, 1998 ($2.95, one-shot)

nn-Wagner-s/Plunkett-a 3.00

STAR WARS: THE LAST COMMAND
Dark Horse Comics: Nov, 1997 - No. 6, July, 1998 ($2.95, limited series)

1-6:Based on the Timothy Zaun novel 4.00

STAR WARS: THE PROTOCOL OFFENSIVE
Dark Horse Comics: Sept, 1997 ($4.95, one-shot)

nn-Anthony Daniels & Ryder Windham-s 5.00

STAR WARS: VADER'S QUEST
Dark Horse Comics: Feb, 1999 - No. 4, May, 1999 ($2.95, limited series)

1-4-Follows destruction of 1st Death Star; Gibbons-a 3.00

STAR WARS: X-WING ROGUE SQUADRON (Star Wars: X-Wing Rogue Squadron-The Phantom Affair #5-8 appears on cover only)
Dark Horse Comics: July, 1995 - No. 35, Nov, 1998 ($2.95)

Steel #48 © DC

Steve Canyon Comics #6 © HARV

Stone Cold Steve Austin #1 © Chaos!

GD2.0 FN6.0 NM9.4

1/2 5.00
1-24,26-35: 1-4-Baron scripts. 5-20-Stackpole scripts 3.00
25-($3.95) 4.00
The Phantom Affair TPB ($12.95) r/#5-8 13.00

S.T.A.T.
Majestic Entertainment: Dec, 1993 ($2.25)
1 2.25

STATIC (Also see Eclipse Monthly)
Charlton Comics: No, 11, Oct, 1985 - No. 12, Dec, 1985
11,12-Ditko-c/a 2.00

STATIC (See Heroes)
DC Comics (Milestone): June, 1993 - No. 45, Mar, 1997 ($1.50/$1.75/$2.50)
1-($2.95)-Collector's Edition; polybagged w/poster & trading card & backing board (direct sales only) 4.00
1-24,26-45: 2-Origin. 8-Shadow War; Simonson silver ink-c. 14-($2.50, 52 pgs.)-Worlds Collide Pt. 14. 27-Kent Williams-c 2.50
25 ($3.95) 4.00

STEALTH SQUAD
Petra Comics: Sept, 1993 ($2.50, unfinished limited series)
1-Super hero team 2.50

STEED AND MRS. PEEL (TV)(Also see The Avengers)
Eclipse Books/ ACME Press: 1990 - No. 3, 1991 ($4.95, limited series)
Books One - Three: Grant Morrison scripts 5.00

STEEL (Also see JLA)
DC Comics: Feb, 1994 - No. 52, July, 1998 ($1.50/$1.95/$2.50)
1-8,0,9-52: 1-From Reign of the Supermen storyline. 6,7-Worlds Collide Pt. 5 & 12. 8-(9/94). 0-(10/94). 9-(11/94). 46-Superboy-c/app. 50-Millennium Giants x-over 2.50
Annual 1 (1994, $2.95)-Elseworlds story 3.00
Annual 2 (1995, $3.95)-Year One story 4.00
...Forging of a Hero TPB (1997, $19.95) r/ early app. 20.00

STEEL: THE OFFICIAL COMIC ADAPTION OF THE WARNER BROS. MOTION PICTURE
DC Comics: 1997 ($4.95, Prestige format, one-shot)
nn-Movie adaption; Bogdanove & Giordano-a 5.00

STEELGRIP STARKEY
Marvel Comics (Epic Comics): June, 1986 - No. 6, July, 1987 ($1.50, limited series, Baxter paper)
1-6 2.00

STEEL STERLING (Formerly Shield-Steel Sterling; see Blue Ribbon, Jackpot, Mighty Comics, Mighty Crusaders, Roly Poly & Zip Comics)
Archie Enterprises, Inc.: No. 4, Jan, 1984 - No. 7, July, 1984
4-7: 6-McWilliams-a 2.00

STEEL, THE INDESTRUCTIBLE MAN (See All-Star Squadron #8)
DC Comics: Mar, 1978 - No. 5, Oct-Nov, 1978
1 2.40 6.00
2-5: 5-44 pgs. 4.00

STEELTOWN ROCKERS
Marvel Comics: Apr, 1987 - No. 6, Sept, 1990 ($1.00, limited series)
1-6: Small town teens form rock band 2.00

STEVE AUSTIN (See Stone Cold Steve Austin)

STEVE CANYON (See Harvey Comics Hits #52)
Dell Publishing Co.: No. 519, 11/53 - No. No. 1033, 9/59 (All Milton Caniff-a except #519, 939, 1033)
Four Color 519 (1, '53) 8.00 25.00 90.00
Four Color 578 (8/54), 641 (7/55), 737 (10/56), 804 (5/57), 939 (10/58), 1033 (9/59) (photo-c) 4.50 13.50 50.00

STEVE CANYON
Grosset & Dunlap: 1959 (6-3/4x9", 96 pgs., B&W, no text, hardcover)
100100-Reprints 2 stories from strip (1953, 1957) 4.25 13.00 28.00
100100 (softcover edition) 4.00 11.00 22.00

STEVE CANYON COMICS
Harvey Publ.: Feb, 1948 - No. 6, Dec, 1948 (Strip reprints, No. 4,5: 52pgs.)
1-Origin; has biography of Milton Caniff; Powell-a, 2 pgs.; Caniff-a 21.00 64.00 150.00
2-Caniff, Powell-a in #2-6 13.50 41.00 95.00
3-6: 6-Intro Madame Lynx-c/story 12.00 36.00 85.00

STEVE CANYON IN 3-D
Kitchen Sink Press: June, 1986 ($2.25, one-shot)
1-Contains unpublished story from 1954 4.00

STEVE DITKO'S STRANGE AVENGING TALES
Fantagraphics Books: Feb, 1997 ($2.95, B&W)
1-Ditko-c/s/a 3.00

STEVE DONOVAN, WESTERN MARSHAL (TV)
Dell Publishing Co.: No. 675, Feb, 1956 - No. 880, Feb, 1958 (All photo-c)
Four Color 675-Kinstler-a 7.00 22.00 80.00
Four Color 768-Kinstler-a 5.50 16.50 60.00
Four Color 880 3.60 11.00 40.00

STEVE ROPER
Famous Funnies: Apr, 1948 - No. 5, Dec, 1948
1-Contains 1944 daily newspaper-r 11.00 33.00 75.00
2 6.70 20.00 40.00
3-5 5.35 16.00 32.00

STEVE SAUNDERS SPECIAL AGENT (See Special Agent)

STEVE SAVAGE (See Captain...)

STEVE ZODIAC & THE FIRE BALL XL-5 (TV)
Gold Key: Jan, 1964
10108-401 (#1) 7.65 23.00 85.00

STEVIE (Mazie's boy friend)(Also see Flat-Top, Mazie & Mortie)
Mazie (Magazine Publ.): Nov, 1952 - No. 6, Apr, 1954
1-Teenage humor; Stevie, Mortie & Mazie begin 6.70 20.00 40.00
2-6 4.15 12.50 25.00

STEVIE MAZIE'S BOY FRIEND (See Harvey Hits #5)

STEWART THE RAT (See Eclipse Graphic Album Series)

ST. GEORGE (See listing under Saint...)

STIGG'S INFERNO
Vortex/Eclipse: 1985 - No. 7, Mar, 1987 ($1.95, B&W)
1-7 ($1.95) 2.00
Graphic Album (1988, $6.95, B&W, 100 pgs.) 7.00

STING OF THE GREEN HORNET (See The Green Hornet)
Now Comics: June, 1992 - No. 4, 1992 ($2.50, limited series)
1-4: Butler-c/a 2.50
1-4 ($2.75)-Collectors Ed.; polybagged w/poster 3.00

STONE
Avalon Studios: Aug, 1998 - No. 4, Apr, 1999 ($2.50, limited series)
1-Portacio-a/Haberlin-s 2.50
1-Alternate-c 5.00
2-4 2.50
2-($14.95) DF Stonechrome Edition 15.00

STONE (Volume 2)
Avalon Studios: Aug, 1999 - Present ($2.50)
1,2-Portacio-a/Haberlin-s 2.50

STONE COLD STEVE AUSTIN (WWF Wrestling)
Chaos! Comics: Oct, 1999 - No. 4 ($2.95)
1-Reg. & photo-c; Steven Grant-s 3.00

Stories of Romance #5 © MAR

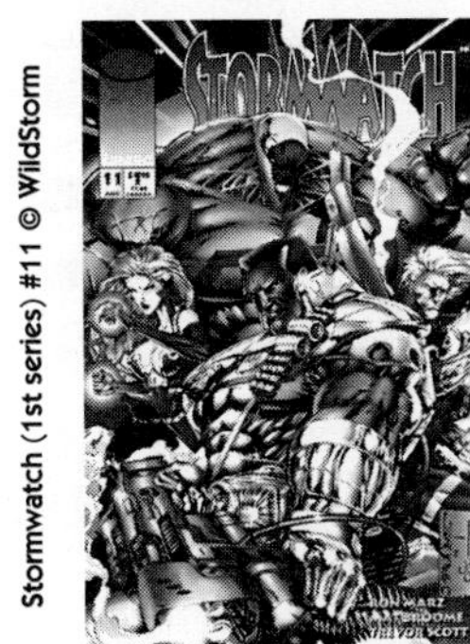
Stormwatch (1st series) #11 © WildStorm

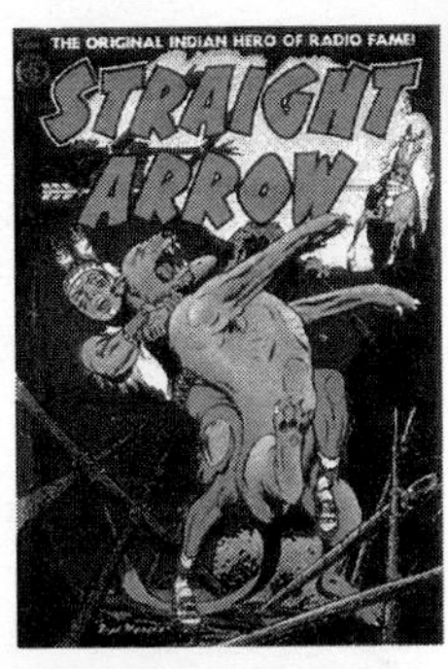

Straight Arrow #16 © ME

	GD2.0	FN6.0	NM9.4
1-Premium Ed. ($10.00)			10.00
Preview ($5.00)			5.00

STONEY BURKE (TV)
Dell Publishing Co.: June-Aug, 1963 - No. 2, Sept-Nov, 1963

1,2-Jack Lord photo-c on both	2.25	6.75	18.00

STONY CRAIG
Pentagon Publishing Co.: 1946 (No #)

nn-Reprints Bell Syndicate's "Sgt. Stony Craig" newspaper strips	6.70	20.00	40.00

STORIES BY FAMOUS AUTHORS ILLUSTRATED (Fast Fiction #1-5)
Seaboard Publ./Famous Authors Ill.: No. 6, Aug, 1950 - No. 13, Mar, 1951

1-Scarlet Pimpernel-Baroness Orczy	34.00	103.00	240.00
2-Capt. Blood-Raphael Sabatini	34.00	103.00	240.00
3-She, by Haggard	40.00	120.00	295.00
4-The 39 Steps-John Buchan	23.00	69.00	160.00
5-Beau Geste-P. C. Wren	23.00	69.00	160.00

NOTE: *The above five issues are exact reprints of Fast Fiction #1-5 except for the title change and new Kiefer covers on #1 and 2. Kiefer c(r)-3-5. The above 5 issues were released before Famous Authors #6.*

6-Macbeth, by Shakespeare; Kiefer art (8/50); used in **SOTI**, pg. 22,143; Kiefer-c; 36 pgs.	30.00	90.00	210.00
7-The Window; Kiefer-c/a; 52 pgs.	21.00	64.00	150.00
8-Hamlet, by Shakespeare; Kiefer-c/a; 36 pgs.	27.00	81.00	190.00
9,10: 9-Nicholas Nickleby, by Dickens; G. Schrotter-a; 52 pgs. 10-Romeo & Juliet, by Shakespeare; Kiefer-c/a; 36 pgs.	23.00	69.00	160.00
11-13: 11-Ben-Hur; Schrotter-a; 52 pgs. 12-La Svengali; Schrotter-a; 36 pgs. 13-Scaramouche; Kiefer-c/a; 36 pgs.	21.00	64.00	150.00

NOTE: *Artwork was prepared/advertised for #14, The Red Badge Of Courage. Gilberton bought out Famous Authors, Ltd. and used that story as C.I. #98. Famous Authors, Ltd. then published the Classics Junior series. The Famous Authors titles were published as part of the regular Classics Ill. Series in Brazil starting in 1952.*

STORIES OF ROMANCE (Formerly Meet Miss Bliss)
Atlas Comics (LMC): No. 5, Mar, 1956 - No. 13, Aug, 1957

5-Baker-a?	10.00	30.00	60.00
6-10,12,13	5.85	17.50	35.00
11-Baker, Romita-a; Colletta-c/a	7.00	21.00	42.00

NOTE: ***Ann Brewster** a-13. **Colletta** a-9(2), 11; c-5, 11.*

STORM
Marvel Comics: Feb, 1996 - No. 4, May, 1996 ($2.95, limited series)

1-4-Foil-c; Dodson-a(p); Ellis-s: 2-4-Callisto;			3.50

STORMQUEST
Caliber Press (Sky Universe): Nov, 1994 - No. 6, Apr, 1995 ($1.95)

1-6			2.00

STORMWATCH
Image Comics (WildStorm Prod.): May, 1993 - No. 50, Jul, 1997 ($1.95/$2.50)

1-8,0,9-36: 1-Intro StormWatch (Battalion, Diva, Winter, Fuji, & Hellstrike); 1st app. Weatherman; Jim Lee-c & part scripts; Lee plots in all. 1-Gold edition.1-3-Includes coupon for limited edition StormWatch trading card #00 by Lee. 3-1st app. Backlash (cameo). 0-($2.50)-Polybagged w/card; 1st full app. Backlash. 9-(4/94, $2.50)-Intro Defile. 10-(6/94), 11,12-Both (8/94). 13,14-(9/94). 15-(10/94). 21-Reads #1 on-c. 22-Direct Market; Wildstorm Rising Pt. 9, bound-in card. 23-Spartan joins team. 25-(6/94, June 1995 on-c, $2.50). 35-Fire From Heaven Pt. 5. 36-Fire From Heaven Pt. 12			2.50
10-Alternate Portacio-c, see Deathblow #5			4.00
22-($1.95)-Newsstand, Wildstorm Rising Pt. 9			2.50
37-(7/96, $3.50, 38 pgs.)-Weatherman forms new team; 1st app. Jenny Sparks, Jack Hawksmoor & Rose Tattoo; Warren Ellis scripts begin; Justice League #1-c/swipe			3.50
38-49: 44-Three covers.			2.50
50-($4.50)			4.50
Special 1 ,2(1/94, 5/95, $3.50, 52 pgs.)			3.50
Sourcebook 1 (1/94, $2.50)			2.50

STORMWATCH
Image Comics (WildStorm): Oct, 1997 - No. 11, Sept, 1998 ($2.50)

	GD2.0	FN6.0	NM9.4
1-Ellis-s/Jimenez-a(p); two covers by Bennett			2.50
1-($3.50)-Voyager Pack bagged w/Gen 13 preview			3.50
2-11: 7,8-Freefall app. 9-Gen13 & DV8 app.			2.50
Change or Die TPB ('99, $14.95) r/V1 #48-50 & V2 #1-3			15.00
A Finer World TPB ('99, $14.95) r/V2 #4-9			15.00

STORMWATCHER
Eclipse Comics (Acme Press): Apr, 1989 - No. 4, Dec, 1989 ($2.00, B&W, limited series)

1-4			2.00

STORMY (Disney) (Movie)
Dell Publishing Co.: No. 537, Feb, 1954

Four Color 537 (...the Thoroughbred)-on top 2/3 of each page; Pluto story on bottom 1/3	2.75	8.00	30.00

STORY OF JESUS (See Classics Illustrated Special Issue)

STORY OF MANKIND, THE (Movie)
Dell Publishing Co.: No. 851, Jan, 1958

Four Color 851-Vincent Price/Hedy Lamarr photo-c	6.40	19.00	70.00

STORY OF MARTHA WAYNE, THE
Argo Publ.: April, 1956

1-Newspaper strip-r	5.00	15.00	30.00

STORY OF RUTH, THE
Dell Publishing Co.: No. 1144, Nov-Jan, 1961 (Movie)

Four Color #1144-Photo-c	9.00	27.00	100.00

STORY OF THE COMMANDOS, THE (Combined Operations)
Long Island Independent: 1943 (15¢, B&W, 68 pgs.) (Distr. by Gilberton)

nn-All text (no comics); photos & illustrations; ad for Classic Comics on back cover (Rare)	29.00	86.00	200.00

STORY OF THE GLOOMY BUNNY, THE (See March of Comics #9)

STRAIGHT ARROW (Radio)(See Best of the West & Great Western)
Magazine Enterprises: Feb-Mar, 1950 - No. 55, Mar, 1956 (All 36 pgs.)

1-Straight Arrow (alias Steve Adams) & his palomino Fury begin; 1st mention of Sundown Valley & the Secret Cave	43.00	128.00	340.00
2-Red Hawk begins (1st app?) by Powell (origin), ends #55	21.00	64.00	150.00
3-Frazetta-c	30.00	90.00	210.00
4,5: 4-Secret Cave-c	19.00	58.00	135.00
6-10	18.00	54.00	125.00
11-Classic story "The Valley of Time", with an ancient civilization made of gold	19.00	58.00	135.00
12-19	13.50	41.00	95.00
20-Origin Straight Arrow's Shield	16.00	47.00	110.00
21-Origin Fury	19.00	58.00	135.00
22-Frazetta-c	21.00	62.00	145.00
23,25-30: 25-Secret Cave-c. 28-Red Hawk meets The Vikings	9.15	27.00	55.00
24-Classic story "The Dragons of Doom!" with prehistoric pteradactyls	11.00	33.00	75.00
31-38: 36-Red Hawk drug story by Powell	6.70	20.00	40.00
39-Classic story "The Canyon Beast", with a dinosaur egg hatching a Tyranosaurus Rex	10.00	30.00	70.00
40-Classic story "Secret of The Spanish Specters", with Conquistadors' lost treasure	10.00	30.00	60.00
41,42,44-54: 45-Secret Cave-c	5.85	17.50	35.00
43-Intro & 1st app. Blaze, S. Arrow's Warrior dog	8.35	25.00	50.00
55-Last issue	10.00	30.00	60.00

NOTE: ***Fred Meagher** a 1-55; c-1, 2, 4-21, 23-55. **Powell** a 2-55. **Whitney** a-1. Many issues advertise the radio premiums associated with Straight Arrow.*

STRAIGHT ARROW'S FURY (Also see A-1 Comics)
Magazine Enterprises: No. 119, 1954 (one-shot)

A-1 119-Origin; Fred Meagher-c/a	13.50	41.00	95.00

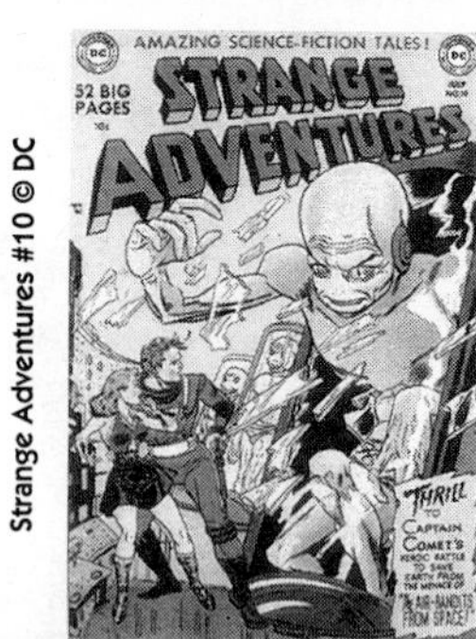

Strange Adventures #10 © DC

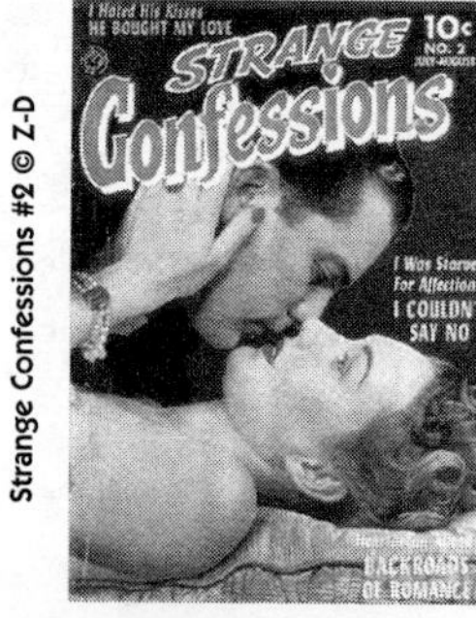

Strange Confessions #2 © Z-D

Strange Fantasy #7 © AJAX

GD2.0 FN6.0 NM9.4

STRANGE (Tales You'll Never Forget)
Ajax-Farrell Publ. (Four Star Comic Corp.): March, 1957 - No. 6, May, 1958

1 19.00 56.00 130.00
2-Censored r/Haunted Thrills 10.00 30.00 65.00
3-6 9.15 27.50 55.00

STRANGE ADVENTURES
National Periodical Publications: Aug-Sept, 1950 - No. 244, Oct-Nov, 1973 (No. 1-12: 52 pgs.)

1-Adaptation of "Destination Moon"; preview of movie w/photo-c from movie (also see Fawcett Movie Comic #2); adapt. of Edmond Hamilton's "Chris KL-99" in #1-3; Darwin Jones begins 250.00 750.00 2600.00
2 110.00 330.00 1200.00
3,4 70.00 210.00 825.00
5-8,10: 7-Origin Kris KL-99 64.00 192.00 675.00
9-(6/51)-Origin/1st app. Captain Comet (c/story). 150.00 450.00 1600.00
11-20: 12,13,17,18-Toth-a. 14-Robot-c 44.00 132.00 475.00
21-30: 28-Atomic explosion panel. 30-Robot-c 35.00 105.00 375.00
31,34-38 34.00 102.00 330.00
32,33-Krigstein-a 34.00 102.00 340.00
39-Ill. in **SOTI** "Treating police contemptuously" (top right) 38.00 114.00 400.00
40-49-Last Capt. Comet; not in 45,47,48 32.00 96.00 300.00
50-53-Last precode issue (2/55) 24.00 72.00 230.00
54-70 17.00 51.00 170.00
71-99 12.50 38.00 125.00
100 14.00 42.00 140.00
101-110: 104-Space Museum begins by Sekowsky. 9.50 28.50 95.00
111-116,118,119: 114-Star Hawkins begins, ends #185; Heath-a in Wood E.C. style 8.50 25.50 85.00
117-(6/60)-Origin/1st app. Atomic Knights. 48.00 144.00 575.00
120-2nd app. Atomic Knights 23.50 70.00 235.00
121,122,125,127,128,130,131,133,134: 134-Last 10¢ issue 7.00 21.00 70.00
123,126-3rd & 4th app. Atomic Knights 13.50 40.00 135.00
124-Intro/origin Faceless Creature 7.50 22.50 75.00
129,132,135,138,141,147-Atomic Knights app. 8.50 25.50 85.00
136,137,139,140,143,145,146,148,149,151,152,154,155,157-159: 159-Star Rovers app.; Gil Kane/Anderson-a. 5.00 15.00 50.00
142-2nd app. Faceless Creature 5.50 16.50 55.00
144-Only Atomic Knights-c (by M. Anderson) 9.50 28.50 95.00
150,153,156,160: Atomic Knights in each. 153-(6/63)-3rd app. Faceless Creature; atomic explosion-c. 160-Last Atomic Knights 6.50 19.50 65.00
161-179: 161-Last Space Museum. 163-Star Rovers app. 170-Infinity-c. 177-Intro/origin Immortal Man 3.50 10.50 35.00
180-Origin/1st app. Animal Man 19.00 51.00 190.00
181-183,185-189: 187-Intro/origin The Enchantress 2.50 7.50 22.00
184-2nd app. Animal Man by Gil Kane 11.50 34.00 115.00
190-1st app. Animal Man in costume 14.00 42.00 140.00
191-194,196-200,202-204 2.25 6.75 18.00
195-1st full app. Animal Man 7.50 22.50 75.00
201-Last Animal Man; 2nd full app. 3.50 10.50 35.00
205-(10/67)-Intro/origin Deadman by Infantino & begin series, ends #216 9.50 28.50 95.00
206-Neal Adams-a begins 6.00 18.00 60.00
207-210 5.00 15.00 50.00
211-216: 211-Space Museum-r. 216-(1-2/69)-Deadman story finally concludes in Brave & the Bold #86 (10-11/69); secret message panel by Neal Adams (pg. 13); tribute to Steranko 3.80 11.40 38.00
217-r/origin & 1st app. Adam Strange from Showcase #17, begin-r; Atomic Knights-r begin 1.50 4.50 12.00
218-221,223-225: 218-Last 12¢ issue. 225-Last 15¢ issue 1.50 4.50 12.00
222-New Adam Strange story; Kane/Anderson-a 2.50 7.50 24.00
226,227,230-236-(68-52 pgs.): 226, 227-New Adam Strange text story w/illos by Anderson (8,6 pgs.) 231-Last Atomic Knights-r. 235-JLA-c/s 1.50 4.50 12.00
228,229 (68 pgs.) 2.00 6.00 16.00
237-243 1.10 3.30 9.00
244-Last issue 1.50 4.50 12.00

NOTE: ***Neal Adams** a-206-216; c-207-216, 228, 235. **Anderson** a-8-52, 94, 96, 99, 115, 117, 119-163, 217r, 218r, 222, 223-225r, 226, 229r, 242i(r); c-18, 19, 21, 23, 24, 27, 30, 32-44(most); c/r-157i, 190i, 217-224, 228-231, 233, 235-239, 241-243. **Ditko** a-188, 189. **Drucker** a-42, 43, 45. **Elias** a-212. **Finlay** a-2, 3, 6, 7, 210r, 229r. **Giunta** a-237r. **Heath** a-116. **Infantino** a-10-101, 106-151, 154, 157-163, 180, 190, 218-221r, 223-244p(r); c-50; c(r)-190p, 197, 199-211, 218-221, 223-244. **Kaluta** c-238, 240. **Gil Kane** a-8-116, 124, 125, 130, 138, 146-157, 173-186, 204r, 222r, 227-231r; c(p)-11-17, 25, 154, 157. **Kubert** a-55(2 pgs.), 226; c-219, 220, 225-227, 232, 234. **Moriera** c-26, 28, 29, 71. **Morrow** c-230. **Mortimer** c-8. **Powell** a-4. **Sekowsky** a-71p, 97-162p, 217p(r), 218p(r); c-206, 217-219r. **Simon & Kirby** a-2r (2 pgs) **Sparling** a-201. **Toth** a-8, 12, 13, 17-19. **Wood** a-154i. Atomic Knights in #117, 120, 123, 126, 129, 132, 135, 138, 141, 144, 147, 150, 153, 156, 160. Atomic Knights reprints by **Anderson** in 217-221, 223-231. Chris KL99 in 1-3, 5, 7, 9, 11, 15. Capt. Comet covers-9-14, 17-19, 24, 26, 27, 32-44.*

STRANGE ADVENTURES
DC Comics (Vertigo): Nov, 1999 - No. 4 ($2.50, limited series)

1-Bolland-c; art by Bolland, Gibbons, Quitely 2.50

STRANGE AS IT SEEMS (See Famous Funnies-A Carnival of Comics, Feature Funnies #1, The John Hix Scrap Book & Peanuts)

STRANGE AS IT SEEMS
United Features Syndicate: 1939

Single Series 9, 1, 2 34.00 103.00 240.00

STRANGE ATTRACTORS
RetroGraphix: 1993 - No. 15, Feb, 1997 ($2.50, B&W)

1-15: 1-(5/93), 2-(8/93), 3-(11/93), 4-(2/94) 2.50
Volume One-($14.95, trade paperback)-r/#1-7 15.00

STRANGE ATTRACTORS: MOON FEVER
Caliber Comics: Feb, 1997 - No. 3, June, 1997 ($2.95, B&W, mini-series)

1-3 3.00

STRANGE COMBAT TALES
Marvel Comics (Epic Comics): Oct, 1993 - No. 4, Jan, 1994 ($2.50, limited series)

1-4 2.50

STRANGE CONFESSIONS
Ziff-Davis Publ. Co.: Jan-Mar (Spring on-c), 1952 - No. 4, Fall, 1952 (All have photo-c)

1(Scarce)-Kinstler-a 44.00 132.00 350.00
2(Scarce, 7-8/52) 33.00 99.00 230.00
3(Scarce, 9-10/52)-#3 on-c, #2 on inside; Reformatory girl story; photo-c 33.00 99.00 230.00
4(Scarce) 33.00 99.00 230.00

STRANGE DAYS
Eclipse Comics: Oct, 1984 - No. 3, Apr, 1985 ($1.75, Baxter paper)

1-3: Freakwave, Johnny Nemo, & Paradax from Vanguard Illustrated; nudity, violence & strong language 2.00

STRANGE DAYS (Movie)
Marvel Comics: Dec, 1995 ($5.95, squarebound, one-shot)

1-Adaptation of film 6.00

STRANGE FANTASY (Eerie Tales of Suspense!)(Formerly Rocketman #1)
Ajax-Farrell: Aug, 1952 - No. 14, Oct-Nov, 1954

2(#1, 8/52)-Jungle Princess story; Kamenish-a; reprinted from Ellery Queen #1 40.00 120.00 300.00
2(10/52)-No Black Cat or Rulah; Bakerish, Kamenish-a; hypo/meathook-c 34.00 103.00 240.00
3-Rulah story, called Pulah 33.00 99.00 230.00
4-Rocket Man app. (2/53) 30.00 90.00 210.00
5,6,8,10,12,14 21.00 64.00 150.00
7-Madam Satan/Slave story 30.00 90.00 210.00
9(w/Black Cat), 9(w/Boy's Ranch; S&K-a)(A rebinding of Harvey interiors; not publ. by Ajax) 26.00 79.00 185.00

GD2.0 FN6.0 NM9.4

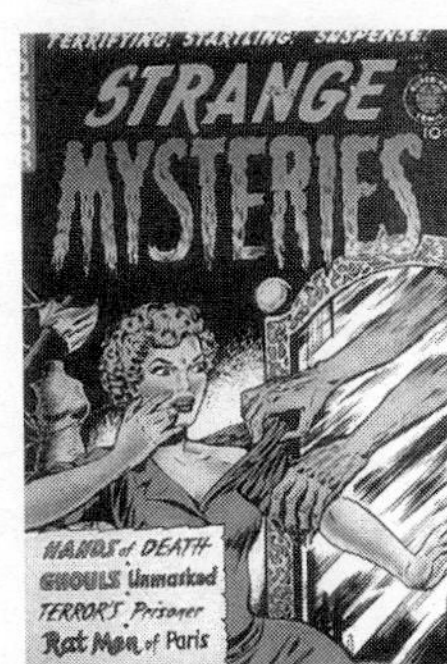

Strange Mysteries #4 © SUPR

Strangers in Paradise V3 #15 © Terry Moore

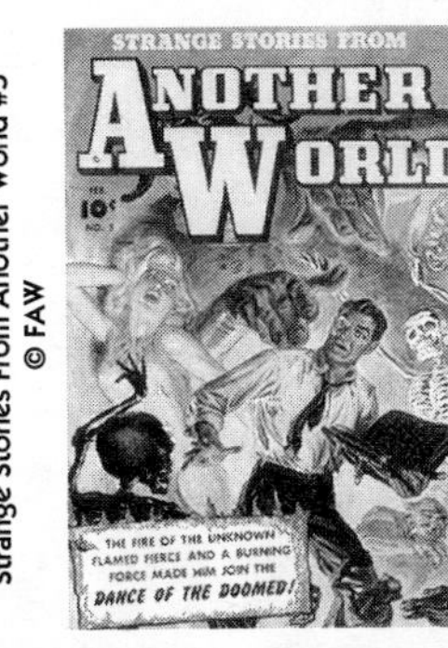

Strange Stories From Another World #5 © FAW

GD2.0 FN6.0 NM9.4

9-Regular issue; Steve Ditko's 3rd published work (tied with Captain 3D) 40.00 120.00 300.00
11-Jungle story 29.00 86.00 200.00
13-Bondage-c; Rulah (Kolah) story 29.00 86.00 200.00

STRANGE GALAXY
Eerie Publications: V1#8, Feb, 1971 - No. 11, Aug, 1971 (B&W, magazine)
V1#8-Reprints-c/Fantastic V19#3 (2/70) (a pulp) 2.60 7.80 26.00
9-11 2.50 7.50 20.00

STRANGEHAVEN
Abiogenesis Press: June, 1995 - Present ($2.95, B&W)
1-12 3.00

STRANGE JOURNEY
America's Best (Steinway Publ.) (Ajax/Farrell): Sept, 1957 - No. 4, Jun, 1958 (Farrell reprints)
1 18.00 54.00 125.00
2-4: 2-Flying saucer-c 12.00 36.00 85.00

STRANGE LOVE (See Fox Giants)

STRANGELOVE
Entity Comics: 1995 ($2.50)
1 2.50

STRANGE MYSTERIES
Superior/Dynamic Publications: Sept, 1951 - No. 21, Jan, 1955
1-Kamenish-a & horror stories begin 52.00 157.00 420.00
2 30.00 90.00 210.00
3-5 26.00 79.00 185.00
6-8 22.00 66.00 155.00
9-Bondage 3-D effect-c 29.00 86.00 200.00
10-Used in **SOTI**, pg. 181 21.00 62.00 145.00
11-18 18.00 54.00 125.00
19-r/Journey Into Fear #1; cover is a splash from one story; Baker-r(2) 20.00 60.00 140.00
20,21-Reprints; 20-r/#1 with new-c 12.00 36.00 85.00

STRANGE MYSTERIES
I. W. Enterprises/Super Comics: 1963 - 1964
I.W. Reprint #9; Rulah-r/Spook #28; Disbrow-a 3.00 9.00 30.00
Super Reprint #10-12,15-17(1963-64): 10,11-r/Strange #2,1. 12-r/Tales of Horror #5 (3/53) less-c. 15-r/Dark Mysteries #23. 16-r/The Dead Who Walk. 17-r/Dark Mysteries #22 3.00 9.00 30.00
Super Reprint #18-r/Witchcraft #1; Kubert-a 3.00 9.00 30.00

STRANGE PLANETS
I. W. Enterprises/Super Comics: 1958; 1963-64
I.W. Reprint #1(nd)-Reprints E. C. Incredible S/F #30 plus-c/Strange Worlds #3 6.00 18.00 60.00
I.W. Reprint #9-Orlando/Wood-r/Strange Worlds #4; cover-r from Flying Saucers #1 8.00 24.00 80.00
Super Reprint #10-Wood-r (22 pg.) from Space Detective #1; cover-r/Attack on Planet Mars 7.50 22.50 75.00
Super Reprint #11-Wood-r (25 pg.) from An Earthman on Venus 9.00 27.00 90.00
Super Reprint #12-Orlando-r/Rocket to the Moon 7.50 22.50 75.00
Super Reprint #15-Reprints Journey Into Unknown Worlds #8; Heath, Colan-r 3.50 10.50 35.00
Super Reprint #16-Reprints Avon's Strange Worlds #6; Kinstler, Check-a 4.00 12.00 40.00
Super Reprint #18-r/Great Exploits #1 (Daring Adventures #6); Space Busters, Explorer Joe, The Son of Robin Hood; Krigstein-a 3.00 9.00 30.00

STRANGERS, THE
Malibu Comics (Ultraverse): June, 1993 - No. 24, May, 1995 ($1.95/$2.50)
1-4,6-12,14-20: 1-1st app. The Strangers; has coupon for Ultraverse Premiere #0; 1st app. the Night Man (not in costume). 2-Polybagged w/trading card. 7-Break-Thru x-over. 8-2 pg. origin Solution. 12-Silver foil logo; wraparound-c. 17-Rafferty app. 2.50
1-With coupon missing 2.00
1-Full cover holographic edition, 1st of kind w/Hardcase #1 & Prime #1 6.00
1-Ultra 5000 limited silver foil 4.00
4-($2.50)-Newsstand edition bagged w/card 2.50
5-($2.50, 52 pgs.)-Rune flip-c/story by B. Smith (3 pgs.); The Mighty Magnor 1 pg. strip by Aragones; 3-pg. Night Man preview 2.50
13-($3.50, 68 pgs.)-Mantra app.; flip book w/Ultraverse Premiere #4 3.50
21-24 ($2.50) 2.50
...:The Pilgrim Conundrum Saga (1/95, $3.95, 68pgs.) 4.00

STRANGERS IN PARADISE
Antarctic Press: Nov, 1993 - No. 3, Feb, 1994 ($2.75, B&W, limited series)
1 5.00 15.00 55.00
1-2nd/3rd prints 5.00
2 (2300 printed) 4.00 12.00 40.00
3 2.50 7.50 25.00
Trade paperback (Antarctic Press, $6.95)-Red -c (5000 print run) 10.00
Trade paperback (Abstract Studios, $6.95)-Red-c (2000 print run) 15.00
Trade paperback (Abstract Studios, $6.95, 1st-4th printing)-Blue- 7.00
Hardcover ('98, $29.95) includes first draft pages 30.00
Gold Reprint Series ($2.75) 1-3-r/#1-3 2.75

STRANGERS IN PARADISE
Abstract Studios: Sept, 1994 - No. 14, July, 1996 ($2.75, B&W)
1 2.00 6.00 16.00
1,3- 2nd printings 4.00
2,3: 2-Color dream sequence. 1.00 3.00 8.00
4-10 4.00
4-6-2nd printings 2.75
11-14: 14-The Letters of Molly & Poo 3.00
Gold Reprint Series ($2.75) 1-13-r/#1-13 2.75
I Dream Of You ($16.95, TPB) r/#1-9 17.00
It's a Good Life ($8.95, TPB) r/#10-13 9.00

STRANGERS IN PARADISE (Volume Three)
Homage Comics #1-8/Abstract Studios #9-on: Oct, 1996 - Present ($2.75, color #1-5, B&W #6-on)
1-Terry Moore-c/s/a in all; dream seq. by Jim Lee-a 5.00
1-Jim Lee variant-c 5.00
2-5 4.00
6-25: 6-Return to B&W. 13-15-High school flashback. 16-Xena Warrior Princess parody; two covers 3.00
...Lyrics and Poems (2/99) 2.75
High School ('98, $8.95, TPB) r/#13-16 9.00
Immortal ('98, $14.95, TPB) r/#6-12 15.00
Love Me Tender ($12.95, TPB) r/#1-5 in B&W w/ color Lee seq. 13.00

STRANGE SPORTS STORIES (See Brave & the Bold #45-49, DC Special, and DC Super Stars #10)
National Periodical Publications: Sept-Oct, 1973 - No. 6, July-Aug, 1974
1 2.50 7.50 24.00
2-6: 2-Swan/Anderson-a 1.85 5.50 15.00

STRANGE STORIES FROM ANOTHER WORLD (Unknown World #1)
Fawcett Publications: No. 2, Aug, 1952 - No. 5, Feb, 1953
2-Saunders painted-c 45.00 135.00 360.00
3-5-Saunders painted-c 37.00 111.00 260.00

STRANGE STORIES OF SUSPENSE (Rugged Action #1-4)
Atlas Comics (CSI): No. 5, Oct, 1955 - No. 16, Aug, 1957
5(#1) 36.00 107.00 250.00
6,9 21.00 64.00 150.00
7-E. C. swipe cover/Vault of Horror #32 22.00 66.00 155.00
8-Morrow/Williamson-a; Pakula-a 23.00 69.00 160.00
10-Crandall, Torres, Meskin-a 22.00 66.00 155.00
11-13: 12-Torres, Pakula-a. 13-E.C. art swipes 18.00 54.00 125.00
14-16: 14-Williamson/Mayo-a. 15-Krigstein-a. 16-Fox, Powell-a 19.00 58.00 135.00

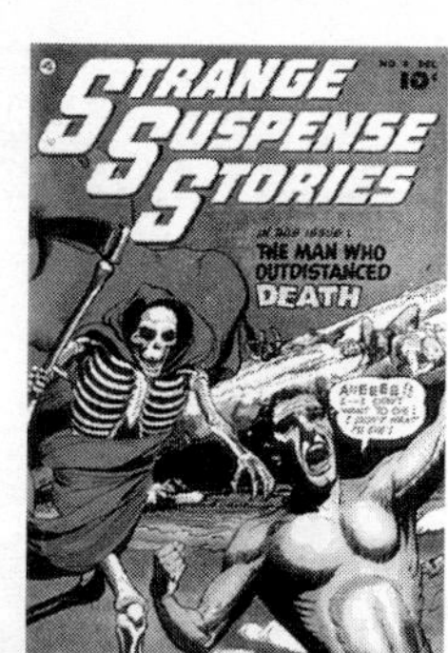

Strange Suspense Stories #4 © FAW

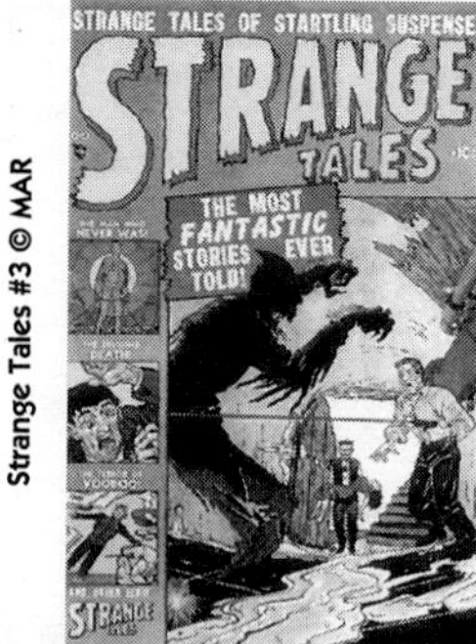

Strange Tales #3 © MAR

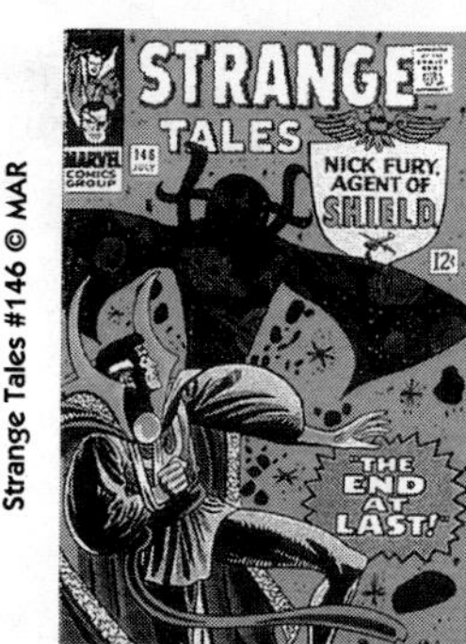

Strange Tales #146 © MAR

GD2.0 FN6.0 NM9.4

NOTE: *Everett a-6, 7, 13; c-8, 9, 11-14. Heath a-5. Maneely c-5. Morisi a-11. Morrow a-13. Powell a-8. Severin c-7. Wildey a-14.*

STRANGE STORY (Also see Front Page)
Harvey Publications: June-July, 1946 (52 pgs.)

1-The Man in Black Called Fate by Powell 28.00 84.00 195.00

STRANGE SUSPENSE STORIES (Lawbreakers Suspense Stories #10-15; This Is Suspense #23-26; Captain Atom V1#78 on)
Fawcett Publications/Charlton Comics No. 16 on: 6/52 - No. 5, 2/53; No. 16, 1/54 - No. 22, 11/54; No. 27, 10/55 - No. 77, 10/65; V3#1, 10/67 - V1#9, 9/69

1-(Fawcett)-Powell, Sekowsky-a 67.00 202.00 540.00
2-George Evans horror story 43.00 128.00 340.00
3-5 (2/53)-George Evans horror stories 40.00 120.00 290.00
16(1-2/54)-Formerly Lawbreakers S.S. 27.00 81.00 190.00
17,21: 21-Shuster-a 21.00 64.00 150.00
18-E.C. swipe/HOF 7; Ditko-c/a(2) 37.00 111.00 260.00
19-Ditko electric chair-c; Ditko-a 45.00 135.00 360.00
20-Ditko-c/a(2) 37.00 11.00 260.00
22(11/54)-Ditko-c, Shuster-a; last pre-code issue; becomes This Is Suspense 31.00 94.00 220.00
27(10/55)-(Formerly This Is Suspense #26) 13.00 39.00 90.00
28-30,38 9.15 27.00 55.00
31-33,35,37,40-Ditko-c/a(2-3 each) 19.00 58.00 135.00
34-Story of ruthless business man, Wm. B. Gaines; Ditko-c/a 40.00 120.00 280.00
36-(15¢, 68 pgs.); Ditko-a(4) 21.00 64.00 150.00
39,41,52,53-Ditko-a 17.00 49.00 115.00
42-44,46,49,54-60 3.50 10.50 35.00
45,47,48,50,51-Ditko-c/a 9.00 27.00 90.00
61-74 2.25 6.75 18.00
75(6/65)-Reprints origin/1st app. Captain Atom by Ditko from Space Advs. #33; r/Severin-a/Space Advs. #24 (75-77: 12¢ issues) 11.00 33.00 110.00
76,77-Captain Atom-r by Ditko/Space Advs. 5.00 15.00 50.00
V3#1(10/67): 12¢ issues begin 2.50 7.50 22.00
V1#2-Ditko-c/a; atom bomb-c 2.25 6.75 18.00
V1#3-9: All 12¢ issues 1.50 4.50 12.00

NOTE: *Alascia a-19. Aparo a-60, V3#1, 2, 4; c-V1#4, 8. Baily a-1-3; c-2, 5. Evans c-3, 4. Giordano c-16, 17p, 24p, 25p. Montes/Bache c-66. Powell a-4. Shuster a-19, 21. Marcus Swayze a-27.*

STRANGE TALES (...Featuring Warlock #178-181; Doctor Strange #169 on)
Atlas (CCPC #1-67/ZPC #68-79/VPI #80-85)/Marvel #86(7/61) on: June, 1951 - #168, May, 1968; #169, Sept, 1973 - #188, Nov, 1976

1-Horror/weird stories begin 255.00 766.00 2600.00
2 95.00 286.00 860.00
3,5: 3-Atom bomb panels 70.00 211.00 625.00
4-Cosmic eyeball story "The Evil Eye" 76.00 230.00 675.00
6-9: 6-Heath-c/a. 7-Colan-a 53.00 159.00 475.00
10-Krigstein-a 58.00 172.00 500.00
11-14,16-20 38.00 114.00 300.00
15-Krigstein-a 39.00 116.00 310.00
21,23-27,29-34: 27-Atom bomb panels. 33-Davis-a. 34-Last pre-code issue (2/55) 30.00 90.00 235.00
22-Krigstein, Forte/Fox-a 31.00 92.00 240.00
28-Jack Katz story used in Senate Investigation report, pgs. 7 & 169 31.00 94.00 245.00
35-41,43,44: 37-Vampire story by Colan 19.00 57.00 190.00
42,45,59,61-Krigstein-a; #61 (2/58) 19.50 58.00 195.00
46-57,60: 51-1st S.A. issue. 53,56-Crandall-a. 60-(8/57) 17.00 51.00 170.00
58,64-Williamson-a in each, with Mayo-#58 17.50 52.00 175.00
62,63,65,66: 62-Torres-a. 66-Crandall-a 16.00 48.00 160.00
67-Prototype ish. (Quicksilver) 18.50 55.00 185.00
68,71,72,74,77,80: Ditko/Kirby-a in #67-80 17.00 51.00 170.00
69,70,73,75,76,78,79: 69-Prototype ish. (Prof. X). 70-Prototype ish. (Giant Man). 73-Prototype ish. (Ant-Man). 75-Prototype ish. (Iron Man). 76-Prototype ish. (Human Torch). 78-Prototype ish. (Ant-Man). 79-Prototype ish. (Dr. Strange) (12/60) 22.00 66.00 220.00

GD2.0 FN6.0 NM9.4

81-83,85-88,90,91-Ditko/Kirby-a in all: 86-Robot-c. 90-(11/61)-Atom bomb blast panel 15.00 45.00 150.00
84-Prototype ish. (Magneto)(5/61); has powers like Magneto of X-Men, but two years earlier; Ditko/Kirby-a 18.50 55.00 185.00
89-1st app. Fin Fang Foom (10/61) by Kirby 40.00 120.00 440.00
92-Prototype ish. (Ancient One); last 10¢ issue 16.00 48.00 160.00
93,95,96,98-100: Kirby-a 14.00 42.00 140.00
94-Prototype ish. (The Thing); Kirby-a 16.00 48.00 160.00
97-1st app. Aunt May & Uncle Ben by Ditko (6/62), before Amazing Fantasy #15; (see Tales Of Suspense #7); Kirby-a 43.00 128.00 340.00

GD2.0 FN6.0 VF8.0 NM9.4

101-Human Torch begins by Kirby (10/62); origin recap Fantastic Four & Human Torch; H. Torch-c begin 73.00 219.00 438.00 875.00

GD2.0 FN6.0 NM9.4

102-1st app. Wizard; robot-c 29.00 87.00 290.00
103-105: 104-1st app. Trapster. 105-2nd Wizard 24.00 72.00 240.00
106,108,109: 106-Fantastic Four guests (3/63) 15.50 47.00 155.00
107-(4/63)-Human Torch/Sub-Mariner battle; 4th S.A. Sub-Mariner app. & 1st x-over outside of Fantastic Four 19.00 57.00 190.00

GD2.0 FN6.0 VF8.0 NM9.4

110-(7/63)-Intro Doctor Strange, Ancient One & Wong by Ditko 88.00 263.00 528.00 1050.00

GD2.0 FN6.0 NM9.4

111-2nd Dr. Strange 29.00 87.00 290.00
112,113 10.50 32.00 105.00
114-Acrobat disguised as Captain America, 1st app. since the G.A.; intro. & 1st app. Victoria Bentley; 3rd Dr. Strange app. & begin series (11/63) 31.00 93.00 325.00
115-Origin Dr. Strange; Human Torch vs. Sandman (Spidey villain; 2nd app. & brief origin); early Spider-Man x-over, 12/63 38.00 114.00 425.00
116-(1/64)-Human Torch battles The Thing; 1st Thing x-over 10.00 30.00 100.00
117,118,120: 120-1st Iceman x-over (from X-Men) 6.50 19.50 65.00
119-Spider-Man x-over (2 panel cameo) 9.00 27.00 90.00
121,122,124,126-134: Thing/Torch team-up in 121-134. 126-Intro Clea. 128-Quicksilver & Scarlet Witch app. (1/65). 130-The Beatles cameo. 134-Last Human Torch; The Watcher-c/story; Wood-a(i) 4.50 13.50 45.00
123-1st app. The Beetle (see Amazing Spider-Man #21 for next app.); 1st Thor x-over (8/64); Loki app. 5.00 15.00 50.00
125-Torch & Thing battle Sub-Mariner (10/64) 5.00 15.00 50.00
135-Col. (formerly Sgt.) Nick Fury becomes Nick Fury Agent of Shield (origin/1st app.) by Kirby (8/65); series begins 8.00 24.00 80.00
136-140: 138-Intro Eternity 3.00 9.00 30.00
141-147,149: 145-Begins alternating-c features w/Nick Fury (odd #'s) & Dr. Strange (even #'s). 146-Last Ditko Dr. Strange who is in consecutive stories since #113; only Ditko Dr. Strange-c this title. 147-Dr. Strange (by Everett #147-152) continues thru #168, then Dr. Strange #169 2.50 7.50 25.00
148-Origin Ancient One 5.00 15.00 50.00
150(11/66)-John Buscema's 1st work at Marvel 3.00 9.00 30.00
151-Kirby/Steranko-c/a; 1st Marvel work by Steranko 4.00 12.00 40.00
152,153-Kirby/Steranko-a 3.00 9.00 30.00
154-158-Steranko-a/script 3.00 9.00 30.00
159-Origin Nick Fury retold; Intro Val; Captain America-c/story; Steranko-a 3.20 9.60 32.00
160-162-Steranko-a/scripts; Capt. America app. 2.50 7.50 25.00
163-166,168-Steranko-a(p). 168-Last Nick Fury (gets own book next month) & last Dr. Strange who also gets own book 2.50 7.50 20.00
167-Steranko pen/script; classic flag-c; last 12¢-c 3.00 12.00 30.00
169-1st app. Brother Voodoo(origin in #169,170) & begin series, ends #173. 1.25 3.75 10.00
170-174: 174-Origin Golem 1.00 3.00 8.00
175-177: 177-Brunner-c 4.00
178-(2/75)-Warlock by Starlin begins; origin Warlock & Him retold; 1st app. Magus; Starlin-c/a/scripts in 178-181 (all before Warlock #9) 1.75 5.25 14.00
179-181-All Warlock. 179-Intro/1st app. Pip the Troll. 180-Intro Gamora. 181-

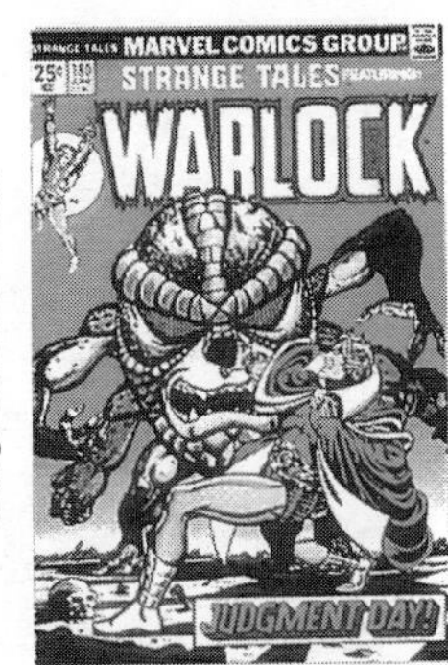

Strange Tales #180 © MAR

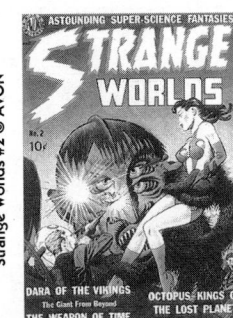

Strange Worlds #2 © AVON

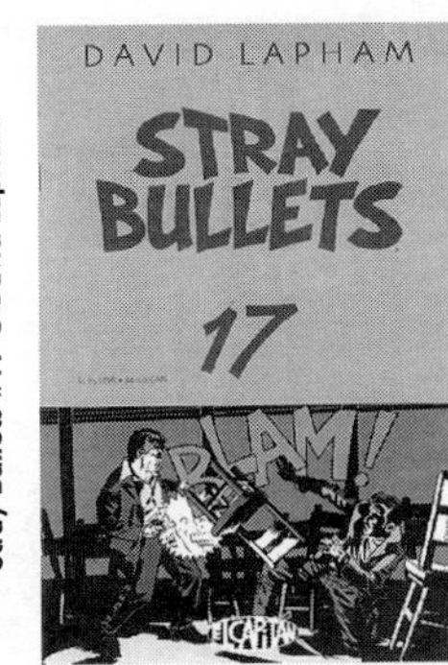

Stray Bullets #17 © David Lapham

GD2.0 FN6.0 NM9.4

(8/75)-Warlock story continued in Warlock #9 1.00 3.00 8.00
32-188: 185,186-(Regular 25¢ editions) 4.00
35,186-(30¢-c variants, limited distribution)(5,7/76) 1.75 5.25 14.00
nnual 1(1962)-Reprints from Strange Tales #73,76,78, Tales of Suspense #7,9, Tales to Astonish #1,6,7, & Journey Into Mystery #53,55,59; (1st Marvel annual?) 42.00 125.00 460.00
nnual 2(7/63)-Reprints from Strange Tales #67, Strange Worlds (Atlas) #1-3, World of Fantasy #16; new Human Torch vs. Spider-Man story by Kirby/Ditko (1st Spidey x-over; 4th app.); Kirby-c
41.00 123.00 500.00

OTE: **Briefer** *a-17.* **Burgos** *a-123p.* **J. Buscema** *a-174p.* **Colan** *a-7, 11, 20, 37, 53, 169-173p, 88p.* **Davis** *c-71.* **Ditko** *a-46, 50, 67-122, 123-125p, 126-146, 175r, 182-188r; c-51, 93, 115, 21, 146.* **Everett** *a-4, 21, 40-42, 73, 147-152, 164i; c-8, 10, 11, 13, 15, 24, 45, 49-54, 56, 58, 60, 1, 63, 148, 150, 152, 158i.* **Forte** *a-27, 43, 50, 53, 54, 60.* **Heath** *a-6; c-6, 18-20.* **Kamen** *a-45.* **. Kane** *c-170-173, 182p.* **Kirby** *Human Torch-101-105, 108, 109, 114, 120; Nick Fury-135p, 41-143p; (Layouts)-135-153; other* **Kirby** *a-67-100p; c-68-70, 72-74, 76-92, 94, 95, 101-114, 16-123, 125-130, 132-135, 136p, 138-145, 147, 149, 151p.* **Kirby/Ayers** *c-101-106, 108-110.* **irby/Ditko** *a-80, 88, 121; c-75, 93, 97, 100. .* **Lawrence** *a-29.* **Leiber/ Fox** *a-110, 111, 113.* **laneely** *a-3, 7, 37, 42; c-33, 40.* **Moldoff** *a-20.* **Mooney** *a-174i.* **Morisi** *a-53, 56.* **Morrow** *a-54.* **rlando** *a-41, 44, 46, 49, 52.* **Powell** *a-42, 44, 49, 54, 130-134p; c-131p.* **Reinman** *a-11, 50, 74, 8, 91, 95, 104, 106, 112i, 124-127i.* **Robinson** *a-17.* **Romita** *c-169.* **Roussos** *c-201i.* **R.Q. Sale** *-56; c-16.* **Sekowski** *a-3, 11.* **Severin** *a(i)-136-138; c-137.* **Starlin** *a-178, 179, 180p, 181p; c-78-180, 181p.* **Steranko** *a-151-161, 162-168p; c-151i, 153, 155, 157, 159, 161, 163, 165, 167.* **orres** *a-53, 62.* **Tuska** *a-14, 166p.* **Whitney** *a-149.* **Wildey** *a-42, 56.* **Woodbridge** *a-59. antastic Four cameos #101-134. Jack Katz app.-26.*

STRANGE TALES
Marvel Comics Group: Apr, 1987 - No. 19, Oct, 1988

/2#1-19 2.00

STRANGE TALES
Marvel Comics: Nov, 1994 ($6.95, one-shot)

/3#1-acetate-c 7.00

STRANGE TALES (Anthology; continues stories from Man-Thing #8 and Verewolf By Night #6)
Marvel Comics: Sept, 1998 - No. 2, Oct, 1998 ($4.99)

1,2: 1-Silver Surfer app. 2-Two covers 5.00

STRANGE TALES: DARK CORNERS
Marvel Comics: May, 1998 ($3.99, one-shot)

1-Anthology; stories by Baron & Maleev, McGregor & Dringenberg, DeMatteis & Badger; Estes painted-c 4.00

STRANGE TALES OF THE UNUSUAL
Atlas Comics (ACI No. 1-4/WPI No. 5-11): Dec, 1955 - No. 11, Aug, 1957

1-Powell-a 40.00 120.00 310.00
2 25.00 75.00 175.00
3-Williamson-a (4 pgs.) 26.00 77.00 180.00
4,6,8,11 18.00 54.00 125.00
5-Crandall, Ditko-a 23.00 69.00 160.00
7,9: 7-Kirby, Orlando-a. 9-Krigstein-a 19.00 58.00 135.00
10-Torres, Morrow-a 18.00 54.00 125.00

NOTE: **Baily** *a-6.* **Brodsky** *c-2-4.* **Everett** *a-2, 6; c-6, 9, 11.* **Heck** *a-1.* **Maneely** *c-1.* **Orlando** *a-7.* **Pakula** *a-10.* **Romita** *a-1.* **R.Q. Sale** *a-3.* **Wildey** *a-3.*

STRANGE TERRORS
St. John Publishing Co.: June, 1952 - No. 7, Mar, 1953

1-Bondage-c; Zombies spelled Zoombies on-c; Fine-*esque* -a
45.00 135.00 360.00
2 27.00 81.00 190.00
3-Kubert-a; painted-c 36.00 107.00 250.00
4-Kubert-a (reprinted in Mystery Tales #18); Ekgren painted-c; Fine-*esque* -a; Jerry Iger caricature 43.00 128.00 340.00
5-Kubert-a; painted-c 36.00 107.00 250.00
6-Giant (25¢, 100 pgs.)(1/53); bondage-c 43.00 128.00 340.00
7-Giant (25¢, 100 pgs.); Kubert-c/a 46.00 139.00 370.00

NOTE: **Cameron** *a-6, 7.* **Morisi** *a-6.*

STRANGE WORLD OF YOUR DREAMS
Prize Publications: Aug, 1952 - No. 4, Jan-Feb, 1953

1-Simon & Kirby-a 60.00 180.00 480.00

GD2.0 FN6.0 NM9.4

2,3-Simon & Kirby-c/a. 2-Meskin-a 47.00 142.00 380.00
4-S&K-c; Meskin-a 40.00 120.00 320.00

STRANGE WORLDS (#18 continued from Avon's Eerie #1-17)
Avon Periodicals: 11/50 - No. 9, 11/52; No. 18, 10-11/54 - No. 22, 9-10/55 (No #11-17)

1-Kenton of the Star Patrol by Kubert (r/Eerie #1 from 1947); Crom the Barbarian by John Giunta 91.00 272.00 725.00
2-Wood-a; Crom the Barbarian by Giunta; Dara of the Vikings app.; used in **SOTI**, pg. 112; injury to eye panel 87.00 262.00 700.00
3-Wood/Orlando-a (Kenton), Wood/Williamson/Frazetta/Krenkel/Orlando-a (7 pgs.); Malu Slave Girl Princess app.; Kinstler-c
169.00 506.00 1350.00
4-Wood-c/a (Kenton); Orlando-a; origin The Enchanted Daggar; Sultan-a; classic cover 87.00 262.00 700.00
5-Orlando/Wood-a (Kenton); Wood-c 55.00 165.00 440.00
6-Kinstler-a(2); Orlando/Wood-c; Check-a 40.00 120.00 300.00
7-Fawcette & Becker/Alascia-a 36.00 107.00 250.00
8-Kubert, Kinstler, Hollingsworth & Lazarus-a; Lazarus Robot-c
36.00 107.00 250.00
9-Kinstler, Fawcette, Alascia-a 34.00 103.00 240.00
18-(Formerly Eerie #17)-Reprints "Attack on Planet Mars" by Kubert
31.00 94.00 220.00
19-r/Avon's "Robotmen of the Lost Planet"; last pre-code issue; Robot-c
31.00 94.00 220.00
20-War-c/story; Wood-c(r)/U.S. Paratroops #1 9.15 27.00 55.00
21,22-War-c/stories. 22-New logo 6.70 20.00 40.00
I.W. Reprint #5-Kinstler-a(r)/Avon's #9 2.50 7.50 24.00

STRANGE WORLDS
Marvel Comics (MPI No. 1,2/Male No. 3,5): Dec, 1958 - No. 5, Aug, 1959

1-Kirby & Ditko-a; flying saucer issue 80.00 240.00 640.00
2-Ditko-c/a 45.00 135.00 360.00
3-Kirby-a(2) 39.00 118.00 275.00
4-Williamson-a 36.00 107.00 250.00
5-Ditko-a 30.00 90.00 210.00

NOTE: **Buscema** *a-3, 4.* **Ditko** *a-1-5; c-2..* **Heck** *a-2.* **Kirby** *a-1, 3.* **Kirby/Brodsky** *c-1, 3-5.*

STRAWBERRY SHORTCAKE
Marvel Comics (Star Comics): Jun, 1985 - No. 7, Apr, 1986 (Children's comic)

1-7: Howie Post-a 3.00

STRAY BULLETS
El Capitan Books: 1995 - Present ($2.95, B&W, mature readers)

1-David Lapham-c/a/scripts 1.50 4.50 12.00
2,3 1.00 3.00 8.00
4-8 5.00
9-14 4.00
15-20-(2.95) 3.00
Volume 1 ($29.95, hardcover) 30.00

NOTE: *Multiple printings of all issues exist & are worth cover price.*

STRAY TOASTERS
Marvel Comics (Epic Comics): Jan, 1988 - No. 4, April, 1989 ($3.50, squarebound, limited series)

1-4: Sienkiewicz-c/a/scripts 3.50

STREET COMIX
Street Enterprises/King Features: 1973 (50¢, B&W, 36 pgs.)(20,000 print run)

1,2: 1-Rip Kirby. 2-Flash Gordon 1.10 3.30 9.00

STREETFIGHTER
Ocean Comics: Aug, 1986 - No. 4, Spr, 1987 ($1.75, limited series)

1-4: 2-Origin begins 2.00

STREET FIGHTER
Malibu Comics: Sept, 1993 - No. 3, Nov, 1993 ($2.95)

1-3: 3-Includes poster; Ferret x-over 3.00

STREET FIGHTER: THE BATTLE FOR SHADALOO

Street Fighter II #3 © Viz

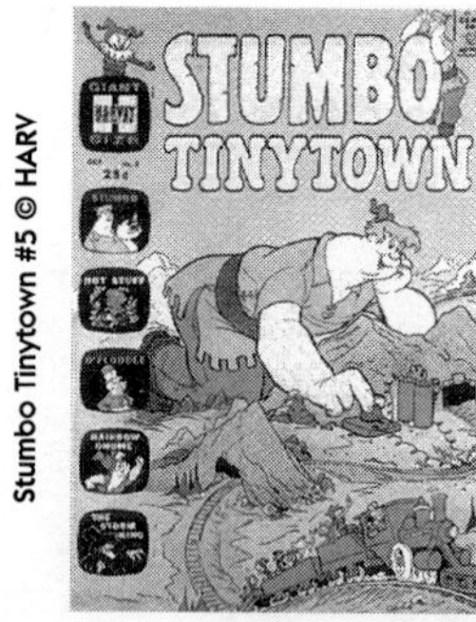

Stumbo Tinytown #5 © HARV

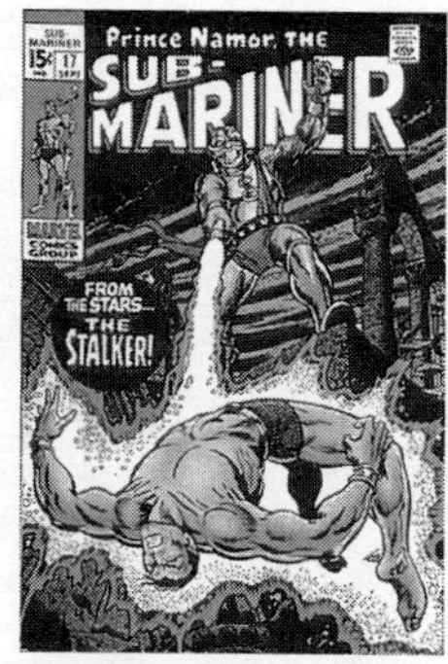

The Sub-Mariner #17 © MAR

GD2.0 FN6.0 NM9.4

DC Comics/CAP Co. Ltd.: 1995 ($3.95, one-shot)
1-polybagged w/trading card & Tattoo 4.00

STREET FIGHTER II
Tokuma Comics (Viz): Apr, 1994 - No. 8, Nov, 1994 ($2.95, limited series)
1-8 3.00

STREET POET RAY
Blackthorne Publ./Marvel Comics: Spring, 1989; 1990 - No. 4, 1990 ($2.95, B&W, squarebound)
1 (Blackthorne, $2.00) 3.00
1-4 (Marvel, $2.95, thick-c & paper) 3.00

STREETS
DC Comics: 1993 - No. 3, 1993 ($4.95, limited series, 52 pgs.)
Book 1-3-Estes painted-c 5.00

STREET SHARKS
Archie Publications: Jan, 1996 - No. 3, Mar, 1996 ($1.50, limited series)
1-3 2.00

STREET SHARKS
Archie Publications: May, 1996 - Present ($1.50, published 8 times a year)
1-6 2.00

STRICTLY PRIVATE (You're in the Army Now)
Eastern Color Printing Co.: July, 1942 (#1 on sale 6/15/42)
1,2: Private Peter Plink. 2-Says 128 pgs. on-c 22.00 66.00 155.00

STRIKE!
Eclipse Comics: Aug, 1987 - No. 6, Jan, 1988 ($1.75)
1-6, ...Vs. Sgt. Strike Special 1 (5/88, $1.95) 2.00

STRIKEBACK! (The Hunt For Nikita)
Malibu Comics (Bravura): Oct, 1994 - No. 3, Jan, 1995 ($2.95, unfinished limited series)
1-3: Jonathon Peterson script, Kevin Maguire-c/a 3.00
1-Gold foil embossed-c 5.00

STRIKEBACK!
Image Comics (WildStorm Productions): Jan, 1996 - No. 5, May, 1996 ($2.50, limited series)
1-5: Reprints original Bravura series w/additional story & art by Kevin Maguire & Jonathon Peterson; new Maguire-c in all. 4,5-New story & art 2.50

STRIKEFORCE: AMERICA
Comico: Dec, 1995 ($2.95)
V2#1-Polybagged w/gaming card; S. Clark-a(p) 3.00

STRIKEFORCE: MORITURI
Marvel Comics Group: Dec, 1986 - No. 31, July, 1989
1-31: 14-Williamson-i. 13-Double size. 25-Heath-c 2.00

STRIKEFORCE MORITURI: ELECTRIC UNDERTOW
Marvel Comics: Dec, 1989 - No. 5, Mar, 1990 ($3.95, 52 pgs., limited series)
1-5 Squarebound 4.00

STRONG GUY REBORN (See X-Factor)
Marvel Comics: Sept, 1997 ($2.99, one-shot)
1-Dezago-s/Andy Smith, Art Thibert-a 3.00

STRONG MAN (Also see Complimentary Comics & Power of...)
Magazine Enterprises: Mar-Apr, 1955 - No. 4, Sept-Oct, 1955
1(A-1 #130)-Powell-c/a 21.00 62.00 145.00
2-4: (A-1 #132,134,139)-Powell-a. 2-Powell-c 17.00 51.00 120.00

STRONTIUM DOG
Eagle Comics: Dec, 1985 - No. 4, Mar, 1986 ($1.25, limited series)
1-4: 4-Moore script. 2.00
Special 1 (1986)-Moore script 2.00

STRYFE'S STRIKE FILE

GD2.0 FN6.0 NM9.4

Marvel Comics: Jan, 1993 ($1.75, one-shot, no ads)
1-Stroman, Capullo, Andy Kubert, Brandon Peterson-a; silver metallic ink-c; X-Men tie-in to X-Cutioner's Song 2.00
1-Gold metallic ink 2nd printing 2.00

STRYKE
London Night Studios: 1995 ($3.00)
0, 0-Alternate-c 3.00

STUMBO THE GIANT (See Harvey Hits #49,54,57,60,63,66,69,72,78,88 & Hot Stuff #2)

STUMBO TINYTOWN
Harvey Publications: Oct, 1963 - No. 13, Nov, 1966 (All 25¢ giants)
1-Stumbo, Hot Stuff & others begin 13.50 41.00 135.00
2 8.00 24.00 80.00
3-5 5.50 16.50 55.00
6-13 4.50 13.50 45.00

STUNT DAWGS
Harvey Comics: Mar, 1993 ($1.25, one-shot)
1 2.00

STUNTMAN COMICS (Also see Thrills Of Tomorrow)
Harvey Publ.: Apr-May, 1946 - No. 2, June-July, 1946; No. 3, Oct-Nov, 1946
1-Origin Stuntman by S&K reprinted in Black Cat #9; S&K-c 100.00 300.00 800.00
2-S&K-c/a; The Duke of Broadway story 65.00 195.00 520.00
3-Small size (5-1/2x8-1/2"; B&W; 32 pgs.); distributed to mail subscribers only; S&K-a; Kid Adonis by S&K reprinted in Green Hornet #37
Estimated value... $250.00-$400.00
(Also see All-New #15, Boy Explorers #2, Flash Gordon #5 & Thrills of Tomorrow)

STUPID HEROES
Mirage Studios: Sept, 1993 - No. 3, Dec, 1994 ($2.75, unfinished limited series)
1-3-Laird-c/a & scripts; 2 trading cards bound in 2.75

STYGMATA
Entity Comics: No. 0, July, 1994 - No. 3, Oct, 1994 ($2.95, B&W, limited series)
0, 1-3: 0,1-Foil-c. 3-Silver foil logo 3.00
Yearbook 1 (1995, $2.95) 3.00

SUBHUMAN
Dark Horse Comics: Nov, 1998 - No. 4, Feb, 1999 ($2.95, limited series)
1-4-Mark Schultz-c 3.00

SUBMARINE ATTACK (Formerly Speed Demons)
Charlton Comics: No. 11, May, 1958 - No. 54, Feb-Mar, 1966
11 2.80 8.40 28.00
12-20 2.50 7.50 24.00
21-30 2.50 7.50 20.00
31-54 2.00 6.00 16.00
NOTE: *Glanzman c/a-25.* ***Montes/Bache*** *a-38, 40, 41.*

SUB-MARINER (See All-Select, All-Winners, Blonde Phantom, Daring, The Defenders, Fantastic Four #4, Human Torch, The Invaders, Iron Man &..., Marvel Mystery, Marvel Spotlight #27, Men's Adventures, Motion Picture Funnies Weekly, Namora, Namor, The..., Prince Namor, The Sub-Mariner, Saga Of The..., Tales to Astonish #70 & 2nd series, USA & Young Men)

SUB-MARINER, THE (2nd Series)(Sub-Mariner #31 on)
Marvel Comics Group: May, 1968 - No. 72, Sept, 1974 (No. 43: 52 pgs.)
1-Origin Sub-Mariner; story continued from Iron Man & Sub-Mariner #1 8.00 24.00 100.00
2-Triton app. 4.00 12.00 40.00
3-7,9,10: 5-1st Tiger Shark (9/68). 6-Tiger Shark-c & 2nd app., cont'd from #5. 7-Photo-c. (1968). 9-1st app. Serpent Crown (origin in #10 & 12) 2.80 8.40 28.00
8-Sub-Mariner vs. Thing 2.80 8.40 28.00
11-13,15: 15-Last 12¢ issue 2.50 7.50 20.00
14-Sub-Mariner vs. G.A. Human Torch; death of Toro (1st modern app. & only app. Toro, 6/69) 2.80 8.40 28.00
16-20: 19-1st Sting Ray (11/69); Stan Lee, Romita, Heck, Thomas, Everett &

Sub-Mariner Comics #6 © MAR

Sugar & Spike #12 © DC

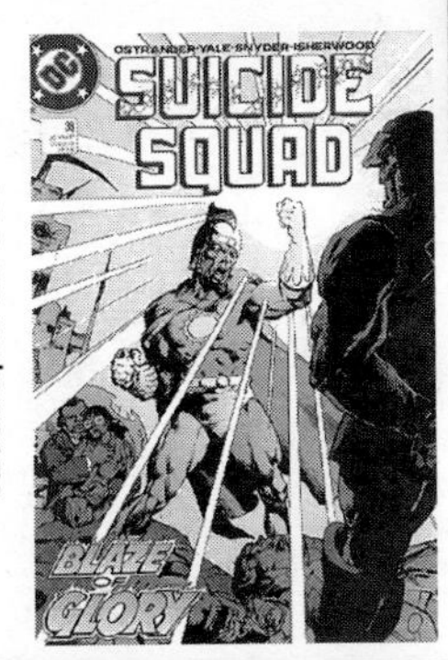

Suicide Squad #36 © DC

GD2.0 FN6.0 NM9.4

Kirby cameos. 20-Dr. Doom app. 1.50 4.50 12.00
21,23-33,36-39,41,42: 25-Origin Atlantis. 30-Capt. Marvel x-over. 37-Death of Lady Dorma. 38-Origin retold. 42-Last 15¢ issue. 1.10 3.30 9.00
22,40: 22-Dr. Strange x-over. 40-Spider-Man x-over 1.25 3.75 10.00
34,35-Prelude to 1st Defenders story. 34-Hulk & Silver Surfer x-over. 35-Namor/Hulk/Silver Surfer team-up to battle The Avengers-c/story (3/71); hints at teaming up again 2.25 6.75 18.00
43-King Size Special (52 pgs.) 2.40 6.00
44,45-Sub-Mariner vs. Human Torch 2.40 6.00
46-49,56,62,64-72: 47,48-Dr. Doom app. 49-Cosmic Cube story. 62-1st Tales of Atlantis, ends #66. 64-Hitler cameo. 67-New costume; F.F. x-over. 69-Spider-Man x-over (6 panels) 5.00
50-1st app. Nita, Namor's niece (later Namorita in New Warriors) 1.00 2.80 7.00
51-55,57,58,60,61,63-Everett issues: .61-Last artwork by Everett; 1st 4 pgs. completed by Mortimer; pgs. 5-20 by Mooney 2.40 6.00
59-1st battle with Thor; Everett-a 1.00 3.00 8.00
Special 1 (1/71)-r/Tales to Astonish #70-73 1.25 3.75 10.00
Special 2 (1/72)-r/T.T.A. #74-76; Everett-a 1.00 3.00 8.00

NOTE: *Bolle a-67i. Buscema a(p)-1-8, 20, 24. Colan a(p)-10, 11, 40, 43, 46-49, Special 1, 2; c(p)-10, 11, 40. Craig a-17i, 19-23i. Everett a-45r, 50-55, 57, 58, 59-61(plot), 63(plot); c-47, 48i, 55, 57-59i, 61, Spec. 2. G. Kane c(p)-42-52, 58, 66, 70, 71. Mooney a-24i, 25i, 32-35i, 39i, 42i, 44i, 45i, 60i, 61i, 65p, 66p, 68i. Severin c/a-38i. Starlin c-59p. Tuska a-41p, 42p, 69-71p. Wrightson a-36i. #53, 54-r/stories Sub-Mariner Comics #41 & 39.*

SUB-MARINER COMICS (1st Series) (The Sub-Mariner #1, 2, 33-42)(Official True Crime Cases #24 on; Amazing Mysteries #32 on; Best Love #33 on)
Timely/Marvel Comics (TCI 1-7/SePI 8/MPI 9-32/Atlas Comics (CCC 33-42)): Spring, 1941 - No. 23, Sum, 1947; No. 24, Wint, 1947 - No. 31, 4/49; No. 32, 7/49; No. 33, 4/54 - No. 42, 10/55

GD2.0 FN6.0 VF8.0 NM9.4
1-The Sub-Mariner by Everett & The Angel begin 1910.00 5730.00 11,460.00 21,000.00

GD2.0 FN6.0 NM9.4
2-Everett-a 450.00 1350.00 4500.00
3-Churchill assassination-c; 40 pg. Sub-Mariner story 355.00 1067.00 3200.00
4-Everett-a, 40 pgs.; 1 pg. Wolverton-a 288.00 862.00 2600.00
5: 5,8-Gabrielle/Klein-c 225.00 675.00 1800.00
6-10: 9-Wolverton-a, 3 pgs.; flag-c 188.00 562.00 1500.00
11-Classic Schomburg-c 156.00 468.00 1250.00
12-15 131.00 394.00 1050.00
16-20 119.00 356.00 950.00
21-Last Angel; Everett-a 97.00 291.00 775.00
22-Young Allies app. 97.00 291.00 775.00
23-The Human Torch, Namora x-over (Sum/47); 2nd app. Namora after Marvel Mystery #82 106.00 319.00 850.00
24-Namora x-over (3rd app.) 97.00 291.00 775.00
25-The Blonde Phantom begins (Spr/48), ends No. 31; Kurtzman-a; Namora x-over; last quarterly issue 116.00 347.00 925.00
26-28: 28-Namora cover; Everett-a 97.00 291.00 775.00
29-31 (4/49): 29-The Human Torch app. 31-Capt. America app. 97.00 291.00 775.00
32 (7/49, Scarce)-Origin Sub-Mariner 150.00 450.00 1200.00
33 (4/54)-Origin Sub-Mariner; The Human Torch app.; Namora x-over in Sub-Mariner #33-42 87.00 261.00 695.00
34,35-Human Torch in each 70.00 210.00 560.00
36,37,39-41: 36,39-41-Namora app. 70.00 210.00 560.00
38-Origin Sub-Mariner's wings; Namora app.; last pre-code (2/55) 79.00 238.00 635.00
42-Last issue 82.00 247.00 660.00

NOTE: *Angel by **Gustavson**-#1, 8. **Brodsky** c-34-36, 42. **Everett** a-1-4, 22-24, 26-42; c-32, 33, 40. **Maneely** a-38; c-37, 39-41. **Rico** c-27-31. **Schomburg** c-1-4, 6, 8-18, 20. **Sekowsky** c-24. 25, 26(w/**Rico**). **Shores** c-21-23, 38. Bondage c-13, 22, 24, 25, 34.*

SUBSPECIES
Eternity Comics: May, 1991 - No. 4, Aug, 1991 ($2.50, limited series)
1-4: New stories based on horror movie 2.50

SUBTLE VIOLENTS
CFD Productions: 1991 ($2.50, B&W, mature)
1-Linsner-c & story 2.50 7.50 25.00
San Diego Limited Edition 10.00 30.00 110.00

SUE & SALLY SMITH (Formerly My Secret Life)
Charlton Comics: V2#48, Nov, 1962 - No. 54, Nov, 1963 (Flying Nurses)
V2#48 2.50 7.50 20.00
49-54 1.75 5.25 14.00

SUGAR & SPIKE (Also see The Best of DC & DC Silver Age Classics)
National Periodical Publications: Apr-May, 1956 - No. 98, Oct-Nov, 1971
1 (Scarce) 225.00 675.00 1800.00
2 81.00 244.00 650.00
3-5: 3-Letter column begins 60.00 180.00 480.00
6-10 40.00 120.00 290.00
11-20 34.00 103.00 240.00
21-29: 26-Christmas-c 23.00 69.00 160.00
30-Scribbly & Scribbly, Jr. x-over 24.00 71.00 165.00
31-40 14.50 43.00 145.00
41-60 8.50 25.00 85.00
61-80: 69-1st app. Tornado-Tot-c/story. 72-Origin & 1st app. Bernie the Brain 6.00 18.00 60.00
81-84,86-95: 84-Bernie the Brain apps. as Superman in 1 panel (9/69) 4.00 12.00 40.00
85 (68 pgs.)-r/#72 5.00 15.00 50.00
96 (68 pgs.) 6.00 18.00 60.00
97,98 (52 pgs.) 4.80 14.40 48.00

NOTE: *All written and drawn by **Sheldon Mayer.***

SUGAR BOWL COMICS (Teen-age)
Famous Funnies: May, 1948 - No. 5, Jan, 1949
1-Toth-c/a 14.00 43.00 100.00
2,4,5 7.00 21.00 42.00
3-Toth-a 10.00 30.00 65.00

SUGARFOOT (TV)
Dell Publishing Co.: No. 907, May, 1958 - No. 1209, Oct-Dec, 1961
Four Color 907 (#1)-Toth-a, photo-c 12.00 37.00 135.00
Four Color 992 (5-7/59), Toth-a, photo-c 11.00 34.00 125.00
Four Color 1059 (11-1/60), 1098 (5-7/60), 1147 (11-1/61), 1209-all photo-c 8.00 25.00 90.00

SUICIDE SQUAD (See Brave & the Bold and Doom Patrol & Suicide Squad Spec., Legends #3 & note under Star Spangled War stories)
DC Comics: May, 1987 - No. 66, June, 1992 (Direct sales only #32 on)
1-66: 9-Millennium x-over. 10-Batman-c/story. 13-JLI app. (Batman). 16-Re-intro Shade The Changing Man. 27-34-Snyder-a. 36,37-Snyder-a. 40-43-"The Phoenix Gambit" Batman storyline. 40-Free Batman/Suicide Squad poster 2.00
Annual 1 (1988, $1.50)-Manhunter x-over 2.00

NOTE: *Chaykin c-1.*

SUIT, THE
Virtual Comics (Byron Preiss Multimedia): Oct, 1996 - No. 3, Dec, 1996 ($2.50, limited series)
1-3 2.50

SUMMER FUN (See Dell Giants)

SUMMER FUN (Formerly Li'l Genius; Holiday Surprise #55)
Charlton Comics: No. 54, Oct, 1966 (Giant)
54 3.00 9.00 30.00

SUMMER FUN (Walt Disney's...)
Disney Comics: Summer, 1991 ($2.95, annual, 68 pgs.)
1-D. Duck, M. Mouse, Brer Rabbit, Chip 'n' Dale & Pluto, Li'l Bad Wolf, Super Goof, Scamp stories 3.00

SUMMER LOVE (Formerly Brides in Love?)
Charlton Comics: V2#46, Oct, 1965; V2#47, Oct, 1966; V2#48, Nov, 1968
V2#46-Beatles-c/story 11.00 33.00 110.00

Sunny, America's Sweetheart #14 © FOX

Superboy #8 © DC

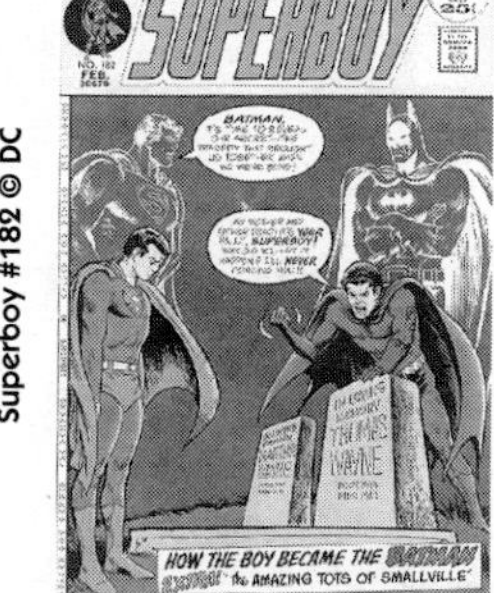

Superboy #182 © DC

GD2.0 FN6.0 NM9.4

47-Beatles story 9.50 28.00 95.00
48 1.00 3.00 8.00

SUMMER MAGIC (See Movie Comics)

SUNDANCE (See Hotel Deparee...)

SUNDANCE KID (Also see Blazing Six-Guns)
Skywald Publications: June, 1971 - No. 3, Sept, 1971 (52 pgs.)

1-Durango Kid; Two Kirby Bullseye-r 1.50 4.50 12.00
2,3: 2-Swift Arrow, Durango Kid, Bullseye by S&K; Meskin plus 1 pg. origin.
3-Durango Kid, Billy the Kid, Red Hawk-r 1.10 3.30 9.00

SUNDAY FUNNIES
Harvey Publications: 1950

1 5.85 17.50 35.00

SUN DEVILS
DC Comics: July, 1984 - No. 12, June, 1985 ($1.25, maxi series)

1-12: 6-Death of Sun Devil 2.00

SUN FUN KOMIKS
Sun Publications: 1939 (15¢, B&W & red)

1-Satire on comics 29.00 86.00 200.00

SUNFIRE & BIG HERO SIX (See Alpha Flight)
Marvel Comics: Sept, 1998 - No. 3, Nov, 1998 ($2.50, limited series)

1-3-Lobdell-s 2.50

SUN GIRL (See The Human Torch & Marvel Mystery Comics #88)
Marvel Comics (CCC): Aug, 1948 - No. 3, Dec, 1948

1-Sun Girl begins; Miss America app. 144.00 431.00 1150.00
2,3: 2-The Blonde Phantom begins 105.00 315.00 840.00

SUNGLASSES
Verotik: Nov, 1995 - No. 6, Nov, 1996 ($2.95, limited series, mature)

1-5: Nancy Collins scripts; adapt. of "Sunglasses after Dark" 3.00
6-($3.95) 4.00

SUNNY, AMERICA'S SWEETHEART (Formerly Cosmo Cat #1-10)
Fox Features Syndicate: No. 11, Dec, 1947 - No. 14, June, 1948

11-Feldstein-c/a 69.00 206.00 550.00
12-14-Feldstein-c/a; 14-Lingerie panels 55.00 165.00 440.00
I.W. Reprint #8-Feldstein-a; r/Fox issue 11.00 33.00 110.00

SUN-RUNNERS (Also see Tales of the...)
Pacific Comics/Eclipse Comics/Amazing Comics: 2/84 - No. 3, 5/84; No. 4, 11/84 - No. 7, 1986 (Baxter paper)

1-7: P. Smith-a in #2-4 2.00
Christmas Special 1 (1987, $1.95)-By Amazing 2.00

SUNSET CARSON (Also see Cowboy Western)
Charlton Comics: Feb, 1951 - No. 4, 1951 (No month) (Photo-c on each)

1-Photo/retouched-c (Scarce, all issues) 82.00 247.00 660.00
2-Kit Carson story; adapts "Kansas Raiders" w/Brian Donlevy, Audie Murphy & Margaret Chapman 60.00 180.00 480.00
3,4 45.00 135.00 360.00

SUNSET PASS (See Zane Grey & 4-Color #230)

SUPER ANIMALS PRESENTS PIDGY & THE MAGIC GLASSES
Star Publications: Dec, 1953 (25¢, came w/glasses)

1-(3-D Comics)-L. B. Cole-c 40.00 120.00 325.00

SUPERBOY (See Adventure, Aurora, DC Comics Presents, DC 100 Page Super Spectacular #15, DC Super Stars, 80 Page Giant #10, More Fun Comics, The New Advs. of... & Superman Family #191, Young Justice)

SUPERBOY (1st Series)(...& the Legion of Super-Heroes with #231)(Becomes The Legion of Super-Heroes No. 259 on)
National Periodical Publications/DC Comics: Mar-Apr, 1949 - No. 258, Dec, 1979 (#1-16: 52 pgs.)

GD2.0 FN6.0 VF8.0 NM9.4

1-Superman cover; intro in More Fun #10 (1-2/45) 680.00 2040.00 4080.00 6800.00

GD2.0 FN6.0 NM9.4

2-Used in **SOTI**, pg. 35-36,226 187.00 562.00 1500.00
3 144.00 431.00 1150.00
4,5: 5-1st pre-Supergirl tryout (c/story, 11-12/49) 97.00 291.00 775.00
6-10: 8-1st Superbaby. 10-1st app. Lana Lang 84.00 253.00 675.00
11-15 65.00 195.00 520.00
16-20 43.00 128.00 340.00
21-26,28-30: 21-Lana Lang app. 39.00 116.00 270.00
27-Low distribution 40.00 120.00 280.00
31-38: 38-Last pre-code issue (1/55) 28.00 84.00 195.00
39-48,50 (7/56) 20.00 60.00 210.00
49 (6/56)-1st app. Metallo (Jor-El's robot) 25.00 74.00 200.00
51-60: 52-1st S.A. issue 16.50 49.00 140.00
61-67 13.00 39.00 110.00
68-Origin/1st app. original Bizarro (10-11/58) 46.00 138.00 460.00
69-77,79: 76-1st Supermonkey 10.00 30.00 85.00
78-Origin Mr. Mxyzptlk & Superboy's costume 17.50 53.00 150.00
80-1st meeting Superboy/Supergirl (4/60) 15.00 44.00 125.00
81,83-85,87,88: 83-Origin/1st app. Kryptonite Kid 8.00 24.00 70.00
82-1st Bizarro Krypto 9.00 26.00 75.00
86-(1/61)-4th Legion app; Intro Pete Ross 15.00 44.00 125.00
89-(6/61)-1st app. Mon-el; 2nd Phantom Zone 27.00 81.00 230.00
90-92: 90-Pete Ross learns Superboy's I.D. 92-Last 10¢ issue 8.00 24.00 70.00
93-10th Legion app.(12/61); Chameleon Boy app. 8.00 24.00 80.00
94-97,99 5.00 15.00 50.00
98-(7/62)-18th Legion app; origin & 1st app. Ultra Boy; Pete Ross joins Legion 9.00 27.00 90.00
100-(10/62)-Ultra Boy app; 1st app. Phantom Zone villains, Dr. Xadu & Erndine. 2 pg. map of Krypton; origin Superboy retold; r-cover of Superman #1 17.00 51.00 170.00
101-120: 104-Origin Phantom Zone. 115-Atomic bomb-c. 117-Legion app. 4.00 12.00 40.00
121-128: 124-(10/65)-1st app. Insect Queen (Lana Lang). 125-Legion cameo. 126-Origin Krypto the Super Dog retold with new facts 3.50 10.50 35.00
129-(80-pg. Giant G-22)-Reprints origin Mon-el 4.50 13.50 45.00
130-137,139,140: 131-Legion statues cameo in Dog Legionnaires story. 132-1st app. Supremo. 133-Superboy meets Robin 2.50 7.50 22.00
138 (80-pg. Giant G-35) 4.00 12.00 40.00
141-146,148-155,157: 145-Superboy's parents regain their youth. 148-Legion app. 157-Last 12¢ issue 1.85 5.50 15.00
147(6/68)-Giant G-47; 1st origin of L.S.H. (Saturn Girl, Lightning Lad, Cosmic Boy); origin Legion of Super-Pets-r/Adv. #293 2.70 8.00 27.00
156,165,174 (Giants G-59,71,83): 165-r/1st app. Krypto the Superdog from Adventure Comics #210 2.50 7.50 20.00
158-164,166-171,175: 171-1st app. Aquaboy? 1.50 4.50 12.00
172,173,176-Legion app.: 172-Origin Yango (Super Ape). 176-Partial photo-c; last 15¢ issue 1.50 4.50 12.00
177-184,186,187 (All 52 pgs.): 182-All new origin of the classic World's Finest team (Superman & Batman) as teenagers (2/72, 22pgs). 184-Origin Dial H for Hero-r. 1.75 5.25 14.00
185-Also listed as DC 100 Pg. Super Spectacular #12; Legion-c/story; Teen Titans, Kid Eternity(r/Hit #46), Star Spangled Kid-r(S.S. #55)
(see DC 100 Pg. Super Spectacular #12 for price)
188-190,192,194,196: 188-Origin Karkan. 196-Last Superboy solo story 2.40 6.00
191,193,195: 191-Origin Sunboy retold; Legion app. 193-Chameleon Boy & Shrinking Violet get new costumes. 195-1st app. Erg-1/Wildfire; Phantom Girl gets new costume. 1.00 3.00 8.00
197-Legion series begins; Lightning Lad's new costume 2.00 6.00 16.00
198,199: 198-Element Lad & Princess Projectra get new costumes 1.25 3.75 10.00
200-Bouncing Boy & Duo Damsel marry; J'onn J'onzz cameo 1.75 5.25 14.00

Superboy #209 © DC

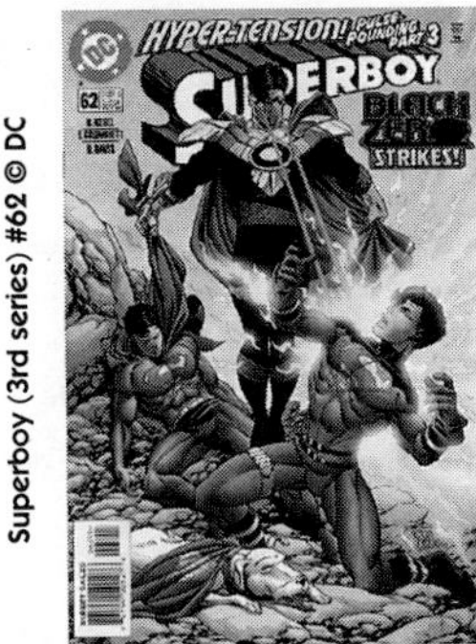

Superboy (3rd series) #62 © DC

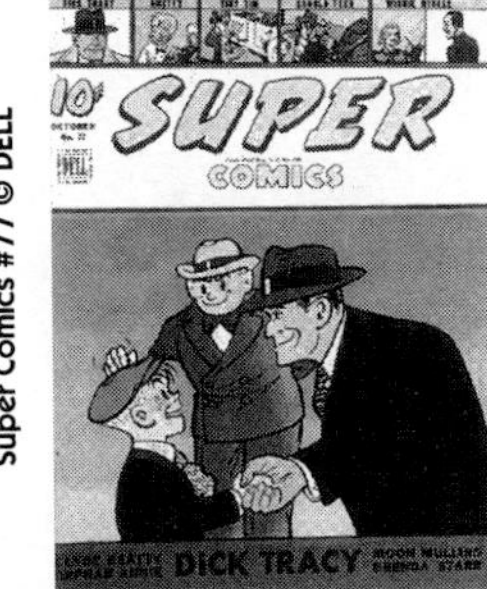

Super Comics #77 © DELL

201,204,206,207,209: 201-Re-intro Erg-1 as Wildfire. 204-Supergirl resigns from Legion. 206-Ferro Lad & Invisible Kid app. 209-Karate Kid gets new costume 1.25 3.75 10.00
202,205-(100 pgs.): 202-Light Lass gets new costume; Mike Grell's 1st comic work-i (5-6/74) 2.90 8.70 29.00
203-Invisible Kid dies 1.75 5.25 14.00
208,210: 208-(68 pgs.). 208-Legion of Super-Villains app. 210-Origin Karate Kid 1.50 4.50 12.00
211-220: 212-Matter-Eater Lad resigns. 216-1st app. Tyroc, who joins the Legion in #218 2.40 6.00
221-230,246-249: 226-Intro. Dawnstar. 228-Death of Chemical King 4.00
231-245: (Giants). 240-Origin Dawnstar. 242-(52 pgs.). 243-Legion of Substitute Heroes app. 243-245-(44 pgs.). 1.00 2.80 7.00
250-258: 253-Intro Blok. 257-Return of Bouncing Boy & Duo Damsel by Ditko 4.00
Annual 1 (Sum/64, 84 pgs.)-Origin Krypto-r 16.50 50.00 165.00
Spectacular 1 (1980, Giant)-Distr. through comic stores; mostly-r 4.00

NOTE: *Neal Adams c-143, 145, 146, 148-155, 157-161, 163, 164, 166-168, 172, 173, 175, 176, 178. M. Anderson a-178,179, 245i. Ditko a-257p. Grell a-202i, 203-219, 220-224p, 235p; c-207-232, 235, 236p, 237, 239p, 240p, 243p, 246, 258. Nasser a(p)-222, 225, 226, 230, 231, 233, 236. Simonson a-237p. Starlin a(p)-239, 250, 251; c-238. Staton a-227p, 243-249p, 252-258p; c-247-251p. Swan/Moldoff c-109. Tuska a-172, 173, 176, 183, 235p. Wood inks-153-155, 157-161. Legion app.-172, 173, 176, 177, 183, 184, 188, 190, 191, 193, 195, 197-258.*

SUPERBOY (TV)(2nd Series)(The Adventures of...#19 on)
DC Comics: Feb, 1990 - No. 22, Dec, 1991 ($1.00/$1.25)

1-22: Mooney-a(p) in 1-8,18-20; 1-Photo-c from TV show. 8-Bizarro-c/story; Arthur Adams-a(i). 9-12,14-17-Swan-p 2.00
...Special 1 (1992, $1.75) Swan-a 2.00

SUPERBOY (3rd Series)
DC Comics: Feb, 1994 - Present ($1.50/$1.95/$1.99)

1-8,0,9-24,26-68: 1-Metropolis Kid from Reign of the Supermen. 6,7-Worlds Collide Pts. 3 & 8. 8-(9/94)-Zero Hour x-over. 0-(10/94). 9-(11/94)-King Shark app. 21-Legion app. 28-Supergirl-c/app. 33-Final Night. 38-41-"Meltdown". 45-Legion-c/app. 47-Green Lantern-c/app. 50-Last Boy on Earth begins. 60-Crosses Hypertime. 69-Demon-c/app. 2.00
25-($2.95)-New Gods & Female Furies app.; w/pin-ups 3.00
#1,000,000 (11/98) 853rd Century x-over 2.00
Annual 1 (1994, $2.95, 68 pgs.)-Elseworlds story, Pt. 2 of The Super Seven (see Adventures Of Superman Annual #6) 3.00
Annual 2 (1995, $3.95)-Year One story 4.00
Annual 3 (1996, $2.95)-Legends of the Dead Earth 3.00
Annual 4 (1997, $3.95)-Pulp Heroes story 4.00
...Plus 1 (Jan, 1997, $2.95) w/Capt. Marvel Jr. 3.00
...Plus 2 (Fall, 1997, $2.95) w/Slither (Scare Tactics) 3.00
.../Risk Double-Shot 1 (Feb, 1998, $1.95) w/Risk (Teen Titans) 2.00

SUPERBOY & THE RAVERS
DC Comics: Sept, 1996 - No. 19, March, 1998 ($1.95)

1-19: 4-Adam Strange app. 7-Impulse-c/app. 9-Superman-c/app. 2.00

SUPERBOY/ROBIN: WORLD'S FINEST THREE
DC Comics: 1996 - No. 2, 1996 ($4.95, squarebound, limited series)

1,2: Superboy & Robin vs. Metallo & Poison Ivy; Karl Kesel & Chuck Dixon scripts; Tom Grummett-c(p)/a(p) 5.00

SUPER BRAT
Toby Press: Jan, 1954 - No. 4, July, 1954

1 6.35 19.00 38.00
2-4: 4-Li'l Teevy by Mel Lazarus 4.00 12.00 24.00
I.W. Reprint #1,2,3,7,8('58): 1-r/#1 1.00 3.00 8.00
I.W. (Super) Reprint #10('63) 1.00 3.00 8.00

SUPERCAR (TV)
Gold Key: Nov, 1962 - No. 4, Aug, 1963 (All painted-c)

1 22.00 65.00 235.00
2,3 10.00 30.00 110.00
4-Last issue 14.00 44.00 160.00

SUPER CAT (Formerly Frisky Animals; also see Animal Crackers)
Star Publications #56-58/Ajax/Farrell Publ. (Four Star Comic Corp.): No. 56, Nov, 1953 - No. 58, May, 1954; Aug, 1957 - No. 4, May, 1958

56-58-L.B. Cole-c on all 20.00 60.00 140.00
1(1957-Ajax)- "The Adventures of..." c-only 9.15 27.00 55.00
2-4 5.35 16.00 32.00

SUPER CIRCUS (TV)
Cross Publishing Co.: Jan, 1951 - No. 5, Sept, 1951 (Mary Hartline)

1-(52 pgs.)-Cast photos on-c 12.00 36.00 85.00
2-Cast photos on-c 9.15 27.00 55.00
3-5 7.00 21.00 42.00

SUPER CIRCUS (TV)
Dell Publ. Co.: No. 542, Mar, 1954 - No. 694, Mar, 1956 (Mary Hartline)

Four Color 542: Mary Hartline photo-c 6.40 19.00 70.00
Four Color 592,694: Mary Hartline photo-c 5.50 16.50 60.00

SUPER COMICS
Dell Publishing Co.: May, 1938 - No. 121, Feb-Mar, 1949

1-Terry & The Pirates, The Gumps, Dick Tracy, Little Orphan Annie, Little Joe, Gasoline Alley, Smilin' Jack, Smokey Stover, Smitty, Tiny Tim, Moon Mullins, Harold Teen, Winnie Winkle begin 266.00 800.00 2000.00
2 100.00 300.00 700.00
3 91.00 275.00 650.00
4,5: 4-Dick Tracy-c; also #8-10,17,26(part),31 73.00 219.00 500.00
6-10 58.00 174.00 400.00
11-20: 20-Smilin' Jack-c (also #29,32) 45.00 137.00 320.00
21-29: 21-Magic Morro begins (origin & 1st app., 2/40). 22,27-Ken Ernst-c (also #25?); Magic Morro c-22,25,27,34 34.00 101.00 290.00
30- "Sea Hawk" movie adaptation-c/story with Errol Flynn 34.00 101.00 290.00
31-40: 34-Ken Ernst-c 31.00 94.00 220.00
41-50: 41-Intro Lightning Jim. 43-Terry & The Pirates ends 25.00 75.00 175.00
51-60 19.00 56.00 130.00
61-70: 62-Flag-c. 65-Brenda Starr-r begin? 67-X-Mas-c 17.00 49.00 115.00
71-80 13.00 39.00 90.00
81-99 11.00 33.00 75.00
100 12.00 36.00 85.00
101-115-Last Dick Tracy (moves to own title) 8.00 24.00 48.00
116-121: 116,118-All Smokey Stover. 117-All Gasoline Alley. 119-121-Terry & The Pirates app. in all 6.70 20.00 40.00

SUPER COPS, THE
Red Circle Productions (Archie): July, 1974 (one-shot)

1-Morrow-c/a 2.40 6.00

SUPER COPS
Now Comics: Sept, 1990 - No. 4, Dec?, 1990 ($1.75)

1-($2.75, 52 pgs.)-Dave Dorman painted-c (both printings) 2.75
2-4 2.00

SUPER CRACKED (See Cracked)

SUPER DC GIANT (25-50¢, all 68-52 pg. Giants)
National Periodical Publications: No. 13, 9-10/70 - No. 26, 7-8/71; V3#27, Summer, 1976 (No #1-12)

S-13-Binky 8.30 25.00 90.00
S-14-Top Guns of the West; Kubert-c; Trigger Twins, Johnny Thunder, Wyoming Kid-r; Moreira-r (9-10/70) 2.80 8.40 28.00
S-15-Western Comics; Kubert-c; Pow Wow Smith, Vigilante, Buffalo Bill-r; new Gil Kane-a (9-10/70) 2.80 8.40 28.00
S-16-Best of the Brave & the Bold; Batman-r & Metamorpho origin-r from Brave & the Bold; Spectre pin-up. 2.80 8.40 26.00
S-17-Love 1970 (scarce) 18.00 55.00 200.00
S-18-Three Mouseketeers; Dizzy Dog, Doodles Duck, Bo Bunny-r; Sheldon Mayer-a 8.00 24.00 80.00
S-19-Jerry Lewis; Neal Adams pin-up 7.50 22.50 75.00

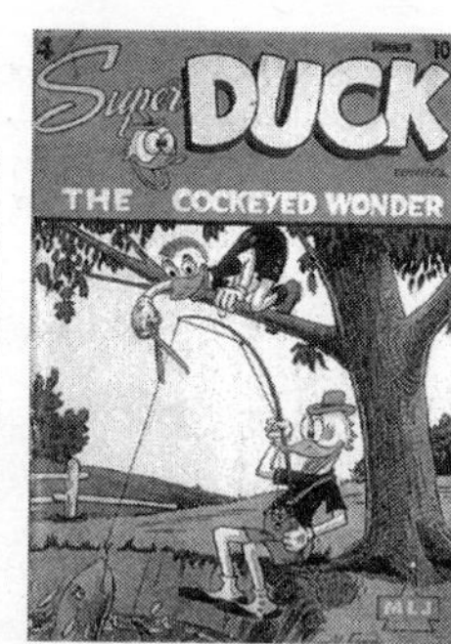

Super Duck Comics #4 © AP

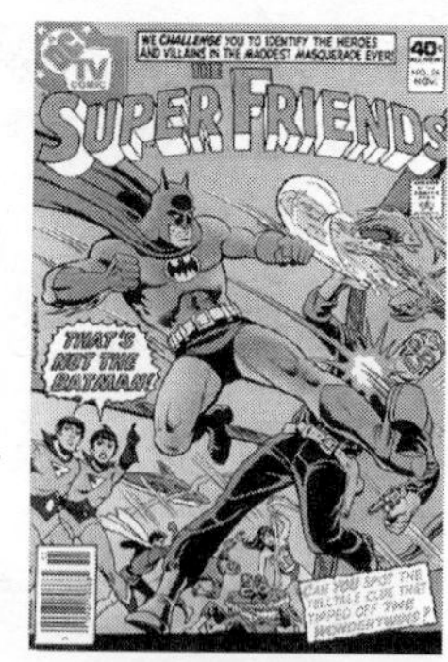

Super Friends #26 © DC

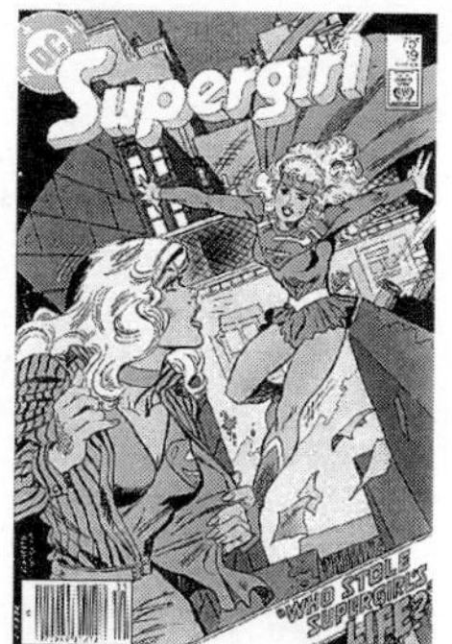

Supergirl #19 © DC

GD2.0 FN6.0 NM9.4

S-20-House of Mystery; N. Adams-c; Kirby-r(3) 4.50 13.50 45.00
S-21-Love 1971 (scarce) 21.50 64.00 235.00
S-22-Top Guns of the West; Kubert-c 2.50 7.50 20.00
S-23-The Unexpected 2.60 7.80 26.00
S-24-Supergirl 2.60 7.80 26.00
S-25-Challengers of the Unknown; all Kirby/Wood-r 2.50 7.50 20.00
S-26-Aquaman (1971)-r/S.A. Aquaman origin story from Showcase #30 2.50 7.50 20.00
27-Strange Flying Saucers Adventures (Sum, 1976) 1.25 3.75 10.00

NOTE: ***Sid Greene*** *r-27p(2),* ***Heath*** *r-27.* ***G. Kane*** *a-14r(2), 15, 27r(p).* ***Kubert*** *r-16.*

SUPER-DOOPER COMICS
Able Mfg. Co./Harvey :1946 - No. 8, 1946 (10¢, 32 pgs., paper-c, #1-4 exist?)

1-The Clock, Gangbuster app. 17.00 51.00 120.00
2 11.00 33.00 75.00
3,4,6 10.00 30.00 65.00
5-Capt. Freedom 11.50 34.00 80.00
7,8-Shock Gibson. 7-Where's Theres A Will by Ed Wheelan, Steve Case Crime Rover, Penny & Ullysses Jr. 8-Sam Hill app. 11.50 34.00 80.00

SUPER DUCK COMICS (The Cockeyed Wonder) (See Jolly Jingles)
MLJ Mag. No. 1-4(9/45)/Close-Up No. 5 on (Archie): Fall, 1944 - No. 94, Dec, 1960 (Also see Laugh #24)(#1-5 are quarterly)

1-Origin; Hitler & Hirohito-c 45.00 135.00 360.00
2-Bill Vigoda-c 21.00 64.00 150.00
3-5: 4-20-Al Fagaly-c (most) 14.00 43.00 100.00
6-10 11.50 34.00 80.00
11-20(6/48) 10.00 30.00 60.00
21,23-40 (10/51) 8.35 25.00 50.00
22-Used in **SOTI**, pg. 35,307,308 9.15 27.00 55.00
41-60 (2/55) 6.35 19.00 38.00
61-94 4.25 13.00 26.00

SUPER DUPER (Formerly Pocket Comics #1-4?)
Harvey Publications: No. 5, 1941 - No. 11, 1941

5-Captain Freedom & Shock Gibson app. 29.00 86.00 200.00
8,11 18.00 54.00 125.00

SUPER DUPER COMICS (Formerly Latest Comics?)
F. E. Howard Publ.: No. 3, May-June, 1947

3-1st app. Mr. Monster 10.00 30.00 70.00

SUPER FRIENDS (TV) (Also see Best of DC & Limited Collectors' Edition)
National Periodical Publications/DC Comics: Nov, 1976 - No. 47, Aug, 1981 (#14 is 44 pgs.)

1-Superman, Batman, Robin, Wonder Woman, Aquaman, Atom, Wendy, Marvin & Wonder Dog begin (1st Super Friends) 2.25 6.75 18.00
2-Penquin-c/sty 1.10 3.30 9.00
3-5 1.00 3.00 8.00
6-10,14:7-1st app. Wonder Twins & The Seraph. 8-1st app. Jack O'Lantern. 9-1st app. Icemaiden. 14-Origin Wonder Twins 2.40 6.00
11-13,15-30,32-46: 13-1st app. Dr. Mist. 25-1st app. Fire as Green Fury. 28-Bizarro app. 36,43-Plastic Man app. 5.00
31,47: 31-Black Orchid app. 47-Origin Fire & Green Fury 2.40 6.00
...Special 1 (1981, giveaway, no ads, no code or price)-r/Super Friends #19 & 36 4.00

NOTE: ***Estrada*** *a-1p, 2p.* ***Orlando*** *a-1p.* ***Staton*** *a-43, 45.*

SUPER FUN
Gillmor Magazines: Jan, 1956 (By A.W. Nugent)

1-Comics, puzzles, cut-outs by A.W. Nugent 3.60 9.00 18.00

SUPER FUNNIES (...Western Funnies #3,4)
Superior Comics Publishers Ltd. (Canada): Dec, 1953 - No. 4, Sept, 1954

1-(3-D, 10¢)-...Presents Dopey Duck; make your own 3-D glasses cut-out inside front-c; did not come w/glasses 40.00 120.00 280.00
2-Horror & crime satire 11.50 34.00 80.00
3-Phantom Ranger-c/s; Geronimo, Billy the Kid app.6.70 20.00 40.00
4-Phantom Ranger-c/story 6.70 20.00 40.00

GD2.0 FN6.0 NM9.4

SUPERGIRL (See Action, Adventure #281, Brave & the Bold, Crisis on Infinite Earths #7, Daring New Advs. of..., Super DC Giant, Superman Family, & Super-Team Family)

SUPERGIRL
National Periodical Publ.: Nov, 1972 - No. 9, Dec-Jan, 1973-74; No. 10, Sept-Oct, 1974 (1st solo title)(20¢)

1-Zatanna back-up stories begin, end #5 2.80 8.40 28.00
2-4,6,7,9 1.50 4.50 12.00
5,8,10: 5-Zatanna origin-r. 8-JLA x-over; Batman cameo. 10-Prez 1.75 5.25 14.00

NOTE: *Zatanna in #1-5, 7(Guest); Prez app. in #10. #1-10 are 20¢ issues.*

SUPERGIRL (Formerly Daring New Adventures of...)
DC Comics: No. 14, Dec, 1983 - No. 23, Sept, 1984

14-23: 16-Ambush Bug app. 20-JLA & New Teen Titans app. 2.00
...Movie Special (1985)-Adapts movie; Morrow-a; photo back-c 3.00

SUPERGIRL
DC Comics: Feb, 1994 - No. 4, May, 1994 ($1.50, limited series)

1-4: Guice-a(i) 2.00

SUPERGIRL (See Showcase '96 #8)
DC Comics: Sept, 1996 - Present ($1.95/$1.99)

1: Peter David scripts & Gary Frank-c/a; DC cover logo in upper left is blue 1.00 3.00 8.00
1-2nd printing-DC cover logo in upper left is red 3.00
2,4-9: 4-Gorilla Grodd-c/app. 6-Superman-c/app. 9-Last Frank-a 4.00
3-Final Night, Gorilla Grodd app. 5.00
10-19: 14-Genesis x-over. 16-Power Girl app. 3.50
20-35: 20-Millennium Giants x-over; Superman app. 23-Steel-c/app. 24-Resurrection Man x-over. 25-Comet ID revealed; begin $1.99-c 3.00
36-38: 36,37-Young Justice x-over 2.00
#1,000,000 (11/98) 853rd Century x-over 3.00
Annual 1 (1996, $2.95)-Legends of the Dead Earth 3.00
Annual 2 (1997, $3.95)-Pulp Heroes; LSH app.; Chiodo-c 4.00
...Plus (2/97, $2.95) Capt.(Mary) Marvel-c/app.; David-s/Frank-a 3.00
.../Prysm Double-Shot 1 (Feb, 1998, $1.95) w/Prysm (Teen Titans) 2.00
TPB-('98, $14.95) r/Showcase '96 #8 & Supergirl #1-9 15.00

SUPERGIRL/LEX LUTHOR SPECIAL (Supergirl and Team Luthor on-c)
DC Comics: 1993 ($2.50, 68 pgs., one-shot)

1-Pin-ups by Byrne & Thibert 2.50

SUPER GOOF (Walt Disney) (See Dynabrite & The Phantom Blot)
Gold Key No. 1-57/Whitman No. 58 on: Oct, 1965 - No. 74, 1982

1 2.60 7.80 26.00
2-5 1.40 4.20 14.00
6-10 1.20 3.60 12.00
11-20 .90 2.70 9.00
21-30 2.40 6.00
31-50 5.00
51-57 4.00
58,59 (Whitman) 5.00
60-62 (8/80-12/80, 3-pack?) 1.20 3.60 12.00
63-66('81) 2.40 6.00
67-69 4.00
70-74 (#90180 on-c; pre-pack? nd, nd code) 1.00 3.00 10.00

NOTE: *Reprints in #16, 24, 28, 29, 37, 38, 43, 45, 46, 54(1/2), 56-58, 65(1/2), 72(r-#2).*

SUPER GREEN BERET (Tod Holton...)
Lightning Comics (Milson Publ. Co.): Apr, 1967 - No. 2, Jun, 1967

1,2-(25¢, 68 pgs) 3.20 9.60 32.00

SUPER HEROES (See Giant-Size... & Marvel...)

SUPER HEROES
Dell Publishing Co.: Jan, 1967 - No. 4, June, 1967

1-Origin & 1st app. Fab 4 3.00 9.00 30.00
2-4 2.50 7.50 20.00

SUPER-HEROES BATTLE SUPER-GORILLAS (See DC Special #16)

Super Magician Comics #8 © Conde nast

Superman #9 © DC

Superman #128 © DC

GD2.0 FN6.0 NM9.4

National Periodical Publications: Winter, 1976 (52 pgs., all reprints, one-shot)
1-Superman, Batman, Flash stories; Infantino-a(p) 1.00 3.00 8.00

SUPER HEROES VERSUS SUPER VILLAINS
Archie Publications (Radio Comics): July, 1966 (no month given)(68 pgs.)
1-Flyman, Black Hood, Web, Shield-r; Reinman-a 5.00 15.00 50.00

SUPERHERO WOMEN, THE - FEATURING THE FABULOUS FEMALES OF MARVEL COMICS (See Fireside Book Series)

SUPERICHIE (Formerly Super Richie)
Harvey Publications: No. 5, Oct, 1976 - No. 18, Jan, 1979 (52 pgs. giants)
5-Origin/1st app. new costumes for Rippy & Crashman 1.10 3.30 9.00
6-18 1.00 2.80 7.00

SUPERIOR STORIES
Nesbit Publishers, Inc.: May-June, 1955 - No. 4, Nov-Dec, 1955
1-The Invisible Man by H.G. Wells 21.00 64.00 150.00
2-4: 2-The Pirate of the Gulf by J.H. Ingrahams. 3-Wreck of the Grosvenor by William Clark Russell. 4-The Texas Rangers by O'Henry 10.00 30.00 70.00
NOTE: *Morisi c/a in all. Kiwanis stories in #3 & 4. #4 has photo of Gene Autry on-c.*

SUPER MAGIC (Super Magician Comics #2 on)
Street & Smith Publications: May, 1941
V1#1-Blackstone the Magician-c/story; origin/1st app. Rex King (Black Fury); Charles Sultan-c; Blackstone-c begin 131.00 394.00 1050.00

SUPER MAGICIAN COMICS (Super Magic #1)
Street & Smith Publications: No. 2, Sept, 1941 - V5#8, Feb-Mar, 1947
V1#2-Blackstone the Magician continues; Rex King, Man of Adventure app. 55.00 165.00 440.00
3-Tao-Anwar, Boy Magician begins 37.00 111.00 260.00
4-7,9-12: 4-Origin Transo. 11-Supersnipe app. 34.00 103.00 240.00
8-Abbott & Costello story (1st app?, 11/42) 37.00 111.00 260.00
V2#1-The Shadow app. 40.00 120.00 280.00
2-12: 5-Origin Tigerman. 8-Red Dragon begins 18.00 54.00 125.00
V3#1-12: 5-Origin Mr. Twilight 18.00 54.00 125.00
V4#1-12: 11-Nigel Elliman Ace of Magic begins (3/46), V5#1-6 14.00 43.00 100.00
7,8-Red Dragon by Edd Cartier-c/a 36.00 107.00 250.00
NOTE: *Jack Binder c-1-14(most). Red Dragon c-V5#7, 8.*

SUPERMAN (See Action Comics, Advs. of..., All-New Coll. Ed., All-Star Comics, Best of DC, Brave & the Bold, Cosmic Odyssey, DC Comics Presents, Heroes Against Hunger, JLA, The Kents, Krypton Chronicles, Limited Coll. Ed., Man of Steel, Phantom Zone, Power Record Comics, Special Edition, Steel, Super Friends, Superman: The Man of Steel, Superman: The Man of Tomorrow, Taylor's Christmas Tabloid, Three-Dimension Advs., World Of Krypton, World Of Metropolis, World Of Smallville & World's Finest)

SUPERMAN (Becomes Adventures of...#424 on)
National Periodical Publ./DC Comics: Summer, 1939 - No. 423, Sept, 1986 (#1-5 are quarterly)

GD2.0 FN6.0 VF8.0 NM9.4

1(nn)-1st four Action stories reprinted; origin Superman by Siegel & Shuster; has a new 2 pg. origin plus 4 pgs. omitted in Action story; see The Comics Magazine #1 & More Fun #14-17 for Superman proto-type app.; cover r/splash page from Action #10; 1st pin-up Superman on back-c - 1st pin-up in comics 13,000.00 39,000.00 78,000.00 140,000.00

1-Reprint, Oversize 13-1/2x10". **WARNING**: This comic is an exact duplicate reprint of the original except for its size. DC published it in 1978 with a second cover titling it as a Famous First Edition. There have been many reported cases of the outer cover being removed and the interior sold as the original edition. The reprint with the new outer cover removed is practically worthless. See Famous First Edition for value.

GD2.0 FN6.0 NM9.4

2-All daily strip-r; full pg. ad for N.Y. World's Fair 1000.00 3000.00 10,000.00
3-2nd story-r from Action #5; 3rd story-r from Action #6 670.00 2010.00 6700.00
4-2nd mention of Daily Planet (Spr/40); also see Action #23; 2nd & 3rd app. Luthor (red-headed; also see Action #23) 500.00 1500.00 5000.00
5-4th Luthor app. (red hair); classic-c 389.00 1167.00 3500.00
6,7: 6-1st splash pg. in a Superman comic. 7-1st Perry White? (11-12/40) 282.00 846.00 2500.00
8-10: 10-5th app. Luthor (1st bald Luthor, 5-6/41) 275.00 825.00 2200.00
11-13,15: 13-Jimmy Olsen & Luthor app. 200.00 600.00 1600.00
14-Patriotic Shield-c classic by Fred Ray 294.00 882.00 2600.00
16,18-20: 16-1st Lois Lane-c this title (5-6/42); 2nd Lois-c after Action #29 162.00 487.00 1300.00
17-Hitler, Hirohito-c 187.00 562.00 1500.00
21-23,25: 25-Clark Kent's only military service; Fred Ray's only super-hero story 122.00 366.00 975.00
24-Classic Jack Burnley flag-c 169.00 506.00 1350.00
26-29: 27,29-31-Lois Lane-c. 28-Lois Lane Girl Reporter series begins, ends #40,42 112.00 337.00 900.00
28-Overseas edition for Armed Forces; same as reg. #28 112.00 337.00 900.00
30-Origin & 1st app. Mr. Mxyztplk (9-10/44)(pronounced "Mix-it-plk") in comic books; name later became Mxyzptlk ("Mix-yez-pit-l-ick"); the character was inspired by a combination of the name of Al Capp's Joe Blyfstyk (the little man with the black cloud over his head) & the devilish antics of Bugs Bunny; he 1st app. in newspapers 3/7/44 187.00 562.00 1500.00
31-40: 33-(3-4/45)-3rd app. Mxyztplk. 35,36-Lois Lane-c. 38-Atomic bomb story (1-2/46); delayed because of gov't censorship; Superman shown reading Batman #32 on cover. 40-Mxyztplk-c 97.00 291.00 775.00
41-50: 42-Lois Lane-c. 45-Lois Lane as Superwoman (see Action #60 for 1st app.). 46-(5-6/47)-1st app. Superboy this title? 48-1st time Superman travels thru time 75.00 225.00 600.00
51,52: 51-Lois Lane-c 62.00 187.00 500.00
53-Third telling of Superman origin; 10th anniversary issue ('48); classic origin-c by Boring 262.00 787.00 2100.00
54,56-60: 57-Lois Lane as Superwoman-c. 58-Intro Tiny Trix 62.00 187.00 500.00
55-Used in **SOTI**, pg. 33 65.00 195.00 520.00
61-Origin Superman retold; origin Green Kryptonite (1st Kryptonite story); Superman returns to Krypton for 1st time & sees his parents for 1st time since infancy, discovers he's not an Earth man 120.00 360.00 960.00
62-70: 62-Orson Welles-c/story. 65-1st Krypton Foes: Mala, Kizo, & U-Ban. 66-2nd Superbaby story. 67-Perry Como-c/story. 68-1st Luthor-c this title (see Action Comics) 59.00 178.00 475.00
71-75: 74-2nd Luthor-c this title. 75-Some have #74 on-c 56.00 169.00 450.00
76-Batman x-over; Superman & Batman learn each other's I.D. for the 1st time (5-6/52)(also see World's Finest #71) 162.00 486.00 1300.00
77-81: 78-Last 52 pg. issue. 81-Used in **POP**, pg. 88 53.00 159.00 425.00
82-87,89,90 50.00 150.00 400.00
88-Prankster, Toyman & Luthor team-up 53.00 159.00 425.00
91-95: 95-Last precode issue (2/55) 43.00 128.00 340.00
96-99: 96-Mr. Mxyztplk-c/story 35.00 106.00 300.00

GD2.0 FN6.0 VF8.0 NM9.4

100 (9-10/55)-Shows cover to #1 on-c 165.00 495.00 990.00 1650.00

GD2.0 FN6.0 NM9.4

101-105,107-110: 109-1st S.A. issue 33.00 99.00 280.00
106 (7/56)-Retells origin 36.00 110.00 310.00
111-120 28.00 85.00 240.00
121,122,124-127,129: 127-Origin/1st app. Titano. 129-Intro/origin Lori Lemaris, The Mermaid 23.00 70.00 200.00
123-Pre-Supergirl tryout-c/story (8/58). 26.00 78.00 220.00
128-(4/59)-Red Kryptonite used. Bruce Wayne x-over who protects Superman's i.d. (3rd story) 25.00 74.00 210.00
130-(7/59)-1st app, Krypto, the Superdog with Superman (all previous app. w/Superboy 23.00 70.00 200.00
131-139: 139-Lori Lemaris app.; "Untold Lois Lane Story " back-up story 19.00 56.00 160.00
140-1st Blue Kryptonite & Bizarro Supergirl; origin Bizarro Jr. #1 20.00 60.00 170.00
141-145,148: 142-2nd Batman x-over 15.00 44.00 125.00
146-(7/61)-Superman's life story; back-up hints at Earth II. Classic-c 19.00 56.00 160.00
147(8/61)-7th Legion app; 1st app. Legion of Super-Villains; 1st app. Adult

Superman #333 © DC

Superman #423 © DC

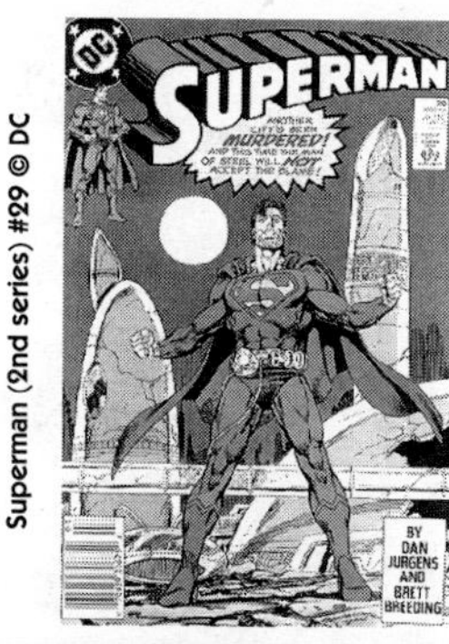

Superman (2nd series) #29 © DC

GD2.0 FN6.0 NM9.4

Legion; swipes-c to Adv. #247 17.50 53.00 150.00
149(11/61)-8th Legion app. (cameo); "The Death of Superman" imaginary story; last 10¢ issue 16.00 48.00 135.00
150,151,153,154,157,159,160: 157-Gold Kryptonite used (see Adv. #299); Mon-el app.; Lightning Lad cameo (11/62) 8.00 24.00 80.00
152,155,156,158,162: 152(4/62)-15th Legion app. 155-(8/62)-Legion app; Lightning Man & Cosmic Man, & Adult Legion app. 156,162-Legion app. 158-1st app. Flamebird & Nightwing & Nor-Kan of Kandor(12/62) 8.00 24.00 80.00
161-1st told death of Ma and Pa Kent 8.00 24.00 80.00
161-2nd printing (1987, $1.25)-New DC logo; sold thru So Much Fun Toy Stores (cover title: Superman Classic) 2.50
163-166,168-180: 166-XMas-c. 168-All Luthor issue; JFK tribute/memorial. 169-Bizarro Invasion of Earth-c/story; last Sally Selwyn. 170-Pres. Kennedy story is finally published after delay from #169 due to assassination. 172,173-Legion cameos. 174-Super-Mxyzptlk; Bizarro app. 6.00 18.00 60.00
167-New origin Brainiac & Brainiac 5; intro Tixarla (later Luthor's wife) 9.00 27.00 90.00
181,182,184-186,188-192,194-196,198,200: 181-1st 2965 story/series. 182-1st S.A. app. of The Toyman (1/66). 189-Origin/destruction of Krypton II. 5.00 15.00 50.00
183,187,193,197 (Giants G-18,G-23,G-31,G-36) 6.00 18.00 60.00
199-1st Superman/Flash race (8/67): also see Flash #175 & World's Finest #198,199 (r-in Limited Coll. Ed. #48) 22.00 66.00 220.00
201,203-206,208-211,213-216: 213-Brainiac-5 app. 216-Last 12¢ issue 3.50 10.50 35.00
202 (80-pg. Giant G-42)-All Bizarro issue 4.00 12.00 40.00
207,212,217,222,239 (Giants G-48,G-54,G-60,G-66,G-84): 207-30th anniversary Superman (6/68) 4.00 12.00 40.00
218-221,223-226,228-231 2.60 7.80 26.00
227,232(Giants, G-72,G-78)-All Krypton issues 4.00 12.00 40.00
233-2nd app. Morgan Edge; Clark Kent switches from newspaper reporter to TV newscaster; all Kryptonite on earth destroyed; classic Adams-c 4.00 12.00 40.00
234-238 2.50 7.50 20.00
240-Kaluta-a; last 15¢ issue 1.50 4.50 12.00
241-244 (All 52 pgs.): 241-New Wonder Woman app. 243-G.A.-r/#38 2.00 6.00 16.00
245-Also listed as DC 100 Pg. Super Spectacular #7; Air Wave, Kid Eternity, Hawkman-r; Atom-r/Atom #3
(see DC 100 Pg. Super Spectacular #7 for price)
246-248,250,251,253 (All 52 pgs.): 246-G.A.-r/#40. 248-World of Krypton story. 251-G.A.-r/#45. 253-Finlay-a, 2 pgs., G.A.-r/#1 2.00 6.00 16.00
249,254-Neal Adams-a. 249-(52 pgs.); origin & 1st app. Terra-Man by Neal Adams (inks) 2.50 7.50 20.00
252-Also listed as DC 100 Pg. Super Spectacular #13; Ray(r/Smash #17), Black Condor, (r/Crack #18), Hawkman(r/Flash #24); Starman-r/Adv. #67; Dr. Fate & Spectre-r/More Fun #57; N. Adams-c
(see DC 100 Pg. Super Spectacular #13 for price)
255-271,273-277,279-283: 263-Photo-c. 264-1st app. Steve Lombard. 276-Intro Capt. Thunder. 279-Batman, Batgirl app. 1.00 3.00 8.00
272,278,284-All 100 pgs. G.A.-r in all. 272-r/2nd app. Mr. Mxyztplk from Action #80 2.50 7.50 24.00
285-299: 289-Partial photo-c. 292-Origin Lex Luthor retold 2.40 6.00
300-(6/76) Superman in the year 2001 2.25 6.75 18.00
301-350: 301,320-Solomon Grundy app. 323-Intro. Atomic Skull. 327-329-(44 pgs.). 330-More facts revealed about I. D. 338-The bottled city of Kandor enlarged. 344-Frankenstein & Dracula app. 4.00
351-399: 353-Brief origin. 354,355,357-Superman 2020 stories (354-Debut of Superman III). 356-World of Krypton story (also #360,367,375). 366-Fan letter by Todd McFarlane. 372-Superman 2021 story. 376-Free 16 pg. preview Daring New Advs. of Supergirl. 377-Free 16 pg. preview Masters of the Universe 3.00
400 (10/84, $1.50, 68 pgs.)-Many top artists featured; Chaykin painted cover, Miller back-c 5.00
401-422: 405-Super-Batman story. 408-Nuclear Holocaust-c/story. 411-Special Julius Schwartz tribute issue. 414,415-Crisis x-over. 422-Horror-c 3.00

GD2.0 FN6.0 NM9.4

423-Alan Moore scripts; Perez-a(i); last Earth I Superman story, cont'd in Action #583 1.00 3.00 8.00
Annual 1(10/60, 84 pgs.)-Reprints 1st Supergirl story/Action #252; r/Lois Lane #1; Krypto-r (1st Silver Age DC annual) 79.00 238.00 950.00
Annual 2(Win, 1960-61)-Super-villain issue; Brainiac, Titano, Metallo, Bizarro origin-r 38.00 114.00 420.00
Annual 3(Sum, 1961)-Strange Lives of Superman 28.00 84.00 280.00
Annual 4(Win, 1961-62)-11th Legion app; 1st Legion origins (text & pictures); advs. in time, space & on alien worlds 22.50 68.00 225.00
Annual 5(Sum, 1962)-All Krypton issue 18.00 54.00 180.00
Annual 6(Win, 1962-63)-Legion-r/Adv. #247 16.50 50.00 165.00
Annual 7(Sum, 1963)-Origin-r/Superman-Batman team/Adv. 275; r/1955 Superman dailies 12.00 36.00 120.00
Annual 8(Win, 1963-64)-All origins issue 10.50 32.00 105.00
Annual 9(8/64)-Was advertised but came out as 80 Page Giant #1 instead
Annual 9(1983)-Toth/Austin-a 2.40 6.00
Annuals 10-12: 10(1984, $1.25)-M. Anderson inks. 11(1985)-Moore scripts. 12(1986)-Bolland-c 4.00
Special 1-3('83-'85): 1-G. Kane-c/a; contains German-r 4.00
The Amazing World of Superman "Official Metropolis Edition" (1973, $2.00, 14x10-1/2")-Origin retold; Wood-r(i) from Superboy #153,161 2.50 7.50 24.00
11195 (2/79, $1.95, 224 pgs.)-Golden Press 1.50 4.50 12.00
NOTE: ***N. Adams** a-249i, 254p; c-204-206, 210, 212-215, 219, 231i, 233-237, 240-243, 249-252, 254, 263, 307, 308, 313, 314, 317. **Adkins** a-323i. **Austin** c-368i. **Wayne Boring** art-late 1940's to early 1960's. **Buckler** a(p)-352, 363, 364, 369; c(p)-324-327, 356, 363, 368, 369, 373, 376, 378. **Burnley** a-252r; c-19-25, 30, 33, 34, 35p, 38p, 39p, 45p. **Fine** a-252r. **Kaluta** a-400. **Gil Kane** a-272r, 367, 372, 375, Special 2; c-374p, 375p, 377, 381, 382, 384-390, 392, Annual 9, Special 2. **Joe Kubert** c-216. **Morrow** a-238. **Mortimer** a-250r. **Perez** c-364p. **Fred Ray** a-25; c-6, 8-18. **Starlin** c-355. **Staton** a-354i, 355i. **Swan/Moldoff** c-149. **Williamson** a(i)-408-410, 412-416; c-408i, 409i. **Wrightson** a-400, 416.*

SUPERMAN (2nd Series)
DC Comics: Jan, 1987 - Present (75¢/$1.00/$1.25/$1.50/$1.95/$1.99)

1-Byrne-c/a begins; intro new Metallo 4.00
2-8,10: 3-Legends x-over; Darkseid-c & app. 7-Origin/1st app. Rampage. 8-Legion app. 3.00
9-Joker-c 4.50
11-15,17-20,22-49,51,52,54-56,58-67: 11-1st new Mr. Mxyzptlk. 12-Lori Lemaris revived. 13-1st app. new Toyman. 13,14-Millennium x-over. 20-Doom Patrol app.; Supergirl cameo. 31-Mr. Mxyzptlk app. 37-Newsboy Legion app. 41-Lobo app. 44-Batman storyline, part 1. 45-Free extra 8 pgs. 54-Newsboy Legion story. 63-Aquaman x-over. 67-Last $1.00-c 2.50
16,21: 16-1st app. new Supergirl (4/88). 21-Supergirl-c/story; 1st app. Matrix who becomes new Supergirl 4.00
50-($1.50, 52 pgs.)-Clark Kent proposes to Lois 5.00
50-2nd printing 2.00
53-Clark reveals i.d. to Lois (Cont'd from Action #662) 3.00
53-2nd printing 2.00
57-($1.75, 52 pgs.) 3.00
68-72: 65,66,68-Deathstroke-c/stories. 70-Superman & Robin team-up 2.00
73-Doomsday cameo 5.00
74-Doomsday Pt. 2 (Cont'd from Justice League #69); Superman battles Doomsday 2.40 6.00
73,74-2nd printings 2.00
75-($2.50)-Collector's Ed.; Doomsday Pt. 6; Superman dies; polybagged w/poster of funeral, obituary from Daily Planet, postage stamp & armband premiums (direct sales only) 1.50 4.50 12.00
75-Direct sales copy (no upc code, 1st print) 5.00
75-Direct sales copy (no upc code, 2nd-4th prints) 2.00
75-Newsstand copy w/upc code 5.00
75-Platinum Edition; given away to retailers 35.00
76,77-Funeral For a Friend parts 4 & 8 3.00
78-($1.95)-Collector's Edition with die-cut outer-c & bound-in mini poster; Doomsday cameo 3.00
78-($1.50)-Newsstand Edition w/poster and different-c; Doomsday-c & cameo 2.00
79-81,83-89: 83-Funeral for a Friend epilogue; new Batman (Azrael) cameo. 87,88-Bizarro-c/story 3.00

Superman (2nd series) #150 © DC

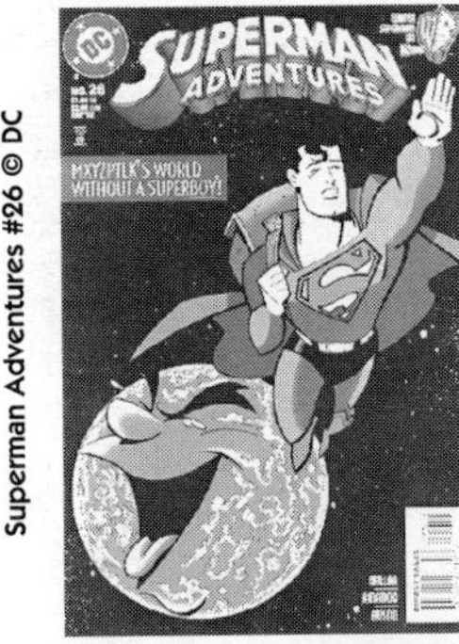

Superman Adventures #26 © DC

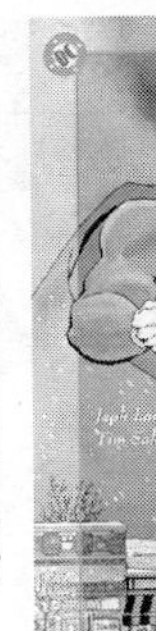
Superman For All Seasons #4 © DC

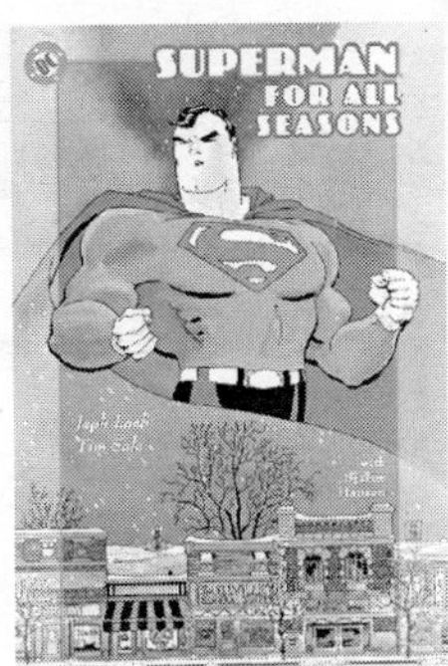

GD2.0 FN6.0 NM9.4

82-($3.50)-Collector's Edition w/all chromium-c; real Superman revealed; Green Lantern x-over from G.L. #46; no ads 2.40 6.00
82-($2.00, 44 pgs.)-Regular Edition w/different-c 2.00
90-93,0,94-99: 93-(9/94)-Zero Hour. 0-(10/94). 94-(11/94). 95-Atom app. 96-Return of Brainiac 2.00
100-Death of Clark Kent foil-c 4.00
100-Newsstand 3.00
101-122: 101-Begin $1.95-c; Black Adam app. 105-Green Lantern app. 110-Plastic Man-c/app. 114-Brainiac app; Dwyer-c. 115-Lois leaves Metropolis. 116-(10/96)-1st app. Teen Titans by Dan Jurgens & George Perez in 8 pg. preview. 117-Final Night. 118-Wonder Woman app. 119-Legion app. 122-New powers 2.00
123-Collector's Edition w/glow in the dark-c, new costume 2.40 6.00
123-Standard ed., new costume 4.00
124-149: 128-Cyborg-c/app. 131-Birth of Lena Luthor. 132-Superman Red/ Superman Blue. 134-Millenium Giants. 136,137-Superman 2999. 139-Starlin-a. 140-Grindberg-a 2.50
150-($2.95) Standard Ed.; Brainiac 2.0 app.; Jurgens-s 3.00
150-($3.95) Collector's Ed. w/holo-foil enhanced variant-c 4.00
151-Loeb-s begins; Daily Planet reopens 2.00
#1,000,000 (11/98) 853rd Century x-over; Gene Ha-c 2.00
Annual 1,2: 1 (1987)-No Byrne-a. 2 (1988)-Byrne-a; Newsboy Legion; return of the Guardian 4.00
Annual 3-6 ('91-'94 68 pgs.): 1-Armageddon 2001 x-over; Batman app.; Austin-c(i) & part inks. 4-Eclipso app. 6-Elseworlds sty 3.00
Annual 3-2nd & 3rd printings; 3rd has silver ink 2.00
Annual 7 (1995, $3.95, 69 pgs.)-Year One story 4.00
Annual 8 (1996, $2.95)-Legends of the Dead Earth story 3.00
Annual 9 (1997, $3.95)-Pulp Heroes story 4.00
Annual 10 (1998, $2.95)-Ghosts; Wrightson-c 3.00
Annual 11 (1999, $2.95)-JLApe; Art Adams-c 3.00
...: 80 Page Giant (2/99, $4.95) Jurgens-c 5.00
...: 80 Page Giant 2 (6/99, $4.95) Harris-c 5.00
...Plus 1(2/97, $2.95)-Legion of Super-Heroes-c/app. 3.00
Special 1 (1992, $3.50, 68 pgs.)-Simonson-c/a 5.00
...: Eradication! The Origin of the Eradicator (1996, $12.95, TPB) 13.00
...: Exile (1998, $14.95, TPB)-Reprints space exile following execution of Kryptonian criminals; 1st Eradicator 15.00
The Death of Clark Kent (1997, $19.95, TPB)-Reprints Man of Steel #43 (1 page), Superman #99 (1 page),#100-102, Action #709 (1 page), #710,711, Advs. of Superman #523-525, Superman:The Man of Tomorrow #1 20.00
The Death of Superman (1993, $4.95, TPB)-Reprints Man of Steel #17-19, Superman #73-75, Advs. of Superman #496,497, Action #683,684, & Justice League #69 1.00 3.00 8.00
The Death of Superman, 2nd & 3rd printings 5.00
The Death of Superman Platinum Edition 15.00
The Trial of Superman ('97, $14.95, TPB) reprints story arc 15.00
...: Time and Time Again (1994, $7.50, TPB)-Reprints 8.00
... :Transformed ('98, $12.95, TPB) r/post Final Night powerless Superman to Electric Superman 13.00
... Vs. The Revenge Squad (1999, $12.95, TPB) 13.00

NOTE: ***Austin*** *a(i)-1-3.* ***Byrne*** *a-1-16p, 17, 19-21p, 22; c-1-17, 20-22; scripts-1-22.* ***Guice*** *c/a-64.* ***Kirby*** *c-37p.* ***Joe Quesada*** *c-Annual 4.* ***Russell*** *c/a-23i.* ***Simonson*** *c-69i. #19-21 2nd printings sold in multi-packs.*

SUPERMAN (one-shots)
Daily News Magazine Presents DC Comics' Superman nn-(1987, 8 pgs.)-Supplement to New York Daily News; Perez-c/a 4.00
...: A Nation Divided (1999, $4.95)-Elseworlds Civil War story 5.00
... & Savage Dragon: Metropolis (11/99, $4.95) Bogdanove-a 5.00
...: At Earth's End (1995, $4.95)-Elseworlds story 5.00
...: Distant Fires (1998, $5.95)-Elseworlds; Chaykin-s 6.00
... For Earth (1991, $4.95, 52 pgs, printed on recycled paper)-Ordway wraparound-c. 5.00
...IV Movie Special (1987, $2.00)-Movie adaptation; Heck-a 3.00
...Gallery, The 1 (1993, $2.95)-Poster-a 3.00
...: Kal (1995, $5.95)-Elseworlds story 6.00
...: Monster (1999, $5.95)-Elseworlds story; Anthony Williams-a 6.00
...Movie Special-(9/83)-Adaptation of Superman III; other versions exist with store logos on bottom 1/3 of-c 4.00
...'s Metropolis-(1996, $5.95, prestige format)-Elseworlds; McKeever-c/a 6.00
...: Speeding Bullets-(1993, $4.95, 52 pgs.)-Elseworlds 5.00
.../Spider-Man-(1995, $3.95)-r/DC and Marvel Presents... 4.00
...: The Earth Stealers 1-(1988, $2.95, 52 pgs, prestige format) Byrne script; painted-c 4.00
...: The Earth Stealers 1-2nd printing 3.00
...: The Legacy of Superman #1 (3/93, $2.50, 68 pgs.)-Art Adams-c; Simonson-a 4.00
...: The Last God of Krypton ('99,$4.95) Hildebrandt Bros.-a/Simonson-s 5.00
...: The Odyssey ('99, $4.95) Clark Kent's post-Smallville journey 5.00
.../Toyman-(1996, $1.95) 2.00
...: 3-D (12/98, $3.95)-with glasses 4.00
...: Under A Yellow Sun (1994, $5.95, 68 pgs.)-A Novel by Clark Kent; embossed-c 6.00
...: War of the Worlds (1999, $5.95)-Battles Martians 6.00

SUPERMAN ADVENTURES, THE (TV)
DC Comics: Oct, 1996 - Present ($1.75/$1.95/$1.99)(Based on animated series)
1-Rick Burchett-c/a begins; Paul Dini script; Lex Luthor app.; silver ink, wraparound-c. 3.00
1-Preview issue distributed at Warner Bros. stores 3.00
2-20,22: 2-Scott McCloud scripts begin; Metallo-c/app. 3-Brainiac-c/app. 6-Mxyzptlk-c/app. 2.50
21-($3.95) 1st animated Supergirl 5.00
23-37: 23-Begin $1.99-c; Livewire app. 25-Batgirl-c/app. 28-Manley-a 2.00
Annual 1 (1997, $3.95)-Zatanna and Bruce Wayne app. 4.00
Special 1 (2/98, $2.95) Superman vs. Lobo 3.00
TPB (1998, $7.95) r/#1-6 8.00

SUPERMAN & BATMAN: GENERATIONS (Elseworlds)
DC Comics: 1999 - No. 4, 1999 ($4.95, limited series)
1-4-Superman & Batman team-up from 1939 to the future; Byrne-c/s/a 5.00

SUPERMAN/BATMAN: ALTERNATE HISTORIES
DC Comics: 1996 ($14.95, trade paperback)
nn-Reprints Detective Comics Annual #7, Action Comics Annual #6, Steel Annual #1, Legends of the Dark Knight Annual #4 15.00

SUPERMAN/DOOMSDAY: HUNTER/PREY
DC Comics: 1994 - No. 3, 1994 ($4.95, limited series, 52 pgs.)
1-3 5.00

SUPERMAN FAMILY, THE (Formerly Superman's Pal Jimmy Olsen)
National Per. Publ./DC Comics: No. 164, Apr-May, 1974 - No. 222, Sept, 1982
164-(100 pgs.) Jimmy Olsen, Supergirl, Lois Lane begin 3.00 9.00 30.00
165-169 (100 pgs.) 2.50 7.50 20.00
170-176 (68 pgs.) 1.75 5.25 14.00
177-190 (52 pgs.): 177-181-52 pgs. 182-Marshall Rogers-a; $1.00 issues begin; Krypto begins, ends #192. 183-Nightwing-Flamebird begins, ends #194. 189-Brainiac 5, Mon-el app. 1.00 3.00 8.00
191-193,195-199: 191-Superboy begins, ends #198 2.40 6.00
194,200: 194-Rogers-a. 200-Book length sty 1.00 3.00 8.00
201-222: 211-Earth II Batman & Catwoman marry 2.40 6.00

NOTE: ***N. Adams*** *c-182-185.* ***Anderson*** *a-186i.* ***Buckler*** *c(p)-190, 191, 209, 210, 215, 217, 220.* ***Jones*** *a-191-193.* ***Gil Kane*** *c(p)-221, 222.* ***Mortimer*** *a(p)-191-193, 199, 201-222.* ***Orlando*** *a(i)-186, 187.* ***Rogers*** *a-182, 194.* ***Staton*** *a-191-194, 196p.* ***Tuska*** *a(p)-203, 207-209.*

SUPERMAN/FANTASTIC FOUR
DC Comics/Marvel Comics: 1999 ($9.95, tabloid size, one-shot)
1-Battle Galactus and the Cyborg; wraparound-c by Alex Ross and Dan Jurgens; Jurgens-s/a; Thibert-a 10.00

SUPERMAN FOR ALL SEASONS
DC Comics: 1998 - No, 4, 1998 ($4.95, limited series, prestige format)
1-Loeb-s/Sale-a/c; Superman's first year in Metropolis 6.00
2-4 5.00

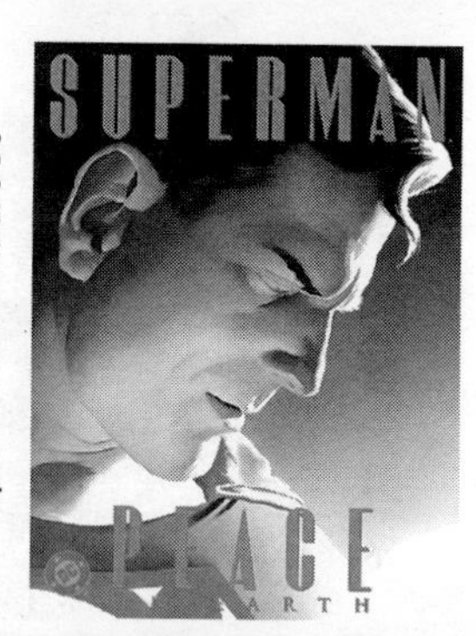

Superman: Peace on Earth © DC

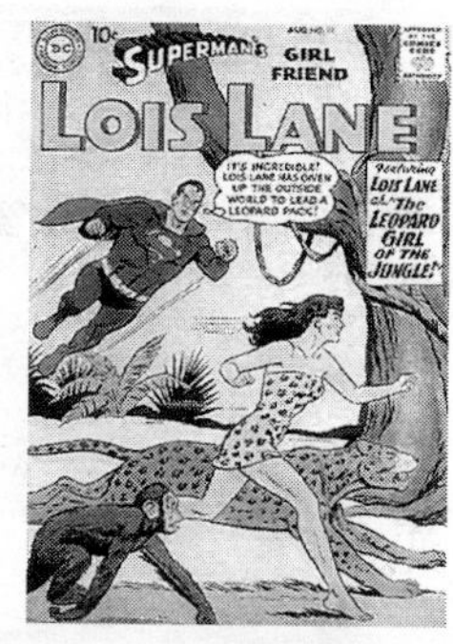

Superman's Girlfriend Lois Lane #11 © DC

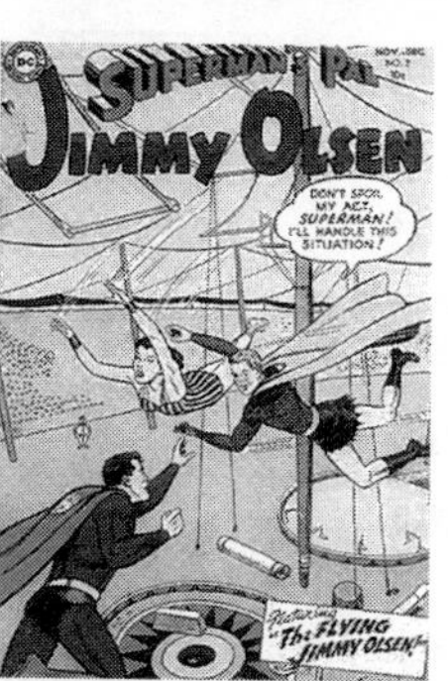

Superman's Pal Jimmy Olsen #2 © DC

GD2.0 FN6.0 NM9.4

Hardcover (1999, $24.95) r/#1-4 25.00

SUPERMAN FOR EARTH (See Superman one-shots)

SUPERMAN FOREVER
DC Comics: Jun, 1998 ($5.95, one-shot)
1-($5.95)-Collector's Edition with a 7-image lenticular-c by Alex Ross; Superman returns to normal; s/a by various 7.00
1-($4.95) Standard Edition with single image Ross-c 5.00

SUPERMAN: KING OF THE WORLD
DC Comics: June, 1999 ($3.95/$4.95, one-shot)
1-($3.95) Regular Ed. 4.00
1-($4.95) Collectors' Ed. with gold foil enhanced-c 5.00

SUPERMAN: LOIS LANE (Girlfrenzy)
DC Comics: Jun, 1998 ($1.95, one shot)
1-Connor & Palmiotti-a 2.00

SUPERMAN/MADMAN HULLABALOO!
Dark Horse Comics: June, 1997 - No. 3, Aug, 1997 ($2.95, limited series)
1-3-Mike Allred-c/s/a 3.00
TPB (1997, $8.95) 9.00

SUPERMAN: PEACE ON EARTH
DC Comics: Jan, 1999 ($9.95, Treasury-sized, one-shot)
1-Alex Ross painted-c/a; Paul Dini-s 12.00

SUPERMAN RED/ SUPERMAN BLUE
DC Comics: Feb, 1998 ($4.95, one shot)
1-Polybagged w/3-D glasses and reprint of Superman 3-D (1955); Jurgens-plot/3-D cover; script and art by various 5.00
1-($3.95)-Standard Ed.; comic only, non 3-D cover 4.00

SUPERMAN: SAVE THE PLANET
DC Comics: Oct, 1998 ($2.95, one-shot)
1-($2.95) Regular Ed.; Luthor buys the Daily Planet 3.00
1-($3.95) Collector's Ed. with acetate cover 4.00

SUPERMAN SCRAPBOOK (Has blank pages; contains no comics)

SUPERMAN: SECRET FILES
DC Comics: Jan, 1998; May 1999 ($4.95)
1,2: 1-Retold origin story, "lost" pages & pin-ups 5.00

SUPERMAN'S GIRLFRIEND LOIS LANE (See Action Comics #1, 80 Page Giant #3, 14, Lois Lane, Showcase #9, 10, Superman #28 & Superman Family)

SUPERMAN'S GIRLFRIEND LOIS LANE (See Showcase #9,10)
National Periodical Publ.: Mar-Apr, 1958 - No. 136, Jan-Feb, 1974; No. 137, Sept-Oct, 1974

	GD2.0	FN6.0	VF8.0	NM9.4
1-(3-4/58)	230.00	690.00	1500.00	3200.00

	GD2.0	FN6.0	NM9.4
2	67.00	200.00	800.00
3	44.00	131.00	525.00
4,5	38.00	114.00	420.00
6,7	31.00	93.00	325.00
8-10: 9-Pat Boone-c/story	27.00	81.00	270.00
11-13,15-19: 12-(10/59)-Aquaman app.	15.00	45.00	150.00
14,20: 14-Supergirl x-over; Batman app. on-c only. 20-Supergirl-c/sty	15.00	45.00	150.00
21-28: 23-1st app. Lena Thorul, Lex Luthor's sister. 27-Bizarro-c/story	11.50	34.00	115.00
29-Aquaman, Batman, Green Arrow cover app. and cameo; last 10¢ issue	12.50	38.00	125.00
30-32,34-46,48,49	6.00	18.00	60.00
33(5/62)-Mon-el app.	7.00	21.00	70.00
47-Legion app.	7.00	21.00	70.00
50(7/64)-Triplicate Girl, Phantom Girl & Shrinking Violet app.	6.50	19.50	65.00
51-55,57-67,69: 59-Jor-el app.; Batman back-up sty	4.50	13.50	45.00
56-Saturn Girl app.	4.50	13.50	45.00

GD2.0 FN6.0 NM9.4

	GD2.0	FN6.0	NM9.4
68-(Giant G-26)	5.50	16.50	55.00
70-Penguin & Catwoman app. (1st S.A. Catwoman, 11/66; also see Detective #369 for 3rd app.); Batman & Robin cameo	22.00	66.00	220.00
71-Batman & Robin cameos (3 panels); Catwoman story cont'd from #70 (2nd app.); see Detective #369 for 3rd app	12.50	38.00	125.00
72,73,75,76,78	2.50	7.50	24.00
74-1st Bizarro Flash (5/67); JLA cameo	3.40	10.20	34.00
77-(Giant G-39)	4.50	13.50	45.00
79-Neal Adams-c or c(i) begin, end #95,108	2.50	7.50	24.00
80-85,87,88,90-92: 92-Last 12¢ issue	2.25	6.75	18.00
86,95 (Giants G-51,G-63)-Both have Neal Adams-c	3.60	10.80	36.00
89,93: 89-Batman x-over; all N. Adams-c. 93-Wonder Woman-c/story	2.25	6.75	18.00
94,96-99,101-103,107-110	2.00	6.00	16.00
100	2.25	6.75	18.00
104-(Giant G-75)	3.60	10.80	36.00
105-Origin/1st app. The Rose & the Thorn.	3.80	11.40	38.00
106-"Black Like Me" sty; Lois changes her color to black	2.25	6.75	18.00
111-Justice League-c/s; Morrow-a; last 15¢ issue	2.25	6.75	18.00
112,114-123 (52 pgs.): 122-G.A. Lois Lane-r/Superman #30. 123-G.A. Batman-r/Batman #35 (w/Catwoman)	2.00	6.00	16.00
113-(Giant G-87) Kubert-a (previously unpublished G.A. story)	3.60	10.80	36.00
124-135: 130-Last Rose & the Thorn. 132-New Zatanna story	1.25	3.75	10.00
136,137: 136-Wonder Woman x-over	1.50	4.50	12.00
Annual 1(Sum, 1962)-r/L. Lane #12; Aquaman app.	18.00	54.00	180.00
Annual 2(Sum, 1963)	12.00	36.00	120.00

NOTE: ***Buckler** a-117-121p. **Curt Swan or Kurt Schaffenberger** a-1-81(most); c(p)-1-15.*

SUPERMAN: SILVER BANSHEE
DC Comics: Dec, 1998 - No. 2, Jan, 1999 ($2.25, mini-series)
1,2-Brereton-s/c; Chin-a 2.25

SUPERMAN'S NEMESIS: LEX LUTHOR
DC Comics: Mar, 1999 - No. 4, Jun, 1999 ($2.50, mini-series)
1-4-Semeiks-a 2.50

SUPERMAN'S PAL JIMMY OLSEN (Superman Family #164 on)
(See Action Comics #6 for 1st app. & 80 Page Giant)
National Periodical Publ.: Sept-Oct, 1954 - No. 163, Feb-Mar, 1974 (Fourth World #133-148)

	GD2.0	FN6.0	VF8.0	NM9.4
1	320.00	960.00	2240.00	4800.00

	GD2.0	FN6.0	NM9.4
2	108.00	325.00	1300.00
3-Last pre-code issue	58.00	174.00	700.00
4,5	43.00	129.00	500.00
6-10	31.00	93.00	340.00
11-20: 15-1st S.A. issue	22.00	66.00	220.00
21-30: 29-1st app. Krypto in Jimmy Olsen	14.00	42.00	140.00
31-Origin & 1st app.Elastic Lad (Jimmy Olsen)	11.00	33.00	110.00
32-40: 33-One pg. biography of Jack Larson (TV Jimmy Olsen). 36-Intro Lucy Lane. 37-2nd app. Elastic Lad & 1st cover app.	9.50	28.50	95.00
41-50: 41-1st J.O. Robot. 48-Intro/origin Superman Emergency Squad	7.50	22.50	75.00
51-56: 56-Last 10¢ issue	6.00	18.00	60.00
57-62,64-70: 57-Olsen marries Supergirl. 62-Mon-el & Elastic Lad app. but not as Legionnaires. 70-Element Boy (Lad) app.	3.50	10.50	35.00
63(9/62)-Legion of Super-Villains app.	4.00	12.00	40.00
71,74,75,78,80-84,86,89,90: 86-Jimmy Olsen Robot becomes Congorilla	3.00	9.00	30.00
72,73,76,77,79,85,87,88: 72(10/63)-Legion app; Elastic Lad (Olsen) joins. 73-Ultra Boy app. 76,85-Legion app. 76-Legion app. 77-Olsen with Colossal Boy's powers & costume; origin Titano retold. 79-(9/64)-Titled The Red-head ed Beatle of 1000 B.C. 85-Legion app. 87-Legion of Super-Villains app. 88-Star Boy app.	3.20	9.50	32.00
91-94,96-98	2.50	7.50	22.00

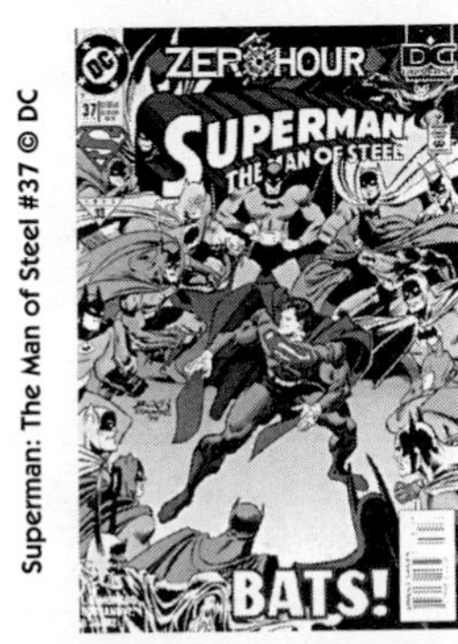
Superman: The Man of Steel #37 © DC

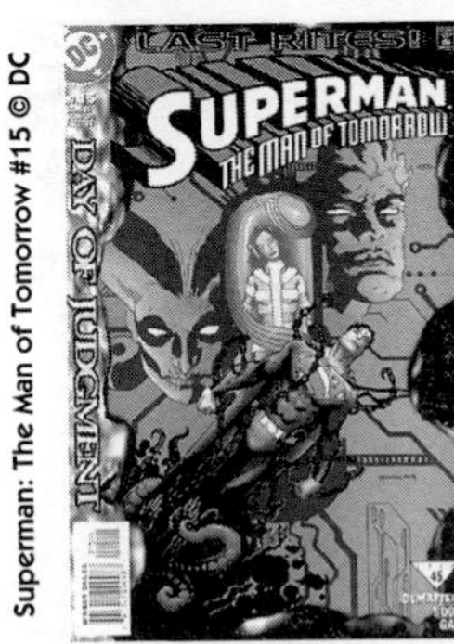
Superman: The Man of Tomorrow #15 © DC

Supermen of America #1 © DC

GD2.0 FN6.0 NM9.4

95,104 (Giants G-25,G-38) 4.00 12.00 40.00
99-Olsen w/powers & costumes of Lightning Lad, Sun Boy & Element Lad 2.50 7.50 24.00
100-Legion cameo 3.40 10.20 34.00
101-103,105-112,114-120: 106-Legion app. 110-Infinity-c. 117-Batman & Legion cameo. 120-Last 12¢ issue 2.00 6.00 16.00
113,122,131,140 (Giants G-50,G-62,G-74,G-86) 3.30 9.90 33.00
121,123-130,132
133-(10/70)-Re-intro Newsboy Legion; Kirby story & art begins; 1st app. Morgan Edge. 5.00 15.00 50.00
134-1st app. Darkseid (1 panel, 12/70) 6.00 18.00 65.00
135-2nd app. Darkseid (1 pg. cameo; see New Gods & Forever People); G.A. Guardian app. 2.80 8.40 28.00
136-139: 136-Origin new Guardian. 138-Partial photo-c. 139-Last 15¢ issue 2.50 7.50 22.00
141-150: (25¢,52 pgs.). 141-Photo-c; Newsboy Legion-r by S&K begin; full pg. self-portrait Kirby; Don Rickles cameo. 149,150-G.A. Plastic Man-r in both; 150-Newsboy Legion app. 2.50 7.50 20.00
151-163 1.50 4.50 12.00
NOTE: *Issues #141-148 contain* ***Simon & Kirby*** *Newsboy Legion reprints from Star Spangled #7, 8, 9, 10, 11, 12, 13, 14 in that order.* ***N. Adams*** *c-109-112, 115, 117, 118, 120, 121, 132, 134-136, 147, 148.* ***Kirby*** *a-133-139p, 141-148p; c-133, 137, 139, 142, 145p.* ***Kirby/N. Adams*** *c-137, 138, 141-144, 146.* ***Curt Swan*** *c-1-14(most)., 140.*

SUPERMAN SPECTACULAR (Also see DC Special Series #5)
DC Comics: 1982 (Magazine size, square binding)
1-Saga of Superman Red/ Superman Blue 1.00 3.00 8.00

SUPERMAN: THE DARK SIDE
DC Comics: 1998 - No. 3, 1998 ($4.95, squarebound, mini-series)
1-3: Elseworlds; Kal-El lands on Apokolips 5.00

SUPERMAN: THE DOOMSDAY WARS
DC Comics: 1998 - No. 3, 1999 ($4.95, squarebound, mini-series)
1-3: Superman & JLA vs. Doomsday; Jurgens-s/a(p) 5.00

SUPERMAN: THE MAN OF STEEL (Also see Man of Steel, The)
DC Comics: July, 1991 - Present ($1.00/$1.25/$1.50/$1.95)
1-($1.75, 52 pgs.)-Painted-c 4.00
2-16: 3-War of the Gods x-over. 5-Reads sideways. 10-Last $1.00-c. 14-Superman & Robin team-up 2.50
17-1st app. Doomsday (cameo) 1.00 2.80 7.00
17,18: 17-2nd printing. 18-2nd & 3rd printings 2.00
18-1st full app. Doomsday 1.10 3.30 9.00
19-Doomsday battle issue (c/story) 4.00
20-22: 20,21-Funeral for a Friend. 22-($1.95)-Collector's Edition w/die-cut outer-c & bound-in poster; Steel-c/story 2.50
22-($1.50)-Newsstand Ed. w/poster & different-c 2.00
23-37,0,38-49,51-94: 30-Regular edition. 32-Bizarro-c/story. 35,36-Worlds Collide Pt. 1 & 10. 37-(9/94)-Zero Hour x-over. 0, 38-44-(10/94). 38-(11/94). 48-Aquaman app. 54-Spectre-c/app; Lex Luthor app. 56-Mxyzptlk-c/app. 57-G.A. Flash app. 58-Supergirl app. 59-Parasite-c/app.; Steel app. 60-Reintro Bottled City of Kandor. 62-Final Night. 64-New Gods app. 67-New powers. 75-"Death" of Mxyzptlk. 78,79-Millennium Giants. 80-Golden Age style. 92-JLA app. 2.00
30-($2.50)-Collector's Edition; polybagged with Superman & Lobo vinyl clings that stick to wraparound-c; Lobo-c/story 2.50
50 ($2.95)-The Trial of Superman 4.00
#1,000,000 (11/98) 853rd Century x-over; Gene Ha-c 2.00
Annual 1-5 ('92-'96,68 pgs.): 1-Eclipso app.; Joe Quesada-c(p). 2-Intro Edge. 3 -Elseworlds story; Mignola-c; Batman app. 4-Year One story. 5-Legends of the Dead Earth story 3.00
Annual 6 (1997, $3.95)-Pulp Heroes story 4.00
...Gallery (1995, $3.50) Pin-ups by various 3.50

SUPERMAN: THE MAN OF TOMORROW
DC Comics: 1995 - No. 15, Fall, 1999 ($1.95, quarterly)
1-15: 1-Lex Luthor app. 3-Lex Luthor-c/app; Joker app. 4-Shazam! app. 5-Wedding of Lex Luthor. 10-Maxima-c/app. 13-JLA-c/app. 2.00
#1,000,000 (11/98) 853rd Century x-over; Gene Ha-c 2.00

SUPERMAN: THE SECRET YEARS
DC Comics: Feb, 1985 - No. 4, May, 1985 (limited series)
1-4-Miller-c on all 2.50

SUPERMAN: THE WEDDING ALBUM
DC Comics: Dec, 1996 ($4.95, 96 pgs, one-shot)
1-Standard Edition-Story & art by past and present Superman creators; gatefold back-c. Byrne-c 5.00
1-Collector's Edition-Embossed cardstock variant-c w/ metallic silver ink and matte and gloss varnishes 5.00
TPB ('97, $14.95) r/Wedding and honeymoon stories 15.00

SUPERMAN 3-D (See Three-Dimension Adventures)

SUPERMAN VILLAINS SECRET FILES
DC Comics: Jun, 1998 ($4.95, one shot)
1-Origin stories, "lost" pages & pin-ups 5.00

SUPERMAN VS. ALIENS
DC Comics/Dark Horse Comics: July, 1995 - No. 3, Sept, 1995 ($4.95, limited series)
1-3: Jurgens/Nowlan-a 5.00

SUPERMAN VS. THE AMAZING SPIDER-MAN (Also see Marvel Treasury Edition No. 28)
National Periodical Publications/Marvel Comics Group: 1976 ($2.00, Treasury sized, 100 pgs.)
1-Andru/Giordano-a; 1st Marvel/DC x-over. 5.50 16.50 60.00
1-2nd printing; 5000 numbered copies signed by Stan Lee & Carmine Infantino on front cover & sold through mail 11.00 33.00 120.00
nn-(1995, $5.95)-r/#1 2.40 6.00

SUPERMAN/WONDER WOMAN: WHOM GODS DESTROY
DC Comics: 1997 ($4.95, prestige format, limited series)
1-4-Elseworlds; Claremont-s 5.00

SUPERMAN WORKBOOK
National Periodical Publ./Juvenile Group Foundation: 1945 (B&W, one-shot, reprints, 68 pgs)
nn-Cover-r/Superman #14 144.00 431.00 1150.00

SUPER MARIO BROS. (Also see Adventures of the..., Blip, Gameboy, and Nintendo Comics System)
Valiant Comics: 1990 - No. 5?, 1991 ($1.95, slick-c) V2#1, 1991 - No. 5, 1991
1-Wildman-a 4.00
2-5, V2#1-5-($1.50), Special Edition 1 (1990, $1.95)-Wildman-a 3.00

SUPERMEN OF AMERICA
DC Comics: Mar, 1999 ($3.95/$4.95, one-shot)
1-($3.95) Regular Ed.; Immonen-s/art by various 4.00
1-($4.95) Collectors' Ed. with membership kit 5.00

SUPERMOUSE (...the Big Cheese; see Coo Coo Comics)
Standard Comics/Pines No. 35 on (Literary Ent.): Dec, 1948 - No. 34, Sept, 1955; No. 35, Apr, 1956 - No. 45, Fall, 1958
1-Frazetta text illos (3) 29.00 86.00 200.00
2-Frazetta text illos 14.00 43.00 100.00
3,5,6-Text illos by Frazetta in all 11.50 34.00 80.00
4-Two pg. text illos by Frazetta 12.00 36.00 85.00
7-10 5.00 15.00 30.00
11-20: 13-Racist humor (Indians) 4.00 12.00 24.00
21-45 3.60 9.00 18.00
1-Summer Holiday issue (Summer, 1957, 25¢, 100 pgs.)-Pines 11.50 34.00 80.00
2-Giant Summer issue (Summer, 1958, 25¢, 100 pgs.)-Pines; has games, puzzles & stories 10.00 30.00 60.00

SUPER-MYSTERY COMICS
Ace Magazines (Periodical House): July, 1940 - V8#6, July, 1949

Super-Mystery Comics V3 #3 © ACE

Supernatural Thrillers #11 © MAR

Supersnipe V3 #7 © S&S

GD2.0 FN6.0 NM9.4 **GD2.0 FN6.0 NM9.4**

V1#1-Magno, the Magnetic Man & Vulcan begins (1st app.); Q-13, Corp. Flint, & Sky Smith begin 175.00 525.00 1400.00
2 81.00 244.00 650.00
3-The Black Spider begins (1st app.) 71.00 212.00 565.00
4-Origin Davy 55.00 165.00 440.00
5-Intro. The Clown & begin series (12/40) 56.00 169.00 450.00
6(2/41) 45.00 135.00 360.00
V2#1(4/41)-Origin Buckskin 45.00 135.00 360.00
2-6(2/42): 6-Vulcan begins again 40.00 120.00 325.00
V3#1(4/42),2: 1-Black Ace begins 40.00 120.00 280.00
3-Intro. The Lancer; Dr. Nemesis & The Sword begin; Kurtzman-c/a(2) (Mr. Risk & Paul Revere Jr.); Robot-c 47.00 142.00 380.00
4-Kurtzman-c/a 40.00 120.00 320.00
5-Kurtzman-a(2); L.B. Cole-a; Mr. Risk app. 46.00 139.00 370.00
6(10/43)-Mr. Risk app.; Kurtzman's Paul Revere Jr.; L.B. Cole-a 46.00 139.00 370.00
V4#1(1/44)-L.B. Cole-a 40.00 120.00 310.00
2-6(4/45): 2,5,6-Mr. Risk app. 29.00 86.00 200.00
V5#1(7/45)-6 30.00 90.00 210.00
V6#1-6: 3-Torture story. 4-Last Magno. Mr. Risk app. in #2,4-6. 6-New logo 23.00 69.00 160.00
V7#1-6, V8#1-4,6 23.00 69.00 160.00
V8#5-Meskin, Tuska, Sid Greene-a 23.00 69.00 160.00

NOTE: ***Sid Greene** a-V7#4. **Mooney** c-V1#5, 6, V2#1-6. **Palais** a-V5#3, 4; c-V4#6-V5#4, V6#2, V8#4. Bondage c-V2#5, 6, V3#2, 5. Magno c-V1#1-V3#6, V4#2-V5#5, V6#2. The Sword c-V4#1, 6(w/Magno).*

SUPERNATURALS
Marvel Comics: Dec, 1998 - No. 4, Dec, 1998 ($3.99, weekly limited series)

1-4-Pulido-s/Balent-c; bound-in Halloween masks 4.00
1-4-With bound-in Ghost Rider mask (1 in 10) 4.00

SUPERNATURAL THRILLERS
Marvel Comics Group: Dec, 1972 - No. 6, Nov, 1973; No. 7, Jul, 1974 - No. 15, Oct, 1975

1-It!; Sturgeon adap. (see Astonishing Tales #21). 2.00 6.00 16.00
2-4,6-15: 2-The Invisible Man; H.G. Wells adapt. 3-The Valley of the Worm; R.E. Howard adapt. 4-Dr. Jekyll & Mr. Hyde; R.L. Stevenson adapt.. 6-The Headless Horseman; last 20¢ issue. 7-The Living Mummy begins 1.25 3.75 10.00
5-1st app. The Living Mummy 4.00 12.00 40.00

NOTE: ***Brunner** c-11. **Buckler** a-5p. **Ditko** a-8r, 9r. **G. Kane** a-3p; c-3, 9p, 15p. **Mayerik** a-2p, 7, 8, 9p, 10p, 11. **McWilliams** a-14i. **Mortimer** a-4. **Steranko** c-1, 2. **Sutton** a-15. **Tuska** a-6p.*

SUPERPATRIOT (Also see Freak Force & Savage Dragon #2)
Image Comics (Highbrow Entertainment): July, 1993 - No. 4, Dec, 1993 ($1.95, limited series)

1-4: Dave Johnson-c/a; Larsen scripts; Giffen plots 2.50

SUPERPATRIOT: LIBERTY & JUSTICE
Image Comics (Highbrow Entertainment): July, 1995 - No. 4, Oct, 1995 ($2.50, limited series)

1-4: Dave Johnson-c/a. 1-1st app. Liberty & Justice 2.50

SUPER POWERS (1st Series)
DC Comics: July, 1984 - No. 5, Nov, 1984

1-5: 1-Joker/Penguin-c/story; Batman app.; all Kirby-c. 5-Kirby c/a 4.00

SUPER POWERS (2nd Series)
DC Comics: Sept, 1985 - No. 6, Feb, 1986

1-6: Kirby-c/a; Capt. Marvel & Firestorm join; Batman cameo; Darkseid storyline in all. 4-Batman cameo. 5,6-Batman app. 4.00

SUPER POWERS (3rd Series)
DC Comics: Sept, 1986 - No. 4, Dec, 1986

1-4: 1-Cyborg joins; 1st app. Samurai from Super Friends TV show. 1-4-Batman cameos; Darkseid storyline in #1-4 2.50

SUPER PUP (Formerly Spotty The Pup) (See Space Comics)
Avon Periodicals: No. 4, Mar-Apr, 1954 - No. 5, 1954

4,5: 5-Robot-c 5.00 15.00 30.00

SUPER RABBIT (See All Surprise, Animated Movie Tunes, Comedy Comics, Comic Capers, Ideal Comics, It's A Duck's Life, Movie Tunes & Wisco)
Timely Comics (CmPl): Fall, 1944 - No. 14, Nov, 1948

1-Hitler & Hirohito-c; war effort paper recycling PSA by S&K; Ziggy Pig & Silly begin? 62.00 187.00 500.00
2 34.00 103.00 240.00
3-5 21.00 64.00 150.00
6-Origin 23.00 69.00 160.00
7-10: 9-Infinity-c 13.00 39.00 90.00
11-Kurtzman's "Hey Look" 13.50 41.00 95.00
12-14 12.00 36.00 85.00
I.W. Reprint #1,2('58),7,10('63): 1-r/#13. 2-r/#10. 2.00 6.00 16.00

SUPER RICHIE (Superichie #5 on) (See Richie Rich Millions #68)
Harvey Publications: Sept, 1975 - No. 4, Mar, 1976 (All 52 pg. Giants)

1 1.60 4.80 16.00
2-4 1.00 3.00 10.00

SUPERSNIPE COMICS (Formerly Army & Navy #1-5)
Street & Smith Publications: V1#6, Oct, 1942 - V5#1, Aug-Sept, 1949 (See Shadow Comics V2#3)

V1#6-Rex King - Man of Adventure (costumed hero, see Super Magic/ Magician) by Jack Binder begins; Supersnipe by George Marcoux continues from Army & Navy #5; Bill Ward-a 78.00 234.00 625.00
7,10-12: 10,11-Little Nemo app. 47.00 141.00 375.00
8-Hitler, Tojo, Mussolini in Hell with Devil-c 51.00 154.00 410.00
9-Doc Savage x-over in Supersnipe; Hitler-c 64.00 191.00 510.00
V2#1-12: Both V2#1(2/44) & V2#2(4/44) has V2#1 on outside-c. 1-Huck Finn by Clare Dwiggins begins, ends V3#5; V2#2 shows V2#1 on cover 37.00 111.00 260.00
V3#1-12: 8-Bobby Crusoe by Dwiggins begins, ends V3#12. 9-X-Mas-c 32.00 96.00 225.00
V4#1-12, V5#1: V4#10-X-Mas-c 23.00 69.00 160.00

NOTE: ***George Marcoux** c-V1#6-V3#4. Doc Savage app. in some issues.*

SUPER SOLDIER (See Marvel Versus DC #3)
DC Comics (Amalgam): Apr, 1996 ($1.95, one-shot)

1-Mark Waid script & Dave Gibbons-c/a. 2.00

SUPER SOLDIER: MAN OF WAR
DC Comics (Amalgam): June, 1997 ($1.95, one-shot)

1-Waid & Gibbons-s/Gibbons & Palmiotti-c/a. 2.00

SUPER SOLDIERS
Marvel Comics UK: Apr, 1993 - No. 8, Nov, 1993 ($1.75)

1-($2.50)-Embossed silver foil logo 2.50
2-8: 5-Capt. America app. 6-Origin; Nick Fury app.; neon ink-c 2.00

SUPERSPOOK (Formerly Frisky Animals on Parade)
Ajax/Farrell Publications: No. 4, June, 1958

4 7.50 22.50 45.00

SUPER SPY (See Wham Comics)
Centaur Publications: Oct, 1940 - No. 2, Nov, 1940 (Reprints)

1-Origin The Sparkler 106.00 319.00 850.00
2-The Inner Circle, Dean Denton, Tim Blain, The Drew Ghost, The Night Hawk by Gustavson, & S.S. Swanson by Glanz app. 66.00 197.00 525.00

SUPER STAR HOLIDAY SPECIAL (See DC Special Series #21)

SUPER-TEAM FAMILY
National Periodical Publ./DC Comics: Oct-Nov, 1975 - No. 15, Mar-Apr, 1978

1-Reprints by Neal Adams & Kane/Wood; 68 pgs. begin, ends #4. New Gods app. 1.75 5.25 14.00
2,3: New stories 1.00 3.00 8.00
4-7: Reprints. 4-G.A. JSA-r & Superman/Batman/Robin-r from World's Finest. 5-52 pgs. begin 1.00 3.00 8.00
8-14: 8-10-New Challengers of the Unknown stories. 9-Kirby-a. 11-14: New stories 1.10 3.30 9.00

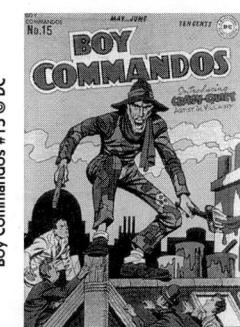

P9-DMO-759

COMICS
GUARANTY, LLC
Charter
Member Dealer

THE BETHLEHEM COLLECTION 2000
COLLECTORS ASSEMBLE!
BUYING and SELLING
COMICS PRE 1966
Collectors Assemble!
ComicCollectors.net
Marnin Rosenberg
P.O. Box 2047
Great Neck, NY 11022-2047
(516) 466-8147
www.ComicCollectors.net
for high grade quality rare vintage comic books!!!
SPECIALIZING IN RARE HIGH GRADE INVESTMENT COMICS
OVERSTREET ADVISOR · CBG CUSTOMER SERVICE AWARD · MEMBER C.G.C.

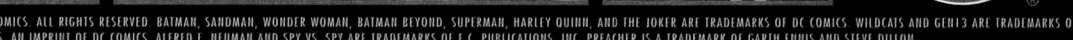

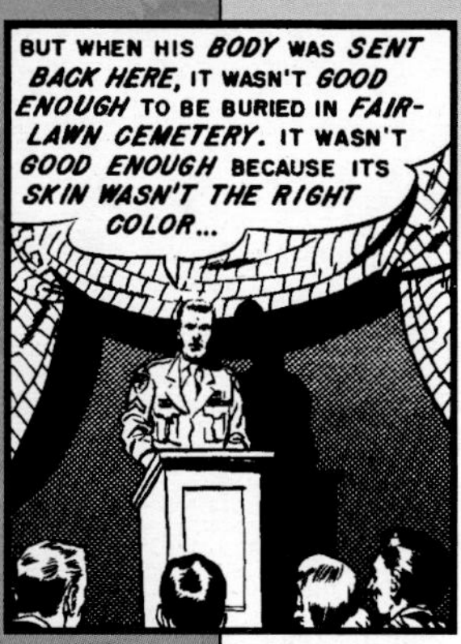

DO YOU COLLECT EC COMICS?
World Press
EXTRA!
REPORTER RISKS LIFE TO NAB RACKETEER
HE-MAN ADVENTURE
TWO-FISTED TALES
No. 21
MAY-JUNE
10¢
WE'RE IN A CROSS-FIRE! GET THIS JEEP OUT OF HERE!
THE ROAD'S BEEN MINED! IT'S A GUERILLA AMBUSH!
SHOCK SUSPENSTORIES
NO. 5
JOLTING TALES OF TENSION IN THE EC TRADITION!

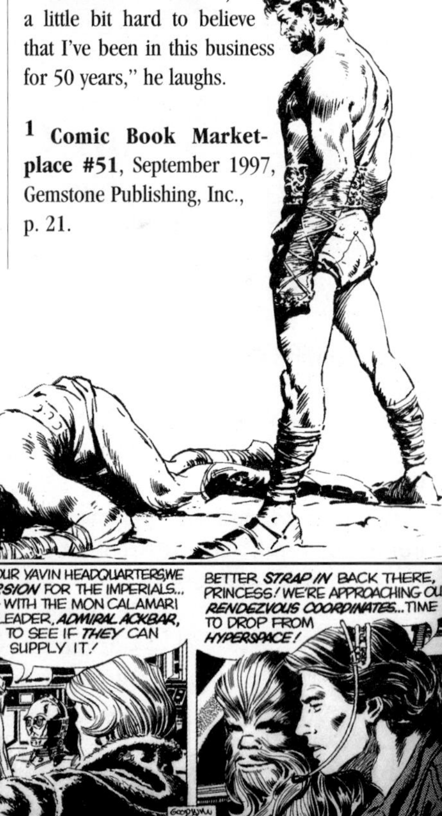

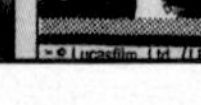

1. Who was the first millionaire comic-strip artist?
2. What was the first direct-sales-only comic book produced by a major publisher?
3. Why did Superman have a 4-F draft classification during World War II?

. . . AND YOU THOUGHT YOU KNEW COMICS!

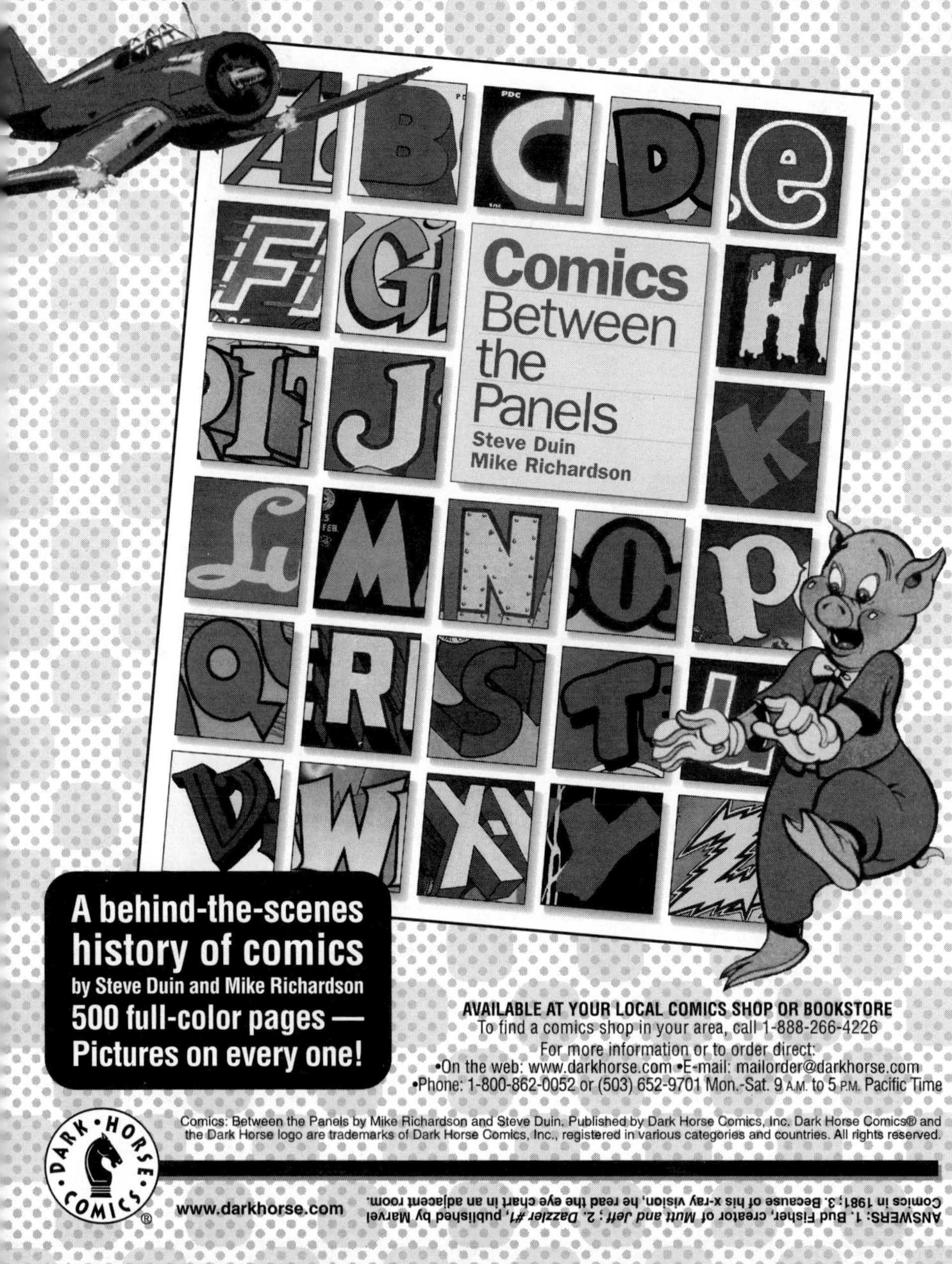

Comics Between the Panels
Steve Duin
Mike Richardson

A behind-the-scenes history of comics
by Steve Duin and Mike Richardson
500 full-color pages — Pictures on every one!

AVAILABLE AT YOUR LOCAL COMICS SHOP OR BOOKSTORE
To find a comics shop in your area, call 1-888-266-4226
For more information or to order direct:
•On the web: www.darkhorse.com •E-mail: mailorder@darkhorse.com
•Phone: 1-800-862-0052 or (503) 652-9701 Mon.-Sat. 9 A.M. to 5 P.M. Pacific Time

www.darkhorse.com

ANSWERS: 1. Bud Fisher, creator of *Mutt and Jeff*; 2. *Dazzler #1*, published by Marvel Comics in 1981; 3. Because of his x-ray vision, he read the eye chart in an adjacent room.

ES
NET WEIGHT 7 OZ.
GET THIS NEW AMAZING
Kix Atomic BOMB Ring
See Scale-Model Plastic Planes on Sides of Box
Kix
READY-TO-EAT CEREAL

Finest Comics #3 recently, I started thinking about those early days back in 1952 when I first met Landon Chesney and became an EC fan. It's all coming back to me now—the correspondence, the price lists, the artwork, all the memories. My god! It was 1952 and Chesney and I were both only 13 years old! Maybe it's fate, but for some reason I did save all my correspondence and price lists from those early years and recently re-read the dozens of letters. Interestingly, fans were a lot more sophisticated than you may realize. The

"BESIDE A WESTERN WATER TANK,ONE COLD NOVEMBER DAY – INSIDE AN EMPTY BOXCAR, A DYING HOBO LAY. – GULP!"
YANK!
Original artwork by Bob Overstreet

The title of the song was "Dying Hobo!" and it was an old railroad song from the 1930s. Ever heard of it?

When I showed up at the theater the piano player asked me what my song was, and then said "that's okay, I can play anything. Just tell me what it is when you go on." Finally my turn came, and there I was standing center stage. The announcer asked me what I was going to sing, and I told him "Dying Hobo!" Well, they had never heard of it and I began to sing the lyrics while the piano tried to catch up. It was a disaster! Very soon, there was this guy on the side of the stage with a big wooden hook and looking very mean. My brother Jerry was sitting in the front row booing and getting the whole audience to do the same. He started throwing tomatoes and the guy with the hook finally got me. How embarrassing! What a kid will do for a quart of ice cream.

We left Tuskaloosa and moved back to Cleveland, Tennessee in 1950, where my older brother and I were both in the same classroom—he was in the eighth grade and I was in the seventh—with the same teacher. We lived in the country and had to ride the bus to this small school on the edge of town. The next year we moved closer to town and I was sent to Arnold School for the eighth grade. It was here that I met Landon Chesney.

BIRTH OF AN EC FAN

Chesney invited me over to his house one day to look at his EC collection, which was a stack of comics carefully stored in a small cardboard box. These comic books were special. As Chesney put it, "ECs were the best written and best drawn comic

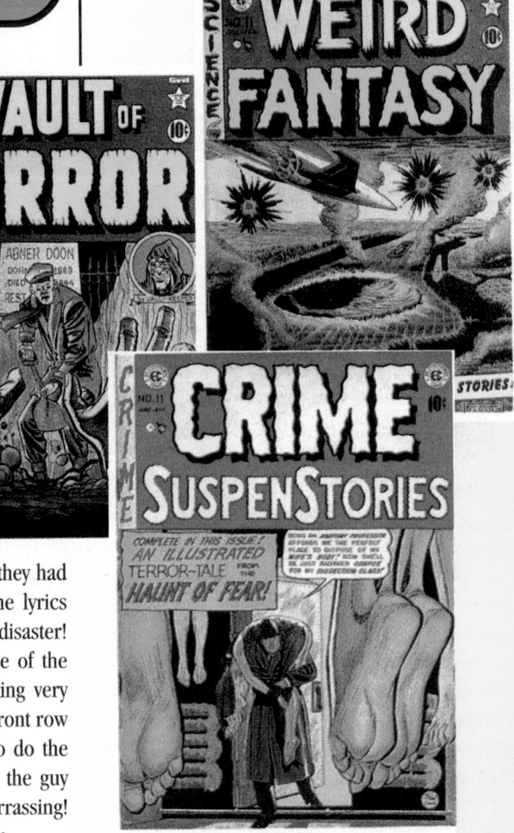

Clockwise: *Weird Fantasy #11*. A long bicycle ride to acquire this baby! *Haunt of Fear #11*. My first back issue! *Crime SuspenStories #11*. My first Crime off the stands! *Vault of Horror #15 (#4)*, found in an old box of comics! All © WMG.

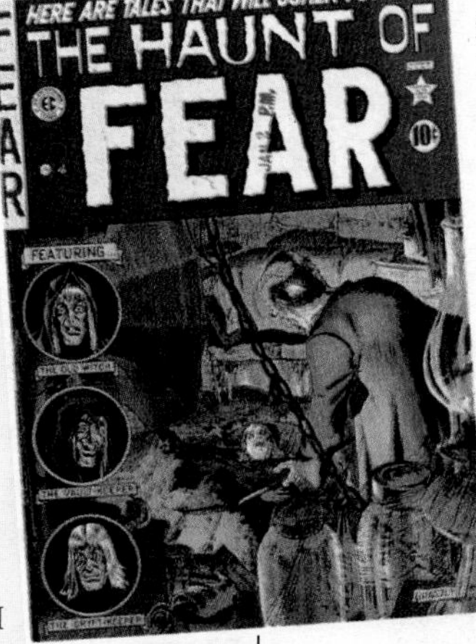

soleum with a decorated iron spiked fence. We sat on top of a large tombstone with pad and pencil in hand sketching out this beautiful scene. This would be just the thing for an opening sequence in one of our horror stories. As we were sketching away, we heard muffled voices coming from behind. The voices came louder and louder. Finally we turned around and there was a large group of people collecting around the very gravestone where we were sitting! We burned leather and didn't stop until we reached our car and made it out of there and back to Cleveland.

Houdini was known for his levitation tricks. He always said that there was an explaination for all of his illusions, although some have never been explained to this very day.

HOUDINI AND THE OCCULT

Chesney also had an interest in magic and was a fan of Houdini. Houdini was an enigma. Not only was he the best escape artist ever, but he prided himself on performing the ultimate illusions, such as levitation and other tricks that could not be easily explained. His interest in the occult was such that he never attended a seance that he couldn't expose. His famous reward of $10,000 to any occultist that could fool him was legendary. He promised his wife that after his death, if there was any way to do it, he would contact her, but he never did. The complexities of Houdini challenged Chesney's mind and we spent many nights talking about it. We were both intrigued and aspired to be like Houdini.

Chesney concocted a straight jacket which he would have a friend put on him. He would suddenly disappear behind a screen and, voila!, come out in seconds completely free (just like Houdini). He also designed a small stock, like the ones from the middle ages, made of two-by-fours that were hinged, opening at the top, with two holes cut out for locking in your hands. He would have a friend put this on him, lock the padlock and hold the key. He would disappear behind a screen and within seconds appear with his hands out, completely free! He would then hand the still locked stock to his astonished friend. Yes, it was fun being an escape artist like Houdini.

WATCH ME DISAPPEAR!!
Original artwork by Bob Overstreet

The secret hideaway!

A rare 1950s shot of Chesney in his cloak and hat.

THE TRUNK ESCAPE

In 1952, Chesney had a black top hat and cloak (like Dracula's) which he wore to play a villain. He found this old bell-top trunk which we decided to set up with a false bottom. We dug this deep ditch at his house, reliving some of the great EC horror stories where someone was digging a grave. Our hole was

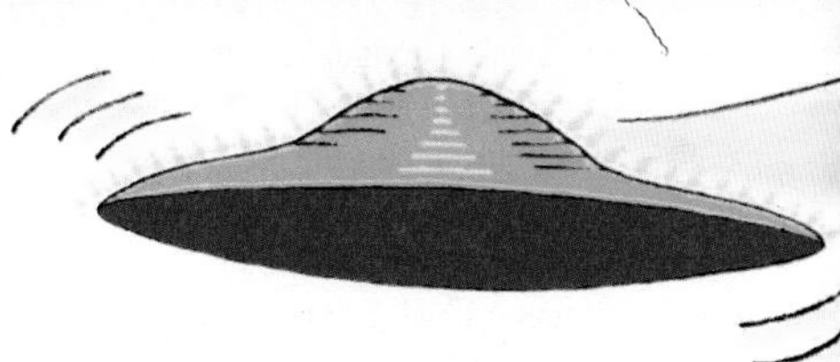

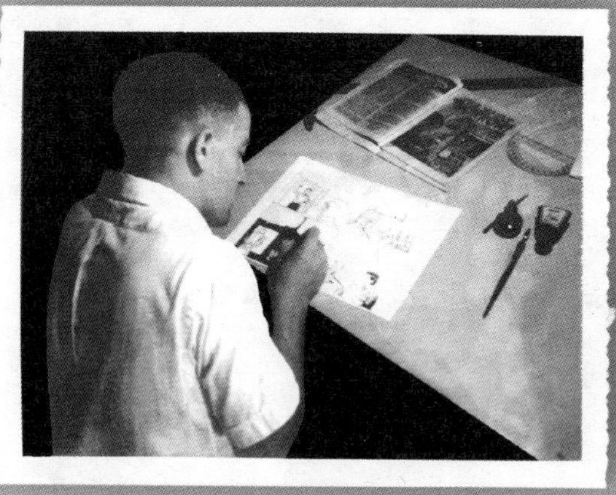

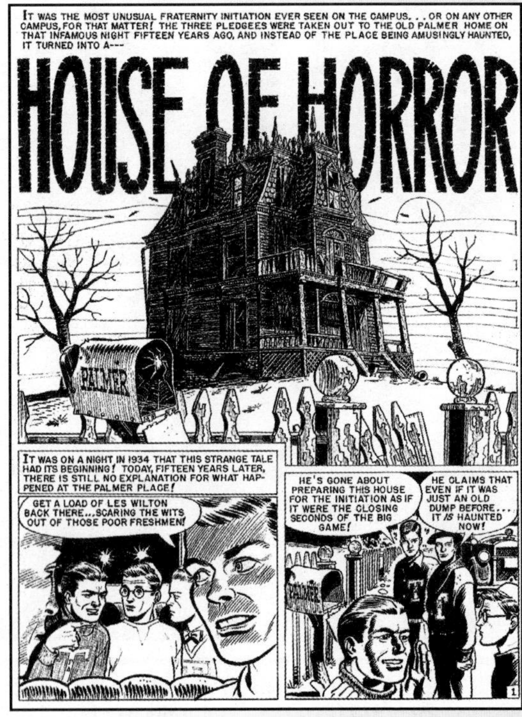

The following story was originally written and drawn back in the 1950s by Chesney and Overstreet and was published in the early 1960s by Bill Spicer in a black and white format. Now as a special treat to our readers, here it is–**IN FULL COLOR FOR THE FIRST TIME**! The storyline was recently rewritten by today's Chesney and Overstreet for two reasons. One was to make the dialog fit better into today's world and the other to create an interesting "twist" on the original theme where the story repeats itself. So, let the story begin.....

ON THE MOONLIT CAMPUS OF A LARGE MIDWESTERN UNIVERSITY, A JOURNALISM MAJOR NAMED SIDNEY PIKE IS INTERRUPTED IN HIS WORK...
HEY SID! GUESS WHAT I FOUND IN A BACK ISSUE OF THE COLLEGE NEWSPAPER!
WHAT IS IT, STEVE?
OKAY... THIS GOES BACK SOME 30 YEARS! "TWO STUDENTS FROM STATE U. DECIDED TO SPEND THE NIGHT IN A HAUNTED HOUSE... ON A DARE! THE NEXT MORNING ONE WAS FOUND INSANE AND THE OTHER HAD VANISHED!"
SAY! LETS SEE THAT!
WELL, I'LL BE DARNED! I ALWAYS THOUGHT THAT STORY WAS A GAG! SOME KIND OF URBAN MYTH OR WHATEVER...
YEAH! A FOLK TALE WITH NO BASIS IN FACT!
YOU KNOW SOMETHING, STEVE? THIS IS REALLY INTRIGUING! LIKE, WHAT REALLY HAPPENED TO THE GUY WHO VANISHED?! I MEAN... C'MON... PEOPLE DON'T JUST VANISH!!
...AND WHAT ABOUT THE GUY WHO WENT BONKERS? DID HE RECOVER?? OR IS HE STILL LOCKED AWAY SOMEWHERE?
ITS HIGH TIME I TESTED MY SKILLS AS AN INVESTIGATIVE REPORTER!! I THINK I'LL FOLLOW UP ON THIS! WHY DON'T YOU COME ALONG?!
W-WHAT?! ME SPEND THE NIGHT IN A HAUNTED HOUSE?!
YEAH!! WHY NOT!
...ASSUMING THE PLACE IS STILL STANDING, THAT'S A GREAT IDEA! SO FAR WE'VE GOT MORE QUESTIONS THAN ANSWERS, BUT I'VE GOT AN IDEA FOR A SHORTCUT! I'M GONNA CONTACT THE ALUMNI OFFICE AND SEE IF THEY HAVE A CURRENT ADDRESS ON ALDOUS MANOR!
WHO'S ALDOUS MANOR?!
TECH
HE OWNS THE PROPERTY!

AS STORM CLOUDS LOOM ON THE HORIZON, SID AND STEVE CONTINUE ON THEIR UNUSUAL JOURNEY TO THE SMALL VILLAGE WHERE ALDOUS MANOR LIVES.
YOU'VE COME TO THE RIGHT PLACE, BOYS!
THANKS FOR SEEING US ON SUCH SHORT NOTICE! THIS SHOULD PROVE INTERESTING FOR MY THESIS ON THE PARANORMAL!!
A.M. MANOR

MAKE YOURSELVES COMFORTABLE, BOYS, AND I'LL SKETCH A LITTLE BACKGROUND ON THE HOUSE FOR YOU!!
WHAT WE'VE HEARD SO FAR IS FACINATING, MISTER MANOR!

FASCINATING—YES—AND PERHAPS A LITTLE MORE THAN THAT—YOU SEE THE HOUSE IS TIED IN DIRECTLY WITH MY FAMILY AND, SINCE THE HOUSE WAS FIRST BUILT OVER 70 YEARS AGO NO LESS THAN 5 MEMBERS OF THE MANORS CLAN HAVE MET... SINGULARLY STRANGE FATES THERE!

HOW-HOW WAS THAT, SIR?

TWO WERE FOUND HANGED IN AN UPPER CHAMBER OF THE HOUSE CALLED THE GREEN ROOM — THE OTHER THREE DISAPPEARED — VANISHED WITHOUT A TRACE— PERHAPS I SHOULD EXPLAIN THAT THEY HAD ALL SLEPT IN THE GREEN ROOM THE NIGHT OF THEIR DISAPPEARANCE—THE NEXT MORNING THERE WAS NO EVIDENCE OF ANYONE EVEN HAVING PASSED THE NIGHT THERE — IT WAS AS IF—AS IF THEY HAD NEVER EVEN--- EXISTED---

BUT SURELY, MR. MANOR—THERE IS SOME EXPLANATION!

NONE—SAVE AN OLD LEGEND THAT HAS BEEN HANDED DOWN THROUGH THE FAMILY—BUT EVEN IT IS SO PREPOSTEROUS THAT ONLY THE MOST SUPERSTITIOUS COULD GIVE IT CREDENCE—

PLEASE GO ON MR. MANOR

THE HOUSE WAS ORIGINALLY BUILT BY SILAS MANOR—MY GREAT-GRANDFATHER—AND IT SEEMS THAT DURING CONSTRUCTION OF THE HOUSE HE CAUSED AN OLD SHACK THAT WAS ON THE PREMISES TO BE TORN DOWN AND MOVED---

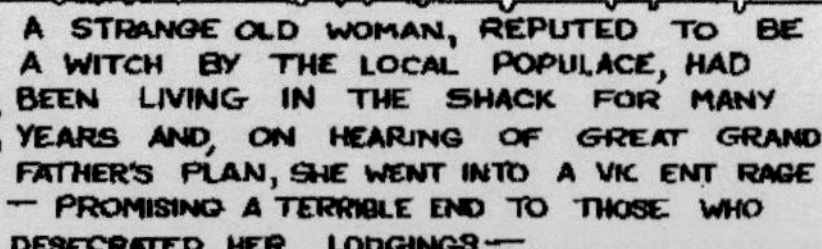
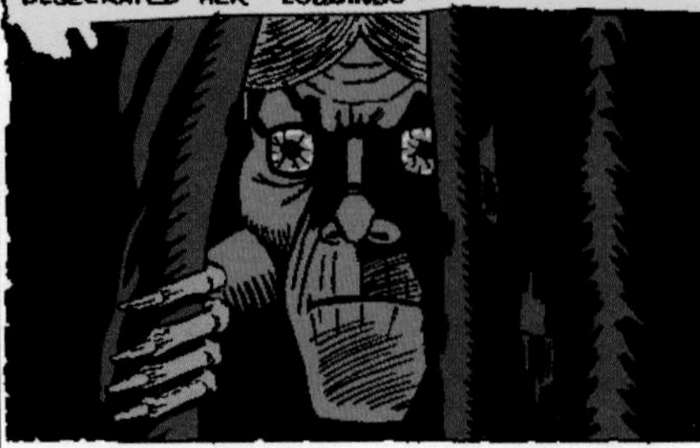

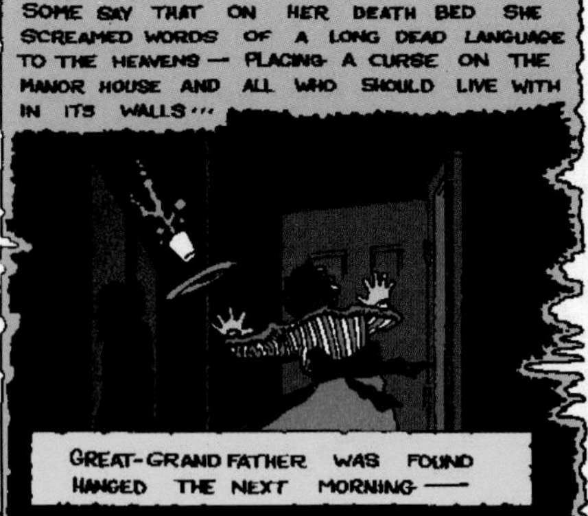
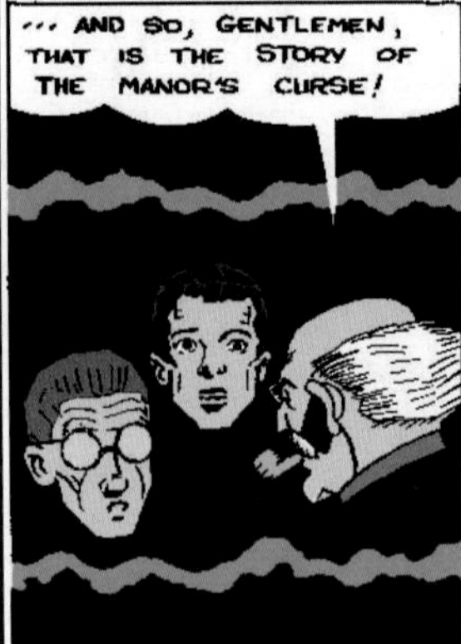
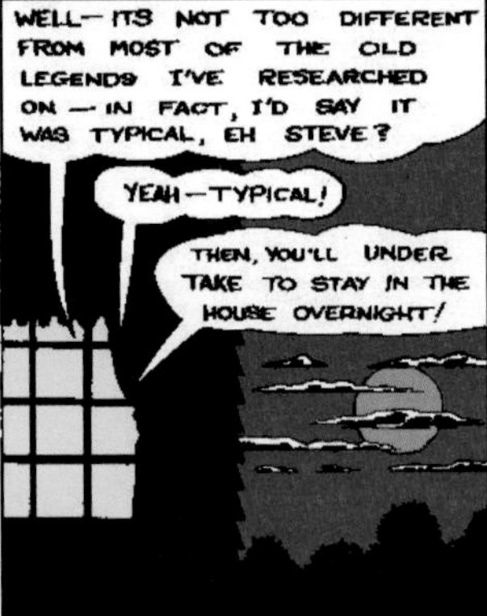
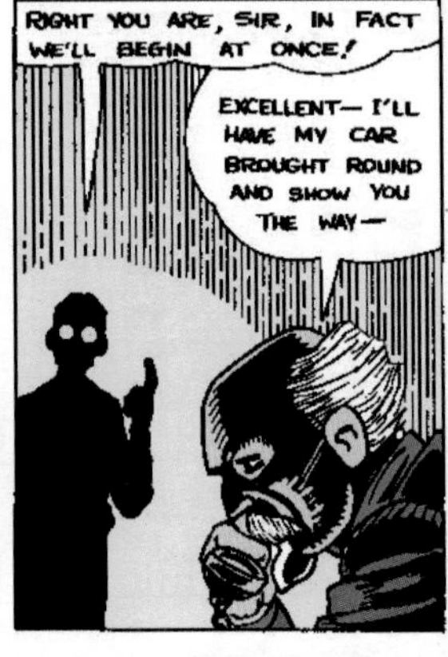
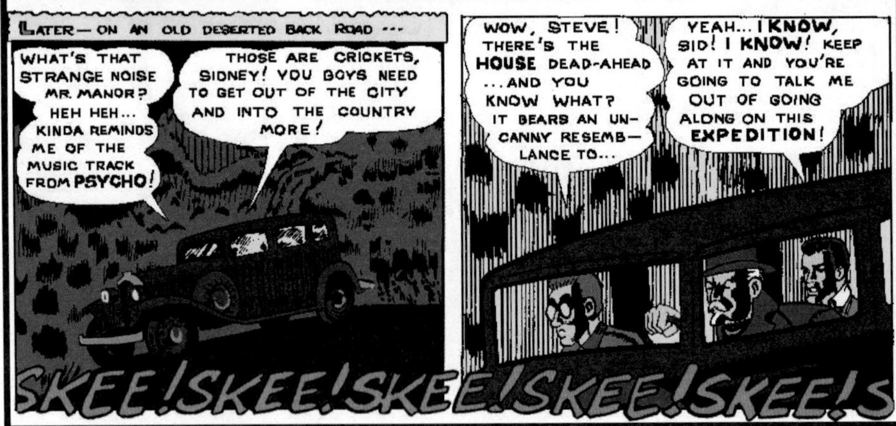

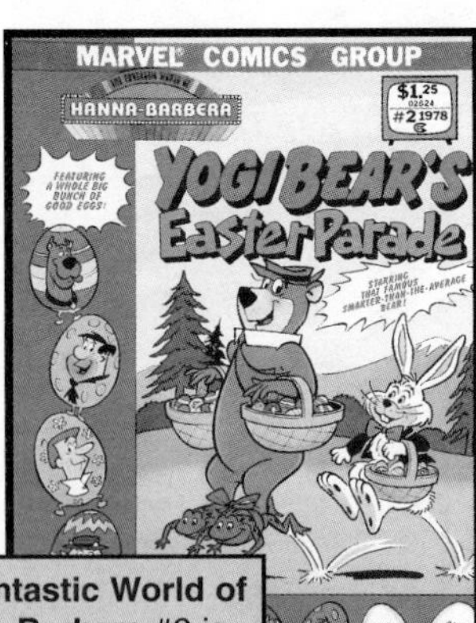

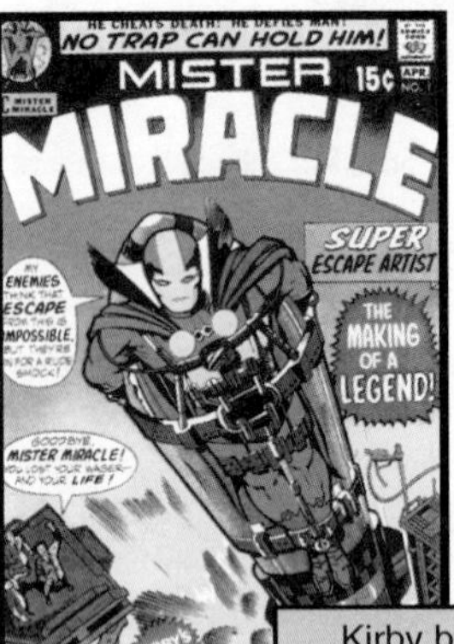

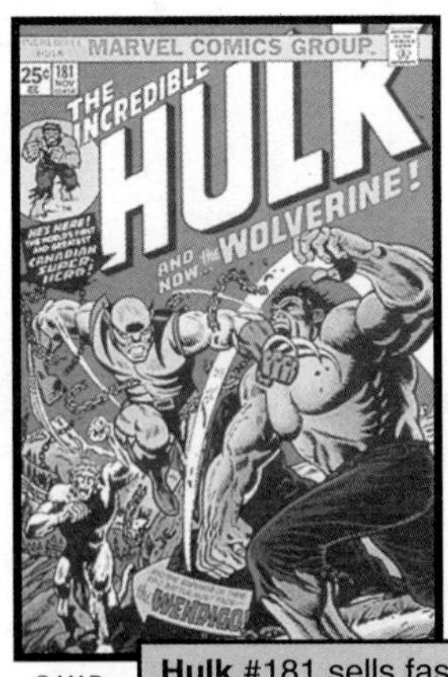

and Atlas is close behind. There are still plenty of bargains to be found here. Our Army at War is sought after, with issues #82-198 in any condition selling above guide. GI Combat is on the increase (#67, 87, 114), as well as Grandenetti and gray tone covers and pre-Code Atlas war comics.

© CC

Charltons are elusive and HOT! **Hot Rods & Racing Cars** #1 shown.

WESTERNS: DC titles are increasing, while Atlas is hot depending on the featured artist. Hopalong Cassidy leads Fawcett, which otherwise has moderate sales, and Dell titles are slow apart from movie and TV tie-ins.

MISCELLANEOUS: Teen comics from the '60s, like Harvey's Bunny or Charlton's Go-Go, with artwork or photos of rock stars, sell at guide when they can be found. Other Charltons in demand are Frank Merriwell at Yale, Hercules and Hot Rods & Racing Cars. Monkeyshines, Calling All Kids, Men of Battle and all King comics are selling, especially cartoons and reading library issues, while ACG horror and superhero titles are steady, with humor and love titles picking up steam,. Other oddball titles that bring 150%-200% of guide include: Fatman, Capt. Marvel (MF Enterprises), Henry Brewster, True Comics & Adventure Stories. All Skywald, both magazine and giant comics, are in short supply and in high demand. Tower special artist issues and Tippy Teen titles are on the move as well. Fast Willie Jackson is in demand for $10 each and up. Solid sales have been reported in pre-Code horror from all publishers except EC, which may be slower due to reprints. High grade material is harder to find and sought after. Although a peripheral category of comic collectible, the venerable pulps have experienced some increased demand. Nice copies of low number classic strip reprints like Sparkler and Popular are experiencing limited demand. Copies of Crackajack and Fritzi Ritz sell steadily.

© AP

Giants are hot: **Archie's Giant Series Magazine** #2 shown.

MARKET REPORT BY COMPANY

As with the genre section, some of our market data focused on many of the major publishers in the hobby both past and present. Here are some examples of 1999 activity in those categories:

ARCHIE COMICS: This company shows steady growth with unknown parodies surfacing. Giants, especially squarebound, are red hot. Sabrina (with its TV connection) and Josie are top sellers (Josie #45-#50 and Sabrina #1-#10 bring over 200% of guide!), and that trend includes any appearances and cameos as well. While teen superheroes are heating up, Betty & Veronica lead the pack in the mainline titles. High demand also reported for Little Archie, '70s digests, Cheryl Blossom, and all Red Circle titles. '80s Mighty Crusaders, Mighty Comics and Shadow are going up, and the Spire issues are hot. '80s Katy Keene issues bring top dollar from paper doll collectors, while Sonic the Hedgehog (based on the Sega Genesis and other video games) is blazing hot, fetching from $5-$20 each!! Christmas and Archie #1 treasuries are rare in any condition, and NM

Black Knight is an Atlas book on top of many want lists. #2 shown.

© MAR

COME VISIT OUR NEW YORK CITY SHOWROOM! OPEN WEEKDAYS, BY APPOINTMENT O
SILVER
WHY YOU SHOULD CALL US BEFOR
YOU SELL YOUR COLLECTION O
COMICS, ARTWORK OR MEMORABILI
We make it easy! No waiting for paymen
No song and dance about grading. We'll com
to you; anywhere, anytime! Four Color Comic
takes the risk out of selling. Treat yourself to a
honest, straight-forward experience—Sell you
collection to us and walk away with more mone
in your pocket and a smile on your face
FOUR COLOR
COMICS
115 West 27th Street, New York, NY 1000
TEL: (212) 675-6990 FAX: (212) 675-6145
1000's
of comics on-line!
SEARCHABLE
DATABASE!
no more scrolling thru
endless listings!
www.fourcolorcomics.com
FAN FORUM
FOUR COLOR COMICS
SEARCH COMICS!
COMPANY INFO.

DID YOU TURN INTO A
MONSTER
THE LAST TIME YOU RECEIVED
A MAIL ORDER?
If this looks familiar, treat yourself to honest grading and fair pricing by buying your Silver and Golden Age comics from us!
At FOUR COLOR COMICS, we specialize in treating the customer right and we unconditionally guarantee every book we sell!
Fantastic Four
10¢
FEATURING: "THE THING!" "MR. FANTASTIC!" "HUMAN TORCH!" "INVISIBLE GIRL!" TOGETHER FOR THE FIRST TIME IN ONE MIGHTY MAGAZINE!
FOUR COLOR
COMICS
NY SHOWROOM (By Appointment Only): 115 West 27th St, New York, NY 10001 (212) 675-6990 Fax:(212) 675-6145
IF YOU'VE GOT BOOKS TO SELL, CALL IMMEDIATELY: (212) 675-6990
DESIGN: ARNIE SAWYER All artwork: © DC COMICS, © MARVEL ENTERTAINMENT GROUP, INC

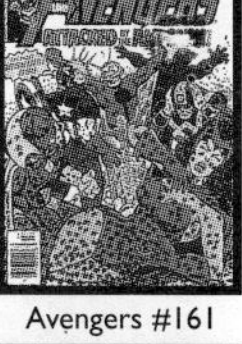

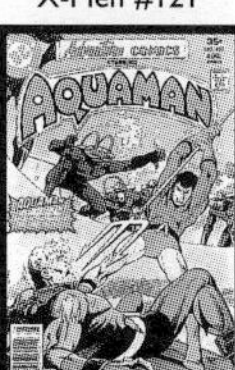

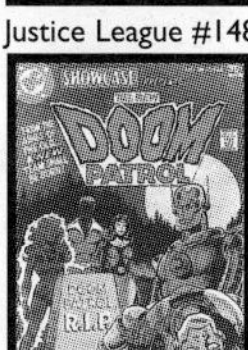

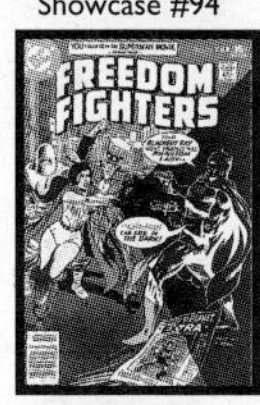

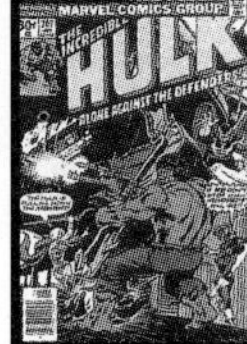

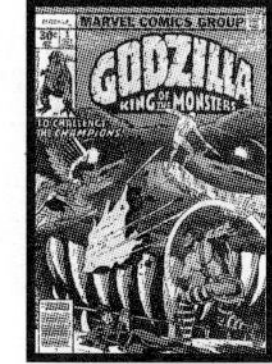

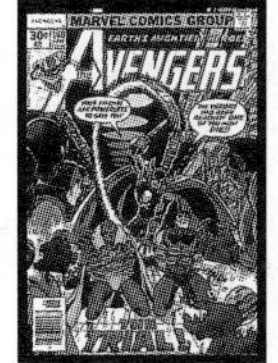

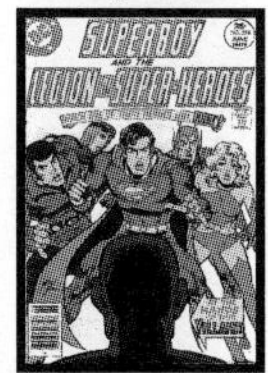

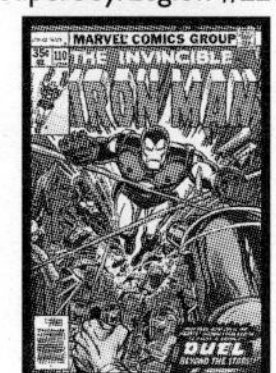

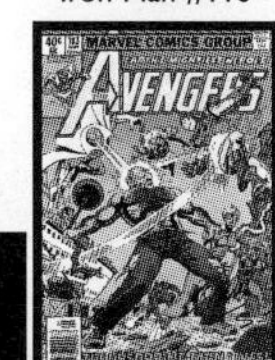

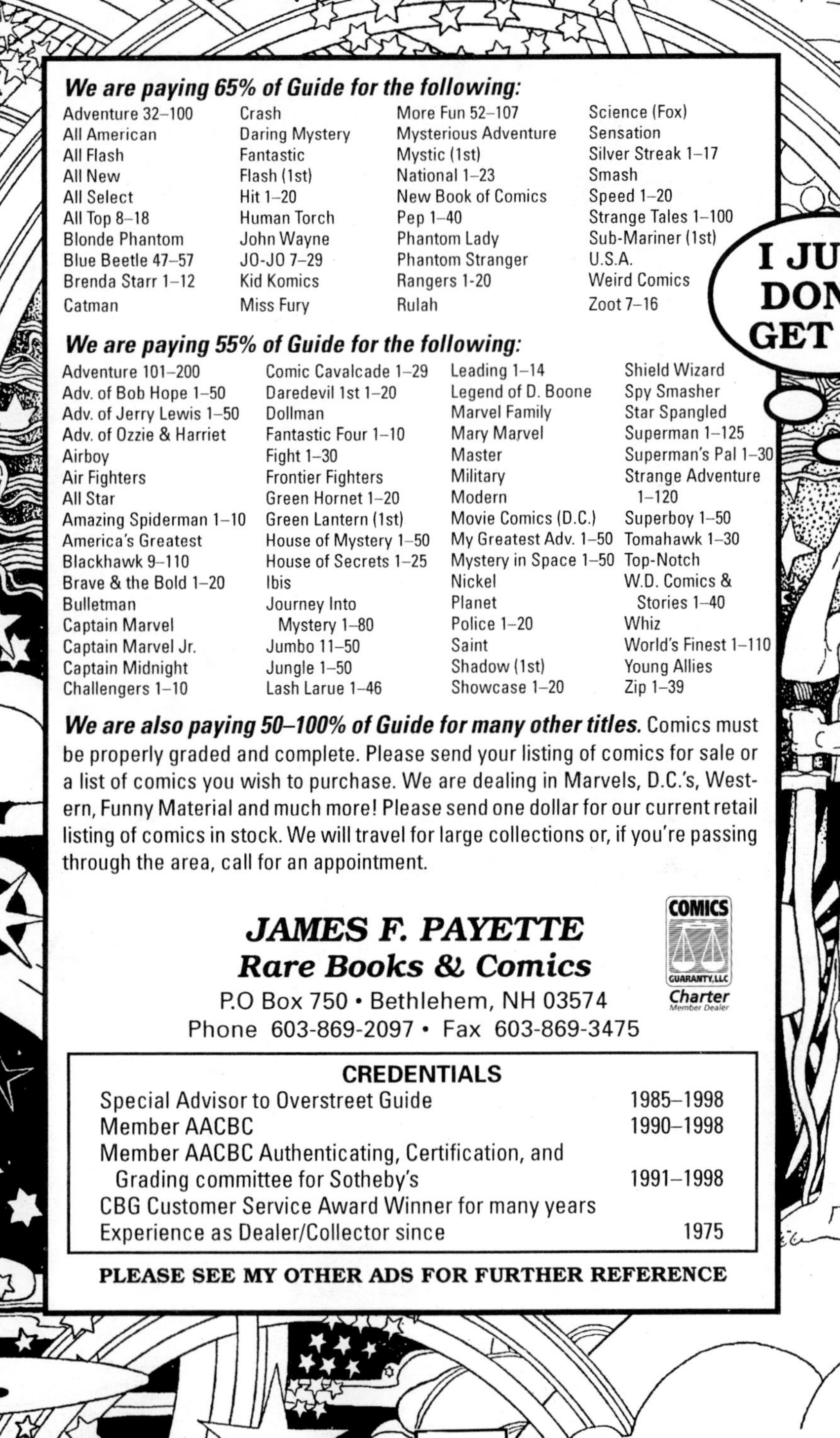

Follow the Leader in Golden and Silver Age Comics with
BEDROCK CITY
COMIC COMPANY
TM
6517 Westheimer
(at Hillcroft)
Houston, Texas 77057
(713) 780-0675
2204-D FM 1960 W.
(at Kuykendahl)
Houston, Texas 77090
(281) 444-9763
fax (713) 780-2366
www.bedrockcity.com
Shazam © 1997 D.C. Comics

Every day thousands of amazing items go up for bid online. Choose from Collectibles, Entertainment Memorabilia, Art and Antiques, and Jewelry. All items are guaranteed. Prices $100 and up.

www.sothebys.amazon.com

PACIFIC COMIC EXCHANGE, INC.

SELLERS: Please contact The Exchange if you would like to *consign* these or other books at full market value or sell your collection directly at competitive prices.

CGSA	M	NM/M	++ + NM --	VFN/NM	++ + VFN --	FN/VFN	+ FN --	VG/FN	+ VG	G/VG	G	Fr/G	Fr	Pr
	100 - 91	90	88,85,80,75	70	68,65,63,60,55	50	45,40,35	30	25,20	15	10	8	6	3
OVERSTREET - 10.0		9.8	97.9.6.9.4.9.2	9.0	8.8.8.5.8.3.8.0.7.5	7.0	6.5.6.0.5.5	5.0	4.5.4.0	3.0	2.0	1.5	1.0	.5

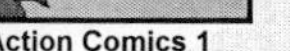
© DC
Action Comics 1

© DC
Detective Comics 27

© MEG
Marvel Comics 1

	G 10	VG 20	FN 40	VFN 60	NM 80	NM/M 90
Action Comics 1	$30,000	$50,000	$100,000	$150,000	$300,000	$600,000
Detective Comics 27	$25,000	$45,000	$85,000	$125,000	$250,000	$450,000
Marvel Comics 1	$12,000	$20,000	$40,000	$60,000	$120,000	$300,000

Wanted Immediately in VFN 60 - NM/M 90

	VFN 60	NM 80	NM/M 90		VFN 60	NM 80	NM/M 90
Action Comics 1	$150,000	$300,000	$600,000	Green Lantern 1 (SA)	$1,250	$4,000	$7,500
Adventure Comics 40	$25,000	$50,000	$120,000	Green Lantern 1 (GA)	$12,500	$30,000	$75,000
Adventure Comics 210	$1,500	$3,500	$7,500	Incredible Hulk 1	$5,000	$12,000	$30,000
Adventure Comics 247	$2,250	$6,000	$12,000	Jimmy Olsen 1	$3,000	$9,000	$15,000
All Star Comics 3	$16,000	$35,000	$120,000	Journey Into Mystery 83	$1,800	$5,000	$12,000
All Star Comics 8	$13,000	$30,000	$100,000	Justice League 1	$1,500	$5,000	$10,000
All-American Comics 16	$40,000	$80,000	$175,000	Lois Lane 1	$2,000	$4,500	$9,000
Amazing Fantasy 15	$10,000	$27,000	$50,000	Marvel Comics 1	$60,000	$120,000	$300,000
Amazing Spider-Man 1	$6,000	$18,000	$35,000	More Fun Comics 52	$30,000	$75,000	$150,000
Batman 1	$33,000	$80,000	$180,000	More Fun Comics 55	$6,500	$13,500	$30,000
Batman 100	$1,350	$2,500	$5,000	Sensation Comics 1	$10,000	$24,000	$65,000
Captain America 1	$30,000	$70,000	$150,000	Showcase 4	$12,000	$30,000	$60,000
Detective Comics 1	$50,000	$100,000	$225,000	Showcase 22	$1,800	$5,500	$11,000
Detective Comics 27	$125,000	$250,000	$485,000	Sub-Mariner Comics 1	$10,000	$20,000	$60,000
Detective Comics 33	$20,000	$45,000	$100,000	Superman 1	$75,000	$150,000	$400,000
Detective Comics 38	$18,000	$35,000	$100,000	Superman 100	$1,200	$3,000	$6,000
Fantastic Four 1	$7,500	$25,000	$50,000	Suspense Comics 3	$8,000	$25,000	$50,000
Flash Comics 1	$30,000	$75,000	$165,000	Wonder Woman 1	$9,000	$25,000	$50,000
Flash Comics 104	$3,500	$8,000	$20,000	X-Men 1	$2,500	$9,000	$20000

See complete catalog at www.pcei.com

Corporate Office:
337 S. Robertson Blvd. Ste 203, Beverly Hills, CA 90211
Tel: (310) 544-4936, Fax: (310) 544-4900

Shipping Address:
P.O. Box 2629 Palos Verdes Pen., CA 90274
E-Mail: sales@pcei.com, www.pcei.com

VISA

MasterCard

PACIFIC COMIC EXCHANGE, INC.

P.O. BOX 2629, Palos Verdes Peninsula, CA 90274 ❖ Tel: (310) 544-4936 ❖ Fax: (310) 544-4900 ❖ E-Mail: sales@pcei.com

Instructions: The following books are currently listed on the Exchange and are available for sale at the prices specified. Prices are subject to change without notice. All orders are subject to a 12% buyers commission.

PgQ: Page Quality (0.0 - 3.0: White; 3.3: Near White; 3.5: Off-White; 4: Beige or Cream, 4.5-6.5: Light to Dark Tan).

The grade listed is the **CGSA** grade (see diagram below). See our full catalog at our web site at **www.pcei.com**

CGSA	M	NM/M	NM	VFN/NM	VFN	FN/VFN	FN	VG/FN	VG	G/VG	G	Fr	Pr
	100,99,98,97,96,95,94,93,92,91	90	88,85,80,75	70	65,60,55	50	45,40,35	30	25,20	15	10	6	3
OVERSTREET -	10.0	9.8	9.7,9.6,9.4,9.2	9.0	8.5,8.0,7.5	7.0	6.5,6.0,5.5	5.0	4.5,4.0	3.0	2.0	1.0	.5

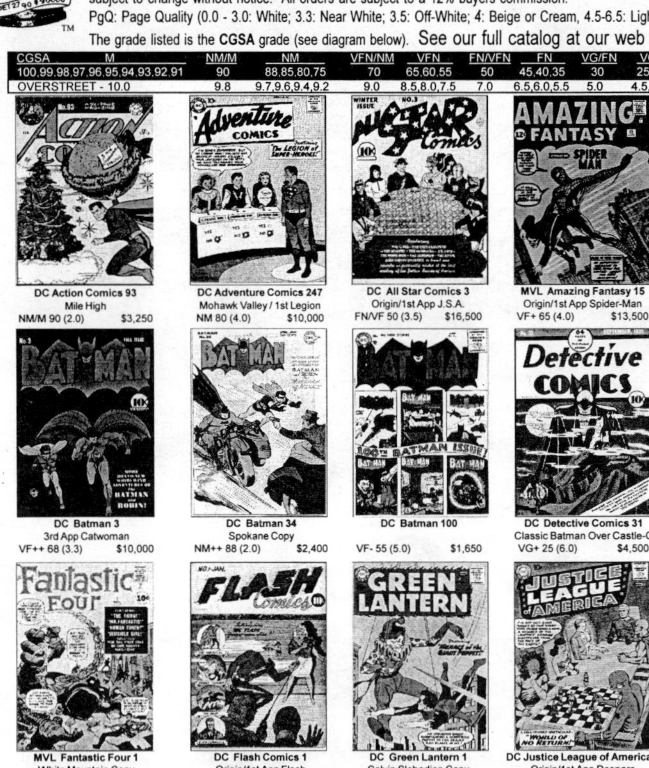

DC Action Comics 93
Mile High
NM/M 90 (2.0) $3,250

DC Adventure Comics 247
Mohawk Valley / 1st Legion
NM 80 (4.0) $10,000

DC All Star Comics 3
Origin/1st App J.S.A.
FN/VF 50 (3.5) $16,500

MVL Amazing Fantasy 15
Origin/1st App Spider-Man
VF+ 65 (4.0) $13,500

DC Batman 1
Origin Batman/1st App Joker
VG+ 25 (3.3) $20,000

DC Batman 3
3rd App Catwoman
VF++ 68 (3.3) $10,000

DC Batman 34
Spokane Copy
NM++ 88 (2.0) $2,400

DC Batman 100
VF- 55 (5.0) $1,650

DC Detective Comics 31
Classic Batman Over Castle-C
VG+ 25 (6.0) $4,500

DC Detective Comics 33
Origin Batman
VG 20 (6.0) $6,000

MVL Fantastic Four 1
White Mountain Copy
NM+ 85 (2.0) $50,000

DC Flash Comics 1
Origin/1st App Flash
VG+ 25 (5.0) $15,000

DC Green Lantern 1
Calvin Slobodian Copy
VF+ 65 (3.5) $3,000

DC Justice League of America 1
Origin/1st App Desparo
VF+ 65 (4.0) $2,750

TIM Marvel Comics 1
Origin Sub-Mariner
VG 20 (6.5) $22,000

DC More Fun Comics 52
Mod. Restored By S. Cicconne
M aVFN 60 (4.0) $17,500

DC Mystery In Space 1
Bethlehem Copy
VF/NM 70 (4.0) $4,000

DC Showcase 4
Origin/1st App SA Flash
NM 80 (4.5) $37,500

DC Superboy 1
Superman-C
VF- 55 (5.0) $4,500

Superman's Pal Jimmy Olsen 1
FN- 35 (5.0) $2,000

DC Superman 53
Origin Superman
NM 80 (3.5) $6,000

MVL Tales of Suspense 39
Origin/1st App Iron Man
NM+ 85 (3.5) $10,000

DC Wonder Woman 17
Mile High
NM/M 90 (3.0) $3,650

MVL X-Men 1
Pacific Coast Collection / 1st X-Men
NM++ 88 (3.5) $20,000

MLJ ZIP Comics 1
Origin Steel Sterling
VF/NM 70 (4.5) $3,500

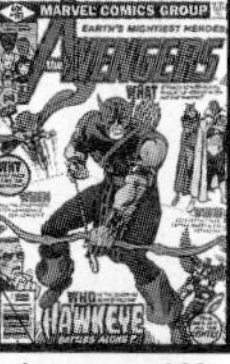
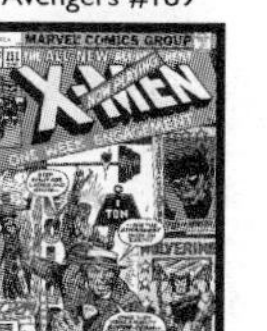
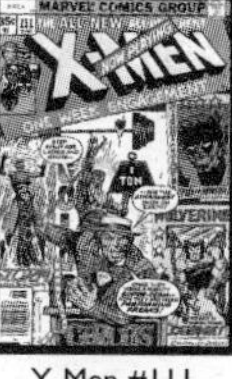
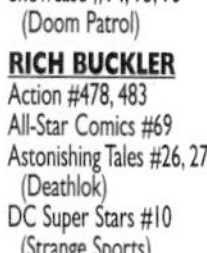
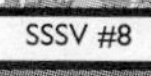
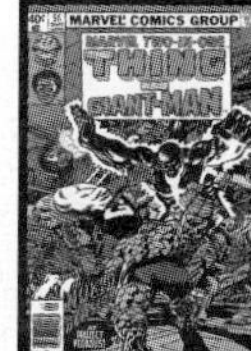
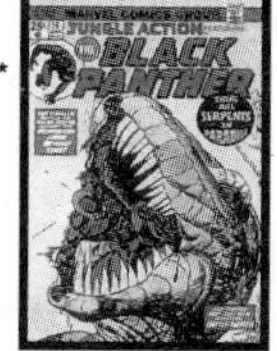
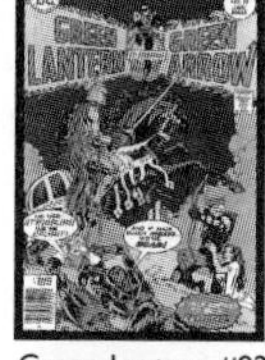
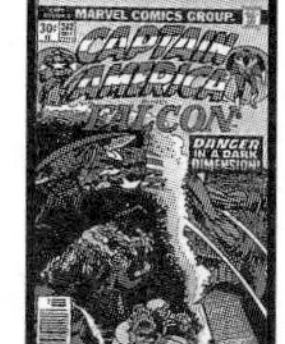
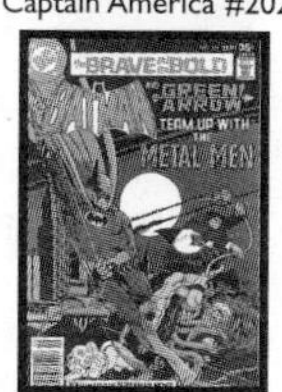
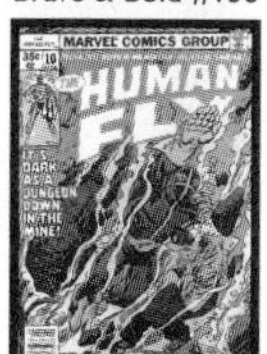
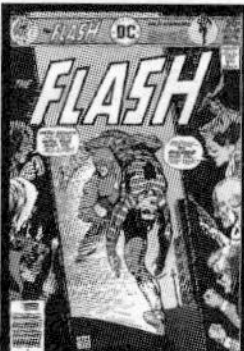

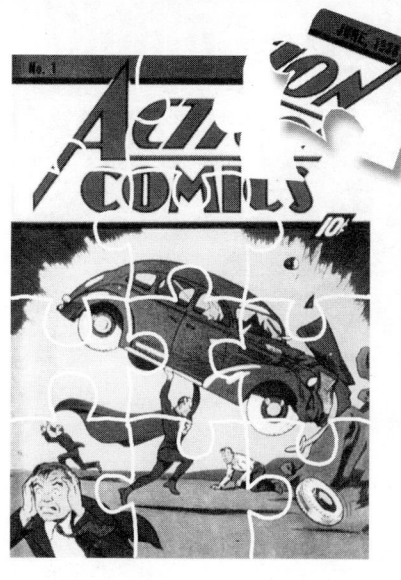

the GOBLIN'S DEN
437 Pinesmoke Cr.
ississauga, Ontario, Canada
Y 3L4
#(905)848-0559 Fax#(416)622-0574
nail:GOBLINS@ionsys.com
ALWAYS
Buying & Selling
Pre-1977
Comics
We also buy: Action Figures, Model Kits &
lemorabilia
Highest Prices Paid for quality pre-code Horror,
rime & Good Girl

BUYING ALL COMICS

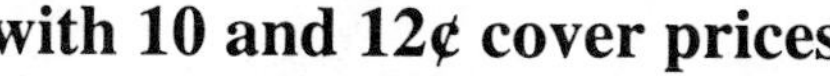
with 10 and 12¢ cover prices

TOP PRICES PAID!

IMMEDIATE CASH PAYMENT

Stop Throwing Away Those Old Comic Books!

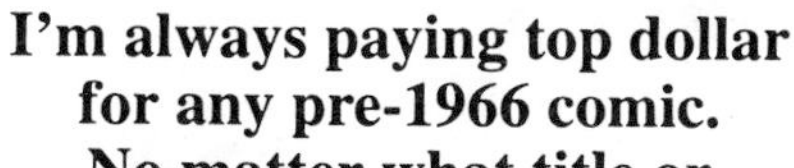
I'm always paying top dollar for any pre-1966 comic. No matter what title or condition, whether you have one comic or a warehouse full.

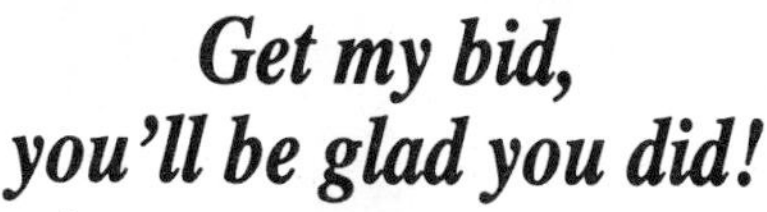
Get my bid, you'll be glad you did!

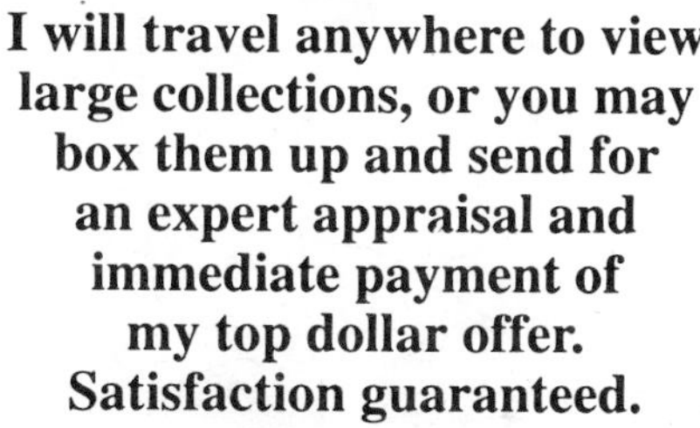
I will travel anywhere to view large collections, or you may box them up and send for an expert appraisal and immediate payment of my top dollar offer. Satisfaction guaranteed.

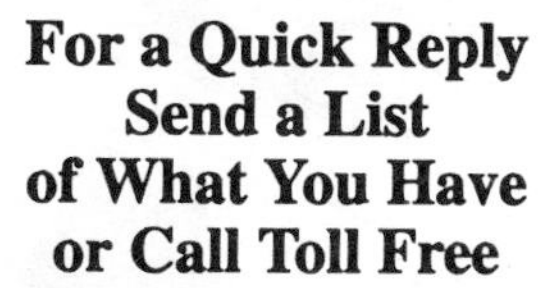
For a Quick Reply Send a List of What You Have or Call Toll Free

1-800-791-3037

or

1-608-277-8750

or Write

Jef Hinds

P.O. Box 44803
Madison, WI 53744-4803

Also available for
Insurance & Estate Appraisals, Strictly Confidential.

NO. 16 JULY
ALL-AMERICAN COMICS 10¢
Introducing the GREEN LANTERN!
SILVER STREAK COMICS
SEPT. No. 6 10¢
THE AVENGING HAND OF THE CLAW REACHES OUT TO DESTROY THE LIVES OF HIS ENEMIES!
No.14
SUPERMAN 10¢

MOTOR CITY COMICS
Gold & Silver Age
NOW OPEN
Come Visit Our Warehouse
by appointment only
WE ALSO DEAL IN PULPS
& ORIGINAL ART
TWICE A MO
OCTOBER
Batman, Spectre, Green Lantern © DC Comics

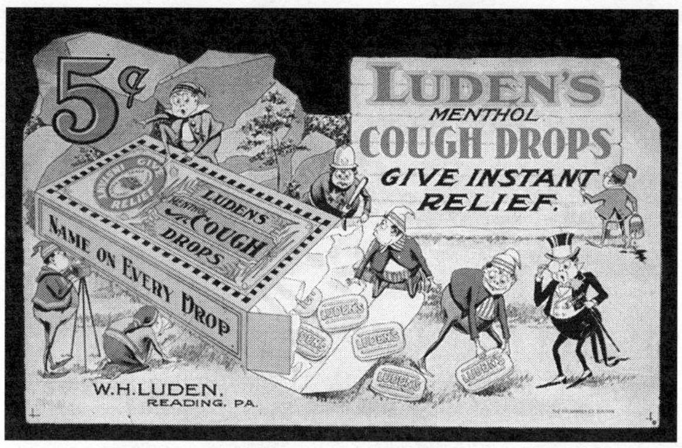

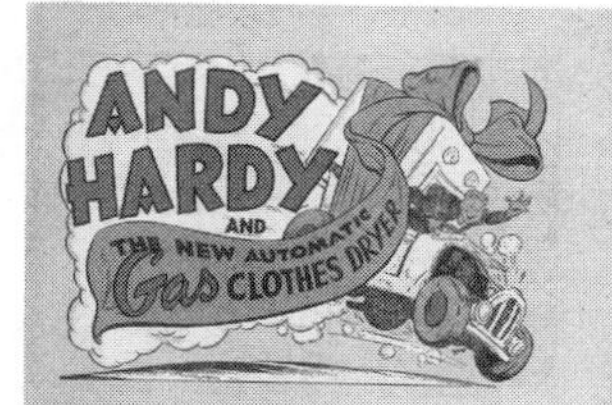

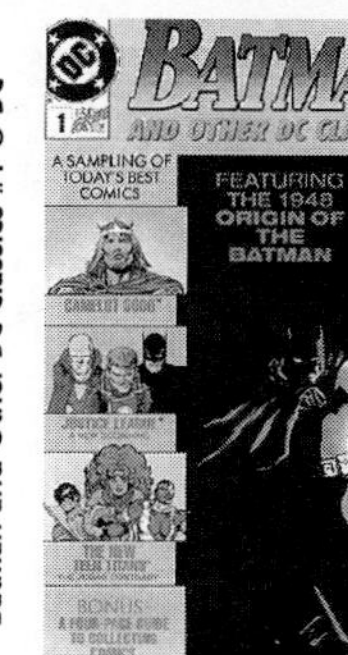

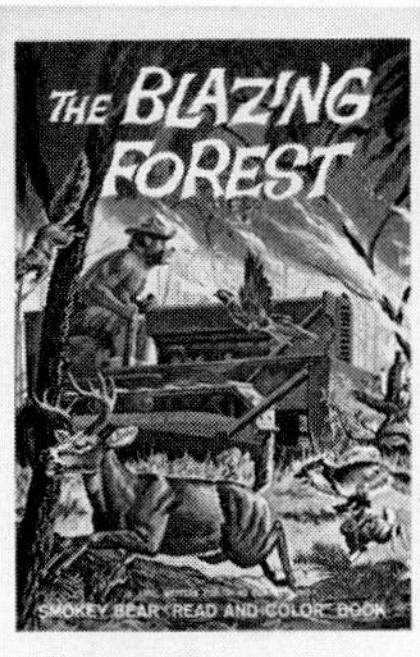

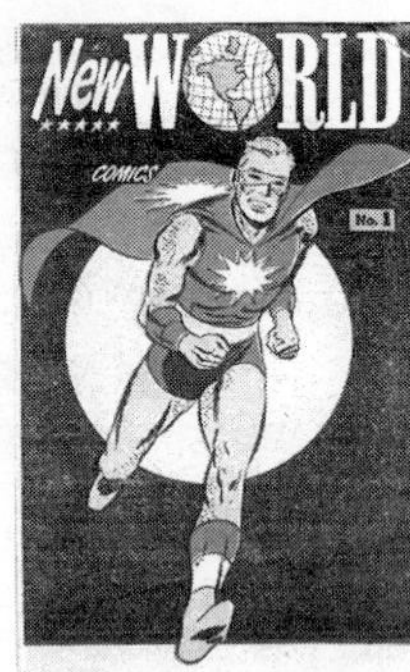

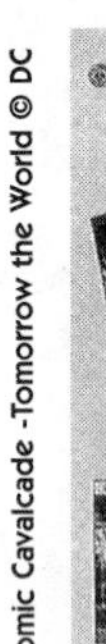
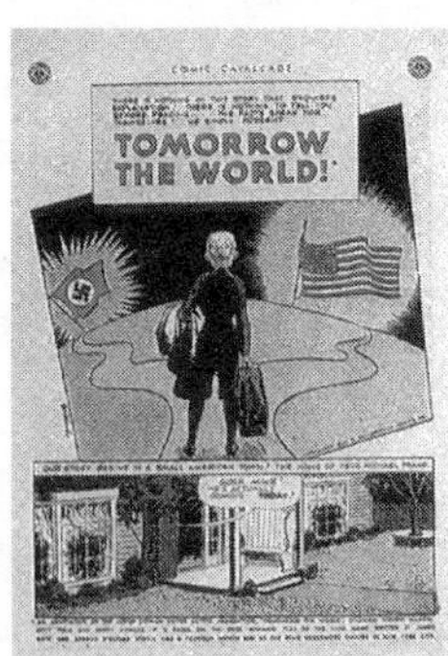

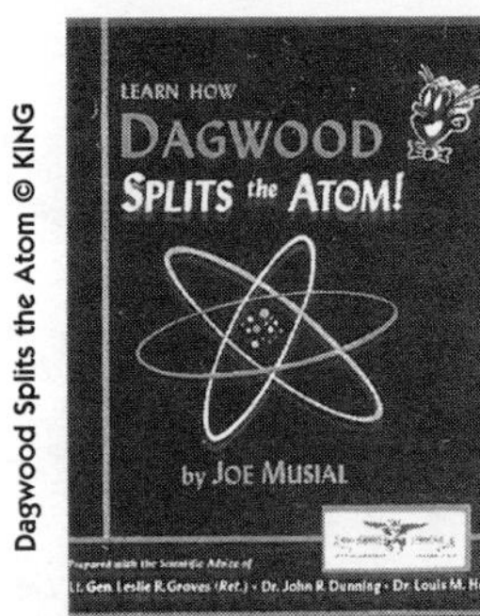

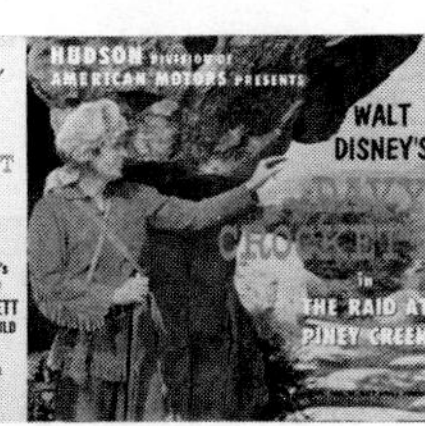

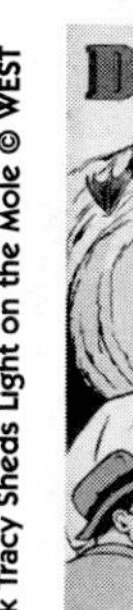

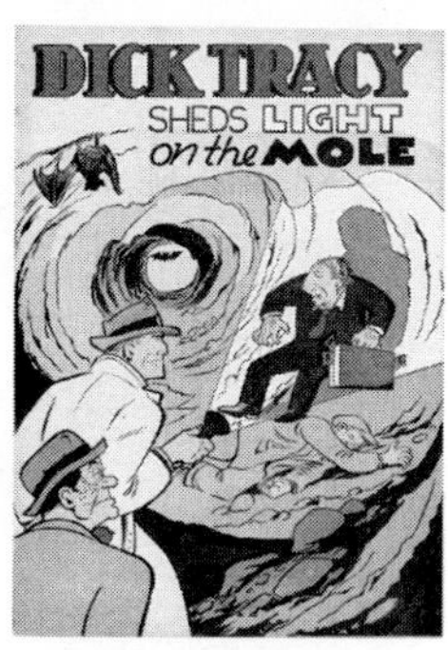

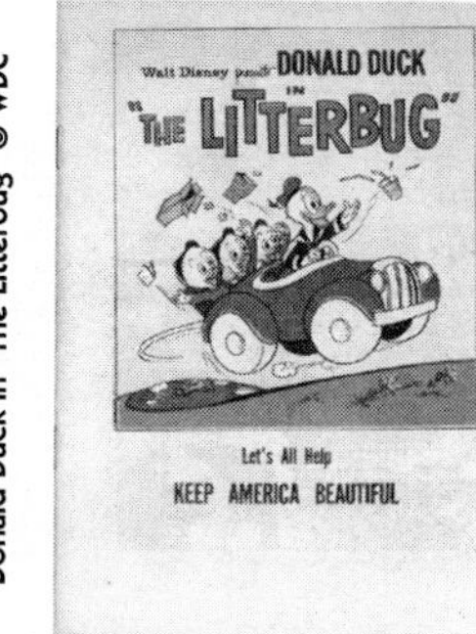

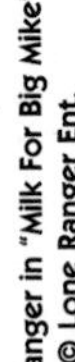

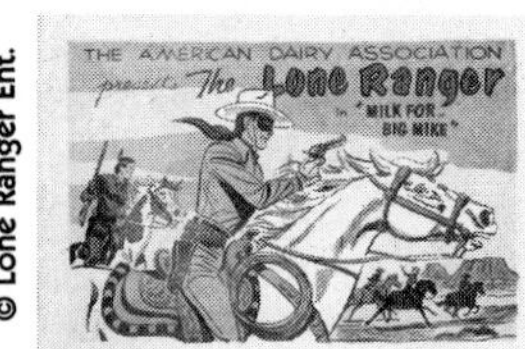

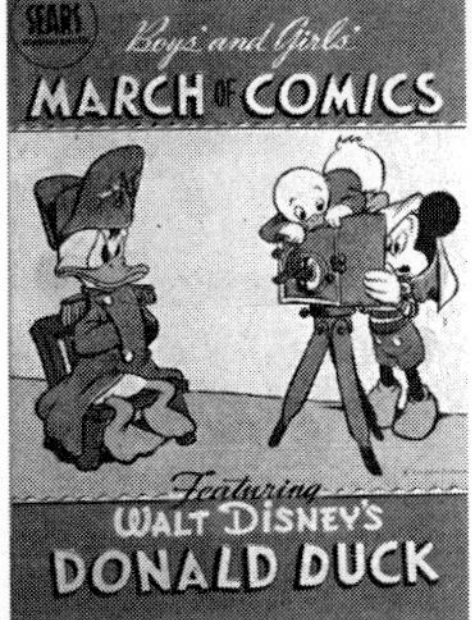

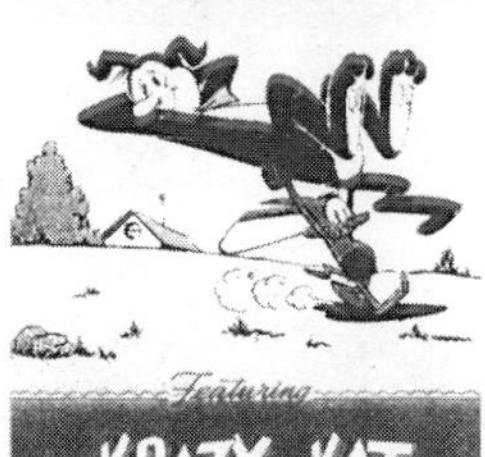

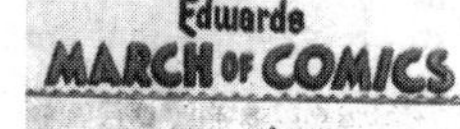

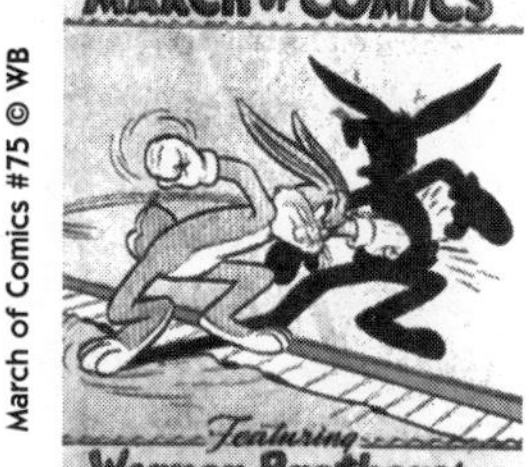

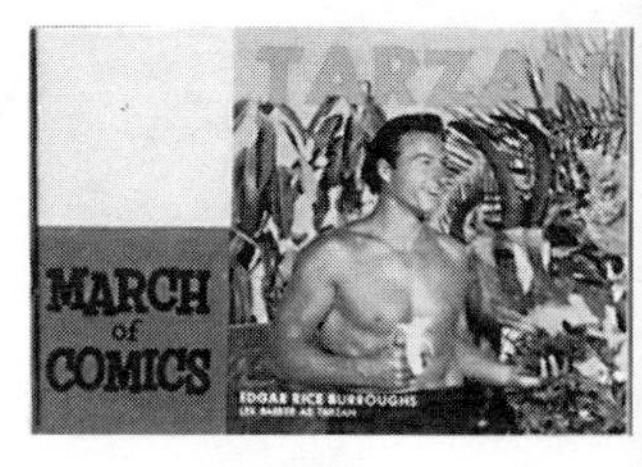

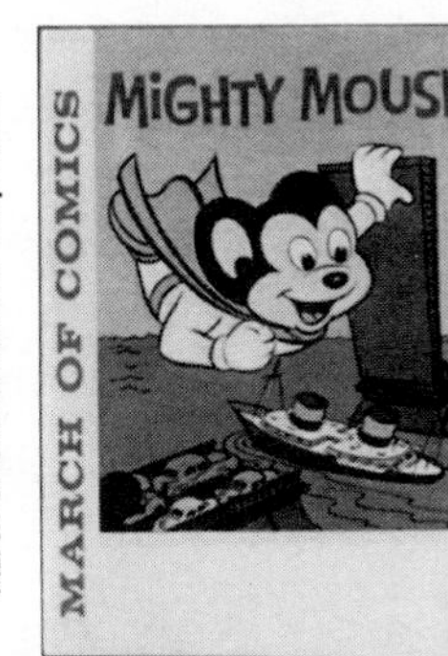

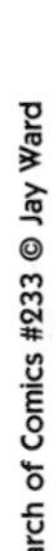
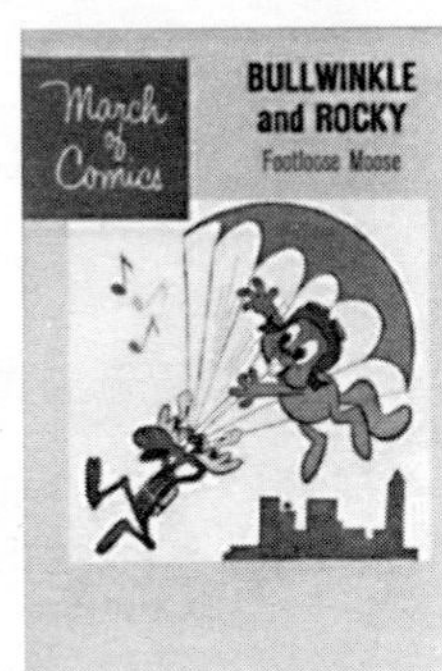

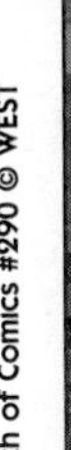
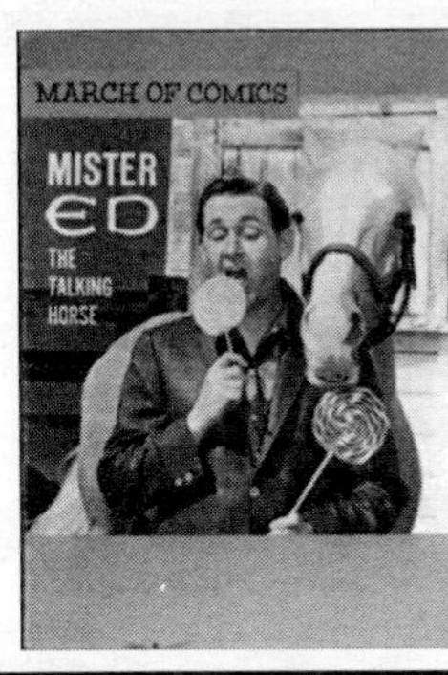

March of Comics #323 © WEST

March of Comics #395 © WEST

March of Comics #439 © WEST

	GD2.0	FN6.0	NM9.4
305-Tom and Jerry	2.00	5.00	10.00
306-Daniel Boone (TV); Fess Parker photo-c	5.85	17.50	40.00
307-Little Lulu; Irving Tripp-a	7.50	22.50	45.00
308-Lassie (TV); photo-c	4.00	11.00	22.00
309-Yogi Bear (TV)	4.25	13.00	28.00
310-The Lone Ranger; Clayton Moore photo-c	12.00	36.00	85.00
311-Santa's Show	2.40	6.00	12.00
312-Christmas Album (1967)	2.40	6.00	12.00
313-Daffy Duck (1968)	2.00	5.00	10.00
314-Laurel and Hardy (TV)	4.70	14.00	28.00
315-Bugs Bunny	2.80	7.00	14.00
316-The Three Stooges	7.50	22.50	45.00
317-The Flintstones (TV)	7.15	21.50	50.00
318-Tarzan	6.70	20.00	40.00
319-Yogi Bear (TV)	4.25	13.00	28.00
320-Space Family Robinson (TV); Spiegle-a	14.00	43.00	100.00
321-Tom and Jerry	2.00	5.00	10.00
322-The Lone Ranger	6.70	20.00	40.00
323-Little Lulu; not by Stanley	4.35	13.00	26.00
324-Lassie (TV); photo-c	4.00	11.00	22.00
325-Fun with Santa	2.40	6.00	12.00
326-Christmas Story (1968)	2.40	6.00	12.00
327-The Flintstones (TV)(1969)	7.15	21.50	50.00
328-Space Family Robinson (TV); Spiegle-a	14.00	43.00	100.00
329-Bugs Bunny	2.80	7.00	14.00
330-The Jetsons (TV)	11.50	34.00	80.00
331-Daffy Duck	2.00	5.00	10.00
332-Tarzan	5.35	16.00	32.00
333-Tom and Jerry	2.00	5.00	10.00
334-Lassie (TV)	4.00	10.00	20.00
335-Little Lulu	4.35	13.00	26.00
336-The Three Stooges	7.50	22.50	45.00
337-Yogi Bear (TV)	4.25	13.00	28.00
338-The Lone Ranger	6.70	20.00	40.00
339-(Was not published)			
340-Here Comes Santa (1969)	2.40	6.00	12.00
341-The Flintstones (TV)	7.15	21.50	50.00
342-Tarzan	5.35	16.00	32.00
343-Bugs Bunny	2.40	6.00	12.00
344-Yogi Bear (TV)	4.15	12.50	25.00
345-Tom and Jerry	2.00	5.00	10.00
346-Lassie (TV)	4.00	10.00	20.00
347-Daffy Duck	2.00	5.00	10.00
348-The Jetsons (TV)	10.00	30.00	70.00
349-Little Lulu; not by Stanley	4.00	11.00	22.00
350-The Lone Ranger	5.00	15.00	30.00
351-Beep-Beep, the Road Runner (TV)	2.80	7.00	14.00
352-Space Family Robinson (TV); Spiegle-a	14.00	43.00	100.00
353-Beep-Beep, the Road Runner (1971) (TV)	2.80	7.00	14.00
354-Tarzan (1971)	4.70	14.00	28.00
355-Little Lulu; not by Stanley	4.00	11.00	22.00
356-Scooby Doo, Where Are You? (TV)	7.15	21.50	50.00
357-Daffy Duck & Porky Pig	2.00	5.00	10.00
358-Lassie (TV)	4.00	10.00	20.00
359-Baby Snoots	2.80	7.00	14.00
360-H. R. Pufnstuf (TV); photo-c	7.15	21.50	50.00
361-Tom and Jerry	2.00	5.00	10.00
362-Smokey the Bear (TV)	2.00	5.00	10.00
363-Bugs Bunny & Yosemite Sam	2.40	6.00	12.00
364-The Banana Splits (TV); photo-c	5.70	17.00	40.00
365-Tom and Jerry (1972)	2.00	5.00	10.00
366-Tarzan	4.35	13.00	26.00
367-Bugs Bunny & Porky Pig	2.40	6.00	12.00
368-Scooby Doo (TV)(4/72)	5.70	17.00	40.00
369-Little Lulu; not by Stanley	3.60	9.00	18.00
370-Lassie (TV); photo-c	4.00	10.00	20.00
371-Baby Snoots	2.40	6.00	12.00

	GD2.0	FN6.0	NM9.4
372-Smokey the Bear (TV)	2.00	5.00	10.00
373-The Three Stooges	6.70	20.00	40.00
374-Wacky Witch	2.00	5.00	10.00
375-Beep-Beep & Daffy Duck (TV)	2.00	5.00	10.00
376-The Pink Panther (1972) (TV)	2.80	7.00	14.00
377-Baby Snoots (1973)	2.40	6.00	12.00
378-Turok, Son of Stone; new-a	16.00	47.00	110.00
379-Heckle & Jeckle New Terrytoons (TV)	2.00	5.00	10.00
380-Bugs Bunny & Yosemite Sam	2.00	5.00	10.00
381-Lassie (TV)	3.20	8.00	16.00
382-Scooby Doo, Where Are You? (TV)	5.00	15.00	30.00
383-Smokey the Bear (TV)	1.60	4.00	8.00
384-Pink Panther (TV)	2.00	5.00	10.00
385-Little Lulu	3.00	7.50	15.00
386-Wacky Witch	1.60	4.00	8.00
387-Beep-Beep & Daffy Duck (TV)	1.60	4.00	8.00
388-Tom and Jerry (1973)	1.60	4.00	8.00
389-Little Lulu; not by Stanley	3.00	7.50	15.00
390-Pink Panther (TV)	1.60	4.00	8.00
391-Scooby Doo (TV)	4.15	12.50	25.00
392-Bugs Bunny & Yosemite Sam	1.20	3.00	6.00
393-New Terrytoons (Heckle & Jeckle) (TV)	1.20	3.00	6.00
394-Lassie (TV)	2.40	6.00	12.00
395-Woodsy Owl	1.20	3.00	6.00
396-Baby Snoots	1.60	4.00	8.00
397-Beep-Beep & Daffy Duck (TV)	1.20	3.00	6.00
398-Wacky Witch	1.20	3.00	6.00
399-Turok, Son of Stone; new-a	13.00	39.00	90.00
400-Tom and Jerry	1.20	3.00	6.00
401-Baby Snoots (1975) (r/#371)	1.60	4.00	8.00
402-Daffy Duck (r/#313)	1.00	2.50	5.00
403-Bugs Bunny (r/#343)	1.20	3.00	6.00
404-Space Family Robinson (TV)(r/#328)	10.00	30.00	70.00
405-Cracky	1.00	2.50	5.00
406-Little Lulu (r/#355)	2.40	6.00	12.00
407-Smokey the Bear (TV)(r/#362)	1.20	3.00	6.00
408-Turok, Son of Stone; c-r/Turok #20 w/changes; new-a	9.30	28.00	65.00
409-Pink Panther (TV)	1.00	2.50	5.00
410-Wacky Witch	.80	2.00	4.00
411-Lassie (TV)(r/#324)	2.40	6.00	12.00
412-New Terrytoons (1975) (TV)	.80	2.00	4.00
413-Daffy Duck (1976)(r/#331)	.80	2.00	4.00
414-Space Family Robinson (r/#328)	9.30	28.00	65.00
415-Bugs Bunny (r/#329)	.80	2.00	4.00
416-Beep-Beep, the Road Runner (r/#353)(TV)	.80	2.00	4.00
417-Little Lulu (r/#323)	2.40	6.00	12.00
418-Pink Panther (r/#384) (TV)	.80	2.00	4.00
419-Baby Snoots (r/#377)	1.00	2.50	5.00
420-Woody Woodpecker	.80	2.00	4.00
421-Tweety & Sylvester	.80	2.00	4.00
422-Wacky Witch (r/#386)	.80	2.00	4.00
423-Little Monsters	1.00	2.50	5.00
424-Cracky (12/76)	.80	2.00	4.00
425-Daffy Duck	.80	2.00	4.00
426-Underdog (TV)	5.00	15.00	30.00
427-Little Lulu (r/#335)	1.60	4.00	8.00
428-Bugs Bunny	.60	1.50	3.00
429-The Pink Panther (TV)	.60	1.50	3.00
430-Beep-Beep, the Road Runner (TV)	.60	1.50	3.00
431-Baby Snoots	.80	2.00	4.00
432-Lassie (TV)	1.20	3.00	6.00
433-437: 433-Tweety & Sylvester. 434-Wacky Witch. 435-New Terrytoons (TV). 436-Wacky Advs. of Cracky. 437-Daffy Duck	.60	1.50	3.00
438-Underdog (TV)	4.15	12.50	25.00
439-Little Lulu (r/#349)	1.60	4.00	8.00
440-442,444-446: 440-Bugs Bunny. 441-The Pink Panther (TV). 442-Beep-			

Story of Harry S. Truman © DNC

No. 3
OMAR
SUPER-BOOK
OF COMICS
featuring
TERRY AND THE PIRATES
Also in this issue
The Adventures of OMAR

Super Book of Comics #3 © WEST

Super Book of Comics #5 © WEST

	GD2.0	FN6.0	NM9.4
	5.00	15.00	38.00
4/8/51-7/29/51,8/12/51-Last Eisner issue	3.50	10.50	26.00
8/5/51,8/19/51-7/20/52-Not Eisner	1.85	5.60	14.00
7/27/52-(Rare)-Denny Colt in Outer Space by Wally Wood; 7 pg. S/F story of E.C. vintage	32.00	95.00	235.00
8/3/52-(Rare)- "Mission...The Moon" by Wood	32.00	95.00	235.00
8/10/52-(Rare)- "A DP On The Moon" by Wood	32.00	95.00	235.00
8/17/52-(Rare)- "Heart" by Wood/Eisner	27.00	81.00	200.00
8/24/52-(Rare)- "Rescue" by Wood	32.00	95.00	235.00
8/31/52-(Rare)- "The Last Man" by Wood	32.00	95.00	235.00
9/7/52-(Rare)- "The Man in The Moon" by Wood	32.00	95.00	235.00
9/14/52-(Rare)-Eisner/Wenzel-a	8.75	27.00	70.00
9/21/52-(Rare)- "Denny Colt, Alias The Spirit/Space Report" by Eisner/Wenzel	11.50	34.00	85.00
9/28/52-(Rare)- "Return From The Moon" by Wood	32.00	95.00	235.00
10/5/52-(Rare)- "The Last Story" by Eisner	11.50	34.00	85.00

Large Tabloid pages from 1946 on (Eisner) - Price 200 percent over listed prices.
NOTE: *Spirit sections came out in both large and small format. Some newspapers went to the 8-pg. format months before others. Some printed the pages so they cannot be folded into a small comic book section; these are worth less. (Also see Three Comics & Spiritman).*

SPY SMASHER
Fawcett Publications

	GD2.0	FN6.0	NM9.4
Well Known Comics (1944, 12 pgs., 8-1/2x10-1/2"), paper-c, glued binding, printed in green; Bestmaid/Samuel Lowe giveaway	15.00	45.00	105.00

STANDARD OIL COMICS (Also see Gulf Funny Weekly)
Standard Oil Co.: 1933 (Giveaway, tabloid size, 4 pgs. in color)

	GD2.0	FN6.0	NM9.4
1-Series has original art	50.00	150.00	400.00
2-5	20.00	60.00	150.00
6-14: 14-Fred Opper strip, 1 pg.	11.00	33.00	75.00

STAR TEAM
Marvel Comics Group: 1977 (6-1/2x5", 20 pgs.) (Ideal Toy Giveaway)

	GD2.0	FN6.0	NM9.4
nn	1.00	3.00	8.00

STEVE CANYON COMICS
Harvey Publications

	GD2.0	FN6.0	NM9.4
Dept. Store giveaway #3(6/48, 36pp)	10.00	30.00	70.00
...'s Secret Mission (1951, 16 pgs., Armed Forces giveaway); Caniff-a	10.00	30.00	65.00
Strictly for the Smart Birds (1951, 16 pgs.)-Information Comics Div. (Harvey) Premium	9.35	28.00	56.00

STORIES OF CHRISTMAS
K. K. Publications: 1942 (Giveaway, 32 pgs., paper cover)

	GD2.0	FN6.0	NM9.4
nn-Adaptation of "A Christmas Carol"; Kelly story "The Fir Tree"; Infinity-c	37.00	111.00	260.00

STORY HOUR SERIES (Disney)
Whitman Publ. Co.: 1948, 1949; 1951-1953 (36 pgs., paper-c) (4-3/4x6-1/2")
Given away with subscription to Walt Disney's Comics & Stories

	GD2.0	FN6.0	NM9.4
nn(1948)-Mickey Mouse and the Boy Thursday	12.00	36.00	85.00
nn(1948)-Mickey Mouse the Miracle Master	12.00	36.00	85.00
nn(1948)-Minnie Mouse and Antique Chair	12.00	36.00	85.00
nn(1949)-The Three Orphan Kittens(B&W & color)	7.50	22.50	45.00
nn(1949)-Danny-The Little Black Lamb	7.50	22.50	45.00
800(1948)-Donald Duck in "Bringing Up the Boys"	18.00	54.00	125.00
1953 edition	11.00	33.00	75.00
801(1948)-Mickey Mouse's Summer Vacation	10.00	30.00	65.00
1951, 1952 editions	4.25	13.00	28.00
802(1948)-Bugs Bunny's Adventures	8.35	25.00	50.00
803(1948)-Bongo	5.70	17.00	35.00
804(1948)-Mickey and the Beanstalk	8.35	25.00	50.00
805-15(1949)-Andy Panda and His Friends	6.70	20.00	40.00
806-15(1949)-Tom and Jerry	7.50	22.50	45.00
808-15(1949)-Johnny Appleseed	5.70	17.00	35.00
1948, 1949 Hard Cover Edition of each....	$3.00 - $5.00 more.		

STORY OF EDISON, THE
Educational Comics: 1956 (16 pgs.) (Reddy Killowatt)

	GD2.0	FN6.0	NM9.4
nn-Reprint of Reddy Kilowatt #2(1947)	8.35	25.00	50.00

STORY OF HARRY S. TRUMAN, THE
Democratic National Committee: 1948 (Giveaway, regular size, soft-c, 16 pg.)

	GD2.0	FN6.0	NM9.4
nn-Gives biography on career of Truman; used in **SOTI**, pg. 311	14.00	43.00	100.00

STRANGE AS IT SEEMS
McNaught Syndicate: 1936 (B&W, 5x7", 24 pgs.)

	GD2.0	FN6.0	NM9.4
nn-Ex-Lax giveaway	4.00	10.00	20.00

SUGAR BEAR
Post Cereal Giveaway: No date, circa 1975? (2-1/2x4-1/2", 16 pgs.)

	GD2.0	FN6.0	NM9.4
"The Almost Take Over of the Post Office", "The Race Across the Atlantic", "The Zoo Goes Wild" each...			5.00

SUPER BOOK OF COMICS
Western Publishing Co.: nd (1942-1943?) (Soft-c, 32 pgs.) (Pan-Am/Gilmore Oil/Kelloggs premiums)

	GD2.0	FN6.0	NM9.4
nn-Dick Tracy (Gilmore)-Magic Morro app.	44.00	132.00	350.00
1-Dick Tracy & The Smuggling Ring; Stratosphere Jim app. (Rare) (Pan-Am)	44.00	132.00	350.00
1-Smilin' Jack, Magic Morro (Pan-Am)	13.00	39.00	125.00
2-Smilin' Jack, Stratosphere Jim (Pan-Am)	13.00	39.00	125.00
2-Smitty, Magic Morro (Pan-Am)	13.00	39.00	125.00
3-Captain Midnight, Magic Morro (Pan-Am)	36.00	107.00	250.00
3-Moon Mullins?	13.00	39.00	125.00
4-Red Ryder, Magic Morro (Pan-Am). Same content as Red Ryder Victory Patrol comic w/diff. cover	21.00	64.00	150.00
4-Smitty, Stratosphere Jim (Pan-Am)	13.00	39.00	125.00
5-Don Winslow, Magic Morro (Gilmore)	21.00	64.00	150.00
5-Don Winslow, Stratosphere Jim (Pan-Am)	21.00	64.00	150.00
5-Terry & the Pirates	25.00	75.00	175.00
6-Don Winslow, Stratosphere Jim (Pan-Am)-McWilliams-a	21.00	64.00	150.00
6-King of the Royal Mounted, Magic Morro (Pan-Am)	21.00	64.00	150.00
7-Dick Tracy, Magic Morro (Pan-Am)	29.00	86.00	200.00
7-Little Orphan Annie	14.00	43.00	100.00
8-Dick Tracy, Stratosphere Jim (Pan-Am)	25.00	75.00	175.00
8-Dan Dunn, Magic Morro (Pan-Am)	14.00	43.00	100.00
9-Terry & the Pirates, Magic Morro (Pan-Am)	25.00	75.00	175.00
10-Red Ryder, Magic Morro (Pan-Am)	21.00	64.00	150.00

SUPER-BOOK OF COMICS
Western Publishing Co.: (Omar Bread & Hancock Oil Co. giveaways)
1944 - No. 30, 1947 (Omar); 1947 - 1948 (Hancock) (16 pgs.)

Note: The Hancock issues are all exact reprints of the earlier Omar issues. The issue numbers were removed in some of the reprints.

	GD2.0	FN6.0	NM9.4
1-Dick Tracy (Omar, 1944)	24.00	73.00	170.00
1-Dick Tracy (Hancock, 1947)	18.00	54.00	125.00
2-Bugs Bunny (Omar, 1944)	8.35	25.00	50.00
2-Bugs Bunny (Hancock, 1947)	6.70	20.00	40.00
3-Terry & the Pirates (Omar, 1944)	13.00	39.00	90.00
3-Terry & the Pirates (Hancock, 1947)	11.50	34.00	80.00
4-Andy Panda (Omar, 1944)	8.35	25.00	50.00
4-Andy Panda (Hancock, 1947)	6.70	20.00	40.00
5-Smokey Stover (Omar, 1945)	6.70	20.00	40.00
5-Smokey Stover (Hancock, 1947)	5.00	15.00	30.00
6-Porky Pig (Omar, 1945)	8.35	25.00	50.00
6-Porky Pig (Hancock, 1947)	6.70	20.00	40.00
7-Smilin' Jack (Omar, 1945)	8.35	25.00	50.00
7-Smilin' Jack (Hancock, 1947)	6.70	20.00	40.00
8-Oswald the Rabbit (Omar, 1945)	6.70	20.00	40.00
8-Oswald the Rabbit (Hancock, 1947)	5.00	15.00	30.00
9-Alley Oop (Omar, 1945)	14.00	43.00	100.00

Swamp Fox © WDC

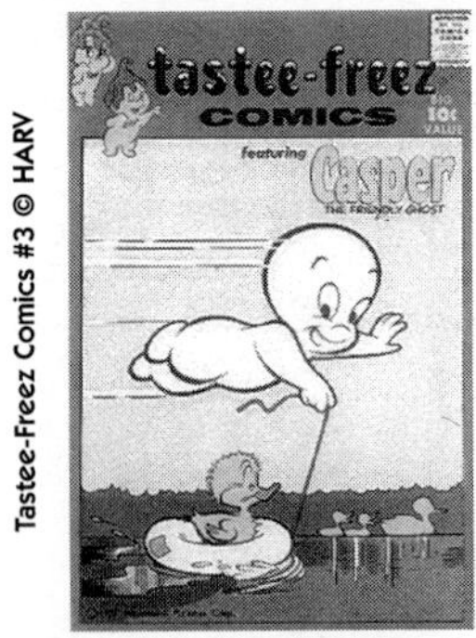

Tastee-Freez Comics #3 © HARV

Tilly and Ted - Tinkertotland © W.T. Grant Co.

	GD2.0	FN6.0	NM9.4
All 36 pgs.	34.00	103.00	240.00
9/47-Stamp album issue & Superman story	44.00	132.00	350.00
10/47, 11/47, 12/47-Superman stories (24 pgs.)	34.00	103.00	240.00
1/48-7/48,10/48, 11/48, 2/49, 4/49-11/49	27.00	81.00	190.00
8/48-Contains full page ad for Superman-Tim watch giveaway	26.00	79.00	185.00
9/48-Stamp album issue	36.00	107.00	250.00
1/49-Full page Superman bank cut-out	26.00	79.00	185.00
3/49-Full page Superman boxing game cut-out	26.00	79.00	185.00
12/49-3/50, 5/50-Superman stories	30.00	90.00	210.00
4/50-Superman story, baseball stories; photo-c without Superman	27.00	81.00	190.00

NOTE: *All issues have Superman illustrations throughout. The page count varies depending on whether a Superman-Tim comic story is inserted. If it is, the page count is either 36 or 24 pages. Otherwise all issues are 16 pages. Each issue has a special place for inserting a full color Superman stamp. The stamp album issues had spaces for the stamps given away the past year. The books were mailed as a subscription premium. The stamps were given away free (or when you made a purchase) only when you physically came into the store.*

SWAMP FOX, THE
Walt Disney Productions: 1960 (14 pgs, small size) (Canada Dry Premiums)

Titles: (A)-Tory Masquerade, (B)-Turnabout Tactics, (C)-Rindau Rampage; each came in paper sleeve, books 1,2 & 3;

	GD2.0	FN6.0	NM9.4
Set with sleeves	6.00	18.00	60.00
Comic only	1.85	5.50	15.00

SYNDICATE FEATURES (Sci/fi)
Harry A. Chesler Syndicate: V1#3, 11/15/37 (Tabloid size, 3 colors, 4 pgs.) (Editors premium)(Came folded)

V1#3-Dan Hastings daily strips-Guardineer-a 500.00 1500.00 2500.00

TASTEE-FREEZ COMICS
Harvey Comics: 1957 (10¢, 36 pgs.)(6 different issues given away)

	GD2.0	FN6.0	NM9.4
1,3: 1-Little Dot. 3-Casper	3.80	11.40	38.00
2,4,5: 2-Rags Rabbit. 4-Sad Sack. 5-Mazie	2.40	7.20	24.00
6-Dick Tracy	3.50	10.50	35.00

TAYLOR'S CHRISTMAS TABLOID
Dept. Store Giveaway: Mid 1930s, Cleveland, Ohio (Tabloid size; in color)

nn-(Very Rare)-Among the earliest pro work of Siegel & Shuster; one full color page called "The Battle in the Stratosphere", with a pre-Superman look; Shuster art thoughout. (Only 1 known copy)
Estimated value... 3000.00

TEE AND VEE CROSLEY IN TELEVISION LAND COMICS
(Also see Crosley's House of Fun)
Crosley Division, Avco Mfg. Corp. : 1951 (52 pgs.; 8x11"; paper cover; in color) (Giveaway)

Many stories, puzzles, cut-outs, games, etc. 5.00 15.00 30.00

TENNESSEE JED (Radio)
Fox Syndicate? (Wm. C. Popper & Co.): nd (1945) (16 pgs.; paper cover; regular size; giveaway)

nn 30.00 100.00 200.00

TENNIS (...For Speed, Stamina, Strength, Skill)
Tennis Educational Foundation: 1956 (16 pgs.; soft cover; 10¢)

Book 1-Endorsed by Gene Tunney, Ralph Kiner, etc. showing how tennis has helped them 5.00 15.00 30.00

TERRY AND THE PIRATES
Dell Publishing Co.: 1939 - 1953 (By Milton Caniff)

	GD2.0	FN6.0	NM9.4
Buster Brown Shoes giveaway(1938)-32 pgs.; in color	29.00	86.00	200.00
Canada Dry Premiums-Books #1-3(1953, 36 pgs.; 2x5")-Harvey; #1-Hot Shot Charlie Flies Again; 2-In Forced Landing; 3-Dragon Lady in Distress)	17.00	51.00	120.00
Gambles Giveaway (1938, 16 pgs.)	10.00	30.00	60.00
Gillmore Giveaway (1938, 24 pgs.)	10.00	30.00	65.00
Popped Wheat Giveaway(1938)-Strip reprints in full color; Caniff-a			5.00
Shoe Store giveaway (Weatherbird)(1938, 16 pgs., soft-c)(2-diff.)	10.00	30.00	60.00
Sparked Wheat Giveaway(1942, 16 pgs.)-In color	10.00	30.00	60.00

TERRY AND THE PIRATES
Libby's Radio Premium: 1941 (16 pgs.; reg. size)(shipped folded in the mail)

	GD2.0	FN6.0	VF8.0
"Adventure of the Ruby of Genghis Khan" - Each pg. is a puzzle that must be completed to read the story	300.00	1000.00	1800.00

THAT THE WORLD MAY BELIEVE
Catechetical Guild Giveaway: No date (16 pgs.) (Graymoor Friars distr.)

	GD2.0	FN6.0	NM9.4
nn	1.60	4.00	8.00

350 YEARS OF AMERICAN DAIRY FOODS
American Dairy Assoc.: 1957 (5x7", 16 pgs.)

nn-History of milk 3.00 7.50 15.00

THUMPER (Disney)
Grosset & Dunlap: 1942 (50 cents, 32pgs., hardcover book, 7"x8-1/2" w/dust jacket)

	GD2.0	FN6.0	NM9.4
nn-Given away (along with a copy of Bambi) for a $2.00, 2-year subscription to WDC&S in 1942. (Xmas offer). Book only	16.00	47.00	110.00
Dust jacket only	9.15	27.00	55.00

TILLY AND TED-TINKERTOTLAND
W. T. Grant Co.: 1945 (Giveaway, 20 pgs.)

nn-Christmas comic 6.35 19.00 38.00

TIM (Formerly Superman-Tim; becomes Gene Autry-Tim)
Tim Stores: June, 1950 - Oct, 1950 (B&W, half-size)

4 issues; 6/50, 9/50, 10/50 known 8.35 25.00 50.00

TIM AND SALLY'S ADVENTURES AT MARINELAND
Marineland Restaurant & Bar, Marineland, CA: 1957 (5x7", 16 pgs., soft-c)

nn-copyright Oceanarium, Inc. 1.60 4.00 8.00

TIM IN SPACE (Formerly Gene Autry Tim; becomes Tim Tomorrow)
Tim Stores: 1950 (1/2 size giveaway) (B&W)

nn 5.35 16.00 32.00

TIM TOMORROW (Formerly Tim In Space)
Tim Stores: 8/51, 9/51, 10/51, Christmas, 1951 (5x7-3/4")

nn-Prof. Fumble & Captain Kit Comet in all 5.35 16.00 32.00

TOM MIX (...Commandos Comics #10-12)
Ralston-Purina Co.: Sept, 1940 - No. 12, Nov, 1942 (36 pgs.); 1983 (one-shot)
Given away for two Ralston box-tops; 1983 came in cereal box

	GD2.0	FN6.0	NM9.4
1-Origin (life) Tom Mix; Fred Meagher-a	300.00	1500.00	3000.00
2	106.00	319.00	850.00
3-9	66.00	197.00	525.00
10-12: 10-Origin Tom Mix Commando Unit; Speed O'Dare begins; Japanese sub-c. 12-Sci/fi-c	53.00	160.00	425.00
1983- "Taking of Grizzly Grebb", Toth-a; 16 pg. miniature	1.85	5.50	15.00

TOM SAWYER COMICS
Giveaway: 1951? (Paper cover)

nn-Contains a coverless Hopalong Cassidy from 1951; other combinations known 4.00 10.00 20.00

TOPPS COMICS PRESENTS
Topps Comics: No. 0, 1993 (Giveaway, B&W, 36 pgs.)

0-Dracula vs. Zorro, Teenagents, Silver Star, & Bill the Galactic Hero 2.00

TOWN THAT FORGOT SANTA, THE
W. T. Grant Co.: 1961 (Giveaway, 24 pgs.)

nn 2.00 6.00 16.00

TOY WORLD FUNNIES (See Funnies On Parade)
Eastern Color Printing Co.: 1933 (36 pgs., slick cover, Golden Eagle and Wanamaker giveaway)

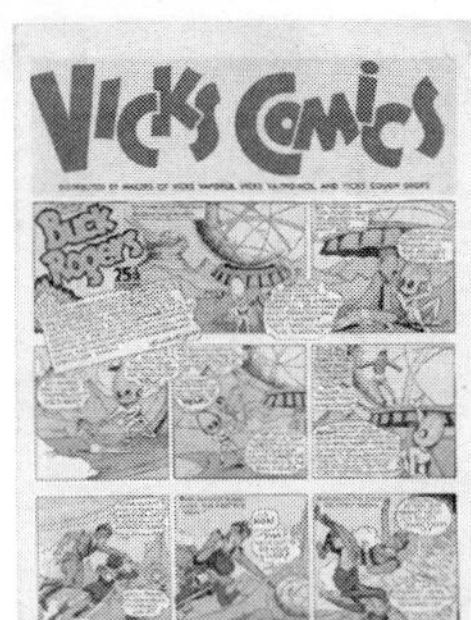

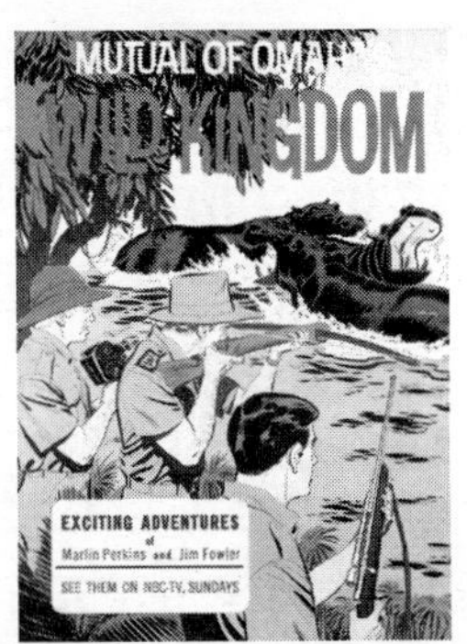

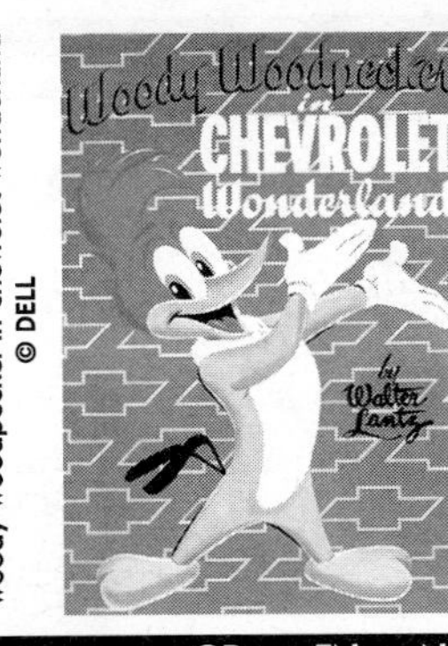

Thus was born the Sunday "comic supplement." Most of the regular favorites were under contract with these magazines; however, there was an artist working for **Truth** who wasn't. Roy L McCardell, then a staffer at **Puck**, informed Morrill Goddard, Sunday editor of **The New York World**, that he knew someone who could fit what was needed at the then largest newspaper in America.

Richard F. Outcault (1863-1928) first introduced his street children strip in the June 2, 1894 issue of **Truth**, somewhat inspired by Michael Angelo Woolf's slum kids single panel cartoons in Life which had begun in the mid 1880s. It's also possible that Outcault's **Hogan's Alley** cast, including the Yellow Kid, was inspired by Charles W. Saalburg's **The Ting Ling Kids** which began in the **Chicago Inter-Ocean** by May 1894. By 1895 Saalburg was Art Director in charge of coloring for the new color printing press at the **New York World**. Edward Harrigan's play "O'Reilly and the Four Hundred," which had a song beginning with the words "Down in Hogan's Alley..." likely provided direct inspiration.

By the November 18, 1894 issue of the **World**, Outcault was working for Goddard and Saalburg. Outcault produced a successful Sunday newspaper sequential comic strip in color with "The Origin of a New Species" on the back page in the World's first colored Sunday supplement. Long time pro Walt McDougall, a famous cartoonist reputed to have turned the 1884 Presidential race with a single cartoon that ran in the **World**, handled the cartoon art on the front page. Earlier, **The World** began running full page color single panels on May 21, 1893. McDougall did various other page panels during 1893, but it was January 28, 1894 when the first sequence of comic pictures in a newspaper appeared in panels in the same format as our comic strips today. It was a full page cut up into nine panels, and the sequence was drawn entirely in pantomime, with no words. This historic page was drawn by Mark Fenderson.

The second page to appear in panels was an eight panel strip from February 4, 1894, also lacking words except for the title. This page was a collaboration between Walt McDougall and Mark Fenderson titled "The Unfortunate Fate of a Well-Intentioned Dog." From then on, many full page color strips by McDougall and Fenderson appeared; they were the first cartoonists to draw for the Sunday newspaper comic section. It was Outcault, however, who soon became the most famous cartoonist featured. After first appearing in black and white in Pulitzer's **The New York World** on February 17, 1895 and again on March 10, 1895, **The Yellow Kid** was introduced to the public in color on May 5, 1895.

Some have erroneously reported in scholarly journals that perhaps it was Frank Ladendorf's "Uncle Reuben," first introduced May 26, 1895, which became the first regularly recurring comics character in newspapers. This is wrong, as even Outcault's "Yellow Kid" began in Pulitzer's paper a good three months before **Uncle Reuben**. Until firm evidence to the contrary comes to light, that honor will forever be enshrined with Jimmy Swinnerton's **Little Bears** cartoon characters, found all over inside Hearst's **San Francisco Examiner** as early as 1892. Though never actually a comic strip, they nonetheless were the earliest presently known recurring comics characters in American newspapers. There

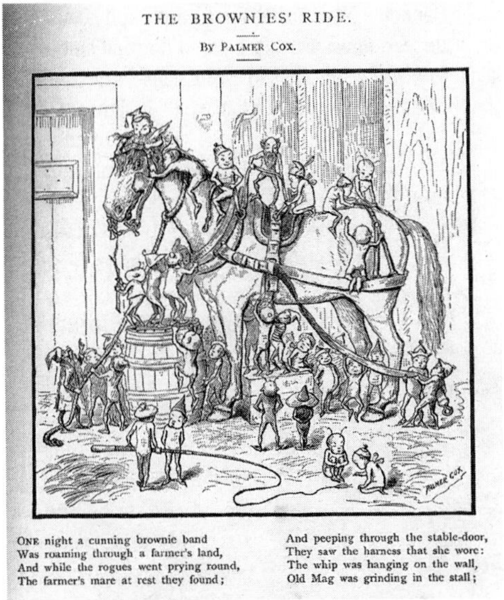

THE BROWNIES' RIDE.

By Palmer Cox.

ONE night a cunning brownie band
Was roaming through a farmer's land,
And while the rogues went prying round,
The farmer's mare at rest they found;

And peeping through the stable-door,
They saw the harness that she wore:
The whip was hanging on the wall,
Old Mag was grinding in the stall;

The Brownies by Palmer Cox, 1883, were the earliest known recurring comic characters merchandised in North America.

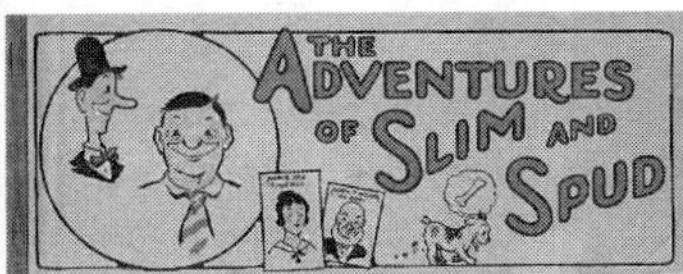

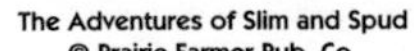
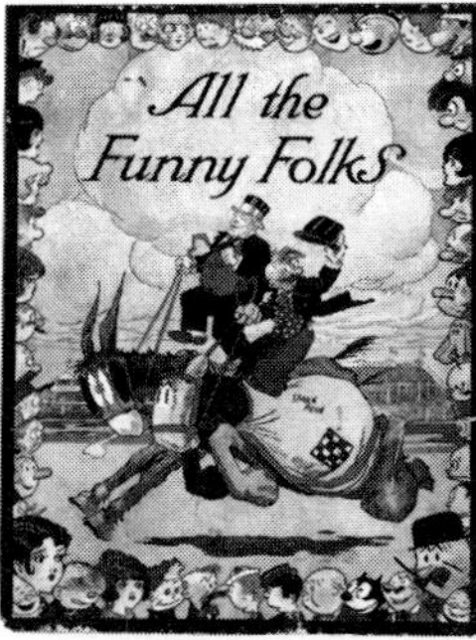

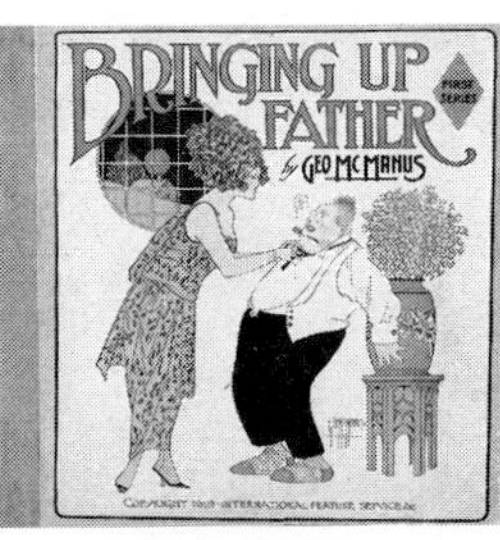

Jimmy
© NY American & Journal

Little Nemo 1906
© Doffield & Co.

Little Orphan Annie #3 - The Haunted House
© C&L

	GD2.0	FN6.0	VF8.0
...The Funny Larks Of (1927) reprints 1916 strips; Halloween-c	82.00	328.00	575.00
...The Funny Larks Of 2(1929)	79.00	316.00	550.00

HAPPY HOOLIGAN (See Alphonse...)
Hearst's New York American & Journal: 1902,1903

	GD2.0	FN6.0	VF8.0
Book 1-(1902)-"And His Brother Gloomy Gus", By Fred Opper; has 1901-02-r; (yellow & black)(86 pgs.)(10x15-1/4")	175.00	700.00	-
50 Pg. Edition(1903)-10x15" 18 pgs. in color	157.00	628.00	-

HAPPY HOOLIGAN (See The Travels of...)
Frederick A. Stokes Co.: 1908 (10x15", cardboard-c)

	GD2.0	FN6.0	VF8.0
1908-"Handy--", 32 pgs, color	93.00	372.00	-
1908?-"--Home Again", 68 pgs., 60¢ in color; by F. Opper; full color-c	112.00	450.00	-

HAPPY HOOLIGAN (Story of...)
McLoughlin Bros.: No. 281, 1932 (9-1/2x12", 16 pgs., soft-c)

	GD2.0	FN6.0	VF8.0
281-Three-color text, pictures on heavy paper	64.00	193.00	450.00

HAROLD TEEN (Adventures of...)
Cupples & Leon Co.: 1929-31 (52 pgs., cardboard-c)

	GD2.0	FN6.0	VF8.0
nn-B&W daily strip reprints by Carl Ed	41.00	164.00	290.00

HAWKSHAW THE DETECTIVE (See Advs. of..., Hans Und Fritz & Okay)
The Saalfield Publishing Co.: 1917 (10-1/2x13-1/2", 24 pgs., B&W Sunday strip-r)

	GD2.0	FN6.0	VF8.0
nn-By Gus Mager	41.00	164.00	290.00

HENRY
David McKay Co.: 1935 (25¢, soft-c)

	GD2.0	FN6.0	VF8.0
Book 1-By Carl Anderson	50.00	200.00	350.00

HOME, SWEET HOME
M.S. Publishing Co.: 1925 (10-1/4x10")

	GD2.0	FN6.0	VF8.0
nn-By Tuthill	33.00	134.00	235.00

HOW THEY DRAW PROHIBITION
Association Against Prohibition: 1930 (10x9-1/2", 100 pgs.)

	GD2.0	FN6.0	VF8.0
nnSingle panel and multi-panel comics (rare)	71.00	285.00	500.00

IT HAPPENS IN THE BEST FAMILIES
Powers Photo Engraving Co.: 1920 (52 pgs.)(9-1/2x10-3/4")

	GD2.0	FN6.0	VF8.0
nn-By Briggs; B&W Sunday strips-r	28.00	112.00	195.00
Special Railroad Edition (30¢)-r/strips from 1914-1920	24.00	96.00	170.00

JIMMIE DUGAN AND THE REG'LAR FELLERS
Cupples & Leon: 1921, 46 pgs. (11"x16")

	GD2.0	FN6.0	VF8.0
nn-By Gene Byrne; Ties with "The Troubles With Bringing up Father" by EmBee (#21) as last of this size	71.00	284.00	500.00

JIMMY (James Swinnerton)
N. Y. American & Journal: 1905 (10x15", 40 pgs., color)

	GD2.0	FN6.0	VF8.0
nn	125.00	500.00	-

JIMMY AND HIS SCRAPES
Frederick A. Stokes: 1908?, (10x15", 60¢, cardboard-c)

	GD2.0	FN6.0	VF8.0
nn-In color	57.00	228.00	400.00

JIMMY, STORY OF
McLoughlin Bros.:1932 (9'1/2"X12", 16 pgs., soft cover)

	GD2.0	FN6.0	VF8.0
nn	64.00	193.00	450.00

JOE PALOOKA
Cupples & Leon Co.: 1933 (52 pgs., B&W daily strip-r)

	GD2.0	FN6.0	VF8.0
nn-(Scarce)-by Fisher	114.00	456.00	800.00

JUST KIDS
McLoughlin Bros.: No. 283, 1932 (9-1/2x12", 16 pgs., paper-c)

	GD2.0	FN6.0	VF8.0
283-Three-color text, pictures on heavy paper	21.00	84.00	145.00

KATZENJAMMER KIDS, THE (Also see Hans Und Fritz)
New York American & Journal: 1902,1903 (10x15-1/4", 86 pgs., color) (By Rudolph Dirks; strip 1st appeared in 1898) © W.R. Hearst

	GD2.0	FN6.0	VF8.0
1902 (Rare)(red & black); has 1901-02 strips	350.00	1400.00	-
1903 (Rare)-reprint	275.00	1100.00	-
1905?-The Cruise of the, 10x15", 60¢, in color	175.00	700.00	-
1905-A Series of Comic Pictures, 10x15", 40 pgs. in color	175.00	700.00	-
1905-Tricks of...(10x15)	175.00	700.00	-
1906-Stokes-10x16", 32 pgs. in color	150.00	600.00	-
1910-The Komical...(10x15)	79.00	316.00	600.00
1921-Embee Dist. Co., 10x16", 20 pgs. in color	64.00	256.00	450.00

KEEPING UP WITH THE JONESES
Cupples & Leon Co.: 1920 - No. 2, 1921 (9-1/4x9-1/4", 52 pgs., B&W daily strip-r)

	GD2.0	FN6.0	VF8.0
1,2-By Pop Momand	37.00	148.00	260.00

LADY BOUNTIFUL
Saalfield Publ. Co./Press Publ. Co.: 1917 (10-1/4x13-1/2", 24 pgs., B&W, cardboard-c)

	GD2.0	FN6.0	VF8.0
nn-By Gene Carr; 2 panels per page	37.00	148.00	260.00

LIFE'S LITTLE JOKES
M.S. Publ. Co.: No date (1924) (52 pgs., B&W)

	GD2.0	FN6.0	VF8.0
nn-By Rube Goldberg	61.00	244.00	425.00

LILY OF THE ALLEY IN THE FUNNIES
Whitman Publishing Co.(one of their first two books)**:** No date (1927) (10-1/4x15-1/2"; 28 pgs., color)

	GD2.0	FN6.0	VF8.0
W936 - By T. Burke (Rare)	57.00	228.00	400.00

LITTLE ANNIE ROONEY
David McKay Co.: 1935 (25¢, soft-c)

	GD2.0	FN6.0	VF8.0
Book 1	43.00	172.00	300.00

LITTLE JOHNNY & THE TEDDY BEARS
Reilly & Britton Co.: 1907 (10x14", 32 pgs.; green, red, black interior color)

	GD2.0	FN6.0	VF8.0
nn-By J. R. Bray-a/Robert D. Towne-s	57.00	228.00	400.00

LITTLE NEMO (...in Slumberland)
Doffield & Co.(1906)/Cupples & Leon Co.(1909): 1906, 1909 (Sunday strip-r in color, cardboard covers)

	GD2.0	FN6.0	VF8.0
1906-11x16-1/2" by Winsor McCay; 30 pgs. (Rare)	700.00	2800.00	-
1909-10x14" by Winsor McCay (Rare)	600.00	2400.00	-

LITTLE ORPHAN ANNIE (See Treasure Box of Famous Comics)
Cupples & Leon Co.: 1926 - 1934 (7x8-3/4", 100 pgs., B&W daily strip-r, hard-c)

	GD2.0	FN6.0	VF8.0
1(1926)-Little Orphan Annie	50.00	200.00	350.00
1(1926)-softback (see Treasure Box...)			
2('27)-In the Circus	36.00	144.00	250.00
2('28)-softback (36 pgs.)	30.00	120.00	210.00
3('28)-The Haunted House	36.00	144.00	250.00
3('28)-softback (36 pgs.)	30.00	120.00	210.00
4('29)-Bucking the World	36.00	144.00	250.00
5('30)-Never Say Die	30.00	120.00	210.00
6('31)-Shipwrecked	30.00	120.00	210.00
7('32)-A Willing Helper	24.00	96.00	170.00
8('33)-In Cosmic City	24.00	96.00	170.00
9('34)-Uncle Dan (Rare)	43.00	172.00	300.00

TILLIE THE TOILER
BY RUSS WESTOVER
BOOK 5
CUPPLES AND LEON COMPANY - PUBLISHERS - NEW YORK

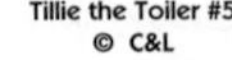
Tillie the Toiler #5
© C&L

TOONERVILLE TROLLEY
1ST SERIES
AND OTHER
CARTOONS
BY
FONTAINE FOX

Toonerville Trolley #1
© C&L

Yellow Kid in McFadden's Flats
© G.W. Dillingham Co.

GD2.0 FN6.0 VF8.0

TAILSPIN TOMMY STORY & PICTURE BOOK
McLoughlin Bros.: No. 266, 1931? (nd) (10-1/2x10", color strip-r)
266-By Forrest 34.00 136.00 240.00

TAILSPIN TOMMY (Also see Famous Feature Stories & The Funnies)
Cupples & Leon Co.: 1932 (100 pgs., hard-c)
nn-(Rare)-B&W strip reprints from 1930 by Hal Forrest & Glenn Claffin 43.00 172.00 300.00

TARZAN BOOK (The Illustrated...)
Grosset & Dunlap: 1929 (7x9", 80 pgs.)
1(Rare)-Contains 1st B&W Tarzan newspaper comics from 1929. Cloth reinforced spine & dust jacket (50¢); Foster-c
with dust jacket... 82.00 328.00 575.00
without dust jacket... 33.00 132.00 230.00
2nd Printing(1934, 25¢, 76 pgs.)-4 Foster pgs. dropped; paper spine, circle in lower right cover with 25¢ price. The 25¢ is barely visible on some copies 31.00 124.00 220.00
1967-House of Greystoke reprint-7x10", using the complete 300 illustrations/ text from the 1929 edition minus the original indicia, foreword, etc. Initial version bound in gold paper & sold for $5.00. Officially titled **Burroughs Biblophile #2**. A very few additional copies were bound in heavier blue paper.
Gold binding... 2.25 6.75 18.00
Blue binding... 2.50 7.50 24.00

TARZAN OF THE APES TO COLOR
Saalfield Publishing Co.: No. 988, 1933 (10-3/4x15-1/4", 24 pgs) (Coloring book)
988-(Very Rare)-Contains 1929 daily reprints with some new art by Hal Foster. Two panels blown up large on each page with one at the top of opposing pages on every other double-page spread. Believed to be the only time these panels appeared in color. Most color panels are reproduced a second time in b&w to be colored 257.00 1028.00 1800.00

THIMBLE THEATRE STARRING POPEYE
Sonnet Publishing Co.: 1931 - No. 2, 1932 (25¢, B&W, 52 pgs.)(Rare)
1-Daily strip serial-r in both by Segar 157.00 628.00 1100.00
2 136.00 544.00 950.00
NOTE: *The very first Popeye reprint book. Popeye first entered Thimble Theatre in 1929.*

THREE FUNMAKERS, THE
Stokes and Company: 1908 (10x15", 64 pgs., color) (1904-06 Sunday strip-r)
nn-Maude, Katzenjammer Kids, Happy Hooligan 275.00 1100.00 -

"TIGE" HIS STORY
Frederick A. Stokes Co.: 1905 (10x8", 63 pgs., B&W) (63 illos.)
nn 125.00 500.00 -

TIGERS (Also see On and Off Mount Ararat)
Hearst's New York American & Journal: 1902, 86pgs. 10x15-1/4"
nn-Funny animal strip-r by Jimmy Swinnerton 125.00 500.00 -

TILLIE THE TOILER
Cupples & Leon Co.: 1925 - No. 8, 1933 (52 pgs., B&W, daily strip-r)
nn (#1) 46.00 184.00 325.00
2-8 34.00 136.00 240.00
NOTE: *First strip appearance was January, 1921.*

TOM SAWYER & HUCK FINN
Stoll & Edwards Co.: 1925 (10-3/4x10", 52 pgs, stiff covers)(Sunday strips in color)
nn-By Dwiggins; 1923, 1924-r 35.00 140.00 245.00

GD2.0 FN6.0 VF8.0

TOONERVILLE TROLLEY
Cupples & Leon Co.: 1921 (52 pgs., B&W, daily strip-r)
1-By Fontaine Fox 54.00 216.00 375.00

TRAVELS OF HAPPY HOOLIGAN, THE
Frederick A. Stokes Co.: 1906 (10-1/4x15-3/4", 32 pgs., cardboard covers)
nn-Contains reprints from 1905 100.00 400.00 -

TREASURE BOX OF FAMOUS COMICS
Cupples & Leon Co.: Mid 1930's (6-7/8x8-1/2", 36 pgs, soft covers) (Boxed set of 5 books)
Little Orphan Annie (1926) 21.00 84.00 150.00
Reg'lar Fellers (1928) 19.00 76.00 130.00
Smitty (1928) 19.00 76.00 130.00
Harold Teen (1931) 19.00 76.00 130.00
How Dick Tracy & Dick Tracy Jr. Caught The Racketeers (1933) 26.00 104.00 185.00
Softcover set of five books in box 160.00 640.00 1125.00
Box only 57.00 228.00 400.00
NOTE: *Dates shown are copyright dates; all books actually came out in 1934 or later. The softcovers are abbreviated versions of the hardcover editions listed under each character.*

TRIALS OF LULU AND LEANDER, THE
William A. Stokes Co.: 1906 (10x16", 32 pgs. in color)
nn-By F. M. Howarth 125.00 500.00 -

TROUBLE OF BRINGING UP FATHER, THE
Embee Publ. Co.: 1921 (9x15", Sunday-r in color)
nn-(Rare) 75.00 300.00 525.00

VAUDEVILLES AND OTHER THINGS
Isaac H. Blandiard Co.: 1900 (10-1/2x13", 22 pgs., color), 1901 (11X13")
nn-By Bunny (Scarce) 200.00 800.00 -
nn-2nd print. "By the creator of Foxy Grandpa" on-c 150.00 600.00 -

WILLIE WESTINGHOUSE EDISON SMITH THE BOY INVENTOR
William A. Stokes Co.: 1906 (10x16", 36 pgs. in color)
nn-By Frank Crane (Scarce) 175.00 700.00 -

WINNIE WINKLE
Cupples & Leon Co.: 1930 - No. 4, 1933 (52 pgs., B&W daily strip-r)
1 39.00 156.00 275.00
2-4 26.00 104.00 185.00

YELLOW KID, THE (Magazine)(becomes The Yellow Kid Book #10 on)
Howard Ainslee & Co., N.Y.: Mar. 20, 1897 - #9, July 17, 1897 (5¢, B&W w/color covers, 52p., stapled)
1-R.F. Outcault Yellow kid on-c only #1-6. The same Yellow Kid color ad app. on back-c #1-6 (advertising the New York Sunday Journal) 650.00 2600.00 -
2 (4/3/97) 350.00 1400.00 -
3-6 (#6, 6/5/97) 243.00 975.00 -
7-9 (Yellow Kid not on-c) 106.00 425.00 -
NOTE: Richard Outcault's Yellow Kid from the Hearst New York American represents the very first successful comic strip in America. Eventually the first prototype comic books appeared reprinting these early strips. This magazine is listed here due to historical importance but is not a comic book.

YELLOW KID IN MCFADDEN'S FLATS, THE
G. W. Dillingham Company, New York: 1897 (50¢, 5 1/2x7 1/2", 196 pgs., B&W, squarebound)
nn-The first "comic" book; E. W. Townsend narrative w/R. F. Outcault Sunday comic page art-r & some original drawings 4750.00 8500.00 -

folded paper, it occurred to him that it was a convenient book size (actually it was late stage "Dime Novel" size, which companies like Street & Smith were pumping out). The format had its heyday from the 1880s through the 1910s, having been invented by the firm of Beadle and Adam in 1860 in more of a digest format. According to a 1942 article by Max Gaines, another contributing factor in the development of the format was an inspection of a promotional folder published by the Ledger Syndicate, in which four-color Sunday comic pages were printed in 7" x 9".

According to a 1949 interview with Wildenberg, he thought "why not a comic book? It would have 32 or 64 pages and make a fine item for concerns which distribute premiums." Wildenberg obtained publishing rights to certain Associated, Bell, Fisher, McNaught and Public Ledger Syndicate comics, had an artist make up a few dummies by hand, and then had his sales staff walk them around to his biggest advertisers. Wildenberg received a telegram from Proctor & Gamble for an order of a million copies for a 32-page color comic magazine called **Funnies on Parade**. The entire print run was given away in just a few weeks in the Spring of 1933.

Also working for Eastern Color at this same time were quite a few future legends of the comics business, such as Max Gaines, Lev Gleason and a fellow named Harold Moore (all sales staff directly underneath the supervision of Wildenberg), Sol Harrison as a color separator, and George Dougherty Sr. as a printer. All of them worked on the **Funnies on Parade** project. Morris Margolis was brought in from Charlton

Publications in Derby, Connecticut to solve binding problems centered on getting the pages in proper numerical sequence on that last fold to "modern" comic book size. All were infected with the comics bug for mostof the rest of their lives.

The success of **Funnies on Parade** quickly led to Eastern publishing additional giveaway books in the same format by late 1933, including the 32 page **Famous Funnies A Carnival of Comics**, the 100 page **A Century of Comics** and **Skippy's Own Book of Comics**; the latter became the first "new" format comic book about a single character. These thicker issues had press runs of up to 500,000 per title. The idea that anyone would pay for them seemed fantastic to Wildenberg, so Max Gaines stickered ten cents on several dozen of the latest premium, **Famous Funnies A Carnival of Comics**, as a test, and talked a couple newsstands into participating in this experiment. The copies sold out over the weekend and newsies asked for more.

Eastern sales staffers then approached Woolworth's. The late Oscar Fitz-Alan Douglas, sales brains of Woolworth, showed some interest, but after several months of deliberation decided the book would not give enough value for ten cents. Kress, Kresge, McCrory, and several other dime stores turned them down even more abruptly. Wildenberg next went to George Hecht, editor of **Parents Magazine**, and tried to persuade him to run a comic supplement or publish a "higher level" comic magazine. Hecht also frowned on the idea.

In Wildenberg's 1949 interview, he

SHELL
GLOBE
VOL. 4
MARCH-APRIL, 1934
NO. 2

Not to be outdone, Shell Oil began a huge comics promotion in March 1934 to compete with Gulf and Standard Oil.

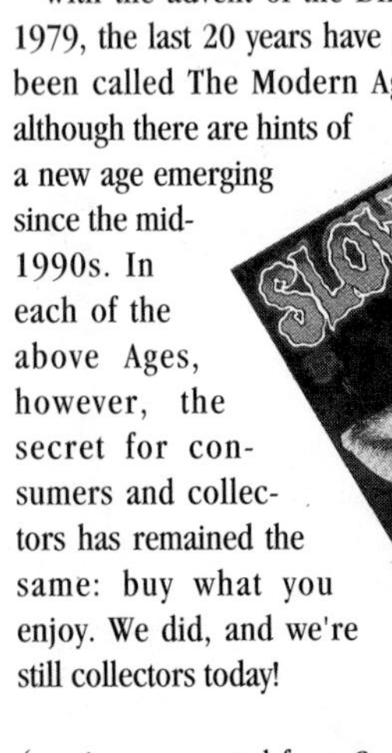

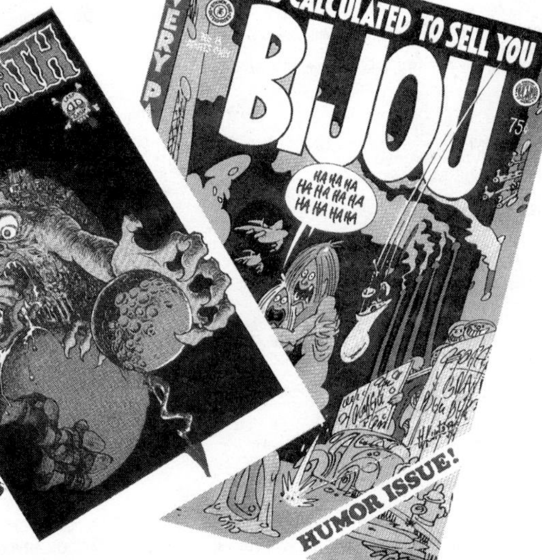

Abbott and Costello #4 © STJ

Ace Comics #50 © DMP

Aces High #4 © WMG

GD2.0 FN6.0 NM9.4

The correct title listing for each comic book can be determined by consulting the indicia (publication data) on the beginning interior pages of the comic. The official title is determined by those words of the title in capital letters only, and not by what is on the cover.

Titles are listed in this book as if they were one word, ignoring spaces, hyphens, and apostrophes, to make finding titles easier. Comic books listed should be assumed to be in color unless noted "B&W".

Comic publishers are invited to send us sample copies for possible inclusion in future guides.

Near Mint is the highest value listed in this price guide. True mint books from the 1970s through the present do exist, so the Near Mint value listed should be interpreted as a Mint value for those books.

A-1 (See A-One)

AARON STRIPS
Image Comics: Apr, 1997 - No. 4, Oct, 1997;
Amazing Aaron Prod.: No. 5, Jan, 1999 - Present ($2.95, B&W)

	GD2.0	FN6.0	NM9.4
1-6-Reprints Adventures of Aaron newspaper strips			3.00

ABBIE AN' SLATS (...With Becky No. 1-4) (See Comics On Parade, Fight for Love, Giant Comics Edition 2, Giant Comics Editions #1, Sparkler Comics, Tip Topper, Treasury of Comics, & United Comics)
United Features Syndicate: 1940; March, 1948 - No. 4, Aug, 1948 (Reprints)

	GD2.0	FN6.0	NM9.4
Single Series 25 ('40)	37.00	111.00	260.00
Single Series 28	31.00	92.00	215.00
1 (1948)	16.00	47.00	110.00
2-4: 3-r/Sparkler #68-72	9.15	27.50	55.00

ABBOTT AND COSTELLO (...Comics)(See Giant Comics Editions #1 & Treasury of Comics)
St. John Publishing Co.: Feb, 1948 - No. 40, Sept, 1956 (Mort Drucker-a in most issues)

	GD2.0	FN6.0	NM9.4
1	50.00	150.00	400.00
2	27.00	81.00	190.00
3-9 (#8, 8/49; #9, 2/50)	17.00	51.00	120.00
10-Son of Sinbad story by Kubert (new)	21.00	62.00	145.00
11,13-20 (#11, 10/50; #13, 8/51; #15, 12/52)	12.00	36.00	85.00
12-Movie issue	13.50	41.00	95.00
21-30: 28-r/#8. 30-Painted-c	10.00	30.00	65.00
31-40: 33,38-Reprints	7.50	22.50	45.00
3-D #1 (11/53, 25¢)-Infinity-c	35.00	105.00	245.00

ABBOTT AND COSTELLO (TV)
Charlton Comics: Feb, 1968 - No. 22, Aug, 1971 (Hanna-Barbera)

	GD2.0	FN6.0	NM9.4
1	6.00	18.00	60.00
2	3.20	9.60	32.00
3-10	2.80	8.40	28.00
11-22	2.50	7.50	20.00

ABC (See America's Best TV Comics)

ABE SAPIEN: DRUMS OF THE DEAD
Dark Horse Comics: Mar, 1998 ($2.95, one-shot)

	GD2.0	FN6.0	NM9.4
1-McDonald-s/Thompson-a. Hellboy back-up; Mignola-s/a/c			3.00

A. BIZARRO
DC Comics: Jul, 1999 - No. 4, Oct, 1999 (2.50, limited series)

	GD2.0	FN6.0	NM9.4
1-4-Gerber-s/Bright-a			2.50

ABOMINATIONS (See Hulk)
Marvel Comics: Dec, 1996 - No. 3, Feb, 1997 (1.50, limited series)

	GD2.0	FN6.0	NM9.4
1-3-Future Hulk storyline			2.00

ABRAHAM LINCOLN LIFE STORY (See Dell Giants)

ABRAHAM STONE
Marvel Comics (Epic): July, 1995 - No. 2, Aug, 1995 ($6.95, limited series)

	GD2.0	FN6.0	NM9.4
1,2-Joe Kubert-s/a	1.00	2.80	7.00

ABSENT-MINDED PROFESSOR, THE
Dell Publishing Co.: Apr, 1961 (Disney)

	GD2.0	FN6.0	NM9.4
Four Color #1199-Movie, photo-c	6.40	19.00	70.00

ABSOLUTE VERTIGO
DC Comics (Vertigo): Winter, 1995 (99¢, mature)

	GD2.0	FN6.0	NM9.4
nn-1st app. Preacher. Previews upcoming titles including Jonah Hex: Riders of the Worm, The Invisibles (King Mob), The Eaters, Ghostdancing & Preacher	1.00	3.00	8.00

ABYSS, THE (Movie)
Dark Horse Comics: June, 1989 - No. 2, July, 1989 ($2.25, limited series)

	GD2.0	FN6.0	NM9.4
1,2-Adaptation of film; Kaluta & Moebius-a			2.25

ACCLAIM ADVENTURE ZONE
Acclaim Books: 1997 ($4.50, digest size)

	GD2.0	FN6.0	NM9.4
1-Short stories of Turok, Troublemakers, Ninjak and others			4.50

ACE COMICS
David McKay Publications: Apr, 1937 - No. 151, Oct-Nov, 1949 (All contain some newspaper strip reprints)

	GD2.0	FN6.0	NM9.4
1-Jungle Jim by Alex Raymond, Blondie, Ripley's Believe It Or Not, Krazy Kat begin (1st app. of each)	300.00	900.00	2700.00
2	94.00	282.00	750.00
3-5	60.00	180.00	485.00
6-10	45.00	135.00	360.00
11-The Phantom begins (1st app., 2/38) (in brown costume)	71.00	213.00	570.00
12-20	40.00	120.00	280.00
21-25,27-30	34.00	102.00	240.00
26-Origin & 1st app. Prince Valiant (5/39); begins series?	90.00	270.00	725.00
31-40: 37-Krazy Kat ends	24.00	72.00	170.00
41-60	18.00	54.00	125.00
61-64,66-76-(7/43; last 68 pgs.)	16.00	48.00	110.00
65-(8/42)-Flag-c	17.00	51.00	115.00
77-84 (3/44; all 60 pgs.)	13.00	39.00	90.00
85-99 (52 pgs.)	11.00	33.00	75.00
100 (7/45; last 52 pgs.)	12.00	36.00	85.00
101-134: 128-(11/47)-Brick Bradford begins. 134-Last Prince Valiant (all 36 pgs.)	9.15	27.50	55.00
135-151: 135-(6/48)-Lone Ranger begins	8.35	25.00	50.00

ACE KELLY (See Tops Comics & Tops In Humor)

ACE KING (See Adventures of Detective...)

ACES
Acme Press (Eclipse): Apr, 1988 - No. 5, Dec, 1988 ($2.95, B&W, magazine)

	GD2.0	FN6.0	NM9.4
1-5			3.00

ACES HIGH
E.C. Comics: Mar-Apr, 1955 - No. 5, Nov-Dec, 1955

	GD2.0	FN6.0	NM9.4
1-Not approved by code	15.50	46.50	155.00
2	9.50	28.00	95.00
3-5	8.00	24.00	80.00

NOTE: *All have stories by* ***Davis, Evans, Krigstein,*** *and* ***Wood. Evans*** *c-1-5.*

ACES HIGH
Gemstone Publishing: Apr, 1999 - No. 5, Aug, 1999 ($2.50)

	GD2.0	FN6.0	NM9.4
1-5-Reprints E.C. issues			2.50
Annual 1 ($13.50) r/#1-5			13.50

ACTION ADVENTURE (War) (Formerly Real Adventure)
Gillmor Magazines: V1#2, June, 1955 - No. 4, Oct, 1955

	GD2.0	FN6.0	NM9.4
V1#2-4	4.00	12.00	24.00

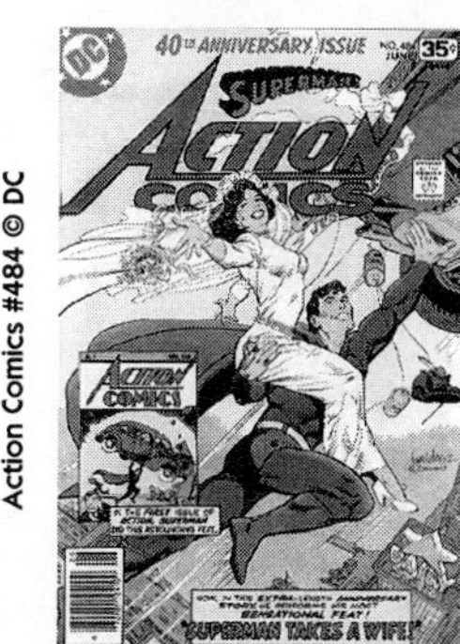

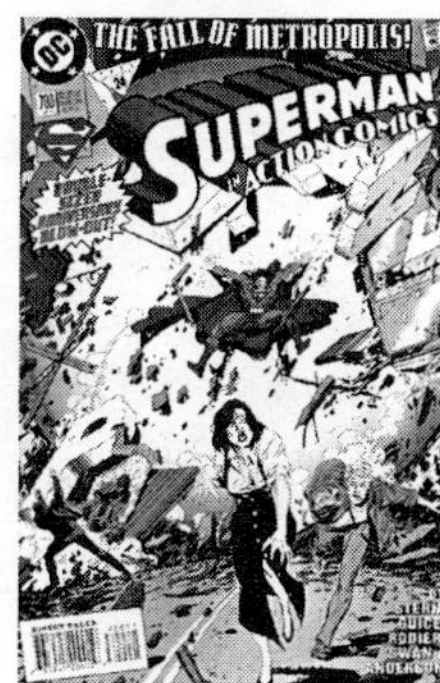

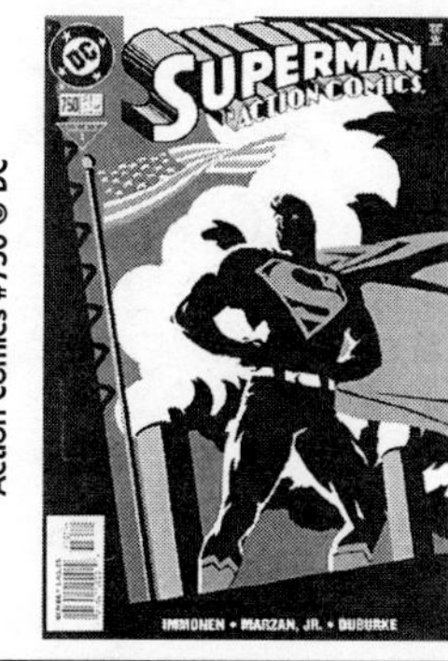

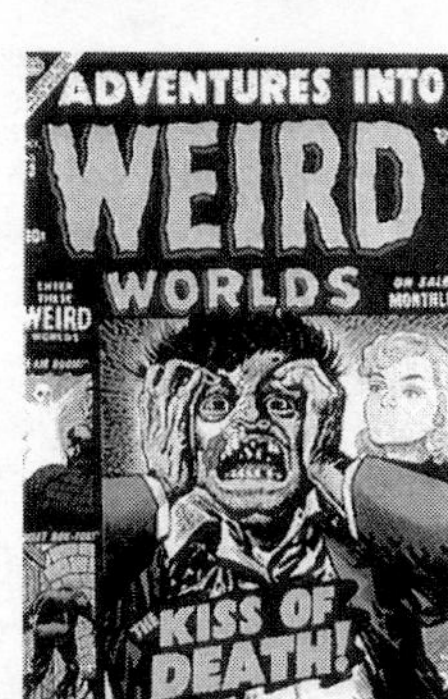

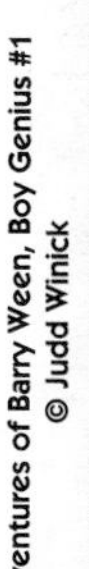
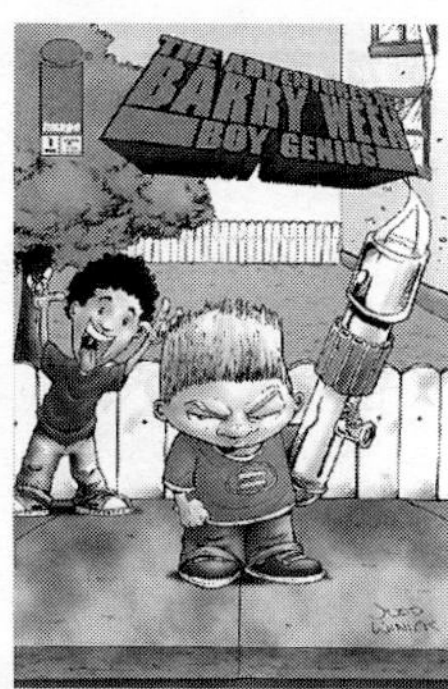

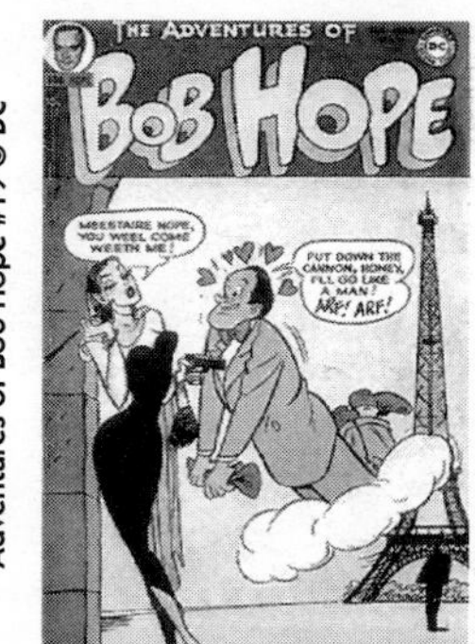

Adventures of Mighty Mouse #7 © STJ

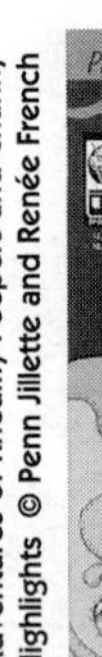

Adventures of Rheumy Peepers and Chunky Highlights © Penn Jillette and Renée French

Adventures of Superman #557 © DC

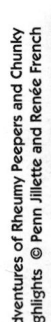

	GD2.0	FN6.0	NM9.4
102-Beatles app.; Neal Adams c/a	6.00	18.00	60.00
105-Superman x-over	3.80	11.40	38.00
106-111,113-116	2.50	7.50	20.00
112,117: 112-Flash x-over. 117-W. Woman x-over	3.60	10.80	36.00
118-124	2.00	6.00	16.00

NOTE: *Monster-c/s-90,93,96,98,101. Wack-A-Buy Camp-c/s-96,99,102,107,108.*

ADVENTURES OF JO-JOY, THE (See Jo-Joy)

ADVENTURES OF LASSIE, THE (See Lassie)

ADVENTURES OF LUTHER ARKWRIGHT, THE
Valkyrie Press/Dark Horse Comics: Oct, 1987 - No. 9, Jan, 1989 ($2.00, B&W) V2, #1, Mar, 1990 - V2#9, 1990 ($1.95, B&W)

	GD2.0	FN6.0	NM9.4
1-9: 1-Alan Moore intro., V2#1-9 (Dark Horse): r-1st series; new-c			4.00
TPB (1997, $14.95) r/#1-9 w/Michael Moorcock intro.			15.00

ADVENTURES OF MIGHTY MOUSE (Mighty Mouse Adventures No. 1)
St. John Publishing Co.: No. 2, Jan, 1952 - No. 18, May, 1955

	GD2.0	FN6.0	NM9.4
2	24.00	73.00	170.00
3-5	12.00	36.00	85.00
6-18	10.00	30.00	60.00

ADVENTURES OF MIGHTY MOUSE (2nd Series)
(Two No. 144's; formerly Paul Terry's Comics; No. 129-137 have nn's)
(Becomes Mighty Mouse No. 161 on)
St. John/Pines/Dell/Gold Key: No. 126, Aug, 1955 - No. 160, Oct, 1963

	GD2.0	FN6.0	NM9.4
126(8/55), 127(10/55), 128(11/55)-St. John	7.15	21.50	50.00
nn(129, 4/56)-144(8/59)-Pines	4.20	12.60	42.00
144(10-12/59)-155(7-9/62) Dell	3.25	10.00	35.00
156(10/62)-160(10/63) Gold Key	3.65	11.00	40.00

NOTE: *Early issues titled "Paul Terry's Adventures of ...."*

ADVENTURES OF MIGHTY MOUSE (Formerly Mighty Mouse)
Gold Key: No. 166, Mar, 1979 - No. 172, Jan, 1980

	GD2.0	FN6.0	NM9.4
166-172			4.00

ADVS. OF MR. FROG & MISS MOUSE (See Dell Junior Treasury No. 4)

ADVENTURES OF OZZIE & HARRIET, THE (See Ozzie & Harriet)

ADVENTURES OF PATORUZU
Green Publishing Co.: Aug, 1946 - Winter, 1946

	GD2.0	FN6.0	NM9.4
nn's-Contains Animal Crackers reprints	4.15	12.50	25.00

ADVENTURES OF PINKY LEE, THE (TV)
Atlas Comics: July, 1955 - No. 5, Dec, 1955

	GD2.0	FN6.0	NM9.4
1	26.00	78.00	185.00
2-5	16.00	48.00	110.00

ADVENTURES OF PIPSQUEAK, THE (Formerly Pat the Brat)
Archie Publications (Radio Comics): No. 34, Sept, 1959 - No. 39, July, 1960

	GD2.0	FN6.0	NM9.4
34	3.20	9.60	32.00
35-39	2.50	7.50	22.00

ADVENTURES OF QUAKE & QUISP, THE (See Quaker Oats "Plenty of Glutton")

ADVENTURES OF REX THE WONDER DOG, THE (Rex...No. 1)
National Periodical Publications: Jan-Feb, 1952 - No. 45, May-June, 1959; No. 46, Nov-Dec, 1959

	GD2.0	FN6.0	NM9.4
1-(Scarce)-Toth-c/a	103.00	309.00	875.00
2-(Scarce)-Toth-c/a	51.00	153.00	435.00
3-(Scarce)-Toth-a	39.00	117.00	335.00
4,5	31.00	93.00	250.00
6-10	23.00	69.00	185.00
11-Atom bomb-c/story	26.00	78.00	210.00
12-19: 19-Last precode (1-2/55)	14.00	42.00	110.00
20-46	10.00	30.00	80.00

NOTE: ***Infantino, Gil Kane** art in 5-19 (most)*

ADVENTURES OF RHEUMY PEEPERS AND CHUNKY HIGHLIGHTS, THE
Oni Press: Feb, 1999 ($2.95, B&W, one-shot)

	GD2.0	FN6.0	NM9.4
nn-Penn Jillette-s/Renée French-a			3.00

ADVENTURES OF ROBIN HOOD, THE (Formerly Robin Hood)
Magazine Enterprises (Sussex Publ. Co.): No. 7, 9/57 - No. 8, 11/57 (Based on Richard Greene TV Show)

	GD2.0	FN6.0	NM9.4
7,8-Richard Greene photo-c. 7-Powell-a	15.00	45.00	105.00

ADVENTURES OF ROBIN HOOD, THE
Gold Key: Mar, 1974 - No. 7, Jan, 1975 (Disney cartoon) (36 pgs.)

	GD2.0	FN6.0	NM9.4
1(90291-403)-Part-r of $1.50 editions	1.50	4.50	12.00
2-7: 1-7 are part-r	1.00	3.00	7.00

ADVENTURES OF SNAKE PLISSKEN
Marvel Comics: Jan, 1997 ($2.50, one-shot)

	GD2.0	FN6.0	NM9.4
1-Based on Escape From L.A. movie; Brereton-c			2.50

ADVENTURES OF SPIDER-MAN, THE (TV cartoon)
Marvel Comics: Apr, 1996 - No. 12, Mar, 1997 (99¢)

	GD2.0	FN6.0	NM9.4
1-12: Based on animated television show.			2.00

ADVENTURES OF SUPERBOY, THE (See Superboy, 2nd Series)

ADVENTURES OF SUPERMAN (Formerly Superman)
DC Comics: No. 424, Jan, 1987 - No. 499, Feb, 1993; No. 500, Early June, 1993 - Present

	GD2.0	FN6.0	NM9.4
424			3.00
425-462: 426-Legends x-over. 432-1st app. Jose Delgado who becomes Gangbuster in #434. 436-Byrne scripts begin. 436,437-Millennium x-over. 438-New Brainiac app. 440-Batman app. 449-Invasion			2.50
463-Superman/Flash race; cover swipe/Superman #199			5.00
464-Lobo-c & app. (pre-dates Lobo #1)			3.00
465-495: 467-Part 2 of Batman story. 473-Hal Jordan, Guy Gardner x-over. 477-Legion app. 491-Last $1.00-c. 480-($1.75, 52 pgs.). 495-Forever People-c/story; Darkseid app.			2.50
496,197: 496-Doomsday cameo. 497-Doomsday battle issue			3.00
496,497-2nd printings			2.00
498,499-Funeral for a Friend; Supergirl app.			2.50
498-2nd & 3rd printings			2.00
500-($2.95, 68 pgs.)-Collector's edition w/card			3.50
500-($2.50, 68 pgs.)-Regular edition w/different-c			2.50
500-Platinum edition	2.25	6.80	25.00
501-($1.95)-Collector's edition with die-cut-c			2.00
501-($1.50)-Regular edition w/mini-poster & diff.-c			2.00
502-516: 502-Supergirl-c/story. 508-Challengers of the Unknown app. 510-Bizarro-c/story. 516-(9/94)-Zero Hour			2.50
505-($2.50)-Holo-grafx foil-c edition			2.50
0,517-523: 0-(10/94). 517-(11/94)			2.00
524-549,551-571: 524-Begin $1.95-c. 527-Return of Alpha Centurion (Zero Hour) 533-Impulse c/app. 535-Luthor-c/app. 536-Brainiac app. 537-Parasite app. 540-Final Night x-over. 541 Superboy-c/app.;Lois and Clark honeymoon. 545-New powers. 546-New costume. 551-Cyborg app. 555-Red & Blue Supermen battle. 557-Millennium Giants x-over, 558-560: Superman Silver Age-style story; Krypto app. 561-Begin $1.99-c. 565-JLA app.			2.00
550-($3.50)-Double sized			3.50
#1,000,000 (11/98) Gene Ha-c; 853rd Century x-over			3.00
Annual 1 (1987, $1.25, 52 pgs.)-Starlin-c & scripts			4.00
Annual 2,3 (1990, 1991, $2.00, 68 pgs.): 2-Byrne-c/a(i); Legion '90 (Lobo) app. 3-Armageddon 2001 x-over			3.00
Annual 4-6 ('92-'94, $2.50, 68 pgs.): 4-Guy Gardner/Lobo-c/story; Eclipso storyline; Quesada-c(p). 5-Bloodlines storyline. 6-Elseworlds sty.			3.00
Annual 7,9('95, '97, $3.95)-7-Year One story. 9-Pulp Heroes sty			4.00
Annual 8 (1996, $2.95)-Legends of the Dead Earth story			3.00

NOTE: ***Erik Larsen** a-431.*

ADVENTURES OF THE DOVER BOYS
Archie Comics (Close-up): September, 1950 - No. 2, 1950 (No month given)

	GD2.0	FN6.0	NM9.4
1,2	8.35	25.00	50.00

ADVENTURES OF THE FLY (The Fly #1-6; Fly Man No. 32-39; See The Double Life of Private Strong, The Fly, Laugh Comics & Mighty Crusaders)
Archie Publications/Radio Comics: Aug, 1959 - No. 30, Oct, 1964; No. 31, May, 1965

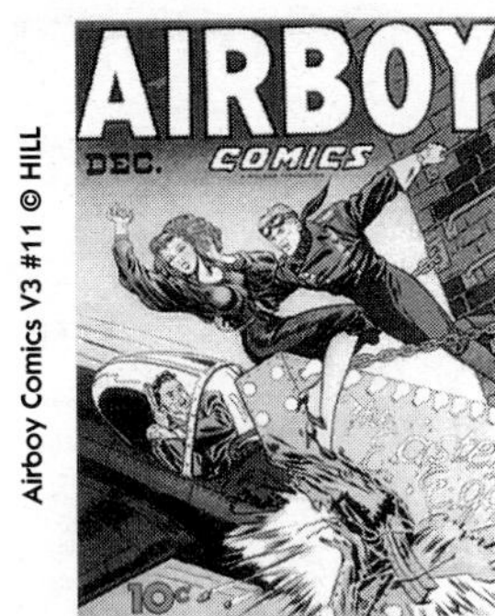

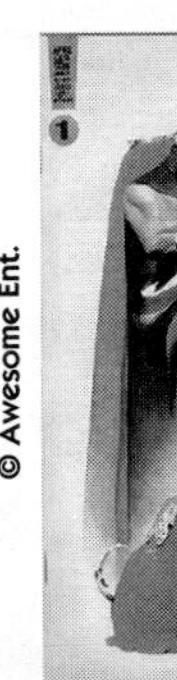
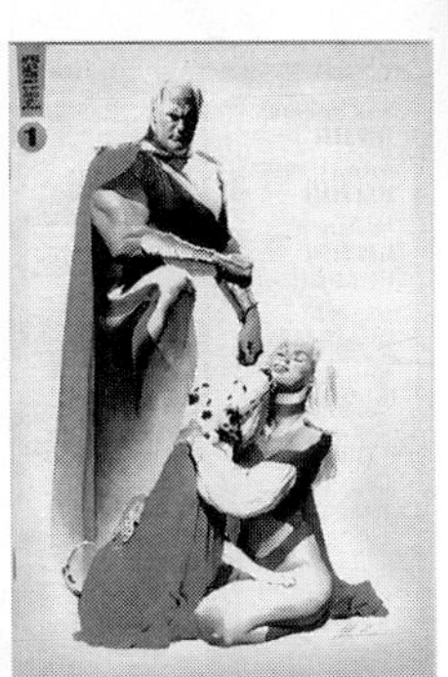

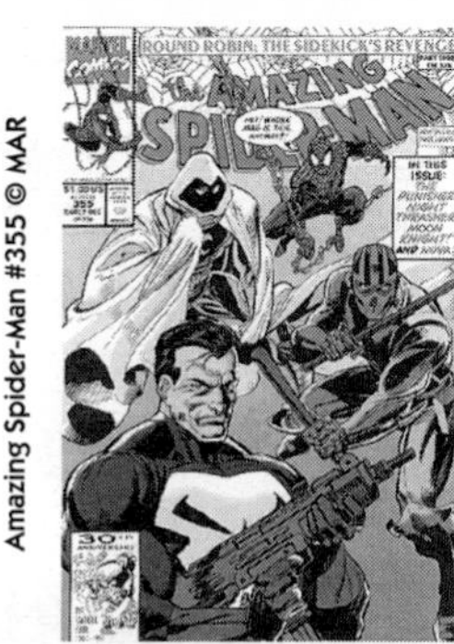

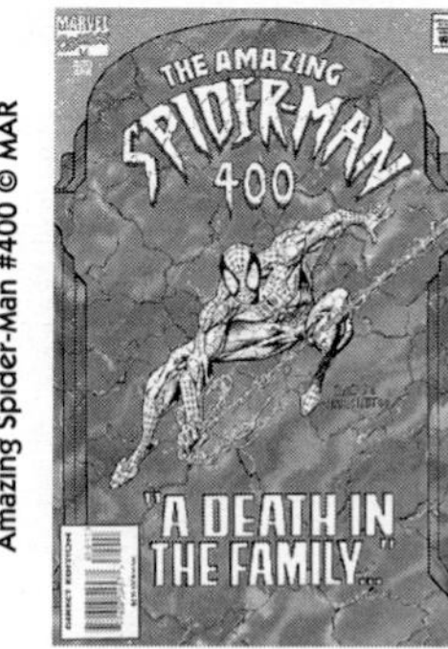

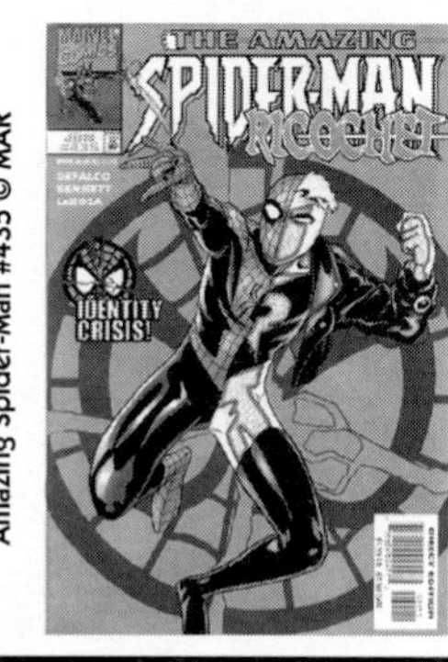

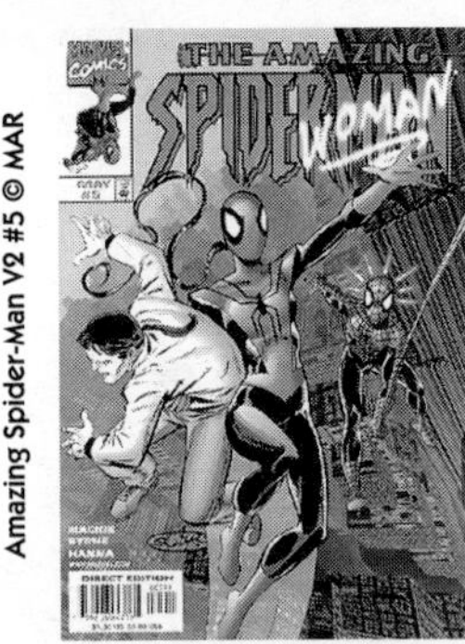

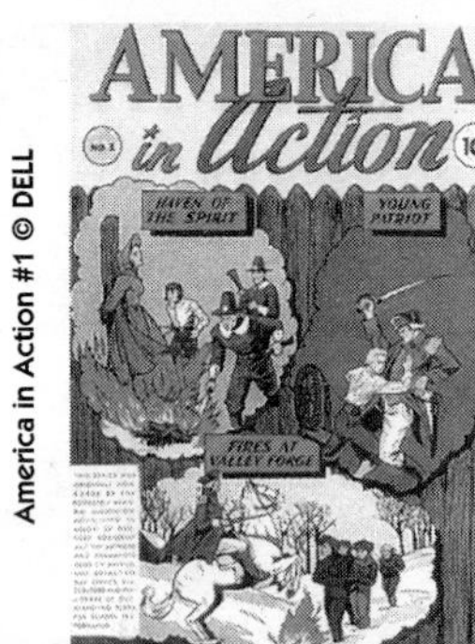

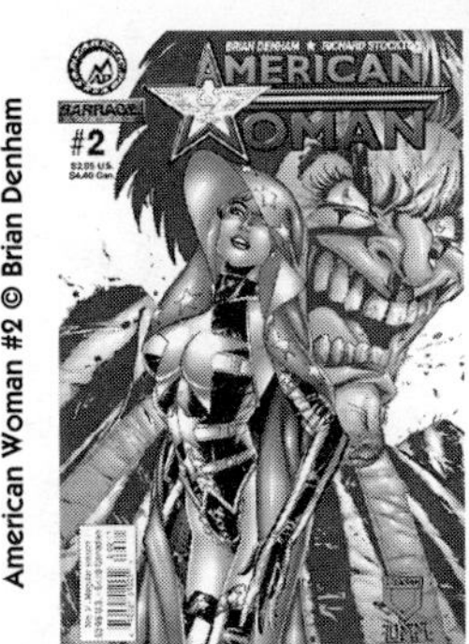

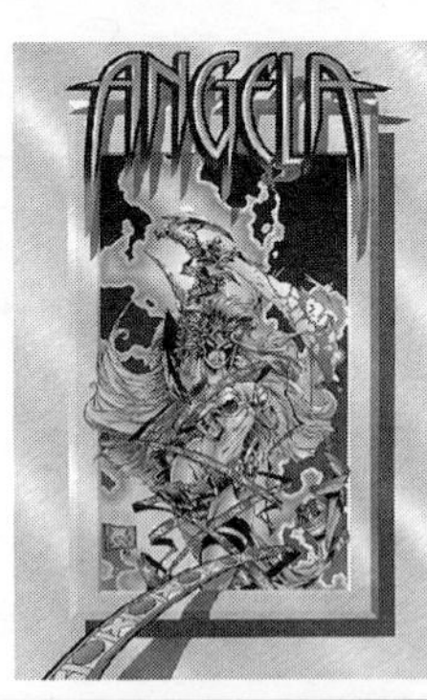

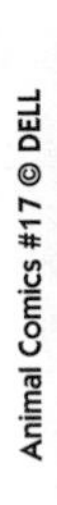

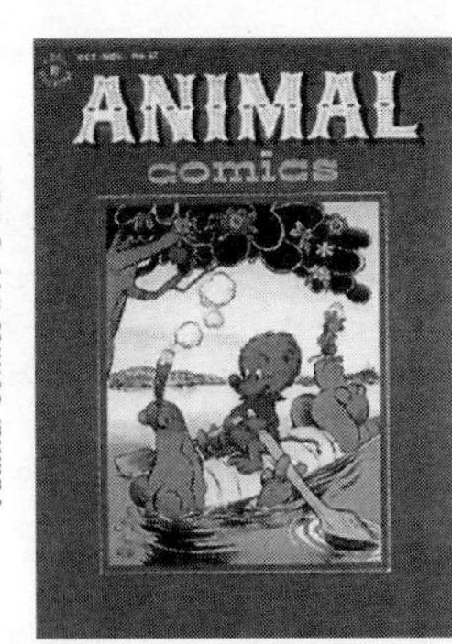

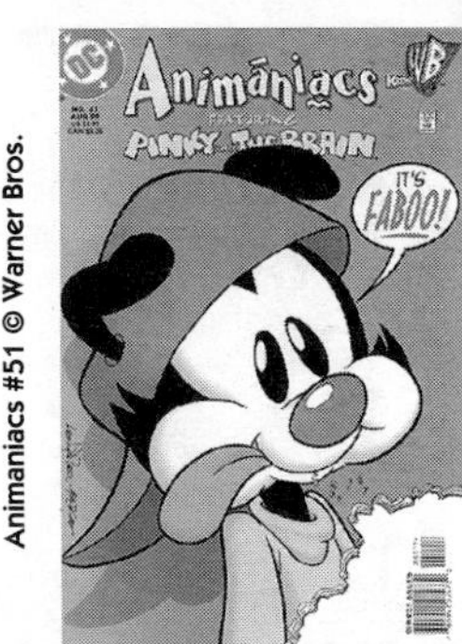

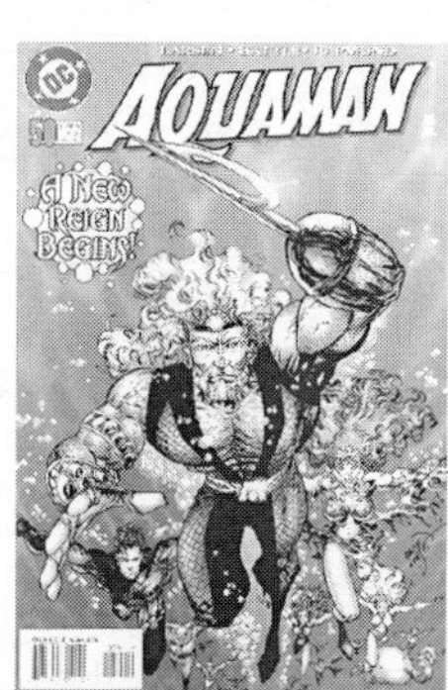
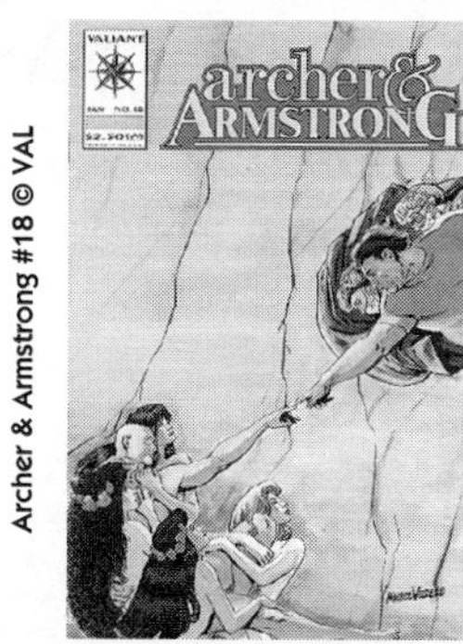
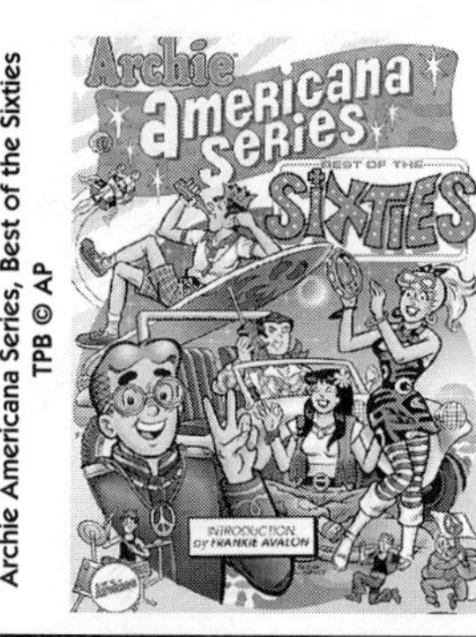

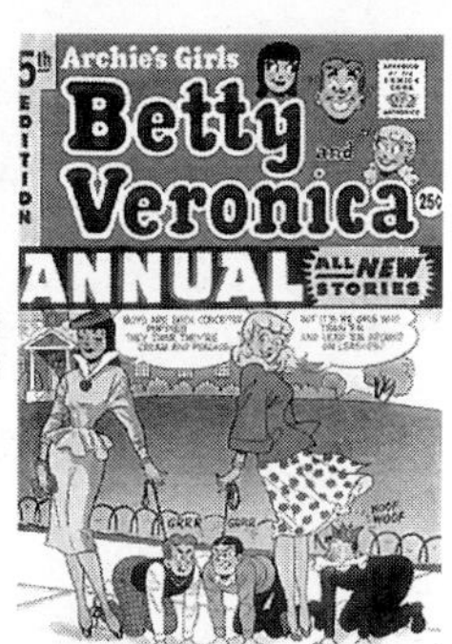

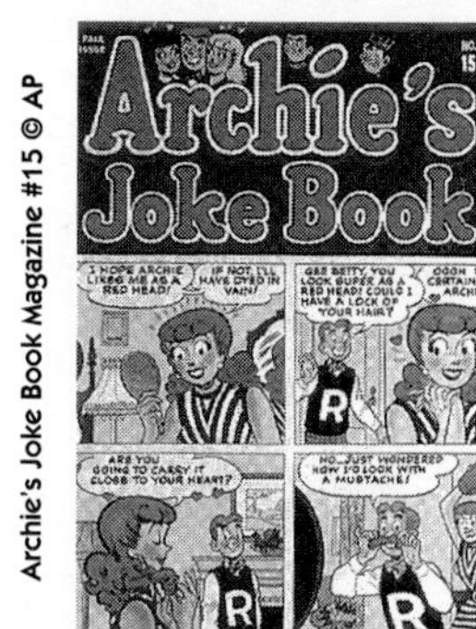

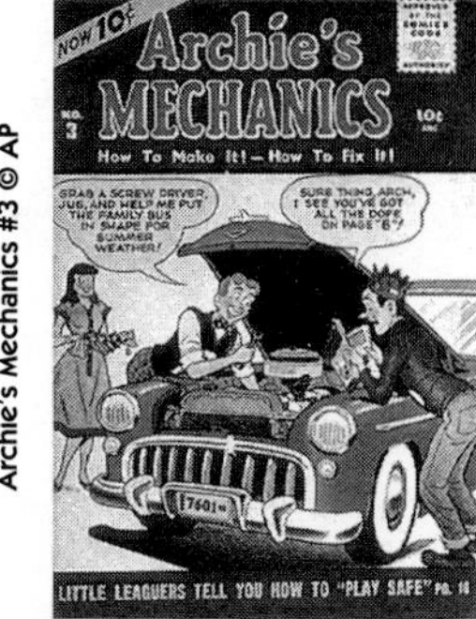

Attack #1 © YM

Authentic Police Cases #10 © STJ

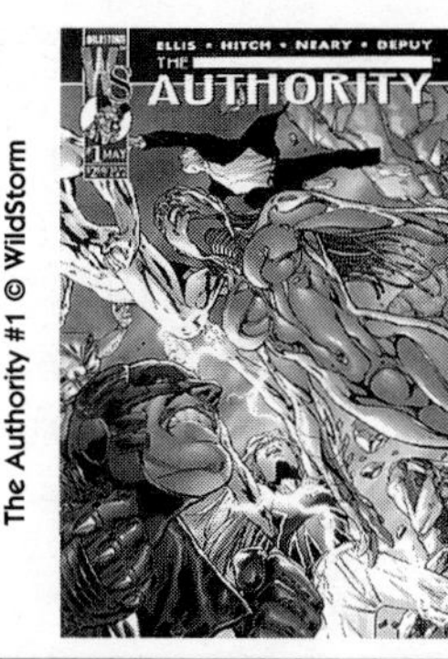

The Authority #1 © WildStorm

Capitol Stories/Charlton Comics: 3/53 - No. 54, 6/63; No. 1, 12/84; V2#10, 9/85 - No. 13, ?/86

	GD2.0	FN6.0	NM9.4
1-Origin & 1st app.; Al Fago-c/a in all?	31.00	94.00	220.00
2	11.50	34.00	80.00
3-10: 5-Timmy The Timid Ghost app.; see Zoo Funnies	10.00	30.00	65.00
11-13,16-25	5.35	16.00	32.00
14,15-Hoppy The Marvel Bunny app.	7.50	22.50	45.00
26-(68 pgs.)	10.00	30.00	70.00
27-40: 36,37-Atom The Cat app.	4.25	13.00	28.00
41-54	3.00	7.50	15.00
1 (1984)-Low print run			4.00
V2#10 (10/85) -13-Fago-r. #12(1/86)-Low print run			3.00

ATOMIC RABBIT (Atomic Bunny #12 on; see Giant Comics #3 & Wotalife)
Charlton Comics: Aug, 1955 - No. 11, Mar, 1958

	GD2.0	FN6.0	NM9.4
1-Origin & 1st app.; Al Fago-c/a in all?	27.00	81.00	190.00
2	11.00	33.00	75.00
3-10	7.50	22.50	45.00
11-(68 pgs.)	11.00	33.00	75.00

ATOMIC SPY CASES
Avon Periodicals: Mar-Apr, 1950 (Painted-c)

	GD2.0	FN6.0	NM9.4
1-No Wood-a; A-bomb blast panels; Fass-a	30.00	90.00	210.00

ATOMIC THUNDERBOLT, THE
Regor Company: Feb, 1946 (one-shot)

	GD2.0	FN6.0	NM9.4
1-Intro. Atomic Thunderbolt & Mr. Murdo	56.00	168.00	450.00

ATOMIC WAR!
Ace Periodicals (Junior Books): Nov, 1952 - No. 4, Apr, 1953

	GD2.0	FN6.0	NM9.4
1-Atomic bomb-c	85.00	255.00	680.00
2,3: 3-Atomic bomb-c	55.00	165.00	440.00
4-Used in **POP**, pg. 96 & illo.	55.00	165.00	440.00

ATOMIK ANGELS
Crusade Comics: May, 1996 - No. 4, Nov. 1996 ($2.50)

	GD2.0	FN6.0	NM9.4
1-4: 1-Freefall from Gen 13 app			3.00
1-Variant-c			4.00
Intrep-Edition (2/96, B&W, giveaway at launch party)-Previews Atomik Angels #1; includes Billy Tucci interview.			4.00

ATOM SPECIAL (See Atom & Justice League of America)
DC Comics: 1993/1995 ($2.50/$2.95)(68pgs.)

	GD2.0	FN6.0	NM9.4
1,2: 1-Dillon-c/a. 2-McDonnell-a/Bolland-c/Peyer-s			3.00

ATOM THE CAT (Formerly Tom Cat; see Giant Comics #3)
Charlton Comics: No. 9, Oct, 1957 - No. 17, Aug, 1959

	GD2.0	FN6.0	NM9.4
9	9.15	27.00	55.00
10,13-17	5.00	15.00	30.00
11,12: 11(64 pgs)-Atomic Mouse app. 12(100 pgs.)	10.00	30.00	70.00

ATTACK
Youthful Mag./Trojan No. 5 on: May, 1952 - No. 4, Nov, 1952; No. 5, Jan, 1953 - No. 5, Sept, 1953

	GD2.0	FN6.0	NM9.4
1-(1st series)-Extreme violence	27.00	81.00	190.00
2,3-Both Harrison-c/a; bondage, whipping	13.00	39.00	90.00
4-Krenkel-a (7 pgs.); Harrison-a (becomes Atomic Attack #5 on)	13.50	41.00	95.00
5-(#1, Trojan, 2nd series)	11.00	33.00	75.00
6-8 (#2-4), 5	8.35	25.00	50.00

ATTACK
Charlton Comics: No. 54, 1958 - No. 60, Nov, 1959

	GD2.0	FN6.0	NM9.4
54 (25¢, 100 pgs.)	10.00	30.00	65.00
55-60	4.00	11.00	22.00

ATTACK!
Charlton Comics: 1962 - No. 15, 3/75; No. 16, 8/79 - No. 48, 10/84

	GD2.0	FN6.0	NM9.4
nn(#1)-('62) Special Edition	3.20	9.60	32.00
2('63), 3(Fall, '64)	2.50	7.50	22.00
V4#3(10/66), 4(10/67)-(Formerly Special War Series #2; becomes Attack At Sea V4#5)	2.00	6.00	16.00
1(9/71)	2.00	6.00	16.00
2-5: 4-American Eagle app.	1.50	4.50	12.00
6-15(3/75):	1.10	3.30	9.00
16(8/79) - 40			3.00
41-47 Low print run			4.00
48(10/84)-Wood-r; S&K-c			5.00
Modern Comics 13('78)-r			3.00

NOTE: ***Sutton*** *a-9,10,13.*

ATTACK!
Spire Christian Comics (Fleming H. Revell Co.): 1975 (39¢/49¢, 36 pgs.)

	GD2.0	FN6.0	NM9.4
nn			5.00

ATTACK AT SEA (Formerly Attack!, 1967)
Charlton Comics: V4#5, Oct, 1968

	GD2.0	FN6.0	NM9.4
V4#5	2.00	6.00	16.00

ATTACK ON PLANET MARS (See Strange Worlds #18)
Avon Periodicals: 1951

	GD2.0	FN6.0	NM9.4
nn-Infantino, Fawcette, Kubert & Wood-a; adaptation of Tarrano the Conqueror by Ray Cummings	70.00	210.00	560.00

ATTITUDE LAD
Slave Labor Graphics: Apr, 1994 - No. 3, Nov, 1994 ($2.95, B&W)

	GD2.0	FN6.0	NM9.4
1-3			3.00

AUDREY & MELVIN (Formerly Little...)(See Little Audrey & Melvin)
Harvey Publications: No. 62, Sept, 1974

	GD2.0	FN6.0	NM9.4
62	1.00	3.00	8.00

AUGIE DOGGIE (TV) (See Hanna-Barbera Band Wagon, Quick-Draw McGraw, Spotlight #2, Top Cat & Whitman Comic Books)
Gold Key: October, 1963 (12¢)

	GD2.0	FN6.0	NM9.4
1-Hanna-Barbera character	17.00	50.00	185.00

AUTHENTIC POLICE CASES
St. John Publishing Co.: 2/48 - No. 6, 11/48; No. 7, 5/50 - No. 38, 3/55

	GD2.0	FN6.0	NM9.4
1-Hale the Magician by Tuska begins	39.00	116.00	270.00
2-Lady Satan, Johnny Rebel app.	24.00	73.00	170.00
3-Veiled Avenger app.; blood drainage story plus 2 Lucky Coyne stories; used in **SOTI**, illo. from Red Seal #16	41.00	124.00	330.00
4,5: 4-Masked Black Jack app. 5-Late 1930s Jack Cole-a(r); transvestism story	24.00	73.00	170.00
6-Matt Baker-c; used in **SOTI**, illo- "An invitation to learning", r-in Fugitives From Justice #3; Jack Cole-a; also used by the N.Y. Legis. Comm.	44.00	132.00	350.00
7,8,10-14: 7-Jack Cole-a; Matt Baker-a begins #8, ends #?; Vic Flint in #10-14. 10-12-Baker-a(2 each)	20.00	60.00	140.00
9-No Vic Flint	16.00	47.00	110.00
15-Drug-c/story; Vic Flint app.; Baker-c	20.00	60.00	140.00
16,18,20,21,23: Baker-a(i)	12.00	36.00	85.00
17,19,22-Baker-c	13.50	41.00	95.00
24-28 (All 100 pgs.): 26-Transvestism	23.00	69.00	160.00
29-32	7.50	22.50	45.00
33-38: 33-Transvestism; Baker-c. 34-Baker-c; r/#95. 35-Baker-c/a(2); r/#10 36-r/#11; Vic Flint strip-r; Baker-c/a(2) unsigned. 37-Baker-c; r/#17. 38-Baker-c/a; r/#18	11.00	33.00	75.00

NOTE: ***Matt Baker*** *c-6-16, 17, 19, 22, 27, 29, 31-38; a-13, 16. Bondage c-1, 3.*

AUTHORITY, THE
DC Comics (WildStorm): May, 1999 - Present ($2.50)

	GD2.0	FN6.0	NM9.4
1-5: 1-Wraparound-c; Warren Ellis-s/Bryan Hitch and Paul Neary-a			3.00

AUTOMATON
Image Comics (Flypaper Press): Sept, 1998 - No. 3, 1998 ($2.95, lim. series)

	GD2.0	FN6.0	NM9.4
1-3-R.A. Jones-s/Peter Vale-a			3.00

AUTUMN

Avengelyne V2 #7 © Rob Liefeld

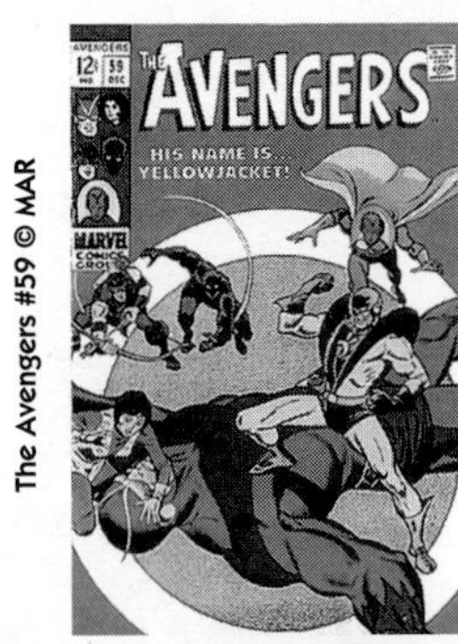

The Avengers #59 © MAR

The Avengers #178 © MAR

Caliber Comics: 1995 - No. 3, 1995 ($2.95, B&W)

	GD2.0	FN6.0	NM9.4
1-3			3.00

AUTUMN ADVENTURES (Walt Disney's...)
Disney Comics: Autumn, 1990; No. 2, Autumn, 1991 ($2.95, 68 pgs.)

	GD2.0	FN6.0	NM9.4
1-Donald Duck-r(2) by Barks, Pluto-r, & new-a			3.50
2-D. Duck-r by Barks; new Super Goof story			3.50

AVATAR
DC Comics: Feb, 1991 - No. 3, Apr, 1991 ($5.95, limited series, 100 pgs.)

	GD2.0	FN6.0	NM9.4
1-3: Based on TSR's Forgotten Realms		2.40	6.00

AVENGEBLADE
Maximum Press: July, 1996 - No. 2, Aug, 1996 ($2.99, limited series)

	GD2.0	FN6.0	NM9.4
1,2: Bad Girls parody			3.00

AVENGELYNE
Maximum Press: May, 1995 - No. 3, July, 1995 ($2.50/$3.50, limited series)

	GD2.0	FN6.0	NM9.4
1/2	1.85	5.50	15.00
1/2 Platinum			20.00
1-Newstand ($2.50)-Photo-c; poster insert	1.00	3.00	8.00
1-Direct Market ($3.50)-Chromium-c; poster	1.10	3.30	9.00
1-Glossy edition	3.00	9.00	30.00
1-Gold			15.00
2-3: 2-Polybagged w/card			4.00
3-Variant-c; Deodato pin-up		2.40	6.00
...Swimsuit (8/95, $2.95)-Pin-ups/photos. 3-Variant-c exist (2 photo, 1 Liefeld-a)			5.00
...Swimsuit (1/96, $3.50, 2nd printing)-photo-c			5.00
Trade paperback (12/95, $9.95)			10.00

AVENGELYNE
Maximum Press: V2#1, Apr, 1996 - No. 14, Apr, 1997 ($2.95/$2.50)

	GD2.0	FN6.0	NM9.4
V2#1-Four covers exist (2 photo-c).			5.00
V2#2-Three covers exist (1 photo-c); flip book w/Darkchylde	2.25	6.75	18.00
V2#0, 3-14: 0-(10/96).3-Flip book w/Priest preview. 4-Cybrid app; w/Darkchylde/Avengelyne poster. 5-Flip book w/Blindside. 6-Divinity-c/app.			4.00
...Bible (10/96, $3.50)			3.50

AVENGELYNE (Volume 3)
Awesome Comics: Mar, 1999 - Present ($2.50)

	GD2.0	FN6.0	NM9.4
1-Fraga & Liefeld-a			2.50

AVENGELYNE: ARMAGEDDON
Maximum Press: Dec, 1996 - No. 3, Feb, 1997 ($2.99, limited series)

	GD2.0	FN6.0	NM9.4
1-3-Scott Clark-a(p)			4.00

AVENGELYNE: DEADLY SINS
Maximum Press: Feb, 1996 - No. 2, Mar, 1996 ($2.95, limited series)

	GD2.0	FN6.0	NM9.4
1,2: 1-Two-c exist (1 photo, 1 Liefeld-a). 2-Liefeld-c; Pop Mhan-a(p).			3.00

AVENGELYNE/GLORY
Maximum Press: Sept, 1995 ($3.95, one-shot)

	GD2.0	FN6.0	NM9.4
1-Chromium-c			5.00
1-Variant-c		2.40	6.00

AVENGELYNE/GLORY: GODYSSEY, THE (See Glory/...)
Maximum Press: Sept, 1996 ($2.99, one-shot)

	GD2.0	FN6.0	NM9.4
1-Two covers (1 photo)			3.00

AVENGELYNE/GLORY SWIMSUIT SPECIAL
Maximum Press: June, 1996 ($2.95)

	GD2.0	FN6.0	NM9.4
1-Pin-ups & photos of Avengelyne and Glory; photo-c (variant illos-c. also exists)			4.00

AVENGELYNE/POWER
Maximum Press: Nov, 1995 - No.3, Jan, 1996 ($2.95, limited series)

	GD2.0	FN6.0	NM9.4
1-3: 1,2-Liefeld-c. 3-Three variant-c. exist (1 photo-c)			3.00
1-Variant-c			3.50

AVENGELYNE • PROPHET
Maximum Press: May, 1996; No. 2, Feb. 1997 ($2.95, unfinished lim. series)

	GD2.0	FN6.0	NM9.4
1,2-Liefeld-c/a(p)			3.00

AVENGELYNE/ WARRIOR NUN AREALA (See Warrior Nun/...)
Maximum Press: Nov, 1996 ($2.99, one-shot)

	GD2.0	FN6.0	NM9.4
1			4.00

AVENGER, THE (See A-1 Comics)
Magazine Enterprises: Feb-Mar, 1955 - No. 4, Aug-Sept, 1955

	GD2.0	FN6.0	NM9.4
1(A-1 #129)-Origin	39.00	116.00	270.00
2(A-1 #131), 3(A-1 #133) Robot-c, 4(A-1 #138)	25.00	75.00	175.00
IW Reprint #9('64)-Reprints #1 (new cover)	2.50	7.50	24.00

NOTE: ***Powell*** *a-2-4; c-1-4.*

AVENGERS, THE (TV)(Also see Steed and Mrs. Peel)
Gold Key: Nov, 1968 ("John Steed & Emma Peel" cover title) (15¢)

	GD2.0	FN6.0	NM9.4
1-Photo-c	22.00	66.00	240.00

AVENGERS, THE (See Essential..., Giant-Size..., Kree/Skrull War Starring..., Marvel Graphic Novel #27, Marvel Super Action, Marvel Super Heroes('66), Marvel Treasury Ed., Marvel Triple Action, Solo Avengers, Tales Of Suspense #49, West Coast Avengers & X-Men Vs....)

AVENGERS, THE (The Mighty Avengers on cover only #63-69)
Marvel Comics Group: Sept, 1963 - No. 402, Sept, 1996

	GD2.0	FN6.0	VF8.0	NM9.4
1-Origin & 1st app. The Avengers (Thor, Iron Man, Hulk, Ant-Man, Wasp); Loki app.	171.00	514.00	1111.00	2400.00

	GD2.0	FN6.0	NM9.4
2-Hulk leaves Avengers	52.00	156.00	620.00
3-1st Sub-Mariner x-over (outside the F.F.); Hulk & Sub-Mariner team-up & battle Avengers; Spider-Man cameo (1/64)	35.00	105.00	385.00
4-Revival of Captain America who joins the Avengers; 1st Silver Age app. of Captain America & Bucky (3/64)	125.00	375.00	1500.00
4-Reprint from the Golden Record Comic set	7.50	22.50	75.00
With Record (1966)	11.00	33.00	110.00
5-Hulk app.	22.50	68.00	225.00
6-8: 6-Intro/1st app. original Zemo & his Masters of Evil. 8-Intro Kang	18.00	54.00	180.00
9-Intro Wonder Man who dies in same story	18.50	55.00	185.00
10-Intro/1st app. Immortus; early Hercules app. (11/64)	15.50	47.00	155.00
11-Spider-Man-c & x-over (12/64)	18.50	55.00	185.00
12-15: 15-Death of original Zemo	11.50	34.00	115.00
16-New Avengers line-up (Hawkeye, Quicksilver, Scarlet Witch join; Thor, Iron Man, Giant-Man, Wasp leave)	12.50	38.00	125.00
17-19: 19-Intro/1st app. Swordsman; origin Hawkeye (8/65)	8.50	25.50	85.00
20-22: Wood inks	5.50	16.50	55.00
23-30: 23-Romita Sr. inks (1st Silver Age Marvel work). 25-Dr. Doom-c/story. 28-Giant-Man becomes Goliath (5/66)	4.00	12.00	40.00
31-40	2.80	8.40	28.00
41-47,49-52,54-56: 43,44-1st app. Red Guardian. 46-Ant-Man returns (re-intro, 11/67) 47-Magneto-c/story. 52-Black Panther joins; 1st app. The Grim Reaper. 54-1st app. new Masters of Evil. 56-Zemo app; story explains how Capt. America became imprisoned in ice during WWII, only to be rescued in Avengers #4	2.50	7.50	24.00
48-Origin/1st app. new Black Knight (1/68)	2.50	7.50	25.00
53-X-Men app.	3.50	10.50	35.00
57-1st app. S.A. Vision (10/68)	7.00	21.00	70.00
58-Origin The Vision	4.80	14.40	48.00
59-65: 59-Intro. Yellowjacket. 60-Wasp & Yellowjacket wed. 63-Goliath becomes Yellowjacket; Hawkeye becomes the new Goliath. 65-Last 12¢ issue	2.50	7.50	22.00
66,67-B. Smith-a	2.60	7.80	26.00
68-70: 70-Nighthawk on cover	1.85	5.50	15.00
71-1st app. The Invaders (12/69); 1st app. Nighthawk; Black Knight joins	3.20	9.60	32.00
72-79,81,82,84-86,88-91: 82-Daredevil app. 88-Written by Harlan Ellison			

The Avengers #254 © MAR

The Avengers #1 1/2 © MAR

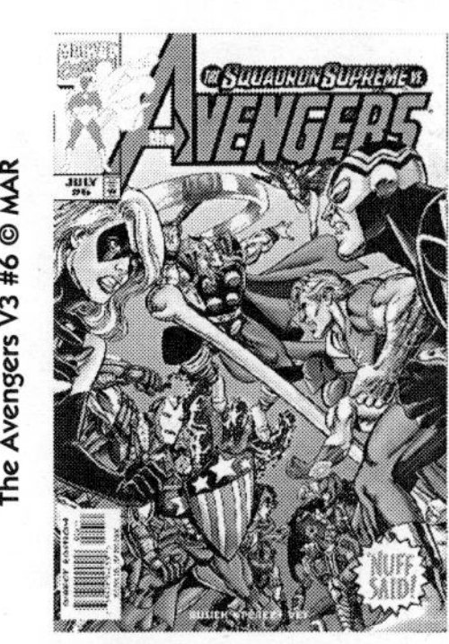

The Avengers V3 #6 © MAR

1.75 5.25 14.00
80-Intro. Red Wolf (9/70) 2.50 7.50 22.00
83-Intro. The Liberators (Wasp, Valkyrie, Scarlet Witch, Medusa & the Black Widow) 2.50 7.50 24.00
87-Origin The Black Panther 2.80 8.40 28.00
92-Last 15¢ issue; Neal Adams-c 2.25 6.75 18.00
93-(52 pgs.)-Neal Adams-c/a 5.00 15.00 55.00
94-96-Neal Adams-c/a 3.50 10.50 35.00
97-G.A. Capt. America, Sub-Mariner, Human Torch, Patriot, Vision, Blazing Skull, Fin, Angel, & new Capt. Marvel x-over 2.25 6.75 18.00
98,99: 98-Goliath becomes Hawkeye; Smith c/a(i). 99-Smith-c, Smith/Sutton-a 2.50 7.50 22.00
100-(6/72)-Smith-c/a; featuring everyone who was an Avenger 6.25 18.50 70.00
101-106,108,109: 101-Harlan Ellison scripts 1.50 4.50 12.00
107-Starlin-a(p) 1.85 5.50 15.00
110,111-X-Men app. 2.50 7.50 22.00
112-1st app. Mantis 2.00 6.00 16.00
113-115,119-124,126-130: 123-Origin Mantis 1.25 3.75 10.00
116-118-Defenders/Silver Surfer app. 2.00 6.00 16.00
125-Thanos-c & brief app. 2.00 6.00 16.00
131-133,136-140: 136-Ploog-r/Amazing Advs. #12 1.00 3.00 8.00
134,135-True origin Vision 1.25 3.75 10.00
141-143,145,152-163 2.40 6.00
144-Origin & 1st app. Hellcat 1.10 3.30 9.00
146-149-(Reg.25¢ editions)(4-7/76) 2.40 6.00
146-149-(30¢-c variants, limited distribution) 1.60 4.80 16.00
150-Kirby-a(r); new line-up: Capt. America, Scarlet Witch, Iron Man, Wasp, Yellowjacket, Vision & The Beast 1.00 3.00 8.00
150-(30¢-c variant, limited distribution) 1.80 5.40 18.00
151-Wonder Man returns w/new costume 1.00 3.00 8.00
160-164-(35¢-c variants, limited dist.)(6-10/77) 2.50 7.50 24.00
164-166: Byrne-a 1.00 2.80 7.00
167-180: 168-Guardians of the Galaxy app. 174-Thanos cameo. 176-Starhawk app. 3.50
181-191-Byrne-a: 181-New line-up: Capt. America, Scarlet Witch, Iron Man, Wasp, Vision, Beast & The Falcon. 183-Ms. Marvel joins. 185-Origin Quicksilver & Scarlet Witch 5.00
192-199,201-213,215-262: 195-1st Taskmaster. 211-New line-up: Capt. America, Iron Man, Tigra, Thor, Wasp & Yellowjacket. 213-Yellowjacket leaves. 215,216-Silver Surfer app. 216-Tigra leaves. 217-Yellowjacket & Wasp return. 221-Hawkeye & She-Hulk join. 227-Capt. Marvel (female) joins; origins of Ant-Man, Wasp, Giant-Man, Goliath, Yellowjacket, & Avengers. 230-Yellowjacket quits. 231-Iron Man leaves. 232-Starfox (Eros) joins. 234-Origin Quicksilver, Scarlet Witch. 236-New logo. 238-Origin Blackout. 239-Avengers app. on David Letterman show. 240-Spider-Woman revived. 250-($1.00, 52 pgs.) 2.50
200-(10/80, 52 pgs.)-Ms. Marvel leaves. 3.50
214-Ghost Rider-c/story 5.00
263-1st app. X-Factor (1/86)(story continues in Fantastic Four #286) 5.00
264-299: 272-Alpha Flight app. 291-$1.00 issues begin. 297-Black Knight, She-Hulk & Thor resign. 298-Inferno tie-in 2.50
300 (2/89, $1.75, 68 pgs.)-Thor joins; Simonson-a 2.50
301-325,327,329-343: 302-Re-intro Quasar. 305-Byrne scripts begin. 314-318-Spider-Man x-over. 320-324-Alpha Flight app. (320-cameo). 327-2nd app. Rage. 341,342-New Warriors app. 343-Last $1.00-c 2.00
326-1st app. Rage (11/90) 3.00
328,344-349,351-359,361,362,364,365,367: 328-Origin Rage. 365-Contains coupon for Hunt for Magneto contest 2.00
350-($2.50, 68 pgs.)-Double gatefold-c showing-c to #1; r/#53 w/cover in flip book format; vs. The Starjammers 2.50
360-($2.95, 52 pgs.)-Embossed all-foil-c; 30th ann. 3.50
363-($2.95, 52 pgs.)-All silver foil-c 3.00
366-($3.95, 68 pgs.)-Embossed all gold foil-c 4.00
368,370-374,376-399: 368-Bloodties part 1; Avengers/X-Men x-over. 374-bound-in trading card sheet. 380-Deodato-a. 390,391-"The Crossing." 395-Death of "old" Tony Stark; wraparound-c. 2.00
369-($2.95)-Foil embossed-c; Bloodties part 5 3.00
375-($2.00, 52 pgs.)-Regular ed.; Thunderstrike returns; leads into Malibu Comics' Black September. 2.00
375-($2.50, 52 pgs.)-Collector's ed. w/bound-in poster; leads into Malibu Comics' Black September. 2.50
400-402: Waid-s; 402-Deodato breakdowns; cont'd in X-Men #56 & Onslaught: Marvel Universe. 4.00
Special 1 (9/67, 25¢, 68 pgs.)-New-a; original & new Avengers team-up 6.50 19.50 65.00
Special 2 (9/68, 25¢, 68 pgs.)-New-a; original vs. new Avengers 3.50 10.50 35.00
Special 3 (9/69, 25¢, 68 pgs.)-r/Avengers #4 plus 3 Capt. America stories by Kirby (art); origin Red Skull 2.50 7.50 24.00
Special 4 (1/71, 25¢, 68 pgs.)-Kirby-r/Avengers #5,6 1.85 5.50 15.00
Special 5 (1/72)-Spider-Man x-over 1.85 5.50 15.00
Annual 6 (11/76) 1.00 3.00 8.00
Annual 7 (11/77)-Starlin-c/a; Warlock dies; Thanos app. 2.25 6.75 18.00
Annual 8 (1978)-Dr. Strange, Ms. Marvel app. 2.40 6.00
Annual 9 (1979)-Newton-a(p) 5.00
Annual 10 (1981)-Golden-p; X-Men cameo; 1st app. Rogue & Madelyne Pryor 2.50 7.50 20.00
Annual 11-18: 11(1982)-Vs. The Defenders. 12('83), 13('84), 14('85),15('86), 16('87), 17 ('88)-Evolutionary War x-over, 18('89)-Atlantis Attacks 3.50
Annual 19-23 (90-'94, 68 pgs.). 22-Bagged/card 3.00
Marvel Double Feature...Avengers/Giant-Man #379 ($2.50, 52 pgs.)-Same as Avengers #379 w/Giant-Man flip book 2.50
The Yesterday Quest ($6.95)-r/#181,182,185-187 1.00 2.80 7.00
Under Siege ('98, $16.95, TPB) r/#270,271,273-277 17.00
...: Visionaries ('99, $16.95)-r/early George Perez art 17.00

NOTE: ***Austin*** *c(i)-157, 167, 168, 170-177, 181, 183-188, 198-201, Annual 8.* ***John Buscema*** *a-41-44p, 46p, 47p, 49, 50, 51-62p, 74-77, 79-85, 87-91, 97, 105p, 121p, 124p,125p, 152, 153p, 255-279p, 281-302p; c-41-66, 68-71, 73-91, 97-99, 178, 256-259p, 261-279p, 281-302p.* ***Byrne*** *a-164-166p, 181-191p, 233p, Annual 13i, 14p; c-186-190p, 233p, 260, 305p; scripts-305-312.* ***Colan*** *a(p)-63-65, 111, 206-208, 210, 211; c(p)-65, 206-208, 210, 211.* ***Ditko*** *a-Annual 13.* ***Guice*** *a-Annual 12p.* ***Don Heck*** *a-9-15, 17-40, 157.* ***Kane*** *c-37p, 159p.* ***Kane/Everett*** *c-97.* ***Kirby*** *a-1-8p, Special 3r, 4r(p); c-1-30, 148, 151-158; layouts-14-16.* ***Ron Lim*** *c(p)-335-341.* ***Miller*** *c-193p.* ***Mooney*** *a-86i, 179p, 180p.* ***Nebres*** *a-178i; c-179i.* ***Newton*** *a-204p, Annual 9p.* ***Perez*** *a(p)-141, 143, 144, 148, 150, 154, 155, 160, 161, 162, 167,168, 170, 171, 194-196, 198-202, Annual 6, 8; c(p)-160-162, 164-166, 170-174, 181,183-185, 191, 192, 194-201, 379-382, Annual 8.* ***Starlin*** *c-121, 135.* ***Staton*** *a-127-134i.* ***Tuska*** *a-47i,48i, 51i, 53i, 54i, 106p, 107p, 135p, 137-140p, 163p. Guardians of the Galaxy app. in #167, 168, 170, 173, 175, 181.*

AVENGERS, THE (Volume Two)
Marvel Comics: V2#1, Nov, 1996 - No. 13, Nov, 1997 ($2.95/$1.95/$1.99)
(Produced by Extreme Studios)

1-($2.95)-Heroes Reborn begins; intro new team (Captain America, Swordsman, Scarlet Witch, Vision, Thor, Hellcat & Hawkeye); 1st app. Avengers Island; Loki & Enchantress app.; Rob Liefeld-p & plot; Chap Yaep-p; Jim Valentino scripts; variant-c exists 4.00
1-($1.95)-Variant-c 5.00
2-12: 2,3-Jeph Loeb scripts begin, Kang app. 4-Hulk-c/app. 5-Thor/Hulk battle; 2 covers. 10,11,13-"World War 3"-pt. 2, x-over w/Image characters. 12-($2.99) "Heroes Reunited"-pt. 2 4.00

AVENGERS, THE (Volume Three)
Marvel Comics: Feb, 1998 - Present ($2.99/$1.99)

1-($2.99, 48 pgs.) Busiek-s/Perez-a/wraparound-c; Avengers reassemble after Heroes Return 5.00
1-Variant Heroes Return cover 1.00 2.80 7.00
1-Rough Cut-Features original script and pencil pages 3.00
2-($1.99)Perez-c, 2-Lago painted-c 3.00
3,4: 3-Wonder Man-c/app. 4-Final roster chosen; Perez poster 2.50
5-11: 5,6-Squadron Supreme-c/app. 8-Triathlon-c/app. 2.00
12-($2.99) Thunderbolts app. 3.00
13-21: 13-New Warriors app. 16-18-Ordway-s/a. 19-Ultron returns 2.00
#1 1/2 (12/99, $2.50) Timm-c/a/Stern-s; 1963-style issue 2.50
.../ Squadron Supreme '98 Annual ($2.99) 3.00
1999 Annual (7/99, $3.50) Manco-a 3.50

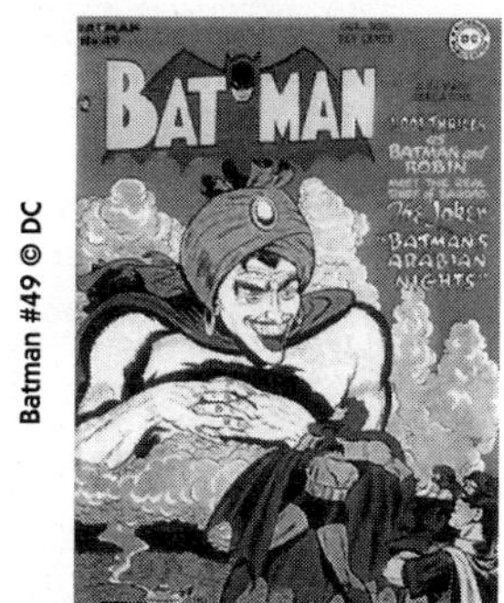

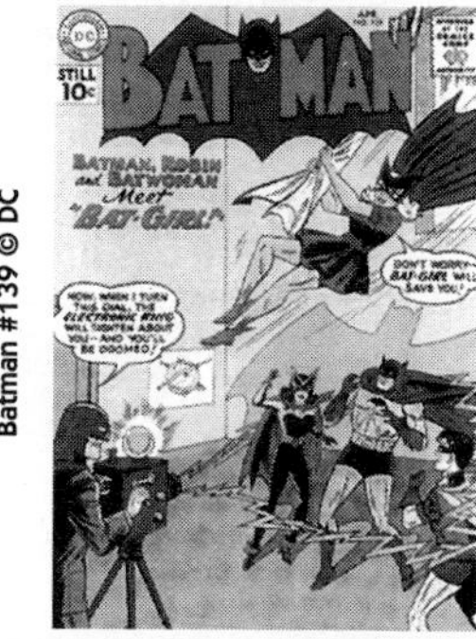

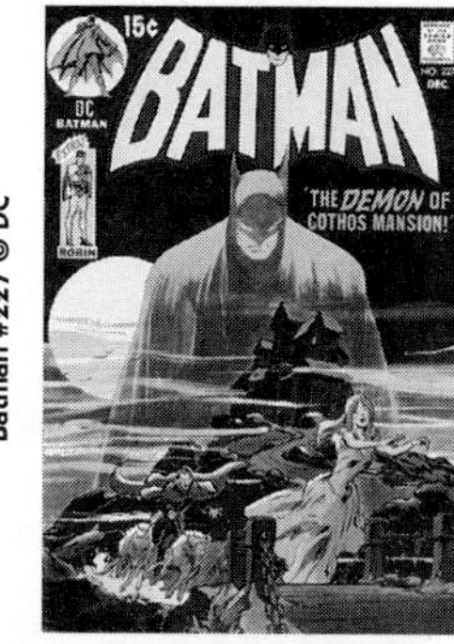

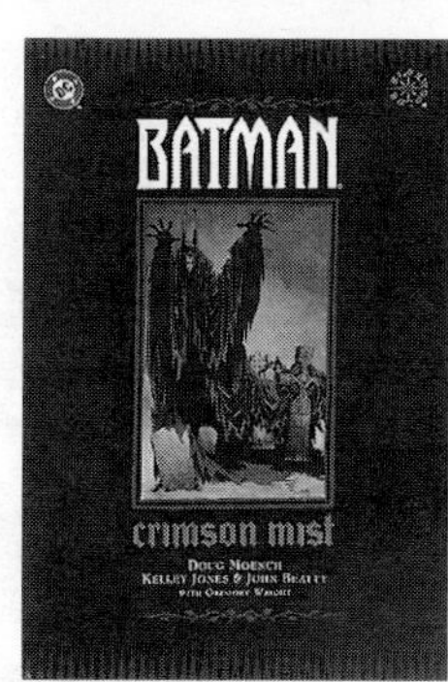

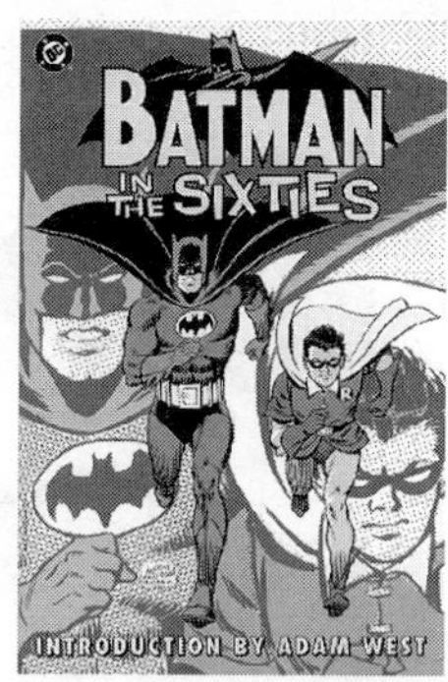

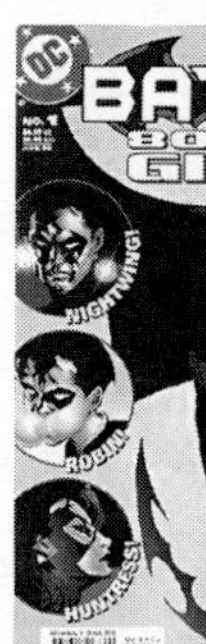
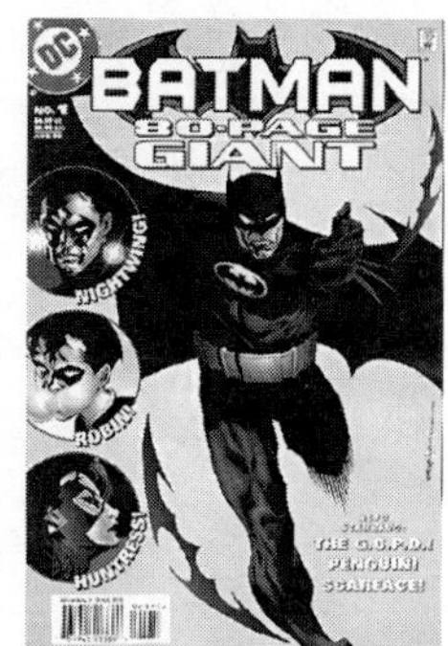

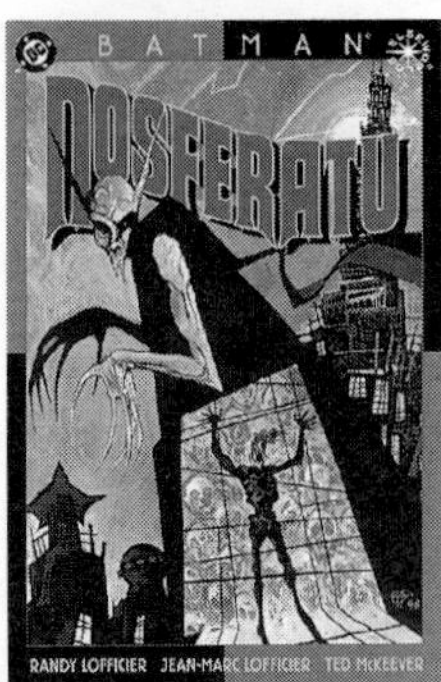

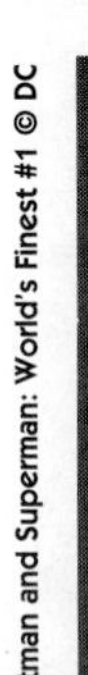

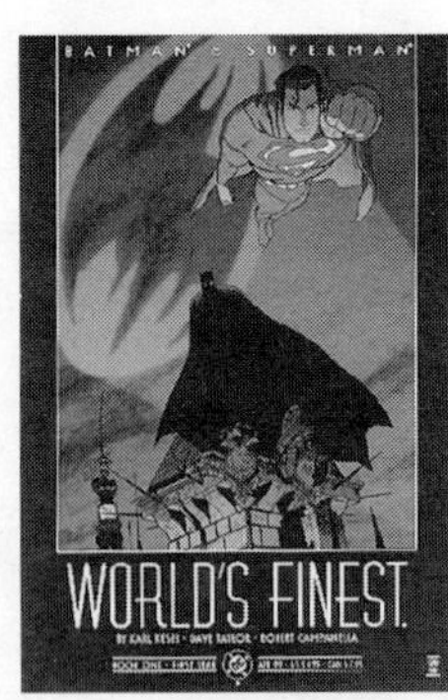

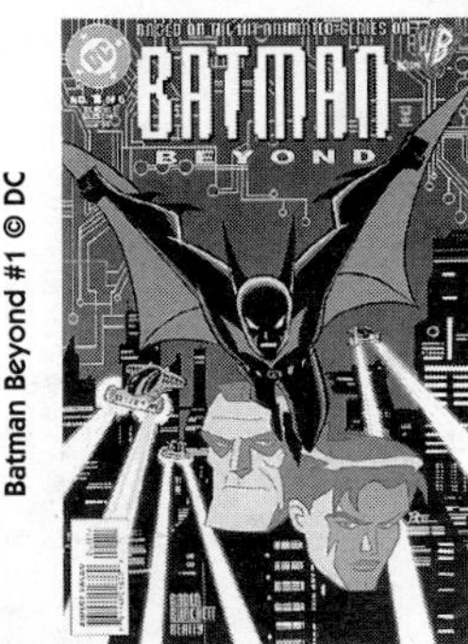

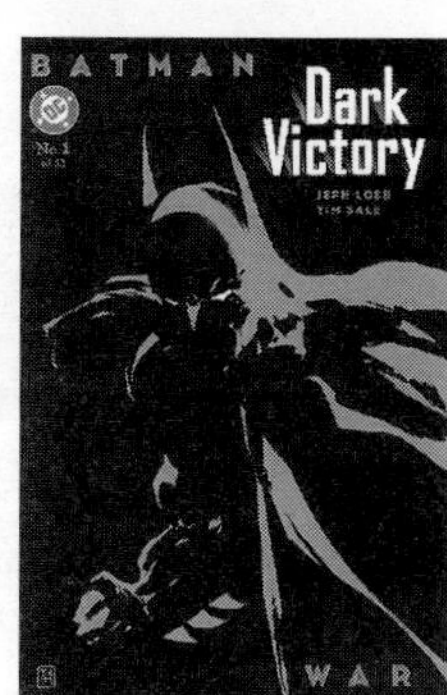

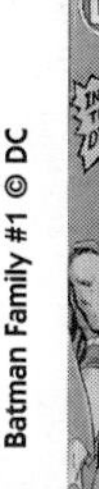

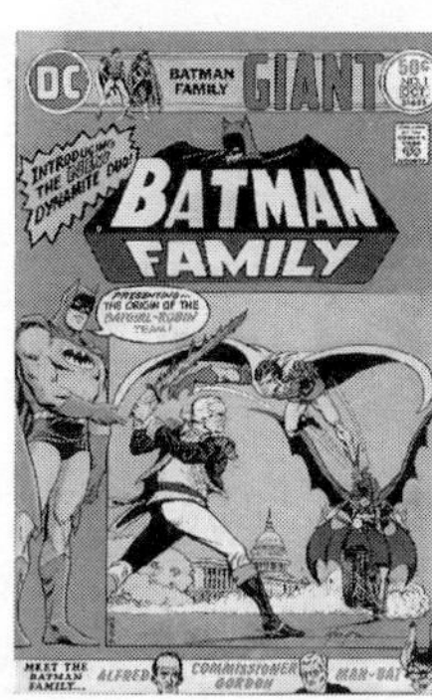

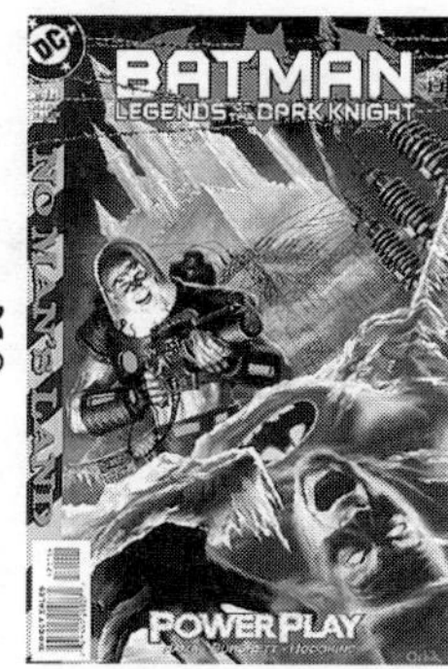

Bewitched #11 © Screen Gems

Big Bang Comics #17 © Image Comics

Big Chief Wahoo #5 © EAS

GD2.0 FN6.0 NM9.4

Finest #249)
National Periodical Publications: May-June, 1968 - No. 6, Mar-Apr, 1969 (All 12¢ issues)

	GD2.0	FN6.0	NM9.4
1-(5-6/68)-Classic Ditko-c; Ditko-a in all	6.50	19.50	65.00
2-6: 2-5-Ditko-c. 6-Gil Kane-c	4.20	12.60	42.00

BEWITCHED (TV)
Dell Publishing Co.: 4-6/65 - No. 11, 10/67; No. 12, 10/68 - No. 13, 1/69; No. 14, 10/69

	GD2.0	FN6.0	NM9.4
1-Photo-c	14.00	41.00	150.00
2-No photo-c	7.00	21.00	75.00
3-13-All have photo-c. 12-Reprints #1	5.00	15.00	55.00
14-No photo-c; reprints #2	3.20	9.50	35.00

BEYOND, THE
Ace Magazines: Nov, 1950 - No. 30, Jan, 1955

	GD2.0	FN6.0	NM9.4
1-Bakerish-a(p)	40.00	120.00	280.00
2-Bakerish-a(p)	24.00	71.00	165.00
3-10: 10-Woodish-a by Cameron	15.00	45.00	105.00
11-20: 18-Used in **POP**, pgs. 81,82	12.00	36.00	85.00
21-26,28-30	11.50	34.00	80.00
27-Used in **SOTI**, pg. 111	12.00	36.00	85.00

NOTE: ***Cameron*** *a-10, 11p, 12p, 15, 16, 21-27, 30; c-20.* ***Colan*** *a-6, 13, 17.* ***Sekowsky*** *a-2, 3, 5, 7, 11, 14, 27r. No. 1 was to appear as Challenge of the Unknown No. 7.*

BEYOND THE GRAVE
Charlton Comics: July, 1975 - No. 6, June, 1976; No. 7, Jan, 1983 - No. 17, Oct, 1984

	GD2.0	FN6.0	NM9.4
1-Ditko-a (6 pgs.); Sutton painted-c	1.85	5.50	15.00
2-6: 2-5-Ditko-a; Ditko c-2,3,6	1.25	3.75	10.00
7-17: ('83-'84) Reprints. 13-Aparo-c(r). 15-Sutton-c (low print run)	2.40		6.00
Modern Comics Reprint 2('78)			3.00

NOTE: ***Howard*** *a-4.* ***Kim*** *a-1.* ***Larson*** *a-4, 6.*

BIBLE TALES FOR YOUNG FOLK (...Young People No. 3-5)
Atlas Comics (OMC): Aug, 1953 - No. 5, Mar, 1954

	GD2.0	FN6.0	NM9.4
1	24.00	73.00	170.00
2-Everett, Krigstein-a	17.00	51.00	120.00
3-5: 4-Robinson-c	13.00	39.00	90.00

BIG (Movie)
Hit Comics (Dark Horse Comics): Mar, 1989 ($2.00)

1-Adaptaiton of film; Paul Chadwick-c — 2.00

BIG ALL-AMERICAN COMIC BOOK, THE (See All-American Comics)
All-American/National Per. Publ.: 1944 (132 pgs., one-shot) (Early DC Annual)

	GD2.0	FN6.0	VF8.0	NM9.4
1-Wonder Woman, Green Lantern, Flash, The Atom, Wildcat, Scribbly, The Whip, Ghost Patrol, Hawkman by Kubert (1st on Hawkman), Hop Harrigan, Johnny Thunder, Little Boy Blue, Mr. Terrific, Mutt & Jeff app.; Sargon on cover only; cover by Kubert/Hibbard/Mayer/others	800.00	2400.00	5950.00	9,500.00

BIG BABY HUEY (Also see Baby Huey)
Harvey Comics: Oct, 1991 - No. 4, Mar, 1992 ($1.00, quarterly)

	GD2.0	FN6.0	NM9.4
1-4			2.50

BIG BANG COMICS (Becomes Big Bang #4)
Caliber Press: Spring, 1994 - No. 4, Feb, 1995 ($1.95, limited series)

0-4: 0-Alex Ross-c. — 2.00
Your Big Book of Big Bang Comics TPB ('98, $11.00) r/#0-2 — 11.00

BIG BANG COMICS (Volume 2)
Image Comics (Highbrow Entertainment): V2#1, May, 1996 - Present ($1.95/$2.50/$2.95)

1-23: 1-Mighty Man app.2-4-S.A. Shadowhawk app.5-Begin $2.95-c. 6-Curt Swan/Murphy Anderson-c. 7-Begin B&W. 12-Savage Dragon-c/app. 15-Bissette-c. 16,17,21-Shadow Lady — 3.00
24,25-($3.95): 24-History of Big Bang Comics Vol. 1 — 4.00

BIG BLACK KISS
Vortex Comics: Sep, 1989 - No, 3, Nov, 1989 ($3.75, B&W, lim. series, mature)

1-3-Chaykin-s/a — 4.00

BIG BLOWN BABY (Also see Dark Horse Presents)
Dark Horse Comics: Aug, 1996 - No. 4, Nov, 1996 ($2.95, lim. series, mature)

1-4: Bill Wray-c/a/scripts — 3.00

BIG BOOK OF ..., THE
DC Comics (Paradox Press): 1994 - Present (B&W)($12.95 - $14.95)

nn-...**BAD**,1998 ($14.95),...**CONSPIRACIES**, 1995 ($12.95), ...**DEATH**,1994 ($12.95), ...**FREAKS**, 1996 ($14.95), ...**GRIMM**, 1999 ($14.95), ...**HOAXES**, 1996 ($14.95), ...**LITTLE CRIMINALS**,1996 ($14.95), ...**LOSERS**,1997 ($14.95), **MARTYRS**, 1997 ($14.95), ...**SCANDAL**,1997 ($14.95), ...**THE WEIRD WILD WEST**,1998 ($14.95), ...**THUGS**, 1997 ($14.95), ...**UNEXPLAINED**, 1997 ($14.95), ...**URBAN LEGENDS**, 1994 ($12.95), ...**VICE**, 1999 ($14.95), ...**WEIRDOS**, 1995 ($12.95) — 12.95 - 14.95 ea.

BIG BOOK OF FUN COMICS (See New Book of Comics)
National Periodical Publications: Spring, 1936 (Large size, 52 pgs.) (1st comic book annual & DC annual)

	GD2.0	FN6.0	VF8.0
1 (Very rare)-r/New Fun #1-5	2083.00	6250.00	12,500.00

BIG BOOK ROMANCES
Fawcett Publications: Feb, 1950 (no date given) (148 pgs.)

	GD2.0	FN6.0	NM9.4
1-Contains remaindered Fawcett romance comics - several combinations possible	36.00	107.00	250.00

BIG BOY (See Adventures of the Big Boy)

BIG BRUISERS
Image Comics (WildStorm Productions): July, 1996 ($3.50, one-shot)

1-Features Maul from WildC.A.T.S, Impact from Cyberforce & Badrock from Youngblood; wraparound-c — 3.50

BIG CHIEF WAHOO
Eastern Color Printing/George Dougherty (distr. by Fawcett): July, 1942 - No. 7, Wint., 1943/44?(no year given)(Quarterly)

	GD2.0	FN6.0	NM9.4
1-Newspaper-r (on sale 6/15/42)	40.00	120.00	315.00
2-Steve Roper app.	22.00	66.00	155.00
3-5: 4-Chief is holding a Katy Keene comic	17.00	49.00	115.00
6-7	11.50	34.00	80.00

NOTE: *Kerry Drake in some issues.*

BIG CIRCUS, THE (Movie)
Dell Publishing Co.: No. 1036, Sept-Nov, 1959

	GD2.0	FN6.0	NM9.4
Four Color 1036-Photo-c	5.50	16.50	60.00

BIG COUNTRY, THE (Movie)
Dell Publishing Co.: No. 946, Oct, 1958

	GD2.0	FN6.0	NM9.4
Four Color 946-Photo-c	6.40	19.00	70.00

BIG DADDY ROTH (Magazine)
Millar Publications: Oct-Nov, 1964 - No. 4, Apr-May, 1965 (35¢)

	GD2.0	FN6.0	NM9.4
1-Toth-a	14.00	42.00	140.00
2-4-Toth-a	10.50	32.00	105.00

BIG GUY AND RUSTY THE BOY ROBOT, THE (Also See Madman Comics #6,7 & Martha Washington Stranded In Space)
Dark Horse (Legend): July, 1995 - No. 2, Aug, 1995 ($4.95, oversize, lim. series)

	GD2.0	FN6.0	NM9.4
1,2-Frank Miller scripts & Geoff Darrow-c/a	1.10	3.30	9.00
Trade paperback (10/96, $14.95)-r/1,2 w/cover gallery			15.00

BIG HERO ADVENTURES (See Jigsaw)

BIG JON & SPARKIE (Radio)(Formerly Sparkie, Radio Pixie)
Ziff-Davis Publ. Co.: No. 4, Sept-Oct, 1952 (Painted-c)

	GD2.0	FN6.0	NM9.4
4-Based on children's radio program	18.00	54.00	125.00

BIG LAND, THE (Movie)
Dell Publishing Co.: No. 812, July, 1957

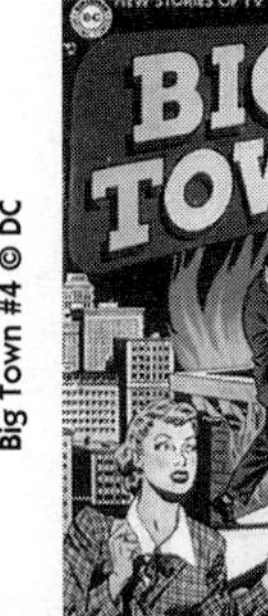

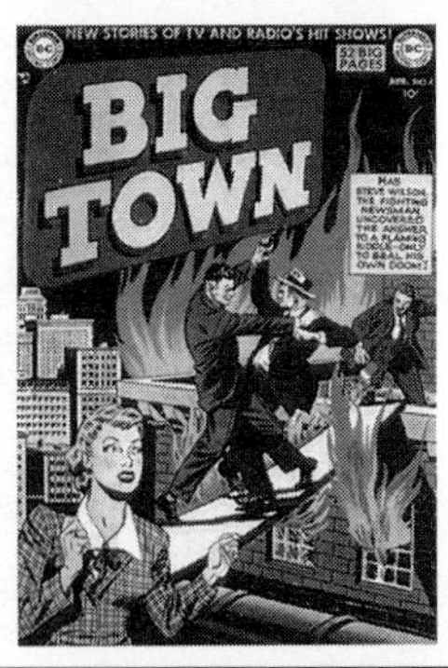

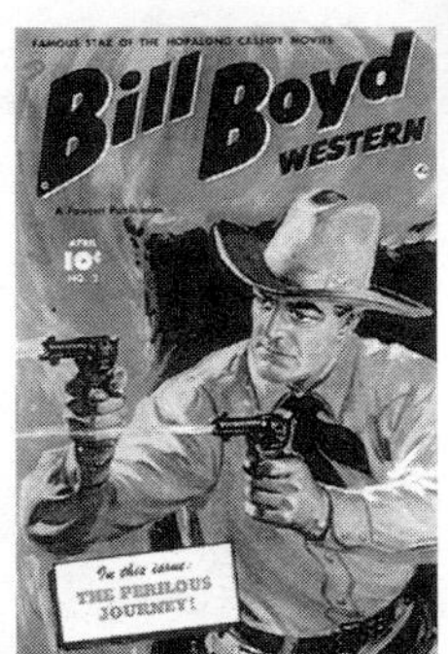

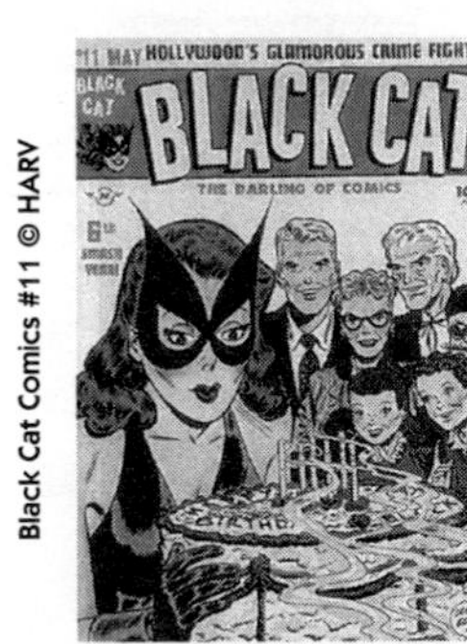

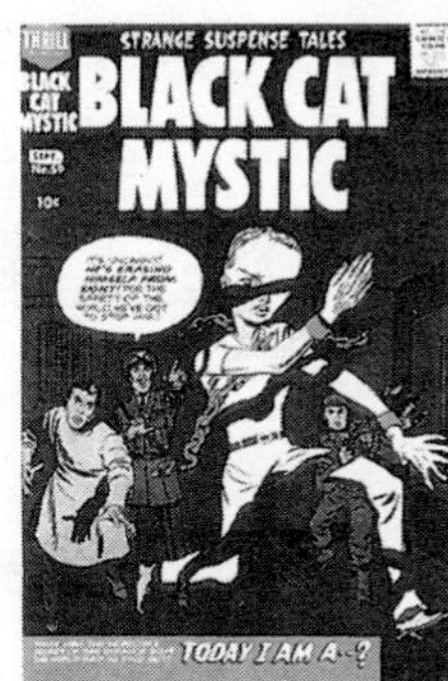

Black Diamond Western #16 © LEV

Black Goliath #1 © MAR

Blackhawk #41 © QUA

BLACK CROSS: DIRTY WORK (See Dark Horse Presents)
Dark Horse Comics: Apr, 1997 ($2.95, one-shot)

	GD2.0	FN6.0	NM9.4
1-Chris Warner-c/s/a			3.00

BLACK DIAMOND
Americomics: May, 1983 - No. 5, 1984 (no month)($2.00-$1.75, Baxter paper)

	GD2.0	FN6.0	NM9.4
1-3-Movie adapt.; 1-Colt back-up begins			2.50
4,5			2.00

NOTE: ***Bill Black** a-1i; c-1. **Gulacy** c-2-5. Sybil Danning photo back-c-1.*

BLACK DIAMOND WESTERN (Formerly Desperado No. 1-8)
Lev Gleason Publ: No. 9, Mar, 1949 - No. 60, Feb, 1956 (No. 9-28: 52 pgs.)

	GD2.0	FN6.0	NM9.4
9-Black Diamond & his horse Reliapon begin; origin & 1st app. Black Diamond	19.00	56.00	130.00
10	10.00	30.00	60.00
11-15	7.50	22.50	45.00
16-28(11/49-11/51)-Wolverton's Bing Bang Buster	10.00	30.00	60.00
29-40: 31-One pg. Frazetta anti-drug ad	5.00	15.00	30.00
41-50,53-59	4.15	12.50	25.00
51-3-D effect-c/story	12.00	36.00	85.00
52-3-D effect story	11.50	34.00	80.00
60-Last issue	5.35	16.00	32.00

NOTE: ***Biro** c-9-35?. **Fass** a-58, c-54-56, 58. **Guardineer** a-9, 15, 18. **Kida** a-9. **Maurer** a-10. **Ed Moore** a-16. **Morisi** a-55. **Tuska** a-10, 48.*

BLACK DRAGON, THE
Marvel Comics (Epic Comics): 5/85 - No. 6, 10/85 (Baxter paper, mature)

	GD2.0	FN6.0	NM9.4
1-6: 1-Chris Claremont story & John Bolton-c/a in all.			2.50

BLACK DRAGON, THE
Dark Horse Comics: Apr, 1996 ($17.95, B&W, trade paperback)

	GD2.0	FN6.0	NM9.4
nn-Reprints Epic Comics limited series; intro by Anne McCaffrey			18.00

BLACK FLAG (See Asylum #5)
Maximum Press: Jan, 1995 - No.4, 1995; No. 0, July, 1995 ($2.50, B&W) (No. 0 in color)

	GD2.0	FN6.0	NM9.4
Preview Edition (6/94, $1.95, B&W)-Fraga/McFarlane-c.			2.00
0-4: 0-(7/95)-Liefeld/Fraga-c. 1-(1/95).			3.00
1-Variant cover			5.00
2,4-Variant covers			3.00

NOTE: ***Fraga** a-0-4, Preview Edition; c-1-4. **Liefeld/Fraga** c-0. **McFarlane/Fraga** c-Preview Edition.*

BLACK FURY (Becomes Wild West No. 58) (See Blue Bird)
Charlton Comics Group: May, 1955 - No. 57, Mar-Apr, 1966 (Horse stories)

	GD2.0	FN6.0	NM9.4
1	6.35	19.00	38.00
2	3.60	9.00	18.00
3-10	2.80	7.00	14.00
11-15,19,20	2.00	5.00	10.00
16-18-Ditko-a	6.35	19.00	38.00
21-30	1.00	2.80	7.00
31-57			5.00

BLACK GOLIATH
Marvel Comics Group: Feb, 1976 - No. 5, Nov, 1976

	GD2.0	FN6.0	NM9.4
1-Tuska-a(p) thru #3		2.40	6.00
2-5: 2-4-(Regular 25¢ editions). 4-Kirby-c			4.00
2-4-(30¢-c variants, limited distribution)(4,6,8/76)	2.00	6.00	16.00

BLACKHAWK (Formerly Uncle Sam #1-8; see Military & Modern Comics)
Comic Magazines(Quality)No. 9-107(12/56); National Periodical PublicationsNo. 108(1/57)-250; DC Comics No. 251 on: No. 9, Winter, 1944 - No. 243, 10-11/68; No. 244, 1-2/76 - No. 250, 1-2/77; No. 251, 10/82 - No. 273, 11/84

	GD2.0	FN6.0	NM9.4
9 (1944)	300.00	900.00	2700.00
10 (1946)	106.00	318.00	850.00
11-15: 14-Ward-a; 13,14-Fear app.	70.00	210.00	560.00
16-20: 20-Ward Blackhawk	56.00	168.00	450.00
21-30 (1950)	44.00	132.00	350.00
31-40: 31-Chop Chop by Jack Cole	36.00	107.00	250.00
41-49,51-60: 42-Robot-c	29.00	86.00	200.00
50-1st Killer Shark; origin in text	31.00	94.00	220.00
61,62: 61-Used in **POP**, pg. 91. 62-Used in **POP**, pg. 92 & color illo	25.00	75.00	175.00
63-70,72-80: 65-H-Bomb explosion panel. 66-B&W & color illos **POP**. 70-Return of Killer Shark; atomic explosion panel. 75-Intro. Blackie the Hawk	23.00	69.00	160.00
71-Origin retold; flying saucer-c; A-Bomb panels	26.00	79.00	185.00
81-86: Last precode (3/55)	21.00	64.00	150.00
87-92,94-99,101-107: 91-Robot-c. 105-1st S.A.	17.00	51.00	120.00
93-Origin in text	18.00	54.00	125.00
100	21.00	64.00	150.00
108-1st DC issue (1/57); re-intro. Blackie, the Hawk, their mascot; not in #115	40.00	120.00	450.00
109-117: 117-(10/57)-Mr. Freeze app.	15.00	45.00	150.00
118-(11/57)-Frazetta-r/Jimmy Wakely #4 (3 pgs.)	16.00	48.00	160.00
119-130 (11/58): 120-Robot-c	10.00	30.00	100.00
131-140 (2/59): 133-Intro. Lady Blackhawk	7.50	22.50	75.00
141-150,152-163,165,166: 141-Catman returns-c/s. 143-Kurtzman-r/Jimmy Wakely #4. 150-(7/60)-King Condor returns. 166-Last 10¢ issue	5.50	16.50	55.00
151-Lady Blackhawk receives & loses super powers	6.00	18.00	60.00
164-Origin retold	6.50	19.50	65.00
167-180	3.00	9.00	30.00
181-190	2.50	7.50	22.00
191-196,199,201,202,204-210: 196-Combat Diary series begins.	2.25	6.75	18.00
197-New look for Blackhawks	2.50	7.50	22.00
198,200: 198-Origin retold	2.50	7.50	22.00
203-Origin Chop Chop (12/64)	2.50	7.50	22.00
211-227,229-243(1968): 230-Blackhawks become superheroes; JLA cameo 242-Return to old costumes	1.75	5.25	14.00
228-Batman, Green Lantern, Superman, The Flash cameos.	2.00	6.00	16.00
244 ('76) -250: 250-Chuck dies			4.00
251-273: 251-Origin retold; Black Knights return. 252-Intro Domino. 253-Part origin Hendrickson. 258-Blackhawk's Island destroyed. 259-Part origin Chop-Chop. 265-273 (75¢ cover price)			2.00

NOTE: ***Chaykin** a-260; c-257-260, 262. **Crandall** a-10, 11, 13, 16?, 18-20, 22-26, 30-33, 35p, 36(2), 37, 38?, 39-44, 46-50, 52-58, 60, 63, 64, 66, 67; c-14-20, 22-63(most except #28-33, 36, 37, 39). **Evans** a-244, 245,246i, 248-250i. **G. Kane** c-263, 264. **Kubert** c-244, 245. **Newton** a-266p. **Severin** a-257.**Spiegle** a-261-267, 269-273; c-265-272. **Toth** a-260p. **Ward** a-16-27(Chop Chop, 8pgs. ea.); pencilled stories-No. 17-63(approx.). **Wildey** a-268. Chop Chop solo stories in #10-95?*

BLACKHAWK
DC Comics: Mar, 1988 - No. 3, May, 1988 ($2.95, limited series, mature)

	GD2.0	FN6.0	NM9.4
1-3: Chaykin painted-c/a/scripts			3.00

BLACKHAWK (Also see Action Comics #601)
DC Comics: Mar, 1989 - No. 16, Aug, 1990 ($1.50, mature)

	GD2.0	FN6.0	NM9.4
1-6,8-16: 16-Crandall-c swipe			2.00
7-($2.50, 52 pgs.)-Story-r/Military #1			2.50
Annual 1 (1989, $2.95, 68 pgs.)-Recaps origin of Blackhawk, Lady Blackhawk, and others			3.00
Special 1 (1992, $3.50, 68 pgs.)-Mature readers			3.50

BLACKHAWK INDIAN TOMAHAWK WAR, THE
Avon Periodicals: 1951 (Also see Fighting Indians of the Wild West)

	GD2.0	FN6.0	NM9.4
nn-Kinstler-c; Kit West story	18.00	54.00	125.00

BLACK HEART ASSASSIN
Iguana Comics: Jan, 1994 ($2.95)

	GD2.0	FN6.0	NM9.4
1			3.00

BLACK HOLE (See Walt Disney Showcase #54) (Disney, movie)
Whitman Publishing Co.: Mar, 1980 - No. 4, Sept, 1980

	GD2.0	FN6.0	NM9.4
11295(#1) (1979, Golden, $1.50-c, 52 pgs., graphic novel; 8 1/2x11") Photo-c; Spiegle-a.	1.50	4.50	16.00
1-4: 1,2-Movie adaptation. 2-4-Spiegle-a. 3-McWilliams-a; photo-c.			

Black Widow #1 © MAR

Blade Runner #1 © MAR

Blazing Comics #3 © Enwil

GD2.0 FN6.0 NM9.4

Noid in 3-D #2 — 4.00

BLACK WIDOW (Marvel Knights)
Marvel Comics: May, 1999 - No. 3, Aug, 1999 ($2.99, limited series)

1-(June on-c) Devin Grayson-s/J.G. Jones-c/a; Daredevil app. — 4.00
1-Variant-c by Jones — 4.00
2,3 — 3.00
...Web of Intrigue (6/99, $3.50) r/origin & early appearances — 3.50

BLACKWULF
Marvel Comics: June, 1994 - No. 10, Mar, 1995 ($1.50)

1-($2.50)-Embossed-c; Angel Medina-a — 2.50
2-10 — 2.00

BLADE (The Vampire Hunter)
Marvel Comics: Mar, 1998 ($3.50, one-shot)

1-Colan-a(p)/Christopher Golden-s — 3.50

BLADE (The Vampire Hunter)
Marvel Comics: Nov, 1998 - No. 3, Jan, 1999 ($3.50/$2.99)

1-($3.50) Contains Movie insider pages; McKean-a — 3.50
2,3-($2.99): 2-Two covers — 3.00
...Sins of the Father (10/98, $5.99) Sears-a — 6.00

BLADE OF THE IMMORTAL (Manga)
Dark Horse Comics: June, 1996 - Present ($2.95/$3.95, B&W)

1-10: 2-#1 on cover in error — 4.00
11,19,20,34-($3.95, 48 pgs.): 34-Food one-shot — 4.00
12-18,21-33,35-37: 12-Begin Dreamsong. 21-Begin On Silent Wings. 29-Begin Dark Shadow. 35-Begin Heart of Darkness — 4.00

BLADE RUNNER (Movie)
Marvel Comics Group: Oct, 1982 - No. 2, Nov, 1982

1,2-r/Marvel Super Special #22; 1-Williamson-c/a. 2-Williamson-a — 2.00

BLADESMEN UNDERSEA
Blue Comet Press: 1994 ($3.50, B&W)

1-Polybagged w/trading card — 3.50

BLADE: THE VAMPIRE-HUNTER
Marvel Comics: July, 1994 - No. 10, Apr, 1995 ($1.95)

1-($2.95)-Foil-c — 4.00
2-10 — 3.00

BLAIR WITCH PROJECT, THE (Movie companion, not adaption)
Oni Press: July, 1999 ($2.95, B&W, one-shot)

1-(1st printing) History of the Blair Witch, art by Edwards, Mireault, and Davis; Van Meter-s; only the stick figure is red on the cover — 15.00
1-(2nd printing) Stick figure and title lettering are red on cover — 5.00
1-(3rd printing) Stick figure, title, and creator credits are red on cover — 3.00
DF Glow in the Dark variant-c ($10.00) — 10.00

BLAST (Satire Magazine)
G & D Publications: Feb, 1971 - No. 2, May, 1971

	GD2.0	FN6.0	NM9.4
1-Wrightson & Kaluta-a/Everette-c	5.50	16.50	55.00
2-Kaluta-c/a	3.80	11.40	38.00

BLAST CORPS
Dark Horse Comics: Oct, 1998 ($2.50, one-shot, based on Nintendo game)

1-Reprints from Nintendo Power magazine; Mahn-a — 2.50

BLASTERS SPECIAL
DC Comics: 1989 ($2.00, one-shot)

1-Peter David scripts; Invasion spin-off — 2.00

BLAST-OFF (Three Rocketeers)
Harvey Publications (Fun Day Funnies): Oct, 1965 (12¢)

	GD2.0	FN6.0	NM9.4
1-Kirby/Williamson-a(2); Williamson/Crandall-a; Williamson/Torres/Krenkel-a; Kirby/Simon-c	4.20	12.60	42.00

BLAZE
Marvel Comics: Aug, 1994 - No. 12, July, 1995 ($1.95)

1-($2.95)-Foil embossed-c — 3.00
2-12: 2-Man-Thing-c/story — 2.00

BLAZE CARSON (Rex Hart #6 on)(See Kid Colt, Tex Taylor, Wild Western, Wisco)
Marvel Comics (USA): Sept, 1948 - No. 5, June, 1949

	GD2.0	FN6.0	NM9.4
1: 1,2-Shores-c	26.00	77.00	180.00
2,4,5: 4-Two-Gun Kid app. 5-Tex Taylor app.	19.00	56.00	130.00
3-Used by N.Y. State Legis. Comm. (injury to eye splash); Tex Morgan app.	20.00	60.00	140.00

BLAZE: LEGACY OF BLOOD (See Ghost Rider & Ghost Rider/Blaze)
Marvel Comics (Midnight Sons imprint): Dec, 1993 - No. 4, Mar, 1994 ($1.75, limited series)

1-4 — 2.00

BLAZE THE WONDER COLLIE (Formerly Molly Manton's Romances #1?)
Marvel Comics(SePI): No. 2, Oct, 1949 - No. 3, Feb, 1950 (Both have photo-c)

	GD2.0	FN6.0	NM9.4
2(#1), 3-(Scarce)	22.00	66.00	155.00

BLAZING BATTLE TALES
Seaboard Periodicals (Atlas): July, 1975

1-Intro. Sgt. Hawk & the Sky Demon; Severin, McWilliams, Sparling-a; Thorne-c — 5.00

BLAZING COMBAT (Magazine)
Warren Publishing Co.: Oct, 1965 - No. 4, July, 1966 (35¢, B&W)

	GD2.0	FN6.0	NM9.4
1-Frazetta painted-c on all	15.00	45.00	150.00
2	4.00	12.00	40.00
3,4: 4-Frazetta half pg. ad	3.00	9.00	30.00
...Anthology (reprints from No. 1-4)	4.20	12.60	42.00

NOTE: *Above has art by* ***Colan, Crandall, Evans, Morrow, Orlando, Severin, Torres, Toth, Williamson,*** *and* ***Wood.***

BLAZING COMBAT: WORLD WAR I AND WORLD WAR II
Apple Press: Mar, 1994 ($3.75, B&W)

1,2: 1-r/Colan, Toth, Goodwin, Severin, Wood-a. 2-r/Crandall, Evans, Severin, Torres, Williamson-a — 3.75

BLAZING COMICS
Enwil Associates/Rural Home: 6/44 - #3, 9/44; #4, 2/45; #5, 3/45; #5(V2#2), 3/55 - #6(V2#3), 1955?

	GD2.0	FN6.0	NM9.4
1-The Green Turtle, Red Hawk, Black Buccaneer begin; origin Jun-Gal	47.00	141.00	375.00
2-5: 3-Briefer-a. 5-(V2#2 inside)	33.00	99.00	230.00
5(3/55, V2#2-inside)-Black Buccaneer-c, 6(V2#3-inside, 1955)-Indian/Japanese-c	13.00	39.00	90.00

NOTE: *No. 5 & 6 contain remaindered comics rebound and the contents can vary. Cloak & Daggar, Will Rogers, Superman 64, Star Spangled 130, Kaanga known. Value would be half of contents.*

BLAZING SIXGUNS
Avon Periodicals: Dec, 1952

	GD2.0	FN6.0	NM9.4
1-Kinstler-c/a; Larsen/Alascia-a(2), Tuska?-a; Jesse James, Kit Carson, Wild Bill Hickok app.	14.00	43.00	100.00

BLAZING SIXGUNS
I.W./Super Comics: 1964

	GD2.0	FN6.0	NM9.4
I.W. Reprint #1,8,9: 1-r/Wild Bill Hickok #26, Western True Crime #? & Blazing Sixguns #1 by Avon; Kinstler-c. 8-r/Blazing Western #?; Kinstler-c. 9-r/Blazing Western #1; Ditko-r; Kintsler-c reprinted from Dalton Boys #1.	1.50	4.50	12.00
Super Reprint #10,11,15,16: 10,11-r/The Rider #2,1. 15-r/Silver Kid Western #?. 16-r/Buffalo Bill #?; Wildey-r; Severin-c. 17(1964)-r/Western True Crime #?	1.50	4.50	12.00
12-Reprints Bullseye #3; S&K-a	3.00	9.00	30.00
18-r/Straight Arrow #? by Powell; Severin-c	1.60	4.85	13.00

BLAZING SIX-GUNS (Also see Sundance Kid)
Skywald Comics: Feb, 1971 - No. 2, Apr, 1971 (52 pgs.)

1-The Red Mask, Sundance Kid begin, Avon's Geronimo reprint by Kinstler;

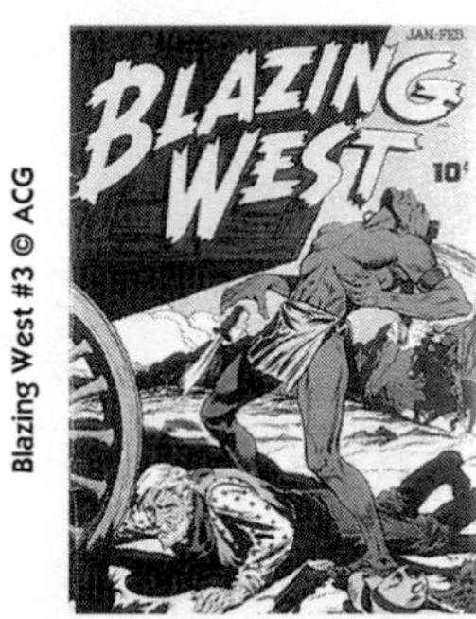

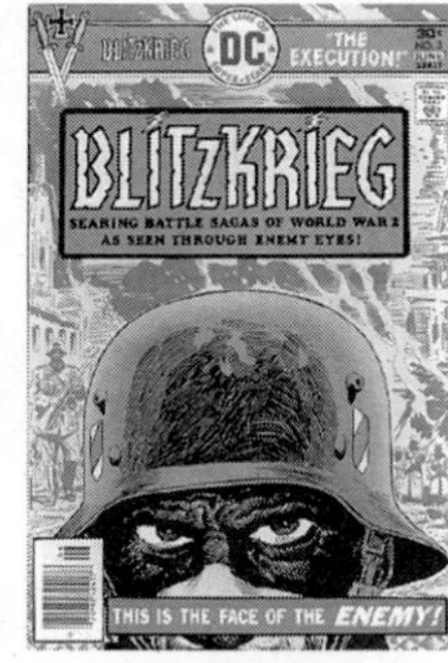

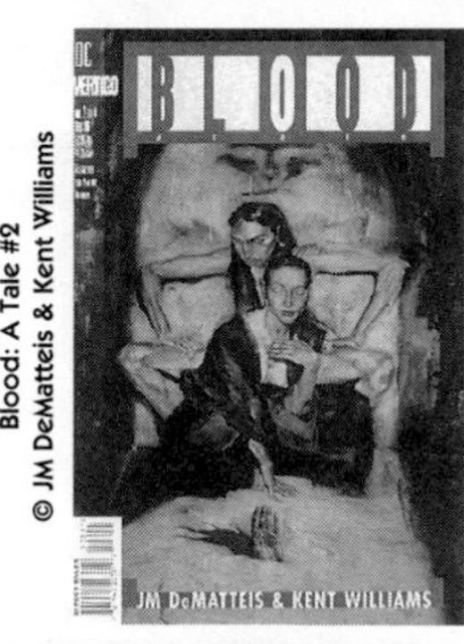

Body Doubles #1 © DC

Bomber Comics #3 © EP

The Book of Night #1 © DH

BODYCOUNT (Also see Casey Jones & Raphael)
Image Comics (Highbrow Entertainment): Mar, 1996 - No. 4, July, 1996 ($2.50, limited series)

	GD2.0	FN6.0	NM9.4
1-4: Kevin Eastman-a(p)/scripts; Simon Bisley-c/a(i); Turtles app.			2.50

BODY DOUBLES (See Resurrection Man)
DC Comics: Oct, 1999 - No. 4 ($2.50, limited series)

	GD2.0	FN6.0	NM9.4
1,2-Lanning & Abnett-s. 2-Black Canary app.			2.50
...(Villains) (2/98, $1.95, one-shot) 1-Pearson-c; Deadshot app.			2.00

BOFFO LAFFS
Paragraphics: 1986 - No. 5 ($2.50/$1.95)

	GD2.0	FN6.0	NM9.4
1-($2.50) First comic cover with hologram			2.50
2-5			2.00

BOHOS
Image Comics (Flypaper Press): June, 1998 - Present ($2.95)

	GD2.0	FN6.0	NM9.4
1-3-Whorf-s/Penaranda-a			3.00

BOLD ADVENTURES
Pacific Comics: Oct, 1983 - No. 3, June, 1984 ($1.50)

	GD2.0	FN6.0	NM9.4
1-Time Force, Anaconda, & The Weirdling begin			2.00
2,3: 2-Soldiers of Fortune begins. 3-Spitfire			2.00

NOTE: ***Kaluta*** *c-3.* ***Nebres*** *a-1-3.* ***Nino*** *a-2, 3.* ***Severin*** *a-3.*

BOLD STORIES (Also see Candid Tales & It Rhymes With Lust)
Kirby Publishing Co.: Mar, 1950 - July, 1950 (Digest size, 144 pgs.)

	GD2.0	FN6.0	NM9.4
March issue (Very Rare) - Contains "The Ogre of Paris" by Wood	120.00	360.00	960.00
May issue (Very Rare) - Contains "The Cobra's Kiss" by Graham Ingels (21 pgs.)	103.00	309.00	825.00
July issue (Very Rare) - Contains "The Ogre of Paris" by Wood	90.00	272.00	725.00

BOLT AND STAR FORCE SIX
Americomics: 1984 ($1.75)

	GD2.0	FN6.0	NM9.4
1-Origin Bolt & Star Force Six			2.00
Special 1 (1984, $2.00, 52pgs., B&W)			2.00

BOMBARDIER (See Bee 29, the Bombardier & Cinema Comics Herald)

BOMBAST
Topps Comics: 1993 ($2.95, one-shot) (Created by Jack Kirby)

	GD2.0	FN6.0	NM9.4
1-Polybagged w/Kirbychrome trading card; Savage Dragon app.; Kirby-c; has coupon for Amberchrome Secret City Saga #0			3.00

BOMBA THE JUNGLE BOY (TV)
National Periodical Publ.: Sept-Oct, 1967 - No. 7, Sept-Oct, 1968 (12¢)

	GD2.0	FN6.0	NM9.4
1-Intro. Bomba; Infantino/Anderson-c	2.50	7.50	22.00
2-7	2.00	6.00	16.00

BOMBER COMICS
Elliot Publ. Co./Melverne Herald/Farrell/Sunrise Times: Mar, 1944 - No. 4, Winter, 1944-45

	GD2.0	FN6.0	NM9.4
1-Wonder Boy, & Kismet, Man of Fate begin	62.00	187.00	500.00
2-Hitler-c	40.00	120.00	300.00
3: 2-4-Have Classics Comics ad to HRN 20	39.00	116.00	270.00
4-Hitler, Tojo & Mussolini-c; Sensation Comics #13-c/swipe; has Classics Comics ad to HRN 20.	50.00	150.00	400.00

BONANZA (TV)
Dell/Gold Key: June-Aug, 1960 - No. 37, Aug, 1970 (All Photo-c)

	GD2.0	FN6.0	NM9.4
Four Color 1110 (6-8/60)	34.00	102.00	375.00
Four Color 1221,1283, & #01070-207, 01070-210	16.00	49.00	180.00
1(12/62-Gold Key)	17.00	52.00	190.00
2	8.75	26.50	95.00
3-10	7.00	20.00	75.00
11-20	5.50	16.50	60.00
21-37: 29-Reprints	4.50	13.50	50.00

BONE
Cartoon Books/Image Comics #21 on: July, 1991 - Present ($2.95, B&W)

	GD2.0	FN6.0	NM9.4
1-Jeff Smith-c/a in all	7.00	21.00	75.00
1-2nd printing	1.50	4.50	12.00
1-3rd thru 5th printings			4.00
2-1st printing	4.00	12.25	45.00
2-2nd & 3rd printings			5.00
3-1st printing	3.50	10.50	35.00
3-2nd thru 4th printings			4.00
4,5	1.85	5.50	15.00
6-10	1.00	3.00	8.00
11-36: 21-1st Image issue			4.00
13 1/2	1.50	4.50	12.00
13 1/2 (Gold)	1.85	5.50	15.00
1-26-($2.95): 1-Image reprints begin w/new-c. 2-Allred pin-up.			3.00
Holiday Special (1993, giveaway)			3.00
Sourcebook-San Diego Edition			3.00
Complete Bone Adventures Vol 1,2 ('93, '94, $12.95, r/#1-6 & #7-12)			13.00
Volume 1-($19.95, hard-c)-"Out From Boneville"			20.00
Volume 1-($12.95, soft-c)			13.00
Volume 2,5-($22.95, hard-c)-"The Great Cow Race" & "Rock Jdaw"			23.00
Volume 2,5($14.95, soft-c)			15.00
Volume 3,4-($24.95, hard-c)-"Eyes of the Storm" & "The Dragonslayer"			25.00
Volume 3,4-($16.95, soft-c)			17.00
Volume 6-($15.95, soft-c)-"Old Man's Cave"			16.00

NOTE: *Printings not listed sell for cover price.*

BONGO (See Story Hour Series)

BONGO & LUMPJAW (Disney, see Walt Disney Showcase #3)
Dell Publishing Co.: No. 706, June, 1956; No. 886, Mar, 1958

	GD2.0	FN6.0	NM9.4
Four Color 706 (#1)	4.50	13.50	50.00
Four Color 886	3.80	11.50	40.00

BON VOYAGE (See Movie Classics)

BOOF
Image Comics (Todd McFarlane Prod.): July, 1994 - No. 6, Dec, 1994 ($1.95)

	GD2.0	FN6.0	NM9.4
1-6			2.00

BOOF AND THE BRUISE CREW
Image Comics (Todd McFarlane Prod.): July, 1994 - No. 6, Dec, 1994 ($1.95)

	GD2.0	FN6.0	NM9.4
1-6			2.00

BOOK AND RECORD SET (See Power Record Comics)

BOOK OF ALL COMICS
William H. Wise: 1945 (196 pgs.)(Inside f/c has Green Publ. blacked out)

	GD2.0	FN6.0	NM9.4
nn-Green Mask, Puppeteer & The Bouncer	39.00	116.00	270.00

BOOK OF ANTS, THE
Artisan Entertainment: 1998 ($2.95, B&W)

	GD2.0	FN6.0	NM9.4
1-Based on the movie Pi; Aronofsky-s			3.00

BOOK OF BALLADS AND SAGAS, THE
Green Man Press: Oct, 1995 - Present ($2.95/$3.50/$3.25, B&W)

	GD2.0	FN6.0	NM9.4
1-4: 1-Vess-c/a; Gaiman story.			3.50

BOOK OF COMICS, THE
William H. Wise: No date (1944) (25¢, 132 pgs.)

	GD2.0	FN6.0	NM9.4
nn-Captain V app.	39.00	116.00	270.00

BOOK OF FATE, THE (See Fate)
DC Comics: Feb, 1997 - No. 12, Jan, 1998 ($2.25/$2.50)

	GD2.0	FN6.0	NM9.4
1-12: 4-Two-Face-c/app. 6-Convergence. 11-Sentinel app.			3.00

BOOK OF LOVE (See Fox Giants)

BOOK OF NIGHT, THE
Dark Horse Comics: July, 1987 - No. 3, 1987 ($1.75, B&W)

	GD2.0	FN6.0	NM9.4
1-3: Reprints from Epic Illustrated; Vess-a			2.25
TPB-r/#1-3			15.00
Hardcover-Black-c with red crest			100.00

Books of Magic #52 © DC

Boots and Her Buddies #5 © STD

The Bouncer #13 © FOX

	GD2.0	FN6.0	NM9.4
Hardcover w/slipcase (1991) signed and numbered			50.00

BOOK OF THE DEAD
Marvel Comics: Dec, 1993 - No. 4, Mar, 1994 ($1.75, limited series, 52 pgs.)

	GD2.0	FN6.0	NM9.4
1-4: 1-Ploog Frankenstein & Morrow Man-Thing-r begin; Wrightson-r/Chamber of Darkness #7. 2-Morrow new painted-c; Chaykin/Morrow Man-Thing; Krigstein-r/Uncanny Tales #54; r/Fear #10. 3-r/Astonishing Tales #10 & Starlin Man-Thing. 3,4-Painted-c			3.00

BOOKS OF FAERIE, THE
DC Comics (Vertigo): Mar, 1997 - No. 3, May,1997 ($2.50, limited series)

	GD2.0	FN6.0	NM9.4
1-3-Gross-a			2.50
TPB (1998, $14.95) r/#1-3 & Arcana Annual #1			15.00

BOOKS OF FAERIE, THE :AUBERON'S TALE
DC Comics (Vertigo): Aug, 1998 - No. 3, Oct,1998 ($2.50, limited series)

	GD2.0	FN6.0	NM9.4
1-3-Gross-a			3.00

BOOKS OF FAERIE, THE :MOLLY'S STORY
DC Comics (Vertigo): Sept, 1999 - No. 4, Dec,1999 ($2.50, limited series)

	GD2.0	FN6.0	NM9.4
1,2-Ney Rieber-s/Mejia-a			3.00

BOOKS OF MAGIC
DC Comics: 1990 - No. 4, 1991 ($3.95, 52 pgs., limited series, mature)

	GD2.0	FN6.0	NM9.4
1-Bolton painted-c/a; Phantom Stranger app.; Gaiman scripts in all	1.10	3.30	9.00
2,3: 2-John Constantine, Dr. Fate, Spectre, Deadman app. 3-Dr. Occult app.; minor Sandman app.		2.40	6.00
4-Early Death-c/app. (early 1991)	1.00	2.80	7.00
Trade paperback-($19.95)-Reprints limited series			20.00

BOOKS OF MAGIC
DC Comics (Vertigo): May, 1994 - Present ($1.95/$2.50, mature)

	GD2.0	FN6.0	NM9.4
1-Charles Vess-c	1.50	4.50	12.00
1-Platinum	2.50	7.50	20.00
2,3	1.00	2.80	7.00
4-Death app.	1.00	2.80	7.00
5-14; Charles Vess-c			4.00
15-50: 15-$2.50-c begins. 22-Kaluta-c. 25-Death-c/app; Bachalo-c			3.00
51-65: 51-Peter Gross-s/a begins. 55-Medley-a			2.50
Annual 1,2 (2/97, 2/98, $3.95)			4.00
Bindings (1995, $12.95, TPB)-r/#1-4			13.00
Girl in the Box (1999, $14.95, TPB)-r/#26-32			15.00
Reckonings (1997, $12.95, TPB)-r/#14-20			13.00
Summonings (1996, $17.50, TPB)-r/#5-13, Vertigo Rave #1			17.50
Transformations (1998, $12.95, TPB)-r/#21-25			13.00

BOONDOGGLE
Knight Press: Mar, 1995 - No. 4 ($2.95, B&W)

	GD2.0	FN6.0	NM9.4
1-4: Stegelin-c/a/scripts			3.00

BOONDOGGLE
Caliber Press: Jan, 1997 - Present ($2.95, B&W)

	GD2.0	FN6.0	NM9.4
1,2: Stegelin-c/a/scripts			3.00

BOOSTER GOLD (See Justice League #4)
DC Comics: Feb, 1986 - No. 25, Feb, 1988 (75¢)

	GD2.0	FN6.0	NM9.4
1			3.00
2-25: 4-Rose & Thorn app. 6-Origin. 6,7,23-Superman app. 8,9-LSH app. 22-JLI app. 24,25-Millennium tie-ins			2.00

NOTE: ***Austin*** *c-22i.* ***Byrne*** *c-23i.*

BOOTS AND HER BUDDIES
Standard Comics/Visual Editions/Argo (NEA Service):
No. 5, 9/48 - No. 9, 9/49; 12/55 - No. 3, 1956

	GD2.0	FN6.0	NM9.4
5-Strip-r	15.00	45.00	105.00
6,8	10.00	30.00	70.00
7-(Scarce)-Spanking panels(3)	11.50	34.00	80.00
9-(Scarce)-Frazetta-a (2 pgs.)	25.00	75.00	175.00
1-3(Argo-1955-56)-Reprints	5.00	15.00	30.00

BOOTS & SADDLES (TV)
Dell Publ. Co.: No. 919, July, 1958; No. 1029, Sept, 1959; No. 1116, Aug, 1960

	GD2.0	FN6.0	NM9.4
Four Color 919 (#1)-Photo-c	7.00	22.00	80.00
Four Color 1029, 1116-Photo-c	4.50	13.50	50.00

BORDERLINE
Friction Press: June, 1992 ($2.25, B&W)

	GD2.0	FN6.0	NM9.4
0-Ashcan edition; 1st app. of Cliff Broadway			2.00
1-Painted-c			3.00
1-Special Edition (bagged w/ photo, S&N)			4.00

BORDER PATROL
P. L. Publishing Co.: May-June, 1951 - No. 3, Sept-Oct, 1951

	GD2.0	FN6.0	NM9.4
1	11.00	33.00	75.00
2,3	8.35	25.00	50.00

BORDER WORLDS (Also see Megaton Man)
Kitchen Sink Press: 7/86 - No. 7, 1987; V2#1, 1990 - No. 4, 1990 ($1.95-$2.00, B&W, mature)

	GD2.0	FN6.0	NM9.4
1-7, V2#1-4: Donald Simpson-c/a/scripts			3.00

BORIS KARLOFF TALES OF MYSTERY (TV) (...Thriller No. 1,2)
Gold Key: No. 3, April, 1963 - No. 97, Feb, 1980

	GD2.0	FN6.0	NM9.4
3-5-(Two #5's, 10/63,11/63): 5-(10/63)-11 pgs. Toth-a.	3.00	9.00	30.00
6-8,10: 10-Orlando-a	2.50	7.50	24.00
9-Wood-a	2.80	8.40	28.00
11-Williamson-a, 8 pgs.; Orlando-a, 5 pgs.	2.80	8.40	28.00
12-Torres, McWilliams-a; Orlando-a(2)	2.50	7.50	22.00
13,14,16-20	2.25	6.75	18.00
15-Crandall	2.50	7.50	20.00
21-Jeff Jones-a(3 pgs.) "The Screaming Skull"	2.50	7.50	20.00
22-Last 12¢ issue	1.75	5.25	14.00
23-30: 23-Reprint; photo-c	1.75	5.25	12.00
31-50: 36-Weiss-a	1.10	3.30	9.00
51-74: 74-Origin & 1st app. Taurus	1.00	2.80	7.00
75-79,87-97: 90-r/Torres, McWilliams-a/#12; Morrow-c			5.00
80-86-(52 pgs.)	1.00	3.00	8.00
Story Digest 1(7/70-Gold Key)-All text/illos.; 148pp.	3.00	9.00	30.00

(See Mystery Comics Digest No. 2, 5, 8, 11, 14, 17, 20, 23, 26)
NOTE: ***Bolle*** *a-51-54, 56, 58, 59.* ***McWilliams*** *a-12, 14, 18, 19, 72, 80, 81, 93.* ***Orlando*** *a-11-15, 21. Reprints: 78, 81-86, 88, 90, 92, 95, 97.*

BORIS KARLOFF THRILLER (TV) (Becomes Boris Karloff Tales...)
Gold Key: Oct, 1962 - No. 2, Jan, 1963 (80 pgs.)

	GD2.0	FN6.0	NM9.4
1-Photo-c	5.90	18.00	65.00
2	4.00	12.00	45.00

BORIS THE BEAR
Dark Horse Comics/Nicotat Comics #13 on: Aug, 1986 - No. 34, 1990 ($1.50/$1.75/$1.95, B&W)

	GD2.0	FN6.0	NM9.4
1, Annual 1 (1988, $2.50)			3.00
1 (2nd printing),2,3,4A,4B,5-12, 14-34: 8-(44 pgs.)			2.00
13-1st Nicotat Comics issue			3.00

BORIS THE BEAR INSTANT COLOR CLASSICS
Dark Horse Comics: July, 1987 - No. 3, 1987 ($1.75/$1.95)

	GD2.0	FN6.0	NM9.4
1-3			2.00

BORN AGAIN
Spire Christian Comics (Fleming H. Revell Co.): 1978 (39¢)

	GD2.0	FN6.0	NM9.4
nn-Watergate, Nixon, etc.			5.00

BOUNCER, THE (Formerly Green Mask #9)
Fox Features Syndicate: 1944 - No. 14, Jan, 1945

	GD2.0	FN6.0	NM9.4
nn(1944, #10?)	26.00	77.00	180.00
11(#1)(9/44)-Origin; Rocket Kelly, One Round Hogan app.	21.00	64.00	150.00
12-14: 14-Reprints no # issue	17.00	51.00	120.00

BOUNTY GUNS (See Luke Short's..., Four Color 739)